Dictionary of Literary Biography

Documentary Series

Walter McDonald, John M. Del Vecchio, edited by Ronald Baughman (1991)

10 *The Bloomsbury Group,* edited by Edward L. Bishop (1992)

11 *American Proletarian Culture: The Twenties and The Thirties,* edited by Jon Christian Suggs (1993)

12 *Southern Women Writers: Flannery O'Connor, Katherine Anne Porter, Eudora Welty,* edited by Mary Ann Wimsatt and Karen L. Rood (1994)

13 *The House of Scribner, 1846-1904,* edited by John Delaney (1996)

14 *Four Women Writers for Children, 1868-1918,* edited by Caroline C. Hunt (1996)

15 *American Expatriate Writers: Paris in the Twenties,* edited by Matthew J. Bruccoli and Robert W. Trogdon (1997)

16 *The House of Scribner, 1905-1930,* edited by John Delaney (1997)

17 *The House of Scribner, 1931-1984,* edited by John Delaney (1998)

18 *British Poets of The Great War: Sassoon, Graves, Owen,* edited by Patrick Quinn (1999)

19 *James Dickey,* edited by Judith S. Baughman (1999)

See also DLB 210

Yearbooks

1980 edited by Karen L. Rood, Jean W. Ross, and Richard Ziegfeld (1981)

1981 edited by Karen L. Rood, Jean W. Ross, and Richard Ziegfeld (1982)

1982 edited by Richard Ziegfeld; associate editors: Jean W. Ross and Lynne C. Zeigler (1983)

1983 edited by Mary Bruccoli and Jean W. Ross, associate editor Richard Ziegfeld (1984)

1984 edited by Jean W. Ross (1985)

1985 edited by Jean W. Ross (1986)

1986 edited by J. M. Brook (1987)

1987 edited by J. M. Brook (1988)

1988 edited by J. M. Brook (1989)

1989 edited by J. M. Brook (1990)

1990 edited by James W. Hipp (1991)

1991 edited by James W. Hipp (1992)

1992 edited by James W. Hipp (1993)

1993 edited by James W. Hipp, contributing editor George Garrett (1994)

1994 edited by James W. Hipp, contributing editor George Garrett (1995)

1995 edited by James W. Hipp, contributing editor George Garrett (1996)

1996 edited by Samuel W. Bruce and L. Kay Webster, contributing editor George Garrett (1997)

1997 edited by Matthew J. Bruccoli and George Garrett, with the assistance of L. Kay Webster (1998)

1998 edited by Matthew J. Bruccoli, contributing editor George Garrett, with the assistance of D. W. Thomas (1999)

Concise Series

Concise Dictionary of American Literary Biography, 7 volumes (1988-1999): *The New Consciousness, 1941-1968; Colonization to the American Renaissance, 1640-1865; Realism, Naturalism, and Local Color, 1865-1917; The Twenties, 1917-1929; The Age of Maturity, 1929-1941; Broadening Views, 1968-1988; Supplement: Modern Writers, 1900–1998.*

Concise Dictionary of British Literary Biography, 8 volumes (1991-1992): *Writers of the Middle Ages and Renaissance Before 1660; Writers of the Restoration and Eighteenth Century, 1660-1789; Writers of the Romantic Period, 1789-1832; Victorian Writers, 1832-1890; Late-Victorian and Edwardian Writers, 1890-1914; Modern Writers, 1914-1945; Writers After World War II, 1945-1960; Contemporary Writers, 1960 to Present.*

Concise Dictionary of World Literary Biography, 20 volumes projected (1999-): *Ancient Greek and Roman Writers; German Writers.*

Concise Dictionary of World Literary Biography

German Writers

Concise Dictionary of World Literary Biography

German Writers

Edited by
James Hardin
University of South Carolina

A Bruccoli Clark Layman Book
The Gale Group
Detroit • San Francisco • London • Boston • Woodbridge, Conn.

CONCISE DICTIONARY OF WORLD LITERARY BIOGRAPHY

Matthew J. Bruccoli and Richard Layman, Editorial Directors
C. E. Frazer Clark Jr., Managing Editor
Karen L. Rood, Senior Editor

Printed in the United States of America

The paper used in this publication meets the minimum requirements
of American National Standard for Information Sciences–Permanence
Paper for Printed Library Materials, ANSI Z39.48-1984. ∞™

Library of Congress Cataloging-in-Publication Data

German writers.
    p. cm.–(Concise dictionary of world literary biography; v. 2)
"A Bruccoli Clark Layman book."
Includes bibliographical references and index.
ISBN 0-7876-4482-X (alk. paper)
ISBN 0-7876-4480-3 (set: alk. paper)
1. Authors, German–Biography–Dictionaries. I. Series.
PT155.G47 1999

          99–39453
          CIP

10 9 8 7 6 5 4 3 2 1

Contents

Rationale

The *Concise Dictionary of World Literary Biography* is a collection of complete essays from the standard *Dictionary of Literary Biography* series selected to serve the needs of students. It was developed in response to requests from high-school and junior-college teachers and librarians, and from small- to medium-sized public libraries, for a *Dictionary of Literary Biography* series for the most-studied authors that would meet their budgets. Entries for the *Concise DWLB* have been selected from the more than 12,000 entries in the 250-volume standard *DLB* as of 1999.

Concise indicates the scope of this series—not the content of the entries. In the *Concise* volumes, original *DLB* entries are published in their entirety; indeed, the *Concise* entries are updated and augmented where required. Entries are grouped by national literature and chronology to preserve the rationale of the original *DLB:* to provide a history of literature in all languages developed through the biographies of writers. *DLB* entries contain five basic types of information: a comprehensive checklist of the author's works, the facts of the author's life, a description of the literary works, a discussion of the critical response to them, and a bibliography of recommended sources for further information. In these entries students will find reliable resources to begin study of an author's literary achievement and to place the author in appropriate literary and social contexts. The *DLB* is prepared according to exacting scholarly standards. Users of the *Concise* series will find the same reliable biographical and bibliographical information as provided by the standard *DLB*.

It is anticipated that this series will not be confined to library uses. Just as the *DLB* has been a tool for stimulating students' literary interest in the college classroom—for comparative studies of authors and, through its ample illustrations, as a means of invigorating literary study—the *Concise DWLB* is a first resource for high-school and junior-college educators. Users of this series will find it advantageous to consult the standard *DLB* for information about those writers omitted from the *Concise DWLB* whose significance to contemporary readers may have faded but whose contribution to the wider literary-cultural heritage remains meaningful.

A Note to Students

The purpose of the *Concise DWLB* is to enlarge the scope of literary study. In their various ways, writers react in their works to the circumstances of their lives, the events of their time, and the culture that envelops them. Literature provides readers with ways to see and understand what writers have observed and experienced. Besides being inherently interesting, biographies of writers provide a basic perspective on literature and social history.

Concise DWLB entries start with the most important facts about writers: what they wrote. The student should start there. The chronological listing of an author's works provides an outline for the examination of his or her career achievement. The critical biographies that follow prepare for the presentation of the writings. Each of the author's important publications and the most reliable critical evaluations of them are discussed in *Concise DWLB*. More information about the author and critical studies of the works is provided in the references section at the end of the entry.

Illustrations are an integral element of *Concise DWLB* entries. Photographs of the author are reminders that literature is produced by writers, whose faces sometimes reveal their minds; facsimiles of the author's working drafts are the best available evidence for understanding the act of composition—the author in the process of refining his or her work and acting as self-editor; and dust jackets and advertisements reveal how literature reaches readers through the marketplace, which may serve to alter present perceptions of the works.

Literary study is a complex and immensely rewarding endeavor. The purpose of the *DLB* and *Concise DWLB* is to provide the information required to make that experience rewarding and useful.

Introduction

German literary history covers a period as long as that of English literature: from around A.D. 750 to the present. The term "German" is misleading, since German literature actually comprises works written in several languages and dialects: Old High German (ca. 750–1050); Latin, used in the "high" literature of the entire medieval period through the Reformation and particularly prominent as a literary language in the writings of the humanists; Middle High German (ca. 1050–1350), the language of the heroic and courtly epics; Early New High German (ca. 1350–1640); and New High German (ca. 1640 to the present). The existence of German neo-Latin literature—in humanist poetry, letters, and drama written under the influence of classical sources, and in virtually all learned works well into the eighteenth century—is a significant but often overlooked fact. German dialects, which have existed from the earliest days of recorded written German, have also played a significant role in the history of German letters. Not only was dialect used to enhance the "realism" or local color of naturalistic drama and nineteenth- and twentieth-century prose, especially in the early dramas of Gerhart Hauptmann, but entire works were, especially in the nineteenth century, written in various dialects—Low German, Silesian, and Bavarian among others—in hopes of preserving a threatened tradition or to convey the quaint quality of a local culture outside the mainstream.

German had its beginnings in a prehistoric, pre-Christian era, when the dialect of German (Deutsch), like English a West Germanic language, was developing from the several Germanic languages and gradually became the leading language in what is now east-central Germany. The few heathen documents in German that survived time and the destructive fervor of the monks are short and fragmentary, such as the famous *Merseburger Zaubersprüche* (Merseburg Charms) of around 750, which provide charms that enable one to escape one's enemies and to cure a horse with a sprained leg. Although the earliest pre-Christian documents and archaeological survivals are characterized by their rarity, that is far from the case in the centuries following the founding of the Holy Roman Empire of the German Nation in 800. From the coronation of Charlemagne in 800 to the time of the writing of the *Nibelungenlied* around 1200, the number of significant literary manuscripts increased rapidly. The enormous flowering of high medieval culture in Europe, with its refined neo-scholastic philosophy, music, and incredible achievements in architecture, brought with it the first great period of German literature. Two centuries later, another event brought about an unprecedented proliferation of the written word: the invention of movable type in the fifteenth century, which enabled printers to reproduce sheets of type rapidly and thus to produce books. The timing of this invention was uncanny, as it came only shortly before the outbreak of the Reformation, which clearly owed much of its revolutionary force to the ability of both warring factions quickly to publish fusillades of polemics and satires during the first half of the sixteenth century. It also enabled the publication of Martin Luther's translation of the Bible.

As German continued to mature as a language and gradually to displace Latin in scholarly books and university lecture halls (in the late seventeenth and eighteenth centuries), and with the rise of Germany as a leading force in European cultural life in the eighteenth century, the number of secular works published came finally to exceed the number of religious works. A literary industry consisting of scholars, writers, and publishers arose that was one of the most active and prolific in Europe.

Any "concise" treatment of German literature is therefore bound to be selective. The present work is no exception. The *Concise Dictionary of World Literary Biography: German Writers* provides entries on writers beginning with the literary efflorescence in the high medieval period around 1200, at a point when the German language and culture had matured and were on a par with the other major European vernaculars. The leading genre was the courtly epic, and its chief practitioners were Hartmann von Aue, Gottfried von Straßbourg, and Wolfram von Eschenbach. Not much is known about any of them, but their works were clearly hugely popular in their time, as can be seen in the large number of extant manuscripts containing their works. The *Concise Dictionary* treats the huge contribution of Luther as reformer and translator in the late medieval or early modern period and then concentrates primarily on the two remaining great epochs of German literature: that lasting from the Sturm und Drang (Storm and Stress, ca. 1765-1781) through German Romanticism (ca. 1790-1830), when such major writers as Johann Wolfgang von Goethe, Friedrich Schiller, and the German Romantics flourished, and, finally, the period 1900-1933, when the best writings of Thomas Mann, Franz Kafka, Hermann Hesse, Bertolt Brecht, Rainer Maria Rilke, and the expressionist poets and dramatists were published. In those decades, Germany and Austria experienced an unprecedented creative ferment, not just in the field of literature, but also in the cinema, musical composition, and plastic arts in the Weimar Republic.

That creative outburst was, as we know all too well, brought to a halt by the rise to power of the Nazi Party. Although German and Austrian literature continued to be written during the Third Reich, largely by impecunious writers in exile in the United States, Switzerland, England, and South America, or in so-called internal exile in Germany and Austria, the readership for authors who had not gained a world reputation was lost. Some of the best German and Austrian writers died in exile (such as Robert Musil, in Switzerland) or barely maintained their existence living on crumbs from various academic tables (Hermann Broch at Yale). A few flourished in America, either because they already had a considerable readership in the English-speaking world (Thomas Mann) or because they could accommodate their works to American cultural institutions such as Hollywood (Erich Maria Remarque). The drain of German artists–actors, directors, and composers as well as writers–to Hollywood in the 1930s and 1940s was in fact a major factor in the strength of American films of that period. And so German literature languished in Germany but continued to be produced, usually under very difficult conditions, in other countries until the end of the war.

It was hoped that after the fall of Nazi Germany in 1945 there would be an outpouring of long-suppressed literature of high quality, but the harvest was at first sparse. Established writers such as Thomas Mann produced the earliest works directly after the war to achieve broad critical acclaim (*Dr. Faustus,* 1947), or the fame of already-dead authors such as Kafka and Musil eclipsed that of a newer generation of writers who had their own creative difficulties in a smashed and literally demoralized country. It was at the time of the establishment in 1947 of a loose association of German writers called the Gruppe 47 (Group 47) that another generation of postwar writers emerged. The most prominent of these were the novelists Heinrich Böll (1917-1985) and Günter Grass (1927-). The primary theme of most prominent German writers in the years immediately after the war was coming to terms with the events

of the Hitler regime. The guilt experienced by German intellectuals after the end of World War II is perhaps without precedent in the history of literature. It is to this day still a leading theme, as are political topics and social attitudes in general. Germany is a very literary country, with a myriad of literary prizes, happenings, university support, and support by radio, television, and newspapers. There are many writers. Few have risen to world prominence. Some who have include Christa Wolf, Uwe Johnson, and Thomas Bernhard, but critics have yet to reach a consensus on the names that will assume a leading position, and maintain it, in the German literary canon.

The Periods of German Literature

The periods of German literature follow roughly the same pattern as all of Europe. The chief exception to this pattern is the Renaissance. Germany naturally experienced the cultural influences that brought about the Renaissance in Italy, France, Spain, and England, but two factors militated against there being a blossoming of secular learning and belles lettres. The first was the Reformation. The humanist achievements of the fifteenth century, the tolerance, erudition, and wit of such figures as Erasmus, could not survive the intense zealotry of the period after 1517 when Luther's steadfast principles and intransigence led to the intolerant outbursts on both sides that split Europe into the Protestant north and Catholic south. The religious controversy led in the following century to the Thirty Years' War (1618-1648) which was, until World War II, the most catastrophic event in German history. Another important factor distinguishes German literature from that of the other major European cultures: its linguistic backwardness. German in the sixteenth and even in the seventeenth centuries was not as nuanced a language as French, English, or Italian. One reason for this was the reliance of the educated classes, especially the clergy and scholars, on Latin as the language of scholarship and theology. German of the early seventeenth century was not as expressive or as flexible as the other major vernaculars. It was a measure of the individual genius of such Baroque writers as Andreas Gryphius and Johann Jacob Christoffel von Grimmelshausen that they were able nonetheless to write masterworks at a point when the language they had to work with was not fully developed. Eric Blackall has argued that German did not come fully of age as a literary language until the late eighteenth century, and that the emergence of the language came about just at the time when such writers as Gotthold Ephraim Lessing, Goethe, and Schiller made Germany a leading literary force in Europe. The linguistic gap that had prevailed since the time of humanism no longer existed, and from the Sturm und Drang period to the present, German literature—with the huge anomaly of the Third Reich—has followed the broad patterns of literary development in the rest of Europe, going through the same periods: Enlightenment (followed by that uniquely German movement, the Sturm und Drang), neoclassicism (also called Weimar Classicism), Romanticism, poetic realism, naturalism, impressionism, expressionism, New Objectivity (largely a reaction to World War I), some monumentally bad neoclassical or folkish Nazi works in the 1930s, and the literature of the war and reaction to the war after 1945.

As stated at the outset, it has been necessary even in a lengthy volume to be quite selective in our choice of representative German writers. Rather than cutting down the articles on each writer, it was decided to treat each in a full-length article, together with a complete bibliography of his or her works, together with the first English translation of each work, if such translations exist. Given this fact, I have tried to select writers who themselves created high literature, to include works that are not traditionally taught in literature courses, such as Nietzsche's *Also sprach Zarathustra*. I have, reluctantly, omitted some admittedly important figures who did not themselves create great literature but pointed the way and were enormously influential, figures such as Johann Georg Hamann and Johann Gottfried Herder. Even highly significant figures had to be omitted in the interest of a full treatment of the representative figures included. Since it was also decided to place more stress on the chief periods of German literature, especially the Age of Goethe and the modern period, it was not possible to treat some interesting writers of German humanism (such as Johannes Reuchlin), of the Baroque (such

as Johann Beer and Daniel Casper von Lohenstein), and many other figures from the nineteenth and twentieth centuries. There is such a richness in German and Austrian literature beginning in the eighteenth century that only the most representative figures could be chosen. Even then some tough decisions had to be made, and I tried to pay attention to the influence a given writer had exercised on readers of the time, to their popularity in other words, and for this reason included Remarque because of his great first war novel, *Im Westen nichts Neues* (1929; translated as *All Quiet on the Western Front,* 1929).

Throughout this introduction I have used the term German literature to denote not only literature written in the German Empire (there being no united Germany until 1871) but also in German-speaking Switzerland and Austria. Austria is a particularly interesting case since that now-small country has produced so many excellent writers. One could certainly argue for a separate treatment of Austrian literature, or at least of Viennese literature, but the cultural world represented by the language that links these countries is, in my view, more important than geographical boundaries. When one thinks of the great German writers, the *Dichter,* one thinks immediately not only of Goethe, Schiller, Annette von Droste-Hülshoff, Thomas Mann, and Hesse, but also of Kafka and Rilke in the provincial capital Prague, and Musil, Broch, and a vast number of lesser but great talents in Vienna. Geopolitical distinctions do need to be made, as the influences of homeland, city, dialect, religious background, landscape, and local history, are undeniable and often decisive. The entries themselves will touch on those points.

—James Hardin

Acknowledgments

This book was produced by Bruccoli Clark Layman, Inc. Karen L. Rood is senior editor for the *Dictionary of Literary Biography* series. R. Bland Lawson was the in-house editor.

Production manager is Philip B. Dematteis.

Administrative support was provided by Ann M. Cheschi, Tenesha S. Lee, and Joann Whittaker.

Accounting was done by Angi Pleasant.

Copyediting supervisor is Phyllis A. Avant. Senior copyeditor is Thom Harman. The copyediting staff includes Ronald D. Aiken II, Brenda Carol Blanton, Worthy B. Evans, Melissa D. Hinton, William Tobias Mathes, Jennifer Reid, and Michelle L. Whitney.

Editorial assistant is Margo Dowling.

Editorial trainee is Carol A. Fairman.

Indexing specialist is Alex Snead.

Layout and graphics supervisor is Janet E. Hill. Graphics staff includes Zoe R. Cook.

Office manager is Kathy Lawler Merlette.

Photography editors are Charles Mims, Scott Nemzek, Alison Smith, and Paul Talbot. Digital photographic copy work was performed by Joseph M. Bruccoli.

SGML supervisor is Cory McNair. The SGML staff includes Tim Bedford, Linda Drake, Frank Graham, and Alex Snead.

Systems manager is Marie L. Parker.

Kimberly Kelly performed data entry.

Typesetting supervisor is Kathleen M. Flanagan. The typesetting staff includes Karla Corley Brown, Mark J. McEwan, and Patricia Flanagan Salisbury. Freelance typesetter is Delores Plastow.

Walter W. Ross and Steven Gross did library research. They were assisted by the following librarians at the Thomas Cooper Library of the University of South Carolina: Linda Holderfield and the interlibrary-loan staff; reference-department head Virginia Weathers; reference librarians Marilee Birchfield, Stefanie Buck, Stefanie DuBose, Rebecca Feind, Karen Joseph, Donna Lehman, Charlene Loope, Anthony McKissick, Jean Rhyne, and Kwamine Simpson; circulation-department head Caroline Taylor; and acquisitions-searching supervisor David Haggard.

Concise Dictionary of World Literary Biography

German Writers

Concise Dictionary of World Literary Biography

Thomas Bernhard

(9 or 10 February 1931 – 12 February 1989)

Steve Dowden
Brandeis University

This entry originally appeared in DLB 124: Twentieth-Century German Dramatists, 1919–1992.

See also the Bernhard entry in *DLB 85: Austrian Fiction Writers After 1914.*

BOOKS: *Auf der Erde und in der Hölle: Gedichte* (Salzburg: Müller, 1957);

In hora mortis (Salzburg: Müller, 1958);

Unter dem Eisen des Mondes: Gedichte (Cologne & Berlin: Kiepenheuer & Witsch, 1958);

die rosen der einöde: fünf sätze für ballett, stimmen, und orchester (Frankfurt am Main: Fischer, 1959);

Frost (Frankfurt am Main: Insel, 1963); excerpt translated by Helene Scher as "Frost," in *Postwar German Culture,* edited by Charles McClelland and Steven Scher (New York: Dutton, 1974), pp. 238–242;

Amras (Frankfurt am Main: Insel, 1964);

Prosa (Frankfurt am Main: Suhrkamp, 1967);

Verstörung (Frankfurt am Main: Insel, 1967); translated by Richard and Clara Winston as *Gargoyles* (New York: Knopf, 1970);

Ungenach: Erzählung (Frankfurt am Main: Suhrkamp, 1968);

Ein Fest für Boris (Frankfurt am Main: Suhrkamp, 1968); translated by Peter Jansen and Kenneth Northcott as *A Party for Boris,* in *Histrionics: Three Plays* (Chicago & London: University of Chicago Press, 1990), pp. 1–71;

An der Baumgrenze: Erzählungen (Salzburg: Residenz, 1969); "An der Baumgrenze" translated by Sophie Wilkins as "At the Timberline," in *Anthology of Modern Austrian Literature,* edited by Adolf

Opel (Atlantic Heights, N.J.: Humanities Press, 1981; London: Wolff, 1981);

An der Baumgrenze: Erzählungen (Salzburg: Residenz, 1969); "An der Baumgrenze" translated by Sophie Wilkins as "At the Timberline," in *Anthology of Modern Austrian Literature,* edited by Adolf Opel (Atlantic Heights, N.J.: Humanities Press, 1981; London: Wolff, 1981);

Ereignisse (Berlin: Literarisches Kolloquium, 1969);

Watten: Ein Nachlaß (Frankfurt am Main: Suhrkamp, 1969);

Das Kalkwerk (Frankfurt am Main: Suhrkamp, 1970); translated by Wilkins as *The Lime Works* (New York: Knopf, 1973);

Der Italiener (Salzburg: Residenz, 1971);

Midland in Stilfs: Drei Erzählungen (Frankfurt am Main: Suhrkamp, 1971);

Gehen (Frankfurt am Main: Suhrkamp, 1971);

Der Ignorant und der Wahnsinnige (Frankfurt am Main: Suhrkamp, 1972);

Die Jagdgesellschaft (Frankfurt am Main: Suhrkamp, 1974), translated by Gitta Honegger as *The Hunting Party,* in *Performing Arts Journal,* 5, no. 1 (1980): pp. 101–131;

Die Macht der Gewohnheit: Komödie (Frankfurt am Main: Suhrkamp, 1974); translated by Neville and Stephen Plaice as *The Force of Habit: A Comedy* (London: Heinemann, 1976);

Der Kulterer: Eine Filmgeschichte (Salzburg: Residenz, 1974);

Thomas Bernhard

Der Präsident (Frankfurt am Main: Suhrkamp, 1975); translated by Honegger as *The President,* in *The President & Eve of Retirement* (New York: Performing Arts Journal Publications, 1982), pp. 17–114;

Die Ursache: Eine Andeutung (Salzburg: Residenz, 1975); translated by David McLintock as "An Indication of the Cause," in *Gathering Evidence: A Memoir* (New York: Knopf, 1985), pp. 75–141;

Korrektur: Roman (Frankfurt am Main: Suhrkamp, 1975); translated by Wilkins as *Correction* (New York: Knopf, 1979);

Der Wetterfleck: Erzählungen (Stuttgart: Reclam, 1976);

Die Berühmten (Frankfurt am Main: Suhrkamp, 1976);

Minetti: Porträt des Künstlers als alter Mann (Frankfurt am Main: Suhrkamp, 1976);

Der Keller: Eine Entziehung (Salzburg: Residenz, 1976); translated by McLintock as "The Cellar: An Escape," in *Gathering Evidence,* pp. 142–213;

Der Atem: Eine Entscheidung (Salzburg & Vienna: Residenz, 1978); translated by McLintock as "Breath: A Decision," in *Gathering Evidence,* pp. 215–275;

Die Kälte: Eine Isolation (Salzburg: Residenz, 1978); translated by McLintock as "In the Cold," in *Gathering Evidence,* pp. 277–340;

Ja (Frankfurt am Main: Suhrkamp, 1978); translated by Ewald Osers as *Yes* (London: Quartet, 1991);

Der Stimmenimitator (Frankfurt am Main: Suhrkamp, 1978);

Immanuel Kant: Komödie (Frankfurt am Main: Suhrkamp, 1978);

Die Erzählungen (Frankfurt am Main: Suhrkamp, 1979);

Vor dem Ruhestand (Frankfurt am Main: Suhrkamp, 1979); translated by Honegger as *Eve of Retirement,* in *The President & Eve of Retirement,* pp. 115–207;

Der Weltverbesserer (Frankfurt am Main: Suhrkamp, 1979);

Die Billigesser (Frankfurt am Main: Suhrkamp, 1980); translated by Osers as *The Cheap-Eaters* (London: Quartet, 1990);

Über allen Gipfeln ist Ruh: Ein deutscher Dichtertag um 1980. Komödie (Frankfurt am Main: Suhrkamp, 1981);

Am Ziel (Frankfurt am Main: Suhrkamp, 1981);

Ave Vergil: Gedicht (Frankfurt am Main: Suhrkamp, 1981);

Wittgensteins Neffe: Eine Freundschaft (Frankfurt am Main: Suhrkamp, 1982); translated by McLintock as *Wittgenstein's Nephew: A Friendship* (New York: Knopf, 1989);

Ein Kind (Salzburg: Residenz, 1982); translated by McLintock as "A Child," in *Gathering Evidence,* pp. 1–73;

Beton (Frankfurt am Main: Suhrkamp, 1982); translated by McLintock as *Concrete* (New York: Knopf, 1984; London: Dent, 1984);

Der Schein trügt (Frankfurt am Main: Suhrkamp, 1983); translated by Honegger as *Appearances are Deceiving,* in *Theater* (Yale University), 15 (Winter 1983): 31–51;

Der Untergeher (Frankfurt am Main: Suhrkamp, 1983); translated by Jack Dawson as *The Loser: A Novel* (New York: Knopf, 1991);

Der Theatermacher (Frankfurt am Main: Suhrkamp, 1984); translated by Jansen and Northcott as *Histrionics,* in *Histrionics,* pp. 179–282;

Holzfällen: Eine Erregung (Frankfurt am Main: Suhrkamp, 1984); translated by McLintock as *Woodcutters* (New York: Knopf, 1987);

Ritter, Dene, Voss (Frankfurt am Main: Suhrkamp, 1984); translated by Jansen and Northcott as *Ritter, Dene, Voss* in *Histrionics,* pp. 73–178;

Alte Meister: Komödie (Frankfurt am Main: Suhrkamp, 1985); translated by Osers as *Old Masters* (London: Quartet, 1989);

Einfach kompliziert (Frankfurt am Main: Suhrkamp, 1986);

Auslöschung: Ein Zerfall (Frankfurt am Main: Suhrkamp, 1986); translated by McLintock as *Extinction: A Novel* (New York: Knopf, 1995);

Elisabeth II (Frankfurt am Main: Suhrkamp, 1987);

Der deutsche Mittagstisch: Dramolette (Frankfurt am Main: Suhrkamp, 1988)–includes *Maiandacht, Freispruch, Eis, Match;* translated by Honegger as *The German*

Lunch Table, in *Performing Arts Journal*, 6, no. 1 (1981): 26–29;

Stücke, 4 volumes (Frankfurt am Main: Suhrkamp, 1988);

Heldenplatz (Frankfurt am Main: Suhrkamp, 1988);

Die Irren; Die Häftlinge (Frankfurt am Main: Insel, 1988);

In der Höhe: Rettungsversuch, Unsinn (Salzburg: Residenz, 1989); translated by Russell Stockman as *On the Mountain* (Marlboro, Vt.: Marlboro Press, 1991);

Claus Peymann kauft sich eine Hose und geht mit mir essen: Drei Dramolette (Frankfurt am Main: Suhrkamp, 1990);

Aus dem Gerichtssaal: Thomas Bernhards Salzburg in den 50er Jahren, edited by Jens Dittmar (Vienna: Edition S, 1992).

PLAY PRODUCTIONS: *Ein Fest für Boris*, Hamburg, Deutsches Schauspielhaus, 29 June 1970;

Der Ignorant und der Wahnsinnige, Salzburg, Festspiele, 29 July 1972;

Die Jagdgesellschaft, Vienna, Burgtheater, 4 May 1974;

Die Macht der Gewohnheit, Salzburg, Festspiele, 27 July 1974;

Der Präsident, Vienna, Burgtheater, 17 May 1975;

Die Berühmten, Vienna, Theater an der Wien, 8 June 1976;

Minetti: Porträt des Künstlers als alter Mann, Stuttgart, Staatstheater, 1 September 1976;

Immanuel Kant, Stuttgart, Staatstheater, 15 April 1978;

Vor dem Ruhestand, Stuttgart, Württembergisches Staatstheater, 29 June 1979;

Der Weltverbesserer, Bochum, Schauspielhaus, 6 September 1980;

Maiandacht, Freispruch, and *Eis*, Bochum, Schauspielhaus, 7 November 1981;

Der Schein trügt, Bochum, Schauspielhaus, 21 January 1984;

Der Theatermacher, Salzburg, Festspiele, 17 August 1985;

Einfach kompliziert, West Berlin, Schiller-Theater, 28 February 1986;

Claus Peymann verläßt Bochum und geht als Burgtheaterdirektor nach Wien, Bochum, Schauspielhaus, 8 June 1986;

Ritter, Dene, Voss, Salzburg, Festspiele, 18 August 1986;

Match, Vienna, Burgtheater, 23 October 1987;

Heldenplatz, Vienna, Burgtheater, 4 November 1988;

Elisabeth II: Keine Komödie, Berlin, Schiller-Theater, 5 November 1989.

OTHER: "Großer, unbegreiflicher Hunger," in *Stimmen der Gegenwart 1954*, edited by Hans Weigel (Vienna: Dürer, 1954), pp. 138–143;

"Der Schweinehüter," in *Stimmen der Gegenwart 1956* (Vienna & Munich: Herold, 1956), pp. 158–179;

"Ein Frühling," in *Spektrum des Geistes 1964: Literaturkalender* (Ebenhausen: Voss, 1963), p. 36;

"Der Italiener," in *Insel-Almanach auf das Jahr 1965* (Frankfurt am Main: Insel, 1964);

"Mit der Klarheit nimmt die Kälte zu," in *Jahresring 65/66* (Stuttgart: DVA, 1965), pp. 243–245;

"Nie und mit nichts fertig werden," in *Deutsche Akademie für Sprache und Dichtung: Jahrbuch 1970* (Heidelberg & Darmstadt: Schneider, 1971), pp. 83–84.

SELECTED PERIODICAL PUBLICATIONS–
UNCOLLECTED: "Eine Zeugenaussage," *Wort in der Zeit*, 10 (1964): 38–43;

"Ein junger Schriftsteller," *Wort in der Zeit*, 11 (1965): 56–59;

"Politische Morgenandacht," *Wort in der Zeit*, 12 (1966): 11–13;

"Unsterblichkeit ist unmöglich: Landschaft der Kindheit," *Neues Forum*, 169/170 (1968): 95–97;

"Der Wahrheit und dem Tod auf der Spur: Zwei Reden," *Neues Forum*, 173 (1968): 347–349;

Ein Fest für Boris, in *Theater heute*, 11 (January 1970): 39–47;

"Der Berg," *Literatur und Kritik*, 46 (1970): 330–352;

"Vor der Akademie," *Frankfurter Allgemeine Zeitung*, 19 October 1970, p. 22;

"Als Verwalter in Asyl: Fragment," *Merkur*, 24 (1970): 1163–1164;

"Protest," *Theater heute*, 13 (September 1972): 14;

Der Ignorant und der Wahnsinnige, in *Theater heute*, 13 (September 1972): 34–47;

Die Jagdgesellschaft, in *Spectaculum*, 20 (1974): 15–79;

Die Macht der Gewohnheit, in *Theater heute*, 15 (September 1974): 37–52;

"Die Komödie der Eitelkeit," *Die Zeit*, 27 February 1976, p. 55;

"Was Österreich nicht lesen soll: Die Kleinbürger auf der Heuchelleiter," *Die Zeit*, 17 February 1978, p. 40;

Der deutsche Mittagstisch: Eine Tragödie für ein Burgtheatergastspiel in Deutschland, in *Die Zeit*, 29 December 1978, p. 33;

Der Weltverbesserer, in *Theater* (1978): 88–102;

"Der doppelte Herr Bernhard," *Die Zeit*, 31 August 1979, pp. 43–44;

Vor dem Ruhestand: Eine Komödie von deutscher Seele, in *Theater heute*, 20 (August 1979): 33–49;

"Zu meinem Austritt," *Frankfurter Allgemeine Zeitung*, 7 December 1979, p. 25;

A Doda: Für zwei Schauspielerinnen und eine Landstraße, in *Die Zeit*, 12 December 1980, p. 40;

"Der pensionierte Salonsozialist," *profil,* 26 January 1981, pp. 5–9;

Alles oder nichts: Ein deutscher Akt, in *Theater heute,* 22 (May 1981): 5–9;

"Am Ziel," *Theater heute,* 22 (October 1981): 35–53;

"Verfolgungswahn?," *Die Zeit,* 11 January 1982, p. 32;

"Goethe schtirbt," *Die Zeit,* 19 March 1982, pp. 41–42;

"Montaigne: Eine Erzählung in 22 Fortsetzungen," *Die Zeit,* 8 October 1982, pp. 1–22;

"Der Schein trügt," *Spectaculum,* 39 (1984): 17–77;

"Vranitzky: Eine Erwiderung," *Die Presse,* 13 September 1985;

Claus Peymann verläßt Bochum und geht als Burgtheaterdirektor nach Wien, in *Die Zeit,* 9 May 1986, p. 51;

"Claus Peymann kauft sich eine Hose und geht mit mir essen," *Theater* (1986): 6–10;

"Claus Peymann und Hermann Beil auf der Sulzweise," *Die Zeit,* 11 September 1987, pp. 53–54;

"Mein glückliches Österreich," *Die Zeit,* 11 March 1988, p. 75;

"Einfach kompliziert," *Spectaculum,* 46 (1988): 7–42;

"Zwei Briefe an Claus Peymann," *Die Zeit,* 3 March 1989, p. 14.

From the production of his first dramas in the early 1970s until his death in 1989, Thomas Bernhard was one of the most prominent and controversial playwrights composing for the German-language theater. His grimly comic works for the stage confront the audience with death, madness, hatred, contempt, and disease. The role of plot, character, and psychology in his dramas is thin; Bernhard concentrates his gift on language. He was a virtuoso in his unique and highly musical prose style, which, though it was more dependent on charismatic stage performers than most theatrical idioms, earned him a substantial international reputation in Europe. Virtuosity of language is all that remains of the dramatic art in Bernhard's vision of the stage. The more humane aspects of theater and acting are allowed to wither: "die Schauspieler müssen Talent haben und müssen eine Maschine sein" (the actors have to have talent and have to be a machine), he once said. Empty virtuosity is also one of his favorite themes.

Bernhard's drama is satirical and antipsychological. His protagonists are individuals isolated beyond recall to the human community, which is only a dim memory to them. The course of modernity, especially World War II, has eroded the spiritual vitality of Austria. And theater, which in the German tradition holds a special and honorable place as the source of moral education for an enlightened public, has not escaped the ravages of modern degeneration. Bernhard's works for the stage embody an idea of theater as a mutilated cadaver bearing little resemblance to the living institution envisioned by Gotthold Ephraim Lessing and Friedrich Schiller, by Franz Grillparzer and Hugo von Hofmannsthal. His idea of theater must be understood as an ironic comment on theirs.

Bernhard's predilection for metaphors of death and disease is partly biographical in origin. Plagued by heart and lung problems from the age of eighteen, Bernhard's life was difficult and unhappy. He was born on 9 or 10 February 1931 to Hertha Bernhard in a Dutch home for unwed mothers in Heerlen, near Maastricht. He never met his father, an itinerant Austrian carpenter named Alois Zuckerstätter. Hertha Bernhard soon returned to Austria, where she married in 1935 and raised her family mostly in Henndorf, a village near Salzburg. Her father, Johannes Freumbichler, a novelist of local reputation who never managed to earn a living as a professional writer, was probably the most significant influence on Bernhard's childhood.

Life was arduous for Bernhard's poverty-stricken clan. He records the details of the hard times in his memoirs, which have been collected and translated under the title *Gathering Evidence* (1985). He spent time at a home for maladjusted children; he did not do well in his Nazi-administered boarding school, nor did he fare well at the hands of the school's Catholic administration after the war. At fifteen he dropped out to become a grocer's apprentice at a store in one of Salzburg's saddest postwar housing projects. He was studying voice on the side and hoped to make a career for himself in music; but in 1949 hard work and poor nutrition caught up with him, and he came down with pneumonia. His doctors did not expect him to recover, and they committed him to a gruesome ward for the terminally ill. Bernhard did not die, but he did contract tuberculosis. During the next few years he was in and out of sanatoriums, and his lungs were scarred for life. The disease put an end to his hope for a singing career. During this same period he lost his mother to cancer and his beloved grandfather to old age. These experiences of disease and death, together with a pessimistic outlook that he learned from his grandfather, shaped Bernhard's literary imagination.

In the course of his slow convalescence Bernhard became increasingly interested in reading literature and in writing poetry. After his release from the public health system he studied music and drama in Vienna and then at Salzburg's Mozarteum, from which he was graduated in 1957 with a qualifying examination on Antonin Artaud and a thesis on Bertolt Brecht. During the 1950s he had some short prose works and three books of verse published, followed by librettos in 1959 and 1960. He did not achieve substantial recognition until the publication of his first novel, *Frost,* in 1963.

His first published work for the theater, *Ein Fest für Boris* (translated as *A Party for Boris,* 1990), appeared as a book in 1968 and premiered two years later. It begins his lifelong assault on the complacent assumptions of modern German theater. Bernhard aims to shock, to confront his audience with "truths" that most people would prefer not to see. An alarmingly tasteless farce, *Ein Fest für Boris* concentrates on several legless and demented invalids who use and abuse one another. Foremost among them is "die Gute" (the Good Woman), a monstrous hypocrite who is bent on humiliating everyone around her. The macabre situation embodies Bernhard's vision of modernity: a morally, spiritually, and physically twisted humanity. The play ends with the sudden death of Boris at his birthday party and the raving laughter of the Good Woman. For Bernhard, death defines the human condition; a joke played by nature, death is both comic and tragic, a brute fact against which all else is measured. Bernhard's subsequent dramatic work hardly deviates from the underlying theme of *Ein Fest für Boris,* that human beings are wretched creatures and death is a certainty. His dramas constitute a series of variations on this basic premise and explore two issues: the loss of genuine art (especially theater) in modernity; and the Austrian historical experience, which Bernhard understands to be a moral and intellectual catastrophe.

By the time his second drama, *Der Ignorant und der Wahnsinnige* (The Ignoramus and the Madman; published, 1972), made its way to the stage in 1972, Bernhard's prestige as a novelist was established. He had begun to accumulate literary awards: the Julius Campe Prize in 1964; the Bremen Prize in 1965; the Austrian State Prize for Literature, the Presentation of the Culture Circle of the Federated League of German Industry, and the Anton Wildgans Prize of the Austrian Industrialists' Association in 1967; the Georg Büchner Prize in 1970; and the Grillparzer Prize, the Franz Theodor Csokor Prize of the Austrian PEN Club, and the Adolf Grimme Prize in 1972. More prizes were to come, in spite of Bernhard's reputation for heaping contempt on his benefactors: the Hannover Dramatists Prize and the Prix Séguier in 1974, the Literature Prize of the Austrian Chamber of Commerce in 1976, the Premio Prato in 1982, the Premio Modello in 1983, and the Prix Medicis in 1988. It was no doubt due to Bernhard's extraordinary prestige that the Salzburg Festival, though in general an aesthetically conservative undertaking, staged *Der Ignorant und der Wahnsinnige,* a parody on the value and meaning of high culture.

The play revolves around a production of Wolfgang Amadeus Mozart's *Die Zauberflöte* (The Magic Flute, 1791) and the figure called the Queen of the Night: she is so steeped in the aria that has made her famous that she has adopted its name. But her celebrated virtuosity is empty and mechanical; and she is tired of Mozart, *Die Zauberflöte,* opera, and theater and is filled with scorn for her audience:

> Wir kennen alle Opern
> alle Schauspiele
> wir haben alles gelesen
> und wir kennen die schönsten Gegenden auf der Welt
> und insgeheim hassen wir das Publikum
> nicht wahr
> unsere Peiniger
> wir treten auf
> und verabscheuen was
> wir kennen
>
> (We know all the operas
> all the plays
> we have read it all
> and we know the world's most beautiful spots
> and secretly we hate the audience
> isn't it so
> our tormentors
> we go on stage
> and despise what
> we know).

The visual image of broken lines on the page suggests that even poetry is crippled; Bernhard withholds from his disabled verse even the modest support of punctuation. There is no rhyme or recurrence of stress patterns to suggest the character of traditional prosody; only repetition remains as a grotesque vestige of lyric and dramatic verse forms. Bernhard uses monotonously recurring phrases to irritate his audience and expresses contempt for theater and for poetry itself.

The director of *Der Ignorant und der Wahnsinnige* was Claus Peymann, one of West Germany's established avant-gardists. Peymann staged the premieres of most of Bernhard's plays, including his next, *Die Jagdgesellschaft* (published, 1974; translated as *The Hunting Party,* 1980), which opened on 4 May 1974 at Vienna's Burgtheater, Austria's most venerable stage. An aging general has gathered a hunting party at his remote lodge; the forest around the lodge is infested with insects and, like the general, is dying. What is diseased here is history itself, personified in the authoritarian, vaguely Austro-Balkan figure of "der General." History has shaped or—more exactly—misshaped him. The general is a veteran of Stalingrad, where his arm (as he constantly reminds everyone) was ripped from his body; the carcasses of frozen game in the forest remind him of the frozen corpses of his soldiers. His antagonist is the voice of art and literature, embodied in "der Schriftsteller" (the writer), who offers a running commentary on death, disease, and ruination: "Das Unheil kommt /

wie wir wissen / aus allen menschlichen Naturen / und die ganze Geschichte / ist nichts als Unheil / Und wenn wir in die Zukunft hineinschauen / sehen wir nichts anderes" (Ruination stems / as we know / from all human natures / and all of history / is nothing but ruination / And if we look into the future / we see nothing else). By the end of the piece the general has committed suicide, and the woodcutters, in an allusion to the end of Anton Chekhov's *The Cherry Orchard* (1904), have begun to raze the diseased forest.

In the same way that *Der Ignorant und der Wahnsinnige* defined Bernhard's sense of art's place in the order of things, *Die Jagdgesellschaft* registers his apocalyptic sense of history. His next play, *Die Macht der Gewohnheit* (1974; translated as *The Force of Habit,* 1976) returns to the futility of art in a comic mode. Written for the Salzburg Festival, *Die Macht der Gewohnheit* indirectly mocks that grand and solemn enterprise in the image of a second-rate family circus. Its tyrannical director, Herr Caribaldi, is obsessed with forcing his unmusical troupe to perform Franz Schubert's *Trout Quintet* (1819) flawlessly. He tortures them with his obsession, and they do all they can to sabotage the daily ritual of rehearsing the piece. His motto, "Wir hassen das Forellenquintett / aber es muß gespielt werden" (We hate the Trout Quintet / but it has to be played), expresses the play's idea that empty ritual has driven out true art. It is nothing but force of habit that, from Bernhard's cantankerous viewpoint, motivates the pretentious middle-class aspirations to Bildung (culture) which, in turn, fuel the empty ritual of high culture in places such as Salzburg. His satirical play *Die Berühmten* (The Big Names, 1976), also commissioned by the Salzburg Festival, reveals an intent similar to that of *Die Macht der Gewohnheit*. But this time the satire was not oblique. When the administrators discovered that it openly lampooned "the big names" (and their lesser successors) on which the festival's reputation and tradition were based, they refused to produce it.

The idea that drives *Die Macht der Gewohnheit* and *Die Berühmten* recurs in Bernhard's dramas and prose with heavy emphasis: in this fallen era, true art is lost forever. *Über allen Gipfeln ist Ruh* (O'er All Mountain Peaks Is Repose, 1981 [the title is an ironic citation of a well-known poem by Johann Wolfgang von Goethe]) and *Der Theatermacher* (published, 1984; performed, 1985; translated as *Histrionics,* 1990) proceed in a similar vein. Yet Bernhard's plays do not claim to recover the squandered patrimony; they merely attempt to call attention to the catastrophe. *Minetti: Porträt des Künstlers als alter Mann* (Minetti: A Portrait of the Artist as Old Man, 1976), written for and about one of Bernhard's favorite stage stars, Bernhard Minetti, deals with a senescent actor banished from the limelight because he

refuses to compromise his artistic vision. His suicide embodies the extinction of art. Minetti appeared in the premieres of *Der Schein trügt* (published, 1983; performed, 1984; translated as *Appearances Are Deceiving,* 1983) and *Einfach kompliziert* (Simply Complicated, 1986), both of which are similar in theme to *Minetti*. Bernhard also wrote a play for three favorite actors from Peymann's troupe in Bochum: Gert Voss, Kirsten Dene, and Ilse Ritter. *Ritter, Dene, Voss* (published, 1984; performed, 1986; translated, 1990) satirizes the sterile elegance of the Viennese upper-middle class.

Vor dem Ruhestand (1979; translated as *Eve of Retirement,* 1982) brought a previously latent concern to the forefront of Bernhard's dramatic imagination: the history and politics of Germany and Austria. An earlier work, *Der Präsident* (1975; translated as *The President,* 1982) had mocked the vanity of political power, but it was an indirect critique with a vaguely Austro-Balkan setting. In contrast, *Vor dem Ruhestand* savagely attacks the afterlife of Nazism in Germany and Austria. Rudolf Höller, a former concentration-camp commandant, is retiring as chief justice of a German court. He and his sister Vera annually celebrate the birthday of Heinrich Himmler. In honor of the occasion Höller dons his old SS uniform, which Vera lovingly cares for, and the two reminisce over a meal. As a final tribute to Himmler, Rudolf and Vera go to bed together. The two monsters are opposed by their paraplegic sister Clara, a leftist. They torment her, shaving her head and forcing her into the role of a concentration-camp victim.

Vor dem Ruhestand was Bernhard's response to a scandal that involved Peymann, who directed its premiere in Stuttgart. The archconservative prime minister of Baden-Württemberg, Hans Filbinger, who was also a likely candidate for president of the Federal Republic of Germany, had severely criticized Peymann's work at the Staatstheater (State Theater) in Stuttgart and was instrumental in forcing Peymann from his post as artistic director. But before Peymann left, it was discovered that Filbinger had concealed a sordid Nazi past. Rolf Hochhuth worked out the details of Filbinger's case in his documentary play *Juristen* (Lawyers; published, 1979; performed, 1980). The difference between Hochhuth's approach and Bernhard's is significant. Characteristically, Bernhard sought not to review and analyze the facts of the Filbinger case but to explore satirically the sensibility that underlay Filbinger's prestige and prosperity in a booming postwar Germany.

In a similar spirit Bernhard's final drama, *Heldenplatz,* offers a histrionic vision of postwar Austria. The play was his offering on the occasion of the Burgtheater's one hundredth anniversary. But 1988 was also the fiftieth anniversary of Austria's union with Nazi Germany. Against the background of the scandal surrounding the Austrian president, Kurt Waldheim, but with little direct reference to it, Bernhard pokes into the sore wound of Austrian anti-Semitism and complicity in Nazism. Professor Josef Schuster, a Jew who had fled Vienna for Oxford in 1938 and had returned in 1955, has committed suicide. His brother, Professor Robert Schuster, who has returned from English exile, is one of Bernhard's most fully achieved misanthropes. He rants artfully and at great length against Austria's politicians and pretensions, against the lowered standards of art and intellect in modern Austria, and above all against Austrian anti-Semitism, symbolized by the Heldenplatz: on 15 March 1938 the Heldenplatz had been the scene of Adolf Hitler's speech to masses of jubilant Viennese shortly after the annexation of Austria to Germany.

The premiere of *Heldenplatz* at the Burgtheater fomented an acrimonious public debate over questions of taste, patriotism, art, self-indulgence, and national conscience. Bernhard and Peymann, who had become artistic director of the Burgtheater in 1986, were denounced by outraged politicians and citizens. But Bernhard advocates no political or social agenda other than absolute resignation. The intention that drives Bernhard's theater is not revolution or social reform or even constructive criticism; it is personal outrage at the course of modern Austrian history. Bernhard, the misanthrope, was an uncompromising moralist.

On 12 February 1989 Bernhard died at his home in Ohlsdorf, near Gmunden in Upper Austria; a lifetime of heart and lung disease had finally claimed him at the age of fifty-eight. He was buried in Vienna's Grinzinger Cemetery on 15 February, before the news of his death was made public. At his request only three close relatives were in attendance. In a posthumous demonstration of his contempt for Austria, Bernhard specified in his will–prepared three days before his death–that none of his novels or plays could be published, produced, or recited in that country for the duration of his copyright, seventy years. The will also forbids access to his private papers, letters, and unpublished manuscripts, which are reported to include two presumably unfinished plays and a novel, "Neufundland" (Newfoundland).

Letters:

Peter Bader and Karl Ignaz Hennetmair, eds., *Thomas Bernhard, Karl Ignaz Hennetmair: Ein Briefwechsel 1965–1974* (Weitra: Publication PN 1, 1994).

Interviews:

"Je remplis le vide avec des phrases," *Nouvelles littéraires,* 22–29 (June 1978): 18;

André Müller, "Thomas Bernhard," in his *Entblößungen* (Munich: Goldmann, 1979), pp. 59–102;

"Ich könnte auf dem Papier jemand umbringen," *Der Spiegel,* 34 (23 June 1980): 172–182;

"Ansichten eines unverbesserlichen Weltverbesserers," *Stern,* 24 (4 June 1981): 160–162;

"Aveux et paradoxes de Thomas Bernhard," *Le Monde,* 7 January 1983, p. 15;

"Ich behaupte nicht, mit der Welt gehe es schlechter: Aus einem Gespräch mit Thomas Bernhard," *Frankfurter Allgemeine Zeitung,* 24 February 1983, p. 23;

"'Es ist eh alles positiv,' Thomas Bernhard über seine Bücher, seine Feinde und sich selbst," *Die Presse,* 22/23 September 1984, "Spektrum" supplement;

"Von einer Katastrophe in die andere," *Süddeutsche Zeitung,* 17/18 January 1987, pp. 169–170;

"Eine groteske Phantomedebatte," *profil,* 17 October 1988;

Kurt Hofmann, ed., *Aus Gesprächen mit Thomas Bernhard* (Vienna: Löcker, 1988);

"Letzte Worte aus der Einsamkeit," *Der Spiegel,* 44 (29 January 1990): 160–170;

André Müller im Gespräch mit Thomas Bernhard (Weitra: Bibliothek der Provinz, 1992);

Interviews (Frankfurt am Main: Suhrkamp, 1992).

Bibliographies:

Charles A. Carpenter, *Modern Drama Scholarship and Criticism 1966–1980: An International Bibliography* (Toronto: University of Toronto Press, 1986), p. 318;

Donald Daviau, "The Reception of Thomas Bernhard in the United States," *Modern Austrian Literature,* 21, nos. 3/4 (1988): 267–276;

Jens Dittmar, *Thomas Bernhard Werkgeschichte,* revised edition (Frankfurt am Main: Suhrkamp, 1990);

Bernhard Sorg and Michael Töteberg, "Thomas Bernhard," in *Kritisches Lexikon sur deutschsprachigen Gegenwartsliteratur,* edited by Heinz Ludwig Arnold (Munich: Edition text + kritik, n.d.), n. pag.

References:

Mark Anderson, "Notes on Thomas Bernhard," *Raritan,* 7 (1987): 81–96;

Arnold Barthofer, "Das Cello und die Peitsche: Beobachtungen zu Bernhards *Die Macht der Gewohnheit,*" *Sprachkunst,* 7 (1976): 294–331;

Barthofer, "King Lear in Dinkelsbühl: Historisch-biographisches zu Thomas Bernhards Theaterstück *Minetti,*" *Maske und Kothurn,* 23 (1977): 158–172;

Barthofer, "The Plays of Thomas Bernhard–A Report," *Modern Austrian Literature,* 11, no. 1 (1978): 21–48;

Barthofer, "Vorliebe für die Kömodie: Todesangst; Anmerkungen zum Kömodienbegriff bei Thomas

Bernhard," *Vierteljahresschrift des Adalbert-Stifter-Instituts,* 31 (1982): 77–100;

Peter von Becker, "Bei Bernhard: Eine Geschichte in 15 Episoden," *Theater heute,* supplement 1977/1978, 19 (1978): 80–87;

Becker, "Die Unvernünftigen sterben nicht aus: Über Thomas Bernhards Vor dem Ruhestand," *Theater heute,* 20 (August 1979): 4–11;

Alexander von Bormann, ed., *Sehnsuchtsangst: Zur österreichischen Literatur der Gegenwart, Kolloquium an der Universität von Amsterdam* (Amsterdam: Rodopi, 1987);

Anneliese Botond, ed., *Über Thomas Bernhard* (Frankfurt am Main: Suhrkamp, 1970);

Denis Calandra, *New German Dramatists* (New York: Grove, 1983), pp. 139–161;

Robert Craft, "Comedian of Horror," *New York Review of Books,* 27 September 1990, pp. 40–48;

Gordon Craig, *The Germans* (New York: Putnam, 1982), pp. 229–230;

Michel Demet, "Le Théâtre de Thomas Bernhard," *Etudes germaniques,* 31 (1976): 58–66;

Peter Demetz, "Thomas Bernhard: The Dark Side of Life," in his *After the Fires: Recent Writing in the Germanies, Switzerland, and Austria* (New York: Harcourt Brace Jovanovich, 1986), pp. 199–212;

A. P. Dierick, "Thomas Bernhard's Austrian Neurosis," *Modern Austrian Literature,* 12, no. 1 (1979): 73–93;

Josef Donnenberg, "Thomas Bernhard und Österreich," *Österreich in Geschichte und Gegenwart,* 14 (1970): 237–251;

Heinz Ehrig, "Probleme des Absurden: Vergleichende Bemerkungen zu Bernhard und Beckett," *Wirkendes Wort,* 29 (1978): 44–64;

Nicholas Eisner, "Theatertheater/Theaterspiele: The Plays of Thomas Bernhard," *Modern Drama,* 30 (March 1987): 104–114;

Ria Endres, *Am Ende angekommen: Dargestellt am wahnhaften Dunkel der Männerporträts des Thomas Bernhard* (Frankfurt am Main: Fischer, 1980);

Martin Esslin, "Beckett and Bernhard: A Comparison," *Modern Austrian Literature,* 18, no. 2 (1985): 67–78;

Esslin, "Contemporary Austrian Playwrights," *Performing Arts Journal,* 3 (Spring/Summer 1978): 93–98;

Esslin, "A Drama of Disease and Derision: The Plays of Thomas Bernhard," *Modern Drama,* 23 (January 1981): 367–384;

Betty Falkenberg, "Thomas Bernhard," *Partisan Review,* 47, no. 2 (1980): 269–277;

Joseph Federico, "Millenarianism, Legitimation, and the National Socialist Universe in Thomas Bernhard's *Vor dem Ruhestand,*" *Germanic Review,* 59 (Fall 1984): 142–148;

Ulrich Gaier, "*Ein Fest für Boris* oder das Ende der Hermeneutik," *Deutschunterricht,* 36 (1984): 31–40;

Herbert Gamper, *Thomas Bernhard* (Munich: Deutscher Taschenbuch Verlag, 1977);

Rüdiger Görner, "Thomas Bernhard," in *A Radical Stage,* edited by W. G. Sebald (Oxford: Berg, 1988), pp. 161–173;

Görner, "Thomas Bernhard as Dramatic Writer," *Neue Rundschau,* 99 (1988): 157–171;

Robert Gross, Jr., "The Perils of Performance in Thomas Bernhard's *Der Ignorant und der Wahnsinnige,*" *Modern Drama,* 23 (January 1981): 385–392;

Götz Großklaus, "Österreichische Mythen: Zu zwei Filmen von Bernhard und Handke," *Lili,* 29 (1978): 40–62;

Bruno Hannemann, "Satirisches Psychogramm der Mächtigen: Zur Kunst der Provokation in Thomas Bernhards *Der Präsident,*" *Maske und Kothurn,* 23 (1977): 147–158;

Hannemann, "Totentanz der Marionetten: Monotonie und Manier bei Thomas Bernhard," *Modern Austrian Literature,* 13, no. 2 (1980): 123–150;

Hannemann, "Vernunft und Irrfahrt: Zu Thomas Bernhards Komödie Immanuel Kant," *Maske und Kothurn,* 27 (1981): 346–359;

"*Heldenplatz*-Skandal: Stille Post," *Wochenpresse* (Vienna), 20 January 1989, pp. 43–44;

Benjamin Henrichs, "Heldenplatz, die Schlacht ums Wiener Burgtheater," *Die Zeit,* 21 October 1988, pp. 67–68;

Henrichs, "Ein Toter wird ermordet: *Elisabeth II.,* die letzte Thomas Bernhard Uraufführung," *Die Zeit,* 10 November 1989, p. 80;

Hannes Höller, "Die Form der Sprache und die Form der Gesellschaft: Zu Bernhards *Ein Fest für Boris,*" *Acta Universitatis Wratislaviensis,* 26 (1976): 203–219;

Gitta Honegger, "Acoustic Masks: Strategies of Language in the Theater of Canetti, Bernhard, and Handke," *Modern Austrian Literature,* 18, no. 2 (1985): 57–66;

Honegger, "How German Is It? Thomas Bernhard at the Guthrie," *Performing Arts Journal,* 6, no. 1 (1981): 7–25;

Honegger, "Wittgenstein's Children: The Writings of Thomas Bernhard," *Theater,* Yale University, 15 (Winter 1983): 58–62;

Werner Jung, "Die Anstrengung des Erinnerns," *Neue Deutsche Hefte,* 35 (1988): 96–104;

Manfred Jurgensen, ed., *Bernhard: Annäherungen* (Bern & Munich: Francke, 1981);

Dieter Kafitz, "Die Problematisierung des individualistischen Menschenbildes im deutschsprachigen Theater der Gegenwart," *Basis,* 10 (1980): 93–126;

Ulrich Klingemann, "Begriff und Struktur des Komischen in Thomas Bernhards Dramen," *Wirkendes Wort,* 34 (1984): 78–87;

Gerhard Knapp, "Der Prozeß hat kaum begonnen: Thomas Bernhard und die Literaturwissenschaften," *Österreich in Geschichte und Gegenwart,* 15 (1971): 347–350;

Wolfgang Kralicek, "Sein Wille geschehe: Thomas Bernhards letzter Text sorgt posthum für Erregung," *Wochenpresse* (Vienna), 24 February 1989, pp. 42–43;

Renate Latimer, "Thomas Bernhard's Image of Woman," *Germanic Notes,* 8, no. 1 (1977): 25–27;

Hans Lietzau, "Zum Tod von Thomas Bernhard," *Theater heute,* 30 (April 1989): 17–20;

Caroline Markolin, *Die Großväter sind die Lehrer: Johannes Freumbichler und sein Enkel Thomas Bernhard* (Salzburg: Müller, 1988); translated by Petra Hartweg as *Thomas Bernhard and His Grandfather Johannes Freumbichler: Our Grandfathers are Our Teachers* (Riverside, Cal.: Ariadne, 1993);

Terrill May, "Thomas Bernhard's *Der Ignorant und der Wahnsinnige:* An Analysis of Dramatic Style," *Modern Language Studies,* 9 (Winter 1978–1979): 60–72;

Siegfried Melchinger, "Das Material ist die Wahrheit der Welt: *Die Jagdgesellschaft,*" *Theater heute,* 15 (June 1974): 8–9;

Franz N. Mennemeier, "Nachhall des absurden Dramas: Thomas Bernhard," in *Modernes deutsches Drama: Kritiken und Charakteristiken,* volume 2, edited by Mennemeier (Munich: Fink, 1975), pp. 307–320;

Michael Merschmeier, "Heldenspatz: Thomas Bernhards Heldenplatz am Wiener Burgtheater: Anmerkungen zu einem Theaterskandal," *Theater heute,* 29 (December 1988): 1–4;

Nicholas J. Meyerhofer, *Thomas Bernhard,* Köpfe des 20. Jahrhunderts, 104 (Berlin: Colloquium, 1985);

Rolf Michaelis, "Mein Salzburg–eine Todesstadt: Das Neueste vom Dauerkrach Thomas Bernhards mit den Salzburger Festspielen," *Die Zeit,* 29 August 1975, p. 33;

Modern Austrian Literature, special Bernhard issue, 21, nos. 3/4 (1988);

Ingrid Petrasch, *Die Konstitution von Wirklichkeit in der Prosa Thomas Bernhards* (Frankfurt am Main: Lang, 1987);

Alfred Pittertschatscher, ed., *Literarisches Kolloquium Linz '84 Thomas Bernhard,* Schriftenreihe literarisches Kolloquium Linz, 1 (Linz: Land Oberösterreich, 1985);

Henning Rischbieter, "Salzburg/Strehler/Bernhard: Die Festspielkrise," *Theater heute,* 15 (September 1974): 31–36;

Amity Schlaes, "Thomas Bernhard and the German Literary Scene," *New Criterion,* 5 (January 1982): 26–32;

Wendelin Schmidt-Dengler, *Der Übertreibungskünstler: Studien zu Thomas Bernhard,* revised edition (Vienna: Sonderzahl, 1989);

Schmidt-Dengler and Martin Huber, eds., *Statt Bernhard: Über Misanthropie im Werk Thomas Bernhards* (Vienna: Edition S, 1987);

Helmut Schödel, "Wenn ihr nicht brav seid, kommt der Bernhard: Ohlsdorf nach dem Tod des Dichters," *Die Zeit,* 11 August 1989, pp. 15–16;

Zdenko Skreb, "Weltbild und Form bei Thomas Bernhard," in *Literatur aus Österreich, österreichische Literatur,* edited by Karl Konrad Polheim (Bonn: Bouvier, 1981), pp. 145–166;

Bernhard Sorg, *Thomas Bernhard,* Autorenbücher, 7 (Munich: Beck, 1977);

Hilde Spiel, "Das Dunkel ist Licht genug: Die Salzburger Festspiele 1972," *Theater heute,* 13 (September 1972): 8–14;

Botho Strauß, "Komödie aus Todesangst: Thomas Bernhard Ein Fest für Boris in Berlin," *Theater heute,* 11 (August 1970): 30–32;

Text und Kontext, special Bernhard issue, 14 (1987);

text + kritik, special Bernhard issue, 43 (1974);

Erika Tunner, "Absolutheitsstreben oder Vernichtungsdrang," *Revue d'Allemagne,* 8 (October/December 1976): 584–600;

Tunner, "Thematik der Regression bei Thomas Bernhard," *Austriaca* (Rouen), 7 (November 1978): 23–36;

Albrecht Weber, "Wittgensteins Gestalt und Theorie und ihre Wirkung im Werk Thomas Bernhards," *Österreich in Geschichte und Literatur,* 25 (1981): 86–104;

Ernst Wendt, "Krankheit als musikalisches Problem," *Theater heute,* 13 (September 1972): 33–34;

Benno von Wiese, "Thomas Bernhard," in *Otium et Negotium,* edited by Folke Sandgren (Stockholm: Kungl, 1972), pp. 632–646.

Heinrich Böll

(21 December 1917 – 16 July 1985)

Reinhard K. Zachau
University of the South

This entry originally appeared in DLB 69: Contemporary German Fiction Writers, First Series.

BOOKS: *Der Zug war pünktlich: Erzählung* (Opladen: Middelhauve, 1949); translated by Richard Graves as *The Train Was on Time* (London: Arco, 1956; New York: Criterion Books, 1956);

Wanderer, kommst du nach Spa . . . : Erzählungen (Opladen: Middelhauve, 1950); translated by Mervyn Savill as *Traveller, If You Come to Spa . . .* (London: Arco, 1956);

Die schwarzen Schafe: Erzählung (Opladen: Middelhauve, 1951);

Wo warst du, Adam? Roman (Opladen: Middelhauve, 1951); translated by Savill as *Adam, Where Art Thou?* (New York: Criterion Books, 1955); translated by Leila Vennewitz as "And Where Were You, Adam?," in *Adam and The Train: Two Novels* (New York: McGraw-Hill, 1970);

Nicht nur zur Weihnachtszeit (Frankfurt: Frankfurter Verlagsanstalt, 1952); published with *Der Mann mit den Messern,* edited by Dorothea Berger (New York: American Book Co., 1959);

Und sagte kein einziges Wort: Roman (Cologne & Berlin: Kiepenheuer & Witsch, 1953); translated by Graves as *Acquainted with the Night: A Novel* (New York: Holt, 1954); translated by Vennewitz as *And Never Said a Word* (New York: McGraw-Hill, 1978);

Haus ohne Hüter: Roman (Cologne & Berlin: Kiepenheuer & Witsch, 1954); translated by Savill as *The Unguarded House* (London: Arco, 1957); translation republished as *Tomorrow and Yesterday* (New York: Criterion Books, 1957);

Das Brot der frühen Jahre: Erzählung (Cologne & Berlin: Kiepenheuer & Witsch, 1955); translated by Savill as *The Bread of Our Early Years* (London: Arco, 1957); translated by Vennewitz as *The Bread of Those Early Years* (New York: McGraw-Hill, 1976);

So ward Abend und Morgen: Erzählungen (Zurich: Arche, 1955);

Unberechenbare Gäste: Heitere Erzählungen (Zurich: Arche, 1956);

Irisches Tagebuch (Cologne & Berlin: Kiepenlieuer & Witsch, 1957); translated by Vennewitz as *Irish*

Journal (New York: McGraw-Hill, 1967; London: Secker & Warburg, 1983);

Im Tal der donnernden Hufe: Erzählung (Wiesbaden: Insel, 1957); edited by James Alldridge (London: Heinemann Educational, 1970);

Abenteuer eines Brotbeutels, und andere Geschichten, edited by Richard Plant (New York: Norton, 1957);

Die Spurlosen: Hörspiel (Hamburg: Hans Bredow-Institut, 1957); published with Leopold Ahlsen, *Philemon und Baukis,* edited by Anna Otten (New York: Odyssey, 1967);

Doktor Murkes gesammeltes Schweigen und andere Satiren (Cologne & Berlin: Kiepenheuer & Witsch, 1958); edited by Gertrud Seidmann (London: Harrap, 1963);

Der Wegwerfer: Erzählung (Alfeld-Gronau: Hannoversche Papierfabriken, 1958);

Im Ruhrgebiet, text by Böll, illustrations by Karl Hargesheimer (Frankfurt am Main: Büchergilde Gutenberg, 1958);

Die ungezählte Geliebte (Zollikofen: Privately printed, 1958);

Die Waage der Baleks und andere Erzählungen (Berlin: Union, 1959);

Billard um halb zehn: Roman (Cologne & Berlin: Kiepenheuer & Witsch, 1959); translated by Patrick Bowles as *Billiards at Half-past Nine* (London: Weidenfeld & Nicolson, 1961; New York: McGraw-Hill, 1962);

Der Mann mit den Messern: Erzählungen (Stuttgart: Reclam, 1959); published with *Nicht nur zur Weihnachtszeit,* edited by Berger (New York: American Book Co., 1959);

Der Bahnhof von Zimpren: Erzählungen (Munich: List, 1959);

Aus unseren Tagen, edited by Gisela Stein (New York: Holt, Rinehart & Winston, 1960);

Menschen am Rhein, text by Böll, illustrations by Hargesheimer (Frankfurt am Main: Büchergilde Gutenberg, 1960);

Brief an einen jungen Katholiken (Cologne & Berlin: Kiepenheuer & Witsch, 1961);

Bilanz; Klopfzeichen: Zwei Hörspiele (Stuttgart: Reclam, 1961);

Erzählungen, Hörspiele, Aufsätze (Cologne & Berlin: Kiepenheuer & Witsch, 1961);

Als der Krieg ausbrach; Als der Krieg zu Ende war: Zwei Erzählungen (Frankfurt am Main: Insel, 1962); translated by Vennewitz as "Enter and Exit," in *Absent without Leave: Two Novellas* (New York: McGraw-Hill, 1965); translation republished in *Absent without Leave and Other Stories* (London: Weidenfeld & Nicolson, 1967);

Ein Schluck Erde: Drama (Cologne & Berlin: Kiepenheuer & Witsch, 1962);

Assisi (Munich: Knorr & Hirth, 1962);

Ansichten eines Clowns: Roman (Cologne & Berlin: Kiepenheuer & Witsch, 1963); translated by Vennewitz as *The Clown* (New York: McGraw-Hill, 1965);

Hierzulande: Aufsätze (Munich: Deutscher Taschenbuch Verlag, 1963);

1947 bis 1951: Erzählungen (Cologne & Opladen: Middelhauve, 1963); translated by Vennewitz as *Children Are Civilians, Too* (New York: McGraw-Hill, 1970);

Die Essenholer und andere Erzählungen, edited by Fritz Bachmann (Frankfurt am Main: Hirschgraben-Verlag, 1963);

Zum Tee bei Dr. Borsig: Hörspiele (Munich: Deutscher Taschenbuch Verlag, 1964);

Entfernung von der Truppe: Erzählung (Cologne & Berlin: Kiepenheuer & Witsch, 1964); translated by Vennewitz as "Absent without Leave," in *Absent without Leave: Two Novellas* (New York: McGraw-Hill, 1965); translation republished in *Absent without Leave and Other Stories* (London: Weidenfeld & Nicolson, 1967);

Der Rat des Weltunweisen: Roman (Gütersloh: Mohn, 1965);

Frankfurter Vorlesungen (Cologne: Kiepenheuer & Witsch, 1966);

Ende einer Dienstfahrt: Erzählung (Cologne: Kiepenheuer & Witsch, 1966); translated by Vennewitz as *End of a Mission* (New York: McGraw-Hill, 1967); translation republished as *The End of a Mission* (London: Weidenfeld & Nicolson, 1968);

Die Spurlosen: Drei Hörspiele (Leipzig: Insel, 1966);

18 Stories, translated by Vennewitz (New York: McGraw-Hill, 1966);

Aufsätze, Kritiken, Reden (Cologne: Kiepenheuer & Witsch, 1967);

Georg Büchners Gegenwärtigkeit: Eine Rede (Berlin: Friedenauer Presse, 1967);

Hausfriedensbruch: Hörspiel; Aussatz: Schauspiel (Cologne: Kiepenheuer & Witsch, 1969);

Leben im Zustand des Frevels: Ansprache zur Verleihung des Kölner Literaturpreises (Berlin: Berliner Handpresse, 1969);

Geschichten aus zwölf Jahren (Frankfurt am Main: Suhrkamp, 1969);

Böll für Zeitgenossen: Ein kulturgeschichtliches Lesebuch, edited by Ralph Ley (New York: Harper & Row, 1970);

Gruppenbild mit Dame: Roman (Cologne: Kiepenheuer & Witsch, 1971); translated by Vennewitz as *Group Portrait with Lady* (New York: McGraw-Hill, 1973);

Erzählungen, 1950–1970 (Cologne: Kiepenheuer & Witsch, 1972);

Gedichte (Berlin: Literarisches Colloquium, 1972);

Versuch über die Vernunft der Poesie: Nobelvorlesung (Stockholm: Norstedt & Söner, 1973);

Neue politische und literarische Schriften (Cologne: Kiepenheuer & Witsch, 1973);

Die verlorene Ehre der Katharina Blum oder wie Gewalt entstehen und wohin sie führen kann: Erzählung (Cologne: Kiepenheuer & Witsch, 1974); translated by Vennewitz as *The Lost Honor of Katharina Blum: How Violence Develops and Where It Can Lead* (New York: McGraw-Hill, 1975);

Drei Tage im März: Ein Gespräch, by Böll and Christian Linder (Cologne: Kiepenheuer & Witsch, 1975);

Berichte zur Gesinnungslage der Nation (Cologne: Kiepenheuer & Witsch, 1975);

Gedichte: Mit Collagen von Klaus Staeck (Cologne: Labbe und Muta, 1975);

Wie kritisch darf engagierte Kunst sein? (Munich: Presseausschuß Demokratische Initiative, 1976);

Einmischung erwünscht: Schriften zur Zeit (Cologne: Kiepenheuer & Witsch, 1977);

Werke: Romane und Erzählungen, edited by B. Balzer, 5 volumes (Cologne: Middelhauve/Kiepenheuer & Witsch, 1977);

Missing Persons and Other Essays, translated by Vennewitz (New York: McGraw-Hill, 1977);

Werke: Essayistische Schriften und Reden, Interviews, edited by Balzer, 4 volumes (Cologne: Kiepenheuer & Witsch, 1978);

Hörspiele, Theaterstücke, Drehbücher, Gedichte, edited by Balzer (Cologne: Kiepenheuer & Witsch, 1978);

Mein Lesebuch (Frankfurt am Main: Fischer, 1978);

Eine deutsche Erinnerung: Interview mit René Wintzen (Cologne: Kiepenheuer & Witsch, 1979);

Du fährst zu oft nach Heidelberg und andere Erzählungen (Bornheim-Merten: Lamuv, 1979);

Fürsorgliche Belagerung: Roman (Cologne: Kiepenheuer & Witsch, 1979); translated by Vennewitz as *The Safety Net* (Franklin Center, Pa.: Franklin Library, 1981; London: Secker & Warburg, 1982);

Ein Tag wie sonst: Hörspiele (Munich: Deutscher Taschenbuch Verlag, 1980);

Was soll aus dem Jungen bloß werden? Oder: Irgendwas mit Büchern (Bornheim-Merten: Lamuv, 1981); translated by Vennewitz as *What's to Become of the Boy? or, Something to Do with Books* (New York: Knopf, 1984);

Eine deutsche Erinnerung: Interview mit René Wintzen (Munich: Deutscher Taschenbuch Verlag, 1981);

Warum haben wir aufeinander geschossen?, by Böll and Lev Kopelev (Bornheim-Merten: Lamuv, 1981);

Der Autor ist immer noch versteckt, by Böll and Jürgen Wallmann (Hauzenberg: Pongratz, 1981);

Vermintes Gelände: Essayistische Schriften 1977–1981 (Cologne: Kiepenheuer & Witsch, 1982);

Verantwortlich für Polen? (Reinbek: Rowohlt, 1982);

Das Vermächtnis: Kurzroman (Bornheim-Merten: Lamuv, 1982); translated by Vennewitz as *A Soldier's Legacy* (New York: Knopf, 1985; London: Secker & Warburg, 1985);

Antikommunismus in Ost und West (Cologne: Bund-Verlag, 1982);

Die Verwundung und andere frühe Erzählungen (Bornheim-Merten: Lamuv, 1983); translated by Vennewitz as *The Casualty* (New York: Farrar, Straus & Giroux, 1987);

Der Angriff (Cologne: Kiepenheuer & Witsch, 1983);

Bild, Bonn, Boenisch (Bornheim-Merten: Lamuv, 1984);

Katholisch und rebellisch: Ein Wegweiser durch, die andere Kirche (Reinbek: Rowohlt, 1984);

Veränderungen in Staech: Erzählungen 1962–1980 (Cologne: Kiepenheuer & Witsch, 1984);

Weil die Stadt so fremd geworden ist (Bornheim-Merten: Lamuv, 1985);

Die Juden von Drove (Berlin: Rütten & Loening, 1985);

Heinrich Böll, on His Death (Bonn: Inter Nationes, 1985);

Frauen vor Flußlandschaft: Roman in Dialogen und Selbstgesprächen (Cologne: Kiepenheuer & Witsch, 1985); translated by David McLintock as *Women in a River Landscape: A Novel in Dialogues and Soliloquies* (New York: Knopf, 1988);

The Short Stories of Heinrich Böll, translated by Vennewitz (New York: Knopf, 1986);

Die Fähigkeit zu trauern (Bornheim-Merten: Lamuv, 1986);

Feindbild und Frieden: Schriften und Reden, 1982–1983 (Munich: Deutscher Taschenbuch, 1987);

Rom auf den ersten Blick: Landschaften, Städte, Reisen (Bornheim-Merten: Lamuv, 1987);

Der Engel schweig: Roman (Cologne: Kiepenheuer & Witsch, 1992); translated by Breon Mitchell as *The Silent Angel* (New York: St. Martin's Press, 1994);

Der blasse Hund: Erzählungen (Cologne: Kiepenheuer & Witsch, 1995);

The Mad Dog: Stories, translated by Mitchell (New York: St. Martin's Press, 1997).

OTHER: Wolfgang Borchert, *Draußen vor der Tür und ausgewählte Geschichten,* afterword by Böll (Hamburg: Rowohlt, 1956);

Ein Artikel und seine Folgen, edited by Böll and Franz Grützbach (Bornheim-Merten: Lamuv, 1982).

TRANSLATIONS: Patrick White, *Zur Ruhe kam der Baum des Menschen nie,* translated by Böll and Annemarie Böll (Cologne: Kiepenheuer & Witsch, 1957);

Bernard Malamud, *Der Gehilfe,* translated by Böll and Annemarie Böll (Cologne: Kiepenheuer & Witsch, 1960);

J. M. Synge, *Ein wahrer Held,* translated by Böll and Annemarie Böll (Berlin: Kiepenheuer & Witsch, 1960);

J. D. Salinger, *Der Fänger im Roggen,* translated by Böll (Cologne: Kiepenheuer & Witsch, 1962);

Salinger, *Franny und Zooey,* translated by Böll and Annemarie Böll (Cologne: Kiepenheuer & Witsch, 1963);

George Bernard Shaw, *Caesar und Cleopatra,* translated by Böll and Annemarie Böll (Frankfurt: Suhrkamp, 1965).

When in the summer of 1972 Heinrich Böll received the news that he had been awarded the Nobel Prize in literature, he responded with the surprised question: "Was, ich, und nicht Günter Grass?" (Really? I, and not Günter Grass?). This reaction summarizes Böll's assessment of his place in West German postwar literature–sometimes referred to as "Grass-Böll-literature"–and it reflects Böll's competition with Grass, who is generally regarded by critics as the superior writer. Böll's sales figures, however, tell a different story: with 31 million books in print and having been translated into forty-five languages, he is by far the most popular of all modern German writers. In his unpretentious style he became a chronologist of the first forty years of the Federal Republic of Germany. The reader recognizes himself and people he knows in Böll's books; the simple ideas of this modest man influenced the way Germans look at their second republic. Böll became an important public figure in Germany–much against his will: when a poll was conducted in the 1970s to determine the ten most influential people in West Germany, Böll was mentioned in fourth place, after the politicians Helmut Schmidt, Willy Brandt, and Franz Josef Strauß as the man who "represents our conscience."

Heinrich Theodor Böll was born in Cologne on 21 December 1917, to Victor Böll and his second wife, Marie Hermanns Böll, during the worst famine year of World War I. Böll had two older brothers and three older sisters. His mother was an energetic, domineering woman from a long line of Catholic farmers and brewers. His father's family, Catholics who had preferred emigration to the state religion of Henry VIII, had come centuries earlier from the British Isles. Victor Böll had moved to Cologne from Essen in 1896, at the age of twenty-six, to "move up" socially and, together with an associate, to start his own business as a carpenter and wood sculptor; he worked ambitiously for fifty years, much like Heinrich Fähmel in Heinrich Böll's novel *Billard um halb zehn* (1959; translated as *Billiards at Half-past Nine,* 1961). Victor Böll was a sensitive, nervous man who liked to tell stories to his sons. His tastes

were neoclassic; he created the kind of sculptures that were in demand during the second German empire, which he supported enthusiastically. During World War I, however, Victor's enthusiasm for the Kaiser–"der kaiserliche Narr" (the imperial fool)–changed to cynicism. It is clear that Böll inherited his anti-Prussian attitude from his father. But if Böll represented the attitude of the citizens of Cologne as far as Prussia was concerned, his postwar antiestablishment position did not reflect the prevailing mood at the time.

The Böll family at first lived in an apartment but soon acquired their own home in Cologne-Raderberg, Kreuznacher Straße 49. Böll recalled his childhood years as happy ones, and some critics see his writings as an attempt to reconstruct his lost childhood experiences in the modern technological world. Böll's parents were broad-minded and never forced their children to join the Catholic Church. They also allowed them to play with the children of socialists in their neighborhood, something that the professors, attorneys, architects, and bank directors strictly forbade their children. This childhood paradise ended when Böll entered a Catholic elementary school in 1924, while most of his friends entered public school. Böll later attended the Kaiser-Wilhelm-Gymnasium, which made him more aware of social distinctions: he could not understand why the "Reds" could not go with him.

In October 1930 Böll's father lost his business in the Great Depression, and the family had to sell the house and their possessions. This experience brought Böll even closer to his parents, especially when he realized "daß meine Eltern völlig hilflos waren gegenüber diesen Umständen" (that my parents were totally helpless in the face of these conditions). The Bölls had to move several times, the bill collector appeared on numerous occasions, and they were forced to rent out rooms in their apartment. The family was slipping out of the middle class but was not really establishing itself in a new class. These experiences explain why Böll sometimes described himself as proletarian, sometimes as "kleinbürgerlich" (lower middle class).

When Adolf Hitler became chancellor in 1933, Böll, in bed with the flu, heard his mother say: "That means war." During his last years at the gymnasium, Böll saw how the Nazis brought the unemployment caused by the Great Depression under control: "Einige Jahre später waren die Arbeitslosen untergebracht, sie wurden Polizisten, Soldaten, Henker, Rüstungsarbeiter–der Rest zog in die Konzentrationslager" (A few years later the unemployed were taken care of: they were given work as policemen, soldiers, executioners, and armament workers–the rest were sent into concentration camps). His parents permitted secret meetings of the illegal Catholic Youth in their apartment, while his teachers tried to remain neutral. Literature became Böll's main interest in those years: he read Leon Bloy, Georges Bernanos, Charles Dickens, Honoré de Balzac, and the German dramatists Heinrich von Kleist and Friedrich Hebbel, who were to become his models. He withdrew into reading to the point of neglecting his studies and having to repeat a grade.

After graduating from the gymnasium in 1937 Böll worked in a bookstore in Bonn, where he catalogued collections of old books for ten marks a month. The job brought him into his first contact with banned books such as the works of Sigmund Freud and Karl Marx. He soon quit, considered becoming a librarian, began writing, and worked as a tutor but essentially did not know what to do. His mother worried: "Was soll aus dem Jungen bloß werden?" (What is to become of the boy?). Everything in those days, Böll later said in an interview, was overshadowed by the prospect of the war that many sensed was coming. Before he could be admitted to a university, Böll had to perform the compulsory labor service to which all high school graduates were called. In the winter of 1938–1939 he dug irrigation ditches and worked in the forests in Hesse. After completion of his labor service he enrolled at the University of Cologne to study German and classical philology and literature. In early 1939 he was called into military service for an eight-week training course. When the war broke out in September, he was called to active duty as an infantryman and served in France, Poland, and then again in France, where his right hand was wounded when the train in which he was traveling struck a mine. In 1942 Böll married Annemarie Cech. That same year his parents' apartment was destroyed in an air raid; the family was evacuated to Ahrweiler, where his mother died during another air raid. The family was then evacuated to the Bergisches Land, a rural area east of Cologne. In the summer of 1943 Böll was sent to the Crimea, where he was wounded in the leg. Shortly afterward he was struck in the head by a shell fragment and was sent to a hospital in Odessa. The front, however, was rapidly approaching the city, and Böll was quickly released from the hospital. He was transferred to Jassy in Romania; eight days after arriving there he was seriously wounded in the back. He managed to stay in a hospital in Hungary until August 1944. By this time he was trying to evade the army by faking illness. He deserted in February or March 1945. In the confusion of the final days of the war, he was able to rejoin the army in time to be taken prisoner by the Americans on 9 April 1945, thereby guaranteeing that he would obtain the proper army release papers. He was imprisoned in France and Belgium until the fall.

In November 1945 Böll and his family returned to Cologne. His first son, Christoph, who had been born earlier that year, died that winter. Cologne was almost totally destroyed; only three hundred buildings were without damage, and there was no transportation, no water, and no electricity. Böll enrolled at the University of Cologne in 1945, not to study but to acquire a ration card. He worked for a while in the family carpentry shop but soon found temporary employment with the statistical office of the City of Cologne; the family was dependent, however, on his wife's income as a middle-school teacher. During this time Böll wrote industriously and in 1947 published two outstanding short stories, "Die Botschaft" (The Message; translated as "Breaking the News") and "Kumpel mit dem langen Haar" (Coal Miner with the Long Hair; translated as "My Pal with the Long Hair"), in the periodical *Karussell*.

These and other stories were printed in newspapers such as the *Rheinischer Merkur* and in Alfred Andersch's magazine *Der Ruf* and were published in book form in 1950 as *Wanderer, Kommst du nach Spa . . .* (translated as *Traveller, If You Come to Spa . . .*, 1956). These stories can be separated into two groups: war stories and stories dealing with the immediate postwar era. The war stories are told in the first person; the narrator is a typical, usually unnamed German soldier who relates Böll's own experiences and dreams of a better world. The latter are normally the unpolitical, middle-class dreams of good books in a quiet home, a family, music, and art. The most common pattern is the fatal outcome; the hero usually does not survive. The mood of these stories is best characterized by a sentence from "Die Botschaft" where the narrator has to tell a woman that her husband has been killed in the war: "Da wußte ich, daß der Krieg niemals zu Ende sein würde, niemals, solange noch irgendwo eine Wunde blutete, die er geschlagen hat" (Then I knew that the war would never be finished, never as long as somewhere a wound was bleeding that it had caused). One of Böll's concerns in these stories was to refute the notion of heroism in war; most men of his generation realized the absurdity of their existence under war conditions.

The tales about the postwar period typically describe returning veterans who do not benefit from the "Wirtschaftswunder" (economic miracle) after the Currency Reform of 1948; these unfortunate men are looking for their niche in the new society. One man counts people crossing a bridge for a statistical office, but he never counts his girlfriend, in order to maintain her "humanity." Such individual forms of resistance constituted a theme which was to become Böll's central message in the next decades.

The stories did not provide enough money to support his family, which by then included three children: Raimund, born in 1947; René, born in 1948; and Vincent, born in 1950. The publication of his first two novels did not change Böll's financial situation significantly, partly because his publisher, Middelhauve, was mainly a publisher of science books and was not interested in promoting literature. In 1949 Middelhauve had published Böll's first book, *Der Zug war pünktlich* (translated as *The Train Was on Time*, 1956), the structure of which closely resembles that of a classical novella. A soldier, Andreas, boards an army train to join a unit in the Ukraine. He travels through Dresden and Krakow, and finally arrives in Lemberg, where two other soldiers take him to an expensive restaurant and a bordello. There he meets the Polish resistance fighter Olina, for whom he develops a platonic affection. Andreas, Olina, and the two other soldiers decide to flee in a general's car, and all are killed when a mortar fired by partisans strikes the vehicle. The tension and atmosphere of the story are created by Andreas's premonition at the beginning of the trip that he will never see Germany again. He knows he will die near Lemberg because his mind goes blank when he thinks of the next town, Stry. This unrealistic element of "fate" gives Böll's style its special quality. The reader is convinced of Andreas's ability to see the future and thus anticipates his death. The novella takes on biblical dimensions: Andreas is seen as Jesus at the Last Supper and as having a Jesus-Mary Magdalene relationship with Olina. He persuades Olina to give up her political undercover war, which he considers immoral and insignificant. In the same way, Andreas is apolitical in his relationship to Nazi Germany. *Der Zug war pünktlich,* with its religious and mystical treatment of the war, shows Böll's own limited understanding during the period 1945 to 1950 of the social aspects and causes of the war. The formal achievement of the novella, however, and its humanistic, antifascist spirit, drew praise. Gert Kalow calls it a "Geniewurf" (stroke of genius), and Theodore Ziolkowski writes: "Never again has Böll written a story of such close perfection and inevitability. . . . It is an artistic tour de force." The success of *Der Zug* can also be seen in the fact that in 1949 Böll was invited to read at a meeting of the Gruppe 47, the major German literary group of the 1950s and 1960s.

Böll's most famous war novel, *Wo warst du, Adam?* (translated as *Adam, Where Art Thou?*, 1955), was published in 1951. Minor characters in earlier chapters become main characters in later ones; except for this aspect, the chapters are not connected and can be seen as independent short stories. The chapter about the building of the bridge at Berczaby, in fact, has been performed separately as a radio play. The Ilona episode is an early treatment of concentration camps in postwar German fiction: when Ilona sings the Litany of the

Saints, the camp commander, Filskeit, comprehends the monstrousness of the death camps. The book's main theme is the absurdity of man's existence; the deaths of Feinhals and his parents at his parents' home caused by German artillery fire show that there is no escape from the senselessness of the war. After publication of *Wo warst du, Adam?,* the Gruppe 47 again invited Böll to one of their meetings. He read his humorous story *Die schwarzen Schafe* (The Black Sheep, 1951), for which he received a prize of 1,000 marks and an invitation to attend subsequent meetings.

A third novel about World War II, written at about the same time as *Der Zug war pünktlich* and *Wo warst du, Adam?,* was published in 1982 by Böll's son René under the title *Das Vermächtnis* (translated as *A Soldier's Legacy,* 1985). It takes place in 1943 in France. The commanding officer, Schelling, is trying to find out why his soldiers' food rations are being illegally withheld. When he discovers that Captain Schnecker is partly responsible, Schnecker kills him. As is often the case in Böll's works, the compassionate die and the heartless survive, eventually to play a leading role in postwar society.

In "Die Waage der Baleks" (The Balek Scales, 1952), one of his most popular stories, Böll introduced the overriding concern in his writing, the criticism of postwar materialism. Here, however, he approaches the subject indirectly, setting the story of capitalist exploitation in a provincial Austrian town around 1900. Although the story involves a failed proletarian revolt, it does not advocate revolution.

With the novel *Und sagte kein einziges Wort* (And Said Not a Single Word, 1953; translated as *Acquainted with the Night,* 1954) Böll switched to the publisher Kiepenheuer and Witsch and achieved an immediate breakthrough; this work, still one of his best-known books, made him financially independent. Poverty causes the protagonist, Fred Bogner, to become ill; it drives him away from the one room he shares with his wife, Käte, and their children. He drifts around the city and meets his wife in cheap hotels on weekends. She is ready to leave him, but in the end they are reconciled. The novel is told in alternating first-person narratives by Fred and Käte. Fred is a drinker, has beaten his children, and is beginning to question the authority of the church. He is not ambitious and feels self-pity for being left out, but he wants no part of the new society. The social criticism is explicit; the author especially criticizes the bigoted landlady, Frau Franke, who refuses to give the family another room, maintaining that she needs it as a reception room for Catholic aid committees. There is corruption in the church: the church offices fail to criticize the pharmaceutical industry for advertising contraceptives because the bishop's cousin is the chairman of the association of druggists. The druggist becomes the personification of modern-day society with its cleanliness, contraception, and mindless consumption. Neither Fred nor Käte accepts these values; Fred sees himself as the only righteous one and defends his own way of life. When he gets back together with Käte, she is expecting another child. The novel demonstrates Böll's meticulously realistic style in its description of the world that surrounds Fred Bogner. Most critics agree that the novel is a preparatory stage to Böll's more political works; many critics deplore its peaceful ending, which, as Günter Wirth points out, is inconsistent with the hostility Fred had shown to society.

Haus ohne Hüter (1954; translated as *The Unguarded House,* 1957) uses film techniques, such as rapid cuts between scenes. The story is told in consecutive chapters by two boys, Martin Bach and Heinrich Brielach; the children's perspective adds an element of alienation, allowing the reader to see the adult world in a different light. Both boys have lost their fathers in the war. Martin's mother, Nella, remains caught in a fantasy world after the death of her husband, the poet Rai. Martin is sent to live in luxury with his grandmother, whose wealth comes from the family's inherited business; Böll rarely depicts a "selfmade" man. Heinrich, on the other hand, has to earn a living for his family on the black market while still attending school. His mother works in a bakery and later moves in with the baker, as she had with several other "uncles" before. The Brielachs are stigmatized because of their poverty and are ashamed to move their modest belongings in front of their curious neighbors.

The novel gains momentum at the end when Gäseler is introduced. During the war Gäseler, who had disliked Rai, had sent the poet on a reconnaissance mission, knowing that he was ill equipped for it and probably would not survive. Since the war Gäseler has become a conformist representative of the new capitalist system; he is vain and opportunistic, not unlike the devil of Nella's fantasies. When Nella asks Gäseler to tell her about the war, he reveals himself as a representative of the times: "Ich denke nicht oft daran. Ich versuche, es zu vergessen, und es gelingt mir. . . . Man muß den Krieg vergessen" (I don't think about it any more. I try to forget it, and I can. . . . People have to forget the war). But he has not forgotten the names of his Nazi heroes; only the death and suffering have been erased from his mind. Nella responds to Gäseler: "Ohrfeigen an Leute verteilen, die den Krieg vergessen haben" (A box on the ears for all the people who have forgotten the war) and walks away.

Das Brot der frühen Jahre (1955; translated as *The Bread of Our Early Years,* 1957) covers time from about eight o'clock in the morning to about eight o'clock in

the evening of a single day in the narrator's life in 1955. Walter Fendrich goes to the train station to meet Hedwig Müller, the daughter of a friend of his father, who is coming to the city to study at the university. Walter has previously found her a room and is to take her there and go back to work. But when he sees Hedwig, his life changes: "Ich sah nur diesen grellgrünen Mantel, sah dieses Gesicht, und ich hatte plötzlich Angst, jene Angst, die Entdecker empfinden, wenn sie das neue Land betreten haben. . . . Dieses Gesicht ging tief in mich hinein . . . es war, als würde ich durchbohrt ohne zu bluten" (I saw only her dazzling green coat, her face, and I was suddenly filled with that fear which explorers have when they enter upon a new land. . . . Her face went deep into me . . . it was as if I had been pierced without bleeding). From this moment on, Walter is a new person. He does not return to his old job, withdraws all his savings from the bank, breaks his engagement to his boss's daughter, and decides to live with Hedwig without the sacrament of the church.

In one of Böll's most beautiful short stories, "Und so ward Abend und Morgen" (And It Became Night and Day, 1955), the relationship between man and woman is symbolized as a cry of a man for company in his lonely life. His wife has stopped talking to him, and on a Christmas evening he makes her say "no" twice and "yes" once—which saves his life.

Böll's treatment of the relationship between the sexes continues in the longer narrative *Im Tal der donnernden Hufe* (In the Valley of the Thundering Hooves, 1957), about the sexual problems of two Catholic boys, Paul and Griff. An atheist girl, Mirzova, helps Paul overcome his anxiety by exposing her breasts; but as a result she has to leave town for a few years to avoid being labeled a prostitute by the narrow-minded townspeople.

In the mid 1950s the Federal Republic of Germany under Chancellor Konrad Adenauer embarked on a rearmament campaign which Böll opposed. Until that time he had been a supporter of Adenauer's Christian Democratic Union (CDU). In response to these developments, Böll "escaped" to Ireland for a few weeks in the summer of 1955. Later, when asked whether Ireland was his second home, he said: "Ich weiß daß es keine zweite Heimat gibt, entweder man emigriert oder behält seine Nationalität—ich bin Deutscher, schreibe deutsch" (I know there is no such thing as a second homeland; either you emigrate, or you keep your nationality—I am a German, I write in German). Böll was a "Kölner" (a person from Cologne); his idea of "home" was centered in Cologne. He could not represent Prussia or the eastern part of Germany.

In 1956 Böll made a second trip to Ireland. His *Irisches Tagebuch* (1957; translated as *Irish Journal,* 1967) resulting from those trips is not a conventional travelogue; rather, Böll uses travel impressions to make moral and historical points about Ireland and Germany. He continues his criticism of German society in this book in a more subtle form.

Another reason for Böll's escape to Ireland was the attacks on some satirical short stories he published in the 1950s, especially *Nicht nur zur Weihnachtszeit* (Not Only at Christmastime, 1952). The mother in a middle-class family has saved Christmas decorations from the prosperous times before the war and protests whenever anybody tries to take the Christmas tree down; so the family celebrates Christmas every day of the year. When Böll was attacked by the church he responded that he had not intended to denounce Christmas but rather the commercialization of it. In "Der Wegwerfer" (The Disposer, 1951) he criticizes the same commercialism by portraying a mailroom clerk whose job is to throw away junk mail, thereby reducing the work load of the others in the office. The satirical story "Doktor Murkes gesammeltes Schweigen" (Dr. Murke's Collected Silences, 1955) is considered by Cesare Cases one of the finest works of European literature since World War II, and Walter Jens claims that Böll's work culminates in this story. The "philosopher" Bur-Malottke wants to change the word *God* in a tape of one of his notorious radio talks to the phrase "jenes höhere Wesen, das wir verehren" (the higher being whom we revere). The word *God* is cut out of the tape and edited into another program, where an atheist's questions are now answered by Bur-Malottke's "God." What is left is cut-out "silence," and the journalist Murke takes the pieces home in a box. Murke shows the absurdity of the procedure when he lets Bur-Malottke say the phrase "the higher being whom we revere" twenty-seven times; he hates Bur-Malottke because of the latter's opportunism. Böll was criticizing the intellectual climate that left religion out of the economic and political restoration of the 1950s: God got "cut out" of social considerations.

Billard um halb zehn, published in 1959, shows the rise of a middle-class family, the Fähmels, through whose perspective the novel presents fifty years of German history from 1907 to 1958. The novel, however, actually covers only a few hours, from about ten o'clock in the morning to about eight o'clock in the evening on 6 September 1958, the eightieth birthday of Heinrich Fähmel, the day his wife shoots at a politician and symbolically destroys corruption. Böll symbolically contrasts those who have partaken of "das Sakrament des Büffels" (the sacrament of the buffalo)—the militarists, Nazis, and the power hungry—to those who have tasted of "das Sakrament des Lamms" (the sacrament of the lamb)—the persecuted, emigrés, and people sensitive to suffering. Böll himself criticized this symbolism later

as being too simplistic to portray the horrors and intricacies of German history. The St. Anton Abbey ties the three generations of Fähmels together: the grandfather built it, the son blew it up, and the grandson does not know whether he wants to reconstruct or demolish it. Some critics claimed that the *nouveau roman* and the psychological novel excluded each other and that Böll failed by trying to combine the two. Böll worked out the novel in a meticulous, almost mathematical, way, using a colored chart divided into three levels: the present, the reflective or memory level, and the symbolic. But the resulting novel is too confusing. Johanna Fähmel's attempt to shoot a high government official with a Nazi past fails to enhance the novel's tension. Walter Jens summarized the views of many critics when he observed that the novel form was too long for Böll, and that he should have stayed with the short story.

In 1961, in one of his fiercest essays, "Hast Du was, dann bist Du was" (You Are What You Have), Böll attacked Cologne's Cardinal Frings for his pastoral letter linking the Bonn government's idea of making stocks available to low-income people to the principles of the Christian Church: "Die Heiligsprechung des Habenichts von Assisi war wohl ein Irrtum" (The canonization of the have-not Francis of Assisi probably was a mistake). Böll also attacked Chancellor Adenauer for too eagerly forgetting Germany's Nazi past and for his socioeconomic policies as outlined in the statement: "Der Erwerb mäßigen Besitzes für alle ehrlich Schaffenden ist zu fördern [und] ist eine wesentliche Sicherung des demokratischen Staates" (The accumulation of a moderate amount of property by all honest workers is to be furthered [and] is an essential guarantee of the democratic state). Böll asked sarcastically: "Was machen wir da bloß mit dem unmäßigen Besitz des unehrlich Schaffenden?" (What are we to do about [the] immoderate property of the dishonest worker [that is, the capitalist]?). In those years Böll also criticized the change by the Social Democrats to a more capitalist ideology, as reflected in the 1959 Godesberg Program of the Social Democratic Party (SPD). An advocate of socialism and even Marxism, Böll wanted two basic sociopolitical concepts to be expressed in the German party system; he was opposed to a system like that of the United States, where both parties advocate capitalism. In his writings Böll tried to change the course of the SPD. In the early 1960s Böll, together with the artist HAP Grieshaber and others, founded the Christian Socialist periodical *Labyrinth*. Here he published his first play, *Ein Schluck Erde* (A Piece of Earth, 1962), about an old man who would like to combine Christianity and communism. In 1960 Böll completed the essay "Karl Marx," which praises the philosopher as a secular saint, and "Assisi," a study of St. Francis. In a 1967 interview with the critic Marcel Reich-Ranicki, Böll confessed his Communist sympathies and wished communism as many years of power as capitalism had already had. He said that if he had not grown up in fascist Germany he would have certainly been a Communist by 1936. Böll also regretted that more Germans had not had the opportunity to become Communists in the 1930s, thereby purifying the political atmosphere.

The *Brief an einen jungen Katholiken* (Letter to a Young Catholic, 1961) reveals that Böll's development toward socialism was related to his disenchantment with the Catholic church. He expresses his disapproval of what he considered the merger of church and government in the Federal Republic at that time. The *Brief an einen jungen Katholiken* started a process that ended with Böll officially leaving the church in 1977 (in Germany this means that he simply stopped paying "church taxes").

In 1962 Böll made his first official trip to the Soviet Union in connection with the new German-Soviet Cultural Exchange Program. At the time he was working on a new book, *Ansichten eines Clowns* (1963; translated as *The Clown*, 1965), one of his most controversial novels. Böll's biographer Klaus Schröter has said that after finishing this book he lost interest in reading Böll for a long time. The novel takes place on one evening in the Bonn apartment of twenty-seven-year-old Hans Schnier, who has left the home of his wealthy parents to earn his living as a clown. Hans is feeling sorry for himself because his girlfriend, Marie, has left him to marry a "Berufskatholik" (professional Catholic). Through phone calls to relatives and friends, Hans learns that Marie is on her honeymoon which will include a visit to the pope. He decides to await her return by singing religious songs at the railroad station while wearing his clown costume. Hans advocates a form of marriage in which the church plays no role and only the mutual consent of the partners matters. With his anarchistic tendencies, it is not surprising that Hans has become a professional clown, entitled, like a medieval court jester, to criticize society.

The novel shows Hans's isolation: he can live only with Marie, and she has left him. Because of his artistic nature, Hans views the living and the dead differently than other people do. His sister Henriette, who died in the war, is alive in his mind, while his mother is dead for him because she adjusts eagerly to the new social conditions and wants to forget. J. D. Salinger's *The Catcher in the Rye* (1951), which Böll and his wife had just translated into German, influenced Böll's writing of the novel; Holden Caulfield's character and his relationship with his sister are clearly reflected in Böll's depiction of Hans.

Ansichten eines Clowns divided the critics into two groups: those who saw it as a lapse in Böll's progress as a writer and those who considered it his best and most straightforward book to that time. Manfred Durzak argued that the novel was an aesthetic dead end for Böll, who had reached his satirical limits. Hans-Joachim Bernhard was of the opinion that the aesthetic balance of the book was disrupted by Böll's subjectivity. But Frank Trommler saw in *Ansichten eines Clowns* a new phase in post–World War II German literary history, characterized by blunt political reasoning instead of formal artistic expression.

The author's detachment from German political life is noticeable in the short novel *Entfernung von der Truppe* (Absent without Leave, 1964). The narrator states that his life as a human being began with his "desertion," his rejection of society. Despite its bleak plot, the story is told in a loose, humorous manner, reminiscent of Laurence Sterne. Böll's effort to experiment with a different style is not completely successful.

In *Frankfurter Vorlesungen* (Frankfurt Lectures, 1966), given at the University of Frankfurt after a long stay in Dugort, Ireland, where he had bought a home, Böll says that love for one's "Heimat" (homeland), memory, and language constitute the human being. Böll criticizes the German rejection of regionalism in the postwar period, pointing out that many important works of art have been created in cities such as Dublin or Prague. Böll's literary position is "engaged": the poet is to analyze the "Abfall der Gesellschaft" (garbage of society) and take the place of a political opposition that no longer exists in West Germany. The Grand Coalition of the CDU and the SPD from 1966 to 1969 confirmed Böll's political fears.

Ende einer Dienstfahrt (1966; translated as *End of a Mission*, 1967), in its depiction of the military as a senseless machine, is reminiscent of *Wo warst du, Adam?* In classical novella form, the book describes the trial of the Gruhls, a father and son who burn the son's army jeep as an act of protest. The case is an embarrassment to the authorities, who play it down by keeping the press out and by giving the case to a lenient judge. The Gruhls are finally sentenced to only six weeks imprisonment. Böll wanted to show that the ruling class understands the danger of the Gruhls' political action; he also wanted to show the goodness of the village people, all of whom support the Gruhls. The critic Jochen Vogt asserted that this support by the villagers reveals too idealized a sense of "Heimat." The novel, he said, excludes the reader who comes from a different background.

In August 1968 Böll happened to be in Czechoslovakia during the Soviet invasion. This event provided an opportunity for him to protest Soviet policies, which increased his political credibility with the right. He campaigned for Willy Brandt and the Social Democrats (SPD) in the national elections of 1969, seeing the victory of the SPD as a unique opportunity to overcome what he considered the authoritarian government Adenauer's CDU had perpetuated. He also welcomed the defeat of the CDU because it had chosen a former Nazi, Kurt Georg Kiesinger, as its candidate for chancellor. Brandt, Böll wrote, was not a Herr (ruler); for the first time a real human being sat in the Chancellery.

In "Epilog zu Stifters *Nachsommer*" (Epilogue to Stifter's *Indian Summer*, 1970; published in *Erzählungen, 1950–1970*, 1972) Böll imitates the language and plots of the nineteenth-century novelist Adalbert Stifter, whose work he admired. Böll, however, destroys the nineteenth-century middle-class world and shows how that society was based on lies.

In 1971 Böll was elected the first German president of the International PEN Club and visited the New York PEN offices. At the time of Böll's election Hans Werner Richter, the founder of the Gruppe 47, said: "Böll can do things that we others cannot even dream of."

When the Swedish Academy awarded Böll the Nobel Prize in literature in 1972, it especially mentioned *Gruppenbild mit Dame* (1971; translated as *Group Portrait with Lady*, 1973). The publishers called the book Böll's "most comprehensive, encompassing work," a "summation of his previous life and work." The heroine, Leni Pfeiffer, joins other tenants in preventing her relatives from tearing down the Cologne apartment house where she lives. Leni is another of Böll's attempts to combine realism with Christian mythology; she is a "pure" soul, without any interest in the consumer and achievement-oriented society. She is helpful, sensual, a "subversive madonna." She and her son Lev introduced Böll's principle of "Leistungsverweigerung" (rejection of the work ethic), a concept attacking the dehumanization of life under capitalism. Their belief in Leistungsverweigerung makes Leni and Lev the center of a counterculture in the city.

The novel offers another dimension, introduced by an inquiring author who collects information about Leni from the people around her and discovers that she was the lover of a Russian prisoner of war during World War II; the Russian, Boris, is Lev's father. Böll contrasts the purity of the couple with the petty reactions of Leni's friends to her affair and the birth of her illegitimate son. Böll said later that he tried to portray Leni as a woman "die die ganze Last dieser Geschichte. . . auf sich genommen hat" (who carried the whole burden of German history).

According to Karl Korn, the novel reveals the "archaeology of Cologne's society," especially of the lower classes. Rainer Nägele said *Gruppenbild mit Dame* was "a much more rambling novel than anything Böll had written previously." Theodore Ziolkowski called it a "secular beatification." The novel struck a responsive chord in Germany during the years of student protests. The reception of *Gruppenbild mit Dame* in the United States, however, is typical of Böll's lack of success there. The *Newsweek* reviewer wrote that he would rather read Günter Grass but read Böll out of "a guilty feeling"; *Time* magazine implied that Böll received the Nobel Prize more for his "idealistic tendency" than for his literary qualities. Böll's failure in the United States is puzzling; he is the most popular German author in England, France, Sweden, and the Soviet Union.

After receiving the Nobel Prize, Böll was an important public figure in Germany, praised by the left as the "conscience of his age" and attacked from the right as a writer without any real talent. Those opposed to Böll claimed that the best writers never received the Nobel Prize. Böll responded that he could not afford not to accept the prize, since Germany had not had many people whom the world could look up to.

In 1972 Böll published an article in the magazine *Der Spiegel* defending the terrorist Baader-Meinhof gang, members of which were then on trial. The tabloid *Bild-Zeitung* had already concluded that the group was guilty; Böll's defense of the gang was based on the belief that everybody is entitled to due process. Böll pointed out that former Nazis were being released from jail but predicted that the Baader-Meinhofs would find no mercy. In reaction to this article, the papers controlled by the West German press czar Axel Springer published a letter by Prime Minister Filbinger of the State of Baden-Württemberg asking for Böll's resignation as International PEN president. On 1 June Böll's house was searched by the police, and on 7 June a CDU member of the West German parliament declared people like Böll to be more dangerous than the Baader-Meinhofs. Böll's literary response to these events was *Die verlorene Ehre der Katharina Blum* (1974; translated as *The Lost Honor of Katharina Blum*, 1975), which first appeared in July 1974 in *Der Spiegel*; it was the first work of fiction ever published by the periodical. The first edition of the book, published in August, sold 100,000 copies in a few weeks and 200,000 by the end of the year; the paperback edition sold more than 1 million copies. The novel has been translated into eighteen languages.

Katharina, a housekeeper who has accumulated some wealth through her frugality, loses her reputation through the practices of the *Zeitung*. The *Zeitung* finds out that Katharina fell in love with an army deserter and bank robber, kept him in her apartment overnight, and let him escape the following morning. Without any justification, the *Zeitung* calls him a "terrorist" and Katharina his accomplice. Details about her love life are fabricated and published. Katharina is so enraged that she decides to shoot Tötges, the journalist who is responsible for the stories. Other citizens are equally appalled by the *Zeitung* and ready for revenge against the slander, which Böll describes as "public violence."

As PEN president, Böll played host to Aleksandr Solzhenitsyn after he was exiled from the Soviet Union in 1974, and later to Wolf Biermann and Lev Kopelev, who were exiled from East Germany and the Soviet Union, respectively. Despite his support for Soviet dissidents, Böll continued to be one of the most popular German writers in the Soviet Union.

In 1977, when the German industrialist Hanns-Martin Schleyer was kidnapped and murdered by terrorists and several terrorists committed suicide in the Stammheim prison, Böll was again accused by conservatives of promoting terrorism. They criticized his 1975 satire *Berichte zur Gesinnungslage der Nation* (Reports on the Attitudinal State of the Nation), which attacks West German bureaucracy because of its surveillance of so-called radicals. They also found fault with his story "Du fährst zu oft nach Heidelberg" (You Go to Heidelberg Too Often, 1977), an indictment of the Berufsverbote (the law that keeps suspected Communists out of government jobs).

In the novel *Fürsorgliche Belagerung* (1979; translated as *The Safety Net,* 1981) the house of the newspaper editor Fritz Tolm is constantly protected by police against a possible terrorist attack. Tolm, a sensitive man, is ready to withdraw into private life and give up his privileged but exposed public position. The same events are recounted from the viewpoints of Tolm, other family members, the guards, and the terrorists, allowing the reader to see the protection system from all sides. Family life is destroyed by the heavy security; there is no privacy for the protected. Finally, after the terrorists burn down the house, the Tolms withdraw into a pastoral idyll in the country.

Böll continued to be involved in political issues, participating in the 1981 Bonn peace demonstration. In 1983 he was made an honorary citizen of the city of Cologne. The local CDU was not opposed to honoring Böll the "great writer" but was opposed to honoring Böll the social critic. In his acceptance speech Böll said it was a mistake to separate the two aspects, asserting that his essays, reviews, and lectures were also literature and had been written with the same kind of moral consciousness as his novels and short stories. Böll called his being regarded as the moral conscience of Germany a sign of the corruption of German society: parliament and press, not a single writer, should constitute the public conscience.

Böll's health had long been poor; diabetes and a liver disorder necessitated several hospital stays, and his smoking aggravated his circulatory problems. On 16 July 1985 he died in his house in Langenbroich/Eifel, having been released from the hospital two days before. His last novel, a book about Bonn and its women titled *Frauen vor Flußlandschaft* (Women with River Landscape), was published in August 1985 in an edition of 100,000 copies. Although the novel was not intended as a roman à clef, it is easy to recognize certain politicians on the Bonn scene.

Heinrich Böll's contribution to postwar German literature was considerable. At a time when Germany was discredited and most Germans, including most writers, were ready to withdraw into introspection, he set an example of social commitment. Although he was a regional writer of the lower Rhineland, his home, Cologne, was the spiritual center of West German political power during the Adenauer years. His writing was at its best when he anticipated a political crisis; it became superior when he was drawn into the turmoil of politics. His ability to maintain his roots, his religion, and his idealism throughout his political involvement made him an exemplary figure among postwar West German writers.

Letters:

Herbert Hoven, ed., *Die Hoffnung ist wie ein wildes Tier: Der Briefwechsel zwischen Heinrich Böll und Ernst-Adolf Kunz, 1945–1953* (Cologne: Kiepenheuer & Witsch, 1994).

Interviews:

Horst Bienek, *Werkstattgespräche mit Schriftstellern* (Munich: Deutscher Taschenbuch, 1965), pp. 168–184;

"Interview von Marcel Reich-Ranicki," in *Heinrich Böll, Aufsätze, Kritiken, Reden* (Cologne: Kiepenheuer & Witsch, 1967), pp. 502–510;

Im Gespräch: Heinrich Böll mit Heinz Ludwig Arnold (Munich: Boorberg, 1971);

"Ich tendiere nur zu dem scheinbar Unpolitischen: Gespräche mit Heinrich Böll," in *Manfred Durzak, Gespräche über den Roman* (Frankfurt: Suhrkamp, 1976), pp. 128–153.

Bibliographies:

Ferdinand Melius, *Der Schriftsteller Heinrich Böll: Ein biographisch-bibliographischer Abriß* (Cologne: Kiepenheuer & Witsch, 1959);

Werner Lengning, ed., *Der Schriftsteller Heinrich Böll: Ein biographisch-bibliographischer Abriß,* third edition (Munich: Deutscher Taschenbuch Verlag, 1972);

Werner Martin, *Heinrich Böll: Eine Bibliographie seiner Werke* (Hildesheim: Olms, 1975).

Biographies:

Christine Gabriele Hoffmann, *Heinrich Böll* (Hamburg: Dressler, 1977);

Christian Linder, *Heinrich Böll* (Reinbek: Rowohlt, 1978);

Alfred Böll, *Bilder einer deutschen Familie: Die Bölls* (Bergisch-Gladbach: Lübbe, 1981);

Klaus Schröter, *Heinrich Böll: In Selbstzeugnissen und Bilddokumenten* (Reinbek: Rowohlt, 1982).

References:

Heinz Ludwig Arnold, ed., *Heinrich Böll* (Munich: Edition text + kritik, 1982);

Albrecht Beckel, *Mensch, Gesellschaft, Kirche bei Heinrich Böll* (Osnabrück: Fromm, 1966);

Hans-Joachim Bernhard, *Die Romane Heinrich Bölls: Gesellschaftskritik und Gemeinschaftsutopie* (Berlin: Rütten & Loening, 1970);

Hanno Beth, ed., *Eine Einführung in das Gesamtwerk in Einzelinterpretationen* (Kronberg: Scriptor, 1975);

Viktor Böll and Yvonne Jürgensen, *Heinrich Böll als Filmautor: Rezensionsmaterial aus dem Literaturarchiv der Stadtbücherei Köln* (Cologne: City of Cologne, 1982);

Robert A. Burns, *The Theme of Non-Conformism in the Works of Heinrich Böll* (Coventry: University of Warwick, 1973);

Michael Butler, ed., *The Narrative Fiction of Heinrich Böll: Social Conscience, and Literary Achievement* (Cambridge & New York: Cambridge University Press, 1994);

Robert C. Conard, *Heinrich Böll* (Boston: Hall, 1981);

Conard, *Understanding Heinrich Böll* (Columbia: University of South Carolina Press, 1992);

Manfred Durzak, *Der deutsche Roman der Gegenwart* (Stuttgart: Kohlhammer, 1971), pp. 19–107;

Frank Finlay, *On the Rationality of Poetry: Heinrich Böll's Aesthetic Thinking* (Amsterdam & Atlanta: Rodopi, 1996);

Hermann Friedmann and Otto Mann, eds., *Heinrich Böll als christlicher Dichter der Gegenwart* (Heidelberg: Rothe, 1955);

Frank Grützbach, ed., *Freies Geleit für Ulrike Meinhof: Ein Artikel und seine Folgen* (Cologne: Kiepenheuer & Witsch, 1972);

Heinrich Herlyn, *Heinrich Böll und Herbert Marcuse: Literatur als Utopie* (Lambertheim: Kübler, 1979);

Walter Jens, *Deutsche Literatur der Gegenwart: Themen, Stile, Tendenzen* (Munich: Piper, 1962);

Manfred Jurgensen, ed., *Böll: Untersuchungen zum Werk* (Bern: Francke, 1975);

Karl Korn, "Heinrich Bölls Beschreibung einer Epoche," *Frankfurter Allgemeine Zeitung,* 28 July 1971;

Enid MacPherson, *A Student's Guide to Böll* (London: Heinemann, 1972);

Materialien zur Interpretation von Heinrich Bölls "Fürsorgliche Belagerung" (Cologne: Kiepenheuer & Witsch, 1982);

Renate Matthaei, ed., *Die subversive Madonna: Ein Schlüssel zum Werk Heinrich Bölls* (Cologne: Kiepenheuer & Witsch, 1975);

Aleidine Kramer Moeller, *The Woman as Survivor: The Evolution of the Female Figure in the Works of Heinrich Böll* (New York: Peter Lang, 1991);

Rainer Nägele, *Heinrich Böll: Einführung in das Werk und in die Forschung* (Frankfurt am Main: Athenäum-Fischer, 1976);

Marcel Reich-Ranicki, *In Sachen Böll: Ansichten und Einsichten* (Munich: Deutscher Taschenbuch, 1971);

James Henderson Reid, *Heinrich Böll, A German for His Time* (Oxford & New York: Berg, 1988);

Reid, *Heinrich Böll: Withdrawal and Re-Emergence* (London: Wolff, 1973);

Klaus Schröter, *Heinrich Böll: In Selbstzeugnissen und Bilddokumenten* (Reinbek: Rowohlt, 1982);

Wilhelm J. Schwarz, *Der Erzähler Heinrich Böll: Seine Werke und Gestalten* (Bern & Munich: Francke, 1967; third edition, 1973); translated by Alexander Henderson and Elizabeth Henderson as *Heinrich Böll: Teller of Tales* (New York: Ungar, 1968);

Jochen Vogt, *Heinrich Böll* (Munich: Beck/edition text + kritik, 1978);

Günter Wirth, *Heinrich Böll: Essayistische Studie über religiöse und gesellschaftliche Motive im Prosawerk des Dichters* (Berlin: Union, 1967);

Reinhard K. Zachau, *Heinrich Böll: Forty Years of Criticism* (Columbia, S.C.: Camden House, 1994).

Papers:

The holdings of the former Böll-Archiv of Kiepenheuer and Witsch and those of the Boston University Library were transferred to the Archives of the City of Cologne on 29 April 1983, when Böll was awarded the honorary citizenship of the City of Cologne; they are administered by a nephew of Böll, Viktor Böll (Literaturarchiv der Stadtbücherei: Köln, Zentralbibliothek, Josef-Hanbrich-Hof, 5000 Köln 1). The former Kiepenheuer and Witsch collection contains all of Böll's printed texts; his manuscripts and letters are in private possession. The former Boston University Library collection contains manuscripts, typescripts, notes, correction sheets, copies of Böll's works, reviews, and articles about Böll; it is described by Robert C. Conard in *The University of Dayton Review,* 10 (Fall 1973): 11–14.

Bertolt Brecht

(10 February 1898 – 14 August 1956)

Herbert Knust
University of Illinois at Urbana-Champaign

This entry originally appeared in DLB 124: Twentieth-Century
German Dramatists, 1919–1992.

See also the Brecht entry in *DLB 56, German Fiction Writers, 1914–1945.*

SELECTED BOOKS: *Baal* (Potsdam: Kiepenheuer, 1922); translated by Eric Bentley as *Baal* in *Baal, A Man's a Man, and The Elephant Calf* (New York: Grove, 1966);

Trommeln in der Nacht: Drama (Munich: Drei Masken, 1922); edited by Volkmar Sander (Waltham, Mass., Toronto & London: Blaisdell, 1969); translated by Anselm Hollo as *Drums in the Night* in *Jungle of Cities and Other Plays* (New York: Grove, 1966);

Leben Eduards des Zweiten von England: Nach Marlowe. Historie, by Brecht and Lion Feuchtwanger (Potsdam: Kiepenheuer, 1924); translated by Bentley as *Edward II: A Chronicle Play* (New York: Grove, 1966);

Taschenpostille: Mit Anleitungen, Gesangsnoten und einem Anhang (Potsdam: Privately printed, 1926);

Im Dickicht der Städte: Der Kampf zweier Männer in der Riesenstadt Chicago. Schauspiel (Berlin: Propyläen, 1927); translated by Hollo as *Jungle of Cities* in *Jungle of Cities and Other Plays;*

Hauspostille: Mit Anleitungen, Gesangsnoten und einem Anhang (Berlin: Propyläen, 1927); translated by Bentley as *Manual of Piety: A Bilingual Edition* (New York: Grove, 1966);

Mann ist Mann: Die Verwandlung des Packers Galy Gay in den Militärbaracken von Kilkoa im Jahre 1925: Lustspiel (Berlin: Propyläen, 1927); translated by Bentley as *A Man's a Man* in *Baal, A Man's a Man, and The Elephant Calf;*

Drei angelsächsische Stücke, by Brecht and Feuchtwanger (Berlin: Propyläen, 1927);

Aufstieg und Fall der Stadt Mahagonny: Oper in drei Akten, text by Brecht, music by Kurt Weill (Vienna & Leipzig: Universal-Edition, 1929); translated by

Bertolt Brecht in 1953

Guy Stern as *Rise and Fall of the City of Mahagonny* (brochure accompanying recorded version, Columbia K3L 243, 1959);

Die Dreigroschenoper, text translated by Elisabeth Hauptmann from John Gay's *The Beggar's Opera,* rewritten by Brecht, music by Weill (Vienna: Universal-Edition, 1929; London: Malik, 1938); translated by Bentley and Desmond Vesey as *The Threepenny Opera* (New York: Grove, 1964);

Versuche, volume 1, edited by Hauptmann (Berlin: Kiepenheuer, 1930)–comprises *Der Flug der Lindberghs:* "Radiotheorie"; "Geschichten vom Herrn Keuner"; *Fatzer, 3;*

Versuche, volume 2, edited by Hauptmann (Berlin: Kiepenheuer, 1930)–comprises *Aufstieg und Fall der Stadt Mahagonny,* "Über die Oper, Aus dem Lesebuch für Städtebewohner," *Das Badener Lehrstück vom Einverständnis; Das Badener Lehrstück vom Einverständnis* translated by Lee Baxandall as *The Baden Play for Learning* in *Drama Review* (Tulane), 4 (May 1960): 118–133;

Versuche, volume 3, edited by Hauptmann (Berlin: Kiepenheuer, 1931)–comprises *Die Dreigroschenoper, Die Beule: Ein Dreigroschenfilm, Der Dreigroschenprozess;*

Versuche, volume 4, edited by Hauptmann (Berlin: Kiepenheuer, 1931)–comprises *Der Jasager und Der Neinsager: Schulopern, Die Maßnahme: Lehrstück; Der Jasager* translated by Gerhard Nillhaus as *He Who Said Yes,* in *Accent,* 7 (Autumn 1946): 14–20; *Die Maßnahme* translated by Carl L. Mueller as *The Measures Taken* in *The Measures Taken and Other Lehrstücke* (London: Methuen, 1977);

Versuche, volume 5, edited by Hauptmann (Berlin: Kiepenheuer, 1932)–comprises *Die heilige Johanna der Schlachthöfe: Schauspiel,* "Geschichten vom Herrn Keuner"; *Die heilige Johanna der Schlachthöfe* translated by Frank Jones as *Saint Joan of the Stockyards* (Bloomington: Indiana University Press, 1969);

Versuche, volume 6, edited by Hauptmann (Berlin: Kiepenheuer, 1932)–comprises "Die drei Soldaten"; "Ein Kinderbuch";

Versuche, volume 7, edited by Hauptmann (Berlin: Kiepenheuer, 1933)–comprises *Die Mutter,* "Geschichten aus der Revolution"; *Die Mutter* translated by Baxandall as *The Mother* (New York: Grove, 1965);

Ballade vom armen Stabschef + 30. Juni 1934 (N.p., 1934);

Dreigroschenroman (Amsterdam: De Lange, 1934); translated by Vesey and Christopher Isherwood as *A Penny for the Poor* (London: Hale, 1937); translation republished as *Threepenny Novel* (New York: Grove, 1956; London: Granada, 1981);

Lieder Gedichte Chöre, music by Hanns Eisler (Paris: Editions du Carrefour, 1934);

Gesammelte Werke, 2 volumes (London: Malik, 1938);

Svendborger Gedichte; Deutsche Kriegsfibel; Chroniken: Deutsche Satiren für den deutschen Freiheitssender (London: Malik, 1939);

Furcht und Elend des III. Reiches (Moscow: Meshdunarodnaja Kniga, 1941; New York: Aurora, 1945); translated by Bentley as *The Private Life of the Master Race* (New York: New Directions, 1944);

Herr Puntila und sein Knecht: Nacherzählungen der Hella Wuolijoki. Volksstück in 9 Bildern (Munich: Desch, 1948); republished as *Herr Puntila und sein Knecht Matti,* edited by Margaret Mare (London: Methuen, 1962); translated by John Willett as *Mister Puntila and His Man Matti* (London: Methuen, 1977);

Kalendergeschichten (Halle: Mitteldeutscher Verlag, 1948); translated by Yvonne Kapp and Michael Hamburger as *Tales from the Calendar* (London: Methuen, 1961);

Versuche, volume 9, edited by Hauptmann (Berlin & Frankfurt am Main: Suhrkamp, 1949)–comprises *Mutter Courage und ihre Kinder: Eine Chronik aus dem Dreißigjährigen Krieg,* "Anmerkungen," "Fünf Schwierigkeiten beim Schreiben der Wahrheit"; *Mutter Courage und ihre Kinder* translated by Bentley as *Mother Courage and Her Children* (New York: Grove, 1966);

Das Zukunftslied: Aufbaulied der FDJ, music by Paul Dessau (Weimar: Thüringer Volksverlag, 1949);

Antigonemodell 1948: Die Antigone des Sophokles, nach der Hölderlinschen Übertragung für die Bühne, bearbeitet (Berlin: Weiss, 1949);

Versuche, volume 10, edited by Hauptmann (Berlin & Frankfurt am Main: Suhrkamp, 1950)–comprises *Herr Puntila und sein Knecht Matti,* "Chinesische Gedichte," *Die Ausnahme und die Regel; Die Ausnahme und die Regel* translated by Bentley as *The Exception and the Rule,* in *Chrysalis,* 14, no. 68 (1961);

Versuche, volume 11, edited by Hauptmann (Berlin: Suhrkamp, 1951)–comprises *Der Hofmeister,* by Jakob Michael Reinhold Lenz, revised by Brecht; "Studien: Neue Technik der Schauspielkunst"; *Übungsstücke für Schauspieler; Das Verhör des Lukullus,* by Brecht and Margarete Steffin; "Anmerkungen über die Oper Die Verurteilung des Lukullus"; *Das Verhör des Lukullus* translated by H.R. Hays as *The Trial of Lucullus* (New York: New Directions, 1943);

Offener Brief an die deutschen Künstler und Schriftsteller (Berlin, 1951);

Die Erziehung der Hirse. Nach dem Bericht von G. Fisch: Der Mann, der das Unmögliche wahr gemacht hat (Berlin: Aufbau, 1951);

Hundert Gedichte, 1918–1950 (Berlin: Aufbau, 1951);

An meine Landsleute (Leipzig: VEB Offizin Haag-Grodru-
gulin, 1951);

Das Verhör des Lukullus: Oper in zwölf Bildern, music by
Dessau (Berlin: Aufbau, 1951);

Die Verurteilung des Lukullus: Oper, music by Dessau (Berlin: Aufbau, 1951);

Versuche, volume 12, edited by Hauptmann (Berlin &
Frankfurt am Main: Suhrkamp, 1953)–comprises
Der gute Mensch von Sezuan, "Kleines Organon für
das Theater," "Über reimlose Lyrik mit
unregelmäßigen Rhythmen," "Geschichten vom
Herrn Keuner"; *Der gute Mensch von Sezuan* trans-
lated by Bentley as *The Good Woman of Setzuan* in
Parables for the Theater: Two Plays by Bertolt Brecht
(Minneapolis: University of Minnesota Press,
1948); translation revised as *The Good Woman of
Setzuan* (New York: Grove, 1966); "Kleines Orga-
non für das Theater" translated by Willett as "A
Short Organum for the Theatre" in *Brecht on Theatre* (New York: Hill & Wang, 1964);

Versuche, extra volume, edited by Hauptmann (Berlin:
Aufbau, 1953)–comprises *Die Gewehre der Frau
Carrar,* "Der Augsburger Kreidekreis," "Neue
Kinderlieder"; *Die Gewehre der Frau Carrar* trans-
lated by Keene Wallis as *Señora Carrar's Rifles,* in
Theatre Workshop, 2 (April–June 1938): 30–50;
retranslated by George Tabori as *The Guns of Car-
rar* (New York: French, 1971);

Versuche, volume 13, edited by Hauptmann (Berlin &
Frankfurt am Main: Suhrkamp, 1954)–comprises
Der kaukasische Kreidekreis, by Brecht and Ruth Ber-
lau; "Weite und Vielfalt der realistischen Schreib-
weise"; "Buckower Elegien"; *Der kaukasische
Kreidekreis* translated by Bentley and Maja Aple-
man as *The Caucasian Chalk Circle* in *Parables for the
Theater;*

Versuche, volume 14, edited by Hauptmann (Berlin:
Suhrkamp, 1955)–comprises *Leben des Galilei,*
"Gedichte aus dem Messingkauf," *Die Horatier und
die Kuriatier; Leben des Galilei* translated by Vesey as
The Life of Galileo (London: Methuen, 1963);
translated by Charles Laughton as *Galileo* (New
York: Grove, 1966);

Gedichte, edited by S. Streller (Leipzig: Reclam, 1955);

Kriegsfibel, edited by Berlau (Berlin: Eulenspiegel, 1955);

Gedichte und Lieder, edited by Paul Suhrkamp (Berlin &
Frankfurt am Main: Suhrkamp, 1956);

Die Geschäfte des Herrn Julius Cäsar: Romanfragment (Berlin: Aufbau, 1957);

Lieder und Gesänge (Berlin: Henschel, 1957);

Versuche, volume 15, edited by Hauptmann (Berlin &
Frankfurt am Main: Suhrkamp, 1957)–comprises
Die Tage der Commune, "Die Dialektik auf dem The-
ater," *Zu Leben des Galilei,* "Drei Reden," "Zwei

Briefe"; *Die Tage der Commune* translated by
Leonard J. Lehrmann as *The Days of the Commune,*
in *Dunster Drama Review,* 10, no. 2 (1971);

Schriften zum Theater: Über eine nicht-aristotelische Dramatik,
edited by S. Unseld (Berlin & Frankfurt am Main:
Suhrkamp, 1957);

Stücke aus dem Exil, 5 volumes (Frankfurt am Main:
Suhrkamp, 1957)–includes *Die Rundköpfe und die
Spitzköpfe; Der aufhaltsame Aufstieg des Arturo Ui; Die
Gesichte der Simone Machard,* by Brecht and Feucht-
wanger; *Schweyk im zweiten Weltkrieg; Die Rundköpfe
und die Spitzköpfe* translated by N. Goold-Ver-
schoyle as *Roundheads and Peakheads* in *Jungle of Cit-
ies and Other Plays; Der aufhaltsame Aufstieg des Arturo
Ui* adapted by Tabori as *The Resistible Rise of Arturo
Ui: A Gangster Spectacle,* music by Hans-Dieter
Hosalla (New York: S. French, 1972); translated
by Ralph Manheim as *The Resistible Rise of Arturo
Ui* (London: Eyre Methuen, 1976); *Die Gesichte der
Simone Machard* translated by Carl Richard Muel-
ler as *The Visions of Simone Machard* (New York:
Grove, 1965); *Schweyk im weiten Weltkrieg* translated
by Peter Sander as *Schweyk in the Second World War*
(Waltham, Mass.: Brandeis University, 1967);

Geschichten vom Herrn Keuner (Berlin: Aufbau, 1958);

Brecht: Ein Lesebuch für unsere Zeit, edited by Hauptmann
and Benno Slupianek (Weimar: Volksverlag
Weimar, 1958);

*Mutter Courage und ihre Kinder: Text; Aufführung; Anmerkun-
gen* (Berlin: Henschel, 1958);

Versuche, volumes 5–8, 1 volume (Berlin & Frankfurt am
Main: Suhrkamp, 1959)–comprises *Die heilige
Johanna der Schlachthöfe,* "Die drei Soldaten," *Die
Mutter, Die Spitzköpfe und die Rundköpfe;*

Der gute Mensch von Sezuan: Parabelstück, by Brecht, Berlau, and Steffin, music by Dessau (Berlin & Frankfurt am Main: Suhrkamp, 1959); edited by Mare
(London: Methuen, 1960);

Schweyk im zweiten Weltkrieg (Berlin & Frankfurt am Main:
Suhrkamp, 1959);

Die sieben Todsünden der Kleinbürger (Frankfurt am Main:
Suhrkamp, 1959); translated by W. H. Auden
and Chester Kallmann as *The Seven Deadly Sins of
the Lower Middle Class,* in *Drama Review* (Tulane), 6
(September 1961): 123–129;

Bearbeitungen, 2 volumes (Frankfurt am Main: Suhrkamp, 1959)–comprises *Die Antigone des Sophokles,
Der Hofmeister, Coriolan, Der Prozeß der Jeanne d'Arc
zu Rouen 1431, Don Juan, Pauken und Trompeten;*

*Kleines Organon für das Theater: Mit einem "Nachtrag zum
Kleinen Organon"* (Frankfurt am Main: Suhrkamp,
1960);

Flüchtlingsgespräche (Berlin: Suhrkamp, 1961);

Me-Ti; Buch der Wendungen—Fragment, edited by Uwe Johnson (Frankfurt am Main: Suhrkamp, 1965);

Einakter: Die Kleinbürgerhochzeit; Der Bettler oder Der tote Hund; Er treibt einem Teufel aus; Lux in Tenebris; Der Fischzug; Dansen; Was kostet das Eisen? (Frankfurt am Main: Suhrkamp, 1966); *Lux in Tenebris, Der Fischzug, Dansen, and Was kostet das Eisen?* translated by Martin and Rose Kastner as *Lux in Tenebris, The Catch, Dansen, and How Much Is Your Iron?,* in *Collected Plays,* 9 volumes, edited by Willett and Manheim (London: Methuen, 1971–1973; New York: Random House, 1971–1973);

Gesammelte Werke, 22 volumes (Frankfurt am Main: Suhrkamp, 1967–1969); volumes 1–7, *Stücke,* translation edited by Willett and Manheim as *Collected Plays,* 9 volumes (London: Methuen, 1971–1973; New York: Random House, 1971–1973); volumes 8–10, *Gedichte,* translated by Willett and Manheim as *Poems 1913–1956* (New York: Methuen, 1976); volume 11, *Prosa I,* translated by Willett and Manheim as *Short Stories 1921–1946* (New York: Methuen, 1983); volumes 15–17, *Schriften zum Theater,* translated by Willett as *Brecht on Theatre* (New York: Hill & Wang, 1964);

Turandot oder Der Kongreß der Weißwäscher (Frankfurt am Main: Suhrkamp, 1968);

Arbeitsjournal 1938–1955, 3 volumes (Frankfurt am Main: Suhrkamp, 1973); translated by Hugh Rorrison and edited by Willett as *Bertolt Brecht Journals* (New York: Routledge, 1993);

Tagebücher 1920–1922: Autobiographische Aufzeichnungen 1920–1954, edited by Herta Ramthun (Frankfurt am Main: Suhrkamp, 1975); translated by Willett as *Diaries 1920–1922* (New York: St. Martin's Press, 1979);

Werke: Große kommentierte Berliner und Frankfurter Ausgabe, 30 volumes projected, 15 volumes published, edited by Werner Hecht, Jan Knopf, Werner Mittenzwei, and Klaus-Detlev Müller (Berlin: Aufbau / Frankfurt am Main: Suhrkamp, 1988–)—included in volume 5, *Leben des Galilei;*

Ich bin aus den schwarzen Wäldern: Seine Anfänge in Augsburg und München, 1913–1924 (Frankfurt am Main: Suhrkamp, 1994);

Der Schnaps ist in die Toiletten geflossen: Seine Erfolge in Berlin, 1924–1933 (Frankfurt am Main: Suhrkamp, 1994);

Unterm dänischen Strohdach: Sein Exil in Skandinavien, 1933–1941 (Frankfurt am Main: Suhrkamp, 1994);

Broadway—the hard way: Sein Exil in den USA, 1941–1947 (Frankfurt am Main: Suhrkamp, 1994);

Der Untergang des Egoisten Johann Fatzer, adapted by Heiner Müller (Frankfurt am Main: Suhrkamp, 1994);

Gedichte, edited by Jan Knopf (Stuttgart: Reclam, 1995).

Editions in English: *Poems & Songs from the Plays,* edited by John Willett (London: Methuen, 1990);

The Good Person of Szechwan; Mother Courage and Her Children; Fear and Misery of the Third Reich, translated by Willett (New York: Arcade, 1993);

The Threepenny Opera; Baal; The Mother, translated by Ralph Manheim (New York: Arcade, 1993);

Life of Galileo; The Resistible Rise of Arturo Ui; The Caucasian Chalk Circle, translated by Willett (New York: Arcade, 1994);

Bad Time for Poetry: 152 Poems and Songs, edited by Willett (London: Methuen, 1995);

The Rise and Fall of the City of Mahagonny; and, The Seven Deadly Sins of the Petty Bourgeoisie, translated by W. H. Auden and Chester Kallman, edited by Willett and Manheim (New York: Arcade, 1996).

PLAY PRODUCTIONS: *Trommeln in der Nacht,* Munich, Kammerspiele, 29 September 1922;

Die rote Zibebe, contributions by Brecht, Munich, Kammerspiele, 30 September 1922;

Im Dickicht, Munich, Residenztheater, 9 May 1923;

Baal, Leipzig, Altes Theater, 8 December 1923;

Leben Eduards des Zweiten von England, by Brecht and Lion Feuchtwanger, Munich, Kammerspiele, 18 March 1924;

Mann ist Mann, Darmstadt, Landestheater, 25 September 1926;

Die Hochzeit (Die Kleinbürgerhochzeit), Frankfurt am Main, Städtische Bühnen, Schauspielhaus, 11 December 1926;

Mahagonny, Baden-Baden, Stadttheater, 17 July 1927;

Kalkutta, 4. Mai, by Brecht and Feuchtwanger, Königsberg, Neues Schauspielhaus, 12 November 1927;

Jaroslav Hašek, *Die Abenteuer des braven Soldaten Schwejk,* dramatized by Max Brod and Hans Reimann, adapted by Brecht, Erwin Piscator, and Leo Lania, Berlin, Theater am Nollendorfplatz, 23 January 1928;

Die Dreigroschenoper, music by Kurt Weill, Berlin, Theater am Schiffbauerdamm, 31 August 1928;

Der Ozeanflug, Baden-Baden, Kurhaus, 27 July 1929;

Das Badener Lehrstück vom Einverständnis, music by Paul Hindemith, Baden-Baden, Kurhaus, 28 July 1929;

Happy End, by Brecht and Elisabeth Hauptmann, music by Weill, Berlin, Theater am Schiffbauerdamm, 31 August 1929;

Aufstieg und Fall der Stadt Mahagonny, music by Weill, Leipzig, Opernhaus, 9 March 1930;

Der Jasager und der Neinsager, music by Weill, Berlin, Zentralinstitut für Erziehung und Unterricht, 23 June 1930;

Die Maßnahme, music by Hanns Eisler, Berlin, Berliner Philharmonie, 13 December 1930;

Die Mutter, music by Eisler, Berlin, Komödienhaus am Schiffbauerdamm, 15 January 1932;

Die sieben Todsünden der Kleinbürger, music by Weill, Paris, Théâtre des Champs-Elysées, Les Ballets, 7 June 1933;

Die Ballade vom Reichstagsbrand, Moscow, Deutsches Theater Kolonne links im Klub ausländischer Arbeiter, March 1934;

Die Rundköpfe und die Spitzköpfe, music by Eisler, Moscow, Thälmann-Klub, Spring 1935;

Die Gewehre der Frau Carrar, Paris, Salle Adyar, 16 October 1937;

Die Ausnahme und die Regel (in Hebrew), Givat Chaim, Palestine, 1 May 1938;

99% (scenes from *Furcht und Elend des Dritten Reiches*), Paris, Salle d'Iéna, 21 May 1938;

Vad kostar järnet? (*Was kostet das Eisen?;* later called *Dansen II*), Stockholm, Volkshochschule Tollare, August 1939;

Mutter Courage und ihre Kinder, music by Paul Dessau, Zurich, Schauspielhaus, 19 April 1941;

Der gute Mensch von Sezuan, Zurich, Schauspielhaus, 4 February 1943;

Leben des Galilei, Zurich, Schauspielhaus, 9 March 1943;

John Webster, *The Duchess of Malfi,* adapted by Brecht and W. H. Auden, Boston, Schubert Theater, 23 September 1946;

Friedrich Hölderlin, *Die Antigone des Sophokles,* adapted by Brecht, Chur, Stadttheater, 15 February 1948;

The Caucasian Chalk Circle, translated by Eric and Maja Bentley, Northfield, Minn., Nourse Little Theatre, 4 May 1948;

Herr Puntila und sein Knecht Matti, Zurich, Schauspielhaus, 5 June 1948;

J. M. R. Lenz, *Der Hofmeister,* adapted by Brecht, Berlin, Berliner Ensemble, 15 April 1950;

Das Verhör des Lukullus, music by Dessau, Berlin, Deutsche Staatsoper, 17 March 1951;

Herrnburger Bericht, Berlin, Deutsches Theater, 5 August 1951;

Die Verurteilung des Lukullus, music by Dessau, Berlin, Deutsche Staatsoper, 12 October 1951;

Molière, *Don Juan,* adapted by Brecht, Rostock, Volkstheater, 25 May 1952;

Anna Seghers, *Der Prozess der Jeanne d'Arc zu Rouen 1431,* adapted by Brecht, Berlin, Berliner Ensemble, 23 November 1952;

George Farquhar, *Pauken und Trompeten,* adapted by Brecht, Berlin, Berliner Ensemble, 19 June 1955;

Die Tage der Commune, music by Eisler, Karl-Marx-Stadt, Städtisches Theater, 17 November 1956;

Schweyk im zweiten Weltkrieg, translated into Polish by Andrzej Wirth, Warsaw, Theater der polnischen Armee, 15 January 1957;

Die Gesichte der Simone Machard, by Brecht and Feuchtwanger, Frankfurt am Main, Städtische Bühnen, 8 March 1957;

Die Horatier und die Kuriatier, music by Kurt Schwaen, Halle, Theater der jungen Garde, 26 April 1958;

Der aufhaltsame Aufstieg des Arturo Ui, Stuttgart, Württembergisches Staatstheater, 10 November 1958;

Die heilige Johanna der Schlachthöfe, Hamburg, Deutsches Schauspielhaus, 30 April 1959;

William Shakespeare, *Coriolan von Shakespeare,* adapted by Brecht, Frankfurt am Main, Schauspielhaus, 22 September 1961;

Flüchtlingsgespräche, Munich, Kammerspiele, 15 February 1962;

Der Messingkauf, Berlin, Berliner Ensemble, 12 October 1963;

Der Ingwertopf, Heidelberg, Städtische Bühne, 9 February 1965;

Der Fischzug, Heidelberg, Städtische Bühne, 11 January 1967;

Der Brotladen, Berlin, Berliner Ensemble, 13 April 1967;

Der Bettler oder der tote Hund, Berlin, Tribüne, 27 September 1967;

Dansen I; Dansen II, Cologne, Kammerspiele der Kölner Bühnen, 4 October 1967;

Turandot oder Der Kongreß der Weißwäscher, music by Eisler, Zurich, Schauspielhaus, 5 February 1969;

Lux in Tenebris, Essen, Städtische Bühnen, 6 December 1969;

Circus-Pantomime, New York, Theatre de Lys, 9 October 1972;

Er treibt einen Teufel aus, Basel, Stadttheater, 3 October 1975;

Der Untergang des Egoisten Johann Fatzer, Berlin, Schaubühne am Halleschen Ufer, 11 March 1976.

OTHER: M. Andersen-Nexö, *Die Kindheit: Erinnerungen,* translated by Brecht (Zurich: Vereinigung "Kultur und Volk," 1945);

Lion Feuchtwanger, *Auswahl,* contributions by Brecht (Rudolstadt: Greifen, 1949);

T. Otto, *Nie wieder: Tagebuch in Bildern,* foreword by Brecht (Berlin: Volk und Welt, 1950);

Wir singen zu den Weltfestspielen: Herrnburger Bericht, edited by Brecht and Paul Dessau (Berlin: Neues Leben, 1951);

Theaterarbeit: Sechs Aufführungen des Berliner Ensembles, edited by Brecht, Ruth Berlau, C. Hubalek, and others (Dresdner: Dresden Verlag, 1952);

Die Kleinbürgerhochzeit, in Spiele in einem Akt. 35 exemplarische Stücke, edited by Walter Höllerer (Frankfurt am Main: Suhrkamp, 1961); translated by Martin and Rose Kastner as *The Wedding,* in volume 1 of *Collected Plays,* edited by Ralph Manheim and John Willett (New York: Random House, 1971).;

Der Bettler oder Der tote Hund, in *Wer zuletzt lacht: Eine Auswahl heiterer Stücke für Laienspielgruppen,* edited by Carl-Ernst Teichmann and Rosemarie Zimmermann (Berlin, 1965); translated by Peter Hertz as *The Beggar, or The Dead Dog,* in volume 1 of *Collected Plays,* edited by Manheim and Willett (New York: Random House, 1971).

RADIO: *Lindberghflug,* music by Kurt Weill and Paul Hindemith, 29 July 1929;

Die heilige Johanna der Schlachthöfe, Berlin Radio, 11 April 1932;

Das Verhör des Lukullus, Studio Bern, 12 May 1940.

Bertolt Brecht is one of the great names not only of twentieth-century German literature but of modern world literature. His contribution, though varied—it includes lyrical, narrative, dramatic, and theoretical works—has a distinct "Brechtian" quality throughout. It has made a virtue out of provocation in the course of Germany's troubled history from World War I to World War II and beyond. But, although Brecht became increasingly committed to analyses of the sociopolitical scene, he was not just a writer for the day, nor did he put topical subjects above artistic considerations. With a keen eye for hypocrisy and injustice, he addressed fundamental issues of humanity with the fervor of a rebellious idealist and the poetic sensitivity of a great artist of the word. Long a figure of ideological controversy, Brecht has emerged as a classic, and he continues to challenge successive generations to take a close look at their world, to note its contradictions, and to weigh the options and actions that might change it to the better.

Eugen Berthold Brecht—he later dropped the first name and changed the spelling of the middle name—was born in Augsburg into a fairly well-to-do bourgeois family on 10 February 1898. His father, Friedrich Berthold Brecht, an employee of a paper factory, advanced to the position of business director; Brecht's mother was Sofie Brezing Brecht. Brecht attended elementary and high school in Augsburg. Having failed to educate his teachers (as he put it), he began to write occasional poems. In 1914 he had a short play, *Die Bibel* (The Bible), published in the school journal. This first drama, a kind of Judith story set in the religious wars of the seventeenth century, reflects not only the beginning of a lifelong critical involvement in the conflicting teachings of the Bible (influenced, perhaps, by a Protestant father and a Catholic mother) but also the victimization of a girl by a warring world—a motif Brecht was to take up again in later plays. Although he wrote a few patriotic poems at the outbreak of World War I, Brecht's antiwar sentiments developed early. His criticism of Horace's dictum "Dulce est et decorum pro patria mori" (It is sweet and honorable to die for the fatherland) almost led to his expulsion from school. Various journals and newspapers printed poems and stories by the fledgling author, who liked to play the guitar, pursue love adventures, and roam through countryside, fairs, and pubs with a group of bohemian friends.

In 1917 Brecht moved to Munich, enrolled at the university, devoured books, scouted the theater scene, became increasingly involved in literary circles, and tried his hand at several projects, among them one-act plays and a full-fledged drama, *Baal* (published, 1922; performed, 1923). Even the one-act plays written in 1919 exhibit features that were to become his trademark. *Die Kleinbürgerhochzeit* (performed, 1926; translated as *The Wedding*) is a stinging exposure of petit bourgeois mentality; *Der Bettler oder Der tote Hund* (translated as *The Beggar, or the Dead Dog*) confronts the extreme opposites of the social scale: the world of the emperor and the world of the beggar; *Der Fischzug* (translated as *The Catch*) is a clever parodistic double adaptation of a Homeric and a biblical "catch" (Ares trapping Aphrodite, Saint Peter fishing for souls); and in *Lux in Tenebris* Brecht uses the theme of prostitution on several levels for his attack on what he considers the physical, spiritual, and social corruption of the bourgeoisie, whose perversion of the spirit, language, and action is highlighted by parodistic allusions to the Bible (which was to become one of his major literary sources). In style these interludelike sketches tend toward farcical satire; they show some influence of the Munich comedian Karl Valentin, whose witty dialogue-sketches Brecht admired and with whom he had performed in sideshows at fairs. The first full-fledged play, *Baal,* glorifies unfettered, amoral individualism, reflecting, to some extent, Brecht's bohemianism and his sympathy for such vitalist-sensualist figures as Frank Wedekind, Paul Verlaine, Arthur Rimbaud, and François Villon. It is both a literary and a social protest. As a "Gegenentwurf" (counterplay) to Hanns Johst's drama *Der Einsame* (1917; *The Solitary*), about a misunderstood poet, Brecht's play "corrects" the expressionist pathos and sentimentalizing "spirituality" of a Christlike, suffering "genius" by his own earthbound, materialist, selfish vagabond-genius named after a heathen deity; Baal (like Brecht) plays the guitar, writes poetry, eats, drinks, dances, makes love, and uses and drops people without any scruples. As an affront against a stale society, Baal breaks conventions at every turn, living only for his own pleasure, indulging until the last moment in the sensual experiences of this world which knows no afterworld. The powerful imagery of this balladlike, dramatic biography has strong ties to Brecht's early poetry, blending Baal's lust for life with the cyclical rhythm of vegetative nature. Like an insatiable animal Baal "grazes" off the world, and he as well as his lyrics are finally consumed in life's "digestive" process. Baal's reckless craving for self-assertion, tantamount to self-deification, seems to express Brecht's own hunger for life in the face of nothingness. (Brecht reworked the play repeatedly—there are five versions altogether. Such reworkings in the light of historical developments became characteristic of his habits as playwright.)

Brecht's early dramatic responses to the world indicate that while he had an eye for things he disliked, he had not yet developed a political or moral philosophy. In the absence of a constructive stance critics have called Brecht's literary beginnings "nihilistic"—a somewhat dubious term if one considers the vigor and keenness of his early poetic statements.

Shortly before the end of World War I Brecht, who had enrolled in medical studies to avoid the draft, was called to military service nevertheless. As a hospital orderly he witnessed the suffering of victims of war and disease. He wrote the satiric "Legende vom toten Soldaten" (Legend of the Dead Soldier), in which a corpse is revived to be declared fit for military service again. This antiwar ballad was sung in the fourth act of *Trommeln in der Nacht* (1922; translated as *Drums in the Night*, 1966) and was one of the reasons Brecht was put on the blacklist of the Nazis as early as 1923. After the war Brecht witnessed the turbulent beginning of the Weimar Republic and the power struggle among political parties, the violent suppression of the 1918–1919 revolution (whose cause he then seemed to consider hopeless), and the murders of political figures such as Rosa Luxemburg, Karl Liebknecht, and Kurt Eisner by reactionaries. While working on *Baal*, Brecht wrote *Trommeln in der Nacht*, which captures a drab postwar milieu. A disillusioned soldier, Andreas Kragler, returns from the front to his faithless bride, Anna. He encounters war profiteers—Anna's father and Murk, the father of her unborn child—and supporters of the communist "Spartacus" uprising. The revolution is thus in the background of the play (which was initially titled "Spartacus") but is hardly the issue of a serious political debate. Brecht called the play a comedy; it certainly is a satire of the bourgeois mentality and of art forms dear to such a mentality, such as bourgeois tragedy, operatic scenes, and sentimental songs played on gramophones. Andreas's in-laws, the Balickes, who had been doing a

thriving war business manufacturing ammunition boxes, now make baby carriages. They have engineered a profitable liaison between their daughter and Murk after telling her that Andreas has been killed in the war. The engagement is celebrated in a dinner scene titled "Fressen" (Goßling)—a suggestive image for their brutal, grabbing mentality—that includes sentimental German songs and patriotic slogans typical of a "good" German family. The postwar bourgeois victory feast is disturbed by the returning soldier, who pops up claiming his rights—an exploited survivor wanting his slice of the pie. As a "have-not" he is linked with the revolutionaries by the wary Balicke; and he seems to be drifting that way out of spite when he falls into the company of proletarians in a pub. But the play does not end with his joining the revolution. He does not have that sort of romantic "red moon" in his head but drums up his own antiromantic mood: Why, he asks, should he risk himself a second time for pure ideas, when he is likely to become damaged just like the purity of his pregnant bride? Let's be a stinker in a stinking world, he decides. He throws his drum at the red moon, which is nothing but a stage prop lantern; "moon" and "drum" fall into a river without water, and off he goes to bed with his prize, Anna.

This stark assessment of reality was a slap in the face to all ideology, and the later, political Brecht reviewed it with some embarrassment. But *Trommeln in der Nacht*, the first Brecht play performed, brought rave reviews—especially from the influential theater critic Herbert Ihering, who discovered Brecht as a new talent and was instrumental in his receiving the Kleist Prize. New were Brecht's pithy language, his strategy of disillusionment, his radical unveiling of false fronts and sentiments. The many noble clichés are undercut by the actions of lowly characters: exploiters, cutthroats, cowards, and opportunists of every persuasion. Brecht's theater dissects reality rather than imitating it. Symbols such as the artificial red moon that lights up each time Andreas comes onstage point to the bourgeoisie's fear of the revolutionary who would threaten their smug existence, and placards saying "Glotzt nicht so romantisch" (Don't gape so romantically) were hung in the auditorium as part of the strategy of disillusionment—early examples of a technique that Brecht would later develop into his dramaturgy of estrangement.

In 1919, while still a student, Brecht had a son by Paula Banholzer, whose parents disliked Brecht and dissuaded their daughter from marrying him. Frank, named after Brecht's idol, Wedekind, was placed in a foster home; he would be killed on the eastern front in 1943. In 1922 Brecht married the actress Marianne Zoff; the following year they had a daughter, Hanne, who would later become an actress as well. While working on his own projects Brecht also wrote stinging theater reviews that indicate his displeasure with fashionable entertainment void of intellectual challenge.

From several trips to the German capital Brecht had learned that Berlin was the cultural metropolis and, especially, the center of the theater scene in Germany, and he made up his mind to move to Berlin. But even before he settled there in 1924 he was engaged in a new project that was obviously influenced by his impression of a cold, chaotic cityscape. Like Upton Sinclair and Johannes Vilhelm Jensen, both of whose works he had read, Brecht set out to portray the city as jungle, filled with struggle and solitude. The result was a confusing play, first titled "Garga," then *Im Dickicht* (In the Jungle; performed, 1923), later *Im Dickicht der Städte* (published, 1927; translated as *Jungle of Cities,* 1966). Set in Chicago, it is Brecht's first American play and an early instance of his practice of addressing the immediate via the distant to allow more objective perceptions. Americanism was fashionable during the 1920s in Berlin; there were many who romanticized American freedom and open spaces as against the drabness and restrictions of German society; and many saw the cities, with skyscrapers, progress, gangsterism, and clashing social extremes, as American models of modern development.

The duel between the two men in the jungle of cities appears to be a duel of principles. Garga, a library clerk, begins as a sensitive individualist who believes in the freedom of the spirit; Shlink, a successful businessman lonely and hardened by the conditions of his profession, challenges Garga to a combat of changing strategies in which they undermine each other's existence. Neither side really wins. Ultimately Garga survives because he is the younger; but in the course of the fight his individualist ideas are compromised and battered. He emerges a changed man: the struggle has made him a thick-skinned city dweller at the expense of his family, which has disintegrated in the process.

Brecht's adaptation of Christopher Marlowe's play *Edward II* (1693), *Leben Eduards des Zweiten von England* (Life of Edward the Second of England, 1924; translated as *Edward II: A Chronicle Play,* 1966), is a bestiary of lusts and passions in which the members of the nobility are at each other's throat during thirteen years of slaughter, leaving the country ravaged and the people starved. Brecht shows that a deep-rooted source of the vicious circle of historical events is the "eye for an eye" obsession posing as justice.

Brecht pushed his criticism of individualism a step further in the comedy *Mann ist Mann* (performed, 1926; published, 1927; translated as *A Man's a Man,* 1966), set in colonial India. Among the motifs he develops are the economic nature of war and the manipulation of the economic nature of the individual. Galy Gay,

a plain dock porter who has almost no passions, goes out to buy a fish for supper and is changed, through calculated triggering of his desire for gain, into an insatiable war machine. Galy takes the place of the soldier Jip, who is changed in a similar way: hungry not for a fish but for a beefsteak (*beefsteak* is a symbolic word in Brecht's play, meaning not only food [existence] for the soldiers but also the soldiers themselves as cannon fodder—war turns them into beefsteak tartare) he is turned into a god in a pagoda, where he is used to exploit the faithful. The interchangeability of the men in the roles that they assume as new identities "proves" that "a man's a man." Galy loses his private self in his uniformed function in a collective that may be used for any purpose. Brecht's transition from anarchic individualism through anti-individualism to collectivism is reflected in this first stage of his dramatic production between 1918 and 1924. By turning his plays into demonstrations of social conditions rather than perpetuating, in traditional fashion, dramatic clashes of great individuals, Brecht laid the groundwork for an innovative kind of theater. With naturalists and expressionists Brecht shared a discontent with society. But he considered purely emotional dramatic effects unproductive. To change social conditions, nothing was to be accepted as natural or inevitable. The audience was to be confronted with a theater that was not an illusion of reality but a detached yet provocative portrayal that would challenge the viewers to use their critical faculties.

Brecht's adaptation of John Gay's *The Beggar's Opera* (1728), translated by his collaborator Elisabeth Hauptmann, was a major theatrical event in 1928 and made Brecht and Kurt Weill, who wrote the music for it, famous. Gay's successful play had parodied fashionable pastorals and had satirized aristocrats and respectable members of the bourgeoisie by representing them as underworld types: rogues, harlots, and thieves. Two hundred years later Brecht updated this formula, letting his beggars, thieves, gangsters, and harlots behave like the members of the bourgeoisie. This depiction was part of his estrangement technique, as were the songs that interrupted the action and commented on the goings-on in a corrupt world. But the experiment had unforeseen effects: the bourgeoisie apparently considered what they saw as natural rather than as striking. They did not feel affronted; they loved the play and never stopped whistling the melody of "Mackie Messer" (Mac the Knife). The wit and the music seemed to diffuse the stinging anti-bourgeois attack rather than to enhance it as intended.

Nevertheless, Brecht's *Die Dreigroschenoper* (published, 1929; translated as *The Threepenny Opera,* 1964) certainly has an aggressive edge. Peachum, king of the beggars, wants to see Macheath, the gentlemanly street robber, hanged because Macheath has married Peachum's alluring daughter Polly. Peachum controls the beggars, whom he trains and exploits, while Mac controls the thieves and burglars in a similar way. During a visit to the brothel Mac is betrayed by Ginny Jenny and jailed, but he is freed by Police Chief Brown's daughter Lucy, who is one of Mac's girlfriends. Peachum puts pressure on Brown, threatening to disrupt the upcoming coronation ceremony with his hordes of beggars. Mac is captured again; his attempts at bribery fail because of lack of money. He is brought to the gallows, and the noose is laid around his neck, when a royal messenger rides up, orders his immediate release, and raises him to the permanent ranks of the nobility.

The trivial operatic story with a happy ending is used as a critical commentary on bourgeois mentality. It is a ravenous mentality: Mac, Brown, and Peachum are the beasts of society, preying on their victims. What is dangerous about them—and Brecht's estrangement technique calls attention to it—is that they cannot be recognized as beasts of prey by sharp teeth, fins, or claws. They hide their true nature under white-gloved manners. They do their preying according to rules: Peachum by the Bible, Mac by bourgeois etiquette, Brown by the law. But while they feast, the poor, living in shacks gnawed by rats, have to eat stone instead of bread. It is a society in which each person lives by maltreating, beating, cheating, or eating someone else. The maxim "Erst kommt das Fressen, dann kommt die Moral" (First comes the belly, then morality) is sung by Macheath and by Jenny, by the bourgeois exploiter and by the tavern harlot—higher and lower circles seem to agree on that fundamental economic issue, and Jenny adds that right and wrong can wait until the stomach of the poor is fed as well. Depending on which side of the double-faced characters speaks, the maxim expresses cynicism or rebellion. The marriage feast in the stable—which is not in Gay's play—unites the trinity: Religion (Reverend Kimball), Law (Brown), and Gangsterism (Mac). A manger in the stable suggests that this society has perverted a gospel of bliss into a gospel of looted blessings. Mac on the gallows parodies Christ on the cross, inverting the message of salvation: Mac, not humanity, is saved, and he will continue to plague mankind as a banker. Brecht later rewrote the play as a novel (1934) and gave a sharper political focus to the subject. But it is *Die Dreigroschenoper,* with its spicy ballads set to Weill's catchy tunes, that has made its mark in the history of modern theater.

Brecht and Weill collaborated on another opera, *Aufstieg und Fall der Stadt Mahagonny* (published, 1929; performed, 1930; translated as *Rise and Fall of the City of Mahagonny,* 1959). Here a fictive American city of pleasure and exploitation is the setting for an indictment of a capitalist world that ends in apocalypse. It is a paradise fed by biblical myth and the myth of the Wild West; but everything hinges on money, turning all value—including freedom—into a commodity. A commercial paradise that knows no mercy becomes hell. Nazi sympathizers disrupted the premiere of this collaboration by a "communist" and a "Jew."

Between 1928 and 1930 Brecht also wrote several brief "Lehrstücke" (didactic plays) as educational practice pieces for actors. The main concerns of these plays—*Der Ozeanflug* (The Flight across the Ocean; performed, 1929; published as *Der Flug der Lindberghs* [Lindbergh's Flight], 1930), *Das Badener Lehrstück vom Einverständnis* (The Baden Didactic Play on Consent; performed, 1929; published, 1930; translated as *The Baden Play for Learning,* 1960), *Die Maßnahme* (performed, 1930; published, 1931; translated as *The Measures Taken,* 1977), *Der Jasager und Der Neinsager* (He Who Says Yes and He Who Says No; performed, 1930; published, 1931; translated as *He Who Said Yes,* 1946), and *Die Ausnahme und die Regel* (performed, 1938; published, 1950; translated as *The Exception and the Rule,* 1961)—are the experimental exploration of human behavior in socioeconomic relationships and the relationship between individual and collective. These experiments were influenced by Marxist doctrine and by questions about the political effectiveness of revolutionary group efforts by the workers.

A full-fledged revolutionary play is *Die Mutter* (performed, 1932; published, 1933; translated as *The Mother,* 1965), derived from Maksim Gorky's novel *Mat'* (Mother, 1907), about the Russian revolution of 1905, which Brecht extends to include the revolution of 1917 against the czarist regime. A loving but apolitical mother, Pelagea Vlassova, is educated by her experiences to join her son and his comrades in the revolution; after her son is killed she continues the fight. The mother has adopted the children of the revolution, and she carries the flag, leading the striking workers. This was the last Brecht play performed before the takeover by the Nazis, who had increasingly harassed leftist productions.

The most ambitious and powerful political play from Brecht's Berlin period is *Die heilige Johanna der Schlachthöfe* (published, 1932; performed, 1959; translated as *Saint Joan of the Stockyards,* 1969), written under the impact of the Great Depression of 1929, the bloody suppression of workers' demonstrations by the police in Berlin, and his reading of Karl Marx and Friedrich Engels's *Das Kapital* (1867-1895; translated as *Capital,* 1887-1896). The play is a variation on the Jeanne d'Arc theme and alludes to classical German authors, George Bernard Shaw, and Upton Sinclair's *The Jungle* (1906), which Brecht had recommended ten years earlier as an antidote to Friedrich Schiller's idea of freedom. Once again an American city is the setting for a general—but particularly German—reality. The stockyards of Chicago become the battleground between the meat packers, whose king is Pierpont Mauler, and the masses of hungry workers, victims of engineered economic crises and recoveries serving monopolist interests. Johanna Dark, leading the Black Straw Hats of the Salvation Army, tries to mediate between the two sides by appealing to philanthropy and religion. She is good but naive about economic and political operations, which Brecht exposes by his estrangement technique. One of the strangest effects is that the meat packers strut around like great individuals in classical drama and speak in noble verse expressing (or covering up) their cutthroat business interests. This work is one of Brecht's bitterest counterplays, in which he demonstrates the dehumanizing power of hunger and the machinations of those in power who cause it. In his *Die Jungfrau von Orleans* (1802; translated as *The Maid of Orleans,* 1824) Schiller had idealized the alliance between the king of France and the God of victorious battle brought about by a self-sacrificial "Saint" Johanna. Brecht parodies this notion with the commercial alliance between the king of the slaughterhouses and the "saint" from the Salvation Army who unwittingly helps him to win his battle. In Brecht's imagery, the world is a bloody slaughterhouse. There is not much difference between cattle and people; both become the objects of consumerism, as symbolically highlighted in the gruesome and grotesque accident of the worker Luckerniddle, who falls into the boiler, is processed through the bacon-maker, and is marketed like the slaughtered oxen, and whose place and coat are desperately grabbed by the next worker.

Johanna wants to help the workers; she preaches religion and feeds them a meager soup. Her actions are useful to the capitalist Mauler, who, "influenced" by her goodness, shows himself as a "humanitarian" and wants to collaborate with the Salvation Army to keep things as they are. When Johanna begins to recognize these machinations she joins the communists; but she fails them because, as a pacifist, she shies away from the use of violence. She cannot prevent the new alliance between the king of the slaughterhouses and the god of the Salvation Army, between capitalism and religion. She was the initiator and becomes victim of this alliance, which provides just enough soup for the poor and hungry to keep them from smashing their tools and rising in rebellion.

Brecht and Marianne Zoff had been divorced in 1927. In 1929 he married the actress Helene Weigel, whom he had met in 1923. Their son, Stefan, had been born in 1924; a daughter, Barbara, was born in 1930. With the Nazis coming into power the exile of the Brecht family began. His works were included in the infamous burning of the books in May 1933, but he had read the signs and escaped one day after the Reichstag fire on 27 February. The stations of his exile, during which he changed countries more often than his shoes (as he once put it), were Czechoslovakia, Austria, Switzerland, France, Denmark, Sweden, Finland, and the United States. Brecht remained active and productive while in exile. He traveled to conferences of writers and emigrants, joined anti-Fascist demonstrations, collaborated on emigrant journals, wrote poems and satires for the German broadcasting station in Moscow, attempted through his publications abroad to strengthen anti-Fascist resolve, and had his works smuggled into Germany for underground circulation. His parable play *Die Rundköpfe und die Spitzköpfe* (performed, 1935; published, 1957; translated as *Roundheads and Peakheads,* 1966) lashes out against Adolf Hitler's racism as a tool of class exploitation. Brecht used more realistic means in the resistance piece *Die Gewehre der Frau Carrar* (performed, 1937; translated as *Señora Carrar's Rifles,* 1938; published, 1953), dedicated to the struggle of the Spanish people against fascism. Beginning in 1935 Brecht worked on a series of one-act sketches about the Nazi terror, which he joined together in the play *Furcht und Elend des III. Reiches* (Fear and Misery of the Third Reich; performed as *99%,* 1938; published, 1941; translated as *The Private Life of the Master Race,* 1944). In 1938 he finished the first version of *Leben des Galilei* (Life of Galileo; performed, 1943). His claim that this play contained no barbs against Germany or Italy was to placate the nervous Danish authorities; its topicality, nevertheless, was apparent. With *Mutter Courage und ihre Kinder* (performed, 1941; published, 1949; translated as *Mother Courage and her Children,* 1966) Brecht warns against imminent war. The one-act plays *Dansen* (performed, 1967; published, 1966; translated, 1971–1973) and *Was kostet das Eisen?* (performed as *Vad kostar järnet?,* 1939; published, 1966; translated as *How Much Is Your Iron?,* 1971–1973) criticize, in parabolic form, Scandinavian trade with Nazi Germany. In *Der aufhaltsame Aufstieg des Arturo Ui* (published, 1957; performed, 1958; translated as *The Resistible Rise of Arturo Ui,* 1976) Brecht chose a Chicago gangster story to indict Nazi methods. In American exile Brecht updated, together with Charles Laughton, the Galileo play in view of new political events. He also wrote *Die Gesichte der Simone Machard* (1957; translated as *The Visions of Simone Machard,* 1965) and *Schweyk im zweiten Weltkrieg* (1957; translated as *Schweyk in the Second World War,* 1967), and the frame story of *Der kaukasische Kreidekreis* (published, 1954; translated as *The Caucasian Chalk Circle,* 1948; translation performed, 1948), all of which take issue with the events of the time and raise keen questions about the kind of society in which such events can occur.

Among the anti-Fascist projects he pursued in Scandinavian exile, *Mutter Courage und ihre Kinder,* written on the eve of World War II, sounded the most intense warning about consenting to—and doing business with—war. Mother Courage, a sutler who follows the armies of the Thirty Years' War to make her living, loses all three of her children in the process. The Thirty Years' War, a low point in German history, had been realistically described by Johann Jacob Christoffel von Grimmelshausen in his novels *Der abentheuerliche Simplicissimus Teutsch* (1669; translated as *The Adventurous Simplicissimus,* 1912) and *Trutz Simplex: Oder Ausführliche und wunderseltzame Lebensbeschreibung der Ertzbetrügerin und Landstörtzerin Courasche* (Simple Defiance; or, Detailed and Curious Biography of the Arch-Cozener and Vagabond Courasche, 1669), which were Brecht's major sources of inspiration. Brecht does not show "great" generals of the "religious" war but rather the plain people who are the cannon fodder for "higher" interests. The ups and downs of the fortunes of war are reflected in the alternatingly prosperous and rundown condition of Courage's wagon, which links the twelve scenes. She does business with war to support her children, and she uses her children to support her business. That this practice cannot lead to success is shown by the horrors of war in which her children perish—at the end it is just Mother Courage who pulls her tattered wagon.

The wagon is the center of all kinds of trading for profit or survival: while Courage sells a belt buckle, the recruiter "buys" her son Eilif; a scrawny capon can be sold to the army cook at a high price because the captain has nothing else to offer to Eilif for his heroic deed; a preacher sells out his ideals to the war; a prostitute sells herself to the highest bidder; because Courage's honest son Schweizerkas (Swiss Cheese) does not trade a military cashbox to the enemy, his mother is forced to trade her wagon for his life, which is then lost anyway because she bargains too long for the best deal; a sudden enemy takeover necessitates a hasty trading of Protestant for Catholic insignia and garb. Such give-and-take is highlighted time and again to show that dealing with war, which is the business of those in power, brings nothing but loss to the lower classes. Mother Courage loses each of her children while she tries to drive some bargain, and the virtues she taught them only contribute to their destruction.

Brecht gives both admirable and despicable traits to Courage—he did not see her as a tragic figure. Some critics see her as a split character in an irreconcilable conflict between mother and businesswoman, while others think that she is more the latter than the former. At one point Courage condemns the war; but she is

quick to get back into it, as it is her source of business. She does not recognize that her little world of opportunism, aggressiveness, scheming, and outsmarting others is a reflection of the tactics of big business. War is made—it does not just happen—and the common people have to pay the bill.

While for Courage business takes priority over family, for her daughter Kattrin the opposite is true. Victimized by the brutalities of war since she was a child, Kattrin is mute, disfigured, and deprived of hope for personal happiness. Yearning for love and sympathizing with the miserable and helpless, she opposes her mother's cold business tactics. One night she witnesses a sneak attack on a city and thinks of all the people—especially innocent children—about to be murdered; she beats a drum to warn them and is promptly shot to death, but she has awakened the city and saved other lives. She has been seen as a rebel and a martyr, a spontaneous activist in contrast to her calculating opportunist mother. But while Brecht endowed her with the qualities of a heroine, he does not glorify martyrdom per se and points out in considerable detail how the unselfish girl was manipulated, time and again, by the selfish people around her.

Der gute Mensch von Sezuan (performed, 1943; published, 1953; translated as *The Good Woman of Setzuan,* 1948) is Brecht's master parable, considered by many to be his most perfect example of epic theater as the art of estrangement. His first plans for the play date back to 1927; he worked on it intermittently during his exile and completed it in the United States in 1941. In a prologue three gods descend to earth; they will allow the world to go on as it is if they can find enough people who live lives worthy of human beings. No one except the poor prostitute Shen Te is willing to put them up overnight; the gods, happy to have found one good soul, remind her to maintain a good life, and they continue their search. But Shen Te, who earns the nickname "Engel der Vorstädte" (angel of the suburbs) by practicing goodness with the money the gods left her, is about to lose her little tobacco shop because parasites and opportunists have descended on her, exploiting her humanitarianism. She finds no other way out but to disguise herself as her "cousin" Shui Ta, a hard-nosed businessman, whenever she needs him. While Shui Ta provides the means through "his" ruthless bargaining methods and factory employment practices, Shen Te remains good to others. As demands on her goodness increase, Shui Ta has to stay longer and longer. Finally, Shen Te cannot keep up the double front and is unmasked in a trial before the gods, who can neither help her nor tell her why the world cannot be different. They hastily beat a retreat to heaven on their theater clouds and leave behind them a split person, an open-ended play, and an audience urged in the epilogue to find its own happy conclusion. Brecht uses the trial scene to confront the gods' judgment of humans with human judgment of the gods. The open ending challenges the old idea of the "theatrum mundi," according to which God observes and judges individuals in their performance of the roles allotted to them in life. Shen Te recognizes that something is wrong with this world; the spectators and readers have also witnessed the negative experiment demonstrated by the parable. By addressing the audience directly, the speaker of the epilogue links the parable to whatever reality the spectators may find themselves in, a reality they are encouraged to shape toward a good end.

Less strident in its exposure of social injustice and more detached from immediate historical reference is the colorful comedy *Herr Puntila und sein Knecht Matti* (1948; translated as *Mister Puntila and His Man Matti*, 1977), based on a story by Hella Wuolijoki, who hosted Brecht during his Finnish exile. The landowner Puntila is humane and fraternizes with his servants only when he is drunk; when he is sober he is a ruthless exploiter. At the end his servant Matti, who has realized that a worthwhile relationship with the upper class is impossible, leaves to become his own master. Once again the conclusion is open-ended; Brecht challenges his audience to determine the meaning and the method of becoming one's "own master."

During his American exile Brecht lived in a colony of German emigrants in Los Angeles and continued with his anti-Fascist theater in a more direct, realistic style. *Die Gesichte der Simone Machard,* written together with Lion Feuchtwanger, is a modern variant of the Jeanne d'Arc theme. A naive young French servant girl, reading the patriotic legend, becomes a resistance fighter against the Nazi occupation of France; she is victimized by her countrymen, who, to save their possessions, collaborate with the invaders.

In *Schweyk im zweiten Weltkrieg* Brecht uses folk comedy and satire to encourage indirect subversiveness. Apparently he hoped to repeat the success of the 1928 Berlin staging of a dramatization of Jaroslav Hašek's antiwar novel *Osudy dobrého vojáka Svejka* (1920–1923; translated as *The Good Soldier Schweik,* 1930) by Erwin Piscator's political theater, a production in which the satirist George Grosz and Brecht himself had collaborated. A cartoon of Hitler, Hermann Göring, Heinrich Himmler, and Joseph Goebbels by the caricaturist Arthur Szyk, published in *Collier's* (17 January 1942), and reprinted in *Look* (8 September 1942), influenced Brecht's prelude set in the higher regions, where preternaturally large gods with grandiose plans for world power talk about the self-denying virtues of the little people on whose faith, love, and work they must rely.

But while the "great ones" proclaim their totalitarian goals, the lowly ones, seemingly fulfilling these plans, actually undermine them. The Good Soldier Schweyk, who has survived World War I, battles to outlive World War II. Brecht sees in him the indestructible vitality of the people: the more oppressive the system, the more devious the defensive tactics. Under the pretense of naïveté, if not idiocy, Schweyk follows orders sometimes to the letter; but by fumbling his assignments he avoids danger. For example, he gives confusing directions to a freight train attendant, who sends a carload of weapons off on the wrong track; his march to the front turns out to be circular, leading him back to base. "Alles hat zwei Seiten" (there are two sides to everything) is Schweyk's motto: he does not accept the absolute or the inevitable but keeps the door open to alternatives. Some see him as an opportunistic fellow traveler, others as a devious opponent. He must be both, for open resistance is simply clobbered down. Brecht's hope of seeing *Schweyk im zweiten Weltkrieg* performed on Broadway with music by his erstwhile collaborator Weill did not materialize; the play was first staged in Warsaw, with music by Hanns Eisler.

Another Broadway prospect, *The Caucasian Chalk Circle,* was not accepted either–Brecht's epic theater style was too unusual for mainstream American stages, and the play premiered in Northfield, Minnesota. With this new play, Brecht once again elaborated a subject that had interested him earlier. It is based on a Chinese fable about a Solomonic judgment that identifies the "true" mother of a child. The main story is a play within a play that is used to demonstrate the solution to a conflict between two collective farms that have survived Nazi aggression and plan to rebuild their economy. One group proposes to return to its old methods of breeding sheep so that the cheese will taste better (a conservative position); the other proposes to build an irrigation system for growing fruit in the valley (a progressive position aimed at communal good). The latter group wins the day and puts on the play, which consists of two parts: the story of Grusha, a kitchen maid; and the story of Azdak, the judge. The stories, presented one after the other, are parallel in time and converge at the end; in Brechtian fashion, the performance is interspersed with narrative comments and songs. During a revolution in a Caucasian city the governor is overthrown and killed. Grusha saves the child left behind by the escaping governor's wife, and protects and educates him. At the end of the first story all her self-sacrificial effort seems for naught: the soldiers of the "Fat Prince" (the governor's rival) capture the child, who is reclaimed by its biological mother; she hopes that after the return of the grand duke to power her properties will be restored to her by virtue of being the blood relative of the governor's heir. While Grusha saved a child, Azdak, a tramp, saved an old man. The old man turns out to be the grand duke, who, after the rebellion fails, rewards Azdak by making him a judge. Azdak settles law cases in a most unorthodox manner: taking from the rich and giving to the poor, he becomes the hero of the people, who at long last see real justice being done. Azdak's situation, however, becomes more and more precarious: feudal society did not change through the revolution, which was merely a power struggle between feudal lords. Azdak finally fades out of the picture, but not before he has decided the dispute between the two "mothers" by way of the chalk-circle test: the real mother is the one who can pull the child out of the circle. While the biological mother pulls him recklessly, Grusha lets go of his hand so that he will not be torn apart. Azdak declares her the "real" mother. The minstrel-narrator summarizes the message that what there is should belong to those who are good for it—the children to the motherly that they may thrive, the valley to those who water it so that it may bring forth fruit. Some performances of the play exclude the socialistic frame story about the valley. A sensitive audience will not miss the modern relevance of an old parable demonstrating how and why injustices occur in society.

To many, *Leben des Galilei* is the most significant of Brecht's dramas, not only because of its fascinating, complex central character but also because of its examination of the difficult pursuit of truth and the problem of applying truth to the well-being of society. Galileo Galilei, one of the great figures of the Renaissance, founder of modern astronomy and pioneer of empirical scientific inquiry, championed the new heliocentric theory of Nicolaus Copernicus against the old geocentric theory of Ptolemy. As Galileo's teaching appeared to contradict certain passages in the Bible, the Inquisition forced him to recant, put him under house arrest for the rest of his life, and policed his further research. This situation set back the pursuit of scientific truth, and men such as René Descartes ceased publishing "dangerous" findings; but the spread of Galileo's works, which were smuggled out of Italy, could not be stopped. As in *Mutter Courage und ihre Kinder,* the situation remote in time becomes a parable for current political events. The first sketches of the play project Galileo as a popular hero amid social upheaval, a courageous and cunning underground fighter. As resistance was more and more suppressed by the Nazis, the first full version of the play, written in Danish exile in 1938–1939, makes Galileo a more controversial character bending under political pressure in order to survive but continuing to write while under arrest. Those who saw the inaugural performance of this play in Zurich in 1943 were clearly aware of its anti-Fascist thrust.

The second version, *Galileo,* was a collaboration between Brecht, who was then in California, and Charles Laughton, who was to play the title role in an American production. The dropping of the atomic bombs on Japan in early August 1945 gave a new meaning to the biography of the founder of modern physics. This version shows more negative traits of the hero; Brecht also left out the last scene, which showed the smuggling of Galileo's work over the border and suggested prospects for a better future. Also, social conflicts are profiled to a larger extent to bring home the message of the scientist's betrayal of society. The most important change, however, is the denial of the ethics of cunning through Galileo's self-accusation, which forms the new conclusion of the play. Galileo is now cast into the role of hero *and* criminal, one who committed the scientist's original sin: selling out truth to the powers that be for irresponsible political use. The play was performed in Beverly Hills in 1947 and later that year in New York, without making a great impression on an audience not used to Brechtian theater.

The third version translated the American version back into German and added material from the first version, including the last (crossing-of-the-border) scene. By this time the race for nuclear weapons had given the arsenals of the super-powers unfathomable potential for destruction. The negative elements in Galileo's character remain and are sharpened by radical additions such as the claim that, if he had held out, scientists might have developed something like the physicians' Hippocratic oath, the vow to use their knowledge only for the good of mankind. But as things stand now, Galileo says to his former student Andrea, the best one can hope for is a generation of inventive dwarfs who can be hired for any purpose. Brecht's molding of distant history into a parable with contemporary relevance, and the autobiographical affinities between Brecht and his Galileo, have elicited critical responses that include indictments of facism, capitalism, and communism, as well as divided opinions about Brecht himself.

In 1947 Brecht returned to Europe. His departure came one day after he and other members of the Hollywood scene were interrogated by the House Committee on Un-American Activities about communist affiliations. The transcript recording of the hearing is a revealing document of the times and of Brecht's cunning performance. After a brief period in Zurich, Brecht settled in 1948 in East Berlin. He and his wife, Weigel, were given a theater and the opportunity to take part in the cultural rebuilding of East Germany—not an easy task for Brecht, who was unwilling to bend to the narrow precepts of socialist realism, the artistic principle dictated by the ruling party. Until his death he was more active as a director than as a playwright. Although he completed such plays as *Die Tage der Commune* (The Days of the Commune; performed, 1956; published, 1957; translated, 1971) and *Turandot oder Der Kongreß der Weißwäscher* (Turandot; or, The Congress of White-washers; published, 1968; performed, 1969), many projects remained unfinished. A substantial part of his theater experimentation focused on adaptations of plays by Molière, Shakespeare, and Sophocles. At last Brecht was able to direct his own plays according to principles he had developed over the years in such works as "Kleines Organon für das Theater" (1953; translated as "A Short Organum for the Theatre," 1964), with a troupe of actors that was to become world famous as the Berliner Ensemble. Brecht died in Berlin on 14 August 1956, during rehearsals of *Leben des Galilei*.

Letters:

Briefe, 2 volumes, edited by Günter Glaeser (Frankfurt am Main: Suhrkamp, 1981); translated by Ralph Manheim and edited by John Willett as *Letters* (New York: Routledge, 1990);

Liebste Bi: Briefe an Paula Banholzer, edited by Helmut Gier and Jürgen Hillesheim (Frankfurt am Main: Suhrkamp, 1992).

Bibliographies:

Walter Nubel, "Brecht Bibliographie," *Sinn und Form: Sonderheft Bertolt Brecht 2* (1957): 479–623;

Klaus-Dietrich Petersen, *Bertolt-Brecht-Bibliographie* (Bad Homburg: Gehlen, 1968);

Reinhold Grimm, *Bertolt Brecht,* third edition (Stuttgart: Metzler, 1971);

Klaus Völker, "Verzeichnis sämtlicher Stücke, Bearbeitungen und Fragmente zu Stücken von Bertolt Brecht," *text + kritik. Sonderband Bertolt Brecht II* (1973): 210–225;

Jan Knopf, *Bertolt Brecht: Ein kritischer Forschungsbericht* (Frankfurt am Main: Athenäum Taschenbuchverlag, 1974);

Gerhard Seidel, *Bibliographie Bertolt Brecht. Titelverzeichnis Band I: Deutschsprachige Veröffentlichungen aus den Jahren 1913–1972* (Berlin & Weimar: Aufbau, 1975);

Stephan Bock, *Brecht, Bertolt: Auswahl- und Ergänzungs-Bibliographie* (Bochum: Brockmeyer, 1979).

Biographies:

Frederic Ewen, *Bertolt Brecht: His Life, His Art and His Times* (New York: Citadel, 1967);

Werner Frisch and K. W. Obermeier, *Brecht in Augsburg: Erinnerungen, Texte, Photos* (Berlin: Aufbau, 1975);

Klaus Völker, *Bertolt Brecht: Eine Biographie* (Munich: Hanser, 1976); translated by John Nowell as

Brecht: A Biography (New York: Seabury Press, 1978);

Lion Feuchtwanger, ed., *Bertolt Brecht: Leben und Werk im Bild* (Frankfurt am Main: Insel, 1979);

James K. Lyon, *Bertolt Brecht in America* (Princeton: Princeton University Press, 1980);

Ernst Schumacher and Renate Schumacher, *Leben Brechts in Wort und Bild,* third edition (Berlin: Henschel, 1981);

Ronald Hayman, *Brecht: A Biography* (New York: Oxford University Press, 1983);

Bruce Cook, *Brecht in Exile* (New York: Holt, Rinehart & Winston, 1983);

Ruth Berlau, *Brechts Lai-tu: Erinnerungen und Notate,* edited by Hans Bunge (Darmstadt: Luchterhand, 1985);

Werner Mittenzwei, *Das Leben des Bertolt Brecht,* 2 volumes (Berlin: Aufbau, 1986);

Werner Hecht, ed., *Brecht: Sein Leben in Bildern und Texten* (Frankfurt am Main: Insel, 1988);

Hanns Otto Münsterer, *The Young Brecht,* translated by Tom Kuhn and Karen J. Leeder (London: Libris, 1992).

References:

Eric Bentley, *The Brecht Commentaries, 1943–1980* (New York: Grove, 1981);

Keith A. Dickson, *Towards Utopia: A Study of Brecht* (Oxford: Clarendon Press, 1978);

Martin Esslin, *Brecht: A Choice of Evils* (London: Eyre & Spottiswoode, 1959); republished as *Brecht: The Man and His Work* (Garden City, N.Y.: Doubleday, 1960); revised as *Brecht: A Choice of Evils. A Critical Study of the Man, His Work and His Opinions* (London: Methuen, 1984);

John Fuegi, *Brecht and Company: Sex, Politics, and the Making of the Modern Drama* (New York: Grove, 1994);

Ronald Gray, *Brecht the Dramatist* (Cambridge: Cambridge University Press, 1976);

Reinhold Grimm, *Bertolt Brecht: Die Struktur seines Werkes,* sixth edition (Nuremberg: Carl, 1972);

Paula Joan Hanssen, *Elisabeth Hauptmann: Brecht's Silent Collaborator* (Bern & New York: Peter Lang, 1995);

Claude Hill, *Bertolt Brecht* (Boston: Twayne, 1975);

Walter Hinck, *Die Dramaturgie des späten Brecht,* sixth edition (Göttingen: Vandenhoeck & Ruprecht, 1977);

Walter Hinderer, ed., *Brechts Dramen: Neue Interpretationen* (Stuttgart: Reclam, 1984);

Helmut Jendreiek, *Bertolt Brecht: Drama der Veränderung,* second edition (Düsseldorf: Bagel, 1973);

Jan Knopf, *Brecht-Handbuch: Theater. Eine Ästhetik der Widersprüche* (Stuttgart: Metzler, 1980);

Hans-Thies Lehmann, Renate Voris, Marc Silberman, and others, eds., *The Other Brecht,* 2 volumes

(Madison: University of Wisconsin Press, 1992, 1993);

James K. Lyon and Hans-Peter Breuer, eds., *Brecht Unbound* (Newark: University of Delaware Press / London: Associated University Presses, 1995);

Siegfried Mews, ed., *Critical Essays on Bertolt Brecht* (Boston: G.K. Hall, 1989);

Mews and Herbert Knust, eds., *Essays on Brecht: Theater and Politics* (Chapel Hill: University of North Carolina Press, 1974);

John Milful, *From Baal to Keuner: The "Second Optimism" of Bertolt Brecht* (Bern & Frankfurt am Main: Peter Lang, 1974);

Michael Morley, *Brecht: A Study* (London: Heinemann, 1977);

Klaus-Detlev Müller, ed., *Bertolt Brecht: Epoche–Werk–Wirkung* (Munich: Beck, 1985);

Chetana Nagavajara, *Brecht and France* (Bern & New York: Peter Lang, 1994);

Jan Needle and Peter Thomson, *Brecht* (Chicago: University of Chicago Press, 1981);

Patty Lee Parmalee, *Brecht's America* (Columbus: Ohio State University Press, 1981);

Herta Ramthun, ed., *Bertolt-Brecht-Archiv: Bestands-verzeichnis des literarischen Nachlasses*, 4 volumes (Berlin: Aufbau, 1969–1973);

Janelle G. Reinelt, *After Brecht: British Epic Theater* (Ann Arbor: University of Michigan Press, 1994);

Claudette Sartiliot, *Citation and Modernity: Derrida, Joyce, and Brecht* (Norman: University of Oklahoma Press, 1993);

Karl-Heinz Schoeps, *Bertolt Brecht* (New York: Ungar, 1977);

Ronald Speirs, *Brecht's Early Plays* (Atlantic Highlands, N.J.: Humanities Press, 1982);

Antony Tatlow, *The Mask of Evil: Brecht's Response to the Poetry, Theatre, and Thought of China and Japan* (Bern: Peter Lang, 1977);

Peter Thomson and Glendyr Sacks, eds., *The Cambridge Companion to Brecht* (Cambridge & New York: Cambridge University Press, 1994);

Michael Thoss, *Brecht for Beginners* (New York: Writers and Readers, 1994);

Klaus Völker, *Brecht Kommentar zum dramatischen Werk* (Munich: Winkler, 1983);

Betty Nance Weber and Hubert Heinen, eds., *Bertolt Brecht: Political Theory and Literary Practice* (Athens: University of Georgia Press, 1980);

Alfred White, *Bertolt Brecht's Great Plays* (New York: Barnes & Noble, 1978);

John Willett, *Brecht in Context: Comparative Approaches* (London & New York: Methuen, 1984);

Willett, *The Theater of Bertolt Brecht: A Study from Eight Aspects* (London: Methuen, 1977).

Papers:

Bertolt Brecht's papers are at the Bertolt Brecht Archive, Berlin, administered by the Deutsche Akademie der Künste (German Academy of the Arts).

Hermann Broch

(1 November 1886 – 30 May 1951)

Paul Michael Lützeler
Washington University

and

John Carson Pettey
University of Nevada, Reno

This entry originally appeared in DLB 85: Austrian
Fiction Writers After 1914.

BOOKS: *Die Schlafwandler: Eine Romantrilogie,* 3 volumes
(Munich & Zurich: Rhein, 1931–1932); translated
by Willa and Edwin Muir as *The Sleepwalkers: A
Trilogy* (New York: Little, Brown, 1932; London:
Secker, 1932);

Die Unbekannte Größe: Roman (Berlin: Fischer, 1933);
translated by Willa and Edwin Muir as *The
Unknown Quantity* (New York: Viking Press, 1935;
London: Collins, 1935);

James Joyce und die Gegenwart: Rede zu Joyces 50. Geburtstag
(Vienna, Leipzig & Zurich: Reichner, 1936); translated by Maria and Eugene Jolas as "James Joyce
and the Present Age," in *A James Joyce Yearbook*
(Paris: Transition Press, 1949), pp. 68–108;

The City of Man: A Declaration on World Democracy, by
Broch, Herbert Agar, and others (New York:
Viking Press, 1940);

Der Tod des Vergil: Roman (New York: Pantheon, 1945);
translated by Jean Starr Untermeyer as *The Death
of Virgil* (New York: Pantheon, 1945; London:
Routledge, 1946);

Die Schuldlosen: Roman in elf Erzählungen (Munich: Weismann, 1950); translated by Ralph Manheim as
The Guiltless (Boston & Toronto; Little, Brown,
1974);

Gesammelte Werke, 10 volumes (Zurich: Rhein, 1952–
1961)–includes volume 1, *Gedichte: Mit 9 Bildern
und 2 Handschriftproben des Autors,* edited by Erich
Kahler (1953); volume 2, *Die Schlafwandler:
Romantrilogie* (1952); volume 3, *Der Tod des Vergil.
Epische Dichtung* (1952); volume 4, *Der Versucher:
Roman,* edited by Felix Stössinger (1953); repub-
lished as *Demeter* (Frankfurt am Main: Suhrkamp,

Hermann Broch in 1942 (photo: Trude Geiringer)

1967); volume 6, *Dichten und Erkennen: Essays,* edited by Hannah Arendt (1955); volume 7, *Erkennen und Handeln: Essays,* edited by Arendt (1955); volume 8, *Briefe: Von 1929 bis 1951,* edited by Robert Pick (1957); volume 9, *Massenpsychologie: Schriften aus dem Nachlaß,* edited by Wolfgang Rothe (1959); volume 10, *Die unbekannte Größe und frühe Schriften,* edited by Ernst Schönwiese, and *Mit den Briefen an Willa Muir,* edited by Eric William Herd (1961);

Nur das Herz ist das Wirkliche, edited by Schönwiese (Graz: Stiasny, 1959);

Die Eutsühnung: Schauspiel, in der Hörspielfassung, edited by Schönwiese (Zurich: Rhein, 1961);

Die Heimkehr: Prosa und Lyrik. Auswahl aus dem dichterischen Werk ergänzl durch den Vortrag Geist und Zeitgeist, edited by Harald Binde (Frankfurt am Main & Hamburg: Fischer, 1962);

Hermann Broch der Dichter: Eine Auswahl aus dem dichterischen Werk, edited by Binde (Zurich: Rhein, 1964);

Hermann Broch der Dichter: Eine Auswahl aus dem essayistischen Werk und aus Briefen, edited by Binde (Zurich: Rhein, 1966);

Short Stories, edited by Herd (London: Oxford University Press, 1966);

Die Idea ist ewig: Essays and Briefe, edited by Binde (Munich: Deutscher Taschenbuch Verlag, 1968);

Zur Universitätsreform, edited by Götz Wienold (Frankfurt am Main: Suhrkamp, 1969);

Bergroman: Die drei Originalfassungen, edited by Frank Kress and Hans Albert Maier, 4 volumes (Frankfurt am Main: Suhrkamp, 1969);

Gedanken zur Politik, edited by Dieter Hildebrandt (Frankfurt am Main: Suhrkamp, 1970);

Barbara und andere Novellen: Eine Auswahl aus dem dichterischen Werk, edited by Paul Michael Lützeler (Frankfurt am Main: Suhrkamp, 1973)—comprises "Eine methodologische Novelle," "Ophelia," "Leutnant Jaretzki," "Hanna Wendling," "Eine leichte Enttäuschung," "Vorüberziehende Wolke," "Ein Abend Angst," "Die Heimkehr," "Der Meeresspiegel," "Esperance," "Barbara," "Die Heimkehr des Vergil," "Die vier Reden des Studienrats Zacharias," "Die Erzählung der Magd Zerline";

Völkerbund-Resolution: Das vollständige politische Pamphlet von 1937 mit Kommentar, Entwurf und Korrespondenz, edited by Lützeler (Salzburg: Müller, 1973);

Kommentierte Werkausgabe, edited by Lützeler, 17 volumes (Frankfurt am Main: Suhrkamp, 1974–1981)—includes volume 1, *Die Schlafwandler: Eine Romantrilogie* (1978); volume 2, *Die Unbekannte Größe: Roman* (1977); volume 3, *Die Verzauberung* (1976); translated by H. F. Broch de Rothermann as *The Spell*

(New York: Farrar, Straus & Giroux, 1987); volume 4, *Der Tod des Vergil: Roman* (1976); volume 5, *Die Schuldlosen: Roman in elf Erzählungen* (1974); volume 6, *Novellen; Prosa; Fragmente* (1980); volume 7, *Dramen* (1979), including *Die Entsühnung,* translated by George E. Wellwarth and Broch de Rothermann as *The Atonement,* in *German Drama between the Wars,* edited by Wellwarth (New York: Dutton, 1972); volume 8, *Gedichte* (1980); volume 9, part 1, *Schriften zur Literatur: Kritik* (1975); "Hugo von Hofmannsthal und seine Zeit," translated by Michael P. Steinberg as *Hugo von Hofmannsthal and His Time: The European Imagination, 1860–1920* (Chicago & London: University of Chicago Press, 1984); volume 9, part 2, *Schriften zur Literatur: Theorie* (1975); volume 10, part 1, *Philosophische Schriften: Kritik* (1977); volume 10, part 2, *Philosophische Schriften: Theorie* (1977); volume 11, *Politische Schriften* (1979); volume 12, *Massenwahntheorie. Beiträge zu Einer Psychologie der Politik* (1979); volume 13, part 1, *Briefe 1913–1938* (1981); volume 13, part 2, *Briefe 1938–1945* (1981); volume 13, part 3, *Briefe 1945–1951* (1981).

OTHER: "Logik einer zerfallenden Welt," in *Wiedergeburt der Liebe: Die unsichtbare Revolution,* edited by Frank Thiess (Berlin: Zsolnay, 1931), pp. 361–380;

"Gedanken zum Problem der Erkenntnis in der Musik," in *Almanach: "Das 48. Jahr"* (Berlin: Fischer, 1934), pp. 53–66;

"Eh ich erwacht," "Über die Felswand," "Helle Sommernacht," "Sommerwiese," "Schon lichtet der Herbst den Wald," "Die Waldlichtung," "Später Herbst," "Nachgewitter," "Lago Maggiore," "Das Nimmergewesene," in *Patmos: Zwölf Lyriker,* edited by Ernst Schönwiese (Vienna: Johannespresse, 1935), pp. 57–67;

"Mythos und Altersstil," in Rachel Bespaloff, *On the Iliad,* translated by Mary McCarthy (New York: Pantheon, 1947), pp. 9–33;

"Vom Altern," in *Frank Thiess: Werk und Dichter. 32 Beiträge zur Problematik unserer Zeit,* edited by Rolf Italiaander (Hamburg: Krüger, 1950), p. 9.

PERIODICAL PUBLICATIONS: "Philistrosität, Realismus, Idealismus der Kunst," *Der Brenner,* 3 (1 February 1913): 399–415;

"Antwort auf eine Rundfrage über Karl Kraus," *Der Brenner,* 3 (15 June 1913): 849–859;

"Mathematisches Mysterium," *Der Brenner,* 4 (1 November 1913): 136;

"Ethik: Unter Hinweis auf H. St. Chamberlains Buch *Immanuel Kant*," *Der Brenner*, 4 (1 May 1914): 684–690;

"Otto Kaus, Dostojewski: Zur Kritik einer Persönlichkeit. Ein Versuch," *Die Aktion*, 6 (1916): 578–579;

"Zolas Vorurteil," *Summa*, 1, no. 1 (1917): 155–158;

"Morgenstern," *Summa*, 1, no. 2 (1917): 150–154;

"Zum Begriff der Geisteswissenschaften," *Summa*, 1, no. 3 (1917): 199–209;

"Eine methodologische Novelle," *Summa*, 2, no. 3 (1918): 151–159;

"Heinrich von Stein: Gesammelte Dichtungen," *Summa*, 2, no. 3 (1918): 166–169;

"Konstruktion der historischen Wirklichkeit," *Summa*, 2, no. 4 (1918): i–xvi;

"Die Straße (Offener Brief an Franz Blei)," *Die Rettung*, 1 (20 December 1918): 25–26;

"Konstitutionelle Diktatur als demokratisches Rätesystem," *Der Friede*, 3 (11 April 1919): 269–273;

"Wasserkräfte und Abfallenergien im Wiener Überlandnetz," *Der Neue Tag* (Vienna), 31 August 1919, p. 11;

"Der Theaterkritiker Polgar," *Die Neue Rundschau*, 31 (May 1920): 655–656;

"Der Kunstkritiker (Dem Theaterkritiker A. P.)," *Die Rettung*, 2, no. 6 (1920): 78–80;

"Der Schriftsteller Franz Blei (zum fünfzigsten Geburtstag)," *Prager Presse*, 20 April 1921;

"Die erkenntnistheoretische Bedeutung des Begriffes 'Revolution' und die Wiederbelebung der Hegelschen Dialektik: Zu den Büchern Arthur Lieberts," *Prager Presse*, 30 July 1922, "Dichtung und Welt," supplement, pp. iii–iv;

"Max Adler: Marx als Denker, Engels als Denker," *Kantstudien*, 27, no. 1/2 (1922): 184–186;

"Albert Spaier: La pensée et la quantité," *Annalen der Philosophie*, 7 (1928): 112;

"Leben ohne platonische Idee," *Die literarische Welt*, 8 (5 August 1932): 1–4;

"Verwandlung, nach Edwin Muir: 'The Threefold Place,'" *Die literarische Welt*, 8 (2 September 1932): 5;

"Eine leichte Enttäuschung," *Die Neue Rundschau*, 44 (April 1933): 502–517;

"Vorüberziehende Wolke," *Frankfurter Zeitung*, 21 April 1933, p. 9;

"Das Böse im Wertsystem der Kunst," *Die Neue Rundschau*, 44 (August 1933): 157–191;

"Ein Abend Angst," *Berliner Börsen-Courier*, 6 August 1933, second supplement, pp. 9–10;

"Neue religiöse Dichtung?," *Berliner Börsen-Courier*, 3 October 1933, p. 7;

"Die Heimkehr," *Die Neue Rundschau*, 44 (December 1933): 765–795;

"Zwei Bücher von Franz Kafka," *Die Welt im Wort*, 21 December 1933, supplement, p. 2.;

"Der Meeresspiegel," *Die Welt im Wort*, 28 December 1933, pp. 3–4;

"Erneuerung des Theaters?" *Wiener Zeitung*, 11 November 1934, p. 3;

"Allein, nach James Joyce 'Alone,'" *das silberboot*, 1 (October 1935): 31;

"Morgen am Fenster, nach T. S. Eliot 'Morning at the Window,'" *das silberboot*, 2 (June 1936): 105;

"Erwägungen zum Problem des Kulturtodes," *das silberboot*, 1 (December 1936): 251–256;

"Alfred Polgar: Handbuch des Kritikers," *Mass und Wert*, 5 (May/June 1938): 817–818;

"Ethische Pflicht," *Saturday Review of Literature*, 22 (19 October 1940): 8;

"Berthold Viertel: Fürchte dich nicht," *Aufbau* (New York), 7 (30 January 1942): 11; (6 February 1942): 25;

"Letzter Ausbruch eines Größenwahnes: Hitlers Abschiedsrede," *Saturday Review*, 27 (21 October 1944): 5–8;

"Robert Pick: The Terhoven File," *Aufbau* (New York), 10 (27 October 1944): 9;

"Hanns Sachs: Freud, Master and Friend," *Aufbau* (New York), 11 (5 January 1945): 273–274;

"Rede über Viertel," *Plan*, 2, no. 5 (1947): 297–301;

"Paul Reiwald: Vom Geist der Massen," *American Journal of International Law*, 41 (January 1947): 358–359;

"Friedrich Torberg: Hier bin ich, mein Vater," *Aufbau* (New York), 14 (2 July 1948): 11–12;

"Erklärung zu Frank Thiess," *Aufbau* (New York), 14 (15 October 1948): 9;

"Elisabeth Langgässer: Das unauslöschliche Siegel," *Literarische Revue*, 4 (1949): 56–59;

"Geschichte als moralische Anthropologie: Erich Kahlers 'Scienza Nuova,'" *Hamburger Akademische Rundschau*, 3, no. 6 (1949): 406–416;

"Werner Richter: Frankreich. Von Gambetta zu Clemençeau," *Schweizer Rundschau*, 48 (March 1949): 1031–1033;

"Trotzdem: Humane Politik. Verwirklichung einer Utopie," *Die Neue Rundschau*, 61, no. 1 (1950): 1–31.

About a year before his death on 30 May 1951 Hermann Broch received a letter from his son, Hermann Friedrich Broch de Rothermann, in which Broch's reception in postwar Austria and Germany was characterized as that of an "unknown quantity"–a reference to Broch's second novel. Though Broch's name was "in the air" his works remained unknown save to a small and select readership; his reputation in literary circles both inside and outside of German-speaking countries, on the other hand, had been firmly established. Commercial popularity and financial success eluded Broch throughout his career, but this failure did not lessen his importance as a philosopher, experimental novelist, and critic of the intellectual and cultural trends of his day. While it was perhaps his philosophical concerns and his penchant for nontraditional narrative techniques in his novels that kept him from gaining a larger readership during his lifetime, these same aspects of his fiction and essays constitute his growing significance for scholars today. Undaunted by his lack of fame and pecuniary reward, Broch worked indefatigably on projects ranging from aesthetics to mass psychology, from epistemology to politics, while repeatedly returning to the literary medium to express his theories and perceptions.

Broch's literary interests had no precedent in his family background, which on both sides consisted of Jewish merchants whose gradually accrued wealth had drawn them from the provinces to Vienna, the commercial center of the Austro-Hungarian Empire. With this integration into the economic center came an attempt at social assimilation, a process that was accompanied by deemphasis on Judaic customs and rituals. Broch was born on 1 November 1886 to Josef Broch, a wholesaler of textiles, and Johanna Schnabel Broch. A brother, Friedrich (Fritz), was born in 1889. Josef Broch's economic aspirations were realized in 1906 with the acquisition of a textile factory at Teesdorf. Broch's interests in humanistic studies were stifled by his father's demand that he pursue an educational regimen befitting an up-and-coming businessman. While his father fostered only feelings of resentment and fear in him, Broch's relationship with his mother was marked by a dutiful affection which was rebuffed by her greater attachment to his younger brother. These family tensions are depicted in the story of the Pasenows in the first novel of his trilogy *Die Schlafwandler* (1931–1932; translated as *The Sleepwalkers,* 1932). In 1906–1907, on the instructions of his father, Broch studied textile engineering at Mülhausen (now Mulhouse, France) in Alsace. In October 1907 he went to the United States to investigate advances in cotton production, about which, he later admitted, he learned little. At the end of the year he became assistant director in charge of administrative affairs at the Teesdorf factory.

At about that time he fell in love with Franziska von Rothermann, the daughter of a well-to-do sugar manufacturer; her family's concern for social position initially stood in the way of the courtship between the two young lovers. But his conversion to Catholicism in May 1909 and his rise in the Teesdorf administration made possible his marriage to Franziska on 11 December 1909. On 4 October 1910 their only child, Hermann Friedrich Maria, affectionately called "Pitz," was born. (In later years the son became estranged from his father, even changing his surname; but most of their differences were resolved by the time of Broch's death.) Broch's increasing dissatisfaction with his unchosen profession drove him to spend most of his free time in the autodidactic study of philosophy. With her growing resentment of the provincial life at Teesdorf, Franziska's affections for her husband grew colder, and after seven years of marriage the relationship had become irreparable; but the prevailing Catholic influence in Austria prevented a divorce until 1923.

When Fritz Broch enlisted in the Austrian air force at the outbreak of World War 1, Broch was compelled to take charge of all administrative duties at Teesdorf. Under his skillful managerial hand the family business prospered, reaching its financial apex in 1915–1916. To escape from the factory he began frequenting the café scene of Vienna, where he came into contact with such prominent literary figures as Willy Haas, Paul Schrecker, Robert Musil, and Franz Blei. In 1918 he published in Blei's journal *Summa* his first fictional piece, "Eine methodologische Novelle" (A Methodological Novella), which Sidonie Cassirer has characterized as a "whimsical satire on bourgeois mediocrity, on philosophical determinism, and, indirectly, on the formal rules governing the *Novelle* itself." The novella describes the love affair between Antigonus, a young teacher of mathematics at a small-town gymnasium, and Philaminthe, the daughter of a petit bourgeois widow. The lovers meet when Antigonus rents a room in the widow's house; they talk, fall in love, and decide to marry. What makes the novella unique is the narrator's invitation to the reader to construct the plausible elements of personality, time, and situation that would allow such love to reach consummation. The novella is intended as a counterargument to the determinism of the naturalists. In his reviews for *Summa* Broch commended Emile Zola for his style and his humanity but criticized his materialism; he attacked Heinrich von Stein as a positivist, linking his ideas with those of Richard Wagner and the philistinism of the previous generation; although he discovered a "gravitätischen Leichtsinn" (grave levity) in Christian Morgenstern's humorous poetry, he felt Morgenstern lacked precision in the formulation of his ideas. These reviews serve as what Cassirer calls a "rough draft" for his subsequent fictional critiques of his time.

In 1925 Broch began five years of study at the University of Vienna, where he attended lectures by Moritz Schlick and Rudolf Carnap of the Wiener Kreis (Vienna Circle) and participated in seminars on mathematics. In 1927 he sold the textile factory and also began a course of psychoanalysis with Hedwig Schaxel, a student of Freud, that would continue until 1935. Gradually Broch became disillusioned with the logical positivist leanings of his professors; he began to feel the members of the Wiener Kreis were ignoring ethics and metaphysics. These subjects, he decided, could more properly be investigated in literature than in philosophy.

Broch's literary career can be said to have begun when he met Frank Thiess in the winter of 1928–1929. Broch and Thiess became close friends despite the differences in their literary leanings: Broch found his paradigm in James Joyce, while Thiess wrote popular novels reminiscent of the realistic style of the nineteenth century. Broch read Thiess's novels as a "corrective" for any extremes in his own style. Thiess took Broch under his wing; Broch called his friend the "Schutzengel der Schlafwandler" (guardian angel of *The Sleepwalkers*) for his constant advice on and public approbation of the novel. In 1930 Broch met the publisher Daniel Brody, whose firm, the Rhein Verlag, had published the German translation of Joyce's *Ulysses* (1922) in 1927. On 26 March 1930 Broch and Brody discussed the first draft of *Die Schlafwandler*. Six weeks later they negotiated the publishing contract for *Pasenow oder die Romantik, 1888* (translated as "The Romantic, [1888]"), the first part of the trilogy. During the summer Broch's confidence in the financial success of his novel grew as he worked on the second draft; but he later felt the need to correct the material, delaying its publication until November 1930 (dated 1931). Part two, *Esch oder die Anarchie 1903* (translated as "The Anarchist [1903]"), arrived at the publishers in April 1931, six months later than originally planned. Brody had wanted the entire trilogy on the market in time for the Christmas shopping season, but Broch's continual reworkings postponed the final novel, *Huguenau oder die Sachlichkeit 1918* (translated as "The Realist [1918]"), until April 1932. Though his desire to perfect his narratives enhanced their literary quality, it proved less beneficial in financial terms as the second and third novels of the trilogy also missed the potentially lucrative Christmas market. Bad timing of publication dates would become the rule for Broch's works.

The tripartite structure of *Die Schlafwandler* reflects three critical stages in the recent historical and cultural development of Germany. Falling back on ideas first espoused in his 1911 essay first published in volume 10, part 1, of the *Kommentierte Werkausgabe* (1977), "Ornamente (Der Fall Loos)" (Ornaments [The Loos Case]), Broch characterizes each period according to its dominant intellectual style: romantic, anarchistic, and objective. Structurally and stylistically the first two novels are conventional, while in *Huguenau* Broch includes lyrical, dramatic, essayistic, and aphoristic elements within the

narrative. The protagonists–Joachim von Pasenow, August Esch, and Wilhelm Huguenau–are differentiated as the aesthetic, the unaesthetic, and the anti-aesthetic, respectively. The actual "hero" of the trilogy is the iconoclastic cotton importer Eduard von Bertrand, whose thoughts and perceptions permeate each novel despite his absence from the third one. The protagonist of the first novel, Joachim von Pasenow, is an officer of noble birth who attempts to render his life meaningful through hopelessly impractical actions, such as confrontations with his father and a defiant love affair with a bar dancer named Ruzena. He is attracted by the cynicism of his friend Bertrand, but is ultimately unable to break with conventional familial duties. His lack of emotional progress exemplifies the degeneration of the Prussian nobility in the face of the modern world. His eventual marriage to Elisabeth Baddensen, a baron's daughter who is his ideal of chastity, underscores in a humorous final scene his lack of harmony with the world around him.

The revolt against convention which Joachim fails to accomplish is achieved in part by the fired bookkeeper August Esch in the second novel; but his attempts at revolution are as ill-fated as Pasenow's emotional longings. Irrationally, he connects all of the world's injustice and evil with the industrialist Bertrand, whom he denounces to the police as a homosexual. Bertrand's subsequent suicide does not end Esch's inner turmoil. Escaping into erotic excesses in his marriage to Mutter Hentjen, the owner of a bar in the working-class section of Cologne, Esch dreams of going to America but finally returns to his work with the new status of chief bookkeeper. His violent, anarchistic rages eventually subside, as reflected in his lessening aggression toward his wife: "Manchmal schlug ersie noch, aber immer weniger und schließlich garnicht mehr" (Sometimes he still hit her, but less and less and finally not at all).

The protagonist of the third novel, Wilhelm Huguenau, is an entrepreneur. His unbridled egocentrism is symbolized by his extreme myopia; the world exists only as an extension of his "Privattheologie" (private theology) of exploitation. After deserting from the army he settles in a small town on the Mosel, where he becomes a partner in a newspaper owned by Esch. He socializes with the town's leading citizens, among them the aging Pasenow. The fates of the three main figures illustrate the "Wertzerfall" (disintegration of values) precipitated by World War I: Pasenow gradually succumbs to his illusions and goes insane; Esch is murdered by his ruthless partner; Huguenau rapes Esch's widow, marries for the sake of social convention, and becomes complacently wealthy. *Huguenau* is by far the most complex of the three novels in that it incorporates multiple subplots, such as that of the doomed love affair of the Salvation Army girl Marie and the Jew Nuchem in Berlin, and essayistic chapters on the decay of values.

The reception of *Die Schlafwandler* by the intelligentsia was most positive. Thomas Mann noted in his diary that the novels were "intellectually rich and stimulating"; Hermann Hesse rated them among the best of contemporary fiction; Hans A. Joachim's review in the *Neue Rundschau* compared Broch's creation to that of God in Genesis. Edwin and Willa Muir's translation of the trilogy, *The Sleepwalkers,* came to the attention of Aldous Huxley, T. S. Eliot, Stephen Spender, and Thornton Wilder. Edwin Muir's review in the *Bookman* described the work as a "masterpiece" because of its experimental form and Broch's "extremely comprehensive, profound, and exact knowledge of the human heart and mind." Writing to Martin Secker, the English publisher of the Muirs' translation of the trilogy, Aldous Huxley was equally impressed by the inventiveness of Broch's style: "I read the trilogy with steadily increasing admiration. It is the work of a mind of extraordinary power and depth, and at the same time of extraordinary subtlety and sensitivity–of a philosopher who is also an artist of exceptional refinement and purity. It is a difficult book that makes great demands of the reader– nothing less than his whole mind at the highest pitch of attention. Not at all a book for tired business men! But I hope, all the same, that it will be widely read; for it is manifestly a work of first-rate importance." Despite such reviews the novels' readers were limited to a group of writers who themselves were part of the literary vanguard; in addition, the political climate of Germany had been so radically altered by the time of their publication that their financial failure was assured. Broch remarked, paraphrasing a German proverb, that "der Verleger denkt, und Hitler lenkt" (the publisher proposes and Hitler disposes). The lack of popular response to the trilogy is an example of the sociopolitical and cultural somnambulance attacked in the work itself.

Throughout the early 1930s, as Broch's reputation increased among the international literary avant-garde, his financial situation grew more precarious. On 22 April 1932 he read his essay *James Joyce und die Gegenwart* (James Joyce and the Present Age, 1936) at the Ottakring Adult Education Center in Vienna, where Heinrich and Thomas Mann, Arnold Schönberg, Franz Werfel, and C. G. Jung had previously spoken. Broch held that Joyce had achieved in *Ulysses* what Goethe had attempted to do in *Wilhelm Meisters Wanderjahre* (1829): to capture through a radical narrative mode the "Totalität" (totality) of an epoch within a single work of art. Four days after his speech, Broch himself was the subject of a lecture by Ernst Schönwiese, who discussed the merits of the recently published trilogy. During the next two years Broch became a regular speaker at the center. There he read his examination of the novel form, "Das Weltbild des Romans" (The Novel's World Image, published in volume 9, part 2 of the *Kommentierte Werkausgabe,* 1975), which again advocated that totality through which the novel could reveal the ethical failings of contemporary society. Broch criticized the anti-intellectual climate promulgated by the National Socialists as fundamentally false in "Leben ohne platonische Idee" (Life without Platonic Form), published in the journal *Die Literarische Welt* in 1932. In April 1934 he approached Brody with the request that these essays be published in a single volume for the general public, but the publisher felt that such a volume would bring little reward for either himself or its author.

In the years 1932 to 1934 Broch began working in the dramatic medium. His first play, *Die Entsühnung* (published in volume 7 of the *Kommentierte Werkausgabe,* 1979; translated as *The Atonement,* 1972), concerns the labor disputes at the Filsmann family factories in the waning days of the Weimar Republic; the picture presented is pessimistic and quasi-tragic. Broch portrays the social strata of the Weimar Republic and its inevitably catastrophic confrontations uncompromisingly and exactly. *Die Entsühnung* also provides evidence of Broch's wrestling with questions of literary tradition and form; he said in a letter to the Muirs that he tried to combine naturalistic with abstract techniques but admitted that the combination was only partially successful. No German theater would perform the unpublished play. It finally had its premiere in Zurich on 15 March 1934, but the producer felt that it needed to be shortened. He therefore excised the elegiac epilogue, the "Totenklage" (lament for the dead) of the mothers, which Broch considered the most essential scene. The play, which was performed under the title *Denn sie wissen nicht, was sie tun* (For They Know Not What They Do), drew small audiences and was canceled after a short run. (The German premiere took place on 3 June 1981 in Osnabrück, almost fifty years after the play's composition). During 1934 Broch wrote the comedy *Aus der Luft gegriffen* (Pure Invention; published in volume 7 of the *Kommentierte Werkausgabe*), but Otto Preminger, the director of the Theater in der Josefstadt in Vienna, considered it "too cold and too literary" to stage.

Broch completed his next novel in only six months. *Die Unbekannte Größe* (1933; translated as *The Unknown Quantity,* 1935) tells the story of the young mathematician Richard Hieck's attempts to counter life's irrational forces through scientific rationality. His love for the lab assistant Ilse and the death of his younger brother Otto bring disorder into the academician's otherwise orderly world. Slowly, through discussions with friends and family, Richard constructs a theory of the "unknown quantity," an underlying religiosity in human perception that connects reason and irrationality in the soul. The novel is too short to deal adequately with such difficult issues, however, and even Broch found his protagonist's resolution unsatisfactory and unconvincing. The novel's poor showing in the German and American marketplace (Broch referred to it as a "worst seller") confirmed his doubts.

At about the same time Broch wrote five novellas, which he attempted in vain to have published in one volume, and some poetry. Ernst Schönwiese included twelve of the poems in his anthology *Patmos: Zwölf Lyriker* (1935). In 1934 Broch was asked to write the screenplay for a film to be directed by Berthold Viertel, a leftist Austrian emigré living in England, but the combination of an antifascist writer and a Marxist director had little chance of success in Austria in the 1930s. Broch wrote a film version of *Die unbekannte Größe* titled "Das unbekannte X: Der Film einer physikalischen Theorie" (X, the Unknown: The Film of a Physical Theory), but nothing came of the venture. Metro-Goldwyn-Mayer approached him about filming *The Sleepwalkers,* but that project was also dropped.

Although Broch had established his name in European literature, his works of the early 1930s were artistic compromises for the sake of barely adequate financial gains. Broch finally decided to leave these compromises behind and to concentrate his efforts on a new novel, *Die Verzauberung* (1976; translated as *The Spell,* 1987). For this novel Broch broke with his model, Joyce, feeling that the radical subjectivity of *Ulysses* bordered on the asocial; he was also determined to avoid what he considered the realist approach of Thomas Mann. Broch wanted to expose the sociopolitical climate that had led to National Socialism, the nadir of European culture. Broch studied some French provincial novels and the contemporary Austrian popular novel. With the rise of nationalism in Austria and Germany there had been an increase in the popularity of "Heimatromane" (provincial novels), and it was in part against this often insipid type of writing that Broch aimed his work. To assure himself of the quiet needed to complete the novel Broch moved to a farm near Mösern in the Tirol; but his work on *Die Verzauberung* was interrupted in late 1935 by the writing of his assessment of cultural decay, "Erwägungen zum Problem des Kulturtodes" (Considerations on the Problem of Cultural Death), which was published the following year in Schönwiese's journal *das silberboot.* Although the essay expressed skepticism about the function of literature in the era of National Socialism, Broch was determined to complete his novel, and in January 1936 he sent Brody the first draft.

Die Verzauberung was originally planned as the first part of another trilogy, to be titled "Bergroman" (Mountain Novel), but the subsequent parts were never written. The novel remains a fragment; the third version, which was never completed, was published after Broch's death. Unlike his other novels, *Die Verzauberung* has a first-person narrator, a country doctor who has fled his urban practice for the serenity of a small mountain village. His dreams of a peaceful existence are disrupted by the arrival of a stranger, Marius Ratti, a demagogue based on Hitler. Ratti uses eloquent turns of phrase to convince the villagers that their salvation lies in recapturing the golden age of preindustrial times; taking his meaning literally, the community reopens its gold mine. The intoxication of this potential new greatness metastasizes into mass hysteria: the gruesome outcome is the ritualistic blood sacrifice of Irmgard, a girl who is in love with Ratti. The counterpoint to Ratti is Mutter (Mother) Gisson, Irmgard's grandmother, who represents an older, more natural order than Ratti's brutal atavism. The doctor realizes the danger inherent in Ratti's demonic magic and is even susceptible to it, but he remains unable to achieve the natural power of self-redemption achieved by the aged Mutter Gisson. The symbolic interplay of nature and politics in this novel is an unusually successful response to the "Blut-und-Boden" (blood and soil) literature endorsed by the National Socialists.

Broch's work on his fiction was also interrupted by his growing interest in the international peace movement. He sent his "Völkerbund-Resolution" (League of Nations Resolution) to Thomas Mann for publication in Mann's journal *Mass und Wert,* but Mann declined it. The article called for a new declaration of human rights and called on the League of Nations to enforce control of those rights and to oversee the armaments industry. The resolution was finally published in 1973.

Since the death of his father in October 1933 there had been a dispute over the estate between Broch and his brother Fritz. Broch had been named executor of the will upon their mother's refusal of those duties, but almost immediately Fritz had filed suit against him. Their mother had been left forty thousand Austrian schillings and two houses; the interest on the money and the rent from the houses were given to Broch, who divided the income into monthly allowances for his mother, his son, and himself. In late December 1936 Broch learned that Fritz was again seeking to wrest his inheritance from him; on receiving the news he had a heart attack. On recovering, Broch, who was thirty-five hundred Swiss francs in debt to Brody, felt compelled to fight his brother in court for the security of his family. These trials consumed a great deal of his time and energy; referring to *Die Verzauberung,* he commented later that they constituted a "Mord an dem Buch" (murder of the book).

While revising *Die Verzauberung* Broch had read Theodor Haecker's *Vergil: Vater des Abendlandes* (Virgil: Father of the West, 1931) after hearing the philosopher speak at the Ottakring Adult Education Center. With his interest in Virgil aroused, he set about studying the *Aeneid* and the *Eclogues*. In Virgil, Broch saw a literary figure who stood at the end of a cultural epoch and whose aversion to the political changes of his day caused him to want to burn his magnum opus, the *Aeneid,* which glorified the Roman state. Broch's skepticism about literature in an era of "cultural death" is paralleled in the thoughts and actions of the dying poet in his novella "Die Heimkehr des Vergil" (Virgil's Return, 1973), which rendered into fiction ideas he had stated in essay form two years earlier. On 11 December 1937 Broch read selections from the novella at the Institute Anderl-Rogge in Graz. He then retired to the rural atmosphere of Alt-Aussee in Styria to revise the work, but the novel which grew from the novella would not be published for another eight years and then not in Europe.

On 13 March 1938, the day following the march of German troops into Austria, Broch was arrested and imprisoned in Alt-Aussee after his postman reported to the authorities that he subscribed to *Das Wort,* the leading organ of literary exiles in the Soviet Union. Because of this subscription Broch was considered a Marxist; the Nazis seemed unaware of his Jewish heritage. In prison his correspondence was limited to postcards, the chronic stomach ailment he had suffered since the 1920s was exacerbated by the stress, and he became increasingly convinced that he faced a death sentence. He worked daily on his Virgil novel, which became more of a diary than a literary project. At Broch's trial in Bad Aussee the judge released him with the stipulation that Broch travel immediately to Vienna and register with the police. In Vienna Broch hid with friends. The necessity of emigration became increasingly apparent to Broch, who, fearing the worst, gave Thiess the typescript of *Die Verzauberung;* Thiess sent it to Edwin Muir in Scotland for safekeeping.

In April 1938 Paul Schrecker, a friend from Broch's early days in Vienna, persuaded Anna Herzog, another longtime friend residing in Paris, to seek assistance for Broch from James Joyce. When he heard of Broch's predicament, Joyce immediately interceded to help him secure an exit visa. In May Edwin Muir, Stephen Hudson, and Aldous Huxley began trying to obtain a British visa for Broch. The papers were finally processed, but with bureaucratic delays in both England and Austria they did not reach Broch until 20 July 1938. Unable to dissuade his mother from remaining in her homeland (she would die in the Theresienstadt concentration camp in 1942), he flew from Vienna to London via Rotterdam, boarding the plane with only twenty Reichsmark in his pocket. In London Broch met Hudson and Stefan Zweig; he was soon invited by the Muirs to stay with them in St. Andrews. There Broch began again to work on his League of Nations resolution; this renewed political activity aroused the consternation of Brody, who wrote Broch that his main task was the completion of his Virgil novel. Brody likened the author to Dante, emphasizing that the Italian poet's contribution to the world came from his poetry and not from his politics. Despite these admonitions Broch continued revising the resolution.

On 21 September Broch received an American visa through the United States consulate in Glasgow, and the following week he booked passage for New York. Arriving on 9 October, Broch met with the writers Richard Bermann and Erich von Kahler; they worked with the American Guild for German Cultural Freedom, an organization established for dealing with the problems facing exiles from National Socialism. Broch traveled to Princeton to thank Albert Einstein for his letter of recommendation in the matter of Broch's visa. He also met with Henry Seidel Canby, the editor of the *Saturday Review of Literature* and professor of English and American literatures at Yale University; through Canby Broch hoped to obtain a position at an American university, but he lacked the necessary academic credentials. Canby was a member of the American Guild, which had been founded by Prince Hubertus zu Löwenstein to preserve German culture in exile; Broch received fifty dollars per month from the guild for a short time to cover his living expenses. Canby procured a six-weeks residency for Broch at the artists' colony Yaddo in Saratoga Springs, New York, beginning in June 1939. At Yaddo Broch became acquainted with the poet Jean Starr Untermeyer, whose translation of the "Schicksals-Elegien" (fate-elegies) in the manuscript of his Virgil novel so impressed him that he chose her to become the translator of the entire work.

During 1939 Broch began work on his studies of mass psychology, even though he had been given a stipend by the Carl Schurz Memorial Association to continue working on his fiction. In September 1939 he was the guest of Thomas Mann in Princeton; Mann helped Broch receive a Guggenheim Fellowship stipend of $2,500 for the fiscal year 1940. The stipend was extended until December 1941 to allow Broch to complete his study of mass psychology. In Princeton Broch met Giuseppe Antonio Borgese, the Italian historian and author of *Goliath: The March of Fascism* (1937), and with him organized other authors for the compilation of a book favoring democracy. *The City of Man: A Declaration on World Democracy* was published in November 1940 by the Viking Press.

The City of Man describes the cataclysmic situation facing the world, argues against the appeasement policy of the past and in favor of America as the last stronghold of democracy, and advocates a peace established and preserved by a universal state with universal representation. *The City of Man* is somewhat utopian; nevertheless, it is an important document representing one of the rare instances of American and European intellectual teamwork. Broch's participation in the project heightened his visibility in the American academic community, and in early 1942 Hadley Cantril of the Office of Public Opinion Research applied to the Rockefeller Foundation for a stipend of $2,000 from May 1942 to April 1943 to make possible Broch's study of mass psychology. Broch was unable to complete the essay in the allotted time and turned to the Bollingen Foundation for further support in late 1944. Even though later he requested an extension of this second funding, he left the study unfinished. Some of the manuscripts and notes, edited by Wolfgang Rothe, were published in 1959 as volume 9 of his collected works.

The Virgil novel had been occupying more and more of his attention since early 1940. At that time he had sent copies to Brody, Muir, and other friends, most of whom urged him not to leave the novel unpublished. On 22 April 1942 Broch received a literary prize from the American Academy of Arts and Sciences for the fourth version of the novel. With that money he was finally able to pay back the debts he had incurred through his assistance to other refugees. Broch then applied himself diligently to the task of completing the novel, while Untermeyer worked on the English translation. *Der Tod des Vergil* (translated as *The Death of Virgil*) was published by Pantheon Books in June 1945 in both German and English editions, reflecting the status of its newly naturalized Austrian-American author.

The novel is divided into four parts, each of which is named for one of the four elements of antiquity. The opening section, "Wasser" (Water), describes the dying poet's return by ship to Italy and his abhorrence at the sight of the jubilant throngs attending the emperor's triumphal procession. The mass hysteria aroused by Augustus makes Virgil conscious of the animal nature of man and leads him to decide to destroy his masterpiece. "Feuer" (Fire) depicts the dying poet's feverish final night, during which images from his past are resurrected in his mind. "Erde" (Earth) brings the novel back to more solid ground: Virgil, epitomizing Roman intellectual life, argues against his antithesis, the emperor, that most political personage, that he has the right to destroy his own work as he deems fit. Augus-

tus, supporting the rights of the state over the individual, tries to dissuade what he considers the rash action of the dying poet. In the final section, "Äther" (Ether), antithetical positions and divergent elements coalesce into a unity with the eternal as Virgil slips into death. Each element suggests the events of the last day of Virgil's life and his respective moods through its associative quality. Perhaps the most striking stylistic invention of the novel is the lyrical passages embedded within the prose; these "eclogues" are especially effective in the long interior monologue sequences. *Der Tod des Vergil* is reminiscent of Joyce in its presentation of the totality of an epoch within a single day; yet there the similarity ends, since, unlike his former model, Broch blends the lyrical and prose genres. *Der Tod des Vergil* deals with the death of the "Wertsystem" (value system) of the Roman Empire and the first glimmerings of the new Wertsystem of Christianity. Broch links the disintegration of the pagan world with that of the modern world, revealing—more clearly than in any of his other works—his cultural pessimism.

Between 1946 and 1948 there were only nine reviews of *Der Tod des Vergil* in German, indicating that Broch's importance had diminished in Germany and Austria. In contrast, in the United States the book elicited some thirty reviews. Aldous Huxley found *The Death of Virgil* stylistically inferior to Broch's trilogy. Günther Anders, who wrote an even less complimentary review for the *Austro-American Tribune,* reiterated some earlier critical assessments of "Joyce imitation" and "themeless mass." Hannah Arendt, on the other hand, wrote in the *Nation* that the book placed Broch firmly in the avant-garde of the twentieth-century novel with Proust and Kafka. In the reviews Broch was compared to such disparate writers as Kafka, Proust, Thomas Wolfe, Hermann Hesse, Thomas Mann, Martin Heidegger, Richard Wagner, and Joyce. Hermann Weigand's suggestion that the idea for the novel had come from Broch's reading of Dante so disturbed Broch that he protested against it in a letter to Weigand and in a sonnet titled "Dantes Schatten" (Dante's Shadow, published in volume 8 of the *Kommentierte Werkausgabe,* 1980). As usual, Broch received little financial gain from his novel.

In November 1948 the Friedrich Schiller University in Jena, East Germany, offered Broch a post in psychology and literature, but Broch rejected the offer. Although Broch was not a Marxist, his work was held in esteem by the leadership of the eastern zone. Beginning in July 1947 Broch received a monthly allowance of $50 from Wilhelm Roth, a wealthy German expatriate. On 17 June 1948 Broch suffered a broken leg and was hospitalized in Princeton. Ironically, with health and accident insurance, he was financially better off in the hospital. Broch said that his convalescence made him a "Kombination von Hiob und Lazarus" (combination of Job and Lazarus)–a remark that might appropriately be applied to the whole of his exile experience since 1938. While in the hospital he began work on a study of Hugo von Hofmannsthal which had originally been planned as an introduction to Hofmannsthal's *Selected Prose* (1952). Broch felt that a mere accounting of his compatriot's literary achievements in vacuo would oversimplify the measure of his works; therefore he felt it necessary to include an analysis of the cultural phenomena surrounding Hofmannsthal's literary production. His discussion centered on the social class he best understood and to which his subject belonged–the bourgeoisie. The middle class had dictated tastes in Austria and Germany in the later half of the nineteenth century; its leading artist was Richard Wagner, in whose operas the desires of the bourgeoisie were collected and articulated. Despite his praise for much of Hofmannsthal's work Broch's study ends by taking a position in favor of the ethics of Karl Kraus over the purely aesthetic predilections of the poet. Such a preference is not surprising, since Hofmannsthal had no influence on Broch's works, whereas the satirical tone of both *Die Schlafwandler* and *Die Schuldlosen* (1950; translated as *The Guiltless,* 1974) resembles Kraus's polemical essays and aphorisms. The Hofmannsthal study was published posthumously as "Hugo von Hofmannsthal und seine Zeit" (1975; translated as *Hugo von Hofmannsthal and His Time,* 1984).

In 1948 Willi Weismann, whose monthly *Die Fähre* had published an entire issue on Broch on the occasion of his sixtieth birthday in 1946, proposed the publication of a collection of his novellas and short stories. Broch sent him five stories, and a few months later Weismann returned the galley proofs. In correcting the proofs Broch decided that the stories–four of which he had written in the early 1930s–could not be printed in their present form. In June 1949 he began work on other stories to supplement the original five, and a month later he had a tentative form for the book: "Elf Novellen und drei Gedichte, beinahe ein Roman" (Eleven novellas and three poems, practically a novel). The novel, *Die Schuldlosen,* was published in mid December 1950–once again too late for the Christmas market.

Die Schuldlosen is introduced with a parable which has its roots in the Hassidic narrative tradition of the *tsadi'kim* (saintly men), reminiscent of much of Martin Buber's work. This enigmatic, paradoxical tale relates the attempts of some shtetl members to comprehend the meaning of the voice of God in Genesis. The rabbi, in accordance with the practices of that tradition, provokes his students to rethink their questions by recasting them as counterquestions; but those seeking a single

definitive answer so convolute the essential question that they lose sight of the original purpose. Finally, after loudly laughing at their muddled theological thinking, the rabbi tells them that it is time, the remembered past, which contains both the Lord's voice and silence in one undifferentiated state. This Talmudic paradox is left unresolved for both the students and the reader. God's creation of the world remains ineffable in human discourse.

Each of the three story sections–the "Vor-Geschichten" (prestories), the "Geschichten" (stories), and the "Nach-Geschichten" (poststories)–is preceded by a poetry section. Recalling the opening parable, these sections are called "Stimmen" (voices) and are assigned the dates 1913, 1923, and 1933, corresponding to the stages of political decay that culminated in Hitler's assumption of power. Each set of poems is a mixture of various lyrical forms, some traditional–the emblem, the ballad, the folk song, the elegy, and the sonnet–and some free verse forms of Broch's own invention. Thematically, *Die Schuldlosen*–the title is ironic–centers on the question of collective German guilt. Andreas, a Dutch diamond dealer, arrives in a small German town and takes up lodging with the Baroness von W. and her daughter Hildegard. Like Huguenau, he cleverly exploits the economic disaster of the post–World War I period, amassing a considerable sum of money through currency fluctuations and real estate investments. After attending a meeting of some local Socialists, Andreas spends a drunken evening with the schoolmaster Zacharias, who gives long diatribes on the future greatness of the German nation. Zacharias's language foreshadows the political rhetoric adopted by the German nationalists who supported Hitler's bid for political control. In a dreamlike episode the young businessman meets Melitta, a poor laundress. Their love affair is thwarted by Hildegard, who tells Melitta that she and Andreas are to be married. Believing this lie, Melitta commits suicide. Hildegard seduces Andreas, but her aggressiveness renders him impotent. Andreas takes the baroness and her chambermaid Zerline to a secluded hunting lodge. Melitta's grandfather, an old beekeeper, confronts Andreas toward the novel's end with his complacency and failure to accept responsibility, and Andreas's depraved desire for the "Nicht- Seiende" (nonbeing) is finally realized with his suicide. Without focusing on actual historical events, Broch has critically depicted the indifference and inertia of Germans of all classes that allowed the National Socialists to rise to power.

Weismann's reaction to the unique form of *Die Schuldlosen* was rather negative; he especially felt that the poetry impaired the rhythm of the narrative. Broch, however, felt that the novel might have been his masterpiece because of the cohesion achieved through the poems; he referred to *Die Schuldlosen* as a "Seiltänzerkunststück" (tight-rope walker's work of art). Critical reaction was varied. The *Times Literary Supplement* of 29 March 1953 characterized the poetry as "some of those homemade verses that German writers for the past century have been so ready to turn out on their sewing machines." Karl August Horst's review in *Merkur* praised the experimental nature of the novel but expressed doubts as to whether Broch had succeeded in achieving his goal. Perhaps the most positive view of *Die Schuldlosen* came from Broch's friend Erich von Kahler, who felt that the importance of examining the phenomenon of guilt and its origins should not be overlooked.

On 5 December 1949 Broch had married Anne Marie Meier-Graefe, whom he had met in Vienna in 1937. On 1 April 1951 he suffered a heart attack while once again reworking *Die Verzauberung*. While convalescing in New Haven, he wrote to an editor at the Alfred A. Knopf publishing house that "the irony of fate sometimes hits the racing horse just going through the goal: that is I." On 30 May 1951 he had another heart attack; this one was fatal.

Broch received only limited recognition for his literary and critical achievements. In spite of efforts by the Austrian PEN Club, he failed to receive the Nobel Prize for Literature in 1950; financially, his efforts were disastrous. Broch's recalcitrant commitment to novelistic experiment and his uncompromising analysis of contemporary issues combined to deny him accolades in his lifetime; but because of these very qualities his place in German letters of the twentieth century has been irrevocably established.

Letters:

Hermann Broch–Daniel Brody: Briefwechsel 1930–1951, edited by Bertold Hack and Marietta Kleiss (Frankfurt am Main: Buchhändler-Vereinigung, 1971);

Hermann Broch. Briefe über Deutschland: Die Korrespondenz mit Volkmar von Zühlsdorff, edited by Paul Michael Lützeler (Frankfurt am Main: Suhrkamp, 1986).

Biography:

Paul Michael Lützeler, *Hermann Broch: Eine Biographie* (Frankfurt am Main: Suhrkamp, 1985); translated by Janice Furness as *Hermann Broch: A Biography* (London: Quartet, 1987).

References:

Günther Anders, "Der Tod des Vergil . . . und die Diagnose seiner Krankheit (Zu Brochs neuem Werk)," *Austro-American Tribune,* 4, no. 2 (1945): 9, 12;

Hannah Arendt, "No Longer and Not Yet," *Nation,* 163 (14 June 1946): 300–302;

Jean-Paul Bier, *Hermann Broch et La Mort de Virgile* (Paris: Larousse, 1974);

Gisela Brude-Firnau, ed., *Materialien zu Hermann Brochs "Die Schlafwandler"* (Frankfurt am Main: Suhrkamp, 1972);

Sidonie Cassirer, "Hermann Broch's Early Writings," *PMLA,* 75 (1965): 453–462;

Dorrit Claire Cohn, *The Sleepwalkers: Elucidations of Hermann Broch's Trilogy* (The Hague & Paris: Mouton, 1966);

Timm Collmann, *Zeit und Geschichte in Hermann Brochs Roman "Der Tod des Vergil"* (Bonn: Bouvier, 1967);

Sverre Dahl, *Relativität und Absolutheit: Studien zur Geschichtsphilosophie Hermann Brochs (bis 1932)* (Bern: Lang, 1980);

Stephen D. Dowden, ed., *Hermann Broch: Literature, Philosophy, Politics. The Yale Broch Symposium* (Columbia, S.C.: Camden House, 1988);

Manfred Durzak, *Hermann Broch: Der Dichter und seine Zeit* (Stuttgart: Kohlhammer, 1968);

Durzak, *Hermann Broch: Dichtung und Erkenntnis* (Stuttgart: Kohlhammer, 1978);

Durzak, *Hermann Broch in Selbstzeugnissen und Bilddokumenten* (Reinbek: Rowohlt, 1966);

Durzak, ed., *Hermann Broch: Perspektiven der Forschung* (Munich: Fink, 1972);

Die Fähre, special Broch issue, 8 (November 1946);

Waldo Frank, "The Novel as Poem," *New Republic,* 113 (20 August 1945): 226–228;

James Hardin, "Das Thema der Erlösung in den Romanen Hermann Brochs," *Schweizer Monatshefte,* 52 (July 1972): 257–261;

Hermann Hesse, "Beim Malen," *Dresdener Neueste Nachrichten,* 29 May 1932;

Hesse, "Die Schlafwandler," *Neue Zürcher Zeitung,* 15 June 1932;

Aldous Huxley, "Why Virgil Offered a Sacrifice," *New York Herald Tribune Weekly Book Review,* 8 July 1945, p. 5;

Hans A. Joachim, "Ausgewählte Romane," *Neue Rundschau,* 44 (January 1933): 129–131;

Erich Kahler, *Die Philosophie von Hermann Broch* (Tübingen: Mohr, 1962);

Kahler, ed., *Dichter wider Willen: Einführung in das Werk von Hermann Broch* (Zurich: Rhein, 1958);

Thomas Koebner, *Hermann Broch: Leben und Werk* (Bern & Munich: Francke, 1965);

Hermann Krapoth, *Dichtung und Philosophie: Eine Studie zum Werk Hermann Brochs* (Bonn: Bouvier, 1971);

Leo Kreutzer, *Erkenntnistheorie und Prophetie: Hermann Brochs Romantrilogie "Die Schlafwandler"* (Tübingen: Niemeyer, 1966);

Paul Michael Lützeler, *Hermann Broch—Ethik und Politik: Studien zum Frühwerk und zur Romantrilogie "Die Schlafwandler"* (Munich: Winkler, 1973);

Lützeler, ed., *Brochs Verzauberung* (Frankfurt am Main: Suhrkamp, 1983);

Lützeler, ed., *Hermann Broch* (Frankfurt am Main: Suhrkamp, 1986);

Lützeler, ed., *Materialien zu Hermann Brochs "Der Tod des Vergil"* (Frankfurt am Main: Suhrkamp, 1976);

Karin Mack and Wolfgang Hofer, eds., *Spiegelungen: Denkbilder zur Biographie Brochs* (Vienna: Sonderzahl, 1984);

Karl Robert Mandelkow, *Hermann Brochs Romantrilogie "Die Schlafwandler": Gestaltung und Reflexion im modernen deutschen Roman* (Heidelberg: Winter, 1962);

D. Meinert, *Die Darstellung der Dimensionen menschlicher Existenz in Brochs "Tod des Vergil"* (Bern & Munich: Francke, 1962);

Karl Menges, *Kritische Studien zur Wertphilosophie Hermann Brochs* (Tübingen: Niemeyer, 1970);

Modern Austrian Literature, special Broch issue, 13, no. 4 (1980);

Edwin Muir, "Hermann Broch," *Bookman,* 75 (1932): 664–668;

Hartmut Reinhardt, *Erweiterter Naturalismus: Untersuchungen zum Konstruktionsverfahren in Hermann Brochs Romantrilogie "Die Schlafwandler"* (Cologne & Vienna: Böhlau, 1972);

Renato Saviane, *Apocalissi e Messianismo nei Romanzi di Hermann Broch* (Padua: Università di Padova, 1971);

Ernestine Schlant, *Hermann Broch* (Boston: Twayne, 1978);

Schlant, *Die Philosophie Hermann Brochs* (Bern & Munich: Francke, 1971);

Grover Smith, ed., *Letters of Aldous Huxley* (New York & Evanston, Ill.: Harper & Row, 1969), pp. 364–365;

Hartmut Steinecke, *Hermann Broch und der polyhistorische Roman: Studien zur Theorie und Technik eines Romantyps der Moderne* (Bonn: Bouvier, 1968);

Joseph Strelka, ed., *Broch heute* (Bern & Munich: Francke, 1978);

Richard Thieberger, ed., *Hermann Broch und seine Zeit* (Bern: Lang, 1980);

Peter Bruce Waldeck, *Die Kindheitsproblematik bei Hermann Broch* (Munich: Fink, 1968);

Hermann J. Weigand, "Broch's Death of Virgil: Program Notes," *PMLA,* 62 (June 1947): 525–554;

Theodore Ziolkowski, *Hermann Broch* (New York & London: Columbia University Press, 1964).

Papers:
Hermann Broch's papers are at the Beinecke Rare Book Library, Yale University. His correspondence with his publisher, Daniel Brody, is in the Deutsches Literaturarchiv, Marbach.

Georg Büchner

(17 October 1813 – 19 February 1837)

Rodney Taylor
Truman State University

This entry was updated by Professor Taylor from his entry in DLB 133: Nineteenth-Century German Writers to 1840.

BOOKS: *Der Hessische Landbote: Erste Botschaft,* anonymous, by Büchner and Friedrich Ludwig Weidig (Offenbach: Preller, 1834); enlarged edition, anonymous, by Büchner, Weidig, and L. Eichelberg (Marburg, 1834); translated by Henry J. Schmidt as *The Hessian Courier* (New York: Continuum, 1986);

Danton's Tod: Dramatische Bilder aus Frankreichs Schreckensherrschaft (Frankfurt am Main: Sauerländer, 1835); translated by Geoffrey Dunlop as *Danton's Death,* in *The Plays of Georg Büchner* (London: Howe, 1927; New York: Viking, 1927);

Mémoire sur le système nerveux du barbeau (Cyprinus barbus L.) (Paris & Strasbourg: Levrault, 1835);

Nachgelassene Schriften, edited by Ludwig Büchner (Frankfurt am Main: Sauerländer, 1850)—includes "Lenz," translated by Stephen Spender in *Great European Short Stories,* edited by Spender (New York: Dell, 1960); *Leonce und Lena,* translated by Walter N. Green as *Leonce and Lena: A Comedy in Three Acts,* in *New Europe,* 13 (1919): 246–254, 275–283;

Sämmtliche Werke und handschriftlicher Nachlaß: Erste kritische Gesammt-Ausgabe, edited by Karl Emil Franzos (Frankfurt am Main: Sauerländer, 1879)—includes *Woyzeck,* translated by Dunlop as *Wozzeck* in *The Plays of Georg Büchner* (1927);

Georg Büchners Werke und Briefe, edited by Fritz Bergemann (Leipzig: Insel, 1926);

Sämtliche Werke, edited by Paul Stapf (Berlin: Tempel, 1959);

Werke, edited by Henri Poschmann (Berlin & Weimar: Aufbau, 1967);

Sämtliche Werke und Briefe: Historisch-kritische Ausgabe mit Kommentar, 2 volumes, edited by Werner R. Lehmann (Hamburg: Wegner, 1967, 1971);

Sämtliche Werke, edited by Gerhard P. Knapp (Munich: Goldmann, 1978);

Georg Büchner (engraving by Auerbach)

Werke und Briefe, edited by Karl Pörnbacher, Gerhard Schraub, Hans-Joachim Simm, and Edda Ziegler (Munich & Vienna: Hanser, 1988).

Editions in English: *Leonce and Lena,* translated by E. R. Bentley, in *From the Modern Repertoire,* edited by Bentley (Bloomington: Indiana University Press, 1956), pp. 1–37;

Danton's Death, translated by Bentley, in *The Modern Theatre,* volume 5, edited by Bentley (New York: Doubleday, 1957), pp. 69–160;

Danton's Death, translated by James Maxwell (San Francisco: Chandler, 1961; London: Methuen, 1968);

Woyzeck, and Leonce and Lena, translated by Carl Richard Mueller (San Francisco: Chandler, 1962);

Complete Plays and Prose, translated by Mueller (New York: Hill & Wang, 1963);

Lenz, translated by Michael Hamburger (Buffalo, N.Y.: Frontier Press, 1969);

Danton's Death, translated by Henry J. Schmidt (New York: Avon, 1971);

Leonce and Lena; Lenz; Woyzeck, translated by Hamburger (Chicago & London: University of Chicago Press, 1972);

Danton's Death, translated by Howard Brenton (London: Methuen, 1982);

Leonce and Lena, translated by Hedwig Rappolt (New York: Time and Space Limited, 1983);

Lenz, translated by Rappolt (New York: Time and Space Limited, 1983);

Complete Works and Letters, translated by Schmidt (New York: Continuum, 1986);

Danton's Death; Leonce and Lena; Woyzeck, translated by Victor Price (London & New York: Oxford University Press, 1988);

Woyzeck and Lenz, translated by Rappolt (New York: Time and Space Limited, 1988);

Woyzeck, translated by John Mackendrick (London: Heinemann, 1988);

Georg Büchner's Woyzeck, translated by Michael Ewans (New York: Lang, 1989).

TRANSLATIONS: Victor Hugo, *Lucretia Borgia; Maria Tudor,* volume 6 of Hugo's Sämtliche Werke (Frankfurt am Main: Sauerländer, 1835).

Although his work is profoundly rooted in the crises, conflicts, and ideals of his time, Georg Büchner's writings have far transcended the intellectual and historical framework of his turbulent age. Büchner, who died at twenty-three, was one of the most significant literary figures in the dark epoch between the Restoration and the Revolution of 1848. His work thus exhibits the deep existential melancholy and Weltschmerz that Friedrich Sengle suggests is an integral characteristic of this age of German realism. On the other hand, Büchner's writings reveal an exalted philosophical vision of human dignity and freedom. His depictions of monumental collisions between *Freiheitsideale* (ideals of freedom) and historical circumstance disclose his deep, often tormented concern for the fate of humanity. They also manifest his intense involvement with the meaning of history. Büchner's writings contain, moreover, highly perceptive critiques of the sociopolitical realities of his time. These critiques anticipate some of the social and political evils of the twentieth century, and Büchner's treatment of the interconnected problems of individual alienation and societal oppression influenced the work of Bertolt Brecht, Friedrich Dürrenmatt, Ingmar Bergman, and Werner Herzog, as well as many other important twentieth-century artists. Subsequent literary movements exhibiting his influence include nineteenth-century German realism, German expressionism, epic theater, theater of the absurd, and documentary theater.

Karl Georg Büchner was born on 17 October 1813 in the village of Goddelau in Hesse; he was the eldest of six children. His father, Ernst Karl Büchner, a successful physician, was an enthusiastic student of the French Revolution, an admirer of French democracy, and a fervent supporter of the social reforms instituted by Napoleon in Germany. Büchner's mother, Caroline Luise Büchner, née Reuß, an impassioned patriot, longed for a unified German state and, unlike her husband, applauded the expulsion of Napoleon. While his father encouraged the young Büchner's interests in natural science and history, his mother fostered his reverence for nature and love of literature. Two of Büchner's siblings were to become leading cultural figures in Germany during the latter half of the nineteenth century, Luise as a writer and intellectual in the women's movement and Ludwig as a philosopher.

When Büchner was three his family moved to Darmstadt, the capital of the Grand Duchy of Hesse. In 1825 he matriculated at the Darmstädter Großherzogliches Gymnasium. This school, known as the "altes Pädagog" (Old Pedagogue), was one of the foremost educational institutions in the German-speaking countries. During his stay Büchner demonstrated outstanding intellectual potential, a tendency toward independent thinking, rebelliousness against authority, and an inchoate political awareness. A recurrent theme in his student essays and school speeches concerns the incontrovertible rights and dignity of the individual. In two of these pieces Büchner describes how heroic persons in history reacted when their moral autonomy was threatened by political oppression. His essays clearly exhibit an ethical as well as an implicitly political critique of the suppression of civil rights in Germany that had resulted from the mandates of the Deutscher Bund (German confederation), the loose confederation of thirty-nine German states set up by the Congress of Vienna in 1815.

Büchner's writings at the gymnasium also disclose a fundamental repugnance toward Christian dogma. In opposition to the traditional Christian strictures against suicide, for example, Büchner argues in "Rede zur Verteidigung des Kato von Utika" (In Defense of Cato of Utika) that suicide for the sake of preserving one's moral dignity is praiseworthy. In "Über den Selbstmord" (On Suicide) an evolutionary conception of nature is developed: life, says Büchner, signifies dynamic development; the great theologian Friedrich Schleiermacher's postulation that earthly existence is little more than an ethical testing ground is a vapid denial of the self-subsisting totality of universal Life. Büchner asserts that a human being who suffers from physical or psychological maladies so severe as to cause his developmental powers to disintegrate has a moral duty to end his own life. Büchner thus touches on a theme that will occupy him for the rest of his life: his vision of nature and humanity as inherently beautiful, noble, and good.

Upon completing his education at the gymnasium in 1831 Büchner embarked on the study of medicine and the natural sciences at the University of Strasbourg. Strasbourg was a hotbed of revolutionary sentiment and activity directed against the conservative government in Paris. The city was also a gathering place for German intellectuals seeking freedom from the increasingly repressive political measures being adopted across the border. As a result of his association with revolutionary student groups in Strasbourg, Büchner became committed to radical democratic reform in Germany. He also participated in protests against the increasingly brutal methods of suppressing political opposition to which the French government was resorting. Nevertheless, Büchner and his fellow expatriates enjoyed considerable freedom of thought and expression, and his stay in Strasbourg was perhaps the happiest period of his life. During this time he met Wilhelmine (Minna) Jaeglé, the daughter of a liberal Protestant pastor, and they were soon engaged.

In Strasbourg, Büchner attended lectures by some of the leading scientists of the age. Constantly expanding his knowledge of the French Revolution, Büchner also read widely in the Greek and Roman classics as well as in French and German literature. His developing capacity for inquiring into the causes of political and economic injustice is exemplified by a letter to his parents dated 5 April 1883: "Man wirft den jungen Leuten den Gebrauch der Gewalt vor. Sind wir denn aber nicht in einem ewigen Gewaltzustand? . . . Was nennt Ihr denn *gesetzlichen Zustand?* Ein *Gesetz,* das die große Masse der Staatsbürger zum fronenden Vieh macht, um die unnatürlichen Bedürfnisse einer . . . verdorbenen Minderzahl zu befriedigen? Und dies Gesetz, unterstützt durch eine rohe Militärgewalt . . . ist eine *ewige, rohe Gewalt,* angetan dem Recht und der gesunden Vernunft, und ich werde mit *Mund und Hand* dagegen kämpfen"

(Young people are accused of using violence. But aren't we in an eternal state of violence? . . . What do you call a *lawful state?* A law that transforms the great masses of citizens into toiling cattle in order to satisfy the unnatural needs of a . . . decadent minority? Supported by raw military might . . . this law is *eternal, brute force,* insulting justice and good sense, and I will fight *tooth and nail* against it). Büchner's evaluation of contemporary society here anticipates Karl Marx's view that the modern capitalist state is founded not on the principles of justice, equality, and human dignity but exists to promote the interests of the ruling elite. Like Marx, Büchner maintains that political power is used by the privileged few to subjugate and exploit the many. Consequently, violence and barbarity come to be institutionalized throughout the entire social hierarchy.

In 1833 Büchner left Strasbourg; following a brief stay with his parents in Darmstadt, he began the study of medicine and philosophy at the provincial University of Gießen in Upper Hesse. In contrast to his life in Strasbourg, Büchner's stay in Gießen was darkened by feelings of despair that were exacerbated by an attack of meningitis. The deep melancholy that permeated this period of Büchner's life became a leitmotif of his literary production.

Through a pastor from Butzbach, Dr. Friedrich Ludwig Weidig, Büchner became a member of one of the covert, loosely organized revolutionary circles then forming throughout the region. Early in 1834 he founded the Gesellschaft der Menschenrechte (Society for Human Rights), a group of students and laborers dedicated to radical social change. Together with Weidig he composed a political leaflet, *Der Hessische Landbote* (1834; translated as *The Hessian Courier,* 1986). While Weidig was convinced that social reform in Germany could only be effected by a wealthy bourgeoisie composed of enlightened industrialists, politicians, and intellectuals, for Büchner reform had to be accomplished through revolutionary activities by the impoverished German peasantry.

Der Hessische Landbote combines an ethical appeal having strong biblical overtones with an exposition of the economic and historical factors involved in the current state of affairs. The disparity between rich and poor in Hesse is for Büchner destructive of the spiritual potential of the people. The government of the Grand Duchy of Hesse exists solely for the benefit of the rich; its purpose is to extort taxes from those who labor and starve to maintain and enhance the luxurious way of life and traditional privileges enjoyed by a decadent, pampered few. The aristocrats justify high taxation as a means of preserving the state, but Büchner asserts that the state should exist only to promote the well-being of its citizens. Büchner's critique includes a striking attempt to demythologize the person of the Grand Duke and thereby to combat the notion that a prince's power is ultimately founded on divine election. This ostensibly superhuman figure, from whom an aura of divine authority seems to radiate, is nothing more than a mortal man: "[Er] ißt, wenn [er] hungert, und schläft wenn sein Auge dunkel wird. Sehet, [er] kroch so nackt und weich in die Welt, wie ihr und wird so hart und steif hinausgetragen, wie ihr, und doch hat [er] seinen Fuß auf eurem Nacken" ([He] eats when [he] is hungry and sleeps when his eyes grow heavy. Behold, like you [he] crept naked and soft into the world and like you [he] will be carried from it hard and stiff, and yet his foot is on your neck).

Because the French king abused his power and betrayed the people, he and many of his decadent aristocratic cohorts were justly executed; because the current governmental system in Germany was set up only to enrich and empower the elite while grinding down the laboring poor, it will inevitably become necessary for the people to overthrow it by force–just as the French did during the revolution.

Distribution of *Der Hessische Landbote* was undertaken by two of Büchner's fellow members in the Gesellschaft der Menschenrechte. One of them, Karl Minnigerode, was soon arrested, and copies of the tract were found sewn into his clothing. On hearing of the arrest, Büchner set out for Butzbach to warn Weidig and the other members. While he was gone his lodging in Gießen was searched by the police. For the time being, however, the authorities were uncertain as to the extent of his involvement in the affair; the authorship of the leaflet had, of course, been left anonymous. Becoming aware of his son's difficulties, Büchner's father forced him to return to Darmstadt in August 1834. The stay with his family was a time of extreme psychological distress for Büchner because of the continuing arrests of the members of his revolutionary group and the constant fear that his own incarceration was imminent. Eventually, Weidig was arrested; he would take his own life in prison in 1837.

Between October 1834 and January 1835 Büchner composed one of the greatest masterpieces of German literature. He submitted the work, a drama titled *Danton's Tod* (1835; translated as *Danton's Death,* 1927), to the prominent literary critic and editor Karl Gutzkow. The latter quickly resolved to publish Büchner's drama in installments in his journal, *Phönix: Frühlingszeitung für Deutschland* (Phoenix: Spring Paper for Germany). In late February, before receiving the news of his literary success, Büchner was summoned to appear in court. He decided to flee the country, returning to Strasbourg.

Danton's Tod is a highly complex historical drama encompassing many levels of meaning, extending from problems relating to the significance and purpose of history to the notion of theodicy: the metaphysical attempt to justify the significance and purpose of suffering in a (presumably) divinely ordered universe. Approximately one-sixth of the drama consists of quotations from documents written during the French Revolution; the play also contains many excerpts from historical studies. The work exhibits a dynamic convergence of supraindividual historical forces and human subjectivity that is particularly evident in the persona of Georges Danton himself. Danton decides to put an end to his life because of the impossibly heavy burden history has laid upon him. The sins he has committed for the sake of the revolution are incessantly reproduced in his memory; one incident in particular, the September Massacres of 1792, tortures him. Danton holds himself responsible for ordering the massacres, in which thousands of persons all over France were slaughtered by angry mobs: "Man hat mir von einer Krankheit erzählt, die einem das Gedächtnis verlieren mache. Der Tod soll etwas davon haben. Dann kommt mir manchmal die Hoffnung, daß er vielleicht noch kräftiger wirke und einen *Alles* verlieren mache. Wenn das wäre!" (I've heard of a sickness that makes one lose one's memory. Death, they say, is like that. Then I hope sometimes that death would be even stronger and make one lose *everything*. If only that were so!).

Büchner's portrayal of Danton as possessing sole responsibility for the September Massacres has the purpose of dramatizing the descent of an overwhelming historical necessity upon a solitary human being. History is not depicted as a blind necessity that acts independently of the subjects of history; Danton's actions originated in a vision of freedom based on the optimistic assumption that the course of history can be altered. But Danton's revolutionary will to freedom engenders a horrifying, irrational necessity that coerces him into mandating the shedding of blood. Danton's wife, Julie, attempts to console him by maintaining that his actions during September 1792 saved the country. But he responds: "Ja, das hab ich; das war Notwehr, wir mußten. Der Mann am Kreuze hat sich's bequem gemacht: es muß ja Ärgernis kommen. . . . Es muß; das war dies Muß. Wer will der Hand fluchen, auf die der Fluch des Muß gefallen? Wer hat das Muß gesprochen, wer? . . . Puppen sind wir, von unbekannten Gewalten am Draht gezogen; nichts, nichts wir selbst!" (Yes, I did. It was self-defense, we had to. The Man on the Cross made it easy for himself: it must needs be that offenses come. . . . It must; it was this 'must.' Who would curse the hand on which the curse of 'must' has fallen? Who has spoken this 'must,' who? . . . We are puppets, our strings are pulled by unknown forces, we ourselves are nothing!). By indicating that Christ "made it easy for himself" by abandoning history instead of remaining in this domain to assume the historical burden of his ethical vision, Danton equates his own importance with that of the Savior. Just as the temporal appearance of Christ effected radical historical changes, Danton asserts, his own revolutionary decisions have forever transformed the course of human history. In contrast to Christ's eschatological otherworldliness, however, Danton's actions were undertaken to save the downtrodden in this world. Christ was powerless to alter the lot of the common people; the kind of freedom he offered was, in the end, not of this world. It consequently remained impervious to the dark necessity that had precipitated Danton's political failure and personal destruction. Danton's subjective torment coincides with the historical result of the September Massacres: the Reign of Terror. Thus, his internal agony is mirrored by and, in turn, mirrors tragic contemporary events that he helped bring into being.

Büchner's return to Strasbourg marked the beginning of a period of relative happiness. He was reunited with his fiancée and resumed his academic studies. He wrote a scientific dissertation, *Mémoire sur le système nerveux du barbeau* (1835); after lecturing on the work in the spring of 1835 he became a member of the professional society of scholars in natural history in Strasbourg. Later he submitted the treatise to the philosophical faculty of the newly founded University of Zurich, which awarded him the doctorate of philosophy in September 1836. During his stay in Strasbourg, Büchner's political activities were minimal. He began once again to study philosophy, particularly Rationalist metaphysics and Georg Wilhelm Friedrich Hegel's *Encyklopädie der philosophischen Wissenschaften* (Encyclopedia of the Philosophical Sciences, 1817; translated as *The Logic of Hegel*, 1874).

During the summer of 1835 Büchner composed another masterpiece, a novella about the incipient stages of acute schizophrenia suffered by the eighteenth-century poet Jakob Michael Reinhold Lenz. "Lenz" (1850; translated, 1960) is the most unpolitical work in Büchner's small oeuvre; in its description of the states of consciousness experienced by the title character, the story is also the most subjective of Büchner's works. The narration of events in the story, both mental and external, is from a third-person standpoint; its recounting of Lenz's psychic turmoil—his suffering as well as his moments of exalted mystical intuition—is dispassionate and objective. The story contains a detailed phenomenological description of the drastic mental isolation symptomatic of schizophrenia: Lenz's illness includes a tormented sense of erosion of subjective

identity. This loss of selfhood, however, is complemented by a passionate mystical longing to embrace what Lenz sees as the munificent oneness of life and nature.

Lenz's painful, often desperate yearning to attain union with the infinite life of nature reflects Büchner's affinity for the Rationalist philosopher Benedict de Spinoza's ontology, as delineated in the *Ethica* (Ethics, 1677). For Büchner and Spinoza, existence is infinite, perfect, and complete. It cannot, therefore, be made to conform to such presumptuous human notions as those postulating that it is designed by a divine creator. In his inaugural doctoral lecture, "Über Schädelnerven der Fische" (On the Cranial Nerves of Fish, 1850), given in 1836, Büchner asserts that nature exists in supreme indifference to human needs and desires. Moreover, nature in its totality is inexplicable by human cognition; it exists for its own sake alone.

While Büchner's perspective on existence manifests the influence of Spinoza, his philosophical notebooks on Spinoza and on Spinoza's Rationalist predecessor René Descartes—written during his second stay in Strasbourg—contain his objections to one of the overriding assumptions of Rationalist metaphysics: that being is ultimately identical with thought. Büchner insists that Spinoza's attempt to deduce existence from an abstract human thought-construction such as the *causa sui* (cause of itself) rests on the mistaken assumption that thought is more perfect than corporeal nature. Büchner's critique of Rationalism anticipates Ludwig Feuerbach's devastating attack on Spinoza and Hegel in his *Grundsätze der Philosophie der Zukunft* (1843; translated as *Principles of the Philosophy of the Future,* 1966).

Büchner's repudiation of purely intellectual attempts to arrive at an adequate comprehension of nature is evident in a passage in his novella where Lenz affirms that "Die einfachste, reinste Natur hinge am nächsten mit der elementarischen zusammen; je feiner der Mensch geistig fühlt und lebt, um so abgestumpfter würde dieser elementarische Sinn; er halte ihn nicht für einen hohen Zustand, er sei nicht selbstständig genug, aber er meine, es müsse ein unendliches Wonnegefühl sein, so von dem eigentümlichen Leben jeder Form berührt zu werden, für Gesteine, Metalle, Wasser und Pflanzen eine Seele zu haben" (The simplest, purest character was closest to elemental nature; the more sophisticated a person's intellectual feelings and life, the duller is this elemental sense; he did not consider it to be an elevated state of being, it was not independent enough, but he believed it must be boundless ecstasy to be touched in this way by the unique life of every form, to commune with rocks, metals, water, and plants). In this passage Büchner attributes his own deep adoration of material nature to his character, who communes in a kind of mystical ecstasy with the manifestations of being in its totality. This vision does not see in nature the dialectical workings of a transcendental Mind, as in the idealism of Hegel or Friedrich Wilhelm Joseph von Schelling. Its source is an awe-filled perception of the immense, majestic totality of organic and inorganic nature. Thus, his unique nature-mysticism is not based on a conception of the universe that seeks to transmute its autonomous existence into a "higher" spiritual reality.

The highly affirmative perception of nature Büchner attributes to Lenz is complemented by the latter's sensitive and loving behavior toward his fellow human beings. Lenz sees in humankind a dignity and beauty that originates in nature itself. Because human beings are manifestations of the universal beauty of nature, one must comport oneself to them with love and respect: "Nur eins bleibt: eine unendliche Schönheit, die aus einer Form in die andre tritt, ewig aufgeblättert, verändert. . . . Man muß die Menschheit lieben, um in das eigentümliche Wesen jedes einzudringen; es darf einem keiner zu gering, keiner zu häßlich sein, erst dann kann man sie verstehen" (Only one thing remains, an endless beauty moving from one form to another, eternally unfolding, changing. . . . One must love humanity in order to penetrate into the unique essence of each individual; no one can be too low or too ugly, only then can one understand them). Lenz also expresses his creator's views on aesthetics: he maintains that only works that are truly realistic, that reveal exacting concentration on the manifold richness of natural and human reality, can be viewed as genuine art.

Lenz's moments of mystical communion with the majestic totality of existence are followed, however, by a horrifying alienation from reality. This alienation brings him progressively nearer the "Abgrund" (abyss), the profound "Leere" (void) that inhabits his thinking and feeling self. Throughout Büchner's narrative, Lenz is harrowed by his sense of a terrifying internal emptiness that he perceives as gradually extinguishing his consciousness. Lenz's horror in experiencing this relentless darkening and disintegration of his self is intensified by his perception that the void will soon isolate him forever from his beloved nature and the human beings he wishes to serve. In his state of sickness and internal desolation Lenz is aware that the mystical plenitude and beauty flowing from nature is inexorably slipping away, dissolving into the nothingness of his advancing insanity and impending death: "Alles, was er an Ruhe aus der . . . Stille des Tals geschöpft hatte, war weg; die Welt, die er hatte nutzen wollen, hatte einen ungeheuern Riß, er hatte keinen Haß, keine Liebe, keine Hoffnung—eine schreckliche Leere und doch eine folternde Unruhe, sie auszufüllen. Er hatte *Nichts*" (All

the peace he had derived from . . . the valley's stillness was gone; the world he had wished to serve had a gigantic crack, he felt no hate, no love, no hope, a terrible void and yet a tormenting anxiety to fill it. He had *nothing*).

Commentators such as Hans Mayer and Gerhard P. Knapp have pointed out that "Lenz" and *Danton's Tod* exhibit the extreme intellectual and spiritual dichotomies that tortured Büchner. During his second stay in Strasbourg, however, his surroundings offered a stable setting for his academic and literary labors. Gutzkow encouraged him to translate two plays by Victor Hugo; published in 1835, both were of mediocre quality. He also began work on an original play, "Pietro Aretino"; the manuscript for the drama, like much of Büchner's correspondence and his diary, has been lost. During the summer of 1836 Büchner received a visit from his mother and older sister; years later, Ludwig Büchner reported that during this visit his older brother told their mother of his foreboding that he would die young. That summer Büchner feverishly completed work on a play for the Cotta publishing house, which had advertised a literary competition with a prize for the best comedy submitted in prose or verse. Büchner's manuscript for *Leonce und Lena* (1850; translated as *Leonce and Lena,* 1927) did not meet the deadline set by the firm and was returned unopened.

A direct literary influence evident in *Leonce und Lena* is William Shakespeare's *As You Like It.* Büchner, however, does not emulate the structural complexity of Shakespeare's comedy; the plot of his play can be delineated in a few sentences. Leonce, a bored and pampered prince, is the victim of a melancholy so profound that it thwarts his every effort to involve himself in the affairs of life. Refusing the arranged marriage—to a princess he has never met—that his father, King Peter, wishes to force on him, he leaves the country with his friend Valerio. Similar events have been occurring in the life of the princess Lena. They meet, neither of them realizing that the other is the preselected mate, and fall in love. Leonce decides not to go through with his plan to commit suicide, and they marry and live happily ever after.

Büchner's comedy satirizes German classical and Romantic literature; it also presents social criticism in the guise of irony and satire. Any more direct critique of the societal status quo would not, Büchner was aware, have escaped the censor. In *Leonce und Lena* he uses a major characteristic of German classical drama: the focus on aristocratic characters. By portraying members of the upper classes, including the king, as boorish, spoiled, and empty-headed, Büchner succeeds both in attacking the absolutism of contemporary German society and in exposing the drama of Classicism as a dead form.

To satirize the totalitarian nature of the aristocratic police states existing under the aegis of the Deutscher Bund, Büchner has his bumbling philosopher-king compare the authority he incarnates with the "substance" that Spinoza describes as the self-subsistent ground upon which all other, lesser entities are contingent. As he is being dressed by his valets, King Peter says: "Der Mensch muß denken und ich muß für meine Untertanen denken; denn sie denken nicht. . . . Die Substanz ist das an sich, das bin ich. (*Er läuft fast nackt im Zimmer herum.*) . . . An sich ist an sich, versteht ihr? Jetzt kommen meine Attribute, Modifikationen, Affektionen und Akzidenzien, wo ist mein Hemd, meine Hose?" (Man must think, and I must think for my subjects, for they do not think. . . . The substance is the "thing-in-itself," that is I. [*He runs around the room almost naked.*] . . . In-itself is in-itself, you understand? Now for my attributes, modifications, affections, and accessories: where is my shirt, my pants?). King Peter perceives his supreme position as exalting him entirely above the subjects over whom he rules; just as Spinozan substance or being is absolutely uncontingent in nature, King Peter views political authority as dwelling within his person alone and as having no relation to the people on whom it is imposed. The indifferent, oafish philosopher-ruler thus embodies the diametrical opposite of Büchner's conviction, expressed in *Der Hessische Landbote,* that a ruler exists only for the benefit of the people.

Another theme in *Leonce und Lena* that resembles ideas developed in *Der Hessische Landbote* is the supercilious attitude adopted by Leonce and Valerio to labor and to those who, unlike themselves, must work to survive. Valerio insists that there are only four ways in which one can earn money—find it, win it, inherit it, or steal it—and that anyone who earns money in any other way is a "Verbrecher" (scoundrel). Leonce adds: "Denn wer arbeitet ist ein subtiler Selbstmörder, und ein Selbstmörder ist ein Verbrecher und ein Verbrecher ist ein Schuft, also, wer arbeitet ist ein Schuft" (Because one who works is subtly committing suicide, and a suicide is a criminal, and a criminal is a scoundrel: therefore whoever works is a scoundrel). The two aristocrats assume that money is a vehicle for securing and multiplying the distractions of luxury; it is a means of survival only for the uncultivated, brutish masses, whose existence is, in any case, superfluous. In *Der Hessische Landbote* Büchner had expressed outrage at how the rich aristocrats of Hesse view those who labor as scarcely better than beasts of burden. Another concept developed in the political leaflet that is touched on in the aristocrats' conversation is Büchner's assertion that the laboring masses in Germany are, in effect, committing suicide by

subjecting themselves to the demands put on them by the ruling elite. *Leonce und Lena* was published posthumously and was first performed in Munich in May 1895.

During the autumn and winter of 1836–1837 Büchner composed what is perhaps the greatest social drama in German literature; the work remained unfinished at his death. In spite of its fragmentary condition, *Woyzeck* (1879; translated as *Wozzeck,* 1927) contains the fullest literary realization of the sophisticated sociocritical analyses found in *Der Hessische Landbote.* In this play, which is based on actual events that took place in the 1820s, Büchner combines analysis of contemporary social conditions with an exposition of the psychological and metaphysical factors that universalize the significance of these conditions.

The title figure of Büchner's play, Franz Woyzeck, ekes out a meager existence as an army barber; his wife, Marie, has recently given birth to a child. The entire meaning of Woyzeck's life is bound up in his relationship with Marie, but he is driven to destroy the person he loves as a result of the intolerable conditions in which he, as the personification of the wretched lower classes, is forced to exist. Degraded to the point of near insanity by an inhuman social environment, Woyzeck is unable to endure Marie's unfaithfulness with a petty army officer, the Tambourmajor (drum major). His murder of Marie mirrors the cruelty and irrationality of a social order that has incessantly exploited him and negated his personhood. His society's denial of human dignity transmogrifies Woyzeck's innate affirmation of life, embodied in his love of Marie, into a hideous act of destruction.

Marie is also a victim of the indifference and cruelty of society. Some commentators have attributed her infidelity to her supposed overwhelming sexual desire for the mindless and brutish Tambourmajor; but as it is for Woyzeck, existence for Marie is a harsh and endless struggle to survive. Although stricken by conscience at her desire, she perceives the higher social status of the Tambourmajor as a way out of her otherwise hopeless poverty. Woyzeck, on the other hand, embodies a future for her and her child that signifies little more than perpetual suffering and want.

In addition to the dehumanization that is inseparable from her poverty, Marie is viewed by the Tambourmajor as a sexual object. Similarly, Woyzeck is treated as a soulless means to an end by his social superiors: the Hauptmann (captain), the Doktor, and the Professor. These figures, who represent the bourgeoisie, are no less callously exploitative than the aristocrats whose indifference and corruption Büchner censures in *Der Hessische Landbote* and *Leonce und Lena.* Their ruthless exploitation of Woyzeck follows from their inhuman ethical, metaphysical, and scientific worldviews. Woyzeck's dialogue with the Doktor, who is examining him, exemplifies this aspect of the play: "DOKTOR. Ich habs gesehn, Woyzeck: Er hat auf die Straß gepißt, an die Wand gepißt wie ein Hund. WOYZECK. Aber Herr Doktor, wenn einem die Natur kommt. . . . DOKTOR. Die Natur kommt! . . . Hab ich nicht nachgewiesen, daß der musculus constrictor vesicae dem Willen unterworfen ist? Die Natur!" (DOCTOR. I saw it, Woyzeck: you pissed on the street, you pissed on the wall like a dog. WOYZECK. But Doctor, the call of nature. . . . DOCTOR. The call of nature! Haven't I proved that the musculus constrictor vesicae is subject to the will? Nature!). His condescending advice to Woyzeck reveals Büchner's sadistic Doktor as a Cartesian for whom the human mind is a "ghost in the machine" of the body. In its conception of the human body as a clocklike mechanical apparatus, Cartesian philosophical anthropology is synonymous, for Büchner, with the reduction of the human being to an automaton. The philosophical anthropology he espouses allows the Doktor to exploit Woyzeck as a guinea pig; thus, while the Doktor kicks Woyzeck repeatedly, he assures the latter that he is doing so only in the service of scientific analysis: "Nein Woyzeck, ich ärger mich nicht, Ärger ist ungesund, ist unwissenschaftlich. . . . Mein Puls hat seine gewöhnlichen 60 und ich sag's Ihm mit der größten Kaltblütigkeit" (No, Woyzeck, I'm not getting angry; anger is unhealthy, it is unscientific. . . . My pulse is beating at its usual sixty, and I'm telling you this in all cold-bloodedness). *Woyzeck* was first performed in November 1913 in Munich; it was the basis for Alban Berg's opera *Wozzeck* (1921).

In October 1836 Büchner assumed a post as Privatdozent (unpaid lecturer) in comparative anatomy at the University of Zurich. His lectures were greeted with enthusiasm by one of the foremost scientists of the age, Lorenz Oken, who was rector of the university. In mid January 1837 a severe cold forced Büchner to interrupt his teaching activities; at the beginning of February symptoms of typhus became apparent. Büchner's condition deteriorated rapidly. Friends who were caring for him informed Minna Jaeglé of the situation; she arrived in Zurich as Büchner was entering into a coma, but he recognized his fiancée and was able to speak with her. Büchner died on 19 February. In 1923 the city of Darmstadt instituted the Georg Büchner Prize for literature, which has become one of the most prestigious literary awards in Germany.

Bibliographies:

Werner Schlick, *Das Georg-Büchner-Schrifttum bis 1965: Eine internationale Bibliographie* (Hildesheim: Olms, 1968);

Monika Rössing-Hager, *Wortindex zu Georg Büchner, Dichtungen und Übersetzungen* (Berlin & New York: De Gruyter, 1970);

Gerhard P. Knapp, *Georg Büchner: Eine kritische Einführung in die Forschung* (Frankfurt am Main: Athenaion, 1975).

Biographies:

Gerhard P. Knapp, *Georg Büchner,* second edition (Stuttgart: Metzler, 1984);

Jan-Christoph Hauschild, *Georg Büchner* (Stuttgart: Metzler, 1993).

References:

Winnifred R. Adolph, *Disintegrating Myths: A Study of Georg Büchner* (New York: Lang, 1989);

Heinz Ludwig Arnold, ed., *Text + Kritik: Georg Büchner I/II* (Munich: Edition text + kritik, 1979);

Alfred Behrmann and Joachim Wohlleben, *Büchner: Danton's Tod. Eine Dramenanalyse* (Stuttgart: Klett-Cotta, 1980);

Maurice B. Benn, *The Drama of Revolt: A Critical Study of Georg Büchner* (Cambridge & New York: Cambridge University Press, 1976);

Fausto Cercignani, ed., *Studia Büchneriana: Georg Büchner 1988* (Milan: Cisalpino, 1990);

Burghard Dedner, ed., *Der widerständige Klassiker: Einleitungen zu Büchner vom Nachmärz bis zur Weimarer Republik* (Frankfurt am Main: Athenäum, 1990);

Dedner, Alfons Glück, Walter Hinderer, and Michael Voges, *Georg Büchner: Dantons Tod, Lenz, Leonce und Lena, Woyzeck. Interpretationen* (Stuttgart: Reclam, 1990);

Heinz Fischer, *Georg Büchner und Alexis Muston: Untersuchungen zu einem Büchner-Fund* (Munich: Fink, 1987);

Reinhold Grimm, *Love, Lust and Rebellion: New Approaches to Georg Büchner* (Madison: University of Wisconsin Press, 1985);

Karlheinz Hasselbach, *Georg Büchner: Lenz. Interpretationen* (Munich: Oldenbourg, 1986);

Jan-Christoph Hauschild, *Georg Büchner: Studien und neue Quellen zu Leben, Werk und Wirkung* (Königstein: Athenäum, 1985);

Ronald Hauser, *Georg Büchner* (New York: Twayne, 1974);

Louis Ferdinand Helbig, *Das Geschichtsdrama Georg Büchners* (Bern: Lang, 1973);

Julian Hilton, *Georg Büchner* (New York: Grove, 1982);

Walter Hinderer, *Büchner Kommentar zum dichterischen Werk* (Munich: Winkler, 1977);

Dorothy James, *Georg Büchner's Dantons Tod: A Reappraisal* (London: Modern Humanities Research Association, 1982);

Gerhard Jancke, *Georg Büchner: Genese und Aktualität seines Werkes* (Kronberg: Skriptor, 1975);

Gerhard P. Knapp, *Georg Büchner: Dantons Tod* (Frankfurt am Main: Diesterweg, 1983);

Knapp, "Der Mythos des Schreckens: Maximilien Robespierre als Motiv in der deutschen Literatur des neunzehnten Jahrhunderts," in *Schreckens-mythen-Hoffnungsbilder: Die Französische Revolution in der deutschen Literatur. Essays,* edited by Harro Zimmermann (Frankfurt am Main: Athenäum, 1989);

Erwin Kobel, *Georg Büchner* (Berlin: De Gruyter, 1972);

Helmut Krapp, *Der Dialog bei Georg Büchner* (Darmstadt: Gentner, 1958);

Herbert Lindenberger, *Georg Büchner* (Carbondale: Southern Illinois University Press, 1964);

Gyorgi Lukács, *Deutsche Literatur in zwei Jahrhunderten* (Neuwied: Luchterhand, 1964);

Wolfgang Martens, ed., *Georg Büchner* (Darmstadt: Wissenschaftliche Buchgesellschaft, 1965);

Hans Mayer, *Georg Büchner und seine Zeit* (Frankfurt am Main: Suhrkamp, 1972);

Albert Meier, *Georg Büchners Ästhetik* (Munich: Fink, 1983);

Henri Poschmann, *Georg Büchner: Dichtung der Revolution und Revolution der Dichtung* (Berlin & Weimar: Aufbau, 1983);

John Reddick, "Georg Büchner and the Agony of Authenticity," *Forum for Modern Language Studies,* 23 (October 1987): 289–324;

Reddick, *Georg Büchner: The Shattered Whole* (Oxford: Oxford University Press, 1994);

William C. Reeve, *Georg Büchner* (New York: Ungar, 1979);

William H. Rey, *Georg Büchners Dantons Tod* (Bern & Las Vegas: Lang, 1982);

David G. Richards, *Georg Büchner and the Birth of the Modern Drama* (Albany: State University of New York Press, 1977);

Henry J. Schmidt, *Satire, Caricature, and Perspectivism in the Works of Georg Büchner* (The Hague: Mouton, 1970);

Friedrich Sengle, *Biedermeierzeit, volume 3: Die Dichter* (Stuttgart: Metzler, 1980);

Rodney Taylor, "Büchner's Danton and the Metaphysics of Atheism," *Deutsche Vierteljahrsschrift,* 2 (June 1995): 231–246;

Taylor, *History and the Paradoxes of Metaphysics in Dantons Tod* (New York: Lang, 1990);

Taylor, "History and the Transcendence of Subjectivity in Büchner's Robespierre," *Neophilologus,* 72 (January 1988): 82–96;

Jan Thorn-Prikker, *Revolutionär ohne Revolution: Interpretationen der Werke Georg Büchners* (Stuttgart: Klett-Cotta, 1978);

Cornelie Ueding, *Denken, Sprechen, Handeln: Aufklärung und Aufklärungskritik im Werk Georg Büchners* (Frankfurt am Main: Lang, 1976);

Karl Vietor, *Georg Büchner: Politik, Dichtung, Wissenschaft* (Bern: Franke, 1949);

Leonard P. Wessell, "Eighteenth-Century Theodicy and the Death of God in Büchner's *Dantons Tod,*" *Seminar,* 8 (October 1972): 198–218;

Raleigh Whitinger, "Echoes of Novalis and Tieck in Büchner's Lenz," *Seminar,* 25 (1989): 324–338;

Benno von Wiese, *Die deutsche Tragödie von Lessing bis Hebbel* (Hamburg: Hoffmann & Campe, 1961);

Wolfgang Wittkowski, *Georg Büchner: Persönlichkeit, Weltbild, Werk* (Heidelberg: Winter, 1978);

U-Tag Yang, *Reflexion und Desintegration: Zur Identitätskrise der Protagonisten im Werk Georg Büchners* (Bern & New York: Lang, 1989).

Papers:

Georg Büchner's papers are at the Goethe-und-Schiller-Archiv, Weimar.

Elias Canetti

(25 July 1905 – 14 August 1994)

Thomas H. Falk
Michigan State University

This entry was updated by Professor Falk from his entry in DLB 85:
Austrian Fiction Writers After 1914.

See also the Canetti entry in *DLB 124: Twentieth-Century German Dramatists, 1919–1992*.

BOOKS: *Die Blendung: Roman* (Vienna, Leipzig & Zurich: Reichner, 1936); translated by C. V. Wedgwood as *Auto-da-Fé* (London: Cape, 1946); republished as *The Tower of Babel* (New York: Knopf, 1947);

Komödie der Eitelkeit: Drama (Munich: Weismann, 1950); translated by Gitta Honegger as *Comedy of Vanity* (New York: Performing Arts Journal Publications, 1983);

Fritz Wotruba (Vienna: Rosenbaum, 1955);

Masse und Macht (Hamburg: Claassen, 1960); translated by Carol Stewart as *Crowds and Power* (London: Gollancz, 1962; New York: Viking, 1962);

Welt im Kopf, edited by Erich Fried (Graz & Vienna: Stiasny, 1962);

Hochzeit: Drama (Munich: Hanser, 1964); translated by Honegger as *The Wedding* (New York: Performing Arts Journal Publications, 1986);

Die Befristeten: Drama (Munich: Hanser, 1964); translated by Honegger as *Life-Terms* (New York: Performing Arts Journal Publications, 1983); translated by Stewart as *The Numbered* (London: Calder & Boyars, 1984);

Dramen (Munich: Hanser, 1964)—comprises *Hochzeit, Komödie der Eitelkeit, Die Befristeten;*

Aufzeichnungen 1942–1948 (Munich: Hanser, 1965);

Die Stimmen von Marrakesch: Aufzeichnungen nach einer Reise (Munich: Hanser, 1967); translated by J. A. Underwood as *The Voices of Marrakesh: A Record of a Visit* (London: Calder & Boyars, 1978; New York: Seabury Press, 1978);

Der andere Prozeß: Kafkas Briefe an Felice (Munich: Hanser, 1969); translated by Christopher Middleton as *Kafka's Other Trial: The Letters to Felice* (London:

Elias Canetti in Stockholm to receive the 1981 Nobel Prize in literature (photograph by Lüfti Özkök)

Calder & Boyars, 1974; New York: Schocken, 1974);

Alle vergeudete Verehrung: Aufzeichnungen 1949–1960 (Munich: Hanser, 1970);

Die gespaltene Zukunft: Aufsätze und Gespräche (Munich: Hanser, 1972);

60

Macht und Überleben: Drei Essays (Berlin: Literarisches Colloquium, 1972);

Die Provinz des Menschen: Aufzeichnungen 1942–1972 (Munich: Hanser, 1973); translated by Joachim Neugroschel as *The Human Province* (New York: Seabury Press, 1978);

Der Ohrenzeuge: Fünfzig Charaktere (Munich: Hanser, 1974); translated by Neugroschel as *Earwitness: Fifty Characters* (New York: Seabury Press, 1979);

Das Gewissen der Worte (Munich: Hanser, 1975; enlarged, 1976); translated by Neugroschel as *The Conscience of Words* (New York: Seabury Press, 1979);

Der Überlebende (Frankfurt am Main: Suhrkamp, 1975);

Der Beruf des Dichters (Munich: Hanser, 1976);

Die gerettete Zunge: Geschichte einer Jugend (Munich: Hanser, 1977); translated by Neugroschel as *The Tongue Set Free: Remembrance of a European Childhood* (New York: Continuum, 1979);

Die Fackel im Ohr: Lebensgeschichte 1921–1931 (Munich: Hanser, 1980); translated by Neugroschel as *The Torch in My Ear* (New York: Farrar, Straus & Giroux, 1982);

Das Augenspiel: Lebensgeschichte 1931–1937 (Munich: Hanser, 1985); translated by Ralph Manheim as *The Play of the Eyes* (New York: Farrar, Straus & Giroux, 1986);

Das Geheimherz der Uhr: Aufzeichnungen 1973–1985 (Munich: Hanser, 1987); translated by Joel Agee as *The Secret Heart of the Clock: Notes, Aphorisms, Fragments 1973–1985* (New York: Farrar, Straus & Giroux, 1989);

Die Fliegenpein: Aufzeichnungen (Munich: Hanser, 1992); translated by H. F. Broch de Rothermann as *The Agony of Flies: Notes and Notations* (Farrar, Straus & Giroux 1994);

Aufzeichnungen 1942–1985 (Munich: Hanser, 1993);

Nachträge aus Hampstead: Aus den Aufzeichnungen 1954–1971 (Zurich: Hanser, 1994); translated by John Hargraves as *Notes from Hampstead: The Writer's Notes 1954–1971* (Farrar, Straus & Giroux, 1998);

Aufzeichnungen 1992–1993 (Munich: Hanser, 1996);

The Memoirs of Elias Canetti (New York: Farrar, Straus & Giroux, 1999).

TRANSLATIONS: Upton Sinclair, *Leidweg der Liebe* (Berlin: Malik, 1930);

Sinclair, *Das Geld schreibt, Eine Studie über die amerikanische Literatur* (Berlin: Malik, 1930);

Sinclair, *Alkohol* (Berlin: Malik, 1932).

Elias Canetti's oeuvre is not extensive, but he wrote with style and wit in all major genres except poetry. When Canetti won the Nobel Prize in Literature in 1981, Dr. Johannes Edfelt said in a speech at the ceremony that the laureate's major concern in his fiction and nonfiction has been to identify "the threat exercised by the 'massman' within ourselves." His one novel, *Die Blendung* (The Deception, 1946; translated as *Auto-da-Fé,* 1946), was identified by the Swedish Academy as a metaphor representing this major problem of modern man. The academy also praised his theoretical study *Masse und Macht* (1960; translated as *Crowds and Power,* 1962) as "a magisterial work" on the origin and nature of the crowd. Canetti was awarded the highest literary prizes but has enjoyed only a small and select readership of writers and scholars. Susan Sontag has quoted Canetti as saying that he set out to "grab this century by the throat," and he has done so with power and grace. His comment on Kafka can be applied to Canetti's own work with equal validity: "Man wird gut, während man ihn liest, aber ohne stolz darauf zu sein" (One turns good while reading him but without being proud of it).

The oldest of three sons, Canetti was born on 25 July 1905 in Rutschuk (now Ruse), Bulgaria. His father's family belonged to that group of Sephardic Jews who had been driven out of Spain at the time of the Inquisition. They had settled in Andrianople, Turkey, for several centuries prior to relocating in Rutschuk, a trading center on the Danube River. His father, Jacques Canetti, always retained his Turkish citizenship; consequently, his children were also Turkish citizens. Canetti's mother, Mathilde Arditti Canetti, belonged to one of Rutschuk's old and distinguished families of Sephardic Jews. Both parents had studied in Vienna, adopting the cosmopolitanism of the old imperial city and becoming totally engrossed in and enamored of the classical German and European theater tradition. If the family had not insisted that Jacques Canetti enter the family's wholesale grocery business, he might have become an actor. The mother used her interest in dramatic literature as the most important educational device during Canetti's early years.

The language the family spoke at home was Ladino, a mixed Spanish and Hebrew dialect spoken by the Jews of Spanish extraction living in the Balkan states. Canetti was also exposed to Bulgarian, Hebrew, Turkish, Greek, Albanian, Armenian, Romanian, and Russian. The parents spoke German when they did not want their children to understand what they were saying. This experience with so many languages undoubtedly led to Canetti's highly sensitive acoustic perception. In later years he would say that each individual has a specific "acoustic mask," a fingerprint of speech. Everything Canetti experienced, even in the earliest years, seemed to find its way into his writings. His earliest memory, the fear of having his tongue cut off if he revealed the truth of his nanny's amorous activities, is integrated into an episode in his novel.

When Canetti was six years old his father escaped the oppressive atmosphere of working in a family business in a small eastern European town by joining his brothers-in-law's business in Manchester, England. There Canetti learned English and started school. But even more important, it was there that his father introduced him to literature and the life of the imagination. After reading a book Canetti would discuss it with his father and would then receive another. He read *The Arabian Nights,* Grimm's fairy tales, *Robinson Crusoe, Gulliver's Travels, Tales from Shakespeare, Don Quixote,* Dante, and *William Tell,* and later said that he was most grateful to his father for never telling him that fairy tales were untrue. This life of youthful joy was shattered in October 1912 with the sudden death of his father from a heart attack. Since Canetti's mother had always been nostalgic for Vienna, she decided in May 1913 to move there. During a three-month sojourn in Lausanne, Switzerland, she intensively taught her son German so that he would be ready to enter the third grade in Vienna. Much to the surprise of everyone but his mother, Canetti was fluent in the language when the family arrived in Vienna in the fall. This experience gave him a language that he would use for all of his major writings; it also provided him with a lifelong cultural identity.

In 1916 the family moved to Zurich to escape the ravages of World War I. The Swiss city was a paradise for Canetti during his formative years. At age fourteen he completed his first literary work, a historical tragedy in five acts of 2,290 lines of blank verse titled "Junius Brutus." He dedicated the unpublished play to his mother, his strictest and most important teacher. Years later Canetti noted that this play, for all its faults, was his first work that confronted the horror of the death penalty, an issue of lifelong concern.

Much to Canetti's dismay, in 1921 the family moved to Frankfurt am Main. If the previous half decade was lived in a dream world, the years in Frankfurt introduced Canetti to the harshness of reality. Although he was not personally affected by the German inflation, he experienced its manifestations when he saw an old woman collapse and die of hunger in the street. On another occasion Canetti had his first experience with the power of a crowd when he saw a mass demonstration against the murder of the Jewish industrialist Walter Rathenau in 1922. For decades thereafter Canetti devoted great energy to gaining an understanding of crowds and power.

In 1924 Canetti matriculated at the University of Vienna as a student of chemistry. He received a doctorate in 1929 but never worked as a chemist. Perhaps the

most important experience of these years was his encounter with Vienna's master polemicist, Karl Kraus. Canetti said at the time he received the Nobel Prize that Kraus taught him to hear the sounds that make up the "acoustic masks" of different individuals; more important, Kraus "hat mich gegen Krieg geimpft" (inoculated me against war).

In 1929 Canetti began writing *Die Blendung.* Originally he planned this work to be one in a series of eight novels which were to make up a "Comédie Humaine an Irren" (Human Comedy of Madmen). Each novel would have as its protagonist a character who lived a life dedicated to the extreme pursuit of a concept or ideal–the man of truth, the visionary who wants to live in outer space, the religious fanatic, the collector, the spendthrift, the enemy of death, the actor, and the bookman. The bookman (Büchermensch), Dr. Peter Kien, is the protagonist of *Die Blendung.* Kien, at age forty, is the greatest living authority on sinology. He has been offered chairs of oriental philology at several major universities but has declined each invitation. He no longer even gives papers at conferences, even though the entire scholarly community relies on his final judgment. He has withdrawn to his personal library of twenty-five thousand volumes on the top floor of an apartment house at No. 24 Ehrlich Straße. (Even though it is never stated specifically, the reader can assume that the locale of the novel is Vienna.) Eight years ago Kien hired Therese Krumbholz, who was then fifty-six, as a housekeeper. Each day she dusts one of the four rooms of the library from floor to ceiling and prepares Kien's meals, which he takes at his desk. Kien, having severed all contact with the world and withdrawn to scholarly activities in his library, is leading the life of "Ein Kopf ohne Welt" (A Head without a World), as the first part of the novel is titled. The reader soon realizes that Kien has a pathological relationship with his books: he speaks to them, he scolds them as one would a recalcitrant child, and on occasion he suspects them of harboring ill will toward him. On other occasions Kien's views seem much more rational: for example, his suggestion that a novel can help the reader to think himself into another person's place seems an acceptable account of what takes place in the reading process.

To assure the continued care of his library, Kien decides to marry his loyal housekeeper; Therese agrees to the marriage because it will provide her with material security in her advancing years. Kien allows Therese to speak to him for only a few minutes during the noon meal, and at that time he concentrates on not listening to her. While Kien remains totally devoted to his scholarly work, Therese sets about securing her future. She assumes that Kien must be rich because he was overly generous in paying her prior to their marriage and now seems to pay no attention to money matters. When she asks for money to buy furniture, for instance, he gives her a large amount. What she does not understand is that he is just trying to get rid of her so that he will not be bothered at his work. From this misunderstanding begins Therese's great search for Kien's bankbook and his will. Not finding either, she assumes that Kien deceived her about his finances. She sets out to get revenge by invading the solitude of Kien's library, making it impossible for him to work. Kien flees from the house.

Homeless and separated from his library, the helpless misogynist and hermit becomes the easy prey of a ruthless exploiter, the dwarf Fischerle, in the section of the novel titled "Kopflose Welt" (Headless World). To continue his sinological studies Kien imagines that he is carrying his library in his head. Each day he adds more imaginary books to his head library, and each evening he imagines himself taking them out and stacking them on the floor of his hotel room. As he accumulates more and more imaginary books, he needs ever larger rooms. When the task becomes too great he hires Fischerle, who introduces himself as the World Chess Champion Siegfried Fischer and plays along with the head-library game. Through a variety of tricks he swindles Kien out of most of his money.

One source Kien uses to build his head library is the municipal pawnshop, the Theresianum (based on the Dorotheum in Vienna). But rather than buying books, he pays would-be customers not to pawn their books. Fischerle enlists four friends who pretend to want to pawn books but just take Kien's money. One day while Kien is standing in the hallway of the Theresianum his wife and the caretaker of his apartment house come to pawn Kien's books. A row breaks out, the police come, and Kien is accused of theft for preventing the sale of his own books. Although he sees Therese, in his disordered mind he believes that she did not throw him out of his apartment but that he locked her in the apartment and that she has died of starvation. When the police tell him that he is accused, he admits that he is his wife's murderer. The caretaker, a retired policeman named Benedikt Pfaff, realizes that he can profit from the situation. He vouches for Kien at the police station and takes him home to his basement apartment. Forcing Kien to live in a totally dark room, Pfaff ensconces himself with Therese in the top-floor apartment.

At this point Kien's brother Georg, a psychiatrist, arrives from Paris. In the third section of the novel, "Welt im Kopf" (World in the Head), a divorce is arranged, and Therese is established as the owner of a dairy store on the other side of town. She and Pfaff will receive generous sums of money from Georg Kien provided that they stay away from the sinologist. Peter Kien's apartment is refurbished, and his library is reclaimed from the pawnshop. By the time Georg returns to Paris he even seems to have cured Peter's psychosis. But suddenly Kien is attacked by his mania. He places all his beloved books in a pile in the center of the room, sets them on fire, and perishes.

Although Canetti never wrote the other seven novels of the "Human Comedy of Madmen," some of the protagonists of those planned works appear in *Die Blendung* in slightly different guises. Peter Kien's extreme pursuit of his sinological studies differs little from the man who would pursue a certain truth, or the visionary, or even the religious fanatic; likewise, Kien represents the collector and the spendthrift. The most fascinating aspect of the book is the meticulous development of the psychological imbalance of the major characters. Kien, Therese, Fischerle, Pfaff, and even Georg Kien each suffers from his or her own brand of madness, and the exposition of each form of madness is finely crafted. In his only major work of fiction, written at the age of twenty-five, Canetti exhibits a mastery of storytelling that his later works, both fiction and nonfiction, confirm.

It took Canetti a long time to convince himself that the book was worthy of publication. Finally, almost five years after he completed the manuscript, Canetti's friend, the writer Stefan Zweig, found a publisher for it. It was well received by some critics and was praised by Hermann Broch, Alban Berg, Thomas Mann, Robert Musil, and Hermann Hesse. But with Hitler in power and the March 1938 annexation of Austria by Germany, Canetti, a Jew, was unable to have his book distributed in most of the German-speaking market. When the novel was translated into English after World War II, many critics and reviewers labeled the work "too difficult." Little effort was made to promote the translation, and it soon went out of print. After Canetti won the Nobel Prize he showed his bitterness for the years of neglect by withholding permission to have his works printed in England until 1985.

In 1932, shortly after completing *Die Blendung,* Canetti wrote his play, *Hochzeit* (1964; translated as *The Wedding,* 1986). After World War II he wrote two other plays, *Komödie der Eitelkeit* (1950; translated as *Comedy of Vanity,* 1983) and *Die Befristeten* (1964; translated as *Life Terms,* 1983). When the first two of these plays premiered in Braunschweig in the Federal Republic of Germany in 1965, they were received with outrage and disapproval; but, productions prepared by the director Hans Hollmann in the late 1970s and early 1980s in Vienna and Basel were highly successful. Hollmann understood these plays of the theater of the absurd and the concept of the "acoustic masks" which Canetti had created.

In February 1934 Canetti married the writer Venetia Toubner-Calderon, whom he had met at Kraus's lectures. In November 1938 they were among the last Jews to flee from Vienna to Paris following the annexation of Austria to Germany. The next year they moved to London.

While in exile Canetti wrote his major nonfiction work, *Masse und Macht*. The impetus for this study can be traced back to 15 July 1927, when Canetti observed firsthand the dynamics of the crowd that set fire to the Palace of Justice in Vienna. (The same event forms the core of Heimito von Doderer's novel *Die Dämonen* [1956; translated as *The Demons,* 1961].) Canetti's further experiences with mob behavior and the inexplicable power of Hitler to incite mass hysteria compelled him to examine the origins, makeup, and behavior of crowds in a vast array of societies from the earliest times to the present.

Venetia Canetti died in May 1963. Canetti married the art historian Hera Buschor in 1971; their daughter, Johanna, was born in 1972. Hera Buschor died in April 1988. During the last decade of his life Canetti divided his residence between Hampstead, England, and Zurich, Switzerland. He died in Zurich on 14 August 1994 at age eighty-nine and is buried there next to James Joyce.

During the war Canetti had begun setting aside an hour or two each day for writing "Aufzeichnungen" (Notes); they eventually covered the years from 1942 to 1993 and were published in several volumes between 1965 and 1996. These aphoristic writings on a host of topics from the myths of various cultures, languages, war and revolutions, and the fate of the Jews to crowds and power are extraordinary miniature essays which, according to some scholars, may someday be regarded as Canetti's most significant contribution to German literature.

Some of Canetti's longer essays were collected in *Das Gewissen der Worte* (1975; enlarged, 1976; translated as *The Conscience of Words,* 1979). These essays deal with people who had a major impact on Canetti's writing and thinking during the decades devoted to the study of crowds and power: Broch, Musil, Kraus, Stendhal, Tolstoy, and Aristophanes. The most important essay in the collection is Canetti's study of the tortured relationship of Franz Kafka and his fiancée Felice Bauer, as it can be read in the letters he sent her while writing *Der Prozeß* (1925; translated as *The Trial,* 1937); the essay had appeared separately in 1969 as *Der andere Prozeß* (translated as *Kafka's Other Trial,* 1974).

The three volumes of Canetti's autobiography, *Die gerettete Zunge: Geschichte einer Jugend* (1977; trans-lated as *The Tongue Set Free: Remembrance of a European Childhood,* 1979), *Die Fackel im Ohr: Lebensgeschichte 1921–1931* (1980; translated as *The Torch in My Ear,* 1982), and *Das Augenspiel: Lebensgeschichte 1931–1937* (1985; translated as *The Play of the Eyes,* 1986), serve not only as a chronicle of the author's life but also as an important contribution to historical writing.

Although Canett was recognized for his work only late in life, he was awarded some of the most distinguished literary prizes: the Grand Prix International du Club Française du Livre in 1949, the Writer's Prize of the City of Vienna in 1966, the Great Austrian State Prize in 1967, the Georg Büchner Prize in 1972, the Franz Nabl Prize of the City of Graz in 1975, the Orden Pour le Mérite in 1980, the Nobel Prize in Literature and the Franz Kafka Prize in 1981, and the Great Service Cross of the Federal Republic of Germany in 1983. He received honorary doctoral degrees from the University of Munich in 1976.

When Canetti was awarded the Nobel Prize there was a curious reaction in the press. *The New York Times* noted that Canetti was "the first native of Bulgaria to win the prize." The *Times* of London identified Canetti as "the first British citizen to win the literature prize since Winston Churchill" and said, "most unusually of all for a British laureate, Dr. Canetti writes, and has always written, in German." At the same time the Austrian literary journal *Literatur und Kritik* wrote that "Canetti ist nicht österreichischer Staatsbürger, aber dank seiner Bekenntnisse dürfen wir ihn unserer Literatur zurechnen. Er ist der erste Autor österreichischen Wesens, der den Nobelpreis erhält" (Canetti is not an Austrian citizen, but in recognition of his acknowledgment we may include him in our literature. He is the first author of truly Austrian spirit who has received the Nobel Prize). It is perhaps understandable that so many countries and language groups wanted to share the honor of the laureate, if only by spurious association. At the Nobel Prize ceremony Edfelt called him an "exiled and cosmopolitan author" who "has one native land, and that is the German language. He has never abandoned it, and he has often avowed his love of the highest manifestations of the classical German culture. . . . With your versatile writings, which attack sick tendencies in our age, you wish to serve the cause of humanity. Intellectual passion is combined in you with the moral responsibility that—in your own words—'is nourished by mercy.'"

References:
Friedbert Aspetsberger and Gerald Stieg, eds., *Elias Canetti: Blendung als Lebensform* (Königsberg: Athenäum, 1985);

Dagmar Barnouw, *Elias Canetti* (Stuttgart: Metzler, 1979);

Barnouw, "Elias Canetti–Poet and Intellectual," in *Major Figures of Contemporary Austrian Literature,* edited by Donald G. Daviau (New York: Lang, 1987), pp. 117–141;

Barnouw, *Elias Canetti zur Einführung* (Hamburg: Junius, 1996);

Kurt Bartsch and Gerhard Melzer, eds., *Elias Canetti: Experte der Macht* (Graz: Droschl, 1985);

Russell A. Berman, "The Charismatic Novel: Robert Musil, Hermann Hesse, and Elias Canetti," in his *The Rise of the Modern German Novel* (Cambridge, Mass.: Harvard University Press, 1986), pp. 179–204;

Alfons-M. Bischoff, *Elias Canetti: Stationen zum Werk* (Bern & Frankfurt am Main: Lang, 1973);

Mechthild Curtius, *Kritik der Verdinglichung in Canettis Roman "Die Blendung" Eine Sozialpsychologische Literaturanalyse* (Bonn: Bouvier, 1973);

Thomas H. Falk, *Elias Canetti* (New York: Twayne / Toronto: Maxwell Macmillan Canada / New York: Maxwell Macmillan International, 1993);

Festschrift, Hüter der Verwandlung: Beiträge zum Werk von Elias Canetti (Munich: Hanser, 1985); translated by Michael Hulse as *Essays in Honor of Elias Canetti* (New York: Farrar, Straus & Giroux, 1987);

Leslie Fiedler, "The Tower of Babel," *Partisan Review,* 3 (May/June 1947): 316–320;

Herbert G. Göpfert, ed., *Canetti lesen: Erfahrungen mit seinen Büchern* (Munich: Hanser, 1975);

Gitta Honegger, "Acoustic Masks: Strategies of Language in the Theater of Canetti, Bernhard, and Handke," *Modern Austrian Literature,* 18, no. 2 (1985): 57–66;

Ortrun Huber, ed., *Wortmasken: Texte zu Leben und Werk von Elias Canetti* (Albany: State University of New York Press, 1997);

Detlef Krumme, *Lesemodelle: Canetti, Grass, Höllerer* (Munich: Hanser, 1983), pp. 31–84;

Richard H. Lawson, *Understanding Elias Canetti* (Columbia: University of South Carolina Press, 1991);

J. W. McFarlane, "The Tiresian Vision," *Durham University Journal,* 49, no. 3 (1957): 109–115;

Modern Austrian Literature, special Canetti issue, 16, no. 3/4; (1983);

Harriet Murphy, *Canetti and Nietzsche: Theories of Humor in Die Blendung* (Albany: State University of New York Press, 1997)

Idris Parry, "Elias Canetti's Novel *Die Blendung,*" in *Essays in German Literature,* edited by F. Norman, volume 1 (London: London University Press, 1965), pp. 145–166;

Edgar Piel, "Herr seines Schicksals ist der Mensch allein: Elias Canettis *Blendung* als eine andere *Comédie humain,*" *Literatur und Kritik,* no. 157/158 (August/September 1981): 444–461;

David Roberts, *Kopf und Welt: Elias Canettis Roman "Die Blendung"* (Munich: Hanser, 1975);

Sidney Rosenfeld, "1981 Nobel Laureate Elias Canetti: A Writer Apart," *World Literature Today,* 56, no. 1 (1982): 5–9;

Peter Russell, "The Vision of Man in Elias Canetti's *Die Blendung,*" *German Life and Letters,* 28 (October 1974): 24–35;

Ingo Seidler, "Who Is Elias Canetti," in *Cross Currents: A Yearbook of Central European Culture, 1982,* edited by Ladislav Matejka and Benjamin Stolz (Ann Arbor: University of Michigan Press, 1982), pp. 107–123;

Walter H. Sokel, "The Ambiguity of Madness: Elias Canetti's Novel *Die Blendung,*" in *Views and Reviews of Modern German Literature: Festschrift for A. D. Klarmann,* edited by Karl S. Weimar (Munich: Delp, 1974), pp. 181–187;

Susan Sontag, "Mind as Passion," in her *Under the Sign of Saturn* (New York: Farrar, Straus & Giroux, 1980), pp. 181–204;

Edward A. Thomson, "Elias Canetti's *Die Blendung* and the Changing Image of Madness," *German Life and Letters,* 26 (October 1972): 38–47;

David Turner, "The Intellectual as King Canute," in *Modern Austrian Writing: Literature and Society after 1945,* edited by Alan Best and Hans Wolfschütz (London: Wolff, 1980), pp. 79–96;

Marion E. Wiley, "Elias Canetti's Reflective Prose," *Modern Austrian Literature,* 12, no. 2 (1979): 129–139.

Paul Celan
(Paul Antschel)
(23 November 1920 – ? April 1970)

James K. Lyon
Brigham Young University

This entry originally appeared in DLB 69: Contemporary
German Fiction Writers, First Series.

BOOKS: *Edgar Jené und der Traum vom Traume* (Vienna:
    Agathon, 1948);

Der Sand aus den Urnen (Vienna: Sexl, 1948);

Mohn und Gedächtnis: Gedichte (Stuttgart: Deutsche Ver-
    lags-Anstalt, 1952);

Von Schwelle zu Schwelle: Gedichte (Stuttgart: Deutsche Ver-
    lags-Anstalt, 1955);

Sprachgitter (Frankfurt am Main: Fischer, 1959);

Gedichte: Eine Auswahl, edited by Klaus Wagenbach
    (Frankfurt am Main: Fischer, 1959);

*Der Meridian: Rede anläßlich der Verleihung des Georg-Büch-
    ner-Preises, Darmstadt, am 22. Oktober 1960* (Frank-
    furt am Main: Fischer, 1961); translated by
    Walter Billeter as "The Meridian," in *Paul Celan:
    Prose Writings and Selected Poems* (Carlton, Victoria,
    Australia: Paper Castle, 1977), pp. 84–93;

Die Niemandsrose (Frankfurt am Main: Fischer, 1963);

Atemkristall (Paris: Brunidor, 1965);

Gedichte (Darmstadt: Moderner Buch-Club, 1966);

Atemwende: Gedichte (Frankfurt am Main: Suhrkamp,
    1967); translated by Pierre Joris as *Breathturn* (Los
    Angeles: Sun & Moon Press, 1995);

Fadensonnen (Frankfurt am Main: Suhrkamp, 1968);

Ausgewählte Gedichte; Zwei Reden (Frankfurt am Main:
    Suhrkamp, 1968);

Lichtzwang (Frankfurt am Main: Suhrkamp, 1970);

Ausgewählte Gedichte, edited by Klaus Reichert (Frankfurt
    am Main: Suhrkamp, 1970);

Speech-grille, and Selected Poems, translated by Joachim
    Neugroschel (New York: Dutton, 1971);

Schneepart (Frankfurt am Main: Suhrkamp, 1971);

Nineteen Poems, translated by Michael Hamburger (South
    Hinksey, U.K.: Carcanet Press, 1972);

Selected Poems, translated by Hamburger and Christo-
    pher Middleton (Harmondsworth, U.K.: Pen-
    guin, 1972);

Paul Celan in 1967 (Ullstein–Heinz Köster)

Gedichte: In zwei Bänden, 2 volumes (Frankfurt am Main:
    Suhrkamp, 1975);

Zeitgehöft: Späte Gedichte aus dem Nachlaß (Frankfurt am
    Main: Suhrkamp, 1976);

Paul Celan: Poems, selected and translated by Hamburger
    (New York: Persea, 1980);

Gesammelte Werke in fünf Bänden, 5 volumes (Frankfurt am Main: Suhrkamp, 1983);

Todesfuge (New York: Edition Gunnar A. Kaldewey, 1984);

65 Poems (Dublin: Raven Arts Press, 1985);

Collected Prose, translated by Rosmarie Waldrop (Manchester, U.K.: PN Review/Carcanet, 1986; Riverdale-on-Hudson, N.Y.: Sheep Meadow Press, 1990);

Last Poems (San Francisco: North Point Press, 1986);

Poems of Paul Celan, translated by Hamburger (London: Anvil Press Poetry, 1988; New York: Persea Books, 1989);

Das Frühwerk, edited by Barbara Wiedemann (Frankfurt am Main: Suhrkamp, 1989);

Eingedunkelt, und Gedichte aus dem Umkreis von Eingedunkelt, edited by Bertrand Badiou and Jean-Claude Rambach (Frankfurt am Main: Suhrkamp, 1991);

Paul Celan: Die Gedichte aus dem Nachlaß, edited by Bertrand Badiou, Jean-Claude Rambach, and Barbara Wiedemann (Frankfurt am Main: Suhrkamp, 1997);

Paul Celan, 18 Gedichte (Hamburg: Maximilian, 1997).

OTHER: "Ansprache anläßlich der Entgegennahme des Literaturpreises der Freien Hansestadt Bremen," in *Ansprachen bei der Verleihung des Bremer Literaturpreises an Paul Celan* (Stuttgart: Deutsche Verlags-Anstalt, 1958), pp. 10–11; translated by Robert Kelly as "Address on Acceptance of the Prize for Literature of the Free Hanseatic City of Bremen," *Origin,* third series, no. 15 (1969): 16–17.

TRANSLATIONS: Jean Cocteau, *Der goldene Vorhang* (Bad Salzburg & Düsseldorf: Rauch, 1949);

Arthur Rimbaud, *Bateau ivre/Das trunkene Schiff* (Wiesbaden: Insel, 1958);

Osip Emil'evich Mandel'shtam, *Gedichte* (Frankfurt am Main: Fischer, 1959);

Jean Cayrol, *Im Bereich einer Nacht: Roman* (Olten: Walter, 1961);

Drei russische Dichter: Alexander Block, Ossip Mandelstamm, Sergej Jessenin (Frankfurt am Main: Fischer, 1963);

Pablo Picasso, *Wie man Wünsche beim Schwanz packt: Ein Drama in sechs Akten* (Zurich: Arche, 1963);

Paul Valéry, *Die junge Parze/La jeune Parque* (Frankfurt am Main: Insel, 1964);

William Shakespeare, *Einundzwanzig Sonette* (Frankfurt am Main: Insel, 1967);

Jules Supervielle, *Gedichte* (Frankfurt am Main: Insel, 1968);

Sergei Aleksandrovich Esenin, *Gedichte* (Leipzig: Reclam, 1970);

René Char, translated by Celan and others (Berlin: Neues Leben, 1973).

PERIODICAL PUBLICATIONS: "Gegenlicht," *Die Tat* (Zurich) (12 March 1949);

"Gespräch im Gebirg," *Neue Rundschau,* 71, no. 2 (1960): 199–202; translated by Joachim Neugroschel as "Conversation in the Mountains," *Antaeus,* no. 7 (1972): 68–71;

"Ansprache vor dem hebräischen Schriftstellerverband," *Die Stimme* (Tel Aviv), no. 246 (August 1970): 7;

"Geräuschlos hüpft ein Griffel . . . ," *Neue Literatur* (Bucharest), 11 (1980): 63–64.

Paul Celan (pronounced say-*lahn*), whom George Steiner has called "almost certainly the major European poet of the period after 1945," is known primarily for his verse. Yet his reputation as a lyric poet overshadows a small but significant body of prose works that deserve attention both for their close links to his poetry and as independent creations.

Paul Antschel, the only child of Jewish parents, Leo Antschel-Teitler and Friederike Schrager, was born in Czernovitz (now Chernivtsi, Ukraine), capital of the Romanian province of Bukovina, on 23 November 1920. He grew up in a multilingual environment. German, the language spoken at home and in some of the schools he attended, remained his mother tongue throughout his life, and Vienna was the cultural lodestar of his youth; but his language of daily speech was Romanian. Before his bar mitzvah he studied Hebrew for three years, and by the time he began a year of premedical studies at the École préparatoire de Médecine in Tours, France, in 1938, he was also fluent in French. Returning to Czernovitz shortly before the outbreak of World War II, he learned Russian at the university and, after Soviet troops occupied Bukovina in 1940, in the streets. When German troops captured the city in 1941 his parents were deported and shot, but he survived. After eighteen months at forced labor for the Germans, he escaped to the Red Army and returned to Czernovitz, which was again under Russian control. There, sometime in late 1944, he wrote the remarkable "Todesfuge" (Death Fugue), perhaps the most powerful poem ever written on the Holocaust. It was included in his first two collections of poems, *Der Sand aus den Urnen* (The Sand from the Urns, 1948) and *Mohn und Gedächtnis* (Poppy and Memory, 1952).

Leaving Czernovitz in 1945 for Bucharest, Antschel joined a surrealist circle, became friends with leading Romanian writers, and worked as a translator and reader in a publishing house. For his prose translations from Russian into Romanian–primarily of Mikhail Lermontov, Konstantin Simonov, and Anton Chekhov–and for publication of his own poems, he used several pseudonyms before transmuting Ancel, the Romanian form of his surname, into Celan in 1947.

Sometime between 1945 and 1947 he wrote a two-page prose fragment that has survived under the title "Geräuschlos hüpft ein Griffel . . ." (A Stylus Noiselessly Hops . . . , 1980). This work reveals his indebtedness to surrealism. In it a noiseless slate pencil or stylus writes under its own power, first on a slate tablet, which is the earth, and then on a "Blatt" (leaf or page) in a treetop. Further surrealistic sequences show a man in a room who finds that the window has been locked by a powerful, unseen external hand, and the same man looking into a mirror, only to see his coat buttons and the carpet transformed into mirrors. At this point the series of dreamlike scenes breaks off.

Late in 1947 Celan went to Vienna, where he joined a circle of leading avant-garde painters, writers, and publishers. His friendship with the painter Edgar Jené gave rise to a brief prose piece, "Die Lanze" (The Lance), which he and Jené wrote jointly early in 1948 and circulated on mimeographed sheets to announce a reading of surrealist texts as part of an exhibition of surrealist painters in Vienna. Like "Geräuschlos hüpft ein Griffel . . . ," "Die Lanze" consists of typical surrealist images: "rainbowfish" flying through the sky, a giant hammer in the air, and waves beating against treetops. It ends with speakers casting nets into the water–an image also found in Celan's early poems. The work contains a dialogue, a format that became a hallmark of his later prose works.

A second prose piece, *Edgar Jené und der Traum vom Traume* (Edgar Jené and the Dream of the Dream, 1948), written at about the same time as "Die Lanze," purports to be a discussion of Jené's paintings but quickly becomes a confessional essay on what happens in the "Tiefsee" (deep sea) of the writer's mind, the "große Kristall der Innenwelt" (huge crystal of the internal world) into which he follows Jené and where he explores his paintings. Aware that language has become false and debased, he seeks to regain a naive view of the world and to recover pristine speech or "truth" that cannot be restored by reason, but only by venturing into the depths of the mind and engaging in dialogue with its "finstere Quellen" (dark sources). With this newfound freedom, he engages Jené's paintings in a dialogue. In the process Celan sketches the contours of "die schöne Wildnis auf der anderen, tieferen Seite des Seins" (the beautiful wilderness on the other, more profound side of existence), the internal world in which most of his poetry takes place, a world of "true" language obscured by lies, an internal darkness that is dispelled only by the light of "true" language. In prose marked by unusual new compound nouns, Celan's many interrogative sentences give

one the sense that he wishes to engage his reader in a direct dialogue.

Leaving Vienna in July 1948, he settled in Paris and began studies in German philology and literature. In March 1949 the Swiss journal *Die Tat* published a collection of his brilliant but enigmatic aphorisms titled "Gegenlicht" (Counter-Light). These aphorisms appear surrealistic in their subversion of conventional time and of space and object relationships–trees fly to birds, hours jump out of the clock, a woman hates a mirror's vanity. Behind them lies a Kafkaesque awareness that the world makes no sense. For Celan it seems that only in the paradox of new language combinations can the world be made coherent, and only in a dialectic of contradictions can truth be rendered. Hence, an aphorism that juxtaposes a battleship and a drowned man might be read as a pacifist statement: "Man redet umsonst von Gerechtigkeit, solange das größte der Schlachtschiffe nicht an der Stirn eines Ertrunkenen zerschellt ist" (One speaks in vain of justice as long as the largest battleship has not been smashed to pieces on a drowned man's brow).

Celan took his Licence des Lettres in 1950. In 1952 he married the graphic artist Gisèle de Lestrange, with whom he had a son, Eric, who was born in 1955. Though he wrote no original prose for almost ten years, the works Celan chose to translate into German were usually prose. For him each translation was a new linguistic creation, a means of establishing his identity and verifying his existence within language. He never gave up German as his mother tongue, telling a friend, "Only in one's mother tongue can one express one's own truth. In a foreign language, the poet lies." Though all of these translations reflect his unique prose style, one reveals almost more of himself than of the original–his rendering of Jean Cayrol's prose narration for Alain Resnais's *Nuit et Brouillard* (Night and Fog, 1956), a film on the Holocaust that Celan endowed with an authentic Jewish voice for German-speaking viewers.

The address he delivered upon receiving the Bremen Literary Prize in 1958 (translated, 1969) is Celan's most personal prose work. After referring to the Bukovinian landscape of his youth and his acquaintance with Martin Buber's Hasidic tales in this world "in der Menschen und Bücher lebten" (where humans and books lived), the address becomes a discussion of his relationship to the German language, one of the few elements of his spiritual existence he did not lose under the Nazis. This language, he says, "mußte nun hindurchgehen . . . durch furchtbares Verstummen, hindurchgehen durch die tausend Finsternisse todbringender Rede" (had to pass . . . through a frightful muting, pass through the thousand darknesses of death-bringing speech). From its miraculous survival, he now attempts to write "um zu sprechen, um mich zu orientieren . . . um mir Wirklichkeit zu entwerfen" (in order to speak, to orient myself . . . to outline reality). He states his views on poetry as dialogue, as a "Flaschenpost" (message in a bottle) cast out and addressed to "etwas Offenstehendes, auf ein ansprechbares Du vielleicht, auf eine ansprechbare Wirklichkeit" (something that stands open, perhaps an addressable Thou, an addressable reality). But he accomplishes this painful task as one who "mit seinem Dasein zur Sprache geht, wirklichkeitswund und Wirklichkeit suchend" (goes to language with his very being, stricken by and seeking reality). Besides being a statement of personal poetics, this piece stands, like Buber's *Ich und Du* (1923; translated as *I and Thou,* 1937), as an expression of man's need for a relation to an "Other."

In 1959 Celan became a reader in German Language and Literature at L'École Normale Superieure, a position he held until his death. While in the Swiss Alps in July 1959 he was to meet Theodor Adorno at Sils-Maria. Forced to return to Paris before they met, Celan composed "Gespräch im Gebirg" (1960; translated as "Conversation in the Mountains," 1972) the following month; it was a reflection on this missed encounter; he later called it a "Mauscheln" (jabber, schmooze) between himself and Adorno. This most distinctly Jewish of his prose works portrays a meeting in the mountains between "Jud-Klein" (Jew-Small) and "Jud-Groß" (Jew-Big). It opens with involved sentences punctuated with dashes, thought fragments, and repetitions as Jew-Small walks through the Alps reflecting on the landscape, his own Jewishness with which he does not feel at ease, the nature of silence, and, finally, the nature of speech. After meeting Jew-Big, he admits that he came there to talk with someone, and immediately they make a distinction between "Reden" (talk) and "Sprechen" (speech) as they reflect on hearing, remembering, and language. Jew-Small, who dominates the conversation, delivers a long reverie on the Jewish dead and on his love for an ancestral candle as it symbolically burns toward extinction: "Auf dem Stein bin ich gelegen, damals, du weißt, auf den Steinfliesen; und neben mir, da sind sie gelegen, die andern, die wie ich waren, die anders, die anders waren als ich und genauso, die Geschwisterkinder; und sie lagen da und schliefen, schliefen und schliefen nicht, und sie träumten und träumten nicht . . ." (On the stone is where I lay, back then, you know, the flagstones; and near me, that's where they were lying, the others, who were different from me and the same, the cousins; and they lay there and slept, sleeping and not sleeping, dreaming and not dreaming . . .). Gradually he realizes that in the dialogue with Jew-Big he is meeting himself, that is, encountering and beginning to accept his people, his heritage, and his Jewish identity.

In 1960 Celan traveled to Darmstadt to receive the Georg Büchner Prize from the German Academy of Language and Literature. His acceptance speech, *Der Meridian* (1961; translated as "The Meridian," 1977), is viewed by critics as a statement of poetic theory, but it is also a literary expression of how Celan attempts to make sense of the world. Written as a dialogue with his listeners, it is punctuated by reservations or uncertainties about the poet's craft, leading the listener/reader through a labyrinth of images relating to the poet's quest for speech in an age when speech has become nearly impossible. After an exposition of Büchner's tragedy *Dantons Tod* (1835) and his short story "Lenz" (1839), both of which for Celan pay homage to the "Majestät des Absurden" (Majesty of the Absurd) characteristic of our era, he expresses doubts about the existence of literary "art"; before anything else, the contemporary writer must radically question the existence of such art. Writing a poem is a search for an "Ort" (place), perhaps a place that does not exist, a "u-topia." Poetic creations do not enjoy universal, a priori existence but arise only through encounters, through the meeting of a voice with an Other, through dialogue that allows an "I" to orient itself through speech and understand itself through contact with a Thou, an act that enables this "I" to discover the "meridian" that connects it through language to the rest of the world.

Before his suicide sometime in April 1970–he had been missing since the middle of April and his body was found in early May–Celan produced only one more prose work, a brief address delivered to the Hebrew Writers' Association on 14 October 1969 during a trip to Israel; it was published in the Tel Aviv magazine *Die Stimme* in August 1970. In the address Celan expresses gratitude for discovering in Israel an "äußere und innere Landschaft" (external and internal landscape) conducive to creating great poetry. He draws an analogy between these two landscapes: "Ich verstehe . . . den dankbaren Stolz auf jedes selbstgepflanzte Grün, das bereitsteht, jeden der hier vorbeikommt zu erfrischen; wie ich die Freude begreife über jedes neuerworbene, selbsterfühlte Wort, das herbeieilt, den ihm Zugewandeten zu stärken" (I understand . . . the grateful pride in every homegrown green thing that stands ready to refresh anyone who comes by; just as I comprehend the joy in every newly won, self-felt word that rushes up to strengthen him who is receptive to it).

Under the heading "Prose," the 1983 edition of Celan's collected works includes three letters he wrote in response to survey questions. Celan wrote brilliant letters; like Rainer Maria Rilke's, they could almost qualify as a separate genre. But so few of them have been published that it is not yet possible to give a general analysis of their style and content.

Creative extensions and elaborations of his poetry, Celan's prose works express the strain of being Jewish, the struggle to reclaim language in a nonpoetic age, and the need for dialogue as a means of connecting oneself with and orienting oneself in the modern world.

Letters:

Paul Celan, Nelly Sachs: Briefwechsel, edited by Barbara Wiedemann (Frankfurt am Main: Suhrkamp, 1993); translated by Christopher Clark as *Paul Celan, Nelly Sachs: Correspondence* (Riverdale-on-Hudson, N.Y.: Sheep Meadow Press, 1995);

Paul Celan, Franz Wurm: Briefwechsel, edited by Wiedemann (Frankfurt am Main: Suhrkamp, 1995).

Bibliographies:

Christiane Heuline, "Bibliographie zu Paul Celan: Werke und Sekundärliteratur," *Zeitschrift für Kulturaustausch,* 3, no. 32 (1982): 245–287;

Heuline, "Bibliographie zu Paul Celan," *text + kritik,* 53/54 (July 1984): 100–149;

Christiane Bohrer, *Paul Celan-Bibliographie* (Frankfurt am Main & New York: Peter Lang, 1989);

Jerry Glenn, *Paul Celan: Eine Bibliographie* (Wiesbaden: Harrassowitz, 1989).

Biography:

Israel Chalfen, *Paul Celan: Eine Biographie seiner Jugend* (Frankfurt am Main: Suhrkamp, 1979); translated by Maximilian Bleyleben as *Paul Celan: A Biography of His Youth* (New York: Persea Books, 1991).

References:

Ewa Borkowska, *From Donne to Celan: Logo(theo)logical Patterns in Poetry* (Katowice, Poland: Wydawn, Uniwersytet Slaskiego, 1994);

Renate Böschenstein-Schäfer, "Anmerkungen zu Paul Celans 'Gespräch im Gebirg,'" *Neue Zürcher Zeitung,* 20 October 1968;

David Brierley, *"Der Meridian": Ein Versuch zur Poetik und Dichtung Paul Celans* (Frankfurt am Main: Peter Lang, 1984);

Beatrice Adrienne Cameron, "Anticomputer: An Essay on the Work of Paul Celan, Followed by Selected Poems in Translation," dissertation, University of California, Berkeley, 1973;

Cameron, "The 'Meridian' Speech: An Introductory Note," *Chicago Review,* 29, no. 3 (1978): 23–27;

Amy Colin, *Paul Celan: Holograms of Darkness* (Bloomington: Indiana University Press, 1991);

Claude David, "Paul Celan, 'Der Meridian,'" *Études Germaniques,* 17 (1962): 101;

Adrian Del Caro, *The Early Poetry of Paul Celan: In the Beginning Was the Word* (Baton Rouge: Louisiana State University Press, 1997);

John Felstiner, *Paul Celan: Poet, Survivor, Jew* (New Haven: Yale University Press, 1995);

Aris Fioretos, ed., *Word Traces: Readings of Paul Celan* (Baltimore: Johns Hopkins University Press, 1994);

Hans Georg Gadamer, *Gadamer on Celan: "Who Am I and Who Are You?" and Other Essays,* translated and edited by Richard Heinemann and Bruce Krajewski (Albany: State University of New York Press, 1997);

Jerry Glenn, "Paul Celan: Edgar Jené and the Dream of the Dream," *Boston University Journal,* 21, no. 1 (1973): 61–63;

John E. Jackson, "Die Du-Anrede bei Paul Celan: Anmerkungen zu seinem 'Gespräch im Gebirg,'" *text + kritik,* 53/54 (1977): 62–68;

Jackson, *La Question du moi* (Neuchâtel: Editions de la Baconnière, 1978), pp. 145–240;

James K. Lyon, "Paul Celan and Martin Buber: Poetry as Dialogue," *PMLA,* 86, no. 1 (1971): 110–120;

Hans Mayer, "Lenz, Büchner und Celan: Anmerkungen zu Paul Celans Georg-Büchner-Preis-Rede 'Der Meridian' vom 22.10.1960," *Vereinzelt Niederschläge: Kritik, Polemik* (Pfullingen: Neske, 1973), pp. 160–171;

Dietlind Meinecke, ed., *Über Paul Celan* (Frankfurt am Main: Suhrkamp, 1973);

Peter Horst Neumann, *Zur Lyrik Paul Celans* (Göttingen: Vandenhoeck & Ruprecht, 1968);

Clarise Samuels, *Holocaust Visions: Surrealism and Existentialism in the Poetry of Paul Celan* (Columbia, S.C.: Camden House, 1993);

Georg-Michael Schulz, "Individuation und Austauschbarkeit: Zu Paul Celans 'Gespräch im Gebirg,'" *Deutsche Vierteljahresschrift für Literaturwissenschaft und Geistesgeschichte,* 53 (1979): 463–477;

George Steiner, "The Loud Silences of Paul Celan," *Jewish Quarterly,* 4 (1980–1981): 49–50;

Steiner, "Songs of a Torn Tongue," *TLS: The Times Literary Supplement,* 28 September 1984, pp. 1093–1094;

Studies in Twentieth Century Literature, special Celan issue (Fall 1983);

Shira Wolosky, *Language Mysticism: The Negative Way of Language in Eliot, Beckett, and Celan* (Stanford: Stanford University Press, 1995).

Papers:

The bulk of Paul Celan's manuscripts is in the possession of his widow, Mme. Gisèle Celan-Lestrange of Paris. Manuscripts of poems and letters are known to exist in the hands of friends in Europe, Israel, and the United States.

Alfred Döblin

(10 August 1878 – 26 June 1957)

Wulf Koepke
Texas A & M University

This entry originally appeared in DLB 66: German Fiction
Writers, 1885–1913.

BOOKS: *Lydia und Mäxchen: Tiefe Verbeugung in einem Akt*
(Strasbourg: Singer, 1906);

Die Ermordung einer Butterblume und andere Erzählungen
(Munich: Müller, 1913);

Das Stiftsfräulein und der Tod: Eine Novelle (Berlin-Wilmers-dorf: Meyer, 1913);

Die drei Sprünge des Wang-lun: Chinesischer Roman (Berlin: Fischer, 1915);

Die Lobensteiner reiten nach Böhmen: Zwölf Novellen und Geschichten (Munich: Müller, 1917);

Wadzeks Kampf mit der Dampfturbine: Roman (Berlin: Fischer, 1918);

Der schwarze Vorhang: Roman von den Worten und Zufällen (Berlin: Fischer, 1919);

Das verwerfliche Schwein: Novelle. Lydia und Mäxchen: Tiefe Verbeugung in einem Akt. Lusitania: Drei Szenen (Vienna: Waldheim-Eberle, 1920);

Wallenstein: Roman, 2 volumes (Berlin: Fischer, 1920);

Der deutsche Maskenball, as Linke-Poot (Berlin: Fischer, 1921);

Staat und Schriftsteller (Berlin: Verlag für Sozialwissenschaft, 1921);

Blaubart und Miß Ilsebill (Berlin: Voegel, 1923);

Die Nonnen von Kemnade: Schauspiel in vier Akten (Berlin: Fischer, 1923);

Berge Meere und Giganten: Roman (Berlin: Fischer, 1924); revised as *Giganten: Ein Abenteuerbuch* (Berlin: Fischer, 1932);

Die beiden Freundinnen und ihr Giftmord (Berlin: Die Schmiede, 1925);

Feldzeugmeister Cratz, Der Kaplan: Zwei Erzählungen (Berlin: Weltgeist-Bücher, 1926);

Reise in Polen (Berlin: Fischer, 1926);

Manas: Epische Dichtung (Berlin: Fischer, 1927);

Das Ich über der Natur (Berlin: Fischer, 1927);

Alfred Döblin: Im Buch-Zu Haus-Auf der Straß, by Döblin and Oskar Loerke (Berlin: Fischer, 1928);

Alfred Döblin

Berlin Alexanderplatz: Die Geschichte vom Franz Biberkopf (Berlin: Fischer, 1929); translated by Eugene Jolas as *Alexanderplatz, Berlin* (New York: Viking, 1931);

Die Ehe: Drei Szenen und ein Vorspiel (Berlin: Fischer, 1931);

Wissen und Verändern! Offene Briefe an einen jungen Menschen (Berlin: Fischer, 1931);

Unser Dasein (Berlin: Fischer, 1933);

Jüdische Erneuerung (Amsterdam: Querido, 1933);

Babylonische Wandrung oder Hochmut kommt vor dem Fall: Roman (Amsterdam: Querido, 1934);

71

Pardon wird nicht gegeben: Roman (Amsterdam: Querido, 1935); translated by Trevor Blewitt and Phyllis Blewitt as *Men without Mercy* (London: Gollancz, 1937; New York: Fertig, 1976);

Flucht und Sammlung des Judenvolkes: Aufsätze und Erzählungen (Amsterdam: Querido, 1935);

Das Land ohne Tod, volume 1: *Die Fahrt ins Land ohne Tod: Roman* (Amsterdam: Querido, 1937);

Das Land ohne Tod, volume 2: *Der blaue Tiger: Roman* (Amsterdam: Querido, 1938);

Die deutsche Literatur (im Ausland seit 1933): Ein Dialog zwischen Politik und Kunst (Paris: Science et Littérature, 1938);

Eine deutsche Revolution: Erzählwerk in drei Bänden, volume 1: *Bürger und Soldaten 1918: Roman* (Stockholm: Bermann-Fischer / Amsterdam: Querido, 1939); revised as *November 1918: Eine deutsche Revolution. Erzählwerk,* volume 1: *Verratenes Volk* (Munich: Alber, 1948);

Nocturno (Los Angeles: Pazifische Presse, 1944);

Sieger und Besiegte: Eine wahre Geschichte (New York: Aurora, 1946);

Der Oberst und der Dichter oder Das menschliche Herz (Freiburg: Alber, 1946);

Der unsterbliche Mensch: Ein Religionsgespräch (Freiburg: Alber, 1946);

Der Nürnberger Lehrprozeß, as Hans Fiedeler (Baden-Baden: Neuer Bücherdienst, 1946);

Die literarische Situation (Baden-Baden: Keppler, 1947);

Auswahl aus dem erzählenden Werk, introduction by E. H. P. Lüth (Wiesbaden: Limes, 1948);

Heitere Magie: Zwei Erzählungen (Baden-Baden: Keppler, 1948);

Das Land ohne Tod, volume 3: *Der neue Urwald: Roman* (Baden-Baden: Keppler, 1948);

November 1918: Eine deutsche Revolution. Erzählwerk, volume 2, *Heimkehr der Fronttruppen* (Munich: Alber, 1949); selections from volumes 1 and 2 translated by John E. Woods as *A People Betrayed* (New York: Fromm International, 1983); volume 3: *Karl und Rosa* (Munich: Alber, 1950); translated by Woods as *Karl and Rosa* (New York: Fromm International, 1983);

Schicksalsreise: Bericht und Bekenntnis (Frankfurt am Main: Knecht-Carolus, 1949);

Die Dichtung, ihre Natur und ihre Rolle (Mainz: Verlag der Akademie der Wissenschaft und der Literatur, 1950);

Hamlet oder Die lange Nacht nimmt ein Ende: Roman (East Berlin: Rütten & Loening, 1956);

Ausgewählte Werke in Einzelbänden, edited by Walter Muschg, Heinz Graber, and Anthony W. Riley, 23 volumes published (Olten & Freiburg: Walter, 1960–1985);

Die Zeitlupe: Kleine Prosa, edited by Muschg (Olten & Freiburg: Walter, 1962);

Die Vertreibung der Gespenster, edited by Manfred Beyer (East Berlin: Rütten & Loening, 1968);

Ein Kerl muß eine Meinung haben, edited by Beyer (Olten & Freiburg: Walter, 1976).

OTHER: Heinrich Heine, *Deutschland: Ein Wintermärchen,* introduction by Döblin (Hamburg & Berlin: Hoffman & Campe, 1923);

Mario von Bucovich, *Berlin,* preface by Döblin (Berlin & Augsburg: Albertus-Verlag, 1928);

Anton Betzner, *Antäus,* postscript by Döblin (Baden-Baden: Merlin, 1929);

August Sander, *Antlitz der Zeit,* preface by Döblin (Munich: Transmare, 1929);

The Living Thoughts of Confucius, edited by Döblin, introductory essay translated by Doris A. Infield (New York & Toronto: Longmans, Green, 1940);

Johann Wolfgang von Goethe, *Belagerung von Mainz 1793,* preface by Döblin (Offenburg & Mainz: Lehrmittel, 1946);

Charles de Coster, *Ulenspiegel: Aus dem Flämischen von K. Wolfskehl,* preface by Döblin (Berlin: Ulenspiegel, 1948);

Arno Holz, *Eine Auswahl,* edited by Anita Holz, introduction by Döblin (Baden-Baden: Keppler, 1949);

Holz, *Die Revolution der Lyrik: Eine Einführung in sein Werk und eine Auswahl,* edited by Döblin (Wiesbaden: Steiner, 1951);

"Mireille oder Zwischen Politik und Religion" and "Großstadt und Großstädter," in *Minotaurus: Dichtung unter den Hufen von Staat und Industrie,* edited by Döblin (Wiesbaden: Steiner, 1953), pp. 9–56, 221–241.

PERIODICAL PUBLICATIONS: "Futuristische Worttechnik: Offener Brief an F. T. Marinetti," *Der Sturm,* no. 150 / 151 (March 1913);

"Zion und Europa," *Neuer Merkur,* 5 (1921–1922): 338–342;

"Der Überfall auf Chao-Lao-Sü," *Genius,* 3 (1921): 275–285;

"Das Wasser," *Neue Rundschau,* 33 (1922): 853–858;

"Doktor Rosinus und seine Abenteuer," by Döblin, Arnold Ulitz, Walter von Molo, and others, *Berliner Tageblatt,* 25 December 1925;

"Sigmund Freud. Zum 70. Geburtstag," *Vossische Zeitung,* 5 May 1926;

"Dichtung und Christentum," *Ostwart-Jahrbuch,* 1 (1926): 148–149;

"Sechs Dichter sehen durch die Zeitlupe," *Vossische Zeitung,* 25 December 1926;

"Kleine Alltagsgeschichte," *Berliner Börsen-Courier,* 20 April 1930;

"Ivar Kreuger lebt!," *Die Literarische Welt,* 8 (1 July 1932): 3–4;

"Jacob Wassermanns letztes Buch," *Die Sammlung,* 1 (1933–1934): 517–523;

"Die letzten Tage der Dichterakademie," *Pariser Tageblatt,* 31 May 1936;

"Persönliches und Unpersönliches," *Die Zukunft,* 1 (12 October 1938): 9;

"Selbstporträt," *Die Zukunft,* 2 (24 February 1939): 8.

Alfred Döblin's reputation as one of the most important German writers of narrative prose in the twentieth century is secure. He was the author of a series of innovative, original, and very diverse works, so diverse that the question has been asked whether he had his own style or changed his style from work to work. In spite of his undisputed reputation among critics, however, few of Döblin's works are known to a wide audience. His early short stories are considered characteristic examples of expressionistic prose and are much anthologized. While his "Chinese novel" *Die drei Sprünge des Wang-lun* (The Three Leaps of Wang-lun, 1915) and—less frequently—*Wallenstein* (1920) are sometimes mentioned, Döblin's fame really rests on a single work: *Berlin Alexanderplatz* (1929; translated as *Alexanderplatz, Berlin,* 1931). It was his only work to become instantly popular, to be recognized by literary critics and the reading public alike, and to endure the passage of time. The works of Döblin's exile period after 1933 have not fared well; scholars have considered most of them to be less weighty and significant than the works written before 1933. When Döblin's last novel, *Hamlet oder Die lange Nacht nimmt ein Ende* (Hamlet; or, The Long Night comes to an End), was belatedly published in 1956, however, it received a surprising popular and critical acclaim; and in 1978 a new paperback edition of *November 1918* (1948–1950) drew attention for the first time to Döblin's intriguing treatment of the failed German revolution.

The lack of popularity of most of Döblin's works is easily explained. They are long; their narrative techniques are unconventional; their meaning is not obvious; they usually do not have unilinear lines of action but branch out into many episodes, and easily move from realistic to imaginary scenes or to surrealistic combinations. They do not facilitate a reader's entrance into their world but are demanding, even misleading. The narrator may not be reliable but may speak in ironic commentaries that only add to the reader's confusion. Yet Döblin's abundant imagination and his narrative power are unmistakable. And it is equally evident that he is a very contemporary writer: fresh, modern, unconventional, challenging–a writer who confronts the reader with fundamental issues, with an intriguing psychological bent, and with views that challenge many "common sense" notions. The reader will rarely totally agree or feel completely comfortable with Döblin's ideas; the author leads the reader into strange, unknown worlds and then leaves him to himself, or else argues with him, teases him, and contradicts him. While these techniques are accepted practice in the tradition of the humorous novel from Cervantes, through Voltaire and Laurence Sterne, to Jean Paul, they are unexpected in Döblin's writings, where the humor and irony, although essential, are usually submerged and not easily recognizable.

While Döblin's "protean" nature is routinely emphasized in the critical literature, there are some characteristic traits of his work that reveal a basic continuity beneath all of his apparent transformations. One such trait is a preoccupation with nature and the position of the human being in nature. This preoccupation includes a religious dimension: Döblin asks whether the divine principle is within nature or beyond it; how the human being lives on after death; whether life is a simple—and eternal—cycle of birth, growth, decay, and death, or whether there is a direction and meaning in this endless resurgence of vital forces. Döblin was always interested in the complexities of close human relationships, such as family relations; and he tried in vain to find a way for human beings to organize themselves into a nonviolent society without political power struggles and social hierarchies. Such major existential questions imposed themselves not only because of Döblin's personal and historical experiences, but most of all because of his unique blend of keen intelligence, extreme sensitivity, and a need for both unlimited freedom and motherly protection, all of which were coupled with an imagination which deeply penetrated historical, geographical, anthropological, and psychological facts.

Döblin was the fourth of five children; his father, Max Döblin, a tailor in Stettin, had artistic leanings, and preferred easy speculations to hard work. His mother, Sophie Freudenheim Döblin, was a tough, materialistic woman who came from a lower-middle-class background but had a firm determination to climb the social ladder. The father, unlucky in his business enterprises due to miscalculations and lack of dedication, grew weary of his responsibilities. In 1888 he ran away with one of his female employees who was much younger than he was to start a new life in America. The plan failed, and he was left stranded in Hamburg. The mother moved with her children to Berlin, where she could count on help from her relatives. The family survived due to the perseverance of the mother;

the help of her brothers; and the success of Döblin's oldest brother, who worked for one of his uncles and later became a factory owner himself.

Döblin's mother's family had come from eastern Europe and had taken advantage of the great economic opportunities in the new German empire; the family had moved from a Jewish orthodox environment to assimilation into German customs and culture. While Döblin's family still observed the Jewish holidays, his religious instruction was sporadic. He knew more of the Jewish religion and traditions than he would admit, but treated this background with ambivalence and some detachment. In 1912 he officially left the Jewish community.

The move to Berlin was catastrophic for Döblin's education. He had just entered the gymnasium in Stettin, but the family could no longer afford the tuition for a gymnasium, and only in 1891 was he able to return with a tuition waiver. In the meantime he had been in contact with boys of the lower classes and had become accustomed to the proletarian section of Berlin where the family lived; when he reentered the gymnasium he was several years older than the other boys and had lost all chance of being integrated. He was a difficult and mediocre student and had to repeat two years because of problems in mathematics. His last years in school were characterized by severe conflicts with his authoritarian teachers. He finally passed his Abitur (school-leaving examination) in 1900 at the age of twenty-two.

Thus, there were three sources of serious conflict during Döblin's youth. First, there was the psychological burden borne by a child from a separated family. Döblin, like his siblings, sided with his mother; but while he accepted her harsh verdict on the failings of the father, she could not understand her son. She had only contempt for his artistic leanings and infected him with a severe distrust of the legitimacy of art and artists. Second, the mother fostered a bourgeois and achievement-oriented spirit in her children while the family lived in a proletarian milieu. Many of Döblin's political attitudes can be attributed to this conflict. Third, Döblin developed an aversion to authority, convention, and conventional wisdom, and began his cultural career in opposition to leading trends and powers. During his school years he read the works of authors who were then outside the canon: Heinrich von Kleist, Friedrich Hölderlin, Friedrich Nietzsche, Arthur Schopenhauer, Fyodor Dostoyevsky, and Benedict de Spinoza. He started writing while in school, but his specific talents needed much time for maturation.

In the fall of 1900 Döblin began to study medicine in Berlin with financial assistance from his uncle and brother. He soon began devoting special attention to psychiatry. Later, his interest shifted to physiology and internal medicine.

Around 1900 Döblin met Herwarth Walden, a musician who became a leading organizer of the modernist movement in literature and the arts. Through Walden, Döblin was introduced to the Berlin avant-garde. Döblin contributed to Walden's many successive magazines, the last and most important of which was *Der Sturm.* Döblin was on friendly terms with Else Lasker-Schüler, Peter Hille, and Samuel Lublinski; he met Frank Wedekind and Arno Holz, two writers whom he particularly respected; and he helped to organize readings for students, among them a reading by Thomas Mann which took place after he had left for Freiburg.

In the fall of 1900 Döblin had finished the manuscript of his first novel, "Jagende Rosse" (Galloping Horses), a "small" novel dedicated to the memory of Hölderlin. Döblin kept his literary production a secret and did not publish any of his output at the time; "Jagende Rosse" was first published in his *Ausgewählte Werke in Einzelbänden* (Selected Works in Single Volumes, 1981). In 1902 and 1903 he wrote *Der schwarze Vorhang* (The Black Curtain), subtitled *Roman von den Worten und Zufällen* (Novel about Words and Chance Happenings), which was not published until 1919. It is a novel about a traumatic man-woman relationship, ending with a sexually motivated murder where the fate of the man is largely determined by his mother fixation. Döblin denied the possibility of causal explanations in psychology; thus he stressed *Zufälle* (accidents)–in which he did not really believe, either–and expressed his feeling that there is a chasm between reality and words.

Döblin concluded his medical studies in Freiburg in 1904–1905; after 1905 he worked in several psychiatric clinics and hospitals near Regensburg and in Berlin. He wrote a most original one-act play, *Lydia und Mäxchen,* produced in 1905, in which the characters rebel against the author and their fictional status. While Döblin's real talent clearly was that of an epic narrator and essayist, it is still a pity that he did not write more for the stage.

While in Regensburg, Döblin tried to define his ideas on art in "Gespräche mit Kalypso: Über die Musik" (Dialogues with Calypso: On Music). Dealing with theoretical questions of music and reflecting the beginnings of modern music, these dialogues demonstrate both Döblin's profound musical understanding and the significance of music and music theory in Walden's circle. But they also touch, directly or by implication, on literature. During the same period, Döblin began to write short stories. Some of these early works, including *Der schwarze Vorhang* and parts of

"Gespräche mit Kalypso," began appearing in 1910 in *Der Sturm*.

Döblin hoped for a career in research and had nearly twenty articles published in medical journals. Due to his impending marriage, however, he started practicing in 1911 as a family doctor and specialist in neurology in a working-class neighborhood. Döblin's marriage to Erna Reiss in 1912 fell into a crisis not only because of the shift in career plans but also because it was preceded by one of Döblin's traumatic love affairs. Döblin's wife resembled his mother in many ways: she was equally family-oriented and domineering, and she constantly thwarted his attempts to leave the house and separate himself from her, either temporarily or permanently. In 1912 a collection of Döblin's short stories was published under the title *Die Ermordung einer Butterblume* (The Assassination of a Dandelion, dated 1913). These twelve stories are important documents of expressionistic prose. Döblin never called himself an expressionist, but it has become customary to consider *Der Sturm* a leading expressionist journal. Döblin shied away from "isms" and never liked labels. He quarreled with the Walden group on the occasion of the exhibitions of Italian futurism in Berlin in 1912. While first enthusiastic about the ideas and works of Marinetti and Boccioni, he soon saw their limitations. In an open letter in *Der Sturm* in March 1913 he criticized Marinetti's ideas on "Worttechnik" (word technique), especially his attempt to dissolve the syntax of language. Döblin recommended that Marinetti cultivate his futurism, while he, Döblin, would cultivate his Döblinismus.

However one chooses to label them, Döblin's early stories are provocative manifestations of a modern type of writing. The title story is one of the most significant in the collection. It is set in Freiburg and begins with a Sunday outing of Michael Fischer, a young businessman. In his Sunday mood, Fischer—who seems to be an authoritarian and somewhat sadistic boss in his office—starts chopping off with his walking stick the heads of dandelions along the path. Suddenly, he is seized by remorse; nature comes alive and he has to fight the trees which place themselves in his way. He arrives at his destination without hat and walking stick and with dirty clothes. He is tortured by guilt, behaves strangely at the office and in social gatherings, and puts a dandelion in a flowerpot at home to atone for the murder. But when his landlady smashes the pot, he is suddenly relieved, and jubilantly sets out for a repeat of the same outing.

The story is told from a subjective narrative perspective; the weeds and trees come alive for the reader as they do for the protagonist, and the psychological background is only hinted at. Do the flowers take on symbolic meaning for Fischer, perhaps representing women he has hurt? While the story is a sociological study of the authoritarian but insecure German male, it also demonstrates a case where reality falls apart, and where the connection between motivation and action seems anything but obvious. The narrator does not clarify the situation but provokes the reader to wonder what the meaning of this strange behavior might be. One unmistakable element is the power of nature, which suddenly manifests itself not as a catastrophic event from the outside but in the form of powerful subconscious urges which may change the course of a human life. The ending is ambiguous; Fischer's jubilation borders on the insane. All of Döblin's work attacks the conventional notion of "normal" versus "abnormal" human beings and describes extreme situations and psychological states.

Images and context suggest that Fischer is subconsciously preoccupied with women and sexual relations. This complex is described more openly from the feminine perspective in two other stories in the collection, "Die Tänzerin und ihr Leib" (The Dancer and Her Body) and "Die Segelfahrt" (The Sailing Trip). "Die Tänzerin und ihr Leib" poses the problem of a girl who has been trained as a dancer to coldly dominate her body. But her body rebels; she falls ill, and the doctors do not know how to cope with her psychosomatic disease. She is finally able to express her sexual problems in a symbolic drawing; she feels that she will be able to dominate her body once more—and she kills herself.

It is evident in this story that the author has been trained to observe people with scientific precision: Döblin's description of physical and psychological processes is based on his scientific knowledge and medical expertise. Döblin always maintained that his two careers did not conflict but complemented each other.

"Die Segelfahrt" makes use of archetypal imagery, especially the water image that is central for Döblin, together with images of trees and forests. A Brazilian gentleman, about fifty years old, arrives in the seaside resort of Ostende after a severe illness. He introduces himself to a woman who is in her thirties and invites her on a sailing trip. She comes back from the trip alone, hurt, and bewildered—the narrator does not describe what happened—leaves for Paris and leads a promiscuous life. Returning to Ostende years later, she is informed that the Brazilian has died. She takes a boat and disappears at sea.

It is not only the psychological dimension—the extreme states which reveal the secrets of human existence beyond the conventional behavior of people—that fascinated Döblin in these stories; it was equally the notion of the human being separated from and returning to nature. The prevailing subjective perspective, even with a third-person narrator, blurs the distinction between facts and imagination, so that in "Das Stiftsfräulein und der Tod" (The Woman in the Women's Home and Death), death seems to be both an event and a mythical person. In all of his stories Döblin explores the border region between facts and the imagination, between normal and abnormal psychological conditions, between explicable data and mysteries, between the subconscious and consciousness, in short: the border regions of human existence that reveal our secret desires, fears, and needs. Döblin respected Sigmund Freud and was attracted by psychoanalysis, but he never considered himself a follower of any of the psychoanalytical schools, probably because he considered physical, organic processes crucial for the understanding of psychological problems. He may also have wondered whether psychoanalysis tried to explain too much and projected the doctor's interpretation into the patient's mind. In any event, Döblin's medical and literary works betray both a familiarity with and a distance from the Freudian approach.

While *Der Sturm* gave Döblin the opportunity to publish the best of the writings he had produced to that time, he had already embarked on a new project: a novel. A newspaper report on a rebellion of Chinese gold miners against Russian troops in Siberia had attracted his interest, and in early 1912 the last emperor of China abdicated, bringing the Mongolian dynasty of the Manchus to an end. Döblin decided to write an historical novel about an eighteenth-century protest movement, led by a man called Wang-lun, which was brutally put down by the Imperial troops. His first long novel, *Die drei Sprünge des Wang-lun,* was written in 1912 and 1913 and offered to several publishers without success. Finally, the prominent S. Fischer house accepted it, but World War I delayed the printing until 1915 and the book was not distributed until 1916. The novel won considerable critical acclaim, and Döblin was awarded the Fontane Prize in 1916. The book had only modest commercial success, but Fischer remained Döblin's publisher until 1933, in spite of disagreements and conflicts.

Wang-lun, the son of a fisherman and drifter, is a strong man who does not fit into the village routine. In his adventures, which include begging and committing crimes, he experiences the brutal injustice of the authorities. He is attracted by the concept of Wu-wei, opposition through nonviolence and nonresistance. Violence, he realizes, will beget violence, and political power cannot exist without violence. When his ideas begin to spread among the disadvantaged, he maintains that he does not want to overthrow the government and seize power. But his movement of "the truly weak ones" degenerates when the followers of Ma-noh begin to practice holy prostitution and also transform their movement into a new political system, provoking the military confrontation Wang-lun had tried to prevent. Before the imperial troops can attack the last stronghold of this group, Wang-lun poisons them with hallucinatory mushrooms; as they die, they imagine a trip into the "Western Paradise" of the goddess Kuan-yin. Wang-lun disappears, begins a new life as a fisherman in the south, marries, and lives for his family. The mass murder greatly perturbs the emperor Khien-lung, who considers it a sign of his failure to keep heaven and earth in harmony. Unable to find an answer to his fears from his advisors and astrologers, he invites the Tashi Lama from Tibet. The lama tells the emperor to be tolerant of the "truly weak ones," but tolerance leads to an expansion of the movement and to disorders. The emperor decides to use force once more, but by this time the movement has gained considerable strength. Wang-lun is rediscovered by his followers and persuaded to lead an armed rebellion against the government. After initial success, the movement is crushed again. Wang-lun takes the last step or "leap": he overcomes the cycle of violence in the moments before he dies. The emperor retires from control of the empire.

Die drei Sprünge des Wang-lun is a work of epic narration which branches out into many episodes. Events and locales are described in minute detail, seemingly without regard to their significance for the story. While Wang-lun is the title figure, large parts of the novel take place without him. It is a novel about the "truly weak ones," about violence and nonviolence, about the balance of heaven and earth, about force and nonresistance, about an entire society. Although some characters show development, it is not a developmental novel. The narrator does not explain the meanings of events. While the novel has a historical setting, and the details show the accuracy of Döblin's research, he contends that historical time is relative and that history should not be considered as a chronological line, leading from the past to the future; instead, it is a circular movement, and the essential elements do not change: "In the life of this earth two thousand years are one year." *Die drei Sprünge des Wang-lun* is a demonstration of the vital forces of nature, and of humankind as part of nature.

Döblin continued to write stories, most of them short, humorous, and playful, with fairytale motifs. Twelve of these stories were collected in the volume *Die Lobensteiner reiten nach Böhmen* (The Men from Lobenstein Are Riding to Bohemia), which appeared in 1917. The title story is a political satire attacking bureaucracy. Other stories, such as "Der Kaplan" or "Linie Dresden-Bukarest," deal with sexuality. These stories refuse to take vexing problems seriously, including the central problem of *Die drei Sprünge des Wang-lun,* violence.

By that time, the question of violence had taken on a contemporary significance. Döblin's involvement in the horrors of World War I was only gradual, however. He volunteered as a doctor in a military hospital and was sent to Lorraine and Alsace. He spent considerable time in the small town of Hagenau, north of Strasbourg. Still largely apolitical, Döblin was not a superpatriot but was not a pacifist, either. He contributed his share of patriotic pronouncements, expressing hostility toward England and justifying German acts of war. Sometimes he was more concerned about his own working conditions, especially the lack of a large library nearby, than about the conduct of the war and the enormous suffering. Yet it is evident that he saw a good deal of the human damage of the war, especially among the wounded from the battle of Verdun. These impressions came into the open only after the war, in his political essays and in novels beginning with *Wallenstein,* but it was not until he wrote *November 1918* between 1937 and 1943 that he gave full expression to what he had experienced so much earlier.

Döblin's works of the period seem remote from his immediate experiences. He wrote *Wadzeks Kampf mit der Dampfturbine* (Wadzek's Struggle with the Steam Turbine) in 1914; it was published in 1918. This novel, which has remained one of Döblin's neglected works, describes the struggles of Wadzek, the owner of a Berlin turbine factory, against his competitor, his wife, his mistress, and his daughter. The two main problems with this work may be the tone used by the narrator and the personality of the protagonist. The narrator considers the story—at least most of it—funny, and uses various forms of humor, irony, and sarcasm which the reader may not always find appropriate for the subject matter. Wadzek is a self-centered entrepreneur, ruthless yet sentimental, a case study rather than a person with whom the reader can identify. Wadzek at first appears to be a clever businessman, but his defeat by his competition is due to his own miscalculations. He develops pathological traits, especially when he retreats to his "fortress" in Reinickendorf; in the end, he has left everything behind and is on his way to a new life in America. The narrator seems to have little respect for his hero, but Wadzek is a survivor in spite of his ineptitude and his strange reactions to conflict situations. Wadzek does not undergo an inner transformation, even if he appears to be doing so at times. The book is a study of the lower-middle-class capitalists of Berlin, and while the author clearly recognizes their vitality, his sympathy with the class seems limited. Döblin had serious problems in rendering the milieu of his family in an appropriate style. The ambiguity, if not hidden hostility, contained in this novel can be found again in *Pardon wird nicht gegeben*

(1935; translated as *Men without Mercy,* 1937), a work of Döblin's early exile days.

While working on his novel Döblin also wrote a number of essays containing pronouncements on his concept of the novel and on what he considered modern. These essays are usually polemical and each accentuates a particular point; therefore, it may seem that Döblin has changed his mind when, in fact, he is merely stressing a different point. He argues against psychology and praises psychiatry, meaning that he rejects cause-and-effect explanations of human behavior in favor of objective descriptions. He considers the contemporary novel anecdotal, too close to the drama, too subservient to "action." He pleads for epic breadth and length, for the description of real events and real people—for "facts." This kind of writing is what he calls "naturalism." Naturalism brings art close to life, breaks out of artificial style and psychology, and returns to natural phenomena. Döblin praises Homer, Dante, Cervantes, and Charles de Coster. He wants to place the human individual in the context of natural processes, conditions, and phenomena. He wants to demonstrate that the human being is part of nature, and that human history is a short episode in the long history of life on earth. He does not deny historical change, but takes a much larger perspective.

Döblin's next historical novel, *Wallenstein,* begun in 1916 and published in 1920, is one of his longest works. It is the book where Döblin, as he was to say later, "plantschte in Fakten" (splashed in facts), where the events and characters take on lives of their own and the narrator has a hard time keeping up with them. It is not really a book about Wallenstein but about the Thirty Years' War; Döblin was originally inspired to write the novel not by the story of Wallenstein but by that of the Swedish king Gustav Adolf. In the book it is the emperor Ferdinand II who emerges as the protagonist, if there is a protagonist. The narrator obviously enjoys describing movements of large armies and roaming through the German geography. He is equally at home at court festivals and in business and diplomatic negotiations, and the majority of the story consists of the dialogues that occur in these situations. The battles do not arouse the narrator's imagination; neither do the many cruelties which occur. Clearly, the narrator is interested not in telling the horror story of the worst war before World War I but in presenting a vast panorama of greed, weakness, lust for power and enjoyment, prejudice, and anxiety, and a model case of a large and wealthy country being destroyed for the benefit of a few profiteers and bigots. Economic and political power struggles remain at center stage. In contrast to *Die drei Sprünge des Wang-lun,* the economic springs of history are stressed; but, in contrast to Marxist theory,

Döblin does not picture a class struggle—history is still in the hands of particular individuals and their followers. The common people rebel at times, but without knowing how and why; and they are usually defeated. It seems to be their lot to suffer and to pay.

Within this web of power struggles, intrigues, and wars, two characters emerge who embody opposite principles. Wallenstein is the man of action who is more and more gripped by restlessness, by the urge to achieve the ultimate, by a blind energy. The other extreme is Ferdinand, the emperor. There are clear parallels with Khienlung in *Die drei Sprünge des Wang-lun:* Ferdinand has a vague notion of a secret balance—not only a balance of power in Europe, but a balance in nature. While he is a good Catholic and is committed to reconquering Protestant lands for the church, he seems to gain a larger view of things and withdraws more and more from action. In the end, Wallenstein frenetically runs to his murder, while Ferdinand disappears into nature and becomes part of it. Döblin does not really deal with the differences between Catholicism and Protestantism, but dismisses the conflict of the two faiths as a purely political struggle. Instead of the question of the true *faith,* Döblin poses the question of the true *religion:* is it the Christianity of the Jesuits, whose power causes so much warfare; or is it a more "pagan" belief in God (or gods), in peace, and in diminishing rather than expanding pain and suffering? *Wallenstein* questions the right of human beings to commit robbery and murder in the name of their convictions. The novel is clearly an indictment of the church and of political religion.

World War I ended with the political breakdown of Germany. Döblin returned to Berlin in November 1918 saddened and bewildered, but curious. The dramatic events in Berlin prompted him to write political commentaries under the pseudonyum "Linke Poot" (Left Hand) for the magazine *Neue Rundschau.* These essays show him to be a sharp observer of people and events, highly interested in politics but not committed to a political faction or cause. His sympathies were apparently with the USPD, the Independent Social Democrats who had broken away from the Sozialdemokratische Partei Deutschlands (SPD) in opposition to the war, and who wanted to introduce true socialism by peaceful means. The USPD did not survive the postwar struggles; its members either joined the new Kommunistische Partei Deutschlands (KPD) or returned to the SPD. Döblin recorded the failure of the peaceful revolution and the reestablishment, with the help of Friedrich Ebert's SPD, of the old powers. He was personally affected when his sister was accidentally killed in the fights in Lichtenberg in March 1919.

The events of 1918–1919 made Döblin a political writer, but one who felt responsible to his own conscience and not to the doctrines of any party. In 1920 he became active in the Schutzverband deutscher Schriftsteller (Protective Association of German Writers), a trade union and political lobby; he became president of the organization in 1924. The inflation of the postwar years cut deeply into Döblin's income from both medicine and writing. Out of economic necessity he began to write theater reviews for the *Prager Tageblatt*—more than eighty between 1921 and 1924—which are highly informative in regard to the cultural life of Berlin in the postwar years. Döblin did not mind criticizing famous writers, directors, and performers; judged by his primary criterion, innovation, very little of what was being produced was worthwhile or significant.

Döblin's new preoccupation with the theater prompted him to write two plays. *Lusitania* (1920) is a "requiem" occasioned by the 1915 sinking of the American passenger liner, an event which played an important role in the psychological preparation of the American people for war. Döblin seems not at all interested in the political aspects of the sinking, nor even in the ethical problem of whether it was defensible to torpedo a neutral vessel full of civilians. Although the play touches on the question of whether the *Lusitania* really was carrying ammunition and other war materials, it mainly deals with life and death as a natural cycle. The passengers are lured into the water by sea spirits. The survivors are bewildered and break down psychologically while the dead in the sea are in harmony with nature. Written in 1920, *Lusitania* was performed in 1926, when the period for expressionist experiments was over. The critics rejected the play, and the first performance caused demonstrations by right-wing nationalists. In 1921 Döblin wrote *Die Nonnen von Kemnade* (The Nuns of Kemnade), which was published and performed in 1923. Set in the twelfth century, the play is a late fruit of Döblin's studies of the Middle Ages during the war. The heroine, Judith, is an abbess who loves life; she is persecuted, deposed, and executed by fanatical crusaders in 1149. Döblin contrasts a religion celebrating the love of life—eating, drinking, sex, and companionship—with fanatical, ascetic Christianity. Even Judith's persecutors are not immune from her spell—they ascribe it to Satan—so the play, while a tragedy, shows the triumph of earthly life over religion. It is a fast-paced play, its style reminiscent of expressionism. But it also has an epic quality; it is more a story told in dialogues than a drama.

Döblin's next large novel, *Berge Meere und Giganten* (Mountains Seas and Giants), was written between 1921 and 1923 and published in 1924. It is a *Zukunftsro-*

man (novel describing the future of humankind); partly science fiction, it is mainly a picture of future history, and not a hopeful one. Taking place during several centuries in the late third millenium, *Berge Meere und Giganten* depicts the exploits and conflicts of the Western world. Asia is left out of the picture, except for the episode of a terrible war in Russia. There is little real story line, although a few leaders emerge in this mass civilization, and some of their fates are interwoven into the historical picture. Movement and countermovement are motivated by attitudes toward nature. The belief of the city dwellers that everything should be left to technology leads to artificial food and thus to an ultimate alienation from nature. This alienation causes, in reaction, a return to the land under the leadership of Marduk in Berlin. But Marduk and his followers do not decide the direction of Western civilization; instead, the faith in technology leads to the harnessing of Iceland's volcanoes, and then to the de-icing of Greenland. This full-scale attack on nature's balance causes dinosaurs to reemerge, and the human race produces giants to fight these creatures. At this point dehumanization is complete; the religion of technology has run its course. Remnants of the human race begin a new life cycle, living in the country far from the ruins of the cities, returning to nature. This return is personified by Venaska, a woman with traits of the South Sea races who becomes a love goddess for the newly emerging society.

While the end is not without hope, the picture of a future based on technology is rather grim. While Döblin did not even imagine the unleashing of nuclear energy, he did envision the generation through biotechnology of new creatures not bound to any tradition of humanism. Döblin foresees much struggle and suffering and little happiness or satisfaction in human relations. Power, greed, and brutality remain dominant. Döblin's reworking of the novel, which was published under the new title *Giganten* in 1932, lays more stress on the significance of the individual.

Berge Meere und Giganten is the last of Döblin's epic sagas on the recurring cycles of life and death. The short novel *Die beiden Freundinnen und ihr Giftmord* (The Two Girl-friends and Their Murder by Poison, 1925), written in 1923, is an account of an actual case which had just come to trial. It was published as part of a series of documentary accounts of criminal cases written by literary figures.

The early 1920s was a period of enormous productivity for Döblin. Besides his novels, plays, and theater reviews, he wrote short stories, political essays and commentaries, book reviews, and essays on literary theory and on philosophical and religious questions. Döblin was by this time very much a part of the literary scene in Berlin, a prominent although not particularly popular writer. S. Fischer continued to publish his works, but reluctantly. The major event in his private life was his intimate friendship with Yolla Niclas, a photographer twenty-two years younger than he, whom he met in 1921. Their relationship continued through the rest of their lives, although mostly in letters in later years. Faced with the decision of leaving his family or staying, Döblin—no doubt remembering his father's desertion of his family—chose to stay.

In the early 1920s Döblin came into contact with Jewish circles, especially emigrants from eastern Europe, and participated in debates on Jewish questions. He was invited to visit Palestine, but refused; instead, he visited Poland in the latter part of 1924. He wrote articles on this trip, mainly for the *Vossische Zeitung,* which were published in 1926 as *Reise in Polen* (Travels in Poland). The book was not the objective account of traditional Jewish life which had been expected from Döblin; it was a subjective description of what he saw when he visited places where Jewish traditions were still intact. Döblin did not restrict his trip to this aspect of Poland; one of his deepest impressions was the altar by Veit Stoß in St. Mary's Church in Cracow. But the encounter with the Jews in Poland changed Döblin's outlook: he became more interested in the life and perspective of the individual than in the large panorama of nature.

This shift becomes evident in Döblin's free-verse "epic poem" *Manas,* written in 1926 and published in 1927. The material for *Manas* is taken from Indian mythology and legends. Manas, son of the king of Udaipur, returns victorious from war but cannot overcome the stupor that so much death and suffering caused for him. He wants to die and makes his Yoga teacher Puto lead him to the field of the dead, where he joins them. Sawitri, Manas's wife, does not accept his death; she calls him back to life, and Shiva grants his revival. But the process of revival is painful: Manas has lost his memory; he devastates the earth with the help of demons and almost becomes a demon himself. In the end, his reemerging memory of Sawitri makes him more human. It takes, however, a last struggle with Shiva to make Manas realize his limits. He changes from a self-confident giant to a beneficial leader obedient to the powers above him. In the course of this struggle, Shiva is also transformed from an unconcerned deity to one who realizes his interdependence with the creatures of this world.

Except for an enthusiastic review by Robert Musil, *Manas* did not find a sympathetic response; it was generally considered one of Döblin's many eccentricities and was little read. Its flowery language and foreign setting obscured the fact that Döblin was dealing with crucial human problems: love, sacrifice, life, death, suffering, happiness, and the transformation of an individual. This last question, how an individual can be transformed and find a new orientation, was to remain one of Döblin's main concerns. It came to the fore in his next and best-known work, *Berlin Alexanderplatz.*

Döblin's publisher, Samuel Fischer, was almost ready to end their contract, but when he heard Döblin read passages from *Berlin Alexanderplatz,* he reconsidered. The novel, published in 1929, has remained Döblin's only popular success. This success is partly due to the novel's subject matter: it is a story of the Berlin "underworld," a topic then popular in movies and books. Franz Biberkopf, a large and powerful man, is released from prison after serving a sentence for manslaughter. He is confused by his new freedom. At first, he is determined to remain on the "right path," but then he comes into contact with a gang of criminals. The self-confident Biberkopf does not know his limits; he is no match for these ruthless criminals. He loses his right arm in one of his exploits, but it takes a heavier blow to make him realize the error of his ways: his girlfriend is murdered by the ringleader. Her death brings Biberkopf to his knees; after some time in a psychiatric hospital he begins another life as a changed man. Most of all, he realizes that he is not alone; he needs others, and they need him. His strength is "broken," but he has found a new basis for life.

In addition to the theme of crime and the underworld milieu, the narrative technique made the book a success. The story is interlaced with newspaper accounts of life in the big city, such as the slaughterhouses, as well as biblical and mythological allusions and stories. Within this montage structure, much of the story is told in the form of interior monologue, depicting Biberkopf's subconscious and half-conscious experiences. Döblin had read the German translation of James Joyce's *Ulysses* (1922) while he was working on his book, but he steadfastly denied having been influenced by Joyce. The similarities of narrative technique, however, are unmistakable. John Dos Passos's *Manhattan Transfer* (1925) is also a possible influence. Another attraction of *Berlin Alexanderplatz* is its language: it is saturated with the living speech of Berlin, but uses the contrast of such different forms of discourse as newspaper reports, documentary style, and biblical language. This polyphonic style adds much to its color.

Berlin Alexanderplatz was written between 1927 and 1929 and published in the fall of 1929. Fischer persuaded Döblin to add the subtitle *Die Geschichte vom Franz Biberkopf* (The Story of Franz Biberkopf). In 1930 Döblin fashioned a radio play from the novel, and a film version was released the following year. Biberkopf was played both on the radio and in the film by Heinrich George.

Döblin was at the height of his reputation. In 1928 he had been elected a member of the section for literature in the Prussian Academy of the Arts. While this office added to a growing hostility of communist writers toward Döblin, it certainly enhanced his status. Döblin had been a good friend of Bertolt Brecht for some years, and Brecht readily acknowledged his debt to Döblin in developing the concept of the Epic Theater. Brecht and Döblin were part of an independent leftist discussion group known as Group 1925. The ideas of Brecht and of Erwin Piscator are manifest in Döblin's epic play, *Die Ehe* (Marriage, 1931), first performed in Munich. The play deals with problems in three different situations: a working-class marriage where the woman dies trying to abort her child; another proletarian family destroyed by the lack of housing; and, in contrast, a marriage among the rich, for money and convenience, which humiliates the woman. The play is sharply critical, often sarcastic, and certainly provocative; it was quickly labeled "communist" and banned by the police. Its literary quality is problematic; any comparison with Brecht would be unfair.

In the Prussian Academy, Döblin entered into an endless fight with the right wing. The temporary victory of the "Republican" wing under the leadership of Heinrich Mann in 1931 was followed by the expulsion or resignation of all non-Nazi members early in 1933. During the short period of activity of Mann and Döblin, the section started initiatives for the reform of textbooks in the schools, attempted to bring universities and writers together, and published manifestos advocating cultural freedom. Döblin contributed several speeches and essays to the academy's program, among them his central essay, "Der Bau des epischen Werks" (The Structure of the Epic Work, 1928). In this piece Döblin summarizes his opposition to the traditional psychological novel, but he also signals his rejection of a purely documentary literature, which was then a leading trend under the label Neue Sachlichkeit (New Objectivity). For Döblin, literature–the work of epic narration in particular–should not just come close to reality but should "pierce through it" to arrive at fundamental truths about human existence. The most important ingredient of the epic work is the narrative language of the author, which has to be an example of the living language of the time.

In 1930 Döblin received a letter from a student, Gustav René Hocke–later a noted essayist–who wanted his advice on how to take a political position and political action during a time of crisis and turmoil. Döblin answered with a series of open letters, first published in the magazine *Das Tagebuch* and later collected under the title *Wissen und Verändern!* (To Know and to

Change!, 1931). Döblin tries to define an independent position for intellectuals toward the working class, and also tries to sketch his own type of socialism in contrast to the Marxist version. Döblin considered capitalism destructive and does not take much space to argue against it; instead, he tries to trace the historical reasons for the lack of freedom in Germany and for the dogmatic nature of the two socialist parties. Surprisingly, he practically ignores the menace from the right—the Nazis, who had just won their great victory in the Reichstag elections of 1930. For Döblin, they were regressive and a passing fad among the lower middle class. Döblin's opposition to communism and his attempt to formulate an alternative to centralized party organizations generated a hot debate that was cut off by the Nazi takeover.

Döblin's philosophical work *Unser Dasein* (Our Existence), which appeared in spring 1933, when Döblin had already left the country, was little read either in Germany or by the exiles. It is a presentation of Döblin's philosophy of nature, with mankind treated as part of nature. As happens in many of Döblin's works, extraneous material, in this case the Jewish question and anti-Semitism, claims more space in the book than it should have. Basically, Döblin's philosophy is still that of life cycles, of Spinozistic pantheism, but in *Unser Dasein* he pays more attention to the individual human being and his response to natural processes and phenomena. Döblin later characterized this period as transitional to his definitive ideas on religion and nature. The writing of his works meant for Döblin a process of self-clarification. Frequently, he starts with a well-defined position, only to arrive at new and unexpected conclusions of a tentative nature.

The tentative character is particularly evident in Döblin's first works in exile. Forced to leave Germany at the end of February 1933, Döblin first had a feeling of relief, even elation. He had felt somewhat uncomfortable before, for private as well as political reasons. At the urging of his wife, Döblin had moved from the working-class district to a middle-class area of Berlin after the success of *Berlin Alexanderplatz,* but he had deeply regretted the separation from his familiar environment and his patients. In his exile, first in Zurich, then in Paris, he felt free. The euphoria is clearly discernible in *Babylonische Wandrung oder Hochmut kommt vor dem Fall* (The Babylonian Migration or Arrogance Precedes the Fall), published in 1934 by Querido, the exile publisher in Amsterdam. The Babylonian god Marduk, whom Döblin calls Konrad, reappears on earth in the present age and finds everything changed; he misses the adoration and sacrifices of human beings. But he adapts and assimilates himself in his wanderings from Baghdad to Istanbul, Zurich, and Paris. As a matter of fact,

the fall announced in the title does not really take place. In contrast with Biberkopf, Konrad never changes and never really understands. He always muddles through and is always rescued from difficult situations. The tone of the book is distinctly Voltairean, reminiscent of *Candide.* Döblin later said that he was dissatisfied with this story of a survivor whose arrogance does not really change. It is true that in Paris, Konrad seems at times to understand the perspective from below, the perspective of the suffering human creature. But he soon settles into a comfortable middle-class life, and the human social and existential problems are not really solved. The novel is commonly considered formless and difficult, but the contrary seems to be the case: it has a definite, though additive, structure, with a clear thesis statement and an easy narrative style, especially compared with Döblin's earlier works. But its conclusion is ambiguous and leaves the reader puzzled. It is a work without real "results."

Like many other exiles, Döblin felt an urgency to participate in Jewish affairs. While he never embraced Zionism, he grew more sympathetic to the "Free Land" movement, the non-Zionist attempt to secure a homeland for the Jews. His 1933 work *Jüdische Erneuerung* (Jewish Renewal) was followed in 1935 by *Flucht und Sammlung des Judenvolkes* (Flight and Collection of the Jewish People). Döblin's readers were surprised to find that his response to the new persecution of Jews seemed to be so nationalistic, with apparent similarities with fascist ideas. Döblin's main point, the need for an Erneuerung (renewal) among the Jews, was never accepted by the Jewish groups. Döblin began to lose interest in the topic and stopped all of his activities in regard to Jewish issues by the end of 1937.

After *Babylonische Wandrung,* Döblin wrote what he later called "einen kleinen Berliner Roman" (a small novel on Berlin), which was published in 1935: *Pardon wird nicht gegeben* (translated as *Men without Mercy,* 1937). Döblin's own somewhat disparaging judgment of this work has colored its evaluation by scholars; the book is significant and is not as exceptional in style and structure as it is generally thought to be. *Pardon wird nicht gegeben* anticipates the style of many parts of Döblin's later works, including *November 1918* and *Hamlet.* The work is Döblin's first attempt to attack his central political concern: the loss of the fight for freedom in Germany and the "betrayal" of the middle classes. Karl, the protagonist, faces the alternatives of becoming part of a revolutionary working-class movement or advancing his personal career and becoming rich. Under the influence of his ambitious mother he chooses the second route. He becomes the owner of a furniture factory, but the pervasive economic collapse takes its toll on him: his family life comes to a crisis; he becomes involved with right-wing groups and falls victim to political intrigues. In a civil war situation, Karl is killed when he tries to cross the lines from the right-wing forces to the left-wing groups.

It is true that the novel deals with individuals rather than with groups, but, contrary to the claims of most scholars, it is less psychological than sociological and political. No place names or dates are given; the novel is intended as an assessment of the reasons for the rise of fascism in general. The autobiographical aspects of the novel are evident only in its first part. Its narrative technique makes the book easy reading, in contrast to Döblin's longer works. Döblin did not repeat the experiment; he quickly returned to his larger epic forms. *Pardon wird nicht gegeben* is significant as his first literary response to Nazism and as a book sympathetic to the independent leftist movements as well as to active, even militant, resistance to the Nazis.

By this time Döblin was exclusively a writer. He missed his medical practice and the income it had provided, but he took full advantage of his free time. In 1935 he began writing his next major work, *Das Land ohne Tod* (The Land without Death), which appeared in two volumes in 1937 and 1938; a postwar edition was published in three volumes. There are three parts to this epic on South America: *Die Fahrt ins Land ohne Tod* (The Journey to the Land without Death) describes the conquest of the continent by the Spaniards and Portuguese; *Der blaue Tiger* (The Blue Tiger) deals with the attempted fusion of European and Indian cultures in the Jesuit state in Paraguay; and *Der neue Urwald* (The New Jungle) concerns the return of twentieth-century Europeans to South America. On the level of action, the novel describes the European colonization of Latin America and the destruction of the native cultures, as well as the heroic attempt by the Jesuits to counteract this spirit of greed, destruction, and murder with true Christian love. On this level, the third part seems irrelevant, and was left out when the novel was reprinted in Döblin's *Ausgewählte Werke* (1960–1985) under the title *Amazonas*. On a sociological level, however, the book attempts an evaluation and critique of modern European civilization; on this level, the third part is crucial. Döblin now, even more than before, regards the spirit of colonization, of technological destruction of nature, as a serious aberration, a self-destructive impulse of humanity. He wants to eliminate the Promethean attitude that tries to remake creation in its own image.

On a more philosophical level, *Das Land ohne Tod* is based on the mythical images of water (the Amazon River system), forest, and mountains, of which human beings are a part and from which they cannot emancipate themselves. Las Casas, the protector of the Indians in the sixteenth century, returns to nature by disappear-

ing in the jungle. *Der blaue Tiger,* however, raises questions about the possibility of this return and ultimately shows the incompatibility of the Europeans and the Indians. *Der neue Urwald* demonstrates the barbarism arising from the civilization of technology, which does not result in a new humanitarianism, as Döblin had earlier hoped, but leads modern man back into the jungle, where he is destined to perish miserably. The novel is a fundamental criticism of the direction of European civilization and regards fascism as only part of a general trend. Part of the then widespread Kulturkritik, it analyzes the present age in historical terms and tries to see Western civilization from the outside. It offers no answers to the questions it raises.

Both *Pardon wird nicht gegeben* and the last part of *Das Land ohne Tod* indirectly approached the question of the origin of National Socialism. Döblin next decided to treat the problem in a direct manner. In 1937 he began writing an Erzählwerk (narrative work) on the failure of the German revolution of 1918–1919. *November 1918* is even less an historical novel than Döblin's previous works, since it uses documents much more extensively and thus becomes a cross between a novel and a history book. Döblin uses a day-by-day narration, from 10 November 1918 to 15 January 1919, the day of the assassinations of Rosa Luxemburg and Karl Liebknecht. This span of hardly more than two months had been, Döblin thought, a unique chance to change the direction of German history, a chance for a true revolution. The decisive moment was missed both because of the ineptitude of the revolutionary leaders and because of the reactionary attitude of the Ebert government.

Döblin had previously reflected on this momentous period in short essays written at the time and in *Wissen und Verändern!* He begins his new epic work with an account, based on his personal recollections, of events in Alsace and Berlin. Historical figures are mixed with fictional characters. Some of these characters begin to assume more importance: Becker and Maus, two wounded former officers in a military hospital; Hilde, a nurse; and a historical figure Liebknecht. In volume 2 Döblin's narrative moves to the centers of power, describing the socialist leaders Ebert, Scheidemann, Barth, Bernstein, and Wels. He enters into the minds of defeated generals, including Hindenburg, Groener, and Schleicher. These passages are interspersed with episodes taken from newspapers and with representative fictional characters, including a working-class family, writers and other intellectuals, criminals, right-wing former soldiers and officers, reactionary government officials, and revolutionary sailors.

Döblin planned a work of three volumes. In 1939 a first volume was published under the title *Bürger und Soldaten 1918* (Citizens and Soldiers 1918). In May

1940, when the German army invaded France, another volume was ready. Döblin had become a French citizen because his sons Wolfgang and Klaus (Claude) were serving in the French army. His citizenship saved him from the French internment camps, but he had to flee Paris in June. He describes his flight in *Schicksalsreise* (Fateful Journey, 1949). In despair while stranded on the road, Döblin had a religious vision in the cathedral of Mende. He later escaped and received a visa for the United States.

Arriving there in late 1940, Döblin was given a one-year contract as a script writer for M-G-M. As he had expected, he had no success in the movie industry, and his contract was not renewed. He was also singularly unsuccessful on the book market: he could not place a single work with an American publisher, despite many attempts. Thus he had to rely on charity, mainly from his fellow exiles. But in spite of these disappointments, numerous illnesses, and his isolation, he continued to produce. He revised *Bürger und Soldaten 1918* as *Verratenes Volk* (Betrayed People, 1948). Then he began work on the concluding volume, which he completed in 1943. Volumes two and three were published under the titles *Heimkehr der Fronttruppen* (Return of the Troops from the Front, 1949; partly translated, with selections from volume 1, as *A People Betrayed,* 1983) and *Karl und Rosa* (1950; translated as *Karl and Rosa,* 1983). In the meantime, Döblin and his family had converted to Catholicism, and his ideas on revolution and history had changed. This new position is evident in *Karl und Rosa.* While the first three volumes of *November 1918* demonstrate the failure of the revolution, this last volume chooses a metaphysical perspective. The dilemma of the revolution is that its aim is to end violence and to begin an age of peace, but it cannot succeed without violence. Thus it fails in Germany, whereas Lenin in the Soviet Union succeeds in establishing a new regime of violence.

Within this historical context, one fictional character gradually assumes a central role: Friedrich Becker, the returning wounded officer. Haunted by guilt feelings over the sufferings of the war, he returns to his Christian faith and tries to live as a Christian in a world of violent ideologies. He is dismissed from his position as a gymnasium teacher of classical studies, and ends up as a penniless vagabond among criminals. Although he errs grievously and should not be taken as an exemplary figure, his story is a manifestation of the struggle of good and evil forces and points to the possibility of a Christian life. Döblin opposes his faith and the idea of Christian responsibility to all political and social solutions. Although still sympathetic to the plight of the poor and the suffering, he rejects organized socialism.

November 1918 is a complex work, grandiose in parts. It is less unified than most of Döblin's works; still, it is a heroic effort to come to grips with the German problem. It is only since the paperback edition of 1978, however, that a discussion of this monumental work has begun.

The end of the war seemed to open up new possibilities. In the fall of 1945 Döblin, then sixty-seven years old, returned to Germany to work for the cultural administration of the French military government in Baden-Baden. He hoped to be able to contribute to a renewal of cultural life in Germany, but his efforts met with disappointment. The main reason for this disappointment was probably Döblin's ideological position. While he professed his Catholicism openly, and while it was fashionable at that time to be a Christian, Döblin's version of the faith was not to the liking of the church and was amalgamated with his socialist convictions, which contradicted the dominant conservative trends. Döblin was staunchly opposed to the communist regimes, but he never accepted the ideology of the Cold War; instead, he pleaded for peace and understanding. Some minor incidents accentuated his isolation in postwar German literary life, especially his campaign against Thomas Mann in the literary magazine *Das Goldene Tor,* which Döblin edited from 1946 to 1951. Döblin was, however, an effective radio commentator. In 1948 he ended his career with the French military government because of age. He was one of the founders of the Akademie der Wissenschaften und der Literatur (Academy of Sciences and Literature) in Mainz in 1949, and became vice president of its section for literature. In 1953 he left Germany for a new exile in Paris.

Döblin's last years were marked by illness. From 1954 until his death in 1957 he needed care in hospitals or rest homes in southwest Germany. While he remained isolated, recognition and assistance from various institutions and individuals in both parts of Germany were not lacking. Döblin's supporters included Theodor Heuß, president of the Federal Republic, and the poet Johannes R. Becher, minister for cultural affairs in the German Democratic Republic.

Döblin's last works are characterized by his discussion of the Christian way of life. Late in 1941, immediately after his conversion, he had begun a Religionsgespräch (religious dialogue) titled *Der unsterbliche Mensch* (Immortal Man), which was published in Germany in 1946. *Der unsterbliche Mensch* provoked intense discussion in both East and West Germany; most of the criticism was negative. Döblin's critics never acknowledged that he had not become a reactionary. His was not a romantic conversion; it was the result of a long process which began around 1925. It may be asked how Catholic Döblin's faith was, as it resulted as much from the influence of Kierkegaard as from that of St. Augustine; but there is no doubt that Döblin was a sincere Christian who practiced what he professed. The "scandalous" point was Döblin's uncompromising sincerity.

Der unsterbliche Mensch offers a dialogue between a younger and an older man, who are commonly taken to be the younger and older Döblin himself. The older Döblin is asked by his previous self for the justification of his conversion. Is it a betrayal? Is it obscurantist blind faith? The older Döblin tries to convey his central message: the Enlightenment, with all its consequences, such as materialism, Marxism, and Nazism, was deficient and self-contradictory. Döblin maintains that modern Western civilization caused an alienation from the balance of nature. In the endless cycle of violence and oppression, peace and freedom can only come from spiritual forces, and ultimately from the love of God. While Döblin enthrones a metaphysical deity beyond the world and emphasizes the crucial role of Jesus as mediator, his view has definite pantheistic, Spinozistic overtones.

The question of material and spiritual forces and their influence on this world is the theme of some narratives written between 1943 and 1945. *Der Oberst und der Dichter* (The Colonel and the Writer, 1946), is a curious hybrid, partly prose, partly verse, arguing for a religious renewal of life; the detective story "Reiseverkehr mit dem Jenseits" (Communication with the Beyond, 1948) provokes the reader to think about other lives after this life, and about the absurdity of superstition. These stories have a light, humorous tone; they are full of irony and try to entertain the reader. Apparently Döblin considered such light fare especially suitable for German readers, as he had these works published before his major exile books, such as *Das Land ohne Tod* and *November 1918*. Döblin's last major literary work is *Hamlet oder Die lange Nacht nimmt ein Ende*. This book, started in Los Angeles in 1945 and completed in Baden-Baden in 1946, was first published in 1956 by Rütten and Loening in East Berlin. There is no doubt that publishers would have accepted it in the postwar years, and it might have been more successful than Döblin's other works; but he held it back until his previous production had been published. In 1950, under economic stress, publishers shied away from this voluminous novel; Döblin suspected a boycott by the West German publishers. *Hamlet* was well received when it finally appeared, and had its West German edition in 1957.

Döblin considered *Hamlet* a new type of novel in his oeuvre and, indeed, it does have new features. The characters tell stories to relieve themselves of tensions and to avoid uncomfortable confrontations—which take place anyway. It is a "family novel": Edward Allison, the son, comes back from World War II to England with an amputated leg and a disturbed mind, not unlike Becker in *November 1918*. Edward wants to know the truth about family relations, about guilt and atonement, about human existence. He never stops asking questions and thus provokes many confrontations. The book consists of dialogues and shorter or longer stories of different kinds. In structure, it is a variation on the model of Boccaccio, but the nature and the function of the stories are fundamentally different: they seem to be an escape from the ugly present, but really serve to lead to the truth. There is a love-hate relationship between Edward's parents, Gordon and Alice; there are also love and hate between father and son, rivalry between mother and daughter, and closeness between mother and son and between father and daughter. Other characters include Alice's brother James and Dr. King, Edward's physician. The decorum of the English country estate cannot prevent the drama. Edward sees himself as Hamlet, facing the fateful mystery and searching for the truth. The truth is elusive; the reader is presented with Gordon's and Alice's sides of the story of their marriage, with no indication of which is the true version. The family breaks up; Gordon and Alice disappear. Gordon, an author, stops writing and wanders restlessly around the country; Alice tries to start a new life. After several adventures, she falls prey to a brutal man and becomes an actress in a cheap show. In a suburb of Paris, she is discovered by Gordon, who dies after a fight with the brutal manager; Alice dies soon afterward, and Edward buries them. Originally, Döblin intended for Edward to enter a monastery, but the published version ends with the vague but hopeful phrase "A new life began." The survivors, Edward, his uncle James, and Dr. King, feel guilt and remorse: they should not have caused or allowed the conflict to develop to the point where the family would break apart and lives would be shattered. The book strongly affirms the value of the family, even if relationships within the family are less than perfect. The end is ambiguous but positive: love is stronger than hate, although it may not be able to determine life on earth.

While it presents a grim picture of human relations, the book offers a religious consolation. The characters are not particularly religious; there is little mention of God, and even less of Jesus Christ. But the truth of divine love dawns on the characters in spite of themselves. The stories told by the characters include new versions of myths and legends, invented tales, and autobiographical accounts; there is evidently no more sincerity or truth in the openly autobiographical stories than in the others. Döblin offers once more a demonstration of the truth of myths and legends as expressions of fundamental human situations.

While the relentless search for truth causes much suffering, the unsatisfactory family situation is not a real alternative either: the members hold each other hostage, as it were, and muddle through by hiding the truth from themselves and others. The situation is truly tragic: the truth causes death, but it also brings love and atonement. There is hope; if not in this life, then certainly beyond the grave.

Döblin did not attempt to write another novel on the scale of *Hamlet*. His last narrative works were "Die Pilgerin Aetheria" (The Pilgrim Aetheria), which Döblin considered the most Christian of his stories, and "Der Kampf mit dem Engel" (The Struggle with the Angel). "Die Pilgerin Aetheria" is the story of an Italian peasant woman whose husband is killed during a robbery. In her quest for revenge she is driven to pilgrimages to Rome and Jerusalem and to a struggle with divine forces. Not only is she seeking God, but it seems that God is seeking her. Thus, there is a mutual attraction (and repulsion) of man and God. Döblin had found the name Aetheria and was fascinated by it; his story has nothing to do with the historical figure of that name. Written between 1947 and 1949, "Die Pilgerin Aetheria" did not appear in print until 1978; "Der Kampf mit dem Engel" was not published until 1980. Both works, which were published in Döblin's *Ausgewählte Werke in Einzelbänden* (Selected Works in Single Volumes, 1960–1985), are documents of his continual and unsuccessful search for certainty in his faith. The remark of Lessing, that man is made for the search for truth, not for its possession, comes to mind; and "Der Kampf mit dem Engel" contains other reminders of Lessing. A commentary on the Bible, it is mostly devoted to the Old Testament and implies a new interpretation of the Jewish heritage. In a second part, the crucial role of Jesus Christ is described, relying most heavily on the gospel of St. John. There is a third part, as there is in Lessing's *Die Erziehung des Menschengeschlechts* (1780, translated as *Education of Mankind*), but the discussion of the religious situation "two thousand years later" is in Döblin's work an affirmation of the message of peace by Jesus Christ, against the spirit of war reemerging in Germany in the early 1950s. Döblin tried to arrive at simple truths. He did not want to invent new aspects of Christianity; he just wanted to bear witness to the fundamental message of peace and the love of God for the world embodied in Jesus Christ. He strongly criticized his own previous "relativistic" and "naturalistic" position as too weak to offer resistance to the evils of the age, including National Socialism. Still, the vexing question remained: how could a loving God create a world that included so much suffering and destruction? This is, of course, the old question of theodicy. Döblin's answer was traditional, and it was an answer which would demand a

continual commitment: man is free to choose the path of love or to avoid it. Life is an opportunity to make the right choice, even if the search for that choice consumes most of one's energy and life span. Even in these last works, Döblin was aware of the tentative nature of his conclusions. He remained open and tolerant in his search for the right path.

In his last years, Döblin continued meditating on life and death and on his own life. When his eyesight failed and arthritis made it impossible for him to write, he dictated some of his thoughts. He had left fiction behind. His "Journal 1952/53," included in his *Ausgewählte Werke,* recounts much of his past life and tries to describe the existence of a sick and lonely old man. It summarizes his postwar efforts in Germany and in this respect is a continuation of *Schicksalsreise*. It ends with ideas on the meaning of history and on death.

Döblin's career was remarkable. Active in public life almost until the end, he was tireless in his efforts to propagate his message and to spread enlightenment. He was disappointed many times. The German revolution of 1918–1919 was a failure; the cultural life of the Weimar Republic did not bring a reorientation of German society; the position of *Wissen und Verändern!* did not take hold in the crisis before 1933; a renewal of the Jewish people after 1933 did not take place; Döblin's efforts to help Germany achieve an inner liberation from Nazism after 1945 did not succeed. Also, he was anything but a successful writer. The popularity of *Berlin Alexanderplatz,* he said, was due to a misunderstanding; for him, it was not a novel about the underworld of Berlin.

Döblin was deeply concerned with the fate of humankind, and he considered it in wide perspectives: natural, historical, and metaphysical. But within the large panorama, he continued to think about the fate of the individual, about his endless suffering and futile search for happiness. Döblin was restless, always ready for new ideas, but always haunted by the same questions. His works are documents of an endless process of questioning and of a piercing search for reality and truth. The "imagination" of his narrative works sprang from observation and tireless questioning, most of all from a hunger for reality. In his exile and his old age, he found that answers from science and history were insufficient to relieve the agony of his search and pain. He turned to a religion of love and salvation beyond physical life, and he tried to reach a position beyond the relativistic cycle of violence and war, a position of real peace. He has had few followers, but there is a growing number of admirers of his literary work, especially his uncanny art of making faraway worlds real and close and making reality transparent in all its complexity.

Language is essential for Döblin's art and message, and it is fitting that his works have had little success in languages other than German. In the English-speaking world even *Berlin Alexanderplatz* found a cool reception. The translation of *Pardon wird nicht gegeben* is a curious exception, and the success of the translation of *November 1918* is still undecided. There are many seeds and suggestions for contemporary writers in Döblin's works, and his message, whether that of the young, the older, or the old Döblin, is certainly worth hearing and debating.

Bibliography:

Louis Huguet, *Bibliographie Alfred Döblin* (Berlin & Weimar: Aufbau, 1972).

References:

Armin Arnold, *Die Literatur des Expressionismus,* second edition (Stuttgart: Kohlhammer, 1971);

Manfred Auer, *Das Exil vor der Vertreibung: Motivkontinuität und Quellenproblematik in den späten Werken Alfred Döblins* (Bonn: Bouvier, 1977);

Hans-Peter Bayerdörfer, "Der Wissende und die Gewalt: Alfred Döblins Theorie des epischen Werkes und der Schluß von *Berlin Alexanderplatz,*" *Deutsche Vierteljahrschrift für Literaturwissenschaft und Geistesgeschichte,* 44, no. 2 (1970): 318–353;

Heinz Graber, *Alfred Döblins Epos "Manas"* (Bern: Francke, 1967);

Graber, "Politisches Postulat und autobiographischer Bericht: Zu einigen Werken Alfred Döblins im Exil," in *Die deutsche Exilliteratur 1933–1945,* edited by Manfred Durzak (Stuttgart: Reclam, 1973), pp. 418–429;

Günter Grass, *Über meinen Lehrer Döblin* (Berlin: LCB Editionen, 1968);

Klaus Kanzog, "Alfred Döblin und die Anfänge des expressionistischen Prosastils," *Jahrbuch der deutschen Schillergesellschaft,* 17 (1973): 63–83;

Otto Keller, *Alfred Döblins Montageroman als Epos der Moderne* (Munich: Fink, 1980);

Helmuth Kiesel, *Literarische Trauerarbeit: Das Exilund Spätwerk Alfred Döblins* (Tübingen: Niemeyer, 1986);

Volker Klotz, "Agon Stadt: Alfred Döblins *Berlin Alexanderplatz,*" in his *Die erzählte Stadt. Ein Sujet als Herausforderung des Romans von Lesage bis Döblin* (Munich: Hanser, 1969), pp. 372–418;

Erwin Kobel, *Alfred Döblin: Erzählkunst im Umbruch* (Berlin: de Gruyter, 1985);

Wolfgang Kort, *Alfred Döblin* (New York: Twayne, 1974);

Leo Kreutzer, *Alfred Döblin: Sein Werk bis 1933* (Stuttgart: Kohlhammer, 1970);

Roland Links, *Alfred Döblin: Leben und Werk* (Berlin: Volk und Wissen, 1963);

Paul E. H. Lüth, ed., *Alfred Döblin zum 70. Geburtstag* (Wiesbaden: Limes, 1948);

Fritz Martini, "Alfred Döblin," in *Deutsche Dichter der Moderne,* edited by Benno von Wiese (Berlin: Schmidt, 1965), pp. 321–360;

Dieter Mayer, *Alfred Döblins Wallenstein: Zur Geschichtsauffassung und zur Struktur* (Munich: Fink, 1972);

Robert Minder, "Alfred Döblin zwischen Osten und Westen," in his *Dichter in der Gesellschaft,* (Frankfurt am Main: Insel, 1966), pp. 155–190;

Minder, "*Die Segelfahrt* von Alfred Döblin: Struktur und Erlebnis," in his *Wozu Literatur?* (Frankfurt am Main: Suhrkamp, 1971), pp. 77–118;

Klaus Müller-Salget, *Alfred Döblin: Werk und Entwicklung* (Bonn: Bouvier, 1972);

Patrick O'Neill, *Alfred Döblin's Babylonische Wandrung: A Study* (Bern: Lang, 1974);

Heinz D. Osterle, "Alfred Döblins Revolutionstrilogie *November 1918,*" *Monatshefte,* 62, no. 1 (1970): 1–23;

Matthias Prangel, *Alfred Döblin* (Stuttgart: Metzler, 1973);

Prangel, ed., *Materialen zu Alfred Döblins Berlin Alexanderplatz* (Frankfurt am Main: Suhrkamp, 1975);

Ernst Ribbat, *Die Wahrheit des Lebens im frühen Werk Alfred Döblins* (Münster: Aschendorff, 1970);

Klaus Schröter, *Alfred Döblin* (Reinbek: Rowohlt, 1978);

Ingrid Schuster and Ingrid Bode, eds., *Alfred Döblin in Spiegel der zeitgenössischen Kritik* (Bern: Francke, 1973);

Dorothee Sölle, "Einübung ins Christentum bei Alfred Döblin," in her *Realisation: Studien zum Verhältnis von Theologie und Dichtung nach der Aufklärung* (Neuwied: Luchterhand, 1973);

Werner Stauffacher, ed., *Internationale Alfred Döblin-Kolloquien 1980–1983* (Bern: Lang, 1986);

Monique Weyembergh-Boussart, *Alfred Döblin: Seine Religiosität in Persönlichkeit und Werk* (Bonn: Bouvier, 1970);

Adalbert Wichert, *Alfred Döblins historisches Denken* (Stuttgart: Metzler, 1978);

Theodore Ziolkowski, *Dimensions of the Modern Novel: German Texts and European Contexts* (Princeton: Princeton University Press, 1969), pp. 99–137;

Victor Zmegac, "Alfred Döblins Poetik des Romans," in *Deutsche Romantheorien,* edited by Reinhold Grimm (Frankfurt am Main & Bern: Athenäum, 1968), pp. 297–320.

Papers:

Alfred Döblin's papers are held by the Schiller-National-Museum, Marbach am Neckar.

Annette von Droste-Hülshoff

(10 January 1797 – 24 May 1848)

Monika Shafi
University of Delaware

This entry originally appeared in DLB 133: Nineteenth-Century German Writers to 1840.

BOOKS: *Gedichte,* anonymous (Münster: Aschendorff, 1838);

Gedichte (Stuttgart & Tübingen: Cotta, 1844);

Das geistliche Jahr: Nebst einem Anhang religiöser Gedichte, edited by Christoph Bernhard Schlüter and Wilhelm Junkmann (Stuttgart & Tübingen: Cotta, 1851);

Letzte Gaben: Nachgelassene Blätter, edited by Levin Schücking (Hannover: Rümpler, 1860);

Gesammelte Schriften, 3 volumes, edited by Schücking (Stuttgart: Cotta, 1878–1879);

Gesammelte Werke, 4 volumes, edited by Elisabeth Freiin von Droste-Hülshoff and Wilhelm Kreiten (Münster & Paderborn: Schöningh, 1884–1887);

Der Familienschild, by Droste-Hülshoff and Schücking (N.p., 1898; reprinted, Münster: Aschendorff, 1960);

Sämtliche Werke, 6 volumes, edited by Eduard Arens (Leipzig: Hesse, 1904);

Sämtliche Werke, 6 volumes, edited by Julius Schwering (Berlin, Leipzig, Vienna & Stuttgart: Bong, 1912);

Sämtliche Werke, 4 volumes, edited by Karl Schulte Kemminghausen (Munich: Müller, 1925–1930);

Sämtliche Werke, in zeitlicher Folge geordnet, edited by Clemens Heselhaus (Munich: Hanser, 1952);

Sämtliche Werke, 2 volumes, edited by Günter Weydt and Winfried Woesler (Munich: Winkler, 1973, 1978);

Werke und Briefe, 2 volumes, edited by Manfred Häckel (Leipzig: Insel, 1976);

Historisch-kritische Ausgabe: Werke, Briefwechsel, 14 volumes, edited by Woesler (Tübingen: Niemeyer, 1978–1985).

Editions in English: "Pentecost," "The House in the Heath," "The Boy on the Moor," "On the Tower," "The Desolate House," "The Jew's Beech-Tree," translated by Charles Wharton Stork and Lillie Winter, in *The German Classics of the Nineteenth and Twentieth Centuries,* volume 7,

Annette von Droste-Hülshoff

edited by Kuno Francke and William Guild Howard (New York: German Publication Society, 1913), pp. 437–496;

The Jew's Beech, translated by Lionel and Doris Thomas (London: Calder, 1958).

OTHER: Ferdinand Freiligrath and Levin Schücking, *Das malerische und romantische Westphalen,* contributions by Droste-Hülshoff (Leipzig: Volckmar, 1841).

Annette von Droste-Hülshoff is regarded as the greatest woman poet of nineteenth-century German literature, and her work has received more critical acclaim and attention than that of any other German woman writer. Her novella "Die Judenbuche" (published in her *Letzte Gaben* [Final Offerings], 1860; translated as "The Jew's Beech-Tree," 1913) is a highly intriguing crime story whose enigmatic plot and complex narrative structure bewildered generations of scholars and readers. Her many ballads and poems cover a wide range of topics and forms and feature a detailed, almost microscopic depiction of nature as well as a fascination with the uncanny, supernatural, and mysterious side of human nature. The depth of psychological insight displayed in these works goes far beyond the scope of the Biedermeier period and connects her writing to modern literature and consciousness.

Droste-Hülshoff's reputation as a leading figure of German literature was established several decades after her death; the public began to notice her only during the last years of her life. This relative anonymity, although to some extent sought by the author, reflects for the most part the many obstacles imposed on Droste-Hülshoff's creative development by her class, her sex, her religion, and her region. Besides struggling with a family that barely tolerated her literary efforts, she was troubled throughout her life by her poetic vocation. Although she never left the narrowly defined boundaries of her existence, she did question and challenge them in her writings.

Anna Elisabeth Franziska Adolfine Wilhelmina Luisa Maria, Freiin Droste-Hülshoff, nicknamed Annette, was born on 10 January 1797 in the castle of Hülshoff in Westphalia; her family could trace its aristocratic lineage as far back as the thirteenth century. She was born several weeks premature and survived thanks to the help of a wet nurse, Maria Katharina Plettendorf. Droste-Hülshoff would always feel a close emotional bond to this simple peasant woman and would take care of her until Plettendorf's death in 1845. Droste-Hülshoff had to cope throughout her life with poor health and frequent illnesses, suffering in particular from weak eyesight.

She was an extraordinarily gifted child, writing her first verses around the age of seven. Her mother, Therese Luise, née Haxthausen, an energetic and dominant woman, took great pride in her daughter's talents. She provided Droste-Hülshoff and the other three children with a thorough and extensive education. After the mother taught the children the elementary subjects, tutors were hired for the boys; Droste-Hülshoff and her older sister, Jenny, were allowed to follow their lessons in classical languages, French, mathematics, and natural history. Moreover, Droste-Hülshoff was introduced to a close observation and study of nature by her father, Clemens August von Droste-Hülshoff, an avid ornithologist and botanist. Visits to the theater in nearby Münster, family readings, and musical activities completed Droste-Hülshoff's education, which was far superior to that which most girls of her class received. Droste-Hülshoff also had an extensive social life. She seems, however, to have been at odds with her role and the behavior expected of her. In a revealing letter written in 1819 to her friend and literary mentor Matthias Sprickmann, she confesses the "wunderliches, verrücktes Unglück" (strange, crazy misery) caused by her desire to travel to exotic, faraway places; at the same time she scolds herself for wanting to be away from her family. This ambivalence between resisting and accepting her gender role, characteristic of much of her early writing, can be seen as a dominant theme connecting a diverse body of texts.

The play *Bertha oder Die Alpen* (Bertha; or, The Alps), written in 1813, of which she completed only one and a half acts; "Walther: Ein Gedicht in sechs Gesängen" (Walther: A Poem in Six Cantos), written in 1818; the prose fragment "Ledwina," written in 1819; some poems and letters; and part 1 of *Das geistliche Jahr* (The Spiritual Year, 1851), a cycle of poems linked to the ecclesiastical year, comprise Droste-Hülshoff's early works (all except *Das geistliche Jahr* were published in volume four [1886] of her *Gesammelte Werke* [1884–1887]). With the exception of *Das geistliche Jahr,* these texts have frequently been dismissed as lacking in originality and substance and as offering only glimpses of her future genius. Droste-Hülshoff seemed to be too incoherent in her choice of genre, plot, and theme. They reveal, however, an amazing awareness and insight into the limitations imposed on females, and in particular into the problems of the woman writer. This awareness is especially apparent in "Ledwina," the most innovative and best-written piece of the early period. Sickness and an intense awareness of the restrictions of her female role have turned Ledwina, a young woman of aristocratic background, into an outsider within her family and class. Droste-Hülshoff juxtaposes the portrayal of aristocratic social life with Ledwina's tormented inner world of wild, intense dreams and fantasies, thus combining romantic themes and motives with a realistically depicted social setting that foreshadows the Gesellschaftsroman (social novel) of late nineteenth-century realism. The many images of death and disease in "Ledwina" indicate the heroine's inability to resolve the conflicts between social expectations of her as a woman and her desire for a self-determined development. Droste-Hülshoff is clearly referring to her own experiences: she struggled to appease her own inner turmoil by seeking refuge in the safety of her family, her Catholic faith, and her native Westphalia. "Ledwina" is not, however, only a thinly veiled autobiographical account; the literary treatment of these conflicts allowed the author to explore alternatives to norms she had to comply with in real life.

While outwardly leading the aristocratic existence expected of her, Droste-Hülshoff tried to fulfill her own artistic needs. This precarious balance between inner and outer existence was severely affected during the summer of 1820, which she spent at Bökendorf, the estate of her maternal step-grandmother, as part of a large circle of young people. Droste-Hülshoff was attracted to two young men: Heinrich Straube, a student of modest means and background, and the aristocrat August von Arnswald. Insecure about her feelings and naive in handling relationships, Droste-Hülshoff fell victim to an intrigue in which she was portrayed as an arrogant and superficial person who deliberately played with the sincere feelings of the two men. Although the episode was rather trivial, it had a deep and lasting effect on Droste-Hülshoff, profoundly affecting her self-image and resulting in an overwhelming sense of guilt. The experience heightened her awareness of being an outsider who had failed not only in the social but also in the divine order. This sentiment is most acutely expressed in the poems of *Das geistliche Jahr,* although they never mention the incident. By the fall of 1820 she had finished the first part, the poems from the first day of the New Year until Easter Monday. But under the influence of the summer's experiences the focus and the purpose of the cycle had changed: it could no longer serve as a prayer book for her grandmother, as was originally intended. As Droste-Hülshoff wrote in a letter to her mother, the book was meant for "jene unglücklichen aber thörichten Menschen, die in einer Stunde mehr fragen, als sieben Weise in sieben Jahren beantworten können" (those unhappy but foolish people who ask more questions in one hour than seven wise men can answer in seven years). A strong confessional tone dominates the poems, which show a human being with an ardent desire to believe and feel worthy of God's love but at the same time overcome by doubt and fear. The mood of the poems is dark and somber. The speaker voices guilt, despair, and anxiety in a way that neither leaves room for hope nor explains the reason for this incredible guilt. *Das geistliche Jahr* shows Droste-Hülshoff's familiarity with baroque liturgical cycles as well as with the religious poetry of the seventeenth and eighteenth centuries. She brings, how-

ever, a strikingly new and original tone to these conventional forms, re-creating the tradition to express an individual religious experience. *Das geistliche Jahr,* which Droste-Hülshoff considered to be her most useful work, contributed in the latter part of the nineteenth century to her reputation as a religious and conservative author firmly rooted in the Catholic faith. While this faith as well as her close ties to her family and class certainly shaped her work, Droste-Hülshoff also struggled with these forces because they hindered her personal and artistic development.

From 1820 until 1825 Droste-Hülshoff withdrew almost completely from the outside world and ceased her literary activities in an attempt to come to terms with the Straube-Arnswald affair. In the fall of 1825 she emerged from her solitude, traveling to the Rhine region to visit relatives and friends in Cologne, Bonn, and Koblenz. The trip provided her with new social and intellectual stimuli; she also made new friends, the most important of whom was Sibylle Mertens-Schaafhausen, the wife of a rich merchant. She resumed her writing during her Rhine journey, making an attempt to finish "Ledwina"; but she finally gave up on the work.

Her father died in 1826, and she moved with her mother and sister to Rüschhaus, a small country manor not far from Hülshoff that was managed by her older brother and his wife. Life in Rüschhaus was uneventful and often lonely. Two years after her father's death Droste-Hülshoff's younger brother Ferdinand died, and Droste-Hülshoff fell seriously ill. Her frail health often left her unable to write for weeks and months, and the relatively small size of her oeuvre has to be understood in the light of these frequent bouts with illness. In addition, she dutifully took care of sick relatives—as expected from an unmarried woman—leaving her with little time for her own work.

Droste-Hülshoff traveled back to the Rhine region in 1828; that year she began to work on a verse epic, "Das Hospiz auf dem großen Sankt Bernhard" (The Hostel on the Great Mountain Saint Bernhard), the story of a rescue in the Swiss mountains. During a last Rhine visit from the fall of 1830 until the spring of 1831 she came to know Johanna and Adele Schopenhauer, the mother and sister of the philosopher Arthur Schopenhauer. Friendships, particularly with women, played an important role throughout Droste-Hülshoff's life, and many of her poems are dedicated to friends. In contrast to her family, these contacts provided her with encouragement and exchanges of ideas that proved beneficial for her writing.

In 1834 Droste-Hülshoff's sister Jenny married Josef von Laßberg, an avid collector of medieval manuscripts; he was also well connected in the literary and publishing world. The couple later moved to Meersburg, near Lake Constance, where Laßberg purchased an old castle that was to become an important retreat for Droste-Hülshoff; she traveled there three times.

In Rüschhaus, Droste-Hülshoff completed "Das Hospiz auf dem großen Sankt Bernhard" and two other verse epics, "Des Arztes Vermächtnis" (The Legacy of the Physician) in 1834 and "Die Schlacht im Loener Bruch" (The Battle in the Loener Marsh)—dealing with an historic event from the Thirty Years' War—in 1838. (Droste-Hülshoff finished all her verse epics, while many of her prose works remained fragments.) Of the three epics "Des Arztes Vermächtnis" is the most innovative and modern. It is a fascinating document of a mental disturbance caused by the mysterious events of a single night. The first-person narrative is a confession that is the "Vermächtnis" (legacy) a physician leaves to his son, who reads it after his father's death. The father describes how, on the night of 12 May, he was taken blindfolded to a robbers' hideout deep in the Bohemian forest to assist a gravely sick man who died in the course of the night. The physician thought that he recognized the dying man, as well as a beautiful woman in his company, as former members of Viennese aristocratic society. He was able to obtain his release from a young man, to whom he refers as "der Dunkle" (the dark one). The narrator is not absolutely sure whether these events really happened or whether they were the imaginations of his troubled mind. Did he, for example, witness the murder of the beautiful woman on his way back home? A hot spot where the dark one touched him has remained on his head after this night, reminding him of the occurrence that has left him a disturbed and guilt-ridden man. The blurring of dream and reality, the element of suspense, and the detailed descriptions of nature and of mental processes make this text a turning point in Droste-Hülshoff's work. Not only had she found themes that were to become hallmarks of her writing but she had also integrated them into a complex narrative that did not allow the reader to clarify the maze of visions, uncertainties, and doubts.

The three epics, together with some poems, a ballad, and a few pieces from *Das geistliche Jahr,* were published in 1838 as *Gedichte* (Poems). The forty-three-year-old author had to ask her mother for permission to have the work published, and it did not appear under her name. This edition turned out, however, to be an ill-fated first attempt. Droste-Hülshoff had no experience with publishing companies and left the negotiations to others, who did not fare much better in the task than she would have. The book did not sell well and received only a limited, albeit positive, reception. But despite its commercial failure, which Droste-Hülshoff found embarrassing, she had finally become a published author.

In her letters during these years Droste-Hülshoff frequently discusses possible new literary projects, revealing herself to be unsure which direction her writing should take. Her friend Christoph Bernhard Schlüter, a blind professor of philosophy whom she had met in 1834, unrelentingly reminded and encouraged her to finish *Das geistliche Jahr.* Even though she was reluctant to return to it, by the beginning of 1840 she had completed the second half (the poems from the first Sunday after Easter until New Year's Eve); but the cycle was not published during her lifetime. Considering the twenty-year interval, the two parts are remarkably coherent. Droste-Hülshoff did not change the tone or mood of the work but enlarged its focus by addressing indirectly matters such as the contemporary decline of religion and morality. The cycle is considered the most important work of religious poetry in the nineteenth century.

For many years members of her family had tried to persuade Droste-Hülshoff to display her sense of humor and comical talents in a literary work. Although she was hesitant to venture in this direction, Droste-Hülshoff succumbed to the pressure and decided "einen Versuch im Komischen zu unternehmen" (to try something in the comic genre). By the end of 1840 she had finished a one-act comedy, *Perdu! oder Dichter, Verleger und Blaustrümpfe* (Lost! or, Poets, Publishers and Bluestockings). A satire, it barely camouflages the personalities and activities of a small literary circle that had formed in the late 1830s in Münster whose gatherings Droste-Hülshoff attended from time to time. The play has not received much critical attention, but it reveals Droste-Hülshoff's perception of the contemporary literary world, particularly of women authors. While reiterating many clichés about women's inferior production, she portrays Frau von Thielen, her fictional alter ego, as a serious, uncompromising artist who feels uneasy about the publishing world. *Perdu!* is thus another example of Droste-Hülshoff's ambivalent attitude about writing and female creativity. According to the critic Gertrud Bauer-Pickar, Droste-Hülshoff viewed authorship as an essentially male prerogative yet tried to establish herself as a writer, thereby implicitly challenging her own beliefs as well as the dominant social norms. Droste-Hülshoff never had the play published, partly because the manuscript received—as was to be expected—a negative response from the members of the literary circle.

During the late 1830s Droste also worked on "Die Judenbuche," the only prose work she ever completed. It was originally part of an ethnographic description of Westphalia to be written in the style of Washington Irving's *Bracebridge Hall* (1822). She never finished the project, out of which only two pieces other than "Die Judenbuche" developed: "Westfälische Schilderungen aus einer westfälischen Feder" (Westphalian Portrayals from a Westphalian Pen), published anonymously in 1845 in the *Historisch-politische Blätter für das katholische Deutschland* (Historic-Political Papers for Catholic Germany), and a short narrative, "Bei uns zu Lande auf dem Lande" (With Us at Home in the Country). Droste-Hülshoff's original title for "Die Judenbuche," "Ein Sittengemälde aus dem gebirgichten Westfalen" (A Picture of Customs and Morals from the Westphalian Mountains), reflects her intention to portray the people, customs, and values of the region she knew so well. The editor of Cotta's *Morgenblatt für gebildete Leser* (Morning Paper for Cultured Readers), where the novella was published in April and May 1842, chose, however, the more eye-catching "Die Judenbuche," using Droste-Hülshoff's phrase as a subtitle. The source of the novella is a document written by Droste-Hülshoff's uncle August von Haxthausen and published in 1818 under the title "Geschichte eines Algierer Sklaven" (Story of an Algerian Slave). It is the true story of a man from the Paderborn region who killed a Jew, fled, spent years in slavery, returned home, and committed suicide under the tree where the murder had happened. Droste-Hülshoff kept the basic plot but reinvented the main character as well as the narrative and thematic framework. Her story opens with a short poem admonishing the reader that a poor man's wrongdoings cannot be judged by people born into more fortunate circumstances. The poem's underlying notion of environmental influences on a person's development is a striking anticipation of modern thinking. The life of the protagonist, Friedrich Mergel, is described by carefully listing all the factors that contribute to his ill-fated destiny. To depict his entire life within the limited framework of a novella, Droste-Hülshoff uses a narrative strategy that has been referred to as "scene-sequencing," that is, showing decisive moments or turning points—a device that is also used in the modern cinema.

Born in 1738 in a remote region where law and order have been undermined by continuous infringement of the forest laws, and growing up in an unhappy family, Friedrich misses from the beginning moral guidance and positive role models. At nine he loses his father, a heavy drinker and social outcast. Three years later his maternal uncle, Simon, offers to take the boy. This uncle is a devious character, and under his influence Friedrich, who works as the village's shepherd, becomes arrogant and sly. Simon seems to be involved in the theft of timber and may have murdered the forester, Brandis, who tried to catch the thieves. But it was Friedrich who, after a heated argument with Brandis, sent him in the direction where he was to encounter the wood thieves. Shocked by the brutal murder, which he

by no means anticipated, Friedrich is briefly plagued by a bad conscience; but he never confesses, and he forgets the incident rather quickly. Brandis's murderer is never identified. Four years later a second murder takes place. A Jew named Aaron is found dead under a beech tree three days after a big wedding at which he publicly accused Friedrich of not having paid for a silver watch. Because of this incident Friedrich is suspected of having committed the crime, but he and his companion Johannes Niemand, who is probably Simon's illegitimate son, have left the village. In this case, too, the murderer is never found. Twenty-eight years later a sick old man returns from Turkish slavery; he says that he is Johannes Niemand. After living for some time in the village the man suddenly disappears; he is discovered two weeks later, hanging from the tree under which Aaron was found dead. On careful examination of the corpse the old squire declares the dead man to be Friedrich Mergel. The last line of the novella reads: "Wenn du dich diesem Orte nahest, so wird es dir ergehen, wie du mir getan hast" (When you near this place, what happens to you will be the same as what you did to me). It is a translation of the Hebrew inscription the leaders of the Jewish community had engraved in the beech tree after Aaron's death.

Owing to the ingenious way in which Droste-Hülshoff simultaneously gives and conceals information, the reader never knows who really committed the murder; it is never explicitly said that Friedrich is Aaron's murderer, and a criminal named Lumpenmoises confesses having murdered a Jew named Aaron. A shift in narrative perspective from documentary description with careful chronicling of dates to the viewpoints of various characters who give subjective accounts of the occurrences further contributes to the enigmatic character of the story. While "Die Judenbuche" unfolds on one level as a suspenseful detective story, it is also a study in crime, guilt, and punishment with a religious or metaphysical dimension. Despite the strong environmental influences on his development, Friedrich is shown as having a choice between good and evil; but he opts for the latter. At the same time, the village experiences a continuous failure of its judicial system, which is unable to render justice in the two murder cases or in the wood theft. Finally, because the corpse is found hanging in the beech tree in September 1789—the eve of the French Revolution—a wider sociopolitical context is established. The continuing fascination of the work results from the multitude of themes integrated into the framework of a detective story and from the tension between appearance and reality that Droste-Hülshoff so masterfully maintains. Despite all its realism there remains a mysterious, opaque atmosphere that challenges every reader anew.

Levin Schücking, one of the members of the Münster literary circle, asked Droste-Hülshoff to contribute to the collection *Das malerische und romantische Westfalen* (Picturesque and Romantic Westphalia, 1841), which he and Ferdinand Freiligrath were editing. As a result, Droste-Hülshoff produced almost a dozen ballads dealing with Westphalian history or legend. The genre of the ballad, with its combination of lyric, epic, and dramatic elements and its climactic structure, lent itself to Droste-Hülshoff's affinity for the uncanny and mysterious, and its focus on destiny allowed her to explore further the themes of crime, punishment, and guilt. In the ballad "Vorgeschichte" (Second Sight) a nobleman belonging to the "gequälte[s] Geschlecht" (tormented dynasty) of people who can foretell their futures wakes up from a nightmare but is unable to free his mind from the swirl of images, hallucinations, and visions that arc beautifully described through moon and water symbols. He then "sees" the preparations for a funeral taking place in the courtyard of his castle and, relieved to recognize the coat of arms as his own and not his wife's, calms down and prepares his will. What is most striking about this poem is Droste-Hülshoff's vivid description of mental processes in which reason no longer prevails, a tormented mind on the brink of insanity. "Das Fräulein von Rodenschild" (Miss von Rodenschild), in which a young countess is confronted with her double, gives another brilliant example of a troubled consciousness. "Die Schwestern" (The Sisters) portrays a woman searching for her sister, who, in pursuing her erotic desires, became a social outcast. The ballad reveals the dual perspective that is a dominant feature in most of Droste-Hülshoff's work and that indicates her ambivalent perception of herself as a woman author in a time of great social and political change.

Droste-Hülshoff arrived in Meersburg for a visit in September 1841. She was joined a month later by Schücking, the person who most decisively influenced her artistic development. Droste-Hülshoff had known his mother, Katharina Busch Schücking, and after the mother's death in 1831 she felt an obligation to take care of Schücking. When Droste-Hülshoff had met him again in 1837, Schücking was an impecunious young poet and journalist. Although initially repelled by Schücking's vanity and dandyish behavior, Droste-Hülshoff soon grew fond of him, and she tried hard to find suitable employment for him. She finally convinced her brother-in-law to invite Schücking to Meersburg to work as a librarian. In Meersburg, Droste-Hülshoff could, for the first time, escape maternal control and satisfy her creative as well as her emotional needs. Much has been speculated about the extent of Droste-Hülshoff's amorous involvement with Schücking, who seemed an unlikely match for the conservative

aristocrat. Not only was Schücking of bourgeois background and seventeen years her junior but he also held decidedly liberal views. Droste-Hülshoff's letters and poems dealing with the relationship and the devastation she felt after Schücking's sudden departure for new employment in February 1842 show a strong attachment and deep affection. Although he was only a modestly gifted writer, Schücking recognized Droste-Hülshoff's genius and was a perceptive critic of her work. He directed her away from the verse epic toward prose and lyric poetry, and he helped to unleash a tremendous creative outburst: during the months they spent together at Meersburg, Droste-Hülshoff prepared the final draft of "Die Judenbuche" and wrote more than fifty poems. Schücking later said that he used a trick to stimulate her creativity: provoked by his claim that the lyric inspiration occurs only rarely, Droste-Hülshoff promised to produce an entire volume of poetry within a few months. Some of these poems were published in journals, but the majority appeared in her *Gedichte* (1844). Published by the prestigious Cotta firm—Schücking had acted as an intermediary between Droste-Hülshoff and the publisher—the edition was a literary as well as a commercial success. It contributed to Droste-Hülshoff's growing reputation as an author, and the honorarium enabled her to buy Fürstenhausle (Prince's Cottage), a small retreat at Meersburg. Droste-Hülshoff's final breakthrough as an author was accompanied by a growing estrangement from the man who had contributed to it. It was difficult for Droste-Hülshoff to overcome the disappointment and loneliness caused by his sudden departure, but Schücking's marriage in 1843 hurt her even more. As the poem "Lebt wohl" (Farewell) shows, Droste-Hülshoff countered the desolation by affirming her poetic vocation. This affirmation, albeit often ambivalent, is manifest in the poems of the 1844 edition. The volume is divided into five sections: political and social issues dominate in "Zeitbilder" (Pictures of the Times); "Heidebilder" (Pictures of the Heath) and "Fels, Wald und See" (Rock, Forest, and Sea) contain nature poetry (the latter section includes some of Droste-Hülshoff's idyllic, genre-painting poetry, such as the small cycles "Die Elemente" [The Elements] and "Der Säntis"); under the heading "Gedichte vermischten Inhalts" (Miscellaneous Poems) verses dealing with personal experiences and occasional poems are grouped together; finally, in "Scherz und Ernst" (Fun and Seriousness) Droste-Hülshoff displays her humorous talent on political, artistic, and general topics.

The poems of "Zeitbilder" show Droste-Hülshoff as a staunch defender of a conservative social and religious order. As titles such as "Alte und neue Kinderzucht" (Old and New Upbringing) and "Vor vierzig

Jahren" (Forty Years Ago) indicate, she contrasts a harmonious past with the present disintegration caused by liberal tendencies and admonishes the reader to follow a conservative, Christian ideology. While the poems in this group never became popular, those in "Heidebilder" as well as poems such as "Am Thurme" (On the Tower), "Im Moose" (On the Moss), and "Das Spiegelbild" (The Reflection in the Mirror) from the following two sections represent some of her best-known work. The striking originality of these poems lies in their observation of nature. Droste-Hülshoff not only chooses new and unusual locales, such as the moor and the marl pit, but she also perceives nature in its most detailed and intricate movements, observing the sound of a berry dropping to the ground or the fearful cry of a fly. Many of these poems feature such an abundance of images and sounds that they have been compared to impressionistic paintings. But despite the intensity of the visual and auditory descriptions these lyrics do not clarify the perception of nature; instead, they render it rather ambiguous and vague. The narrator of "Die Mergelgrube" (The Marl Pit) in "Heidebilder" is caught, for example, between dream and reality while exploring the pit and is unable to distinguish his inner vision from outer appearances. The nightly wanderer in "Der Hünenstein" (The Giant Stone), another poem in "Heidebilder," is at once attracted and repelled by a prehistoric cave, with its atmosphere of death and decay. Giving free play to his fantasies, he is drawn further and further into the past and is almost overcome with horror. "Der Knabe im Moor" (The Boy on the Moor), the concluding poem of "Heidebilder," is a striking example of the combination of detailed description of nature with supernatural figures such as ghosts. The ghosts frighten the child crossing the moor almost to death and cause him to lose his direction and footing. Fear and anxiety reign even in seemingly idyllic places, reflecting the troubled inner world of the poem's narrator. In the many poems dealing explicitly or implicitly with the poet's vocation, Droste-Hülshoff explores her painful struggle with her identity as a woman author. Their double structures and double figures, often presented as mirror images or hallucinations, echo similar constellations in her early works. They attest to the extent to which Droste-Hülshoff perceived her life and work as torn between opposite forces that spring not only from gender-specific constraints but also from Droste-Hülshoff's deep-seated feelings of inexpiable sin and guilt.

Droste-Hülshoff was unable to repeat the creative eruption that occurred during her first stay in Meersburg. She finished another verse epic, "Der Spiritus Familiaris des Roßtäuschers" (The Familiar Spirit of the Horse Dealer), which recounts an old folk legend. In the fall of 1844 she began another crime story, "Josef," but never completed it. Of the other poems she wrote, eighteen appeared during her lifetime; but most of this work was published posthumously by Schücking. By 1846, however, Droste-Hülshoff had broken off all relations with him. She strongly disapproved of Schücking's liberal-minded poems, in which he advocated freedom of the press and a more democratic form of government. What upset her most was the publication of his novel *Die Ritterbürtigen* (Of Noble Birth, 1846), an attack on the outmoded aristocratic class that drew much of its material from Droste-Hülshoff's intimate knowledge of the Westphalian aristocracy. She felt that Schücking had violated her trust and misused their friendship.

The final two years of her life were overshadowed by growing isolation and severe illness. Droste-Hülshoff suffered from overagitated nerves and sleeplessness; she was so overcome by weakness that she was unable to walk. Hoping for an improvement in the more favorable southern climate, in the fall of 1847 she traveled once again to Meersburg. Her health remained poor, and she died on 24 May 1848 at Meersburg. She is buried in the cemetery there.

Letters:
Briefe der Freiin Annette von Droste-Hülshoff, edited by Christoph Bernhard Schlüter (Münster: Russel, 1877);
Briefe von Annette von Droste-Hülshoff und Levin Schücking, edited by Theo Schücking (Leipzig: Grunow, 1893); enlarged edition, edited by Reinhold Conrad Muschler (Leipzig: Grunow, 1928);
Die Briefe der Dichterin Annette v. Droste-Hülshoff, edited by Hermann Cardauns (Münster: Aschendorff, 1909);
Die Briefe der Annette von Droste-Hülshoff: Gesamtausgabe, 2 volumes, edited by Karl Schulte-Kemminghausen (Jena: Diederich, 1944).

Bibliographies:
Eduard Arens and Karl Schulte Kemminghausen, *Droste-Bibliographie* (Münster: Aschendorff, 1932);
Clemens Heselhaus, "Droste-Bibliographie 1932–1948," *Droste Jahrbuch,* 2 (1948–1950): 334–352;
Hans Thiekötter, *Annette von Droste-Hülshoff: Eine Auswahlbibliographie* (Münster: Aschendorff, 1963);
Helmut Dees, *Annette von Droste-Hülshoffs Dichtungen in England und Amerika* (Tübingen: Fotodruck Präzis, 1966);
Winfried Theiss, "Droste-Bibliographie 1949–1969," *Droste-Jahrbuch,* 5 (1972): 147–244;
Walter Huge, "Annette von Droste-Hülshoff: Die Judenbuche. Ein Sittengemälde aus dem gebirgigten Westphalen," dissertation, University of Münster, 1977;

Aloys Haverbusch, "Droste-Bibliographie 1838–1900," in *Modellfall der Rezeptionsforschung: Droste-Rezeption im 19. Jahrhundert. Dokumentation, Analysen, Bibliographie,* edited by Winfried Woesler, 1 volume (Frankfurt am Main: Peter Lang, 1980), pp. 1331–1582.

Biographies:

Levin Schücking, *Annette von Droste: Ein Lebensbild* (Hannover: Rümpler, 1862);

Hermann Hüffer, *Annette v. Droste-Hülshoff und ihre Werke* (Gotha: Perthes, 1887);

Mary Lavater-Sloman, *Einsamkeit: Das Leben der Annette von Droste-Hülshoff* (Zurich: Artemis, 1950);

Margaret Mare, *Annette von Droste-Hülshoff* (London: Methuen, 1965);

Peter Berglar, *Annette von Droste-Hülshoff in Selbstzeugnissen und Bilddokumenten* (Reinbek: Rowohlt, 1967);

Clemens Heselhaus, *Annette von Droste-Hülshoff: Werk und Leben* (Düsseldorf: Bagel, 1971);

Doris Maurer, *Annette von Droste-Hülshoff: Ein Leben zwischen Auflehnung und Gehorsam* (Bonn: Keil, 1982);

Mary E. Morgan, *Annette von Droste-Hülshoff: A Biography* (Bern, Frankfurt am Main & New York: Peter Lang, 1984);

John Guthrie, *Annette von Droste-Hülshoff: A German Poet between Romanticism and Realism* (Oxford: Berg, 1989);

Walter Godden, *Annette von Droste-Hülshoff: Leben und Werk: eine Dichterchronik* (Bern & New York: Peter Lang, 1994).

References:

Clifford Albrecht Bernd, "Clarity and Obscurity in Annette von Droste-Hülshoff's 'Judenbuche,'" *Studies in German Literature of the Nineteenth and Twentieth Centuries: Festschrift for Frederic E. Coenen,* edited by Siegfried Mews (Chapel Hill: University of North Carolina Press, 1970), pp. 64–77;

Stephan Berning, *Sinnbildsprache: Zur Bildstruktur des Geistlichen Jahres der Annette von Droste-Hülshoff* (Tübingen: Niemeyer, 1975);

Sylvia Bonati-Richner, *Der Feuermensch: Studien über das Verhältnis von Mensch und Landschaft in den erzählenden Werken der Annette von Droste-Hülshoff* (Bern: Francke, 1972);

Renate Böschenstein-Schäfer, "Die Struktur des Idyllischen im Werk der Annette von Droste-Hülshoff," *Kleinere Beiträge zur Drosteforschung,* 3 (1974–1975): 25–49;

Artur Brall, *Vergangenheit und Vergänglichkeit: Zur Zeiterfahrung und Zeitdeutung im Werk Annette von Droste-Hülshoffs* (Marburg: Elwert, 1975);

Edson Chick, "Voices in Discord: Some Observations of 'Die Judenbuche,'" *German Quarterly,* 42 (March 1969): 147–157;

Elke Frederiksen and Monika Shafi, "Annette von Droste-Hülshoff (1797–1848): Konfliktstrukturen im Frühwerk," in *Out of Line/Ausgefallen: The Paradox of Marginality in the Writings of Nineteenth-Century German Women,* edited by Ruth-Ellen Boetcher Joeres and Marianne Burkhard (Amsterdam: Rodopi, 1989), pp. 115–136;

Wilhelm Gössmann, *Annette von Droste-Hülshoff: Ich und Spiegelbild. Zum Verständnis der Dichterin und ihres Werkes* (Düsseldorf: Droste, 1985);

Gössmann, *Heine und die Droste : Eine literarische Zeitgenossenschaft* (Düsseldorf: Grupello, 1996);

Gössmann, "Trunkenheit und Desillusion: Das poetische Ich der Droste," *Zeitschrift für deutsche Philologie,* 101, no. 4 (1982): 506–525;

Gotthard Guder, "Annette von Droste-Hülshoff's Conception of Herself as Poet," *German Life and Letters,* 11 (1957): 13–24;

Günter Häntzschel, "Annette von Droste-Hülshoff," in *Zur Literatur der Restaurationsepoche 1815–1848: Forschungsreferate und Aufsätze,* edited by Jost Hermand and Manfred Windfuhr (Stuttgart: Metzler, 1970), pp. 151–199;

Häntzschel, *Tradition und Originalität: Allegorische Darstellung im Werk Annette von Droste-Hülshoffs* (Stuttgart: Kohlhammer, 1968);

Wolfgang Kayser, "Sprachform und Redeform in den 'Heidebildern' der Annette von Droste-Hülshoff," in *Interpretationen I: Deutsche Lyrik von Weckherlin bis Benn,* edited by Jost Schillemeit (Frankfurt am Main: Fischer, 1965), pp. 212–244;

Janet K. King, "Conscience and Conviction in *Die Judenbuche,*" *Monatshefte für den deutschen Unterricht,* 64 (1972): 349–355;

Bernd Kortländer, *Annette von Droste-Hülshoff und die deutsche Literatur: Kenntnis, Beurteilung, Beeinflussung* (Münster: Aschendorff, 1979);

Herbert Kraft, *Annette von Droste-Hülshoff* (Reinbek bei Hamburg: Rowohlt, 1994);

Kraft, *Mein Indien liegt in Rüschhaus* (Münster: Regensberg, 1987);

Mary Morgan, *Annette von Droste-Hülshoff: A Woman of Letters in a Period of Transition* (Bern: Peter Lang, 1981);

Ortrun Niethammer and Claudia Belemann, eds., *Ein Gitter aus Musik und Sprache: feministische Analysen zu Annette von Droste-Hülshoff* (Paderborn: Schöningh, 1993);

Brigitte Peucker, "Droste-Hülshoff's Ophelia and the Recovery of Voice," *Journal of English and Germanic Philology,* 82 (July 1983): 374–391;

Peucker, "The Poetry of Regeneration: Droste-Hülshoff's Ophelia as Muse," in her *Lyric Descent in the German Romantic Tradition* (New Haven: Yale University Press, 1987), pp. 71–118;

Gertrud Bauer Pickar, *Ambivalence Transcended: A Study of the Writings of Annette von Droste-Hülshoff* (Columbia, S.C.: Camden House, 1997);

Pickar, "Perdu Reclaimed: A Reappraisal of Droste's Comedy," *Monatshefte für den deutschen Unterricht*, 76 (Winter 1984): 409–421;

Pickar, "'Too manly is your spirit': Annette von Droste-Hülshoff," *Rice University Studies*, 64 (Winter 1978): 51–68;

Wolfgang Preisendanz, "'. . . und jede Lust, so Schauer nur gewähren mag': Die Poesie der Wahrnehmung in der Dichtung Annette von Droste-Hülshoffs," *Droste-Forschung*, 4 (1976–1977): 9–21;

Ernst Ribbat, ed., *Dialoge mit der Droste: Kolloquium zum 200. Geburtstag von Droste-Hülshoff* (Paderborn: Schöningh, 1998);

Irmgard Roebling, "Weibliches Schreiben im 19. Jahrhundert: Untersuchungen zur Naturmetaphorik der Droste," *Der Deutschunterricht*, 18 (1986): 36–56;

Heinz Rölleke, "Erzähltes Mysterium: Studien zur 'Judenbuche' der Annette von Droste-Hülshoff," *Deutsche Vierteljahrsschrift für Literaturwissenschaft und Geistesgeschichte*, 42 (August 1968): 399–426;

Ronald Schneider, *Annette von Droste-Hülshoff* (Stuttgart: Metzler, 1977);

Schneider, *Realismus und Restauration: Untersuchungen zu Poetik und epischem Werk der Annette von Droste-Hülshoff* (Kronberg: Scriptor, 1976);

Walter Silz, "Annette von Droste-Hülshoff, 'Die Judenbuche,'" in his *Realism and Reality: Studies in the German Novelle of Poetic Realism* (Chapel Hill: University of North Carolina Press, 1954), pp. 36–51;

Emil Staiger, *Annette von Droste-Hülshoff* (Frauenfeld: Huber, 1967);

Manfred Weiss-Dasio, *Heidewelt: Eine Einführung in das Gedichtwerk der Annette von Droste-Hülshoff* (Bonn: Bouvier, 1996);

Larry D. Wells, "Indeterminacy as Provocation: The Reader's Role in Annette von Droste-Hülshoff's 'Die Judenbuche,'" *Modern Language Notes*, 94 (April 1979): 475–492;

Zeitschrift für deutsche Philologie, special issue on Droste-Hülshoff, edited by Walter Huge and Winfried Woesler (1980).

Papers:

Eighty percent of Annette von Droste-Hülshoff's papers are in public libraries and museums. The most important are the Universitätsbibliothek (University Library), Bonn; the Stadt- und Landesbibliothek (City and State Library), Dortmund; the Deutsches Literaturarchiv/ Schiller-Nationalmuseum (German Literature Archives/ Schiller National Museum), Marbach; the Fürstenhäusle, Meersburg; and the Annette von Droste-Gesellschaft (Annette von Droste Society), the Franziskanerkloster (Franciscan Cloister), the Universitätsbibliothek, and the Westfälisches Landesmuseum für Kunst und Kulturgeschichte (Westphalian State Museum for Art and Culture History), all in Münster.

Friedrich Dürrenmatt

(5 January 1921 – 14 December 1990)

Edson M. Chick
Williams College

This entry was updated by Professor Chick from his entry in DLB 124:
Twentieth-Century German Dramatists, 1919–1992.

See also the Dürrenmatt entry in *DLB 69: Contemporary German Fiction Writers, First Series.*

BOOKS: *Es steht geschrieben: Ein Drama* (Klosterberg & Basel: Schwabe, 1947); revised as *Die Wiedertäufer: Eine Komödie in zwei Teilen* (Zurich: Arche, 1967);

Der Blinde: Ein Drama (Berlin: Bühnenverlag Bloch Erben, 1947);

Pilatus (Olten: Vereinigung Oltner Bücherfreunde, 1949);

Der Nihilist (Horgen: Holunderpresse, 1950); republished as *Die Falle* (Zurich: Arche, 1952);

Das Bild des Sisyphos (Zurich: Arche, 1952); translated by Michael Bullock as "The Picture of Sisyphos," *Mundus Artium,* 1, no. 3 (1968): 53–69;

Der Tunnel (Zurich: Arche, 1952); republished in *Die Panne and Der Tunnel,* edited by F. J. Alexander (London: Oxford University Press, 1967); translated by Carla Coulter and Alison Scott as "The Tunnel," *Evergreen Review,* 5, no. 17 (1961): 32–42;

Die Stadt: Prosa I–IV (Zurich: Arche, 1952);

Der Richter und sein Henker (Einsiedeln, Zurich & Cologne: Benziger, 1952); edited by William Gillis and John J. Neumaier (Cambridge, Mass.: Riverside Press, 1961); edited by Leonard Forster (London: Harrap, 1962); translated by Cyrus Brooks as *The Judge and His Hangman* (London: Jenkins, 1954); translated by Theresa Pol as *The Judge and His Hangman* (New York: Harper, 1955);

Die Ehe des Herrn Mississippi: Eine Komödie in zwei Teilen (Zurich: Oprecht, 1952; revised edition, Zurich: Arche, 1966); translated by Bullock as *The Marriage of Mr. Mississippi,* in *The Marriage of Mr. Mississippi: A Play and Problems of the Theatre: An Essay* (New York: Grove, 1966); German version edited by Reinhold Grimm and Helene Scher (New York: Holt, Rinehart & Winston, 1973);

Friedrich Dürrenmatt (photograph by Margarete Redl-von Peinen)

Der Verdacht (Einsiedeln, Zurich & Cologne: Benziger, 1953); edited by Gillis (Boston: Houghton Mifflin, 1964); edited by Forster (London: Harrap, 1965); translated by Eva H. Morreale as *The*

96

Quarry (New York: Grove, 1961; London: Cape, 1962);

Ein Engel kommt nach Babylon: Eine Komödie in drei Akten (Zurich: Arche, 1954; revised, 1958); translated by William McElwee as *An Angel Comes to Babylon,* in *An Angel Comes To Babylon and Romulus the Great* (New York: Grove, 1964);

Herkules und der Stall des Augias: Mit Randnotizen eines Kugelschreibers (Zurich: Arche, 1954);

Theaterprobleme (Zurich: Arche, 1955); translated by Gerhard Nellhaus as "Problems of the Theatre," in *Four Plays* (London: Cape, 1964; New York: Grove, 1965);

Grieche sucht Griechin: Eine Prosakomödie (Zurich: Arche, 1955); translated by Richard and Clara Winston as *Once a Greek . . .* (New York: Knopf, 1965; London: Cape, 1966);

Die Panne: Eine noch mögliche Geschichte (Zurich: Arche, 1956); republished in *Die Panne and Der Tunnel,* edited by Alexander (London: Oxford University Press, 1967); translated by Richard and Clara Winston as *Traps* (New York: Knopf, 1960); translation republished as *A Dangerous Game* (London: Cape, 1960);

Romulus der Große: Eine ungeschichtliche historische Komödie (Basel: Reiss, 1956; revised edition, Zurich: Arche, 1958); edited by Hugh Frederic Garten (Boston: Houghton Mifflin, 1962; London: Methuen, 1962); translated by Nellhaus as *Romulus the Great,* in *An Angel Comes to Babylon and Romulus the Great;*

Der Besuch der alten Dame: Eine tragische Komödie (Zurich: Arche, 1956); adapted by Maurice Valency as *The Visit: A Play in Three Acts* (New York: Random House, 1958); German version edited by Paul Kurt Ackermann (Boston: Houghton Mifflin, 1961); translated by Patrick Bowles as *The Visit: A Tragicomedy* (New York: Grove, 1962; London: Cape, 1962);

Komödien (Zurich: Arche, 1957);

Nächtliches Gespräch mit einem verachteten Menschen: Ein Kurs für Zeitgenossen (Zurich: Arche, 1957); translated by Robert D. Macdonald as *Conversation at Night with a Despised Character: A Curriculum for Our Times* (Chicago: Dramatic Publishing Co., 1957);

Der Prozeß um des Esels Schatten: Ein Hörspiel nach Wieland—aber nicht sehr (Zurich: Arche, 1958);

Das Unternehmen der Wega: Ein Hörspiel (Zurich: Arche, 1958); translated by Alfred Schild as "The Mission of the Vega," *Texas Quarterly,* 5, no. 1 (1962): 125–149;

Das Versprechen: Requiem auf den Kriminalroman (Zurich: Arche, 1958); translated by Richard and Clara Winston as *The Pledge* (New York: Knopf, 1959;

London: Cape, 1959); German version edited by Forster (London: Harrap, 1967);

Abendstunde im Spätherbst: Ein Hörspiel (Zurich: Arche, 1959); translated by Gabriel Karminski as *Episode on an Autumn Evening* (Chicago: Dramatic Publishing Co., 1959);

Stranitzky und der Nationalheld: Ein Hörspiel (Zurich: Arche, 1959);

Der Doppelgänger: Ein Spiel (Zurich: Arche, 1960);

Friedrich Schiller: Eine Rede (Zurich: Arche, 1960);

Frank der Fünfte: Oper einer Privatbank, music by Paul Burkhard (Zurich: Arche, 1960; revised, 1964);

Die Ehe des Herrn Mississippi: Ein Drehbuch mit Szenenbildern (Zurich: Sanssouci, 1961);

Die Panne: Ein Hörspiel (Zurich: Arche, 1961);

Gesammelte Hörspiele (Zurich: Arche, 1961);

Die Physiker: Eine Komödie in zwei Akten (Zurich: Arche, 1962); translated by James Kirkup as *The Physicists* (London: French, 1963; New York: Grove, 1964); German version edited by Robert E. Helbling (New York: Oxford University Press, 1965); edited by Arthur Taylor (London: Macmillan, 1966);

Die Heimat im Plakat: Ein Buch für Schweizer Kinder (Zurich: Diogenes, 1963);

Herkules und der Stall des Augias: Eine Komödie (Zurich: Arche, 1963); translated by Agnes Hamilton as *Hercules and the Augean Stables* (Chicago: Dramatic Publishing Co., 1963);

Komödien II und frühe Stücke (Zurich: Arche, 1963);

Drei Hörspiele, edited by Henry Regensteiner (New York: Holt, Rinehart & Winston, 1965)—comprises *Abendstunde im Spätherbst, Der Doppelgänger, Die Panne;*

Theaterschriften und Reden, 2 volumes, edited by Elisabeth Brock-Sulzer (Zurich: Arche, 1966–1972); translated by H. M. Waidson as *Writings on Theatre and Drama,* 1 volume (London: Cape, 1976);

Der Meteor: Eine Komödie in zwei Akten (Zurich: Arche, 1966); translated by Kirkup as *The Meteor* (Chicago: Dramatic Publishing Co., 1966; London: Cape, 1973);

Vier Hörspiele (Berlin: Volk und Welt, 1967);

König Johann: Nach Shakespeare (Zurich: Arche, 1968);

Play Strindberg: Totentanz nach August Strindberg (Zurich: Arche, 1969); translated by Kirkup as *Play Strindberg* (Chicago: Dramatic Publishing Co., 1970; London: Cape, 1972);

Monstervortrag über Gerechtigkeit und Recht nebst einem helvetischen Zwischenspiel: Eine kleine Dramaturgie der Politik (Zurich: Arche, 1969); translated by John E. Woods as "A Monster Lecture on Justice and Law Together with a Helvetian Interlude: A Brief Discussion on the Dramaturgy of Politics," in

Friedrich Dürrenmatt: Plays and Essays, edited by Volkmar Sander (New York: Continuum, 1982), pp. 263–312;

Sätze aus Amerika (Zurich: Arche, 1970);

Titus Andronicus: Eine Komödie nach Shakespeare (Zurich: Arche, 1970);

Der Besuch der alten Dame: Oper in 3 Akten nach Friedrich Dürrenmatts tragischer Komödie, music by Gottfried von Einem, German text with English translation by Norman Tucker (London & New York: Boosey & Hawkes, 1971);

Der Sturz (Zurich: Arche, 1971);

Porträt eines Planeten (Zurich: Arche, 1971);

Komödien III (Zurich: Arche, 1972);

Gespräch mit Heinz Ludwig Arnold (Zurich: Arche, 1976);

Zusammenhänge: Essay über Israel. Eine Konzeption (Zurich: Arche, 1976);

Der Mitmacher: Ein Komplex. Text der Komödie, Dramaturgie, Erfahrungen, Berichte, Erzählungen (Zurich: Arche, 1976); play republished as *Der Mitmacher: Eine Komödie* (Zurich: Arche, 1978);

Die Frist: Eine Komödie (Zurich: Arche, 1977);

Dürrenmatt: Bilder und Zeichnungen, edited by Christian Strich (Zurich: Diogenes, 1978);

Friedrich Dürrenmatt Lesebuch (Zurich: Diogenes, 1978);

Albert Einstein: Ein Vortrag (Zurich: Diogenes, 1979);

Die Panne: Komödie (Zurich: Diogenes, 1979);

Werkausgabe in 30 Bänden, 30 volumes (Zurich: Diogenes, 1980)—includes final versions of *Romulus, Mississippi, Ein Engel kommt nach Babylon, Der Besuch, Frank der Fünfte, Die Physiker, Herkules, Der Mitmacher,* and *Die Frist,* and the previously unpublished *Untergang und neues Leben;*

Stoffe I–III (Zurich: Diogenes, 1981);

Die Welt als Labyrinth (Vienna: Deuticke, 1982);

Achterloo: Eine Komödie in zwei Akten (Zurich: Diogenes, 1983; revised, 1988);

Die Erde ist zu schön . . . . : Die Physiker; Der Tunnel; Das Unternehmen der Wega (Zurich: Arche, 1983);

Minotaurus: Eine Ballade mit Zeichnungen des Autors (Zurich: Diogenes, 1985);

Justiz (Zurich: Diogenes, 1985); translated by Woods as *The Execution of Justice* (New York: Random House, 1989);

Varlin, 1900–1977 (New York: Claude Bernard Gallery, 1986);

Der Auftrag oder Vom Beobachter des Beobachters der Beobachter (Zurich: Diogenes, 1986); translated by Joel Agee as *The Assignment; or, On the Observing of the Observer of the Observers* (New York: Random House, 1988);

Rollenspiele: Protokoll einer fiktiven Inszenierung und Achterloo III, by Dürrenmatt and Charlotte Kerr (Zurich: Diogenes, 1986);

Gesammelte Werke, 7 volumes, edited by Franz Josef Goertz (Zurich: Diogenes, 1988);

Versuche (Zurich: Diogenes, 1988);

Durcheinandertal: Roman (Zurich: Diogenes, 1989);

Turmbau: Stoffe IV–IX (Zurich: Diogenes, 1990);

Kants Hoffnung: Zwei politische Reden, zwei Gedichte aus dem Nachlaß (Zurich: Diogenes, 1991);

Midas, oder, Die schwarze Leinwand (Zurich: Diogenes, 1991);

Gedankenfuge (Zurich: Diogenes, 1992);

Das Mögliche ist ungeheuer: Ausgewählte Gedichte (Zurich: Diogenes, 1993);

Der Pensionierte: Fragment eines Kriminalromans, edited by Anna von Planta and Ulrich Weber (Zurich: Diogenes, 1995);

Die Schweiz, ein Gefängnis: Rede auf Vaclav Havel, with an interview of Dürrenmatt by Michael Haller (Zurich: Diogenes, 1997).

Editions in English: *Four Plays,* translated by Nellhaus and others (London: Cape, 1964; New York: Grove, 1965)—comprises *Romulus the Great, The Marriage of Mr. Mississippi, An Angel Comes to Babylon, The Physicists;*

Friedrich Dürrenmatt: Plays and Essays, edited by Volkmar Sander (New York: Continuum, 1982).

PLAY PRODUCTIONS: *Es steht geschrieben,* Zurich, Schauspielhaus, 19 April 1947;

Der Blinde, Basel, Stadttheater, 10 January 1948;

Romulus der Große, Basel, Stadttheater, 25 April 1949;

Die Ehe des Herrn Mississippi, Munich, Kammerspiele, 26 March 1952;

Nächtlicher Besuch (Nächtliches Gespräch mit einem verachteten Menschen), Zurich, Kammerspiele, 26 July 1952;

Ein Engel kommt nach Babylon, Munich, Kammerspiele, 22 December 1953;

Der Besuch der alten Dame, music by Gottfried von Einem, Zurich, Schauspielhaus, 29 January 1956;

Frank der Fünfte, music by Paul Burkhard, Zurich, Schauspielhaus, 19 March 1959;

Abendstünde im Spätherbst, Berlin Renaissancetheater, 19 November 1959;

Die Physiker, Zurich, Schauspielhaus, 20 February 1962;

Herkules und der Stall des Augias, Zurich, Schauspielhaus, 20 March 1963;

Der Meteor, Zurich, Schauspielhaus, 20 January 1966;

Die Wiedertäufer, Zurich, Schauspielhaus, 16 March 1967;

König Johann, Basel, Stadttheater, 18 September 1968;

Play Strindberg, Basel, Komödie, 8 February 1969;

Urfaust, Zurich, Schauspielhaus, 22 October 1970;

Porträt eines Planeten, Düsseldorf, Schauspielhaus, 10 November 1970;

Titus Andronicus, Düsseldorf, Schauspielhaus, 12 December 1970;

Der Mitmacher, Zurich, Schauspielhaus, 8 March 1973;

Ein Engel kommt nach Babylon: Opera in Three Acts, music by Rudolf Kelterborn, Zurich, Opera House, 5 June 1977;

Die Frist, Zurich, Kino Korso, 6 October 1977;

Die Panne, Wilhelmsbad, 13 September 1979;

Achterloo, Zurich, Schauspielhaus, 6 October 1983.

Friedrich Dürrenmatt was the leading German-language dramatist of the generation after Bertolt Brecht. He dominated German, Austrian, and Swiss repertoires and was familiar to audiences throughout Europe and North and South America. His plays reach everyone; they teem with brilliant ideas and fantastic inventions; and behind the comic-grotesque satire lies a deeply humane, urgently felt philosophical and religious impetus. He wrote not book dramas but plays to be performed. When not directing the plays himself, he regularly participated in their production, revising and rewriting in consultation with actors up to the last moment; if the performance failed to affect the audience as he thought it should, he cast the text in a new version.

His most popular plays, especially *Der Besuch der alten Dame* (The Visit of the Old Lady, 1956; adapted as *The Visit,* 1958) and *Die Physiker* (1962; translated as *The Physicists,* 1963), made him the darling of theater people and critics. But as directing styles changed and texts came to be seen as mere raw material, Dürrenmatt began to complain of inadequate performances of his works. He also found reviewers rejecting his work because it seemed uncommitted when compared to the activist message plays and documentaries that began to appear in the late 1960s. Such criticism was particularly galling to Dürrenmatt, who never tired of demonstrating in his plays the untold damage done by ideologies and their true believers.

Dürrenmatt was born on 5 January 1921 in Konolfingen, in the Emmental region of the canton of Bern, Switzerland, to Reinhold and Hulda Zimmermann Dürrenmatt. A sister, Vroni, followed in 1924. His father was pastor of the Konolfingen church, and his grandfather Ulrich Dürrenmatt had been a member of Parliament and a militantly conservative newspaper publisher who was proud to have served ten days in jail for printing a particularly vicious satiric poem on the front page. Father and grandfather left their imprint on "des Pastors Fritzli" (the pastor's boy Fritzli), as he was called by the townspeople, in his intense preoccupation with religion, his conservative cast of mind, and the hard-hitting, Swiftian satire of his plays. The tales his father recounted from classical mythology and the Bible

stories his mother told him provided material for many of his major works.

In 1933 Dürrenmatt entered the secondary school in the neighboring village of Großhochstetten; he spent his spare time in the studio of a local painter, who encouraged him to indulge his passion for painting and drawing. He pursued this activity all his life, producing undisciplined, highly dramatic pictures first of natural catastrophes and great battles of Swiss history and later of the Tower of Babel and astronomical phenomena. He was twenty-three before he decided to concentrate on writing stories and plays and to make visual art an avocation.

The family moved in 1935 to the city of Bern, where Dürrenmatt's father was appointed pastor of the Salem Hospital and the deaconess house. Dürrenmatt was enrolled at the Freies Gymnasium, a Christian secondary school, where he lasted two and a half years. A bad student, he was invited to leave. He transferred to a less rigorous private school, the Humboldtianum, from which he regularly played hooky.

In his school years he was plagued by a tyrannical and chaotic imagination. Frequent attendance at the City Theater of Bern, where his uncle, a high government official, had a loge, provided fuel for these fantasies. In 1941 a summer of concentrated work on neglected subjects—he was good at classical languages but had to make up ground in the sciences—equipped him to pass his final exams. Having been rejected by the Institute of Art, he enrolled at the University of Zurich, where for one semester he studied philosophy, literature, and natural science. He then became a student of philosophy at the University of Bern for a semester, tutoring in Greek and Latin to earn pocket money. His studies were interrupted when he was called to military duty. During basic training his bad eyesight became evident when, according to his own account, he began saluting mailmen, and he was assigned to such tasks as lettering identification tags by hand.

In 1942 he returned to the University of Zurich for two semesters, spending most of his time in the company of painters and writing plays and stories. In 1943 he fell sick with hepatitis and returned home to Bern. He spent his final four semesters of university study there, concentrating on philosophy and contemplating the possibility of a doctoral dissertation on Søren Kierkegaard and tragedy.

In 1946 he married Lotti Geißler, an actress. They settled in Basel the following year, at about the time he was completing his first radio play, *Der Doppelgänger* (The Double, 1960), which was turned down by Swiss Radio, and his first drama, *Es steht geschrieben* (It Is Written, 1947). Opening night spectators in Zurich booed the play; but reviewers recognized Dürrenmatt's powerful talent and potential, and he received a cash prize from the Welti Foundation to encourage him to continue writing plays.

Es steht geschrieben is set in Münster during the period 1534 to 1536, when the city was transformed by Anabaptists into their "New Jerusalem" and was then besieged, defeated, and sacked by a coalition of Catholic and Protestant troops. The play is a panoramic, tumultuous *theatrum mundi,* or universal theater, in the seventeenth-century mode, with more than thirty scenes and a large cast. It mixes monologues, crowd scenes, political intrigue, and religious-existential soul-searching. The language ranges from the biblically hymnic to the grotesque; it is by turns solemn, prophetic, cynical, highly figurative, apocalyptic, and disillusioning. At the center of the action are two starkly contrasting figures: Johann Bockelson, an actor, confidence man, and voluptuary who has himself crowned King David; and Bernhard Knipperdollingck, a wealthy merchant who renounces his earthly goods and, in the final scene, experiences God's grace as his limbs are broken on the wheel. The play can be read as an allegory of Nazism's rise and fall and of the suicidal fanaticism of the Germans under Hitler, or as an expression of deep pessimism over the course of Western history and of anger at the ruling powers' betrayal of the cause of peace and humanity in the sixteenth century as well as at the beginning of the post-1946 Cold War.

Es steht geschrieben is a passionate and immoderate play that poses insuperable problems for directors and actors, and in 1948 Dürrenmatt decreed that rights for its performance would no longer be granted.

Twenty years later, hoping to make it as stage-worthy as his recent successes, he reworked it as a comedy under the title *Die Wiedertäufer* (The Anabaptists, 1967). It was received without enthusiasm by audiences. The play includes large chunks of the earlier drama rearranged and reworded in a more obviously artistic way. Dürrenmatt pared away much of the figurative language and pathos and de-emphasized the play's historicity, with the effect that the farce and cruelty of real life are aesthetically transformed into dramatic satire. The religious utopia of Münster created in part 1 and its downfall in part 2 are presented as theatrical events: Bockelson is a second-rate actor who is able to persuade people, because they are so eager to believe, that he is King David; the whole thing is his show, and he is both star and director. In the end he walks away from the sack of Münster to accept an acting job, leaving the Anabaptist fools who took his fictions so seriously to their bloody fate at the hands of mercenaries who lack religious convictions but cannot tolerate the existence of a Christian community where all property is equally shared. The Anabaptists' overwrought imaginations have been fired by Bockelson's mediocre theatrical performance; but in a moment of clarity near the end they

recognize that they must believe in their ultimate victory, for otherwise all their suffering will have proven meaningless. In accord with the laws of Dürrenmattian satiric theater, events take the worst imaginable turn: greed, indifference, and unreason are victorious. The last word no longer belongs to Knipperdollingck in his mystical transport but to the one-hundred-year-old bishop of Münster, who comments in despair on this monstrous, unjust world.

When he forbade the performing of *Es steht geschrieben,* Dürrenmatt extended the interdiction, with greater justification, to his second play, *Der Blinde* (The Blind Man; published, 1947; performed, 1948). It had aroused neither outrage nor much interest in its initial production, despite outstanding direction and a fine cast, and was removed from the Basel repertoire after nine performances. Productions at two other theaters fared no better.

Where *Es steht geschrieben* is theater of the world, *Der Blinde* is theater of the mind. It revolves around the duke, whose realm lies in ruins and whose people have been killed by the ravages of the Thirty Years' War. The parallels to the Germany of the late 1940s, three hundred years later, are obvious. The duke is blind and has chosen to live according to the principle of absolute credulity; for if a blind person does not believe everyone, he must doubt everything. His antagonist is Negro da Ponte, who carries out an elaborate plot to disillusion the duke and force him to renounce his faith. Da Ponte's elaborate deceptions–having a whore play the role of an abbess and an inarticulate African native play General Wallenstein–have little effect, and his most sadistic hoax backfires: the corpse he presents to the duke as that of his daughter Octavia is revealed, to the surprise of all, to be in fact Octavia and not, as planned, the body of another. The duke's guilt and remorse–he believes himself responsible for her death–paradoxically move him to reaffirm his Christian faith. The play has not been revived or revised because it would inevitably sink under the weight of its philosophical and theological pretension. Dürrenmatt's study of the works of Kierkegaard, Karl Barth, and Jean-Paul Sartre led him to supply his characters with speeches that are paradoxical, wooden, overly metaphysical, and undramatic.

On 6 August 1947 the Dürrenmatts' first child, Peter, was born. After the failure of *Der Blinde* they could no longer afford to live in Basel; they moved to Schernelz, above the Lake of Biel, where Lotti Dürrenmatt's mother, Frau Falb, had a home. Dürrenmatt was helped financially by friends and anonymous patrons who wanted to foster his talent.

Before the move he had agreed to provide the Basel theater with a play titled "Der Turmbau zu Babel" (The Building of the Tower of Babel); the cast had been selected, and the manuscript had grown to four acts. But mature consideration forced him to destroy it. The play he quickly wrote to fulfill his obligation, *Romulus der Große* (performed, 1949; published, 1956; translated as *Romulus the Great,* 1964), became the first of his enduring theatrical successes. It is a neatly structured, fast-paced, tragicomic piece composed with the theater audience in mind and having at its center the most appealing of all Dürrenmatt's protagonists, the calm, relaxed, clear Emperor Romulus, who bears no relation to the martyrs, cynics, and overwrought ideologues of the earlier plays. It is his humane sanity that makes him great and leads to his downfall.

Romulus has reigned over Rome for twenty years as the play opens. He has been inactive, preferring to breed poultry on his country estate and to ignore the empire's deterioration. This inaction is his calculated way of bringing the Roman Empire, an institution he views as founded on war and inhumanity, to an end. The Goths are marching on Rome, and he hopes to surrender the empire to them and die at their hands. But in the greatest of the play's anticlimaxes and the worst turn of events for Romulus, the Gothic king Odoacer turns out to be his equal in intelligence and humane wisdom, hoping to surrender to Romulus and so keep the history of the Germanic nations from following its foreseeable disastrous and bloody course. The leaders are forced to accept their impotence and live on with the bitter knowledge that human affairs are being guided by the unreason of history.

The play is filled with comic ideas. Through much of it anticlimax and frustration make for laughter, and the encounters between Romulus and the shortsighted, ambitious fanatics and bureaucrats who assume that Rome must be saved provide funny and even heartwarming scenes. There is humor also in the anachronisms of this "ungeschichtliche historische Komödie" (unhistorical historical comedy), even when they are allusions to Nazi and postwar Germany.

Romulus der Große was also produced in Zurich in 1948, and in 1949 it became the first major Dürrenmatt production in Germany when the Göttingen theater performed it. Critics were stingy with praise, objecting to the anachronisms and some of the comic effects; but the play became a standard in the German-speaking theater and beyond.

Royalties did not yet amount to much, however, and the Falb household was becoming cramped as the family grew by two daughters: Barbara, born in 1949, and Ruth, born in 1951. Adding to expenses was Dürrenmatt's hospitalization for diabetes. To pay the rent on a house in Ligerz on the Lake of Biel, he turned with great success to writing detective novels. His income, augmented by royalties from radio plays, was great enough to make possible the purchase in 1952 of a house above the city of Neuchâtel in which he lived until his death.

Dürrenmatt had completed the manuscript for *Die Ehe des Herrn Mississippi* (1952; translated as *The Marriage of Mr. Mississippi,* 1966) in 1950, only to have it rejected by Swiss theaters. In 1952, however, Hans Schweikart, manager of the Munich Kammerspiele (Intimate Theater), directed the premiere, establishing Dürrenmatt in Germany as an avant-garde dramatist.

The play opens with the cliché of a political assassination carried out by men in trench coats, after which the victim stands up and notes that his death actually takes place at the end of the drama. His long monologue is one of several with which Dürrenmatt interrupts the action, breaks theatrical illusion, provides exposition, and lets his characters criticize the play itself. The stage setting, too, is designed to break illusions. Everything takes place in one room, furnished in bad taste with decorations in styles from Gothic to art deco. In the course of the play these objects are destroyed, with the exception of the coffee table set for two at center stage. Seated at this table State's Attorney Florestan Mississippi proposes marriage to Anastasia. He has murdered his wife because of her infidelity and knows that Anastasia has murdered her husband—by pouring him poisoned coffee at this table—for the same reason. His fanatical and distorted sense of justice tells him that the hell of this marriage will be fitting punishment for both of them.

Mississippi has set new records for the implementation of the death penalty and has chosen as his life's goal the institution of a perfect system of justice in the form of the Law of Moses. To match him Dürrenmatt introduces the fanatic Marxist Frédéric René Saint-Claude, who is killed at the beginning of the play and is later to be eliminated a second time, and Count Bodo von Übelohe-Zabernsee, medical missionary and fool in Christ, fanatic in regard to Christian charity and self-sacrifice. The utopian schemes of these three allegorical figures with their outlandish names are defeated when they encounter the real world. The nemesis of the three true believers, Anastasia, is an amoral femme fatale who goes to her death reaffirming her lies about her love and fidelity. Another of Dürrenmatt's memorable inventions, she is the modern counterpart of the whore of Babylon and of the medieval church's emblematic Dame World, beautiful face-on, but ugly and diseased when viewed from behind. Diego, the unscrupulous and opportunistic minister of justice, the only character to survive, emerges all-powerful from the chaos of revolution. Dürrenmatt demonstrates the bankruptcy of today's dominant ideologies by showing their adherents to be destructive fools and by giving them speeches that, in their pompous clichés and hyperbole, expose the senselessness of the doctrines. Through Anastasia and the course of affairs, the three fanatics learn that what they have done and said is without meaning or effect.

The play was praised by critics; but the next common undertaking of Dürrenmatt, Schweikart, and the ensemble of the Munich Kammerspiele, *Ein Engel kommt nach Babylon* (performed, 1953; published, 1954; translated as *An Angel Comes to Babylon,* 1964), did not measure up to the first. Productions in Düsseldorf, Zurich, and Vienna fared no better, and the premiere of the revised version in Berlin in 1957 was also a failure.

God's gift of perfect beauty and divine grace, the angel Kurrubi (Cherub), is sent to Earth to become the companion of the poorest mortal in Babylon. Things take the worst imaginable turn when her mission leads her to King Nebuchadnezzar, who, working to carry through his social reforms, is going about disguised as a beggar and falls in love with her. The paradoxical point is that Nebuchadnezzar, for all his wealth and power, is spiritually the poorest of the poor and the lowest of mortals. Kurrubi's overwhelming presence destroys all order in Babylon, and her marriage to the king is seen as the sole way to restore it. But she cannot marry a king, and he will not renounce his power for her sake. She leaves Babylon, and he, in frustration and rage against a seemingly unjust God, determines to avenge his hurt and disgrace by building the Tower. (A sequel to the drama, never completed, was to show how the Tower comes into being even though all are opposed to it.) The third major figure in this fairy-tale play is the city's last remaining beggar, Akki, who is the wisest of all Babylonians and would be the richest if he did not continually throw his earnings into the Euphrates. He makes the king, his bureaucratic henchmen, and all civic institutions look ridiculous.

The central figure of *Der Besuch der alten Dame,* the outlandish Claire Zachanassian, is a Fury from hell and the polar opposite of Kurrubi. Contrary to Dürrenmatt's own view, *Der Besuch der alten Dame* is generally regarded as his best-made play. With its simple and sharply pointed dialogue and its compressed, watchlike intricacy it is both a surefire stage success and a literary masterpiece.

Forty-five years before the play opens Claire, then known as Klari Wäscher, lost a paternity suit against Alfred Ill on the basis of perjured testimony by witnesses he bribed. Pregnant and disgraced, she was forced to leave Güllen (the name means liquid manure) and make her living as a prostitute. Since then she has, by marrying men of wealth and influence, become the richest, most notorious, and most powerful woman in the world. She has divorced husbands and taken new ones so often that she has lost count of them. The sole survivor of a plane crash in Afghanistan, she has an artificial leg and a hand made of ivory. She has secretly bought up Güllen's industries, closed them down, and so brought the town to its knees. The play opens with her triumphant return as a putative benefactress of the town. At the end of act 1, after the welcoming ceremony, she does offer the citizens one billion (in

an unspecified currency) but imposes a condition: that someone kill Alfred. In the name of humanism and humanity, the citizens indignantly reject the offer. Acts 2 and 3 show, at first in a comic way but with increasingly grotesque gruesomeness, how the Gülleners, precisely because they are only human, succumb to the temptation to live better and buy on credit and must ultimately commit the murder none of them wanted. The rationalizations and devices the townspeople contrive to justify and carry out the act make up the substance of Dürrenmatt's satiric gem.

To compel his audiences to face their own potential complicity, Dürrenmatt removes all possibility of making moral judgments and laying blame on an individual. Claire, with her vengeful misanthropy, is potentially a villain, but toward the end of the play she shows a softer, almost sentimental side; and Alfred, a thoughtless, amoral shopkeeper and Güllen's scapegoat, emerges in act 3 ennobled and ethically transformed by the recognition of his personal guilt.

The climactic scene, in which Alfred is sentenced by a vote of the men of the town and killed, is a triumph of satiric writing, presenting in a manner both comic and horrible a travesty of piety, democracy, justice, and Western values, made doubly false by the presence of press and television. Dürrenmatt is savagely castigating Europeans and Americans for their failure to create a just peace after World War II, for drifting into the Cold War, and then for losing their souls to affluence. This dismay and anger over moral depravity and religious indifference informs most of Dürrenmatt's writing after *Der Besuch der alten Dame.* His plays take on a cool, uncompromising, sometimes misanthropic tone; impersonal murderers and their stoically resigned victims speak a language stripped of poetry and rhetorical decoration.

Frank der Fünfte (Frank the Fifth; performed, 1959; published, 1960), written in collaboration with the Swiss operetta composer Paul Burkhard, represents a step in this direction. Owners and employees of the Frank family's gangster bank justify their crimes—no depositor ever gets to withdraw a penny, and those who complain are eliminated—with the excuse that they are committed to escaping the firm and leading a decent life. But all their efforts bind them closer to the institution that they despise and that has become an arena for betrayal and bloodshed. The crushing irony of the conclusion is that the widowed Ottilie Frank, who has desperately attempted to destroy the bank by confessing its criminal nature, must stand by as the government reorganizes and strengthens it and puts it in the hands of her son, Frank VI; it is now all the more pernicious and inhuman because it is run on soulless principles of law and order.

Audiences and reviewers found little to enjoy in the grotesque cruelties of this perverse world—as when the chief of personnel, Egli, is obliged to kill his fiancée for the sake of the company, and she cooperates to spare him another attack of ulcers. Frank V's end—being locked in the vault by his son—is gentle by comparison. The reviews of the Zurich premiere ranged from neutral to negative. Critics looking for leftist political commitment rejected the piece as empty of serious social comment and as a weak imitation of Brecht's *Die Dreigroschenoper* (performed, 1928; published, 1929; translated as *The Threepenny Opera,* 1964), while more conservative reviewers found it in bad taste, blasphemous, and nihilistic. On the other hand, *Frank der Fünfte* reaped nothing but praise in East Bloc countries, particularly Poland and Czechoslovakia. One can only speculate on how members of the Swiss banking industry in the Zurich audience may have felt.

Die Physiker has been second only to *Der Besuch der alten Dame* in its theatrical success in both the East and the West. Its premiere starred Therese Giehse, the original Claire Zachanassian, as Fräulein Doktor Mathilde von Zahndt; Dürrenmatt dedicated the text to Giehse and created the part for her.

Comedy, murder mystery, spy drama, love story, and a play about the problems presented by nuclear technology, *Die Physiker* is couched in straightforward language that fits its taut Aristotelian structure. Dürrenmatt artfully lures his audience into the trap of enjoying what seems a heart warming happy ending, only to show it to be mere wishful thinking and a misperception of the hard truth that events will always take the worst imaginable turn.

The nuclear physicists of the title are patients in Dr. von Zahndt's private sanatorium, each pretending to be insane. Johann Wilhelm Möbius is the scientific genius of the age; the other two, affecting to take themselves for Albert Einstein and Sir Isaac Newton, are undercover agents of the superpowers and are competing for Möbius's formulas. They fail in their mission because he has destroyed his papers; all three, in an outburst of guilt and altruism, solemnly agree to go on pretending to be insane, spend their lives in the sanatorium, and so save the world from nuclear destruction. These heroics are shown to be deluded when Dr. von Zahndt reveals herself to be a megalomaniac madwoman and boasts that she has copied the crucial formulas, giving her the power to rule the world. To make sure that the physicists can do nothing to stop her she turns the sanatorium into a high-security prison. All the physicists' careful planning, artful dissembling, and high-mindedness, and even the murder each had to commit to try to keep his identity secret, are meaningless.

In 1963 appeared *Herkules und der Stall des Augias* (translated as *Hercules and the Augean Stables,* 1963), Dürrenmatt's stage adaptation of his 1954 radio play of the same title. The transfer from one medium to the other did not make for good theater; the growing mountains of manure are not a problem on the radio but are hard to reproduce onstage, and spectators will not stand for frequent, lenghty narrative expositions. The play's burlesque of myth, realistic and sometimes anachronistic topical detail, poetry, criticism of Swiss provincialism, and flat sermonizing did not combine well.

To the original radio play Dürrenmatt added new scenes and characters, a depressing conclusion, and many ingenious theatrical ideas, indicated in lengthy stage directions. The premise is that the life of a national hero is much harder than one thinks. Hercules is no match for the caution and vacillation of King Augeas's administration: because official permission is never granted, the Augean stables never get cleaned, and Hercules is reduced to joining the circus to make ends meet. The most poignant consequence is that, owing to their inertia, the people of the Kingdom of Elis forfeit their one opportunity to bring order and beauty to their land: they cannot imagine a life without manure.

In *Der Meteor* (1966; translated as *The Meteor,* 1966), a mix of farce and *danse macabre,* the Nobel prize-winning playwright Wolfgang Schwitter is twice declared dead by medical authorities and resurrected. This situation dismays Schwitter, who is eager to die; elicits reactions ranging from the jubilation of Pastor Lutz to the rage of Schwitter's son; and leads to the demise of seven other persons. Audiences were kept breathless by the pace of the play's action and its surprise twists. On a seemingly endless hot, sunny midsummer day visitors climb the stairs to the stuffy garret where Schwitter starved as a young artist and where he has chosen to try to die after failing to do so in the hospital. He is irascible and says unexpected and hurtful things to those who confront him; it seems that the resurrected behave in an unfettered, demonic way, bringing out the worst in others. A bitter exchange between father and son is followed by the act 1 finale, in which Schwitter orders Auguste Nyffenschwander, wife of the garret's present tenant, to make love to him while her husband pounds on the locked door. Act 2 begins with the obsequies beside his bier, after which Schwitter sits up, takes off the chin support, and drinks brandy and smokes cigars while the just and the unjust continue to die around him. In the play's final scene, a manic variant of the opening one, the Salvation Army, playing and singing the Hallelujah Chorus, comes to Schwitter's bedside led by Major Friedli, who brings Schwitter's anger to the exploding point by solemnly pronouncing that he is called to eternal life. Schwitter curses all life in the vilest imaginable way, throttles the major, and runs off as darkness falls.

The Zurich premiere and the two major German productions that followed were successes, and *Der Meteor* was played soon thereafter on the major stages of the world, bucking the growing trend toward documentary political activism. The play offers one magnificent role in its central character and several challenging secondary ones. Most critics admired Dürrenmatt's imaginative power, even those who did not know what to make of the final scene: one thought it a failed effort at profundity, others found it anticlimactic, and a few objected to the irreverence toward the Salvation Army.

In late 1967 Dürrenmatt became comanager with Werner Düggelin at the Basel Stadttheater (City Theater). The collaboration continued until April 1969, when, after a long and severe illness and because of disagreements with the Basel administration, he withdrew. After that he declined to accept a position with responsibilities of that sort, being content to sit on the board of directors of the Zurich theater and occasionally to direct a production of his own work.

König Johann (1968), based on William Shakespeare's *The Life and Death of King John* (circa 1595), transforms an historical play chronicling events of the thirteenth century into a comedy dealing with power politics within any system, be it feudalism, communism, capitalism, or Cold War maneuvering. Dürrenmatt shows how the machinery functions at the top and refers only in passing to the thousands who are slaughtered for the benefit of royal houses, the church, or other institutions.

Dürrenmatt's title figure is not the weak and cruel monarch of the original, thanks to the influence of Philipp the Bastard—who, again like his high-living Shakespearean counterpart, is a clear-eyed reformer urging his king to see reason. Each of their combined efforts to improve the world backfires as it elicits reaction from entrenched powers, and Johann finally pronounces his own death sentence by proclaiming the birth of an heir. With the king poisoned and replaced by an infant, the lords of the realm are free to pillage and kill. Dürrenmatt's point, as in many of his plays, is that even those who see and understand are powerless to alter the catastrophic and bloody course of history, for any action they take only makes matters worse.

Dürrenmatt used Shakespearean blank verse, eliminated some characters, tightened up the action, shortened and eliminated speeches, and changed characters and motivations. Under his hand the drama becomes transparent and compelling to modern audiences, applicable to any historical situation. To transform Shakespearean tragedy into Dürrenmattian comedy he added ludicrous situations and farcical stage business. Deals are made while characters are being shaved or sitting in bathtubs; Johann crawls under the covers with the cardinal to escape the cold of an unheated English castle, illustrating the German figure of speech "unter einer Decke stecken" (to be under the same blanket—that is, in cahoots—with someone). Audiences and reviewers greeted the premiere enthusiastically.

Dürrenmatt's other Shakespeare adaptation, *Titus Andronicus* (1970), was a failure. The audience booed during the performance, and critical rejection was unanimous.

Shakespeare's play includes episodes of such unmitigated horror—mutilation, rape, murder, and cannibalism—that some scholars have argued that it must be attributed to a lesser playwright. Dürrenmatt has made the play even more shocking by condensing the five acts into nine scenes, thereby eliminating the lamentations of the victims and their loved ones and leaving only the brutality. At the close of the final scene, in which Tamora has been served her two sons in a meat pie and five murders of vengeance have been committed, Alaric, King of the Goths, a figure added by Dürrenmatt, provides a bitter commentary on the brevity and meaninglessness of human existence that replaces the optimistic closing lines delivered by Lucius in Shakespeare's play.

Dürrenmatt's most successful adaptation was *Play Strindberg* (1969; translated, 1970), subtitled *Totentanz nach August Strindberg* (Dance of Death, after August Strindberg) and based on part 1 and the end of part 2 of Strindberg's *Dödsdansen* (Dance of Death, 1901). The piece has been played on major stages in Europe and America. Using a rough translation and keeping the key dramatic situation of two people trapped in the hell of their marriage, Dürrenmatt strips the original of all psychology, pathos, and philosophizing. He transforms the action into a cooled-down, ritualistic combat between Alice and Edgar played on an arena stage and divided like a boxing match into rounds, each beginning and ending with a bell. As codirector of the premiere Dürrenmatt worked closely with the cast and made revisions on the basis of their experience at rehearsals. The play is a challenge for actors: the speeches are seldom longer than five words, and frequent pauses give the actors the chance to fill the gaps with inventions of their own. It seems painfully difficult for Alice, Edgar, and their guest Kurt to keep their conversations from foundering on a gratuitous insult, indifference, or boredom. Dürrenmatt's text is filled with ideas for stage business—Alice's needlepoint, card games, piano playing, dancing, painting fingernails, building a house of cards, telegraphy—that often seem incommensurate with the words spoken. The effect of burlesque artificiality is heightened by the formal announcement of title and number for each round. There is a photo album scene, a visit scene, and two laughably insipid philosophy scenes. Edgar suffers a stroke and lacks the power of speech for the last four rounds, but his wife fluently translates his babbling into phrases he has earlier used over and over. *Play Strindberg* seems to be an expression of unmitigated misanthropic malice; but it is, at the same time, quite funny, particularly if the performers have a good sense of timing.

Like *Play Strindberg, Porträt eines Planeten* (Portrait of a Planet; performed, 1970; published, 1971) has a tone of heartless ferocity. The play is framed by opening and closing scenes set in a timeless infinity. Four gods, one of them hard of hearing, note with total detachment in the first scene that a once stable sun is turning into a supernova and in the last scene that it has disappeared. Inside this frame Dürrenmatt presents, with no blackouts, curtains, or intermission, a series of vignettes showing that life on Earth is doomed because the sun is exploding and because its inhabitants are governed by the death instinct; in Dürrenmatt's words, the play is a dance of death within a dance of death. At the outset a group of European women are trying to wean cannibals from human flesh to the meat of animals through sexual bribery, only to have a shipwreck defeat their efforts. Further sketches, delimited by slight changes in costume or the introduction of new props and all played by the same eight actors, deal with genocide, racial hatred, the Vietnam War, the drug culture, and two astronauts stranded on the moon whose dying words are of interest to the government only if they can be exploited in the promotion of a grandiose Mars program. Everything under this sun is futile and perverse: soldiers die in vain in the jungle, families squabble over nothing, and the earth is on the verge of annihilation.

Porträt eines Planeten is subverted *theatrum mundi* in radically abbreviated form. Its twenty-five scenes give the impression of a comprehensive panorama of human life, but its curt diction and impersonality of tone convey a message that is the opposite of seventeenth-century theater of the world: human nature is incurably perverse and human events are governed by chance and unreason. It is this nihilistic pessimism, unleavened by comedy, that put off audiences and critics at the premiere in Düsseldorf and again in Zurich, where Dürrenmatt himself directed a revised version.

In 1972 the Zurich Schauspielhaus offered Dürrenmatt the position of managing director. He declined and simultaneously resigned from its board of directors on the grounds that he was occupied with a new play, *Der Mitmacher* (The Accomplice; performed, 1973; published, 1976).

In mood *Der Mitmacher* is even bleaker than its predecessor. Rather than universal and cosmic, it is theater at its most spare and hermetic, set in a cell-like chamber deep underground in Manhattan, where the central figure, Doc, lives and works. The remaining characters, all with monosyllabic names such as Boss, Cop, Ann, and Joe, call on him, introducing themselves and providing exposition at length to the audience and then engaging in dialogues as terse and telegraphic as any Dürrenmatt has written. All these people are caught up in the operation of a business somewhat like Murder Incorporated. In the course of the play all are killed except for Doc, the accomplice, who suffers the most severe punishment: he must go on living in the worst of all conceivable worlds, stripped of human dignity and servicing the mass-producing death machine he invented and installed. The others were annihilated while

trying to stop it; on the other hand, Doc's escape attempts have only trapped him more firmly, like a fly on flypaper.

A biochemist and intellectual, even though he reads comic books, Doc has a grudge against the world that moves him to offer the firm his services and his invention, the necrodialysator, which eliminates the dead bodies that have been creating a pollution problem and threatening the company with bankruptcy. The machine dissolves and flushes away the cadavers and so opens the way for an increased volume of business. The company is treated like any other business by the government because everyone up through the Supreme Court is on the take. The world of *Der Mitmacher* is several shades darker than the one Claire Zachanassian saw operating on the principles of a brothel; in his later years Dürrenmatt viewed prostitution and procuring as honest professions in contrast to the absolute corruption of modern society. In the end the company, like Frank VI's rehabilitated gangster bank, becomes so essential to the nation's social and economic health that it must be nationalized.

Doc's workshop is sparsely furnished and glaringly illuminated by neon lights. Twice the audience hears recorded strains of Vivaldi, but the main sound effect is a repeated flushing noise. The most prominent props are the crates in which the bodies are delivered. Toward the end the refrigerating system stops functioning while corpses accumulate. As these decompose, the stage becomes a stinking charnel house, attracting flies and rats, a far worse place than Güllen or the Augean Stables. Doc survives, but to do so he has had to necrodyalize both his beloved, Ann, and his son, Bill.

Reviews of the Zurich premiere and of the Mannheim performance eight months later commended the cast but found the play disappointing, some making the obvious comparison with the more humane Samuel Beckett. The Zurich production was plagued by disagreements between its director—the Polish filmmaker Andrzej Wajda, whose German was not strong—and the author. Wajda ultimately withdrew; Dürrenmatt replaced him shortly before the first performance, which proved incomprehensible to the audience. In addition, Boss delivers some lines scourging the hypocrisy of intellectuals—and, by implication, of reviewers—which called forth an ovation on opening night but did little to improve Dürrenmatt's strained relationship with the critics.

On 20 November 1975 Generalissimo Francisco Franco, the Spanish dictator, finally succumbed after his death had been held at bay for weeks by the efforts of thirty doctors so that the transfer of power could take place without civil war. These events provide the framework for Dürrenmatt's *Die Frist* (The Moratorium, 1977), in which he comments on the lust for power, the medical profession, the Church, the Holocaust, the use and abuse of television, and feminism in a manner that is at once farcical, mythical, and grotesque.

The drama is haunted throughout by the unseen presence of the Generalissimo and by the ground bass of his groans carried over a loudspeaker as doctors perform a heart transplant and a stomach resection without anaesthesia. The action is dominated by Exzellenz, the chief executive, who bears a strong resemblance to Henry Kissinger. In part 1, set in the throne room that has been the Generalissimo's office, Exzellenz outmaneuvers the secret service thanks to his tactical acumen and sense of realpolitik. Part 2 takes place in the same room, which has been totally transformed by the installation of medical devices and television control apparatus with monitors and technical directors. The second part, which deals with the general's death, is a triumph of theatrical ingenuity and satiric imagination, mixing European Cup soccer and the rite of supreme unction, the dying process and its exploitation as a media event, farcical family bickering and the battle for power between two dynasties. Like so many of Dürrenmatt's talented politicians, Exzellenz checkmates himself in the end. As he dies, he sees to it that Dr. Goldbaum—a concentration camp survivor, Nobel laureate patterned after Andrey Sakharov, and one of two decent persons in the play and therefore not the ideal candidate—is made head of the new government. Exzellenz's dying words of advice, that if Goldbaum does not become inhuman, then the country will become even more monstrous than it is, offer little hope.

Even more unsettling is the play's finale, which belongs to the Immortals, the most fantastic and grotesque of all the drama's inventions. These bloated, Furylike figures, dressed in tattered costumes taken from a Goya painting, are the Generalissimo's female ancestors. They have haunted the background throughout the play, carrying off a cameraman and trying to kill the heiress to the throne. These metaphysical, manhating hags, resembling the Graeae of Greek mythology, pronounce their curses on everything male, including God the Father, in a rhymed line form reminiscent of the last choruses of Johann Wolfgang von Goethe's *Faust II* (1832) and ending with a vicious travesty of the concluding Chorus Mysticus, distorting Goethe's hymn to the feminine principle into the nihilistic proclamation that the feminine aspires only to eternity and sterility—whereupon they collapse and die, and the curtain falls.

The premiere in Zurich and a second production in Basel not long after pleased neither audiences nor reviewers. The director Kazmierz Dejmek, not fluent in German and working with a weak cast, presented an unimaginative mise-en-scène in Zurich; and in Basel, Hans Neuenfels, a believer in directorial theater, distorted the text, using it as an occasion to realize his idiosyncratic theatrical conceptions.

On 16 January 1983 Dürrenmatt's wife, Lotti, died. In October of that year he met Charlotte Kerr, a former actress who had become a filmmaker and journalist; they were married on 8 May 1984. Together they made a four-and-a-half-hour film titled *Porträt eines Planeten: Von und mit Friedrich Dürrenmatt* (Portrait of a Planet: By and with Friedrich Dürrenmatt), a documentary about Dürrenmatt at work and at leisure, broadcast on German television on 26 December 1984.

Dürrenmatt's final drama, *Achterloo* (1983)—the title is a place-name from a children's rhyme—underwent four revisions, the definitive one prepared especially for the 1988 Schwetzingen Festival. It is Dürrenmatt's last word and his most ambitious play, an intricately woven, all-encompassing, fantastic work in the *theatrum mundi* tradition. The characters are inmates of a psychiatric hospital for whom the play serves as therapy. From this narrow base it reaches out, as patients assume various identities, to cover Western history since 1300; the conclusion goes back as far as Old Testament times. To keep this profusion from flying apart, Dürrenmatt bases the plot on events in Poland on 12 and 13 December 1981, when, to prevent the Solidarity labor union from challenging the communist system, to keep Soviet tanks from invading Poland, and to avert any consequent American retaliation, Prime Minister Wojcieck Jaruzelski declared a national emergency and installed a military government. The patient dressed as Napoleon plays Jaruzelski, a master political tactician like Exzellenz in *Die Frist*. He makes the best of a bad situation, maintains the status quo, and spares the world a nuclear war by exploiting the corruption and delusions of the opposing powers. Two patients costumed as Karl Marx represent the Soviets, while "Benjamin Franklin" stands for the United States, "Jan Hus" for Lech Walesa, "Cardinal Richelieu" for Josef Cardinal Glemp, and "Georg Büchner" for Dürrenmatt; another patient plays Joan of Arc. Thus, the Cold War, nuclear warfare, the Roman Catholic church's political activity, Marxism, capitalism, and feminism are allegorically linked to the French Revolution, the persecution of the Huguenots, and the Reformation. Both Büchner and Dürrenmatt have given eloquent expression to a deeply pessimistic view of human history; the play's Büchner-Dürrenmatt figure, who has spent most of his time at a desk writing the play as it goes along, takes this sense of despair and futility to heart. Exiting for the last time he announces that he will write nothing more.

The play's concluding episode is the most visionary, tantalizing, and depressing of all, because it is a parable of the defeat of love by the instinct of aggression. The patients costumed as Joan of Arc and Napoleon reenact the Old Testament story in which Judith, the Israelite heroine, wins the love of the Babylonian general Holofernes and then, according to plan, decapitates him. Just as it seems that the Achterloo couple has broken the spell of the historical archetype that calls for blood revenge, just as they seem ready to let their love lead to peace between nations, he unaccountably throws her to the ground, and she shoots him in the back. Then, for the first time in a Dürrenmatt theater-of-the-world play, the normally obligatory figure of God appears on stage. The woman who has been playing Cardinal Richelieu, now attired in a dinner jacket, announces that she is God and that she has died. Hers is the play's last line: "Ich war der Liebe Gott," a double entendre meaning either "I was the dear God" or "I was the God of love."

In 1988 Dürrenmatt announced his decision to abandon the theater. He died at his home on 14 December 1990. *Der Besuch der alten Dame* and *Die Physiker* are still among the most frequently performed plays in Germany, showing that vintage Dürrenmatt continues to be successful. It remains for perceptive directors, players, and critics to help audiences appreciate his later work. Dürrenmatt won the Literature Prize of the City of Bern for *Ein Engel kommt nach Babylon* in 1954; the Radio Play Prize of the War Blind for *Die Panne* in 1957; the Prix Italia for *Abendstunde im Spätherbst* and the Literature Prize of the *Tribune de Lausanne* for *Die Panne* in 1958; the New York Theater Critics' Prize for *The Visit* and the Schiller Prize from the city of Mannheim in 1959; the Great Prize of the Swiss Schiller Foundation in 1960; the Grillparzer Prize of the Austrian Academy of Sciences in 1968; the Great Literature Prize of the Canton of Bern and an honorary doctorate from Temple University in 1969; honorary membership in Ben-Gurion University, Israel, in 1974; the Buber-Rosenzweig Medal of the German Coordinating Council for Christian-Jewish Cooperation and honorary doctorates from the University of Nice and Hebrew University in Jerusalem in 1977; the Great Literature Prize of the City of Bern in 1979; an honorary doctorate from the University of Zurich in 1983; the Carl Zuckmayer Medal of the State of Rheinland-Pfalz in 1984; the Bavarian Prize for Literature (Jean Paul Prize) in 1985; the Premio Letterario Internatione Monello (Sicily) for *Justiz*, the Georg Büchner Prize of the German Academy for Language and Literature, and an honorary Schiller Memorial Prize from the State of Baden-Württemberg in 1986; the International Prize for Humor and Satire, "Hitar Petar," awarded by the Bulgarian International Museum of Humor and Satire, Gabrovo, in 1987; and the Prix Alexei Tolstoi for his total oeuvre from Association internationale des Ecrivains de Romans Policiers in 1988.

Letters:

Peter Rüedi, ed., *Briefwechsel: Max Frisch, Friedrich Dürrenmatt* (Zurich: Diogenes, 1998).

Interviews:

Horst Bieneck, *Werkstattgespräche mit Schriftstellern* (Munich: Deutscher Taschenbuch Verlag, 1965), pp. 120–136;

Violet Ketels, "Friedrich Dürrenmatt at Temple University: Interview," *Journal of Modern Literature,* 1, no. 1 (1971): 88–108;

Heinz Ludwig Arnold, *Friedrich Dürrenmatt im Gespräch mit Heinz Ludwig Arnold* (Zurich: Arche, 1976);

Dieter Fringeli, *Nachdenken mit und über Friedrich Dürrenmatt: Ein Gespräch* (Breitenbach: Jeger-Moll, 1977);

Fritz Raddatz, "Ich bin der finsterste Komödienschreiber, den es gibt: Ein Zeit-Gespräch mit Friedrich Dürrenmatt," *Die Zeit,* 23 August 1985, pp. 13–14;

Michael Haller, ed., *Über die Grenzen: Friedrich Dürrenmatt* (Zurich: Pendo, 1990);

Arnold, ed., *Gespräche, 1961–1990,* 4 volumes (Zurich: Diogenes, 1996).

Bibliographies:

Elly Wilbert-Collins, *A Bibliography of Four Contemporary German-Swiss Authors: Friedrich Dürrenmatt, Max Frisch, Robert Walser, Albin Zollinger* (Bern: Francke, 1967);

Johannes Hansel, *Friedrich Dürrenmatt: Bibliographie* (Bad Homburg: Gehlen, 1968).

References:

Armin Arnold, *Friedrich Dürrenmatt* (Berlin: Colloquium, 1969);

Arnold, ed., *Zu Friedrich Dürrenmatt: Interpretationen* (Stuttgart: Klett, 1982);

Heinz Ludwig Arnold, *Querfahrt mit Dürrenmatt* (Göttingen: Wallstein, 1990);

Arnold, ed., *Friedrich Dürrenmatt I,* second edition (Munich: Beck, 1980);

Arnold, ed., *Friedrich Dürrenmatt II* (Munich: Beck, 1977);

Gottfried Benn, Elisabeth Brock-Sulzer, Fritz Buri, Reinhold Grimm, Hans Mayer, and Werner Oberle, *Der unbequeme Dürrenmatt* (Basel & Stuttgart: Basilius, 1962);

Thomas Berger, *Friedrich Dürrenmatt: Der Verdacht, Die Panne: Interpretationen und Materialien* (Hollfeld/Ofr.: Beyer, 1990);

Ned Bobkoff, "After the Visit, the Ruins," in *New Theatre Vistas,* edited by Judy Lee Oliva (New York: Garland, 1996), pp. 135–147;

Véronique Brandner, *Der andere Dürrenmatt: auf der Brücke zwischen zwei Welten* (Frankfurt am Main & New York: Peter Lang, 1993);

Brock-Sulzer, *Dürrenmatt in unserer Zeit: Eine Werk-interpretation nach Selbstzeugnissen* (Basel: Reinhardt, 1968);

Brock-Sulzer, *Friedrich Dürrenmatt: Stationen seines Werkes* (Zurich: Arche, 1960);

Martin Burkard, *Dürrenmatt und das Absurde: Gestalt und Wandlung des Labyrinthischen in seinem Werk* (Bern & New York: Peter Lang, 1991);

Edson M. Chick, *Dances of Death: Wedekind, Brecht, Dürrenmatt and the Satiric Tradition* (Columbia, S.C.: Camden House, 1984), pp. 107–133;

Mark E. Cory, "Shakespeare and Dürrenmatt: From Tragedy to Tragicomedy," *Comparative Literature,* 32 (Summer 1981): 253–273;

Roger A. Crockett, *Understanding Friedrich Dürrenmatt* (Columbia: University of South Carolina Press, 1998);

Donald Daviau, "Justice in the Works of Friedrich Dürrenmatt," *Kentucky Foreign Language Quarterly,* 9, no. 4 (1962): 181–193;

Daviau, "The Role of *Zufall* in the Writings of Friedrich Dürrenmatt," *Germanic Review,* 47 (November 1972): 281–293;

Peter Demetz, *Postwar German Literature: A Critical Introduction* (New York: Schocken, 1972), pp. 147–162;

Ernst S. Dick, "Dürrenmatts Dramaturgie des Einfalls: *Der Besuch der alten Dame* und *Der Meteor,*" in *Europäische Komödie,* edited by H. Mainusch (Darmstadt: Wissenschaftliche Buchgesellschaft, 1990), pp. 389–435;

Edward Diller, "Aesthetics and the Grotesque: Friedrich Dürrenmatt," *Wisconsin Studies in Contemporary Literature,* 7 (Autumn 1966): 328–335;

Diller, "Friedrich Dürrenmatt's Chaos and Calvinism," *Monatshefte,* 63 (1971): 28–40;

Diller, "Friedrich Dürrenmatt's Theological Concept of History," *German Quarterly,* 40 (May 1967): 363–371;

Joseph A. Frederico, "The Political Philosophy of Friedrich Dürrenmatt," *Göttingen Studien zur Rechtsgeschichte,* 12 (February 1989): 91–109;

Bodo Fritzen and Heimy F. Taylor, eds., *Friedrich Dürrenmatt: A Collection of Critical Essays* (Normal, Ill.: Applied Literature Press, 1979);

Heinrich Goertz, *Friedrich Dürrenmatt: Mit Selbstzeugnissen und Bilddokumenten* (Reinbek: Rowohlt, 1987);

Sigrun Gottwald, *Der mutige Narr im dramatischen Werk Friedrich Dürrenmatts* (New York: Peter Lang, 1983);

Todd C. Hamlin, "The English Translations of Friedrich Dürrenmatt and Max Frisch: Evolution and Evaluation," *Translation Review,* 40 (1992): 30–43;

Robert B. Heilman, "Tragic Elements in a Dürrenmatt Comedy," *Modern Drama,* 10 (May 1967): 11–16;

Robert E. Helbling, "The Function of the 'Grotesque' in Dürrenmatt," *Satire Newsletter,* 4 (Fall 1966): 11–19;

Urs Jenny, *Friedrich Dürrenmatt* (Velber: Friedrich, 1965);

Gerhard Knapp, *Friedrich Dürrenmatt,* second edition (Stuttgart: Metzler, 1993);

Knapp, ed., *Friedrich Dürrenmatt: Studien zu seinem Werk* (Heidelberg: Stiehm, 1976);

Knapp and Gerd Labroisse, eds., *Facetten: Studien zum 60. Geburtstag Friedrich Dürrenmatts* (Bern: Lang, 1981);

Jan Knopf, *Friedrich Dürrenmatt* (Munich: Beck, 1980);

Moshe Lazar, ed., *Play Dürrenmatt* (Malibu, Cal.: Undena, 1983);

Hans Mayer, *Dürrenmatt und Frisch: Anmerkungen* (Pfullingen: Neske, 1963);

Erna K. Neuse, "Das Rhetorische in Dürrenmatts Besuch der alten Dame: Zur Funktion des Dialogs im Drama," *Seminar,* 11 (November 1975): 225–241;

Murray B. Peppard, *Friedrich Dürrenmatt* (New York: Twayne, 1969);

Eli Pfefferkorn, "Dürrenmatt's Mass Play," *Modern Drama,* 12 (May 1969): 30–37;

Ulrich Profitlich, *Friedrich Dürrenmatt: Komödienbegriff und Komödienstruktur: Eine Einführung* (Stuttgart: Kohlhammer, 1973);

Margaret Scanlan, "Terror as Usual in Friedrich Dürrenmatt's *The Assignment,*" *Modern Language Quarterly,* 52 (March 1991): 86–99;

Hans-Jürgen Syberberg, *Zum Drama Friedrich Dürrenmatts: Zwei Modellinterpretationen zur Wesensdeutung des modernen Dramas* (Munich: Uni-Druck, 1974);

Timo Tiusanen, *Dürrenmatt: A Study in Plays, Prose, Theory* (Princeton: Princeton University Press, 1977);

Hans Wagener, ed., *Friedrich Dürrenmatt, Romulus der Große: Erläuterungen und Dokumente* (Stuttgart: Reclam, 1985);

Kenneth S. Whitton, *Der Besuch der alten Dame and Die Physiker* (London: Grant & Cutler, 1994);

Whitton, *Dürrenmatt: Reinterpretation in Retrospect* (New York: Berg, 1990);

Whitton, *The Theatre of Friedrich Dürrenmatt: A Study in the Possibilities of Freedom* (Atlantic Highlands, N.J.: Humanities Press, 1980);

Peter Wyrsch, "Die Dürrenmatt-Story," *Schweizer Illustrierte,* no. 12 (18 March 1963): 23–25; no. 13 (25 March 1963): 23–25; no. 14 (1 April 1963): 23–25; no. 15 (8 April 1963): 23–25; no. 16 (15 April 1963): 37–39; no. 17 (22 April 1963): 37–39.

Papers:

Friedrich Dürrenmatt's papers are at the Schwizerische Literaturarchiv (Swiss Literature Archive) in Bern. The Reiss AG, Theaterverlag, Zurich, has an archive of reviews of his works and other materials.

Theodor Fontane

(30 December 1819 – 20 September 1898)

Glenn Guidry
Saint Meinrad Seminary

This entry originally appeared in DLB 129: Nineteenth-Century
German Writers, 1841–1900.

BOOKS: *Männer und Helden: Acht Preußenlieder* (Berlin: Hayn, 1850);

Von der schönen Rosamunde: Gedicht (Dessau: Katz, 1850);

Gedichte (Berlin: Reimarus, 1851; enlarged edition, Berlin: Hertz, 1875; enlarged, 1889; enlarged, 1891; enlarged edition, Berlin: Besser, 1898);

Ein Sommer in London (Dessau: Katz, 1854);

Aus England: Studien und Briefe über Londoner Theater, Kunst und Presse (Stuttgart: Ebner & Seubert, 1860);

Jenseit des Tweed: Bilder und Briefe aus Schottland (Berlin: Springer, 1860); translated by Brian Battershaw as *Across the Tweed: A Tour of Mid-Victorian Scotland* (London: Phoenix House, 1965);

Balladen (Berlin: Hertz, 1861);

Wanderungen durch die Mark Brandenburg: Die Grafschaft Ruppin; Barnim-Teltow (Berlin: Hertz, 1862);

Wanderungen durch die Mark Brandenburg: Zweiter Teil Das Oderland; Barnim; Lebus (Berlin: Hertz, 1863);

Deutsche Inschriften an Haus und Gerät: Zur epigrammatischen Volkspoesie, anonymous, attributed to Fontane (Berlin: Hertz, 1865);

Der Schleswig-Holsteinische Krieg im Jahre 1864 (Berlin: Decker, 1866);

Der deutsche Krieg von 1866, 3 volumes (Berlin: Decker, 1870–1871);

Kriegsgefangen: Erlebtes 1870 (Berlin: Decker, 1871);

Aus den Tagen der Occupation: Eine Osterreise durch Nordfrankreich und Elsaß-Lothringen, 1871, 2 volumes (Berlin: Decker, 1872);

Wanderungen durch die Mark Brandenburg: Dritter Teil. Havelland; die Landschaft um Spandau, Potsdam, Brandenburg (Berlin: Hertz, 1873);

Der Krieg gegen Frankreich, 1870–1871, 2 volumes (Berlin: Decker, 1873–1876);

Vor dem Sturm: Roman aus dem Winter 1812 auf 13, 4 volumes (Berlin: Hertz, 1878); translated by R. J. Hollingdale as *Before the Storm: A Novel of the Winter of 1812–13* (Oxford: Oxford University Press, 1985);

Grete Minde: Nach einer altmärkischen Chronik (Berlin: Hertz, 1880);

Ellernklipp: Nach einem Harzer Kirchenbuch (Berlin: Hertz, 1881);

Wanderungen durch die Mark Brandenburg: Vierter Teil. Spreeland; Beeskow-Storkow und Barnim-Teltow (Berlin: Hertz, 1882);

L'Adultera: Novelle (Breslau: Schottländer, 1882); translated by Gabriele Annan as *The Woman Taken in Adultery,* in *The Woman Taken in Adultery and The Poggenpuhl Family* (Chicago: University of Chicago Press, 1979);

Schach von Wuthenow: Erzählung aus der Zeit des Regiments Gensdarmes (Leipzig: Friedrich, 1883); translated by E. M. Valk as *A Man of Honor* (New York: Ungar, 1975);

Graf Petöfy: Roman (Dresden & Leipzig: Dürselen, 1884);

Christian Friedrich Scherenberg und das literarische Berlin von 1840 bis 1860 (Berlin: Hertz, 1885);

Unterm Birnbaum (Berlin: Grote, 1885);

Cécile: Roman (Berlin: Dominik, 1887);

Irrungen, Wirrungen: Roman (Leipzig: Steffens, 1888); translated by Katherine Royce as *Trials and Tribulations,* in *German Fiction: J. W. von Goethe, Gottfried Keller, Theodor Fontane, Theodor Storm* (New York: Collier, 1917); translated by Sandra Morris as *A Suitable Match* (London & Glasgow: Blackie, 1968);

Fünf Schlösser: Altes und Neues aus der Mark Brandenburg (Berlin: Hertz, 1889);

Gesammelte Romane und Novellen, 12 volumes (volumes 1–5, Berlin: Deutsche Verlagshandlung; volumes 6–12, Berlin: Fontane, 1890–1891);

Stine (Berlin: Fontane, 1890); translated by Harry Steinhauer as *Stine,* in *Twelve German Novellas* (Berkeley: University of California Press, 1977);

Quitt: Roman (Berlin: Hertz, 1891);

Unwiederbringlich: Roman (Berlin: Hertz, 1892); translated by Douglas Parée as *Beyond Recall* (London & New York: Oxford University Press, 1964);

Frau Jenny Treibel oder "Wo sich Herz zum Herzen find't": Roman (aus der Berliner Gesellschaft) (Berlin: Fontane, 1893); translated by Ulf Zimmermann as *Jenny Treibel* (New York: Ungar, 1976);

Meine Kinderjahre: Autobiographischer Roman (Berlin: Fontane, 1894);

Von, vor und nach der Reise: Plaudereien und kleine Geschichten (Berlin: Fontane, 1894);

Effi Briest: Roman (Berlin: Fontane, 1895); translated by William A. Cooper as "Effi Briest," in *The German Classics of the Nineteenth and Twentieth Centuries,* volume 12, edited by Kuno Francke and William Guild Howard (New York: German Publication Society, 1914), pp. 217–451;

Die Poggenpuhls: Roman (Berlin: Fontane, 1896); translated by Annan as *The Poggenpuhl Family,* in *The Woman Taken in Adultery and The Poggenpuhl Family* (Chicago: University of Chicago Press, 1979);

Von Zwanzig bis Dreißig: Autobiographisches (Berlin: Fontane, 1898);

Der Stechlin: Roman (Berlin: Fontane, 1899);

Causerien über Theater, edited by Paul Schlenther (Berlin: Fontane, 1905); enlarged as *Plaudereien über Theater: 20 Jahre Königliches Schauspielhaus 1870–1890,* edited by Theodor and Friedrich Fontane (Berlin: Fontane, 1926);

Gesammelte Werke, 22 volumes (Berlin: Fontane, 1905–1911);

Aus dem Nachlaß von Theodor Fontane, edited by Josef Ettlinger (Berlin: Fontane, 1908)—comprises "Mathilde Möhring: Roman," "Gedicht-Nachlese," "Literarische Studien und Eindrücke," "Das Märker und das Berlinertum: Ein kultur-historisches Problem";

Theodor Fontanes engere Welt: Aus dem Nachlaß, edited by Mario Krammer (Berlin: Collignon, 1920);

Gesammelte Werke: Jubiläumsausgabe, 10 volumes, edited by Schlenther (Berlin: Fischer, 1920);

Gesamtausgabe der erzählenden Schriften, 9 volumes, edited by Schlenther (Berlin: Fischer, 1925);

Allerlei Gereimtes, edited by Wolfgang Rost (Dresden: Reißner, 1932);

Kritische Jahre–Kritikerjahre: Autobiographische Brüchstücke aus den Handschriften, edited by Conrad Höfer (Eisenach: Kühner, 1934);

Bilderbuch aus England, edited by Hanns Martin Elster (Berlin: Grote, 1938);

Aus meiner Werkstatt: Unbekanntes und Unveröffentlichtes, edited by Albrecht Gaertner (Berlin: Das Neue Berlin Verlags-Gesellschaft, 1949);

Sämtliche Werke, 28 volumes, edited by Edgar Gross (Munich: Nymphenburger Verlagshandlung, 1959–1962);

Schriften zur Literatur, edited by Hans-Heinrich Reuter (Berlin: Aufbau, 1960);

Sämtliche Werke, 6 volumes, edited by Walter Keitel (Munich: Hanser, 1962);

Gesamtausgabe, 10 volumes, edited by Reuter (Berlin: Aufbau, 1970).

Edition in English: *Journeys to England in Victoria's Early Days,* translated by Dorothy Harrison (London: Massie, 1939).

OTHER: *Deutsches Dichter-Album,* edited by Fontane (Berlin: Jancke, 1852);

Argo Belletristisches Jahrbuch für 1854, edited by Fontane and Friedrich Kugler (Dessau: Katz, 1854);

Wilhelm von Merckel, *Kleine Studien,* preface by Fontane (Berlin: Enslin, 1863).

SELECTED PERIODICAL PUBLICATIONS–UNCOLLECTED: "Das schottische Hochland und seine Bewohner," *Europa,* 16, no. 2 (1860): 509;

"Die alten englischen und schottischen Balladen," *Morgenblatt für Gebildete Leser,* 10 January 1861, pp. 6–10;

"Reisebrief aus Jütland," *Neue Preußische Zeitung,* 6 March 1864, pp. 3–5;

"Paul Heyse: Ein Liebling der Musen," *Gartenlaube,* 15, no. 36 (1867): 9–34;

"Gustav Freytag: *Die Ahnen,*" Vossische Zeitung, 21 February 1875, pp. 8–9;

"Heinrich Seidel: *Aus der Heimat,*" *Vossische Zeitung,* 14 March 1875, pp. 4–5;

"Zwei Bilder in der Commandantenstraße," *Die Gegenwart,* 5, no. 51 (1876): 406–412;

"Gesammelte Schriften von Theodor Storm," *Vossische Zeitung,* 14 January 1877, pp. 13–14;

"Baltisches Leben in Romanen von Thomas H. Pantenius," *Die Gegenwart,* 7, no. 27 (1878): 198–217;

"Julius Rodenberg: *Die Grandidiers,*" *Vossische Zeitung,* 22 November 1879, pp. 26–29;

"Über Wilhelm Raabes Roman *Das Horn von Wanza,*" *Magazin,* 50, no. 27 (1881): 411–423;

"Wilhelm Raabe: *Fabian und Sebastian,*" *Magazin,* 51 no. 25 (1882): 339–351;

"Otto Brahm: *Gottfried Keller,*" *Vossische Zeitung,* 8 April 1883, p. 14;

"Cafés von heute und Konditoreien von ehemals," *Das neue Berlin,* 20, no. 12 (1886): 8–16;

"Die Märker und die Berliner und wie sich das Berlinerthum entwickelte," *Deutsches Wochenblatt,* 2, no. 47 (1889): 560–564;

"Die gesellschaftliche Stellung der Schriftsteller," *Magazin,* 60, no. 52 (1891): 818–842;

"Das Schlachtfeld von Groß-Beeren," *Deutsche Dichtung,* 16, no. 3 (1894): 60–72;

"Adolph Menzel," *Zukunft,* 3, no. 10 (1895): 441–444.

Theodor Fontane is generally considered the most significant realistic novelist of the German-speaking countries. For these lands Fontane consummated the development of the type of novel, the *Gesellschaftsroman* (novel of society), that is characteristic of such great European realists as Charles Dickens, Gustave Flaubert, and Leo Tolstoy. Fontane also paved the way for modernist trends in the novel genre: as the plots of his novels became more and more spare, he placed them more and more in the background and emphasized conversations among characters, who are grouped in socially and symbolically significant constellations.

Thomas Mann, who acknowledged his debt to Fontane, developed this form of the novel with even greater complexity and profundity, summing up the epoch-making intellectual and political movements of the early twentieth century in his *Der Zauberberg* (1924; translated as *The Magic Mountain,* 1927) and *Doktor Faustus* (1947; translated as *Doctor Faustus,* 1948). But Fontane's conversational scenes reflect and comment on political, philosophical, and aesthetic preoccupations of his time without abandoning a style and tone of simple spontaneity, natural charm, and engaging wit. He also placed increasing emphasis on the device of the interior monologue, a tendency that was furthered in the twentieth century with the development of the literary technique of "stream of consciousness."

Fontane was descended from French Huguenots, Protestants who were driven from France by the revocation of the Edict of Nantes in 1685. Encouraged by Friedrich Wilhelm, the Great Elector, to come to Prussia, many Huguenots settled in Berlin and made an important contribution to the city's economy, notably through their proficiency in silk weaving.

Henri Théodor Fontane–it was not until much later that he shed his first name and germanized his second–was born in Neuruppin, a small town in the Brandenburg March of Prussia, on 30 December 1819 to Louis Henri and Emilie Labry Fontane. His father, the owner of a small apothecary store, sold the shop in 1827 and moved to Swinemünde, where Fontane studied at the public school and later received instruction from his father as well as from tutors of families with whom the Fontanes were acquainted. With an awakening interest in history, he began writing historical tales in a school notebook. In 1832 he was sent back to Neuruppin to attend secondary school. There he began to write poems, mostly of a lyrical nature, and joined literary clubs dedicated to the poets Nikolaus Lenau and August von Platen.

These alternating residencies in Neuruppin and Swinemünde had a formative influence on Fontane that he recognized and attested to in the autobiographical novel *Meine Kinderjahre* (My Childhood Years, 1894). Whereas Neuruppin was narrowly bourgeois and dull but practical and realistic, Swinemünde was a romantic city whose population consisted largely of bankrupt merchants. Similarly contrasting traits were presented by Fontane's parents: his mother was strong-willed, principled, and practical, his father congenial, whimsical, but impractical. Fontane vacillated between these poles in his personal life but brought them into a complementary, mutually enhancing relationship in the style of his best novels, which is often termed "poetic realism."

From 1836 until 1840 Fontane served his apothecary apprenticeship in Berlin; he was then an apothecary's assistant in Burg in 1840, in Leipzig in 1841, in Dresden in 1842, and in Leipzig again in 1843. He performed his military service in a grenadier regiment in Berlin in 1844; on a two-week furlough he made his first visit to England. He then practiced pharmacy in Berlin. Although he pursued the profession of his father to support himself, Fontane's first love was still lyric poetry; but as the political climate among the poets of Fontane's generation became increasingly revolutionary, his poetry echoed more and more the rhetorical, heroic tone of others. Finally, toward the end of 1847 Fontane wrote to a friend that he had renounced lyric poetry because he realized that he lacked the gift for it.

Although he was an active member of the conservative literary club "Tunnel über der Spree" (Tunnel over the Spree), Fontane always observed his society with a critical eye. As he tried to establish himself as a freelance writer he accommodated himself to the status quo; but as the bourgeois revolution became imminent he went along with the changing tide and participated in the street fights of 18 March 1848. With the failure of the revolution, Fontane adapted to the ensuing conservative ambience.

Fontane gave up the practice of pharmacy in October 1849. By this time he had become thoroughly familiar with the English ballad tradition, and he turned to writing his own ballads in German. It was in this genre that Fontane first achieved a reputation. The historical and romantic-heroic elements of ballads fit his own interests as well as those of readers during the Prussian ascendancy. His ballads on figures from Prussian history in *Männer und Helden: Acht Preußenlieder* (Men and Heroes: Eight Prussian Songs, 1850) attracted a wide audience. Fontane continued to write ballads for the rest of his life; during his lifetime he was known primarily as a balladeer. Though many of his ballads and some of his lyric poems are still familiar in German-speaking countries, his poems are mostly conventional. The small body of poetry written much later, after he had become a novelist, contains some notable exceptions.

On 16 October 1850 he married Emilie Rouanet-Kummer; that same year he secured a position in the newly founded press headquarters of the Prussian government. The Fontanes' first child was born in November 1851 and named George (the English form, rather than the German Georg) Emile. Continued participation in the Tunnel über der Spree brought Fontane into contact with many prominent writers, including the poet and realist fiction writer Theodor Storm.

In 1855 the Prussian press headquarters took advantage of Fontane's Anglophilia by making him the leader of a group of foreign correspondents assigned to London. His wife and son accompanied him, and a second son, Theodor, was born in November 1856. Fontane wrote reports and feuilletons for German and English newspapers and magazines and also began to write theater reviews. The love of the theater that Fontane acquired at this time is reflected in the settings and characters of some of his novels and the predominance of dialogue over narrative and the theatrical metaphors throughout his novelistic oeuvre.

Fontane resigned his position as foreign correspondent and returned to his homeland in 1859; homesickness and bad health contributed to his decision. The Fontanes had a daughter, Martha, in 1860, and a third son, Friedrich, in 1864. Aside from covering the war in Schleswig-Holstein in 1864 and 1866 and the Franco-Prussian War in 1870–1871 (during which he spent October to December 1870 as a prisoner of war) and two trips with his family to Italy in 1874 and 1875, the only other travels Fontane undertook were a series of journeys through Prussia's Brandenburg March from 1859 to 1882. From 1860 to 1870 he was the editor of the English section of *Kreuz-Zeitung* (Cross Newspaper), and from 1870 until 1889 he was theater critic for the *Vossische Zeitung* (Voss's Newspaper). During the period of his Brandenburg wanderings Fontane stopped writing ballads; it was not until after he had firmly developed his talents as a novelist that he returned to the genre—but with a change of material from the romantic-historical to the realistic-contemporary.

Fontane's *Wanderungen durch die Mark Brandenburg* (Wanderings through the Brandenburg March) appeared in four volumes, in 1862, 1863, 1873, and 1882; in 1889 a fifth volume was published titled *Fünf Schlösser: Altes und Neues aus der Mark Brandenburg* (Five Castles: Old and New from the Brandenburg March). These volumes were Fontane's second most popular works after the ballads; they also signified a shift from a primary interest in the past, imagined as heroic and romantic, to a concern for the present, viewed critically, and the everyday, transformed into art with subtle symbolism, irony, and humor. Fontane's raconteur style and detailed yet ironic observations, developed in his travel books, laid the foundation for his novels. Berlin and much of the rest of the Brandenburg landscape and its lore play significant roles in Fontane's fiction.

The idea of journeying through Brandenburg and describing it had occurred to Fontane earlier; but it was not until his 1858 visit to Scotland—the native country of Sir Walter Scott, whose ballads and novels Fontane had long admired—that he had resolved to carry out his plan. During a trip across Loch Leven, Fontane had had a vision of the Rheinsberg Lake in his homeland. His identification with Scott seems to have stimulated in

Fontane an almost mystical merging of Prussia and Scotland, and the rest of his literary career seems to imitate Scott's: after reestablishing a connection with his geographical roots and abandoning the composition of ballads, Fontane turned to writing novels, just as Scott wrote novels after having begun his literary career by composing ballads.

The *Wanderungen* volumes are affectionate yet critical portrayals of the topography, economy, ethnography, history, and politics of the Prussian province. Fontane begins the first volume with the Ruppin landscape from which he hails, sketching the biographies of Prussian generals who also came from the area and recounting the history of his hometown, Neuruppin. As in all of his travel books, historical chronicles alternate with narration of and commentary on current events and scenes, suggesting parallels and contrasts between Prussia's past and present. The second volume opens with a description of a steamboat ride from Frankfurt to Schwedt an der Oder. The area's settling, its sagas, and its legends are treated. The third volume tells of the founding of several historically and culturally important cloisters by Cistercian monks and nuns, followed by a portrayal of the landscape around Potsdam and Spandau. The fourth volume relates a series of journeys through the Spree forest to Teltow and from Cöpenick to Teupitz. The final volume contains essays on five castles located throughout Brandenburg. Fontane's intention, expressed in the preface, is to sum up emblematically the five hundred years of Brandenburg history in the histories of these castles. Fontane's affection for the old Prussian aristocracy mingles with criticism of its less admirable contemporary representatives and with an awareness of its gradual obsolescence through quickly growing industrialization.

After serving as secretary of the Academy of the Arts in 1876, Fontane devoted most of his time to writing novels. His career as a novelist began with *Vor dem Sturm: Roman aus dem Winter 1812 auf 13* (1878; translated as *Before the Storm: A Novel of the Winter of 1812–13,* 1985), a panorama of the Prussian aristocracy, bourgeoisie, and peasantry just before the outbreak of the Wars of Liberation against Napoleon. Despite the obvious parallels, it does not merit being called a German *War and Peace* (1864–1869)—even though it is one of the best historical novels in German literature. It is characteristic of Fontane's approach that he avoids the "storm" itself and portrays the less dramatic events that preceded the great campaign of 1813. The plot is rather slender for a novel of six hundred pages. Since Fontane was a writer of long experience yet a novice in the field of the novel, it is not surprising that his first effort should demonstrate his skill as a writer while revealing narrative and structural inadequacies. The novel's

sketches of cultural history, similar to those in the Brandenburg *Wanderungen,* as well as character analyses that appear as ends in themselves lessen the work's artistic effect.

Three more historical novels followed *Vor dem Sturm* in fairly rapid succession: *Grete Minde* (1880); *Ellernklipp* (1881), whose title is the name of a cliff in the Harz mountains; and *Schach von Wuthenow* (1883; translated as *A Man of Honor,* 1975). The first two are based on historical chronicles Fontane had discovered in Brandenburg and the Harz mountain region; both examine crimes of past ages and explore with insight the state of mind of the criminal. The third work, which discloses the hollowness of the Prussian military code of honor, is set in 1806; Fontane's historical and topographical studies for *Vor dem Sturm* provided the background.

Grete Minde and *Ellernklipp* are usually referred to as Fontane's balladesque novels, implying not only that they have a structural and stylistic affinity to the ballads Fontane wrote but also that they have less merit than his later Gesellschaftsromane. It is true that in these early fictional works the romantic, balladic elements impose themselves rather ungracefully, and that there is a development in Fontane's oeuvre from a highly colored poetic or balladic mode to a more complex, realistic treatment of social relations. Nonetheless, the novels of society also benefit from the lessons Fontane learned in his long apprenticeship to the ballad form. They, too, contain such elements as the refrain, or leitmotivic repetition of words, phrases, and symbols; the tendency of the story to return to its beginnings; narrative leaps that leave much unsaid and engage the reader's imagination; presentiment or prefiguration; exposition through conversation; and a colloquial manner. On a thematic level, the motif of infidelity that is so often paired in Fontane's works with the themes of guilt and retribution can be traced back to the author's own ballads as well as to the English ballads that served him as models. These balladic elements contribute to the transformation of reality Fontane called "Verklärung" (transfiguration)—the essential ingredient in his poetic realism, one Fontane found lacking in the fiction of Ivan Turgenev and the works of the naturalistic playwright Gerhart Hauptmann. The real distinction in regard to the balladic elements in Fontane's oeuvre is that they are not interwoven subtly and seamlessly into the narrative fabric until his novels of society.

The first of Fontane's novels of society, which have as their background the Berlin of the Bismarckian era, was *L'Adultera* (1882; translated as *The Woman Taken in Adultery,* 1979); like his *Cécile* (1887), *Unwiederbringlich* (1892; translated as *Beyond Recall,* 1964), and *Effi Briest* (1895; translated, 1914), it portrays the gradual decay of a marriage between people who are unequally matched in temperament and age. Each novel is based on an actual scandal in the respectable bourgeois society of contemporary Berlin.

With *Irrungen, Wirrungen* (Confusions, Entanglements, 1888; translated as *Trials and Tribulations,* 1917) Fontane produced his first true masterpiece of fiction: it has no superfluous sentence; its critical vision is clear and steady, its style is relaxed and fluent, and its plot avoids the romantic and melodramatic tendencies to which the author gave partial or complete rein in other works. Unlike his earlier novels, it was long in the making: after drafting the first few chapters in 1882, Fontane picked it up again in the spring of 1884; it reached its final polished form in 1887, appeared as a serial in the *Vossische Zeitung* in July and August of that year, and was published in book form early in 1888. The writing of it overlapped the composition of five other novels, all of which have tragic climaxes; *Irrungen, Wirrungen* is the odd one out. It may wring the heart, but its ending is neither tragic nor happy. The element of resignation in the tone stems from Fontane's reading of the philosophy of the great pessimist Arthur Schopenhauer. The synthesis of resignation, irony, and humor in the novel is characteristic of all of Fontane's greatest works.

Irrungen, Wirrungen is set in Berlin in the 1870s. Lene Nimptsch, the daughter of a washerwoman, has a summer love affair with the young Baron Botho von Rienäcker. The lovers know that their relationship cannot become permanent because of their class differences. Lene is the stronger and more realistic of the pair and does not yield to even the most fleeting of illusions. The two live for their present happiness, the high point of which is a journey up the Spree. Botho's family reminds him of his duties to them and their class, which he is to fulfill by marrying a wealthy distant cousin. Botho and Lene are convinced that they cannot and should not defy the existing social order—reflecting Fontane's conviction of the necessity of order and respect even for its imperfect realization in contemporary social conditions. Botho's marriage to his cheerful but superficial cousin is conventional, yet not unhappy. Lene also marries someone of her own class, a lay preacher whose love for her is strong enough to help her overcome the past—about which she tells her husband everything—but not to forget it. Botho and Lene's short-lived happiness and the sorrow of their separation remain with them for the rest of their lives.

Cut down to these essentials, the plot may seem rather trivial. The achievement in each of Fontane's major novels recalls that of Flaubert's *Madame Bovary* (1857). Flaubert claimed that he deliberately chose the most trivial and mundane subject to highlight the skill of his writing and the aesthetic quality of his prose; in emphasizing the writer's virtuosity and form over content, Flaubert and Fontane point ahead to the modernist and postmodernist writers of the twentieth century. The content of *Irrungen, Wirrungen* was, however, more important to its first readers than stylistic or formal considerations. The novel met with fierce criticism from the reading public. Many took offense at the positive portrayal of a love affair between a nobleman and a woman from the lower class—especially at the author's description of her feelings as simple, true, and natural, which gave them as well as the lovers' relationship a value the reigning middle-class morality would not attribute to what was called a "ghastly whore story." Fontane's social criticism, camouflaged by his acknowledgement of the class hierarchy, is aimed precisely at this moral code that forces people to sacrifice their personal happiness to popular prejudices and social conventions.

George, Fontane's first son, had died at the age of thirty-six in 1887. The following year his youngest son, Friedrich, founded the English-named Fontane and Company, which published Fontane's next work, *Stine* (1890; translated, 1977); *Irrungen, Wirrungen* had made Fontane too controversial for most other publishers. *Stine,* which also deals with the subject of lovers from different social classes, is one of the least-well-constructed of his novels.

During the three years that followed *Irrungen, Wirrungen,* Fontane wrote important reviews of Hauptmann's first two dramas. These extensive pieces, which are more like formal essays than newspaper reviews, reveal many of Fontane's own artistic principles in expressing his antipathy for the movement of naturalism that was then gaining ascendancy. At the same time, Fontane produced two novels that seemed to confirm what he had been saying in letters to friends after his recent setbacks: that he was finished with novels set in contemporary Berlin. *Quitt* (A Settling of Accounts, 1891) is set in Silesia and in the United States, while *Unwiederbringlich* alternates between Danish-ruled Schleswig and Denmark. The first novel begins promisingly but breaks down in the latter half; the tragic conclusion of the second falls short on motivation.

Each of these works is a tragedy, and neither takes place in Berlin; but Fontane's next novel is a comedy set in the capital. *Frau Jenny Treibel* (1893; translated as *Jenny Treibel,* 1976) rates for many as an even greater masterpiece than *Irrungen, Wirrungen, Effi Briest,* or *Der Stechlin* (1899). It is appropriate to use the dramatic terms *comedy* and *tragedy* in describing Fontane's novels, particularly *Frau Jenny Treibel:* including the letters and interior monologues in the text, approximately three quarters of the novel is in direct speech; and the work is easily divided into three "acts." (A dramatization by Christian Hammel was produced in East Berlin in 1964 and in Darmstadt in 1976.) Besides linguistic brilliance and versatility, the novel has a plot that is deceptively simple yet perfectly contrived for its comic purpose and a range of comic characters presented for the most part without caricature. It satirizes middle-class hollowness, pretentiousness, falseness, arrogance, and hardheartedness with incisive urbanity.

The exponent of the middle-class standpoint is the titular figure. Jenny Treibel is a social climber, a grocer's daughter who is married to a Berlin industrialist. A self-styled lover of poetry and a romantic idealist, Jenny never forgets that material security is the only value to be taken seriously. She is not a hypocrite but is unaware of the contradiction between her attitudes and behavior. At the beginning of the novel she invites Corinna Schmidt, the daughter of Professor Willibald Schmidt—who was romantically involved with Jenny in their youth—to dinner. The intelligent and witty Corinna displays her charm ostensibly for the benefit of the guest of honor, the young Englishman Mr. Nelson; in actuality, she is trying to capture the heart of Leopold Treibel, the hosts' son. Corinna's cousin, Marcell Wedderkopp, observes the execution of her strategy with painful jealousy, for he is deeply in love with her. On the way home, Corinna admits to Marcell that she is determined to marry Leopold, who she knows is weaker and less intelligent than she, simply to gain entrée to the affluence and ease of the bourgeoisie.

A few weeks later, on a country outing sponsored by the Treibels, Jenny promenades on the arm of Willibald Schmidt, who views his former lover with characteristically good-humored irony. She sentimentally recalls past times, claiming that she probably would have been happier if she had married a man devoted to the world of ideas and ideals. Meanwhile, Corinna skillfully evokes from Leopold a confession of love and a proposal of marriage. That evening, when Leopold informs his mother of the engagement, Jenny recognizes Corinna's motives and expresses indignation. A tug-of-war between the two pertinacious women ensues; Jenny wins, but only at the price of accepting as a daughter-in-law Helga Monk, a young woman of a wealthy banking family whom Jenny has always disliked. By this time Corinna is happy to relinquish Leopold: she has gained a new perspective on her own motives by seeing them reflected in her opponent. Rather than become another Jenny Treibel, Corinna agrees to marry Marcell, an archaeologist. The Treibel and Schmidt families, their long-standing friendship restored, hold a double wedding; all is forgiven and forgotten.

From March through September 1892 Fontane suffered from anemia of the brain, which caused him to despair of all further artistic creation; his family thought that he was beginning to show signs of mental derangement. He gradually recovered, however, and began to write *Meine Kinderjahre*. This novel became his only narrative work to attain widespread success during his lifetime.

It was also during this time that Fontane resumed writing ballads and lyric poetry. This late poetry is quite different from the poems Fontane had written before. As he points out in the poem "Auch ein Stoffwechsel" (Even a Change of Material), he began his literary career in the land of legends and knights but is finishing it in the everyday world. In his late poems Fontane creates a decidedly unconventional lyric poetry, one that is matter-of-fact, humorous, and ironic in tone—a lyric poetry that is self-consciously unlyrical. In 1894 he was awarded an honorary doctorate by the University of Berlin.

In 1895 *Effi Briest* was published. Effi, who lives with her parents in the Havelland district of Brandenburg, is sought in marriage by an ambitious civil servant, the thirty-eight-year-old Geert von Innstetten. He had once wished to marry Effi's mother, but she had married an older man of more adequate means. Effi scarcely knows Innstetten but accepts him because the offer flatters her and her parents favor the match. Married at seventeen, she moves to Kessin on the Baltic, where her husband is Landrat (prefect). There is no social life, the house is reputed to be haunted, and Innstetten, intent on his career, does not give her much attention. The new territorial district commander, Major von Crampas, has a reputation for success with women and for recklessness in pursuit of them. Mainly out of loneliness and boredom, Effi enters into a brief liaison with him. To her relief the dangerous link with Crampas is broken when Innstetten is promoted to a post in Berlin.

After six pleasant years Innstetten discovers a bundle of old letters from Crampas. Though inclined to forgive his wife and her former lover, Innstetten yields to the Prussian code of honor, kills Crampas in a duel, and divorces Effi. She receives financial support from her parents, though they will not permit her to live with them until illness compels her doctor to urge the Briests that she be allowed to return home. Innstetten, though once again promoted, finds that his career has lost its flavor and is led to question the rightness of his past conduct. A reconciliation with Effi is impossible, even though she has forgiven him; he is, she says, as good as anyone who does not really know how to love could have been. After a serene year at her parents' home, Effi dies of consumption.

Effi Briest is unique among Fontane's masterpieces. Considered the German equivalent of *Madame Bovary* and Leo Tolstoy's *Anna Karenina* (1873–1876) both in subject and in artistic achievement, it is Fontane's only narrative to contain a richly woven plot. There is a corresponding dearth of dialogue. This is a novel of significant silences: things that should be critically examined—above all, the social values and norms the characters allow to dictate their behavior—are never brought up for discussion. As is true even in the novels where Fontane's art of dialogue shines forth, what is not said is always of equal importance to, and sometimes of greater importance than, what is openly stated. In *Effi Briest* Fontane poses a series of problems, leaving the reader to supply possible solutions.

Die Poggenpuhls (translated as *The Poggenpuhl Family,* 1979), Fontane's small-scale portrayal of the dying Prussian aristocracy which he was to portray on a large scale in his last novel, appeared in book form in 1896. During its serialization Fontane finished the first draft of a work that remained unpublished during his lifetime; "Mathilde Möhring," a character study of an emancipated woman, did not appear until 1908. His second autobiographical work, *Von Zwanzig bis Dreißig* (From Twenty to Thirty, 1898), was published in the year of his death. The following year brought the publication of what many consider his greatest work, *Der Stechlin.* According to Thomas Mann (in *Theodor Fontane* [1973], edited by Wolfgang Preisendanz), this work artistically extends far beyond its epoch; yet in content *Der Stechlin* is a summation of its epoch. An extended conversation piece in which virtually nothing "happens," it is a novel of matchless humanity and remarkable technical achievement.

The minimal action of the novel is largely set in a country house and a Berlin residence. The work focuses on the aristocracy, but a wider world—especially that of the growing proletariat—is visible in the background. Dubslav von Stechlin runs for a parliamentary seat, which is won by a member of the recently founded Social Democratic party. Dubslav's son, Woldemar, is faced with a choice between two sisters, daughters of Count Barby in Berlin. He opts for Armgard's youth and simplicity in preference to Melusine's maturity and sophistication. Fontane's position seems to be represented most closely in the Christian Socialism of Pastor Lorenzen, Woldemar's mentor. Dubslav represents "eine aus dem Herzen kommende Humanität" (a humaneness that comes from the heart) incorporated (according to Fontane) in the best examples of the old Brandenburg nobility; the pastor nourishes this trait in himself while at the same time propagating the political ideas and social reforms of socialism.

Dubslav lives on the shore of Lake Stechlin, a small body of water that is reputed to possess an amazing property: whenever some abnormal seismic happening occurs anywhere in the world, Lake Stechlin, in mysterious communication, becomes turbulent; if the event is truly sensational a water-spout forms, at the summit of which a flaming red rooster appears. The lake appealed to Fontane, who had visited it during his Brandenburg travels, as a symbol; Fontane termed it the "Leitmotif" of the novel. It figures sparingly in the work, being inspected twice, discussed twice, and mentioned in the final words of the final sentence, spoken by Pastor Lorenzen at Dubslav's burial: "Es ist nicht nötig, daß die Stechline weiterleben, aber es lebe *der* Stechlin" (It is not necessary that the Stechlin live on, but long live *the* Stechlin). Although once, in jest, one of the characters calls it "ein richtiger Revolutionäre" (a real revolutionary), thus touching the political spheres, the lake's exact symbolic significance is never defined—consistent with Fontane's usual practice of leaving symbols ambiguous.

The Fontanes spent a month at a spa near Dresden, returning to Berlin for the publication of *Von Zwanzig bis Dreißig.* They then went to the spa at Karlsbad, where the author made final corrections for the book edition of *Der Stechlin.* On their return to the capital the Fontanes celebrated their daughter Martha's engagement. Martha was with Fontane when he died around nine o'clock in the evening of 20 September 1898. He was buried in the cemetery of the French Reformed Congregation in Berlin. Two months later, the book edition of *Der Stechlin* was put out by Fontane.

Letters:

Theodor Fontane's Briefe an seine Familie, 2 volumes, edited by K. E. O. Fritsch (Berlin: Fontane, 1905);

Der Briefwechsel von Theodor Fontane und Paul Heyse, 1850–1897, edited by Erich Petzet (Berlin: Weltgeist-Bücher, 1929);

Theodor Fontane und Bernhard von Lepel: Ein Freundschafts-Briefwechsel, 2 volumes, edited by Julius Petersen (Munich: Beck, 1940);

Theodor Fontane: Briefe an seine Freunde, 2 volumes, edited by Friedrich Fontane and Hermann Fricke (Berlin: Fontane, 1943);

Storm–Fontane: Briefe der Dichter, edited by Erich Gülzow (Bern: Lang, 1948);

Theodor Fontane: Briefe an Friedrich Paulsen, edited by Fricke (Bern: Lang, 1949);

Theodor Fontane: Briefe an Georg Friedlaender, edited by Kurt Schreinert (Heidelberg: Quelle & Meyer, 1954);

Theodor Fontane: Von Dreißig bis Achtzig. Sein Leben in seinen Briefen, edited by Hans-Heinrich Reuter (Leipzig: Steffens, 1959);

Fontane: Unbekannte Briefe, edited by Schreinert (Berlin: Aufbau, 1964);

Briefe an Julius Rodenberg, edited by Reuter (Berlin & Weimar: Aufbau, 1969);

Briefe aus den Jahren 1856–1898, edited by Christian Andree (Berlin: Berliner Handpresse, 1975);

Briefe in zwei Bänden, edited by Gotthard Erler (Munich: Nymphenburger Verlagshandlung, 1980);

Die Fontanes und die Merckels: ein Familienbriefwechsel, 1850–1870, edited by Gotthard Erler (Berlin: Aufbau, 1987);

Briefe an den Verleger Rudolf von Decker, edited by Walter Hettche (Heidelberg: Decker, 1988);

Theodor Fontanes Briefwechsel mit Wilhelm Wolfsohn, edited by Christa Schultze (Berlin: Aufbau, 1988);

Theodor Fontane und Friedrich Eggers: der Briefwechsel, edited by Roland Berbig (Berlin & New York: De Gruyter, 1997).

Bibliography:

Charlotte Jolles, *Theodor Fontane* (Stuttgart: Metzler, 1976).

Biographies:

Conrad Wandrey, *Theodor Fontane* (Munich: Beck, 1919);

Mario Krammer, *Theodor Fontane* (Berlin: Fontane, 1922);

Gustav Radbruch, *Theodor Fontane oder Skepsis und Glaube* (Leipzig: Steffens, 1945);

Herbert Roch, *Fontane, Berlin und das 19. Jahrhundert* (Berlin: Schöneberg, 1962);

Elisabeth Moltmann-Wendel, *Hoffnung—jenseits von Glaube und Skepsis: Theodor Fontane und die bürgerliche Welt* (Munich: Nymphenburger Verlagshandlung, 1968);

Hans-Heinrich Reuter, *Fontane* (Munich: Nymphenburger Verlagshandlung, 1968);

Helmut Ahrens, *Das Leben des Romanautors, Dichters und Jounalisten Theodor Fontane* (Düsseldorf: Droste, 1985);

Gustav Sichelschmidt, *Theodor Fontane: Lebensstationen eines großen Realisten* (Munich: Heyne, 1986).

References:

John S. Andrews, "The Reception of Fontane in Nineteenth-Century Britain," *Modern Language Review,* 52 (July 1957): 403–406;

Hugo Aust, ed., *Fontane aus heutiger Sicht: Analysen und Interpretationen seines Werkes* (Munich: Nymphenburger Verlagshandlung, 1980);

George C. Avery, "The Language of Attention: Narrative Technique in Fontane's *Unwiederbringlich,*" in *Formen realistischer Erzählkunst: Festschrift für Charlotte Jolles,* edited by Jörg Thunecke and Eda Sagarra (Nottingham, U.K.: Sherwood Press, 1979), pp. 526–534;

Ehrhard Bahr, "Fontanes Verhältnis zu den Klassikern," *Pacific Coast Philology,* 11 (1976): 15–22;

Marianne Bonwit, "Effi Briest und ihre Vorgängerinnen Emma Bovary und Nora Helmer," *Monatshefte,* 40 (December 1948): 445–456;

Richard Brinkmann, *Über die Verbindlichkeit des Unverbindlichen* (Munich: Piper, 1967);

W. H. Bruford, "Theodor Fontane: Frau Jenny Treibel," in his *The German Tradition of Self-Cultivation: "Bildung" from Humboldt to Thomas Mann* (London: Cambridge University Press, 1975), pp. 190–205;

T. E. Carter, "A Leitmotif in Fontane's *Effi Briest,*" *German Life and Letters,* 10 (October 1956): 38–42;

Harry E. Cartland, "The 'Old' and the 'New' in Fontane's *Stechlin,*" *Germanic Review,* 54 (Winter 1979): 20–28;

Cartland, "The Prussian Officers in Fontane's Novels: A Historical Perspective," *Germanic Review,* 52 (May 1977): 183–193;

Helen Elizabeth Chambers, *The Changing Image of Theodor Fontane* (Columbia, S.C.: Camden House, 1997);

Ernst Correll, "Theodor Fontane's *Quitt,*" *Mennonite Quarterly Review,* 16 (1942): 221–222;

Arthur Davis, "Fontane and the Revolution of 1848," *Modern Language Notes,* 50 (January 1935): 1–9;

Peter Demetz, *Formen des Realismus: Theodor Fontane* (Munich: Hanser, 1964);

Marion Doebeling, ed., *Cultural Codes in Flux: New Approaches to Theodor Fontane* (Columbia, S.C.: Camden House, 1999);

Henry B. Garland, *The Berlin Novels of Theodor Fontane* (Oxford: Clarendon Press, 1980);

Christian Grawe, ed., *Fontanes Novellen und Romane* (Stuttgart: Reclam, 1991);

Glenn A. Guidry, "Fontane's *Frau Jenny Treibel* and 'Having' a Conversation," *Germanic Review,* 64 (Winter 1989): 2–9;

Guidry, *Language, Morality, and Society: An Ethical Model of Conversation in Fontane and Hofmannsthal* (Berkeley: University of California Press, 1989);

Guidry, "Myth and Ritual in *Effi Briest,*" *Germanic Review,* 59 (Winter 1984): 19–25;

Henry C. Hatfield, "Realism in the German Novel," *Comparative Literature,* 3 (Summer 1951): 234–252;

Peter Uwe Hohendahl, "Bemerkungen zum Problem des Realismus," *Orbis Litterarum,* 23, no. 3 (1968): 183–191;

Charlotte Jolles, "Zu Fontanes literarischer Entwicklung im Vormärz," *Jahrbuch der Deutschen Schillergesellschaft,* 13 (1969): 419–425;

Mark Lehrer, "The Nineteenth-Century 'Psychology of Exposure' and Theodor Fontane," *German Quarterly,* 58 (1985): 501–518;

Ingrid Mittenzwei, *Die Sprache als Thema: Untersuchungen zu Fontanes Gesellschaftsromanen* (Bad Homburg: Gehlen, 1970);

Katharina Mommsen, *Hofmannsthal und Fontane* (Bern: Lang, 1978);

Walter Müller-Seidel, *Theodor Fontane: Soziale Romankunst in Deutschland* (Stuttgart: Metzler, 1975);

Wolfgang Paulsen, "Zum Stand der heutigen Fontane-Forschung," *Jahrbuch der Deutschen Schiller-Gesellschaft,* 25 (1981): 474–508;

Wolfgang Preisendanz, ed., *Theodor Fontane* (Darmstadt: Wissenschaftliche Buchgesellschaft, 1973);

Karl Richter, *Resignation: Eine Studie zum Werk Theodor Fontanes* (Stuttgart: Kohlhammer, 1966);

Kurt Schober, *Theodor Fontane in Freiheit dienen* (Herford: Mittler, 1980);

Lambert A. Shears, *The Influence of Walter Scott on the Novels of Theodor Fontane* (New York: Columbia University Press, 1922);

J. P. M. Stern, "'Effi Briest': 'Madame Bovary': 'Anna Karenina,'" *Modern Language Review,* 52 (July 1957): 363–375;

Erika Swales, "Private Mythologies and Public Unease: On Fontane's 'Effi Briest,'" *Modern Language Review,* 75 (January 1980): 114–123;

Reinhard H. Thum, "Symbol, Motif, and Leitmotif in Fontane's *Effi Briest*," *Germanic Review,* 54 (Summer 1979): 115–124;

Hans Rudolf Vaget, "Schach in Wuthenow: 'Psychographie' und 'Spiegelung' im 14. Kapitel von Fontanes 'Schach von Wuthenow,'" *Monatshefte,* 61 (Spring 1969): 1–14;

Marianne Zerner, "Zur Technik von Fontanes 'Irrungen, Wirrungen,'" *Monatshefte,* 45 (January 1953): 25–34.

Papers:

The Theodor Fontane Archive is at the Landes- und Hochschulbibliothek (Provincial and University Library) in Potsdam. In addition, the Märkisches Museum, Berlin, has novel manuscripts; the Handschriftenabteilung (Manuscript Department) of the Deutsche Staatsbibliothek (German State Library), Berlin, has drafts and notebooks; the Deutsches Literaturarchiv at the Schiller-Nationalmuseum, Marbach, has letters and manuscripts of poems; the Cotta-Archiv at the Schiller-Nationalmuseum has letters; the Universitäts-Bibliothek (University Library), Berlin, has manuscripts of novels and poems and magazine and newspaper articles; and the Stiftung Preuscher Kulturbesitz (Foundation for Prussian Cultural Property), Berlin, has letters, manuscripts of poems, and school notebooks.

Max Frisch

(15 May 1911 – 4 April 1991)

Ehrhard Bahr
University of California, Los Angeles

This entry originally appeared in DLB 124: Twentieth-Century
German Dramatists, 1919–1992.

See also the Frisch entry in *DLB 69: Contemporary German Fiction Writers, First Series.*

BOOKS: *Jürg Reinhart: Eine sommerliche Schicksalsfahrt. Roman* (Stuttgart: Deutsche Verlags-Anstalt, 1934); revised as *J'adore ce qui me brûle oder Die Schwierigen: Roman* (Zurich: Atlantis, 1943); revised as *Die Schwierigen oder j'adore ce qui me brûle* (Zurich: Atlantis, 1957);

Antwort aus der Stille: Eine Erzählung aus den Bergen (Stuttgart & Berlin: Deutsche Verlags-Anstalt, 1937);

Blätter aus dem Brotsack (Zurich: Atlantis, 1940);

Bin oder die Reise nach Peking (Zurich: Atlantis, 1945);

Marion und die Marionetten: Ein Fragment (Basel: Gryff-Presse, 1946);

Nun singen sie wieder: Versuch eines Requiems (Klosterberg & Basel: Schwabe, 1946); edited by W. F. Tulasiewicz and K. Scheible (London: Harrap, 1967); translated by David Lommen as *Now They Sing Again,* in *Contemporary German Theatre,* edited by Michael Roloff (New York: Avon, 1972);

Tagebuch mit Marion (Zurich: Atlantis, 1947); enlarged as *Tagebuch 1946–1949* (Frankfurt am Main: Suhrkamp, 1950); translated by Geoffrey Skelton as *Sketchbook 1946–1949* (New York: Harcourt Brace Jovanovich, 1977);

Santa Cruz: Eine Romanze (Klosterberg & Basel: Schwabe, 1947);

Die chinesische Mauer: Eine Farce (Klosterberg & Basel: Schwabe, 1947; revised edition, Frankfurt am Main: Suhrkamp, 1955); translated by James L. Rosenberg as *The Chinese Wall* (New York: Hill & Wang, 1961); German version revised (Frankfurt am Main: Suhrkamp, 1972);

Als der Krieg zu Ende war: Schauspiel (Klosterberg & Basel: Schwabe, 1949); edited by Stuart Friebert (New York: Dodd, Mead, 1967);

Max Frisch in 1948 (photograph by Marie-Agnes Schürenberg)

Graf Öderland: Ein Spiel in zehn Bildern (Berlin: Suhrkamp, 1951); revised as *Graf Öderland: Eine Moritat in zwölf Bildern* (Frankfurt am Main: Suhrkamp, 1963); edited by George Salamon (New York: Harcourt, Brace & World, 1966);

Don Juan oder Die Liebe zur Geometrie: Eine Komödie in 5 Akten (Frankfurt am Main: Suhrkamp, 1953);

Stiller: Roman (Frankfurt am Main: Suhrkamp, 1954); translated by Michael Bullock as *I'm Not Stiller* (London & New York: Abelard-Schumann, 1958; New York: Random House, 1962);

Herr Biedermann und die Brandstifter: Hörspiel (Hamburg: Hans Bredow-Institut, 1955); adapted for the stage as *Biedermann und die Brandstifter: Ein Lehrstück ohne Lehre. Mit einem Nachspiel* (Frankfurt am Main: Suhrkamp, 1958; edited by Paul Kurt Ackerman, Boston: Houghton Mifflin, 1963; London: Methuen, 1963); translated by Bullock as *The Fire Raisers: A Morality without a Moral with an Afterpiece* (London: Methuen, 1962); translated by Mordekai Gorelik as *The Firebugs: A Learning Play without a Lesson* (New York: Hill & Wang, 1963);

Achtung: Die Schweiz. Ein Gespräch über unsere Lage und ein Vorschlag zur Tat, by Frisch, Lucius Burckhardt, and Markus Kutter (Basel: Handschin, 1955);

Die neue Stadt: Beiträge zur Diskussion, by Frisch, Burckhardt, and Kutter (Basel: Handschin, 1956);

Homo faber: Ein Bericht (Frankfurt am Main: Suhrkamp, 1957); edited by Ackermann and Constance Clarke (Boston: Houghton Mifflin, 1973); translated by Bullock as *Homo Faber: A Report* (London & New York: Abelard-Schumann, 1959; New York: Random House, 1962);

Ausgewählte Prosa (Frankfurt am Main: Suhrkamp, 1961); edited by Stanley Corngold (New York: Harcourt, Brace & World, 1968);

Andorra: Stück in zwölf Bildern (Frankfurt am Main: Suhrkamp, 1961); edited by H. F. Garten (London: Methuen, 1964); translated by Bullock as *Andorra: A Play in Twelve Scenes* (New York: Hill & Wang, 1964; London: Methuen, 1964);

Stücke, 2 volumes (Frankfurt am Main: Suhrkamp, 1962);

Mein Name sei Gantenbein: Roman (Frankfurt am Main: Suhrkamp, 1964); translated by Bullock as *A Wilderness of Mirrors* (London: Methuen, 1965; New York: Random House, 1966);

Zürich-Transit: Skizze eines Films (Frankfurt am Main: Suhrkamp, 1966);

Biografie: Ein Spiel (Frankfurt am Main: Suhrkamp, 1967; revised 1968); translated by Bullock as *Biography: A Game* (New York: Hill & Wang, 1969);

Öffentlichkeit als Partner (Frankfurt am Main: Suhrkamp, 1967);

Erinnerungen an Brecht (Berlin: Friedenauer Presse, 1968);

Dramaturgisches: Ein Briefwechsel mit Walter Höllerer (Berlin: Literarisches Colloquium, 1969);

Rip van Winkle: Hörspiel (Stuttgart: Reclam, 1969);

Der Mensch zwischen Selbstentfremdung und Selbstverwirklichung, by Frisch and Rudolf Immig (Stuttgart: Calwer, 1970);

Wilhelm Tell für die Schule (Frankfurt am Main: Suhrkamp, 1971);

Glück: Eine Erzählung (Zurich: Brunnenturm-Presse, 1972);

Tagebuch 1966–1971 (Frankfurt am Main: Suhrkamp, 1972); translated by Skelton as *Sketch-book 1966–1971* (New York: Harcourt Brace Jovanovich, 1974; London: Methuen, 1974);

Dienstbüchlein (Frankfurt am Main: Suhrkamp, 1974);

Montauk: Eine Erzählung (Frankfurt am Main: Suhrkamp, 1975); translated by Skelton as *Montauk* (New York: Harcourt Brace Jovanovich, 1976);

Stich-Worte, selected by Uwe Johnson (Frankfurt am Main: Suhrkamp, 1975);

Zwei Reden zum Friedenspreis des Deutschen Buchhandels 1976, by Frisch and Hartmut von Hentig (Frankfurt am Main: Suhrkamp, 1976);

Gesammelte Werke in zeitlicher Folge, 6 volumes, edited by Hans Mayer and Walter Schmitz (Frankfurt am Main: Suhrkamp, 1976);

Triptychon: Drei szenische Bilder (Frankfurt am Main: Suhrkamp, 1978); translated by Skelton as *Triptych: Three Scenic Panels* (New York: Harcourt Brace Jovanovich, 1981);

Der Mensch erscheint im Holozän: Eine Erzählung (Frankfurt am Main: Suhrkamp, 1979); translated by Skelton as *Man in the Holocene: A Story* (New York: Harcourt Brace Jovanovich, 1980);

Erzählende Prosa 1939–1979 (Berlin: Volk und Welt, 1980);

Stücke, 2 volumes (Berlin: Volk und Welt, 1980);

Blaubart: Eine Erzählung (Frankfurt am Main: Suhrkamp, 1982); translated by Skelton as *Bluebeard* (New York: Harcourt Brace Jovanovich, 1984; London: Methuen, 1984);

Forderungen des Tages: Porträts, Skizzen, Reden 1943–1982 (Frankfurt am Main: Suhrkamp, 1983);

Gesammelte Werke in zeitlicher Folge: Jubiläumsausgabe in 7 Bänden, 7 volumes, edited by Mayer and Schmitz (Frankfurt am Main: Suhrkamp, 1986);

Schweiz ohne Armee?: Ein Palaver (Zurich: Limmat, 1989);

Schweiz als Heimat?: Versuche über 50 Jahre, edited by Walter Obschlager (Frankfurt am Main: Suhrkamp, 1990);

Der Aufruf zur Hoffnung ist heute ein Aufruf zur Widerstand (Saint Gall: Erker, 1991);

Tagebücher, 2 volumes (Frankfurt am Main: Suhrkamp, 1991).

Editions in English: *Three Plays,* translated by Michael Bullock (London: Methuen, 1962)—comprises *The Fire Raisers, Count Oederland, Andorra;*

Three Plays, translated by James L. Rosenberg (New York: Hill & Wang, 1967)—comprises *Don Juan; or,*

The Love of Geometry; The Great Rage of Philipp Hotz; When the War Was Over;

Four Plays: The Great Wall; Don Juan; or, the Love of Geometry; Philipp Hotz's Fury; Biography, A Game, translated by Bullock (London: Methuen, 1969);

Novels, Plays, Essays, edited by Rolf Kieser (New York: Continuum, 1989).

PLAY PRODUCTIONS: *Nun singen sie wieder: Versuch eines Requiems,* Zurich, Schauspielhaus, 29 March 1945;

Santa Cruz: Eine Romanze, Zurich, Schauspielhaus, 7 March 1946;

Die chinesische Mauer: Eine Farce, Zurich, Schauspielhaus, 10 October 1946; second version, Berlin, Theater am Kurfürstendamm, 28 October 1955; third version, Hamburg, Schauspielhaus, 26 February 1965; fourth version, Paris, Jeune Théâtre National des Théâtres de l'Odéon, 8 November 1972;

Als der Krieg zu Ende war: Schauspiel, Zurich, Schauspielhaus, 8 January 1949; revised version, Freiburg, Städtische Bühnen, 8 May 1965;

Graf Öderland: Ein Spiel in zehn Bildern, Zurich, Schauspielhaus, 10 February 1951; second version, Frankfurt am Main, Städtische Bühnen, 4 February 1956; third version, Berlin, Schiller-Theater, 25 October 1961;

Don Juan oder die Liebe zur Geometrie, Zurich, Schauspielhaus; Berlin, Schiller-Theater, 5 May 1953; revised version, Hamburg, Schauspielhaus, 12 September 1962;

Biedermann und die Brandstifter: Ein Lehrstück ohne Lehre, Zurich, Schauspielhaus, 29 March 1958;

Die große Wut des Philipp Hotz, Zurich, Schauspielhaus, 29 March 1958;

Andorra: Stück in zwölf Bildern, Zurich, Schauspielhaus, 2 November 1961;

Biografie: Ein Spiel, Zurich, Schauspielhaus, 1 February 1968; revised version, Ludwigshafen, "Das Ensemble," Theater im Pfalzbau, 15 October 1984;

Triptychon (in French translation), Lausanne, Centre Dramatique de Lausanne, 9 October 1979; (German-language premiere) Vienna, Akademietheater, 1 February 1981;

Jonas und sein Veteran, Zurich, Schauspielhaus, 19 October 1989.

OTHER: Robert S. Gessner, *Sieben Lithographien,* annotations by Frisch (Zurich: Hürlimann, 1952);

Markus Kutter and Lucius Burckhardt, *Wir selber bauen unsere Stadt: Ein Hinweis auf die Möglichkeit staatlicher Baupolitik,* foreword by Frisch (Basel: Handschin, 1956);

Bertolt Brecht, *Drei Gedichte,* afterword by Frisch (Zurich, 1959);

"Nachruf auf Albin Zollinger, den Dichter und Landsmann, nach zwanzig Jahren," in Albin Zollinger, *Gesammelte Werke,* volume 1 (Zurich: Atlantis, 1961), pp. 7–13;

Teo Otto, *Skizzen eines Bühnenbildners: 33 Zeichnungen,* texts by Frisch, Kurt Hirschfeld, and Oskar Wälterlin (St. Gallen: Tschudy, 1964);

Alexander J. Seiler, *Siamo italiani/Die Italiener: Gespräche mit italienischen Arbeitern in der Schweiz,* contribution by Frisch (Zurich: EVZ, 1965), pp. 7–10;

Gody Suter, *Die großen Städte: Was sie zerstört und was sie retten kann,* preface by Frisch (Bergisch-Gladbach: Lübbe, 1966);

Andrei D. Sakharov, *Wie ich mir die Zukunft vorstelle: Gedanken über Fortschritt, friedliche Koexistenz und geistige Freiheit,* translated by E. Guttenberger, postscript by Frisch (Zurich: Diogenes, 1969);

Adolf Hitler, *Mein Kampf: Mit Zeichnungen von Clement Moreau,* preface by Frisch (Munich: Neue Galerie, 1974);

"Why Don't We Have the Cities We Need?," in *The Aspen Papers: Twenty Years of Design Theory from the International Design Conference in Aspen* (New York: Praeger, 1974), pp. 41–46;

"Büchner-Preisrede 1958," in *Büchner-Preisreden 1951–1971* (Stuttgart: Reclam, 1981), pp. 57–72.

SELECTED PERIODICAL PUBLICATIONS–UNCOLLECTED: "Was bin ich?" *Zürcher Student,* 10 (1932/1933): 9–11;

"Kurzgeschichte," *Neue Zürcher Zeitung,* 28 May 1934, pp. 513–514;

"Vorbild Huber: Ein novellistischer Beitrag," *Zürcher Illustrierte,* no. 35 (31 August 1934): 1103, 1104–1106; no. 36 (7 September 1934): 1136–1137, 1139; no. 37 (14 September 1934): 1162–1163;

"Ist es eine Schande?" *Neue Zürcher Zeitung,* 9 September 1934;

"Ausflug aus der Zeit: Skizze," *Neue Zürcher Zeitung,* 7 April 1935;

"Prag, die Stadt zwischen Ost und West," *Neue Zürcher Zeitung,* 30 April 1935, p. 5; 7 May 1935, p. 6; 20 May 1935, p. 6;

"Ein Roman, zweimal besprochen," *Neue Zürcher Zeitung,* 22 November 1940;

"Blätter aus dem Brotsack: Neue Folge," *Neue Zürcher Zeitung,* 23 December 1940, p. 5; 25 December 1940, p. 2; 27 December 1940, p. 4; 29 December 1940, p. 1; 30 December 1940, p. 4;

"Die andere Welt," *Atlantis,* no. 1/2 (1945): 2–4;

"Über Zeitereignis und Dichtung," *Neue Zürcher Zeitung,* 22 March 1945, p. 7;

"Stimmen eines anderen Deutschland? Zu den Zeugnissen von Wiechert und Bergengrün," *Neue Schweizer Rundschau,* 13 (1945/1946): 537–547;

"Death is so permanent," *Neue Schweizer Rundschau,* 14 (1946/1947): 88–110;

"Kleines Nachwort zu einer Ansprache von Thomas Mann," *Zürcher Student,* 25 (1947): 57–59;

"Drei Entwürfe zu einem Brief nach Deutschland," *Die Wandlung,* 2 (1947): 478–483;

"Judith: Ein Monolog," *Die Neue Zeitung,* 25 August 1948, p. 3;

"Friedrich Dürrenmatt: Zu seinem neuen Stück 'Romulus der Große,'" *Die Weltwoche,* 6 May 1949, p. 5;

"Orchideen und Aasgeier: Ein Reisealbum aus Mexico. Oktober/November 1951," *Neue Schweizer Rundschau,* 20 (1952/1953): 67–88;

"Unsere Arroganz gegenüber Amerika," *Neue Schweizer Rundschau,* 20 (1952/1953): 584–590;

"Begegnung mit Negern: Eindrücke aus Amerika," *Atlantis,* 26 (1954): 73–78;

"Brecht als Klassiker," *Dichten und Trachten: Jahresschau des Suhrkamp Verlages,* 5 (1955): 35–37;

"Brecht ist tot," *Die Weltwoche,* 24 August 1956, p. 5;

"Die große Wut des Phillip Hotz: Sketch," in *Hortulus,* 8 (1958): 34–62;

"Öffentlichkeit als Partner," *Börsenblatt für den deutschen Buchhandel,* 14 (1958): 1331–1334;

"Das Engagement des Schriftstellers heute," *Frankfurter Allgemeine Zeitung,* 14 November 1958, p. 8;

"Erinnerungen an Brecht," *Kursbuch,* 7 (1966): 54–79;

"Politik durch Mord," *Die Weltwoche,* 26 April 1968, pp. 49, 51;

"Die Schweiz als Heimat! Dankrede für die Verleihung des Großen Schillerpreises," *National-Zeitung Basel,* 19 January 1974, pp. 1, 6;

"Notizen von einer kurzen Reise nach China 28.10–4.11.1975," *Der Spiegel,* 30 (9 February 1976): 110–132;

"Ohnmächtiger Poet," *Süddeutsche Zeitung,* 1 September 1981;

"Wohnen mitten in der Stadt," *Tages-Anzeiger,* Zurich, 7 September 1984;

"Weinprobe," *Zeit-Magazin,* 22 February 1985;

"Protest von Frisch und Dürrenmatt: Zur Chilenen-Ausweisung," *Tages-Anzeiger,* 1 November 1985;

"Gruß eines Tintenfisches aus der Schweiz," *Tintenfisch,* no. 25 (1986): 8–9;

"Am Ende der Aufklärung steht das Goldene Kalb: Max Frischs Rede an die Kollegen, gehalten an den 8. Solothurner Literaturtagen im Rahmen einer Geburtstagsfeier," *Weltwoche,* 15 May 1986;

"Hat die Hoffnung noch eine Zukunft," *Die Zeit,* 26 December 1986;

"Votum in Moskau," *einspruch: Zeitschrift der Autoren,* no. 2 (1987): 1;

"Wort zum Sonntag (5 May 1987): Zum Asylgesetz," *Die Wochenzeitung* (Zurich), 3 April 1987;

"'America' über alles?: Lesung zur Verleihung des Neustadt-Preises," *Die Wochenzeitung* (Zurich), 22 May 1987.

German drama during the 1950s would be unthinkable without the works of Max Frisch and Friedrich Dürrenmatt; the lack of postwar drama in West Germany was made up for by these two Swiss playwrights between 1945 and 1960. They were the best qualified to fill this vacuum because they were writing in German and were so close to the situation in postwar Germany, yet they were not politically compromised by previous accommodation with the Nazi regime. Furthermore, they had stayed in close contact with the development of modernist drama–in particular German exile drama, which had found a haven at the Zurich Schauspielhaus (Playhouse). Plays by exiled dramatists such as Bertolt Brecht, Ferdinand Bruckner, Ödön von Horvàth, Friedrich Wolf, and Carl Zuckmayer had been produced there during the 1930s and 1940s, and some of the best German actors and directors had found employment in Zurich after 1933. The Zurich Schauspielhaus was thus an ideal place for young dramatists to learn their trade. Dürrenmatt and Frisch made use of the opportunity offered to them in the 1940s, and they found inspiration for their own works from the plays produced at the Schauspielhaus. By the 1960s Frisch and Dürrenmatt were internationally recognized dramatists whose plays were translated into many languages and performed in many countries. Although Frisch became increasingly disappointed with the inertia of the technical apparatus of the theater and neglected drama in the 1970s and 1980s in favor of prose, he never abandoned it.

Max Frisch was born in Zurich on 15 May 1911 to Franz Frisch, an archictect, and Lina Wildermuth Frisch. His mother's family had immigrated to Switzerland from Württemberg, Germany. Frisch studied German literature at the University of Zurich from 1931 until his father died in 1933; he then left school and became a freelance journalist, writing mainly for the *Neue Zürcher Zeitung* (New Zurich Newspaper). In 1936 he took up the study of architecture at the Eidgenössische Technische Hochschule (Federal Institute of Technology) in Zurich. After receiving his degree in 1941 he opened an architectural office. He married Gertrud Anna Constance von Meyenburg in 1942; they had three children. In 1944 Frisch was invited to assist at rehearsals and write for the Schauspielhaus. After World War II, in which he served as a gunner on the Swiss border, Frisch won an architectural competition for a public outdoor swimming pool in Zurich, the Freibad Letzigraben, which was built from 1947 to 1949. The first play he wrote, *Santa Cruz*, was performed in 1946 and was published in 1947; his first play to be performed and published was *Nun singen sie wieder* (performed, 1945; published, 1946; translated as *Now They Sing Again*, 1972). They were followed by *Die chinesische Mauer* (performed, 1946; published, 1947; translated as *The Chinese Wall*, 1961).

Santa Cruz is a dream play. Santa Cruz is not a geographical place but a realm of dreams and self-fulfillment. Its opposite is a castle in a wintry European landscape that stands for reality, marriage, and renunciation. Past and present are synchronized in the dream action of the play. An adventurer and a cavalry officer court the same woman; she opts for marriage and reality but cannot give up her dreams. Neither can her husband, whose alter ego is the adventurer. Only when the adventurer within him dies can the officer and his wife find peace in their life in the castle. Frisch's first play shows the influence of Hugo von Hofmannsthal and Paul Claudel.

Nun singen sie wieder, subtitled *Versuch eines Requiems* (Attempt at a Requiem), deals with war crimes and the vain hope of a moral change. After ordering the shooting of twenty-one hostages, Karl deserts from the army and hangs himself. His wife and child perish in an air raid. The members of the enemy air force are killed in action. The dead celebrate their symbolic requiem with bread and wine. They are committed to a change in spirit, but the survivors do not hear their message. Their deaths will have been in vain unless the audience listens to the song of the hostages, who died singing. Frisch's stage directions specified that scenery was to be present only to the extent that the actors needed it; in no case was it to simulate reality. The impression of a play on a stage was to be preserved throughout. Showing the influence of Thornton Wilder's *Our Town* (1938), the play fails as a *Zeitstück* (play dealing with current events) because neither time nor place is defined.

Die chinesische Mauer, revised in 1955, 1965, and 1972, is a farce. Its subject is the endless cycle of human self-destruction. The construction of the Great Wall of China around 200 B.C. is an allegory for the atomic bomb. Anachronism is the main principle of the play; the characters include "Der Heutige" (Today's Man), Romeo and Juliet, Napoleon Bonaparte, Christopher Columbus, Don Juan, Pontius Pilate, Brutus, Philip of Spain, Cleopatra, Emile Zola, and Ivan the Terrible. Instead of traditional dramatic conflict, there is a constant exchange of quotations, referring to events of the past. Even with his knowledge of history, Der Heutige cannot stop the cycle.

In 1948 Frisch met Brecht, whose theory of the epic or anti-Aristotelian theater would continue to exercise considerable influence on Frisch's dramatic production until the early 1960s. Frisch's fourth play, *Als der Krieg zu Ende war* (When the War was Over, 1949), is set after the fall of Berlin in 1945. Agnes, a German woman, plans to kill a Soviet colonel while her German husband hides in the cellar. Although neither understands the language of the other, the colonel and Agnes overcome prejudice and fall in love. When the colonel learns that Agnes's husband had participated in the massacre of Jews in the Warsaw Ghetto in 1943, he leaves rather than arresting her husband as a war criminal. Brecht wanted Frisch to take a stand in favor of the Soviet "liberation" of Germany, but Frisch considered the conflict between humanity and inhumanity the main theme of the play.

Frisch spent 1951 and 1952 in the United States and Mexico on a Rockefeller grant. His next two plays were *Graf Öderland* (1951; translated as *Count Oederland,* 1962) and *Don Juan oder Die Liebe zur Geometrie* (1953; translated as *Don Juan; or, The Love of Geometry,* 1967). *Biedermann und die Brandstifter* (1958; translated as *The Fire Raisers,* 1962), first written as a radio drama, is one of Frisch's most provocative plays.

Graf Öderland, which underwent two revisions after its premiere in 1951, was a failure because it does not provide convincing motivation for the protagonist's actions. An ambitious state prosecutor changes into an ax murderer with romantically anarchistic notions. But as he overthrows power in order to be free, he is taking over the opposite of freedom: power. Finally the revolutionary takes over as dictator of a new government. At the end Öderland desperately wants to wake up from the nightmare of murder and anarchy he has created. Frisch expressly rejected an interpretation of the play as an allegory about Adolf Hitler or a critique of modern democracy.

In *Don Juan oder Die Liebe zur Geometrie* Don Juan is an intellectual in search of his identity. He tries to escape his destined role as a seducer by loving geometry more than women, but the power of the myth catches up with him. He stages his death and descent into hell so as to escape to his first love, geometry. This escape is denied to him, but he experiences his own hell after he marries Miranda, a former prostitute. He becomes a prisoner in his own castle: he cannot leave the castle because he would then have to live as Don Juan again. He ends up as a henpecked husband and father, reading about his own legend in the 1630 version by Tirso de Molina.

Biedermann und die Brandstifter, subtitled *Ein Lehrstück ohne Lehre* (A Didactic Play without a Lesson), is the first of Frisch's parable plays. Biedermann is not an individual but a type: the businessman who combines pleasant behavior with ruthless brutality in order to succeed in the capitalist world; he is an opportunist and a coward. Because of lack of courage Biedermann allows two suspicious vagrants to camp in his attic, even though there have been newspaper reports about arsonists disguised as peddlers asking for a place to sleep. The vagrants store gasoline barrels in Biedermann's attic and openly handle detonators and fuses in front of him. He cooperates because he does not want to make them his enemies. On the other hand, he has no scruples about driving his employee Knechtling to suicide, because he has nothing to fear from Knechtling. Concerned only with saving himself and his house, Biedermann serves the arsonists a sumptuous dinner; in the end he provides them with the matches they use to set his house on fire. Biedermann and his wife perish in the flames. A chorus of firemen provides commentary in a parody of Greek tragedy. In 1959 Frisch added a "Nachspiel" (epilogue) showing Biedermann and his wife in hell, unchanged and as foolish as ever. Frisch rejected any political interpretation of his "didactic play" as an allegory of the Nazi burning of the Reichstag in 1933 or the Communist takeover of Czechoslovakia in 1948. Unlike Brecht, who wanted to change the world with his theater, Frisch did not believe in the revolutionizing effect of the stage. Also, in spite of the absurd aspects of the plot, Frisch did not want his play to be understood as theater of the absurd. Denouncing Eugène Ionesco and his followers, Frisch declared in 1964 that a public that finds satisfaction in absurdity would be a dictator's delight.

Die große Wut des Philipp Hotz (The Great Madness of Philipp Hotz, published, 1958) is a "Schwank" (slapstick farce) that premiered together with *Biedermann und die Brandstifter* in 1958. The conventional stereotype of the intellectual who is unable to act, Philipp Hotz attempts to break out of the prison of his daily life by locking his wife in a closet, destroying the furniture that symbolizes the bourgeois existence from which he wants to escape, and enlisting in the French foreign legion. Hotz even fabricates an adultery that he has not committed. All his efforts to be taken seriously end in failure. Rejected by the foreign legion because he is nearsighted, he returns to his wife and home and the routines of his daily life.

In 1958 Frisch was awarded the Georg Büchner Prize by the German Academy of Literature in Darmstadt, the Literature Prize of the City of Zurich, and the Veillon Prize of Lausanne. In 1959 he was divorced from his first wife. In 1961 he moved to Rome. That year he had his greatest success on the stage with *Andorra* (published, 1961; translated, 1964). The twelve scenes of *Andorra* are linked by statements made by various characters as they step out of the action of the play to give accounts of their deeds and motivations from a witness box in the foreground of the stage. With the exceptions of Andri and Barblin, the characters are mere types without names. Andri is a young man who is thought to be a Jew who was rescued from persecution by the Schwarzen (Blacks) across the frontier and adopted by the local teacher. Andri is, however, the teacher's illegitimate son by the Señora, a woman from across the border. Although he is not Jewish, the prejudices of his social environment impress on Andri the supposedly Jewish characteristics that he finally accepts, even after he learns of his non-Jewish origin. When he falls in love with Barblin, who—unknown to him—is his half sister, Andri believes that his foster father objects to the affair because he is Jewish. Andri perishes as a Jew when the Schwarzen invade Andorra and take him away, while Barblin's head is shaved because she is considered the Judenhure (Jew's whore). Nobody offers any resistance to the invasion by the Schwarzen. Everybody is guilty, including the teacher, who invented the pious lie of adopting a Jewish child instead of confessing to his illegitimate son; he hangs himself in the schoolroom. The Andorra of this play has nothing to do with the actual state of this name; Frisch said in his notes to the play that Andorra is the prototype of a society ruled by prejudice and fear. There are unmistakable allusions to Switzerland and its relationship to Nazi Germany, even though Frisch stressed in his stage directions that, for example, in the uniform of the Schwarzen any resemblance to the uniforms of the past should be avoided. *Andorra* was criticized for "obscuring rather than analyzing the aberration of anti-Semitism" and of minimizing the Holocaust.

In 1965 Frisch moved to the Ticino, in southern Switzerland. That same year he received the Schiller Prize of Baden-Württemberg. His comedy *Biografie: Ein Spiel* (published, 1967; translated as *Biography: A Game,* 1969) was first produced in 1968. The play, whose subtitle means both "A Play" and "A Game," is introduced by a "Registrator" (chronicler), who reads the stage directions at a lectern. Kürmann, a professor of psychology, wants to start his life over again, like an actor repeating a scene during a rehearsal. He is convinced that he knows exactly what he would do differently. The Registrator and Kürmann's wife Antoinette agree to let him repeat the scene, but it leads to the same result. All other attempts to change the outcome of his life also fail: he is invariably confronted by death from cancer within seven years. Kürmann is limited by his own identity; any particular scene of his life could have been different, but Kürmann cannot adopt a different personality. As Frisch said in his notes to the play, the theater grants an opportunity that reality denies: to repeat, to rehearse, to change.

In 1969 Frisch married Marianne Oellers; the marriage ended in divorce a few years later. After traveling to Japan he was a guest lecturer at Columbia University in New York in 1970–1971. In 1974 he received the Great Schiller Prize of the Swiss Schiller Foundation and became an honorary member of the American Academy of Arts and Letters and the National Institute of Arts and Letters. In 1975 he traveled to China. He received the Peace Prize of the German Book Trade in 1976. His *Triptychon: Drei szenische Bilder* (translated as *Triptych: Three Scenic Panels,* 1981) was published in 1978 and premiered in 1979. *Triptychon* consists of three loosely connected scenes dealing with a common theme, that of death. The first scene deals with the embarrassment caused by the death of a seventy-year-old man; the second is a conversation among the dead, who find eternity banal; the last scene deals with the insoluble relationship between a man and his dead lover.

In November 1989 there was to be a referendum on the abolition of the military. Frisch had been a critic of the Swiss army and its ideology since 1974, when he attacked the Swiss arms industry, Swiss resistance to the immigration of political refugees, and the concept of defense by withdrawal behind an Alpine Maginot Line in his *Dienstbüchlein* (Service Booklet, 1974). His extended dialogue *Jonas und sein Veteran* (Jonas and His Veteran), which premiered in 1989, and his pamphlet *Schweiz ohne Armee?: Ein Palaver* (Switzerland without an Army? A Palaver), published the same year, were Frisch's contribution to the debate on the future of the Swiss army. *Jonas und sein Veteran* consists of a ninety-minute conversation between a Swiss army veteran of 1918 and his grandson Jonas, who faces the alternatives of army service or civil disobedience and emigration. Neither alternative appeals to the young man, who is more interested in a career in computer science. His grandfather is of no help, because his advice consists of historical reminders of Swiss failures and sarcastic analyses of the army as part of Swiss folklore, as an elite unit to protect Swiss capitalism, or as a prop to shore up Swiss national identity. The dramatic dialogue discusses alternatives but does not provide a conclusion. Passages from Frisch's *Dienstbüchlein* are quoted at great length by the grandfather. The proposal to abolish the military was defeated; but it was supported by 35.6 percent of the voters, forcing the army to consider reforms.

In 1989 Frisch was awarded the Heinrich Heine Prize of the City of Düsseldorf. He died in Zurich on 4 April 1991. Although he wrote extensive notes and suggestions for staging his plays, Frisch never provided a comprehensive theory of drama. He questioned the didactic effectiveness of Brecht's epic theater, doubting that anyone would ever change his or her viewpoint as a result of a stage performance. What Frisch had in common with Brecht was his rejection of attempts to imitate reality; the audience is never supposed to forget that what is happening on the stage is make-believe. Throughout his career Frisch was concerned with reminding his audience that his plays were not representations of the world but of our consciousness of the world.

Letters:

"Briefwechsel zwischen Karl Schmid und Max Frisch," in *Unbehagen im Kleinstaat,* by Schmid (Zurich: Artemis, 1977), pp. 255–268.

Interviews:

Gody Suter, "Max Frisch: 'Ich habe Glück gehabt.' Von *Nun singen sie wieder bis zu Andorra,*" *Weltwoche,* 3 November 1961;

Alfred A. Häsler, "Wir müssen unsere Welt anders einrichten: Gespräch mit Max Frisch," in his *Leben mit dem Haß: Gespräche* (Reinbek: Rowohlt, 1969), pp. 40–46;

Peter André Bloch and Bruno Schoch, "Gespräch mit Max Frisch," in their *Der Schriftsteller und sein Verhältnis zur Sprache, dargestellt am Problem der Tempuswahl* (Bern: Francke, 1971), pp. 68–81;

Rolf Kieser, "An Interview with Max Frisch," *Contemporary Literature,* 13 (Winter 1972): 1–14;

Heinz Ludwig Arnold, "Gespräch mit Max Frisch," in his *Gespräche mit Schriftstellern* (Munich: Beck, 1975), pp. 9–73;

Rudolf Ossowski, ed., *Jugend fragt–Prominente antworten* (Berlin: Colloquium, 1975), pp. 116–135;

Jon Barak, "Max Frisch Interviewed," *New York Times Book Review,* 19 March 1978, pp. 3, 36–37;

Peter Rüedi, "Die lange Ewigkeit des Gewesenen: Max Frisch schrieb ein Stück vom Tod, das nicht gespielt wird," *Deutsche Zeitung,* 21 April 1978, p. 15;

Heinz Sichrovsky, "'Da müssen sie einfach lesen lernen!' Max Frisch über sein jüngstes Stück Triptychon und ein paar Probleme, die er mit dem Theater hat," *Deutsche Bühne,* 3 (1981): 16–17;

Fritz Raddatz, "Ich singe aus Angst–das Unsagbare: Ein Zeit-Gespräch mit Max Frisch," *Die Zeit,* 17 April 1981;

Stephan Bosch, "Max Frischs neue Welt," *Schweizer Illustrierte,* 4 May 1981;

Georges Waser, "Jedes Wort ist falsch und wahr: Der Schweizer Schriftsteller über den Sinn des Schreibens, sinnlose Geschichten, die Wahrheit und den Tod," *Rheinischer Merkur/Christ und Welt,* 2 October 1981.

Bibliographies:

Alexander Stephan, "Max Frisch [1934–1988]," in *Kritisches Lexikon zur deutschsprachigen Literatur,* edited by Heinz Ludwig Arnold, volume 3 (Munich: Edition text + kritik, 1978), pp. A–Z8;

"Selected Bibliography [1934–1986]," *World Literature Today,* 60 (Autumn 1986): 549–551.

References:

Heinz Ludwig Arnold, ed., *Max Frisch* (Munich: Edition text + kritik, 1975);

Hans Bänziger, *Dürrenmatt und Frisch,* sixth edition (Bern: Francke, 1971);

Bänziger, *Frisch und Dürrenmatt: Materialien und Kommentare* (Tübingen: Niemeyer, 1987);

Bänziger, *Zwischen Protest und Traditionsbewutsein: Arbeiten zum Werk und zur gesellschaftlichen Stellung Max Frischs* (Bern: Francke, 1975);

Thomas Beckermann, ed., *Über Max Frisch I* (Frankfurt am Main: Suhrkamp, 1971);

Begegnungen: Eine Festschrift für Max Frisch zum siebzigsten Geburtstag (Frankfurt am Main: Suhrkamp, 1981);

Marianne Biedermann, *Das politische Theater von Max Frisch* (Lampertheim: Schäuble, 1974);

John T. Brewer, "Max Frisch's *Biedermann und die Brandstifter* as the Documentation of an Author's Frustration," *Germanic Review,* 46 (March 1971): 119–128;

Michael Butler, *Frisch: Andorra,* Critical Guides to German Texts, 2 (London: Grant & Cutler, 1985);

Butler, *The Plays of Max Frisch* (London: Macmillan, 1985);

Erna M. Dahms, *Zeit und Zeiterlebnis in den Werken Max Frischs: Bedeutung und technische Darstellung* (Berlin: De Gruyter, 1976);

Peter Demetz, "Max Frisch," in his *Postwar German Literature: A Critical Introduction* (New York: Schocken, 1970), pp. 112–125;

Demetz, "Max Frisch: The Last Romantic," in his *After the Fires: Recent Writing in the Germanies, Austria, and Switzerland* (San Diego & New York: Harcourt Brace Jovanovich, 1986), pp. 293–312;

Martin Esslin, "Max Frisch," in *German Men of Letters,* edited by Alex Natan, volume 3, second edition (London: Wolff, 1968), pp. 307–320;

Wolfgang Frühwald and Walter Schmitz, eds., *Max Frisch: Andorra/Wilhelm Tell: Materialien, Kommentare* (Munich: Hanser, 1977);

Heinz Gockel, *Max Frisch: Drama und Dramaturgie* (Munich: Oldenbourg, 1989);

Peter Gontrum, "Max Frisch and the Theatre of Bertolt Brecht," *German Life and Letters,* 33 (January 1980): 163–171;

Gontrum, "Max Frisch's Don Juan: A New Look at a Traditional Hero," *Comparative Literature Studies,* 2 (1965): 117–123;

Klaus Haberkamm, "Die alte Dame in 'Andorra': Zwei Schweizer Parabeln des nationalsozialistischen Antisemitismus," in *Gegenwartsliteratur und Drittes Reich: Deutsche Autoren in der Auseinandersetzung mit der Vergangenheit,* edited by Hans Wagener (Stuttgart: Reclam, 1977), pp. 95–110;

Tildy Hanhart, *Max Frisch: Zufall, Rolle und literarische Form: Interpretationen zu seinem neueren Werk* (Kronberg: Scriptor, 1976);

Walter Hinck, "Abschied von der Parabel: Frisch," in his *Das Moderne Drama in Deutschland* (Göttingen: Vandenhoeck & Ruprecht, 1973), pp. 170–180;

Ferdinand van Ingen, "Max Frischs Don-Juan-Komödie im Rahmen des Gesamtwerks," in *Einheit in der Vielfalt: Festschrift für Peter Lang zum 60. Geburtstag,* edited by Gisela Quast (Bern: Lang, 1988), pp. 249–269;

Manfred Jurgensen, *Max Frisch: Die Dramen* (Bern: Francke, 1968);

Jurgensen, ed., *Frisch: Kritik-Thesen-Analysen* (Bern: Francke, 1977);

Hellmuth Karasek, *Max Frisch* (Munich: Deutscher Taschenbuch Verlag, 1976);

Gerhard P. Knapp, ed., *Max Frisch: Aspekte des Bühnenwerks* (Bern: Lang, 1979);

Knapp and Mona Knapp, *Max Frisch: Andorra* (Frankfurt am Main: Diesterweg, 1980);

Wulf Koepke, *Understanding Max Frisch* (Columbia: University of South Carolina Press, 1991);

Hans Mayer, *Über Friedrich Dürrenmatt und Max Frisch,* second edition (Pfullingen: Neske, 1977);

Doris F. Merrifield, *Das Bild der Frau bei Max Frisch* (Freiburg: Hecksmann, 1971);

Carol Petersen, *Max Frisch,* translated by Charlotte LaRue (New York: Ungar, 1972);

Jürgen H. Petersen, *Max Frisch* (Stuttgart: Metzler, 1978);

Gertrud B. Pickar, *The Dramatic Works of Max Frisch* (Frankfurt am Main & Bern: Lang, 1977);

Gerhard F. Probst and Jay F. Bodine, eds., *Perspectives on Max Frisch* (Lexington: University Press of Kentucky, 1982);

Claus Reschke, *Life as a Man: Contemporary Male-Female Relationships in the Novels of Max Frisch* (New York: Peter Lang, 1990);

Peter Ruppert, "Brecht and Frisch: Two Theaters of Possibility," *Mosaic,* 15, no. 3 (1982): 109–120;

Albrecht Schau, ed., *Max Frisch: Beiträge zur Wirkungsgeschichte* (Freiburg: Becksmann, 1971);

Walter Schmitz, ed., *Frischs Don Juan oder die Liebe zur Geometrie* (Frankfurt am Main: Suhrkamp, 1985);

Schmitz, ed., *Materialien zu Max Frischs Biedermann und die Brandstifter* (Frankfurt am Main: Suhrkamp, 1979);

Schmitz, ed., *Über Max Frisch II* (Frankfurt am Main: Suhrkamp, 1976);

M. E. Schuchmann, *Der Autor als Zeitgenosse: Gesellschaftliche Aspekte in Max Frischs Werk* (Frankfurt am Main & Bern: Lang, 1979);

Eduard Stäuble, *Max Frisch: Gesamtdarstellung seines Werks,* fourth edition (Saint Gall: Erker, 1971);

Horst Steinmetz, *Max Frisch: Tagebuch; Roman; Drama* (Göttingen: Vandenhoeck & Ruprecht, 1973);

Alexander Stephan, *Max Frisch* (Munich: Beck, 1983);

Adelheid Weise, *Untersuchungen zur Thematik und Struktur der Dramen von Max Frisch,* Göppinger Arbeiten zur Germanistik, 7 (Göppingen: Kümmerle, 1975);

Ulrich Weisstein, *Max Frisch* (New York: Twayne, 1967);

Ernst Wendt and Walter Schmitz, eds., *Materialien zu Max Frischs Andorra* (Frankfurt am Main: Suhrkamp, 1978);

Alfred D. White, *Max Frisch, the Reluctant Modernist* (Lewiston, N.Y.: Mellen, 1995);

Monika Wintsch-Spieß, *Zum Problem der Identität im Werk Max Frischs* (Zurich: Juris, 1965);

Arthur Zimmermann, ed., *Max Frisch* (Bern: Pro Helvetia, 1981).

Papers:

Max Frisch's papers are in the Max Frisch Archives, Eidgenössische Technische Hochschule (Federal Institute of Technology), Zurich.

German Literature and Culture from Charlemagne to the Early Courtly Period

Francis G. Gentry
Pennsylvania State University

This entry originally appeared in DLB 148: German Writers and Works of the
Early Middle Ages: 800–1170.

Translated by Wayne K. Wilson

Translated and revised from Deutsche Literatur: Eine Sozialgeschichte, *volume 1, edited by Horst Albert Glaser (Reinbek: Rowohlt, 1988).*

The Disintegration of the Roman Empire in the West

The disintegration of the Western Roman Empire in 476 had a greater influence on modern Europe than on the populations in Italy and Gaul that were immediately affected. The fall of the empire may have been a shock for many contemporaries, but whether they perceived the event as the end of their civilization—perhaps of their culture—is questionable. The reason is that, with few exceptions, conditions in the western part of the empire had been chaotic for quite some time. In 476 the Roman army was already Germanic, as can be seen, for example, in the large number of mercenaries (*foederati*) who were paid to fight for Rome. The refusal of the fifth-century mercenary soldier Odoacer, who had been declared king, to accept the title of emperor and his return of the imperial regalia to Byzantium is evidence of the "usurpatory" Germanic tribes' sense of justice as well as of their realistic assessment of the condition of the Western Roman Empire. The eastern part had become economically and politically superior to the western part long before the definitive collapse. In 476 the Roman Empire still had an emperor in Byzantium, whose influence on the affairs of the western empire was gradually diminishing; that influence virtually vanished with the coronation of Charlemagne as emperor in 800. A few centuries had to pass, nonetheless, before the West felt strong enough to free itself symbolically and politically from the authority of the Eastern Roman emperor.

Although there was no longer an emperor in the West, one institution survived that maintained the continuity with the past: the Christian Church. Its importance for European history of the Middle Ages cannot be overestimated. Political continuity was reestablished only on the basis of the Romano-Christian past when Charlemagne was crowned emperor.

Papal and Secular Theories of Government

Since the decrees of the emperors Theodosius I and Valentinian II in 390 proclaiming Christianity the state religion of the Roman Empire, the pope in Rome exercised governing functions, although the Roman church itself was neither officially established nor proclaimed authoritative; that is, the church in Rome could make no claim to a higher position among the other Christian churches. The special position of the Roman church and of the papacy developed slowly but also quite systematically. Not until the fifth century was the papal doctrine of the special rights of the Roman bishop within the church proclaimed: the Leonic thesis, named for Leo I (pope from 440 to 461), grew out of the assumption that since Peter had suffered martyrdom in Rome, at the beginning of the Christian church a special symbolic relationship between the first pope and Rome had been formed. The biblical confirmation of this special function of the church can be found in the well-known passage in Matthew 16:18–19, where Christ raised Peter to be the head of his church and gave him the right to bind and loose. According to the church, Christ founded thereby not only a distinct *societas* but also gave it an appropriate form of government–a unique event in the history of states and governments. Leo based his thesis of papal authority on a forged letter of Pope Clement I to Saint James, a Greek document from the second century that was translated into Latin in the fifth century. In this letter Clement reports that Peter, before his death and in the presence of the Christian community of Rome, passed on his right of binding and loosing to Clement. It seemed obvious, therefore, that Clement's successors had the right to exercise the power that Christ gave exclusively to Peter, because Peter had publicly given it to Clement. To counter the objection that Christ gave this power to Peter alone because Peter had been the first to recognize Christ as God at Caesarea Philippi, Leo devised a new formulation of the papal office: he admitted that no successor of Peter deserved to share the merit of having been the first to recognize Christ as God; this honor is reserved for Peter. In this sense, every successor is an *indignus haeres beati Petri* (an unworthy heir of Saint Peter). Every new pope is, therefore, a direct successor of *Peter,* not of the pope's immediate predecessor. The merit of Peter is reserved for Peter alone, but his power is constantly passed on anew, through him, to each succeeding Roman bishop. By this means the authority residing in the papal office was separated from the person holding that office. As an unworthy heir to the first pope each new pope receives his power and authority from God, as did Saint Peter himself–not from other humans. The Church, that is, the entire Christian *societas,* is like a minor child that the pope rules for God. The pope, therefore, acted on his own authority; he was not responsible to anyone but God. Thus, one finds, as early as the fifth century, the basis of the papal theory of empire. At this point, however, the pope was too weak to transform this thesis into reality and legitimize it. It was only in the eleventh century that the Roman bishop was able to make these imperial claims and, for a time, to realize them.

The basis of the secular theory of empire can be found in the concept of the monarchy held by the Byzantine emperors. The Eastern Roman emperor, too, considered himself the representative of Christ on earth, chosen by God to rule. Only he was entitled to uphold the sacred beliefs of Christianity. He was priest as well as emperor and participated in important liturgical ceremonies. Only he was entitled to convene church councils; only he was entitled to legislate; and when he did, the laws were given the attribute "holy." Christ was the "pantocrat" (ruler of all); the emperor was the autocrat, the "cosmocrat" (ruler of the created world), chosen by God himself to rule God's people and realm. From the vantage point of the pope, the weakness of the secular theory of the rule was

that it was based in secular history, while the papal thesis found its validation in "true"–that is, divine–history, which must take precedence.

It was to be expected that the papal claims would find little resonance at the imperial court in Constantinople (today Istanbul, Turkey), and as long as the Eastern Roman Empire remained relatively strong the popes were not able to realize them effectively. The great turning point in the politics of the Roman church and in the history of western Christianity came during the papacy of Gregory the Great from 590 to 604. Gregory, who before his selection as pope was an ambassador to the imperial court in Constantinople, recognized that at that time it was impossible to transform the imperial form of government into a papal one. Gregory was farsighted enough to know that if the claims of the papacy were to have a chance to be realized, the pope had to attempt to spread his theories and gain acceptance for them in regions that were not under the hegemony of the eastern emperor. Those regions were in the West. For this reason Gregory sent his monks to Gaul and to England with the mission of proclaiming the papal imperial theory along with the gospel of Christ. The monks succeeded in awakening sympathy for the claims of the papacy, and it is at that point that the actual history of the European Latin West begins. Since the monks brought the Latin Bible with them, Latin became the leading scholarly language of Europe. At the same time, the papal theory of empire was reinforced; after all, Latin was also the language of Rome. Barely one and a half centuries later the papacy harvested the first fruits of these monastic efforts in the Frankish empire.

From Odoacer to Charlemagne

In 493 Odoacer was murdered near Ravenna, either by Theodoric the Great himself or at his behest. Theodoric then ruled Italy until his death in 526. Although the Goths were Christians, they followed the Arian heresy while those they ruled confessed to orthodox Christianity. For this reason an assimilation of the two ethnic populations never came about. The future belonged to another Germanic tribe, the Franks. On Christmas 497 or 498 the Frankish tribal chief Clovis of the Merovingian dynasty (named for its founder, Merovech, who died in 458), submitted to baptism, along with his people, as orthodox–that is, Roman–Christians. His orthodoxy made it possible for Clovis to assimilate the Gallo-Romans into his newly conquered regions and to found a united state; such an accomplishment was not possible for his Ostrogoth neighbor Theodoric, and after Theodoric's death the Goths would disappear as a power in Italy.

In accordance with Frankish custom, after Clovis's death in 511 his empire was divided among his sons. In spite of various attempts to reunite the empire, the power and reputation of the Merovingian dynasty steadily declined; a corresponding decline occurred in religious, moral, and cultural life. Only with the rise of the Carolingian mayors of the palace–beginning with Pépin I around 635, and continuing from 714 with his grandson Charles Martel–did the period of great expansion and prestige of the Frankish kingdom begin, a period that reached its high point in the reign of Charlemagne. By the middle of the eighth century the Merovingian monarchy had become powerless, and the mayor of the palace had long wielded the power of government. Charles Martel's son, Pépin III, sent a message to the pope asking whether he had the right to become king. Pope Zacharias replied that whoever exercises the actual power of government should also be the king. This response was cause enough for Pépin III to send the last Merovingian king, Childeric III, to a monastery and have himself anointed king by the pope. That act was the decisive step on the part of the papacy to free itself of the claims of supreme authority of the eastern emperor and to realize the papal theory of empire: later it would be assumed that the king only became king by being anointed by the pope and that, therefore, the king actually received his power from the pope. Pépin was certainly not aware of the fateful nature of his action, and it did not take long before the great conflict between pope and king threatened to tear apart the empire. But in the meantime, to lend this interpretation the appearance of legitimacy the pope could cite the so-called Donation of Constantine, which–mirabile dictu–appeared in Rome at about this time.

According to this document–which was dated in the fourth century but actually composed in the middle of the eighth century–shortly before moving to Constantinople the emperor Constantine delivered to Pope Sylvester I all the insignia of the empire because he recognized the pope as the true head of Romano-Christian society; Constantine even wanted to put the imperial crown on Sylvester's head, but the pope declined. The symbols of empire, through this purported action by Constantine, thus became the property of the pope. And, as Constantine wore a crown in Constantinople, one had to assume that the pope had lent him papal property–that is, the crown. The pope, therefore, was the actual head of the empire, and the emperor only received his office from the pope. As long as the emperor obeyed the Roman church and protected it, he could remain Roman emperor. If he did not, he was just a Greek king. The eastern emperor was unable to counter this interpretation effectively because western Europe had long been Latin and, therefore, looked to Rome and not to Constantinople. With this forgery began a new period in the Latin West.

Cultural and Literary Life before Charlemagne

In the Frankish empire of the sixth century a cultural life like the one that was to flourish under the Carolingians hardly existed. There were, it is true, men and women who produced literature (in the broadest sense of the word), but their number was small. For that reason the voices of the women of late antiquity and the early Merovingian period stand out in particular. In recent years many studies have revealed that the later development of the European Middle Ages is inconceivable without the active involvement of these important women of the fourth to the sixth centuries.

In spite of Saint Paul's strict admonitions (for example, in 1 Timothy 2:11–12), several women of late antiquity succeeded in raising their voices in the praise of God. Even Saint Jerome (circa 345–420) recognized that the education of women had to be counted among the duties of a true teacher. According to Jerome, women–meaning, of course, women of the upper classes–had to receive such instruction from wise men. They needed to learn Latin and Greek early, so that their speech would not be corrupted by the vernacular and so that they could understand the word of God and the Psalms. In addition, they should become literate so that they could understand Holy Scripture and the writings of the fathers of the church. It should not be surprising, then, that the writings of women of this period that have survived are of an exemplary and didactic character. The travel account of the Spanish nun Egeria, who lived around the end of the fourth century and the beginning of the fifth, can serve as an example. Egeria's *Itinerarium* is, at first glance, a report of her pilgrimage to the Holy Land directed to her "sisters" (perhaps nuns at home in Galicia). Aside from the stylistic characteristics of her description, which show similarities to the later chanson de geste, the *Itinerarium* is remarkable for the confident, almost joyfully naive attitude of the writer. Egeria's reports are full of admiration of the holy places she visited. Again and again she stresses that the reality actually does agree with the descriptions she had read in the Bible. Her report is animated by curiosity and by the happiness she feels when her observations confirm her faith. The reader learns few personal details about Egeria from her account, and she reports only the joys of the trip, not its difficulties: she was not writing for posterity but for a circle of people with whom she was well acquainted, so she did not have to give information about herself; and her "sisters" would have been aware of the hardships of a pilgrimage from Spain to the Holy Land in the late fourth and early fifth centuries. Egeria's objective was not to keep a travel journal in which all sorts of remarkable and extraordinary details were recorded but to assure her readers that the image of the biblical home that they had gained from the Bible and other religious writings was correct. It is, nonetheless, possible to form an image of this pious pilgrim. One can picture Egeria as a woman of education, enterprise, and courage, a convinced and confident Christian who is happy to find confirmation of everything that she has held as true. Egeria awakens in later readers sympathy and admiration that are not lessened by the great temporal distance that separates her from them.

More than a span of time separates Egeria from Radegunda, the Germanic queen and founder of many monasteries and abbeys. Radegunda, a Thuringian princess, was taken prisoner in 529 by the Frankish king Chlotar I after his victory over her uncle, King Herminafrid, and shortly thereafter she was forced to marry her captor. Although Radegunda resisted the marriage from the beginning—Chlotar often complained he had obviously married a nun instead of a queen—she remained with the king until he had her brother murdered. After that she retreated to Sainte Croix, the convent she had founded near Poitiers, where she lived until her death. In her time Sainte Croix became one of the few centers of intellectual life in the Merovingian Frankish empire: kings and bishops came to Radegunda for advice and support; some of the most productive years of the poet Venantius Fortunatus were spent in her presence there. Few men among the Franks were interested in monastic life or scholarly learning; it was, above all, the women who embraced monastic life, and they did so for a practical reason: to escape the bloody power struggles that were the order of the day. Of course, not every woman who took the veil was filled with the same religious fervor as Radegunda, who was later canonized. Rebellions of nuns, even at Sainte Croix after Radegunda's death, are no rarity in contemporary reports (for example, in Gregory of Tours's *Historiarum libri X*, book 10, chapters 15–16). Nonetheless, Sainte Croix was a genuine institution of learning. Radegunda introduced the rule, devised by Saint Caesarius of Arles (circa 470–542), according to which it was mandatory for girls entering the convent to have had some previous education: they were supposed to be further educated at the convent, not to start their education there. While the others worked, one of the sisters would read to the girls; when they were not being read to, the girls were to think about the Scriptures. In convents such as Sainte Croix the noble ladies of the Merovingians were able to enjoy a standard of living commensurate with their place in society while serving God and retreating from the troubles of their times.

The writings that have been preserved from this time are in Latin, although it can be assumed that there was also a wealth of popular secular songs and heroic epics that were part of an oral tradition and not written down. Among the writers of the period was Radegunda's friend Venantius Fortunatus. Coming from upper Italy, Fortunatus studied rhetoric and grammar in Ravenna. In 565 he hiked over the Alps to make a pilgrimage to the grave of Saint Martin in Tours, where he sought healing for his sight (accounts say that he was in fact healed). Thereafter he went from one Merovingian court to another, where he was always well received. To show his gratitude for the friendly treatment, he composed poems in honor of the various kings until he made the acquaintance of Radegunda. He remained in the service of the abbey for several years; from his time there come many occasional poems, poems written in the name of Radegunda, lives of saints, hymns, and satiric verse. Some of his works show great poetic gifts, among them his Martinsvita (Life of Saint Martin) and two hymns that quickly gained entrance into the liturgy, the passion hymn *Pange, lingua, gloriosi* and the processional hymn *Vexilla regis prodeunt*. After his being named bishop of Poitiers around 600 he apparently ceased writing. Nevertheless, his poetic fame lived on, first with the Anglo-Saxons, through whom it reached the Frankish empire of the Carolingians, where Fortunatus became the model for Carolingian authors.

The second great literary personality of the sixth century was Gregory, who came from a well-respected Gallo-Roman family, became bishop of Tours in 573, and remained at that post until his death in 594. In his ambitious work *Historiarum libri X* (History in Ten Books) he paints in rather glaring colors the raw and barbaric conditions that characterized the Merovingian empire; thanks to Gregory posterity possesses generally reliable information regarding the early days of the Merovingian dynasty. His history treats a succession of kings, queens, concubines, pious men and women, bishops, and abbesses, as well as lesser-known people, against the background of an age of change in which the basis of the later Germanic and Roman society of the Middle Ages was created. His history reads much like a modern novel; it is filled with intrigues, murders, bloody revenge, and such. Nonetheless, the reader cannot overlook the quiet humor, sincerity, and zeal of the author. Above all, Gregory wants to report the truth about his time. In his preface he gives his reason for undertaking this task: "As the cultivation of the arts is in a state of decline, possibly even of collapse, no grammarian experienced in the art of rhetoric can be found to portray in prose or in verse what has transpired among us, and yet much has in fact happened . . . . Some have complained and said: 'It is a pity that in our days the cultivation of learning has declined to such an extent, and there is no one of us to write down what has happened in these times.' When I considered that such things are often said, I could not help but try to bring to light both as a commemoration of the past and for the information of future generations even the struggles of the dastardly and the life of the righteous."

Gregory is exaggerating the extent of the decline of learning; in any case, he especially regrets the lack of educated grammarians who would be capable of writing correctly, that is, in the classical style and without errors. He also notes that his contemporaries are not capable of understanding philosophizing orators but only understand the speech of the simple man. Therefore, untalented though he is (he can only express himself, he says, in simple and unadorned speech), he must write his history not only for contemporaries but, above all, for those who will come after. In the first two books he briefly presents the history of the world from the Creation to the death of Clovis. The nearer he comes to his own time in the last eight books, the more extensively he describes historical events and personalities as well as all sorts of miraculous occurrences. The history ends with the year 591. In the last paragraphs he names himself and his writings and implores his unknown successors not to destroy his work. They could perhaps rewrite it in verse form, he says, but otherwise the work should remain intact. Whether Gregory's report on his age is historically reliable or not, it presents a lively picture of his society and its customs without which an understanding and appreciation of the Carolingians would not be possible.

The Anglo-Saxons

The cultural neglect about which Gregory complained was not to be found everywhere. In 597 Saint Augustine (not to be confused with the church father and bishop of Hippo, who died in 430) and some companions landed in England. After initial difficulties Augustine, who became the first archbishop of Canterbury in 601, and his successors spread the Christian religion among the population. The uninterrupted history of the English church up to the Reformation of the sixteenth century begins with the synod of Whitby in 663, where the primacy of the Roman over the Celtic church was established. The next centuries brought a flourishing of scholarly and literary activity the like of which one seeks in vain on the Continent. Above all, these centuries are noteworthy for the production of literature in the vernacular. In addition to the epic *Beowulf* (circa 700), the period brought forth countless primarily religious compositions: biblical epics, lives of saints, allegorical and didactic poetry, chronicles, and so forth. The unique development in England of the vernacular into a literary language can be attributed to the insight of leading scholars–above all, Bede–that it was not enough for only those fluent in Latin to be instructed in

the Christian religion; there should also be priests and teachers who could impart the basic tenets of the Christian message to the people in their own language. How important this idea was to Bede is shown in his life of the natural talent Caedmon in book 4, chapter 24 of his *Historia ecclesiastica gentis Anglorum* (Ecclesiastical History of the English People, 731). Caedmon, who died around 680, was a simple shepherd; he was not known to be poetically gifted until the night he was divinely inspired to compose a hymn of praise to his Creator. He recited it the next day, to the astonishment of all present, and Hilda, the great abbess of Whitby, became his patroness and convinced him to enter the abbey. That God helped Caedmon to compose his hymn not in Latin but in the vernacular shows that the vernacular is a suitable vehicle for praising God. The full effect of Bede's efforts to promote the use of the vernacular is found with his pupils–above all, Bishop Egbert of York, who founded a school that soon became one of the most important educational centers in England. His greatest pupil was Alcuin, who became a scholar and adviser at the court of Charlemagne.

The Educational Reform of Charlemagne

It was important to the Carolingian rulers–above all, to Charlemagne, who became king in 768 and emperor in 800–to reform the Frankish church and its institutions and to establish a program of education to spread the word of God among the people. Charlemagne's promotion of these reforms was motivated not solely by religious zeal but also by the political idea of a Christian empire. The prerequisite for a unified empire was a unified religion, and this unity was to be strengthened through close cooperation between king or emperor and the Frankish church. On the basis of this alliance bloomed first the Frankish and later, with the appearance of the Saxon Ottonian dynasty, the German empire. The long period of stability and relative peace ended only when, as a result of the Investiture Struggle, the German church had to yield to the authority of the Roman church. The rule of Charlemagne formed the beginning of a period of cultural and theological renewal whose high point was reached under his successors, especially his grandson Charles the Bald.

Charlemagne gained the assistance of the best-known scholars from Italy, Gaul, England, and Ireland. Men such as the rhetorician Peter of Pisa, who instructed Charlemagne in grammar; Paul the Deacon, who wrote the history of the Langobards; Theodulf of Orléans; Paulinus of Aquileia; and Einhard, who composed the first biography of Charlemagne, the *Vita Karoli Magni Imperatoris* (830), spent time at the court of Charlemagne and taught at the so-called palace school in Aachen. But the most influential among the scholars at Charlemagne's court and, next to Charlemagne, the driving force behind the educational and monastic reform in the Frankish empire was the Anglo-Saxon Alcuin of York, the student of Egbert who had, in turn, been Bede's student. Alcuin composed many Latin theological works, some lives of saints (for example, the *Vita Willibrordi* and *Vita Martini*), and important didactic works on the cultivation of language (for example, *Dialogus Saxonis et Franconis* and *De orthographia*), on rhetoric, and on the Christian virtues; he also wrote dialogues between himself and Charlemagne (*De rhetorica et virtutibus, De dialectica*) and between himself and Charlemagne's son Pépin (*Disputatio regalis et nobilissimi iuvenis Pépini cum Albino scholastico*). Like most other scholars at Charlemagne's court, he wrote many letters, and he composed several hundred poems.

Although an active cultural life flourished at the court, most of these famous teachers stayed at Charlemagne's court for only a few years. The greatest work was done by unknown scholars who led the schools that Charlemagne commanded to be founded; by anonymous scribes who copied the precious manuscripts in an artistic but quite legible script, the Carolingian minuscule; and by writers of sermons, saints' lives, and schoolbook collections. These obscure persons carried out the educational program of the ruler and his advisers, spread it, and continued it long after the death of Charlemagne.

But it was Charlemagne himself who set the educational project in motion. The two documents that contain an outline of his plans, the *Admonitio generalis* (789) and *De litteris colendis* (circa 780–800), show clearly that his efforts for the cultivation of (above all, Latin) language were aimed at church and monastic reform. Although Charlemagne hesitated to interfere with the sphere of action of his clergy, he considered himself a Christian king who was responsible for the church in his realm–indeed, who was called by God to do so, just as his biblical predecessor Josiah (whom he mentions in the preface to his *Admonitio generalis*), through the introduction of the Deuteronomic law, caused the Israelites to turn away from heathen gods and customs and return to the true faith. Charlemagne admonished bishops to send priests out into all regions of their dioceses to baptize and confirm believers and hear their confessions. Priests should not only forbid heathen practices but actively fight against them. They should teach the people the Lord's Prayer and the correct singing of the Psalms. Believers should be taught to show respect to God's house, to help the priest in cleaning and repairing it, to go to mass regularly, and to wait until the end of the sermon before leaving the church. Schools should be available so that children of every class could learn to read and, perhaps, to write. There were well-known

schools before the Carolingian era, such as the *domus ecclesiae* of Caesarius of Arles, the *Vivarium* of Cassiodorus, and Bede's school at Wearmouth-Jarrow in the British Isles; the new development was that the schools in the Carolingian empire were under the supervision of the ruler. This engagement of the Carolingian rulers ensured the success of the reforms. Even if–or, rather, because the ninth century was peaceful neither within the empire nor outside it, the rulers kept a watchful eye on the welfare of the church and the other institutions of state where their subjects were taught how a Christian empire should function.

Vernacular Literature

In his *Vita Karoli Magni Imperatoris* Einhard reports Charlemagne's order to collect the old "barbaric" songs in a so-called *Heldenliederbuch* (Book of Heroic Songs). According to tradition, the book was later destroyed by Charlemagne's son Louis the Pious. Whether such a book ever actually existed is disputed; it is possible that Einhard invented the incident. Whatever the truth of this matter may be, this passage in Einhard's work is proof of the existence of an oral tradition of worldly poetry in the vernacular, of which only a fragmentary example has survived: the *Hildebrandslied* (Lay of Hildebrand, circa 825).

The *Hildebrandslied* stands at the end of the development of the heroic song, a genre that had its origin with the Germanic peoples of the time of the "migration of the peoples"–that is, between the defeat of the Ostrogoths by the Huns in 375 and the sixth century. Aside from the Old High German *Hildebrandslied,* the only other works that permit insight into the original form of the heroic song are to be found in the old Icelandic collection, the *Edda Saemundar* (after 1220). The extant examples tell primarily about historic events of the heathen early period. Yet the poets did not just want to report facts but also to teach and entertain. The heroic songs are works of art, not examples of folk literature. The poets were warriors at the courts, and the songs were composed for the king and his entourage. Since they were transmitted orally rather than written down, it is difficult, if not impossible, to determine the original text of any heroic song. The song was altered each time it was sung, and sometimes significant changes were made in the text. Only with the written recording of the text does the song become fixed in form and content. But the written mode of presentation did not dominate even then: the heroic song remained primarily an oral tradition until the late Middle Ages.

The heroic song portrays the exceptional warrior hero who, on behalf of his tribe or people, undertakes tasks or withstands hardships that far exceed the normal demands placed on individuals and that call forth admiration and terror in the hearer or reader. The form of the heroic poem, alliterative long-line verse, is well suited to oral transmission. This form was also used for the Old High German biblical epics, which had the same goal of instruction and entertainment and of which many more examples in the vernacular have survived.

The *Hildebrandslied* was written down at the end of the eighth or beginning of the ninth century by two monks at the monastery of Fulda, on the first and the last pages of a Latin theological codex. The monks only wrote down as much as would fit on the two pages, so that the end of the song is missing. In the song Dietrich of Bern (Theodoric the Great), the rightful king of Italy, is driven out of the land by the usurper Otacher (Odoacer). After thirty years in exile at the court of Etzel (Attila), Dietrich returns to Italy to fight Otacher and try to reconquer his realm. The two armies meet at Ravenna, where the leaders choose champions to represent them in single combat: Hildebrand is Dietrich's man, and Hadubrand is Otacher's. From their conversation—a standard element of the heroic encounter, which permits the opponents to learn each other's background, social class, and standing—Hildebrand discovers that he and Hadubrand are *Sunufaterungo* (son and father), respectively. Hildebrand attempts to convince his son Hadubrand of their relationship but is unsuccessful. Finally, Hadubrand reproaches Hildebrand by saying that the latter is not willing to fight because he is too old and too cowardly. This insult to his honor leaves Hildebrand no choice. He laments the hard fate that forces him to fight his own son: "welaga nu, waltant got, wewurt skihit!" (Oh ruling God, fate must run its course!). The song breaks off in the middle of the fight, but there can be no doubt about the outcome: in the old Icelandic *Hildebrands Sterbestrophe* (Hildebrand's Death Strophe, circa 1200) Hildebrand, on his deathbed, laments the fact that he had to kill his own son. According to the Germanic ethos Hildebrand has no choice but to fight his own son: if he does not fight, he proves Hadubrand's accusations correct; but if he does fight and is victorious, he not only takes on the great stigma of blood guilt, of murdering someone from his own family or tribe, but—since Hadubrand is his only child and has no offspring—he also destroys his own posterity. To show this dilemma was the task of the poet of the *Hildebrandslied*.

There still remains the question of why the historical facts were altered in the song. For an answer, one might look to the presumably Gothic origin of the work. The first singer probably wanted to show that Theodoric had a right to rule Italy; but Odoacer, who had been recognized as the king of Italy by the Eastern Roman emperor, was killed by the Ostrogoths during an armistice. The version of events in the *Hildebrandslied* is much more agreeable to the Germanic sense of justice and shows Theodoric as well as the Ostrogoths in a more favorable "ethical" light. That this consideration did not interest the Fulda monks can be seen by the fact that they left off the end of the poem. In all probability, the writing down of the *Hildebrandslied* was a penmanship exercise and not a conscious attempt to preserve a secular poem for posterity.

Secular vernacular literature was—as can be seen from Alcuin's admonition to the monks of Lindisfarne, "Quid Hinieldus cum Christo?" (What has Ingeld [a Heathobardic king and a character in *Beowulf*] to do with Christ?)—largely neglected and despised by the leading representatives of culture; the reading of it was considered useless as a guide to Christian conduct, if not positively sinful. This view continued to be dominant until the courtly period. It was quite different with the vernacular literature of a religious content. This tradition was brought to the Continent by the Anglo-Saxon monks and nuns, above all by Hrabanus Maurus, abbot of Fulda from 822 until 847 and bishop of Mainz from 847 until his death in 856.

With the exception of the *Hildebrandslied* and the *Merseburger Zaubersprüche* (Merseburg Charms, before 750), the Christian religion determined the content of Old High German literature. The purpose of the literature was initially to promote the process of conversion and later to strengthen believers in their faith. But if Old High German was to be used for missionary purposes, priests, monks, and preachers had to have a sufficient command of the language to recognize in translations of Latin writings possibilities of new word formations, of investing existing words with new connotations, and of the necessity, on occasion, of borrowing foreign words. Therefore, it should not be surprising that the first known German writing is a glossary: the *Abrogans* (circa 790–800) is a list of words that was found in a manuscript from the monastery of Saint Gall and is named after the first Latin key word, which means "to ask for forgiveness." The *Vocabularius Sancti Galli,* constructed around 790 in Saint Gall, is a Latin-Greek word list that has been changed into a Latin–Old High German list. In the ninth century glossaries became somewhat more sophisticated, including complete interlinear texts. Among the best known are the *Murbacher Hymnen,* the Saint Gall *Benediktiner Regel* (Benedictine Rule), the *Kasseler Glossen,* and, in the tenth century, the *Pariser Glossen,* which was intended for travelers in the German linguistic area.

While the glossaries served to help the monks in the composition of vernacular texts, the texts themselves were intended for a wider audience. One of the oldest is the eighth-century *Weißenburger Katechismus,* which contains the Lord's Prayer, a confessional, and a creed, all of which the new Christian was expected to memorize. In view of the various theological controversies the creed was of special significance.

At the end of the eighth century, perhaps to fight against the Adoptionism heresy (which held that one had to make a distinction between the divine and the human nature of Christ), the so-called *Old High German Isidor* was written; the work is a translation, with the Latin and German in parallel columns, of the *De fide catholica contra Iudaeos* (On the Catholic Faith, against the Jews) of the bishop Isidore of Seville (circa 575–636). Old Testament references to the divinity of Christ form the center of this work. It cannot be determined with certainty whether the translation was made in one of the well-known monastic scriptoria or elsewhere; the effortless reproduction of the original in the vernacular and the consistent orthography create a great stylistic distance between the *Old High German Isidor* and other glossaries of its time. It is assumed that the *Old High German Isidor* originated in the inner circle of Charlemagne's court, where the doctrine of the Trinity was much discussed. Although the teachings of the *Isidor* were quite suitable for sermons to the congregation, its immediate audience was probably not the common people but the educated class of the empire. Remarkably, the *Isidor* had no immediate successors; only about two hundred years later, with Notker Labeo, is such a subtle and gifted translator found again on German soil.

The ambitious prose translation of the period is the Old High German *Tatian*. Tatian was a Syrian Christian of the second century, to whom is attributed a Gospel harmony that was translated several times over the centuries and found a wide reception. The German translation was completed between 825 and 830 in the Fulda monastery under the direction of its abbot, Hrabanus Maurus. Since its founding in 744 by Saint Boniface I, Fulda was an important educational center of the empire and was influential in the cultivation of the vernacular. This promotion of the vernacular was fostered by the first abbot, Sturmi, and by many Bavarian monks, as well as by Alcuin's student Hrabanus Maurus. Stylistically the *Tatian* is not on the same high level as the *Old High German Isidor,* but it is important for linguistic studies of Old High German because it attempts to define a form of Old High German that is not strongly influenced by dialect. Significant, too, is the enhancement of the language through its rich vocabulary.

While the vernacular efforts of the eighth century—other than the *Old High German Isidor*—are glossaries and interlinear works, the ninth century was a time of poetic creativity, especially in the area of the biblical epic. This genre goes back to Juvencus, who might be considered the founder of the Christian epic in general. Around 330 this Spanish priest wrote his *Evangelium*

Libri IV (Gospel in Four Books) in Latin as a Christian answer to heathen literature. His example was followed in several vernacular languages; in Old High German the primary examples are Otfried von Weißenburg's *Evangelienbuch* (Gospel Book, between 863 and 871) and some important fragments of biblical epics. In the Old Saxon there exists, other than the mighty *Heliand* (Savior, circa 850), only a Genesis fragment. All biblical epics and fragments were either composed or written down in Fulda or inspired by the efforts of the Fulda monks on behalf of the vernacular. All, with the exception of Otfried's *Evangelienbuch,* are in long-line verse with alliteration.

The *Wessobrunner Gebet* (Wessobrunn Prayer, circa 775–825) is written in a Latin codex from the monastery of Wessobrunn in Bavaria. The title is misleading, because the first nine alliterating long lines are definitely the beginning of a biblical epic which has the Creation as its theme. After these nine lines the epic breaks off, and there follows a modest prose prayer that has nothing in common with the previous lines. There can be no doubt that the poem is based on an Anglo-Saxon model, which indicates Fulda as a possible place of composition. The epic part describes the universe before the Creation, portraying the chaos that existed when the natural order of the cosmos was lacking (italics indicate conjectures made where the manuscript is illegible):

Dat gafregin ih mit firahim firiuuizzo meista,
Dat ero ni uuas noh ufhimil,
noh paum, noh pereg ni uuas,
ni *sterro* nohheinig, noh sunna ni scein,
noh mano ni liuhta, noh der mareo seo.
Do dar niuuiht ni uuas enteo ni uuenteo,
enti do uuas der eino almahtico cot,
manno miltisto, enti dar uuarun auh manake mit inan
cootlihhe geista, enti cot heilac.

(This I have found to be the greatest wonder,
that there was no earth, no sky,
no tree, no mountain,
not a single star shone, not even the sun,
neither the moon shone nor the sparkling sea,
when there was nothing that could be understood as the beginning or the end,
there had been the almighty God for a long time
who is rich in grace. There were many
magnificent spirits, but before them [was] the holy God.)

As a text for those to be converted, the *Wessobrunner Gebet* was well suited. The emphasis on the eternity of the Christian God had as its goal to demonstrate the Christian God's primacy over the Germanic gods. Borrowing a typical formula from the heroic epic, the prayer presents God as a ruler with his entourage (the

St. Radegunda entering the monastic life (top) and holding a book in her cell, an illustration from
an eleventh-century manuscript (Poitiers, Bibliothèque Municipale, MS 250, fol. 31v)

angels) in an attempt to express this difficult concept in terms that would be understood by the listeners.

The *Muspilli,* on the other hand, has the end, rather than the beginning, of the world as its theme. Originating in the late ninth century, the *Muspilli* (the title may mean "world fire") is directed to a quite different audience than the *Wessobrunner Gebet.* If the *Wessobrunner Gebet* can be understood as an example of conversion literature, the *Muspilli* can be considered literature for the already converted. Its theme is just actions on earth; only through correct behavior can a person hope to attain the heavenly reward:

> Pidiu ist de*mo* manne so guot, denner ze demo mahale quimit, daz er rahono *uu*eliha re*h*to arteile.
>
> Den*n*e ni dar*f* er sorgen, den*n*e er ze deru suonu qui*mit.*

> (Therefore it is good for a person who goes before the Last Judgment
>
> [himself previously] to have judged righteously in all things.
>
> Then he need not worry when he stands before this court.)

The poet admonishes the judges, probably the secular nobility, to practice their office on earth justly, especially with regard to the needs of the poor and the socially weak, if their hope for paradise is to be fulfilled. This connecting of just actions on earth with the promised heavenly reward became a firm part of literature intended for the nobility. A sense of justice was counted among the most important attributes of the ruler, who was conventionally called *rex iustus et pacificus* (just and peaceful king), as of the nobility in general, and this theme increased in importance in later centuries. The appearance of this theme in the late ninth century was a sure sign that vernacular literature no longer stood just in the service of conversion efforts but rather served the deepening of belief. The *Muspilli* contrasts two groups who are contending in a theological controversy, the so-called Elias struggle: the "experts of secular law," presumably the laity, and the "servants of God," presumably the clergy. The experts of secular law say that the prophet Elias will win the fight with the Antichrist; they interpret the struggle as a divine judgment, while the servants of God believe that Elias will be injured in the fight: "so daz Eliases pluot in erda kitriufit, so inprinnant die perga" (when Elias's blood drops to the earth the mountains will begin to burn), and the world will go up in flames. That in the ninth century a circle of laymen could defend its position with as much energy as the clerics shows the increasing intellectual maturity in the land. In this respect the experts of secular law are worthy heirs of the Carolingian rulers, who, since the

time of Charlemagne, intervened in such matters and thereby enriched the intellectual climate of the time.

An Old Saxon Intermezzo

A fascinating chapter of German literary history was written not in Old High German but in Old Saxon. A massive biblical epic, the *Heliand* (Savior, circa 850) and a biblical epic fragment known as *Genesis A* (circa 850), are the only surviving records of an Old Saxon Christian literature. Of the two works, the *Heliand* is of greater interest. Although the conclusion and some other lines are missing, the *Heliand* still contains 5,983 lines in which the life of Christ is narrated in alliterative epic verse with many stylistic devices borrowed from the Germanic heroic epic. One is tempted to view the *Heliand* as the "Germanization" of the Christian message, revealing mainly a Germanic-heathen ethos and only subliminally a Christian one. But this view would completely misrepresent the purpose of the work. It is true that Christ is described in such Germanic feudal terms as *drohtin* (lord), *uualdand* (ruler), *uualdandes barn* (child of the ruler), *thiodo drohtin* (lord of the peoples), and *mildi mundboro* (generous protector) and that the Apostles—with the exception of Judas—are characterized as excellent noble attendants; but one should interpret these designations as an attempt to reach a compromise with the expectations and literary tastes of the heathen Saxons who lived on the outer edges of the empire and who only yielded to conversion after a violent struggle with the Carolingian Franks. The work's Christian message of love for one's neighbor, justice, and peace remains unaltered by the Germanic-heathen form.

Virtually nothing is known about the poet or the place of composition of the *Heliand.* The latest scholarship points to the monastery Werden on the Ruhr, although one may assume that the *Heliand* was created under the influence of the literary and theological works from Fulda: one of the main sources for the poet is the commentary on the Gospel of Saint Matthew by Hrabanus Maurus, and Fulda was at this time the center of poetic efforts in the vernacular language.

Two Latin prefaces, one in prose and one in verse, may give clues as to the background of the author and his reason for writing the work. These prefaces became known only in 1562, when the humanist Matthias Flacius Illyricus printed them in the second edition of his *Catalogus testium veritatis.* The prose preface says that a poet, a man who was not unknown among the Saxons, in response to the decree of "Ludouuicus piissimus Augustus" (Louis the Pious?) had taken upon himself the task of translating the Old and New Testaments into German. In the verse preface this poet—in an apparent allusion to Bede's Caedmon story—is described as a simple shepherd who was instructed by God in a dream to write of holy things. It is uncertain whether this preface refers to the *Heliand* poet and possibly to the *Genesis* poet, but it can be stated with some certainty that the prefaces are not forgeries by Matthias Flacius: they are written in Carolingian Latin, not in the Latin of the humanists.

Otfried von Weißenburg and His Time

During the time–about 863 until 871–in which Otfried von Weißenburg was creatively active, political conditions were quite different from those that existed during the time of the author of the *Heliand*. The sons of Louis the Pious had divided the Frankish empire into an eastern empire, a middle empire, and a western empire. The *Strasbourg Oaths,* sworn on 14 February 842, cemented an alliance between Charles the Bald, ruler of the western empire, and Louis the German, of the eastern empire, against their brother Lothar, of the middle empire. They also demonstrate that the empires were linguistically divided. Each recited the oath to his brother in the latter's language. First Louis the German spoke his oath in West Frankish (Old French): "Pro deo amur et pro christian poblo et nostro commun saluament, d'ist di in auant, in quant deu sauir et podir me dunat, si saluarai eo cist meon fradre Karlo et in aiuhda et in cadhuna cosa, so cum om per dreit son fradra saluat dist. . . ." Then Charles recited the same oath in East Frankish (Old High German): "In godes minna ind in thes christianes folches ind unser bedhero gehaltnissi, fon thesemo dage frammordes, so fram so mir got geuuizci indi maht furgibit, so haldih thesan minan bruodher, soso man mit rethu sinan bruodher scal. . . ." Each ruler promised not to attack the other and to give the other support in the struggle against Lothar. Similar oaths were sworn by their respective armies in the language of their counterparts.

Hrabanus Maurus's student Otfried von Weißenburg was justifiably regarded as the most illustrious vernacular poet of this period. Influenced by Latin hymns, he was the first to use end rhyme rather than alliteration. In his seven-thousand line Old High German *Evangelienbuch* he selects mainly episodes from the Gospel of Saint John and explains them allegorically, revealing the hidden sense that lies beneath the literal meaning of the text. Discussing the wedding in Cana, for example, he explains that the stone jugs represent the hearts of the disciples of God; they are hollow inside and filled with Holy Scripture so that they always offer something delectable to drink. The audience addressed by such an interpretation would have been a monastic one. As Max Wehrli says in his *Geschichte der deutschen Literatur vom frühen Mittelalter bis*

zum Ende des 16. Jahrhunderts (History of German Literature from the Early Middle Ages until the End of the Sixteenth Century [Stuttgart: Reclam, 1980], p. 79): "Die Dichtung gründet auf der klösterlichen Praxis der Bibellektüre und Meditation, anhand der Lehren der Väter und vertieft durch das Gebet, in welchem sich erst der Kreis zwischen dem Sprechen des Menschen und dem Sprechen Gottes schließt. Letztes Ziel ist die Kontemplation, als Vorbereitung auf die ewige Seeligkeit" (Literature was based on the monastic practice of reading from the Bible and meditation, with the teachings of the church fathers and deepened by prayer, in which the circle between the speaking of the person and the speaking of God is only then completed. The final goal is contemplation as a preparation for eternal bliss).

The *Evangelienbuch* is, however, quite the opposite of a dry reading for a monastic circle. A humane, benevolent spirit accompanied by deep piety informs the work. Of great interest culturally are Otfried's prefaces to Louis the German, Archbishop Liutbert of Mainz, and Bishop Salomon of Constance, as well as his comments on why he wrote his Gospel book in the vernacular. In the dedication to Louis, whom he considers a model ruler, Otfrid enumerates the most important characteristics of a monarch: as a special favorite of God, who chose him to lead his people as he had once chosen David, he overcomes all difficulties with God's help; and like Job, the much-tested king bears his trials with patience and becomes a servant of God. The undivided empire of Charlemagne no longer exists, and his grandchildren are fighting one another; yet the picture of the ruler as the representative of God, as head of a Christian *societas,* remains unaltered.

In the Latin preface to Liutbert, Otfried mentions that his work was undertaken at the bidding of a certain "venerandae matronae" named Judith, who is not further identified, and several "probatissimorum virorum" to counter the pernicious influence of the secular vernacular songs. To accomplish this goal he had to write in the vernacular himself. His declaration at the beginning of the *Evangelienbuch* itself is even more significant: all culturally advanced peoples, such as the Greeks and the Romans, have, according to Otfrid, presented and preserved their deeds in books. They have shown their grand abilities by mastering the rules of literature. Why should only the Franks refrain from singing God's praise in their own language? The Franks are not inferior to the Romans or the Greeks in courage, intelligence, or riches. No one dares to lead a war against the Franks, who belong to the lineage of Alexander the Great. It appears that Otfried is attempting to rekindle the glow of the great, powerful, and unified empire in the consciousness of his contemporaries.

A similar intent is to be found in the *Ludwigslied* (Song of Louis), which was composed around 881 or 882. The song in praise of the West Frankish king is written in the East Frankish dialect (Old High German) and is found in a West Frankish manuscript that also contains the Old French *Eulalia* sequence. Therefore, one may assume that the language of the eastern part of the empire was still alive in the western part at this time, at least in the noble circles.

The picture of Louis the German shows evidence of the Christian concept of the role of a ruler. The relationship between God and the ruler is immediate and direct; God does not just appear to the ruler, he speaks with him. The Franks are the new Israelites, the new chosen people, and Louis is the new Moses. Louis was orphaned as a child, and God became his *magenzogo*. This word, which is usually translated as "master," signifies much more; it implies someone from the same family or clan, a relative—perhaps an uncle—on the maternal side. Therefore, God and Louis are, metaphorically, related by blood. Louis is "rex dei gratia" (king by the grace of God) because the Lord called him and gave him industriousness, magnificent liege men, and the throne in Franconia. Because the Frankish people had sinned, God let them be sorely tested (that is, he let the Normans invade the empire), then had mercy on them and commanded Louis to save them: "'Hluduig, kuning min, Hilph minan liutin!'" ("Louis, my king, help my people!"). The Christian warriors do not go into battle like the old Germans, who, according to Tacitus, had the *barditus* on their lips; instead, they sing the Kyrie Eleison.

Among the many vernacular works of the Old High German period, such as prayers, baptismal vows, and confessional forms, the magic incantations stand out. Most of them show the fusing of the Christian religion with orally transmitted pre-Christian folk wisdom. That they were collected at a relatively late time—the ninth and tenth centuries—shows that they were able to adjust and maintain their popularity in a Christian but largely rural and conservative society. Instead of the Germanic gods, the powers appealed to are Christ, the Virgin Mary, or a saint. The magic is no longer contained in a formula (although these can still be found; for example, in the *Wurmsegen* [Worm Blessing]) but in a supplication to the divinity, perhaps to protect a shepherd's dog or to heal a lame horse. Only the *Merseburger Zaubersprüche,* in a tenth-century manuscript from the Merseburg cathedral, provide insight into the magical world of Germanic antiquity. For example, the second charm reads:

P*h*ol ende Uuodan uuorun zi holza.
du uuart demo Balderes uolon sin uuoz birenki*t*.

thu biguol en Sin*th*gunt, Sunna era suister,
thu biguol en Friia, Uolla era suister,
thu biguol en Uuodan, so he uuola conda:
sose benrenki, sose bluotrenki, sose lidirenki,
ben zi bena, bluot zi bluoda,
lid zi geliden, sose gelimida sin!

(Phol and Wodan rode into the forest.
Then Balder's foal sprained his leg.
Then Singund spoke a magic verse to heal it [and] Sunna, her sister,
then Frija spoke a magic verse to heal it [and] Volla, her sister,
then Wodan spoke a magic verse to heal it, as well as only he could:
Just as the sprain of the leg so the irregularity of the blood and that of the whole limb!
Bone to bone, blood to blood, limb to limb, as if they had been melded together!)

The first section (lines 1–5), containing the anaphors, reports a situation in epic form. The second section (lines 6–8) contains the magic charm. The power of the charm depends on the magical power of the words, which are expressed as a command. It is through this command that such charms differ from Christian prayer and other sayings that were influenced by Christianity. With the *Merseburger Zaubersprüche* one is still in a Germanic-heathen landscape, and they permit a modest glance into the otherwise closed cult life of the pre-Christian era.

Latin Literature of the Carolingian and Ottonian Empires

Though the emphasis here has been on the vernacular literature, one should not conclude that the vernacular was the typical language for literary production during the early Middle Ages. On the contrary, Latin was still the medium for cultivated international communication. While many important Old High German works have been handed down only in fragmentary form, rather insignificant Latin works exist in multiple, even hundreds of manuscripts. The monastic scriptoria produced a flood of manuscripts. Some contain original texts, such as Bible commentaries, theological tracts, sequences, and hymns, while others contain copies of the writings of the church fathers, of the Bible, or of other such documents. In many manuscripts works of Latin authors of antiquity are to be found. The Saint Gall monastic library contains, in addition to the oldest Alcuin Bible and the oldest copy of the pure text of the Benedictine Rule, an especially impressive collection of the great writers of antiquity: Terence, Lucretius, Sallust, Cicero, Caesar, Virgil, Horace, Ovid, Vitruvius, Persius, Lucan, Quintilian, Statius, and Juvenal. The exchange of manuscripts among scholars and monasteries for the purpose of copying was commonplace. It is, unfortunately, not possible to reconstruct the manuscript collections of all of the sixteen significant cathedrals and thirty most important monasteries in the greater Carolingian empire of the ninth century; manuscript catalogs from this time are available only for the Freising, Cologne, and Würzburg cathedrals and the Saint Gall, Reichenau, Murbach, Lorsch, Fulda, Saint-Riquier, and Saint Wandrille monasteries. Nevertheless, one may assume that the other institutions could also claim respectable collections.

That the Carolingian rulers and the women of the ruling houses, especially Empress Judith, the second wife of Louis the Pious, promoted literature through their patronage is attested by the many dedications of works to them. In addition, there were many nonliterary accomplishments during this epoch, such as the book illuminations and the extraordinary building activity: between 768 and 855, 27 cathedrals, 417 monasteries, and 100 royal castles were constructed.

The rich Latin literature of the Carolingian age includes two outstanding works: Einhard's biography of Charlemagne, the *Vita Karoli Magni Imperatoris,* and Dhuoda's *Liber Manualis* (Handbook, 843). The son of a nobleman, Einhard was born around 770 in Maingar, educated at the monastery in Fulda, and then sent, around the end of the century, to the royal court in Aachen. There he studied with Alcuin, was soon elevated to the position of teacher in the court school, and became the emperor's adviser in literary and mathematical matters. He remained in favor with Charlemagne's son Louis the Pious, but when the relationship between Louis and his sons became increasingly strained and Einhard's attempts at reconciliation failed, he withdrew in 830 to Seligenstadt am Main. He died there on 14 March 840.

Written after 830, the *Vita Karoli Magni Imperatoris* is probably the most mature product, in the field of historiography, of the Carolingian cultural reform. Suetonius's biographies of the Roman emperors serve as Einhard's model as he depicts Charlemagne as an ideal ruler. To stress the uniqueness of his lord, Einhard implies that Charlemagne became emperor by God's grace, not as the result of anointing or coronation by the pope. He writes of the coronation of the emperor in 800 that Charlemagne came to Rome, and "quo tempore imperatoris et augusti nomen accepit" (at that time he received the appellations emperor and Augustus). This passage says that Charlemagne received the title, not the office, in Rome. And in another passage one finds the following words: "Post susceptum imperiale nomen . . ." (After accepting the title of emperor. . .). For Einhard, Charlemagne was the highest lord of

Roman Christianity; the title he received from the pope confirmed but did not confer that status. Einhard's descriptions of Charlemagne's efforts on behalf of the church and his charitable activities create the image of a Christian ruler who not only honors and protects the church but rules as a representative of God. This concept of the ruler was maintained and expanded by the Ottonian dynasty and the early Salian kings. In the Investiture Struggle it would be shaken and would undergo a fundamental change.

Dhuoda's *Liber Manualis* is a book of advice for her son. The manual reveals much about conditions in the Carolingian Empire and about the life of a woman in that time. She reports that she married Bernard of Septimania on 29 June 824. Shortly after her marriage she was taken to an estate of her husband in Uzès on the lower Rhône, where she lived in exile. On 29 November 826 her first son, William, was born; on 22 March 841 she bore a second son, Bernard. Her husband took the second child away from her even before the christening; it is not known why he treated her in this fashion. In the summer of 841 her husband sent William as a sort of hostage to the court of Charles the Bald, a custom of that time meant to ensure peace. She wrote the book for William between 30 November 841 and 2 February 843. It is not known when she died.

Although the manual represents an early form of a Prince's Mirror, it really is a work sui generis that gives the modern reader insight into the way of thinking of the Carolingian era. Aside from telling her son how to behave in society and how to serve his lord, Charles, she tries to explain the meaning of the Christian religion. She often discusses the hidden meaning behind numbers and names; for example, she interprets the name *Adam* by using Greek words for the letters: *A* stands for *anathole* (the east), *D* for *dysis* (the west), *A* for *arktos* (the north), and *M* for *mesembrios* (the south). If one adds up the numbers that are associated in Greek with these letters, the sum, forty-six, is exactly the number of years that were needed to rebuild the temple in Jerusalem. One recognizes that Dhuoda was an educated woman who was familiar not only with the Bible but also with the writings of scholars such as Alcuin and Isidore of Seville. She is an impressive product of the Carolingian educational reforms. William must also have been able to read, for she often admonishes him to read her little book, although he already owns many books and will own even more in the future. She also hopes that others after William may read her manual and profit from it.

The work ends with the final words of Christ on the cross, "consumatum est" (It is finished); and with the death of Louis the Child in 911 one can say the same of Frankish influence in the eastern part of the former greater empire of the Carolingians. With the selection of Heinrich I as king in 919, the hegemony in the future German empire went from the Franks to the Saxons. Although it can be assumed that vernacular literature continued in oral form, from 918 until about 1050 literature was mainly written in Latin. In this period the impetus for literary activity came from the monasteries, and women at the imperial court played a significant role as patronesses. From the convents came magnificent illuminated manuscripts, such as the *Hitda Codex* from Meschede, the *Evangeliar* of the abbess Svanhild of Essen, the *Quedlinburger Evangelienbuch,* and the precious processional crosses of the Ottonian abbesses Saint Matilda and Saint Theophano of Essen. These abbeys were led by women of the Saxon aristocracy; Matilde, the mother of the emperor Otto I, made the convent in Quedlinburg an important cultural center; Adelaid, the second wife of Otto I, was the patroness of Ekkehard II of Saint Gall; her daughter Mathilde was also abbess of the Quedlinburg convent; Gerberga, the niece of Otto I, was the abbess of Gandersheim at the time of Hrotsvit. The role of noblewoman in the religious and cultural life of the Saxon imperial period was, clearly, an important one.

With the reigns of Otto I, II, and III from 936 to 1002 came a renaissance in literature. Latin was still the language of literary communication, and secular themes came to be expressed in Latin. The *Carmina Cantabrigensa* (Cambridge Songs, circa 1050), so named from the location of the manuscript, comprises forty-seven songs, some of which are of German origin. Among them are secular *sequentiae* (sequences), such as the *Modus Ottinc,* which proclaims the deeds of the three Ottos, and the *Modus Liebinc* (The Snow-Baby), a farce about a clever Swabian. The poetic *sequentia* was developed by Notker Balbulus, a monk of Saint Gall, from a mnemonic device for monks who had to sing the long final *a* of the *Alleluia* after the gradual of the Mass; the melody of the *a* was complicated, and the sequence provided the monks a way to remember it. Such texts existed long before Notker, but he created a new poetic form with his texts. (From this form the Middle High German *Leich* [lay] developed.) An example of a religious sequence that is still known today is the *Dies Irae.*

Another Notker from Saint Gall was Notker III (circa 950–1022), also known as Notker Labeo (the Thick-lipped) or Notker Teutonicus (the German). He was the leader of the Saint Gall monastery school and a brilliant translator from Latin into German. He begins with a Latin sentence that he sometimes changes syntactically to make it easier to understand. He differentiates in the German between long and short vowels and adorns the stressed syllables with an acute accent. He tried to introduce a uniform orthography and invented

the "Notker Anlautgesetz") (initial-sound law), which says that initials *b, d,* and *g* alternate with *p, t,* and *k,* respectively, according to whether the final sound of the previous word is voiced or unvoiced. He translated *The Consolation of Philosophy* of Boethius, the *Categories* and *Hermeneutics* of Aristotle, the first two books of the *Marriage of Mercury with Philology* of Martianus Capella, and the Psalms. In 1022 he died of the plague just after completing his translation of the commentary on Job that was probably written by Pope Gregory the Great; this work has been lost. Especially appealing in Notker's work are his clear and idiomatic translations and a syntax that is German, not Latin. Notker had no successors in his efforts on behalf of the German language, and it would be 150 years before the "barbarica lingua" achieved new expressive possibilities.

Two Latin epics, the *Waltharius* and *Ruodlieb* (circa 1075), frame the Ottonian epoch. Ekkehard IV (980–1060) reports in his chronicle of Saint Gall that a monk named Ekkehard I (circa 909–973) wrote in his youth a Latin Waltharius epic on this basis, the work has been dated about 930. But in three of the twelve manuscripts there is a prologue by one Geraldus, who says that he presented the epic to Bishop Erchambaldus. It is not clear whether Geraldus meant that he composed the epic or that he merely gave it to the bishop; if the former is the case, there are several persons named Geraldus and Erchambaldus who could be the individuals involved, and the dating of the work would vary from around 850 to 918.

There is some controversy as to whether the *Waltharius* is a heroic poem that has been reworked in a Christian manner and, therefore, is an excellent example of the monastic reception of secular, probably originally vernacular, literature. There are allusions to classical mythology, as well as detailed reports of the bellicose exploits of the hero, Walther, that are related with obvious relish. The *Waltharius* theme of conflict between faithfulness to friend and loyalty of vassals has its origin in the Nibelung legends. As children, Walther, Hagen, and Hiltgunt are sent from their respective homelands—Aquitaine, Francia, and Burgundy—as hostages to the court of Attila the Hun for the purpose of achieving peace. There the three grow up together, and the two boys swear an oath of friendship to one another. The two achieve great fame as commanders of Attila's armies, while Hiltgunt watches over Attila's treasure. One night Hagen escapes to enter the service of the new Frankish king, Gunther. Soon thereafter Walther and Hiltgunt also escape, taking the treasure of the Huns with them. To reach Spain they have to ride through Francia, where Gunther, over Hagen's objections, leads a band of warriors in an attempt to steal the treasure. After much hand-to-hand combat, Walther has killed all the Franks except Gunther and Hagen. The latter had not taken part in the battle because of the oath of friendship he and Walther had sworn. Only when the king begs for his help does he agree to fight, but he makes it clear to Gunther that he is prepared to break the oath of friendship only because of his vassal loyalty. On the other hand, he tells Walther that he is fighting only because the latter has slain his sister's son—in other words, out of loyalty to his kin. The inexorable tragedy of the typical heroic song is lacking at the end of the epic: instead, the three severely wounded men sit around the campfire, make grotesque jokes about their injuries, and make peace with one another—a Christian element that is quite foreign to the ethos of the heroic song.

Ruodlieb is the product of a different historical and literary epoch. It is no longer concerned with Germanic heroes but with German knighthood a century before the rise of French courtly culture; for this reason it has been called the first medieval novel. Incomplete at 2,300 lines, *Ruodlieb* provides many insights into medieval life. One learns detailed information about social classes, table manners, conditions of village streets, the importance of farming, marriage customs, diplomacy, the life of rich peasants, judicial procedures, forms of punishment (including death by fire, drowning, burial alive, and maiming), jewelry, games, and life at court.

The work portrays the ideal secular ruler through the example of the *rex maior* (Greater King). Ruodlieb enters the latter's service after being treated disloyally by his lords at home. In contrast to Ruodlieb's former lords, the *rex maior* is the embodiment of the *rex iustus et pacificus* who always returns good for evil. After winning a devastating war against the unjust *rex minor* (Lesser King), the *rex maior* offers the *rex minor* an honorable and generous peace; the rex minor humbly and gratefully accepts. His message to the *rex maior* is the best expression of the secular-ruler thesis that had gradually taken form in the West from Charlemagne through the Saxon emperors and reached its peak in the Salian dynasty on the eve of the Investiture Struggle: the *rex minor* proclaims through a messenger that in Christ's stead, the *rex maior* is the strong pillar of society (line 154). When the two kings meet at the former scene of battle to celebrate the peace, an altar stands ready for mass, adorned with the diadem and cross of the *rex maior,* symbolizing the close relationship of the king to God. When Ruodlieb finally wants to return to his former lords with an offer of reconciliation, the *rex maior* gives him two silver bowls. One of them is filled with gold coins on which is engraved Christ placing his hand in blessing on the symbol of imperial power. The secular concept of the ruler could not be stated more clearly.

The Investiture Struggle

Ruodlieb shows the direction that literature probably would have taken around the middle of the eleventh century had it not been for the confrontation between the papacy and the emperor known as the Investiture Struggle. This struggle had deep and far-reaching effects on Germany that are today hardly imaginable; it was a blow from which the empire would suffer long after the "official" end of the struggle in the Concordat of Worms in 1122. The struggle cannot be understood in terms of a modern struggle between church and state, because at that time the institutions were not clearly distinguished. It was, rather, a contest between pope and emperor for primacy in the leadership of Christian society. Through the Investiture Struggle the theocratic side of the German monarchy was put to an end once and for all. The result was a twofold emancipation—the church freed itself from secular domination, and the monarchy was released from archaic bonds—and the dawn of a new age.

From this long and bloody struggle, however, it was neither the monarchy nor the church but the German nobility that really profited: it gained about fifty years to free itself of the authority of the emperor. By 1100 Germany was the most feudal country in Europe, with a colorful multiplicity of territorial fiefdoms that were wholly independent of both the monarchy and the church. The strivings of the Saxon and Salian emperors for a centralized authority had been shattered; the real power in the land was with the princes.

Early Middle High German Religious Literature

The designation *early Middle High German religious literature* is applied to about ninety works written from about 1060—after nearly 150 years from which no written works in the vernacular, with the exception of Notker III's translations, have survived—to about 1180. Among them are biblical epics, commentaries on the Song of Songs, penitential sermons, laments for sin, moral-allegorical tracts, historical literature, zoological treatises, minstrel epics, litanies, and commentaries on the Mass.

The ascendancy of vernacular literature at this time is related to the changed role of the church after the Investiture Struggle. Instead of being concerned with the afterlife, as it had been previously, the church directed its attention to life in this world and claimed the right to lead secular society; therefore, it was forced to come to terms with questions about the duties of the various social classes, especially of the nobility, and these are the main themes of the literature of this period. To influence the laity, the church had to use the vernacular language. In addition, the circle of patrons of literature expanded: in the twelfth century the great princely houses began commissioning works; the Latin-speaking imperial court and great imperial monasteries were no longer the most important centers of literary production.

The first known German work of the period is the so-called *Ezzolied* (Song of Ezzo, circa 1060), written by a cleric named Ezzo at the behest of Bishop Gunther of Bamberg. The *Ezzolied* is preserved in two manuscripts: the earlier one, in Strasbourg, contains only the first seven stanzas; the later one, in Vorau, contains thirty-four stanzas. In the Strasbourg manuscript Ezzo directs his work to "iu herron" (my lords)—that is, to an aristocratic audience. He says that he wants to tell a true story, in contrast to the secular literature that is filled with lies. The song moves rapidly from the Creation and the Fall of Man to the birth, miracles, passion, death, and resurrection of Christ. The focus is on Christ's act of redemption, because through it the kingdom of Heaven is assured to all believers. Still, the mood is not one-sidedly otherworldly. The ultimate goal of life is to attain paradise, but the world is valued positively.

A completely different tone predominates in the short work (seventy-three long lines in nineteen stanzas), written around 1080 by an author named Noker, which bears the misleading title used by its discoverer: *Memento mori.* It was probably intended for a noble audience during a time of fasting. Noker begins with the admonition: "nu denchent, wib unde man, war ir sulint werdan" (Now think, woman and man, where you want to end up). The theme, however, is not redemption in the hereafter but the dangers one encounters on the journey through life. Noker complains that the poor do not get *reht* (that which they deserve). The rich and powerful, who fail to follow the command of God to love their neighbors, are to blame for this deplorable state of affairs. If they do not change their lives, they will be condemned forever. In spite of this threat (which is made only twice, in two contiguous stanzas), Noker observes a moderate tone throughout the work. The rich and powerful must fulfill the command to love one's neighbor by using their wealth to help the poor; only in this way can they lead a Christian life and attain Paradise.

These two works express the most important themes of the moral-didactic literature of this epoch: worldly affairs are not evil in themselves, but the purpose of earthly existence is more than just to live a pleasant and self-centered life; and the weaker members of society have certain rights that must be respected. The duty of the powerful is to help them secure their *reht* so that people will be able to live in harmony.

The anonymous author of the so-called *Summa theologiae* (circa 1100) incorporates the second theme into his portrayal of the story of Redemption. He uses, probably for the first time in German literature, the metaphor of the body to demonstrate the unity of humanity. God, he writes, has created our limbs to serve one another. The members that are apparently of the least worth, such as the feet, are needed the most, because the sublime members such as the eyes would be able to accomplish little without the mobility that is provided by the feet. The author concludes that there are gradations of rank in society and that the higher could exercise their functions in only a limited way without the lower ones.

The biblical epic enjoyed some popularity at this time. From the Old Testament come works based on Genesis and Exodus, as well as the *ältere* and *jüngere Judith* (The Older and Younger Judith) and the *Drei Jünglinge im Feuerofen* (Three Youths in the Oven). The earliest work based on Genesis is the *Wiener Genesis* (Vienna Genesis, 1060–1070); the latest is the *Millstätter Genesis* (Millstatt Genesis, presumably from the late twelfth century), and the middle position is occupied by the *Vorauer Bücher Mosis* (Vorau Books of Moses, circa 1120–1140). (*Vienna, Millstätt,* and *Vorau* refer to the locations of the manuscripts in which the works are written.) In the *Wiener Genesis,* which served as a model for the others, the author relates biblical events to the present and speaks to his listeners, who presumably came from noble circles, in images that were familiar to them from their own experiences. He describes the Garden of Eden, for example, as an ideal medieval tree and herb garden. As the chosen people of God, the Israelites prefigure the Germans. The Old Testament figures are portrayed as heroes and princes in a service-and-reward relationship to God, not as the simple peasants and shepherds that they actually were; the armies could just as well be knightly crusaders. The obvious joy in storytelling which already points to the pre-courtly epic writers is not to be mistaken and is a sure sign of the new age.

The history of salvation and the history of the world are interwoven in two works of this period, the *Annolied* (Song of Anno, between 1077 and 1081) and the *Kaiserchronik* (Chronicle of the Emperors, circa 1147). The *Annolied,* which has survived only in the printed version of Martin Opitz (1639), tells of the deeds of the eleventh-century bishop Anno of Cologne, who was one of the most powerful imperial princes and, as a result of the abduction of the minor Heinrich IV, ruled in the king's stead from 1062 to 1065. He was a controversial political personality, a sponsor of the monastic reform movement and an avid founder of churches and monasteries. The *Annolied,* which originated at the Siegburg monastery, can be considered as propaganda for Anno's beatification; the bishop is frequently referred to in the song as "sent Anno" (Saint Anno). As the canonization did not take place until 1183, this designation is rather premature.

According to the song, Anno was the thirty-third bishop of Cologne, and the actual story of Anno begins with the thirty-third stanza (thirty-three was the number of years of Christ's life). In the previous thirty-two stanzas the author describes the history of the world and the story of Redemption, which cannot be separated from one another: the Creation, the fall of Lucifer, original sin, and the birth of Christ. This history is complemented by secular events: founding of the city (Nineveh), construction of the Tower of Babel, episodes from the Alexander material, Daniel's dream of the four animals (in the interpretation of which the lion, bear, leopard, and boar signify the four realms of the world—the Babylonian, Persian, Macedonian-Greek, and Roman, respectively, of which each had historically succeeded the previous one), and the origin of the four significant German tribes in Franconia, Saxony, Bavaria, and Swabia (perhaps in an echo from the time of the great struggles between Charlemagne and the Saxons, the Saxons come off badly). Anno is portrayed as the ideal ruler because he combines the most important attributes of justice and love of one's neighbor. Like a lion, writes the poet, he had the first place among the princes, but like a lamb he goes among the poor. In this way he serves God and the world.

Wehrli describes the monumental (17,283 lines) *Kaiserchronik*, written in Regensburg, as the "großartige[n] Versuch, die Geschichte des Reichs von der Gründung Roms und speziell von Caesar an bis zur Gegenwart [1147] durch eine Sammlung der verschiedensten Überlieferungen darzustellen, als systematische Zusammenfassung des offiziellen abendländischen Erzählstoffs überhaupt" (grand attempt to present the history of the empire from the founding of Rome, and especially from Caesar, until the present [1147] through a collection of diverse records, as a systematic compilation of all the official western narrative material). The author introduces his audience to the idea of a Christian empire in which the imperial and papal powers are one. Attention is always focused on the moral dimension, especially on the virtue of justice. Even heathen emperors were capable of possessing the necessary virtues: Trajan was saved because he "rehtes gerihtes phlegete" (judged righteously), and all kings should take him as an example if they want to attain the heavenly kingdom. Salvation, thus, does not depend on outward membership in the Christian Church but on the inner moral substance of the individual. This emphasis

on the individual is a sign of the new spirit of the twelfth century. The traditional wisdom of antiquity is admired in the work of Otto von Freising, the arme Hartmann's *Rede vom heiligen Glauben* (Tract Concerning [Our] Sacred Faith, between 1140 and 1160) and Priester Arnold's *Loblied auf den Heiligen Geist* (Song of Praise of the Holy Ghost, circa 1150); earthly wisdom, even if it is not sufficient to open the heavenly gates, is still important. This new attitude toward earthly and individual matters is far from the early Christian view that earthly knowledge is useless and vain, if not sinful. Worldly knowledge and the products of human effort are valued within the limits set by Christian belief.

This relaxed attitude with respect to worldly matters is also to be found in the works of the first woman poet in the German language who is known by name, Frau Ava. Ava probably came from a noble family and, as a widow, withdrew to a hermit's cell at the monastery in Melk; she died in 1127. Her oeuvre consists of four works, totaling 3,338 short lines, that form a whole: *Johannes, Leben Jesu* (The Life of Jesus), *Antichrist,* and *Das Jüngste Gericht* (The Last Judgment). Her work is a song of praise by a pious Christian of Christ's act of Redemption. She does not take the rhetorical approach of lamenting the modest poetic gifts she, as a woman, possesses; the humility formulas that one frequently encounters in the writings of other medieval poets are not found in Ava's writings. She considers her poetic activity a natural outcome of her beliefs, and this view was no doubt shared by the noble audience that she addresses as "lieben mine herren" (my dear lords).

The subjectivity found in Ava's writings pervades the great prose work of pious introspection of the twelfth century, the *Sankt Trudperter Hohelied* (Saint Trudpert Song of Solomon), which was presumably written in the upper German linguistic area around 1160. The manuscript was preserved in the Benedictine monastery of Saint Trudpert in the Black Forest. The anonymous poet interprets the seemingly erotic Song of Solomon by stressing the significance of the concept of the bride. First Christianity is the bride, then the Virgin Mary, and finally the soul of the believing individual. As a didactic exegesis for a Benedictine congregation of nuns, this interpretation fits in quite well. These women regarded themselves as brides of God who yearned for union with the Divine Bridegroom. The work is freed from the reserved erudition of earlier interpretations of the Song of Solomon; the erotic language and sensuous images of the biblical text now enter the vernacular. This work's equal in the portrayal of the inner person and of the soul that passionately loves God is not found in German until that of Mechthild von Magdeburg in the thirteenth century.

Johann Wolfgang von Goethe

(28 August 1749 – 22 March 1832)

Jane K. Brown
University of Washington

This entry was updated by Professor Brown from her entry in DLB 94: German Writers
in the Age of Goethe: Sturm und Drang to Classicism.

SELECTED BOOKS: *Neue Lieder in Melodien gesetzt von Bernhard Theodor Breitkopf* (Leipzig: Breitkopf, 1770);

Positiones juris (Strasbourg: Heitzius, 1771);

Von deutscher Baukunst. D.M. Ervini a Steinbach, anonymous (Frankfurt am Main, 1773);

Brief des Pastors zu *** an den neuen Pastor zu ***: Aus dem Französischen, anonymous (Frankfurt am Main, 1773);

Zwo wichtige bisher unerörterte Biblische Fragen zum erstenmal gründlich beantwortet, von einem Landgeistlichen in Schwaben, anonymous (Lindau am Bodensee, 1773);

Götz von Berlichingen mit der eisernen Hand: Ein Schauspiel, anonymous (Darmstadt, 1773); translated by Sir Walter Scott as *Goetz von Berlichingen* (London: Bell, 1799);

Prolog zu den neusten Offenbarungen Gottes verdeutscht durch Dr. Carl Friedrich Bahrdt, anonymous (Giessen, 1774);

Götter Helden und Wieland: Eine Farce, anonymous (Leipzig, 1774);

Clavigo: Ein Trauerspiel (Leipzig: Weygand, 1774); translated by Carl Leftley as *Clavidgo: A Tragedy in 5 Acts* (London: Johnson, 1798);

Neueröffnetes moralisch-politisches Puppenspiel, anonymous (Leipzig & Frankfurt am Main, 1774);

Die Leiden des jungen Werthers, anonymous (Leipzig: Weygand, 1774); translated by Richard Graves as *The Sorrows of Werther,* 2 volumes (London: Dodsley, 1779);

Erwin und Elmire: Ein Schauspiel mit Gesang, anonymous (Frankfurt am Main & Leipzig, 1775);

Nicht ich, sondern Heinrich Leopold Wagner hat den Prometheus gemacht (Frankfurt am Main: Goethe, 1775);

Stella: Ein Schauspiel für Liebende in fünf Akten (Berlin: Mylius, 1776); translated anonymously as *Stella* (London: Hookham & Carpenter, 1798);

Claudine von Villa Bella: Ein Schauspiel mit Gesang (Berlin: Mylius, 1776);

Proserpina: Ein Monodrama, anonymous (N.p., 1778);

Johann Wolfgang von Goethe; oil painting by Heinrich Kolbe, circa 1822–1826 (Goethe-Museum, Düsseldorf)

Aufzug des Winters mit seinem Gefolge (N.p., 1781);

Aufzug der vier Weltalter (N.p., 1782);

Die Fischerinn: Ein Singspiel. Auf dem natürlichen Schauplatz zu Tiefurth vorgestellt (N.p., 1782);

Goethe's Schriften, 8 volumes (Leipzig: Göschen, 1787–1790)—includes in volume 2 (1787), *Die Mitschuldigen: Ein Schauspiel;* in volume 3 (1787), *Die Geschwister: Ein Schauspiel,* translated anonymously as *The Sister,* in *Dramatic Pieces from the German* (Edinburgh & London: Printed for William Creech and

T. Cadell, 1792); *Iphigenie auf Tauris: Ein Schauspiel,* translated by W. Taylor as *Iphigenia: A Tragedy* (London: Johnson, 1793); in volume 4 (1787), *Der Triumph der Empfindsamkeit: Eine dramatische Grille; Die Vögel: Nach dem Aristophanes;* in volume 5 (1788), *Egmont: Ein Trauerspiel in fünf Aufzügen,* translated anonymously as *Egmont* (London: Saunders & Otley, 1848); in volume 6 (1790), *Torquato Tasso: Ein Schauspiel,* translated by J. Cartwright as *Torquato Tasso* (London: Nutt, 1861); in volume 7 (1790), *Faust: Ein Fragment; Jery und Bätely: Ein Singspiel; Scherz, List und Rache: Ein Singspiel;*

Das Römische Carneval, anonymous (Berlin: Unger/ Weimar & Gotha: Ettinger, 1789);

Versuch die Metamorphose der Pflanzen zu erklären (Gotha: Ettinger, 1790);

Beyträge zur Optik, 2 volumes (Weimar: Industrie-Comptoir, 1791–1792);

Goethe's Neue Schriften, 7 volumes (Berlin: Unger, 1792–1800)–includes in volume 1 (1792), *Der Groß-Cophta: Ein Lustspiel in fünf Aufzügen;* as volume 2 (1794), *Reineke Fuchs,* translated by Thomas Arnold as *Reynard the Fox* (London: Natali & Bond, 1855; New York: Appleton, 1860);

Der Bürgergeneral: Ein Lustspiel in einem Aufzuge. Zweyte Fortsetzung der beyden Billets, anonymous (Berlin: Unger, 1793);

Wilhelm Meisters Lehrjahre: Ein Roman, 4 volumes (Berlin: Unger, 1795–1796); translated by Thomas Carlyle as *Wilhelm Meister's Apprenticeship* (Edinburgh: Oliver & Boyd / London: Whittaker, 1824; Boston: Wells & Lilly, 1828);

Epigramme: Venedig 1790 (Berlin: Unger, 1796);

Taschenbuch für 1798: Hermann und Dorothea (Berlin: Vieweg, 1798); translated by Thomas Holcroft as *Hermann and Dorothea* (London: Longmans, 1801; Richmond, Va.: Enquirer Press, 1805);

Neueste Gedichte (Berlin: Unger, 1800);

Was wir bringen: Vorspiel, bey Eröffnung des neuen Schauspielhauses zu Lauchstädt (Tübingen: Cotta, 1802);

Taschenbuch für das Jahr 1804: Die natürliche Tochter. Trauerspiel (Tübingen: Cotta, 1804);

Goethe's Werke, 13 volumes (Tübingen: Cotta, 1806–1810)–includes in volume 4 (1806), *Die Laune des Verliebten;* in volume 7 (1808), *Der Zauberflöte zweyter Theil;* in volume 8 (1808), *Faust: Eine Tragödie,* translated by Lord Francis L. Gower as *Faust,* in *Faust; and Schiller's Song of the Bell* (London: Murray, 1823); in volume 10 (1808), "Achilleis";

Sammlung zur Kenntniß der Gebirge von und um Karlsbad (Carlsbad: Franiecki, 1807);

Die Wahlverwandtschaften: Ein Roman, 2 volumes (Tübingen: Cotta, 1809); translated anonymously

as "Elective Affinities," in *Novels and Tales* (London: Bohn, 1854);

Maskenzug zum 30sten Januar 1810 (N.p., 1810);

Pandora: Ein Taschenbuch für das Jahr 1810 (Vienna & Trieste: Geistinger, 1810);

Zur Farbenlehre, 2 volumes (Tübingen: Cotta, 1810); translated by Sir Charles L. Eastlake as *Goethe's Theory of Colours* (London: Murray, 1840);

Philipp Hackert: Biographische Skizze, meist nach dessen eigenen Aufsätzen entworfen (Tübingen: Cotta, 1811);

Aus meinem Leben: Dichtung und Wahrheit, 3 volumes (Stuttgart & Tübingen: Cotta, 1811–1813); translated anonymously as *Memoirs of Goethe: Written by Himself,* 2 volumes (London: Colburn, 1824; New York: Collins & Hannay, 1824);

Gedichte (Tübingen: Cotta, 1812);

Des Epimenides Erwachen: Ein Festspiel (Berlin: Duncker & Humblot, 1815);

Gedichte, 2 volumes (Stuttgart & Tübingen: Cotta, 1815);

Goethe's Werke, 20 volumes (Stuttgart & Tübingen: Cotta, 1815–1819)–includes in volume 10 (1817), *Die Aufgeregten;*

Aus meinem Leben, zweyter Abtheilung erster Theil, zweyter Theil: Italienische Reise, 2 volumes (Stuttgart & Tübingen: Cotta, 1816–1817); translated by Alexander James W. Morrison as *Travels in Italy* (London: Bohn, 1846);

Bey Allerhöchster Anwesenheit Ihro Majestät der Kaiserin Mutter Maria Feodorowna in Weimar Maskenzug, anonymous (Stuttgart: Cotta, 1818);

West-östlicher Divan (Stuttgart: Cotta, 1819);

Wilhelm Meisters Wanderjahre oder Die Entsagenden: Ein Roman. Erster Theil (Stuttgart & Tübingen: Cotta, 1821); translated by Carlyle as *Wilhelm Meister's Travels; or, The Renunciants* (Edinburgh & London: Tait, 1827);

Aus meinem Leben, zweyter Abtheilung fünfter Theil: Campagne in Frankreich 1792; Belagerung von Mainz (Stuttgart & Tübingen: Cotta, 1822); translated by Robert Farie as *The Campaign in France in the Year 1792* (London: Chapman & Hall, 1849);

Werke: Vollständige Ausgabe letzter Hand, 60 volumes, volumes 41–60 edited by Johann Peter Eckermann and Friedrich Wilhelm Riemer (Stuttgart & Tübingen: Cotta, 1827–1842)–includes in volume 15 (1828), "Novelle," translated by Carlyle as "Goethe's Novel," *Fraser's Magazine,* 6, no. 34 (1832): 383–393; in volumes 21–23 (1829), revised and enlarged version of *Wilhelm Meisters Wanderjahre oder Die Entsagenden;* as volume 41 (1832), *Faust: Eine Tragödie. Zweyter Theil in fünf Akten,* translated anonymously, with Part I, as *Faust Rendered into English Verse,* 2 volumes (London: Printed by Arthur Taylor, 1838); as volume

48 (1833), *Aus meinem Leben: Dichtung und Wahrheit. Vierter Theil;*

Faust in ursprünglicher Gestalt nach der Göchenhausenschen Abschrift, edited by Erich Schmidt (Weimar: Böhlau, 1887);

Werke: Hg. im Auftrage der Großherzogin Sophie von Sachsen. Weimarer Ausgabe, 143 volumes (Weimar: Böhlau, 1887–1919)–includes in Part I, volume 37, "Buch Annette";

Goethe über seine Dichtungen: Versuch einer Sammlung aller Äußerungen des Dichters über seine poetischen Werke, 9 volumes, edited by Hans Gerhard Gräf (Frankfurt am Main: Literarische Anstalt, 1901–1914; reprinted, Darmstadt: Wissenschaftliche Buchgesellschaft, 1968);

Sämtliche Werke: Jubiläums-Ausgabe, edited by Eduard von der Hellen, 40 volumes (Stuttgart: Cotta, 1902–1912);

Sämtliche Werke: Propyläen-Ausgabe, 48 volumes (Munich & Berlin: Propyläen, 1909–1932);

Wilhelm Meisters theatralische Sendung (Stuttgart: Cotta, 1911);

Gedenkausgabe der Werke, Briefe und Gespräche: 28 August 1949, edited by Ernst Beutler, 24 volumes (Zurich: Artemis, 1948–1964);

Werke: Hamburger Ausgabe, edited by Erich Trunz and others, 14 volumes (Hamburg: Wegner, 1949–1964; revised edition, Munich: Beck, 1982);

Gesamtausgabe der Werke und Schriften, 22 volumes (Stuttgart: Cotta, 1950–1968);

Corpus der Goethezeichnungen, edited by Gerhard Femmel, 6 volumes (Leipzig: Seemann, 1958–1970);

Sämtliche Werke nach Epochen seines Schaffens, edited by Karl Richter, 20 volumes in 32 and index volume (Munich: Hanser, 1985–1998);

Sämtliche Werke, Briefe, Tagebücher und Gespräche, 40 volumes (Frankfurt am Main: Deutscher Klassiker Verlag, 1985–1999).

Selected Editions in English: *Autobiography and Works,* translated anonymously, 3 volumes (London: Bohn, 1848–1850);

Works, translated anonymously, 14 volumes (London: Bohn, 1848–1890);

Dramatic Works, translated by Anna Swanwick and Sir Walter Scott (London: Bohn, 1850);

Poems of Goethe, translated by Edgar Alfred Bowring (London: Parker, 1853; revised and enlarged edition, London: Bohn, 1874; New York: Lovell, 1884)–revised edition includes "Hermann and Dorothea" and "West-Eastern Divan";

Novels and Tales, translated by R. Dillon Boylan and others (London: Bohn, 1854);

Works: People's Edition, 9 volumes, edited by F. H. Hedge and Leopold Noa (Boston: Cassino, 1882);

Works: Illustrated by the Best German Artists, 5 volumes, edited by Hjalmar Hjorth Boyesen (Philadelphia & New York: Barrie, 1885);

Reineke Fox, West-eastern Divan, and Achilleid: Translated in the Original Metres, translated by Alexander Rogers (London: Bohn, 1890);

Works: Weimar Edition, 14 volumes, edited by Nathan Haskell Dole (Boston: Niccolls, 1902);

Goethe's Literary Essays, edited by Joel E. Spingarn (London: Milford / New York: Harcourt, Brace, 1921);

Faust, translated by Philip Wayne, 2 volumes (Harmondsworth, U.K.: Penguin, 1949, 1959);

The Sorrows of Young Werther and Selected Writings, translated by Catherine Hutter (New York: New American Library, 1962);

Elective Affinities, translated by Elizabeth Mayer and Louise Bogan (Chicago: Regnery, 1963);

Goethe, edited by David Luke (Harmondsworth, U.K.: Penguin, 1964);

Elective Affinities, translated by R. J. Hollingdale (Harmondsworth, U.K.: Penguin, 1971);

The Sorrows of Young Werther and Novella, translated by Mayer, Bogan, and W. H. Auden (New York: Vintage, 1973);

Goethe's Collected Works, 12 volumes, edited by Victor Lange, Eric Blackall, and Cyrus Hamlin (New York: Suhrkamp, 1983–1989)–comprises volume 1, *Selected Poems,* edited by Christopher Middleton, translated by Middleton, Michael Hamburger, Luke, J. F. Nims, V. Watkins (1983); volume 2, *Faust I & II,* edited and translated by Stuart Atkins (1984); volume 3, *Essays on Art and Literature,* edited by John Gearey, translated by E. and E. H. von Nardhoff (1986); volumes 4 & 5, *From My Life: Poetry and Truth; Campaign in France 1792; Siege of Mainz,* edited by Thomas Saine and Jeffrey Sammons, translated by Saine and R. Heitner (1987); volume 6, *Italian Journey,* edited by Saine and Sammons, translated by Heitner (1989); volume 7, *Early Verse Drama and Prose,* edited by Hamlin and F. Ryder, translated by R. M. Browning, Hamburger, Hamlin and Ryder (1989); volume 8, *Verse Plays and Epic,* edited by Hamlin, and Ryder, translated by Hamburger, Luke, and H. Hannum (1987); volume 9, *Wilhelm Meister's Apprenticeship,* edited by Lange, translated by Blackall and Lange (1989); volume 10, *Wilhelm Meister's Journeyman Years,* edited by Jane K. Brown, translated by Krishna Winston, J. van Heurck, and Brown (1989); volume 11, *The Sorrows of Young Werther; Elective Affinities; Novella,* edited by D. Wellbery, translated by Lange and J. Ryan (1988); volume 12, *Scientific Studies,* edited and translated by D. Miller (1988); reprinted as *Goethe's Collected Works,*

12 volumes (Princeton, N.J.: Princeton University Press, 1994–1995);

Faust, Part 1, translated by Luke (Oxford & New York: Oxford University Press, 1987);

Faust: A Tragedy, second edition, translated by Walter Arndt, edited by Cyrus Hamlin (New York: Norton, 2000).

OTHER: James Macpherson, 4 volumes, *Works of Ossian,* edited anonymously by Goethe and J. H. Merck (volumes 1–2, N.p.; volumes 3–4, Leipzig: Fleischer, 1773–1777);

Die Propyläen: Eine periodische Schrift, 3 volumes, edited by Goethe (Tübingen: Cotta, 1798–1800);

Voltaire, *Mahomet: Trauerspiel in fünf Aufzügen,* translated by Goethe (Tübingen: Cotta, 1802);

Voltaire, *Tancred: Trauerspiel in fünf Aufzügen,* translated by Goethe (Tübingen: Cotta, 1802);

Benvenuto Cellini, *Leben des Benvenuto Cellini Florentinischen Goldschmieds und Bildhauers von ihm selbst geschrieben: Übersetzt und mit einem Anhange,* translated by Goethe, 2 volumes (Tübingen: Cotta, 1803);

Taschenbuch auf das Jahr 1804, edited by Goethe and Christoph Martin Wieland (Tübingen: Cotta, 1803);

Winckelmann und sein Jahrhundert: In Briefen und Aufsätzen herausgegeben, edited by Goethe (Tübingen: Cotta, 1805);

Denis Diderot, *Rameaus Neffe: Ein Dialog von Diderot. Aus dem Manuskript übersetzt und mit Anmerkungen begleitet,* translated by Goethe (Leipzig: Göschen, 1805);

Ueber Kunst und Alterthum, 6 volumes, edited by Goethe (Stuttgart: Cotta, 1816–1832);

Zur Naturwissenschaft überhaupt, besonders zur Morphologie: Erfahrung, Betrachtung, Folgerung, durch Lebensereignisse verbunden, 2 volumes, edited by Goethe (Stuttgart & Tübingen: Cotta, 1817, 1824);

Hans Sachs, *Der deutsche Gilblas oder Leben, Wanderungen und Schicksale Johann Christoph Sachse's, eines Thüringers: Von ihm selbst verfaßt,* introduction by Goethe (Stuttgart & Tübingen: Cotta, 1822);

N. A. von Salvandy, *Don Alonzo oder Spanien: Eine Geschichte aus der gegenwärtigen Zeit,* foreword by Goethe, 5 volumes (Breslau: Max, 1825–1826);

J. C. Mämpel, *Der junge Feldjäger in französischen und englischen Diensten während des Spanisch-Portugiesischen Kriegs von 1806–1816,* introduction by Goethe, 6 volumes (volumes 1–4, Leipzig: Fleischel; volumes 5–6, Brunswick: Verlags-Comptoir, 1826–1831);

Memoiren Robert Guillemard's verabschiedeten Sergeanten: Begleitet mit historischen, meisten Theils ungedruckten Belegen von 1805 bis 1823. Aus dem Französischen, introduction by Goethe, 2 volumes (Leipzig: Weygand, 1827);

Alessandro Manzoni, *Opere poetiche,* introduction by Goethe (Jena: Frommann, 1827);

Manzoni, *Der fünfte May: Ode auf Napoleons Tod,* translated by Goethe and others (Berlin: Maurer, 1828);

Thomas Carlyle, *Leben Schillers: Aus dem Englischen,* introduction by Goethe (Frankfurt am Main: Wilmans, 1830).

PERIODICAL PUBLICATIONS: "Römische Elegien," *Die Horen* (1795); translated by Leopold Noa as *Roman Elegies Translated in the Original Metres* (Boston: Schoenhof & Moeller, 1876);

"Unterhaltungen deutscher Ausgewanderten," *Die Horen* (1795);

"Xenien," by Goethe and Friedrich Schiller, *Musenalmanach auf das Jahr 1797* (1796);

Madame de Staël, "Versuch über die Dichtungen," translated by Goethe, *Die Horen,* 5 (1796): 20–55;

"Zum Schäkespears Tag," *Allgemeine Monatsschrift für Wissenschaft und Literatur* (April 1854): 247ff.

Johann Wolfgang von Goethe is widely recognized as the greatest writer of the German tradition. The Romantic period in Germany (the late eighteenth and early nineteenth centuries) is known as the Age of Goethe, and Goethe embodies the concerns of the generation defined by the legacies of Jean-Jacques Rousseau, Immanuel Kant, and the French Revolution. His stature derives not only from his literary achievements as a lyric poet, novelist, and dramatist but also from his often significant contributions as a scientist (geologist, botanist, anatomist, physicist, historian of science) and as a critic and theorist of literature and of art. He was, finally, such an imposing personality that for the last thirty years of his life he was Germany's greatest cultural monument, serving as an object of pilgrimage from all over Europe and even from the United States and leaving the small town of Weimar a major cultural center for decades after his death. Out of this extraordinary personal presence; out of his overwhelming, almost threatening, literary stature; and out of the rejection of his political position in the turbulence of nineteenth-century German politics, a tradition developed that Goethe's greatness lay in his wisdom rather than in his literary achievement. Nevertheless, the continuing fascination with his works, especially with *Faust* (1808, 1832; translated, 1823, 1838), confirms his position as one of the most important writers of the European tradition.

Most of the available information about Goethe's earliest years comes from his autobiography, *Aus meinem*

Leben: Dichtung und Wahrheit (From my Life: Poetry and Truth, 1811–1813; translated as *Memoirs of Goethe: Written by Himself,* 1824). Written when the poet was in his sixties, long after he was established as the great man of German letters, the work must be recognized as Goethe's deliberately chosen image of himself for posterity. Goethe was born into the Frankfurt patriciate in 1749. His mother, Katharina Elisabeth Textor Goethe, was the daughter of the mayor; his father, Johann Caspar Goethe, was a leisured private citizen who devoted his energies to writing memoirs of his Italian journey (in Italian), patronizing local artists, and, above all, educating his two surviving children, the future poet and his sister, Cornelia. At an early age Goethe studied several languages, as well as art and music. By his early teens he was casting his school exercises in the form of an epistolary novel written in German, French, Italian, English, Latin (with occasional postscripts in Greek), and Yiddish; in his free time he wrote plays in French and poems for all occasions. Goethe attributed great importance for his early development to the social and political situation in Frankfurt, where the busy trade, the annual fairs, the ceremonials associated with the crowning of the Holy Roman Emperor, and the occupation by the French during the Seven Years' War of 1756 to 1763 brought a wealth of cosmopolitan experiences to his very doorstep.

At sixteen he was sent by his father to the University of Leipzig to study law, despite his own desire to study ancient literature in Göttingen. Since the beginning of the century Leipzig had been the major center for those Germans who looked to France for their cultural models. Johann Christoph Gottsched, ardent neoclassicist and doyen of German letters for much of the first half of the century, had taught at the university since 1730 and still determined the theater repertoire in Goethe's day. Goethe met Gottsched and studied with Christian Fürchtegott Gellert, the leading poet of the day. Neither had any significant influence on the young poet, despite his admiration for Gellert as a moralist. By the end of his second semester Goethe had lost interest in legal studies and felt he had exhausted the limited literary resources to be found at the university. He devoted his energy to learning the manners of polite society, to studying art privately with Adam F. Oeser, and to cultivating his talent on his own, especially in conversations with his cynical friend Ernst Wolfgang Behrisch, later tutor to the princes of Dessau. However much he admired the writings of Johann Joachim Winckelmann, who was promulgating a new classical ideal, Goethe's main interest in both art and literature was for the real and natural; when he visited the famous art collections in Dresden, he reacted with greatest enthusiasm to the Dutch school, dutifully admired the works of the Italian school, and failed to visit the classical antiquities. In literature he admired the works of Gotthold Ephraim Lessing and Christoph Martin Wieland.

Dichtung und Wahrheit describes the development of this concern for the real and natural as the most important advance Goethe made in Leipzig. His earliest surviving works date from this period: two collections of unpretentious social poems with mythological imagery in the style of the Greek poet Anacreon—the "Buch Annette" (Book for Annette), a manuscript discovered in 1895, and the *Neue Lieder* (New Songs, 1770), both inspired by Anna Katharina Schönkopf, daughter of the landlord in the inn where Goethe dined—and two short plays in alexandrines. The first play, *Die Laune des Verliebten* (The Wayward Lover, 1806), is a pastoral comedy in which a jealous lover is cured when he learns that he, too, can be unfaithful; its naturalness resides in its simplicity. The second, *Die Mitschuldigen* (Fellow Culprits, 1787), was written soon after Goethe returned to Frankfurt but is still in the style of the Leipzig works. At the end of this brief farce each of the four characters discovers that all of the others have committed some crime equivalent to his own, so that they can all forgive one another. The setting in a German inn and the topical political allusions lend a superficial realism to the play; its true naturalness, however, lies in the bittersweet ending, in which all the characters are forgiven, but it is hard to imagine what future happiness could possibly be in store for them. In this respect the ending is like that of a middle comedy of Shakespeare, to whom Goethe was turning as the embodiment of nature in literature.

In the fall of 1768 Goethe returned to Frankfurt, suffering from a serious illness. His primary comforter during his year-long convalescence was Susanna Catharina von Klettenberg, a pietist mystic who was to serve as the model for the "schöne Seele" (beautiful soul) in *Wilhelm Meisters Lehrjahre* (1795–1796; translated as *Wilhelm Meister's Apprenticeship,* 1824). Together they read the literature of alchemical Neoplatonism, a popular activity at the time in radical Protestant circles, and performed alchemical experiments. From there Goethe's reading extended into medicine. At the same time he was also reading the works of Shakespeare, Lessing, and Rousseau, and continued to do so after he was sent to Strasbourg in March 1770 to finish his law degree.

Goethe's seventeen months in Strasbourg are usually identified as one of the major turning points in his career, although the changes that took place were clearly prepared by his activities and reading of the preceding year. Strasbourg was more German culturally than Leipzig; Goethe made it represent for himself and for German literary history the birthplace of a new, thoroughly German literature. The first step in this process was his "discovery" of the Strasbourg Cathedral and enthusiastic identification of the Gothic style as German. The second and more important step was his encounter with Johann Gottfried Herder, who arrived in Strasbourg in September. The rather difficult Herder imparted to Goethe his enthusiasm for popular poetry, primitivism, recent speculation on the origins of poetry, the works of Johann Georg Hamann, the poems of Ossian (James Macpherson), and above all the novels of Henry Fielding, Laurence Sterne, and Oliver Goldsmith. Everything Goethe learned from Herder was of decisive importance for him, and not just for his Sturm und Drang period, of which Strasbourg marks the beginning; in the last decade of his life Goethe would still be fond of asserting that Sterne and Goldsmith were among the handful of writers from whom he had learned the most. The liberating impact of these new influences was visible almost immediately in the grace, power, and freedom of the folk-songlike poems he wrote for his Alsatian beloved, Friederike Brion; some of them remain among his most popular lyrics: "Mailied" (May Song) and "Willkommen und Abschied" (Welcome and Farewell), both included in volume 8 of *Goethe's Schriften* (Goethe's Writings, 1787–1790). Forty years later, when Goethe described Friederike's family in *Dichtung und Wahrheit,* he proclaimed that his treatment of the episode, even as he was experiencing it, was stylized in terms of Goldsmith's *The Vicar of Wakefield* (1766), all the way down to the names of the minor figures.

In September 1771 Goethe returned to Frankfurt, ostensibly to begin a law career but in fact to begin the most visible literary career in German history. The four years between his return and his departure for Weimar contain the first flowering of his genius and constitute for many critics the high point of his career. During this time Goethe began to practice law both in Frankfurt and in Wetzlar, seat of the supreme court of the Holy Roman Empire; he also wrote book reviews, engaged in constant visiting with literary friends, functioned as the center of the Sturm und Drang movement, and traveled on the Rhine and in Switzerland. The autobiography describes three emotional entanglements in this period. In Wetzlar in 1772 he met Charlotte (Lotte) Buff and fell in love with her before discovering that she was engaged to his friend Johann George Christian Kestner. In 1774 he became involved in an uncomfortably close friendship with Maximiliane Euphrosine von La Roche Brentano, daughter of the novelist Sophie von La Roche and future mother of the poet Clemens Brentano, while she was adjusting with difficulty to her marriage to Peter Anton Brentano, a wealthy Frankfurt merchant. The following year he became engaged to

Anna Elisabeth (Lili) Schönemann, the daughter of a wealthy banker; although it inspired a spate of wonderful poems, the engagement was broken off in September 1775. Goethe had begun his career both as a great personality and as a great writer.

The Sturm und Drang movement aimed at establishing new political, cultural, and literary forms for Germany. Following the intellectual lead of Rousseau, Herder, and Hamann, it looked to the ancients, to England, and to the German past for models to replace the French neoclassical tradition. Hence, Goethe studied Shakespeare, Homer, Pindar, and Hans Sachs (a sixteenth-century German writer of farces) and rejected the classicism of his former hero, Wieland. In 1773 Goethe published an essay on the Strasbourg Cathedral, *Von deutscher Baukunst* (On German Architecture), in which he praised the Gothic style; it also appeared the same year in the manifesto of the Sturm und Drang movement, *Von deutscher Art und Kunst* (On German Culture and Art), edited by Herder. Besides Herder Goethe's collaborators included Johann Heinrich Merck, Johann Georg Schlosser (who married Cornelia Goethe in 1773), Friedrich Maximilian Klinger, Jakob Michael Reinhold Lenz, and Heinrich Leopold Wagner. There was a dimension of religious and moral concern in the movement, which resulted in Goethe's two pleas for religious tolerance, *Brief des Pastors zu *** an den neuen Pastor zu **** (Letter from the Pastor of *** to the New Pastor of ***, 1773) and *Zwo wichtige bisher unerörterte Biblische Fragen* (Two Biblical Questions Not Previously Expounded, 1773). He studied the works of Emmanuel Swedenborg and Benedict de Spinoza and established connections with the theologian Johann Caspar Lavater, the educator Johann Bernhard Basedow, and the philosopher Friedrich Heinrich Jacobi, and with such members of the older generation of poets as Friedrich Gottlieb Klopstock, Heinrich Christian Boie, and Matthias Claudius.

His first contribution in the 1771–1775 period was to unleash the Shakespeare mania for which the Sturm und Drang movement is famous. His speech "Zum Schäkespears Tag" (For Shakespeare's Day, 1854) was presented two months after his return from Strasbourg; a dithyrambic celebration of Shakespeare as a poet of nature, it has remained one of the great milestones of German Shakespeare criticism. Even more influential was the Shakespearean history play *Götz von Berlichingen mit der eisernen Hand* (Götz von Berlichingen with the Iron Hand; translated as *Goetz von Berlichingen,* 1799), first drafted in November 1771 and published in a revised version two years later. The play is based on a sixteenth-century chronicle in which the old baron Götz tries to maintain his independence in the face of the encroaching empire. In the resulting conflict between tradition and law Götz's side degenerates, against his will, into open rebellion. The evil of the court is embodied in the beautiful Adelheid, who seduces Götz's old friend Weislingen into breaking his engagement to Götz's sister Marie. After Weislingen marries Adelheid, she poisons him. Götz dies in prison, welcoming the freedom of a higher world. The play is written in prose (the form of Wieland's translation of Shakespeare), with explosive diction and many short scenes. The emphasis on the prosaic aspects of Shakespearean diction and structure shows that the play is not only a statement in favor of Shakespeare but also a rejection of the orderly elegance of French neoclassical form for German drama.

Goethe's other dramas of the early 1770s are of three types: short satires, mostly from 1773, on literary and cultural themes in prose or in Knittelverse, the doggerel couplets made popular by Hans Sachs; incomplete poetic dramas on great figures such as Caesar, Mahomet, Prometheus, Egmont, and Faust, the extant fragments of which are among Goethe's finest poems of the period; and a group of completed plays of more conventional form—the tragedy *Clavigo* (1774; translated as *Clavidgo*, 1798), the drama *Stella* (1776; translated, 1798), and the operettas *Erwin und Elmire* (1775) and *Claudine von Villa Bella* (1776). *Clavigo* and *Stella* both deal with men like Weislingen who cannot be decisively faithful to a woman. In the first version of *Stella* the shaky hero is finally shared peacefully by the two women he has married; in 1787 Goethe gave the play a more conventional tragic ending. These four plays mark the beginning of a long series of operettas and operatic plays in Goethe's oeuvre.

Goethe's poems of this period set new standards for the genre in Germany. There are ballads, such as "Der König in Thule" (The King of Thule, 1782; later included in *Faust*); love poems, many of which were later set to music by Beethoven and Schubert; and occasional poems, such as the masterpiece "Auf dem See" (On the Lake), written in response to a boat trip on the Lake of Zurich in the summer of 1775. There are also, finally, the great Pindaric hymns—among them "Wanderers Sturmlied" (Wanderer's Storm Hymn, included in volume 2 of *Goethe's Werke* [Goethe's Works, 1815–1819], 1815), "Prometheus," and "Ganymed" (both included in volume 8 of *Goethe's Schriften*, 1789).

Goethe's most famous work of the 1771–1775 period is *Die Leiden des jungen Werthers* (translated as *The Sorrows of Werther*, 1779), published in 1774. In this paradigmatic novel of eighteenth-century sensibility, Werther traces in a series of letters the course of his love for Lotte, who is already engaged to a solid young official when Werther meets her. Misled by the warmth of Lotte's friendship but most of all by his own intense

imagination—which projects upon Lotte all the ideals garnered from his reading of Homer, Goldsmith, and Ossian—Werther gradually loses touch with the world around him, ceases to narrate coherently (an editor takes over the narration), and finally shoots himself. The novel is based on Goethe's relationship with Charlotte Buff and her fiancé, Kestner; the suicide for love of an acquaintance, Karl Wilhelm Jerusalem, provided the model for Werther's death. As important as the personal experiences for the novel are the literary experiences: the epistolary novel of sensibility from Samuel Richardson through Rousseau reaches its zenith in this novel. Through the passion of Werther the basic patterns of eighteenth-century subjectivity are called into question. The same conflicts and torments that Werther suffers in his relationship with Charlotte he also suffers in his relationships with nature and God. Through Werther's destructive preoccupation with himself Goethe offers a sympathetic yet penetrating commentary on the effusive introspectiveness of eighteenth-century consciousness, with its burgeoning psychology and crumbling metaphysics. By dramatically shortening the form, composing with a tight but elaborate symmetrical structure, incorporating foreign material such as translations from Ossian, inserting subordinate narratives, and especially by allowing Werther no respondents and then interrupting the flow of letters with a third-person narrator, Goethe simultaneously brought the epistolary tradition to its peak and to an end. The novel established Goethe as a European celebrity virtually overnight. To his distress it was widely misunderstood to glorify, rather than criticize, the fashionable melancholy of the age; he revised it extensively for the 1787 edition, the version in which it is now read. For his entire lifetime and beyond, *Die Leiden des jungen Werthers* was the work by which Goethe was known to the non-German world; only *Faust* has come to command the same kind of attention.

In the fall of 1775 Goethe left Frankfurt to visit Weimar at the invitation of the young duke Karl August. He quickly became the duke's close personal friend, the general court wit, and the organizer of court theatricals. In 1776 he was awarded the rights of citizenship and assigned administrative responsibilities in the tiny duchy. Weimar was already a center for the arts, since the duke's mother, Anna Amalia, had brought Wieland to be her son's tutor; Goethe soon persuaded Herder to accept a position there as well. Much of Goethe's time was spent traveling, either for official reasons or in company with the duke. He also made two journeys of literary interest: to the Harz mountains in the winter of 1777 and to Switzerland in the fall of 1779. Shortly after his arrival in Weimar he had entered into an intense friendship with Charlotte von Stein, the wife of a court official; this relationship dominated his emotional life for the next twelve years, transforming him from the ebullient Sturmer und Dranger of the 1770s into the reserved, polished courtier of his last four decades. Humanity, virtue, and self-control were the code words of this relationship, as they were to be for much of Goethe's subsequent writing. By the early 1780s Goethe was in charge of mines, roads, war, and finance; in 1782 the duke procured for him a patent of nobility (allowing him to add "von" to his name). Just as important for his future development as the new location, occupation, and personal relationships was the broadening of Goethe's intellectual interests in Weimar: for the first time he became consistently interested in science. As when he studied alchemy, his interest extended beyond reading to collecting and experimenting; but unlike his alchemical studies and some phrenological work he had undertaken for Lavater, his work in geology, anatomy, and botany led not only to literary results but to discoveries and scientific publications. In 1784 he demonstrated the existence of the human intermaxillary (premaxillary) bone and thereby the continuity of anatomical structures across species (unbeknownst to him the discovery had already been made in Paris in 1780), and in 1787 he conceived an influential theory of metamorphosis in plants.

The productivity of the early 1770s abated in Weimar—not surprisingly, given Goethe's many other responsibilities—but it by no means collapsed. Here he wrote many of his best-loved ballads, songs, reflective nature lyrics, and love poems. While the sublimity, irony, folk-song qualities, pathos, and broad humor of his earlier poetry often persist, there is also a new reflectiveness that moderates the emotion of the earlier poems. Goethe continued to write operetta librettos and occasional satires for court entertainments; to his repertory of "minor" drama he added court masques, which he continued to write until late in his life; he also wrote a free adaptation of Aristophanes' *The Birds* (1787). He worked intermittently on *Egmont* (1787; translated, 1848), which he had begun shortly before leaving Frankfurt; on successive versions, mainly in prose, of *Iphigenie auf Tauris,* published in its final blank verse version in 1787 (translated as *Iphigenia: A Tragedy,* 1793); and on *Torquato Tasso* (1790; translated, 1861). He also wrote *Wilhelm Meisters theatralische Sendung* (Wilhelm Meister's Theatrical Mission, 1911), a lively fragment about the state of the German theater.

The pressure of all these competing interests finally became too great, and Goethe fled to Italy, leaving Carlsbad in secret early in the morning of 3 September 1786. He recorded his impressions at the time in a diary for Frau von Stein; later he drew heavily on this diary for his *Italienische Reise* (1817; translated as *Travels in Italy,* 1846). In his reflections on Italy and his experiences there the interests and developments of the previous twelve years coalesce and become clearly articulated. Goethe had always expected to complete his education with a journey to Italy, as his father had, and twice before he had almost set out on that journey. The trip came to signify for him a rebirth, not only into a new life but into what he was always going to become: at several levels it was a journey of self-recovery. But it was in no sense a journey into himself, for his main concern was to look at objects as much as possible for themselves—at the rocks and the plants; the customs, theatricals, and festivals of the people (but never their feelings or political concerns); architecture, sculpture, and, to a lesser extent, painting. His Italy was the Italy of the high Renaissance, which included and subsumed ancient Roman Italy. Apart from brief stays in Venice and Naples and a tour of Sicily, Goethe spent all of his time in Rome, visiting galleries and monuments to study painting and sculpture. For most of his stay he socialized only with the German art colony, especially with Wilhelm Tischbein and Angelika Kauffmann. He revised and completed *Egmont, Iphigenie auf Tauris,* and part of *Torquato Tasso* for the edition of his works that was under way (1787–1790); he also added two scenes to the version of *Faust* that he had composed before he left Frankfurt for Weimar, and selected from his *Faust* materials scenes that he published in preliminary form as *Faust: Ein Fragment* (1790).

The three plays Goethe revised are usually considered the core of his "classical" works, the first efflorescence of the objective style he developed in Italy. *Egmont* is still concerned with the tragedy of the genius too great for the world around him and with the problem of his consciousness, but from the opposite point of view from that of *Die Leiden des jungen Werthers.* If the latter portrays tragic preoccupation with the self, *Egmont* articulates the tragedy of what Goethe called "das Dämonische" (the demonic), that pure unconsciousness that is in direct contact with the wellsprings of being. Comparing himself to a sleepwalker, Egmont, prince of Garve, refuses to be self-conscious, refuses to be interpretable, or to interpret the behavior of others. Immensely popular with the people of the Netherlands, who are suffering under the rule of Philip II of Spain, Egmont ignores warnings that neither his rank, his record of service, nor his standing with the people can save him when the regime decides he is too dangerous. Rejecting all intrigue, he walks blindly into a trap set by the wily Duke of Alba; but, like Götz von Berlichingen, he finds freedom just before his death in a vision of his mistress, Klärchen, as Freedom personified. The classicism of this play may best be identified in its symbolic, operatic, yet still intensely psychological language and themes.

The play, which is in rhythmic prose, ranges in tone from Shakespearean mob scenes to what Friedrich Schiller called a "salto mortale in eine Opernwelt" (somersault into opera) at the end; actually, in their choral effects and the way that they symbolize the situation of the hero, the mob scenes are already operatic. Goethe was no longer imitating Shakespeare but had absorbed him into a new dramatic form of his own making.

Iphigenie auf Tauris combines the same intense psychological concerns with a symbolic form derived less from Shakespeare than from Euripides. Goethe is generally understood to have internalized and psychologized Euripides' drama, in which Orestes comes to barbarian Tauris in search of a statue of Apollo's sister and finds his own sister there. By making the Furies invisible and by reinterpreting the oracle so that Orestes and Iphigenie do not have to steal the statue of Diana, Goethe has indeed collapsed the mythological level of the action into the human level; but at the same time by replacing Euripides' deus ex machina with humans telling the truth, interpreting, and granting grace, he has raised the human level to the mythological: by their acts Iphigenie, Orestes, and the king of Tauris have civilized the world. The end of this play anticipates *Faust* in its celebration of the creative power of the human mind and will. In Italy Goethe recast the play into blank verse. The meter had been established in German drama by Lessing in *Nathan der Weise* (1779; translated as *Nathan the Wise*, 1781); Goethe showed it capable of a sublimity and complexity of diction previously achieved only in the classical meters of Klopstock and of his own Pindaric hymns.

The power and flexibility of Goethe's new dramatic language emerges fully in *Torquato Tasso*, which he finished revising after he returned from Italy in the spring of 1788. The play shows the Renaissance poet Tasso when he has just completed his great epic, *La Gerusalemme liberata*. He is unable to come to terms either with the real political world embodied in the statesman Antonio Montecatino, or to find a satisfactory relationship with his inspiring ideal, the princess Leonore d'Este, sister of his patron, Duke Alfonso. Caught in complex intrigues, both real and imagined, Tasso attempts to fight a duel with Antonio and is placed under arrest by the duke; later, he impulsively embraces the princess. Seemingly abandoned by the duke and the princess, he turns to Antonio for support as he sinks into madness. The blank verse and the Renaissance setting frame a much more objective version of the problem of *Egmont*. Egmont's freedom and lack of self-consciousness appear here as the idealism of the poet, who is above the vagaries and political demands of the real world. Tasso's opposite, the consummate courtier Antonio, is not seen as evil, as Alba

was in *Egmont*, but rather as the other half of Tasso's incomplete personality. (Faust was later to speak of the two souls in his breast, the one that sought the heavens and the other that clung to the world.) The two women in the play, both named Leonore, are likewise complementary personalities; bound together by their love for Tasso and for one another they seek to draw Tasso in opposite directions. By placing his hero between embodiments of his own drives toward the ideal and the real, Goethe transformed his earlier realistic psychology into a symbolic representation of psychological analysis. As a result, he was able to dispense with the Shakespearean mob scenes he used so effectively in *Egmont*; in *Torquato Tasso* the psychological aspects appear visibly on the stage instead of being mirrored in minor characters. Thus it is that despite their seeming lack of stage action *Iphigenie auf Tauris* and *Torquato Tasso* are among the most compelling plays in the German language.

Goethe returned from Italy as, he declared, an artist. Karl August relieved him of all official obligations except the directorship of the court theater, which was officially established in 1791, and of libraries and natural-historical and artistic collections in the duchy, including those at the University of Jena. Goethe returned to emotional dislocations and resentments occasioned both by the changes he had undergone and by his decision to go to Italy alone and in secret. Most severe among these was the rupture with Frau von Stein, who could not forgive his having left her side—let alone his open installation of a mistress, Christiane Vulpius, in his house shortly after his return. Only in the mid 1790s was any relationship with Frau von Stein reestablished, and then on a rather distant basis. Christiane bore Goethe several children, only one of whom—Julius August Walther, born in 1789—survived, and remained his companion until her death. Their marriage in 1806 did little to moderate the Weimar court's disapproval of Goethe's scandalous liaison with his uneducated "dicke Hälfte" (fatter half), as she was cruelly called, but their persistence in this situation is a measure both of their devotion to one another and of Goethe's distance from his immediate circle.

Indeed, he lived thereafter in a world of ideas and intellectual activities rather than in a world of events. Even the Italian journey, which he treasured for the rest of his life, was important to him as a remembered experience: he was not at all pleased when the duke dispatched him to Venice in 1790, though he used the time to learn more about Venetian painting. In Weimar he devoted his energy to studies of all sorts. In addition to his earlier interests in geology, botany, and comparative anatomy he became passionately interested in optics, and in 1790 he began publishing increasingly anti-Newtonian essays about the theory of color and scientific method in general. Much of his time was devoted to studying Kant, Plato, and Homer. His other major area of interest was art. This more academic development of his interests was reflected in his new friendships with the educator and statesman Wilhelm von Humboldt and the art historian Hans Meyer; the latter, whom he had met in Italy, lived in his house from 1791 until 1802. The French Revolution was the one political event that necessarily impinged on Goethe's life, not only because it was a topic of constant interest in all circles but also because the duke, who had entered the Prussian army, insisted that Goethe accompany him on campaigns to France in 1792 and to the Rhine in 1793. Goethe reported on these events in "Campagne in Frankreich 1792" (translated as *The Campaign in France in the Year 1792,* 1849) and "Belagerung von Mainz" (Siege of Mainz), published together in 1822. He continued his optical and artistic studies while trudging around after the army; his refusal to be submerged in military activity enabled him to present a clear picture of the daily reality of the campaigns.

Goethe's literary output in the early 1790s was relatively sparse. Two short plays, *Der Groß-Cophta* (The Great Cophta, 1792) and *Der Bürgergeneral* (The Citizen General, 1793), and a dramatic fragment, *Die Aufgeregten* (The Excited Ones, published in 1817), deal with the French Revolution in poetic terms. The verse epic *Reineke Fuchs* (1794; translated as *Reynard the Fox,* 1855), does so more effectively. This translation and adaptation into hexameter of a Low German version of the old story of the fox at the court of the lion is the first result of Goethe's study of Homer. But the most important poetry of these years is the cycle of love poems "Römische Elegien" (1795; translated as *Roman Elegies Translated in the Original Metres,* 1876), written in the first year of his relationship with Christiane. The poems describe the gradual acceptance of a German visitor into the Roman world of history, love, art, and poetry. As the poet takes possession of his Roman beloved, so too does he enter into the cultural heritage represented by Rome to the eighteenth century and everything represented by the south to the Gothic north. Written in the elegiac couplets of Propertius, Catullus, and Ovid, and in their frank manner, the poems transmute their Roman predecessors with the same facility and success as Goethe's classical plays appropriate their predecessors. They created something of a scandal when they were published but are now recognized as the greatest love poems of the generation.

The year 1794 marks the beginning of Goethe's friendship with Schiller. Schiller had come to Jena in 1789 as professor of history on an appointment arranged by Goethe, but the older poet had had two

reasons for keeping his distance from the newcomer: not only had Schiller made his reputation as a powerful Sturm und Drang poet a decade after Goethe had renounced the movement, but he had recently given up poetry for immersion in Kant. Only in 1794 did a conversation after a lecture in Jena bring the two together into what rapidly became a mutually supportive and productive relationship. Much of Goethe's energy in the following years was devoted to Schiller's journal *Die Horen,* published from 1795 to 1797, and then to his own successor journal, *Die Propyläen,* published from 1798 to 1800. The program of these journals and of the poets' other work together was nothing less than the establishment of a classical German literature in the sense that the literature of fifth-century Athens had been classical: a literature that both represented and shaped a nation. While neither poet ever really spoke for or influenced the nation in the way to which they aspired, their mutual encouragement and criticism resulted in the greatest masterpieces of both men's careers.

Their excitement and productivity derived, however, not only from their friendship but also from the simultaneous emergence, largely under Goethe's supervision, of the University of Jena as the major center in Germany for the study of philosophy and science. Johann Gottlieb Fichte, Friedrich Wilhelm Joseph Schelling, and Georg Wilhelm Friedrich Hegel spent substantial parts of the 1790s in Jena, Fichte and Schelling in appointments arranged in part by Goethe. Drawn to Jena by their presence and by Goethe's presence in nearby Weimar were, at various times, the major Romantic poets—August Wilhelm and Friedrich Schlegel, Ludwig Tieck, Clemens Brentano, Novalis (Friedrich von Hardenberg), Friedrich Hölderlin, and Heinrich von Kleist. Drawn there also for frequent visits were Wilhelm von Humboldt and his brother, the naturalist Alexander von Humboldt. Goethe himself frequently visited Jena to attend lectures and discussions on philosophy, science, and literature. His scientific and literary studies continued unabated, with extensive reading in Greek literature, and, under the influence of A. W. Schlegel, renewed study of Shakespeare and the discovery of Calderón. He also devoted much time to running the court theater—producing, directing, and training the company both in the great modern repertory created by Mozart, Lessing, Schiller, and himself and also in the classics from the Greeks through Shakespeare and Racine. Even more than in Frankfurt in the 1770s Goethe was at the center of German intellectual life. His poetic achievement in all areas in this period is staggering. Against a rich background of "minor" works—scientific papers; important theoretical essays on art and literature; translations of works by Madame de Staël, Denis Diderot, Benvenuto Cellini, and Voltaire; a fragmentary sequel to Mozart's *Die Zauberflöte* (The Magic Flute); and a spectacular torso of a drama about the French Revolution, *Die natürliche Tochter* (The Natural Daughter, 1804)—Goethe produced masterpieces which set the standards for most of the nineteenth century in lyric poetry, prose narrative, and drama.

In addition to the flow of occasional and personal poems, Goethe and Schiller wrote a large collection of satiric epigrams titled "Xenien" (Xenias, 1796) and a series of famous ballads. Goethe also continued his study and practice of classical meters with a series of elegies and "Achilleis" (1808; translated as "Achilleid," 1890), a fragment in hexameter on the death of Achilles. But his most important work in this genre is *Hermann und Dorothea* (1798; translated as *Hermann and Dorothea,* 1801) a hexameter idyll in nine cantos. About an innkeeper's son in a small German town who courts a refugee fleeing the French, the poem constitutes Goethe's most important poetic response to the revolution. At the same time its delicately ironic double vision, in which its characters appear both as limited, very German bourgeois and yet also as Homeric figures, makes the poem the paradigmatic achievement of Goethe's classicism.

Goethe's prose narratives of the 1790s are no less remarkable. For Schiller's *Die Horen* he wrote "Unterhaltungen deutscher Ausgewanderten" (1795; translated as "The Recreations of the German Emigrants," 1854), a collection of novellas in a frame narrative about refugees—this time aristocrats instead of bourgeois—from the French Revolution; the cycle focuses on the development of individual virtues such as cooperativeness and self-control as the basis for social order. But it is more important for formal reasons than for its content: it established the novella as a significant genre in German literature, and the fairy tale with which it concludes was the inspiration and model for similar works into the twentieth century. Nevertheless, in the context of the 1790s "Unterhaltungen deutscher Ausgewanderten" ranks as one of Goethe's minor works, for the great narrative of the decade was *Wilhelm Meisters Lehrjahre* (1795–1796; translated as *Wilhelm Meister's Apprenticeship,* 1824), the revision of the novel Goethe had drafted before he went to Italy. He had begun the revision in 1791, but the most significant part was completed in 1795 in the first flush of his friendship with Schiller. As the new title suggests, the novel no longer deals just with the theater but explores the modes of being that are open to a thoughtful member of the middle class at the close of the eighteenth century. In this respect the novel is like *Die Leiden des jungen Werthers,* but Wilhelm's problem is not the destructive unity of a world projected by his own solipsism; it is, rather, how to make sense out of a world and circumstances which seem to lack any coherence whatsoever. The paradigmatic example of the European Bildungsroman, *Wilhelm Meisters Lehrjahre* follows its hero through a series of love affairs from late adolescence to early manhood as he flees his wealthy middle-class home to become an actor, outgrows the narrow circumstances of the German theater, and joins a secret society composed mainly of landed aristocrats committed to developing new forms of stability in a changing world. As in *Torquato Tasso,* the various figures he encounters embody different possible modes of being for Wilhelm himself—ranging from the loose actress Philine to the poetic child Mignon to the pious "schöne Seele" (beautiful soul) to the ideal woman Natalie, to whom he becomes engaged. First the theater, a traditional metaphor for life, then the mysterious secret society of the tower provide the focus for Wilhelm's journey through art and poetry toward active participation in the world. The novel encompasses a vast range of individuals, character types, settings, episodes, and kinds of narrative, as well as inserted songs. The Romantics immediately hailed the novel as an immeasurably great achievement and then, in a series of imitations, struggled with the challenges it posed. The novel sums up and combines, as no single English novel before Charles Dickens's late works did, the achievements of Fielding, Sterne, and Goldsmith; although it was fashionable for English novelists in the nineteenth century to deplore Goethe's novel for its loose morals, it established the tradition of the Bildungsroman on which they all depended.

Faust is Goethe's best-known work of the 1790s. The core of the tragedy of Margarete had been written in prose before Goethe left Frankfurt; a manuscript of this version, known as the *Urfaust* (original *Faust*), was discovered and published in 1887. Parts of this version plus the two scenes composed in Italy had been published in 1790 as *Faust: Ein Fragment.* From 1797 to 1801, with Schiller's encouragement, Goethe rewrote the existing scenes, expanding some of them, and added the prologues, the pact scenes, and the Walpurgis Night segment to complete Part I of the drama, which was published in 1808. He introduces several important changes in the old legend of the scholar who makes a pact with the devil Mephistopheles: his Faust seeks not power through knowledge but access to transcendent knowledge denied to the human mind; the pact is transformed into a bet under the terms of which Faust will be allowed to live as long as Mephistopheles fails to satisfy his striving for transcendence. Most significantly, Goethe makes the second half of Part I into a love tragedy: Faust seduces Margarete, an innocent young girl who embodies for him the transcendent ideal that he seeks; she is condemned to death for killing their infant, but at the last moment, as Faust and Mephistopheles abandon her in prison, a voice from above declares that she is saved. *Faust,* in typical Romantic fashion, conflates Neoplatonism, which opposes a transcendent mind to an immanent world, with Kantianism, which opposes an internal subject to an external object; thus, sometimes Faust has two souls, one of which longs for transcendence, the other for the world (the Neoplatonist version of the Romantic dialectic), and at other times he feels imprisoned within himself and unable to apprehend the world outside his mind (the Kantian version of the Romantic dialectic). Both sets of oppositions are resolved in play or art. Faust's pact with the devil commits him, a striver after transcendent absolutes rather like Werther, to submerge himself restlessly in the reality of the world, like Wilhelm Meister. His opposing souls come into brief moments of harmony with one another but in moments that, by the terms of his pact with Mephistopheles, must not last. The tragedy of Part I, and the tragedy of Margarete, is that the eternities of the spirit must be subject to the destruction of time if they are to be perceived in the world. The intellectual complexity is matched by the stylistic complexity: Goethe transformed the unreflected, rather primitive Shakespeareanism of the early Sturm und Drang version into the highly sophisticated, "classical," thoroughly catholic text of Part I, which appropriates and transmutes vast numbers of texts from the entire Western tradition (excepting only the Greeks, whom Goethe reserved for Part II). Similarly, the Faust theme, which Lessing and after him the Sturm und Drang movement had identified as the quintessential German theme, becomes in Goethe's treatment a bond to link Germany to the European tradition. At the same time the unreflected neoclassical definition of tragedy in the early version is transformed into a renovation of non-Aristotelian forms, ranging from mystery play and Corpus Christi play to eighteenth-century operetta. In *Faust* Goethe established yet again a new genre, a world theater of such complexity that it has had few successors—certainly none of equal stature.

The death of Schiller in 1805 and the defeat of the Prussians at Jena in 1806 mark another major turning point in Goethe's life. The concentration of leading German intellectuals at the University of Jena gradually dispersed, so that Goethe's loose ties to the younger Romantic generation were maintained at an increasing distance. Furthermore, his sympathy with Napoleon, his insistence on the independence of art from politics, and his unorthodox social and religious attitudes alienated him from an ever-increasing portion of his public; by the time of his death he was clearly Germany's greatest, but not its most popular, writer. For most of the nineteenth century, in fact, Heinrich Heine's label

for Goethe, "der große Heide" (the great pagan) stuck, with *pagan* generally understood in its most pejorative sense. Nevertheless, for the next thirteen years Goethe continued his activities in art, history, science, and literature at what for anyone else would be considered a prodigious rate. He maintained his interest in classical art, wrote a biography (1811) of Philipp Hackert, an artist he had known in Italy, and took great interest in the emerging talents of Caspar David Friedrich and Philipp Otto Runge. Through his friendship with Sulpiz Boisserée, his early interest in Gothic art was reawakened; from 1816 until his death he edited a journal, *Ueber Kunst und Alterthum* (On Art and Antiquity), devoted to these interests. He collected manuscripts and coins, and began reading more widely in history.

He also became more conscious of his own historic role, perhaps partly as a result of being summoned to meet Napoleon in 1808. Around this time his friend Friedrich von Müller began keeping records of his conversations with Goethe, and Goethe started writing his autobiography. The first installment, *Dichtung und Wahrheit,* appeared in 1811. Apart from the information this work offers about Goethe and his interpretation of himself, it is important for the view of his times that it contains. Goethe's great contribution to the development of autobiography was his recognition that the individual can only be understood in his historical context and that all autobiographical writing is historiography.

Goethe worked steadily in the five years following Schiller's death to complete his vast *Zur Farbenlehre* (1810; translated as *Goethe's Theory of Colours,* 1840), which he sometimes called his single most important work. It consists of three parts: an exposition of Goethe's own theory of color, a polemic against the Newtonian theory that white light is a mixture of colors, and a collection of materials on the history of color theory from antiquity to Goethe's own time. While Goethe's theory has never been accepted by physicists, his insights on the perception of color have been influential, as has his recognition that scientific ideas are conditioned by their historical contexts.

As in art, Goethe's tastes in literature remained open to Romantic influence; to his continuing interest in Shakespeare and Calderón he added the medieval German epic the *Nibelungenlied.* He also followed the work of the new generation of poets, inside and outside of Germany, with great interest. In the theater he produced a series of plays by Calderón, stimulating thereby a lasting revival of his works; in addition, he produced plays by younger Romantic dramatists, such as Heinrich von Kleist and Zacharias Werner. He continued writing court masques, but only one major dramatic work, the operatic fragment *Pandora* (1810). He wrote poems steadily, experimenting with new forms in his first group of sonnets and trying out Persian attitudes and forms in the *West-östlicher Divan* (1819; translated as "West-Eastern Divan," 1874), a book of poems composed in response to the German translation of Hafiz. Like the "Römische Elegien," these poems, many of them masterpieces, are arranged into a sketchy plot that articulates the poet's encounter with Hafiz and the culture he represents. The collection embodies better than any of his work except *Faust* the aging poet's passionate concern for "Weltliteratur" (world literature), by which term Goethe summarized his belief in a literary tradition that transcended national boundaries. The *West-östlicher Divan* also contains "Noten und Abhandlungen" (Notes and Treatises), brief essays on the history of Persian life and letters. As in his autobiographical and scientific writings, historical context had become indispensable to Goethe.

Before Schiller's death Goethe had begun planning a sequel to *Wilhelm Meisters Lehrjahre* that was, however, to be a cycle of novellas rather than a novel. Several of these novellas were written in the succeeding decade, but one of them so absorbed Goethe's interest that it developed into a novel in its own right: *Die Wahlverwandtschaften* (1809; translated as "Elective Affinities," 1854). The title refers metaphorically to the capacity of certain elements to displace others during chemical reactions. A young girl, Ottilie, and an unnamed captain arrive at the estate of Eduard and Charlotte, and a double displacement ensues: Eduard and Ottilie are attracted to each other, as are Charlotte and the captain. When Charlotte gives birth to her and Eduard's child, it bears, paradoxically, the features of Ottilie and the captain, with whom the spouses have committed adultery only in spirit. The situation is resolved only when Ottilie forbids Eduard to divorce Charlotte and then starves herself to death. The novel retraces the concerns of *Die Leiden des jungen Werthers,* but in a more abstract and symbolic fashion, as a third-person narrative with only inserted, impersonal diary passages and a full-scale inserted novella. Eduard is a middle-aged Werther who has survived the loss of his beloved Charlotte to marry her on the rebound from her first marriage. Confronting his selfishness and subjectivity is an inscrutable moral law embodied in a powerful natural environment and in the equally inscrutable Ottilie. The novel subtly leaves open to question the extent to which this law is not inherent in nature, but projected by the characters themselves. With its paradoxical double adultery, its frank treatment of divorce, its suicide, and its apparent apotheosis, the novel scandalized most of its readers; despite its undeniable and significant influence in the nineteenth century, especially in England and America, it only became a respectable object of study in the twentieth. It is now considered one of Goethe's major works.

Goethe's wife died in 1816; the following year their son August married Ottilie von Pogwisch, who then ran the household she and August shared with Goethe. Also in 1817 Goethe resigned as director of the court theater after some forty years of supervising Weimar's theatrical life. In the wake of the Wartburg celebration of 1817, an expression of German liberal and national sentiment, Goethe became even more alienated from the political aspirations of his younger countrymen. He spent his last years almost as a living monument to himself, sitting for portraits and busts and receiving the visits of young intellectuals from near and far. This impression is heightened by his extensive autobiographical activities in his last decade. He completed *Dichtung und Wahrheit* and *Italienische Reise* and wrote "Campagne in Frankreich 1792" and "Belagerung von Mainz," as well as shorter reports of his activities year by year. He also organized his papers; published what he could; supervised the early stages of a complete edition of his works, the *Werke: Vollständige Ausgabe letzter Hand* (Works: Complete Edition with Final Touches, 1827–1842); and arranged for the publication of other papers after his death. Finally, he spent much time in conversations that he knew were being recorded for posterity; the most famous of these are the ones with Johann Peter Eckermann, beginning in 1823.

But these last years were not devoted only to fixing the image of the great personality. Goethe read widely and voluminously: classical authors, Shakespeare, Calderón, his beloved English novelists, and contemporary writers such as Lord Byron, Alessandro Manzoni, Sir Walter Scott, and Victor Hugo. Between 1817 and 1824 he published essays on morphology and general scientific topics in two series, continued his work in optics, read extensively in medicine, and began reading and writing about meteorology. He continued to write literary essays, reviews, and major poems. The most important among the latter are "Urworte Orphisch" (Orphic Utterances), "Trilogie der Leidenschaft" (Trilogy of Passion), "Chinesisch-Deutsche Jahres und Tageszeiten" (Sino-German Seasons and Times of Day), and the poems written in Dornburg after the death of Karl August in 1828. A masterly novella, called simply "Novelle" (Novella, 1828; translated as "Goethe's Novel," 1832), was written in 1826–1827. But Goethe also completed two major large-scale works, *Wilhelm Meisters Wanderjahre oder Die Entsagenden* (1821; translated as *Wilhelm Meister's Travels; or, The Renunciants,* 1827) and *Faust,* Part II (1832; translated, 1838).

Like Goethe's other novels, *Wilhelm Meisters Wanderjahre* represents a significant advance in the nature and structure of the European novel, though it took a long time for its true importance to be recognized. Goethe had begun planning sequels to both *Wilhelm*

Meisters Lehrjahre and *Unterhaltungen deutscher Ausgewanderten* before Schiller's death. The result was *Wilhelm Meisters Wanderjahre*, which appeared in a first version in 1821 and in a substantially revised and expanded version in 1829. The frame is a loose narrative of Wilhelm's journeymanship, his travels to increase his mastery of life in company with his son Felix. On his way he is offered innumerable novellas, reports, and collections of aphorisms to read, all of which are included and many of whose characters, along with old friends from *Wilhelm Meisters Lehrjahre*, wander in and out of the frame narrative. The end of Wilhelm's journey, his reunion with his beloved Natalie, is delayed to some indefinite time beyond the end of the novel. With this loose structure Goethe questions the possibility of individual development in the fragmented society that Europe had become during his lifetime and thus calls into question the ideals of his earlier novel and of his cultural program of the 1790s. It no longer seems possible for individual development and education to lead to social cohesion and order. Sympathetic parodies of eighteenth-century writers in the novel mourn the loss of subjectivity imposed by the new historical conditions: the problem is exactly the reverse of that in *Die Leiden des jungen Werthers*. Its complex ironies of tone and structure made the novel inaccessible to early audiences. Only in the twentieth century, as the accuracy of Goethe's reading of the nineteenth century became clear, was it taken seriously; and only since World War II have its literary merits begun to be appreciated.

The second part of *Faust,* completed in 1831 and published posthumously at Goethe's desire, has had a similar—though, perhaps because of its undeniable stylistic virtuosity, not quite so extreme—pattern of reception. Begun in the later stages of composition of Part I but completed only between 1825 and 1831, it is an elaborate unfolding and historicizing of the first part. It shows Faust first at the imperial court, then at the "Klassische Walpurgisnacht" (classical witches' sabbath), where he ransacks Greek mythology to find Helena, who bears him a son. Later he returns to the wars of the emperor, then spends his old age supervising land-reclamation projects. Satisfied that he is working for the benefit of humanity, despite the murder of an elderly couple (killed in a fire started by Mephistopheles' henchmen), Faust renounces magic and dies, still striving to improve his lands. Divine Grace, however, saves his soul, which is shown ascending in pursuit of an ever-receding ideal embodied once more in Margarete, "das Ewig-Weibliche" (the eternal feminine). Most of the play, from the middle of Act I to the beginning of Act IV, grounds both itself and all of modern European literature in the classical tradition, going back to what was understood at the time as the oldest levels of classical mythology. This undertaking is possible only on the basis of Goethe's extensive learning, his ability to absorb and recreate literary styles, and his understanding of the nature of allegory, a mode of writing that had been virtually lost in the eighteenth century. But not only does the play sum up Goethe's and Europe's relation to the classical tradition; it also reflects, like *Wilhelm Meisters Wanderjahre,* on the state of European culture and politics in Goethe's last years, and on the human condition in general. Despite the richness of the text, it never loses sight of the central issues of Part I. Over and over it makes the points that pure truth cannot be permanently manifested in time—the tragedy of the historicist; that truth can be known only temporally and imperfectly in the world—the tragedy of the Platonist; and that truth can only be known through the mental projections of the seeker himself—the tragedy of the Kantian. Nowhere are the central concerns of European Romanticism more cogently summed up in all their ramifications than in Goethe's last masterpiece. On 22 March 1832, less than two months after making his final revisions of *Faust,* Goethe died, probably of a heart attack.

Like all Romantics, Goethe was a profoundly dialectical thinker. For a variety of reasons, including the power of his personality, his preference for concrete detail over broad abstraction, the complexity of his views, and the uncongeniality of some of his attitudes in the prevailing political and social climate, his dialectic was disassembled and his works fragmented into the separate statements of a sage. Thus, opposing readings of Goethe have developed—as serene Olympian or tortured nihilist, as the embodiment of nineteenth-century culture or as utterly out of touch with the world around him, as concerned or indifferent—and there has been a long tradition of ambivalence toward him in Germany. The nineteenth century had strong reservations about the unconventionality of his moral stance and about his rejection of a strong nationalist position, while later generations have had more difficulty with his lack of direct political engagement. But both the vehemence of these reactions and the continuing vitality of his work testify to a power of thought that he was aware of from the earliest years of his career. An acquaintance speaks of his drive in the early 1770s "die Gedanken selbst, wie sie wären, zu denken und zu sagen" (to think and say the thought itself as it really is). This effort to articulate "the thought itself as it really is" is the challenge his writing still presents.

Letters:

Werke: Hg. im Auftrage der Großherzogin Sophie von Sachsen. Weimarer Ausgabe, Part 4, 50 volumes (Weimar: Böhlau, 1887–1912).

Interviews:

Johann Peter Eckermann and Frédéric Jacob Soret, *Gespräche mit Goethe in den letzten Jahren seines Lebens: 1823–1832,* 3 volumes (Leipzig: Brockhaus, 1837–1848); translated by John Oxenford as *Conversations of Goethe with Eckermann and Soret,* 2 volumes (London: Smith, Elder, 1850);

Flodoard Freiherr von Biedermann, Max Morris, Hans Gerhard Gräf, and Leonhard L. Mackall, eds., *Goethes Gespräche: Gesamtausgabe,* 5 volumes (Leipzig: Biedermann, 1909–1911);

Ernst and Renate Grumach, eds., *Goethe: Begegnungen und Gespräche,* 5 volumes (Berlin: De Gruyter, 1965–1985);

Conversations and Encounters, edited and translated by David Luke and Robert Pick (Chicago: Regnery, 1966; London: Wolff, 1966).

Bibliographies:

Karl Goedeke, *Grundriß zur Geschichte der deutschen Dichtung,* third edition, volume 4, part 3 (Dresden: Ehlermann, 1912); volume 4, part 5 (Berlin: Akademie, 1957);

Hans Pyritz, Heinz Nicolai, and Gerhard Burkhardt, *Goethe-Bibliographie,* 2 volumes (Heidelberg: Winter, 1965–1968); continued in *Goethe: Neue Folge des Jahrbuchs der Goethe Gesellschaft* (1955–);

Waltraud Hagen, *Die Drucke von Goethes Werken* (Berlin: Akademie, 1971).

Biographies:

George Henry Lewes, *The Life and Works of Goethe,* 2 volumes (London: Nutt, 1855);

Albert Bielschowsky, *Goethe: Sein Leben und seine Werke,* 2 volumes (Munich: Beck, 1896–1904); translated by W. Alpha Cooper as *The Life of Goethe,* 3 volumes (New York & London: Putnam's, 1905–1908; reprinted, 1970);

Richard Friedenthal, *Goethe: Sein Leben und seine Zeit* (Munich: Piper, 1963); published simultaneously in English as *Goethe: His Life and Times* (Cleveland: World, 1963);

Robert Steiger, ed., *Goethes Leben von Tag zu Tag,* 8 volumes to date (Zurich: Artemis, 1982–1996);

References:

Frederick Amrine, Francis Zucker, and Harvey Wheeler, eds., *Goethe and the Sciences: A Reappraisal,* Boston Studies in the Philosophy of Science, no. 97 (Boston: Reidel, 1987);

Stuart P. Atkins, *Essays on Goethe* (Columbia, S.C.: Camden House, 1995);

Atkins, *Goethe's Faust: A Literary Analysis* (Cambridge: Harvard University Press, 1958);

Atkins, *The Testament of Werther in Poetry and Drama* (Cambridge: Harvard University Press, 1949);

Benjamin Bennett, *Goethe's Theory of Poetry: Faust and the Regeneration of Language* (Ithaca, N.Y.: Cornell University Press, 1986);

Eric A. Blackall, *Goethe and the Novel* (Ithaca, N.Y.: Cornell University Press, 1976);

Jane K. Brown, *Goethe's Cyclical Narratives: The Unterhaltungen deutscher Ausgewanderten and Wilhelm Meisters Wanderjahre,* University of North Carolina Studies in the Germanic Languages and Literatures, no. 82 (Chapel Hill: University of North Carolina Press, 1975);

Brown, *Goethe's Faust: The German Tragedy* (Ithaca, N.Y.: Cornell University Press, 1986);

Brown, *Goethe's Faust: Theater of the World* (New York: Twayne, 1992);

Walter H. Bruford, *Culture and Society in Classical Weimar, 1775–1806* (Cambridge: Cambridge University Press, 1962);

Pietro Citati, *Goethe,* translated by Raymond Rosenthal (New York: Dial, 1974);

Allan P. Cottrell, *Goethe's Faust,* University of North Carolina Studies in the Germanic Languages and Literatures, no. 86 (Chapel Hill: University of North Carolina Press, 1976);

Wilhelm Emrich, *Die Symbolik von "Faust II": Sinn und Vorformen* (Frankfurt am Main & Bonn: Athenäum, 1957);

Barker Fairley, *A Study of Goethe* (Oxford: Clarendon Press, 1947);

John Gearey, *Goethe's Faust: The Making of Part I* (New Haven: Yale University Press, 1981);

Gearey, *Goethe's Other Faust: The Drama Part II* (Toronto & Buffalo: University of Toronto Press, 1992);

Ilse Graham, *Goethe: A Portrait of the Artist* (Berlin & New York: De Gruyter, 1977);

Ronald D. Gray, *Goethe the Alchemist: A Study of Alchemical Symbolism in Goethe's Literary and Scientific Works* (Cambridge: Cambridge University Press, 1952);

Harry G. Haile, *Invitation to Goethe's Faust* (University: University of Alabama Press, 1978);

Harold Jantz, *The Form of Faust: The Work of Art and Its Intrinsic Structures* (Baltimore: Johns Hopkins University Press, 1978);

Elise von Keudell, *Goethe als Benutzer der Weimarer Bibliothek* (Weimar: Böhlau, 1931);

Victor Lange, *The Classical Age of German Literature, 1740–1815* (New York: Holmes & Meier, 1982);

Lange, ed., *Goethe: Twentieth Century Views* (Englewood Cliffs, N.J.: Prentice-Hall, 1968);

Meredith Lee, *Studies in Goethe's Lyric Cycles,* University of North Carolina Studies in the Germanic Languages and Literatures, no. 93 (Chapel Hill: University of North Carolina Press, 1978);

Wolfgang Leppmann, *The German Image of Goethe* (Oxford: Clarendon Press, 1961);

Karl Robert Mandelkow, *Goethe im Urteil seiner Kritiker,* 4 volumes (Munich: Beck, 1975–1984);

Eudo C. Mason, *Goethe's Faust: Its Genesis and Purport* (Berkeley: University of California Press, 1967);

Hans Mayer, ed., *Spiegelungen Goethes in unserer Zeit* (Wiesbaden: Limes, 1949); revised and enlarged as *Goethe im XX. Jahrhundert* (Hamburg: Wegner, 1967);

Clark S. Muenzer, *Figures of Identity: Goethe's Novels and the Enigmatic Self* (University Park: Pennsylvania State University Press, 1984);

Ernst M. Oppenheimer, *Goethe's Poetry for Occasions* (Toronto: University of Toronto Press, 1974);

T. J. Reed, *The Classical Centre: Goethe and Weimar 1775–1832* (London: Croom Helm / New York: Barnes & Noble, 1980);

Paul Requadt, *Goethes "Faust I": Leitmotivik und Architektur* (Munich: Fink, 1972);

Hans Ruppert, *Goethes Bibliothek* (Weimar: Arion, 1958);

Emil Staiger, *Goethe,* 3 volumes (Zurich: Atlantis, 1952–1959);

Fritz Strich, *Goethe und die Weltliteratur* (Bern: Francke, 1946); translated by C. A. M. Sym as *Goethe and World Literature* (London: Routledge & Kegan Paul, 1949; reprinted, 1972);

Karl Viëtor, *Goethe: Dichtung, Wissenschaft, Weltbild* (1949); translated by Moses Hadas as *Goethe, the Poet* (Cambridge: Harvard University Press, 1949; reprinted, 1970), and by Bayard Quincy Morgan as *Goethe, the Thinker* (Cambridge: Harvard University Press, 1950);

Elizabeth M. Wilkinson and Leonard A. Willoughby, *Goethe: Poet and Thinker* (New York: Barnes & Noble, 1962);

Bernd Witte and others, eds., *Goethe-Handbuch: In Vier Bänden* (Stuttgart: Metzler, 1996–1998).

Papers:

The bulk of Goethe's papers are in the Goethe-und-Schiller-Archiv, Weimar. The Goethe Museum, Düsseldorf, houses a major collection of manuscripts, portraits, and first editions. A smaller collection of Goethe manuscripts is at the Freies Deutsches Hochstift Frankfurter Goethemuseum (the museum is the house in which Goethe grew up), Frankfurt am Main. The Speck Collection in the Beinecke Rare Books Library, Yale University, contains first editions and a substantial collection of Goetheana.

Gottfried von Straßburg

(died before 1230)

Michael S. Batts
University of British Columbia

This entry was updated by Professor Batts from his entry in DLB 138: German Writers
and Works of the High Middle Ages: 1170–1280.

MAJOR WORK: *Tristan und Isolde* (circa 1210)

Manuscripts: There are eleven complete manuscripts
of this work: B (Cologne, Historisches Archiv, no.
*88), E (Modena, Biblioteca Estense, MS. Est.
57), F (Florence, Biblioteca Nazionale Centrale,
MS. B. R. 226), H (Heidelberg, Universitätsbibliothek, cod. pal. germ. 360), M (Munich, Bayerische Staatsbibliothek, cod. germ. 51), N
(Berlin, Staatsbibliothek Preuischer Kulturbesitz,
MS. germ. qu. 284), P (Berlin, Staatsbibliothek
Preußischer Kulturbesitz, MS. germ. fol. 640), R
(Brussels, Bibliothèque Royale de Belgique, M.S.
14967), S (Hamburg, Staats-und Universitätsbibliothek, MS. germ. 12), and W (Vienna, Österreichische Nationalbibliothek, cod. vindob. 2707, 3).
Two of these manuscripts date from the thirteenth
century (M, H), four from the fourteenth (F, W,
B, N), and four from the fifteenth (D, E, R); S is
an eighteenth-century copy of a fifteenth-century
manuscript. Manuscripts B, H, M, N, R, and S
include the continuation by Ulrich von Türheim;
E, F, and O include the continuation by Heinrich
von Freiberg; P includes a continuation adapted
from one by Eilhard von Oberge. There are also
fragments of thirteen other manuscripts dating
from the thirteenth, fourteenth, and fifteenth centuries.

First publication: "Tristan, ein Rittergedicht aus dem
XIII. Jahrhundert," in *Samlung deutscher Gedichte
aus dem XII., XIII. und XIV. Jahrhundert,* edited by
Christoph Heinrich Müller, volume 2 (Berlin:
Printed by C. S. Spener, 1785).

Standard editions: *Tristan: Erster Teil. Text,* edited by
Karl Marold (Leipzig: Avenarius, 1906); revised
by Werner Schröder (Berlin: De Gruyter, 1969);
Tristan und Isold, edited by Friedrich Ranke (Berlin: Weidmann, 1930).

*Miniature of Gottfried von Straßburg (with diptych on knee)
reciting from his* Tristan und Isolde *(Heidelberg,
Universitätsbibliothek, cpg 360, f.364a)*

Editions in modern German: *Tristan und Isolde,* 2 vol-
umes, translated by Karl Simrock (Leipzig:
Brockhaus, 1855); *Tristan,* 2 volumes, edited by
Reinhold Bechstein (Leipzig: Brockhaus, 1869–
1870); *Tristan und Isolde: Gedicht,* translated by Her-
mann Kurz (Stuttgart: Cotta, 1844); *Tristan und
Isolde: Neu bearbeitet und nach den altfranzösischen
Tristanfragmenten des Trouvère Thomas ergänzt,* edited

161

by Wilhelm Hertz (Stuttgart: Kröner, 1877); *Tristan und Isolde: Hofisches Epos. Aus dem Mittelhochdeutschen übersetzt,* 2 volumes, translated by Karl Pannier (Leipzig: Reclam, 1903); *Tristan und Isolt: A Poem,* edited by August Closs (Oxford: Blackwell, 1944); *Tristan und Isold: In Auswahl,* edited by Friedrich Ranke (Berlin: Francke, 1946); *Tristan: Nach dem Text von Friedrich Ranke neu herausgegeben, ins Neuhochdeutsche übersetzt mit einem Stellenkommentar und einem Nachwort von Rüdiger Krohn,* fourth edition, Universal-Bibliothek, 4473 (Stuttgart: Reclam, 1995).

Editions in English: *The Story of Tristan and Iseult,* 2 volumes, translated by Jessie L. Weston (London: Nutt, 1889; New York: New Amsterdam, 1900); *The "Tristan and Isolde" of Gottfried von Strassburg,* edited and translated by Edwin H. Zeydel (Princeton: Princeton University Press, 1948); *Tristan, Translated Entire for the First Time: With the Surviving Fragments of the Tristan of Thomas, Newly Translated,* edited and translated by A. T. Hatto (Harmondsworth, U.K.: Penguin, 1960; Baltimore: Penguin, 1960); *Tristan and Isolde,* edited and revised by Francis G. Gentry (New York: Continuum, 1988).

Gottfried von Straßburg was highly regarded by writers who came after him, and his reputation was never greater than it is today. His work, like that of most writers of the high medieval period, was lost from sight with the advent of the Renaissance and was only rediscovered in the latter part of the eighteenth century. During the first half of the eighteenth century Gottfried's *Tristan und Isolde* (circa 1210; translated as *The Story of Tristan and Iseult,* 1889) was appreciated for its virtuosity, but the moral codes of the day, coupled with the belief that the actions and statements of literary figures represented the philosophy of the author, led to condemnation of the work on moral grounds. Today *Tristan und Isolde* is recognized not simply as the height of stylistic virtuosity in its genre but as a masterpiece of characterization, a subtle and moving portrayal of the psychological forces that move men and women. Superior to all other poets of the German High Middle Ages as a versifier, Gottfried also outshines them in his knowledge of the human psyche and can be said to constitute one of the twin peaks of this period in German literature—the other being Wolfram von Eschenbach, who takes not individuals but the whole of German society, if not the whole world, as his subject.

As is the case with so many other poets of this time, and despite the evident popularity of his work, there is no documentary evidence about Gottfried's life. One must, therefore, seek biographical data in his literary works and in those of his contemporaries and successors. Gottfried is almost always referred to as *meister* (master); this title has traditionally been taken to mean that he was of bourgeois rather than noble birth, but the term may also imply that he was a learned man, a master of arts. The initial letters of the quatrains with which *Tristan und Isolde* begins are G, D, I, E, T, E, R, I, C, H, T, and I; the G presumably stands for *Gottfried,* while T and I are the first letters of *Tristan* and *Isolde.* The remaining letters of the names of the protagonists occur at irregular intervals throughout the remainder of the work, as do also—possibly—some further letters of Gottfried's name. The name *Dieterich* is likely that of a patron.

The existence of the incomplete acrostic is evidence that a much longer work was planned than the approximately 19,500 lines that have been preserved. Ulrich von Türheim completed the work from 1230 to 1235; his comment "that death interrupted his living days unfortunately before his time" may mean that Gottfried died at an early age. Rudolf von Ems eulogizes Gottfried in his *Alexander the Great,* a poem written probably around 1230. It is, therefore, clear that Gottfried died before 1230, but there is no evidence as to when he was born.

The only evidence for the date of composition of *Tristan und Isolde* is to be found in the poem itself. When Tristan is knighted by his uncle, King Mark, Gottfried refuses to describe the ceremony; such events traditionally involved great pomp and pageantry, and their depiction was frequently an excuse for poets to display their virtuosity. Instead, Gottfried provides a brief overview of recent literary history in which he refers to Hartmann von Aue in the present tense and to the minnesinger Reinmar der Alte as having fallen silent (died) and castigates an unnamed poet who is presumed to be Wolfram. Since Reinmar had died by 1210 and Hartmann did not die until after that year, possibly not until about 1220, it can be assumed that Gottfried wrote *Tristan und Isolde* between these dates—certainly earlier rather than later in the decade, since he knew Wolfram's *Parzival* (completed around 1210) well enough to criticize it and since Wolfram responded to Gottfried's criticism in his *Willehalm,* which was commenced around 1212.

There is sufficient evidence in *Tristan und Isolde* to indicate that, whether bourgeois or not, Gottfried was, for his time, well educated. He knew a good deal about the literature of his own country (besides his discussions of Hartmann, Reinmar, and Wolfram, he gives high praise to Bligger von Steinach, of whom today virtually nothing is known); in addition, he had a thorough knowledge of French, for he makes no errors in using his French source and claims to have seen other French versions of the same story. He was familiar with the standard works of classical antiquity and seems to have had some acquaintance with the law. He was well versed in theology, even making use for secular purposes of a form of allegorical interpretation that had previously been applied only in the religious sphere. And while he may have had bourgeois origins, he was fully cognizant of the lifestyle of the nobility, from court ceremony and hunting techniques to political councils. Above all, it is evident that Gottfried studied literature and composition: he rhymes with apparent ease and employs, with great skill and evident enjoyment, all manner of rhetorical and stylistic devices.

The historical origins of the story of Tristan and Isolde are obscure. A Prince Drust (Drostan), son of a Pictish king Talorc (the names Trystan and Tallwch are found in Welsh literary works), lived at the end of the eighth century, and a King Mark is recorded by a ninth-century chronicler as having lived in Cornwall in the sixth century. There is no evidence of an historical Isolde, and the etymology of her name is unknown. How these figures came to be associated with one another and with this story is impossible to tell, but the basic plot is Celtic and originally resembled the story of Potiphar's wife, who tried to seduce Joseph, her husband's head servant. In the evolution of the Tristan and Isolde story Isolde's unsuccessful attempt to seduce Tristan was replaced by a successful one and finally by a love potion that draws them irresistibly to one another. Various stock elements were also added to the story as time passed, such as the fight of the young man against a giant or dragon, the poisoned sword for which only one person has the cure, the life in the forest, and the black and white sails; and the work was extended at one end by the stories of the protagonists' parents (primarily those of Tristan) and at the other by the introduction of a second Isolde. Such elements may have been borrowings from myth, from the literature of classical antiquity, or from oriental sources. By the middle of the twelfth century the story was largely complete; there existed, in addition, short works that recounted episodes from the story, it being assumed that the listener or reader would know the general outline of the story as a whole.

This version of approximately 1150, on which the extant works are assumed to have been based, is commonly referred to as the *estoire* and was written in French. The link between the Celtic peoples and the European continent was provided by Henry II of England, who, as Count Henry of Anjou, had married Eleanor of Aquitaine. From the *estoire* derive, on the one hand, the works of Eilhard von Oberge and Béroul, and, on the other, that of Thomas of Brittany. It is gen-

erally assumed that Béroul wrote around 1170 and Eilhard at the same time or ten to twenty years later; the version by Thomas may have been written as early as 1150 or as late as 1190. No complete manuscript of any of these works has been preserved. Gottfried makes a strong point of having selected Thomas's version as the true one, but Gottfried's work ends just after the point at which the surviving text of Thomas's work begins. A comparison of Gottfried's work with its source must therefore be carried out on the basis of a reconstruction of Thomas's, using primarily a Norwegian translation of Thomas's made in 1226 that is somewhat abbreviated, and an even more abbreviated English stanzaic poem of about 1300, *Sir Tristrem*.

It is, however, fairly evident why Gottfried chose Thomas's work rather than that of the Frenchman Béroul or the German Eilhard. In the latter works the effect of the potion wears off after some years; also the flight of the lovers into the forest is occasioned by their being caught in flagrante delicto and condemned to death. In Eilhard's version they are to be burned at the stake; when Tristan escapes, the king is so furious that he orders Isolde to be given over to a crowd of lepers—a fate worse than death. Such uncourtly behavior is not acceptable to Gottfried, who is concerned not only with the proprieties but also with verisimilitude: he is critical, for example, of Eilhard's story of the golden hair, dropped by a swallow, which prompts the king to send Tristan out to find the owner of the hair so that the king can marry her. In Thomas's version the material is organized much more carefully and consistently, and with due regard for courtly convention. The lovers are banished from court rather than fleeing to escape execution; their sojourn in the forest is an idyll rather than a period of suffering; and the permanence of the effect of the potion makes Tristan's continued love for Isolde while in exile, despite his entanglement with the second Isolde, understandable and meaningful. The whole plot hangs together.

Gottfried's *Tristan und Isolde* is much more than the story of the love of two individuals. Rather, it is an analysis of the quality of love in various forms, of the role of love in society, and of the relationship of love to life and death. Precisely what lesson, if any, Gottfried intended his audience to draw from his work is by no means clear, and interpretation has perhaps been hindered rather than assisted by the involved introduction and frequent authorial interpolations.

The story of Tristan and Isolde in Gottfried's version is preceded by a brief history of Tristan's parents. Rivalin, Lord of Parmenie, after successfully waging war against his neighbor, Morgan, sets off to visit the famed court of King Mark at Tintagel in Cornwall. Here he meets Mark's sister, Blancheflor; they fall in love, but neither at first understands what is happening. Rivalin is a man of action, untutored in the arts, though not entirely without social graces, while Blancheflor has been brought up, to judge by her comments about her brother, largely in seclusion. Blancheflor takes the initiative in their relationship; Gottfried allows his female figures a far more active role than is customary in chivalric literature. They declare their love to each other but keep it secret from the outside world. Rivalin is severely wounded in a battle against Mark's enemies; Blancheflor gains entry to his sickroom, and their love is consummated while Rivalin is apparently dying. Their blind passion is symbolized by their union in the darkness of the sickroom. The power of love brings her at first "geliche als ob si waere tot" (almost to the point of death), but the same power revives her and enables him to consummate their love and to recover from what had seemed a mortal wound. Their union takes place in concealment, foreshadowing the union of Tristan and Isolde in the cabin of their ship and later in the grotto. The sexual union of Rivalin and Blancheflor also takes place in the shadow of Rivalin's expected death; it results in his recovery, but she now carries the child that will be brought into the world in the shadow of both their deaths. Tristan's life and death are prefigured in and to be understood in relationship to the lives and deaths of Rivalin and Blancheflor. When Rivalin recovers, he is forced to return to Parmenie to protect his property against renewed attacks by Morgan, secretly taking Blancheflor with him. In the fighting Rivalin is killed, and Blancheflor dies giving birth to a son. The son is named Tristan, from the French *triste* (sad), and is brought up as the child of a couple faithful to Rivalin, Rual and Floraete, to protect him from Morgan.

The early life of Tristan is described in great detail and is intended to qualify him for the experience of a much deeper kind of love. Although he acquires the chivalric skills to a high degree, much greater emphasis is placed on his knowledge and appreciation of the arts. He is a skilled linguist, versed in literature, and above all a musician; his understanding of human nature is based both on these arts and on personal experience gained during the travels that are part of his education. In the guise of the minstrel Tantris, Tristan will transmit much of his knowledge and understanding to Isolde; thus, in her case too, there is emphasis on her ability as a musician, and she is clearly a fitting companion for Tristan. When the moment comes, she, like Blancheflor, will take the initiative.

In the flower of his youth Tristan is abducted by a visiting Norwegian merchant but hastily put ashore on the coast of Cornwall when a storm breaks out that seems to be the wrath of God for this crime. Tristan makes his way, unknown and unknowingly, to the court of Mark at Tintagel, where he becomes a great favorite on account of his many accomplishments. Finally Rual, who has searched everywhere for him, arrives at Tintagel and reveals the story of Tristan's parentage. Mark, his uncle, knights Tristan and sends him back to Parmenie, where he kills Morgan and regains the lands of his father.

Tristan leaves the land in Rual's charge and returns to Cornwall, where he finds that the "giant" champion of Ireland, Morold, has arrived to demand the tribute laid on the country by the Irish king when Mark was a child. The alternative to paying the tribute is single combat with Morold, which only Tristan dares to undertake. He kills Morold but receives a poisoned wound, which only Morold's sister, Isolde, queen of Ireland, can cure.

Tristan goes to Ireland disguised as the minstrel Tantris and is so successful as a teacher of the younger Isolde, the daughter of the queen, that the queen cures him. He returns to Cornwall, where he becomes more popular than ever with his uncle, who wants to make him his heir. But the barons insist that Mark take a wife. When Mark agrees, they select the princess Isolde, whose beauty and nobility have been so highly praised by Tristan, as the only possible wife and Tristan as the best person to undertake the embassy.

Arriving in Ireland for the second time, Tristan finds the countryside ravaged by a dragon and hears that the reward for killing the beast is the hand of the princess. He kills the dragon, cuts out its tongue, and conceals it on his person, but he is overcome by the fumes from the tongue and falls unconscious. A steward, enamored of the princess, finds the dead dragon and claims to have killed it. Neither mother nor daughter believes him; they search for and find the real hero, convey him secretly to the palace, and revive him. He promises to appear and confound the steward, but before he can do so Princess Isolde notices that "Tantris's" sword has a piece missing that exactly fits the piece found in Morold's skull when his body was returned to Ireland, and she realizes that the minstrel is Tristan. Unable to take revenge herself and caught in a dilemma because of the steward, she abandons the idea of revenge. The steward is confounded by the evidence of the tongue, and Tristan claims Isolde on behalf of his uncle. Through their marriage the old enmity between the two kingdoms will be ended.

On the voyage back to Cornwall, Tristan and Isolde inadvertently drink a love potion that was put in the safekeeping of Brangane, Isolde's maidservant, and intended for Isolde and Mark. They subsequently consummate their love. The love potion has been interpreted as necessary to justify an otherwise unacceptable adultery; this view was taken in the sixteenth century and related in part to versions in which Mark also partakes of the potion (Gottfried, however, insists that the remainder of the potion was destroyed and not given to Mark) or the efficacy is of limited duration. Alternatively, the potion has been interpreted as symbolic of a love that has already sprung up between the two. The prevailing modern view is that Gottfried does not depict Tristan and Isolde as falling in love before drinking the potion, but that its function is, nevertheless, largely symbolic. The position can, however, be taken that the potion is meant to be taken literally and that no symbolism is intended; belief in such things was, after all, current in Gottfried's day and remained so for a long time to come. Gottfried portrays Tristan and Isolde as being made for one another; but the potion initiates their relationship, and it may, therefore, be taken as symbolic both of the unpredictability of love and of the dangers love may bring: "ezn was niht mit wine / . . . / ez was diu wernde swaere, / die endelose herzenot, / von der si beide lagen tot" (it was no wine / . . . / it was their lasting sorrow, / their never-ending anguish, / from which they both found death).

Isolde takes the initiative in a manner similar to that of Blancheflor, but the physical union with Tristan is delayed. Brangane realizes that their love, if it remains unconsummated, could lead to their deaths, and she therefore allows them their will. After they have admitted their love to Brangane and obtained her consent to their union, it is Tristan who comes to Isolde; he is led by love, which, as the narrator Gottfried puts it, is acting as their physician: sexual union is the medicine prescribed by love as a cure for their sickness. When Brangane later tells them of the potion and suggests that it will bring about their deaths, Tristan claims that if Isolde is to be his death in this manner, he would wish to die eternally. They willingly embrace the risk. Life, love, and death, linked involuntarily in the union of Rivalin and Blancheflor, are consciously accepted as inextricably linked in the future of Tristan and Isolde.

Tristan and Isolde persuade Brangane, who is a virgin, to take Isolde's place on the wedding night, since the wedding must take place as planned. Subsequently Isolde plots to have Brangane killed; but the plot fails, and the two are reconciled. That neither Tristan nor Isolde for a moment considers that Isolde's marriage to Mark should not take place has nothing to do with fears for their personal safety or concern for the political situation, but everything to do with the medieval concept of society. An existence outside society, which any form of elopement—such as that described in similar Celtic tales—would entail, was simply unthinkable. The noble hearts to whom Gottfried dedicates the work in his prologue understand the quality of true love and accept that it brings both pleasure and pain. Both emo-

tions are experienced by the lovers as they meet in secret or are foiled in their attempts to do so.

There follows a series of episodes in which suspicions of infidelity are aroused in the king—primarily by his followers Melot and Marjodo—and then allayed, until the king becomes so confused that he insists on a formal trial: Isolde is to swear an oath of innocence while holding a red-hot iron. The purpose of these episodes, which are closely linked with major themes running throughout the work—darkness and light, blindness and seeing, hunter and quarry—is to contrast the true love of Tristan and Isolde with false kinds of love and to portray the difficulties encountered by true lovers in a society where love has become salable. There is a distinct progression in these episodes, inasmuch as the circle of those involved widens and the dispute is eventually carried into the public arena. The trouble begins with Tristan's "friend," the steward Marjodo, who discovers Tristan's affair with Isolde and tries to betray them to the king—not out of loyalty to the latter, but because he himself is in love with Isolde and is jealous of Tristan. The king is also in love with Isolde, but his love does not go beyond the desire for physical possession: he was unable to distinguish on the wedding night between Brangane and Isolde, and his concern is the safeguarding of his property.

As Isolde approaches the place where the oath is to be taken, she asks a pilgrim—Tristan in disguise—to lift her from the boat and carry her ashore. He stumbles and falls down with her, so that she is able to swear an oath never to have lain with any man except her husband and the person in whose arms she just fell. Isolde passes the test (occasioning a sarcastic comment from the author about the way God blows with the wind), but the lovers are now kept apart as much as possible, and the king sees that Isolde loves Tristan better than she loves him. He banishes them, and they retire to a grotto far out in the wilderness. In this grotto, which is described in great detail as the abode of true love, they remain for some time, playing, singing, telling tales of love, and hunting for pleasure but not for food; they need no sustenance besides the presence of the other.

Mark's lack of any deeper feeling for Isolde is not criticized by Gottfried, and Mark gains the reader's sympathy to some extent: first by his desire not to suspect his wife and nephew of wrongdoing, and second by sending them away when he thinks that their love for each other is greater than their love for him and that his situation is, consequently, ignominious. In so doing, he overrides the official and public evidence of the trial by ordeal, an episode that has caused a great deal of discussion over the years. The so-called false oath (the oath is literally true but deceptive) was long considered blasphemous but is now generally accepted as Gottfried's criticism of the manner in which individuals take the name of the Lord in vain in the pursuit of their own ends. Although there are other references to matters religious, Gottfried attacks neither the church nor individual representatives of the church, and he does not set up a "religion of love" as a substitute for Christianity.

Banished from a situation of hardship and suffering into paradise, the lovers remain aware of society beyond the wilderness that surrounds them (they send Curvenal, Tristan's faithful servant, back to keep an eye on things for them). In this idyllic situation they pass the time with all manner of pleasures, especially with music and the telling of tales of lovers of the past. The grotto is described as dating from heathen times, but the detailed description and the allegorical interpretation of its shape, dimensions, and colors (for example, the roundness and smoothness of the chamber signify the simplicity of love, the breadth of its power, and the height of its aspiration) are derived from Christian interpretations of the fabric of church buildings, and the recognition of this derivation in Friedrich Ranke's *Die Allegorie der Minnegrotte in Gottfrieds "Tristan"* (The Allegory of the Love Grotto in Gottfried's "Tristan," 1925) has been the most important factor in the modern interpretation of this episode. Other interpretations range from the religious (the grotto as a temple in a religion of love) to the Freudian (the grotto as womb), some of which are summarized in Vlastimil Vrablik's "Die Minnegrotte in Gottfrieds von Strassburg 'Tristan und Isolde': Ein Versuch zur Typologie der Liebe" (The Love Grotto in Gottfried von Straßburg's "Tristan und Isolde": An Attempt at a Typology of Love, 1989). Vrablik's comment that Gottfried's concept of love flies in the face of the *Minnesang* tradition, however, is mistaken: sexual love is a constant factor in *Minnesang*. The traditional dawn song, for example, is based on what is in effect a brief sojourn in a love grotto.

The specific details of the grotto contribute to an understanding of the nature of true love, but its most important aspect is its location. Gottfried describes it at first as in Cornwall and attainable only across a pathless wilderness (which reminds one of the wilderness through which Hartmann's Gregorius passes on his way to a different epiphany). He later claims to have reached the grotto himself and to have known it since his early days, but he also says he has never been in Cornwall. In other words, the grotto represents a state of existence rather than a real place, a state that can be attained only with commitment and suffering and only for a limited time. The ultimate experience of love is akin to the mystic's momentary experience of union with God; the connection is, presumably, deliberately made when Gottfried refers to the grotto as a "kluse" (hermit's cell) and to the lovers as "klusenaere" (anchorites).

When Tristan and Isolde fear that they are about to be discovered by the king, they lie down on their bed with a sword between them. The king, who wants Isolde back, interprets this act as evidence of their innocence, and they return to court. Their deception of Mark and his response to it make it evident that he is compelled by the desire for the physical possession of Isolde to blind himself to the truth. Nevertheless, he surrounds Isolde with watchers to prevent her and Tristan from coming together, and she is impelled to circumvent the restrictions imposed upon her.

The lovers become careless, however, and are one day seen by the king sleeping in each others' arms. They awaken as he leaves to fetch witnesses, and by the time the king returns with the witnesses Tristan has fled. Mark cannot, therefore, prove Isolde's guilt, and she remains with him. The scene in which Mark finds Tristan and Isolde sleeping together in broad daylight in the orchard is prefaced by a diatribe in which Gottfried criticizes those who feel it necessary to lay down rules to protect their honor and argues that Eve would never have offered Adam the fruit if God had not expressly forbidden it. By drawing this parallel Gottfried suggests that Isolde, by inviting Tristan to bed in the orchard, is sinning against true love. Their love has been dragged down to Mark's level, to the level of physical desire. Their discovery by Mark means for him the end of all doubt. Although by the time the witnesses arrive Isolde is alone, Mark knows the truth and can no longer deceive himself. For the lovers, separation cannot mean the end of love, for true love such as theirs survives it.

In exile Tristan meets another woman named Isolde—Isolde Whitehands—and is tempted to fall in love with her, persuading himself that "his" Isolde is happy with her husband. It is at this point that Gottfried's poem breaks off. Tristan becomes involved in yet another kind of love when he meets the second Isolde. It is true that he is initially attracted to her by her name, but the manner in which he behaves is reminiscent of *Minnesang*, of love as a social game. In the playful wooing of Isolde Whitehands, Gottfried depicts Tristan's deviation from the true path of love, a path to which he later would return, just as Isolde has returned to it after the brief lapse in the orchard.

There is sufficient evidence that Gottfried was following his source fairly closely and that the poem would, therefore, have continued, as Thomas's version does, with Tristan's unconsummated marriage to Isolde Whitehands, with Tristan's visits in disguise to his first love, and with his receipt of a second poisoned wound. The first Isolde, who has inherited her mother's skills, is sent for, and the messenger is told to hoist a white sail if she is on board, a black sail if she is not. She does come; but out of jealousy Isolde Whitehands tells Tristan that the sail is black, and he dies. When Isolde arrives and finds Tristan dead, she dies over his corpse. They are buried together. The episodes in which Tristan makes brief visits to Isolde would again exemplify the mixture of joy and suffering experienced by true lovers and together with the second poisoned wound would provide a kind of mirror image of the first stages of their love; the end, which was prefigured in the beginning, is their union in death.

No discussion of Gottfried's great work would be complete without some reference to the vast number of works of literature, art, and music that have been based on it. Gottfried took over the work of his predecessors, of course, and to that extent he is only a link, if one of the greatest, in a long and broad European tradition. But it is undoubtedly his work that made the story so popular in Germany that motifs from it were used in the following centuries to decorate domestic objects, carpets, and tapestries. Since the rediscovery of his work in the eighteenth century there has been an uninterrupted succession of translations, reworkings in literary form, and adaptations into other media. In music the best-known example is, of course, Richard Wagner's music drama *Tristan und Isolde* (1859; translated as *Tristan and Isolde,* 1889). Hans Werner Henze's *Tristan: Preludes für Klavier, Tonbänder und Orchester* (Tristan: Preludes for Piano, Tapes, and Orchestra, 1973) was subsequently used as the score of a ballet on the same subject. Thomas Mann's novella "Tristan" (1903; translated, 1925) is fairly well known, as is Georg Kaiser's play *König Hahnrei* (King Cuckold, 1913), a Freudian version of the story. Mann also drafted an outline for a film on Tristan and Isolde that was never produced. There have been film versions of this story, however, among them Veith von Fürstenberg's *Feuer und Schwert* (Fire and Sword).

Bibliography and Concordance:

Hans-Hugo Steinhoff, *Bibliographie zu Gottfried von Straßburg,* 2 volumes (Berlin: Schmidt, 1971, 1986);

Clifton D. Hall, *A Complete Concordance to Gottfried von Straßburg's Tristan* (Lewiston, N.Y.: Mellen, 1992).

References:

Michael S. Batts, *Gottfried von Strassburg* (New York: Twayne, 1971);

Otfried Ehrismann, "Isolde, der Zauber, die Liebe–der Minnetrank in Gottfrieds Tristan zwischen Symbolik und Magie," in *Ergebnisse und Aufgaben der Germanistik am Ende des 20. Jahrhunderts: Festschrift für Ludwig Erich Schmidt zum 80. Geburtsag,* edited by Elisabeth Feldbusch (Hildesheim: Olms, 1989), pp. 282–301;

Michael Huby, *Prolegomena zu einer Untersuchung von Gottfrieds "Tristan,"* 2 volumes (Göppingen: Kümmerle, 1984);

William T. H. Jackson, *The Anatomy of Love: The "Tristan" of Gottfried von Strassburg* (New York: Columbia University Press, 1971);

Stephen Jaeger, *Medieval Humanism in Gottfried von Strassburg's "Tristan und Isolde"* (Heidelberg: Winter, 1977);

Alain Kerdehelue, "Feuer und Schwert," in *Tristan et Iseut, mythe européen et mondial,* edited by Danielle Buschinger (Göppingen: Kümmerle, 1987);

Lambertus Okken, *Kommentar zum Tristan-Roman Gottfrieds von Straßburg,* second edition, 2 volumes (Amsterdam: Rodopi, 1996);

Friedrich Ranke, *Die Allegorie der Minnegrotte in Gottfrieds "Tristan"* (Berlin: Deutsche Verlagsgesellschaft für Politik und Geschichte, 1925);

Ranke, "Die Überlieferung von Gottfrieds Tristan," *Zeitschrift für deutsches Altertum,* 55 (1917): 157–278, 381–438;

Neil Thomas, *Tristan in the Underworld: A Study of Gottfried von Strassburg's "Tristan" together with the "Tristan" of Thomas* (Lampeter, Wales: Mellen, 1991);

Tomas Tomasek, *Die Utopie im "Tristan" Gotfrids von Straßburg* (Tübingen: Niemeyer, 1985);

Vlastimil Vrablik, "Die Minnegrotte in Gottfrieds von Strassburg 'Tristan und Isolde': Ein Versuch zur Typologie der Liebe," in *Ist zwivel herzen nâchgebûr: Günther Schweikle zum 60. Geburtstag,* edited by Rüdiger Krüger, Jürgen Kühnel, and Joachim Kuolt (Stuttgart: Helfant, 1989), pp. 181–192;

Franziska Wessel, *Probleme der Metaphorik und die Minnemetaphorik in Gottfrieds von Strasburg "Tristan und Isolde"* (Munich: Fink, 1984);

Alois Wolf, *Gottfried von Strassburg und die Mythe von Tristan und Isolde* (Darmstadt: Wissenschaftliche Buchgesellschaft, 1989).

Günter Grass

(16 October 1927 –   )

Alan Frank Keele
Brigham Young University

This entry was updated by Professor Keele from his entry in DLB 75:
Contemporary German Fiction Writers, Second Series.

See also the Grass entry in *DLB 124: Twentieth-Century German Dramatists, 1919–1992.*

BOOKS: *Die Vorzüge der Windhühner* (Berlin-Frohnau & Neuwied: Luchterhand, 1956);

Die Blechtrommel: Roman (Darmstadt, Berlin-Spandau & Neuwied: Luchterhand, 1959); translated by Ralph Manheim as *The Tin Drum* (London: Secker & Warburg, 1962; New York: Pantheon, 1963);

Gleisdreieck (Darmstadt, Berlin-Spandau & Neuwied: Luchterhand, 1960);

Katz und Maus: Eine Novelle (Neuwied & Berlin-Spandau: Luchterhand, 1961); translated by Monheim as *Cat and Mouse* (New York: Harcourt, Brace & World, 1963; London: Secker & Warburg, 1963); German version, edited by Edgar Lohner (Waltham, Mass.: Blaisdell, 1969); German version, edited by H. F. Brookes and C. E. Fraenkel (London: Heinemann Educational, 1971);

Die bösen Köche: Stück (Berlin: Kiepenheuer, 1961); translated by Manheim and A. Leslie Willson as *The Wicked Cooks* in Grass, *Four Plays* (New York: Harcourt, Brace & World, 1967; London: Secker & Warburg, 1968);

Hundejahre: Roman (Neuwied: Luchterhand, 1963); translated by Manheim as *Dog Years* (New York: Harcourt, Brace & World, 1965; London: Secker & Warburg, 1965);

Hochwasser: Ein Stück in zwei Akten (Frankfurt am Main: Suhrkamp, 1963); translated by Manheim and Willson as *Flood* in *Four Plays;*

Die Ballerina (Berlin: Wolff, 1963);

Onkel, Onkel! Ein Spiel in vier Akten (Berlin: Wagenbach, 1965); translated by Manheim and Willson as *Mister, Mister* (*Onkel, Onkel!* in British edition) in *Four Plays;*

Günter Grass (photograph by Sven Simon–Ullstein Bilderdienst)

Rede über das Selbstverständliche (Neuwied & Berlin: Luchterhand, 1965);

Dich singe ich, Demokratie (Neuwied & Berlin: Luchterhand, 1965);

Die Plebejer proben den Aufstand: Ein deutsches Trauerspiel (Neuwied & Berlin: Luchterhand, 1966); translated by Monheim as *The Plebeians Rehearse the*

Uprising: A German Tragedy (New York: Harcourt, Brace & World, 1966; London: Secker & Warburg, 1967); German version, edited by Brookes and Fraenkel (London: Heinemann Educational, 1971);

Selected Poems, translated by Michael Hamburger and Christopher Middleton (London: Secker & Warburg, 1966; New York: Harcourt, Brace & World, 1966);

Ausgefragt: Gedichte und Zeichnungen (Neuwied & Berlin: Luchterhand, 1967);

Der Fall Axel C. Springer am Beispiel Arnold Zweig: Eine Rede, ihr Anlaß und die Folgen (Berlin: Voltaire, 1967);

Über meinen Lehrer Döblin und andere Vorträge (Berlin: Literarisches Colloquium, 1968);

New Poems, translated by Hamburger (New York: Harcourt, Brace & World, 1968);

Über das Selbstverständliche: Reden, Aufsätze, offene Briefe, Kommentare (Neuwied: Luchterhand, 1968);

Briefe über die Grenze: Versuch eines Ost-West-Dialogs, by Grass and Pavel Kohout (Hamburg: Wegner, 1968);

Speak Out! Speeches, Open Letters, Commentaries, translated by Manheim and others (London: Secker & Warburg, 1969);

Davor: Ein Stück in 13 Szenen (Berlin: Kiepenheuer, 1969); edited by Victor Lange and Frances Lange (New York: Harcourt Brace Jovanovich, 1973); translated by Willson and Manheim as *Max: A Play* (New York: Harcourt Brace Jovanovich, 1972);

örtlich betäubt: Roman (Neuwied: Luchterhand, 1969); translated by Manheim as *Local Anaesthetic* (New York: Harcourt, Brace & World, 1970; London: Secker & Warburg, 1970);

Die Schweinekopfsülze (Hamburg: Merlin, 1969);

Freiheit: Ein Wort wie Löffelstiel [by Grass]; *Gegen Gewalt und Unmenschlichkeit* [by Paul Schallück]: *Zwei Reden zur Woche der Brüderlichkeit* (Cologne: Schäuble, 1969);

Poems of Günter Grass, translated by Hamburger and Middleton (Harmondsworth, U.K.: Penguin, 1969);

Theaterspiele (Neuwied: Luchterhand, 1970)—comprises *Hochwasser; Onkel, Onkel!; Noch zehn Minuten bis Buffalo; Die bösen Köche; Die Plebejer proben den Aufstand;* and *Davor; Noch zehn Minuten bis Buffalo* translated by Manheim and Willson as *Only Ten Minutes to Buffalo* in *Four Plays;*

Gesammelte Gedichte (Neuwied: Luchterhand, 1971);

Aus dem Tagebuch einer Schnecke (Neuwied: Luchterhand, 1972); translated by Manheim as *From the Diary of a Snail* (New York: Harcourt Brace Jovanovich, 1973; London: Secker & Warburg, 1974);

Der Schriftsteller als Bürger—Eine Siebenjahresbilanz (Vienna: Dr. Karl Renner-Institut, 1973);

Mariazuehren; Hommage à Marie; Inmarypraise (Munich: Bruckmann, 1973); *Inmarypraise* translated by Middleton (New York: Harcourt Brace Jovanovich, 1973);

Liebe geprüft: Sieben Gedichte mit sieben Radierungen (Bremen: Schünemann, 1974); translated by Hamburger as *Love Tested: Seven Poems with Seven Etchings* (New York: Harcourt Brace Jovanovich, 1975);

Der Bürger und seine Stimme: Reden, Aufsätze, Kommentare (Darmstadt & Neuwied: Luchterhand, 1974);

In the Egg and Other Poems, translated by Hamburger and Middleton (New York: Harcourt Brace Jovanovich, 1977; London: Secker & Warburg, 1978);

Der Butt: Roman (Darmstadt & Neuwied: Luchterhand, 1977); translated by Manheim as *The Flounder* (New York: Harcourt Brace Jovanovich, 1978; London: Secker & Warburg, 1978);

Denkzettel: Politische Reden und Aufsätze (Darmstadt & Neuwied: Luchterhand, 1978);

Das Treffen in Telgte: Eine Erzählung (Darmstadt & Neuwied: Luchterhand, 1979); translated by Manheim as *The Meeting at Telgte* (New York: Harcourt Brace Jovanovich, 1981; London: Secker & Warburg, 1981);

Die Blechtrommel als Film, by Grass and Volker Schlöndorff (Frankfurt am Main: Zweitausendeins, 1979);

Kopfgeburten oder Die Deutschen sterben aus (Darmstadt & Neuwied: Luchterhand, 1980); translated by Manheim as *Headbirths; or, The Germans Are Dying Out* (New York: Harcourt Brace Jovanovich, 1982);

Aufsätze zur Literatur (Darmstadt & Neuwied: Luchterhand, 1980);

Danziger Trilogie (Darmstadt & Neuwied: Luchterhand, 1980)—comprises *Die Blechtrommel, Katz und Maus,* and *Hundejahre;* translated by Manheim as *The Danzig Trilogy* (San Diego: Harcourt Brace Jovanovich / New York: Pantheon, 1987);

Zeichnen und Schreiben, volume 1: *Zeichnungen und Texte 1954–1977* (Darmstadt & Neuwied: Luchterhand, 1982); translated by Hamburger and Walter Arndt as *Drawings & Words Nineteen Fifty-Four to Nineteen Seventy-Seven* (San Diego: Harcourt Brace Jovanovich, 1983);

Bin ich nun Schreiber oder Zeichner? (Regensburg: Schürer, 1982);

Kinderlied (Northridge, Cal.: Lord John Press, 1982);

Ach Butt, dein Märchen geht böse aus: Gedichte und Radierungen (Darmstadt & Neuwied: Luchterhand, 1983);

Widerstand lernen: Politische Gegenreden 1980–1983 (Darmstadt & Neuwied: Luchterhand, 1984);

Zeichnen und Schreiben, volume 2: *Radierungen und Texte 1972–1982* (Darmstadt & Neuwied: Luchterhand, 1984); translated by Hamburger and others as *Etchings & Words Nineteen Seventy-Two to Nineteen Eighty-Two* (San Diego: Harcourt Brace Jovanovich, 1985);

Geschenkte Freiheit: Rede zum 8. Mai 1945 (Berlin: Akademie der Künste, 1985);

On Writing and Politics 1967–1983, translated by Manheim (San Diego: Harcourt Brace Jovanovich, 1985; London: Secker & Warburg, 1985);

In Kupfer, auf Stein: das grafische Werk, edited by G. Fritze Margull (Göttingen: Steidl, 1986; enlarged edition, 1994);

Die Rättin (Darmstadt & Neuwied: Luchterhand, 1986); translated by Manheim as *The Rat* (San Diego: Harcourt Brace Jovanovich, 1987);

Ausstellung anlässlich des 60. Geburtstages von Günter Grass: Hundert Zeichnungen 1955 bis 1987, edited by Jens Christian Jensen (Kiel: Kunsthalle zu Kiel und Schleswig-Holsteinischer Kunstverein, 1987);

Mit Sophie in die Pilze gegangen (Göttingen: Steidl, 1987);

Werkausgabe in Zehn Bänden, edited by Volker Neuhaus (Darmstadt: Luchterhand, 1987);

Calcutta: Zeichnungen (Bremen: Kunsthalle Bremen, 1988);

Die Gedichte 1955–1986 (Darmstadt: Luchterhand, 1988);

Zunge zeigen (Darmstadt & Neuwied: Luchterhand, 1988); translated by John E. Woods as *Show Your Tongue* (San Diego: Harcourt Brace Jovanovich, 1989);

Meine grüne Wiese: Kurzprosa (Zurich: Manesse, 1989);

Skizzenbuch (Göttingen: Steidl, 1989);

Wenn wir von Europa sprechen: Ein Dialog, by Grass and Françoise Giroud (Frankfurt am Main: Luchterhand, 1989);

Deutscher Lastenausgleich: Wider das dumpfe Einheitsgebot: Reden und Gespräche (Frankfurt am Main: Luchterhand, 1990);

Deutschland, einig Vaterland? Ein Streitgespräch, by Grass and Rudolf Augstein (Göttingen: Steidl, 1990); translated by Krishna Winston and A. S. Wensinger as *Two States–One Nation?* (San Diego: Harcourt Brace Jovanovich, 1990);

Kahlschlag in unseren Köpfen (Göttingen: Steidl, 1990);

Ein Schnäppchen namens DDR: Letzte Reden vorm Glockengeläut (Frankfurt am Main: Luchterhand, 1990);

Tierschutz: Gedichte (Ravensburg: Maier, 1990);

Schreiben nach Auschwitz: Frankfurter Poetik-Vorlesung (Frankfurt am Main: Luchterhand, 1990);

Totes Holz: Ein Nachruf (Göttingen: Steidl, 1990);

Brief aus Altdöbern (Remagen: Rommerskirchen, 1991);

Gegen die verstreichende Zeit: Reden, Aufsätze und Gespräche, 1989–1991 (Hamburg & Zurich: Luchterhand, 1991);

Vier Jahrzehnte: Ein Werkstattbericht, edited by Margull (Göttingen: Steidl, 1991);

Rede vom Verlust: Über den Niedergang der politischen Kultur im geeinten Deutschland (Göttingen: Steidl, 1992);

Unkenrufe: Eine Erzählung (Göttingen: Steidl, 1992); translated by Manheim as *The Call of the Toad* (New York: Harcourt Brace Jovanovich, 1992);

The Future of German Democracy, with an Essay on Loss, edited by Robert Gerald Livingston and Volkmar Sander (New York: Continuum, 1993);

Novemberland: 13 Sonette (Göttingen: Steidl, 1993);

Studienausgabe, 12 volumes (Göttingen: Steidl, 1993–1994);

Angestiftet, Partei zu ergreifen, edited by Daniela Hermes (Munich: Deutscher Taschenbuch, 1994);

Die Deutschen und ihre Dichter, edited by Hermes (Munich: Deutscher Taschenbuch, 1995);

Ein weites Feld: Roman (Göttingen: Steidl, 1995);

Novemberland: Selected Poems, 1956–1993, translated by Hamburger (New York: Harcourt Brace, 1996);

Der Schriftsteller als Zeitgenosse, edited by Hermes (Munich: Deutscher Taschenbuch, 1996);

Fundsachen für Nichtleser (Göttingen: Steidl, 1997);

Günter Grass: Ohne die Feder zu wechseln: Zeichnungen, Druckgraphiken, Aquarelle, Skulpturen (Göttingen: Steidl, 1997);

Rede über den Standort (Göttingen: Steidl, 1997);

Werkausgabe, edited by Neuhaus and Hermes, 16 volumes (Göttingen: Steidl, 1997);

Auf einem anderen Blatt: Zeichnungen (Göttingen: Steidl, 1999);

Mein Jahrhundert (Göttingen: Steidl, 1999).

Günter Grass is more than a writer; he is a phenomenon. Recognized in Germany by friend and foe alike as a formidable artistic and political force, abroad he is viewed almost as a personification of Germany and of postwar German literature. Yet, Grass has never pandered to his own popularity: what he writes, says, and does is just as likely to strike an open nerve as a responsive chord. His fame and his infamy are both by-products of his single-minded pursuit of his mission: to make Germany's Nazi experience a moral yardstick—a kind of ethical absolute zero–against which to measure all other movements and ideologies. Beginning his artistic career as a sculptor, he has become a writer of lyric poetry, drama, fiction, ballet libretti, and political tracts; he is also a painter, graphic designer, and etcher. Many of his ideas seem to have been worked out across the various genres in his repertory and reduced to a system of durable symbols which have informed his oeuvre for more than three decades.

For Günter Wilhelm Grass no symbols are more durable than those crafted from his immediate experience. Danzig, now Gdansk, Poland, was at the time of Grass's birth in 1927 a free city, a German-speaking island in the Polish Corridor to the Baltic created after World War I. After the Nazis came to power in Germany in 1933, they began to organize in Danzig; bringing Danzig home to the Reich became one of their most popular rallying cries. In the early morning of 1 September 1939 the first shots of World War II were fired in the attack on the Polish post office in Danzig. Grass has said that in Danzig the Nazis' rise to power occurred slowly, so that one could take notes.

From his perspective as a child, the impressionable and gifted boy simultaneously noted minute details of life in a petit-bourgeois family in the Danzig suburb of Langfuhr and the making of world war and holocaust. Grass's artistic search for the causes of global evil still concentrates on minutiae: subtleties of language, prejudice, political accommodation, misplaced sexual and religious fervor.

His mother, Helena, was descended from the Kashubians, a Slavic people distinct from the Poles. Members of her family were mostly small farmers who lived near the village of Karthaus, southwest of Danzig. Willy Grass, his father, was German. Grass's paternal grandparents owned a moderately large cabinet-making shop, and his parents kept a small neighborhood grocery store. These environments and those of the schools and churches Grass attended became microcosmic mise-en-scènes for his aesthetic reconstructions of the genesis of evil.

His view of this genesis is that of an insider: he does not exempt himself from guilt. Only his youth prevented Grass from being more responsible for Nazi atrocities. If he had been born earlier, he says, he would have been just as zealous as any other Nazi. As it was, even as a child he was quite involved: at ten he was a member of the Jungvolk, the "cubs" of the Nazi party; at fourteen he became a Hitler Youth; at fifteen a helper at an antiaircraft battery; and at seventeen a tank gunner. Wounded near Cottbus in late April 1945, he was taken to a field hospital in Marienbad, Czechoslovakia, where he was captured by the advancing American forces and placed in a prisoner-of-war camp in Bavaria. As a reeducation measure he was taken to visit the concentration camp at Dachau; the experience led him to question for the first time the validity of the Nazi point of view.

After he was released from the POW camp in the spring of 1946, Grass worked on a farm, then spent a year laboring in a potash mine. In 1947 he moved to

Düsseldorf to study art, but the academy was temporarily closed because of a shortage of coal. One of the professors suggested that he become a stonemason instead. When he had completed his apprenticeship, he went to the academy to study sculpting and graphics. In the evenings he was a drummer in a jazz band. Following a trip through Italy in 1951 and a hitchhiking tour of France in 1952, Grass moved to Berlin to study metal sculpture. In 1954 he married a Swiss dancer, Anna Schwarz, through whom he became interested in dance and began to write ballets.

Grass, whose efforts at writing had begun at age thirteen when he entered a "novel" entitled "Die Kaschuben" (The Kashubians) in a contest sponsored by a Nazi school magazine, was awarded the third prize in a poetry contest sponsored by South German Radio in 1955. Subsequently Walter Höllerer published some of Grass's poems, short plays, and essays in his literary magazine *Akzente*. Grass's first book, the poetry volume *Die Vorzüge der Windhühner* (The Advantages of Windchickens), appeared in 1956. His early surrealistic plays *Hochwasser* (1963; translated as *Flood*, 1967) and *Onkel, Onkel!* (1965; translated as *Mister, Mister*, 1967) and his ballet "Stoffreste" (Cloth Remnants) had their premieres in small and experimental theaters around Germany.

In 1955 he read some of his works at the Berlin meeting of Gruppe 47 (Group 47), an informal but extremely influential association of politically engaged writers organized in 1947 by Hans Werner Richter. Grass's talent was recognized by the group, and he received encouragement to try his hand at a novel. In 1956 he and Anna moved to Paris, she to study dance and he to work in earnest on the novel. In 1958 Höllerer arranged for Grass to return to Gdansk to research the attack on the Polish post office and other material for the novel. The trip was partially financed by the 5,000-mark prize of the Gruppe 47, which he won by reading to the group the manuscript for the beginning of the novel, which appeared the next year as *Die Blechtrommel* (translated as *The Tin Drum*, 1962).

Critical reception of *Die Blechtrommel* was polarized: for each of the many literary prizes it was awarded the book elicited protests alleging obscenity and blasphemy. A characteristic case was that of the City of Bremen, whose literary prize was awarded to Grass by the judges but blocked by the Social Democratic municipal senate—by no means a reactionary body—out of concern that the city might be perceived as having given official sanction to a literary anarchist or pornographer.

In a cursory or unsophisticated reading *Die Blechtrommel* might appear to consist merely of the scurrilous, self-indulgent rantings of the misbegotten gnome Oskar Matzerath, an inmate of an institution for the criminally insane. Not only does Grass seem to show the most sympathy toward this character, but it is obvious that the novel is fundamentally autobiographical: Oskar was born in Danzig, where his parents own a neighborhood grocery store, and after the war he moves to Düsseldorf, where he works as a stonemason and a jazz drummer and studies at the Art Academy. But the autobiographical aspects are totally subordinate to the essential intent of the work, which is to investigate the rise of dictatorship, war, and holocaust in the twentieth century. The genius of the novel is that the story of Oskar Matzerath, while based to a certain extent on the biography of Grass, is really a visible, microscopic scratching of an artistic seismograph needle recording not only the violent global upheavals of the twentieth century but also all the subtle foreshocks and aftershocks. Each beat of the sticks on Oskar's mnemonic drum, each jiggle of Oskar's pen recorded on the pages of *Die Blechtrommel,* is a reaction to ever larger forces in the ever widening spheres of his family, his neighborhood, Danzig, Germany, and the world.

But Oskar does not simply record these forces; he is a creation and, at the same time, a victim of them. He is a blue-eyed drummer with a messiah complex because Hitler had blue eyes, was known as "the drummer" for his tub-thumping oratory, and believed himself to be the savior of Germany. His voice breaks glass because he lives in an age that could produce the "Kristallnacht" (Night of Broken Glass), 9–10 November 1938, when Jewish shops and synagogues were destroyed across Germany. He is a liar and murderer because he mirrors the lying and murderous time and place in which he lives. He becomes a Jesus to a gang of vandals because he lives in a society of true believers seeking a Führer. He is a dwarf because he lives in an age of moral dwarfs. He grows into a misshapen hunchback in 1945 because it is his fate to reflect the distorted boundaries and values of postwar Germany and the postwar world. *Die Blechtrommel* is not the story of an obscene dwarf based on the autobiography of a vulgar author; it is the story of historical obscenity in the twentieth century, told by an incarnation of the Zeitgeist whose curriculum vitae corresponds to that of the author only to the extent that the author feels that he, too, is typical of his age.

Book 1, the first third of the novel, covers the period from the birth of Oskar's mother in 1900 to the burning of the Danzig synagogue and other violent anti-Semitic acts connected with the Kristallnacht. This part ends with a surrealistic evocation of the Advent, not of the Prince of Peace, but of a deadly counterfeit—a kind of Hitlerian Santa Claus: the heavenly gasman, who, as soon as his believers declare faith in him to be the state religion, will unleash the great war and the holocaust. And he will return in the future, hiding behind a false beard, with more frightening things in his bag: cyanide instead of almonds (Grass has elsewhere noted the similarity of their aromas) and Christmas sausages stuffed with mincemeat made not *for* humanity but *of* humanity.

Book 2 begins with the first official act of World War II: the German attack on the Polish post office in Danzig. Within the two chapters which form the exact center of this book the major turning points of the war occur: German armies are halted in Africa and in the Soviet Union, and the Allied invasion of Normandy begins. Book 2 ends with the collapse of Germany in 1945, after Soviet armies capture Danzig and proceed to Berlin. Book 3 deals with the postwar world from 1945 to 1953. In the latter year narrated time catches up with narrative time, and the Jesus figure Oskar turns thirty—the age at which Christ began to preach.

The links between Oskar's private microcosm and the historical macrocosm are sophisticated and subtle, often appearing to be the accidental result of Oskar's hyperbolic literary style. For example, to the sentence near the beginning of the novel in which he reports his mother's birth Oskar adds an apparently irrelevant interjection to the effect that Germany was deciding at that time to double the size of the building program for its imperial fleet. He then describes his mother's horoscope, which involves confused marital relationships, fish, eels, illness, a celebration of annihilation, and a dwelling in the deadly house. These elements presage his mother's unhappy ménage à trois with her German husband and her Polish cousin Jan Bronski, her death by self-inflicted fish-and-eel poisoning, and, by a system of ever widening symbolic circles, the future of Danzig and of Germany. The beginning of Book 2 provides a further example of this linkage. After Oskar's mother's death her two former lovers, the German Nazi cell leader Matzerath and the Polish post-office employee Bronski, embarrassed and concerned that they might be seen together, meet at midnight to play a symbolic game of Skat: "Polen hat einen Grand Hand verloren; die Freie Stadt Danzig gewann soeben für das Großdeutsche Reich bombensicher einen Karo einfach" (Poland has lost a grand slam; the Free City of Danzig has just won a blockbuster diamond full house for the Greater German Reich).

The experiences most clearly linked to historical events are often also the most obscene, grotesque, and shocking. Grass apparently wishes to offend his readers' codes of private sexual morality in the hope of making them offended at global political immorality. Thus, Oskar begins the chapter "Fünfundsiebzig Kilo" (translated as "165 Lbs.") with an account of the problems of the German armies in the east, which he links to a particularly graphic description of his unnatural sexual involvement (he uses his drumsticks as a penis) with Lina Greff, the neglected wife of a homosexual greengrocer and former scoutmaster. As the radio falsely reports that the German Sixth Army is conquering Stalingrad (the radio is often used by Grass as the link between microcosm and macrocosm), Lina's husband works single-mindedly on the construction of a contraption resembling a large balance scale and then hangs himself on it by causing exactly his own weight in potatoes to roll down into baskets suspended from the opposite end. Greff's long history of using dishonest scales and his ensuing trouble with the bureau of weights and measures—hence the macabre manner of his death—as well as a summons by the morals squad on charges of pederasty, compounded by grief at the news of the death on the eastern front of his favorite former boy scout, drive him to suicide. In the microcosm of Oskar's street in a suburb of Danzig, a tangle of dishonest and perverse behavior leading to catastrophe is linked to the larger question of the fortunes of Germany on the eastern front. Weighed in a macabre balance, entangled in a web of dishonest and perverted behavior, Germany, like Greff, commits suicide amid the complexities of the bizarre war machine it has created.

The scene in Greff's cellar when his corpse is discovered is imbued with such a frightening, primal nihilism that Oskar drums out the song he reserves for his encounters with the most absolute evil: "Ist die schwarze Köchin da? Jajaja!" (Is the black cook here? Yesyesyes!). The black cook (called "the black witch" in the English translation), the personification of evil, haunts Oskar throughout the novel. She casts her shadow when the neighborhood children make Oskar drink their concoction of urine and frog's legs and when Greff commits suicide; when the members of the Stäuberbande (Duster Gang) make Oskar their Jesus and perform a vandalistic black mass, they are betrayed by Luzie Rennwand, one of the incarnations of the black cook. Her spirit permeates the Kristallnacht and the Nazi program of euthanasia, from which Oskar is saved only by the Soviet advance; and she stands behind the Zeitgeist Oskar when he causes the death of his mother, when he leads his presumptive father Jan to his death at the Polish post office, when he makes his other presumptive father Matzerath choke to death—significantly—on his Nazi party pin, and when he (probably) murders the nurse Dorothea Köngetter in Düsseldorf.

As his thirtieth birthday approaches, Oskar is about to be released from the insane asylum, where he has blackened the "unschuldiges" (innocent) paper he asked for at the beginning of the novel with the sordid story of his past in the shadow of the black cook. What will the cook, who is getting blacker and blacker, have in store in the future? Will Oskar be pressed into service as a Führer, as a Jesus to the disciples of some future Duster Gang? As in all of his novels, Grass leaves the ending open.

Looking back on the creation of *Die Blechtrommel*, Grass admits to having been obsessed. From the moment he wrote its first sentence, he recounts, the characters of the novel, a wildly expanding family, came to life for him and sat around his typewriter. For his real family, his wife and their twin sons, Franz and Raoul, born in 1957, he was present during these years less as a husband and father than as a cloud of tobacco smoke.

Grass moved to Berlin, partly for health reasons, in 1959. On top of his heavy smoking, he had written the book in the damp ground-floor studio which doubled as the furnace room of his flat on the Avenue d'Italie, and he discovered that he had developed tubercles in his lungs. He was also uncomfortable about the nationalist Charles de Gaulle, who had come to power in France. He was made even more uneasy when, for unexplained reasons, he was detained overnight by the French authorities—an experience which, he says, made him downright homesick for the West German police. This event seems to have found its way into *Die Blechtrommel:* on the penultimate page of the novel Oskar recounts that he was arrested on the Avenue d'Italie (at Maison Blanche, the Metro stop closest to Grass's flat at number 111) and that in several faces in the crowd he saw the horrible visage of the black cook.

Before leaving Paris, Grass had written a ballet, *Fünf Köche* (Five Cooks), which was produced in 1959 in Aix-les-Bains and in Bonn; a radio play, "Zweiunddreiig Zähne" (Thirty-two Teeth), which was broadcast in 1959 by South German Radio; and two one-act plays, *Noch zehn Minuten bis Buffalo* (translated as *Only Ten Minutes to Buffalo,* 1967), produced in 1959 in Bochum, and *Beritten hin und zurück* (Mounted There and Back Again), produced in 1959 in Frankfurt. He had also written more poems, which appeared in 1960 in the volume *Gleisdreieck* (Three Rail Junction [a dreary railway stop between East and West Berlin]).

And he had begun another large novel, for which he used the working title "Kartoffelschalen" (Potato Peelings) but which was published in 1963 as *Hundejahre* (translated as *Dog Years,* 1965). Grass says that it was the growth of one episode from this novel into a separate novella of almost two hundred pages that helped him to solidify his concept and change "Kartoffelschalen" into *Hundejahre*. In 1961 the novella was published as *Katz und Maus* (translated as *Cat and Mouse,* 1963).

Katz und Maus is set in Danzig during the war. Some of its characters, such as Störtebeker, the leader of the Duster Gang, who returns in *örtlich betäubt* (1969; translated as *Local Anaesthetic,* 1970), also appear in *Die Blechtrommel* and *Hundejahre.* Oskar also puts in several brief appearances in *Katz und Maus.*

Ostensibly, the main character of the novella is the gangling, devout Catholic Joachim Mahlke, who becomes a tank gunner, wins the Knight's Cross, suffers anxiety, and goes AWOL. And yet, interesting as he is, Mahlke may be only the foil to the real subject of the book, the narrator Pilenz. *He* is the character whose mind Grass seems to wish to explore, a mind which sees in Mahlke's life a whole succession of religious symbols. Pilenz draws the reader's attention, sometimes apparently inadvertently, to connections between Mahlke's life, these religious symbols, and historical events.

Pilenz is the archetypal true believer, a disciple in search of his Jesus, whom he finds in Mahlke. That Mahlke's father is dead becomes for Pilenz something akin to a virgin birth. Mahlke's gaunt face and long hair parted in the middle give him, for Pilenz, an "Erlösermiene" (saviour countenance); and when Mahlke plays the *Ave Maria* on a gramophone aboard the partially sunken minesweeper where the boys spend their summers, the sea, Pilenz claims, is stilled. When Mahlke returns from the war, Pilenz sees in his Knight's Cross a symbol of the ineffable Cross, and believes that the Virgin has made Mahlke bulletproof. On the day—which Pilenz goes to some trouble to point out is a Friday—when Mahlke goes AWOL, Pilenz describes a crucifixion, complete with thorns in the form of unripe "Stachelbeeren" (thornberries [that is, gooseberries]) which cause Mahlke intense stomach pains when he eats them. Mahlke is entombed in the sunken minesweeper, but—unlike Jesus—he does not rise again.

Pilenz is ridden with guilt about the demise of his friend, and with good reason: Mahlke went down into the minesweeper as a result of Pilenz's lies. Mahlke intended to hide in the ship until dark and then have Pilenz row him across the harbor to what he thought was a Swedish vessel and escape from Germany, but Pilenz had a more mythical ending in mind. As Mahlke, with his cans of food, dove into the wreck to swim to his boyhood hideout in the radio shack, which is still above water, Pilenz, the Judas figure, hid the can opener, and he did not return that evening as arranged. It is possible that Mahlke swam away during the night, but it is more likely that, ill and weighted down with cans of food, he drowned before reaching the radio shack. In any case, in his own mind Pilenz has contributed to Mahlke's death, and he seeks a resurrected

Mahlke whom he can repay for his perfidy and venerate anew.

Pilenz's misguided religious discipleship stands as a symbol for the misguided political discipleship that saw in Hitler the military saviour of Germany. An important clue to this symbolic link between religious and political faith is found in Mahlke's large Adam's apple, the "mouse" of the book's title, which fascinates the "cat," Pilenz, who says that he is forced by the book's author to lead it to each locality "der ihn siegen oder verlieren sah" (which witnessed its victories and defeats). In addition to his odd use of military vocabulary in connection with the Adam's apple, Pilenz connects the growth of this symbol of guilt and of the Fall to the beginning of the war in 1939. Mahlke's Adam's apple, then, is a symbol of Germany's fall. Mahlke's Knight's Cross, normally a symbol of military victory, is here a symbol for Mahlke's and Germany's total defeat. There are two earlier Knight's Crosses in *Katz und Maus,* belonging to an air force pilot and a submariner who visit their old school and give speeches glorifying war. In 1944 Mahlke becomes a tank gunner. With this succession of Knight's Crosses, the stages of Germany's defeat are described: initial superiority in the air and under the sea changes to inferiority, just as Germany's land arm—its armor—will be the next, and the last, to crumble.

In October 1959 Pilenz travels to a reunion of the order of the Knight's Cross in Regensburg. A military band of the Bundeswehr (West German armed forces) is playing, and during a break Pilenz asks the lieutenant guarding the door to have Mahlke paged. Mahlke does not appear, of course, but the point is clear: Pilenz and the others are true believers seeking a remnant of their Nazi past, celebrating a supposed glory which was in reality a calamity. That the event is supported by the Bundeswehr is a bitter indictment by Grass of postwar militarism, a suggestion that the Bundeswehr is a vehicle for those who seek a resurrection of the messianic glory of the Nazi era.

In 1961, the year his daughter Laura was born, Grass began to involve himself in politics by supporting Willy Brandt and the Social Democratic party (SPD). Over the next dozen years Grass became a major adviser, campaigner, and speechmaker for Brandt and the SPD.

Another of his short plays, *Die bösen Köche* (1961; translated as *The Wicked Cooks,* 1967), like the ballet *Fünf Köche* a spin-off of *Die Blechtrommel* and the idea of the black cook, was produced in 1961 in Berlin. But Grass concentrated most of his literary efforts during this period on *Hundejahre,* which finally grew to nearly seven hundred pages, about the same length as *Die Blechtrommel.* In *Hundejahre* Grass continues to develop the themes, localities, characters, and narrative techniques of *Die Blechtrommel* and *Katz und Maus;* the three books were republished in one volume in 1980 as the *Danziger Trilogie* (translated as *The Danzig Trilogy,* 1987). But *Hundejahre* deals even more specifically than the other two books with the role of the artist in understanding how the past informs the present and thereby determines the future.

In some ways *Hundejahre* demands more of the reader than *Die Blechtrommel,* which, for all its complexity, is unified by the mesmerizing mono- and megalomania of the narrator, Oskar. Here there are three narrators. Herr Brauxel, the owner of a former potash mine—in place of potash he now dredges up the past—who also spells his name Brauksel and Brauchsel, narrates the first of the three books of *Hundejahre,* which is titled "Frühschichten" (Morning Shifts); book 2, written by Harry Liebenau to his cousin Tulla Prokriefke, is titled "Liebesbriefe" (Love Letters); and book 3 is titled "Materniaden" (Materniads) after its narrator, the actor Walter Matern.

Brauxel is the leader of this collective of authors, who solicits and pays for Liebenau and Matern's contributions. Brauxel is also the subject of their writings, for he is in reality Eddi Amsel—alias Brauxel, alias Hermann Haseloff, alias Goldmäulchen (Goldmouth)—the childhood friend of Matern and childhood acquaintance of Liebenau. From the multiple narrative points of view a unified story emerges of two "blood brothers" growing up in and around Danzig and experiencing the rise of National Socialism, the war, and the war's aftermath.

Though they are "blood brothers," Eddi and Matern are also opposites: Eddi is sensitive and artistic, a fine singer, portly but skilled at games requiring intelligence and finesse; Matern is more emotional than rational, physically powerful, and prone to brutality. Eddi is half Jewish (his very assimilated, patriotic father dies at Verdun); Matern is Catholic, the descendant of a feared robber.

At first, Matern joins the other children in persecuting Eddi; as often as not, he is the one who calls Eddi "Itzig" (Sheeny). Later, Matern uses his fists to protect his weaker friend, whose artistic creations and Jewishness continue to evoke persecution. But after he joins the Nazi Sturmabteilung (Storm Troopers [SA]), Matern turns on Eddi again and, with eight other brown-shirted members of the SA, beats him up, knocking out all thirty-two of his teeth. Eddi disappears and has his teeth replaced with gold ones—hence the alias Goldmouth and the symbolic thirty-two chapters of his part of the novel. After the war he reappears under the alias Brauxel and engages Matern and Liebenau to help write his story.

It is the story of a gifted mimetic artist. Like Oskar, Eddi is precocious, and like Grass, he begins as a sculptor, making his first significant piece at age five. Eddi's unique gift lies in his ability to see the essences of phenomena and to recreate those essences in sculptures made of the flotsam he fishes out of the river Vistula, which serves as a symbol of the flow of time. His peculiar gift is only intensified by his persecution: even as he is beaten, his tears lend him "eine verschwommene und dennoch übergenaue Optik" (blurred and yet overly precise optical powers). Two or three days after each beating one of Eddi's sculptures, depicting the very essence of the brutality of his tormentors, appears in the landscape. It is because Matern sees a statue of himself, multiplied ninefold, striking out in blind rage—a premonition of his attack as an SA man—that he turns from beating Eddi to protecting him. Such is the power of Eddi's vision and of its expression in his art.

For the farmers in his village, who know little and care less about art, Eddi Amsel is a manufacturer of scarecrows. His creations are so startling that they have the power to frighten horses, cows, and even people—not to mention the birds, who fly up in a great cloud at his christening, covering the sun and casting a foreboding shadow upon him. One old crow is so scared that it falls to the ground dead. It is the frightening essence of the things Eddi sees that strikes terror into the hearts of birds, creatures highly sensitive to dangers in the atmosphere (hence their use in mines like Brauxel's).

Young Eddi decides to create something apparently contradictory: a giant bird that has the effect of scaring birds. Made with tar and feathers, it is so terrifying that even the farmers are not interested in purchasing it: hardened fishwives avoid it, and men allow their pipes to go out as they stare at it. Every misfortune which occurs in the village, including the death of Matern's grandmother, is blamed on "der große Vogel Piepmatz" (the great cuckoo bird), as one of the villagers calls it. Eventually, Eddi is told that he must destroy the bird and all of his collected raw materials. A great mound is heaped up by eager volunteers, the bird is placed on top, and the whole is ignited. As Eddi watches this ritualistic burning, taunted by cries of "Itzig!", his eyes narrow into "Sehschlitze" (seeing slits) and he has an apocalyptic vision of ritualistic tarrings and featherings, pogroms, autos-da-fé, and holocausts; and he sees that when he is older he will be forced to make an artistic copy of this vision in the form of another giant bird which will burn eternally, "apokalyptisch und dekorativ zugleich" (apocalyptic and decorative at the same time).

Eddi and Matern leave the village and go to high school in Danzig, where they encounter the Matzeraths, Bronski, and Pilenz, as well as Harry Liebenau and his cousin Tulla Prokriefke. Tulla, who also appears in *Katz und Maus,* is a reptilian female temptress, a black cook figure—a double of Luzie Rennwand of *Die Blechtrommel.*

The blood brothers also meet their teachers: the brutal Mallenbrand, a physical-education instructor, and the gentle Brunies, a humanist addicted to sweets who collects stones containing gleaming flakes of mica. While the boys and their teachers are on a trip to the school's retreat in the forest, some gypsies give Brunies a baby girl, whom he names Jenny and who grows up to become a ballerina.

The dramatis personae of *Hundejahre* is completed by the dogs. In the dark beginnings there was a Lithuanian she-wolf, whose grandson, the black dog Perkun, sired the bitch Senta, who belongs to Walter Matern's father. A dog named Pluto is brought from Stutthof, the site of the death camp, to service Senta; and Senta whelps six pups, among them Harras. Harras is purchased by Harry Liebenau's father to be a guard dog in his cabinet-making shop. Later, Harras will sire Prinz, Hitler's favorite black German shepherd.

The visionary Eddi, sensing an historical mythological symbol, asks Liebenau's permission to sketch Harras, whom he calls Herr Pluto—the hound of hell—and with whom he uses (unheard-of for dogs) the polite form of German address. But Tulla soon chases Eddi away by calling him "Itzig." Thereafter Eddi begins to make brown-shirted sculptures of SA men with pig-bladder heads, pasted-on faces of pro-Nazi celebrities cut from magazines, and a clockwork mechanism which enables them to march and salute. The uniforms for the sculptures are obtained by Matern, who now joins the SA.

Matern is unhappy about Eddi's SA robot-sculptures, especially because of their pig-bladder heads, and accuses Eddi of representing his comrades as "Schweinehunde" (swinish sons-of-bitches). Eddi replies that he merely reproduces with artistic means what life shows him, and he begins to build a replica of Matern. The beating Eddi predicted when he made the scarecrow of Matern striking out ninefold in blind anger now occurs as Matern and eight of his SA friends beat Eddi up and roll him into a snowman in his garden.

Not far away, the sinister Tulla and eight of her followers are making a parallel attack on Jenny Brunies, who is also beaten and rolled into a snowman. Both emerge when a thaw sets in. Eddi leaves for Berlin with a forged passport in the name of Hermann Haseloff. There he becomes the chief of a propaganda company under Josef Goebbels and an important *maître de ballet* who entertains the troops and makes strange, humanoid machines in his basement studio.

After Oswald Brunies is denounced by Tulla and disappears into the death camp at Stutthof, Haseloff

comes to Danzig in his black Mercedes and takes Jenny back to Berlin. He sends a truck for Brunies's furniture and collection of micaceous rocks, which are taken to the site of his future potash mine in Lower Saxony. Around the time of the Allied invasion of June 1944 he begins to produce a ballet on which he had been working since childhood, *Die Vogelscheuchen* (The Scarecrows).

The ballet employs the remnants of a troupe of midgets with whom Oskar Matzerath had entertained the troops in occupied France in *Die Blechtrommel.* As described by Jenny in her letters to Harry Liebenau, the ballet is a fantastic allegory of Germany, a microcosmic reproduction of all of Eddi Amsel's apocalyptic visions, with robot scarecrows, a sinister gardener, and a twelve-legged black dog. The ballet ends with the total destruction of the garden in which it is set. The only survivor is the evil old gardener, who is changed into a scarecrow as the curtain falls.

Two officials from the propaganda ministry who attend the dress rehearsal find the plot too sinister and lacking in the life-affirming element for the soldiers at the front. Haseloff is allowed to add a happy ending in which the scarecrows are bound, brought to the surface from their underground lair, and placed in the service of the now wonderfully virtuous gardener. Eddi's art has always truly reflected and predicted reality, however: as the troupe rehearses the new ending, a bomb falls on the rehearsal room, smashing Jenny's feet, confirming the correctness of the original finale.

Germany, like the garden of the ballet, is eventually destroyed. At the end of the war Prinz, having deserted Hitler, swam across the river Elbe near Magdeburg "und suchte sich westlich des Flusses einen neuen Herrn" (and sought on the west side of the river a new master). Prinz finds Matern as he is being released from a British antifascist camp and follows him everywhere, despite Matern's attempts to frighten him away. The violent, irrational Matern, former SA thug turned belligerent antifascist, is the new master of the hound of hell, whom he calls Pluto. Matern goes around Germany as the personification of the denazification process, meting out absurd punishments to innocent people—he infects the daughters and wives of his old comrades with gonorrhea—while covering up the guilt in his own soul. But the artist Eddi Amsel—Grass's alter ego—will not allow Matern or Germany to cover up the guilt. As Brauxel, using a variety of devices, he dredges up all of Matern's evil deeds.

One such device is the toy Erkenntnisbrille (perception eyeglasses) which Brauxel & Co. places on the market in 1955. Made with cheap plastic frames and simple flat lenses—to which are added mica chips from Brunies's rocks, making them miniature crystal balls—these eyeglasses impart to the wearer something of the powers of Eddi Amsel: when young people from seven to twenty-one put them on, they see what their parents were doing during the war. Unwittingly, Matern buys a pair of these glasses for Walli Sawatzki, the ten-year-old daughter of his SA friend Jochen Sawatzki. When Walli puts them on she sees her father and Matern, along with seven other SA men, beating out Eddi's teeth.

After completely encircling him with reminders of his past—artistic proofs of his essential identity with Hitler—Brauxel brings Matern to his mine for a final confrontation. Here he is bringing into existence scenes from his sketchbook, *Pandämonium* (the dwelling place of all the demons), which he keeps in his safe. Even the hardened, violent Matern is horrified by the bedlam: by the countless varieties and psychotic activities of the most bizarre scarecrows; by the monstrousness of the fiery gods Perkunos, Pikollos, and Potrimpos; by the desensitized birds; by the hellish laughter and the gnashing teeth; by the scarecrow sporting events and religious services; and by the scarecrow emotions of hate, anger, and revenge. "Das ist die Hölle!" (This is hell!) Matern says over and over again. Not so, Brauxel maintains: "Der Orkus ist oben!" (Orcus [Hades] is above ground), and he reminds Matern of Eddi's motto: "Die Vogelscheuche wird nach dem Bild des Menschen erschaffen" (The scarecrow is created in the image of man).

For all its complexities *Hundejahre* has, at bottom, a simple and clear meaning: in Eddi/Brauxel, Grass has created a visionary artist who, like Grass himself, re-creates in his art the hidden and hideous essence of evil. Brauxel's scarecrows are simply copies of the *Schweine-hunde* he sees around him. And like Grass's works—the sales patterns and legal problems connected with Brauxel's magical eyeglasses are identical to those of *Die Blechtrommel* and *Katz und Maus*—Brauxel's works are shocking and horrifying because they reveal real abuses, not imaginary ones. Thus, his fiery atomic gods are Old Prussian artistic models of atomic weapons, like the ballistic missiles to which men attach the names of gods: Poseidon, Atlas, Nike. Scarecrows populate the globe, from Africa to the atomic testing grounds of Nevada. And yet, as the day of nuclear wrath draws ever nearer, and Brauxel prepares to mirror the event in the great cuckoo bird, the artist focuses his visionary powers primarily on Germany, since it is the primary heir of the hound of hell, and secondarily on the Jews, the blood brothers to the Germans, fated by their common past to write together the history of the future. Near the end of *Hundejahre* the half-Jew Eddi says to the German Matern, "Aber unter allen Völkern, die als Vogelscheuchenarsenale dahinleben, ist es mit Vorzug das deutsche Volk, das, mehr noch als das jüdische, alles Zeug in sich hat, der Welt eines Tages die Urvo-

gelscheuche zu schenken" (But among all peoples which exist as scarecrow arsenals, it is first and foremost the German people, which, even more than the Jewish, has within it all the right stuff to bestow one day the arch scarecrow upon the world).

There were several artistic spinoffs from *Hundejahre,* including a play, *Goldmäulchen,* which was produced in Munich in 1964; the dramatic "öffentliche Diskussion" (public discussion) from book 3, which was broadcast in 1963 by Hessian Radio; and the ballet *Die Vogelscheuchen,* which was produced at the German Opera in Berlin in 1970. In 1965, the year his son Bruno was born, Grass was awarded an honorary doctorate from Kenyon College in Ohio and the Georg Büchner Prize. That year he made more than fifty appearances on a campaign tour for the SPD, during which a firebomb charred his front door. Also that year he wrote his first full-scale drama, *Die Plebejer proben den Aufstand* (1966; translated as *The Plebeians Rehearse the Uprising,* 1966), which was produced in Berlin in 1966.

The play is the story of an East German dramaturge called "der Chef" (the chief)—a figure clearly based on Bertolt Brecht—who is rehearsing a class-conscious, revolutionary version of Shakespeare's *Coriolanus* when the workers' rebellion of 17 June 1953 erupts on the streets outside his theater. The workers appeal to the chief to lend his intellect, his language, and his credibility to their cause, but he refuses, too busy with his art to see the political reality outside. As the uprising fails due to its lack of leadership and is ultimately crushed by Soviet armor, the chief stands alone on the stage, echoes of the workers' words in his ears, and realizes that he has allowed the historic moment to slip away. He resigns and goes into retirement, where voices will haunt him for the rest of his life.

Die Plebejer proben den Aufstand is not an attack on Brecht, as some have supposed; it is a defense of Grass and his political activities, for which he has been widely criticized. Grass's thesis is that the purpose of engaged art is the discovery of truth so that one can then act in reality. To the extent that Brecht slipped into art for art's sake, this play implies, he missed an irretrievable opportunity to change the world.

The number and variety of Grass's activities in the late 1960s show that he was determined not to miss any such chances, artistic or political. In 1966 he traveled to the meeting of the Gruppe 47 in Princeton, to Czechoslovakia, and to Hungary. He campaigned during the state elections in Bavaria. *Katz und Maus* was filmed. With Elisabeth Borchers and Klaus Roehler he edited a poetry series called *Luchterhand Loseblatt Lyrik.* He continued to write and deliver political messages, a small portion of which were published in 1968 as *Über das Selbstverständliche: Reden Aufsätze, offene Briefe, Kommen-*

tare (On the Self-evident: Speeches, Essays, Open Letters, Commentaries). He began a column for the *Süddeutsche Zeitung* in Munich. A volume of poetry and drawings, *Ausgefragt* (Thoroughly Interrogated), appeared in 1967. That year Grass campaigned in Schleswig-Holstein and Berlin, traveled to Israel, carried on a correspondence with the Czech writer Pavel Kohout that was published in 1968 as *Briefe über die Grenze: Versuch eines Ost-West-Dialogs* (Letters across the Border: An Attempt at an East-West Dialogue), and won the Carl von Ossietzky Medal. The next year he won the Fontane Prize, gave a major speech at the Social Democratic party convention in Nuremberg, and worked on a citizens' committee in Berlin. All during these busy years the indefatigable Grass was preparing a new literary work which appeared in 1969 both as the novel *örtlich betäubt* and as a play, *Davor* (Before That; translated as *Max: A Play,* 1972).

Many critics were perplexed by Grass's new work. Appearing to deal almost entirely with contemporary problems, it did not seem to fit the pattern of the Danzig Trilogy, with its heavy emphasis upon the past. Yet, *örtlich betäubt* is a most logical extension of Grass's earlier work: it has its roots in the juvenile milieu of Oskar and the Duster Gang in prewar and wartime Danzig; and, like the previous works, it follows its characters and the legacy of that violent period into the present.

The narrator, Eberhard Starusch, is identical with the boy nicknamed "Störtebeker," the leader of the Duster Gang in the Danzig Trilogy. Now a forty-year-old secondary-school teacher of history and German in Berlin, Starusch experiences something like déjà vu as he and his students, who are the same age he was under Nazism, are confronted with a familiar set of problems: a former Nazi, Kurt Georg Kiesinger, is chancellor of West Germany; the country has rearmed; and its major ally, the United States, is engaged in what the students consider an unjust, genocidal war of aggression in Southeast Asia. There is something rotten in the state of affairs.

And there is literally something rotten in Starusch: his carious teeth require extensive dental work. Grass had used teeth and tooth decay before as symbols of hidden moral or social putrescence: Pilenz is suffering from a toothache on the first pages of *Katz und Maus;* Matern knocks out all of Eddi Amsel's teeth; Brauxel opens a restaurant called "Die Leichenhalle" (The Morgue), at which tooth pudding is served to a shocked and nauseated Matern. A poem in *Gleisdreieck* associates the putrescence which is only temporarily masked by toothpaste with the horrible gold teeth of the holocaust: to get rid of the decay lingering from the past, the poem concludes, we must open our mouths.

The question for the characters in *örtlich betäubt* is what to do about present and future decay. Should the treatment of society's ills be "radical" or "moderate"? Should all the teeth be pulled? Should metaphorical bulldozers (which Starusch imagines on the television screen in the dentist's office) be set in motion to clear the world of its corrupt systems? Or should frustration be resisted and more moderate methods of fighting dental and societal decay be used? The dentist argues for moderation and prophylaxis. Ironically, however, he is not above threatening Starusch with pain when Starusch defends violent radicalism. The spineless Starusch immediately recants, for he is really only a verbal anarchist indulging in middle-aged fantasies.

The issue becomes acute, however, when Philipp Scherbaum, Starusch's most gifted student, decides to protest the use of napalm in Vietnam by burning his beloved dachshund Max in front of the Hotel Kempinski on Berlin's Kurfürstendamm. Scherbaum's radical girlfriend Vero Lewand, a disciple of Mao and Che Guevara—and a reincarnation of Tulla Prokriefke, who helped Matern kill a dog in *Hundejahre*—urges him to go ahead with the immolation.

The teacher is not much help. Like Pilenz, he feels frustrated and impotent; he would like to relive his own exciting past vicariously through Philipp's deed. He is even tempted by his fiancée, Irmgard Seifert, another guilt-ridden teacher at the school, to see Philipp as a messiah. On the other hand, he knows better. He is a mature, rational man. He realizes that Philipp is no messiah, that Irmgard is a religious fanatic, and that violence will reap violence. He may even get into trouble himself if his student goes through with the plan. So he lectures Philipp, graphically describing how he will be beaten to death by the matrons eating pastry at Kempinski's when they see him set fire to the dog. Rather than deterring him, however, this lecture convinces Philipp that he is right: people must be shocked into seeing what a violent world they have created.

The solution comes from an unexpected quarter: from history, from the era of the Duster Gang, from the history teacher's own generation. In a trade-union newspaper seventeen-year-old Philipp discovers an account of seventeen-year-old Helmuth Hübener, the leader of a nonviolent resistance group, who composed and distributed antifascist leaflets and was beheaded by the Nazis in 1942. Hübener's photo soon hangs on Philipp's wall, as that of Che Guevara hangs on Vero's. Now it is Philipp who lectures his history teacher about how Hübener did not waste his time demolishing churches like the Duster Gang, could take stenography, and even knew Morse code. Starusch vaguely recalls once reading something about Hübener, and he is stricken with professional guilt for not teaching his students about Hübener's group instead of regaling them with stories about his own glory days with the Duster Gang.

Later, when the teacher invites him to an antiwar demonstration, Philipp declines because he has a short-hand class. He takes over the editorship of the school paper, which he had previously refused to do, and renames it *Morsezeichen* (Morse Code). His first article will deal with Hübener's resistance group and contrast the activities of Kiesinger and Hübener in 1942. He has given up the idea of burning Max and is having his teeth fixed.

Philipp Scherbaum is Grass's new contemporary hero. This hero looks the present clearly in the face. He does not mythologize; he does not seek to be or to follow a messiah; and he rejects easy, violent solutions, patterning his actions after Hübener, who patiently sought to educate and enlighten the German people about Hitler. His heraldic animal could be the snail: representing the slow, patient progress of democracy, freedom, and reason, this animal is Grass's chosen symbol for himself and for his political models.

From the spring to the fall of 1969 Grass participated in a campaign tour for the SPD throughout the Federal Republic, involving almost two hundred appearances and one hundred speeches. An account of this campaign; of Grass's involvement with the archetypal snail Willy Brandt, the heir of the prototypal snail August Bebel, founder of the SPD; of trips to Yugoslavia, France, and Czechoslovakia; of Grass's participation in the Lutheran Church Conference in Stuttgart; and of Brandt's election as chancellor in September 1969 forms the basis for *Aus dem Tagebuch einer Schnecke* (1972; translated as *From the Diary of a Snail,* 1973).

Aus dem Tagebuch einer Schnecke is addressed to Grass's children as an object lesson in history and its application to modern problems. At the beginning of the book Grass tells the twins Franz and Raoul, eleven, Laura, eight, and Bruno, four, that when he observed the election of Gustav Heinemann as federal president in March 1969 he narrowed his eyes into Sehschlitze and saw a giant snail creeping slowly through the hall. She (in German snails are feminine) hesitated, with her feelers out, not wishing to arrive at her goal, not wishing to win. But when Grass promised her a new goal, when he baited her with slices of the future, she crossed the finish line—Heinemann won by a narrow margin—and crept toward the victory of Brandt in September.

The rigors of the campaign include daily confrontations with radical young people, "zugutbehauste Söhne, die vom Proletariat wie von einer Marienerscheinung schwärmen . . . neuerdings berufsmäßige Gottesstreiter, die Christi Blut in hegelförmige Flaschen abfüllen" (too-well-housed sons who rave about the proletariat like it was a manifestation of the Virgin Mary . . . lately, professional gladiators for God, who pour the blood of Christ into Hegel-shaped bottles). Grass encounters some of these political mystics at the Lutheran Church Conference, where he reads to them about Philipp Scherbaum wanting to burn his dachshund. Their counterpart from an earlier generation is August, a former SS man who takes the microphone at the conference, salutes his old SS comrades, and drinks a flask of potassium cyanide. Eventually Grass visits August's family, hoping to understand his motivation.

As Grass prepares a speech on Albrecht Dürer's engraving "Melencolia I," which he has been invited by the City of Nuremberg to give in 1971 for the celebration of the five-hundredth anniversary of Dürer's birth, he recounts a fictional narrative about Hermann Ott, a teacher in a Jewish school in prewar Danzig and collector of snails who is nicknamed "Zweifel" (Doubt) because of his disposition to question commonly accepted "facts." After the destruction of the Danzig synagogue Ott flees from Danzig and takes refuge in occupied Poland in the dank cellar of a rural house owned by a sadistic bicycle repairman named Stoma. Stoma's daughter Elisabeth suffers from aphasia brought on by severe melancholy stemming from the death of her child, who was crushed beneath the wheels of a military vehicle during the invasion in September 1939.

Ott's snails, symbols of healing and progress, gradually help erase the psychological damage of the war. A special purple snail which Elisabeth finds in a graveyard magically draws out her melancholy, providing a model for the healing of an entire society, which is the subject of Grass's Dürer speech. Titled "Vom Stillstand im Fortschritt, Variationen zu Albrecht Dürers Kupferstich 'Melencolia I'" (On Standing Still in Progress, Variations on Albrecht Dürer's Etching "Melencolia I"), the speech forms the book's final chapter. It is a brilliant summary of Grass's engagement with political problems and of the writing of his snail diary; an imaginative, often fantastic exploration of the psychosocial roots of depression in suburban housewives and assembly-line workers; and an analysis of the dark side of utopian expectations, whether in the planned societies of the Eastern bloc or in the artificial "say-cheese!" smiles of consumerism and "the American way of life." It is an inventory of the legacies of the black cook, of modern malaises and their historical roots, and it prescribes the snail of patient progress as a cure.

Most of *Aus dem Tagebuch einer Schnecke* was written during 1969; only a few episodes at the end date from 1970 and 1971, an indication that Grass delayed its publication to coincide with the federal elections in 1972.

Thus, a literary account of one election campaign became a political tool released just in time to aid in the next.

Grass made about 130 appearances during the 1972 campaign. The elections strengthened the mandate for Brandt and his policies, including improved relations with the Communist bloc. Grass accompanied Brandt on his trips in 1970 to East Germany and to Poland—where Brandt knelt before the Warsaw memorial to the victims of Nazism—as well as to Israel and the United States in 1973.

Yet, Grass was prepared to criticize Brandt and the SPD, as he had earlier when they agreed to form the "Grand Coalition" with Kiesinger as chancellor. When Grass perceives present parallels to past errors, he speaks out—even when his evidence may be too subtle to convince many others, and even when speaking out may offend his friends and closest allies. A case in point occurred in 1972 when Heinar Kipphardt produced in Munich a play by Wolf Biermann on the subject of dragon slaying. The program, which was never released, included pictures of prominent civic leaders. For Grass, the implication was clear: here were dragons that needed to be slain—a veiled call for political assassination. Grass harshly lectured Kipphardt in his column in the *Süddeutsche Zeitung*. The ensuing imbroglio resulted in Kipphardt being replaced as dramaturge, but it also made enemies for Grass on the left—especially among the literati and intelligentsia, many of whom had assumed that the stalwart antifascist Grass was their natural ally.

The passage of time has demonstrated that Grass's fears of the revival of something like a Duster Gang of the left may have been well founded. German terrorist groups such as that of Andreas Baader and Ulrike Meinhof began to arise in the early 1970s, in precisely those quarters Grass had predicted: among disenchanted utopian leftists, many of them women, who were impatient with the snail's pace of progress, wanted a new religion of revolution, and felt that humanistic ends justified violent means. While other antifascist authors, such as Nobel laureate Heinrich Böll, were flirting with the allure of violent revolution—Böll's heroes, particularly his female heroes (one of whom, Katharina Blum in *Die verlorene Ehre der Katharina Blum* [1974, translated as *The Lost Honor of Katharina Blum*, 1975], is directly based on Meinhof), are prone to solve their problems with firearms—Grass makes the antifascist Walter Matern the heir of Hitler's dog; analyzes the frustration of middle-aged intellectuals in Eberhard Starusch and the need to find a new messiah and join a crusade in Pilenz, Vero Lewand, and Irmgard Seifert; suggests the alternative nonviolent model of Helmuth Hübener; and reemphasizes in *Aus dem Tagebuch einer Schnecke* his belief in the essential identity and futility of all violent behavior, whether of the left or of the right.

In the middle of his snail diary the campaign-weary Grass inserted four wistful lines saying that someday he would like to rest from his political travails for a while and write about something he really enjoys: "Ich will ein erzählendes Kochbuch schreiben" (I want to write a narrating cookbook). And though he kept up his busy schedule even after the 1972 elections—participating in regional campaigns; making speeches and writing political essays; taking trips to the Soviet Union, Greece, France, Italy, Israel, the United States, Canada, Poland, India, Asia, and Africa; founding with Böll and Carola Stern the journal *L'76 Demokratie und Sozialismus: Politische und Literarische Beiträge* (L'76 Democracy and Socialism: Political and Literary Contributions) as well as, later, the publishing firm L'80 (thereafter the journal was also called *L'80*); supervising the publication of collected editions of his poems, his plays, and a volume of his speeches and essays titled *Der Bürger und seine Stimme* (The Citizen and His Voice, 1974); receiving an honorary doctorate from Harvard in 1976; and working to develop with Luchterhand publishers a model agreement to provide authors with greatly increased rights of participation in important publication decisions—Grass did in fact begin to turn away somewhat from the crush of everyday political affairs to write his cookbook. It was well under way in 1974 when Brandt resigned as chancellor following the revelation that his assistant, Günther Guillaume, was an East German spy. Saddened but more determined than ever, Grass proclaimed that the snail had left the people behind and they must work harder to catch up to her.

The cookbook appeared in 1977 as *Der Butt* (translated as *The Flounder*, 1978). At seven hundred pages, almost the same length as *Die Blechtrommel* and *Hundejahre*, it has an even more complex narrative fabric and an even wider epic scope than the earlier books. Oskar puts in a token appearance, and there are many eyeglasses—reminiscent of Brauxel's Erkenntnisbrille—belonging to the most visionary characters. The narrator is a writer living in Berlin.

A study in yin and yang, *Der Butt* begins with a double impregnation: the narrator physically impregnates his wife Ilsebill, who emotionally impregnates him. Both pregnancies, as well as the parallel development of world history from the stone age to the 1970s, proceed to term in the book's nine sections, which are labeled months. At the end of the ninth month, as history gives birth to the modern world and Ilsebill bears a child—clearly based on Grass's daughter Helena, who was born in 1974 and to whom *Der Butt* is dedicated—the narrator brings forth his emotional "headbirth": the novel itself and its central insight, an extrapolative prediction from the history of male dominance that the future of life on Earth rests with the female.

One strand of the narrative deals with previous embodiments of the narrator and his women, the cooks, from neolithic times to the present. Another strand involves the flounder: he is the fish of the Grimms' fairy tale "Vom Fischer un syner Fru" (The Fisherman and His Wife). A reification of the Weltgeist (world spirit), the flounder advises the male narrator in his various incarnations down through the centuries until, in modern times, it changes sides and begins to advise the women, who place the flounder on trial for his male chauvinist crimes against humanity. A third important strand of narration, then, involves the empaneling of a feminist tribunal, or "feminal," and the interrogation of the fish.

His dual role as advisor, like the double impregnation, has its analog in what Grass claims were dual versions of the Grimms' fairy tale: the familiar one, in which the insatiably ambitious and acquisitive person is a woman, and another in which it is a man. The latter version was destroyed by the Brothers Grimm, who feared that it might undermine the prevailing pattern of male dominance.

The first cook is Aua, who has three breasts. Actually, all women in the tribe in that age were named Aua and had three breasts. That modern mortals have only two breasts is a symbol of the fact that some third dimension, perhaps a third political possibility, is missing. In fact, the narrator maintains, some feminists, like the mythical Amazons, have only one breast. The Auas amply nurse, nourish, and nurture the tribe, including the adult males, all of whom are named Edek. Thus, their plethora of breasts, which "hügelten landschaftlich" (rose as hills in the landscape), is a symbol of their identity with the earth mother.

Aua has stolen fire from the sky wolf (an adaptation of South American Indian myths), but she uses the fire only for cooking. It is the talking fish–the masculine principle–caught by Edek, the narrator, which suggests that the cooking fires can be used also for smelting metals for weapons. These stone-age hunters already have stone weapons, but whenever they encounter the men of another tribe they hastily confer with Aua, as the other men confer with their Eua or Eia, and hostilities cease as dinner invitations are exchanged.

When the women discover that the men have perverted the cooking fire, they perform a ritual dance around an image of the three-breasted goddess and then throw the new metal weapons into the river. But it is a woman–Mestwina, the tenth-century incarnation of Aua–who commits the first murder: she

kills Bishop Adalbert of Prague with a cast-iron cooking spoon. Thus, the metallic, life-taking male principle infringes the organic, life-giving female principle, even in the realm of nourishment. The cooks introduce the potato to Prussia under Friedrich II, thus staving off hunger, and feed poisonous mushrooms to French occupation troops under Napoleon. They smother a lover in bed during the Reformation and feed Jews and other prisoners in the death camp at Stutthof during the Third Reich.

But the bankruptcy of the male principle is at hand: as predicted in the destroyed version of the fairy tale, after man has built bridges over the widest rivers and towers which reach to the clouds, has learned to fly, and wants to journey to the distant stars, all his efforts will collapse as old Mother Earth shakes off his dominion. Even the flounder is disgusted and deserts his sons, who have used their knowledge and power only to create war, misery, and increased hunger.

But who will take over history from the men? It will certainly not be those women who merely imitate men, *Der Butt* maintains. Such a scenario is graphically anticipated in the eighth month, subtitled "Vatertag" (Father's Day). Here the cook is Sibylle Miehlau, the granddaughter of Lena Stubbe, the heroic old Social Democrat who fed the prisoners at Stutthof and was beaten to death while trying to prevent the theft of her supplies. Sibylle is the narrator's former fiancée and the mother of his child; but she has given the child to her mother to raise, has become a lesbian, and has masculinized her name to Billy. On Ascension Day she goes to the lake for a picnic with three other women, Fränki, Siggi, and Mäxchen; all of them are dressed in men's clothing. Fränki, Siggi, and Mäxchen rape Billy with a dildo, an act linked to Ascension Day by being portrayed as a grotesque little crucifixion. A motorcycle gang in black leather observes this atrocity from their metallic cycles. When, newly awakened to her woman- and motherhood, Billy runs away from her "friends" crying "Ich bin eine Frau, eine Frau, eine Frau!" (I am a woman, a woman, a woman!), the seven bikers gang-rape her and then run their heavy machines repeatedly over her body, which is reduced to a pulp.

This episode, the starkest and most shocking thing Grass has ever written, closely parallels the scene in *Hundejahre* where Eddi and Jenny are attacked by the male and female personifications of evil. It demonstrates the bankruptcy of the male principle and the extent to which the male has corrupted the female principle. But it also suggests that in extremis, when the absurdity of male and one-breasted Amazonian violence is most clearly revealed, the fundamental three-breasted female impulse to feed and nurture, inherited by Sibylle from her grandmother Lena Stubbe and from all the cooks back to Aua, may emerge again. If it could take control of history it could provide the third possibility.

It will be opposed by violent women such as the minority on the feminal who vote for the death penalty for the flounder and then throw stones at the others as they return the fish to the sea. For these female terrorists history has simply gone back to the stone age, with masculinized women using stone weapons to take life. For the life-giving women such as Maria Kuczorra, the last cook in *Der Butt,* whose husband is shot down by troops in front of the Lenin shipyards in Gdansk during the 1970 strikes over food prices, history moves ahead, not backward; it does not leap to utopia but progresses slowly and surely with the help of a new flounder, a new Zeitgeist.

At the end of the novel the narrator visits Maria in Gdansk. They walk along the beach; have sex, which she initiates; and eat the food she has cooked. Then she runs into the sea and calls out a Kashubian word, loudly, three times, whereupon a new flounder leaps into her arms and speaks with her for a considerable time. The narrator sits on the beach, "fallen out of history," as he describes himself. When she returns she is neither Maria, though she appears to be, nor any of the other earlier cooks, whom she resembles, but Ilsebill. The ending, like that of *Die Blechtrommel,* points to the future. Oskar feared that he would always have the black cook, the personification of the evil principle, coming after him. Here, the male narrator runs after a white cook, the personification of the nourishing principle, who has broken out of the cycle of war and starvation and begun to make the future history of the world a history of peace and plenty.

Reception of *Der Butt* was anything but unanimous or blasé. Many were shocked by such graphic treatment of violence, scatology, and sex. And though it is clearly much more critical of men than of women, many feminists were offended by it. Yet, the novel was so widely acclaimed and sold so many copies that Grass was able in 1978 to endow a rich literary award in the name of his admired "teacher" Alfred Döblin which is administered by the Berlin Academy of Art.

This fictional account of the battle of the sexes was in part suggested by real life: during the writing of *Der Butt* Grass's marriage had been crumbling, and in 1978 it ended in divorce. The next year he married the Berlin organist Ute Ehrhardt, the model for Ulla Witzlaff in the novel. With her he made a

trip through Asia which provided the basis for a shorter diary on the model of *Aus dem Tagebuch einer Schnecke* titled *Kopfgeburten oder Die Deutschen Sterben aus* (1980; translated as *Headbirths; or, The Germans Are Dying Out,* 1982).

In the meantime he had won several important literary prizes, including the International Mondello Prize in 1977 and the Viareggio Prize in 1978, and had worked on a motion picture version of *Die Blechtrommel;* preparing to film on location necessitated some of the trips to Gdansk fictionalized in *Der Butt.* The director, Volker Schlöndorff, also accompanied the Grasses to the Orient. When the movie appeared in 1979 it won the Golden Palm at Cannes.

In 1979 Grass published *Das Treffen in Telgte* (translated as *The Meeting at Telgte,* 1981) as a tribute to Hans Werner Richter and the Gruppe 47. Set in the last year of the Thirty Years' War, three hundred years before the founding of the Gruppe 47, *Das Treffen in Telgte* is a fictional account of a meeting of war-weary German baroque poets at an inn outside the small Westphalian town of Telgte. Grass had carefully researched this era and these poets for the corresponding section of *Der Butt.* Now he projects onto their time the analogous concerns of the postwar era, including the political factionalism and generational conflicts that racked the Gruppe 47. Simon Dach is the wise, long-suffering analog of Hans Werner Richter; but who, if anyone, is Grass cannot be answered with certainty: the book is not simply a roman à clef. One poet, however, does stand out from all the rest because of his breaking of taboos, his involvement in practical political matters, and his advising of heads of state: the swashbuckling Grimmelshausen, later to become the author of *Der abenteuerliche Simplicissimus Teutsch* (1669; translated as *The Adventurous Simplicissimus,* 1912), the first great German novel and, in part, a remarkable fictional history of the Thirty Years' War, which is certainly a fitting analogy to Grass's Danzig novels.

Kopfgeburten deals with the problems of world hunger and overpopulation. To accompany him and Ute on their journey to the Orient, Grass creates a fictional couple, Harm and Dörte Peters, teachers in Itzehoe, a town north of Hamburg near which Grass's second home at Wewelsfleth is located. In the narrative, which is written in the style of a film script for Schlöndorff, Harm and Dörte try to decide whether to have a child. The overpopulation and the squalor of slums in the Asian countries argue against it. Primitive rituals associated with various mother goddesses, however, awaken deep maternal instincts in Dörte, and she throws her birth-control pills into the toilet. The matter is complicated by the xenophobic political speeches of the Bavarian Christian Socialist leader Franz Josef Strauss, who warns that the Germans are dying out, that Turks and other foreigners are taking over the country, and that Germans must increase their birthrate.

In Shanghai, Grass tries to imagine what it would be like if the first and third worlds were reversed: what if there were a billion Germans? How does German efficiency compare with Chinese efficiency? Could the developed nations feed people as efficiently as they can kill them? The upshot of Grass's musings is that people in the advanced countries can transcend nationalism and begin to exist on a global scale for the first time. They can turn from war and harness their efficiency as well as their maternal instincts to help fight world hunger. They can stop worrying about dying out and begin to prevent dying. They can stop worrying about having a child and begin to worry about children.

The last paragraph of the book is a symbolic cinematographic summary of the whole argument: back home in Germany, as they drive along in their Volkswagen, Harm and Dörte almost hit a small Turkish boy who runs in front of their car. They stop in time, and the boy and his friends—other Turkish boys—celebrate his survival. Then, in a visionary scene, happy Indian, Chinese, and African children stream out from neighboring streets and yards; they increase and become numberless. They all celebrate with the little Turk whose life has been spared. As the children cheerfully knock on the VW, the childless couple inside "does not know what to say in German"; and the very language Grass uses to describe their speechlessness is pidginized, pulled away from standard German in the direction of that of the children: "und nicht weiß, was sagen auf deutsch."

Grass helped organize meetings of writers from East and West in East Berlin in 1981, The Hague in 1982, and West Berlin in 1983 to promote the cause of peace; made a fact-finding trip to Nicaragua in 1982; participated in 1983 in a conference on the future of democratic socialism; and made a speech at the Social Democratic admonitory commemoration of the fiftieth anniversary of Hitler's rise to power on 30 January 1933. He published the collection *Aufsätze zur Literatur* (Essays on Literature, 1980); two large volumes of graphic art accompanied by selected passages from his writings, *Zeichnen und Schreiben* (1982, 1984; translated as *Drawings & Words Nineteen Fifty-four to Nineteen Seventy-seven*, 1983, and *Etchings & Words Nineteen Seventy-two to Nineteen Eighty-two,* 1985); a volume of etchings and poems, *Ach Butt, dein Märchen geht böse aus* (Alas, Flounder, Your Fairy Tale Has An Unhappy Ending, 1983); and a volume of political

rebuttals, *Widerstand lernen* (Learn to Resist, 1984). His graphic art was exhibited in well over one hundred galleries worldwide. In Rome in 1982 he was awarded the Antonio Feltrinelli Prize, at the equivalent of approximately $85,000 one of the most richly endowed cultural awards after the Nobel Prize. In 1983 he was elected president of the Berlin Academy of Arts.

In his acceptance speech for the Feltrinelli Prize, "Die Vernichtung der Menschheit hat begonnen" (The Annihilation of Humanity Has Begun), Grass says that literature, even more than the other arts, has always had one reliable ally: the future. Even though Brecht and Döblin were persecuted by Nazism and the Soviet writers Isaac Babel and Ossip Mandelstam by Stalinism, their works outlived these movements; time was on their side. Now, Grass says, the future is not so secure and cannot be taken for granted in the book which he is writing.

The book referred to in this speech appeared in 1986 under the title *Die Rättin* (The She-Rat; translated as *The Rat,* 1987). It is informed with an air of eschatology but also with irony and self-parody. Characters from his previous works are here reunited and come full circle to their beginnings. Oskar reappears in time for his sixtieth birthday. "Ist abermals die Zeit für ihn reif?" (Is the time ripe for him once more?), asks the narrator, who is nearly identical with Grass. Oskar Matzerath-Bronski, as he now signs his name, is a movie (and erstwhile pornographic video) producer, whom the narrator engages to make a silent movie about acid rain and the death of the forests.

Meanwhile, Oskar's grandmother Anna Koljaiczek, still alive on her farm near Gdansk, is preparing to celebrate her 107th birthday. She invites the far-flung family, all of them characters from earlier novels, to attend. Since it is his gift to foresee the future (his firm is called Postfuturum), Oskar makes a video of the event before he leaves Düsseldorf. He loads his Mercedes with this prophetic video and other gifts, including some plastic Smurfs, and sets out for Poland.

Interwoven with these strands of narrative is an account of the adventures of five women, including the narrator's wife Damroka—an organist, like Ute Grass—on a boat named *Die Neue Ilsebill* (The New Ilsebill). They set out on a scientific expedition into the Baltic to study the link between pollution and an explosion in the population of jellyfish.

The main story concerns the she-rat of the title, which the narrator asks for and receives as a Christmas gift; this incident is a barb aimed at the conservative Bavarian politician Franz Josef Strauss, who had called writers like Grass "Ratten und Schmei-fliegen" (rats and blowflies). The narrator recalls that in Grass's early play *Hochwasser* two speaking rats had commented on human calamity; and now the she-rat does the same. While the narrator circles the earth in a space capsule, the she-rat stands on a pile of human refuse and gives a nightmarish speech modeled on Jean Paul's "Rede des toten Christus vom Weltgebäude herab, daß kein Gott sei" (Speech of the Dead Christ from the Top-of-the-World-Building, That There Is No God) in his novel *Siebenkäs* (1796–1797). She says that the human race is gone; only its refuse survives. As the she-rat describes the end of mankind—"Ultimo," as she calls it—the narrator sees the events happening before him on his video screen.

The she-rat claims that rats gnawed their way into the giant computers in the East and the West into which doomsday was programmed. Or perhaps it was mice, she concedes. At any rate, it was the humans who had programmed the computers and the missiles, euphemistically called "Peacemakers" and "Friends of the People." Any small, unexpected problem could have set them off.

Ultimo occurs at noon on a Sunday, just as Oskar's video reaches its end, where it shows the birthday guests watching the video of the birthday party, at which the guests are watching a video of the party. The women and the wooden superstructure of their boat are vaporized; the steel hull drifts aimlessly across the Baltic. Oskar seeks refuge under the skirts of his grandmother, but he and the other birthday guests are desiccated, reduced to shriveled gnomes by the enhanced radiation of the low-blast neutron weapons with which Gdansk is hit. Only the already shriveled 107-year-old Anna Koljaiczek survives.

When she eventually dies, her mummy and that of Oskar—which is found under her skirts and is taken for that of a newborn—are not eaten as others are but are moved into Gdansk and placed on the altar of St. Mary's church. Here Anna becomes a kind of fertility goddess to the hungry rats, a grotesque new Virgin with Oskar as the Child, the role he played in this very church with the Dusters. The Smurfs are assembled about her in a kind of crèche scene. When one of her fingers breaks off, it seems to point at a group of Smurfs who are tilling the soil. Taking this as a sign, the rats begin to plant and harvest. They subdue mutant pests such as mammalian blowflies and flying snails, and soon they live in abundance.

Shortly before they were vaporized, the five women docked *The New Ilsebill* at Visby, Sweden, and

went ashore for the afternoon. There they joined a group protesting the use of animals in medical research. Rocks were thrown—some of these people are the same violent women who stoned the members of the feminal who acquitted the flounder—and glass was shattered. The women returned to their boat and cast off in haste before the police arrived.

Now, from his vantage point in orbit, the narrator watches the hulk of *The New Ilsebill* moving under its own power into the harbor of Gdansk, again called Danzig. When it docks, human-rats or rat-humans, the products of gene manipulations in the laboratory at Visby who have stowed away on the boat, emerge. They are blond, blue-eyed dwarves with the heads of rats and three fingers on each hand like the Smurfs, whose language they speak. Like Eddi Amsel's scarecrows, these monsters retrace the stages of human development: they reinvent fire, drink beer, and march in formation. Naturally, these new evil humanoids exploit the rats, who are finally forced to eliminate them. Thus, the last monstrous creation of the human race is eradicated, the she-rat says.

Like Jean Paul's story, in the end the tale of the she-rat is only a dream. Oskar returns safely from Gdansk, having suffered nothing worse than a minor traffic accident and an attack of prostatism. Everyone, including Volker Schlöndorff, attends Oskar's sixtieth birthday party. Oskar has begun to make the story of the rat-humans into a film titled *Davor und Danach* (Before That and After That) which will end with the total destruction of the forest and the ecological "romantics" who try to save it; but the film is postponed. Humanity has a second chance. It was all just a bad dream. Or was it?

In the end the narrator dreams that there may be a glimmer of hope that humans can act humanely. Though the rats laugh at this hope, he perseveres, saying, "diesmal wollen wir füreinander und außerdem friedfertig, hörst du, in Liebe und sanft, wie wir geschaffen sind von Natur" (this time we want to be for each other and peace-loving besides, do you hear, loving and gentle, as we are created by nature). "Ein schöner Traum" (a beautiful dream), replies the she-rat before she disappears.

In some ways *Die Rättin* can be seen as Grass's culminating work. It represents a conscious return to his beginnings in *Die Blechtrommel,* a tying-up of loose ends. As a final warning to humanity about the dangers of global cataclysm, it is a very tough act to follow. Still, Grass has not been idle since *Die Rättin.*

In 1988 he documented his gripping trip to India in a book of dark pencil drawings and texts titled *Zunge Zeigen* (translated as *Show Your Tongue,*

1989), in which the third world's hunger and poverty are shown to cast profound shame on wealthy countries. The dying forests of the world are eulogized in a similarly dark volume of drawings called *Totes Holz* (Dead Wood, 1990).

In 1989 an event occurred which electrified Grass anew. After the unforeseen fall of the Berlin Wall in November of that year, Germany under Chancellor Helmut Kohl moved quickly toward unification, in fact toward a ruthless annexation of the socialist East by the capitalist West, Grass would say. His nearly eight-hundred-page novel *Ein weites Feld* (A Far Field, 1995) attempts to explain in literary terms what he tirelessly repeated in speeches and essays leading up to and following unification in 1990.

The novel explores the impact of unification on an East German family, the Wuttkes. The father, Theodor, or Theo, born exactly one hundred years after the nineteenth-century German novelist Theodor Fontane and in the same town, believes himself to be a kind of reincarnation of the writer. Fontane experienced the first German wars of unification leading, in Grass's view, to the world wars of the twentieth century.

Ein weites Feld (the title is a quotation from a Fontane novel) is a difficult read, short on plot or action and long–presumably in imitation of Fontane–on reminiscence and discussion. It may be one of the most-purchased and least-read books in history. Billed in Germany as the novel of the century, advance orders and other immediate sales totaled more than 250,000 copies in the first two months alone. Then a great critical outcry against the book arose. There were very few dissenting voices in support of the novel.

For those who do read their way into *Ein weites Feld,* the characters become like old friends, and the various odd fictional conceits, such as a nosy collective of near-omniscient narrators who work at the Fontane archives in Potsdam, seem almost normal. Certainly the book provides a profoundly insightful psychological portrait of aging and the human condition in the presence of evil.

Shorter fictional works also shaped by the fall of the Berlin Wall, such as *Unkenrufe* (1992; translated as *The Call of the Toad,* 1992), help to place Grass's views on unification in perspective: he has not opposed German or European unification per se, only the ruthless and one-sided methods of the Kohl government. In fact, as *Unkenrufe* demonstrates, Grass envisions a gradual and peaceful European unity, symbolized by an older couple. Alexandra, a Polish widow, and Alexander, a German widower, unite in Grass's birthplace, Danzig/ Gdansk, to open a cemetery of reconciliation where expatriate Danzigers can be buried in their native soil.

At the close of the century Grass published *Mein Jahrhundert* (My Century, 1999), a collection of one hundred short narratives told by various characters, beginning with a German soldier sent to help put down the Boxer Rebellion in 1900 and ending with an account ostensibly written in 1999 by Grass's late mother. Recalling that *Die Blechtrommel* also begins with the birth of Oskar's mother in 1900, and with historical events such as the Boer War that marked "his century" as the century of violence, reading *Mein Jahrhundert* one understands how Grass has come to view himself as a chronicler and artistic mirror of the twentieth century.

Letters:

Gestern, vor 50 Jahren: Ein deutsch-japanischer Briefwechsel, by Grass and Kenzaburo Oe, edited by Otto Putz (Göttingen: Steidl, 1995).

Interview:

Regine Hildebrandt, *Schaden begrenzen, oder auf die Fuße treten: Ein Gesprach* (Berlin: Volk & Welt, 1993).

Bibliographies:

Jean M. Woods, "Günter Grass Bibliography," *West Coast Review,* 5, no. 3 (1971): 52–56; 6, no. 1 (1971): 31–40;

George A. Everett, *A Select Bibliography of Günter Grass (From 1956 to 1973)* (New York: Franklin, 1974);

Patrick O'Neill, *Günter Grass: A Bibliography 1955–1975* (Toronto: University of Toronto Press, 1976);

Daniela Hermes, "Günter Grass: Auswahl-Bibliographie," in *Kritisches Lexikon zur deutschsprachigen Gegenwartsliteratur,* edited by Heinz Ludwig Arnold (Munich: Edition text + kritik, 1994).

References:

Susan C. Anderson, *Grass and Grimmelshausen: Günter Grass's "Das Treffen in Telgte" and Rezeptionstheorie* (Columbia, S.C.: Camden House, 1986);

Heinz Ludwig Arnold, ed., *Text + Kritik, Heft 1/1a: Günter Grass* (Munich: Edition text + kritik, 1978);

Arnold and Franz Josef Görtz, eds., *Günter Grass: Dokumente zur politischen Wirkung* (Munich: Edition text + kritik, 1971);

Philip Brady, Timothy McFarland, and John J. White, eds., *Günter Grass's Der Butt: Sexual Politics and the Male Myth of History* (Oxford: Clarendon Press, 1990);

Hanspeter Brode, *Günter Grass* (Munich: Beck, 1979);

Nicole Casanova, *Günter Grass: Atelier des métamorphoses* (Paris: Belfond, 1979);

W. Gordon Cunliffe, *Günter Grass* (New York: Twayne, 1969);

Edward Diller, *A Mythic Journey: Günter Grass's "Tin Drum"* (Lexington: University Press of Kentucky, 1974);

Manfred Durzak, ed., *Interpretationen zu Günter Grass: Geschichte auf dem poetischen Prüfstand* (Stuttgart: Klett, 1985);

Rolf Geissler, ed., *Günter Grass: Ein Materialienbuch* (Neuwied: Luchterhand, 1976);

Franz Josef Görtz, ed., *Günter Grass: Auskunft für Leser* (Neuwied: Luchterhand, 1984);

Ronald Hayman, *Günter Grass* (London: Methuen, 1985);

Michael Hollington, *Günter Grass: The Writer in a Pluralist Society* (London: Marion Boyars, 1980);

Manfred Jurgensen, *Über Günter Grass* (Bern: Francke, 1974);

Jurgensen, ed., *Grass: Kritik–Thesen–Analysen* (Bern: Francke, 1973);

Alan Frank Keele, *Understanding Günter Grass* (Columbia: University of South Carolina Press, 1988);

Detlef Krumme, *Günter Grass: Die Blechtrommel* (Munich: Hanser, 1986);

Richard H. Lawson, *Günter Grass* (New York: Ungar, 1985);

Irène Leonard, *Günter Grass* (New York: Barnes & Noble, 1974);

Gert Loschütz, ed., *Von Buch zu Buch–Günter Grass in der Kritik: Eine Dokumentation* (Neuwied: Luchterhand, 1968);

Ann L. Mason, *The Skeptical Muse: A Study of Günter Grass' Conception of the Artist* (Bern: Lang, 1974);

Siegfried Mews, ed., *"The Fisherman and His Wife": Günter Grass's "The Flounder" in Critical Perspective* (New York: AMS Press, 1983);

Keith Miles, *Günter Grass* (New York: Barnes & Noble, 1975);

Volker Neuhaus, *Günter Grass* (Stuttgart: Metzler, 1979; revised and enlarged, 1993);

Neuhaus and Daniela Hermes, eds., *Günter Grass im Ausland* (Frankfurt am Main: Luchterhand, 1990);

Patrick O'Neill, ed., *Critical Essays on Günter Grass* (Boston: Hall, 1987);

O'Neill, *Günter Grass Revisited* (New York: Twayne, 1999);

Gertrude Bauer Pickar, ed., *Adventures of a Flounder: Critical Essays on Günter Grass' "Der Butt"* (Munich: Fink, 1982);

John Reddick, *The "Danzig Trilogy" of Günter Grass* (New York: Harcourt Brace Jovanovich, 1975);

Kurt Lothar Tank, *Günter Grass* (New York: Ungar, 1969);

Noel Thomas, *The Narrative Works of Günter Grass: A Critical Interpretation* (Amsterdam: Benjamins, 1982);

Heinrich Vormweg, *Günter Grass, mit Selbstzeugnissen und Bilddokumenten* (Reinbek: Rowohlt, 1986; revised, 1993);

Alexander Weber, *Günter Grass's Use of Baroque Literature* (Leeds: Maney, 1995);

Theodor Wieser, ed., *Günter Grass: Porträt und Poesie* (Neuwied: Luchterhand, 1968);

A. Leslie Willson, ed., *A Günter Grass Symposium* (Austin: University of Texas Press, 1971).

Papers:

The Günter Grass Archive is located in the Deutsches Literaturarchiv, Marbach am Neckar.

Franz Grillparzer

(15 January 1791 – 21 January 1872)

Hinrich C. Seeba
University of California, Berkeley

This entry originally appeared in DLB 133: Nineteenth-Century
German Writers to 1840.

BOOKS: *Die Ahnfrau: Ein Trauerspiel in fünf Aufzügen*
(Vienna: Wallishausser, 1817); translated by Leti-
tia Elizabeth Landon as *The Ancestress: A Dramatic
Sketch,* in her *The Venetian Bracelet, The Lost Pleiad, A
History of the Lyre, and other Poems* (London: Long-
man, Rees, Orme, Brown & Green, 1828);

Sappho: Trauerspiel in fünf Aufzügen (Vienna: Wallishausser, 1819); translated by John Bramsen as *Sappho:
A Tragedy, in Five Acts* (London: Black, 1820);

Das goldene Vließ: Dramatisches Gedicht in drei Abtheilungen
(Vienna: Wallishausser, 1822)–comprises *Der Gast-
freund; Die Argonauten; Medea; Medea* translated by
F. W. Thurstan and Sidney A. Wittmann as
Medea: A Tragedy (London: Nisbet, 1879); entire
work translated by Arthur Burkhard as *The
Golden Fleece* (Yarmouth Port, Mass.: Register,
1942)–comprises *The Guest-Friend; The Argonauts;
Medea;*

König Ottokar's Glück und Ende: Trauerspiel in fünf Aufzügen
(Vienna: Wallishausser, 1825); translated by
Henry H. Stevens as *King Ottocar, His Rise and Fall*
(Yarmouth Port, Mass.: Register, 1938);

Ein treuer Diener seines Herrn: Trauerspiel in fünf Aufzügen
(Vienna: Wallishausser, 1830); translated by
Burkhard as *A Faithful Servant of His Master*
(Yarmouth Port, Mass.: Register, 1941);

Melusina: Romantische Oper in drei Aufzügen, music by C.
Kreutzer (Vienna: Wallishausser, 1833);

Des Meeres und der Liebe Wellen: Trauerspiel in fünf Aufzügen
(Vienna: Wallishausser, 1840); translated by
Stevens as *Hero and Leander* (Yarmouth Port,
Mass.: Register, 1938);

Der Traum ein Leben: Dramatisches Mährchen in vier Aufzügen
(Vienna: Wallishausser, 1840); translated by
Stevens as *A Dream Is Life* (Yarmouth Port, Mass.:
Register, 1946);

Weh' dem, der lügt!: Lustspiel in fünf Aufzügen (Vienna:
Wallishausser, 1840); translated by Stevens as

*Franz Grillparzer; painting by Heinrich Hollpein, 1836 (Österreichische
Nationalbibliothek)*

Thou Shalt Not Lie (Yarmouth Port, Mass.: Register, 1939);

Sämmtliche Werke, 10 volumes, edited by Heinrich Laube
and Josef Weil (Stuttgart: Cotta, 1872)–includes
in volume 6, *Esther: Dramatisches Bruchstück,* translated by Burkhard as *Esther,* in *The Jewess of Toledo;*

187

Esther (Yarmouth Port, Mass.: Register, 1953); *Libussa: Trauerspiel in fünf Aufzügen,* translated by Stevens as *Libussa* (Yarmouth Port, Mass.: Register, 1941); in volume 7, *Ein Bruderzwist in Habsburg: Trauerspiel in fünf Aufzügen,* translated by Burkhard as *Family Strife in Hapsburg* (Yarmouth Port, Mass.: Register, 1940); *Die Jüdin von Toledo: Historisches Trauerspiel in fünf Aufzügen,* translated by George Henry Danton and Annina P. Danton as *The Jewess of Toledo,* in *The German Classics of the Nineteenth and Twentieth Centuries,* volume 6, edited by Kuno Francke and William Guild Howard (New York: German Publication Society, 1913), pp. 337–408; in volume 8, "Der arme Spielmann," translated by A. Remy as "The Poor Musician," in *The German Classics of the Nineteenth and Twentieth Centuries,* volume 6, pp. 409–454; in volume 10, "Selbstbiographie (1791–1836)," excerpt translated by Remy as "My Journey to Weimar," in *The German Classics of the Nineteenth and Twentieth Centuries,* volume 6, pp. 455–463;

Sämmtliche Werke, 16 volumes, edited by August Sauer (Stuttgart: Cotta, 1887);

Sämtliche Werke: Historisch-kritische Ausgabe, 42 volumes, edited by Sauer and Reinhold Backmann (Vienna: Gerlach & Wiedling, 1909–1916; Vienna: Schroll, 1916–1948);

Sämtliche Werke: Ausgewählte Briefe, Gespräche, Berichte, 4 volumes, edited by Peter Frank and Karl Pörnbacher (Munich: Hanser, 1960–1965);

Dichter über ihre Dichtungen: Franz Grillparzer, edited by Pörnbacher (Munich: Heimeran, 1970);

Tagebücher und Reiseberichte, edited by Klaus Geiler (Berlin: Verlag der Nation, 1980);

Sämtliche Werke: Text und Kommentar, 6 volumes, edited by Helmut Bachmaier (Frankfurt am Main: Deutscher Klassiker Verlag, 1986–1993).

Neither Romantic nor purely realist, Franz Grillparzer has been difficult to place in the established periods of literary historiography. The foremost Austrian writer in the nineteenth century, a time when Austrian literature was trying to define its own identity separate from the rest of literature written in German, Grillparzer soon came to serve as the Austrian classic, comparable only to Johann Wolfgang von Goethe and Friedrich Schiller, the twin heralds of German classicism. He himself unabashedly says in his "Selbstbiographie" (Autobiography, 1872; excerpt translated as "My Journey to Weimar," 1913), written in 1853, that "ich mich nämlich denn doch, trotz allem Anstande, für den Besten halte, der nach ihm [Goethe] und Schiller gekommen ist" (I consider myself, in all due respect, the best who has come after him [Goethe] and Schiller). To many anxious observers who had witnessed the collapse of

European Enlightenment into Viennese gemütlichkeit, Grillparzer, who dealt with topics from Greek mythology in classical form, represented the literary counterpart to the musical classicism of Joseph Haydn and Ludwig van Beethoven. Grillparzer would eventually command the unqualified respect of critics within and outside Austria for combining the musicality of Viennese folklore, the tragic genre of classical antiquity, and the quest for a distinctly Austrian history. He endowed the form of classical drama with a psychological depth that anticipates the discovery of the unconscious by Sigmund Freud two generations later. He has been credited by Claudio Magris with creating the "Hapsburg myth," the myth of an idealized imperial dynasty that helped integrate the multiethnic Austro-Hungarian Empire in the face of growing nationalism. The disintegration of the Soviet Empire gave new political significance to the Hapsburg myth, which is believed by some to have inspired the Eastern European countries' drive for independence, and drew new attention to Grillparzer, the major literary advocate of the myth.

In his 1837 essay "Worin unterscheiden sich die österreichischen Dichter von den übrigen?" (In Which Way Are Austrian Writers Different from Others?) Grillparzer defined an Austrian brand of German literature based on what he perceived as virtues of the Austrian character: "Bescheidenheit, gesunder Menschenverstand, und wahres Gefühl" (modesty, common sense, and true feeling). Always contrasting German and Austrian attitudes, Grillparzer saw as underlying art not so much the strain of philosophical reflection he found and detested in the German followers of Friedrich von Schlegel and Georg Wilhelm Friedrich Hegel as the images that enlivened his imagination ever since a maid introduced him as a boy to the wonders of Wolfgang Amadeus Mozart's opera *Die Zauberflöte* (The Magic Flute, 1791). Trying to define a specifically Austrian identity without giving in to the excesses of nationalism that increasingly threatened the survival of the Austrian empire, Grillparzer performed a balancing act that secured his reputation as an Austrian classic. In literary histories Grillparzer is usually classified as a "Biedermeier" writer. The Biedermeier period extended from the Congress of Vienna in 1815 to the March Revolutions of 1848 and is characterized by the idyllic portrayal of the private sphere of salons, waltzes, happy bourgeois families, and neatly framed landscapes. The political reality of the time, however, was quite different. In the wake of Napoleon's defeat at Waterloo the Austrian chancellor, Prince Wenzel von Metternich, fearing all political or social change modeled on the French Revolution, established at the Congress of Vienna the thirty-nine-state German Confederation and a system of repression characterized by strict censorship and the persecution of dissidents.

Grillparzer's fascination with the power and pitfalls of language began with uneasiness about his own name:

"Der verfluchte Name hat mich immer geärgert" (The damned name has always irritated me), he wrote in his diary on 21 December 1831. After Lord Byron read Grillparzer's drama *Sappho* (1819; translated, 1820) in Italian translation, he remarked in his diary for 12 January 1821: "Grillparzer–a devil of a name, to be sure, for posterity, but they *must* learn to pronounce it." For a long time the name was believed to be a pseudonym combining the word for crickets (Grillen), evoking whimsical moodiness, and the word for the Fates (Parzen) of classical mythology, and it was easy for critics to ridicule the aspiring tragic playwright. Johann Heinrich Voss reacted to Grillparzer's *Die Ahnfrau* (1817; translated as *The Ancestress,* 1828) by scoffing "daß die Parzen, die diese Tragödie gesponnen, eitel Grillen sind" (that the Fates which spun this tragedy are nothing but vain fantasy). After *Die Ahnfrau* was successfully staged at Goethe's theater in Weimar to mark the birthday of Duchess Luise in February 1819, Karl Ludwig von Knebel remarked in a letter to Goethe: "Der Name ist etwas ominös und die Musen scheinen ihn eben nicht eingesegnet zu haben" (The name is somewhat ominous and the Muses do not seem to have blessed it). The plays on Grillparzer's "devilish" name were not limited to his own time: in John Irving's novel *The World According to Garp* (1978) the name sounds so amusing to Garp that he uses it to signify a dance as well as having sex ("to Grillparzer").

The latter use of his name is rather ironic in that Grillparzer's own relationships with women were generally unhappy. He was in love with his cousin's wife, Charlotte von Paumgartten; with Marie von Smolenitz, who married the painter Moritz Michael Daffinger; and, most notably, with his "ewige Braut" (eternal bride) Katharina Fröhlich, to whom he became engaged in 1821 but never married. Fröhlich eventually became his housekeeper, his nurse, and, finally, his sole heiress and literary executor. The dominant image of Grillparzer the man is that of a grumbling recluse, a gloomy loner–a "Raunzer" in untranslatable Viennese–whose outlook on life was as grim as his face in a photograph taken shortly before his death. It is a faithful portrait of a man whose potential for happiness was stifled by the severe restrictions of his time.

Grillparzer was born in Vienna on 15 January 1791 to the court lawyer Wenzel Grillparzer and Anna Franziska Grillparzer, née Sonnleithner. Following a family tradition, Grillparzer studied law at the University of Vienna from 1807 to 1811. In 1814, after brief assignments as a private tutor for an aristocratic family and an unpaid probationer in the court library, he became an administrator at the Imperial Archives; he would be appointed director in 1832.

The problem of identity is a recurring theme in Grillparzer's works. First performed on 31 January 1817 at the Theater an der Wien, *Die Ahnfrau* combines motifs of the Gothic tale, the fate tragedy, and robber and ghost sto-ries to present a psychological study of the protagonist, Jaromir. It is Jaromir's "fate" to return unknowingly to the Bohemian castle of his ancestors as a robber; ignorant of his origin, he falls in love with his sister, Bertha, and kills their father, Count Borotin; only then does he learn who he really is. Grillparzer shows that one's identity can be established only by accepting one's history, even if it is a bloody family history that becomes visible as the image in a mirror of the vengeful ancestress, the ghostly "Ahnfrau," whose name was also Bertha.

The search for identity of an artist who is forced to relinquish her needs as a woman is the theme of *Sappho.* The poet takes the infatuation of the adolescent Phaon with Sappho the artist to be love for Sappho the woman. When she realizes that her jealousy has driven Phaon to a young girl, Melitta, she commits suicide by jumping from a high rock into the sea, thus creating the classical image of the artist who shuns life in favor of eternal fame: "Dort oben war mein Platz, dort an den Wolken, / Hier ist kein Ort für mich, als nur das Grab" (Up there is my place, there in the clouds. Here is no place for me but the grave). Grillparzer's play is ranked alongside Goethe's tragedy of an artist, *Torquato Tasso* (1790; translated, 1861), and Thomas Mann's depiction of the dichotomy of life and art in "Tonio Kröger" (1903; translated, 1914). The success of the first performance, at the Burgtheater on 21 April 1818, led to an audience with Chancellor Metternich and to Grillparzer's appointment as court playwright at an annual salary of two thousand gulden. His writing would often bring him into conflict with his role as a civil servant, with ever watchful censors probing the propriety of the views he expressed in literary form. Josef Schreyvogel, who had succeeded Grillparzer's uncle Josef von Sonnleithner as secretary of the Burgtheater in 1814, became his mentor and protector and put several more of Grillparzer's plays on the Burgtheater stage.

Grillparzer's next attempt to deal with Greek antiquity was the trilogy *Das goldene Vließ* (1822; translated as *The Golden Fleece,* 1942), consisting of *Der Gastfreund* (translated as *The Guest-Friend*), *Die Argonauten* (translated as *The Argonauts*), and *Medea* (translated, 1879). Grillparzer juxtaposes two cultures, Greek and barbarian, and dismisses the very classicism whose images are invoked. Medea fails to suppress her wild instincts when she finds herself betrayed by her Greek husband, Jason. Unlike Sappho, Medea does not sacrifice her emotions to an idealized spirituality. In an excessive act of revenge she reaffirms her identity as a barbarian woman who will not allow herself to be "colonized" by a Greek man. The ideal of balanced harmony so much promoted in classical aesthetics is exploded. The trilogy is dedicated to Paumgartten, Grillparzer's cousin's wife, with whom Grillparzer was desperately in love at the time. The first two plays were first performed at the Burgtheater on 26 March 1821 and

Medea the following night; later, *Medea* was usually performed without the other two plays.

Grillparzer's group of historical dramas begins with *König Ottokar's Glück und Ende* (1825; translated as *King Ottocar, His Rise and Fall,* 1938), a rather patriotic depiction of the beginning of the Hapsburg dynasty as it was recorded in the *Österreichische Reimchronik* (Austrian Rhyming Chronicle, 1318), by Ottokar von Steiermark and in the *Österreichischer Plutarch* (Austrian Plutarch, 1807–1814), by Josef von Hormayr. But as the ascent of Rudolf von Hapsburg to the throne in 1273 was bound to the decline of the Bohemian king Ottokar II, the censors were concerned about the nationalist sensitivities of the Slavic minority. Another concern was the obvious similarity between Ottokar, who divorces his wife, Margarethe, to marry the granddaughter of the just-defeated Hungarian king, Kunigunde, and Napoleon, who had celebrated his victory over Austria by replacing his wife, Josephine, with Marie-Louise, the daughter of Emperor Franz I of Austria; such a reminder of Austria's humiliation did not seem opportune only two years after Napoleon's death. The censors therefore refused the permit for the performance. Only the emperor himself could clear the way to the stage, and the play premiered at the Burgtheater on 19 February 1825. Grillparzer endorses Rudolf's pride in the eternal grandeur of his office: "Was sterblich war, ich hab es ausgezogen, / Und bin der Kaiser nur, der niemals stirbt" (What was mortal I have abandoned, / And am nothing but the emperor who never dies). Yet this emperor is lovingly portrayed as a human being who can be addressed as "Herr Kaiser," as if the title were a bourgeois name, and he gracefully asks a bourgeois woman not to bend her knee before him. Such folksy popularity joins with the claim to immortality to create the utopian Hapsburg myth that was to withstand the destructive forces of growing nationalism in the course of the nineteenth century.

Grillparzer was arrested in 1826 as a member of the writers' and artists' club Ludlamshöhle (Ludlam's Cave), which was falsely suspected of secretly promoting subversive ideas. Even though the charges were dropped, the incident proved to Grillparzer the arbitrariness of the repressive system. He escaped from this degrading experience by traveling to Germany to visit Ludwig Tieck in Dresden, Hegel in Berlin, and Goethe in Weimar.

The title of his next historical drama, *Ein treuer Diener seines Herrn* (1830; translated as *A Faithful Servant of His Master,* 1941), seems to invoke an idealized attitude that had outlived its social value. The subordination of a loyal servant to his master was the moral message the play was expected to convey at the coronation of the empress Karoline Auguste as queen of Hungary in Preßburg in September 1825. But Grillparzer refused such loyal service to the court and instead used his research in Ignaz Aurel Feßler's *Geschichte der Ungarn* (History of Hungary, 1812–1825) and Hormayr's *Österreichischer Plutarch* to write a psychological portrayal of the suffering victim of a political power game. Bancbanus, counselor to the Hungarian king Andreas II in the thirteenth century, proves himself a "Hüter der Ruhe" (guardian of calm), as if he were a civil servant in the Biedermeier period. While looking after the state's affairs during the absence of the king, he preserves an almost unreal sense of moral duty under extreme and most cruel pressure from the queen's brother, the unscrupulous Otto von Meran, who requires complete self-denial from Bancbanus and then exploits it. Gone mad from unrequited love, yet calculating the conquest with psychological acuity, Otto tries to seduce and humiliate Bancbanus's wife, Erny, who can remain faithful to her husband only by killing herself. Offering, as Grillparzer emphasized in his autobiography, not "eine Apologie der knechtischen Unterwürfigkeit" (a defense of servility) but "den Heroismus der Pflichttreue" (the heroism of responsibility), the play can be read as an indictment of the misuse of political power. The performance at the Burgtheater on 28 February 1828 was a great success—possibly too great a success for such a delicate subject. The emperor, who attended the first three performances, claimed to be so enthralled by the drama of loyalty that he wanted to be "alleiniger Besitzer desselben" (its sole owner) for a price to be determined by Grillparzer. But Grillparzer resisted the attempt at censorship through bribery by claiming that copies of the play were already circulating outside of Austria and were thus beyond his control. It is ironic that in writing and defending this drama of extreme loyalty, Grillparzer twice successfully withstood the pressure of becoming himself "der treue Diener seines Herrn."

Grillparzer had outlined his fifth Greek drama, *Des Meeres und der Liebe Wellen* (Waves of the Sea and of Love, 1840; translated as *Hero and Leander,* 1938), when he was revising *Das goldene Vließ* in the summer of 1820, but he completed his first two historical dramas before he took it up again in 1826. Grillparzer chose the peculiar title for his drama, which is based on the classical myth of Hero and Leander, to suggest the natural power of love and its deadly potential for those who are swept up by it. The romantic fairy tale of two lovers separated by the sea is presented mainly as a psychological profile of the young priestess, Hero, who awakens from the dreams of her childhood and begins a tragic search for an adult identity. Rather than devoting her life to the service of the goddess of love she becomes a loving woman, only to be severely punished for betraying her holy office: while she is asleep her lover, Leander, drowns when her uncle, the priest, puts out the lamp that was to guide Leander on his swim through the stormy seas of the Hellespont to join her. Due to the death of the actress who was to play Hero, *Des Meeres und der Liebe Wellen* did not premiere at the Burgtheater until 5 April 1831; it was not successful.

In *Der Traum ein Leben* (1840; translated as *A Dream Is Life,* 1946) the Biedermeier notion of "Ruhe" (calm) as the utmost virtue of a good citizen is the background for Rustan's escape into an exotic dream of action that turns so violent that he gladly returns to the reality of his unexciting, idyllic life of conformity: "Eines nur ist Glück hienieden, / Eins, des Innern stiller Frieden / Und die schuldbefreite Brust!" (Only one thing is happiness down here, / Only one: quiet peace inside / And a heart free of guilt!). After tasting the dangerous glamour of usurped power in the dream, he will never again stray from the proper path to private happiness. Based on Voltaire's story *Le Blanc et noir* (1764; translated into German in 1790) and adopting its title from Pedro Calderón de la Barca's *La vida es sueño* (1635), the play presents any attempt at political involvement as a nightmare. A dramatized psychoanalysis of a dream that acts out suppressed desires, the play also effectively reflects its own time of political suppression, censorship, torture, and murder: in the central scene a deaf-mute is so outraged about the system of lies and deceit that he miraculously regains the power of speech to identify Rustan as a murderer. But the fairy tale of Samarkand seemed too far removed in time and space, and its moral too close to the dominant ideology, to arouse the suspicion of the authorities. It was successfully performed at the Burgtheater on 4 October 1834 and long remained a favorite on many stages.

In 1836 Grillparzer escaped from an unhappy love affair by taking a trip to Paris–where he met Alexandre Dumas, Ludwig Börne, and Heinrich Heine–and to London. During his stay in London he was introduced to Edward Bulwer-Lytton, but the author of *The Last Days of Pompeii* (1834) failed to recognize his colleague from Germany. Grillparzer bitterly remarked in his autobiography almost two decades later: "Wenn ein Deutscher nicht Goethe oder Schiller heißt, geht er unbekannt durch die ganze Welt" (If a German's name is not Goethe or Schiller, he wanders through the world unknown).

The last of Grillparzer's completed dramas to be performed during his lifetime was *Weh' dem, der lügt!* (1840; translated as *Thou Shalt Not Lie,* 1939). The performance of his sole comedy at the Burgtheater on 6 March 1838 was a devastating failure due to a mostly aristocratic audience that was offended by the character of the idiotic nobleman, Galomir, and the misalliance between a count's daughter and Leon, a mere cook. Leon's creative playfulness in mixing truth, white lies, and deceit is always well-intentioned and directed at the moral good. His employer, Bishop Gregor, asks Leon to free the bishop's nephew Attalus from imprisonment by Kattwald, an enemy count; but he makes

Leon promise not to tell any lies in carrying out the task. While the man of the church has a dogmatic notion of truthfulness that does not allow for any linguistic ambivalence, the man of the palate enjoys the taste of his verbal concoctions and believes that the end justifies the means. He brings to his task an understanding of the cultural difference between the educated French, who know how to enjoy a good meal, and the barbaric Germans, who, like Count Kattwald, long to be educated in Western culture. In their quest for the art of cooking these savages let themselves be tricked into becoming servants to the irreverent foreigner, who, with his culinary and verbal charades, not only frees the bishop's nephew but also rescues Kattwald's daughter Edrita from an arranged marriage with Galomir. Based on the French translation of the sixth-century *Historia Francorum* of Gregory of Tours and set in the Middle Ages, this comedy is also a polemical pronouncement of Grillparzer's aesthetics directed against German critics of the Hegelian persuasion. In contrasting the principle of absolute truth with the reality of ambivalent language and perspectival truths, Grillparzer is implicitly arguing for the superiority of pragmatic, visual, and sensual perception, which he values as characteristically Austrian, over abstract ideas. But his inability to get his philosophical point across in the dramatic imagery of his comedy led him to withdraw completely from the stage: if he could not solve the problem of representing concepts through strong visual images, he would put his plans and sketches for new dramas aside.

Therefore, three major dramas that were outlined early but completed only after the failure of *Weh' dem, der lügt!* never reached the stage during Grillparzer's lifetime "weil ihnen jenes Lebensprinzip fehlt, das nur die Anschauung gibt und der Gedanke nie ersetzen kann" (because they lack the principle of life that lies only in visual perception and can never be replaced with thought), as he said in his diary in 1849. He had begun *Libussa* (1872; translated, 1941) in 1822 and *Ein Bruderzwist in Habsburg* (1872; translated as *Family Strife in Hapsburg,* 1940) in 1827; in his will of 1848 Grillparzer ordered that both manuscripts be destroyed because he felt that they were nothing but conceptual debates in need of visual execution. The dramas undertake the enormous task of representing a historic shift of paradigm, from the mythical to the historical age symbolized in the founding of Prague in *Libussa,* and from medieval authority to the challenge of diversity on the eve of the Thirty Years' War in *Ein Bruderzwist in Habsburg.* The contrast between Libussa and Primislaus in the first drama and the fraternal quarrel between Emperor Rudolf II and Mathias in the second seem to be rationally constructed contests of ideas rather than visually imagined theatrical agons. The first drama is a nostalgic look at the waning power of poetic imagination in matriarchy, the second a warning against the advancing power of vulgar calculation that threatens the order of the world. In Rudolf's prophetic vision the future is ruled by the masses, who like a monster, destroy everything in their path: "Aus eignem Schoß ringt los sich der Barbar, / Der, wenn erst ohne Zügel, alles Groe, / Die Kunst, die Wissenschaft, den Staat, die Kirche / Herabstürzt von der Höhe, die sie schützt, / Zur Oberfläche eigener Gemeinheit, / Bis alles gleich, ei ja, weil alles niedrig" (From its own womb breaks away the barbarian, / Who, when no longer reined, / Pulls everything that is great—art, science, state, church—From the protective height down to the surface of its own vulgarity, / Until everything is equal, yes, because everything is base). In these dramas a growing concern Grillparzer nurtured about himself is projected onto changes in history. In 1826 he noted in his diary: "Mein Gemüt verhärtet sich, meine Phantasie erkaltet" (My mind hardens, my imagination cools down). The passing on of power in these historical dramas symbolizes the loss of power, both personal and political, creative and authoritative. *Ein Bruderzwist in Habsburg* successfully premiered in two separate productions, at the Vienna Stadttheater under the direction of Heinrich Laube on 24 September 1872 and at the Burgtheater on 28 September 1872; *Libussa,* whose first act was performed in 1840, had its first complete and little-noticed performance at the Burgtheater on 21 January 1874.

The third drama Grillparzer withheld from the public was *Die Jüdin von Toledo* (1872; translated as *The Jewess of Toledo,* 1913). Based on Lope de Vega's drama *La Judia de Toledo* (1616), this tragedy of illicit love shows how the lure of sensuality undermines political power. The beautiful, spirited Jewess Rahel enters the forbidden royal garden to play the role of the queen in carnival costume and to draw the inexperienced King Alphons of Castile into a game of erotic obsession involving the exchange of pictures. But while Alphons eventually comes to his senses, reaffirming his identity as king and man, Rahel is murdered by the queen and her followers. It seems that Grillparzer is subjecting to moral judgment the very magic of poetic imagery that he tried to uphold in his aesthetic pronouncements. The violent ending of the play also marked Grillparzer's end as a writer: *Die Jüdin von Toledo* was the last drama he completed. It was first performed in Prague on 21 November 1872.

A playwright who can no longer rely on his dramatic imagination and therefore frantically searches for new material in real life is the narrator of Grillparzer's story "Der arme Spielmann" (1848; translated as "The Poor Musician," 1913), which is considered one of the masterpieces of German realism. The narrator's "anthropologischer Heißhunger" (insatiable anthropological curiosity) discovers Jakob, a poor, yet highly educated street fiddler, who is committed to his private religion of music. Like Grillparzer, Jakob is a loner on the margin of society who failed to bring order to his unhappy life. While telling the narrator about his life, he succeeds in imposing order

on it. The fiddler's sentimental story becomes a portrayal of alienation in the Biedermeier era on the eve of the revolution of March 1848. The fiddler dies in one of the frequent Danube floods which, in the opening frame of the narrative, is associated with a possible revolution.

Escapism was a trademark of the Biedermeier era, with its exotic travels abroad and its musical soirées at home; Grillparzer escaped into the fantasies of his asocial mind as his creative powers increasingly failed him. The constant battles against suspicion and mediocrity and the lack of support and recognition from his superiors at the archives eventually rendered him an embittered and unproductive hypochondriac. Not only did he never submit any of his later plays to the theater but he only agreed to have his earlier plays performed again after Laube became director of the Burgtheater in 1849. As he confessed in his autobiography, Grillparzer fell into a lifelong depression when he realized "daß unter diesen Umständen in dem damaligen Österreich für einen Dichter kein Platz sei" (that under the circumstances of Austria at the time there was no place for a writer). But unlike Heinrich von Kleist, who had found himself in a similar predicament in Prussia, Grillparzer—whose mother and youngest brother had committed suicide—did not give in to the temptation to take his own life. He lived to receive, with characteristic skepticism, the honors bestowed on him. He was appointed a member of the newly founded Austrian Academy of Science by Metternich in 1847, was named Hofrat (privy councillor) on his retirement from the archives in 1856, received honorary doctorates from the Universities of Vienna and Leipzig in 1859, was appointed a member of the Upper House by Emperor Franz Joseph in 1861, and became an honorary citizen of Vienna in 1864; his eightieth birthday was celebrated as a grand state event with congratulations coming from Versailles, where the German princes were gathering to found the German Empire—Austria's future partner in defeat.

Without ever again inventing a story or play to express the concerns of his life or to re-create his country's history, Grillparzer died on 21 January 1872 at the age of eighty-one. Tens of thousands of people lined the streets of Vienna as his body was carried to the cemetery of Hietzing, which borders on the imperial park of Schönbrunn.

Bibliographies:

Kurt Vancsa, "Grillparzer-Bibliographie: 1905–1937," *Jahrbuch der Grillparzer-Gesellschaft,* 34 (1937): 102–166;

O. Paul Straubinger, "Grillparzer-Bibliographie: 1938–1952," *Jahrbuch der Grillparzer-Gesellschaft,* 1 (1953): 33–80;

Joachim Müller, *Franz Grillparzer* (Stuttgart: Metzler, 1963);

Herbert Seidler, "Grillparzer-Bibliographie," *Grillparzer Forum Forchtenstein* (1965): 95–98; (1966): 114–116; (1968): 131–134; (1969): 100–103; (1970): 97–99; (1971): 123–124; (1972): 162–168; (1973): 196–198; (1974): 153–155; (1975): 137–138; (1976): 236–241; (1978): 113–115;

Heinz Kindermann, ed., *Das Grillparzer-Bild des 20. Jahrhunderts. Festschrift der österreichischen Akademie der Wissenschaften zum 100. Todestag von Franz Grillparzer* (Vienna: Böhlau, 1972), pp. 109–121, 263–284.

Biographies:

August Sauer, *Franz Grillparzer* (Stuttgart: Metzler, 1941);

Douglas Yates, *Franz Grillparzer: A Critical Biography* (Oxford: Blackwell, 1946);

Raoul Auernheimer, *Franz Grillparzer: Der Dichter Österreichs* (Vienna: Ullstein, 1948);

Josef Nadler, *Franz Grillparzer* (Vaduz: Liechtenstein, 1948);

Gerhard Scheit, *Franz Grillparzer* (Reinbek: Rowohlt, 1989);

Humbert Fink, *Franz Grillparzer* (Innsbruck: Pinquin / Frankfurt am Main: Umschau, 1990).

References:

Helmut Bachmaier, *Franz Grillparzer* (Salzburg: Andreas & Andreas, 1980);

Bachmaier, ed., *Franz Grillparzer* (Frankfurt am Main: Suhrkamp, 1990);

Clifford Albrecht Bernd, ed., *Grillparzer's Der arme Spielmann: New Directions in Criticism* (Columbia, S.C.: Camden House, 1987);

Wilhelm Bietak, *Das Lebensgefühl des "Biedermeier" in der österreichischen Dichtung* (Vienna & Leipzig: Braumüller, 1931);

Arthur Burkhard, *Franz Grillparzer in England und Amerika* (Vienna: Bergland, 1961);

Burkhard, *Grillparzer im Ausland* (Cambridge, Mass.: Published by the author, 1969);

Ernst Fischer, "Franz Grillparzer," in his *Von Grillparzer zu Kafka: Sechs Essays* (Frankfurt am Main: Suhrkamp, 1975), pp. 9–65;

Elke Frederiksen, *Grillparzers Tagebücher als Suche nach Selbstverständnis* (Frankfurt am Main: Peter Lang / Bern: Herbert Lang, 1977);

Ulrich Fülleborn, *Das dramatische Geschehen im Werk Franz Grillparzers: Ein Beitrag zur Epochenbestimmung der deutschen Literatur im 19. Jahrhundert* (Munich: Fink, 1966);

Norbert Fürst, *Grillparzer auf der Bühne* (Vienna & Munich: Manutiuspresse, 1958);

Joachim Kaiser, *Grillparzers dramatischer Stil* (Munich: Hanser, 1961);

Claudio Magris, *Der habsburgische Mythos in der österreichischen Literatur* (Salzburg: Müller, 1966);

Walter Naumann, *Franz Grillparzer: Das dichterische Werk* (Stuttgart: Kohlhammer, 1967);

Elfriede Neubuhr, ed., *Begriffsbestimmung des literarischen Biedermeier* (Darmstadt: Wissenschaftliche Buchgesellschaft, 1974);

Heinz Politzer, *Grillparzer oder Das abgründige Biedermeier* (Vienna, Munich & Zurich: Molden, 1972);

Hinrich C. Seeba, "Franz Grillparzer: Der arme Spielmann (1847)," in *Romane und Erzählungen zwischen Romantik und Realismus: Neue Interpretationen,* edited by Paul Michael Lützeler (Stuttgart: Reclam, 1983), pp. 386–422;

Seeba, "Franz Grillparzer: Der arme Spielmann. 'Wie es sich fügte–': Mythos und Geschichte in Grillparzers Erzählung," in *Interpretationen: Erzählungen und Novellen des 19. Jahrhunderts,* volume 2 (Stuttgart: Reclam, 1990), pp. 99–131;

Seeba, "Das Schicksal der Grillen und Parzen: Zu Grillparzers 'Ahnfrau,'" *Euphorion,* 65 (June 1971): 132–161;

Seeba, "Vormärz: Zwischen Revolution und Restauration," *Geschichte der deutschen Literatur,* volume 2: *Von der Aufklärung bis zum Vormärz,* edited by Ehrhard Bahr (Tübingen: Francke, 1988), pp. 411–501;

Herbert Seidler, *Studien zu Grillparzer und Stifter* (Vienna, Cologne & Graz: Böhlau, 1970);

Friedrich Sengle, *Biedermeierzeit: Deutsche Literatur im Spannungsfeld zwischen Restauration und Revolution 1815–1848,* 3 volumes (Stuttgart: Metzler, 1971–1980);

J. P. Stern, "Beyond the Common Indication: Grillparzer," in his *Re-interpretations: Seven Studies in Nineteenth-Century German Literature* (New York: Basic Books, 1964), pp. 42–77;

Bruce Thompson, *Franz Grillparzer* (Boston: Twayne, 1981);

Thompson and Mark G. Ward, eds., *Essays on Grillparzer* (Hull, U.K.: German Department, Hull University, 1981);

Claus Träger, "'Geschichte,' 'Geist' und Grillparzer: Ein klassischer Nationalautor und seine Deutungen," *Weimarer Beiträge,* 7 (1961): 449–519;

Annalisa Viviani, *Grillparzer-Kommentar,* 2 volumes (Munich: Winkler, 1972–1973);

George A. Wells, *The Plays of Grillparzer* (London & New York: Pergamon, 1969);

W. E. Yates, *Grillparzer: A Critical Introduction* (Cambridge: Cambridge University Press, 1972).

Papers:

Franz Grillparzer's papers are in the Stadtbibliothek (City Library), Vienna.

Wilhelm Grimm

(24 February 1786 – 16 December 1859)

Ruth B. Bottigheimer
State University of New York at Stony Brook

This entry was updated by Professor Bottigheimer from her entry in DLB 90:
German Writers in the Age of Goethe, 1789–1832.

BOOKS: *Kinder- und Hausmärchen,* by Grimm and Jacob Grimm (2 volumes, Berlin: Realschulbuchhandlung, 1812–1815; revised and enlarged seven times, 1819–1857); translated by Edgar Taylor as *German Popular Stories, Translated from the Kinder und Haus Marchen,* 2 volumes (London: Baldwyn, 1823, 1826);

Deutsche Sagen, by Grimm and Jacob Grimm, 2 volumes (Berlin: Nicolai, 1816, 1818); edited and translated by Donald Ward as *The German Legends of the Brothers Grimm,* 2 volumes (Philadelphia: Institute for the Study of Human Issues, 1981);

Über deutsche Runen (Göttingen: Dieterich, 1821);

Zur Literatur der Runen: Nebst Mittheilung runischer Alphabete und gothischer Fragmente aus Handschriften (Vienna: Gerold, 1828);

Bruchstücke aus einem Gedichte von Assundin (Lemgo, 1829);

Die deutsche Heldensage (Göttingen: Dieterich, 1829);

De Hildebrando antiquissimi carminis teutonici fragmentum edidit (Göttingen: Published by the author, 1830);

Die Sage vom Ursprung der Christusbilder (Berlin: Königliche Akademie der Wissenschaften, 1843);

Exhortatio ad plebem christianam Glossae Cassellanae: Über die Bedeutung der deutschen Fingernamen. Gelesen in der Königlichen Akademie der Wissenschaften am 24. April 1845 und 12. November 1846 (Berlin: Königliche Akademie der Wissenschaften, 1848);

Über Freidank: Zwei Nachträge. Gelesen in der Königlichen Akademie der Wissenschaften am 15. März 1849 (Berlin: Königliche Akademie der Wissenschaften, 1850);

Altdeutsche Gespräche: Nachtrag (Berlin: Königliche Akademie der Wissenschaften, 1851);

Zur Geschichte des Reims: Gelesen in der Königlichen Akademie der Wissenschaften, am 7. März 1850 (Berlin: Königliche Akademie der Wissenschaften, 1852);

Deutsches Wörterbuch, by Grimm, Jacob Grimm, and others, 32 volumes (Leipzig: Hirzel, 1854–1961);

Wilhelm Grimm (drawing by Ludwig Emil Grimm, 1837; by permission of the Brüder Grimm Museum)

Nachtrag zu den Casseler Glossen (Berlin: Dümmler, 1855);

Thierfabeln bei den Meistersängern (Berlin: Dümmler, 1855);

Die Sage von Polyphem (Berlin: Dümmler, 1857);

Kleinere Schriften, edited by Gustav Hinrichs, 4 volumes (volumes 1–3, Berlin: Dümmler; volume 4, Gütersloh: Bertelsmann, 1881–1887).

OTHER: *Altdänische Heldenlieder, Balladen und Märchen,* translated by Grimm (Heidelberg: Mohr & Zimmer, 1811); translated anonymously as *Old Danish Ballads* (London: Hope, 1856);

Die beiden ältesten deutschen Gedichte aus dem achten Jahrhundert: Das Lied von Hildebrand und Hadubrand und das Weißenbrunner Gebet, edited by Grimm and Jacob Grimm (Cassel: Thurneissen, 1812);

Drei altschottische Lieder im Original und Übersetzung aus zwei neuen Sammlungen: Nebst einem Sendschreiben an Herrn Professor F. D. Gräter, edited and translated by Grimm (Heidelberg: Mohr & Zimmer, 1813);

Altdeutsche Wälder, edited by Grimm and Jacob Grimm, 3 volumes (volume 1, Cassel: Thurneissen, 1813; volumes 2–3, Frankfurt am Main: Körner, 1815–1816);

Lieder der alten Edda: Band I, edited by Grimm and Jacob Grimm (Berlin: Realschulbuchhandlung, 1815);

Hartmann von Aue, *Der arme Heinrich: Aus der Straßburgischen und Vatikanischen Handschrift,* edited by Grimm and Jacob Grimm (Berlin: Realschulbuchhandlung, 1815);

C. Croker, *Irische Elfenmärchen,* translated by Grimm and Jacob Grimm (Leipzig: Fleischer, 1826);

Grâve Ruodolf: Ein altdeutsches Gedicht, edited by Grimm (Göttingen: Dieterich, 1828);

Vrîdankes Bescheidenheit, edited by Grimm (Göttingen: Dieterich, 1834);

Der Rosengarten, edited by Grimm (Göttingen: Dieterich, 1836);

Konrad der Pfaffe, *Ruolandes liet,* edited by Grimm (Göttingen: Dieterich, 1838);

Ludwig Achim's von Arnim sämmtliche Werke, edited by Grimm, 19 volumes (volumes 1–3, 5–8, Berlin: Veit; volumes 9–12, Grünberg & Leipzig: Levysohn; volume 13, Charlottenburg: Bauer; volumes 14–20, Berlin: Arnim, 1839–1848);

Wernher vom Niederrhein, edited by Grimm (Göttingen: Dieterich, 1839);

Konrads von Würzburg Goldene Schmiede, edited by Grimm (Berlin: Klemann, 1840);

Konrads von Würzburg Silvester, edited by Grimm (Göttingen: Dieterich, 1841);

Athis und Prophilias: Mit Nachtrag, edited by Grimm, 2 volumes (Berlin & Göttingen: Dieterich, 1846–1852);

Altdeutsche Gespräche: Mit Nachtrag, edited by Grimm, 2 volumes (Göttingen: Dieterich, 1851, 1852);

Bruchstücke aus einem unbekannten Gedicht vom Rosengarten, edited by Grimm (Berlin: Dümmler, 1860).

Wilhelm Grimm's lasting contribution to German life and letters was the *Kinder- und Hausmärchen* (Children's and Household Tales, 1812–1815; translated as *German Popular Stories,* 1823, 1826; generally known as *Grimm's Fairy Tales*), to which both contemporaries and subsequent generations turned to find sources of German folk identity. Although both Wilhelm Grimm and his brother Jacob were initially responsible for assembling the raw material for the collection, it was Wilhelm who, especially in the later editions, shaped the narratives' content and style. An accomplished storyteller, Wilhelm Grimm imbued the tales with a straightforward, spare style. Because it was widely believed that the collection exhibited a sure grasp of the historical German folk spirit, the *Kinder- und Hausmärchen* found favor in many quarters. Within a few years of its first publication it had been translated into several European languages, and in both content and style it significantly influenced folk tale collections in other countries.

Born in Hanau on 24 February 1786 to Philipp Wilhelm and Dorothea Zimmer Grimm, Wilhelm Grimm spent idyllic childhood years in Steinau, where his father represented the Count of Hanau. After Philipp Grimm's death in 1796, Wilhelm studied at the Cassel lyceum from 1798 until 1803. During this period he began to suffer from the ill health that would plague him intermittently for the rest of his life. Nonetheless, Grimm's schoolboy diligence gave his teachers grounds to expect that he would one day become a distinguished scholar. Grimm studied law at Marburg from 1803 to 1806, passing his final examinations (pro advocatura) in 1806. From his legal studies, and especially from the lectures of Friedrich Carl von Savigny, to whom he was deeply devoted, he gained insight into the value of the historical method for his subsequent literary studies.

Grimm devoted the first years of his scholarly life to the transcription and translation of ancient manuscripts and to writing articles and book reviews for a variety of journals, including Achim von Arnim and Clemens Brentano's *Zeitung für Einsiedler.* From honoraria for his scholarly writing, Grimm was able to contribute to his family's support. His first published book was a translation titled *Altdänische Heldenlieder, Balladen und Märchen* (1811; translated into English as *Old Danish Ballads,* 1856). Its occasional imperfections were counterbalanced by the volume's effectiveness in acquainting German readers with the folk literature of another nation.

Since the early 1800s Wilhelm and Jacob Grimm had been collecting tales from their friends and acquaintances in Cassel. Their efforts were given further impetus after Napoleon installed his brother Jérôme as King of Westphalia, an act that both accentuated France's humiliating occupation of German territory and fostered deeply nationalistic sentiment. Published in 1812 as the *Kinder- und Hausmärchen* with eighty-four tales and several fragments, the first volume of the collection reflected published sources and bourgeois taste. Nonetheless, the preface to volume one put forth the brothers' flawed conviction that the tales resulted from an unbroken oral folk tradition which had borne the stories unchanged from their earliest tellings to their day. The second volume appeared in 1815 and incorporated a larger proportion of tales with folk provenance, a direction which Grimm followed in subsequent reworkings. Through the seven "Large Editions" intended for an adult readership, the collection slowly grew to a total of two hundred numbered tales and ten religious legends. Beginning in 1825, Grimm also put together ten "Small Editions" for children. Despite the scholarly acclaim accorded the *Kinder- und Hausmärchen* and the collection's ultimate success, initial sales were slow.

The tales represent many different genres, including magic tales, burlesques, tales of origins, morality tales, and literary fairy tales. Except for the tales about fairies, they are generally brief and are told in a spare style with a set of formulaic adjectives such as *beautiful* and *ugly, good* and *evil, diligent* and *lazy*. The heroes and heroines suffer humiliation and hunger until their woes are relieved by magical intervention occasioned by evidence of their inherent virtues, such as compassion, piety, or bravery. The rewards are typically the acquisition of great wealth or power, often through marriage, although on occasion the protagonists receive assurance of an abundance of food for the rest of their lives.

Soon after publication of the *Kinder- und Hausmärchen,* individual tales from it were incorporated into schoolbooks, broadsheets, and children's annuals, though often in substantially edited and reworked form, so that specific tales circulated much more widely than sales of the collection would suggest. In the first edition, scholarly notes demonstrating distribution patterns and variant forms of individual tales were appended to each volume; beginning with the second edition (1819–1822), Wilhelm Grimm removed the notes to a separate volume. Initially the Small Editions of the tales were illustrated by the Grimms' younger brother, Ludwig Emil, but over the years the *Kinder- und Hausmärchen* attracted the efforts of hundreds of illustrators, both within Germany and beyond its borders.

Continuing his efforts to bring the ancient literature of other nations within the orbit of the German scholarly public, Grimm published a translation entitled *Drei altschottische Lieder* (Three Ancient Scottish Songs) in 1813. In the same year Wilhelm and Jacob Grimm initiated a short-lived journal, *Altdeutsche Wälder* (Old German Forests), which appeared in three volumes in 1813, 1815, and 1816. Here they presented their own essays over the entire range of their interests—mythology, literature, folklore, linguistics, and history—as well as documents they had unearthed in their archival research.

After the French were driven out of German territory in 1813 and Jacob Grimm was sent to Paris in 1814 as legation secretary for Hessian diplomats, Wilhelm Grimm was appointed assistant librarian in the electoral library in Cassel. He continued to transcribe and publish medieval manuscripts, thus contributing to the retrieval of Germany's medieval literary past—an effort in which many nineteenth-century scholars were active. His collaboration with Jacob on the two volumes of *Deutsche Sagen* (1816, 1818; edited and translated as *The German Legends of the Brothers Grimm,* 1981) continued his work in reviving the German past, in this instance using mostly materials published from the sixteenth through the eighteenth centuries. During the same period Wilhelm also collaborated with Jacob in editing *Lieder der alten Edda* (Songs of the Ancient Edda), published in 1815. Wilhelm Grimm's publications reaffirmed the cultural basis of the emerging German nation.

In 1819 both Wilhelm and Jacob Grimm received honorary doctorates from Marburg University. In 1825 Wilhelm married Henriette Dorothea (Dortchen) Wild, with whom he had four children: Jacob, Herman Friedrich, Rudolf Georg Ludwig, and Auguste Luise Pauline Marie. In 1829 he resigned his position at the electoral library in Cassel, where his service had been unappreciated and undercompensated, and accepted a call to a professorship at Göttingen, the same year that Jacob Grimm was appointed to a chair at Göttingen.

In 1830 Wilhelm Grimm was married with one child and another on the way. His health was precarious, and his family's welfare was not secured should he fall ill or die. When he was appointed Ordentlicher Professor (full professor) in 1835, he enjoyed financial security for the first time in his life. The Göttingen years were fruitful ones for Grimm, who published editions of *Vrîdankes Bescheidenheit* (Freidank's Wisdom) in 1834, *Der Rosengarten* (The Rose Garden) in 1836, and *Ruolandes liet* (The Song of Roland) in 1838. The third edition of *Kinder- und Hausmärchen* appeared in 1837. At the university his lectures covered similar material: *Bescheidenheit,* Walther von der Vogelweide, the *Nibelungenlied, Iwein* and *Kudrun*.

When the Grimms first arrived in Göttingen they gloried in the freedom of expression they found there, so different from the mute reserve that had been necessary in Cassel. Wilhelm spent much time with the historian Friedrich Christoph Dahlmann, who embodied the tradition of classic political liberalism in early nineteenth-century Germany. An admirer of the English constitution, Dahlmann was in the process of working out the basis for constitutional monarchy within a German context. In 1837 the Grimms, Dahlmann, and four other Göttingen professors clashed with the newly crowned king, Ernst August of Hannover, when they refused to acquiesce in his suspension of the Constitution of 1833, to which they had sworn fealty. The seven professors were summarily dismissed; Jacob Grimm was exiled from Göttingen on three days' notice; but Wilhelm was allowed to remain for several months for reasons of family and health.

Wilhelm Grimm wanted his and Jacob's participation in the protest against the king's abrogation of the constitution to be understood not politically but in terms of personal honor and ethics, a point which he made in his editorial amendments to Jacob's pamphlet *Jacob Grimm über seine Entlassung* (Jacob Grimm on His Dismissal, 1838). Both brothers were outraged by Ernst August's arbitrary exercise of power, and Wilhelm demonstrated his sense of solidarity with the protesters by rejecting overtures to be rehired at Göttingen unless such an offer were to include all seven protesters. That offer never materialized, and Wilhelm returned to Cassel, living with his wife, children, and Jacob for two years in the home of their youngest brother, Ludwig Emil Grimm.

In late 1840 when Friedrich Wilhelm IV acceded to the throne, Bettina von Arnim's efforts to secure the brothers positions at the Humboldt University in Berlin were finally successful. Berlin was a great city growing by leaps and bounds, very different from the rolling Hessian countryside as well as from the placid, small-town atmosphere of Göttingen. Wilhelm Grimm, fifty-five years old when he arrived in Berlin in the spring of 1841, was regarded with affection by students and colleagues and had an active social life.

As a scholar Grimm was characterized by intensive rather than extensive labors. His work habits were conditioned by his poor health (he suffered from tachycardia, asthma, erysipelas, rheumatism, and myocarditis), which curtailed his ability in later life to travel to libraries and archives. He commanded fewer foreign languages than did Jacob, and rather than working with the original language, he preferred to translate foreign texts into German, as he did in *Altdänische Heldenlieder, Balladen und Märchen, Drei altschottische Lieder,* and *Irische Elfenmärchen* (Irish Folktales). Similarly, his many scholarly editions of medieval manuscripts involved faithful transcription and painstaking collation of variants. Grimm was a master of reworking and polishing, techniques perhaps most notable in successive editions of *Grimm's Fairy Tales.* The remainder of Wilhelm's scholarly oeuvre consists of critical editions, scholarly articles on Germanic philology, and his collaboration with Jacob on the monumental *Deutsches Wörterbuch* (German Dictionary), which eventually ran to thirty-two volumes, the first of which appeared in 1854. Throughout his life Grimm demonstrated a decidedly artistic bent. Repeated references to landscapes and paintings in his autobiography of 1839 (in *Kleinere Schriften* [Minor Writings], volume 1, 1881) mirror his scholarly concern for

the visual arts, evident, for example, in his use of medieval paintings to support philological argument.

In order to appreciate Grimm's worldview, it is essential to understand the religious divisions which existed within Germany and the nature of the fragmented society in which he grew up. When Landgrave Karl of Hesse invited Huguenots and Waldensians to Cassel and built a new city for them south of the city walls in the 1680s, his action united a significant French Calvinist presence with an already existing German Reformed, or Zwinglian Protestant, group of Swiss theological origin. It also made Hesse-Cassel one of the relatively few German states with a Reformed monarch ruling a subject population, a large proportion of whom were also Reformed, rather than Lutheran. The Grimms, who came from a long line of Reformed pastors, were acutely aware of their confessional heritage: as young children in Hanau they learned religion and reading from the catechism that had belonged to their great-grandfather, a Reformed pastor; in Steinau they attended the Reformed school and continued their study of religion from the Reformed school preceptor; they also learned to despise Lutherans, whom they mocked as "Dickköpfe" (blockheads). In embracing German folk culture, however, they necessarily regarded Lutheran Protestantism positively. Without ever overtly describing the sea change that must have taken place in his awareness of his own religious identity, Grimm incorporated into *Kinder- und Hausmärchen* values of the Lutheran culture that had been defined for him as alien when he was a child.

One of the earliest assessments of Grimm's character came from his maternal grandfather, Johann Hermann Zimmer, who described the twelve-year-old boy as extremely self-confident. His brother Jacob once declared him his alter ego. Through his family and friendships Wilhelm supplied the sociable half of the scholar's personality, while Jacob remained a solitary figure, pursuing research and writing. Wilhelm Grimm came to intellectual maturity in the early years of the nineteenth century with an acute sense of a heroic German past which contrasted starkly with Germany's divided and subjugated present. This perception kindled a lifelong interest in reviving and securing traditional national culture through Germanic philology. By studying Germany's past, Grimm believed, one might be able to reconstitute and restore to the present an enduring sense of wholeness.

Letters:

Freundesbriefe von Wilhelm und Jacob Grimm: Mit Anmerkungen, edited by Alexander Reifferscheid (Heilbronn: Henninger, 1878);

Briefwechsel zwischen Jacob und Wilhelm Grimm aus der Jugendzeit, edited by Herman Grimm and Gustav Hinrichs (Weimar: Böhlau, 1881);

Briefwechsel der Gebrüder Grimm mit nordischen Gelehrten, edited by Ernst Schmidt (Berlin: Dümmler, 1885);

Briefwechsel zwischen Jacob und Wilhelm Grimm, Dahlmann und Gervinus, edited by Eduard Ippel, 2 volumes (Berlin: Dümmler, 1885–1886);

Briefe der Brüder Jacob und Wilhelm Grimm an Georg Friedrich Benecke aus den Jahren 1808–1829, edited by Wilhelm Müller (Göttingen: Vandenhoeck & Ruprecht, 1889);

Briefe der Brüder Grimm an Paul Wigand, edited by Edmund Stengel (Marburg: Elwert, 1910);

Briefwechsel der Brüder Jacob und Wilhelm Grimm mit Karl Lachmann, edited by Albert Leitzmann, 2 volumes (Jena: Frommann, 1927);

Briefe der Brüder Grimm, edited by Leitzmann and Hans Gürtler (Jena: Frommann, 1928);

Briefwechsel zwischen Jenny von Droste-Hülshoff und Wilhelm Grimm, edited by K. Schulte (Münster: Aschendorff, 1929);

Briefe der Brüder Grimm an Savigny: Aus dem Savignyschen Nachlaß, edited by Wilhelm Schoof and Ingeborg Schnack (Berlin: Schmidt, 1953);

Brüder Grimm: Werke und Briefwechsel (Cassel: Verlag der Brüder Grimm-Gesellschaft, 1998–).

Bibliographies:

Ludwig Denecke, "Bibliographie der Briefe von und an Wilhelm und Jacob Grimm: Mit einer Einführung," *Aurora: Jahrbuch der Eichendorff-Gesellschaft,* 43 (1983): 169–227;

Brüder Grimm Bibliographie (Cassel: Brüder Grimm-Museum, 1991–1994).

Biographies:

Wilhelm Schoof, *Wilhelm Grimm: Aus seinem Leben* (Bonn: Dümmler, 1960);

Schoof, *Die Brüder Grimm in Berlin* (Berlin: Hande & Spener, 1964);

Ruth Michaelis-Jena, *The Brothers Grimm* (London: Routledge & Kegan Paul, 1970);

Ludwig Denecke, *Jacob Grimm und sein Bruder Wilhelm* (Stuttgart: Metzler, 1971);

Murray B. Peppard, *Paths through the Forest: A Biography of the Brothers Grimm* (New York: Holt, Rinehart & Winston, 1971);

Hermann Gerstner, *Brüder Grimm* (Reinbek: Rowohlt, 1973);

Gabriele Seitz, *Die Brüder Grimm: Leben–Werk–Zeit* (Munich: Winkler, 1985);

Hans-Bernd Harder and Ekkehard Kauffmann, eds., *Die Brüder Grimm in ihrer Zeit* (Cassel: Röth, 1985);

Dieter Hennig and Bernhard Lauer, eds., *Die Brüder Grimm: Dokumente ihres Lebens und Wirkens* (Cassel: Weber & Weidemeyer, 1985).

References:

Ruth B. Bottigheimer, *Grimms' Bad Girls and Bold Boys: The Moral and Social Vision of the Tales* (New Haven & London: Yale University Press, 1987);

Monika Köstlin, *Im Frieden der Wissenschaft: Wilhelm Grimm als Philologe* (Stuttgart: M & P Verlag für Wissenschaft und Forschung, 1993);

James M. McGlathery, ed., *The Brothers Grimm and the Folktale* (Urbana: University of Illinois Press, 1988);

Maria M. Tatar, *The Hard Facts of the Grimms' Fairy Tales* (Princeton: Princeton University Press, 1987);

Jack Zipes, *The Brothers Grimm* (London: Routledge, 1988).

Papers:

The library of the Humboldt University, Berlin, has a large part of the Grimms' personal library; the Brüder Grimm-Archiv, Cassel, has editions of the *Kinder- und Hausmärchen,* personal copies with marginal notations, and related secondary literature; the Brüder Grimm-Museum, Cassel, has editions of the *Kinder- und Hausmärchen* and personal effects; the Staatsbibliothek Preußischer Kulturbesitz, Berlin, has personal copies of Wilhelm Grimm's publications and those of others with extensive marginal notes, memorabilia, copies of journal publications, diaries, lecture notes, letters, and published and unpublished manuscripts; Grimm's lecture notes for the summer semester of 1836 are in the Germanisches Nationalmuseum, Nuremberg.

Johann Jacob Christoffel von Grimmelshausen

(1621 or 1622 – 17 August 1676)

Hans Wagener
University of California, Los Angeles

This entry originally appeared in DLB 168: German
Baroque Writers, 1661–1730.

BOOKS: *Satyrischer Pilgram, Das ist: Kalt und Warm, Weiß und Schwartz, Lob und Schand, über guths und böß, Tugend und Laster, auch Nutz und Schad vieler Ständt und Ding der Sichtbarn und Unsichtbarn der Zeitlichen und Ewigen Welt. Beydes lustig und nützlich zulesen, von Neuem zusammen getragen durch Samuel Greifnson, vom Hirschfeld* (Leipzig: Printed by Hieronymus Grisenius for Georg Heinrich Frommann, 1666);

Exempel der unveränderlichen Vorsehung Gottes. Unter einer anmutigen und ausführlichen Histori vom Keuschen Joseph in Egypten, Jacobs Sohn. Vorgestellt so wol aus Heiliger als anderer Hebreer, Egyptier, Perser, und Araber Schrifften und hergebrachter Sag, erstlich Teutsch zusammen getragen durch den Samuel Greifnson vom Hirschfeld (Nuremberg: Wolf Eberhard Felsecker, 1667 [i.e., 1666]); enlarged as *Des Vortrefflich Keuschen Josephs in Egypten, Erbauliche, recht ausführliche und vielvermehrte Lebensbeschreibung, zum Augenscheinlichen Exempel der unveränderlichen Vorsehung Gottes, so wol aus heiliger Schrifft, als anderen der Hebreer, Perser und Araber Büchern und hergebrachter Sage auf das deutlichste vorgestellet, und erstesmals mit grosser und unverdroßner Mühe zusammen getragen von Samuel Greifnson von Hirschfeld. Nunmehro aber wiederumb aufs neue vom Autore übersehen, verbessert, und samt des unvergleichlichen Josephs getreuen Schaffners Musai Lebens-Lauff. Vermehrt, dem Curiosen Leser sehr anmuthig, lustig und nutzlich zu betrachten wolmeinend mitgetheilet* (Nuremberg: Wolf Eberhard Felsecker, 1670);

Satyrischer Pilgram Anderer Theil, Zusammen getragen durch Samuel Greifnson vom Hirschfelt (Leipzig: Printed by Hieronymus Grisenius for Georg Heinrich Frommann, 1667);

Der Abentheurliche Simplicissimus Teutsch, das ist: Die Beschreibung deß Lebens eines seltzamen Vaganten, genant Melchior Sternfels von Fuchshaim, wo und welcher gestalt Er nemlich in diese Welt kommen, was er darinn gesehen, gelernet, erfahren und außgestanden, auch warumb er solche wieder freywillig quittirt. Überauß lustig und männiglich nutzlich zu lesen. An Tag geben von German Schleifheim von Sulsfort* (Monpelgart: Printed by Johann Fillion, 1669 [i.e., Nuremberg: Wolf Eberhard Felsecker, 1668]); translated by A. T. S. Goodrick as *The Adventurous Simplicissimus: Being the Description of the Life of a Strange Vagabond Named Melchior Sternfels von Fuchshaim* (London: Heinemann, 1912; New York: Dutton, 1913);

Continuatio des abentheurlichen Simplicissimi oder Schluß desselben, as German Schleifheim von Sulsfort (Monpelgart: Johann Fillton [sic] [i.e., Nuremberg: Wolf Eberhard Felsecker], 1669);

Dietwalds und Amelinden anmutige Lieb- und Leids-Beschreibung, sammt erster Vergrösserung des Weltberühmten Königreichs Franckreich. Den Gottseeligen erbaulich curiosen lustig Historicis annemlich Betrübten tröstlich Verliebten erfreulich Politicis nützlich und der Jugend ohnärgerlich zulesen zusammen gesucht und hervorgegeben von H. J. Christoffel von Grimmelshausen, Gelnhusano (Nuremberg: Wolf Eberhard Felsecker, 1670);

Simplicianischer Zweyköpffiger Ratio Status, lustig entworffen unter der Histori des waidlichen Königs Saul, des sanfftmütigen König Davids, des getreuen Printzen Jonathae, und deß tapffern Generalissimi Joabi (Nuremberg: Wolf Eberhard Felsecker, 1670);

Trutz Simplex: Oder Ausführliche und wunderseltzame Lebensbeschreibung der Ertzbetrügerin und Landstörtzerin Courasche, wie sie anfangs eine Rittmeisterin, hernach eine Hauptmännin, ferner eine Leutenantin, bald eine Marcketenterin, Mußquetirerin, und letzlich eine Ziegeunerin abgegeben, meisterlich agiret, und ausbündig vorgestellet: Eben so lustig, annemlich und nutzlich zu betrachten, als Simplicissimus selbst. Alles miteinander von der Courasche eigner Person dem weit und breitbekanten Simplicissimo zum Verdruß und Widerwillen, dem Autori in die Feder dictirt, der sich vor dißmal nennet Philarchus Grossus von Trommenheim, auf Griffsberg, &c. (Utopia: Printed by

Felix Stratiot [i.e., Nuremberg: Wolf Eberhard Felsecker], 1670);

Der seltzame Springinsfeld, das ist kurtzweilige, lusterweckende und recht lächerliche Lebens-Beschreibung. Eines weiland frischen, wolversuchten und tapffern Soldaten, nunmehro aber ausgemergelten, abgelebten, doch dabey recht verschlagnen Landstörtzers und Bettlers, samt seiner wunderlichen Gauckeltasche. Aus Anordnung des weit und breit bekanten Simplicissimi verfasset und zu Papier gebracht von Philarcho Grosso von Tromerheim (Paphlagonia: Printed by Felix Stratiot [i.e., Nuremberg: Wolf Eberhard Felsecker], 1670);

Der erste Beernhäuter, nicht ohne sonderbare darunter verborgene Lehrreiche Geheimnus, so wol allen denen die so zuschelten pflegen, und sich so schelten lassen, als auch sonst jedermann (vor dißmal zwar nur vom Ursprung dieses schönen Ehren-Tituls) andern zum Exempel vorgestellet, sampt Simplicissimi Gauckeltasche. Von Illiterato Ignorantio, zugenannt Idiota (Nuremberg: Wolf Eberhard Felsecker, 1670);

Des Abenteuerlichen Simplicissimi Ewig-währender Calender, worinnen ohne die ordentliche Verzeichnus der unzehlbar vieler Heiligen Täge auch unterschiedliche curiose Discursen von der Astronomia, Astrologia, Jtem den Calendern, Nativitäten, auch allerhand Wunderbarlichen Wahr- und Vorsagungen, mit untermischter Bauren-Practic, Tag- und Zeitwehlungen, &c. Nicht weniger Viel Seltzame, jedoch Warhaffte Wunder-Geschichten, und andere Merckwürdige Begebenheiten, samt Beyfügung etlicher Künst- und Wissenschaften befindlich, anonymous (Nuremberg: Published by Wolf Eberhard Felsecker, printed by Marcus Bloß in Fulda, 1670 [i.e, 1671]);

Des Abenteuerlichen Simplicii Verkehrte Welt. Nicht, wie es scheinet, dem Leser allein zur Lust und Kurtzweil: Sondern auch zu dessen aufferbaulichem Nutz annemlich entworffen von Simon Lengfrisch von Hartenfels (Nuremberg: Wolf Eberhard Felsecker, 1672);

Rathstübel Plutonis oder Kunst Reich zu werden, durch vierzehen unterschiedlicher namhafften Personen richtige Meynungen in gewisse Reguln verabfasset, und auß Simplicissimi Brunnquell selbsten geschöpfft, auch auffrecht Simplicianisch beschrieben von Erich Stainfels von Grufensholm, sambt Simplicissimi Discurs, Wie man hingegen bald auffwannen; und mit seinem Vorrath fertig werden soll (Samaria [i.e., Nuremberg: Wolf Eberhard Felsecker or Strasbourg: Georg Andreas Dolhopff], 1672);

Der stoltze Melcher, sambt einer Besprecknuß von das Frantzoß Krieg mit der Holland. Welches durch Veranlassung eines Saphoyers der Fridens-satten- vnd gern-kriegenden teutschen Jugend zum Meßkram verehret wird, anonymous (Strasbourg?: Georg Andreas Dolhopff?, 1672);

Des Durchleuchtigen Printzen Proximi, und seiner ohnvergleichlichen Lympidæ Liebs-Geschicht-Erzehlung (Strasbourg: Georg Andreas Dolhopff, 1672);

Das wunderbarliche Vogel-Nest, der Springinsfeldischen Leyrerin, voller Abentheurlichen, doch Lehrreichen Geshcichten, auff Simplicianische Art sehr nutzlich und kurtzweilig zu lesen auß gefertigt durch Michael Rechulin von Sehmsdorff (Monpelgart: Printed by Johann Fillion [i.e., Strasbourg: Georg Andreas Dolhopff?], 1672);

Bart-Krieg, oder Des ohnrecht genanten Roht-Barts Widerbellung gegen den welt-beruffenen Schwartz-bart deß Simplicissimi darinnen er zu Erhaltung der reputation aller zwar fälschlich Rohtgenanten Bärt die Goldfarb, wie billich, dem Kühnruß, das frewdenreiche Gelb, des Teuffels Leibfarb vorziehet (Strasbourg: Georg Andreas Dolhopff, or Nuremberg: Wolf Eberhard Felsecker, 1673);

Deß Weltberuffenen Simplicissimi Pralerey und Gepräng mit seinem Teutschen Michel, jedermänniglichen, wanns seyn kan, ohne Lachen zu lesen erlaubt von Signeur Meßmahl (Nuremberg: Wolf Eberhard Felsecker, 1673);

Simplicissimi Galgen-Männlin, oder Ausführlicher Bericht, woher man die so genannte Allräungen oder Geldmännlin bekommt, und wie man ihrer warten und pflegen soll; auch was vor Nutzen man hingegen von ihnen eigentlich zugewarten. Erstlich durch Simplicissimum selbsten seinem Sohn und allen andern, so die Reichthum dieser Welt verlangen, zum besten an tag geben. Nachgehends mit nutzlichen Anmerck- und Erinnerungen erläutert durch Israël Fromschmidt von Hugenfeß (Strasbourg: Georg Andreas Dolhopff, or Nuremberg: Wolf Eberhard Felsecker, 1673);

Deß Wunderbarlichen Vogelnessts Zweiter theil, an tag geben von A c eee ff g hh ü ll mm nn oo rr sss t uu (Strasbourg: Georg Andreas Dolhopff, 1675);

Deß possirlichen, weit und breit bekannten Simplicissimi sinnreicher und nachdencklicher Schrifften Zweiten Theils (Nuremberg: Johann Jonathan Felsecker, 1683);

Der aus dem Grab der Vergessenheit wieder erstandene Simplicissimus; dessen abentheurlicher, und mit allerhand seltsamen, fast unerhörten Begebenheiten angefüllter Lebens-Wandel (Nuremberg: Johann Jonathan Felsecker, 1684 [i.e., 1683]);

Deß aus dem Grabe der Vergessenheit wieder erstandenen Simplicissimi, mit kostbaren, zu dieser Zeit hochwerthen und dero Liebhaber fest an sich ziehenden Waaren an- und ausgefüllter Staats-Kram, statt deß auf seinen jüngsthin hervorgegebenen Lebens-Wandel, nunmehr ordentlich folgenden dritten und letzten Theils, by Grimmelshausen, Balthasar Venator the Younger, and Johannes Scheffler (Nuremberg: Johann Jonathan Felsecker, 1684).

Editions and Collections: *Der Abentheuerliche Simplicissimus und andere Schriften,* 4 volumes, edited by Adelbert Keller, Bibliothek des Litterarischen Vereins, volumes 33, 34, 65, 66 (Stuttgart: Litterarischer Verein, 1854–1862);

Simplicianische Schriften, 4 volumes, edited by Heinrich Kurz, Deutsche Bibliothek, volumes 3–6 (Leipzig: Weber, 1863–1864);

Werke, 4 volumes, edited by Julius Tittmann, Deutsche Dichter des 17. Jahrhunderts, volumes 7, 8, 10, and 11 (Leipzig: Brockhaus, 1874–1877);

Der abenteuerliche Simplicissimus, edited by Rudolf Kögel (Halle: Niemeyer, 1880);

Werke, 3 volumes, edited by Felix Bobertag (Berlin: Spemann, 1882–1883);

Werke, 4 volumes, edited by Hans Heinrich Borcherdt (Berlin: Bong, 1922);

Werke, 6 volumes, edited by Jan Hendrik Scholte (Halle: Niemeyer, 1923–1943);

Simplicianische Schriften, 2 volumes, edited by Franz Riederer (Naunhof: Hendel, 1939);

Der abenteuerliche Simplicissimus, edited by Alfred Kelletat (Munich: Winkler, 1956);

Simplicianische Schriften, edited by Kelletat (Munich: Winkler, 1958);

Der abenteuerliche Simplicissimus Teutsch, edited by Borcherdt (Stuttgart: Reclam, 1961);

Werke, 4 volumes, edited by Siegfried Streller (Berlin: Aufbau, 1964);

Des Abentheuerlichen Simplicissimi Ewigwährender Calender, 2 volumes, edited by Klaus Haberkamm (Constance: Rosgarten, 1967);

Gesammelte Werke in Einzelausgaben, 17 volumes, edited by Rolf Tarot, Wolfgang Bender, and Franz Günter Sieveke (Tübingen: Niemeyer, 1967–1976);

Lebensbeschreibung der Ertzbetrügerin und Landstörtzerin Courasche, edited by Haberkamm and Günther Weydt (Stuttgart: Reclam, 1976);

Der seltzame Springinsfeld, edited by Haberkamm (Stuttgart: Reclam, 1976);

Der abenteuerliche Simplicissimus, edited by Kelletat (Darmstadt: Wissenschaftliche Buchgesellschaft, 1985);

Der Teutsche Michel, edited by Gunther Kleefeld (Ebenhausen: Langewiesche-Brandt, 1986);

Der Abentheurliche Simplicissimus Teutsch, edited by Martin Bircher (Weinheim: VCH, Acta Humaniora, 1988);

Werke, 2 volumes published, edited by Dieter Breuer (Frankfurt am Main: Deutscher Klassiker-Verlag, 1989–).

Editions in English: *The Adventures of a Simpleton,* translated by Walter Wallich (New York: Ungar, 1963);

Simplicius Simplicissimus, translated by Hellmuth Weissenborn and Lesley MacDonald (London: Calder, 1964);

Frontispiece for Johann Jacob Christoffel von Grimmelshausen's Simplicianischer Zweyköpffiger Ratio Status. *The winged head is thought to be a portrait of the author.*

Courasche, The Adventures & The False Messiah, translated by Hans Speier (Princeton: Princeton University Press, 1964);

Simplicius Simplicissimus, translated by George Schulz-Behrend (Indianapolis, New York & Kansas City: Bobbs-Merrill, 1965; revised edition, Columbia, S.C.: Camden House, 1993);

The Runagate Courage, translated by Robert L. Hiller and John C. Osborne (Lincoln: University of Nebraska Press, 1965);

Mother Courage, translated by Walter Wallich (London: Folio Society, 1965).

OTHER: "Anhang Etlicher wunderlicher Antiquitäten, so der fliegende Wandersmann Zeit seiner wehrenden Reiß, in einer abgelegenen Vestung an dem Meer gelegen, und von den Türcken bewohnet, gesehen und verzeichnet" and "Extract. Der ansehnlichen Tractamenten samt deren Expens, welche den Herrn von Hirschau in vergangener Fastnacht aufgesetzt, und von denselben ritu solenni verzehret worden," in *Der fliegende Wandersmann nach dem Mond,* by Balthasar Venator the Younger (Nuremberg: Wolf Eberhard Felsecker, 1667), pp. 130–142;

Claus von und zu Schauenburg, *Teutscher Friedens-Raht, oder Deutliche Vorstellung, wie im Teutschland by erwünschten Friedenszeiten eine wohlersprießliche Regierung allenthalben wiederumb anzuordnen und einzuführen. Erstlich, mitten in dem Lands-verderblichen grossen Krieg auffgesetzt, von Weyland dem Reichs-Frey-Hoch-Edel Gebohrnen, Gestrengen Herrn Clausen, von- und zu Schauenburg, &c. Nunmehro aber auff Ansinnen guter Leuthe in Truck gegeben, durch Herrn Philipp Hannibalen von- und zu Schauenburg, deß Authoris Sohn,* edited by Grimmelshausen and Philipp Hannibal von und zu Schauenburg (Strasbourg: Printed by Johann Wilhelm Tidemann, 1670).

Next to Johann Beer, Johann Jacob Christoffel von Grimmelshausen was the greatest German novelist of the seventeenth century; today he is probably the most widely read and translated German baroque author. His picaresque novels *Der Abentheurliche Simplicissimus Teutsch* (1668; translated as *The Adventurous Simplicissimus,* 1912), *Trutz Simplex: Oder Ausführliche und wunderseltzame Lebensbeschreibung der Ertzbetrügerin und Landstörtzerin Courasche* (Spite Simplex; or, Detailed and Wondrous Life History of the Female Archfraud and Runagate Courasche, 1670; translated as "Courasche," 1964), and *Der seltzame Springinsfeld* (The Curious Tale of Springinsfeld, 1670) paint such a vivid picture of the Thirty Years' War that most people who have an image of this time acquired it by reading his novels. The instant popularity of *Der Abentheurliche Simplicissimus Teutsch* inspired Grimmelshausen to write several sequels—the so-called Simplician writings—and the work has had a tremendous influence on twentieth-century German authors from Thomas Mann to Günter Grass and beyond. Moreover, *Trutz Simplex* prompted Bertolt Brecht to write his drama *Mutter Courage und ihre Kinder* (performed, 1941; published, 1949; translated as *Mother Courage and Her Children,* 1966). It is astonishing that this former soldier and regimental secretary was able to publish a sizable oeuvre of novels, popular theoretical writings, and calendars within a ten-year period. While earlier critics, citing the poet's deficient formal education, often characterized Grimmelshausen as a natural narrative genius, more recent research has shown that he was relatively well educated and familiar with and able to draw extensively on the fictional, scholarly, and theological literature of his time and to use it in highly creative ways.

Grimmelshausen was probably born in 1621, although, on the basis of clues in *Der Abentheurliche Simplicissimus Teutsch,* earlier research gave preference to 1622. (By applying astrological speculation, some scholars assume

that 17 March was the most likely date.) His birthplace was the small imperial city of Gelnhausen in Hessia, east of Frankfurt am Main. His family came originally from the town of Suhl in Thuringia and belonged to the low nobility. In 1597 the writer's grandfather, Melchior Christoph Grimmelshausen, a baker and innkeeper, gave up his noble title. The author's father, Johannes Christoph, probably worked in his father's bakery.

In April 1627, after his father's early death, Grimmelshausen's mother, Gertraud, whose maiden name is unknown, married the son of a book dealer and moved to Frankfurt am Main. Grimmelshausen stayed behind in Gelnhausen, probably with his grandfather. Between 1627 and 1634 he most likely attended the town's Latin school, which was under Lutheran supervision and emphasized instruction in religion, the classical languages, and rhetoric. After the Protestant defeat at Nördlingen on 8 September 1634 the Spanish army conquered and plundered Gelnhausen, murdered most of its inhabitants, and burned many of its houses. Grimmelshausen and his grandparents fled to the well-fortified neighboring town of Hanau, which had a Swedish-Hessian garrison under the Scottish governor, James Ramsay. Presumably at the beginning of 1635 Hans Christoffel, as he called himself, and several companions were kidnapped on the frozen-over moats that surrounded the city by Croatian troops—then part of the imperial army—and taken to the camp of their leader, Col. Manfred von Corpus, in the convent of Hersfeld. Grimmelshausen probably only stayed with the Croatians for a month, accompanying them as they raided farms and villages. On 25 February 1635 he was captured by Hessian troops, who took him to Kassel.

Theories about Grimmelshausen's life from that point until 1639 are derived from the adventures of his hero in *Der Abentheurliche Simplicissimus Teutsch* and on what is known about the movements of the regiments in which he served. From May to August 1636 he was probably with the imperial force besieging the city of Magdeburg, moving at the beginning of August to Wittstock, where the imperial and Saxon armies were defeated by the Swedes on 4 October. His lively descriptions in *Der Abentheurliche Simplicissimus Teutsch* of the conquest of Magdeburg and the battle of Wittstock go beyond the literary and historiographical sources that would have been at his disposal, suggesting that he was an eyewitness to, or even a participant in, the events. He then may have become a stable boy in the Bavarian light cavalry regiment assigned to the imperial force commanded by the Bavarian field marshal, Count Johann von Götz, which spent the winter garrisoned in the Westphalian city of Soest. The following year he is thought to have participated in some of the campaigns of the Bavarian artillery commander, Count Joachim

Christian von der Wahl, and his general, Alexander von Vehlen. In the meantime, Duke Bernhard of Saxe-Weimar was besieging the imperial Upper Rhine fortress of Breisach, and Götz was ordered to relieve the fortress. Several attempts failed, and after he was decisively defeated at the battle of Wittenweier, Götz was arrested and replaced by Maximilian von Goltz.

Grimmelshausen participated in all these troop movements, first as a wagoner and stable boy, later as a musketeer and dragoon. In the middle of 1639 he became a soldier in the regiment of Col. Hans Reinhard von Schauenburg that was being assembled for the defense of the strategically important imperial city of Offenburg, south of Strasbourg. Schauenburg held the city until the end of the war. During this time—at the latest, in 1645—Grimmelshausen was promoted to clerk in the regimental headquarters under the supervision of the regimental secretary, the highly educated Magister Johannes Witsch. Between February and May 1648 Grimmelshausen joined the regiment of Johann Burkhard von Elter, Schauenburg's brother-in-law, where he obtained the position of regimental secretary. After several campaigns in Bavaria he left military service in July 1649 and returned to Offenburg. Thus, instead of completing Latin school and attending various universities, as most other seventeenth-century poets did, Grimmelshausen had experienced the Thirty Years' War firsthand and had gained invaluable insights into the lives of all social strata.

On 30 August 1649 Grimmelshausen married Catharina Henniger in Offenburg; she was the daughter of a lieutenant of the guard with whom Grimmelshausen had served in the Schauenburg regiment. The entry in the church registry indicates that Grimmelshausen had converted to Catholicism. From this time he used his title of nobility again, calling himself "von Grimmelshausen." By 1669 he and his wife had ten children, at least six of whom lived to maturity.

On 7 September 1649 Grimmelshausen became a *Schaffner* (steward) for Schauenburg and the latter's cousin, Carl Bernhard von Schauenburg, in the village of Gaisbach (today part of the city of Oberkirch) in the Rench Valley. His tasks included reorganizing the administration of the Schauenburg estates, rebuilding the farming economy after the destruction of the Thirty Years' War, and collecting interest and tithes from the Schauenburgs' tenants. In 1653 he bought a large lot in Gaisbach, the "Spitalbühne," on which he erected two houses. In one of them he opened an inn, "Zum silbernen Sternen" (The Silver Star [that is, the moon]), which he ran from 1656 to 1658 while retaining his position as steward. It is unclear why he left the Schauenburgs' service in the fall of 1660; at the time he owed the Schauenburgs a considerable sum of money, leading some researchers to assume that there had

been a disagreement over Grimmelshausen's accounting. This theory is unlikely to be correct, however, because he later dedicated many of his works to members of the Schauenburg family.

Grimmelshausen remained in Gaisbach without employment from 1660 to 1662; from 1662 to 1665 he became steward and castellan of the Ullenburg, a nearby castle that was the summer residence of the wealthy and fashionable Strasbourg physician, Johannes Küffer. Dr. Küffer had a keen interest in the arts and was friendly with important German-Alsatian writers, including Johann Matthias Schneuber, Jesaias Rompler von Löwenhalt, and Johann Michael Moscherosch. From 1665 to 1667 Grimmelshausen resumed the running of his inn. It was during his time as an innkeeper that he became active as an author; his first short literary productions began to appear, and he also must have begun work on his magnum opus, *Der Abentheurliche Simplicissimus Teutsch*.

Since the inn alone could not provide a living for his large family, Grimmelshausen applied for the vacant office of mayor in Renchen, a village of seven hundred inhabitants; his father-in-law provided part of the required bond. Around July 1667 Grimmelshausen assumed the office, which he was to occupy until his death. The mayor's duties combined the functions of judge, police chief, notary public, and tax collector. One wonders how all of these responsibilities could have left him time for writing, but an incredible quantity of publications, totaling more than three thousand printed pages, appeared in the ten years that were left to him. It is tempting to speculate that he had been toiling on his works for years, and that he prepared them for publication during this final decade.

Grimmelshausen usually hid his identity behind pseudonyms, most of which are anagrams of his full name: German Schleifheim von Sulsfort, Samuel Greiffnsohn vom Hirschfeld, Melchior Sternfels von Fuchshaim, Philarchus Grossus von Trommenheim auf Griffsberg, Michael Rechulin von Sehmsdorff, Erich Stainfels von Grufensholm, Simon Leugfrisch von Hertenfels, Israel Fromschmidt von Hugenfelß, and Signeur Messmahl. Only three of his writings were published under his real name. As a result, it was not until 1837 that the authorship of some of his major works was determined.

Grimmelshausen's first known publication, *Satyrischer Pilgram* (The Satiric Pilgrim, 1666), is a didactic, satiric tract, based for the most part on *Piazza Universale* (1585), an encyclopedic compilation by the Italian writer Tommaso Garzoni. In a series of discussions, *Satyrischer Pilgram* deals with the most diverse subjects: in part 1, God, humanity, farmers, money, dancing, wine, beauty, priests, and women; in part 2, poetry, guns, love, tobacco, rulers, philosophy and philosophers, masquerade, medicine and doctors, beggars, and war. Each discussion is subdivided into three parts: a thesis, an antithesis, and an "echo," in which the author gives his own opinion. In its more relaxed style, which is much closer to that of *Der Abentheurliche Simplicissimus Teutsch* and its successors, part 2 shows Grimmelshausen's quick development as a writer who is increasingly able to adapt the material he found in his sources. Social and moral criticism and religious-didactic messages are delivered in a folksy manner. The comments of the literary newcomer are mostly not innovative but are in the satiric tradition of the fifteenth and sixteenth centuries: he assigns negative qualities to the peasants, shows himself to be an antifeminist, and rejects the right of resistance to tyrants.

Exempel der unveränderlichen Vorsehung Gottes. Unter einer anmutigen und ausführlichen Histori vom Keuschen Joseph in Egypten, Jacobs Sohn (Example of the Unchanging Providence of God. In a Pleasant and Full History of the Chaste Joseph in Egypt, Jacob's Son, 1666), Grimmelshausen's first work of fiction, is based on the biblical story of Joseph, which had been highly popular in sixteenth-century drama and was later taken up by Philipp von Zesen in *Assenat* (1670). It includes many of the characteristic elements of his writing: a popular style, humor, moralizing, discussion of humanity's relation to God, contrasting of positive and negative figures, and, in the appended sequel, a story about an adventurer–a literary influence of the picaresque novel. In addition to the Bible, Grimmelshausen uses such sources as Flavius Josephus's *Jewish Antiquities,* which had been translated into German in 1625, as well as Sa'dī's *Golestsān,* which had been translated by Adam Olearius as *Persianischer Rosenthal* (Persian Rose Valley, 1654).

Grimmelshausen uses the story of Joseph in Egypt to demonstrate the operation of divine Providence. Human beings are God's tools; their actions are directed by God's higher intent; even Joseph's brothers are used by God so that, later, Joseph can provide food for them and his father. Joseph is an exemplary human being who excels by his ability to maintain his moral integrity. He possesses the baroque virtues of magnanimity and constancy and, therefore, does not give in to the temptation of Potiphar's wife, Selicha. Secure in his prophesied knowledge that God has a plan for him, he endures the changes from favorite son of the powerful Jacob to slave, to supervisor and favorite of Potiphar, to a smith's helper in prison, and finally to the second most powerful man in the state. At this point he becomes an exemplary statesman who, against public opinion, does what is best, planning for the years of great need at a time when food is plentiful. Joseph's ideal character is brought out when Grimmelshausen, in the reworked edition of 1670, repeatedly describes him as a precursor of Christ–a savior of Egypt and of his own people.

Grimmelshausen contrasts his virtuous hero with a person who is driven by emotion: Potiphar's young wife, Selicha, who is unable to control herself and becomes increasingly bestial. She cannot resist lust or temptation; while he remains constant and true to himself, she is transformed into a devilish fury who dies in despair. She is torn by anger, love, passion, remorse, and fear that her crime might be discovered–the whole baroque arsenal of destructive emotions. She lacks constancy and trust in God.

In the character of Musai, the leader of the Ismaili caravan who buys Joseph from his brothers and later becomes Joseph's personal manager, Grimmelshausen introduces many of the picaresque traits that he would use in his Simplician writings. Musai saves the caravan from Arab robbers through cunning and trickery; he experiences the inconstancy of the human lot, going from wealthy merchant and leader of caravans to slave and ending up as a prince after he finds the "true God." Picaresque elements also reveal themselves in the bluntness of Grimmelshausen's realistic, folksy style: in lapses, proverbial sayings, and sensual or obscene metaphors and comparisons that clearly remove this novel from the courtly-historical genre.

Der Abentheurliche Simplicissimus Teutsch, whose title page claims 1669 as its year of publication but which actually appeared in 1668, is *the* work about the Thirty Years' War in Germany. It is Grimmelshausen's undoubted masterpiece, the novel that not only made him popular in his own time but also made him an author of world literature. It appeared in six editions during his lifetime; by 1976 approximately two hundred editions, including translations into Russian and Japanese, had been published. The novel is divided into five books that show its hero going from innocent simplemindedness through ever-increasing involvement in worldly affairs until, at the end, he withdraws from the world and becomes a hermit. A sixth book, the *Continuatio,* was published in 1669.

In book 1 the hero is growing up in total innocence as the son of a peasant in the Spessart Mountains. After his father's farm is ransacked by soldiers the boy flees into the forest, where he is found by a hermit. He names the boy Simplicius and instructs him in the teachings of Christianity. After the hermit's death Simplicius leaves the forest and makes his way to the Swedish fortress of Hanau, where the governor, Ramsey, makes him a page.

In book 2 Simplicius is made a court jester because of his foolish behavior. Soon thereafter he is kidnapped by Croatian troops, but he escapes and unknowingly participates in a witches' Sabbath. Serving again as a jester, this time in the imperial camp during the siege of Magdeburg, he becomes friends with a young man named Herzbruder. To escape his role as a jester, Simplicius dresses as a girl and becomes a maid to a colonel in the imperial army and his wife. Suspected of spying, he is imprisoned; but Herzbruder, who is now serving in the Swedish army, frees him in a surprise attack. Simplicius then becomes the servant of a stingy and simpleminded dragoon, who is sent to guard a monastery called "Paradies" (Paradise) in Westphalia. After the death of his master he becomes a daring soldier whose exploits earn him the nickname "der Jäger von Soest" (the Hunter of Soest).

In book 3, after committing various pranks, Simplicius is captured by the Swedes and brought to L. (Lippstadt), where he courts various girls, leaving each of them with child. After being forced to marry one of them, he rides away to Cologne to retrieve a treasure that he had found and had entrusted to a merchant there.

When book 4 opens, Simplicius is a chaperon of young noblemen. His duties take him to Paris, where he becomes the servant of the fashionable Doctor Canard. He is successful as a singer in the Royal Opera and amasses a considerable fortune as the lover of wealthy ladies. Since he is afraid of being caught in one of these escapades, he flees, but all his money is stolen when he contracts smallpox. He makes his way back to Germany, cheating farmers as a traveling quack until he is caught and made a musketeer in the fortress of Philippsburg. He is freed again by Herzbruder, who is now a high-ranking officer. In a forest Simplicius meets the wicked Olivier, whom he recognizes from the camp at Magdeburg. Olivier, who has become a robber, relates his life story to Simplicius. Soon afterward, Olivier is killed by soldiers, whom Simplicius kills in turn. He uses Olivier's money to support the wounded Herzbruder, who quickly recovers.

In book 5 Herzbruder and Simplicius make a pilgrimage to Einsiedeln. Frightened by the devil, Simplicius decides to change his life. He and Herzbruder go to Vienna, where Simplicius becomes a captain. Both are wounded; they journey to a spa to recover, but Herzbruder dies. Simplicius, whose first wife has died, marries a country lass but continues to court other girls. He meets his supposed father, the peasant from the Spessart Mountains, who tells him that his real father is the hermit, a former officer and a member of the Scottish nobility. The novel takes a fantastic turn when Simplicius visits Mummel Lake and its sylphic inhabitants. After making a trip through Russia and Asia, Simplicius returns to his home and becomes a hermit on Mooskopf Mountain.

In the *Continuatio* Simplicius has a dream about a competition in hell between Avarice and Prodigality, who ruin the wealthy Englishman Iulus and his servant, Avarus. Leaving his hermitage in the forest, Simplicius

becomes a pilgrim. In Egypt he is captured by robbers and exhibited as a wild man. On his way home, after his release, his ship is wrecked in a storm, and only he and a carpenter are able to reach a paradisiacal island. An Ethiopian woman who is washed ashore turns out to be the devil. The carpenter cannot resist the palm wine with which the devil tempts him, and he soon dies. A Dutch ship lands at the island, but Simplicius refuses to return to Europe. Instead, he entrusts his life history, written on palm fronds, to the captain for publication.

Grimmelshausen borrowed descriptions of historic events, and a large part of the scholarly discourses he includes in his novel, from printed sources. His main sources were Garzoni's *Piazza Universale* and Pierre Boaystuau's *Le Théâtre du Monde* (1561; translated as *Theatrum Mundi: The Theatre or Rule of the World*, 1566?), which had been translated into German in 1659. (The discourse on the Merode Brothers in book 4, chapter 13, for example, is virtually copied from Garzoni.) Saints' legends are the basis for the novel's accounts of hermits; and an Italian novella, which Grimmelshausen probably read in one of Georg Philipp Harsdörffer's collections of short stories, is the inspiration for Simplicius's erotic escapades in Paris. Most of the pranks, such as the ones Simplicius commits as the Jäger von Soest, can be found in sixteenth-century collections of merry tales. In describing historic events such as battles and sieges, the former musketeer Grimmelshausen did not rely on his memory but consulted *Theatrum Europaeum* (1633–1738), a monumental historical compilation that appeared in many volumes, and Eberhard Wassenberg's *Ernewerter Teutscher Florus* (Renewed German Florus, 1647).

Among other fictional works, Grimmelshausen drew on Johann Michael Moscherosch's *Gesichte Philanders von Sittewald* (Visions of Philander of Sittewald, 1642); on the Spanish picaresque novel, particularly Aegidius Albertinus's 1615 adaptation of Mateo Alemán's *La Vida del Pícaro Guzmán de Alfarache* (The Life of the Rogue Guzmán de Alfarache, 1599); and on Charles Sorel's *Histoire comique de Francion* (1623–1633), translated into German in 1662. From the picaresque tradition he took the use of the first-person narrator; the technique of enumerating adventures, episodes, and merry talelike episodes; the insertion of moral discourses and treatises; and the tendency to satirize and criticize one's own age. The character of Simplicius is in many ways identical to that of the Spanish picaro. After Simplicius, as a page in Hanau, first becomes a victim of his colleagues' pranks, he gains his wits through the governor's attempt to change him into a fool. He even attains a kind of superiority over the world, which in turn enables him to be the perpetrator of many pranks. Again like the picaro, Simplicius is driven hither and thither by fate, which raises human beings to the peak of happiness and then lets them fall again. Finally, like the picaro Simplicius exists in a disorderly world, where anarchy rules and each individual must protect himself and prove his own worth.

On the other hand, there are several features that distinguish *Der Abentheurliche Simplicissimus Teutsch* from the picaresque genre: in sixteenth-century Spain, the setting for the picaresque novel, there was certainly much poverty and moral decay, but these conditions did not reach the proportions they did during the disastrous Thirty Years' War in Germany. *Der Abentheurliche Simplicissimus Teutsch* includes eyewitness descriptions of battles and sieges; of devastation of every kind; of looting soldiers who rob and torture farmers; of farmers taking revenge on the soldiers; of life in the fortresses of Hanau, Philippsburg, and Lippstadt and in the military camps; of the general decay of moral values in the army; and of the infiltration of Germany by French culture. Whereas the hero of the Spanish picaresque novel is concerned with physical survival, Simplicius's primary concern is his spiritual state. Simplicius does not merely accept his fate; he reflects on and interprets it. *Der Abentheurliche Simplicissimus Teutsch* thus reveals a reflective attitude that the Spanish picaresque novel does not display. Grimmelshausen's obvious compassion for the peasants, who carry the main burden of the war, opens a new perspective in German literature; up to this time peasants had almost exclusively assumed the role of cheated fools in Shrovetide plays and merry tales.

The events of *Der Abentheurliche Simplicissimus Teutsch* and, therefore, of Simplicius's life, can be dated exactly. The battle of Höchst, which occurred on 10 June 1622, has just taken place when Simplicius is born. The battle of Nördlingen on 8 September 1634 forces the twelve-year-old boy out of the forest, following his stay with the hermit. The siege of Magdeburg, from May to August 1636, brings Simplicius into contact with two opposite types, the good Herzbruder and the wicked Olivier; and the battle of Wittstock, on 4 October 1636, releases him from military arrest. The Peace of Westphalia, concluded on 24 October 1648, is alluded to. On the whole, then, Grimmelshausen locates the action between 1622 and approximately 1650. *Der Abentheurliche Simplicissimus Teutsch* is not an historical novel, however; Grimmelshausen focuses not on the historical background but on the hero and his fate.

The characters in the novel serve as bearers of ideas. For example, Herzbruder and Olivier accompany Simplicius on his journey through life and reappear as embodiments of good and evil at every decisive point. Olivier represents the man who has fallen into earthly snares, who adapts to the world and plays its game; he

is Grimmelshausen's absolutely negative example. Herzbruder is the man who has remained untouched by the world and does not make ethical compromises. Olivier's life history has a deterrent effect on Simplicius because it reveals the consequences of a worldly existence. The example set by Herzbruder repeatedly compels Simplicius to measure his own actions by the standards of Christian morality. Simplicius can be viewed as a kind of specimen who has been placed in the world to test its moral character. Just as Simplicius stands between Herzbruder and Olivier, humanity is stationed between God and the devil; thus, Grimmelshausen's novel is a fundamentally religious depiction of humanity's eternal struggle with good and evil. In spite of the many entertaining features of the book, its basic message is that the world is evil. The moralist Grimmelshausen compels his readers to open their eyes to the ever-present danger of entanglement in the world's snares. Since a positive—that is, Christian—existence is impossible in this world, Simplicius withdraws from it as a hermit at the end of book 5 and by refusing to return to Europe at the end of the *Continuatio*.

Grimmelshausen often engages in a satiric critique of society. He deconstructs the masks the world has donned and endeavors to describe worldly matters as they really are. The frontispiece, which may be seen as substituting for a preface, depicts a monster that is part man, part animal, part bird, and part fish and has the goat's horns of a satyr. It holds an open book that can only be interpreted as the book of life, on the pages of which are symbols from the novel: a crown, a cannon, a tower, a goblet, a fool's cap, a set of dice, a sword, a ship, and so on. Masks lie at the feet of the satyr, and a poem is inscribed beneath it:

> Ich wurde durchs Fewer wie *Phoenix* geborn.
> Ich flog durch die Lüffte! wurd doch nit verlorn,
> Ich wandert durchs Wasser, Ich raißt über Landt,
> in solchem Umbschwermen macht ich mir bekandt
> was mich offt betrüebet und selten ergetzt,
> was war das? Ich habs in diß Büche gesetzt
> damit sich der Leser gleich wie ich itzt thue,
> entferne der Thorheit und lebe in Rhue.

> (I was born out of fire like the *Phoenix*.
> I flew through air! but was not lost,
> I made my way through water, I traveled over land,
> by such journeys I made the acquaintance
> of what often saddened and rarely gladdened me,
> what was that? I have set it down in this book,
> so that the reader may, like myself,
> avoid folly and live in peace.)

The poem evinces a desire to remove the masks from the world by having his hero experience reality in its totality, as shown by mention of the four elements of fire, air, water, and earth. In addition, the poet stresses the moralistic-didactic character of his work: he intends to censure the evil and unhealthy aspects of his age. Grimmelshausen accomplishes this censuring in several ways. First, he directly condemns various deplorable aspects of the period, such as the fashionable French-imitative culture in book 1, chapter 19; gluttony in book 1, chapter 30; and gambling in book 2, chapter 20. Second, he uses the dream or visionary satire; for example, in an allegorical dream in book 1, chapter 15, doubtless written under the influence of Moscherosch's work, that depicts society at the time of the Thirty Years' War in the form of a tree and demonstrates the uselessness of the "little man's" striving and the corruption of powerful men. To this category also belongs the dream allegory about avarice and wastefulness in the *Continuatio* and Simplicius's description of his foster father's farmhouse in the Spessart Mountains in terms of a nobleman's palace. Third, he uses the utopia to establish an absolute, positive norm with which to contrast the politically and socially deplorable state of affairs of his own time when he visits the sylphs in the Mummel Lake, a world deep inside the earth where there is no original sin and where he describes worldly affairs to the king of the sylphs in idealized terms; and in book 2 when, as the Jäger von Soest, he apprehends a fool who pretends to be the god Jove and says that he will send a German hero who will establish religious unity, peace, wealth, governmental and social order, proliferation of the arts, and an overall strengthening of the German nation. This utopian program is presented in the form of a satire, but Simplicius's idea of an ideal human society is fulfilled in the community of the Hungarian Anabaptists in book 5, chapter 19. This ideal community is depicted as the realization of the positive Christian norm, in contrast to the satiric unmasking of contemporary society. The desire for peace at the time of the Thirty Years' War is expressed in these utopias. Finally, Simplicius's life as a hermit on the island in book 6—the first German-language robinsonade, based on *The Isle of Pines* (1618; translated into German, 1668), by the British satirist Henry Neville—describes an ideal life that is only possible because of its remoteness from European society.

By using these various satiric forms Grimmelshausen exposes various deficiencies of the world, both moral and material. Another failing of the world, one that permeates the entire novel and of which Simplicius's life is exemplary, is the inconstancy or transitoriness of everything earthly. The fluctuations in Simplicius's life, the constant changes in his fate, are the heritage of the Spanish picaresque novel. In the *Continuatio,* during a walk in the forest Simplicius meets the allegorical figure of Baldanders (Soon-different), an invention of the sixteenth-century poet Hans Sachs that personifies transitoriness and that changes before his eyes into various objects and then flies away in the shape of a bird. The inconstancy of the world is also demonstrated in the same book by a piece of paper hanging in a privy with which Simplicius converses. It relates to him the sad story of its life, from flax to cloth to paper. When these episodes are taken together with the dream vision at the beginning of the book of the competition between avarice and wastefulness, it is obvious that the *Continuatio* is dominated by dream allegories, while the background of the Thirty Years' War is totally excluded. Therefore, it may have been intended as a commentary on the first five books, assuming the function of the missing preface by providing clues for their interpretation.

There have been many attempts to assign *Der Abentheurliche Simplicissimus Teutsch* to one of the classic novel types. Many scholars, particularly during the 1920s and 1930s, regarded it as a bildungsroman. But to use terms such as *bildungsroman* or *Entwicklungsroman* (novel of development) to characterize *Der Abentheurliche Simplicissimus Teutsch* is to apply concepts from eighteenth- and nineteenth-century literature to a work of the seventeenth century. Such later novels depict the unfolding of innate qualities, a continuous, organic process of maturing, while Simplicius never goes beyond the simple Christian principles taught to him by the hermit; he does not undergo a psychological development into a multifaceted personality.

It is also tempting to view the work, as Jan Hendrik Scholte has done, in terms of a five-act classical drama, but such an interpretation would necessitate a separation of the *Continuatio* from the original five-book novel. The many inconsistencies of character development make it more plausible to see, as Johannes Alt has done, just a sequence of certain types—hermit, fool, Jäger von Soest, gallant adventurer, disciple of Olivier and Herzbruder, hermit; but this interpretation does not do justice to the complexity of the novel or to the unity of Simplicius's life, a unity that is created through the fictional autobiography that integrates various traditional literary forms and types. Other structural theories include Siegfried Streller's attempt to use the cabala and number mysticism to prove that *Der Abentheurliche Simplicissimus Teutsch* and the subsequent Simplician writings were composed according to numbers and Clemens Heselhaus's interpretation of *Der Abentheurliche Simplicissimus Teutsch* in terms of notion of the fourfold meaning of a text that was used in medieval Bible exegesis. More recent research, by Helmut Rehder and particularly by Günter Weydt and his students, has tried to find a structure based on astrology; the text does seem to support various associations that Grimmelshausen's time made between planetary positions, on the one hand, and events and character qualities, on the other. This theory is, however, still hotly debated.

After *Der Abentheurliche Simplicissimus Teutsch,* Grimmelshausen published a work of an entirely different type: *Dietwalds und Amelinden anmuthige Lieb- und Leids-Beschreibung, sammt erster Vergrösserung des Weltberühmten Königreichs Franckreich* (The Pleasant Story of Dietwald and Amelinde through Thick and Thin, Together with the First Enlargement of the World-Famous Kingdom of France, 1670). He also used his own name on the title page. Although the lack of devotional formulae and the address to the audience on the title page make it obvious that Grimmelshausen was not writing for a courtly readership, many motifs—the slaying of robbers, pirates, the separation of the lovers, kidnapping—go back to the courtly-historical novel and its precursor, the late Greek novel of Heliodorus; Grimmelshausen's novel is also closely related to saints' legends. The action is based on the *Magelone* chapbook and even more on the *Meisterlied Dy history des grafen von soffey* (The History of the Count of Savoy, 1497). In fifth-century France the young Prince Dietwald meets and marries Princess Amelinde. To cure their hubris they follow the advice of an angel, who appears to them in the form of a beggar, to spend ten years in disguise and in a lowly condition, after which they are returned to their former exalted status. Although Grimmelshausen does not always achieve the full integration of the history of fifth-century France, which he reports in detail, with the story of his hero and heroine, the book presents Grimmelshausen's ideal of a Christian ruler who has overcome the lure of earthly wealth and power. The work also treats contemporary political problems, such as the question of a strong central power, in historical guise.

Trutz Simplex is the first sequel to *Der Abentheurliche Simplicissimus Teutsch.* In the foreword to *Deß Wunderbarlichen Vogelnessts Zweiter theil* (The Miraculous Bird's Nest, Part Two, 1675) he says that the work to follow is the tenth part of the life of the adventurous Simplicissimus, if *Trutz Simplex* is considered the seventh, *Der seltzame Springinsfeld* the eighth, and the first part of *Das wunderbarliche Vogel-Nest* (1672) the ninth. All of these Simplician writings are connected, and neither *Der Abentheurliche Simplicissimus Teutsch* nor any of the shorter works can be sufficiently understood without connecting it to the others. Scholars disagree as to whether Grimmelshausen was creating this impression in hindsight for commercial purposes, or whether he had conceived a ten-part work from the outset.

Trutz Simplex is a negative counterpart to *Der Abentheurliche Simplicissimus Teutsch.* It does not start where the *Continuatio* left off but resembles the first five books of

Der Abentheurliche Simplicissimus Teutsch. Courage, as her name is spelled in the text itself, was Simplicius's lover at the Sauerbrunnen in book 5 of *Der Abentheurliche Simplicissimus Teutsch,* and in this novel she takes revenge on Simplicius for describing her there as more *mobilis* (agile) than *nobilis* (noble) by telling the world what an unsavory character she is, thereby tainting Simplicius's reputation for having associated with her. Thus, she is relating her life story to spite Simplicius. Her many references to the spite motif serve as a structural device, tying together the many episodes into an epic whole.

Again, the reader is thrown into the middle of the Thirty Years' War: Courage tells of her upbringing in Bragowitz, Bohemia; her involvement in the war; her marriages to a series of officers and soldiers; her acts of bravery and prowess; her pranks; her life as a prostitute; and other adventures until she ends up as the common-law wife of a gypsy leader. The description, in the novel's subtitle, of her fate as a continuous social decline—*wie sie anfangs eine Rittmeisterin, hernach eine Hauptmännin, ferner eine Leutenantin, bald eine Marcketenterin, Mußquetirerin, und letzlich eine Ziegeunerin abgegeben* (How She First Was the Wife of a Cavalry Captain, Then the Wife of an Infantry Captain, Furthermore the Wife of a Lieutenant, Soon Thereafter The Wife of a Sutler, the Wife of a Musketeer and Finally the Wife of a Gypsy)—is not borne out by the plot itself: on several occasions Courage marries someone whose status is equal to or higher than that of her previous husband. To be sure, these situations are only temporary, and there is no doubt that Grimmelshausen wanted to concentrate on her descent. Her downhill slide is not all her own fault, however; the war keeps killing her husbands, thwarting her attempts to regain respectability. In the first part of the novel she displays many weaknesses of character, but she tries to achieve a respectable life the only way a woman at her time could: through an appropriate marriage. In the second part she takes matters into her own hands, stands up to the men, and tries to succeed through her own intelligence, bravery, and boundless will to survive. At the end of the work she has learned nothing from her experiences; she has no regrets and does not repent. Nor does she relate her life story to gain greater self-understanding, as Simplicius did. Thus, Courage is an example of the moral corruption brought about by the Thirty Years' War; a modern version of the medieval incarnation of worldliness, *Frau Welt;* and an indication of the traditional negative view of women that Grimmelshausen held. Courage has tampered with the traditional relationship between men and women by taking over the role of a soldier, by working as an enterprising female sutler, and by gaining a considerable fortune through prostitution and marriage. The possibly ironic moral Grimmelshausen attaches at the end of the novel is that men should beware of women like her—indeed, of women in general. Thus, Courage's redeeming qualities and the bad luck she suffers are negated by Grimmelshausen's reductionistic antifeminism. Nevertheless, Brecht's use of her in his drama *Mutter Courage und ihre Kinder* (Grimmelshausen's Courage is not a mother: she is barren) testifies to the vitality of the character.

In writing *Trutz Simplex* Grimmelshausen again used various historiographical works about the Thirty Years' War as sources, including the *Theatrum Europaeum* and Wassenberg's *Erneuerter Teutscher Florus,* as well as several of Harsdörffer's stories. He also took from a Spanish picaresque novel, Andreas Perez's (pseudonym of Francisco de Ubeda) *Picara Justina* (1605)—which he probably knew in its German translation, *Landstörtzerin Justina Dietzin* (1620)—the idea for a female rogue.

A religious-political tract, *Simplicianischer Zweyköpffiger Ratio Status* (Simplician Two-Headed Ratio Status) appeared in the same year as *Trutz Simplex.* One of the few works published under Grimmelshausen's real name, it attempts to demonstrate what a Christian ruler may and may not do in the interest of the state. Grimmelshausen, largely adhering to Garzoni's opinions in the first discourse of the *Piazza Universale,* sees *ratio status* (justification of the existence of the state) as based on the right of self-preservation. By paraphrasing the biblical stories of Saul, David, Jonathan, and Joab, Grimmelshausen demonstrates the devastating results of Machiavellian principles, which, in his opinion, lead to arrogant behavior on the part of the ruler. His prime negative example is Saul, while David is characterized as a model ruler who, because he trusts in God, is unassailable by Saul's reprehensible machinations. Even David succumbs to ratio status, but he repents and, consequently, is still a ruler to be emulated. Like many of his contemporaries, Grimmelshausen tries to counteract the separation of politics from Christian behavior. The tract is Grimmelshausen's contribution to the theoretical discussions of seventeenth-century absolutism.

Grimmelshausen continued his Simplician writings with *Der seltzame Springinsfeld.* A lengthy narrative frame is established: in the middle of winter the narrator, who is the secretary who wrote down Courage's story, enters an inn. There he meets Simplicius, who has returned to Europe, and, ultimately, Springinsfeld (whose name means "Hop-into-the-Field"), Courage's former common-law husband, who, after losing a leg in the war against the Turks, roams the countryside posing as a beggar playing the violin; in reality, he is carrying a large amount of money. Chapters 4 to 6 are devoted to the secretary's encounter with Courage; chapters 7 to 9 deal with Simplicius, who is no longer a hermit but a wise old man who conducts himself as a moral teacher of the

countryfolk. Chapters 10 through 27 consist of Springinsfeld's relation of the story of his life to the narrator. The son of a Greek noblewoman and an Albanian juggler and tightrope walker, he became a soldier in the Thirty Years' War, committed all sorts of pranks, and mercilessly killed a wounded officer who cried out to him for help (he rationalizes the murder by criticizing the officers' conduct toward the common soldiers). During the war he was briefly married to Courage. After the war he married an innkeeper's widow, was widowed himself, fought the Turks in Hungary, married a minstrel girl who had a bird's nest that rendered her invisible and who was later killed, and lost his leg fighting the Turks in Candia (Crete). At the end of his narration Simplicius pays the secretary to write down Springinsfeld's story and takes Springinsfeld to his farm. He persuades Springinsfeld to lead a Christian life, which Springinsfeld does until his death the next year.

Through Springinsfeld, Grimmelshausen gives a kind of chronicle of the Thirty Years' War and the following Turkish wars, based, again, on *Erneuerter Teutscher Florus* and *Theatrum Europaeum.* At first, Springinsfeld appears to be a picaresque character, that is, one who is morally reprehensible but not a villain; but when he kills the officer, it becomes obvious that he has been brutalized through his life as a soldier. Like Courage, Springinsfeld has experienced fortune's vicissitudes without learning anything. An allegorical scene in chapters 16 and 17 in which Springinsfeld is hiding on a rooftop in a deserted village, surrounded by a pack of ravenous wolves, symbolizes the human being's situation in the world, particularly during the Thirty Years' War. His conversion at the end indicates that humanity can still be redeemed.

Der erste Beernhäuter (The First Sluggard, 1670) was probably written as early as 1666. It tries to explain the folk etymology of *Beernhäuter,* which literally means someone who wears or lies on a bearskin, by telling the legend of a mercenary who, after the battle of Nicropolis in 1396, promises a ghost that he will wear a bearskin, not wash himself, and not pray for seven years; he is rewarded with riches and a pretty bride. The illustration for *Der erste Beernhäuter* is taken from a printing block for a card-game book by Jost Ammann, published in 1588; the same source is used for the appended "Simplicissimi Gauckeltasche" (Simplicissimus's Bag of Tricks), which consists of illustrations with accompanying rhymed texts designed to point out various vices and to admonish people to mend their ways.

A quite different sort of work, *Des Abentheuerlichen Simplicissimi Ewig-währender Calender* (The Adventurous Simplicissimus's Perpetual Calendar), appeared in 1671. Probably written between 1666 and 1669, it is an almanac that offers, in six columns, a calendar, folk literature, meteorology, prophesies, miraculous stories, and astronomy and astrology; one of the columns includes a conversation between Simplicius and an astrologer.

Des Abenteuerlichen Simplicii Verkehrte Welt (The Adventurous Simplicius's Topsy-Turvy World, 1672) is inspired by Moscherosch's *Gesichte Philanders von Sittewald.* During a walk in the mountains Simplicius takes shelter from the rain in a tree; the bottom of the tree falls out, and he lands in hell. There he meets sinners who are being punished according to their trespasses. Just as in the conversation with the king of the sylphs in the Mummel Lake, Simplicius tells them of supposedly ideal moral circumstances on earth. The work is a satire, much less serious and more ironic in tone than Moscherosch's work.

In *Rathstübel Plutonis* (Plutus's Council Chamber, 1672) Simplicius and two members of his family, Knan and Meuder, are in a valley near the spa of Peterstal, where they engage in a dialogue with people who represent all strata of society, including a merchant, a prince who is traveling in disguise, a Jew, and an actress; in the middle of the book they are joined by Courage and Springinsfeld. The format of politely discussing a problem—in this case, money and ways of accumulating, saving, and wasting it, its corrupting effect as well as the effect of its absence—in the form of a social conversation is derived from Harsdörffer's *Frauenzimmer-Gesprächsspiele* (Playful Colloquies for the Ladies, 1641–1649) and the first volume of Johann Rist's *Monatsgespräche* (Monthly Conversations, 1668). As in those works, a discussion leader is appointed; a topic of discussion is determined; and each member of the group makes his or her contribution. But in Grimmelshausen's book the contributions increase in length during each of the nine rounds of conversation, growing from brief theses to short novels. At the end Simplicius displays his satiric wit and irony by instructing the prince in how to rid himself of his wealth by indulging in various extravagances. Simplicius's admonitions to the prince are related to the traditional genre of the *Fürstenspiegel* (princes' mirror). They are a critique of the wasteful practices of absolute princes that lead to their countries' impoverishment.

In *Der stoltze Melcher* (Proud Melchior, 1672) an idler takes a walk outside his village and, hiding behind a bush, witnesses the homecoming of Proud Melchior, the son of a rich farmer, who had run away from home a year earlier to become a soldier. On his return, accompanied by two equally sick and ragged comrades, Melchior is at first rejected and scolded by his father. Then a nobleman and a minister join the group, and the nobleman reconciles father and son. The narration by the three former soldiers of their experiences in the French army are designed as a polemic against French expansionist politics and as antiwar propaganda

intended to discourage young Germans from following the recruiters of Louis XIV, who were seeking soldiers for France's war against Holland.

With *Des Durchleuchtigen Printzen Proximi, und seiner ohnvergleichlichen Lympida Liebs-Geschicht-Erzehlung* (The Love Story of the Illustrious Prince Proximus and His Incomparable Lympida, 1672) Grimmelshausen returns to the genre of the courtly-historical novel, writing a kind of Middle Eastern counterpart to *Dietwald und Amelinde;* the source of the story is a saint's legend. In sixth-century Constantinople, Proximus, the son of the rich Modestus, distinguishes himself by his bravery in the war against the Persians. He also carries out his father's will by sharing his large inheritance with the poor. He is richly rewarded for his Christian deeds: the parents of the chaste and beautiful Lympida, who has secretly loved Proximus for a long time, have decided to give her hand in marriage to the first youth they encounter coming to church in the morning; Proximus is that youth. He is also rewarded with the principality of Thessaly, but he renounces it. As a contrasting figure Grimmelshausen introduces Proximus's avaricious uncle Orontaeus, who cheats Proximus out of his remaining inheritance, only to be eaten up by bitter remorse before his death. As in *Dietwald und Amelinde,* the rulers are presented as chess figures in a game of political power, afraid of being toppled or murdered by powerful vassals or military leaders. By praising the lives of farmers and artisans in contrast to those of courtiers and rulers, Grimmelshausen has secretly introduced an anticourtly element into his seemingly courtly-historical novel. But the emphasis lies in the depiction of the exemplary Christian lives of Proximus, Lympida, and their parents.

The first part of *Das wunderbarliche Vogel-Nest* also appeared in 1672. The hero is the halberdier who, at the end of *Der seltzame Springinsfeld,* catches the bird's nest when the minstrel girl is killed. The halberdier sets out to acquire money with the help of the nest, which renders him invisible. In this condition he watches as an impoverished nobleman tries to give the impression of wealth to catch a rich bride, while the bride and her mother, who are actually poor, try to do the same to him. He observes beggars who are, in reality, well off. He observes a quarrel between Protestants and Catholics in a village inn. He prevents a clergyman from seducing a girl, witnesses a seduction in a stable, and keeps a herdsman from committing sodomy. In some cases he prevents acts of injustice: he keeps two students from being killed by robbers; and he thwarts a burglary attempt, with the result that one burglar kills the other. In a monastery the halberdier witnesses a plot that succeeds in getting young Simplicius ousted from the community; he then saves Simplicius after the latter is falsely accused of adultery. Later, he hears the older Simplicius, who admits to being the author of *Exempel der unveränderlichen Vorsehung Gottes. Unter einer anmutigen und ausführlichen Histori vom Keuschen Joseph in Egypten, Jacobs Sohn,* attack Zesen's novel *Assenat.* After the halberdier is stung by a swarm of bees and has to save himself by jumping into a filthy puddle, he decides that the nest is an evil influence and tears it to pieces; but a rich merchant, with the help of a magician, finds the important parts of the nest, which ants have reassembled. At the end of the story the merchant discovers the minstrel girl's money hidden in a tree.

Nowhere else does Grimmelshausen paint such a complete picture of contemporary society as in *Das wunderbarliche Vogel-Nest,* the first of the Simplician writings that does not take place during a war. The same principle seems to be operative at all levels of society: people see what they want to see and believe that they can get away with their misdeeds if nobody else sees them. By means of his invisibility, the nest-bearer is able to see through the masks people put on to deceive themselves and others. The themes of the book are expressed in the frontispiece, in which a satyr looks through a bird's nest at a globe walking a meandering path. A cherubic child tries to look at the world through a telescope, but a pile of masks obstructs the view. Grimmelshausen's argument is that people should realize that God sees everything they do and should behave accordingly, as the halberdier points out to a peasant girl who is trying to seduce a peasant boy by telling him that no one can see what they are about to do. In many instances, such as this one, Grimmelshausen's nest-bearer is more than an observer; he intervenes, most of the time to promote justice or to prompt people to gain insight into their wrongdoing; but at the end he realizes that he is playing God and thereby committing the sin of pride. In one instance, he himself gets drunk and takes advantage of a girl who believes that she is in bed with her beloved. The halberdier finally understands that his invisibility does not protect him from God's view; he sees that the bird's nest constitutes a threat to the salvation of his soul when he relies on it instead of God's help.

Like Simplicius, therefore, the nest-bearer comes to self-understanding and insight into the deceptive nature of the world. The Christian perspective of the work appears allegorically when the halberdier, after being stung by the bees, bathes in the filthy puddle, signifying the soiling of the soul by sin. He then washes himself in clear water, symbolizing baptism, repentance, and atonement. In contrast to the end of *Der Abentheurliche Simplicissimus Teutsch,* however, *Das wunderbarliche Vogel-Nest* advocates Christian behavior in the world and not a withdrawal from the world.

In *Bart-Krieg* (Beard-War, 1673) the author, who has a red beard, debates the old Simplicius, who, in a conversation in an inn, had called his own gold-colored beard red. This satiric praise of red beards, as compared to black ones, is dated 1 January 1673 and is thus presented as a New Year's joke.

In *Deß Weltberuffenen Simplicissimi Pralerey und Gepräng mit seinem Teutschen Michel* (The World-Reputed Simplicissimus's Boasting and Ostentation with His German Michael, 1673) Grimmelshausen expresses his ideas about the German language, thus contributing to the discussions of the reform-minded literati of his time such as Zesen. He does not present his thoughts in a logically structured argument, as he did in *Satyrischer Pilgram,* but in humorously written chapters dealing with issues such as the integrity of languages and dialect influence, defense of those who only speak their mother tongue, the advantages of knowing a foreign language, and the ridiculousness of extreme and pedantic orthographic reforms including the attempt to invent German terms for all loanwords. Quotes from literary sources, such as Garzoni, Harsdörffer, and Moscherosch, are mixed with observations of his own. The basic tenor of his tract is conservative.

Simplicissimi Galgen-Männlin (Simplicissimus's Mandrake, 1673) is a continuation of *Deß Weltberuffenen Simplicissimi Pralerey und Gepräng mit seinem Teutschen Michel* that humorously applies the language reform advocated in the previous work, such as the elimination of the supposedly superfluous *e.* According to the title page, the work is a report on how to obtain a mandrake, how to care for it, and how to use it to obtain money. It takes the form of a letter from Simplicius to his son, interrupted by the annotations of the "editor," Israel Fromschmidt von Hugenfelß. The booklet provides, in an entertaining fashion, the information that the title page promises, but in typical Grimmelshausen manner it is combined with moralistic warnings against sorcery and other devilish arts.

During the final years of his life Grimmelshausen's productivity abated; the only further work to appear before his death was the ingenious *Deß Wunderbarlichen Vogelnessts Zweiter theil,* which was published in 1675. The new nest-bearer, the merchant from the end of part 1, is a quite different person from the halberdier: he is rich, and he does not try to correct injustice but uses the nest to pursue selfish ends. In contrast to the many short stories and merry tales of the first part, the second part is divided into three sections. In the first section the merchant gets revenge for his wife's intention to commit adultery with a young doctor by cheating on her with one of her relatives. In the second section, which is set in Amsterdam, he uses the Jews' hopes for the coming of the Messiah by playing the prophet Elijah and, in this guise, enjoying the favors of the beautiful Esther; the Messiah, who is supposed to be born from this union, turns out to be a girl. In the third section the merchant serves as a soldier in the 1672 war between Holland and France, using not only his invisibility but also black magic to gain invulnerability for himself and to kill his enemies until, himself becoming the victim of such magic, he is severely wounded and trampled underfoot by horses. With the help of a priest he finally sees the error of his ways, and he throws the nest into the Rhine.

A collection of French love stories, *Les faveurs et les disgraces de l'amour,* and Giovanni Boccaccio's *Decameron* (1351–1353) were probably the source for the first section; the second section was mainly based on the appearance in Amsterdam in 1666, as reported in *Theatrum Europaeum* (1673), of a certain Sabbatai Zwi, who claimed to be the Messiah. Parts of this episode might also have been taken from Moscherosch's *Gesichte Philanders von Sittewald.* Albertinus's adaptation ofj Alemán's *Guzmán de Alfarache* may have contributed to the third section.

In his foreword Grimmelshausen says that the message of the work is a warning against any connection or familiarity with the devil. The ubiquitousness of God in part 1 thus finds a counterpart here in the omnipresence of the devil. His use of the powers of the bird's nest to further enrich himself and to satisfy his carnal desires places the merchant's soul in extreme danger. Whereas in part 1 the halberdier's insight into the deceptive character of society and into his own sinfulness leads to greater self-knowledge, the merchant in part 2 becomes more and more ensnared by devilish forces, magic, and sorcery and becomes increasingly sinful. Just as *Trutz Simplex* and *Der seltzame Springinsfeld* present negative examples following the positive example of *Der Abentheurliche Simplicissimus Teutsch,* so *Deß Wunderbarlichen Vogelnessts Zweiter theil* serves as a negative example after the positive example of part 1. Nevertheless, even the merchant's soul is saved. Because of the magnitude of his sins, however, his salvation cannot come about through a gradual understanding of his situation; instead, it occurs by means of a catastrophe: he is wounded on the battlefield by a poisoned magic bullet, and a priest absolves him from his sins before he dies.

There are indications that during the last years of his life Grimmelshausen had to take up arms again, though without giving up his office as mayor; it is uncertain whether he served in an imperial regiment or in a citizens' militia organized to protect the citizenry from French or imperial forces. After Louis XIV attacked the Netherlands, the German emperor in 1673 and the imperial diet in 1674 went to war with France. Both French and imperial soldiers were billeted in

Grimmelshausen's area until 1675, when the imperial troops defeated the French under Marshall Henri de Turenne in the battle of Sasbach. During the war the poet tried to effect a fair distribution of the burdens imposed on the population. Grimmelshausen died on 17 August 1676; the entry in the church register of Renchen calls him "Honestus et magno ingenio et eruditione" (an honorable man, of talent and erudition) and a good Catholic.

Bibliography:

Gerhard Dünnhaupt, *Personalbibliographien zu den Drucken des Barock,* volume 3 (Stuttgart: Hiersemann, 1991), pp. 1825–1851.

Biography:

Gustave Könnecke, *Quellen und Forschungen zur Lebensgeschichte Grimmelshausens,* 2 volumes, edited by Jan Hendrik Scholte (Weimar: Gesellschaft der Bibliophilen, 1926, 1928).

References:

Johannes Alt, *Grimmelshausen und der Simplicissimus* (Munich: Beck, 1936);

Susan C. Anderson, *Grass and Grimmelshausen,* Studies in German Literature, Linguistics and Culture, volume 28 (Columbia, S.C.: Camden House, 1987);

Argenis, special issue on Grimmelshausen, 1, no. 1–4 (1977);

R. P. T. Aylett, *The Nature of Realism in Grimmelshausen's Simplicissimus Cycle of Novels,* European University Studies, Series I: German Language and Literature, volume 479 (Bern & Frankfurt am Main: Peter Lang, 1982);

Italo Michele Battafarano and Hildegard Eilert, *Grimmelshausen-Bibliographie 1666–1972: Werk–Forschung–Wirkungsgeschichte,* Quaderni degli Annali dell'Instituto universitario orientale, Sezione germanica, volume 9 (Naples: Istituto universitario orientale, 1975);

Artur Bechtold, *Johann Jacob Christoph von Grimmelshausen und seine Zeit* (Munich: Musarion, 1919);

Rudolf Behrle, *Hans Jacob Christoph von Grimmelshausen: Leben und Werk* (Bühl & Baden: Kondordia, 1971);

Mathias Feldges, *Grimmelshausens "Landstörtzerin Courasche": Eine Interpretation nach der Methode des vierfachen Schriftsinns,* Basler Studien zur deutschen Sprache und Literatur, volume 38 (Bern: Francke, 1969);

Friedrich Gaede, *Substanzverlust: Grimmelshausens Kritik der Moderne* (Tübingen: Francke, 1987);

Hans Dieter Gebauer, *Grimmelshausens Bauerndarstellung: Literarische Sozialkritik und ihr Publikum,* Marburger

Beiträge zur Germanistik, volume 53 (Marburg: Elwert, 1977);

Hubert Gersch, *Geheimpoetik: Die "Continuatio des abentheurlichen Simplicissimi" interpretiert als Grimmelshausens verschlüsselter Kommentar zu seinem Roman,* Studien zur deutschen Literatur, volume 35 (Tübingen: Niemeyer, 1973);

Hans Geulen, *Erzählkunst der frühen Neuzeit: Zur Geschichte epischer Darbietungsweisen und Formen im Roman der Renaissance und des Barock* (Tübingen: Rotsch, 1975);

"Grimmelshausen und seine Zeit: Die Vorträge des Münsteraner Symposions zum 300. Todestag des Dichters," *Daphnis: Zeitschrift für Mittlere Deutsche Literatur,* 5, no. 2–4 (1976): 183–737;

Kenneth C. Hayens, *Grimmelshausen* (London: Oxford University Press, 1932);

Gisela Herbst, *Die Entwicklung des Grimmelshausenbildes in der wissenschaftlichen Literatur,* Bonner Arbeiten zur deutschen Literatur, volume 2 (Bonn: Bouvier, 1957);

Clemens Heselhaus, "Hans Jacob Christoffel von Grimmelshausen: Der abenteuerliche Simplicissimus," in *Der deutsche Roman: Vom Barock bis zur Gegenwart,* edited by Benno von Wiese (Düsseldorf: Bagel, 1963), pp. 15–63;

Peter Heßelmann, *Gaukelpredigt: Simplicianische Poetologie und Didaxe. Zu allegorischen und emblematischen Strukturen in Grimmelshausens Zehn-Bücher-Zyklus* (Frankfurt am Main, Bern & New York: Peter Lang, 1988);

Curt Hohoff, *Johann Jacob Christoph von Grimmelshausen in Selbstzeugnissen und Bilddokumenten* (Reinbek: Rowohlt, 1978);

Jan Knopf, *Frühzeit des Bürgers: Erfahrene und verleugnete Realität in den Romanen Wickrams, Grimmelshausens, Schnabels* (Stuttgart: Metzler, 1978);

Ilse-Lore Konopatzki, *Grimmelshausens Legendenvorlagen,* Philologische Studien und Quellen, volume 28 (Berlin: Erich Schmidt, 1965);

Manfred Koschlig, *Grimmelshausen und seine Verleger,* Palaestra, volume 218 (Leipzig: Akademische Verlagsanstalt, 1939; New York & London: Johnson, 1967);

Koschlig, *Das Ingenium Grimmelshausens und das "Kollektiv": Studien zur Entstehungs- und Wirkungsgeschichte des Werkes* (Munich: Beck, 1977);

Eberhard Mannack, "Hans Jacob Christoffel von Grimmelshausen," in *Deutsche Dichter des 17. Jahrhunderts: Ihr Leben und Werk,* edited by Benno von Wiese and Harald Steinhagen (Berlin: Erich Schmidt, 1984), pp. 517–552;

Volker Meid, *Grimmelshausen: Epoche–Werk–Wirkung* (Munich: Beck, 1984);

Kenneth Negus, *Grimmelshausen* (New York: Twayne, 1974);

Wolfdietrich Rasch and others, eds., *Rezeption und Produktion zwischen 1570 und 1730: Festschrift für Günter Weydt zum 65. Geburtstag* (Bern & Munich: Francke, 1972);

Helmut Rehder, "Planetenkinder: Some Problems of Character Portrayal in Literature," *Graduate Journal,* 8, no. 1 (1968): 69–97;

Günter Rohrbach, *Figur und Charakter: Strukturuntersuchungen an Grimmelshausens Simplicissimus,* Bonner Arbeiten zur deutschen Literatur, volume 3 (Bonn: Bouvier, 1959);

Hans Georg Rötzer, *Picaro–Landstörtzer–Simplicius: Studien zum niederen Roman in Spanien und Deutschland,* Impulse der Forschung, volume 4 (Darmstadt: Wissenschaftliche Buchgesellschaft, 1972);

Jan Hendrik Scholte, *Der Simplicissimus und sein Dichter: Gesammelte Aufsätze* (Tübingen: Niemeyer, 1950);

Scholte, *Zonagri Discurs von Waarsagern: Ein Beitrag zu unserer Kenntnis von Grimmelshausens Arbeitsweise in seinem Ewigwährenden Calender mit besonderer Berücksichtigung des Eingangs des Abentheuerlichen Simplicissimus* (Amsterdam: Müller, 1921);

Christoph Stoll, *Hans Jacob Christoffel von Grimmelshausen. 1676/1976* (Bonn & Bad Godesberg: Inter Nationes, 1976);

Siegfried Streller, *Grimmelshausens simplicianische Schriften: Allegorie, Zahl und Wirklichkeitsdarstellung,* Neue Beiträge zur Literaturwissenschaft, volume 7 (Berlin: Rütten & Loening, 1957);

Peter Tiefenbach, *Der Lebenslauf des Simplicius Simplicissimus: Figur–Initiation–Satire* (Stuttgart: Klett-Cotta, 1979);

Hans Wagener, *The German Baroque Novel* (New York: Twayne, 1973);

Werner Welzig, *Beispielhafte Figuren: Tor, Abenteurer und Einsiedler bei Grimmelshausen* (Graz & Cologne: Böhlau, 1963);

Günter Weydt, *Hans Jacob Christoffel von Grimmelshausen* (Stuttgart: Metzler, 1971);

Weydt, *Nachahmung und Schöpfung im Barock: Studien um Grimmelshausen* (Bern & Munich: Francke, 1968);

Weydt, ed., *Der Simplicissimusdichter und sein Werk,* Wege der Forschung, volume 153 (Darmstadt: Wissenschaftliche Buchgesellschaft, 1969);

Weydt and Peter Berghaus, *Simplicius Simplicissimus: Grimmelshausen und seine Zeit. Westfälisches Landesmuseum für Kunst und Kulturgeschichte Münster in Zusammenarbeit mit dem Germanistischen Institut der Westfälischen Wilhelms-Universität* (Münster: Landschaftsverband Westfalen-Lippe, 1976).

Andreas Gryphius

(2 October 1616 – 16 July 1664)

Blake Lee Spahr
University of California, Berkeley

This entry originally appeared in DLB 164: German Baroque Writers, 1580–1660.

BOOKS: *Herodis Furiae, et Rachelis lachrymae* (Glogau: Wigand Funck, 1634);

Dei Vindicis Impetus et Herodis Interitus (Danzig: Georg Rhete II, 1635);

Parnassus . . . virtute . . . domini G. Schönborneri a Schönborn . . . renovatus (Danzig: Georg Rhete II, 1636);

Sonnete (Lissa: Wigand Funck, 1637);

Fewrige Freystadt (Lissa: Wigand Funck, 1637);

Brunnen Discurs bey dem hochkläglichen Leichbegängnß, des WolEdlen, Gestrengen Hoch vnd großachtbaren Herrn George Schönborners (Danzig, 1638?);

Son- undt Freyrtags-Sonnete (Leiden: Bonaventura & Abraham Elzevier, 1639);

Sonnete: Das erste Buch (Leiden, 1643);

Oden: Das erste Buch (Leiden, 1643);

Epigrammata: Das erste Buch (Leiden: Frans Heger, 1643);

Epigrammatum Liber I (Leiden, 1643);

Olivetum Libri tres (Florence, 1646; revised edition, Lissa: Daniel Vetter, 1648);

Teutsche Reim-Gedichte Darein enthalten I. Ein Fürsten-Mörderisches Trawer-Spiel, genant. Leo Armenius. II. Zwey Bücher seiner Oden. III. Drey Bücher der Sonnetten denen zum Schluß die Geistvolle Opitianische Gedancken von der Ewigkeit hinbey gesetzet seyn (Frankfurt am Main: Johann Hüttner, 1650);

Thränen über das Leiden Jesu Christi (N.p., 1652);

Deutscher Gedichte, Erster Theil, 10 volumes (Breslau: Johann Lischke, 1657)—comprises volume 1, *Leo Armenius, oder Fürsten-Mord: Trauerspiel;* volume 2, *Catharina von Georgien. Oder Bewehrte Beständigkeit: Trauerspiel;* volume 3, *Ermordete Majestät. Oder Carolus Stuardus König von Großbrittanien: Trauer-Spiel;* volume 4, *Nicolaus Caussinus, Beständige Mutter, oder Die Heilige Felicitas. Aus dem Lateinischen Nicolai Causini übersetztes Trauer-Spiel,* translated and adapted by Gryphius; volume 5, *Cardenio vnd Celinde, oder Unglücklich Verliebete: Trauer-Spiel;* volume 6, *Majuma, Freuden-Spiel. Auff dem Schauplatz Gesangsweise vorgestellet;* volume 7, *Kirchhoffs-Ged-*

Andreas Gryphius; engraving by Philipp Kilian

ancken; volume 8, *Oden;* volume 9, *Thränen über das Leiden Jesu Christi. Oder seiner Oden, Das Vierdte Buch;* volume 10, *Sonette;*

Absurda Comica. Oder Herr Peter Squentz, Schimpff-Spiel (Breslau: Veit Jacob Trescher, 1658);

Freuden vnd Trauer-Spiele auch Oden vnd Sonnette samt Herr Peter Squentz Schimpff-Spiel (Breslau: Johann Lischke & Veit Jacob Trescher, 1658);

Großmüttiger Rechts-Gelehrter, oder Sterbender Aemilius Paulus Papinianus (Breslau: Georg Baumann's heirs, 1659);

Letztes Ehren-Gedächtniß der Hoch-Edelgebohrnen Hoch-Tugend-Zucht und Ehrenreichen Jungfrawen Jungfr. Marianen von Popschitz aus dem hause Crantz auff Gröditz v.d.g. welche den Tag vor Himmelfahrt, des Erlösers der Welt jn dem XV. Tag des Mey Monats, des M D CLX. Jahres seeligst die Welt gesegnet (Steinau an der Oder: Printed by Johann Kuntze, 1660);

Verlibtes Gespenste, Gesang-Spiel (Breslau: Georg Baumann's heirs, 1660); enlarged as *Verlibtes Gespenste, Gesang-Spil. Die gelibte Dornrose, Schertz-Spill* (Breslau: Jesaias Fellgiebel, 1661);

Mumiae Wratislavienses (Breslau: Veit Jacob Trescher, 1662);

Freuden vnd Trauer-Spiele, auch Oden vnd Sonette (Breslau: Veit Jacob Trescher, 1663);

Epigrammata oder Bey-Schriften (Jena: Veit Jacob Trescher, 1663);

Horribilicribrifax Teutsch (Breslau: Veit Jacob Trescher, 1663);

Dissertationes Funebres, oder Leich-Abdanckungen, bey vnterschiedlichen hoch-und ansehnlichen Leich-Begängnüssen gehalten. Auch nebenst seinem letzten Ehren-Gadächtnüß und Lebens-Lauff (Breslau: Veit Jacob Trescher, 1666);

Teutsche Gedichte, edited by Christian Gryphius (Breslau: Jesaias Fellgiebel's heirs, 1698).

Editions and Collections: *Andreas Gryphius: Werke,* 3 volumes, edited by Hermann Palm, Bibliothek des literarischen Vereins Stuttgart, volumes 138, 162, 171 (Tübingen: Hiersemann, 1878-1884); republished as *Andreas Gryphius: Werke in drei Bänden mit Ergänzungsband,* 4 volumes, edited by Friedrich-Wilhelm Wentzlaff-Eggebert (Darmstadt: Wissenschaftliche Buchgesellschaft, 1961);

Cardenio und Celinde, edited by Hugh Powell (Leicester, U.K.: Leicester University Press, 1961);

Carolus Stuardus, edited by Powell (Leicester, U.K.: Leicester University Press, 1963);

Verliebtes Gespenst; Die Geliebte Dornrose, edited by Eberhard Mannack, Komedia: Deutsche Lustspiele vom Barock bis zur Gegenwart, no. 4 (Berlin: De Gruyter, 1963);

Andreas Gryphius: Gesamtausgabe der deutschsprachigen Werke, 12 volumes published, edited by Powell, Marian Szyrocki, Karl-Heinz Habersetzer, and others (Tübingen: Niemeyer, 1963–);

Leo Armenius: Trauerspiel, edited by P. Rusterholz, Reclams Universal-Bibliothek, no. 7960 (Stuttgart: Reclam, 1971);

Horribilicribrifax Teutsch: Scherzspiel, edited by Gerhard Dünnhaupt, Reclams Universal-Bibliothek, no. 688 [2] (Stuttgart: Reclam, 1976);

Absurda Comica. Oder Herr Peter Squentz, edited by Dünnhaupt and Habersetzer, Reclams Universal-Bibliothek, no. 7982 (Stuttgart: Reclam, 1983);

Gebroeders. Die Gibeoniter. Die Rache zu Gibeon, edited by Egbert Krispyn, Nachdrucke deutscher Literatur des 17. Jahrhunderts, volume 28 (Bern: Peter Lang, 1987).

OTHER: *Glogauisches Fürstenthumbs Landes Privilegia aus denn Originalen an tag gegeben,* edited by Gryphius (Lissa: Wigand Funck, 1653);

Andrea Gryphii Ubersetzete Lob-Gesänge, oder Kirchen-Lieder, translated by Gryphius (Breslau: Georg Baumann's heirs, 1660);

Thomas Corneille, *Der Schwermende Schäfer Lysis,* translated by Gryphius (Brieg: Christoff Tschorn, 1661);

Girolamo Razzi, *Seugamme oder Untreues Haußgesinde. Lust-Spiel,* adapted by Gryphius (Jena: Veit Jacob Trescher, 1663);

Sir Richard Baker, *Frag-Stück und Betrachtungen über das Gebett des Herren,* translated by Gryphius (Leipzig: Veit Jacob Trescher, 1663);

Josua Stegmann, *Himmel Steigente HertzensSeüfftzer ubersehen und mit newen Reimen gezieret,* edited by Gryphius (Breslau: Veit Jacob Trescher, 1665).

Andreas Gryphius was the greatest lyric poet, as well as the greatest dramatist, of seventeenth-century Germany. In lyric poetry his voice is the voice of the century. He gives unforgettable utterance to the horrors of the Thirty Years' War, during which he grew up; to the fears of the plague, which raged throughout Germany during his lifetime; and to the personal uncertainty of a tortured soul held fast by the fetters of a strict Protestant faith while witnessing the miracles of the new scientific discoveries in which he participated. On the other hand, his dramas are not dramatic but are based on the rhetorical principles that dominated the form of the baroque drama. At the same time, he is a trailblazer, one of the first in his country to compose stage productions in the vernacular that are playable and can still be appreciated today in spite of their often ponderous language and lack of dramatic qualities. In his own day his dramatic prowess far outweighed, in the public eye, his reputation as a lyric poet; in fact, he was hailed as the greatest dramatist in the history of his country, as the "German Sophocles." His tragedies provided ample opportunity for his natural penchant for staid, dignified (today one might say bombastic) language, while his comedies, though rather unsophisticated, are amusing. He is one of the few baroque poets whose reputation did not suffer oblivion in the ensuing period. Although he is no longer on a pedestal, even a dusty one, his image has been paid that obscure respect afforded venerable but rarely read pioneers. This situation persisted until the middle of the nineteenth century, when the literary historian Georg Gervinus characterized him as the high point of German literature of the seventeenth century. From that time on, scholarly interest has grown.

Gryphius's life is a catalogue of misfortune punctuated by intervals of patronage, accomplishment, and recognition. He was born on 2 October 1616 to the fifty-six-year-old Lutheran archdeacon of Glogau in Silesia, Paul Gryphius, and his third wife, Anna, née Erhard, who was thirty-two years younger than her husband. (Both 29 September and 11 October are listed in the secondary literature as the birth date of the poet. The first of these erroneous dates stems from a sonnet in which Gryphius moved his birthday forward three days, presumably so that it might coincide with the feast of the archangel Michael; the second may be attributed to a misreading of the Roman numeral II.) During this time Silesia was a hotbed of religious strife, and Glogau was particularly affected. Nominally in the hands of the Roman Catholics, who were supported by the emperor, the town was populated by a majority of Lutherans, and there were constant altercations between the two camps. As archdeacon, Gryphius's father must have played a leading role in the disturbances.

On 5 January 1621 Paul Gryphius died unexpectedly. Twenty years later the poet said in a sonnet that the cause of death had been poison administered by a false friend, but it has been assumed that this was poetic hyperbole to intimate that the staunch old Lutheran archdeacon had been betrayed by a supposed ally and had been so perturbed that he died of a heart attack. The circumstances might bear out this theory: Friedrich V von der Pfalz (of the Palatinate), the so-called Winter King, on his retreat after his defeat in the decisive Battle of the White Mountain, spent the night of 4 January 1621 in Glogau. The next day the king, a Calvinist, stripped the Lutheran church of its silver treasures and continued his march. One may well imagine that the archdeacon might have been driven to death's door by this action, although his tombstone claims that the cause of death was "catharrho, proh! suffocativo extinctus" (a pulmonary disorder resulting from a cold).

Two months after his father's death Gryphius entered the school in Glogau; a year later Gryphius's mother married one of the teachers there, Michael Eder. In 1622 some eight thousand mercenaries passed through the city, while others were quartered in and about the area. The military atrocities that were normal for this period added to the financial ills of the city, which was only slowly recovering from a fire that had destroyed much of it in 1616. In 1628 Gryphius's mother died of tuberculosis. That year a dispute over the repossession of the Lutheran church by the Catholics caused the city to be occupied by the infamous Lichtensteiner dragoons, who forcefully converted some six thousand Protestants and drove the rest, including Gryphius's stepfather, to take refuge across the Polish border.

The Catholics demanded that all boys under the age of fifteen and all girls under the age of thirteen remain in the city, along with any inheritance due them. Gryphius was able to join his stepfather a few months later in Driebitz. Since the town lacked an adequate school, Eder tutored Gryphius at home. In 1629 Eder married the eighteen-year-old Maria Rissmann, daughter of a prominent judge. She bore him six children, but all died or were born dead. She seems to have been drawn ever closer to Gryphius, who was only a little more than four years younger than she. It is possibly through her love of music and literature that Gryphius gained his inclination to the arts, while his erudition certainly had its roots in the teaching of Eder.

In 1631 Gryphius traveled to Görlitz, where he hoped to enter the gymnasium, but, perhaps because of the threat of nearby troop movements, he retreated to Rückersdorf, where his elder brother, Paul, was pastor. For unknown reasons he soon returned to Glogau, where another tremendous fire broke out and reduced the city to a mere sixty houses. On the heels of the fire came the plague, which claimed fifty victims a day. Gryphius fled to his brother's house, where he spent the summer immersed in Latin studies.

At this time Eder acquired the position of pastor in the Polish town of Fraustadt, and Gryphius enrolled in the school there in 1632. Fraustadt and neighboring Lissa offered a haven for Silesian Protestants driven from their homes by the Catholics, who were becoming ever more powerful. Gryphius rapidly acquired a reputation as a brilliant student, a powerful and convincing orator, and an actor, winning a competition for a principal role in a Latin drama.

In 1634 his first published work appeared: *Herodis Furiae, et Rachelis lachrymae* (Herod's Rage and Rachel's Tears), the first part of an epic on the birth and passion of Christ. The second part, *Dei Vindicis Impetus et Herodis Interitus* (The Attack of God the Avenger and the Death of Herod), was published in Danzig (today Gdansk, Poland) the following year. Part 1, begun in 1633, shows the influence of Gryphius's Latin schooling. It is almost a cento, borrowing extensively from other authors—especially Virgil, from whom whole sentences are taken. In staid yet vivid Latin hexameters it tells of the bloodbath when Herod slaughtered the innocent children at the birth of Christ. That in the year of the poem's composition the plague carried off more than eighteen thousand innocent inhabitants of Breslau (today Wrocław, Poland) may have influenced Gryphius. The work opens in hell, where the news of Christ's birth has been announced. The devils confer among themselves, and Beelzebub claims that Herod is the antithesis of the Savior. The slaughter takes place, and the piece ends with Herod and the forces of hell triumphant. A magnificent litany, the lament of Rachel over her lost children, concludes part 1.

Gryphius created in his first work a prototype that would follow him throughout his career. His favorite genre is the martyr drama, which combines the Stoic and Christian attitudes and in which the constancy of the victim is opposed to the supreme evil of the tyrant, the passive resistance of the hero to the active malevolence of the persecutor. Herod is the baroque tyrant par excellence, a personification of evil into whom hell itself has entered. If the first part of the epic shows this villain in triumph, then the second must portray his downfall. Borrowing from the Jewish historian Flavius Josephus, Gryphius gives a picture of the dying Herod, a depiction that has been characterized as the most lurid of this period. Herod lies in bed, his head dripping with pus and blood, his decaying flesh melting away from his bones, exposing his vitals, as he fondles the severed head of his murdered son, Hyrcan, whom he mocks by summoning him to take revenge for his murder by devouring his father's flowing intestines.

What is remarkable in this early work is not Gryphius's mastery of Latin—which is, however, amply demonstrated—but his use of the language to a vivid dramatic end and his portrayal of one of the most impressive baroque villains of the age. His technique has been formed. He uses the baroque antithesis as a schematic device for descriptions, portrayal, and structure. His rhetorical flow of language is evident in the litany of Rachel, and all of the baroque devices, so typical of the age, are employed with consummate skill by the sixteen-year-old poet.

In May 1634 Gryphius entered the academic high school in Danzig, a trade center that was one of the richest and most significant cities in Europe. He supported himself by tutoring. *Parnassus . . . renovatus* (Parnassus Renewed), a rather pedestrian Latin panegyric to the political scientist Georg Schönborner, whom Gryphius had probably met while visiting his brother, Paul, in Freistadt, appeared in 1636.

After a severe illness, the nature of which has not been determined, Gryphius returned to Fraustadt in 1636. On the way he apparently fell from the stagecoach and was disabled for a time; but, presumably in

August of the same year, he went on to Schönborner's estate near Freistadt, where he had been summoned as tutor to Schönborner's sons. Apparently the rich and influential Schönborner regarded Gryphius almost as an adopted son. He shared his extensive library with Gryphius and involved him in frequent discussions of political theory. On the appearance of Gryphius's *Sonnete* (Sonnets) in 1637 Schönborner, exercising his rights as Kaiserlicher Pfalzgraf (imperial count palatine), conferred on his protégé the title of master of philosophy, which implied the *venia legendi* (right to lecture at a university), and had his fourteen-year-old daughter, Elisabeth, crown the young man as poet laureate. Gryphius was undoubtedly in love with Elisabeth, and she is probably the "Eugenia" to whom he addressed several love poems. (The Greek etymology of this covert designation yields, in German, *schöngeboren* [born beautiful].) It is possible that this love affair was what motivated her father, visualizing a future match between his daughter and his favorite, to raise Gryphius to the ranks of the nobility—a distinction of which Gryphius never made use. During this period a bitter blow for the young poet was the death of his stepmother, for whom he seems to have had greater affection than for his real mother. His poem in her memory rings with sincerity.

The *Sonnete,* generally known as the *Lissaer Sonettbuch* (Lissa Sonnet Book), is a collection of thirty-one poems that includes some of Gryphius's best-known sonnets. He would revise and polish the poems through later editions; most of the changes seem to have been dictated by the new fashion of qualitative meter and by the observance of the strict prescriptive rules that had been introduced by the young poet and theoretician Martin Opitz, whose influential *Buch von der Deutschen Poeterey* (Book of German Poetry, 1624) was to become Gryphius's manual for the writing of verse throughout his life. Twenty-nine of the sonnets are repeated in succeeding editions, and there are few changes for the better. Among the best known of the poems is "Vanitas, Vanitatum . . . ," dealing with the ills of the war and the transitoriness of human existence, a favorite theme that is also evident in "Menschliches Elende" (Human Misery) and "Trawrklage des verwüsteten Deutschlandes" (Lament of Devastated Germany). There are eulogies of friends, patrons, teachers, and relatives, as well as epigrammatic castigations of probable real-life subjects. The collection demonstrates, both in language and form, the consummate skill of the poet.

Shortly after the appearance of the volume fire destroyed virtually the entire city of Freistadt. Gryphius commemorated the event in a long poem, *Fewrige Freystadt* (Fiery Freistadt), which appeared as a pamphlet in 1637. In the same year his patron, yielding to a short illness, died in his arms. Gryphius wrote a moving funeral sermon, the *Brunnen Discurs* (Discourse at the Fountain), which was published the following year.

Accompanied by Schönborner's two sons, Gryphius went to Leiden to study law. The University of Leiden was one of the most illustrious in Europe: René Descartes was lecturing in philosophy, as was Justus Lipsius, who was renowned also for his studies in classical philology. Gryphius struck up a close acquaintance with the humanists Daniel Heinsius and Claudius Salmasius (Claude de Saumaise) and associated with his countryman Christian Hoffmann von Hoffmannswaldau, one of the celebrated poets of the century, a lifelong friend whom he had first met in Danzig. He also came into contact with various members of the ruling house of the Palatinate, a connection that was to stand him in good stead in the future. His acquaintance with the works of the leading Dutch dramatists, Joost von den Vondel, Pieter Hooft, and Gerbrand Bredero, was to be important for his later dramatic production. Gryphius's studies ranged from law, through philosophy, rhetoric, and medicine, to mathematics, while the lectures he gave, possibly as private tutorials, cover the fields of astronomy, geography, metaphysics, physiognomy, trigonometry, and even chiromancy. But he also experienced an illness so severe that the doctors gave him up for lost.

In 1639 Gryphius published *Son- undt Freyrtags-Sonnete* (Sonnets for Sundays and Holidays), a collection of one hundred sonnets: one or more for each Sunday of the church year—sixty-five in all—and one for each of the thirty-five church holidays. This second sizable collection of poems, although highly rhetorical in style, demonstrates the skill and facility Gryphius had acquired in the writing of verse. Bound by the rigid sonnet form and restricted to the religious themes of the pericopes, the poems nonetheless flow freely and show little or no sign of constraint.

In 1643 the earlier sonnet book, thoroughly revised and increased by nineteen sonnets, was republished; two of the former sonnets were omitted. Some of the revisions show a distinct improvement, while other poems are polished at the expense of their freshness. Gryphius contributed to the development of the ode by employing the Pindaric form for religious purposes; previously it had been almost exclusively used for encomiums. A collection of one hundred German epigrams and one of sixty-eight Latin epigrams also appeared in 1643. The epigrams are undoubtedly the most inferior of all Gryphius's verses. The petty and often vindictive use to which they are put gives evidence of a spitefulness that was all too common in the age.

During Gryphius's stay in Leiden the Netherlands' greatest dramatist, Vondel, wrote *De Gebroeders* (The Brothers); it premiered in 1641. Gryphius translated the work into German as *Die sieben Brüder, oder Die Gibeoniter* (The Seven Brothers; or, The Gibeonites). He probably did so toward the end of his stay in Leiden, for his mastery of Dutch is quite impressive; but, like many of Gryphius's works, the translation was not published until many years later—in this case, in a posthumous edition of 1698. Gryphius may well have been present at the premiere of Vondel's play, for he adds stage directions that seem to have been derived from an actual production. The source of the play is the biblical account in 2 Sam. 21: 1–14 of David's revenge on Saul's children for Saul's treatment of the Gibeonites. Gryphius has tried to remain as close to the Dutch original as possible, and there are many examples of a too-literal rendition. There are also, however, instances where he has added descriptive adjectives or expanded the sentence structure; a prologue and an epilogue have also been added. (Christian Gryphius, the poet's son, mentioned that his father had, at some unspecified date, completed an original drama, *Die Gibeoniter,* as far as the fifth act.)

Two more translations may have been completed in Leiden, although they were both published much later. In 1634 Gryphius acquired a collection of Latin dramas by the Jesuit Nicolaus Caussinus, father confessor to Louis XII. In this collection is the story of the martyr Saint Felicity, a tale filled with the most grisly descriptions of tortures and dismemberment, a reflection of which would later appear in Gryphius's *Catharina von Georgien. Oder Bewehrte Beständigkeit* (Catharine of Georgia; or, Constancy Maintained, 1657). The poet translated the drama from Latin under the title *Beständige Mutter, oder Die Heilige Felicitas* (The Constant Mother; or, Saint Felicity). Scholars differ greatly in assigning a date to this composition; in any case, it did not appear until 1657, and it was produced by students eight times in the following year in Breslau. While Gryphius's translation of Vondel's work was faithful to the original, this translation strays far enough from its source to be termed a re-creation. There is not really an alteration in substance, but there is certainly a change of emphasis and a stylization. The rather cool and staid humanist Latin yields to the exaggerated, dynamic style of the German baroque.

The other translation is of the Italian comedy *La Balia* (The Nursemaid), by the Florentine Renaissance writer Girolamo Razzi. Although the translation would appear only in the collected edition of 1663, Gryphius mentions that he had begun it in his early youth. *Seugamme oder Untreues Hausgesinde* (The Wet Nurse; or, Unfaithful Servants) is a completely faithful translation into German prose. The plot is complex, including a supposed incest that turns out to be a spoof. The many devices of the commedia dell'arte are all present, culminating in a happy ending consisting of a series of marriages. Gryphius prefixes the translation with a stodgy prologue in which he claims that the immorality of the times reminded him of this *comédie des mœurs,* but this statement seems to be an attempt to justify translating a work containing such libertinage rather than an explanation of his motivation for doing so. The play affords convincing evidence that Gryphius, in addition to French, Dutch, and Latin, was also adept in Italian.

The poet remained in Leiden until June 1644, when he departed for the tour of France and Italy that was part of the education of all well-brought-up young noblemen of the day. As to the source of his finances for the journey, one may assume that he was a paid traveling companion to Wilhelm Schlegel, son of a well-to-do Pomeranian merchant, and four young noblemen who had become his friends as well as his charges. Details of his trip are sparse. He was in Paris in July, where he visited the legal authority Hugo Grotius and where he was particularly interested in the extensive library of the late Cardinal Richelieu. From Paris he traveled via Angers to Marseilles and then to Florence, where he viewed the art collection of the grand duke; in 1646 he arrived in Rome, where he met the well-known Jesuit writer and scholar Athanasius Kircher. He probably came into closer contact with the commedia dell'arte and the Italian opera, evidence of both of which is to be found in his works.

His return led through Florence, Bologna, and Ferrara to Venice, where he presented his second Latin epic, *Olivetum* (The Mount of Olives, 1646), to the republic of Venice. The first edition was printed in Florence; a second, slightly revised, followed in 1648. It, too, was dedicated to Venice but also to the prince elector of Brandenburg, Friedrich Wilhelm, and to his cousin the Countess Palatine Elisabeth, daughter of the Winter King. There is doubt about the date of its composition, but the earliest date that has been suggested, 1637, is almost certainly incorrect.

While still dependent on classical style, *Olivetum* shows considerable differences from the earlier Herod epic. If Gryphius painted a prototypical villain in Herod, here he creates Herod's opposite in the prototypical martyr figure of Christ. No longer the biblical passive sufferer, Gryphius's Christ is a baroque hero, beset by all possible goads to a betrayal of his mission. Hunger, thirst, sickness, care, even desire and lust assail him until the Angel of Divine Love rescues him from his temptations. Abstractions are personified; Treachery and Greed speak to Judas; Peter becomes a larger-than-life braggart as he boasts of his loyalty to his master. On the cross Jesus assumes the form of a favorite image of the baroque age, a *Wundchristus* (wounded Christ) covered with blood, sweat, and wounds oozing

pus, as he faces the hour of his Passion. Some of Gryphius's most powerful poetic effects are evident in these graphic descriptions.

How long Gryphius remained in Italy is not known. On his return through Germany he took up residence in Strasbourg, where he was in contact with some of the most celebrated scholars at the university. There, too, he completed his first and, in the opinion of many, his best drama, *Leo Armenius, oder Fürsten-Mord* (Leo Arminius; or, Regicide). He left the manuscript for this play, along with expanded versions of his other youthful works (with the exception of the Latin epics), in the hands of a Strasbourg publisher, who, because of financial difficulties, did not produce the edition. The works came into the hands of a Frankfurt publisher, Johann Hüttner, who published them in 1650, without Gryphius's knowledge, along with works of other poets as *Teutsche Reim-Gedichte* (German Rhymed Poems).

Gryphius's tragedies differ vastly from the modern concept of the drama and, hence, are often criticized on the basis of false criteria. Derivative from Seneca but immediately dependent on the Dutch theater, they reflect a Stoic attitude within a Christian framework. There is no real concept of the dramatic, of creating suspense, or even of tragic guilt. The Christian parameter permits only martyrdom or the violation of God's social, political, or religious order as causes of tragedy, and the Christian virtue of constancy coupled with Stoic acceptance of the world are the heroic qualities most highly valued. Historical events may be interpreted but not altered in a substantive way. Thus, the dramatist's only chore is to present the facts about his subject in a manner worthy of that subject. Since tragedy is limited to the higher social order, members of the royalty or the high nobility are featured as both heroes and villains, and the language and style must be of an elevated nature, rhetorical, and replete with gnomic sentiments. There is often little action—in fact, much of the action takes place between the acts—while the dialogue consists of long monologues, sometimes merely relating the historical background or delineating the state of mind of the character, but always composed of noble—or, equally, ignoble—sentiments that can be quoted out of context. Gryphius borrowed from Dutch drama the concept of the *Reyen,* a combination of the classical chorus with a moralizing summation of the events depicted. These *Reyen,* which usually appear after each act, may be in the form of a recitative chorus or a short sketch.

The impetus for *Leo Armenius* may well have come from the work of a Jesuit author, Joseph Simon, who treated the same material in his drama *Leo Armenus seu Impietas punita* (Leo Armenus; or, Impiety Punished); the play had been performed in Rome during the spring of

1646, a time when Gryphius was probably in the city. It is the story of a Byzantine emperor who, having acquired the rule from the former emperor by an army coup, was deposed and assassinated by his general, Michael Balbus; the original source was the account by the Byzantine historians Johannes Zonaras and Georgios Cedrenus. By a daring analogy of the emperor Leo to Christ, Gryphius provides powerful support for the divine right of kings, or at least of those kings who acquired their power lawfully. Gryphius's patron, Schönborner, had taught that tyrants who came to their rule by lawful means could be deposed or resisted only by such means, whereas those who had usurped the power could be removed by force. In Gryphius's play the former emperor is represented as having abdicated the throne on hearing that Leo had been chosen by the army to assume the imperial power; thus, Leo could be considered the rightful emperor. Gryphius sets the play on Christmas Eve and calls attention to the symbolism of Leo, the lion, as an icon of Christ; moreover, he has Leo murdered before the high altar while clinging to the true cross. Running somewhat athwart this analogy is the justification for Leo's actions: the pretender, Michael Balbus, has been taken prisoner and condemned to death. But in view of the holy festival, Leo's wife begs Leo to postpone the execution. Leo yields to sentiment, which he places before his duty as emperor, thus violating his role as governing power ordained by God: the ruler is the sword of God, destined to carry out the execution as part of the divine order. The postponement gives Michael Balbus the opportunity to escape from prison and organize a conspiracy that results in Leo's death. It is suggested that Leo's wife is merely the tool of the priests, thus injecting into the play the concept of the church as a political power—perhaps a blow of the Protestant Gryphius against the Roman Catholic Church, whose power he had felt, and was to feel again, in his native Silesia.

In spite of the highly rhetorical style and long declamatory passages the play is successful as a drama and closely corresponds to the modern notion of high tragedy. The striking scene in the church, which occurs offstage but is vividly reported; a soothsayer, with his eerie magic charms, who is consulted by the conspirators and who delivers an ambiguous prediction; and the final scene, in which Leo's wife (reminiscent of Ophelia in William Shakespeare's *Hamlet* [circa 1600–1601]) delivers a declamation of fantasy that may be either insanity or prophetic clairvoyance—all make for good drama in the modern sense. The message of the work is clearly expressed in the prophecy of the soothsayer that Michael Balbus will possess what the emperor now possesses—that is, his crown—and the certainty of his forthcoming death: the emperor is dead; long live the

emperor, who will also die. History is a circle: the good fortune of today turns to death on the morrow, but the successor will suffer the same fate; the glories of this world are transient. These are baroque clichés, but Gryphius illustrates them most effectively.

Gryphius departed Strasbourg in May 1647 for Leiden, whence he returned via ship to the North German port of Stettin, arriving in his home country on 25 July after an absence of nine years. In Stettin he stayed at the home of his friend and traveling companion Schlegel and worked on his second drama, *Catharina von Georgien,* which he probably completed before his departure in November for Frauenstadt. It did not appear in print until 1657.

Catharina von Georgien has its origin in an event that transpired during Gryphius's lifetime. In 1624 the queen of Armenian Georgia was killed by the shah of Persia after being held prisoner for several years. Gryphius was so impressed with her unwavering constancy that he composed this "martyr drama" to narrate the last day of her life. Gryphius depicts the shah as madly in love with Catharina and determined to make her his wife. He swears that she will be "free" by the evening either by becoming his wife and espousing his religion or by suffering torture and death. She rejoices at this opportunity of gaining immortal life via martyrdom. Her tortures are described in gruesome detail, and in the final scenes her severed head is brought in to be kissed by the Russian emissary who had been sent to procure her release. The shah, meanwhile, is tortured by remorse and by the prophecy that he will have to live through war and disgrace, a hell on earth, whereas she will go to her eternal reward.

The play, aside from the sensationalism of the tortures reported and the ghastly spectacle of the severed head, is a tedious recitation of historic events rather than a representation of any semblance of dramatic action. Act 3 opens on a long monologue, more than three hundred lines of alexandrine verse that provide all the details of the historical background—most of which are already known from an equally tedious recitation in the first act. As a martyr drama, the play's weakness lies in the fact that Catharina really has no choice: she cannot give in to the shah, for she would thereby become an object of scorn in the eyes of her son and her people and yet would gain nothing thereby; the shah could give her nothing that she does not have already, and she realizes that she would, at best, become just another of his concubines. And the betrayal of her religion, her country, and the memory of her husband, who had been killed by the Persians, would be unthinkable. But by the death sentence, she gains eternal life. Martyrdom is only conferred by free choice, and in Catharina's case there is no alternative to her decision.

Gryphius arrived in Fraustadt to find his stepfather, Eder, in bad health and worse financial condition. But the poet's fame and influential connections were widespread by this time. He received calls to the University of Frankfurt an der Oder and the University of Heidelberg as professor of mathematics; the Swedish ambassador to Holland had promised him a professorship at the University of Uppsala, as well. He refused all of these positions, probably because he already had the prospect of becoming Syndikus (syndic)–roughly, the legal adviser and juristic representative of the landed nobility–in Glogau. As such, he would be the legal go-between for Silesian Protestants and imperial Catholics, a position demanding diplomacy and tact.

A year and a week after his return to Silesia he became engaged to Rosine Deutschländer, the daughter of a well-to-do merchant in Fraustadt. He married her in January 1649. They would have seven children, four of whom would die young. A son would live to the age of twenty-four, and a precocious daughter would fall prey to a strange malady that would rob her of speech and understanding. The eldest son, Christian, would become a poet and the editor of a posthumous edition of his father's works.

After his return to Germany, Gryphius had another period of productivity. His drama *Cardenio und Celinde* (1657) was written at this time, as well as his tragedy about the recently executed English king, *Ermordete Majestät. Oder Carolus Stuardus König von Großbrittannien* (Murdered Majesty; or, Charles Stuart, King of Great Britain, 1657). He probably also completed in these few years two comedies, *Absurda Comica, Oder Herr Peter Squentz* (Absurd Comedy; or, Mr. Peter Squentz, 1658) and *Horribilicribrifax* (The Horrible Sieve-maker, 1663).

The impetus to the composition of *Cardenio und Celinde* had come during Gryphius's stay in Amsterdam, on his way back to Germany, in the summer of 1647: a nocturnal walk with friends through a graveyard inspired him to tell a ghost story that he claimed to have heard in Italy as a true occurrence, and his narration made such an impression on his friends that they demanded that he commit it to written form just as he had related it. A few years later he acceded to their request but converted the material into a "tragedy"– even though the participants, as he notes, are too low in social status for so exalted an art form and the language is scarcely more elevated than that of real life. Actually, it is not a tragedy but a ghost story recast in declamatory form. The source was a *novela* from a 1624 Spanish collection by Juan Pérez de Montalbán. A young Spanish nobleman studying at the University of Bologna falls in love with the beautiful Olympia, who returns his love. His fiery temperament, which leads him into fre-

quent swordplay, robs him of his love, who becomes betrothed to the opportunistic Lysander. Out of despair Cardenio takes up with a "kept woman," Celinde, murders her lover, and plots to kill his rival. But finally God's order is realized: Olympia and Lysander are married, while the title figures retire to an improbable cloistered life. Most of the action takes place before the play begins; only the murder plot, which never materializes, is depicted onstage. And the ending, in which the unworthy Lysander gains the hand of Olympia, a less than ideal heroine, is decidedly unsatisfactory. A macabre scene in which Celinde, at the behest of a sorceress, attempts to cut out the heart of her dead lover, who is partially decayed in the grave, and another in which Cardenio, about to embrace Olympia, sees her turn into a skeleton pointing a deadly arrow at his heart, impart a ghostly atmosphere to the play. The poet's attempt to remain faithful to his source was no doubt responsible for at least some of the work's defects.

The beheading of Charles I of England in 1649 was an event of world-shaking proportions in the absolutist Hapsburg empire–especially for Gryphius, who had been schooled by his mentor, Schönborner, in the divine right of kings. He must have set to work immediately on hearing the news, for *Ermordete Majestät* was certainly finished in 1650. For unknown reasons he withheld it from publication, complaining in 1652 that the work, which he had wanted to keep to himself, had somehow come into the hands even of royalty. Only in 1657, in his collected works, did he release the drama, but he revised it drastically for the next edition of the collected works in 1663. It is not clear whether this revision was a result of additional information that reached him in the interim, or whether artistic considerations were the motivating forces.

The earlier version is a somewhat tedious recitation of the facts as Gryphius knew them. Charles is ready to die and is presented as a true martyr, for he rejects willingly all attempts to rescue him. Oliver Cromwell, on the other hand, is weak and wavering, whereas Gen. Thomas Fairfax is depicted as a staunch defender of the king. There is a hint of a conspiracy to save the king, but it comes to nothing. Religion, personified, appears in a chorus to bemoan the crimes committed in her name. After many declarations of the sad state of affairs, Charles is executed onstage while a chorus of the spirits of murdered English kings calls out for revenge. The ponderous mass of continuous recitation gives a sermonlike quality to the piece.

In the second version a plot to save the king, directed by Fairfax's wife, produces some dramatic interest. There is an entirely new first act, and the former second and third acts are combined. Fairfax is transformed into a weak, vacillating personality, while

Cromwell becomes the staunch opponent, and this change is accomplished simply by exchanging their lines. The plot to save the king is somewhat reminiscent of *Leo Armenius,* in that the wife is the power behind the machinations. A new character, the mad regicide Poleh, is introduced. The new version has led some to believe that Gryphius was presenting Charles as an analogue to Christ, Fairfax to Pontius Pilate, and Poleh to Judas. The drama can be read as overt political support for divine right, in spite of the opposition in Silesia to Hapsburg Catholicism.

In *Absurda Comica* Peter Squentz is Peter Quince, from the play-within-the-play of Shakespeare's *A Midsummer Night's Dream* (circa 1595–1596), although it is fairly certain that Gryphius did not know Shakespeare's work. The original was probably a farce by Daniel Schwenter, a professor at the University of Altdorf, to whom Gryphius accords the credit, although Schwenter's play, if it existed, is lost. This circumstance has led to controversy concerning the real authorship of the piece, but the extant version is certainly the work of, or a drastic reworking by, Gryphius. Using the spectacle of ignorant village artisans producing Ovid's *Pyramus and Thisbe,* Gryphius satirizes the traditional productions of such popular comedies as those of Hans Sachs. The refined noble audience is duly amused at the slapstick production. The work has remained the most popular comedy of the German baroque and has been frequently produced.

The title character of *Horribilicribrifax* is so called for his propensity of making his opponents look like sieves when he duels with them. It is not surprising that Gryphius should take up the theme of the braggart soldier back from the wars, for Germany must have been full of them. The ultimate source was the *Miles Gloriosus* of Plautus, but the theme was not new to Germany. Around 1594 Heinrich Julius, Duke of Brunswick, had produced a typical example in *Vincentius Ladislaus,* but Gryphius was undoubtedly more directly influenced by the figure of Capitano Spavento of the commedia dell'arte. He doubles the figure of the braggart by presenting a foil to him in the person of Daradiridatumtarides, differentiating between them only by having the one lard his language with Italian, the other with French phrases, both distorted and mispronounced. An extremely complicated plot involves such other stock figures as the schoolmaster who constantly cites Latin and Greek phrases and an old crone whose linguistic stock-in-trade is folkloristic phrases and popular nonsense. In fact, the main source of the humor is a continual give-and-take dependent on characters misunderstanding one another's learned or foreign phrases. A series of marriages ties up the strands of the various subplots. There are strong indications that the play never reached its final form, for it is full of contradictions, including variant forms of the names of some of the characters. It consists of five acts and was included in the collected works in 1663.

In 1650 appeared the collection of Gryphius's works that he had left in Strasbourg but that had been handed over to Hüttner in Frankfurt am Main. In the same year he assumed his office as syndic for the Glogau estates. Not much is known of the final years of his life. In 1653 he published a collection of legal papers, *Glogauisches Fürstenthumbs Landes Privilegia aus den Originalen* (The Rights and Privileges of the Landed Aristocracy in the Principality of Glogau, from the Original Version). They are in Latin, German, and Czech. Also in 1653 he wrote *Majuma, Freuden-Spiel,* a mini-operetta to which the music has been lost. It was in honor of the coronation of Ferdinand IV as king and was probably produced in June of that year. It uses a rather hackneyed mythological setting to encomiastic ends. The most that can be said of it is that it is typical of such frilly occasional pieces.

Fleeing from a new onslaught of the plague, Gryphius and his family took refuge at the estate of his former patron, Schönborner. The first part of his collected works appeared in 1657; it was completed in 1658 by an edition that was identical except for the title page and the inclusion of *Absurda Comica.* In the 1657 edition appears a short rumination on death and the vanities of human existence, "Kirchhoffs-Gedancken" (Cemetery Thoughts), which contains some of the most drastic and macabre descriptions of decaying corpses to be found in Gryphius's writings. A small collection of translated Latin hymns and a tripartite cantata also appeared in 1657. Possibly around this time was conceived "Weicher-Stein" (Smooth Stone–the name of a rock formation), in which Gryphius and his friends J. C. von Gersdorff and J. C. von Schönborner, the son of his patron, each contributed a commemoration of an afternoon picnic's entertainment; it would be included in his *Epigrammata oder Bey-Schriften* (Epigrams; or, Annotations, 1663).

The greatest event of the 1650s for Gryphius was undoubtedly the composition of his tragedy *Großmüttiger Rechts-Gelehrter, oder Sterbender Aemilius Paulus Papinianus* (The Courageous Jurist; or, The Death of Paulus Papinianus, 1659). Written between 1657 and 1659, it tells in compressed form the story of the emperor Caracalla, who murders his half brother Geta, then attempts to gain legal justification of the murder via the testimony of the great legal scholar Paulus Papinianus. The latter refuses to compromise his principles and chooses death for himself and his family rather than accede to the wishes of the emperor. The play is, in the opinion of some, a secularized martyr drama in which morality rather than religion motivates the choice of death. But Gryphius seems to have fused a Lutheran attitude with a Stoic morality, both of which he presents within the framework of the martyr. A problem is that, by deliberately going to his death, Papinianus deprives the corrupt empire of his staunch, righteous voice. There are several subplots, such as the possible revenge of the empress Julia for the murder of her son, and the evil plans of the counselor Laetus, who has cast his envious eye on the imperial throne. Papinianus is offered several ways out of his dilemma—joining the empress to seize the throne, or taking over the military in a coup d'etat, or simply acquiescing passively in the emperor's request to condone the murder. Since the sixteenth century this case had been a quandary for legal thinkers, an object lesson of the end justifying the means. As a stage production, its lurid horrors surpass even those of *Catharina von Georgien:* the heart is torn from the living body of Laetus and trodden underfoot by the raging empress; Papinianus holds up the severed head of his son; on his own beheading, his wife kisses the hands and head of her husband and of her son before collapsing on the truncated corpse of her husband.

The work is generally recognized as the most mature of Gryphius's dramas. The language as well as the actions of the personalities are not so tightly contained within a rhetorical straitjacket as in his earlier plays. And the philosophical problem may well reflect Gryphius's own situation as syndic, representing the Protestant estates yet owing at least passive obedience to the Catholic emperor. Judging from its reception, it was also the most popular of Gryphius's tragedies: in 1660 it was produced seven times on the stage of the Elisabeth Gymnasium in Breslau.

Gryphius had become a well-known and respected figure, not only in the political sphere as an important functionary of the estates and in literary circles as a poet and dramatist of the greatest fame, but also as a man of erudition in the most widely divergent areas. In 1658 the city of Breslau came into the possession of three Egyptian mummies, two of them well preserved and one fragmented. Gryphius was called on to take part in their dissection. In 1662 he published a detailed description of the dissection under the title *Mumiae Wratislavienses* (Breslau Mummies).

In 1660 Gryphius wrote a *Lust-und Gesangspiel* (comic operetta) titled *Piastus,* concerning the dynastic origin of the dukes of Brieg, Liegnitz, and Wohlau. The occasion was probably the pregnancy of Duchess Luise, wife of Duke Christian of Wohlau, who was hoping to produce an heir to the line of Silesian Piast rulers, the last descendants of the first Polish royal dynasty; the duchies would fall prey to Bohemia if a male heir were not born. (The son, Georg Wilhelm, would die at

fifteen, ending the line.) It is an active little piece, featuring fireworks, a wild Tartar dance, a comic interchange, and a final dance to which provisions for an additional ballet are appended. It was only published in the posthumous edition of 1698.

An occasional piece, written for the marriage celebration of Duke Georg III of Liegnitz and Brieg and the Countess Palatine, Elisabeth Maria Charlotte, was perhaps Gryphius's most accomplished comedy, which has been considered worthy even of a Gotthold Ephraim Lessing: the double playlet *Verlibtes Gespenste, Gesang-Spiel* (The Amorous Ghost: Operetta) and *Die gelibte Dornrose, Schertz-Spill* (Beloved Dornrose: Farce). The first edition appeared in 1660 and included only *Verlibtes Gespenste;* in 1661 both playlets were published together. The operetta, while in no sense a translation or even a reworking, nonetheless shows the influence of the French writer Philippe Quinault's *Le Fantôme amoureux* (The Amorous Ghost, 1658). Gryphius's playlets are interwoven, the acts alternating between the works, a traditional technique perhaps originating in the necessity to provide time for changes of scenery and costume. While there is no attempt at contrived parallelism, the juxtaposition of the individual acts, as well as that of the two plays as a whole, creates a skillful mirror image. The operetta presents a kind of daisy-chain series of love affairs, with each character loving someone who loves someone else. The title is derived from a climactic scene in which the principal lover, playing dead, is conjured "back to life" by the tears of his beloved. The language is that of the alexandrine line in elevated discourse; the framework is classical mythology interspersed with Christian references; and the personnel are of a high social order. On the other hand, *Die gelibte Dornrose* is in many ways a parody of the operetta. The poetic line has yielded to prose, the elevated speech becomes dialect, and the aristocracy has changed places with the peasantry. Within this framework there is a Romeo-and-Juliet plot, with the lovers separated by the feuding of their guardians. Only when the heroine's lover saves her from being raped by a crude bumpkin is the way paved for a happy ending. Both plays are graceful and light. Either could stand on its own as an individual work, but the combination of the two is a mark of genius.

The play *Der Schwermende Schäfer Lysis* (The Rapturous Shepherd Lysis, 1661) is a translation of *Le Berger extravagant* (The Extravagant Shepherd, 1639), by Thomas Corneille, who in his day shared at least equal fame with his brother Pierre. It was a commissioned occasional piece for the first birthday of the last duke of the Piast dynasty, Georg Wilhelm. Gryphius adheres closely to the original text but moves the locale to his homeland. Originally intended as a satire of the pastoral mode, the French original is sufficiently exaggerated to make it difficult to differentiate between intended satire and "normal" affectation.

It was part of the devotional exercises of many poets during the seventeenth century to compose works of meditation from a religious standpoint. In 1663 Gryphius translated, probably from a Dutch translation of the original English, a large collection of the religious writings of Sir Richard Baker. In 1665 he reworked *Himmel steigente HertzensSeüfftzer* (Sighs from the Heart Ascending to Heaven, 1626), by the theologian Josua Stegmann. Throughout his life Gryphius was invited or commissioned to write and deliver funeral orations on the deaths of prominent patrons or acquaintances. These works were published as individual editions and collected as *Dissertationes Funebres, oder Leich-Abdanckungen* (Funeral Dissertations; or, Funeral Orations, 1666). Typically an allegorical theme is developed via emblematic iconography, and many of the images are also to be found in Gryphius's dramas. Recent scholarship has established the importance of these lugubrious works for the development of his prose style and for the understanding of his imagery.

In 1662, in a somewhat belated recognition of his stature as a writer, Gryphius was accepted into the most celebrated literary society in Germany, the Fruchtbringende Gesellschaft (Fruit-bringing Society). The sobriquet accorded to him, after the practice of the society, attests to the respect in which he was held: he was called "der Unsterbliche" (the Immortal). He is, indeed, one of the few baroque poets whose fame persisted through the succeeding eras of literary criticism. On 16 July 1664, while attending a session of the landed estates in his capacity as syndic, he suffered a fatal heart attack. He is remembered as Germany's greatest poet of the seventeenth century.

Bibliographies:

Victor Manheimer, *Die Lyrik des Andreas Gryphius: Studien und Materialien* (Berlin: Weidmann, 1904);

M. Johannes Theodor Leubscher, "Andreas Gryphius," *Text + Kritik,* 7/8 (March 1980): 112–128;

Gerhard Dünnhaupt, *Personalbibliographien zu den Drucken des Barock,* volume 3 (Stuttgart: Hiersemann, 1991), pp. 1855–1883.

Biographies:

Marian Szyrocki, *Der junge Gryphius,* Neue Beiträge zur Literaturwissenschaft, volume 9 (Berlin: Rütten & Loening, 1959);

Szyrocki, *Andreas Gryphius: Sein Leben und Werk* (Tübingen: Niemeyer, 1964);

Baltzer Siegmund von Stosch, "Danck-und Denck-Seule des Andreae Gryphii (1665)," *Text + Kritik,* 7/8 (March 1980): 2–11;

Christian Stieff, "Andreae Gryphii Lebens-Lauf," *Text + Kritik,* 7/8 (March 1980): 24–31;

Conrad Wiedemann, "Andreas Gryphius," in *Deutsche Dichter des 17. Jahrhunderts: Ihr Leben und Werk,* edited by Harald Steinhagen and Benno von Wiese (Berlin: Erich Schmidt, 1984), pp. 435–472;

Eberhard Mannack, *Andreas Gryphius,* Sammlung Metzler, volume 76 (Stuttgart: Metzler, 1986).

References:

Judith P. Aikin, "The Audience within the Play: Clues to Intended Audience Reaction in German Baroque Tragedies and Comedies," *Daphnis,* 13, no. 1–2 (1984): 187–201;

Aikin, "The Comedies of Andreas Gryphius and the Two Traditions of European Comedy," *Germanic Review,* 63 (Summer 1988): 114–120;

J. R. Alexander, "A Possible Historical Source for the Figure of Poleh in Andreas Gryphius's *Carolus Stuardus,*" *Daphnis,* 3, no. 2 (1974): 203–207;

Günter Berghaus, *Die Quellen zu Andreas Gryphius' Trauerspiel "Carolus Stuardus": Studien zur Entstehung eines historisch-politischen Märtyrerdramas der Barockzeit,* Studien zur deutschen Literatur, no. 79 (Tübingen: Niemeyer, 1983);

Werner Eggers, *Wirklichkeit und Wahrheit im Trauerspiel von Andreas Gryphius,* Probleme der Dichtung, volume 9 (Heidelberg: Winter, 1967);

Willi Flemming, *Andreas Gryphius: Eine Monographie* (Stuttgart: Kohlhammer, 1965);

Flemming, *Andreas Gryphius und die Bühne* (Halle: Niemeyer, 1921);

Gerhard Fricke, *Die Bildlichkeit in der Dichtung des Andreas Gryphius: Materialien und Studien zum Formproblem des deutschen Literaturbarock* (Darmstadt: Wissenschaftlich Buchgesellschaft, 1967);

Maria Fürstenwald, *Andreas Gryphius. Dissertationes Funebres: Studien zur Didaktik der Leichabdankungen,* Abhandlungen zur Kunst-, Musik-und Literaturwissenschaft, volume 46 (Bonn: Bouvier, 1967);

Herbert Heckmann, *Elemente des barocken Trauerspiels: Am Beispiel des "Papinian" von Andreas Gryphius* (Darmstadt: Gentner, 1959);

Gerd Hillen, *Andreas Gryphius: Cardenio und Celinde,* De Proprietatibus litterarum: Series Practica, no. 45 (The Hague: Mouton, 1971);

Dietrich Walter Jöns, *Das "Sinnen-Bild": Studien zur allegorischen Bildlichkeit bei Andreas Gryphius* (Stuttgart: Metzler, 1966);

Gerhard Kaiser, ed., *Die Dramen des Andreas Gryphius: Eine Sammlung von Einzelinterpretationen* (Stuttgart: Metzler, 1968);

Hans-Henrik Krummacher, "Andreas Gryphius und Johann Arndt: Zum Verständnis der 'Sonn-und Feiertagssonette,'" in *Formenwandel: Festschrift für Paul Böckmann* (Hamburg, 1964);

Krummacher, *Der junge Gryphius und die Tradition: Studien zu den Perikopensonetten und Passionsliedern* (Munich: Fink, 1976);

W. Kühlmann, "Der Fall Papinian: Ein Konfliktmodell absolutistischer Politik im akademischen Schrifttum des 16. und 17. Jhs.," *Daphnis,* 11, no. 1–2 (1982): 223–252;

Henri Plard, "Gryphiana," *Text + Kritik,* 7/8 (February 1965): 37–53;

Plard, "Gryphius und noch immer kein Ende," *Etudes germaniques* (January–March 1973): 61–85; (April–June 1973): 185–204;

Plard, "De Heiligheid van de Koninklijke Macht in de Tragedie van Andreas Gryphius," *Tijdschrift van de Vrije Universiteit van Brussel,* 2 (1960): 202–229;

Plard, "Sur la jeunesse d'Andreas Gryphius," *Etudes germaniques* (January–March 1962): 34–40;

Hugh Powell, "Andreas Gryphius and the 'New Philosophy,'" *German Life and Letters,* new series 5 (July 1952): 275–278;

Powell, "Observations on the Erudition of Andreas Gryphius," *Orbis Litterarum,* 25, no. 1–2 (1970): 115–125;

Powell, "Probleme der Gryphius-Forschung," *Germanisch-romanische Monatschrift,* new series 7 (1957): 328–343;

Sibylle Rusterholz, *Rostra, Sarg und Predigtstuhl: Studien zur Form und Funktion der Totenrede bei Andreas Gryphius,* Studien zur Germanistik, Anglistik und Komparatistik, no. 16 (Bonn: Bouvier, 1974);

Marvin S. Schindler, *The Sonnets of Andreas Gryphius: Use of the Poetic Word in the Seventeenth Century* (Gainesville: University of Florida Press, 1971);

Hans-Jürgen Schings, *Die patristische und stoische Tradition bei Andreas Gryphius: Untersuchungen zu den Dissertationes funebres und Trauerspielen* (Cologne: Böhlau, 1966);

Albrecht Schöne, *Emblematik und Drama im Zeitalter des Barock* (Munich: Beck, 1964);

Blake Lee Spahr, "Gryphius and the Holy Ghost," "Cardenio und Celinde," "Herod and Christ:

Gryphius' Latin Epics," in his *Problems and Perspectives: A Collection of Essays on German Baroque Literature* (Frankfurt am Main: Peter Lang, 1981), pp. 111–122, 131–150, 151–159;

Janifer Gerl Stackhouse, *The Constructive Art of Gryphius' Historical Tragedies,* Berner Beiträge zur Barockgermanistik, no. 6 (Bern: Peter Lang, 1986);

Stackhouse, "The Mysterious Regicide in Gryphius' Stuart Drama: Who is Poleh?," *Modern Language Notes,* 89 (1974): 797–811;

Harald Steinhagen, *Wirklichkeit und Handeln im barocken Drama: Historisch-ästhetische Studien zum Trauerspiel des Andreas Gryphius,* Studien zur deutschen Literatur, no. 51 (Tübingen: Niemeyer, 1977);

Adolf Strutz, *Andreas Gryphius: Die Weltanschauung eines deutschen Barockdichters,* Wege zur Dichtung, 11 (Zurich: Münster-Presse, 1931);

Elida Maria Szarota, *Geschichte, Politik und Gesellschaft im Drama des 17. Jahrhunderts* (Bern: Francke, 1976);

Szarota, *Künstler, Grübler und Rebellen: Studien zum europäischen Märtyrerdrama des 17. Jahrhunderts* (Bern: Francke, 1967);

Erich Trunz, "Andreas Gryphius: Über die Geburt Jesu," "Tränen des Vaterlandes," "Es ist alles eitel," in *Die deutsche Lyrik: Form und Geschichte,* edited by Benno von Wiese (Düsseldorf: Bagel, 1957), pp. 139–151;

Wilhelm Vosskamp, *Untersuchungen zur Zeit- und Geschichts-auffassung im 17. Jahrhundert bei Gryphius und Lohenstein,* Literatur und Wirklichkeit, no. 1 (Bonn: Bouvier, 1967);

Mara R. Wade, *The German Baroque Pastoral "Singspiel,"* Berner Beiträge zur Barockgermanistik, no. 7 (Bern: Peter Lang, 1990);

F. Meyer von Waldeck, "Der Peter Squenz von Andreas Gryphius, eine Verspottung von Hans Sachs," *Vierteljahrsschrift für Litteraturgeschichte,* 1 (1888): 195–212;

Friedrich-Wilhelm Wentzlaff-Eggebert, *Dichtung und Sprache des jungen Gryphius* (Berlin: De Gruyter, 1966);

Günther Weydt, "Sonettkunst des Barocks: Zum Problem der Umarbeitung bei Andreas Gryphius," *Jahrbuch der deutschen Schillergesellschaft,* 9 (1965): 1–32;

Louis G. Wysocki, *Andreas Gryphius et la tragédie allemande aux xviie siècle* (Paris: Bouillon, 1893).

Hartmann von Aue

(circa 1160 – circa 1205)

Will Hasty
University of Florida

This entry originally appeared in DLB 138, German Writers
and Works of the High Middle Ages: 1170–1280.

MAJOR WORKS: *Die Klage* or *Das Büchlein* (circa 1180)

Manuscript: This work is preserved only in the Ambraser Heldenbuch (Österreichische National-bibliothek, Vienna; cod. Vind. ser. nov. 2663), a large parchment manuscript containing twenty-five works by Hartmann and other authors that was commissioned by Emperor Maximilian I and completed by his secretary, Hans Ried of Bozen, between 1504 and 1516; the title *Das Büchlein* is based on an error by its first editor, Moriz Haupt, who mistakenly associated this poem with another poem in the Ambraser Heldenbuch (*Das zweite Büchlein*).

First publication: In *Die Lieder und Büchlein und Der arme Heinrich,* edited by Moriz Haupt (Leipzig: Weidmann, 1842).

Standard editions: *Die Klage–Das (zweite) Büchlein,* edited by Herta Zutt (Berlin: De Gruyter, 1968); *Das Klagebüchlein Hartmanns von Aue und das zweite Büchlein,* edited by Ludwig Wolff (Munich: Fink, 1972); *Hartmann von Aue: Das Büchlein; nach den Vorarbeiten von Arno Schirokauer zu Ende geführt und herausgegeben,* edited by Petrus W. Tax (Berlin: Schmidt, 1977).

Eighteen Songs (circa 1180)

Manuscripts: Strophes of Hartmann's songs are transmitted in the three major manuscripts containing *Minnesang* which were all assembled around the year 1300; sixty strophes in Die große Heidelberger (or Die Mannessiche) Liederhandschrift (Universitätsbibliothek, Heidelberg; cpg 848), ten strophes in Die kleine Heidelberger Liederhandschrift (Universitätsbibliothek, Heidelberg; cpg 357), and twenty-eight strophes in Die Weingart-ner Liederhandschrift (Württembergische Landes-bibliothek, Stuttgart; cod. HB XIII 1); the number of strophes and their order differ from one manuscript to another; formal characteristics

Miniature depicting Hartmann von Aue as a knight, from the Große Heidelberger Liederhandschrift (Heidelberg, Universitätsbibliothek, cpg. 848, f. 184v)

of the strophes indicate eighteen different melodies, or Töne.

First publication: In *Sammlung von Minnesingern aus dem schwaebischen Zeitpuncte, CXL Dichter enthältend: durch*

Ruedger Manessen, weiland des Rathes der uralten Zyrich, aus der Handschrift der königlich-französischen Bibliothek herausgegeben, 2 volumes, edited by Johann Jakob Bodmer and Johann Jakob Breitinger (Zurich: Orell, 1758, 1759).

Standard edition: *Des Minnesangs Frühling,* edited by Karl Lachmann and Moriz Haupt (Leipzig: Hirzel, 1857); revised by Hugo Moser and Helmut Tervooren, 2 volumes (Stuttgart: Hirzel, 1987).

Edition in modern German: *Lieder: Mittelhochdeutsch/ Neuhochdeutsch,* edited and translated by Ernst von Reusner (Stuttgart: Reclam, 1985).

Editions in English: Translated by Frank C. Nicholson, in *Old German Love Songs* (London: Unwin, 1907); translated by Jethro Bithell, in *The Minnesingers,* volume 1 (New York: Longmans, 1909); translated by M. F. Richey, in *Medieval German Lyrics* (Edinburgh: Oliver & Boyd, 1958); translated by Barbara G. Seagrave and J. W. Thomas, in *The Songs of the Minnesingers* (Urbana: University of Illinois Press, 1966).

Erec (circa 1180)

Manuscripts: The only complete version, which lacks several lines from the beginning of the poem, is preserved along with *Die Klage, Iwein,* and works by other authors in the Ambraser Heldenbuch. There are also fragments of manuscripts in Wolfenbüttel (Herzog August Bibliothek, cod. 19.26.9 Aug.4⁰ and in Koblenz (Landeshauptarchiv, Best.701 Nr.759,14) from the thirteenth century, and in Vienna (Nordösterreichisches Landesarchiv, Nr.821) from the fourteenth century.

First publication: *Erec: Eine Erzählung von Hartmann von Aue,* edited by Moritz Haupt (Leipzig: Weidmann, 1839).

Standard edition: *Hartmann von Aue: Erec,* edited by Albert Leitzmann (Halle: Niemeyer, 1939); revised by Christoph Cormeau and Kurt Gärtner (Tübingen: Niemeyer, 1985).

Edition in modern German: *Erec,* edited and translated by Wolfgang Mohr (Stuttgart: Kümmerle, 1980).

Editions in English: Translated by J. Wesley Thomas as *Erec* (Lincoln: University of Nebraska Press, 1982); translated by R. W. Fischer as "Erec" in *The Narrative Works of Hartmann von Aue* (Göppingen: Kümmerle, 1983); translated by Michael Resler as *Erec* (Philadelphia: University of Pennsylvania Press, 1987).

Gregorius (circa 1187)

Manuscripts: Six manuscripts and five fragments are preserved from the thirteenth to the fifteenth century; the prologue, in which the author introduces himself and his story, is preserved in only two of the manuscripts, designated *J* (Staatsbibliothek Stiftung Preußischer Kulturbesitz, Berlin; Ms. germ. qu. 979) and *K* (Stadtarchiv, Constance; Hs. A I 1), and its relationship to Hartmann is questionable.

First publications: *Gregorius: Eine Erzählung von Hartmann von Aue,* edited by Karl Lachmann (Berlin: Reimer, 1838); in *Spicilegium Vaticanum: Beiträge zur näheren Kenntnis der Vaticanischen Bibliothek für deutsche Poesie des Mittelalters,* edited by Carl Greith (Frauenfeld, 1838), pp. 135–303.

Edition in modern German: *Gregorius der gute Sünder,* edited by Friedrich Neumann, translated by Burkhard Kippenberg (Stuttgart: Reclam, 1976).

Editions in English: Translated by Edwin H. Zeydel and Bayard Q. Morgan as *Gregorius: A Medieval Oedipus Legend* (Chapel Hill: University of North Carolina Press, 1955; New York: AMS Press, 1966); translated by Sheema Z. Buehne as *Gregorius: The Good Sinner* (New York: Ungar, 1966).

Der arme Heinrich (circa 1191)

Manuscripts: This work is preserved in three manuscripts, a fragment, and a dozen verses in a Latin manuscript from the fourteenth century, and in two fragments from the thirteenth century; the manuscripts present two widely divergent versions of the work.

First publication: In *Samlung deutscher Gedichte aus dem XII., XIII. und XIV. Jahrhundert,* edited by Christoph Heinrich Myller, volume 1 (Berlin: Printed by C. S. Spener, 1784).

Standard editions: *Der arme Heinrich von Hartmann von Aue,* edited by Hermann Paul (Halle: Niemeyer, 1882); revised by Gesa Bonath (Tübingen: Niemeyer, 1984); *Der arme Heinrich: Überlieferung und Herstellung,* edited by Erich Gierach (Heidelberg: Winter, 1913).

Edition in modern German: *Der arme Heinrich: Mittelhochdeutscher Text und Übertragung,* edited and translated by Helmut de Boor (Frankfurt am Main & Hamburg: Fischer, 1967).

Editions in English: Paraphrased by Dante Gabriel Rossetti as *Henry the Leper,* 2 volumes (Boston: Printed for the Members of the Bibliophile Society, 1905); translated by C. H. Bell in *Peasant Life in Old German Epics: Meier Helmbrecht and Der arme Heinrich* (New York: Columbia University Press, 1931); translated by J. Wesley Thomas as "Poor Heinrich," in *The Best Novellas of Medieval Germany* (Columbia, S.C.: Camden House, 1984).

Iwein (circa 1203)

Manuscripts: Fifteen complete manuscripts and seventeen fragments have been preserved from the thirteenth to the sixteenth century; more than 40 percent of the manuscripts are from the thirteenth century, another 30 percent are from the fourteenth century; this is the best preserved of Hartmann's works.

First publication: In *Samlung deutscher Gedichte aus dem XII., XIII. und XIV. Jahrhundert,* edited by Christoph Heinrich Myller, volume 2 (Berlin, 1784).

Standard editions: *Iwein der riter mit dem lewen getihtet von dem hern Hartmann dienstman ze Ouwe,* edited by G. F. Benecke and Lachmann (Berlin: Reimer, 1827); revised by Ludwig Wolff (Berlin: De Gruyter, 1968).

Edition in modern German: *Iwein: aus dem Mittelhochdeutscher übertragen,* translated by Max Wehrli (Zurich: Manesse, 1988).

Editions in English: Translated by J. Wesley Thomas as *Iwein* (Lincoln: University of Nebraska Press, 1982); edited and translated by Patrick McConeghy as *Iwein* (New York: Garland, 1984).

Hartmann von Aue stands out as one of the most significant authors of the flourishing of literary activity that occurred in German-speaking lands at the end of the twelfth and the beginning of the thirteenth centuries. Hartmann is a seminal figure: his versions of works by the French author Chrétien de Troyes introduced what is regarded as the classical form of the Arthurian epic to subsequent German authors. During an age when many authors concentrated their efforts on a single epic or lyrical genre, Hartmann is also a rarity in the variety of his literary production. Next to his worldly works dealing with Arthur and the Round Table, *Erec* (circa 1180) and *Iwein* (circa 1203), are two works of a spiritual, if not ascetic, tone: *Gregorius* (circa 1187) and *Der arme Heinrich* (circa 1191) as well as a relatively large group of songs in the *Minnesang* tradition. No other author of this period so distinguished himself both by the variety and by the significance of his literary work. Perhaps the best testimony to the importance of Hartmann comes from another author of the same period, Gottfried von Straßburg, who in his *Tristan und Isolde* (circa 1210) speaks highly of his predecessor while passing review on several of the significant poets of his age:

> ahi, wie der diu mære
> beid uzen unde innen
> mit worten und mit sinnen
> durchverwet und durchzieret!
> wie er mit rede figieret
> der aventiure meine!

(Oh, how he
colors and adorns the tales
Both inside and out
With words and with wit!
How he grasps with words
the meaning of the adventure!)

These words are not only a tribute to Hartmann's literary style, which is regarded as a model by later authors; they portray him as a prime example of what an author of his day and age is supposed to be: a combination of craftsman, entertainer, and pedagogue, whose skillful renditions of existing literary traditions convey their true meaning.

Despite Hartmann's literary importance, almost nothing is known about his life; there is no historical documentation of his existence. This situation is the rule rather than the exception even for the major authors of court literature. It is possible to say some things about Hartmann's life based on a few passages in literary works, but doing so involves interpretive problems. When Hartmann sings about his participation in a Crusade, for example, should one understand this as an autobiographical statement, or is he merely availing himself of the purely literary possibilities afforded by the Crusade song, a subgenre within the *minne* (love) lyrics? In other words, is it possible to separate the biographical Hartmann from the Hartmann who is stylized according to the demands of different literary traditions? Despite such problems and many differences of opinion among scholars with regard to the details, there exists a consensus concerning the rough outline of Hartmann's life.

The beginning point for establishing when Hartmann lived and worked is a passage from Wolfram von Eschenbach's *Parzival* (circa 1200–1210). To illustrate the consequences of a rowdy knightly tournament he has portrayed, Wolfram makes an extremely rare allusion to an historical event: "Erffurter wîngarte giht / von treten noch der selben nôt: / maneg orses fuoz die slâge bôt" (The vineyards at Erfurt still show the effects of trampling from the foot of many a horse). Thanks to this offhand comparison between Wolfram's fictional knightly tournament and an actual conflict at Erfurt in 1203 between two rivals for the crown of the empire, Philipp von Schwaben and Otto IV, it is possible to determine that Wolfram's work was composed around 1205. In an earlier section of the work a reference is made to *Iwein,* which for stylistic reasons is presumed to be Hartmann's last work. Hence, all of Hartmann's works were likely written before the year 1205. It is impossible to say whether Hartmann lived beyond this year or whether he produced other works after *Iwein* which have been lost. Establishing the approximate year of his birth and the beginning of Hartmann's literary activity is much more difficult. *Erec,* which is presumed to be among Hartmann's first works, contains a reference to a place called Connelant, or Ikonium, with which diplomatic contacts were made by the emperor Friedrich I ("Barbarossa") by 1179 or 1180 in preparation for the third Crusade, from 1189 to 1192. The approximate date of Chrétien's first Arthurian work, *Erec et Enide,* is 1165, but it is improbable that Hartmann would have been able to get a manuscript and produce his own work until many years later. For lack of a better clue, the connection to Ikonium suggests that Hartmann's first works were written around 1180. Assuming that he was twenty years old at the time, his date of birth would be around 1160. Consequently, Hartmann's literary activity must have occurred for the most part during the last two decades of the twelfth century. The chronology of his works during this period is tenuous; it is based on the criterion of literary style as well as on certain assumptions about Hartmann's philosophy or psychology that ultimately remain conjectural.

The language of Hartmann's works indicates an Alemannic origin, meaning that he probably came from a region that today encompasses parts of Baden-Württemberg and Bavaria in Germany, the Thurgau and Zürichgau in Switzerland, and the French Alsace. Hartmann's Alemannic origin is supported by a later medieval author, Heinrich von dem Türlîn, who designates this region when he says that Hartmann was "von der Swâbe lande" (from the land of Swabians). In *Der arme Heinrich* Hartmann refers to himself as a *dienstman*; this designation means that he belonged to the unfree class of *ministeriales,* a social class consisting of functionaries, administrators, and servants who performed duties of various kinds at the larger courts. In the prologues of *Iwein* and *Der arme Heinrich,* Hartmann calls himself a *rîter* (knight) who can read and write, indicating that the combination of knighthood and literacy is not self-evident. During this age an education could only be obtained in a cloister or a cathedral school. Hence, sometime during his youth, perhaps before entering the service of his feudal lord(s) and literary patron(s), Hartmann may have received teaching in the liberal arts; if so, he would have known Latin. On the basis of a passage in *Die Klage* (circa 1180) that mentions a *Krûtzouber von Kärlingen* (magical root from France), some scholars have posited that Hartmann may have spent some time in France. Although a stay in France cannot be confirmed, Hartmann's intimate knowledge of works by Chrétien makes it fairly certain that he was familiar with the French language.

Two manuscripts of *Minnesang* containing illustrations of singers, Die große Heidelberger and Die Weingartner, depict Hartmann with a coat of arms consisting of white eagles' heads on a blue or black background. The same coat of arms is documented for the Wespersbühler family in Thurgau as of 1238. Unfortunately, this family reveals no connection to the name Aue. An association has also been made to the coat of arms of the Zähringer, a powerful noble family in the Swabian region of Germany that can be connected to families named Aue. Another clue about Hartmann may be contained in *Der arme Heinrich,* whose protagonist is named Heinrich von Aue. Scholars have considered this similarity of names too striking to be merely coincidental and have theorized that this literary figure may have been one of Hartmann's ancestors. Heinrich, who at the work's beginning is a rich and powerful noble, marries the daughter of a peasant at the end of the work. In the Middle Ages marriage tended to be a matter of political alliance rather than personal preference. A good marriage could bolster the fortunes of a family for generations, while a bad one could result in a loss of economic and political power. Some scholars perceive the rough outlines of Hartmann's own family history in the events described in *Der arme Heinrich:* the Aues may have been free nobles who fell into feudal servitude (that is, into the *ministeriales*) as the result of a bad marriage. Such a conclusion involves, of course, the questionable assumptions that the Heinrich depicted in this work really existed, that he was related to Hartmann, and that his actions had a direct influence on Hartmann's existence, none of which can be proved.

Another assumption can be made on the preconditions of literary activity in general. Manuscripts of source works, such as the works of Chrétien, had to be obtained; the high cost of parchment and the financial support of scribes and authors had to be paid. The activity of an author such as Hartmann could only be supported by a lord and patron with connections at high levels of the nobility and a great deal of financial wherewithal. In the region in question there would appear to be only three families that would have been in a position to employ an author such as Hartmann: the Staufer, the Welfs, and the Zähringer. Links to any or all of these families are possible. Nevertheless, associations between the Zähringer and the patrons of Chrétien, the source of Hartmann's Arthurian works, provide good reason for viewing this family as Hartmann's patrons. The similarity of the coat of arms carried by Hartmann in the illustrations to that of the Zähringer gives further support to this link. The name Aue is found in association with that of the Zähringer in three places, any one of which might have been the locus of Hartmann's literary activity: Obernau, Owen/Teck, and Au bei Freiburg. The last place is especially interesting because there are records of a Heinricus de Owen or Owon as of 1112, and it is possible that this family fell into the status of servitude characteristic of the *ministeriales.*

Almost everything that is known about Hartmann is based on literary works. Each of these works belongs to a specific literary tradition that shapes and limits what Hartmann says about himself. While it is certainly possible to define Hartmann in a literary rather than biographical way in terms of the contributions he makes to these literary traditions, it is difficult to relate the lives and personal experiences of medieval authors to their literary works in the same way one might relate Johann Wolfgang von Goethe to *Die Leiden des jungen Werthers* (The Sorrows of Young Werther, 1774) or Thomas Mann to *Buddenbrooks* (1901). Literature is not, in the Middle Ages, the vehicle of self-expression or catharsis for the author that it was to become later. Hence, in turning to the works of Hartmann one turns primarily to these literary traditions and Hartmann's versions of them. At the same time, one must remain open to the possibility that Hartmann may reveal something about himself despite the dictates of the literary traditions within which he worked.

Die Klage is considered Hartmann's first work. Like all of Hartmann's narrative poems, it is composed in rhymed couplets, except for the final part (from line 1645), when a crossing-rhyme pattern is employed. The source of the poem is unknown, but it shows similarities to the traditions of the French *complaintes d'amour* and *saluts.* The poem takes the form of an allegorical disputation between personifications of the *herz* (heart) and the *lîp* (body) of a certain unnamed *jungelinc* (youth), and it consists of four parts. In the first (lines 1–484) the body reproachfully addresses the heart for forcing it to seek the love of a lady who repudiated it. As a result the body has suffered unending torment and has lost its desire to continue living. In the second part (lines 485–972) the heart responds that the body shares responsibility for falling in love, since it was through the eyes of the body that the image of the beloved reached the heart. This notion of love as the result of an image that passes through the eyes to the heart is standard in medieval love literature and is found, for example, in André le Chapelain's treatise *De amore.* The heart also chastises the body for not pursuing the lady's love with greater diligence and provides a bit of advice: "swer ahte hât ûf minne / der darf wol schœner sinne" (whoever values love / must refine himself). This advice on the part of the heart allows this work to be placed in the tradition of courtly love because of its conception of love as an ennobling force. During the third section of the poem (lines 973–1644), which is a dialogue between the heart and the body, the advice of the heart to the body culminates in the *krûtzouber von Kärlingen,* which is a formula for achieving the love of God and of fellow man. The

krûtzouber consists of *milte* (generosity), *zuht* (appropriate behavior), *diemut* (modesty), *triuwe* (loyalty), *staete* (constancy), *kiuscheit* (purity), and *gewislîchiu manheit* (dependable manhood) mixed in a heart without hatred. The elements of this recipe are qualities that describe the ideal courtly lover and are found everywhere in the literature of this period. The body promises to avail itself of the *krûzouber* and is sent back to the beloved lady to renew the suit in the fourth and final section of the work (lines 1645–1914). By this time it is abundantly clear that the outcome of the suit is not as important as the manner in which it is pursued.

This disputation is a highly conventional literary form, and it would be an error to see in this debate between the body and the heart a reflection of the psychology of Hartmann. What is at stake is the value of love, which is portrayed not as a personal or subjective emotion, as a modern reader might expect, but as a principle that leads to the self-perfection of the lover not only in the eyes of his beloved but also in the eyes of God and his fellow man. The heart/body dialogue would seem to be a secularized version of soul/body dialogues encountered in many religious treatises. The position has been taken that this work reveals close ties to early Scholasticism, which would support the thesis that Hartmann attended a cathedral or cloister school in his youth.

Erec was probably completed within a few years of *Die Klage.* Hartmann names Chrétien as his source; but he takes many liberties with his stated source, leaving open the possibility that he may have consulted other versions of this tale, such as the ones contained in the Welsh *Gereint* and *Enid* and the Norse *Erexsaga.* In all likelihood Hartmann's differences from Chrétien have more to do with his own literary conception than with other versions of the Erec tale. With his *Erec,* Hartmann introduces into German literature the "classical" bipartite structure of Chrétien's Arthurian works.

The beginning of Hartmann's *Erec* is missing, but in all likelihood it would not have been much different from that of Chrétien. Hartmann would have introduced himself in the prologue and begun his tale by describing the court of King Arthur. The court resolves at the beginning of the work to embark on a hunt for a white stag. The hunter who brings down the stag will enjoy the honor of bestowing a kiss upon the most beautiful lady at court. For reasons that are not explained, the young knight Erec, the son of King Lac, is not with the other knights on the hunt but rather accompanies the queen and a lady attendant. It is at this point that the preserved verses of Hartmann's work take up the tale. The three come across an unknown knight, his lady, and a dwarf. The queen's attendant, sent to discover who the strangers are, receives a whipping at the hands of the dwarf, and Erec receives the same rough treatment when he attempts to find out their identity. Because he is without armor and weapons Erec is unable to react and must content himself with following the strangers in the hope that he will have an opportunity to overcome this insult to his honor.

The strangers lead Erec to a castle called Tulmein. The castle and surrounding town are full of people, and Erec, who has no money with him, is forced to accept the hospitality of a destitute count named Koralus, who possesses little more than his humble abode, a suit of armor, and a pretty young daughter named Enite. From Koralus, Erec discovers the identity of the unknown knight he has followed as well as the reason for the multitude of people at Tulmein: there is to be a beauty contest on the following day. The lady of the unknown knight has won the contest for the last two years, and if she wins again this year, she will receive a sparrow hawk to symbolize her ultimate victory and the conclusion of the contest. This lady's success has been based not so much on her beauty as on the strength of her knight, Iders, who has intimidated the competition. The old count provides Erec with armor and weapons, in exchange for which Erec promises to marry the beautiful Enite. On the appointed day, when Ider's lady moves to take possession of the falcon, Erec protests her claim and insists that Enite is the more beautiful. The sought-after battle between Iders and Erec ensues, and the victory of the latter overcomes the insult to Erec's honor. Iders's dwarf is given a sound beating, and Iders is sent back to the court of Arthur to announce what has transpired. The importance of Arthur's court as the source of courtly values such as honor is underscored by the practice, visible here and in other Arthurian works of this period, of sending defeated knightly opponents back to that court. There they spread the fame of the knights who have defeated them, ask for forgiveness, and are generally taken into the fold of the king's court. In the meantime, it was Arthur who succeeded in bringing down the white stag. Because of concern about Erec, he has not yet bestowed the distinguishing kiss. When the victorious Erec returns to court with Enite, the two narrative strands are tied neatly together: Enite receives the kiss due the most beautiful lady. A knightly tournament, in which Erec further distinguishes himself, follows Erec and Enite's wedding. The first segment of the work nears its end when Erec returns to his homeland with his bride.

Erec's knightly fame and courtly honor, at their apogee on his return to the family castle, are short-lived. Erec is so enamored of his wife that he spends the entire day in bed with her and neglects the activities that make him a lord to be respected and a knight to be honored.

Eros disrupts the socially responsible attitude that previously characterized Erec's actions:

> Êrec wente sînen lîp
> grôzes gemaches durch sîn wîp.
> die minnete er sô sêre
> daz er aller êre
> durch si einen verphlac,
> unz daz er sich sô gar verlac
> daz niemen dehein ahte ûf in gehaben mahte. (2966–2973)

> (Erec turned to a life of ease
> because of his wife,
> whom he loved with such passion
> that, to be with her,
> he gave up all striving for honor
> and became indolent
> to the point where no one could respect him.)

The second segment of the work is instigated by the shame Erec's lying around in bed with his wife brings upon him. It is not the distracted Erec but Enite who discovers the disrepute into which her husband has fallen. While in bed one sunny day she sighs and utters words of regret at a moment when she assumes Erec to be asleep. Erec overhears his wife and, after forcing her to reveal the source of her unhappiness and the cause of his shame, abruptly resolves to depart with Enite from the castle and seek adventures. At the outset of their mutual adventure, Erec commands Enite to ride ahead of him. By so doing, Enite will be in a position to perceive dangers before Erec. But she is also commanded by her husband to hold her tongue, on pain of death, no matter what she may see.

The second segment is divided into two parts that mirror each other structurally. In the first part Erec and Enite confront a group of robber knights, a count who attempts to take Enite away from Erec, and a knightly opponent named Guivreiz le petiz. In the second part Erec encounters two rampaging giants, a count named Oringles who wishes to wed Enite against her will, and Guivreiz le petiz for a second time. The two parts of the second segment are divided by a short stay at the court of Arthur, to which Erec is unwittingly led by his knightly friend Gawein. The latter two adventures are the most significant. At Oringles's castle Enite suffers physical abuse at the hands of the count because she will not stop grieving for her husband. Erec, whom all believe to be dead after his battle with the giants, hears the cries of his wife, arises from his deathlike stupor, and falls with sword in hand upon the surprised Oringles and his men, killing the importunate count and escaping with Enite into the forest. This episode underscores Enite's loyalty to Erec in an exemplary way, and it is also suggested that Erec's former identity has been shed and that a new and wiser Erec has arisen to replace the old. Above all, the relationship between Erec and Enite seems to have gained a depth that it did not possess before, and it is not coincidental that Erec chooses this moment to reconcile with his wife.

The second battle with the dwarf-king Guivreiz seems by its outcome to suggest that Erec's single-minded pursuit of adventures and knightly activity has been as unbalanced as the erotic activity that resulted in his *verligen*. The two knights meet in the forest; neither recognizes the other. Erec insists on battle, although he is still weak from his wounds and has nothing to gain from the fight. After losing the contest and discovering the identity of his opponent, who swore allegiance and friendship to him after their first battle, Erec seems to question the value of knighthood pursued for its own sake when he says of himself: "swelh man tœrlîche tuot, / wirts im gelônet, daz ist guot" (If a man behaves foolishly, it is fitting that he receive a fool's reward). Nevertheless, despite this apparent insight, Erec does not put an end here to his knightly pursuit of honor.

The adventures of the second segment, however interesting and colorful in themselves, have two basic functions. One of these is to demonstrate the *triuwe* of Enite to her husband. Despite her fear of punishment, she breaks Erec's command to silence and warns her husband every time she perceives imminent danger to him. She also spurns the advances of the two counts, who promise to deliver her from her tribulations. Enite's loyalty to her husband, despite his harsh treatment of her, transcends even life itself in one memorable instance. After Erec has apparently died in his battle with the giants, Enite chastises God for taking a husband away from his wife when the two, according to God's own law, are of one flesh. Enite sets about to commit suicide to rejoin her husband, but God mercifully sends the count Oringles to stop her before she can carry out her intention. The only puzzling thing about the demonstration of Enite's loyalty, which is clearly a concern of the work, is why such a demonstration should be necessary. It is difficult to locate any grave lapse on her part that would justify such a grueling test. It is probable that the remnants of a literary tradition dealing with the test of a wife who is presumed to be unfaithful may have found their way into Hartmann's work.

More significant than the proven loyalty of Enite is the test that Erec has passed. Hartmann's increased emphasis on Erec's rehabilitation is the most important difference between this work and that of Chrétien. Most scholars believe that the honor and fame so quickly achieved by Erec in the first segment of the work were hollow and incomplete. The socially destructive eruption of erotic *minne* that ensued was not an indictment of love per se but served to demonstrate

that his social standing had not yet been placed on a solid foundation. There is a broad critical consensus that the second segment of adventures, although involving an extreme devotion to knightly activity that is itself faulty, provides him with a depth he did not possess before—a depth that carries over into his social standing and his marriage. This depth is exemplified in the final adventure of the work, "Joie de la curt" (Joy of the Court), which receives special emphasis because it occurs after the end of the second structural segment. In it Erec meets the formidable knight Mabonagrin, who has sworn to his wife to live in total isolation with her until he has suffered defeat at the hands of another knight. The garden in which he lives with his beloved is surrounded with stakes on which are impaled the heads of his defeated opponents. The isolation of Mabonagrin and his wife from courtly society seems to allude to the earlier erotic lapse of Erec and Enite, which also isolated them from the court. Erec's victory over Mabonagrin achieves what has been present at this castle in name only: the joy of the court. Mabonagrin is able to return to court society and place his formidable knightly talents at its disposal. It would appear that the lesson learned by Erec, which is transferred to Mabonagrin in somewhat abbreviated fashion, has something to do with recognizing one's responsibilities to society. "'Bî den liuten ist sô guot'" (It is so good to be with other people), says Erec to Mabonagrin after their battle, apparently divulging an insight that has caused him and his wife a good deal of pain during the course of their joint adventure.

Concurrently with the writing of these early narrative works it is likely that Hartmann was also composing songs. Sixty strophes composed for eighteen separate melodies have been preserved in the three major manuscripts of *Minnesang*. Important in this context are several songs that have been understood as a demonstration of a psychological or philosophical transformation on the part of the poet, if not of biographical events. This presumed transformation is based, in turn, on a hypothetical chronology of Hartmann's songs. Peter Wapnewski, for example, speaks of a "seelische Entwicklung" (spiritual development) and distinguishes four chronological phases in Hartmann's lyrical poetry. In the first phase Hartmann more or less directly emulates the conventions of the Provençal and German lyrical traditions that preceded him. This attitude shows the same uncritical acceptance of the conventions of courtly love that are visible in *Die Klage*. The second phase is characterized by a loss of the feeling of joy stemming from love's ennobling power that elsewhere in the *minne* tradition accompanies the pain of unrewarded service. In this phase falls a song that shatters for a brief and rare moment the conventionality of the lyrical language of *Minnesang*. In this song Hartmann laments the death of his overlord: "mich hât beswæret mînes herren tôt" (the death of my liege has saddened me). This line almost certainly refers to a real event in the life of Hartmann and allows a rare glimpse of individual sentiment in the otherwise opaque and conventional language of the courtly love lyric. It is possible that such a moving event in Hartmann's life may have gradually led him to regard *Minnesang* and the values conveyed in it as vain and frivolous. The third phase of Hartmann's lyrical development involves what Wapnewski calls a rejection of *minne* based on practical reason. This rejection of a love that holds no promise whatsoever of fulfillment, which anticipates the songs of *niedere minne* (low love) by Walther von der Vogelweide, is exemplified by the so-called *Unmutslied* (song of discontent), in which the singer Hartmann arrives at a highly unusual conclusion after being rejected by a highborn lady: "ich mac baz vertrîben / die zî mit armen wîben" (I can spend my time better with low-born women). *Unmut* is certainly not exceptional in the German love lyrics of this time, but Hartmann is the first to suggest that the challenges posed by *minne* in its classical or "high" form (characterized by unrequited love) are simply not worth the trouble and that ladies of a lower social status offer the possibility of a satisfying love that is mutual rather than hopelessly one-sided. In Hartmann's Crusade songs Wapnewski perceives a final rejection of *minne* and of the worldly values propagated by the love and service of highborn ladies in favor of the love of God. Wapnewski views the Crusade songs as the last in Hartmann's lyrical oeuvre, positing that there is no way back to the worldly lyric once this spiritualized form of *minne* has been adopted. At this point Hartmann may have participated in a Crusade. Two of them come into question, the Third Crusade (1189 to 1192) and the Fourth Crusade (1197 to 1198). The determination hinges on a passage that seems to indicate that the great Muslim leader Saladin is still alive (218, 19ff.). The meaning of this passage is disputed, however, and either Crusade appears to be possible. Despite the plausibility of many of the points made by Wapnewski with regard to this proposed spiritual development on the part of Hartmann, it is important to recognize that this development posits a chronology of the songs that cannot be proved.

The spiritual development posited for Hartmann is based not only on his lyrics but also on *Gregorius*, which is presumed to be his next narrative work. The oldest preserved version of the Gregorius story is the French *Vie du Pape Gregoire*. Whether one of the six preserved versions of this work served as Hartmann's source or whether he based his work on a lost manuscript is a matter of debate. The Gregorius story, which

reveals broad similarities to the story of Oedipus, is one of many tales in the Middle Ages that revolve around the theme of incest. It is not known upon whom the story is based: the protagonist cannot be identified with any of the historical popes named Gregorius.

It is somewhat convenient to think that *Gregorius* was written at about the same time Hartmann wrote his Crusade songs. In the same way that the singer's higher love of God is construed by some as a rejection of the courtly love of ladies that characterized his earlier lyrical work, the religious theme of *Gregorius* is seen as a turn away from the worldly themes of Hartmann's early narrative works. Such a turn is suggested in a direct way in the prologue of the work:

> Mîn herze hât betwungen
> dicke mîne zungen
> daz si des vil gesprochen hât
> daz nâch der werlde lône stât:
> daz rieten im diu tumben jâr. (1–5)
>
> (My heart has often
> induced my tongue
> to speak of many matters
> that attract the rewards of this world:
> in this it was persuaded by youthful inexperience.)

These lines have been taken both as an overt reference to Hartmann's earlier works–that is, as a sort of biographical statement–and as a literary trope that belongs to all works with a religious theme. However its relationship to Hartmann's other works is viewed, there is little doubt that this work presents a clear departure from the themes present in the Arthurian works and in *Die Klage*. The story is supposed to exemplify the power of God's grace in an exceptional case of human sinfulness. A brother and sister share a relationship of special fondness after the death of their parents, the rulers of the land of Aquitaine. Due to the power of *minne* (here portrayed most negatively), the devil's evil designs, and his own inexperience, the brother begins to desire his sister sexually; their relationship culminates in incest. To atone for this deed, the brother eventually embarks on a Crusade and dies of lovesickness for his sister along the way. The sister, now princess of Aquitaine, gives birth secretly to a son, whom she places in a boat and leaves at the mercy of God and the waves. Into the boat she places twenty marks of gold and an ivory tablet on which the baby's noble status and sinful origin are written. She also imparts a message to her son: he should devote his life to atonement for the sins of his mother and father. Because she has devoted her life to God, the princess rejects the suit of a powerful neighbor who seeks her hand in marriage. The neighbor responds by attacking Aquitaine and taking nearly all her lands and castles. Still the princess rejects marriage, and she holds out in her capital city in the only castle that has not been taken by the invader.

The baby is found after three days by fishermen of an island cloister. The abbot gives the child his own name, Gregorius, and places him in the care of a fisher family. After he has grown to manhood, Gregorius's foster mother reveals to him in a moment of anger that he is a foundling, and from the abbot he discovers the full truth about himself. Although shattered by the story of his sinful origin, Gregorius is encouraged by the news of his noble heritage to adopt a profession to which he has long felt a deep inner affinity. Against the advice of the abbot, who admonishes him to follow the wish of his mother that he spend his life atoning for his parents' sins, Gregorius becomes a knight and sets out into the world, taking with him the ivory tablet to remind him of his sinful origin. In a series of events that closely resemble episodes in Hartmann's Arthurian works, Gregorius helps to free a city ruled by a lady from the siege of an undesirable suitor. As a reward Gregorius receives the hand of the lady. A crucial difference makes the distance of this work from the Arthurian ones quite clear: the lady is the princess of Aquitaine; unbeknownst to Gregorius, the lady he has won is his own mother. The adoption of the profession of knighthood has preceded, if not caused, a relapse into the sinfulness to which Gregorius owes his existence. The tablet on which Gregorius's story is written is eventually discovered by the mother, and thus the two become aware of this recurrence of incest. They resolve to devote their lives to atonement. Gregorius's atonement takes a most unconventional and extreme form: he has a fisherman chain him to a rock in the sea, where he miraculously lives for seventeen years on nothing but water. After this long atonement he is sought by two legates from Rome, who have been told by God in a vision that Gregorius is to succeed the recently deceased pope. A miracle aids them in their attempt to find Gregorius and provides another proof of his beatitude: while the legates are dining with the fisherman who chained Gregorius to the rock, the key to the chains, which the fisherman had thrown into the waves some seventeen years earlier, is found in the stomach of a fish. A final miracle occurs three days before Gregorius enters Rome to take up the holy scepter, when all the bells of the city begin to chime (Thomas Mann's *Der Erwählte* [translated as *The Holy Sinner,* 1951], which is based on this work, begins with the miraculous chiming of Rome's bells). The new pope is visited by a woman who carries such a horrible sin that only the pontiff himself could grant her absolution. Mother and son recognize each other a final time, not in sinfulness but in the grace of God.

From the lowest depths of sinfulness, Gregorius is raised by God's grace to the position of God's highest earthly servant. Nobody disputes that the power of grace is a central theme, but there is a good deal of scholarly debate concerning the kind of religiosity that manifests itself in this work. In the prologue Hartmann makes use of concepts (for example, *buoze* [atonement], *bîhte* [confession], *zwîvel* [doubt]) that have their place in official church doctrine. The story itself, however, seems to be characterized by a religiosity that more closely corresponds to the values and customs of the lay nobility than to the practices of the church. The most striking example of this religiosity is the "sinfulness" of Gregorius: according to church doctrine, a necessary prerequisite of sin is the *voluntas* (will) of the sinner; since Gregorius never knowingly committed incest, his sinfulness would appear to be questionable from a theological standpoint. Despite the vocabulary used by Hartmann in the prologue, it would seem that the stigma attached to incest is more social than religious in nature. According to medieval law, the son of an incestuous relationship was a social nonperson, incapable of owning or inheriting property. Related to this point, and important for assessing Hartmann's presumed religious development, is the status of worldly values in general. Does the work present a categorical condemnation of worldly values such as *minne* and *êre* (honor)? Or does it invoke a realm of spiritual experience which only qualifies the validity of worldly values? Although even less is known about Hartmann's audience than about the author, it is unlikely that this work was written for monks or priests. If it was written for lay nobility, as is generally assumed, then it seems improbable that he wished categorically to reject worldly values, even if his primary goal was to get his listeners to think about the welfare of their souls.

A spiritual concern is also visible in what is presumed to be Hartmann's penultimate work, *Der arme Heinrich*. It is not known if the author had a particular source for this work (its relationship to two Latin exempla from the fourteenth and fifteenth centuries—*Heinricus pauper* and *Albertus pauper*—is unclear), but it is clear that he availed himself of two literary traditions that involve the medieval belief that leprosy can be cured by the blood of a human sacrifice. One tradition, the so-called Sylvester legend, is linked to the Roman emperor Constantine, who, after contracting leprosy, forgoes the sacrifice of young boys to achieve a cure. Subsequently he is healed in the sacrament of baptism administered by Pope Sylvester. The other tradition focuses on the individual who has to make the sacrifice. Konrad von Würzburg's *Engelhard* (circa 1260?), for example, presents a situation in which the protagonist must sacrifice his children to achieve the cure of a friend. While it is possible that Hartmann's source had already combined these two traditions, there is no good reason to assume that the combination was not Hartmann's own achievement. Although the preservation of *Der arme Heinrich* does not indicate that it was popular in the Middle Ages, it is perhaps the best known of Hartmann's works among modern readers. One of the more noteworthy of these was Goethe, who found it "ein an und für sich betrachtet höchst schätzenswerthes Gedicht" (all things considered a most estimable poem), which nevertheless caused him "physisch-ästhetischen Schmerz" (physical–aesthetic pain).

In contrast to *Gregorius,* the short prologue of this work does not prepare its audience for the religious theme that is to come. After alluding to his literacy and naming himself, Hartmann sets about to relate "ein rede die er geschriben vant" (a written story that he has found). The only indication that the work is of a religious nature is Hartmann's request that his audience reward him by praying for his soul. The story proper begins with an introduction of Heinrich von Aue, who is in every respect exemplary of the values of the lay nobility. He is by birth equal to princes and possesses great wealth. These qualities that come automatically with high birth are complemented by more-individual accomplishments. Heinrich possesses *êre, tugent* (chastity), *stæte, zuht,* and *milte.* Described in the most glowing terms, Heinrich's ideal existence comes to an abrupt end that shows that it is seemingly rotten to the core: he is stricken by leprosy, a disease that attacks in a most visible way the things this world holds dearest. In the Middle Ages lepers were considered unclean in both a physical and a spiritual sense. It was also thought that the disease was a form of divine punishment that not only attacked the flesh of lepers but also their souls; this belief resulted in the exclusion of lepers from society.

Heinrich, who is not immediately willing to accept the new "identity" that leprosy involves, responds with denial and attempts in consultations with several doctors to find a cure for his ailment. Not until he discovers that he can only be cured by the sacrifice of a young maiden who is willing to give her life freely for him does he accept the apparent impossibility of a cure and the social ramifications of his illness. He empties his treasury in alms to the poor and to the church, leaves behind his life among noble peers, and moves in with a free peasant family that lives in his territory. His friendship with the eight-year-old daughter of the peasant couple deepens to the point of containing an erotic element. Heinrich gives her little gifts that one would ordinarily associate with *Minne* at court: a ring, a sash, a mirror. He calls her, curiously, his *gemahel* (bride). After three years the girl learns from Heinrich what is necessary to achieve his cure, and she resolves to make the ultimate sacrifice for him. She reveals her resolution to her parents and, against their objections, defends it with great rhetorical skill. The parents, believing that God is speaking through her, finally acquiesce to her wish. Heinrich departs with the girl to Salerno, where her sacrifice is to be performed. The doctor who is to perform the procedure first verifies that the girl is acting of her own free will. In an attempt to dissuade her, he explains that the procedure involves cutting the still-beating heart out of her body. Finding her resolute, the doctor takes her into a room, where she is bound naked to a large table. Struck by the great beauty of her body, the doctor takes pity on the girl and begins to sharpen the knife so that the ordeal will at least be over quickly. Outside the door Heinrich, hearing the sound of the blade against the stone, suddenly realizes that he will never see the girl again. He finds a hole in the wall and looks into the other room. The beauty of the girl's body, perhaps increased by her proximity to death and by the selflessness of her sacrifice, causes a transformation within Heinrich, which is described by Hartmann as "eine niuwe güete" (a new sense of charity). At this moment Heinrich decides to accept the illness as God's will and to reject the sacrifice of the girl.

The girl's ranting and raving fail to reverse Heinrich's decision not to allow the sacrifice. The position has been taken that the girl's fanatical desire to die and her belief that she is predestined for a life of glory in heaven indicate a degree of self-aggrandizement that is equivalent to that revealed by Heinrich's former desire to cling to his earthly existence. Although the story is clearly oriented toward Heinrich, the girl's importance as a protagonist is underscored by the fact that she, too, has a lesson to learn. This lesson is not stated directly but seems to follow from the program of the work: the goal is neither to become wrapped up in this world nor to escape from it but to find the proper manner of living in it. The two begin their return home, and while they are en route, God's mercy manifests itself: he has tested Heinrich and the girl as he once tested Job and has found them worthy of his grace. Heinrich is cured of his disease and rejuvenated. The girl, who was in a condition near death after being deprived of her heavenly crown, is also restored to health. As miraculous as the cure itself is Heinrich's immediate resumption of his former life, now with even more wealth and honor than before. There is, however, one crucial difference in Heinrich's attitude—one that sheds light on all the events of this work:

> er wart rîcher vil dan ê
> des guotes und der êren.
> daz begunde er allez kêren
> stateclîchen hin ze gote

und warte sînem gebote
baz dan er ê tate.
des ist sîn êre state. (1430–1436)

(He became much wealthier than before
in possessions and in prestige.
All this he proceeded to devote
faithfully to God and observed his command
better than he did before.
Thus his honor is now secure.)

Like the empty glory of Erec before his fall into erotic excess, Heinrich's life before leprosy was only externally correct. It lacked the substance that comes only from a proper relationship to the Source of All Things.

Restored to power, Heinrich rewards the peasant family by giving them the piece of land on which they live. Finally, at the urging of his advisers to marry, he takes the peasant girl as his bride. One need not fall back on the thesis that Heinrich may have been a real ancestor of Hartmann, and that this unfavorable marriage may have been a part of the author's own family history, to understand the marriage in its literary context. The utopian, fairy-tale ending of this work, in which everything is contingent on the proper personal attitude, occurs independently of realistic concerns involving social class.

There is some difference of opinion with regard to the status of worldly/courtly values in this work. Wapnewski is of the opinion that Hartmann's critique of these values in this work is "unerbittlicher" (more relentless) than in *Gregorius:* "anders als im Erec, im Iwein und im Gregorius versagt hier nicht einer in der höfischen Welt, sondern in ihm versagt die höfische Welt!" (as opposed to *Erec, Iwein,* and *Gregorius,* this work is not about a hero who fails in the courtly world but about the courtly world failing in the hero!). Nevertheless, in light of the generally positive depiction of worldly values, one tends to agree with Christoph Cormeau and Wilhelm Störmer, who view the spirituality postulated by Hartmann not as antithetical but rather as a necessary complement to worldly values.

Probably around 1200 Hartmann composed *Iwein,* a work that shows the author at the height of his artistic ability. Indeed, it is this work's merits that have led many scholars to view it as Hartmann's final and most significant achievement. Nowhere is his simple elegance of style and aesthetic conception more evident than in *Iwein.* Its medieval popularity is demonstrated by the many manuscripts of the work and by the many representations of episodes from this work in tapestries and frescoes. It seems more than appropriate to regard *Iwein* as what Helmut de Boor and Richard Newald call "das klassische Werk der hochhöfischen, staufischen Zeit" (*the* classical work of the courtly period of the Hohenstauffen dynasty). With *Iwein* Hartmann returns to the literary world of King Arthur and the knights of the Round Table and to the source of his first Arthurian work, Chrétien, whom he follows much more closely than in *Erec.* At the beginning of the Iwein tradition stands a historical Owen, son of King Uriens, who lived in the sixth century; but it is unlikely that Iwein shares much with this historical figure beyond his name. As is the case with *Erec,* the Iwein story is present in many versions during this period. Besides the works of Chrétien and Hartmann, there is the story of Owen and Lunet in the Welsh "Mabinogion," a Norse *Ivens Saga,* and a Middle English poem, *Ywain and Gawein.* The latter two works, along with that of Hartmann, are all dependent on the version of Chrétien.

Iwein shares with *Erec* the bipartite structure that is definitive of the classical Arthurian works following in the tradition of Chrétien. In the first segment Iwein achieves honor and fame as he wins a wife and land. An ensuing crisis demonstrates that this initial glory is insubstantial and initiates the second segment of adventures, in which a solid foundation for Iwein's achievements is established. In contrast to Erec, however, whose insufficiency was manifested by a socially irresponsible sexual excess, it is difficult to define where Iwein's fault lies. Despite the acclaim that *Iwein* has enjoyed, it has proved to be an extremely difficult work to interpret. A reason for this difficulty may be that the Iwein story incorporates many magical elements from Celtic mythology. Such elements are inherent to all of the stories within the *matière de Bretagne* (matter of Britain; that is, Arthurian legends), but the Iwein tradition seems to be especially replete with them. The land of the fountain, for example, is similar to an enchanted, fairy-tale landscape; the queen of the land, Laudine, may originally be related to a race of water nymphs; the drawbridge across which Iwein pursues his opponent shows similarities to a mythical bridge into the realm of the dead; and the year given by Laudine to Iwein for knightly adventures may correspond to conditions issued by fairies to people returning to a former life. These and other mythical elements, which are discussed by Wapnewski, operate according to rules that are not always in accord with the values and priorities of Arthurian knighthood, which are more social and ethical in nature. The killing of the watchman of the fountain, for example, may be a necessary step in a fairy tale, but it involves moral issues in the world of Arthur.

The tale begins at the court of Arthur, during a festival in celebration of Whitsuntide. Knights and ladies are amusing themselves in a typically ideal Arthurian scenario. The harmony is almost predictably deceptive. While the king is napping, the queen comes upon a group of knights that includes Iwein, his cousin Kalogreant, and Sir Kay, the marshal of the court. The last is a stock character in the Arthurian tradition, whose abrasiveness and disgraceful manners contribute to the motivations of the heroes in their adventures. After some verbal sparring mainly involving the queen and Kay, Kalogreant begins to tell of an adventure that he undertook ten years earlier.

His adventure began at the castle of a most courtly host, where he was generously wined and dined. On the following day Kalogreant left these comfortable surroundings and came upon a clearing where a wild man, who looked more like an animal than a human, held scores of wild beasts at his beck and call. The wild man turned out to be congenial, despite his appearance, but he did not know what knightly *aventiure* (adventure) was, so Kalogreant defined it for him: two armed men fight, and the winner becomes more honorable than he was before. Some scholars have considered this crude definition to be an implicit criticism by Hartmann of the motivations that guide Kalogreant here and that will guide Iwein later. It is also possible that the exchange concerning the meaning of adventure serves to illustrate that Kalogreant's path has taken him into a magical realm where the rules and customs are different from those to which the Arthurian knight is accustomed.

Despite his ignorance about the meaning of adventure, the wild man was able to direct Kalogreant to the land of the fountain and to instruct him how to achieve his goal of combat. Kalogreant followed these instructions on his arrival at the fountain by pouring water onto a stone, thus triggering a magical sequence of events. A terrible storm was unleashed, which Kalogreant barely survived. Following the storm, the original harmony and beauty of the place was immediately restored. The watchman of the land, Ascalon, then appeared, accused Kalogreant of causing the storm, and challenged him to combat. Kalogreant was summarily unhorsed by his opponent, who, according to the rules of knightly combat, led away his steed. Horseless and with a bruised ego, Kalogreant made his way back to the court of Arthur and has remained quiet about his disgrace until this moment.

The story undermines the harmony of the festive situation. Iwein immediately declares his intention to avenge the disgrace of his cousin, an intention that draws the derision of Kay. When Arthur discovers the shame inflicted upon a member of his court, he resolves to travel two weeks later to the fountain with his entire retinue. Because Iwein fears that the renowned Gawein will be given first permission to undertake the adventure, he secretly departs from the court and follows the same path taken by Kalogreant. This time, after receiv-

ing a stunning blow from Iwein, Ascalon flees. Concerned that he will have no proof that he has won the contest, Iwein pursues his opponent over the drawbridge of the castle. As he leans forward to deal a mortal blow to his fleeing opponent, a trap-door falls down behind him, splitting his horse in two but leaving Iwein unscathed. Another door falls in front of Iwein and behind the dying Ascalon, leaving the victor confined in the castle of his enemies.

Iwein gains the assistance of a servant named Lunete, who protects him from the castle's angry inhabitants by giving him a ring that makes him invisible. She eventually achieves a reconciliation between Iwein and the lady of the castle, Laudine, with whom Iwein has fallen in love at first sight. Concerned about the defense of her land and honor and aware of the planned invasion by Arthur, Laudine agrees, after some resistance, to marry the killer of her husband. Medieval and modern sensibilities have been disturbed by this marriage of mutual convenience, but Hartmann himself does not criticize it. It seems more likely that this marriage is determined by fairy-tale elements in the Iwein tradition than that a criticism of Laudine or Iwein is intended. As lord of the land Iwein responds to the invading Arthur. Narrative logic dictates that none other than Kay is granted permission to try the adventure by pouring water on the stone. Iwein duly avenges himself on Kay, reveals his identity, and basks in the fame and honor his adventure has won for him in the eyes of Arthur's court.

The first segment of Iwein's adventures ends with an episode which structurally parallels the episode in which Erec's erotic excess occurred. On the advice of his friend Gawein, the paragon of Arthurian knighthood, who warns about the dangers of inactivity and even brings up the example of Erec, Iwein resolves to depart from his newly won wife and land to seek more adventures. From Laudine he receives permission to be absent for one year. She states that she will wait no longer for him, however, since her honor and the defense of their land are at stake. As a token of these words she gives him a ring. Caught up in knightly activity in the company of Gawein, Iwein forgets about his promise to return until several months after the deadline. While at the court of Arthur, enjoying the increased honor his adventures have won for him, Iwein suddenly realizes that he has not returned to his wife on time. The resulting regret makes him dumb to the world. Iwein's fall from the high position he has reached begins with the arrival of Lunete, who takes back his lady's ring and formally rejects Iwein on the basis of his lack of *triuwe*. The sudden, apparently irrevocable loss of wife, land, and honor are too much for

Iwein: he becomes insane, strips off his clothing, runs into the forest, and lives as a wild beast.

The cause of Iwein's fall is a matter of debate. Some scholars say that the killing of Ascalon violated the spirit of knighthood, which is supposed to be self-less service on behalf of others and not merely a vehicle for obtaining honor for oneself. This interpretation is supported by the words "âne zuht" (unscrupulously), which Hartmann uses to describe Iwein's relentless pursuit of the fleeing Ascalon. The argument has also been made, however, that Iwein's motivations during this battle correspond in every way to accepted practices of knighthood. Iwein's failure to return to his wife during the allotted year has also been viewed as the main reason for his fall; but although it would be an error to expect psychological realism in this work, the overstepping of a deadline would seem to be a purely formal offense that could hardly hurl the protagonist into madness. The deadline has even been viewed as an egotistical whim on the part of Laudine.

The second segment of Iwein's adventures provides evidence for both his pursuit of Ascalon and his neglect of Laudine's deadline as the reason for his fall. After he has been cured by the magic salve of the Lady of Narison, Iwein undertakes six adventures: the liberation of the Lady of Narison from the count Aliers, of a lion from a dragon, of some relatives of Gawein from a vicious giant named Harpin, of Lunete from death by fire at the hands of two angry marshals, of three hundred ladies from demeaning labor imposed by two other giants, and of a young lady from the tyranny of an elder sister who attempts to deprive her of her inheritance. The adventures involving Lunete and the younger sister were preceded by promises on the part of Iwein to appear at an appointed hour, and he did so despite conflicting engagements. The logic and order of these adventures are determined both by the principle of knightly service on behalf of others and by the necessity of fulfilling promises. Underlying both these priorities is the principle of *triuwe,* for which the lion that becomes Iwein's companion and helper is a symbol. Whether Iwein's original lack of *triuwe* was exemplified by the knightly pursuit of fame for himself that resulted in the death of Ascalon, by his overstepping of Laudine's deadline, or by both of these actions, the general emphasis of the second segment indicates that it is Iwein's *triuwe* that had to be put to the test. It is noteworthy—and indicative of the elusiveness of a satisfactory interpretation of this work—that Iwein achieves a final reconciliation with his wife by leading her to believe that her land is being invaded again. Closure is achieved not by *triuwe,* but by force.

If there is a single principle underlying all of Hartmann's works, despite their diversity, it is the necessity of being pleasing both to God and to one's fellow man. This principle, which is a defining characteristic of court literature, is formulated at the end of Wolfram's *Parzival:*

> swes lebn sich sô verendet,
> daz got niht wirt gepfendet
> der sêle durch des lîbes schulde,
> und der doch der werlde hulde
> behalten kan mit werdekeit,
> daz ist ein nütziu arbeit. (827, 19–24)

> (A life that ends in such a way
> that God is not deprived
> of the soul through the guilt of the body,
> and that can still obtain the praise of the world
> with dignity,
> that is a worthy task.)

Besides the elegant clarity of his style, Hartmann's individual mark on German courtly literature may well be the social concern of his works. Even those works addressing religious questions deal with one's obligations to others, with conflicts that can result from such obligations, and with false and legitimate solutions to these conflicts. Although clothed in the garb of medieval knights and popes, the social orientation of Hartmann's works is frequently general enough to address the experience of modern readers.

Bibliographies:

Ingrid Klemt, *Hartmann von Aue: Eine Zusammenstellung der über ihn und sein werk von 1927–1965 erschienenen Literatur* (Cologne: Greven, 1968);

Elfriede Neubuhr, *Bibliographie zu Hartmann von Aue* (Berlin: Schmidt, 1977).

Biographies:

Ludwig Schmidt, *Des Minnesängers Hartmann von Aue. Stand, Heimat und Geschlecht: Eine kritisch-historische Untersuchung* (Tübingen: Fues, 1874);

Hendricus Spaarnay, *Hartmann von Aue: Studien zu einer Biographie,* 2 volumes (Halle: Niemeyer, 1933, 1938).

References:

Hans Blosen, "Noch einmal: Zu Enites Schuld in Hartmanns Erec," *Orbis Litterarum,* 31, no. 2 (1976): 81–109;

Helmut de Boor and Richard Newald, *Geschichte der deutschen Literatur,* volume 2, *Die höfische Literatur: Vorbereitung, Blüte, Ausklang (1170–1250),* fifth edition (Munich: Beck, 1953);

M. A. Bossy, "Medieval Debates of Body and Soul," *Comparative Literature,* 28 (Spring 1976): 144–163;

Saul Nathaniel Brody, *The Disease of the Soul: Leprosy in Medieval Literature* (Ithaca, N.Y.: Cornell University Press, 1974);

Susan Clark, *Hartmann von Aue: Landscapes of Mind* (Houston: Rice University Press, 1989);

Christoph Cormeau, "Hartmann von Aue," in *Die deutsche Literatur des Mittelalters: Verfasserlexikon,* volume 3, edited by Kurt Ruh (Berlin: De Gruyter, 1987);

Cormeau and Wilhelm Störmer, *Hartmann von Aue: Epoche-Werk-Wirkung* (Munich: Beck, 1985);

Thomas Cramer, "Saelde und êre in Hartmanns Iwein," *Euphorion,* 60, no. 1-2 (1966): 30–47;

Otfried Ehrismann, "Höfisches Leben und Individualität–Hartmanns *Erec,*" in *Aspekte der Germanistik,* edited by Walter Tauber (Göppingen: Kümmerle, 1989);

Humbertus Fischer, *Ehre, Hof und Abenteuer in Hartmanns Iwein: Vorarbeiten zu einer historischen Poetik des höfischen Epos* (Munich: Fink, 1983);

Wolf Gewehr, *Hartmanns Klage-Büchlein im Lichte der Frühscholastik* (Göppingen: Kümmerle, 1975);

Gewehr, "Der Topos 'Augen des Herzens'–Versuch einer Deutung durch die scholastische Erkenntnistheorie," *Deutsche Vierteljahrsschrift,* 46 (November 1972): 626–649;

D. H. Green, "Hartmann's Ironic Praise of Erec," *Modern Language Review,* 70 (October 1975): 795–807;

Gudrun Haase, *Die germanistische Forschung zum Erec Hartmanns von Aue* (Frankfurt am Main: Lang, 1988);

Beate Hennig, *"Maere" und "werc": Zur Funktion von erzählerischem Handeln im "Iwein" Hartmanns von Aue* (Göppingen: Kümmerle, 1981);

Gert Kaiser, *Textauslegung und gesellschaftliche Selbstdeutung: Aspekte einer sozialgeschichtlichen Interpretation von Hartmanns Artusepen* (Frankfurt am Main: Athenäum, 1973);

Marianne Kalinke, "Hartmann's *Gregorius:* A Lesson in the Inscrutability of God's Will," *Journal of English*

and Germanic Philology, 74 (October 1975): 485–501;

Irmgard Klemt, *Hartmann von Aue: Eine Zusammenstellung der über ihn und sein Werk von 1929 bis 1965 erschienenen Literatur* (Cologne: Greven, 1968);

Hugo Kuhn, "Erec," in *Dichtung und Welt im Mittelalter* (Stuttgart: Metzler, 1959);

Timothy McFarland and Silvia Ranawake, eds., *Hartmann von Aue: Changing Perspectives* (Göppingen: Kümmerle, 1988);

Volker Mertens, *Laudine: Soziale Problematik im "Iwein" Hartmanns von Aue* (Berlin: Schmidt, 1978);

Kurt Ruh, *Höfische Epik des deutschen Mittelalters,* volume 1 (Berlin: Schmidt, 1967);

Paul Salmon, "The Wild Man in *Iwein* and Medieval Descriptive Technique," *Modern Language Review,* 56 (October 1961): 520–528;

Thomas Perry Thornton, "Love, Uncertainty, and Despair: The Use of *zwîvel* by the *Minnesänger,*" *Journal of English and Germanic Philology,* 60 (April 1961): 213–227;

Frank Tobin, "Fallen Man and Hartmann's *Gregorius,*" *Germanic Review,* 50 (March 1975): 85–98;

Tobin, *Gregorius and Der arme Heinrich: Hartmann's Dualistic and Gradualistic Views of Reality* (Frankfurt am Main: Lang, 1973);

Frederic C. Tubach, "Postulates for an Approach to Medieval German Lyric Poetry," *Journal of English and Germanic Philology,* 70 (July 1971): 458–467;

Rudolf Voß, "Handlungsschematismus und anthropologische Konzeption–Zur Ästhetik des klassischen Artusromans am Beispiel des Erec und Iwein Hartmanns von Aue," *Amsterdamer Beiträge zur älteren Germanistik,* 18 (1982): 95–114;

Peter Wapnewski, *Hartmann von Aue,* fourth edition (Stuttgart: Metzler, 1969).

Gerhart Hauptmann

(15 November 1862 – 6 June 1946)

Roy C. Cowen
University of Michigan

This entry originally appeared in DLB 118: Twentieth-Century German Dramatists, 1889–1918.

See also the Hauptmann entry in *DLB 66: German Fiction Writers, 1885–1913*.

BOOKS: *Liebesfrühling: Ein lyrisches Gedicht* (Salzbrunn: Privately printed, 1881);

Promethidenloos: Eine Dichtung (Berlin: Ißleib, 1885);

Das bunte Buch: Gedichte, Sagen & Märchen (Leipzig & Stuttgart: Meinhard, 1888);

Vor Sonnenaufgang (Berlin: Conrad, 1889); translated by Leonard Bloomfield as *Before Dawn* (Boston: Badger, 1909);

Das Friedensfest: Eine Familienkatastrophe. Bühnendichtung (Berlin: Fischer, 1890); translated by Janet Achurch and C. E. Wheeler as *The Coming of Peace: A Family Catastrophe* (Chicago: Sergel, 1900);

Einsame Menschen (Berlin: Fischer, 1891); translated by Mary Morison as *Lonely Lives* (New York: De Witt, 1898);

Der Apostel; Bahnwärter Thiel: Novellistische Studien (Berlin: Fischer, 1892); "Bahnwärter Thiel," translated by A. S. Seltzer as "Flagman Thiel," in *Great German Short Novels and Stories,* edited by Bennett A. Cerf (New York: Modern Library, 1933);

College Crampton: Komödie (Berlin: Fischer, 1892); translated by Roy Temple House and Ludwig Lewisohn as *Colleague Crampton,* in *The Dramatic Works of Gerhart Hauptmann,* edited by Lewisohn, volume 3 (New York: Huebsch, 1914);

Die Weber: Schauspiel aus den vierziger Jahren (Berlin: Fischer, 1892); translated by Morison as *The Weavers* (New York: Russell, 1899); translated by F. Marcus as *The Weavers* (London: Methuen, 1980);

Der Biberpelz: Eine Diebskomödie (Berlin: Fischer, 1893); translated by Lewisohn as *The Beaver Coat,* in *The Dramatic Works of Gerhart Hauptmann,* edited by Lewisohn, volume 1 (New York: Huebsch, 1912);

Hannele Matterns Himmelfahrt (Berlin: Fischer, 1893); republished as *Hannele: Traumdichtung in zwei Teilen* (Berlin: Fischer, 1894); translated by William

Archer as *Hannele* (London: Heinemann, 1894); original republished as *Hanneles Himmelfahrt: Traumdichtung* (Berlin: Fischer, 1896); translated by Charles Henry Meltzer as *Hannele* (New York: Doubleday, Page, 1908);

Florian Geyer (Berlin: Fischer, 1896); translated by Bayard Quincy Morgan as *Florian Geyer,* in *The Dramatic Works of Gerhart Hauptmann,* edited by Lewisohn, volume 9 (New York: Viking, 1929);

Die versunkene Glocke (Berlin: Fischer, 1897); translated by Mary Harned as *The Sunken Bell* (Boston: Badger, 1898);

Fuhrmann Henschel: Schauspiel (Berlin: Fischer, 1899); translated by Marion A. Redlich as *Drayman Henschel* (Chicago: Dramatic Publishing, 1910);

Helios: Fragment eines Dramas (N.p., 1899); translated by Lewisohn as *Helios (Fragment),* in *The Dramatic Works of Gerhart Hauptmann,* edited by Lewisohn, volume 7 (New York: Huebsch, 1917);

Michael Kramer: Drama in vier Akten (Berlin: Fischer, 1900); translated by Lewisohn as *Michael Kramer,* in *The Dramatic Works of Gerhart Hauptmann,* edited by Lewisohn, volume 3 (New York: Huebsch, 1914);

Schluck und Jau: Spiel zu Scherz und Schimpf (Berlin: Fischer, 1900); translated by Lewisohn as *Schluck and Jau,* in *The Dramatic Works of Gerhart Hauptmann,* edited by Lewisohn, volume 5 (New York: Huebsch, 1916);

Der rote Hahn: Tragikomödie in vier Akten (Berlin: Fischer, 1901); translated by Lewisohn as *The Conflagration,* in *The Dramatic Works of Gerhart Hauptmann,* edited by Lewisohn, volume 1 (New York: Huebsch, 1912);

Der arme Heinrich: Eine deutsche Sage (Berlin: Fischer, 1902); translated by Lewisohn as *Henry of Auë,* in *The Dramatic Works of Gerhart Hauptmann,* edited by Lewisohn, volume 4 (New York: Huebsch, 1915);

Rose Bernd: Schauspiel in fünf Akten (Berlin: Fischer, 1903); translated by Lewisohn as *Rose Bernd,* in *The Dramatic Works of Gerhart Hauptmann,* edited by Lewisohn, volume 2 (New York: Huebsch, 1913);

Elga (Berlin: Fischer, 1905); translated by Harned as *Elga* (Boston: Badger, 1909);

Und Pippa tanzt! Ein Glashüttenmärchen in vier Akten (Berlin: Fischer, 1906); translated by Harned as *And Pippa Dances* (Boston: Badger, 1909);

Gesammelte Werke, 6 volumes (Berlin: Fischer, 1906);

Die Jungfern von Bischofsberg: Lustspiel (Berlin: Fischer, 1907); translated by Lewisohn as *The Maidens of the Mount,* in *The Dramatic Works of Gerhart Hauptmann,* edited by Lewisohn, volume 6 (New York: Huebsch, 1916);

Griechischer Frühling (Berlin: Fischer, 1908);

Kaiser Karls Geisel: Legendenspiel (Berlin: Fischer, 1908); translated by Lewisohn as *Charlemagne's Hostage,* in *The Dramatic Works of Gerhart Hauptmann,* edited by Lewisohn, volume 5 (New York: Huebsch, 1916);

Griselda (Berlin: Fischer, 1909); translated by Alice Kauser as *Griselda* (Binghampton, N.Y.: Binghampton Book Manufacturing, 1909);

Der Narr in Christo Emanuel Quint (Berlin: Fischer, 1910); translated by Thomas Seltzer as *The Fool In Christ Emanuel Quint* (New York: Huebsch, 1911);

Die Ratten: Berliner Tragikomödie (Berlin: Fischer, 1911): translated by Lewisohn as *The Rats,* in *The Dramatic Works of Gerhart Hauptmann,* edited by Lewisohn, volume 2 (New York: Huebsch, 1913);

Atlantis: Roman (Berlin: Fischer, 1912); translated by Adele and Thomas Seltzer as *Atlantis* (New York: Huebsch, 1912);

Gabriel Schillings Flucht: Drama (Berlin: Fischer, 1912); translated by Lewisohn as *Gabriel Schilling's Flight,* in *The Dramatic Works of Gerhart Hauptmann,* edited by Lewisohn, volume 6 (New York: Huebsch, 1916);

Gesammelte Werke: Volksausgabe in 6 Bänden, 6 volumes (Berlin: Fischer, 1912);

The Dramatic Works of Gerhart Hauptmann, edited by Lewisohn, 9 volumes (volumes 1–8, New York: Huebsch, 1912–1917, 1924; volume 9, New York: Viking, 1929);

Festspiel in deutschen Reimen (Berlin: Fischer, 1913); translated by Morgan as *Commemoration Masque,* in *The Dramatic Works of Gerhart Hauptmann,* edited by Lewisohn, volume 7 (New York: Huebsch, 1917);

Lohengrin (Berlin: Ullstein, 1913);

Der Bogen des Odysseus (Berlin: Fischer, 1914); translated by Lewisohn as *The Bow of Odysseus,* in *The Dramatic Works of Gerhart Hauptmann,* edited by Lewisohn, volume 7 (New York: Huebsch, 1917);

Parsival (Berlin: Ullstein, 1914); translated by Oakley Williams as *Parsifal* (New York: Macmillan, 1915);

Winterballade: Eine dramatische Dichtung (Berlin: Fischer, 1917); translated by Willa and Edwin Muir as *A Winter Ballad,* in *The Dramatic Works of Gerhart Hauptmann,* edited by Lewisohn, volume 8 (New York: Huebsch, 1924);

Der Ketzer von Soana (Berlin: Fischer, 1918); translated by Morgan as *The Heretic of Soana* (New York: Huebsch, 1923; London: Secker, 1923);

Der weiße Heiland: Dramatische Phantasie (Berlin: Fischer, 1920); translated by Willa and Edwin Muir as *The White Saviour,* in *The Dramatic Works of Gerhart Hauptmann,* edited by Lewisohn, volume 8 (New York: Huebsch, 1924);

Indipohdi: Dramatisches Gedicht (Berlin: Fischer, 1920); translated by Willa and Edwin Muir as *Indipohdi,* in *The Dramatic Works of Gerhart Hauptmann,* edited by Lewisohn, volume 8 (New York: Huebsch, 1924);

Anna: Ein lädliches Liebesgedicht (Berlin: Fischer, 1921);

Peter Brauer: Tragikomödie (Berlin: Fischer, 1921);

Das Hirtenlied: Ein Fragment (Berlin: Holten, 1921); translated by Lewisohn as *Pastoral (Fragment),* in *The Dramatic Works of Gerhart Hauptmann,* edited by Lewisohn, volume 7 (New York: Huebsch, 1917);

Für ein ungeteiltes deutsches Oberschlesien: Öffentliche Protestversammlung zu Berlin (Berlin: Zentralverlag, 1921);

Sonette (Berlin: Voegel, 1921);

Deutsche Wiedergeburt: Vortrag (Vienna: Heller, 1921);

Gesammelte Werke: Große Ausgabe, 12 volumes (Berlin: Fischer, 1922);

Rußland und die Welt, by Hauptmann, Fridtjof Nansen, and Maksim Gorki (Berlin: Verlag für Politik und Wirtschaft, 1922);

Phantom: Aufzeichnungen eines ehemaligen Sträflings (Berlin: Fischer, 1923); translated by Morgan as *Phantom* (New York: Huebsch, 1922; London: Secker, 1923);

Fasching (Berlin: Holten, 1923);

Ausblicke (Berlin: Fischer, 1924);

Festaktus zur Eröffnung des Deutschen Museums, text by Hauptmann, music by H. Zilcher (Munich: Knorr & Hirth, 1925);

Die Insel der Großen Mutter oder Das Wunder von I'le des Dames (Berlin: Fischer, 1925); translated by Willa and Edwin Muir as *The Island of the Great Mother; or, The Miracle of I'le des Dames* (New York: Huebsch, 1925);

Veland: Tragödie (Berlin: Fischer, 1925); translated by Edwin Muir as *Veland,* in *The Dramatic Works of Gerhart Hauptmann,* edited by Lewisohn, volume 9 (New York: Viking, 1929);

Dorothea Angermann: Schauspiel (Berlin: Fischer, 1926);

Die blaue Blume (Berlin: Fischer, 1927);

Till Eulenspiegel: Ein dramatischer Versuch (Leipzig: Klinkhardt, 1927);

Des großen Kampffliegers, Landfahrers, Gauklers und Magiers Till Eulenspiegel Abenteuer, Streiche, Gauheleien, Gesichte und Träume (Berlin: Fischer, 1928);

Gedanken an Walther Rathenau, by Hauptmann, Wilhelm Marx, Arnold Brecht, and Edwin Redslob (Dresden: Reißner, 1928);

Ansprache bei der Eröffnung der internationalen Buchkunst-Ausstellung Leipzig (Leipzig, 1928);

Wanda (Der Dämon): Roman (Berlin: Fischer, 1928);

Der Baum von Gallowayshire (Heidelberg: Kampmann, 1929);

Spuk: Die schwarze Maske, Schauspiel; Hexenritt: Ein Satyrspiel (Berlin: Fischer, 1929);

Buch der Leidenschaft, 2 volumes (Berlin: Fischer, 1930);

Drei deutsche Reden (Leipzig: Gesellschaft der Freunde der Deutschen Bücherei, 1930);

Die Spitzhacke: Ein phantastisches Erlebnis (Berlin: Fischer, 1931);

Die Hochzeit auf Buchenhorst: Erzählung (Berlin: Fischer, 1932);

Vor Sonnenuntergang: Schauspiel (Berlin: Fischer, 1932);

Um Volk und Geist: Ansprachen (Berlin: Fischer, 1932);

Das dramatische Werk: Gesamtausgabe zum siebzigsten Geburtstag des Dichters, 2 volumes (Berlin: Fischer, 1932);

Die goldene Harfe: Schauspiel (Berlin: Fischer, 1933);

Das Meerwunder: Eine unwahrscheinliche Geschichte (Berlin: Fischer, 1934);

Hamlet in Wittenberg: Schauspiel (Berlin: Fischer, 1935);

Das epische Werk, 2 volumes (Berlin: Fischer, 1935);

Im Wirbel der Berufung: Roman (Berlin: Fischer, 1936);

Das Abenteuer meiner Jugend, 2 volumes (Berlin: Fischer, 1937);

Ährenlese: Kleinere Dichtungen (Berlin: Fischer, 1939);

Die Tochter der Kathedrale: Schauspiel (Berlin: Fischer, 1939);

Ulrich von Lichtenstein: Komödie (Berlin: Fischer, 1939);

Iphigenie in Delphi: Tragödie (Berlin: Suhrkamp, 1941);

Der Schuß im Park: Novelle (Berlin: Fischer, 1941);

Der Dom (Dramenfragment) (Chemnitz: Gesellschaft der Bücherfreunde, 1942);

Magnus Garbe: Tragödie (Berlin: Fischer, 1942);

Der große Traum: Dichtung (Leipzig: Insel, 1942); enlarged, edited by Hans Reisiger (Gütersloh: Bertelsmann, 1956);

Das gesammelte Werk: Ausgabe letzter Hand zum achtzigsten Geburtstag des Dichters, 17 volumes (Berlin: Fischer, 1942);

Der neue Christophorus: Ein Fragment (Weimar: Gesellschaft der Bibliophilen, 1943); enlarged, edited by H.-E. Hass (Berlin: Propyläen-Verlag, 1965);

Iphigenie in Aulis: Tragödie (Berlin: Suhrkamp, 1944);

Neue Gedichte (Berlin: Aufbau, 1946);

Die Finsternisse: Ein Requiem, introduction by Walter A. Reichart (Aurora, N.Y.: Hammer, 1947);

Mignon: Novelle (Berlin: Suhrkamp, 1947);

Agamemnons Tod; Elektra: Tragödien (Berlin: Suhrkamp, 1948);

Galahad oder Die Gaukelfuhre: Dramatische Fragmente, edited by C. F. W. Behl (Lichtenfels: Fränkische Bibliophilengesellschaft, 1948);

Die Atriden-Tetralogie: Tragödie (Berlin: Suhrkamp, 1949);

Herbert Engelmann: Drama in vier Akten, Aus dem Nachlaß, completed by Carl Zuckmayer (Munich: Beck, 1952);

Winckelmann: Das Verhängnis. Roman, edited and completed by Frank Thiess (Gütersloh: Bertelsmann, 1954);

Der große Traum, edited by Reisiger (Gütersloh: Bertelsmann, 1956);

Sämtliche Werke: Centenar-Ausgabe zum hundertsten Geburtstag des Dichters 15. November 1962, edited by Hass, Martin Machatzke, and W. Bungies, 11 volumes

(Frankfurt am Main & Berlin: Propyläen-Verlag, 1962–1974);

Italienische Reise: Tagebuchaufzeichnungen, edited by Machatzke (Berlin: Propyläen-Verlag, 1976);

Diarium 1917 bis 1933, edited by Machatzke (Berlin: Propyläen-Verlag, 1980);

Notiz-Kalender 1889 bis 1891, edited by Machatzke (Frankfurt am Main, Berlin & Vienna: Propyläen-Verlag, 1982);

Tagebuch 1892 bis 1894, edited by Machatzke (Frankfurt am Main, Berlin & Vienna: Propyläen-Verlag, 1985);

Tagebücher 1897–1905, edited by Machatzke (Frankfurt am Main: Propylaen-Verlag, 1987).

PLAY PRODUCTIONS: *Vor Sonnenaufgang,* Berlin, Lessingtheater, 20 October 1889;

Das Friedensfest, Berlin, Ostendtheater, 1 June 1890;

Einsame Menschen, Berlin, Residenztheater, 11 January 1891;

Kollege Crampton, Berlin, Deutsches Theater, 16 January 1892;

Die Weber, Berlin, Neues Theater, 26 February 1893;

Hanneles Himmelfahrt, Berlin, Königliches Schauspielhaus, 14 September 1893;

Der Biberpelz, Berlin, Deutsches Theater, 21 September 1893;

Florian Geyer, Berlin, Deutsches Theater, 4 January 1896;

Die versunkene Glocke, Berlin, Deutsches Theater, 2 December 1896;

Fuhrmann Henschel, Berlin, Deutsches Theater, 5 November 1898;

Schluck und Jau, Berlin, Deutsches Theater, 3 February 1900;

Michael Kramer, Berlin, Deutsches Theater, 21 December 1900;

Der rote Hahn, Berlin, Deutsches Theater, 27 November 1901;

Der arme Heinrich, Vienna, Hofburgtheater, 29 November 1902;

Rose Bernd, Berlin, Deutsches Theater, 31 October 1903;

Elga, Berlin, Lessingtheater, 4 March 1905;

Und Pippa tanzt!, Berlin, Lessingtheater, 19 January 1906;

Die Jungfern von Bischofsberg, Berlin, Lessingtheater, 2 February 1907;

Kaiser Karls Geisel, Berlin, Lessingtheater, 11 January 1908;

Griselda, Berlin, Lessingtheater, and Vienna, Hofburgtheater, 6 March 1909;

Die Ratten, Berlin, Lessingtheater, 13 January 1911;

Gabriel Schillings Flucht, Bad Lauchstedt, Goethes Theater, 14 June 1912;

Festspiel in deutschen Reimen, Breslau, Jahrhunderthalle, 31 May 1913;

Der Bogen des Odysseus, Berlin, Deutsches Künstlertheater, 17 January 1914;

Winterballade, Berlin, Deutsches Theater, 17 October 1917;

Der weiße Heiland, Berlin, Groes Schauspielhaus, 28 March 1920;

Peter Brauer, Berlin, Lustspielhaus, 1 November 1921;

Indipohdi, Dresden, Staatliches Schauspielhaus, 23 February 1922;

Festaktus zur Eröffnung des Deutschen Museums in München, Munich, Deutsches Museum, 7 May 1925;

Veland, Hamburg, Deutsches Schauspielhaus, 19 September 1925;

Dorothea Angermann, Vienna, Theater in der Josefstadt; Munich, Kammerspiele; Leipzig, Schauspielhaus; Brunswick, Landestheater; and thirteen other theaters, 20 November 1926;

Shakespeare: Hamlet, adapted by Hauptmann, Dresden, Staatliches Schauspielhaus, 8 December 1927;

Spuk: Die schwarze Maske and *Hexenritt,* Vienna, Burgtheater, 3 December 1929;

Vor Sonnenuntergang, Berlin, Deutsches Theater, 16 February 1932;

Die goldene Harfe, Munich, Kammerspiele, 15 October 1933;

Hamlet in Wittenberg, Leipzig, Altes Theater; Altona, Stadttheater; and Osnabrück, Deutsches National-altheater, 19 November 1935;

Die Tochter der Kathedrale, Berlin, Staatliches Schauspielhaus, 3 October 1939;

Ulrich von Lichtenstein, Vienna, Burgtheater, 11 November 1939;

Iphigenie in Delphi, Berlin, Staatliches Schauspielhaus, 15 November 1941;

Iphigenie in Aulis, Vienna, Burgtheater, 15 November 1943;

Agamemnons Tod and *Elektra,* Berlin, Deutsches Theater, 10 September 1947;

Herbert Engelmann, adapted by Carl Zuckmayer, Vienna, Akademietheater, 8 March 1952;

Die Finsternisse, Göttingen, Studio, 5 July 1952;

Magnus Garbe, Düsseldorf, Schauspielhaus, 4 February 1956;

Herbert Engelmann (original version), Putbus/Rügen, Theater, 12 November 1962.

OTHER: Franz Stelzhamer, *Charakterbilder aus Oberösterreich,* foreword by Hauptmann (Vienna: Wiener Verlag, 1906);

Herman Georg Fiedler, ed., *The Oxford Book of German Verse,* foreword by Hauptmann (London: Oxford University Press, 1911);

Ludwig von Hofmann, *Rhythmen: Neue Folge. Zehn Steinzeichnungen,* foreword by Hauptmann (Leipzig: Dehne, 1921);

Heinrich Grünfeld, *In Dur und Moll: Begegnungen und Erlebnisse aus fünfzig Jahren,* introduction by Hauptmann (Leipzig: Grethlein, 1923);

Kurt Hielscher, *Deutschland: Baukunst und Landschaft,* foreword by Hauptmann (Berlin: Wasmuth, 1924);

Käthe Kollwitz, *Abschied und Tod: Acht Zeichnungen,* introduction by Hauptmann (Berlin: Propyläen-Verlag, 1924);

William Shakespeare, *Die tragische Geschichte von Hamlet Prinzen von Dänemark in deutscher Sprache,* translated and adapted by Hauptmann (Weimar: Cranachpresse, 1929);

Johann Wolfgang von Goethe, *Werke,* introduction by Hauptmann, 2 volumes (Berlin: Knaur, 1931);

R. Voigt, *Das Gesicht des Geistes,* introduction by Hauptmann (Berlin: Metzner, 1944).

SELECTED PERIODICAL PUBLICATIONS–UNCOLLECTED: "Deutschland und Shakespeare," *Jahrbuch der deutschen Shakespeare-Gesellschaft,* 51 (1915): vii–xii;

"Hamlet: Einige Worte zu meinem Ergänzungsversuche," *Sächsische Stadttheater: Schauspielhaus Dresden 1927* (1927);

"Goethe," *Germanic Review,* 7 (1932): 101–122;

"Die Wiedertäufer: Romanfragment," *Gerhart Hauptmann-Jahrbuch,* 1 (1936): 12–37;

"Über Tintoretto," *Die neue Rundschau,* 49 (1938): 209–226;

"Johann Winckelmanns letzte Jahre: Novelle (Fragment)," *Das XX. Jahrhundert,* 2 (1940): 331–334, 337;

"Das Märchen," *Die neue Rundschau,* 52 (1941): 686–694;

"Die Wiedertäufer," *Die neue Rundschau,* 53 (1942): 488–494.

Gerhart Hauptmann first attempted to express himself artistically as a sculptor. But once he had discovered his literary talents he explored, after a somewhat epigonic beginning, all possible literary forms: novellas, novels, epic and lyrical poetry, and drama. While he had artistic and popular success with his novellas and novels, Hauptmann achieved his broadest recognition as a playwright. He rapidly became the most prolific and most imitated dramatist since Friedrich Schiller, whose plays dominated German thinking about this genre up to the advent of naturalism. Without its success on the stages in Berlin, naturalism would probably have remained only a mildly disruptive occurrence on the German literary scene; and this success would have been impossible without Hauptmann's plays. On the other hand, without the emergence of naturalism, Hauptmann might never have found the proper vehicle for his talents, let alone gained such prominence and influence.

Today Hauptmann remains for most theatergoers and literary historians alike the outstanding representative of strongly realistic, character-oriented, socially critical plays. Not only did he achieve his first triumphs with them, but he continued to succeed in writing such dramas–interspersed with works in other genres and modes–long after radical realism had ceased to be in fashion. He gradually expanded the potential of realistic drama far beyond that recognized by his contemporaries during and after the period of naturalism. He accommodated it to his own changing views of human existence and incorporated into it elements of such subsequent developments as neoromanticism, symbolism, Jugendstil (art nouveau), and expressionism.

Robert and Marie Straehler Hauptmann, who were already the parents of three other children–Georg, Johanna (Lotte), and Carl–have never been viewed as being directly influential on the later artistic success of their youngest child, who was born on 15 November 1862 and was baptized in 1863 Gerhard (*sic*) Johann Robert Hauptmann. Nor did his formal education contribute to his receiving, in 1912, the Nobel Prize in literature as a successor to such learned countrymen as Theodor Mommsen, Rudolf Eucken, and Paul Heyse. Hauptmann's elementary schooling, which began in his birthplace, Ober-Salzbrunn (now Szczawno, Poland), and continued in Breslau (now Wrocław, Poland), ended abruptly in 1878 as a consequence of his father's loss of the resort hotel he owned.

Nonetheless, the indirect influence of these early years proved to be lasting. Hauptmann would gain literary immortality through his depiction of flesh-and-blood characters from all classes and environments. In his diary he wrote on 29 November 1898: "Erst Menschen, hernach das Drama. An ein Drama von Puppen kann niemand glauben" (First the people, then the drama. No one can believe a drama of puppets). Hauptmann was convinced that realistically portrayed characters would necessarily evoke a plot, and he always made his characters as heterogeneous as possible. At his father's hotel he was exposed as a child to such a mixed bag of social classes, the wealthy bourgeoisie and to members of the German, Polish, and Russian nobility. Ober-Salzbrunn, situated in a rural area, provided Hauptmann's first contact with simpler people and farmers, which was augmented in 1878–1879 by his work as an agricultural trainee on the estates of his uncle Gustav Schubert in Lohning and Lederose. There he fell in love for the first time and was subjected to the pietism of the Herrnhut sect. During his formative years Hauptmann made the acquaintance of many people who would provide models for literary characters, such as Alfred Ploetz, the model for Loth in *Vor Sonnenaufgang* (1889; translated as *Before Dawn,* 1909), Alf in *Helios* (1899; translated, 1917), and Schmidt in *Atlantis* (1912; translated, 1912). Since these characters, albeit based on one real person, are so different, it is obvious that Hauptmann, when drawing on people he had known, would utilize only those traits he needed or could show within the confines of a given work.

In 1880 Hauptmann resumed his formal education at the Royal Art and Trade School in Breslau. He also tried his hand at writing; his products—poems, an alliterative epic, and several dramatic fragments—all betray the then-fashionable obsession with the Germanic and the influence of the very writers against whom the naturalists would soon take up arms. His efforts in art school resulted in failure and expulsion. He then began private instruction with the sculptor Robert Haertel, who first helped him to reenter the art school and then assisted him in enrolling at the University of Jena, where Hauptmann heard lectures by Eucken, Ernst Haeckel, and other eminent scholars. His studies remained unsystematic and ended after a year.

In 1883 his fiancée, Marie Thienemann, whose sisters married his brothers Georg and Carl, financed Hauptmann's trip to the Mediterranean; Málaga, Barcelona, Marseilles, Naples, Pompeii, Rome, and Florence were among the cities he visited. He went back to Germany only to return soon afterward to Rome, where he took up residence as a sculptor. But his efforts ended in failure in 1884, and six weeks of study at the Dresden Academy of Arts in the summer of that year likewise produced nothing. Two semesters at the University of Berlin in 1884–1885 provided no academic inspiration; thereafter, Hauptmann turned once and for all to creative writing. In retrospect one can recognize that academic success would have had little direct effect on his eventual achievement, for Hauptmann's most salient asset would prove to be his ability to observe and listen to the persons around him as human beings, not as representatives of ideas. In his greatest plays Hauptmann does let his characters express ideas and principles that transcend their immediate situations; nonetheless, these ideas are not necessarily Hauptmann's own beliefs. Instead, they are means of portraying a character with a definite personality and sometimes quite unique views. Moreover, Hauptmann never produced any theoretical writings of significance on his own or other writers' works. Art as life, not as art or as a vehicle for his own philosophical notions, would remain his strength. Yet the lack of a formal education left its mark on Hauptmann,

who developed typically autodidactic strengths and weaknesses: great learning and many allusions in his works to both well-known and obscure subjects that serve primarily intuitive associations, not a systematic, logical approach.

On 5 May 1885 Hauptmann married Marie Thienemann and moved with her to Berlin. In September they moved to Erkner, a suburb of Berlin, where Hauptmann met many of the people who would reappear in his plays. He also encountered young writers such as Max Kretzer (later called the "Berlin Zola"); Wilhelm Bölsche, whose *Die naturwissenschaftlichen Grundlagen der Poesie* (The Scientific Foundations of Literature, 1887) would be one of the most important manifestos of German naturalism; and Bruno Wille, a strong advocate of the Social Democratic party. Since 1884 Hauptmann had been taking acting lessons from Alexander Heßler, who would provide the model for the politically and artistically conservative theater director Hassenreuter in *Die Ratten* (1911; translated as *The Rats,* 1913). This instruction, which lasted until 1886, offered Hauptmann insights into conventional modes of acting, the practical demands of the theater, and, as *Die Ratten* reveals, a clearly defined target against which his own first plays could be directed. In his mature years Hauptmann would direct many of his own and other playwrights' works, and he always demonstrated a concern for the practicalities of the stage.

In 1887 Hauptmann visited the new literary club "Durch" (Through), where he met yet more representatives of what later became known as naturalism. Although the theoretical discussions of this club—like those of the others springing up all over Berlin at that time—achieved little more than to keep alive the younger generation's demand for a new, modern, realistic literature, Hauptmann made an outstanding contribution befitting his own nontheoretical, practice-oriented thinking: he read to the members from the little-known works of Georg Büchner, one of the most important precursors of naturalism and subsequent literary movements such as expressionism and the theater of the absurd. Also in 1887 Hauptmann wrote his first two successful novellas: "Fasching" (Carnival) was based on a newspaper account and appeared the same year in *Siegfried,* an obscure magazine (it would be published in book form in 1923). "Bahnwärter Thiel" (1892; translated as "Flagman Thiel," 1933) appeared in 1888 in the first important journal of naturalism, *Die Gesellschaft* (Society), founded in 1885 in Munich. "Bahnwärter Thiel," strongly influenced by Büchner, proved to be a masterpiece and is still read in schools today.

Always interested less in the rational side of humanity than in its irrational side—emotions, psychological problems, mystical leaning—Hauptmann spent several weeks in 1888 studying under Auguste Forel, a prominent psychiatrist and director of a clinic in Zurich. There Hauptmann also associated with the playwright Frank Wedekind, who would later accuse Hauptmann of using in *Das Friedensfest: Eine Familienkatastrophe* (1890; translated as *The Coming of Peace: A Family Catastrophe,* 1900) intimate details he had recounted from his own life. Wedekind would then seek revenge in his comedy *Die junge Welt* (The Young World, 1898), in which he satirized Hauptmann's "notebook" technique and naturalism in general.

The year 1889 was a turning point in the development of naturalism and also in Hauptmann's career. First came the publication of some of the most radically "realistic" prose thus far seen in Germany: *Papa Hamlet,* by Arno Holz and Johannes Schlaf. Until then, Hauptmann had been reading the works of foreign models for the new "realists" (the German naturalists seldom called themselves "naturalists"): Leo Tolstoy, Emile Zola, Ivan Turgenev, Fyodor Dostoyevsky, and Walt Whitman. Then came the founding of the "Freie Bühne" (Free Stage), a club devoted to the performance of "modern" (naturalist) drama (a year later a periodical of the same name was founded, which later became the *Neue Rundschau* [New Review]; one member of the board was Samuel Fischer, whose publishing house brought out many plays of the young naturalists and published Hauptmann's works for many years). Its first chairman was Otto Brahm, who developed the naturalist style of stage direction and production that would dominate the German theater until Max Reinhardt came on the scene at the end of the century. Since the Freie Bühne was a private club, it could stage plays forbidden by the censor. With an eye for a proven theatrical success, Brahm began on 15 September 1889 with a production of *Ghosts* (1881), by Henrik Ibsen, whose *A Doll's House* (1879) had already become a rallying point for advocates of woman's emancipation. In August 1889 Hauptmann's own first mature, modern play, the social drama *Vor Sonnenaufgang,* had been published in Berlin and had caught the attention of many literary figures there. Needing a German playwright to make his undertaking a success, Brahm premiered Hauptmann's play on 20 October 1889. The work launched not only a series of imitations but also a frenzied conflict between conservative forces and the naturalists.

In some respects *Vor Sonnenaufgang* incorporates the innovations of Ibsen that characterize much of subsequent German naturalist drama; in other respects, however, Hauptmann goes far beyond Ibsen both in subject and in style. Ibsen's influence can be seen in the structure, which uses "analytic exposition"—the practice of beginning with a situation and gradually exposing what has led to it. A second technique, closely allied with the first and likewise perfected by Ibsen, is the use of a "messenger from the outside," a stranger who serves as a catalyst for the analytic

exposition, sometimes without intending to do so. Alfred Loth, a journalist with an education in sociology and economics and an impassioned believer in social justice, abstinence, and the power of heredity, arrives at the farm of the Krause family, which has suddenly become wealthy through the discovery of coal and the exploitation of the other residents of the area. Loth looks up his old friend from his university days, the engineer Hoffmann. This reunion provides a "realistic" setting for revelations regarding their respective activities and changes in character since they last met: Loth's abortive attempt to establish a utopian community in the New World resulted in his imprisonment for supposedly collecting money for the socialists; Hoffmann, who now denies ever sharing Loth's idealism, has by devious means married into the Krause family and has been the driving force behind the manipulation and exploitation of the farmers and workers. Loth falls in love with Helene, Hoffmann's sister-in-law, who is apparently the sole uncorrupted member of the household. She falls in love with him, seeing in him the opportunity to escape her situation. But through Dr. Schimmelpfennig, another former friend from the university, Loth learns that Helene's sister and father are alcoholics. Believing first in his social mission, which includes not only the emancipation of women but also handing down his healthy genes to future generations, Loth writes a note to Helene and leaves. True to naturalist principles, Hauptmann strives for the greatest possible realism, which does not allow him to reveal any more about a character's thoughts and motives than a real person would reveal under the given circumstances. Thus, the characters are trapped in a closed, almost suffocating atmosphere, and the audience must watch for subtle gestures or chance words to gain insights into their various motives and intentions. Personalities, not principles, evoke most of the conflicts. Loth's fanaticism, coupled with his inability to effect any social reform, removes him from the conventional role of the playwright's spokesman. The play has remained a subject of lively critical debate mainly because of the questionable motives of Loth, Helene, and all the other characters. In fact Hauptmann scarcely ever created a "hero" or "heroine" who might be interpreted as his spokesperson; at the same time, as he himself said, he never created a true "villain."

What distinguishes *Vor Sonnenaufgang* from Ibsen's plays is, first, the frankness and crassness with which sexual and other manifestations of decadence and moral corruption are presented, as when Helene's drunken father grasps her in an lustful manner. Many contemporary naturalists in Germany had been calling for "truth" rather than beauty, and Hauptmann's play seems to respond to this demand. Second, Hauptmann incorporates the working-class and rural elements and lets them speak in dialect, a device he also uses with the Krause family to reveal how thin the veneer of culture acquired through wealth is. Hauptmann reveals his models for these innovations in his autobiography, *Das Abenteuer meiner Jugend* (The Adventure of My Youth, 1937): "Dieses Drama würde ohne *Thérèse Raquin* von Zola, ohne die *Macht der Finsternis* von Tolstoi und die Vehemenz des *Buches der Zeit* und seines Dichters wohl kaum entstanden sein" (This play would probably never have come about without *Thérèse Raquin* by Zola, *The Power of Darkness* by Tolstoy and the vehemence of the *Book of Time* and its author [Arno Holz]). It was especially Tolstoy's play, which was later performed by the Freie Bühne, that inspired Hauptmann to expand his realistic social drama to include not only the bourgeois hypocrisy that had been the subject of Ibsen's dramas but also the lot of farmers and laborers. Until then the general public had gleaned its literary images of country life from the Dorfnovellen and Dorfromane (village novellas and novels) that had flourished since the 1830s. In selecting locales for his works Hauptmann returns frequently to rural life in Silesia, but he does not idealize it.

During his lifetime Hauptmann had forty-one plays published, and five more appeared posthumously. His plays can be divided into three categories: at least seven have remained uncontested as literary masterpieces; twenty-two have evoked some degree of favorable critical and popular response or maintain interest because of their historical importance. Only seventeen have had relatively little popular or critical impact. While one might dispute the numbers in each category, one would certainly confer masterpiece status on *Die Weber* (published 1892; performed, 1893; translated as *The Weavers,* 1899), *Der Biberpelz* (1893; translated as *The Beaver Coat,* 1912), *Hannele Matterns Himmelfahrt* (Hannele Mattern's Ascension; published, 1893; performed as *Hanneles Himmelfahrt,* 1893; translated as *Hannele,* 1894), *Fuhrmann Henschel* (1899; translated as *Drayman Henschel,* 1910), *Rose Bernd* (1903; translated, 1913), *Die Ratten,* and *Vor Sonnenuntergang* (Before Sundown, 1932). Five of these works appeared before 1906, the year Hauptmann's seventeenth play, *Und Pippa tanzt!* (1906; translated as *And Pippa Dances,* 1909), was published. By this time Hauptmann had averaged one drama per year since his first appearance as a playwright. While he would complete another twenty-nine stage works, every one of these first seventeen falls into one of the first two categories. Given Hauptmann's succession of controversial or aesthetically interesting plays, it was only natural that the theatergoing public after 1906 awaited with enthusiasm every new drama from his pen. Only infrequently did his audience leave the theater disappointed. Nonetheless, Hauptmann's enduring fame depends primarily on the plays written by 1906. When Oxford University awarded him an honorary doctorate in 1905, it confirmed that Hauptmann's fame had become an international phenomenon.

Hauptmann's first six plays conform to the general goal of naturalism: to show people as products of their heredity and milieu. Yet *Die Weber* is both the extreme example of a supposedly strict adherence to such principles and is also theatrically unique. Throughout his life Hauptmann would be known not only as the foremost realist but also, more specifically, as the author of *Die Weber.* The naturalists had, from the beginning, denounced historical drama, a genre that dominated the serious stage following Schiller's death in 1805. *Die Weber* portrays the lot of Silesian weavers in the days leading up to their revolt on 3 June 1844, but it was considered by its first audiences a dramatization of almost contemporary events. The weavers' revolt had been crushed by government troops after only a few days, and their situation had not changed by 1891, when Hauptmann completed the first version of his play. Various literary works had kept alive the memory of the revolt, and newspapers throughout Germany were still publishing articles on the misery of the weavers. True to the naturalist tendency toward ascertaining and reproducing all the sociopolitical details of a situation, Hauptmann traveled to the site of the revolt, where he spoke with survivors. He later recorded his impressions of what he saw on these visits: "Der Menschheit ganzer Jammer, wie man sagt, faßte mich nicht zum ersten Male an. Ich hatte in dieser Beziehung, wie das Buch meiner Jugend beweist, schon in Salzbrunn vieles gesehen. Grimmiger Treffendes dann in Zürich unter den Kranken des Burghölzli, der Kantonalirrenanstalt. Was sich in diesen Weberhütten enthüllte, war, ich möchte sagen: das Elend in seiner klassischen Form" (The entire suffering of humanity, as one says, did not seize me for the first time. In this connection I had, as the book of my youth proves, already seen much in Salzbrunn. More horribly moving things then in Zurich among the patients of Burghölzli, the Canton Insane Asylum. What was revealed in these huts of the weavers was, I would like to say, misery in its classical form). After recounting many details, he admits that he could never show the true depths of this misery in his play.

The censor, aware that the plight of the weavers was a live political issue, forbade Hauptmann's play as dangerous—first in its almost incomprehensible original version in the Silesian dialect, then in the second version, which, as a concession to the Berliners, was written according to Hauptmann in a dialect "approaching High German" (dem Hochdentschen angenähert). The second version was performed by the Freie Bühne on 26 February 1893 and, after a court trial, elsewhere. A ban by the censor was not in itself remarkable; bans were often deliberately sought by the naturalists, who were intent on shocking contemporary audiences. What made—and still makes—*Die Weber* less political propaganda than a work of art is its aesthetic quality and its dramaturgical daring. There is no traditional "hero"; only one relatively minor character, who serves as a barometer for the rising emotional pressure among the weavers, appears in all five acts. The acts take place without any regard for the temporal and spatial limitations typical of most naturalist drama. At first glance, the play seems to consist of five individual one-act dramas, each with a different locale and with only occasionally recurring characters. Yet there is more than thematic unity, for the play does have a hero, albeit a new type: the weavers themselves as a collective, whose rising feelings of indignation lead to the revolt and whose heartbeat is heard throughout in the song "Das Blutgericht" (The Blood-Court), which was actually sung by the weavers in the 1840s. Hauptmann shows, through the collective, "misery in its classical form"; and, as in classical drama, the climax comes at the end of the third act, when one of the weavers says, "A jeder Mensch hat halt 'ne Sehnsucht" (Everyone has something he yearns for). Almost every character, even those speaking only a few lines, comes across as an individual. Yet despite its subtle, underlying adherence to traditional dramaturgical principles, *Die Weber,* unlike classical drama, ends on a note of ambiguity befitting the naturalist commitment to a "slice of life" having neither a real beginning nor a true conclusion. *Die Weber* is probably the greatest mass-drama in German literature and influenced all subsequent writers of such dramas, including the expressionists.

Hauptmann violates the rules of a well-made play by introducing a major character in the fifth act: Old Hilse, who voices trust in God and opposition to the no longer restrainable revolt occurring around him. In no other work does Hauptmann better show his ability to have a character express a thought that, while it purports to transcend the limitations of the immediate situation and the speaker, remains firmly anchored in the speaker's personality. Since Old Hilse's notions are typical of the religious attitudes prevalent among the weavers as a group, not the ideas but only their most persevering exponent can be seen as "new." Often interpreted as a representative of religion's function as what Karl Marx called an "opiate of the people," Old Hilse is killed by a stray bullet. Being accidental, his death cannot be viewed as a symbolic renunciation of the old ways that have kept the weavers in a state of self-enslavement. Hauptmann concludes his play on an ironic note that leaves the impression that the weavers will now triumph, but everyone in his audience knew that the real weavers were quickly defeated and forced back into their former life. While Hauptmann portrays

the revolt as unavoidable, the play cannot be interpreted as a call for another revolt—unless deeper changes occur first in the people themselves.

Nonetheless, *Die Weber* was considered by many to be virtually seditious. When it was publicly performed for the first time, Kaiser Wilhelm II canceled his loge at the Deutsches Theater. And when Hauptmann was suggested for the prestigious Schiller Prize in 1896 and again in 1899, Wilhelm personally rejected him both times. But Hauptmann had already exacted his revenge against the intolerance and stupidity of Wilhelminian officialdom with his masterful comedy *Der Biberpelz,* which uses as its heroine a washerwoman, Frau Wolff. Hauptmann changed his model, an honest washerwoman, into a petty thief who first poaches, then takes home carelessly stored firewood, and finally steals and sells a beaver coat—progressively greater crimes, which, because the victim is both wealthy and ludicrous, do not transgress the limits of a comedy. She commits them under the eyes of a local official, who is more concerned with the supposed danger of socialists, especially with one patently harmless character modeled after Hauptmann himself. The role of the thieving washerwoman is one of the most famous, and this comedy one of the most frequently performed, in German theatrical history.

Yet the initial reaction to *Der Biberpelz* was far from auspicious. The censor's office, substantiating Hauptmann's low opinion of public officials, allowed the play to be presented only because it was considered too boring to have a long run. The first audience remained in its seats after the last curtain because it expected a fifth act in which Frau Wolff would be discovered and punished. But the comedy ends with the official's reiteration of his belief in her innocence and good character and his reassertion of the danger of the suspected "socialist."

Der Biberpelz was Hauptmann's second comedy; the first was *Kollege Crampton* (performed 1892; published as *College Crampton,* 1892; translated as *Colleague Crampton,* 1914), a study of a drunken painter and teacher whose real-life counterpart Hauptmann had met in 1880 at the Breslau Art Academy. But the focus in the first comedy remained relatively narrow, and at the end the audience questions only the protagonist's ability to fulfill his good resolutions, not the social and political background. In his second comedy Hauptmann expands the comic potential of naturalism beyond the depiction of individual characters. While Crampton is an outsider or even a victim, Frau Wolff asserts her mastery over her environment. Always one step ahead of other characters and able to manipulate them, Frau Wolff appears as the rogue figure of many traditional comedies. At the same time she is always a realistically portrayed individual with a specific background and discernible limitations.

It was not popular morality, with its desire to see this "thief" punished, but the dictates of realism that led Hauptmann to write a sequel, *Der rote Hahn* (1901; translated as *The Conflagration,* 1912)—but as a tragicomedy, not a comedy. In the sequel Hauptmann shows that Frau Wolff's seemingly harmless, victimless crimes were motivated by capitalistic avarice; in the time since the end of the first play she has committed arson for profit. An innocent man is punished for her crime, but she refuses to confess. She dies at the end with the words: "Ma langt . . . Ma langt nach was" (One reaches . . . One reaches for something). Here is the culmination of Hauptmann's vision of his characters as individuals obeying their own instincts, drives, and emotions to the end, for the final, truly criminal acts of Frau Wolff were already implied by her personality in *Der Biberpelz.* The sequel has enjoyed neither the favorable critical reception nor the popularity of the original; but the consistency of thought and character connecting the two plays was noted by Bertolt Brecht, who tried to mold them into a single drama in his stage production *Bieberpelz und Roter Hahn* (1951).

To many, *Hanneles Himmelfahrt* seemed to initiate Hauptmann's break with naturalism. After *Die Weber* and *Der Biberpelz,* the lesser exponents of naturalism assumed that little else remained to be done technically and that subsequent works would distinguish themselves solely through new subjects and issues. *Hanneles Himmelfahrt,* however, reveals that Hauptmann had not abandoned the fundamental goals of naturalism but had expanded its artistic means.

The initial reception of *Hanneles Himmelfahrt* was not favorable. Paul Schlenther, one of the cofounders of the Freie Bühne and a close friend as well as first biographer of Hauptmann, commented that the overly pious members of the audience wanted to ascribe the play to the Social Democrats, while the Social Democrats found it too religious. The first of the two acts depicts in thoroughly naturalistic manner a poorhouse whose inhabitants take in the freezing young girl Hannele; a victim of poverty and maltreatment by her drunken stepfather, she has attempted to drown herself. In the second act the audience shares in Hannele's dream, in which Christ appears looking like her schoolteacher, and Hannele is prepared by angels for her wedding with him. At the end of the play the action returns to the real world, and the audience learns that Hannele has died.

Hauptmann incorporates in this play many aspects of the very literary tendencies—neoromanticism and Jugendstil—that were developing as reactions against naturalism's exclusion of everything not recognized by science and its emphasis on the banal and ugly side of life. Hannele's hallucination fulfills all the expectations of heaven that are implied by the traditional reli-

gious views of Old Hilse; consequently, there is some truth in those interpretations that consider *Hanneles Himmelfahrt* the second part of *Die Weber.* On the other hand, the irrationality of an obviously delirious dreamer, the erotic fantasies of an adolescent girl, and the sociological basis of her religious expectations do not exhaust the significance of the dream. Hauptmann's intention is to dramatize the creation of a work of art. In an April 1894 letter replying to one of his critics, Hauptmann asserts: "Wie das Märchen ist, suchte ich mir ein Aschenbrödel, um es, wiederum wie das Märchen tut, aus tiefstem Elend zu höchstem Glück zu führen. Gleich dem Märchen, welches nach Möglichkeit real zu sein versucht, suchte ich nun aber innerhalb des Märchenrahmens ebenfalls so viel mir möglich, real zu sein. . . . Das Kind stellte für mich gleichsam ein Stückchen des Urbodens dar, aus dem alle Religion und alle Poesie entkeimt ist" (As in a fairy tale, I looked for a Cinderella in order to lead her, as a fairy tale does, out of the deepest misery to the highest happiness. Like the fairy tale, which tries as far as possible to be real, I now, however, likewise sought to be as real as possible within the framework of a fairy tale. . . . That child represented for me more or less a small piece of the mother earth from which all religions and all poetry have sprung). Hannele's dream, to be sure, represents the extreme example of personal escapism; but a similar desire to manipulate and transcend reality motivates all poetic expression.

Hauptmann's next attempt to dramatize such a line of thought, *Die versunkene Glocke* (performed, 1896; published, 1897; translated as *The Sunken Bell,* 1898), was more accessible to contemporary audiences. One of his most popular plays and the first one to earn a substantial amount of money for Hauptmann, *Die versunkene Glocke,* which bears the subtitle *Ein deutsches Märchendrama* (a German Fairy-Tale Drama) and is in verse, was its author's concession to bourgeois taste and to the fashion set by Maurice Maeterlinck; it is considered today to be a weak work. Of far greater scope and of more lasting critical interest would, however, be the still frequently puzzling *Und Pippa tanzt!,* which begins almost as naturalistically as *Hanneles Himmelfahrt* but allows its nonrealistic elements even more autonomy. In fact, its almost allegorical tendencies mark it as a forerunner of expressionist drama.

After moving in 1889 to Charlottenburg, another suburb of Berlin, Hauptmann made a trip in 1890 to Zurich, Italy, and Monaco; in 1891 he traveled to Silesia for studies for *Die Weber.* By this time he and Marie had three sons—Ivo, born in 1886; Eckart, born in 1887; and Klaus, born in 1889—and she had inherited enough money to make the family financially secure. In 1891 the Hauptmanns moved to Schreiberhau (now Szklarska Poreba, Poland) in Silesia. Hauptmann soon fell in love with the sister of Max Marschalk, the composer of the music for *Hanneles Himmelfahrt* and later for more of Hauptmann's works. Hauptmann had met Margarete Marschalk in 1889, when she was fourteen. She had later studied violin under Joseph Joachim but had had to give up a musical career. Hauptmann, who knew Gustav Mahler, Richard Strauss, and other prominent musical figures, was undoubtedly drawn to Margarete in part because of her musical talent. She reentered his life as a guest at the dinner Hauptmann gave after the premiere of *Hanneles Himmelfahrt* in September 1893. After spending the following days with Margarete in Berlin, he returned to his wife and children, who had remained in Silesia. Hauptmann confessed his new love to his wife. He returned shortly thereafter to Berlin, where he saw Margarete again. When he went to Paris for the opening of *Hanneles Himmelfahrt* there, Marie left for America, where she stayed with Alfred Plots in Meriden, Connecticut. Hauptmann hurried after her and a reconciliation was reached. Hauptmann gained mostly unfavorable impressions of the United States. Shortly after the failure of *Hanneles Himmelfahrt* in New York on 1 May 1894, he returned with his family to Germany.

The reconciliation did not last long; but Marie refused to give the playwright a divorce, even though Margarete gave birth to Hauptmann's son Benvenuto on 1 June 1900. In the fall of that year Marie and the children moved into a house in Dresden that Hauptmann had built for them, and he moved with Margarete into Wiesenstein, a house he had constructed for himself and his new family in Agnetendorf. Finally, in 1904, Marie divorced him, and in September of that year he married Margarete.

In September 1905 he met a sixteen-year-old girl, Ida Orloff, who became a threat to the new marriage. Hauptmann broke off his affair in 1906 or 1907. But while there are few figures in his works reminiscent of Margarete, Ida Orloff recurs frequently in his plays and fiction—sometimes in a positive, sometimes in a negative light—even long after he had stopped seeing her. One should not, however, ascribe such figures to her alone, for their occurrence in Hauptmann's works coincides with the obsession of many Jugendstil and symbolist poets for the *femme-enfant* and femme fatale. One could almost suggest that Hauptmann, through this affair, was unconsciously living out a current literary motif.

During these years Hauptmann suffered some artistic disappointments. The most notable came with the premiere of *Florian Geyer* (published, 1896; translated, 1929) on 4 January 1896. Although it has a "hero," this play about the Peasant Wars of 1524–1525 has much in common with *Die Weber;* to this day it represents the best attempt to write a thoroughly naturalistic drama on an historical subject of such remoteness in time. Hauptmann had begun his preliminary studies in 1891, while he was working on *Die Weber;* as in the case

of *Die Weber* he went to the areas concerned, this time southern Germany. As a naturalist, Hauptmann always strives for a rigorously accurate phonetic reproduction of linguistic peculiarities and dialects, which allows his audience to pinpoint the educational and social level and regional background of a character. Opinions vary on Hauptmann's success in reproducing the language of the sixteenth century, but if he had not tried to reproduce it—including differentiations among the various characters and classes—then *Florian Geyer* would have been merely another costume piece, yet another play of the type the naturalists consciously rejected.

Moreover, the naturalist seeks the "complete" truth, not a "higher" or more poetic one. Hauptmann gathered an enormous amount of material on Geyer, his friends and enemies, and the times in general. Nonetheless, the play, admittedly not well staged or acted, was rejected by critics and public alike at its premiere. But in 1904 it was successfully performed with Rudolf Rittner in the title role, and thereafter it served as a vehicle for several other actors of stature. Yet such successes have, paradoxically, only emphasized a fundamental dilemma: did Hauptmann make a politically inactive and historically unimportant historical figure too central to the work? Or do the events overcome and obscure not only the central character but also the myriad of others? In any case, *Florian Geyer* remains the only historical drama of note produced by naturalism.

Before 1906 Hauptmann created two more masterpieces, *Fuhrmann Henschel* and *Rose Bernd*. Both represent a refinement of naturalist technique rather than an expansion of it to previously untried subjects. At the same time, in both plays Hauptmann lets his audience feel that more than the forces of biological and sociological determinism produces the tragic outcome.

Returning to the themes of "Bahnwärter Thiel" and the Silesian milieu and dialect of *Vor Sonnenaufgang, Fuhrmann Henschel* portrays against the background of the industrial and economic changes of the contemporary world the unhappy marriage of a man to his former maid, a sexually active, domineering woman, after he promises his dying first wife that he will not marry her. Many contemporaries heard echoes in the play of the so-called fate tragedies of the early nineteenth century. But Hauptmann avoids the crudity of such plays' emphasis on a vague concept of fate: his protagonist commits suicide only after the audience has seen him destroyed by his guilt, the changes in the socioeconomic world, and his unfaithful second wife. The tragedy, which premiered on 5 November 1898 in Berlin, was an immediate success there and in Paris, where André Antoine, founder of the "théâtre libre," the model for the Freie Bühne, praised not only the presentation of the milieu but also the play's "clarity and sobriety." Many critics have subsequently likened it to Attic tragedy.

In 1897 and again in 1898 Hauptmann traveled to Italy, where he began several works on exotic subjects that, with the exception of material that was later integrated into *Der arme Heinrich* (Poor Henry, 1902; translated as *Henry of Auë,* 1915) and *Und Pippa tanzt!,* would not appear on the stage. Another drama in a realistic manner, if not a great one, followed: *Michael Kramer* (1900; translated, 1914) was rejected at its premiere on 21 December 1900, yet the fourth act, with Kramer's almost lyrical comments on death, found admirers in Rainer Maria Rilke and Thomas Mann.

Then another masterpiece, *Rose Bernd,* premiered on 31 October 1903 in Berlin. Although the theme of an unmarried mother killing her child had been a favorite of the Storm and Stress writers of the 1770s and had been given its most famous treatment by Johann Wolfgang von Goethe in *Faust I* (1808), Hauptmann's direct inspiration can be found neither in the past nor in the contemporary naturalist concern for fallen or victimized women. Instead, it came from his participation as a juror from 15 to 17 April 1903 at the trial of a waitress accused of murdering her child.

A criticism made of virtually all of Hauptmann's strongly realistic character dramas surfaced again in the case of *Rose Bernd:* that the play is too epic, that is, not "dramatic" enough. By 1903 the naturalist style of acting had dominated the stages of Germany for several years, and *Rose Bernd* seemed to many critics an anachronism. Moreover, despite the artistic liberties introduced by naturalism since 1889, the subject of *Rose Bernd* was still considered controversial enough for the play to be removed by royal order from the repertoire in Vienna.

Nevertheless, the tragedy gained in popularity and in 1919 became the first of Hauptmann's plays to be filmed (his novel *Atlantis* had been filmed in 1913). There followed films of *Elga* (1905; translated, 1909) in 1919, *Die Ratten* and *Schluck und Jau* (1900; translated as *Schluck and Jau,* 1916) in 1921, *Die Weber* in 1927, and *Der Biberpelz* in 1928. After these silent films *Hanneles Himmelfahrt* initiated in 1934 a series of movies with sound: *Der Herrscher* (loosely adapted from *Vor Sonnenuntergang*), *Der Biberpelz,* and *The Rats* (based on *Die Ratten*) in 1937, and *Die Jungfern von Bischofsberg* (1907; translated as *The Maidens of the Mount,* 1916) in 1943. The years after the fall of the Nazi dictatorship, when a reborn German film industry was looking for uncontroversial but proven subjects, brought forth *Der Biberpelz* in 1949, *Die Ratten* in 1955, *Vor Sonnenuntergang* and *Fuhrmann Henschel* in 1956, *Rose Bernd* in 1957, and *Dorothea Angermann* (1926) in 1959. But none of the films contribute much toward an assessment of Hauptmann as a playwright. Almost without exception they take great liberties with his texts. Most are based on Hauptmann's realistic

plays; yet despite the ability of the camera to show gestures and facial expressions crucial to naturalist acting but often not discernible to those seated at the back of a theater, most of these films are visually disappointing. Unlike Carl Zuckmayer, Brecht, and other playwrights, Hauptmann never wrote an original screenplay.

In 1907 Hauptmann traveled to Greece. The most immediate result of his sojourn there was his diary, *Griechischer Frühling* (Grecian Spring, 1908). In the years to come many critics would see this work as a turning point in Hauptmann's career, and one not in the right direction. Yet what Hauptmann says in *Griechischer Frühling* about Greek tragedy obviously stems from seeing it through the eyes of a dramatist schooled in the perspective and expectations of naturalism: "Tragödie heißt: Freundschaft, Verfolgung, Haß und Liebe als Lebenswut! Tragödie heißt: Angst, Not, Gefahr, Pein, Qual, Marter, heißt Tücke, Verbrechen, Niedertracht, heißt Mord, Blutgier, Blutschande, Schlächterei" (Tragedy means: friendship, persecution, hate and love as existential passion! Tragedy means: fear, misery, danger, anguish, torment, torture; means deception, crime, depravity; means murder, bloodthirstiness, incest, butchery). Hauptmann's works reflecting the forms and themes of antiquity remained for a long time mainly nondramatic ones; his only play on a classical source to appear before his old age would be *Der Bogen des Odysseus* (1914; translated as *The Bow of Odysseus,* 1917), which he began during this trip but completed only after much work. The long genesis produced a play that relies more on characterization and the bucolic than on Homer, from whom Hauptmann takes only the plot. Despite its originality, the play enjoyed only moderate success.

By 1907 Hauptmann had become financially successful, although, as his correspondence reveals, he spent all his income. Public honors became more frequent: after an honorary doctorate from Oxford in 1905, he received another from the University of Leipzig in 1909. Invitations to lecture in major cities came frequently, and in 1912 he received the Nobel Prize in literature. The literary winds had turned increasingly away from naturalism, yet Hauptmann was frequently admired by and developed friendships with younger writers representing new literary movements, such as Hugo von Hofmannsthal, Rilke, Thomas Mann, and Georg Kaiser; James Joyce is said to have learned German just to read Hauptmann. During this time, however, his published works were mainly in fiction, and up to the advent of the Nazi dictatorship, his stage triumphs would become increasingly rare and would never duplicate those before 1906. He could, however, still create controversy. For example, he was commissioned to write a festival play to commemorate the centenary of the Wars of Liberation in 1813. The result, *Festspiel in deutschen Reimen* (Festival Performance in German Rhymes, 1913; translated as *Commemoration Masque,* 1917), applied not the expected blind reverence but a note of irony toward the revered figures of German history and caused a scandal. Nonetheless, at the outbreak of World War I in 1914 Hauptmann joined other writers in composing patriotic poems. While Hauptmann's attitudes and statements frequently contradict each other, on balance he is usually patriotic but not nationalistic or sycophantic toward the rulers.

In the years between *Rose Bernd* and World War I, Hauptmann, albeit largely occupied with fiction, wrote another truly great work for the stage, a tragicomedy that perhaps remains his most "modern" play. *Die Ratten* is the most complex and subtle play in Hauptmann's oeuvre. Its main plot is strongly naturalistic: Frau John, a cleaning woman who lives in a rat-infested former barracks, adopts the illegitimate child of a Polish maid but convinces her husband, a bricklayer, that she has given birth to it. She is discovered despite her brother's murder of the true mother and commits suicide. The time of the play is 1884–1885–that is, before the theatrical breakthrough of naturalism with *Vor Sonnenaufgang*–and a second plot revolves around the acting school of Hassenreuter, which is housed in the same building. It provides an ironic, largely comic foil to the plot about Frau John. Hassenreuter, who is something of a philanderer, provides a sharp contrast to the cleaning woman, who tries to attain middle-class stability and happiness in her marriage but is driven to suicide by her husband's inflexible attitude toward her "crime." Hassenreuter is an exponent of Friedrich Schiller's classical, declamatory style of acting. His opponent in a series of arguments is his student Spitta, who advocates more reality–the naturalism that would soon put such people as Frau John on the stage as tragic heroes and heroines. Neither Hassenreuter nor Spitta notices that Frau John's plight has all the qualities of a tragedy in both the naturalistic and the classical senses, and they remain as ludicrous in their theoretical arguments as Frau John remains tragic in her real life. *Die Ratten* represents a reckoning both with the forces that made naturalism necessary and with the ultimate impotence of the naturalist as a reformer.

Few plays are recognized immediately as having the qualities of lasting greatness, and *Die Ratten* was no exception. After Hauptmann gained a court decision against a petty objection by the censor, the premiere took place on 13 January 1911 in Berlin. The reaction was subdued. Even Alfred Kerr, one of the most brilliant and perceptive theater critics, an exponent of naturalism, and an enthusiastic supporter of Hauptmann, had little to say about *Die Ratten* that was good. But five

years later, when the play was performed again, another critic, Siegfried Jacobsohn, wrote: "Kritik ist Selbskritik. Weswegen bin ich 1911 vor diesen Ratten durchgefallen?" (Criticism is self-criticism. Why did I flop in 1911 when confronted by *Die Ratten?*). In retrospect, it can be seen that the cause of the rejection in 1911 is the very "modernity" and relevance of *Die Ratten:* its complex intertwining of the tragic and comic and its ironic, disquieting view of human existence and social values.

During World War I Hauptmann wrote little of note for the stage and certainly no overtly patriotic works. When peace came in 1918, Hauptmann welcomed it; the following year he also welcomed the Weimar Republic, which, in turn, lionized him to an extent previously unknown in Germany or elsewhere. His sixtieth and seventieth birthdays became events of national importance. Honorary doctorates from the German University in Prague in 1921 and Columbia University in 1932 show that his fame grew in foreign countries as well.

Between 1925 and 1936 Hauptmann was intensely preoccupied with William Shakespeare's *Hamlet*. He wrote an original play, *Hamlet in Wittenberg* (1935), which portrays the years before the beginning of Shakespeare's play. He also wrote an adaptation of the Shakespeare play (performed, 1927; published, 1929) and a novel, *Im Wirbel der Berufung* (Following My Calling, 1936), about staging the play. The purpose of all of these works was to show that Hamlet could not have been as passive and indecisive as he seems to be in Shakespeare's play. Hauptmann later said: "Überall ist er [Hamlet] um mich gewesen und hat sich dabei allmählich von den schönen Fesseln der Shakespearischen Dichtung ganz befreit. In unzähligen Stunden, Wanderungen durch Feld und Wald, Vigilien der Nächte meiner Gebirgsheimat, haben wir miteinander gesprochen und Meinungen ausgetauscht: Wo dann der Gedanke, ihn auch für andere nochmals sichtbar zu machen, sich beinahe mit Notwendigkeit ergab" (Everywhere he [Hamlet] was around me and thereby gradually freed himself from the fetters of the Shakespearean play. In countless hours, wanderings through field and forest, nocturnal vigils in my mountainous homeland, we spoke with one another and exchanged opinions: where then the thought of once again making him visible for others arose almost as a necessity). Here one can recognize a reversal of his creative process as a naturalist, where a character modeled after a real person reveals only a portion of his real-life counterpart; in contrast, Hauptmann sees Hamlet as only a portion of a real person and tries to conjure up the complete person that must have been on Shakespeare's mind. Yet his long study of *Hamlet* (including philological studies) and his "personal" relationship with its protagonist bore little fruit, for the critical reception of the Hamlet works was unfavorable.

Hauptmann's last unquestionably great and popular play, *Vor Sonnenuntergang,* which premiered in the midst of his Hamlet studies on 16 February 1932, grew out of an interest in another Shakespearean play. Hauptmann had set out to write a new *King Lear,* but soon the play embraced a multitude of other influences and stimuli. *Vor Sonnenuntergang* portrays the family conflicts that arise when Matthias Clausen, a dignified, cultured, and sensitive man of seventy, falls in love with his gardener's niece, Inken Peters, fifty years his junior. The main parallels to *King Lear* stem from the opposition of Clausen's sons and daughters to this union, which they oppose for financial reasons. In the printed version there is a fifth act in which Clausen commits suicide, but in the premiere and in many subsequent performances he dies of a heart attack in the fourth act.

The model for Matthias Clausen was Max Pinkus, a bibliophile and longtime friend of the author. Clausen quotes Goethe, has named his children after Goethe or Goethe's characters or friends, and is celebrating his seventieth birthday on the hundredth anniversary of Goethe's death. Moreover, everyone in the audience at the premiere probably remembered that the seventy-three-year-old Goethe had fallen in love with an eighteen-year-old girl. These parallels and allusions to Goethe are intended to reinforce the impression of Clausen as the last representative of a bygone concept of culture and humanism.

Vor Sonnenuntergang had its premiere the year before Adolf Hitler became chancellor. The more perceptive writers did not have to wait until the Nazis had actually assumed power to predict the manner and consequences of their rule. For example, in Thomas Mann's *Mario und der Zauberer* (1930; translated as *Mario and the Magician,* 1930) the stage technique of the demonic magician Cipolla shows great similarity to Hitler's observations on political rallies in *Mein Kampf* (My Struggle, 1925–1926). Also in 1932 Brecht was already working on his anti-Nazi play *Die Rundköpfe und die Spitzköpfe* (1957; translated as *Roundheads and Peakheads,* 1966). In his novella Mann proves himself to be especially adept in evoking the atmosphere that breeds a Cipolla and allows him to succeed. In the same way, Hauptmann's minor figures in *Vor Sonnenuntergang* represent an entire society's role in bringing about the "sundown" of traditional forms of family relationships and cultural values.

The "sundown" in the title of the play obviously alludes to Hauptmann's first success, which came just before a "dawn." On 20 July 1933, not quite five months after the burning of the Reichstag and less than a week after the creation of a oneparty state in Germany, Hauptmann said to C. F. W. Behl: "Meine Epoche beginnt mit 1870 und endigt mit dem Reichstagsbrand" (My epoch begins with 1870 [the establishment of the Second Reich] and ends with the burning of the Reichstag). In other words, his time, the time that understood and revered culture, was over. Even if its

prophetic implications had not been fulfilled through the dictatorship of the Nazis, *Vor Sonnenuntergang* would still capture the atmosphere of an era that bred radical opponents of traditional cultural values.

Many Jews and intellectuals left Germany in 1933 and the following years. But Hauptmann, who had turned seventy in 1932, felt himself too old to follow their lead. His remaining in Germany, his "inner emigration," subjected him to attacks from exiles such as his old friend Kerr. Even today this issue is occasionally raised as a stigma on his reputation. Hauptmann's attitude toward the new rulers can, however, be inferred from their policy toward him: he and his works were relegated to the status of museum pieces. Hauptmann did not publish a single artistic work that could be called an homage to the new masters.

Hauptmann and his wife were the only gentiles at the funeral of his Jewish friend Pinkus in 1934. Although Pinkus had been the model for the protagonist of *Vor Sonnenuntergang,* Hauptmann had ignored Pinkus's Jewishness in the play–even though Hauptmann had long wanted to write a drama about the mysteries of Judaism. In 1937 he finally accomplished this goal with *Die Finsternisse* (The Darknesses), which was inspired by Pinkus's funeral. In the last year of the war Hauptmann, fearing a police search, had the manuscript burned. But a copy found its way to the United States, where it was published in 1947 by Walter A. Reichart; it was first performed in 1952. Dramatically, this work leaves much to be desired, but it is an eloquent statement of Hauptmann's humanity. This play about a Jewish funeral documents not only Hauptmann's lifelong preoccupation with the "Magic des Todes" ("magic of death") but also his increasing tendency toward religious mysticism and interest in a "Zwischenreich" (middle kingdom between the real and mythical worlds).

During the Nazi years Hauptmann wrote a couple of minor stage works and some fiction. Then, almost eighty years old, he seemed to rise up like an awakening giant for one last great effort as a dramatist. This last creative surge began with *Iphigenie in Delphi* (1941). His inspiration was a passage in Goethe's *Italienische Reise* (1816–1817; translated as *Travels in Italy,* 1846) describing how Goethe would have written a sequel to his *Iphigenie auf Tauris* (1800; translated as *Iphigenia on Tauris,* 1851). But Hauptmann's Iphigenia, although she sacrifices herself to atone for the crimes committed by the house of Atreus, bears little resemblance to the Goethean personification of the all-too-human. Goethe adhered to J. J. Winckelmann's concept of Greek culture and art as representative of "edle Einfalt und stille Größe" (noble simplicity and quiet grandeur). Hauptmann, on the other hand, remains true to what he said about Greek tragedy in *Griechischer Frühling:* that regardless of how it might be disguised, a human sacrifice is "die blutige Wurzel der Tragödie" (the bloody root of tragedy). Hauptmann in the meanwhile expanded this view of Greek tragedy to include *Hamlet* as well: he says in the novel *Im Wirbel der Berufung* that Hamlet is "ein antik-heroisches Leichenspiel" (an antique-heroic play about a body) and that the ghost of Hamlet's father can be propitiated only by blood. Nonetheless, *Iphigenie in Delphi* ends on a conciliatory note, with the crimes of Agamemnon, Orestes, Klytemnestra, and Electra expiated. This outcome would seem to be consistent with Goethe's view that in his *Iphigenie auf Tauris* pure humanity atones for all human feelings.

Once he had completed his play, Hauptmann felt compelled to portray the events for which Iphigenia atones. He completed *Iphigenie in Aulis* (performed, 1943; published, 1944) in 1943, *Agamemnons Tod* (Agamemnon's Death; performed, 1947; published, 1948) in 1944, and *Elektra* (performed, 1947; published, 1948) in 1945 as the first three parts of a tetralogy. Of all the plays in the tetralogy, *Iphigenie in Aulis,* the second to be written but first in terms of the chronology of the plot, proved the most difficult for Hauptmann to complete and exists in the most manuscript versions; the two one-act dramas that fill out the intervening action of the tetralogy followed rather quickly. Hauptmann needed so long to finish *Iphigenie in Aulis* because he was freeing himself of Goethe's influence and rethinking the implications of the legend within the framework of his own conception of Greek tragedy.

No critic has denied that the tetralogy represents a remarkable accomplishment for any playwright, especially for one in his eighties. But this has been the sole point of general agreement. Critics have condemned the language, the lack of dramatic qualities, and the naturalistic approach to the characters. The most damning criticism concerns the obvious differences in tone and in underlying attitude toward the human condition between *Iphigenie in Delphi,* which is usually interpreted as optimistic, and the three subsequently written parts, which take an essentially pessimistic view of the human ability to avert or rectify disaster.

Many critics see in the tetralogy Hauptmann's reckoning with the Nazi dictatorship and the war it brought about; in 1962 the director Erwin Piscator tried to stage the tetralogy (in much shortened form) as a symbolic representation of Nazi rule. But the texts themselves refute any direct equations of individual characters with contemporary historical personages. One can also demonstrate that Hauptmann was most interested in the Greek legend in itself, not as a vehicle for expressing essentially modern views.

When World War II ended, Hauptmann was a broken, tired man, although the Russians occupying Silesia treated the author of *Die Weber* with respect. He died on 6 June 1946 and was buried on the island of Hiddensee, where he had spent some of the most enjoyable times of his life and had, in 1930, bought the house "Seedorn" in Kloster. There are now Hauptmann museums in Kloster and Erkner maintained by the German government.

Letters:

Gerhart Hauptmann und Ida Orloff: Dokumentation einer dichterischen Leidenschaft (Berlin: Propyläen-Verlag, 1969);

Walter A. Reichart, "Gerhart Hauptmann and his British Friends: Documented in Some of Their Correspondence," *German Quarterly,* 50 (November 1977): 424–451;

Klaus Bohnen, "Briefwechsel zwischen Gerhart Hauptmann und Georg Brandes," *Jahrbuch der deutschen Schiller-Gesellschaft,* 23 (1979): 55–68;

Klaus W. Jonas, "Gerhart Hauptmann und Hans von Seeckt: Erinnerungen eines Sammlers und Bibliographen. Mit unveröffentlichten Briefen," *Imprimatur,* 9 (1980): 216–239;

Gerhart Hauptmann–Ludwig von Hofmann: Briefwechsel 1894–1944, edited by Herta Hesse-Frielinghaus (Bonn: Bouvier, 1983);

Otto Brahm–Gerhart Hauptmann: Briefwechsel 1889–1912, edited by Peter Sprengel (Tübingen: Narr, 1985).

Bibliographies:

Max Pinkus and Viktor Ludwig, *Gerhart Hauptmann: Werke von ihm und über ihn* (Neustadt: Privately printed, 1922; revised by Ludwig, 1932);

Walter Requardt, *Gerhart Hauptmann Bibliographie,* 3 volumes (Berlin: Selbstverlag, 1931);

C. F. W. Behl, "Gerhart Hauptmann-Bibliographie," *Gerhart Hauptmann-Jahrbuch,* 1 (1936): 147–162; 2 (1937): 150–160;

Walter A. Reichart, "Fifty Years of Hauptmann Study in America (1894–1944): A Bibliography," *Monatshefte,* 37 (1945): 1–31; 54 (1962): 297–310;

Reichart, "Bibliographie der gedruckten und ungedruckten Dissertationen über Gerhart Hauptmann und sein Werk," *Philobiblon,* 11 (June 1967): 121–134;

Reichart, *Gerhart-Hauptmann-Bibliographie* (Bad Homburg: Gehlen, 1969);

Klaus W. Jonas, "Gerhart Hauptmanns Manuskripte in Europa," *Börsenblatt für den deutschen Buchhandel,* 26 (28 July 1970): A121–A139;

Jonas, "Gerhart Hauptmann Collections in America and England," *Stechert-Hafner Book News,* 26 (February 1971): 77–82;

H. D. Tschörtner, *Gerhart-Hauptmann-Bibliographie* (Berlin: Deutsche Staatsbibliothek, 1971);

Rudolf Ziesche, *Der Manuskriptnachlaß Gerhart Hauptmanns* (Wiesbaden: Harrassowitz, 1977);

Sigfrid Hoefert, *Internationale Bibliographie zum Werk Gerhart Hauptmann,* 2 volumes (Berlin: Schmidt, 1986–1989).

Biographies:

Paul Schlenther, *Gerhart Hauptmann: Sein Lebensgang und seine Dichtung* (Berlin: Fischer, 1898; revised, 1912; revised by A. Eloesser, 1922);

C. F. W. Behl and F. A. Voigt, *Chronik von Gerhart Hauptmanns Leben und Schaffen* (Munich: Korn, 1957);

Wolfgang Leppmann, *Gerhart Hauptmann: Leben, Werk und Zeit* (Munich: Scherz, 1986).

References:

Neville Edward Alexander, *Studien zum Stilwandel im dramatischen Werk Gerhart Hauptmanns* (Stuttgart: Metzler, 1964);

Hermann Barnstorff, *Die soziale, politische und wirt-schaftliche Zeitkritik im Werke Gerhart Hauptmanns* (Jena: Frommann, 1938);

Peter Bauland, Introduction to *Before Daybreak,* by Hauptmann, translated by Bauland (Chapel Hill: University of North Carolina Press, 1978), pp. i–xxiv;

C. F. W. Behl, *Wege zu Gerhart Hauptmann* (Goslar: Verlag Deutsche Volksbücherei, 1948);

Behl, *Zwiesprache mit Gerhart Hauptmann: Tagebuchblätter* (Munich: Desch, 1949);

Hans von Brescius, *Gerhart Hauptmann: Zeitgeschehen und Bewusstsein in unbekannten Selbstzeugnissen* (Bonn: Bouvier, 1976);

Joseph Chapiro, *Gespräche mit Gerhart Hauptmann* (Berlin: Fischer, 1932);

W. A. Coupe, "An Ambiguous Hero: In Defence of Alfred Loth," *German Life and Letters,* new series 31 (October 1977): 13–22;

Roy C. Cowen, *Das deutsche Drama im 19. Jahrhundert* (Stuttgart: Metzler, 1988);

Cowen, *Hauptmann-Kommentar zum dramatischen Werk* (Munich: Winkler, 1980);

Cowen, *Hauptmann-Kommentar zum nichtdramatischen Werk* (Munich: Winkler, 1981);

Cowen, *Der Naturalismus: Kommentar zu einer Epoche* (Munich: Winkler, 1973);

Hans Daiber, *Gerhart Hauptmann oder der letzte Klassiker* (Vienna: Molden, 1971);

C. T. Dussère, *The Image of the Primitive Giant in the Work of Gerhart Hauptmann* (Stuttgart: Heinz, 1979);

Gustav Erdmann, "Einige pommersch-rügensche Motive in Gerhart Hauptmanns Schaffen: Quellenkundliche Untersuchungen," *Greifswald- Stralsunder Jahrbuch,* 5 (1965): 211–277;

Ralph Fiedler, *Die späten Dramen Gerhart Hauptmanns* (Munich: Korn, 1954);

Hugo F. Garten, "Formen des Eros im Werk Gerhart Hauptmanns," *Zeitschrift für deutsche Philologie,* 90 (1971): 242–258;

Garten, *Gerhart Hauptmann* (Cambridge: Bowes & Bowes, 1954);

Garten, "Gerhart Hauptmann: A Revaluation," *German Life and Letters,* 3 (1949): 32–41;

Joseph Gregor, *Gerhart Hauptmann: Das Werk und unsere Zeit* (Vienna: Diana-Verlag, 1951);

Karl S. Guthke, *Gerhart Hauptmann: Weltbild im Werk* (Göttingen: Vandenhoeck & Ruprecht, 1980);

Frederick W. J. Heuser, *Gerhart Hauptmann: Zu seinem Leben und Schaffen* (Tübingen: Niemeyer, 1961);

Klaus Hildebrandt, *Gerhart Hauptmann und die Geschichte* (Munich: Delp, 1968);

Hildebrandt, *Naturalistische Dramen Gerhart Hauptmanns* (Munich: Oldenbourg, 1983);

Eberhard Hilscher, *Gerhart Hauptmann* (Berlin: Verlag der Nation, 1988);

James L. Hodge, "The Dramaturgy of 'Bahnwärter Thiel,'" *Mosaic,* 9 (Spring 1976): 97–116;

Sigfrid Hoefert, *Gerhart Hauptmann* (Stuttgart: Metzler, 1982);

Josef Hofmiller, *Zeitgenossen* (Munich: Süddeutsche Monatshefte, 1910);

Karl Holl, *Gerhart Hauptmann: His Life and His Work 1862–1912* (London: Gay & Hancock, 1913; Chicago: McClurg, 1913);

Jenny Christa Hortenbach, *Freiheitsstreben und Destruktivität: Frauen in den Dramen August Strindbergs und Gerhart Hauptmanns* (Oslo: Universitetsforlaget, 1965);

K. G. Knight and F. Norman, eds., *Hauptmann Centenary Lectures* (London: University of London Institute of Germanic Studies, 1964);

Ward B. Lewis, "O'Neill and Hauptmann: A Study in Mutual Admiration," *Comparative Literature Studies,* 22 (Summer 1985): 231–243;

Thomas Mann, *Gerhart Hauptmann* (Gütersloh: Bertelsmann, 1953);

Ludwig Marcuse, ed., *Gerhart Hauptmann und sein Werk* (Berlin & Leipzig: Schneider, 1922);

Alan Marshall, *The German Naturalists and Gerhart Hauptmann* (Frankfurt am Main & Bern: Lang, 1982);

Warren R. Maurer, *Gerhart Hauptmann* (Boston: Twayne, 1982);

Hans Mayer, *Gerhart Hauptmann* (Velber bei Hannover: Friedrich, 1972);

Edward McInnes, *Das deutsche Drama des 19. Jahrhunderts* (Berlin: Schmidt, 1983);

McInnes, *German Social Drama 1840–1900: From Hebbel to Hauptmann* (Stuttgart: Heinz, 1976);

Philip Mellen, *Gerhart Hauptmann and Utopia* (Stuttgart: Heinz, 1976);

Mellen, *Gerhart Hauptmann: Religious Syncretism and Eastern Religions* (Bern, Frankfurt am Main & New York: Lang, 1984);

Rolf Michaelis, *Der schwarze Zeus: Gerhart Hauptmanns zweiter Weg* (Berlin: Argon, 1962);

Rudolf Mittler, *Theorie und Praxis des sozialen Dramas bei Gerhart Hauptmann* (Hildesheim, Zurich & New York: Olms, 1985);

Irmgard Müller, *Gerhart Hauptmann und Frankreich* (Breslau: Priebatsch, 1939);

Siegfried H. Muller, *Gerhart Hauptmann und Goethe* (New York: King's Crown Press, 1949);

Muller, "Gerhart Hauptmann's Relation to American Literature and His Concept of America," *Monatshefte*, 44 (1952): 333–339;

Gerdt Oberembt, *Gerhart Hauptmann: Der Biberpelz* (Paderborn, Munich, Vienna & Zurich: Schöningh, 1987);

John Osborne, *The Naturalist Drama in Germany* (Manchester: Manchester University Press / Totowa, N.J.: Rowman & Littlefield, 1971);

Jill Perkins, *Joyce and Hauptmann: Before Sunrise* (San Marino, Cal.: Huntington Library, 1978);

Gerhart Pohl, *Bin ich noch in meinem Haus? Die letzten Tage Gerhart Hauptmanns* (Berlin: Lettner, 1953); translated as *Gerhart Hauptmann and Silesia* (Grand Forks: University of North Dakota Press, 1962);

Walter A. Reichart, *Einheben für Gerhart Hauptmann: Aufsätze aus dem Jahren 1929–1990* (Berlin: Schmidt, 1991);

Reichart, "Gerhart Hauptmann, War Propaganda, and George Bernard Shaw," *Germanic Review*, 33 (October 1958): 176–180;

Reichart, "Gerhart Hauptmann's Dramas on the American Stage," *Maske und Kothurn*, 8 (1962): 223–232;

Reichart, "Grundbegriffe im dramatischen Schaffen Gerhart Hauptmanns," *PMLA*, 82 (March 1967): 142–151;

Ilse H. Reis, *Gerhart Hauptmanns Hamlet-Interpretationen in der Nachfolge Goethes* (Bonn: Bouvier, 1969);

Walter Requardt and Martin Machatzke, *Gerhart Hauptmann und Erkner* (Berlin: Schmidt, 1980);

Hermann Schreiber, *Gerhart Hauptmann und das Irrationale* (Aichkirchen: Schönleiter, 1946);

Hans Joachim Schrimpf, ed., *Gerhart Hauptmann* (Darmstadt: Wissenschaftliche Buchgesellschaft, 1976);

Leroy R. Shaw, *Witness of Deceit: Gerhart Hauptmann as Critic of Society* (Berkeley & Los Angeles: University of California Press, 1958);

Peter Sprengel, *Gerhart Hauptmann: Epoche, Werk, Wirkung* (Munich: Beck, 1984);

Sprengel, "Todessehnsucht und Totenkult bei Gerhart Hauptmann," *Neue Deutsche Hefte*, 189, no. 33 (1986): 11–34;

Sprengel, "'Vor Sonnenuntergang'–ein Goethe-Drama? Zur Goethe-Rezeption Gerhart Hauptmanns," *Goethe-Jahrbuch* (Weimar), 103 (1986): 31–53;

Sprengel, *Die Wirklichkeit der Mythen: Untersuchungen zum Werk Gerhart Hauptmanns aufgrund des handschriftlichen Nachlasses* (Berlin: Schmidt, 1982);

Sprengel and Philip Mellen, eds., *Hauptmann-Forschung: Neue Beiträge–Hauptmann Research: New Directions* (Bern, Frankfurt am Main & New York: Lang, 1986);

J. L. Styan, *Modern Drama in Theory and Practice,* volume 1: *Realism and Naturalism* (Cambridge, New York & Melbourne: Cambridge University Press, 1981);

Kurt Lothar Tank, *Gerhart Hauptmann in Selbstzeugnissen und Bilddokumenten* (Hamburg: Rowohlt, 1959);

Günther Taube, *Die Rolle der Natur in Gerhart Hauptmanns Gegenwartsdramen bis zum Anfang des 20. Jahrhunderts* (Berlin: Ebering, 1936; reprint, Nendeln, Liechtenstein: Kraus, 1967);

H. D. Tschörtner, "Bertolt Brecht und Hauptmann," *Weimarer Beiträge*, 32, no. 3 (1986): 386–403;

Tschörtner, *Ungeheures erhofft: Zu Gerhart Hauptmann–Werk und Wirkung* (Berlin: Der Morgen, 1986);

Felix A. Voigt, *Antike und antikes Lebensgefühl im Werke Gerhart Hauptmanns* (Breslau: Maruschke & Berendt, 1935);

Voigt, *Gerhart Hauptmann der Schlesier* (Breslau: Schlesien-Verlag, 1942; revised, Goslar: Deutsche Volksbücherei, 1947);

Voigt, *Hauptmann-Studien: Untersuchungen über Leben und Schaffen Gerhart Hauptmanns* (Breslau: Maruschke & Berendt, 1936);

Voigt, "Die Schaffensweise Gerhart Hauptmanns," *Germanisch-Romanische Monatsschrift,* 32 (1950): 93–106;

Voigt and Reichart, *Hauptmann und Shakespeare* (Breslau: Maruschke & Berendt, 1938; revised, Goslar: Deutsche Volksbücherei, 1947);

Benno von Wiese, "Gerhart Hauptmann," in *Deutsche Dichter der Moderne,* edited by Wiese (Berlin: Schmidt, 1965), pp. 27–48;

Bernhard Zeller, ed., *Gerhart Hauptmann: Leben und Werk: Eine Gedächtnisausstellung des Deutschen Literaturarchivs zum 100. Geburtstag des Dichters* (Stuttgart: Turmhaus-Druckerei, 1962);

Theodore Ziolkowski, "Hauptmann's Iphigenie in Delphi: A Travesty?" *Germanic Review,* 34 (February 1959): 105–123;

Carl Zuckmayer, *Ein voller Erdentag: Zu Gerhart Hauptmanns hundertstem Geburtstag* (Frankfurt am Main: Fischer, 1962).

Papers:

Manuscript materials of Gerhart Hauptmann are at the Staatsbibliothek Preußischer Kulturbesitz, Berlin.

Friedrich Hebbel

(18 March 1813 – 13 December 1863)

A. Tilo Alt
Duke University

This entry was updated by Professor Alt from his entry in DLB 129:
Nineteenth-Century German Writers, 1841–1900.

BOOKS: *Judith: Eine Tragödie in fünf Acten* (Hamburg: Hoffmann & Campe, 1841); translated by Carl van Doren as *Judith: A Tragedy in Five Acts* (Boston: Badger, 1914);

Gedichte (Hamburg: Hoffmann & Campe, 1842);

Genoveva: Tragödie in fünf Acten (Hamburg: Hoffmann & Campe, 1843);

Mein Wort über das Drama!: Eine Erwiderung an Professor Heiberg in Copenhagen (Hamburg: Hoffmann & Campe, 1843); translated by Moody Campbell as "My View on the Drama," in his *Hebbel, Ibsen and the Analytic Exposition* (Heidelberg: Winter, 1922), pp. 78–85;

Maria Magdalene: Ein bürgerliches Trauerspiel in drei Acten. Nebst einem Vorwort, betreffend das Verhältnis der dramatischen Kunst zur Zeit und verwandte Puncte (Hamburg: Hoffmann & Campe, 1844); translated by Paul Bernard Thomas as *Maria Magdalena,* in *The German Classics of the Nineteenth and Twentieth Centuries,* volume 9, edited by Kuno Francke and William Guild Howard (New York: German Publication Society, 1914), pp. 22–80;

Der Diamant: Eine Komödie in fünf Acten (Hamburg: Hoffmann & Campe, 1847);

Neue Gedichte (Leipzig: Weber, 1848);

Herodes und Mariamne: Eine Tragödie in fünf Acten (Vienna: Gerold, 1850); translated by Edith J. R. Isaacs and Kurt Rahlson as *Herod and Mariamne: A Tragedy in Five Acts,* in *Drama: A Quarterly Review of Dramatic Literature,* no. 6 (May 1912): 3–168;

Schnock: Ein niederländisches Gemälde (Leipzig: Weber, 1850);

Ein Trauerspiel in Sicilien: Tragicomödie in einem Act, nebst einem Sendschreiben an H. T. Rötscher (Leipzig: Geibel, 1851);

Friedrich Hebbel; painting by Karl Rahl, 1851 (Freies Deutsches Hochstift, Frankfurter Goethemuseum)

Julia: Ein Trauerspiel in drei Akten. Nebst einer Vorrede und einer Abhandlung: "Abfertigung eines ästhetischen Kannegießers" (Leipzig: Weber, 1851);

Der Rubin: Ein Märchen-Lustspiel in drei Acten (Leipzig: Geibel, 1851);

Agnes Bernauer: Ein deutsches Trauerspiel in fünf Aufzügen (Vienna: Tendler, 1855); translated by Loueen Pattee as *Agnes Bernauer (a German Tragedy in Five Acts),* in *Poet Lore,* 20, no. 1 (1909): 1–60;

Erzählungen und Novellen (Pest: Heckenast, 1855)—comprises "Matteo," "Herr Haidvogel und seine Familie," "Anna," "Pauls merkwürdige Nacht," "Die Kuh," "Der Schneidermeister Nepomuk Schlägel auf der Freudenjagd," and "Eine Nacht im Jägerhaus"; "Anna" translated by Frances H. King in *The German Classics of the Nineteenth and Twentieth Centuries,* volume 9, pp. 166–173;

Michel Angelo: Ein Drama in zwei Akten (Vienna: Tendler, 1855);

Gyges und sein Ring: Eine Tragödie in fünf Acten (Vienna: Tendler, 1856); translated by L. H. Allen as *Gyges and His Ring,* in *Three Plays by Friedrich Hebbel* (London: Dent / New York: Dutton, 1914);

Gedichte: Gesamt-Ausgabe, stark vermehrt und verbessert (Stuttgart & Augsburg: Cotta, 1857);

Mutter und Kind: Ein Gedicht in sieben Gesängen (Hamburg: Hoffmann & Campe / New York: Westermann, 1859);

Die Nibelungen: Ein deutsches Trauerspiel in drei Abtheilungen, 2 volumes (Hamburg: Hoffmann & Campe, 1862); translated by G. H. McCall as *The Niebelungs: A Tragedy in Three Acts* (London: Siegle, 1903);

Demetrius: Eine Tragödie (Hamburg: Hoffmann & Campe, 1864);

Sämmtliche Werke, 12 volumes, edited by Emil Kuh (Hamburg: Hoffmann, 1865–1867);

Tagebücher, 2 volumes, edited by Felix Bamberg (Berlin: Grote, 1885, 1887); excerpts translated by King as "Extracts from the Journals of Friedrich Hebbel," in *The German Classics of the Nineteenth and Twentieth Centuries,* volume 9, pp. 253–267;

Sämtliche Werke: Historisch-Kritische Ausgabe, 24 volumes, edited by Richard Maria Werner (Berlin: Behr, 1901–1907);

Friedrich Hebbel: Sämtliche Werke nebst Tagebüchern und einer Auswahl der Briefe, 6 volumes, edited by Paul Bornstein (Munich: Müller, 1911–1925);

Werke, 5 volumes, edited by Gerhard Fricke, Werner Keller, and Karl Pörnbacher (Munich: Hanser, 1963–1967).

Edition in English: *Three Plays, by Friedrich Hebbel* (London: Dent / New York: Dutton, 1914)—comprises *Gyges and His Ring,* translated by L. H. Allen; *Herod and Mariamne,* translated by Allen; and *Maria Magdalena,* translated by Barker Fairley.

OTHER: *Ernst Freiherrn von Feuchtersleben's sämtliche Werke: Mit Ausnahme der rein medicinischen,* edited by Hebbel (Vienna: Gerold, 1853).

SELECTED PERIODICAL PUBLICATIONS–UNCOLLECTED: "Über den Styl des Dramas," *Jahrbücher für dramatische Kunst und Literatur,* 1 (1847): 35–40;

"Wie verhalten sich im Dichter Kraft und Erkenntnis zu einander?," *Jahrbücher für dramatische Kunst und Literatur,* 1 (1847): 310–313;

"Aus meiner Jugend," *Unterhaltungen am häuslichen Herd,* 2, no. 40 (1854): 625–626; translated by Frances H. King as "Recollections of My Childhood (1846–1854)," in *The German Classics of the Nineteenth and Twentieth Centuries,* volume 9, edited by Kuno Francke and William Guild Howard (New York: German Publication Society, 1914), pp. 221–254.

Friedrich Hebbel had to overcome formidable odds to achieve greatness. Not only did he have a most difficult start in life, but he also lived in an epoch that regarded greatness as dangerous and modesty and moderation as virtues. At the beginning of the age of science and technology, the idealistic and spiritual side of life had been replaced with materialistic concerns.

Although Hebbel's misappropriation by the Nazis as a "Nordic" poet and dramatist on the one hand and his rejection by Marxist critics on the other have made him a controversial figure, there is agreement among admirers and critics alike that he was the most significant playwright to follow Johann Wolfgang von Goethe and Friedrich Schiller. His poetry, too, though to a lesser degree, commands a place of high regard in the annals of German letters, and a good deal of it is part of the canon. Hebbel has been labeled a poet of the conservative Biedermeier restoration period between 1815 and 1848, a neoclassicist, an early realist, a prophet of German national unity, as well as an advocate of a league of nations. These contradictory classifications make Hebbel a difficult but fascinating figure in German cultural history.

Hebbel's posthumous road to fame proved as rocky as the reception of his work during his lifetime. His friend Emil Kuh hoped to publicize Hebbel's work by bringing out an edition of his collected works (1865–1867) shortly after the writer's death in 1863; in 1877 Kuh's biography of Hebbel was published in two volumes. Neither effort produced the desired result. Interest in Hebbel's works was not to gather momentum until Felix Bamberg, Hebbel's friend and admirer from his Paris days, edited Hebbel's diaries (1885, 1887) and letters (1890–1892). Bamberg's commentaries, his article on the poet in the *Allgemeine Deutsche Biographie* (Universal German Biography) of 1880, and his publication of the correspondence between Hebbel and Theodor Rötscher, a disciple of the philosopher Georg Wilhelm Friedrich Hegel, alerted academicians that here was a man of both artistic and philosophical significance. Finally, after the completion of Richard Maria Werner's critical edition of Hebbel's works (1901–1907), the poet gained admission to the pantheon of German literature. The Hebbel centenary in 1913 brought the unveiling of his monument in Wesselburen and the publication of new editions of his works, including diaries. Hebbel had become a "classic," part of the curriculum of schools and universities and of the repertory of most important theaters in the German-speaking countries.

Christian Friedrich Hebbel was born on 18 March 1813 in Wesselburen, a small town near the North Sea in the region of Dithmarschen in Holstein. Since the duchies of Schleswig and Holstein belonged to Denmark, Hebbel was a Danish citizen by birth and remained so throughout his life. His father, Claus Friedrich, was a poor bricklayer; his mother, Antje Margarete Schubert, worked as a domestic. Hebbel's "Aus meiner Jugend" (translated as "Recollections of my Childhood [1846–1854]," 1914), published in 1854 in Karl Gutzkow's popular magazine *Unterhaltungen am häuslichen Herd* (Fireside Chats) as the first part of a planned but soon abandoned autobiography, is the main source of information about his youth. Most critics, including the author himself, have regarded this fragment as his best prose work; his forte was dramatic dialogue and verse. His account passes over the unhappy moments of his youth in favor of experiences that had a positive effect on him and that might inspire others. In this effort Hebbel's ambition to be a classical writer asserted itself.

Hebbel's father died in 1827 at the age of thirty-seven, leaving Hebbel and his brother, Johann, to be brought up by their mother. On the recommendation of Hebbel's schoolteacher, the fourteen-year-old was hired as an errand boy and clerk by J. J. Mohr, the magistrate of the parish of Wesselburen. Without this stroke of good fortune Hebbel would not have had the opportunity to continue his education. In later years he complained bitterly about Mohr's treatment of him—he had to share a bed under the stairs with Mohr's coachman, even when the latter was sick, and he had to take his meals with the servants—but Hebbel's duties were light, and he was permitted to use the magistrate's library. Although Mohr's library lacked Goethe's works, those of Schiller, Heinrich von Kleist, Friedrich Klopstock, E. T. A. Hoffmann, and—momentously—Ludwig Uhland were well represented. After Hebbel made some poetic attempts in the manner of Schiller's reflective lyric, Uhland's natural simplicity struck the boy as a revelation. As late as 1857 Hebbel would dedi-cate his collected poems to Uhland, "dem ersten Dichter der Gegenwart" (premier poet of the present). By the time Uhland died in 1862, however, Hebbel had come to recognize the poet's mediocrity.

During his self-education Hebbel also became acquainted with Immanuel Kant's ethical theory, Hegel's dialectic, and Ludwig Feuerbach's materialism. The vehicles for these ideas were Christoph Tiedge's poem "Urania: Über Gott, Unsterblichkeit und Freiheit" (Urania: Of God, Immortality, and Freedom, 1800), Gotthilf H. Schubert's "Ansichten von der Nachtseite der Naturwissenschaft" (Views on the Dark Side of Natural Science, 1808) and "Symbolik des Traums" (Dream Symbolism, 1814), and Feuerbach's "Gedanken über Tod und Unsterblichkeit" (Reflections on Death and Immortality, 1830). These texts did not come to light as sources of his philosophical ideas until nearly a century later. The philosophy of Friedrich Wilhelm Joseph von Schelling and Hegel's aesthetics also exercised a lasting but unacknowledged influence on the poet. With the exception of Friedrich Theodor von Vischer's *Ästhetik oder Wissenschaft des Schönen* (Aesthetics; or, the Science of the Beautiful, 1847–1858), he endeavored to conceal the sources of his ideas.

In 1832 Amalie Schoppe, a popular writer of trivial novels, published some poems and stories Hebbel had sent her in the two Hamburg journals she edited: *Iduna: Eine Zeitschrift für die Jugend beiderlei Geschlechts, belehrenden, erheiternden und geistbelebenden Inhalts* (Iduna: A Journal of Didactic, Amusing and Stimulating Contents for the Youth of Both Sexes) and *Neue Pariser Modeblätter* (New Parisian Fashion Journal). One of the poems he sent her subsequently, the patriotic "Die Schlacht bei Hemmingstedt" (The Battle of Hemmingstedt, 1833), was timely because the 1830s were a period of unrest in the duchies, where the populace sought to free itself from Danish rule in the wake of uprisings in Poland and France. The poem commemorates the victory of the Dithmarschen peasants over Danish and German troops in the sixteenth century. It prompted Schoppe to invite Hebbel to come to Hamburg to prepare himself for admission to a university. One of the requirements for admission was proficiency in Latin, and Schoppe arranged for Latin lessons for him. Hebbel arrived in Hamburg in February 1835. He was given free room and board in the home of a ship's carpenter, whose stepdaughter, Elise Lensing, a seamstress, became his lover, even though she was eight and a half years his senior. In March 1835 Hebbel began to keep a journal, a practice he continued until his death.

Hebbel failed his Latin examinations; furthermore, Schoppe disapproved of his liaison with Lensing, and his relationship with his benefactress became strained. Therefore, after collecting the funds she had set aside for his studies, on 27 March 1836 he left for the University of Heidelberg. He arrived in Heidelberg on 3 April. Shortly thereafter he began attending lectures without matriculating.

Hebbel remained in Heidelberg until September 1836. The most important aspect of his life then was his friendship with Emil Rousseau, a law student. After Rousseau's death in 1838 Hebbel remarked that Rousseau had been the only real friend he had ever had. He was to keep up a regular correspondence with Rousseau's father and sister.

From Heidelberg, Hebbel traveled to Munich on foot to continue his studies. To supplement his meager resources he had accepted a position as correspondent for the *Morgenblatt für gebildete Leser* (Morning Paper for Educated Readers). On the way to Munich he visited his revered poetic mentor Uhland, but he came away disappointed in what he regarded as Uhland's banal nature. In Munich he stayed with the family of the master joiner Schwarz. He and Schwarz's daughter Beppi became lovers.

In March 1839 Hebbel ran out of money and returned to Hamburg on foot. There he took a job as correspondent for the *Telegraph für Deutschland* (German Telegraph).

At the end of 1839 Hebbel began writing his first drama, *Judith* (1841; translated, 1914), based on the apocryphal Book of Judith. The play depicts the clash between paganism, represented by the mighty general Holofernes, and Judaism, represented by Judith of Bethulia. Since, according to Hebbel, the nature of woman is to love rather than to hate, the virgin Judith faces a tragic conflict when she is called on by the deity to kill Holofernes, the enemy of her people. In the end she has a personal reason to kill Holofernes: she stabs him to death for raping her even though she longed for the encounter with Holofernes, a man of imposing physical attributes and great power. If she should become pregnant, she tells her people, they must kill her. Hegel's dialectic is visible here in that Judith functions as the guilty tool of history: she produces the downfall of Holofernes, which results in the rise of monotheism. The play premiered on 6 July 1840 at the Berlin court theater and was a great success.

Hebbel summarized his ideas about drama in the essay *Mein Wort über das Drama!* (1843; translated as "My View on the Drama," 1922) and in the preface to his tragedy *Maria Magdalene* (1844; translated as *Maria Magdalena,* 1914). They reveal Hebbel's near-total dependence on Hegel's aesthetic paradigm, despite his repeated denials of any Hegelian influence. With Hegel, Hebbel accepts the need to "regenerate" Western tragedy as the highest form of poetic expression and as the vehicle for establishing a divine presence in the world,

the original raison d'être of tragedy. Hebbel opposed the view of history as an objective phenomenon, as the concrete result of human activity. For Hebbel and Hegel, history has a religious source that manifests itself in ethical values. Hebbel claimed that his historical dramas had a higher, more universal purpose than the historical tragedies of his contemporaries, which served narrow nationalistic interests. Hebbel sought to establish a synthesis of the cultural achievements of the West in a symbolic way. In Hebbel's concept of tragic guilt, guilt arises not by accident but by necessity, because life exists only individually while—at the same time—the individual remains a part of the Whole. Through separation from the Whole, the individual unavoidably incurs guilt. Tragic guilt is part of what is known as Hebbel's concept of pantragedy. Finally, Hebbel says that the task of drama is to help overcome the alienation that he saw taking place between the individual and social institutions, such as the emerging metropolis and the state.

In the summer of 1840 Hebbel had a brief affair with Emma Schröder, the daughter of a Hamburg senator. Lensing, who knew of the affair, was expecting a child by him. He was beset by feelings of guilt and remorse, and the figure of Golo in the drama *Genoveva* (1843), which he had begun writing, reflects those feelings. On 5 November 1840 Lensing gave birth to a son, Max. Hebbel's financial situation had become desperate despite the royalties he received from *Judith*. He decided to petition King Christian VIII of Denmark, who was known for his support of the arts, for a professorship at the University of Kiel or some other position. In the winter of 1842 he journeyed to Copenhagen, where the poet Adam Oehlenschläger was his advocate at court. In the spring of 1843 Hebbel obtained from the king a two-year travel grant of twelve hundred talers, a stipend that was larger than customary and that entailed no obligation on his part. He returned to Hamburg and gave Lensing half of the grant to help support herself and their child. After completing *Genoveva,* one of his lesser plays, he set sail for France on 9 September 1843. His knowledge of French was poor, and he came to depend on the services and the subsequent friendship of Bamberg, the Prussian consul in Paris. During his stay in Paris Hebbel met the poet Heinrich Heine and, through Heine, the philosopher and socialist Arnold Ruge, coeditor with Karl Marx of the *Deutsch-Französische Jahrbücher* (German-French Annals). Hebbel lived extremely frugally in Paris, and he felt inadequate because of his poverty, his humble origins, and his lack of social graces.

His stay in Paris was marred even further when he learned of his son's death on 2 October 1843 and Lensing's despondency over the loss. She was expecting their second child, and Hebbel feared for her life. He despaired over her inability to put the loss behind her. For Hebbel, pain caused by the state of the world outweighs pain suffered because of the loss of an individual; the death of the individual is necessary for the preservation and progress of humanity as a whole. At one point, however, he was so gripped by guilt and remorse that he offered to marry her and share the rest of his stipend with her. Bamberg prevented him from doing so by reminding him of his creative mission. In May 1844 she gave birth to their second son, Ernst.

In September 1844 Hebbel's *Maria Magdalene, a* "bürgerliches Trauerspiel" (middle-class tragedy) in the tradition of Gotthold Ephraim Lessing's *Miß Sara Sampson* (1755) and *Emilia Galotti* (1772), was published. It was to become his most influential and most frequently staged tragedy. In many ways Hebbel's most personal work, it depicts the misery of an individual in social and economic circumstances not unlike those of the playwright's youth. He modeled the characters Klara and Meister Anton on the Schwarzes, the family with whom he had stayed when he was a student in Munich. The tragedy arises not from conflict between social classes but from conflict within the same class. The destruction of the family is the result of the harshness of Meister Anton, the master joiner and father of Klara. Klara becomes pregnant by her fiancé, the villainous clerk Leonhard, whom she does not love and who wants to marry her only for her dowry. She commits suicide so as not to "disgrace" her father. When it is explained to her father that he and the secretary Friedrich—Klara's former fiancé, who had neglected her—must bear the guilt for her death, Meister Anton is moved to utter the final and often-quoted line of the play: "Ich verstehe die Welt nicht mehr" (I no longer understand the world). Not only do the men in Klara's environment fail to understand her, but, in the last analysis, she agrees with their assessment because she has internalized the values of her father's patriarchal world. Hebbel's interest in character and environment and his keen psychological insight make *Maria Magdalene* an unusual middle-class tragedy. Anticipating the naturalists, Hebbel depicts the social milieu as the reason for the actions of his characters: the rigid moral standards of his class make Meister Anton a tyrant, even though he loves his children. A dramatic technique that Hebbel employs with great success and that had been used by Lessing, Schiller, and Kleist is that of analytic exposition: opening the drama not long before the catastrophe and then showing the events that led up to it.

Because he was afraid he had represented the everyday milieu of a contemporary small-town family too graphically, Hebbel, at Bamberg's urging, added to the play a preface in which he asserts his noble intentions and great regard for the drama as the highest form of artistic expression. The Greeks had as their purpose the representation of fate; Shakespeare showed the destruction of the individual through the individual's inherently demonic nature. The drama of Hebbel's time is to make visible the struggle of the extraordinary individual with God or history. Drama must serve the highest and truest interests of its own time, even if the plot is taken from ancient myths. Hebbel came to regret adding the preface because it was frequently used to attack him by pointing to the contradiction between his idealistic goals and naturalistic results.

On 26 September 1844 Hebbel left Paris for Italy. His stays in Rome and Naples yielded some poems, epigrams, and the plot for his tragicomedy *Ein Trauerspiel in Sicilien* (A Tragedy in Sicily, 1851), about the rape and murder of a young woman by two policemen who are convicted on the testimony of a witness. In Rome he met the painter Louis Gurlitt, with whom he was to enter into a lengthy correspondence, and the literary historian Hermann Hettner. And he broke with Lensing in harsh and uncompromising letters from Rome.

In October 1845, after the Danish king sent him additional money for his return home—Hebbel had spent every penny of his grant—he left for Berlin via Vienna. The author of three tragedies, he was no longer unknown, and the papers in Vienna reported his arrival in early November. The wealthy brothers Julius and Wilhelm Zerboni, admirers of Hebbel's work, organized a grand party in his honor and showered him with attention and presents. Book dealers began to order his works, and Christine Enghaus, the leading actress at the Vienna Burgtheater, let it be known that she was interested in playing the roles of Judith and Klara. Like Hebbel, Christine was from northern Germany and was the parent of a child born out of wedlock. On 26 May 1846 she and Hebbel were married. Vienna, which was to have been a stop on his way to Berlin and an uncertain future, had become his home. That same year, through the good offices of his deceased friend Rousseau's father, who advanced him the money for the fee, Hebbel was granted a doctorate in philosophy by the University of Erlangen. He had submitted *Mein Wort über das Drama!* in lieu of a dissertation.

Christine's relative financial security enabled Hebbel to concentrate on his writing, and her generosity allowed him to resolve his relationship with Elise Lensing in an amicable if unconventional way. The couple invited Elise to visit them in Vienna; the death of Ernst, Hebbel and Elise's second son, on 12 May 1847 was the immediate reason for the invitation. Hebbel's marriage had caused Elise much bitterness at first, but her good nature prevailed over her rancor; she accepted the invitation and stayed with the Hebbels for more than a year in an innocent menage à trois. Christine's illegitimate son, Carl, whom Hebbel had adopted but whom he had come to resent, was placed in Elise's care as a substitute for Ernst. Christine and Hebbel's first child, Emil, was born on 27 December 1846 and died a few months later. On Christmas Eve of 1847 their second child, Christine (Titi), was born; she was Hebbel's only child to grow to adulthood. Elise and Christine kept up a correspondence until Elise's death in 1854.

Hebbel's *Herodes und Mariamne* (1850; translated as *Herod and Mariamne,* 1912) was based on Flavius Josephus's history of the Jewish people (circa A.D. 65); Hebbel knew nothing of the previous dramatic treatments of the story by Hans Sachs (1552), Pedro Calderón de la Barca (1637), Voltaire (1730), and Friedrich Rückert (1844). Herodes (Herod), an Edomite forcibly converted to Judaism, marries Mariamne, a descendant of the royal house of the Maccabees. With the help of the Romans, Herodes becomes king of Judea. Josephus reports that Herodes' love for Mariamne was directly proportionate to her hatred for him, but in Hebbel's tragedy Mariamne loves Herodes as passionately as he loves her. But Mariamne learns that Herodes has twice given orders that she is to be killed should he fail to return from Alexandria, where he fears death at the hands of his Roman superiors. She is hurt and outraged at his lack of trust in her to take her own life out of devotion to him, and she decides to force him to execute her. When he returns from his second journey, he finds her celebrating his supposed death. She is tried and sentenced to die. Above all, the tragedy is another variant of Hebbel's representation of the battle of the sexes. The reduction of Mariamne to the status of an object is a sin, and a world that permits it to happen is doomed. Mariamne reveals her true feelings to the Roman captain Titus not long before her death; she has resolved that Herodes should be her executioner. Titus must promise not to reveal Mariamne's reasons for acquiescing in her death sentence. When Herodes learns of his wife's innocence after her execution, it is the Roman, Titus, who steadies the fainting king, thus symbolizing the greater stability represented by imperial Rome. After the arrival of the three wise men and their announcement of the birth of the King of Kings, Herodes issues his infamous order to have all the male infants of Bethlehem killed.

In keeping with Hegel's dialectics of history and aesthetics, the drama ends on a hopeful note: the arrival of the three kings from the Orient heralds the dawning of a more humane age. The three wise men symbolize the Christian gospel of love, forgiveness, and redemption. This new age is a synthesis that was produced by the clash of the antithetical cultures of paganism and Judaism and is a stage in the inevitable progress of history toward its ultimate goal of reunion with the Absolute. Hebbel was criticized for superimposing this conciliatory and idealistic perspective on the tragic events rather than having it flow naturally from them; this criticism seems justified.

Hebbel felt that he had to subordinate realistic psychological details, such as those in *Maria Magdalene,* to his abstract view of history: the spectator was to ponder the subordination of the individual to the general tragic order of the universe. The open-ended, relativistic tragedies of the realists and naturalists no longer admitted of such cosmic vistas; it was Hebbel's ambition to renew the ancient Attic tragedy. The price he had to pay for his untimely ambition was the slight theatrical success of the drama. *Herodes und Mariamne* premiered in April 1849 at the Burgtheater in Vienna. Hebbel's wife played Mariamne, a role he had written for her; despite a stellar performance by Christine, the play did not meet with a warm reception and to this day lags far behind *Maria Magdalene* as a stage success.

With his tragedy *Agnes Bernauer* (1855; translated, 1909) Hebbel hoped to gain access to the circle of literary neoclassicists around King Maximilian II of Bavaria and his flourishing Hoftheater (court theater) in Munich under the direction of Franz Dingelstedt. As Friedrich Sengle has pointed out, Hebbel sought to overwhelm the king and his coterie with a tragedy that was to demonstrate his sympathy with the restoration of aristocratic rule in the sense of medieval feudalism. But he was naive in his assumption that Munich was the residence of a feudal king rather than that of an enlightened constitutional monarch.

The play is based on actual events from the fifteenth century. Albrecht, the son of Duke Ernst of Bavaria, marries Agnes Bernauer, the beautiful daughter of a barber-surgeon in Augsburg. Ernst fears that Agnes's beauty and rightful claims as the wife of the heir to the Bavarian throne will drive a wedge between the people and the dynasty, and during Albrecht's absence the duke signs her death warrant in the name of the widows and orphans that would be created and the cities and towns that would be reduced to cinders if civil war broke out. She is drowned in the Danube. When Albrecht learns of this legal murder he goes to war against his father. They meet on the battlefield, and the duke offers to acknowledge the dead Agnes as his son's legitimate wife and to establish a requiem to commemorate her sacrifice for all time. Ernst abdicates the throne and retires to a monastery, and father and son are reconciled.

Ludwig of Bavaria, who had been forced to abdicate in 1848 because of the scandal that arose from his attempt to have his mistress, Lola Montez, elevated to the peerage, granted Hebbel an audience after the drama's premiere in Munich on 25 March 1852. Horror-struck by the cruelty of his medieval ancestor, the former king said that he himself could never have contemplated such an act. Hebbel replied that the king would have had to act in this manner if he had been in power at that time. The Munich audience responded favorably to the play because of the historical pomp and colorful setting provided by Dingelstedt and because of the parallels it drew between Agnes and Montez.

In *Gyges und sein Ring* (1856; translated as *Gyges and His Ring,* 1914) Hebbel sought to revive the tradition of French classical theater in Germany. He based the plot on the account of Herodotus; the ring episode was taken from Plato's *Republic;* and the source of the oriental customs depicted was a book on Indian legends that Hebbel had reviewed in 1848. In a note appended to the list of characters Hebbel points out that his drama has a prehistoric and mythical plot and that it observes the Aristotelian unities by taking place within a period of two days. It was Hebbel's ambition to prove that, like Schiller and Goethe, he could produce a synthesis of antiquity and modernity.

Rhodope, the wife of Kandaules, King of Lydia, comes from a place where Indian and Greek customs blend and where women, on pain of death, must not be seen except by their fathers and husbands. Gyges, a young Greek who is Kandaules' guest, gives the king a magic ring that has the power to make its wearer invisible. Kandaules boasts to Gyges of Rhodope's beauty and urges Gyges to enter her chamber with the help of the magic ring. On glimpsing Rhodope, Gyges is overwhelmed by her beauty and falls in love with her. Rhodope senses that something is amiss, and she sends for Gyges the next day. He confesses his love for her. The breach of time-honored custom cannot be forgiven, and Rhodope insists that Kandaules and Gyges fight a duel. Gyges prevails, and Rhodope pledges herself to be his consort. She demands the ring from Gyges, who replies that it is still on the dead king's finger. She says that the ring has found its proper place and continues: "Ich bin entsühnt, / Denn Keiner sah mich mehr, als dem es ziemte, / Jetzt aber scheide ich mich so von Dir!" (I have been cleansed, / For no one has seen me except the one who had a right to, / But now I am leaving you, thus!). She then stabs herself to death. By ignoring what custom and tradition demand of Rhodope and by attempting to be "modern" before the time is ripe, Kandaules has violated what he calls the "Schlaf der Welt" (sleep of the world). The world needs its "sleep" in order to "digest" previous changes, to recover from and to consolidate them. By the same token, Hebbel did not think that the Austrian revolution of 1848 should have demanded a republic; he felt

that the radical changes advocated by the communists and socialists were premature. He believed that, at most, Austria should become a constitutional monarchy, and he had been a member of the delegation of Viennese writers dispatched to Innsbruck, where the royal family had fled, to persuade Archduke Johann to accept the office of constitutional monarch. In Hebbel's view the new does not have the right to supplant the old unless it is stronger than the old. In the case of Austria, he felt that neither the educational level of the populace nor the influence of the educated was sufficient to allow for a form of government more liberal than a constitutional monarchy. In Hegelian terms the clash between the forces of absolutism (thesis) and democracy (antithesis) results in a synthesis in which the rights and privileges of the ruling classes are preserved while being limited through a new constitution. King Kandaules has no new and better values with which to replace the old customs; hence, he should have respected the old values.

Gyges und sein Ring could not be performed in the age of realism, and the playwright had to be content with giving a public reading of the drama in April 1855. The play was not staged until 1889.

Hebbel purchased a modest summer home on the Traunsee in Gmunden, Upper Austria, in 1855. Grand Duke Karl Alexander of Saxe-Weimar awarded him a high decoration for his dramas in 1858, as did the Bavarian king in 1860. His plays were staged at the court theaters in Munich and Weimar. On his fiftieth birthday Hebbel was awarded the honorary title of private librarian to the grand duke.

At the Weimar court he befriended Princess Caroline Sayn-Wittgenstein, the wife of the Russian ambassador, and their daughter Marie. Through the Wittgensteins, Hebbel met Franz Liszt. Marie Wittgenstein became Hebbel's confidante and was the first person to read the manuscript for his *Die Nibelungen: Ein deutsches Trauerspiel in drei Abtheilungen* (1862; translated as *The Niebelungs: A Tragedy in Three Acts,* 1903).

In addition to royal patronage, Hebbel enjoyed friendships with the leading liberal Jewish journalists and writers in Vienna. His relations with such great Austrian writers of his day as Franz Grillparzer, Adalbert Stifter, and Johann Nepomuk Nestroy and the German composer Richard Wagner were fraught with hostility and mutual lack of understanding, but the poets Ludwig Tieck and Eduard Mörike and the composers Liszt and Robert Schumann thought highly of the playwright.

Hebbel's lengthy epic poem *Mutter und Kind* (Mother and Child, 1859) is composed in the manner of Goethe's *Hermann und Dorothea* (1798), which, in turn, harks back to the tradition of the Greek idyll. While still in manuscript, the poem was awarded the Tiedge Prize in December 1857. It concerns motherly love, economic hardship, and the tendency of the wealthy to regard their wishes as everyone else's command. A poor couple is offered land in exchange for their infant son by a wealthy childless couple, but in the end they are allowed to keep both. The two couples are not portrayed in simplistic terms of good and evil but are represented with all their weaknesses.

Hebbel's first collection of lyrics, *Gedichte* (Poems), had appeared in 1842, followed by *Neue Gedichte* (New Poems) in 1848; his own rearrangement of all his poetry into cycles was published in 1857. The critical evaluation of his poetry has, by and large, focused on a comparison with the lyrical tradition begun by Goethe, the lyric of the private experience, and the mid-century realism exemplified by Theodor Storm and Gottfried Keller. There is little in Hebbel's lyrics that can be called realistic; his shorter verse reflects a Romantic and Goethean orientation in keeping with the residual romanticism of the Biedermeier period as well as the residual classicism (in a formal sense) typical of this pre-realistic period. He experimented with many sounds and rhythms; his emotional palette ranged from happy to serene to sad to sarcastic, from the folk song to the intellectual and reflective lyric. Metrically, the classical, stately, occasionally somber measures of trochees and dactyls predominate; among the strophic forms the sonnet and distich are the most frequent.

In 1857 Hebbel traveled to Frankfurt am Main to meet the philosopher Arthur Schopenhauer and to Stuttgart to meet Mörike. While Mörike was an admirer of Hebbel's works, Schopenhauer did not reciprocate Hebbel's enthusiasm for the philosopher's ideas. The poet and herald of a metaphysics of pain and suffering expected his cycle of poems "Dem Schmerz sein Recht" (The Legitimacy of Pain) to strike a responsive chord in the philosopher. Instead, Schopenhauer argued with Hebbel about his preface to *Maria Magdalene,* which Schopenhauer regarded as unnecessary.

Hebbel also traveled to Kraków, Poland, with his friend and future biographer Kuh to gather Slavic material for the drama *Demetrius* (1864)—which, however, like Schiller's play of the same title, was to remain a fragment. In January 1861 Hebbel and his wife went to Weimar, where the first two parts of his most ambitious and impressive project, *Die Nibelungen,* were performed. Christine played Brunhild on the first evening and Kriemhild on the second. More than any of his other works, this German heroic epic in new and typically Hebbelian guise helped establish his fame among the educated throughout Germany. It received acclaim during a time

of rising nationalism, even though Hebbel was a Danish subject and wished to remain so.

Hebbel's interest in this most German of all legends, *Das Nibelungenlied* (The Lay of the Nibelungs), had begun in 1847, when he saw his wife in the role of Kriemhild in Ernst Raupach's dramatization of the epic. He had started working on his own version in earnest in October 1855 and, with many interruptions, completed the drama at the end of 1860. The great success of the Weimar performance helped thaw the icy atmosphere at the Burgtheater (Hebbel and Heinrich Laube, the director at the Burgtheater, had had differences concerning Hebbel's dramas as well as his wife, who in Hebbel's opinion had consistently been slighted by Laube in the roles she was given), and the first two parts were staged there in February 1863. Its success was attributable to the popularity of the national myth, which continued into the Nazi period. In post–World War II Germany *Die Nibelungen* has rarely been staged; it received an avant-garde and "denationalized" treatment in 1973, when it was performed in Cologne under the direction of Hansgünther Heyme.

In keeping with Hebbel's Hegelian view of history, the drama brings into relief a point of crisis when barbaric German paganism yields to the more civilized Christian view of the world. As in *Gyges und sein Ring,* Hebbel sought to create an entirely human tragedy on the foundation of a mythical subject. The heroic pagan figures—Siegfried, Brunhild, Kriemhild, Frigga, the Burgundians, and the Huns—are governed by an ethic of loyalty, bravery, and revenge that inevitably leads to their downfall. Rüdeger, Dietrich von Bern, and the chaplain represent the emerging norms of Christianity: self-control, compassion, and forgiveness.

Hebbel's major change from the epic revolves around the conflict between the sexes. After her betrothal to Gunther, Brunhild wonders why Siegfried, destined by a prophecy to be hers, has married Kriemhild instead. Siegfried explains to the kings of Burgundy that when he first saw Brunhild in her castle on Isenland he was unmoved by her beauty, and he felt that he must not court one whom he could not love. In the world of human conventions Siegfried's attitude is praiseworthy, but in the irrational, primordial, mythical sphere he has committed a grave sin. Siegfried should have recognized Brunhild as preordained for him and should have loved her.

He compounds his sin of omission with one of commission by using his mysterious powers to subdue Brunhild for Gunther. Again, the cardinal sin of the male—of Siegfried, Holofernes, Herod, Kandaules, and of Hebbel himself in his relationship with Elise Lensing—is to degrade a woman to the status of an object. Only in the abdication of Etzel (Attila), the king of the

Huns, in favor of Dietrich von Bern is the chain of revenge broken.

In March 1863 Hebbel became ill with what was misdiagnosed as rheumatism; his real ailment was osteoporosis. At the end he could not walk or even hold his head erect. On 7 November 1863 the king of Prussia awarded him the Schiller Prize for *Die Nibelungen.* The prize had been established in 1859 but had never been awarded; Hebbel was the first writer considered worthy of what was to become Germany's most prestigious literary award. Later that month he contracted pneumonia, and on 13 December he died. He was buried in Vienna's Protestant cemetery at Matzleinsdorf.

Letters:

Briefwechsel mit Freunden und berühmten Zeitgenossen, 2 volumes, edited by Felix Bamberg (Berlin: Grote, 1890–1892);

Aus Friedrich Hebbels Korrespondenz, edited by Friedrich Hirth (Munich & Leipzig: Müller, 1913);

Neue Hebbel-Dokumente, edited by Dietrich Kralik and Fritz Lemmermayer (Berlin: Schuster & Loeffler, 1913);

Hebbel-Dokumente: Unveröffentlichtes aus dem Nachlaß, edited by Rudolf Kardel (Heide: Westholsteinische Verlagsanstalt, 1931);

Neue Hebbel-Briefe, edited by Anni Meetz (Neumünster: Wachholtz, 1963);

Friedrich Hebbel: Briefe, edited by Henry Gerlach (Heidelberg: Winter, 1975);

Briefe von und an Friedrich Hebbel, edited by Gerlach (Heidelberg: Winter, 1978);

Hebbel-Briefe, edited by A. Tilo Alt (Berlin: Schmidt, 1989);

Friedrich Hebbel: Briefwechsel 1829–1863, 5 volumes, edited by Günter Häntzschel and others (Munich: Iudicium, 1999).

Bibliographies:

Hans Wütschke, *Hebbel-Bibliographie: Ein Versuch* (Berlin: Behr, 1910);

Henry Gerlach, *Hebbel-Bibliographie 1910–1970* (Heidelberg: Winter, 1973);

Gerlach, "Hebbel-Bibliographie 1970–1980," *Hebbel Jahrbuch* (1983): 157–189.

Biographies:

Emil Kuh, *Biographie Friedrich Hebbels,* 2 volumes (Vienna: Braumüller, 1877);

Thomas Campbell, *The Life and Works of Friedrich Hebbel* (Boston: Badger, 1919);

Paul Bornstein, *Friedrich Hebbels Persönlichkeit,* 2 volumes (Berlin: Propyläen, 1924);

Edna Purdie, *Friedrich Hebbel: A Study of His Life and Work* (London: Oxford University Press, 1932);

Anni Meetz, *Friedrich Hebbel* (Stuttgart: Metzler, 1962);

Friedrich Sengle, "Friedrich Hebbel," in his *Biedermeierzeit,* volume 3: *Die Dichter* (Stuttgart: Metzler, 1980), pp. 332–414;

Heinz Stolte, *Friedrich Hebbel–Leben und Werk* (Husum: Druck-und Verlagsgesellschaft, 1987);

Barbara Wellhausen, *Friedrich Hebbel: Sein Leben in Texten und Bildern. Eine Bildbiographie* (Heide: Boyens, 1988).

References:

A. Tilo Alt, "Hebbel's 'Die Muschel im Ozean' as Metaphor and Motto," in *Essays in Honor of Clifford Albrecht Bernd on the Occasion of His Sixtieth Birthday,* edited by John Fetzer and others (Stuttgart: Heinz, 1989), pp. 11–21;

Alt, "Die kritische Rezeption Friedrich Hebbels in den USA," *Hebbel Jahrbuch* (1978): 163–180;

Alt, "Zum Humanismus Friedrich Hebbels," *Monatshefte,* 76 (Winter 1984): 441–456;

Patricia Boswell, "The Hunt as a Literary Image in Hebbel's 'Die Nibelungen,'" *Hebbel Jahrbuch* (1977): 163–194;

Otfrid Ehrismann, "Tod und Erkenntnis. Hebbels Polenbild," *Hebbel Jahrbuch* (1983): 9–40;

Sten Flygt, *Friedrich Hebbel* (New York: Twayne, 1968);

Paul G. Graham, "Hebbel's Study of King Lear," *Smith College Studies in Modern Languages,* 21 (October 1939): 81–90;

Graham, "The Principle of Necessity in Hebbel's Theory of Tragedy," *Germanic Review,* 15 (December 1940): 258–262;

Graham, *The Relation of Drama to History in the Works of Friedrich Hebbel* (Northampton, Mass.: Smith College, 1934);

Hilmar Grundmann, ed., *Friedrich Hebbel: Neue Studien zu Werk und Wirkung* (Heide: Boyens, 1982);

A. E. Hammer, "The Comic Element in Hebbel's Plays," *German Life and Letters,* new series 26 (April 1973): 192–201;

Elizabeth Heptner, "Two Nineteenth-Century Conceptions of Womanhood: A Comparison of the Attitudes of Kleist and Hebbel," dissertation, Washington University, 1975;

Harvey W. Hewitt-Thayer, "Ludwig Tieck and Hebbel's Tragedy of Beauty," *Germanic Review,* 2 (January 1927): 16–25;

Edith Isaacs, "Concerning the Author of Herod and Mariamne," *Theatre Arts Monthly,* 22 (December 1938): 886–890;

Lee B. Jennings, "Treasure and the Quest for the Self in Wagner, Grillparzer, and Hebbel," in *Myth and*

Reason: A Symposium, edited by Walter Wetzels (Austin: University of Texas Press, 1973), pp. 71–100;

Herbert Kaiser, *Friedrich Hebbel: Geschichtliche Interpretation des dramatischen Werks* (Munich: Fink, 1983);

Ida Koller-Andorf and Hilmar Grundmann, eds., *Hebbel: Mensch und Dichter im Werk. Neue Wege zu Hebbel. Internationales Hebbel Symposium in Wien* (Vienna: VWGÖ, 1990);

Helmut Kreuzer, ed., *Hebbel in neuer Sicht* (Stuttgart: Kohlhammer, 1963);

Wolfgang Liepe, "Ideology Underlying the Writings of Friedrich Hebbel," *American Philosophical Society Year Book 1953* (1954): 221–225;

Alfred D. Low, *Jews in the Eyes of the Germans: From Enlightenment to Imperial Germany* (Philadelphia: Institute for the Study of Human Issues, 1979), pp. 217–218, 234–240;

Ludger Lütkehaus, *Friedrich Hebbel, "Maria Magdalene"* (Munich: Fink, 1983);

Ludwig Marcuse, "Der Hegelianer Friedrich Hebbel–gegen Hegel," *Monatshefte,* 39 (December 1947): 506–514;

W. John Niven, *The Reception of Friedrich Hebbel in Germany in the Era of National Socialism* (Stuttgart: Heinz, 1984);

Hannelore and Heinz Schlaffer, *Studien zum ästhetischen Historismus* (Frankfurt am Main: Suhrkamp, 1975), pp. 121–139;

Betty Nance Weber, "Bertolt Brecht and Friedrich Hebbel: A Study in Literary Influence and Vandalism," dissertation, University of Wisconsin–Madison, 1973;

Benno von Wiese, *Die deutsche Tragödie von Lessing bis Hebbel,* 2 volumes (Hamburg: Hoffman & Campe, 1948), II: 334–461;

James D. Wright, "Hebbel's Klara: The Victim of a Division in Allegiance and Purpose," *Monatshefte,* 38 (May 1946): 304–316;

Klaus Ziegler, *Mensch und Welt in der Tragödie Friedrich Hebbels* (Darmstadt: Wissenschaftliche Buchgesellschaft, 1966).

Papers:

The Hebbel Archives are at the University of Kiel; the Hebbel Museum in Wesselburen, Schleswig-Holstein; and the Goethe and Schiller Archive in Weimar.

Christoph Hein

(8 April 1944 –   )

Phillip S. McKnight
University of Kentucky

This entry was updated by Professor McKnight from his entry in DLB 124:
Twentieth-Century German Dramatists, 1919–1992.

BOOKS: *Einladung zum Lever Bourgeois: Prosa* (Berlin &
Weimar: Aufbau, 1980)–includes "Der Sohn";

Cromwell und andere Stücke (Berlin & Weimar: Aufbau,
1981)–comprises *Cromwell; Lasalle fragt Herrn Herbert nach Sonja: Die Szene ein Salon; Schlötel oder Was
solls; Der Neue Menoza oder Geschichte des kumbanischen
Prinzen Tandi: Komodie nach Jakob Michael Reinhold
Lenz;*

Der fremde Freund: Novelle (Berlin & Weimar: Aufbau,
1982); republished as *Drachenblut* (Darmstadt &
Neuwied: Luchterhand, 1983); translated by
Krishna Winston as *The Distant Lover* (New York:
Pantheon, 1989);

Nachtfahrt und früher Morgen (Hamburg: Hoffmann &
Campe, 1982);

*Das Wildpferd unterm Kachelofen: Ein schönes dickes Buch von
Jakob Borg und seinen Freunden* (Berlin: Altberliner
Verlag, 1984);

Die wahre Geschichte des Ah Q.: Stücke und Essays (Darmstadt & Neuwied: Luchterhand, 1984)–includes
*Lasalle fragt Herrn Herbert nach Sonja: Die Szene ein
Salon;* "Anmerkungen zu *Lasalle fragt Herrn Herbert
nach Sonja: Die Szene ein Salon*";

Horns Ende: Roman (Berlin & Weimar: Aufbau, 1985);

Schlötel oder Was solls: Stücke und Essays (Darmstadt & Neuwied: Luchterhand, 1986)–includes *Cromwell,*
"Anmerkungen zu *Cromwell*";

Öffentlich arbeiten: Essais und Gespräche (Berlin & Weimar:
Aufbau, 1987);

Passage: Ein Kammerspiel in drei Akten (Darmstadt:
Luchterhand, 1987);

Die wahre Geschichte des Ah Q: Passage (Berlin: Henschel,
1988);

Der Tangospieler: Roman (Berlin & Weimar: Aufbau,
1989); translated by Philip Boehm as *The Tango
Player* (New York: Farrar, Straus & Giroux, 1992);

Christoph Hein (photograph by Isolde Ohlbaum)

Die Ritter der Tafelrunde: Komödie (Frankfurt am Main:
Luchterhand, 1989)–includes *Die wahre Geschichte
des Ah Q, Passage, Britannicus;*

Als Kind habe ich Stalin gesehen: Essais und Reden (Berlin &
Weimar: Aufbau, 1990);

Die fünfte Grundrechenart: Aufsätze und Reden (Frankfurt
am Main: Luchterhand, 1990);

Bridge Freezes before Roadway (Berlin: Berliner Handpresse, 1990);

Die Vergewaltigung (Leipzig: Faber & Faber, 1991);

Das Napoleon-Spiel: Ein Roman (Berlin: Aufbau, 1993);

Exekution eines Kalbes und andere Erzählungen (Berlin: Aufbau, 1994);

Randow: Eine Komödie (Berlin: Aufbau, 1994);

Die Mauern von Jericho: Essais und Reden (Berlin: Aufbau, 1996);

Von allem Anfang an (Berlin: Aufbau, 1997);

Bruch/In Acht und Bann/Zaungäste/Himmel auf Erden: Stücke (Berlin: Aufbau, 1999).

PLAY PRODUCTIONS: Molière, *Der fliegende Arzt,* translated and adapted by Hein, Berlin, Volksbühne, 11 May 1973;

Vom Furz, translated and adapted by Hein, Berlin, Volksbühne, 11 May 1973;

Vom hungrigen Hennicke, Berlin, Volksbühne, 25 September 1974;

Schlötel oder Was solls, Berlin, Volksbühne, 25 September 1974;

Die Geschäfte des Herrn John D., Neustrelitz, Stadttheater, 21 April 1979;

Cromwell, Cottbus, Theater der Stadt Cottbus, 4 May 1980;

Lasalle fragt Herrn Herbert nach Sonja: Die Szene ein Salon, Düsseldorf, Schauspielhaus, 9 November 1980;

Der Neue Menoza oder Geschichte des kumbanischen Prinzen Tandi: Komödie nach Jakob Michael Reinhold Lenz, Schwerin, Staatliche Bühnen, 29 May 1982;

Die wahre Geschichte des Ah Q, Berlin, Deutsches Theater, 22 December 1983;

Passage, Essen, Grillo-Theater, 25 October 1987; Zürich, Schauspielhaus, 15 November 1987; Dresden, Staatschauspiel, 28 November 1987;

Die Ritter der Tafelrunde, Dresden, Staatschauspiel, 12 April 1989;

Ma . . . Ma . . . Marlene: Szenen aus "Horns Ende," Berlin, Maxim-Gorki-Theater, 22 March 1990;

Randow: Eine Komödie, Dresden, Staatschauspiel, 21 December 1994;

Bruch, Düsseldorf, Schauspielhaus, 27 February 1999;

In Acht und Bann, Weimar, Deutsches Nationaltheater, 29 April 1999;

Himmel auf Erden, Chemnitz, Städtisches Theater, 9 October 1999;

Zaungäste, Chemnitz, Städtisches Theater, 9 October 1999.

OTHER: "Von der Magie und den Magiern," in *Windvogelviereck: Schriftsteller über Wissenschaften und Wissenschaftler,* edited by John Erpenbeck (Berlin: Der Morgen, 1987), pp. 11–34;

"Die Zensur ist überlebt, nutzlos, paradox, menschen-und volksfeindlich, ungesetzlich und strafbar: Rede auf dem X. Schriftstellerkongreß der DDR," in *X. Schriftstellerkongreß der DDR: Arbeitsgruppen,* edited by the Schriftstellerverband der DDR (Berlin & Weimar: Aufbau, 1988), pp. 224–247;

Johann Wallbergen, *Sammlung natürlicher Zauberkünste oder aufrichtige Entdeckung vieler bewährter, lustiger, und nützlicher Geheimnisse,* edited by Hein (Leipzig & Weimar: Kiepenheuer, 1988);

"Leserpost oder Ein Buch mit sieben Siegeln," in *Christa Wolf: Ein Arbeitsbuch,* edited by Angela Drescher (Berlin & Weimar: Aufbau, 1989), pp. 398–413;

Gustav Just, *Zeuge in eigener Sache,* foreword by Hein (Berlin: Der Morgen, 1990);

"Rede am Berliner Alexanderplatz," in *Der Weg zur Demonstration auf dem Alexanderplatz in Berlin,* edited by Initiativgruppe 4.11.89 (Cologne: Kölnische Verlagsdruckerei, 1990), pp. 55–57;

"Die Zeit, die nicht vergehen kann oder Das Dilemma des Chronisten," *Kopfbahnhof: Das falsche Dasein,* edited by Andreas Tretner (Leipzig: Reclam, 1990): 245–269;

"Erinnerung an eine Zeit," in *Und diese verdammte Ohnmacht: Report der Untersuchungskommission zu den Ereignissen vom 7. und 8. Oktober 1989 in Berlin,* edited by Daniela Dahn and Fritz-Jochen Kopka (Berlin: Basis, 1991), pp. 9–13.

SELECTED PERIODICAL PUBLICATIONS–
UNCOLLECTED: "Laudatio auf den Heinrich-Mann-Preisträger Friedrich Dieckmann," *Neue Deutsche Literatur,* 7 (1983): 159–161;

"Massa Sloterdijk und der linke Kolonialismus," *Konkret Literatur* (Fall 1983): 36–41;

"Damit Lessing nicht resigniert: Rede," *Frankfurter Rundschau,* 8 October 1983;

"Das Verschwinden des künstlerischen Produzenten im Zeitalter der Reproduzierbarkeit," *Freibeuter,* 31 (1987): 63–71; 32 (1987): 11–19;

"Literatur und Publikum: Ein Briefwechsel mit Elmar Faber," *Sinn und Form,* 3 (1988): 672–678;

"Nachdenken über Deutschland," *Die Weltbühne,* 6 March 1990, pp. 295–298;

"No Sea Route to India," *Time,* 135 (25 June 1990): 68;

"Unbelehrbar–Erich Fried: Rede zur Verleihung des Erich-Fried-Preises am 6. Mai 1990 in Wien," *Freibeuter,* 44 (1990): 24–33;

"Kein Krieg ist heilig, kein Krieg ist gerecht," *Berliner Zeitung,* 13 February 1991;

"Ansichten einer deutschen Kleinstadt, leicht retuschiert," *Neue Deutsche Literatur,* 40, no. 4 (1992): 9–30.

Few in the West had heard of Christoph Hein in 1982 when he received the prestigious Heinrich Mann Prize for Literature. Unlike many East German writers who were equally critical of censorship and of the authoritarian Socialist Party regime of the German Democratic Republic (GDR) and who were forcibly expatriated, compelled to exercise "self-censorship" or simply remained silent, Hein stood out as his small country's most eloquent and respected advocate of freedom of speech, press, and artistic expression.

Hein established himself early as an author of world literature, one who wrote in the historical context of the culture in which he lived without being limited by the standard critical reception that forced most East German writers into one of two simple categories: dissident or writer for the State. Unlike the works of most East German writers, Hein's writing continues to be well received in unified Germany, including both his earlier and recent work. It is perhaps no accident, therefore, that Hein's position of respect both in the East and in the West led to his election as president of the unified German PEN in 1998, after eight years of bitter haggling between representatives of both East and West German PEN organizations had left both sides divided, as though no Berlin wall had been dismantled. The primary task of the international organization PEN, to aid writers in all parts of the world in prison and exile, was seriously neglected in Germany during this struggle. Although Hein repeatedly expressed disdain towards this bitter dispute, perhaps no other German writer from either of the two Germanies could have taken the job by consensus and served in such a manner as to unify the groups.

Hein was recognized as one of the most important European writers of the late twentieth century with his long novella, *Der fremde Freund* (1982; translated as *The Distant Lover,* 1989), which was translated into more than twenty languages within a short time of its original publication in 1982 and became an international best-seller in both eastern and western Europe. His controversial play, *Die wahre Geschichte des Ah Q* (The True Story of Ah Q; published, 1984), which premiered at the Deutsches Theater in Berlin in 1983, ran for the next six years throughout Europe.

The chief merit of Hein's literary work lies in his relentless search for truth in language. He has said that "Poesie ist keine Sklavensprache" (poesy is not a slave language)—that is, it manifests no tacit agreement with the rulers. He exposes his characters as speakers of "Sklavensprache." He avoids imposing his own attitude on the reader of his prose or the audience at his plays. Social, political, and individual choices, with their various implied consequences, are left open. Hein's plays are a forum in which the audience participates in a continuing dialogue with the author. Hein sought to counteract the spoon-fed dogmatism of the state, which had perpetuated a condition of mental dependency throughout large sections of the population.

Hein was born on 8 April 1944 in Heinzendorf, Silesia (now in Poland), the third of six children of Günther Hein and Lonny Weber Hein. After World War II the family fled the Red Army and took up residence in Bad Düben, near Leipzig, where Hein's father became the town parson and began a long career characterized by resistance to the state's efforts to discredit and suppress religion. From his father, Hein learned resilience, perseverance, and the ability to face adversity without compromising his values. He attended elementary school in Bad Düben from 1950 to 1958, and by the age of twelve he knew he wanted to be a playwright.

Determined that the brightest of his children should not suffer because of his own dedication to his ministry, Günther Hein sent Christoph to join his brother Gottfried at the West Berlin Evangelisches Gymnasium zum grauen Kloster (Evangelical Gymnasium at the Gray Cloister), a humanistic preparatory school which took the sons of East German pastors, doctors, and intellectuals who were not members of the Socialist Unity party.

In 1960 Günther Hein went to East Berlin to lead his church's youth organization. Hein moved in with his parents and commuted to school until August 1961, when the construction of the Berlin Wall forced a decision. Günther Hein was determined to remain in the East with his congregation, and Christoph chose to stay with his family. He was refused entry into the elite preparatory schools, and his application to learn a trade as a cabinetmaker was rejected as well. Between 1961 and 1964 he attended the Vocational School for the German Book Trade, including two years as an apprentice in a bookstore on the Alexanderplatz. In 1964 he began attending evening school at the Volkshochschule (People's High School). He passed his Abitur (school-leaving examination) in 1966 and married Christiane Zauleck in May of the same year.

At the age of nineteen Hein had introduced himself to Benno Besson, a prominent director from Switzerland. Besson had taken Hein under his wing at the Deutsches Theater, and in the 1965–1966 season Hein worked for eight months as the director's assistant without pay, scraping by with honoraria from literary contributions and interviews for weeklies such as *Sonntag* (Sunday) and *Junge Welt* (Young World). Occasionally he picked up ten marks for playing bit parts or forty marks for small singing roles at the theater.

In the summer of 1966 he enrolled at the Cinema College in Babelsberg, but the government ordered the school to invalidate his registration. The intrigues, fictionalized in his short story "Der Sohn"

(The Son, 1980), continued when he tried to switch to the College of Theatrical Arts in Leipzig, only to receive a letter of rejection directly from the central Ministry of Culture.

With the birth of his first son, Georg, imminent, Hein moved to Leipzig to be with Christiane and found work as a waiter. Georg was born on 20 October 1966. In January 1967 Hein worked as an assembler in an adding machine factory. In September he finally gained admittance to the Karl-Marx-University in Leipzig. He studied philosophy, but his steadfast adherence to his principles and his biting wit caused an uproar among the faculty and students. After he presented a provocative oral report in 1970, he was advised to change universities or be expelled. He completed his studies at the Humboldt University in Berlin, with a senior thesis on pluralistic logic, in June 1971.

By this time Besson had moved to the Volksbühne (People's Stage) in Berlin, where he and Heiner Müller were leading the venerable theater to its heyday. After Christiane gave birth on 25 October 1971 to their second son, Jakob, Hein went to work as dramaturge and director's assistant at the Volksbühne. He was promoted to house author in 1974.

In his early years at the Volksbühne, Hein translated and adapted Molière's *Le médicin volant* as *Der fliegende Arzt* (The Flying Physician) and the anonymous farce *Du pect* as *Vom Furz* (Of Farts), both of which were first performed on 11 May 1973. Other adaptations were of Jean Racine's tragedy *Britannicus* (1669), staged in 1975, and J. M .R. Lenz's comedy *Der neue Menoza oder die Geschichte des cumbanischen Prinzen Tandi* (1774), performed in 1982. His first original plays were both performed at the Volksbühne on 25 September 1974: *Vom hungrigen Hennike* (Hungry Henneke), a short piece for children's theater that questions the heroization of the legendary East German miner Adolf Henneke, was directed by Thomas Valentin; *Schlötel oder Was solls* (Schlötel; or, What's the Use) was directed by Manfred Karge. *Schlötel* was published in 1981 in *Cromwell und andere Stücke* (Cromwell and Other Plays).

Schlötel is set in a factory, but it is not a typical socialist realist work in which solutions to social and economic problems are found by an energetic, heroic worker who then convinces his fellow workers to adopt his ideas. The play examines the conflict of interests between utopian intellectuals and the working class, with its considerably less ambitious needs. The original script portrays Schlötel as a late-1960s radical student who moves from West to East Germany and expects to show the workers what is good for them; in the published version Schlötel is a brilliant sociologist who has just graduated from the University of Leipzig. The new text places more emphasis on the changes brought about by the Neues ökonomisches System (New Economic System), initiated by the Politburo in 1966 to increase productivity.

Schlötel sets out to convince the workers to vote for a system of "Objektlohn" (incentive pay for completed projects), which had been suggested by party leaders. The issue for Schlötel—for which he sacrifices the happiness of his private life with his wife and newborn child—is for the workers to exercise self-determination instead of slavishly accepting the party's orders. But the workers want neither incentive pay, which disrupts the leisurely pace of work, nor emancipation, and they have him fired and banned from the premises. In despair, Schlötel drowns himself in the Baltic Sea. Shortly thereafter, the party decrees the implementation of the incentive pay system. Whether the workers are engaged or apathetic, the party still decides. Hein calls his play a comedy in the vein of Lenz's *Der Hofmeister* (1774; translated as *The Tutor,* 1972). Both plays are replete with humorous dialogue and comic situations, but in each the main character comes to a tragic end while the ruling class continues to do as it pleases.

The West German premiere of *Schlötel,* which was also the first staging of the published version, took place in 1986 in Kassel under the direction of Mathias Fontheim. Many of Hein's references to everyday life in the German Democratic Republic were omitted, and Fontheim's decision to portray Schlötel as a "Storm and Stress" figure undermined the sophisticated intellectual superiority that had lent Hein's character the universal appeal of the idealistic, brooding, and enlightened outsider.

In 1978 Besson and Hein left the Volksbühne due to official harassment over the repertoire. Hein decided to commit himself to full-time writing; by then Christiane had a decent income working on documentary films for DEFA, the East German television consortium. Hein's next stage production was the satirical revue for actors' ensembles, *Die Geschäfte des Herrn John D.* (The Deals of John D., 1979), which premiered on 21 April 1979 in the provincial town of Neustrelitz. The "Drei-Dollar-Operetta" (Three-Dollar Operetta), as it was dubbed by one critic, was favorably reviewed in the West when it was produced at the Vagantenbühne in Berlin in 1983 and at the Theater im Depot in Recklinghausen in 1986 where it was directed by Doris Heliand. The play, which included a medley of American blues, country music, and Dixieland jazz, was a reworking of a 1930 radio play by Friedrich Wolf about John D. Rockefeller's monopolization of the oil-refining industry.

In July 1978 *Cromwell,* Hein's first work to be published in the GDR, appeared in *Theater der Zeit* (Theater Times), the monthly theater journal that held the monopoly on all play manuscripts in the country. The historical Oliver Cromwell was a small landowner who was driven by Puritan fundamentalism, which Hein incorporates in the figure of his mother, and was forced into a coalition with the Levellers to prevent the revolution from failing. A faction that arose in the army of the Long Parliament around 1647, the Levellers embodied pure communistic ideals, advocating the leveling of all ranks and the establishment of a more democratic government. It was their influence that pushed Cromwell to execute Charles I in 1649 and to have himself named Lord Protector of the Puritan Republic. Hein's *Cromwell* is sprinkled with anachronisms taken from the French Revolution, czarist Russia, and speeches by Joseph Stalin, and with references to cigarettes, Mauser pistols, Datschas, Red Brothers, Compañeros, and colloquialisms from everyday East German life. The most stunning anachronism is the fate of the Levellers, who are loaded into train cars for the west coast. Ten miles from the Irish Sea the train is stopped, the boxcar doors are thrown open, and the entire "counterrevolutionary" contingent of soldiers is liquidated by forty-three machine guns.

The play was blocked in a dozen other cities before it premiered at the Theater der Stadt (City Theater) in Cottbus on 4 May 1980, directed by Peter Röll. It was cut extensively, and the revisions incorporated references to the Nazis. The West German premiere in Essen on 24 October 1986 went to the opposite extreme by clothing Cromwell's soldiers in East German army uniforms and Cromwell's son in the blue shirt of the Communist Young Pioneers. Han Günther Heyme's version, which premiered on 24 October 1986, focused on the tension between Cromwell's Puritan background, the political impact of the Levellers, and the business interests of Parliament. In 1984 East German productions directed by Klaus Krampe in Gera and by Michael Grosse in Eisenach succeeded in portraying Cromwell's corruption, self-indulgence, and arbitrary exercise of power.

The conflict between public achievement and private values depicted in *Schlötel* and *Cromwell* is the focal point of *Lasalle fragt Herrn Herbert nach Sonja: Die Szene ein Salon* (Lasalle Asks Mr. Herbert about Sonja: The Scene a Salon; published in *Cromwell und andere Stücke*), which Hein described as both a critique and a continuation of *Cromwell. Lasalle fragt Herrn Herbert nach Sonja* is based on the founder of the General German Workers' Union, Ferdinand Lasalle (1825–1864). Hein sets the play in a salon, representative of a stagnating, superficial society. Lasalle, by his own admission, is unable to overcome his own petit bourgeois indulgences and Jewish intellectual background to the point of being able to identify with the workers he purports to represent. His decadence is revealed by his womanizing, which ultimately becomes more important to him than his political program. He dies from a wound to the genitals received in a foolish duel over a woman.

Hein decided to give *Lasalle fragt Herrn Herbert nach Sonja* to a West German theater, and it premiered in Düsseldorf on 9 November 1980, directed by Heinz Engels. It was the first work by Hein to be performed in the West. Aside from antagonizing the West German left, the play was relatively well received. It was more than six years before the play was allowed to be performed in East Germany, opening in Erfurt on 2 February 1987 under the direction of Ekkehard Emig.

Hein has often described himself as a chronicler, a writer interested in recording the historical veracity of contemporary events in poetic form. Like the chronicle plays that flourished in the Elizabethan period, Hein's plays are characterized by a free treatment of the official and popular histories of his society and culture. The same is true of his prose: the novel *Horns Ende,* printed and ready for distribution in 1984 and but not released until 1985, is a free chronicle presenting a devastating nutshell history of the GDR. *Der fremde Freund* makes what Hein refers to as a "precise social inventory" of his society, an inventory that serves as an explosive provocation for change. The narrator, Claudia, is a successful physician who suppresses her self-alienation and becomes a compassionless, empty person, unable to recognize or to experience simple human feelings and attitudes, all the while proclaiming herself to "have it made." Claudia's proclamations of her invulnerability compel the reader to think the opposite of what she states to be true, especially in the context of her psychological well-being.

The turning point which changed Claudia's life came at age twelve or thirteen, when she denounced her friend Katharina in front of the school class for refusing to renounce her religious beliefs and join the socialist youth club. In language quoted from the rejection Hein himself received when he applied to the elite level of the East German school system, the judgment against Katharina stated that it "was inappropriate that she be allowed to attain the educational goals of an accredited high school in our Republic." The breakdown of the girls' friendship introduced psychological stresses in Claudia's life that resurface in her estranged love affair with Henry, who is killed in a senseless bar fight, and in her refusal to permit herself to have meaningful relationships with anyone else. Historical forces played a role in Claudia's psychological crippling as well: during the height of the Cold War a tank was stationed in her hometown, and it was made clear to all the children that they were never to discuss the presence of the tank. This event taught her the expediency of keeping silent and fostered her ability to repress her awareness of important social issues. Claudia's repression stands as a repudiation of the political mandate for the "new human being" in the GDR. The novella, which was quickly translated into twenty-eight languages, implied that the socialist system was failing because its utopian goals were negated by self-contradictory political measures.

Plays that treated alienation or the loss of definitive certainties were virtually nonexistent on the East German stage; thus, when *Die wahre Geschichte des Ah Q* premiered on 22 December 1983–this time not in the provinces but at the Deutsches Theater in East Berlin under the direction of Alexander Lang–it created a sensation. The West German premiere in Kassel, directed by Valentin Jeker, took place a month after the French premiere at the Théâtre National de Strasbourg in November 1984. The play went on to be a tremendous success in Paris, Bordeaux, Bern, Zurich, Vienna, Graz, West Berlin, Düsseldorf, Hamburg, Tübingen, Paderborn, Nuremberg, and Wiesbaden.

The play is an adaptation of the Chinese writer Lu Xun's 1921 short story of the same title, a tale of the Boxer Revolution in China in 1911. Hein incorporated dialogue from the story but changed the central character from a village beggar to a self-centered bourgeois intellectual. Ah Q and Wang, intellectuals and self-styled anarchists, are waiting for a revolution which does, in fact, come, but they do not notice it until after it is over. They are locked in a room in a dilapidated building by the Temple Guard, a bureaucrat who follows orders and official policy unquestioningly. Ah Q rapes and kills the nun who has brought them milk soup every Thursday. He is depicted as not quite realizing what he is doing; the analogy to be drawn is the unwitting destruction by bureaucracy of humane values. On two occasions Ah Q addresses the audience. In the first instance he goes into the sixth or seventh row of seats in an attempt to find a single statement that expresses the essence of existence. He stops, returns to the stage, and declares, "ich habe keine Botschaft" (I have no message to give); the audience will have to think of one on its own. The other instance has Wang and Ah Q claiming that they are only performing scenes from the world of bureaucrats and professionals and that the audience members are all bureaucrats.

While the youthful members of the audience responded with glee at the premiere, the bureaucrats and dignitaries invited to the show walked out in protest. Nevertheless, the play ran for six years at the Deutsches Theater, a remarkable run for a contemporary play and strongly indicative of public support in the face of official disapproval.

Many consider Hein's historical novel *Horns Ende* to be his best prose work. After a long period of difficulty with the censorship bureau, the book became the only belletristic work in the GDR to be released without official permission. The novel presents the life and suicide of the former history professor and museum director Horn from the viewpoints of several different characters. Horn, Kruschkatz and Dr. Spodeck are historical philosophers. Horn himself insists on the truth, no matter how trivial or damaging it might be. Kruschkatz, who had denounced Horn and caused him to lose his position at the University of Leipzig, is a Socialist Party functionary and mayor of Bad Guldenberg, a town very reminiscent in detail of Bad Düben, where Hein grew up. Kruschkatz regards history as open to subjective interpretations which distort the truth and believes the goals of the party can only be met by not dwelling on historical facts and their implications. Spodeck, damaged by his Nazi father, sees history as unreliable because human beings can falsify it. Hein connects the mentality of the townspeople both with the Nazi past, during which they anonymously denounced a mentally impaired individual, and with the cold-war socialist period of the 1950s, when many innocent people–who were good communists besides–were subjected to show trials and false recriminations. The carryover of the story into the early 1980s implies that the Socialist regime has compromised history to preserve power, thereby creating a state of stagnation. To his credit, Kruschkatz thwarts the aims of a group of ambitious people engaged in an intrigue to overthrow him and regenerate the old Nazi discrimination against gypsies and other minority groups; on the other hand, he denounces Horn a second time, leading to Horn's suicide. Kruschkatz is unable to prevent the town from forgetting its earlier atrocities during the Nazi years.

In the spring of 1987, after a year's delay due to the mishandling of his travel documents by the GDR's Writer's Union, Hein accepted an invitation from the University of Kentucky to visit the United

States. He spent a month traveling with an interpreter under the auspices of the United States Information Agency, visiting dramatists, workshops, and theaters in Virginia, New Orleans, San Francisco, and New York, and a second month conducting workshops and lecturing at the University of Kentucky, Amherst College, New York University, Vanderbilt University, the University of Texas, and UCLA. His return to the GDR was followed by one of his most productive periods, with the publication of many essays, two plays, and the novel *Der Tangospieler* (1989; translated as *The Tango Player,* 1992), which portrays an academic who passes up a chance to become independent and returns to his career under terms that compromise his integrity. It is a bitter commentary on the distortion of the socialist dream by the corrupt Stalinist structure of East German society.

Der fremde Freund and *Horns Ende* were set in the historical framework of the East German workers' uprising on 17 June 1953 and during the Hungarian revolt of 1956; *Der Tangospieler* completes the trilogy with a setting during the "Prague Spring" of 1968 that led to the invasion of Warsaw Pact troops and the elimination of democratic reforms in Czechoslovakia. Hans-Peter Dallow, a history professor at the University of Leipzig, has left the sanctity of prison, where he was serving time for playing the piano part in a satirical cabaret performance. Dallow loves his car and is a womanizer. He claims he was innocent, since he was only engaged when the regular piano player became ill. Dallow is apolitical, a man without convictions, claiming innocence in a matter which was of no concern to him in the first place. After a series of trivial misadventures he is reinstated in his job. The secret police figures who shadow Dallow throughout the story think he would be an ideal professor of history in such trying times, since they can depend on him to write up historical events according to the Party's interpretation with out suffering any pangs of conscious.

The two plays Hein wrote following his return to the GDR were *Passage* (performed, 1987; published, 1988) and *Die Ritter der Tafelrunde* (The Knights of the Round Table, 1989). In *Passage,* as in *Horns Ende,* he refined the use of historicism in drama and prose to define the present. In Hein's view, to forget the past would be to deprive oneself of the kind of experience which provides cultural depth and continuity to life. According to Walter Benjamin, whose works Hein studied intensely during this period of his life, the consequences of history are more important than the facts and, in any case, historical consciousness defines the present.

Passage is set in the back room of a café in the south of France in 1940. The play depicts the anxiety, hope, and despair of a group of Jewish refugees seeking to get across the border into Spain before the Gestapo closes in on them. If they succeed, they hope to find passage on a ship taking Jewish refugees to America. When the Gestapo does find them, it causes a break from their lethargic condition of waiting and hoping for the impossible. The catalyst for the existential choices the group faces is Hugo Frankfurter—a character based on Benjamin—who stuns the group by poisoning himself as the Gestapo is inspecting their papers. The town's mayor, Paul Joly, who had been protecting the refugees, decides to go to Paris to join the Resistance. The others attempt to escape but are turned back for one more day until the Spanish border opens. The key figure of the play is a seventy-five-year-old retired German officer, Alfred Hirschburg, who is subject to the scorn of the group for his insistence on retaining his identity as a German. In his mind his Jewish origin is of no consequence, and his problems are attributable to a misunderstanding. He breaches the fragile security of the village hideaway by inviting an old comrade in arms to join him. When his friend shows up leading a group of fifteen old Jewish men in traditional caftans who had made a dreamlike trek from Zator, the old duchy of Auschwitz, Hirschburg's historical consciousness is jolted, and his adamant Germanness is transformed. To the awe of the others, Hirschburg leads the old men by night out of the village on a surrealistic trek over the mountains. As the director of the play at the Dresdner Staatsschauspiel (State Playhouse) viewed it, the image of the fifteen Jews was a challenge to everyone to contemplate the limits of the possible.

Hein's last play before the end of the German Democratic Republic in many ways predicted the fall of the Communist regime. It showed the stagnation and senility of the older generation and its inability to cope with change. Directed by Klaus Dieter Kirst, *Die Ritter der Tafelrunde* was scheduled to premiere on 24 March 1989 in Dresden. As officials became aware of its content, a controversy ensued about staging it. A "preview" was staged on 24 March and was followed by five or six additional previews, all sellouts. The official premiere took place on 12 April 1989, but the play was performed only once more that season. After the opening of the Berlin Wall, however, the play appeared in theaters all over East Germany and, beginning in Kassel, in many theaters in West Germany as well.

King Artus (Arthur) and his knights represent the old Communist rulers who maintained that history was mistaken, and not they themselves. The knights believe that they must uphold their faith in the Holy Grail—symbolizing the utopian ideals of communism—even though they have given up hope of ever finding it. One of the knights exhorts Artus to kill his own son, Mordret, in order to preserve the old order. Lancelot, returning from his quest, reports that the people think of their leaders as fools and criminals. Mordret says that he has no interest in assuming the throne, but indicates that he would put the Round Table in a museum. The play ends with Mordret's outspoken intention to destroy everything associated with his father's regime.

A controversial speech Hein gave opposing censorship at the East German Writers Congress in November 1987 contributed to the end of censorship in the German Democratic Republic. He was active in the demonstrations of 1989, giving speeches and interviews in both East and West. Having publicly denounced the GDR attorney general for his failure to act, Hein then worked directly with the committee established to investigate police brutality during the national celebrations on 7 and 8 October 1989, which preceded the massive November demonstrations and the opening of the Berlin Wall. Hein's hopes for a democratic form of socialism were dashed as the two Germanies were unified under the constitution of West Germany. He had once said that if he were to move to the West it would take him years before he could write again; but the West had come to him. Having sold his Bergsdorf farmhouse in 1988, he found a new home near Kraków, an eastern German town near the Polish border, where he could work and collect his thoughts.

Considering Hein's output in the years following the reunification of Germany, it is safe to say that he made the transition much better than most East German authors, in spite of a stroke suffered in 1992 that led to two surgical procedures and over a year of recuperation. In the 1990s he published two novels, *Das Napoleon-Spiel* (The Napoleon-Game, 1993) and *Von allem Anfang an* (From the very Beginning, 1997); a short-story collection, *Exekution eines Kalbes* (Execution of a Calf, 1994); three essay collections, *Als Kind habe ich Stalin gesehen* (I saw Stalin when I was a Child, 1990), *Die fünfte Grundrechenart* (The Fifth Math Function, 1990), and *Die Mauern von Jericho* (The Walls of Jericho, 1996); and five plays, *Randow* (1994), *Bruch* (1999), *In Acht und Bann* (Outlawed and Banned, 1999), *Zaungäste* (Fence Guests, 1999), and *Himmel auf Erden* (Heaven on Earth, 1999).

Das Napoleon-Spiel is one of the most difficult of Hein's works to read. The malicious language the character Friedel Wörle uses to describe his "com-

pulsory manslaughter" of a department store clerk during a subway ride consists of legalese, bureaucratic formulations, and intentionally misleading statements made to his lawyer, Fiarthes. Fiarthes, whose sense of decency amuses Wörle, becomes an inextricable part of the game Wörle plays to manipulate people and events to gratify his insatiable self-interest and arrogant ego. Guilt and innocence are subjected to a legal game, to the manipulation of language according to established court procedures that themselves become more decisive than the facts. Image, show, and manipulative language render merit, real character, and truth secondary considerations. The novel consists of two letters, the first covering Wörle's cynical defense of his cold-blooded murder and a description of his life as a "player," and the second describing how he succeeds in manipulating his half brother from East Germany into forcing Fiarthes against his will into a "game" with Wörle. The killer goes free in the end and chooses Fiarthes as his opponent in order to raise the stakes measurably and justify his triumph over boredom. Wörle may symbolize the specter of fascism—always linked with capitalism in socialist ideology—raising its head again in Germany during and after unification, duping Germans like Fiarthes into defending it. On the other hand, Wörle's language also echoes that employed by GDR government officials in their own defense. The consequences of a successful manipulation of history are embodied in the disturbing figure of Wörle and his justification of murder as a pardonable action.

Hein's comedy *Randow* is a postreunification drama which presents the absurdity and desolateness of individuals experiencing the problems of unemployment, alcoholism, and generational conflicts, not only between younger people and the old communist party members, but also between those who were active dissidents during the GDR regime and their children, who accuse them of having been unrealistic in their dissent. Anna Andress has moved to the Randow valley near the Polish border to pursue her art while her daughter remains in Berlin and her former husband, an unemployed alcoholic, continually breaks the court order to stay away from her. At the other end of the spectrum is an unscrupulous wheeler-dealer in East German properties, Fred P. Paul, and his helper, Stadler, a former GDR secret police agent and border guard. They serve their clients without moral consideration and with the intention of rebuilding German patriotism, with all this implies of extreme right-wing nationalism. Two Romanian refugees are shot fleeing over the border into Germany by Stadler and his buddies, although the blame seems for a time to rest with the local mayor and forest ranger, who want Anna to sell her property. Their bodies are found burned beyond recognition in an abandoned home like Anna's and the mayor uses the incident to frighten her into selling. She does not sell out to the radical conservatives, however, until her dog is mysteriously poisoned. The land associated with Randow had been used to train doctors for biological warfare and for the "final solution" of the Jewish population during the Nazi period. This heritage, coupled with the broken East German family situation, the failure of the local farmers and sport hunters to claim the property, the presence of neo-Nazis, and xenophobia, presents the situation in Randow as a return to ugly thinking, a topic Hein has addressed in several essays. The play captures the atmosphere shortly after reunification when the radical right attempt to gain some political control, a small amount of which it succeeded in doing for two or three years.

Perhaps the best-received book by Hein since *Der fremde Freund* is his novel of puberty, *Von allem Anfang an,* a charming collection of anecdotes of a pastor's son, Daniel. Set in the 1950s in the GDR, the novel is probably Hein's most autobiographical work. The story concerns Daniel's experiences in the time leading up to his departure to attend a preparatory school in West Berlin. His aunt Magdalena tells him that he must always face up to reality, beginning with classmates and townspeople. The book is notable for its complete lack of a political agenda, with the exception of the discussions of the Hungarian revolution in the last chapter shortly before Daniel leaves for Berlin. He is chastised for having an "indifferent" political viewpoint. But the bulk of the book represents Daniel's normalcy as a teenager struggling with first kisses, an unexpected and strange first orgasm, and an encounter with a young girl during a trip to Dresden, where their classes have gone to present plays in a dramatic competition. In some respects, the lack of overt political action is a political statement in itself, and caught by surprise many Western reviewers, long schooled in political reactions to literature by East German authors even after reunification. But why should children and teenagers growing up in the GDR should be any different from those anywhere else in the world? The answer Hein provides is that they are not and, in contrast to most of his other works, he presents a figure in Daniel who is neither damaged nor drawn into the psychological and material damage of others around him.

The same cannot be said for the characters in the four plays that followed *Randow. Bruch* is the story of a famed German surgeon, Theodor Bruch, who has been forcibly retired from his clinic but refuses to accept his retirement. He also refuses to fill out the papers to begin collecting his pension, leading his housekeeper to cut expenses by not heating the house and by accepting groceries from Bruch's loyal friend, Sterling. Sterling has followed his friend's wishes and attempted to organize the building of a new clinic named after Bruch, but the financial capitalist he has engaged turns out to be incompetent and threatens to lead them all into ruin. This Bruch accomplishes on his own by operating on a former patient at home—who refused the care of any other doctor—ending in her death and his impending arrest. The time periods are unclear: Bruch claims to have operated on Hindenburg, and the hospital under his direction was La Charité, the most prominent East Berlin hospital. The present time of the play seems clearly to be after reunification, but this would make Bruch almost ninety years old. He represents a viewpoint opposite to that of Aunt Magdalena, who advised Daniel that he should always confront reality. Bruch cannot even accept that he has been retired and that the car coming for him will not take him to his hospital but to the police station following his arrest; he is symptomatic of people unable to let go of their past under any circumstances.

In Acht und Bann presents most of the Knights of the Round Table from Hein's earlier play, *Die Ritter der Tafelrunde,* serving out life sentences, or, in Parzival's case, twenty years, for crimes committed during their reign. The characters are slightly different from those in *Die Ritter der Tafelrunde.* Parzival has become an opportunist who believes he can be useful to the new democratic government under Mordret, and Orilus has converted to Christianity, although his final decision on whether to join a Catholic or a Protestant church is dependent on which of the two is willing to provide the most pomp and ceremony at his conversion. Keie, the self-proclaimed chief of state in exile, Orilus, and Lancelot form a group of old hard-liners who hold fast to the dogmatic doctrines of the old Socialist regime, much as Bruch clings to his past life. These hard-liners despise Artus, whom they blame for the fall of their empire, and Parzival, who betrayed them. They conduct "cabinet meetings" in which they discuss foreign affairs, the misery of the people, the dishonorable condition to which they have been brought, and, lastly, plans for the reinstatement of electronic eavesdropping and the criminalization of demonstrations upon their return to power. Artus, here somewhat reminiscent of Mikhail Gorbachev, recognizes that the old regime was never able to achieve its goal of creating better human beings and rejects the idea of young knights on the outside breaking him out of jail, as well as any notion of reviving the old regime. The other knights are all chasing windmills in a play that treats the remaining nostalgia of Eastern Germans for the old GDR with wit, irony, and humor.

Zaungäste and *Himmel auf Erden* are one-act comedies written in dialect, *Zaungäste* in the Saxon dialect of Leipzig and *Himmel auf Erden* in the dialect of Mecklenburg. In the first play Berger, hired by the secret police to watch over a student demonstration in 1968 the day before the Pauliner church in Leipzig is torn down, is unhappy because he is missing his chance to buy spare parts for his "Trabi" (Trabant, a car manufactured in the GDR), which will be sold out by the end of the day and will not be available again for probably a year. Luise and Lotte have just come from the funeral of Lotte's husband, Willi, and are drinking their seventh and eighth schnapps. A waiter is disgruntled that the destruction of the church is costing him paying customers; his one regular customer, an old World War II veteran, provides advice for countering the demonstration with tanks. In the end Berger runs out to attack the demonstrators, but is caught by the water canons and drenched as the demonstrators disperse safely. The destruction of the church, which took place just a short time before the invasion of Czechoslovakia, was an extremely unpopular act and left a great deal of bitterness toward the Socialist regime. Hein presents the situation in the context of people who do not care about the church but rather find the whole incident to be an intrusion into their trivial lives.

Himmel auf Erden takes place in an exotic dance bar in a small town in Mecklenburg. Two tradesmen, Horst and Heinz, get off work at eleven in the morning and decide to visit the bar for some excitement. The situation comedy revolves around how out of place the two married men are in such a setting. They try to order the standard fare of the Mecklenburg blue-collar worker, a schnapps and a beer, but the bar serves only high-priced cocktails, which they refuse to drink. Horst finally orders a glass of water, but Heinz refuses to do so because it costs roughly the equivalent of fifteen dollars. In the end the exotic dancer does not dance. The comedy suggests that the old ways of the East German Mecklenburger population, a poor agricultural area for hundreds of years, are out of step with the new ways of the West, which include a decadence heretofore unknown to them.

Interviews:

"Interview mit Christoph Hein," *Theater der Zeit,* 7 (1978): 51–52;

Gregor Edelmann, "'Ansonsten würde man ja aufhören zu schreiben . . .': Interview mit Christoph Hein," *Theater der Zeit,* 10 (1983): 54–56;

Janice Murray and Mary-Elizabeth O'Brian, "Interview mit Christoph Hein," *New German Review,* 3 (1987): 53–66;

Krzystof Joachimczak, "Gespräch mit Christoph Hein," *Sinn und Form,* 2 (1988): 342–359;

Günter Gaus, "Christoph Hein: Gespräch vom 14. März 1990," in *Zur Person,* edited by Gaus (Berlin: Volk und Welt, 1990), pp. 95–114.

Bibliographies:

Manfred Behn, "Christoph Hein," in *Kritisches Lexikon zur deutschsprachigen Gegenwartsliteratur,* volume 3, edited by Heinz Ludwig Arnold (Munich: Edition text + kritik, n.d.), n.pag.;

Lothar Baier, ed., *Christoph Hein: Texte, Daten, Bilder* (Frankfurt am Main: Luchterhand, 1990);

Arnold, ed., *Christoph Hein* (München: Edition text + kritik, 1991);

Klaus Hammer, ed., *Chronist ohne Botschaft, Christoph Hein: Ein Arbeitsbuch: Materialien, Auskünfte, Bibliographie* (Berlin: Aufbau, 1992).

References:

Terrance Albrecht, *Fremde Blicke: Zeitlichkeit und Rezeptionserfahrung im Werk Christoph Heins* (Hamburg: Bockel, 1998);

Wolfgang Albrecht, "Christoph Hein: Dramatiker und Erzähler," *Deutsch als Fremdsprache: Zeitschrift für Theorie und Praxis des Deutschunterrichts für Ausländer,* 21 (1984): 41–54;

Matthias Altenburg, "Dem Leben kann man nur davonlaufen," *Konkret Literatur* (Fall 1985): 88–89;

Lothar Baier and others, *Christoph Hein: Texte, Daten, Bilder* (Frankfurt am Main: Luchterhand, 1990);

Rudiger Bernhardt and others, "Fur und wider: *Der fremde Freund,*" *Weimarer Beiträge,* 9 (1983): 1635–1655;

Brigitte Böttcher, "Diagnose eines unheilbaren Zustands," *Neue Deutsche Literatur,* 6 (1983): 145–149;

Fabrizio Cambi, "Jetztzeit und Vergangenheit: Ästhetische und ideologische Auseinandersetzung im Werke Christoph Heins," in *Die Literatur der DDR: Akten der internationalen Konferenz, Pisa, Mai,* edited by Anna Chiarloni and others (Pisa: Giardini, 1988), pp. 79–86;

Günther Cwordrak, "Ah Q oder was solls," *Weltbühne,* 1 (1984): 26–28;

Jürgen Engler, "Moralität ohne Rückhalt," in *DDR-Literatur '85 im Gespräch,* edited by Siegfried Rönisch (Berlin & Weimar: Aufbau, 1986), pp. 130–136;

Adolf Fink, "Ein Lindenblatt der Verletzlichkeit," in *Deutsche Literatur 1983* (Stuttgart: Reclam, 1984), pp. 134–138;

Bernd Fischer, *Christoph Hein: Drama und Prosa im letzten Jahrzehnt der DDR* (Heidelberg: Winter, 1990);

Fischer, "Christoph Heins *Die wahre Geschichte des Ah Q* (zwischen Hund und Wolf) nach Luxun: Zum komischen Traditionsbezug im Drama der DDR," in *Crossings-Kreuzungen: Festschrift für Helmut Kreuzer,* edited by Edward R. Haymes (Columbia, S.C.: Camden House, 1990), pp. 10–31;

Fischer, "*Drachenblut:* Christoph Heins 'fremde Freundin,'" *Colloquia Germanica,* 21, no. 1 (1988): 46–57;

Fischer, "*Einladung zum Lever Bourgeois:* Christoph Hein's First Prose," in *Studies in GDR Culture and Society 4,* edited by Margy Gerber (Lanham, Md.: University Press of America, 1984), pp. 125–136;

Christoph Funke, "Spiel mit der Geschichte," *Neue Deutsche Literatur,* 10 (1981): 149–152;

Ilse-Marie Gates, "Christoph Heins Novelle *Der fremde Freund*–ein fiktionaler Bericht moderner Kommunikationsschwierigkeiten," *Carleton Germanic Papers,* 18 (1990): 51–73;

Bernhard Greiner, "Bürgerliches Lachtheater als Komödie in der DDR: J.M.R. Lenz' *Der neue Menoza,* bearbeitet von Christoph Hein," in *Die Literatur der DDR: Akten der internationalen Konferenz, Pisa,* edited by Chiarloni and others (Pisa: Giardini, 1988), pp. 329–345;

Antonia Grunenberg, "Geschichte und Entfremdung: Christoph Hein als Autor der DDR," *Michigan Germanic Studies,* 8, nos. 1–2 (1985): 229–251;

Hélène Guibert-Yèche, *Christoph Hein–L'oeuvre romanesque des années 80. De la provocation au dialogue* (Bern: Lang, 1998);

Peter Hacks, "Heinrich-Mann-Preis 1982: Laudatio," *Neue Deutsche Literatur,* 6 (1982): 159–163;

Klaus Hammer, "Christoph Hein: *Horns Ende,*" *Weimarer Beiträge,* 8 (1987): 1358–1369;

Ursula Heukenkamp, "Die fremde Form," *Sinn und Form,* 3 (1983): 625–632;

Andrea Hilbk, *Von Zirkularbewegungen und kreisenden Utopien: Zur Geschichtsdarstellungen in der Epik Christoph Heins* (Augsburg: Wißner, 1998);

Karin Hirdina, "Das Normale der Provinz," *Neue Deutsche Literatur,* 8 (1989): 138–143;

Frank Hörnigk, "*Cromwell,*" *Weimarer Beiträge,* 1 (1983): 33–39;

Hörnigk, "*Die wahre Geschichte des Ah Q*–ein Clownspiel mit Phantasie," in *DDR-Literatur '83 im Gespräch* (Berlin & Weimar: Aufbau, 1984), pp. 41–51;

Michael Hulse, "Tumult, Horn and Double Bass," *Antigonish Review,* nos. 66–67 (Summer–Autumn 1986): 247–257;

Siegfried Jäkel, "Das Prinzip des Eklektizismus in Christoph Heins Roman *Horns Ende,*" *Jahrbuch für finnisch-deutsche Literaturbeziehungen: Mitteilungen aus der Deutschen Bibliothek,* 21 (1989): 193–201;

Antje Janssen-Zimmermann, *Gegenwürfe: Untersuchungen zu Dramen Christoph Heins* (Frankfurt, Bern, New York & Paris: Lang, 1988);

Klaus Jarmatz, "Vorführung eines dialogischen Prinzips," *Neue Deutsche Literatur,* 9 (1988): 135–140;

Hans Kaufmann, "Christoph Hein in der Debatte," in *DDR-Literature '83 im Gespräch,* pp. 41–51;

Christl Kiewitz, *Der stumme Schrei: Krise und Kritik der sozialistischen Intelligenz im Werk Christoph Heins* (Tübingen: Stauffenburg, 1995);

Heinz Klunker, "Der Revolutionär endet im Salon," *Theater heute,* 2 (1981): 8–10;

Gabriele Kreis, "In diese Haut wird nichts eindringen," *Konkret Literatur* (Fall 1983): 82–83;

Hartmut Krug, "Ritter von der traurigen Gestalt," *Theater heute,* 7 (1989): 23–26;

Marianne Krumrey, "Gegenwart im Spiegel der Geschichte," *Temperamente,* 4 (1981): 143–147;

Gabriele Lindner, "Ein geistiger Widergänger," *Neue Deutsche Literatur,* 10 (1986): 155–161;

Dietrich Löffler, "Christoph Hein: *Öffentlich arbeiten,*" in *DDR-Literatur '87 im Gespräch* (Berlin & Weimar: Aufbau, 1988), pp. 252–258;

Löffler, "Christoph Heins Prosa–Chronik der Zeitgeschichte," *Weimarer Beiträge,* 9 (1987): 1484–1487;

Bärbel Lücke, *Christoph Hein, Drachenblut: Interpretation* (München: Oldenbourg, 1989);

Lücke, *Christoph Hein, Horns Ende: Interpretation* (München: Oldenbourg, 1994);

Phillip S. McKnight, "Alltag, Apathy, Anarchy: GDR Everyday Life as a Provocation in Christoph Hein's Novelle *Der fremde Freund,*" in *Studies in GDR Culture and Society 8,* edited by Gerber (Lanham, Md., New York & London: University Press of America, 1988), pp. 179–190;

McKnight, "Ein Mosaik zu Christoph Heins Roman *Horns Ende,*" *Sinn und Form,* 2 (1987): 413–425;

McKnight, *Understanding Christoph Hein* (Columbia: University of South Carolina Press, 1995);

Georg Menchén, "Verlorene Geschichtlichkeit," *Theater der Zeit,* 5 (1987): 52–53;

Timm Menke, "Der Literat als Politiker: Zur Vorwärtsverteidigung der Kunst in den Essays von Christoph Hein," *Germanic Review,* 64 (Fall 1989): 177–181;

Karl-Heinz Müller, "Wem nützen Ideale?," *Theater der Zeit,* 8 (1980): 12–13;

Jirí Munzar, "Die Dramen Christoph Heins und einige Gattungsprobleme der jüngeren Dramatik der DDR," *Brücken* (1986/1987): 144–155;

Heinz-Peter Preußer, *Zivilisationskritik und literarische Öffentlichkeit. Strukturale und wertungstheoretische Untersuchungen zu erzählenden Texten Christoph Heins* (Frankfurt am Main, Bern, New York & Paris: Lang, 1991);

Peter Reichel, "'En passant': Zitate und Notate zu Christoph Heins *Passage,*" *Theater der Zeit,* 5 (1987): 50–53;

Lutz Richter, "Christoph Hein: Auf eine neue Art zum Nachdenken zwingen," *Deutsch als Fremdsprache: Zeitschrift für Theorie und Praxis des Deutschunterrichts für Ausländer,* 24 (1987): 79–89;

Andreas Roßmann, "Kein leichtes Spiel: DDR-Dramatik im Westen," *Deutschland-Archiv,* 12 (1986): 1255–1259;

Roßmann, "Die Revolution als Geisterschiff," *Theater heute,* 3 (1984): 53;

Roßmann, "Die Revolution frißt ihre Ideale," *Theater heute,* 10 (1980): 64–66;

Holger Rudolf, "Subjektive Gefühlsevidenzen und allgemienes Teilnehmungsgefühl. Anmerkungen zu literarischen Texten von Peter Handke, Christoph Hein und Robert Gernhardt," *Diskussion Deutsch,* 20 (1989): 252–261;

Jirina Saavedrová, "Möglichkeiten einer linguostilistischen Analyse literarisch-künstlischer Texte. Dargestellt an Christoph Heins Novelle *Der fremde Freund,*" *Brücken* (1986/1987): 156–165;

Saavedrová, "Christoph Hein: *Horns Ende.* Versuch einer kommunikativ-pragmatisch orientierten Stilanalyse," *Brücken* (1987/1988): 106–214;

Michael Schenkel, *Fortschritts- und Modernitätskritik in der DDR-Literatur: Prosatexte der achtziger Jahre* (Tübingen: Stauffenburg, 1995);

Dieter Schlenstedt and others, "DDR-Literaturentwicklung in der Diskussion," *Weimarer Beiträge,* 10 (1984): 1589–1616;

Joscha Schmierer, "Das Menschliche, der Mann, der Funktionär und die Frauen," *Kommune,* 3 (1986): 65–68;

Galina Snamenskaja, "Die geistig-seelische Suche im Werk Christoph Heins," *Weimarer Beiträge,* 3 (1990): 506–511;

Erika Stephan, "Christoph Heins Kammerspiel Passage im Verständnis des Theaters," in *DDR-Literatur '87 im Gespräch,* pp. 259–272;

Jürgen Stötzer, "Lenz–ein Schatten nur einer ungesehenen Tradition? Aspekte der Rezeption J.M.R. Lenz' bei Christoph Hein," *Zeitschrift für Germanistik,* 9 (1989): 429–441;

Text + Kritik, special Hein issue, 111 (1991);

Hans-Georg Werner and others, "*Der fremde Freund* von Christoph Hein," *Ginkgobaum,* 5 (1986): 34–44;

Ines Zekert, *Poetologie und Prophetie: Christoph Heins Prosa und Dramatik im Kontext seiner Walter-Benjamin-Rezeption* (Frankfurt am Main: Lang, 1993).

Heinrich Heine

(13 December 1797 – 17 February 1856)

Robert C. Holumb
University of California, Berkeley

This entry originally appeared in DLB 90: German Writers
in the Age of Goethe, 1789–1832.

BOOKS: *Gedichte* (Berlin: Maurer, 1822);

Tragödien, nebst einem lyrischen Intermezzo (Berlin: Dümmler, 1823);

Reisebilder, 4 volumes (Hamburg: Hoffmann & Campe, 1826–1831)–comprises volume 1, "Die Heimkehr," "Die Harzreise," "Die Nordsee I"; volume 2, "Die Nordsee II," "Die Nordsee III," "Ideen: Das Buch Le Grand," "Briefe aus Berlin"; volume 3, "Reise von München nach Genua," "Die Bäder von Lucca"; volume 4, *Nachträge,* "Die Stadt Lucca," "Englische Fragmente"; translated by Charles Godfrey Leland as *Pictures of Travel,* 1 volume (Philadelphia: Weik, 1855; London: Trübner, 1856);

Buch der Lieder (Hamburg: Hoffmann & Campe, 1827); translated by Leland as *Heine's Book of Songs* (Philadelphia: Leypoldt / New York: Christern, 1864); translated by Henry Sullivan Jarrett (under the pseudonym Stratheir) as *The Book of Songs* (London: Constable, 1913); German version republished (New York: Ungar, 1944);

Französische Zustände (Hamburg: Hoffmann & Campe, 1833);

Vorrede zu Heinrich Heines französischen Zuständen: nach der französischen Ausgabe ergänzt (Leipzig: Heideloff & Campe, 1833);

Zur Geschichte der neueren schönen Literatur in Deutschland, 2 volumes (Paris & Leipzig: Heideloff & Campe, 1833); republished as *Die romantische Schule,* 1 volume (Hamburg: Hoffmann & Campe, 1836); translated by S. L. Fleishman as *The Romantic School* (New York: Holt, 1882);

Der Salon, 4 volumes (Hamburg: Hoffmann & Campe, 1834–1840)–comprises volume 1, "Französische Maler: Gemäldeausstellung in Paris 1831," "Gedichte," "Aus den Memoiren des Herrn von Schnabelewopski"; volume 2, "Zur Geschichte der Religion und Philosophie in Deutschland," "Frühlingslieder"; volume 3, "Florentinische

Heinrich Heine (Heinrich-Heine-Institut, Düsseldorf)

Nächte," "Elementargeister"; volume 4, "Der Rabbi von Bacharach," "Gedichte," "Über die französische Bühne"; "Zur Geschichte der Religion und Philosophie in Deutschland," translated by John Snodgrass as *Religion and Philosophy in Germany: A Fragment* (New York: Houghton, Mifflin, 1882; London: Trübner, 1882);

De l'Allemagne, 2 volumes (Paris: Renduel, 1835); enlarged edition, 2 volumes (Paris: Lévy, 1855);

Über den Denunzianten: Eine Vorrede zum dritten Theile des Salons (Hamburg: Hoffmann & Campe, 1837);

Shakespeares Mädchen und Frauen: Mit Erläuterungen (Paris & Leipzig: Brockhaus & Avenarius, 1838 [dated 1839]);

Heinrich Heine über Ludwig Börne (Hamburg: Hoffmann & Campe, 1840);

Neue Gedichte (Hamburg: Hoffmann & Campe / Paris: Dubochet, 1844);

Deutschland: Ein Wintermärchen (Hamburg: Hoffmann & Campe, 1844);

Atta Troll: Ein Sommernachtstraum (Hamburg: Hoffmann & Campe, 1847); translated by Thomas Selby Egan as "Atta Troll" in *Atta Troll and Other Poems* (London: Chapman & Hall, 1876); translated by Herman Scheffauer as *Atta Troll* (London: Sidgwick & Jackson, 1913; New York: Huebsch, 1914);

Der Doktor Faust: Ein Tanzpoem Nebst kuriosen Berichten über Teufel, Hexen und Dichtkunst (Hamburg: Hoffmann & Campe, 1851); translated by Basil Ashmore as *Doktor Faust: A Dance Poem; Together with Some Rare Accounts of Witches, Devils, and the Ancient Art of Sorcery* (London: Nevill, 1952);

Romanzero (Hamburg: Hoffmann & Campe, 1851);

Les Dieux en exil (Brussels & Leipzig: Kiessling, 1853);

Vermischte Schriften, 3 volumes (Hamburg: Hoffmann & Campe, 1854)–comprises volume 1, "Geständnisse," "Gedichte 1853 und 1854," "Die Götter im Exil," *Die Göttin Diana;* volumes 2–3, *Lutezia;*

Heinrich Heine's Sämmtliche Werke, 7 volumes (Philadelphia: Weik, 1855–1861);

Heinrich Heine's Sämmtliche Werke: Rechtmäßige Original-Ausgabe, edited by Adolf Strodtmann, 24 volumes (Hamburg: Hoffmann & Campe, 1861–1895);

Memoiren und neugesammelte Gedichte, Prosa und Briefe: Mit Einleitung, edited by Eduard Engel (Hamburg: Hoffmann & Campe, 1884);

Sämtliche Werke, edited by Ernst Elster, 7 volumes (Leipzig: Bibliographisches Institut, 1887–1890);

Sämtliche Schriften, edited by Klaus Briegleb, 6 volumes (Munich: Hanser, 1968–1976);

Werke, Briefwechsel, Lebenszeugnisse: Säkularausgabe, edited by the Nationale Forschungs- und Gedenkstätten der klassischen deutschen Literatur in Weimar and the Centre National de la Recherche Scientifique in Paris, 5 volumes published (Berlin & Paris: Aufbau, 1970–);

Sämtliche Werke, edited by Manfred Windfuhr, 13 volumes published (Hamburg: Hoffmann & Campe, 1973–).

Editions in English: *The Poems of Heine, Complete: Translated in the Original Metres*, translated by Edgar Alfred Bowring (London: Bohn, 1861)–comprises "Memoir," "Book of Songs," "Pictures of Travel," "Atta Troll," "Germany, a Winter Tale," "Romancero," and "Latest Poems";

The Works of Heinrich Heine, translated by Leland and others, 12 volumes (London: Heinemann, 1891–1905; New York: Dutton, 1906)–comprises volume 1, "Florentine Nights," "The Memoirs of Herr von Schnabelewopski," "The Rabbi of Bacharach," "Shakespeare's Maidens and Women"; volumes 2–3, *Pictures of Travel;* volume 4, *The Salon; or, Letters on Art, Music, Popular Life and Politics;* volumes 5–6, *Germany;* volumes 7–8, *French Affairs;* volume 9, *The Book of Songs,* translated by Thomas Brooksbank; volume 10, *New Poems,* translated by Margaret Armour; volume 11, "Germany," "Romancero, Books I–II," translated by Armour; volume 12, "Romancero, Book III," "Last Poems," translated by Armour;

Heinrich Heine: Paradox and Poet, volume 2: *The Poems,* translated by Louis Untermeyer (New York: Harcourt, Brace, 1937);

The Poetry and Prose of Heinrich Heine, translated by Untermeyer, Aaron Kramer, Frederic Ewen, and others, edited by Ewen (New York: Citadel Press, 1948);

Selected Works, translated and edited by Helen M. Mustard and Max Knight (New York: Random House, 1973);

The Complete Poems of Heinrich Heine: A Modern English Version, translated by Hal Draper (Cambridge, Mass.: Suhrkamp/Insel, 1982; Oxford: Oxford University Press, 1982);

Poetry and Prose, edited by Jost Hermand and Robert C. Holub (New York: Continuum, 1982);

The Romantic School and Other Essays, edited by Hermand and Holub (New York: Continuum, 1985).

OTHER: *Kahldorf über den Adel in Briefen an den Grafen M. von Moltke,* edited by Heine (Nuremberg: Hoffmann & Campe, 1831);

Miguel de Cervantes, *Der sinnreiche Junker Don Quichote von La Mancha,* translated by Heine, 2 volumes (Stuttgart: Verlag der Klassiker, 1837–1838).

From the generation following Johann Wolfgang von Goethe there is perhaps no writer more controversial than Heinrich Heine. Although best known now for his early lyrics–which have been set to music more often than those of any other poet–during most of his life he was renowned for his witty prose, his political journalism, and his caustic satires. These were the writings which earned him a controversial reputation among his contemporaries and after his death. Frequently censored for his liberal views and his attacks on religion, he was despised by narrow-minded German nationalists for his cosmopolitan feelings and discriminated against by a bigoted German society for his Jewish origins. While his writings became extremely popular among enlightened sectors of the European intelligentsia, in his native land he was often subjected to scorn or ridicule. This prejudice against Heine culminated in the period of National Socialism, when he was retroactively stripped of his German background; during the Third Reich the author of the "Loreley," Heine's most celebrated poem, was listed as "an unknown poet."

This blatant discrimination on the part of fanatical racists is somewhat balanced, however, by Heine's tremendous impact on the most innovative minds of the nineteenth century. He was a close friend of Karl Marx during his Parisian exile in 1843–1844, and it is quite likely that the radical socialist was influenced by both Heine's wit and his political views. Richard Wagner used motifs from two of Heine's works for his operas *Der fliegende Hollander* (The Flying Dutchman, 1841) and *Tannhäuser* (1843–1844). Friedrich Nietzsche admired him as one of the greatest poets of the century and considered him to be one of the superior German stylists of all times. And Sigmund Freud was obviously thoroughly acquainted with his writings; many of the illustrations he uses in *Wit and Its Relation to the Unconscious* (1905) are taken from Heine's works. With regard to his reputation, then, Heine has been a subject of considerable dispute. Hailed as a genial poet and innovative prose writer by some, he has been vilified as a flighty poetaster and traitor to the fatherland by others.

In fact, controversy entered into Heine's life from–and around–the very moment of his birth. Although it is now presumed that he was born on 13 December 1797, this elementary biographical fact is by no means certain. No official record exists, and Heine himself, for unknown reasons, never confirmed this date. Indeed, he most often asserted that he was born two years later. Previous defamatory speculation that he lied in order to cover up his illegitimacy or to avoid service in the Prussian army has proven to be false. But no one has been able to ascertain why Heine consistently felt compelled to hide his actual age.

Heine's birth is not the only fact about his early life which is shrouded in mystery. Little information is available about his early years, and what there is is often of somewhat dubious validity. This much seems certain, however. Heine was one of four children–three sons and a daughter–born to Samson and Betty (van Geldern) Heine. He was named Harry by his parents, apparently to honor one of his father's associates. His childhood appears to have been rather uneventful. He attended a nursery school and a Hebrew school before entering the public school system in 1807. He was accepted into the lyceum in 1810 but never graduated, partially because of the turbulence surrounding the Napoleonic Wars, and partially because his family had planned for him to become a businessman. Accordingly he was enrolled in a business school in 1814. In 1816 he

was apprenticed to a bank in Hamburg under the auspices of his uncle, Salomon Heine, one of the wealthiest financiers in Germany. Two years later his uncle set him up in his own business, but it was liquidated by early 1819, apparently because Salomon discovered that Samson was drawing money against his son's accounts.

After this brief and unsuccessful business career it was decided, probably by Uncle Salomon, that Heine should study law. In the autumn of 1819 he enrolled at the recently founded university in Bonn. Although he was several years older than the usual student, his behavior appears to have been quite typical for a young man of his times. He participated in a demonstration to commemorate the Battle of Leipzig shortly after his arrival in town, joined a nationalist student club in his first semester, and attended lectures on topics relating to German history and literature. After a year at Bonn, he transferred to the university in Göttingen, which had a fine reputation, particularly in the field of law. Here he was terribly unhappy, chiefly because both the faculty and the students lacked the nationalist enthusiasm he had experienced in Bonn. Heine joined a student club but was expelled, probably because of his Jewishness, which no doubt contributed to his dissatisfaction with the university. The misery of his first stay in Göttingen, however, lasted less than four months. Because he engaged in a duel with a fellow student, he was expelled from the university for a minimum of half a year.

After a short visit with his family in Hamburg, Heine was sent to Berlin to continue his studies. Berlin, like Bonn, was a relatively new university (founded in 1810), but it had already acquired a fine reputation. Heine seems to have enjoyed seminars there more than in Göttingen, and he attended lectures by some of the most eminent intellectuals of his times. Chief among these was Georg Wilhelm Friedrich Hegel, perhaps the most influential philosopher on the Continent. But more important than his studies were the social connections he made in the Prussian capital. He gained entrance to the salon of Rahel Varnhagen von Ense, a Jewish woman married to a liberal Prussian former diplomat, and mingled there with the important literati of Berlin society. He was also successful in finding a publisher for his first book, *Gedichte* (Poems, 1822). But perhaps most significant for him was his association with the Verein für Cultur und Wissenschaft der Juden (Society for Culture and Scholarship of the Jews). In association with other young Jewish intellectuals, Heine explored the role Jews had played in European culture and came to appreciate his own heritage. From his own researches Heine began a novel, "Der Rabbi von Bacherach" (The Rabbi from Bacherach, 1840), of which he completed less than three chapters.

Fortified by his sojourn in Berlin, Heine returned to Göttingen in 1824 to complete his degree in law. Aside from a two-month journey on foot through the Harz mountains in the fall of that year, he appears to have applied himself diligently to his studies. In May 1825 he passed his oral defense, and in July the title of doctor of law was conferred on him. Between these two dates another momentous change occurred in his life. In June he converted to Protestantism and was baptized Heinrich. For Jews who had any aspirations to hold governmental (including academic) positions, such a conversion was hardly unusual. Eduard Gans, who later became Hegel's successor in Berlin, and Heinrich Marx, Karl Marx's father, converted at about the same time. Heine himself insisted that it was his "Entreebillet zur europäischen Kultur" (entrance ticket to European culture). Still, considering his recent encounters with the Jewish tradition in Berlin and his reactions against others who converted, it is safe to assume that the decision was not made lightly.

By this time in his life Heine had already gained some notoriety as a writer. He had composed two dramas in the early 1820s, *Almansor* and *William Ratcliff,* first published in *Tragödien, nebst einem lyrischen Intermezzo* (Tragedies, with a Lyrical Intermezzo, 1823), but these were epigonic works which are largely forgotten today. His real talent lay in lyric poetry. Starting in 1817 he had begun to publish his verse in literary journals, and two small books appeared in 1822 and 1823. His literary reputation, however, rests largely on the collection of verse published in 1827 under the title *Buch der Lieder* (Book of Songs). It contained chiefly poems Heine had written during the late 1810s and early 1820s, revised and arranged in five sections or cycles: "Junge Leiden" (Young Sorrows), "Lyrisches Intermezzo" (Lyrical Intermezzo), "Die Heimkehr" (Homecoming), "Aus der Harzreise" (From the Harz Journey), and "Die Nordsee" (The North Sea). Although the second edition did not appear until a decade later, by the end of the nineteenth century it had become one of the best-selling books of poetry in the German language. Heine's most familiar poems, including those that so enchanted the composers of Romantic Lieder, are found in this volume.

Most of these early poems deal with the theme of unrequited love. Although they appear to be simply constructed from familiar romantic motifs, closer inspection reveals meticulous poetic craft and insight. Their outstanding feature is the turn or ironic twist which frequently concludes a poem. The reader is lulled into a false sense of security when he or she encounters the familiar imagery of lyrics from the Age of Goethe. But in the final lines Heine calls this imagery—and the ideology behind it—into question with a note of discord or ironic distancing. In this way the poem becomes a vehicle for self-reflection upon the role of the poet, the use of poetic motifs, and romantic poetry in general. To achieve their effect these poems therefore depend on subtle techniques of playing with and often disappointing the expectations of the reader. They are carefully designed to destroy the harmony they initially seem to posit, and thus they reaffirm in the form the thematic emphasis on unhappy love. Unfortunately, many of the most famous musical compositions for the poetry in *Buch der Lieder* fail to appreciate Heine's essentially ironic stance. These poems implicitly challenge the ideal of harmony and the idyllic world found in the literature of the preceding period. In accord with an era of turbulence and change in the social, political, and intellectual realm, they explore, on the level of emotions, dissonance and strife.

Although this poetry would later become an enormous success, Heine was unable to live by writing verse. In fact, the *Buch der Lieder* brought him no money at all for at least a decade after its publication. Since poetry was not a promising way to earn a living, Heine was forced to pursue other avenues. During the period between the attainment of his law degree in 1825 and his immigration to Paris in 1831 he traveled about Europe—journeying to England in 1827 and to Italy in 1828—while contemplating various career options. At the beginning of 1828 he assumed the only regularly paying position he ever held, editor of the *Neue allgemeine politische Annalen,* but he resigned after six months. He then ingratiated himself with a Bavarian minister of the interior in hopes of securing a professorship in Munich. He apparently wanted to lecture on German history, but a competitor was chosen above him. Heine even thought about entering the political arena. Toward the end of 1830 he waged an unsuccessful and half-hearted campaign to be appointed to a high post in the Hamburg city government. Since he had no experience and scant qualifications, it is not surprising that nothing ever came of this attempt.

Much more important for Heine during these years was his writing; it was during this period that he established himself as a major author on the German literary scene. In 1826 he met Julius Campe, a progressive publisher in Hamburg who recognized his genius and did much to promote his works. Heine sold him the rights to "Die Harzreise" (The Harz Journey), a prose work that had appeared in a literary journal, and Campe saw the opportunity to publish more than just an isolated travel description. He conceived the idea of using it and other similar works in a series; each volume would thus serve as advertisement for subsequent volumes. Accordingly, he brought out *Reisebilder I* (Travel Pictures I) in 1826, followed by second, third, and fourth volumes in 1827, 1829, and 1831. Although the sales were unimpressive at first, by the time Heine left Germany in 1831 the *Reisebilder* had made him a relatively famous writer, especially in the circles of young, liberal intellectuals.

The success of this series can be attributed largely to its controversial content and innovative form. Heine takes up matters of current concern and comments upon them in a witty and critical fashion. Because of censorship he had to be extremely cautious. Rarely does one find a sustained or direct treatment of an issue or personality. Most often Heine operates with an apparently free-floating technique of associating ideas. Something he witnesses or experiences will remind him of a politically more sensitive topic which he then discusses with humor, allusions, and innuendos. Heine had developed this technique earlier in the 1820s in a set of correspondence articles, "Briefe aus Berlin" (Letters from Berlin, 1822), and in a short travel description, "Über Polen" (On Poland; 1823), but by the end of the decade he had obviously perfected his art.

"Die Harzreise" is the first and probably the best-known work in the *Reisebilder*. The framework is the journey through the Harz mountains which Heine undertook as a break from his studies in late 1824. In this work his attitudes are more clearly tied to the German Romantic tradition. Some of the main targets for his ironic barbs are those individuals and institutions which maintain senseless cultural conventions. Heine's narrative persona is presented as a friend of nature, love, and authentic feeling, someone who disdains poetic prescriptions and aesthetic pretentiousness. In this work the philistine, a frequent object of ridicule for Romanticism, is the epitome of all that Heine detests. But Heine's criticism, unlike that of most Romantics, extends beyond the realm of art into societal relations. He is concerned with restrictions not only to artistic creativity, but to human potential as well. Thus he takes society to task wherever it confines individual liberty. For this reason Heine frequently mocks rigid class distinctions and orthodox religious attitudes. Both serve to maintain a conservative order inimical to his progressive, emancipatory desires.

Perhaps the most imaginative work in the *Reisebilder* is "Ideen: Das Buch Le Grand." Consisting of twenty chapters of varying length, this work may be conveniently divided into four sections. In the first and last quarter of the work Heine assumes various personae: an Italian knight, an Indian count, a brokenhearted lover. In these parts the dominant themes are familiar from the Romantic canon: love, death, and suicide. At the close of the fifth chapter and throughout the next quarter of the book, the loosely structured narration shifts focus; the narrative persona, who is a somewhat

distorted mirror of the author, begins to talk of his youth. The major event he discusses is the invasion of the French army into the German Rhineland at the beginning of the nineteenth century. Napoleon and the drum major Le Grand become symbols of emancipation for a backward, biased, and anesthetized Germany. In the third quarter of the work, after the demise of Napoleon and the death of Le Grand, the narrator reflects on a variety of themes including academic scholarship, the writing profession, and the political absurdities following the Congress of Vienna in 1815. The result is an amusing but critical collage of culture and society in an age of reactionary politics.

With the exception of "Die Nordsee I" and "Die Nordsee II" (The North Sea), the first cycles of German poetry written about the sea, the rest of the works in the *Reisebilder* exhibited similar tendencies. In their form an apparently loose association of ideas, they deliver nonetheless a powerful and decisive liberal message. Because of the conservative political and cultural establishment these works were bound to be seen as a challenge to the status quo. But the most controversial of the works in the *Reisebilder* is known less for its political critique than for its personal character assault. In "Die Bäder von Lucca" (The Baths of Lucca) Heine's penchant for literary polemics led him to lash out fiercely at a fellow writer, August Graf von Platen-Hallermünde. The feud between them apparently began when Heine published some epigrams ridiculing Platen at the end of "Nordsee III." Although they were composed by Heine's friend Karl Immermann, a noted playwright and novelist of the period, it appears that Platen was offended that Heine would dare to print them. He therefore countered with *Der romantische Oedipus* (The Romantic Oedipus, 1829), a satire of German literary life which included a few anti-Semitic swipes at Heine's Jewish background. Heine, who was especially sensitive about this matter anyway, suspected—wrongly, it turns out—that Platen was part of a Catholic-reactionary conspiracy which had prevented him from obtaining the professorship he had wanted in Munich. His assault was therefore especially harsh and all encompassing. Platen was taken to task for his metrical fastidiousness, his lack of originality, his aristocratic origins, and his bragging. But Heine also attacked him rather shamelessly for his homosexuality. In the prudish moral climate of the times such openness was unusual and attracted a great deal of attention. Heine was severely censured for this impropriety, even by some of his friends.

Although by 1830 Heine had acquired quite a reputation as a writer of both verse and prose, his future was nonetheless uncertain. Unable to live from his writings and unsuccessful at finding a secure position, hounded by the censors for his moral and political views and constantly fearing detention or incarceration, he decided to leave his native land for Paris. In May 1831 he arrived in the French capital, and outside of two visits to Germany in the 1840s and an occasional vacation, it remained his home until his death a quarter of a century later. Heine was exceedingly pleased with what he found there. Shortly after his arrival he remarked that if a fish in water were asked how it felt, it would reply, "Like Heine in Paris." It is not difficult to understand his enthusiasm. In Paris he found the stimulating political environment which was totally lacking in Germany. The French Revolution of 1830 had brought Louis Philippe, the bourgeois king, to the throne, but a spectrum of political parties from royalists to socialists thrived in a relatively open climate. Heine was also able to pursue his interests in Saint-Simonism, a philosophically based utopian doctrine which he had begun to study in Germany. But another reason he felt at home in Paris was because he fit well into the cultural life of the city. Several good translations of his work facilitated his acceptance into the best salons and literary circles. By the mid 1830s he had become acquainted with some of the most celebrated musicians and writers of the era, and in time he himself became a cultural figure to whom visitors flocked.

One of Heine's principal activities in the Parisian capital was to mediate French cultural and political events to the German public. During the first decade and a half of what began as a self-imposed exile, he was an on-the-scene correspondent for some of the more popular German newspapers and journals. One of the first projects he undertook after arriving in Paris was a series of reports on an art exhibit in 1831. Although many of the paintings on display were conceived before the July Revolution, Heine seeks to uncover the spirit of the new era in these works. The articles, originally published in the *Morgenblatt* in 1831, were collected under the title "Französische Maler" (French Painters) in the first volume of *Der Salon* (1834–1840). In the second half of the 1830s Heine performed a similar task for French theater. In the form of letters to August Lewald, the editor of the *Allgemeine Theater-Revue,* Heine dealt with recent trends on the French stage. "Über die französische Bühne" (Concerning the French Stage; in volume 4 of *Der Salon*), like "Französische Maler," praises progressive trends in France, while questioning German backwardness. Heine's most successful writings about France were collections of correspondence articles he wrote during the 1830s and 1840s. *Französische Zustände* (Conditions in France, 1833) consists of reports published originally in early 1832 in the *Augsburg Allgemeine Zeitung,* while *Lutezia,* which appeared in book form in 1854 and is the longest work published by Heine, is an edition of articles composed in the early 1840s. In both works Heine shows himself to be an acute observer of the political and cultural scene. Using more intuition than investigative procedures, and writing in the witty, sometimes associative style that was his trademark, Heine analyzes various aspects of cultural and political progress in the most revolutionary European city of the early nineteenth century.

But Heine also endeavored to mediate German culture to the French. His two most important essays of the early 1830s, *Die romantische Schule* (The Romantic School) and "Zur Geschichte der Religion und Philosophie in Deutschland" (Concerning the History of Religion and Philosophy in Germany; published in volume 2 of *Der Salon*) attempt to correct the view of German intellectual life found in Mme de Staël's influential book *De l'Allemagne* (1813). It was especially important for Heine to combat de Staël's favorable portrayal of German Romanticism, and Heine's first essay contains a sustained discussion of and attack upon this current in German letters. *Die romantische Schule,* however, is more encompassing than its title suggests. For it includes observations on most of the major figures in German literature during the Age of Goethe. Indeed, the title under which this work was first published, *Zur Geschichte der neueren schönen Literatur in Deutschland* (Concerning the History of Recent Belles Lettres in Germany, 1833), is much more appropriate. What emerges from this literary history—which was one of the first of its kind to be written in German—is a view of two antagonistic tendencies in German culture. The first is identified with the Enlightenment, sensualism, Protestantism, and progressive politics; Gotthold Ephraim Lessing, Johann Gottfried von Herder, Friedrich von Schiller, Johann Heinrich Voß, and the Young Germans are placed in this tradition. Opposing it is a mystical, spiritualist, Catholic, and politically regressive turn to the Middle Ages that Heine associates with the Romantic movement. Towering above both of these, although definitely allied with the Enlightenment heritage, is Goethe. By introducing this typology to deal with German literary history, Heine is attempting to discourage French intellectuals from their admiration of the German Romantics, while simultaneously showing them that Germany, too, possesses a critical and forward-looking literature.

The identical set of dichotomies structures Heine's essay on German religious and philosophical thought. Heine sets up an historical narrative according to which the spiritualism of the Catholic Middle Ages is gradually eroded by advances in the domain of German intellectual life. The major stages in this erosion process, which is also the path of political emancipation, are the focal points of the three sections. In the first Heine treats Martin Luther's clash with the Roman

Catholic Church as a pivotal point in breaking the hegemony of spiritualism. By opposing this foreign, intellectual oppression, Luther managed to assist in the creation of a positive and liberating national identity. Benedict de Spinoza appears as the hero of the second section because of his doctrine of pantheism, "the clandestine religion of Germany." Here Heine traces the materialist roots of pantheistic teachings and points to their potentially revolutionary implications. Although the final book deals with German idealist philosophy in general, there is little doubt that Immanuel Kant is the central figure. His *Kritik der reinen Vernunft* (Critique of Pure Reason, 1781) is likened to the French Revolution; it destroyed the last remnants of deism in German philosophy and made theology in any traditional sense a dead issue. Heine's reading of intellectual life in this work thus posits a basically emancipatory trajectory, and his exegetical practice elucidates the hidden stations on the enlightened road as well as the intellectual detours.

Heine's views were inherently oppositional, especially when one considers the repressive atmosphere in Germany at that time. But he appears to have limited his opposition to acts of the pen. He seems never to have been a member of any organized political group. It must have come as a surprise to him, therefore, when in 1835 the German Diet marked him as one of the leaders of the Young Germans and banned the sales of all his past and future works. The others mentioned in this official decree (Karl Gutzkow, Heinrich Laube, Theodor Mundt, and Ludolf Wienbarg) were also liberal writers; the conspiracy against the state which the Diet perceived was clearly nonexistent, the result of either mistaken identity or extreme paranoia. Heine–and most of the others–protested vehemently against this prohibition, and although total censorship was soon lifted, the ban definitely had a deleterious effect on the intellectual climate for the rest of the decade. Certainly this is part of the reason that the following five years were the least productive in Heine's literary career. Aside from a polemic against Wolfgang Menzel, a rabid nationalist who was one of the most vituperative critics of the Young Germans, and an attack on a group of Swabian poets, Heine published only a novel fragment, "Florentinische Nächte" (Florentine Nights), an essay on folklore entitled "Elementargeister" (Elementary Spirits)–both in volume 3 of *Der Salon*–and a preface to an edition of illustrations from Shakespeare, *Shakespeares Mädchen und Frauen* (Shakespeare's Maidens and Ladies, 1838). When he collected a few miscellaneous works for a volume which appeared in 1837, he suggested "das stille Buch" (the quiet book) or "Märchen" (fairy tales) as the title; either would have been appropriate.

Toward the end of the decade, however, Heine once again turned to bolder themes. Perhaps the most controversial of these dealt with the writer Ludwig Börne. On the surface Börne and Heine had much in common. Both were liberal Jews residing in France, and both wielded particularly sharp pens. During the early part of the decade they seem to have recognized these affinities and admired one another's work, but a process of estrangement obviously occurred. By the time Börne died in 1837 he and Heine were no longer on friendly terms. Some unfavorable remarks which Börne made in reviews of Heine's work and in private had increased the acrimony between the two men, and Heine soon seized the opportunity to distinguish his views from Börne's. The result was a book which was supposed to be titled "Ludwig Börne: Eine Denkschrift" (Ludwig Börne: A Memorial). To fuel the fires of controversy, however, Heine's publisher Campe gave it the unauthorized title *Heinrich Heine über Ludwig Börne* (1840)–a pun, since the German word *über* means both "about" and "over." In the Denkschrift Heine sets up two different types of radical positions. The Nazarene, associated with Börne, is narrowly political, antiartistic, petty, and Catholic. The Hellene, on the other hand, appreciates aesthetic excellence and understands that a true revolution must encompass more than political upheaval. Although it is never explicitly stated, Heine identifies himself with this preferred position.

Because of Börne's sterling reputation, even among adversaries, Heine's strategy backfired. He was almost universally condemned for what was perceived as an unjustified assault on a man of unimpeachable integrity. What made matters worse was that Heine had also cast aspersions on Jeanette Wohl; for a time Börne had lived with her and her husband, Salomon Strauss. Heine's innuendos concerning this ménage à trois occasioned a public scandal which led to a duel between Heine and Strauss; Heine escaped with a mere wounded hip. The more lasting outcome of this escapade was Heine's marriage to Crescence Eugénie Mirat. Mathilde, as Heine renamed her, was a poor salesgirl whom he had met in 1834 and with whom he had been living since 1836. Recognizing that he could be killed in his confrontation with Strauss, he decided to provide some measure of security for her, and they were wed a week before the duel in August 1841.

Despite the reception of the Börne book and its disastrous consequences, its appearance marks a positive turning point in Heine's literary career. Although in this book he consciously separated himself from the Republican oppositional party with which Börne was associated, his writing once again became more radical and more political during the early 1840s. This turn is partially due to the altered political atmosphere in Germany during the period known as the Vormärz (pre-March), which refers to the eight years directly preceding the March Revolution in 1848. With the death of Friedrich Wilhelm III of Prussia in 1840 and the ascension to the throne of his successor, Friedrich Wilhelm IV, progressive forces hoped for a fundamental change in German political life. These hopes were kindled during the initial years of his reign by reforms in censorship and an apparent willingness to tolerate oppositional views. But perhaps more important for the intellectual climate was the appearance of a strong contingent of left or young Hegelians, who attacked conservative bastions with journalistic enterprises and philosophically informed arguments. Heine was acquainted with the writings of many members of this diverse group, and he befriended for a time the most celebrated young Hegelian, Karl Marx, while he was in his Parisian exile during 1843–1844. Some of Heine's most rousing political verse was written for the radical newspaper *Vorwärts,* to which Marx was also a frequent contributor.

The culmination of Heine's political poetry occurred in 1844 with the mock epic *Deutschland: Ein Wintermärchen* (Germany: A Winter's Tale). In twenty-seven brief chapters containing clever rhymes and witty barbs the poem describes a fictitious coach trip from the French border to Hamburg. Heine had traveled to Hamburg in late 1843 to visit his mother, and the stations on his return home correspond, in reverse order, to the central episodes in the poem. Heine's biting satire has three major objects. First, he attacks the German government, especially Prussian bureaucracy and the limitations placed on individual freedom. Second, he criticizes a rabid nationalism which advocated political revolution without a liberation from religious and ethical bondage. And finally Heine takes to task the German people themselves for their Romantic quietism and political acquiescence to authority. To some extent all three are assailed in the central chapters (14–17), where in a dream the poet confronts the former kaiser of the Holy Roman Empire, Friedrich Barbarrosa. According to legend Barbarrosa and his army are asleep in the Kyffhäuser Mountain waiting for the proper moment to rise up and save Germany. Heine mocks this nationalist myth and the people who would place false hopes on revolutionary leadership coming from royalty. After arousing Barbarrosa's anger by mentioning the French Revolution, he concludes that the German people do not need a kaiser at all.

Atta Troll (1847), the other mock epic Heine wrote during the 1840s, has a somewhat different target. The title figure is a dancing bear who escapes from captivity only to be tracked down and killed by a team of odd hunters whose symbolic significance remains obscure.

Atta Troll represents everything Heine objected to most in the German opposition. Prone to long-winded, empty speeches about freedom and equality, this "Tendenzbär" (tendentious bear) personifies the politically limited, religiously tainted, and ethically backward personality Heine had ridiculed in his caricature of Börne. And indeed, this work performs a function similar to that of the book on Börne. While in the earlier work he sought to distinguish his views from those of an apparent political ally, in *Atta Troll* he endeavors to separate his notions of political poetry from the crudities of the poetasters during the Vormärz. In defending fantasy and the imagination as imperative for successful verse, Heine criticizes the trend during the 1840s to create poems consisting of revolutionary platitudes in rhyme.

Heine's radical phase came to an end toward the close of the decade, and three factors were generally responsible for this change. First was his growing preoccupation with what has been called the Erbschaftstreit (inheritance controversy). Salomon Heine had helped to support his nephew with a modest annual allowance, but when he died in 1844, his son Carl balked at continuing these payments. A huge struggle ensued, and the battle of the cousins was carried out on Heine's part with all the public pressure and private leverage he could muster. Heine eventually secured the money he wanted on the condition that he not print anything injurious to the reputation of his family. Far more important was Heine's rapidly deteriorating health, a condition which may have been exacerbated by the stress of the inheritance controversy. Although the precise identity of Heine's ailment is uncertain—most commentators feel that it was some variety of syphilis—its effects were all too evident. He had suffered from severe headaches even as a young man, but during the mid 1840s he began to experience more serious symptoms. Among these were paralysis in various parts of his body, including his eyelids, severe spinal cramps, and tormenting pain. During the last eight years of his life he was completely bedridden, and this period has therefore come to be known as the Matratzengruft (mattress grave). Finally, the failure of the 1848 revolutions to achieve any of the political goals he so cherished probably dampened his spirits even further.

In this state of physical decay and spiritual depression, Heine underwent a conversion of sorts. Although he had been one of the harshest critics of religion all his life, during his final years he expresses a strong belief in a supreme being. Perhaps more significant for his writing was the abandonment of the sensualist position which had characterized his thought from the early 1820s. While his two ballet scenarios, *Der Doktor Faust* (1851) and *Die Göttin Diana* (published in volume 1 of

Vermischte Schriften, 1854), the first of which was commissioned in 1846 for Her Majesty's Theatre in London, still advocate a pagan materialism, his later works tend to reject both sensualism and spiritualism as philosophical doctrines. Thus the tenor and content of his poetry from the Matratzengruft, the two collections *Romanzero* (1851) and "Gedichte 1853 und 1854" (in volume 1 of *Vermischte Schriften*), stand in marked contrast to both his early love poetry and his activist verse from the 1840s. While there is no decline in poetic craft or composition, thematically his verse now most often deals with the futility of existence and the ultimate victory of evil over good. That each collection contains a Lazarus cycle says much about the mood and content. Despite this pessimism in his later years, Heine did not completely relinquish his progressive political stance; his later lyrics still evidence a sense of moral outrage at social injustice, and quite a few treat contemporary topics with the satirical wit for which he had become so famous. But a sense of melancholy pervades even these poems, and like the soldier in the war for liberation in "Enfant Perdu," Heine knows that he must count on others who are younger and stronger to fight future battles.

The sufferings of Heine's final years were mitigated somewhat by a woman acquaintance, Elise Krinitz, who is better known by her pen name, Camille Selden, and whom Heine called La Mouche. He met her in 1855, and although Heine's physical state made a passionate affair impossible, the six poems he wrote to her demonstrate his genuine feelings. By the time she had appeared in his life, however, his condition had much deteriorated. Severe cramps and hemorrhaging became frequent occurrences; his pain was regularly relieved by rubbing morphine in an open wound. An end to his torment finally came on 17 February 1856. Three days later he was buried in Montmartre Cemetery on the outskirts of Paris.

Bibliographies:

Arnmin Arnold, *Heine in England and America: A Bibliographical Check-List* (London: Linden Press, 1959);

Gottfried Wilhelm and Eberhard Galley, *Heine Bibliographie,* 2 volumes (Weimar: Arion, 1960);

Franz Finke, "Heine-Bibliography 1954–1959," *Heine-Jahrbuch,* 3 (1964): 80–94;

Eva D. Becker, "Heinrich Heine: Ein Forschungsbericht 1945–1965," *Deutschunterricht,* 18, no. 4 (1966): 1–18;

Siegfried Seifert, *Heine-Bibliographie 1954–1964* (Berlin: Aufbau, 1968);

Jost Hermand, *Streitobjekt Heine: Ein Forschungsbericht 1945–1975* (Frankfurt am Main: Athenäum, 1975);

Jeffrey L. Sammons, *Heinrich Heine: A Selected Critical Bibliography of Secondary Literature, 1956–1980* (New York: Garland, 1982);

Seifert and Albina A. Volgina, *Heine-Bibliographie 1965–1982* (Berlin: Aufbau, 1986).

Biographies:

Adolf Strodtman, *H. Heines Leben und Werke,* 2 volumes (Berlin: Duncker, 1867–1869);

Louis Untermeyer, *Heinrich Heine: Paradox and Poet,* volume 1: *The Life* (New York: Harcourt, Brace, 1937);

E. M. Butler, *Heinrich Heine: A Biography* (London: Hogarth Press, 1956);

Hans Kaufmann, *Heinrich Heine: Geistige Entwicklung und künstlerisches Werk* (Berlin: Aufbau, 1967);

Manfred Windfuhr, *Heinrich Heine: Revolution und Reflexion* (Stuttgart: Metzler, 1969);

Fritz Mende, *Heinrich Heine-Chronik seines Lebens und Werkes* (Berlin: Akademie-Verlag, 1970);

Joseph A. Kruse, *Heines Hamburger Zeit* (Hamburg: Hoffmann & Campe, 1972);

Michael Werner, ed., *Begegnungen mit Heine: Berichte der Zeitgenossen,* 2 volumes (Hamburg: Hoffmann & Campe, 1973);

Eberhard Galley, *Heinrich Heine,* 4th revised edition (Stuttgart: Metzler, 1976);

Jeffrey L. Sammons, *Heinrich Heine: A Modern Biography* (Princeton: Princeton University Press, 1979);

Mende, *Heinrich Heine: Studien zu seinem Leben und Werk* (Berlin: Akademie-Verlag, 1983);

Wolfgang Mädecke, *Heinrich Heine: Eine Biographie* (Munich: Hanser, 1985);

Ritchie Robertson, *Heine* (London: Holban, 1988).

References:

Akademie der Wissenschaften der DDR, eds., *Heinrich Heine und die Zeitgenossen: Geschichtliche und literarische Befunde* (Berlin: Aufbau, 1979);

Karl Wolfgang Becker, and others, eds., *Heinrich Heine: Streitbarer Humanist und volksverbundener Dichter* (Weimar: Nationale Forschungsund Gedenkstätten der klassischen deutschen Literatur in Weimar, 1973);

Albrecht Betz, *Ästhetik und Politik: Heinrich Heines Prosa* (Munich: Hanser, 1971);

Klaus Briegleb, *Opfer Heine?: Versuche über Schriftzüge der Revolution* (Frankfurt am Main: Suhrkamp, 1986);

Jürgen Brummack, ed., *Heinrich Heine: Epoche—Werk—Wirkung* (Munich: Beck, 1980);

Barker Fairley, *Heinrich Heine: An Interpretation* (Oxford: Clarendon Press, 1954);

Wilhelm Grössmann, ed., *Geständnisse: Heine im Bewußtsein heutiger Autoren* (Düsseldorf: Droste, 1972);

Grössmann, ed., *Der späte Heine 1848–1856: Literatur–Politik–Religion* (Hamburg: Hoffmann & Campe, 1982);

Heinz Hengst, *Idee und Ideologieverdacht: Revolutionäre Implikation des deutschen Idealismus im Kontext der zeitkritischen Prosa Heinrich Heines* (Munich: Fink, 1973);

Jost Hermand, *Der frühe Heine: Ein Kommentar zu den "Reisebildern"* (Munich: Winkler, 1976);

Laura Hofrichter, *Heinrich Heine* (Oxford: Clarendon Press, 1963);

Gerhard Höhn, *Heine-Handbuch: Zeit, Person, Werk* (Stuttgart: Metzler, 1987);

Robert C. Holub, *Heinrich Heine's Reception of German Grecophilia: The Function and Application of the Hellenic Tradition in the First Half of the Nineteenth Century* (Heidelberg: Winter, 1981);

Rolf Hosfeld, ed., *Signaturen: Heinrich Heine und das 19. Jahrhundert* (Berlin: Argument, 1986);

Raymond Immerwahr and Hanna Spencer, eds., *Heinrich Heine: Dimensionen seines Wirkens* (Bonn: Bouvier, 1979);

Wolfgang Kuttenkeuler, *Heinrich Heine: Theorie und Kritik der Literatur* (Stuttgart: Kohlhammer, 1972);

Sol Liptzin, *The English Legend of Heinrich Heine* (New York: Bloch, 1954);

Willfried Maier, *Leben, Tat, Reflexion: Untersuchungen zu Heinrich Heines Asthetik* (Bonn: Bouvier, 1969);

Günter Oesterle, *Integration und Konflikt: Die Prosa Heinrich Heines im Kontext oppositioneller Literatur der Restaurationsepoche* (Stuttgart: Metzler, 1972);

Klaus Pabel, *Heines "Reisebilder": Ästhetisches Bedürfnis und politisches Interesse* (Munich: Fink, 1977);

S. S. Prawer, *Franken-Stein's Island: England and the English in the Writings of Heinrich Heine* (Cambridge: Cambridge University Press, 1986);

Prawer, *Heine's Jewish Comedy: A Study of His Portraits of Jews and Judaism* (Oxford: Clarendon Press, 1983);

Prawer, *Heine the Tragic Satirist: A Study of the Later Poetry 1827–1856* (Cambridge: Cambridge University Press, 1961);

Wolfgang Preisendanz, *Heinrich Heine: Werkstrukturen und Epochenbezüge* (Munich: Fink, 1973);

Nigel Reeves, *Heinrich Heine: Poetry and Politics* (Oxford: Oxford University Press, 1974);

William Rose, *The Early Love Poetry of Heinrich Heine: An Inquiry into Poetic Inspiration* (Oxford: Clarendon Press, 1962);

Jeffrey L. Sammons, *Heinrich Heine: The Elusive Poet* (New Haven: Yale University Press, 1969);

A. I. Sandor, *The Exile of Gods: Interpretation of a Theme, a Theory and a Technique in the Work of Heinrich Heine* (The Hague: Mouton, 1967);

Hanna Spencer, *Heinrich Heine* (Boston: Twayne, 1982);

Dolf Sternberger, *Heinrich Heine und die Abschaffung der Sünde* (Düsseldorf: Claassen, 1972);

Benno von Wiese, *Signaturen: Zu Heinrich Heine und seinem Werk* (Berlin: Schmidt, 1976);

Stefan Bodo Wurffel, *Der produktiver Widerspruch: Heinrich Heines negative Dialektik* (Bern: Francke, 1986);

Susanne Zantop, ed., *Paintings on the Move: Heinrich Heine and the Visual Arts* (Lincoln: University of Nebraska Press, 1989).

Papers:

The Heine Archive is at the Landes- und Stadtbibliothek, Düsseldorf.

Hermann Hesse

(2 July 1877 – 9 August 1962)

Joseph Mileck
University of California, Berkeley

This entry was updated by Professor Mileck from his entry in
DLB 66: German Fiction Writers, 1885–1913.

BOOKS: *Romantische Lieder* (Dresden & Leipzig: Pierson, 1899);

Eine Stunde hinter Mitternacht (Leipzig: Diederichs, 1899);

Hinterlassene Schriften und Gedichte von Hermann Lauscher: Herausgegeben von Hermann Hesse (Basel: Reich, 1901);

Gedichte (Berlin: Grote, 1902); republished as *Jugendgedichte* (Hamm: Grote, 1950);

Boccaccio (Berlin & Leipzig: Schuster & Loeffler, 1904);

Franz von Assisi (Berlin & Leipzig: Schuster & Loeffler, 1904);

Peter Camenzind (Berlin: Fischer, 1904); translated by W. J. Strachan (London: Owen, 1961); translated by Michael Roloff (New York: Farrar, Straus & Giroux, 1969);

Unterm Rad (Berlin: Fischer, 1906); translated by Strachan as *The Prodigy* (London: Owen, Vision, 1957); translated by Roloff as *Beneath the Wheel* (New York: Farrar, Straus & Giroux, 1968);

Diesseits: Erzählungen (Berlin: Fischer, 1907; enlarged, 1930);

Selma Lagerlöf (Munich: Langen, 1907);

Nachbarn: Erzählungen (Berlin: Fischer, 1908);

Gertrud: Roman (Munich: Langen, 1910); translated by Adèle Lewisohn as *Gertrude and I* (New York: International Monthly, 1915); translated by Hilde Rosner as *Gertrude* (London: Owen, 1955);

Unterwegs: Gedichte (Munich: Müller, 1911; enlarged, 1915);

Umwege: Erzählungen (Berlin: Fischer, 1912);

Aus Indien: Aufzeichnungen von einer indischen Reise (Berlin: Fischer, 1913);

Roßhalde (Berlin: Fischer, 1914); translated by Ralph Manheim as *Rosshalde* (New York: Farrar, Straus & Giroux, 1970);

Am Weg (Konstanz: Reuss & Itta, 1915);

Musik des Einsamen: Neue Gedichte (Heilbronn: Salzer, 1915);

Hermann Hesse

Knulp: Drei Geschichten aus dem Leben Knulps (Berlin: Fischer, 1915); translated by Manheim as *Knulp: Three Tales from the Life of Knulp* (New York: Farrar, Straus & Giroux, 1971);

Brief ins Feld (Munich-Pasing: Lang, 1916);

289

Zum Gedächtnis: Nachruf auf seinen Vater (Zurich: Polygraphisches Institut, 1916);

Hans Dierlamms Lehrzeit: Vorfrühling (Berlin: Künstlerdank-Gesellschaft, 1916);

Schön ist die Jugend: Zwei Erzählungen (Berlin: Fischer, 1916);

Alte Geschichten: Zwei Erzählungen (Bern: Bücherzentrale für deutsche Kriegsgefangene, 1918);

Zwei Märchen (Bern: Bücherzeutrale für deutsche Kriegsgefangene, 1918);

Demian: Die Geschichte einer Jugend von Emil Sinclair (Berlin: Fischer, 1919); translated by N. H. Priday as *Demian* (New York: Boni & Liveright, 1923);

Kleiner Garten: Erlebnisse und Dichtungen (Vienna: Tal, 1919);

Märchen (Berlin: Fischer, 1919);

Zarathustras Wiederkehr: Ein Wort an die deutsche Jugend. Von einem Deutschen (Bern: Stämpfli, 1919);

Gedichte des Malers: Zehn Gedichte (Bern: Seldwyla, 1920);

Blick ins Chaos. Drei Aufsätze (Bern: Seldwyla, 1920);

Klingsors letzter Sommer: Erzählungen (Berlin: Fischer, 1920); "Klingsors letzter Sommer" translated by Richard and Clara Winston as *Klingsor's Last Summer* (New York: Farrar, Straus & Giroux, 1970);

Wanderung: Aufzeichnungen (Berlin: Fischer, 1920); translated by James Wright as *Wandering: Notes and Sketches* (New York: Farrar, Straus & Giroux, 1972);

Elf Aquarelle aus dem Tessin (Munich: Recht, 1921);

Ausgewählte Gedichte (Berlin: Fischer, 1921);

Siddhartha: Eine indische Dichtung (Berlin: Fischer, 1922); translated by Rosner as *Siddhartha* (New York: New Directions, 1951; London: Owen, 1956);

Die Offizina Bodoni in Montagnola (Hellerau: Hegner, 1923);

Im Pressel'schen Gartenhaus: Eine Zeichnung aus dem alten Tübingen (Stettin, 1923);

Italien: Verse (Berlin: Euphorion, 1923);

Sinclairs Notizbuch (Zurich: Rascher, 1923);

Psychologia Balnearia oder Glossen eines Badener Kurgastes (Montagnola: Privately printed, 1924); republished as *Kurgast: Aufzeichnungen von einer Badener Kur* (Berlin: Fischer, 1925);

Aufzeichnungen eines Herrn im Sanatorium: Fragment aus einem nicht ausgeführten Roman (Vienna: Phaidon, 1925);

Erinnerung an Lektüre (Vienna: Braumüller, 1925);

Piktors Verwandlungen: Ein Märchen (Chemnitz: Gesellschaft der Bücherfreunde, 1925);

Bilderbuch: Schilderungen (Berlin: Fischer, 1926);

Die Nürnberger Reise (Berlin: Fischer, 1927);

Der schwere Weg (Leipzig: Wolf, 1927);

Der Steppenwolf (Berlin: Fischer, 1927); translated by Basil Creighton as *Steppenwolf* (New York: Holt,

1929; translation revised by Joseph Mileck, New York: Holt, Rinehart & Winston, 1963);

Verse im Krankenbett (Bern: Stämpfli, 1927);

Krisis: Ein Stück Tagebuch (Berlin: Fischer, 1928); translated by Manheim as *Crisis: Pages from a Diary* (New York: Farrar, Straus & Giroux, 1975);

Betrachtungen (Berlin: Fischer, 1928);

Eine Bibliothek der Weltliteratur (Leipzig: Reclam, 1929);

Trost der Nacht: Neue Gedichte (Berlin: Fischer, 1929);

Der Zyklon und andere Erzählungen (Berlin: Fischer, 1929);

Zum Gedächtnis unseres Vaters, by Hesse and A. Hesse (Tübingen: Wunderlich, 1930);

Narziss und Goldmund: Erzählung (Berlin: Fischer, 1930); translated by Geoffrey Dunlop as *Death and the Lover* (New York: Dodd, 1932); translated by Ursule Molinaro as *Narcissus and Goldmund* (New York: Farrar, Straus & Giroux, 1968);

Jahreszeiten: Zehn Gedichte (Zurich: Fretz, 1931);

Weg nach Innen: Vier Erzählungen (Berlin: Fischer, 1931);

Kastanienbäume: Übungsarbeit der Kunstgewerbeschule Aachen (Aachen: Kunstgewerbeschule, 1932);

Herman Hesse, edited by A. Simon (Munich: Reinhardt, 1932);

Die Morgenlandfahrt: Eine Erzählung (Berlin: Fischer, 1932); translated by Rosner as *The Journey to the East* (London: Owen, Vision, 1956; New York: Noonday, 1957);

Kleine Welt: Erzählungen (Berlin: Fischer, 1933);

Schön ist die Jugend (Darmstadt: Winklers, 1933);

Vom Baum des Lebens: Ausgewählte Gedichte (Leipzig: Insel, 1934);

Besinnung: Aufgezeichnet am 20. Nov. 1933 in Baden (Berlin: Erasmusdruck, 1934);

Fünf Gedichte (Zurich: Fretz, 1934);

Magie des Buches (Berlin: Privately printed, 1934);

Fabulierbuch: Erzählungen (Berlin: Fischer, 1935);

Das Haus der Träume: Eine unvollendete Dichtung (Olten: Vereinigung Oltner Bücherfreunde, 1936);

Stunden im Garten: Eine Idylle (Vienna: Bermann-Fischer, 1936);

Tragisch: Eine Erzahlung (Vienna: Reichner, 1936);

Der Brunnen im Maulbronner Kreuzgang (Leipzig: Poeschel & Trepte, 1937);

Gedenkblätter (Berlin: Fischer, 1937; enlarged, Zurich: Fretz & Wasmuth, 1947);

Neue Gedichte (Berlin: Fischer, 1937);

Der lahme Knabe: Eine Erinnerung aus der Kindheit (Zurich: Fretz, 1937);

Ein Traum Josef Knechts: Zum 2. Juli 1937 (Montagnola: Privately printed, 1937);

Zehn Gedichte (Bern: Stämpfli, 1939);

Der Novalis: Aus den Papieren eines Altmodischen (Olten: Vereinigung Oltner Bücherfreunde, 1940);

Kleine Betrachtungen: Sechs Aufsätze (Bern: Stämpfli, 1941);

Die Gedichte (Zurich: Fretz & Wasmuth, 1942);

Das Glasperlenspiel: Versuch einer Lebensbeschreibung des Magister Ludi Josef Knecht samt Knechts hinterlassene Schriften, 2 volumes (Zurich: Fretz & Wasmuth, 1943); translated by Mervyn Savill as *Magister Ludi* (New York: Holt, 1949);

Stufen: Noch ein Gedicht Josef Knechts. Herman Hesse zum 2. Juli 1943 (Pößneck: Bezirksschule für das graphische Gewerbe in Thüringen, 1943);

Sechs Gedichte aus dem Jahre 1944 (Zurich: Fretz & Wasmuth, 1944);

Nachruf auf Christoph Schrempf (Zurich: Fretz & Wasmuth, 1944);

Zwischen Sommer und Herbst (Zurich: Fretz, 1944);

Zwei Aufsätze (Zurich: Fretz, 1945);

Berthold: Ein Romanfragment (Zurich: Fretz & Wasmuth, 1945);

Der Blütenzweig: Eine Auswahl aus den Gedichten (Zurich: Fretz & Wasmuth, 1945);

Zwei Briefe, by Hesse and Thomas Mann (St. Gallen: Tschudy, 1945);

Friede 1914; Dem Frieden entgegen 1945: Zwei Friedens-Gedichte (Murnau: Polyphylus-Presse, 1945);

Maler und Schriftsteller (N.p., 1945);

Der Pfirsichbaum und andere Erzählungen: Werbegabe (Zurich: Büchergilde Gutenberg, 1945);

Rigi-Tagebuch 1945 (Bern: Stämpfli, 1945);

Traumfährte: Neue Erzählungen und Märchen (Zurich: Fretz & Wasmuth, 1945);

Ansprache in der ersten Stunde des Jahres 1946 (Zurich: Neue Zürcher Zeitung, 1946);

Eine Bibliothek der Weltliteratur: Mit den Aufsätzen "Magie des Buches" und "Lieblingslektüre" (Zurich: Classen, 1946);

Brief an Adele: Februar 1946 (Zurich: Neue Zürcher Zeitung, 1946);

Ein Brief nach Deutschland (Basel: National-Zeitung, 1946);

Statt eines Briefes (Montagnola: Privately printed, 1946);

Dank an Goethe (Zurich: Classen, 1946);

Danksagung und moralisierende Betrachtung (N.p., 1946);

Der Europäer (Berlin: Suhrkamp, 1946);

Feuerwerk: Aufsatz aus dem Jahre 1930 (Olten: Vereinigung Oltner Bücherfreunde, 1946);

Gedichte (Stuttgart & Bad Cannstatt: Cantz, 1946);

Späte Gedichte (St. Gallen: Tschudy, 1946);

Krieg und Frieden: Betrachtungen zu Krieg und Politik (Zurich: Fretz & Wasmuth, 1946);

Antwort auf Bittbriefe (Montagnola: Privately printed, 1947);

Der Autor an einen Korrektor (Bern: Kantonales Amt für berufliche Ausbildung, 1947);

Beschreibung einer Landschaft: Ein Stück Tagebuch (Bern: Stämpfli, 1947);

Gedichte (Marbach am Neckar: Schiller-Buch-handlung, 1947);

Geheimnisse (Montagnola: Privately printed, 1947);

Haus Zum Frieden: Aufzeichnungen eines Herrn im Sanatorium (Zurich: Johannes-Presse, 1947);

An einen jungen Kollegen in Japan (Montagnola: Privately printed, 1947);

Eine Konzertpause (Zurich: Neue Zürcher Zeitung, 1947);

Spätsommer: Zum neuen Jahr (Karlsruhe: Kindt, 1947);

Spaziergang in Würzburg: Zugunsten der Stadt Würzburg, edited by F. X. Münzel (St. Gallen: Tschudy, 1947);

Stufen der Menschwerdung (Olten: Vereinigung Oltner Bücherfreunde, 1947);

Berg und See: Zwei Landschaftsstudien (Zurich: Büchergilde Gutenberg, 1948);

Blätter vom Tage (Zurich: Fretz, 1948);

Legende vom indischen König (Burgdorf: Jenzer, Berner Handpresse, 1948);

Frühe Prosa (Zurich: Fretz & Wasmuth, 1948);

Musikalische Notizen (N.p., 1948);

Notizen aus diesen Sommertagen (Basel: National-Zeitung, 1948);

Preziosität (N.p., 1948);

Die Stimmen und der Heilige: Ein Stück Tagebuch (N.p., 1948);

Alle Bücher dieser Welt: Ein Almanach für Bücherfreunde, 1950, edited by K. H. Silomon (Murnau: Die Waage, 1949);

Gedenkblatt für Adele: 15. August 1875; 24. September 1949 (Zurich: Fretz, 1949);

Gerbersau (Tübingen: Wunderlich, 1949);

Glück (St. Gallen: Tschudy, 1949);

Aus vielen Jahren: Gedichte, Erzählungen und Bilder (Bern: Stämpfli, 1949);

An einen jungen Künstler (Montagnola: Privately printed, 1949);

Stunden am Schreibtisch (N.p., 1949);

Brief an einen schwäbischen Dichter, edited by W. Matheson (Olten: Vereinigung Oltner Bücherfreunde, 1950);

Zwei Briefe: An einen jungen Künstler; Das junge Genie (St. Gallen: Tschudy, 1950);

Gartenfreuden: Eine Bilderfolge, edited by K. Jud (Zurich: Die Arche, 1950);

An einen "einfachen Mann aus dem arbeitenden Volk" (N.p., 1950);

Eine Auswahl, edited by R. Buchwald (Bielefeld, Hannover & Berlin: Velhagen & Klasing, 1951);

Bericht aus Normalien: Ein Fragment aus dem Jahre 1948 (Gelterkinden: Lustig, 1951);

Erinnerung an André Gide (St. Gallen: Tschudy, 1951);

Zwei Gedichte (St. Gallen: Tschudy, 1951);

Glückwunsch für Peter Suhrkamp: Zum 28. März 1951 (Montagnola: Privately printed, 1951);

Nörgeleien (Basel: National-Zeitung, 1951);

Aus einem Notizbuch (St. Gallen: Tschudy, 1951);

Späte Prosa (Berlin: Suhrkamp, 1951);

Die Verlobung und andere Erzählungen (Berlin & Darmstadt: Deutsche Buchgemeinschaft, 1951);

Dank für die Briefe und Glückwünsche zum 2. Juli 1952 (Montagnola: Privately printed, 1952);

Gesammelte Dichtungen, 6 volumes (Berlin & Frankfurt am Main: Suhrkamp, 1952); enlarged as *Gesammelte Schriften,* 7 volumes (Frankfurt am Main: Suhrkamp, 1957); enlarged again as *Gesammelte Werke in Zwölf Bänden,* 12 volumes (Frankfurt am Main: Suhrkamp, 1970);

Herbstliche Erlebnisse: Gedenkblatt für Otto Hartmann (St. Gallen: Tschudy, 1952);

Geburtstag: Ein Rundbrief. Juli 1952 (Montagnola: Privately printed, 1952);

Großväterliches (St. Gallen: Tschudy, 1952);

Hermann Hesse als Badener Kurgast, by Hesse, Robert Mächler, and Uli Münzel (St. Gallen: Tschudy, 1952);

Lektüre für Minuten: Ein paar Gedanken aus meinen Büchern und Briefen. Zu Ehren des fünfundsiebzigsten Geburtstages von Hermann Hesse (Bern: Stämpfli, 1952);

Rückblick: Ein Fragment aus der Zeit um 1937 (Zurich: Fretz, 1952);

Engadiner Erlebnisse: Ein Rundbrief (Zurich: Fretz, 1953);

Kaminfegerchen (St. Gallen: Tschudy, 1953);

Nachruf für Marulla: 1880–1953 (St. Gallen: Tschudy, 1953);

Über das Alter (Olten: Vereinigung Oltner Bücherfreunde, 1954);

Beschwörungen: Rundbrief im Februar 1954 (St. Gallen: Tschudy, 1954);

Die Nikobaren (Basel: National-Zeitung, 1954);

Notizblätter um Ostern (Montagnola: Privately printed, 1954);

Rundbrief aus Sils-Maria (St. Gallen: Tschudy, 1954);

Aquarelle aus dem Tessin (Baden-Baden: Klein, 1955);

Beschwörungen: Späte Prosa, neue Folge (Berlin: Suhrkamp, 1955);

Knopf-Annähen (Basel: National-Zeitung, 1955);

Abendwolken: Zwei Aufsätze; Abendwolken: Bei den Massageten (St. Gallen: Tschudy, 1956);

Weltanschauliche Briefe politischer Richtung (N.p., 1956);

Zwei jugendliche Erzählungen (Olten: Vereinigung Oltner Bücherfreunde, 1956);

Zum Frieden (Thal: Christ, 1956);

Wanderer im Spätherbst (Montagnola: Privately printed, 1956);

Weihnachtsgaben und anderes (Montagnola: Privately printed, 1956);

Freunde: Erzählung (Olten: Vereinigung Oltner Bücherfreunde, 1957);

Malfreude, Malsorgen (N.p., 1957);

Der Trauermarsch: Gedenkblatt für einen Jugendkameraden (St. Gallen: Tschudy, 1957);

Wenkenhof: Eine romantische Jugenddichtung (Basel: National-Zeitung, 1957);

Antworten (St. Gallen: Tschudy, 1958);

Klein und Wagner: Erzählung (Berlin: Suhrkamp, 1958);

Vier späte Gedichte (St. Gallen: Tschudy, 1959);

Chinesische Legende (St. Gallen: Tschudy, 1959);

Freund Peter (Zurich: Fretz, 1959);

Sommerbrief (St. Gallen: Tschudy, 1959);

Ein paar Aufzeichnungen und Briefe (St. Gallen: Tschudy, 1960);

Bericht an die Freunde: Letzte Geditche (Olten: Vereinigung Oltner Bücherfreunde, 1960);

An einen Musiker (Olten: Vereinigung Oltner Bücherfreunde, 1960);

Rückgriff (St. Gallen: Tschudy, 1960);

Aus einem Tagebuch des Jahres 1920 (Zurich: Arche, 1960);

Stufen: Alte und neue Gedichte in Auswahl (Frankfurt am Main: Suhrkamp, 1961);

Aerzte: Ein paar Erinnerung (Olten: Vereinigung Oltner Bücherfreunde, 1963);

Die späten Gedichte (Frankfurt am Main: Insel, 1963);

Geheimnisse: Letzte Erzählungen (Frankfurt am Main: Suhrkamp, 1964);

Erwin (Olten: Vereinigung von Freunden der Oltner Liebhaberdrucke, 1965);

Der vierte Lebenslauf Josef Knechts: Zwei Fassungen, edited by Ninon Hesse (Frankfurt am Main: Suhrkamp, 1966);

Aus Kinderzeiten und andere Erzählungen (Frankfurt am Main: Suhrkamp, 1968);

Politische Betrachtungen (Frankfurt am Main: Suhrkamp, 1970);

Mein Glaube (Frankfurt am Main: Suhrkamp, 1971);

Eigensinn: Autobiographische Schriften (Frankfurt am Main: Suhrkamp, 1972);

Die Erzählungen, 2 volumes (Frankfurt am Main: Suhrkamp, 1973);

Glück: Späte Erzählungen, Betrachtungen (Frankfurt am Main: Suhrkamp, 1973);

Iris: Ausgewählte Märchen (Frankfurt am Main: Suhrkamp, 1973);

Die Kunst des Müßiggangs: Kurze Prosa aus dem Nachlaß, edited by Volker Michels (Frankfurt am Main: Suhrkamp, 1973);

Das erste Abenteuer: Erzählungen, edited by Michels (Frankfurt am Main: Suhrkamp, 1975);

Die Fremdenstadt im Süden (Frankfurt am Main: Suhrkamp, 1975);

Legenden (Frankfurt am Main: Suhrkamp, 1975);

Eine Literaturgeschichte in Rezensionen und Aufsätzen (Frankfurt am Main: Suhrkamp, 1975);

Musik: Betrachtungen, Gedichte, Rezensionen und Briefe, edited by Michels (Frankfurt am Main: Suhrkamp, 1976);

Die Gedichte, 2 volumes (Frankfurt am Main: Suhrkamp, 1977);

Gesammelte Erzählungen, 4 volumes (Frankfurt am Main: Suhrkamp, 1977);

Kleine Freuden: Prosa aus dem Nachlaß, edited by Michels (Frankfurt am Main: Suhrkamp, 1977);

Magie des Buches: Betrachtungen (Frankfurt am Main: Suhrkamp, 1977);

Politik des Gewissens: die Politischen Schriften 1914–1962, edited by Michels, 2 volumes (Frankfurt am Main: Suhrkamp, 1977);

Von Wesen und Herkunft des Glasperlenspiels: Die vier Fassungen der Einleitung zum Glasperlenspiel, edited by Michels (Frankfurt am Main: Suhrkamp, 1977);

Die Welt der Bücher: Betrachtungen und Aufsätze zur Literatur, edited by Michels (Frankfurt am Main: Suhrkamp, 1977);

Aus Indien: Aufzeichnungen, Tagebücher, Gedichte, Betrachtungen und Erzählungen (Frankfurt am Main: Suhrkamp, 1980);

Italien: Schilderungen, Tagebücher, Gedichte, Aufsätze, Buchbesprechungen und Erzählungen, edited by Michels (Frankfurt am Main: Suhrkamp, 1983);

Bericht aus Normalien: Humoristische Erzählungen, Gedichte und Anekdoten (Frankfurt am Main: Suhrkamp, 1986);

Bodensee: Betrachtungen, Erzählungen, Gedichte, edited by Michels (Frankfurt am Main: Suhrkamp, 1986);

Mit Hermann Hesse durch Italien: Ein Reisebegleiter durch Oberitalien, edited by Michels (Frankfurt am Main: Suhrkamp, 1988);

Die Welt im Buch: Lesererfahrungen 1: Rezension und Aufsätze aus den Jahren 1900–1910, edited by Michels (Frankfurt am Main: Suhrkamp, 1988).

OTHER: *Der Lindenbaum: Deutsche Volkslieder,* edited by Hesse, Martin Lang, and Emil Strauß (Berlin: Fischer, 1910);

Ludwig Achim von Arnim and Clemens Brentano, *Des Knaben Wunderhorn: Alte deutsche Lieder, gesammelt,* edited by Hesse (Berlin: Deutsche Bibliothek, 1913);

Joseph, Freiherr von Eichendorff, *Gedichte und Novellen,* edited by Hesse (Berlin: Deutsche Bibliothek, 1913);

Jean Paul, *Titan,* 2 volumes, edited by Hesse (Leipzig: Insel, 1913);

Justinus Kerner, *Die Reiseschatten,* introduction and afterword by Hesse (Weimar: Kiepenheuer, 1913);

Christian Wagner, *Gedichte,* edited by Hesse (Munich: Müller, 1913);

Der Zauberbrunnen: Die Lieder der deutschen Romantik, edited by Hesse (Weimar: Kiepenheuer, 1913);

Johann Gottfried Herder and August Jakob Liebeskind, eds., *Morgenländische Erzählungen (Palmblätter),* reedited by Hesse (Leipzig: Insel, 1914);

Lieder deutscher Dichter: Eine Auswahl der klassischen deutschen Lyrik von Paul Gerhardt bis Friedrich Hebbel (Munich: Langen, 1914);

Gesta Romanorum: Das älteste Märchen–und Legendenbuch des christlichen Mittelalters, translated by Johann Georg Theodor Graesse, edited by Hesse (Leipzig: Insel, 1915);

Zum Sieg: Ein Brevier für den Feldzug, introduction by Hesse (Stuttgart: Die Lese, 1915);

Matthias Claudius, *Der Wandsbecker Bote: Eine Auswahl aus den Werken,* edited by Hesse (Leipzig: Insel, 1916);

Albert Welti, *Gemälde und Radierungen,* introduction by Hesse (Berlin: Furche, 1917);

Arthur Bonus, *Isländerbuch: Zwei Geschichten aus dem Isländerbuch,* foreword by Hesse (Bern: Bücherzentrale für deutsche Kriegsgefangene, 1918);

Dichtergedanken, foreword by Hesse (Bern: Bücherzentrale für deutsche Kriegsgefangene, 1918);

Arthur Fürst and Alexander Moszkowski, *Das kleine Buch der Wunder* (Bern: Bücherzentrale für deutsche Kriegsgefangene, 1918);

Aus dem Mittelalter, edited by Hesse (Bern: Bücherzentrale für deutsche Kriegsgefangene, 1918);

Wilhelm Schäfer, *Anekdoten und Sagen,* foreword by Hesse (Bern: Bücherzentrale für deutsche Kriegsgefangene, 1918);

Emil Strau, *Der Laufen: Musik,* foreword by Hesse (Bern: Bücherzentrale für deutsche Kriegsgefangene, 1918);

Alemannenbuch, edited by Hesse (Bern: Seldwyla, 1919);

Ein Badisches Buch, edited by Hesse and Richard Woltereck (Bern: Bücherzentrale für deutsche Kriegsgefangene, 1919);

Ein Schwabenbuch für die deutschen Kriegsgefangenen, edited by Hesse and Walter Stich (Bern: Bücherzentrale für deutsche Kriegsgefangene, 1919);

Ein Luzerner Junker vor hundert Jahren: Aus den Lebenserinnerungen des X. Schnyder von Wartensee, edited by Hesse (Bern: Benteli, 1920);

Monika Hunnius, *Mein Onkel Hermann: Erinnerungen aus Alt-Estland,* foreword by Hesse (Heilbronn: Salzer, 1921);

Geschichten aus Japan, edited by Hesse (Bern: Seldwyla, 1922);

Salomon Gessner, *Dichtungen,* edited by Hesse (Leipzig: Insel, 1922);

Jean Paul, *Der ewige Frühling,* edited by Carl Seelig, foreword by Hesse (Vienna: Tal, 1922);

Jean Paul, *Die wunderbare Gesellschaft in der Neujahrsnacht: Erzählungen,* edited by Hesse (Bern: Seldwyla, 1922);

Heinrich Leuthold, *Der schwermütige Musikant,* edited by Seelig, foreword by Hesse (Vienna: Tal, 1922);

Mordprozesse, edited by Hesse (Bern: Seldwyla, 1922);

Novellino: Novellen und Schwänke der ältesten italienischen Erzähler, edited by Hesse (Bern: Seldwyla, 1922);

Aus Arnims Wintergarten, edited by Hesse (Bern: Seldwyla, 1922);

Johann Wolfgang von Goethe, *Wilhelm Meisters Lehrjahre,* introduction by Hesse (Berlin: Ullstein, 1923);

Adelbert von Keller, *Zwei altfranzösische Sagen,* afterword by Hesse (Bern: Seldwyla, 1924);

Luigi da Porto and Matteo Bandello, *Die Geschichte von Romeo und Julia,* edited by Hesse (Berlin: Fischer, 1925);

Geschichten aus dem Mittelalter, translated and edited by Hesse (Konstanz & Landschlacht: Hönn, 1925);

Hölderlin: Dokumente seines Lebens, edited by Hesse and Karl Isenberg (Berlin: Fischer, 1925);

Novalis: Dokumente seines Lebens und Sterbens, edited by Hesse (Berlin: Fischer, 1925);

Sesam: Orientalische Erzählungen, edited by Hesse (Berlin: Fischer, 1925);

Jonathan Swift, *Lemuel Gullivers Reisen in verschiedene ferne Länder der Welt,* translated by Seelig, foreword by Hesse (Leipzig: List, 1925);

Jean Paul, *Siebenkäs,* afterword by Hesse (Leipzig: List, 1925);

Blätter aus Prevorst: Eine Auswahl von Berichten über Magnetismus, Hellsehen, Geistererscheinungen usw. aus dem Kreise Justinus Kerners und seiner Freunde, edited by Hesse (Berlin: Fischer, 1926);

Schubart: Dokumente seines Lebens, edited by Hesse and Isenberg (Berlin: Fischer, 1926);

Frans Masereel, *Die Idee Masereel,* introduction by Hesse (Munich: Wolff, 1927);

Hugo Ball: Sein Leben in Briefen und Gedichten, edited by Emmy Ball-Hennings, foreword by Hesse (Berlin: Fischer, 1930);

Goethe, *Dreißig Gedichte: Festgabe zum hundertsten Todestag, 22. März 1932,* edited by Hesse (Zurich: Lesezirkel Hottingen, 1932);

Masereel, *Geschichte ohne Worte: Ein Roman in Bildern,* afterword by Hesse (Leipzig: Insel, 1933);

Eichendorff, *Aus dem Leben eines Taugenichts und anders,* edited by Hesse (Berlin: Deutsche Bibliothek, 1934);

Falterschönheit: Exotische Schmetterlinge, foreword by Hesse (Leipzig: Iris-Druck, 1936);

Ernst Morgenthaler, edited by Hesse (Zurich: Niehans, 1936);

Ball-Hennings, *Blume und Flamme: Geschichte einer Jugend,* foreword by Hesse (Einsiedeln: Benziger, 1938);

Bunte Feier: Erzählungen und Gedichte, edited by "Kreis junger Autoren," foreword by Hesse (St. Gallen: Widmer, 1938);

Jean Paul, *Ausgewählte Werke,* introduction by Hesse (Zurich: Scientia, 1943);

Der Autorenabend: Dichteranekdoten von Rabelais bis Thomas Mann, introduction by Hesse (Zurich: Diogenes, 1953);

Alfredo Baeschlin, *Ein Künstler erlebt Mallorca,* foreword by Hesse (Schaffhausen: Lemper, 1953);

Ein paar Leserbriefe an Hermann Hesse, edited by Hesse (Montagnola: Privately printed, 1955);

Leopold Zahn, *Künstler auf der Höri am Bodensee,* foreword by Hesse (Konstanz: Simon & Koch, 1956);

Ernst Morgenthaler: Zum siebzigsten Geburtstag des Künstlers, foreword by Hesse (Bern: Scherz, 1957);

Ernst Morgenthaler, *Ein Maler erzählt: Aufsätze, Reiseberichte, Briefe,* foreword by Hesse (Zurich: Diogenes, 1957).

Only a few German writers of the twentieth century have enjoyed worldwide acclaim. Undisputably numbered among these are Thomas Mann, Franz Kafka, Bertolt Brecht, and Hermann Hesse. Hesse's major works have been translated into some thirty-five languages. Of all foreign countries, the United States, followed closely by Japan, has been most taken with Hesse. The 15 million or so books that had been published in the United States by 1987 equaled the number that had been sold in Germany, and exceeded 14 million or more that readers had bought in Japan. Only Romain Rolland has attracted more attention in Japan than Hesse. In the West, Hesse has, since the 1950s, enjoyed his most widespread popularity in the English- and Spanish-speaking countries.

Hesse's father, Johannes Hesse, was born in Weissenstein, Estonia; his mother, Marie, daughter of the missionary and Indologist Hermann Gundert, was born in Talatscheri, India. Both branches of the family were given to a severe form of Pietism. Following his studies at the Basler Missionsanstalt (Mission Society of Basel), Johannes, like Hermann Gundert before him, served as a missionary in India. Brought back to Europe by ill health, he settled in Calw, a little town at the edge of the Black Forest, to assist Gundert, then director of the Calwer Verlagsverein, a Pietist publishing house. There Johannes met and married Marie, and there Hermann Hesse was born on 2 July 1877, the second of six children.

A hypersensitive, imaginative, lively, and extremely headstrong child, Hesse was long a source of annoyance and anxiety. He tyrannized his parents;

school held little attraction for him, and his teachers even less. In January 1890 Hesse was sent off to the Latin School in nearby Göppingen; in September 1891 he began his studies at the exclusive Protestant church school in Maulbronn, ostensibly in preparation for the pulpit. His stay was unexpectedly brief: the deeply disturbed youngster took French leave in March 1892 and was withdrawn in May, much to the relief of the school authorities, who had begun to doubt his sanity. He fared no better at schools for retarded and emotionally disturbed children in Bad Boll and Stetten or at a secondary school in Bad Cannstatt. Acceding to the pleas of their wayward and truculent son, Hesse's parents finally permitted him to return home in the autumn of 1893. He spent the next six months gardening, assisting his father in the publishing house, and reading avidly in his grandfather's library. In early June 1894, after his father had denied him permission to leave home to prepare himself for a literary career, Hesse became an apprentice machinist in Calw. This was a trade, he believed, that would afford him a livelihood, that he could some day ply abroad, and that would permit him ample time for his literary interests. Fifteen months of grimy labor disabused the young dreamer of his romantic notions. In October 1895 he began a more appropriate apprenticeship in a bookshop in Tübingen.

Hesse's four years in Tübingen were relatively tranquil. He continued to be a lonely outsider, applying himself diligently in the bookshop and otherwise preoccupied with his writing and self-education. During his preceding two years in Calw he had steeped himself in the German literature of the eighteenth and nineteenth centuries; in Tübingen he continued his prodigious reading but narrowed its scope drastically. For a time he devoted himself almost exclusively to Goethe. Then he fell under the spell of the German romantics, Novalis in particular. Under their influence and that of the late-nineteenth-century aestheticism, he created his own beauty-worshiping realm of the imagination, a retreat from and substitute for the crass outer world in which he was an unappreciated misfit. Hesse was tolerably content; he had found a niche and a way of life.

According to his mother's letters and diaries, Hesse began to compose ditties before he was able to wield a pencil, and at the age of thirteen he had decided to become a poet or nothing at all. In Tübingen, no longer in the shadow of home or school, Hesse was finally able to pursue his literary interests as he pleased. His poems began to appear in a Viennese periodical in 1896; *Romantische Lieder* (Romantic Songs), his first book of poetry, was published at the beginning of 1899; and *Eine Stunde hinter Mitternacht* (An Hour After Midnight), his first book of prose, followed in mid 1899. Poetry and prose tales, reveries, and monologues bask in the

sweetly scented atmosphere, the muted sounds, and the brilliant colors of an uncontained romanticism. A lonely and aristocratic outsider indulges in melodramatic fantasies and melodic lament, is morbidly preoccupied with love and death, seeks his retreat in temples and castles, communes with his muse, consorts with ethereal maidens, and burns incense at the altar of beauty far from the profane world. Neither book attracted more than a modicum of attention.

In September 1899 Hesse left Tübingen for more cosmopolitan Basel, where he made a determined effort to learn the art of living with his fellow humans to escape the loneliness that had begun to plague him. He soon found his way into Basel's intellectual and art circles, and became a frequent guest of some of the city's culturally most prominent families. Even so, Hesse remained essentially an outsider, distinctly uncomfortable at social gatherings, a loner who preferred the company of nature to that of his fellow humans. In the spring of 1900—while writing "Lulu," his fairy-tale paean to Julie Hellmann, whom he had courted hesitantly and vainly with flowers and verse while vacationing in Kirchheim unter Teck the previous August—Hesse fell in love with Elisabeth La Roche, the "Elisabeth" of his poems and prose of the time. When the hopelessness of his shyly pursued love became apparent, he began a more successful courtship of Maria Bernoulli, of Basel's mathematically celebrated Bernoulli family.

Long hours in a bookshop and few holidays left Hesse with neither time nor energy for his literary career, and little opportunity for travel. With enough money to tide him over for some months, he quit his job in February 1901, returned to Calw, wrote the first four of his many brief recollections of his childhood, left for northern Italy at the end of March, returned to Calw in mid May, and went back to Basel later in the summer. Hesse's diary notes, rewritten soon after his return from Italy and published in the *Basler Anzeiger* that autumn, were the first of his many travel journals.

Aestheticism peaked and began to ebb in the poeticized recollections and ruminations, the diary excerpts, and the poems of *Hinterlassene Schriften und Gedichte von Hermann Lauscher* (Posthumous Writings and Poems of Hermann Lauscher, 1901), which Hesse called "Dokumente der eigentümlichen Seele eines modernen Ästheten und Sonderlings" (documents of the peculiar soul of a modern aesthete and eccentric). Three of these "documents" look to the past in both their sentiment and manner, and three are telling intimations of things to come in Hesse's life and art. "Meine Kindheit" (My Childhood), a recollection of childhood in Bern, anticipates the more realistic narrative style that Hesse was soon to cultivate, and is the beginning of what became–and until *Demian* (1919; translated, 1923) remained–an obsessive preoccupation with childhood and youth. "Lulu," a fictionalized recollection of his vacation in Kirchheim unter Teck, foreshadows Hesse's fairy tales and his novels *Demian, Der Steppenwolf* (1927; translated as *Steppenwolf,* 1929), and *Die Morgenlandfahrt* (1932; translated as *The Journey to the East,* 1956) in both their novel blending of the magic realm of the imagination and the commonplace world, and their focus upon the pendulation between isolation and contact, spirituality and sensuality, and the ideal and the real–the fluctuation that was to remain the characteristic rhythm of Hesse's life and the lives of his protagonists. An embryonic Harry Haller, protagonist of *Der Steppenwolf,* just discernible in the allegory of "Lulu," assumes a clear outline in "Tagebuch 1900" (Diary 1900). Lauscher emerges a potential Steppenwolf, like Haller a sensitive misfit, an observer of life and not a participant, an extreme individualist dedicated to the ideal and disdainful of the real.

Gedichte (Poems), a second volume of romantic poetry, appeared in 1902. Hesse made another trip to northern Italy in April 1903; following his return on 24 April he gave the finishing touches to his first novel. Hesse had begun *Peter Camenzind* (translated 1961) in November 1901 but had progressed slowly until the end of 1902. With the novel scheduled to be published in January 1904, Hesse decided in September 1903 to quit the bookselling trade and become a full-time author.

Peter Camenzind marks the beginning of the second stage in the evolution of Hesse's writings. His preceding shorter prose characteristically reflects the author-protagonist's inner self almost to the exclusion of any interaction with the physical world, and his prevailing aesthetic concerns find appropriate expression in an ornate narrative manner. *Peter Camenzind,* in contrast, mirrors both inner and outer circumstances, and Hesse's incipient cultivation in Bern of the art of life and of love finds expression in the blending of romanticism and realism. The shades and airy worlds of the earlier works yield to living people involved in real events. Emotive adjectives and adverbs become less profuse, abstractions less common, imagery less choice, and narrative less punctured by rhetorical questions and exclamatory outbursts. But Hesse's characters and settings continue to be felt rather than seen, and nature continues to be for Camenzind the mirror for moods and the setting for protracted reflection that it has always been for romantics. Nor did a writer of vignettes suddenly emerge a full-fledged storyteller. Camenzind's spotty memory, unevenly developed recollections, and propensity for rumination make his story less a smooth continuum of evolving action firmly anchored in space and time than a series of loosely juxtaposed reminiscences with liberally interspersed self-contemplation, nature description, and social comment. Camenzind, left an embittered loner, frustrated writer, misanthropist, and caustic sociocultural critic by his feeble and futile efforts to learn to live and love and by his disenchanting exposure to a shoddy world of culture, seeks solace in wine and a refuge in nature, finds a new ideal in the love and service exemplified by St. Francis of Assisi, then returns to his native Alpine peasant village prepared, though still in his prime, to turn his back upon life, to shelve his writing, and to become a simple innkeeper. Relenting enough to resume what had for him become a "miserable métier," Camenzind tells his narratively frail story. In his unhurried musing, he recalls his idyllic childhood, dwells sentimentally and at length on his love of nature, alludes to his early interest in books and writing, brushes by his formative years in high school, then turns his attention to his errant ambling through life and his disenchanting exposure to the cultural world. This story is Hesse's own veiled literary self-disclosure, prompted by his psychological need to dwell on his attempted new adjustment to life in Basel, to account for its failure, and to lend approbation to his decision to forgo any further efforts to socialize. The gauche and inhibited misfit Camenzind is what Hesse was in 1901–1903; his affable, happy, and carefree friend Richard is the man of the world Hesse aspired to become. Richard's death is Hesse's symbolic realization of the hopelessness of this aspiration. But for his successful courtship of Maria Bernoulli, Hesse might indeed, like his protagonist, have sought his comfort in solitary withdrawal.

While Hesse spent the autumn of 1903 and the winter and spring of 1904 in Calw writing the novel *Unterm Rad* (Beneath the Wheel, 1906; translated as *The Prodigy,* 1957) and monographs on Boccaccio and St. Francis of Assisi, Maria, to whom he had become engaged in the spring of 1903, scoured the countryside around the Bodensee for an appealing rural retreat. Both had had their fill of sophisticated city life. She found an old farmhouse for rent in the secluded and picturesque village of Gaienhofen on the German side of the Untersee. They were married on 2 August 1904, moved immediately to Gaienhofen, and began a Rousseauesque experiment in simple living.

Hesse continued to cultivate the poetic-realistic narrative manner of *Peter Camenzind* in his three remaining pre–World War I novels. *Unterm Rad* is more realistic than poetic, *Gertrud* (1910; translated as *Gertrude and I,* 1915) is as realistic as it is poetic, and *Roßhalde* (1914; translated as *Rosshalde,* 1970) is again more realistic than poetic; and all three, like *Peter Camenzind,* remain more study than story. Autobiography continues to be the matrix of Hesse's narration, psychological need is still the creative thrust, and protagonists remain reflections of the discontented loner Hesse had become.

Unterm Rad was Hesse's contribution to the tendentious literature fashionable in German letters at the turn of the century. Like most of these school novels and dramas, it is a severe indictment of the adult world. Parents, teachers, and pastors are upbraided for their lack of understanding, neglect, and victimization of their wards, and for their smugness, incompetence, and hypocrisy. Only the thick-skinned children escape relatively unscathed by their mistreatment; the sensitive and gifted are brushed aside or ground under. Hesse's acrid social satire is an overstatement less intent on exposing and reforming social institutions than on purging painful memories and venting latent anger. Like Hesse, Hans Giebenrath takes the state examination in Stuttgart in mid July, then proceeds to Maulbronn in September. Hesse's schoolmates and teachers, only slightly disguised, become Giebenrath's, and Giebenrath takes the same courses Hesse took and is the same relatively docile student that Hesse was until his French leave. But the temperamental and self-assertive Hermann Heilner, Giebenrath's close friend, is also a self-projection, a recollection of the discontented truant and rebellious youngster Hesse became. Giebenrath is what Hesse was, and Heilner is the person he had to become to make something of his life. The former's suicide and the latter's survival are Hesse's symbolic depiction of an actual change in his life. This double self-projection in the guise of intimate friends was to be used in all of Hesse's major works.

Hesse's first son, Bruno, was born in December 1905. In the autumn of 1907 the family moved into a larger and more comfortable home on a knoll overlooking Gaienhofen and the lake. A second son, Heiner, was born in March 1909.

Gaienhofen marked a new chapter in Hesse's life, a new period in his career, and a new phase in his writing. With the publication of *Peter Camenzind* in 1904, an unknown aspirant suddenly became a celebrity. That same year his maiden novel was awarded the Bauernfeld Prize of Vienna, the first of many literary awards. Before Gaienhofen, Hesse's poetry and prose were intimately personal and highly lyrical. With his marriage and increased concern with everyday life, he became less obviously personal and more prose conscious, and began to cultivate a more down-to-earth literary style. The novella became his favorite medium of expression.

The writing of *Unterm Rad* not only purged Hesse of painful school recollections but also evoked treasured memories of Calw. His birthplace, alias Gerbersau, became a persistent preoccupation which gave his art fresh impetus and new direction. This little provincial community was his wonderful world of childhood, where he had been part of a social complex and not yet the lonely outsider he was to become. In Gaienhofen, this "Heimat" (home) transfigured in Hesse's memory, became the very stuff of his art: a mythicized community reminiscent of Gottfried Keller's Seldwyla. Together with *Unterm Rad,* Hesse's three volumes of Gerbersau tales–*Diesseits* (In This World, 1907), *Nachbarn* (Neighbors, 1908) and *Umwege* (Byways, 1912)– represent the Swabian period of his career, when he chose to look to the past and tell traditional stories.

Hesse's traditional stories were not confined to his Swabian tales. While still in Basel, fascinated by both Boccaccio and St. Francis of Assisi, he had begun to write stories in the manner of the Italian novella and legends in the manner of traditional hagiography. He continued this practice in Gaienhofen. Many of these Italianate tales and legends were republished in *Fabulierbuch* (Book of Fables, 1935). His literary essays, personal ruminations, nature sketches, diary-like recollections, and travel reports were published in newspapers and magazines and republished in such miscellanies as *Aus Indien* (From India, 1913), *Bilderbuch* (Book of Pictures, 1926), and *Betrachtungen* (Observations, 1928). In Gaienhofen Hesse also continued to write his romantic poems, but in drastically reduced number. Some of these appeared in *Unterwegs* (Under Way, 1911) and *Musik des Einsamen* (Music of the Lonely One, 1915).

Hesse's third novel, *Gertrud,* written in the winter of 1908–1909, was as much a self-appraisal as *Peter Camenzind* had been. In Camenzind's story Hesse was primarily intent upon accounting for the asocial withdrawal he had briefly courted after his futile efforts in Basel to become sociable; in *Gertrud* he was eager to account for his passive adjustment to life in Gaienhofen. The inner world of the violinist-composer Kuhn, like that of Camenzind, remains intimately autobiographical; and Kuhn's outer world, albeit decidedly more fictive than Camenzind's, draws freely upon the personal for its filler detail. Kuhn starts out as the person Hesse had been in Basel, the lonely misfit-observer knocking timidly on the door of life, and he becomes Hesse the disenchanted artist-bourgeois of Gaienhofen desperately intent upon making self-acceptance possible and life palatable. To this end, Kuhn embraces a fatalistic philosophy, evolves a Nietzschean theory of art, argues a Schopenhauerian conception of love, and advocates, as had Camenzind, a St. Francis of Assisi adjustment: fate is responsible for the unalterable circumstances of life; loneliness and suffering are the sine qua non for creativity; love between man and woman is essentially a flighty, brutal, and painfully demeaning passion; and social love, with its commitment to service, is man's ultimate solace. In so arguing, Kuhn achieves, as had

Hesse, if not an ideal, at least a functional adjustment to a thwarted self, cruel life, and unkind fate. Reflecting upon this capricious, ineluctable fate, upon possible composed acceptance of it, and upon the possibility of a Schillerian type of self-fashioned inner fate, Kuhn recalls and comments upon the highlights of his life: lonely youth; refuge and solace in music; disappointing years at a conservatory; the accident that left him crippled; friendship with the handsome opera singer and voluptuary Heinrich Muoth; preference for solitude despite his chronic loneliness; persistent shy and distant worship of women; unrequited love for Gertrud; success as a composer; Muoth's suicide; growing devotion to his work; and gradual acceptance of life's meager offerings, persuaded that humans can counter fickle fate in mutual understanding, love, and service and can find comfort in art and religion. Just as in *Peter Camenzind,* this frail narration is fragmented by protracted dialogue, copious rumination, and epistolary and verse inclusions, and ends just as limply, abruptly, and unconvincingly. That Hesse himself was as little convinced by Kuhn's assessment of, and adjustment to, life as he had been by Camenzind's is clearly reflected in the last of his prewar novels, *Roßhalde.*

As the novelty of marriage and his new way of life wore off, Hesse became convinced that he had given up too much for too little. He and Maria, who was not only nine years his senior, but just as strong willed and self-preoccupied as he, began to drift apart. Hesse's growing discontent became chronic wanderlust, which culminated in September 1911 in a trip to the East.

Accompanied by the Swiss painter Hans Sturzenegger, Hesse visited Ceylon, Malaya, and Sumatra. He vaguely expected to find the wisdom of India, a more innocent community, and answers to his personal problems, but found only appalling poverty and depressingly commercialized Buddhism. Disenchanted, suffering from dysentery, and exhausted by the oppressive heat, Hesse left for home in December without visiting India proper. Nine months later, the Hesses settled in a spacious and elegant seventeenth-century country house on the outskirts of Bern. Remote Gaienhofen had lost its attraction and was no place for schoolchildren, and Hesse and his wife hoped that a return to Switzerland would be salutary for their crumbling marriage.

Roßhalde, a depiction of the climactic stage of an infelicitous marriage written between July 1912 and January 1913, drew as heavily on Hesse's life as had each of his preceding major works. Veraguth, a painter, is the temperamental individual that Hesse was–the lonely romantic who lives in dreamy anticipation, is quickly sated by realization, and carefully nurtures his chronic disillusionment. His wife, Adele, staid and humorless, possessive mother and unresponsive wife, is patterned after Maria. Veraguth's decision to terminate his marriage and to begin life anew, on a different basis, and alone, anticipates Hesse's separation from his wife and children; and his planned interim trip to India with his carefree friend Burkhardt recalls Hesse's own flight and quest. *Roßhalde* is Hesse's frank confession not only of the failure but even more of the folly of his attempt in marriage to achieve an intimate relationship with life and to find a place for himself in society. Hesse had become convinced that the artist was essentially an observer and a creator, and that to try to be a participant, to be in and of life, was to play a role and not to live as oneself. For the artist, therefore marriage was per se mismarriage. Like Hesse, Veraguth had only compounded his error by long resigning himself to it. Unlike Lauscher, who had settled for aestheticism, Camenzind, who had settled for nature, and Kuhn, who had settled for resigned retirement, Veraguth, left an embittered recluse by his initial Kuhnian approach to life, decides belatedly to settle for nothing less than the self. This resolve is supported by a new concept of fate. Until *Roßhalde,* Hesse's protagonists characteristically assume that everything happens or does not happen to them; adjustment to circumstances is their primary concern, and minimal involvement is their ideal. Until his decision to leave family, home, and false identity behind him, Veraguth belongs to these timorous bystanders. Convinced finally that fate is not intrusive but inherent, he becomes determined to seek his own medium and to try only to be himself. He now recognizes that he is by nature an outsider and an observer, that art is his destiny and not just his consolation, and that loneliness is his element and not something to be feared. Reluctant acceptance of circumstances yields to joyous self-acceptance, and bitter renunciation will become self-realization. On this note Veraguth's story, like Camenzind's and Kuhn's, ends abruptly and inconclusively. A new and more meaningful way of life is proposed but left untested. Hesse again took his protagonist no farther than the point he himself had reached.

Hesse's move to Bern in the hope of resolving his personal and family problems proved to be as abortive as his trip to the East. The novelty of change quickly wore thin and life resumed its troubled course. Unable to cope with their extremely irritable youngest son following his severe illness in the spring of 1914, Hesse and his wife put the boy into a foster home. The outbreak of World War I left an already unsettled Hesse badly shaken. His initial ambiguous political stance–he was nationalistic enough to sympathize with Germany and to hope for German victory, but he also argued for internationalism and abhorred war–at first attracted only scattered suspicion, but by the autumn of 1915 it elicited not only denunciation by militarists but also rebuke by pacifists. That Hesse had volunteered his services to the German embassy in Bern and was collecting books and coediting two weeklies for German prisoners of war did little to dissuade his detractors. The death of Hesse's father in March 1916 added an acute sense of guilt to his growing despair. Exhausted, Hesse sought help in psychoanalysis. From the end of April 1916 to November 1917, he had some seventy-two sessions with Dr. J. B. Lang, who had become one of C. G. Jung's students. This encounter with psychoanalysis provided Hesse with the incentive to appraise himself and his adjustment to life, and afforded him the insights necessary to begin his long "Weg nach Innen" (inward path), that tortuous road that he hoped would lead to self-knowledge and ultimately to greater self-realization.

By the beginning of 1916 Hesse was so distressed by the criticism of militarists and pacifists and by the futility of his own protests that he stopped writing about the war. The lull that followed was a period of resolute reconsideration and incubation, the beginning of what Hesse was later to call his "Erwachen" (awakening) and his "Wandlung" (transformation). In the middle of 1917 Hesse began again to address himself publicly to politics, excoriating proponents of war and pleading for immediate peace. He continued his berating and exhorting in the immediate postwar period, shifting gradually from international and national politics to the individual and from the outer to the inner world. Hesse's words were primarily directed to youth: a challenge to emulate Nietzsche in an acceptance of the self and of life's inherent loneliness and suffering, and an invitation to undertake the self-scrutiny and self-realization he himself had just embarked upon.

The concluding thoughts of *Roßhalde* were a portent of things to come in Hesse's life and art. Veraguth is determined to end his timorous adjustment to life and to "live what he is," but he does not–just as Hesse did not yet–give any thought to the demanding implications of this new way of life. *Roßhalde* represents the enthusiastic and ingenuous initial stage of Hesse's conversion to a new ideal. Serious reflection followed during the critical period of Hesse's political change of mind from 1915 to mid 1917. Hesse concluded that to "live the self" would involve emancipation from traditional religion and morality and the cultivation of a personal ethos. Responding to these necessities, a withdrawn, mild-mannered traditionalist at odds with himself and the world became a thoroughly Nietzschean individualist, iconoclast, and moralist. Heeding his "Eigensinn" (self-will) and not the "Herdensinn" (herd-will), Hesse was determined to follow Nietzsche's path of individuation, prepared not only to accept but to extol loneliness and suffering in the manner of the Nietzschean elect. Ours was a world of and for the "Herdenmensch" (herd man), a dated society. A better world could be ushered in by an enlightened few girded for a Nietzschean transvaluation of values. Christianity became the focal point of this transvaluation for Hesse, just as it had for Nietzsche. Due to Christianity, the here and the beyond had become an unnecessary and trying duality of incompatibles. A religion with a deity who was both God and Satan and a morality beyond absolutist good and evil, a credo appreciative of wholesome self-love and tolerant of self-expression and self-realization would be more in accord with the nature of things. The old would give way to the new: a new God, a new morality, a new man, and a new world.

This Nietzschean sentiment found its immediate expression in *Demian,* written in September and October 1917. The novel depicts emancipation from traditional belief and thought and the crystallization of his own ethos, ascribed to precocious Emil Sinclair in his passage from youth to young manhood. The ten-year-old Sinclair is the sensitive and unruly youngster Hesse had been; his home and family are modeled on Hesse's; the streets through which he strolls are the Calw Hesse had never forgotten; his "helle Welt" (light world) is Hesse's cloistered world of childhood; and this childhood paradise ends for Sinclair, as it had for Hesse, with a growing awareness of and painful involvement with seductive and profane life at large, "die dunkle Welt" (the dark world). Sinclair's first encounter with evil in the person of the young blackmailer Kromer, his own first lies and theft, his awareness of sin and torment by guilt, his unhappy and dissolute school years, his despair and thoughts of suicide, his distant worship of an older girl, his disenchantment with academia, and his attraction to Nietzsche had all been Hesse's early experiences. The mystagogic Pistorius's tutoring of Sinclair in gnosticism and the interpretation of dreams reflects Hesse's indebtedness to his psychiatrist, Dr. Lang. Sinclair's belief that war is the birth pangs of a new and better age had also been Hesse's. Nevertheless, *Demian,* like all of Hesse's preceding tales, is not strictly autobiography. Hesse's past and present were only the matrix of his art; his recollection was always selective and his imagination remained vivid. Max Demian, Sinclair's mentor, and Demian's mother, Eva– the novel's prime enigmas and its two most important figures excepting the protagonist–were products of this fertile imagination: pivotal points around which Hesse structured a tale in which psychic experiences are rendered visible and actuality is conceptualized. Demian and Frau Eva are multidimensional symbols, concepts thinly actualized. Demian is Sinclair's Socratic *daimon,* his admonishing inner self, but he is also a Jungian imago, Sinclair's mental image of the ideal self, and is also the reflective, culturally unconditioned alter ego Sinclair must become before he can begin to "live himself." Frau Eva is Sinclair's Jungian anima, the soul, the unconscious with which his conscious mind must establish rapport in the process of individuation, and also life in all its fullness, heaven and earth, an actualized Magna Mater, mankind's origin and destiny. Demian's and Frau Eva's actions and Sinclair's interactions with them are primarily psychic experience externalized: Demian's disposing of Kromer is Sinclair's own mental neutralizing of his tormentor by acknowledging and accepting the evil that he represents; Demian's death is not an end but a beginning in which Sinclair has become his projected better self, fully emancipated and ready to "live himself." While Demian and Frau Eva arc conccpts bccome persons, the remaining personae are actuality become concepts: all are more universally typical than real, more timeless representation than being. To make interpretation even more tantalizingly elusive, the tale's psychic experience rendered visible is artfully extended to an interplay of Sinclair's dreams and paintings: psychoanalytical interests become literary devices. Sinclair's dream of the heraldic hawk that Demian compels him to swallow and that he subsequently paints and sends to Demian for explanation, and his dream of a love embrace with his own mother, his painting of the recurrent sexual fantasy and ingestion of the painting's ashes are thought process externalized: his emancipation from traditional Christian-bourgeois belief and thought to accept an ethic affirming both good and evil, an ethic represented by Abraxas, the gnostic deity that is both god and devil. Sinclair's cerebral breakthrough is now complete: no longer encased in tradition, he is finally ready to "live himself." By the end of 1917, Hesse had gotten no further than this in his own emancipation. Hesse was awarded the Theodore Fontane Prize of Berlin for *Demian* in 1919.

Hesse's six and a half years in Bern were quite productive. His essays on war and politics, sundry recollections, literary studies, travel reports, congratulatory articles, and general observations on the human condition written during the period were collected in *Kleiner Garten* (Small Garden, 1919), *Wanderung* (1920; translated as *Wandering,* 1972), *Sinclairs Notizbuch* (Sinclair's Notebook, 1923), *Bilderbuch,* and *Betrachtungen.* He edited thirty-nine books and two weeklies and maintained a continuous flow of book reviews. He also added considerably to his fiction: besides *Roßhalde* and *Demian,* he published *Knulp: Drei Geschichten aus dem Leben Knulps* (translated as *Knulp: Three Tales from the Life of*

Knulp, 1971) in 1915, and *Märchen* (Fairy Tales), seven stories written between 1913 and 1917, in 1919. Many of the poems written in Bern became part of the second edition of *Unterwegs* (1915), of *Musik des Einsamen,* and of *Ausgewählte Gedichte* (Selected Poems, 1921). In 1916 he took up watercolor painting, a diversion he pursued for the rest of his life.

After Maria became psychotic in October 1918, Hesse put Bruno and Heiner into a boarding school. When he was released from his wartime job in March 1919 he immediately left for the canton of Ticino in southern Switzerland. Domesticity had not agreed with Hesse: his Rousseauesque adventure in Gaienhofen had ended in tedium and frustration, and his life in Bern had become a nightmare. Neither his early aestheticism nor his rise into the bourgeoisie had served Hesse well. In the Ticino he was determined just to be himself, come what might.

By the beginning of May Hesse had settled in a Spartan apartment in the Casa Camuzzi, a baroque country house in Montagnola, a village on the outskirts of Lugano, where he lived until August 1931. From 1919 to 1923 Hesse emerged rarely and only reluctantly from his retreat. Since his postwar royalties from Germany had little monetary value in Switzerland, he was compelled to give sporadic public readings of his works. While in Zurich for this purpose in May 1921 he had a few analytic sessions with Jung. After 1923 his lecture tours were extended to Germany and continued until the late 1920s. The generosity of Fritz Leuthold, a wealthy friend, enabled Hesse to spend his winters from 1925 to 1931 in a small apartment in Zurich.

Hesse had hardly settled in Montagnola before he became acquainted with twenty-two-year-old Ruth Wenger, daughter of the Swiss writer Lisa Wenger, who lived in nearby Carona. Hesse terminated his marriage in July 1923 and married Wenger on 11 January 1924. His second marital misadventure was short-lived: distraught and ill, Ruth returned to her parents in April. Hesse's efforts to achieve a reconciliation were futile, and Ruth was granted a divorce in April 1927. A shy outsider, most at home in his study, in the concert hall, and in nature, Hesse became a desperate frequenter of Zurich's bars and dance halls. By late 1926 this sensual eruption had run its course. Early that year, while in Zurich, Hesse had met Ninon Dolbin, née Ausländer, a longtime devotee of his writing from Czernowitz, Rumania. She joined him in the Casa Camuzzi in June 1927.

Politically, the period from 1919 to 1931 was no less discouraging for Hesse than the preceding years in Bern. Persuaded that a disenchanted postwar Germany would be susceptible to changes for the better, he helped to found and edit *Vivos Voco,* a periodical devoted to social reform, pacifism, and internationalism.

Quickly disabused of his hopes by resurgent nationalism and spreading communism, Hesse terminated his association with the monthly in the autumn of 1921, only two years after its first issue. By then he had again become a favorite target of invective, and public self-defense was again futile. Continued indignities and waning faith in Germany's political future persuaded Hesse to become a citizen of Switzerland in November 1924 and to resign from the Prussian Academy of Art in November 1930.

Hesse's twelve years in the Casa Camuzzi were the most exciting chapter of his life and the most productive period in his art. In his relentless quest of himself, his writing received fresh impetus and assumed new directions. A traditionalist before the war, he emerged an exciting innovator. Hesse's fictive documentation of his self-quest started with "Klein und Wagner" (Klein and Wagner), begun immediately after he arrived in Montagnola and completed by mid July 1919; it was serialized in *Vivos Voco* from October to December 1919. "Klingsors letzter Sommer" (translated as *Klingsor's Last Summer,* 1970) was ready for publication by the beginning of September. It was published together with "Klein und Wagner" as *Klingsors letzter Sommer: Erzählungen* (1920). The first eight chapters of *Siddhartha* (1922; translated, 1951) were written from December 1919 to the end of July 1920, the last four from March to May 1922. *Kurgast: Aufzeichnungen von einer Badener Kur* (Guest at a Spa: Notes of a Water Cure in Baden, 1925), the ironic psychologizing and philosophizing of an embittered rheumatic, was written in October 1923, and *Die Nürnberger Reise* (The Journey to Nuremberg, 1927), acerbic memoirs of a reading tour, in the late autumn of 1925. *Der Steppenwolf* (1927; translated as *Steppenwolf,* 1929), a surrealistic self-exposure that began to preoccupy Hesse in November 1924, was finished at the end of 1926. *Narziss und Goldmund* (1930; translated as *Death and the Lover,* 1932), begun in mid 1927, was completed by the end of 1928, and *Die Morgenlandfahrt* (1932; translated as *The Journey to the East,* 1956), started during the latter half of 1929, was finished by April 1931. These major works were accompanied by Hesse's usual stream of poetry, most of which was included in *Krisis* (1928; translated as *Crisis,* 1975) and *Trost der Nacht* (The Solace of the Night, 1929), and by his continued output of shorter tales, literary essays, and recollections, many of which were brought together in his miscellanies. During these years Hesse also managed to edit sixteen volumes and to continue his prolific reviewing of books.

Roßhalde boldly proclaims a new way of life: the protagonist will be what he is and live as he was meant to live. *Demian* depicts the emancipation from traditional religion and morality necessary for this new style of life. "Klein und Wagner" proceeds from the brash manifesto of *Roßhalde* and the optimistic celebrations of *Demian* to an actual venture, a venture that is an astonishingly faithful rendition of Hesse's separation from his family in the spring of 1919, his trip, and the mental and emotional anguish of his first few weeks in the Ticino. Klein is a respectable member of society, a conscientious employee, a faithful husband, a good father, and a reliable provider. He is also a man who has never taken the trouble to find himself. Disillusionment, frustration, and resultant murderous impulses compel him to bolt. He embezzles, forges documents, procures a revolver, and flees. Distraught, he tries desperately to assess himself and his actions, to ponder life and morality, and to become an authentic human being. His belated efforts to establish his own identity, to fashion his own values, and to "live himself" are futile. Long hours of excruciating thought, a bout of gambling, and a whirl of sex only add to his agitation. The blissful moments when he is at peace with himself and with life are too few and too elusive to sustain him. Guilt and anxiety plague him, his new way of life leaves him wallowing in self-contempt, and destructive impulses once more become urgent. Klein begins to falter, and flight again becomes imperative. Since life no longer holds any attraction for him and since his own inner resources are depleted, just one week after his flight he succumbs to his long-nurtured passion for suicide. Klein's attempt to emancipate himself from the Christian-bourgeois ethos as Sinclair does, and to "live himself" as Veraguth proposes to do, fails. His suppressed and omniscient real and innermost self can make itself heard, but is unable, except for brief interludes, to prevail over his socialized self. Except for Klein's theft and cloak-and-dagger behavior and for the inclusion of the worldly Teresina, all of this is autobiography that could have hardly been veiled more thinly. Even Klein's death had its actual precedent in the demise of the Klein Hesse had temporarily become and had quickly overcome. Whereas actual experience had almost persuaded Hesse—as it does persuade Klein—that this new ideal was more pipe dream than possibility, a surge of faith in the essential oneness, eternity, and meaningfulness of life convinced Hesse to the contrary. This faith finds its expression in the epiphanic concluding moments of Klein's life. Given this faith, the individual has only to "sich fallen lassen" (let himself fall), to surrender himself to himself and to life, fully and with no regard for consequences. Hesse's pictorial and highly gripping depiction of this mystical moment of grace, experienced in the very process of dying, is a most appropriate finale for a narrative that is pure psychic drama in classically dramatic form. Of Hesse's major tales, Klein's encompasses the shortest span of time, involves the smallest cast, and presents the most concentrated treatment of theme. This control and concentration finds deliberate and appropriate expression in the classical structure of drama: in the progression from the abrupt and jolting expository beginning, to development, climax, and denouement. (The Wagner of the title refers both to the composer of whose music Klein was once fond, and to a schoolteacher who murdered his family–something Klein was afraid he would also do unless he fled the scene.)

Autobiography was mythicized in *Demian* and dramatized in "Klein und Wagner"; it is fantasized in "Klingsors letzter Sommer." While Klein is what Hesse was in the spring of 1919, Klingsor's story, decidedly more portrait than narrative, is a memorial to the summer of 1919, Hesse's first in Ticino. Klingsor, born on 2 July, forty-two years old and unattached, painter, poet, philosopher, and hypochondriac troubled by the thought of death, possessed by a passion for life and art, and given to revelry and depression, is obviously Hesse. The setting is clearly Lugano and its vicinity; actual place names are only playfully distorted. Klingsor's July excursion to Kareno with his coterie of friends to meet the Queen of the Mountains is Hesse's fantasized depiction of his first visit to Carona to meet Ruth Wenger. A night with Jup der Magier, a night given to revelry and morbid preoccupation with cultural decline and death, is based on Hesse's frequent night bouts of alcohol and argument with his astrologer friend Josef Englert. In this transmutation of autobiography, Hesse is, as usual, intent upon more inner portraiture than upon narration. Actually, a double portrait is executed: that which emerges as the work proceeds along its erratic course, and the unusual self-portrait described in the conclusion. Hesse's characterization of the painting–as a marvelously harmonized tapestry in brilliant hues, an exercise in surrealism, a self-analysis unsparing in its psychological insights, and a ruthless, screaming confession–applies just as much to the tale itself. That "Klingsors letzer Sommer" is self-analysis and confession in a surrealistic vein, replete with colors and sounds reflecting and accentuating the turbulence of Klingsor's emotions and the feverishness of his thoughts, is obvious. At first sight however, it seems to be anything but a "marvelously harmonized tapestry," comprising as it does ten disparate segments, jarringly juxtaposed, assigned to one summer but otherwise only vaguely related in time. This fractured structure with its romantic confusion of genres (descriptive prose, dramatic dialogue, poetry, and letters) suggests an uncontrolled effervescence, imagination on the rampage. The work was indeed written in this eruptive fashion; but closer examination discloses that Hesse, like Klingsor given madly to his self-portrait, has proceeded intu-

itively and unerringly to produce a work that is indeed a "marvelously harmonized tapestry," in which all elements of form are consonant with each other, and of which the form as a whole is completely in accord with the matter. The tale's splintered structure and its lack of homogeneity mirror and highlight Klingsor's inner discord and the chaotic structure of his lifestyle. The hectic flow and rhythm of the sentences reflect Klingsor's alternately frantic and ecstatic inner state. Nature, evocatively depicted and excitingly animated by garish color and brilliant sound, becomes an accentuating mirror for frenzied thoughts. Hesse's very language assumes a vitality that derives from its lively colors and symphony of sounds, its lavish figures of speech, and its restive rhetorical questions and exclamations, and that lends Klingsor's story gripping immediacy. This work represents Hesse's intuitively controlled artistry at its best. The cacophony of the last summer of Klingsor's life finds expression in a consistent cacophony of form. Klingsor begins where Klein left off: like Klein, he has broken through the shell of traditional values and beliefs; unlike Klein's, his emancipation is complete. He has left society and his socialized self behind without any moral compunctions. But he has not come to terms with death: he tries to blot out the reality of death by rushing headlong into an oblivion of intoxicating experience. But sex, alcohol, and painting prove to be ineffectual weapons against death. He is not capable of letting himself "fall into life" until he is finally able to come to terms fully with both life and death. This rare moment is depicted symbolically in Klingsor's struggle with his self-portrait, an undertaking that is not just the culminating artistic experience of an exciting summer but the crowning achievement of his life. A lifetime of thinking, feeling, and acting the self and a concomitant learning to know the self climax in a bold confrontation with the self and with life at large. Klingsor's painting of his self-portrait symbolizes this confrontation and his resultant affirmation of the self, life, and death. He is now in accord with all, no longer suffers from anxiety, and is finally able to let himself fall into life. At this critical juncture, Hesse's narration terminates in its usual abrupt manner: Klingsor dies mysteriously soon after putting the finishing touches to his self-portrait. As usual, Hesse took the protagonist only to the point he himself had reached.

What had become a passionate ideal for Hesse finally received its full expression in *Siddhartha*. Just as for Klein and Klingsor, life for Hesse's new standard-bearer consists primarily of two areas of experience: "Geist," the world of the mind and thought, and "Natur," the world of the body and physical action. Klein is at home in neither realm; Klingsor lives in the intoxication of each; Siddhartha exhausts both possibilities and, in their exhaustion, transcends them and finds himself miraculously in a third realm: that of the soul, the ultimate stage of being in which the individual lives in complete accord with himself and life, when he is finally able, fully and not just for chance moments, to experience the essential oneness and meaningfulness of everything. After his encounter with the Buddha, and with his subsequent awakening to the realization that the incidental I of his senses is no less he than the incidental I of his thoughts, Siddhartha, the Brahmin once dedicated to ritual and speculation and the *Samana* (ascetic) once given to self-denial, leaves the realm of the mind behind. Through his affair with Kamala the courtesan, his partnership with Kamaswami the businessman, his reveling in wealth, power, and sloth, his constant self-disgust, and his attempt to commit suicide, he leaves the realm of the flesh behind. And after his return to the river and Vasudeva the ferryman, his encounter with his son, and his last bout with anxious love and fearful concern, Siddhartha emerges transfigured, a wise saintly figure given to his fellow humans in love and service; paradoxically, he has achieved self-transcendence through self-realization. Hesse's idea is an exemplary Western approach to life, opposed to the exemplary Eastern approach advocated by the Gautama Buddha. To accord his literary credo something of timeless, mythic validity, Hesse locates his tale in remote India of a time long past. To enhance the gospel quality of the tale, Hesse cultivates an antiquated, liturgical mode of expression reminiscent of both Pali scriptures and the Bible. And to stress his equal concern with, and approbation of, each of the three areas of human experience, Hesse carefully adjusts manner to matter. Structurally the tale is a balanced tripartite, in keeping with Siddhartha's balanced progression from the realm of the mind, through that of the body, to that of the soul. Each of the three stages of Siddhartha's life comprises a series of three-beat patterns of action. This triadic structure is extended to the very mechanics of expression: to sentences, clauses, phrases, words, and paragraphs. And in keeping with this three-beat pulsation, Hesse even extends his customary projection of the actual self and one alternative to the actual self and three possibilities. Siddhartha is Hesse's fictionalized self and Govinda, Buddha, and Vasudeva are the possibilities: Govinda is the self-effacing, institution-oriented person Siddhartha should not become; Buddha represents a laudable but undesirable life-denying model; and Vasudeva is an exemplary life-affirming ideal. And when Siddhartha becomes this ideal, Vasudeva leaves the scene, just as Demian vanished when Sinclair became his ideal self. Just as "Klingsors letzter Sommer" is intuitively controlled artistry at its best, *Siddhartha* is conscious craftmanship at its best.

The third major crisis in Hesse's life began when he and Ruth separated at the end of March 1924. Withdrawal, bitter self-hatred, a lusting for both death and raw life, and an experiencing of the bars and dance halls of Zurich in early 1926 were followed in mid 1926 by a return to Montagnola, his art, his ideals, and his solitude. It was of this crisis, the most radical of Hesse's characteristic swings from spirituality to sensuality and back, that *Der Steppenwolf* was born. Harry Haller's story and *Krisis*, its poetic counterpart, are also the most painfully honest of Hesse's literary renditions of these sporadic ordeals. *Krisis*, in particular, is a brutally sincere reflection of Hesse's attempted drowning of the self in sex, jazz, and alcohol, and of his agonizing recognition that he was at best a shy guest at life's feast and would remain a troubled stranger in the community of man. Hesse has his prose counterpart recount his experience in less strident detail and buffered by a touch of fantasy. Haller, intellectual, writer, and uncompromising idealist, too long ascetically devoted to mental pursuits, becomes emotionally unhinged. His aloneness has become a torment, his freedom repugnant, and all his interests and ideals questionable. He is unable to continue in his estrangement, is tempted but not prepared to commit suicide, and will not compromise and join the throng, find a comfortable place among the many. He has no choice but to relax, to emerge from his isolation, and to seek relief in the world of the senses. Late one night, Haller meets Hermine, a well-groomed prostitute who responds sympathetically to his plight. At the very outset of their involvement she informs him that she will make him fall in love with her, then will order him to kill her and will expect him to comply. In the interim she teaches Haller to dance, laugh, and live. She introduces him to handsome young Pablo, a jazz-band saxophonist, and arranges a bedroom friendship for him with the sensual Maria. At a masked ball only four weeks after their first meeting, Haller and Hermine dance a passionate wedding dance and then accept Pablo's invitation to his quarters for a climactic drug party, an introduction to his Magic Theater. Awakening slightly from his drug-induced fantasizing and finding Pablo and Hermine side by side, exhausted from their sexual intercourse, Haller hallucinates that he plunges a knife into Hermine's heart. Slipping back into a deep daze, he imagines a conversation with Mozart about the necessity of learning to laugh at the apparently real and to remain mindful only of the ideal, then a trial in which he is sentenced to eternal life for his imagined murder of an imaginary figure. Mozart suddenly returns and becomes Pablo, who likewise chides Haller for his confusion of the ideal and real and then vanishes, with Hermine in his vest pocket, leaving Haller to his thoughts. Sober again, Haller is prepared to resume the game of life, to suffer its agonies and senselessness once more, hopeful that he will someday be able, like Mozart, Goethe, and their fellow Immortals, to distinguish between ideas and appearance and to rise above it all and laugh. Thus, like every major tale before it, *Der Steppenwolf* ends abruptly and on a note of optimism: like Sinclair in Demian's death, Haller in Hermine's death absorbs and becomes his guiding alter ego and can look forward to better things to come. And like each of the tales beginning with Sinclair's, Haller's is yet another of Hesse's experiments in narrative possibility: from *Demian's* literary integration of psychoanalysis to the dramatic psychological realism of *Klein und Wagner,* the fantasia of *Klingsors letzter Sommer,* the exotically stylized art of *Siddhartha,* and the surrealistic admixture of psychological realism and symbolism, fantasy, and hallucination of *Der Steppenwolf.* As usual, too, Hesse the storyteller plays second fiddle to Hesse the portraitist. Recounting is characteristically overshadowed by copius reflective accounting, and from this accounting there emerge four complementary pairs of portraits of Haller and his age: the preface depicts two physical portraits, the tract inserted in the novel two psychological portraits, the tale proper two portraits of action, and the Magic Theater's review studies of Haller and the bourgeois world complement each of the preceding pairs of portraits. Together these pairs of portraits furnish a full psychologically penetrating study of a man and a detailed, trenchant analysis of a bourgeois-dominated culture. What could have been a tediously long treatise becomes a tale fascinating in its exposition and unique in its tetrapartite structure.

By the beginning of 1927 Hesse's crisis had run its course, and in the relative tranquillity of the lull that followed he looked to the past, reviewed his thoughts, and permitted himself to dream. The embittered Haller was forgotten, a more amiable Goldmund was espoused, and the dramatic tempo of *Der Steppenwolf* yielded to the more epic flow of *Narziss und Goldmund.* Just as in Siddhartha's exotic tale, also written during a period of relative equanimity following considerable agitation, there is little in the outer detail of Goldmund's medieval world that is discernibly autobiographical. Goldmund's schooling, friendships, experiences in the Mariabronn monastery, and eventual stealthy departure from the monastery are a colorful reflection of Hesse's sojourn in and flight from the monastery in Maulbronn. All that follows—Goldmund's restless peregrinations from forest to forest and village to village; parade of brief sexual encounters; restrictive years of sculpturing under the tutelage of Master Niklaus; happy return to the open road, exposure to the horrors of the plague; last dangerous dalliance; apprehension; rescue from death by his boyhood friend and mentor Narziss, now

abbot of Mariabronn; return to the monastery; dedication to his art; last worldly sally; and self-but not life-affirming death that gives Narziss cause to reflect upon himself and life—was born of Hesse's wishful imagination. On the other hand, Goldmund's thoughts, feelings, basic problems, and aspirations, like Siddhartha's, are no less self-projections than those of all of Hesse's other protagonists. Like most of Hesse's tales, *Narziss und Goldmund* juxtaposes and scrutinizes two human possibilities; the ideal possible and the dubious actual: Goldmund is the possible and Narziss the actual. Protagonist and intimate friend are yet another variation of Hesse's customary double self-projection: Goldmund is the ingratiating artist-voluptuary he would have liked to be, and Narziss is the retiring thinker-ascetic he knew himself to be. Like all of Hesse's self-projections, and particularly those following World War I, both Goldmund and Narziss are caught up in life's polar tug of war. Each adjusts in a manner that most accords with his psychology. Neither adjustment is without its drawbacks and each has its virtues. Goldmund swings freely and with no compunctions between sensuality and spirituality, is both a disciplined artist and a roving voluptuary, and is as much at home in the monastery as in the world. His rewards are life's intensities, and the price he pays is equanimity. Narziss chooses to deny the body, to turn his back upon the world, and to cultivate things spiritual in the seclusion of the monastery. His reward is peace and its price is human warmth. Though Hesse gives preference to Goldmund's resolution of this dichotomy, he condones both approaches to life; both are psychological necessities, not caprices, and both can unveil life's mysteries. It was not given to Hesse to live and to create as spontaneously and unconcernedly as Goldmund, but he could dream. Narziss, like Haller, was Hesse's real predicament and lot. Tripartite substance had in *Siddhartha* found accordant rhythmic expression in triadic structure, action, and syntax. *Narziss und Goldmund's* focus upon life's basic dichotomy with its constellation of polarities finds its equally conscious expression in a thoroughly contrapuntal structure. The antithetical setting of the tale immediately directs attention to dichotomy and polarity. Ten of the novel's twenty chapters are given to the monastery and ten to the world, and Goldmund moves twice from one to the other. Dichotomy and polarity are accentuated no less by the tale's pervasive two-beat rhythm of action, persistent pairing of characters, linking and opposing attitudes and emotions, and frequent syntactical coupling of sentences, clauses, and phrases. In *Kurgast* Hesse had expressed the desire someday to give simultaneous expression to the two voices of life's melody in both the substance and the form of his prose. *Narziss und Goldmund* approaches this envisaged verbal counterpoint as closely as prose ever can.

In December 1928, while putting the finishing touches to *Narziss und Goldmund,* Hesse began again to experience sharp qualms about himself, life, and art: he was a crippled human being, life was an incomprehensible horror, and writing was a pursuit of disturbingly limited possibility. This new attack of doubt and Hesse's usual determination to find order and meaning in apparent chaos provided the impetus and matter for *Die Morgenlandfahrt.* Autobiography had been poetically fantasized in "Klingsors letzter Sommer" and surrealistically fantasized in *Der Steppenwolf;* it is playfully fantasized, mystified, and metaphorized in *Die Morgenlandfahrt.* H. H.'s acceptance into the Order of the Eastern Wayfarers, his year of probation, his initiation, his participation in the order's Journey to the East, his defection after a few months, his ten-year period of lonely suffering and suicidal despair, his months of grueling effort to recall and record his association with the order, and his culminating readmission into its ranks extend over some twelve years. This time frame represents Hesse's twelve years of quest, despair, and new hope following his departure from Bern in the spring of 1919. Content is no less autobiographical than structure: H. H. is what Hesse was during the years 1919–1931, undisguised even in name. His background, friends, interests, inclinations, aspirations, and conflicts reflect Hesse's own life. H. H.'s serpentine journey with its tantalizing enigmatic receptions and the romantically fantastic festival in Bremgarten are just as rooted in autobiography as is his personality: trek and highlights are but a transfigured amalgam of Hesse's five or six reading trips to south Germany from 1923 to 1929 and of the many festive receptions in the homes of his wealthy patrons in Zurich, Winterthur, and Bern. On the other hand, H. H.'s relationship with the supreme head of the Eastern Wayfarers and his ceremonious admission and readmission into the order are not fictionalized actuality but psychic process externalized in pure fantasy and playful mystification. H. H. and Leo are another of Hesse's double self-projections: the distraught individualist he actually was, and the confident master-servant he hoped he might become. Like Demian and Hermine, Leo is both the admonishing and enlightening "*daimon*" and the more ideal alter ego, rendered visible. And Leo's order is another of Hesse's ideal communities, another Kingdom of the Spirit accorded visibility. Admission to the order and Leo's presence symbolize H. H.'s awareness of and faith in a noumenal reality, and represent the first stage in his progression from an anxious seeker to a blithe Eastern Wayfarer. Leo's disappearance and H. H.'s defection from the order are tantamount to a disturbing loss of this vision and belief, a relapse to self-centered and troubled individualism, and a return to everyday reality and its agonies. Leo's reappearance, H. H.'s readmission to the order, and Leo's ultimate absorption and displacement of H. H., promised by the double-bodied figurine, connote faith restored and anticipate H. H.'s emergence as a master-servant and his selfless dedication to the transcendent world of art and thought, Hesse's own latest wish. Hesse's focus of interest had shifted from his characteristic self-concern and adjustment to the self to self-justification and adjustment to a community, a transcendent world. With this shift Hesse's renascent aestheticism, a blending of Lauscher's romanticism and Haller's Platonism, was complete.

In the summer of 1931, after four years together in their inadequate quarters in the Casa Camuzzi, Hesse and Ninon Dolbin moved into a house built nearby for their lifelong use by Hans C. Bodmer, another wealthy patron. They were married on 14 November. Hesse's third marriage afforded him the comfort and contentment that neither of his previous marriages had. His life began to revolve almost ritually around his writing, reading, extensive correspondence, music, painting, and gardening. With Adolf Hitler's rise to power in 1933, Hesse quickly became host and benefactor to a steady flow of German and Austrian refugee artists and intellectuals.

Hesse had permitted World War I to divert him from his conviction that an artist should divorce himself from politics, tend to his art, and nurture his humanitarian ideals; but his political activism had been of no advantage to himself, his art, or Germany. He remained more mindful of his better judgment during the political mayhem of the 1930s and World War II. Because of his public silence, Hesse's works continued to be published freely in Germany until he began to feature Catholic and Protestant writers in bad standing, and Jews in his reviews. Newspapers and periodicals throughout Germany suddenly lost interest in his literary comments. In 1935, when he began to contribute to Sweden's *Bonniers Litterära Magasin* surveys of contemporary German literature in which he continued to feature writers who had become silenced undesirables in Germany, he was assailed by the thoroughly Nazified journal *Die Neue Literatur* as a Jew-loving traitor. A letter written to the journal in self-defense only attracted more invective. While Nazis in Germany maligned Hesse for promoting the cause of Jewry in literature, émigré German Jews in Paris took him to task for abetting National Socialism by allegedly writing for the *Frankfurter Zeitung.* Hesse's public statement that he had stopped contributing to the paper when Hitler came to power was ineffectual, and he again lapsed into silence. Due to this silence, some of his older and politically innocuous works continued to be published throughout the war; but after the war broke out in 1939, rationed paper was suddenly no longer available for his new books.

What had been novelty and abundance in the Casa Camuzzi became primarily recollection and collection in the Casa Bodmer. Hesse's flood of tales, poetry, essays, and reviews gave way to a slow flow. From 1931 to 1945 new books appeared at regular intervals but consisted largely of earlier prose and poetry: *Vom Baum des Lebens* (From the Tree of Life, 1934), *Fabulierbuch* (1935), *Gedenkblätter* (Commemorations, 1937), *Neue Gedichte* (New Poems, 1937), and *Die Gedichte* (The Poems, 1942). During these fourteen years Hesse added to his fiction only a fairy tale, "Vogel" (Bird, 1932), and the last of his novels, *Das Glasperlenspiel* (The Glass Bead Game, 1943; translated as *Magister Ludi,* 1949). He received the Gottfried Keller Prize of Zurich in 1936.

It was in 1927 that it had first occurred to Hesse that a narrative in which a protagonist experiences the great epochs of history in several reincarnations, a biography both individual and archetypal, might give apt expression to the stable in life's flux, to the continuity of man's spiritual-intellectual tradition. *Die Morgenlandfahrt* expressed Hesse's unqualified extolment of and commitment to this timeless realm of the soul and the mind. Returning to his originally envisaged series of biographies soon after completion of *Die Morgenlandfahrt* in the spring of 1931, and reflecting further upon and almost immediately questioning and modifying his unconditional homage and dedication of 1931, Hesse proceeded slowly and tenaciously from segment to segment of the most challenging of his many literary ventures until *Das Glasperlenspiel* was completed in 1942. The book, purportedly written in the year 2400, comprises an introductory history of the Glass Bead Game; a biography of Josef Knecht, the celebrated Master of the Game in the educational province Castalia circa 2200; a cluster of his poems; and three of his conjectural autobiographies, official assignments preceding his admission to the Order of the Glass Bead Game. Exotic though Hesse could wax, his life and personal problems, interests, and convictions never ceased to be the stuff of his art. Autobiography had become the matrix of his tales of the past and the present; in *Das Glasperlenspeil,* the final installment of his serial projection of the self, it furnished the matter for a world of tomorrow. Although the last of Hesse's tales is less conspicuously personal than many of its predecessors, it is actually as autobiographical as, if not more autobiographical than, many of them. It not only highlights a particular period of Hesse's life but also draws heavily upon all of the preceding years. Young Knecht at the Latin School in Berolfingen, then at Castalia's elite school in Escholz, receives Hesse's schooling at Göppingen's Latin School

and at Maulbronn's exclusive church school. The little town of Waldzell owes its physical profile to Maulbronn, the Benedictine abbey Mariafels is indebted for its history and structural detail to Maulbronn's former Cistercian monastery, and Castalia and its order are derived from Hesse's impressions of Maulbronn and its monasticism. Knecht's following ten years of independent study and preparation for admission into the order equate with Hesse's journeyman years as a writer from *Peter Camenzind* to *Roßhalde.* Knecht treasures seclusion during this period in his career as much as had Hesse; the game becomes the passion for him that writing became for Hesse; and he achieves the fame that Hesse gained before World War I. The three to four years after Knecht's admission to the order and before his elevation to Castalia's most exalted magistery correspond to World War I in Hesse's career. This interim is for Knecht the hiatus of sociopolitical involvement it had been for Hesse: Knecht commits himself to a reconciliation of Castalia and the Catholic Church just as Hesse had committed himself to the cause of peace. The eight years between Knecht's investiture and his resignation and departure from Castalia correspond to the period in Hesse's life from the end of the war to the mid 1930s. These are for Knecht the years of dedicated application, major achievements, severe conflict, and drastic decision they had been for Hesse. Knecht now dedicates himself wholeheartedly to the bead game as Hesse had devoted himself to his writing: his seven grand annual games are counterparts to the seven major tales published by Hesse from *Demian* to *Die Morgenlandfahrt.* Success notwithstanding, life's polar possibilities gradually became for Knecht the crucial and disturbing concern they had become for Hesse. He is caught between isolation and contact, reflection and involvement, and the mind and the body, just as Hesse had been. He, like Hesse, is left convinced that he has become an artist but not a human among humans. He also becomes convinced that Castalia is less than the impeccable ideal he had believed it to be, just as Hesse had lost his unqualified faith in the timeless realm of art and thought courted in *Der Steppenwolf* and extolled in *Die Morgenlandfahrt.* And Knecht's eventual departure from Castalia is Hesse's farewell to Haller's Platonic Immortalia and to H. H.'s Order of Eastern Wayfarers, his commitment to social involvement is Hesse's final rejections of long-espoused aestheticism, and his hoped-for harmonious interplay of *vita contemplativa* and *vita activa* had become Hesse's latest and last ideal possibility. Nor did the novel's other main characters or even its supernumeraries draw any less heavily upon life than did its protagonist. The novel is one more of Hesse's appraisals of the self and life; the last stage of his preoccupation with self-realization and the climax of his serial quarrel with the real world. Each of the Knecht stories, like Sinclair's, Siddhartha's, Haller's, Goldmund's, and H. H.'s, is also a variant of what Hesse believed to be the timeless predicament of the artistically, intellectually, or spiritually gifted few vis-à-vis the mediocre many or the world at large. With their protagonists located in widely dispersed times and places, but similarly engrossed in thought and moved by ideals, the novels from *Demian* to *Die Morgenlandfahrt* were an unwitting expression of a growing interest and deepening belief in a universal spiritual-intellectual continuum. What is only intimated by this series of separate works and symbolically expressed by the timeless and widespread membership of Haller's Immortalia and H. H.'s Order of Eastern Wayfarers, is clearly illustrated and deliberately argued by Hesse's organized cluster of concluding tales with their common protagonist, who in several reincarnations experiences some of the major epochs of human history from the Stone Age to a distant future, and who in each reincarnation partakes of an appropriately different but analogous spiritual-intellectual tradition. In this novel, Hesse adds a philosophy of history to the psychology of history that he had proposed in the essays in *Blick ins Chaos* (A Glance into Chaos, 1920) to account for what he believed to be the inevitable and imminent cultural collapse of Western Europe. Immediately after World War I Hesse had been primarily intent upon the behavioral dynamics of culture; in *Das Glasperlenspiel* he fixed his attention upon the generative thrust behind all culture: the innate spiritual impulse of man. Cultures and cultural institutions are transitory, but the universal impulses of which these are temporary manifestations is a continuum that guarantees a constant flow of culture. Hesse's view of Knecht's resignation from the order and from Castalia to tutor Tito, his friend Designori's son, and his death plunge into a glacial lake in response to his ward's challenge was no less optimistic than this philosophy of history. Knecht's apparent defection is not caprice, panic, chance, or even choice, but dispositional inevitability. He, like every other of Hesse's protagonists, is essentially a nomad nowhere permanently at home, a seeker never satisfied, and a loner intolerant of ties and plagued by life's polarities. Once Knecht has tried all that Castalia has to offer and new possibility becomes insistent, the confines of the order turn intolerable. Synthesis, Knecht's old dream, emerges as a new pursuit. Life for Knecht will be no longer in Castalia or the world, *vita contemplativa* or *vita activa,* spirituality or sensuality, but both. Since this new possibility is an impossibility within the province, Knecht has no choice but to go beyond it. The Magister Musicae had been Knecht's model for self-realization in terms of the order, and Peter Jacobus had then become his model for self-realization in terms

of the world at large. In the characteristic manner of Hessean wards, Knecht had virtually absorbed both and become more than either. Like Knecht, Tito has two polar models: he is heir to his father's worldly heritage, and in Knecht's death he falls heir to his teacher's Castalian heritage. Like Knecht, Tito promises to become more than either of his models. He will not only realize the personal synthesis of life's polarities that his actual and spiritual fathers could only court but also will help achieve something of that synthesis of Castalia and the world to which Knecht and Designori could only look forward. Thus, thanks to Knecht, neither order nor Castalia succumbs to moral dry rot, and thanks to his impact on Tito they do not collapse for want of further support from the outside world. Castalia again emerges a conscientious guardian of cultural heritage and spiritual values, again becomes the socially responsible educational authority it formerly was, and again stocks the world's schools with dedicated teachers.

The final seventeen years of Hesse's life were relatively uneventful and tranquil. He gave his mornings and afternoons to gardening, painting, and his enormous correspondence, and his evenings to books, music, and writing. He left Montagnola as infrequently as he had in the 1930s; and then only briefly, and never for places beyond Switzerland, not even when awarded the Goethe Prize of Frankfurt am Main and the Nobel Prize for literature in 1946. With this national and international recognition, Hesse suddenly became the dean of German letters, a celebrity feted in Germany, Switzerland, and Austria upon the occasion of his seventieth birthday and on every fifth anniversary thereafter. But Hesse was far less elated by this official and popular acclaim than he was troubled by gradually declining health. Though quite fragile by the late 1950s, he continued to paint and to write.

For the septuagenarian Hesse, the world of memory gradually became the fascination and consolation that the world of the imagination had been at the beginning of his career, and that *Der Steppenwolf*'s Platonic realm of life's Immortals had become in mid career. Remembrance of things past produced a steady flow of memorials, congratulatory articles, reminiscences, ruminations, and circular letters. Many of these were brought together in such miscellanies as *Krieg und Frieden* (War and Peace, 1946), *Späte Prosa* (Late Prose, 1951), and *Beschwörungen* (Conjurations, 1955). No fiction was written during these final years, and only some fifty poems, some of which appear in *Stufen* (Stages, 1961) and *Die späten Gedichte* (The Late Poems, 1963). The last period of Hesse's life was also one of literary entrenchment. A lifetime's work was sifted and made more readily available in numerous reprints, in new editions, and particularly in such collections as *Traumfährte* (Dream Trail, 1945), *Frühe Prosa* (Early Prose, 1948), and the *Gesammelte Dichtungen* (Collected Writings, 1952).

This lively publication of old and new material became even livelier following Hesse's death of leukemia on 9 August 1962. A new edition of his collected works appeared in 1970 and another in 1977, and these were complemented by more than a dozen volumes of letters and several dozen volumes of miscellanies in the series Suhrkamp Taschenbuch and Biliothek Suhrkamp.

Hesse arrived in 1904 with the publication of *Peter Camenzind,* and his following grew with each subsequent book. German readers felt comfortable with his traditional stories and poetry and looked forward eagerly to his next publication and, by 1914, he had become a pleasant reading habit. But his wartime essays with their disparagement of militarism and nationalism and their censure of Germany quickly reduced him to an undesirable draft dodger and traitor.

If the older generations brushed Hesse aside during the war, youth extolled him in the sociopolitically chaotic postwar years. *Demian's* apotheosizing of the individual and its apolitical gospel of self-knowledge and self-realization struck respondent chords. Youth was offered a new credo and new possibility; Hesse became its idol and *Demian* its bible. But youth's exaltation was short-lived: spreading communism on the one hand and budding National Socialism on the other proved to be too enticing. Hesse's popularity declined slowly but steadily in the 1920s, then rapidly after the Nazis came to power in 1933. Hesse now became a rank "Jew-lover" and a classical example of the insidious poisoning of the German soul by Freud's psychoanalysis. By the mid 1930s Hesse was on the blacklist of virtually every newspaper and periodical in Germany, and by the outbreak of World War II Switzerland and Austria were the only outlets for his new book publications.

Literary history repeated itself after the war. A Germany in physical and spiritual shambles again turned to Hesse for moral guidance; notoriety again became celebrity. Hesse was awarded the Wilhelm Raabe Prize of Braunschweig in 1950, was appointed a member of the Friedensklasse des Ordens Pour le Merité in 1955, and received the Peace Prize of the German Book Trade, also in 1955; he was feted nationally on his birthdays; and his books could not be published fast enough to meet the swelling demand. This reverential acclaim peaked in the mid 1950s, then declined rapidly. By the early 1960s, Hesse was again relegated to the limbo of spent writers. A relatively small following of enthusiasts continued to read him, but the postwar generation of Germans remained unresponsive to his world of private concerns, preferring such sociopolitically committed authors as Bertolt Brecht, Günter Grass, and Peter Weiss.

Yet another wave of interest in Hesse began to spread in Germany in the early 1970s, occasioned in large part by America's Hesse boom of the 1960s. His books again became best-sellers, and in 1977, on his hundredth birthday, he was again publicly celebrated throughout Germany. But by the early 1980s, despite the vigorous promotion of his publisher, another wave of popularity had spent itself.

Until World War I, Hesse was acclaimed by German literary critics and scholars no less than he was enjoyed by the German reading public. He was a writer with a soul, a lyricist reminiscent of Joseph von Eichendorff, an observer of life's little comedies and tragedies in the manner of Gottfried Keller, and an author with a most promising future. During the Weimar Republic from 1919 to 1933, scholarly interest became progressively less widespread and less favorable, and politically tainted negative criticism began to be heard. This trend culminated in the strident political and literary rejection of Hesse in Hitler's Germany between 1933 and 1945. By the mid 1930s new editions of older works and new book publications virtually ceased even to be reviewed, let alone given scholarly attention, and whatever modicum of consideration university professors had accorded Hesse in the 1920s ended abruptly.

With the collapse of National Socialism in 1945 and Hesse's Nobel Prize in 1946, German critics and scholars, like Germany's reading public, suddenly rediscovered Hesse. For the next decade he enjoyed both political and literary approval as never before. The swell of books, pamphlets, dissertations, articles, and reviews surpassed by far, in both quality and quantity, all the secondary literature of the preceding four decades. An undesirable German of questionable literary merits had become a man of insight, foresight, and humanity, an heir to the noblest heritage of the German people, a guide and inspiration for his fellow humans, and a worthy addition to Germany's pantheon of illustrious authors. Contrary views were almost as rare and muted as those of Hesse's defenders had been during the preceding twelve years. But Germany's literary industry continued to be fickle. Almost immediately after Hesse's eightieth birthday in 1957, there was just as sudden and sharp a decrease in every manner of scholarly interest, and by the mid 1960s it was again virtually dead. Another reversal in fortune was in full swing by the mid 1970s. An elitist, solipsistic, asocial epigone romantic, ignorant of the ways of the world, was again worthy of intense and appreciative scholarship, and remained so on into the early 1980s. Many of the most discerning of Germany's Hesse studies belong to this last and not yet fully exhausted Hesse revival.

By 1946 only three of Hesse's major works had been translated into English. Reviews were politely condescending or by and large superciliously negative, and none of the books found a reading public. When *Demian* appeared in 1923, it was brushed aside in the *Boston Transcript* of 14 April as "a nightmare of abnormality, a crazed dream of a paranoiac." In *Bookman*, October 1929, *Steppenwolf* was disposed of as "a peculiarly unappetizing conglomeration of fantasy, philosophy, and moist eroticism." *Death and the Lover (Narziss und Goldmund)* elicited polite praise in 1932 but, like the other two books, did little more for decades than gather dust in a few bookshops and warehouses. Little wonder that the English-speaking world raised its eyebrows when Hesse was awarded the Nobel Prize. Few knew who Hesse was, and to most of these few he was but another odd and suspect German writer. For the next fifteen years the critics were generally unimpressed, and the reading public apparently had better things to do than to read Hesse, Nobel Prize winner though he was.

Publishers, however, alerted to a potential market by the prize, began to scramble for translations that had previously gone begging. *Magister Ludi (Das Glasperlenspiel)* appeared in 1949, *Siddhartha* in 1951, *Gertrude* in 1955, *The Journey to the East* in 1956, *The Prodigy (Unterm Rad)* in 1957, and *Peter Camenzind* in 1961. Despite this commercial priming of Hesse's pump, his works continued to sell relatively poorly until the beginning of the Hesse boom in the mid 1960s. Now suddenly, what had long been inconsequential became acutely relevant. Almost everyone seemed to be reading or talking about Hesse. Book after book became a best-seller, and their author was a sensation, by far the most popular of foreign writers.

Unprepared for this sudden swell of interest in Hesse, with no backlog of unpublished translations, publishers had to make do with the nine novels available in English by 1961. Hesse's remaining novels, as well as many short stories, essays, poetry, and letters, did not appear in English translation until the 1970s; fourteen volumes of this material were published from 1970 to 1976. By 1976 the tide that had begun to sweep across America in the mid 1960s and that had peaked in 1970 had spent itself. The deluge was over, but not before almost fifteen million copies of Hesse's works had been sold within a single decade—a literary phenomenon without precedent in America.

American Hesse scholarship followed in the wake of the general public's attraction to and the publishers' financial interest in Hesse. Before 1946 the scholarly field was oblivious of Hesse; in the years following it gradually picked up momentum with the appearance of half a dozen books and pamphlets, twenty-seven dissertations, and some sixty articles. Scholarly activity accelerated in the mid 1960s and crested in 1973–1974, a few years after the reading community had already begun to lose its interest in Hesse. As many dissertations, more articles, and four times as many books and pamphlets were written from the mid 1960s to the mid 1970s as in the preceding two decades. Scholarly activity then tapered off to become a slow but steady flow. American Hesse scholarship is now second in quantity only to its German counterpart and has in quality outstripped it.

In America Hesse was a pied piper whose song was heard and heeded from the Atlantic to the Pacific. It knew no age or social barriers. It attracted high school and university students and their parents, beatniks, hippies, real estate agents, car salesmen, tradesmen, and bankers. The rush of readers was followed by a rash of journalistic articles in leading periodicals, sporting such telling titles as: "Hermann Hesse: Poet of the Interior Journey," "The Flowering of the Hippies," "The New Mendicants," "The Outsider," "Eastward Ho," "Connoisseur of Chaos," "Saint Hesse among the Hippies," and "The Hesse Trip." While the journalistic world advertised Hesse, the world of scholarship began to scrutinize him, and professors from Princeton to Berkeley proceeded to spread the gospel in English translation in their foreign literature courses.

Nor did the business world or the world of entertainment remain immune to what was called "the Hesse virus." Demian's Rathskeller appeared in Princeton, Siddhartha's Pad in Bloomington, a Magic Theater coffee shop in Philadelphia, a Siddhartha restaurant and Glass Bead Game boutique in New York, and a Steppenwolf bookshop in Aspen; Siddhartha's began to sell waterbeds in San Francisco, and Berkeley got its Magic Theater, Steppenwolf bar, Castalia school supply store, and its Siddhartha with oriental rugs and exotica; the world of music inherited the Steppenwolf Rock Quintet, the Demian Singers, and Abraxas records; television paid its respects with "American Dream" (1971); and the movies *Siddhartha* (1973) and *Steppenwolf* (1974); Siddhartha found his way into the comic strips and the dog Snoopy of "Peanuts" became a Hesse fan. Hesse's impact was both wide and powerful. He remained a conspicuous part of the cultural scene of "new America" for almost a decade.

In the mid 1950s Hesse expressed the belief that America was not likely ever to be taken with his inward-directed individualism and his almost exclusive preoccupation with the individual. Hesse was wrong: it was precisely his brand of extreme individualism with its focus on the inner self and his concern for the individual more than for the world at large that found sudden favor in America. This individualism, together with Hesse's related disparagement of modern society but firm faith in life and his touch of Orientalism, account in great part for the Hessomania that swept the country. America in the 1960s was as though primed for this type of fare. Its middle-aged were disenchanted, its youth were rebellious, and skepticism and cynicism were widespread. For many, and for youth in particular, America had become a stifling, mass-oriented, excessively materialistic, morally and culturally bankrupt society. Hesse's social criticism confirmed this spreading conviction, his individualism offered new possibilities, and his unshakable belief in the ultimate meaningfulness of life was a welcome antidote to the twentieth century's bleaker view of things. Hesse became a rallying point for protest and change, a kindred soul, a support, and an inspiration for an enthusiastic following of dissidents, seekers, and estranged loners drawn from both the establishment and the counterculture.

Espousal of the individual, social criticism, a positive view of life, and propitious cultural moment notwithstanding, Hesse's name would hardly have become a byword in America but for his ability to universalize autobiography. His tales depict his life and his concerns, but they also mirror the lives and concerns of his readers. It is this ready identification of reader with protagonist and in turn with author that makes Hesse a life and not just a literary experience. Hesse's motley array of American enthusiasts were all troubled people drawn to a troubled writer. Each found something of the self in Hesse's works, and all found needed or attractive new possibilities.

This widespread personal commitment to Hesse has been the case no less in countries other than German- and English-speaking ones, and Hesse's popularity worldwide has been no less fluctuating than it has been in Germany and in the United States. The Nobel Prize briefly reawakened an earlier interest in Hesse in Denmark, France, Holland, and Sweden; America's Hesse boom had brief cultish reverberations in Denmark, Holland, Sweden, and Finland in the early 1970s; and in the late 1970s the international celebration of the hundredth anniversary of Hesse's birth occasioned a broad and again brief Hesse renaissance. Worldwide interest in Hesse continued to simmer in the eighties and nineties. The success of the biennial *Intrenationales Hermann-Hesse-Kolloquium Calw* (1977–) is reflective of this continued interest. The ninth meeting of the colloquium in May 1997 attracted the usual large crowd of enthusiastic laymen and scholars.

Hesse excelled in the depiction of personal crisis and private agony; such literature seems to be particularly popular during periods of cultural crisis, which accounts by and large for Hesse's idolization in Germany immediately after two devastating wars no less than for his similar idolization in America during the politically and socially chaotic 1960s and 1970s. Similar swells of popularity at future times are not unthinkable. Hesse's fortunes will probably continue to rise and fall with the times. It is this ebb and flow that is likely to secure his place in both German and world literature.

Letters:

Briefe (Berlin & Frankfurt am Main: Suhrkamp, 1951);

Ein Handvoll Briefe (Zurich: Büchergilde Gutenberg, 1951);

Hermann Hesse/Romain Roland: Briefe (Zurich: Fretz & Wasmuth, 1954);

Kindheit und Jugend vor Neunzehnhundert: Hermann Hesse in Briefen und Lebenszeugnissen, 2 volumes, edited by Ninon Hesse and Gerhard Kirchhoff (Frankfurt am Main: Suhrkamp, 1966, 1978);

Hermann Hesse/Thomas Mann: Briefwechsel, edited by Anni Carlsson (Frankfurt am Main: Suhrkamp, 1968);

Hermann Hesse/Peter Suhrkamp: Briefwechsel, edited by Siegfried Unseld (Frankfurt am Main: Suhrkamp, 1969);

Hermann Hesse/Helene Voigt-Diederichs: Zwei Autorenporträts in Briefen, edited by Bernhard Zeller (Düsseldorf & Cologne: Diederichs, 1971);

Hermann Hesse/Karl Kerényi: Briefwechsel aus der Nähe, edited by Magda Kerényi (Munich & Vienna: Langen-Müller, 1972);

Gesammelte Briefe, 4 volumes, edited by Volker Michels (Frankfurt am Main: Suhrkamp, 1973, 1979, 1982, 1986);

Briefe an Freunde: Rundbriefe 1946–1962, edited by Michels (Frankfurt am Main: Suhrkamp, 1977);

Christian Wagner/Hermann Hesse: Ein Briefwechsel, edited by Friedrich Pfäfflin (Stuttgart-Bad Cannstatt: Dr. Cantz'sche Druckerei, 1977);

Hermann Hesse/R. J. Humm: Briefwechsel, edited by Michels and Ursula Michels (Frankfurt am Main: Suhrkamp, 1977);

Herman Hesse/Heinrich Wiegand: Briefwechsel, edited by Klaus Pezold (Berlin & Weimar: Aufbau, 1978);

Der kuriose Dichter Hans Morgenthaler: Briefwechsel mit Ernst Morgenthaler und Hermann Hesse, edited by Roger Perret (Basel: Lenos, 1983);

Hermann Hesse/Hans Sturzenegger: Briefwechsel, edited by Kurt Bächtold (Schaffhausen: Meili, 1984).

Bibliographies:

Horst Kliemann and Karl H. Silomon, *Hermann Hesse: Eine Bibliographische Studie* (Frankfurt am Main: Bauersche Giesserei, 1947);

Joseph Mileck, *Hermann Hesse and His Critics: The Criticism and Bibliography of Half a Century* (Chapel Hill: University of North Carolina Press, 1958);

Helmut Waibler, *Hermann Hesse: Eine Bibliographie* (Bern & Munich: Francke, 1962);

Otto Bareiss, *Hermann Hesse: Eine Bibliographie der Werke über Hermann Hesse,* 2 volumes (Basel: Maier-Bader, 1962–1964);

Martin Pfeifer, *Hermann-Hesse-Bibliographie: Primär- und Sekundärschriftum in Auswahl* (Berlin: Schmidt, 1973);

Mileck, *Hermann Hesse: Biography and Bibliography,* 2 volumes (Berkeley: University of California Press, 1977).

Biographies:

Hugo Ball, *Hermann Hesse: Sein Leben und sein Werk* (Berlin: Fischer, 1927; revised edition, Zurich: Fretz & Wasmuth, 1947);

Bernhart Zeller, ed., *Hermann Hesse: Eine Chronik in Bildern* (Frankfurt am Main: Suhrkamp, 1960);

Zeller, *Hermann Hesse in Selbstzeugnissen und Bilddokumenten* (Reinbek bei Hamburg: Rowohlt, 1963); translated by Mark Hallebone as *Portrait of Hesse: An Illustrated Biography* (New York: Herder & Herder, 1971);

Volker Michaels, ed., *Hermann Hesse: A Pictorial Biography* (New York: Farrar, Straus & Giroux, 1975);

Michaels, ed., *Hermann Hesse: Sein Leben in Bildern und Texten* (Frankfurt am Main: Suhrkamp, 1979);

Gisela Klein, *Ninon und Hermann Hesse: Leben als Dialog* (Sigmaringen: Thorbecke, 1982);

Herbert Schnierle-Lutz, *Literaturreisen auf den Spuren Hermann Hesses von Calw nach Montagnola* (Stuttgart & Dresden: Klett, 1991);

Uli Rothfuss, *Hermann Hesse privat: In Texten, Bildern und Dokumenten* (Berlin: edition q, 1992).

References:

Ursula Apel, ed., *Hermann Hesse: Personen und Schlüsselfiguren in seinem Leben,* 2 volumes (Munich & London: Saur, 1989);

Sunil Bansal, *Das mönchische Leben im Erzählwerk Hermann Hesses* (Frankfurt am Main & Bern: Lang, 1992);

Günter Baumann, *Hermann Hesses Erzählungen im Lichte der Psychologie C. G. Jungs* (Rheinfelden: Schäuble, 1989);

Fritz Böttger, *Hermann Hesse: Sein Leben und sein Werk* (East Berlin: Verlag der Nation, 1974);

Mark Boulby, *Hermann Hesse: His Mind and Art* (Ithaca, N.Y.: Cornell University Press, 1967);

Friedrich Bran and Martin Pfeifer, eds., *Begegnungen mit Hermann Hesse* (Bad Liebenzell: Gengenbach, 1984);

Bran and Pfeifer, eds., *Hermann Hesse Glasperlenspiel* (Bad Liebenzell: Gengenbach, 1987);

Bran and Pfeifer, eds., *Hermann Hesse und die Religion* (Bad Liebenzell: Gengenbach, 1990);

Bran and Pfeifer, eds., *Hermann Hesse und seine literarischen Zeitgenossen* (Bad Liebenzell: Gengenbach, 1982);

Bran and Pfeifer, eds., *Wege zu Hermann Hesse: Dichtung, Musik, Malerei, Film* (Bad Liebenzell: Gengenbach, 1988);

Gert E. Bruhn, *Hermann Hesse: Biographer of the Soul* (New York: Regina, 1975);

Edwin F. Casebeer, *Hermann Hesse* (New York: Warner Paperback Library, 1972);

Kyung Yang Cheong, *Mystische Elemente aus West und Ost im Werk Hermann Hesses* (Frankfurt am Main & Bern: Lang, 1991);

Ursula Chi, *Die Weisheit Chinas und "Das Glasperlenspiel"* (Frankfurt am Main: Suhrkamp, 1976);

Werner Dürr, *Hermann Hesse: Vom Wesen der Musik in der Dichtung* (Stuttgart: Silberberg, 1957);

Helga Esselborn-Krumbiegel, *Hermann Hesse: "Der Steppenwolf"* (Munich: Oldenbourg, 1985);

G. W. Field, *Hermann Hesse* (New York: Twayne, 1970);

Field, *Hermann Hesse: Kommentar zu sämtlichen Werken* (Stuttgart: Hans-Dieter Heinz, 1977);

Ralph Freedman, *Hermann Hesse: Pilgrim of Crisis* (London: Cap, 1979);

Vridhagiri Ganeshan, *Das Indienerlebnis Hermann Hesses* (Bonn: Bouvier, 1974);

Edmund Gnefkow, *Hermann Hesse* (Freiburg im Breisgau: Kirchhoff, 1952);

Siegfried Greiner, *Hermann Hesse: Jugend in Calw* (Sigmaringen: Thorbecke, 1981);

Richard C. Helt, *A Poet or Nothing at All: The Tübingen and Basel Years of Hermann Hesse* (Providence, R.I. & Oxford: Berghahn, 1996);

Adrian Hsia, *Hermann Hesse und China* (Frankfurt am Main: Suhrkamp, 1974);

Hsia, ed., *Hermann Hesse heute* (Bonn: Bouvier, 1980);

Walter Jahnke, *Hermann Hesse: Ein Erlesener Roman* (Paderborn: Schöningh, 1984);

Claudia Karstedt, *Die Entwicklung des Frauenbildes bei Hermann Hesse* (Bern & Frankfurt am Main: Lang, 1983);

Astrid Khera, *Hermann Hesses Romane der Krisenzeit in der Sicht seiner Kritiker* (Bonn: Bouvier, 1978);

Andreas Kiryakakis, *The Idea of Heimat in the Works of Hermann Hesse* (New York & Bern: Lang, 1988);

Rudolf Koester, *Hermann Hesse* (Stuttgart: Metzlersche Verlagsbuchhandlung, 1975);

Annette Kym, *Hermann Hesses Rolle als Kritiker: Eine Analyse seiner Buchbesprechungen in März, Vivos Voco, und Bonniers Litterära Magasin* (Bern & Frankfurt am Main: Lang, 1984);

Judith Lieberman, ed., *Hermann Hesse: A Collection of Criticism* (New York: McGraw-Hill, 1977);

Michael Limberg, ed., *Hermann Hesse in seinen Briefen* (Bad Liebenzell: Gengenbach, 1994);

Limberg, ed., *Kunst als Therapie: Hermann Hesse und die Psychoanalyse* (Bad Liebenzell: Gengenbach, 1997);

Hans Jürg Lüthi, *Hermann Hesse: Natur und Geist* (Stuttgart: Kohlhammer, 1970);

Carlee Marrer-Tising, *The Reception of Hermann Hesse by the Youth in the United States* (Bern & Frankfurt am Main: Lang, 1982);

Richard B. Matzig, *Hermann Hesse in Montagnola: Studien zu Werk und Innenwelt* (Basel: Amerbach, 1947);

Gerhart Mayer, *Die Begegnung des Christentums mit den asiatischen Religionen im Werk Hermann Hesses* (Bonn: Röhrscheid, 1956);

Volker Michels, ed., *Materielen zu Hermann Hesses "Demian,"* 2 volumes (Frankfurt am Main: Suhrkamp, 1996–1997);

Michels, ed., *Materielen zu Hermann Hesses "Das Glasperlenspiel,"* 2 volumes (Frankfurt am Main: Suhrkamp, 1973–1974);

Michels, ed., *Materielen zu Hermann Hesses "Siddhartha,"* 2 volumes (Frankfurt am Main: Suhrkamp, 1975–1976);

Michels, ed., *Materielen zu Hermann Hesses "Der Steppenwolf"* (Frankfurt am Main: Suhrkamp, 1972);

Michels, ed., *Über Hermann Hesse,* 2 volumes (Frankfurt am Main: Suhrkamp, 1976–1977);

Joseph Mileck, *Hermann Hesse: Life and Art* (Berkeley: University of California Press, 1978);

Martin Pfeifer, ed., *Hermann Hesse und die Politik* (Bad Liebenzell: Gengenbach, 1992);

Pfeifer, ed., *Hermann Hesses weltweite Wirkung: Internationale Rezeptionsgeschichte,* 2 volumes (Frankfurt am Main: Suhrkamp, 1977–1979);

Pfeifer, *Hesse Kommentar zu sämtlichen Werken* (Munich: Winkler Verlag, 1980);

Edmund Remys, *Hermann Hesse's Das Glasperlenspiel: A Concealed Defence of the Mother World* (Bern & Frankfurt am Main: Lang, 1983);

David G. Richards, *Exploring the Divided Self: Hermann Hesse's "Steppenwolf" and its Critics* (Columbia, S.C.: Camden House, 1996);

Richards, *The Hero's Quest for the Self: An Archetypal Approach to Hesse's Demian and Other Novels* (Lanham, Md.: University Press of America, 1987);

Ernest Rose, *Faith from the Abyss: Hermann Hesse's Way from Romanticism to Modernity* (New York: New York University Press, 1965);

Uli Rothfuss, ed., *Erinnerungen der Söhne an ihren Vater Hermann Hesse* (Calw: Kreissparkasse Calw, 1996);

Jörg Röttger, *Die Gestalt des Weisen bei Hermann Hesse* (Bonn: Bouvier, 1980);

Hans Rudolf Schmid, *Hermann Hesse* (Frauenfeld: Huber, 1928);

Max Schmid, *Hermann Hesse: Weg und Wandlung* (Zurich: Fretz & Wasmuth, 1947);

Klaus von Seckendorff, *Hermann Hesses propagandische Prosa: Selbstzerstörerische Entfaltung als Botschaft in seinen Romanem vom Demian bis zum Steppenwolf* (Bonn: Bouvier, 1982);

Eugene L. Steltzig, *Hermann Hesse's Fictions of the Self* (Princeton: Princeton University Press, 1988);

Heinz Stolte, *Hermann Hesse: Weltscheu und Lebensliebe* (Hamburg: Hansa, 1971);

text + kritik: Zeitschrift für Literatur, special Hesse issue, 10/11 (May 1977);

Lewis W. Tusken, *Understanding Hermann Hesse: The Man, His Myth, His Metaphor* (Columbia: University of South Carolina Press, 1998);

Siegfried Unseld, *Begegnungen mit Hermann Hesse* (Frankfurt am Main: Suhrkamp, 1975);

Unseld, *Hermann Hesse: Werk und Wirkungsgeschichte* (Frankfurt am Main: Suhrkamp, 1985);

Kurt Weibel, *Hermann Hesse und die deutsche Romantik* (Winterthur: Keller, 1954);

Uwe Wolff, *Hermann Hesse: Demian–Die Botschaft vom Selbst* (Bonn: Bouvier, 1979);

Helmut W. Ziefle, *Hermann Hesse und das Christentum* (Wuppertal & Zurich: Brockhaus, 1994);

Theodore Ziolkowski, ed., *Hesse: A Collection of Critical Essays* (Englewood Cliffs, N.J.: Prentice-Hall, 1973);

Ziolkowski, *The Novels of Hermann Hesse: A Study in Theme and Structure* (Princeton: Princeton University Press, 1965);

Ziolkowski, *Der Schriftsteller Hermann Hesse* (Frankfurt am Main: Suhrkamp, 1979).

Papers:

Hermann Hesse's extensive *Nachlaß* (literary remains) is housed in the Hermann-Hesse-Archiv of the Schiller-Nationalmuseum, Marbach am Neckar. Significant additional Hesseana is housed in the Hermann-Hesse-Museum in Calw and in the Höri-Museum in Gaienhofen, Switzerland.

Das Hildebrandslied

(circa 820)

Brian Murdoch
University of Stirling

This entry originally appeared in DLB 148: German Writers and
Works of the Early Middle Ages: 800–1170.

Manuscript: The work is preserved (incomplete) on the front and back pages (1r and 76v) of a collection of ecclesiastical writings in Kassel, Landesbibliothek, Cod. theol. fol. 54. Facsimile: In Hanns Fischer, *Schrifttafeln zum althochdeutschen Lesebuch* (Tübingen: Niemeyer, 1966), pp. 12–13.

First publication: J. G. Eckhart, *Commentarii de rebus Francio* (Würzburg: Magenav, 1729).

Standard editions: In *Denkmäler deutscher Poesie und Prosa aus dem VIII.–XII. Jahrhundert,* edited by K. Müllenhoff and W. Scherer, third edition, edited by Elias von Steinmeyer (Berlin: Weidmann, 1892); in *Die kleineren althochdeutschen Sprachdenkmäler,* edited by Steinmeyer (Berlin: Weidmann, 1916); in Georg Baesecke, *Das Hildebrandslied: Eine geschichtliche Einleitung für Laien, mit Lichtbildern der Hs., alt-und neuhochdeutschen Texten* (Halle: Niemeyer, 1945); in Siegfried Gutenbrunner, *Von Hildebrand und Hadubrand* (Heidelberg: Winter, 1976), pp. 11–33; in *Althochdeutsches Lesebuch,* edited by Wilhelm Braune, sixteenth edition, edited by Ernst Ebbinghaus (Tübingen: Niemeyer, 1979).

Editions in modern German: In *Älteste deutsche Dichtungen,* edited by Karl Wolfskehl and Friedrich von der Leyen (Frankfurt am Main: Insel, 1964), pp. 6–9; in *Deutsche Balladen,* edited by Konrad Nussbacher (Stuttgart: Reclam, 1967), pp. 3–8; in *Althochdeutsche Literatur,* edited by Horst Dieter Schlosser (Frankfurt am Main: Fischer, 1970), pp. 264–267; in *Älteste deutsche Dichtung und Prosa,* edited by Heinz Mettke (Leipzig: Reclam, 1976), pp. 78–83.

Editions in English: Translated by Bruce Dickins, in *Runic and Heroic Poems of the Old Teutonic Peoples* (Cambridge: Cambridge University Press, 1915), pp. 78–85; translated by Brian Murdoch as

"From the Old High German: Hildebrand," *Lines Review* (Edinburgh), 109 (June 1989): 20–22.

The author of *Das Hildebrandslied* (The Lay of Hildebrand, circa 820) is not known, nor is it known why it was written down on the blank front and back pages of a Latin manuscript from the monastery of Fulda in northern Germany in the early ninth century. Its immediate origin is also unknown, although the extant version clearly stands at the end of a long and complex process of transmission. It is incomplete; the story lacks the last few lines, although it is not difficult to reconstruct what is missing. It is written in an impossible mixture of High and Low German because someone has tried, but failed, to translate a High German original into Low German. This feature presents less of a problem for understanding the work than does its incompleteness and the misplacement of some lines toward the end. The poem, thus, requires a certain amount of editorial work before it is readable, but it then emerges not only as the sole surviving example in Old High German of a heroic warrior poem in alliterative verse–a genre that survives far more fully in Anglo-Saxon and Old Norse–but also as an extremely well-presented and tightly told narrative that deals with universal problems.

The story is simple and is told mostly in dialogue between the two protagonists. Two groups of warriors face each other, and from each a champion comes forward to fight in single combat. The winner will be entitled to the armor and battle gear of the other. Although the two armies do not play an active role in the narrative, they are always present and should never be forgotten: they are the social background that forces each man to fight, whether he wants to or not. Finally, the two champions are father and son; the audience of the poem knows the situation, but neither the champions nor their armies are aware of it at the beginning. The two champions parley before the combat, and Hildebrand realizes that Hadubrand is his son when Hadubrand tells him that his father was called Hildebrand, that he was a great warrior, and that he had fled with Dietrich (Theoderic) from the wrath of Odoacer, leaving a bride and a baby. This information has come to him from people who are now dead, and passing sailors have told him that Hildebrand died in battle.

Hildebrand tells his son who he is and offers him a token of friendship:

> want her do ar arme   wuntana bauga,
> cheisuringu gitan,   so imo se der chuning gap,
> Huneo truhtin. . . . (lines 33–35)

> (He took from his arm   a torque of twisted gold,
> of imperial gold   given him by the king,
> lord of the Huns. . . .)

It is significant that the narrator speaks these lines, since the protagonists are usually left to speak for themselves; only the scene setting at the start and the battle at the end are fully in the hands of an objective narrator. After telling the audience in line 4 that the pair are father and son (using the single Old High German word *sunufaturungo*) the poem launches almost at once into dialogue. Thus the description of the arm ring is shown to be crucial in the work. Apparently Hildebrand has fought, under Theoderic's command, for the Huns and has been rewarded for his bravery. But Hadubrand assumes that the older man is trying to throw him off his guard and that, since he is wearing Hunnish gold, he *is* a Hun who has survived so long only because he cheats in this way. Hadubrand's response is a sharp one:

> mit geru scal man   geba infahan,
> ort widar orte. (lines 37–38)

> (you should take such gifts   with a spear,
> point against point.)

He accuses Hildebrand of trying to trick him and (if a textual emendation is correct) goes on to say that Hildebrand can never have been the exile he claims to be. Hildebrand realizes that his situation and the presence of the silent watchers and listeners give him no choice; he will have to fight, either killing his son or being killed by him. Almost with a shrug, he bows to the inevitable:

> welaga nu, waltant got . . . wewurt skihit (line 49)

> (alas, God above . . . cruel fate will take its course)[.]

The son reinforces his rejection of the trickery of this supposed Hun by restating, rather than surmising, that his father is dead, killed in battle, since the sailors had told him so. Once the older man realizes the impossibility of identifying himself to his son, he comments that only the most cowardly of the Eastern people—a reference to the Huns, perhaps—would refuse to fight, and the battle has to begin. Once again, as so often before, the only way Hildebrand can prove who he is— Hildebrand, the most famous warrior—is by fighting, and this time he has to do so by killing his only son. He can prove his identity only by destroying his family line. The winner in such a contest would have the right to take the armor from his dead adversary, and there is a massive irony in the father's final words: that the son can take his armor if he has any right to it, for the son has a legal right to the old man's belongings once Hildebrand is dead, but he now stands to obtain this inheritance by unknowingly killing his father. He speculates that this feat should be easy for the son, since he— Hildebrand—is so old. These words are the most poignant of the whole work, in which there are several expressions of the role of tragic necessity.

The poem breaks off in the midst of a brief (since the various stages are covered quickly) and somewhat stylized battle description. Some critics have taken the piece to be self-contained and not a fragment at all; at all events, it is not primarily a battle poem. Although theoretically various conclusions are possible—death of the son, death of the father, death of both men, or some kind of mediation that stops the fight—only the first fits into the context of the work. The story of the father/son conflict is an archetype in world literature—the best-known examples are the death of Sohrab in battle with Rustum in the Persian epic, known in English through Matthew Arnold's 1853 poem, and the killing of his son by Cuchullain in the Old Irish tale—and almost invariably ends this way, even though a thirteenth-century German version, the so-called *Jüngeres Hildebrandslied* (Later Lay of Hildebrand), has a reconciliation brought about by the mother. For the son to kill the father would be tragic, but not a tragedy, because the son has no reason to believe that this man is his father and is convinced that he has a Hun as an opponent. The pair could kill each other, but for the poem to end with a double death would be horror, not tragedy. Hildebrand clearly kills his son, his actual posterity, so that his reputation can live on. A series of strophes attached to a manuscript of the Old Norse *Saga of Asmund* and known in German as "Hildebrand's Sterbelied" (Death Song of Hildebrand) refers to the speaker's having killed his son, his own heir, against his will. That he is the greatest of warriors has at the last told against him; the gifts of the gods are always two-edged.

The only thing that mitigates the tragedy is the one thing that—according to another Old Norse poem, the *Havamal* (Words of the High One)—does not die: the reputation of the warrior. The real inheritance left by Hildebrand is the *Hildebrandslied* itself, the song composed after the battle.

The monastery had Anglo-Saxon connections, which perhaps accounts for the use of Anglo-Saxon characters in the text (most notably the runic sign for *w*). The *Hildebrandslied* was probably written down in the third or fourth decade of the ninth century, seemingly by two different scribes, at Fulda. That the language was originally Old High German and that the attempt was made to adapt it into Low German (and not vice versa) was established only after years of scholarly debate when it was noted that one part alliterates only in Old High German. Furthermore, the extant text is clearly a copy of a written work, not a transcription of an oral one: when the scribe wrote the name Deotrihhe (Theoderic) in line 26 his eye obviously went back to the last occurrence of the name, in line 23, and he repeated a few words from that line.

The basic verse form is the heroic alliterative long line, found in Old Norse and Anglo-Saxon on a far greater scale than in Old High German, where there are only a few examples and where the form soon gave way to the Latin-influenced end-rhyming verse demonstrated so fully in Otfried von Weißenburg's *Evangelienbuch* (Gospel Book, between 863 and 871). The Germanic alliterative long line falls into two parts, with a strong caesura, and each half line typically contains two strong beats. The first beat of the second half line is the most important, and it carries the alliteration; that is, at least one and sometimes both of the strong beats in the first half line will begin with the same sound (an identical consonant or group of consonants, or any vowel alliterating with others). The final strong beat of the whole line rarely alliterates. The form is a regular and forceful one, and the weight of sense placed on the first strong beat of the second half is considerable:

mit *g*éru scál man   *g*éba infáhan

(literally: with a spear should one   gifts accept)[.]

The poem also uses formulas—set phrases that fit the meter and are convenient to use when no major point is being made. Some of the description of the arming of the two men and of the battle is told in lines that can be matched in Anglo-Saxon or Old Norse, and Hildebrand's asking the younger man about his father contains phrases used by Otfried for the Devil's attempt to find out who Christ is. Some lines are repeated within the work itself.

In the version that has survived many lines are corrupt, parts seem to be missing or have been changed, and additions have been made. Just when these modifications were made is not known, nor is it known precisely when the translation into Low German was attempted. Any assertions about the earlier stages of the poem have to be speculative, since this is the only version in existence. Although some critics have insisted on keeping the text exactly as it stands, one particular editorial problem needs noting. Most of the poem is in dialogue, the speeches of the father alternating with those of the son. At one point, however, this alternation seems confused. Hadubrant says that his father is definitely dead (line 43):

tot ist Hiltibrant,   Heribrantes suno

(dead is Hildebrand,   Heribrand's son)[.]

The next line is a repeated formula that underscores, with the alliteration and the similar names (Heribrant, Hiltibrant, Hadubrant), the family relationship that is the point of the piece:

Hiltibrant gimahalta   Heribrantes suno

(Hildebrand spoke,   Heribrand's son)[.]

The placing is effective, but Hildebrand now apparently says that he can see from his adversary's armor that he has never been an exile. If this is really Hildebrand speaking, it is rather self-pitying; the argument has been made that these words really belong to Hadubrand and are part of his expression of disbelief that the man he sees before him can be his exiled father. Indeed, the line that follows this brief speech inserts, in addition to the somewhat anomalous reference to God, a metrically impossible indication of the fact that this is still Hildebrand speaking, as if the scribe or his predecessor realized at this point that things were confused. Just how the lines should be rearranged has never been established, but the comments on exile do look as if they should be spoken by the son and not the father.

The poem clearly has a long ancestry. The names Theoderic (Dietrich) and Odoacer (Ottokar) and the reference to the king of the Huns (Attila) place the story into the context of the Goths in the fifth century. The Goths, a Germanic tribe in southeastern Europe, were divided into two groups. The Visigoths (West Goths) moved westward and eventually took Rome. By the end of the fifth century Rome was under the rule of Odoacer. He was killed in 493 at Ravenna by the Ostrogoths (East Goths) under Theoderic; a generation earlier the Ostrogoths had been allied with the Huns under Attila. Theoderic ruled the western part of the

First page of the manuscript for the Hildebrandslied *(Kassel, Landesbibliothek, Cod. theol. fol. 54)* old Roman Empire until 526. His success led to a revision of the actual events that appears regularly in Germanic heroic stories for many centuries. In the literary tradition Theoderic had a right to rule in Rome but was wrongfully supplanted by Odoacer and went into exile with a few men (including Hildebrand) at the court of Attila. This distorted and anachronistic version is the background of the *Hildebrandslied*. A Gothic original has been presumed, and it is thought that the poem moved to Italy, where it was taken up by the Germanic successors of the Goths, the Lombards; the names of the central characters are Lombardic (Hildebrand's name, for instance, is spelled at least once as Hiltibraht). From northern Italy the poem might well have passed to Bavaria, and thence to Fulda in its final and least successful linguistic leap, to the would-be Low German form in which it now exists.

The poem is, in essence, fatalistic and pre-Christian; the few references to God are exclamatory and usually fail to fit the meter, and there is no afterlife in the poem except that of fame and reputation. Hildebrand does not even live on in his son. The work bears a straightforward interpretation as a tragedy, and within the context of father/son conflicts it is striking in the tightness of the noose drawn by fate around Hildebrand. Other interpretations of the work have been offered, however, which are linked with the attempt to explain why it was written down in Fulda in the first decades of the ninth century at a time when its style and content were clearly antiquated.

The work has been seen as the expression of a legal conflict (emphasizing the word *dinc* in line 32 as an equivalent to the Latin *causa* [case, legal dispute]). The proffered gift has been considered an attempt on Hildebrand's part to rejoin his clan. From another point of view the theme is Hadubrand's revenge for his father's abandonment of him and his mother. According to another related interpretation, the song may have been written down as a document to be used in the settlement of family feuds, indicating the possible consequences of neglecting one's familial responsibilities.

While Hildebrand's acceptance that he must kill his own son in the service of his overlord, Theoderic, has sometimes been viewed as the ultimate expression of the warrior virtue of loyalty, it has also been taken as a warning *against* the heroic ideal, which can lead to tragedies of this nature. Further, Hadubrand's obdurate refusal to accept this man as his father has been taken as a condemnation of the Germanic warrior ethos, with Hildebrand's conciliatory attempt a rejection of those values and an embodiment of the Christian virtues of *sapientia et fortitudo* (wisdom and fortitude). This interpretation, however, overlooks the fact that Hadubrand has no reason to believe Hildebrand and every reason—

probability, hearsay evidence, and the offer of an armband that associates his opponent with the Huns—not to do so. Also, the Lay of Hildebrand confirms, simply by existing, the reputation of the heroic warrior. In an Old Norse poem a character who knows that his life will be a tragic one seeks reassurance that the right songs will be sung about him after his death; he is comforted when he is told that this will be the case.

The style and content of the *Hildebrandslied* clearly look back to a time far earlier than the ninth century, possibly bespeaking an antiquarian interest on the part of the monks who wrote the work down, but the heroic ideal and the style of the poem were not quite as antiquated in the Saxon north as in the south. At all events the tragic necessity, the problem of identity, and the irony of fame are universals that have allowed the work to hold its literary value, even if the reasons for its appearance in Fulda remain obscure.

Bibliographies:

H. van der Kolk, *Das Hildebrandslied: Eine forschungsgeschichtliche Darstellung* (Amsterdam: Scheltema & Holkema, 1967);

J. Sidney Groseclose and Brian O. Murdoch, *Die althochdeutschen poetischen Denkmäler* (Stuttgart: Metzler, 1976), pp. 31–41.

References:

J. Knight Bostock, *A Handbook on Old High German Literature,* second edition, revised by K. C. King and D. R. McLintock (Oxford: Clarendon Press, 1976), pp. 43–82;

Ernst Ebbinghaus, "The End of the Lay of Hiltibrant and Hadubrant," in *Althochdeutsch,* volume 2, edited by Rolf Bergmann, Heinrich Tiefenbach, and Lothar Voetz (Heidelberg: Winter, 1987), pp. 670–676;

Ebbinghaus, "Some Heretical Remarks on the Lay of Hiltibrant," in *Festschrift Taylor Starck* (The Hague: Mouton, 1964), pp. 140–147;

A. T. Hatto, "On the Excellence of the *Hildebrandslied:* A Comparative Study in Dynamics," *Modern Language Review,* 68 (1973): 820–838;

Wolfgang Haubrichs, *Die Anfänge,* volume 1/i of *Geschichte der deutschen Literatur,* edited by Joachim Heinzle (Frankfurt am Main: Athenaeum, 1988), pp. 147–159;

Joachim Heinzle, "Rabenschlacht und Burgundenuntergang im *Hildebrandslied?,*" in *Althochdeutsch,* volume 2, pp. 667–684;

Werner Hoffmann, "Das *Hildebrandslied* und die indo-germanische Vater-Sohn-Kampf-Dichtung," *Beiträge* (Tübingen), 92 (1970): 26–42;

Hoffmann, "Zur geschichtlichen Stellung des *Hildebrandsliedes*," in *Festschrift M.-L. Dittrich* (Göppingen: Kümmerle, 1976), pp. 1–17;

Herbert Kolb, "Hildebrands Sohn," in *Studien zur deutschen Literatur des Mittelalters,* edited by Rudolf Schützeichel and Ulrich Fellmann (Bonn: Bouvier, 1979), pp. 51–75;

Willy Krogmann, *Das Hildebrandslied in der langobardischen Urfassung hergestellt* (Berlin: Schmidt, 1959);

Hugo Kuhn, "Stoffgeschichte, Tragik und formaler Aufbau im *Hildebrandslied*" and "Hildebrand, Dietrich von Bern und die Nibelungen," in his *Text und Theorie* (Stuttgart: Metzler, 1969), pp. 113–140;

Richard H. Lawson, "The *Hildebrandslied:* Originally Gothic?," *Neuphilologische Mitteilungen,* 74 (1973): 333–339;

W. P. Lehmann, "*Das Hildebrandslied,* ein Spätzeitwerk," *Zeitschrift für deutsche Philologie,* 81 (1962): 24–29;

Rosemarie Lühr, *Studien zur Sprache des Hildebrandsliedes* (Frankfurt am Main & Bern: Lang, 1982);

Friedrich Maurer, "*Hildebrandslied* und *Ludwigslied,*" *Der Deutschunterricht,* 9, no. 2 (1957): 5–15;

William C. McDonald, "Too Softly a Gift of Treasure: A Re-reading of the Old High German *Hildebrandslied,*" *Euphorion,* 78 (1984): 1–16;

D. R. McLintock, "The Language of the *Hildebrandslied,*" *Oxford German Studies,* 1 (1966): 1–9;

McLintock, "Metre and Rhythm in the *Hildebrandslied,*" *Modern Language Review,* 71 (1976): 565–576;

McLintock, "The Politics of the *Hildebrandslied,*" *New German Studies,* 2 (1974): 61–81;

H. H. Meier, "Die Schlacht im *Hildebrandslied,*" *Zeitschrift für deutsches Altertum,* 119 (1990): 127–138;

Birgit Meineke, *Chind und Barn im Hildebrandslied vor dem Hintergrund ihrer althochdeutschen Überlieferung* (Göttingen: Vandenhoek & Ruprecht, 1987);

Brian Murdoch, *Old High German Literature* (Boston: Twayne, 1983), pp. 55–64;

Frederick Norman, *Three Essays on the Hildebrandslied* (London: Institute of Germanic Studies, 1973);

K. Northcott, "*Das Hildebrandslied:* A Legal Process?," *Modern Language Review,* 56 (1961): 342–348;

W. Perrett, "On the *Hildebrandslied,*" *Modern Language Review,* 31 (1936): 532–538;

Alain Renoir, "The Armor of the *Hildebrandslied,*" *Neuphilologische Mitteilungen,* 78 (1977): 389–395;

Renoir, "The Kassel Manuscript and the Conclusion of the *Hildebrandslied,*" *Manuscripta,* 23 (1979): 104–108;

Renoir, *A Key to Old Poems: The Oral-Formulaic Approach to the Interpretation of West Germanic Verse* (University Park & London: Pennsylvania State University Press, 1988), pp. 133–156;

Werner Schröder, "Hildebrands tragische Blindheit und der Schluß des *Hildebrandsliedes,*" *Deutsche Vierteljahresschrift,* 37 (1963): 481–497;

Schröder, "Ist das germanische Heldenlied ein Phantom?," *Zeitschrift für deutsches Altertum,* 120 (1991): 249–256;

Rudolf Schützeichel, "Zum *Hildebrandslied,*" in *Festschrift Max Wehrli* (Zurich & Freiburg: Atlantis, 1969), pp. 83–94;

Ute Schwab, *Arbeo laosa: philologische Studien zum Hildebrandslied* (Bern: Francke, 1972);

Heather Stuart, "The *Hildebrandslied:* An Anti-heroic Interpretation," *German Life and Letters,* 32 (1978–1979): 1–9;

W. F. Twaddell, "The *Hildebrandslied* Manuscript in the USA," *Journal of English and Germanic Philology,* 73 (1974): 157–168;

Jan de Vries, "Das Motiv des Vater-Sohn-Kampfes im *Hildebrandslied,*" *Germanisch-romanische Monatsschrift,* 34 (1953): 257–274;

N. Wagner, "*Cheisuringu gitan,*" *Zeitschrift für deutsches Altertum,* 104 (1975): 179–188;

Roswith Wisniewski, "Hadubrands Rache: Eine Interpretation des *Hildebrandsliedes,*" *Amsterdamer Beiträge zur älteren Gemanistik,* 9 (1975): 1–12.

E. T. A. Hoffmann

(24 January 1776 – 25 June 1822)

Steven Paul Scher
Dartmouth College

*This entry was updated by Professor Scher from his entry
in* DLB 90: German Writers in the Age of Goethe, 1789–1832.

BOOKS: *Fantasiestücke in Callot's Manier: Blätter aus dem Tagebuche eines reisenden Enthusiasten,* anonymous, 4 volumes (Bamberg: Kunz, 1814–1815)—comprises volume 1, "Jacques Callot," "Ritter Gluck," "Kreisleriana Nro. 1–6," "Don Juan"; volume 2, "Nachricht von den neuesten Schicksalen des Hundes Berganza," "Der Magnetiseur"; volume 3, "Der goldene Topf: Ein Märchen aus der neuen Zeit," translated by Thomas Carlyle as "The Golden Pot," in his *German Romance: Specimens of Its Chief Authors* (Edinburgh: Tait, 1827; Boston: Munroe, 1841); volume 4, "Die Abenteuer der Silvester-Nacht," "Kreisleriana"; revised (1819);

Die Vision auf dem Schlachtfelde bei Dresden: Vom Verfasser der Fantasiestücke in Callots Manier, anonymous (Bamberg: Kunz, 1814);

Die Elixiere des Teufels: Nachgelassene Papiere des Bruders Medardus, eines Capuziners. Herausgegeben von dem Verfasser der Fantasiestücke in Callots Manier, anonymous (Berlin: Duncker & Humblot, 1815–1816); translated anonymously as *The Devil's Elixir,* 2 volumes (Edinburgh & London: Blackwood, 1824); translated by Ronald Taylor as *The Devil's Elixirs* (London: Calder, 1963);

Kinder-Mährchen, by Hoffmann, Karl Wilhelm Contessa, and Friedrich de la Motte Fouqué, 2 volumes (Berlin: Realschulbuchhandlung, 1816–1817);

Nachtstücke, herausgegeben von dem Verfasser der Fantasiestücke in Callots Manier, anonymous, 2 volumes (Berlin: Realschulbuchhandlung, 1817)—comprises volume 1, "Der Sandmann," translated by J. Oxenford as "The Sandman," in Oxenford and C. A. Feiling's *Tales from the German* (New York: Harper, 1844; London: Chapman & Hall, 1844); "Ignaz Denner"; "Die Jesuiterkirche in G.," translated by Oxenford as "The Jesuits Church in G-," in *Tales from the German;* "Sanctus"; volume 2, "Das öde

E. T. A. Hoffmann in 1821 (drawing by Wilhelm Hensel; by permission of the Nationalgalerie, Berlin)

Haus"; "Das Majorat," translated by Robert Pierce Gillies as "Rolaudsitten; or, The Deed of Entail," in his *German Stories* (Edinburgh: Blackwood, 1826); "Das Gelübde"; "Das steinerne Herz";

Seltsame Leiden eines Theater-Direktors: Aus mündlicher Tradition mitgeteilt vom Verfasser der Fantasiestücke in Callots Manier, anonymous (Berlin: Maurer, 1819);

Klein Zaches genannt Zinnober: Ein Mährchen herausgegeben von E. T. A. Hoffmann (Berlin: Dümmler, 1819);

Die Serapions-Brüder: Gesammelte Erzälungen und Mährchen. Herausgegeben von E. T. A. Hoffmann, 4 volumes (Berlin: Reimer, 1819–1821)–comprises volume 1, "Der Einsiedler Serapion"; "Rat Krespel," translated anonymously as "The Cremona Violin," in *Stories by Foreign Authors,* 2 volumes (New York: Scribners, 1898); "Die Fermate"; "Der Dichter und der Komponist"; "Ein Fragment aus dem Leben dreier Freunde"; "Der Artushof"; "Die Bergwerke zu Falun"; "Nußknacker und Mausekönig," translated by Mrs. Saint Simon as *Nutcracker and Mouse-king* (New York: Appleton, 1853); volume 2, "Der Kampf der Sänger"; "Eine Spukgeschichte"; "Die Automate"; "Doge und Dogaresse"; "Alte und neue Kirchenmusik"; "Meister Martin der Küfner und seine Gesellen," translated anonymously as "Master Martin and His Workmen," in *Beauties of German Literature: Selected from Various Authors* (London: Burns, 1847); "Das fremde Kind," translated anonymously as *The Strange Child: A Fairy Tale* (London: Rivington, 1852); volume 3, "Nachricht aus dem Leben eines bekannten Mannes"; "Die Brautwahl"; "Der unheimliche Gast"; "Das Fräulein von Scuderi," translated by Gillies as "Mademoiselle de Scuderi," in *German Stories;* "Spielerglück"; "Baron von B."; volume 4, "Signor Formica," translated anonymously as *Signor Formica: A Tale, in Which Are Related Some of the Mad Pranks of Salvator Rosa and Don Pasquale Capuzzi* (New York: Taylor, 1845); "Erscheinungen"; "Der Zusammenhang der Dinge"; "Die Königsbraut"; translated by Alexander Ewing as *The Serapion Brethren,* 2 volumes (London: Bell, 1886–1892);

Lebens-Ansichten des Katers Murr nebst fragmentarischer Biographie des Kapellmeisters Johannes Kreisler in zufälligen Makulaturblättern, 2 volumes (Berlin: Dümmler, 1820–1822); translated by A. R. Hope as "The Educated Cat," in *Nutcracker and Mouse King, and, The Educated Cat* (London: Unwin, 1892);

Prinzessin Brambilla: Ein Capriccio nach Jacob Callot (Breslau: Max, 1821);

Meister Floh: Ein Mährchen in sieben Abenteuern zweier Freunde (Frankfurt am Main: Wilmans, 1822); translated by G. Sloane as "Master Flea," in *Specimens of German Romance, Selected and Translated from Various Authors,* volume 2 (London: Printed for Whittaker, 1826); unexpurgated edition (Berlin: Bard, 1908);

Geschichten, Mährchen und Sagen, by Hoffmann, H. von den Hagen, and Heinrich Steffens (Breslau: Max, 1823);

Aus Hoffmann's Leben und Nachlass, edited by Julius Eduard Hitzig, 2 volumes (Berlin: Dümmler, 1823);

Die letzten Erzählungen von E. T. A. Hoffmann, edited by Hitzig, 2 volumes (Berlin: Dümmler, 1825)–comprises volume 1, "Haimatochare"; "Die Marquise de la Pivardiere"; "Die Irrungen: Fragment aus dem Leben eines Fantasten"; "Die Geheimnisse: Fortsetzung des Fragments aus dem Leben eines Fantasten"; "Der Elementargeist," translated by Oxenford as "The Elementary Spirit," in *Tales from the German;* "Die Räuber: Abenteuer zweier Freunde auf einem Schlosse in Böhmen"; volume 2, "Die Doppeltgänger"; "Datura fastuosa," translated anonymously as "The Datura Fastuosa: A Botanical Tale," *Dublin University Magazine,* 13 (1839): 707; "Meister Johannes Wacht"; "Des Vetters Eckfenster"; "Die Genesung: Fragment aus einem noch ungedruckten Werke";

Ausgewählte Schriften, 10 volumes (Berlin: Reimer, 1827–1828);

E. T. A. Hoffmann's Erzählungen aus seinen letzten Lebensjahren, sein Leben und Nachlaß, edited by Micheline Hoffmann, 5 volumes (Stuttgart: Brodhag, 1839);

Lied von E. T. A. Hoffmann (Altona: Hammerich, 1839);

E. T. A. Hoffmann's gesammelte Schriften, 12 volumes (Berlin: Reimer, 1844–1845);

E. T. A. Hoffmanns musikalische Schriften: Mit Einschluß der nicht in die gesammelten Werke aufgenommen Aufsätze über Beethoven, Kirchenmusik, etc. nebst Biographie, edited by H. vom Ende (Leipzig: H. vom Ende, 1889);

E. T. A. Hoffmann, Sämtliche Werke in 15 Bänden, edited by Eduard Greisbach, 15 volumes (Leipzig: Hesse, 1900);

Das Fräulein von Scuderi: Erzählung aus dem Zeitalter Ludwig des Vierzehnten, edited by Gustav Gruener (New York: Holt, 1907);

Meister Martin der Küfner und seine Gesellen: Erzählung, edited by Robert Herndon Fife Jr. (New York: Holt, 1907);

E. T. A. Hoffmanns Sämtliche Werke: Historischkritische Ausgabe, edited by Carl Georg von Maassen, 9 volumes (volumes 1–4, 6–7, Munich: Müller; volume 8, Berlin: Propyläen; volumes 9–10, Munich: Müller, 1908–1928);

E. T. A. Hoffmanns Werke in fünfzehn Teilen, edited by Georg Ellinger, 5 volumes (Berlin: Bong, 1912; revised, 1927);

E. T. A. Hoffmanns Tagebücher und literarische Entwürfe: Mit Erläuterungen und ausführilichen Verzeichnissen, edited by Hans von Müller (Berlin: Paetel, 1915);

Sämmtliche Werke: Serapions-Ausgabe, edited by Leopold Hirschberg, 14 volumes (Berlin: De Gruyter, 1922);

E. T. A. Hoffmann: Musikalische Werke, edited by Gustav Becking, 3 volumes (Leipzig: Linnemann, 1922–1927);

Die Maske: Ein Singspiel in 3 Akten (1799), edited by Friedrich Schnapp (Berlin: Verlag für Kunstwissenschaft, 1923);

Dichtungen und Schriften sowie Briefe und Tagebücher: Gesamtausgabe, edited by Walther Harich, 15 volumes (Weimar: Lichtenstein, 1924);

Handzeichnungen E. T. A. Hoffmanns in Faksimileleichtdruck nach den Originalen, mit einer Einleitung: E. T. A. Hoffmann als bildender Künstler, edited by Walter Steffen and Müller (Berlin: Propyläen, 1925); revised edition, edited by Schnapp (Hildesheim: Gerstenberg, 1973);

Der goldene Topf: Ein Märchen aus der neuen Zeit, edited by William Faulkner Mainland (Oxford: Blackwell, 1942);

E. T. A. Hoffmann: Poetische Werke, edited by Klaus Kanzog, 12 volumes (Berlin: De Gruyter, 1957–1962);

Gesammelte Werke: Neuausgabe, edited by Walter Müller-Seidel and others, 5 volumes (Munich: Winkler, 1960–1965); volume 5, part 1, revised by Schnapp as *Schriften zur Musik: Aufsätze und Rezensionen* (Munich: Winkler, 1977); volume 5, part 2, revised by Schnapp as *Nachlese: Dichtungen, Schriften, Aufzeichnungen und Fragmente* (Munich: Winkler, 1981);

Liebe und Eifersucht (Die Schärpe und die Blume): Ein Singspiel-Libretto in drei Aufzügen, nach dem Spanischen des Calderón und der Schlegelschen Übersetzung, edited by Schnapp (Munich: Winkler, 1970);

E. T. A. Hoffmann: Ausgewählte musikalische Werke, edited by Georg von Dadelsen and others, 8 volumes published (Mainz: Schott, 1970–)–comprises volumes 1–3, *Undine;* volumes 4–5, *Die lustigen Musikanten;* volume 10b, *Miserere;* volume 11, *Sinfonia Es-dur; Recitativo ed Aria "Prendi, l'acciar ti rendo";* volume 12b, *Quintett c-moll für Harfe, zwei Violinen, Viola und Violoncello; Grand Trio E-dur für Klavier, Violine und Violoncello;*

Tagebücher: Nach der Ausgabe Hans von Müllers mit Erlauterungen, edited by Schnapp (Munich: Winkler, 1971);

Juristische Arbeiten, edited by Schnapp (Munich: Winkler, 1973);

E. T. A. Hoffmann, edited by Schnapp (Munich: Heimeran, 1974);

Gesammelte Werke in Einzelausgaben, edited by Rudolf Mingau and Hans-Joachim Kruse, 8 volumes in 9 published (Berlin & Weimar: Aufbau, 1976–);

Der Musiker E. T. A. Hoffmann: Ein Dokumentenband, edited by Schnapp (Hildesheim: Gerstenberg, 1981);

Sämtliche Werke, edited by Hartmut Steinecke, Wulf Segebrecht, and others, 3 volumes in 4 published (Frankfurt am Main: Deutscher Klassiker Verlag, 1985–).

Editions in English: *Hoffmann's Strange Stories: From the German,* translated by Lafayette Burnham (Boston: Burnham, 1855)–comprises "Life of Hoffmann," "The Cooper of Nuremberg" ("Meister Martin, der Küfner, und seine Gesellen"), "The Lost Reflection" ("Die Abenteuer der Sylvester-Nacht"), "Antonia's Song" ("Rat Krespel"), "The Walled-up Door" ("Das Majorat"), "Berthold, the Madman" ("Die Jesuiterkirche in G–"), "Coppelius, the Sandman" ("Der Sandmann"), "Salvator Rosa" ("Signor Formica"), "Cardillac, the Jeweler" ("Das Fräulein von Scuderi"), "The Pharo-bank" ("Spielerglück"), "Fascination" ("Der Magnetiseur"), "The Agate Heart" ("Das steinerne Herz"), "The Mystery of the Deserted House" ("Das öde Haus");

Hoffmann's Fairy Tales, translated by Burnham (Boston: Burnham, 1857)–comprises "The Adventures of Traugott" ("Der Artushof"), "Annunziata" ("Doge und Dogaressa"), "The Chain of Destiny" ("Der Zusammenhang der Dinge"), "Ignaz Denner" ("Nachtstücke," part 1), "Little Zack" ("Klein Zaches");

Weird Tales by E. T. A. Hoffmann: A New Translation from the German, translated by John Thomas Bealby, 2 volumes (London: Nimmo, 1885; New York: Scribners, 1885)–comprises volume 1, "The Cremona Violin," "The Fermata," "Signor Formica," "The Sand-man," "The Entail," "Arthur's Hall"; volume 2, "The Doge and Dogess," "Master Martin the Cooper," "Mademoiselle de Scudéri," "Gambler's Luck," "Master Johannes Wacht";

Tales of Hoffmann, translated by Frederick MacCurdy Atkinson (London: Harrap, 1932; New York: Dodd, Mead, 1933)–comprises "The Interdependence of Things," "The Sandman," "The Mystery of the Deserted House," "The Lost Reflection," "The Walled in Door";

The Tales of Hoffmann: Stories by E. T. A. Hoffmann, translated out of the German by Various Hands (New York: Heritage Press, 1943)–comprises "The Sandman," translated by Bealby; "The Mines of Falun," translated by E. N. Bennett; "Councillor Krespel," translated by Barrows Munsey; "Don Juan," translated by Jacques Le Clercq; "The Mystery of the Deserted House," translated by Maria Labocceta; "The Vow," translated by F. E. Pierce; "Mademoiselle De Scudéry," translated by

Bealby; "The Entail," translated by Bealby; "The Uncanny Guest," translated by Alexander Ewing; "Gambler's Luck," translated by Bealby;

Tales of Hoffmann, edited by Christopher Lazare (New York: Wyn, 1946; republished, New York: Grove Press, 1959)–comprises "Mademoiselle de Scudéry," "Don Juan," "Antonia's Song," "The Golden Pot," "The Doubles," "The Vow," "The Fermata," "Berthold the Madman," "Salvator Rosa," "The Legacy";

Tales from Hoffmann: Translated by Various Hands, edited by J. M. Cohen (London: Bodley Head, 1950; New York: Coward-McCann, 1951)–comprises "The Golden Pot," "The Sandman," "The Deed of Entail," "The Story of Krespel," "Mlle de Scudéri";

Eight Tales of Hoffmann, Newly Translated, translated by Cohen (London: Pan, 1952)–comprises "The Lost Reflection," "The Sandman," "The Jesuit Church in Glogau," "The Deserted House," "Councillor Krespel," "The Mines of Falun," "A Ghost Story," "Gamblers' Luck";

The King's Bride, translated by Paul Turner (London: Calder, 1959);

The Tales of Hoffmann: Newly Selected and Translated from the German, translated by Michael Bullock (New York: Ungar, 1963)–comprises "The Sandman," "Mademoiselle de Scudery," "Datura Fastuosa," "The King's Bride," "Gambler's Luck";

The Best Tales of Hoffmann, edited by E. F. Bleiler (New York: Dover, 1967)–comprises "The Golden Flower Pot," "Automata," "A New Year's Eve Adventure," "Nutcracker and the King of Mice," "The Sand-man," "Rath Krespel," "Tobias Martin, Master Cooper, and His Men," "The Mines of Falun," "Signor Formica," "The King's Betrothed";

Selected Writings of E. T. A. Hoffmann, edited and translated by Leonard J. Kent and Elizabeth C. Knight, 2 volumes (Chicago: University of Chicago Press, 1969)–comprises volume 1, "Ritter Gluck," "The Golden Pot," "The Sandman," "Councillor Krespel," "The Mines of Falun," "Mademoiselle de Scuderi," "The Doubles"; volume 2, "The Life and Opinions of Kater Murr," books 1 & 2;

Three Märchen of E. T. A. Hoffmann, translated by Charles E. Passage (Columbia: University of South Carolina Press, 1971)–comprises "Little Zaches, Surnamed Zinnober," "Princess Brambilla," "Master Flea";

Tales, edited by Victor Lange (New York: Continuum, 1982)–comprises "The Golden Pot," "Councillor Krespel," "Mademoiselle de Scudéri," "The Mines of Falun," "The Fermata," "The Deed of Entail," "The Sandman";

Tales of Hoffmann, edited and translated by R. J. Hollingdale (Harmondsworth, U.K. & New York: Penguin,

1982)–comprises "Mademoiselle de Scudery," "The Sandman," "The Artushof," "Councillor Krespel," "The Entail," "Doge and Dogaressa," "The Mines of Falun," "The Choosing of the Bride";

Nutcracker, translated by Ralph Manheim (New York: Crown, 1984; London: Bodley Head, 1984);

E. T. A. Hoffmann's Musical Writings: Kreisleriana, The Poet and the Composer, Musical Criticism, translated by Martyn Clarke, edited, with an introduction, by David Charlton (Cambridge: Cambridge University Press, 1989);

The Golden Pot and Other Tales, edited and translated by Ritchie Robertson (Oxford: Oxford University Press, 1992)–comprises "The Golden Pot," "The Sandman," "Princess Brambilla," "Master Flea," "My Cousin's Corner Window."

An ironist and humorist par excellence, the prolific storyteller E. T. A. Hoffmann occupies a prominent place in the canon of nineteenth-century European literature. He is regarded today as the influential, eccentric genius of German Romanticism, whose distinctive fictional universe foreshadows late-twentieth-century sensibility. Sophisticated as well as entertaining, Hoffmann's fiction is quintessentially Romantic in thematic orientation, milieu, aesthetic and philosophical outlook, and narrative stance–and yet it also strikes contemporary readers as astonishingly modern. At the height of his writing career, Hoffmann was a best-selling author in Germany, and soon after his premature death at age forty-six he became known on the Continent through translation as the author of "weird" and fantastic tales–particularly in France and Russia, but also in England. The prominent poets and writers demonstrably inspired by Hoffmann's oeuvre include Gerard de Nerval, Honoré de Balzac, Victor Hugo, Alfred de Musset, George Sand, Alexandre Dumas père, Prosper Mérimée, and Charles Baudelaire in France; Sir Walter Scott, Thomas Carlyle, Charles Dickens, Robert Louis Stevenson, the Brontës, Oscar Wilde, and G. K. Chesterton in England; Samuel Beckett in Ireland; Edgar Allan Poe, Nathaniel Hawthorne, and Washington Irving in America; Alexander Pushkin, Nikolai Gogol, Ivan Turgenev, Fyodor Dostoyevsky, and Leo Tolstoy in Russia; Søren Kierkegaard, Hans Christian Andersen, Henrik Ibsen, and filmmaker Ingmar Bergman in Scandinavia; and Heinrich Heine, Hugo von Hofmannsthal, Thomas Mann, and Franz Kafka in German-speaking countries.

E. T. A. Hoffmann
born Königsberg in Prussia
on 24 January 1776
died Berlin on 25 June 1822
Court of Appeal Councillor

excellent
in office
as writer
as composer
as painter
Dedicated by his friends.

Perhaps this concise inscription on his tombstone captures best the existential dilemma that plagued the uncommonly talented Hoffmann throughout his life and shaped the all-pervasive dualistic worldview that he so consistently espoused: can one and the same individual live and work as an integral part of bourgeois society and be a free-spirited creative artist as well? Today it is little known that Hoffmann was a multiply gifted man and artist: he was not only the successful author of fantastic and grotesque tales but also an eminent jurist, a Romantic composer of considerable merit, a talented painter, draftsman, and caricaturist, as well as an experienced man of the theater. Ironically, it is the inauthentic, trivializing nineteenth-century image of the "Hoffmann of the Tales" that lives on in public consciousness, perpetuated by Jacques Offenbach's popular opera *Les Contes d'Hoffmann* (The Tales of Hoffmann, 1881) which portrays the title hero as a self-dramatizing Romantic fabulist, notorious drinker, and womanizer. And while Tchaikovsky's *Nutcracker* continues to be a perennial favorite of audiences the world over, few of its admirers realize that the scenario for the ballet is based on Hoffmann's tale "Nußknacker und Mausekönig" (1816; translated as *Nutcracker and Mouse-king,* 1853). Typically, even Hoffmann's tombstone stands to remind posterity of his accomplishment as a legal official first and not as the writer and composer E. T. A. Hoffmann who, in honor of Mozart, his idol, substituted Amadeus for his third given name, Wilhelm. "Es ist in meinem Leben etwas recht Charakteristisches," he wrote to a friend in 1814, contemplating his new appointment as a judge in Berlin, "daß immer das geschieht was ich gar nicht erwartete, sey es nun Böses oder Gutes, und daß ich stets das zu thun gezwungen werde, was meinem eigentlichen tieferen Prinzip widerstrebt." (It is something genuinely characteristic of my life that what happens is invariably what I least expect, whether for the worst or for the best, and that I am always compelled to do what runs counter to my deepest convictions.)

Ernst Theodor Wilhelm Hoffmann spent the first twenty years of his life in Königsberg, a university town on the Baltic Sea known chiefly for its most famous son, the philosopher Immanuel Kant. Hoffmann was born into troubled family circumstances: his parents, Christoff Ludwig and Luise Albertine Doerffer Hoffmann, divorced when he was barely two years old. Hoffmann endured a lonely childhood in the depressing household of his maternal grandmother, a religious fanatic, where he lived with his neurotic and perennially ill mother, two spinster aunts, and his uncle Otto Wilhelm Doerffer, a pedantic philistine who was dismissed from legal practice for incompetence. Hoffmann's psychologically unstable father, a descendant of lawyers and a civil servant himself, moved away and was not heard from again. The desolate family atmosphere did not, however, altogether stifle the boy's budding intellectual and artistic curiosity. Oddly enough, it was Uncle Otto, an avid amateur chamber musician, who gave the precocious child his first music lessons and thus planted the seeds of Hoffmann's lifelong passion for music. More systematic musical study followed, and soon he became quite proficient in music theory; learned to play the piano, violin, harp, and guitar; and—at age thirteen—began to compose. During these formative years he received instruction in the visual arts as well and developed his talent for drawing and painting. His reading habits were also formed in his early teens. Hoffmann and his playmate Theodor Gottlieb von Hippel, later a leading Prussian legal administrator and lifelong loyal friend, devoured contemporary adventure stories and popular novels along with the classics of European literature, among them the works of Johann Wolfgang von Goethe, Friedrich von Schiller, Jean Paul, William Shakespeare, Jonathan Swift, Laurence Sterne, Miguel de Cervantes, Jean-Jacques Rousseau, and Denis Diderot. Their particular favorites were Goethe's *Die Leiden des jungen Werthers* (The Sorrows of Young Werther, 1787), Sterne's *Sentimental Journey* (1768) and *Tristram Shandy* (1759–1767), and Rousseau's *Confessions* (1770).

In spite of his inclination toward the arts, Hoffmann yielded to family pressures and at age sixteen enrolled as a law student at Königsberg University. He pursued his legal studies conscientiously, passed his first law examination in 1795, and started working as a judicial aide at a local court. But, characteristically, when not on the job, he devoted himself totally to artistic pursuits—a double lifestyle he juggled throughout his career: "Sontag blühn bey mir Künste und Wissenschaften. . . . Die Wochentage bin ich Jurist und höchstens etwas Musiker, Sontags am Tage wird gezeichnet und Abends bin ich ein sehr witziger Autor bis in die späte Nacht." (On Sundays the arts and sciences are in flower for me. . . . Weekdays I am a jurist and at most a bit of a musician. In the daytime on Sundays I draw; in the evening and far into the night I am a very witty author.) Indeed, already in his late teens, in addition to musical composition, caricature drawing, and portrait and historical painting, the budding jurist experimented with writing fiction, though neither of the two novels he wrote at the time—the three-volume "Cornaro" and "Der Geheimnisvolle" (The Mystery Man)—survives.

While a law student, Hoffmann supported himself by giving music lessons. He fell in love with one of his pupils, Dora ("Cora") Hatt, an unhappily married woman ten years his senior. Though in 1796 he left Königsberg for a two-year stint as judiciary aide in the provincial Silesian town of Glogau, the passionate but hopeless affair was not terminated until 1798; it reappeared later in fictionalized form as the core of one of Hoffmann's best-known stories, "Das Majorat" (1817; translated as "Rolaudsitten; or, The Deed of Entail," 1826). In this narrative, which demonstrably inspired Edgar Allan Poe's famous 1839 ghost story "The Fall of the House of Usher," the young lawyer-narrator Theodor visits a haunted castle and falls unhappily in love with the baroness Seraphine, who shares his passion for music.

In Glogau, Hoffmann stayed with the family of another lawyer uncle and continued to compose and paint in his spare time. After the break with Cora he became engaged, however halfheartedly, to his first cousin Minna Doerffer. Upon passing his second judicial examination in 1798, with the help of his uncle he received a transfer to a new legal post in Berlin. For the first time in his life, Hoffmann was in his element: the Prussian capital offered him the intellectual and cultural excitement provincial Glogau so sorely lacked. He threw himself with a vengeance into Berlin's rich opera, concert, and theater life, frequented literary salons, and even found time to study composition with Johann Friedrich Reichardt, a central figure of contemporary German music who was also Goethe's friend and consultant in musical matters.

In 1799 Hoffmann completed his first substantial creative effort, a singspiel titled *Die Maske* (The Mask), which was discovered and published in 1923. That he wrote both the text and the music is an early confirmation of the musico-literary aspirations that he sustained throughout his life. Clearly indebted to the Italian opera buffa tradition and particularly to Mozart's *Don Giovanni* (1787), Hoffmann's favorite opera, the music is competently crafted. The libretto anticipates many of his later thematic preoccupations such as the split personality, the occult, insanity, inherited sin, and the demonic.

Hoffmann's first Berlin stay was cut short in 1800 by his promotion, after his final law examination, to a new legal post in the Prussian administration, this time in the Polish provinces at a higher court in Posen. Once again, life in the hinterlands had an adverse effect on the urbane young man, who sought solace in drinking and socializing. The bitterly satirical caricatures he drew of fellow legal officials and members of the local military elite earned him a disciplinary transfer to Plock, a tiny and even more provincial Polish town totally devoid of culture. Shortly before leaving Posen for Plock, Hoffmann broke off his engagement to Minna Doerffer, and on 26 July 1802 he married Michaelina ("Mischa") Rorer, a good-natured, stable, and loyal twenty-three-year-old Polish woman with whom he enjoyed lasting domestic bliss. Mischa's unfal-

tering devotion and support could, however, only partially mitigate the interminable two years in Plock; his diary entries record continued drinking, illnesses, a persecution complex, death visions, and doppelgänger fantasies. Yet, at night Hoffmann continued to compose and write. In 1803 he made it into print for the first time with a piece of musico-literary criticism, a short essay entitled "Schreiben eines Klostergeistlichen an seinen Freund in der Hauptstadt" (Letters from a Friar to His Friend in the Capital), which discusses the function of declamation and singing in drama. He also won honorable mention in a playwriting competition with a comedy called *Der Preis* (The Prize).

In 1804 the intervention of his friend Hippel rescued Hoffmann at last from his provincial "exile": he was appointed as government councillor in Warsaw. The Polish capital was a cultural haven at the time, and Hoffmann took full advantage of its offerings. His lasting friendship with Julius Eduard Hitzig, a fellow lawyer from Berlin and later his first biographer, also dates from the happy Warsaw years. Hitzig introduced him to the best of contemporary German literature, the writings of Friedrich and August Wilhelm von Schlegel, Novalis, Ludwig Tieck, and Clemens Brentano. Hoffmann resumed composition in earnest and even got a chance to conduct regularly in public orchestral concerts a sampling of his own music, along with works by Christoph Willibald von Gluck, Franz Joseph Haydn, Wolfgang Amadeus Mozart, Luigi Cherubini, and Ludwig van Beethoven. For a while Hoffmann's musical career seemed well under way. He composed some of his best works during the Warsaw period, among them a singspiel based on Brentano's comedy *Die lustigen Musikanten* (The Merry Minstrels, 1805); a mass in D minor (1805); his only symphony, in E-flat major (1806); a quintet for harp and string quartet in C minor (1807); and an opera entitled *Liebe und Eifersucht* (Love and Jealousy, 1807), for which he also wrote a libretto inspired by Spanish dramatist Pedro Calderón de la Barca.

In October 1806 Napoleon's armies occupied the Polish capital and dissolved the Prussian administration. Hoffmann, along with other legal officials, suddenly found himself without a livelihood and had to leave Warsaw. He sent his wife and infant daughter Cäcilia (who died shortly after at the age of two) to stay with relatives in Posen and decided to try his luck in Berlin, where he returned in the summer of 1807. His brief second Berlin stay turned out to be disappointing. The Napoleonic invasion had left the Prussian capital in shambles, and Hoffmann, who was penniless, was unable to make ends meet either as a jurist or a freelance artist. Finally, after a period of despair and even starvation, during which he nevertheless continued composing, painting, and drawing, he responded to a newspaper advertisement and accepted a position as music director of the theater in Bamberg in southern Germany. It seemed at last that Hoffmann might have a fair chance to fulfill his lifelong ambition to pursue the career of a professional musician.

Upon arrival in Bamberg in 1808, however, he found the theater nearly bankrupt, the artistic conditions debilitating, and the management fraught with internal strife. A few weeks after he assumed his duties as conductor and music director, he was unemployed once again. Though he retained his title, at the theater he merely functioned as artistic consultant and occasional composer of incidental music. To eke out a living, he gave piano and singing lessons. In 1810 he became hopelessly infatuated with fourteen-year-old Julia Mark, one of his voice pupils. The affair remained strictly one-sided, internalized, and sublimated in passionate diary entries. Julia was soon married off to a boorish Hamburg merchant, and Hoffmann never saw her again. But this all-consuming emotional experience, transfigured and poeticized, came to permeate many of Hoffmann's major narratives as a recurrent theme of the artist's idealized, unattainable beloved, forever the object of his infinite yearning and unfulfilled desire. For example, the Julia Mark affair forms the core of the 1814 story "Nachricht von den neuesten Schicksalen des Hundes Berganza" (An Account of the Latest Fortunes of the Dog Berganza), a fictionalized reminiscence about Hoffmann's time in Bamberg from the ironic perspective of a Cervantes-inspired talking dog. The motif also figures prominently as the Julia-Giulietta constellation in the tale "Die Abenteuer der Silvester-Nacht" (1815; translated as "A New Year's Eve Adventure," 1967) and in the Julia-Kreisler relationship of the novel *Lebens-Ansichten des Katers Murr nebst fragmentarischer Biographie des Kapellmeisters Johanes Kreisler in zufälligen Makulaturblättern* (1820–1822; translated as "The Life and Opinions of Kater Murr," in *Selected Writings of E. T. A. Hoffmann,* 1969).

Despite the emotional turmoil and pecuniary difficulties, the Bamberg years (1808–1813) were crucial for Hoffmann's evolving artistic career as musician, music critic, and writer of fiction. To be sure, throughout his Bamberg stay Hoffmann still regarded himself primarily as a musician. He composed here some of his finest music, such as the piano trio in E major (1809), a *Miserere* in B-flat minor (1809), the operas *Trank der Unsterblichkeit* (Potion of Immortality, 1808) and *Aurora* (1812), and began working on his musical magnum opus, the opera *Undine* (composed in 1813–1814). But while still composing, he turned increasingly to writing critical essays on the contemporary musical scene for the *Leipzig Allgemeine musikalische Zeitung,* the leading musical journal at the time. It was an ingenious blend of satirical music criticism and fantastic fiction that in February 1809 launched Hoffmann's career as both music critic and man of letters: the narrative "Ritter Gluck" (literally Sir Gluck, translated as "Ritter Gluck," 1969).

Hoffmann scholars unanimously agree that "Ritter Gluck," though a literary first, is an unusually accomplished piece which provides the key to understanding this multiply gifted writer: it embodies most of the traits and narrative strategies of his fictional universe that the term "Hoffmannesque" has come to signify. An extended anecdote rather than a short story, "Ritter Gluck"–subtitled "Eine Erinnerung aus dem Jahre 1809" (A Recollection from the Year 1809)–offers no real plot. In a Berlin outdoor café, the first-person narrator meets a curious old man, who claims to be a musician and raves mysteriously about having just been banished from the "kingdom of dreams," hospitable to true artistic talent, and condemned to reconcile his higher vision of truth with living in the philistine confines of the Prussian capital. The two become acquainted through a conversation praising the music of Mozart and Gluck and disparaging contemporary musical life in Berlin. Back at his lodgings, the stranger amazes the narrator by playing Gluck's 1777 opera *Armide* on the piano from a score of blank pages. Then, in the italicized concluding line of the story, the stranger at last reveals his identity: "*Ich bin der Ritter Gluck!*" (I am Chevalier Gluck!). The German title "Ritter" corresponds to the English "Sir" and implies knighthood, an honor that was indeed conferred on the composer Christoph Willibald Gluck, who died in 1787 in Vienna. But who, then, is Ritter Gluck, roving the streets of Berlin in 1809? A revenant, a mad musician who believes he is the great composer, or simply a creation of the daydreaming narrator? Who is the inquisitive narrator? And what about the parallel between the fictitious author of this musical reminiscence and the real author of the story, the struggling composer and budding writer E. T. A. Hoffmann? Typically, these and countless other questions remain unresolved, signifying that there are simply no clear-cut solutions to Hoffmann's puzzling narratives; ambiguity and multiple meanings reign supreme.

"Ritter Gluck" established Hoffmann's reputation as the author of a refreshingly original kind of music criticism. The numerous reviews of contemporary as well as earlier music that he regularly contributed to the *Allgemeine musikalische Zeitung* until 1815 combined broad aesthetic assessment and informed value judgments with competent yet not overly technical analysis. His insights into the creative process of the musical giants Giovanni Pierluigi da Palestrina, Johann Sebastian Bach, Gluck, Haydn, Mozart, and Beethoven are valid today and earned him recognition as the founder of modern music criticism. His Beethoven reviews, particularly that of the Fifth Symphony (1810), stand out as pioneering critical achievements. That Hoffmann considered reviewing music as a genuinely literary activity is borne out by the fact that his famous interpretive essay entitled "Beethovens Instrumental-Musik" (1814)– a recasting, without the analytical sections, of his reviews of the Fifth Symphony and two piano trios into a flowing narrative–became part of the first volume of his first literary publication in book form, the *Fantasiestücke in Callot's Manier: Blätter aus dem Tagebuche eines reisenden Enthusiasten* (Fantasy Pieces in the Manner of Callot: Sheets from the Diary of a Travelling Enthusiast, 1814–1815). It was in this epoch-making essay that Hoffmann, for the first time in the history of musical aesthetics, conjoined Haydn, Mozart, and Beethoven as the musical trinity that still perdures, pronounced Beethoven as a quintessentially Romantic artist, and formulated his influential definition of music as "die romantischste aller Künste, [. . .] denn nur das Unendliche ist ihr Vorwurf" (the most romantic of all the arts, [. . .] for its sole subject is the infinite). For Hoffmann, the term "Romantic" was a value judgment rather than a period designation. He interpreted Haydn, Mozart, and Beethoven as Romantic composers because he regarded them as the greatest, because in their works he could discern an unmediated aura of the demonic, the supernatural, and the inexpressible. A characteristic, musically inspired literary manifestation of Hoffmann's elusive romantic aura is the well-known fantasy piece "Don Juan" (1813; translated 1943), which has profoundly influenced critical appraisals of Mozart's opera, *Don Giovanni*. This enigmatic narrative oscillates between an autobiographically charged fictional frame and a partial analysis of the opera based on a curiously biased interpretation of the ambivalent Don Giovanni-Donna Anna relationship.

In the spring of 1813 Hoffmann accepted an offer to become music director of an opera company that performed alternately in Dresden and Leipzig. Just before he left Bamberg, he signed a contract for the publication of his *Fantasiestücke*, the first two volumes of which were to collect most of his writings to date. Since he was still determined to make a name for himself as a musician, he requested that his publisher print the work anonymously: "Ich mag mich nicht nennen, indem mein Name nicht anders als durch eine gelungene musikalische Composition der Welt bekannt werden soll." (I do not wish to be named, for my name should become known to the world by means of a successful musical composition and not otherwise.) Even after he had become a best-selling author, Hoffmann adhered to this resolution: not one of his literary works appeared under his own name until 1816, when his opera *Undine* was successfully staged and enthusiastically received in Berlin.

Hoffmann's brief stint as opera conductor in Dresden and Leipzig (1813–1814) was also his last employment as a professional musician. As his notoriously bad luck would have it, once again he found himself in the midst of the Napoleonic wars: he had to shuttle between the two besieged cities and conduct performances between battles. Yet, during his hectic, nine-month tenure as commuting conductor, Hoffmann managed to complete his operatic masterpiece *Undine* and the first part of the two-volume novel *Die Elixiere des Teufels: Nachgelassene Papiere des Bruders Medardus, eines Capuziners. Herausgegeben von dem Verfasser der Fantasiestücke in Callots Manier* (1815–1816; translated as *The Devil's Elixir*, 1824). In Dresden he also wrote his best-known tale, "Der goldene Topf: Ein Märchen aus der neuen Zeit" (1814)–which was translated by Carlyle in 1827 as "The Golden Pot"–and contributed two major pieces of music criticism to the *Allgemeine musikalische Zeitung*: "Der Dichter und der Komponist" (The Poet and the Composer, 1813) and "Alte und neue Kirchenmusik" (Ancient and Modern Church Music, 1814).

Hoffmann himself considered "Der goldene Topf" his best piece of writing. It is also perhaps his most representative work, for it illustrates best his poetics of storytelling: a characteristic fusion of fabulistic inventiveness, reader manipulation, and biting social satire imbued with humor and irony. Already the narrative's startling subtitle "A Modern Fairy Tale" signals the Hoffmannesque confrontation between the poetic fairy-tale world and the prosaic confines of every day. Like "Ritter Gluck," "Der goldene Topf" opens in a commonplace setting and concludes with an intimation of the supernatural as the realm of "true reality." Hoffmann formulates the principle for this paradigmatic story-telling strategy in a famous passage from the conversational frame of his *Die Serapions-Brüder: Gesammelte Erzählungen und Mährchen. Herausgegeben von E. T. A. Hoffmann* (1819–1821; translated as *The Serapion Brethren*, 1886–1892):

Ich meine, daß die Basis der Himmelsleiter, auf der man hinaufsteigen will in höhere Regionen, befestigt sein müsse im Leben, so daß jeder nachzusteigen vermag. Befindet er sich dann immer höher und höher hinaufgeklettert, in einem fantastischen Zauberreich, so wird er glauben, dies Reich gehöre auch noch in sein Leben hinein, und sei eigentlich der wunderbar herrlichste Teil desselben.

(I believe that the foot of the heavenly ladder, upon which we want to climb into higher regions, has to be anchored in life, so that everyone may be able to follow. If then, having climbed higher and higher, people find themselves in a fantastic, magical world, they will think that this realm, too, still belongs in their life and is actually its most wonderfully glorious part.)

"Der goldene Topf" is novelistic in form, dimension, and narrative technique. Hoffmann divides his tale into twelve vigils and gives each vigil elaborate and humorously elliptical headings that anticipate plot details intelligible only later in the appropriate narrative context. The basic story line is both disarmingly transparent and wondrously blurred; it revolves around the typically romantic protagonist Anselmus, a young, handsome, and talented social misfit. Amiably shy and clumsy, the student Anselmus shuttles between ordinary life in contemporary Dresden and the supernatural realm of snakes, salamanders, fire lilies, witches, enchanted gardens, and exotic birds. He spends his leisure time in the company of pedantic bureaucrats like Registrar Heerbrand and Dean Paulmann, courting Paulmann's lovely, blue-eyed daughter Veronica, who is not disinclined. But Anselmus, given to poetic reverie, also leads an entirely different sort of existence in the world of myth and magic. Here his adventures are remote-controlled by Lindhorst, a salamander and prince of the spirits who, as the eccentric Privy Archivarius, is also a respected citizen of Dresden. In the mythical fairy-tale realm Anselmus's beloved and muse is Serpentina, the little blue-eyed golden-green snake, who also happens to be one of Lindhorst's marriageable daughters. By the end of the tale Anselmus has become a poet: his quest for knowledge and self-realization is fulfilled as he symbolically graduates from Veronica's philistine world into Serpentina's redemptive realm of the imagination and attains "life in poetry" in mythical Atlantis. His reward is a golden flowerpot that signifies endurance and growth. Hoffmann's poetic allegory of the fundamental "dualism of being" has come full circle.

Hoffmann had to wait for public recognition as composer and storyteller until he was offered a chance—through the intervention of his influential friend Hippel—to return to Berlin, where he spent the remaining eight years of his life as a literary celebrity and respected civil servant. In February 1814 the destitute and disillusioned thirty-eight-year-old composer-conductor was ready to opt for a more settled lifestyle: however reluctantly, he decided to abandon his dream of a musical career and accepted a position in the Prussian judicial system. Within a mere two years he acquired a reputation as a brilliant jurist and rose in the legal hierarchy from unpaid court councillor to judge on the supreme court of appeals.

By 1816 Hoffmann was well known as the author of Fantasiestücke, the four-volume collection of his narratives including "Ritter Gluck," "Don Juan," "Der goldene Topf," the famous Beethoven essay, and other "Kreisleriana" pieces (featuring his musician alter ego, the eccentric and opinionated Kapellmeister Johannes Kreisler); and his first novel, Die Elixiere des Teufels, became a best-seller overnight. This intriguingly complex, ingeniously constructed forerunner of the sophisticated crime thriller and the modern psychological novel–replete with violence, lust, inherited guilt, rape, murder, incest, insanity, persecution complex, mistaken identities, split personalities, and doppelgänger–conjures up the demonic powers that emanate from the darkest recesses of the subconscious. The story of the runaway monk Medardus is a suspenseful spine-chiller from start to finish: cursed by the sins of his degenerate ancestors and led by Satan, Medardus becomes inextricably entangled in a series of lurid criminal adventures, for which he atones by recording his experiences before he dies.

With fourteen performances the hit of the 1816–1817 Berlin theater season, the opera Undine–one of the long line of German Romantic operas which includes Karl Maria von Weber's Der Freischütz (1821) and Richard Wagner's Lohengrin (1850)–established at last Hoffmann's reputation as a composer, and he began to publish his writings under his own name. The Undine libretto, however, was provided by Friedrich de la Motte Fouqué, the author of the well-known fairy tale of the same title (1811): the erotic story of the water nymph Undine, frustrated in her attempt to become a loved and loving woman. But Hoffmann's long-awaited operatic success was soon eclipsed by his literary fame as the best-selling author of the Fantasiestücke, the Elixiere des Teufels, and the dozens of diverse narratives he published during his remaining six years. By 1818 he commanded such a devoted reading public that despite his phenomenal productivity he could not keep up with the ever-increasing requests and commissions from publishers for new works. Encouraged by the success of his Fantasiestücke model, Hoffmann gathered the enormous literary harvest of his last years in two multivolume collections: Nachtstücke, herausgegeben von dem Verfasser der Fantasiestücke in Callots Manier (Night Pieces, edited by the Author of the Fantasy Pieces in the Manner of Callot, 1817) and Die Serapions-Brüder. Only his second and last novel, Kater Murr, and three longer narratives were published separately in book form: Klein Zaches genannt Zinnober: Ein Mährchen herausgegeben von E. T. A. Hoffmann (1819; translated as "Little Zaches, Surnamed Zinnober," 1971), Prinzessin Brambilla: Ein Capriccio nach Jacob Callot (1821; translated as "Princess Brambilla," 1971), and Meister Floh: Ein Mährchen in sieben Abenteuern zweier Freunde (1822; translated as "Master Flea," 1826).

The two volumes of Nachtstücke contain eight suspenseful stories, among them "Der Sandmann" (translated as "The Sandman," 1844), which inspired Sigmund Freud's celebrated essay on the "uncanny" that led to his formulation of the Oedipal castration complex, and "Das Majorat." The title for his collection Hoffmann borrowed from painting terminology: "night piece" fittingly conveys the uncanny, nocturnal aura of mystery and impending doom that permeates these tales of horror, replete with telepathy, hallucinations, and optical illusions and populated with ghosts, villains, murderers, and madmen. That throughout the nineteenth century the supreme mastery of narration evident in these stories went unnoticed seems inexplicable today. It was chiefly on account of the *Nachtstücke* (and the novel *Die Elixiere des Teufels*) that for years the author was labeled "Gespenster-Hoffmann" (Hoffmann of the ghosts) and his entire oeuvre degraded by insensitive critics as inferior, trivial literature.

With twenty-eight narratives in four volumes, *Die Serapions-Brüder* constitutes Hoffmann's largest collection. Like the *Nachtstücke,* this last collection includes some of his best-known tales such as "Nußknacker," "Rat Krespel" (translated as "Councillor Krespel," 1943), "Die Automate" (translated as "Automata," 1967), and "Das Fräulein von Scuderi" (translated as "Mademoiselle de Scuderi," 1826). But unlike the *Nachtstücke,* which is unified by a prevailing spooky atmosphere, *Die Serapions-Brüder* brings together many different kinds of fiction. In seemingly random succession, stories based on mesmerism, animal magnetism, somnambulism, and clairvoyance alternate with genuine fairy tales; chronicle-inspired narratives follow critical essays on musical aesthetics and the poetics of opera; and the first example of modern crime fiction ("Scuderi") coexists with stories exploring the creative process in music, painting, and literature. The underlying fictional frame that interrelates the diverse narratives is Hoffmann's unobtrusive device for integrating his poetics of storytelling into his own fiction: a series of sophisticated conversations in which six friends, members of the literary Serapion Brotherhood, first narrate and then discuss their works. Ingeniously enough, all of this is fictional: the narratives as well as the frame which presents criticism of fiction that is itself fiction.

The extraordinary narrative virtuosity that Hoffmann attained in *Kater Murr* secures this truly Romantic yet astonishingly modern novel a prominent place among the handful of outstanding epic monuments in nineteenth-century European literature. That Hoffmann's favorite double-optics principle propels this unique novelistic experiment is hinted at in his elaborate, ironic title echoing Sterne's title *The Life and Opinions of Tristram Shandy, Gentleman.* Clearly, in *Kater Murr* there are two seemingly unrelated protagonists and two distinct narratives that are also generically different: the memoirs of Tomcat Murr and an anonymous biography of the musician Kreisler promise to converge under the same cover. Moreover, Hoffmann signs himself as the editor of the work. Meister Abraham, Murr's owner and Kreisler's close friend, the only figure who appears in both narratives, may also be Kreisler's unidentified biographer. The complex fictionalizing process comes full circle when the reader begins to suspect that Abra-

ham and Kreisler are antithetical alter egos of the book's real author, E. T. A. Hoffmann.

Tomcat Murr's hilarious autobiographical disquisitions allow for plenty of vintage Hoffmannesque humor, parody, and satire. A delightfully unaware pseudointellectual with an overblown ego, Murr "unintentionally" unmasks contemporary society's pretentions, hypocrisy, and ignorance concerning the function and value of education, culture, and the arts. The feline author's "informed" account of cat and dog society evokes bourgeois societal conditions in Hoffmann's Germany so vividly that the two worlds virtually merge and animals become paradigmatic of humans. As Hoffmann's fictional musician alter ego, Johannes Kreisler figures prominently in the earlier *Kreisleriana* pieces. In *Kater Murr* he is an unappreciated composer-conductor in residence at the tiny court of an insignificant, intrigue-laden German principality. Like his creator, an ironist out of self-preservation, Kreisler embodies Hoffmann's conception of the exalted, disillusioned, and unfulfilled yet forever striving Romantic artist at odds with his social milieu.

By contrasting specific plot details in the Murr and Kreisler sections, Hoffmann skillfully integrates the heterogeneous narrative strains and character constellations of the novel. The complacent tomcat's reminiscences unfold in a coherent chronological sequence, while Kreisler's biography is presented in desultory, episodic fragments that reflect his eccentric, disjointed personal and artistic traits in tone, syntax, diction, and narrative structure. Kreisler's name (circler) subtly points to the circular compositional design underlying the Kreisler sections: though positioned first in the cycle of episodes, the opening Kreisler fragment is actually meant to conclude it as well. In a postscript to *Kater Murr,* "editor" Hoffmann reports Murr's death (his own real-life cat was also called Murr) and promises more of both stories to follow in a third volume, which he never wrote. Ironically, this purported openendedness, too, is part of the novel's overall fictional design.

During his last years, the constitutionally fragile Hoffmann continued to lead his precarious double existence and somehow managed to sustain simultaneously his literary and legal careers while also frequenting Berlin's salons and cafés. But once more politics interfered with his life. After the Napoleonic wars a period of reaction set in and Prussia became a police state. In 1819 Hoffmann was appointed to a newly formed legal commission to investigate subversive and demagogic activities, an added burden that must have hastened the onset of final illness. As a member of the commission, he courageously defended liberal intellectuals and students charged with fabricated crimes. When it leaked out that in the humorous tale

Meister Floh Hoffmann himself satirized police methods, the powerful and humorless chief of police started proceedings against him. The satirical passages had to be deleted before publication in the spring of 1822, and Hoffmann was interrogated and had to compose his own legal defense while on his deathbed. He escaped persecution only through his death from total paralysis of the nervous system on 25 June 1822.

E. T. A. Hoffmann is recognized today as a major nineteenth-century writer. But beyond his well-established literary fame as the "author of the tales," he will also be remembered as a distinguished jurist and an important figure in music history, a pioneer of modern music criticism.

Letters:

E.T. A. Hoffmann im persönlichen und brieflichen Verkehr: Sein Briefwechsel und die Erinnerungen seiner Bekannten, edited by Hans von Müller, 4 volumes (Berlin: Paetel, 1912);

Briefe: Eine Auswahl, edited by Richard Wiener (Vienna: Rikola, 1922);

E. T. A. Hoffmann Briefwechsel, edited by Müller and Friedrich Schnapp, 3 volumes (Munich: Winkler, 1967–1969);

Selected Letters of E. T. A. Hoffmann, edited and translated by Johanna C. Sahlin (Chicago: University of Chicago Press, 1977).

Bibliographies:

Klaus Kanzog, "Grundzüge der E. T. A. Hoffmann-Forschung seit 1945: Mit einer Bibliographie," *Mitteilungen der E. T. A. Hoffmann-Gesellschaft,* 9 (1962): 1–30;

Kanzog, "E. T. A. Hoffmann-Literatur 1962–1965: Eine Bibliographie," *Mitteilungen der E. T. A. Hoffmann-Gesellschaft,* 12 (1966): 33–39;

Jürgen Voerster, *160 Jahre E. T. A. Hoffmann-Forschung: Eine Bibliographie 1805–1965* (Stuttgart: Eggert, 1967);

Hartmut Steinecke, "Zur E. T. A. Hoffmann-Forschung," *Zeitschrift für deutsche Philologie,* 89 (1970): 222–234;

Kanzog, "E. T. A. Hoffmann-Literatur 1966–1969: Eine Bibliographie," *Mitteilungen der E. T. A. Hoffmann-Gesellschaft,* 16 (1970): 28–40;

Steinecke, "E. T. A. Hoffmann: Dokumente und Literatur 1973–1975," *Zeitschrift für deutsche Philologie,* 95 (1976): 160–163;

Kanzog, "Zehn Jahre E. T. A. Hoffmann-Forschung: E. T. A. Hoffmann-Literatur 1970–1980: Eine Bibliographie," *Mitteilungen der E. T. A. Hoffmann-Gesellschaft,* 27 (1981): 55–103;

Gerhard Salomon, *E. T. A. Hoffmann Bibliographie* (Hildesheim: Olms, 1983);

Jörg Petzel, "Auswahlbibliographie zu E. T. A. Hoffmann," *E. T. A. Hoffmann,* edited by Heinz Ludwig Arnold (Munich: Text + Kritik, 1992): 188–210;

Andreas Olbrich, "E. T. A. Hoffmann: Bibliographie der Werke 1981–1993," *E. T. A. Hoffmann-Jahrbuch,* 3 (1995): 95–133;

Olbrich, "Bibliographie der Sekundärliteratur über E. T. A. Hoffmann 1981–1993, Teil 1: 1981–1987," *E. T. A. Hoffmann-Jahrbuch,* 4 (1996): 91–141;

Olbrich, "Bibliographie der Sekundärliteratur über E. T. A. Hoffmann 1981–1993, Teil 2: 1981–1993," *E. T. A. Hoffmann-Jahrbuch,* 5 (1997): 67–119;

Olbrich and Anja Pohsner, "Bibliographie der Sekundärliteratur über E. T. A. Hoffmann 1994–1996," *E. T. A. Hoffmann-Jahrbuch,* 6 (1998): 72–112.

Biographies:

Georg Ellinger, *E. T. A. Hoffmann: Sein Leben und seine Werke* (Hamburg: Voss, 1894);

Walter Harich, *E. T. A. Hoffmann: Das Leben eines Künstlers,* 2 volumes (Berlin: Reiss, 1920);

Theo Piana, *E. T. A. Hoffmann als bildender Künstler* (Berlin: Das neue Berlin, 1954);

Gabrielle Wittkop-Ménardeau, *E. T. A. Hoffmann in Selbstzeugnissen und Bilddokumenten* (Reinbek: Rowohlt, 1966);

Friedrich Schnapp, ed., *E. T. A. Hoffmann in Aufzeichnungen seiner Freunde und Bekannten* (Munich: Winkler, 1974);

Ulrich Helmke, *E. T. A. Hoffmann: Lebensbericht mit Bildern und Dokumenten* (Cassel: Wenderoth, 1975);

Klaus Günzel, *E. T. A. Hoffmann: Leben und Werk in Briefen, Selbstzeugnissen und Zeitdokumenten* (Berlin: Verlag der Nation, 1976);

Arwed Blomeyer, *E. T. A. Hoffmann als Jurist. Eine Würdigung zu seinem 200. Geburtstag* (Berlin: De Gruyter, 1978);

Marcel Schneider, *Ernest Théodore Amadeus Hoffmann: Biographie* (Paris: Julliard, 1979);

Rüdiger Safranski, *E. T. A. Hoffmann: Das Leben eines skeptischen Phantasten* (Munich: Hanser, 1984);

Eberhard Roters, *E. T. A. Hoffmann* (Berlin: Stapp, 1985);

Marianne Beese, *E. T. A. Hoffmann* (Leipzig: Bibliographisches Institut, 1986);

Eckart Klessmann, *E. T. A. Hoffmann oder Die Tiefe zwischen Stern und Erde: Eine Biographie* (Stuttgart: DVA, 1988).

References:

Gerhard Allroggen, *E. T. A. Hoffmanns Kompositionen: Ein chronologisch-thematisches Verzeichnis seiner musikalischen Werke mit einer Einführung* (Regensburg: Bosse, 1970);

Horst S. Daemmrich, *The Shattered Self: E. T. A. Hoffmann's Tragic Vision* (Detroit: Wayne State University Press, 1973);

Hermann Dechant, *E. T. A. Hoffmanns Oper "Aurora"* (Regensburg: Bosse, 1975);

Klaus Deterding, *Die Poetik der inneren und äusseren Welt bei E. T. A. Hoffmann: Zur Konstitution des Poetischen in den Werken und Selbstzeugnissen* (Frankfurt am Main & New York: Peter Lang, 1991);

Klaus-Dieter Dobat, *Musik als romantische Illusion: Eine Untersuchung zur Bedeutung der Musikvorstellung E. T. A. Hoffmanns für sein literarisches Werk* (Tübingen: Niemeyer, 1984);

E. T. A. Hoffmann-Jahrbuch (1992–);

Hans Ehinger, *E. T. A. Hoffmann als Musiker und Musikschriftsteller* (Olten: Walter, 1954);

Heide Eilert, *Theater in der Erzählkunst: Eine Studie zum Werk E. T. A. Hoffmanns* (Tübingen: Niemeyer, 1977);

Brigitte Feldges and Ulrich Stadler, eds., *E. T. A. Hoffmann: Epoche–Werk–Wirkung* (Munich: Bcck, 1986);

Paul Greeff, *E. T. A. Hoffmann als Musiker und Musikschriftsteller* (Cologne: Staufen, 1958);

Ernst Heilborn, *E. T. A. Hoffmann: Der Künstler und die Kunst* (Berlin: Ullstein, 1926);

Harvey Hewett-Thayer, *Hoffmann: Author of the Tales* (Princeton: Princeton University Press, 1948);

Gerhard Kaiser, *E. T. A. Hoffmann* (Stuttgart: Metzler, 1988);

Werner Keil, *E. T. A. Hoffmann als Komponist: Studien zur Kompositionstechnik an ausgewählten Werken* (Wiesbaden: Breitkopf & Härtel, 1986);

Lothar Köhn, Vieldeutige Welt: Studien zur Struktur der Erzählungen E. T. A. Hoffmanns und zur Entwicklung seines Werkes (Tübingen: Niemeyer, 1966);

Detlef Kremer, *E. T. A. Hoffmann zur Einführung* (Hamburg: Junius, 1998);

Kremer, *Romantische Metamorphosen: E. T. A. Hoffmanns Erzählungen* (Stuttgart: Metzler, 1993);

Claudia Liebrand, *Aporie des Kunstmythos: Die Texte E. T. A. Hoffmanns* (Freiburg: Rombach, 1996);

Peter von Matt, *Die Augen der Automaten: E. T. A. Hoffmanns Imaginationslehre als Prinzip seiner Erzählkunst* (Tübingen: Niemeyer, 1971);

Hans Mayer, "Die Wirklichkeit E. T. A. Hoffmanns," in his *Von Lessing bis Thomas Mann* (Pfullingen: Neske, 1959), pp. 198–246;

James M. McGlathery, *E. T. A. Hoffmann* (New York: Twayne, 1997);

McGlathery, *Mysticism and Sexuality: E. T. A. Hoffmann,* 2 volumes (Bern: Lang, 1981–1985);

McGlathery, ed., *Journal of English and German Philology,* special Hoffmann issue, 75 (1976);

Mitteilungen der E. T. A. Hoffmann-Gesellschaft (1938–1991);

Alain Montandon, ed., *E. T. A. Hoffmann et la musique* (Bern: Lang, 1987);

Elena Nährlich-Slatewa, *Das Leben gerät aus dem Gleis: E. T. A. Hoffmann im Kontext karnevalesker Überlieferungen* (Frankfurt am Main & New York: Peter Lang, 1995);

Kenneth Negus, *E. T. A. Hoffmann's Other World: The Romantic Author and His "New Mythology"* (Philadelphia: University of Pennsylvania Press, 1965);

Lothar Pikulik, *E. T. A. Hoffmann als Erzähler: Ein Kommentar zu den "Serapions-Brüdern"* (Göttingen: Vandenhoeck & Ruprecht, 1987);

Helmut Prang, ed., *E. T. A. Hoffmann* (Darmstadt: Wissenschaftliche Buchgesellschaft, 1976);

Jean F. A. Ricci, *E. T. A. Hoffmann, l'homme et l'oeuvre* (Paris: Corti, 1947);

Elke Riemer, *E. T. A. Hoffmann und seine illustratoren* (Hildesheim: Gerstenberg, 1978);

R. Murray Schafer, *E. T. A. Hoffmann and Music* (Toronto & Buffalo, N.Y.: University of Toronto Press, 1975);

Steven Paul Scher, ed., *Zu E. T. A. Hoffmann* (Stuttgart: Klett, 1981);

Wulf Segebrecht, *Autobiographie und Dichtung: Eine Studie zum Werk E. T. A. Hoffmanns* (Stuttgart: Metzler, 1967);

Segebrecht, *Heterogenität und Integration: Studien zu Leben, Werk und Wirkung E. T. A. Hoffmanns* (Frankfurt am Main & New York: Peter Lang, 1996);

Hartmut Steinecke, *E. T. A. Hoffmann* (Stuttgart: Reclam, 1997);

Steinecke, ed., *Zeitschrift für deutsche Philologie,* special Hoffmann issue, 95 (1976);

Ronald Taylor, *Hoffmann* (London: Bowes & Bowes, 1963);

Gerhard Weinholz, *E. T. A. Hoffmann: Dichter, Psychologe, Jurist* (Essen: Die blaue Eule, 1991);

Hans-Georg Werner, *E. T. A. Hoffmann: Darstellung und Deutung der Wirklichkeit im dichterischen Werk* (Berlin & Weimar: Aufbau, 1971);

Johannes Wiele, *Vergangenheit als innere Welt: Historisches Erzählen bei E. T. A. Hoffmann* (Frankfurt am Main & New York: Peter Lang, 1996);

Ilse Winter, *Untersuchungen zum serapiontischen Prinzip E. T. A. Hoffmanns* (The Hague: Mouton, 1976);

Achim Würker, *Das Verhängnis der Wünsche: Unbewusste Lebensentwürfe in Erzählungen E. T. A. Hoffmanns. Mit Überlegungen zu einer Erneuerung der psychoanalytischen Literaturinterpretation* (Frankfurt am Main & New York: Peter Lang, 1993).

Papers:

Only a few of E. T. A. Hoffmann's original papers and manuscripts, including letters, musical scores, and drawings, survived World War II. Most are in the Märkisches Museum der Stadt Berlin; the E. T. A. Hoffmann-Sammlung der Staatsbibliothek Bamberg; and the Handschriftenabteilung, Staatsbibliothek Preußischer Kulturbesitz, Berlin.

Hugo von Hofmannsthal
(1 February 1874 – 15 July 1929)

Michael Winkler
Rice University

This entry was updated by Professor Winkler from his entry in DLB 118:
Twentieth-Century German Dramatists, 1889–1918.

BOOKS: *Gestern: Studie in einem Akt, in Reimen,* as Theophil Morren (Vienna: Verlag der "Modernen Rundschau," 1891);

Theater in Versen (Berlin: Fischer, 1899)—comprises *Die Frau im Fenster, Die Hochzeit der Sobeide, Der Abenteurer und die Sängerin; Die Hochzeit der Sobeide* translated by Bayard Quincy Morgan as *The Marriage of Sobeide,* in *The German Classics of the Nineteenth and Twentieth Centuries,* edited by Kuno Francke and William G. Howard, volume 20 (New York: German Publishing Society, 1914), pp. 234–288;

Der Kaiser und die Hexe (Berlin: Insel, 1900);

Der Thor und der Tod (Berlin: Insel, 1900); translated by Elisabeth Walter as *Death and the Fool* (Boston: Badger, 1914);

Der Tod des Tizian: Ein dramatisches Fragment (Berlin: Insel, 1901); translated by John Heard as *The Death of Titian* (Boston: Four Seas, 1920);

Studie über die Entwickelung des Dichters Victor Hugo (Vienna: Verlag von Dr. Hugo von Hofmannsthal, 1901); republished as *Victor Hugo* (Berlin: Schuster & Loeffler, 1904); republished as *Versuch über Victor Hugo* (Munich: Bremer Presse, 1925);

Ausgewählte Gedichte (Berlin: Verlag der Blätter für die Kunst, 1903);

Das kleine Welttheater oder Die Glücklichen (Leipzig: Insel, 1903); translated by Walter Rather Eberlein as *The Little Theater of the World* (Aurora, N.Y.: Printed by Victor & Jacob Hammer, 1945);

Elektra: Tragödie in einem Aufzug frei nach Sophokles (Berlin: Fischer, 1904); translated by Arthur Symons as *Electra: A Tragedy in One Act* (New York: Brentano's, 1908);

Unterhaltungen über literarische Gegenstände, edited by Georg Brandes (Berlin: Bard, Marquardt, 1904);

Das gerettete Venedig: Trauerspiel in fünf Aufzügen (Berlin: Fischer, 1905); translated by Walter as *Venice Pre-*

Hugo von Hofmannsthal, ca. 1924

served: A Tragedy in Five Acts (Boston: Badger, 1915);

Das Märchen der 672. Nacht und andere Erzählungen (Vienna & Leipzig: Wiener Verlag, 1905)—comprises "Das Märchen der 672. Nacht," "Reitergeschichte," "Erlebnis des Marschalls von Bassompierre," "Ein Brief," "Reitergeschichte" translated by Basil Creighton as "Cavalry Patrol" in *Tellers of Tales,* edited by W. Somerset Maugham

331

(New York: Doubleday, Doran, 1939), pp. 860–867; "Ein Brief" translated by Francis C. Golffing as "The Letter," *Rocky Mountain Review,* 6, no. 3–4 (1942): 1, 3, 11–13;

Ödipus und die Sphinx: Tragödie in drei Aufzügen (Berlin: Fischer, 1906); translated by Gertrude Schoenbohm as *Oedipus and the Sphinx,* in *Oedipus: Myth and Drama,* edited by Martin Kalisch and others (New York: Odyssey, 1968);

Kleine Dramen, 2 volumes (Leipzig: Insel, 1906–1907)–volume 1 comprises *Gestern, Der Tor und der Tod, Der weiße Fächer;* excerpt from *Der weiße Fächer* translated by Maurice Magnus as *The White Fan* in *Mask: The Journal of the Art of the Theater* (Florence), 1 (February 1909): 232–234; volume 2 comprises *Das Bergwerk zu Falun, Der Kaiser und die Hexe, Das kleine Welttheater;*

Die gesammelten Gedichte (Leipzig: Insel, 1907); translated by Charles Wharton Stork as *The Lyrical Poems of Hugo von Hofmannsthal* (New Haven: Yale University Press / London: Milford, 1918);

Die prosaischen Schriften gesammelt, 3 volumes (Berlin: Fischer, 1907–1917);

Vorspiele (Leipzig: Insel, 1908);

Hesperus: Ein Jahrbuch, by Hofmannsthal, Rudolf Alexander Schröder, and Rudolf Borchardt (Leipzig: Insel, 1909);

Cristinas Heimreise: Komödie (Berlin: Fischer, 1910; revised, 1910); translated by Roy Temple House as *Cristina's Journey Home: A Comedy in Three Acts* (Boston: Badger, 1917); German version revised as *Florindo* (Vienna & Hellerau: Avalun, 1923);

Jedermann: Das Spiel vom Sterben des reichen Mannes. Erneuert (Berlin: Fischer, 1911); translated by M. E. Tafler as *The Salzburg Everyman: The Play of the Rich Man's Death* (Salzburg: Mora, 1911); German version edited by Margaret Jacobs (London & Edinburgh: Nelson, 1957);

Grete Wiesenthal in Amor und Psyche und Das fremde Mädchen: Szenen (Berlin: Fischer, 1911);

Alkestis: Ein Trauerspiel nach Euripides (Leipzig: Insel, 1911);

Der Rosenkavalier: Komödie für Musik, music by Richard Strauss (Berlin: Fischer, 1911); translated by Kalisch as *The Rose-Bearer* (Berlin & Paris: Fürstner, 1912);

Die Gedichte und kleinen Dramen (Leipzig: Insel, 1911);

Ariadne auf Naxos: Oper in einem Aufzuge. Zu spielen nach dem "Bürger als Edelmann" des Molière, music by Strauss (Berlin & Paris: Fürstner, 1912); revised as *Ariadne auf Naxos: Oper in einem Aufzug nebst einem Vorspiel* (Berlin & Paris: Fürstner, 1916); translated by Kalisch as *Ariadne on Naxos: Opera in One Act, with a Prelude* (New York: Boosey & Hawkes, 1924);

Die Wege und die Begegnungen (Bremen: Bremer Presse, 1913);

Josephslegende, by Hofmannsthal and Harry Graf Kessler, music by Strauss (Berlin: Fürstner, 1914); translated by Kalisch as *The Legend of Joseph* (Berlin & Paris: Fürstner, 1914);

Prinz Eugen der edle Ritter: Sein Leben in Bildern, lithographs by Franz Wacik (Vienna: Seidel, 1915);

Die Frau ohne Schatten: Oper in drei Akten, music by Strauss (Berlin: Fürstner, 1916; London: Boosey & Hawkes, 1964);

Der Bürger als Edelmann: Komödie mit Tänzen von Molière. Freie Bühnenbearbeitung in drei Aufzügen, music by Strauss (Berlin: Fürstner, 1918);

Rodauner Nachträge, 3 volumes (Vienna: Amalthea, 1918);

Lucidor: Figuren zu einer ungeschriebenen Komödie (Berlin: Reiss, 1919); translated by Kenneth Burke as *Lucidor: Characters for an Unwritten Comedy,* in *Dial,* 73, no. 2 (1922): 121–132;

Die Frau ohne Schatten: Erzählung (Berlin: Fischer, 1919);

Der Schwierige: Lustspiel in drei Akten (Berlin: Fischer, 1921; edited by W. E. Yates, Cambridge: Cambridge University Press, 1966);

Reden und Aufsätze (Leipzig: Insel, 1921);

Gedichte (Leipzig: Insel-Verlag, 1922);

Das Salzburger große Welttheater (Leipzig: Insel, 1922);

Buch der Freunde (Leipzig: Insel, 1922); enlarged as *Buch der Freunde: Tagebuch-Aufzeichnungen* (Leipzig: Insel, 1929);

Die grüne Flöte: Ballettpantomime, music by Wolfgang Amadeus Mozart (Vienna & Leipzig: Universal-Edition, 1923);

Augenblicke in Griechenland (Regensburg & Leipzig: Habbel & Naumann, 1924);

Der Turm: Ein Trauerspiel in fünf Aufzügen (Munich: Bremer Presse, 1925; revised edition, Berlin: Fischer, 1927);

Die Ruinen von Athen: Ein Festspiel mit Tänzen und Chören, music by Strauss and Ludwig van Beethoven (Berlin: Fürstner, 1925);

Gedichte (Vienna: Johannes-Presse, 1926);

Szenischer Prolog zur Neueröffnung des Josefstädtertheaters (Vienna: Johannes-Presse, 1926);

Früheste Prosastücke (Leipzig: Gesellschaft der Freunde der Deutschen Bücherei, 1926);

Das Schrifttum als geistiger Raum der Nation (Munich: Bremer Presse, 1927);

Drei Erzählungen (Leipzig: Insel, 1927);

Die ägyptische Helena: Oper in zwei Aufzügen, music by Strauss (Berlin: Fürstner, 1928); translated by Kalisch as *Helen in Egypt* (Berlin: Fürstner / New York: Ricordi, 1928);

Loris: Die Prosa des jungen Hugo von Hofmannsthal (Berlin: Fischer, 1930);

Die Berührung der Sphären (Berlin: Fischer, 1931);

Wege und Begegnungen (Leipzig: Reclam, 1931);

Fragment eines Romans (Munich: Privately printed, 1931); enlarged as *Andreas oder Die Vereinigten: Fragmente eines Romanes* (Berlin: Fischer, 1932); translated by Marie D. Hottinger as *Andreas; or, The United: Being Fragments of a Novel* (London: Dent, 1936);

Arabella: Lyrische Komödie, music by Strauss (Berlin: Fürstner, 1933); translated by John Gutman as *Arabella: A Lyrical Comedy in Three Acts* (New York: Boosey & Hawkes, 1955; London: Boosey & Hawkes, 1965);

Semiramis; Die beiden Götter (Munich: Rupprechtpresse, 1933);

Prolog zur Feier von Goethes 50. Geburtstag am Burgtheater zu Wien (Vienna: Officina Vindobonensis, 1934);

Nachlese der Gedichte (Berlin: Fischer, 1934);

Dramatische Entwürfe aus dem Nachlaß, edited by Heinrich Zimmer (Vienna: Johannes-Presse, 1936);

Beethoven: Rede gehalten an der Beethovenfeier des Lesezirkels Hottingen in Zürich am 10. Dezember 1920, edited by Willi Schuh (Vienna: Reichner, 1938);

Festspiele in Salzburg (Vienna: Bermann-Fischer, 1938);

Gesammelte Werke in Einzelausgaben, 15 volumes, edited by Herbert Steiner (volumes 1–2, Stockholm: Bermann-Fischer, 1945–1948; volumes 3–15, Frankfurt am Main: Fischer, 1950–1959); reedited by Bernd Schoeller and Rudolf Hirsch as *Gesammelte Werke in zehn Einzelbänden,* 10 volumes (Frankfurt am Main: Fischer, 1979);

Das Theater des Neuen: Eine Ankündigung (Vienna: Edition Komödie im Bindenschildverlag, 1947);

Dem Gedächtnis des Dichters Theodor Storm, in der Handschrift des Dichters, edited by Lothar Hempe (Stuttgart: Hempe, 1951);

Aus dem Jugendwerk Hugo von Hofmannsthals (Loris), edited by Emmy Rosenfeld (Pavia, Italy: Editrice viscontia, 1951);

Danae oder die Vernunftheirat: Szenarium und Notizen, edited by Schuh (Frankfurt am Main: Fischer, 1952);

Österreichische Aufsätze und Reden, edited by Helmut A. Fiechtner (Vienna: Bergland, 1956);

Natur und Erkenntnis: Essays (Berlin: Deutsche Buch-Gemeinschaft, 1957);

Ausgewählte Werke, 2 volumes, edited by Hirsch (Berlin & Frankfurt am Main: Fischer, 1957);

Silvia im "Stern": Auf Grund des Manuskriptes, edited by Martin Stern (Bern & Stuttgart: Haupt, 1959);

Komödie (Graz & Vienna: Stiasny, 1960);

Das erzählerische Werk (Frankfurt am Main: Fischer, 1969);

Ausgewählte Werke, edited by Eike Middell (Leipzig: Insel, 1975);

Sämtliche Werke: Kritische Ausgabe, 31 volumes published, 38 volumes projected, edited by Rudolf Hirsch, Clemens Köttelwesch, Heinz Rölleke, and Ernst Zinn (Frankfurt am Main: Fischer, 1975–).

Editions in English: *Selected Writings,* volume 1: *Selected Prose,* translated by Mary Hottinger and Tania and James Stern (London: Routledge & Kegan Paul, 1952); volume 2: *Poems and Verse Plays: Bilingual Edition,* edited by Michael Hamburger, translated by John Bednall, Arthur Davidson, and others (London: Routledge & Kegan Paul, 1961; New York: Pantheon, 1961); volume 3: *Selected Plays and Libretti,* edited by Hamburger (New York: Pantheon, 1963; London: Routledge & Kegan Paul, 1964);

Three Plays, translated by Alfred Schwarz (Detroit: Wayne State University Press, 1966)–comprises *Death and the Fool, Electra, The Tower.*

PLAY PRODUCTIONS: *Madonna Dianora: Eine Ballade dramatisiert,* Berlin, Deutsches Theater, 15 May 1898;

Der Thor und der Tod, Munich, Theater am Gärtnerplatz, 13 November 1898;

Der Abenteurer und die Sängerin oder Die Geschenke des Lebens: Ein Gedicht in zwei Aufzügen, Berlin, Deutsches Theater and Vienna, Burgtheater, 18 March 1899;

Die Hochzeit der Sobeide: Dramatisches Gedicht in einem Aufzug, Berlin, Deutsches Theater and Vienna, Burgtheater, 18 March 1899;

Der Tod des Tizian: Ein dramatisches Fragment, Munich, Künstlerhaus, 14 January 1901;

Jules Renard, *Fuchs: Schauspiel in einem Akt,* translated by Hofmannsthal, Vienna, Burgtheater, 14 February 1901;

Elektra: Tragödie in einem Akt frei nach Sophokles, Berlin, Kleines Theater, 30 October 1903; revised as an opera, with music by Richard Strauss, Dresden, Hofoper, 25 January 1909;

Das gerettete Venedig: Trauerspiel in fünf Aufzügen, Berlin, Lessingtheater, 21 January 1905;

Oedipus und die Sphinx: Tragödie in drei Aufzügen, Berlin, Deutsches Theater, 2 March 1906;

Cristinas Heimreise: Komödie in drei Akten, Berlin, Deutsches Theater, 11 February 1910;

Sophocles, *König Ödipus: Tragödie,* translated and adapted by Hofmannsthal, Munich, Neue Musikfesthalle auf dem Ausstellungsgelände, 25 September 1910;

Die Heirat wider Willen: Komödie in einem Akt von Molière, neu übersetzt, Berlin, Deutsches Theater, 7 October 1910;

Der Rosenkavalier: Komödie für Musik in drei Aufzügen, music by Strauss, Dresden, Opernhaus, 26 January 1911;

Jedermann: Das Spiel vom Sterben des reichen Mannes erneuert, Berlin, Zirkus Schumann, 1 December 1911;

Molière, *Der Bürger als Edelmann: Komödie mit Tänzen,* adapted by Hofmannsthal, music by Strauss, Stuttgart, Kleines Haus des Königlichen Hoftheaters, 25 October 1912;

Josephslegende, by Hofmannsthal and Harry Graf Kessler, music by Strauss, Paris, Opéra, 14 May 1914;

Die Schäferinnen, Berlin, Kammerspiele, 14 March 1916;

Alkestis: Ein Trauerspiel nach Euripides, Munich, Kammerspiele, 14 April 1916;

Die grüne Flöte: Ballettpantomime, music by Wolfgang Amadeus Mozart, Berlin, Deutsches Theater, 27 April 1916;

Die Lästigen: Ein Lustspiel, frei nach Molière, Berlin, Deutsches Theater, 27 April 1916;

Die Frau ohne Schatten: Oper in drei Akten, music by Strauss, Vienna, Staatsoper, 10 October 1919;

Dame Kobold: Lustspiel in drei Aufzügen von Calderon. Freie Bearbeitung für die neuere Bühne, Berlin, Deutsches Theater, 3 April 1920;

Der Schwierige: Lustspiel in drei Akten, Munich, Residenztheater, 8 November 1921;

Carnaval, getanzt nach der Schumann'schen Musik, Vienna, Opertheater, 12 June 1922;

Das Salzburger große Welttheater, music by Einar Nilson, Salzburg, Collegienkirche, 12 August 1922;

Der Unbestechliche: Lustspiel in fünf Akten, Vienna, Raimundtheater, 16 March 1923;

Szenischer Prolog zur Neueröffnung des Josefstädter Theaters, Vienna, Theater in der Josefstadt, 1 April 1924;

Die Ruinen von Athen: Ein Festspiel mit Tänzen und Chören, music by Strauss and Ludwig van Beethoven, Vienna, Opertheater, 20 September 1924;

Achilles auf Skyros: Ballett in einem Aufzug, music by Egon Wellesz, Stuttgart, Großes Haus des Landestheaters, 4 March 1926;

Das Theater des Neuen: Eine Ankündigung, Vienna, Theater in der Josefstadt, 21 March 1926;

Der Kaiser und die Hexe: Ein Spiel, music by Hans Pleß, Vienna, Urania, 16 December 1926;

Der weiße Fächer: Ein Zwischenspiel, Vienna, Akademietheater, 13 May 1927;

Der Turm: Ein Trauerspiel in fünf Aufzügen, Munich, Prinzregententheater and Hamburg, Schauspielhaus, 4 February 1928;

Gestern: Studie in einem Akt, in Reimen, Vienna, Die Komödie, 25 March 1928;

Die ägyptische Helena: Oper in zwei Aufzügen, music by Strauss, Dresden, Staatsoper, 6 June 1928;

Das kleine Welttheater oder Die Glücklichen, Munich, Residenztheater, 6 October 1929;

Das Bergwerk zu Falun, Vienna, Akademietheater, 20 December 1932;

Arabella: Lyrische Komödie in drei Aufzügen, music by Strauss, Dresden, Staatsoper, 1 July 1933;

Die Liebe der Danae, music by Strauss, Salzburg, Festspielhaus, 14 August 1952.

OTHER: Arthur Schnitzler, *Anatol,* introduction by Hofmannsthal (Berlin: Fischer, 1901); translated by Trevor Blakemore in *Playing with Love (Liebelei),* by Schnitzler, translated by P. Morton Shand (London: Gay & Hancock, 1914);

Sophocles, *König Ödipus,* translated by Hofmannsthal (Berlin: Fischer, 1910);

Deutsche Erzähler, 4 volumes, edited by Hofmannsthal (Leipzig: Insel, 1912);

Österreichischer Almanach auf das Jahr 1916, edited by Hofmannsthal (Leipzig: Insel, 1915);

Franz Grillparzer, *Grillparzers politisches Vermächtnis,* edited by Hofmannsthal (Leipzig: Insel, 1915);

Pedro Calderón de la Barca, *Dame Kobold: Lustspiel in drei Aufzügen,* translated by Hofmannsthal (Berlin: Fischer, 1920);

Die Erzählungen aus den Tausendundeinen Nächten, 6 volumes, translated by Enno Littmann, introduction by Hofmannsthal (Leipzig: Insel, 1921–1928);

Griechenland: Baukunst, Landschaft, Volksleben, photographs by Hanns Holdt and others, introduction by Hofmannsthal (Berlin: Wasmuth, 1922); translated by L. Hamilton as *Picturesque Greece: Architecture, Landscape, Life of the People* (New York: Architectural Book Publishing, 1922; London: Unwin, 1923);

Neue Deutsche Beiträge, 6 volumes, edited by Hofmannsthal (Munich: Bremer Presse, 1922–1927);

Deutsches Lesebuch, 2 volumes, edited by Hofmannsthal (Munich: Bremer Presse, 1922–1923; enlarged, 1926);

Deutsche Epigramme, edited by Hofmannsthal (Munich: Bremer Presse, 1923);

Adalbert Stifter, *Der Nachsommer: Eine Erzählung,* afterword by Hofmannsthal (Leipzig: List, 1925);

Friedrich Schiller, *Schillers Selbstcharakteristik aus seinen Schriften,* edited by Hofmannsthal (Munich: Bremer Presse, 1926);

Wert und Ehre deutscher Sprache, in Zeugnissen, edited by Hofmannsthal (Munich: Bremer Presse, 1927).

What is perhaps most striking about Hugo von Hofmannsthal are contradictions that characterize his creative imagination. His poetic laboratory was filled with an ever-increasing multiplicity of images, themes, ideas, situations, and dramatis personae. In changing disguises and in new contexts they constitute a large repertoire of works in progress, some of which, often after long delays, came to fruition. Much more of his material, however, never developed beyond the stage of arrested inventiveness and was forced into shapes and patterns that defied the poet's quest for grace and civility. Hofmannsthal's plays, especially, either move along with an altogether irresistible ease and an unobtrusively natural momentum, every inflection of their dialogue perfectly coordinated, every character a convincing embodiment of his or her dramatic function, every scene a full realization of its inherent conflict; or they strike even the casual reader as laborious and stilted—as the futile products of a refined sensibility struggling against its better inclinations.

These contradictions haunted Hofmannsthal all his life and colored much of his posthumous reputation. They were a consequence both of his particular talent and, perhaps more so, of the cultural role he was expected if not forced to play, a role that was defined by the social and historical pressures of fin de siécle Vienna. To his early admirers Hofmannsthal represented the prodigiously talented aesthete; later critics saw in him the melancholy embodiment of an old order that had ceased to live long before its political demise, and his detractors attacked him as the propagator of a conservative ideology of cultural elitism. The brilliantly versatile virtuoso of the "beautiful life" had turned into an anachronism. What was missing between the artistic exuberance of his beginnings and the debilitating insecurities—even despair—of his final decade was an extended time of self-assured maturity. Hofmannsthal, like most of his literary creations, appears to have had an extended youth, during which he experienced all the privileges of a prodigy; and then he had to face the gravity of premature old age, with its agitated determination to maintain dignity or at least to preserve a posture of dignified resignation, perhaps even wisdom. He had to live with the awareness that at the age of forty he had become a part of history, and he had to turn this knowledge into a new source of inspiration. As early as the turn of the century, when he had reached the midpoint of his short life, Hofmannsthal's existence was defined by two contradictory burdens: that of an unfinished youth and that of representing the values of an old heritage. This paradox shaped his public persona and much of his creative work.

Hugo Laurenz August Hofmann, Edler von Hofmannsthal was born on 1 February 1874 in Vienna and was the only child of prosperous bourgeois parents. His father, Hugo August Peter Hofmann, was heir to part of a fortune that his own father, Isaak Löw Hofmann, had accumulated during the first half of the nineteenth century, primarily through improvements in the manufacture of silk and in the production of potash. Hugo August Peter Hofmann was a director of the Central-Bodencreditanstalt, a prominent investment bank. In 1873 he married Anna Maria Josefa Fohleutner, whose family came from Bavaria and the Sudetenland and whose wealth derived from agriculture and the brewing business. The Hofmanns' house at 12 Salesianergasse, a prestigious neighborhood, was four stories high and had an elegant neoclassical facade; it represented social solidity, urbane civility, discreet self-assurance, and the restrained opulence of old money. Hofmannsthal's paternal grandfather had converted from Judaism to Roman Catholicism on marrying the daughter of an Austrian court official in Milan. Hofmannsthal's parents considered themselves fully assimilated and put their confidence in religious tolerance, economic liberalism, the beneficence of the monarchy, and the inevitability of progress. They doted on the child, the mother often with nervous protectiveness and excessive solicitude; the father, a man of diverse cultural interests with a broad education and urbane manners, discreetly supervised his emotional and intellectual development and encouraged his precocious talents and artistic aspirations.

Hofmannsthal grew up in a world of undisturbed security and in an atmosphere of privileged insularity. Outside reality, in the forms of anti-Semitism, working-class poverty, nationalist extremism, and political demagoguery, seemed far away. But in the stock-exchange crash of 1873, a result of speculative manipulations of the bond market in connection with the Vienna World's Fair, Hofmannsthal's parents lost a major portion of their investments. They were still able, nevertheless, to give their son the best education, social contacts, and artistic experiences that established prominence in the cosmopolitan capital of the Austro-Hungarian Empire could provide, including riding and fencing lessons, opera tickets, a box at the Burgtheater (Imperial Theater), summer vacations in the Alps, and trips to the centers of Italian art.

Vienna's profusion of architectural traditions, its salons and cafés, and its divers other entertainments, as well as the atmosphere of its summer resorts, shaped the young Hofmannsthal no less than did his rigorous education. After preliminary studies with private tutors he was enrolled from 1884 until 1892 at the Akademisches Gymnasium, a public school with a tradition of Jesuit discipline and one of the three prominent institutions of humanistic learning in the city. He completed the study of law at the University of Vienna with his first juristisches Staatsexamen on 13 July 1894, then signed up for military service. He spent his obligatory year as a Freiwilliger (volunteer) with a regiment of dragoons garrisoned in the Moravian border town of Göding. He then resumed his academic career, which, after October 1895, centered around French literature. His dissertation on the language of the "Pléiade" poets was accepted in 1897, but he withdrew his study of Victor Hugo's development as a poet (1901) from consideration for an appointment to the faculty of the university. He had decided instead to make his living as a playwright and essayist.

Hofmannsthal's first publications were poems and analytical essays, often impressionistic in character, on the art and psychology of modern *décadence;* they are mellifluous and highly perceptive effusions of extraordinary versatility that describe various aspects of the mentality of fin de siècle Europe. Although they had to appear under pseudonyms (Loris, Loris Melikow, and Theophil Morren) because of university regulations, they quickly made him a literary sensation and gained him access to the circle of literati that became known as Young Vienna. The author and actor Gustav Schwarz-kopf introduced him in the fall of 1890 to the writers gathering at Café Griensteidl, among them Arthur Schnitzler, Richard Beer-Hofmann, and Felix Salten (Siegmund Salzmann). Hermann Bahr, whom he met on 27 April 1891, was the most conspicuous spokesman of the group. Their artistic and cultural affinities, fostered in almost daily conversations of mutual encouragement and criticism, though hardly ever free of misunderstandings, personality conflicts, and jealousies, brought about a rejuvenation of Austrian letters and helped to introduce the style and attitudes of European symbolism to German literature.

The essential impulse behind their work was a predilection for refined sensations, nobly subdued and graceful gestures, and clusters of melodious words; such charms were expected to play out their most intoxicating effects on the stage of an intimate theater. Hofmannsthal's earliest symbolist playlet, written under the inspiration of this Viennese aestheticism, *Gestern* (Yesterday), was begun in early summer 1891 and was printed at his own expense in October of that year; it was not performed until 1928. In the Italian Renaissance, Andrea proclaims the attitude of hedonistic impressionism: he lives only for each moment's fleeting pleasures, fully conscious of every quickly changing mood and never able to preserve any sensory experience as an enduring value. He changes his attitude when Arlette, through a small act of infidelity, forces him to admit that past experience is an ineradicable part of his self. In

this work the amorality of art for art's sake is subjected to criticism.

During his formative years as a poet Hofmannsthal was repeatedly frightened by the prospect of losing his inspiration. Periods of sustained and seemingly effortless creativity and enjoyment of life alternated with times of depression, even panic, and feelings of profound inadequacy. The ever-present reality of death, its accidental appearance in the midst of all the splendors of life and as the final intensification of life in a Dionysiac burst of vital energy, became a recurring preoccupation: in the fragmentary play *Der Tod des Tizian* (The Death of Titian, 1901), written during March and April 1892, in which a group of the old master's disciples experience the plague in Venice and their own voluntary deaths as an orgy of life heightened to its utmost sensuality; in *Der Thor und der Tod* (1898; published, 1900; translated as *Death and the Fool,* 1914), written in March and April 1893, a one-act comedy in which the young nobleman Claudio, in melancholy withdrawal from the demands imposed on him by the world, at last welcomes death as the only true encounter among his fleeting contacts and one who teaches him to honor the value of life and fidelity; and in *Alkestis* (published, 1911; performed, 1916), written in February 1894, an adaptation of Euripides' play in which the rebirth of the noble king Admetos is made possible by his wife Alkestis's self-sacrificial death.

Hofmannsthal's personal life during these years was enriched by friendships with the poet Stefan George, whom he met in December 1891; with Marie Herzfeld, whom he met in March 1892; with the aged Josephine von Wertheimstein, whose death in July 1894 affected him deeply; and with the young poet and prospective diplomat Leopold von Andrian, whom he met in autumn 1893. Vacation trips took him to Switzerland and the south of France in September 1892, to the Salzkammergut region of Austria and Bavaria from August through October 1893; and to Venice in September 1895. He wrote an amazing variety of short pieces and read voraciously recent European and classical German literature, Latin poetry, the works of Honoré de Balzac and Guy de Maupassant, and Walter Pater on the Renaissance. During a bicycle tour through the Italian Alps in August 1897, many of his plans came to fruition in what he experienced as a miraculous outburst of lyrical intuition. Dramatic projects that had lingered during an earlier "very strong inner petrification and disorder" (letter to George of 3 June 1897) and were completed at this time include *Die Frau im Fenster* (The Woman in the Window, performed under the title *Madonna Dianora,* 1898; published, 1899); *Das kleine Welttheater oder Die Glücklichen* (The Little Theater of the World; or, The Happy Ones; published, 1903; performed, 1929; translated as *The Little Theater of the World,* 1945), completed by the end of August 1897 and inspired in part by Pedro Calderón de la Barca, a performance of whose *El gran teatro del mundo* (1655) in front of Vienna's courthouse Hofmannsthal had attended in June of that year; *Der weiße Fächer* (published, 1906; performed, 1927; excerpt translated as *The White Fan,* 1909); *Die Hochzeit der Sobeide* (1899; translated as *The Marriage of Sobeide,* 1914); and *Der Kaiser und die Hexe* (The Emperor and the Witch, published, 1900; performed, 1926).

All of these playlets portray characters who are connected to life with varying degrees of self-conscious hesitation and tentativeness and who must learn how to become worthy of fidelity and elicit trust. The most important of them is the *Das kleine Welttheater oder Die Glücklichen.* In a sequence of lyrical monologues different stages of humanity's removal from the "stream of life" are revealed. The play's central archetypal figure is "der Wahnsinnige" (the one who has lost his senses), who has surrendered his individuality to the mystery of an all-encompassing order.

By 1900 Hofmannsthal had found two publishers who would prove to be reliable advocates of his art: Samuel Fischer, who printed a collection of three of his verse plays as *Theater in Versen* (Theater in Verse, 1899); and Alfred Walter Heymel and Rudolf Alexander Schröder, the founders of the Insel Verlag (Island Publishing House), to whose journal, the *Insel,* Hofmannsthal frequently contributed and whose Insel-Bücherei, a series of exquisitely printed and illustrated small volumes, provided an appropriate format for his shorter theatrical works. *Der Thor und der Tod* became one of Insel's most successful titles. On the stage, however, Hofmannsthal's plays encountered many obstacles, hardly ever satisfied their author's expectations, and failed to meet with even a moderate measure of popular acclaim. A matinee performance of *Der Thor und der Tod* directed by Otto Brahm in Munich in 1898 was anything but memorable; the next attempt, the year after, proved even more disappointing: a presentation of *Die Hochzeit der Sobeide* together with a new "serious comedy," *Der Abenteurer und die Sängerin* (The Adventurer and the Singer, published, 1899), was canceled after three nights due to hostile reviews in the Berlin press. But Hofmannsthal's brief stay in Germany's theater and publishing capital was not without its benefits. He met Count Harry Kessler, a dilettante in various arts, energetic promoter of many cultural projects, diplomat, and man of the world; he renewed his acquaintance with Gerhart Hauptmann; and he solidified his friendship with Eberhard von Bodenhausen, a lawyer who would rise to prominent positions in German industry (including a directorship at Krupp), would acquire an expert knowledge of art history, and had served since 1895 as

head of the literary society that financed the lavish art nouveau publication *Pan.* Through these connections Hofmannsthal was introduced to a world beyond Vienna that he was to cherish as personifying old Europe's cultural nobility at the time of its final glow. He was attracted to Helene and Alfred von Nostitz and to the much younger Ottonie von Degenfeld because of their moral integrity and their refined appreciation of the arts. The discreet elegance of Chateau Neubeuern, a possession of the Bodenhausen and Degenfeld families in the serenely beautiful countryside above the Inn River in southern Bavaria, became a congenial refuge from the pressures of his public life. It was there that Hofmannsthal, who was never able to fully free himself of snobbish affectations, preferred to meet his friends for year-end gatherings.

Der Abenteurer und die Sängerin, written between 22 September and 10 October 1898 in Venice, was inspired by an episode in Giovanni Giacomo Casanova's memoirs. The adventurous seducer Baron Weidenstamm is the first of several Casanova variations in Hofmannsthal's works. He persuades the musician Vittoria to overcome her submission to commercial success and bourgeois propriety and to rediscover the fire of inspiration that is his legacy as a "Lebenskünstler" (one who has made living a form of art). In finding herself she makes her music into a sublime elixir: the gift of life for others. The power of lyrical art to reverse the loss of identity and facilitate an imaginative access to the confusing multiplicity of worldly phenomena is advocated here for the last time.

By this point Hofmannsthal had become intensely suspicious of his own symbolist practice. This suspicion becomes apparent in a project which had begun to occupy him at the end of June 1899: a fairy-tale tragedy in five acts, *Das Bergwerk zu Falun* (The Mine at Falun, published, 1907; performed, 1932), based on a novella from E. T. A. Hoffmann's *Die Serapions-Brüder* (The Serapion Brotherhood, 1819–1821). The miner Elis Fröbom abandons his bride, Anna, for the Mountain Queen. His descent into the mountain from which he will not return symbolizes an intense process of introversion in which the reality of dreams obliterates all other possibilities of experience. Though revised several times, the play never achieved what Hofmannsthal was striving for: dramatic plasticity, the richness and immediacy of life, and external conflict. Its preponderance of subjectivity was a fundamental shortcoming. This failure is the central concern of "Ein Brief" (translated as "The Letter," 1942), written in 1901, published in the journal *Tag* (Day) in 1902 and in the collection *Das Märchen der 672. Nacht und andere Erzählungen* (The Tale of the 672nd Night and Other Stories) in 1905 and better known as the "Chandos Letter": the loss of coherent perception, conceptual systematization, and communicative competence when language represents only its own wealth of suggestive associations and abandons its discursive function.

Hofmannsthal embarked on a period of experimentation during which he sought to revitalize earlier genres of drama. He turned to ancient Greek tragedy, to the medieval mystery play, to the Spanish baroque practice of showing the world as a play before God *(teatro del mundo)*, to the character comedies of Molière, to the Italian commedia dell'arte, to the Austrian Volkstheater, and to the opera buffa. In modernizing material from previous eras, Hofmannsthal at first relied heavily on elaborate stage designs and an excessive use of rhetorical language. These shortcomings disappeared as his mastery of the dramatic medium increased.

One of Hofmannsthal's most exhilarating experiences of this time was his sojourn from 10 February through 2 May 1900 in Paris, where his friend Georg Freiherr zu Franckenstein introduced him to the diplomatic elite and another friend, the painter Hans Schlesinger, introduced him to leading artists, among them Maurice Maeterlinck, Auguste Rodin, and Anatole France. On 8 June 1901 he married Gertrud Schlesinger, his friend's sister and the daughter of a bank official, with whom he had been acquainted for more than five years. The couple bought a villa in Rodaun, near Vienna, where they brought up their three children: Christiane, born in 1902; Franz, born in 1903; and Raimund, born in 1906. Apart from a small apartment in the city at Stallburggasse 2, the "Fuchsschlössel" (named after Countess Fuchs, the tutor of Empress Maria Theresa) became the place where he entertained such friends as Rudolf Alexander Schröder, Rudolf Borchardt, and Rudolf Kassner.

Hofmannsthal's turn away from the symbolist lyrical drama and his need to write plays of a larger compass—what he called "das große Stück" (the large play)—engendered a variety of projects: a never-completed tragedy, "Pompilia oder Das Leben" (Pompilia; or, Life), which was to have been built around a crime provoked by an act of marital infidelity (its plot, borrowed from Robert Browning, proved overcomplex because too many points of view had to be incorporated); *Elektra* (published, 1904; translated as *Electra,* 1908), conceived early in September 1901, finished two years later, and produced in 1903 by Max Reinhardt with Gertrude Eysoldt playing the title role at the Kleines Theater (Little Theater) in Berlin to strong critical and popular acclaim; a free adaptation of Calderón's *La vida es sueño* (1636) as "Das Leben ein Traum" (Life a Dream); a recasting of Thomas Otway's *Venice Preserved* (1682) as *Das gerettete Venedig* (1905), a first draft of which was finished at the end of November

1902, the final version in August 1904. Other plans included dramatizations of the myth of Jupiter and Semele; of an episode from the chapbook *Fortunatus* (1509); and an Oedipus trilogy, of which only one part, *Oedipus und die Sphinx* (1906; translated as *Oedipus and the Sphinx,* 1968) was finished. Plays dealing with King Kandaules, with Leda and the swan, and with Euripides' *The Bacchants* (circa 405 B.C.) were never completed. A plan to rewrite the English *Everyman* was first conceived in April 1903 and was revived in April 1906: the old morality play had become a drama in doggerel verse, *Jedermann: Das Spiel vom Sterben des reichen Mannes* (1911; translated as *The Salzburg Everyman: The Play of the Rich Man's Death,* 1911).

Two new contacts Hofmannsthal made during this period developed into cooperative associations of lasting importance. In Reinhardt, whom he had met in Vienna in May 1903, he found an impresario and director who made the premieres of *Elektra* and *Jedermann* rousing successes. In Richard Strauss, whom he met on 2 February 1906 in Berlin, he found a composer with the talent to visualize what makes for effective theater; their cooperation during the next twenty years, though often tested by differences of temperament, style, and purpose, proved durable as Strauss coaxed and pushed the hesitant, fidgety, and ever-sensitive Hofmannsthal to complete some of his most balanced works for the opera stage. The need for frequent consultations with Reinhardt and Strauss made Berlin rather than Vienna his artistic headquarters. It was there that, at the end of February 1912, he met Sergey Diaghilev of the Russian Ballet; he attended the company's performances in Paris, most notably the premiere of Vaslav Nijinsky's *Afternoon of a Faun,* during his stay there from 25 March through 7 June. Their modernist dancing had such a strong impact on him that he wanted to become their principal scenarist, but the association did not materialize. He also failed to interest Strauss in writing the music for a tragic symphony for the company, to be titled "Orest und die Furien" (Orestes and the Furies). In partnership with Kessler, however, he wrote a short ballet, *Josephslegende* (1914; translated as *The Legend of Joseph,* 1914), that was performed at the Paris Opéra on 14 May 1914.

By this time several other projects had taken hold of his imagination. A comedy, "Silvia im Stern" (Sylvia in the Star), was first outlined in August 1907 and occupied him intermittently during the following years; some of its themes were taken over into a new Casanova play in four acts, "Florindo," which was abandoned in December 1908 after its female protagonist, Cristina, had assumed central importance. *Cristinas Heimreise* (1910; translated as *Cristina's Journey Home,* 1917), completed on 6 December 1909, had to be shortened after its Berlin opening on 11 February 1910 for its performance by the troupe of Reinhardt's Deutsches Theater (German Theater) in Vienna, where in May 1910 it became a great success. By then, work on *Der Rosenkavalier* (1911; translated as *The Rose-Bearer,* 1912), which originated in a conversation with Kessler during the first half of February 1909 and which profited greatly from his suggestions, had progressed satisfactorily. Since its premiere on 26 January 1911 in Dresden, it has been the work with which Hofmannsthal's international reputation is most intimately connected. But new material pushed to the fore immediately thereafter: an opera about Ariadne replaced a plan for a drama to be titled "Das steinerne Herz" (The Heart of Stone). *Ariadne auf Naxos* (1912; translated as *Ariadne on Naxos,* 1924) was first performed as a one-act opera within Molière's *Le bourgeois gentilhomme* (1670)—translated into German as *Der Bürger als Edelmann*—on 25 October 1912 in Stuttgart; in later performances the play became a prelude to the opera. Work on *Die Frau ohne Schatten* (The Woman without a Shadow; published, 1916; performed, 1919) had not progressed much beyond the completion of act 2 when World War I broke out in 1914, but by the end of September 1915 the whole libretto was in Strauss's hands.

It may appear that during the decade before 1914 Hofmannsthal was exclusively absorbed in his work with Strauss. But this impression overlooks his concurrent fiction and essays. It also slights his attempts to write not only for the urban *haute bourgeoisie* who could afford to buy opera tickets and whose approval had made him a moderately wealthy man. He also wanted to speak to a broad audience of ordinary people, whom he called "die Menge" (the multitude) and "das Volk" (the people), and do so in a language that was simple without being condescending and complex without being idiosyncratic. He wanted to reclaim for the playwright and for the stage as a public institution something of their earlier relevance as sources of political education. Such a revitalization of art was not to be confused either with partisan sloganeering or with the nostalgic evocation of past cultural riches. Eschewing both naturalism and modernist experimentation, Hofmannsthal tried to recapture "Elementarer-fahrungen" (fundamental human experiences) that he found most essentially expressed in religious mysteries and rituals. He knew how difficult it would be to resuscitate their mythic power in a secular society, but for Hofmannsthal the preservation of traditional religious values in the face of a general revaluation of all values was at stake. He came to consider it the poet's special obligation to show ways in which a mindless confidence in exter-

nal possessions and materialism could be overcome. Christian allegory became his preferred means for expressing this concern.

As early as April 1903 he had read *Everyman,* and he consulted further relevant material, including Hans Sachs's Reformation play *Von dem reichen sterbenden Menschen* (Of the Rich Dying Man, 1549) as well as woodcuts and many other sources, throughout its slow transformation into *Jedermann: Das Spiel vom Sterben des reichen Mannes.* Its criticism of humanity's servitude to mammon owes a good deal to the sociologist Georg Simmel's *Philosophie des Geldes* (Philosophy of Money, 1900), which analyzes the destruction of individual differences and of subjectivity wrought by money as the mediating agency of all aspects of modern life. After experiencing how unreliable are the friendships that he had bought, Jedermann recognizes that what is required for a meaningful existence are the beauty of good deeds and faith in God's mercy.

The allegorical structure of *Jedermann* and its poetic archaisms reflect a dubious shift in Hofmannsthal's dramatic technique. He admitted that these features were impossible to duplicate in other plays. They were complemented by Reinhardt's highly modern directorial style, which absorbed the audience in a stunning display of meticulously coordinated effects of light, sound, movement, and costumes. In the final analysis, though, *Jedermann* was a dead end rather than a breakthrough to a sustainable new dramatic style. Linking *Elektra* with *Jedermann,* Hofmannsthal said that both plays ask what is left of human beings after everything has been taken away from them and that their answer is: "die Tat oder das Werk" (what one does or accomplishes). This affirmation of a law beyond the merely personal is the principal impulse behind his preoccupation with the theme of sacrifice; but Elektra's obsessions render her unable to act, and Jedermann's death has at best a minimal effect on the petrified world of objects around him.

Hofmannsthal turned to a form of drama whose peculiar mixture of styles and changing character constellations suggest that all things, even the most antagonistic and divergent elements, are connected with each other. In blending the ordinary with the fantastic and the sublime, in combining the humble with the pathetic, he wanted to show that in the midst of tumult and confusion it is still possible to find oneself. Persuaded that a pious Volksgeist (Spirit of the people) was groping for modern confirmation, and encouraged by the popular acclaim of *Jedermann* after its performance on the Domplatz (Cathedral Square) on 22 August 1920 as part of the Salzburg

Festival, he completed *Das Salzburger große Welttheater* (The Salzburg Great World Theater, 1922) in six weeks (1 October to 14 November 1921). Its central figure is the Beggar, who refuses to accept his position at the bottom of the secular hierarchy and whose rebellion threatens to turn the world upside down. But Wisdom raises her hands in prayer, neither for her own salvation nor for the protection of a corrupt order but to testify to the spiritual insignificance of wealth and power. The Beggar, converted by a miraculous insight, renounces revolutionary violence and becomes an obedient Christian.

This proclamation of conventional Christian morality was Hofmannsthal's answer to the dissolution of the Hapsburg empire, to Austria's impoverishment, and to uncertainty about the future. But his advocacy of traditional values and of the social institutions that make their survival possible goes back beyond 1914 and can be traced nowhere more clearly than in the various revisions of the Florindo-Cristina material, which was originally conceived as a comedic vindication of the artist-seducer. Florindo is a person without attachments who leaves his lovers with nothing but their memory of a moment of perfect erotic bliss; he arranges suitable marriages for them so that he can escape the responsibilities of a husband. But more and more the naive country girl Cristina, secure in her moral convictions even though she becomes a victim of the seducer's designs, gains prominence. She overcomes the temptations of profligacy or despair by returning to her mountain village, where she will marry an old sea captain, Tomaso, a Ulysses figure. Their union will not fulfill her earlier expectations of love and happiness, but it is meant to be less a source of personal satisfaction than a testimony to the ethical values of marriage as an institution, of a covenant as permanent as the Alps where they will make their home.

Such a transformation of a somewhat frivolous idea into metaphysical seriousness overtaxed the potential of comedy. For this reason Hofmannsthal turned again to narrative prose, which proved to be a more appropriate form in which to express his concern with the need for loyalty and a willingness to subordinate personal desires to higher goals. The prose version of *Die Frau ohne Schatten* (1919), the story of an emperor's redemption through his wife's charitable honesty, is his most ambitious exemplification of what he meant by the "Triumph des Allomatischen" (triumph of the allomatic principle), the recovery of one's true self in another person. This principle is also a sustaining theme of Hofmannsthal's only novel, the fragmentary *Andreas oder Die Vereinigten* (1932; translated as *Andreas; or, The United*, 1936), which he worked on from 1907 to 1927 but most of which was written during 1912–1913. Such convictions also inspired his activities in support of the Austrian war effort. Hofmannsthal served in the Kriegsfürsorgeamt, a propaganda branch of the War Ministry, largely free to set his own agenda and convinced that his many articles, lectures, diplomatic missions, and especially his editions of representative documents from Austrian history would have a beneficial effect on the country's rapidly declining morale. For a while he believed that at last he had found a role that would satisfy his desire to contribute to the public good. In the end he realized that his cultural politics of a "konservative Revolution" and of a "schöpferische Restauration" (creative restoration) were the product of an idealistic illusion. But as late as 1927, in his speech of 10 January at Munich University that was published as *Das Schrifttum als geistiger Raum der Nation* (Literature as the Spiritual Homeland of the Nation, 1927), he suggested that literature would be able to replace the political institutions that had formerly united the various German nations. His suspicion, however, that he was chasing a phantom had arisen long before the end of World War I made the full extent of the European catastrophe apparent. His ever more debilitating awareness that he was far removed from the forces that shaped the postwar world, that he had become an anachronism, was the cause of his increasingly frequent fits of depression. His correspondence between 1917 and 1922 with Rudolf Pannwitz, whose *Die Krisis der europäischen Kultur* (The Crisis of European Culture, 1917) made a profound impression on him, and the letters he exchanged with the young diplomat-scholar Carl Jakob Burckhardt reveal the depth of his disorientation.

The last decade of Hofmannsthal's life, when none of his new works found a responsive public, was characterized by a tenacious desire to show how social conflicts can be resolved. His premise was that such conflicts result from impulses and desires that, while disparate and antagonistic on the surface, converge at a deeper level. He achieved his purpose best in a type of comedy that combines three aspects in perfect fusion: the subtly ironic study of an inimitable character; a social portrait of that character's class, particularly of the evasive mannerisms of the aristocracy; and a conversational language that hides serious, even potentially tragic concerns behind a superficial ease. *Der Schwierige* (The Difficult One, 1921) is his only play set in the present. Its rather uneventful story takes place just after the war. Count Hans Karl Bühl decides to end his affair with Countess Antoinette Hechingen because he knows that her husband, his comrade during the war, is profoundly devoted to her. Bühl's sister, the widowed Countess Crescence Freudenberg, is afraid that Antoinette may seek to entrap her naively arrogant son Stani, and she asks Bühl to intervene as the young man's protector. Stani, meanwhile, reveals his intention of marrying Countess Helene Altenwyl, whose shy sensitivity has also attracted Bühl's affection. At a soiree at the Altenwyls' Bühl bids farewell to a desolate Antoinette and then, hesitant to put his feelings into words, speaks to Helene of an ideal marriage without mentioning that he would like to be the ideal husband. Tragic disappointments appear to be the order of the evening. But Helene puts an end to these confusions with a discreet confession of her love for Bühl, only to give rise to a new comedy of errors when Crescence assumes that her "irresistible" son is the cause of Helene's happiness—a mistake that an embarrassed Bühl must tactfully rectify.

With a perfectly balanced economy of means Hofmannsthal had realized, for the first time in his career, the theatrical potential inherent in his type of comedy, a comedy that reflects the futility of language and straightforward action at the same time as it shows their necessity. He had also succeeded in capturing the intimate interplay of the comedic with the tragic, a seemingly paradoxical amalgam that for him characterized the Austria—particularly its nobility—of his time.

No doubt in an attempt to capitalize on the mastery he had achieved in this genre, Hofmannsthal wrote another comedy during 1922. *Der Unbestechliche* (The Incorruptible One; performed, 1923) is a variation on the "servant as master" theme. Theodor, a Bohemian lackey who combines a crafty interest in his own advantages with virtuous dignity, has left the service of Baron Jaromir, a nobleman of questionable morals, to join the household of the latter's mother. When the presence of two of Jaromir's "prenuptial" lady friends on her estate endangers the baron's marriage, Theodor discreetly arranges events that impel the speedy departure of the unwelcome guests. Using the bedroom Jaromir had prepared for an amorous encounter for his own rendezvous with a young widow, the wily servant enjoys a double reward for his intervention on behalf of familial virtue. But his belief that he alone is in control of the little intrigues that save his master's marriage turns out to be erroneous. Ultimately a transcendent power, whose instrument he is, has to intervene at the critical moment to restore order to Jaromir's affairs.

At this time Hofmannsthal was concentrating on a drama in five acts that he had begun in the summer of 1902 as an adaptation of Calderón's *La vida es sueño*. It was originally intended to be an exploration of the "Höhlenreich des Selbst" (cavernous kingdom of the self), but the political implications of the plot assumed importance as early as 1904. *Der Turm* (The Tower, published, 1925; performed, 1928), as the play was renamed, appeared to have found its final shape in October 1924. But Reinhardt had reservations, especially considering its conclusion—the entrance of a child-king as the messianic representative of a new generation—unconvincing. At Reinhardt's residence, Schloß Leopoldskron near Salzburg, the author and the director discussed a less mythic ending that gives prominence to Olivier, the unscrupulous master of power politics.

The play is set in a legendary Poland of the seventeenth century. Sigismund, the son of King Basilius, is imprisoned in a remote tower because of a prophecy that he will overthrow his father; he is unaware of his actual identity. Revolutionary upheavals persuade his guard, Julian, to conspire with a doctor to confront the king with his son. During the confrontation Sigismund questions the prerogatives of the old regime and strikes the king. Overpowered by courtiers, Sigismund and Julian are condemned to death. As the nobles turn against their absolutist monarch and the impoverished people accept the demagogue Olivier as their leader, a rebellion frees Sigismund as he is about to be executed. After the king's abdication, Sigismund, the new ruler, makes Julian his principal councillor. Julian warns the nobles not to oppose his plan of building a new kingdom with the support of the peasants. Even the new king rejects this program, fearing that it would lead to anarchy. When Olivier's masses turn against him, he realizes that Julian's attempt to restore legitimacy to the monarchy has failed. The divorce of power and spiritual values is absolute. Olivier, representing raw power without self-control, offers Sigismund a symbolic role in the victory parade; the king declines with aristocratic disdain. This assertion of his spiritual superiority seals his fate. He is discarded like a useless commodity after an assassin's bullet kills him from ambush. The play's language is freighted with an artificial seriousness and at the same time tries to appear simple and natural. It lacks dramatic intensity, precision, and concreteness.

During his last years Hofmannsthal traveled to the premieres of his plays, to Sicily, to northern Italy, to Paris, to Morocco, and to London and Oxford. There were bursts of renewed creativity, and he continued his involvement with the Salzburg Festival, but ever more frequently he complained of nervous exhaustion, depression, and of an inability to concentrate. While the general public respected him as a dignified representative of the "world of yesterday," he also could not help but notice that the next generation of writers barely knew his name. He died on 15 July 1929 of a stroke as he was preparing to go to his older son's funeral.

Letters:

Richard Strauss: Briefwechsel mit Hugo von Hofmannsthal, edited by Franz Strauss (Berlin & Leipzig: Zsolnay, 1926); translated by Paul England as *Correspondence Between Richard Strauss and Hugo von Hofmannsthal, 1907–1918* (London: Secker, 1927; New York: Knopf, 1927);

Briefwechsel zwischen George und Hofmannsthal, edited by Robert Boehringer (Berlin: Bondi, 1938; enlarged edition, Munich: Küpper, 1953);

Briefwechsel: Richard Strauss/Hugo von Hofmannsthal. Gesamtausgabe, edited by Franz and Alice Strauss and Willi Schuh (Zurich: Atlantis, 1952); translated by Hanns Hammelmann and Edward Osers as *A Working Friendship: The Correspondence between Richard Strauss and Hugo von Hofmannsthal* (New York: Random House, 1961);

Hugo von Hofmannsthal/Eberhard von Bodenhausen: Briefe der Freundschaft, edited by Dora von Bodenhausen (Düsseldorf: Diederichs, 1953);

Hugo von Hofmannsthal/Rudolf Borchardt: Briefwechsel, edited by Marie Luise Borchardt and Herbert Steiner (Frankfurt am Main: Fischer, 1954);

Hugo von Hofmannsthal/Carl Jakob Burckhardt Briefwechsel, edited by Carl J. Burckhardt (Frankfurt am Main: Fischer, 1956);

Hugo von Hofmannsthal/Arthur Schnitzler: Briefwechsel, edited by Therese Nickl and Heinrich Schnitzler (Frankfurt am Main: Fischer, 1964);

Hugo von Hofmannsthal/Helene von Nostitz: Briefwechsel, edited by Oswalt von Nostitz (Frankfurt am Main: Fischer, 1965);

Hugo von Hofmannsthal/Edgar Karg von Bebenburg: Briefwechsel, edited by Mary E. Gilbert (Frankfurt am Main: Fischer, 1966);

Briefe an Marie Herzfeld, edited by Horst Weber (Heidelberg: Stiehm, 1967);

Hugo von Hofmannsthal/Leopold von Andrian: Briefwechsel, edited by Walter H. Perl (Frankfurt am Main: Fischer, 1968);

Hugo von Hofmannsthal/Harry Graf Kessler: Briefwechsel 1898–1929, edited by Hilde Burger (Frankfurt am Main: Insel, 1968);

Hugo von Hofmannsthal/Willy Haas: Ein Briefwechsel, edited by Rolf Italiaander (Berlin: Propyläen, 1968);

Hugo von Hofmannsthal/Josef Redlich: Briefwechsel, edited by Helga Fußgänger (Frankfurt am Main: Fischer, 1971);

Hugo von Hofmannsthal/Anton Wildgans: Briefwechsel, edited by Norbert Altenhofer (Heidelberg: Stiehm, 1971);

Hugo von Hofmannsthal/Richard Beer-Hofmann: Briefwechsel, edited by Eugene Weber (Frankfurt am Main: Fischer, 1972);

Briefwechsel mit Max Rychner; mit Samuel und Hedwig Fischer, Oscar Bie und Moritz Heimann, edited by Claudia Mertz-Rychner (Frankfurt am Main: Fischer, 1973);

Briefwechsel: Hugo von Hofmannsthal/Ottonie Gräfin Degenfeld, edited by Marie Thérèse Miller-Degenfeld and Weber (Frankfurt am Main: Fischer, 1974); revised as *Briefwechsel mit Ottonie Gräfin Degenfeld und Julie Freifrau von Wendelstadt* (Frankfurt am Main: Fischer, 1986);

Hugo von Hofmannsthal/Rainer Maria Rilke: Briefwechsel, edited by Rudolf Hirsch and Ingeborg Schnack (Frankfurt am Main: Insel, 1978);

Hugo von Hofmannsthal/Max Mell: Briefwechsel, edited by Margret Dietrich and Heinz Kindermann (Heidelberg: Lambert Schneider, 1982);

Ria Schmujlow-Claassen und Hugo von Hofmannsthal: Briefe-Aufsätze-Dokumente, edited by Claudia Albrecht (Marbach: Marbacher Schriften, 1982);

Hugo von Hofmannsthal/Paul Zifferer: Briefwechsel, edited by Burger (Vienna: Verlag der öster-reichischen Staatsdruckerei, 1983);

Hugo von Hofmannsthal: Briefwechsel mit dem Insel-Verlag 1901–1929, edited by Gerhard Schuster (Frankfurt am Main: Buchhändler-Vereinigung, 1985;

Hugo von Hofmannsthal/Rudolf Pannwitz: Briefwechsel 1907–1926, edited by Gerhard Schuster (Frankfurt am Main: Fischer, 1994).

Bibliographies:

Horst Weber, *Hugo von Hofmannsthal: Bibliographie des Schrifttums 1892–1963* (Berlin: De Gruyter, 1966);

Weber, *Hugo von Hofmannsthal: Bibliographie. Werke, Briefe, Gespräche, Übersetzungen, Vertonungen* (Berlin & New York: De Gruyter, 1972);

James E. Walsh, *The Hofmannsthal Collection in the Houghton Library: A Descriptive Catalogue of Printed Books* (Heidelberg: Stiehm, 1974);

Hans-Albrecht Koch, *Hugo von Hofmannsthal* (Darmstadt: Wissenschaftliche Buchgesellschaft, 1989);

Mathias Meier, *Hugo von Hofmannsthal* (Stuttgart: Metzler, 1993).

Biographies:

Günther Erken, "Hofmannsthal-Chronik: Beitrag zu einer Biographie," *Literaturwissenschaftliches Jahrbuch,* new series 3 (1962): 239–313;

Werner Volke, *Hugo von Hofmannsthal in Selbstzeugnissen und Bilddokumenten* (Reinbek: Rowohlt, 1967).

References:

Richard Alewyn, *Über Hugo von Hofmannsthal* (Göttingen: Vandenhoeck & Ruprecht, 1958);

Norbert Altenhofer, *Hofmannsthals Lustspiel "Der Unbestechliche"* (Bad Homburg: Gehlen, 1967);

Gerhard Austin, *Phänomenologie der Gebärde bei Hugo von Hofmannsthal* (Heidelberg: Winter, 1981);

Lowell A. Bangerter, *Hugo von Hofmannsthal* (New York: Ungar, 1977);

Sibylle Bauer, ed., *Hugo von Hofmannsthal* (Darmstadt: Wissenschaftliche Buchgesellschaft, 1968);

Benjamin Bennett, *Hugo von Hofmannsthal: The Theatres of Consciousness* (Cambridge: Cambridge University Press, 1988);

Carlpeter Braegger, *Das Visuelle und das Plastische: Hugo von Hofmannsthal und die bildende Kunst* (Bern & Munich: Francke, 1979);

Gisa Briese-Neumann, *Ästhet-Dilettant-Narziss: Untersuchungen zur Reflexion der fin de siècle-Phänomene im Frühwerk Hofmannsthals* (Frankfurt am Main: Lang, 1985);

Hermann Broch, "Hofmannsthal und seine Zeit: Eine Studie," in his *Kommentierte Werkausgabe,* volume 9, edited by Paul M. Lützeler (Frankfurt am Main: Suhrkamp, 1975), pp. 111–275; translated by Michael P. Steinberg as *Hugo von Hofmannsthal and His Time: The European Imagination, 1860–1920* (Chicago & London: University of Chicago Press, 1984);

Brian Coghlan, *Hofmannsthal's Festival Dramas* (London: Cambridge University Press, 1964);

Károly Csúri, *Die frühen Erzählungen Hofmannsthals: Eine generativ-poetische Untersuchung* (Kronberg: Scriptor, 1978);

Donald G. Daviau and George J. Buelow, *The "Ariadne auf Naxos" of Hugo von Hofmannsthal* (Chapel Hill: University of North Carolina Press, 1975);

Adrian Del Caro, *Hugo von Hoffmansthal: Poets and the Language of Life* (Baton Rouge: Louisiana State University Press, 1993);

Manfred Diersch, *Empiriokritizismus und Impressionismus: Über Beziehungen zwischen Philosophie, Ästhetik und Literatur um 1900 in Wien* (Berlin: Aufbau, 1977);

Günter Erken, *Hofmannsthals dramatischer Stil: Untersuchungen zur Symbolik und Dramaturgie* (Tübingen: Niemeyer, 1967);

Karl G. Esselborn, *Hofmannsthal und der antike Mythos* (Munich: Fink, 1969);

Karen Forsyth, *"Ariadne auf Naxos" by Hugo von Hofmannsthal and Richard Strauss: Its Genesis and Meaning* (London: Oxford University Press, 1982);

Hanns Hammelmann, *Hugo von Hofmannsthal* (New Haven & London: Yale University Press, 1957);

Edgar Hederer, *Hugo von Hofmannsthal* (Frankfurt am Main: Fischer, 1960);

Hofmannsthal-Blätter: Veröffentlichungen der Hugo-von-Hofmannsthal-Gesellschaft, 1– (1968–);

Hofmannsthal-Forschungen, 1– (1971–);

Manfred Hoppe, *Literatentum, Magie und Mystik im Frühwerk Hofmannsthals* (Berlin: De Gruyter, 1968);

Corinna Jaeger-Trees, *Aspekte der Dekadenz in Hofmannsthals Dramen und Erzählungen des Frühwerks* (Bern & Stuttgart: Haupt, 1988);

Alan Jefferson, *Richard Strauss* (London: Macmillan, 1975);

Douglas A. Joyce, *Hugo von Hoffmansthal's "Der Schwierige": A Fifty-Year Theater History* (Columbia, S.C.: Camden House, 1993);

Peter Christoph Kern, *Zur Gedankenwelt des späten Hofmannsthal: Die Idee einer schöpferischen Restauration* (Heidelberg: Winter, 1969);

Jacob Knaus, *Hofmannsthals Weg zur Oper "Die Frau ohne Schatten": Rücksichten und Einflüsse auf die Musik* (Berlin: De Gruyter, 1971);

Erwin Kobel, *Hugo von Hofmannsthal* (Berlin: De Gruyter, 1970);

Thomas A. Kovach, *Hofmannsthal and Symbolism: Art and Life in the Work of a Modern Poet* (New York: Lang, 1985);

Eva-Maria Lenz, *Hugo von Hofmannsthals mythologische Oper "Die ägyptische Helena"* (Tübingen: Niemeyer, 1972);

Wolfram Mauser, *Hugo von Hofmannsthal. Konfliktbewältigung und Werkstruktur: Eine psychosoziologische Interpretation* (Munich: Fink, 1977);

H. Jürgen Meyer-Wendt, *Der frühe Hofmannsthal und die Gedankenwelt Nietzsches* (Heidelberg: Quelle & Meyer, 1973);

David Holmes Miles, *Hofmannsthal's Novel "Andreas": Memory and Self* (Princeton: Princeton University Press, 1972);

Wolfgang Nehring, *Die Tat bei Hofmannsthal: Eine Untersuchung zu Hofmannsthals großen Dramen* (Stuttgart: Metzler, 1966);

Eva-Maria Nüchtern, *Hofmannsthals "Alkestis"* (Bad Homburg: Gehlen, 1968);

Sherill Halm Pantle, *"Die Frau ohne Schatten" by Hugo von Hofmannsthal and Richard Strauss: An Analysis of Text, Music and Their Relationship* (Bern: Lang, 1978);

Karl Pestalozzi, *Sprachskepsis und Sprachmagie im Werk des jungen Hofmannsthal* (Zurich: Atlantis, 1958);

Gerhardt Pickerodt, *Hofmannsthals Dramen: Kritik ihres historischen Gehalts* (Stuttgart: Metzler, 1968);

Benno Rech, *Hofmannsthals Komödie: Verwirklichte Konfiguration* (Bonn: Bouvier, 1971);

William H. Rey, *Weltentzweiung und Weltversöhnung in Hofmannthals griechischen Dramen* (Philadelphia: University of Pennsylvania Press, 1962);

Hermann Rudolph, *Kulturkritik und konservative Revolution: Zum kulturellpolitischen Denken Hofmannsthals und seinem problemgeschichtlichen Kontext* (Tübingen: Niemeyer, 1971);

Rudolf H. Schäfer, *Hugo von Hofmannsthals "Arabella"* (Bern: Lang, 1967);

Friedrich Schröder, *Die Gestalt des Verführers im Drama Hugo von Hofmannsthals* (Frankfurt am Main: Haag & Herchen, 1988);

Jürgen Schwalbe, *Sprache und Gebärde im Werk Hofmannsthals* (Freiburg: Schwarz, 1971);

Egon Schwarz, *Hofmannsthal und Calderon* (Cambridge, Mass.: Harvard University Press, 1962);

Hinrich C. Seeba, *Kritik des ästhetischen Menschen: Hermeneutik und Moral in Hofmannsthals "Der Tor und der Tod"* (Bad Homburg: Gehlen, 1970);

Steven P. Sondrup, *Hofmannsthal and the French Symbolist Tradition* (Bern: Lang, 1976);

Uwe C. Steiner, *Die Zeit der Schrift: Die Krise der Schrift und die Vergänglichkeit der Gleichnisse bei Hofmannsthal und Rilke* (Munich: Fink, 1996);

Rolf Tarot, *Hugo von Hofmannsthal: Daseinsformen und dichterische Struktur* (Tübingen: Niemeyer, 1970);

Cynthia Walk, *Hugo von Hofmannsthals großes Welttheater: Drama und Theater* (Heidelberg: Winter, 1980);

Waltraud Wiethölter, *Hofmannsthal oder die Geometrie des Subjekts: psychostrukturelle und ikonographische Studien zum Prosawerk* (Tubingen: Niemeyer, 1990);

Lothar Wittmann, *Sprachthematik und dramatische Form im Werke Hofmannsthals* (Stuttgart: Kohlhammer, 1966);

Michael Worbs, *Nervenkunst: Literatur und Psychoanalyse im Wien der Jahrhundertwende* (Frankfurt am Main: Athenäum, 1983);

Gotthart Wunberg, *Der frühe Hofmannsthal: Schizophrenie als dichterische Struktur* (Stuttgart: Kohlhammer, 1965);

W. E. Yuill and Patricia Howe, ed., *Hugo von Hofmannsthal (1874–1929): Commemorative Essays* (London: Institute of Germanic Studies, 1981).

Papers:

Hugo von Hofmannsthal's papers are at the Bibliothek des Freien Deutschen Hochstifts (Library of the Free German Academy), Frankfurt am Main; at the Houghton Library at Harvard University; and in various private collections.

Friedrich Hölderlin

(20 March 1770 – 7 June 1843)

Lawrence Ryan
University of Massachusetts, Amherst

This entry originally appeared in DLB 90: German Writers
in the Age of Goethe, 1789–1832.

BOOKS: *Hyperion oder Der Eremit in Griechenland,* 2 volumes (Tübingen: Cotta, 1797–1799); translated by Willard R. Trask as *Hyperion; or, The Hermit in Greece* (New York: Ungar, 1965); facsimile edition of German version (Frankfurt am Main: Stroemfeld/Roter Stern, 1979);

Gedichte, edited by Gustav Schwab and Ludwig Uhland (Stuttgart & Tübingen: Cotta, 1826)—includes *Der Tod des Empedokles,* translated by Michael Hamburger as *The Death of Empedocles, Quarterly Review of Literature,* 13 (1964): 93–121;

Sämtliche Werke, edited by Christoph Theodor Schwab, 2 volumes (Stuttgart & Tübingen: Cotta, 1846);

Sämtliche Werke: Historisch-kritische Ausgabe, edited by Norbert von Hellingrath, Friedrich Seebaß, and Ludwig von Pigenot, 6 volumes (volumes 1, 4, 5, Munich & Leipzig: Müller; volumes 2, 3, 6, Berlin: Propyläen, 1913–1923);

Sämtliche Werke, edited by Friedrich Beißner and Adolf Beck, 8 volumes (Stuttgart: Cotta/Kohlhammer, 1943–1985);

Sämtliche Werke und Briefe, edited by Günter Mieth, 2 volumes (Munich: Hanser, 1970);

Sämtliche Werke: Frankfurter Ausgabe, edited by Dietrich Sattler, 13 volumes to date (Frankfurt am Main: Roter Stern, 1975–);

Homburger Folioheft, facsimile edition, edited by Sattler and Emery E. George (Basel: Stroemfeld/Roter Stern, 1986);

Stuttgarter Foliobuch, facsimile edition, edited by Sattler (Frankfurt am Main: Stroemfeld/Roter Stern, 1989);

Bevestigter Gesang: Die neu zu entdeckende hymnische Spätdichtung bis 1806, facsimile edition, edited by Dietrich Uffhausen (Stuttgart: Metzler, 1989).

Editions in English: Poems and Fragments, translated and edited by Michael Hamburger (London: Routledge & Kegan Paul, 1967; Ann Arbor: University of Michigan, 1967; 2nd enlarged edition, Cambridge: Cambridge University Press, 1980);

Hyperion; Thalia Fragment, 1794, translated and edited by Karl W. Maurer (Winnipeg: Hölderlin Society, 1968);

Friedrich Hölderlin in 1792 (pastel by Franz K. Hiemer; by permission of the Schiller-Nationalmuseum, Marbach)

Friedrich Hölderlin, Eduard Mörike: Selected Poems, translated by Christopher Middleton (Chicago: University of Chicago Press, 1972);

"On Tragedy: Notes on the *Oedipus;* Notes on the *Antigone,*" translated by Jeremy Adler, *Comparative Criticism,* 5 (1983): 205–244;

"Philosophical Archaeology: Hölderlin's *Pindar Fragments,*" translated, with an interpretation, by Adler, *Comparative Criticism,* 6 (1984): 23–46;

Hymns and Fragments, translated by Richard Sieburth (Princeton: Princeton University Press, 1984);

"On Tragedy, Part 2: 'The Ground of Empedocles'; On the Process of Becoming in Passing Away," translated by Adler, *Comparative Criticism,* 7 (1985): 147–173;

Selected Verse, edited and translated by Hamburger (London & Dover, N.H.: Anvil Press, 1986);

Essays and Letters on Theory, translated and edited by Thomas Pfau (Albany: State University of New York Press, 1988).

OTHER: *Die Trauerspiele des Sophokles,* translated by Hölderlin, 2 volumes (Frankfurt am Main: Wilmans, 1804)—comprises volume 1, *Ödipus der Tyrann;* volume 2, *Antigonä;* facsimile edition (Frankfurt am Main: Stroemfeld/Roter Stern, 1986);

"On the Process of the Poetic Mind," translated by Ralph R. Read, in *German Romantic Criticism,* edited by A. Leslie Willson (New York: Continuum, 1982), pp. 219–237.

Denied recognition during his lifetime, Friedrich Hölderlin has come to be regarded as a central figure of the German Classical-Romantic period. Despite his achievements in the fields of the novel, drama, and poetic theory, and despite the important influence he exerted on the development of the philosophy of German Idealism, he is best known for his lyric poetry. Hölderlin's verse represents both the culmination of the German classical tradition, with its thematic and formal indebtedness to the literature of antiquity, and the highest expression of the German Romantic glorification of the poet, combining veneration of nature with the development of a national poetic ideal.

Johann Christian Friedrich Hölderlin was born in Lauffen, near Nürtingen, in Swabia, to Heinrich Friedrich Hölderlin and Johanna Christiana Heyn Hölderlin on 20 March 1770. His father died in 1772, and his mother remarried in 1774; her second husband, Johann Christoph Gock, Mayor of Nürtingen, died in 1779. Hölderlin's mother was a constant admonishing presence throughout most of his life, forcing him continually to defend his preoccupation with poetry. After attending the local school in Nürtingen, Hölderlin enrolled in 1788 in the Tübinger Stift, the theological seminary which has counted among its pupils such thinkers and poets as Johannes Kepler, Johann Albrecht Bengel, Friedrich Christoph Oetinger, Eduard Mörike, Wilhelm Hauff, and Friedrich Theodor Vischer. Georg Wilhelm Friedrich Hegel and Friedrich Wilhelm Joseph von Schelling, two of the leading figures of German Idealism, were fellow students of Hölderlin, and their exchange of ideas continued for some years after they left the seminary. At Tübingen Hölderlin was instructed in theology, Greek literature, and contemporary philosophy, all of which laid the groundwork for his later writings. He graduated from the seminary in 1793 on the basis of two theses, "Parallele Zwischen Salomons Sprüchwörtern und Hesiods *Werken und Tagen*" (Parallel Between the Proverbs of Solomon and Hesiod's *Works and Days*) and "Geschichte der schönen Künste unter den Griechen" (History of the Fine Arts among the Greeks). An important influence was the French Revolution, which aroused in the seminarians high hopes for the realization of revolutionary political ideals in Germany. While still in Tübingen, Hölderlin wrote hymnic poems with such titles as "Hymne an die Freiheit" (Hymn to Freedom) and "Hymne an die Göttin der Harmonie" (Hymn to the Goddess of Harmony). They are lengthy, somewhat prolix rhymed poems that owe much to the example of Hölderlin's Swabian compatriot Friedrich Schiller, whom the younger poet revered and with whom he occasionally corresponded. Although several of these poems were published in various almanacs, they attracted little attention and are by no means characteristic of Hölderlin's most important work.

After graduating from the seminary, Hölderlin was unwilling to pursue the career of clergyman for which his training had befitted him, and instead, on Schiller's recommendation, took a position as private tutor with Schiller's friend Charlotte von Kalb at Waltershausen, in Thuringia. Although this position afforded him an opportunity to devote himself to the poetic and philosophical studies that were already his main concern, he soon encountered difficulties with his pedagogical duties, which led to termination of his employment. In early 1795 he moved to Jena, where he attended lectures at the university with the intention either of preparing himself for an academic career or of supporting himself by his writing. There he was in contact with Schiller, and also met Johann Wolfgang von Goethe and Johann Gottfried von Herder, but he was influenced most particularly by the philosopher Johann Gottlieb Fichte, whom he called "die Seele von Jena" (the soul of Jena). Fichte's epoch-making lectures on his "Wissenschaftslehre" (Theory of Knowledge), which laid the foundation of German Idealist philosophy, affected Hölderlin deeply. But Fichte's theory of the self-positing ego, inimical to nature as it was, plunged Hölderlin into a turmoil of self-doubt from which he had to struggle to emancipate himself. It is generally considered that his precipitous return from Jena to his native Nürtingen in mid 1795 was largely an attempt to escape from what he called the "Luftgeister mit den metaphysischen Flügeln" (airborne spirits with metaphysical wings).

Hölderlin's philosophical differences with Fichte first found expression in two jottings (unpublished until the 1960s) titled "Sein" (Being) and "Urteil" (Judgment), in which he questions Fichte's concept of the manifest self-consciousness of the "absolute ego" as the starting point of philosophy. For Hölderlin, self-consciousness is the establishment of an identity that presupposes a foregoing difference and is therefore by definition distinct from the ultimate oneness of Being, so that self-consciousness and the Absolute are mutually exclusive. (He expressed a similar idea in a letter to Hegel of 26 January 1795.) "Sein" and "Urteil" probably represent the first articulation of a criticism of Fichte that gave a new turn to the whole philosophy of Idealism; they also suggest the important influence that Hölderlin exerted on Hegel and Schelling, as does the document generally known as "Das älteste Systemprogramm des deutschen Idealismus" (The Oldest System-Program of German Idealism; unpublished until 1917), a two-page outline of a philosophic program which culminates in the call for "eine neue Mythologie" (a new mythology). It is in Hegel's handwriting but its authorship has been much disputed, and it has been variously attributed to Hegel, Schelling, and Hölderlin; the input of Hölderlin seems in any case to have been paramount.

Late in 1795 Hölderlin accepted a position as tutor with the family of Jakob Friedrich Gontard, a banker in Frankfurt am Main. Although disaffected by the stiffness of the city's social life, he soon developed a deep attachment to Susette Borkenstein Gontard, the wife of his employer. Under the name of Diotima, taken from that of the priestess of love in Plato's *Symposium,* she began to figure in Hölderlin's writings as the object of his love and as the incarnation of eternal beauty. He describes himself as being in a "neue Welt" (new world), where his "Schönheitssinn" (sense of beauty) is assured beyond all uncertainty. In 1796, owing to the unrest caused by the Napoleonic Wars, he accompanied Susette Gontard on a trip to Cassel and Bad Driburg in Westfalia, where he also made the acquaintance of the author Wilhelm Heinse. By September 1798, however, his relationship with Susette Gontard had created such tensions in the household that he was forced to give up his position and leave Frankfurt am Main for the nearby town of Homburg. He seems seldom to have seen Susette after his departure, but her letters to him, published in 1921 as *Die Briefe von Diotima* (Letters from Diotima) and often reprinted, constitute a moving testimony to their love.

The main work of this period is the novel *Hyperion oder Der Eremit in Griechenland* (2 volumes, 1797–1799; translated as *Hyperion; or, The Hermit in Greece,* 1965). Hölderlin had begun the novel during his student days in Tübingen and had revised it continually during his stays in Waltershausen and Jena. In 1794 a preliminary version was published under the title "Fragment von *Hyperion*" (Fragment of *Hyperion*) in Schiller's literary journal *Neue Thalia.* This version of the novel is cast in the form of letters from Hyperion, a young late-eighteenth-century Greek, to his German friend Bellarmin. The letters depict his constant struggle to attain the moment of transcendent experience in which all conflict is resolved and temporality is suspended: "Was mir nicht Alles, und ewig Alles ist, ist mir Nichts" (What for me is not All, and eternally All, is nothing). In nature, in love, in a visit to Homeric sites, Hyperion experiences momentary intimations of his ideal, which constantly eludes him, so that his aspirations remain unfulfilled. The image of the "exzentrische Bahn" (eccentric path), which constantly diverges from the center of Being that it always seeks but can never permanently attain, becomes a symbol of the course of human existence.

In Jena, Hölderlin had revised this version, partly in order to take account of his attempt to come to terms with the philosophy of Fichte. In a metrical version and a fragment entitled "Hyperions Jugend" (Hyperion's Youth), he abandoned the epistolary format in favor of a retrospective technique in which the older Hyperion looks back on his youth. The narrator, relating his story to a young visitor, acknowledges that the process of reflection has made him "tyrannisch gegen die Natur" (tyrannical toward nature), in that he has reduced nature to the material of self-consciousness. This theme echoes Hölderlin's criticism of Fichte's philosophy and its preoccupation with the autonomy of the "absolute ego." Hölderlin's new orientation finds expression in the Platonic view of love as the longing of the imperfect for the ideal, and in a new conception of beauty, which emerges as the only form in which the unity of Being, unattainable precisely because it is the object of striving, is incarnated: "jenes Sein, im einzigen Sinne des Worts . . . ist vorhanden–als Schönheit" (Being, in the unique sense of the word . . . is present–as Beauty). With this subordination of self-consciousness to the realization of beauty, Hölderlin establishes the conceptual framework that he follows in completing the novel.

The final version of the novel, the greater part of which was completed during the period he was in

Frankfurt am Main, shows Hölderlin's increasing stylistic and formal mastery. He returns to the epistolary form of the first version, but now endows it with a particularly sophisticated structure. Hyperion presents a retrospective view of his life, beginning at the stage at which, after having lost his beloved and his friends, he returns bitterly disappointed to his native land, intending to take up the life of a hermit. The main focus is not the sequence of events but the act of narration itself. The seemingly disconnected fragments of his experience are integrated through the process of reflective recapitulation and gradually assume a dialectical structure in which union and separation, joy and suffering come to be seen as inseparable parts of a complex unity.

The first book of volume 1 presents fleeting moments of a joyous hope that is inevitably dashed: "Auf dieser Höh steh ich oft, mein Bellarmin! Aber ein Moment des Besinnens wirft mich herab. . . . O ein Gott ist der Mensch, wenn er träumt, ein Bettler, wenn er nachdenkt" (On these heights I stand often, Bellarmin! But a moment of reflection casts me down. O man is a god when he dreams, and a beggar when he thinks). This pattern is repeated in Hyperion's relationship with his mentor Adamas, who introduces him to the world of the ancient Greeks, and especially with his friend Alabanda, who is a political revolutionary. Together, Hyperion and Alabanda aspire to change the world, but their ways soon part, as Hyperion becomes disillusioned with the violence that is inseparable from revolutionary action. He accuses Alabanda of placing too much emphasis on the state, which has but a restrictive and regulatory function, and too little on the "unsichtbare Kirche" (invisible church) of all-enveloping enthusiasm, which is the only means of comprehensive regeneration. The conclusion of the first book laments the illusory nature of human fulfillment with a consistent hopelessness that is reminiscent of that expressed by Goethe's Werther. It is at this point that the theme of beauty transforms Hyperion's strivings. The encounter with Diotima (narrated in the second book of the first volume) transports him to a realm of experience in which the ideal that is otherwise sought beyond the stars or at the end of time has become reality in the here and now. As such, it is not lost when no longer immediately present, but merely hidden, and can be recovered through the process of memory. Not only the person of Diotima, but also the culture of ancient Athens is an embodiment of the divine in this sense. In this view Athenian culture was a self-realization of divine beauty by virtue of the fact that God and man were ultimately one, and the forms of human self-expression—art, religion, political freedom, and even philosophy—were manifestations of their unity. The principle of "das Eine in sich unterschiedne" (the

one that is differentiated within itself), which Hölderlin adapted from a formulation of Heraclitus, defines at once the essence of the Athenian and the nature of beauty—as opposed to the one-sidedness and fragmentation characteristic of the Egyptians and the Spartans, and, in Hölderlin's view, also of modern times.

Thus at the beginning of the second volume Hyperion thinks he has found in the Athenian realization of beauty a model that can be re-created in his own epoch. The belief enables him to take up again the political cause that he had previously rejected. He allies himself once more with Alabanda and participates in the Greek war of liberation against the Turks, hoping to forge a free state as a pantheon of beauty. Such a project is, however, doomed to failure, as the discrepancy between the high ideal and the reality of warfare and violence becomes apparent, and he is forced to recognize that it is folly to entrust a "Räuberbande" (band of robbers) with the founding of his Elysium. In despair, Hyperion plunges recklessly into battle, where death seems certain. In fact, he is merely wounded, and spends several days in a coma. At this stage, Hyperion's relationships with both Alabanda and Diotima, who had represented opposite poles of his being, have undergone radical transformation. Whereas they had previously been dominant influences on him, their essential impulses are now subsumed in Hyperion himself, who combines the activism of the one with the harmony of the other. As a result, both characters recognize that Hyperion has absorbed into himself and thus superseded the essence of their being. Alabanda submits himself to the harsh judgment of the revolutionary confederates that he has betrayed by his association with Hyperion, and Diotima, caught up in Hyperion's passion for change, is fatally estranged from the innocent harmony that she had once embodied. A visit to Germany brings further disappointment, as Hyperion discovers the Germans' total lack of aesthetic sensibility. His "Letter on the Germans" has become a famous example of German cultural self-criticism.

When he returns to his native land from Germany, Hyperion has returned to the point at which the novel begins. Now, however, his past has become for him the consequence of a necessary interplay of forces, rather than of a series of isolated setbacks. He is "ruhig" (calm) as he realizes that suffering and death are inseparable from life, and is able through recollection to resolve dissonances into the harmony of song. Diotima's parting words, that he is neither crowned with the laurel wreath of fame nor decorated with the myrtle leaves of love, but that his "dichterische Tage" (poetic days) as priest of nature are now assured, provide a justification for his future poetic vocation that concludes the novel and lays the groundwork for the overriding theme of Hölderlin's later work.

From 1798 until 1800 Hölderlin was in Homburg. There he was befriended by Isaak von Sinclair, who had studied law in Tübingen and Jena, had been expelled from the University of Jena in 1795 because of his involvement with Jacobin political circles, and was now in the service of the Landgraf (count) of Hessen-Homburg. Hölderlin called Sinclair his "Herzensfreund (bosom friend) *instar omnium*" and accompanied him to the Congress of Rastatt in 1798–1799. The theme of the affinity of poet and hero (man of action), which occurs in several of Hölderlin's poems of this period, reflects his relationship to Sinclair. The ode "An Eduard" (To Edward) is actually addressed to Sinclair, to whom Hölderlin later dedicated "Der Rhein" (The Rhine), one of his major poems. While in Homburg, Hölderlin made every effort to establish himself by his writing. Hoping for recognition from the court, he addressed an ode to the princess ("Der Prinzessin Auguste von Homburg") and some years later dedicated his translation of Sophocles' tragedies to her; his poem "Patmos," furthermore, was presented to the Landgraf. Hölderlin attempted to establish himself in the literary world by founding a journal called "Iduna," which would contain both original literary works and critical and historical essays; although he solicited the support of several literary figures, including Schiller, Schelling, and Goethe, the response was negligible. Indeed, his isolation and lack of recognition were such that he has become almost a prototype of the poet who fails to regain renown in his own time.

Hölderlin's major literary project in Homburg was his verse drama *Der Tod des Empedokles* (1826; translated as *The Death of Empedokles*, 1964), on which he had begun work while he was still in Frankfurt am Main. Its theme was taken from a legend of the pre-Socratic natural philosopher Empedocles, who was said to have thrown himself to his death in the volcano Etna. Empedocles is for Hölderlin the figure of a seer who, endowed with the ability to be the mouthpiece of nature, is, in his attempt to exploit his prophetic gifts, guilty of a hubris that can only be expiated by his return to nature through the act of his freely chosen death. His guilt is the "guilt of language," which desecrates the divine by articulating it in human words. The play is also the vehicle for Hölderlin's criticism both of established religion and of political rule, in that the priest Hermokrates and the archon Kritias are cast as opponents who endeavor to have Empedocles expelled and condemned. But in anticipation of his death, which is a spiritual reconciliation with nature, Empedocles regains the support of his people by articulating the prophetic vision of a coming festival of the gods at which his

"einsam Lied" (lonely song) is to become a "Freudenchor" (chorus of joy) uniting the whole people.

The play is on the one hand an attempt to recreate the tragic drama of the Greeks, on the other a statement of Hölderlin's position in relation to questions of his own time. The declaration "Dies ist die Zeit der Könige nicht mehr" (This is no longer the time of kings), with which Empedocles rejects the crown proffered to him, is an affirmation of the republican principle derived ultimately from the French Revolution. But the problem of establishing an overriding "objective" necessity of Empedocles' death, according to the Greek conception of tragedy, caused Hölderlin considerable difficulty and led him to recast the play several times. After leaving the (comparatively extensive) first version and a shorter second version incomplete, he set down his reflections in an essay, "Ground zum Empedokles" (translated as "The Ground of Empedocles" 1985), which attempts to establish that, as Empedocles is a son of his time and of his country and conditioned by a particularly virulent conflict between nature and culture, his death is the means of reconciliation of this conflict: he is "ein Opfer seiner Zeit" (a victim of his time), who must be sacrificed so that the reconciliation achieved in him as an individual can be carried over into the life of his people. He is in a way a Christ figure, the prophet of a new age of peace that he cannot himself live to see. This conception finds expression in a third version of the play, which, however, also remains unfinished. One of the reasons Hölderlin abandoned his play, without publishing any of it, may be that he came to see that the prophetic vision of a new age was not really a theme suitable for tragic drama, the quintessentially Greek form, but was more appropriate to the lyric, whose origin is rather the isolation of the individual in a still-godless age.

It is in the lyric that Hölderlin was able to express himself most freely at all stages of his literary career. Whereas in Tübingen he had, until 1792, largely imitated the loose, rhymed forms of Schiller's poetry, he soon turned predominantly to the classical ode. The ode, as it is understood in German literary history, is not the so-called Pindaric ode cultivated by English Romantic writers, but the Horatian ode, whose basic form is a four-line stanza, unrhymed, with an intricate metrical pattern. It had been adapted to the German language by Friedrich Gottlieb Klopstock and others, and gained in Hölderlin's work a new level of flexibility and expressiveness. In contrast to Klopstock, who experimented with many traditional ode forms and even invented new ones, Hölderlin confined himself almost entirely to the alcaic and the (third) asclepiadeic stanzas. In Frankfurt am Main he had written several short, almost epigrammatic odes, some of which were published in various journals and almanacs, but in the more mature odes written in Homburg he expanded the form to accommodate the full range of his themes. The odes are mostly apostrophes to divine, natural, or heroic beings, elevated in tone, and borne by a conviction to the poet's vocation: "Beruf ist mirs, zu rühmen Höhers" (It is my profession to extol higher things). The programmatic ode "Natur und Kunst, oder Saturn und Jupiter" (Nature and Art, or Saturn and Jupiter), for example, calls upon the Olympian god Jupiter, who embodies the rule of law and has banished his own father, the god of the Golden Age, to reinstate the latter and acknowledge his supremacy. In terms of the poem's metaphorical dimension, art must recognize its origin in and indebtedness to nature as the ground of its being. The poem "Der Abschied" (Leave-taking) laments the poet's parting from Diotima, which, anguishing though it is at first, ultimately yields to a poetic recollection of past happiness that transcends the sense of loss. "Der gefesselte Strom" (The Icebound Stream) depicts the river that in the spring bursts out of its frozen state to become the harbinger of regeneration, although it must lose itself as it flows into the sea. In this poem (as elsewhere) the river, the demigod of divine birth whose life-bringing sojourn on earth is but a prelude to his return to his origins, is a central image. Several odes—"Dichterberuf" (The Poet's Vocation), "Dichtermut" (The Courage of the Poet), "Der blinde Sänger" (The Blind Singer)—outline the theme of the poetic vocation with its immediacy to the divine and its consequent perils and blessings. An experimental poem written in Pindaric meters, "Wie wenn am Feiertage . . ." (As when on a Feast Day . . .), presents the situation of the poet in the figure of Semele, who, according to the myth, wished to see Jupiter with her own eyes but was fatally consumed by his radiance, giving birth to Dionysus. Just so should the poet stand bareheaded in the storms of the divine, in order to transmit the sacred fire to other human beings in the form of song. It is characteristic of Hölderlin's odes of the Homburg period to conclude with an affirmation of poetry.

During this time he also drafted several essays, which for the most part remained unfinished and were probably not intended for publication in their present form, but which contain the outline of a comprehensive theory of poetry. He was concerned on the one hand to define poetry as the articulation of the "infinite moment" of transcendent experience, and on the other hand to construct a system of poetic genres and forms. The essay "Über die Verfahrungsweise des poetischen Geistes" (On the Procedure of the Poetic Spirit) defines the "free choice" of poetic subject matter and the creation of a "Welt in der Welt" (World in the World) as the only means of attaining self-consciousness. Thus

poetry provides the answer to the philosophical question raised by Fichte and becomes for Hölderlin—as for other Romantic writers of his time—the highest expression of the human spirit. By shaping the relationship of the human to the divine, it also in a sense supersedes "positive" religion: "So wäre alle Religion ihrem Wesen nach poetisch" (Thus all religion is essentially poetic), as Hölderlin asserts in the essay "Über Religion" (On Religion).

The "Romantic" glorification of poetry was balanced by a "classical" adherence to formal clarity and exactitude. Not only did Hölderlin write mainly in classical meters, but in addition his whole conception of genres was based on ancient Greek literature, with its three great models: Homer for epic poetry, Sophocles for tragedy, and Pindar—"das Summum der Dichtkunst" (the ultimate perfection of poetry), as Hölderlin had put it while still in Tübingen—for the lyric. In Hölderlin's essay "Über den Unterschied der Dichtarten" (On the Difference of Poetic Genres), each kind of poetry is defined in terms of a basic opposition: the underlying "heroic" impulse of epic poetry is expressed all the more powerfully because of its contrast with the "naive" concreteness of Homeric language; lyric poetry is "naive" in its origin, in that it speaks with the voice of an individual, but it soars to the expression of a suprasensual, "idealistic" harmony; tragic poetry is grounded in an "idealistic" intellectual perception of the whole, which can only be expressed in the depiction of "heroic" conflict. It is apparent from the use of the terms *naive, heroic,* and *idealistic* that Hölderlin's theory, while based on traditional divisions into genre, is also a self-contained system in the spirit of idealist thinking. He further proceeds to define poetic structure in terms of these same three tones, which he even sets out as a "Wechsel der Töne" (modulation of tones) in tabular form. The tables also establish an overall structure: by returning to its starting point at a higher level of reflection, the poem effects a dialectical resolution of dissonances.

In mid 1800 Hölderlin moved to Stuttgart, where he spent an unusually happy half year with a friend he had first met in Jena, Christian Landauer. He earned some money by giving lessons in philosophy, but soon sought another position as a children's tutor. In January 1801 he accepted a post with the family Gonzenbach in Hauptwil, Switzerland, which he gave up after only three months in order to return to Nürtingen. The exact reason for the termination of his employment is not known, but there are indications that his growing restlessness may have been a first sign of the mental illness that later befell him. His experience of the Swiss landscape left traces in the elegy "Heimkunft" (Homecoming) and other poems.

At about this time, Hölderlin composed several lengthy poems in the elegiac form. In the German tradition, the elegy is not just a poem of lamentation, but is written in elegiac couplets (consisting of an alternation of hexameter and pentameter) adapted from Greek and Roman literature. Building upon the work of such predecessors as Goethe and Schiller, who had already adapted this form to the needs of the German language, Hölderlin was able to render it with consummate mastery. His first elegy, "Menon's Klagen um Diotima" (Menon's Lament for Diotima), takes its starting point in the separation of the lovers, but opens into an enthusiastic invocation of a new age of bliss. "Brod und Wein," perhaps his best known elegy, explores the historical progression from Greek antiquity to the present: the disappearance of the gods from Greece leads to a premonition of their reappearance in present-day Germany, which—in a conflation of the classical and the Christian traditions centered in Dionysus and Christ respectively—is embodied in the symbols of bread and wine, common to both traditions. The elegies "Stuttgart" and "Heimkunft" take this process further and celebrate German heroes. More and more the elegies, which had begun by turning to the past, shift in emphasis toward the national future. The same applies to the long hexameter poem "Der Archipelagus" (The Archipelago), which celebrates the Greek victory over the Persians but ultimately evokes a development that encompasses Greek antiquity and the present day in a single grandiose sequence of the seasons, so that the "köstliche Frühlingszeit im Griechenlande" (precious springtime of Greece) is due to return the coming autumn in the perfection of maturity.

The elegies can thus be regarded as an intermediate stage leading to the later hymns, which are perhaps Hölderlin's most lasting achievement. In 1801 he began a series of poems in free rhythms in the tradition of the "hymn" (in the German sense), for which the obvious model was Pindar—though less in respect to meter (which in Pindar, as Hölderlin already knew, is closely regulated) than in the overall structure, specifically in the tripartite form that is characteristic of Pindar's poems. Most of Hölderlin's hymns contain six, nine, twelve, or fifteen stanzas, which are arranged in groups of three in a complex dialectical pattern. From various statements in his letters, it is clear that he regarded this new style—"das hohe und reine Frohlocken vaterländischer Gesänge" (the pure noble jubilation of patriotic songs)—as the attainment of his poetic goal, indeed as a fusion of nature and history that was previously achieved only in ancient Greece: "die Sangart überhaupt wird einen andern Character nehmen" (poetry altogether will take on a new character). It should be noted that the "patriotic" element does not so much involve the narrowly German as the modern, "sofern es von dem Griechischen verschieden ist" (insofar as it is

distinct from the Greek). Hölderlin's view of the *querelle des anciens et des modernes* is one of the more significant variations of this theme, which was so prevalent in the literature of his time.

The later hymns conform to this conception. The poem "Der Rhein" combines the depiction of the river as a demigod that bursts its banks in order to transform the divine impulse into fruitful human activity with a reflection on the nature of genius and with a consideration of Jean-Jacques Rousseau, a problematical figure who in his closeness to the harmony of nature seems no longer to typify the heroic existence, and of Socrates, who retained sobriety when all around him were succumbing. The poem combines the immediate presence of the divine in nature with the timeless transcendence of the spirit in a vast panorama that embraces the whole range of interaction of the human and the divine in a concerted set of images. In "Patmos" the poet is transported to the isle of Patmos, site of the composition of the Gospel of John, which inaugurates a tradition that points from the Orient to the West, from the original revelation of the divine to its transmission in the form of the "fester Buchstabe" (the fixed letter) of biblical tradition. The poem "Friedensfeier" (Festival of Peace), whose final version was not discovered and published until 1953, celebrates a truce in the Napoleonic Wars, but at the same time envisages the coming of a somewhat mysterious "Fürst des Fests" (Prince of the Feast), who seems to combine elements of Napoleon, Christ, and other figures. But however controversial the question of the identity of Hölderlin's unnamed figure has remained, it is clear that his coming signals a reconciliation of nature and humanity, a new millenium. In the poem "Der Einzige" (The Unique One) the sweeping overview of the whole philosophical and religious tradition is called into question by what seems to be an irreconcilable conflict between the claims of Christ to a uniqueness that excludes the worship of all other gods (hence the title of the poem), and the mutual mediability of the polytheistic gods—and demigods—of antiquity. If Heracles as the conquering inaugurator and Dionysus as the purveyor of the communal spirit can be regarded as successive stages in the development of human culture, then the Christian claim to uniqueness threatens to disrupt continuity: thus the poem circles incessantly about the theme of the comparability of Heracles, Dionysus, and Christ, who ideally should be conceivable as forming a kind of three-leafed clover but whose respective claims tend to cause dissension rather than unity. That the poem remains unfinished, despite having been recast several times, is testimony to the vastness of Hölderlin's ambition: to reconcile the Greek and the Christian traditions in one comprehensive vision, to rewrite mythology, to dissolve the fixity of traditional names in order to recreate them out of their common matrix. More and more, the ambitiousness of Hölderlin's attempt to present the coming fulfillment as the culmination of European history strained his poetic capacities and led to a continual process of revision which affected several of his poems of this period.

After his return to Nürtingen from Switzerland in April 1801, Hölderlin had gained provisional consent from the publisher Johann Friedrich Cotta to bring out a collection of his poems. But the project was interrupted (and in effect aborted) by Hölderlin's decision to take yet another position as private tutor, this time with the family of D. C. Meyer, German consul in Bordeaux. He set out on foot for Strasbourg in December 1801, arriving in Bordeaux on 28 January 1802. Again, the circumstances of his stay and the reasons for its premature termination remain unclear. He left Bordeaux on 10 May and arrived in Strasbourg in early June, evidently after extensive wanderings that took him by way of Paris. On his arrival in Germany he received the shattering news of the death of Susette Gontard, who had succumbed to an infection she had caught from her children. He arrived home in Nürtingen in a distraught state, and from this time reports of his mental instability increased.

The poems that Hölderlin completed after his return show a certain shift, which has often been attributed to a growing doubt in the validity of his prophetic vision. The poem "Andenken" (Remembrance) is clearly influenced by the scenery of Bordeaux; although it culminates in the apparent definitiveness of the oft-quoted final verse "Was bleibet aber, stiften die Dichter" (But what lasts is founded by the poets), it is characterized by an uneasy alliance of private remembrance and gnomic utterance that gives it a hauntingly mysterious, not clearly definable tone. The same applies to "Mnemosyne," in which the theme of the death of Mnemosyne, the muse of memory, suggests that Hölderlin had reached a breaking point, at which the constituent elements of his unifying vision were threatened by disintegration. His later poems, which remain largely unfinished, attempt to incorporate ever more modern figures.

While his poetic production yielded few tangible results in the form of complete poems at this stage, Hölderlin turned his attention increasingly to translations from the Greek, and had his versions of Sophocles' *Oedipus Rex* and *Antigone* published in 1804. His concern, however, was allied to that of his own poetry, in that he wished to make of his translations a kind of reinterpretation that would reestablish continuity between antiquity and the present. Indeed, he expressed the intention of "correcting" the artistic failing of Sophocles, who had underplayed the "Feuer vom Himmel" (fire from heaven) in which the "Oriental" origins of Greek culture are reflected. Hölderlin's translations are notable in that, despite certain inaccuracies, they convey more of the elemental power of the original than other German translations; they have often been performed on the stage. (The translation of *Antigone* forms the basis of a play by Bertolt Brecht and an opera by Carl Orff.) Hölderlin elaborated his views in several letters written in 1803 and 1804 to his publisher Friedrich Wilmans, and also in the commentaries that accompany his versions of Sophocles' plays. Here he suggests that Oedipus, who is driven out of his mind by the inability to comprehend his own origins, is the prototype of Greek tragedy, whereas Antigone, who asserts her own independence in defiance of the established order, anticipates the transition from the ancient Greek to the modern. At much the same time, Hölderlin translated some fragments from Pindar, which he supplied with comments that are less an explanation of Pindar's poems than a rather enigmatic exposition of some of Hölderlin's own concepts.

A request from the publisher Wilmans to contribute to his almanac for the year 1805 provided Hölderlin with the opportunity to publish several of his poems. He submitted a group of nine poems that had been written after his return from Bordeaux in 1802 and that he now collected under the title "Nachtgesänge" (Night Songs). The six odes among them are in the main reworkings of earlier poems which introduce a harsher and more discordant note. The well-known poem "Hälfte des Lebens" (Middle of Life), which contrasts a summer scene of peace and bliss with the windswept emptiness of portending wintry desolation, has often been read as a portrayal of Hölderlin's recognition of a turning point in his own life.

Following the publication of the Sophocles translations in 1804 and the "Night Songs" in 1805, several other poems by Hölderlin appeared in print, if not always with his permission: an old friend, Leo von Seckendorf, brought out the poems "Stuttgart" and "Die Wanderung" (The Journey) in his *Musenalmanach für das Jahr 1807* (Almanac for the Muses for 1807) and other poems–"Der Rhein," "Patmos," and "Andenken" (Remembrance)–in the corresponding volume for 1808. But Hölderlin was able to work only sporadically by this time, and in June 1804 his friend Sinclair took him to Homburg once more and obtained for him a position (more of a sinecure, as Hölderlin's salary was paid out of Sinclair's pocket) as court librarian. Hölderlin was further unsettled by events of early 1805, when one Alexander Blankenstein denounced Sinclair for having allegedly conspired against the life of the Elector Friedrich II of Württemberg; Sinclair was accused of high treason and imprisoned for a time before being brought to trial (he was later acquitted), and Hölderlin was tangentially involved through his association with Sinclair. Although medical testimony to his insanity saved him from having to stand trial, he was deeply disturbed by the whole affair, which also unfavorably affected his friendship with Sinclair. Because the state of Hesse-Homburg was dissolved in 1806, Sinclair could no longer provide for Hölderlin in Homburg and asked Hölderlin's mother to take him back. By this time considered quite insane by most people who knew him, Hölderlin was forcibly removed from Homburg in September 1806 and delivered to the tender mercies of Ferdinand Autenrieth, who ran a clinic in Tübingen for the mentally ill. (It lies on the bank of the Neckar just above the Hölderlin Tower, and now houses various university departments.) Autenrieth is best known as the inventor of a face mask named after him, whose function was to present patients from screaming, and his treatment of Hölderlin did little to alleviate the latter's condition. In May 1807 Hölderlin was released as incurable, with the prognosis of having no more than about three years to live, and given over to the care of the carpenter Ernst Zimmer and his family, who lived just below the clinic. Hölderlin's room was in a tower by the riverbank, which (after having been burned down and rebuilt) is now known as the Hölderlin Tower and houses the Hölderlin-Gesellschaft (Hölderlin Society).

The three years allotted to Hölderlin became thirty-six. During that time he was lovingly cared for by the Zimmer family and treated in niggardly fashion by his mother, who, although living close by, did not once visit him and contrived to limit his access to the patrimony due to him. Hölderlin became an object of some notoriety to students and younger writers. Writers such as Justinus Kerner, Mörike, and Wilhelm Waiblinger have left accounts, with Waiblinger making him the subject of an essay titled *Friedrich Hölderlins Leben, Dichtung und Wahnsinn* (Friedrich Hölderlin's Life, Poetry and Madness, 1947). Although he may have continued to write for a short time in his previous style, most of the poetry that Hölderlin wrote during this period represents a distinct break: he reverted to simple rhyming four-line stanzas, devoted largely to stereotypical evocations of the seasons and reflections on the human condition, devoid of the intensity and breadth of vision of his earlier work. Many of the poems he distributed to visitors were signed with imaginary names—most often: Scardanelli—and provided with impossible dates. Hölderlin died peacefully in his sleep on 7 June 1843, at the age of seventy-three.

Although Hölderlin achieved comparatively little recognition during his lifetime, and during his final stay in Tübingen was unable to supervise the publication of his own work, there was some slight local interest in his writings. His novel *Hyperion* was republished in 1822, and in 1826 Gustav Schwab and Ludwig Uhland brought out an edition of some of the poems. The first edition with any claim to comprehensiveness was prepared by Christoph Theodor Schwab; comprising a larger selection of poetry, some letters, and the "Fragment von *Hyperion*," it appeared in 1846. Other editions appeared around the turn of the century, without exciting great resonance. The first real breakthrough occurred in the years preceding World War I, when Norbert von Hellingrath, who as a student in Munich had written a doctoral dissertation on Hölderlin's translations of Pindar, inaugurated an historical-critical edition. The fourth volume, which appeared in 1916 and for the first time designated the later poems as "Herz, Kern und Gipfel" (heart, core and pinnacle) of Hölderlin's work, had a sensational impact that established his reputation as a major poet. Several German Expressionist poets—Georg Trakl, Georg Heym, Johannes R. Becher, Ernst Stadler—as well as Stefan George and Rainer Maria Rilke felt a close affinity to him. Hölderlin's prophetic poetry came to be regarded by many as a proclamation for modern times, or as a timeless manifestation of the poetic essence. An influential case is that of the philosopher Martin Heidegger, who in the 1930s, after he had disassociated himself from the National Socialist order that he had at first embraced, turned to the glorification of Hölderlin.

After Hellingrath's death in World War I, the edition he had begun was completed by others. The fact that so many poems exist only in heavily reworked but not finally revised manuscripts has made the editing of Hölderlin's works a test of the editor's craft. The standard critical edition is the Große Stuttgarter Ausgabe (Large Stuttgart Edition), edited by Friedrich Beißner (eight volumes, published from 1943 to 1985), which breaks new ground in its presentation of variant readings; the letters and extensive biographical documents are edited by Adolf Beck. The more recent Frankfurt Edition (to date thirteen volumes, the first of which appeared in 1975) includes photocopies of manuscripts; and facsimile collections of manuscripts—the *Homburger Folioheft* (1986) and the *Stuttgarter Foliobuch* (1989)—have also been published in recent years, attesting to Hölderlin's now-established renown as a poet and thinker of international importance.

In 1943 the Hölderlin-Gesellschaft was established in Tübingen. It is responsible for the *Hölderlin-Jahrbuch* (Hölderlin Yearbook), the twenty-fifth volume of which appeared in 1987, and also conducts biennial meetings. The Hölderlin Archive, which has originals or copies of all extant manuscripts and a comprehensive collection of literature on Hölderlin, was founded in Tübingen in 1941; moved to Bebenhausen, near Tübingen, in 1943; and in 1970 was incorporated into the Württembergische Landesbibliothek (Württemberg State Library) in Stuttgart.

Letters:

Ausgewählte Briefe, edited by Wilhelm Böhm (Jena: Diederichs, 1910);

Briefe, edited by Erich Lichtenstein (Weimar: Lichtenstein, 1922);

Friedrich Hölderlins gesammelte Briefe, edited by Ernst Bertram (Leipzig: Insel, 1935);

Briefe, edited by Friedrich Seebaß (Vienna: Kirschner, 1944);

Briefe zur Erziehung, edited by K. Lothar Wolf (Hamburg: Simons, 1950);

Einundzwanzig Briefe, edited by Bertold Hack (Frankfurt am Main: Beyer, 1966);

Dokumente seines Lebens: Briefe, Tagebücher, Aufzeichnungen/ Hölderlin, edited by Hermann Hesse and Karl Isenberg (Frankfurt am Main: Insel, 1976).

Bibliography:

Maria Kohler, ed., *Internationale Hölderlin-Bibliographie* (Stuttgart: Frommann-Holzboog, 1985).

References:

Adolf Beck and Paul Raabe, *Hölderlin: Eine Chronik in Text und Bild* (Frankfurt am Main: Insel, 1970);

Friedrich Beißner, *Hölderlins Übersetzungen aus dem Griechischen* (Stuttgart: Metzler, 1933);

Beißner, *Reden und Aufsätze* (Weimar: Böhlau, 1961);

Maurice Benn, *Hölderlin and Pindar* (The Hague: Mouton, 1962);

Paul Bertaux, *Friedrich Hölderlin* (Frankfurt am Main: Suhrkamp, 1978);

Wolfgang Binder, *Friedrich Hölderlin: Studien* (Frankfurt am Main: Suhrkamp, 1987);

Binder, *Hölderlin-Aufsätze* (Frankfurt am Main: Insel, 1970);

Bernhard Böschenstein, *Hölderlins Rheinhymne* (Zurich: Atlantis, 1959);

Böschenstein, *Konkordanz zu Hölderlins Gedichten nach 1800* (Göttingen: Vandenhoeck & Ruprecht, 1964);

David Constantine, *Hölderlin* (Oxford: Clarendon Press, 1988);

Martin Dannhauer, Hans Otto Horch, and Klaus Schuffels, eds., *Wörterbuch zu Friedrich Hölderlin,* volume 1: *Die Gedichte* (Tübingen: Niemeyer, 1983);

Howard Gaskill, *Hölderlin's "Hyperion"* (Durham, U.K.: University of Durham, 1984);

Robin Harrison, *Hölderlin and Greek Literature* (Oxford: Clarendon Press, 1975);

Martin Heidegger, *Erläuterungen zu Hölderlins Dichtung* (Frankfurt am Main: Klostermann, 1951);

Dieter Henrich, *Der Gang des Andenkens: Beobachtungen zu Hölderlins Gedicht* (Stuttgart: Klett-Cotta, 1986);

Henrich, "Hegel und Hölderlin," in his *Hegel im Kontext* (Frankfurt am Main: Suhrkamp, 1971), pp. 9–40;

Alfred Kelletat, *Hölderlin: Beiträge zu seinem Verständnis in unsrem Jahrhundert* (Tübingen: Mohr, 1961);

Werner Kirchner, *Der Hochverratsprozeß gegen Sinclair* (Marburg: Simons, 1949);

Günter Mieth, *Friedrich Hölderlin: Dichter der bürgerlich-demokratischen Revolution* (Berlin: Rütten & Loening, 1978);

Ernst Müller, *Hölderlin: Studien zur Geschichte seines Geistes* (Stuttgart: Kohlhammer, 1944);

Ronald Peacock, *Hölderlin* (London: Methuen/New York: Barnes & Noble, 1973);

Allesandro Pellegrini, *Friedrich Hölderlin: Sein Bild in der Forschung* (Berlin: De Gruyter, 1965);

Lawrence Ryan, *Friedrich Hölderlin* (Stuttgart: Metzler, 1961; revised, 1967);

Ryan, *Hölderlins "Hyperion": Exzentrische Bahn und Dichterberuf* (Stuttgart: Metzler, 1965);

Ryan, *Hölderlins Lehre vom Wechsel der Töne* (Stuttgart: Kohlhammer, 1960);

Eric L. Santner, *Friedrich Hölderlin: Narrative Vigilance and the Poetic Imagination* (New Brunswick, N.J.: Rutgers University Press, 1986);

Jochen Schmidt, *Hölderlins Elegie "Brot und Wein"* (Berlin: Schmidt, 1968);

Schmidt, *Über Hölderlin* (Frankfurt am Main: Insel, 1970);

Richard Ungar, *Friedrich Hölderlin* (Boston: Twayne, 1984);

Wilhelm Waiblinger, *Friedrich Hölderlins Leben, Dichtung und Wahnsinn* (Hamburg: Ellermann, 1947).

Papers:

The Hölderlin Archive is located at the Württembergische Landesbibliothek, Stuttgart.

Uwe Johnson

(20 July 1934 – 23? February 1984)

Robert K. Shirer
University of Nebraska at Lincoln

This entry originally appeared in DLB 75: Contemporary German Fiction
Writers, Second Series.

BOOKS: *Mutmaßungen über Jakob: Roman* (Frankfurt am Main: Suhrkamp, 1959); translated by Ursule Molinaro as *Speculations about Jakob* (London: Cape, 1963; New York: Grove Press, 1963);

Das dritte Buch über Achim: Roman (Frankfurt am Main: Suhrkamp, 1961); translated by Molinaro as *The Third Book about Achim* (New York: Harcourt, Brace & World, 1967);

Karsch und andere Prosa (Frankfurt am Main: Suhrkamp, 1964); "Eine Reise wegwohin, 1960" translated by Richard and Clara Winston as *An Absence* (London: Cape, 1969);

Zwei Ansichten (Frankfurt am Main: Suhrkamp, 1965); translated by Richard and Clara Winston as *Two Views* (New York: Harcourt, Brace & World, 1966; London: Cape, 1967);

Jahrestage: Aus dem Leben von Gesine Cresspahl, 4 volumes (Frankfurt am Main: Suhrkamp, 1970–1973, 1983); translated by Leila Vennewitz as *Anniversaries: From the Life of Gesine Cresspahl,* 2 volumes (New York & London: Harcourt Brace Jovanovich, 1975, 1987);

Eine Reise nach Klagenfurt (Frankfurt am Main: Suhrkamp, 1974);

Berliner Sachen: Aufsätze (Frankfurt am Main: Suhrkamp, 1975);

Begleitumstände: Frankfurter Vorlesungen (Frankfurt am Main: Suhrkamp, 1980);

Skizze eines Verunglückten (Frankfurt am Main: Suhrkamp, 1982);

Ingrid Babendererde: Reifeprüfung 1953 (Frankfurt am Main: Suhrkamp, 1985);

Der 5. Kanal (Frankfurt am Main: Suhrkamp, 1987);

Porträts und Erinnerungen, edited by Eberhard Fahlke (Frankfurt am Main: Suhrkamp, 1988);

Entwöhnung von einem Arbeitsplatz: Klausuren und frühe Prosatexte, edited by Bernd Neumann (Frankfurt am Main: Suhrkamp, 1992);

Uwe Johnson at about the time he began writing his four-volume novel
Jahrestage *(Kindermann)*

Inselgeschichten, edited by Fahlke (Frankfurt am Main: Suhrkamp, 1995);

Heute neunzig Jahr: Aus dem Nachlaß herausgegeben, edited by Norbert Mecklenburg (Frankfurt am Main: Suhrkamp, 1996).

OTHER: Herman Melville, *Israel Potter: Seine fünfzig Jahre im Exil,* translated by Johnson (Leipzig: Dietrich'sche Verlagsbuchhandlung, 1961);

John Knowles, *In diesem Land,* translated by Johnson (Frankfurt am Main: Suhrkamp, 1963);

Bertolt Brecht, *Me-ti: Buch der Wendungen, Fragment,* edited by Johnson (Frankfurt am Main: Suhrkamp, 1965);

"Einer meiner Lehrer," in *Hans Mayer zum 60. Geburtstag,* edited by Walter Jens and Fritz J. Raddatz (Reinbek: Rowohlt, 1967), pp. 118–126;

Das neue Fenster: Selections from Contemporary German Literature, compiled by Johnson (New York: Harcourt, Brace & World, 1967);

"Dead Author's Identity in Doubt: Publishers Defiant," in *Vorletzte Worte: Schriftsteller schrieben ihren eigenen Nachruf,* edited by Karl Heinz Kramberg (Frankfurt am Main: Bärmeier & Nikel, 1970), pp. 116–124;

"Brief an Walser," in *Leporello fällt aus der Rolle: Zeitgenössische Autoren erzählen das Leben von Figuren der Weltliteratur weiter,* edited by Peter Härtling (Frankfurt am Main: Fischer, 1971), pp. 216–217;

"Nachforschungen in New York: Rede bei der Entgegennahme des Georg-Büchner-Preises," in *Büchner-Preis-Reden,* 1951–1971, edited by Ernst Johann (Stuttgart: Reclam, 1972), pp. 217–240;

"Einatmen und hinterlegen," in *Günter Eich zum Gedächtnis,* edited by Siegfried Unseld (Frankfurt am Main: Suhrkamp, 1973), pp. 74–77;

"Erste Lese-Erlebnisse," in *Erste Lese-Erlebnisse,* edited by Unseld (Frankfurt am Main: Suhrkamp, 1975), pp. 101–110;

"Vorschläge zur Prüfung eines Romans," in *Romantheorie: Dokumentation ihrer Geschichte in Deutschland seit 1880,* edited by Eberhard Lämmert and Hartmut Eggert (Cologne: Kiepenheuer & Witsch, 1975), pp. 398–403;

Max Frisch, *Stich-Worte,* edited by Johnson (Frankfurt am Main: Suhrkamp, 1975);

Das Werk von Samuel Beckett: Berliner Colloquium, edited by Johnson and Hans Mayer (Frankfurt am Main: Suhrkamp, 1975);

"Zu Montauk," in *Über Max Frisch II,* edited by Walter Schmitz (Frankfurt am Main: Suhrkamp, 1976), pp. 448–450;

Von dem Fischer un syner Fru: Ein Märchen nach Philipp Otto Runge mit sieben Bildern von Marcus Behmer, einer Nacherzählung und einem Nachwort, translated by Johnson (Frankfurt am Main: Insel, 1976);

Margret Boveri, *Verzweigungen: Eine Autobiographie,* edited by Johnson (Munich & Zurich: Piper, 1977).

PERIODICAL PUBLICATIONS: "Mir ist gelegen an Fairness: Erklärung von Uwe Johnson auf der Pressekonferenz des Suhrkamp Verlages am 5. Dezember 1961," *Deutsche Zeitung mit Wirtschaftszeitung* (Cologne), 7 December 1961;

"Ich nenne Hermann Kesten einen Lügner: Uwe Johnsons Erklärung in Frankfurt," *Die Welt,* 9 December 1961;

"Pro Wolf Biermann: Erklärungen von Heinrich Böll, Peter Weiss und Uwe Johnson," *Der Tagesspiegel,* 18 December 1965;

"Beisetzung Giangiacomo Feltrinelli," *Kürbiskern,* 8 (1972): 367–371;

"Besuch im Krankenhaus: Erinnerung an Margret Boveri–Zum 75. Geburtstag der Schriftstellerin," *Die Zeit,* 15 August 1975;

"Ich habe zu danken," *Frankfurter Allgemeine Zeitung,* 8 December 1975;

"Gast war ich gerne: Keine Mafia, sondern Tagung meiner Innung," *Die Zeit,* 15 July 1977;

"Ich über mich," *Die Zeit,* 4 November 1977;

"Ach! Sind Sie ein Deutscher?" *Die Zeit,* 6 February 1978;

"Lübeck habe ich ständig beobachtet," *Vaterstädtische Blätter* (Lübeck), 30 (March / April 1979): 51–57;

"Ein Vorbild," *Literaturmagazin,* 10 (1979): 167–170;

"Ein unergründliches Schiff," *Merkur,* 33 (1979): 537–550;

"Seien Sie vielmals bedankt! Mitteilungen aus der alltäglichen Nachbarschaft eines Schriftstellers," *Die Zeit,* 13 August 1980.

When *Mutmaßungen über Jakob* (translated as *Speculations about Jakob,* 1963), Uwe Johnson's first published novel, appeared in 1959, Johnson immediately became one of the most discussed and most controversial German authors. The novel displayed a virtuosity of language and narrative technique that was remarkable in a first publication, and it incorporated the fact of the division of Germany–and Europe–in a manner that was unprecedented in postwar German literature. Johnson's subsequent work maintained the technical brilliance and linguistic sophistication of *Mutmaßungen über Jakob,* and it continued to examine the juxtaposition of what Johnson called the "beiden Ordnungen, nach denen heute in der Welt gelebt werden kann" (two systems under which one can live in the world today). His persistence in examining the effects of this division on his characters garnered him the titles "poet of both Germanies" and "poet of divided Germany," labels Johnson loathed and rejected. With an insistence on precision of language characteristic of him, he refused to associate himself with the political and ideological connotations these titles carried: "Peinlich ist in solcher Nachrede die Vermutung wahrzunehmen, er befasse sich mit den für ihn vorliegenden 'beiden Deutschland,' weil die Mehrzahl in verstimme und er einen Singular vorziehe in einer Wieder-Vereinigun" (It is embarrassing in such slander to perceive the assumption that he concerns himself with the "two Germanies" he confronts, because the plural distresses him and he would prefer a singular in a reunification). Moreover, Johnson insisted that his thematic concerns were merely a function of his biography and that it was this biography that provided him not only with his themes but also with the skeptical attitude toward language and ideology from which he fashioned his narrative techniques.

Uwe Johnson was born in Cammin in the province of Pomerania on 20 July 1934. His father, Erich Johnson, was a Mecklenburg farmer who became the administrator of a large estate; his mother, Erna Sträde Johnson, was the daughter of a west Pomeranian farmer. He grew up in the small town of Anklam an der Peene. There, by his own account in *Begleitumstände* (Attendant Circumstances, 1980), he learned from his family to be skeptical of the values and the rhetoric of the Nazis. During the last months of the war Johnson, then in his first year of secondary school, was chosen by a state examination commission to attend a National Socialist "Deutsche Heimschule" (German home school) in Koscian, in what is now Poland. When the advance of the Red Army forced a mass exodus to the west, Johnson was young enough to go; the older students had to stay behind to fight, and many of them died.

Johnson's father was interned after the war and died in a camp in Belorussia in 1947 or 1948. Johnson and his mother and sister settled in a village in Mecklenburg; the mother found work as a train conductor. In the difficult year after the war Johnson worked in the village and on the farms around it for food and other necessities. In 1946, following his father's wishes, he began to attend the John Brinkman-Oberschule in Güstrow. At school Johnson wrote and recited a series of connecting texts for a program of folk songs performed by his school choir, and the "junger Güstrower Poet" received his first review in a local newspaper. In *Begleitumstände* he recounts how, as a seventeen-year-old, he felt the need to shape his own unique experience of the conflict between life and art in the form of a story—until he read Thomas Mann's "Tonio Kröger" (1903; translated, 1914): "Dem etwas hinzuzufügen, das erübrigte sich" (Adding anything to that was unnecessary). For the next few years his literary activity was restricted to reading.

During the years Johnson was in Güstrow the division of Germany grew more sharply defined. The Western occupation zones merged into an economic unit and then, in 1949, became the Federal Republic of Germany (FRG). In the Soviet zone the eastern Social Democrats were merged with the Communists to form the Socialist Unity party, which began to consolidate its power under the watchful eye of the Soviet Military Administration. In 1949, Shortly after the birth of the FRG, the German Democratic Republic (GDR) was proclaimed in the East.

Johnson was a leader of his school's chapter of the party youth group, the Freie Deutsche Jugend (Free German Youth [FDJ]), and he supported the policies of the new administration—land reform, opening of the schools to the children of workers and farmers, and exposing schoolchildren to the evils of National Socialism. But his enthusiasm was tempered by the discrepancies he perceived between the version of reality served up by his teachers and representatives of the party and what he could observe himself: "Andere Lehrer wissen, daß der Schüler lügt beim Aufsagen von Lügen, die er von Niemandem weiß als von ihnen selber, und eine Eins schreiben sie ihm an, und der Schüler sieht ihnen zu dabei" (Other teachers know that the student is lying as he recites lies that he knows from no one other than them, and they give him a one—the highest mark—for it, and the student watches them do it).

There was no lack of opportunity to wonder about the meanings of words and descriptions. *Flüchtlinge* (refugees) and *Vertriebene* (those driven out of the former Eastern provinces) became officially *Umsiedler* (resettlers), and the use of any of these terms brought with it a considerable baggage of ideological connotations. Johnson himself benefited from an exercise in redefinition, for he had been classified as the son of middle-class parents and, as such, not eligible for preferential treatment in gaining entrance to a university; but when his mother switched jobs from passenger-train to freight-train conductor he found himself the son of a worker, possessed of new opportunities. Johnson's suspicion of the relationship between observable reality and the words used to describe it never left him, for he found it affirmed in his experiences in both East and West. It forms one of the most significant elements in his development as a writer.

In 1952, after completing the Abitur (school-leaving exam), Johnson became a student at the University of Rostock. In early 1953 he felt the effects of the nationwide effort by the party to discredit the Christian youth organization, the Junge Gemeinde (Young Congregation). This group was accused of being a "Tarnorganisation für Kriegshetze, Sabotage, und Spionage im USA-Auftrag" (front organization in the service of the USA for agitation to war, sabotage, and espionage). All over the GDR members of the Junge Gemeinde were being expelled from the FDJ and from schools and universities. Johnson was called upon to describe to a meeting of the Rostock FDJ a violent attack by two young Christians upon a recruit of the Red Army which allegedly had taken place in Güstrow. He refused, but when ordered to speak he defended the

Christians and cited many violations of the GDR constitution by the government. As a result, he was expelled from school and barred from all universities in the GDR. During the upheavals in June 1953, however, the government reached a rapprochement with the church, and those who had been punished and banished during the Junge Gemeinde incident were quietly rehabilitated and reinstated.

Johnson was thus able to continue his university studies. He was no longer comfortable in Rostock, and in 1954 he moved to Leipzig. Over the next two years he worked and reworked his Rostock experiences into his first novel. *Ingrid Babendererde: Reifeprüfung 1953* (Ingrid Babendererde: School-leaving Examination 1953), which was published posthumously in 1985, is set in a small Mecklenburg town during the week prior to the school-leaving exam in April 1953. The intrusion of the Junge Gemeinde campaign into the lives of Ingrid Babendererde; her boyfriend, Klaus Niebuhr; their good friend Jürgen Peterson, the leader of the school FDJ chapter; and their other friends has devastating effects. The students know that to associate the local Christian youth with the charges against the national organization is patently ridiculous, but the party presses forward with its accusations. Ingrid is called upon to denounce the young Christians, and after first refusing, she makes a speech which results in her being expelled from school and shadowed by state security agents. Klaus, who had stayed away from the proceedings and had implored Ingrid to do the same, withdraws from school the next day, citing violations of the GDR constitution. Jürgen, at odds with his party and with himself, helps Klaus and Ingrid make their way to West Berlin, where "sie umsteigen in jene Lebensweise, die sie ansehen für die falsche" (they transfer over to the way of life they consider to be the wrong one). Much of what concerned Johnson as a writer for the rest of his life is prefigured in this youthful novel: the gap between reality and the language various ideologies use to reconstruct it; the inability of those who insist upon saying what they mean to find a home in social environments where such directness is rare in public discourse; the celebration of Mecklenburg; and the fear of losing its language and its landscapes.

In July 1956, during the brief period of more tolerant cultural policies between Khrushchev's condemnation of Stalin at the Twentieth Soviet Party Congress and the Hungarian intervention, Johnson submitted the manuscript of *Ingrid Babendererde* to the Aufbau publishing house. The editors showed interest in the book and admiration for the talents of the young writer, but they were unable to resolve their ideological reservations. Over the next year several other prominent East German publishers—Hinstorff, Paul List, and the Mitteldeutscher Verlag—agreed that the novel could not be published. Late in

1956 the cultural-political newspaper *Sonntag* showed interest in the manuscript, but shortly thereafter its editor was arrested for sedition. *Ingrid Babendererde* would, for its time, have been a truly remarkable East German novel, raising issues that were not explored in the GDR until over a decade later by writers such as Christa Wolf and Hermann Kant.

As it became increasingly clear that publication in the GDR was unlikely, Johnson pursued a contact made possible by his Leipzig professor Hans Mayer with the Frankfurt publisher Peter Suhrkamp. Suhrkamp showed initial enthusiasm for *Ingrid Babendererde,* but the novel was ultimately rejected. The contract remained open, however, and, although Suhrkamp did not live to see it, his house became Johnson's sole German publisher.

His studies with Mayer exposed Johnson to some of the great writers of modern world literature, many of whom were rejected by official GDR cultural policies as bourgeois, decadent, and formalist. He read Samuel Beckett, Alfred Döblin, James Joyce, and William Faulkner; he encountered the work of Walter Benjamin; and his respect for Bertolt Brecht deepened.

Johnson continued to have problems with the authorities. He wrote an examination in which he took the part of the writers who had criticized official cultural policies at the Sixth Writers' Congress of the GDR in 1956. The exam was declared unacceptable, and Johnson only grudgingly agreed to write another. His thesis on Ernst Barlach's novel *Der gestohlene Mond* (The Stolen Moon, 1948) was rejected. And when he finally received his diploma in 1956, no job offers were forthcoming. While a student Johnson had a practicum with the Leipzig publisher Recalm, and he had hoped for an editorial position when his studies were completed. His political files were so problematic, however, that he remained "'arbeitslos' in einem Lande, das solchen Zustand abgeschafft haben wollte" ("unemployed" in a country that claimed to have eliminated such a condition). Supporting himself with literary odd jobs on commission from various publishers, he did editorial work for a modern German translation of the medieval epic, the *Nibelungenlied* (1961); translated Herman Melville's *Israel Potter* (1961); and prepared evaluations of manuscripts. During this time he was working on his second novel. In late 1956 his mother and sister left the GDR and moved to Karlsruhe, and Johnson was able to retain their former room in Güstrow in addition to his room in Leipzig. He traveled frequently by train between the two cities and became intrigued by the world of railway workers his mother had left behind.

The central character of *Mutmaßungen über Jakob* is Jakob Abs, a Dresden train dispatcher who, as can be inferred from the opening sentences of the novel, has been struck and killed by a locomotive while crossing the tracks on his way through the freight yards to work. The reader encounters a puzzling variety of narrative elements as the people who were close to Jakob try to understand his death. There are fragments of three conversations in which it only gradually becomes clear who is speaking, three stream-of-consciousness monologues, and a third-person narrative. These elements are combined, often in mid-sentence, into a recounting of various versions and interpretations of the events leading up to Jakob's death. The reader is forced to piece these events together and draw his own conclusions about the death. This process is further challenged by the language used in these narrative strands: fragments of Mecklenburg dialect, English, and Russian are mixed together; highly unusual syntax combines with idiosyncratic punctuation; and the narrator constantly disassembles conventional compound words or assembles unconventional ones. In a 1962 interview with the magazine *konkret* Johnson explained: "Ich habe das Buch so geschrieben, als würden die Leute es so langsam lesen, wit ich es geschrieben habe" (I wrote the book in such a way that people would read it as slowly as I wrote it).

In the fall of 1956 Jakob Abs learns that his mother has left the Mecklenburg town of Jerichow, where she and Jakob had settled with the family of Heinrich Cresspahl after the war, and has gone to the West. Jakob is contacted by Rohlfs, an officer of the East German State Security Service, and learns that Rohlfs had approached Frau Abs in the hope of establishing a working relationship with Cresspahl's daughter Gesine, who has been in the West since 1953 and works as a secretary and interpreter for NATO. Although Frau Abs's response had been to bolt, Jakob agrees to consider Rohlfs's proposal and to meet with him again.

His mother's departure and his encounter with the world of the secret police and espionage intrude into Jakob's well-integrated social role as a responsible worker. When Jakob goes to Jerichow to put his mother's affairs in order he is confronted by another, equally disturbing point of view, for there he meets Gesine's former lover Jonas Blach, a dissident intellectual who has sought refuge with Cresspahl to work on a manuscript critical of the East German political system.

After he returns to work, Jakob's situation is further complicated by the unexpected arrival of Gesine, who makes a clandestine visit to the GDR to check on her father—and perhaps for other reasons. Jakob meets Rohlfs and tells him that he will not approach Gesine. He then makes his way with her to Jerichow, with Rohlfs close on their heels. It is the night of the Soviet intervention in Hungary, and Jakob is worried that Gesine's visit will be seen as part of a plot to stir up trouble in the GDR. He arranges a meeting with Rohlfs, who agrees to guarantee Gesine's safe passage back to the West if she will meet with him later in West Berlin.

After Gesine's visit Jakob returns briefly to work, where he must help dispatch Soviet military trains on their way to Hungary. He obtains leave, ostensibly to visit his mother but in reality to see Gesine, for during her return to the GDR they fell in love. But Jakob does not feel that he belongs in the West, and despite her request that he stay with her, he returns to the GDR. There, as he crosses the tracks in foggy weather on his way back to work, he is struck by a train and killed.

This story leaves the reader with much to ponder. Jakob was clearly a man of exemplary integrity who was disturbed by both personal and political events. His death, whether an accident, suicide, or murder, prevented him from confronting life under the altered circumstances he would have had to face. The perspectives of those who remain—of Gesine, the ex-GDR citizen; of Jonas, the dissident; of Jöche, a worker and friend of Jakob's who participates in one of the conversations; and of Rohlfs, the representative of the state—are all given their due; limited by ideology and interest, none can give a complete or trustworthy account. The narrator can do no more than contribute what he knows and use his skill as editor to weave together the other narrative strands. The reader is invited to join the narrator in his exercise in "Wahrheitsfindung" (discovery of the truth).

Mutmaßungen über Jakob was published by Suhrkamp in July 1959. Johnson chose the same time to move to West Berlin. He had made it a point to have his publishers arrange a residency permit for him in advance, and for the remainder of his life he flatly refused to allow the term Flüchtling (refugee) to be applied to him. Over and over he insisted, "Ich bin umgezogen" (I moved).

Mutmaßungen über Jakob attracted enormous critical attention. Although some critics were disturbed by the radical use of language and the modernistic narrative techniques, there was admiration for the virtuosity of this first publication and considerable enthusiasm for a young author who had dared to address the important and neglected theme of the division of Europe. Critics as varied in outlook as Günter Blöcker, Reinhard Baumgart, Gerd Semmer, and Marcel Reich-Ranicki praised the book and saw great promise in Johnson.

Johnson's emergence as an important German literary figure was soon confirmed by various honors. In 1959 he received an invitation to participate in the meetings of the Gruppe (Group) 47, the association of writers organized in 1947 by Hans Werner Richter, at which most of the leading literary personalities of West Germany, Switzerland, and Austria read and discussed their work. In 1960 he was awarded the Fontane Prize of the City of West Berlin for *Mutmaßungen über Jakob*. In 1961 he made his first trip to the United States for an extensive tour of lectures, public readings, and university visits that lasted for four months.

He was already at work on his second published book, *Das dritte Buch über Achim* (1961; translated as *The Third Book About Achim*, 1967). In this novel Johnson continues to examine the effects of divisions, borders, and distance on his protagonist. Because this character is a journalist trying to work outside the limits of his own political and ideological experience, the questions about the relationship of language and reality and about the possibilities of narration that were implicit in the complex form of *Mutmaßungen über Jakob* become explicit—become, in fact, the central theme—in *Das dritte Buch über Achim*.

Karsch, a West German journalist, accepts an invitation from his former lover Karin S., an actress, to visit her in the GDR. There he encounters the cyclist Achim T., Karin's current lover and a national sports hero, and begins to write an article about him. An East German publisher approaches Karsch about expanding the project into a third full-fledged biography of Achim; the other two have been rendered obsolete by Achim's continual triumphs and the expansion of his social and political role. Karsch is intrigued by the idea, and Achim is initially enthusiastic and cooperative.

Karsch prepares to write a biography of the sort that he understands. Endeavoring to comprehend the development of the individual Achim, he gathers material about the cyclist's childhood and youth, his apprenticeship, and early love affair, and the beginnings of his sports career. At the same time he reads books about cycling, watches Achim's training sessions, and accompanies him to his many public appearances.

As his work progresses, Karsch continually encounters problems in reconciling the personality that emerges from his investigation of Achim's past with the Achim he observes fulfilling the role of national sports hero. What Karsch considers to be important for understanding Achim—his background and development—is often discounted or denied by Achim and the publishers, who are interested only in Achim's current role in East Germany. Anything that calls that role into question has no place in the biography they envision. Karsch finds precisely such contradictory and problematic elements of Achim's development essential for comprehending Achim as an individual, and he is unwilling to ignore them. Ultimately, work on the biography breaks down over apparently incontrovertible evidence that Achim participated in the June 1953 uprising in Leipzig. Karsch returns home and, in an attempt to explain his failure to his friends and to himself, writes

an account of his efforts which becomes *Das dritte Buch über Achim*.

This account is carried forward by a series of questions which serve as chapter headings and allow Karsch to reflect upon his experience in the GDR. Karsch's cool, detached descriptions of his literary failure—his research, the rejected drafts of portions of the book, his futile attempts to work out an approach acceptable to Achim, to the publishers, and to himself—repeatedly force him back to the problem of the border: he simply cannot fit his view of an individual identity into a political and social context the presuppositions of which he neither shares nor understands.

Critical response to the novel was largely favorable. Walter Jens felt that Johnson was on the way to greatness, Martin Walser praised his unique prose style, and Blöcker was convinced that Johnson had consolidated his position as the "Dichter der beiden Deutschland" (poet of both Germanies). There were, however, dissenting voices. Karl August Horst called the novel a "trojanisches Pferd" (Trojan horse) and worried about the implications of Johnson's skepticism toward language, while Karlheinz Deschner deprecated Johnson's prose as the ugliest German of its day.

Johnson's efforts to find a voice beyond ideology extended into his public pronouncements and embroiled him in a series of controversies. In the late 1961 he went on an extensive reading tour which included a stop in Milan. There he participated in a public round-table discussion at which the keynote speaker was the German writer Hermann Kesten. Kesten's account of the evening, which characterized Johnson as a supporter of the Berlin Wall and an apologist for the GDR, appeared two weeks later in the newspaper *Die Welt*. During the remainder of his tour Johnson found himself besieged by questions and accusations. After obtaining a tape recording of the discussion in Milan, Johnson and the Suhrkamp house held a press conference at which the author took great care to demonstrate how distorted and self-serving Kesten's account had been. In Milan, Johnson had discussed the Wall and the reasons it had been built and, characteristically, had tried to keep the discussion free of emotion and polemic. Kesten's denunciation and its appearance in a newspaper well known for its polemical anti-Communism represented precisely the kind of linguistic abuse that Johnson so abhorred and strove to avoid in his own writing. It even led to a discussion in the Bundestag, where the former foreign minister, Heinrich von Brentano, who had previously demonstrated his literary sensitivies by a witless comparison of Brecht to the Nazi hero and "poet" Horst Wessel, demanded that Johnson's 1962 fellowship at the Villa Massimo in Rome be revoked. Eighteen years later Johnson still considered this incident so important that he resigned from the German Academy for Language and Literature in Darmstadt after a catalogue it published characterized the incident as a "Streit" (controversy), a term that infuriated Johnson by its neutrality.

Shortly after the Wall was constructed, Johnson began to take an interest in a group of young people who were engaged in helping those who wanted to leave East Berlin. In *Begleitumstände* he discusses an attempt, which he ultimately abandoned, to document the work of this group. In spite of the failure of this project, Johnson's research and association with the group served him well in the novels *Zwei Ansichten* (1965; translated as *Two Views,* 1966) and *Jahrestage: Aus dem Leben von Gesine Cresspahl* (1970-1973, 1983; translated as *Anniversaries: from the Life of Gesine Cresspahl,* 1975, 1987) when he described illegal departures from the GDR. He also drew on this experience for his 1965 essay "Eine Kneipe geht verloren" (A Tavern Is Lost).

In 1962 Johnson married Elisabeth Schmidt, whom he had met in Leipzig and who had just completed a semester studying in Prague. A year later they had a daughter, Katherina.

To use his fellowship at the Villa Massimo Johnson traveled in 1962 to Rome; there he associated with Ingeborg Bachmann and Max Frisch, writers whose work he admired. Also, in 1962 he received the International Publisher's Prize for *Das dritte Buch über Achim.* This prize carried the stipulation that he serve on the jury that would determine the following year's award.

Johnson's service on this jury caused more controversy. The jury, which consisted of critics and publishers from all over Europe, met on the island of Corfu in a luxury hotel located in an area where the local people were extremely poor. Although Johnson fulfilled his obligation as a jury member, he publicly criticized the meetings after the prize was awarded, contending that contemporary literature was inappropriately celebrated in such opulent surroundings. His criticism and his refusal to participate in the gala banquet which ended the jury's week of deliberations garnered him considerable unfavorable publicity.

In 1964 Suhrkamp published Johnson's *Karsch und andere Prosa* (Karsch and Other Prose), a collection of three short texts featuring Gesine Cresspahl of *Mutmaßungen über Jakob;* a brief piece about the biblical Jonah written in 1957; and a long text, "Eine Reise wegwohin, 1960" (translated as *An Absence,* 1969), which returns, from quite a different perspective, to Karsch's attempt to write about Achim.

The critics did not respond as positively to the collection as most had to Johnson's first two books. Reich-Ranicki, for example, dismissed the Gesine pieces as sketches from the material for *Mutmaßungen über Jakob* and found the Karsch piece a distressingly conventional retelling of the admired original. In retrospect, however, the collection is important for several reasons. The Gesine pieces demonstrate Johnson's continuing involvement with the Cresspahl family, an involvement that lasted for the rest of his life and produced his masterpiece, *Jahrestage.* The Karsch piece offers a new dimension in Johnson's investigation of the relationship between what one can say and what is perceived: moving beyond the impossibility of writing Achim's biography, it follows Karsch back to the West and portrays the frustrations he experiences trying to write there about the GDR. The ideological barriers Karsch encounters when he tries to describe in print or over the air what he felt and observed in the East are no less onerous than those he had experienced when trying to write about Achim.

Toward the middle of 1964 Johnson began a brief career as a television critic. Believing that the refusal of the West Berlin newspapers to print the schedule of GDR television programs was a foolish denial of reality, he approached the independent Berliner Tagesspiegel and proposed that if the paper would print the schedules, he would review the shows. In the next six months Johnson reviewed over a hundred GDR broadcasts. In 1987 Suhrkamp published a collection of these reviews under the title *Der 5. Kanal* (Channel Five).

In 1965 a short novel appeared which returned once again, this time with a narrower focus, to the problems of division, distance, and borders. *Zwei Ansichten* (Two Views) examines the relationship between B., a West German photographer, and D., a nurse from East Germany. B. encounters D. at a party in West Berlin, and the two have what might have remained a brief, casual affair. They have little in common: B. is a rather unremarkable young man from a small town in Schleswig-Holstein who has a passion for automobiles; D. is a quiet woman who regularly travels back and forth between her parents' home in Potsdam and East Berlin, where she lives and works. She has friends in the West and often visits there, but she is content with her life in the East.

The construction of the Berlin Wall, however, adds a new dimension to the relationship of this unlikely pair. After the Wall is erected, B. plans to visit D. in East Berlin and hopes to impress her with his newly acquired foreign sports car. But their meeting does not take place because the car is stolen from in front of his West Berlin hotel and, as he later discovers, is used in a foolhardy attempt to escape from East Berlin. Afraid that he will be suspected of participating in the escape plot, B. decides not to go to the East.

The Wall gives the relationship an increasingly compelling aura. B. feels an ill-defined, simplistically romantic responsibility to "do something" for D., a feeling which alternately irritates him and puts him in a sentimental frame of mind. D.'s memories of B. are vague, and only when her anger at losing the option of choosing to stay in the East combines with a frustrating professional situation at her hospital does she accept B.'s offer of help.

That offer is made in an almost comically offhand manner. The lure of the Wall, the loss of his car, and the personal myth B. has made of D. repeatedly draw B. back to West Berlin from his home in Schleswig-Holstein. He spends much of his time in a bar that happens to be the meeting place for a group of young men and women who help people leave East Berlin. The young female bartender reminds him of his vision of D., and during an evening of too much drinking he writes a letter to D. which he leaves on the bar, a letter that he probably would not have mailed. The group hand-delivers the letter, establishing the contact that leads to D.'s escape.

D. leaves the East by posing as an Austrian tourist on her way to Denmark. Her preparations for flight and the journey itself generate considerable suspense, especially because B. had forgotten the color of D.'s eyes; consequently, the passport provided to D. would not have stood up under close scrutiny.

When B. hears that D. has arrived in Denmark and will be in West Berlin the next day, he makes a hurried trip to Stuttgart to pick up the new sports car with which he wants to greet and to impress her. B. frantically tries to return to Berlin in time, but the car breaks down. When he finally does arrive, he discovers that D. no longer wants to see him. Exhausted and dazed, B. stumbles against a moving bus and suffers a mild concussion. D. visits him in the hospital, but they have little to say to one another. Thereafter they go their separate ways. The shallow reality of their relationship has little to do with the expectations B. or D. had developed in the absence of the other.

The title, *Zwei Ansichten,* identifies the narrative program. The story of B. and D. is told alternately from the perspective of each of the two main figures, with each chapter marking a shift to the other view. The narration, especially when compared with Johnson's earlier works, appears almost traditional; but the two straightforward, chronological, third-person accounts are set against one another. The border is once again a literary category.

Toward the end of the novel the narrator accounts for his acquaintance with the material: he had been on the scene when B. stumbled against the bus, and he had gotten to know D. after her arrival in West Berlin. She recounted her story to the narrator and suggested that he write it down. But, she said, "das Müssen Sie alles erfinden, was Sie Schreiben. Es ist erfunden" (You have to make up everything that you write. It is made up).

The reduction of the protagonists' names to initials underscores their fundamental anonymity and ordinariness. Many critics were quick to note the correspondence between B. and D. and the German initials for the Federal Republic (Bundesrepublik [BRD]) and the German Democratic Republic (Deutsche Demokratische Republik [DDR]) and to suggest that the characters were somehow representatives of their countries. Johnson denied that he had intended any such association and, in the English translation, rather pointedly provided his characters first names—Dietbert and Beate—which reversed the initials. Johnson wanted to present the different perspectives of ordinary people from both sides of the border.

The critical reception of *Zwei Ansichten* was far less positive than the response to Johnson's earlier work had been. Although critics such as Heinrich Vormweg appreciated the exciting evocation of an illegal exit from East Berlin, they lamented what they perceived as a regression to conventionality; they compared the later with the earlier Johnson and were disappointed. Johnson was unmoved by such criticism: "Es ist eben eine einfachere Geschichte . . ." (It is just a simpler story . . .), he said.

In 1965 the Suhrkamp firm asked Johnson to edit *Me-ti: Buch der Wendungen,* one of the unpublished works in the Brecht archives in East Berlin; the volume was published within the year. Johnson's intense involvement with the manuscript increased his already strong affinity for Brecht's work, and the assignment afforded him the opportunity to meet with writers and other friends in East Berlin. His visits with the singer and writer Wolf Biermann, whose performances and publications had been banned by the East German authorities, resulted in Johnson's being denied access to East Berlin in January 1966.

Johnson had made his second trip to the United States in mid 1965 and, while there, looked for an opportunity to return for at least a year to immerse himself in the American milieu. He did not, however, want an invitation as a writer in residence or guest professor; he was not interested in the isolated, artificial environment of the university but wanted a more conventional job. Helen Wolff, Johnson's American editor, responded with an offer of an editorship in the textbook division of Harcourt, Brace and World, charged with producing an anthology of contemporary German literary texts for high school use. In June 1966 Johnson and his family moved to New York, where they lived on Riverside Drive on the upper West side of Manhattan.

During the first year Johnson completed the anthology *Das neue Fenster* (1967).

Johnson's New York stay provided him with material that would sustain him until his death. By his own account, he "renewed his acquaintance" with Gesine Cresspahl; he began to imagine her as a resident of the upper West side and to consider how she had come to be there. This renewed interest in Gesine and her background led Johnson to the project that would consume most of the rest of his life, the writing of *Jahrestage*. With the help of his American publisher and a grant from the Rockefeller foundation he was able to remain in New York for a second year and to begin work on the novel.

Jahrestage: Aus dem Leben von Gesine Cresspahl is a massive novel of nearly nineteen hundred pages in four volumes that goes far beyond an examination of the implications of the border between the two Germanies. Gesine seeks to come to terms with her identity in the present—as a German who was born in the Third Reich, was educated under the Nazis and in the formative years of the GDR, left the East in the 1950s and the West in the 1960s, and now lives in Manhattan. She must examine the child that she was, that child's antecedents, and the series of identities she has moved through as the child became the adult.

This extraordinarily ambitious undertaking is presented in the form of a diary with entries for each day from 21 August 1967 to 20 August 1968—a year in the life of Gesine Cresspahl. In these entries Gesine—and often a writer named Uwe Johnson, whom, the reader eventually learns, she has asked to assist her—reflects on her job, on her relationships with her ten-year-old daughter Marie and the other people she encounters, and on the city. The entries reveal Gesine's interest in political and social behavior through her intensive reading of *The New York Times* as she quotes, paraphrases, or simply reacts to the news items that she finds particularly arresting.

This complex evocation of her contemporary life is interwoven with an account of Gesine's background, from her birth in 1933 back to her parents' courtship and marriage and forward through her childhood and education to the present. The narrative, written mostly in the third person but sometimes in the first, is usually straightforward. It also, however, occasionally takes the form of reports of conversations Gesine has with Marie, and imaginary ones with long-dead relatives and acquaintances. Sometimes it represents a transcription of tapes Gesine has made about her life for her daughter "für wenn ich tot bin" (for when I am dead). The interaction of past and present allows Gesine to examine the patterns of behavior that she developed as a child and young adult and to ponder how they operate in her present life. These patterns derive from the continuing influence exerted by the powerful and conflicting figures of her mother and father and their responses to the extreme social and political climate in which they lived.

Gesine was only five years old when her mother, Lisbeth Cresspahl, committed suicide. But the absolute moral standards, the fanatical piety, that drove Lisbeth to take her life had already had a powerful effect on Gesine. When Lisbeth married Heinrich Cresspahl, a cabinetmaker who had immigrated to England and had met her on a visit to his native Mecklenburg, she had agreed to live with him in Richmond, where he had a thriving business. She was unable to feel at home in England, however, and when she became pregnant with Gesine she insisted on returning to Jerichow. There she conspired with her father to force Cresspahl to move back permanently to Mecklenburg, and Cresspahl acquiesced. But the return to Germany and Gesine's birth coincided with the Nazi accession to power, a fact which was an increasingly disturbing source of guilt for Lisbeth. As the Nazis began to implement their policies Lisbeth realized that she could not reconcile what was happening around her with her absolute moral standards. She also realized that she was trapped: her inability to live in England meant that there was no escape from her guilt. To shield herself and her child from this guilt she tried to kill Gesine and twice tried to take her own life. Finally, on 9 November 1938, the Kristallnacht (Night of Broken Glass), in the absence of Cresspahl and the child, she succeeded in killing herself. Gesine sees in herself the legacy of her mother's moral absolutism, and she wishes fervently "daß ich nicht werde wie meine Mutter" (that I not become like my mother).

Heinrich Cresspahl provided a very different example for Gesine. Left responsible for his small daughter, the taciturn craftsman developed a close relationship with her. While conducting his business in apparent harmony with the authorities, he served throughout the war as a British agent. After Germany's surrender he became the mayor of Jerichow and had to struggle with the Soviet military occupation—a struggle which ultimately resulted in a lengthy and debilitating internment. Although Gesine did not always understand the precise nature of his activities, Cresspahl showed her that it was legitimate, even essential, to separate a private sphere of moral and political convictions from the identity one assumes in public.

As an adolescent Gesine had to apply this lesson. Like Johnson, Gesine found the new ideological climate in the Soviet occupation zone both attractive and disturbing. Through the example of her father—and, after his internment, of the young refugee Jakob Abs, who became the head of the Cresspahl household–Gesine developed an abiding belief in progressive socialism. She regarded as essential policies such as redistributing land, providing educational and social opportunities for the children of workers and farmers, and confronting the people with the realities of the Nazi crimes. Her early experience on Johnny Schlegel's prototypical collective farm helped to form her vision of a society of people doing meaningful work and sharing in the benefits of their production.

Gesine could not, however, fail to notice the often appalling disparity between the socialist vision and the reality of the Soviet occupation zone and later of the fledgling GDR. The internment of her father and many other examples of capricious "justice" and heavy-handed rule discredited the ideological claims of the new regime. The 1953 riots in East Germany provided the final blow to Gesine's relationship with the GDR, and she moved to the West.

But neither West Germany nor, later, the United States could provide Gesine with the home she sought. Until 1956 and the ill-fated visit to Jerichow that served as the central event in *Mutmaßungen über Jakob,* she worked as a secretary and interpreter for NATO. After Jakob's visit to West Berlin, when Marie was conceived, and Jakob's subsequent mysterious death, Gesine went to work for a bank. In 1961 she relocated to Manhattan.

Gesine's socialist vision provides her with moral and political principles as rigorous and as uncompromising as those of her mother. But Gesine, who, like her father, must bear responsibility for a small child, cannot afford to allow her moral absolutism free rein. She must be Mrs. Cresspahl, employee of a bank, resident alien in a country of whose political and social policies she does not approve. And she must watch her daughter's steady socialization into a society in which she herself will never feel at home.

She reserves within herself a private sphere in which she can retain her hope, where she can continue to seek the answer to her question, "Wo ist die moralische Schweiz, in die wir emigrieren könnten?" (Where is the moral Switzerland to which we could emigrate?). Initially, there appears to be little prospect of a concrete answer to that question. She is distressed by the careless rhetoric and the radical chic of the American protest movement against the Vietnam war and is painfully aware of her own modest role in the financial and economic system that supports the war. What she can do is to bear witness: "Es ist was mir übriggeblieben ist: Bescheid zu lernen. Wenigstens mit Kenntnis zu leben" (That is what is left to me: to learn what is going on. At least to live with awareness).

During the year chronicled in *Jahrestage,* however, a focus for Gesine's hope emerges. She is made responsible for her bank's efforts to establish a financial agreement with Czechoslovakia. At first this assignment is merely another aspect of her job. But in the early weeks of 1968 she begins increasingly to note the news from Prague. The rapidly developing promise she sees in the reforms of the Prague Spring captures her imagination, and she begins to believe that her work might also contribute to the establishment of a dynamic socialism under the rule of law. "Für den würde ich arbeiten, aus freien Stücken" (That I would work for freely), she says.

But Gesine is not to have the chance to work for the realization of her socialist vision. The date which, from the beginning of Johnson's work on the novel, had been projected as the last day to be chronicled marked the violent end of the Prague Spring. The ending of the novel is left open; the reader last sees Gesine on a Danish beach shortly before her departure for Prague. It is clear, though, "daß diese Dame und diese Armee notwending auf einander stoen würden in dieser Nacht" (that this woman and this army would necessarily collide with one another during this night). Whether this devastating blow to her hopes will cause Gesine to yield to the despair that destroyed her mother, or whether she will continue to bear witness, to maintain her vision as an act of defiance against silence and acquiescence, remains unknown. In any event, the hundreds of pages of *Jahrestage* give voice to that spirit of defiance and stand as a lasting monument to Gesine's–and Johnson's–vision.

Because Johnson's novel appeared in four installments, the last volume nearly ten years after it was originally scheduled to appear, critical response to it also came in stages. After reading the first volume some critics were repelled by the puzzling combination of the daily entries, the shifts between past and present and between first and third person, the large sections of text paraphrasing or quoting *The New York Times,* and the huge cast of characters. Reich-Ranicki and Helmut Heißenbüttel sought in vain to discern a whole in this first part and failed to see unity between the various levels of narration. Rolf Becker and Hans Mayer, however, showed more awareness of the fragmentary nature of the first volume; they were impressed by the volume in its own right and intrigued by the promise of what was to come. Mayer praised the delicate and complex relationship Johnson was working to establish between past and present, and Becker felt that Johnson's voice had grown stronger, more mature, and more confident.

With the appearance of the second volume in 1971 and the third volume in 1973, critical voices were increasingly respectful. After the second volume was published, Blöcker wrote in the *Frankfurter Allgemeine Zeitung* that Johnson had attained a mastery that left "nahezu alle der mit ihm angetretenen Autoren seiner Generation hinter sich zurück, einen Grass ebenso wie einen Walser, von anderen gar nicht zu reden" (behind nearly all the authors of his generation who had debuted with him, a Grass as well as a Walser, to say nothing of the others).

Although the final volume of the novel had been promised for 1974, what followed was ten years of silence. Rumors of Johnson's personal and physical problems contributed to the growing conviction that *Jahrestage* would remain a monumental and, in the eyes of many, a masterful fragment. When the weekly newspaper *Die Zeit* chose its library of the one hundred best works of world literature in 1978, it included the unfinished novel.

In 1983 the final volume did appear, and the critics were nearly unanimous in their respect for Johnson's accomplishment. To be sure, many critics had individual quibbles—Peter Demetz liked the youthful Gesine far better than the adult; Fritz J. Raddatz felt that Johnson's language had lost its intensity in the final volume; some critics still complained about his alleged overuse of *The New York Times* or about Marie's precocity. These caveats served only to temper the overwhelmingly positive response to the novel as a whole. Seeking adequate comparisons, the critics looked back to Balzac, Fontane, Proust, Joyce, and Thomas Mann. The sense of virtually all the reviews of the final volume is that *Jahrestage* will stand as one of the remarkable literary achievements of the twentieth century.

In 1968, after two years in the United States, Johnson and his family returned to West Berlin, where he continued to work on *Jahrestage*. The following year he joined the P.E.N. Club of the Federal Republic. He also became a member of the Academy of Arts in West Berlin, of which he became vice president in 1972. In 1971, after publication of the first two volumes of *Jahrestage,* Johnson received the George Büchner Prize. Other major literary awards followed: in 1975 the Wilhelm Raabe Prize from the City of Brunswick, in 1978 the Thomas Mann Prize from the City of Lübeck, and in 1983 the Literary Prize of the City of Cologne.

Following the death of Ingeborg Bachmann in late 1973 Johnson spent four days in Klagenfurt, the city of her birth and burial, a city in which she had chosen not to live. The next year he published *Eine Reise nach Klagenfurt* (A Journey to Klagenfurt, 1974), a compilation of statistics, documents, quotations and observations which form a curious obituary for the poet. By creating an image of Klagenfurt out of the contradictions between its past and present and between the self-image of tourist brochures and the picture that

emerges from less flattering statistics, Johnson seeks to identify the city in which Bachmann spent her childhood and to re-create the tensions this place continued to cause for her long after she had left it. Heinrich Böll said in the *Frankfurter Allgemeine Zeitung* for 23 November 1974 that this modest book could be "ein Modell . . . für Biographien—besser noch: auch für Autobiographien" (a model for biographies—better yet: also for autobiographies).

In 1975 Suhrkamp published *Berliner Sachen* (Berlin Affairs), a collection of Johnson's short prose pieces from 1961 to 1970. Most of these had been previously published but were relatively difficult to find. Included were the important theoretical essay "Berliner Stadtbahn" (The Berlin Elevated Railway, 1961); the 1965 account of the "travel agency" that helped people leave East Berlin after the construction of the Wall, "Eine Kneipe geht verloren"; and Johnson's fascinating afterword to a collection of interviews with former citizens of the GDR, "Versuch eine Mentalität zu erklären" (Attempt to Explain a Mentality, 1970).

In 1974 Johnson had moved to the island of Sheerness-on-Sea, Kent, in the mouth of the Thames River. There he intended to find the peace and quiet he needed to finish *Jahrestage*. In 1975, however, he experienced a personal crisis that had lasting physical and psychological consequences and proved to be a serious obstacle to the completion of his novel. Johnson learned that his wife had had an affair and remained in contact with "einem Vertrauten des S.T.B., des tschechoslowakischen Staatssicherheitsdienstes" (a confidant of the S.T.B., the Czechoslovakian state security agency). The author felt that it was thus possible "seine berufliche Integrität in Frage zu stellen" (to call his professional integrity into question) when he wrote about political developments in Czechoslovakia or the GDR. Johnson experienced serious heart trouble and, after his recovery, a long-lasting writer's block. Johnson and his wife attempted for two years to continue with their marriage; but rumors about their problems became public, and in 1977 they separated.

In the years during and immediately after this crisis Johnson's literary activities were limited to short contributions to German periodicals, a translation into modern German of the Low German fairy tale *Von dem Fischer un syner Fru* (The Fisherman and His Wife, 1976), and the editing of the journalist Margret Boveri's autobiography *Verzweigungen* (Ramifications, 1977). In 1977 Johnson became a member of the German Academy of Language and Literature in Darmstadt, from which he resigned in protest two years later over the Kesten affair.

In 1978 Johnson began slowly to work his way back into *Jahrestage*. He also accepted his publisher's invitation to give a series of lectures that would reestablish the poetics chair at the University of Frankfurt. These lectures, which were given in 1979 and published in 1980 as *Begleitumstände,* provide a fascinating account of Johnson's "Erfahrungen im Berufe des Schriftstellers" (experiences in the writer's profession). Throughout the lectures Johnson's almost obsessive concern with concrete, dispassionate language emerges as the unifying theme. His study of German language and literature, he says, awakened in him "eine Vorliebe für das Konkrete . . . für das, was man vorzeigen, nachweisen, erzählen kann" (a preference for the concrete . . . for that which one can exhibit, authenticate, narrate). He reveals important information about his years in the GDR, his beginnings as a writer, and his decision to move to the West. He also examines many of the public controversies that marked his first years in West Berlin and provides detailed documentation supporting and explaining his positions. He concludes the final lecture with a cryptic acknowledgment of the personal crisis that impeded his progress on *Jahrestage* and makes clear his intention to complete the novel.

The short narrative *Skizze eines Verunglückten* (Sketch of a Casualty, 1982) is an account of marital problems similar to those that had proved so destructive for the author. Johnson's narrator, Joe Hinterhand, is a writer living in New York City after serving time in prison for the murder of his wife. Hinterhand had been an exile from the Third Reich, and his wife had betrayed him with a representative of his political enemies. An attempted reconciliation had failed when the private tragedy threatened to become public scandal. The book did not generate a great deal of critical comment, and those who did review it saw it as a thinly veiled account of the unhappy conclusion of the author's own marriage.

After the completion of *Jahrestage* in 1983 Johnson began to make new plans. He wanted to probe more deeply into the family history of the Cresspahls, and he wanted to return to the United States. In September 1983 he made a brief trip to New York, and he planned to go back for a year beginning in June 1984. By the time of his planned departure, Johnson was dead.

The circumstances surrounding Johnson's death underscore the sad, troubled isolation that characterized the last few years of his life. To be sure, he maintained his literary contacts and friendships in West Germany, traveling frequently to the Continent to give readings, attend meetings, or accept prizes. But in Sheerness he spent most of his time alone in his house, striving to finish *Jahrestage* or planning further investigations of the Cresspahl family. His only regular contact with other people on the island was at the local pub, where he usually sat silently at the bar for a few hours every evening.

Reports of Johnson's heavy consumption of alcohol are too numerous to discount, and, given the weakened condition of his heart, his drinking must have hastened his end. On or about 23 February 1984 he suffered heart failure and died in his house; his body was not discovered for nearly three weeks.

Uwe Johnson's death deprived contemporary German literature of one of its most original, interesting, and idiosyncratic voices. Johnson, perhaps more than any of his contemporaries, sought a language beyond ideology with which he could present his readers a story that would encourage—or provoke—a reexamination of their preconceived notions. When that quest was most successful, in *Mutmaßungen über Jakob* and in *Jahrestage,* he produced novels that will stand among the finest achievements of postwar German literature.

Letters:

Die Katze Erinnerung: Uwe Johnson, eine Chronik in Briefen und Bildern, edited by Eberhard Fahlke (Frankfurt am Main: Suhrkamp, 1994).

Interviews:

Horst Bienek, "Uwe Johnson," in his *Werkstattgespräche mit Schriftstellern* (Munich: Hanser, 1962), pp. 86–98;

Arnhelm Neusüss, "Über die Schwierigkeiten beim Schreiben der Wahrheit: Gespräch mit Uwe Johnson," *konkret,* 8 (1962): 18–19;

Michael Roloff, "Interview mit Uwe Johnson," *Metamorphosis,* 4 (1963): 33–42;

Phyllis Meras, "Talk with Uwe Johnson," *New York Times Book Review,* 23 April 1967, pp. 42–43;

Reinhard Baumgart, "Gespräch mit Uwe Johnson (1968)," in *Selbstanzeige: Schriftsteller im Gespräch,* edited by Werner Koch (Frankfurt am Main: Fischer Taschenbuch Verlag, 1971), pp. 47–56;

Gertrud Simmerding and Christof Schmid, "Bichsel, Grass, Johnson, Wohmann: Wie ein Roman ensteht," in their *Literarische Werkstatt* (Munich: Oldenbourg, 1972), pp. 63–72;

Matthias Prangel, "Gespräch mit Uwe Johnson," *Deutsche Bücher* (1974): 45–49;

Manfred Durzak, "Dieser langsame Weg zu einer größeren Genauigkeit: Gespräch mit Uwe Johnson," in his *Gespräche über den Roman: Formbestimmungen und Analysen* (Frankfurt am Main: Suhrkamp, 1976), pp. 428–460;

Ree Post-Adams, "Antworten von Uwe Johnson," *German Quarterly,* 50 (March 1977): 241–247;

A. Leslie Willson, "'An Unacknowledged Humorist': An Interview with Uwe Johnson," *Dimension,* 15 (1982): 401–413;

Martin Meyer and Wolfgang Strehlow, "Das sagt mir auch mein Friseur: Film- und Fernsehäuerungen von Uwe Johnson," *Sprache im technischen Zeitalter,* no. 95 (1985): 170–183;

Heinz D. Osterle, "Todesgedanken?: Gespräch über die *Jahrestage,*" *German Quarterly,* 58 (Fall 1985): 576–584;

Ich überlege mir die Geschichte: Uwe Johnson im Gespräch, edited by Eberhard Fahlke (Frankfurt am Main: Suhrkamp, 1988).

Bibliographies:

Nicolai Riedel, *Uwe Johnson: Bibliographie 1959–1975. Zeitungskritik und wissenschaftliche Literatur* (Bonn: Bouvier, 1976); revised as *Uwe Johnson: Bibliographie 1959–1980. Das schriftstellerische Werk und seine Rezeption in literaturwissenschaftlicher Forschung und feuilletonistischer Kritik in der Bundesrepublik Deutschland. Mit Annotationen und Exkursen zur multimedialen Wirkungsgeschichte* (Bonn: Bouvier, 1981);

Riedel, *Uwe Johnson: Bibliographie 1959–1977. Das schriftstellerische Werk in fremdsprachigen Textausgaben und seine internationale Rezeption in literaturwissenschaftlicher Forschung und Zeitungskritik* (Bonn: Bouvier, 1978).

References:

Derek van Abbe, "From Proust to Johnson: Some Notes after *Das dritte Buch über Achim,*" *Modern Languages,* 55 (1974): 73–79;

Heinz Ludwig Arnold, ed., *Uwe Johnson* (Munich: Edition text + kritik, 1980);

Reinhard Baumgart, "Eigensinn: Ein vorläufiger Rückblick auf Uwe Johnsons *Jahrestage,*" *Merkur,* 37 (1983): 921–927;

Baumgart, "Ein Riese im Nebel," *Neue deutsche Hefte,* 7 (1960): 967–969;

Baumgart, "Kleinbürgertum und Realismus: Überlegungen zu Romanen von Böll, Grass und Johnson," *Neue Rundschau,* 70 (1964): 650–664;

Baumgart, "Uwe Johnson: *Das dritte Buch über Achim,*" *Neue deutsche Hefte,* 9 (1962): 146–148;

Baumgart, ed., *Über Uwe Johnson* (Frankfurt am Main: Suhrkamp, 1970);

Sigrid Bauschinger, "Mythos Manhattan: Die Faszination einer Stadt," in *Amerika in der deutschen Literatur,* edited by Bauschinger, Horst Denkler, and Wilfried Malsch (Stuttgart: Reclam, 1975), pp. 382–397;

Rolf Becker, "Jerichow in New York," *Der Spiegel,* 24 (5 October 1970): 228–230;

Michael Bengel, ed., *Johnsons "Jahrestage"* (Frankfurt am Main: Suhrkamp, 1985);

Günter Blöcker, "Du hast Auftrag von uns, Gesine: Der zweite Band von Uwe Johnsons *Jahrestage,*" *Frankfurter Allgemeine Zeitung,* 23 October 1971;

Blöcker, "Roman der beiden Deutschland, *Frankfurter Allgemeine Zeitung,* 31 October 1959;

Blöcker, "Roman der deutschen Entfremdung," *Frankfurter Allgemeine Zeitung,* 16 September 1961;

Hamida Bosmajian, *Metaphors of Evil: Contemporary German Literature and the Shadow of Nazism* (Iowa City: University of Iowa Press, 1979);

Mark Boulby, "Surmises on Love and Family Life in the Work of Uwe Johnson," *Seminar,* 10 (1974): 131–140;

Boulby, *Uwe Johnson* (New York: Ungar, 1974);

Peter Demetz, "Uwe Johnsons Blick in die Epoche: 'Aus dem Leben von Gesine Cresspahl'–der vierte Band der *Jahrestage,*" *Frankfurter Allgemeine Zeitung,* 12 November 1983;

Karlheinz Deschner, "Uwe Johnson: *Das dritte Buch über Achim,*" in his *Talente, Dichter, Dilettanten* (Wiesbaden: Limes, 1964), pp. 187–202;

Robert Detweiler, "*Speculations about Jacob:* The Truth of Ambiguity," *Monatshefte,* 58 (1966): 24–32;

Edward Diller, "Uwe Johnson's *Karsch:* Language as a Reflection of the Two Germanies," *Monatshefte,* 60 (1968): 35–39;

Darko Dolinar, "Die Erzähltechnik in drei Werken Uwe Johnsons," *Acta Neophilologica,* 3 (1970): 27–47;

Manfred Durzak, "Mimesis und Wahrheitsfindung: Probleme des realistischen Romans: Uwe Johnsons *Jahrestage,*" in his *Gespräche über den Roman: Formbestimmungen und Analysen* (Frankfurt am Main: Suhrkamp, 1976), pp. 461–481;

Durzak, "Wirklichkeitserkundung und Utopie: Die Romane Uwe Johnsons," in his *Der deutsche Roman der Gegenwart,* third edition (Stuttgart: Kohlhammer, 1979), pp. 328–403;

Eberhard Fahlke, "Gute Nacht, New York–Gute Nacht, Berlin . . . : Anmerkungen zu einer Figur des Protestierens anhand der *Jahrestage* von Uwe Johnson," in *Literatur und Studentenbewegung: Eine Zwischenbilanz,* edited by W. Martin Lüdke (Opladen: Westdeutscher Verlag, 1977), pp. 186–218;

Fahlke, *Die "Wirklichkeit" der Mutmaßungen: Eine politische Lesart der "Mutmaßungen über Jakob" von Uwe Johnson* (Bern: Lang, 1981);

Kurt J. Fickert, "Biblical Symbolism in *Mutmaßungen über Jakob,*" *German Quarterly,* 54 (January 1981): 59–62;

Fickert, *Neither Left nor Right: The Politics of Individualism in Uwe Johnson's Work* (New York: Lang, 1987);

Fickert, "Symbol Complexes in *Mutmaßungen über Jakob*," *Germanic Review,* 61 (Summer 1986): 105–108;

John Fletcher, "The Themes of Alienation and Mutual Incomprehension in the Novels of Uwe Johnson," *International Fiction Review,* 1 (1974): 81–87;

Erhard Friedrichsmeyer, "Quest by Supposition: Johnson's *Mutmaßungen über Jakob*," *Germanic Review,* 42 (1968): 215–226;

Hans-Jürgen Geisthardt, "Das Thema der Nation und zwei Literaturen: Nachweis an Christa Wolf–Uwe Johnson," *Neue Deutsche Literatur* 13 (June 1966): 48–69;

Ingeborg Gerlach, *Auf der Suche nach der verlorenen Identität: Zu Uwe Johnsons "Jahrestagen"* (Kronberg: Athenäum, 1980);

Rainer Gerlach and Matthias Richter, eds., *Uwe Johnson* (Frankfurt am Main: Suhrkamp, 1984);

Colin Good, "Uwe Johnson's Treatment of the Narrative in *Mutmaßungen über Jakob*," *German Life and Letters,* 24 (1971): 358–370;

Werner Gotzmann, "Detektiv, Inquisitor und Don Quichotte: Bemerkungen zu Uwe Johnsons *Jahrestage*," *Sprache im technischen Zeitalter,* no. 95 (1985): 184–195;

Jürgen Grambow, "Heimat im Vergangenen," *Sinn und Form,* 38 (1986): 134–157;

Christian Grawe, "Literarisch aktualisierte Bibel: Uwe Johnsons Kurzgeschichte 'Jonas zum Beispiel,'" *Der Deutschunterricht,* 25 (February 1973): 34–39;

Michael Hamburger, "Uwe Johnson–eine Freundschaft," *Sprache im technischen Zeitalter,* no. 93 (1985): 2–12;

Ingeborg Hoesterey, "Die Erzählsituation als Roman: Uwe Johnsons *Jahrestage*," *Colloquia Germanica,* 16 (1983): 13–26;

Karl August Horst, "Im Bauch des trojanischen Pferdes," *Neue Züricher Zeitung,* 7 October 1961;

Sharon Edwards Jackiw, "The Manifold Difficulties of Uwe Johnson's *Mutmaßungen über Jakob*," *Monatshefte,* 65 (1973): 126–143;

Walter Jens, "Johnson auf der Schwelle der Meisterschaft," *Die Zeit,* 6 October 1961;

Jens, "Privatroman statt Lagebericht," *Die Zeit,* 8 October 1965;

Herbert Kolb, "Rückfall in die Parataxe: Anläßlich einiger Satzbauformen in Uwe Johnsons erstveröffentlichtem Roman," *Neue Deutsche Hefte,* 10 (1963): 42–74;

Anita Krätzer, *Studien zum Amerikabild in der neueren deutschen Literatur: Max Frisch–Uwe Johnson–Hans Magnus Enzensberger und das "Kursbuch"* (Bern: Lang, 1982);

Vera Zuzana Langerova, "Women Characters in the Works of Uwe Johnson," Ph.D. dissertation, Vanderbilt University, 1976;

Sara Lennox, "Die New York Times in Uwe Johnsons *Jahrestagen*," in *Die USA und Deutschland: Wechselseitige Spiegelungen in der Literatur der Gegenwart,* edited by Wolfgang Paulsen (Bern & Munich: Francke, 1976), pp. 103–109;

Lennox, "Yoknapatawpha to Jerichow: Uwe Johnson's Appropriation of William Faulkner," *Arkadia,* 14 (1979): 166–176;

K. H. Lepper, "Dichter im geteilten Deutschland: Bemerkungen zu Uwe Johnsons Erzählung 'Eine Kneipe geht verloren,'" *Monatshefte,* 60 (1968): 23–34;

Eberhard Mannack, *Zwei deutsche Literaturen? Zu Günter Grass, Uwe Johnson, Hermann Kant, Ulrich Plenzdorff und Christa Wolf* (Kronberg: Athenäum, 1977);

Hans Mayer, "Das erste Buch über Gesine," *Die Weltwoche,* 4 December 1970;

Mayer, "Versuch, eine Grenze zu beschreiben: Zu Uwe Johnsons Roman Mutmaßungen über Jakob," in his *Vereinzelt Niederschläge: Kritik und Polemik* (Pfullingen: Neske, 1973), pp. 137–146;

Norbert Mecklenburg, "Großstadtmontage und Provinzchronik: Die epische 'Aufhebung' des regionalen Romans in Uwe Johnsons *Jahrestage*," in his *Erzählte Provinz: Regionalismus und Moderne im Roman* (Königstein: Athenäum, 1982), pp. 180–224;

Mecklenburg, "Zeitroman oder Heimatroman? Uwe Johnsons *Ingrid Babendererde*," *Wirkendes Wort,* 36 (1986): 172–189;

Rolf Michaelis, *Kleines Adreßbuch für Jerichow und New York: Ein Register zu Uwe Johnsons Roman "Jahrestage"* (Frankfurt am Main: Suhrkamp, 1983);

Karl Migner, "Uwe Johnson," in *Deutsche Literatur seit 1945 in Einzeldarstellungen,* edited by Dietrich Weber (Stuttgart: Kröner, 1968), pp. 484–504;

Migner, *Uwe Johnson: "Das dritte Buch über Achim." Interpretation* (Munich: Oldenbourg, 1974);

Migner, "Uwe Johnson *Das dritte Buch über Achim*: Methodische Hinweise zu seiner Erarbeitung," *Der Deutschunterricht,* 16 (1964): 17–25;

Leslie L. Miller, "Uwe Johnson's *Jahrestage*: The Choice of Alternatives," *Seminar,* 10 (February 1974): 50–70;

Richard Allen Murphy, "The Dilemma of the Artist-Writer in the Novels of Uwe Johnson," Ph.D. dissertation, Cornell University, 1967;

Bernd Neumann, *Utopie und Mimesis: Zum Verhältnis von Ästhetik, Geschichtsphilosophie und Politik in den Romanen Uwe Johnsons* (Kronberg: Athenäum, 1978);

Heinz D. Osterle, "Uwe Johnsons *Jahrestage:* Das Bild der U.S.A.," *German Quarterly,* 48 (November 1975): 505–518;

Karl Pestalozzi, "Achim alias Täve Schur: Uwe Johnsons zweiter Roman und seine Vorlage," *Sprache im technischen Zeitalter,* no. 6 (1962-1963): 479–486;

Hansjürgen Popp, "Einführung in Uwe Johnsons Roman *Mutmaßungen über Jakob,*" supplementary issue of *Der Deutschunterricht* (1967);

Ree Post-Adams, *Uwe Johnson: Darstellungsproblematik als Romanthema in Mutmaßungen über Jakob und Das dritte Buch über Achim* (Bonn: Bouvier, 1977);

Fritz J. Raddatz, "Ein Märchen aus Geschichte und Geschichten: Uwe Johnson: *Jahrestage* 4: Zum Abschluß eines großen Romanwerks," *Die Zeit,* 14 October 1983;

Werner Joachim Radke, "Untersuchungen zu Uwe Johnsons *Mutmaßungen über Jakob,*" Ph.D. dissertation, Stanford University, 1966;

Marcel Reich-Ranicki, "Dichter der beiden Deutschland?" *Die Zeit,* 24 September 1965;

Reich-Ranicki, "Ein Mann fährt ins andere Deutschland," Die Zeit, 16 September 1961;

Reich-Ranicki, "Mutmaßungen wurden Gewißheit: Uwe Johnson macht es sich zu leicht," *Die Zeit,* 13 March 1964;

Reich-Ranicki, "Registrator Johnson," in his *Deutsche Literatur in Ost und West* (Munich: Piper, 1963), pp. 231–246;

Reich-Ranicki, "Uwe Johnsons neuer Roman: Der erste Band des Prosawerks *Jahrestage,*" *Die Zeit,* 2 October 1970;

Nicolai Riedel, *Determinanten der Rezeptionssteuerung: Dargestellt am Beispiel der multimedialen Rezeption des schriftstellerischen Werks Uwe Johnsons: Materialien und Grundlagenstudien zu einer kritischen Einführung in die Forschung* (Mannheim: Selbstverlag N. Riedel, 1978);

Riedel, *Untersuchungen zur Geschichte der internationalen Rezeption Uwe Johnsons: Ein Beitrag zur empirischen Forschung* (Hildesheim: Olms, 1985);

Riedel, ed., *Uwe Johnsons Frühwerk: Im Spiegel der deutschsprachigen Literaturkritik* (Bonn: Bouvier, 1987);

Eva Schiffer, "Politsches Engagement oder Resignation: Weiteres zu Uwe Johnsons *Jahrestage,*" in *Der deutsche Roman und seine historischen und politischen Bedingungen,* edited by Wolfgang Paulsen (Bern & Munich: Francke, 1977), pp. 236–246;

Walter Schmitz, *Uwe Johnson* (Munich: Beck / edition text + kritik, 1984);

Franz Schonauer, "Uwe Johnson," in *Schriftsteller der Gegenwart: 53 literarische Porträts,* edited by Klaus Nonnemann (Olten: Walter, 1963);

Peter Schreiner, "Uwe Johnson und seine Welt: Weltsicht, epische Grundform und Sprachstruktur," *Die Zeit im Buch* (1967): 1–8;

Wilhelm Johannes Schwarz, *Der Erzähler Uwe Johnson,* third edition (Bern & Munich: Francke, 1973);

Robert K. Shirer, *Difficulties in Saying "I": The Narrator as Protagonist in Uwe Johnson's "Jahrestage" and Christa Wolf's "Kindheitsmuster"* (Bern: Lang, 1988);

Hugo Steger, "Rebellion und Tradition in der Sprache von Uwe Johnsons *Mutmaßungen über Jakob,*" in his *Zwischen Sprache und Literatur: Drei Reden* (Göttingen: Sachse & Pohl, 1967), pp. 43–69;

Gisela Ullrich, *Identität und Rolle: Probleme des Erzählens bei Johnson, Walser, Frisch und Fichte* (Stuttgart: Klett, 1977);

Siegfried Unseld, "Nachwort: Die Prüfung der Reife im Jahre 1953," in *Ingrid Babendererde: Reifeprüfung 1953,* by Uwe Johnson (Frankfurt am Main: Suhrkamp, 1985), pp. 249–264;

Heinrich Vormweg, "Uwe Johnsons Bestandaufnahmen vom Lauf der Welt," in *Zeitkritische Romane des 20. Jahrhunderts: Die Gesellschaft in der Kritik der deutschen Literatur,* edited by Hans Wagener (Stuttgart: Reclam, 1975), pp. 362–380;

Martin Walser, "Was Schriftsteller tun können," *Süddeutsche Zeitung,* 26 and 27 August 1961;

Roland H. Wiegenstein, "Die Grenze des Uwe Johnson," *Frankfurter Hefte,* 16 (1961): 633–634;

Wiegenstein, "Johnson lesen: Vorschläge zu den *Jahrestagen* 1–4," *Neue Rundschau,* 95 (1984): 128–144;

Gotthard Wunberg, "Struktur und Symbolik in Uwe Johnsons Roman *Mutmaßungen über Jakob,*" Neue Sammlung, 2 (1962): 440–449;

Erich Wunderlich, *Uwe Johnson* (Berlin: Colloquium, 1973);

Richard E. Ziegfeld, "Exilautor / Exilverleger: Uwe Johnson und Helen Wolff," in *Das Exilerlebnis: Verhandlungen des vierten Symposiums über deutsche und österreichische Exilliteratur,* edited by Donald G. Daviau and Ludwig M. Fischer (Columbia, S.C.: Camden House, 1982), pp. 505–516.

Papers:

The Uwe Johnson Archive is at the University of Frankfurt am Main.

Ernst Jünger

(29 March 1895 – 17 February 1998)

Carl Steiner
George Washington University

This entry originally appeared in DLB 56:German
Fiction Writers, 1914–1945.

BOOKS: *In Stahlgewittern: Aus dem Tagebuch eines Stotrup-
pführers von Ernst Jünger. Kriegsfreiwilliger, dann Leutnant und Kompanieführer im Füsilier-Regiment "Prinz
Albrecht von Preußen" (Hannov. Nr. 73)* (Hannover:
Privately printed, 1920; revised, Berlin: Mittler,
1922); translated by Basil Creighton as *The Storm
of Steel: From the Diary of a German Storm-Troop Officer*
(London: Chatto & Windus, 1929; New York:
Doubleday, Doran, 1929);

Der Kampf als inneres Erlebnis (Berlin: Mittler, 1922;
revised, 1926);

*Das Wäldchen 125: Eine Chronik aus den Grabenkämpfen
1918* (Berlin: Mittler, 1925); translated by Creighton as *Copse 125: A Chronicle from the Trench Warfare
of 1918* (London: Chatto & Windus, 1930);

Feuer und Blut: Ein kleiner Ausschnitt aus einer großen Schlacht
(Magdeburg: Stahlhelm, 1925; revised, Ham-
burg: Hanseatische Verlagsanstalt, 1929);

Das abenteuerliche Herz: Aufzeichnungen bei Tag und Nacht
(Berlin: Mittler, 1925); republished as *Das aben-
teuerliche Herz: Figuren und Capriccios* (Hamburg:
Hanseatische Verlagsanstalt, 1938);

Die totale Mobilmachung (Berlin: Verlag für Zeitkritik,
1931);

Der Arbeiter: Herrschaft und Gestalt (Hamburg: Hanseatische
Verlagsanstalt, 1932);

Blätter und Steine (Hamburg: Hanseatische Verlagsanstalt, 1934);

Geheimnisse der Sprache: Zwei Essays (Hamburg: Hanseatische
Verlagsanstalt, 1934);

Afrikanische Spiele (Hamburg: Hanseatische Verlagsanstalt, 1936); translated by Stuart Hood as *African
Diversions* (London: Lehmann, 1954);

Auf den Marmorklippen (Hamburg: Hanseatische Verlagsanstalt, 1939); translated by Hood as *On the Marble Cliffs* (London: Lehmann, 1947; New York:
New Directions, 1947);

*Gärten und Straßen: Aus den Tägebüchern von 1939 und
1940* (Berlin: Mittler, 1942);

*Myrdun: Briefe aus Norwegen. Einmalige Feldpostausgabe für
die Soldaten . . . in Norwegen* (N.p., 1943);

*Der Friede: Ein Wort an die Jugend Europas und an die
Jugend der Welt* (Hamburg: Hanseatische Verlags-
anstalt, 1945); translated by Hood as *The Peace*
(Hinsdale, Ill.: Regnery, 1948);

Atlantische Fahrt: Nur für Kriegsgefangene gedruckt (London: Kriegsgefangenenhilfe des Weltbundes der Christlichen Vereine Junger Männer in England, 1947); republished as *Atlantische Fahrt* (Zurich: Arche, 1948);

Sprache und Körperbau (Zurich: Arche, 1947; revised, Frankfurt am Main: Klostermann, 1949);

Im Granit (Olten, 1947);

Ein Inselfrühling: Ein Tagebuch aus Rhodos, mit den sizilischen Tagebuchblättern "Aus der goldenen Muschel" (Zurich: Arche, 1948);

Strahlungen (Tübingen: Heliopolis, 1949);

Heliopolis: Rückblick auf eine Stadt (Tübingen: Heliopolis, 1949);

Über die Linie (Frankfurt am Main: Klostermann, 1950);

Das Haus der Briefe (Olten: Vereinigung Oltner Bücherfreunde, 1951);

Der Waldgang (Frankfurt am Main: Klostermann, 1951);

Am Kieselstrand: Gedruckt als Gabe des Autors an seine Freunde, Weihnachten 1951 – Neujahr 1952 (Frankfurt am Main: Klostermann, 1951);

Besuch auf Godenholm (Frankfurt am Main: Klostermann, 1952);

Drei Kiesel: Gedruckt als Gabe des Autors an seine Freunde, Weihnachten 1952 – Neujahr 1953 (Frankfurt am Main: Klostermann, 1952);

Ernst Jünger: Eine Auswahl, edited by Arnim Mohler (Bielefeld, Hannover, Berlin & Darmstadt: Velhagen & Klasing, 1953);

Der gordische Knoten (Frankfurt am Main: Klostermann, 1953);

Das Sanduhrbuch (Frankfurt am Main: Klostermann, 1954);

Geburtstagbrief: Zum 4. November 1955 (Olten: Vereinigung Oltner Bücherfreunde, 1955);

Die Herzmuschel (N.p., 1955);

Sonnentau: Pflanzenbilder (Olten: Vereinigung Oltner Bücherfreunde, 1955);

Am Sarazenenturm (Frankfurt am Main: Klostermann, 1955);

Rivarol (Frankfurt am Main: Klostermann, 1955);

Serpentara (Zurich: Bösch-Presse, 1957);

San Pietro (Olten: Vereinigung Oltner Bücherfreunde, 1957);

Gläserne Bienen (Stuttgart: Klett, 1957; revised, Hamburg: Rowohlt, 1960); translated by Louise Bogan and Elizabeth Mayer as *The Glass Bees* (New York: Noonday, 1960);

Mantrana: Einladung zu einem Spiel (Stuttgart: Klett, 1958);

An der Zeitmauer (Stuttgart: Klett, 1959);

Der Weltstaat: Organismus und Organisation (Stuttgart: Klett, 1960);

Ein Vormittag in Antibes (Olten: Vereinigung Oltner Bücherfreunde, 1960);

Sgraffiti (Stuttgart: Klett, 1960);

Werke, 10 volumes (Stuttgart: Klett, 1960–1965);

Fassungen (Munich: Gotteswinter, 1963);

Sturm (Olten: Oltner Liebhaberdruck, 1963);

An Friedrich Georg zum 65. Geburtstag (Frankfurt am Main: Klostermann, 1963);

Subtile Jagden (Stuttgart: Klett, 1967);

Annäherungen: Drogen und Rausch (Stuttgart: Klett, 1970);

Sinn und Bedeutung: Ein Figurenspiel (Stuttgart: Klett, 1971);

Die Zwille (Stuttgart: Klett, 1973);

Zahlen und Götter; Philemon und Baucis: Zwei Essays (Stuttgart: Klett, 1974);

Eumeswil (Stuttgart: Klett, 1977); translated by Joachim Neugroschel (New York: Marsilio, 1993);

Siebzig verweht, 2 volumes (Stuttgart: Klett-Cotta, 1980–1981);

Aladins Problem (Stuttgart: Klett-Cotta, 1983); translated by Neugroschel as *Aladdin's Problem* (New York: Marsilio, 1992);

Autor und Autorschaft (Stuttgart: Klett-Cotta, 1984);

Eine gefährliche Begegnung (Stuttgart: Klett-Cotta, 1985); translated by Hilary Barr as *A Dangerous Encounter* (New York: Marsilio, 1993);

Zwei Mal Halley (Stuttgart: Klett-Cotta, 1987);

Die Schere (Stuttgart: Klett-Cotta, 1990);

Siebzig verweht III (Stuttgart: Klett-Cotta, 1993).

OTHER: *Der Aufmarsch: Eine Reihe deutscher Schriften,* edited by Jünger, 2 volumes (Leipzig: Aufmarsch-Verlag-Gesellschaft, 1926);

Die Unvergessenen, edited, with contributions, by Jünger (Berlin: Andermann, 1928);

Luftfahrt ist not!, edited by Jünger (Leipzig: Rudolph, 1928);

Der Kampf um das Reich, edited, with contributions, by Jünger (Berlin: Andermann, 1929);

Das Antlitz des Weltkrieges: Fronterlebnisse deutscher Soldaten, edited by Jünger (Berlin: Neufeld & Henius, 1930);

Krieg und Krieger, edited by Jünger (Berlin: Junker & Dünnhaupt, 1930);

Der gefährliche Augenblick: Eine Sammlung von Bildern und Berichten, edited by F. Buchholtz, introduction by Jünger (Berlin: Junker & Dünnhaupt, 1931);

Hier spricht der Feind: Kriegserlebnisse unserer Gegner, edited by Jünger (Berlin: Neufeld & Henius, 1931);

Die veränderte Welt: Eine Bilderfibel unserer Zeit, edited by E. Schultz, introduction by Jünger (Breslau: Korn, 1933);

A. Horion, *Käferkunde für Naturfreunde,* foreword by Jünger (Frankfurt am Main: Klostermann, 1949);

H. Speidel, *Invasion 1944: Ein Beitrag zu Rommels und des Reiches Schicksal*, foreword by Jünger (Tübingen: Wunderlich, 1949).

The soldier-philosopher, a combination with which ancient civilizations such as those of Greece and Rome were quite comfortable, has become a rarity in the modern age of progressive overspecialization. If one adds the categories of naturalist, writer, and essayist, one moves into even more rarified circles. Ernst Jünger, blending the courage of the soldier with the curiosity of the student of life forms, the skill and imagination of the literary stylist with the probing intellect of the researcher, was such an exceptional individual. What made him even more special is the fact that he was still writing in his nineties. His represents the longest life span of any major figure in the annals of German literature. To call him the doyen of twentieth-century German letters is indeed no exaggeration.

Born into the soaring Second German Reich, nurtured on its ideals of expansive nationalism and imperialism, he experienced as a soldier its last days of glory and its downfall and demise. He lived through the ill-fated Weimar Republic, in which he began to expand his role from soldier to student and lover of nature, writer, essayist, and political thinker. He braved and survived the twelve years of the Third Reich, with which he may have sympathized at first; but as soon as he became aware of the fatal flaws of its rulers, he turned intellectual critic if not outright enemy. He saw his homeland almost completely destroyed, tragically divided, and miraculously rebuilt. In the course of an active life that included extensive traveling, he was able to create a voluminous literary opus. Yet in spite of—or perhaps because of—his endeavors, he remains a controversial figure. His life, almost from the beginning, has been immersed in controversies paralleling those that have embroiled his nation.

Jünger was born in Heidelberg on 29 March 1895; soon after his birth, his family moved to Hannover. His father, Dr. Ernst Georg Jünger, a basically kind but authoritarian man, was well versed in the humanities but developed a liking for the sciences, and, like the father of the first German novelist of the modern era, Theodor Fontane, he became a chemist and apothecary. Unlike Fontane, Jünger never harbored any intention of entering his father's profession; nonetheless, he developed a considerable interest in and knowledge of the sciences later in life. Jünger's mother, Karoline Lampl Jünger, was called "Lily" by her husband; the lily was to become one of the most important symbols in Jünger's fiction. His mother was a beautiful, intelligent, cultured woman whose interests included literature and such controversial issues as the emancipation of women.

Jünger was the oldest of seven children, of whom two died in childhood. His younger brother Friedrich Georg, nicknamed "Fritz," was also to become a well-known writer. The two brothers had a special relationship that lasted until Friedrich Georg's death in 1977. Otherwise, Ernst was much of a loner in his formative years. Highly intelligent, but a dreamer and underachiever in school, he very early developed a strong dislike for the established order. As a result, he and Friedrich Georg joined the Wandervögel (Boy Scouts), a group of middle-class youths banding together to escape what they perceived as a life of artificiality, bourgeois mediocrity, and decadence. Their aim was to find a new meaning in life through discussion, poetry, folk songs, and contact with nature on weekend hikes—very much in the mood of the then popular neo-romantic movement. Friedrich Georg Jünger described their shared feelings at the time in his book of remembrances *Grüne Zweige* (Green Branches, 1951): "Reisepläne beschäftigten uns. Die Unrast, der Wunsch, in eine sehr ferne Ferne zu gehen, der zugleich eine erste Regung von Selbständigkeit in sich birgt, setzte mir zu. Ernst wurde von diesem Wunsche sehr geplagt und entwickelte mir in dieser Zeit neue Pläne über Reisen in ferne Länder" (We were preoccupied with travel plans. I was troubled by unrest, by the desire to go to very distant lands, a wish which at the same time harbors a first impulse for independence. The desire tormented Ernst very much and caused him at that time to discuss with me plans for travel to faraway countries).

At the age of eighteen Jünger went to France, where he signed up for a five-year enlistment in the French foreign legion. His intent from the very beginning, though, was to desert from the legion once he had arrived in Africa, in order to assure himself of full freedom of action there. More than twenty years later, Jünger wrote an autobiographical novel based on his adventures, *Afrikanische Spiele* (1936; translated as *African Diversions*, 1954). In this somewhat romanticized version of his first attempt to gain independence from paternal supervision, Jünger tells the story of an adolescent, fascinated with danger and evil and filled with the hope of conquering all difficulties, who overcomes his earlier disappointments and disillusionment. The novel focuses on the two failed attempts by the narrator, Herbert Berger, to desert from the legion and on his encounter with the misfits and outcasts of society. It also marvels at the mysteries and natural wonders of parts of the Dark Continent. In real life, Dr. Jünger succeeded in having Ernst, who was still a minor, returned home. The magnanimous father promised to finance an extended excursion to Africa for Jünger once he had completed secondary school. Jünger agreed, but the outbreak of World War I in August 1914 intervened.

The nineteen-year-old Jünger enthusiastically signed up with the Seventy-third Hannoverian Fusiliers. Five days later he was allowed to take an emergency Abiturium (comprehensive examination) at his Gymnasium. After passing the examination, he enrolled at the University of Heidelberg. At the beginning of October he was inducted into his regiment, with which he served the entire four years of the war on the western front, advancing from cadet to first lieutenant and leader of elite assault troops; he received seven double wounds and was awarded the highest German medal of the time, the Pour le mérite, for exceptional bravery. His wish to leave his homeland and to face the challenges of the adventurous life had finally been realized, but the price and the pain were extremely high. The young warrior's first feelings of glory and enthusiasm soon gave way to an awareness of the reality of modern mass warfare. In his first book, *In Stahlgewittern* (1920; translated as *The Storm of Steel,* 1929), which became the most successful German book of its time and established the international fame of its author, Jünger conveyed the loss of illusion which was experienced by a whole generation of young German soldiers: "Nach kurzem Aufenthalt beim Regiment hatten wir alle Illusionen verloren, mit denen wir ausgezogen waren. Statt der erhofften Gefahren hatten wir Schmutz, Arbeit und schlaflose Nächte vorgefunden, zu deren Bezwingung ein uns wenig liegendes Heldentum gehörte" (After a short stay with the regiment, we lost almost all the illusions with which we had departed. Instead of the hoped-for dangers we found dirt, work and sleepless nights, which could only be overcome with a kind of heroism that was alien to us).

In spite of such pronouncements, Jünger neither denigrated war nor slighted the bravery of the soldier; occasionally he glorified both. In contrast to Erich Maria Remarque's international best-seller *Im Westen nichts Neues* (1929; translated as *All Quiet on the Western Front,* 1929) and other pacifistic books of the time, Jünger's book tells of the heroism of the warrior who is willing to sacrifice his life for his country and inspire his fellow soldiers. Jünger dedicated the book, which is written in diary form and gives a personal account of trench warfare, to his fallen comrades in arms. Due to the strong antiwar sentiments in German publishing circles in the 1920s, he had difficulty in finding a publisher for the book; the first edition had to be printed privately.

Appearing in the heyday of German literary expressionism, the realistic matter-of-fact tone and the simple but artistic style of *In Stahlgewittern* anticipated the era of the Neue Sachlichkeit (New Objectivity). Yet one can also detect in this work the beginnings of what Volker Katzmann calls Jünger's "magic realism." Already in this text, the author's rendering of the devastating reality of modern war is marked by a sense of form and style reminiscent of eighteenth- and nineteenth-century classicism and romanticism. His other works of the 1920s were of similar nature and sentiment. *Der Kampf als inneres Erlebnis* (Combat as an Inner Experience, 1922) is an essay on the psychology of combat; *Feuer und Blut* (Fire and Blood, 1925) describes the German offensive on the Somme River of March 1917, again from a personal vantage point; *Das Wäldchen 125* (1925; translated as *Copse 125,* 1930) chronicles the trench warfare of 1918.

Jünger was among the first to portray the reactions and emotions of a young, cultured European trying to cope with modern warfare. He related not just the physical but also the psychological effects of his experiences. The short novel *Sturm* (Storm) deals with the feelings of a young leader when he must order his men to attack. Remarkable for its experimental form and style, the novel was first published in installments in the daily *Hannoverscher Kurier* in 1923. The author had little recollection of the work later on; considered lost, it was found in 1960 and published in 1963. Its plot appears to be patterned somewhat after Rainer Maria Rilke's romanticized version of a soldier's life and death in war, *Die Weise von Liebe und Tod des Cornets Christoph Rilke* (1903; translated as *The Tale of the Love and Death of Cornet Christopher Rilke,* 1932). Longer and much less poetic in style than Rilke's popular tale, Jünger's account also ends with the death of the hero in battle. Nonetheless, the experiences of its main character, Lieutenant Sturm, are largely autobiographical. How important this character was to Jünger is attested to by the fact that when his essays which were later collected as *Das abenteuerliche Herz: Aufzeichnungen bei Tag und Nacht* (The Adventurous Heart: Notations by Day and by Night, 1925) first appeared in the journal *Arminius,* they were published under the pseudonym Hans Sturm.

Das abenteuerliche Herz was published in a revised and expanded version in 1938 as a collection of sixty-three short prose pieces, which Gerhard Loose has characterized as "adventures of the spirit, as the heart, the organ of consummate cognition, understands them." Jünger's intention was to encompass and convey the whole external picture as well as the inner core of the organic life of man, animal, and plant, a Goethean undertaking.

Yet the primary influence on Jünger's early works remained his war experiences. He continued his military service after November 1918 in the Reichswehr, a limited defensive force permitted the Weimar Republic by the Treaty of Versailles, until 1923. After his discharge, he studied biology in Leipzig and later in Naples, financing his schooling through the sale of his books. On 3 August 1925 he married Gretha von Jeinsen, with whom he had fallen in love at proverbial first sight, and decided to end his academic pursuits and make a living as a writer. Gretha bore him two sons, Ernst Johann Friedrich Oskar and Alexander Joachim.

In 1927 Jünger moved to Berlin, where he became involved with a revolutionary movement which espoused a doctrine of "national bolshevism" aimed at linking Germany with Russia against the West. Jünger shared the movement's romantic notion of a hierarchical military state in which an elite force of workers and soldiers was to exercise supreme power.

His fame as a writer of war experiences and as an officer and war hero made him not only the darling of some fringes of the political left but also a favorite of the right. As a result of his political flirtations with the extremist circles of the right, Jünger became a contributor and later also a coeditor, well into the early 1930s, of the right-wing, antidemocratic political magazines *Standarte, Arminius, Widerstand, Der Vormarsch,* and *Die Kommenden.* He also edited compilations dealing with World War I, including *Die Unvergessenen* (The Unforgotten, 1928), *Der Kampf um das Reich* (The Struggle for the Empire, 1929), *Das Antlitz des Weltkrieges* (The Face of the World War, 1930), and *Krieg und Krieger* (War and Warrior, 1930).

Jünger's attempts to effect social change through the power of his pen and his intellect resulted in two important works: *Die totale Mobilmachung* (Total Mobilization, 1931) and *Der Arbeiter: Herrschaft und Gestalt* (The Worker: Rule and Form, 1932).

Die totale Mobilmachung, written in Berlin in 1929 and 1930, advocates the total mobilization of society for total warfare. Peace is a time during which society has to go "all out" to prepare for war. Since the ideal of a permanent peace is an illusion, a futile dream to be abandoned, the notion of attaining a life of ease and comfort is equally spurious. Such false hopes have to be replaced by a new willingness for service and sacrifice. Jünger envisaged the society of the future and its ruling class in the subsequent work *Der Arbeiter,* an essay of more than three hundred pages. While the worker as a type was considered downtrodden and exploited in the nineteenth century, the present age, according to Jünger, is in desperate need of developing a different type, whose destiny is to become a leader and ruler. Unimpeded by prejudices, political theories, and divisions, the worker can determine the shape of society and the world. The ultimate goal is the "Ablösung der liberalen Demokratie durch den Arbeiterstaat" (replacement of liberal democracy by a workers' state). The

worker is both building block for and representative of the new order. To fulfill his destiny, he has to be militant and radical, a warrior and a destroyer. As a result of his radicalism and militancy, the old order will disintegrate, giving life to a new world arising like a phoenix from the ashes of the moribund system. The worker, the progenitor of the new world, will then fully unfold his creative and constructive powers and become its actual builder. Jünger saw the worker not just as a member of a special class or social category but as a metaphysical being who appears to be not too distant a relative of Friedrich Nietzsche's Übermensch (superman). Some thirty years after the appearance of *Der Arbeiter,* Jünger wrote an addition, titled "Maxima-Minima," to supplement and expand the earlier work and bring it up to date. This text contains new explanations about methodology as well as new insights and reflections.

With *Der Arbeiter,* Jünger reached the end of the first stage of his development as a writer of major importance. In all these early years, and in spite of his support for right-wing causes, he avoided party affiliations. He did not want to be bound by narrow party doctrines, especially those of the most forceful and powerful group of all, the National Socialist German Workers (Nazi) Party under Adolf Hitler. Jünger's stance vis-à-vis the Nazi movement in the 1920s and 1930s has been a topic of much investigation and deliberation, especially in connection with the reception of the author and his work after the demise of the Third Reich. The truth seems to be that Jünger, like Hitler, rejected the Weimar Republic and the democratic process. In their view, democracy was an ineffective form of government, lacking in authority if not in integrity. Both men criticized liberalism, the free press, the parliamentary system, the bourgeois mentality, and the exploitation of the workers and the public by unscrupulous capitalist entrepreneurs. Both propagated, in Roger Woods's words, "a blood-based community, and a state founded upon nationalism, socialism, authority, and a fitness to fight." Both proclaimed the supremacy of the will in partial adaptation of Nietzsche's vitalism and agreed with Oswald Spengler's contention that the inevitable decline of Western civilization could only be stopped by a unified nationalistic front within Germany asserting its supremacy.

Jünger's initial enthusiasm for National Socialism quickly gave way to disillusionment. The virulent anti-Semitism of the Nazis was a major stumbling block in Jünger's attempt to make common cause with the party. In the final analysis, Jünger acknowledged Hitler's effectiveness as an orator but rejected his claim to sole and supreme leadership of the envisaged conservative and nationalistic revolution. As a result, Jünger began to distance himself from the Nazis and in time shunned all political affiliations. In 1927 he refused to run as a Nazi candidate for a seat in the Reichstag. After Hitler came to power in 1933, Jünger went so far as to write a letter of protest to the official newspaper and main propaganda organ of the Third Reich, *Der Völkische Beobachter,* for having published from his work without his permission; and he let the Deutsche Akademie der Dichtung (German Academy of Literature), the literary section of the prestigious Prussian Academy of Arts, know in unmistakable terms that he was not interested in demonstrating solidarity with the Nazi regime by accepting membership in the body.

When concerted efforts by the regime to make Jünger an adherent proved futile, he found himself more and more in a state of intellectual and professional isolation. On 12 December 1933 he and his family moved to Goslar. Three years later, they moved to Überlingen, and in April 1939 they established themselves in Kirchhorst.

Although Jünger was reinstated in the army at the beginning of World War II, he was given the rather lowly rank of captain, which was not at all commensurate with his previous record as a battlefield commander of elite troops and a war hero. Consequently, his years of service at the Westwall (Siegfried Line) and with occupation forces in France were rather undistinguished in light of his military potential. He saw relatively little battlefield action, spending most of the war years in Paris as a member of the staff of Generals Speidel and Stülpnagel with vague responsibilities, pursuing his private and intellectual interests. His novel *Auf den Marmorklippen* (On the Marble Cliffs, 1939) and the first part of his World War II diary, *Gärten und Straßen* (Gardens and Streets, 1942), were banned by government censors. Jünger's mood in 1940 can be gleaned from a letter to Alfred Kubin, with whom he had been in correspondence for many years: "Man reist heute lange, um einen Menschen zu sehen" (One has to travel far today to meet a genuine human being).

Auf den Marmorklippen, Jünger's first novel held together by a continuous story, established its author as one of the leading writers of the Innere Emigration, those authors who, instead of going into exile during the Hitler years, remained in Germany and published works that criticized fascism either openly or in symbolic and allegorical form. The group included Werner Bergengruen, Reinhold Schneider, Ernst Wiechert, and Hans Carossa. Even though Jünger's novel betrays many autobiographical features, it is essentially a denunciation and philosophical critique in allegorical form of the Nazi government. The surrealistic, futuristic novel relates the experiences of the anonymous narrator and his brother Otho, who leave military service

and withdraw from a totalitarian organization called Mauretania to seek a peaceful life of contemplation and the pursuit of botanical and linguistic studies in a hermitage atop the marble cliffs of the lake of Marina. But their retreat is threatened by the charismatic leader of the Mauretanians, the Chief Ranger, who has come to power by spreading terror and fear. His aim is to reduce the social order to anarchy and primitivism, and ultimately to impose absolutist rule. The opposing forces, led by the Chief Ranger's principal opponent, Braquemart, a disciple of Nietzsche; Prince Sunmyra, the head of the conservatives; and Belovar, the protector of the farmers and herdsmen, are too divided and weak to ward off the destruction of the social order. The brothers are eventually drawn into the fighting and oppose the forces of the Chief Ranger openly. Although they are able to escape annihilation through the timely help of the narrator's son Erio, the child of a brief love affair, the atmosphere of impending doom and the symbolic ending hint that civilization will be destroyed. But there is hope, as in the ancient Germanic myth, that out of utter destruction new life will arise: the brothers leave for another shore after their hermitage is consumed in flames.

The novel is clearly a Zeit und Schlüsselroman (novel of contemporary history and roman à clef), describing the factional strife among the various political forces prior to Hitler's assumption of absolute power through ruthlessness and violence. It attacks the intelligentsia for their cowardly betrayal of the humanistic tradition and pillories the military for its equally cowardly neutrality during the struggle for power and its opportunistic declaration of loyalty to the victorious Führer. On the other side there appears Father Lampros, "the radiant one," the symbolic and heroic representative of Christianity. Beyond its references to the political scene of the 1920s and 1930s, *Auf den Marmorklippen* is a mythical conception of the history of humankind that shows the ultimate battle between the forces of good and evil.

Gärten und Straßen contains entries from as early as April 1939, when Jünger and his family had just moved from Überlingen on Lake Constance to Kirchhorst near Hannover; it conveys the tranquil picture of Jünger tending his garden and engaging in botanical studies. When the war began, he "took to some of the highways of Western Europe" as an officer of the German army.

Jünger was discharged from the army because of what was officially called "Wehruntüchtigkeit" (unfitness for service) in 1944, the same year his oldest son, Ernst, was killed in action in Italy. Jünger's dismissal was actually due to his suspected association with some of those involved in the plot to assassinate Hitler in July

1944. In April 1945 he was made commanding officer of the Kirchhorst District Volkssturm (people's militia), part of a last-ditch effort to summon to arms everybody who could possibly carry a rifle; Jünger ordered his men to put down their weapons.

During the period of denazification in Germany after the war, strong denunciations were made by literary critics of Jünger's nationalistic past. He was called a Nazi collaborator, and some demanded that he be tried as a war criminal. Typically, Jünger not only ignored these charges but refused to fill out the official denazification papers. This refusal led to a ban on the publication of his books in occupied Germany for several years. Yet Jünger, the former soldier and perennial adventurer, went even further, attacking the accusers by stating: "Nach dem Erdbeben schlägt man auf die Seismographen ein. Man kann jedoch die Barometer nicht für die Taifune büßen lassen, falls man nicht zu den Primitiven zählen will" (After the earthquake, people tend to attack the seismographs. However, they should not punish the barometers for the fact that there are typhoons, provided that they do not want to be counted among the primitives).

Jünger's *Der Friede: Ein Wort an die Jugend Europas und an die Jugend der Welt* (Peace: An Appeal to the Youth of Europe and to the Youth of the World, 1945; translated as *The Peace,* 1948), had originally been written between the winter of 1941 and the spring of 1942. Dissatisfied with this version as too personal, Jünger destroyed it and wrote a second, more political piece between July and October 1943. He had the manuscript read by fellow officers and superiors whom he could trust, among them Field Marshal Erwin Rommel. Conceived originally as an attempt to clarify the situation that the war had brought about and as an "Übung in Gerechtigkeit" (exercise in justice), Jünger intended to have the document printed and distributed in large quantities after the overthrow of the Nazi regime. Part 1, "Die Saat" (The Seed), expounds prevailing philosophical ideas and envisages the achievement of peace. Part 2, "Die Frucht" (The Fruit), develops a political program for peace that is to serve as a guideline not only for Europe but for the entire world. Before such a program can go into effect, the war has to end decisively: Germany has to suffer utter defeat. But if a lasting peace is to be achieved, everybody will have to benefit somehow: "Der Krieg muß von allen gewonnen werden" (The war has to be won by all). Jünger envisaged a culturally diverse but politically unified Europe as the ultimate goal, a political "Vaterland" of the various ethnic "Mutterländer," in which the worker was to play a central role by virtue of his constructive talents: "Die Erde muß für alle Brot haben" (The world must have bread for all). The creative forces thus released

must include religion: peace cannot be secured unless it becomes a sacred compact to lessen violence, "zu trösten, zu mildern, Schutz zu verleihen" (to comfort, to mitigate, to grant protection). Only by these means could the forces of nihilism be banished. Ironically, Jünger's plan to have his treatise widely distributed among the German people after the collapse of the Hitler regime came to naught. Since his works were prohibited from publication in Germany by order of the Allied occupation forces, only a limited number of copies came out illegally. The essay is significant not only as Jünger's political manifesto of the war years but also, along with such works as Wiechert's *Der Totenwald* (1945; translated as *The Forest of the Dead,* 1947), as one of the most courageous documents of resistance to the tyranny of the Third Reich.

In 1949 the publication restrictions on Jünger's works were lifted. That year he published his nine-hundred-page diary detailing his war experiences and his reflections on the three years of occupation of his homeland under the title *Strahlungen* (Emanations). The diary had been his only way, in a totalitarian state, to engage in meaningful discussion. Yet while writing it, he seems to have been disturbingly oblivious to the suffering that the regime he served was wreaking on the world. The first part of *Strahlungen* comprises the previously published *Gärten und Straßen.* Parts 2 and 4 are titled "Pariser Tagebuch" (Parisian Diary) and deal with his experiences in occupied Paris, where he associated with French writers, artists, and intellectuals such as Pierre Drieu la Rochelle, Jean Giraudoux, Jean Cocteau, Georges Braque, Pablo Picasso, and Banine, who later wrote *Rencontres avec Ernst Jünger* (Encounters with Ernst Jünger, 1951). In Paris, Jünger also read the Bible thoroughly for the first time because of his growing interest in religion. The third part of the diary, "Kaukasische Aufzeichnungen" (Caucasian Notes), relates a special mission by order of General Stülpnagel to the southern part of occupied Russia from October 1942 to February 1943 to provide a firsthand account of the German campaign there. Jünger was also looking for reliable fellow officers at the eastern front who might join him in a conspiracy against the Führer. Part 5 of the diary, "Kirchhorster Blätter" (Kirchhorst Journal), records Jünger's discharge from the army and command of the Kirchhorst District Volkssturm. The final part of the diary, "Jahre der Okkupation" (Years of Occupation), deals with the period from 1945 to 1948.

Jünger's second full-fledged novel, the futuristic *Heliopolis: Rückblick auf eine Stadt* (Heliopolis: Reflections on a City), also appeared in 1949. This ambitious epic work of universal scope deals with man's past and his possible future development. Heliopolis is an imaginary place, what Loose calls "a timeless prototype of a city," bearing no relationship to the ancient Egyptian city of that name. The novel is set in an epoch that postdates "the second nihilism" and the disappearance of the global workers' state. As in *Auf den Marmorklippen,* there are several opposing powers in the city. The Governor, an unscrupulous tyrant ruling on behalf of the extraterrestrial Regent, keeps the masses spellbound. His ultimate aim is "die Perfektion der Technik" (the perfection of technology). He is opposed by the Proconsul, who is supported by the army and conservative forces. The Proconsul strives for a "historische Ordnung" (historical order) and "die Vollkommenheit des Menschen" (the perfection of man). A third, smaller group is made up of the closely knit nihilistic Mauretanians, who adroitly exploit the standoff between the major powers. The protagonist, Lucius de Geer, commander of the war college, is a cultured humanist as well as a man of action. A diplomat, philosopher, teacher, and a skilled officer, as well as attractive to the opposite sex, he is the personification of the "adventurous heart." Intermittent acts of terror have taken the place of open warfare, yet a clash between the two main forces seems inevitable. Lucius is drawn into the action but tries to keep a measure of independence and follow the dictates of his conscience. Hence, rather than persecuting the beautiful Budur Peri, as he is ordered to do, he saves her and falls in love with her, and she becomes his intellectual counterpart. This most exquisite female character that Jünger has ever conceived belongs to an outcast people, the Parsen, who, like the Jews in past ages, are subjected to constant persecution because of their aloofness and their beliefs. In the end, Lucius gives up his military and political ambitions and resolves to leave the violent and corrupt city of Heliopolis with Budur for the distant Hesperides, his original home.

Like *Auf den Marmorklippen,* this symbolic and allegorical narrative shows that Jünger's visions of the future are dystopian rather than utopian. But in both novels there is some hope at the end that man may be able to begin anew after the inevitable destruction of his civilization. As in the earlier novel, philosophical reflections and the exposition of ideas do more than fill out the framework of the narrative: they are the actual core of the work. Extraordinary figures such as Halder the painter, Ortner the poet, Serner the philosopher, and Father Foelix the enlightener open up significant aesthetic and philosophical questions to discussion in the manner of ancient symposia. These characters are joined by a geologist with philosophical inclinations and an historian, Orelli. Orelli represents the genuine scholar, who is not just in command of the facts but also possesses sensitivity and intuitive insight. They all act as mystagogues, verbalizing and clarifying de Geer's understanding of the eternal verities. Even though the

hero falters in his political undertakings, he gains intellectually and spiritually. Clearly, Jünger has broken away from what Alfred von Martin calls the "heroic realism" and "heroic nihilism" of his early and middle years. He expresses belief in a "theological humanism" that celebrates free will and altruistic individualism, rejecting collectivism and the heartless worship of power.

In 1950 Jünger moved to the hamlet of Wilflingen in Württemberg, which has been his home ever since. A dedicated student of plant, animal, and insect life, his study of man always takes into account man's natural environment. In the reflective piece *Der Waldgang* (Walk through the Forest, 1951), he deals symbolically with the rootlessness of modern man, who has lost his homeland but is determined to transgress the metaphorical "Nullmeridian" (zero longitude) and to hold on to his newly gained freedom. This theme is expanded in the essayistic prose poem *Besuch auf Godenholm* (Visit on Godenholm, 1952). In this work, a physician, representing modern man and his dilemma, is helped through a mental crisis by a mysterious magician on a Nordic island; the physician comes to the realization that "der Mensch trägt alles Nötige in sich" (Man carries all that is necessary within himself).

During the 1950s Jünger, who was already one of the most widely traveled German writers, undertook a series of extensive journeys. He continued his wanderings well into his ninth decade, visiting the Mediterranean, northern Europe, the Americas, the Canary Islands, Asia Minor, Ceylon, and the Far East. These experiences have led to the publication of more than a dozen travel books as well as countless reflections on faraway lands in his diaries and essayistic works. In the philosophical essay *Der gordische Knoten* (The Gordian Knot, 1953), he analyzes the areas of contact and contrast between East and West. Orient and occident are, he says, fundamentally separated from one another by their different attitudes toward freedom. Despotism is the inherent rule of the east; it tends to extinguish all impulses toward freedom. In the West, on the other hand, freedom remains deeply ingrained in man's psyche. Jünger refrains from giving specific definitions of freedom: "Sie führen zu unfruchtbarem Streit" (They lead to unproductive bickering). One of his most celebrated works in the travel genre is the 1955 diary of his journey to Sardinia, *Am Sarazenenturm* (At the Tower of the Saracens), which was awarded the literary prize of the city of Bremen. Here the author learns among shepherds, hunters, fishermen, and gardeners that man is happy while living the simple, natural life but saddened when he forsakes nature for artificiality. In 1955 Jünger was awarded the Kulturpreis (Culture Prize) of the city of Goslar.

Junger's complex science-fiction constructions in *Heliopolis* are greatly simplified in the short novel *Gläserne Bienen* (1957; translated as *The Glass Bees,* 1960). The plot of this work does not revolve around the fantastic mechanical insects of the title, which perform their task of nectar gathering by remote control; they merely serve as background. The story focuses on Captain Richard, a retired army officer who, having fallen on hard times, is forced to seek civilian employment. He is out of touch with the new age of automation; his world has disappeared. Put to a series of tests by the great Zapparoni, the industrial czar of modern automation, he is bound to fail. In the epilogue to the second edition (1960), *Gläserne Bienen* is revealed to be a lecture given by Captain Richard in a seminar on historical topics, which one of the participants has published in drastically abbreviated form. Evidently, Jünger wished to deemphasize the novelistic aspect of the work in order to focus attention on the conflict between humanity and technology, sensitivity and automation. In peace as in war, the machine has made fallible man appear obsolete and useless. Perfection is no longer an ideal to be striven for, but an achieved reality, a perennial state of matter-of-factness. The altar on which it is worshipped is that of efficiency and productivity, the modern gods of man's industrial enterprises.

In 1959 Jünger received the Großes Bundesverdienstkreuz (Great Order of Merit of the Federal Republic of Germany) and became cofounder and coeditor of the periodical *Antaios: Zeitschrift für eine freie Welt*. In the same year the sequel to *Der Arbeiter, An der Zeitmauer* (At the Wall of Time), was published. Whereas the earlier essay was polemical in nature, dealing with the political issues of the age in a futuristic guise, *An der Zeitmauer* is concerned with metaphysics. Jünger has forsaken the role of political activist and become an objective observer of man and his institutions, a kind of detached prophet and cosmic visionary. A second volume of essays, *Sgraffiti,* appeared in 1960 as a follow-up to *Das abenteuerliche Herz*. The topics of discussion in *Sgraffiti* are nearly as broad as in the earlier volume, but there is a dearth of inventiveness; no fewer than fourteen pieces are given the title "Mosaik." These pieces present an interconnected pattern of short observations, personal commentary, aphorisms, and sayings.

Jünger's wife died in 1960. That year he received the Lituraturpreis des Bundesverbandes der deutschen Industrie (Literature Prize of the Federal League of German Industry) and produced an essay on global political structure, *Der Weltstaat: Organismus und Organisation* (The World State: Organism and Organization), as a sequel to *Der Friede*. Jünger contends that the national state determines the type of society it comprises, all the way down to the family unit. But even the great countries are limited in their freedom of action. Global decision-making is more and more a juggling act, especially since the world is divided into powerful western and eastern halves. The severity of the division is indicated by such slogans as "Cold War" and "Iron Curtain." Yet the two superpowers are much more alike than is generally believed; hence it would not be too farfetched to assume that these two halves are the casting-mold for the formation of a universal state. The possibility of its genesis augurs well for the prospect of ultimate world peace. The idea that the state is the source of all evil is the core of anarchism. The anarchist in his purest form is one whose recollections go back to prehistoric, indeed premythical ages: he believes that man at that time already fulfilled his destiny. In this sense, anarchists are ultraconservatives who seek the salvation of society in its origins. Pure anarchists are almost an extinct species today; the present world is overrun by nihilists. Yet the anarchist has been instrumental in bringing about the great revolutions. His protests against the state and its institutions come from the heart. He shows us a better, more just, and more natural mode of existence. Today, the character of each state is determined by other states, which serve as models; but this has not always been true and need not be the case in the future. In an ideal state, which once existed in an insular or a similar type of secluded setting, no defensive or war-making forces are necessary. In it alone, the human organism, truly humane and freed from the coercive forces of organization, could appear in a more nearly pure form.

On 3 March 1962 Jünger married Dr. Liselotte Lehrer, an archivist and publisher's reader twenty-two years younger than he. During the decade following his second marriage Jünger again undertook extensive travels. He received the Immermann Prize from the city of Düsseldorf in 1964.

In 1970, at the age of seventy-five, Jünger produced a book about drugs and drug-taking titled *Annäherungen: Drogen und Rausch* (Approach: Drugs and Intoxication). This book of some five hundred pages is another of his travelogues, but this time the journey is an inward one in which he penetrates, in Loose's phrase, "the uncharted seas of the soul." Jünger was no novice in dealing with drugs: from 1918 to 1922 he had experimented with the mind-altering effects of ether, cocaine, opium, and hashish; thirty years later, he acquainted himself with mescaline, ololuiqui (a Mexican mushroom), and LSD. Scientific and literary sources, including Thomas De Quincey's *Confessions of an English Opium-Eater* (1822), Charles Baudelaire's *Les paradis artificiels* (1860), and Aldous Huxley's *The Doors of Perception* (1954), supplement his personal experiences in *Annäherungen*. In contrast to some of his literary predecessors, however, Jünger has never been addicted to drugs.

In the novel *Die Zwille* (The Slingshot, 1973) Jünger reminisces about his schooldays in Hannover and Braunschweig. But *Die Zwille* is less an autobiographical novel than a psychological study of the relationship between pupil and teacher. It is also an exposé of secondary education as well as of village and city life in the Wilhelminian era. The two protagonists, Clamor and Teo, are both endowed with certain traits of the author. Ten-year-old Clamor, the loner and dreamer who has lost his lowly parents, feels constantly threatened and considers himself a failure. Yet he desperately wants to belong, to be a member of a group. He shares these characteristics with Teo's father, the minister of Oldhorst, who has become his protector. Teo, on the other hand, is the exact opposite of both. Seven or eight years older than Clamor, he is as strong as his own father and Clamor are weak; consequently, he is cast in the role of lord and master over Clamor. The same hierarchical spirit prevails in the Gymnasium, where there is moreover a strong sense of antagonism and distrust between teachers and pupils. A prank conceived and directed by the domineering Teo results in the clumsy Clamor being nabbed and expelled from school, although it was really Teo who had shattered an unpopular vice principal's window with a slingshot. But the novel comes to a conciliatory ending. A benevolent art teacher to whom Clamor has become devoted takes the distraught youngster under his wing, giving him what he has needed most all along: parental love and understanding as well as sensitive preceptorship.

Jünger's next book, *Zahlen und Götter; Philemon und Baucis: Zwei Essays* (Numbers and Gods; Philemon and Baucis: Two Essays, 1974), deals with nothingness, chaos, creation, myths, and man's attempt to understand these concepts in mathematical terms. In the first essay, the author says that he subscribes to the Pythagorean principle: "Die Zahl ist das Wesen aller Dinge" (Numbers are the essence of all things). But Jünger modifies this notion by stating: "Die Zahl ist eine Erfindung: sie kommt im Universum nicht vor" (Numbers are an invention: they do not appear in the universe). Jünger discusses the special mystique and fascination of the number Null (zero). The second essay, "Philemon und Baucis," expounds the theme of death in the mythical and the technological worlds. It was written as a memorial to René and Blanka Marcic, two close friends who perished in an airplane crash in Belgium on 2 October 1971.

In 1977 the futuristic novel *Eumeswil* (translated, 1993) was published. It is cut from the same cloth as *Auf den Marmorklippen* and *Heliopolis* and is, in a sense, a sequel to both. The narrator of the new novel, Manuel Venator, is not a hunter or warrior, however, but a "Forscher" (researcher) and "Lauscher" (quiet listener). His main occupation is that of night steward in the Kasbah of Eumeswil, an imaginary place somewhere in the Near East. The government there seems to be dictatorial but not despotic. There is a ruling class, consisting of the Condor, the Consuls, and the Domo. Hunting appears to be one of the main pursuits of the rulers. Eumeswil also has a Luminar, a kind of time machine that is a relic from the days of high technology, which permits the narrator, who has been trained as an historian, to study images from the past. Venator calls himself an "Anarch," a term he defines not without humor as follows: "Der Anarch unterscheidet sich . . . vom Anarchisten, daß er einen ausgesprochenen Sinn für Vorschriften besitzt" (The anarch differentiates himself from the anarchist in that he has a pronounced fondness for regulations). In spite of all his occupations and callings, Venator, who is not quite thirty, is unimpressive. He is unheroic, subservient toward the ruling clique, dependent, and pleasant. He confesses: "Ich bin also dabei, als ob Eumeswil ein Traum, ein Spiel oder auch ein Experiment wäre" (I am thus part of it as though Eumeswil were a dream, a game or even an experiment). On the other hand, he is philosophical and playful. At the end, Venator is invited by the members of the ruling group to participate in a great hunt. Fearing the worst, he prepares himself for death; but he survives. His brother Martin, though, perishes in the retinue of the tyrants. (Jünger's own brother Friedrich Georg died the year the novel was published.)

This novel is more reflective than the two earlier works set in the future and displays considerable detachment from the woes of the future. Jünger finally seems to feel at ease in a world in which the hunger for equality has devoured personal freedom and conformity has supplanted individualism. All that is left for those indulging in the anachronistic pursuit of personal uniqueness is the power to disengage, to veer toward the anarchic, and above all to be playful. Here Jünger's versatile Manuel Venator shares some characteristics with Hermann Hesse's Magister Ludi, with Thomas Mann's doomed iconoclast Adrian Leverkühn, and even with Günter Grass's diabolic dwarf Oskar Matzerath.

At the age of eighty-five, Jünger directed the publication of the first volume of his diary, *Siebzig verweht* (Gone past Seventy). This volume, which was published in 1980, covers the period from 30 March 1965 to 12 December 1970. The fragmentary form of the diary and its focus on observations of the moment are part of the author's design, yet it is his ambition to be a cosmographer and to convey universals. Jünger continues here in a vein which he successfully employed in

Das abenteuerliche Herz, focusing his gifts of observation with equal ardor on man and his artistic and technical products as well as on animals, flowers, and even minerals. His insights into the mysteries of organic and inanimate forms of creation are related in a style that only the wisdom acquired by many decades of observation and reflection can dictate. The entries were written in the garden or surrounding forests of his "Wilflingen Klause" (Wilflingen refuge); during sojourns in Rome, Portugal, the Canary Islands, Angola, and east Asia; or on ships or airplanes en route. "Ein Letzter aus Humboldts Schule" (one of the last of Humboldt's school), he notes while passing the coast of the island of Sokotra in the Indian Ocean. The reference is to Georg Schweinfurth, the explorer-scientist who gave an explanation of the island "aus den Fundamenten" (from the foundation upward). Jünger venerates Schweinfurth because in this extraordinary individual "treffen sich welt-und naturhistorische Einsichten als Frucht ausgedehnter Reisen und Studien" (philosophical and scientific insights come to fruition as a result of extended travels and studies). The same statement could be applied to Jünger himself. There are many personal letters to old friends and acquaintances such as Martin Heidegger and Henri Plard, reflections on philosophers and artists such as Nietzsche and Goya, letters to publishers such as Rowohlt and Klett. Jünger exposes a vast panoply of topics from the "drug scene" to fairy tales, from World War I to the Portuguese involvement in Angola.

The second volume of *Siebzig verweht,* covering the period from 1971 to 1980, was published in 1981. Jünger has the reader witness and partake in his own development, a method he advocated in the preface to *Strahlungen.* Yet in contrast to the earlier journals, Jünger, chastened by old age, tries now to observe the highest standards of objectivity. He remarks: "Die abendländische Geschichtsschreibung eines Thukydides, eines Tacitus, eines Ranke hat ihre Grenzen, ihre Voraussetzungen. Sie hat ein Zentrum, von dem, wie von der Sternwarte von Greenwich aus, gemessen wird. Von daher wird das Geschehen in Geschichte transformiert. Der Begriff der Freiheit, vor allem der Willensfreiheit, zählt zu den Maßstäben. Das Schicksal wird durch den Willen, und zwar durch den Willen des Menschen, geformt. Der Historiograph prüft und beurteilt die Entscheidungen" (The western historiography of a Thucydides, a Tacitus, a Ranke has its limits, its presuppositions. It has a center, from which, as from the Greenwich observatory, measurements are taken. From there, occurrence is transformed into history. The concept of freedom, above all that of the freedom of the will, becomes one of the yardsticks. Fate is shaped by the will, that is, by the will of man. The historiographer checks and evaluates the decisions).

In volume 2 of *Siebzig verweht,* Jünger jots down his impressions of people, books, paintings, animals, plants, and landscapes as he encounters them. On some occasions his observations are compressed into aphorisms; at other times they set into motion chain reactions of reflections and associations, which, in spite of their multiple topics and themes, somehow converge at the end. His trips take him to Sardinia, Sicily, Malta, Tunisia, Corfu, Crete, Turkey, Liberia, and Sri Lanka and end in Wilflingen. Both volumes also contain direct and indirect social and political criticism. Jünger examines the age and its political and social developments in the same penetrating way in which he observes natural phenomena. These diaries, like Jünger's earlier ones, are timely documentation of an unfolding era.

Aladins Problem (1983; translated as *Aladdin's Problem,* 1992), a volume of short aphoristic essays in four parts completed in Wilflingen on 6 January 1982, deals with the problem of the self. Part 1 focuses on personal confessions: "Nun bin ich kein Dichter; das muß ich zugeben, obwohl ich, 'was ich leide,' ausdrücken kann—freilich nur im Selbstgespräch" (After all, I am not a poet; that I must confess, although I can express "my suffering"—to be sure, only by talking to myself). The narrator also reflects on his war experiences and on his close relationship with a senior fellow officer by the name of Jagello. In part 2, he reminisces about his family, but also focuses on literature, philosophy, and religion: "Vor allem die Götter ändern sich. Entweder wechseln sie Gestalt und Gesicht, oder sie verschwinden ganz und gar" (Above all, the gods change. Either they alter their shape and face, or they disappear altogether). The third part deals in more detail with his friends, such as the former sculptor Kornfeld and the banker Sigi Jersson, whom he met at a Jewish cemetery. In the concluding fourth part, the narrator reflects on the themes of the brotherhood of all men, history, and nihilism. He explains the mysterious title of the book by establishing a relationship between himself and the Arabian fairy-tale figure of Aladdin: "Auch Aladin war ein erotischer Nihilist. Er begehrte die unerreichbare Prinzessin Budûr. . . . Und er berührte sie nicht als sie neben ihm lag. . . . Aladins Problem war die Macht mit ihren Genüssen und Gefahren" (Aladdin, too, was an erotic nihilist. He lusted for the unattainable princess Budûr. . . . And he did not touch her when she lay by his side. . . . Aladdin's problem was power with its pleasures and dangers).

The collection of aphorisms and short essays *Autor und Autorschaft* (Author and Authorship) appeared in 1984. Jünger, who called these short compositions "notes," seemed deeply concerned with the mark the creative writer leaves behind. The book begins with a reflection about the significance of Goethe's death for the history of thought and literature and ends with a maxim that states in its conclusion that "Verehrung und Liebe in hohen Graden sich ausschließen" (veneration and love are to a large extent mutually exclusive). In contrast to Goethe, Jünger does not feel that an author has to be loved to be esteemed.

On 29 March 1985 Jünger turned ninety. He celebrated his birthday by readying for publication his latest diaries and a new novel, *Eine gefährliche Begegnung* (translated as *A Dangerous Encounter,* 1993), in which his skill as a storyteller is unimpeded by the passage of time. His keen eye for reality combines, as in his first books, with his classical sense of stylistic proportion and his romantic proclivity for adventure, wonderment, and the irrational forces of life. The plot takes the reader to the Paris of 1889, the year in which the Eiffel Tower was built. The young diplomat Gerhard zum Busche, nephew of the German ambassador, is drawn into an amorous relationship with Irene, a married woman of higher Parisian society. Her husband, Count Kargané, although no longer in love with her, takes this occasion to plot her murder. By chance, however, another woman of rather questionable reputation occupies the suite which Irene had used for past indiscretions and is murdered by mistake. Accused of the crime by the police, Kargané commits suicide. The story of the unfaithful wife and her equally unfaithful husband, who wants her dead and pays with his own life instead, is only outwardly an Alfred Hitchcock thriller. Jünger's inner theme is the superficiality, shallowness, and decadence of the pleasure-seeking society of the turn of the century. It was a world "die der Liebe und den heiteren Genüssen gewidmet war" (which was given to the pursuit of sex and pleasure)—a world not all that remote, the author implies, from our own time.

Without question, Jünger, who died on 17 February 1998, was one of the most prolific writers in modern German literature. His literary production included diaries and travelogues, science fiction and futuristic novels, and political and philosophical essays and aphorisms on a wide variety of topics. But it could also be said that he was one of those authors who writes one or two basic books over and over again in ingenious variation. Ludwig Marcuse's description of Heinrich Heine as "armer Subjektivling" (pitiable chap immersed in his own subjectivity) could have been coined for Jünger, for the latter's depiction of the world, whether in diary form or through fiction, was always filtered through his overpowering ego. A confirmed individualist, he reacted to the drastically changing world of his long life with vigor, vehemence, and occasional scorn. His strong conservatism notwithstanding, however, there is a detectable development in his Weltanschauung through the years. The "heroic nihilism" of his early work, which found the highest values in nationalism,

militancy, discipline, and defiance of death and glorified war as a mythical and metaphysical end in itself, gives way gradually to a cosmopolitan outlook that embraces the Western tradition of benevolent individualism, freedom of expression, and universal peace. In this drastically changed worldview, the warrior and the worker—manifestations of the antibourgeois and antidemocratic "neuer Mensch" (new man), subordinating themselves to the demands of the collective spirit—are replaced by the researcher and the teacher—the seeker and the conveyor of universal truths, acting to uphold the sanctity of benign individualism and constantly probing for inner meaning.

Jünger's style has been characterized by Joseph Peter Stern as a "fusion, perfect and unique . . . , of the language of the battlefield and the language of nature-study; . . . a fusion of command and aestheticism." The universal, almost Goethean quality of his style—which could be called "European"—results from his having synthesized not just "command and aestheticism" but also the essence of German and French culture as well as the stylistic fashions of the century from impressionism to existentialism and from neo-romanticism to surrealism.

As perhaps no other author, Jünger reflected nearly the entire development of the mainstream of German conservative intellectual and political thought of the twentieth century. Ironically, however, Jünger always saw himself in the Nietzschean vein as a nonconformist and an antiestablishment writer. Again and again he pointed out the disproportion between nature and technology, the individual and the might of government, and saw in these disparities the unresolved if not insoluble, destructive, and even fatal debacle of our age.

The critical and analytical approach to Jünger's work has fluctuated over the decades from lavish praise and adulation to rejection and condemnation. Although critics of all persuasions have had to acknowledge the breadth and depth of his encyclopedic intellect, the largely political nature of his writing has made it almost impossible for a detached and impartial literary criticism to evolve. A truly objective interpretation of his voluminous, complex, and still incomplete literary opus will have to await the passing of time.

Letters:

Ernst Jünger, Alfred Kubin: Eine Begegnung (Frankfurt am Main, Berlin & Vienna: Propyläen, 1975);

Ernst Jünger, Rudolf Schlichter: Briefe 1935–1955, edited by Dirk Heisserer (Stuttgart: Klett-Cotta, 1997).

Bibliographies:

Karl O. Paetel, *Ernst Jünger: Eine Bibliographie* (Stuttgart: Lutz & Meyer, 1953);

Hans Peter des Coudres and Horst Mühleisen, *Bibliographie der Werke Ernst Jüngers* (Stuttgart: Klett, 1970; revised and enlarged editions, Stuttgart: Cotta, 1985, 1996);

Alain de Benoist, *Ernst Jünger: une bio-bibliographie* (Paris: Tredaniel, 1997).

Biography:

Thomas R. Nevin, *Ernst Jünger and Germany: Into the Abyss, 1914–1945* (Durham, N.C.: Duke University Press, 1996).

References:

Ad hoc: Zum 75. Geburtstag Ernst Jüngers (Stuttgart: Klett, 1970);

Heinz Ludwig Arnold, *Ernst Jünger* (Berlin: Steglitz, 1966);

Arnold, ed., *Wandlung und Wiederkehr: Festschrift zum 70. Geburtstag Ernst Jüngers* (Aachen: Georgi, 1965);

Banine, *Rencontres avec Ernst Jünger* (Paris: René Julliard, 1951);

Franz Baumer, *Ernst Jünger* (Berlin: Colloquium, 1967);

Max Bense, *Ptolemäer und Mauretanier oder die theologische Emigration der deutschen Literatur* (Cologne & Berlin: Kiepenheuer, 1950);

Karl Heinz Bohrer, *Die Ästhetik des Schreckens: Die pessimistische Romantik und Ernst Jüngers Frühwerk* (Munich & Vienna: Hanser, 1978);

Erich Brock, *Ernst Jünger und die Problematik der Gegenwart* (Basel: Schwabe, 1943);

Marcel Decombis, *Ernst Jünger: L'homme et l'oeuvre jusqu'en 1936* (Paris: Aubier, 1943);

Farbige Saüme: Ernst Jünger zum 70. Geburtstag, special issue of *Antaios,* 7 (1965);

Marjatta Hietala, *Der neue Nationalismus in der Publizistik Ernst Jüngers und des Kreises um ihn 1920–1933* (Helsinki: Suomalaison Tiedeakatemian Toimituksia, 1975);

Friedrich Georg Jünger, *Die Spiele: Ein Schlüssel zu ihrer Bedeutung* (Frankfurt am Main: Klostermann, 1953);

Volker Katzmann, *Ernst Jüngers magischer Realismus* (Hildesheim: Olms, 1975);

Arnim Kerker, *Ernst Jünger–Klaus Mann: Gemeinsamkeit und Gegensatz in Literatur und Politik* (Bonn: Bouvier, 1974);

Helmut Konrad, *Kosmos: Politische Philosophie im Werk Ernst Jüngers* (Vienna & Augsburg: Blasaditsch, 1972);

Gerhard Loose, *Ernst Jünger* (New York: Twayne, 1974);

Loose, *Ernst Jünger: Gestalt und Werk* (Frankfurt am Main: Klostermann, 1957);

Alfred von Martin, *Der heroische Nihilismus und seine Überwindung: Ernst Jüngers Weg durch die Krise* (Krefeld: Scherpe, 1948);

Arnim Mohler, ed., *Freundschaftliche Begegnungen: Festschrift für Ernst Jünger zum 60. Geburtstag* (Frankfurt am Main: Klostermann, 1955);

Mohler, ed., *Die Schleife: Dokumente zum Weg von Ernst Jünger* (Zurich: Arche, 1955);

Hans-Rudolf Müller-Schwefe, *Ernst Jünger* (Wuppertal: Barmen, 1951);

Gerhard Nebel, *Ernst Jünger und das Schicksal des Menschen* (Wuppertal: Marées, 1948);

Karl O. Paetel, *Ernst Jünger in Selbstzeugnissen und Bilddokumenten* (Reinbek & Hamburg: Rowohlt, 1962);

Paetel, *Wandlungen eines deutschen Dichters und Patrioten* (New York: Krause, 1946);

Hans Peter Schwarz, *Der konservative Anarchist: Politik und Zeitkritik Ernst Jüngers* (Freiburg: Rombach, 1962);

Joseph Peter Stern, *Ernst Jünger* (New Haven: Yale University Press, 1953);

Roger Woods, *Ernst Jünger and the Nature of Political Commitment* (Stuttgart: Heinz, 1982).

Papers:

Archives of Ernst Jünger's papers have been started by Hans Peter des Coudres in Hamburg and Karl O. Paetel in New York.

Franz Kafka

(3 July 1883 – 3 June 1924)

Richard H. Lawson
University of North Carolina at Chapel Hill

This entry originally appeared in DLB 81: Austrian
Fiction Writers, 1875–1913.

BOOKS: *Betrachtung* (Leipzig: Rowohlt, 1913);

Der Heizer: Ein Fragment (Leipzig: Wolff, 1913);

Die Verwandlung (Leipzig: Wolff, 1915); translated by
Eugene Jolas as "Metamorphosis," *Transition*
(Paris), no. 25 (Autumn 1936): 27–38; no. 26
(Winter 1937): 53–72; no. 27 (April/May 1938):
79–103; translated by A. L. Lloyd as *The Metamor-
phosis* (London: Parton, 1937; New York: Van-
guard, 1946); German version edited by Marjorie
L. Hoover (New York: Norton, 1960; London:
Methuen, 1962);

Das Urteil: Eine Geschichte (Leipzig: Wolff, 1916); translated by Jolas as "The Sentence," *Transition* (February 1928): 35–47; translated by Rosa M.
Beuscher as "The Judgment," *Quarterly Review of
Literature,* 2, no. 3 (1945): 189–198;

In der Strafkolonie (Leipzig: Wolff, 1919); translated by
Jolas as "In the Penal Colony," *Partisan Review,* 8
(March 1941): 98–107; (April 1941): 146–158;

Ein Landarzt: Kleine Erzählungen (Munich & Leipzig:
Wolff, 1919); translated by Vera Leslie as *The
Country Doctor: A Collection of Fourteen Short Stories*
(Oxford: Counterpoint, 1945);

Ein Hungerkünstler: Vier Geschichten (Berlin: Die
Schmiede, 1924)—comprises "Erstes Leid"; "Ein
Hungerkünstler," translated by Harry Steinhauer
and Helen Jessiman as "The Hunger-Artist," in
Modern German Short Stories, edited by Steinhauer
and Jessiman (New York & London: Oxford Uni-
versity Press, 1938), pp. 203–217; "Eine kleine
Frau," translated by Francis C. Golfing as "A Lit-
tle Woman," *Accent* (Summer 1943): 223–227;
"Josefine, die Sängerin, oder das Volk der
Mäuse," translated by Clement Greenberg as
"Josephine, the Songstress; or, The Mice Nation,"
Partisan Review, 9 (May/June 1942): 213–228;

Der Prozeß: Roman (Berlin: Die Schmiede, 1925); translated by Willa and Edwin Muir as *The Trial* (Lon-

Franz Kafka

don: Gollancz, 1937; New York: Knopf, 1937);
translation revised, with additional chapters and
notes (definitive edition), by E. M. Butler (Lon-

don: Secker & Warburg, 1956; New York: Knopf, 1957);

Das Schloß: Roman (Munich: Wolff, 1926); translated by Willa and Edwin Muir as *The Castle: A Novel* (London: Secker & Warburg, 1930; New York: Knopf, 1930); translation revised, with additional materials (definitive edition), by Eithne Wilkins and Ernst Kaiser (London: Secker & Warburg, 1953; New York: Knopf, 1954);

Amerika: Roman (Munich: Wolff, 1927); translated by Willa and Edwin Muir as *America* (London: Routledge, 1938; Norfolk, Conn.: New Directions, 1940);

Beim Bau der chinesischen Mauer: Ungedruckte Erzählungen und Prosa aus dem Nachlaß, edited by Max Brod and Hans Joachim Schoeps (Berlin: Kiepenheuer, 1931); translated by Willa and Edwin Muir as *The Great Wall of China and Other Pieces* (London: Secker & Warburg, 1933);

Gesammelte Schriften, edited by Brod and Heinz Politzer, 6 volumes (volumes 1–4, Berlin: Schocken, 1935; volumes 5–6, Prague: Mercy, 1936–1937); volume 1, *Erzählungen und kleine Prosa* (1935), translated by Kaiser and Wilkins as *In the Penal Settlement: Tales and Short Prose Works* (London: Secker & Warburg, 1973); volume 5, *Beschreibung eines Kampfes: Novellen, Skizzen, Aphorismen aus dem Nachlaß* (1936), translated by Willa and Edwin Muir and Tania and James Stern as *Description of a Struggle and The Great Wall of China* (London: Secker & Warburg, 1960);

Parables in German and English, translated by Willa and Edwin Muir (New York: Schocken, 1947);

The Penal Colony: Stories and Short Pieces, translated by Willa and Edwin Muir and C. Greenberg (New York: Schocken, 1948; London: Secker & Warburg, 1949);

The Diaries of Franz Kafka, edited by Brod, translated by Joseph Kresh, Martin Greenberg, and Hannah Arendt, 2 volumes (New York: Schocken, 1948–1949);

Gesammelte Werke, edited by Brod, 11 volumes (Frankfurt am Main: Fischer, 1950–1974); volume 4, *Briefe an Milena,* edited by Willy Haas, translated by Tania and James Stern as *Letters to Milena* (New York: Farrar & Straus, Schocken/London: Secker & Warburg, 1953); volume 7, *Hochzeitsvorbereitungen auf dem Lande und andere Prosa aus dem Nachlaß,* translated by Kaiser and Wilkins as *Wedding Preparations in the Country, and Other Posthumous Prose Writings* (London: Secker & Warburg, 1954); translation republished as *Dearest Father: Stories and Other Writings* (New York: Schocken, 1954); volume 9, *Briefe 1902–1904,* translated, with addi-

tional material, by Richard and Clara Winston, edited by Beverly Colman and other as *Letters to Friends, Family, and Editors* (New York: Schocken/London: Calder, 1977); volume 10, *Briefe an Felice und andere Korrespondenz aus der Verlobungszeit,* edited by Erich Heller and Jürgen Born, translated by James Stern and Elisabeth Duckworth as *Letters to Felice* (New York: Schocken, 1973); volume 11, *Briefe an Ottla und die Familie,* edited by Hartmut Binder and Klaus Wagenbach, translated by Richard and Clara Winston, edited by Nahum N. Glatzer, as *Letters to Ottla and the Family* (New York: Schocken, 1982);

Selected Short Stories, translated by Willa and Edwin Muir (New York: Modern Library, 1952);

Parables and Paradoxes, in German and English, translated by Willa and Edwin Muir (New York: Schocken, 1958);

Erzählungen und Skizzen, edited by Wagenbach (Darmstadt: Moderner Buch-Club, 1959);

Die Erzählungen, edited by Wagenbach (Frankfurt am Main: Fischer, 1961);

Metamorphosis and Other Stories, translated by Willa and Edwin Muir (Harmondsworth, U.K.: Penguin, 1961);

Er: Prosa, edited by Martin Walser (Frankfurt am Main: Suhrkamp, 1963);

Short Stories, edited by J. M. S. Pasley (London: Oxford University Press, 1963);

Der Heizer; In der Strafkolonie; Der Bau, edited by Pasley (Cambridge: Cambridge University Press, 1966);

Sämtliche Erzählungen, edited by Paul Raabe (Frankfurt am Main: Fischer, 1970);

The Complete Stories, edited by Glatzer (New York: Schocken, 1971);

Shorter Works, translated and edited by Malcolm Pasley (London: Secker & Warburg, 1973);

I Am a Memory Come Alive: Autobiographical Writings, edited by Glatzer (New York: Schocken, 1974).

PERIODICAL PUBLICATIONS: "Betrachtung," *Hyperion,* 1, no. 1 (1908): 91–94;

"Gespräch mit dem Beter," *Hyperion,* 1, no. 8 (1909): 126–131;

"Gespräch mit dem Betrunkenen," *Hyperion,* 1, no. 8 (1909): 131–133;

"Brief an den Vater," *Die Neue Rundschau,* 63, no. 2 (1952): 191–231; translated by Ernst Kaiser and Eithne Wilkins as *Letter to His Father/Brief an den Vater* (New York: Schocken, 1953).

Franz Kafka is one of the founders of modern literature. His claim to greatness includes his service in completely collapsing the aesthetic distance that had traditionally separated the writer from the reader. In what is probably his most famous work of fiction, *Die Verwandlung* (1915; translated as "Metamorphosis," 1936–1938), the protagonist, Gregor Samsa, is presented to the reader as a man who has become an insect; Gregor's condition is never suggested to be an illusion or dream (although many critics have commented on its dreamlike qualities). In his shock at the result of Kafka's unmediated aesthetic distance, the reader is led to forgo his usual reflective and explicative function. Kafka has his characters perform that explicative function– hectically, repeatedly, self-contradictorily, and with a new kind of irony that has come to characterize modern literature. Finally, in an age that celebrates the mass, Kafka redirects the focus to the individual. His characters stand for themselves as individuals; in the case of the male protagonists–and almost all of his protagonists are male–they stand for Kafka himself.

Kafka was born on 3 July 1883 in Prague, a large provincial capital of the Austro-Hungarian Empire that was home to many Czechs, some Germans, and a lesser number of German-cultured, German-speaking Jews. His father, Hermann Kafka, of humble rural origin, was a hardworking, hard-driving, successful merchant. His mother tongue was Czech, but he spoke German, correctly seeing the language as an important card to be played in the contest for social and economic mobility and security. Kafka's mother, Julie Löwy Kafka, came from a family with older Prague roots and some degree of wealth. She proved unable to mediate the estrangement between her brusque, domineering husband and her quiet, tyrannized, oversensitive son.

The boy and his three younger sisters were largely cared for by a transient staff of mostly Czech-speaking household servants, for when Julie was not pregnant she helped her husband in his fancy-goods and haberdashery business. At the age of six Kafka began attending the German school, and thereafter he spoke more German than Czech. When he was ten he entered the Altstädter Deutsches Gymnasium, the German preparatory school in Old Town. Kafka, despite his indifferent attitude, was an excellent student. He was conspicuously not one of the gang; while he was not entirely unsociable, he shrank from taking social initiatives.

As a youngster, Kafka, like his father, had no more than the most perfunctory relationship with Judaism. He dutifully memorized what was necessary for his bar mitzvah, but he was already an atheist–as was perhaps to be expected of a youthful fan of the naturalistic drama then in vogue in the German theater in Prague. His interest in drama led him to write scenarios to be acted out by his sisters at home. He also wrote

fragments of a novel. Writing early became an issue in the antagonism between Kafka and his father; the latter continued to disdain writing as an unworthy occupation long after Kafka became a published author.

Kafka entered the German Karl-Ferdinand University in Prague in 1901. (The university was divided into a German part and a Czech part.) After enrolling in chemistry and taking one semester of Germanics he switched to law, a field that had his father's blessing because it afforded the prospect of future employment. Kafka began to reach out socially a bit more: among his new friends was Max Brod, who was to be his lifelong friend and literary executor. At this time, too, he had a sexual relationship with a young woman and then with an older one.

He received his doctorate in law on 18 June 1907. On 1 October he joined the staff of the Assicurazioni Generali, an insurance office in Prague. As if the overcrowded Kafka residence were not already daunting enough to the budding writer, the Assicurazioni Generali contributed a six-day, fifty-hour week of extremely dull work together with an abrasive environment. Nonetheless, in March 1908 he published his first short prose pieces in the Munich literary magazine *Hyperion.*

In July he received the opportunity to move to the Workers' Accident Insurance Institute for the Kingdom of Bohemia, a semigovernmental agency. Kafka's command of Czech proved useful in the job, which involved the settlement of workmen's compensation claims. The occasional brief trips out of Prague required by the new job were welcome to Kafka; his salary was better; his hours were shorter; and his advancement was gratifying. The din and the harassment from his father at home continued to make writing difficult, but he could have moved out had he resolved to do so.

Early in 1907 he had begun work on a novel titled "Beschreibung eines Kampfes" (1936; translated as "Description of a Struggle," 1960). There were two versions, neither of which was completed. It is a dialogue between the narrator, who is a young artist engaged to be married, and a bachelor; both are obvious projections of Kafka. Among the themes broached, as they hike in and about Prague on a clear, freezing February day, two are of primary interest: the artist suffers psychological discomfort under the spell of his bachelor acquaintance, and the artist casually orders the bachelor to commit suicide.

Within the episodic framework of "Beschreibung eines Kampfes," are two tales that were extracted and, at Brod's urging, published in *Hyperion* in 1909: "Gespräch mit dem Beter" (Conversation with the Supplicant) and "Gespräch mit dem Betrunkenen" (Conversation with the Drunkard). In the former the supplicant is a romantic young man hobbled by self-consciousness in striving to strike up party conversation with a girl. Although he does not know how to do so, the supplicant insists on playing the piano; the girl acts as if he has played excellently. The supplicant dearly wants to believe that he is not awkward, that he is just as graceful as the other guests. His departure from the party is marked by his host's helping him into someone else's topcoat. The central idea of "Gespräch mit dem Betrunkenen" is a cliché, but an amusing one: the presumed benefit to the thinker in learning from the drunkard. Reality and fantasy–vignettes of an imagined Paris–are juxtaposed in both stories. This juxtaposition, along with a striking self-consciousness and an episodic structure, indicate the direction Kafka's mature fiction was to take.

Coincident with his work on "Beschreibung eines Kampfes"–that is, from 1907 to 1910–Kafka worked on another embryonic novel, "Hochzeitsvorbereitungen auf dem Lande" (1953; translated as "Wedding Preparations in the Country," 1954). In this case there were three uncompleted versions, again written primarily for the benefit of the author himself, although Brod was allowed to read the work in progress. The narrator, Eduard Raban, an exhausted Prague businessman thirty years of age, is a persona of Kafka; the name Raban, Czech for raven, is a cryptogram of Kafka's name, which in the form *kavka* means jackdaw in Czech. Raban, having committed himself to visit his fiancée Betty and her mother in the country, hesitates to undertake the trip. When he does undertake it he is beset by rain, the physical discomfort of the train, awkward conversations with fellow travelers, and a yearning to return to the city. He is uneasy about the darkness; the uncanny atmosphere of the countryside; and the circumstances of his lonely arrival, which is as far as any of the three versions of the story goes.

"Hochzeitsvorbereitungen auf dem Lande" incorporates narrative features that are beginning to emerge as typical of Kafka: a first-person narrator as a persona of the author, an episodic structure, an ambivalent quester on an ambiguous mission, and pervasive irony. Kafka is moving toward a more subtle split projection of his persona; in "Beschreibung eines Kampfes" the artist and the bachelor were separate persons, each representing one side of the author's psyche; in "Hochzeitsvorbereitungen auf dem Lande" the split is implied within the narrator, Raban, who suggests at one point that he is just dispatching his clothed body to the country: most of the time his mind is in a comfortable bed in Prague while his body is suffering the rigors of travel and rurality. As he lies in bed he further splits himself mentally and identifies part of himself with a bug. Pressing his tiny insect legs to his bulging belly he imagines himself whispering instructions to his body, which is standing close by. Raban has not really become an insect, as Gregor Samsa will in *Die Verwandlung;* he is *imagining* that part of him is an insect. But Kafka has traveled at least half of the conceptual distance between the inchoate "Beschreibung eines Kampfes" and the masterpiece that is *Die Verwandlung.*

While writing his drafts of "Hochzeitsvorbereitungen auf dem Lande" and completing several short pieces, Kafka was also writing the first draft of another novel, "Der Verschollene" (He Who Was Lost without Trace). From the point of view of publication history "Der Verschollene" consists of two parts: the first chapter, *Der Heizer* (The Stoker), with which Kafka was satisfied and which was published separately in May 1913; and the entire but never completed novel, as assembled and published by Brod in 1927 as *Amerika* (translated as *America,* 1938). By the time Kafka published *Der Heizer* he abhorred the other five hundred pages. The reason is not difficult to surmise, for in those pages he had employed many of the conventions of nineteenth-century realistic fiction, a mode he rejected wholeheartedly. As a critic, Kafka was extremely hard on himself, but his estimate of *Der Heizer* vis-à-vis *Amerika* is close to the mark–which is not to say that the latter is bad fiction.

Der Heizer begins in realistic fashion. Karl Rossmann, a fifteen or sixteen-year-old immigrant, is on the deck of a steamer entering New York harbor. The story becomes increasingly surrealistic when he dashes through an unfamiliar part of the ship on his way back to steerage to retrieve his umbrella. He falls in with a disaffected stoker, and the two make their way to the captain's stateroom. There Karl eloquently, but ineffectively, pleads the stoker's grievance. One of the many dignitaries who have boarded is Karl's long-lost wealthy uncle, who recognizes Karl. Accompanying his uncle to his magnificent home, Karl abandons the stoker's lost cause.

The gap between presumed reality and the actual state of things is so pervasive as to be thematic. It is true that Karl has been expelled from his parents' house in Prague for impregnating a thirty-five-year-old cook. But his parents are not poor, as the narrator early declared; they are well-to-do and inhumane. Uncle Jacob, who rescued Karl because the cook wrote to him, gives out a romanticized version of Karl's seduction by the cook which Karl has to correct. Mostly, however, it is Karl who lacks an accurate perception of reality. His naiveté is profound and stubborn. He accepts his parents' cruelty with an untarnished devotion, fondly imagining how he would rise in their esteem if only they could see him valiantly pleading the cause of justice for the stoker. This point brings up another theme, which is more important for the novel than for the story. The stoker noisily proclaims his Germanness; he is a German fighting the machinations of his Romanian superior. Karl's abrupt and instinctive rapport with the stoker, with whom he would seem to have little in common, lies in the stoker's symbolizing the German world that, for Karl, is forever lost. He has been thrown upon the alien shores of an unknown new world. Just how alien is emphasized by the conspicuous and self-conscious Americanism of his Uncle Jacob. If Karl is an unnested German fledgling, Uncle Jacob is a mature American entrepreneurial raptor in quest of ever more money.

Each of the seven chapters that follow "Der Heizer," as they are arranged by Brod, coincides with an expulsory episode. Karl is brought to one fall after another in an America that remains an enigma to him from beginning to end—even an apparently utopian end in which he precipitately finds acceptance. In addition, there are two incomplete chapters, which Brod places in an appendix; narratively they belong between the penultimate and final chapters.

For a while Karl lives in luxury with Uncle Jacob; Jacob's business friends, Mr. Green and Mr. Pollunder; and the latter's hoydenish daughter, Clara, who attempts to seduce him. In fact, it is Karl's unwillingly prolonged—by Clara—stay at the Pollunders that prompts his sudden, apparently capricious expulsion from Jacob's house. Karl is forbidden ever to contact his uncle again. On the streets Karl meets a pair of vagabond machinists, Delamarche and Robinson, who exploit him through much of the novel. Their exploitation results in Karl's expulsion from his employment as an elevator boy at the Hotel Occidental. The pair contrive for Karl to be a slave in a tacky ménage à trois that includes Delamarche's grotesquely fat mistress, Brunelda. Between this exploitation and the final chapter in which Karl discovers unconditional acceptance in the Theater of Oklahoma, there is a narrative gap that is less than completely bridged by the two fragmentary chapters with their indication of Karl's degradation in the filthy and sexually charged Delamarche household and in a shabbily splendid whorehouse where he has some sort of job as a factotum.

Exploitation and expulsion are so often linked with seduction as to make the latter a motif. The very first sentence of the novel informs the reader that the servant girl seduced Karl and had a child by him; this seduction severed him from his previous life and deposited him in America, where the pattern was to be repeated over and over. By no means are all of Karl's subsequent seducers as successful or thorough as Johanna Brummer, the servant girl; most are not, Clara Pollunder among them. Therese Berchtold, a secretary-typist at the Hotel Occidental, is no more than a charmingly innocent flirt who brings Karl a gift apple. But

Karl's guilt is, on the whole, simply existential; he does not have to do anything, he does not have to bite into an apple to validate his guilt.

Responding to a recruiting poster of the Theater of Oklahoma, which assertedly has a post for every applicant, Karl meets his old friend, Fanny—except that the reader is in the dark about their past friendship, which is not recounted in the published novel. Fanny is already a member of the company, one of hundreds of women dressed as angels, mounted on a tall pedestal, playing trumpets. After the initial reunion, however, Karl never sees Fanny again; he is hired as a technical assistant, and they are posted to different troupes of the Theater of Oklahoma. As Karl is on the train headed for Oklahoma the novel breaks off with a description of mountain streams and the chill breath rising from them. Definitive as this imagery may sound as a symbol of death, the reader ought to remember that this is simply where Kafka stopped writing.

The atmosphere of fantasy about the Theater of Oklahoma inheres partly in the fact that it is, precisely, a theater, the realm of fantasy, and partly in the reader's perception that it is a very unusual sort of theater: huge, friendly, socially beneficent, open-armed in its hiring policy, and inscrutable. If you want to be an artist, its sign proclaims, come and join us. In this theater even a technical assistant is an artist. Kafka, a highly self-conscious artist holding down a mundane job, may be intimating that fantasy is essential to the salvation of the artist.

Is the reader to imagine that Karl's novel-long probity (even though he does give an alias to the theater interviewer), his naiveté blended with pride, his submissiveness, his slightly ridiculous desire to oblige, are really going to enable him to find redemption for whatever he is guilty of? This is the gist of the eschatological reading promulgated by Brod and reflected in his editing and subtitling of Kafka's unfinished work. It is a remarkably durable view, especially among Americans attuned to happy endings. There is little in *Amerika* to warrant such a reading, even in the final chapter. In what seems a parodistic finale the chief themes of the preceding chapters are stood on their heads. Where Karl had encountered hostility, now he finds amicability. Where life had consisted of one exploitation after another, from Johanna Brummer forward, now he finds acceptance. Where injustice had everywhere prevailed, now there is sweet justice. And there is the promise, under the benign and expansive wing of the Theater of Oklahoma, of always more amicability, acceptance, and justice.

Now and then it is suggested that *Amerika* is a bildungsroman, a picaresque novel, or a naturalistic novel of social reform. It is in fact none of these. No additional insight is to be gained by analyzing it as a novel in which the developing hero is formed by his experiences in such a way as to successfully enter and prevail in the middle-class world. For despite the topsy-turvy milieu in which he finds himself in the Theater of Oklahoma, Karl himself is unchanged. He seemingly learns nothing, or exceedingly little, from his travails in alien America. He remains a European throughout, with a guileless, immature European's perceptions and expectations. Tellingly, in the last chapter he is still categorized as a European intermediate school pupil.

Nor is Karl the streetwise picaro surviving by playing dirty tricks on the members of bourgeois society. He does not play tricks, others play tricks on him. He does not act upon his environment, he is acted upon by it—and scarcely to his benefit. Karl's social world, it is true, is that common to picaresque novels, where the middle class and the proletarian and petty criminal worlds intersect. But he plays there a role quite the reverse of the picaro's.

Nor is *Amerika* a naturalistic novel of social reform. Somewhat naturalistic it is—much to Kafka's distress; and, from his thoroughly bourgeois perspective, Kafka was indeed sympathetic with the victims of urban industrialization in and around Prague and insightfully depicted the plight of the exploited. Political and social reform, however, was not the motivating tendency of his art, which has a much more individual basis.

In Prague in May 1910 Kafka discovered with Brod, and was fascinated by, the Polish Yiddish Musical Drama Company of Lemberg (now Lvov, Ukraine). Another troupe of Yiddish actors, also from Lemberg, played in Prague in the winter of 1911–1912; Kafka attended some twenty performances and became a friend of Jizchok Löwy, one of the actors. These austere Yiddish theaters enabled Kafka to see, in a way that memorizing for his halfhearted bar mitzvah never did, the living and pervasive interrelationships of Jewish tradition and culture.

On 13 August 1912 Kafka met Felice Bauer, who was visiting the Brods from her home in Berlin. Attracted to her to the point of being even more than usually conscious of his supposed awkwardness, he nevertheless soon afterward described with quite unromantic, even unflattering objectivity how she first appeared to him. A short time later he wrote and dedicated to her the novella *Das Urteil* (1916; translated as "The Sentence," 1928), his first masterpiece. Its basis is highly autobiographical, although the theme of the internal conflict inherent in assimilationist Jewry owes something to Brod's 1912 novel *Arnold Beer: Das Schicksal eines Juden* (Arnold Beer: The Fate of a Jew).

In the first part of the twelve-page novella, which Kafka wrote in a single sitting on 22–23 September 1912 between 10:00 P.M. and 6:00 A.M., Georg, a prosperous young businessman, writes a long letter telling a bachelor friend in St. Petersburg (now Leningrad) that he has become engaged to a girl named Frieda Brandenfeld; it is Frieda who has insisted that Georg convey this news. In the course of the letter it is revealed that Georg has taken over the family firm and guided it to dazzling success, relegating his widowed father, with whom he lives, to sterile retirement.

The Westernized reversal of father-son roles—with all that it implies for the traditional hierarchical Jewish family organization—is the meat of the second part of the story. Georg confronts his father in the airless back room and tells the old man that he has written his friend with news of his engagement. The old man at first dismisses the existence of the friend as a joke. But then he is seemingly endowed with a spectacular resurgence of strength and dominance, proclaims that *he* is in touch with the Petersburg friend, whose representative he is and who would be a son after his own heart. Georg is getting married, the old man suggests, because his fiancée lifted her skirts. When Georg retaliates with invective, the father sentences his son to death by drowning. Georg promptly complies by running out and jumping off a nearby bridge, asserting his filial love.

The autobiographical component is amply supported by Kafka's diary entries: Georg is Franz Kafka, Georg's father is Hermann Kafka, Frieda Brandenfeld is Felice Bauer. An Oedipal theme suggests itself: when his mother was still living, Georg seems to have been a dutiful and diligent son. But now that he is engaged—that is, sexually potent—he is also commercially potent: he has displaced his father and permits himself to imagine the father's death. A further thematic possibility besides those of the family dissolution in assimilated Jewry and the dynamics in the Kafka family is that of the lonely artist caught up by mundane responsibilities: Georg, a writer reduced to writing letters, may regard bourgeois marriage as a powerful threat to further writing; thus his unreluctant compliance with his father's judgment of death.

Whichever of the thematic possibilities the reader prefers, he should probably reexamine his natural tendency to identify with Georg, the ostensible victim. In fact, Georg is far from admirable. His manipulativeness is revealed by the letter: he is trying to give the appearance of extending an invitation without really doing so. He also manipulates his father, who is probably fed up with it. His chief concern about Frieda is not related to love and—despite his father's coarse innuendo—perhaps not to sex either, but to the fact that she comes from a prosperous family.

In November and December 1912 Kafka wrote *Die Verwandlung.* The writing took about three weeks; two of them overlapped with extra duties as a substitute superintendent of the family's recently acquired asbestos factory, and of course his duties at the insurance office went on as usual. From this uncongenial mélange of preoccupations came one of the most widely read and discussed works of world literature: a shocking and yet comic tragedy of modern man's isolation, inadequacy, and existential guilt. *Die Verwandlung* represents a substantial advance in technique over *Das Urteil,* and even more over *Amerika,* which still lay incomplete in Kafka's drawer.

While *Amerika* is loose and episodic, never intended by Kafka to be published, *Die Verwandlung* is compact, artistically and formally structured, and at least for a short while it had the approbation of its author. After some equivocation Kafka agreed to its publication in *Die Weißen Blätter* and in book form by Kurt Wolff in 1915–although by then he had again changed his mind about its quality: he found the story as a whole to be imperfect and the ending unreadable.

Like the name Raban in "Hochzeitsvorbereitungen auf dem Lande," the surname of the protagonist in *Die Verwandlung,* Gregor Samsa, is a cryptogram of the name Kafka. While Gregor Samsa shares with his fictional predecessor Raban the distinction of turning into an insect, Gregor's metamorphosis is quite different in that it is unwilled, total, and irrevocable. A traveling salesman, Gregor awakens at home one dreary morning after a night of troubled dreams to find himself transformed into a monstrous, beetlelike bug. Unable to go to the tedious job that has provided financial support for his parents and sister, he is held prisoner in a room and subjected to violent persecution by his father and to progressively lessened care and solicitude by his sister. Failing to find satisfaction or nourishment in the fresh food she initially brings him, and gradually taking less interest in sustenance of any sort, alternately ignored and persecuted, he starves and dies, then is swept up and disposed of by the cleaning woman.

Die Verwandlung comprises three Roman-numbered sections, each with its own climax. The first climax occurs when Gregor, having unwisely ventured from his bedroom, is attacked by his father–who, not incidentally, has resumed his role as the family breadwinner. In the second climax Gregor is again driven back to his bedroom; this time his father throws an apple at him which lodges in his back and rots. In the third section, attracted to the living room by his sister's violin playing, Gregor for the last time is driven back to his room, where death comes. After the prompt disposal of his remains his family, buoyant with joy, goes on a spring outing in the country. Although Kafka later found this ending unreadable, it is nonetheless a well-motivated conclusion, lending the story a sense of integrated completeness rarely found in Kafka's previous fiction.

As in *Das Urteil,* the father-son estrangement is thematically fundamental in *Die Verwandlung;* at one point Kafka had the idea of publishing the two novellas together with *Der Heizer* in a single volume to be titled "Söhne" (Sons). In *Die Verwandlung,* however, he achieves a firmer artistic grip on his personal estrangement. Still, the lurking Oedipal component, as well as a counterbalancing sense of humor, are both on view when Gregor is obliged to witness the one scene that he would above all prefer not to see: his mother, stumbling in a mass of hurriedly removed petticoats, hurling herself on his father, with whom she shares perfect sexual congress.

It is not only the father's sexual energy that revives; in the economic sphere his revival is no less marked. From premature retirement he reemerges, coincident with Gregor's transformation, to the fiscal leadership of his beleaguered family, proud in his new role as bank messenger. Even at home he wears the smart uniform of his new calling, with its gold buttons and accumulated grease spots. On resuming the management of the family purse, he finds the latter not to be in such bad shape after all: it contains a reserve that inexplicably had escaped the collapse of the former family business, and Gregor's long and arduous labors have largely liquidated a family debt to his employer. Restored to his proper petty-bourgeois authority, Samsa senior even feels expansive enough to allow Gregor's bedroom door to be left ajar so that he may have the solace of seeing the family grouped about the lamp-lit table.

Grete is the only Samsa with whom the metamorphosed Gregor has any rapport. Her feelings, however, can survive neither the awful disparity between their personal situations nor her emergence from adolescence. At first she serves Gregor his food conscientiously and does her best to make him comfortable in his new circumstances. She becomes the family expert on Gregor, his representative to their uncomprehending mother and to their antagonistic and revitalized father. But dealing with the unpredictabilities of an insect brother proves too much for the idealistic girl, who at about sixteen years of age undergoes her own metamorphosis into a clear-sighted, practical-minded young woman. She honors the memory of her lost brother, but she no longer objects to the notion of ridding her and her parents' lives of the bug that now dwells in his room.

The climax of Grete's metamorphosis and of Gregor's plight comes when she plays an impromptu violin concert for her parents and the family's three lodgers, all of whom become bored and hostile. On the other hand, Gregor is deeply moved, as if discovering the spiritual nourishment he longed for, and crawls from his room. As a human being he had never had the slightest interest in music, but now, shed of his human materialism, he finds himself propelled toward a mystical union with the music and fantasizes imprisoning his sister and her violin in his room with him forever; his fantasy suggests latent incestuous desire, set free as the music liberates his spiritual desire.

When the lodgers excitedly demand explanations for Gregor's presence and his advance toward the music, the violin recital ends. While the lodgers give notice, Grete rushes into their room and in a flurry of blankets and pillows dexterously makes up their beds. Her violin slips onto the floor with a loud clang, symbolizing her definitive rejection of Gregor. Her whirlwind bedmaking suggests acceptance of her domestic adult function in the real world—the essence of her metamorphosis. It is Grete who has taken to referring to Gregor as "it" and who locks him in his room shortly before the end. The insect's last glance as it is being forced back into its room is at its mother, whom the tumult of the scene has left in a state of exhausted sleep.

While Gregor has metamorphosed and his father and sister have been fundamentally, if less spectacularly, transformed, his mother remains unchanged and somewhat peripheral to the action. Less hostile than the father and with occasional flashes of insight superior to the sister's, she is for the most part unsure of herself, overexcited, subject to asthmatic seizure, all too anxious to indulge her husband—the veritable picture of the harried middle-class housewife.

The reader is not required to grieve for Gregor. Whether before or after his transformation, Gregor is unsuited for the burdensome existence that he was obliged to lead; he is incapable of articulating his desire for a different sustenance, and thus he comes to see that he ought to disappear. With an apple—the fruit of knowledge—stuck in his back, he simply dries up from a not very strongly willed self-starvation of himself. Or maybe his death is not really willed at all but simply an acquiescence. Outside his window dawn is beginning to lighten the world as his head sinks to the floor and he breathes his last. Last-minute illumination from a window or doorway occurs at the moment of expiration of more than one Kafka hero. It is a subject of critical debate whether this light is to be taken as a sign of eschatological hope or is to be taken ironically.

Running parallel with the largely autobiographical theme of the father-son relationship is the theme of losing and then regaining bourgeois status. The reestablishment of the family under the father's dominance is ironically confirmed by the narrator's giving the parents back their proper bourgeois titles: after Gregor's body is certified to be lifeless his parents again become Herr and Frau Samsa rather than father and mother. Shortly thereafter, they note that their daughter Grete is shapely and marriageable; having sacrificed Gregor on the altar of middle-class respectability they are prepared to do the same—only the mechanics are different—to Grete. Everyone, even Grete, is in a good mood as they embark on their Sunday outing. Not only has Gregor departed, but his departure permits more extensive bourgeois self-authentication than the Samsas had ever known.

In 1913 and 1914 Kafka carried on an intense correspondence with Felice Bauer. He was a prolific letter writer and seemed in his element in courting by mail, although he included generous helpings of self-doubt about marriage. He doubted that he could combine the roles of writer and bourgeois husband, and the former was more important to him. He visited Felice three times in 1913, and early in 1914 he went to Berlin to see her again. The two-day visit, however, resulted in even greater doubt and mutual misunderstanding. Yet only four months later, on 12 April, their engagement was officially announced—only to be broken, at Kafka's insistence, on 12 July. His letters and diaries show that in addition to perceiving the incompatibility between writing and the demands of middle-class domesticity, he regarded writing as the means of escaping the intolerabilities of a life so awful that he likened it to an underworld. Kafka's uncertain relationship with Felice during this trying period was mediated by a girlfriend of Felice's, Grete Bloch, who later asserted that Kafka was the father of her son.

In August 1914 the thirty-one-year-old Kafka, having completed the novella *In der Strafkolonie* (1919; translated as "In the Penal Colony," 1941) and begun working on the novel *Der Prozeß* (1925; translated as *The Trial*, 1937), finally moved out of his parents' home. He moved a second time after only a month; nowhere, it seemed, could he escape the distraction of noise and disturbance.

World War I, which broke out in August 1914, seems to have had a remarkably remote effect on Kafka. Owing to his position with the semigovernmental insurance company he was initially exempted from the mobilization. After a trip to war-torn Hungary in 1915 he attempted to enlist in the army but was rejected: in 1914 his incipient tuberculosis had been diagnosed as bronchitis.

In der Strafkolonie is set in a maritime and tropical locale; because it seems to be so much like the formerly notorious French penal colony on Devil's Island, the reader tends to make that identification. Kafka, celebrated otherwise for the absence of distance between the narrative point of view and the events narrated, here interposes a noteworthy distance between the explorer-narrator and the shocking events that he describes. The effect is one of coolness, contrasting effectively with both the tropical heat and the ardor of the executioner and his former superior, the old commandant, for summary judgments of guilt and execution. The judgments are carried out by an officer who presides over a horrible execution machine, which under a new commandant has suffered from a lack of replacement parts and is just barely serviceable. The renowned foreign explorer is witness first to an aborted execution and then to one he could hardly have expected. A simple, animal-like soldier has been ordered to awaken every night each hour on the hour to salute his captain's door. At two o'clock one morning he failed to wake up and did not thereafter take kindly to being lashed in the face, nor did he beg the captain's pardon. The judgment pronounced on him is that he shall be killed on the execution machine. He has not been allowed to know the charge against him, to offer a defense, or even to comprehend his sentence. In any case, guilt in Kafka's work is never subject to doubt.

The officer in charge of the execution machine, evidently hoping that a well-impressed foreign dignitary might induce the new commandant to support the renovation and retention of the machine, delivers a long, tendentious explanation while he prepares the machine for the condemned. It is not designed to work quickly. Its victims give up the ghost in twelve hours, during which time their sentence is inscribed into their flesh by the apparatus—the disobedient soldier is to have the legend "Ehre deine Vorgesetzten" (Honor thy Superiors) stitched into his body. Before death, the officer believes, the victims arrive at an insight into their guilt and their sentence—they experience a transfiguration.

In its present, jury-rigged state the apparatus presents a decided contrast to its former efficient operation. In the days of its splendor, under the aggressive sponsorship of the old commandant, huge throngs turned out to witness and be enlightened by its work. Now no one attends; even the new commandant stays away. The decrepitude of the machine is signaled by the loud creaking of a badly worn cogwheel.

In spite of the lobbying by the officer, the explorer declines to promise his support of this method of execution before the new commandant. At that, the execution is halted, the condemned man is removed from the apparatus, and the officer takes his place. He cannot reach the starter, but the machine starts itself and even runs for a while without the noise from the worn cogwheel. Soon, however, the gear assembly comes completely apart; the summary sentence of the officer on

himself is accomplished in much less than twelve hours. The expression on his corpse suggests no hint of the advertised insight and transfiguration.

The apparently anachronistic status of the officer, an obviously unfavored, even imperiled survivor from the predecessor administration, suggests a Nietzschean theme. This theme requires the reader to perceive the old commandant—who is now dead but whose tombstone prophesies his resurrection and recovery of the old colony—in a positive light, as the representative of a tough and righteous era whose values have been supplanted by a less rigorous, soft order with overtones of feminine weakness and compassion. The new commandant's ladies supply the doomed prisoner with candy before his date with the machine, as well as diverting the commandant from properly exercising his authority. There is a suggestion that the ladies have even softened up the officer in charge of the execution machine, for several ladies' handkerchiefs are to be seen within the neckband of his inappropriately nontropical uniform, helping to soak up the sweat produced by the performance of his office. The work of the machine in making its victims see the light suggests Nietzsche's valuing of pain as a teacher, although the suggestion is free of parodistic implication: the officer's contention that the final expression of the victims reveals transfiguration fails to be verified in his own case.

The story can be interpreted as an analogue to the crucifixion of Christ, with the execution machine standing for the cross. Early critics of Kafka often supported this interpretation, and it has returned to favor despite the obstacle that Kafka was not a Christian. Assertions that Kafka, heir to an assimilationist tradition but increasingly interested in Judaism, flirted with becoming a Christian are quite incorrect. Furthermore, the quite nondivine officer in *In der Strafkolonie* shows no sign of resurrection, and his features fail to reflect the transfiguration that he attributed to the machine's victims in the course of their torture-execution. It is tempting to suggest that the execution of the officer is a parody of the crucifixion; that interpretation seems questionable, however, for the same reason that an exclusively religious interpretation is unlikely: a paucity of sufficient identifying detail.

Kafka's later fiction dispenses with the distanced narrative perspective represented here by the visiting explorer. In the later works there is a closer relationship—even a complete identity—between the narrative point of view and the protagonist. What is sacrificed in narrative tension is replaced by a subtly complex psychology.

Within weeks of terminating his engagement to Felice Bauer in 1914 Kafka had written all but the last chapter of *Der Prozeß;* that chapter was completed in

1916. Kafka gave the manuscript to Brod in 1920. Despite the author's wish that it be destroyed, Brod took it upon himself to have the novel published after Kafka's death.

Brod arranged the unnumbered chapters of the novel according to a sequence based on his memory of Kafka's having read the novel aloud before a group of friends; nonetheless, internal evidence has suggested a different sequence to many critics. (Kafka enjoyed reading *Der Prozeß* to his friends; the first chapter especially gave rise to hearty laughter on the part of author and audience. Conditioned to the mystifying and grotesque elements in Kafka's fiction and to the solemnity that characterizes his Anglo-American reception, one may find it difficult to keep in mind the mirthful first reception of the novel. But there is indeed humor there and elsewhere in Kafka. He had not become enamored of the Yiddish theater for nothing: he knew the comedy of domestic situation, and he was not above using one-liners and burlesque-style skits.)

The novel is fundamentally autobiographical. The hero, Joseph K., shares many characteristics with his author: he is a businessman in Prague whose surname begins with a K; further, Joseph K. has just passed his watershed thirtieth birthday as Kafka had just observed his thirty-first. The events of the novel cover one year, and Joseph K. is assassinated on the eve of his thirty-first birthday.

The structure is episodic, hardly less so than that of *Amerika*. Characters frequently disappear, never to return or at most to reappear fleetingly. But *Der Prozeß* is not a detective story with characters and strands to be traced and neatly resolved. The focus of the novel is not the Law that hounds Joseph K. to death but rather Joseph K. himself and his flawed responses to the machinations of the Law.

One morning Joseph K. is arrested without having done anything wrong. He is still in bed in his quarters at Frau Grubach's lodging house when two warders, the lowest rank of Court officials, burst in to arrest him. The warders, Franz and Willem, do not know what he is charged with; they know only that his arrest has been preceded by an adequate investigation and that the Law is not given to frivolous accusation. The officials of the Law, higher officials than the warders, do not go hunting for crime; rather, they are drawn to the guilty. In giving one of the warders his own first name, Kafka calls attention—whether ironically or not—to the compromised authenticity of his "autobiographical" hero, K.

As a high-ranking bank officer Joseph K. knows more than a smattering of law. (In a discarded draft he is shown as a confidant and friend of lawyers and judges. Kafka's deletion of this chapter demonstrates his penchant for economy of narration.) But his arrest so throws him off guard that he fails to use even his mother wit very sensibly: he looks a bit of a fool madly rummaging around after his bicycle license, with the intention of presenting it to the warders as documentation that should lead to the dropping of his case. The warders eat his breakfast, then offer to get a takeout breakfast for him from an apparently—in K.'s haughty view—not very clean coffeehouse across the street.

The arrival of the inspector to afford K. a preliminary hearing right on Frau Grubach's premises does nothing to apprise K. of the charge against him. The inspector recommends that instead of trying so hard to find out what his offense was, he ought to be thinking more about himself. The context of his recommendation tends to reinforce its theme: it is K.'s thirtieth birthday, life's dividing point. As a true adult, K. ought to abandon his argumentative and rationalizing responses and engage in serious contemplation of his self. He may be a wunderkind in the banking business, but in his personal life he is distinctly immature. Doubtless the omniscient Court that has ordered K.'s arrest already knows that K. has given short shrift to his family responsibilities and that his entire emotional life consists of once-a-week appointments to have sex with Elsa, a cabaret waitress.

The hearing itself is a comedy of irregularity, conducted in the bedroom of another of Frau Grubach's tenants, Fräulein Bürstner, who is absent during the day. Fräulein Bürstner's nightstand is pressed into service as a desk. The two bumbling warders are joined by three anemic young men who stand about idly, regard K. gravely, and display an improper curiosity about Fräulein Bürstner's personal photographs. This motley group is witnessed from the window across the way by a curious and salacious old couple.

The reader does not get to know Fräulein Bürstner well, even when, much later in the novel, she appears in person. K. obviously has a crush on her in which gallant friendship and a desire to talk are mixed with lust and jealousy about her being out on a date after 11:00 P.M. She is the fictional persona of Felice Bauer, with whom Kafka had just broken his engagement. Kafka never gives Bürstner's first name; in the published novel she is consistently referred to as Fräulein Bürstner and in the manuscript by the initials F. B.

It is an odd form of arrest under which Joseph K. finds himself. He is not to be hauled away, decrees the inspector; he is not to be hindered from pursuing his ordinary life, including returning to work at the bank as soon as the hearing is over. To accompany him there the inspector has detained the three anemic young men, who, it suddenly dawns on K., are his subordinates at the bank. His earlier failure to identify them can of course be attributed to the shock of his arrest and the unusual circumstances surrounding it. Something additional, however, is reflected here: the hermetic separateness of his personal and professional worlds, the rigid compartmentalization of his perceptions. Flexibility is not among the advantages that K. takes with him in his contest with the Law and the Court. For example, if K.'s disposition were of a less rigid, preconceived cast, he might have derived useful guidance from Frau Grubach's unsophisticated but clear-sighted advice. Freely admitting that she does not understand K.'s arrest, she goes on to assert that there is no need to understand it. K. is unable to accept such a simple suggestion, since Frau Grubach is a stupid woman. Kafka is inviting the reader to ponder who is really stupid, the uncomplicated Frau Grubach or the sophisticated Joseph K.

On receiving a summons to his first formal interrogation, K. is impelled to attend by his desire to find out the identity of his adversary and the nature of the charge against him. While that desire may strike the reader as perfectly normal, the point is that it is not knowledge of his opponent but knowledge of himself that K. needs. The facts that the place of his hearing is in an unlikely tenement district and that the date is on a Sunday, with no hour specified, should give K. pause. But he is resolved to fight; he is strong and determined. Yet a physical toll is exacted from him even on his first confrontation with his adversary, and it will be increased during subsequent encounters. The Court, when he finally finds it, is in the attic room of a tenement, overcrowded with workers on their day off, airless, dirty, and hot. The fetid atmosphere weakens him.

K. makes fine speeches in his defense before the tenement Court, dwelling on the impropriety, the unfairness of the charge against him—whatever that charge might be. In front of the assembly—only somewhat later does he realize that they are all, no matter how shabbily dressed, officials of the Court—K. makes it his tactic to humiliate the examining magistrate. He denounces the warders and the whole organization behind his arrest. When he starts to stalk out, the magistrate informs him that he has flung away all the advantages that an interrogation confers on an accused. Naturally that comment is ironic, but it also has a measure of truth in the case of K., who has overreacted and will do so more and more as his plight worsens and his energy wanes.

Kafka is plainly intent on establishing a social chasm between K. and his adversary. In an earlier version of the novel the Court session is a socialist meeting; even in the final version the reader is not permitted to forget that the Court is a court of proletarians in proletarian territory and that K. is a middle-class striver

interloping in that territory. It is probably difficult for an American reader to keep this severe class distinction in focus; but in thematic importance it is second only to K.'s existential guilt and is connected with the latter to it.

Despite Marxist interpretations, Kafka was not concerned to write a novel of social protest, let alone revolution. Rather, and as almost invariably, his concern is with the individual. The constantly reiterated social gulf, even as it stirs K.'s repugnance and discomfort, also feeds his self-satisfaction and props up his self-righteous ego, blinding him to the necessity of forgetting his legal innocence and the traducers thereof and of confessing his existential guilt.

K.'s unbidden second visit to the Court on the following Sunday reiterates the social gulf between him and his tormentors and indicates the attrition of his resistant energy. (The German noun *Prozeß* means process as well as trial.) Touring the upstairs offices of the Court with an usher, K. realizes that the many accused persons waiting in the lobby belong to the same social class as he. When he queries a gray-haired man as to what he is waiting for, he receives a confused answer that hardly relates to the question. This response is reminiscent of K.'s own slightly ridiculous confusion on first being arrested, and it anticipates his confusion a moment later at suddenly feeling overwhelmingly tired and faint, wanting only to get out to some fresh air. Just as suddenly, K. becomes passive; unable to either make or find his way, he has to be accompanied to an exit. In his passivity K. hears a voice declaring that even though he is told a hundred times that the way out is right in front of him, he still fails to respond to the information.

The fifth chapter, "Der Prügler" (The Whipper), clarifies the thematic importance of K.'s having failed to recognize his bank subordinates at the scene of his arrest. He is worried that word of his case will be leaked at the bank, that his exalted station as putative successor to the managership will be threatened; thus he resorts to subconscious—the nonidentification—as well as conscious stratagems to keep his personal and professional worlds isolated from each other. The maintenance of this separation becomes especially difficult when he hears convulsive sighs issuing from a storage room at the bank. On entering the little-used room he encounters a stranger clad in dark leather beating two other men on their bare backs with a whip. It takes a while before he recognizes the victims as the bumbling warders, Franz and Willem, who had originally placed him under arrest. He had complained to the presiding magistrate about their unprofessional conduct, which is why, the victims shout, they are being whipped. K. honestly declares that he had not asked that they be punished. Forget the excuses, replies the whipper; the punishment is proper and inevitable. That declaration, of course, has a powerful relevance for K.'s own case.

K. has not comprehended that relevance. He is, in any event, less motivated by humane consideration than by the threat to his position posed by the cruel and indecent scene occurring on the bank premises. K.'s attempt to bribe the whipper to stop having proved unsuccessful and the victims' shrieks having become too loud to be ignored, he hurriedly abandons the storage room and assures the two concerned clerks rushing to the scene that the noise is a dog howling in the courtyard. The next day he finds the unsavory tableau in the storage room unchanged, except that the unhappy workers are now completely naked. Distancing himself from the proceedings, he orders the clerks to clean out the room, which he declares is smothered in filth. His order is at odds with his desire to conceal the goings-on in the storage room; perhaps that is why he accedes to the clerks' notion of performing the task the next day. But again, K.'s peremptory cleanup campaign is not so much related to a repugnance toward filth—though he is in fact fastidiously sensitive to dirt—as to an enforcement of the mutual exclusivity between his legal case and his profession. While K. allows himself to imagine that his security remains unbreached, actually the word is out. When his Uncle Karl in the country is informed, he hurries to the aid of his nephew; but K. refuses help from a person he associates with his childhood. The latter is one more walled-off compartment in K.'s psyche.

In spite of the increasing signs, K. is unable to grasp just how serious his plight is. He affects an insouciance quite at variance with what is going on around him. While he fears for his position at the bank enough to take defensive measures, at the same time he underestimates the strength and resourcefulness of his adversaries.

The theme of underestimation dominates chapter 6. K. is by no means enthusiastic about going with his Uncle Karl to consult the lawyer Huld, who was his uncle's classmate (his name, ironically, means grace or mercy in German). Huld, ill though he is, is nevertheless well informed about K.'s case, for he has remained in touch with his colleagues and their professional gossip. More than that, he is at the moment receiving a visit from the chief clerk of the Court that is K.'s nemesis. Uncle Karl joins the discussion, while K. goes off to the study and makes love with Leni, the lawyer's nurse and mistress.

Not only is Leni an exhilarating sexual partner—a fantasized sex object in the manner of many of Kafka's fictional young women—but she is bright and is disposed to use her intelligence in K.'s behalf. From the professional confabulation she has heard that K. is

excessively unyielding. She accordingly advises him to confess his guilt. K., having almost willfully damaged his case by making love to his lawyer's mistress, does not believe that a confession might render his case moot. But he does believe that the sick lawyer can do little effective work for his case.

K.'s position at the bank daily becomes more tenuous, dangerous, and complicated. In his growing preoccupation he finds it more and more difficult to clear his mind to serve the needs of the bank's clients. The assistant manager, who is also ambitious for the managership, practically kidnaps K.'s clients. One such client, however, more sympathetic than most, recommends that K. get in touch with a certain Titorelli. Titorelli is not a lawyer, but an artist; yet he has worked for the Court and is well versed in its operations. Such an advocate could prove most useful; even K. is beginning to be aware of his diminishing alertness and vitality, and of the risk entailed thereby. He is helped to this awareness after casually proposing to write Titorelli, a step that, as the helpful client points out to him, could easily prove self-incriminating.

Titorelli's combined studio and living quarters, cramped and stifling, are in a shabby tenement. The painter sympathetically acquaints K. with details of Court procedure, with the kind of justice the Court dispenses, and with the three types of acquittal that are theoretically possible. He volunteers to represent K.'s interests before the Court. Hopeful as all of this sounds, it does not advance K.'s real, though unadmitted interest; it merely facilitates his inquiry into the essence of the Court, whereas he ought to be directing his efforts into self-inquiry. Titorelli is pragmatic where Huld was obscure; where Huld was inconclusive, Titorelli proposes an active defense. He distinguishes between what is written in the Law and the practices he has discovered behind the facade. With good luck, personal connections and influence may prevent a case from achieving formal status before the higher Court. Insusceptible to being shaken from its prior persuasion of guilt, such a higher Court has never been known to issue a decree of definite acquittal. A lower Court is empowered to issue only two decrees: if the defendant and his counsel engage in a concentrated defensive effort, they may receive a decree of ostensible acquittal, in which case the charges may be reinstituted at any time; continual but less concentrated defense activity may be answered by a decree of indefinite postponement, with the risks obviously inherent in such a verdict. How much simpler it would be for K. to turn inward and confess his guilt, even though he knows of no offense that he has committed. Titorelli's establishment proves to be adjacent to Court offices—which, he assures K., are in almost every attic. The stifling air in

Titorelli's place was the indicator. Even the band of juvenile harlots that besets K. when he emerges is owned by the Court, which indeed owns everything.

Titorelli's instruction impresses K. enough to make him decide to dismiss Huld, and, in the unfinished eighth chapter, he visits the lawyer to inform him that his services are no longer needed. Naturally, Leni is at Huld's, and she assumes cheerfully that K. is going to spend the night with her. But also there is Huld's client Block, whose case has dragged on before the Court for five and a half years—K.'s is at the six-month mark. Block has been reduced to a subhuman figure by the wear and tear of his case, as conducted by Huld and at intervals, with especially sad results, by himself. He is broke, depleted physically and spiritually, and humiliated by Huld, who has converted him into a fawning animal. The last is reflected in a spectacle enacted for K.'s benefit after K. has dismissed the lawyer. This cruel humiliation demonstrates what sort of treatment is reserved for the accused who try to free themselves from the entanglement of Huld's counsel: they are tortured by rumor, subjected to cruel and teasing innuendo, and then despised for their cringing fear. Ironically, it is K.'s despised avuncular connection that saves him from Block's pitiful fate.

The chapter breaks off, to be followed by the chapter "Im Dom" (In the Cathedral), which revolves around the parable "Vor dem Gesetz" (Before the Law). This parable is the key not only to the chapter containing it but to the entire novel. Kafka sets up the parable, which is the only passage in *Der Prozeß* that has a specifically Jewish resonance, with a skill that transcends the episodic nature of the novel. K. is dragooned into serving as guide and quasi-art expert for a visiting Italian client of the bank. He possesses a modest command of Italian and an equally modest layman's knowledge of the artworks displayed in the cathedral, but he is reluctant to commit his time and energies to the project when they are needed to reduce the number of mistakes he is making with ever greater frequency at the bank. Still, his cooperation in serving as companion to the visitor may help compensate for his errors. On top of everything else, he has a severe cold and an even more severe headache. The day is cold, rainy, and dark.

There are further indications that K. is losing his grip. For half of the preceding night he had buried himself in his Italian grammar, laboriously copying, reciting, and memorizing words and phrases that he supposed might be useful on the tour of the cathedral the next day. But now he has forgotten it all; his usually excellent memory has deserted him. To add to K.'s woes the Italian speaks a southern dialect that K. can understand only fragmentarily. Inexplicably K.'s manager understands it well, forcing K. to strain to tune out the Italian's ceaseless babble while he strives to focus on his manager's concise German summaries.

Just before his departure from his office to meet the Italian, K. receives a phone call from Leni. She is calling, she says, to wish him a good morning. When K. mentions his appointment at the cathedral (which, based on what follows, she may already know about), she maintains that "sie" (they) are goading K. He agrees. Superficially, "they" could mean the bank and its manager, attempting to goad K. into improving his professional performance. But K. reconsiders: Leni works for and lives with Huld, who undertakes cases before the Court. "They" could be the Court. More ambiguously, "they" could be both the bank and the Court, between which, for K., the dividing line is shortly to be dissolved.

The Italian fails to keep his appointment to meet K. at the cathedral. K. feels compelled to wait a bit in case the visitor should arrive late. It is raining so hard that he could hardly leave in any case; on the other hand, the urge to get back to the bank gives him no peace. He could be trying to catch up on his work. He begins to examine the finely wrought great pulpit. It is not likely that the reader has imagined K. to be a pious person; and the latter's study of the great pulpit confirms that his interest in religion is small while his interest in art is considerable.

K. is signaled by a verger to a small, cramped pulpit, above which the lamp is on. When a priest ascends the stairs, apparently to give a sermon, although only a couple of people besides K. are present, K. prepares to leave. But he is brought up short when the priest sharply cries his name. It emerges that the priest, who is the prison chaplain and thus an official of the Court, had K. summoned to the cathedral. The mechanism of the summoning is not further explained. What role—if any—did the Italian client play? The reader tends to follow K.'s false concerns by trying to identify his adversary and its modus operandi. But that is not the problem; K. is the problem.

When the priest relays the information that K.'s case before the Court is going badly, K. proclaims his innocence; he is not guilty, it is all a mistake. How can anyone be guilty? After all, we are merely here in this world. The priest declares that that is how guilty men talk. He has other complaints: K. has too much outside help in this case, especially from women. Shrieking, the priest asks if K. cannot see one pace before him. The implication is that K. is forever focusing on the far distance, on irrelevancies such as what the Court is and why it is pursuing him.

Validating the priest's observation that K. is too dependent, K. is quick to imply his dependency on the priest himself, whom he imagines to be more sympathetic than other minions of the Court. You are entertaining a delusion about the Court, replies the priest. To clarify the delusion he tells the parable of the man from the country and the doorkeeper. The man from the country begs the doorkeeper to admit him to the Law. The doorkeeper asserts that at the moment that is impossible; he may be allowed to enter later, but not now. The doorkeeper dares him to try to get in, warning that inside there is a succession of further doorkeepers, each more powerful than the last. The man decides to wait; the doorkeeper provides a stool. Bribing does not work; the doorkeeper accepts the bribes but does not relent. The man grows old, finally senile, waiting. At length the dying old man asks why it is that in all the years no one else had sought admission. The doorkeeper replies that no one else could gain admittance through this door because the door was intended for the man from the country; and it is now going to be closed.

A difficulty with this parable is that, like practically all Kafka parables, it does not explicate the truth but simply offers a metaphor of truth. K., not surprisingly, holds that it inveighs against deception, such as that perpetrated by the doorkeeper; the priest regards it as a summons to penetrate delusion. Neither of these readings, however, comes to grips with the apparently assumed identity between externally imposed deception and inwardly generated delusion. K. blames the doorkeeper for withholding crucial information from the man. The priest denies any contradiction between the doorkeeper's early refusal to allow the man to enter and the information he reveals at the end of the man's days; there would, accordingly, be no deception.

The disputants reach a shaky common ground in the possibility that both the doorkeeper and the man from the country were deluded. But the priest objects that it is not permissible to render a judgment on the doorkeeper, who, as a representative of the Law, is beyond judgment. The priest concludes by saying that one must not look for truth but should accept necessity. K. objects that such a principle merely licenses lying. K. is by now worn down by the stress of work, the preparation for the Italian's visit, the failure of the guest to show up, and finally by the strenuous argument with the aggressive priest; but his desire to leave the cathedral is countervailed by a desire to talk further with the priest. The latter, however, withdraws his apparent friendliness. That K. has not noticed its superficiality before is further evidence of his capacity for delusion. K.'s need for guidance in getting out of the cathedral reminds one of his earlier need for assistance in evacuating the Court's offices. What has happened over the course of the chapter "Im Dom" is the dissolution of the dividing line between K.'s two fundamentally opposed spheres: the bank, the focus of his professional world, and the Court, the focus of his public world.

Following somewhat abruptly after "Im Dom"– Kafka may well have intended to write intervening chapters–is "Das Ende," the final chapter. It is the eve of K.'s thirty-first birthday; thus one year, less a few hours, has elapsed since K. was accosted by the warders in his bed at Frau Grubach's. As with his arrest, K. has no inkling of his execution. True, he is dressed in black, but that is because he is awaiting other visitors–visitors who will arrive to find him gone, marched by his assassins to a quarry at the edge of town. Grotesque, bumbling, fat, and pallid, wearing top hats, his executioners strike K. as resembling tenth-rate actors from a provincial theater. But they have a butcher knife. On the walk that comes to an end at the quarry, K. seems to discern the figure of Fräulein Bürstner approaching the nearby square. K. resolves to keep his composure and to show that he has learned something from his trial. Whether he really saw Fräulein Bürstner is not the point; whether he has experienced an epiphany or undergone gradual change over the year is of thematic importance.

The motif of darkness and occasionally brief and limited light, prevalent in the cathedral, is replicated on K.'s death walk to the quarry–the reader never knows if the quarry was a prearranged destination or if the executioners just became tired at that point. The night is dark, the street is dark, the windows on the other side of the street are dark. The assassins dispute politely with each other who shall plunge the knife into K.'s breast. K. is supposed to do it himself as a redemptive act of autonomy. But redemption is rarely granted a Kafka hero. Finally, one assassin chokes him while the other wields the knife. Just before the knife-thrust K. discerns a flicker of light in a nearby house. It is as if a light were being turned on at the moment the shutters are thrown open and a human figure stretches forward. Whatever the import of the figure–humanity? succor?– no light actually goes on; rather, like the flash of a light, the shutters burst open.

K. has changed only in that his vitality is worn down. For that reason he can be forgiven for his refusal to take the bravura step with the knife that his executioners keep tossing back and forth. The predominant sense to be derived from this scene is not that it takes more heroism not to be a hero–if indeed heroism may be invoked at all in connection with one's own compulsory suicide–but rather that a macabre comedy is being played about a man's life. The effect is thus one of irony. K.'s eagerness to assert to himself that he has learned something is simply pitiable, and is made more so by his wish that people be left with the correct idea of his change. In other words, he is as concerned with image as with substance. It does come as a surprise that

K., who has not previously consulted God, should do so in his final moment. But he invokes God only to lay at His door the responsibility for his own final failure to act: God had failed to leave him sufficient strength for the deed. K. gives up the ghost with his hands raised, fingers spread, in what might or might not be supplication.

Der Prozeß brims with paradoxes, but the most basic one is that K., burdened with existential guilt, is both guilty and innocent. He thus both receives and is denied justice. The ending of the story is closed: he is murdered. Yet it is open if one prefers to think him redeemed. The use of religious categories is encouraged by the finale; on the other hand, the belated proliferation of devotional attitudes suggests irony. The Court is indisputably K.'s adversary. Yet at the same time K. and the Court are members of a symbiotic relationship in which the Court reflects what is going on in K.'s mind but lacks the will or the power to bring K. to look within himself.

Moving, gripping, paradoxical, humorous, and tragic, *Der Prozeß* is not a closely wrought novel. Still, even though Kafka never prepared it for publication, it is more closely structured than *Amerika.* The penultimate chapter that so persuasively anticipates the end may be penultimate only fortuitously, but the obviously final chapter is in fine balance with the opening chapter. The most prominent detail of this balance lies in the two pairs of bumbling Court officials, one pair initiating K.'s misguided relationship with the Court, the other terminating it.

Kafka and Felice Bauer agreed in July 1917 to marry after the war was over and to live in Berlin, but Kafka's incipient tuberculosis was diagnosed as such in September. Resorting to a psychosomatic explanation, he saw his disease as the triumph of evil in the five-year battle for and against Felice. After five months the second engagement went the way of the first. By this time Kafka was on medical leave with pay from his insurance post and living with his youngest and favorite sister, Ottla, and her husband on their farm in Zürau, a village in northwestern Bohemia. There, while blocking out his third novel, *Das Schloß* (1926; translated as *The Castle,* 1930), he wrote a profusion of stories and parables, including "Ein Landarzt" (translated as "The Country Doctor"), "Beim Bau der chinesischen Mauer" (translated as "The Great Wall of China"), "Ein Bericht für eine Akademie" (translated as "A Report for an Academy") and "Der Jäger Gracchus" (1936; translated as "The Hunter Gracchus," 1960). A collection of fourteen stories and sketches was published by Wolff in 1919 under the title *Ein Landarzt: Kleine Erzählungen* (translated as *The Country Doctor: A Collection of Fourteen Short Stories,* 1945). Even so, Kafka was by no means free of his usual concern that his work fell short of his expectations.

On a blizzardy night the country doctor in "Ein Landarzt" receives an urgent summons to make a house call ten miles away. As he laments his lack of transportation—the harsh winter has claimed his horse—two splendid horses and an unknown groom emerge from a supposedly uninhabited pigsty. The doctor drives off to fulfill his duty, while the oafish groom, intent on raping the servant girl Rosa, insists on remaining behind. Speeded by compression of time, as in a dream, the doctor is instantly at the bedside of his patient, a boy who whispers that he desires to die. The doctor at first accuses the boy of malingering, then sees that he has an awful rose-pink wound on his hip, clotted with worms wriggling out toward the light. The doctor falsely assures the boy that his wound is not so bad; in fact, it is incurable. The doctor's supernatural horses peer through the windows, whinnying to remind him that he must return home. Taking curt leave of the young patient's family and friends, he escapes to his sleigh. But the return trip is infinitely labored and slow. He fears that he may never reach home, where he has left poor Rosa to endure the assault of the groom. The night bell to which he had responded was a false alarm, he declares in his desperation—false in that it summoned him to a case beyond his powers: a false era, having abandoned its priests, expects its doctors to save it. Inspired by Kafka's favorite uncle, Siegfried Löwy, who was in fact a country doctor, the doctor is a perplexed Good Samaritan. The quandary in which he finds himself is: shall he save Rosa from the groom or shall he minister to a patient he knows is dying? The groom, indispensable in harnessing the unearthly horses, knows his power, and the doctor cannot neutralize it. He is now prepared, reluctantly, to sacrifice Rosa. If only, he laments, he had been less indifferent over the years that this helpful and pretty girl had lived in his house. He had hardly noticed her, and now. . . . The crisis has stimulated the doctor to a human awareness that had fallen victim to the professional obligations heaped on him by his ungrateful contemporaries. The horns of the doctor's dilemma are joined in the word *rosa* (pink). It is both the girl's name and the color of the patient's wound. The German word, like its English counterpart, also suggests the flower, and, sure enough, the boy's wound is rose-shaped as well as pink. Sexual overtones, heretofore confined to the groom's designs on Rosa, are apparent when, at the boy's house, the boy's family and the village elders strip the doctor naked and put him in bed with the patient, next to the wound. He cannot cure the wound; he is, so to speak, impotent.

"Ein Landarzt" has elicited many Freudian interpretations, most of which point out that the doctor, having ignored Rosa for years, is for all practical purposes impotent with her as well. In any case, the reader is aware that the doctor is beset by failure on every front, a consequence of being obliged to be a shaman as well as a medical man. The most suggestive contribution of Freudian interpretation is in positing the groom as the doctor's long-suppressed id. The dreamlike ambiance, of which the most striking elements are the compression of time and the doctor's final naked flight, also obviously lends itself to Freudian treatment. But Kafka was not writing case histories in "Ein Landarzt" or elsewhere; exhaustive Freudian explication is apt to become mere reductivism. The youngster's flowerlike fatal wound reminds some critics of the wound of King Amfortas in the legend of Parsifal; as such, it would be a mark of the human condition which is beyond the doctor's powers to remedy. Interpretation in Christian terms usually takes its starting point from the wound, which may suggest the wounds of Christ; but redemption is conspicuously absent from the story. The doctor, who is perplexed at the start of the story, feels betrayed toward the end. He has been betrayed by the groom, maybe by his own id, by the false summons of his night bell, but most of all by his incapacity for coping with new demands that exceed his limited—thus human—competence.

"Beim Bau der chinesischen Mauer" appears at first to have as its theme the social benefit of huge public works. A feared incursion of nomads from the north provides ample reason for erecting the wall. The high command, however, ignoring a fundamental tenet of military defense, has ordered that the wall be built not continuously but in scattered thousand-yard segments. Because each segment requires five years for completion, the wall offers a very porous defense. Even as total completion is proclaimed, word persists that gaps still remain. The subtle Chinese scholar who is the narrator advises against too much diligence in trying to fathom the decreese of the high command, which has, after all, existed for eternity, as has its decision to build the wall. The narrator continues with a discussion of vastness. What is the defense of distant Peking to the people of southeast China? Why should they have to leave their native place to train in unfathomably remote Peking? The people in the remote province hardly know the name of the reigning dynasty, not to speak of that of the emperor. The empire itself is a vague institution; they cannot really conceive of it. Further, the people, rooted in the past and its glories, have allowed themselves to be bypassed by history. The thematic strand that began as one of spatial vastness has evolved into one of time, and it is similar to one of the chief themes of *In der Strafkolonie:* the past is more unrestrained and more vigorous than, and therefore superior to, the present.

The final story in the *Ein Landarzt* collection is "Ein Bericht für eine Akademie." The report, compiled by an ape called Red Peter, chronicles his successful aspiration to become a human being. His transformation commences after his capture on Africa's Gold Coast. In a cage on board ship he perceives that his best interest is served not by escaping and jumping overboard but by learning to imitate the humans around him. Because they are sailors, learning to drink, though revolting to him, is high on his list. He has the wisdom to opt for the vaudeville stage rather than a more commodious cage in a zoo. While being captured, Red Peter received two wounds—one to his cheek, the other to his private parts. In later days, to show visitors where the shot entered, he has the habit of calmly taking down his trousers, knowing even as he does so that what he calls "Windhunde" (windbag commentators) will declare such behavior to be evidence of his still untamed ape nature. Actually, the habit is less a lapse than a provocation. From Red Peter's unhappy assertion that the eye of his ape girlfriend reveals a bewildered, insane look, one may conclude that she, too, has made some progress down the road to becoming human.

Not a part of the *Ein Landarzt* collection is the fragmentary "Der Jäger Gracchus." It is more directly autobiographical than the other stories of the period and thus more reflective of Kafka's state of mind. The name of the hunter appears to be a Latinization of the Italian *gracchio,* which, like the Czech *kavka,* means jackdaw. Gracchus, a German hunter killed in a hunting accident in the Black Forest in the fourth century, was put into a winding sheet and laid in his death boat for transport to the realm of the dead. But the death boat went off course and has been sailing earthly waters with its dead but garrulous passenger for fifteen centuries. Apprised by an advance dove, the mayor of Riva has gone to the harbor to chat with Gracchus. (Riva, by Lake Garda in northern Italy, was a resort town frequently visited by Kafka; he had a brief love affair there in 1913 with an unnamed eighteen-year-old Swiss girl.) All he knows, Gracchus tells the mayor, is that he is forever en route to the other world but never quite attains it. He is a link between men of the present and their forebears—an ineffective link, because no one in the living world is sufficiently interested in the connection to take time to learn about it. And Gracchus is incapable of comprehending the living world. The fundamental incommensurability runs both ways.

In 1918 Kafka contracted influenza, an epidemic of which was then raging worldwide. After three weeks' confinement to bed he obtained further medical leave from his job, during which he convalesced at Schelesen, in the countryside north of Prague.

At Schelesen Kafka met and became engaged to Julie Wohryzek, the keen-witted daughter of a shoemaker and synagogue official in Prague. Kafka's father was outraged that his only son should propose a marital alliance with a socially and economically inferior family. The wedding, scheduled for November 1919, did not take place, for the familiar reason of Kafka's fear that marriage would have an adverse effect on his ability to write. Nevertheless, Kafka continued to see Julie well into the inflammatory period of his next romance.

"Brief an den Vater" (1952; translated as *Letter to His Father,* 1953), which Kafka's father never received (either Kafka never sent it or it was intercepted before it reached his father—accounts vary), dates from that troubled November of 1919 when the wedding with Julie Wohryzek failed to occur. It failed to occur because, Kafka says in the letter, for a bourgeois marriage to be successful the man must be forceful, unreflective, healthy, and knowledgeable, all of which he is not. Those are rather the qualities of his father, whereas the son is shy, quiet, bookish, a bit out of place in the bourgeois milieu. Kafka acknowledges his oversensitive fear of his father's noisy, domineering, ridiculing manner, which brought about the loss of whatever filial self-confidence there may have been. In its stead he has only a sense of guilt. It has been an unfair fight: on the one side the defenseless son, on the other a bloodsucking vermin. In spite of the impassioned metaphor, the letter is a rather keen analysis of what went wrong between father and son, with the son's fearfulness readily admitted as a prime ingredient in the bitter brew. "Brief an den Vater" seems to certify the final deterioration of personal contact.

After a somewhat paternal relationship with the much younger Minze Eisner, Kafka's next love affair—typically initiated by letter—was with Milena Jesensá Poláková. She had been the translator of *Der Heizer* into Czech, and Kafka was impressed with the quality of her work. When at length they met he fell madly in love with her. Rendezvous were stormy and passionate. Although Milena's husband physically abused her, she would not leave him. Kafka eventually had to see that, despite the uncustomary ease of his relationship with Milena, it was a love that had nowhere to go. Perhaps it blossomed as it did because he was exempt from the threat of marriage and its feared deleterious effect on his writing.

By 1920 Kafka was almost continually on sick leave. Toward the end of that year, after a creative period that produced several short tales and parables, he was sent to a sanatorium at Matliary in the mountains of Slovakia. Released in September 1921, he returned to his job. In October he was placed on a sick leave of three months. Aware of his deteriorating health, he had already advised Brod that he wanted all of his unpublished work destroyed after his death. In January 1922, at about the time his sick leave expired and its renewal began, he started writing *Das Schloß*.

One inevitably compares its protatonist, K., with the protagonists of *Amerika* and *Der Prozeß*, Karl Rossmann and Joseph K. The K. of *Das Schloß* is more forceful, more aggressive, more consistently tenacious in his quest than the other two. The object of his pursuit is the castle. To be sure, he comes not unbidden: the castle has asked him to come in the capacity of land surveyor. Or has it? Signs are abundant—but far from clear—that he may be an impostor. All the same, he insists on the castle's making good on its presumed offer to him, and he is dogged—if at the same time inwardly uncertain—in his pursuit of his redoubtable target through the maze of its protective bureaucracy.

The circumstances of K.'s arrival near the castle are not propitious. It is evening, it is snowing, he has no surveying equipment, and he is unaccompanied by any assistant such as is essential for land surveying, so that his commitment to surveying is not overwhelmingly convincing. Nor for that matter is his very authenticity: the denotation of his profession, *Landvermesser,* contains not only the suggestion of *messen* (to measure) but also the suggestion of *vermessen* (to strike a presumptuous pose).

Unlike the previous novels, *Das Schloß* does not introduce themes that are never further iterated or developed. Thus, K.'s fatigue on his first evening in the village, where he awaits permission to proceed to the castle, will be often replicated, then become less prominent for a while, to reappear toward the end in full force: K. will be too worn down to take advantage of an opportunity to finally effect a useful connection with the castle.

From the novel's second, terse sentence the reader learns that the village is deep in snow, whereas the castle itself is almost entirely free of snow. That contrast persists: the village seems consistently half-buried in snow. It has always just snowed or is snowing—K. early feels the power of the snow by imprudently getting bogged down in it. Adapting to the all but yearlong snow—summer is ephemeral—defines physical existence in the village. Life there is oppressive, whereas the virtually snow-free castle holds out the promise of a better existence.

Not that the castle is a particularly splendid edifice: it is a rambling pile apparently composed of several small buildings. It is not new, but it is not old, either. If it is meant to symbolize God, as some critics have maintained, it is a singularly unprepossessing structure to serve that purpose. It has but one tower, about which fly flocks of crows. It could as well be a symbol of death—that has been critically suggested, too—as of divinity. Days are short, darkness pervasive.

Two fellows named Artur and Jeremias, wearing the uniforms of the castle (which K. does not yet recognize), present themselves as his assistants. K. puts a strange question: are they his old assistants? Surely he would know if they were. They assure him that they are, and he seems to believe them. They say that they have come a long way; in fact, they have come from the castle—which, for K., does turn out to be a terribly long way. Despite tantalizing appearances of cooperation, such as the dispatch of the assistants, the castle is basically characterized by impenetrability. After hearing something like the humming of children's voices on the phone, K. has no difficulty in discerning the "Niemals" (never) pronounced by a castle official with a slight speech defect. The castle appears, however, to evince a further cooperativeness in dispatching Barnabas as a messenger for K.'s use. Barnabas brings K. a letter, signed by a department chief named Klamm, recognizing K.'s appointment as land surveyor. The trouble is that the recognition is ambiguous: K. is left with the options of becoming a village worker with a merely apparent connection with the castle, or an ostensible village worker whose real occupation will be determined by the castle and relayed to him by Barnabas.

He falls in love with Frieda, the barmaid at the Herrenhof—the inn favored by the gentlemen of the castle when on business in the village. Frieda is also the mistress of Klamm. Frieda is gregarious and coquettish; she seems an odd match for the reserved, secretive, imperious Klamm. Indeed, when Klamm calls her from his room near the bar it is difficult to determine whether he desires beer or sex. That perfunctoriness—on both sides—may help make her amenable to an affair with K. The latter's motivation, besides that of amorous attraction, is clear: Frieda can influence Klamm to intercede in K.'s behalf at the castle.

Frieda, like K., is intelligent, ambitious, and energetic; having begun as a stable-girl, she was quickly promoted to barmaid and shows promise as a future manager. Instantly in tune with each other, inflamed by a single desire, they sink into an embrace among the puddles of spilled beer on the floor behind the bar and remain so for hours. Kafka's account of their lovemaking has impressed some critics as a lyric description of selfless, unifying love unique in his oeuvre. More likely, however, it is a satire of the sort of European love story rendered obsolete by a novel of modernism like *Das Schloß* itself. Together with the clichés, the locale of this tableau vivant suggests other than idealized love.

During the marathon Klamm calls for Frieda. K., whose chief interest promptly becomes nonerotic, repeats the summons into Frieda's ear as he helpfully

refastens her blouse. When Frieda shouts to Klamm that she is with the land surveyor, K. naturally thinks that her role as Klamm's mistress, the role in which she can be of most value to K., will come to an end.

K. is more human—though not necessarily in the most admirable sense—than the heroes of Kafka's other novels. Above all, K. is readier to exploit his fellows. Karl Rossmann in *Amerika* is brought to one fall after another by female seductiveness, but he is in no sense the exploiter; rather, the contrary. Joseph K. in *Der Prozeß* is quite willing to abandon his own benefit, dubious as it may be, at the legal conference at the lawyer Huld's for the pleasure of making love with the eager Leni—but again, he does not exploit her. K. does exploit. He may love Frieda, but he loves her the more because she is a conduit to Klamm. On the other hand, he will marry her, even without the opportunity of having a talk with Klamm first.

K.'s tenuous position as ignorant but tolerated outsider is threatened less by his marriage to Frieda than by his socializing with the outcast family of Barnabas. Barnabas himself, it is true, is a castle messenger, but he has insinuated himself into the job, and his family is not thereby relieved from the role of village pariahs. The castle official Sortini once sent a letter to Barnabas's sister, Amalia, by whom, without her doing anything, he had suddenly been smitten at the fire brigade picnic. The letter contained a lewd proposal, which Amalia ignored. By spurning the castle she condemned her family to ruin—not by any dramatic, overt, hostile act, but by the gradual effect of ostracism and deprivation of a livelihood. Now it is clearer why the castle assigned Barnabas as the messenger between itself and K.: the assignment assured that K. would socialize with the pariah family and thus contaminate himself in the eyes of the village. That contamination will scarcely facilitate his quest to penetrate the castle.

K. calls on the mayor, his nominal superior, for enlightenment as to his status. His status, the mayor tells him, is the most insignificant of all petty matters. Further, from an official point of view, his cherished letter of entitlement from Klamm is meaningless; as if to underline that discouraging analysis the mayor's wife folds the letter into a paper boat. Nor do the mayor's voluminous files contain any entry whatsoever under the heading *Landvermesser*. Far from attaining access to the highest reaches of the castle bureaucracy, K. will be lucky to get a part-time job of the lowest rank. And he cannot leave, because he has come from such a long way off, and he is going to marry a local girl.

Momus, Klamm's village secretary, disabuses K. of any remaining grounds for hope. But then comes a second letter from Klamm, lauding K.'s surveying and encouraging continuation of the work. Since K. has performed no surveying at all, his concerns are hardly alleviated. The bureaucracy does offer K. and Frieda a job of sorts: at starvation wages they are signed on as custodians at the schoolhouse, where they are given quarters in one of the two classrooms. This unlikely venue for lovemaking, with classes bursting in on them before they are out of bed, is the castle's way of trivializing sex as a weapon against K. The scene is farce, approaching burlesque, and was perhaps inspired by Kafka's memories of Yiddish theater.

If only, Frieda laments, we had gone off somewhere that first night, then we might always be together. Her only dream has been to have K.'s company, but that has proved an impossible dream. For K. to leave with Frieda, and thus be always in her company without the intrusion of schoolchildren and schoolmasters, is precisely what K. cannot do. He can only stay and try to accomplish his self-imposed mission. Having thus reiterated her love for K. and strongly implied the reason it could not be, Frieda leaves him for Jeremias, an insider like herself.

At this point, in chapter 18, the text of the first edition of *Das Schloß* ends. The rest of chapter 18 and two further chapters, added in the fourth edition, provide, if not an ending, at least a more rounded-off sense of integration. For example, the thematic tiredness of K., lost sight of in the middle chapters, is reintroduced with some effect. K.'s overwhelming fatigue is responsible for the failure of his most promising attempt to establish a connection with the castle. Through Barnabas, K. learns that Erlanger, one of Klamm's chief secretaries, wants K. to report to him in room fifteen of the Herrenhof. Except by appointment, all of the Herrenhof but the barroom is off-limits to K. and the villagers. K. is so exhausted that he fails to keep the appointment. Even so, fate makes possible a second chance. His fatigue intensified by the lateness of the hour–Erlanger holds office hours at night–K. is wandering around the Herrenhof at four in the morning in search of an empty bed. Blundering into the room of an insomniac secretary named Bürgel, K. is invited to stay and chat. Bürgel is not one of Klamm's secretaries, so he can help K. in no direct way; but he informs K. that the castle personnel start getting up at about five o'clock, which might be a good time for him to make belated contact with Erlanger.

Meanwhile, Bürgel is genially disposed to talk out his insomnia, with K. as a taciturn audience. Bürgel's admitted ignorance of K.'s case does not prevent him from grandiloquently volunteering to do something that will result in K.'s actually being employed as a surveyor. Sometimes, Bürgel assures him after a tedious bureaucratic discourse, even though a miracle cannot happen it does happen. But K. is too sleepy to follow him.

In the next room Erlanger, kept awake by the noise of Bürgel's unrelenting discourse, gives loud vent to a renewal of the summons to K. Sleepily staggering into the next room, K. suffers Erlanger's reproach for his tardiness. Erlanger makes him aware of the futility of his attempts to effect a relationship with the castle. Klamm, he says, may be disturbed by the presence of a new barmaid, Pepi, who was brought in to take Frieda's place when the latter left to join K. That potential disturbance could suffice to dash K.'s hopes forever. Still, K.'s cooperation might yet prove helpful to his aspiration.

Dismissed curtly by Erlanger, and therefore supposedly obliged to promptly vacate the premises of the Herrenhof, K. nonetheless loiters in the corridor. A servant is distributing files from a cart to the castle secretaries in the various rooms. But the servant is angry, some doors hardly open, mistakes are made, one secretary is shouting, a buzzer goes off–all because everyone except K., in his ignorance and fatigue, knows that a trespasser is hanging around in the corridor. So much is his general guilt taken for granted that no one could imagine that he was there by mistake, in perfectly good faith.

After the distribution is apparently concluded, a single small piece of paper remains in the file cart. K. cannot escape the suspicion that it is his file. The servant signals his assistant to remain silent about the forthcoming breach of bureaucratic protocol, tears the remaining paper to bits, and puts the pieces into his pocket.

The twentieth and last chapter is devoted primarily to the retrospective story of Pepi, Frieda's replacement as barmaid during her four-day idyll with K. Pepi correctly attributes her installation as barmaid to K.'s influence on Frieda. By the same token, she holds him responsible for her demotion, because his love was insufficient to keep Frieda from returning to the post. In her jealousy, malevolence, and vituperation, Pepi provides the reader with a different view of Frieda, heretofore seen only from the infatuated point of view of K. If one is to credit Pepi, Frieda is no great beauty, nor is she free of character defects. Frieda was a great favorite of the customers, yet she had always to worry about the possibility that they, and Klamm, would grow tired of her. To strengthen her position as barmaid and mistress, Pepi concludes, Frieda needed to provide a spectacle of some sort; she therefore decided to have an affair. K., the stranger, proved the ideal respondent. In other words, Frieda was using K. quite as much as K. was using Frieda.

It has struck many critics that K.'s failure with Frieda presages his failure with the castle. Similarly, if Frieda is unattractive, both physically and as to character, then the castle may be so, too. Neither Frieda nor the castle are what they purport to be, and neither is worth aspiring to; K. should desist. Maybe that is what K. has in mind when he implies that he will join Pepi and the other chambermaids, Emilie and Henriette, in their snug little room in the Herrenhof, where he will be their helper and protector. Yet K., wondering aloud if spring will ever come, seems unlikely to simply relinquish the quest and adopt the peasant lifestyle of the ever-snowy village in the shadow of the less-snowy castle.

There is a recurrent critical urge to equate the castle with God, despite the almost total absence of textual indicators. One wonders if it is the business of God to be granting rights to surveying jobs, especially to such an unrepentant petitioner as K. He would not be a very estimable God, either, to judge from the castle's indifference, pettiness, cruelty, lechery, and fallibility.

Since the castle does not represent God, K.'s quest can scarcely symbolize a religious pilgrimage. Far from contrition or self-knowledge, let alone admission of guilt—in contrast to the guiltladen protagonists of *Amerika* and *Der Prozeß*—K. comes to demand his rights, not to abjure them. He is a quester, which is by no means the same as a pilgrim. In contrast to a pilgrim's approach, K. is exactly as far from his goal at the end of the novel as at the beginning. Furthermore, the scene is set for another in-house sexual affair, this time with Pepi. The maids' cozy room seems a curious place for a religious pilgrimage to end.

It is all too easy to apply Freudian categories to *Das Schloß*—for example, K. as an Oedipal avenger against the paternal castle. Such efforts may be enlightening or suggestive; any attempt, however—and there have been a few—to impose a Freudian system on the novel will leave merely an eviscerated case study, a poor remnant from a magnificent and ambiguous novel. The reader ought to be able to enjoy and savor those allusive ambiguities without feeling compelled to force them onto the procrustean bed of any single category of reductive criticism.

While writing *Das Schloß*, Kafka continued to write parables, including his perhaps best-known ones, "Gibs auf!" (1936; translated as "Give It Up!," 1960) and "Von den Gleichnissen" (1936; translated as "About Parables," 1960). The purport of the former is summed up in its title. The narrator, lost, appeals to a policeman for directions and is mocked in reply. This is what comes from reposing faith and trust in another; thus the titular admonition to give up the quest. "Von den Gleichnissen" is Kafka's final parable. Its gist is that

parables only intend to say that the incomprehensible is incomprehensible, which we already know. This incomprehensibility or inexplicability is a hallmark of the Kafkaesque parable, as opposed to the New Testament parable, which typically concludes with an elucidation to make certain that the hearer gets the point. Familiarity with the latter type probably accounts for the tendency of zealous explicators to force Kafka's parables into the more familiar, but alien, mold.

After June 1922 there were no more renewals of Kafka's sick leaves from the insurance company, and in July he retired on pension. He left Prague to live with his sister Ottla in southern Bohemia for several months and then returned to Prague. Along with work on *Das Schloß* in 1922 he devoted himself to a story called "Ein Hungerkünstler" (translated as "The Hunger-Artist," 1938). In the summer of 1923 he vacationed on the Baltic coast with his sister Elli and her family. There he met Dora Diamant, a young girl of Hasidic roots. Her family background and her competence in Hebrew appealed to Kafka equally with her personal attractiveness. He lived with her in Berlin until the spring of 1924, when she accompanied him to Austria. There he entered Kierling sanatorium near Klosterneuburg. In 1923 and 1924, when able, Kafka worked on three stories that were published posthumously: "Eine kleine Frau" (1924; translated as "A Little Woman," 1943), "Der Bau" (1936; translated as "The Burrow," 1960), and "Josefine, die Sängerin, oder das Volk der Mäuse" (1924; translated as "Josephine, the Songstress; or, The Mice Nation," 1942). After horrible suffering, he died on 3 June 1924 of tuberculosis of the larynx.

The eponymous "hunger artist" is an artist of dubious authenticity, whose art is to starve himself. At the end he dies unnoticed in a pile of dirty straw. His dying reply to the question of why he pursued his unusual—but in nineteenth-century Europe not unique—profession is that he could not find the food he liked; if he had, he would have made no fuss but would have eaten just like anyone else. He fails to disclose what sort of food *would* have appealed to him, an omission that has given rise to the critical suggestion that it is spiritual provender that he is talking about. Add to this speculation the fact that his fasts endure for forty days—thus recalling the temptation of Christ in the wilderness—and the notion grows that the story is a Christian allegory. The problem with this interpretation is that the hunger artist, unlike a hermit in a cave or Christ in the wilderness, was not resisting temptation at all; far from depriving himself of what he wanted, he was, by his lights, indulging his desires in a way unthinkable for an authentic saint. After his sad end, his remains are swept away with the straw and he is replaced in the cage by a sleek and hungry leopard, which draws huge and enthusiastic crowds. The leopard celebrates the joy of life as the hunger artist never had and *that* now attracts the crowds. Thus the theme, as in *In der Strafkolonie* and "Ein Landarzt," has to do with the contrast between former times and the present; in "Ein Hungerkünstler," however, the schema is stood on its head, for it is the present era that is the hardier and the more vigorous. The leopard is by far the healthier act.

"Eine kleine Frau" is a monologue in which a male narrator discusses at somewhat tedious length a highly critical woman and the torment caused him by her gratuitous criticisms. There seems to be no way for him to mute her criticism, which has been going on for years. Their incompatibility is total. In the end he resolves to ignore the little woman as best he can and quietly lead his own life. This fictional little woman is probably a projection of Kafka's unrelenting self-criticism; in any event, there are only occasionally lively narrative passages in the monologue, which is spun out longer than its slight premise can comfortably support. It is conceivable that Kafka's physical exhaustion was taking an artistic toll.

On the other hand, "Der Bau," the next-to-last story Kafka wrote and a monologue of much greater length, does not sag. The species of the fictional burrower Kafka withholds; the burrower no doubt stands for the author. Now past his prime, the burrower in his years of vigor constructed for his protection an elaborate burrow. He does not confine himself to it; he does most of his hunting aboveground. He is tempted to spend the rest of his life on the surface, contemplating the entrance to his burrow. Being aboveground carries risk of confrontation, but being underground does not entirely eliminate danger. For he built his underground works before he adequately comprehended the principles of defense. Sure enough, the burrower returns to his underground castle and perceives a barely audible whistling noise through the earthen walls. At first he dismisses it as unimportant, but the noise does not go away. The burrower wavers between ignoring it and agitatedly weighing methods of confronting it; like Kafka, he is given to neurotic reflection. As the noise changes in volume and quality, he concludes that it must be a large beast digging toward him. The ending of the story is lost. The threat, if one pursues the autobiographical relationship, would be that posed by Kafka's fatal disease. Critics have also detected in "Der Bau" a sexual metaphor—hardly less suggestive than that in "Ein Landarzt"—which is considerably more apparent in the original German than in translation. Language aside, burrowing is clearly susceptible to interpretation as sexual penetration, especially with so much narrative attention focused on the entrance to the burrow. In conjunction with the sterility of the burrow—

the burrower has no mate, no offspring—the sexual metaphor must be taken ironically.

"Josefine, die Sängerin, oder das Volk der Mäuse" is Kafka's last story, written just three months before his death. Like "Eine kleine Frau," it is more a discussion than a narration. The narrator, apparently a fellow mouse of Josefine, is anything but polished: his report is rife with internal qualifications and contradictions, so that it is difficult for the reader to get an accurate perception of Josefine, the idiosyncratic and spurious musical artist, and her relationship with the mouse community. Josefine, for all the glitz of her singing performances, really only makes the whistling sound that all mice make, many of them without even knowing it; and the mouse community for whom she performs lacks a sense of music, for their lives are too fraught with worry, danger, and terror to permit the leisure or the reflectiveness necessary for art. The mice are said to revere Josefine and her singing, yet at times they must be rounded up and coerced into attending her concerts—some given when the mood strikes her, others scheduled in advance, such as the one a day or two ago at which she failed to show up. On previous occasions she has had to be persuaded to perform, but now she has disappeared without a trace. Her habit has been to insist on and feed on the appreciation of her fellow mice even as she disdains it. She gives herself the airs of a prima donna—and yet the question is constantly posed by the narrator: is Josefine an artist at all?

Brod was responsible for the notion that the mouse nation was Kafka's metaphor for the Jewish people. This interpretation probably reflects Brod's Zionist interests more than Kafka's artistic intention, for Kafka causes his narrator to repeatedly deny any historical memory to the mouse people, whereas Jews are singularly rich in historical memory. Marxist interpretation points out that the mass, the community, endures eternally, whereas the individual, represented by Josefine, vanishes. This formulation ignores the final paragraph, which dwells on Josefine's redemption. That redemption will take place in the collective unconscious of the mouse people; she will be forgotten, yet she will have contributed to that collective unconscious.

Perhaps the interpretative line suggested by Kafka's other late stories is the most likely: the problematic authenticity of the artist in an environment not conducive to art. This interpretation makes Josefine a colleague of the hunger artist, of the narrator of "Eine kleine Frau," and of the burrower, all of them personae of the dying and not very hopeful, but still humorously ironic Kafka. It would not do to suggest that these final stories, conceived and written under the most harrowing personal circumstances, are Kafka's best. But like the best, which signal the beginning of the era of literary modernism, they enlist the reader directly, without mediation, into the work. They embrace deformation, whether physical or spiritual, as an inducement to doubt or to ambiguity; they focus on an individual who is a fictional persona of the author, who is, in turn, not Everyman, and they do all of it with ambiguity and irony that invite, but rarely validate, a single interpretation.

Bibliographies:

Rudolf Hemmerle, *Franz Kafka: Eine Bibliographie* (Munich: Lerche, 1958);

Angel Flores, *A Kafka Bibliography* (New York: Gordian Press, 1976);

Maria Luise Caputo-Mayr and Julius M. Herz, *Franz Kafkas Werke: Eine Bibliographie der Primärliteratur (1908–1980)* (Bern & Munich: Francke, 1982);

Ludwig Dietz, *Franz Kafka: Die Veröffentlichungen zu seinen Lebzeiten (1908–1924): Eine textkritische und kommentierte Bibliographie* (Heidelberg: Stiehm, 1982);

Malcolm Pasley, *Catalogue of the Kafka Centenary Exhibition 1983* (Oxford: Bodleian Library, 1983).

Biographies:

Max Brod, *Kafka: A Biography,* translated by G. Humphreys-Roberts (New York: Schocken, 1947; revised, translated by Humphreys-Roberts and Richard Winston, 1960);

Klaus Wagenbach, *Franz-Kafka: Eine Biographie seiner Jugend, 1883–1912* (Bern: Francke, 1958);

Daryl Sharp, *The Secret Raven: Conflict and Transformation in the Life of Franz Kafka* (Toronto: Inner City Books, 1980);

Ronald Hayman, *Kafka: A Biography* (New York: Oxford University Press, 1982);

Joachim Unseld, *Franz Kafka: Ein Schriftstellerleben* (Munich & Vienna: Hanser, 1982);

Rotraut Hackermüller, *Das Leben, das mich stört: Eine Dokumentation zu Kafkas letzten Jahren 1917–1924* (Vienna & Berlin: Medusa, 1984);

Ernest Pawel, *The Nightmare of Reason: A Life of Franz Kafka* (New York: Farrar, Straus & Giroux, 1984);

Klaus Wagenbach, *Franz Kafka: Pictures of a Life,* translated by Arthur S. Wensinger (New York: Pantheon, 1984).

References:

Jürg Johannes Amann, *Das Symbol Kafka: Eine Studie über den Künstler* (Bern & Munich: Francke, 1974);

Günther Anders, *Franz Kafka,* translated by A. Steer and A. K. Thorlby (London: Bowes & Bowes, 1960);

Evelyn W. Asher, *Urteil ohne Richter: Psychische Integration oder Charakterentfaltung im Werke Franz Kafkas* (New York: Lang, 1984);

Evelyn Torton Beck, *Kafka and the Yiddish Theater: Its Impact on His Work* (Madison, Milwaukee & London: University of Wisconsin Press, 1971);

Peter U. Beicken, *Franz Kafka: Eine kritische Einführung in die Forschung* (Frankfurt am Main: Athenaion, 1974);

Beicken, *Franz Kafka. Leben und Werk* (Stuttgart: Klett, 1986);

Friedrich Beiner, *Der Erzähler Franz Kafka* (Stuttgart: Kohlhammer, 1961);

Charles Bernheimer, *Flaubert and Kafka: Studies in Psychopoetic Structure* (New Haven & London: Yale University Press, 1982);

Chris Bezzel, *Kafka-Chronik* (Munich & Vienna: Hanser, 1975);

Hartmut Binder, *Kafka: Der Schaffensproze* (Frankfurt am Main: Suhrkamp, 1983);

Binder, *Kafka-Handbuch,* 2 volumes (Stuttgart: Kröner, 1979);

Binder, *Kafka in neuer Sicht* (Stuttgart: Metzler, 1976);

Binder, *Kafka-Kommentar zu den Romanen, Rezensionen, Aphorismen und zum Brief an den Vater* (Munich: Winkler, 1976);

Binder, *Kafka-Kommentar zu sämtlichen Erzählungen* (Munich: Winkler, 1975);

Binder, *Motiv und Gestaltung bei Franz Kafka* (Bonn: Bouvier, 1966);

Jürgen Born, *Franz Kafka: Kritik und Rezeption 1924–1938* (Frankfurt am Main: Fischer, 1983);

Born and others, eds., *Franz Kafka: Kritik und Rezeption zu seinen Lebzeiten* (Frankfurt am Main: Fischer, 1979);

Patrick Bridgwater, *Kafka and Nietzsche* (Bonn: Bouvier, 1974);

Max Brod, *Über Franz Kafka* (Frankfurt am Main: Fischer, 1966);

Brod, *Verzweiflung und Erlösung im Werk Franz Kafkas* (Frankfurt am Main: Fischer, 1959);

Elias Canetti, *Kafka's Other Trial: The Letters to Felice,* translated by Christopher Middleton (New York: Schocken, 1974);

Michel Carrouges, *Kafka versus Kafka,* translated by Emmett Parker (University: University of Alabama Press, 1968);

Peter Cersowsky, *"Mein ganzes Leben ist auf Literatur gerichtet": Franz Kafka im Kontext der literarischen Dekadenz* (Würzburg: Königshausen + Neumann, 1983);

Jules Chaix-Ruy, *Kafka, la peur de l'absurde* (Paris: Centurion, 1968);

Stanley Corngold, *The Commentator's Despair: The Interpretation of Kafka's "Metamorphosis"* (Port Washington, N.Y. & London: Kennikat Press, 1973);

Claude David, ed., *Franz Kafka: Themen und Problemen* (Göttingen: Vandenhoeck & Ruprecht, 1978);

Gilles Deleuze and Félix Guattari, *Kafka: Toward a Minor Literature,* translated by Dana Polan (Minneapolis: University of Minnesota Press, 1986);

Ludwig Dietz, *Franz Kafka* (Stuttgart: Metzler, 1975);

Pavel Eisner, *Franz Kafka and Prague,* translated by Lowry Nelson and René Wellek (New York: Arts, 1950);

Wilhelm Emrich, *Franz Kafka: A Critical Study of His Writings,* translated by Sheema Z. Buehne (New York: Ungar, 1968);

Rose-Marie Ferenczi, *Kafka, subjectivité, histoire et structures* (Paris: Klincksieck, 1975);

Kurt J. Fickert, *Kafka's Doubles* (Bern, Frankfurt am Main & Las Vegas: Lang, 1975);

Karl-Heinz Fingerhut, *Die Funktion der Tierfiguren im Werke Franz Kafkas* (Bonn: Bouvier, 1969);

Brigitte Flach, *Kafkas Erzählungen: Strukturanalyse und Interpretation* (Bonn: Bouvier, 1967);

Angel Flores, ed., *Explain to Me Some Stories of Kafka: Complete Texts with Explanations* (New York: Gordian Press, 1983);

Flores, ed., *The Kafka Debate: New Perspectives for Our Time* (New York: Gordian Press, 1977);

Flores, ed., *The Kafka Problem* (New York: Octagon Books, 1963);

Flores, ed., *The Problem of "The Judgment"* (New York: Gordian Press, 1977);

Flores and Homer Swander, eds., *Franz Kafka Today* (Madison: University of Wisconsin Press, 1964);

A. P. Foulkes, *The Reluctant Pessimist: A Study of Franz Kafka* (The Hague & Paris: Mouton, 1967);

Nahum N. Glatzer, *The Loves of Franz Kafka* (New York: Schocken, 1986);

Eduard Goldstücker, ed., *Franz Kafka aus Prager Sicht* (Berlin: Voltaire, 1965);

Maja Goth, *Franz Kafka et les lettres françaises* (Paris: Corti, 1956);

Ronald Gray, *Franz Kafka* (Cambridge: Cambridge University Press, 1973);

Gray, *Kafka's Castle* (Cambridge: Cambridge University Press, 1956);

Martin Greenberg, *The Terror of Art: Kafka and Modern Literature* (New York & London: Basic Books, 1968);

Karl Erich Grözinger, Stéphane Mosès, and Hans Dieter Zimmermann, eds., *Kafka und das Judentum* (Frankfurt am Main: Jüdischer Verlag bei Athenäum, 1987);

Jirí Grusa, *Franz Kafka of Prague,* translated by Eric Mosbacher (London: Secker & Warburg, 1983);

Calvin S. Hall and Richard E. Lind, *Dreams, Life, and Literature: A Study of Franz Kafka* (Chapel Hill: University of North Carolina Press, 1970);

Leo Hamalian, comp., *Franz Kafka: A Collection of Criticism* (New York: McGraw-Hill, 1974);

Günter Heintz, *Franz Kafka: Sprachreflexion als dichterische Einbildungskraft* (Würzburg: Königshausen + Neumann, 1983);

Erich Heller, introduction to *The Basic Kafka* (New York: Pocket Books, 1979);

Heller, *Franz Kafka* (New York: Viking, 1975);

Peter Heller, *Dialectics and Nihilism: Essays on Lessing, Nietzsche, Mann, and Kafka* (Amherst: University of Massachusetts Press, 1966);

Klaus Hermsdorf, *Kafka: Weltbild und Roman* (Berlin: Rütten & Loening, 1961);

John Hibberd, *Kafka in Context* (London: Studio Vista, 1975);

Hans Helmut Hiebel, *Die Zeichen des Gesetzes: Recht und Macht bei Franz Kafka* (Munich: Fink, 1983);

Heinz Hillmann, *Franz Kafka: Dichtungstheorie und Dichtungsgestalt* (Bonn: Bouvier, 1964);

Kenneth Hughes, ed. *Franz Kafka: An Anthology of Marxist Criticism,* translated by Hughes (Hanover & London: University Press of New Zealand, 1981);

Adrian Jaffe, *The Process of Kafka's "Trial"* (Lansing: Michigan State University Press, 1967);

Wolfgang Jahn, *Kafkas Roman "Der Verschollene" ("Amerika")* (Stuttgart: Metzler, 1965);

Gustav Janouch, *Conversations with Kafka,* translated by Goronwy Rees (New York: New Directions, 1969);

Harry Järv, *Die Kafka Literatur: Eine Bibliographie* (Malmö & Lund: Bo Cavefors, 1961);

Jean Jofen, *The Jewish Mystic in Kafka* (New York, Bern & Frankfurt am Main: Lang, 1987);

Norbert Kassel, *Das Groteske bei Franz Kafka* (Munich: Fink, 1969);

Lida Kirchberger, *Franz Kafka's Use of Law in Fiction* (New York, Bern & Frankfurt am Main: Lang, 1986);

Jörgen Kobs, *Kafka: Untersuchungen zu Bewutsein und Sprache seiner Gestalten,* edited by Ursula Brech (Bad Homburg: Athenäum, 1970);

Herbert Kraft, *Mondheimat-Kafka* (Pfullingen: Neske, 1983);

Franz Kuna, *Franz Kafka: Literature as Corrective Punishment* (Bloomington & London: Indiana University Press, 1974; London: Elek, 1974);

Kuna, ed., *On Kafka: Semi-Centenary Perspectives* (New York: Barnes & Noble, 1976);

Richard H. Lawson, *Franz Kafka* (New York: Ungar, 1987);

Mijal Levi, *Kafka and Anarchism* (New York: Revisionist Press, 1972);

René Marill (R. M. Albérès) and Pierre de Boisdeffre, *Kafka: The Torment of Man,* translated by Wade Baskin (New York: Philosophical Library, 1968);

Eric Marson, *Kafka's "Trial": The Case against Josef K.* (St. Lucia: University of Queensland Press, 1975);

Ramón G. Mendoza, *Outside Humanity: A Study of Kafka's Fiction* (Lanham, Md.: University Press of America, 1986);

Weiyan Meng, *Kafka und China* (Munich: Iudicium, 1986);

Modern Austrian Literature, special Kafka issue, 11, no. 3/4 (1978);

Mosaic, special Kafka issue, 3, no. 4 (1970);

Bert Nagel, *Kafka und die Weltliteratur* (Munich: Winkler, 1983);

Ralf R. Nicolai, *Ende oder Anfang: Zur Einheit der Gegensätze in Kafkas "Schloß"* (Munich: Fink, 1977);

Nicolai, *Kafkas Amerika-Roman "Der Verschollene"* (Würzburg: Königshausen + Neumann, 1981);

Margot Norris, *Beasts of the Modern Imagination: Darwin, Nietzsche, Kafka, Ernst, and Lawrence* (Baltimore: Johns Hopkins University Press, 1985);

Charles Osborne, *Kafka* (New York: Barnes & Noble, 1967);

Roy Pascal, *Kafka's Narrators: A Study of His Stories and Sketches* (Cambridge: Cambridge University Press, 1982);

Heinz Politzer, *Franz Kafka: Parable and Paradox* (Ithaca & London: Cornell University Press, 1966);

Elizabeth M. Rajec, *Namen und ihre Bedeutungen im Werke Franz Kafkas* (Bern, Frankfurt am Main & Las Vegas: Lang, 1977);

Phillip H. Rhein, *The Urge to Live: A Comparative Study of Franz Kafka's "Der Prozeß" and Albert Camus' "L'Etranger"* (Chapel Hill: University of North Carolina Press, 1964);

Helmut Richter, *Franz Kafka: Werk und Entwurf* (Berlin: Rütten & Loening, 1962);

Marthe Robert, *Franz Kafka's Loneliness,* translated by Ralph Manheim (London: Faber & Faber, 1982); republished as *As Lonely as Franz Kafka* (New York & London: Harcourt Brace Jovanovich, 1982);

Ritchie Robertson, *Kafka: Judaism, Politics, and Literature* (Oxford: Clarendon Press, 1985);

James Rolleston, *Kafka's Narrative Theater* (University Park & London: Pennsylvania State University Press, 1974);

Rolleston, ed., *Twentieth Century Interpretations of "The Trial"* (Englewood Cliffs, N.J.: Prentice-Hall, 1976);

Richard Sheppard, *On Kafka's "Castle": A Study* (New York: Barnes & Noble, 1973);

Walter H. Sokel, *Franz Kafka* (New York: Columbia University Press, 1966);

Meno Spann, *Franz Kafka* (Boston: Twayne, 1976);

Mark Spilka, *Dickens and Kafka: A Mutual Interpretation* (Bloomington: Indiana University Press, 1963);

J. P. Stern, ed., *The World of Franz Kafka* (New York: Holt, Rinehart & Winston, 1980);

Roman Struc and J. C. Yardley, eds., *Franz Kafka (1883–1983): His Craft and Thought* (Waterloo, Ont.: Wilfrid Laurier University Press, 1986);

Jörg Thalmann, *Wege zu Kafka: Eine Interpretation des Amerikaromans* (Frauenfeld & Stuttgart: Huber, 1966);

Anthony Thorlby, *Kafka: A Study* (London: Heinemann, 1972);

Ruth Tiefenbrun, *Moment of Torment: An Interpretation of Franz Kafka's Short Stories* (Carbondale & Edwardsville: Southern Illinois University Press, 1973);

Alan Udoff, ed., *Kafka and the Contemporary Critical Performance* (Bloomington: Indiana University Press, 1987);

Johannes Urzidil, *There Goes Kafka,* translated by Harold A. Basilius (Detroit: Wayne State University Press, 1968);

Martin Walser, *Versuch über Franz Kafka* (Munich: Hanser, 1961) ;

Kurt Weinberg, *Kafkas Dichtungen* (Bern & Munich: Francke, 1963);

Melvin Wilk, *The Jewish Presence in T. S. Eliot and Franz Kafka* (Atlanta: Scholars Press, 1986).

Papers:

Most of Franz Kafka's manuscript materials are in the Bodleian Library, Oxford. Two pages of "Der Verschollene" (*Amerika*) are in the Österreichische Nationalbibliothek in Vienna. Most of the "Dorfschullehrer" (Village Schoolmaster—an incomplete tale probably dating from after World War I) papers are in the Deutsches Literaturarchiv in Marbach, together with some of Kafka's letters. The letters to Felice Bauer and Milena Jesenská are in the possession of Schocken Books, New York. The manuscript of *Der Prozeß* was purchased at auction at Sotheby's in London for $1.98 million on 17 November 1988 by a West German book dealer reportedly acting on behalf of the German government. He said that the manuscript would be displayed at the Deutsches Literaturarchiv.

Georg Kaiser

(25 November 1878 – 4 June 1945)

Ernst Schürer
Pennsylvania State University

and

Wiebke Strehl
Pennsylvania State University

This entry was updated by Professor Schürer from his and Professor Strehl's entry in
DLB 124: Twentieth-Century German Dramatists, 1919–1992.

BOOKS: *Hochzeits-Chansons: Verliebte Lautenschläge oder Neue Unterlagen zu alten Vertonungen* (Magdeburg: Friese & Fuhrmann, 1905);

Die jüdische Witwe: Biblische Komödie (Berlin: Fischer, 1911);

Hyperion (Weimar: Dietsch & Brückner, 1911)—comprises *Ballade vom schönen Mädchen, La Fanciulla, Mona Lisa;*

König Hahnrei: Tragödie in fünf Akten (Berlin: Fischer, 1913);

Hyperion: Die Gabe an die Freunde (Weimar: Wagner, 1913)—comprises *Claudius, Mona Nanna;*

Der Fall des Schülers Vehgesack: Eine kleine deutsche Komödie in fünf Akten (Weimar: Wagner, 1914);

Rektor Kleist: Vier komitragische Akte (Weimar: Wagner, 1914); revised as *Rektor Kleist: Tragikomödie in vier Akten* (Berlin: Fischer, 1918);

Großbürger Möller: Ein gewinnendes Spiel in vier Akten (Weimar: Wagner, 1914); republished as *Großbürger Möller: Lustspiel in vier Akten* (Berlin: Fischer, 1915); republished as *David und Goliath: Lustspiel in vier Akten* (Potsdam: Kiepenheuer, 1921);

Der Kongress: Komödie in drei Akten (Weimar: Wagner, 1914); revised as *Der Präsident: Komödie in drei Akten* (Potsdam: Kiepenheuer, 1927);

Die Bürger von Calais: Bühnenspiel in drei Akten (Berlin: Fischer, 1914); translated by Rex Last and J. M. Ritchie as *The Burghers of Calais in Five Plays* (London: Calder & Boyars, 1970);

Europa: Spiel und Tanz in fünf Aufzügen (Berlin: Fischer, 1915);

Georg Kaiser

Der Zentaur: Komödie in fünf Aufzügen (Berlin: Fischer, 1916); revised as *Der Zentaur: Lustspiel in fünf Aufzügen* (Berlin: Fischer, 1918); revised as *Konstantin Strobel (Der Zentaur): Lustspiel in fünf Aufzügen* (Potsdam: Kiepenheuer, 1920); revised as *Marga-*

rine: Lustspiel in vier Akten (Potsdam: Kiepenheuer, 1925);

Von morgens bis mitternachts: Stück in zwei Teilen (Berlin: Fischer, 1916); translated by Ashley Dukes as *From Morn till Midnight: A Play in Seven Scenes* (London: Hendersons, 1920; New York: Brentano's, 1922);

Die Versuchung: Eine Tragödie unter jungen Leuten aus dem Ende des vorigen Jahrhunderts in fünf Akten (Berlin: Fischer, 1917);

Die Sorina: Komödie in drei Akten (Berlin: Fischer, 1917);

Die Koralle: Schauspiel in fünf Akten (Berlin: Fischer, 1917); translated by Winifred Katzin as *The Coral, in Modern Continental Plays,* edited by S. M. Tucker (New York: Harper, 1929), pp. 469–497; translated by B. J. Kenworthy as *The Coral, in Five Plays;*

Gas: Schauspiel in fünf Akten (Berlin: Fischer, 1918); translated by Hermann Scheffauer as *Gas: A Play in Five Acts* (Boston: Small, Maynard, 1924; London: Chapman & Dodd, 1924);

Das Frauenopfer: Schauspiel in drei Akten (Berlin: Fischer, 1918);

Drei Einakter: Claudius; Friedrich und Anna; Juana (Potsdam: Kiepenheuer, 1918);

Hölle, Weg, Erde: Stück in drei Teilen (Potsdam: Kiepenheuer, 1919);

Der Brand im Opernhaus: Ein Nachtstück in drei Aufzügen (Berlin: Fischer, 1919); translated by Katzin as *The Fire in the Opera House: A Nightpiece, in Eight European Plays,* edited by Katzin (New York: Brentano's, 1927), pp. 139–186;

Gas: Zweiter Teil. Schauspiel in drei Akten (Potsdam: Kiepenheuer, 1920); translated by Katzin as *Gas, Part II, in Modern Continental Plays,* edited by Tucker;

Der gerettete Alkibiades: Stück in drei Teilen (Potsdam: Kiepenheuer, 1920); translated by Bayard Quincy Morgan as *Alkibiades Saved, in An Anthology of German Expressionist Drama,* edited by Walter H. Sokel (Garden City, N.Y.: Doubleday, 1963);

Der Protagonist: Einakter (Potsdam: Kiepenheuer, 1921); translated by Hugo F. Garten as *The Protagonist, in Tulane Drama Review,* 5, no. 2 (1960); republished in *Seven Expressionist Plays,* edited by Ritchie (London: Calder & Boyars, 1969);

Noli me tangere: Stück in zwei Teilen (Potsdam: Kiepenheuer, 1922);

Kanzlist Krehler: Tragikomödie in drei Akten (Potsdam: Kiepenheuer, 1922);

Der Geist der Antike: Komödie in vier Akten (Potsdam: Kiepenheuer, 1923);

Gilles und Jeanne: Bühnenspiel in drei Teilen (Potsdam: Kiepenheuer, 1923);

Nebeneinander: Volksstück 1923 in fünf Akten (Potsdam: Kiepenheuer, 1923);

Die Flucht nach Venedig: Schauspiel in vier Akten (Berlin: Die Schmiede, 1923);

Kolportage: Komödie in einem Vorspiel und drei Akten nach zwanzig Jahren (Berlin: Die Schmiede, 1924);

Gats: Drei Akte (Potsdam: Kiepenheuer, 1925);

Zweimal Oliver: Stück in drei Teilen (Berlin: Die Schmiede, 1926);

Der mutige Seefahrer: Komödie in vier Akten (Potsdam: Kiepenheuer, 1926);

Der Zar läßt sich photographieren: Opera buffa in einem Akt, music by Kurt Weill (Vienna: Universal-Edition, 1927);

Papiermühle: Lustspiel in drei Akten (Potsdam: Kiepenheuer, 1927);

Der Präsident, Komödie in drei Akten (Potsdam: Kiepenheuer, 1927);

Oktobertag: Schauspiel in drei Akten (Potsdam: Kiepenheuer, 1928); translated by Hermann Bernstein and Adolph E. Meyer as *The Phantom Lover: A Play in Three Acts* (New York: Brentano's, 1928);

Die Lederköpfe: Schauspiel in drei Akten (Potsdam: Kiepenheuer, 1928);

Gesammelte Werke, 3 volumes (Potsdam: Kiepenheuer, 1928–1931);

Hellseherei: Gesellschaftsspiel in drei Akten (Berlin: Kiepenheuer, 1929);

Zwei Krawatten: Revuestück in neun Bildern (Berlin: Kiepenheuer, 1929);

Mississippi: Schauspiel in drei Akten (Berlin: Kiepenheuer, 1930);

Es ist genug: Roman (Berlin: Transmare, 1932);

Der Silbersee: Ein Wintermärchen in drei Akten (Berlin: Kiepenheuer, 1933);

Der Gärtner von Toulouse: Schauspiel in fünf Akten (Amsterdam: Querido, 1938);

Der Schuß in die Öffentlichkeit: Vier Akte (Amsterdam: Querido, 1939);

Rosamunde Floris: Schauspiel in drei Akten (Zurich & New York: Oprecht, 1940);

Alain und Elise: Schauspiel in drei Akten (Zurich & New York: Oprecht, 1940);

Der Soldat Tanaka: Schauspiel in drei Akten (Zurich & New York: Oprecht, 1940);

Villa Aurea: Roman (Amsterdam: Querido, 1940); translated by R. Wills Thomas as *A Villa in Sicily* (London: Dakers, 1939); translation republished as *Vera* (New York: Alliance Book Corp./ Longmans, Green, 1939);

Griechische Dramen (Zurich: Artemis, 1948)–comprises *Zweimal Amphitryon, Pygmalion, Bellerophon;*

Das Floß der Medusa, edited by Walther Huder (Cologne: Kiepenheuer & Witsch, 1963); translated by Ulrich Weisstein as *The Raft of the Medusa*, in *First Stage*, 1 (Spring 1962): 35–48;

Stücke, Erzählungen, Aufsätze, Gedichte, edited by Huder (Cologne & Berlin: Kiepenheuer & Witsch, 1966)—includes *Schellenkönig: Eine blutige Groteske; Napoleon in New Orleans: Tragikomödie in neun Bildern; Die Spieldose: Schauspiel in fünf Akten;*

Werke, 6 volumes, edited by Huder (Frankfurt am Main: Propyläen, 1970–1972)—includes in volume 5 (1972): *Singspiel zum Weihnachtsball am 2.1.1897; Faust; König Heinrich: Ein Bühnenvorgang; Die Pfarrerwahl: Ein hochzeitlich, aber gar ernst und empfindsam Spiel; Ein Feierabend: Skizze; Die melkende Kuh: Tragikomödie; Hete Donat: Drama in fünf Akten; Die Dornfelds: Eine Hauskomödie in drei Akten;* in volume 6 (1972): *Das Los des Ossian Balvesen: Komödie in fünf Akten; Adrienne Ambrossat: Schauspiel in drei Akten; Agnete: Schauspiel in drei Akten; Pferdewechsel; Vincent verkauft ein Bild: Neun Szenen; Das gordische Ei; Klawitter: Komödie in fünf Akten; Der englische Sender;*

Werke in drei Bänden, 3 volumes, edited by Klaus Kändler (Berlin & Weimar: Aufbau, 1979).

Edition in English: *Five Plays*, translated by B. J. Kenworthy, Rex W. Last, and J. M. Ritchie (London: Calder & Boyars, 1971)—comprises *From Morning to Midnight, The Burghers of Calais, The Coral, Gas I, Gas II.*

PLAY PRODUCTIONS: *Der Fall des Schülers Vehgesack,* Vienna, Neue Bühne, 11 February 1915;

Großbürger Möller, Düsseldorf, Schauspielhaus, 20 November 1915; revised as *David und Goliath,* Minden, Stadttheater, 19 March 1922;

Die Bürger von Calais, Frankfurt am Main, Neues Theater, 29 January 1917;

Die Sorina, Berlin, Lessing-Theater, 6 March 1917;

Von morgens bis mitternachts, Munich, Kammerspiele, 28 April 1917;

Die Versuchung, Hamburg, Thalia-Theater, 31 May 1917;

Der Zentaur, Frankfurt am Main, Schauspielhaus, 23 October 1917; revised as *Margarine,* Berlin, Komödienhaus, 4 September 1925;

Die Koralle, Frankfurt am Main, Neues Theater, 27 October 1917;

Rektor Kleist, Königsberg, Neues Schauspielhaus, 26 January 1918;

Das Frauenopfer, Düsseldorf, Schauspielhaus, 23 March 1918;

Drei Einakter: Claudius, Friedrich und Anna, Juana, Frankfurt am Main, Neues Theater; *Baden-Baden,* Städtische Schauspiele, 21 October 1918;

Der Brand im Opernhaus, Hamburg, Kammerspiele; Nuremberg, Intimes Theater des Stadttheaters; Berlin-Charlottenburg, Kleines Schauspielhaus, 16 November 1918;

Gas, Frankfurt am Main, Neues Theater; Düsseldorf, Schauspielhaus, 28 November 1918;

Hölle, Weg, Erde, Frankfurt am Main, Neues Theater; Munich, Kammerspiele; Berlin, Lessing-Theater, 5 December 1919;

Der gerettete Alkibiades, Munich, Residenztheater, 29 January 1920;

Gas: Zweiter Teil, Brünn, Vereinigte deutsche Theater, 29 October 1920;

Europa, music by Werner Robert Heymann, Berlin, Großes Schauspielhaus, 5 November 1920;

Die jüdische Witwe, Meiningen, Landestheater, 31 January 1921;

Kanzlist Krehler, Berlin, Kammerspiele des Deutschen Theaters, 14 February 1922;

Der Protagonist, Breslau, Lobe Theater, 16 March 1922;

Die Flucht nach Venedig, Nuremburg, Intimes Theater des Stadttheaters, 9 February 1923;

Gilles und Jeanne, Leipzig, Altes Theater, 2 June 1923;

Nebeneinander, Berlin, Die Truppe, 3 November 1923;

Kolportage, Berlin, Lessing-Theater; Frankfurt am Main, Neues Theater, 27 March 1924;

Juana, Nuremberg, Intimes Theater des Stadttheaters, 7 January 1925;

Gats, Vienna, Deutsches Volkstheater, 9 April 1925;

Der mutige Seefahrer, Dresden, Staatliches Schauspielhaus, 12 November 1925;

Der Protagonist, music by Kurt Weill, Dresden, Staatsoper, 25 March 1926;

Zweimal Oliver, Dresden, Staatliches Schauspielhaus; Krefeld, Stadttheater; Hamburg, Thalia-Theater; Karlsruhe, Landestheater; Oldenburg, Landestheater; Mannheim, Nationaltheater; Düsseldorf, Schauspielhaus, 15 April 1926;

Papiermühle, Dresden, Alberttheater; Krefeld, Stadttheater; Aachen, Stadttheater; Leipzig, Schauspielhaus, 26 January 1927;

Der Präsident, Frankfurt am Main, Schauspielhaus, 28 January 1928;

Der Zar läßt sich photographieren, music by Weill, Leipzig, Neues Theater, 18 February 1928;

Oktobertag, Hamburg, Kammerspiele, 13 March 1928;

Die Lederköpfe, Frankfurt am Main, Neues Theater, 24 November 1928;

Zwei Krawatten, music by Mischa Spolianski, Berlin, Berliner Theater, 5 September 1929;

Hellseherei, Stuttgart, Landestheater; Lübeck, Kammerspiele des Stadttheaters; Düsseldorf, Schauspielhaus; Würzburg, Stadttheater; Giessen, Stadttheater; Brieg, Stadttheater; Oldenburg, Landestheater, 19 October 1929;

Mississippi, Munich, Prinzregenten-Theater; Frankfurt am Main, Schauspielhaus; Mainz, Stadttheater; Mannheim, Nationaltheater; Darmstadt, Hessisches Landestheater; Bremen, Schauspielhaus; Kassel, Staatstheater; Magdeburg, Wilhelmstheater; Karlsruhe, Landestheater; Würzburg, Stadttheater; Hamburg, Deutsches Schauspielhaus; Stuttgart, Landestheater; Konstanz, Stadttheater; Oldenburg, Landestheater; Düsseldorf, Schauspielhaus; Dresden, Schauspielhaus, 20 September 1930;

König Hahnrei, Berlin, Staatliches Schauspielhaus, 5 May 1931;

Der Silbersee, music by Weill, Leipzig, Altes Theater; Erfurt, Stadttheater; Magdeburg, Stadttheater, 18 February 1933;

Adrienne Ambrossat, Vienna, Theater in der Josefsstadt, 5 February 1935;

Das Los des Ossian Balvesen, Vienna, Burgtheater, 26 November 1936;

Der Soldat Tanaka, Zurich, Schauspielhaus, 2 November 1940;

Die Spieldose, Basel, Stadttheater, 12 October 1943;

Zweimal Amphitryon, Zurich, Schauspielhaus, 29 April 1944;

Das Floß der Medusa, Basel, Stadttheater, 24 February 1945;

Der Gärtner von Toulouse, Mannheim, Nationaltheater, 22 December 1945;

Klawitter, Brandenburg, Städtische Bühnen, 19 September 1949;

Der Schuß in die Öffentlichkeit, Magdeburg, Städtische Bühnen, 10 December 1949;

Agnete, Mannheim, Nationaltheater, 16 December 1949;

Napoleon in New Orleans, Karlsruhe, Badisches Staatstheater, 28 January 1950;

Rosamunde Floris, Stuttgart, Kammertheater des Württembergischen Staatstheaters, 6 February 1953;

Bellerophon, Saarbrücken, Großes Haus des Stadttheaters, 21 November 1953;

Pygmalion, Munich, Studio Fink, 16 December 1953;

Alain und Elise, Frankfurt am Main, Städtische Bühnen, 1 September 1954;

Das gordische Ei, Marburg, Schauspiel, 21 November 1958;

Rosamunde Floris, Berlin, Städtische Oper, 21 September 1960.

RADIO: *Der englische Sender,* London, German Programme of the BBC, 26 November 1947.

OTHER: Georg Birnbacher, Lyonel Feininger, Walter Grammatté, Walther Ruttman, and Fritz Schaef-

ler, *Die Fibel,* text by Kaiser and Hans Theodore Joel (Darmstadt: Lang, 1921);

"Wie ich es sehe," in *Das Altenbergbuch,* edited by Egon Friedel (Leipzig, Vienna & Zurich: Wiener Graphische Werkstätte, 1921);

Iwan Goll, *Methusalem oder Der ewige Bürger,* introduction by Kaiser (Potsdam: Kiepenheuer, 1922);

"Photographie Atelier Riess," in *Das Querschnittbuch,* edited by Hermann von Wedderkop (Berlin: Propyläen, 1924), p. 232;

"Über Alexander Moissi," in *Moissi,* edited by Hans Böhm (Berlin: Eigenbrödler, 1927), p. 59;

"Der platonische Dialog," in *25 Jahre Frankfurter Schauspielhaus* (Frankfurt am Main, 1927), p. 96; translated by Bayard Quincy Morgan as "Plato as Dramatist," *Tulane Drama Review,* 7, no. 1 (1962): 188–189.

SELECTED PERIODICAL PUBLICATIONS–
UNCOLLECTED: "Notiz über mein Leben," *Das Programm: Blätter der Münchener Kammerspiele,* 3, no. 14 (1917): 4–6;

"Vorwort zu 'Die Muttergottes,'" *Das Programm: Blätter der Münchener Kammerspiele,* 3, no. 14 (1917): 13;

Die Erneuerung: Skizze für ein Drama, in *Das Programm: Blätter der Münchener Kammerspiele,* 4, no. 2 (1917): 2–4;

"Biographische Notiz," *Das Literarische Echo,* 20, no. 6 (1917): 320;

"Wedekind und seine Zeit," *BZ am Mittag,* 42, no. 60 (1918); republished as "Zum Tode Wedekinds," *Die literarische Gesellschaft,* 4, no. 7/8 (1918): 255;

"Vision und Figur," *Das junge Deutschland,* 1, no. 10 (1918): 314–315;

"Offener Brief an den Herausgeber Hans Theodor Joel," *Die neue Bücherschau,* 1, no. 3 (1919): 1–2;

"Dramatischer Dichter und Zuschauer," *Der Zuschauer: Blätter des Neuen Theaters,* 1, no. 1 (1919): 2–3;

"Mythos," *Theaterzeitung der Staatlichen Bühnen Münchens,* 1, no. 4 (1920): 8–9;

"Europa," *Blätter des Deutschen Theaters,* 7, no. 4 (1920): 5–6;

"Brief über sich selbst: Aus dem Münchener Gefängnis an Max Schach," *Das Tagebuch,* 2, no. 9 (1921): 264–267;

"Ein Dichtwerk in der Zeit," *Blätter des deutschen Theaters,* 8, no. 12 (1922): 92–93; republished as "Ein Dichterwerk in der Zeit," *Masken,* 22, no. 4 (1928): 65–66;

"Der kommende Mensch," *Hannoverscher Anzeiger,* 9 April 1922, p. 9; republished as "Dichtung und Energie," *Berliner Tageblatt,* 25 December 1923, p. 6; translated as "The Energetics of Poetry," *English Review,* 35 (December 1922): 533–537;

"Rezension zu 'Raumsturz' von Fred Antoine Anger-mayer," *Prager Presse,* 12 April 1922;

"Ein neuer Naturalismus?? Antwort auf eine Rund-frage," *Das Kunstblatt,* 6, no. 9 (1922): 406;

"Die französisch-deutsche Annäherung und die deut-schen Schriftsteller," *L'Indépendance Belge* (Brus-sels), 13 October 1922, p. 1;

"Formung von Drama," *Deutsches Bühnen-Jahrbuch,* 33 (1922): 53;

"Brief an Gustav Kiepenheuer," *Die Tabatière,* 17 Janu-ary 1923;

"Die Krise des Theaters," *Neue Freie Presse,* 2 March 1923, p. 10;

"Historientreue: Am Beispiel der Flucht nach Venedig," *Berliner Tageblatt,* 4 September 1923, p. 3;

"Der Mensch im Tunnel," *Das Kunstblatt,* 8, no. 1 (1924): 5-6; translated by Eric Bentley as "Man in the Tunnel," *Tulane Drama Review,* 7, no. 1 (1962): 194-195;

"Beitrag," *Volkszeitung Plauen,* 8 March 1924;

"Unreifezeugnis," *Volkszeitung für das Vogtland,* 20 April 1924;

"Brief an Hans Theodor Joel," *Die Kassette* (April 1924): 1;

"Gibt es noch eine Gesellschaft," *Berliner Börsen-Courier,* 25 December 1924, p. 5;

"Bericht vom Drama," *Der Zuschauer: Blätter der Salten-burg-Bühnen,* 2, no. 2 (1925): 1-3;

"Welche Stoffe liefert die Gegenwart dem Drama-tiker?," *BZ am Mittag,* 10 December 1925;

"Theater und Publikum," *Berliner Börsen-Courier,* 603 (1925): 21;

"Die zwölf unsterblichen Dichter," *Ostseezeitung,* 19 August 1926;

"Georg Kaiser und die Entstehung des deutschen Dra-mas: Ein Briefwechsel," *Das Stachelschwein,* 1 December 1926, pp. 20-21;

"Wie ein Theaterstück entsteht," *Svenska Dagbladet* (Stockholm), 19 December 1926, pp. 42-43;

"Zu Heinrich von Kleists 150. Geburtstag," *Vossische Zei-tung,* 16 October 1927;

"Zur Psychologie des dichterischen Schaffens: Inspira-tion und Arbeitsweise," *Die literarische Welt,* 4, no. 39 (1928): 4;

"Tendenz im Drama?," *Der Scheinwerfer,* 2, no. 4 (1928): 10;

"Warum ich keine Filme schreibe," *Vossische Zeitung,* 31 March 1929;

"Das Lieblingsbuch meiner Knabenjahre," *Die literarische Welt,* 5, no. 26 (1929): 3;

"Von Magdeburg nach Magdeburg," *Der Querschnitt,* 10, no. 5 (1930): 296-301;

"Brief an Karl Otto," *blickpunkt,* 4, no. 5 (1961): 30.

Georg Kaiser is best known as the leading expo-nent of German expressionism. Kaiser burst upon the German stage with his play *Die Bürger von Calais,* (pub-lished, 1914; translated as *The Burghers of Calais,* 1970) which premiered in Frankfurt am Main on 29 January 1917. During the heyday of expressionism, Kaiser's Sta-tionendramen (dramas in "stations"), such as *Von mor-gens bis mitternachts* (published, 1916; performed, 1917; translated as *From Morn till Midnight,* 1920), and his vision of modern technology in the *Gas* trilogy (1917–1920) were considered the very embodiment of the form and ideas of expressionist drama. But even after the demise of expressionism around 1923 Kaiser's suc-cess continued: during the following decade he had the largest number of premieres of any German playwright. He was not only the most widely performed but also the most controversial German playwright during the Weimar Republic, which was cut short in 1933–as was Kaiser's career–when the Nazis silenced all political and cultural dissent. They prohibited the staging of Kaiser's plays because they could not tolerate his antiauthoritar-ian views and his pacifism. For them he was a promi-nent representative of the hated Weimar Republic, which they saw as controlled by Jews and Bolsheviks. Kaiser was forced into "inner emigration"; in 1938 he went into exile in Switzerland, where he died in 1945. During those twelve years of isolation Kaiser continued writing, although there was little chance that his new dramas would be staged. He left behind an enormous number of plays as well as novels, poems, and letters. Kaiser's oeuvre mirrors the development of German lit-erature between naturalism and literature in exile–the period from 1889 to 1945. During the 1920s his come-dies found a large audience, but today he is remem-bered mainly for his expressionist plays.

Kaiser was born on 25 November 1878 in Magde-burg, the fifth of six sons of Friedrich and Antonie Anton Kaiser. An energetic and vivacious woman six-teen years younger than her husband, who was forty-nine years old at the time of Kaiser's birth, Antonie Kaiser bore most of the responsibilities for edu-cating her children; as chief agent of the Bavarian Loan Association and the Allianz insurance company, Friedrich Kaiser was on the road most of the time. The Kaisers led a comfortable bourgeois existence. Kaiser's childhood was untroubled by the friction and enmity between father and son that afflicted many expression-ists and is an important element in many of their plays, including Kaiser's *Die Koralle* (1917; translated as *The Coral,* 1929). Kaiser never said an unkind word about his father, who apparently did not have the authoritar-ian tendencies typical of the heads of bourgeois families in Wilhelmian society.

Kaiser entered elementary school in 1885 and the gymnasium three years later. He was a bright but unenthusiastic student and, although he suffered from nervous disorders, a passionate soccer player and bicyclist. He showed an early interest in literature and loved to go to the theater and the opera. He organized a literary club at the meetings of which the members presented their own poetic attempts and read the works of European classical writers as well as modern authors such as Georg Büchner, Henrik Ibsen, Jens Peter Jacobsen, Stefan George, Hugo von Hofmannsthal, Johannes Schlaf, Arno Holz, and Gerhart Hauptmann.

Kaiser developed such an aversion to the gymnasium that he left it in 1895 after attaining his Einjährige (first certificate at the end of the tenth grade) and became an apprentice in a bookshop. Appalled by the tastes of the customers, he left the bookstore in disgust and began a new apprenticeship in 1896 at an import-export firm. To get ahead in this branch of commerce he studied Italian and Spanish; it is not known whether he passed the Handlungsgehilfenprüfung (journeyman's examination). In August 1899 he sailed to Buenos Aires, where he worked as a clerk in the local office of the German electrotechnical company AEG. At night he studied philosophy and started reading the works of Fyodor Dostoyevski. Arthur Schopenhauer's subjectivism and pessimism, Friedrich Nietzsche's call for a revaluation of all values and a new, strong, and independent individual, and the humanism and love for the poor and downtrodden in Dostoyevski's works exerted a lasting influence on Kaiser. His return from South America after two years (not three, as is usually asserted) was occasioned as much by his failing health—he had contracted malaria on a horseback trip across the pampas to the Brazilian border—as by his desire for fame.

After his return to Germany, Kaiser lived with his parents and with his brothers. In 1902 he suffered a nervous breakdown and spent half a year in a sanatorium in Berlin, where he worked in the carpenter shop and in the garden. He also tried to get in touch with the literary circle around Stefan George, but without success. He did not look for a job, since he felt that he would never fit into the world of business. He believed so strongly in his mission as a poet that he accepted financial assistance from his parents and brothers and, after his marriage to Margarethe Habenicht in 1908, from his wife and in-laws as his due. His wife's dowry was substantial, and with it Kaiser bought a house at Seeheim, near Darmstadt; in addition, in 1911 he rented a villa in Weimar, the city of Johann Wolfgang von Goethe and Friedrich Schiller. He maintained that he had to live in beautiful and luxurious surroundings

to be able to write. Any doubt as to his ultimate success as a writer he suppressed rigorously.

Although Kaiser deprecates Hauptmann in his letters, it is apparent that he took Hauptmann's work as one of the models for his own early literary attempts. A good example is his sketch *Ein Feierabend* (An Evening; published, 1971), written in 1903, with an epilogue consisting of excerpts from a rather romantic poem by Holz that evokes a peaceful evening in a small town. The poem stands in sharp contrast to the depressing situation in the family of a poverty-stricken bricklayer who, after drinking, has fallen from a scaffold and seriously injured himself. All of the thematic and formal principles of naturalist drama are observed in this dramatic finger exercise. The influence of Holz and Schlaf's *Die Familie Selicke* (The Selicke Family, 1890), of Schlaf's *Meister Oelze* (Master Oelze, 1892), and of Hauptmann's plays is in evidence, as it is in Kaiser's first full-length drama, *Die melkende Kuh* (The Milking Cow; published, 1971), written in 1906. In this play Frau Roland wishes her husband to become the proprietor of the mess hall for the workers constructing the Teltow Canal near Berlin. Frau Roland is ruthless in the pursuit of her goal: she lies, manipulates her husband, blackmails the engineer, and causes the death of her father-in-law in the process. Her plans are defeated when her husband, shaken by his wife's brutality, commits suicide. In naturalistic fashion Kaiser uses dialect in his play, and his characters are determined by their environment. Society is portrayed as corrupt.

Kaiser wrote other plays in the naturalist manner that were not performed until his fame had been established through his expressionist plays. One such play, *Die Versuchung* (Temptation, 1917), written around 1910, is a tragedy dealing with the important naturalistic topic of heredity. The heroine, Karla Axthelm, is inspired by Nietzsche's doctrine of the superman. Since her husband, Albert, drinks wine and smokes cigarettes, she does not want him to be the father of her dream child. She selects for this purpose a wanderer who shuns the decadent cities with their materialism and superficiality and raves about the beauty of nature and the Nordic races. But when she learns that the father of her child does not believe in his own theories, she feels betrayed and defiled and kills herself.

The first plays by Kaiser to be performed were comedies modeled on the works of Frank Wedekind and Carl Sternheim. Nietzsche's vitalistic philosophy, with its praise of the Dionysian elements of life, elevating of instinct above intellect, and attack on the educated but narrow-minded German bourgeoisie, was brought to life in the theater by Wedekind and Sternheim, who espoused the cult of a strong life and attacked the complacency, conventions, and institutions of Wilhelmian society. In Kaiser's plays, however, the Nietzschean vitalism is often countermanded by Schopenhauer's pessimism and nihilism–his denial of the will to live and his wish for salvation in death. Kaiser often presents diametrically opposed ideas in his plays–such as Nietzsche's vitalism and Schopenhauer's pessimism, or compassion for the weak and downtrodden and admiration for the superman–without creating a synthesis.

Wedekind's *Frühlings Erwachen* (1891; translated as *The Awakening of Spring,* 1909) pioneered a topic that became rather fashionable: the attack on the outmoded and repressive school system in Wilhelmian Germany. The students in the play are driven to suicide by the bigoted attitude of their parents and the hypocrisy and brutality of their teachers. Written in 1905, Kaiser's first play to be performed, *Der Fall des Schülers Vehgesack* (Student Vehgesack's Case; published, 1914; performed, 1915), was clearly inspired by Wedekind's tragedy. But while Wedekind shows his students as victims, Kaiser's pupils are quite able to hold their own. (Kaiser probably learned more about school between 1903 and 1908, during his many stays with his brother Bruno, than he did during his own school days. Bruno, a teacher at Schulpforte near Naumburg, had students boarding with his family.) The play is a coarse and heavy-handed farce, with the stock characters found in most school comedies presented as caricatures. The students are an overworked but boisterous and merry gang; the teachers are well-meaning fools, easily duped by their students; and the teachers' wives are sexually starved and lewd. The teacher Hornemann has neglected his wife to devote all his time and financial resources to his research on Homer's *Odyssey;* she seduces Vehgesack, the student who has been ordered to accompany her on her bicycle rides. When the other lusty wives hear about Vehgesack's sexual prowess he becomes a veritable rooster in a henhouse. Hornemann wants Vehgesack expelled from school, but the principal must avoid scandal because the prince has just announced that his son will attend the institution. To placate Hornemann he finds a different reason for dismissing the student: Vehgesack has written a play, which is strictly forbidden by school regulations. Unfortunately, a publisher already has the manuscript, and, seeing in Vehgesack a new genius, he visits the school. The prince hears about Vehgesack, proclaims him the friend of his son, and extends his special protection to the student: "Es soll der König mit dem Sänger gehen!" (The king shall walk together with the poet!).

Kaiser's second play about school life, the tragicomedy *Rektor Kleist* (Principal Kleist; published, 1914; performed, 1918), written in 1905, focuses on the dichotomy between body and mind, vitality and the intellect; the influence of Nietzsche is dominant. Principal Kleist is a sensitive and intelligent but sickly hunchback who tries to hide his bodily weakness. His rival is the self-assured and vital physical education teacher Kornmüller. The plot revolves around Kornmüller's attempt to find the student responsible for throwing an inkwell against a dormitory wall. He considers Fehse the culprit, while Fehse knows that Kleist had hurled the inkwell at a caricature of himself drawn and pinned to the wall by another student. Kleist privately admits to Kornmüller that he is guilty, but Kornmüller refuses to believe him. Fehse is brought before the faculty and declares his innocence, but Kleist does not own up to his guilt since he fears the ridicule of his colleagues. When Fehse breaks down under the strain and commits suicide after confessing his guilt in a letter, Kleist announces that the culprit has been found and has passed sentence on himself. Because of this cowardly action Kleist is the real villain of the play. He is the perfect example of a Nietzschean intellectual who has recognized the relativity of all values; but he is afraid of this awareness and would prefer to be like Kornmüller, who sees everything as black and white.

In the comedy *Der Geist der Antike* (The Spirit of Antiquity; published, 1923), written in 1905, Professor Nehrkorn, the very picture of the hyperintellectual scientist who lives only for his research, suddenly realizes during excavations in Greece that his life has been one-sided and impulsively decides to start a new and more practical one. His wife, however, recognizes that Nehrkorn has only exchanged one extreme for another and must realize that a healthy balance is necessary. When Nehrkorn's invention, a superior mousetrap, turns out to be a failure, he returns to his profession.

Even more fanatical than Nehrkorn is the main character in Kaiser's grotesque comedy *Der Zentaur* (The Centaur; performed, 1917), written in 1906 and published under this title in 1916, revised as *Konstantin Strobel* in 1920, and republished as *Margarine* (performed, 1925) in 1925. In *Der Zentaur* the narrowminded and overly conscientious teacher Strobel seems devoid of all common sense. When he learns that the grandmother of his fiancée, Judith, has left them a fortune that will go to a foundation if Judith does not bear a child within one year after their wedding, Strobel naively feels duty bound to prove his masculinity by experimentation. He seduces the servant girl and is delighted when she tells him that she is expecting. Judith's petty-bourgeois father, however, is horror-struck when he hears about Strobel's affair and has his daughter break off the engagement. Strobel's mother is so disgraced by her son's immoral behavior that she dies. Strobel is dismissed from his teaching position. His sense of duty, which had won him the respect of the community, has caused his downfall: he has carried it to extremes without taking feelings and social customs into consideration. In *Konstantin Strobel* Kaiser adds a totally unexpected and grotesque ending: a rich widow hears about Strobel's affair and comes to claim this prize stud for herself; as a teacher Strobel had caused the suicide of her son by his excessive pedantry, and she marries him to have a new child. Practically all reviewers pointed to Sternheim as the spiritual father of this satire; many also noted that the idea was revolting.

Two comedies that were published and staged in 1927 and 1928, when Kaiser was in financial difficulties, were written between his return from Argentina and his marriage. *Papiermühle* (Paper Mill, 1927), written in 1905, focuses on the opportunistic critic Raymond Duchut, who is writing a study of the successful playwright Ernest Ollier. Duchut wants to prove that Ollier's most recent and unusually passionate play, *Francesca da Rimini,* is based on fact. He discovers to his mortification that his own wife, Francine, served as a model for the title character. She spent her vacation with Ollier, and the two have fallen deeply in love. The triangle is resolved when Duchut, who had only married Francine because of her good social connections, relinquishes her to Ollier. *Papiermühle* was treated harshly by the critics. *Der Präsident* (The President; published, 1927; performed, 1928), written in 1906, is also a rather flimsy comedy about an ambitious lawyer who hopes to advance his career by fighting the white-slave traffic but ends up losing his money and his daughter.

In general, Kaiser's comedies that deal with the lives of ordinary people are witty and entertaining; they can be staged successfully if they are played at a fast pace and if the dialogue is pruned carefully. Kaiser tends to be too verbose and to overdo the humor so that it degenerates into farce.

Kaiser's first play to be published commercially rather than privately printed was his "biblical comedy" *Die jüdische Witwe* (The Jewish Widow; published, 1911; performed, 1921). The legend of Judith has been treated by many playwrights, among them Friedrich Hebbel and Johann Nestroy, as a tragedy or comedy. Kaiser portrays Judith as an amoral, strong-willed, modern emancipated woman, much like the heroines of George Bernard Shaw. She is searching for a man since neither her husband, Manasse, a senile and impotent voyeur, nor the weakened defenders of the besieged city are interested in her. In desperation she visits the Assyrian camp. She is attracted to the vital, animal nature of the general Holofernes; but when the intellectual King Nebukadnezar demands Judith for himself, she kills the general, whereupon the horrified king and his army flee in terror. Judith is sent to Jerusalem to become a vestal virgin, and it seems that she will never attain her objective. But the high priest who leads her into the temple is a virile man, and her wish is ultimately fulfilled. The stage in *Die jüdische Witwe,* although still naturalistic, also has a symbolic function. In the first act, for instance, the towering structure of the temple with its huge pillars symbolizes the might of the community and the laws of Jewish society that Judith should obey. Kaiser is here well on his way to expressionist drama.

Another pseudohistorical play by Kaiser in which the language can be called expressionistic in parts is *König Hahnrei* (King Cuckold; published, 1913; performed, 1931). This play reflects the influence of neo-Romantic literature on Kaiser. Neo-Romantic artists tried to escape from the modern world of industry, big cities, social problems, and ugliness into a self-contained haven of art and a cult of aestheticism; the younger neo-Romantics called for a return to nature and for free love. All of Kaiser's works in this genre have either a garden or a room in a castle as their setting. The time is a historical or mythical past, such as ancient Greece, the Middle Ages, or the Renaissance. Three one-act plays, *Claudius* (published, 1913; originally titled *La Fanciulla,* 1911), *Friedrich und Anna* (published, 1918; also published as *Mona Lisa,* 1911, and *Monna Nanna,* 1913), and *Juana* (published, 1918), are linked thematically and stylistically; their topic is love and jealousy. Claudius, the black knight, sallies forth from his castle every night to battle imaginary rivals and loses his wife. Friedrich, on the other hand, overcomes his jealousy: instead of challenging a former lover of his bride to a duel he invites him to dinner because he had made Friedrich's wife happy at a time when Friedrich did not even know her. And Juana, caught between two friends, commits suicide so that they may remain friends and continue to pursue their careers. When the plays were produced in 1918 the critics reacted negatively to their somewhat abstract nature and to the contrived and improbable plots. *König Hahnrei* is the tragedy of King Marke, Isolde's husband. The play is a long monologue in which Marke exposes his jealousy, hatred, and frustration. He refuses to believe what he sees and creates an imaginary world in which he can live happily. While the play's setting and erotic atmosphere and the king's decadent narcissism, introspectiveness, and self-delusion are clearly neo-Romantic, Kaiser's detached attitude, ironic perspective, and tense language turn the medieval legend into a modern play.

In *Europa* (Europe; published, 1915; performed, 1920) the symbolism of color, the stylized movements, and the pantomime are already expressionistic. The play is a satire on the cult of dancing and the Jugendbewegung (youth movement) in Germany. The ending of the play shows that Kaiser was not impervious to the patriotism and militarism that engulfed the peoples of

Europe at the beginning of World War I: the warriors carry off the daughter and maidens of King Agenor, whose men have become so effeminate that they cannot defend the country. Thus, Nietzschean Dionysian vitalism triumphs over decadent aesthetic pacifism. With music by Werner Robert Heymann, the play was a great success.

In 1917 *Die Bürger von Calais* caught the attention of critics and the public in war-weary Germany as a call to pacifism and a denunciation of war. The historical background of the play is the siege of Calais by the troops of Edward III of England in 1347, during the Hundred Years' War. An English officer brings an ultimatum: the city will be spared from destruction if six citizens, in sackcloths and with a rope around their necks, turn themselves over to the English king to be executed, bringing the keys to the city with them. Duguesclins, the constable of France, is determined to fight until Calais is destroyed. His opponent is Eustache de Saint-Pierre, a wealthy merchant who pleads for submission to save the rest of the townspeople. His pacifist ethos is taken up by the other citizens. Eustache is the first to volunteer as a hostage, and six other citizens follow his example–making a total of seven, one more than the English demanded.

If Kaiser had wanted to write an historical play to celebrate the heroism of the citizens, the play could have ended there. But he saw the sacrifice as only the first step in the renewal and regeneration of the human being, a central concept of expressionism. Irrationality and the beastly aspects of human nature must be overcome by rational thinking and behavior. Eustache recognizes that the six have volunteered impulsively, that they are not yet ready to act freely, without regret, and from inner conviction. Eustache orchestrates a conversion of their thinking so that a "neuer Mensch" (new human being) will come into existence. One of the seven volunteers will be reprieved, and Eustache keeps the others–and the audience–in suspense to achieve their inner transformation. At the end of the second act the seven draw balls from an urn to determine who is to live and who is to die; but they all draw blue balls. Eustache then informs them that they have until the next morning to consider their decision, and that the one who arrives last at the marketplace shall be free.

In the final act, the other six volunteers arrive at the marketplace before Eustache. They are calm and prepared to die. The assembled citizens accuse Eustache of trying to save his own life when he does not appear. In the midst of their outcry his body is carried onto the stage, and his blind old father announces that he has committed suicide to show them the way. But the six are pardoned by the English king, to whom a

son was born during the night. Is this son a reincarnation of Eustache?

By his example and through his teaching Eustache has changed the volunteers; they have become his disciples and will help their fellow citizens establish a kingdom of peace. Eustache has not died in vain, but, like Christ, for the sins of his fellowmen. The secularized religious aspects of the play, such as the last supper of Eustache and the volunteers, the resurrection of Eustache through the birth of the king's son, and the discipleship of the volunteers led critics to refer to the play as a "Verkündigungsdrama" (drama of annunciation) or "Erlösungsdrama" (play of redemption).

The play was influenced by the operas of Richard Wagner: the settings are monumental and the stylized mass scenes have an operatic quality. The play is tightly structured; Kaiser's language is rhythmical and dynamic but rather abstract. With its pathos, this "Ideen-drama" (play of ideas) is clearly aimed at the indoctrination of the audience. Through repetitions, parallel constructions, and other rhetorical devices the message is hammered home, and it is further underscored by the setting, the lighting, and the music. The production by Arthur Hellmer at the Frankfurt am Main Neues Theater marked the beginning of the so-called Frankfurt Expressionism.

Großbürger Möller (Bourgeois Möller; published, 1914; performed, 1915), set in a small Danish town, is a tightly constructed comedy after the manner of Sternheim. All members of the Möller family except Sophus believe that they have won eight hundred thousand crowns in the lottery; unfortunately, Sophus has not played the number for the last ten years, instead spending the money collected for the ticket on the musical education of his daughter, Dagmar. He pretends, however, that the money will be coming their way, and all start carrying out their plans as if they were already in possession of the wealth. The brewery owner Magnussen hears about their windfall and sets out to lay his hands on the money. Sophus, however, manipulates him in such a deft manner that in the end everybody has reached his or her goal except Magnussen: he has spent his money in the hope of being richer in the end by eight hundred thousand crowns, only to learn that Sophus's ten-year-old lottery ticket has expired. In danger of becoming the laughingstock of the community, he has to make the best of a bad situation and acquiesce in Sophus's plans. His son Axel, however, is overjoyed, since he loves Dagmar but had vowed never to marry a rich girl. The play has been staged successfully many times.

Von morgens bis mitternachts and two later plays, *Kanzlist Krehler* (Clerk Krehler, 1922) and *Nebeneinander* (Side by Side, 1923), were linked by Kaiser, who called them a trilogy connected by characters but not by plot. The main characters of the three plays—the Kassierer (cashier), the Kanzlist, and the Pfandleiher (pawnbroker)—are men who one day realize that life has passed them by. Their reactions to this realization are so exaggerated that the plays take on tragicomic aspects.

Van morgens bis mitternachts was Kaiser's first Stationendrama; with Reinhard Sorge's *Der Bettler* (The Beggar, 1912) and Walter Hasenclever's *Der Sohn* (The Son, 1914) it is one of the first examples of this genre. In such plays the central character is living a meaningless existence when he suddenly receives an Anstoß (impetus), which leads to his Aufbruch (departure) to a new Ziel (goal). On his Weg (way) to this more or less nebulous goal he goes through many stations led by his vision of a new meaning in life. His action is as much a Flucht (flight) from his past as it is a Marsch (march) to a better future. In the end, the goal eludes his grasp; but the search is more important than the goal. The action of the play is seen through the eyes of the central character; Stationendramen are subjective. The characters are types—they do not have names but carry generic designations such as "Kassierer," "Frau" (wife), "Mutter" (mother), "Tochter" (daughter), and "Dame" (lady) that point to their position in the social environment.

In *Von morgens bis mitternachts* the monotonous and machinelike life of the cashier is changed when a beautiful Italian lady comes into the bank to withdraw three thousand marks. He and the bank director consider her an impostor intent on defrauding the bank. This incident is the beginning of a series of events that will lead to the cashier's death. He takes sixty thousand marks and goes to the lady, planning to flee with her to start a new life. But he soon realizes that she is not a confidence woman but a respectable rich widow traveling with her son, an art historian, who needs the money to buy a painting he has discovered. It is too late for the cashier to return to the bank and confess his mistake. Crossing a snowfield, he sees what appears to be a skeleton formed by the bare branches of a tree—a memento mori. But he knows the value of the money he has embezzled and believes that he can master his fate, and he defiantly challenges the Grim Reaper to return at midnight.

The cashier's respectable bourgeois family is disturbed when he returns home earlier than usual. He relates his experience of a rebirth on the snowfield, but the allegory is lost on the family; they are only interested in getting him back into his old image with his slippers, long pipe, and nightcap, the symbolic utensils of the German philistine. When he takes a forceful leave before lunch his old mother becomes so upset that she dies of a heart attack.

The cashier departs from his provincial town and travels to the big city; he leaves the private sphere of workplace and family and enters the public world of sports, politics, amusement, and religion. His next station is a six-day bicycle race where he gets the idea that by betting on the racers he will drive the spectators into unrestrained behavior; he desires to experience passionate life at least vicariously. But the ecstasy of the crowd is cut short when the crown prince appears and the national anthem is played. The cashier leaves the race disappointed: tradition is stronger than vibrant life. He goes to a private room in a cabaret, but his desire for sensual pleasures is disappointed as well. The last stage in his desperate journey is the Salvation Army, where he hears the confessions of various sinners and recognizes them as his own. When he confesses and throws the money into the prayer hall, a wild scramble ensues in which everybody grabs what he or she can and flees. The cashier's last hope is the Salvation Army girl, but she turns him over to the police for the reward.

Now the cashier has his second vision of death; this time he sees no escape, and he shoots himself. His journey toward redemption and renewal had to remain unsuccessful because he was only looking for self-realization without consideration for anyone else. He was also following his accustomed thought patterns by trying to buy immaterial goods that cannot be purchased. He drew the conclusion that money is worthless and that there is nothing to live for; he did not recognize the purely functional value of money.

Thematically, *Von morgens bis mitternachts* is a Wandlungsdrama (play of regeneration). Although the cashier does not achieve such a regeneration, the audience can learn from his mistakes. This aspect of the play appealed to Bertolt Brecht, who considered Kaiser one of his teachers. The play was successfully produced by the director of the Munich Kammerspiele (Intimate Theater), Otto Falckenberg, on 28 April 1917. It was later performed in many other German theaters and was translated and produced all over the world. A film version was also released.

In *Kanzlist Krehler* the title character is thrown out of his sterile routine when he is given a Monday off following the wedding of his daughter, Ida. Since he has never experienced a free weekday he becomes disoriented; he cannot even find his way home. This experience makes him realize that he is in a rut and is not really alive any more, and it inspires him to try to make a new start: he wants to give up his job and his pension and face the adventures the globe—an important symbolic stage prop—seems to offer. But his wife rejects his ideas and wants him back to normal. She gets support from Krehler's boss, who does not want to lose a valuable employee; he tells Krehler the story of the cashier from *Von morgens bis mitternachts*. Krehler realizes that he is no longer young and that rebirth is impossible, but he does not want to go back to his old life. He turns his desperation and anger against his wife, accusing her of having stolen his life. He wants her to die with him. When she refuses he kills his son-in-law by throwing him off the balcony of a high rise before following him into death. Because of its mixture of naturalistic and expressionistic elements the work did not find favor in the eyes of most critics, who considered it too abstract and contrived.

In the last play in the trilogy, *Nebeneinander,* three plots unfold simultaneously; they are connected only through a letter. The main plot revolves around the pawnbroker and his daughter, who find the letter in a suit that has been pawned. The address has been obliterated, but they read that the intended recipient of the letter, a woman named Lu, is threatening suicide. They try to find her to deliver the letter. In the process they lose their business, and they take their own lives. In the second plot Lu receives a copy of the letter since the man who had written it realized that he left the original in the suit that he took to the pawnbroker. She leaves the city, finds a new life, and finally marries a friend of her sister. In the third plot the man who wrote the letter, Neumann, becomes the director of a film company.

The title and structure of the play are intended to show that society has fallen apart, that people live isolated existences. The play gives dramatic expression to the misery and the economic and moral degradation brought on by a lost war, inflation, corruption, and opportunism. The alienated individual finds no support structure in the lonely crowd, where everybody is intent only on his or her own survival. The pawnbroker, who has exploited the misery of others, is suddenly transformed into a neuer Mensch and sets out to save a fellow human being. He has experienced a moral rebirth, but people do not understand him. Like the cashier in *Von morgens bis mitternachts* he goes from station to station, but in contrast to the cashier he acts for unselfish and humanitarian reasons. His expressionist passion comes to the same end as that of the cashier, but at least he dies with his daughter and not alone. The Lu plot, on the other hand, has a Hollywood happy ending in the idyllic countryside far from the hectic modern city. For Neumann, the unscrupulous and amoral but witty and vital entrepreneur, the city is the ideal backdrop. His phenomenal rise in the new world of the film is matched in the personal sphere by his conquest of a beautiful film star. Both he and Lu find the happiness they have been looking for. The audience in Berlin wildly applauded the Neumann character; the expressionist era was drawing to a close, and the public was tired of being preached to.

Die Sorina (1917) is a satire in the tradition of Nikolay Gogol and Anton Chekhov on corrupt petty bureaucracy in Russia. The setting is a provincial Russian town, and the plot is predictable. The police inspector Barssukoff courts the famous actress Sorina. He tries to subject her to his will by using his authority to ban all plays with a part she could play. Sorina is saved by the dashing young playwright Barin, who is loved by Barssukoff's wife. In the end the Barssukoffs are duped, and the lovers leave town.

Die Koralle; Gas (1918; translated 1924); and *Gas: Zweiter Teil* (1920; translated as *Gas, Part II,* 1929) constitute a trilogy. The principal characters belong to four generations of the family of the Milliardär (billionaire), and the plays cover a period of about seventy years. In *Die Koralle* the protagonist is the billionaire, who rules over a vast industrial empire and ruthlessly exploits his laborers but acts like a philanthropist by endowing hospitals, schools, and convalescent homes. Every Thursday he holds an open house at which people can come and ask for help, which is usually granted. But the billionaire does not want to be reminded of his own poverty-stricken past, and therefore his identical double, his secretary, takes his place. A coral attached to the secretary's watch chain identifies him to the billionaire's bodyguards. Not even the billionaire's children know about this double. For them the billionaire tries to arrange a happy and carefree life to protect them from traumatic experiences such as he suffered on the way to the top. In his children he vicariously experiences a sunny youth without worries. But the billionaire's plans go awry. His son chooses to become a stoker on a steamer and learns about hard work and exploitation, and his daughter decides to serve the needy by becoming a nurse. When his son admits that he almost killed his father because of the latter's brutality in suppressing a workers' protest after an explosion in the mines, the billionaire is deeply shaken and considers suicide; but when he hears about the secretary's happy childhood he shoots him and takes his identity by clipping the coral to his own watch chain. He is arrested and signs a statement that he is the secretary; he has exchanged the secretary's happy past for his own nightmarish childhood and youth, and he is willing to die for this happiness. His last three visitors before the execution—his son, a socialist, and a priest—cannot help him, since joining his son's struggle for a better life or the socialist movement would be as much a betrayal of his philosophy as to believe in God. That philosophy is molded by Schopenhauer's idea that the individual is separated from nature and suffers accordingly; only through abnegation of the will and negation of life will the pain be alleviated and the individual become part of the universe again.

Die Koralle was hailed as a truly expressionist drama, and its powerful poetic language was praised. But while the social concerns of the first three acts were easy to understand, the psychological problems of the protagonist and the complex symbolism of the last two acts confused many critics. Most directors were not yet familiar with the language and style of expressionism, resulting in attempts to present Kaiser's play in a realistic manner.

In *Gas* the billionaire's son now owns his father's factories. He has put his socialist ideas into practice and shares all profits with the workers. The firm's product is gas, a source of energy that has become indispensable for the economies of the world's industrial nations. But it is also potentially destructive, and one day a devastating explosion destroys the main plant and kills many workers. The survivors regard the Ingenieur (engineer) as responsible for the explosion and want him fired before they will return to work. The son thinks that they have become slaves of their machines and have lost their human nature; he wants them to return to a simple life in the country. But the engineer convinces the workers that they cannot turn their backs on industrial progress and become peasants again. They decide to follow him back into the factory, but the billionaire's son has locked them out. At this point the government steps in since it needs gas for the production of weapons. The only hope at the end of the play comes from the daughter of the billionaire's son, who promises to give birth to the New Man.

The protagonist in *Gas: Zweiter Teil* is this New Human Being, the great-grandson of the billionaire, called the *Milliardärarbeiter* (billionaire-worker). He does not own the factories but is a moral leader. The world is now divided into two camps, the *Gelbfiguren* (Yellows) and the *Blaufiguren* (Blues), who are engaged in an arms race and a war of attrition that can only end in total destruction unless there is a spiritual reorientation of humanity. When the workers proclaim a general strike, the billionaire-worker hopes to convince the enemy to conclude a peace treaty. But the Yellow forces occupy the country and force the workers to return to their soul-killing jobs. In the final act the chief engineer incites the workers to rebellion: he has invented poison gas and urges them to use it against their oppressors even if it means total annihilation. The billionaire-worker urges them to submit and calls for a spiritual renewal, but the masses continue to follow the chief engineer. In desperation the billionaire-worker drops the ball containing the poison gas among the workers, and the world is annihilated.

The isolation and alienation of the characters in the trilogy are expressed through their language. The engineer is concerned with formulas, control stations, machines, and the production of gas, while the capitalists speak of strikes, profits, losses, and meetings. In *Gas: Zweiter Teil* the vocabulary of most of the figures has become extremely limited, consisting of a few basic words. Only the speeches of the protagonists rise above this abstract style and at times even show a lyrical quality. Stage settings and color are used in a symbolic manner; in *Gas: Zweiter Teil* the workers wear either blue or yellow—they have become uniform and have lost their multicolored liveliness.

The theme of these plays is the unpreparedness of the masses for regeneration, an unpreparedness that causes their extinction. It is the enlightened leader who must chart the course for the workers, but they refuse to follow his ideas. Kaiser, whose idea of leadership was based on his reading of the workers of Nietzsche never had the faith in the intelligence of the masses that other expressionists professed.

In the *Gas* trilogy Kaiser portrays the inhumanity and injustice of capitalist Wilhelmian society toward the less-privileged classes, and he shows the military-industrial complex of European society that was responsible for World War I. But more important is Kaiser's vision of the dehumanization of an industrial society and the dangers inherent in an unchecked growth of technology. The *Gas* trilogy has remained topical; Fritz Lang's film *Metropolis* (1927) is based on it, and following the atomic accidents at Three Mile Island in Pennsylvania in 1979 and at Chernobyl in the Soviet Union in 1986 there were revivals of the plays.

A group of nine plays by Kaiser can be called "Frauenstücke" (plays about women). They are written for small casts in intimate theaters; the backgrounds are usually artificial settings, such as greenhouses or winter gardens; they are centered around female protagonists who are isolated and live in a fantasy world; and the protagonists do anything to protect the world of their dreams, even commit murder. Kaiser poses the problem of subjective and objective truth, and in most cases the illusion emerges triumphant. The plots revolve around the relationship between a woman and a man, and absolute love and the purity of the woman are seen as the ideal.

In the earliest play in this group, *Das Frauenopfer* (Sacrifice of a Woman, 1918), the wife of Count Lavalette, one of Napoleon's generals, changes places with her imprisoned husband to save him from execution after the fall of Napoleon. He had married her on the orders of the emperor; now, when he sees her sacrifice, he realizes how much she loves him. He eagerly awaits her release so that they may start a new life together. But when they are reunited and she tells him that she had given herself frequently to the guards to buy their silence, he is repelled and calls her a whore. He cannot accept her actions as a sacrifice performed on his behalf, and he wants to return to prison. To rescue him a second time she tells him that she did not save him for love but because she wanted him to become emperor so that she could be empress. He now hates her, and he decides to join Napoleon, who has returned from Elba. His wife disguises herself as her husband a second time and is shot by the gendarmes who are looking for the escaped prisoner. With her dying words she condemns Lavalette because he had never been ready to live only for her as she was ready to suffer and die for him. When Lavalette realizes what she has done for him he can no longer fight for Napoleon. He ends up a lonely man who, however, now has an understanding of true human values. The critics could not make up their minds whether or not the play was an expressionistic work; they objected to the countess's explicit description of a rape; and they found fault with the overly complex and contrived plot and the stilted language. The controversy seems to have kept the play from being forgotten, and by the time it was staged in Berlin in 1923 the critics praised it as one of Kaiser's best dramas.

Der Brand im Opernhaus, (performed, 1918; published, 1919; translated as *The Fire in the Opera House,* 1927) has as its background the burning of the Paris Opera in 1763. The play centers around the orphan girl Sylvette and her husband, who has retired from the decadent life of the rich upper class at the time of Louis XV. He lives isolated with his wife, whom he had married because of her chastity and purity. On the evening of the fire he learns that his wife has led a promiscuous life. When she confesses to her husband after escaping from the fire at the opera house, where she was attending a ball, he refuses to recognize her. He clings to his belief in her purity and pretends that she died in the fire. He orders his servants to bring to his house the body of any woman killed in the fire, which he will then claim to be his wife. But, when the body is identified as the king's mistress by a ring she is wearing, he persuades Sylvette to put on the ring and jump into the flames to purify herself. He wants to go on believing in the purity of his wife.

Hölle, Weg, Erde (Hell, Way, Earth, 1919), based on a sketch by Kaiser titled *Die Erneuerung* (Regeneration, 1917), revolves around an artist's desire to lead the masses in Nietzschean fashion and the expressionist visionary longing for the brotherhood of all mankind. The protagonist, Spazierer, is a wanderer on his "way" from "hell" to "earth." When the friend he is trying to help kills himself, Spazierer tries to press charges against a rich woman who had the means to save him but refused to do so. But nobody takes him seriously. In desperation he stabs a jeweler, considering him

responsible for a society that is consumer-oriented instead of stressing human concerns. This act of violence makes people think about social conditions, and when Spazierer leaves prison after serving his sentence for attempted murder he finds a changed world. Now all feel guilty and innocent at the same time since they are all victims of society, and all want to give up their old lives and start anew. After crossing a bridge they arrive on a stony plain, where, under the rays of the morning sun, they are going to build a new society. Even if the road is rocky and the work hard, regenerated humanity will establish paradise on earth. The critics called *Hölle, Weg, Erde* one of Kaiser's weakest dramas; they especially criticized the language, which is mechanistic and impersonal and does not change during the course of the play.

In spite of his success as a playwright and the help of his relatives, Kaiser's debts mounted during and after World War I. His son Dante Anselm had been born in 1914; Laurent followed in 1918; and a daughter, Eva Sybille, was born in 1919. Kaiser's expenses were rising, but he and his wife were not willing to change their lifestyle, and they lost their houses in Seeheim and Weimar in 1918 and were forced to live in rented apartments and later a furnished country house. To meet living expenses Kaiser sold or pawned furniture and art objects.

In *Der gerettete Alkibiades* (1920; translated as *Alkibiades Saved,* 1963), Kaiser questions the traditional portrayal of Socrates. Since knowledge of the ancient Greek language and Greek history and philosophy were the foundation of a German classical education, Kaiser's view was sharply attacked. The playwright boasted that he had toppled Goethe's and Johann Joachim Winckelmann's interpretation of classical Greece as the land of noble simplicity and serene grandeur. Alkibiades, the ideal of strength and beauty, is contrasted with Socrates, the great thinker. During a battle Socrates saves Alkibiades; Socrates was only in the battle because he stepped on a thorn and could not flee like the others, but he claims that it was his superior intellectual powers that enabled him to save the stronger man. Vitality is discredited. Now Socrates has to hide the fact that it was not his intelligence but the weakness of his body that had induced him to fight. In consequence, he has to invent new philosophical interpretations for all phenomena that confront him. When he is condemned to death he looks forward to it: only in the separation of his soul from his body can he achieve the synthesis of vitality and intellect.

In October 1920 Kaiser was arrested in Berlin and charged with embezzlement. He was transferred to a prison in Munich, where he was examined for weeks in the psychiatric ward. Before the court Kaiser identified himself with Georg Büchner and Heinrich von Kleist, great German writers who had also suffered persecution. He maintained that the laws did not apply to him, that as a genius he stood above the common crowd. He saw himself as an instrument for the creation of great works of art that benefited all of humanity. What he had done was not criminal because he had done it not for himself or his family but for his work, which had to be created at all costs. In February 1921 he was sentenced to a year in prison, but he was released after serving six months—including the time since his arrest—and placed on probation for the remaining half of his sentence. On his release Kaiser settled in Grünheide, a suburb of Berlin.

The conflict between "Schein" (illusion) and "Sein" (reality) that dominates Kaiser's Frauenstücke becomes the main topic in his Künstlerdramen (plays about artists). The first of these Künstlerdramen is the one-act play *Der Protagonist* (published, 1921; performed, 1922; translated as *The Protagonist,* 1960), in which an actor is unable to distinguish between the roles he plays and his real life. His sister is the only one who can call him back to the real world because he has complete trust in her. One evening after he has acted in a comedy she tells him that she has a lover. The brother, in a good mood from a happy play, wants to meet him. While the sister goes to get her lover, the actor is asked by his patron to perform the role of a jealous husband in another play. When his sister returns he confuses her with his faithless wife in the play and stabs her. In her dying moments she brings him back to reality one last time. He asks his patron not to have him arrested until after that evening's performance, when he will play his part so convincingly that nobody will be able to draw the line between real and feigned madness. The actor had tried to sublimate his incestuous feelings for his sister by turning her into a paragon of virtue and chastity. When she destroyed his idea of her by behaving like a normal woman he killed her and took refuge in madness.

In 1926 Kurt Weill—a student of Ferruccio Busoni, who had revitalized modern opera—set *Der Protagonist* to music. He stayed in Kaiser's home in Grünheide and there met his future wife, Lotte Lenya. The opera was staged successfully in March 1926 at the Dresden Staatsoper.

In prison Kaiser had sketched *Noli me tangere* (Do Not Touch Me; published, 1922). The story of Jesus' betrayal by Judas is presented here in the utmost abstract expressionist fashion; none of the characters has a name. A prison is the place of action, and prisoners 5, 15, and 16 are the main protagonists. 5 was arrested when he tried to steal some carrots because he was hungry; 15 is a well-dressed bourgeois artist; and 16 is the Christ figure. With the arrival of 16 there is one prisoner too many in the cell, which is meant to hold only twelve inmates. The beginning of part 2 shows the prisoners at dinner—a kind of Last Supper. When it is time to sleep, 16 does not have a bed. 16 tries to convince 15 that poets have to set attainable goals and must become part of the people again. 15 offers 16 his bed and in return receives 16's coat. With this exchange a personality change takes place and 15 becomes Christ-like. The change of coat leads to the release of 15, who is mistaken for 16. 5, who has witnessed the exchange, tells the guards the truth for some food. 16 is taken away and punished, and 5 commits suicide. With this play Kaiser repudiates his previous utopian expressionist plays. He pleads for a more realistic approach to a better society through love of one's neighbor and decent behavior. It is not sufficient to have a vague idea of the good society; one must also have the means and concrete plans for building this new kingdom. Kaiser's play is so abstract that it is almost unintelligible; it has never been performed.

Gilles und Jeanne (1923) is based on the Jeanne d'Arc legend. The main character is Gilles de Rais, who in the course of the play is transformed into a neuer Mensch. Gilles is erotically obsessed with Jeanne, who rejects him; he therefore causes her death at the stake by accusing her of witchcraft. Later he kills six innocent young women who are presented to him under the pretense that they are Jeanne brought back to life. He defends himself before the same church court that sentenced Jeanne and is acquitted for lack of evidence; but as he leaves he has a vision of Jeanne in her silver armor. He suddenly confesses and, feeling that he has been saved, gladly submits to his execution. Through his confession Gilles has been not only redeemed but has been elevated above the common people and has become a second Christ. One can consider the play Kaiser's contribution to the mystical trend in expressionism represented by Ernst Barlach. When the play was performed in 1923 and 1924 in Leipzig and Berlin it had mostly negative reviews; the illogical plot and the exaggerated language met with general disapproval.

In the Künstlerdrama *Die Flucht nach Venedig* (The Flight to Venice, 1923) the central figures are the writers George Sand and Alfred de Musset. Musset has left Paris and his lover, George Sand, because he feels exploited by the way she integrates all her experiences, including her love affairs, into her works. He also cannot cope with her bisexual nature, which is expressed in her pseudonym. George Sand, who is desired by men and women alike, follows Musset to Venice, accompanied by a German girl who loves her. Musset confronts George Sand with the accusation that she is exposing his deepest feelings for the whole world to read about.

Torn between his love and his revulsion for her, he collapses. George Sand is deeply shaken and wants to prove to herself and to Musset that she can love with total self-abandonment. The young Italian doctor summoned to tend Musset becomes the object of her experiment. She wins him from his English lover, then spends the night with him. In the morning the husband of the Englishwoman arrives to challenge the doctor to a duel, but George Sand convinces him that his wife did not betray him because she was so filled with her new love that the outside world ceased to exist for her. She then tells Musset that she herself experienced this feeling when she slept with the doctor. Musset takes his revenge by asking her to narrate her experiences; the doctor is thus transformed into a literary figure, and when he returns she no longer loves him. George Sand leaves to continue her career, leaving her two lovers behind. The play closes with the doctor's line: "Das Wort tötet das Leben" (The word [literature] kills life).

Kolportage (Colportage, 1924) is a tightly constructed satire on bourgeois life and the literary trends of the time—especially "Trivialliteratur"—set in Sweden. It centers around the exchange of a count's son for the son of a beggar woman to prove that class behavior is not genetically acquired but learned. In the end the once-poor Acke, who is now the noble heir to the Stjernenhö estate, begins a new life with his love, Alice. They depart for America, where there are no class distinctions and everyone can make an honest living. Erik, the count's son, has become a wealthy American businessman who is only interested in making his money work for the good of society. The play was successful because the audience enjoyed the humor and the clichés about the arrogant Swedish aristocracy, the wealthy American, and the good-hearted proletarian mother, and because the plot is not as convoluted and contrived as most of Kaiser's others.

With *Nebeneinander* and *Kolportage* Kaiser moved away from his expressionist excesses to a kind of idealistic realism. It is with these plays that he finally conquered Berlin, and they continued to be produced throughout the 1920s. In 1935 the plot of *Kolportage* was used as a scenario for a film titled *Familienparade* (Family Parade). The banning of Kaiser's works two years earlier prevented his name from being mentioned in connection with the film. *Kolportage* experienced a renaissance after 1945.

Gats (1925) focuses on the problem of overpopulation. The Kapitän der Union für weltweiche Kolonalization (captain of the Union for Worldwide Colonization) has been sent out to look for new land for the masses of the unemployed. When he returns he announces that he has found a better solution in the form of a drink called "gats" that induces infertility. In a civilization he

discovered in the jungle gats is administered to newly-wed couples once a certain population size has been reached. He proposes that the settlers give up the colonization idea in favor of sterilization. But they have dreams of owning land and having families, and they rise in rebellion against the captain and try to kill him. The riots are suppressed by the military, but the captain has to go into hiding. He administers gats to the woman he loves; but when he tells her what he has done, her love turns to hate, and she hands him over to the police. They are not able to protect him and he is lynched by an angry mob. Birth control is a sound idea, but the captain is a radical and megalomanic like most of Kaiser's reformers and does not take human feelings into account. The captain fails to consider that the settlers want children; he also offends the settlers' sense of justice by placing the burden of sterilization on the shoulders of the poor while permitting the rich to have as many children as they wish. Since Gats so clearly resembles Kaiser's expressionist plays, most critics compared it unfavorably to these plays. The drama is of interest today, however, because of its topical themes of birth control, overpopulation, and exploitation of the poor by the rich and of the underdeveloped countries by the industrial nations.

In the comedy *Der mutige Seefahrer* (The Brave Seafarer; performed, 1925; published, 1926) three Danish brothers learn that they will inherit the fortune of a schoolmate who has grown rich in America if one of them travels across the Atlantic to visit the dying friend before his end. Lars goes, but his ship is lost with no survivors. The friend regains his health and travels to Denmark to share his wealth with the two surviving brothers and Lars's family. But Lars is alive: he never boarded the ship because of his fear of the ocean. He decides to disappear for good so that his relatives may benefit from the American money. In the end, however, everything turns out happily.

The protagonist in Kaiser's Künstlerdrama *Zweimal Oliver* (Two Olivers, 1926) is an actor who flees the world of reality and takes on a double identity. He is unemployed on the stage but is being paid for playing the lover of a rich woman named Olivia. He cannot tell his insanely jealous wife how he is earning the money. With his problems mounting he withdraws more and more into a dream world. He falls in love with Olivia, and when a rival appears he decides to commit suicide. In reality, however, he shoots his rival and escapes into madness. In an insane asylum he becomes the czar of Russia.

Following the success of *Der Protagonist,* Kaiser asked Weill to write the music for a one-act comic opera titled *Der Zar läßt sich photographieren* (The Czar Has His Picture Taken; published, 1927; performed, 1928). On a visit to Paris the czar goes to a famous photographer to have a portrait of himself made. Meanwhile, a group of Russian conspirators who are looking for a chance to assassinate the ruler have occupied the photographer's studio. One of them, Angèle, takes the photographer's place and hides a gun in the camera. The czar, however, turns out to be a pleasant man and starts flirting with Angèle. She cannot force herself to pull the trigger and is apprehended by the police, who have learned of the plan. Humanity triumphs over politics.

Oktobertag (October Day, 1928; translated as *The Phantom Lover,* 1928) is another of Kaiser's Frauenstücke. Catherine is expecting a child but does not want to reveal the name of the father. In childbirth, however, she screams out the name Jean-Marc Marrien. Her uncle finds the man, a lieutenant from a good family, and questions him about the night Catherine claims to have spent with him. Marrien at first asserts that he does not know her, but she finally convinces him of her love. He agrees to marry her and consider himself the father of the child. The real father, the butcher Leguerche, claims paternity and tries to blackmail the family. Marrien kills him, and he and Catherine retire into a fantasy world.

Kaiser's antimilitaristic play *Die Lederköpfe* (The Leatherheads, 1928) is based on the siege and conquest of Babylon by the Persian King Darius as told by Herodotus. Zopyrus, one of the Persian officers, mutilates himself in such a horrible manner that he has to wear a leather hood at all times. He pretends to desert to the Babylonians, whom he convinces that he has been mistreated by Darius. He distinguishes himself in the defense of the city until he is able to secretly admit the Persians. Darius is so delighted with the success of his "Feldhauptmann" (field commander) that he wants to turn all his soldiers into "Leatherheads." He also promises his daughter to Zopyrus. But she rejects him, telling him that he has forfeited his humanity for military glory. Struck by her accusations, Zopyrus realizes his guilt and sacrifices himself by leading an uprising in which both he and Darius are killed. The play ends with the daughter's appeal to the soldiers to join forces with the townspeople to rebuild the destroyed city. Kaiser's expressionist treatment of Herodotus did not find favor with the audience or the critics; his expressionist pathos, his rather general condemnation of tyranny, and his call for a more humanistic attitude were considered superficial. The Nazis attacked Kaiser for his pacifism. *Die Lederköpfe* played mainly in the provinces.

Hellseherei (Clairvoyance, 1929) is another Frauenstück. With the help of the clairvoyant Sneederhan, Vera wins back the love of her husband, Viktor, an architect who had an affair with a client. In contrast to Catherine in *Oktobertag,* Vera lives in the real world and does not try to flee it. When she is confronted with the truth about her husband's affair by his lover she accepts the facts and takes steps that will prevent further problems. The critics dismissed the play as trite, superficial, and boring.

After finishing the score for *Der Zar läßt sich photographieren,* Weill collaborated with Bertolt Brecht on *Die Dreigroschenoper* (published, 1929; translated as *The Threepenny Opera,* 1964), which became the great Berlin hit of 1928. For his next musical, *Zwei Krawatten,* (Two Neckties, 1929) Kaiser turned to Mischa Spolianski, a popular composer. The revue features a love story that includes a winning lottery ticket, an inheritance, and a comparison of Europe and America. Although Jean is successful beyond all dreams in the land of unlimited opportunities and is set to marry Mabel, a rich American heiress, he suddenly remembers Trude, his true love, and returns to her. His loyalty is richly rewarded, since Trude has also just inherited a fortune. The play was a popular success because of the lavish production it received. It featured dancing girls and variety acts and included actors such as Hans Albers and Marlene Dietrich and the dancer Sammy Lewis. The critics did not know whether Kaiser's intent was a parody like *Kolportage* or whether he was simply presenting a Volksstück (folk play). Spolianski's music also came in for criticism, and the lack of political content was noted.

Zwei Krawatten was produced one month before the stock-market crash in 1929. After a peaceful and prosperous interval between 1924 and 1929 the economic situation in Germany deteriorated rapidly, millions of people became unemployed, and Communists and Nazis battled each other in the streets. Kaiser's *Mississippi* (1930), which premiered at sixteen theaters simultaneously, was inspired by a newspaper article which Kaiser had read about a flood that threatened New Orleans; indirectly, it was influenced by the economic crisis. Doris Thompson had divorced her husband, Noel Kehoe, because of his religious fanaticism and his call to Franciscan poverty. Noel's religiously inspired experiment in communal living has been going on for twelve years. He and the other members of the "Bruderschaft der freiwilligen Armut" (Brotherhood of Voluntary Poverty) have rejected greed and materialism and have established a Christian community in the Louisiana countryside, where they grow only enough food for survival. This subsistence farming will lead, Noel hopes, to the starving of the inhabitants of the sinful city of New Orleans and to the overthrow of capitalist institutions in general. When a flood seems to spell doom for New Orleans, Noel is jubilant; but then the governor decides to blow up the dam in the vicinity of the commune to relieve the pressure on the dikes and save the city. Noel tries to sabotage this plan but is shot in the attempt. Dying, he realizes that he had no right to play God. He and Doris, who has rejoined him, perish as regenerated individuals who have rejected violence and reaffirmed their love. The reception of the play was reserved; the third act and the ending especially came in for criticism from both ends of the political spectrum, and the transformation of Doris was considered unbelievable. In Oldenburg the Nazis tried to disrupt the performance.

Adolf Hitler was appointed chancellor of the Reich on 30 January 1933. When the Reichstag (parliament building) was set on fire in February the Nazis blamed the Communists; the opposition parties were dissolved and the press was taken over. Since Kaiser had not been politically active his plays could still be produced, and *Der Silbersee* (The Silver Lake; published, 1933) premiered on 18 February 1933 simultaneously in Leipzig, Erfurt, and Magdeburg. In *Der Silbersee* Kaiser alludes pointedly to contemporary events. The songs, especially, reveal Kaiser's antifascist stance, but his message remains the same: the individual must be renewed before society can be changed. The policeman Olim and the unemployed Severin overcome their prejudices and try to help each other. When they are cheated out of their homes and money by two ruthless aristocrats they see no escape other than drowning themselves. But when they reach the Silver Lake they find it frozen over, and they conclude that they are meant to remain alive and continue their struggle. They wander off into the mist over the lake into an unclear future.

The Magdeburg production was attacked by the Nazis, and Kaiser was notified on 5 May that he had been expelled from the Prussian Academy of Arts. When he approached Gustaf Gründgens, the new director of the Berlin Staatliches Schauspielhaus (state playhouse), about possible productions of his works he was rebuffed by Gründgens's superior, Joseph Goebbels, the minister of propaganda and public enlightenment. Kaiser went into "inner exile" at his home in Grünheide, where he continued to write. Two of his plays were produced in Vienna in 1935 and 1936, but his royalties were meager.

Adrienne Ambrossat (performed, 1935; published, 1972) is based on a story by Guy de Maupassant. Adrienne tries to hide the loss of a borrowed pearl necklace; the truth is revealed when a man with whom she has had an affair comes looking for her. Her husband almost leaves her, but when she is released from prison he is waiting for her so that they may start a new life together. The afflictions they had to endure are a trial from which their love emerges stronger and purer than before. While the Vienna production, with a star-studded cast including Paula Wessely and Ernst Deutsch,

was a success, the play itself was criticized for its contrived plot and stilted dialogue.

In the comedy *Das Los des Ossian Balvesen* (The Lottery Ticket of Ossian Balvesen; performed, 1936; published, 1972) Ossian convinces Glynn that he, Ossian, has a moral right to a winning lottery ticket because he had played the number for twenty-four years, while Glynn only played it this year. Ossian realizes, however, that he will have to give up his career and his happy lifestyle once he becomes a millionaire. He returns the ticket to Glynn, who sends it back to Ossian; he does not want the money, either. It ends up in the wastebasket. Ossian and Glynn are not well differentiated; they act in a similar manner and even use the same arguments in refusing the money. Nevertheless, the play was received favorably when it was produced in Vienna in 1936.

Agnete (performed, 1949; published, 1972), written in 1935, is a Frauenstück. When Heinrich returns from a prisoner-of-war camp in Siberia he learns that he is the father of Agnete's child, which was conceived during Agnete's visit to him in the hospital; Heinrich, in a feverish delirium, did not know that he was making love to the sister of his fiancée, Lena. Agnete had gone there to tell him of Lena's death. Agnete's husband, Stefan, knows that he is not the child's father but loves the boy as if he were his own. When Heinrich demands that Agnete and his child go with him to start a new life in Chile, Stefan is willing to let his wife go but not his son. Unable to leave the boy behind, Agnete stays with her husband, and Heinrich leaves alone. The child represents hope for a better world.

Der Gärtner von Toulouse (The Gardener of Toulouse; published, 1938; performed, 1945), another Frauenstück, has great similarities to *Der Brand im Opernhaus* and *Das Frauenopfer* with their male protagonists who fanatically protect their ideal of female purity. The gardener Francois marries Janine to obtain a position with Mrs. Teophot; he does not know that his wife once worked in a brothel owned by his new employer. When Mrs. Teophot, after seducing Francois, tells him about his wife's past, he strangles her. Then he forces his wife to accept the blame for the murder since he believes that she can never atone for her sinful life. Francois is afraid of his sensuality, which he tries to hide by condemnation and punishment; he shows no sympathy for his wife, who had been forced into prostitution by dire necessity. He can only live in an ideal world, which for him is the greenhouse with its pure plants.

In the summer of 1938 Kaiser traveled to Amsterdam and then to Switzerland. For the remaining seven years of his life he lived in hotels or with friends in Zurich, Montana-Vermala, Morcote, Männedorf, Saint Moritz, and Ascona. Until 1941 he tried to procure a visa for the United States; although his application was supported by Albert Einstein and Thomas Mann, his attempt was not successful.

In *Pferdewechsel* (Changing Horses; published, 1972) written in 1938, the disillusioned Napoleon is on his way into exile on Elba when Marie Roux, the widow of one of his soldiers who perished in Russia, convinces him that he must not succumb to despair since it is not the fame he won in battle but his greatness in defeat that counts. He will remain a model for his followers, and his soldiers, including her husband, will not have died in vain; his creative genius will continue to change humanity for the better. Nietzsche's ideas still held such sway over Kaiser that he did not see the contradiction between the glorification of the great leader and his expressionist belief in equality.

The Künstlerdrama *Der Schuß in die Öffentlichkeit* (The Shot into the Public; published, 1939; performed, 1949) is a detective story set in London. The writer Alan Flanagan has been found shot to death in the woods. The first suspect is his publisher, Unwin, who is in financial difficulties because of huge advances he has made to Flanagan. He was also jealous of Flanagan because the writer was paying too much attention to Unwin's young wife, Helen. After a meeting he had accompanied Flanagan on a walk through the very woods where his body was later found. To top it all off, a gun is found in his possession. As it turns out, however, the murderer is Unwin's bookkeeper, Burns, who had learned about the financial problems of his employer and feared that a bankruptcy would cost him his job; he hoped that the sensational murder would increase the sales of Flanagan's books. He did not commit the murder for selfish reasons but to help his ailing wife. Now that Flanagan's books have become best-sellers, Unwin assures Burns that he will assume all financial responsibilities for his wife. Burns then gladly accepts his punishment.

In Switzerland Kaiser could be more outspoken in his criticism of the Nazis and their allies, the Japanese. In *Der Soldat Tanaka* (Private Tanaka, 1940) the title character is an enthusiastic soldier who venerates the emperor until he finds his sister in a brothel; his parents had sold her to pay the taxes on their home. In a rage, he kills her and his sergeant, who had asked for her services. Condemned to death, he is told that he will be pardoned because of his excellent military record if he begs the emperor for mercy. But Tanaka demands that the emperor apologize to him: he has recognized that the government can only support an army by enslaving the rest of the population, and he knows that some sections of society profit from war while others are exploited. The shots of the execution end the play. *Der Soldat Tanaka* was produced at the Zurich Schauspiel-haus, which served as a home for the plays of exiled German dramatists during the Third Reich. The production was successful but was discontinued because of a protest by the Japanese embassy.

Rosamunde Floris (published, 1940; performed, 1953) is yet another of Kaiser's Frauenstücke. Rosamunde and William had a three-week love affair and then went on with their separate lives. When Rosamunde learns that she is pregnant she tries to seduce Erwin so that she will have a father for her child, but he falls to his death trying to escape from her. She then confronts his family, claiming that she is expecting his child, and his brother, Bruno, breaks off his engagement to marry her. When Bruno's former fiancée finds out who the real father of the child is, Rosamunde kills her and Bruno. Finally she smothers her child because it has begun to look like its father. Now the secret of her pure love for William is safe forever. With the strength of this freedom Rosamunde confesses to a murder she did not commit–that of Erwin–and is sentenced to death. She lives and dies for a subjective reality with its own laws.

In the Frauenstück *Alain und Elise* (Alain and Elise; published, 1940; performed, 1954), Elise, the wife of the wealthy industrialist Dapperre, sits for the painter Alain. Inspired by her beauty he creates a masterpiece and is so elated that he refuses to accept payment for the painting. Elise believes that he has fallen in love with her, and she loves him in return. When she tells Alain about her love he admits that he does not share her feelings. The scorned Elise tells her husband that Alain had kissed her during the painting sessions. He invites Alain to their home and confronts him with the accusation in the presence of Elise. Elise shoots her husband and hands the weapon to Alain, who is arrested and tried for murder. During Elise's testimony Alain realizes that he is responsible for her action since he had aroused her feelings for him. He takes on this responsibility and accepts his life sentence. Like Rosamunde Floris, he finds a new freedom in this acceptance of guilt. He will be deported to Devil's Island, where he will transmute his suffering into art that will save the world. The complicated and illogical plot of this drama is hard to follow, and the paradox of how Alain can save the world by leaving it remains unsolved. The audience is asked to believe that a feeling which originates from the basest of crimes should suddenly acquire a high moral value.

In *Klawitter* (performed, 1949; published, 1972), written in 1940, Ernst Hoff, a proscribed author, has submitted a new play to the Staatstheater under the pseudonym Klawitter. When the play is accepted Hoff has to produce the author, and he is lucky to find one Klawitter in the telephone book. The vulgar and greedy Klawitter is only too happy to cooperate with Hoff, since he will earn a substantial amount of money. The play is a hit, but when Hoff asks Klawitter for his share of the royalties he is rebuffed. To add insult to injury, his wife becomes Klawitter's mistress. Sitting in a café, the dejected Hoff becomes furious when he hears on the radio that the prize for the best play of the year is presented to Klawitter. He hurls his cup at the radio and is arrested for sabotaging state approved cultural activities. Contrary to Kaiser's intention, the play does not focus on the policies and actions of the Nazi party; although Hoff's desperate financial situation is certainly the result of Nazi censorship of his plays, he is betrayed by Klawitter, who is not a Nazi. Also, the audience never learns about Hoff's political views or why he is opposed to the Nazis.

Hero worship like that of Marie Roux in *Pferdewechsel* is condemned in Kaiser's *Napoleon in New Orleans* (performed, 1950; published, 1966), written in 1941. Kaiser constructed his play around a legend according to which Napoleon had spent his last years in New Orleans after being abducted from Saint Helena, where a double took his place; according to this legend his grave can still be seen in Louisiana. In actuality, the Napoleon House in the French Quarter was the home of the mayor, Nicholas Girod, an admirer of Napoleon who planned an expedition to Saint Helena to liberate the emperor and bring him to New Orleans; Napoleon died before Girod could realize his plans. The protagonist of Kaiser's play, Baron Dergan, is modeled on Girod. His infatuation with Napoleon is exploited by a criminal gang that sells him fake relics and arranges for Napoleon's "abduction." One of the members then impersonates Napoleon and tells Dergan that he is going to establish a new empire on American soil. He also marries Dergan's daughter Gloria, who adores the emperor. By telling Dergan that he needs weapons for his new army, the false Napoleon swindles him out of all his wealth. When news reaches New Orleans that the real Napoleon has died, Dergan is cruelly awakened from his dreams of conquest and glory. He realizes, however, that he has been justly punished for his unquestioning hero worship. He perishes with his daughter in the flames of his house, which he has set afire. In his last moments he has a vision of a democratic and peaceful America that will be a model for all nations. When Kaiser wrote the play he anticipated immigrating to the United States, where it would be translated and staged. But just as it was completed the United States entered the war and the borders were closed.

In the Künstlerdrama *Das gordische Ei* (The Gordian Egg; performed, 1958; published, 1972), written in 1941, the playwright Abel Oberon and his daughter

Marjorie are forced to leave London because Oberon's publisher is demanding a new play that Oberon is unable to write. After hiding out in Scotland they return home to find that a new drama under Oberon's name is playing with great success. Oberon discovers that two students are the authors, but they do not claim the play as their own nor do they ask for royalties. They are idealists whose reward is the enjoyment the drama brings to the audience. Through this lucky turn of events Oberon is freed of all his debts.

Der englische Sender (The English Broadcast; performed, 1947; published, 1972), written in 1941, is based on Heinrich von Kleist's play *Der zerbrochne Krug* (1811; translated as The Broken Jug, 1939). Like the village judge Adam, the corrupt and lecherous protagonist of Kleist's comedy, the local Nazi leader Schmutz (Dirt) uses his official position to seduce innocent girls. But Schmutz is such a grotesque figure that he cannot be taken seriously by the audience, and the satire is so heavy-handed that all credibility is lost. When Schmutz learns that some villagers have listened to an English broadcast he threatens dire consequences unless Alma agrees to marry him. To protect the villagers, Alma goes along with Schmutz's plans; but during the wedding his former wife appears and exposes him as a swindler, thief, and bigamist, and he flees into the woods. The play was not produced onstage but was broadcast by the German Programme of the British Broadcasting Corporation.

In *Die Spieldose* (The Music Box; performed, 1943; published, 1966) Paul Chaudraz and his father, Pierre, are poor peasants in Brittanny who wrest a meager living from the soil. Paul has just married Noelle when World War II erupts and he is called up. In the turmoil of the defeat of the French army he is reported killed, and Pierre and Noelle can only find solace by marrying each other. When their child is born they look on it as a replacement for their beloved Paul. But Paul has survived and returns from a German prisoner-of-war camp. When he is told about the marriage he becomes so jealous that he kills his own father. Noelle is horrified and rejects him. Paul now recognizes the enormity of his crime; when he hears that the Germans will execute ten hostages for one of their soldiers killed by a guerrilla unless the killer surrenders, he turns himself in so that the hostages may go free.

The title of *Das Floß der Medusa* (performed, 1945; published, 1963; translated as *The Raft of the Medusa*, 1962) was inspired by Théodore Géricault's painting, but the plot is based on an actual incident in which a ship carrying children from the bombed cities of England to Canada in September 1940 was torpedoed; only a few of the children survived. Allan and Ann are the leaders of the children in the lifeboat. While Allan does everything he can to raise their spirits and improve their chances of survival, Ann insinuates that they will never be rescued because there are thirteen children in the boat. With this evil omen she terrifies the other children and persuades them to throw the youngest child overboard while she distracts Allan so that he cannot interfere. Because of Ann's ability to corrupt the other children, Allan can no longer believe in human goodness: the world is thoroughly immoral, and children are no better than their parents. Allan refuses to be rescued and is shot when a German plane strafes the boat. The play shows marked similarities to *Die Bürger von Calais:* there is a number game, a version of a communion, a lottery, and the self-sacrifice of the protagonist while the other characters are saved. But while the six volunteers in *Die Bürger von Calais* had become regenerated human beings, the rescued children are murderers just like their warring parents.

The last three plays Kaiser wrote are based on classical Greek mythology and are written in blank verse. In *Zweimal Amphitryon* (Twice Amphitryon; performed, 1944; published, 1948) Amphitryon is more interested in power and glory than in his beautiful bride, Alkmene, and he makes war on his peaceful neighbors. Alkmene prays to Zeus to bring him back to her. Zeus is moved by the purity of Alkmene's love and visits her in the form of Amphitryon. Afterward he tells her that she will bear a divine son, Herakles, who will cleanse the earth and establish the Olympic games for the purpose of peaceful contests of strength. Amphitryon must work as a goatherd until he is purified.

In *Pygmalion* and *Bellerophon,* both of which were published in 1948 and performed in 1953, Kaiser is concerned with a topic that took on ever greater importance for him toward the end of his life, the loneliness of the artist. The protagonist of *Pygmalion* is a sculptor; when Athene grants him a wish he asks that his statue, Chaire, come to life. Chaire is a creation of Pygmalion's spirit and embodies perfect aesthetic beauty, and he has fallen in love with her. When Pygmalion and Chaire become lovers in the real world, Pygmalion is sued by his fiancée, Korinna, and by Konon, who had originally ordered the statue. When the jury hears Pygmalion's story they believe he is joking, and he is released; but the judge decides that Chaire must be returned to the brothel from which the people believe she came. Pygmalion is about to commit suicide when Athene intervenes again: she turns Chaire back into stone and returns the statue to Pygmalion. Konon claims her as the work of art he has paid for, and Pygmalion follows Korinna to Korinth. He has come to under-stand that his works spring not from happiness but from suffering. Pygmalion marries Korinna, but she is not his true love; he remains a lonely man who creates his art to protect himself from life's realities.

The theme of the loneliness of the artist is carried to its logical conclusion in *Bellerophon.* The title character is a musician who was raised by Apollo, the god of music. When he prefers his music over the charms of Anteia, the wife of King Proitos, her pride is hurt. To get revenge, she tells her husband that Bellerophon tried to seduce her. The king sends the young man to his governor, Jobates, with a sealed message that contains instructions to kill him. But Jobates does not immediately look at the letter Bellerophon presents to him. Bellerophon meets Jobates' daughter, Myrtis, a wonderful singer, and falls in love with her. Marriage arrangements are being made when her father finally reads the king's message. He sends Bellerophon to a cave where a dragon lives, but Bellerophon kills the monster. He then searches for his fiancée on his winged horse, Pegasus, and they are united. He and Myrtis are placed among the stars where he will delight the gods with his music. Thus Bellerophon overcomes the difficulties of the artist's life by leaving this world altogether.

In his final years in exile in Switzerland, Kaiser worked on novels that were never completed and wrote lyrical poems. As he did in his last plays, Kaiser bemoans in these poems the fate of the poet in a hostile world.

Following the defeat of the Third Reich in May 1945 Kaiser made plans to found a publishing house in Germany to be called Lenz (Spring). As the newly elected honorary president of the Association of Exiled German Writers in Switzerland, Kaiser intended to promote the work of returning German antifascist writers. But before he could realize his plans he died on Monte Verita in Ascona on 4 June 1945 of an embolism caused by an infected tooth. His body was cremated on 6 June at Lugano, and his urn was interred in the cemetery at Morcote on Lake Lugano.

Letters:

Briefe, edited by Gesa M. Valk (Frankfurt am Main, Berlin & Vienna: Propyläen, 1980);

Georg Kaiser in Sachen Georg Kaiser: Briefe 1916–1933, edited by Valk (Leipzig & Weimar: Kiepenheuer, 1989).

Interviews:

Karl Marilaun, "Gespräch mit Georg Kaiser," *Neues Wiener Journal,* 21 December 1921, p. 4;

Iwan Goll, "Georg Kaiser über Georg Kaiser," *Das Tagebuch,* 5, no. 17 (1924): 573–574;

Hermann Kasack, "Der Kopf ist stärker als das Blut," *Berliner Börsen-Courier,* 25 December 1928;

O. K., "Interview mit Georg Kaiser: Ein Autor, der auf seine Stücke nicht neugierig ist," *Neues Wiener Journal,* 30 October 1930, pp. 6–7.

Bibliography:

Marianne Henn, ed., *Bibliography of The Georg Kaiser Collection at The University of Alberta,* compiled by Erika Radenovich-Banski (Edmonton: Division of Germanic Languages, Literatures, and Linguistics, University of Alberta, 1998).

Biography:

Brian J. Kenworthy, *Georg Kaiser* (Oxford: Blackwell, 1957).

References:

Wilfried Adling, "Georg Kaisers Drama *Von morgens bis mitternachts* und die Zersetzung des dramatischen Stils," *Weimarer Beiträge,* 5 (1959): 369–386;

Arnim Arnold, ed., *Interpretationen zu Georg Kaiser* (Munich: Klett, 1980);

Helmut Arntzen, "Wirklichkeit als Kolportage: Zu drei Komödien von Georg Kaiser und Robert Musil," *Deutsche Vierteljahresschrift,* 36 (1962): 544–561;

Renate Benson, *Deutsches expressionistisches Theater: Ernst Toller und Georg Kaiser* (New York: Lang, 1987);

Heinrich Breloer, *Georg Kaisers Drama "Die Koralle": Persönliche Erfahrung und ästhetische Abstraktion* (Hamburg: Lüdke, 1977);

John O. Buffinga, "From 'Bocksgesang' to 'Ziegenlied': The Transformation of a Myth in Georg Kaiser's *Zweimal Amphitryon,*" *German Studies Review,* 9 (October 1986): 475–495;

Rudolf Bussmann, *Einzelner und Masse: Zum dramatischen Werk Georg Kaisers* (Kronberg: Scriptor, 1978);

Susan C. Cook, "*Der Zar läßt sich photographieren:* Weill and Comic Opera," in *A New Orpheus: Essays on Kurt Weill,* edited by Kim H. Kowalke (New Haven: Yale University Press, 1986), pp. 83–101;

Paul Davies, "The Political and Social Aspects of Georg Kaiser's Drama in the Context of Expressionism," *Revue Frontenac Review,* 14 (1985): 314–336;

Horst Denkler, *Georg Kaiser "Die Bürger von Calais": Drama und Dramaturgie* (Munich: Oldenbourg, 1967);

Bernhard Diebold, *Der Denkspieler Georg Kaiser* (Frankfurt am Main: Frankfurter Verlagsanstalt, 1924);

Manfred Durzak, *Das expressionistische Drama: Carl Sternheim–Georg Kaiser* (Munich: Nymphenburger, 1978);

Anna Margarethe Elbe, *Technische und soziale Probleme in der Dramenstruktur Georg Kaisers* (Hamburg: GEG Druckerei, 1959);

Eric Albert Fivian, *Georg Kaiser und seine Stellung im Expressionismus* (Munich: Desch, 1947);

Max Freyhan, *Georg Kaisers Werk* (Berlin: Die Schmiede, 1926);

H. F. Garten, "Georg Kaiser," in *German Men of Letters,* volume 2, edited by Alex Natan (London: Wolff, 1963), pp. 155–172;

Garten, "Georg Kaiser and the Expressionist Movement," *Drama,* 37 (1955): 18–21;

Garten, "Georg Kaiser Re-Examined," in *Essays in German and Dutch Literature,* edited by William Douglas Robson-Scott (London: University of London, 1973), pp. 41–48;

Werner Geifrig, *Georg Kaisers Sprache im Drama des expressionistischen Zeitraums* (Munich: 1968);

Richard C. Helt and John Carson Pettey, "Georg Kaiser's Reception of Friedrich Nietzsche: The Dramatist's Letters and Some Nietzschean Themes in His Works," *Orbis Litterarum,* 38, no. 3 (1983): 215–234;

Peter Uwe Hohendahl, *Das Bild der bürgerlichen Welt im expressionistischen Drama* (Heidelberg: Winter, 1967);

Walter Huder, "Gedenkwort für Georg Kaiser," *Sinn und Form,* 11 (1959): 257–268;

Huder, "Symbol und Perspektive in Georg Kaisers *Schellenkönig,*" *Theater und Zeit,* 10 (June 1958): 13–16;

Erwin Ihrig, "*Die Bürger von Calais:* Auguste Rodins Denkmal–Georg Kaisers Bühnenspiel," *Wirkendes Wort,* 11 (1961): 290–303;

Marianne R. Jetter, "Some Thoughts on Kleist's *Amphitryon* and Kaiser's *Zweimal Amphitryon,*" *German Life and Letters,* 13 (1960): 178–189;

Robert Alston Jones, "German Drama on the American Stage: The Case of Georg Kaiser," *German Quarterly,* 37 (January 1964): 17–25;

Klaus Kändler, "Georg Kaiser, der Dramatiker des neuen Menschen," *Wissenschaftliche Zeitschrift der Karl-Marx-Universität Leipzig: Gesellschafts- und Sprachwissenschaftliche Reihe,* 7 (1957/1958): 297–303;

Robert Kauf, "Georg Kaiser hundert Jahre," *Neue Deutsche Hefte*, 159 (1978): 663–666;

Kauf, "Georg Kaiser's Social Tetralogy and the Social Ideas of Walther Rathenau," *PMLA*, 77 (1962): 311–317;

Kauf, "*Schellenkönig:* An Unpublished Early Play by Georg Kaiser," *Journal of English and German Philology*, 55 (1956): 439–450;

Brian J. Kenworthy, *Georg Kaiser* (Oxford: Blackwell, 1957);

Rolf Kieser, Erzwungene Symbiose: Thomas Mann, Robert Walser, *Georg Kaiser und Bertolt Brecht im Schweizer Exil* (Bern: Haupt, 1984);

Hans-Jörg Knobloch, "Zur Datierung der Komoedien Georg Kaisers," *Zeitschrift für deutsche Philologie*, 109, no. 2 (1990): 217–238;

Hugo F. Koenigsgarten, "Georg Kaiser: The Leading Playwright of Expressionism," *German Life and Letters*, 3 (1939): 195–205;

Koenigsgarten, *Georg Kaiser: Mit einer Bibliographie von Alfred Loewenberg* (Potsdam: Kiepenheuer, 1928);

Rudolf Koester, "Kaiser's *Von morgens bis mitternachts* and Hesse's *Klein und Wagner:* Two Explorations of Crime and Human Transcendence," *Orbis Litterarum*, 24 (1969): 237–250;

Silvia Konecny, "Georg Kaisers *König Hahnrei*," *Zeitschrift für deutsche Philologie*, 97 (1976): 27–35;

Manfred Kuxdorf, *Die Suche nach dem Menschen im Drama Georg Kaisers* (Bern & Frankfurt am Main: Lang, 1971);

Eberhard Lämmert, "Georg Kaiser: *Die Bürger von Calais*," in *Das deutsche Drama vom Barock bis zur Gegenwart: Interpretation*, volume 2, edited by Benno von Wiese (Düsseldorf: Bagel, 1960), pp. 305–324;

Rex W. Last, "Kaiser, Rodin and the *Burghers of Calais*," *Seminar*, 5 (Spring 1969): 36–44;

Last, "Kaiser's *Bürger von Calais* and the Drama of Expressionism," in *Periods in German Literature II: Texts and Contexts* (London: Wolff, 1968), pp. 247–264;

Last, "Symbol and Struggle in Georg Kaiser's *Die Bürger von Calais*," *German Life and Letters*, 19 (1966): 201–209;

Ludwig Lewin, *Die Jagd nach dem Erlebnis: Ein Buch über Georg Kaiser* (Berlin: Die Schmiede, 1926);

Leroy Marion Linick, *Der Subjektivismus im Werke Georg Kaisers* (Strasbourg: Heitz, 1938);

Ian C. Loram, "Georg Kaiser's *Der Soldat Tanaka:* 'Vollendeter Woyzeck'?," *German Life and Letters*, 10 (1956): 43–48;

Loram, "Georg Kaiser's Swan Song: Griechische Dramen," *Monatshefte*, 49 (1957): 23–30;

Arnold Meese, *Die theoretischen Schriften Georg Kaisers* (Fürstenfeldbruck: Loher, 1965);

Willibald Omanowski, *Georg Kaiser und seine besten Bühnenwerke: Eine Einführung* (Berlin, Leipzig & Vienna: Siedentop, 1922);

Wolfgang Paulsen, *Georg Kaiser: Die Perspektiven seines Werkes. Mit einem Anhang: Das dichterische und essayistische Werk Georg Kaisers. Eine historisch-kritische Bibliographie* (Tübingen: Niemeyer, 1960);

Holger A. Pausch und Ernest Reinhold, eds., *Georg Kaiser: Studien zu seinem Werk und Leben* (Berlin: Agora, 1980);

Klaus Petersen, *Georg Kaiser: Künstlerbild und Künstlerfigur* (Bern, Frankfurt am Main & Munich: Lang, 1976);

Petersen, "Georg Kaisers *Rosamunde Floris:* Der Engel mit dem Flammenschwert," *Seminar*, 13 (1977): 13–28;

Petersen, "Mythos in Gehalt und Form der Dramen Georg Kaisers," *Neophilologus*, 60 (April 1976): 266–279;

Petersen, "Das Wort tötet das Leben!: Möglichkeiten des Künstlertums in Georg Kaisers Drama *Die Flucht nach Venedig*," *Colloquia Germanica*, 11, no. 2 (1978): 149–165;

Herbert W. Reichert, "Nietzsche and Georg Kaiser," *Studies in Philology*, 61 (January 1964): 85–108;

Steven P. Scher, "Georg Kaiser's *Von morgens bis mitternachts:* Isolation as Theme and Artistic Method," in *Theatrum Mundi: Essays on German Drama and German Literature Dedicated to Harold Lenz on his Seventieth Birthday, September 11, 1978*, edited by Edward R. Haymes, Houston German Studies, no. 2 (Munich: Fink, 1980), pp. 125–135;

H. J. Schueler, "The Symbolism of Paradise in Georg Kaiser's *Von morgens bis mitternachts*," *Neophilologus*, 68, no. 1 (1984): 98–104;

Ernst Schürer, *Georg Kaiser* (New York: Twayne, 1971);

Schürer, *Georg Kaiser und Bertolt Brecht: Über Leben und Werk* (Frankfurt am Main: Athenäum, 1971);

Schürer, *Georg Kaiser "Von morgens bis mitternachts": Erläuterungen und Dokumente* (Stuttgart: Reclam, 1975);

Schürer, "Verinnerlichung, Protest und Resignation: Georg Kaisers Exil," in *Die Deutsche Exilliteratur, 1933–1945*, edited by Manfred Durzak (Stuttgart: Reclam, 1973), pp. 263–281;

Adolf Munke Schütz, *Georg Kaisers Nachlass: Eine Untersuchung über die Entwicklungslinien im Lebenswerk des Dichters* (Basel: Frobenius, 1949);

Harro Segeberg, "Simulierte Apokalypsen: Georg Kaisers 'Gas' Dramen im Kontext expressionistischer Technik-Debatten," in *Literatur in einer industriellen Kultur,* edited by Götz Großklaus and Eberhard Lämmert (Stuttgart: Cotta, 1989), pp. 294–313;

Leroy R. Shaw, "Georg Kaiser auf der deutschsprachigen Bühne 1945–1960," *Maske und Kothurn,* 9 (1963): 68–86;

Shaw, "Georg Kaiser (1878–1945): A Bibliographical Report," *Texas Studies in Literature and Language,* 3 (1961): 399–408;

Shaw, *The Playwright and Historical Change* (Madison, Milwaukee & London: University of Wisconsin Press, 1970);

Richard William Sheppard, "Unholy Families: The Oedipal Psychopathology of Four Expressionist Ich-Dramen," *Orbis Litterarum,* 41, no. 4 (1986): 355–383;

M. Helena Goncalves da Silva, *Character, Ideology, and Symbolism in the Plays of Wedekind, Sternheim, Kaiser, Toller, and Brecht* (London: Modern Humanities Research Association, 1985);

Wilhelm Steffens, *Georg Kaiser* (Velber: Friedrich, 1969);

G. C. Tunstall, "The Turning Point in Georg Kaiser's Attitude towards Friedrich Nietzsche," *Nietzsche Studien: Internationales Jahrbuch für die Nietzsche-Forschung,* 14 (1985): 314–336;

Peter K. Tyson, "Georg Kaiser's Breakthrough as an Expressionist in Berlin," *Neophilologus,* 67, no. 4 (1983): 575–581;

Tyson, *The Reception of Georg Kaiser 1915–1945,* 2 volumes (New York, Bern, Frankfurt am Main & Nancy: Lang, 1984);

Ulrich Weisstein, "Was noch kein Auge je gesehen: A Spurious Cranach in Georg Kaiser's *Von Morgens bis Mitternachts,*" in *The Comparative Perspective on Literature: Approaches to Theory and Practice,* edited by Clayton Koelb and Susan Noakes (Ithaca, N.Y.: Cornell University Press, 1988), pp. 233–259;

Edith Welliver, "Georg Kaiser's *Kolportage:* Commentary on Class in the Weimar Republic," *Germanic Review,* 64 (Spring 1989): 73–78;

Peter von Wiese, "Georg Kaiser: *Pygmalion,*" in *Das deutsche Drama,* volume 2 (Düsseldorf: 1960): 325–337;

Audrone B. Willeke, *Georg Kaiser and the Critics: A Profile of Expressionism's Leading Playwright* (Columbia, S.C.: Camden House, 1995);

Rhys W. Williams, "Culture and Anarchy in Georg Kaiser's *Von morgens bis mitternachts,*" *Modern Language Review,* 83 (April 1988): 364–374;

Andrzej Wirth, "Kaiser und Witkiewicz: Der Expressionismus und seine Zurücknahme," in *Aspekte des Expressionismus,* edited by Paulsen (Heidelberg: Stiehm, 1968), pp. 153–164.

Papers:

Manuscripts, letters, and other materials by and about Georg Kaiser are in the Georg Kaiser Archives at the Akademie der Künste (Academy of Arts), Berlin. Duplicates of these materials are in the Georg Kaiser Archives at the University of Alberta, Edmonton, and at the University of Texas, Austin.

Gottfried Keller

(19 July 1819 – 15 July 1890)

Gail K. Hart
University of California, Irvine

This entry was updated by Professor Hart from her entry
in DLB 129: Nineteenth-Century German Writers, 1841–1900.

BOOKS: *Gedichte* (Heidelberg: Winter, 1846);

Neuere Gedichte (Brunswick: Vieweg, 1851; enlarged, 1854);

Der grüne Heinrich: Roman, 4 volumes (Brunswick: Vieweg, 1854–1855; revised edition, Stuttgart: Göschen, 1879–1880); translated by A. M. Holt as *Green Henry* (London: Calder, 1960; New York: Grove, 1960);

Die Leute von Seldwyla: Erzählungen (Brunswick: Vieweg, 1856)—comprises "Pankraz, der Schmoller," "Frau Regel Amrain und ihr Jüngster," "Romeo und Julia auf dem Dorfe," "Die drei gerechten Kammacher," "Spiegel, das Kätzchen"; enlarged edition, 2 volumes (Stuttgart: Göschen, 1874)—volume 2 comprises "Kleider machen Leute," "Der Schmied seines Glückes," "Die mißbrauchten Liebesbriefe," "Dietegen," "Das verlorene Lachen"; excerpts translated by Wolf von Schierbrand as *Seldwyla Folks: Three Singular Tales by the Swiss Poet Gottfried Keller* (New York: Brentano's, 1919)—comprises "Three Decent Combmakers," "Dietegen," "Romeo and Juliet of the Village";

Sieben Legenden (Stuttgart: Göschen, 1872); translated by Martin Wyness as *Seven Legends* (London & Glasgow: Gowans & Gray, 1911);

Züricher Novellen, 2 volumes (Stuttgart: Göschen, 1878);

Das Sinngedicht: Novellen (Berlin: Hertz, 1882 [i.e., 1881]);

Gesammelte Gedichte (Berlin: Hertz, 1883);

Martin Salander: Roman (Berlin: Hertz, 1886); translated by Kenneth Halwas as *Martin Salander* (London: Calder, 1964);

Gesammelte Werke, 10 volumes (Berlin: Hertz, 1889);

Sämtliche Werke, 22 volumes, edited by Jonas Fränkel and Carl Helbling (Bern & Leipzig: Benteli, 1926–1949);

Gottfried Keller in 1886 (photograph by Karl Stauffer-Bern)

Sämtliche Werke und ausgewählte Briefe, 4 volumes, edited by Clemens Heselhaus, fourth edition (Munich: Hanser, 1978–1979);

Sämtliche Werke, 6 volumes, edited by Thomas Böning, Gerhard Kaiser, and Dominik Müller (Frankfurt

430

am Main: Deutscher Klassiker Verlag, 1985–
1990);

Die Fugenddramen, edited by Laurence A. Rickels (Zurich: Ammann, 1990).

Editions in English: *Legends of Long Ago* ("Sieben Legenden"), translated by Charles Hart Handschin (Chicago: Abbey, 1911; reprinted, Freeport, N.Y.: Books for Libraries Press, 1971);

"The Governor of Greifensee," translated by Paul Bernard Thomas; "The Company of the Upright Seven," "Ursula," translated by Bayard Quincy Morgan, in *The German Classics of the Nineteenth and Twentieth Centuries,* volume 14, edited by Kuno Francke and William Guild Howard (New York: German Publication Society, 1914), pp. 96–319;

The People of Seldwyla and Seven Legends, translated by M. D. Hottinger (London & Toronto: Dent / New York: Dutton, 1929)—comprises "The People of Seldwyla: 'Spiegel the Cat,' 'A Village Romeo and Juliet,' 'The Three Righteous Combmakers,' 'Clothes Make the Man'; Seven Legends: 'Eugenia,' 'The Virgin and the Devil,' 'The Virgin as Knight,' 'The Virgin as Nun,' 'Vitalis, the Holy Rogue,' 'Dorothea's Rose-Basket,' 'A Little Legend of the Dance'";

The Misused Love Letters, translated by Michael Bullock, and Regula Amrain and Her Youngest Son, translated by Anne Fremantle: Two Novellas (New York: Ungar, 1974);

Gottfried Keller: Stories, edited by Frank Ryder (New York: Continuum, 1982).

Gottfried Keller—poet, critic, and Switzerland's most prominent writer of fiction—aspired initially to be a landscape painter; it was only after his reluctant and costly determination that he lacked the talent to support himself as such that he began to produce the moderately successful poems and the great novels and novellas that have established him as one of the major figures of German "poetic realism," as the dominant style of the period from approximately 1850 to 1880 is known. Though his subject matter was wide-ranging, he consistently focused on themes of individual development, paying close attention to the role of childhood experience in the formation of character. As Heinrich Lee, the hero of Keller's autobiographical novel *Der grüne Heinrich* (1854–1855; revised, 1879–1880; translated as *Green Henry,* 1960), explains: "Wenn ich nicht überzeugt wäre, daß die Kindheit schon ein Vorspiel des ganzen Lebens ist und . . . schon die Hauptzüge der menschlichen Zerwürfnisse im Kleinen abspiegele . . . so würde ich mich nicht so weitläufig mit den kleinen Dingen jener Zeit beschäftigen" (If I were not convinced that childhood is a foretaste of the rest of life and . . . that it

reflects the main characteristics of human struggle in miniature . . . I would not occupy myself to such an extent with the minor matters of childhood). This conviction, as well as a tendency to represent the movements of the unconscious mind in symbols and images strikingly similar to those recognized by psychoanalysis, endeared Keller's neurotic prose to Sigmund Freud, who cites him twice in *Die Traumdeutung* (1900; translated as *The Interpretation of Dreams,* 1913), and to psychoanalytic critics.

Another conspicuous aspect of Keller's output is its educational mission. Keller, who regularly affirmed his morally or socially didactic intentions in letters and essays, wrote mainly of errant souls and dreamers who blunder into situations that force a confrontation with a reality that contradicts their desires. Those who are enlightened by such confrontations tend to prosper, whereas those who persist in erring or dreaming suffer some sort of punishment. Poetic justice generally prevails, and the recommendation is that the reader avoid lingering in a subjectively or selfishly defined world of dreams and emerge as an active member of the family or social community. Thus, Keller's thematics fit the general pattern of nineteenth-century realism, which pits individual fantasy against an overwhelming "objective reality" that negates it; but Keller's texts tend to undercut this process with ironic humor. A lingering regret at the loss of the dream or of the dreamer colors the apparently conventional conclusion of most of Keller's prose works and reflects the author's own experience as a man caught between self-involvement and social responsibility. Unfortunately, Keller's irony does not always survive translation, and this circumstance may account for the relative obscurity of this important author in the English-speaking world.

Keller was born on 19 July 1819 in Zurich to Elisabeth Scheuchzer Keller, a pious woman from Glattfelden with a sharp mind and conservative values, and Rudolf Keller, a master lathe turner. Rudolf, also from Glattfelden, was a farmer's son, but he was, by Glattfelden standards, well traveled and cosmopolitan in his tastes. As a journeyman he had lived for four years in Vienna, and he spoke High German rather than Swiss dialect. He was an astute businessman who devoted long hours to community service, an ardent supporter of public education who favored national unity over cantonal sovereignty, and a relatively cultured man who wrote poetry and organized amateur theatrical presentations in his spare time. Always overextended and often working himself to exhaustion, he died in 1824, leaving Elisabeth with Gottfried and a daughter, Regula, who was two. The only one of Keller's five siblings to survive early childhood, Regula would live her entire life in the shadow of her brother, working as a seamstress and later as a salesclerk to replenish family funds spent on his prolonged professional training; after the death of Elisabeth in 1864 Regula would keep house for her brother. Neither Gottfried nor Regula ever married.

Keller always felt that the early death of his father deprived him of a role model who might have taught him steadfast devotion to duty and helped him make more rational career choices. Though his mother's second marriage, to a journeyman worker named Hans Heinrich Wild, lasted from 1826 to 1834, Keller only once mentions his stepfather in his writings and then as "ein fremder Mann, der bei uns wohnt" (a strange man who lives in our house). His intense possessiveness of his mother, who, like Regula, devoted her life and savings to him, seems to have resulted in the absolute effacement of the challenger. Nowhere in Keller's largely autobiographical fiction does a stepfather occur, though "Frau Regel Amrain und ihr Jüngster" (1856; translated as "Regula Amrain and Her Youngest Son," 1951) contains a scene in which the heroine, deserted by her husband, must fend off the advances of the foreman of the family stone quarry; at the moment she considers yielding, her youngest son, Fritz, emerges from the bedroom armed with a curtain rod, calls the intruder a thief, clobbers him with the rod, and repossesses his mother. She resolves to devote all her energies to raising this son, choosing him over his colorless brothers, who slept through the attack, because of his resemblance to his father. Keller extracted similar loyalty from his mother after her divorce.

The other major setback of Keller's childhood occurred in 1834, when he was permanently expelled from the cantonal trade school. Keller, who already had been disciplined for lack of concentration in class—when asked to name the capital of Italy he had answered, "camera obscura"—was singled out for punishment for his role in a student demonstration against an unpopular teacher. Since his family did not possess the means to send him to private or boarding school, his formal education was at an end for the time being. Keller never recovered from the insult and the exclusion. In *Der grüne Heinrich,* where the hero suffers the same fate, Keller uses the word *köpfen* (decapitate) to describe the effect on Heinrich's spiritual development.

After his expulsion Keller began the serious study of painting, repairing to rural Glattfelden to sketch the natural scenery. Through the efforts of his mother he was eventually apprenticed to the lithographer Peter Steiger in Zurich. Steiger, who emphasized rapid reproduction over sound composition and refinement, failed to impart the basic principles of landscape art to his pupil, and in 1838 Elisabeth Keller engaged the talented but mentally unbalanced artist Rudolf Meyer to tutor

her son. Meyer was an effective teacher who expanded Keller's horizons in many directions; but he soon succumbed to paranoid delusions, and the relationship ended bitterly when Keller and his mother demanded a refund. Steiger and Meyer have their fictional counterparts in *Der grüne Heinrich* in Meister Habersaat and Römer, respectively.

In 1840, after demanding and obtaining a large part of the money that had been held in trust for him from his grandfather's estate, Keller enrolled at the great art academy in Munich. Though the stay in a large urban center with a thriving artistic and literary culture augmented the young man's store of experience, he was unable to lay the foundations of a painting career—largely because of a strong inclination to drink and socialize. Like many students who find themselves on their own for the first time in a big city, Keller spent beyond his means and neglected his training. His letters to his mother from this period, each containing a request for more money, recount the factors that impeded his study: from a four-week bout with typhus to the need to get out and enjoy himself (lest his spirit become impoverished) to lack of funds for proper food, shelter, and artistic supplies—a problem that resulted in part from a decision to eat in better restaurants (for the sake of his health). The German word *Schuld* means both monetary debt and personal guilt, and it sums up the legacy of Keller's Munich years: he incurred vast debts and drained his family's finances while refusing to take available work as a colorist, causing his mother great worry and sorrow. That Keller recognized the extent of his callousness is suggested by the ending of the first version of *Der grüne Heinrich:* the hero returns to Switzerland after spending several years in a German urban art center at great cost to his overindulgent mother, whom he has, as it turns out, literally worried to death. Heinrich arrives as his mother's funeral is in progress, and his guilt over her death and his failure is so great that he himself dies a short time afterward.

Frau Keller was alive when her dejected son returned in November 1842. He spent the winter in the kitchen reading, sulking, and writing. While in Munich, Keller had had brief articles and essays published in a local newspaper for Swiss residents; in Zurich he continued writing poems and occasional pieces, ultimately coming to the conclusion that he could express himself "rascher und bequemer" (more quickly and easily) in words than in pictorial images.

Having made his choice, Keller, inspired by the revolutionary ferment in post–Restoration Europe and by the large group of illustrious political refugees who had come to live in liberal Zurich, began writing political poetry as well as occasional and nature poems. One of the refugees, A. A. L. Follen, published a selection of

Keller's poems in two issues of his *Deutsches Taschenbuch* (German Notebook) in 1845 and 1846 under the heading "Lieder eines Autodidakten" (Songs of an Autodidact) to the resounding approval of critics and readers. Keller was greeted as "das bedeutendste lyrische Talent, das in der Schweiz laut geworden" (the most important poetic talent to be heard from in Switzerland). The enthusiastic reception led to the publication of a volume of his poetry, *Gedichte* (Poems), in Heidelberg in 1846. A second volume, *Neuere Gedichte* (Recent Poems), appeared in Brunswick in 1851, and an enlarged edition of that collection came out in 1854.

Keller's poetry encompasses a broad range of themes, from brief reflections on love, patriotism, lost youth, and nature to extended narrative poetry such as the parody of Heinrich Heine, "Der Apotheker von Chamounix" (The Pharmacist of Chamonix) and the long poem "Gedanken eines Lebendig-Begrabenen" (Thoughts of One Buried Alive), which realistically records the thoughts of a man who finds himself in this situation. Though formally flawed, Keller's poems are appreciated for their immediacy of expression and the humor and irony with which he often treats his subject matter. One further volume, *Gesammelte Gedichte* (Collected Poems, 1883), appeared during Keller's lifetime, and many other poems from his personal papers have been published in critical editions since his death.

In Zurich, Keller experienced the first of a series of demoralizing rejections by women. By most standards unattractive—gruff, diminutive, and oddly proportioned—he was awkward and resentful toward the women he loved, almost as if he mistrusted or feared them for the influence they exerted on his feelings. He repeatedly chose tall, beautiful women, and they consistently rebuffed this small, impecunious, and unpleasant suitor. The first documented case is that of Luise Rieter, to whom Keller confessed his love in a letter of 16 October 1847: "Ich bin noch gar nichts und muß erst werden, was ich werden will, und bin dazu ein unansehnlicher armer Bursche, also habe ich keine Berechtigung, mein Herz einer so schönen und ausgezeichneten jungen Dame anzutragen, wie Sie sind, aber wenn ich einst denken müßte, daß Sie mir doch ernstlich gut gewesen wären und ich hätte nichts gesagt, so wäre das ein sehr großes Unglück für mich, und ich könnte es nicht wohl ertragen. . . . Wollen Sie so gütig sein und mir mit zwei Worten sagen, ob Sie mir gut sind oder nicht?" (I am as yet nothing at all and still have to become what I wish to become, and besides that I am a poor unattractive lad and therefore I have no right to offer my heart to such a beautiful and distinguished young lady, but if I had to think someday that you really had liked me and that I had said nothing, that would be a very great misfortune for me and I would

not be able to bear it. . . . Would you please be so kind and tell me plainly whether you love me or not?). She did not, nor did Johanna Kapp in 1849 or Betty Tendering in 1855. Finally, in 1866 Keller became engaged to a much younger woman, the twenty-three-year-old Luise Scheidegger; but Scheidegger, depressed by tales of his drinking escapades, drowned herself in July of that year to avoid marrying him. As far as can be determined, he never again proposed to a woman.

In 1848 several Zurich politicians who had taken an interest in Keller's poetry awarded him a scholarship to help him acquire a university education. Keller chose the University of Heidelberg, and left Zurich in October. In Heidelberg, Keller attended the lectures of the atheist philosopher Ludwig Feuerbach, an experience that permanently altered his worldview. In *Das Wesen des Christentums* (The Essence of Christianity, 1841) Feuerbach sought to expose the Christian God as a mere projection of the virtues and talents of human beings: "Die Religion zieht die Kräfte, Eigenschaften, Wesensbestimmungen des Menschen vom Menschen ab und vergöttert sie als selbstständiges Wesen" (Religion draws the strengths, qualities, and essential determinations of man away from mankind and deifies them as an independent being). Thus, in worshiping their own good qualities, abstracted and reconstituted as God, men and women failed to recognize the value of humanity; and in their yearning for heaven and immortality—a second, superior "reality" beyond experience—they devalued their own finite lives. Feuerbach, best known today for the observation "Der Mensch ist, was er ißt" (You are what you eat), preached a doctrine of "Diesseitigkeit" (this-worldliness), exhorting his listeners and readers to find fulfillment in the material world and to abandon the distractions of preparing for an imagined eternity. Over the course of the Heidelberg lectures Keller enjoyed frequent personal contact with Feuerbach and grew ever more convinced of the truth of the philosopher's message, though he rarely displayed the quasi-religious zeal with which Feuerbach proclaimed the new materialism.

Keller left Heidelberg in 1850 for Berlin, where he hoped to establish himself as a tragedian. Though he never completed a drama that was worthy of being published or produced, his five years in Berlin, during which he produced *Der grüne Heinrich,* the first volume of *Die Leute von Seldwyla* (1856; excerpts translated as *Seldwyla Folks,* 1919), and many sketches for later novellas, were the most fruitful of his career.

Der grüne Heinrich, which is regarded as one of the most important works in the genre of the bildungsroman after Johann Wolfgang von Goethe's *Wilhelm Meisters Lehrjahre* (1795–1796; translated as *Wilhelm Meister's Apprenticeship,* 1824), begins as the twenty-year-old Heinrich Lee, described as an ungrateful child, leaves Switzerland for Germany and the art academy. The "green" of the title derives from Heinrich's green coat and refers to the hero's youth and inexperience as well as to hope for the future. Heinrich has written a lengthy account of his youth, "Eine Jugendgeschichte," and the third-person narrator of the novel's first four chapters suggests that "wir" (we) read it while Heinrich is getting settled in Germany. The first-person account follows the adventures of the child Heinrich, who enlivens mundane events with flourishes of fantasy while resisting assimilation into the social order that threatens to overwhelm him. When he cannot grasp the spiritual nature of God as described by his mother, Heinrich selects the weathercock on top of the church steeple and later a drawing of a tiger from one of his picture books to serve as the material objects of his worship: "Es waren ganz innerliche Anschauungen und nur wenn der Name Gottes genannt wurde, so schwebte mir erst der glänzende Vogel und nachher der schöne Tiger vor" (These were entirely subjective perceptions and when someone spoke the name of God, first the image of the shimmering bird came to me and later that of the beautiful tiger). His habit of appropriating and personalizing elements of the external order persists and has a dual and contradictory purpose in the novel as a regrettable retardant of his socialization and as a compelling demonstration of his imagination.

A later incident allows Heinrich actually to shape objective events. When caught uttering profanities, he spontaneously invents a tale of four older boys, whom he names, luring him into the forest and forcing him to use foul language. This testimony results in severe punishment of the alleged offenders and in great satisfaction for Heinrich: "ich fühlte . . . eine Befriedigung in mir, daß die poetische Gerechtigkeit meine Erfindung so schön und sichtbarlich abrundete, daß etwas auffallendes geschah, gehandelt und gelitten wurde und das infolge meines schöpferischen Wortes" (I felt . . . great satisfaction that poetic justice had completed my invention so palpably and so well, that something remarkable had happened and that suffering had occurred and that it was all a consequence of my creative words). Heinrich's participation in the schoolboys' heckling of their least favorite teacher (a close parallel to Keller's own experience, as are many of the events in "Eine Jugendgeschichte") does not turn out as he might have wished: he is reprimanded and expelled from school by a teachers' committee.

As Heinrich matures, his dualistic worldview finds corroboration in his two loves, the fragile and ethereal Anna and the wise, frank, and earthy Judith, who appeal, respectively, to his soul and his body. When the delicate Anna dies of consumption, Heinrich,

like Feuerbach's Christian, swears eternal allegiance to the departed and lives in anticipation of joining her after death. When he rejects Judith on the grounds that he cannot have a harem in eternity, she asks slyly whether he is sure that there is such a thing as eternity. "Eine Jugendgeschichte," which is the heart of the novel, ends as Heinrich and Judith separate, and the third-person narrator returns to chronicle Heinrich's failure as a painter, his subsequent reflections on vocation and the purpose of life, and his conversion to atheism shortly before his departure from Germany. While making his way home Heinrich encounters a liberal-minded count and his adopted daughter, Dortchen Schönfund, both of whom are disciples of Feuerbach and patrons of the arts. With their help and encouragement he produces and exhibits paintings and earns money that is augmented by an unexpected inheritance. Heinrich returns too late to benefit his long-suffering mother. Having botched his personal life, despairing of becoming an asset to his community through public service, and knowing he cannot encounter his mother in an afterlife, Heinrich dies. His corpse is found clutching a slip of paper on which Dortchen had written a poem about hope. Beautiful green grass grows on his grave.

Keller's first novel was well received by contemporary critics and writers; they enjoyed the many ancillary narratives, such as the child who could not pray and the family of readers, that punctuate Heinrich's life story, though most complained that Heinrich's death was unmotivated and incongruous. Keller initially defended his "tragic" conclusion as preferable to a tidy ending in which the hero finds love and marries; but he ultimately relented and in 1878–after buying and burning all remaining copies of the original printing, which had not sold well–set about rewriting his great novel. The second version of *Der grüne Heinrich*, which was published in 1879–1880, is considered the standard version, and it is the one that has been translated into English. The second version has the author's endorsement as the definitive one, and it contains certain improvements in style and organization. Nonetheless, many critics believe that Keller traded the frank immediacy of the original language for a more polished and less expressive idiom. The second version of *Der grüne Heinrich* begins with the account of Heinrich's youth, in which Keller made few significant changes. The rest of the novel is also related in the first person by Heinrich. Significantly, Heinrich now returns just as his mother is dying–she is able to give her son a single "fragenden Blick" (questioning look) before expiring. In his deep despair over the death of his mother and his inability to rid his office of corruption–he has been managing the chancery of a small district near his hometown–Heinrich takes to a mountain path, where he casts to the winds the paper containing Dortchen's hope verses. At this moment Judith appears, having returned from America because she has heard that Heinrich is in trouble, and becomes his guide, his platonic friend, and his companion for life. It is her death many years later that inspires Heinrich to review the account of his youth and to record the further course of his life, "die alten grünen Pfade der Erinnerung zu wandeln" (to wander down the old green paths of memory).

While finishing the first version of *Der grüne Heinrich* Keller conceived a collection of novellas set against the backdrop of life in the fictional town of Seldwyla. *Die Leute von Seldwyla* describes Seldwyla as a pleasant sunny spot, home to a community of fun-loving, failure-prone fools. Seldwyla men all go bankrupt between the ages of thirty and thirty-six, and the major local "product" is Gemütlichkeit, an untranslatable German word that indicates good fellowship or conviviality. The first of the five novellas, "Pankraz, der Schmoller" (Pankraz, the Sulker), describes a lazy, bitter boy who deserts the widowed mother and the sister who supported him and travels the world learning to work and to adjust to "eine feste außer mir liegende Ordnung" (a fixed order external to me). He returns to relate his adventures to his mother and sister, but the women hear only the beginning and end of his tale: how he ran away and was ultimately socialized during a standoff with a man-eating lion. They mysteriously fall asleep during Pankraz's narration of the central experience of his life: the baffling encounter with Lydia, a beautiful woman who appeared to be kind, wise, and sincerely interested in him but was actually a crass and indifferent flirt who solicited a declaration of love for the sake of ego gratification. Pankraz neither solves nor comes to terms with "das Rätsel der Schönheit" (the mystery of beauty), but he does stop sulking and becomes a good son and brother.

"Romeo und Julia auf dem Dorfe" (translated as "Romeo and Juliet of the Village," 1919) is the most widely read and the most controversial of Keller's works. The narrator stresses that the adaptation of Shakespeare's theme to village life is the fictional reflection of a real occurrence—Keller had read of two young peasants who shot themselves because their feuding families refused to let them marry—and evidence that the great plots of fiction derive from human behavior rather than detached imaginings or literary borrowings. Sali and Vrenchen are the children of farmers whose dispute over property rights results in the ruin of both families. When they fall in love and can find no socially acceptable means of marrying, they spend a festive day together and drown themselves rather than separate when the day is over. The tale closes with a report of a newspaper article deploring their "gottverlassene" (god-

less) action. The fairy-tale romanticism of the lovers' idylls seems to enshrine them in the starry firmament of fantasy, but it coexists—eerily at times—with a realistic rendering of the families' debasement, an unappealing social portrait, and reminders of the grim finality of suicide. Such unresolved tensions, as well as the suicide and the richly symbolic character of the narrative, have made it unusually popular with scholars, who have produced more than fifty essays on "Romeo und Julia auf dem Dorfe." Most of these essays undertake to demonstrate that the suicide was inevitable, suggesting that critics are still uncomfortable with Keller's harsh conclusion.

"Frau Regel Amrain und ihr Jüngster" follows Fritz Amrain's exemplary upbringing, which culminates in Fritz's overcoming his errant father and ejecting him from the family business. "Die drei gerechten Kammacher" (The Three Righteous Combmakers; translated as "Three Decent Combmakers," 1919) is the humorous history of three ascetic journeyman combmakers who lead lives they consider to be beyond reproach, even though they hoard all their money and benefit no one. Each hopes to purchase the master's workshop when the latter predictably goes bankrupt, but they end grotesquely when forced to race each other for the privilege. The final tale, "Spiegel, das Kätzchen" (Mirror, the Cat; translated as "Spiegel the Cat," 1929), features a Faustian cat who strikes a bargain with the evil sorcerer Pineiß. Pineiß will give Spiegel a life of perfect ease and abundance, and in return the cat will deliver up his skin at the end of a specified period so that the sorcerer can use the attached fat in his spells. When the day of reckoning comes, Spiegel becomes Scheherezade and literally saves his skin by entangling the sorcerer in a lengthy tall tale. As a consequence of his gullibility, Pineiß blunders into marriage with a domineering witch, and Spiegel regains his freedom.

Though Keller had already finished two more Seldwyla novellas by 1855 and had composed significant parts of another three by the early 1860s, it was not until 1874 that he submitted final revisions of a second volume to the publisher. The town has changed drastically since the first volume appeared. Along with industrialization, a capitalist economy has taken hold in Seldwyla, and the citizens, as born speculators, are ideally suited to this kind of economic system because of their love of empty activity and their abhorrence of honest work. Prosperity, however, has taken its toll: the Seldwylers laugh less frequently, and they are too busy to play pranks on each other. In other words, nothing happens there anymore, so the narrator proposes to return to the old days for narrative material and offers five tales from the past.

"Kleider machen Leute" (translated as "Clothes Make the Man," 1929) was inspired by various contemporary reports of commoners masquerading as nobles for profit. Wenzel Strapinski, a well-dressed but impoverished journeyman tailor whose master has gone bankrupt, hitches a ride to the next town, Goldach, with a coachman who is delivering an elegant carriage to its aristocratic purchaser. When Wenzel emerges from the coach in his fine clothes, the Goldachers take him for a Polish count, and every awkward move he makes reinforces this perception. Eventually Wenzel catches on and plays along, providing the Goldachers with the excitement their dreary lives lack. Inevitably, Wenzel is unmasked by the merry Seldwylers; but his fiancée, Nettchen, who had fallen in love with Count Strapinski, decides that she loves the man and not the clothes, and the two marry and move to Seldwyla to make clothes for the Seldwylers. In the end, Wenzel proves to be as much a Philistine as any Goldacher–he works hard and drains the Seldwylers' pockets without reinvesting in the town's economy. "Kleider machen Leute" is one of Keller's signature pieces and has often been cited for its "Sein und Schein" (essence and appearance) thematics, which many believe are central to Keller's program as a writer.

Anthologies and single editions have helped to popularize individual Seldwyla stories, such as "Romeo und Julia auf dem Dorfe," "Die drei gerechten Kammacher" and "Kleider machen Leute." "Der Schmied seines Glückes" (The Smith of His Own Fortune) is rarely singled out, but it has one of the most interesting plots. John Kabys, determined to become rich without working, agrees to be "adopted" by Adam Litumlei, a rich old man who fears that he will die without an heir and will thus appear to have been impotent. It is agreed that Kabys will act as if he were a long-lost illegitimate son of Litumlei and inherit the latter's riches. The plan backfires because Kabys cannot resist the charms of Litumlei's young wife. When she becomes pregnant by him, her "stepson" is displaced by a "true" heir; Kabys realizes that he has collaborated in the manufacture of his *mis*fortune. When he claims to be the father of his "father's" son, he is cast out and forced to make his living as a nailsmith.

"Die mißbrauchten Liebesbriefe" (translated as "The Abused Love Letters," 1891) and "Dietegen" (translated, 1919) are less compelling than the other Seldwyla tales. The first is a graceless and immoderate literary satire, taking broad stabs at contemporary writers who wish to recapture the ferment of the Sturm und Drang (Storm and Stress) years; "Dietegen" is an endless and intricately plotted fifteenth-century period piece about concealment and revelation of emotions, wealth, and truth. The final tale, "Das verlorene Lachen" (translated as "The Lost Smile," 1982), is a compendium of Keller's social-didactic concerns into which is woven the love and marriage of Justine Glor and Jukundus Meyenthal, whose suitedness to one another is indicated by their identical smiles. "Das verlorene Lachen" attempts to shore up declining values by demonstrating the shallowness of caste consciousness, the dangers of religious orthodoxy, the fragility of the natural environment in an age of increasing industrialization, the folly of ignoring tradition, the vanity of faith in progress, and the destructive effects of greed. At least one of these factors threatens the lovers' relationship at any given time, and they must navigate a treacherous course and learn many lessons before they come to a true and lasting understanding. "Das verlorene Lachen," which begins at a folk festival, is a tapestry of Swiss life.

In 1855 Keller left Berlin for Zurich. There he made his living as a freelance writer, contributing articles and essays to journals and writing patriotic and political poems and essays that were widely praised–especially by those in the government. In 1861 cantonal officials encouraged him to apply for the position of "Erster Staatsschreiber" (first secretary) of Zurich, and on 14 September he was elected to that prestigious and demanding post. He was forty-two, and it was his first job. On 22 September, the evening before he was to take office, he attended a party for the German socialist agitator Ferdinand Lassalle. After much drinking and a lengthy demonstration of magic tricks by Lassalle, Keller lost his temper and attacked the guest of honor with a stool. He was seized and ejected before he could do any damage, and Lassalle was not offended; but Keller did not show up at eight the next morning at his office, where accounts of his drunken brawling were already circulating. Finally, at ten, one of Keller's supporters went to his house, woke him up, and brought him in. Since Keller's excesses had been an issue in the discussion of his application, his future in government did not look bright; but the reprimand he received his first day on the job was the last. For the next fifteen years he was a model civil servant. When he stepped down in 1876, it was to return to his fiction, which he had neglected as Staatsschreiber.

Sieben Legenden (translated as *Seven Legends,* 1911), which appeared in 1872, was conceived during the Berlin years and, like the second volume of Seldwyla stories, took final form during Keller's years in office. It was intended as an ironic counterpart or profane rejoinder to *Legenden* (1804), a book of sentimental legends of the saints by Ludwig Kosegarten. The first piece, "Eugenia," concerns an early Christian bluestocking whose intellectual vanity leads her to masquerade as a man–Keller's prose abounds with women in men's clothing and men in women's clothing–so as to become a monk. She is saved from this folly by the man who loves her. The next three legends relate the adventures of the Virgin Mary in medieval times: she wrestles with the devil in "Die Jungfrau und der Teufel" (translated as "The Virgin and the Devil"); wins a jousting contest disguised as a knight in "Die Jungfrau als Ritter" (translated as "The Virgin as Knight"); and substitutes in a cloister for a nun who goes out to enjoy civilian life in "Die Jungfrau als Nonne" (translated as "The Virgin as Nun"). "Der schlimm-heilige Vitalis" (translated as "The Naughty Saint Vitalis) describes a monk who tries to convert prostitutes by paying for their time and praying for them. "Dorotheas Blumenkörbchen" (translated as "Dorothea's Flower-Basket") follows two lovers who forgo happiness on earth to spend eternity together in heaven. Postponement of pleasure is also the theme of the final piece, "Das Tanzlegendchen" (translated as "A Legend of the Dance"), where King David convinces the young Musa to take a vow to cease dancing on earth so that she may dance forever in the afterlife. She achieves sainthood by denying herself her favorite pleasure and arrives in heaven, where she finds that the souls long for earthly music and dancing. Keller renders his parodies of saints' legends with great control and finesse. Barely touched by the author's will to educate readers to social utility, they are among the most subtle examples of his narrative style.

By the time Keller stepped down from office he had also finished his *Züricher Novellen* (Zurich Novellas, 1878), a collection of tales from Zurich history; most of the stories deal with themes of originality and the belatedness of the epigone writer. The frame narrative of the first cycle follows the career of Herr Jacques, a young boy who understands the strange stirrings of puberty to be "der unbewußte Trieb, ein Original zu sein oder eines zu werden" (the unconscious drive to be an original or to become one). Jacques wishes to write highly original literature but fails to produce anything, and his well-meaning godfather finds it necessary to tell him several didactic tales so that he might recognize that "good" originality is exemplary behavior or conduct that deserves imitation.

"Hadlaub" is the account of an epigone minnesinger of late medieval times, Johannes Hadlaub, whose legendary contribution to culture was his copying of old minnesongs to compile the Codex Manesse–a secondary phenomenon that is original as well. "Der Narr auf Manegg" (The Fool of Manegg) depicts the negative originality of the deranged and cruel Buz Falätscher, for whom death is a relief. "Der Landvogt von Greifensee" (translated as "The Governor of Greifensee," 1914) chronicles the romantic life of the historical Salomon Landolt, whose fruitful bachelorhood would never have

been if he had married one of the five women whose stories he relates. Keller's tendency to embed stories within stories within stories is especially apparent in "Der Landvogt von Greifensee." Jacques, who had been bidden to copy "Der Landvogt von Greifensee" from a manuscript his godfather had written, is ultimately unaffected by the tales offered as tonic for his disturbance. He continues to pursue the arts as a patron or cocreator and renounces his aspirations only after his shocking discovery that a sculptor he had sponsored in Rome has produced an illegitimate child rather than the marble statue Jacques had expected. The tale closes with the suggestion that the recently married Jacques will imitate the sculptor and produce or originate progeny.

Two more tales are appended to the "Jacques" cycle. "Ursula" (translated, 1914) is the account of a victim of religious fanaticism and the loyal lover who rescues her amid post-Reformation factional strife. "Das Fähnlein der sieben Aufrechten" (The Banner of the Upright Seven; translated as "The Company of the Upright Seven," 1914) remains one of Keller's most popular tales. Seven patriotic master craftsmen prepare for a great folk festival at which they will arrive under their own banner and present a silver cup. One of them must make a speech for the presentation, but none of them has a gift for oratory. This situation and the developing romance between the son of one of the craftsmen and the daughter of another–which the fathers oppose–constitute the plot, but the main intent of the novella is to convey vignettes of exemplary citizenship and admirable social behavior.

Less tendentious and more pluralistic in its appeal to the educated reader was Keller's last collection of tales, *Das Sinngedicht* (The Epigram), which appeared in late autumn of 1881 with the publication date 1882 on the title page. His contemporaries greeted it as the finest of his works, and even today it is considered the best example of Keller's mature writing. The philosopher Friedrich Nietzsche praised it in a letter to the author of 14 October 1886 ("so rein, frisch und körnig schmeckte uns dieser Honig" [so pure, fresh, and crystalline does this honey taste to us]), and *Das Sinngedicht* does have the quality of an elegantly wrought refreshment.

Das Sinngedicht, the frame story of which is essentially a battle of the sexes leading to reconciliation and betrothal, is free of the social-didactic theme of the earlier works and also of the unrelenting misogyny that Keller had up to this point displayed in his authorial comments on women and in his characterizations of them. Though many have praised Keller for his "strong woman characters," closer inspection reveals that the few "strong women" he produced–Judith in *Der grüne Heinrich* is an example–are pure projections of the needs of male protagonists, who suffer from existential problems that the strong women cannot fathom. Their "strength" thus derives from their relative ignorance. Yet Lucie seems to have full rights and privileges in *Das Sinngedicht*–that is, she has strengths and weaknesses. Her past is as troubled and error-ridden as that of any man in Keller's works, and she often appears to be the wiser of the two protagonists.

The premise of *Das Sinngedicht* is playful and "aesthetic" to the highest degree. A young scientist, Herr Reinhart, notices one day that he has been pursuing the study of light (in the dark) to excess and that his eyes need a rest; light is the dominant metaphor of the collection, and Lucie, whose nickname is "Lux," is the light the myopic Reinhart seeks. As a first step toward reentering the world of human concerns he seeks advice in a volume of Karl Lachmann's edition of Gotthold Ephraim Lessing's edition of Friedrich Logau's epigrams and finds: "Wie willst du weiße Lilien zu roten Rosen machen? / Küß eine weiße Galathee: sie wird errötend lachen!" (How do you turn white lilies to red roses? / Kiss a white Galatea: she will laugh and blush!). Reinhart vows to enact this imperative and sets off on a quest for his Galatea. The circumstances of his discovery of the epigram and the multiply mediated nature of the text (Logau edited by Lessing edited by Lachmann) make it clear that his is a purely fanciful mission that has less to do with the epigram itself than with a frivolous urge to experiment outside the walls of his laboratory. Reinhart is thus able to kiss several of the women he encounters without arousing their anger–but also without eliciting the combined reaction predicted by Logau. But when he stumbles on Lucie in a white gown, next to a marble fountain, sorting roses, he betrays his purpose; and she, angered by the presumption of a man seeking his Galatea, enters into a round of competitive storytelling with him. All the tales they tell are loosely related to the Pygmalion theme: "Regine" depicts a wealthy man who educates a servant girl to be his wife; "Die arme Baronin" (The Poor Baroness) concerns the efforts of a young boarder to revive his sullen, aristocratic landlady to life's joys; and "Don Corea" relates the adventures of a Portuguese admiral who finds happiness with an African woman, whom he grooms to be his good Catholic wife. These tales are told by Reinhart. Lucie's tales are more inclined to show the failure of the Pygmalion projects and the losses incurred by those who attempt them. In "Die Berlocken" (The Trinkets), for example, Thibaut, a French soldier and rake, spends many years acquiring a superb collection of trinkets, only to lose them to an Indian woman in America. Trusting in her savage simplicity, Thibaut gives his treasures to the woman, whom he wishes to marry, only to find them dangling from the nose of her fearsome Indian fiancé the next day. Thibaut's colonialist construction of a naive and artless Indian maiden is a delusion of superiority that makes him her dupe. The

analogy to Reinhart, hoping to breathe life into his blushing Galatea, is subtly established.

Whereas Reinhart strives to preserve an objective historical style in his narratives, Lucie favors empathic penetration of her figures' states of mind. These differences give rise to many methodological arguments that deepen their knowledge of one another and fuel their growing affection. Eventually they join hands, Lucie laughs and blushes when Reinhart kisses her, and he professes to have forgotten his original purpose.

Keller, who acknowledged that his collection might appear "leer und skurril" (empty and farcical) to some, defended in letters to his publisher and friends his right to produce something that was purely poetic and unrelated to social utility. Despite his protests, he seems to have had compensatory intentions when, in 1881, the same year in which *Das Sinngedicht* appeared, he began writing a "relevant" novel. *Martin Salander* (1886; translated, 1964) represents an emphatic return to social themes. Keller's last work (he never wrote the intended sequel), it reflects all of the aging author's bitterness about the political and social changes wrought by industrial capitalism in Switzerland. Martin Salander, an upstanding merchant, is legally swindled out of his fortune by an old friend, Louis Wohlwend. To rebuild, Salander goes off to work in Brazil for seven years, leaving his wife and children behind. The poignancy of their difficult separation is nicely rendered and becomes all the more heartbreaking when Martin, having returned with ample funds, is again swindled by Wohlwend and must again go off to work in South America. He returns and establishes a healthy business; but he suffers great disappointment when his indistinguishable daughters, Setti and Netti, marry the worthless and unscrupulous Weidelich twins. Figures who are profoundly dull or nearly subhuman tend to occur in twos or threes in Keller's works; the Weidelichs "haben keine Seelen" (have no souls) because, like the three combmakers, they are motivated by personal gain and make no contribution to the society that sustains them.

Martin suffers further during his brief fascination with the beautiful Myrrha Glawicz, who turns out to be mindless, but he remains with his loyal Marie after learning that appearances can be deceiving. He must also learn to accept that the democratic system, which he supports so passionately, makes no distinction between a Salander and a Wohlwend and thus abets the destructive dishonesty of the latter and his ilk. With the exception of Marie, the only positive force in the novel is their son, the upstanding Arnold Salander, who was to be the subject of the sequel.

Though it has a few bright moments, *Martin Salander* is flat and disappointing. It lacks humor, and Keller himself admitted that there was too little poetry in it. The great socialist literary critic Georg Lukács wrote that Keller's poetic vein dried up with his increasing awareness of and disappointment in the capitalistic industrialization of Switzerland, and *Martin Salander* tends to confirm this suspicion. Keller was extremely worried about economic trends and suspicious of those in power. He saw the world of his youth deteriorating in his later years, but instead of returning to the past, as in the second volume of Seldwyla stories, he brooded about the present. Emil Ermatinger, the preeminent biographer of Keller, notes that the effects of aging as well as having to write *Martin Salander* in new lodgings above a lively tavern on a noisy street may have also taken their toll on Keller's poetic vein.

Keller spent his final years reaping the benefits of his poetic labors. He had attained widespread fame in German-speaking lands by the mid 1870s and spent much of his time corresponding with critics, publishers, and other authors—notably with Theodor Storm and Conrad Ferdinand Meyer, two other important realist writers. He also received distinguished visitors and accepted awards as befitted a writer of his renown and advancing age. By the early 1880s his beloved sister was ill with heart disease, and he began to care for her as she had once cared for him. He was deeply shaken by her death in 1888.

In 1889 Keller began arrangements for the publication of his collected works in ten volumes, a great achievement for a living poet and confirmation of his stature. His seventieth birthday brought further confirmation. Along with trophies, medals, awards, telegrams, books, and paintings came official recognition from the German government and a proclamation from the Swiss legislature declaring Keller the best living German-language writer and recognizing him for his many contributions to Swiss society and culture. Keller was by then too feeble to attend the celebrations or respond energetically to the panegyrics. He received only the representatives of the legislature, preferring to be alone for most of the day. When he was honored with a gold medal in September, he wept and told those present that the award signified the end for him. In January 1890 he contracted influenza; he never recovered from its complications. Several strokes followed. Keller seems to have been barely alert during his last months; though he was attended by many friends and literary acquaintances, they report no profound deathbed conversations. There is testimony from his nurses that Keller asked them to read to him from the Bible and to say the Lord's Prayer, but one is tempted to take these reports with a grain of salt. A return to the Christian faith would have pleased most of Keller's admirers, inasmuch as it would have rounded out the popular image of a benign, humorous, happy—and by this time religious—man that so many of his readers cherished. It is, however, unclear how Keller stood on theological mat-

ters at the time of his death on 15 July 1890, and his posthumous "deification" (as one critic puts it) tends to distort the record of Keller's life and achievement by effacing his dark side. The dual image of Keller as benevolent, pious national poet, on the one hand, and bitter, misogynistic, alcoholic atheist, on the other, cannot be resolved by forcing a choice. Keller's brave recognition of his limits—including his difficult personality—and his passionate wish that these limits did not exist constitute a contradiction that was mediated time and again by his unique ironic humor. Only in the experience of this contradiction, or tension, between the desired and the available did Keller's genius emerge, enabling him to produce some of the finest poetic fiction of the nineteenth century.

Letters:

Gottfried Keller und J. V. Widmann: Briefwechsel, edited by Max Widmann (Zurich: Füli, 1922);

Gesammelte Briefe, 4 volumes, edited by Carl Helbling (Bern: Benteli, 1950–1954);

Der Briefwechsel zwischen Theodor Storm und Gottfried Keller, edited by Peter Goldammer, second edition (Berlin: Aufbau, 1967);

Aus Gottfried Kellers glücklicher Zeit: Der Dichter im Briefwechsel mit Marie und Adolf Exner, edited by Irmgard Smidt (Stafa: Gut, 1981);

Kellers Briefe, edited by Goldammer, second edition (Berlin: Aufbau, 1982);

Mein lieber Herr und bester Freund: Gottfried Keller im Briefwechsel mit Wilhelm Petersen, edited by Smidt (Stafa: Gut, 1984);

Gefährdete Künstler: Der Briefwechsel zwischen Gottfried Keller und Johann Salomon Hegi, edited by Fridolin Stahli (Zurich: Artemis, 1985);

Gottfried Keller–Emil Kuh Briefwechsel, edited by Smidt and Erwin Streitfeld (Stafa: Gut, 1988).

Bibliographies:

Jakob Baechthold, *Gottfried Keller Bibliographie (1844–1897)* (Berlin: Hertz, 1897);

Charles Zippermann, *Gottfried Keller Bibliographie* (Zurich: Rascher, 1935);

Hermann Boeschenstein, *Gottfried Keller* (Stuttgart: Metzler, 1969).

Biographies:

Jakob Baechthold, *Gottfried Kellers Leben: Seine Briefe und Tagebücher* (Berlin: Hertz, 1894–1897);

Marie Hay, *The Story of a Swiss Poet: A Study of Gottfried Keller's Life and Works* (Bern: Wyss, 1920);

Emil Ermatinger, *Gottfried Kellers Leben,* eighth revised edition (Zurich: Artemis, 1950);

James Lindsay, *Gottfried Keller: Life and Works* (London: Wolff, 1968);

Adolf Muschg, *Gottfried Keller,* second edition (Munich: Kindler, 1977);

Bernd Breitenbruch, *Gottfried Keller in Selbstzeugnissen und Bilddokumenten,* third edition (Reinbek: Rowohlt, 1983);

Hans Wysling, ed., *Gottfried Keller 1819–1890* (Zurich: Artemis, 1990).

References:

Walter Benjamin, "Gottfried Keller: Zu Ehren einer kritischen Gesamtausgabe seiner Werke," in his *Angelus Novus: Ausgewählte Schriften,* volume 2 (Frankfurt am Main: Suhrkamp, 1966), pp. 384–395;

John M. Ellis, "Die drei gerechten Kammacher," in his *Narration in the German Novelle* (Cambridge: Cambridge University Press, 1974), pp. 136–154;

William Harrison Faulkner, *Keller's Der grüne Heinrich: Anna and Judith and Their Predecessors in Rousseau's Confessions* (Charlottesville: University of Virginia, 1912);

John L. Flood and Martin Swales, eds., *Gottfried Keller 1819–1890: The London Symposium 1990* (Stuttgart: Heinz, 1991);

Gail K. Hart, *Readers and Their Fictions in the Novels and Novellas of Gottfried Keller* (Chapel Hill: University of North Carolina Press, 1989);

Eduard Hitschmann, *Gottfried Keller: Psychoanalyse des Dichters, seiner Gestalten und Motive* (Leipzig: Internationaler psychoanalytischer Verlag, 1919);

Hugo von Hofmannsthal, "Unterhaltung über die Schriften von Gottfried Keller," in his *Gesammelte Werke,* volume 2 (Berlin: Fischer, 1924), pp. 266–275;

T. M. Holmes, "Poetry Against Realism: The Divided Structure of Gottfried Keller's *Das verlorene Lachen,*" *Forum for Modern Language Studies,* 19 (July 1983): 249–260;

Robert C. Holub, "Realism, Repetition, Repression: The Nature of Desire in *Romeo und Julia auf dem Dorfe,*" *Modern Language Notes,* 100 (April 1985): 461–497;

David Jackson, "*Pankraz, der Schmoller* and Gottfried Keller's Sentimental Education," *German Life and Letters,* 30 (October 1976): 52–64;

Lee B. Jennings, "The Model of the Self in Gottfried Keller's Prose," *German Quarterly,* 56 (March 1983): 196–230;

Gerhard Kaiser, *Gottfried Keller: Das gedichtete Leben* (Frankfurt am Main: Insel, 1981); Kaiser, *Gottfried Keller: Eine Einführung* (Munich: Artemis, 1985);

Lucie Karcic, *Light and Darkness in Gottfried Keller's "Der grüne Heinrich"* (Bonn: Bouvier, 1976);

Priscilla Kramer, *The Cyclical Method of Composition in Gottfried Keller's Sinngedicht* (New York: Ottendorfer, 1939);

Victor Lemke, "The Deification of Gottfried Keller," *Monatshefte,* 48 (1956): 119–126;

Kaspar T. Locher, *Gottfried Keller: Der Weg zur Reife* (Bern: Francke, 1969);

Rätus Luck, *Gottfried Keller als Literaturkritiker* (Bern: Francke, 1970);

Georg Lukács, *Gottfried Keller: Mit einer Einleitung* (Berlin: Aufbau, 1946);

Bernd Neumann, *Gottfried Keller: Eine Einführung in sein Werk* (Königstein: Athenäum, 1982);

Wolfgang Preisendanz, *Poetischer Realismus als Spielraum des Grotesken in Gottfried Kellers "Der Schmied seines Glückes"* (Constance: Universitätsverlag Konstanz, 1989);

Herbert W. Reichert, *Basic Concepts in the Philosophy of Gottfried Keller,* second edition (New York: AMS Press, 1966);

Heinrich Richartz, *Literaturkritik als Gesellschaftskritik: Darstellungsweise und politisch-didaktische Intention in Gottfried Kellers Erzählkunst* (Bonn: Bouvier, 1975);

B. A. Rowley, *Keller: Kleider machen Leute* (London: Arnold, 1960);

Richard R. Ruppel, *Gottfried Keller and His Critics: A Case Study in Scholarly Criticism* (Columbia, S.C.: Camden House, 1998);

Ruppel, *Gottfried Keller: Poet, Pedagogue, and Humanist* (New York: Lang, 1988);

Erika Swales, *The Poetics of Scepticism: Gottfried Keller and Die Leute von Seldwyla* (Oxford: Berg, 1994);

Bruno Weber, *Gottfried Keller: Landschaftsmaler* (Zurich: Neue Zürcher Zeitung, 1990);

Kurt Wenger, *Gottfried Kellers Auseinandersetzung mit dem Christentum* (Bern: Francke, 1971);

Hans Wysling, ed., *Gottfried Keller: Elf Essays zu seinem Werk* (Munich: Fink, 1990).

Papers:

Gottfried Keller's papers are in the Zentralbibliothek (Central Library) in Zurich, the Goethe-und Schiller-Archiv in Weimar, and the Cotta-Archiv in the Schiller Nationalmuseum in Marbach.

Heinrich von Kleist

(18 October 1777 – 21 November 1811)

James M. McGlathery
University of Illinois at Urbana-Champaign

This entry was updated by Professor McGlathery from his entry in DLB 90:
German Writers in the Age of Goethe, 1789–1832.

BOOKS: *Die Familie Schroffenstein: Ein Trauerspiel in fünf Aufzügen,* anonymous (Bern & Zurich: Gessner, 1803); translated by Mary J. and Lawrence M. Price as *The Feud of the Schroffensteins* (London: Badger, 1916);

Amphitryon: Ein Lustspiel nach Molière, edited by Adam H. Müller (Dresden: Arnold, 1807); translated by Marion Sonnenfeld as *Amphitryon: A Comedy* (New York: Ungar, 1962);

Penthesilea: Ein Trauerspiel (Tübingen: Cotta, 1808); translated by Humphry Trevelyan as *Penthesilea,* in *Five German Plays,* volume 2 of *The Classic Theatre,* edited by Eric Bentley (London: Mayflower, 1959; New York: Doubleday, 1959);

Erzählungen, 2 volumes (Berlin: Realschulbuchhandlung, 1810–1811)—comprises volume 1, "Michael Kohlhaas: Aus einer alten Chronik," translated by J. Oxenford as "Michael Kohlhaas," in *Tales from the German* (London: Chapman & Hall, 1844; New York: Harper, 1844); "Die Marquise von O . . . ," translated by Heinrich Roche as "The Marquise of O . . . ," in *Great German Stories* (London: Benn, 1929); "Das Erdbeben in Chili," translated by Norman Brown as "Earthquake in Chile," in *The Blue Flower* (New York: Roy, 1946); volume 2, "Die Verlobung in St. Domingo," translated by Martin Greenberg as "The Engagement in Santo Domingo," in *The Marquise of O-, and Other Stories* (New York: Criterion, 1960); "Das Bettelweib von Locarno," translated by Ernest N. Bennett as "The Beggar Woman of Locarno," in *German Short Stories* (London: Oxford, 1934); "Der Findling," translated by Greenberg as "The Foundling," in *The Marquise of O-, and Other Stories* (New York: Criterion, 1960); "Die heilige Cäcilie oder Die Gewalt der Musik, Eine Legende," translated by J. Oxenford as "St. Cecilia; or, The Power of Music: A Catholic Leg-

Miniature (1801) of Heinrich von Kleist by Peter Friede, the only likeness known to have been executed from life (private collection)

end," in *Tales from the German* (London: Chapman & Hall, 1844; New York: Harper, 1844); "Der Zweikampf," translated by Greenberg as "The Duel," in *The Marquise of O-, and Other Stories* (New York: Criterion, 1960);

Das Käthchen von Heilbronn oder Die Feuerprobe: Ein großes historisches Ritterschauspiel (Berlin: Realschulbuchhandlung, 1810); translated by Elijah B. Impey as *Kate of Heilbronn,* in *Illustrations of German Poetry*

(London: Simkin, Marshall, 1841); translated by Frederick E. Pierce as *Kaethchen of Heilbronn or The Test of Fire: Great Historical Chivalric Drama in 5 Acts,* in *Romantic Drama,* volume 2 of *Fiction and Fantasy of German Romance: Selections from the German Romantic Authors, 1790–1830 in English Translation* (New York: Oxford, 1927);

Der zerbrochne Krug: Ein Lustspiel (Berlin: Realschulbuchhandlung, 1811); translated by J. Krumpelmann as *The Broken Jug: A Comedy, Poet Lore,* 45 (1939): 146–209;

Germania an ihre Kinder (N.p., 1813);

Das erwachte Europa (Berlin: Achenwall, 1814);

Hinterlassene Schriften, edited by Ludwig Tieck (Berlin: Reimer, 1821)–includes *Die Hermannsschlacht: Ein Drama; Prinz Friedrich von Homburg: Ein Schauspiel,* translated by Francis Lloyd and William Newton as *Prince Frederick of Homburg,* in *Prussia's Representative Man* (London: Trübner, 1875); translated by Hermann Hagedorn as *The Prince of Homburg,* in *The German Classics of the Nineteenth and Twentieth Centuries,* edited by Kuno Francke and W. G. Howard, volume 4 (New York: German Publications Society, 1913); and "Fragment aus dem Trauerspiel Robert Guiskard, Herzog der Normänner";

Gesammelte Schriften, edited by Tieck, 3 volumes (Berlin: Reimer, 1826);

Gesammelte Schriften, edited by Tieck, revised by J. Schmidt (Berlin: Reimer, 1859);

Politische Schriften und andere Nachträge zu seinen Werken, edited by Rudolf Koepke (Berlin: Charisius, 1862);

Werke: Kritisch durchgesehene und erl. Gesamtausgabe, edited by E. Schmidt, G. Minde-Pouet, and R. Steig, 5 volumes (Leipzig: Bibliographisches Institut, 1904–1905);

Sämtliche Werke und Briefe, edited by Helmut Sembdner, 2 volumes (Munich: Hanser, 1985);

Sämtliche Werke und Briefe, edited by Ilse-Marie Barth, Klaus Müller-Salget, and Hinrich C. Seeba, 4 volumes (Frankfurt am Main: Deutscher Klassiker Verlag, 1987–1997).

OTHER: *Phöbus: Ein Journal für die Kunst,* edited by Kleist and Adam H. Müller (volume 1, nos. 1–10, Dresden: Gärtner, 1808; nos. 11–12, Dresden: Walther, 1808);

Berliner Abendblätter, edited by Kleist (first quarter, nos. 1–77, Berlin: Hitzig, 1810; second quarter, nos. 1–76, Berlin: Kunst-und Industrie-Comptoir, 1811).

PERIODICAL PUBLICATION: "Über das Marionettentheater," *Berliner Abendblätter,* 12–15 December 1810; translated by Christian Albrecht-Gollub as "On the Marionette Theater," in *German Romantic Criticism: Novalis, Schlegel, Schleiermacher, and Others,* edited by A. Leslie Willson (New York: Continuum, 1982).

One of the most enigmatic of German writers, Heinrich von Kleist has been the object of critical debate and controversy from his appearance on the literary scene, in the first decade of the nineteenth century, to the present day. That his creative genius was of an exceptionally high order has never been disputed. It was rather the extremity and immoderation of his depictions that shocked his contemporaries, denying him the public and critical acclaim he coveted and believed he deserved. In his plays and stories, raging passions result in shattered skulls with brains oozing from them and suitors slain and devoured in the name of love. This very propensity has contributed to maintaining interest in his works, as have the shocking circumstances of his suicide.

Kleist's short life is almost as much a puzzle as his works. (His death came just a month after his thirty-fourth birthday; he never married.) In his plays and stories, the facts at least are clear; only their meaning is in doubt. Regarding his life, however, there is a dearth of information.

He was born in Frankfurt an der Oder on 18 October 1777. On his father's side the men in the family mostly served as officers in the Prussian army, some having risen to the rank of general; the Kleists thus were known throughout German-speaking countries as a military family. The expectation was, therefore, that Heinrich would follow that career, or at least one in the Prussian civil service. His father, Joachim Friedrich von Kleist, a captain in the Leopold von Braunschweig Regiment, died in June 1788, when Kleist was ten; the youth was sent to the Prussian capital Berlin to be educated. His mother, Juliane Ulrike von Kleist (née von Pannwitz) died in February 1793, by which time Kleist was a corporal in the King's Guard Regiment based at Potsdam. When he had his first experience of military service in an area of combat, with allied armies opposing French revolutionary forces at the Rhine, he was thus largely out in the world on his own; his mother's sister, an officer's widow, presided over the orphaned family back home in Frankfurt an der Oder.

In the spring of 1799 he turned his back on the secure military career that was expected of him to return home and take up studies at the small university there, with the intention possibly of becoming a professor. He attended the university only one year, 1799–1800, and never completed his studies. At the time of his resignation from the military there was no indication that he was thinking of pursuing a literary career. He threw himself instead into study of science and philosophy, and tried out his pedagogical skills by organizing and teaching a private course for a dozen aristocratic young women.

This attempt at pedagogy led at the end of the year to his proposal of marriage to one of the students, Wilhelmine von Zenge, two years his junior and the elder of two daughters of Kleist's neighbor, the local regimental commander. His engagement to Wilhelmine made the choice of a career more pressing. Her family would not consent to the marriage until his ability to support her properly was assured. It was for this reason that he broke off his studies at the university the year after having begun them, and went to Berlin in the summer of 1800 to seek a civil position in the Prussian bureaucracy. Late that August he interrupted this stay to embark on a mysterious journey.

The purpose of this trip, about which Kleist engaged in deliberate mystification, has remained one of the great secrets in his life. The journey led to a protracted visit in the Catholic, Franconian university city of Würzburg, on the Main river. The chances are that the goal was medical treatment, and probably for a sexual deficiency; but Kleist created the impression in letters to his fiancée and to his half sister Ulrike, the only member of his immediate family in whom he confided, that he was on a secret diplomatic or commercial mission related to the aim of his securing a civil position.

Not long after Kleist's return to Berlin he was writing to Ulrike that a career in the civil service would be impossibly uncongenial for him and to Wilhelmine that their marriage might need to be postponed—perhaps for as long as six years, until he could support them by writing about Kantian philosophy (much discussed at the time) or by teaching. He would need, he wrote, to go to Paris; Ulrike, whom he asked to help pay for the journey, accepted his perhaps only half-hearted invitation to join him. In justifying his need to get away, he reported that Kant's assertion that the existence of God and thus of any absolute could never be shown had destroyed his belief in man's ability to know the truth; he needed time to rethink his aims and purposes.

While there was in the winter of 1800 and early spring of 1801 still no hint that he was thinking of a literary career, the ensuing trip to Paris that spring and early summer carried him first to the Saxon capital Dresden, known as Florence on the Elbe, with its impressive architecture and cultivation of the arts. The famous Dresden gallery attracted him so strongly that he could hardly be persuaded to continue the journey. Then, as he and Ulrike traveled on toward Paris, they stopped to visit the elderly author Johann Wilhelm

Gleim, who had been a friend of their distant relative Ewald Christian von Kleist, a poet who died from wounds received in the battle of Kunersdorf during the Seven Years' War. Paris itself was, of course, a center for artists and poets. By the end of his stay there, it was clear that Kleist, now just turned twenty-four, had determined to support himself and achieve fame as an author.

Kleist wrote to his fiancée that he would never return to his Prussian fatherland until he could do so honorably crowned with poetic laurels. He therefore begged her to join him in Switzerland, where he planned to take up farming while he strove for literary fame; but she declined, and their engagement was broken off. In Bern he was encouraged in his writing by a circle of three literary friends: Heinrich Zschokke, a young author and pedagogue prominent in Swiss politics; Heinrich Gessner, publisher and son of Salomon Gessner, the celebrated Swiss writer of idylls; and Ludwig Wieland, son of the well-known German author Christoph Martin Wieland. That winter of 1802 and spring of 1803, Kleist read to them from a play he was completing, the lovers' tragedy *Die Familie Schroffenstein* (1803; translated as *The Feud of the Schroffensteins,* 1916), which takes from Shakespeare's Romeo and Juliet its theme of family enmity standing in the way of young love.

This first of Kleist's works already bears the stamp of his peculiar genius. The dramatic tension is located so deeply and completely in the characters' emotions that there is essentially no reflection, only action. Thus, even the soliloquies are almost wholly expressions of passion, not contemplations of ideas; and in the dialogues, the characters' responses are often fragmentary or enigmatic, suggesting mental confusion or emotional conflict. Intensity of feeling produces frequent lapses of comprehension on the part of the characters, and occasional faintings. The spectator or reader is left with uncertainty, too, about the characters' intentions, motivations, and emotions, which often are indicated not by words, but by gestures. One of the marks of Kleist's greatness is thus that he does not tell his audience what to think about the action or how to understand it. The emotions of each character form a drama within the drama, because the characters typically know no more what to make of their own feelings and actions than they do of those around them.

The enmity between the families of the two lovers Ottokar and Agnes von Schroffenstein—they are first cousins, their mothers being sisters, while their fathers are more distantly related—has resulted from mistrust owing to the provision that if one of the lines of the family is left without an heir its estate falls to the other line. The situation enables Kleist to exploit the possibilities of confused perceptions about the motives of others, and inner doubt and uncertainty about the purity of one's own feelings and motivations. Also, since the tension between the families renders the young lovers' passion a forbidden one, the intensity of their romantic desire is that much greater, as in *Romeo and Juliet*. Kleist emphasizes this point by commingling, to a far greater extent than Shakespeare did, erotic passion and thoughts of suicide. In addition, Kleist makes his heroine the object of passion on the part of the hero's illegitimate brother, Johann, and of less intense attraction for two older men as well, her middle-aged suitor and relative Jeronimus and her blind old grandfather, Sylvius. The veiled role of erotic desire in motivating the characters' actions contributes significantly to the mysteriousness of their behavior and their mystification of themselves, one another, and Kleist's audience.

Kleist may have brought this play with him to Switzerland in almost completed form. It was, in any case, published there anonymously by Gessner's firm in 1803, not long after Kleist had returned to Germany. Still in Switzerland in the spring of 1802, he repaired to an island on the lake at Thun to devote himself to writing, perhaps the play that became the comedy *Der zerbrochne Krug* (1811; translated as *The Broken Jug,* 1939), but especially historical drama, probably including "Robert Guiskard, Herzog der Normänner" (Robert Guiskard, Duke of the Normans), which became for him, at this early stage, the test of his calling to poetic greatness.

The effort at proving his talent for historical drama perhaps contributed to his falling ill that summer, so that he had to leave the island to put himself under a physician's care in Bern. There he was joined in September by Ulrike, who rushed to his aid when she learned he was sick and needing money. By the time she reached Bern he had recovered; and they soon departed for Germany with Wieland, who had incurred the displeasure of the revolutionary government in Bern and been ordered to leave. The intention was to accompany Wieland home to visit his famous father; and although Wieland changed his plans and Ulrike journeyed homeward to Prussia, Kleist went on by himself to meet the elderly poet and stayed with him as his guest on his estate near Weimar. During this visit Kleist again struggled to progress with writing the play about the medieval Norman ruler, and remained with Wieland through the winter of 1802 to the following spring, when the romantic passion that the old author's youngest daughter conceived for the young poet occasioned his departure. He moved to Leipzig, and then on to Dresden, still unhappy with the results of his labors on "Robert Guiskard."

In Dresden a friend from his youth in the military, Ernst von Pfuel, who in later years was to become a high Prussian official, encouraged Kleist to turn his talents to comedy to distract himself from his torment with the serious play. When that remedy failed, Pfuel arranged to travel with him to Switzerland. From there they went to Paris, where, in October 1803, Kleist suffered a complete collapse of his hopes and, after arguing with Pfuel, set out for Normandy intending to seek death in the invasion of England Napoleon was planning. Instead, this crisis of suicidal despair ended with his being persuaded to return to Paris, once his identity was discovered, and then to accede to the Prussian ambassador's stipulation that, in view of his attempt to join the French forces, he accept a passport constraining him to return by direct route to his homeland. For unknown reasons, perhaps having to do with secret missions or activities of a political nature, but more likely because of despair over the prospect of having to explain himself to government authorities on his return to Prussia and over his failed ambitions for the Guiskard play, when he reached Germany, Kleist, who was ailing, remained in the Rhineland through the following spring, spending most of the time in Mainz as houseguest of a physician named Georg Christian Gottlob Freiherr von Wedekind, a friend of Wieland's, who took him in so that he could keep him under observation.

When Kleist finally presented himself to officials in Berlin in the summer of 1804, he was sharply reprimanded for his behavior; but, aided by intercession from friends and relatives, he was offered an appointment in the finance ministry. The following spring, he accepted an offer to be allowed to study in Königsberg, at government expense, under the leading economist Christian Jakob Kraus, and arrived there the first week of May 1805. At this juncture he enjoyed the encouragement and support of highly placed officials. Karl Freiherr vom Stein zum Altenstein, particularly, who was soon to become finance minister, took a special interest in him as a promising prospective public servant. Yet Kleist continued to be devoted to his writing, which he likely had never ceased except for the period of despair in France. In Berlin, while waiting to receive civil appointment, he had attended the literary salons and worked on his manuscripts. Now in Königsberg, he increasingly withdrew to his writing and neglected the study of finance. During his second summer in Königsberg, he sought and received a leave of absence for health reasons, as a way of easing out of his commitment to pursue a career in civil service. He wrote at the time to Otto August Rühle von Lilienstern, a friend from his military youth who shared Kleist's interest in literature, that he intended for the rest of his life, "as long as that lasts," to do tragedies and comedies: "Du weißt, daß ich meine Karriere wieder verlassen habe. . . . Ich will mich jetzt durch meine dramatischen Arbeiten ernähren; und nur, wenn Du meinst, daß sie auch dazu nicht taugen, würde mich Dein Urteil schmerzen, und auch das nur, weil ich verhungern müßte. Sonst magst Du über ihren Wert urteilen, wie Du willst" (You know that I have left my career [in government service] again. . . . I want to support myself now through my dramatic works; and only if you think that they are not even good enough for that would your verdict pain me, and then only because I would have to starve to death. Otherwise, you may judge them as you wish).

Prussia's crushing defeat by Napoleon at Jena and Auerstedt on 14 October 1806 found Kleist still in Königsberg, to which the Prussian court fled in the face of Berlin's capture by the French. Civilian and military refugees followed the king and queen to East Prussia, so that Königsberg soon became overcrowded. Already having planned to move to a center of publishing to help further his aim of supporting himself from his writings, Kleist the following January set out for Dresden by way of Berlin. In the occupied Prussian capital, however, he was arrested and sent as a war prisoner to Châlons-sur-Marne, in France, evidently under the suspicion that as former military officers he and his traveling companions were on a mission for the Prussian government. During this captivity, which lasted until early July 1807, when the peace treaty was signed at Tilsit in East Prussia, Kleist was able for the most part to continue his writing, and enjoyed the satisfaction of learning that a second book of his had been published, the first since *Die Familie Schroffenstein* four years before.

This new work of Kleist's was the play *Amphitryon* (1807; translated as *Amphitryon: A Comedy,* 1962), an adaptation of Molière's comedy of the same title, in turn derived from Plautus's *Amphitruo.* As contemporary critics were quick to observe, Kleist transformed the French farce into something quite sublime, and introduced an element of idealization, transcendence, and mystery into the play's previously matter-of-fact sensuality. In particular, he deepened the relationship between the heroine Alkmene and the god Jupiter, who took the form of her husband Amphitryon in order to spend a night of love with her. Goethe, who read the play at the baths in Carlsbad that summer and was both fascinated and bothered by it, remarked in his diary (13 July 1807) that Kleist aimed at depicting a "Verwirrung des Gefühls" (confusion of emotions) in the main figures.

Following his release from prison at Châlons-sur-Marne, Kleist finally was able to reach his journey's original goal, Dresden, where Rühle von Lil-

ienstern, to whom he had entrusted several of his completed manuscripts, was living and where *Amphitryon* had been published. Rühle had just had a much-discussed book published on a military subject; and the two friends, reckoning that they could make far more from their writings by publishing the books themselves, joined in a venture with Adam Heinrich Müller, a lecturer and publicist, who had been instrumental in the publication of *Amphitryon* and had written the preface for it. The positive critical reception of that play, together with the news that Goethe had accepted Kleist's other finished comedy, *Der zerbrochne Krug,* for production at the court theater in Weimar, contributed to Kleist's being lionized by literary circles in Dresden. Thus, with his thirtieth birthday in the fall of 1807, his dream of literary fame and of supporting himself from his writings appeared about to be fulfilled, after six years of ardent striving and of doubt and despair.

Almost immediately, these high hopes were dashed. An ambitious literary periodical, *Phöbus,* edited by Kleist and Müller, was announced and promoted with a pretentious exuberance that won it only enemies and no friends, so that long before 1808 was out the enterprise was doomed, and the issues of that first and only year were brought to completion late and with great difficulty. Goethe's production of *Der zerbrochne Krug* failed in Weimar; and Kleist's resulting attacks on Goethe, blaming him for the failure, further cast a shadow over him with the public. The underlying reason for the defeat of Kleist's hopes, however, surely was the peculiar nature of his poetic gift. He was simply a problematic genius.

The failure of Kleist's comedy on the stage was attributed to what Goethe and others viewed as a lack of a truly dramatic plot. The scene is set entirely in the courtroom of a Dutch village magistrate; and the drama revolves around the gradual revelation that the judge himself is the culprit in the case at hand, which involves a broken jug and an attempt on a maiden's honor. Like all of Kleist's plays and stories, the comedy is a masterpiece of finely drawn psychological depiction, which was undoubtedly a reason for Goethe's having wanted to produce it. The audience in Weimar rejected the play chiefly because they found it boring; but there were also complaints about offenses against good taste and propriety, perhaps because of the eroticism expressed in some of the characters' emotional outbursts.

The tragedy *Penthesilea* (1808; translated, 1959), excerpted in the first issue of *Phöbus* and published as a book that same year, most strikingly reveals Kleist's unsettling peculiarities as an author. Kleist wrote at the time, to his relative by marriage Marie von Kleist, his intimate, older friend and benefactress at the Prussian court, that the play contained "der ganze Schmutz zuglcich und Glanz meiner Seele" (the whole filth as well as splendor of my soul; it has been debated whether Kleist wrote Schmutz , filth, or Schmerz, pain). The drama is a depiction of intense romantic passion, rendered extreme because the heroine, the title character, is queen of the Amazons, and is therefore prohibited from choosing a lover instead of merely accepting the one that falls to her by the luck of battle. While her society dictates that Penthesilea shall capture a warrior solely to mate with him to produce daughters who will guarantee the survival of the all-female state, feminine vanity coupled with erotic desire makes her yearn to captivate Achilles with her charms, as much or more than to vanquish him on the battlefield. Faced with her inability to defeat him, she complains to her sister Amazons that they should allow her to become his captive and concubine; but ashamed at having thus impulsively divulged her secret wish, she reacts to Achilles' renewed invitation to combat by calling forth the whole machinery of destruction at her command to run him down like a hunted animal and then to eat the flesh of his corpse. When she learns that he called her out to battle only to surrender to her, she dies of a broken heart, but happy that her charms had moved him after all. The play's bizarre eroticism, especially in association with murder, lust, and suicidal urges, turned public favor away from Kleist. The enigmatic behavior of his characters in *Die Familie Schroffenstein* and *Amphitryon* had fascinated his readers; but Penthesilea's desperate passion struck them as offending against decency and propriety.

In 1807 the first of Kleist's stories to be published, "Das Erdbeben in Chili" (collected in *Erzählungen* [Stories], volume 1, 1810; translated as "Earthquake in Chile," 1946), appeared–under the title "Jeronimo und Josephe," the names of the hero and heroine–in a leading periodical, the publisher Johann Friedrich Cotta's *Morgenblatt für gebildete Stände* (Morning Paper for the Cultivated Classes), shortly after Kleist's arrival in Dresden. It tells of the tragic fate of a young couple who, on the verge of death and suicide, are spared by a terrible earthquake only to be slain by an angry crowd of churchgoers eager to find scapegoats for the sinfulness that they believe has brought God's judgment on the city in the form of the natural disaster. The tale appears to have been favorably received and certainly did not detract from Kleist's positive, enthusiastic reception in his first months in Dresden. The same cannot be said of his next published story when it appeared in his journal *Phöbus* in 1808. Opinions on "Die Marquise von O . . . " (collected in *Erzählungen,* volume 1; translated as "The Marquise of O . . . ," 1929) were divided, with women readers in particular finding embarrassing or revolting this tale about a rape that occurs while the heroine is in a faint, and about which she and the

reader learn only after she has become pregnant. Here Kleist aimed once again at depicting the "confusion of emotions" of which Goethe spoke in regard to *Amphitryon;* but as with *Penthesilea,* his focus on uncontrolled erotic passion alienated many in his audience.

Following the failure of his publishing venture centered around the journal *Phöbus,* and the disappointing reception given *Penthesilea* and "Die Marquise von O . . . " by readers and *Der zerbrochne Krug* in Goethe's production, Kleist set his hopes on a play better suited for success in the theater. This was the "Grand Historical Chivalric Play" *Das Käthchen von Heilbronn oder Die Feuerprobe* (Katie of Heilbronn; or, The Trial by Fire, 1810; translated as "Kate of Heilbronn," 1841), which he tailored especially for the Vienna stage, hoping to make use of the good contacts with the Austrian court he had established in Dresden through the embassy secretary Joseph von Buol-Mühlingen and the connections he had made, via Adam Müller, with the author and government official Friedrich von Gentz. Though *Das Käthchen von Heilbronn* is thoroughly Kleistian, particularly in the emotional violence attendant upon the aristocratic hero's struggle to suppress his passion for the beautiful burgher heroine, it is still quite recognizable as a romantic and extremely tender love story and remains a popular favorite with theater audiences. This success did not become assured until after Kleist's death, however, and then at first only with texts substantially adapted for the stage.

Das Käthchen von Heilbronn was performed during Kleist's lifetime, and in Vienna, but not until early spring of 1810. One reason for the delay was the outbreak of hostilities between Austria and France. Anticipating that turn of events, on the first day of 1809 Kleist sent the manuscript of another play, the patriotic drama *Die Hermannsschlacht* (The Battle of Teutoburg Forest, published in *Hinterlassene Schriften* [Posthumous Writings], 1821), to his contact with the Viennese theaters, Heinrich Joseph von Collin, secretary to the court and a writer himself, suggesting that the play might be performed first, before *Das Käthchen von Heilbronn,* because its topicality would make its success more certain. On 9 April Austria declared war on France; and at the end of the month Kleist left Dresden with an Austrian passport and headed via Prague for Vienna, but failed to reach there because Napoleon captured the Austrian capital on 13 May. In Prague, Kleist and his traveling companion, the young scholar Friedrich Christoph Dahlmann (later, with Jacob and Wilhelm Grimm one of the seven Göttingen professors who protested the revocation of Hannover's constitution in 1837), sought, with others, to establish a journal, *Germania,* to agitate for Napoleon's defeat. Austria was decisively beaten on 5 July at Wagram, however; and Kleist was prevented from making a name for himself as a patriotic publicist, and thus from joining the ranks of others in his Romantic generation, including Friedrich Schlegel in Vienna and Ernst Moritz Arndt in Berlin, who found employment through their enthusiasm for the cause of liberation from French domination.

Information is scant about Kleist's life from July 1809 to the following February. Clearly, though, his travels in this period home to Frankfurt an der Oder, to Berlin, and westward to the other Frankfurt, on the Main, concerned his financial plight and his desperate need to secure a future for himself as a writer.

In the end, Kleist returned to the capital of his native Prussia. Arriving in Berlin at the beginning of February 1810, he renewed contacts with literary friends and made new ones, drawing especially close to Achim von Arnim and Clemens Brentano. Again he frequented the literary salons, particularly that of Rahel Levin (better known as Rahel Varnhagen von Ense because of her marriage a few years later), and met such important publishers as Georg Andreas Reimer, Johann Daniel Sander, and Julius Eduard Hitzig. *Penthesilea* had been published by Cotta in the fall of 1808; and at the beginning of 1810, Kleist had sent the manuscript of *Das Käthchen von Heilbronn* to him. When Cotta indicated, though, that he would not be able to publish the volume by the end of the year, Kleist offered it to Reimer, whose Realschulbuchhandlung produced it that autumn, followed by *Der zerbrochne Krug* in February 1811. Reimer likewise published a volume of Kleist's tales in fall 1810, and the next summer brought out a second one.

Kleist's hopes for financial survival, though, came in the fall of 1810, pinned on a publishing project of a new sort, a daily newspaper edited by him and called *Berliner Abendblätter* (Berlin Evening Newspages). The venture was initially greeted with enthusiasm, partly because the paper was the only one in the city to appear each weekday, and was thus able to provide brief reports of events such as crimes and fires almost immediately after they happened. Entertaining anecdotes and other short pieces of excellent quality were offered, too, as well as essays on contemporary economic, political, and cultural matters of interest, most of them authored by Kleist and his collaborators, who included Arnim, Brentano, Friedrich de la Motte Fouqué, Wilhelm Grimm, and Adam Müller, among others. The first issue of the *Abendblätter* appeared on 1 October 1810. Before the end of the year, Hitzig withdrew as its publisher; and with the new firm, August Kuhn, publisher of the established journal *Der Freimüthige* (The Frank Talker), the *Abendblätter* limped along through the second quarter of its first year before ceasing publication at the end of March 1811. Though the venture failed, it

occasioned some of Kleist's finest prose, from his masterful recastings of material from other journals to brilliantly ironic satirical pieces and the enigmatic fictional dialogue "Über das Marionetten-theater" (1810; translated as "On the Marionette Theater," 1982), of which dozens of critical and scholarly interpretations have appeared.

A major reason for Kleist's turn to the newspaper venture was that the Berlin stage seemed to be closed to his plays; and except for the three-evening, heavily attended run of *Das Käthchen von Heilbronn* in Vienna, he was not making headway in other major theater cities either. About the time of the performance of *Das Käthchen von Heilbronn* in Vienna in the spring of 1810, it was planned that Kleist's new play, *Prinz Friedrich von Homburg* (published in *Hinterlassene Schriften;* translated as *Prince Frederick of Homburg,* 1875), would be performed at the private theater of Anton Heinrich, Prince of Radziwill, husband of Princess Luise of Prussia, and then at Berlin's Nationaltheater; but when it was learned that the hero and title character, a young Prussian officer, becomes terrified at the sight of the grave being dug for him, prominent persons in the army and at court became indignant, and the plan to perform the play was abandoned. Then, that summer, the much-celebrated actor and playwright August Wilhelm Iffland, director of the Nationaltheater, rejected *Das Käthchen von Heilbronn* for performance there.

Prinz Friedrich von Homburg was Kleist's third play on a historical subject, after the unfinished "Robert Guiskard" and *Die Hermannsschlacht.* Only the first ten scenes of "Robert Guiskard," a play about the Norman leader's plan to conquer Constantinople in 1085, have survived, and only in the version published in Kleist's journal *Phöbus* in the double issue for April and May 1808 (and later included in *Hinterlassene Schriften*). This fragment, though, suffices to demonstrate how powerful a drama it might have become had he been able to finish it. These scenes again reveal Kleist's use of dramatic gesture and unfinished utterance paired with Homeric similes, hyperbolic metaphor, convoluted rhetoric, and disrupted word order—all to indicate the emotional conflicts and secret thoughts and feelings of the characters. Yet "Robert Guiskard" is anomalous in having no romantic interest, only a moral and political one. Moreover, the central figure is dying of the plague and is much debilitated at the opening of the play. These differences may explain why, of all of Kleist's major works that have survived, "Robert Guiskard" is the only one he never finished. He did complete *Die Hermannsschlacht,* for example, a consummately political drama (indeed, very much a propaganda piece, using the German defeat of Roman legions in the Teutoburg forest in A.D. 9 to urge revolt against Napoleonic influence and rule in Germany). But in this play the central figure, far from being sickly, is entirely robust and in condition thoroughly to savor his triumph in the end. Romantic drama, too, is not lacking in the play. The work's poetic interest is owing largely to the susceptibility of the German leader's wife to the flattering attentions of a young Roman diplomat and the–typically Kleistian–emotional conflict this produces in her.

Prinz Friedrich von Homburg is as much a love story as a piece about political and moral issues. With this drama, which may have supplanted or superseded "Robert Guiskard" in Kleist's poetic imagination, he largely returned to depiction of erotic desire and its sublimations evident in the earlier plays, from *Die Familie Schroffenstein* to the comedies *Amphitryon* and *Der zerbrochne Krug* and on to the romantic dramas *Penthesilea* and *Das Käthchen von Heilbronn*. To be sure, the issue in *Prinz Friedrich von Homburg* is whether the young prince is guilty of insubordination and treason for disobeying orders to delay his cavalry charge and whether he should be executed for it. Yet the prize of which he dreams and which makes him yearn to win laurels on the battlefield is quite specifically marriage to the elector's pretty niece; and that is the very reward Brandenburg's ruler apparently accords him, once Homburg has shown his greater heroism by proving he is ready to accept death as punishment for his questionable deed.

Among Kleist's stories, "Michael Kohlhaas," of which the beginning was published in *Phöbus*, is the most political, especially with the completion he gave it for the first volume of *Erzählungen*, where it appeared with "Das Erdbeben in Chili" and "Die Marquise von O . . . ," both of which had appeared in finished form earlier. Kohlhaas, a subject of the elector of Brandenburg, is a horse trader who doggedly, single-mindedly, and violently seeks restitution for a cruel wrong done him by a member of the neighboring Saxon nobility. The tale, based on a chronicle from Luther's time, has been a favorite with readers for its historical realism and narrative objectivity, but has been criticized for the seemingly pointless, drawn-out story toward the end about a gypsy woman and a mysterious capsule containing a secret prophecy concerning the future of Saxony's ruling family. Often overlooked is that the tale is also a love story. The immediate occasion for Kohlhaas's murderous rampage is his wife's death as a consequence of his efforts to win justice (this is where the fragment in *Phöbus* broke off); grief over her loss is uppermost in his mind in the climactic scene when he visits Luther to justify his behavior; and the dead wife herself proves to have sought to protect him from beyond the grave as his guardian angel, in the form of the gypsy woman.

Political history and romance are mixed, too, in the first story of the second volume of Kleist's *Erzählungen*, "Die Verlobung in St. Domingo," (translated as "The Engagement in Santo Domingo," 1960), set during the black Haitians' revolt against the whites in the wake of the refusal to accept freedom and equality for the blacks as ordered by the revolutionary government in France in 1794. (Kleist's interest in these events was aroused evidently by his having been imprisoned in 1807 temporarily in the same Fort Joux in France where the black Haitian leader Toussaint l'Ouverture had been held captive and died in 1804.) The second tale of the volume, "Das Bettelweib von Locarno" (translated as "The Beggar Woman of Locarno," 1934), while not political, does contain an element of class resentment, in that the woman has been treated gruffly by an Italian aristocrat and returns from the grave to haunt his castle; but the short piece is chiefly a masterful ghost story, memorable in its lack of explanation of the apparition and for the suicidal horror and despair it produces in the central figure. "Der Findling" (translated as "The Foundling," 1960), the third of these five stories, likewise involves class tension. A rich Roman merchant, widowed and still more recently grieving over the death of his child by his first wife, rescues a youth from the plague and adopts him to replace the dead son. When the youth reaches maturity he attempts to rape the benefactor's young wife, taking advantage of her romantic love for an aristocratic Genovese youth who had died as a result of his heroic rescue of her when she was a girl and whom the adopted foundling resembles, especially when dressed in appropriate costume. The succeeding tale, "Die heilige Cäcilie oder Die Gewalt der Musik, Eine Legende" (translated as "St. Cecilia; or, The Power of Music: A Catholic Legend," 1844), has a religious rather than a political or social subject. Four young Dutch brothers involved in a planned attack on a convent in Aix-la-Chapelle during the period of iconoclasm in the wake of the Reformation fall strangely insane after a young nun, pale from having just arisen from her sickbed, has appeared in the convent church to direct the playing of an old Italian Mass. As in Kleist's ghost story, there is no single, satisfactory explanation of this mystery. The concluding story, "Der Zweikampf" (translated as "The Duel," 1960), which is the last work from Kleist's pen that has been preserved, has a religious subject, too. A duel is fought to seek God's judgment of a woman's virtue; and as a consequence, a tender love story unfolds and competes for the reader's attention with the question of whether God's hand is evident in the duel's result.

Volume 2 of Kleist's *Erzählungen* appeared at the beginning of August 1811; but this gratification was not enough to sustain him. He was unable to earn enough from publication of his plays and stories to survive financially. A last, desperate hope for supporting himself was reinstatement as a military officer (that request was languishing in the files at the time of his death). Ulrike had lent or given him money time and again over the years, much to his shame; but when he visited her in September to ask for enough to outfit himself for the prospective officer's commission, he met with a rebuke from her and several relatives who were with her in the family home in Frankfurt an der Oder.

Kleist's financial plight and other disappointments deepened his sense of loneliness. After the breaking off of his engagement to Wilhelmine von Zenge he had resolved never to marry and to devote himself entirely to his writing. In Dresden, on the way to Paris with Ulrike in the spring of 1801, he had drawn close to the two von Schlieben sisters, Caroline and Henriette, impoverished aristocrats; and during his later residence in Dresden, from late summer 1807 to spring 1809, he and Adam Müller reportedly quarreled over Sophie von Haza, the wife of Müller's former employer (Müller married her soon after she divorced her husband). Other women also played roles in Kleist's life; most were concerned for his welfare and survival and drawn to him because of his poetic genius. Of all of them, he was closest to his relative by marriage, Marie von Kleist, and felt that she best understood his poetic aspirations. When he died, however, it was in the company of a friend's wife who suffered from an incurable uterine cancer, and who accepted his offer to end her life and then his own. In the late afternoon of 21 November 1811, beside Lake Wannsee near Potsdam, Kleist shot Henriette Vogel through the chest and then discharged a second pistol in his mouth. Both died instantly; and after the investigation of the deaths, they were buried side by side at the spot the following evening.

The double suicide was reported throughout Europe and attracted much attention and debate, thereby helping to keep Kleist's memory alive and ultimately to stimulate critical interest in his works. Later in the century Prussia's political ascendance caused him to be praised for patriotic reasons. It was not until the vogue of literary naturalism in Germany in the 1880s and 1890s, though, that analysis of his works began in earnest, in this case emphasizing his depiction of the characters as creatures of biology and society. In the early decades of the twentieth century, during the period of expressionism and with the rise of intellectual history, interest became focused first on death mysticism in his works, and then on the crisis he suffered over Kant's philosophy and reported in his letters to his fiancée in the spring of 1801. The arrival of existentialism in the late 1920s and early 1930s caused this crisis

to assume new importance in criticism of Kleist's work, showing him to be a poet of man's struggle with an incomprehensible universe. Under Hitler, both the Prussian patriotic and existentialist views of Kleist were appropriated by National Socialists to portray him as a poet of Germany's tragic mission and destiny for greatness. Kleist criticism after World War II has largely reflected the existentialist approach; but since the 1960s there has been increasing emphasis on social, political, and historical aspects of his works. This orientation has moved Western criticism closer to the Marxist approach of Eastern European scholars, whose views in turn arose in reaction and response to earlier nationalist and existentialist perspectives. In the huge literature on Kleist that numbers books in the hundreds and articles in the thousands (a complete bibliography has not yet been prepared), many other critical viewpoints are also represented, including psychoanalytically oriented studies.

Letters:

Heinrich von Kleists Leben und Briefe: Mit einem Anhange, edited by Eduard von Bülow (Berlin: Besser, 1848);

Briefe an seine Schwester Ulrike, edited by August Koberstein (Berlin: Schroeder & Hermann Kaiser, 1860);

Briefe an seine Braut: Zum ersten Male nach den Originalhandschriften, edited by Karl Biedermann (Breslau: Schottlaender, 1884);

Letters of Heinrich von Kleist: With a Selection of Essays and Anecdotes, edited by Philip B. Miller (New York: Dutton, 1982).

Bibliographies:

Richard Kade, "Heinrich von Kleist," in Karl Goedeke, *Grundriß zur Geschichte der deutschen Dichtung aus den Quellen,* revised by Edmund Goetze, volume 6 (Leipzig, Berlin & Dresden: Ehlermann, 1898), pp. 96–104;

Alexander von Weilen, "Zur Kleist-Literatur des Jahres 1911," *Zeitschrift für die österreichischen Gymnasien,* 63 (1912): 198–218;

Georg Minde-Pouet, "Neue Kleistliteratur," *Das literarische Echo,* 15 (1912–1913): columns 968–978;

Minde-Pouet, "Kleist-Bibliographie 1914–1921," Jahrbuch der Kleist-Gesellschaft, 1 (1921): 89–169;

Minde-Pouet, "Kleist-Bibliographie 1922," *Jahrbuch der Kleist-Gesellschaft,* 2 (1922): 112–163;

Minde-Pouet, "Kleist-Bibliographie 1923 und 1924 mit Nachträgen," *Jahrbuch der Kleist-Gesellschaft,* 3–4 (1923–1924): 181–230;

Paul Kluckhohn, "Das Kleistbild der Gegenwart: Bericht über die Kleistliteratur der Jahre 1922–25,"

Deutsche Vierteljahrsschrift für Literaturwissenschaft und Geistegeschichte, 4 (1926): 798–830;

Minde-Pouet, "Kleist-Bibliographie 1925–1930 mit Nachträgen," *Jahrbuch der Kleist-Gesellschaft,* 11–12 (1929–1930): 60–193;

Minde-Pouet, "Kleist Bibliographie 1931 bis 1937 mit Nachträgen," *Jahrbuch der Kleist-Gesellschaft,* 17 (1933–1937): 186–263;

Roger Ayrault, *La Légende de Heinrich von Kleist: Un poéte devant la critique* (Paris: Nizet et Bastard, 1934);

Kluckhohn, "Kleist-Forschung 1926–1943," *Deutsche Vierteljahrsschrift für Literaturwissenchaft und Geistesgeschichte,* 21 (1943): 45–87;

Helmut Kreuzer, "Kleist-Literatur 1955–1960," *Der Deutschunterricht,* 13, no. 2 (1961): 116–135;

Eva Rothe, "Kleist-Bibliographie 1945–60," *Jahrbuch der Deutschen Schiller-Gesellschaft,* 5 (1961): 414–547;

Horst Schiller, ed., *Heinrich von Kleist 1777–1811: Auswahlbibliographie über Leben, Werk und Zeit* (Frankfurt an der Oder & Berlin: Zentralinstitut für Bibliothekswesen, 1962);

Werner Preuss, "Hundertfünfzig Jahre Kleist-Forschung," *Wissenschaftliche Zeitschrift der Pädagogischen Hochschule Potsdam: Gesellschaftsund Sprachwissenschaftliche Reihe,* 10 (1966): 243–262;

Helmut Sembdner, *Kleist-Bibliographie 1803–62: Heinrich von Kleists Schriften in frühen Drucken und Erstveröffentlichungen* (Stuttgart: Eggert, 1966);

Manfred Lefèvre, "Kleist-Forschung 1961–1967," *Colloquia Germanica,* 3 (1969): 1–86;

Helmut G. Hermann, "Der Dramatiker Heinrich von Kleist: Eine Bibliographie," in *Kleists Dramen: Neue Interpretationen,* edited by Walter Hinderer (Stuttgart: Reclam, 1981), pp. 238–289.

Biographies:

Max Morris, *Heinrich von Kleists Reise nach Würzburg* (Berlin: Skopnik, 1899);

Reinhold Steig, *Heinrich von Kleists Berliner Kämpfe* (Berlin & Stuttgart: Spemann, 1901);

Steig, *Neue Kunde zu Heinrich von Kleist* (Berlin: Reimer, 1902);

Otto Brahm, *Das Leben Heinrichs von Kleist,* fourth revised edition (Berlin: Egon Fleischl, 1911);

Heinrich Meyer-Benfey, *Kleists Leben und Werke: Dem deutschen Volke dargestellt* (Göttingen: Hapke, 1911);

Heinz Ide, *Der junge Kleist* (Würzburg: Holzner, 1961);

Heinz Politzer, "Auf der Suche nach Identität: Zu Heinrich von Kleists Würzburger Reise," *Euphorion,* 61 (1967): 383–399; reprinted in his *Hatte Ödipus einen Ödipus-Komplex?: Versuche zum Thema Psychoanalyse und Literatur* (Munich: Piper, 1974), pp. 182–202;

Helmut Scmbdncr, *Heinrich von Kleists Nachruhm: Eine Wirkungsgeschichte in Dokumenten* (Berlin: Schünemann, 1967);

Sembdner, *Dichter über ihre Dichtungen: Heinrich von Kleist* (Munich: Heimeran, 1969);

Katharina Mommsen, *Kleists Kampf mit Goethe* (Heidelberg: Stiehm, 1974);

Sembdner, *In Sachen Kleist: Beiträge zur Forschung* (Munich: Carl Hanser, 1974);

Joachim Maass, *Kleist: Die Geschichte seines Lebens* (Bern & Munich: Scherz, 1977); abridged as *Kleist: A Biography,* translated by Ralph Manheim (New York: Farrar, Straus & Giroux, 1983);

Sembdner, *Heinrich von Kleists Lebensspuren: Dokumente und Berichte der Zeitgenossen,* revised and enlarged edition (Frankfurt: Insel, 1977);

Hermann F. Weiss, *Funde und Studien zu Heinrich von Kleist* (Tübingen: Niemeyer, 1984).

References:

Ruth K. Angress, "Kleist's Treatment of Imperialism: 'Die Hermannsschlacht' and 'Die Verlobung in St. Domingo,'" *Monatshefte für deutschen Unterricht, deutsche Sprache und Literatur,* 69 (1977): 17–33;

Hermann Behme, *Heinrich von Kleist and C.M. Wieland* (Heidelberg: Winter, 1914);

John C. Blankenagel, *The Dramas of Heinrich von Kleist: A Biographical and Critical Study* (Chapel Hill: University of North Carolina Press, 1931);

Günter Blöcker, *Heinrich von Kleist oder das absolute Ich,* second edition (Berlin: Argon, 1962);

Friedrich Bruns, "Die Motivierung aus dem Unbewußten bei Heinrich von Kleist," in *Studies in Honor of Alexander Rudolph Hohlfeld* (Madison: University of Wisconsin Press, 1925), pp. 47–77;

Sigurd Burckhardt, *The Drama of Language: Essays on Goethe and Kleist,* edited by Bernhard Blume and Roy Harvey Pearce (Baltimore: Johns Hopkins University Press, 1970);

Ernst Cassirer, *Heinrich von Kleist und die kantische Philosophie* (Berlin: Reuther & Reichard, 1919); republished in his *Idee und Gestalt: Goethe, Schiller, Hölderlin, Kleist: Fünf Aufsätze* (Berlin: Bruno Cassirer, 1921), pp. 153–200;

Dorrit Cohn, "Kleist's 'Marquise von O . . .': The Problem of Knowledge," *Monatshefte für deutschen Unterricht, deutsche Sprache und Literatur,* 67 (1975): 129–144;

Josef Collin, "Heinrich von Kleist, der Dichter des Todes: Ein Beitrag zur Geschichte seiner Seele," *Euphorion,* 27 (1926): 69–112;

Donald H. Crosby, "Psychological Realism in the Works of Kleist: 'Penthesilea' and 'Die Marquise von O . . . ,'" *Literature and Psychology,* 19, no. 1 (1969): 3–16;

Peter Dettmering, *Heinrich von Kleist: Zur Psychodynamik seiner Dichtung* (Munich: Nymphenburger Verlagshandlung, 1975);

Denys Dyer, *The Stories of Kleist: A Critical Study* (New York: Holmes & Meier, 1977);

John Martin Ellis, *Heinrich von Kleist: Studies in the Character and Meaning of His Writings* (Chapel Hill: University of North Carolina Press, 1979);

Ellis, *Kleist's "Prinz Friedrich von Homburg": A Critical Study* (Berkeley: University of California Press, 1970);

Gerhard Fricke, *Gefühl und Schicksal bei Heinrich von Kleist: Studien über den inneren Vorgang im Leben und Schaffen des Dichters* (Berlin: Junker & Dünnhaupt, 1929);

Franziska Füller, *Das psychologische Problem der Frau in Kleists Dramen und Novellen* (Leipzig: Haessel, 1924);

John Gearey, *Heinrich von Kleist: A Study in Tragedy and Anxiety* (Philadelphia: University of Pennsylvania Press, 1968);

Ilse Graham, *Heinrich von Kleist: Word into Flesh: A Poet's Quest for the Symbol* (Berlin: De Gruyter, 1977);

Friedrich Gundolf, *Heinrich von Kleist* (Berlin: Bondi, 1922);

Dieter Harlos, *Die Gestaltung psychischer Konflikte einiger Frauengestaltungen im Werk Heinrich von Kleists: Alkmene, Die Marquise von O, Penthesilea, Käthchen von Heilbronn* (Frankfurt am Main: Lang, 1984);

Ingeborg Harms, "'Wie feilgender Sommer': Eine Untersuchung der Höhlenszene' in Heinrich von Kleists *Familie Schroffenstein,*" *Jahrbuch der Deutschen Schiller-Gesellschaft,* 28 (1984): 270–314;

Robert E. Helbling, *The Major Works of Heinrich von Kleist* (New York: New Directions, 1975);

Hanna Hellmann, *Heinrich von Kleist: Darstellung des Problems* (Heidelberg: Winter, 1911);

Walter Hinderer, ed., *Kleists Dramen: Neue Interpretationen* (Stuttgart: Reclam, 1981);

Johannes Hoffmeister, "Beitrag zur sogenannten Kantkrise Heinrich von Kleists," *Deutsche Vierteljahresschrift für Literaturwissenschaft und Geistesgeschichte,* 33 (1959): 574–587;

Werner Hoffmeister, "Die Doppeldeutigkeit der Erzählweise in Heinrich von Kleists 'Die heilige Cäcilie oder die Gewalt der Musik,'" in *Festschrift für Werner Neuse,* edited by Herbert Lederer and Joachim Seyppel (Berlin: Die Diagonale, 1967), pp. 44–56;

Hans Heinz Holz, *Macht und Ohnmacht der Sprache: Untersuchungen zum Sprachverständnis und Stil Heinrich von Kleists* (Frankfurt am Main: Athenäum, 1962);

Peter Horn, "Hatte Kleist Rassenvorurteile?: Eine kritische Auseinandersetzung mit der Literatur zur 'Verlobung in St. Domingo,'" *Monatshefte für deutschen Unterricht, deutsche Sprache und Literatur,* 67 (1975): 117–128;

Jahresgabe der Heinrich von Kleist-Gesellschaft, 1962, 1964, 1965–1966, 1968, edited by Walter Müller-Seidel (Berlin: Schmidt, 1962–1969);

Klaus Kanzog, *Edition und Engagement: 150 Jahre Editionsgeschichte der Werke Heinrich von Kleists,* 2 volumes (Berlin: De Gruyter, 1979);

Kleist-Jahrbuch (1980–);

Friedrich Koch, *Heinrich von Kleist: Bewusstsein und Wirklichkeit* (Stuttgart: Metzler, 1958);

Max Kommerell, "Die Sprache und das Unaussprechliche: Eine Betrachtung über Heinrich von Kleist," in his *Geist und Buchstabe der Dichtung: Goethe, Schiller, Kleist, Hölderlin,* fourth edition (Frankfurt am Main: Klostermann, 1956), pp. 243–317;

Helmut Koopmann, "Das 'rätselhafte Faktum' und seine Vorgeschichte: Zum analytischen Charakter der Novellen Heinrich von Kleists," *Zeitschrift für deutsche Philologie,* 84 (1965): 508–550;

Hans Joachim Kreutzer, *Die dichterische Entwicklung Heinrich von Kleists: Untersuchungen zu seinen Briefen und zu Chronologie und Aufbau seiner Werke* (Berlin: Schmidt, 1968);

Clara Kuoni, *Wirklichkeit und Idee in Heinrich von Kleists Frauenerleben* (Leipzig: Huber, 1937);

Robert Labhardt, *Metapher und Geschichte: Kleists dramatische Metaphorik bis zur 'Penthesilea' als Widerspiegelung seiner geschichtlichen Position* (Kronberg im Taunus: Scriptor, 1976);

Örjan Lindberger, *The Transformations of Amphitryon* (Stockholm: Almqvist & Wiksell, 1956);

Georg Lukács, "Die Tragödie Heinrich von Kleists," in his *Deutsche Realisten des 19. Jahrhunderts* (Bern: Francke, 1951), pp. 19–48;

Thomas Mann, "Kleists 'Amphitryon': Eine Wiedereroberung," in his *Gesammelte Werke in zwölf Bänden,* volume 9: *Reden und Aufsätze,* part 1 (Frankfurt am Main: Fischer, 1960), pp. 187–228;

Hans Mayer, *Heinrich von Kleist: Der geschichtliche Augenblick* (Pfullingen: Neske, 1962);

James M. McGlathery, *Desire's Sway: The Plays and Stories of Heinrich von Kleist* (Detroit: Wayne State University Press, 1983);

Heinrich Meyer-Benfey, *Das Drama Heinrich von Kleists,* 2 volumes (Göttingen: Hapke, 1911–1913);

Walter Müller-Seidel, *Versehen und Erkennen: Eine Studie über Heinrich von Kleist* (Cologne & Graz: Böhlau, 1961);

Müller-Seidel, ed., *Heinrich von Kleist: Aufsätze und Essays* (Darmstadt: Wissenschaftliche Buchgesellschaft, 1967);

Heinz Politzer, "Kleists Trauerspiel vom Traum: 'Prinz Friedrich von Homburg,'" *Euphorion,* 64 (1970): 200–220; republished in Politzer's *Hatte Ödipus einen Ödipus-Komplex?: Versuche zum Thema Psychoanalyse und Literatur* (Munich: Piper, 1974), pp. 156–181;

William C. Reeve, *In Pursuit of Power: Heinrich von Kleist's Machiavellian Protagonists* (Toronto: University of Toronto Press, 1987);

Reeve, *Kleist's Aristocratic Heritage and Das Kätchen von Heilbronn* (Montreal: McGill-Queen's University Press, 1991);

Ewald Rösch, "Bett und Richterstuhl: Gattungsgeschichtliche Überlegungen zu Kleists Lustspiel *Der zerbrochene Krug,*" in *Kritische Bewahrung: Beiträge zur deutschen Philologie: Festschrift für Werner Schröder zum 60. Geburtstag,* edited by Ernst-Joachim Schmidt (Berlin: Schmidt, 1974), pp. 434–475;

Alfred Schlagdenhauffen, *L'Univers Existentiel de Kleist dans le Prince de Hombourg* (Paris: Société d'Édition les Belles Lettres, 1953);

Jochen Schmidt, *Heinrich von Kleist: Studien zu seiner poetischen Verfahrensweise* (Tübingen: Niemeyer, 1974);

Schriften der Kleist-Gesellschaft, 1 (1921)–19 (1939);

Gerhard Schulz, "Kleists 'Bettelweib von Locarno': Eine Ehegeschichte?," *Jahrbuch der Deutschen Schiller-Gesellschaft,* 18 (1974): 431–440;

Walter Silz, *Heinrich von Kleist: Studies in His Works and Literary Character* (Philadelphia: University of Pennsylvania Press, 1961);

Ernst Ludwig Stahl, *Heinrich von Kleist's Dramas* (Oxford: Blackwell, 1948);

Anthony Stephens, "'Eine Träne auf den Brief': Zum Status der Ausdrucksformen in Kleists Erzählungen," *Jahrbuch der Deutschen Schiller-Gesellschaft,* 28 (1984): 315–348;

Stephens, *Heinrich von Kleist: The Dramas and Stories* (Oxford: Berg, 1994);

Siegfried Streller, *Das dramatische Werk Heinrich von Kleists* (Berlin: Rütten & Loening, 1966);

Rudolf Unger, *Herder, Novalis und Kleist: Studien über die Entwicklung des Todesproblems in Denken und Dichten vom Sturm und Drang zur Romantik* (Frankfurt am Main: Diesterweg, 1922), pp. 88–143;

Ulrich Vohland, *Bürgerliche Emanzipation in Heinrich von Kleists Dramen und theoretischen Schriften* (Bern: Herbert Lang/Frankfurt am Main: Peter Lang, 1976);

Hermann J. Weigand, "Das Motiv des Vertrauens im Drama Heinrichs von Kleist," *Monatshefte für deutschen Unterricht, deutsche Sprache und Literatur,* 30 (1938): 233–245;

Weigand, "Das Vertrauen in Kleists Erzählungen," *Monatshefte für deutschen Unterricht und deutsche Sprache und Literatur,* 34 (1942): 49–63, 126–144;

David E. Wellbery, ed., *Positionen der Literaturwissenschaft: Acht Modellanalysen am Beispiel von Kleists "Das Erdbeben in Chili"* (Munich: Beck, 1985);

Hans Wolff, *Heinrich von Kleist als politischer Dichter* (Berkeley: University of California Press, 1947).

Papers:

Heinrich von Kleist's papers are in the West-deutsche Bibliothek, Marburg; the Staatsbibliothek Berlin; the Universitätsbibliothek Tübingen; the Universitätsbibliothek Heidelberg; and the Jagiellonian Library of the University of Cracow, Poland.

Gotthold Ephraim Lessing

(22 January 1729 – 15 February 1781)

Gerd Hillen
Unversity of California, Berkeley

This entry originally appeared in DLB 97: German Writers from the
Enlightenment to Sturm und Drang: 1720–1764.

BOOKS: *Der Eremite: Eine Erzehlung,* anonymous (Kerapolis [actually Stuttgart: Mezler], 1749);

Die alte Jungfer: Ein Lustspiel in drei Aufzügen, anonymous (Berlin: Voß, 1749);

Tarantula: Eine Poszen Oper, anonymous (Teltow an der Tyber [actually Berlin], 1749);

Weiber sind Weiber: Ein Lustspiel in fünf Aufzügen, anonymous (Berlin, 1749);

Critische Nachrichten aus dem Reiche der Gelehrsamkeit, 2 volumes, anonymous (Berlin: Haude & Spener, 1750–1751);

Palaion: Comédie en un Acte, anonymous (Berlin, 1750);

Kleinigkeiten, anonymous (Frankfurt am Main & Leipzig [actually Stuttgart: Mezler], 1751);

Das Neueste aus dem Reiche des Witzes, anonymous (Berlin, 1751);

Schrifften, 6 volumes (Berlin: Voß, 1753–1755)–volume 6 (1755) includes *Der junge Gelehrte in der Einbildung: Ein Lustspiel in drey Aufzügen, Die Juden, Der Freygeist, Der Schatz, Mi Sara Sampson, Der Misogyne oder Der Feind des weiblichen Geschlechts: Ein Lustspiel in zwey Aufzüge;*

Ein Vade Mecum für den Hrn. Sam. Gotth. Lange, Pastor in Laublingen, in dessen Taschenformate angefertigt (Berlin: Voß, 1754);

Theatralische Bibliothek, 4 volumes (Berlin: Voß, 1754–1758);

Miß Sara Sampson: Ein Trauerspiel in fünf Aufzügen (Berlin: Voß, 1755);

Pope–ein Metaphysiker!, anonymous, by Lessing and Moses Mendelssohn (Danzig: Schuster, 1755);

Philotas: Ein Trauerspiel, anonymous (Berlin: Voß, 1759);

Fabeln: Drey Bücher. Nebst Abhandlungen mit dieser Dichtungsart verwandten Inhalts (Berlin: Voß, 1759); translated anonymously as *Fables: In Three Books* (London: Taylor, 1829); German version republished, edited by Walther Killy (Hamburg: Maximilian-Gesellschaft, 1979);

Painting by O. May, circa 1766 (Gleimhaus, Halberstadt)

Sophokles: Erstes Buch, anonymous (Berlin: Voß, 1760);

Laokoon: Oder Über die Grenzen der Mahlerey und Poesie. Erster Theil. Mit beiläufigen Erläuterungen verschiedener Punkte der alten Kunstgeschichte (Berlin: Voß, 1766); translated by William Ross as *Laocoon; or, The Limits of Poetry and Painting* (London: Ridgway, 1836); translated by Ellen Frothingham as *Laocoon: An Essay upon the Limits of Painting and Poetry* (London: Low, 1874; Boston: Roberts, 1874; reprinted,

New York: Noonday Press, 1957); German version republished, edited by Dorothy Reich (London: Oxford University Press, 1965);

Lustspiele, 2 volumes (Berlin: Voß, 1767)–includes *Minna von Barnhelm oder das Soldatenglück,* translated by Fanny Holcroft as *Minna von Barnhelm: A Comedy in 5 Acts,* in *The Theatrical Recorder,* volume 2 (London: Holcroft, 1806), pp. 217–258;

Hamburgische Dramaturgie, 2 volumes (Hamburg & Bremen: Cramer, 1767–1769; reprinted, 1 volume, edited by Friedrich Schröter and Richard Thiele, Halle: Waisenhaus, 1878; reprinted, Hildesheim & New York: Olms, 1979); translated by Helen Zimmern as *Hamburg Dramaturgy,* 1 volume (New York: Dover, 1962);

Brief, antiquarischen Inhalts, 2 volumes (Berlin: Nicolai, 1768–1769);

Wie die Alten den Tod gebildet: Eine Untersuchung (Berlin: Voß, 1769);

Berengarius Turonensis: oder Ankündigung eines wichtigen Werkes desselben, wovon in der Herzoglichen Bibliothek zu, Wolfenbüttel ein Manuscript befindlich, welches bisher völlig unbekannt geblieben (Brunswick: Waisenhaus, 1770);

Vermischte Schriften, 14 volumes, edited by Karl Gotthelf Lessing and Johann Joachim Eschenberg (volumes 1–10, 13–14, Berlin: Voß; volumes 11–12, Berlin: Nicolai, 1771–1793);

Sinngedichte (Berlin: Voß, 1771; republished, edited by Helmut Hirsch, Berlin: Der Morgen, 1980);

Trauerspiele: Mi Sara Sampson; Philotas; Emilia Galotti (Berlin: Voß, 1772); *Emilia Galotti* translated by Benjamin Thompson (London: Vernor & Hood, 1800);

Emilia Galotti: Ein Trauerspiel in fünf Aufzügen (Berlin, Voß, 1772);

Zur Geschichte und Litteratur: Aus den Schätzen der Herzoglichen Bibliothek zu Wolfenbüttel, 6 volumes (Brunswick: Waisenhaus, 1773–1781);

Vom Alter der Oelmalerey: Aus dem Theophilus Presbyter, anonymous (Brunswick: Waisenhaus, 1774);

Zwey Lustspiele: Damon; Die alte Jungfer (Frankfurt am Main & Leipzig: Fleischer, 1775);

Über den Beweis des Geistes und der Kraft an den Herrn Director Schumann, zu Hannover, anonymous (Brunswick: Waisenhaus, 1777);

Das Testament Johannis: Ein Gespräch, anonymous (Brunswick: Waisenhaus, 1777);

Anti-Goeze: Das ist, Nothgedrungener Beytrag zu den freiwilligen Beyträgen des Hrn. Past. Goeze, anonymous (Brunswick: Waisenhaus, 1778);

Von dem Zwecke Jesu und seiner Jünger: Noch ein Fragment des Wolfenbüttelschen Ungenannten (Brunswick: Waisenhaus, 1778);

Nöthige Antwort auf eine sehr unnöthige Frage des Herrn Hauptpastor Goeze in Hamburg (Wolfenbüttel, 1778);

Der nöthigen Antwort auf ein sehr unnöthige Frage des Herrn Hauptpastor Goeze in Hamburg: Erste Folge (N.p., 1778);

Axiomata, wenn es deren in dergleichen Dingen giebt, wider den Herrn Pastor Goeze in Hamburg, anonymous (Brunswick: Waisenhaus, 1778);

Eine Duplik, anonymous (Brunswick: Waisenhaus, 1778);

Eine Parabel: Nebst einer kleinen Bitte und einem eventualen Absagungsbriefe an Herrn Pastor Goeze, in Hamburg, anonymous (Brunswick: Waisenhaus, 1778); translated by Henry Crabb Robinson as "A Parable from the German of Lessing," *Monthly Repository of Theology and General Literature,* 1 (1806): 183–185;

Neue Hypothese über die Evangelisten als blos menschliche Geschichtschreiber betrachtet (Wolfenbüttel, 1778);

Ernst und Falk: Gespräche für Freymäurer, 2 volumes, anonymous (volume 1, Wolfenbüttel & Göttingen: Dieterich, 1778; volume 2, Frankfurt am Main: Brönner, 1780; republished, Hamburg: Bauhütten, 1980); translated by A. Cohn as *Masonic Dialogues* (London: Baskerville Press, 1927);

Noch nähere Berichtigung des Mährchens von 1000 Ducaten oder Judas Ischarioth dem Zweyten (N.p., 1778);

Nathan der Weise: Ein dramatisches Gedicht in fünf Aufzügen (Berlin: Voß, 1779); translated by William Taylor as *Nathan the Wise* (Norwich, U.K.: Stevenson & Matchett, 1791); translated by Frothingham as *Nathan the Wise* (New York: Holt, 1867); German version republished, edited by Peter Demetz (Frankfurt am Main & Berlin: Ullstein, 1966);

Die Erziehung des Menschengeschlechts (Berlin: Voß, 1780); translated by Frederick William Robertson as *The Education of the Human Race* (London: Smith, Elder, 1858; New York: Collier, 1909); German version republished, edited by Louis Ferdinand Helbig (Bern: Lang, 1980);

Theatralischer Nachlaß, 2 volumes, edited by Karl Gotthelf Lessing (Berlin: Voß, 1784–1786);

Theologischer Nachlaß, edited by Karl Gotthelf Lessing (Berlin: Voß, 1784);

Analekten für die Litteratur, 4 volumes (Bern & Leipzig: Haller, 1785–1786);

Der Schlaftrunk: Ein Lustspiel in drey Aufzügen von Gotthold Ephraim Lessing, zu Ende gebracht vom Verfasser der Jugendgeschichte Karl und Sophie (Regensburg: Montag, 1785);

Übrige noch ungedruckte Werke des Wolfenbüttlischen Fragmentisten: Ein Nachlaß, edited by C. A. E. Schmidt (N.p., 1787);

Kollektaneen zur Literatur, 2 volumes, edited and enlarged by Johann Joachim Eschenburg (Berlin: Voß, 1790);

Die Matrone von Ephesus: Ein Lustspiel in einem Aufzuge, completed by K. L. Rahbek (Mannheim: Schwann & Götz, 1790);

Sämmtliche Schriften, 32 volumes, edited by Johann Friedrich Schink (volumes 1–28, Berlin: Voß; volumes 29–32, Berlin & Stettin: Nicolai, 1825–1828);

Sämmtliche Schriften 13 volumes, edited by Karl Lachmann (Berlin: Voß, 1838–1840); revised and enlarged by Franz Muncker, 23 volumes (volumes 1–22, Stuttgart & Leipzig: Göschen; volume 23, Berlin: De Gruyter, 1886–1924; reprinted, Berlin: De Gruyter, 1968);

Werke: Vollständige Ausgabe, 25 volumes, edited by Julius Petersen and Waldemar von Olshausen (Berlin: Bong, 1925–1935; reprinted, Hildesheim & New York: Olms, 1970);

Gesammelte Werke, 10 volumes, edited by Paul Rilla (Berlin: Aufbau, 1954–1958);

Werke, 8 volumes, edited by Herbert G. Göpfert, Karl Eibl, and others (Munich: Hanser, 1970–1979).

Editions in English: *Three Comedies,* translated by J. J. Holroyd (Colchester, U.K.: Totham, 1838)–comprises *The Freethinker, The Treasure, Minna von Barnhelm; or, The Soldier's Fortune;*

Dramatic Works, 2 volumes, translated by Ernest Bell and R. Dillon Boylan, edited by Bell (London: Bell, 1878)–comprises in volume 1 *(Tragedies),* "Memoir," *Miss Sara Sampson, Philotas, Emilia Galotti, Nathan the Wise;* in volume 2 *(Comedies), Damon; or, True Friendship, The Young Scholar, The Old Maid, The Woman-Hater, The Jews, The Freethinker, The Treasure, Minna von Barnhelm;*

Select Prose Works, translated by E. C. Beasley and Helen Zimmern (London: Bell, 1879; revised, 1890)–comprises "Laocoön," "How the Ancients Represented Death," "Dramatic Notes";

Nathan the Wise: A Dramatic Poem in Five Acts, translated and edited by Leo Markun (Girard, Kans.: Haldeman-Julius, 1926);

Laocoön; Nathan the Wise; Minna von Barnhelm, translated by William A. Steel and Anthony Dent, edited by Steel (London: Dent / New York: Dutton, 1930; reprinted, 1959);

Nathan the Wise: A Dramatic Poem in Five Acts. Translated into English Verse, translated by Bayard Quincy Morgan (New York: Ungar, 1955; reprinted, 1975);

Theological Writings, translated by Henry Chadwick (London: Black, 1956; Stanford: Stanford University Press, 1957);

Emilia Galotti: A Tragedy in Five Acts, translated by Anna Johanna Gode von Aesch (Great Neck, N.Y.: Barron's, 1959);

Emilia Galotti: A Tragedy in Five Acts, translated by Edward Dvoretzky (New York: Ungar, 1962);

Laocoön: An Essay on the Limits of Painting and Poetry, translated by Edward Allen McCormick (Indianapolis: Bobbs-Merrill, 1962);

Minna von Barnhelm: A Comedy in Five Acts, translated by Kenneth J. Northcott (Chicago: University of Chicago Press, 1972);

Nathan the Wise, translated by Walter Frank Charles Ade (Woodbury, N.Y.: Barron's, 1972);

Miss Sara Sampson: A Tragedy in Five Acts, translated by G. Hoern Schlage (Stuttgart: Heinz, 1977);

Philotas, translated by Dvoretzky (Stuttgart: Heinz, 1979).

OTHER: Crébillon, *Catalina: Ein Trauerspiel. Aus dem Französischen,* translated anonymously by Lessing (Berlin, 1749);

Charles Rollin, *Römische Historie von der Erbauung der Stadt Rom: Theile 4–6,* 3 volumes, translated anonymously by Lessing (Leipzig & Danzig: Rüdiger, 1749–1752);

Beyträge zur Historie und Aufnahme des Theaters, edited by Lessing and Christlob Mylius (Berlin & Stuttgart: Metzler, 1750);

Pedro Calderón de la Barca, *Das Leben ist ein Traum,* translated anonymously by Lessing (Berlin, 1750);

Titus Maccias Plautus, *Die Gefangenen,* translated by Lessing (Stuttgart: Metzler, 1750);

Voltaire, *Kleinere historische Schriften: Aus dem Französischen,* translated anonymously by Lessing (Rostock: Koppe, 1752);

Juan Huarte de San Juan, *Johann Huarts Prüfung der Köpfe zu den Wissenschaften: Aus dem Spanischen,* translated anonymously by Lessing (Wittenberg & Zerbst: Zimmermann, 1752);

Johann Gotthilf Vockerodt, *An impartial Foreigner's Remarks upon the present Dispute between England and Prussia, in a Letter from a Gentleman at the Hague to his Friend in London: Amerkungen [sic] eines unpartheyischen Fremden über die gegenwärtige Streitigkeit zwischen England und Preußen; in einem Brief eines Edelmanns in dem Haag an seinen Freund in London. Aus dem Englischen,* translated anonymously from the French by Lessing (Berlin, 1753);

Francois Augier de Marigny, *Geschichte der Araber unter der Regierung der Califen,* volumes 1–2, translated by Lessing (Berlin & Potsdam: Voß, 1753–1754);

Frederick II, *Schreiben an das Publicum: Aus dem Französischen,* translated anonymously by Lessing (Berlin: Voß, 1753);

William Hogarth, *Zergliederung der Schönheit, die Schwankenden Begriffe von dem Geschmack festzusetzen: Aus dem Englischen,* translated by Mylius, foreword by Lessing (Berlin & Potsdam: Voß, 1754);

Mylius, *Vermischte Schriften,* edited by Lessing (Berlin: Haude & Spener, 1754);

Elizabeth Rowe, *Geheiligte Andachts-Ubungen in Betrachtung, Gebet, Lobpreisung und Herzens-Gesprächen,* translated anonymously by Lessing and Christian Felix Weiße (Erfurt: Nonnen, 1754);

Francis Hutcheson, *Sittenlehre der Vernunft: Aus dem Englischen übersetzt,* 2 volumes, translated anonymously by Lessing (Leipzig: Wendler, 1756);

William Law, *Eine ernsthafte Ermunterung an alle Christen zu einem frommen und heiligen Leben: Aus dem Englischen übersetzt,* translated anonymously by Lessing (Leipzig: Weidmann, 1756);

James Thomson, *Sämtliche Trauerspiele: Aus dem Englischen übersetzt,* translated by a scholarly society in Stralsund, foreword by Lessing (Leipzig: Weidmann, 1756);

Bibliothek der schönen Wissenschaften und der freyen Künste, 3 volumes, edited by Lessing, Moses Mendelssohn, and Friedrich Nicolai (Leipzig: Dyck, 1757–1758);

Samuel Richardson, *Sittenlehre für die Jugend in den auserlesensten Aesopischen Fabeln mit dienlichen Betrachtungen zur Beförderung der Religion und der allgemeinen Menschenliebe vorgestellt,* translated by Lessing (Leipzig: Weidmann, 1757);

Johann Wilhelm Ludwig Gleim, *Preußische Kriegslieder in den Feldzügen 1756 und 1757: Von einem Grenadier. Mit Melodien,* edited by Lessing (Berlin: Voß, 1758);

Briefe, die Neueste Litteratur betreffend, parts 1–4, edited anonymously by Lessing, Mendelssohn, and Nicolai (Berlin: Nicolai, 1759; reprinted, Hildesheim: Olms, 1971);

Friedrich von Logau, *Sinngedichte: Zwölf Bücher. Mit Anmerkungen über die Sprache des Dichters,* edited by Lessing and Karl Wilhelm Ramler (Leipzig: Weidmann, 1759);

Denis Diderot, *Das Theater des Herrn Diderot: Aus dem Französischen,* 2 volumes, translated anonymously by Lessing (Berlin: Voß, 1760; revised, 1781);

Jean-Georges Noverre, *Briefe über die Tanzkunst und über die Ballette: Aus dem Französischen übersetzt,* translated by Lessing and Johann Joachim Christoph Bode (Hamburg & Bremen: Cramer, 1769);

Andreas Scultetus, *Gedichte: Aufgefunden,* edited by Lessing (Brunswick: Waisenhaus, 1771);

Karl Wilhelm Jerusalem, *Philosophische Aufsätze,* edited by Lessing (Brunswick: Waisenhaus, 1776; edited by Paul Beer, Berlin: Behr, 1900; reprinted, New York & Nendeln, Liechtenstein: Kraus, 1966);

Hermann Samuel Reimarus, *Von dem Zwecke Jesu und seiner Jünger: Noch ein Fragment des Wolfenbüttelschen Ungenannten,* edited by Lessing (Brunswick: Waisenhaus, 1778);

Pedro Cudena, *Beschreibung des Portugiesischen Amerika: Ein Spanisches Manuskript in der Wolfenbüttelschen Bibliothek,* translated by Christian Leiste, edited by Lessing (Brunswick: Waisenhaus, 1780);

Reimarus, *Fragmente des Wolfenbüttelschen Ungenannten: Ein Anhang zu dem Fragment von Zweck Jesu und seiner Jünger,* edited by Lessing (Berlin: Weber, 1784);

G. E. Lessings Übersetzungen aus dem Französischen Friedrichs des Großen und Voltaires, edited by Erich Schmidt (Berlin: Hertz, 1892; reprinted, Munich: Kraus, 1980).

To the extent that the eighteenth century in Germany was indeed an age of the unfettered critical spirit, as Immanuel Kant assured his contemporaries it was, it found its most articulate voice in Gotthold Ephraim Lessing. As a scholar of classical antiquity he rivals Johann Joachim Winckelmann. In his extended controversy with leading Protestant theologians on the nature of Christianity and the truth of its teachings, a topic of singular importance to the European Enlightenment, he presented the more convincing arguments until he was silenced by ducal decree. But his most significant contribution was the rejuvenation of German literature, especially the drama.

Lessing's devastating attack on Johann Christoph Gottsched's theater reform put an end to the attempt to establish a classicist literature in Germany. Reinterpreting Aristotle's *Poetics,* Lessing subordinated aesthetic "laws" and "rules" to the effect which a specific genre is to have on its recipients, thus replacing the normative poetics that governed French classical literature and that, in turn, were espoused by Gottsched and his followers. The new theoretical orientation, especially in its application to dramatic theory, marks the beginning of "modern" German literature; it led to works which have maintained their place in the canon of German literature ever since. Among them are some of Lessing's own: his plays continue to evoke a considerable amount of critical attention, and his dramatic masterpieces, *Minna von Barnhelm* (1767; translated, 1806), *Emilia Galotti* (1772; translated, 1800), and *Nathan der Weise* (1779; translated as *Nathan the Wise,* 1791), can still be found in the repertoire of the German theater. Lessing reasoned that if the purpose of tragedy is to evoke "Mitleid" (pity), the stoic hero and the related set of aristocratically tinged values cease to be a proper subject for the drama. Stoic endurance may elicit admiration, but not pity. Witnessing human suffering will evoke pity, and the experience will intensify if the protagonist shares common bonds with his audience. With this argument Lessing opened the stage to the social realities of his time.

Lessing's conviction that pity is the cardinal virtue and the ultimate goal of tragedy did not prevent him from using the theater as an instrument for the more general purposes of the Enlightenment. He attacks anti-Semitism in *Die Juden* (1755; translated as *The Jews,* 1878), exposes cruelty and egocentricity in the guise of patriotism in *Philotas* (1759; translated, 1878), demonstrates the failings of "enlightened" absolutism and bourgeois passivity in *Emilia Galotti,* and crowns his dramatic work with a plea for religious tolerance in *Nathan der Weise,* one of the noblest documents of the European Enlightenment.

Lessing was born in Kamenz, Saxony, on 22 January 1729, the third of twelve children of Johann Gottfried Lessing, a Protestant minister, and Justina Salome Lessing, née Feller. His unusual talents were recognized early. In 1741 he was admitted to St. Afra in Meißen, one of the elite secondary schools endowed by the dukes of Saxony. In 1746, complying with his father's wishes and equipped with a stipend from his native city, he enrolled as a student of theology at the University of Leipzig. At this center of eighteenth-century scholarship, the unusual alliance of Gottsched, then rector of the university, and Frederike Caroline Neuber, the leader of a theatrical troupe, had given the stage a new respectability. Lessing's lifelong fascination with the theater began in Leipzig. His first play, *Der junge Gelehrte* (1755; translated as *The Young Scholar,* 1878), was performed there in January 1748; it is a comedy in which he lampoons an arrogant young scholar engaged in meaningless philological squabbles totally divorced from real learning, as well as from the world around him. With his friend Felix Weiße, who was to become a minor playwright, Lessing translated Marivaux; wrote poetry in the anacreontic vein; and wrote outlines for several plays, most of which remained fragmentary. Such activities caused his parents some consternation. Although the errant student was allowed to change the focus of his studies to medicine and philology, Lessing left the university in 1748 to seek his fortune in Berlin. In a letter to his mother (20 January 1749), he blames this move on debts he had incurred; it is likely that the bankruptcy of Neuber's troupe in the summer of 1748 was a contributing factor.

Lessing survived in Berlin as a struggling writer. He became review editor of the *Berlinische Priveligierte Zeitung* and received a masters in theology during a stay

in Wittenberg in 1751–1752 and gradually built a reputation as a literary critic. He did not eschew formidable targets: he took Friedrich Gottlieb Klopstock to task for his religious fervor, and Samuel Gotthold Lange, Horace translator and respected head of the Halle school of poets, was ridiculed for incompetence in *Ein Vade Mecum für den Hrn. Sam. Gotth. Lange* (A Primer for Mr. Samuel G. Lange, 1754). But although he was a prolific writer–his collected works, *Schrifften* (Writings, 1753–1755), began to appear before he was twenty-five years old–the Prussian capital and the literary market in Germany did not afford him, or any other independent writer, a comfortable existence. The success of his first bourgeois tragedy, *Miß Sara Sampson,* (1755; translated, 1878), increased his stature as a playwright and drew new attention to his early comedies, but it did not alleviate his financial problems. The play depicts Sara's elopement with Mellefont, a young man who finds himself torn between her and a former lover. Above all he is motivated by a deep-rooted urge to maintain his personal freedom. The sophistication of Sara's reasoning as to why she cannot accept her distraught father's forgiveness has persuaded critics to interpret the play as a commentary on the Third Commandment. But the indictment of rigid bourgeois morality, specifically with regard to sexual ethics, is equally prominent. The tearful reunion of errant daughter and regretful father, who blames himself and his own strict moralistic stance for Sara's poisoning by Mellefont's former lover, set the stage for domestic tragedies well into the nineteenth century.

The play's English model–Restoration drama–and the London setting had a provocative edge: in no German city was the dominance of French culture felt more keenly than in the Berlin of Frederick II. Yet Lessing's attitude can hardly be called chauvinistic; for while ridiculing Corneille, he praised Diderot, and in Voltaire he admired the philosopher but belittled the playwright. However, his squabble with the great French philosopher over a manuscript Lessing should have returned earlier than he did may well have ruined his chances for an appointment at the Prussian court–if indeed the king needed such a pretext to prefer a French intellectual to a German one. Lessing found support elsewhere. His circle of friends included Moses Mendelssohn, accountant by profession and philosopher by inclination; Friedrich Nicolai, publisher and staunch supporter of Enlightenment causes; and Karl Wilhelm Ramler, author and instructor at the military academy. Travel plans–he had agreed to accompany the son of a rich Leipzig merchant on a tour of Holland, northern Germany, and England–came to an abrupt halt in Amsterdam with the outbreak of the Seven Years' War in August 1756. Lessing returned with his charge from Holland to Leipzig, which was occupied by Prussian troops.

Lessing remained in Leipzig until May 1758, when he returned to Berlin. In Leipzig he barely supported himself by translating works by Francis Hutcheson (1756), William Law (1756), and Samuel Richardson (1757), and collaborating with Mendelssohn and Nicolai on the journal *Bibliothek der schönen Wissenschaften und der freyen Künste* (Library of Liberal Arts, 1757–1758). But it was not only economically that his position was a tenuous one. Although it was rumored in Berlin that he had written against the interest of the Prussian state, he estranged his Leipzig friends by consorting with officers of the Prussian army who had just levied an extraordinarily heavy tax on the city. A true cosmopolitan, he assured Nicolai that he considered himself neither a Saxon nor a Prussian patriot. And Johann Wilhelm Ludwig Gleim, whose *Preußische Kriegslieder* (Prussian War Songs, 1758) Lessing had edited, was finally taken to task for his blatant nationalism: "Vielleicht zwar ist auch der Patriot bey mir nicht ganz erstickt, obgleich das Lob eines eifrigen Patrioten, nach meiner Denkungsart, das allerletzte ist, wonach ich geitzen würde; des Patrioten nehmlich, der mich vergessen lehrt, daß ich ein Weltbürger seyn sollte" (It is possible that the patriot is also not quite stifled in me, although the reputation as a fervent patriot is the last thing I crave, as a patriot, that is, who makes me forget that I should be a citizen of the world). He also made the price of heroic greatness the theme of a one-act play: the self-sacrifice of the title character in *Philotas* is an indictment of a society that educates its youth to accept death on the battlefield as the ultimate goal and unquestioningly to place the interest of the state over all human concerns. The setting of the play in classical antiquity does not blur the obvious analogy to Prussia's acquisition of Silesia through war.

Despite this anticipation of the spirit that characterized the great minds of the following generation, Lessing was not totally unaffected by the upsurge of pro-Prussian sentiments triggered by the Seven Years' War. He looked forward to his return to Berlin, "wo ich es nicht länger nötig haben werde, es meinen Bekannten nur ins Ohr zu sagen, daß der König von Preußen dennoch ein großer König ist" (where I will no longer be obliged to whisper into my friends' ears that the King of Prussia is a great king in spite of it all), he wrote to Gleim in May 1757.

Among the projects Lessing completed during his second stay in Berlin were an edition of the all but forgotten works of the seventeenth-century poet Friedrich von Logau (1759) and a collection of his own fables, *Fabeln: Drey Bücher* (1759; translated as *Fables: In Three Books*, 1829). Of more immediate impact was his *Briefe, die Neueste Litteratur betreffend* (Letters, on the Most Recent Literature, 1759), a journal of literary criticism to which Nicolai and Mendelssohn also contributed. The fictional framework of these "letters"–they are addressed to an officer recovering from wounds received in the battle of Zorndorf–allowed Lessing the elegant informality that characterizes most of his critical writings. Moving beyond the traditional form of reviewing individual publications, he used the journal to exert influence on the entire spectrum of contemporary literature. The famous seventeenth letter (16 February 1759) contains an attack on Gottsched's efforts to reform the German stage. It is based on arguments which were later to be more fully developed by Johann Gottfried Herder: that literary models should be akin to the national character; that indigenous traditions are preferable to imported themes and forms; and that Shakespearean theater is superior to classical French drama, even though the latter adheres to the letter of Aristotelian poetics while the former violates it.

Lessing's theoretical stance placed him between the two established and feuding camps in Leipzig and Zurich. His rejection of Gottsched may have endeared him to the Swiss critics Johann Jakob Bodmer and Johann Jakob Breitinger, but, because their revision of Gottsched's theories was only a modest one, the feeling was not mutual. Lessing saw the danger of forming yet another literary clique. His decision to withdraw from the journal may also have been prompted by his financial situation, which remained as uncertain as ever; he was unable to respond to pleas from Kamenz that he support two of his brothers attending the University of Wittenberg. In September 1760 Lessing resigned; a month later he left for Breslau to join the staff of the Prussian general Bogislaw Friedrich von Tauentzien as regimental secretary.

Less is known about his years in Silesia than about any other part of his life. According to a local schoolmaster, J. B. Klose, he slept late, went to every book auction in town, and, after performing his secretarial duties, attended theatrical performances. Often leaving before the last act, he spent the better part of the night gambling with fellow Prussian officers. Even though Klose's account, cited by Lessing's brother and first biographer Karl Gotthelf, may be slanted, it seems obvious that these were relatively carefree years for Germany's foremost critic.

It is unclear what Lessing expected for himself after he proclaimed the end of the long war to the citizenry of Breslau in 1763. But his hopes, hinted at in a letter to his father, were not fulfilled: "Ich warte noch einen einzigen Umstand ab, und wo dieser nicht nach meinem Willen ausfällt, so kehre ich zu meiner alten Lebens Art wieder zurück" (I am only waiting for one decision. Should that be contrary to expectations, then I will return to my old way of life). Von Tauentzien was appointed governor of Silesia, and Lessing returned to his old and rather insecure way of life. But unlike his dramatic figure, the Baltic nobleman Tellheim in *Minna von Barnhelm,* who had also joined the Prussian cause for reasons he finds difficult to explain after his sudden and unjust dismissal, Lessing was not destitute. Although many of his personal effects were lost in transit from Breslau to Berlin, he was able to send a significant amount of money to his family, and his library at this time contained some six thousand volumes.

The literary results of his four years in Silesia were two major works: *Minna von Barnhelm* and *Laokoon: Oder Über die Grenzen der Mahlerey und Poesie* (1766; translated as *Laocoon; or, The Limits of Poetry and Painting,* 1836).

The plot of Lessing's great comedy reflects the aftermath of the war. In a humane and generous gesture, Major von Tellheim had asked for smaller reparations from the defeated Saxons than were expected. When the vanquished proved unable to pay even these at short notice, he advanced them some of his own money to meet the minimum demands of the Prussians. While this selfless deed wins him the love of Minna, an aristocratic Saxon heiress, the Prussian ministry suspects bribery. The play opens with Tellheim dismissed, dishonored, and about to be evicted from his hotel room. It ends with his honor rehabilitated by the king, his fortune restored, and his impending marriage to Minna. Despite this seeming conventionality, Lessing's play is a radical departure from the genre as established on the German stage. More significant than the true-to-life characters and idiosyncratic diction of the dramatis personae was the public discussion of social problems caused by the war and high-handed Prussian administrative measures. Instead of following the traditional pattern of exposing some aberrant form of behavior to ridicule, Lessing subjects the aristocratic concept of honor to scrutiny. When his honor is questioned, Tellheim, although innocent, refuses to marry Minna. When she claims to be dishonored in the eyes of Saxon patriots for loving a Prussian officer, and disinherited as well, he reverses his position; the now-eager suitor is forced to invalidate his own earlier arguments, which Minna quotes back to him. Neither the plausibility of her fictitious misfortune nor the superiority of "Mitleid" over honor as a vir-

tue inspiring moral action could have been lost on the audience. The play rapidly became the most popular of Lessing's dramatic works. Its first performance, in Hamburg on 30 December 1767, was followed before the end of the decade by productions in Frankfurt am Main, Vienna, Leipzig, Berlin, and Breslau. That the king's letter ultimately solves Tellheim's dilemma led to a reading of the play as a glorification of Frederick II; the opposite interpretation points to the arbitrariness of Tellheim's rehabilitation and finds a general indictment of Prussia and its ruler. More recent scholarship has focused on aesthetic and sociopolitical issues.

With *Laokoon* Lessing participated in a larger European debate on the specific differences among the individual arts and the nature of aesthetic perception. His plan was to include music and dance, but the published work is restricted to the pictorial arts (painting and sculpture) and literature. A discussion of theories presented by Joseph Spence in *Polymetis* (1747) and by Anne Claude Philippe de Tubières, comte de Caylus in *Tableaux tirés de L'Iliade* (1757) precedes the introduction of his true target: Winckelmann. In his *Gedanken über die Nachahmung der griechischen Werke in der Malerei und Bildhauerkunst* (On Imitating Greek Artworks in Painting and Sculpture, 1755) Winckelmann analyzed the Laocoön sculpture and concluded that the Greeks avoided the artistic expression of extreme emotions: the priest and his sons, about to be strangled by snakes, display only muted and controlled suffering. This stoic ideal was diametrically opposed to Lessing's own views; yet he disputes Winckelmann's famous dictum that no inner turmoil would disturb the Greeks' "edle Einfalt and stille Größe" (noble simplicity and calm grandeur) not on moral but on aesthetic grounds. Since Homer and Sophocles allow their heroes to scream, he argues, different laws must apply for the writer and the sculptor. In his search for these laws he establishes several principles which have proved to be extraordinarily fruitful for all subsequent theory in this area, among them the structural analysis of the medium to determine its representational possibilities, the distinction of natural and arbitrary signs, and the participatory role of the reader or viewer. Literature uses successive signs in time; the pictorial arts employ coexisting figures and colors in space. Therefore, the proper subject of literature is "Handlungen" (action) while "Körper" (objects) are the most adequate subjects for the painter and the sculptor. Limited to re-creating a single moment in time, the artist must select one that leaves the most latitude for the imagination. It is not the pinnacle of an emotion but an earlier or later stage that allows viewer participation. For this reason Laocoön is depicted as suffering, but not screaming. Lessing concludes that literature is superior to pictorial art because it can represent the entire spectrum of human emotions. It achieves its highest form by translating its arbitrary signs into natural signs, by turning words into the spoken dialogue of drama.

The impact of the work was considerable. Even Winckelmann's great admirer Goethe remembered in his autobiography "daß dieses Werk uns aus der Region eines kümmerlichen Anschauens in die freien Gefilde des Gedankens hinriß" (that this work lifted us from the level of meager perception to the unencumbered regions of thought). But Lessing had to defend himself in *Brief, antiquarischen Inhalts* (Letters on Classical Matters, 1768–1769) against an attack by Christian Adolf Klotz, a professor of rhetoric in Halle; the entire first volume of Herder's *Kritische Wälder* (Critical Essays, 1769) was a critique of *Laokoon*–by and large Herder sided with Winckelmann; and Goethe presented his own views as a third position in the journal *Propyläen* in 1798.

Lessing's hopes for employment as royal librarian in Berlin or at the art gallery in Dresden ended in disappointment. In the spring of 1767 he accepted a position as theater critic at the newly founded German National Theater in Hamburg. He may well have shared the high expectation embodied in the idea of a national theater; his involvement in a similar venture in Mannheim in 1776 and his interest in plans for a national academy in Vienna to be presided over by Friedrich Gottlieb Klopstock would point in that direction. But regional interests and petty rivalries and intrigues foiled all of these attempts to establish an intellectual center of national significance. The Hamburg enterprise, underfunded and mismanaged, folded before the end of the year. Lessing stayed to complete his contribution: the *Hamburgische Dramaturgie* (1767–1769; translated as *Hamburg Dramaturgy*, 1962).

It is not a systematic work. When the original plan to review each play, all of the actors, and every performance had to be abandoned because of personal sensitivities, Lessing broadened his theme to include all matters pertaining to the contemporary debate on drama: the nature of the tragic hero–he is to be "vom gleichen Schrot und Korn" (of like kind) as the audience in order to affect them; the concept of genius; and the problem of historical accuracy in drama are among the issues treated. An overriding concern is the critique of French classical drama, and Shakespeare is used to substantiate its devaluation. But the greatest attention is devoted to a reinterpretation of Aristotle's comments on tragedy. In the light of modern scholarship Lessing's reading of the crucial passage may be faulty: he translates *eleos* and *phobos* as *Furcht* (fear) and *Mitleid* (pity), declares *Furcht* to be pity we feel for ourselves, and sees both emotions as the object of the cathartic experience of tragedy.

Eminently sociable, Lessing acquired a large circle of friends in Hamburg. With Johann Bode he entered into a short-lived publishing business; in the house of the merchant Engelbert König he met his future wife, Eva, who was then married to König; the children of Hermann Samuel Reimarus, professor of oriental languages, provided him with the manuscript of their father's radically deistic "Apologia oder Schutzschrift für die vernünftigen Verehrer Gottes" (Apology or Defense of the Rational Worshipers of God). He became acquainted with Carl Philipp Emanuel Bach, then musical director of the Hamburg parish, and played chess with Klopstock. He also met Johann Arnold Ebert, professor at the Carolinum in Brunswick, who secured for him his last position: the librarianship at the ducal library in Wolfenbüttel, then and now one of the most significant libraries in Europe.

Financial difficulties and poor health delayed his departure from Hamburg, and he did not assume his new duties until May 1770. His years in Wolfenbüttel were overshadowed by the provinciality of the duchy of Braunschweig-Lüneburg and the social and intellectual isolation in which he found himself. Although his relationship with the court in Brunswick was strained from the beginning, he was not treated ungenerously. His prolonged absences from Wolfenbüttel were tolerated, and he was asked to accompany a member of the ducal family on a tour of Italy from April to December 1775; the duke also exempted his publications from censorship and approved his plan to make the treasures of the library available to the public. Lessing's work on Berengar of Tours (1770) and the six-volume *Zur Geschichte und Litteratur: Aus den Schätzen der Herzoglichen Bibliothek zu Wolfenbüttel* (On History and Literature: From the Collections of the Ducal Library in Wolfenbüttel, 1773–1781) are efforts in this direction. Most of his commentaries on rare or forgotten texts take the form of righting an old wrong. Thus he defends the heretic Berengar against his orthodox critics, Leibniz against the accusation of religious hypocrisy, and the sixteenth-century apostate Adam Neuser as a victim of religious intolerance. The third volume of *Zur Geschichte und Litteratur* (1774) includes the first of a series of fragments from Reimarus's "Apologie," which were to involve Lessing in an extended theological controversy with the Hamburg theological Johann Melchior Goeze and others, and which culminated in the publication of *Nathan der Weise* in 1779.

But before the quarrel over the "Reimarus Fragments" dominated his life, he was able to complete *Emilia Galotti*. In a letter to his brother, Lessing describes the play as "eine modernisierte, von allem Staatsinteresse befreite *Virginia*" (a modernized *Virginia,* devoid of all political concerns). He provided his ducal employer with a similar description, and it is likely that he deemphasized the play's sociopolitical content to avoid censorship. *Emilia Galotti* is an indictment of an immoral prince, Hettore Gonzaga. The prince's designs on Emilia, who is unaccustomed to the amorality of the court and unable to defend herself against it, seem to leave her no alternative but to seek her own death. On her wedding day she finds herself trapped at the prince's retreat after her bridegroom has been murdered. The prince, indirectly the perpetrator of this crime, now acts as judge and orders a full investigation, thus preventing Emilia's escape. That Emilia is less afraid of the political and judicial power of the prince than of the power of seduction has inspired many psychological analyses. That her father, Odoardo, urged by Emilia, kills her and spares the prince seems to expose the passivity and frustrations of the middle class.

The play was hailed as the prototype of a German drama with true-to-life characters, but Matthias Claudius found the heroine's fear of her own sensuality difficult to understand; Goethe called the play a masterpiece yet found it "nur gedacht" (too contrived); and Friedrich Schlegel, who influenced future commentaries on Lessing by praising the philosopher at the expense of the poet, described the play as "ein großes Exempel der dramatischen Algebra" (a great example of dramatic algebra).

Even though more recent commentaries have deemphasized the play's sociopolitical edge, it is clear that Lessing's view of the Prussian state, which during his lifetime had emerged as a major military power in Europe, had undergone considerable change. In response to an ironic remark by Nicolai regarding censorship in Vienna, Lessing belittled a presumed freedom of the press that allows inane attacks on religion but excludes all critical review of social and political conditions. In this respect, he calls Prussia "das sklavischste Land Europas" (the most slavish country in Europe). Having joined the Freemasons in Hamburg, and possibly disappointed by the "secrets" imparted to him at his initiation, he published *Ernst und Falk: Gespräche für Freymäurer* (1778; translated as *Masonic Dialogues,* 1927). The work maps out the duties of the citizen in an imperfect state.

In 1771, after the death of her husband, Eva König had become engaged to Lessing. Returning from his Italian journey, he intensified his efforts to have his position upgraded, for he considered his own financial independence an essential prerequisite to marriage, despite Eva's considerable fortune. Embittered by

delays, Lessing was ready to resign when his conditions were finally met. A few months later, on 8 October 1776, the wedding took place on the estate of friends near Hamburg. Lessing's marital life was short. His son Traugott survived for only one day after a difficult birth, from which the mother never fully recovered. Eva Lessing died on 10 January 1778.

In his grief, Lessing submerged himself in the increasingly polemical debate triggered by his second installment of segments from the Reimarus manuscript. The first portion, "Von der Duldung der Deisten" (On Tolerating Deists) in 1774, had gone widely unnoticed; but the radical questioning of the New Testament accounts of Christ's death and resurrection in *Von dem Zwecke Jesu und seiner Jünger* (On the Purpose of Jesus and His Disciples, 1778) triggered a vociferous response from the already embattled orthodox Protestant camp. Its main spokesman, Goeze, was no match for Lessing's satirical pen, but he succeeded in rousing the established ecclesiastic and secular hierarchies into action. Lessing's publisher, the Waisenhaus-Buchhandlung in Brunswick, was ordered by ducal decree to halt the distribution of all writings pertaining to the controversy; and Lessing, whose efforts to persuade the court otherwise were ignored, was advised to cease all further publications on matters of religion.

To shield Reimarus's children from public wrath, Lessing had presented Reimarus's text as "Fragmente eines Ungenannten" (Fragments by an unnamed author). Furthermore, he had introduced the deistic arguments with counterarguments of his own. Despite these precautions, he was soon publicly suspected of being himself the "unnamed" author. In defiance of his ducal employer's order, Lessing published simultaneously in Hamburg and Berlin; his penultimate response to the ultraconservative Goeze then turned to his old forum, the theater, to present his last word on the matter.

A posthumously published preface to *Nathan der Weise* says: "daß der Nachteil, welchen geoffenbarte Religionen dem menschlichen Geschlechte bringen, zu keiner Zeit einem vernünftigen Manne müsse auffallender gewesen sein, als zu den Zeiten der Kreuzzüge" (the disadvantage which revealed religions bring to mankind can never have been more obvious to a rational man than at the time of the Crusades). The play shows intolerance and inhumanity to be the result of the conviction that a single religion is the sole recipient of transcendental truth. But the principal representatives of the warring factions–a young Templar captured and pardoned by Saladin (the Muslim ruler of Jerusalem), and the wise Jewish merchant Nathan–overcome their religious as well as their political and racial differences. Even before the play's utopian ending, which reveals that they are related to each other, they become friends. This friendship is brought about by several educational processes which permeate the play and culminate in the famous Parable of the Rings. Questioned by Saladin regarding the truth which all religions claim, Nathan responds with Lessing's adaptation of one of Boccaccio's tales from the *Decameron* (1351–1353). Under the veil of allegory Nathan allows all revealed religions the same degree of "truth." They are indistinguishable from one another in that they all base their claims on reported historical events; such "historical proofs" are judged to be insufficient in the court of reason, and therefore their mutually exclusive claims would have to be rejected. But the judge in Nathan's parable moves beyond this deist position; instead of a judgment, he offers advice: although the validity of religious beliefs cannot be demonstrated, their value can be established through the virtuous life of the believer. The absence of transcendental certainty becomes the incentive to strive toward moral autonomy.

In *Die Erziehung des Menschengeschlechts* (1780; translated as *The Education of the Human Race,* 1858) Lessing seems to provide a more definitive answer regarding his stand toward Christianity. He sent the manuscript to his publisher, Voß, with the condition that his authorship be withheld; instead, he was described on the title page as the book's editor. The work describes the Old and New Testaments as schoolbooks that have served their purpose in the continuing progress of mankind toward ultimate enlightenment; Christianity is an imperfect but necessary stage along the way. The work does not focus on the irrelevance or the absence of divine guidance in the education of mankind, however, but on those accomplishments which man, individually or collectively, has achieved for himself. It ends with the conviction that the ultimate goal, the moral autonomy of man, will be reached: "sie wird gewiß kommen, die Zeit der Vollendung, da der Mensch . . . das Gute tun wird, weil es das Gute ist" (the time of perfection will surely come, when man . . . will act virtuously for virtue's sake).

Lessing died in Brunswick on 15 February 1781, in the presence of his stepdaughter Amalie and his friend Alexander Daveson.

Letters:

Briefe von und an Gotthold Ephraim Lessing: In fünf Bänden, volumes 17–21 of *Gotthold Ephraim Lessings sämtliche Schriften,* edited by Karl Lachmann, third edition, edited by Franz Muncker (Berlin & Leipzig: De Gruyter, 1904–1907; reprinted, Berlin: De Gruyter, 1968);

Lessings Briefwechsel mit Mendelssohn und Nicolai über das Trauerspiel: Nebst verwandten Schriften Nicolais und Mendelssohns, edited by Robert Petsch (Leipzig: Durr, 1910; reprinted, Darmstadt: Wissenschaftliche Buchgesellschaft, 1967);

Lessings Briefe in einem Band, edited by Herbert Greiner-Mai (Berlin: Aufbau, 1967);

Briefwechsel über das Trauerspiel: Gotthold Ephraim Lessing, Moses Mendelssohn, Friedrich Nicolai, edited by Jochen Schult-Sasse (Munich: Winkler, 1972);

Briefe Lessings aus Wolfenbüttel, edited by Günter Schulz (Bremen & Wolfenbüttel: Jacobi, 1975);

Meine liebste Madam!: Gotthold Ephraim Lessings Briefwechsel mit Eva König, 1770–1776, edited by Günter and Ursula Schulz (Munich: Beck, 1979);

Dialog in Briefen und andere ausgewählte Dokumente zum Leben Gotthold Ephraim Lessings mit Eva Catharina König: Zur 200. Wiederkehr des Todestages von Gotthold Ephraim Lessing am 15. Februar 1981, edited by Helmut Rudloff (Kamenz: Lessing-Museum, 1981).

Bibliography:

Siegfried Seifert, *Lessing Bibliographie* (Berlin: Aufbau, 1973).

Biographies:

Karl Gotthelf Lessing, *Gotthold Ephraim Lessings Leben, nebst seinem noch übrigen Nachlasse* (Berlin: Voß, 1793);

Erich Schmidt, *Lessing: Geschichte seines Lebens und seiner Schriften* (Berlin: Weidmann, 1899);

Henry B. Garland, *Lessing, the Founder of Modern German Literature,* second edition (London & New York: St. Martin's Press, 1962);

Wolfgang Drews, *Gotthold Ephraim Lessing in Selbstzeugnissen und Bilddokumenten* (Reinbek: Rowohlt, 1962);

Kurl Wölfel, *Lessings Leben und Werk in Daten und Bildern* (Frankfurt am Main: Insel, 1967);

Gerd Hillen, *Lessing Chronik: Daten zu Leben und Werk* (Munich: Hanser, 1979).

References:

Henry E. Allison, *Lessing and the Enlightenment: His Philosophy of Religion and its Relation to Eighteenth-Century Thought* (Ann Arbor: University of Michigan Press, 1966);

Ehrhard Bahr and others, eds., *Humanität und Dialog: Lessing und Mendelssohn in neuer Sicht* (Detroit: Wayne State University Press / Munich: Edition text + kritik, 1982);

Wilfried Barner, *Produktive Rezeption: Lessing und die Tragödien Senecas* (Munich: Beck, 1973);

Barner and Albert M. Reh, eds., *Nation und Gelehrtenrepublik: Lessing im Europäischen Zusammenhang* (Detroit: Wayne State University Press / Munich: Edition text + kritik, 1984);

Barner and others, eds., *Lessing: Epoche, Werk, Wirkung*, fourth edition (Munich: Beck, 1981);

Martin Bollacher, *Lessing: Vernunft und Geschichte. Untersuchungen zum Problem religiöser Aufklärung in den Spätschriften* (Tübingen: Niemeyer, 1978);

Manfred Durzak, *Poesie und Ratio: Vier Lessing-Studien* (Bad Homburg: Athenäum, 1970);

Helmut Göbel, *Bild und Sprache bei Lessing* (Munich: Fink, 1971);

F. J. Lamport, *Lessing and the Drama* (Oxford: Clarendon Press, 1981);

Lessing Yearbook! (1969–);

Volker Nölle, *Subjektivität und Wirklichkeit in Lessings dramatischem und theologischem Werk* (Berlin: Schmidt, 1977);

George Pons, *Gotthold Ephraim Lessing et le Christianisme* (Paris: Didier, 1964);

J. G. Robertson, *Lessing's Dramatic Theory* (Cambridge: University Press, 1939);

Victor A. Rudowski, *Lessing's Aesthetica in Nuce: An Analysis of the May 26, 1769 Letter to Nicolai* (Chapel Hill: University of North Carolina Press, 1971);

Jürgen Schröder, *Gotthold Ephraim Lessing: Sprache und Drama* (Munich: Fink, 1972);

Harald Schultze, *Lessings Toleranzbegriff: Eine theologische Studie* (Göttingen: Vandenhoeck & Ruprecht, 1969);

Hinrich C. Seeba, *Die Liebe zur Sache. Öffentliches und privates Interesse in Lessings Dramen* (Tübingen: Niemeyer, 1973);

Gisbert Ter-Nedden, *Lessings Trauerspiele: Der Ursprung des modernen Dramas aus dem Geist der Kritik* (Stuttgart: Metzler, 1986).

Papers:

Manuscripts of Gotthold Ephraim Lessing are in various European libraries, notably in the Herzog-August-Bibliothek, Wolfenbüttel, and the Deutsche Staatsbibliothek, Berlin.

Martin Luther

(10 November 1483 – 18 February 1546)

Jeffrey Jaynes
Methodist Theological School in Ohio

This entry was updated by Professor Jaynes from his entry in DLB 179: German
Writers of the Renaissance and Reformation 1280–1580.

SELECTED BOOKS: *Dispvtatio D. Martini Lvther Theologi, pro declaratione virtutis indulgentiarum* (Basel: Adam Petri, 1517);

Eynn Sermon von dem Ablasz vnnd Gnade (Wittenberg: Johann Grunenberg, 1518);

Resolutiones disputationem de Indulgentiarum virtute (Wittenberg: Johann Rhau-Grunenberg, 1518);

Eyn Sermon von der Bereytung zum Sterbenn (Wittenberg: Johann Rhau-Grunenberg, 1519);

Eyn Sermon von den Wucher (Wittenberg: Johann Rhau-Grunenberg, 1519);

Eyn Sermon von dem Bann (Wittenberg: Johann Rhau-Grunenberg, 1520);

An den Christlichen Adel deutscher Nation: von des Christlichen Standes Besserung (Wittenberg: Melchior Lotter the Younger, 1520);

De captivate babylonica ecclesiae, præludium (Wittenberg: Melchior Lotter the Younger, 1520);

Von der Freyheyt einiß Christen menschen (Wittenberg: Johann Rhau-Grunenberg, 1520);

De votis monasticis (Wittenberg: Johann Rhau-Grunenberg, 1521);

Eyn trew Vormanung Martini Luther tzu allen Christen. Sich tzu vorhuten fur auffruhr vnnd Emporung (Wittenberg: Melchior Lotter the Younger, 1522);

Eyn bett buchlin der tzehen gepott. Des glawbens. Des vatter vnßers und des Ave Maria (Wittenberg: Johann Rhau-Grunenberg, 1522);

Das eyn Christliche Versamlung odder Gemeyne: recht und macht habe: alle lere tzu urteylen und lerer tzu berufen, ein- und abzusetzen (Wittenberg: Lucas Cranach the Elder & Christian Döring, 1523);

Uon welltlicher vberkeytt, wie weytt man yhr gehorsam schuldig sey (Wittenberg: Nickel Schirlentz, 1523);

Formvla missae et communionis pro Eccelsia Vuitembergensi (Wittenberg: Nickel Schirlentz, 1523);

Ordenung eyns gemeynen kastens (Wittenberg: Lucas Cranach the Elder & Christian Döring, 1523);

*Martin Luther in 1526; portrait by Lucas Cranach the Elder
(Lutherhalle, Wittenberg)*

Das Ihesus Christus eyn geborner Iude sey (Wittenberg: Lucas Cranach the Elder & Christian Döring, 1523);

An die Radherrn aller stedte deutsches lands: das sie christliche Schulen auffrichten vnd hallten sollen (Wittenberg: Lucas Cranach the Elder & Christian Döring, 1524);

Von Kauffshandlung vnd wucher (Wittenberg: Hans Lufft, 1524);

Geystliche Gesangk Buchlein (Wittenberg: Joseph Klug, 1524);

Ermanunge zum fride auff die zwelff artikel der Bawrschafft ynn Schwaben (Wittenberg: Joseph Klug, 1525);

Wider die rewbischen vnnd mördischen rotten der anderen bawren (Erfurt: Melchior Sachse, 1525);

De servo arbitrio Mar. Lutheri ad D. Erasmum Roterodamum (Wittenberg: Hans Lufft, 1525);

Widder die hymelischen propheten, von den bildern vnd Sacrament (Wittenberg: Lucas Cranach the Elder & Christian Döring, 1525);

Deudsche Messe vnd ordnung Gottis diensts (Wittenberg: Melchior Lotter, 1526);

Das diese Worte Christi (Das ist mein leib etce) noch fest stehen widder die Schwerm geister (Wittenberg: Melchior Lotter, 1527);

Vnterricht der Visitatoren an die Pfarhern ym Kurfurstenthum zu Sachsen, by Luther and Philipp Melanchthon (Wittenberg: Nickel Schirlentz, 1528);

Vom abendmahl Christi, Bekendnis (Wittenberg: Melchior Lotter, 1528);

Enchiridion. Der kleine Catechismus für die gemeine Pfarher vnd Prediger, gemehret und verbessert (Wittenberg: Nickel Schirlentz, 1529);

Deudsch Catechismus (Wittenberg: Georg Rhau, 1529);

Vom kriege widder die Türken (Wittenberg: Hans Wei, 1529);

Eine Heerpredigt widder die Türken (Wittenberg: Nickel Schirlentz, 1529);

Vermanung an die geistlichen versamlet auf dem Reichstag zu Augsburg (Wittenberg: Hans Lufft, 1530);

Warnunge D. Martini Luther, An seine lieben Deudschen (Wittenberg: Hans Lufft, 1531);

Ein sendbrieff D. M. Lutthers. Vom Dolmetzschen vnd Fürbit der heiligenn (Nuremberg: Georg Rottmaier, 1531);

Eine einfeltige weise zu Beten, für einen guten Freund (Wittenberg: Hans Lufft, 1535);

Beelzebub an die Heilige Bepstliche Kirche (Wittenberg: Nickel Schirlentz, 1537);

Artickel, so da hetten sollen auffs Concilion zu Mantua, oder wo es würde sein, vberantwortet werden (Wittenberg: Hans Lufft, 1538);

Ein Brieff D. Mart. Luther wider die Sabbather an einen guten Freund (Wittenberg: Nickel Schirlentz, 1538);

Von den Concilijs vnd Kirchen (Wittenberg: Hans Lufft, 1539);

Der Erste Teil der Bücher D. Mart. Luth. vber etliche Epistel der Aposteln (Wittenberg: Hans Lufft, 1539);

Wider Hans Worst (Wittenberg: Hans Lufft, 1541);

Vermanunge zum Gebet, Wider den Türeken (Wittenberg: Nickel Schirlentz, 1541);

Der XXIX. Psalm ausgelegt, durch Doctor Iohan Bugenhagen . . . Ein trost D. Martini Luthers den Weibern, welchen es vngerade gegangen ist mit Kindergeberen (Wittenberg: Joseph Klug, 1542);

New Zeitung vom Rhein (Wittenberg: Hans Lufft, 1542);

Von den Iüden vnd jhren Lügen (Wittenberg: Hans Lufft, 1543);

Hauß postil D. Martin Luther (Nuremberg: Johann vom Berg & Ulrich Neuber, 1544);

Wider das Bapstum zu Rom vom Teuffel gestifft (Wittenberg: Hans Lufft, 1545);

Tomus Primus Omnium Operum . . . Martini Lutheri (Wittenberg: Hans Lufft, 1545);

Tomus Secundus Omnium Operum . . . Martini Lutheri (Wittenberg: Hans Lufft, 1546);

Der ander Teil der Bücher D. Mart: Luth: Darin alle Streitschriften, sampt etlichen Sendbrieuen, an Fürsten vnd Stedte (Wittenberg: Hans Lufft, 1548);

Tomus Tertius Omnium Operum . . . Martini Lutheri (Wittenberg: Hans Lufft, 1549);

Der Dritte Teil der bücher des . . . Martini Lutheri, darin zusamen gebracht sind christliche vnd tröstliche Erklerung vnd auslegung der furnemesten Psalmen (Wittenberg: Hans Lufft, 1550);

Der Vierdte Teil der Bücher des . . . Mart. Luth. darin . . . Christliche vnd tröstliche erklerung vnd auslegung vber etliche fürneme Capitel vnd Sprüche aus göttlicher Schrifft (Wittenberg: Hans Lufft, 1551);

Der Fünffte Teil der Bücher des . . . Martini Lutheri, darinnen . . . die Auslegung vber das erste Buch, vnd folgend vber etliche Capitel der andern Bücher Mose (Wittenberg: Hans Lufft, 1552);

Tomus Quartus Omnium Operum . . . Martini Lutheri (Wittenberg: Hans Lufft, 1552);

Der Sechste teil der Bücher des . . . Martini Lutheri, darinnen begriffen etliche auslegung der heiligen Schrifft im newen Testament, auch die Bücher vom Ehestand, Kauffshendel vnd Wucher, Vermanung vnd Trostschifften (Wittenberg: Hans Lufft, 1553);

Der Siebend Teil der bücher des . . . Mart. Lutheri, Darinnen begriffen, die Bücher vom Christlichen stand, wider den Bapst, vnd die Bischoue . . . Item, von der Kirchen vnd den Concilijs (Wittenberg: Hans Lufft, 1554);

Tomus Quintus Omnium Operum . . . Martini Lutheri (Wittenberg: Hans Lufft, 1554);

Tomus Sextus Omnium Operum . . . Martini Lutheri (Wittenberg: Peter Seitz's heirs, 1555);

Der Achte teil der Bücher des . . . Martini Lutheri: darinnen die verdeutschte Auslegunge begriffen vber die Psalmos graduum, vnd den 110 Psalm, Das fünffte buch Mose, vnd dies Propheten (Wittenberg: Hans Lufft, 1556);

Der Neundte Teil der Bücher des—Martini Lutheri: darinnen die Propositiones vom Ablas . . . samt vielen Sendbrieun an Bapst, Keiser, Fürstn vnd Bischoue, vnd andern schrifften von dem 17. bis in das 33. jar (Wittenberg: Hans Lufft, 1557);

Tomvs Septimvs Omnivm Opervm . . . Martini Lutheri (Wittenberg: Thomas Klug, 1557);

Der Zehende Teil der Bücher des . . . Martini Lutheri, Nemlich, die herrliche Auslegung vber das Erste Buch Mosi (Wittenberg: Thomas Klug, 1558);

Der Eilffte Teil der Bücher des . . . Martini Lutheri, Nemlich die herrliche Auslegung vber das Erste Buch Mosi (Wittenberg: Thomas Klug, 1558);

Der Zwelffte vnd letzte Teil der Bücher des . . . Mart. Lutheri: Nemlich die erste Auslegung vber die Epistel an die Galater, Ecclesiastes oder Prediger Salomonis, sampt etlichen Trostschriften, Sendbrieuen vnd handlungen (Wittenberg: Hans Lufft, 1559);

Tischreden, oder colloquia Doct. Mart. Luthers, so er in vielen Jaren gegen gelarten leuten auch frembden Gesten, und seinen Tischgesellen gefüret, edited by Johannes Aurifaber (Eisleben: Urban Gaubisch, 1566); translated by Henri Bell as *Dris. Martini Lutheris colloquia mensalia; or . . . divine discourses at his table* (London: William Du Gard, 1652).

Collections: *Dr. Martin Luthers sämmtliche Schriften,* 23 volumes, edited by Johann Georg Walch (Saint Louis: Concordia, 1880–1910);

D. Martin Luthers Werke: Kritische Gesamtausgabe, 104 volumes (Weimar: Böhlau, 1883–1984).

Editions in English: *Watchwords for the Warfare of Life,* translated by Mrs. Elizabeth Charles (New York: Dodd, 1868);

The First Principles of the Reformation: The 95 Theses and the Three Primary Works, translated by Henry Wace (London: Murray, 1883);

Luther's Works, edited by Jaroslav Pelikan and Helmut T. Lehmann (Philadelphia: Fortress, 1955);

Martin Luther: Selections from His Writings, edited by John Dillenberger (Garden City, N.Y.: Doubleday, 1961);

Selected Writings of Martin Luther, edited by Theodore G. Tappert (Philadelphia: Fortress, 1967);

Martin Luther, edited by E. G. Rupp and Benjamin Drewery (New York: St. Martin's Press, 1970).

OTHER: *Eyn geystlich edles Buchleynn. von rechter vnderscheyd vnd vorstand. was der alt vnd new mensche sey. Was Adams vnd gottis kind sey. vnd wie Adam ynn vns sterben vnnd Christus ersteen sall,* introduction by Luther (Wittenberg: Johann Rhau-Grunenberg, 1516);

Sylvester de Prierio, *Epitoma responsionis ad Martinvm Lvtherum,* introduction and critical glosses by Luther (Wittenberg: Melchior Lotter the Younger, 1520);

Das Newe Testament Deutzsch, translated by Luther (Wittenberg: Melchior Lotter, 1522; revised, 1522);

Das Allte Testament deutsch, translated by Luther (Wittenberg: Melchior Lotter the Younger, 1523);

Der Psalter teutsch (Strasbourg: Johann Knobloch, 1524);

Das tauffbuchlin verdeudscht, auffs new zu gericht, translated and revised by Luther (Wittenberg: Hans Weiß, 1526);

Biblia: das ist, die gantze Heilige Schrifft Deudsch, translated by Luther (Wittenberg: Hans Lufft, 1534; revised, 1541);

Aesop, *Hundert Fabeln aus Esopo,* translated by Luther and others, edited by Nathan Chytraeus (Rostock: Jacob Lucius, 1571).

Early in the 1520s Hans Holbein, the great German artist and illustrator, depicted Martin Luther as Hercules Germanicus. In this image the vigorous Luther, clothed in his Augustinian cowl and wielding a deadly club, stands triumphant over several vanquished proponents of Scholastic theology. It is appropriate that Luther should be associated with the mythology of antiquity, since his life and influence have been so susceptible to characterizations of mythical proportions. Champion of German liberties, reviler of the Jews, source of modern High German, seed of dogmatic intolerance, herald of the Protestant Reformation, heretic of the Catholic Church, friend of God and foe of the devil—these and countless other descriptions embrace some aspect of the man. Regardless of personal perspective, however, one would have to judge Luther's efforts in publishing and his literary achievements as truly herculean: from 1516 to 1546 he wrote a treatise nearly every other week—some sixty thousand printed pages that today fill the 104 volumes published thus far in the Weimar edition (1883) of his works. It has been estimated that Luther's writings account for 20 percent of all the literature printed in Germany from 1500 to 1530. The breadth of his literary accomplishments is also impressive, as his works include theological tracts, hymns, poetry, liturgies, sermons, *postillae* (preaching aids), commentaries, translations, and polemics. Luther may have written more than any of his predecessors, and more has probably been written about him than about almost any other religious figure in history.

Despite his accomplishments, Luther came from modest origins—a fact that he never ceased to mention. He was born in Eisleben in the county of Mansfeld on 10 November 1483. His father, Hans, rose from the status of copper miner to become a *Hüttenmeister* (copper smelter) and owner of a few small mines. These mining interests led him to move his family in 1484 from Eisleben to the town of Mansfeld, where he parlayed his business success into a position on the town council in 1508. Luther's mother, Margareta, née Lindemann, came from a burgher family that was well established in the Thuringian city of Eisenach.

After completing his primary Latin education in the Mansfeld town school, Luther moved in 1497 to Magdeburg, where he lived and studied at a foundation school established by the Brethren of the Common Life. He completed his pre-university education in Eisenach, living in the vicinity of his mother's family and boarding with the family of Heinrich Schalbe. The quasi-monastic lifestyle of the Brethren in Magdeburg, and his experience with an informal collegium in Eisenach, introduced Luther to life in a religious community. Next, encouraged by his father, Luther enrolled at the University of Erfurt: the university matriculation register for May 1501, listing Martinus Ludher ex Mansfeldt, is the first documented reference to the Reformer. Humanist influence was strong at Erfurt; although Luther's accomplishments as a classical scholar would never rival those of such humanist luminaries as Conrad Celtis, Ulrich von Hutten, Mutianus Rufus, Eobanus Hessus, and Crotus Rubeanus, he would retain a commitment to original languages and sources that reflected their agenda.

The prevailing philosophical tradition at Erfurt, however, was nominalism, and it was in this context that Luther learned to think about the nature of the world and of God. The nominalist *via moderna* (modern way), in contrast to the realist *via antiqua* (ancient way) of Thomas Aquinas and Duns Scotus, emphasized personal experience and observation as opposed to speculation on abstract universal truths. Nominalist preachers such as Gabriel Biel of Strasbourg argued that God will not deny grace to one who makes a sincere effort. Jodokus Trutfetter and Bartholomaeus Arnoldi von Usingen, Luther's instructors in the arts faculty at Erfurt, were aligned with the nominalist tradition. Luther received his bachelor of arts in 1502 and his masters in 1505, graduating near the top of his class.

Erfurt was the scene of the first pivotal crisis in Luther's life. Plagued by spiritual doubts and by what he called *Anfechtungen* (moral trials), he abandoned his intention of pursuing studies in law. During a thunderstorm on the Feast Day of the Visitation of Mary he vowed to Anne, patron saint of miners, to become a monk. He subsequently entered the order of the Observant Augustinians at the Black Cloister in Erfurt. Johann von Staupitz, vicar general of the order in Germany, sought to provide spiritual

consolation to the scrupulous friar in the midst of his Anfechtungen; but Staupitz was frequently exasperated by Luther's confessions, characterizing them as "Humpelwerk und Puppensünden" (weak excuses and play sins). Luther found little comfort in the exercise of his religious office after he was ordained a priest in 1507, trembling in terror as he celebrated the Mass. At Staupitz's instigation, however, he began to study the Scriptures, and he found consolation there. Luther had seen his first Bible as a twenty-year-old university student in Erfurt, and he received one during the year of his novitiate. In addition to his Bible studies, Luther continued his training as a theologian and began to lecture on the *Sententiae libri quatuor* (Four Books of Sentences, circa 1160) of Peter Lombard. In 1508 he lectured on moral philosophy at Elector Friedrich's recently established University of Wittenberg, using Aristotle's *Nichomachean Ethics* as his text. He dabbled in mystical theology, reading works by Bridget of Sweden and Saint Bonaventura and, eventually, the early-fifteenth-century *Theologia Deutsch* (German Theology). Luther's exceptional level of commitment at the Erfurt cloister was recognized by his peers, and in the winter of 1510 they sent him to Rome as their representative in negotiating a settlement between rival factions of the Augustinian order. Luther returned from his trip disillusioned by the religious laxity that he encountered in Rome, where seven masses could be crammed into an hour, and disappointed over his failure to gain recognition for his faction.

Tensions in the Erfurt cloister encouraged Luther to follow Staupitz to the University of Wittenberg in the fall of 1511. With Staupitz's retirement as professor of theology in 1512, Luther began to lecture on the subject, and he was promoted to doctor of theology in October of that year. In Wittenberg, Luther resided with the other canons in the Augustinian monastery that would later be presented to him and his family as a gift from the elector. In 1513 Staupitz insisted that Luther assume duties as preacher at the city church in Wittenberg.

At the university Luther lectured on the Psalms from 1513 to 1515, Paul's Epistles to the Romans in 1515–1516, and the Epistle to the Galatians in 1516–1517. Rejecting his nominalist training, he came to a new understanding of God's righteousness. His first significant published work was a short introduction to a new edition of the *Theologia Deutsch* in 1516. The following year he prepared a series of theses against scholastic theology for his student Franz Günther to defend at a disputation on 4 September. Shortly afterward Luther presented a series of arguments that would eventually shatter the medieval Church Catholic: on 31 October 1517 he dispatched his *Diputatio pro declaratione virtutis indulgentiarum* (Disputation on the Declaration Concerning the Power of Indulgences), better known as his Ninety-five Theses, to Albrecht of Brandenburg, archbishop of Mainz and German elector, calling for a debate on the practice of selling indulgences—conditional promises of divine forgiveness and of diminished time in purgatory. (Much later, Philipp Melanchthon would claim that Luther posted the theses on the door of the Castle Church in Wittenberg.) Luther was incensed with the way indulgences were being hawked by the Dominican preacher Johann Tetzel with the jingle "Sobald als das Geld im koffer klingt, sofort die Seele aus dem Fegefeur springt" (As soon as coin in the money box rings, the soul from purgatory springs); this sort of inappropriate extension of the sacrament of penance had been condemned at the Sorbonne in 1482. Even though a debate never occurred, Luther attracted the attention of an influential German audience. He expanded his discussion of the issue in his *Resolutiones disputationem de Indulgentiarum virtute* (Resolutions on the Disputation Concerning the Power of Indulgences, 1518).

In 1518 Luther was invited to defend his developing theology before a gathering of fellow Augustinians in Heidelberg. In the "Disputatio Heidelberg habita" (Theses of the Heidelberg Disputation), published in the first volume of his collected Latin works (1545), he did not refer to the matter of indulgences, but, in what he believed represented the spirit of Saint Augustine, he appealed to divine grace and branded his nominalist heritage as a Pelagian error leading to damnation. While Luther won over many supporters at Heidelberg, including the Dominican Martin Bucer of Strasbourg and the educator Georg Simmler of Heidelberg, he also alienated many and found himself embroiled in a growing series of controversies. The Dominican Sylvester Prierias's *In Praesumptuosas Martini Lutheri conclusiones de potestate Papae dialogus* (Dialogue against the Presumptuous Conclusions of Martin Luther Concerning the Authority of the Pope, 1518) argued that Luther's position on indulgences threatened the Pope's authority and must be rejected. That same year the papal legate, Cardinal Cajetan (Tommaso de Vio), summoned Luther to the Diet of Augsburg to make the same point. The following year, at a debate in Leipzig, the theologian Johannes Eck not only forced Luther to acknowledge his defiance of the authority of the bishop of Rome but got Luther to equivocate on the authority of ecclesiastical councils. For Luther, Scripture was the final authority; for Eck, this position was tantamount to spiritual anarchy.

Luther was making enemies; but he was also gaining friends through the publication of his sermons, which dealt with a wide range of controversial social and religious topics. *Eynn Sermon von dem Ablasz vnnd Gnade* (A Sermon on Indulgences and Grace, 1518) was a popular restatement of his condemnation of indulgences; *Eyn Sermon von der Bereytung zum Sterbenn* (A Sermon on Preparation for Dying, 1519) contributed to the literature of *ars moriendi* (the art of dying); *Eyn Sermon von den Wucher* (A Sermon on Usury, 1519) attacked economic inequality; and *Eyn Sermon von dem Bann* (A Sermon on the Ban, 1520) defended church discipline but rejected papal excommunication.

In 1520 Luther, learning that a papal bull of excommunication, *Exsurge Domine,* had been issued against him, published *An den Christlichen Adel deutscher Nation: von des Christlichen Standes Besserung* (To the Christian Nobility of the German Nation: Concerning the Improvement of the Christian Estate). The work calls on the princes to serve as *Nötbishofe* (emergency bishops) and make the cause of church reform a concern of the German nation. Luther blasts what he identifies as the three *Mauer* (walls) of papal tyranny—the separation of the clerical from the lay estates and the exclusive authority of the Pope to interpret Scripture and to call a council—and argues for what would come to be called the priesthood of all believers. He also calls for reducing ecclesiastical revenues, forbidding pilgrimages to Rome, and eliminating masses for the dead. In *De captivate babylonica ecclesiae* (On the Babylonian Captivity of the Church, 1520) Luther insists that the church's sacramental practices have no sound scriptural basis and serve only the interests of the hierarchy; he concludes that only baptism and the Eucharist should be practiced as sacraments, for they alone had both the mandate of Scripture (the Word of promise) and a visible sign. In *Von der Freyheyt einiß Christen menschen* (On the Freedom of a Christian, 1520) Luther offers his clearest statement to that time on the principle of justification by faith, arguing that no amount of good works can make a person righteous before God; righteousness comes as a gift of divine grace through faith. Nevertheless, Luther maintains, the needs of the outer person for moral restraints and the need to live in a loving relationship to one's neighbor require one to live as servant as well as lord. Law and Gospel belong together, and good works should proceed naturally from a faith that makes one righteous *coram deo* (before God).

On the morning of 10 December 1520 Luther marked the expiration of his sixty-day grace period for responding to the papal bull of excommunication by gathering with Melanchthon and several university students to burn the bull, along with the writings of several Scholastic theologians and a copy of the *Corpus Iuris Canonici* (Body of Canon Law). In January 1521 Luther was excommunicated in Rome, and in April he was summoned to appear before Emperor Charles V at the Diet of Worms. The emperor had one request: recant. Luther's response was equally straightforward: he would retract nothing unless convinced to do so by the Word of God or by reasonable argument. In contrast to the popular image of the Augustinian friar standing defiant before the emperor at Worms, Luther reported that he was so shaken by the experience that he was nauseated nearly to the point of incapacitation. Luther was guaranteed safe passage to return home, but Elector Friedrich decided that he would be safer in Friedrich's castle at the Wartburg, outside Eisenach. Meanwhile, in Augsburg, Charles V issued the Edict of Worms, calling for Luther's arrest and banning his writings. Enforcement of the edict, however, was nearly impossible because of the myriad political entities into which the empire was divided.

Although he resented the isolation from his Wittenberg associates, the Wartburg proved to be a productive and invigorating environment for Luther. In this setting he expanded his critical assault on the institutions of the Roman Church with the attack on the whole structure of monastic life, *De votis monasticis* (On Monastic Vows, 1521). Here he holds that monastic vows violate the principles of Christian freedom and rejects the traditional monastic counsels of perfection, insisting on a uniform Christian estate. By 1523 he would be calling for the closing of monasteries and convents. He also turned his attention to a project that would consume the rest of his life: the translation of the Bible into German. During this exile period he devoted himself to the translation of the New Testament, completing the task in less than three months by averaging some fifteen hundred words a day. The resulting *Das Newe Testament Deutzsch* was published in Wittenberg in September 1522, thereby coming to be known as the *September-testament*; it was followed by a slightly modified *Dezembertestament* when the three thousand copies of the first edition sold out almost immediately. Subsequently Luther would translate the rest of the Bible, providing a translation of the Psalms in 1524 and completing the rest of the Old Testament in 1534; in the latter year Luther's entire German Bible was published. He would continue to revise his translation until his death.

His work was, indeed, one of translation; it was no mere paraphrase or modification of the Vulgate but was based on the best available Greek and Hebrew sources. In completing his work on the New Testament, Luther relied on Desiderius Erasmus's 1519 edition of the Greek New Testament. Luther was not, however, content with a word-for-word, literal rendition of the text, which he called a mere *Buchstabieren* (spelling exercise); he sought to provide equivalent words that captured the sense and spirit of the original. He insisted that the effective translator "mus die mutter jhm hause, die kinder auff der gassen, den gemeinen man auff dem marckt drumb fragen, und den selbigen auff das maul sehen, wie sie reden und darnach dolmetszschen, so verstehen sie es auch und mercken, das man Deutsch mit jn redet" (must ask the mother at home, children in the street, the common man in the market and look them in the mouth, and listen to how they speak, then translate accordingly. They will understand it that way, too, and will notice that one is speaking German with them). There is a rustic or earthy quality to his work that hearkens back to the peasant ancestry that Luther seemed to cherish. The *Septembertestament* also includes some stunning illustrations, especially in the Book of Revelation; one of the most provocative is an image of the Whore of Babylon wearing a three-tiered papal tiara. Luther's translation was anything but theologically neutral, whether for the unlettered or for the literate.

Beyond simplicity, Luther cultivated an appreciation for the aesthetic dimensions of the Bible. In a letter to Georg Spalatin he insisted that people must learn that German nightingales can sing as beautifully as Roman goldfinches. Nowhere is his elegance of expression more evident than in his translation of the Psalms, based on the Hebrew texts. In Psalm 51 he has King David confess:

Gott sey mir gnedig, nach deiner Güte
Und tilge meine Sünde, nach deiner grossen Barm-
    hertzigkeit . . .
An dir allein hab ich gesündiget
Und übel fur dir gethan.
Auff das du recht behaltest in deinen worten,
Und rein bleibest, wenn du gerichtet wirst.

(God be gracious to me, according to thy goodness;
And blot out my sins, according to your great mercy . . .
Against thee alone have I sinned
And done this evil in thy sight.
That thou might be justified when thou speakest
And remain pure when thou judgest.)

Here Luther has retained the parallelism of the Hebrew text, yet he has couched this penitential outburst of the fallen king in language that would be clear to any German. The translators of the King James Bible in the next century would draw much of their inspiration from Luther's German text, especially from the Psalms, as they attempted to match gracious speech with economy of expression. Moreover, Luther's Psalms would provide inspiration to Johann Sebastian Bach, whose many oratorios and cantatas would give the language of the *Lutherbibel* a permanent place in German culture.

Luther's Bible also played a pivotal role in the linguistic evolution of Modern High German. Early-modern Germany was a hodgepodge of principalities, ecclesiastical territories, and imperial free cities with a confusing array of regional and territorial dialects, but the court speech of Saxony was emerging as a universal diplomatic language because it could be generally understood from the Low Countries to Switzerland and Bohemia. Luther realized the advantage living in Wittenberg gave him: "Ich red nach der sächsischen Canzeley, welcher nachfolgen alle fürsten und könige im teutsch lande" (I speak the language of the Saxon chancellery that all the princes and kings of Germany seek to imitate). Luther had no interest in replicating the frivolities of court speech, but he wanted to employ language that would be comprehensible to the largest number of people. Thus, Luther took the modified German of the princes to the people, and the vast dissemination of the *Lutherbibel* gave permanence to this linguistic form as literary New High German.

Luther's passion for the text of the Bible should not be misconstrued as a worship of the Bible. In his preface to the translation of the New Testament he indicates that he does not regard all of the books to be of equal worth. He recognizes the Gospel of John, Paul's letters to the Romans, and the first letter of Peter as exceptionally valuable, but he says that the book of James is full of straw and has serious questions about the canonical authority of Revelations. Thus Luther brought his own critical judgments to the Scriptures, a reflection of his humanist heritage. He expected and hoped that ordinary people would read the Scriptures frequently, even daily, and his later interest in education was inspired by a desire to expand this literate audience. Moreover, the prefaces Luther wrote for the various books of the Bible were meant as guides for the common folk. Yet, he would always maintain that the text was insufficient without the proclamation of the Word through preaching. Therefore, he spent much time during his stay at the Wartburg in composing postillae.

Luther's absence from Wittenberg afforded him the opportunity to think, write, and translate, but he was aware of what his absence meant to the tumultuous movement that was beginning to surface at home. Melanchthon could provide adequate intellectual leadership to the cause of Reform, as was evident in his *Loci communes rerum theologicarum* (1521; translated as *The Loci Communes of Philip Melanchthon*, 1944), a work that Luther praised as the best systematic theology of its time. Melanchthon did not, however, possess the personal force necessary to rally public sentiment. The most popular Wittenberg leader during Luther's exile was Andreas Karlstadt, dean of the theology faculty and Luther's companion in the Leipzig disputation. Yet, in Luther's mind, Karlstadt introduced ecclesiastical innovations, such as dispensing with the Mass, advocating clerical marriage, and offering two kinds of Communion, merely for the sake of fomenting rebellion. Receiving permission from the elector to return home, Luther gave a series of sermons in March 1522 that restored order to the community.

Luther understood that introducing reform measures too rapidly could unravel social constraints that he wanted to preserve. Accordingly, he composed a treatise against sedition, *Eyn trew Vormanung Martini Luther tzu allen Christen. Sich tzu vorhuten fur auffruhr vnnd Emporung* (A Faithful Admonition from Martin Luther to All Christians to Guard Themselves against Insurrection and Disorderliness, 1522). He followed it with a more extensive treatise on his understanding of the proper relationship between church and state, *Uon welltlicher vberkeytt, wie weytt man yhr gehorsam schuldig sey* (On Secular Authority: To What Extent It Should Be Obeyed, 1523). Luther maintains the Augustinian distinction between the Kingdom of God (the divine realm) and the Kingdom of the World (the secular realm), but he goes further than Augustine in laying out specific duties for secular rulers. He defends the right of secular authorities to wield the sword in the midst of a wicked world, but he chastises princes who "vermessen auch ynn Gottis Stuel zu setzen, und die gewissen und glauben zu meisten, und nach yherm tollen gehyrn, den helige geist zur schulen furren" (put themselves in the place of God, lord it over conscience and faith, and put the Holy Spirit to school according to their mad brains). Duke Georg's prohibition of the printing of Luther's German New Testament in Albertine Saxony was the kind of transgression that, according to Luther, confused the proper spheres of secular and spiritual authorities.

Practical issues of Reform began to consume more of Luther's attention. In *Formula missae et communionis* (Form of the Mass and Communion, 1523) he retained the traditional Latin vocabulary but eliminated references to the mass as a sacrifice and offered two kinds of communion to the laity. Vernacular liturgical resources appeared in his guide for personal prayer and confession, *Eyn bett buchlin der tzehen gepott. Des glawbens. Des vatter unßers und des Ave Maria* (A Little Prayer Book on the Ten Commandments, the Creed, the Lord's Prayer, and the Hail Mary, 1522) and in his *Das tauffbuchlin verdeudscht* (The German Baptism Book, 1526). Sharing with his humanist supporters the conviction that any significant changes, whether social or religious, must be undergirded by sufficient learning, Luther issued an appeal for universal public education in *An die Radherrn aller stedte deutsches lands: das sie christliche Schulen auffrichten vnd hallten sollen* (To the Councillors of All Cities in Germany: That They Should Establish and Maintain Christian Schools, 1524). In regard to relief for the poor, he recommended community action in *Ordenung eyns gemeynen kastens* (Community Chest Order, 1523). His preface to these regulations makes an explicit connection between *gottes dienst* (service to God, or worship) and service to one's needy neighbor.

On 13 June 1525 Luther, who had set aside his Augustinian cowl the previous October, married a former Cistercian nun, Katherine von Bora, sixteen years his junior. Their first child, Johannes—named after Johannes Bugenhagen, the Wittenberg city pastor who had performed the marriage ceremony—was born the next summer and was followed by five more children: Elisabeth in 1527, Magdelena in 1529, Martin in 1531, Paul in 1533, and Margarete in 1534. Katherine ran their household in the former cloister with efficiency and even managed a small pig farm.

The year of his marriage brought one of the greatest intellectual challenges Luther would ever experience: the need to respond to Erasmus's treatise *De libero arbitrio* (On the Freedom of the Will, 1524). In his *De servo arbitrio* (On the Bondage of the Will, 1525) Luther rightly observed that "Unus tu et solus cardinem rerum uidisti, et iugulum petisti" (You and you alone [Erasmus] have seen to the heart of the matter and seized the jugular). The disputants marshaled many scriptural passages to support their respective positions, Erasmus defending human freedom and Luther claiming that the fallen condition of humankind resulted in the loss of freedom. Above all, Luther insisted on the certainty of theological assertions for "Spiritus sanctus non est Scepticus" (the Holy Spirit is not a skeptic). The contrast between the cautious Erasmus and the dogmatic Luther is symptomatic of the gap that was growing between humanist and Protestant Reformers in this generation.

Beyond the rhetoric of the debate, Erasmus believed that Luther's grace-laden theology sacrificed moral responsibility, undercut ethics, and was at least partially responsible for the social tragedies that erupted in the Peasants' War of 1524–1525. The message of Christian liberty had obvious social as well as spiritual implications, and whether intended or not by the theologians, it affirmed the longings of many for a different kind of reformation. *Gemeindereformationen* (communal Reform movements) capitalized on the climate of religious discontent to argue for local control of ecclesiastical affairs. Luther's own treatise *Das eyn Christliche Versamlung odder Gemeyne: recht und macht habe: alle lere tzu urteylen und lerer tzu berufen, ein- und abzusetzen* (That a Christian Assembly Has the Right and Authority to Judge All Teaching and to Call, Appoint, and Dismiss Teachers, 1523) identified a central element of this communal reform: the right to call a pastor. Luther's response to the early stages of the peasant rebellion in 1524, *Ermanunge zum fride auff die zwelff artikel der Bawrschafft ynn Schwaben* (Admonitions on Peace from the Twelve Articles of the Swabian Peasantry, 1525), urged both peasants and princes to exercise restraint. But when a more full-scale revolution broke out in the spring of 1525, Luther, in his *Wider die rewbischen vnnd mördischen rotten der anderen bawren* (Against the Robbing and Murdering Hordes of Other Peasants, 1525), called on the princes to crush the rebels; they did so with great ferocity.

The events of 1525 fueled the magisterial, as opposed to the popular, wing of the Reformation, and the meeting of the imperial diet at Speyer in 1526 set the stage for the *landesherrliche Kirchenregiment* (territorial church system). Since Charles V's issuance of the Edict of Worms, Lutheranism had technically been a renegade movement. After the diet at Speyer, however, the estates of the empire were allowed to proceed with their own programs of reform in anticipation of the convening of a general church council. The process of implementing reform assumed a more official posture as princes and their advisers sought to introduce ecclesiastical changes. In Luther's Saxony, as in many other German territories, teams of clergy and lay authorities designated by the prince visited the parishes; in Saxony they used the visitation protocols drafted by Melanchthon. After the preliminary round of visitations was completed, Luther and Melanchthon collaborated on a summary set of instructions, *Vnterricht der Visitatoren an die Pfarhern ym Kurfürstenthum zu Sachsen* (Instructions for the Parish Visitors to the Congregations in Electoral Saxony, 1528), that was adopted as the first church ordinance for Electoral Saxony. Reforms in worship were one important element of this visitation process, and Luther's vernacular *Deudsche Messe vnd ordnung Gottis diensts* (German Mass and Order of Service, 1526) was introduced as the norm for Saxony.

An important consequence of these early rounds of visitations was Luther's commitment to providing basic instruction in Christian faith in the form of a catechism. In his preface to his *Enchiridion. Der kleine Catechismus für die gemeine Pfarher vnd Prediger, gemehret und verbessert* (Handbook: Small Catechism for the Common Pastor and Preacher, Expanded and Improved, 1529), Luther explained the urgency of the task after hearing the reports of the visitors: "Hilf, lieber Gott, wie manchen Jammer habe ich gesehen, daß der gemeine Mann doch so garnichts weiß von der christliche Lehre, sonderlich auf den Dörfen" (Good God, what wretchedness I beheld! The common people, especially those who live in the country, have no knowledge whatsoever of Christian teaching). The Small Catechism, first published as a broadsheet, sought to address this deficiency with an emphasis on belief over religious practice. As Luther discussed the prescriptions of the Ten Commandments, he focused on faith, placing each commandment in the context of a relationship with the divine: "Wir sollen Gott fürchten, lieben und vertrauen, daß . . ." (We should fear, love and trust God, so that . . .). His discussions of the Lord's Prayer and the Apostles' Creed and his explanations of the sacraments of Communion and baptism maintained this accent on what one should know as opposed to what one should do. The Small Catechism was designed for simple family instruction; Luther's subsequent *Deudsch Catechismus* (German Catechism, 1529), known as the *Großer Katechismus* (Large Catechism), provided more elaborate explanations of basic Christian doctrines for pastors and teachers.

Another aid to Reform at the popular level were the many hymns that Luther composed or edited. The first of his hymnbooks, the *Geystliche Gesangk Buchlein* (Spiritual Hymn Book), appeared in 1524; it was followed by nearly one hundred other collections over the course of his life. Luther's hymns were effective because their melodies captured the soul of the simple folk and their texts expressed the depths of his theological insights. In "Vom himmel hoch" (From Heaven on High) Luther marvels at the majesty and simplicity of the Incarnation:

> Ach Herr, du Schöpfer aller Ding,
> wie bist du worden so gering,
> daß du da liegt auf dürrem Gras
> davon ein Rind und Esel aß.

> (Ah Lord and Creator of all,
> How art thou become so small
> lying there on withered grass,
> whereof ate a cow and ass.)

The hymn "Nun freut euch lieben Christen gmein" (Rejoice Now, Beloved Christian Congregation) recalls his dispute with Erasmus over free will:

> Dem Teufel ich gefangen lag
> im Tod war ich verloren,
> mein Sund mich qulte Nacht und Tag,
> darin ich war geboren.

> (I lay captured by the Devil,
> lost in death,
> my sinfulness tormented me day and night,
> in which I was born.)

The pervasive battle for Luther was with the devil and cosmic evil. Hymns provided him the opportunity to exult in victories already won, even though the comfort proved personally elusive as he continued to struggle with his Anfechtungen. The familiar stanzas of his "Ein feste Burg ist unser Gott" (A Mighty Fortress Is Our God) recognize this demonic opposition yet affirm the power of the divine Word:

> Und wenn die Welt voll Teufel wär
> und wolt uns gar verschlingen
> so fürchten wir uns nicht so sehr
> es soll uns doch gelingen.
> Die fürst dieser Welt
> wie saur er sich stellt
> tut er uns doch nicht
> das macht, er ist gericht
> ein Wörtlein kann ihn fällen.

> (And though this world with devils filled,
> should threaten to undo us,
> We will not fear for God has willed,
> his truth to triumph through us,
> the prince of darkness grim,
> we tremble not for him.
> His rage we can endure,
> for lo his doom is sure,
> one little word shall fell him.)

These powerful hymns and the simple teaching of the Small Catechism may represent Luther's most enduring and universal religious contributions.

In 1529 the imperial diet, meeting again in Speyer, suspended previously granted concessions to the evangelical–that is, Lutheran–states. This action resulted in an official protest by representatives of the cities and territories, and, hence, to the generic title *Protestant* for these estates of the empire. When it came to negotiating territorial arrangements, Luther was a terrible politician. His participation in the colloquy that Landgrave Philip of Hesse sponsored at his castle in Marburg in 1529 demonstrates his disdain for political expediency and unswerving commitment to theological positions. These meetings with the south German and Swiss representatives, the most important of whom was Huldrych Zwingli of Zurich, foundered on an issue Luther regarded as critical: the understanding of Christ's presence in the Eucharist. Luther had addressed this matter on countless occasions, beginning with *Widder die hymelischen propheten, von den bildern vnd Sacrament* (Against the Heavenly Prophets in the Matter of Images and Sacraments, 1525), then again in his *Das diese Worte Christi (Das ist mein leib etce) noch fest stehen widder die Schwerm geister* (That the Words of Christ [This Is My Body, etc.] Still Stand Firm against the Fanatics, 1527). Moreover, in his *Vom abendmahl Christi, Bekendnis* (Confession on the Lord's Supper, 1528) Luther had again made the point that insisting on the real presence of Christ distinguished his thinking from the errors he associated with Zwingli and Johann Oecolampadius. When the parties met at Marburg agreement was reached on every article except the one on Christ's presence in the Eucharist. This doctrine alone was sufficient to separate the Swiss Reformed movement from the German Lutherans.

The next summer the imperial diet convened again, this time in Augsburg. The emperor was present, but Luther was not; he remained close to the proceedings but safe at Coburg Castle, trusting Melanchthon to carry out the critical negotiations at the diet. He communicated with the participants in *Vermanung an die geistlichen versamlet auf dem Reichstag zu Augsburg* (Admonition to the Clergy Assembled at Augsburg, 1530), outlining his doctrinal proposals and calling on the clergy to heed the Gospel. In Coburg, Luther continued to work on his lectures on the Psalms and completed a series of translations of Aesop's fables that would be published in 1571. The most important consequence of the Diet of Augsburg for Luther was the completion of *Confessio fidei exhibita invictissimo Imperatori Carolo V.* (1531; translated as *The confessyon of the fayth of the Germaynes exhibited to . . . Emperour Charles the v in the councell . . . holden at Augusta 1530,* 1536)–the Augsburg Confession–submitted by Melanchthon on 25 June but written under Luther's supervision. The Catholic and imperial response to the confession, the *Confutatio* (Confutation

of the Augsburg Confession), defended the orthodox positions of Rome and labeled the Protestants theologically deviant. The Augsburg Confession, however, remains the definitive expression of the Lutheran Reformation.

After Augsburg a foreboding, even apocalyptic, tone would characterize many of Luther's writings. It is evident in *Warnunge D. Martini Luther, An seine lieben Deudschen* (Address of Dr. Martin Luther to His Beloved Germans, 1531), in which he expresses disgust at the outcome of the diet, argued that he would never counsel rebellion, and made it clear that he believed that conflict was imminent and that the Protestants would offer resistance. Furthermore, Luther insisted, "Man muß nicht alles auffrürisch sein lassen, was die bluthunde auffrürisch schelten" (One cannot take for rebellion everything that the bloodhounds designate as rebellion). The treatise reveals an important shift in Luther's thinking: hitherto he had opposed any attempt to legitimize resisting the emperor, but now he was willing to support the rights of a defensive alliance. Luther's arguments bore fruit in the formation of the Protestant Schmalkaldic League in 1531.

The simple caricatures of "old man" Luther–boorish, dogmatic, bigoted, constipated, and outdated–have been challenged as scholars have turned greater attention to the later stages of his career. Luther continued to be prolific as a writer, although the freshness of his ideas and the vigor of his presence had begun to wane. Students and Wittenberg associates such as Veit Dietrich, Georg Rörer, and Conrad Cordatus began to collect anecdotes of the lives of Luther and his family in 1531 and continued doing so until the year before his death; for some, the crude and satiric Luther who was captured in these *Tischreden* (Table Talks, 1566; translated as *Dris. Martini Lutheris colloquia mensalia; or . . . divine discourses at his table,* 1652) had an almost endearing quality. Luther could also be conciliatory in the continual attempts to secure political alliances through confessional negotiations. His 1536 meeting with the Strasbourg representatives Bucer and Wolfgang Capito produced the Wittenberg Concord, in which the parties compromised on their understandings of the Lord's Supper. Moreover, linking the south Germans with Saxony provided an important partner in the network of the Schmalkaldic estates. The following year Luther composed his own confession of faith, *Artickel, so da hetten sollen auffs Concilion zu Mantua, oder wo es würde sein, vberantwortet werden* (Articles that Should Have Been Addressed Either at the Council of Mantua or Wherever It Might Be, 1538), generally known as *Die Schmalkaldischen Artikel* (The Schmalkaldic Articles), in response to an urgent request from Elector Johann Friedrich. Pope Paul III's Council of Mantua was scheduled to meet during 1537, and the elector and other German Protestant leaders wanted a concise expression of their faith to offer at it. Although the council was never convened, it provided Luther the opportunity to outline clearly where he would and would not compromise with the Church of Rome. Luther still had the capacity to offer lucid theological arguments, and the Lutheran church incorporated the Schmalkaldic Articles into the *Book of Concord* (1580), the foundational document of the church.

Nevertheless, there is something to the observation that the later Luther was known more by his enemies than by his friends. Of particular concern to Luther was an unholy trinity of the Turks, the Jews, and the Pope and his allies. To the Christian citizens of the German Empire the Turk was a terrifying "other" whose armies had besieged Vienna in 1529 and whose alleged atrocities made for frightening bedtime tales. Beginning with the military advances of the Ottoman Empire in the early 1520s, polemical pamphlets known collectively as the *Türkenbücher* circulated throughout the German Empire. These writings tended to wax and wane, depending upon the perceived imminence of a Turkish invasion. Luther contributed directly to this literature on a couple of occasions. His initial writings, *Vom kriege widder die Türken* (On War against the Turks, 1529) and *Eine Heerpredigt widder die Türken* (A Military Sermon against the Turks, 1529) concerned the propriety of a military response. Later he wrote *Vermanunge zum Gebet, Wider den Türeken* (An Admonition to Pray against the Turk, 1541), in which he describes the Turks both as a demoniacal agent of God's wrath and as a schoolmaster sent to stimulate honorable worship. Luther's real purpose in writing these works was to shame lax German Christians into obedient service to God.

While the Turks were an alien outsider, the Jews were an alien insider—at least in those territories that had not driven them into exile. Luther's early thinking about the Jews demonstrates guarded optimism: he believed that the emancipation of the Gospel and of true preaching would result in the salvation—that is, the conversion—of the Jews. In *Das Ihesus Christus eyn geborner Iude sey* (That Jesus Christ Was Born a Jew, 1523) he argued that Jews should be treated in a friendly fashion so that many of them would become true Christians and return to the faith of their fathers, the prophets and patriarchs. This fanciful thinking about Jewish conversions to Christianity was not, of course, borne out in reality, and Luther became increasingly bitter about what he regarded as this lost opportunity for the Jews. His exasperation is evident in *Ein Brieff D. Mart. Luther wider die Sabbather an einen guten Freund* (A Letter of Dr. Martin Luther against the Sabbatarians, to a Good

Friend, 1538), in which he seeks to demonstrate the error of the false Jewish hopes for a Messiah and to make the case for the fulfillment of Old Testament prophecies in Christ. The pamphlet is generally cordial and self-confident, and occasionally rude.

Luther's harshest comments were reserved for his scandalous *Von den Iüden vnd jhren Lügen* (On the Jews and Their Lies, 1543). In this treatise Luther abandons the treatment of the Jews in a friendly fashion for a rather different response: "Wir müssen mit gebet und Gottes furcht eine scharffe barmhertzigkeit uben, ob wir doch etliche aus der flammen und glut erretten kündten" (We must, with prayer and the fear of God, exercise a harsh mercy, in hopes that we can save some from the flames and embers). He goes on to argue that those Jews who remain obstinate in their religious tradition should have their schools and synagogues burned and razed, their houses destroyed, their books confiscated, and their livelihoods stripped away. Although some have argued that Luther should be considered religiously intolerant rather than anti-Semitic, these belligerent statements represent the most negative aspect of his legacy.

Luther's final assaults on the papacy and affiliated parties contained nothing new; they were simply expressed in a more comical or coarse fashion. For pure invective and ad hominem attack Luther never surpassed his reply to Duke Heinrich of Brunswick, *Wider Hans Worst* (Against Hans Wurst, 1541). The treatise is a farce based on Hans Wurst, a clownish character who appeared at fairs and marketplaces with a sausage around his neck. For Luther, Duke Heinrich was the fool Hans Wurst; in addition, he referred to the duke as a devil, an archprostitute, and a harem guard. For any who might differ with Luther's assessment, he had a suggestion: "so thut in die Bruch und hengt sie an den hals, und macht davon euch ein galreden und fresset ir groben Esel und Sewe" (so do it in your pants, and hang it around your neck and make it into a sausage, then gobble it down like the gross asses and sows you are). Although scatalogical language was an element of Luther's rhetoric throughout his life, this mode of expression seemed to occur more often in his later works. Duke Heinrich was an adversary of the Saxon elector and the Hessian landgrave and a persecutor of faithful Lutherans in his territory; thus, Luther's assault was motivated by religious concerns, however difficult that dimension may be to discern in this particular exchange. When it came to attacking the papacy directly, Luther still preferred the appropriately colorful language of Scripture that spoke of Antichrists and Great Whores of Babylon. One of Luther's last published treatises was this kind of work, *Wider das Bapstum zu Rom vom Teuffel gestifft* (Against the Papacy at Rome,

Founded by the Devil, 1545). He was shocked and dismayed when he learned that Pope Paul III had taken upon himself the responsibility of delaying the first meeting of the church council scheduled to open in Trent. For Luther, it was but one final example that the authority of Rome was entirely out of proportion.

Luther's battles with an array of foes, and his struggles with his personal Anfechtungen, concluded on 18 February 1546. Luther's life ended where it began, in the town of Eisleben in the county of Mansfeld. He had been summoned there to aid the counts in their dispute regarding the division of their territory. He should not have made the journey, given the state of his health, but he believed that it was important to attempt to mediate in this situation. His body was returned to Wittenberg for the funeral service on 22 February. His pastor Bugenhagen preached the funeral sermon, and Melanchthon offered the eulogy. Luther was buried in front of the pulpit of the Castle Church.

The year before his death Luther had provided a preface to the complete edition of his Latin writings (1545–1547). He refers to the controversies and experiences that surrounded his earliest works–the debate over indulgences; the battles with Tetzel, Cajetan, and Eck; and his increasing alienation from the Roman Church. He describes a theological breakthrough that later came to be called his *Turmerlebnis* (tower experience), when he felt as though "apertis portis in ipsam paradisum intrasse" (he had entered into paradise itself with the gates flung open). Luther's life, however, had manifested many breakthroughs as he abandoned one system of philosophical and religious commitments and developed a theology and a church suitable to his new understanding. The literary output that accompanied this feat was truly staggering and remains an accomplishment with few if any rivals. In the Latin preface Luther offers a more humble assessment: "cupiebam omnes libros meos perpetua oblivione sepultos, ut melioribus esset locus" (I wished that all my books were consigned to perpetual oblivion, so that better ones could take their place). Luther's writings, hymns, translations, sermons, and liturgies, however, continue to inform religious practice throughout the Christian community, both Protestant and Catholic. Luther's own caution is appropriate: too much can be and has been made of his influence. Yet, the language of his Bible, and the literature he addressed to so many different audiences of his day, make it impossible to overlook his contributions.

Bibliographies:

Josef Benzing and Helmut Claus, *Lutherbibliographie: Verzeichnis der gedruckten Schriften Martin Luther's bis zu dessen Tod* (Baden-Baden: Heitz, 1966);

Herbert Wolf, *Germanistische Luther-Bibliographie: Martin Luthers deutsches Sprachschaffen in Spiegel des internationalen Schrifttums der Jahre 1880–1980* (Heidelberg: Winter, 1985).

Biographies:

Julius Köstlin, *Martin Luther the Reformer* (London: Cassell, 1883);

Preserved Smith, *The Life and Letters of Martin Luther* (Philadelphia: Lutheran Publication Society, 1913);

Paul J. Reiter, *Martin Luther: Umwelt, Charakter und Psychose* (Copenhagen: Levin & Munksgaard, 1937);

Heinrich Boehmer, *Road to Reformation: Martin Luther to the Year 1521,* translated by John W. Doberstein and Theodore G. Tappert (Philadelphia: Muhlenberg, 1946);

Roland Herbert Bainton, *Here I Stand: A Life of Martin Luther* (New York: Abingdon-Cokesbury, 1950);

Erik H. Erikson, *Young Man Luther: A Study in Psychoanalysis and History* (New York: Norton, 1958);

John Murray Todd, *Martin Luther: A Biographical Study* (New York: Paulist Press, 1964);

Erwin Iserloh, *Luther zwischen Reform und Reformation: Der Thesenanschlag fand nicht statt* (Münster: Aschendorff, 1966);

A. G. Dickens, *Martin Luther and the Reformation* (London: English Universities Press, 1967);

James Atkinson, *Martin Luther and the Birth of Protestantism* (Baltimore: Penguin, 1968);

Hartmann Grisar, *Martin Luther: His Life and Work,* translated and adapted by Frank J. Eble (New York: AMS, 1971);

Heinrich Bornkamm, *Martin Luther in der Mitte seines Lebens: Das Jahrzehnt zwischen dem Wormser und dem Augsburger Reichstag,* edited by Karin Bornkamm (Göttingen: Vandenhoeck & Ruprecht, 1979); translated by E. Theodore Bachman as *Luther in Mid-Career, 1521–1530* (Philadelphia: Fortress, 1983);

H. G. Haile, *Luther: An Experiment in Biography* (Garden City, N.Y.: Doubleday, 1980);

Bernhard Lohse, *Martin Luther: Eine Einführung in sein Leben und sein werk* (Munich: Beck, 1981);

Peter Manns, *Martin Luther: An Illustrated Biography,* translated by Michael Shaw (New York: Crossroad, 1982);

James Arne Nestingen, *Martin Luther: His Life and Teachings* (Philadelphia: Fortress, 1982);

Wilhelm Fleschendranger, *Martin Luther: Bildbiographie* (Leipzig: Bibliographisches Institut, 1982);

John Todd, *Luther: A Life* (New York: Crossroad, 1982);

Eric W. Gritsch, *Martin–God's Court Jester: Luther in Retrospect* (Philadelphia: Fortress, 1983);

Helmar Junghans, ed., *Leben und Werk Martin Luthers von 1526 bis 1546: Festgabe zu seinem 500. Geburtstag,* 2 volumes (Göttingen: Vandenhoeck & Ruprecht, 1983);

Marc Lienhard, *Martin Luther: Un Temps, une Vie, un Message* (Geneva: Labor et Fides, 1983);

Joachim Rogge, *Martin Luther: Sein Leben, seine Zeit, sein Wirkungen* (Berlin: Evangelische Verlagsanstalt, 1983);

Martin Brecht, *Martin Luther,* 3 volumes, translated by James L. Schaff (Philadelphia: Fortress, 1985–1992);

James Kittelson, *Luther the Reformer: The Story of the Man and His Career* (Minneapolis: Augsburg, 1986);

Heiko Oberman, *Luther: Man between God and the Devil,* translated by Eileen Walliser-Schwarzbart (New Haven: Yale University Press, 1989);

Albrecht Beutel, *Martin Luther* (Munich: Beck, 1991);

Junghans, *Martin Luther und Wittenberg* (Munich: Koehler & Amelang, 1996);

Reinhard Schwarz, *Luther* (Göttingen: Vandenhoeck and Ruprecht, 1998).

References:

Kurt Aland, *Hilfsbuch zum Lutherstudium,* third edition (Wittenberg: Luther-Verlag, 1970);

Paul Althaus, *The Ethics of Martin Luther,* translated by Robert C. Schultz (Philadelphia: Fortress, 1972);

Althaus, *The Theology of Martin Luther* (Philadelphia: Fortress, 1966);

David V. N. Bagchi, *Luther's Earliest Opponents: Catholic Controversialists, 1518–1525* (Minneapolis: Fortress, 1991);

Oswald Bayer, *Promissio: Die Geschichte der reformatorischen Wende in Luthers Theologie* (Göttingen: Vandenhoeck & Ruprecht, 1971);

Ernest Bizer, *Fides ex Auditu: Eine Untersuchung über die Entdeckung der Gerechtigkeit Gottes durch Martin Luther* (Neukirchen: Kreis Moers, 1958);

Bizer, *Studien zur Geschichte des Abendmahlstreits in 16. Jahrhundert* (Gütersloh: Bertelsmann, 1940);

Peter Blickle, *Communal Reformations: The Quest for Salvation in Sixteenth Century Germany* (Atlantic Highlands, N.J.: Humanities, 1992);

Heinz Bluhm, *Martin Luther, Creative Translator* (Saint Louis: Concordia, 1965);

Heinrich Bornkamm, *Thesen and Thesenanschlag Luthers: Geschehen und Bedeutung* (Berlin: Topelmann, 1967);

Carl Braaten and Robert Jensen, eds., *Union With Christ: the New Finnish Interpretation of Luther* (Grand Rapids, Mich.: Eerdmans, 1998);

Thomas A. Brady, "Settlements: The Holy Roman Empire," in *Handbook of European History 1400–1600,* edited by Brady, Heiko A. Oberman, and James D. Tracy (Leiden: Brill, 1995), pp. 349–384;

Martin Brecht, *Luther als Schriftsteller* (Stuttgart: Calwer, 1990);

A. G. Dickens, *The German Nation and Martin Luther* (New York: Harper & Row, 1974);

Gerhard Dünnhaupt, ed., *Martin Luther Quincentennial* (Detroit: Wayne State University Press, 1984);

Gerhard Ebeling, *Luther: An Introduction to His Thought* (Philadelphia: Fortress, 1970);

Mark U. Edwards, *Luther and the False Brethren* (Stanford, Calif.: Stanford University Press, 1975);

Edwards, "Luther's Biography," in *Reformation Europe: A Guide to Research,* 2, edited by William S. Maltby (Saint Louis: Center for Reformation Studies, 1992), pp. 5–20;

Edwards, *Luther's Last Battles: Politics and Polemics, 1531–1546* (Ithaca, N.Y.: Cornell University Press, 1983);

Edwards, *Printing, Propaganda, and Martin Luther* (Berkeley: University of California Press, 1994);

Stephen Fischer-Galati, *Ottoman Imperialism and German Protestantism, 1521–1555* (Cambridge, Mass.: Harvard University Press, 1959);

George W. Forell, *Faith Active in Love: An Investigation of the Principles Underlying Luther's Social Ethics* (Minneapolis: Augsburg, 1954);

Leif Grane, *Martinus Noster: Luther in the German Reform Movement, 1518–1521* (Mainz: Zabern, 1994);

Grane, *Modus loquendi Theologicus: Luthers Kampf um die Erneuerung der Theologie* (Leiden: Brill, 1975);

H. G. Haile, "The Great Martin Luther Spoof," *Yale Review,* 65 (1976): 43–57;

Haile, "Luther and Literacy," *PMLA,* 49 (1976): 816–828;

Haile, "Martin Luther and the Art of the Gloss," *Georgia Review,* 24 (Summer 1980): 323–333;

Scott Hendrix, *Ecclesia in Via: Ecclesiological Developments in the Medieval Psalms Exegesis and the Dictata super Psalterium (1513–1515) of Martin Luther* (Leiden: Brill, 1974);

Erwin Iserloh, *The Theses Were Not Posted: Luther between Reform and Reformation,* translated by Jared Wicks (Boston: Beacon Press, 1968);

Helmar Junghans, *Der junge Luther und die Humanisten* (Göttingen: Vandenhoeck & Ruprecht, 1985);

Steffen Kjeldgaard-Pedersen, *Gesetz, Evangelium, und Bue: Theologiegeschichtliche Studien zum Verhältnis zwischen dem jungen Johann Agricola (Eisleben) und Martin Luther* (Leiden: Brill, 1983);

Walter Köhler, *Zwingli und Luther: Ihr Streit über das Abendmahl nach seinen politischen und religiösen Bezie-*

hungen, 2 volumes, Quellen und Forschungen zur Reformationsgeschichte, volumes 6–7 (volume 1, Leipzig: Heinsius, 1924; volume 2, Gütersloh: Bertelsmann, 1953);

Hans-Walter Krumwiede, *Zur Entstehung des landesherrlichen Kirchenregiments in Kursachsen und in Braunschweig-Wolfenbüttel* (Göttingen: Vandenhoeck & Ruprecht, 1967);

Kurt Löcher, ed., *Martin Luther und die Reformation in Deutschland* (Schweinfurt: Weppert, 1988);

Bernard Lohse, *Mönchtum und Reformation: Luthers Auseinandersetzung mit dem Mönchsideal des Mittelalters* (Göttingen: Vandenhoeck & Ruprecht, 1963);

Joseph Lortz and Erwin Iserloh, *Kleine Reformationsgeschichte: Ursachen, Verlauf, Wirkung* (Freiburg im Breisgau: Herder, 1969);

Martin E. Marty, ed., *The Place of Trust: Martin Luther on the Sermon on the Mount* (San Francisco: Harper & Row, 1983);

Alistair E. McGrath, *Luther's Theology of the Cross: Martin Luther on Justification, 1509–1519* (London: Blackwell, 1985);

Karl Heinz zur Mühlen, *Nos extra Nos: Luthers Theologie zwischen Mystik und Scholastik* (Tübingen: Mohr, 1972);

Gerhard Müller, *Causa Reformationis: Beiträge zur Reformationsgeschichte und zur Theologie Martin Luthers* (Gütersloh: Mohn, 1989);

Heiko A. Oberman, *The Roots of Anti-Semitism in the Age of the Renaissance and Reformation* (Philadelphia: Fortress, 1984);

Daniel Olivier, *Le procès luther* (Paris: Fayard, 1971);

Steven Ozment, *When Fathers Ruled: Family Life in Reformation Europe* (Cambridge, Mass.: Harvard University Press, 1983);

Otto Pesch, *Hinführung zu Luther* (Mainz: Matthias-Grünewald, 1982);

Gordon Rupp, *The Righteousness of God* (London: Hodder & Stoughton, 1953);

Heinz Schilling, "Confessional Europe," in *Handbook of European History, 1400–1600,* edited by Thomas A. Brady, Heiko A. Oberman, and James D. Tracy (Leiden: Brill, 1995);

Robert W. Scribner, *For the Sake of Simple Folk: Popular Propaganda for the German Reformation* (Oxford: Clarendon Press, 1994);

Ralph Smith, *Luther, Ministry, and Ordination Rites in the Early Reformation Church* (New York: Peter Lang, 1996);

David C. Steinmetz, *Luther and Staupitz: An Essay on the Intellectual Origins of the Protestant Reformation* (Durham, N.C.: Duke University Press, 1980);

Gerald Strauss, *Luther's House of Learning: Indoctrination of the Young in the German Reformation* (Baltimore: Johns Hopkins University Press, 1978);

Jared Wicks, *Cajetan Responds: A Reader in Reformation Controversy* (Washington, D.C.: Catholic University of America Press, 1978);

Herbert Wolf, *Martin Luther: Eine Einführung in germanistische Luther-Studien* (Stuttgart: Metzler, 1980);

Eike Wolgast, *Die Wittenberger Theologie und die Politik der evangelischen Stände: Studien zu Luthers Gutachten in politischen Fragen* (Gütersloh: Mohn, 1977).

Thomas Mann

(6 June 1875 – 12 August 1955)

Dieter W. Adolphs
Michigan Technological University

and

Egon Schwarz
Washington University

This entry was updated by Professor Adolphs from his and Professor Schwarz's entry in
DLB 66: German Fiction Writers, 1885–1913.

BOOKS: *Der kleine Herr Friedemann: Novellen* (Berlin: Fischer, 1898); title story translated by Herman George Scheffauer as "Little Herr Friedemann" in *Children and Fools* (New York: Knopf, 1928);

Buddenbrooks: Verfall einer Familie, Roman, 2 volumes (Berlin: Fischer, 1901); translated by H. T. Lowe-Porter as *Buddenbrooks,* 2 volumes (New York: Knopf, 1924);

Tristan: Sechs Novellen (Berlin: Fischer, 1903); title story translated by Kenneth Burke in *Death in Venice* (New York: Knopf, 1925); "Tonio Kröger" translated by B. Q. Morgan in *The German Classics of the 19th and 20th Centuries,* edited by Kuno Francke and William Guild Howard, volume 19 (New York: German Publications Society, 1914);

Fiorenza (Berlin: Fischer, 1906);

Bilse und ich (Munich: Bonsels, 1906);

Königliche Hoheit (Berlin: Fischer, 1909); translated by A. Cecil Curtis as *Royal Highness: A Novel of German Court Life* (New York: Knopf, 1916);

Der kleine Herr Friedemann und andere Novellen (Berlin: Fischer, 1909);

Der Tod in Venedig: Novelle (Munich: Hyperion, 1912); translated by Burke as *Death in Venice* (New York: Knopf, 1925);

Das Wunderkind: Novellen (Berlin: Fischer, 1914); title story translated by Scheffauer as "The Infant Prodigy" in *Children and Fools* (New York: Knopf, 1928);

Friedrich und die große Koalition (Berlin: Fischer, 1915);

Thomas Mann in May 1955 (Conti-Press, Hamburg)

Betrachtungen eines Unpolitischen (Berlin: Fischer, 1918); translated by Walter D. Morris as *Reflections of a Nonpolitical Man* (New York: Ungar, 1983);

Herr und Hund; Gesang vom Kindchen: Zwei Idyllen (Berlin: Fischer, 1919); translated by Scheffauer as *Bashan and I* (London: Collins, 1923); translation republished as *A Man and His Dog* (New York: Knopf, 1930);

Wälsungenblut (Munich: Phantasus, 1921);

Bekenntnisse des Hochstaplers Felix Krull: Buch der Kindheit (Vienna: Rikola, 1922; enlarged, Amsterdam: Querido, 1937); enlarged as *Bekenntnisse des Hochstaplers Felix Krull: Der Memoiren erster Teil* (Frankfurt am Main: Fischer, 1954); translated by Denver Lindley as *Confessions of Feliz Krull, Confidence Man: The Early Years* (New York: Knopf, 1955);

Novellen, 2 volumes (Berlin: Fischer, 1922);

Rede und Antwort: Gesammelte Abhandlungen und kleine Aufsätze (Berlin: Fischer, 1922);

Goethe und Tolstoj: Vortrag (Aachen: Verlag "Die Kuppel," 1923); revised as *Goethe und Tolstoj: Zum Problem der Humanität* (Vienna: Bermann-Fischer, 1932);

Von deutscher Republik (Berlin: Fischer, 1923);

Okkulte Erlebnisse (Berlin: Häger, 1924);

Der Zauberberg: Roman, 2 volumes (Berlin: Fischer, 1924); translated by Lowe-Porter as *The Magic Mountain,* 2 volumes (New York: Knopf, 1927);

Bemühungen: Neue Folge der gesammelten Abhandlungen und kleinen Aufsätze (Berlin: Fischer, 1925);

Gesammelte Werke in zehn Bänden, 10 volumes (Berlin: Fischer, 1925);

Lübeck als geistige Lebensform (Lübeck: Quitzow, 1926);

Kino: Romanfragment (Gera: Blau, 1926);

Pariser Rechenschaft (Berlin: Fischer, 1926);

Unordnung und frühes Leid (Berlin: Fischer, 1926); translated by Scheffauer as *Early Sorrow* (London: Secker, 1929);

Ausgewählte Prosa, edited by J. van Dam (Groningen & The Hague: Wolters, 1927);

Die erzählenden Schriften, 3 volumes (Berlin: Fischer, 1928);

Zwei Festreden (Leipzig: Reclam, 1928);

Children and Fools, translated by Scheffauer (New York: Knopf, 1928);

Hundert Jahre Reclam: Festrede (Leipzig: Reclam, 1928);

Sieben Aufsätze (Berlin: Fischer, 1929);

Mario und der Zauberer: Ein tragisches Reiseerlebnis (Berlin: Fischer, 1930); translated by Lowe-Porter as *Mario and the Magician* (London: Secker, 1930; New York: Knopf, 1931);

Lebensabriß (Paris: Harrison, 1930); translated by Lowe-Porter as *A Sketch of My Life* (New York: Knopf, 1960);

Die Forderung des Tages: Reden und Aufsätze aus den Jahren 1925–1929 (Berlin: Fischer, 1930);

Deutsche Ansprache: Ein Appell an die Vernunft (Berlin: Fischer, 1930);

Goethe als Repräsentant des bürgerlichen Zeitalters: Rede (Vienna: Bermann-Fischer, 1932);

Goethes Laufbahn als Schriftsteller: Vortrag (Munich: Oldenbourg, 1933);

Die Geschichten Jaakobs (Berlin: Fischer, 1933); translated by Lowe-Porter as *Joseph and His Brothers* (New York: Knopf, 1934);

Past Masters and Other Papers, translated by Lowe-Porter (New York: Knopf, 1933);

Der junge Joseph (Berlin: Fischer, 1934); translated by Lowe-Porter as *Young Joseph* (New York: Knopf, 1935; London: Secker, 1935);

Leiden und Größe der Meister (Berlin: Fischer, 1935);

Freud und die Zukunft: Vortrag (Vienna: Bermann-Fischer, 1936);

Joseph in Ägypten (Vienna: Bermann-Fischer, 1936); translated by Lowe-Porter as *Joseph in Egypt* (New York: Knopf, 1938; London: Secker, 1938);

Stories of Three Decades, translated by Lowe-Porter (New York: Knopf, 1936);

Ein Briefwechsel (Zurich: Oprecht, 1937); translated by Lowe-Porter as *An Exchange of Letters* (New York: Knopf, 1937);

Freud, Goethe, Wagner: Three Essays, translated by Lowe-Porter (New York: Knopf, 1937);

Stockholmer Gesamtausgabe der Werke, 12 volumes (Stockholm: Bermann-Fischer, 1938–1956);

Dieser Friede (Stockholm: Bermann-Fischer, 1938); translated by Lowe-Porter as *This Peace* (New York: Knopf, 1938);

Schopenhauer (Stockholm: Bermann-Fischer, 1938);

Vom künftigen Sieg der Demokratie (Zurich: Oprecht, 1938); translated by Agnes E. Meyer as *The Coming Victory of Democracy* (London: Secker & Warburg, 1938);

Achtung, Europa! Aufsätze zur Zeit (Stockholm: Bermann-Fischer, 1938);

Einführung in den Zauberberg für Studenten der Universität Princeton (Stockholm: Bermann-Fischer, 1939);

Lotte in Weimar (Stockholm: Bermann-Fischer, 1939); translated by Lowe-Porter as *The Beloved Returns* (New York: Knopf, 1940); translation republished as *Lotte in Weimar* (London: Secker & Warburg, 1940);

The Problem of Freedom (New Brunswick, N.J.: Rutgers University Press, 1939); translated into German as *Das Problem der Freiheit* (Stockholm: Bermann-Fischer, 1939);

Die vertauschten Köpfe: Eine indische Legende (Stockholm: Bermann-Fischer, 1940); translated by Lowe-Porter as *The Transposed Heads: A Legend of India* (New York: Knopf, 1941);

Dieser Krieg: Aufsatz (Stockholm: Bermann-Fischer, 1940); translated by Eric Sutton as *This War* (New York: Knopf, 1940; London: Secker & Warburg, 1940);

War and Democracy (Los Angeles: The Friends of the Colleges at Claremont, 1940);

Order of the Day: Political Essays and Speeches of Two Decades, translated by Lowe-Porter, Meyer, and Eric Sutton (New York: Knopf, 1942);

Deutsche Hörer! 25 Radiosendungen nach Deutschland (Stockholm: Bermann-Fischer, 1942); translated by Lowe-Porter as *Listen, Germany! Twenty-five Radio Messages to the German People over B.B.C.* (New York: Knopf, 1943); German version enlarged as *Deutsche Hörer! 55 Radiosendungen nach Deutschland* (Stockholm: Bermann-Fischer, 1945);

Joseph, der Ernährer (Stockholm: Bermann-Fischer, 1943); translated by Lowe-Porter as *Joseph the Provider* (New York: Knopf, 1944);

Das Gesetz: Erzählung (Stockholm: Bermann-Fischer, 1944); translated by Lowe-Porter as *The Tables of the Law* (New York: Knopf, 1945);

The War and the Future (Washington, D.C.: Library of Congress, 1944);

Adel des Geistes: Sechzehn Versuche zum Problem der Humanität (Stockholm: Bermann-Fischer, 1945); translated by Lowe-Porter as *Essays of Three Decades* (New York: Knopf, 1947); German version enlarged as *Adel des Geistes: Zwanzig Versuche zum Problem der Humanität* (Berlin: Aufbau, 1955);

Leiden an Deutschland: Tagebuchblätter aus den Jahren 1933 und 1934 (Los Angeles: Pazifische Presse / New York: Rosenberg, 1946);

Ein Streitgespräch über die äußere und innere Emigration, by Mann, Frank Thieß, and Walter von Molo (Dortmund: Druckschriften-Vertriebsdienst, 1946);

Deutschland und die Deutschen: Vortrag (Stockholm: Bermann-Fischer, 1947);

Doktor Faustus: Das Leben des deutschen Tonsetzers Adrian Leverkühn, erzählt von einem Freunde (Stockholm: Bermann-Fischer, 1947); translated by Lowe-Porter as *Doctor Faustus: The Life of the German Composer, Adrian Leverkühn, as Told by a Friend* (New York: Knopf, 1948);

Nietzsches Philosophie im Lichte unserer Erfahrung: Vortrag (Berlin: Suhrkamp, 1948);

Neue Studien (Stockholm: Bermann-Fischer, 1948);

Die Entstehung des Doktor Faustus: Roman eines Romans (Amsterdam: Bermann-Fischer, 1949); translated by Richard and Clara Winston as *The Story of a Novel: The Genesis of Doctor Faustus* (New York: Knopf, 1961);

Goethe und die Demokratie (Zurich: Oprecht, 1949);

Ansprache im Goethe-Jahr 1949 (Frankfurt am Main: Suhrkamp, 1949; Weimar: Thüringer Volksverlag, 1949);

Goethe / Wetzlar / Werther (Copenhagen: Rosenkilde og Bagger, 1950);

Michelangelo in seinen Dichtungen (Cellerina: Quos Ego Verlag, 1950);

Meine Zeit: 1875–1950. Vortrag (Frankfurt am Main: Fischer, 1950);

Der Erwählte: Roman (Frankfurt am Main: Fischer, 1951); translated by Lowe-Porter as *The Holy Sinner* (New York: Knopf, 1951);

Lob der Vergänglichkeit (Frankfurt am Main: Fischer, 1952);

Die Begegnung: Erzählung (Olten: Vereinigung Oltner Bücherfreunde, 1953);

Die Betrogene: Erzählung (Frankfurt am Main: Fischer, 1953); translated by Willard R. Trask as *The Black Swan* (New York: Knopf, 1954);

Gerhart Hauptmann: Rede, gehalten am 9. November 1952 im Rahmen der Frankfurter Gerhart-Hauptmann-Woche (Gütersloh: Bertelsmann, 1953);

Der Künstler und die Gesellschaft: Vortrag (Vienna: Frick, 1953);

Altes und Neues: Kleine Prosa aus fünf Jahrzehnten (Frankfurt am Main: Fischer, 1953);

Ansprache im Schillerjahr 1955 (Berlin: Aufbau, 1955);

Das Eisenbahnunglück: Novellen (Munich: Piper, 1955);

Gesammelte Werke in zwölf Bänden, 12 volumes (Berlin: Aufbau, 1955);

Versuch über Schiller: Seinem Andenken zum 150. Todestag in Liebe gewidmet (Frankfurt am Main: Fischer, 1955);

Nachlese: Prosa 1951–1955 (Frankfurt am Main: Fischer, 1956);

Meerfahrt mit Don Quijote (Wiesbaden: Insel, 1956);

Das erzählerische Werk: Taschenbuchausgabe in zwölf Bänden, 12 volumes (Frankfurt am Main: Fischer, 1957);

Sorge um Deutschland: Sechs Essays (Frankfurt am Main: Fischer, 1957);

Erzählungen (Frankfurt am Main: Fischer, 1958);

Last Essays, translated by Richard and Clara Winston, Tania and James Stern, and Lowe-Porter (New York: Knopf, 1959);

Gesammelte Werke in dreizehn Bänden, 13 volumes (Frankfurt am Main: Fischer, 1960–1974);

Stories of a Lifetime, translated by Lowe-Porter, 2 volumes (London: Secker & Warburg, 1961);

Das essayistische Werk, edited by Hans Bürgin, 8 volumes (Frankfurt am Main: Fischer, 1968);

Notizen: Zu Felix Krull, Königliche Hoheit, Versuch über das Theater, Maja, Geist und Kultur, Ein Elender, Betrachtungen eines Unpolitischen, Doktor Faustus und anderen

Werken, edited by Hans Wysling (Heidelberg: Winter, 1973);

Wagner und unsere Zeit: Aufsätze, Betrachtungen, Briefe, edited by Erika Mann (Frankfurt am Main: Ficher, 1963); translated by Allan Blunden as *Pro and Contra Wagner* (Chicago: University of Chicago Press, 1985);

Romane und Erzählungen, 10 volumes (Berlin: Aufbau, 1974–1975);

Thomas Mann: Tagebücher 1918–1921; 1933–1934; 1935–1936; 1937–1939; 1940–1943, 5 volumes, edited by Peter de Mendelssohn (Frankfurt am Main: Fischer, 1977–1982); partially translated by Richard, Clara, and Krishna Winston, edited by Hermann Kesten as *Thomas Mann Diaries: 1918–1939,* 1 volume (New York: Abrams, 1982);

Gesammelte Werke in Einzelbänden, edited by de Mendelssohn, 14 volumes published (Frankfurt am Main: Fischer, 1980–);

Thomas Mann: Tagebücher 1944–1.4.1946, 28.5.1946–31.12.1948, 1949–1950, 1951–1952, 1953–1955, 5 volumes, edited by Inge Jens (Frankfurt am Main: Fischer, 1986–1995);

Notizbücher: Edition in zwei Bänden, edited by Wysling and Yvonne Schmidlin (Frankfurt am Main: Fischer, 1991–1992);

Essays, 6 volumes, edited by Hermann Kurzke and Stefan Stachorski (Frankfurt am Main: Fischer, 1993–1997);

On Myself and Other Princeton Lectures: An Annotated Edition Based on Mann's Lecture Typescripts, edited by James N. Bade (New York: Peter Lang, 1996; revised, 1997);

Theodor Storm: Essay, edited by Karl Ernst Laage (Heide: Boyens, 1996).

Editions in English: *Thomas Mann's "Goethe and Tolstoy": Notes and Sources,* edited by Clayton Koelb, translated by Koelb and Alcyone Scott (University, Ala.: University of Alabama Press, 1984);

Death in Venice and Other Stories, translated by David Luke (New York: Bantam, 1988; London: Secker & Warburg, 1990);

Buddenbrooks: The Decline of a Family, translated by John E. Woods (New York: Knopf, 1993);

Doctor Faustus, translated by Woods (New York: Knopf, 1997);

Death in Venice and Other Tales, translated Joachim Neugroschel (New York: Viking, 1998);

Death in Venice: Complete, Authoritative Text with Biographical and Historical Contexts, Critical History, and Essays from Five Contemporary Critical Perspectives, edited by Naomi Ritter (Boston: Bedford Books, 1998);

Death in Venice, Tonio Kröger, and Other Writings, edited by Frederick A. Lubich (New York: Continuum, 1999).

OTHER: E. von Mendelssohn, *Nacht und Tag: Roman,* edited by Mann (Leipzig: Verlag der weißen Bücher, 1914);

Johann Wolfgang von Goethe, *Die Wahlverwandtschaften,* afterword by Mann (Leipzig: List, 1925);

Theodor Fontane, *Ausgewählte Werke,* introduction by Mann, 6 volumes (Leipzig: Reclam, 1929);

M. Karlweis, *Jakob Wassermann: Bild, Kampf und Werke,* introduction by Mann (Amsterdam: Querido, 1935);

Erika Mann, *Zehn Millionen Kinder: Die Erziehung der Jugend im Dritten Reich,* foreword by Mann (Amsterdam: Querido, 1938);

Martin Niemöller, *"God is My Fuehrer": Being the Last 28 Sermons,* preface by Mann (New York: Philosophical Library and Alliance Book Corp., 1941);

The Short Novels of Dostoevsky, translated by Constance Garnett, introduction by Mann (New York: Dial Press, 1945);

Adelbert von Chamisso, *Gedichte; Peter Schlemihls wundersame Geschichte,* introduction by Mann (Oldenburg & Mainz: Lehrmittel-Verlag, 1947);

Frans Masereel, *Jeunesse,* introduction by Mann (Zurich: Oprecht, 1948);

Arthur Schopenhauer, *Die Welt als Wille und Vorstellung,* edited by Mann (Zurich: Claassen, 1948);

Alfred Kantorowicz, *Suchende Jugend: Briefwechsel mit jungen Leuten,* introduction by Mann (Berlin: Kantorowicz, 1949);

Klaus Mann zum Gedächtnis, foreword by Mann (Amsterdam: Querido, 1950);

Sigmund Freud, *Abriß der Psychoanalyse; Das Unbehagen in der Kultur,* afterword by Mann (Frankfurt am Main & Hamburg: Fischer, 1953);

José María Corredor, *Gespräche mit Casals,* foreword by Mann (Bern: Scherz, 1954);

Die schönsten Erzählungen der Welt: Hausbuch unvergänglicher Prosa, introduction by Mann, 2 volumes (Munich, Vienna & Basel: Desch, 1955–1956);

Alexander Moriz Frey, *Kleine Menagerie,* foreword by Mann (Wiesbaden: Limes, 1955);

Und die Flamme soll euch nicht versengen: Letzte Briefe zum Tode Verurteilter aus dem europäischen Widerstand, edited by Piero Malvezzi and Giovanni Pirelli, translated by U. Muth and P. Michael, foreword by Mann (Zurich: Steinberg, 1955);

Heinrich von Kleist, *Die Erzählungen,* foreword by Mann (Frankfurt am Main: Fischer, 1956);

Masereel, *Mein Stundenbuch,* foreword by Mann (Munich: List, 1957).

Thomas Mann is one of the most celebrated German writers in history, and he owes part of this fame to the United States, where he held citizenship when he died in 1955 at the age of eighty. In 1929 he received the Nobel Prize in literature. Until then, he had spent most of his life in Germany and had never left Europe. Even when Mann took a trip to Egypt and Palestine a year later in preparation for writing a tetralogy of novels based on the biblical story of Joseph, he could not imagine ever residing anywhere but in Germany. He also regarded himself merely as an unpolitical artist who preferred not to concern himself with the order of the day. When Hitler came to power in 1933, however, Mann decided not to return to Germany from a trip to Switzerland. In the next few years, he became a frequent visitor to the United States. During his second visit there, in 1935, Harvard University awarded him an honorary doctorate, President Roosevelt received him in the White House, and, on the occasion of his sixtieth birthday, he was celebrated as "the most eminent living man of letters." In 1938, the year he left Europe for exile in the United States, he had seventeen years of great productivity ahead of him.

Mann was one of the few German-speaking intellectuals who received a warm welcome in the United States; within a short time he was fully integrated into American society. His decision to settle in the United States was influenced by an invitation to become an honorary faculty member at Princeton University. He traveled all over the continent, delivering widely publicized speeches. One of the most prestigious American publishers, Alfred A. Knopf, had already hired Helen T. Lowe-Porter to translate Mann's works into English, enabling him to address himself to a large circle of people who were interested in both his literary works and his political views. Consequently, as a political exile and later as an American citizen, he accepted the responsibilities of the artist to take public stances. As an articulate and passionate opponent of fascism and an outspoken partisan of Roosevelt's policies at home and abroad, Mann exercised a considerable influence on the country he had chosen as his residence, and in many respects Americans could consider him their own.

The reasons Mann gave students at Princeton for the success of his novels in Germany help to explain the enormous interest he elicited in the United States. Characterizing his novel *Der Zauberberg* (1924; translated as *The Magic Mountain,* 1927), which had been placed next to the works of Cervantes and Voltaire in a course on world literature, Mann explained that "the subject matter of *The Magic Mountain* was not by its nature suitable for the masses. But with the bulk of the educated classes these were burning questions, and the national crisis had produced in the general public precisely that alchemical keying up in which had consisted the actual adventure of young Hans Castorp. Yes, certainly the German reader recognized himself in the simple-minded but shrewd young hero of the novel. He could and would be guided by him."

Mann's works represent a successful synthesis of the artist's egotistical need to produce and the world citizen's desire to express his ideas in a universally intelligible way. He saw *Der Zauberberg* as a document of the "europäischen Seelenverfassung und geistigen Problematik im ersten Drittel des zwanzigsten Jahrhunderts" (European mentality and intellectual dilemma of the first third of the twentieth century). He realized that for a work to be successful, the artistic wishes of the author and the concerns of the times must be fused into one whole. To achieve this aim, Mann consciously assumed the task of representing Germany's venerable cultural tradition in the intellectual world.

After receiving the Nobel Prize Mann regarded it as his responsibility to play the role of diplomat for the "good" Germany, particularly in the face of the historical catastrophe he saw coming. Americans harbored no suspicion that Mann might be a National Socialist, and, unlike many contemporary intellectuals, he did not look to Moscow for a utopian solution, either. His hopes were dependent on the "American model" that he was more willing to embrace than many of his fellow immigrants. No other German-speaking author, with the exception perhaps of Goethe, knew how to exploit the position of representative of German culture as well as Mann.

Mann's public role as representative of the German culture and his aim to express his ideas in a universally intelligible way did not allow him openly to admit his bisexuality. The only authority to which he confided his homoerotic fantasies was his diary, and he burned most of the journals he had written before 1933. Twenty years after Mann's death the remaining diaries were unsealed and subsequently published. It was only then that his readers were provided with clear evidence of the autobiographical nature of the homoerotic elements in his novels and novellas. The diaries point out that several characters in his works secretly commemorate young men to whom Mann had been erotically attracted. However, his artistic practice of encoding such autobiographical elements into cryptographic references, secretly identifying with literary figures who are disguised as women, and symbolically depicting homoeroticism as a universally human trait discourages one from regarding his works as gay literature.

During the Middle Ages Mann's hometown of Lübeck, a port in the extreme southwest corner of the Baltic Sea, had been one of the most important cities of the Hanse, a commercial association whose power extended from England to Scandinavia to Russia. Even after the collapse of the Hanse in the seventeenth century, Lübeck maintained its political independence and commercial significance. Since trade was at the core of the city's life, it was the wealthy merchant families who determined its political and financial fate, and it was from them that the members of the city parliament were selected. The wealthy Bürger (upper-class citizens) often functioned as the consuls of other European states and their colonies. Business and residential quarters were united under one roof in the larger homes, whose imposing, gabled facades dominated the city.

Johann Siegmund Mann moved from Mecklenburg to Lübeck in 1775; fifteen years later he established a small business. Through his marriage to the daughter of a Hamburg grain merchant he furthered his professional relationships and established the basis for the success of his firm, which was primarily achieved by delivering grain to the Prussian troops during the Napoleonic Wars from 1804 to 1814. In 1825 his son, Johann Siegmund II, married the daughter of the future mayor. It was not long before the Mann family was well established in Lübeck. After the death of his first wife, Johann Siegmund II married Elisabeth Marty; his first son from this marriage was Thomas Mann's father, Thomas Johann Heinrich Mann, who was born in 1840. One year later the house on Mengstraße, which Thomas Mann was to make famous in his novel *Buddenbrooks* (1901; translated, 1924), was built.

In 1863 Thomas Johann Heinrich Mann took over the family business and also assumed the position of consul of the Netherlands. In 1869 he became a member of the city's parliament. The same year he married Julia da Silva-Bruhns, who had been born in Brazil to a wealthy former citizen of Lübeck and his Portuguese wife; after her mother's death she had been raised in Lübeck by her father's relatives. Their first son, Luiz Heinrich, was born in 1871; their second son, officially named Paul Thomas, was born on 6 June 1875. In 1877 Thomas Johann Heinrich Mann was elected to a lifetime position as senator of the city. The same year his daughter Julia Elisabeth was born.

In the early 1870s a great economic upsurge, known as the Gründerjahre, took place in Germany. Reparations from France, which had lost the Franco-Prussian War, fueled a period of wild financial speculation. Lübeck began to industrialize; the old firms had already lost their privileges by 1866, and their anachronistic system of business was replaced by new institutions such as stock corporations. In spite of the insecure future of his firm, Mann's father was able until his death to provide his children with a glamorous lifestyle, including summers at Travemünde on the Baltic Sea; the state of mind created by the sea is found again and again in Mann's works. In 1881, the year his daughter Carla Augusta Olga Maria was born, he built a house at Beckergrube 52. A final child, Viktor, was born in 1890.

Mann believed that his own ability to create long novels was strengthened by the lasting impression his reliable and ambitious father had made on him. Mann also observed the pleasure his father took in outer appearances and later assumed this characteristic himself. His mother exercised the primary artistic influence on both Thomas and Heinrich: she had a large repertoire of songs that she enjoyed performing for the children; she also liked to read aloud to them and told them stories from her childhood in Brazil. Thus, Julia Mann not only awakened artistic interests in her sons but also introduced them to a world foreign to their existence in Lübeck, providing them experiences and feelings beyond the horizon of other boys their own age.

The family firm was dissolved upon the death of Mann's father in 1891. At about the same time his grandmother died. Her house on Mengstraße, which had provided for Mann not only refuge from the social turmoil of his parents' home but also a retreat from the pressures of school, was sold. A year after her husband's death, Julia Mann moved to the culturally and artistically active city of Munich with her younger children. Heinrich had left home in 1888 to pursue a career as a writer. Thomas, who was not quite seventeen, remained in Lübeck to complete the sixth form at the Katharineum, which entitled him to a shortened term of military service.

In spite of these profound changes and the experience of death, which left a deep imprint on Mann, he felt a sense of liberation. He no longer had to spend long hours studying to please his father, who had hoped that he would eventually take over the family business, and could devote himself to his real interests. His closest friend was Otto Grautoff, who was a social outcast because of the bankruptcy of his father; Mann's letters to Grautoff between 1894 and 1900 are the only autobiographical source of importance for the significant period in the author's life before the appearance of *Buddenbrooks*. It was together with Grautoff that Mann published his first works in the school paper, *Frühlingssturm,* of which the two were coeditors. Two issues of this short-lived effort appeared in 1893. After he had made several attempts at poetry, Mann's superior narrative talent became evident. His first literary endeavors portray an inexperienced person who feels frustrated by the inability of others to respond to his feelings of love.

In Lübeck Mann had his first and immediately intense encounter with the operatic music of Richard Wagner. At the same time he was reading everything available, particularly Friedrich Schiller and Heinrich Heine.

Immediately upon receiving his diploma in 1894 Mann left Lübeck to join his family in Munich. The move marked his dissociation from the upper-class mores and values of the nineteenth century and his entry into the modern era. In contrast to Lübeck, Munich was one of the great centers of a developing Germany. The suburb of Schwabing, where farmers and tradesmen lived in close proximity to the well-to-do middle class, was being invaded by artists, who brought with them an atmosphere of liberalism. Elite circles such as that around the poet Stefan George believed themselves exempt from conventional social mores on account of their aesthetic superiority and developed an ideology of "art for the sake of art." This atmosphere provided the basis for what is known as "decadent" art and literature.

Within a short time Mann was well acclimated to life in Munich; through his mother's circle of friends he came to know many artists and intellectuals. He took a position with a fire-insurance company, the Süddeutsche Feuerver-sicherungsbank. During office hours he secretly wrote a short story, "Gefallen" (Fallen).

Although Mann later rejected this piece, it marks a significant step in his career since it was published in October 1894 in the respected periodical *Die Gesellschaft,* where it attracted the attention of the influential writer and editor Richard Dehmel. Dehmel wrote to Mann, praising his work, and later visited him. Such recognition strengthened Mann's standing in the artistic circles of Munich and encouraged him to embark on a literary career unencumbered by gainful but time-consuming employment. He gave notice at the insurance company and registered for several courses at the Technische Universität in Munich. The lectures and seminars he attended more or less regularly from November 1894 to June 1895 provided important material for many of his future writings; Professor Wilhelm Hertz's lectures on German mythology and literature of the Middle Ages inspired as late a novel as *Der Erwählte* (The Chosen One, 1951; translated as *The Holy Sinner,* 1951).

Mann's short story "Der Wille zum Glück" (The Will to Be Happy) appeared in the August/September 1896 issue of the recently founded magazine *Simplicissimus.* Two other stories, which were later lost, were sent to Dehmel, who offered encouragement but failed to publish them. Mann, however, was little concerned with immediate success, and concentrated on sharpening his writing skills and expanding his literary knowledge; his notebooks from this period document a strong interest in Friedrich Nietzsche and Arthur Schopenhauer.

The success of "Gefallen" improved Mann's relationship with his older brother. During his last school years Mann had not felt that he was taken seriously by Heinrich, who had already established himself as a writer; but in 1895 the brothers traveled to Italy, returning there in October 1896 for what would become an eighteen-month stay. In Rome Thomas finished a short story, "Der kleine Herr Friedemann" (translated as "Little Herr Friedemann," 1928), which he sent to the periodical *Neue*

deutsche Rundschau of the influential S. Fischer publishing house. The editor, Oskar Bie, accepted the piece and requested that Mann send him all his previously written works so that they could be published as a collection. Before his return to Munich in the spring of 1898 the collection appeared under the title *Der kleine Herr Friedemann.*

In these stories two spheres are presented in opposition to one another. On the one hand, there is the world of the successful hero who follows traditional, socially acceptable paths. The action serves primarily to show how he improves his position in society, catering to well-tested societal norms. This type strives for what is acknowledged by all as good and right. Within his limited realm of family and professional life, he searches for happiness. This is the "banale Bürger" (commonplace citizen). The second world is that of the outsider who expects something more from life. He looks down on the commonplace citizen, but at the same time admires his strength and the naive self-confidence. The perspective of the outsider reveals that the concepts of happiness and love are empty ideals in view of the "normal" social reality. The story "Enttäuschung" (Disillusionment) is paradigmatic for the entire collection: disillusionment stems from the realization that life does not correspond to commonly held ideals. The aesthetics of decadence requires the rejection of banal social reality and concentration on the feelings of the sensitive individual. To the extent that they do not correspond to the "average," Mann's main characters can be seen as decadent; but they do not fill the bill completely because they do not make a cult of their heightened awareness or create an artistic principle out of their choice of lifestyle. They suffer because they are aware of an unbridgeable gap between their own lives and normal existence. They can enjoy neither the pleasures of narcissistic reflection nor the pathos of art for the sake of art; they are always in a state of gnawing self-doubt. Hardly have they been confronted with the outside world when they feel that their weaknesses have been exposed: they have removed themselves so completely from society that they can no longer participate in its life; at the same time, their search for inner fulfillment has been equally unsuccessful.

The stories of *Der kleine Herr Friedemann* present varied perspectives on the outsider's existence. Johannes Friedemann in "Der kleine Herr Friedemann" is physically an outsider from the very outset; a cripple, he attempts to find happiness outside of family and work. For a time he finds pleasure in nature and music. The narrator of "Der Bajazzo" (The Dilettante) intentionally distances himself from others because he feels superior to them. His artistic tendencies, however, are unproductive. Socially prominent women always see through the Bajazzo and Friedemann. These childless females enjoy success without having fulfilled the traditional female role; they are cruel and without compassion for weakness. They relentlessly show their superiority, giving men a feeling that their happiness is based on lies and deceit. The love, hate, and rage of the male characters in Mann's early works are initially directed at life, then toward the female characters, and finally internalized as doubt, disgust, and self-hate.

As the eminent Mann scholar Hans Rudolf Vaget has shown, already in these early short stories Mann employs a technique of implicitly referring to other works of art as well as to the lives of their creators. Consequently, what may appear to the uninformed reader as a simple or at times convoluted plot is in fact an invitation to recognize such references. Without such insight, the reader will not grasp the strong sense of humor that is peculiar to Mann's works.

The stories in *Der kleine Herr Friedemann* reveal a thematic and structural unity through which Mann presents a common world. This unity is characteristic of all of his works. It is accomplished by various means, among them the stylistic element that has become famous through Mann's oeuvre: the leitmotiv. The linking of individual pieces of Mann's first collection by common settings, such as Lübeck, Munich, and Italy, and the repetition of names, such as Gerda for Johannes Friedemann's mother as well as for the mother of Hanno in *Buddenbrooks,* can be seen as the beginning of the leitmotiv.

A parallel between Mann's literary leitmotiv and Wagner's musical one has often been pointed out by critics. Both devices serve a similar function: to create thematic and structural unity by guiding the reader or listener's attention to an artificial connection between details. While the musical leitmotiv can link a new and old theme by combining the two, the literary leitmotiv lacks this possibility because only one theme can be developed within the narration at a time. Mann's peculiar use of the leitmotiv turns this apparent disadvantage into a powerful means of narration. By using motifs which contradict each other, Mann undermines and exposes as an illusion the supposed omniscience of the narrator. The reader always has to be aware of the dialectical function of the stereotypes Mann uses: to first create powerful images, and then, in a second step, to mercilessly unmask these images as illusions.

Mann had begun writing *Buddenbrooks* in 1897, completing it in August 1900. In October he began a one-year enlistment in the Royal Bavarian Infantry but was discharged as unfit in December. The publisher Samuel Fischer was appalled at the length of the manuscript of *Buddenbrooks* and demanded radical cuts, but the young author insisted on an unabridged printing. The publisher's agreement to do so was one of the most important decisions in the company's history. While the first two-volume edition of 1,000 copies sold slowly, the second printing, in an inexpensive one-volume edition, exploded like a bombshell.

In *Buddenbrooks* the characters represent different generations as they develop within an historical framework. The novel, which tells the story of a merchant's family, begins with the founding of the Johann Buddenbrook firm and ends with the death of Hanno, the only heir of the fourth generation. The details are generally those of Mann's family's history and the social life of Lübeck. The story opens in 1835, just after the Buddenbrook family has moved into a house on Mengstraße. Three generations are living together: the founder of the family firm is seventy years old and heads the business together with his twenty-five-year-old son, Johann II. Nine-year-old Thomas, his brother Christian, and his sister Tony participate in the celebration of the new home in the company of friends and members of the two older Buddenbrook generations. These festivities are described in great detail; through this gathering the basic themes of the novel are revealed and the differences of the three generations are emphasized. The founder of the firm still thinks in a way that reflects the ideals of the Napoleonic era. His son, Consul Johann Buddenbrook, is completely adapted to modern times and follows the practical ideals of his position. But his father senses the potential for evil in this practice. He regrets the fading away of the classical education based on the humanities and its replacement by a technical, goal-oriented system. His grandson Thomas is brought up under the new system: his father sends him to the Realgymnasium (a school combining a classical with a practical modern education), which prepares him to be a businessman.

The subtitle of the novel is *Verfall einer Familie* (Decline of a Family): the Buddenbrooks are subject to an inner dynamic which brings about the demise of the family and makes its final collapse inevitable. Johann Buddenbrook establishes a tradition by founding a family firm that requires different generations to work together. The principles of this tradition secure the success of the business; the symbol of the tradition is the house on Mengstraße, where the most important achievements in the family history are recorded chronologically in the Gutenberg Bible. But the succeeding generations have increasing difficulty abiding by the traditional laws of the firm. The leitmotiv of bad teeth makes it easier to comprehend this change: when bad teeth are mentioned, other difficulties are sure to follow. This leitmotiv is well illustrated by the fate of Thomas Buddenbrook. He is prosperous—he breaks all records in the firm's history, in the face of many obstacles, and also becomes a senator. Thus it is apparent that the Buddenbrooks do not decline because of financial trouble but because of their physical and mental weakness. In the first part of the novel the reader learns that Thomas has bad teeth; later, before his fiftieth birthday, he goes to the dentist and dies on the way home of a complete physical breakdown, symbolized by a decayed, hollow tooth.

The house on the Mengstraße also serves as a leitmotiv. It first belongs to the wealthy Ratenkamp family, who experience their decline within its shelter. This fate is inherited by the Buddenbrooks when they move in, and the reader can only assume that the ever-growing Hagenström family will die out just like the Ratenkamps and Buddenbrooks after they buy the house in 1871.

Another leitmotiv in *Buddenbrooks* is happiness. To an ever-increasing degree the interests of the firm force the family members to renounce their personal happiness. The main victim of this denial of happiness and love is Thomas's sister Tony, who was modeled after Mann's aunt, Elisabeth Amalia Hyppolitha. The greatest happiness in Tony's life is her love for Morten Schwarzkopf, who comes from a modest background. Together with him Tony experiences the beauty of the sea, and from him she learns about the political liberation movements stirring in the country. Cruelly torn away from this relationship by her family, she is forced into two unfortunate marriages that cause financial loss as well as loss of prestige. Yet it is Tony herself who feels the need to protect the family tradition. She upholds the principles of the firm even though they have become empty of meaning; just how blind Tony is to reality is revealed by the fact that she continues to repeat the leftist slogans of her young love, Schwarzkopf, which are quite incongruous with her otherwise patrician worldview.

In Hanno's education the prophecy of his grandfather is fulfilled: the new school system, representing modern times, is incompatible with the cultivated spirit and intellect of the Buddenbrooks. The classical education that had fused a refined lifestyle with class consciousness has disintegrated—all that is left is an empty striving for success. The somewhat morbid Hanno suffers under the narrow-minded perspective of his teachers and seeks escape in nature during vacations at the Baltic Sea and through the music of Wagner. He perceives school as never-ending harassment. Hanno's education marks the end of the days of the patricians and the point of departure for art in the coming twentieth century. The second chapter of the last section of the novel, which ends with the words "Dies war ein Tag aus dem Leben des kleinen Johann" (This was one day in the life of little Johann), is a literary document of intellectual oppression through education. Hanno dies at the age of fifteen.

Only women remain alive at the conclusion of the novel; they represent a static element in contrast to the male characters. Gerda, Thomas's widow, with her passion for music and her symbolic origins on the edge of the North Sea, is subtly stylized into a harbinger of dissolution and death. After her husband and her son have died she

leaves the culturally inactive city of Lübeck. Tony remains the only proof of the Buddenbrooks' former existence.

While the protagonists of Mann's early works do not overtly disclose any homoerotic desire, their unsuccessful attempts to be accepted point decisively to the societal pressures that were also directed against deviant sexual orientation. The novella "Tonio Kröger" (published in *Tristan: Sechs Novellen,* 1903; translated, 1914) depicts a character who shares many traits with Hanno Buddenbrook, yet manages to live beyond his adolescence. As a schoolboy he has only one friend, Hans Hansen. Hans's name, his blond hair, and his blue eyes make him a stereotypical German, while Tonio's first name and southern European appearance are indications of his "foreignness" to the dominant society. Hans is the first of Mann's fictional characters to be based on someone to whom he had been homoerotically attracted. A few months before his death, Mann confessed in a letter to a former fellow student, Hermann Lange, that the model for Hans Hansen was their classmate Armin Martens: "[Armin] was my first love, and never again in my life was I granted an equally tender, blissful, and grievous love." While Martens did not acknowledge Mann's affection, Hans does at least concede to a distant friendship with Tonio.

Tonio shares his last name with the in-laws of Thomas Buddenbrook; his first name represents the Latin heritage of Mann's mother. For Mann the South symbolized a purely aesthetic world. Tonio's mother is musical and inspires her son to write at a very early age. His Latin appearance and literary interests contribute to his outsider status at school. Later in life he must fight inner conflicts: he could follow the path of the artist and completely remove himself from society; this choice, however, would deny the Nordic and social side of his heritage. In accepting the fact that he is an outsider and yet remaining within society, Tonio has a chance to find love and happiness. The love which the average person experiences presupposes a certain naiveté which Tonio has lost. Instead, he strives for a sublimated form of love, a special kind of art that expresses social sympathy.

Mann identified with the bourgeois tradition of humanism as defined in this story. In *Buddenbrooks* he showed that the traditional ideals of the upper classes were either an illusion or a reflection of self-interest; at the same time, he was unable to renounce the need to portray ideals that were so much a part of his heritage. He wanted to speak for everyone, without a fixed point of view. He belonged neither to the capitalists, as represented by the Hagenströms, nor to the left-leaning liberals such as Morten Schwarzkopf. After his father's death and the demise of his social group Mann lost any firm political orientation; art remained his only means of speaking out. "Tonio Kröger" documents Mann's path away from the disillusioned romanticism of his first collection of stories toward a new artistic intellectualism.

In his letter to Lange, Mann also defines the artistic importance of his homoerotic experiences as the "rousing of a feeling which is destined to be transformed into a lasting work of art." What he does not disclose, though, is the fact that "Tonio Kröger" was written during the time of his intensely homoerotic bonding with the painter Paul Ehrenberg.

Mann's relationship with Ehrenberg came to an end in 1903, when he was introduced to the wealthy Pringsheim family. Alfred Pringsheim, of Jewish descent, was a mathematician at the University of Munich and a member of a group of Wagner worshippers. His mansion was one of the most significant sites for intellectual and artistic meetings in Munich. Pringsheim's daughter Katharina (Katia) was nineteen years old when Mann met her. They were married on 11 February 1905 and had six children: Erika was born in 1905, Klaus in 1906, Golo in 1909, Monika in 1910, Elisabeth in 1918, and Michael in 1919.

Mann's marriage enabled him to resume the way of life he had loved so much during his childhood. In *Lebensabriß* (1930; translated as *A Sketch of My Life,* 1960) he says: "Die Atmosphäre des großen Familienhauses, die mir die Umstände meiner Kindheit vergegenwärtigte, bezauberte mich. Das im Geist kaufmännischer Kultureleganz Vertraute fand ich hier ins Prunkhaft-Künstlerische und Literarische modänisiert und vergeistigt" (The atmosphere of the large home, which brought back my childhood memories as if they were real again, totally enchanted me. The familiar spirit of the elegance of the cultured businessman's world was enhanced and transmuted into the luxurious glamor of artistic and literary life). Through the Pringsheim family Mann was introduced to the most affluent circles of Munich and Berlin society. In addition, Katia's father presented the young couple with a royally furnished apartment in Schwabing and supported them financially for years.

Katia Mann became Mann's partner in his intellectual enterprise. Her self-assured personality complemented his ambitious but sensitive nature. She assumed the social responsibilities for her famous husband, kept his mornings free from intrusions so that he could work on his literary projects, managed his financial affairs, and even intervened when she felt that he was being manipulated or was simply saying too much in interviews. Life without Katia seemed utterly unimaginable to Mann. His new social role of a family man and cultural exponent not only impeded future erotic relationships with men, but it also determined and limited his choice of literary subjects. He abandoned plans for a novel called "Maya," an artistic reflection of his friendship with Ehrenberg.

In 1905 Mann finished his next major work, the drama *Fiorenza* (1906), which deals with the intellectual and political conflict between Lorenzo the Magnificent, the glorious figure of the Florentine High Renaissance, and Girolamo Savonarola, the prior of San Marco, who condemns the humanists' excessive enjoyment of life and "decadent" art. While Savonarola is seen as an ascetic and a rigid moralist who is about to draw the masses away from Lorenzo, the latter seems to be an aesthete who supports art for art's sake and lacks any responsibility to lead his people to a moderate and moral life. Only at the end do the opponents meet, when Savonarola visits Lorenzo on his deathbed. Now it becomes apparent that the two men have much in common. In Lorenzo's view, Savonarola and he are brothers through an elective affinity: their fragile natures, which are only to be overcome by means of artistic fame or political power.

Lorenzo says, "Wär' ich schön geboren, nie hätte ich zum Herrn der Schönheit mich gemacht. Die Hemmung ist des Willens bester Freund" (Had I been born beautiful, I would never have made myself the lord of beauty. Hindrance is the will's best friend). He has no sense of smell and calls himself a cripple who does not know the scent of the rose or of a woman. His will to rule over the people's aesthetic taste stems from this personal shortcoming, just as Savonarola's desire for ethical and political leadership is a reaction to his personal weakness; the artist's work is seen as a form of sublimation. Shortly before his death Lorenzo identifies with the prior's confession: "Das Leiden darf nicht umsonst gewesen sein. Ruhm muß es bringen!" (My sufferings must not have been in vain. They must bring me fame!).

For the first time, Mann is openly confessing his own need for recognition. He accepts his new role as the famous man admired by the masses, but at the same time wants to make clear that glory and power are dangerous illusions. Thus, he links these themes with the leitmotiv of the great figure who is physically handicapped from birth and suffers from illness.

Fiorenza was Mann's only experiment with the dramatic form. It was performed in Frankfurt and Munich and was a moderate success; but Mann referred to it as a "dramatic novella," realizing that it was not well suited for the traditional stage. In its depiction of the confrontation between opposing artistic and ideological tenets, portrayed as a debate between individuals who represent these contradictory attitudes, *Fiorenza* prefigures *Der Zauberberg*.

In 1906 Mann wrote *Wälsungenblut* (The Blood of the Walsungs), which deals with incestuous love. He was forced to retract the work before the copies of *Die neue Rundschau* which contained it had arrived in the bookstores. He had used the stereotype of the rich Jew and his tastelessly "bedecked" wife, and even before publication the news spread around Munich that Mann had written the story as a satire of his wife's family. The public could not believe that Katia Mann's father was not identical with the Jewish Wagner-worshiper in *Wälsungenblut;* and even though his mother-in-law had approved the publication, her husband, who was not fond of his son-in-law's "loose" literary career, became so outraged that Mann had no choice but to withdraw the work. The story did not appear until 1921, and then only in a private edition.

In *Königliche Hoheit* (1909; translated as *Royal Highness,* 1916) Mann once again varies two of his favorite themes, the outsider and happiness. Like Tonio Kröger, Prince Klaus Heinrich experiences exclusion from his peer group; once again, the protagonist is suffering from a physical handicap, this time atrophy of his left hand. He is able to turn his feelings as an outsider into a positive attitude: when he assumes the throne he does not become a cynical tyrant but a kindhearted ruler. He finds happiness in marriage to Imma Spoelmann, who is also an outsider because of her American Indian ancestry. His wife's wealth enables Klaus Heinrich to reform his destitute land. *Königliche Hoheit* marks the turning point in Mann's development from an apolitical aesthete and pessimistic critic of culture to a nationalistic monarchist—an orientation to which he held for ten years out of loyalty to traditional values.

The novella *Der Tod in Venedig* (1912; translated as *Death in Venice,* 1925) depicts the last few weeks of the life of Gustav von Aschenbach, who is presented as the celebrated author of the novel "Maya." His works have become part of the school curriculum and are presented to Germany's youth as a model of stylistic discipline and moral integrity. In spite of his extraordinary success, he is yet another protagonist who is excluded from mainstream society: he is an outsider by virtue of his role as a national idol. A widowed and intellectually solitary man in his fifties, Aschenbach finds it increasingly difficult to live up to these public and self-imposed expectations. He frequently seeks refuge from his artistic and public duties through traveling, especially to Venice and the nearby elegant beach resort, Lido.

The erotic excitement of decaying Venice and the allure of a handsome boy named Tadzio render Aschenbach incapable of leaving. As a result of his decision to stay in the cholera-infested city he becomes a victim of the disease. *Death in Venice* reveals the homoerotic fantasies of an author who could never openly admit his sexual propensity. The moral standards of his time did not allow Mann actual fulfillment of his desires; instead, the boys and young men who aroused his fantasies repeatedly found entrance into his literary works. Even though Tadzio, whose family is staying in the same luxurious hotel as Aschenbach, will never engage in a conversation with his worshiper, he is well aware of Aschenbach's infatuation with him, enjoys the older man's adoration of his body, and engages in an exchange of secret glances with

him. Aschenbach's obsession is so strong that he makes light of all warnings about the cholera outbreak in Venice; one day it is too late, and the city is placed under quarantine. He has lost any self-control and pursues his beloved Tadzio, helplessly roaming about the death-stricken streets and canals of Venice.

At the end of the novella Aschenbach dies in his canopied beach chair while watching his beloved Tadzio, who seems to be summoning him into the sea. The public will remember the great man as a model of artistic and personal self-discipline, while his actual end is rather undignified. Artistic beauty has revealed itself to be an illusion; it is the basis for the artist's fame, but not a true picture of his inner self.

Aschenbach succumbs to the erotic impulses which he had repressed in the interest of a disciplined classical art. The taming of the artist's drives by means of a rigorous self-discipline may result in a purified classicism—for a while; but beauty, no matter how spiritualized, is inextricably bound up with the artist's erotic subconscious. Mann's modern-day Venice is imperceptibly transformed into a classical landscape where the ancient gods Apollo and Dionysus wage a battle for Aschenbach's soul.

Like Hans Hansen in "Tonio Kröger," Tadzio was based on an actual youth to whom Mann had been homoerotically attracted. During a stay in Lido in May of 1911, he had glimpsed the Polish boy Wadyslaw ("Adzio"), Baron Moes. In the essay "Die Ehe im Übergang" (Marriage in the State of Transition, 1925), Mann presents his view of homoeroticism and its symbolic meaning in his own works, especially *Death in Venice*. He draws a parallel between art and Eros: homoerotic love is like art for art's sake, self-serving, childless, and without the potential for commitment and faithfulness. In this regard, Aschenbach's demise is the price modern art must pay for its newly gained independence and loss of social responsibility. However, by largely straying from the ostensible subject, marriage, the essay pays homage to homoeroticism, and it also serves as an apologia for homoerotic love as the true origin of artistic creativity.

The outbreak of World War I forced Mann to deal explicitly with politics. He became an ally of the patriotic monarchists with his essay *Friedrich und die große Koalition* (Frederick and the Great Coalition, 1915), in which he demonstrated the qualities of the German spirit as exemplified by Frederick the Great. He was suddenly identified with a group of loyalist writers who saw Germany as a country with high moral qualities that was being unfairly attacked.

While Mann was making plans for a book which would reawaken the ideals of the nineteenth century and celebrate the moral and apolitical characteristics of the German spirit, he encountered an unexpected opponent in his own brother, Heinrich, whose 1915 essay "Zola" cast France as an ally in the struggle for democracy. Heinrich Mann felt that it was the responsibility of all intellectuals to lend support for democratization and thereby accelerate a process hampered by autocratic Germany. Artists such as his brother Thomas were depicted as parasites who could not break away from their old financial supporters. This criticism hurt Thomas Mann deeply. He wanted to be right at any cost, even without being fully convinced of his own position. But as it became increasingly clear that Germany would lose the war, Mann realized that the time for support for conservatism was over. The only thing yet to be done was to secure his personal integrity; there were no longer any political interests worth defending. Thus, his book was finally completed as the intellectual retreat of an artist who could no longer defend traditional values politically but rather as a reflection of his own apolitical conscience.

When the voluminous work appeared in 1918 under the title *Betrachtungen eines Unpolitischen* (translated as *Reflections of a Nonpolitical Man,* 1983), its great success was an irony of fate. The book was enthusiastically adopted by the antidemocratic forces in Germany at a moment when its author was trying to adjust to the coming of democracy. In 1922 he publicly declared his allegiance to the new system in the speech *Von deutscher Republik* (Of the German Republic, 1923). From that day forward he was placed in a difficult position between the disappointed conservatives, on the one hand, and the German Democrats, who would hold him suspect for a long time to come, on the other.

After a relatively unproductive period, Mann completed *Der Zauberberg* in 1924. When he had first planned it in 1912, he had thought of it as a brief humorous pendant–he called it a "satyr play"–to the tragic novella *Der Tod in Venedig*. But the doom signaled by Gustav Aschenbach's downfall had become reality at the end of the war. Thus, what was originally conceived as a short story became Mann's third swan song; this time not to the upper class of Lübeck nor to the nineteenth-century artist, but to the entire prewar culture.

The beginning of the novel is indicative of the complex interplay it presents between the past, the present, and the future. The narrator points out a special feature of the German language: while the simple past tense can be used in English to refer to recent events, its German equivalent is mainly reserved for storytelling purposes. The narrator emphasizes the irrecoverability of the world depicted in his story by calling himself "den raunenden Beschwörer des Imperfekts" (the murmuring conjurator of the simple past tense). He points out that the era portrayed in the story is not separated from the present by a long period of time–in fact, it is rather recent–but by the cataclysm of World War I, which has ushered in a new and completely different era.

The novel is more than a mourning of the past; it also attempts to remind the new culture of its historical dimensions. It begins in 1907 at the tuberculosis sanatorium Berghof in Davos, a luxurious resort for the upper classes in a remote area of the Swiss Alps. Its inhabitants represent the various national mentalities and intellectual currents of the prewar period. The protagonist, the inexperienced young German engineer Hans Castorp, is so absorbed by the uncanny atmosphere of the Berghof that he feels as if he is caught in a magical circle. Initially, he intends to stay only three weeks to visit his cousin Joachim Ziemßen, whose military career has been interrupted by tuberculosis. Ziemßen returns to the army, but he has to come back to the sanatorium, where he dies. Castorp, entranced by the Magic Mountain, remains in Davos; seven years later, long after the death of his cousin, it is only World War I that can remove him from this world. He is called back to everyday life to fight in the Great War.

In many respects *Der Zauberberg* can be compared to the classical German bildungsroman or educational novel. Like Goethe's Wilhelm Meister, Castorp becomes a more educated and responsible individual after the years of exposure to all the trends of his time and culture. First of all, he experiences the difference between objective and subjective time: the former can be measured mechanically and subjects the human being to the law of cause and effect; the latter depends on the intensity of feelings and alternately stagnates and rushes. Subjective time is the basis for human perception, enabling Castorp to broaden his horizon and understand the intellectual heritage of his culture. The Magic Mountain with its international atmosphere enables him to realize that Germany's fate is bound to a common European tradition. Castorp gains a perspective from which he can appreciate what initially was completely strange and forbidding to his pragmatic and technically oriented mind.

During the first year of his stay Castorp becomes completely part of the Berghof routine. Wrapped in blankets, he rests for hours on his private balcony, just like the patients, who are acclimated to such a degree that their former lives in the lower altitudes have become unimaginable. While the original purpose of their stay was to escape death from tuberculosis, they are caught in a vicious circle: the Berghof can prolong their lives to a degree, but they are still hopelessly in the clutches of death. The luxurious lifestyle deceives them and serves the interest of the Berghof management, which quietly removes the corpses of the deceased on sleds at night, unnoticed by survivors.

There are frequent festivities, some of them carried to bacchanalian excess. But the main social events are the regular meals, which are too opulent to qualify as a healthy diet. As in the outside world, the patients are divided into social and ethnic groups, represented by seven dinner tables. When he leaves the sanatorium, Castrop will have eaten at every table, even the "schlechten Russentisch" (the bad Russian table).

Castorp's most significant insights stem from his increasingly active inclusion in the intellectual battles between the Italian humanist Settembrini and the rigid dogmatist and ascetic Naphta. Mann's descriptions of Settembrini and Naphta are suffused with irony and humor: the hedonistic humanist's lifestyle is extremely modest, while the radical ascetic lives in a stylish and comfortable apartment. Their ideological confrontation cannot be settled by arguments: in a pistol duel, Naphta shoots himself after Settembrini refuses to aim at him. It is not the rigid moralist who survives, as in *Fiorenza,* but the physically weakened humanist with self-doubts that derive from his commitment to a cosmopolitan intellectualism.

In addition to the seven dinner tables and the intellectual dispute, Castorp is exposed to three other powerful influences. First, he develops a critical attitude toward science as a result of his observations of Dr. Behrens, the head physician, a traditional medical doctor who apparently acts more in the interest of the institution's management than in that of his patients, and his assistant, Dr. Krokowski, a follower of a popularized form of psychoanalysis that Ziemßen calls "Seelenzergliederung" (dismemberment of the soul), an approach that only reinforces his patients' illusions.

The appearance of Clawdia Chauchat is another key experience for Castorp. Her Eastern heritage and fluent knowledge of French upset the balance Mann's previous works had established between "Northern" and "Southern" values, the German tradition of self-command and the Latin dedication to art. Clawdia's unpunctuality and sensuality irritate Castorp, who tries to hide his insecurity behind a feeling of cultural superiority. He harbors a chauvinistic prejudice against Clawdia's native Russia, and finds her behavior uncivilized and uncouth. Clawdia tries to avenge herself by forcing Castorp to speak in French, but she cannot destroy his self-respect; she only strengthens him by refuting his initial prejudice. Castorp's love affair with Clawdia is indicative of Mann's enormous intellectual development in the years between the *Betrachtungen eines Unpolitischen* and the completion of *Der Zauberberg.*

Finally, Castorp is extremely impressed with his successor as Clawdia's lover, the giant Mynheer Peeperkorn. Peeperkorn is the epitome of the strong personality. His lack of intellectuality, symbolized by his incapacity for articulate speech, is compensated for by his cult of vitalism. Peeperkorn commits suicide when he feels his sexual powers falter; Castorp is repulsed by this demeaning death and realizes that the ideal of a great personality stems from the exaggeration of the individual.

Before Castorp leaves the Magic Mountain to become a foot soldier in the chaos of World War I he has a vision during a snowstorm of a peaceable mankind, civilized and humane, albeit with a sinister, indeed murderous, secret under the pleasant surface. The vision gives way to daydreaming and finally the verbalization of problems central to the novel. In the course of these musings the reader finds the only italicized sentence in the book; it says that for the sake of love, man is not to grant death power over his thoughts. Stripped of its symbolism, this passage contains Mann's confession that in *Der Zauberberg* he has subjected his romantic German heritage to a final scrutiny, deciding to relegate it to second place behind the democratic and life-enhancing virtues of western European culture. It can be argued that the impact of this message is weakened by the narrator's explicit assertion that shortly after escaping from the storm Castorp forgets the vision, and by the fact that the book continues for several more chapters. But in the course of these chapters the message turns up again in only slightly modified form, so that the conclusion is permissible that it retains its validity even if Castorp himself cannot live up to it. At the end of the novel he is left to an uncertain fate in the midst of a merciless battle.

Der Zauberberg shows the self-destructive powers hidden in culture; at the same time, it appeals to the moral values of culture, without which the world would be totally lost. In this work Mann's narrative techniques sparkle at their most brilliant. The narrator, the characters, and the world created are constantly relativized through irony so that it is impossible for the reader to maintain any fixed point of reference. The characters exist behind masks: their individual fates seem to adhere to historically predetermined roles. But even these roles receive a new individuation through the narration. The story is an exercise in dialectical hermeneutics: without tradition the people would have no identity, but the tradition must incessantly be reinterpreted and related to the present lest it become a simple stereotype.

All of this does not make it easy for the reader, particularly if he must rely on a translation. The constant switching between historical patterns and individual fates is achieved through Mann's use of language, which is significant to the smallest detail. Certain references, such as the one to the function of the German simple past tense, have to be left out unless the text is to be encumbered by lengthy footnotes (in *The Magic Mountain* "den raunenden Beschwörer des Imperfekts" is translated as "the rounding wizard of times gone by").

Another difficulty is caused by the use of the leitmotiv. Repeated phrases such as "blond und blauäugig" (blond and blue-eyed) connect parts of the text; they often have not been recognized by the translator, or their different contexts did not allow for the exact repetition of the former phrase. The names of characters, such as Clawdia Chauchat (hotcat) or Hermine Kleefeld (cloverfield), are related to their personalities in ways that are only apparent in the original German. Some passages imitate the language of special social groups or particular styles of art to such an extent that it is impossible to determine the line between parody and seriousness. Every translation of Mann's works is necessarily an interpretation that limits and reduces the vast and rich tapestry of his language. The English translations by Lowe-Porter concentrate almost exclusively on the story line and, consequently, do not let the reader see how resolutely the German text relativizes the plot through irony. Newer translations of some of Mann's works–such as David Luke's rendition of *Death in Venice* and John E. Woods's translations of *Buddenbrooks* and *Der Zauberberg*–have tried to overcome these limitations.

Today, even German-speaking readers are separated from Mann's text by a great historical and cultural distance. The original readers of the work were privileged bourgeois citizens educated in the humanities in a style that no longer exists. They were well acquainted with mythology and texts of world literature as well as the biographies of people such as Goethe and Nietzsche. The modern reader is often unaware of the allusions to this tradition, nor will he suspect, for example, that Peeperkorn is modeled on the dramatist Gerhart Hauptmann. This cultural distance does not make the story less interesting than it was for the reader of 1924, but it reduces the significance of the intended irony. Even if the modern reader is aware of the cultural background, he will experience the humor in a different way than Mann intended–in analogy to a joke which requires extensive explanation to be appreciated. In spite of these obstacles to full understanding, Mann's texts retain much of their original luster and, on the whole, their many levels of significance.

In 1926 Mann was elected a member of the Literary Section of the Prussian Academy of Art. After *Der Zauberberg* he returned to the present, the era of the Weimar Republic, which is reflected in two of his works. The economic depression and the rise of National Socialism provided the background for these short stories. In *Unordnung und frühes Leid* (Disorder and Early Sorrow, 1926; translated as *Early Sorrow,* 1929), the economic crisis forms the background. The story centers on a family whose lifestyle has been severely reduced and which is undergoing a generational conflict. The children see in their magnificent villa only the relic of a bygone time; the values their parents associate with the house are foreign to them. The inner tensions of the father, Abel Cornelius, a history professor who has to reconcile his rigorous self-expectations as a scholar with his mystical inclinations, constitute a subtheme. The main theme is the painful process of his separation from the youngest daughter, Lorchen; he is forced to witness her loss of childish naiveté without being able to keep the distance between them from growing. Lorchen is Mann's typical child figure: she lacks the "normal" childlike characteristics. In the eyes of her brothers and sisters she is too young to be taken seriously; in reality, she already possesses the self-awareness and eros that tragically separate her from her siblings and her father, whom she loves dearly.

The story *Mario und der Zauberer* (1930; translated as *Mario and the Magician,* 1931) is based on experiences Mann and his family had as vacationers in Mussolini's Italy. In the story a family witnesses a murder: a magician/hypnotist humiliates his audience of vacationers and townspeople until the uneducated young waiter Mario draws a revolver and puts an end to the terror. The narrator, who confesses that he, too, had come under the hypnotic spell of the demogogic entertainer, hopes that his children have misunderstood the episode as a simple stunt. The story does not answer the question whether the parents have done the right thing by protecting the children from the truth of the situation. *Mario und der Zauberer* was later acknowledged as Mann's warning against fascism, already in power in Italy and threatening to take over Germany.

Mario und der Zauberer reflects an incident of injured vanity Mann suffered in Italy, when his family was refused permission to dine on the same hotel terrace as the Italian aristocracy. Something similar happened on 10 December 1929, when Mann was awarded the Nobel Prize in Stockholm: King Gustav V gave preferential treatment to the one aristocrat among the winners. Fifty years later Katia Mann still remembered this event as a grievous insult. Mann had defended democracy undauntedly throughout the Weimar period, but he had to experience what it meant to be discriminated against before he could really stand up for it emotionally.

In 1921 and 1925 Mann had written essays on Goethe and Tolstoy in which he attempted to bind the realism of the nineteenth century to the older tradition of German classicism. In the course of this work he became receptive to the suggestion in Goethe's autobiography *Aus meinem Leben: Dichtung und Wahrheit* (From My Life: Poetry and Truth, 1811–1814, 1833; translated as *Autobiography of Goethe,* 1846) that the biblical story of Joseph be recast as an historical novel. In 1926 Mann began a project based on a section of Genesis that resulted in his mammoth tetralogy. Seventeen years would be devoted to this effort. He made an intensive study of the era in question and took a three-month tour of the historical sites referred to in the Bible. In 1933 the first of the four volumes appeared: *Die Geschichten Jaakobs* (The Tales of Jacob; translated as Joseph and His Brothers, 1934), in which the origin of the historical tradition from which Joseph derives is described. *Der junge Joseph* (translated as *Young Joseph,*

1935) and *Joseph in Ägypten* (translated as *Joseph in Egypt,* 1938) followed in 1934 and 1936, respectively. The final volume, *Joseph, der Ernährer* (translated as *Joseph the Provider,* 1944), was not published until 1943.

The last three works were written abroad. Mann left Germany on 11 February 1933 on a lecture tour and remained in exile. Despite his great influence during the Weimar years, which he had repeatedly used to warn his countrymen against the rising tide of National Socialism, at heart Mann had remained the "unpolitical German." His political ideas strike the modern reader as alarming in their optimistic naiveté. When one reads his interviews of the period one is amazed to see the extent to which he minimized the dangers of militarism and political extremism. In 1928 he had still believed that National Socialism, in spite of all the bloody rioting, need not be taken seriously. As late as 1932 he was still of the opinion that the Nazi threat would be short-lived. Soon after Hitler became chancellor, Mann gave a lecture in Munich on Richard Wagner titled "Leiden und Größe Richard Wagners" (Sufferings and Greatness of Richard Wagner), in which he upheld the essence of German culture against ideological abuse. The speech greatly fanned the hostility of the new regime and its sympathizers. Still, Mann might have returned to Germany after his foreign lecture tour had it not been for the warnings of his oldest children, Klaus and Erika, who were fervent antinationalists. A letter of March 1933 reveals the depth of his fear that he would never be able to "breathe the air" of Germany again. In exile he regarded it as his mission to represent Germany's "good element" against the destructive powers of its current rulers.

At first he stayed in Sanary-sur-Mer on the French Riviera, where many refugee writers had taken up residence; in the early fall of 1933 he moved to Küsnacht, near Zurich, where he lived until his move to the United States in 1938. On 19 December 1936 his honorary doctorate, which he had received in 1919, was revoked by the philosophical faculty of Bonn University; Mann published the letter informing him of the revocation, along with his reply, as *Ein Briefwechsel* (1937; translated as *An Exchange of Letters,* 1937). In 1937 he was awarded Czechoslovakia's Herder Prize for exiled writers. In Küsnacht he began a novel about Goethe, *Lotte in Weimar* (translated as *The Beloved Returns,* 1940), which was completed at Princeton and published in 1939. Goethe is portrayed as an isolated intellectual giant in the small-town atmosphere of eighteenth-century Weimar who is visited by a woman he had loved and lost forty years earlier: Charlotte Kestner (neé Buff), who served as the model for Charlotte in his novel *Die Leiden des jungen Werthers* (1774; translated as *The Sorrows of Werther,* 1786). At an early stage of his life, impressed with the sage's productivity, Mann had taken Goethe as a model. He had especially been inspired by

Goethe's ability to balance his often contradictory inner forces and achieve mental harmony even in his most trying moments.

In *Lotte in Weimar,* Mann paints a picture of Goethe as an older man who, in spite of his great fame and many social amenities, is intellectually isolated. He has not overcome the loss of his only intellectual equal, Schiller, and is surrounded by a group of jealous worshipers. The central part of this work, however, departs from the description of these external circumstances and puts the reader into the protagonist's own perspective, thereby disclosing the processes of a creative mind. It is here that Mann reveals his view of bisexuality as the driving force of artistic creativity.

Before resuming his work on the Joseph novels, which he had interrupted with *Lotte in Weimar,* Mann also wrote the novella *Die vertauschten Köpfe* (1940; translated as *The Transposed Heads,* 1941). While *Lotte in Weimar* limits its idolization of bisexuality to the artistic and creative realm, *Die vertauschten Köpfe* takes advantage of the supernatural elements of its model, an Indian legend, in order to visualize the consequences of transposing the heads of different characters onto the bodies of others they desire. Thus, Nanda, a beautiful and sensual herdsman, has his body exchanged with the trunk of his sophisticated and highly intellectual bosom-friend, Schridaman. In some respect, this novella overcomes the dichotomy of life and art, as presented in "Tonio Kröger": both men gain from the transposition of their bodies, in that Nanda's mere physical beauty becomes spiritually refined and Schridaman's intellect is enriched with sensuality. However, both must realize that their mutual attraction was based on the fact that each desired in the other the qualities he lacked. Consequently, they both lose their quarrel over Schridaman's wife, Sita. Whoever she considers to be her husband cannot satisfy her desires: Schridaman's new body has lost its attraction of being secretly desired, and when she is united with his former body, she misses his intellect. Finally, all three agree to commit suicide, since they realize that they have destroyed the basis for their happiness on earth, as limited as it may have been.

The Joseph project corresponded well to the concerns of the time. Joseph is banned by his brothers to Egypt. Having grown up in the mythical world of Israel, he is struck by the modernity and complexity of the Egyptian civilization. Thanks to this new horizon he can free himself from the mythical entanglement. He does not give up his own culture, but his new experiences make it possible for him to show his people a way into the future. Like Prince Klaus Heinrich, he avoids becoming a despotic patriarch and finds his identity as a wise statesman. Thus, the ending of the fourth Joseph novel, *Joseph, der Ernährer,* elaborates on a theme Mann had used thirty-five years previously in *Königliche Hoheit;* by 1943 he had given up the idea of an elitist and aristocratic leadership. While *Königliche Hoheit* was the literary prelude to an ideological defense of nationalistic politics, the Joseph novels try to work against the nationalists' attempt to use a distorted view of history and culture as a support for their ideology.

Joseph is destined to become a cofounder of the chosen people of Israel. In order to fulfill this destiny, he follows in the steps of his forefathers. However, Mann goes beyond this mythical symbolism by emphasizing the psychological aspects of the plot: Joseph relies on the support of several father figures, but he must also learn to cope with an ever-present majority of male enemies, beginning with his half brothers who resent his naive pride in being their father's favorite son. After a long series of setbacks, he finally assumes the role of Egypt's protector. He becomes a wise statesman who resembles Mann's political idol, Roosevelt. Joseph's fateful tenacity is symbolized by his long-lasting chastity. However, when Mut-em-enet, the wife of his earlier Egyptian master, Potiphar, develops an irresistible passion for Joseph, she comes very close to seducing him. Mann's diaries reveal that Mut-em-enet's passion commemorates the "central love experience of [his] first twenty-five years," his relationship with Ehrenberg.

From 1940 until 1952 Mann lived in a luxurious home in Pacific Palisades, California. He became an American citizen on 23 June 1944. On 25 January 1947 his honorary doctorate was restored by Bonn University. He received many other honorary doctorates and awards from American and European institutions between 1939 and his death in 1955, including membership in the Accademia Nazionale dei Lincei in Rome in 1947, the Goethe Prize of Weimar in 1949, membership in the Academy of Arts and Letters in New York City in 1951, and the Officer's Cross of the Legion of Honor of France in 1952.

Even though Mann was highly respected during his American exile and regarded as the "most eminent living man of letters," he later confessed that, while he had become an American citizen and was very impressed with Roosevelt's social reforms, he never felt that he belonged intellectually to American culture ("Ich bin geistig niemals Amerikaner geworden"). He had, however, become close friends with several Americans, among them his publisher, Knopf, and Agnes E. Meyer, the journalist and writer who was married to Eugene Meyer, the influential banker, statesman, and owner/publisher of *The Washington Post*. In addition to the six volumes of Mann's diaries, his correspondence with Meyer is the most compelling documentation of his American exile.

With the completion of *Joseph, der Ernährer* and a short story about Moses, *Das Gesetz* (1944; translated as *The Tables of the Law*, 1945), Mann's biblical writings were finished. His next novel, *Doktor Faustus: Das Leben des deutschen Tonsetzers Adrian Leverkühn, erzählt von einem Freunde*

(1947; translated as *Doctor Faustus: The Life of the German Composer, Adrian Leverkühn, as Told by a Friend,* 1948), was his last swan song–a farewell to German culture and its intellectual tradition. In this story Germany's downfall is reflected in the fate of the composer Adrian Leverkühn.

The initiated reader of Mann's works will immediately recognize Lübeck society in the fictional town of Kaisersaschern. Mann completes the circle of his personal development by describing the upbringing of a young man with artistic ambitions in a traditional German environment, surroundings just like Hanno Buddenbrook's and Tonio Kröger's in the stories completed more than forty years before. Many themes are used again in the fashion of the leitmotiv, but the intellectual framework has changed completely.

This change is particularly reflected by the narrative perspective: for the first time, Mann uses a first-person narrator for a novel. Adrian Leverkühn's friend Serenus Zeitblom, Ph.D., a professor of literature, represents the educated German who is well versed in history and aware of the coming catastrophes of National Socialism and World War II but is paralyzed when it comes to taking action against these developments. A comparison of *Doktor Faustus* with *Mario und der Zauberer* shows that Mann's criticism of German intellectuals remained the same during the entire period of European fascism.

The hope he had expressed in *Der Zauberberg* that Germany could maintain a cooperative and mediating position in the middle of Europe had been cruelly disappointed. Mann's predominantly aesthetic comprehension of history did not allow for new explanations of Germany's Nazi aberration. Instead, he returned to his older concept of tragic fate: Leverkühn's end appears to be as inevitable as Thomas Buddenbrook's or Gustav Aschenbach's.

In contrast to Zeitblom, who is a passive intellectual with a bourgeois lifestyle and modest scholarly ambitions, Leverkühn is driven to produce art that has never existed before; and he is not afraid of unleashing self-destructive forces to do so. Leverkühn is the prototype of the German character who has to go his own way without concern for his own destruction or that of others.

Mann always had conflicting feelings about music, especially about the love of his childhood and youth, Wagner. He could not withstand the stunning power of Wagner's music, but at the same time, he realized the danger of its overwhelming sensuality and irrationality. In 1903 he had expressed this concern in literary form in "Tristan" (translated, 1925), the title story in the collection that included "Tonio Kröger." Adrian Leverkühn strongly opposes Wagner. Arnold Schönberg's rationalistic twelve-tone music, which attempts to exclude any element of arbitrariness, is attributed in the novel to Leverkühn.

His striving to reach this goal stands for the desire of the German character to accomplish the impossible.

To emphasize Leverkühn's dilemma as specifically German, Mann uses the greatest theme contributed by Germany to world literature, the Faust motif stemming from the Middle Ages. Leverkühn, the new Faust, has to seal a pact with the devil if he is to create great music. Unlike Goethe in his basically optimistic *Faust,* Mann has grave doubts about the redemption of Leverkühn's soul. Like the characters in *Buddenbrooks* whose dedication to the firm entails a denial of love and happiness, Leverkühn will create great music at the price of the same renunciation. Thus, Mann reverts to the medieval view that Faust is damned. By making love to a prostitute Leverkühn contracts syphilis, which stimulates and ultimately destroys his genius: the modern version of hell is insanity.

As remarkable as the reinterpretation of the Faust legend in the light of German history is the method Mann employs, a technique he called "Montage." He had always been fond of overtly or covertly quoting from various sources in his narrative works; in this novel the propensity is carried to such lengths that practically no passage is independent of some written model. The poetry of Shakespeare and the German romantics, epistolary literature, musicians' biographies, and newspaper and magazine articles on space and deep-sea exploration, medicine, and theology are quoted verbatim or in slight adaptation to surrounding passages. It thus turns out that Adrian Leverkühn "is" not only Faust (and Zeitblom his traditional assistant, Wagner) but also Nietzsche, whose stages in life Leverkühn replicates; Luther (which makes Zeitblom an Erasmus figure); and Beethoven, Schönberg, Alban Berg, and other musicians. Leverkühn's life embodies the entire cultural development of Germany. Mann's next work, *Die Entstehung des Doktor Faustus* (1949; translated as *The Story of a Novel,* 1961), retells the circumstances under which *Doktor Faustus* was written. This book-length text is the principle account of Mann's American exile that was published during his lifetime. Although it does not express the disillusion of its author with the country, it does reveal his disappointment with the lack of understanding with which *Doctor Faustus* was met by German as well as American reviewers. It also pays tribute to Theodor W. Adorno, the music theorist and philosopher who would later become one of Germany's most important cultural critics. It was Adorno who provided Mann with the extensive insight into modernist music and musical history that was crucial for the composition of *Doctor Faustus.* In fact, entire passages of the novel can be considered Adorno's writing. *Die Entstehung des Doktor Faustus* avoids criticizing McCarthyism and America's role in the Cold War; it also remains silent about the fact that Adorno's co-authorship was not met with sympathy by

Mann's family, especially by Erika Mann, who had been yet another "secret adviser" to the novelist.

In 1949, on the occasion of Goethe's 200th birthday, Mann made speeches in both the western and the eastern parts of Germany in which he spoke out for a united nation. This message was not well received in the West. It was not understood that by preferring one side over the other Mann would have compromised his deepest convictions about Germany's indivisible tradition. Mann was deeply shocked by the cold war that followed the end of World War II in 1945 and by Senator Joseph McCarthy's persecution of liberal intellectuals. The hysteria unleashed by McCarthyism drove him from the United States, and in 1952 he moved to Kilchberg, near Zurich.

His last two novels once more brought to the fore the optimistic Thomas Mann. In *Der Erwählte,* based on Hartmann von Aue's medieval work *Gregorius,* one of the worst sinners is chosen by God to become pope. The second novel was a work Mann had left unfinished after publishing the first chapter as a novella in 1922: *Bekenntnisse des Hochstaplers Felix Krull: Der Memoiren erster Teil* (1954; translated as *Confessions of Felix Krull, Confidence Man: The Early Years,* 1955). At the end of his life he possessed the serenity to portray the artist as a confidence man who fools both himself and society by hiding behind a succession of masks in an effort to maintain his intellectual integrity, all the while admitting the illusionary nature of his acts.

Mann's last work was the voluminous essay *Versuch über Schiller* (On Schiller, 1955). He completed the manuscript in time for it to be used for the addresses he gave in Stuttgart and Weimar in May 1955 on the occasion of the 150th anniversary of Schiller's death. In this essay Mann appeals to the optimistic side of the German character. Consequently, his last word is a manifestation of hope–in favor of Schiller's *An die Freude* (Ode to Joy, 1786) and not Leverkühn's symphony "Dr. Fausti Weheklag" (Lamentation of Dr. Faustus). When Mann returned to his hometown of Lübeck on 20 May 1955 to receive an honorary citizenship from the city, he had already returned to Tonio Kröger's enthusiasm for Schiller. Mann was conciliatory at last, in accordance with the good German character he had always tried to emulate.

At first glance, the works of Mann's old age seem to convey three rather distinct frames of mind: his last fictional works appear as youthful as "Tonio Kröger," yet they are further enriched by self-parody. In his late essays, Mann once again displays rhetorical brilliance, yet he shies away from the political engagement and fearless verve of the late Weimar years and his American exile. Even more surprisingly, the diaries of this time reveal that the most highly acclaimed author of such masterpieces as *Der Zauberberg* was beset with gnawing self-doubt as well as despair over a political world and culture that were a far cry from his dreams of humanism and universal sympathy. However, these disparities found in his late writing can be understood as the last reverberation of Mann's artistic self-understanding. Although he enjoyed being celebrated as a representative and spokesperson for the virtues of the educated burgher culture and humanism, he had devoted his life to writing fiction. He could not imagine a life without writing. Toward the end of his life, it became harder and harder for him to meet this expectation. Without the help of his family, above all Katia and Erika Mann, he would not have had the strength to carry out his writing plans. Consequently, rather than taking these late works at face value and assuming that Mann was taken from this world at the height of his intellectual power, one must consider them the subtly melancholic swan song of an artist who has outlived his own time.

Mann died in Zurich on 12 August 1955 at eighty years of age, just two days after being elected to the Peace Class of the Order *Pour le mérite* by West Germany. Almost half a century after his decease, his artistic works have strengthened their reputation as masterpieces of world literature. While Mann's essays will most likely never rank as highly as his novels and novellas, they certainly hold their own in the history of German nonfiction; moreover, together with his letters and diaries, they are among the most compelling historical documents of the twentieth century. The S. Fischer publishing house is in the process of issuing a new edition of his collected works in more than fifty volumes, with *Buddenbrooks* as the first volume, to commemorate Mann's one-hundred-twenty-fifth birthday. The new English translations of his novels and novellas will make his works accessible to more American readers as well. In the 1990s, several comprehensive biographies of Mann have appeared both in German and in English. However, no single account of his life and works will ever solve the mystery of his creativity and of his intellect—it is his own works that will captivate readers for many generations to come.

Letters:

Briefe an Paul Amann 1915–1952, edited by Herbert Wegener (Lübeck: Schmidt-Römhild, 1959);

Thomas Mann–Karl Kerényi: Gespräch in Briefen, edited by Karl Kerényi (Zurich: Rhein, 1960);

Thomas Mann an Ernst Bertram: Briefe aus den Jahren 1910–1955, edited by Inge Jens (Pfullingen: Neske, 1960);

Briefe, 1889–1955, 3 volumes, edited by Erika Mann (Frankfurt am Main: Fischer, 1961–1965);

Thomas Mann–Heinrich Mann: Briefwechsel 1900–1949, edited by Hans Wysling (Frankfurt am Main: Fischer, 1968; enlarged, 1984); translated by Don Reneau, Richard Winston, and Clara Winston as

Letters of Heinrich and Thomas Mann, 1900–1949 (Berkeley: University of California Press, 1998);

Letters of Thomas Mann, 1889–1955, edited and translated by Richard and Clara Winston (London: Secker & Warburg, 1970; New York: Knopf, 1971);

Thomas Mann: Briefwechsel mit seinem Verleger Gottfried Bermann Fischer 1932–1955, edited by Peter de Mendelssohn (Frankfurt am Main: Fischer, 1973);

Hermann Hesse–Thomas Mann: Briefwechsel, edited by Anni Carlsson and Volker Michels (Frankfurt am Main: Suhrkamp, 1975; revised and enlarged, 1999); first edition translated by Ralph Manheim as *The Hesse / Mann Letters, 1910–1955* (New York: Harper & Row, 1975);

An Exceptional Friendship: The Correspondence of Thomas Mann and Erich Kahler, translated by Richard and Clara Winston (Ithaca, N.Y. & London: Cornell University Press, 1975);

Thomas Mann: Briefe an Otto Grautoff, 1894–1901, und Ida Boy-Ed, 1903–1928, edited by de Mendelssohn (Frankfurt am Main: Fischer, 1975);

Die Briefe Thomas Manns: Regesten und Register, 5 volumes, edited by Hans Bürgin, Hans-Otto Mayer, and Yvonne Schmidlin (Frankfurt am Main: Fischer, 1976–1987);

Thomas Mann–Alfred Neumann: Briefwechsel, edited by de Mendelssohn (Darmstadt: Schneider, 1977);

Briefwechsel mit Autoren, edited by Wysling (Frankfurt am Main: Fischer, 1988);

Dichter oder Schriftsteller?: der Briefwechsel zwischen Thomas Mann und Josef Ponten 1919–1930, edited by Wysling and Werner Pfister (Bern: Francke, 1988);

Thomas Mann und Alfred Baeumler: eine Dokumentation, edited by Marianne Baeumler, Hubert Brunträger, and Hermann Kurzke (Würzburg: Königshausen & Neumann, 1989);

Jahre des Unmuts: Thomas Manns Briefwechsel mit Rene Schickele, 1930–1940, edited by Wysling and Cornelia Bernini (Frankfurt am Main: Klostermann, 1992);

Thomas Mann–Agnes E. Meyer: Briefwechsel, 1937–1955, edited by Hans Rudolf Vaget (Frankfurt am Main: Fischer, 1992);

Thomas Mann–Erich von Kahler, Briefwechsel, 1931–1955, edited by Michael Assmann (Hamburg: Luchterhand, 1993);

Thomas Mann–Félix Bertaux: Correspondence, 1923–1948, edited by Biruta Cap (New York: Peter Lang, 1993);

Thomas Mann, Käte Hamburger: Briefwechsel, 1932–1955, edited by Hubert Brunträger (Franfurt am Main: Klostermann, 1999).

Interviews:

Frage und Antwort: Interviews mit Thomas Mann 1909–1955, edited by Volkmar Hansen and Gert Heine (Hamburg: Knaus, 1983).

Bibliographies:

Hans Bürgin, *Das Werk Thomas Manns,* edited by Walter A. Reichart and Erich Neumann (Frankfurt am Main: Fischer, 1959);

Georg Potempa, ed., *Thomas Mann: Beteiligung an politischen Aufrufen und anderen kollektiven Publikationen: eine Bibliographie* (Morsum: Cicero, 1988);

Potempa, *Thomas Mann-Bibliographie: Das Werk,* 2 volumes (Morsum: Cicero, 1992, 1997);

Potempa, *Thomas Mann: Konkordanzen der Bibliographien zur Primärliteratur* (Morsum: Cicero, 1993).

Biographies:

Klaus Mann, *The Turning-Point: Thirty-Five Years in This Century* (New York: Fischer, 1943);

Viktor Mann, *Wir waren fünf: Bildnis der Familie Mann* (Konstanz: Südverlag, 1949);

Hans Mayer, *Thomas Mann: Werk und Entwicklung* (Berlin: Volk und Welt, 1950);

Erika Mann, *The Last Year of Thomas Mann,* translated by Richard Graves (New York: Farrar, Straus & Cudahy, 1958);

Julia Mann, *Aus Dodos Kindheit* (Konstanz: Rosgarten-Verlag, 1958);

Klaus Schröter, ed., *Thomas Mann in Selbstzeugnissen und Bilddokumenten* (Reinbeck: Rowohlt, 1964);

Eike Midell, *Thomas Mann: Versuch einer Einführung in Leben und Werk* (Leipzig: Reclam, 1966);

J. P. Stern, *Thomas Mann* (London & New York: Columbia University Press, 1967);

Hans Bürgin and Hans-Otto Mayer, *Thomas Mann: A Chronicle of His Life,* translated by Eugene Dobson (University: University of Alabama Press, 1969);

Schröter, ed., *Thomas Mann im Urteil seiner Zeit* (Hamburg: Wegner, 1969);

André von Gronicka, *Thomas Mann: Profile and Perspectives* (New York: Random House, 1970);

Katia Mann, *Unwritten Memories,* translated by Hunter and Hildegarde Hannum (New York: Knopf, 1975);

Peter de Mendelssohn, *Der Zauberer: Das Leben des deutschen Schriftstellers Thomas Mann,* 3 volumes (Frankfurt am Main: Fischer, 1975–1996);

Inge Diersen, *Thomas Mann: Episches Werk, Weltanschauung, Leben* (Berlin: Aufbau, 1975);

Nigel Hamilton, *The Brothers Mann: The Lives of Heinrich and Thomas Mann, 1871–1950, 1875–1955* (New Haven: Yale University Press, 1979);

Richard Winston, *Thomas Mann: The Making of an Artist, 1875–1911* (New York: Knopf, 1981);

Eberhard Hilscher, *Thomas Mann: Sein Leben und sein Werk* (Berlin: Das europäische Buch, 1983);

Marcel Reich-Ranicki, *Thomas Mann and His Family,* translated by Ralph Manheim (London: Collins, 1989);

Thomas Sprecher, *Thomas Mann in Zürich* (Zurich: Neue Zürcher Zeitung, 1992);

Hans Wysling and Yvonne Schmidlin, eds., *Thomas Mann: ein Leben in Bildern* (Zurich: Artemis, 1994);

Klaus Harpprecht, *Thomas Mann: eine Biographie* (Reinbek bei Hamburg: Rowohlt, 1995);

Ronald Hayman, *Thomas Mann: A Biography* (New York: Scribners, 1995);

Donald Prater, *Thomas Mann: A Life* (Oxford & New York: Oxford University Press, 1995);

Anthony Heilbut, *Thomas Mann: Eros and Literature* (New York: Knopf, 1996);

Erika Mann, *Mein Vater, der Zauberer,* edited by Irmela von der Lühe and Uwe Naumann (Reinbek bei Hamburg: Rowohlt, 1996);

Hans Wisskirchen, *Spaziergänge durch das Lübeck von Heinrich und Thomas Mann* (Zurich: Arche, 1996);

Hermann Kurzke, *Thomas Mann: Das Leben als Kunstwerk: eine Biographie* (Munich: Beck, 1999);

Wisskirchen, *Familie Mann* (Reinbek bei Hamburg: Rowohlt, 1999).

References:

Dieter W. Adolphs, *Literarischer Erfahrungshorizont: Aufbau und Entwicklung der Erzählperspektive im Werk Thomas Manns* (Heidelberg: Winter, 1985);

T. E. Apter, *Thomas Mann: The Devil's Advocate* (New York: New York University Press, 1979);

Hendrik Balonier, *Schriftsteller in der konservativen Tradition: Thomas Mann 1914–1924* (Frankfurt am Main: Lang, 1983);

Reinhard Baumgart, *Das Ironische und die Ironie in den Werken Thomas Manns* (Munich: Hanser, 1964);

Baumgart, *Selbstvergessenheit: drei Wege zum Werk: Thomas Mann, Franz Kafka, Bertolt Brecht* (Munich: Hanser, 1989);

Michael Beddow, *Thomas Mann, Doctor Faustus* (Cambridge & New York: Cambridge University Press, 1994);

Gunilla Bergsten, *Thomas Mann's Doctor Faustus: The Sources and Structure of the Novel,* translated by Krishna Winston (Chicago & London: University of Chicago Press, 1969);

Jeffrey B. Berlin, ed., *Approaches to Teaching Mann's Death in Venice and Other Short Fiction* (New York: Modern Language Association, 1992);

Harold Bloom, ed., *Thomas Mann* (New York: Chelsea House, 1986);

Bloom, ed., *Thomas Mann's The Magic Mountain* (New Haven, Conn.: Chelsea House, 1986);

Beatrix Bludau, Eckhard Heftrich, and Helmut Koopmann, eds., *Thomas Mann 1875–1975: Vorträge in München, Zürich, Lübeck* (Frankfurt am Main: Fischer, 1977);

Bernhard Blume, *Thomas Mann und Goethe* (Bern: Francke, 1949);

Karl Werner Böhm, *Zwischen Selbstzucht und Verlangen: Thomas Mann und das Stigma Homosexualität: Untersuchungen zu Frühwerk und Jugend* (Wurzburg: Königshausen & Neumann, 1991);

Hubert Brunträger, *Der Ironiker und der Ideologe: die Beziehungen zwischen Thomas Mann und Alfred Baeumler* (Würzburg: Königshausen & Neumann, 1993);

Francis Bulhof, *Transpersonalismus und Synchronizität: Wiederholung als Strukturelement in Thomas Manns "Zauberberg"* (Groningen: Van Dederen, 1966);

James Cleugh, *Thomas Mann: A Study* (New York: Russell, 1933);

Peter de Mendelssohn, ed., *Thomas Mann: 1875/1975* (Munich: Moos, 1975);

Deutsche Blätter (Santiago de Chile), special supplement, "Huldigung an Thomas Mann zum 70. Geburtstag–Homenaje a Thomas Mann," 3 (May/June 1945);

Ulrich Dittmann, *Sprachbewußtsein und Redeform im Werk Thomas Manns: Untersuchungen zum Verhältnis des Schriftstellers zur Sprachkrise* (Stuttgart: Kohlhammer, 1969);

Stephen D. Dowden, ed., *A Companion to Thomas Mann's The Magic Mountain* (Columbia, S.C.: Camden House, 1999);

John F. Fetzer, *Changing Perceptions of Thomas Mann's Dr. Faustus: Criticism, 1947–1992* (Columbia, S.C.: Camden House, 1996);

Fetzer, *Music, Love, Death, and Mann's Doctor Faustus* (Columbia, S.C.: Camden House, 1990);

Ignace Feuerlicht, *Thomas Mann* (New York: Twayne, 1968);

Martin Flinker, ed., *Hommage de la France à Thomas Mann à l'occasion de son 80e anniversaire* (Paris: Flinker, 1955);

Christoph Geisler, *Naturalismus und Symbolismus im Frühwerk Thomas Manns* (Bern & Munich: Francke, 1971);

Germanic Review, special Mann issue, 25 (December 1950);

Harvey Goldman, *Max Weber and Thomas Mann: Calling And The Shaping of The Self* (Berkeley: University of California Press, 1988);

Goldman, *Politics, Death, and the Devil: Self and Power in Max Weber and Thomas Mann* (Berkeley: University of California Press, 1992);

Bernd Hamacher, *Thomas Manns letzter Werkplan "Luthers Hochzeit": Edition, Vorgeschichte und Kontexte* (Frankfurt am Main: Klostermann, 1996);

Käthe Hamburger, *Thomas Manns biblisches Werk: Der Joseph-Roman, die Moses-Erzählung "Das Gesetz"* (Munich: Nymphenburger Verlagshandlung, 1981);

Gerhard Härle, *Die Gestalt des Schönen: Untersuchung zur Homosexualitätsthematik in Thomas Manns Roman "Der Zauberberg"* (Königstein: Hain, 1986);

Härle, *Männerweiblichkeit: zur Homosexualität bei Klaus und Thomas Mann* (Frankfurt am Main: Athenäum, 1988);

Härle, ed., *Heimsuchung und süsses Gift: Erotik und Poetik bei Thomas Mann* (Frankfurt am Main: Fischer, 1992);

Henry Hatfield, *From the Magic Mountain: Mann's Later Masterpieces* (Ithaca, N.Y. & London: Cornell University Press, 1979);

Hatfield, *Thomas Mann: An Introduction to His Fiction* (New York: New Directions, 1962);

Hatfield, ed., *Thomas Mann: A Collection of Critical Essays* (Englewood Cliffs, N.J.: Prentice-Hall, 1964);

Hellmut Haug, *Erkenntnisekel: Zum frühen Werk Thomas Manns* (Tübingen: Niemeyer, 1969);

Eckhard Heftrich, *Geträumte Taten: Joseph und seine Brüder* (Frankfurt am Main: Klostermann, 1993);

Heftrich, *Zauberbergmusik: Über Thomas Mann* (Frankfurt am Main: Klostermann, 1975);

Heftrich and Koopmann, eds., *Thomas Mann und seine Quellen: Festschrift für Hans Wysling* (Frankfurt am Main: Klostermann, 1991);

Erich Heller, *The Ironic German: A Study of Thomas Mann* (Boston & Toronto: Little, Brown, 1958);

Margit Henning, *Die Ich-Form und ihre Funktion in Thomas Manns "Doktor Faustus" und in der deutschen Literatur der Gegenwart* (Tübingen: Niemeyer, 1966);

Frank Donald Hirschbach, *The Arrow and the Lyre: A Study of the Role of Love in the Works of Thomas Mann* (The Hague: Nijhoff, 1955);

R. J. Hollingdale, *Thomas Mann: A Critical Study* (Cranbury, N.J.: Associated University Press, 1971);

Klaus W. Jonas, *Fifty Years of Thomas Mann Studies: A Bibliography of Criticism* (Minneapolis: University of Minnesota Press, 1955);

Jonas, ed., *Die Thomas-Mann-Literatur*, 2 volumes (Berlin: Schmidt, 1972, 1979); volume 3, edited by

Jonas and Koopmann (Frankfurt am Main: Klostermann, 1997);

Fritz Kaufman, *Thomas Mann: The World as Will and Representation* (Boston: Beacon, 1957);

Ernst Keller, *Der unpolitische Deutsche: Eine Studie zu den "Betrachtungen eines Unpolitischen" von Thomas Mann* (Bern & Munich: Francke, 1965);

Helmut Koopmann, *Die Entwicklung des "intellektualen" Romans bei Thomas Mann* (Bonn: Bouvier, 1962);

Koopman, *Der schwierige Deutsche: Studien zum Werk Thomas Manns* (Tübingen: Niemeyer, 1988);

Koopman, *Thomas Mann: Konstanten seines literarischen Werkes* (Göttingen: Vandenhoeck, 1975);

Koopman, ed., *Thomas Mann* (Darmstadt: Wissenschaftliche Buchgesellschaft, 1975);

Koopman, ed., *Thomas-Mann-Handbuch* (Stuttgart: Kröner, 1990);

Børge Kristiansen, *Thomas Manns Zauberberg und Schopenhauers Metaphysik,* revised and enlarged edition (Bonn: Bouvier, 1986);

Hermann Kurzke, *Auf der Suche nach der verlorenen Identität: Thomas Mann und der Konservatismus* (Würzburg: Königshausen & Neumann, 1980);

Kurzke, *Thomas Mann: Epoche–Werk–Wirkung,* third edition (Munich: Beck, 1997);

Kurzke, *Thomas-Mann-Forschung 1969–1976: Ein kritischer Bericht* (Frankfurt am Main: Fischer, 1977);

Herbert Lehnert, *Thomas Mann: Fiktion, Mythos, Religion* (Stuttgart: Kohlhammer, 1965);

Lehnert, *Thomas-Mann-Forschung: Ein Bericht* (Stuttgart: Metzler, 1969);

Lehnert, "Thomas Mann in Exile 1933–1938," *Germanic Review,* 38 (1963): 277–294;

Lehnert and Peter C. Pfeiffer, eds., *Thomas Mann's Doctor Faustus: A Novel at the Margin of Modernism* (Columbia, S.C.: Camden House, 1991);

Frederick Alfred Lubich, *Die Dialektik von Logos und Eros im Werk von Thomas Mann* (Heidelberg: Winter, 1986);

Martin H. Ludwig, *Thomas Mann: Gesellschaftliche Wirklichkeit und Weltsicht in den Buddenbrooks* (Hollfeld: Beyer, 1979);

Georg Lukács, *Essays on Thomas Mann,* translated by Stanley Mitchell (London: Merlin Press, 1964; New York: Grosset & Dunlap, 1965);

Judith Marcus, *Georg Lukács and Thomas Mann: A Study in the Sociology of Literature* (Amherst: University of Massachusetts Press, 1987);

E. L. Marson, *The Ascetic Artist: Prefigurations in Thomas Mann's "Der Tod in Venedig"* (Bern, Frankfurt am Main & Las Vegas: Peter Lang, 1979);

Harry Matter, *Die Literatur über Thomas Mann: Eine Bibliographie 1896–1969,* 2 volumes (Berlin & Weimar: Aufbau, 1972);

James R. McWilliams, *Brother Artist: A Psychological Study of Thomas Mann's Fiction* (Lanham, Md.: University Press of America, 1983);

Gertrude Michielsen, *The Preparation of the Future: Techniques of Anticipation in the Novels of Theodor Fontane and Thomas Mann* (Bern, Frankfurt am Main & Las Vegas: Peter Lang, 1978);

Michael Minden, ed., *Thomas Mann* (London & New York: Longman, 1995);

Modern Language Notes, special issue, "Thomas Mann, 1875–1975," 90, no. 3 (1975);

Ken Moulden and Gero von Wilpert, eds., *Buddenbrooks-Handbuch* (Stuttgart: Kröner, 1988);

Charles Neider, ed., *The Stature of Thomas Mann* (New York: New Directions, 1947);

Neue Rundschau (Stockholm), special issue, "Sonderausgabe zu Thomas Manns 70. Geburtstag" (6 June 1945);

Hans W. Nicklas, *Thomas Manns Novelle "Der Tod in Venedig": Analyse des Motivzusammenhangs und der Erzählstruktur* (Marburg: Elwerz, 1968);

Ronald Peacock, *Das Leitmotiv bei Thomas Mann* (Bern: Haupt, 1934);

Heinz-Peter Pütz, *Kunst und Künstlerexistenz bei Nietzsche und Thomas Mann: Zum Problem des ästhetischen Perspektivismus in der Moderne* (Bonn: Bouvier, 1963);

Pütz, *Thomas Mann und die Tradition* (Frankfurt am Main: Athenäum, 1971);

T. J. Reed, *Death in Venice: Making and Unmaking a Master* (New York: Twayne / New York : Maxwell Macmillan, 1994);

Reed, *Thomas Mann: The Uses of Tradition,* revised edition (Oxford: Clarendon Press, 1996);

Joachim Rickes, *Der sonderbare Rosenstock: eine werkzentrierte Untersuchung zu Thomas Manns Roman Königliche Hoheit* (Frankfurt am Main & New York: Peter Lang, 1998);

Hugh Ridley, *Thomas Mann: Buddenbrooks* (Cambridge & New York: Cambridge University Press, 1987);

Klaus-Jürgen Rothenberg, *Das Problem des Realismus bei Thomas Mann: Zur Behandlung der Wirklichkeit in den "Buddenbrooks"* (Cologne & Vienna: Böhlau, 1969);

Heinz Sauereßig, *Die Entstehung des Romans Der Zauberberg: Zwei Essays und eine Dokumentation* (Biberach: Wege und Gestalten, 1965);

Sauereßig, ed., *Besichtigung des Zauberbergs* (Biberach: Wege und Gestalten, 1974);

Jürgen Scharfschwerdt, *Thomas Mann und der deutsche Bildungsroman: Eine Untersuchung zu den Problemen einer literarischen Tradition* (Stuttgart: Kohlhammer, 1967);

Oskar Seidlin, *Von Goethe zu Thomas Mann: Zwölf Versuche* (Göttingen: Vandenhoeck, 1963);

Sinn und Form, special Mann issue (1965);

Ellis Shookman, *Thomas Mann's Death in Venice: A Novella and Its Critics* (Columbia, S.C.: Camden House, 1999);

Martin Swales, *Buddenbrooks: Family Life as the Mirror of Social Change* (Boston: Twayne, 1991);

Richard Thieberger, *Der Begriff der Zeit bei Thomas Mann: Vom Zauberberg zum Joseph* (Baden-Baden: Kunst und Wissenschaft, 1952);

John C. Thirwall, *In Another Language: A Record of the Thirty-Year Relationship between Thomas Mann and His English Translator, Helen Tracy Lowe-Porter* (New York: Knopf, 1966);

Thomas Mann Jahrbuch (Frankfurt am Main: Klostermann, 1988–);

Frédérick Tristan, ed., *Thomas Mann: Cahier dirigé par Frédérick Tristan* (Paris: Edition de l'Herne, 1973);

Hans Rudolf Vaget, *Thomas Mann: Kommentar zu sämtlichen Erzählungen* (Munich: Winkler, 1984);

Vaget and Dagmar Barnouw, *Thomas Mann: Studien zu Fragen der Rezeption* (Bern & Frankfurt am Main: Peter Lang, 1975);

Hermann Weigand, *Thomas Mann's Novel "Der Zauberberg"* (New York & London: Appleton-Century, 1933);

Weimarer Beiträge, special Mann issue, 21, no. 9 (1975);

George Wenzel, ed., *Betrachtungen und Überblicke: Zum Werk Thomas Manns* (Berlin & Weimar: Aufbau, 1966);

Wenzel, ed., *Thomas Mann zum Gedenken* (Potsdam: Thomas-Mann-Arbeitskreis des Kulturbundes zur demokratischen Erneuerung Deutschlands, 1956);

Wenzel, ed., *Vollendung und Größe Thomas Manns: Beiträge zu Werk und Persönlichkeit* (Halle: Sprache und Literatur, 1962);

Hermann Wiegmann, *Die Erzählungen Thomas Manns: Interpretationen und Realien* (Bielefeld: Aisthesis, 1992);

Wissenschaftliche Zeitschrift der Friedrich-Schiller-Universität Jena, Gesellschafts- und Sprachwissenschaftliche Reihe, special Mann issue, 25, no. 3 (1976);

Dierk Wolters, *Zwischen Metaphysik und Politik: Thomas Mann Roman "Joseph und seine Brüder" in seiner Zeit* (Tübingen: Niemeyer, 1998);

Hans Wysling, *Narzissmus und illusionäre Existenzform: zu den Bekenntnissen des Hochstaplers Felix Krull,* second edition (Frankfurt am Main: Klostermann, 1995);

Wysling, *Thomas Mann heute: Sieben Vorträge* (Bern & Munich: Francke, 1976);

Michael Zeller, *Bürger oder Bourgeois? Eine literatur-soziologische Studie zu Thomas Manns "Buddenbrooks" und Heinrich Manns "Im Schlaraffenland"* (Stuttgart: Klett, 1976).

Papers:

Thomas Mann's papers are in the Thomas Mann Collection, Yale University; the Thomas-Mann-Archiv, Berlin; the Thomas-Mann-Archiv, Lübeck; the Sammlung Ida Herz, Nuremberg; and the Sammlung Hans-Otto-Meyer, Düsseldorf. The main center for Thomas Mann research is the Thomas-Mann-Archiv, Eidgenössische Technische Hochschule Zürich, Schönberggasse 15, CH-8001 Zurich. The Thomas-Mann-Archiv publishes the *Blätter der Thomas Mann Gesellschaft Zürich* and the *Thomas-Mann-Studien.*

Robert Musil

(6 November 1880 –15 April 1942)

Michael W. Jennings
Princeton University

This entry originally appeared in DLB 81: Austrian
Fiction Writers, 1875–1913.

BOOKS: *Die Verwirrungen des Zöglings Törleß* (Vienna:
Wiener Verlag, 1906); translated by Ernst Kaiser
and Eithne Wilkins as *Young Törless* (London:
Secker & Warburg, 1955; New York: Pantheon,
1955);

Vereinigungen: Zwei Erzählungen (Berlin: Fischer, 1911)–
comprises "Die Vollendung der Liebe," "Die Versuchung der stillen Veronika";

Die Schwärmer: Schauspiel in drei Aufzügen (Dresden: Sibyl-
len, 1921); translated by Andrea Simon as *The
Enthusiasts* (New York: Performing Arts Journal
Publications, 1983);

Die Portugiesin (Berlin: Rowohlt, 1923);

Grigia: Novelle (Potsdam: Müller, 1923);

Vinzenz und die Freundin bedeutender Männer (Berlin:
Rowohlt, 1924);

Drei Frauen: Novellen (Berlin: Rowohlt, 1924; enlarged,
Reinbek: Rowohlt, 1968);

Rede zur Rilke-Feier in Berlin am 16. Januar 1927 (Berlin:
Rowohlt, 1927);

Der Mann ohne Eigenschaften: Roman, 3 volumes (volumes
1 and 2, Berlin: Rowohlt, 1930–1933; volume 3,
edited by Martha Musil, Lausanne: Imprimerie
Centrale, 1943); translated by Kaiser and Wilkins
as *The Man without Qualities,* 3 volumes (London:
Secker & Warburg, 1953–1960; New York: Coward-McCann, 1953–1960);

Nachlaß zu Lebzeiten (Zurich: Humanitas, 1936); translated by Peter Wortsman as *Posthumous Papers of a
Living Author* (Hygiene, Colo.: Eridanos Press,
1987);

Über die Dummheit (Vienna: Bermann-Fischer, 1937);

Gesammelte Werke in Einzelausgaben, edited by Adolf Frisé,
3 volumes (Hamburg: Rowohlt, 1952–1957);

Das hilflose Europa: Drei Essays (Munich: Piper, 1961);

Aus den Tagebüchern (Berlin: Suhrkamp, 1963);

Tonka, and Other Stories, translated by Wilkins and Kaiser
(London: Secker & Warburg, 1965); republished

Robert Musil (photograph by Staub)

as *Five Women* (New York: Delacorte, 1966)–comprises translations of *Drei Frauen* and *Vereinigungen;*

Theater: Kritisches und Theoretisches (Reinbek: Rowohlt,
1965);

Der deutsche Mensch als Symptom: aus dem Nachlaß, edited by
Karl Corino, Elisabeth Albertsen, and Karl Dinklage (Reinbek: Rowohlt, 1967);

Die Amsel: Bilder (Stuttgart: Reclam, 1967);

Sämtliche Erzählungen, edited by Frisé (Reinbek: Rowohlt, 1968);

Three Short Stories, edited by Hugh Sacker (London: Oxford University Press, 1970);

Tagebücher, edited by Frisé, 2 volumes (Reinbek: Rowohlt, 1976);

Gesammelte Werke in neun Bänden, edited by Frisé, 9 volumes (Reinbek: Rowohlt, 1978–1981);

Beitrag zur Beurteilung der Lehren Machs, edited by Frisé (Reinbek: Rowohlt, 1980); translated by Kevin Mulligan as *On Mach's Theories* (Washington, D.C.: Catholic University of America Press / Munich: Philosophia, 1983);

Selected Writings, edited by Burton Pike (New York: Continuum, 1986).

Edition in English: *The Man without Qualities,* two volumes, translated by Sophie Wilkins (New York: Knopf, 1995).

PERIODICAL PUBLICATIONS: "Politisches Bekenntnis eines jungen Mannes," *Die Weißen Blätter,* 1, no. 3 (1913): 237–244;

"Anmerkung zu einer Metaphysik," *Die neue Rundschau,* (April 1914);

"Skizze der Erkenntnis des Dichters," *Summa,* 1918;

"Die Nation als Ideal und als Wirklichkeit," *Die neue Rundschau,* (December 1921);

"Symptomen-Theater," *Der neue Merkur,* 6, no. 3 (1922): 179–186; no. 10/12 (1923): 587–594;

"Isis und Osiris," *Die neue Rundschau,* 34, no. 5 (1923): 464;

"Das Fliegenpapier," *Das Tage-Buch,* 4, no. 4 (1923): 122–123;

"Robert Müller," *Das Tage-Buch,* 5, no. 37 (1924): 1300–1304;

"Zur deutschen Literatur: Aus dem Nachruf für Rilke," *Die literarische Welt,* 3, no. 4 (1927): 1;

"Literat und Literatur: Randbemerkungen dazu," *Die neue Rundschau,* 42, no. 9 (1931): 390–412.

Robert Musil belongs to that small group of twentieth-century novelists who strove to capture in fictional form the definitive image of their age. His early works, the novel *Die Verwirrungen des Zöglings Törleß* (The Confusions of Young Törless, 1906; translated as *Young Törless,* 1955) and the novella collection *Vereinigungen* (Unions, 1911; translated in *Tonka, and Other Stories,* 1965), are unsurpassed examples of an innovative, modernist prose style adequate to the representation of complex psychological states. Like his contemporaries James Joyce, Thomas Mann, and Marcel Proust, Musil gradually broadened the scope of his literary investigations to include an entire society. His achievement in

some ways parallels that of another contemporary, the painter Wassily Kandinsky: both brought an exceptionally thorough training in philosophy and the physical sciences to the practice of art, and both turned that education to a revolutionary end. Just as Kandinsky opened the way for nonrepresentational painting in the twentieth century, Musil in *Der Mann ohne Eigenschaften* (1930–1943; translated as *The Man without Qualities,* 1953–1960) pointed the modern novel on its path beyond narrative. In this novel Musil emerges as the twentieth century's greatest ironist and one of its premier writers.

Musil's paternal grandfather, Matthias Musil, was born into a peasant family and used his training as a military physician to rise into the bourgeoisie. Musil also had a paternal uncle and several maternal uncles and cousins who became high-ranking staff officers in the imperial army.

His father, Alfred Musil, was trained as an engineer. He worked in Klagenfurt, where Musil was born in 1880; in Komotau, Bohemia; in Steyr, Upper Austria; and achieved appointment as a Professor at the Technical Institute at Brünn (now Brno, Czech Republic) in Moravia in 1891. Alfred Musil regarded family life, and in particular attention to Robert, as impediments to his research. The author of a long list of scholarly works and a reliable servant of the emperor, he was elevated to the lower nobility in 1917. Alfred Musil clearly furnished a model for certain prominent characteristics in his son: the exactitude with which he analyzed even the most apparently marginal of his insights and observations and the compulsive necessity to work and to write.

The father's "soft, easily intimidated disposition" was balanced by a mother, Hermine Bergauer Musil, who was passionate, emotional, and often willful. Early in her marriage she entered into a relationship with another engineer, Heinrich Reiter, which was unusual even in the open atmosphere of late imperial Austria. Reiter accompanied the family on their vacations and finally moved in with them in 1900. Musil's writings reflect the family tensions which resulted from this ménage à trois, as well as the atmosphere of illicit eroticism that must have dominated the household.

For the most part Musil distinguished himself both in the classroom and on the athletic field; he was given, though, to lapses into lethargy. When he was about ten he began to reject his parents' values. His father, an advocate of late-nineteenth-century rational positivism, remained basically irreligious and apolitical throughout his life; Musil was critical of what he called an "aufgeklärtes Haus, in dem man nichts glaubt und nichts als Ersatz dafür gibt" (enlightened household, in which no one believes in anything and no one offers anything as a replacement for that belief). His mother's relationship to Reiter became an increasingly bitter source of contention.

His mother solved the problem by convincing Alfred Musil to send Robert to the military academies at Eisenstadt from 1892 to 1894, and at Mährisch-Weisskirchen from 1894 to 1897. Those five years saw an unbroken series of academic successes but also a growing impatience with the intellectual limits of military life. Nevertheless, Musil enrolled in September 1897 in the Technical Military Academy in Vienna, where he intended to study ballistics. In early 1898 he transferred to his father's institution, the Technical Institute in Brünn.

Musil had begun to write in 1897. These sketches, aesthetic pronouncements, reflections on his experiences, and excerpts from his reading were recorded in a scrics of notcbooks, a practicc Musil would continuc for the rest of his life. Published in full for the first time in 1976, the notebooks comprise over fifteen hundred pages of closely set text.

Musil's initial literary efforts were colored by his reading of Austrian authors such as Peter Altenberg and Richard Schaukal, but also by his enthusiasm for Stéphane Mallarmé, Ralph Waldo Emerson, and, above all, Friedrich Nietzsche. The problem of possibility, the key category of Musil's mature work, derives from his reading of Nietzsche. "Das Charakteristische liegt darin," Musil wrote, "daß er sagt: dies könnte so sein und jenes so. Und darauf könnte man dies und darauf jenes bauen. Kurz: er spricht von lauter Möglichkeiten, lauter Combinationen, ohne eine einzige uns wirklich ausgeführt zu zeigen" (It is characteristic of Nietzsche that he says: this could be so and that could be so. And one could build one thing on one assumption, something else on the latter. In short: he speaks of pure possibilities, pure combinations, without showing us how any single one could really be carried out). Also, the experimental quality of Musil's fiction is the result of a deep reading of Nietzsche's call for new forms of language capable of denoting previously uncharted aspects of human life. Finally, Musil began to grope toward a new conception of the self predicated on Nietzsche's attack on the notion of subjectivity. In his early notebooks Musil stresses the discontinuous, random aspects of human thought and action, anticipating his later notion of a man wholly without salient or defining characteristics.

Musil remarks in the notebooks that no one, including the naturalists, has yet found the form to capture the random, structureless nature of life, while still representing it as beautiful. He styles himself "Monsieur le vivisecteur," a Nietzschean "brain-man" who dissects contemporary culture. Yet this cold modernism is tempered in Musil's early years by a form of the neoromanticism so prevalent in Austria at the turn of the century. Even while thinking of himself as a remorseless vivisectionist, Musil portrays himself at a window, observing the change from day to night. This is the classical romantic figure for a voyage beyond reason into the depths of the unconscious. The notebooks contain excerpts from Eduard von Hartmann's pioneering study of the unconscious, from Ricarda Huch, from Novalis, and from Franz von Baader, one of the central figures in the importation of mystical motifs into German romantic thought.

Musil's fascination with romanticism finally took a different turn from that of other writers of his generation. Whereas for Hugo von Hofmannsthal, for example, the mixture of hermetic symbols derived from French symbolism and German romantic thinking on the possibilities dormant in the unconscious was of primary interest, for Musil it was the more radical fringe of romanticism, the direct line to the German mystical tradition, which was of concern. "Das Ich des Cartesius ist der letzte feste Punkt im erkenntnis-kritischen Gedankengange, es ist die gewisse augenblickliche Einheit. Das Ich, von dem die Mystiker sprechen, ist das komplexe Ich" (The Cartesian "ego" is the last firm point in the epistemological train of thought, it is the certain, momentary unity. The "I" of which the mystics speak is the complex I). Often portrayed as a dualist who opposed mystical cognition to discursive reason, Musil actually wanted to explore the relations between reason and those aspects of life that are not yet penetrated by reason. Convinced of the importance of mystical experience, Musil tried to discover a rational faculty capable of articulating that experience. His wariness of instrumental reason is characteristic of many of the best minds of his generation, including Mann, Benedetto Croce, Georg Lukács, Walter Benjamin, and Ernst Bloch.

The early years of the century were marked for Musil by attempts to break free of his social class. An attempt to become the theater critic of the Brünn socialist paper and the establishment of a long-term relationship with Herma Dietz, a girl of proletarian origins, were steps on Musil's path to the idiosyncratic form of socialism that characterized his later political convictions. A year of compulsory military service in 1901–1902 also left its mark on Musil: he retained throughout the rest of his life something of the posture and dress of the young officer who is also a dandy. The officer's ethos had one other effect: Musil plunged headlong into a series of sexual adventures. One of the key themes of his notebooks from then on was sensuality.

In 1902, with the help of his father, Musil obtained a position as an assistant in one of the leading mechanical engineering laboratories in Europe, that of Julius Carl von Bach at the Technical University in Stuttgart. Ironically, it was there, at the height of his career as an engineer, that Musil made the final turn from science and toward humanism. In the winter of 1902–1903 he formulated a plan to study philosophy and psychology in Berlin. He also began writing a novel.

Die Verwirrungen des Zöglings Törleß, one of the great first novels in German, is nominally a portrait of adolescent life in a military academy. Such "school stories" were a common literary form at the time, with Frank Wedekind's *Frühlings Erwachen* (1891; translated as *The Awakening of Spring*, 1909), Emil Strauß's *Freund Hein* (Friend Hein, 1902), and Hermann Hesse's *Unterm Rad* (Under the Wheel, 1906; translated as *The Prodigy*, 1957) the most obvious comparisons. Yet this generic description hardly does justice to Musil's work. While *Die Verwirrungen des Zöglings Törleß* does depict the coming to adolescent consciousness of the young cadet Törleß, with the attendant painful experiences of awakening sexuality and the struggle for independent critical intelligence, the significance of the concepts and problems with which Törleß struggles far exceed those normally confronted in a novel of puberty.

Sent to an exclusive academy, Törleß enters into a difficult relationship with two classmates, Beineberg and Reiting. The three discover that another, Basini, has stolen from his peers, and they turn this knowledge into a form of brute power over him. Humiliated, subjected to a series of homoerotic episodes, and finally tortured, Basini confesses to the theft in order to escape Beineberg and Reiting. Törleß occupies an ambivalent position in these events. He is frequently present while Basini is being tortured, and he has his own homosexual encounters with him in the absence of Beineberg and Reiting. Yet Törleß remains removed from his fellows and their activities by his confusions, by a pervasive sense that the world before him and the world within himself somehow remain inaccessible to him. "Nein, ich irrte mich nicht, wenn ich von einem zweiten, geheimen, unbeachteten Leben der Dinge sprach! . . . Es ist etwas Dunkles in mir, unter allen Gedanken, das ich mit den Gedanken nicht anmessen kann, ein Leben, das sich nicht in Worten ausdrückt und das doch mein Leben ist" (No, I wasn't wrong when I spoke of a second, secret unnoticed life in things! . . . There is something dark in me, beneath all thoughts, that I can't measure with thoughts, a life that can't be expressed in words and yet is still my life). When Törleß flees from the academy, he is running less from his role in the Basini affair than the intensity and complexity of his attempt to regulate his thoughts and feelings. He realizes that his two worlds—that which is "hell" (bright) and "täglich" (everyday) and that which is "leidenschaftlich, nackt, vernichtend" (passionate, naked, destructive)—intermingle, that he must search "nach einer Brücke, einem Zusammenhange, einem Vergleich . . . zwischen sich und dem, was wortlos vor seinem Geiste stand" (for a bridge, a context, a comparison—between himself and that which stood wordlessly before his spirit). Much of the book's power stems from the carefully maintained tension between the naturalistic description of milieu and action on the one hand and the variegated portrayal of Törleß's inner life on the other. The novel frequently verges on essayism in its attempts to describe the relations between thought and feeling; the narration spreads out into a morass of description, the formal counterpart to Törleß's reaction to events. Yet the world around Törleß is evoked in a way that is convincing and occasionally frightening.

For all its originality, Musil's novel is a product of its age. The intensive preoccupation with eroticism ties it closely to the work of the psychologist Sigmund Freud, the writer Arthur Schnitzler, and the painters Gustav Klimt and Egon Schiele; and its exploration of the limits of language's ability to give shape to inner states points to the more general "crisis of language" perceived in turn-of-the-century Austria, a crisis best described in Hofmannsthal's "Ein Brief" (1905; translated as "The Letter," 1942). The novel's mixture of innovation and tradition led to an enthusiastic critical response. Alfred Kerr's long review on 21 December 1906 in the Berlin journal *Der Tag* was the first of a long series of positive evaluations. Volker Schlöndorff's 1965 film adaptation attests to the staying power of Musil's first work.

When *Die Verwirrungen des Zöglings Törleß* was published in 1906, Musil had been studying in Berlin for three years under the philosopher and psychologist Carl Stumpf, whose early integration of experimental psychology and phenomenology paved the way for Gestalt psychology.

One of Musil's earliest Berlin acquaintances, Johannes von Allesch, also a student of Stumpf's, proved to be a lifelong friend. Musil also began to move in Berlin's literary circles. Through his contact with Kerr he came to know the writers associated with the journals *Hyperion* and *Die neue Rundschau*. It was also through Kerr that Musil met Martha Marcovaldi.

Martha Heimann Marcovaldi had been raised in an assimilated Jewish family in Berlin, had studied painting with Lovis Corinth, and had attracted considerable attention in the Italian artistic community. When Musil met her in 1907 at the Baltic resort town of Graal, she had been married twice and was separated from her second husband. Seven years older than Musil, Martha was an outspoken feminist and an advocate of sexual freedom. Musil's letters to his parents and to Allesch were soon full of references to Martha as his "married sister."

Musil concluded his studies in 1908 with a dissertation on the Austrian physicist and philosopher Ernst Mach. His interest in Mach centered on Mach's pragmatic, experimental approach to science: in attempting to overcome the Kantian dualism which divides the world into phenomena and noumena and which had dominated nineteenth-century German science, Mach had asserted that only sensations are real; the distinction between mind and body is inappropriate, since neither is anything more than "a relatively stable complex of sensational elements."

More than two years passed between the completion of the dissertation and the publication of Musil's next works, the novellas "Die Vollendung der Liebe" (translated as "The Perfecting of a Love," 1965) and "Die Versuchung der stillen Veronika" (translated as "The Temptation of Quiet Veronika," 1965), which were published together in 1911 under the title *Vereinigungen* (Unions). The long gestation of these short works points to Musil's struggle to discover a formal vocabulary adequate to the expression of his ideas on psychology, one in which the boundary between affectivity and rationality becomes indiscernible. The result was two of the most radically experimental of all modernist texts.

The plots of the novellas consist of little more than the evocation of situations which are in themselves quite banal. In "Die Vollendung der Liebe" a woman travels by train to a distant town and betrays her husband. In "Die Versuchung der stillen Veronika" a woman rejects the advances of the more spiritual of two brothers in favor of his animalistic sibling; ultimately, even this temptation is rejected in favor of an autoeroticism of astonishing intensity. In place of action and even of character, the reader encounters an attempt to make transparent the awakening self-consciousness of the protagonists. The stream of traditional narrative comes to a standstill, to be replaced by a unique combination of figurative language and philosophical reflection on the psyche: "Sie wußte nicht mehr, was sie dachte, nur ganz still faßte sie eine Lust am Alleinsein mit fremden Erlebnissen; es war wie ein Spiel leichtester, unfaßbarster Trübungen und großer, danach tastender, schattenhafter Bewegungen der Seele. Sie suchte sich ihres Mannes zu erinnern, aber sie fand von ihrer fast vergangenen Liebe nur eine wunderliche Vorstellung wie von einem Zimmer mit lange geschlossenen Fenstern" (She no longer knew what she thought; a desire for being alone with alien experiences quietly took hold of her. It was like the play of the lightest, most incomprehensible disturbances and of great, shadowy movements of the soul grasping for them. She tried to remember her husband, but she found of her almost past love only a curious image, like that of a room with long-shut windows). In *Vereinigungen* Musil experiments with the possibilities of the simile, a device which captures the neither/nor, both/and character of certain moments of being. In "Die Vollendung der Liebe" alone Musil employs 337 similes; the combination of this thicket of similes and the static, patient narrative representation of consciousness lends to these novellas a unique, oneiric quality. "Die Versuchung der stillen Veronika" and "Die Vollendung der Liebe" are not easy to read: they have the density and complexity of other classic works of high modernism, qualities reminiscent of Arnold Schönberg's music or Pablo Picasso's cubist canvases.

In 1910, thirty years old and the author of two books, Musil was still being supported by his parents. Contemplating marriage and seeing no possibility of earning a living through literary activity in Berlin, Musil returned with extreme reluctance to Vienna, where his father had obtained for him a position in the library of the Technical Institute. Musil began work in January 1911; he and Martha were married in April, after her divorce became final. What was to have been a brief return home turned into three years of well-paid but exhausting and frustrating employment. The period during which he worked at the library is marked by repeated bouts of illness and by an almost total failure to write; there are almost no notebook entries for the year 1912. Musil's isolation and resentment were exacerbated not only by his work; he also found intellectual life in Vienna stifling. The efflorescence of the arts which Vienna had enjoyed at the turn of the century was on the wane; the important strands of German-language modernism were tied increasingly to Berlin.

Between 1911 and 1921, when his drama *Die Schwärmer* (translated as *The Enthusiasts,* 1983) appeared, Musil completed not a single work of imaginative literature. This is not to say that he was not productive: the notebooks again swelled with drafts and materials for an array of later works. In 1913 alone Musil published eleven important essays in the journals *Der lose Vogel* and *Die neue Rundschau*. One of the finest of these, "Über Robert Musils Bücher" (On Robert Musil's Books), offers incisive commentary on his first two books. These essays show Musil moving away from the fascination with decadence and aestheticism that had characterized his early work and, indeed, that of his generation. The relentless introspection of *Die Verwirrungen des Zöglings Törleß* and *Vereinigungen* would be supplanted in years to come by a highly developed sense for the dialectical relationship between the individual and society. In the essay "Moralische Fruchtbarkeit"(Moral Fruitfulness) Musil hints at a new understanding of literature as a tool of moral and not simply psychological analysis. Such essays as "Politisches Bekenntnis eines jungen Mannes"(Political Confession of a Young Man, 1913) and "Europäertum, Krieg, Deutschtum" (Europeanness, War, Germanness) point toward Musil's new consciousness of political responsibility. These attempts at political commentary lack the sovereign overview of the European situation, not to mention the ironic, brilliantly satirical voice, that characterizes both his later essays and *Der Mann ohne Eigenschaften,* but they mark Musil's emergence as a writer who would devote enormous time and energy to cultural politics.

Musil visited Berlin whenever possible, and the chance to return for what promised to be an extended stay came in December 1913. Samuel Fischer, the publisher of *Die neue Rundschau,* the leading literary journal of the period, offered Musil a position as editor. An emergent German modernism, with authors such as Mann and Hesse, appeared in its pages alongside the work of established foreign writers such as Hofmannsthal, Oscar Wilde, Maurice Maeterlinck, and Henrik Ibsen. Musil immediately resigned from the Austrian civil service and returned to Berlin. The new position proved short-lived.

A reserve officer since 1911, Musil was called up at the outbreak of World War I in August 1914. He served with distinction, first in command of a company and then as a battalion adjutant, in the southern Tirol. His notebook entries for these years alternate between a sober recounting of the routine of military service and the reworking of individual observations for subsequent use in literary works; the novellas *Grigia* (1923; translated, 1965) and *Die Portugiesin* (1923; translated as "The Lady from Portugal," 1965) are deeply colored by Musil's war experiences. In March 1916 his active service was brought to an end by a stomach ulcer; after six weeks in various hospitals he was reassigned to the headquarters of the southwestern army group in Bozen, Austria.

Musil's new assignment was as editor of the *Soldaten-Zeitung,* the soldiers' newspaper of the southwest front. The "newspaper" had been little more than a newsletter containing a loose and anecdotal collection of reports from the front; under Musil's direction, and at the express wish of the general staff, the publication took shape as a professional and highly sophisticated organ for the dissemination of information and propaganda. Charged primarily with combating irredentism and the spread of nationalist tendencies among the troops of the Austrian Empire, the journal far exceeded

this mandate in the prominent position it lent to social and political criticism. Musil's contributions are notable largely for the first appearance of that mode of literature which was to characterize much of his later production: satire. The command to discontinue the paper came in March 1917. Musil was transferred to Adelsberg, near Trieste, and then to Vienna, where he served on the staff of the propaganda journal *Heimat.* He remained an imperial functionary until December 1918, transferring his services to the new Austrian Republic in January 1919. His work in the press section of the Austrian Foreign Office consisted of collecting and indexing newspaper reports relevant to the foreign policy of the new nation. Musil ironically styled himself the "archivist of newspaper cuttings," a vocation which found its way into *Der Mann ohne Eigenschaften.*

The end of the war, the dissolution of the empire, and the creation of the Austrian Republic prompted a series of essays from Musil. "Skizze der Erkenntnis des Dichters" (Sketch of the Poet's Cognition, 1918), "Der Anschluß an Deutschland" (The Union with Germany, 1919), and "Die Nation als Ideal und als Wirklichkeit" (The Nation as Ideal and as Reality, 1921) are political essays only in a limited sense. They deal, to be sure, with the contemporary problems confronting Europe—the peace of Versailles, the establishment of a new identity for Austria, the nature of the state under democracy—but Musil's approach remains that of a humanist primarily concerned with cultural issues. For Musil, the question of European direction remains a radically individual one: what will the new European person be like? Individuals, not collectives and certainly not states, which are for Musil little more than abstract categories invested with brutal power, will determine the shape of the new civilization. Musil described his politics as "conservative anarchy"; he held that the state could only serve as a repressive force, inhibiting the individual's development.

Musil regarded himself as the heir of Emerson and Nietzsche, the advocate of the strong, self-reliant individual; his repeated insistence on the absolute uniqueness of each human, however, points to a Kierkegaardian element in his thinking which is seldom acknowledged. In differentiating the poet from the man of reason Musil points to the ability to recognize the radically individual, the exception to the rule of regularity and law. In "Skizze der Erkenntnis des Dichters" he distinguishes between the "ratioïd" and the "non-ratioïd," that is, the distinction between that which is susceptible to rational understanding due to its regularity and that which eludes rational comprehension because of its endlessly variable and individual character. The poet must above all be sensitive to individual human reactions to the world and to other humans. "Die Aufgabe ist: immer neue Lösungen, Zusammenhänge, Konstellationen, Variable zu entdecken, Prototypen von Geschehensabläufen hinzustellen, lockende Vorbilder, wie man Mensch sein kann, den inneren Menschen *erfinden*" (The task is: always to discover new solutions, contexts, constellations, variables, to suggest prototypes of courses of events, to *invent* the inner man, tempting models of how to be human).

In August 1920 Musil gave up his job in the Foreign Ministry and returned to Berlin, hoping to find an editorial position similar to the one he had occupied so briefly at *Die neue Rundschau* before the war. He met with a total lack of success. Neither Fischer at *Die neue Rundschau* nor any other publisher was in a financial position to enlarge his staff. Musil returned to Vienna in September and assumed a position in the War Ministry, charged with the education and integration of Austrian officers into the ways of a peacetime democratic army. This well-paid job made relatively few demands on his time, making possible a great outpouring of literary production. Musil's position was, however, eliminated for budgetary reasons in December 1922, although his salary was paid until the following summer.

While working at the ministry, Musil also assumed the role of theater critic. The sixty reviews he wrote for the *Prager Presse* between March 1921 and August 1922 and for the Prague magazine *Bohemia* between September and December 1922 constitute one of the most remarkable bodies of theater criticism of the century. The additions to Musil's salary from his literary activity contributed to an unprecedented and never wholly recaptured period of economic security. He was able to buy a large, comfortable apartment at Rasumofskygasse 20 in Vienna's third district.

In the drama *Die Schwärmer,* for which he won the Kleist Prize, and in the novella collection *Drei Frauen* (Three Women, 1924), Musil establishes several of the experimental, prototypical forms of life called for in his essays. He also, for the first time, allows for the interaction of these inventions and a sociopolitical environment.

Like the novellas in *Vereinigungen, Die Schwärmer* turns on a banal situation: seduction and the breakup of marriage. Anselm, a philosophical seducer, has taken Regine away from her husband, the professor Josef. They have sought refuge in the home of Regine's sister Maria and her husband Thomas. Thomas, the protagonist, is a typical Musil hero, characterized by pure possibility, unpredictability, the refusal to be frozen by concepts or ideals. "Ideale sind toter Idealismus" (Ideals are dead idealism), he says. This same lack of qualities applies to his opponent, Anselm. The two figures are finally differentiated by their language: Thomas emerges as the champion of an intellect intensely, almost morbidly aware of the complexity of human ethical behavior and of the difficulty of finding linguistic forms adequate to express this complexity; Anselm shows himself in his speech to be less fluid than simply unstable, less distanced from the conventions and repression of society than compulsively driven to destroy them. Thomas's language retains a beautifully unfixed quality which stands in stark contrast to the increasingly debased language of the seducer Anselm.

In Josef, Musil caricatures the unthinking bourgeois adherence to moral norms and ideals. Josef is the twentieth-century man of reason who applies tools appropriate to the ratioïd realm to the non-ratioïd sphere of morals. Stringent moral judgments blind him to the complexity and nuance which characterize the relationships in the play. Stader, the detective hired by Josef to unmask Anselm as a fraud and thus to bring Regine back, represents an even more extreme example of the dangers arising from the false application of rationality. A "scientific" detective, Stader believes that the problems of life can be sorted out through the amassing and analysis of factual evidence. The judgmental hubris of Josef and Stader contrasts sharply with Thomas's absolute refusal to judge. Even as Anselm gradually takes Maria away from him, Thomas proves incapable of stopping or condemning him.

Musil's play stands alongside Hofmannsthal's *Der Schwierige* (The Difficult One, 1921) as one of the great German-language comic dramas of the century. Like Hofmannsthal, Musil examines the position of the outsider in a society unwilling to address the changes necessitated by new political, social, and economic conditions, a society content to fall back on the mores and language of the fallen empire. The challenges for theatrical performance of Musil's play are considerable: the almost total absence of action, the extreme subtlety of the language, and the play's resolutely cerebral nature. The first production, in Berlin in 1929, was a bowdlerization, with the play cut in half. Musil, enraged, afterwards stormed through the Berlin streets and could be calmed only as morning approached. The play has since then found its place in the repertory of Germany's and Austria's major theaters.

Although *Drei Frauen* appeared three years later than *Die Schwärmer,* the materials for its three novellas came from Musil's past. "Tonka" makes use of notebook entries from as early as 1903, while sketches for *Grigia* and *Die Portugiesin*–both of which appeared separately in 1923–appear in the notebooks from the war years. The novellas have a common theme: in each, a strong male protagonist discovers in the encounter with the titular female figure what Musil calls "der andere Zustand" (the other condition), the dimension of life which is "beweglich, singulär, irrational" (mobile, singular, irrational). In each case eroticism is the trigger for this turn inward to an epiphanic mystical experience. The three novellas can be seen as Musil's answer to his own challenge, expressed in "Skizze der Erkenntnis des Dichters," to "invent the inner human"; the protagonists represent three radically different experimental instantiations of the "other condition." In search of a firm sense of identity, each of the three emerges instead with a deep sense of the shifting, deeply unsettling character of the self.

The protagonist of *Grigia,* Homo, is an engineer at work in a remote Italian valley whose inhabitants preserve primitive cultural and social practices. Separated from his wife, he satisfies his sexual desires with Grigia, a peasant woman. His encounters with an eroticism both real and imagined open him to a mystical experience: "Er sank zwischen den Bäumen mit den giftgrünen Bärten aufs Knie, breitete die Arme aus, . . . und ihm war zu Mut, als hätte man ihm in diesem Augenblick sich selbst aus den Armen genommen. Er fühlte die Hand seiner Geliebten in seiner, ihre Stimme im Ohr, alle Stellen seines Körpers waren wie eben erst berührt, er empfand sich selbst wie eine von einem anderen Körper gebildete Form" (He sank to his knees between the trees with the poison-green beards, spread out his arms, . . . and he felt as if someone had at that moment taken him out of his own arms. He felt the hand of his lover in his, her voice in his ear, it was as if every place on his body had just been touched for the first time, he sensed himself as a form shaped by another body). As the subtle negative description of Homo's natural surroundings indicates, though, the preconditions for a productive encounter with the irrational are absent: a parallel is established between the capitalistic exploitation of the valley and its inhabitants on the one hand and Homo's sexual subjugation of Grigia on the other. Homo understands his epiphanic insight as a revelation to him alone, and his messianic pretensions lead him to amorality and to death at the hands of Grigia's husband. In Homo, Musil shows that a mere openness to the irrational is insufficient and dangerous.

"Tonka" is a reworking of Musil's relationship with Herma Dietz between 1905 and 1907. The nameless protagonist, a young engineering student, is confronted with apparently insoluble contradiction: the young proletarian woman with whom he lives has contracted a venereal disease and has become pregnant; for either condition he cannot be responsible, yet she insists that she has never betrayed him. The contradiction between the evidence against Tonka, which from a scientific point of view is decisive, and the protagonist's growing conviction of Tonka's deeply rooted simplicity and honesty leads him to call into question the applica-

bility of rational explanations of the world. He discovers, as will Ulrich in *Der Mann ohne Eigenschaften,* that another world exists, "die wir aber nicht bloß im Herzen tragen oder im Kopf, sondern die genau so wirklich drauen steht wie die geltende" (which we don't merely carry in our heart or in our head, but which stands out there exactly as real as the world in force). He is able to transcend, if only temporarily, the rational limits set to knowledge and to perceive something of that "other world" behind appearances. "Wollen, Wissen und Fühlen sind wie ein Knäuel verschlungen; man merkt es erst, wenn man das Fadenende verliert; aber vielleicht kann man anders durch die Welt gehen als am Faden der Wahrheit? In solchen Augenblicken, wo ihn von allen ein Firnis der Kälte trennt, war Tonka mehr als ein Mädchen, da war sie fast eine Sendung" (Volition, knowledge, and feeling are all intertwined like a knot; one notices this only when one has lost the end of the thread; but is it perhaps possible to go through the world other than on the thread of truth? At such moments, when a varnish of coldness separated him from all others, Tonka was more than a girl; then she was almost a revelation). Of all Musil's texts, "Tonka" employs the most radically innovative use of narrative perspective. The point of view is free-floating, attaching itself now to the protagonist, now to a narrator, now to an unidentifiable perspective–though never to Tonka. This feature, together with the jumbled chronology of the novella, evokes in the reader a sense of the epistemological crisis experienced.

The protagonist of *Die Portugiesin* is Lord von Ketten, a medieval robber knight engaged in an endless and draining war with the neighboring bishop. Having won his wife after an assiduous courtship in her native Portugal, von Ketten has spent all but one day and night of each of the succeeding eleven years away from home. The death of the bishop changes this pattern. Von Ketten's sense of the purpose and meaning of his life had been defined by his war with the bishop; the loss of this meaning is symbolized by von Ketten being bitten by a fly and contracting an apparently fatal illness. The pitiful nature of his new existence is brought home to him as a friend of his wife, recently arrived from Portugal, seems gradually to usurp his place. A soothsayer tells von Ketten that he will be cured only if he accomplishes something. One day a small cat, similarly afflicted with a wasting sickness, enters the castle and draws the sympathy of von Ketten, his wife, and the visitor. Unable to watch it suffer further, von Ketten has it killed. In an apparent attempt to avoid the fate of the cat, von Ketten rises from his bed and tries to scale the sheer cliff below the castle–a superhuman task. When he arrives at the top, he finds his strength and will restored to him. He believes that the stranger may be in his wife's room, and intends to kill him. Instead, he finds her sleeping alone and learns that the visitor has departed.

Die Portugiesin mediates between the negative experience of Homo and the largely positive one of the protagonist of "Tonka." The key feature of the central novella is its undecidability. Musil's irony cuts through the lush, exotic quality of the tale, weighing against the unequivocal interpretation of any of its elements, and in particular of the value assigned to von Ketten's encounter with the "other condition." Of all Musil's texts, *Die Portugiesin* conforms most closely to his own demand for fluidity and lack of definition; the novella stubbornly resists assimilation to a unifying interpretation.

Drei Frauen and *Die Schwärmer* appeared to enthusiastic reviews. Musil, who won the Literature Prize of the City of Vienna in 1924, was again a literary celebrity, an important voice not only in Austria but in Weimar Germany as well. Many of his most significant essays appeared in Weimar journals, and his work has affinities with the best Weimar literature, such as Mann's *Der Zauberberg* (1924; translated as *The Magic Mountain,* 1927) and Alfred Döblin's *Berlin Alexanderplatz* (1929; translated as *Alexanderplatz, Berlin,* 1931);

Yet Musil's inability to secure a living in Germany and his resulting continued presence in Austria exacerbated his innate tendency to play the role of the passive outside observer who felt that his work was "als ein Fremdes bekämpft, mißverstanden, oder gering geschätzt" (contested, misunderstood, or undervalued as something alien).

In contrast to the war and the period immediately following it, when Musil's engagement with his society and culture were intensive, after 1923 his life became synonymous with the writing of his one great novel. The story of this period is largely that of Musil sitting at his desk in the Rasumofskygasse, wrestling with the enormous amount of material he had assembled for the book. The only significant breaks in this routine were periodic difficulties with Ernst Rowohlt, his Berlin publisher. Rowohlt agreed to pay Musil a monthly stipend against the eventual completion of the great novel, and the late 1920s offered the repeated dance of Musil promising the first volume, his dissatisfaction with the finished material, his decision to work on, and Rowohlt's threats to suspend his payments. Musil shared with Proust more than the will to complete a definitive work of art: his habit of returning proofs with new text written in every available space recalls Proust's similarly endless marginal scribbling.

The struggle with the novel and his economic circumstances took a terrible toll on Musil. In 1929 he had a nervous breakdown, complicated by nicotine poisoning. His sessions with Hugo Lukács, an Adlerian ana-

lyst, apparently had some effect, since the novel began to move forward again. The receipt in autumn 1929 of the Gerhart Hauptmann Prize brought confirmation of his stature, but, owing to the German economic crisis, only a fraction of the monetary award found its way to Musil.

The first volume finally appeared in November 1930 to immediate and unanimous critical acclaim. The widespread recognition that *Der Mann ohne Eigenschaften* was the definitive modern German novel led rapidly to the improvement of Musil's financial and emotional situation. The Robert Musil Society, led by Professor Kurt Glaser, the director of the State Art Library in Berlin, was established in 1931 to provide a stipend to allow Musil to work undisturbed on his novel. Musil and Martha moved to Berlin in November 1931. But residence in Berlin, for all its positive aspects, also led to more direct pressure from Rowohlt; the second volume of the novel was published, with some reservations on the part of the author, in March 1933.

In *Der Mann ohne Eigenschaften* Musil attempted to write the representative novel of his era, an all-encompassing account of the situation of the European intellectual in the new social, political, cultural, scientific, and technological conditions at the end of the war. Although the action of the novel takes place in the years 1912 to 1914 in "Kakanien"–Musil's name for Austria under the monarchy–it is clear that nothing less than the fate of the individual in twentieth-century Europe is the focus. Ulrich, the protagonist, is a representative modern individual whose identity and behavior are in constant flux; he has no defining traits and no permanent core. In contrast to those other great encyclopedic novels of high modernism–Joyce's *Ulysses* (1922), Proust's *A la recherche du temps perdu* (1913–1927; translated as *Remembrance of Things Past,* 1922–1931), and *Der Zauberberg*–Musil's novel conceives this erasure of identity, this lack of definition, as something positive and even difficult to attain. Ulrich comes to the realization that the maintenance of *possibility* outweighs any involvement with, and inevitable fixedness within, the real.

The primary sign of the essential fluidity and lack of definition which characterize Ulrich is the stylistic device of essayism. Ulrich is finally nothing more than a momentary nexus in a larger field made up of the prevalent ideas in Western philosophy, politics, psychology, and literature. Essayism is more than a narrative mode; it is the principle of characterization in the novel. "Ungefähr wie ein Essay in der Folge seiner Abschnitte ein Ding von vielen Seiten nimmt, ohne es ganz zu erfassen,–denn ein ganz erfaßtes Ding verliert mit einem Male seinen Umfang und schmilzt zu einem Begriff ein–glaubte [Ulrich], Welt und eigenes Leben am richtigsten ansehen und behandeln zu können"

([Ulrich] believed it was best to regard and treat the world and one's own life approximately as an essay, which examines, in the sequence of its sections, a thing from many sides, without wholly comprehending it—for a thing wholly comprehended instantly loses its contours and melts into a concept).

Der Mann ohne Eigenschaften remains a fragment. The first volume contains two parts. "Eine Art Einleitung" (A Sort of an Introduction) comprises a brief account of Ulrich's early attempt to become a man of significance by beginning, successively, careers as a soldier, an engineer, and a mathematician. The six-hundred-page second part, "Seinesgleichen Geschieht" (Something Like It Happens), shows that the society is in search of that same identity and definition which had been of such importance to the young Ulrich. This part narrates the foundation and activities of the Parallelaktion (Parallel Action), a committee attempting to organize a celebration of the jubilee of Franz Josef's rule that is conceived as a parallel to the celebration of the German Kaiser's reign. Musil depicts a society which is not so much exhausted as ossified, locked by a rigid structure of beliefs onto a path toward war and defeat. The most prominent figure on this vast stage is Ulrich's opponent, the industrialist Arnheim. Like Anselm in *Die Schwärmer,* Arnheim bears a striking resemblance to the protagonist. Like Ulrich, he is concerned with the balance of "Ratio und Seele" (rationality and soul) in human affairs. Unlike Ulrich, though, Arnheim claims to have found that mystical balance; based loosely upon the industrialist and statesman Walther Rathenau, Arnheim becomes the prophet of a new European order. Ulrich's call for the establishment of a secretariat for "Genauigkeit und Seele" (exactitude and soul) is intended as a rebuttal to Arnheim, as an assertion that these matters admit of no definitive resolution.

Ulrich's infrequent attempts to imbue the Parallelaktion with his own lack of principles are not the only suggested alternatives to the present course of society; Moosbrugger, an apparently insane sex murderer, figures as the window onto another possible form of reality: he exists at "the edge of possibility." But all attempts to open the committee to new courses of action meet with defeat. Having received no response to his call for the creation of the secretariat, Ulrich withdraws from the movement into a liaison with his own sister, Agathe. The novel's second volume, which recounts this relationship, is titled "Ins tausendjährige Reich" (Into the Thousand Year Empire).

Ulrich and Agathe voyage together toward a state—the "other condition"—in which exteriority and interiority might be bridged. The other condition is more than mystical ecstasy; it is a form of self-love open to infinite possibility and variation. Ulrich and Agathe are spiritual Siamese twins in whom the separation between individual identities becomes increasingly blurred. Like Moosbrugger, they journey beyond the border of that which is held to be morally permissible. But their actions are less important than their linguistic attempts to get at the essence of their actions. It is not clear whether the completed novel would have included a portrayal of the consummation of their union.

The meaning of the novel turns on the manner in which the reader constructs the connection between the Parallelaktion and Ulrich and Agathe's love. Both are marked by an intense, always frustrated longing for wholeness and unity. Both are possible modes through which to experience the world, to bridge the gap between feeling and perception. The novel exemplifies Lukács's characterization of the path of the European novel from the nineteenth-century "big world" of society and its complicated net of relationships toward the "small world" of the individual and his subjectivity, a movement Lukàcs viewed negatively.

Musil labored in his final years to complete the novel. His papers contain hundreds of pages of fragments and completed chapters which would have gone into the completion of the second volume and into the conclusion, "Eine Art Ende" (A Sort of an Ending). But the resistance to closure evident at every level of the novel—in Ulrich's incompleteness, in the destabilizing effect of the narrator's ironic voice, and in the characteristic eschewal of plot in favor of reflection and analysis—strongly suggest that even a completed *Der Mann ohne Eigenschaften* would have remained radically open. Musil once said that he wanted the novel to end in the middle of a sentence, with a comma.

Hitler's ascent to power in Germany was followed in early summer 1933 by Musil's return to Vienna and to renewed financial worries. The Musil Society ceased to exist, its members either in exile or unable to continue their financial contributions. Voices—among them that of Mann—were immediately raised in support of Musil, and Bruno Fürst was able to form a new Musil Society in Vienna in spring 1934.

In 1935 Musil traveled to Paris to address the International Writers' Congress for the Defense of Culture. His speech met a hostile reception from the largely leftist audience. Somewhat ingenuously, Musil had taken the title of the congress literally and limited himself to the problem of the defense of culture in an age dominated by ideological conflict. He refused to restrict his critique of the dangers of ideology to fascism, and his talk was attacked as an implicit criticism of socialist and communist political activity. Musil's sympathy for socialism could not prevent him from delivering an essentially apolitical speech at a political congress. For him, culture remained the sole repository of hope in the modern world, and any threat to the furtherance of culture was to be scorned. His stance was underlined in 1938 when he turned down an offer by the French Communist Party of a villa.

Soon after his return to Vienna, Musil had again been beset with problems with his health and his psychological state. Dr. Lukács was again able to help him overcome his inhibitions regarding his work, but in 1936 Musil suffered a stroke. Although he recovered to a large extent, he never again felt that his health could support the work he needed to accomplish.

In 1936 appeared Musil's last significant publication, *Nachlaß zu Lebzeiten* (translated as *Posthumous Papers of a Living Author,* 1987), a collection of short pieces most of which had appeared in newspapers and journals. Best known for its inclusion of the novella "Die Amsel" (The Blackbird), *Nachlaß zu Lebzeiten* has been consistently undervalued by Musil's critics and readers. His mastery of the very short prose piece in such texts as "Das Fliegenpapier" (Flypaper) and "Triedere" places him alongside Franz Kafka as the authors who have best opened the short, almost fragmentary sketch to the possibilities of modernity.

In 1937 Musil delivered two of his best-known speeches, "Der Dichter in dieser Zeit" (The Poet in These Times) and *Über die Dummheit* (On Stupidity, 1937), further attempts to define the character of the age and to awaken Europe to the threat posed to its culture. *Über die Dummheit* in particular aroused considerable interest as a definitive characterization of the age; Musil repeated it several times in Vienna, and the Bermann-Fischer Verlag, which had purchased the rights to Musil's works from Rowohlt, published it that same year.

The Anschluß of Austria into the Third Reich occurred in March 1938. That summer, following a visit from a representative of the Propaganda Ministry who requested his services, Musil and Martha quietly left Vienna for Italy, purportedly to restore his health. In September they established themselves in a small hotel in Zurich. Musil continued to labor over the novel, maintaining correspondence with the circle of readers and friends without whose intellectual sustenance he was unable to work, and, as always, seeking financial support. Of Musil's Zurich acquaintances, Pastor Robert LeJeune stands out. LeJeune's aesthetic proclivities and critical insight replaced some of the intellectual and cultural stimulation the Musils had left behind.

Yet the letters and notebooks of the period record Musil's increasing feeling of isolation. Like other German literary figures living in exile, Musil found himself deprived of publishers and readers; his situation was in

many ways worse, though, than that of a Mann or a Bertolt Brecht. Musil's readership had in the best of times been limited to a narrow segment of the intelligentsia. Musil moved again after only ten months in Zurich, this time to Geneva, definitively severing his ties to German-language culture. In Geneva he moved four times in two years in search of ideal working conditions for the completion of his novel. In Zurich there had at least been some connection to the community; in Geneva Musil was alone and unknown. He emerged from his retreat only once, for a reading from his works organized by LeJeune in Winterthur. One of the greatest living German-language authors of his age found fifteen listeners awaiting him. One last hope, for immigration to America, was shattered in 1940: Albert Einstein and Mann attempted to persuade the Rockefeller Foundation to grant Musil a stipend, but since he lacked scholarly credentials, nothing could be done.

Martha Musil found her husband on the floor of the bathroom on 15 April 1942, the victim of a massive stroke. Eight friends attended the funeral, after which Musil was cremated. Martha retained his ashes until her departure for America, when she scattered them in the woods near Geneva.

Musil had worked feverishly on *Der Mann ohne Eigenschaften* to the very end but left behind no indication of how the drafts and completed chapters were to be ordered. Martha published a tentative reconstruction of the continuation of the story of Ulrich and Agathe in 1943. In 1952 Rowohlt published the novel as the first volume of Musil's collected works, edited by Adolf Frisé. This edition, which contains a new ordering of the posthumous material, met with violent criticism from Musil scholars. A third edition, also edited by Frisé, appeared in 1978; it includes a much larger but by no means complete selection from the posthumous papers and still another ordering of the more polished material. A new two-volume English translation of the novel was published by Knopf in 1995; it includes about six hundred pages of material that was not used in the original English edition. The uncertain textual status of Musil's masterpiece has not, however, detracted from its acknowledged position as a major monument of twentieth-century European culture; and the very openness of his novel in its final form will continue to remind Musil's readers that he was the author of the possible.

Letters:

Briefe nach Prag, edited by Barbara Köpplová and Kurt Krolop (Reinbek: Rowohlt, 1971);

Briefe, edited by Adolf Frisé and Murray G. Hall, 2 volumes (Reinbek: Rowohlt, 1981);

Briefe, Nachlese: Dialog mit dem Kritiker Walther Petry, edited by Frisé (Saarbrücken: Internationale Robert-Musil-Gesellschaft, 1994).

Bibliographies:

Ulrich Karthaus, "Musil-Forschung und Musil-Deutung: Ein Literaturbericht," *Deutsche Vierteljahrsschrift für Literaturwissenschaft und Geistesgeschichte,* 39 (1965): 441–483;

Jürgen C. Thöming, *Robert-Musil-Bibliographie* (Bad Homburg: Verlag Dr. Max Gehlen, 1968);

Robert L. Roseberry, *Robert Musil: Ein Bericht* (Frankfurt am Main: Fischer Athenäum Taschenbücher, 1974);

Wolfgang Freese, "Zur neueren Musil-Forschung. Ausgaben und Gesamtdarstellungen," *Text und Kritik,* 21/22 (1983): 86–148.

Biography:

David S. Luft, *Robert Musil and the Crisis of European Culture 1880–1942* (Berkeley: University of California Press, 1980).

References:

Helmut Arntzen, *Musil Kommentar sämtlicher zu Lebzeiten erschienener Schriften außer dem Roman "Der Mann ohne Eigenschaften"* (Munich: Winkler, 1980);

Arntzen, *Musil Kommentar zum Roman "Der Mann ohne Eigenschaften"* (Munich: Winkler, 1982);

Dagmar Barnouw, "Skepticism as Literary Mode: David Hume and Robert Musil," *MLN,* 93 (1978): 852–870;

Gerhart Baumann, *Robert Musil: Zur Erkenntnis der Dichtung* (Berne: Franke, 1965);

Wilfried Berghahn, *Robert Musil in Selbstzeugnissen und Bilddokumenten* (Hamburg: Rowohlt, 1963);

Dorrit Cohn, "Psyche and Space in Musil's 'Die Vollendung der Liebe,'" *Germanic Review,* 49 (1974): 154–168;

Karl Corino, "Ödipus oder Orest? Robert Musil und die Psychoanalyse," *Musil-Studien,* 4 (1973): 123–235;

Karl Dinklage, ed., *Robert Musil: Leben, Werk, Wirkung* (Hamburg: Rowohlt, 1960);

Peter Henninger, *Der Buchstabe und der Geist: Unbewute Determinierung im Schreiben Robert Musils* (Frankfurt am Main: Lang, 1980);

Henninger, "On Literature and Condensation: Robert Musil's Early Novellas," *Glyph,* 5 (1979): 114–132;

Hannah Hickman, *Robert Musil and the Culture of Vienna* (La Salle, Ill.: Open Court, 1984);

Michael Jennings, "Mystical Selfhood, Self-Delusion, Self-Dissolution: Ethical and Narrative Experimentation in Musil's 'Grigia,'" *MAL,* 17, no. 1 (1984): 59–78;

Ernst Kaiser and Eithne Wilkins, *Robert Musil: Eine Einführung in das Werk* (Stuttgart: Kohlhammer, 1962);

Jörg Kühne, *Das Gleichnis: Studien zur inneren Form von Robert Musils Roman "Der Mann ohne Eigenschaften"* (Tübingen: Niemayer, 1968);

Frederick G. Peters, *Robert Musil: Master of the Hovering Life* (New York: Columbia University Press, 1978);

Burton Pike, *Robert Musil: An Introduction to his Work* (Ithaca: Cornell University Press, 1961);

Annie Reniers-Servranckx, *Robert Musil: Konstanz und Entwicklung von Themen, Motiven und Strukturen in den Dichtungen* (Bonn: Bouvier, 1972);

Marie-Louise Roth, *Robert Musil: Ethik und Ästhetik. Zum theoretischen Werk des Dichters* (Munich: List, 1972);

Albrecht Schöne, "Der Gebrauch des Konjunktivs bei Robert Musil," *Euphorion,* 55 (1961): 196–220;

Walter Sokel, "Kleist's *Marquise of O.,* Kierkegaard's *Abraham,* and Musil's *Tonka:* Three stages of the Absurd as the Touchstones of Faith," in *Festschrift für Bernhard Blume: Aufsätze zur deutschen und europäischen Literatur,* edited by Egon Schwarz, Hunter G. Hannum, and Edgar Lohner (Göttingen: Vandenhoeck & Ruprecht, 1967), pp. 323–332;

Sokel, "The Problem of Dualism in Hesse's *Demian* and Musil's *Törless,*" *MAL,* 9, no. 3/4 (1976): 35–42.

Papers:

The Robert Musil Archive is in Klagenfurt, Austria.

Friedrich Nietzsche

(15 October 1844 – 25 August 1900)

Adrian Del Caro
University of Colorado

This entry was updated by Professor Del Caro from his entry in DLB 129:
Nineteenth-Century German Writers, 1841–1900.

BOOKS: *Die Geburt der Tragödie aus dem Geiste der Musik* (Leipzig: Fritzsch, 1872; revised, 1874); revised as *Die Geburt der Tragödie: Oder Griechenthum und Pessimismus. Neue Ausgabe mit dem Versuch einer Selbstkritik* (Leipzig: Fritzsch, 1886); translated by William A. Haussmann as *The Birth of Tragedy* (1909), volume 1 of *The Complete Works of Friedrich Nietzsche,* 18 volumes, edited by Oscar Levy (London: Foulis, 1909–1913);

Unzeitgemäße Betrachtungen. Erstes Stück: David Strau der Bekenner und der Schriftsteller (Leipzig: Fritzsch, 1873); translated by Anthony Ludovici as "Thoughts out of Season: David Strauss the Confessor and the Writer," in volume 4 (1910) of *The Complete Works of Friedrich Nietzsche;*

Unzeitgemäße Betrachtungen. Zweites Stück: Vom Nutzen und Nachtheil der Historie für das Leben (Leipzig: Fritzsch, 1874); translated by Adrian Collins as "On the Use and Disadvantage of History," in volume 5 (1909) of *The Complete Works of Friedrich Nietzsche;*

Unzeitgemäße Betrachtungen. Drittes Stück: Schopenhauer als Erzieher (Chemnitz: Schmeitzner, 1874); translated by Collins as "Schopenhauer as Educator," in volume 5 (1909) of *The Complete Works of Friedrich Nietzsche;*

Unzeitgemäße Betrachtungen. Viertes Stück: Richard Wagner in Bayreuth (Chemnitz: Schmeitzner, 1876); translated by Ludovici as "Richard Wagner in Bayreuth," in volume 4 (1910) of *The Complete Works of Friedrich Nietzsche;*

Menschliches, Allzumenschliches: Ein Buch für freie Geister, 3 volumes (Chemnitz: Schmeitzner, 1878–1880)—includes as volume 2, *Menschliches, Allzumenschliches: Ein Buch für freie Geister. Anhang: Vermischte Meinungen und Sprüche* (1879); as volume 3, *Der Wanderer und sein Schatten* (1880); revised edition, 2 volumes (Leipzig: Fritzsch, 1886); translated by Helen Zimmern and Paul V. Cohn as *Human,*

Nietzsche as a philology professor at the University of Basel, 1872

All-Too-Human, volumes 6 and 7 (1909, 1911) of *The Complete Works of Friedrich Nietzsche;*

Morgenröthe: Gedanken über die moralischen Vorurtheile (Chemnitz: Schmeitzner, 1881; enlarged edition, Leipzig: Fritzsch, 1887); translated by Johanna Volz as *The Dawn of Day* (London: Unwin, 1903; New York: Macmillan, 1903);

Die fröhliche Wissenschaft (Chemnitz: Schmeitzner, 1882; enlarged edition, Leipzig: Fritzsch, 1887); translated by Thomas Common as *The Joyful Wisdom*, in volume 10 (1910) of *The Complete Works of Friedrich Nietzsche;*

Also sprach Zarathustra: Ein Buch für Alle und Keinen, 4 volumes (volumes 1–3, Chemnitz: Schmeitzner, 1883–1884; volume 4, Leipzig: Naumann, 1885); translated by Alexander Tille as *Thus Spake Zarathustra: A Book for All and None* (London: Henry, 1896; New York: Macmillan, 1896);

Jenseits von Gut und Böse: Vorspiel einer Philosophie der Zukunft (Leipzig: Naumann, 1886); translated by Zimmern as *Beyond Good and Evil*, volume 12 (1909) of *The Complete Works of Friedrich Nietzsche;*

Zur Genealogie der Moral: Eine Streitschrift (Leipzig: Naumann, 1887); translated by Haussmann as "A Genealogy of Morals," in *A Genealogy of Morals; Poems*, translated by Haussmann and John Gray (New York: Macmillan, 1897; London: Unwin, 1899);

Der Fall Wagner: Ein Musikanten-Problem (Leipzig: Naumann, 1888); translated by Common as "The Case of Wagner," in *The Case of Wagner, Nietzsche contra Wagner, The Twilight of the Idols, The Antichrist* (London: Henry, 1896; New York: Macmillan, 1896);

Götzen-Dämmerung oder Wie man mit dem Hammer philosophirt (Leipzig: Naumann, 1889); translated by Common as "The Twilight of the Idols," in *The Case of Wagner, Nietzsche contra Wagner, The Twilight of the Idols, The Antichrist;*

Nietzsche contra Wagner: Aktenstücke eines Psychologen (Leipzig: Naumann, 1889); translated by Common as "Nietzsche contra Wagner," in *The Case of Wagner, Nietzsche contra Wagner, The Twilight of the Idols, The Antichrist;*

Nietzsches Werke: Gesamtausgabe, edited by Peter Gast (Leipzig: Naumann, 1892–1894);

Nietzsches Werke: Großoktavausgabe, 15 volumes, edited by the Nietzsche Archive (Leipzig: Naumann, 1894–1904)–includes in volume 8 (1895), "Der Antichrist: Fluch auf das Christenthum," translated by Common as "The Antichrist," in *The Case of Wagner, Nietzsche contra Wagner, The Twilight of the Idols, The Antichrist;* in volume 15 (1901), "Der Wille zur Macht," translated by Ludovici as *The Will to Power*, volumes 15 and 16 (1909, 1910) of *The Complete Works of Friedrich Nietzsche;*

Gedichte und Sprüche, edited by Elisabeth Förster-Nietzsche (Leipzig: Naumann, 1908);

Ecce homo: Wie man wird, was man ist (Leipzig: Insel, 1908); translated by Ludovici as "Ecce Homo," in

The Complete Works of Friedrich Nietzsche, volume 17 (1911);

Friedrich Nietzsche: Werke, 4 volumes, edited by Karl Schlechta (Munich: Hanser, 1954);

Kritische Gesamtausgabe, 30 volumes, edited by Giorgio Colli and Mazzino Montinari (Berlin: De Gruyter, 1967–1978);

Kritische Studienausgabe: Sämtliche Werke, 15 volumes, edited by Colli and Montinari (Berlin & Munich: De Gruyter & Deutscher Taschenbuch Verlag, 1980).

Editions in English: *The Complete Works of Friedrich Nietzsche*, 18 volumes, edited by Oscar Levy (New York: Macmillan, 1909–1911; Edinburgh & London: Foulis, 1909–1913);

The Portable Nietzsche, edited and translated by Walter Kaufmann (New York: Viking, 1954);

The Will to Power, edited by Kaufmann, translated by Kaufmann and R. J. Hollingdale (New York: Random House, 1967);

Basic Writings of Nietzsche, edited and translated by Kaufmann (New York: Modern Library, 1968);

The Gay Science, translated by Kaufmann (New York: Random House, 1974);

Daybreak: Thoughts on the Prejudices of Morality, translated by Hollingdale (Cambridge & New York: Cambridge University Press, 1982);

Untimely Meditations, translated by Hollingdale (Cambridge & New York: Cambridge University Press, 1983)–comprises *David Strauss, the Confessor and the Writer, On the Uses and Disadvantage of History for Life, Schopenhauer as Educator, Richard Wagner in Bayreuth.*

Human, All Too Human, translated by Hollingdale (Cambridge & New York: Cambridge University Press, 1986);

The Poetry of Friedrich Nietzsche, translated by Philip Grundlehner (New York: Oxford University Press, 1986).

Virtually unknown and ignored during his productive life, Friedrich Nietzsche lapsed into insanity in the first days of 1889 and only glimpsed the beginning of his rapid ascent to fame and controversy throughout the world. By 1900 Nietzsche's thoughts were resonating in the works of George Bernard Shaw, Hugo von Hofmannsthal, August Strindberg, and Thomas Mann. The writer who advocated bringing "Heroismus in die Erkenntnis" (heroism into knowledge) waged spirited campaigns against intellectual smugness, metaphysics, Christianity, romanticism, nationalism, idealism, and a host of modern society's chief ills. Nietzsche earned the distinction of being history's most eloquent wielder of the *anti* while, paradoxically, serving as a champion of life-affirmation. To a greater extent than any predecessor Nietzsche elevated philosophical expression to an art. His approach to issues was influenced by comparisons between ancients and moderns; his overriding concern for the condition of the modern individual, forced to come to terms with egalitarian institutions and principles, provides coherence to his writings, which he refused to systematize. Nietzsche rejected the age-old academic standard of comprehensive philosophical systems purporting to illuminate "reality" but resulting only in metaphors; the will to systematize, he said in his typically succinct style, shows a lack of integrity. After a hundred years of debate in a variety of disciplines, Nietzsche's mastery of language and his psychological insights continue to fascinate commentators and expand the horizons of art and theory.

Born on 15 October 1844 in the small town of Röcken, Friedrich Wilhelm Nietzsche (he was named for the Prussian king Friedrich Wilhelm IV, whose birthday he shared) was expected to follow in the footsteps of his father, the Lutheran pastor Karl Ludwig Nietzsche. The father's death in 1849 at thirty-five, due to a condition diagnosed as Gehirnerweichung (softening of the brain), left Nietzsche with his mother, Franziska (née Oehler); his younger sister, Elisabeth; and a brother, born in 1848, who died in 1850. The family resettled in 1850 in nearby Naumburg, where they lived with Nietzsche's grandmother Erdmuthe Nietzsche and two maiden aunts. In Naumburg, Nietzsche was tutored along with two other boys; one of them was Gustav Krug, whose father was a music patron and a friend of the composer Felix Mendelssohn-Bartholdy. Nietzsche's earliest exposure to music took place in this setting. His boyhood penchant for setting psalms to music and writing religious poems stands in stark contrast to his writing in 1888 of "Der Antichrist" (1895; translated as "The Antichrist," 1896). Beginning around his twelfth year Nietzsche was stricken by severe headaches; the condition grew worse as he aged.

After three years at the local gymnasium Nietzsche transferred in 1858 to the Latin school Schulpforta, from which such notables as Friedrich Gottlieb Klopstock and Johann Gottlieb Fichte had graduated. There he received rigorous training in Latin, Greek, and German. Throughout his adolescence Nietzsche's major interests were music and literature; by the time he left Schulpforta for the University of Bonn in 1864 he was no longer committed to theological study, and a year later he informed his mother that he was switching to philology. Under the auspices of growing Prussian strength, Germany was on the road to nationhood at the same time that Nietzsche was entering adulthood; the sense of destiny fermenting

within the diverse German lands was bound to infect Nietzsche's generation.

At Bonn, Nietzsche joined the Franconia, a fraternity popular among aspiring philologists, but demonstrated his independence by preferring lectures and discussions to the drinking and carousing of his peers. Nietzsche behaved more soberly and thoughtfully than other young men; his sense of responsibility probably resulted from being the only male in his family. During a visit to nearby Cologne in 1865 he engaged a guide to take him on a walking tour of the city; at the end of the tour he instructed the man to take him to a restaurant. Instead, Nietzsche found himself in a bordello, where, as he explained to his friend Paul Deussen the next day, he was at such a loss when surrounded by the scantily clad prostitutes that he instinctively approached the piano (the only creature in the place with a soul, he said), struck a few chords, and, as if liberated by the music, walked out. This incident was richly detailed and embellished by Thomas Mann in his novel *Doktor Faustus* (1947; translated as *Doctor Faustus*, 1948), in which the protagonist, Adrian Leverkühn, is partly based on Nietzsche. It is possible that Nietzsche later visited a brothel and contracted syphilis: the disease that plunged him into madness may have resulted from an infection sustained during his student years.

When the prominent philologist Friedrich Ritschl left Bonn in 1865 for the University of Leipzig, Nietzsche also transferred to Leipzig and began a close association with Ritschl. Following Ritschl's advice, Nietzsche helped to establish a philology club at Leipzig. Beside the real mentor, Ritschl, stood a spiritual mentor who was to compete with the philologist for Nietzsche's attention: Arthur Schopenhauer, whose masterpiece, *Die Welt als Wille und Vorstellung* (1819; translated as *The World as Will and Idea*, 1883–1886), Nietzsche discovered in a secondhand bookstore. Nietzsche served a compulsory stint in the military from 1867 to 1868, but he injured himself while mounting his horse and required several weeks to convalesce. When he made the acquaintance of Richard Wagner in 1868, through a meeting arranged by Ritschl's wife, Sophie, the major ingredients of Nietzsche's future philosophical thought were in place: philology, with a focus on Greek drama; philosophy in the manner of the Romantic Schopenhauer; and the music of Wagner, whom Nietzsche came to regard as the apotheosis of Schopenhauerian genius. Nietzsche's interest in literature and music had seduced him away from theology, and now a growing passion for philosophy and music was beginning to weaken his commitment to philology.

During his years at Leipzig, Nietzsche began to see himself as a continuator of the tradition of German idealism fueled by the philosophy of Immanuel Kant, promulgated in the highly idealistic writings of Friedrich Schiller and Schopenhauer, and culminating in Wagner's concept of the Gesamtkunstwerk (total work of art). Nietzsche was blessed with two powerful and influential patrons, each representing a different side of his character: Ritschl appealed to the scholar in Nietzsche, who was a gifted student of languages and an ardent admirer of ancient Greek culture; Wagner appealed to the artist in him and also satisfied his craving for philosophical substance, since Wagner was not only a composer but also a theorist and avowed Schopenhauerian. It began to seem to Nietzsche that philology was too narrow a field for him, and he entertained the idea of writing a dissertation on the concept of the organic in philosophy since Kant.

Whatever wavering Nietzsche might have experienced came to an end in 1869, when Ritschl recommended him for a position at the University of Basel. Nietzsche had had articles published in a philology journal, but he had not written a dissertation; yet he became a professor of Greek language and literature in February 1869. In the spring he was awarded the doctoral degree by the University of Leipzig.

His teaching duties in Basel included advanced courses at the university on the literature and philosophy of the Greeks and language courses at the local gymnasium. He volunteered to serve in the Franco-Prussian War in 1870 but spent less than a month as a medical orderly before contracting diphtheria. After convalescing in Naumburg for a month he returned to Basel. Nietzsche's firsthand experience of the ravages of warfare would not keep him from claiming in *Also sprach Zarathustra* (1883–1885; translated as *Thus Spake Zarathustra,* 1896) that it is not the good cause that justifies war but the good war that justifies the cause—one of the many transvaluations or reversals of values that are signatures of his later philosophical writings.

The Basel years are considered Nietzsche's early Romantic phase; many of his writings from this period are devoted to Wagner's rising fame, Schopenhauerian philosophy, and Germany's emergence as a military and political power. Wagner was living in Tribschen, Switzerland, where Nietzsche frequently visited him. Nietzsche still felt constrained by his profession; his application in 1871 for a vacancy in philosophy at Basel was politely declined.

The tension that to Nietzsche was a fundamental principle of all life was at work in him before it surfaced in his writings, and he was fond of pointing out that his writings spoke only of things he had overcome. His first major published work, *Die Geburt der Tragödie aus dem Geiste der Musik* (The Birth of Tragedy from the Spirit of Music, 1872; translated as *The Birth of Tragedy,* 1909),

embodied this tension and immediately gained notoriety for Nietzsche. The book, for which Wagner had secured his own publisher, is dedicated to Wagner and contains a panegyric foreword about him. Ostensibly a work of classical philology, the treatise combines Schopenhauerian, Wagnerian, and earlier theoretical Romantic elements in a complex argument intended to demonstrate the relationship between music and word that culminated among the early Greeks in the tragic dramas of Aeschylus and Sophocles. The relationship was represented in the worship of Dionysus, the god of wine, regeneration, death, madness, and resurrection. During the Dionysian festivals, revelers became free of their individual identities and merged with the Primal Unity, Nietzsche's metaphor for all-encompassing nature. The Dionysian principle represents the unrestrained and unbounded life force; on the other hand, the Apollinian principle derived from the worship of Apollo and the other Olympian deities represents the calm, individuated, and orderly perception of the universe. These principles interact to sustain a tension, and tragedy evolved from a form of worship into the highest expression of Greek art and a direct reflection of the Greek soul. In the tragedies of Aeschylus and Sophocles, but no longer in those of Euripides, Nietzsche saw the vitality and wisdom of mythology contributing to the Greeks' sophisticated understanding of the world as a fertile, burgeoning chaos. The triumphant sublimation momentarily reconciling the states of individuation and Primal Unity was celebrated in tragic drama, wherein the hero symbolizes the fate of Dionysus. Ultimately, Nietzsche argues for a rebirth of tragedy and a revitalization of modern culture through the music of Wagner. Nietzsche is writing in the tradition of German Romantic theory, which was sympathetic toward mythologically based cultures and their unifying spirit, as opposed to knowledge-based, optimistic, and theoretical cultures that contribute to fragmentation. In *Die Geburt der Tragödie* Nietzsche's main quarrel is with Socrates, whom he sees as a metaphor for the momentous historical shift from mythology to cognition: Nietzsche opposes the symbol of the dying Socrates, who sacrificed himself for knowledge, with the symbol of the music-playing Socrates, who acknowledged the importance of the Dionysian aspect of Greek culture by playing the flute. German writers, philosophers, and poets such as Fichte, Schiller, Friedrich Schlegel, and Friedrich Hölderlin had addressed themselves to the role that Germany and moderns in general would play in the wake of the French Revolution and the rapidly vanishing old world order. Nietzsche adopted the model of cultural unity suggested by the ancient Greeks at the precise time that Germany was unified and became a modern state with the establishment of the Second Reich in 1871.

Responses to the publication of *Die Geburt der Tragödie* were swift and emotional; by the time Nietzsche again received such attention he would be insane and thus unaware of it. Rivals attacked the work as a product of the imagination and ridiculed it as Wagnerian propaganda; Wagnerians and Nietzsche's friends came to its defense. But Nietzsche had not intended to win the favor of his colleagues; he wanted to make a case for the culture of antiquity as a rich source of inspiration for moderns who were increasingly falling under the yoke of utilitarian values, specialization, alienation, and fragmentation. He had presented the ancient Greek aesthetic through the eyes not only of the philologist but those of the philosopher Schopenhauer and the artist Wagner as well. One effect of this painful intellectual debut was a rift between Nietzsche and Ritschl, who dismissed the book as "geistreiche Schwiemelei" (genial dissipation). Nietzsche's resentment toward his profession and its constraints deepened; he also resented Wagner for having lured him into the dangerous zone of artistic metaphysics. Years later, when bitter enmity had developed between the two, Nietzsche would refer to Wagner as a clever old Minotaur who feasted on German youths delivered to him as human sacrifices. For his part, he would never again sacrifice his independence. His later theory of resentment as the motivating factor in "slave morality" carried, as usual, the bitter flavor of those obstacles that Nietzsche had had to overcome in himself.

The controversy surrounding *Die Geburt der Tragödie* subsided, but Nietzsche had become aware of the distance between himself and his society. Migraine headaches and their accompanying nausea continued to afflict him, and writing became a means of therapy. The four book-length essays collectively titled *Unzeitgemäße Betrachtungen* (Untimely Meditations, 1873–1876) were devoted to issues of the day rather than to classical philology. Nietzsche felt out of step with the times, but this feeling had been disguised in *Die Geburt der Tragödie* because of his devotion to Wagner. The age was rife with stirrings of nationalism and cultural chauvinism brought on by Prussia's decisive defeat of France and by the unification of Germany under Prussian hegemony. Nietzsche continued to visit Wagner and write favorably about him, but he observed with disdain that Wagner was allowing himself to become the symbol of a new Germany that represented a self-righteous blend of Christian and nationalistic sentiments. The Wagner to whom Nietzsche had devoted himself had been a cosmopolitan spirit struggling against the smugness of his age, a fellow Schopenhauerian whose aesthetic vision had been animated by respect for the culture of pagan Greece.

The most original and widely studied essay of *Unzeitgemäße Betrachtungen* is the second volume, *Vom Nutzen und Nachtheil der Historie für das Leben* (1874; translated as "On the Use and Disadvantage of History," 1909), a treatise on modern society's preoccupation with history. The health of individuals and of peoples, Nietzsche maintains, is determined not only by the historical sense, recollection, but also by the unhistorical sense, the ability to forget. Moreover, the unhistorical sense is more important because it is the foundation of human growth, enabling us to experience change unencumbered by the static effect of the past. The best sense, however, would be the suprahistorical: historical people look to the past and believe in progress, while unhistorical types concentrate on deeds and act without guidance from the past. The suprahistorical type would combine both, bringing together a healthy regard for deeds as well as the ability to bring memory to bear on great historical events. *Vom Nutzen und Nachtheil der Historie für das Leben* was clearly influenced by the writings of Johann Wolfgang von Goethe and the example he provided as an individual; Nietzsche says that the goal of humanity cannot lie at its end but only in its highest representatives, such as Goethe, Michelangelo, Julius Caesar, or William Shakespeare.

Since 1873 Nietzsche had suffered increasingly from migraines, and on the advice of his family and friends he decided to find a suitable spouse to look after him. In 1876 he proposed marriage to Mathilde Trampedach, a woman he had known for only a few hours, through an intermediary; she declined. That year his illness became severe; his sister Elisabeth had to care for him, as she had done on several occasions since 1873. In October he was granted a year's leave from the university.

The final volume of *Unzeitgemäße Betrachtungen, Richard Wagner in Bayreuth* (1876; translated, 1910), concerns the transformation of Bayreuth into a Wagnerian mecca and festival center, and Wagner's place in German cultural history. Though the work is favorable to the composer, Nietzsche's experiences at the first festival in 1876 were grueling and tiresome. Surrounded by Wagnerian devotees and the increasing nationalism of the German scene, he felt out of place.

When the first volume of *Menschliches, Allzumenschliches* (1878–1880; translated as *Human, All-Too-Human,* 1909, 1911) was published, Nietzsche's situation had changed considerably. First, the friendship with Wagner was over, and hostility would prevail between Wagner and Nietzsche until Wagner's death in 1883. *Menschliches, Allzumenschliches* announced his debut as a writer no longer affiliated with Wagner, since all the writings

Nietzsche had undertaken between 1872 and 1876 had been devoted to Wagner or at least enjoyed Wagner's blessing. Second, Nietzsche had developed a new style: the essayistic works of the years 1872 to 1876 had yielded to a collection of philosophical aphorisms. Third, Nietzsche had wanted to retire from academic life since 1874, but he had to wait for a medical pension that was granted in 1879. Free of both Wagner and academe, he would never again be distracted from his vocation of writing. Another significant factor contributing to the new Nietzsche was his friendship with Paul Rée, a writer, and Peter Gast (pseudonym of Heinrich Köselitz), a struggling composer. Nietzsche had met them when they took courses at Basel. Having found a kindred spirit in Rée and an ardent disciple in Gast, Nietzsche could feel better about himself than the minuscule sale of his books would have allowed. The publication of *Menschliches, Allzumenschliches,* whose subtitle, *Ein Buch für freie Geister* (A Book for Free Spirits), was Nietzsche's gesture of independence. He would write in his foreword to the second edition (1886) that *Menschliches, Allzumenschliches* had been the chronicle of his anti-Romantic self-treatment, his declaration of independence and convalescence from his physical illness and from the insidious disease of romanticism that he had contracted from Wagner.

Menschliches, Allzumenschliches was not only Nietzsche's longest work to date, amounting to more than seven hundred pages, it was also the most baffling. The hundreds of aphorisms comprising each volume cover a wide range of concerns including metaphysics, the origin of morals, religious faith, cultural values, the state, democratic institutions, and the nature of the artist. *Menschliches, Allzumenschliches* is Nietzsche's first attempt to work out his philosophical priorities and spell out his agenda as a thinker no longer hemmed in by German concerns. Significant for this work and all those to follow was Nietzsche's solitary, nomadic life-style. Constantly searching for a comfortable climate and an abode that was not beyond his humble means, he lived at various times in Genoa; Sils-Maria, Switzerland; Nice; and Turin, and stayed for a few months at a time at other locations in southern Switzerland and northern Italy. Themes of wandering, homelessness, an unfettered existence, and exploration are hallmarks of his writings, and he once said that one must never trust a thought that originates from behind a desk. Nietzsche had given up his Prussian citizenship in 1869 to accept his position at Basel; however, because he did not live without interruption for a long enough period of time in Basel, he never did qualify for Swiss citizenship. Thus, technically, Nietzsche had been a man without a country since 1869.

The "freie Geister" (free spirits) whom Nietzsche invented as his spiritual allies were enlightened individuals who accepted nothing without close scrutiny, especially in the realm of values. They were opponents of Christianity and nationalism. They remained aloof from politics, disavowing nationalism, socialism, and causes in general. The dominant feature of the free spirits was an aversion to egalitarian principles and liberalism, which Nietzsche traced to decadent Christianity or "Platonismus fürs Volk" (Platonism for the people). *Menschliches, Allzumenschliches* contains Nietzsche's first reflections on the concepts of good, bad, and evil: in early tribal society the good were the powerful, and the bad were the powerless; the resentment of the powerless inspired them to create a new moral category, evil, which they ascribed to the powerful. In a similar way, Nietzsche analyzed other concepts whose origins had become dim. Revenge, for example, depends on a complicated set of circumstances including time for reflection, sufficient intelligence to feel offended, the need to restore honor, and the need to demonstrate lack of fear in restoring the balance between two parties. Justice is society's revenge on behalf of the individual. Viewing linear progress and an ultimate goal for humanity as biases of Socratic optimism, Nietzsche defined progress as "Veredelung" (ennoblement). For its spiritual and cultural ennoblement a society must be inoculated by the introduction of a pathogen that rallies the forces of the collective first to fight off and then eventually to embody the outsider. Nietzsche's consistent advocacy of the presence of artists to test the collective's stability through creative behavior was based on his understanding that society cannot thrive without tension.

In 1881 a collection of 575 aphorisms titled *Morgenröthe* (translated as *The Dawn of Day,* 1903) appeared. The subtitle, *Gedanken über die moralischen Vorurtheile* (Thoughts on Moral Prejudice), indicates the thrust of Nietzsche's late work: an aggressive, radical campaign against modern decadence. In *Morgenröthe* Nietzsche says that there are two basic denials of morality: first, one can deny that people's alleged motives actually contribute to their actions; second, one can deny that moral judgments are based on truth. Nietzsche opts for the second choice: he admits that many actions generally considered immoral should be avoided and that many actions considered moral should be encouraged; the challenge is to perform right actions and avoid wrong ones for different reasons than those that have proven to be in error. We have to learn anew in order to be able to feel anew later on. The words Nietzsche used to convey "learning anew" and "feeling anew" are *umlernen* and *umfühlen.* The prefix um indicates reversal of the action denoted by the stem verb, so that in these acts of relearning and refeeling Nietzsche is suggesting his later campaign to revaluate all values (Umwertung aller Werte). An aphorism near the conclusion of *Morgenröthe* expresses Nietzsche's philosophy of development: a snake that cannot shed its skin must die; minds that are not permitted to change their opinions cease to be minds.

In 1882 another collection of aphorisms, *Die fröhliche Wissenschaft* (The Gay Science; translated as *The Joyful Wisdom,* 1910), appeared. By this time Nietzsche had met Lou Salomé, a young Russian friend of Rée's. Nietzsche's attraction to her was profound and was both intellectual and sexual. Salomé, however, preferred Rée's company to Nietzsche's. As a result Nietzsche became embittered toward Rée and Salomé.

In his aphorism "Der tolle Mensch" (The Madman) Nietzsche depicts a madman who rushes about in broad daylight with a lantern, desperately trying to illuminate the way for humanity in the appalling darkness that follows the death of God. But the people are not aware of the darkness; they remain indifferent to the ravings of the madman and continue to act complacently. In the infancy of the species gods, and later God, provided life with meaning; but in the absence of belief in God, religion and its institutions are hollow. The nothingness that accumulates in the absence of God, in the absence of absolute meaning, is insidious but inevitable. Nietzsche uses the analogy of light traveling from distant stars to make his point: by the time we see starlight, it has been on its way for years; in time humanity will receive the awesome and devastating news that it has been worshipping a God who died years ago. Meanwhile, should we persist in going through the motions as if God were a living concept? Should we passively stand by while the foundations of faith erode, refusing to create new values because the old ones have not been questioned?

This intense focus on living well in the here and now is related in *Die fröhliche Wissenschaft* in a parable that became one of Nietzsche's most celebrated ideas. "Das größte Schwergewicht" (The Greatest Stress) presents a scenario in which an individual–Nietzsche uses the familiar pronoun *du* (you)–finds himself in the depths of abject depression. A demon pursues you into your isolation and utters a horrifying proposition; your entire life in every detail, including this very moment of horror, will recur eternally–there is no end to look forward to, no heaven, no hell, no oblivion, no redemption from the weight of the eternal recurrence of the same events. You must now live with the consequences of this knowledge. Do you curse the demon and sink deeper into misery and denial, or do you affirm your existence for all eternity? Nietzsche intended the parable of the eternal recurrence to lay the greatest possible stress on living in the here and now; if we believe that we will live the same life in every detail over and over, then it is incumbent on us to create a life that we can *will* to recur eternally.

In his advocacy of adding style to one's character, of achieving selfhood, and of living dangerously in the absence of God, Nietzsche had rounded the corner from the criticism of prevailing values to positing new ones. This development reaches fruition in *Also sprach Zarathustra,* a work that deviates from Nietzsche's usual aphoristic style.

In *Also sprach Zarathustra* dramatic, exuberant expression is given to Nietzsche's own experience of that fateful moment of affirmation called for by the demon in "Das größte Schwergewicht," so that the work is even more confessional than Nietzsche's earlier writings. Hymnic in tone, prophetic in vision, and brimming with metaphors, *Also sprach Zarathustra* defies all standards of philosophical discourse and blurs the distinction between philosophy and poetry. The protagonist of the work is the mythical prophet Zarathustra (German for Zoroaster), Nietzsche's alter ego. Zarathustra's experiences are not uniformly joyous, and, like most prophets, he is not accepted in his own land. Nietzsche animated his later ego with the tensions of his own life, providing sometimes lyrical and sometimes biting testimony about the journey through suffering to affirmation. The tone of the book was influenced by his disappointment in Rée and Salomé: *Also sprach Zarathustra* is the work of a lonely and sometimes bitter man.

Nietzsche wrote volumes one through three, which appeared in 1883, in a matter of less than two weeks each. The final part was published in a private, limited edition in 1885. In *Ecce homo* (Behold the Man, 1908; translated, 1911) Nietzsche described the inspiration under which he wrote the work, explaining that revelation would be an appropriate term: suddenly, and with undeniable certainty, those things that had shaken and convulsed him on the inside became visible and audible. He heard but did not have to seek, he took but did not have to ask the source; thoughts flashed like lightning, by necessity, and without hesitation: "Ich habe nie eine Wahl gehabt" (I never had a choice). (Carl Gustav Jung devoted a seminar to a psychological analysis of *Also sprach Zarathustra,* claiming that during the hectic weeks of writing Nietzsche was taken over by the archetype represented by the wise old prophet.)

Also sprach Zarathustra is full of parables, proclamations, metaphors, and lyrical-hymnic writing. Zarathustra comes down the mountain after ten years of solitude to share his overabundant wisdom with the people. He learns on his way down that the people have not heard that God is dead, so his first message proclaims the death of all gods. In tandem with this news, however, he exhorts the people to prepare for the "Übermensch" (overman or superman), who represents an "Übergehen" (going over) from current man, hindered by misplaced faith, to a future man who will represent the fulfillment of man's destiny on earth. Humanity has historically perceived itself as a creation of a god and cast itself in the image of a god; it is now incumbent on humans to determine their own image, free of all gods. This existential mission requires the exploration of uncharted, dangerous territory: man, Zarathustra says, is a rope tied between animal and "overman," with an abyss below. The "going over" from one to the other will not occur overnight, it will not come about easily, and many will perish in the abyss before the hour of the great noon—the moment when, without the cover of shadow, man experiences the transition from Mensch (human) to overman. Nietzsche is adamant that mankind must face its condition without the false comfort of gods, ideals, and religions. The greatness of humanity is that we are a bridge, not a goal; mankind is a constant journey toward fulfillment.

The people, of course, reject or at best misunderstand Zarathustra's teachings. The prophet must tell even his disciples that they should strive to overcome their master and demonstrate their own growth by denying him. This commandment is a direct transvaluation of Matt. 10:24–25, 33: "The disciple is not above his master, nor the servant above his lord. / It is enough for the disciple that he be as his master, and the servant as his lord. / But whosoever shall deny me before men, him will I also deny before my Father which is in heaven." Throughout *Also sprach Zarathustra* there are allusions to the Bible because Zarathustra is diametrically opposed to Christ, who preached about the afterlife, renunciation, and humility and therefore contributed to man's inauthentic relation to the here and now. Nietzsche's alter ego voices his concerns about the rabble and its uninspired, unconscious life in speeches, tales, and parables. In one parable the three metamorphoses of the spirit are described: mankind's spirit is first a camel that allows itself to be burdened, and it is practiced in surviving in harsh climes; the camel becomes a lion and does battle against the dragon Thou Shalt, but the lion can only annihilate, it cannot create; finally, the lion becomes a child, representing a new beginning, a promise, and a potential once the field has been cleared of decadent obstacles.

All of the concepts of Nietzsche's later philosophy appear in *Also sprach Zarathustra*. The eternal recurrence appears in the third part, when Zarathustra summons the strength to affirm his own eternal existence. The will to power is presented in the context of self-overcoming: wherever Zarathustra finds life, he finds a will to power ceaselessly struggling to overcome itself. The concept of the Übermensch is presented early in the

work and contrasted with that of the "letzter Mensch" (last man) who can no longer harbor ambitions but prefers to cultivate tiny virtues and remain happy. The first three parts of the work illustrate Zarathustra's inability to communicate with the people because the distance between his message and their spiritual condition is too great. In the fourth part, which is more pessimistic in tone than the hymnic early parts, Zarathustra no longer even tries to function among ordinary humans. The "höhere Menschen" (higher men) visit Zarathustra on his mountain, but they have not yet reached a high enough level of growth and enlightenment to have earned the privilege of staying with him. They rely too strongly on Zarathustra and take his words literally, so that they are not capable of surviving on their own in Zarathustra's harsh environment.

Though Nietzsche poured his heart into *Also sprach Zarathustra,* the work did not attract many readers; the fourth part was published in only forty copies. Undeterred by his failure to win a large readership for his works, or perhaps emboldened by the challenge of espousing his new philosophy against all odds, Nietzsche launched the final phase of his writing with *Jenseits von Gut und Böse* (1886; translated as *Beyond Good and Evil,* 1909). In this carefully structured, aphoristic work, which is divided into chapters, Nietzsche spells out the implications of ideas that had emerged with eruptive force in *Also sprach Zarathustra.* Many of the 296 aphorisms are a page or more in length; hence, they deviate from the traditional aphorism, which is a concise statement of a principle or a terse formulation of a truth. Nietzsche retained this style of single paragraphs of varying length in the remainder of his works, and beginning with *Jenseits von Gut und Böse* the paragraphs are more closely related than the aphorisms of the pre-*Zarathustra* works. This style afforded him both the conceptual rigor and the open-ended freedom that characterize his thought.

After *Also sprach Zarathustra* Nietzsche had little to say about the Übermensch, but he retained a vision of the emerging individual. The new philosopher, Nietzsche claimed, is one who prepares the way for a nonidealized consummation of life. In aphorism 212 of *Jenseits von Gut und Böse* he explains that the philosopher's work requires him to establish a presence in opposition to the times, to exist as the thorny question mark within a society that is losing the strength to ask questions. Modern society encourages narrowness, specialization, and lack of will disguised as objectivity; the philosopher should demonstrate strength of will, hardness, and the capacity for long-range decisions as a means of countering the nihilistic Christian values of renunciation, humility, and selflessness. The closing words of the aphorism summarize the fate of

Nietzsche's alter ego Zarathustra, the prophet of the Übermensch: the greatest human being will be the one who is loneliest, most concealed, most deviant, living beyond good and evil as the master of his own virtues, overly rich in will, and capable of being as manifold as he is whole.

Nietzsche had taken legal action against his publisher, Ernst Schmeitzner, in 1884 to collect royalties from the sale of *Also sprach Zarathustra*. His old publisher, E. W. Fritzsch, bought the rights to *Menschliches, Allzumenschliches, Morgenröthe,* and *Die fröhliche Wissenschaft* from Schmeitzner in 1886, and also brought out a new edition of *Die Geburt der Tragödie*. For *Jenseits von Gut und Böse* and all the works that followed, Nietzsche paid for publication under an agreement with the publisher C. G. Naumann. By 1886 only sixty to seventy copies of *Also sprach Zarathustra* had been sold.

To supplement and clarify *Jenseits von Gut und Böse,* Nietzsche wrote *Zur Genealogie der Moral* (1887; translated as "A Genealogy of Morals," 1897). In number 260 (an "aphorism" of four pages) Nietzsche discusses the differences between "Herrenmoral" (master morality) and "Sklavenmoral" (slave morality). Master morality observes a distinction between noble and contemptible, calling the noble "good" and the contemptible "bad." The close-knit group of masters feels responsibilities only to itself. Modern slave morality, on the other hand, advocates sympathy, responsibility for others, and altruism. Slave morality is created by the oppressed, the victimized, the weak, and the disenfranchised. Of prime importance to this group is the alleviation of suffering, and it promotes virtues that contribute to making existence bearable. Slave morality applies the term *good* to whatever is not dangerous; wherever there is a preponderance of slave morality, language has a tendency to equate the word *good* with *stupid. Evil* is invented by the powerless and victimized, and those who arouse fear are regarded as evil. In master morality, on the other hand, those who arouse fear are regarded as good, because they are capable of inflicting harm and are therefore worthy of respect, while *bad* designates those who, being powerless, are contemptible. It is the ressentiment (resentment; Nietzsche preferred the French term) of the slaves toward the masters that drives them to invent the category of evil. The French Revolution was a triumph of ressentiment over the classical aristocratic ideals of seventeenth- and eighteenth-century France, "die letzte politische Vornehmheit, die es in Europa gab" (the last political noblesse that existed in Europe). The ideals of the French Revolution, which Nietzsche often vilified in the person of Jean-Jacques Rousseau, are the renunciatory values of slave morality; the appearance of the last great representative of the noble ideal, Napoleon, was the single factor that justified the revolution. Modern society is basically the society of Rousseau, the Enlightenment, and the French Revolution.

In November 1887 the influential Danish scholar and critic Georg Brandes, who had received a copy of *Jenseits von Gut und Böse* from Nietzsche's publisher in 1886, wrote to Nietzsche. Brandes expressed his admiration for Nietzsche, pointed out affinities between their views, and said he was surprised at not having learned of Nietzsche earlier. Nietzsche replied to Brandes in a letter of 2 December 1887: "Verehrter Herr, ein paar Leser, die man sich selbst in Ehren hält und sonst keine Leser—so gehört es in der Tat zu meinen Wünschen" (Dear Sir, a few readers whom I can hold in honor and otherwise no readers—this indeed is my wish). In 1888 Brandes gave the first lectures on Nietzsche's philosophy at the University of Copenhagen. By this time Nietzsche had endured much depression owing to his ill health; to his friend and former Basel colleague Franz Overbeck, Nietzsche explained that writing had become alchemy, a process whereby he turned the mud of his painful experiences into the gold of his works. Not only did Nietzsche have to contend with solitude and frail health; he was constantly feuding with his mother and sister, who meddled in his affairs at every opportunity.

Buoyed by the dialogue he enjoyed with Brandes and, through him, with Strindberg, Nietzsche experienced his most productive—and final—year of writing in 1888. *Der Fall Wagner* (1888; translated as "The Case of Wagner," 1896), a polemic detailing the differences between healthy taste and healthy values, on the one hand, and the decadence associated with romanticism in general and with Wagner as the personification of romanticism in particular, on the other hand, is much more than a debate about music. Wagner stands for the modern spirit and modern taste: frenetic, nervous, emotional, obscure, Germanic; in contrast, Georges Bizet is extolled as a representative of the healthy, lucid, light, and Mediterranean character—Nietzsche frequently praises the French at the expense of the Germans. "Der Antichrist: Fluch auf das Christenthum" (The Antichrist: A Curse on Christianity) was finished in 1888 but did not appear until 1895. The Germans are taken to task in this work for having sabotaged Europe's chances for a great cultural revival: the Renaissance revalued Christian values by offering its own aristocratic ones, but Martin Luther, concerned only with his own salvation, attacked the Catholic church and restored its power at the same time. According to Nietzsche, Christianity was on the verge of collapsing at precisely the moment when Luther decided to save it; the corruption of the popes actually signaled a triumph of life's affirmative values.

Also written in 1888 was *Götzen-Dämmerung* (1889; translated as "The Twilight of the Idols," 1896), in which Nietzsche returns to his major concerns and makes final formulations of his positions; the title is yet another barb directed at Wagner, a play on Wagner's *Gotterdämmerung* (1863; translated as *The Twilight of the Gods,* 1900). The critique of Socrates begun in *Die Geburt der Tragödie* concludes in *Götzen-Dämmerung:* the Socratic dialectic, aimed against aristocratic authority, represents the modern spirit of mob rule. By attacking the instincts and elevating the pursuit of knowledge through reason alone, Socrates took a step backwards, since ascending vitality is accompanied by an affirmation of the instincts. In *Götzen-Dämmerung* and other writings of 1888 Nietzsche referred to himself as "der letzte Jünger des Philosophen Dionysos" (the last disciple of the philosopher Dionysus), the deity symbolic of the values of ascending life and eternal recurrence.

Nietzsche contra Wagner (1889; translated, 1896) is a brief essay that continues Nietzsche's critique of Wagner; it relies heavily on passages from earlier works. *Ecce homo* is Nietzsche's ironic and self-parodistic autobiography; the title is the words Pontius Pilate used to indicate the flogged and humiliated Christ, and in the work Nietzsche distinguishes between his teachings and those of Christ. Nietzsche gives expression in *Ecce homo* to the euphoria he experienced in his last year of writing: "Wie sollte ich nicht meinem ganzen Leben dankbar sein?–Und so erzähle ich mir mein Leben" (How should I not be grateful to my whole life?–And so I will recount my life to myself). Nietzsche spent the latter part of 1888 in a condition of physical and mental exhaustion; he was also subject to uncontrollable facial contortions–grins and grimaces. His feelings of euphoria probably enabled him to work beyond his normal endurance. *Ecce homo* is frequently cited along with other late works as the product of madness, but it exhibits typical Nietzschean boldness. *Ecce homo* also offers Nietzsche's reviews of his own works, in which ample doses of arrogance are mixed with self-parody.

Nietzsche suffered a mental breakdown on 3 January 1889 in the Piazza Carlo Alberto in Turin. From 3 to 7 January he wrote brief, ecstatic notes to various people, signing himself "Der Gekreuzigte" (The Crucified One) to Gast and Brandes and "Dionysos" to Wagner's wife, Cosima, and the historian Jakob Burckhardt. Burckhardt, a former colleague of Nietzsche's at Basel, also received a long, rambling letter dated 6 January that begins: "Lieber Herr Professor, zuletzt wäre ich sehr viel lieber Basler Professor als Gott; aber ich habe es nicht gcwagt, mcincn Privat-Egoismus so weit zu treiben, um seinetwegen die Schaffung der Welt zu unterlassen. Sie sehen, man muß Opfer bringen, wie und wo man lebt" (Dear Professor, ultimately I would much rather be a Basel professor than God, but I did not dare to push my private egoism so far as to neglect the creation of the world. You see, one has to make sacrifices however and wherever one lives). Burckhardt took the letter to Overbeck, who sped down to Turin by train to fetch Nietzsche and return him to Basel. He was diagnosed as suffering from progressive paralysis. On 17 January 1889 his mother and two orderlies took him to Jena, where he was committed to the psychiatric clinic at the university. In 1890 he was released to the care of his mother in Naumburg.

In 1885 Nietzsche's sister had married Dr. Bernhard Förster, an outspoken anti-Semite who had tried to establish a colony of "Aryans" in Paraguay and had committed suicide in 1889 when the colony collapsed financially. After Elisabeth Förster-Nietzsche returned from Paraguay in 1893, she devoted all her energy to acquiring sole possession and control of Nietzsche's literary estate. In 1894 Nietzsche's works finally began to bring in considerable royalties. Förster-Nietzsche manipulated Neitzsche's late unpublished writings and letters to present her own version of his ideas, and she represented herself as his greatest supporter. In 1896 she moved the Nietzsche archive to Weimar to profit from the association with the Goethe Archive located there. After their mother died in 1897, Förster-Nietzsche moved her brother to Weimar. Nietzsche never recovered from his total nervous breakdown. He died on 25 August 1900.

Nietzsche's madness and his sister's unprofessional behavior as the executor of his literary estate contributed to the myths, half-truths, and intrigues that swirled around his reputation. She dismissed Gast as editor of the first collected edition of Nietzsche's works even though he was infinitely better prepared to perform the work than those chosen by her. In 1901 she began to publish Nietzsche's notes from the 1880s, even though Nietzsche had already used this material in the published works. It was thus that "Der Wille zur Macht" (1901; translated as *The Will to Power,* 1909, 1910) was put together. Förster-Nietzsche claimed that her brother had intended to write such a work and had finished the first part, "Der Antichrist." Nietzsche had indeed referred to a work with that title, and to "Der Antichrist" as its first installment, but he frequently made plans for books that he later abandoned. The projected "Der Wille zur Macht" was never completed by Nietzsche, but his notes of the 1880s were published under that title by Förster-Nietzsche.

Nietzsche's works are difficult to translate, since he uses wordplay and coinages. The iconoclastic nature of the late writings, such as "Der Antichrist" and *Ecce homo,* caused the editors, frequently under the inept guidance of Förster-Nietzsche, to postpone their publication while instead publishing discarded notes that appeared more "philosophical." Nietzsche's reception in the English-speaking world was hampered by the fact that his late works were translated before the early ones; hence, his ideas were construed as unfounded and eccentric. An additional drawback was the poor quality of the English translations. Furthermore, Nietzsche's ideas were given an anti-Semitic, nationalistic, and prowar slant by Nazi propagandists. Nietzsche's message, then, reached the English-speaking world in a distorted form.

In the 1950s the American philosopher Walter Kaufmann began translating Nietzsche's major writings into English; Kaufmann also argued forcefully in his own publications against the misinterpretations of Nietzsche's thought. Today a consensus exists among philosophers, literary theorists, and historians of ideas that Nietzsche was a watershed figure of Western culture. His criticisms of metaphysics and values have influenced theorists who are committed to exposing bias, hypocrisy, and false assumptions. Deconstructionist followers of Jacques Derrida lionize Nietzsche for what they perceive as his disavowal of the "ideal" of meaning; other thinkers, however, claim that Nietzsche saw his task as a philosopher to be that of rescuing the concept of meaning from the chaos of collapsing values.

Letters:

Selected Letters of Friedrich Nietzsche, edited by Oscar Levy, translated by Anthony Ludovici (New York: Doubleday, 1921);

Selected Letters of Friedrich Nietzsche, translated and edited by Christopher Middleton (Chicago: University of Chicago Press, 1969);

Briefwechsel: Kritische Gesamtausgabe, 24 volumes, edited by Giorgio Colli and Mazzino Montinari (Berlin: De Gruyter, 1975–1984).

Bibliographies:

Herbert Reichert and Karl Schlechta, *International Nietzsche Bibliography* (Chapel Hill: University of North Carolina Press, 1960; revised and enlarged, 1968);

Reichert, "International Nietzsche Bibliography 1968–1971," *Nietzsche-Studien,* 2 (1973): 320–339;

Reichert, "International Nietzsche Bibliography 1972–1973," *Nietzsche-Studien,* 4 (1975): 351–373.

Biographies:

Lou Andreas-Salomé, *Friedrich Nietzsche in seinen Werken* (Vienna: Konegan, 1894); edited and translated by Siegfried Mandel as Nietzsche (Redding Ridge, Conn.: Black Swan, 1988);

Georg Brandes, *Friedrich Nietzsche,* translated by A. G. Chater (London: Heinemann, 1914);

Charles Andler, *Nietzsche: Sa vie et sa pensée,* 6 volumes (Paris: Bossard, 1920–1931);

Erich Podach, *Nietzsches Zusammenbruch: Beiträge zu einer Biographie auf Grund unveröffentlichter Dokumente,* (Heidelberg: Kampmann, 1930); translated by Fritz August Voigt as *The Madness of Nietzsche* (New York: Putnam's, 1930);

Crane Brinton, *Nietzsche* (Cambridge, Mass.: Harvard University Press, 1941);

Frederick Copleston, *Friedrich Nietzsche: Philosopher of Culture* (London: Burns, Oates & Washbourne, 1942);

H. A. Reyburn, *Nietzsche: The Story of a Human Philosopher* (London: Macmillan, 1948);

Frederick Love, *Young Nietzsche and the Wagnerian Experience* (Chapel Hill: University of North Carolina Press, 1963);

R. J. Hollingdale, *Nietzsche: The Man and His Philosophy* (Baton Rouge: Louisiana State University Press, 1965);

Curt Paul Janz, *Friedrich Nietzsche,* 3 volumes (Munich: Hanser, 1978);

Ronald Hayman, *Nietzsche: A Critical Life* (London: Weidenfeld & Nicolson, 1980);

Sander L. Gilman, ed., *Begegnungen mit Nietzsche,* second edition (Bonn: Bouvier, 1985); translated by David J. Parent as *Conversations with Nietzsche: A Life in the Words of His Contemporaries* (Oxford: Oxford University Press, 1987);

Peter Bergmann, *Nietzsche: "The Last Antipolitical German"* (Bloomington: Indiana University Press, 1987);

Carl Pletsch, *Young Nietzsche: Becoming a Genius* (New York: Free Press, 1991).

References:

David Allison, ed., *The New Nietzsche: Contemporary Styles of Interpretation* (New York: Dell, 1977);

Steven E. Aschheim, *The Nietzsche Legacy in Germany 1890–1990* (Berkeley: University of California Press, 1992);

Ernst Behler, "Deconstruction versus Hermeneutics: Derrida and Gadamer on Text and Interpretation," *Southern Humanities Review,* 21 (Summer 1987): 201–223;

Behler, *Derrida–Nietzsche, Nietzsche–Derrida* (Munich: Schöningh, 1988);

Ernst Bertram, *Nietzsche: Versuch einer Mythologie,* eighth edition (Bonn: Bouvier, 1965);

Harold Bloom, ed., *Friedrich Nietzsche* (New York: Chelsea House, 1987);

William M. Calder III, "The Wilamowitz-Nietzsche Struggle: New Documentation and a Reappraisal," *Nietzsche-Studien,* 12 (1983): 214–254;

Daniel W. Conway, *Nietzsche and the Political* (New York: Routledge, 1997);

Conway, ed., *Nietzsche: Critical Assessments,* 4 volumes (New York: Routledge, 1998);

Adrian Del Caro, *Nietzsche contra Nietzsche: Creativity and the Anti-Romantic* (Baton Rouge: Louisiana State University Press, 1989);

Del Caro, "Nietzsche, Sacher-Masoch, and the Whip," *German Studies Review,* 21, no. 2 (1998): 241–261;

Del Caro, "Nietzschean Self-Transformation and the Transformation of the Dionysian," in *Nietzsche, Philosophy and the Arts,* edited by Salim Kemal, Ivan Gaskell, and Conway (Cambridge: Cambridge University Press, 1998), pp. 70–91;

Del Caro, "Reception and Impact: The First Decade of Nietzsche in Germany," *Orbis Litterarum,* 37, no. 1 (1982): 32–46;

Jacques Derrida, *Spurs: The Styles of Nietzsche,* translated by Barbara Howell (Chicago: University of Chicago Press, 1979);

Linda Duncan, "Heine and Nietzsche," *Nietzsche-Studien,* 19 (1990): 336–345;

Volker Dürr, Reinhold Grimm, and Kathy Harms, eds., *Nietzsche: Literature and Values* (Madison: University of Wisconsin Press, 1988);

Ivo Frenzel, ed., *Friedrich Nietzsche in Selbstzeugnissen und Bilddokumenten* (Hamburg: Rowohlt, 1968);

Michael A. Gillespie and Tracey B. Strong, eds., *Nietzsche's New Seas: Explorations in Philosophy, Aesthetics, and Politics* (Chicago: University of Chicago Press, 1988);

Robert Gooding-Williams, "Literary Fiction as Philosophy: The Case of Nietzsche's 'Zarathustra,'" *The Journal of Philosophy,* 83, no. 11 (1986): 667–676;

Reinhold Grimm, "Antiquity as Echo and Disguise," *Nietzsche-Studien,* 14 (1973): 201–249;

Martin Heidegger, *Nietzsche,* 2 volumes (Pfullingen: Neske, 1961); volume 1 translated by David Krell as *The Will to Power as Art* (New York: Harper & Row, 1979);

Erich Heller, *The Artist's Journey Into the Interior and Other Essays* (New York: Random House, 1965);

Heller, *The Disinherited Mind* (Philadelphia: Dufour & Saifer, 1952);

Heller, *The Importance of Nietzsche: Ten Essays* (Chicago: University of Chicago Press, 1988);

Kathleen Higgins, *Nietzsche's "Zarathustra"* (Philadelphia: Temple University Press, 1987);

Carl G. Jung, *Nietzsche's Zarathustra: Notes of the Seminar Given in 1934–1939,* 2 volumes, edited by James L. Jarrett (Princeton: Princeton University Press, 1988);

Walter Kaufmann, *Nietzsche: Philosopher, Psychologist, Antichrist* (Princeton: Princeton University Press, 1950; revised, 1974);

Rudolf Kreis, *Nietzsche, Wagner und die Juden* (Würzburg: Königshausen & Neumann, 1995);

Richard Krummel, *Nietzsche und der deutsche Geist* (Berlin: De Gruyter, 1974);

Laurence Lampert, *Nietzsche and Modern Times: A Study of Bacon, Descartes, and Nietzsche* (New Haven: Yale University Press, 1993);

Lampert, *Nietzsche's Teaching: An Interpretation of "Thus Spoke Zarathustra"* (New Haven: Yale University Press, 1986);

György Lukács, *Die Zerstörung der Vernunft* (Berlin: Aufbau, 1962);

Jürgen Manthey, ed., *Literaturmagazin XII: Nietzsche* (Reinbek: Rowohlt, 1980);

James C. O'Flaherty, ed., *Studies in Nietzsche and the Classical Tradition* (Chapel Hill: University of North Carolina Press, 1976);

John Pizer, "The Use and Abuse of 'Ursprung': On Foucault's Reading of Nietzsche," *Nietzsche-Studien,* 19 (1990): 462–478;

Matthias Politycki, *Umwertung aller Werte?: Deutsche Literatur im Urteil Nietzsches* (Berlin: De Gruyter, 1989);

Stanley Rosen, *The Mask of Enlightenment: Nietzsche's "Zarathustra"* (Cambridge: Cambridge University Press, 1995);

Richard Schacht, *Nietzsche* (London: Routledge & Kegan Paul, 1985);

M. S. Silk and Joseph Peter Stern, *Nietzsche on Tragedy* (Cambridge: Cambridge University Press, 1981);

Joan Stambaugh, *Nietzsche's Thought of Eternal Recurrence* (Baltimore: Johns Hopkins University Press, 1972);

Henry Staten, *Nietzsche's Voice* (Ithaca and London: Cornell University Press, 1990);

Wolfgang F. Taraba, "Friedrich Nietzsche," in *Deutsche Dichter der Moderne,* edited by Benno von Wiese, third edition (Berlin: Schmidt, 1975), pp. 11–26;

David S. Thatcher, *Nietzsche in England 1890–1914: The Growth of a Reputation* (Toronto: University of Toronto Press, 1970).

Papers:

Friedrich Nietzsche's papers are in the Goethe- und Schillerarchiv in Weimar.

Novalis

(2 May 1772 – 25 March 1801)

William Arctander O'Brien
University of California, San Diego

This entry originally appeared in *DLB 90: German Writers in the Age of Goethe, 1789–1832.*

BOOKS: *Schriften,* edited by Friedrich Schlegel and Ludwig Tieck, 2 volumes (Berlin: Realschulbuch-handlung, 1802)–includes *Heinrich von Ofterdingen: Ein nachgelassener Roman,* translated by Palmer Hilty as *Henry von Ofterdingen* (New York: Ungar, 1964); "Geistliche Lieder"; and *Die Lehrlinge zu Sais,* translated by Ralph Manheim as *The Novices of Sais* (New York: Valentin, 1949);

Schriften, edited by Tieck and Schlegel, 2 volumes (Berlin: Realschulbuchhandlung, 1826)–includes "Die Christenheit oder Europa";

Schriften, edited by Paul Kluckhohn, Richard Samuel, Hans-Joachim Mähl, and Gerhard Schulz, 6 volumes (Stuttgart: Kohlhammer, 1975–1983);

Werke, Tagebücher und Briefe Friedrich von Hardenbergs, edited by Mähl and Samuel, 3 volumes (Munich: Hanser, 1978–1987).

Editions in English: "The Story of Hyacinth and Rose-blossom," translated by Lillie Winter, in *German Classics of the Nineteenth and Twentieth Centuries,* edited by Kuno Francke and W. G. Howard, volume 4 (New York: German Publications Society, 1913);

Hyacinth and Rosebud, Eros and Fabel, translated by Florence Bryan and Kathe Roth (Aberdeen: Selma, 1955);

Sacred Songs of Novalis, translated by Eileen Hutchins (Aberdeen: Selma, 1956);

Hymns to the Night and Other Selected Writings, translated by Charles E. Passage (New York: Liberal Arts Press, 1960)–includes "Hymns to the Night," "Christianity or Europe," "Klingsohr's Fairy Tale," and selected aphorisms;

"Selected Aphorisms and Fragments," translated by Alexander Gelley, in *German Romantic Criticism,* edited by A. Leslie Willson (New York: Continuum, 1982), pp. 62–83–includes selections from "Pollen," "Miscellaneous Observations," "Logolog-

Novalis as a young man (oil portrait by Franz Gareis; photograph by Foto-Kind, Weißenfels, used by permission of the Museum Weißenfels)

ical Fragments," "Dialogues 1 & 2," and "Monologue";

Selections from "Miscellaneous Writings," 6 "Dialogues," "Monologue," and the fragment "On Goethe," in *The Romantic Ironists and Goethe,* edited by Kathleen Wheeler (Cambridge: Cambridge University Press, 1984), pp. 83–111;

Hymns to the Night, translated by Dick Higgins, revised edition (New Paltz, N.Y.: McPherson, 1984).

PERIODICAL PUBLICATIONS: "Klagen eines Jünglings," *Der Neue Teutsche Merkur,* 37 (April 1791): 410–413;

"Blüthenstaub," *Athenaeum: Eine Zeitschrift,* 1 (April 1798): 70–106;

"Blumen," *Jahrbücher der Preußischen Monarchie unter der Regierung von Friedrich Wilhelm III.,* 2 (June 1798): 184ff;

"Glauben und Liebe, oder der König und die Königin," *Jahrbücher der Preußischen Monarchie unter der Regierung von Friedrich Wilhelm III.,* 2 (July 1798): 269–286;

"Hymnen an die Nacht," *Athenaeum: Eine Zeitschrift,* 3 (August 1800): 188–204; translated by Charles E. Passage as "Hymns to the Night" in *Hymns to the Night and Other Selected Writings* (New York: Liberal Arts Press, 1960).

Poet, aphorist, novelist, mystic, literary and political theoretician, student of philosophy and the natural sciences, Friedrich von Hardenberg–best known by his pen name, Novalis–was one of the most striking figures of German Romanticism. Hardenberg's theoretical writings helped establish the program of Early or Jena Romanticism, and his literary compositions rank among the most radical examples of Romantic experimentation in form. His best-known works remain the fragment collection "Blüthenstaub" (1798; selections translated as "Pollen," 1982), the rhapsodic essay "Die Christenheit oder Europa" (1799; translated as "Christianity or Europe," 1960), the poetic cycle "Hymnen an die Nacht" (1800; translated as "Hymns to the Night," 1960), and the unfinished novel *Heinrich von Ofterdingen* (1802; translated as *Henry von Ofterdingen,* 1964). The last two writings especially have secured Hardenberg's place in the history of letters, although his voluminous notebooks, which comprise the greatest part of his literary remains, have attracted much recent critical attention for their imaginative and often strikingly advanced treatment of literary, scientific, and philosophical issues. Both practical and enthusiastic, Hardenberg regarded his work in letters as a mere avocation beside his career in the Saxon civil service, and he published scarcely eighty pages of writings before his death at the age of twenty-eight. Celebrated or condemned in the nineteenth and early twentieth centuries primarily as the sweet poet of "the blue flower" (a striking image from *Heinrich von Ofterdingen* that came to symbolize the Romantic movement), Hardenberg has come to be recognized not only as an expressive and innovative poet of the German

language, but as a daring, resourceful, and rigorous thinker at the threshold of modernity.

A direct descendant of twelfth-century Saxon nobility, the Freiherr (Baron) Georg Friedrich Philipp von Hardenberg was the second oldest of eleven children born into the quiet Pietistic household of Auguste Bernhardine (née von Bölzig) and Heinrich Ulrich Erasmus Freiherr von Hardenberg. Raised on the family estate of Oberwiederstedt, about eighty kilometers north of the cultural and academic centers of Leipzig and Jena, Hardenberg was a weak and slow child, who suddenly emerged as a sensitive and imaginative boy upon recovery from a prolonged case of dysentery in his ninth year. A brief visit for instruction with the religious Herrnhuter community in Neudietendorf appears to have ended unsuccessfully, and he was sent to live for a year with his uncle, a prestigious aristocrat of the ancien régime and Commander of the Teutonic Order at the opulent Lucklum castle. After having acquainted himself with the good library and more worldly society of his uncle, in 1785 Hardenberg rejoined his family at their new home in Weißenfels. At about this time he began to write poetry in the style of Friedrich Klopstock, Christoph Martin Wieland, and Gottfried August Bürger. In May 1789 a meeting with Bürger followed a correspondence in which the young admirer had exulted that a letter was written to him by the same hand that once wrote "Lenore" and wrestled with Homer.

In 1790, after studying at the Eisleben gymnasium under the distinguished classicist C. D. Jani, Hardenberg moved to Jena to begin university studies in jurisprudence. He quickly attached himself to the professor of Kantian philosophy, Karl Leonhard Reinhold, and to his history professor, the thirty-one-year-old Friedrich Schiller. Schiller, a lifelong acquaintance and influence, encouraged Hardenberg's interest in history, philosophy, poetry, and–at the request of the boy's father–his foundering study of jurisprudence. Hardenberg idolized his teacher, helped nurse him through severe illness in the winter of 1792, and followed his advice to transfer to the university at Leipzig in the fall. His feelings of inferiority before Schiller led directly to Hardenberg's first publication, the poem "Klagen eines Jünglings" (A Youth's Lament). A sentimental prayer for more manly "Sorgen, Elend und Beschwerden" (cares, misery and hardships), the poem was printed under the signature v. H***g. in Wieland's *Der Neue Teutsche Merkur* of April 1791.

At Leipzig, Hardenberg met Friedrich Schlegel, who, though only two months older, assumed the role of mentor for his provincial friend. The two neglected their formal studies and abandoned themselves to a raucous student life, while Schlegel led Hardenberg deeper into the study of Kant, introduced him to more contemporary literature and criticism, and awakened his delight in the wit and paradox that would henceforth enliven his writing. In

1792 Hardenberg transferred to the University of Wittenberg. There he finally applied himself to his studies, and in the summer of 1794 he passed the state examinations in jurisprudence with the highest grade.

Having made little headway in securing a government post through a distant relative, the Prussian minister Karl August von Hardenberg, in October Hardenberg accepted a position as administrative assistant for the district director Coelestin August Just in Tennstedt. By November Hardenberg had embarked upon the experience that would prove decisive in his life: on a business trip to nearby Grüningen, he met and fell deeply in love with the twelve-year-old Sophie von Kühn. Everyone who met her, including Goethe, Schlegel, and Ludwig Tieck, would later agree that Sophie was a remarkable girl, and in his most detailed description of her, a sketch titled "Klarisse," Hardenberg notes that she was devoted to her family, rather formal, fond of tobacco, not overly fond of poetry, and, perhaps most important: "Sie *will nichts seyn*–Sie *ist* etwas" (She *wants to become nothing*–She *is* something). The two became secretly engaged in March, but in November Sophie fell ill with a tuberculosis-related liver tumor. A series of painful operations ensued, and after much suffering she died on 19 March 1797, followed a month later by Hardenberg's favorite brother, Erasmus. The deaths plunged Hardenberg into a prolonged period of mourning and a meditation on death that would decisively alter the nature of his work.

The two years with Sophie had been intellectually fruitful. Hardenberg had immersed himself in the philosophy of Johann Gottlieb Fichte and produced the long "Fichte-Studien" (Fichte Studies) notebooks of 1795 and 1796. Here Hardenberg grapples with problems of the self, perception, religion, ontology, and semiotics, and makes the statement central to all his work: "Spinotza stieg bis zur Natur–Fichte bis zum Ich, oder der Person. Ich bis zur These Gott" (Spinoza ascended to Nature, Fichte to the Ego or Person; I to the thesis, God). In the summer of 1795 he met Fichte along with the poet Friedrich Hölderlin at a gathering where, his host noted, much was spoken about how many questions still remained open for philosophy in regard to religion. After Sophie von Kühn's death, by which time he had returned to Weißenfels to assist his father's directorate of the Saxon salt mines, he studied Spinoza, Kant, Schelling, Goethe, the pietistic writer Nikolaus Ludwig Zinzendorf, the mystical philosophers Johann Kasper Lavater and Tiberius Hemsterhuis, the Scottish physician John Brown, and other philosophical, mystical, and alchemical writers.

In December 1797, after stopping on the way to meet Schelling, Hardenberg arrived at the Mining Academy in Freiberg for a year and a half of studies. Under the direction of Abraham Gottlob Werner and W. H. Lampadius, two of the foremost scientists of the day, he studied geology, mineralogy, chemistry, surveying, mining, and mining law, and worked in the mines three or four times a week. Hardenberg, who during his stay at the academy often slept only five hours a night and planned his time to the quarter hour, managed to continue his other readings and his notebooks, as well as to socialize with Fichte, Schiller, Goethe, Friedrich Schlegel and his brother August Wilhelm, and his friends in the Saxon Diet, Hans Georg von Carlowitz and Dietrich von Miltitz. In the summer of 1798 he produced his first major publications, the fragment collections "Blüthenstaub" and "Glauben und Liebe, oder der König und die Königin" (Faith and Love, or the King and Queen). In both, Hardenberg took up the pseudonym Novalis, a name derived from the phrase *de novali* and used by his early forebears from the estate Von der Rode.

"Blüthenstaub" filled thirty-seven pages of the first issue of the Schlegel brothers' epochmaking journal, the *Athenaeum,* with 114 prose fragments–a genre raised to new heights by the Romantics. Ranging in length from two lines to two pages, the fragments address issues in philosophy, literature, religion, and politics. This diversity is explained by the collection's motto: "Freunde, der Boden ist arm, wir müßen reichlichen Samen / Ausstreuen, daß uns doch nur mäßige Erndten gedeihn" (Friends, the soil is poor, we must richly scatter seeds to produce even a modest harvest). Enthusiastic over the French Revolution and the rapid literary development of Germany, the contributors to the *Athenaeum* had great ambitions, as Hardenberg programmatically states in "Blüthenstaub": "Wir sind auf einer Mißion: zur Bildung der Erde sind wir berufen" (We are on a mission: we are called to the education of the world). Such a project, which would now inform all of Hardenberg's work, clearly shows a debt to the enlightened pedagogy of Schiller and Gotthold Ephraim Lessing, but also the change it has undergone in its "Romanticization." No longer elaborated in a discursive treatise but in a fragmentary and disparate text, the Romantic project of "universal education" rejects an enlightened, totalizing concept of history, and instead envisions a pervasive reevaluation of values and institutions for which the goal–playfully called by Hardenberg "the Golden Age"–remains infinitely deferred. The "end of history" is no longer an historical goal for Hardenberg but a question of personal salvation. As he states in one of the most famous and "Fichtecizing" fragments of "Blüthenstaub": "Nach Innen geht der geheimnißvolle Weg. In uns, oder nirgends ist die Ewigkeit mit ihren Welten, die Vergangenheit und Zukunft" (Inward goes the mysterious path. In us or nowhere is eternity with its worlds, the past and future).

The political and personal, practical and mystical, revolutionary and reactionary task set forth by the Early Romantics at first provoked general incomprehension, a response that greeted Hardenberg's "Glauben und Liebe, oder der König und die Königin" even from the Prussian throne. Forty-three political aphorisms preceded by two pages of poetic "Blumen" (Flowers), "Glauben und Liebe" was printed in the 1798 *Jahrbücher der Preußischen Monarchie unter der Regierung von Friedrich Wilhelm III.* (Journal of the Prussian Monarchy under Friedrich Wilhelm III), a monthly magazine devoted to the young Prussian monarch and Queen Louise, both of whom had been greeted as paragons of political and domestic virtue upon succession to the throne in 1797. "Glauben und Liebe" puts forth a complex and highly metaphorical theory of political institutions. Praising the Prussian king and queen in their own right, it also presents them as educating their subjects for the eventual replacement of monarchy with new, republican institutions—which Hardenberg still describes with metaphors of monarchial rule. Thus, while Hardenberg heaps exorbitant praise on the actual king and queen, he simultaneously uses them as figures for political conceptualization, as in the claim: "Der König ist das gediegene Lebensprinzip des Staats; ganz dasselbe, was die Sonne im Planetensystem ist" (The king is truly the principle of life in the state; quite the same as the sun in the planetary system). Paradoxes abound in formulations such as: "kein König" (No king without a republic, and no republic without a king) and: "Alle Menschen sollen thronfähig werden" (All men should become fit for the throne). Notwithstanding Hardenberg's disclaimer that he was writing in a "Tropen und Räthselsprache" (language of tropes and riddles), the court made its disapproval known, the censor stopped publication of the final installment titled "Politische Aphorismen" (Political Aphorisms), and even Friedrich Schlegel voiced his disapproval, advising his friend either to find a new pseudonym or to abandon hopes for publishing ever again.

While in Freiberg, Hardenberg greatly expanded his reflections on the underlying linguistic and cognitive structures that permitted something like "a language of tropes and riddles" or even scientific language. In groups of fragments with titles such as "Logologische Fragmente" (translated as "Logological Fragments," 1982) and "Poëticismen" (Poeticisms), he develops a theory of "Magic Idealism." Extending the thought of Kant and Fichte, Hardenberg claims, "Die Welt . . . ist überhaupt a priori von mir belebt" (The world . . . is animated by me a priori), and he seeks to control this animation through the magic of language: "Magie ist = Kunst, die Sinnenwelt willkührlich zu gebrauchen" (Magic is = the art of using the world of the senses arbitrarily). To systematize these observations further, he embarked on a large encyclopedic project, the "Allgemeine Brouillon" (General Notebooks) of 1798–1799. Differing from the encyclopedias of the eighteenth century, which present individual fields of knowledge under separate headings, the "Allgemeine Brouillon" tries to show the underlying unity of all knowledge through analogical discussions of "chemische Musik"

(chemical music), "poetische Physiologie" (poetic physiology), "mathematische Philosophie" (mathematical philosophy), and "physicalische Geschichte" (physical history), among many other similarly combinative topics.

While Hardenberg's theoretical studies reached their most abstract point in Freiberg, he soon established relationships with two people who would rivet his attention more closely than ever to his professional career and to literature. In January 1798 Hardenberg met Julie von Charpentier, the daughter of the Freiberg official and former mineralogy instructor Johann Friedrich Wilhelm von Charpentier. A year later they were engaged, a step Hardenberg seems to have undertaken not entirely without calculation and with a pronounced ambivalence (he wrote to Friedrich Schlegel that a very interesting life appeared to await him—still, he would rather be dead). In any case, he energetically returned to work in Weißenfels in May 1799, filled with hopes for financial independence and marriage. The following month on a visit to Jena he met the young Ludwig Tieck, already a popular writer. The two instantly struck up a close friendship, read the mystical writings of Jakob Böhme together, and even planned joint literary projects. Hardenberg entered upon his most intense period of professional and literary activity, producing by the following fall the essay "Die Christenheit oder Europa," the novelistic fragment *Die Lehrlinge zu Sais* (translated as *The Novices of Sais,* 1949), and the first of the poems known as "Geistliche Lieder" (Spiritual Songs, translated as *Sacred Songs of Novalis,* 1956).

Die Lehrlinge zu Sais is an essay-length prose text composed of first- and third-person meditations on nature that are loosely bound together by the general narrative setting of novices arriving in the ancient Egyptian city of Sais in search of the *Ursprache,* or primeval language. In the brief first part, "Der Lehrling" (The Novice), a first-person narrator muses on nature as a "große Chiffernschrift" (great script of ciphers) written in a language no one understands, "weil sich die Sprache selber nicht verstehe, nicht verstehen wolle" (because the language does not understand itself, nor want to understand). He compares it to "die ächte Sanscrit" (genuine Sanskrit), which only speaks "um zu sprechen, weil Sprechen ihre Lust und ihr Wesen sey" (in order to speak, because speaking is its pleasure and its essence). This simultaneously skeptical and mystical conception of language—which Hardenberg also expounds in his brief poetical manifesto "Monolog" (translated as "Monologue," 1982)—receives amplification in the longer second part of *Die Lehrlinge zu Sais,* "Die Natur" (Nature). Here a marginal narrator introduces soliloquies on nature and language that echo the views of Hardenberg's own teachers. One of the voices makes the extreme claim—especially remarkable given the Romantics' supposed cult of nature: "Man kann nicht sagen, daß es eine Natur gebe, ohne etwas überschwengliches zu sagen, und alles Bestreben nach Wahrheit in den Reden und Gesprächen von der Natur entfernt nur immer mehr von der Natürlichkeit" (One cannot say that nature exists, without saying something excessive; and all striving after truth in speeches and conversations about nature only progressively distances one from naturalness). Yet if in *Die Lehrlinge zu Sais* one voice denies the ability of language truthfully to represent nature, the teacher's voice claims at its conclusion that nature still serves as an instrument of higher understanding if it provokes an overwhelming feeling of *Sehnsucht,* of longing for a transcendent unity that never appears as such, but only in diversity, difference, and change. This desire for a lost unity is succinctly dramatized within the second part of *Die Lehrlinge zu Sais* by the story "Hyacinth und Rosenblüthe" (translated as "The Story of Hyacinth and Roseblossom," 1913), an allegorical fairy tale in which Hyacinth abandons his childhood home and his beloved to search for knowledge, only to recover Roseblossom far from home, in a dream within the temple of Isis.

Hardenberg's skepticism regarding language as a medium of truthful representation and his by no means contradictory belief in its practical power coalesced in his attempts to generate new cultural mythologies in "Die Christenheit oder Europa" and the "Geistliche Lieder." Opening with the words, "Es waren schöne, glänzende Zeiten" (They were beautiful, sparkling brilliant times), "Die Christenheit oder Europa" is cleverly posed between historical account and fairy tale. In presenting a mythical history of Europe from the Middle Ages to the present, Hardenberg strives to incite readers both to a reevaluation of modern European history and to personal transformation. Employing the triadic structure of unity, fall, and redemption, the essay rhapsodically recalls the Catholic Middle Ages as a time of cultural and spiritual integration, laments Europe's spiritual disintegration through the Reformation and Enlightenment, and announces the imminent return of "die Regierung Gottes auf Erden" (God's reign upon earth), which it sees foreshadowed in the political turmoil of the French Revolution and in the cultural growth of Germany. "Die Christenheit oder Europa" ends with the insistence that this political and cultural renewal can take place only through religion: "Nur die Religion kann Europa wieder aufwecken" (Only religion can reawaken Europe). The text produced great embarrassment among Hardenberg's friends. In presenting the Middle Ages not as the Dark Ages but as a period of high culture to inspire Germany, Hardenberg was building upon the groundwork of a new, Romantic appreciation of the past that Tieck and Heinrich Wackenroder had already laid in place; but in his effusive celebration of Catholicism and the Counter-Reformation, his hyperbolic criticism of the Reformation, Protestantism, and the Enlightenment, and his explicit fusion of republican politics with mystical religion, Hardenberg went beyond the pale of even the most liberal Romantic propriety. Acting on the advice of Goethe and the Berlin theologian Friedrich Schleiermacher, the Schlegels refused to publish the manuscript in the *Athenaeum*–and it was first printed twenty-five years later, probably through an error.

The twelve poetical songs now grouped together as the "Geistliche Lieder" were undertaken as a more modest project and met with more immediate success. Having found the church songs of the eighteenth century to be overly intellectual, dogmatic, and obscure, Hardenberg set about the composition of more accessible and evocative ones. He succeeded in producing poems that express tender religious sentiments in an imaginative, mystical, and at times erotic language, poems that preserve their popular appeal with a deceptively simple style and vocabulary. Although their orthodoxy remains a matter of debate, several of the songs quickly found their way into church songbooks, where they can still be found today.

The fall of 1799 marked the high point of Early Romanticism, as Hardenberg, Tieck, Schleiermacher, the scientist J.W. Ritter, and Friedrich and Dorothea Schlegel met regularly at the home of August and Caroline Schlegel in Jena. Hardenberg, a brilliant speaker and, according to Tieck, a virtuoso in the social arts, read his new works aloud to this group, who spurred him on to his most productive year. Although professional duties in Tennstedt occupied most of his attention, and his health continued to deteriorate from the tuberculosis that had begun to afflict him the previous year, Hardenberg began work on his two most ambitious literary projects: the poetic cycle "Hymnen an die Nacht" and the quintessentially Romantic novel *Heinrich von Ofterdingen.*

"Hymnen an die Nacht," published in the final issue of the *Athenaeum* in August 1800, immediately became Hardenberg's most successful work in his lifetime, and continues to be his most-read work to the present day. The first four hymns, written almost entirely in rhythmic prose, elaborate the basic argument of the text. In the first hymn, after initially praising the light as a "König der irdischen Natur" (king of earthly nature), the poet announces a turn "Abwärts . . . zu der heiligen, unaussprechlichen, geheimnißvollen Nacht" (downward . . . to the holy, ineffable, mysterious night). The poet's nostalgia for the daylight is overcome by the appearance of a mediatrix, his "zarte Geliebte" (tender beloved) with whom he experiences a sexual-mystical union, which proves at first to be only transitory. In the second hymn, the poet returns to day and laments the transitoriness of the night. The brief third hymn, perhaps Hardenberg's most famous piece of writing, recounts the central experience of the "Hymnen an die Nacht," a vision with striking–and artfully reworked–similarities to his 1796 diary account of an experience at Sophie von Kühn's grave. The poet tells how he once stood, overcome with grief, at the burial mound of the "Gestalt meines Lebens" (shape of my life). Suddenly he feels a "Dämmerungsschauer" (twilight shudder). A heavenly sleep overcomes him, the mound seems to rise up, time to blow away, and the beloved almost to resurrect before him. The poet claims that this vision was "der erste, einzige Traum" (the first and only dream), after which he feels only an "ewigen, unwandelbaren Glauben an den Himmel der Nacht und sein Licht, die Geliebte" (eternal, immutable faith in the heavenly Night and in its light, the beloved). The fourth hymn, after affirming the poet's now cheerful return to the day and his inner fidelity to the night, concludes by breaking forth with jubilant song in praise of the night and "des Todes / Verjüngende Flut" (death's rejuvenating flood). The fifth hymn sharply changes the direction of the "Hymnen an die Nacht" by translating this history of personal salvation into a mythical history of Western religion from ancient Greece to Christianity. After alternating between prose and verse, it ends with a song in praise of the Resurrection as mankind's victory over death, and of the Virgin Mary as the eternal mother who awakens the human longing for immortality. The sixth and final hymn, the ten-stanza poem "Sehnsucht nach dem Tode" (Longing for Death) recapitulates the major themes of the "Hymnen an die Nacht" and ends with the poet's yearning for his celestial home, where "Ein Traum bricht unsre Banden los / Und senkt uns in des Vaters Schoß" (A dream at last our bonds does snap / And lays us in our Father's lap).

Heinrich von Ofterdingen, a Bildungsroman based freely on accounts of the medieval poet Heinrich von Ofterdingen, was Hardenberg's final and most extensive literary production. It traces the growth of its protagonist through adolescence on his way to becoming a poet—a goal never attained in the incomplete novel. Formally daring, *Heinrich von Ofterdingen* mixes a realistic and morally elevated narration with dreams, fairy tales, operatic songs, mystical dialogues, discourses on poetry, and fantastic adventures. The first part, "Die Erwartung" (Anticipation), begins with Heinrich's dream within a dream of the blue flower—a vision that fills him with a longing he cannot understand. The second through fifth chapters trace Heinrich's journey to Augsburg with his mother and their encounters with businessmen, former crusaders, an Arabian woman, and a wise miner, all of whom share their stories with the boy. In the sixth chapter the pair arrives at his grandfather's house in Augsburg, where Heinrich falls in love with Mathilde, the daughter of his grandfather's friend and adviser, the poet Klingsohr. Heinrich and Klingsohr discuss poetry, history, and politics into the eighth chapter, in which Heinrich and Mathilde promise eternal love in a series of avowals that would later become the clichés of Romantic love, but are here spoken with a fairy-tale simplicity. The first part of the novel ends with "Klingsohrs Märchen" (Klingsohr's Fairy Tale), an obscure allegory of universal renewal filled with scientific, alchemical, mystical, philosophical, and literary allusions. When the novel's second, unfinished part, "Die Erfüllung" (Fulfillment), begins, Mathilde has died, and Heinrich is roaming the world as a pilgrim. The novel abruptly breaks off as Heinrich speaks with Sylvester, his father's former teacher, about nature, education, and religion.

Although Hardenberg had detailed plans for the continuation of the novel and wrote some of his finest poetry to include within it, his rapidly deteriorating health prevented him from finishing it. While writing the first part, Hardenberg had continued to make literary and professional plans, and even obtained a promotion as district director for the area around Weißenfels. Yet while he remained free from pain, he grew progressively weaker. In October 1800, when he received word that a younger brother had drowned, Hardenberg suffered a severe hemorrhage and was forced to cease virtually all professional and literary activity. Over the winter of 1800–1801, even speaking became tiring for him, and in the spring he sent for his friends. On 25 March 1801, as Friedrich Schlegel sat beside him in Weißenfels, Hardenberg fell asleep listening to his brother Karl play piano and died peacefully at noon. Less than a year and a half later Tieck and Schlegel issued the first two-volume collection of his works, including *Heinrich von Ofterdingen, Die Lehrlinge zu Sais,* "Geistliche Lieder," and some unpublished fragments. By 1837 the collection had gone through five editions and had assured Novalis's place in the world of letters.

Letters:
Friedrich Schlegel und Novalis: Biographie einer Romantikerfreundschaft in ihren Briefen, edited by Max Preitz (Darmstadt: Gentner, 1957).

Bibliography:
Richard Samuel, "Zur Geschichte des Nachlasses Friedrich von Hardenberg (Novalis)," *Jahrbücher der deutschen Schillergesellschaft,* 2 (1958): 301–347;

Samuel, *Novalis (Friedrich von Hardenberg): Der handschriftliche Nachlaß des Dichters. Zur Geschichte des Nachlasses* (Hildesheim: Gerstenberg, 1973).

Biographies:
Sophie von Hardenberg, *Friedrich von Hardenberg (genannt Novalis): Eine Nachlese aus den Quellen des Familienarchivs* (Gotha: Perthes, 1873);

Heinz Ritter-Schaumburg, *Novalis und seine erste Braut* (Stuttgart: Urachhaus, 1986);

Hermann Kurzke, *Novalis* (Munich: Beck, 1988).

References:
Heinz Bollinger, *Novalis: Die Lehrlinge zu Sais. Versuch einer Erläuterung* (Winterthur: Keller, 1954);

Kenneth S. Calhoon, "Language and Romantic Irony in Novalis' *Die Lehrlinge zu Sais,*" *Germanic Review,* 56 (Spring 1981): 51–61;

Manfred Dick, *Die Entwicklung des Gedankens der Poesie in den Fragmenten des Novalis* (Bonn: Bouvier, 1967);

Martin Dyck, *Novalis and Mathematics* (Chapel Hill: University of North Carolina Press, 1960);

Manfred Frank, *Das Problem "Zeit" in der deutschen Romantik* (Munich: Winkler, 1972);

Richard W. Hannah, *The Fichtean Dynamic of Novalis' Poetics* (Bern: Lang, 1981);

Klaus Hartmann, *Die freiheitliche Sprachauffassung des Novalis* (Bonn: Bouvier, 1987);

Josef Haslinger, *Die Ästhetik des Novalis* (Königstein: Hain, 1981);

J. F. Haussmann, "Die deutsche Kritik über Novalis von 1850–1900," *Journal of English and Germanic Philology,* 12 (1913): 211–244;

Haussmann, "German Estimates of Novalis from 1800 to 1850," *Modern Philology,* 9 (January 1911): 399–415;

Bruce Haywood, *Novalis: The Veil of Imagery. A Study of the Poetic Works of Friedrich von Hardenberg* (Cambridge, Mass.: Harvard University Press, 1959);

Friedrich Hiebel, *Novalis: German Poet, European Thinker, Christian Mystic* (Chapel Hill: University of North Carolina Press, 1954);

Frank and Gerhard Kurz, "Ordo inverus: Zu einer Reflexionsfigur bei Novalis, Hölderlin, Kleist und Kafka," in *Geist und Zeichen,* edited by H. Anton and others (Heidelberg: Winter, 1977), pp. 75–97;

Alice Kuzniar, *Delayed Endings: Nonclosure in Novalis and Hölderlin* (Athens: University of Georgia Press, 1987);

Nikolaus Lohse, *Dichtung und Theorie: Der Entwurf einer dichterischen Transzendentalpoetik in den Fragmenten des Novalis* (Heidelberg: Winter, 1988);

György Lukács, "On the Romantic Philosophy of Life: Novalis," in his *Soul and Form,* translated by Anna Bostock (Cambridge: Massachusetts Institute of Technology Press, 1974);

Hans-Joachim Mähl, *Die Idee des goldenen Zeitalters im Werk des Novalis* (Heidelberg: Winter, 1965);

Mähl, "Novalis," in *Deutsche Dichter der Romantik,* edited by Benno von Wiese (Berlin Schmidt, 1971), pp. 190–224;

Wilfried Malsch, *"Europa": Poetische Rede des Novalis, Deutung der französischen Revolution und Reflexion auf die Poesie in der Geschichte* (Stuttgart: Metzler, 1965);

Géza von Molnár, "Another Glance at Novalis' 'Blue Flower,'" *Euphorion,* 67 (1973): 273–286;

Von Molnár, *Novalis' "Fichte Studies"* (The Hague: Mouton, 1970);

Von Molnár, *Romantic Vision, Ethical Context. Novalis and Artistic Autonomy* (Minneapolis: University of Minnesota Press, 1987);

John Neubauer, *Bifocal Vision: Novalis' Philosophy of Nature and Disease* (Chapel Hill: University of North Carolina Press, 1971);

Neubauer, *Novalis* (Boston: Twayne, 1980);

William Arctander O'Brien, "Twilight in Atlantis: Novalis' *Heinrich von Ofterdingen* and Plato's *Republic,*" *Modern Language Notes,* 95, no. 5 (1980): 1292–1332;

Heinz Ritter, *Novalis' Hymnen an die Nacht* (Heidelberg: Winter, 1974);

Gerhard Schulz, *Novalis in Selbstzeugnissen und Bilddokumenten* (Reinbek: Rowohlt, 1969);

Schulz, "Die Poetik des Romans bei Novalis," *Jahrbuch des Freien Deutschen Hochstifts* (1964): 120–157;

Schulz, ed., *Novalis: Beiträge zu Werk und Persönlichkeit Friedrich von Hardenbergs,* second edition (Darmstadt: Wissenschaftliche Buchgesellschaft, 1986);

Elisabeth Stopp, "'Übergang vom Roman zur Mythologie': Formal Aspects of the Opening Chapters of *Heinrich von Ofterdingen,* Part II," *Deutsche Vierteljahrsschrift für Literaturwissenschaft und Geistesgeschichte,* 48 (1974): 318–341;

Friedrich Strack, *Im Schatten der Neugier: Christliche Tradition und kritische Philosophie im Werk Friedrich von Hardenbergs* (Tübingen: Niemeyer, 1982).

Papers:

The Freies Deutsches Hochstift, Frankfurt am Main, holds the largest collection of Novalis's extant manuscripts. The Biblioteka Jagielloska of Kraków University has collections of his poetic juvenilia and professional writing. The Museum Weißenfels has a collection of Hardenberg family correspondence, several of Novalis's personal possessions, and the oil portrait of Novalis by Franz Gareis.

Old High German Charms and Blessings

Brian Murdoch
University of Stirling

This entry originally appeared in DLB 148: German Writers
and Works of the Early Middle Ages: 800–1170.

Manuscripts: The *Merseburger Zaubersprüche* are preserved in Merseburg, Domstift, Codex 136, fol. 85r. The *Contra vermes* is in Munich Bayerische Staatsbibliothek, Clm 18, 524, fol. 203v. The epilepsy charm is in Munich, Bayerische Staatsbibliothek, clm 14, 763, fol. 88v. Those for a sore throat and for sore eyes are in Munich, Bayerische Staatsbibliothek, clm 23,390, fol. 59v. The Zurich blood charm is in Zurich, Kantonalbibliothek, ms. 51, fol. 23v. Horse charms are in Vienna, Österreichische Nationalbibliothek, cod. 751, fol. 188v; Trier, Stadtbibliothek, Hs. 40, vol. 36v; and Vatican, Palatine Library, Cod. Pal. 1158, fol. 68. The *Lorscher Bienensegen* is in the Vatican, Palatine Library, Cod. 220, fol. 58r. The *Wiener Hundsegen* is in Vienna, Österreichische Nationalbibliothek, cod. 552, fol. 107r. The *Innsbruck Pharmacopoeia* is in Innsbruck, Universitätsbibliothek, ms. 652. The *Zurich Pharmacopoeia* is in Zurich, Stadtbibliothek, Hs. C 58/275. The *Cambridge Eye-Charm* is in Cambridge, Peterhouse College, Cambridge University, ms. 130, fol. 219v. The *Graz Hail-Blessing* is in Graz, Universitätsbibliothek, ms. 41/12, fol. ult. The *Zurich House-Blessing* is in Zurich, Kantonalbibliothek, ms. C 176, fol. 154r. Various charms and blessings are in Paris, Bibliothèque Nationale nouv. acq. lat. 229. The *Bamberger Blutsegen* is in Bamberg, Dombibliothek, Cod. med. 6, fol. 139. The *Weingartner Reisesegen* is in Stuttgart, Landesbibliothek, Bibl. 25.

Standard editions: In *Denkmäler deutscher Poesie und Prosa aus dem VIII.–XII. Jahrhundert,* edited by Karl Müllenhoff and Wilhelm Scherer, third edition, edited by Elias von Steinmeyer (Berlin: Weidmann, 1892; reprinted, Berlin & Zurich: Weidmann, 1964); *Die kleineren althochdeutschen Sprachdenkmäler,* edited by Steinmeyer (Berlin: Weidmann, 1916); in *Denkmäler deutscher Prosa des 11. und 12. Jahrhunderts,* edited by Friedrich Wilhelm (Munich: Call-

wey, 1916); in *Frühmittelalterliches Deutsch,* edited by Fritz Tschirch (Halle: Niemeyer, 1955), pp. 35–38; in Carol Ann Miller, "The Old High German and Old Saxon Charms and Blessings," Ph.D. dissertation, Washington University, 1963; in *Altdeutsche Texte,* edited by Heinz Mettke (Leipzig: Bibliographisches Institut, 1970), pp. 45–50, 97; in *Althochdeutsches Lesebuch,* edited by Wilhelm Braune, sixteenth edition, edited by Ernst Ebbinghaus (Tübingen: Niemeyer, 1979); in *Sammlung kleinerer althochdeutscher Sprachdenkmäler,* edited by Gerhard Köbler (Gießen: Arbeiten zur Recht- sund Sprachwissenschaft, 1986), pp. 116–117, 262–263, 508–510, 528–529, 544–545, 570–575, 592–593.

Editions in modern German: In *Älteste deutsche Dichtungen,* edited by Karl Wolfskehl and Friedrich von der Leyen (Frankfurt am Main: Insel, 1964), pp. 30–41; in *Althochdeutsche Literatur,* edited by Horst Dieter Schlosser (Frankfurt am Main & Hamburg: Fischer, 1970), pp. 251–261; in *Älteste deutsche Dichtung und Prosa,* edited by Heinz Mettke (Leipzig: Reclam, 1976), pp. 84–101; in *Althochdeutsche Literatur,* edited by Hans Joachim Gernentz (Berlin: Union, 1979), pp. 84–89.

The Old High German charms and blessings, the best known of which are preserved in a manuscript of the tenth century now in the library of the Bishopric of Merseburg, are short pieces of prose or poetry designed either to ameliorate a situation that already exists—for example, curing an ailment—or to prevent something unpleasant from happening. About thirty such texts are extant. Those designed to cure are usually referred to as *Zaubersprüche* (magic charms), those whose intent is prevention as *Segen* (blessings)—a genre virtually impossible to distinguish from the *Gebet* (prayer). Indeed, the overlap among all three terms in the Old High German period is considerable, and the terminology applied to these pieces is confused and often artificial. All the works are designed, however, to have an effect through the power of the word. They may be contrasted with recipes or prescriptions, with which they are often found side by side in the manuscripts and which are also designed to ameliorate; the difference is that recipes require the use of ingredients and do not work by the power of the word alone. Nor is it always helpful to insist on the distinction between healing and prophylaxis, which is sometimes used to separate charms from blessings or prayers: insofar as they are written down, the Old High German charms, even when ostensibly concerned with a situation that already obtains, are obviously for use at a future time when such a situation will arise again.

All the surviving Old High German charms and blessings are Christian; a few of the earliest contain references to Germanic gods; but even those pieces are found in monastic manuscripts, and their context is invariably Christian. The manuscripts in which the charms are recorded are rarely earlier than the tenth century; most are later and are, therefore, from a Christian culture that had been established for many centuries.

Although anthologies, especially those that offer modern German translations, invariably highlight the Old High German parts of any given charm, the Old High German charms all contain integral Latin elements that must not be ignored. The two *Merseburger Zaubersprüche* (Merseburg Charms), for example, are accompanied by a Latin prayer that is rarely printed. An early charm that exists in High German and in Low German has the Latin title *Contra vermes* or *Pro nessia,* both of which literally mean "against worms" but actually mean "against disease." The precise meaning of the German portion is not quite clear, since the last word may refer to a horse's hoof or to an arrow that was, perhaps, to be fired away, taking the disease with it:

Ganz uz, Nesso, mit niun nessichilinon,
uz fonna marge in deo adra, vonna den adrun in daz fleisk,
fonna demu fleiske in daz fel, fonna demo velle in diz tulli.

(Go out, worm, with your nine little ones
out from the marrow into the vein, from the vein into the flesh,
from the flesh into the skin, from the skin into this hoof [or arrow].)

(There are parallels to this section of the charm in an ancient Indian work, the *Atharva-veda.*) But the charm is not just these three lines of German: not only is the Latin title part of the work, but at the end are the words *Ter Pat nr,* which mean that the Paternoster, the Latin version of the Lord's Prayer, has to be repeated three times as part of the charm. These words have sometimes been minimized as the "sole Christian element" in the text, but three full repetitions of the Lord's Prayer would far outweigh the three lines of German. Although the German seems to prescribe an action and include a command for the disease to leave by magic, the Latin Lord's Prayer is the dominant element; and that prayer does not contain a command but, rather, the request "fiat voluntas tua" (Thy will be done). The Old High German charm preserves what is probably older pagan material, but as it exists it is entirely Christian. The Low German form of the charm ends with the words "Drohtin, werthe so" (Let it be, O Lord), which is equivalent to the liturgical *amen,* which means "so be it."

The church was not against magic of this kind. There are frequent condemnations in religious literature of black magic, storm raising, cursing, and so on, but there is nothing of this kind in Old High German; the charms and blessings are invariably for positive purposes. The role of the church is important in determining the possible use of the Old High German charms. There are, for example, similarities between the charms and the collects—prayers used in the liturgy to make special requests, such as for the healing of sickness or the prevention of misfortune. These prayers were read, sometimes in groups of three or seven, before the lesson at certain masses. The pattern of the collects corresponds well to that of many of the Old High German charms. Critics examining only the German portions of the charms have stressed the supposedly magical command, by which the healing was supposed to be effected. In the surviving pieces, that command is modified by an invocatory request that God should permit the healing.

The pre-Christian Germanic elements preserved in some of the charms were presumably for oral use, and since the charms usually contain a liturgical prayer they, too, were probably intended to be spoken—perhaps by a priest—like the collects. That some of the charms for curing horses call for the user to whisper the charm in the horse's ear does not mean, as some scholars have surmised, that all the charms were whispered; there seems to be a difference in this regard between veterinary and human charms. A charm against epilepsy prescribes certain actions in addition to the speaking of the words; these actions have a distinctly ritual character.

It is possible that some of the charms were used as amulets. In Latin many charms exist in which nonsense or abracadabra words were written down to be carried as talismanic protection. In Christian societies names (for example, the traditional names of the Three Wise Men) and prayers were written down for this purpose;

and to an illiterate person, of course, all written words would be nonsense words. There are some Old High German charms containing nonsense words; but there is no clear evidence of a periaptic (talismanic) intent, and the Old High German charms and blessings depend on speech. These pieces of practical literature are the first stage of a continuum in German; precisely similar charms to those found in Old High German are found also, and in larger numbers, in Middle High German and, indeed, in modern German.

The two Merseburg Charms are a tenth-century addition to a ninth-century manuscript (now in the Cathedral Chapter in Merseburg) that includes liturgical material, including a Franconian baptismal oath. The German portions of the two charms contain references to pagan deities, but the Christian context is clear. Critics have for many years confidently described the first of the two as a charm to conjure magically the release of prisoners and the second as designed to cure a horse's sprained foot; both views are questionable. Neither piece is given a title. The Old High German material is followed by a lengthy Latin prayer (in a neater version of what is probably the same scribal hand) asking God to help a person whose name can be inserted at specific points and to guard the congregations of the faithful. This prayer presumably makes respectable the references in the Old High German part to the pagan gods.

The first charm describes how *idisi,* women roughly equivalent to the Norse Valkyries, took prisoners, harrowed an army, and picked at fetters. This triadic description, which is not very clear, is followed by a command: "insprinc haptbandun / inuar uigandun" (burst asunder fetters, / escape the foe). Taken at face value, this phrase seems to be associated with an escaping prisoner, and there are references in Old Norse literature to prisoners escaping by magic; but such references are, precisely, in *literature*. Later in the Middle Ages amulets were carried into battle by soldiers to protect them from death or capture, but prisoners did not escape in that way. It is far more plausible to see the fetters and captivity as metaphors for disease. There is at the end of this part of the text what might be the letter *N* for *nomen* (name), indicating that the sick person is to be named here.

The German portion of the second Merseburg Charm is also built on a triadic pattern. In alliterative verse, like the first charm, it describes Phol and Wodan riding in the woods. The first name is obscure; it might be Apollo or Paul, although in neither case would the alliteration of the line work. (In fact, the scribe who wrote the charm down was unsure himself, since the *h* has been added later.) In the next line Balder's horse goes lame, leading one to assume that Phol and Balder,

a known Germanic god, are one and the same. There follows a three-line section in which goddesses try to conjure a cure by incantation, and then Wodan does so. Five names are mentioned, not all of them recognizable from other sources. The first two pairs of names may be appositional: for example, "Friia Uolla ira suester" may mean "Freya, who is Folla's sister" rather than "Freya and Folla, her sister"; thus three rather than five goddesses may be involved. The third section makes a general statement about the healing of any kind of disorder, whether of humans or of horses:

> sose benrenki, sose bluotrenki, sose lidirenki:
> ben zi bena, bluot zi bluoda,
> lid zi geliden, sose gelimida sin!

> (be it bone-wrench, be it blood-wrench, be it limb-wrench:
> bone to bone, blood to blood,
> limb to limb, let them be locked!)

Versions of the same charm may be found all over Europe, though the male participants in the narrative vary; often they are Saint Peter and Christ, with Christ effecting the cure, and these versions complete the Christianization process begun, perhaps, in the Merseburg manuscript. The triadic "bone to bone, blood to blood, limb to limb" formula appears in many other languages and is clearly of some antiquity. Not all of the similar charms refer to the cure of horses, and there is no need to link the Merseburg Charm with horses only. A parallel Old High German example from Trier is directed against an equine ailment called *spurihalz,* presumably some kind of lameness; here Christ cures Saint Stephen's horse, but the "bone-to-bone" passage is not present. The Trier charm, like that from Merseburg, adds two Christian prayers, the standard Latin Paternoster and a German prayer asking Christ to cure the present horse as he did Saint Stephen's. The second Merseburg Charm has been interpreted in many ways, even as the reflection of a horse sacrifice. It is not known whether the Merseburg scribe understood the real sense of the Germanic parts or whether he just felt them to be of impressive antiquity and acceptable in a Christian society as long as a Christian element was attached.

It is worth asking at this point whether the charms worked. In general terms the Old High German charms (and a good many in other languages, such as Anglo-Saxon) are preserved together with medical recipes, and this supports the idea that they were felt to be efficacious. Most of the Old High German pieces are to do with bleeding (which does stop), sprains (which again improve with rest), epileptic attacks (which, though frightening, are temporary and can actually be helped by soothing the patient, with familiar prayers, for example), or perhaps for general sickness. More specifically prophylactic pieces and prayers—those designed to prevent misfortunes that have not yet happened—will, of course, always be felt to be useful if the misfortune does not happen or does not last.

Only one other charm seems to preserve some elements of pre-Christian thought: the charm against epilepsy, which has the Latin title *Contra caducum morbum* (Against the Falling Sickness) in one of its two surviving versions. Both versions are in relatively late manuscripts, one currently in Paris, the other in Munich. In the Paris manuscript the charm is attached to a medical tract; the Munich manuscript is a miscellany in which the charm, together with some Latin charms against bleeding and against fevers, follows a grammatical treatise. The content of the German portion of the charm, which is in prose, seems to indicate that neither scribe was entirely sure what he was writing. In the Paris version Latin instructions follow the title, telling the practitioner to stand over the patient and to say the charm three times. The charm itself opens with what may be the name of the Germanic god Donar but might have become an abracadabra word by the time the charm was written down. The rest seems to be Christian, although the sense is unclear: the Devil's son came to Adam's bridge, but Adam's son defeated him; Peter sent Paul, his brother, to heal the sick (Peter and Paul appear as brothers in some apocryphal writings and are often in conflict with the pagan archmagician, Simon Magus); a garbled Latin phrase, *pontum patum,* might refer to a bridge or to Pontius Pilate; the help of Christ is asked for the patient; there are instructions to touch the sides of the patient, who is to be commanded in God's name to stand up ("got der gebot dir ez" [God bids you do so]). The charm is completed by the Our Father, with its request that God's will be done. By the time this charm had been completed the patient would probably have recovered from the seizure on his or her own, and the charm would have received the credit.

References are found to genuine biblical incidents, such as the piercing of Christ's side, but much use is made of nonbiblical stories: legends of the infancy of Christ, the tale of how the Jordan ceased to flow at Jesus' baptism, additional miracles such as the restoring to life of a fish. Besides Peter and Paul, other saints play a role in charms, just as they do in liturgical prayers, specific saints being invoked for particular illnesses. The *Münchener Halsentzündungssegen* (Munich Charm for the Healing of a Sore Throat) invokes Saint Blaise, who saved the life of a child who was choking. On the other hand, a hemostatic charm from a now-lost Strasbourg manuscript, the *Straßburger Blutsegen* (Strasbourg Blood Charm) invokes "ter heilego Tumbo" (Saint Dumb), whose name plays on the Latin *stupidus,*

which in turn plays on *stupere* (to step). The Strasbourg manuscript contained another charm that presumably refers in garbled form to an incident from Christ's youth.

Many extant charms are designed to stop bleeding, and quite often nosebleeds are specified. A medical recipe from the eleventh century, the end of the Old High German period, in an Innsbruck medical manuscript calls for ground eggshell to be inhaled through a hollow reed; it is followed by a charm, and the juxtaposition of these texts indicates their intended similarity of function. (The recipe would probably work.) The charms against bleeding in Old High German are of three main types, although they are by no means always clearly distinguished. One group refers to an incident in the youth of Jesus, in which Jesus and someone else—often Judas—are playing with spears; they cut themselves, and Jesus heals his own wound. The second group, the Longinus charms, refers to the soldier who pierced Christ's side in John 19:34 and was, according to legend, himself healed of blindness. Third are the Jordan charms, alluding to the apocryphal story that the river stopped flowing when Jesus was baptized in it. All are common in Latin and in other languages, and all are contained in the *Bamberger Blutsegen* (Bamberg Blood Blessing), a composite or extended charm in another medical manuscript in which the charms are headed "pro pauperes" (for the poor). The Old High German text first gives the Judas and Jesus story (which is probably that which is found in garbled form in the Strasbourg text), then refers to the river Jordan. There follows a verse about the healing of Christ, and then a conjuration of the blood to stop flowing in the name of the five wounds of Christ.

A succinct version of the wounding and healing of Christ appears in a Low German blood charm in the same Trier manuscript as the Christ and Saint Stephen piece against *spurihalz:*

> Ad catarrum dic:
> Christ uuarth giuund to uuarth he hel gi ok gesund
> that bluod forstuond so duo thu bluod
> 　　　　amen Ter Pater noster Ter
>
> (For nosebleeds, say:
> Christ was wounded, he became whole and
> healthy again that blood stopped, do you likewise, o blood.
> 　　　　three amens, three Our Fathers)

There is an Old High German version of the Jordan charm in the same Paris manuscript that contains the epilepsy charm; the Latin heading specifies that the charm is for a nosebleed. Christ commands the Jordan to stop flowing until he and Saint John have crossed it, a

Manuscript page including the Lorscher Bienensegen, *written upside down at the bottom (Vatican, Palatine Library, Cod. Pal. 220, fol. 58r)* story reminiscent of the parting of the Red Sea by Moses. The Longinus story is found in several charms, including the eleventh-century *Innsbruck pharmacopoeia* and as part of the *Münchener Wundsegen* (Munich Wound Charm), written in the latter part of the twelfth century, where it is combined with a soteriological nonbiblical narrative much used in blood charms, the story of the "three good brothers" who meet Christ, the healer, when they are out looking for herbs. Sometimes the various stories merge, and the mixture of Latin and German in the charms is well illustrated by what Elias von Steinmeyer calls "ein ziemlich unverständlicher Blutsegen" (a pretty well incomprehensible blood charm) in a tenth-century manuscript in Zurich that also contains Latin sermons. Between two Latin fever charms and the story of the woman with an issue of blood in Matt. 9:20–22 is a composite charm that includes German words (the Latin abbreviations are resolved as far as possible, sometimes by guesswork, and in the translation the Latin is in italics):

> Longinus miles. lango zile. cristes thegan ast astes. Adiuro sanguis per patrem et filium. et spiritum sanctum vt ne fluas. plus quam iordanis aha . . . quando Christus. In ea baptizatus est et a . . . a [alleluia?]. III uicibus Pater noster cum gloria.

> (*Longinus the soldier.* long [?]. Christ's warrior . . . grace [?] *I abjure you, blood, in the name of the father and the Son and the Holy Spirit to stop flowing like Jordan* river . . . *when Christ was baptized and . . . [?]. Three times Our Father with the Gloria.*)

The language and the content seem equally confused, but this state of affairs is not unusual with the charms.

Other Old High German charms are concerned with various, not always identifiable, misfortunes. *Contra malum malannum* (Against a Tumor[?]) invokes the Father and the Son; the precise nature of the disease is unclear. One against *uberbein* (bone spur), which Steinmeyer groups with some recipes against gout, invokes the Holy Cross. An early piece preserved in Munich and a twelfth-century charm in Cambridge deal with sore eyes. The first adds an *amen* to the injunction to bathe the eyes in running water; the second offers a litany—no action is prescribed, but the amen is again present. The even later *Gothaer Fiebersegen* (Gotha Fever Charm) invokes all the saints and concludes with a selection of triple prayers. Charms against diseases in general, thought to be caused by worms, are sometimes accompanied by specific instructions in Latin on their use. Their closeness to recipes is apparent.

Some charms clearly refer to animal diseases, frequently of horses; here, too, the use of the Our Father and the *amen* are normal. The German text is some-

times incomprehensible, being reduced to a series of magic words. Such is the case in the confused *Contra rehin,* directed presumably against a kind of lameness, in a group of animal charms added to the twelfth-century *Zurich Pharmacopeia;* three Our Fathers are clearly called for, however. Identifying the horse diseases is not always easy, but many seem concerned with lameness or stiffness. One notable example, found in the same Paris manuscript as the epilepsy charm, has the title *Ad equum errehet* (For a Lame Horse). Three rhymed German quatrains describe a man with a lame horse who encounters Christ; the latter instructs the man to perform various actions, including whispering in the horse's ear and stepping on its hoof. Instructions in Latin call for the same actions; the words to be spoken to the horse are in German but are preceded by a Paternoster. Another series of charms in a medical manuscript, also in Paris, contains little German; these charms specify various actions, as well as the repetition of the Paternoster ten times. There are warnings against the use of the charm (or *Medicina,* the medicine, as it is called in the text) on other animals. Other charms are concerned with the banishing of worms—that is, disease—from horses and from animals in general, and some are supposed to banish worms from human beings; there are Latin and German examples of the last type, usually with the repeated Paternoster. One of these charms in the Paris group invokes Saint Germain, asking that the sun should not shine until the worms leave the animal.

Spurihalz is the subject of a horse charm in a ninth-century manuscript in Vienna that calls for a preliminary Paternoster (or perhaps three of them) and a concluding *amen.* The text refers to Christ's healing of a fish, perhaps alluding to one of the apocryphal stories in which a dried fish is brought back to life. Two horse charms written in the twelfth century in a manuscript that is now in the Vatican ask for the cure of an unknown equine disease, *morth;* the first gives a rudimentary narrative of a previous healing, the second invokes Christ, and both demand a threefold Paternoster.

The distinction between charms and blessings is, at best, one of intent: the former are aimed at situations that have already come into being, the latter at preventing situations from arising. It is not possible to distinguish between blessings and prayers; the collects, for example, are prayers that can request both healing and prevention. There are Old High German blessings that exhibit the same mixture of Latin and German, and add the same official prayers or liturgical utterances as the charms. Possibly the earliest general request for a blessing is the runic inscription on the Osthofen fibula, which may ask God for protection against the Devil.

Mixed in with a series of Latin charms of a particularly liturgical nature in a tenth-century manuscript now in Zurich is the enigmatic *Hausbesegnung* (House Blessing)—a Latin title indicates that the piece protects the home against demons. Two alliterative long lines in German exorcise the demon by making use of its inability to say the word *chnospinci;* what the word means has been long and inconclusively debated. Two blessings have to do with animals: the *Wiener Hundesegen* (Viennese Dog Blessing) invokes Christ and Saint Martin to protect dogs, and the *Lorscher Bienensegen* (Lorsch Bee Blessing) asks bees, in the name of the Virgin, not to swarm. Bee charms are found in various early cultures—not surprisingly, given the enormous importance of honey in those cultures.

One group of pieces comes close to liturgical prayers. Old and early Middle High German has preserved several *Reisesegen* (travel blessings), the best known being one from Weingarten, in a twelfth-century prayer book that also includes litanies. The *Weingartner Reisesegen* is quite impressive in literary terms. It opens with a formal Latin blessing (and instructions to make the sign of the cross) and asks for the safety of the traveler in the name of Christ, the Virgin, and Saint Ulrich. Later in the Middle Ages come the longer *Tobiassegen* (Tobias Blessings), which read like litanies of protection, and the similar double Munich *Ausfahrtssegen* (Departure Blessing). Blessings and whole masses for those undertaking a journey are common in missals and sacramentaries in the Old High German period (the fragmentary Saint Gall sacramentary is one example), as are invocations regarding the weather. In addition to Latin collects on the latter theme there is a brief and sometimes incomprehensible piece in German against hailstorms in a manuscript in Graz dating from the twelfth century: the *Grazer Hagelsegen* (Graz Hail Blessing) contains the usual demands for Paternosters.

Distinctions among charms, blessings, and prayers are hard to make; it is easier to distinguish between charms, blessings, and prayers, on the one hand, and recipes, on the other, although all are closely related, in aim at least, and it must be recalled that charms and blessings often survive in medical manuscripts. Judgments of what the form and function of charms might have been in pre-Christian Germanic society have to be speculative, because no pre-Christian charms survive as such. Virtually all the surviving Old High German charms have been Christianized.

References:

Jean Paul Allard and Jean Haudry, "Du second charme de Mersebourg au Viatique de Weingarten," *Études Indoeuropéenes,* 14 (September 1985): 33–59;

Peter Assion, *Altdeutsche Fachliteratur* (Berlin: Schmidt, 1973), pp. 133–151;

Isaac Bacon, "Versuch einer Klassifizierung altdeutscher Zaubersprüche und Segen," *Modern Language Notes,* 67 (April 1952): 224–232;

Georg Baesecke, "*Contra caducum morbum,*" *Beiträge,* 62 (1938): 456–460;

J. Knight Bostock, *A Handbook on Old High German Literature,* second edition, edited by K. C. King and D. R. McLintock (Oxford: Clarendon Press, 1976), pp. 26–42;

Wilhelm Boudriot, *Die altgermanische Religion in der christlichen kirchlichen Literatur* (Bonn: Rohrscheid, 1928);

Gerhard Eis, *Altdeutsche Zaubersprüche* (Berlin: De Gruyter, 1964);

Eis, "Der Millstätter Blutsegen in einer Memminger Handschrift," *Studia Neophilologica,* 36 (1964): 207–210;

Marianne Elsakkers, "*Contra caducum morbum:* 2 maal vallen en opstaan," *Amsterdamer Beiträge zur älteren Germanistik,* 29 (1989): 49–60;

Oskar Erdmann, *Blut-und Wundsegen in ihrer Entwicklung dargestellt* (Berlin: Mayer & Müller, 1903);

Adolph Franz, *Die kirchlichen Benediktionen im Mittelalter* (Freiburg: Herder, 1909);

Susan D. Fuller, "Pagan Charms in Tenth-Century Saxony?: The Function of the Merseburg Charms," *Monatshefte,* 72 (Summer 1980): 162–170;

Manfred Geier, "Die magische Kraft der Poesie: Zur Geschichte, Struktur und Funktion des Zauberspruchs," *Deutsche Vierteljahresschrift,* 56 (1982): 359–385;

Felix Genzmer, "Germanische Zaubersprüche," *Germanisch-Romanische Monatshefte,* 1 (October 1950): 21–35;

Genzmer, "Die Götter des zweiten Merseburger Zauberspruchs," *Arkiv for Nordisk Fililogi,* 63 (1948): 55–72;

T. Grienberger, "Althochdeutsche Texterklärungen," *Beiträge,* 45 (1921): 212–238;

J. Sidney Groseclose and Brian O. Murdoch, *Die althochdeutschen poetischen Denkmäler* (Stuttgart: Metzler, 1976), pp. 48–58;

Barbara Kerewsky Halpern and John Miles Foley, "The Power of the Word: Healing Charms as an Oral Genre," *Journal of American Folklore,* 91 (October–December 1978): 903–924;

Irmgard Hampp, "Vom Wesen des Zaubers im Zauberspruch," *Der Deutschunterricht,* 13, no. 1 (1961): 58–76;

Wolfgang Haubrichs, *Die Anfänge,* volume 1, part 1 of *Geschichte der deutschen Literatur,* edited by Joachim Heinzle (Frankfurt am Main: Athenaeum, 1988), pp. 412–436;

R-M. S. Heffner, "The Third Basel Recipe (BaIII)," *Journal of English and Germanic Philology*, 46 (1947): 248–253;

Karl Helm, "Zur althochdeutschen 'Hausbesegnung,'" *Beiträge* (Halle), 69 (1947): 358–360;

J. A. Huisman, "*Contra caducum morbum:* Zum althochdeutschen Spruch gegen Fallsucht," *Amsterdamer Beiträge zur älteren Germanistik*, 17 (1982): 39–50;

Adolf Jacoby, "Der Bamberger Blutsegen," *Zeitschrift für deutsches Altertum*, 54 (1913): 200–209;

Wolfgang Jungandreas, "*God fura dih, deofile*," *Zeitschrift für deutsches Altertum*, 101, no. 1 (1972): 84–85;

Rolf Ködderitzsch, "Der Zweite Merseburger Zauberspruch und seine Parallelen," *Zeitschrift für celtische Philologie*, 33 (1974): 45–57;

H. W. J. Kroes, "Zum Lorscher Bienensegen," *Germanisch-Romanische Monatsschrift*, new series, 10 (1960): 86–87;

Willy Krogmann, "*Pro cadente morbo*," *Archiv*, 173 (1938): 1–11;

Georg Manz, *Ein St Galler Sakramentar-Fragment (Cod. Sangall. No. 350)* (Münster: Aschendorff, 1939);

Achim Masser, "Zum Zweiten Merseburger Zauberspruch," *Beiträge* (Tübingen), 94 (1972): 20–25;

Hermann Menhardt, "Der sogenannte Millstätter Blutsegen aus St. Blasien," *Zeitschrift für deutsches Altertum*, 85 (1954–1955): 197–202;

Hugo Moser, "Vom Weingartner Reisesegen zu Walthers Ausfahrtsegen," *Beiträge* (Halle), 82 (1961): 69–89;

Murdoch, "But Did They Work?: Interpreting the Old High German *Merseburg Charms* in Their Medieval Context," *Neuphilologische Mitteilungen*, 89, no. 3 (1988): 358–369;

Murdoch, "Drohtin, uuerthe so!: Funktionsweisen der altdeutschen Zauberspüche," *Literaturwissenschaftliches Jahrbuch der Görres-Gesellschaft*, 32 (1991): 11–37;

Murdoch, *Old High German Literature* (Boston: Twayne, 1983), pp. 45–54;

Murdoch, "*Peri hieres nousou:* Approaches to the Old High German Medical Charms," in "*Mit regulu bithuungan*": *Neue Arbeiten zur althochdeutschen Poesie und Sprache*, edited by John L. Flood and David N. Yeandle (Göppingen: Kümmerle, 1989), pp. 142–160;

Kenneth Northcott, "An Interpretation of the Second Merseburg Charm," *Modern Language Review*, 54 (January 1959): 45–50;

F. Ohrt, *Die ältesten Segen über Christi Taufe und Christi Tod in religionsgeschichtlichem Lichte* (Copenhagen: Levin & Munksgaard, 1938);

Robert Priebsch, "A Rhymed Charm against 'Mort' in Horses," *Modern Language Review*, 17 (October 1922): 415–417;

Rainer Reiche, *Ein rheinisches Schulbuch aus dem 11. Jahrhundert* (Munich: Arbeo-Gesellschaft, 1976);

Lynn L. Remly, "Murder at a Gallop: The Second Merseburg Charm," *Midwestern Journal of Language and Folklore*, 2 (Spring 1976): 31–39;

Hellmut Rosenfeld, "*Phol ende Wuodan Vuorun zi holza:* Baldermythe oder Fohlenzauber?," *Beiträge* (Tübingen), 95 (1973): 1–12;

Hubert Schiel, "Trierer Segensformeln und Zaubersprüche," *Trierisches Jahrbuch* (1953): 23–36;

Arno Schirokauer, "Der Eingang des Lorscher Bienensegens," *Modern Language Notes*, 57 (January 1942): 62–64;

Schirokauer, "Form und Formel einiger altdeutscher Zaubersprüche," *Zeitschrift für deutsche Philologie*, 73, no. 3 (1954): 353–364;

Bernhard Schnell, "Das 'Prüler Kräuterbuch': Zum ersten Herbar in deutscher Sprache," *Zeitschrift für deutsches Altertum*, 120, no. 2 (1991): 184–202;

Anton Schönbach, "Segen," *Zeitschrift für deutsches Altertum*, 24 (1880): 65–84;

Carl Selmer, "An Unpublished Old German Blood Charm," *Journal of English and Germanic Philology*, 51 (1952): 345–354;

Gerd Sieg, "Zu den Merseburger Zaubersprüchen," *Beiträge* (Halle), 82 (1960): 364–370;

Stefan Sonderegger, *Althochdeutsch in St Gallen* (Saint Gall, 1970), pp. 75–77;

Heather Stuart and F. Walla, "*Eoris sazun idisi*–or did they?," *Germanic Notes*, 14, no. 3 (1983): 35–37;

Stuart and Walla, "Die Überlieferung der mittelalterlichen Segen," *Zeitschrift für deutsches Altertum*, 116, no. 1 (1987): 53–79;

Wolf von Unwerth, "Der Zweite Trierer Zauberspruch," *Zeitschrift für deutsches Altertum*, 54 (1913): 195–199;

Heinrich Wesche, *Der althochdeutsche Wortschatz im Gebiete des Zaubers und der Weissagung* (Halle: Niemeyer, 1940);

K. A. Wipf, "Die Zaubersprüche im Althochdeutschen," *Numen*, 22 (1975): 42–69.

Erich Maria Remarque

(22 June 1898 – 25 September 1970)

Charles W. Hoffmann
Ohio State University

This entry originally appeared in DLB 56: German Fiction Writers, 1914–1945.

BOOKS: *Die Traumbude: Ein Künstlerroman* (Dresden: Schönheit, 1920);

Im Westen nichts Neues (Berlin: Propyläen, 1929); translated by A. W. Wheen as *All Quiet on the Western Front* (Boston: Little, Brown, 1929; London: Putnam, 1929);

Der Weg zurück (Berlin: Propyläen, 1931); translated by Wheen as *The Road Back* (Boston: Little, Brown, 1931; London: Putnam, 1931);

Drei Kameraden (Amsterdam: Querido, 1937); translated by Wheen as *Three Comrades* (Boston: Little, Brown, 1937);

Flotsam, translated by Denver Lindley (Boston: Little, Brown, 1911; London: Hutchinson, 1941); German version published as *Liebe deinen Nächsten: Roman* (Batavia: Querido / Stockholm: Bermann-Fischer, 1941);

Arch of Triumph, translated by Lindley and Walter Sorell (New York & London: Appleton-Century, 1945; London: Hutchinson, 1946); original German version published as *Arc de Triomphe: Roman* (Zurich: Micha, 1946);

Der Funke Leben (Cologne: Kiepenhener & Witsch, 1952); translated by James Stern as *Spark of Life* (New York: Appleton-Century-Crofts, 1952);

A Time to Love and a Time to Die, translated by Lindley (New York: Harcourt, Brace, 1954); original German version published as *Zeit zu leben und Zeit zu sterben* (Cologne: Kiepenheuer & Witsch, 1954);

Der schwarze Obelisk: Geschichte einer verspäteten Jugend (Cologne: Kiepenheuer & Witsch, 1956); translated by Lindley as *The Black Obelisk* (New York: Harcourt, Brace, 1957; London: Hutchinson, 1957);

Der Himmel kennt keine Günstlinge (Cologne: Kiepenheuer & Witsch, 1961); translated by Richard and Clara Winston as *Heaven Has No Favorites* (New York: Harcourt, Brace & World, 1961); translation

Erich Maria Remarque (Ullstein)

republished as *Bobby Deerfield* (Greenwich, Conn.: Fawcett, 1961);

Die Nacht von Lissabon (Cologne: Kiepenheuer & Witsch, 1963); translated by Ralph Manheim as *The Night in Lisbon* (New York: Harcourt, Brace & World, 1964; London: Hutchinson, 1964);

Schatten im Paradies (Munich: Droemer Knaur, 1971); translated by Manheim as *Shadows in Paradise* (New York: Harcourt Brace Jovanovich, 1972);

Full Circle, translated by Peter Stone (New York: Harcourt Brace Jovanovich, 1974).

It is sometimes claimed that next to the Bible, Erich Maria Remarque's *Im Westen nichts Neues* (1929; translated as *All Quiet on the Western Front,* 1929) has sold more copies than any other book in history. Whether that claim is true or not, the enormous popularity of this best-seller has made the name Remarque a household word for over half a century; and without much question that name is recognized by more readers around the world than that of any other modern German writer. For serious observers of literature he does not rank with Thomas Mann, Heinrich Böll, or Bertolt Brecht; but generations of young people continue to form their attitudes toward war from *Im Westen nichts Neues,* and it is difficult to find a literate person anywhere who has not read the novel.

In spite of such success, however, Remarque is not very well known today if one considers not just *Im Westen nichts Neues* but the whole of his output. Readers who consider themselves fans because of this first book are often surprised to learn that it was followed by ten more novels. This surprise is in turn surprising, for when the later works first appeared, several of them were also best-sellers; and from the 1930s through the 1960s the appearance of "a new Remarque" was a major publishing event—especially outside of Germany, where the author's reputation was never as high as it was abroad.

His books have appeal on several counts. They are generally well-crafted novels with clear plot lines; they are easy to read; and they mix adventure, suspense, social comment, and some violence with a central love story. At the same time, they were clearly intended as documents of their age, telling in presumably realistic fashion what was happening to Germans in the chaotic 1920s, during the Hitler years and the war, and in exile. No doubt it was Remarque's vivid chronicling of at least one side of the German experience in this momentous century that once made up a major part of the appeal for non-German readers; and his episodic style and his use of the first person and the present tense gave several of the later novels the same appearance of eyewitness authenticity that *Im Westen nichts Neues* had had.

Remarque lived a colorful life, and most of his works are autobiographical, though seldom in much more than an incidental way. His protagonists like to recall boyhood haunts and pleasures that were also Remarque's own: they, too, collected butterflies and read Arthur Schopenhauer, Friedrich Nietzsche, Jack London, Friedrich Hölderlin, and Thomas Mann. Streets and houses where the author lived and places

where he worked appear again and again in the novels; and characters are often named directly after or modeled in thinly disguised fashion on people he had known. Recognizing such real-life references increases one's enjoyment of the works and, perhaps, one's sense of their authenticity, though it is not necessary for understanding the novels themselves. In the infrequent interviews he granted, Remarque always insisted that the events of his life were not important for his fiction and that, like any decent novelist, he wanted to be known for the latter. Nevertheless, Remarque was a successful, famous, and colorful man.

He was born in Osnabrück on 22 June 1898 as Erich Paul Remark. He later took the middle name Maria from his mother, Anna Maria Remark, and the spelling *Remarque* from French ancestors. His father, Peter Franz Remark, was a bookbinder and the family, which included two sisters, was poor. By the time Remarque left for the army the family had had to move some eleven times, and yet the clearly autobiographical reminiscences of his later heroes suggest that his childhood was happy. He was close to his mother, less so to his father, and fond of roaming the streets of Osnabrück and exploring the nearby countryside. His early education was Catholic, and at the time he was drafted he was preparing for a career as an elementary school teacher. His interest in music, which is so well documented in the novels, began in these early years— Remarque played both the organ and the piano and gave lessons in the latter. At the age of sixteen or seventeen he also made his first attempts at writing: essays, poems, and the beginnings of an eminently forgettable novel. Finished later and published in 1920 as *Die Traumbude* (The Dream Room or Dream Den), this first novel was written in a flowery art nouveau style and was an embarrassment to Remarque after he turned seriously to literature. To his great relief, the Ullstein publishing house bought up and destroyed the unsold copies when it published *Im Westen nichts Neues* a decade later.

Although some of his own war experiences are reflected in *Im Westen nichts Neues,* Remarque did not, like his hero Paul Bäumer, volunteer enthusiastically for military service. He was drafted in November 1916; and, because his mother was seriously ill (she died in September 1917), he was given frequent leave to visit her at home and was not sent to France until the following summer. Nor did he see much fighting or front line service. In the battle of Flanders in July his unit was attacked by the British; and while carrying a wounded comrade back from the attack, Remarque suffered shrapnel wounds which sent him to a hospital in Germany. There he spent most of the rest of the war recuperating, writing music, and working on *Die Traumbude.*

In 1919 he returned to school to finish his teacher training and for a little over a year served as substitute teacher in several small-town schools near Osnabrück. Accused of lack of cooperation with the local authorities and of having played a role in the revolutionary Spartacist movement–he steadfastly denied the latter charge–he was in constant trouble during his brief teaching career and in 1920 decided that the education of the nation's youth was better left in other hands. He turned to a variety of odd jobs which are mirrored in the later novels, especially in *Der schwarze Obelisk* (1956, translated as *The Black Obelisk,* 1957): he was an itinerant peddler, a salesman for a gravestone firm, an organist in an insane asylum, and an advertising copywriter. In 1925 he moved to Berlin, where he edited the magazine *Sport im Bild* and began to establish a reputation for high living, fancy clothes, hard drinking, and as an aficionado of automobile racing. He married his first wife, the actress Jutta Zambona, in 1925. He made a second literary start with the story "Stationen am Horizont" (Stations on the Horizon), which was serialized in the sports journal for which Remarque was working but was never published in book form.

Im Westen nichts Neues was written in a few months in 1927, but Remarque was not immediately able to find a publisher. Ullstein eventually decided to bring out the work, and it appeared first in serial form during November and December 1928 in the *Vossische Zeitung*. Book publication followed in January 1929, and *Im Westen nichts Neues* proved to be an instant best-seller. Within three months a half million copies were sold in Germany, and the book was quickly translated into fourteen languages. A year after publication the figure had jumped to a million copies at home and the number of translations to twenty-three, not counting a half dozen pirated editions. After eighteen months the worldwide sales totaled three-and-a-half million copies.

Such phenomenal and immediate success was spurred by the fact that the publishers aggressively promoted the book with a media campaign that might not seem unusual today but that was unprecedented in the 1920s. But the main reason was that readers ten years after the Armistice found their own perceptions of the Great War confirmed by Remarque's portrayal of a new kind of war which seemed to mark a turning point in man's history. Remarque allows this theme to emerge indirectly and without much direct editorial comment.

Paul Bäumer, eighteen years old and fresh from school at the beginning of the novel, is sent after skimpy but brutal basic training to the trenches in France. The plot consists of Paul's experiences at the front, at home on leave, and in the hospital where he twice recuperates from wounds. The novel ends with his death just before the cessation of hostilities, on a day when all is otherwise "quiet on the front." What happens between the beginning and the end is divided almost exactly into two halves. In the first half the action takes place largely behind the lines; the fighting is only sporadic; and Paul and the other soldiers spend much of their time thinking about home, school, and what life might be like after the war is over. This half ends with the first great battle, and the second half begins with Paul's subsequent leave at home. After he returns to France, the book depicts unrelieved fighting. Most of the main characters die in quickening succession, and life is reduced to a primitive struggle for survival where instinct is crucial and reason meaningless, reaction and luck are everything, and thinking or planned action are at best irrelevant and at worst disastrous.

This construction of the novel mirrors the actual course of the war, in which the German troops had to fight against the growing material superiority of the Allies, though Remarque does not really present the conflict as war between Germans and Allies. The battles are almost never identified and dates are rarely given; he writes of "the troops over there" more often than he does of the French or the British or the Americans, for they are not the real enemy. Speaking in a foxhole in no-man's-land to the Frenchman he has killed, Paul blames the carnage on the desire for profit and on "national interest" as defined by authorities and institutions on both sides. Little men ruled by forces over which they have no control, those doing the fighting are all victims and have too much in common to be enemies. The rhythm established by the book's structure also underlines the theme of the lost generation, to whom *Im Westen nichts Neues* is dedicated. In the beginning the young recruits are still closely tied to the past; and in their conversations with the older soldiers, who look forward to returning to jobs and family, they struggle to imagine a future for themselves. When Paul is home on leave, he realizes that the war has cut him and his comrades off from a past that is forever lost; and back at the front he recognizes that the war has made concern for the future meaningless. The only thing that counts is the present and surviving from one moment of that present to the next. Survival becomes increasingly more difficult as the book progresses and the technological nature of the war is made more evident. From the start Remarque stresses that living or dying has little to do with one's prowess as a soldier, except as "prowess" is equated with conditioned reflex. Death comes from afar in the artillery shells and the bombs; and as the trenches offer less and less refuge from the other side's new tanks and airplanes and its better guns, survival becomes little more than a matter of chance.

Im Westen nichts Neues is, of course, a book about the war, but in its insistence that life has been reduced to reaction and instinct it goes beyond the war. Remarque means more than just the trenches when he has Paul say that "das Leben ist nur auf einer ständigen Lauer gegen die Bedrohung des Todes,–es hat uns zu denkenden Tieren gemacht, um uns die Waffe des Instinktes zu geben,–es hat uns mit Stumpfheit durchsetzt, damit wir nicht zerbrechen vor dem Grauen, das uns bei klarem, bewußtem Denken überfallen würde . . ." (life is simply one continual watch against the menace of death,–it has transformed us into unthinking animals in order to give us the weapon of instinct–it has reinforced us with dullness, so that we do not go to pieces before the horror which would overwhelm us if we had clear, conscious thought . . .). Nowhere in the novel is the real meaning of the war brought home to Paul more clearly than in the military hospital where he is recovering from his wounds: the war is a new outbreak of man's inherent primitivism and makes a lie of his belief in culture and civilization and progress. "Wie sinnlos ist alles, was je geschrieben, getan, gedacht wurde, wenn so etwas möglich ist! Es muß alles gelogen und belanglos sein, wenn die Kultur von Jahrtausenden nicht einmal verhindern konnte, daß diese Ströme von Blut vergossen wurden, daß diese Kerker der Qualen zu Hunderttausenden existieren. Erst das Lazarett zeigt, was Krieg ist" (How senseless is everything that can ever be written, done, or thought, when such things are possible. It must be all lies and of no account when the culture of a thousand years could not prevent this stream of blood being poured out, these torture-chambers in their hundreds of thousands. A hospital alone shows what war is). A. F. Bance points out that *Im Westen nichts Neues* "is a novel of Weimar Germany," written not immediately after the war but in the late 1920s, when "the individual became fully aware of his limited freedom of action in the face of social, industrial and political forces." It would be going too far to suggest that Remarque's intention was to present World War I as a metaphor for what has happened to man in the twentieth century, yet the theme of the individual struggling against but clearly determined by forces beyond his control–technology, institutions, politics, social conventions, disease, death–remained central in his later work. So did the importance of chance and accident and of the one thing that retains its positive value in the novel: comradeship. Finally, the straightforward, relatively unadorned, realistic style of *Im Westen nichts Neues*, with its division into succinct short episodes and a heavy reliance on conversation, remained characteristic of Remarque's writing.

Despite the instant acclaim that greeted the novel, its appearance also caused a tidal wave of controversy–which did nothing to harm book sales. While most of the early critics and reviewers praised *Im Westen nichts Neues* as the ultimate antiwar statement, others attacked its view of the war, its inherent pacifism, its "outrageous" popularity, the quality of the writing, and Remarque himself. His role in the war, and thus the authenticity of his portrayal of it, were called into doubt. Even the author's identity was questioned in a book-length satire, *Hat Erich Maria Remarque wirklich gelebt?* (Does Erich Maria Remarque Really Exist?), and Remarque's novel was blasted as both mediocre writing and bad propaganda. The most outspoken revilers were the Nazis, by 1930 the second most important party in the nation. Literally everything about *Im Westen nichts Neues,* but particularly its pacifism and its "defamatory" picture of the German soldier, aroused their ire. Late in 1930, when Lewis Milestone's American film version played in Berlin, Nazi gangs roughed up spectators waiting in line for tickets and disrupted performances. In a Germany buffeted by the shock waves of the stock market crash, precariously close to civil chaos, and already ruled in large measure by emergency decree, the film was banned as too controversial and a threat to law and order. The Nazis' ultimate verdict was pronounced in 1933 when *Im Westen nichts Neues* was one of the first books to be burned publicly. Propaganda Minister Joseph Goebbels himself consigned it to the flames with the words: "For his literary betrayal of the soldiers of the First World War and so that our people may be educated in the spirit of truthfulness, I give to the flames the writings of Erich Maria Remarque."

Remarque was not on hand to see the novel so honored. After his unprecedented first success he was able to devote himself exclusively to writing, and he had immediately begun work on a sequel. But he recognized that the political reaction to *Im Westen nichts Neues* had made him a marked man; and in 1931, after finishing *Der Weg zurück* (1931; translated as *The Road Back,* 1931) and making sure that his money was out of the country, he left Germany. He bought a villa in Porto Ronco in Switzerland and lived both there and in France until 1939, when he left Europe for the United States. Sometime during the early 1930s he divorced his wife (sources disagree as to the date) but subsequently remarried her so that she could remain in Switzerland and avoid having to return to Hitler's Germany. In 1938 the Third Reich took away his citizenship.

Der Weg zurück takes up where *Im Westen nichts Neues* ended: on the battlefields of France in the final days before the Armistice. All of the principal characters are veterans of the trenches; some of them are known to the reader from *Im Westen nichts Neues* but most, including the narrator, Ernst Birkholz, are new. The book traces their return from France and their attempts to get a footing in a world which they find alien and hostile. Some seek this footing in reestablished relationships with parents, wives, friends, or school, others in jobs and new commitments. Most are unsuccessful: two commit suicide; one disappears with a wife who had been unfaithful while he was away and with whom there can now be no more love; another is sent to prison for murder; and the few who manage to find a niche in the postwar world do so by becoming profiteers and opportunists.

Though the fact is not made explicit, the novel is set in the Osnabrück to which Remarque himself returned after demobilization. The time span is kept indefinite: not long before the end it is mentioned that the characters were at the front "a year ago"; but there is also reference to the rapidly falling value of the mark, which suggests that the work ends closer to 1923. In any event, the novel is set primarily in 1919 and 1920, the fateful years when the seeds of the ultimate death of Weimar democracy and the victory of fascism were sown. These were months of civil strife, of unsuccessful revolution both from the left and from the right, of economic deprivation, of acrid division on national goals and national identity, of humiliation from the peace treaty, and of groping experimentation with a new form of democratic government for which there was neither the necessary tradition nor sufficient popular support. This historical background is all part of *Der Weg zurück,* and the novel is a fascinating chronicle of the period.

Historical event is not really the issue, however, for Remarque is primarily interested in private concerns. His theme is the inability of the lost generation to function in the civilian world, and it is made abundantly clear that this failure stems from the war. The characters' values and motivations, their actions, and their reactions to the current situation are all determined by their wartime experience. "Halt die Ohren steif, Junge, der Krieg ist noch nicht zu Ende" (That's right, keep smiling, lad; the war's not over yet), "Aber für den Frieden? Taugen wir dazu? Passen wir Überhaupt noch zu etwas anderm, als Soldaten zu sein?" (But for peace? Are we suitable? Are we fit for anything but soldiering?), "Wir sind immer noch Soldaten, ohne es gewußt zu haben" (We are soldiers still without having been aware of it), "Wir haben den Krieg noch in den Knochen. . . . Wir werden ihn auch nie mehr los" (We have the war in our bones still. . . . Yes, and we'll never get it out again)–these quotations taken from various places in the novel could be multiplied many times over. In *Im Westen nichts Neues* the past had been wiped out; the future did not exist; the present was all that was real. In *Der Weg zurück* it is only the past that counts;

and as much as the veterans struggle against the past and lament the fact that they have been permanently crippled by it, they continually affirm its significance. The horrors of the war must not be glossed over or forgotten, they tell their teachers, their parents, the court, and a troubled society that would like to get back to business as usual; otherwise the sacrifices and the losses will have been in vain. But their stubborn clinging to the wartime past makes *Der Weg zurück* as much a novel of resentment as the commitment to a new beginning that Remarque claimed he wanted it to be.

This commitment is nowhere more evident than in his continuing emphasis on the one thing that had remained a positive value in the otherwise pessimistic *Im Westen nichts Neues:* comradeship. In the sequel the pronoun *wir* (we) is by far the most important one, and it means "we, the veterans" vis-á-vis "them, the rest of the world." The characters are scarcely home before they seek each other out, and only when they are together do they feel a sense of belonging and a bit of hope. As some adjust and others disappear, as social distinctions and civilian ties gradually erode the old solidarity from the front, Birkholz sees that the one positive thing which the war had given him is now lost: "Alles andere ist kaputgegangen im Kriege, aber an die Kameradschaft hatten wir geglaubt. Und jetzt sehen wir: was der Tod nicht fertiggebracht hat, das gelingt dem Leben: es trennt uns" (All else went west in the war, but comradeship we did believe in; now only to find that what death could not do, life is achieving; it is driving us asunder). The inability to fit into civilian life confirms his feeling that he and his friends are ruined, that they are helpless to do much about the problems that now confront them, and that others are responsible for making it so.

Remarque had not intended for *Der Weg zurück* to be quite the pessimistic work that it is. "We want to begin once more to believe in life," he said in correspondence when he was working on the novel, and its title means not just "the road back" to postwar Germany but explicitly "the road back to life." For a time Ludwig Breyer, a veteran who has recognized that the real enemy is not the past but the reactionary trend of the present, seems to be on the right road. And in the novel's brief epilogue, which is–uncharacteristically for Remarque–filled with metaphors, Birkholz assures the reader that he will find his way back to vital living just as surely as "ein Baum oder die atmende Erde" (a tree or the breathing earth) do every spring. But Breyer has committed suicide; Birkholz has suffered a nervous breakdown; and the overwhelming prior evidence of the book argues for skepticism that the lost generation can ever find new meaning.

As in the case of *Im Westen nichts Neues,* it is well to remember that *Der Weg zurück* was written a decade after the period it depicts and to ponder what the text reveals about German thinking in the late 1920s and early 1930s. The conviction that private identity is determined by external factors and that the individual is powerless to do much but react to the social, economic, and political forces that impinge on him is characteristic of the last years before Hitler. This conviction turned out to have fatal consequences; and some early critics, hitting on this point, blamed Remarque for not warning openly of the dangers in such thinking. The left particularly criticized the novel for dwelling so exclusively in the realm of private fate and for failing to pay sufficient attention to the historical context. Remarque himself considered *Der Weg zurück* a better novel than *Im Westen nichts Neues* and was disappointed when it did not sell as well. Reviewers abroad, especially in the United States, tended to agree with the author; but German critics generally found the work repetitive in style, lacking in focus, given to sentimentality and sensationalism (a charge Remarque went on to hear again and again), and poorly written.

Remarque's next novel, *Drei Kameraden* (1937; translated as *Three Comrades,* 1937) spans the years from the inflation of 1923 to the end of the decade. The book was begun in Berlin, finished in Switzerland after he had emigrated, and published by the Querido Verlag in Amsterdam, by this time the leading publisher for the works of German writers in exile.

The three comrades of the title—the narrator Robert Lohkamp, Otto Köster, and Gottfried Lenz—run an auto repair shop and garage. The novel is made up of a series of episodes in which they confront the economic problems of the times and the institutions and values of the society in which they live—or, one might better say, in which they do their best to exist *despite* these "values," for Lohkamp and his friends are outsiders. They vehemently reject the demands of normal living, which they consider false, meaningless, and stupid, and insist instead on living according to a self-determined code that brings them into constant conflict with the rest of their world. To make ends meet they also use as a taxi a magnificent old souped-up car named Karl, which functions almost as a fourth comrade in the novel. A fifth comrade is Patricia Hollmann, a glamorous but fragile woman with whom Lohkamp falls in love. The tale of this love, from hesitant first approach to Pat's death from tuberculosis at the end, gives the novel its plot; and this use of a love story to provide the principal action and structure—which marks a distinct break from the two earlier, essentially all-male books—sets the model for the rest of Remarque's writing.

Like Remarque's previous novels, *Drei Kameraden* is a first-person narrative, told this time in the past tense. The plot is once more developed in episodes which are strung together loosely and can often stand as semi-independent stories. Characterization and dialogue remain more important than action, relationships more important than historical background. While the role of the war in making the principal characters what they are is now less decisive, it still gets a major share of the blame for their unwillingness to adjust, their lack of purpose, their indifference, and even—in the case of Pat—for their inability to survive: chronic malnutrition during the war years is responsible for her frailty and ultimate death. The basic tone of this book, like that of the earlier ones, is pessimistic. Lenz is murdered by a rival political group after a rally which he attends more out of curiosity and for the excitement than out of conviction. Karl is sold to pay for Pat's stay in the sanatorium even though it is clear that this sacrifice of the means of the comrades' livelihood will do nothing but buy a few more days together for her and Lohkamp. Lohkamp and Köster are left at the end with no particular reason, and surely without the wherewithal, to go on living.

In a variety of ways, however, *Drei Kameraden* points ahead to the author's later works more than it does back to his earlier ones. Themes, motifs, and settings that later became Remarque trademarks are developed here: the fascination of his characters with auto racing and fast cars, the prodigious amounts of alcohol they drink and the number of pages they spend doing it, the conspicuous role played by a colorful but often seamy variety of social outcasts and misfits as secondary characters. Much more significant is Remarque's building the action around an intense but doomed love story, and Pat Hollmann is the first of a kind of heroine for which he would become famous. Like Patricia ("Patrice" in the German version), several of these heroines have names which are strange to the German ear; they are beautiful but usually not in the way their world customarily defines beauty; they are passionate but at the same time aloof, fragile, and somehow even artificial. They are different from other women and seem to come, as Remarque says about Pat, "from another world." In this "foreignness" they are fit lovers for outsiders like Lohkamp and Remarque's other loners. They have a greater willingness to belong to the society around them than do the men; but they also recognize that because of illness or personality or (in the later novels) external circumstance, they will never belong. Though not necessarily resigned to their fate, they accept their feelings of separateness and loneliness and their need for a like partner. These qualities are also characteristic of Remarque's male protagonists in his later novels.

Shortly before Pat dies she has an exchange with Lohkamp which states the view of existence that drives most of Remarque's later figures. After reviewing their brief time together and granting that it has brought a happiness he never really expected to find, Lohkamp says of life, "Die Einzelheiten sind wunderbar, aber das Ganze hat keinen Sinn. Als wenn es von einem Irren gemacht ist, dem auf die wunderbare Vielheit des Lebens nichts anderes eingefallen ist, als es wieder zu vernichten" (The details are wonderful, but the whole has no sense. As if it had been made by a madman who could think of nothing better to do with the marvelous variety of life that he had created but to annihilate it again). Pat replies, "Doch, Liebling, mit uns, das hat er schon gut gemacht. Besser gings gar nicht. Nur zu kurz. Viel zu kurz" (Anyway, darling, he hasn't done so badly by us. That couldn't have been better. Only too short. Far too short). Remarque's characters are isolated and alone either because they reject the expectations and lifestyle of the world around them or because they are forced (by exile, internment, or war) to live as outsiders. They seek companionship, usually with others who also rebel against the accepted values. But they do not believe that happiness can be found and do not trust it when it does sometimes come, because they "know" that ultimately happiness, like life itself, will not last. They are convinced that chance is more important than their own planned actions, and their perception of life's brevity leads them to pessimism and resignation. They drink to avoid confronting reality. They welcome risk and danger as ways of combating stagnation, and the fast pace at which they live helps them to avoid confronting existential fear. Their cynicism is often a cover for inner hurt, their flippancy for insecurity. They long to have something–or, more frequently, someone–to believe in, but their hope for success is outweighed by the conviction that the world in which they live offers only the shakiest basis for trust and confidence.

Because *Drei Kameraden* was published by an émigré press, the original German version did not receive much attention, but Remarque's name was enough to get a good reception for the English translation in the United States. *The New York Times* reviewer said: "I found Remarque's novel the most moving, the hardest to put down, that I have read in a long time. He is that rarity, a born storyteller with something to say." In 1938 M-G-M made a movie of the work for which F. Scott Fitzgerald wrote the significantly changed film script (his only screen credit) and with an all-star cast including Robert Taylor as Lohkamp, Franchot Tone, Robert Young, and Monty Woolley; Margaret Sullavan was nominated for an Academy Award for her por-

trayal of Pat. Though the film did not fare well at the box office, it helped prepare the way for the American phase of the author's exile.

Remarque wrote three novels that depict most vividly the fate of those who fled from the Nazis and their persecution as stateless persons in the countries where they sought refuge. Remarque himself experienced little of their misery: his stay in Switzerland was legal and relatively comfortable; and he seems to have had no great trouble in getting to the United States once it became clear that war in Europe was inevitable. President Roosevelt himself saw to it that the author of *All Quiet on the Western Front* was allowed legal entry under the immigrant quota. From 1939 to 1942 Remarque lived in Hollywood, where he had a celebrated affair with Marlene Dietrich, a close friendship with Greta Garbo, and working associations with Charlie Chaplin and Cole Porter. He applied for American citizenship in 1941; in 1942 he moved to New York, where he maintained a residence until his death, although after the war he spent a part of each year in his villa in Switzerland.

The war years were not without tragedy: in 1943 the Nazis executed his youngest sister, Elfriede, for her involvement with the White Rose resistance group, and Remarque was convinced that the fact that she was his sister had something to do with her death. But exile in America was good to him, and he suffered few of the disappointments that were the general rule for German authors living in the United States during the Hitler years. Far from being unknown, he was celebrated in America; he moved in exciting circles; he had money; he continued to write and to enjoy success with his work.

Remarque's fourth novel, *Flotsam,* appeared in a serial version in English translation in *Collier's* magazine in 1939, and Remarque spent another year revising the text for its book publication in 1941; the German version, *Liebe deinen Nächsten,* was published the same year. It is episodic and made up in large part of dialogue, but it differs from most of Remarque's earlier work in that it is a third-person narrative with frequent flashbacks. This style was dictated by the fact that the novel has two central heroes, rather than one, and an omniscient narrator was needed to report their separate fates. The one who is followed most closely is Ludwig Kern. In his early twenties, he has fled from Germany to Austria after his Jewish father was forced out of his pharmacy and imprisoned. From older and more seasoned refugees Kern learns the hazardous business of living without papers in a foreign country which is hostile toward the émigrés from across the border. He learns the most from Josef Steiner, who had earlier escaped from a concentration camp and has been in Austria long enough to be thoroughly familiar with the tricks of survival, the best ways of avoiding police and bureaucracy, and the elaborate networking which enables the refugees to keep in contact and to provide each other what meager help they can. Kern's and Steiner's paths cross frequently but they are never together long, for the nature of living in exile is that one is always on the move, always essentially in hiding, and regularly separated from others by deportation or imprisonment. Though this isolation now stems not from choice but from circumstance, Remarque's refugees are thus, once again, outsiders who know that relationships can only be temporary and that existence itself is constantly threatened.

The title page of *Flotsam* bears the motto "To live without roots takes a stout heart," to which the author might well have added "and continued good luck." Most of the characters who people his émigré novels soon run out of one or the other or both, but Kern is an exception. In Vienna he falls in love with Ruth Holland, a Jewish student at the university until the imminent German annexation of Austria forces her, too, into exile. Ruth and Kern make their way to Switzerland, and eventually to Paris; at the end of the novel, after all sorts of perils, they secure visas and ship tickets for immigration to Mexico, where they hope to begin a new life together. The money that makes this escape (and the happy ending, unusual for Remarque) possible comes from Steiner. He has gone to Berlin to be with his dying wife; knowing that return to Germany means almost certain death, he has left the money he had set aside for his own passage abroad for Kern. Steiner is apprehended in Berlin by an SS officer who is his longtime enemy; and in a final, satisfying gesture he kills the officer by pushing him out of the hospital window and plunging to death with him.

Such incidents are the stuff of melodrama, and in *Flotsam* Remarque pulls out all the stops. The novel is essentially a thriller, and its basic story is less memorable than is the endless series of escapes, illegal border crossings, arrests, imprisonments, beatings, acts of persecution, and betrayals. Readers today are likely to be most impressed by the portraits of the other refugees with whom the protagonists come in fleeting contact: Jews, political émigrés who have to worry not just about the local authorities but also about German spies and Gestapo agents, White Russians who have already lived in exile for two decades, and a host of others. All live a hand-to-mouth existence; all survive from one day to the next with the conviction that they are merely "corpses on parole."

Flotsam was not particularly popular, either as a book or as the movie *So Ends Our Night* (1941); but the novel *Arch of Triumph,* first published in 1945 in English translation and republished in German as *Arc de Tri-*

omphe in 1946, was another instant best-seller and reached worldwide sales of nearly five million copies. *Arch of Triumph* also has a large cast and a wealth of journalistic detail that is at times confusing. Its characters philosophize a great deal–and when Remarque lets his characters do that, he becomes pretentious and they do not ring true. There is more than a touch of the soap opera in the central love story, and the role played by coincidence taxes the reader's credulity. But the novel is far better artistically than *Flotsam.* The plot is less diffuse; the things that happen to the principal actors are not there just for their own sake but add up to a larger meaning for a culture on the verge of collapse. The novel is set in Paris in the months immediately preceding the fall of France and concludes at the moment of occupation. The characters live with the growing realization that an end is just ahead and, since the Parisians are unwilling and the exiles are unable to do anything but watch it come, with a paralyzing fatalism.

In *Arch of Triumph* the surface story takes on a metaphoric quality that Remarque's work had not had since *Im Westen nichts Neues.* The novel is about Ravic (his current name, anyway, thanks to the false passport he holds), once a successful surgeon in Germany, who earns his meager and illegal keep by checking the health of the whores in a brothel and by doing "ghost operations" for Parisian surgeons who take the credit for his work and all but a fraction of the money. At the beginning of the book he prevents another classic Remarque heroine, Joan Madou, from committing suicide; and the story of the love that soon develops between them is the main thread of the narrative. It is not an easy love and both know it will not last, but for a time at least it gives them a reason to go on living in a world that is coming apart around them. At the end Joan leaves Ravic and is shot by a jealous new lover; unable to save her, Ravic watches her die in the hospital. With the only thing that has given his life some brief meaning now gone, Ravic stays in Paris to be arrested and presumably to be sent to a concentration camp by the Nazi invaders.

Ravic is the most complex, least one-dimensional hero Remarque had created to this point. "A stranger everywhere," he is, to be sure, much like his predecessors in believing that the only thing that really counts in a threatened and transitory world is the intensity with which one can live the moment. But though he essentially remains a cynic, Ravic does change and things other than self and survival become important to him. Though he tries to get over it quickly–usually with Calvados, the apple brandy made famous by the novel–it matters to him when a patient dies; and when a difficult operation is successful he is pleased not only with his own skill but also because of the saved life. He can go out of his way to help others, and at one point doing so leads to his arrest and deportation to Switzerland. Above all, he changes as a result of his love for Joan. At the beginning of the tale Ravic is burned out, utterly without hope, and capable of emotion only when he dreams of exacting revenge on Haake, the Gestapo man who tortured him and sent him to a concentration camp in 1933. With Joan he learns that there are other feelings which can at least help to fill his spiritual vacuum and are worth having even if one is doomed to lose them. Amazed that he is jealous when she has left him, he discovers that he is "nicht mehr wie ein Toter auf Urlaub mit Kleinem Zynismus, Sarkasmus und etwas Mut, nicht mehr kalt; lebendig wieder, leidend meinetwegen, aber offen wieder den Gewittern des Lebens, zurückgeboren in seine schlichte Gewalt!" (no longer like a dead man on furlough with his small cynicism, sarcasm, and portion of courage, no longer cold: alive again, suffering if you like, but again open to all the thunderstorms of life, reborn into its own simple strength!). This "rebirth" is not strong enough to give him the will to resist his eventual betrayal to the Germans, but it brings a precarious sort of fulfillment that none of Remarque's earlier heroes had achieved—not even Kern, who survives at the end of *Flotsam* but is pale as a character compared to Ravic. Ravic also experiences fulfillment in revenge: just before the fall of the city he kills Haake; after the deed he feels at peace, as he had not since before their first encounter years ago—"leicht und gelöst . . . als wenn ein Schloß von seiner Vergangenheit abgefallen wäre" (easy and as if a padlock had fallen from his past). So great is this sense of finished business that Ravic decides not to flee again when the Germans reach Paris but to suffer whatever comes his way: "Er hatte Rache gehabt und Liebe. Das war genug. Es war nicht alles, aber es war so viel, wie ein Mann verlangen konnte. Er hatte beides nicht mehr erwartet" (He had had revenge and love. That was enough. It was not everything, but it was as much as a man could ask for. He had not expected either one again).

As had been the case with each of Remarque's four previous novels, a Hollywood film version of *Arch of Triumph* followed soon after book publication, starring Ingrid Bergman as Joan, Charles Boyer as Ravic, and Charles Laughton as Haake. Even with this cast the film was a box office failure. It emphasized the love story to the virtual exclusion of all else and failed particularly to capture the desperate atmosphere of existence in exile which the novel had depicted so vividly. Remarque would return a third time to this subject in *Die Nacht von Lissabon* (1963; translated as *The Night in Lisbon,* 1964), but not until nearly twenty years later. First he wrote a novel about the more immediate past in

Germany, a task which necessitated considerable research. There was a gap of seven years—a long silence for Remarque—between *Arch of Triumph* and his next work, *Der Funke Leben* (translated as *Spark of Life*), which appeared both in German and in English in 1952.

Der Funke Leben is the author's literary tribute to the suffering and determination of the victims of the concentration camps. The novel is set in a camp in Germany called Mellern and in a town in a valley below the camp; it begins in March 1945 and ends after the camp has been liberated by American troops. Like *Flotsam* and *Arch of Triumph,* it is written in the third person so that the author can trace the fates of a number of characters. The principal focus is on an inmate who is called "509" throughout and is not identified by name until well into the work. But the reader also gets to know a number of other prisoners and several of their SS guards—especially the camp commandant, Neubauer, whose complex personality is developed more fully than that of any other character in the book. In some respects the structure recalls that of *Im Westen nichts Neues:* the central figure is less a binding force than elsewhere in Remarque's works, and the plot is less important than the individual episodes which it ties together.

German critics have long contended that the subject of the concentration camps is all but impossible to treat effectively in fiction. The historical facts familiar to everyone from eyewitness accounts, pictures, and newsreels, it is argued, have left an impact that literature cannot hope to match. Fact is so vividly real that fiction is certain to seem a pale imitation; and unless the horror is presented through stylization and metaphor, literary treatments run the dangers of trivializing atrocity and of sensationalism. In *Der Funke Leben* Remarque in no way departs from his usual stark realism, and some of his descriptions of life and especially of death in Mellern certainly earn the charge of sensationalism. Mellern is not an extermination camp, but a forced-labor camp; it has no gas chambers, but it does have a crematorium which is kept busy day and night. Death, brutality, and terror are depicted on every page, and some of the descriptions seem to be there for their own gruesome sake rather than because they are needed to make the book's point.

These flaws are not fatal, however, for Remarque's theme is that death and horror will end and life will return, even for the skeletal inmates of Mellern. The first event in the book is an Allied bombing raid on the town below the camp, and thus from the beginning the prisoners have a sign that their liberation may be coming closer. This and other signs gradually kindle in them a new "spark of life" and a hesitant determination to survive a while longer. The spark causes 509, who has been in the camp for ten years and is near death when the story opens, to defy the SS by refusing to "volunteer" for medical experiments; his example leads his young friend Bucher to refuse as well. The two are savagely tortured and given up for lost by the rest; but their return, just barely alive, is a further indication that holding out may yet be worth the effort. Plans are made to take over the barracks when the Americans arrive; Bucher and Ruth Holland from the women's camp begin to think of a life not separated by barbed wire but together; and the Communist prisoners talk of a new political order for Germany once the Nazis are gone.

Although 509 is touched by the growing determination of the others to live and begins to remember a name and a past he had all but forgotten, he dies in a senseless bloodbath staged by the SS hours before the camp is liberated. By killing one of the most sadistic guards who is shooting prisoners as they try to escape a burning building, however, he saves the lives of many more inmates. This is a melodramatic and not exactly happy ending, yet 509 accomplishes something no other Remarque protagonist does: he comes to believe that betterment may be possible, at least for others, and he is willing to act for the common good. In a sense, Steiner had done the same thing in *Flotsam;* but his leaving money for Kern was a private deed, done as a contingency, and the reader knows nothing beyond the fact that it will enable Kern to escape Europe. In 509 Remarque portrays for the only time a central character whose actions have a demonstrated positive effect on others that lasts beyond his own death. Dozens of fellow prisoners live to see freedom as a result of his death, particularly Bucher. The book's final pages tell of his leaving Mellern with Ruth: the spark fanned by 509 has sprung to life in their new beginning.

While he was writing *Der Funke Leben* Remarque was also working on a novel he called *Zeit zu leben und Zeit zu sterben* (Time to Live and Time to Die). Published first in English translation in 1954 with the not-quite-literal title *A Time to Love and a Time to Die,* it is a novel with clear echoes of *Im Westen nichts Neues:* this time the story is of a soldier who falls in love while home on leave from the Russian front at the end of World War II and who dies when he returns to the battlefield. Like *Im Westen nichts Neues,* the book begins and ends at the front, and many of the themes and motifs of the first novel are repeated: the all-important role of chance, the ruling of the world by inhumanity and unreason, the soldiers' realization that the war is lost and they are lost with it. Unlike Paul Bäumer, however, the hero, Graeber, cannot escape despair in comradeship, for in *Zeit zu leben und Zeit zu sterben* Remarque has again created a lone protagonist who is at odds with most of his surroundings. Nor can Graeber fall back on instinct,

since—at least at the end—he is much more aware than Paul had been of what is happening to him and what it means. Above all, the books differ in that here Remarque uses a love story to structure the main plot: four fifths of the novel is devoted to Graeber's three week furlough; and though his love for Elisabeth Kruse does not develop until nearly a week of the leave is over and ends with his death a few days after his return to Russia, the love story is what the book is about.

In many ways this is a typical Remarque love: although Elisabeth is a more wholesome and normal heroine than many of the others, the "life" together of the two characters is again brief, intense because they know it will be brief, and lived essentially in isolation from the world around them. There is something new here, however: their isolation from others has a strongly underlined idyllic quality, and they share an eagerness to make their love last even as they recognize that it is not likely to do so. In the book's early sections the word *Verzweifelung* (despair) is used again and again to characterize Graeber's attitude toward his existence; yet by the end of his leave he and Elisabeth have married, talk of having a child (a most unusual notion for Remarque characters), and dream of normalcy and permanence once the war is over. This, of course, is not to be. Back at the front, Graeber is soon forced to realize that, strong though his love for Elisabeth is, "es reichte nicht weit genug. Es rührte sein Herz, aber es hielt ihn nicht. Es versank, es war ein kleines Privatglück, es konnte sich nicht halten in dem endlosen Moor des allgemeinen Elends und der Verzweifelung" (it could not extend far enough. It touched his heart but it did not hold him. It was swallowed up; it was a small, private happiness that could not support itself in the limitless morass of general misery and despair).

In good Remarque fashion his death is both dramatic and ironic. After killing a fanatical German comrade who is about to gun down a group of Russian civilians, Graeber is himself shot by one of the Russians whom he has freed. Christine R. Barker and R. W. Last, who are among the best critics of Remarque's work, find "at least a suggestion of hope for the future" in this death, since Graeber "has come to realize the necessity for involving himself in wider issues than his own personal survival." They also conclude that, because Elisabeth may be pregnant, the novel "marks a huge advance on the bleak negativity" of *Im Westen nichts Neues* and other earlier works. There is truth in this judgment and one does hear faint echoes of expressionism's symbolic "new man" optimism in the hint that Graeber may be survived by the child he and Elisabeth discussed when they talked of the future. But Graeber's last word on his leave demonstrates that Remarque has not mellowed very much: "Es war zu kurz gewesen, und das andere war zu lang. Es war ein Urlaub gewesen; aber das Leben eines Soldaten rechnet nach der Zeit an der Front und nicht nach Urlauben" (It had been too short and the other was too long. It had been a furlough; but a soldier's life is reckoned by his time at the front and not by furloughs).

The best part of *A Time to Love and a Time to Die* is not the central story but the picture of life in Germany during the late days of the Third Reich. When Graeber arrives home he finds destruction and loss, distrust and fear everywhere. The physical destruction from the bombing is bad, but worse is the destruction of old values and relationships under Nazi rule. Pervasive fear is both the result of this rule and the tool it uses to maintain control as its power crumbles. As he had done in *Der Funke Leben,* the author stresses that the bulk of Hitler's support came not from gangsters or unusually evil people but from everyday Germans. As a major source of the regime's tyranny he cites its passion for organization, its manipulation of a normal respect for authority and institutions, its overburdening bureaucracy.

There is a final tie between *Im Westen nichts Neues* and *A Time to Love and a Time to Die* in the fact that the later work once again made Remarque the subject of controversy. Written, as were all his novels, in German, it appeared first in English translation; publication in Germany followed the same year, but only after the author had made a number of changes in the text. Critics claimed that these changes amounted to censorship forced on Remarque by his German publisher and were intended to blunt the potential political impact of the novel. It was charged that the publisher was afraid that the original version would stir up memories which German readers of the 1950s were trying hard to forget and even that the book's depiction of Nazi tyranny could embarrass the many former Nazis who held powerful positions in the Federal Republic. Remarque dismissed the criticism as an unfounded attack on his publisher and maintained, as he had always done, that his novels were not political. It is possible, however, that the furor helped to rule out any plans he may have had of returning to Germany.

Actually, he probably had no such plans. The firm conviction that "you can't go home again" is expressed in one way or another in every one of his novels; besides, Remarque liked living in a country which had been good to him, especially in New York. He had become an American citizen in 1947; and though he made occasional trips to Germany during the postwar years, they were always short. After 1945 he spent part of the year in New York and part in his villa in Switzerland or in Italy until, in the last years of his life, illness kept him entirely in Europe.

Although Remarque is known almost exclusively as a novelist, he did try his hand briefly at dramatic forms during his later years and did so with considerable success. In 1955 he wrote the screenplay for an Austrian movie, *Der letzte Akt* (The Last Act), about Hitler's final days in the bunker of the Chancellery in Berlin, which was based on the book *Ten Days to Die* (1950) by Michael A. Musmanno, one of the American judges at the Nuremberg Trials. Directed by G. W. Pabst, the film played to large audiences and favorable reviews in its English version, *Ten Days to Die.* Two years later Remarque was also persuaded by Universal Studios to write the screenplay for Douglas Sirk's Hollywood adaptation of *A Time to Love and a Time to Die;* this script was the only work he ever wrote in English. Except for a few scenes, his script was not actually used in the film. In the movie, however, the author himself played the secondary but important role of a former schoolteacher with whom Graeber discusses the war and the meaning of Nazism for Germany, and his acting was praised by the critics as more convincing than the performances turned in by the stars, John Gavin and Lilo Pulver. In 1956 Remarque wrote a drama for the stage, *Die letzte Station* (The Last Station), which played successfully both in Germany and on Broadway; it was never published in German, but an English translation, *Full Circle,* appeared in 1974.

After *Zeit zu leben und Zeit zu sterben* Remarque wrote four more novels, but none of them broke significant new ground. Two return to settings and themes familiar from earlier novels and are among his more effective works; the other two are clearly his weakest books. *Der schwarze Obelisk* (translated as *The Black Obelisk,* 1957), published in 1956 and set in the inflation year 1923, belongs in the former category. The most autobiographical of all Remarque's novels and the one in which the historical background is most precisely documented, it depicts a small German city in a time of reviving nationalism and rising anti-Semitism, of unemployment, and above all of racing inflation—"der große Ausverkauf des Sparers, des ehrlichen Einkommens und der Anständigkeit" (the great sellout of thrift, honest effort, and respectability). From his postwar vantage point Remarque sees in this combination the fertile soil from which National Socialism was able to grow.

There is another doomed love story, though this time it is depicted with a lighter touch that is in keeping with the book's satirical intent. *Der schwarze Obelisk* has a greater measure of humor than one finds in Remarque's other works; but it is very black humor, for the main concern of the novel is death. The narrator, Ludwig Bodmer, works for a gravestone company, and the black obelisk of the title is a monument which is too costly to sell and which functions throughout the book as a fairly heavy-handed symbol of death. Although at the end it is finally sold, the inflation is brought under control, and Bodmer leaves for a new life as a journalist in Berlin, fear of "the great dark," with which the author's protagonists had wrestled ever since *Im Westen nichts Neues,* is what makes the characters what they are and is the issue that drives the plot.

Der schwarze Obelisk is a rambling narrative, the individual episodes of which are better than the story itself. The principal settings, which include a whore-house and an insane asylum as well as the office and sales lot of the tombstone firm, are bizarre, and the secondary characters are colorful, some of them grotesquely so. The best feature of the book is the uncertain atmosphere it captures of loss and struggle and change in one of the decisive years of the 1920s.

In 1958 Remarque married the film star Paulette Goddard. After 1960 he spent more and more of his time in Italy and at his villa in Switzerland, returning less frequently to the United States as increasing ill health made overseas travel more difficult. Aside from his health, he lived comfortably and enjoyed a life that was quiet in comparison to the fast pace of his earlier years.

German reviewers could always be counted on to greet the appearance of a new Remarque novel with the charge that he had written "yet another" overly sentimental book that was ridden with clichés. This criticism was often undeserved, but it was certainly appropriate for *Der Himmel kennt keine Günstlinge* (1961; translated as *Heaven Has No Favorites,* 1961), and for once most of the foreign critics agreed. The characters were universally seen as Hollywood caricatures of real people and the story as far-fetched. The author's habit of repeating and even of quoting himself, which is evident in all his books, was found to be particularly annoying here, and his penchant for facile philosophizing was held to have gone beyond all bounds of good taste. Remarque himself apparently had a different opinion of the novel's worth, since he dedicated it "to Paulette Goddard Remarque"; and his readers must have disagreed, too, for the book sold better than any work since *Arch of Triumph.*

Attention is fairly evenly divided between Clerfayt, a professional racing car driver, and Lillian Dunkerque, but for a change the heroine is really the principal character. The first third of the story is set in a sanatorium where she awaits death, the rest in Paris, Venice, and glamorous stops on the racing circuit where she seeks to spend the time she has left in adventure and fast living with Clerfayt. She is attracted to him because his lifestyle represents vitality, risk, and intensity. When he starts to talk of settling down and of the future, she hears bourgeois stagnation—"the prison of

mediocrity"—and realizes that she must break with him. In a typically ironic ending the author makes this action unnecessary: Clerfayt is killed in a crash and Lillian dies soon after returning to the sanatorium. The novel ends with the judgment that "sie glücklich gewesen sei, soweit man einen Menschen jemals glücklich nennen könne" (she had been happy, insofar as any human being can ever be called happy).

Die Nacht von Lissabon, published in 1963 and a year later in English as *The Night in Lisbon,* is the last work Remarque finished and a far better novel than its predecessor. In it the author returns to subjects and techniques which had worked well for him in the past: to the time of Nazi persecution and the fate of those who fled from it, to suspense, and to the first-person narrative with its sense of immediacy and authenticity. German reviews were mixed but generally much more favorable than reviews of Remarque's previous novel had been; and though it was feared that the reading public would resent being reminded of the Nazi past, the book actually contributed to the public discussion of that past which had begun to take place in the early 1960s. The novel sold some 900,000 copies in Germany and was a modest best-seller abroad as well.

There is nothing very new about *Die Nacht von Lissabon.* Those who knew *Flotsam* and *Arch of Triumph* were long since familiar with its motifs and the events it describes: the inhuman treatment suffered by the émigrés, the impossibility of living without papers or work, the never-ending cycle of imprisonment and release or escape, accident and bad luck. (*The New York Times* reviewer, who felt that *Die Nacht von Lissabon* was Remarque's best book, called it "almost a manual of underground refugee existence.") The tone is somber; the overall mood is hopeless; the atmosphere is charged with suspense that is only rarely relieved, and then never for long. The core of the novel is, as always, a tragic love story.

The only new feature is the framing structure the author employs. The narrative present, Lisbon in 1942, is only a small part of the book. The essential matter is the tale of how he got to Lisbon told by "Josef Schwarz" (the passport is again false) to the unnamed narrator, himself a German emigrant, during the course of a long night in one refugee bar after another. The first-person flashback is a technique Remarque had tried before but never to the extent that it is used here. The need to compress the story so that it could be related in a single night makes this book shorter than Remarque's other novels, and the writing is much tighter; together with the considerable restraint with which Schwarz's tale is developed, these qualities make *Die Nacht von Lissabon* one of Remarque's better novels.

In 1967 Remarque was awarded the Großes Verdienstkreuz (Great Order of Merit) of the Federal Republic of Germany. In 1968 his postwar German publishers, Kiepenheuer & Witsch and Kurt Desch, issued a slim volume of tributes to mark his seventieth birthday; in it his friend and fellow novelist Hans Habe praised Remarque as "the last *grandseigneur* of literature." But discussion of his work virtually ceased. Though slowed by several heart attacks, the author continued to work quietly on his last novel, *Schatten im Paradies,* right up to his death in the hospital at Locarno on 25 September 1970 at the age of seventy-two. After a Catholic funeral he was buried in the cemetery above the village of Porto Ronco.

His death was prominently noted in newspapers around the world, but neither the obituaries nor the reawakened critical comment that followed them did anything to change the well-established views of Remarque and his place in literature. In Germany he was still described as the successful (and therefore suspect) writer of popular thrillers and pulp love stories, abroad as the chronicler of German destiny from 1914 through 1945. Everywhere he remained, above all, the author of *Im Westen nichts Neues.*

Schatten im Paradies confirms much of the criticism given his other books over the years and is virtually a compilation of the author's weaknesses: superficiality, pretentiousness, stereotyped characters, an unlikely plot with inconsistencies and too many coincidences, sentimentality, and sensationalism. In addition there is artistic bad taste in the somewhat lurid eroticism which invades the love story and which had been absent from the earlier works. Published in 1971 and a year later in English translation as *Shadows in Paradise,* the novel pleased no one, not even longtime Remarque fans; one should keep in mind, however, that it was not a finished piece and that the author would surely have changed it a good deal had he lived. The draft he was working on when he died was complete, but Remarque was notorious for rewriting and tinkering with his manuscripts.

Remarque's intention in the novel was to follow the émigrés to America. Both *Flotsam* and *Die Nacht von Lissabon* end at the moment of departure for the promised land overseas; in *Schatten im Paradies,* which was clearly meant to be a sequel to *Die Nacht von Lissabon,* the reader is told that life in "paradise" is not really so different for the émigrés from what it was elsewhere, that paradise does not exist. The protagonist, Robert Ross, and the many other displaced Germans with whom he comes in contact in New York and Los Angeles suffer no physical brutality and are free of the old persecution. They work; they can earn money, some of them a lot of it; and they are allowed the pursuit of private happiness. But though they are no longer dead men on leave, they remain outsiders. The weight of the past is too great to permit them

any real trust in other people or in permanence, any real hope for fulfillment and a future.

Although the book is less autobiographical than has generally been claimed, there is obviously much of Remarque's own experience in it, and the style reminds one as much of the diary as it does of the novel. More important than the plot is the author's desire to document what it was like for "us refugees" who managed to reach a shadowy paradise that could not live up to its promise.

The constant underlying theme for Remarque, as for so many other writers of his generation, was the breakdown of Western civilization and order that World War I brought to the surface of European consciousness and that the following decades served to substantiate, especially in Germany. Lacking the belief of earlier ages in something absolute to fall back on in the face of such dissolution, Remarque found himself with few alternative responses. On the one hand there was anarchy, nihilism, and despair. At the other end of the scale there was political ideology, but for Remarque ideology was the enemy and not a solution. Somewhere in the middle there was the individual self, and this is what he wrote about. The characters in his novels are essentially always alone; and though they seek to escape isolation in the companionship of others like themselves or in love, the attempt is born of panic and is successful only in the short run. If external circumstances and political events have not done so already, death can always be counted on to make sure that success does not last. Because living is a brief and hazardous undertaking, Remarque's characters prize the intensity of the moment above all else, for it, at least, is real.

This Remarque—the cultural pessimist—and the other Remarque who wanted to write popular and entertaining novels did not always get along well with each other. Three or four of the novels that resulted from their collaboration, however, will remain vivid documentation of the desperate times they depict and moving statements of the power of the human spirit to endure and conquer such times.

Biographies:

Franz Baumer, *E. M. Remarque* (Berlin: Colloquium, 1976);

Christine R. Barker and R. W. Last, *Erich Maria Remarque* (London: Wolff,1979);

Alfred Antkowiak, *Erich Maria Remarque: Leben und Werk* (Berlin: Das Europäische Buch, 1983).

References:

A. F. Bance, "Im Westen nichts Neues: A Bestseller in Context," *Modern Language Review,* 72 (April 1977): 359–373;

Hans-Werner Baum, "E. M. Remarque und seine Zeitromane," *Der Bibliothekar,* 11 (1957): 509–604;

S. E. Cernyak, "The Life of a Nation: The Community of the Dispossessed in Erich Maria Remarque's Emigration Novels," *Perspectives on Contemporary Literature,* 3, no. 1 (1977): 15–22;

"The End of the War? A Correspondence between the Author of All Quiet on the Western Front and General Sir Ian Hamilton," *Life and Letters,* 3 (November 1929): 399–411;

Erich Maria Remarque zum 70. Geburtstag am 22. Juni 1968 (Cologne: Kiepenheuer & Witsch, 1968);

M. Feldmann, "Gespräch mit C. [*sic*] M. Remarque," *Europäische Rundschau,* 1, no. 2 (1946): 228–230;

Armin Kerker, "Zwischen Innerlichkeit und Nacktkultur: Der unbekannte Remarque," *Die Horen,* 96, no. 1 (1974): 3–23;

Hermann Kesten, "Gedenkwort für Erich Maria Remarque," *Deutsche Akademie für Sprache und Dichtung Darmstadt: Jahrbuch 1970* (1971): 99–102;

Manfred Kuxdorf, "Mynona versus Remarque, Tucholsky, Mann, and Others: Not So Quiet on the Literary Front," in *The First World War in German Narrative Prose,* edited by Charles H. Genno and Heinz Wetzel (Toronto:University of Toronto Press, 1980), pp. 71–92;

Frédéric LeFèvre, "An Hour with Erich Remarque," *Living Age,* 339 (December 1930): 344–349;

Helmut Liedloff, "Two War Novels: A Critical Comparison," *Revue de Littérature Comparée,* 42 (July–September 1968): 390–406;

P. J. Middleton, "The Individual, Society, and the Contemporary Background in the Novels of Erich Maria Remarque," Ph.D. dissertation, University of Southampton, 1969;

Hanns–Gerd Rabe, "Erich Maria Remarque 1898–1970," *Niedersächsische Lebensbilder,* 8 (August 1973): 193–211;

John F. Riddick, "Erich Maria Remarque: A Bibliography of Biographical and Critical Material, 1929–1980," *Bulletin of Bibliography,* 39, no. 4 (1982): 207–210;

Helmut Rudolf, "Helden in der Krise: Zu Erich Maria Remarques, Emigrationsromanen," *Arbeiten zur deutschen Philologie,* 2 (1966): 83–93;

Hubert Rüter, *Erich Maria Remarque: "Im Westen nichts Neues." Ein Bestseller der Kriegsliteratur im Kontext* (Paderborn: Schöningh, 1980);

Helena Szépe, "Der deklassierte Kleinbürger in den Romanen Erich Maria Remarques," *Monatshefte,* 65 (Winter 1973): 385–392;

Harley U. Taylor, "Autobiographical Elements in the Novels of Erich Maria Remarque," *West Virginia University Philological Papers,* 17 (1970): 84–93;

Taylor, "Humor in the Novels of Erich Maria Remarque," *West Virginia University Philological Papers,* 29 (1983): 38–45;

Pawel Toper and Alfred Antkowiak, *Ludwig Renn: Erich Maria Remarque: Leben und Werk* (Berlin: Volk & Wissen, 1965);

Robert Van Gelder, "An Interview with Erich Maria Remarque," in his *Writers and Writing* (New York: Scribners, 1946), pp. 377–381;

Hans Wagener, "Erich Maria Remarque," in *Deutsche Exilliteratur seit 1933. I: Kalifornien,* edited by John M. Spalek and Joseph Strelka (Bern: Francke, 1976), pp. 591–605;

Irene Wegner, "Zur Rezeption der Romane Erich Maria Remarques," in *Erzählte Welt: Studien zur Epik des 20. Jahrhunderts,* edited by Helmut Brandt and Nodar Kakabadse (Berlin: Aufbau, 1978), pp. 384–399.

Johann Paul Friedrich Richter
(Jean Paul)
(21 March 1763 – 14 November 1825)

Wulf Koepke
Texas A & M University

This entry was updated by Professor Koepke from his entry in DLB 94: German Writers in
the Age of Goethe: Sturm und Drang to Classicism.

BOOKS: *Grönländische Prozesse oder Satirische Skizzen,*
anonymous, 2 volumes (Berlin: Voß, 1783;
revised edition, Berlin: Vossische Buchhandlung,
1822);

Auswahl aus des Teufels Papieren, nebst einem nöthigen Aviso
vom Juden Mendel, as J. P. F. Hasus (Gera: Beck-
mann, 1789);

Die unsichtbare Loge: Eine Biographie, 2 volumes (Berlin:
Matzdorff, 1793; revised edition, Berlin: Reimer,
1822); translated by Charles T. Brooks as *The*
Invisible Lodge (New York: Holt, 1883);

Hesperus, oder 45 Hundsposttage: Eine Biographie (3 volumes, Berlin: Matzdorff, 1795; revised and
enlarged, 4 volumes, 1798); translated by Brooks
as *Hesperus; or, Forty-five Dog-post-days: A Biography,*
2 volumes (New York: Lovell, 1864; London:
Trübner, 1865);

Leben des Quintus Fixlein, aus fünfzehn Zettelkästen gezogen:
Nebst einem Mustheil und einigen Jus de tablette
(Bayreuth: Lübeck, 1796; revised and enlarged,
1801); translated by Thomas Carlyle as "Life of
Quintus Fixlein, Extracted from Fifteen Let-
ter-Boxes," in his *German Romance: Specimens of Its*
Chief Authors, with Biographical and Critical Notices,
volume 3 (Edinburgh & London: Tait, 1827); volume 2 (Boston: Munroe, 1841);

Blumen- Frucht- und Dornenstücke oder Ehestand, Tod und
Hochzeit des Armenadvokaten F. St. Siebenkäs im Reichs-
marktflecken Kuhschnappel (3 volumes, Berlin: Matzdorff, 1796–1797; revised and enlarged edition, 4
volumes, Berlin: Realschulbuchhandlung, 1818);
translated by Edward Henry Noel as *Flower, Fruit,*
and Thorn Pieces; or, The Married Life, Death, and
Wedding of the Advocate of the Poor, Firmian Stanislaus
Siebenkäs, 2 volumes (London: Smith, 1845; Boston: Munroe, 1845);

Engraving by Adrian Schluch of a painting of Richter by Friedrich
Meier, 1811

Jean Paul's biographische Belustigungen unter der Gehirnschale
einer Riesin: Erstes Bändchen (Berlin: Matzdorff,
1796);

Geschichte meiner Vorrede zur zweiten Auflage des Quintus Fix-
lein (Bayreuth: Lübeck, 1797);

Der Jubelsenior: Ein Appendix (Leipzig: Beygang, 1797);

Das Kampaner Thal oder Über die Unsterblichkeit der Seele:
Nebst einer Erklärung der Holzschnitte unter den 10

Geboten des Katechismus (Erfurt: Hennings, 1797); translated by Juliette Bauer as *The Campaner Thal; or, Discourses on the Immortality of the Soul* (London: Gilpin, 1848);

Palingenesien, 2 volumes (Leipzig & Gera: Heinsius, 1798);

Jean Pauls Briefe und bevorstehender Lebenslauf (Gera & Leipzig: Heinsius, 1799);

Titan, 4 volumes (Berlin: Matzdorff, 1800–1803); translated by Brooks as *Titan: A Romance,* 2 volumes (Boston: Ticknor & Fields, 1862; London: Trübner, 1863);

Komischer Anhang zum Titan, 2 volumes (Berlin: Matzdorff, 1800–1801);

Clavis Fichtiana seu Leibgeberiana: Anhang zum I. komischen Anhang des Titans (Erfurt: Hennings, 1800);

Das heimliche Klaglied der jezigen Männer: Eine Stadtgeschichte; und Die wunderbare Gesellschaft in der Neujahrsnacht (Bremen: Wilmans, 1801);

Vorschule der Aesthetik, nebst einigen Vorlesungen in Leipzig über die Parteien der Zeit, 3 volumes (Hamburg: Perthes, 1804; revised and enlarged edition, Stuttgart & Tübingen: Cotta, 1813); translated by Margaret R. Hale as *Horn of Oberon: Jean Paul Richter's School for Aesthetics* (Detroit: Wayne State University Press, 1973);

Flegeljahre: Eine Biographie, 4 volumes (Tübingen: Cotta, 1804–1805); translated by Eliza Buckminster Lee as *Walt and Vult; or, The Twins,* 2 volumes (Boston: Munroe / New York: Wiley & Putnam, 1846);

Jean Paul's Freiheits-Büchlein oder Dessen verbotene Zueignung an den regierenden Herzog August von Sachsen-Gotha; dessen Briefwechsel mit ihm;-und die Abhandlung über die Preßfreiheit (Tübingen: Cotta, 1805);

Levana oder Erziehungslehre (2 volumes, Brunswick: Vieweg, 1807; revised and enlarged edition, 3 volumes, Stuttgart & Tübingen: Cotta, 1814); translated by "A. H." as *Levana; or, The Doctrine of Education* (London: Longman, Brown, Green & Longmans, 1848; Boston: Ticknor & Fields, 1861);

Ergänzungs-Blatt zur Levana (Brunswick: Vieweg, 1807);

Friedens-Predigt an Deutschland gehalten von Jean Paul (Heidelberg: Mohr & Zimmer, 1808);

Des Feldpredigers Schmelzle Reise nach Flätz mit fortgehenden Noten: Nebst der Beichte des Teufels bey einem Staatsmanne (Tübingen: Cotta, 1809); translated by Carlyle as "Army Chaplain Schmelzle's Journey to Flaetz," in his *German Romance,* volume 3 (volume 2 of American edition);

Dr. Katzenbergers Badereise: Nebst einer Auswahl verbesserter Werkchen, 2 volumes (Heidelberg: Mohr & Zimmer, 1809; revised and enlarged edition, Breslau: Max, 1823);

Dämmerungen für Deutschland (Tübingen: Cotta, 1809);

Herbst-Blumine oder Gesammelte Werkchen aus Zeitschriften, 3 volumes (Stuttgart & Tübingen: Cotta, 1810–1820);

Leben Fibels, des Verfassers der Bienrodischen Fibel (Nuremberg: Schrag, 1812);

Museum (Stuttgart & Tübingen: Cotta, 1814);

Mars und Phöbus: Thronwechsel im J. 1814. Eine scherzhafte Flugschrift (Tübingen: Cotta, 1814);

Politische Fastenpredigten während Deutschlands Marterwoche (Stuttgart & Töbingen: Cotta, 1817);

Ueber die deutschen Doppelwörter: Eine grammatische Untersuchung in zwölf alten Briefen und zwölf neuen Postskripten (Stuttgart & Tübingen: Cotta, 1820);

Der Komet oder Nikolaus Marggraf: Eine komische Geschichte, 3 volumes (Berlin: Reimer, 1820–1822);

Kleine Bücherschau: Gesammelte Vorreden und Rezensionen, nebst einer kleinen Nachschule zur ästhetischen Vorschule, 2 volumes (Breslau: Max, 1825);

Wahrheit aus Jean Paul's Leben, edited by Christian Otto and Ernst Förster, 8 volumes (Breslau: Max, 1826–1833)—includes, as volume 1, *Selberlebensbeschreibung;*

Jean Paul's sämmtliche Werke, 65 volumes (Berlin: Reimer, 1826–1838);

Selina oder Über die Unsterblichkeit (Stuttgart & Tübingen: Cotta, 1827);

Politische Nachklänge: Wiedergedrucktes und Neues, edited by Förster (Heidelberg: Winter, 1832);

Der Papierdrache: Jean Paul's letztes Werk. Aus des Dichters Nachlaß, edited by Forster, 2 volumes (Frankfurt am Main: Literarische Anstalt, 1845);

Jean Paul's Werke, 60 volumes (Berlin: Hempel, 1867–1879);

Jean Paul's sämtliche Werke: Historisch-kritische Ausgabe, herausgegeben von der Preußischen Akademie der Wissenschaften in Verbindung mit der Akademie zur wissenschaftlichen Erforschung und zur Pflege des Deutschtums (Deutsche Akademie) und der Jean-Paul-Gesellschaft, edited by Eduard Berend, 33 volumes (Weimar: Böhlau, 1927–1964);

Werke, edited by Norbert Miller, 10 volumes (Munich: Hanser, 1959–1980);

Jean Paul: Ideen-Gewimmel: Texte und Aufzeichnungen aus dem unveröffentlichten Nachlaß, edited by Thomas Wirtz and Kurt Wölfel (Frankfurt am Main: Eichhorn, 1996).

Editions in English: *The Death of an Angel and Other Pieces,* translated by A. Kenney (London, 1829);

Reminiscences of the Best Hours of Life for the Hour of Death, translated anonymously (Boston: Dowe, 1841);

Extracts from the Works of Jean Paul F. Richter, selected and translated by Georgiana Lady Chatterton (London: Parker, 1859);

The Campaner Thal, and Other Writings, translated by Juliette Bauer, Thomas Carlyle, and Thomas De Quincey (Boston: Ticknor & Fields, 1864);

"Life of the Cheerful Schoolmaster Maria Wutz," translated by John D. Grayson, in *Nineteenth-Century German Tales,* edited by Angel Flores (New York: Doubleday, 1959), pp. 1–37;

Jean Paul: A Reader, edited by Timothy J. Casey, translated by Erika Casey (Baltimore & London: Johns Hopkins University Press, 1992).

OTHER: *Taschenbuch für 1801,* edited by Richter, F. Genz, and Johann Heinrich Voß (Brunswick: Vieweg, 1800);

Sinngrün: Eine Folge romantischer Erzählungen, edited, with contributions by Richter and others (Uthe-Spazier & Berlin: Enslin, 1819).

PERIODICAL PUBLICATIONS: "Saturnalien, den die Erde 1818 regierenden Hauptplaneten Saturn betreffend; in sieben Morgenblättern mitgetheilt von Dr. Jean Paul Fr. Richter," 9 installments, *Morgenblatt für gebildete Stände,* 1–3, 5–10 January 1818;

"Traum eines bösen Geistes vor seinem Abfalle," *Taschenbuch für Damen auf das Jahr 1819* (1818): 251–257;

"Unternacht-Gedanken über den magnetischen Weltkörper im Erdkörper; nebst heun magnetischen Gesichten," 10 installments, *Morgenblatt für gebildete Stände:* January 1819;

"Briefblättchen an die Leserinnen des Damen-Taschenbuchs bey gegenwärtiger Uebergabe meiner abgerissenen Gedanken vor dem Frühstück und dem Nachtstück in Löbischau," *Taschenbuch für Damen auf das Jahr 1821* (1820): 285–318;

"Gesichte einer griechischen Mutter: Ein Traum; in den letzten Tage des Juli-Monats," *Morgenblatt für gebildete Stände,* 14 August 1821, pp. 773–774;

"Politisches und poetisches Allerlei," *Taschenbuch für Damen auf das Jahr 1822* (1821): 150–175;

"Die Anbeter des Luzifers und des Hesperus. Ein Beytrag zur ältesten Kirchengeschichte," *Morgenblatt für gebildete Stände,* 1–7 January 1822;

"Jean Paul's Wetterprophezeiungen zum Beßten der Reisenden, Spazierengehenden und Gartenbauenden. Höchst wahrscheinliche Mutmaßungen über das Wetter der nächsten 6 Monate, an meinem Geburtstage, den 21. März, mildthätig, an Wetter-Laien ausgetheilt," *Abend-Zeitung,* 19 June 1823, p. 583;

"Ausschweife für künftige Fortsetzungen von vier Werken," 9 installments, *Morgenblatt für gebildete*

Stände, 20, 22–24, 26–27, 29, 31 December 1823, 1 January 1824.

Johann Paul Friedrich Richter created for his first published novel, *Die unsichtbare Loge* (1793; translated as *The Invisible Lodge,* 1883), a narrator called "Jean Paul," and that name has been transferred to Richter himself. German patriots who considered Richter's work very "German" never liked this name and at least pronounced Paul in the German and not in the French way. "Jean Paul" is a clear allusion to Richter's great model, Jean-Jacques Rousseau. It is not really a pseudonym, since Richter never wanted to hide his authorship. But the creation of a narrator both identical and nonidentical with his author made possible a series of role-playing games in which fiction and reality merged. The narrator "Jean Paul" could meet the characters of his novels; on the other hand, Richter's audience, the women in particular, identified him as "Jean Paul" and carried the novels over into real life. Thus, while his book sales do not bear out the legend that Richter was the most popular writer of his time—far from it—he and his novel *Hesperus, oder 45 Hundsposttage* (1795; translated as *Hesperus; or, Forty-five Dog-post Days,* 1864) had real fans who cut off locks of his or his dog's hair, proposed marriage to "Jean Paul," and named their daughters after his heroine.

Although he lived at the time of German Classicism and Romanticism, Richter did not belong to any group or "school." His novels and shorter narratives can be seen in the context of the European humoristic novel from François Rabelais's *Gargantua* and *Pantagruel* (1532–1564) and Miguel de Cervantes's *Don Quixote* (1605–1615) to Jonathan Swift's *Gulliver's Travels* (1726) and Laurence Sterne's *Tristram Shandy* (1760–1767). Noteworthy among Richter's German predecessors is Theodor Gottlieb von Hippel with his *Lebensläufe nach aufsteigender Linie* (Biographies in an Ascending Line, 1778–1781). Richter's popularity in his own time rested mainly on his novel *Hesperus.* Other works, notably *Titan* (1800–1803; translated, 1862) and *Flegeljahre* (Adolescence, 1804–1805; translated as *Walt and Vult; or, The Twins,* 1846), had a considerable impact on the younger Romantics. Richter's fame faded away in the late nineteenth century; but he was rediscovered around 1900, and the modernity of his narrative style and structures has been recognized ever since. While he continues to impress writers and individual readers and is acknowledged by scholars as one of the truly important writers of his age, his work remains unknown to a general audience; and its complexity has prevented most of it from being included in school reading lists. Thus his novels with their interesting narrative style, their many-layered depictions of German life in the late eighteenth century, and their portrayal of the aspirations of the best people of the time are left to the specialists and the few fans. Richter's life can be divided into three periods: his early career of starvation and frustration, until around 1790; his writing of his best-known works from *Die unsichtbare Loge* to *Flegeljahre;* his family life and writing in Bayreuth from 1804 to his death in 1825.

Richter was born on 21 March 1763 in Wunsiedel, the oldest son of Johann Christian Christoph Richter, who taught at the local school, and Sophia Rosina Kuhn Richter, the daughter of a well-to-do textile manufacturer from Hof. Wunsiedel is a small town east of the Fichtel mountains in the northeast corner of Bavaria. Richter's father, the son of a village schoolmaster, was a gifted musician and an impressive conversationalist. In 1765 he was able to find patronage to be appointed minister of the Lutheran church in the village of Joditz, and by 1776 he had risen to the position of head pastor in the town of Schwarzenbach. But his earlier life of poverty and his inability to pursue a career in music resulted in increasingly severe spells of depression. He became aloof and dogmatic, and he inflicted the worst possible private education on the two oldest of his five sons: memorizing meaningless grammatical items in Latin. In spite of clear indications of musical talent, "Fritz," the eldest, never received any instruction in music. Endowed with a vivid imagination, the boy began to create his own inner world, nourished by books. *Robinson Crusoe* (1719) was one of his earliest and most lasting impressions.

In Schwarzenbach a colleague of Richter's father, Johann Samuel Völkel, taught him some geography, gave him Johann Christoph Gottsched's *Erste Gründe der gesamten Weltweisheit* (First Elements of Philosophy, 1734), and introduced him to enlightened Lutheran theology. Erhard Friedrich Vogel, a vicar in a neighboring village, opened his personal library to the boy. Around 1778, Richter began to write down excerpts from Vogel's journals and books—which he could never afford to own himself—and collected them in bound volumes (not in *Zettelkästen* [filing cabinets], as legend has it). He later established elaborate indexes and thus had a ready-to-use reservoir of quotations for all possible topics. He also began to compose his own aphorisms and ideas, indexing them in the same way. The majority of his aphorisms, one of the largest collections of any German writer, remain unpublished.

Early in 1779 Richter was sent to the gymnasium in Hof to prepare for university studies. While he became the butt of the jokes of his classmates because of his naive trust in people, he was an outstanding student who even embarrassed the teachers with his intelligence and knowledge. In April 1779 his father died,

leaving behind a mountain of debts. Richter went to the University of Leipzig in spring 1781 with a *testimonium paupertatis* in hand. Realizing after one semester of theology that he would never follow in the footsteps of his father, he decided to become a writer. Had he not lived such an isolated life, he would have seen the misery of the many writers who were trying to make a living in the city of book fairs.

In 1780 Richter wrote a series of brief essays on issues in philosophy, theology, and popular science which he called "Übungen im Denken" (Exercises in Thinking). He then imitated Johann Martin Miller's sentimental novel *Siegwart* (1776) in an immature epistolary novel, "Abelard und Heloise" (published in 1928 in Eduard Berend's edition of Richter's collected works). In the spring of 1781 he wrote a long essay, "Über den Menschen" (On Man), with many echoes from the second epistle of Alexander Pope's *Essay on Man* (1733–1734); it seems to have been the first piece he submitted for publication–without success. He reworked and condensed his "Übungen im Denken" as "Rhapsodien" (Rhapsodies), including some ideas which came to him through the only professor at Leipzig who made an impression on him: Ernst Platner, a then-popular philosopher. But life in poverty and the constant struggle with what he considered mediocre, bigoted people had changed his initial confidence and trust. He began to diagnose the dominant ill of society as "Dummheit" (stupidity) and to fight for the legitimate place of extraordinary people, even if they appear to be "Narren" (fools). Taking his cue from Erasmus, he wrote a satirical work titled "Lob der Dummheit" (Praise of Stupidity) but found it unsatisfactory. Then he produced a collection of satirical essays which he called *Grönländische Prozesse* (Greenland Trials) since in Greenland, he had read somewhere, disputes were settled by the opponents satirizing each other. Broad attacks on the nobility, courtiers, women, hack writers, and the clergy, the satires are harsh and radical, with details intended to shock the readers; the language abounds in imagery, metaphors, and similes, a style that makes it hard to follow the author's arguments. It is obvious to the reader that the author has read many books, from Juvenal to Swift, but does not know much about the real world.

Unlikely though it was that such a book could attract a large audience, the respected publisher Christian Friedrich Voß of Berlin accepted the manuscript and paid Richter a generous honorarium. The first volume appeared in spring 1783, the second in the fall. After the second volume, Voß refused to continue. The few reviews were hostile, noting the negativism and the sometimes shocking and overcharged language; sales must have been minimal. Richter continued to write in the same vein but had extreme difficulty placing his manuscripts. His mounting debts finally led him to flee from Leipzig under an assumed name on 12 November 1784 and return to his family, then living in Hof.

The fortunes of his family had gone from bad to worse. Richter's grandfather had died, but his estate had been squandered through litigation brought by spiteful relatives. The family lived in cramped quarters and abject poverty. The next-oldest brothers showed few signs of working toward stable careers. The family's situation was so bad that it drove Heinrich, the second youngest, to suicide in April 1789. Nobody in Hof understood why Richter kept on writing under such conditions. His unusual clothes–including open shirts "à la Hamlet"–and refusal to wear a wig in the fashion of the day kept the "society" of Hof away from him. In 1787 he became the tutor of the younger brother of a deceased friend in nearby Töpen, and from 1790 to 1794 he taught a group of seven children of friends in Schwarzenbach.

In the meantime, he continued to write. A new collection went through several versions and after many delays was published in 1789 as *Auswahl aus des Teufels Papieren* (Selection from the Devil's Papers) by an obscure publishing house. This collection contained satires with more narrative elements and more direct social criticism than *Grönländische Prozesse* and also included some serious essays. The book was published under the pen name "J. P. F. Hasus." As grim as Richter's life was, there were moments of joy in it, especially with friends such as Vogel and Christian Otto. Richter had an uncanny ability to maintain his hope and good spirits, although he had not really regained the belief in the existence of God and the progress of humankind that he had lost in Leipzig. To stimulate himself to write he began to drink strong coffee; he later switched to alcohol, especially beer, which became indispensable for his writing for the rest of his life.

During the fall and winter of 1790 and 1791 Richter weathered a psychological crisis; on 15 November–which he afterward called the most important evening of his life–he had a vision of his death. Among the pieces he wrote for a planned collection to be titled "Bairische Kreuzerkomödie" (Bavarian Penny Theater) was a horrifying speech in which the dead Shakespeare tells dead listeners in a church that there is no God. The collection was never completed, but the speech would later become the famous "Rede des toten Christus vom Weltgebäude herab, daß kein Gott sei" (Speech of the Dead Christ from the Top of the Universe that There Is No God, 1797). This somber mood is discernible in Richter's first novel, which he wrote from spring 1791 to spring 1792. He finished the manuscript in a state of exhaustion, feeling only partially satisfied with the novel's incomplete plot. He sent the manuscript, which

he titled "Mumien" (Mummies), to one of his favorite writers, Karl Philipp Moritz, in Berlin, and asked him to help in finding a publisher. Moritz responded enthusiastically and gave the manuscript to his brother-in-law, the publisher Matzdorff. It appeared in two little volumes in 1793 under the title *Die unsichtbare Loge,* with the innovative story "Das Leben des vergnügten Schulmeisterlein Wuz in Auenthal" (translated as "Life of the Cheerful Schoolmaster Maria Wutz," 1959), written in early 1791, as one of its appendices.

The plot of *Die unsichtbare Loge* would have required another volume to be completed. But considering its similarities with *Tristram Shandy,* completion may have been doubtful from the beginning. The book shows the influences of Rousseau's *Émile* (1762), Christoph Martin Wieland's *Bildungsroman Geschichte des Agathon* (Story of Agathon, 1766–1767), Swift's satire, Johann Wolfgang von Goethe's novel *Die Leiden des jungen Werthers* (The Sorrows of Young Werther, 1774), and Sterne's humor. In spite of these and other discernible influences, *Die unsichtbare Loge* is an original work that sets a new tone in German literature. For the first eight years of his life Gustav, the protagonist, is educated in a cave by a genius from Herrnhut, the center of the Moravians; during this time Gustav has no contact with anyone other than his teacher. Later he receives instruction from a second tutor, the narrator Jean Paul. As a young man he is brought to the court of Scheerau, a fictitious German state, where he is subjected to many intrigues, first as an officer, then as a diplomat. He falls in love with a girl named Beata but is seduced by a lady at the court; and it is only at the end, in a new spring–the seasons are of great significance in Richter's stories–that he is reunited with Beata, with Jean Paul, and with his friend Ottomar, half brother of the prince. The novel ends with Gustav being caught in a cave with a conspiratorial group and taken prisoner. If one can judge from the plots of Richter's later novels *Hesperus* and *Titan,* Gustav might have turned out to be the prince's son and the successor to the throne had the work been completed.

The book receives its distinctive character through its narrative tone. The narrator Jean Paul is a humorist capable both of satire and of sublime vision, but he is always good-hearted. Jean Paul adds quite a few materials that are not directly related to the plot: mostly satires but also serious essays such as "Vom hohen Menschen" (Of High People), which maintains that extraordinary human beings such as Plato and Shakespeare are not characterized by greatness in the traditional sense but by their elevation above ordinary life and their expectation of a "zweites Leben" (second life). These sections foreign to the plot are called "Extrablätter" (extra pages). They are more numerous in the first volume, less conspicuous and much better structurally integrated in the second. Richter continued to adorn his stories with such materials, but after *Hesperus* he put them into appendixes rather than interrupting the plot. The digressive manner of the narrator with his flowery imagery may confuse the reader more than the "Extrablätter."

Equally important are the extraordinary scenes Richter brings about: the "resurrection" of Gustav from his life in the cave and his first experience of a sunrise; the death of Gustav's friend Amandus during an eclipse of the moon; Ottomar's awakening in a grave after having been believed dead; declarations of friendship and love, usually in a park. Such sublime moments prefiguring a second life were the favorites of his readers. All his novels combine sublimity, satire, a politically revolutionary spirit, a humorous view of the insignificance of this life, and tolerance for human weakness.

Matzdorff's honorarium ended the years of starvation for Richter's family, but Richter continued to teach. When his oldest pupils in Schwarzenbach were ready for the gymnasium in 1794, he returned to Hof. There he finished his second novel, *Hesperus, oder 45 Hundsposttage,* which appeared in 1795. *Die unsichtbare Loge* had not done well commercially, so Matzdorff offered him a less favorable contract. Richter did not stipulate the number of copies to be printed for the first edition, so although *Hesperus* became a popular success, it is uncertain how many books were actually sold. A second edition appeared in 1798, a third in 1819.

In *Hesperus* the narrator Jean Paul lives on a small artificial island in a lake. He receives the materials for his "Biographie"–Richter tended to call his fictional works "biographies" rather than novels–from an unknown correspondent who sends them via a dog ("Hundspost"). In the principality of Flachsenfingen, an English aristocrat, Lord Horion, is in charge of the education of the prince's five sons and wants to ensure a transition to a better rule. The story of separated and reunited brothers, interwoven with an account of the dawn of a new social system, is reminiscent of the complex plot of an anonymous novel, *Dya-Na-Sore* (1787–1789), part of which Richter had read in 1787. The protagonist is the young doctor Viktor, presumably the son of the lord, to whom the lord entrusts his affairs at court. Viktor becomes embroiled in a complex court intrigue; falls in love with Klotilde, who thinks she is a courtier's daughter; develops a friendship with Flamin, who is supposedly the son of a Lutheran minister; and becomes the target of Flamin's jealousy when Flamin also falls in love with Klotilde. Viktor early on learns that Klotilde is Flamin's half sister, but Flamin and Klotilde do not know this. Flamin is drawn into a political conspiracy by triplets from England. In the end, those

triplets, Flamin, and the narrator Jean Paul all turn out to be the sons of the prince, and Flamin the heir to the throne. Viktor finds out that he is really the Lutheran minister's son; thus there is a huge social difference between him and Klotilde, who is really the illegitimate daughter of the prince. Social standing, however, will not matter in the new world of Flachsenfingen, and Viktor and Klotilde will be married.

Hesperus, while continuing in the vein of *Die unsichtbare Loge,* was more accessible, more sentimental, even more realistic; the audience could more easily identify with its characters, and Flachsenfingen was perceived as a typical German court. Many readers, especially women, enjoyed the escape the novel afforded them from the miseries of life. For them, Richter was Jean Paul, and they treated him as such. He responded in kind, playing the role of the witty and sentimental narrator he had created.

Richter distinguished three types of stories in his oeuvre. The first type, exemplified by *Die unsichtbare Loge, Hesperus,* and later *Titan,* revolves around a small court in Germany, a "hidden prince" who is the successor to the throne, and a change of the social system for the better. It also involves love and friendship on a high level and visions of a "second life." In contrast, the second type is a village story, describing the life of humble and poor people, especially schoolmasters and vicars. The third type takes place in a small town and shows an idealistic young man struggling with bourgeois prejudice and pettiness and with poverty. The second type is best exemplified by the story of the Schulmeisterlein Wuz, who survives incredible poverty by his imagination and his talent for finding the sunny side of every moment. He is a "Kauz" (odd character): he likes to read, but since he is too poor to buy books he obtains the catalog of the book fair, finds titles that interest him, then writes books to go with the titles: thus there are Wuz's versions of Friedrich Gottlieb Klopstock's *Der Messias* (The Messiah), Immanuel Kant's *Kritik der reinen Vernunft* (Critique of Pure Reason), and the like.

Wuz's first successor in Richter's work was Quintus Fixlein, described in *Leben des Quintus Fixlein* (1796; translated as "Life of Quintus Fixlein," 1827). Fixlein, a poor teacher, receives a vicarage through a clerical error. His idyllic life is disturbed by a prediction that he will die in his thirty-second year, as his ancestors did. He survives to that age and marries, but then documents are found which prove that his birthdate is really later than had been thought, and the critical time is impending. Initially almost insane with fear, Fixlein is calmed by the narrator, who is able to persuade him that he is a child playing with toys. Richter provides some counterpoints to this heartwarming story with two satires written earlier, and collected with it: the story of Freudel, whose life is made unbearable by his extreme absentmindedness; and the story of an excursion to the Fichtel mountains by the school principal Fälbel and his students. Fälbel is as inhumane a pedagogue as possible, the very model of the "Schultyrann" (school tyrant) well known in modern German literature. Richter also added a significant essay, "Über die natürliche Magie der Einbildungskraft" (On the Natural Magic of Imagination), which gives clues to his ideas on poetic imagination and its close relationship to dream language. Although Richter was for some time chiefly known for these "idyllic" village stories, he actually did not write many of them. The year after *Leben des Quintus Fixlein* appeared he published *Der Jubelsenior* (The Senior's Anniversary Celebration, 1797), an idyllic story about a village Lutheran minister's silver anniversary; in a comedy-of-errors subplot the minister tries to discover whether or not his son has been approved to be appointed as his vicar. Also involved is a visit from the narrator, Jean Paul, in his role as a prince from Flachsenfingen.

Richter's next major work after *Leben des Quintus Fixlein* was a novel of the third type, describing life in a small town. He gave it a long and baroque title, *Blumen-Frucht- und Dornenstükke oder Ehestand, Tod und Hochzeit des Armenadvokaten F. St. Siebenkäs im Reichsmarktflecken Kuhschnappel* (1796–1797; translated as *Flower, Fruit, and Thorn Pieces; or, The Married Life, Death, and Wedding of the Advocate of the Poor, Firmian Stanislaus Siebenkäs*, 1845). Kuhschnappel is a republican "free city"; but it is too small really to be called a city and is ruled not by its citizenry but by a clique of wealthy businessmen. Siebenkäs returns to his hometown with his law degree and marries Lenette, a simple woman from Augsburg. Their prospects for happiness are shattered when Siebenkäs's guardian, the privy counselor von Blaise, one of the most prominent citizens, denies him his inheritance of 1,200 gulden plus interest, on the grounds that Siebenkäs has exchanged names with his friend and look-alike Leibgeber. Siebenkäs's suit against Blaise becomes his only activity as a lawyer. Living from occasional book reviews and from pawning possessions, Siebenkäs writes a collection of satires titled *Auswahl aus des Teufels Papieren*. Siebenkäs is rescued in the spring, the season of hope and new beginnings, by Leibgeber, who invites him to Bayreuth; there he meets and falls in love with Blaise's niece, Natalie. The designated fiance of Natalie, Everard Rosa von Meyern, a lothario, tries to seduce Lenette while Siebenkäs is competing for the title of Schützenkönig (best marksman). Rosa von Meyern's actions contribute to the estrangement of the couple, but other factors—their poverty and Lenette's love for the school superintendent Stiefel—are more important in driving them apart. Leibgeber and Siebenkäs tell

Natalie about Rosa von Meyern's true character, and she cancels her engagement to him. Leibgeber conceives a plan whereby Siebenkäs fakes his own death and then takes Leibgeber's place as a counselor to the count of Vaduz; Leibgeber goes off to wander around the world. A year later Siebenkäs is passing through Kuhschnappel and learns that after a second, happier marriage to Stiefel, Lenette has died in childbirth. At her graveside (and supposedly his own) he meets Natalie, who believed him dead. United at last, Siebenkäs and Natalie look forward to a happy life together.

Critics found the mock death with its grotesque details objectionable. They even charged Richter with condoning insurance fraud: Siebenkäs had taken out a life insurance policy in Natalie's favor, and she, of course, had collected on it. On the other hand, they were favorably impressed—though sometimes shocked—by the depletion of the two friends. Leibgeber is a radical humorist, a free spirit who shuns all conventions, who criticizes all social institutions, who does not believe in God but would like to, and who laughs about humankind and himself, sometimes with a laughter of despair. Siebenkäs, on the other hand, while he considers the world as ridiculous and insignificant as Leibgeber does, empathizes with the ordinary people and smiles at their weaknesses and prejudices. He is an amiable humorist, while Leibgeber scorns ordinary life and people in a Swiftian manner. Richter appended to the novel "Rede des toten Christus vom Weltgebäude herab, daß kein Gott sei." The narrator carefully declares that this nightmare vision is indeed a dream and says that it shocked him into believing in God again. But this declaration can hardly offset the impact of the speech, in which Jesus Christ comes to tell humankind that there is no God, no father for them all. "Rede des toten Christus" has remained one of Richter's most anthologized pieces. Through a translation of parts of it into French in Madame de Staël's seminal book *De l'Allemagne* (On Germany, 1813), it found a large international audience and had an impact especially on French Romantics.

In June 1796 Richter sent off the last part of the manuscript of *Siebenkäs* to his publisher. The next day he departed on foot for a visit to Weimar at the invitation of Charlotte von Kalb, Friedrich Schiller's former friend. For Richter, Weimar was the holy city of the great geniuses of his age. Next to Goethe, he wanted to meet Johann Gottfried Herder, whose works had deeply impressed him since his student days in Leipzig. Richter must have envisioned Weimar as a community of "hohe Menschen," but what he found was a small town rife with gossip and literary and political disputes. Goethe and Herder were not on speaking terms. Richter was well received by Goethe and Schiller but quickly sided with Herder, whose friendship he treasured. The acquaintance with important men and women gave a new quality to his writing. Herder introduced him to great literary works, such as the Greek classics, and to a new understanding of history, and he began to moderate his digressive style in favor of more unified structures. Weimar was also the beginning of the end of Richter's idealistic view of people and his hope for a future utopian society.

In 1796 appeared the novel fragment *Jean Paul's biographische Belustigungen unter der Gehirnschale einer Riesin* (Jean Paul's Biographical Enjoyments under the Skull of a Female Giant), a tale of a Scottish nobleman disappointed in the outcome of the French Revolution, his return to Scotland, and his marital problems. It was followed in 1797 by *Das Kampaner Thal oder Über die Unsterblichkeit der Seele* (translated as *The Campaner Thal; or, Discourses on the Immortality of the Soul,* 1848). The narrator Jean Paul goes to the valley of Campan in the Pyrenees, where a group of friends are engaging in platonic dialogues on immortality; Jean Paul is especially intent on refuting the Kantian position that there is no proof for the immortality of the soul, that the idea is only helpful in a moral sense. The work ends with a rise in a balloon at sunset, a lofty image of sublimity.

After his mother's death in July 1797 Richter left Hof to look for a place to settle. Leipzig, where he stayed from 1797 to 1798, disappointed him. During this time his youngest brother, Samuel, whose university studies Richter was financing, became a gambler and fled with all of Richter's money. Richter lived in Weimar from 1798 to 1800, enjoying Herder's friendship and instruction. In *Palingenesien* (Palingeneses, 1798), a work that grew out of the offer for a second edition of *Auswahl aus des Teufels Papieren,* Richter combined a small selection of reworked satires with the story of a trip to Nuremberg, where the narrator Jean Paul and his wife meet Siebenkäs and Natalie–Siebenkäs, according to the novel *Siebenkäs,* being the author of the original *Auswahl aus des Teufels Papieren.* The same narrator couples a collection of essays in the form of letters with an enthusiastic description of his future life with Hermine in an idyllic countryside in *Jean Pauls Briefe und bevorstehender Lebenslauf* (Jean Paul's Letters and Future Biography, 1799). For a time, this inviting picture of married life was a favorite among Richter's women readers.

In 1799 Richter wrote a political essay, "Der 17. Juli oder Charlotte Corday" (The 17th of July; or Charlotte Corday), in which he defended Charlotte Corday's assassination of Jean Paul Marat and the position of the Girondists against the Jacobins. Over the years this essay attracted much attention, some of it unwanted: the university student Karl Ludwig Sand declared that

he was inspired by the essay to kill the playwright August von Kotzebue in 1819. During this time Richter attracted many women, several of whom proposed marriage to him; he was engaged several times. Finally, in Berlin, where he lived from 1800 to 1801, he met Karoline Mayer, who was fourteen years younger than he. They were married in 1801. The couple moved to Meiningen in 1801 and to Coburg in 1803.

Since 1792 Richter had been planning and writing what he called his "Kardinalroman" (principal novel), *Titan.* In his impatience to see it finally in print he published it in four individual volumes from 1800 to 1803. This mode of publication was one of the reasons for the work's lack of commercial success. Originally, Richter wanted to write a novel about a genius who was both good and evil, like the protagonist of Friedrich Heinrich Jacobi's epistolary novel *Eduard Allwill's Briefsammlung* (Eduard Allwill's Correspondence, 1792) about the young Goethe. Subsequently, Richter separated the good and evil aspects into two characters, Albano and Roquairol, and integrated into the novel his experiences in Weimar. His reading of Goethe's *Wilhelm Meisters Lehrjahre* (Wilhelm Meister's Apprenticeship, 1795–1796) also had its impact. For Richter, the age was characterized by self-centered titanic tendencies overreaching the limits of human existence: classicistic aestheticism, which implies moral indifference; excessive emotionalism; a creation of the world in one's own image through Kantian and Fichtean idealism. Such one-sided attacks on organic order and harmony were "einkräftig" (single-powered) and were to be countered by a new breed of active people whom Richter called "allkräftig" (all-powered).

Albano, the protagonist of *Titan,* is once more the hidden prince, the successor to the throne brought up with an assumed identity. His supposed father, Gaspard von Zesara, a count with Spanish connections and a Goethelike figure, wants to rule Hohenfließ through Albano and his presumed ward Linda, who is actually his own daughter. Even more complicated intrigues surround this plan, giving occasion for many elements of the gothic novel to be used. Albano's real education comes mainly through Dian, a Greek architect and Herderlike figure who introduces him to Shakespeare and Rousseau and Herderian ideas; and through the humorist Schoppe, who is actually Leibgeber from *Siebenkäs.* Before meeting Linda, his destined bride, however, Albano falls in love with the oversensitive Liane and becomes close friends with her brother Roquairol. Diabolical court intrigues intervene, and Liane dies after being told that Albano is not to be hers. Albano's rage and sorrow are soothed by a trip to Italy, where he decides to go to France to fight for the revolution. But then he meets Linda and falls in love with her. In Pestiz, the capital of Hohenfließ, he encounters the enmity of Roquairol, who loved Linda but was rebuffed. Meanwhile Schoppe, suspecting Albano's true identity, disturbs Gaspard's plans; and Gaspard's brother, a frightful bald-headed ventriloquist, pursues him and finally drives him insane. Roquairol seduces Linda one night by imitating Albano's voice; then he performs his own life onstage and commits suicide at the end of the play. The novel ends with Albano's succession to the throne and a palingenesis of his former companions: he will marry Idoine, Liane's look-alike, and will be counseled by Siebenkäs, who arrives when Schoppe dies. Gaspard and Linda leave Hohenfließ for an unknown destination.

An expression of Schoppe's insanity, and one of its causes, is his adherence to the idealistic philosophies of Johann Gottlieb Fichte and Friedrich Wilhelm Joseph Schelling. Richter attacked these philosophies in his satirical *Clavis Fichtiana seu Leibgeberiana* (The Leibgeberian Key to Fichtiana), which he published separately in 1800 but considered part of *Titan*. *Titan* has several comic appendices, the most notable being "Des Luftschiffers Giannozo Seebuch" (The Logbook of the Balloonist Giannozzo), the diary of a friend of Schoppe's. Giannozzo, another wild humorist, roams Europe in a balloon until he meets his death in a thunderstorm over the waterfalls of the Rhine at Schaffhausen. The diary is "edited" by the narrator Jean Paul, who has found it. The perspective from the air, between sublimity and satire, gives rise to some of Richter's most unusual scenic descriptions.

In political terms, the utopian society of Hohenfließ at the end of *Titan* may have been obsolete in 1803, when Napoleon was bringing an end to the small German principalities and when people's aspirations were oriented toward a constitutional government rather than a philosopher-king. The work's message, directed against self-centered titanic arrogance, never stirred any debate. In literary terms, the last volume of *Titan* may be Richter's most outstanding achievement in style, character development, and presentation of tragic conflicts. Readers were most impressed by the tragic figures of Schoppe, Linda, and Roquairol.

During his work on *Titan* Richter thought of appending a contrasting story of idyllic character in the manner of *Leben des Quintus Fixlein*. This story grew into one of his major novels, *Flegeljahre*. It is a hilarious and melancholy tale of the twins Walt and Vult Harnisch, who cannot live without each other but cannot live together either; they are too close to be friends. A rich man, van der Kabel (whose real name is Richter), leaves his fortune to poor young Walt instead of to his seven distant relatives, stipulating that Walt has to accomplish a series of tasks before the fortune will be

his. There are penalties for mistakes, and it is foreseeable that the young poet Walt, in his naive trust of people, will incur so many penalties that little or nothing will be left in the end. After four volumes, however, most of the tests still lie ahead. Vult, who has tried in vain to make his brother more realistic, grows bitter and jealous when they both fall in love with Wina and she prefers Walt. All that is left of their friendship is the novel they wrote together, which was rejected by a publisher because it reminded him too much of the novels of Jean Paul.

After a climactic masked ball and a grandiose dream which Walt relates to Vult, the disappointed if not desperate Vult leaves Walt and the novel breaks off. Vult, the humorist, will never find a home; Walt, the poet, will never understand reality. The novel is serene, but it is also a farewell to the hopes and illusions of youth. There is a constant irony from this double perspective on life, and there are also scenes of elementary comic power. One of the best known is the opening scene, in which van der Kabel declares in his will that he will leave his house to whichever of his disinherited relatives is the first to shed tears over his death. Walt, the idealistic dreamer, often seems to be a Don Quixote who cannot distinguish fantasy from reality. Nevertheless, he is a real poet, and the reader likes him even while laughing at him. The narrator recreates Walt's enthusiasm and poetic power while keeping an ironic distance from his protagonist. *Flegeljahre* is possibly Richter's best book; it is certainly one of his most complex (for example, during the story he tells how it was written). It is also one of Richter's most accessible books. It was, however, anything but a success, which may have discouraged its author from completing it.

In 1804 Richter moved to Bayreuth, where he was to live for the rest of his life. He was at the height of his powers. He had thought about literature for more than twenty years, and he brought his thoughts together in *Vorschule der Aesthetik* (School for Aesthetics, 1804). Richter first defines the ascending scale of creative powers from imitation to creative genius; one category is that of the "passive Genie" (passive genius), that of the writer like Herder who is creative through receptivity rather than original production. Richter contrasts antique and modern poetry and art and defends modern Romantic poetry: Romanticism, he says, has created "das romantisch Komische" (the romantic comic), which is humor. Richter offers a penetrating analysis of humor, excluding satire from "poetic" literature although he includes in his definition of humor much of what is commonly called satire—Swift, for instance. Equally important are Richter's reflections on imagery, especially metaphor. Metaphors are anything but embellishments of style; metaphorical comparisons and combinations are "heuristic," a means of finding truth through the creation of images. *Vorschule der Aesthetik* itself states many of its results in images rather than in "scientific" terms.

After the theoretical first two parts of *Vorschule der Aesthetik,* Richter offers a third, narrative part in which Jean Paul tries to give lectures on contemporary literature during a book fair in Leipzig. With his first lecture, on poetic "materialists"–prosaic realists such as Friedrich Nicolai–he drives away most of the crowd. His second lecture deals with poetic "nihilists" whose concern for poetic form annihilates all real-life substance and makes their works, like those of some younger Romantics, poetry about poetry. For the third lecture, on real poetic poetry that uses the elements of real life to make the "second life" reflected in ordinary life, only one listener shows up: Albano from Titan. He is the lone recipient not only of Jean Paul's thoughts on literature in general but also of his moving eulogy of Herder, who had died at the end of 1803.

Vorschule der Aesthetik is a valiant attempt to give an account of the achievements of German literature; it offers assessments of Gotthold Ephraim Lessing, Klopstock, Wieland, Herder, Schiller, and especially Goethe. It is less fair to Schiller than to the others, for he considered Schiller's style pedestrian and too apolitical, and he did not personally like Schiller. While critical of trends of the Romantic school, it recognizes quality in individual writers, such as Novalis and Heinrich von Kleist.

Levana oder Erziehungslehre (1807; translated as *Levana; or, The Doctrine of Education,* 1848), Richter's response to Rousseau's *Émile,* is based on his experiences as a student, teacher, and father. The book deals primarily not with institutional instruction but with teaching by parents and tutors. It contains much concrete and practical advice, especially for the education of younger children, and mothers at the time found it useful. It also offers an ideal view of what a human being should be, and thus is part of the new definition of "Bildung" (education) by German neohumanism. In contrast to Rousseau's "natural man," Richter defines the goal of education as an "Idealmensch" (ideal person) who lives in and for society but has developed his own ideas and the willpower to resist the temptations of fashion and corruption. Firmness of character rather than the development of the powers of emotion and imagination is the main purpose of the educational process. While Richter advocates education for girls, he, like almost everybody else in his time, sees their role as essentially tied to the household. For this reason he thought their education should be practical, not abstract. Although he is keenly aware of the momentous reforms going on in the gymnasium and the university, Richter stresses, as Rousseau does, the personal relationship of teacher and pupil and the responsibilities of parents and tutors. An outstanding feature of his work, which he shared with the Swiss educator Johann Heinrich Pestalozzi, is respect for the child's mentality and world.

Richter had three children: Emma, born in 1802, who became the wife of the painter and art historian Ernst Förster; Maximilian, born in 1803; and Odilie, born in 1804. He decided to have only three children and apparently stopped having sexual intercourse at that point. His marriage, happy at first, went through several crises, and he and his wife were more than once on the verge of separation or divorce. Until he was close to forty years old Richter had been slim and youthful looking; but rather suddenly he became fat and looked much older than his years, certainly not least because of his heavy consumption of beer. The excellence of local beer had been a major factor in the choice of Bayreuth as his final residence.

Bayreuth was then Prussian territory and was affected by the war between France and Prussia in 1806 and 1807. The following years brought French occupation, much soul-searching and attempts at reorientation in German intellectual circles, and a severe economic crisis that directly affected a freelance writer with family obligations. Richter took an active interest in the events of the time, but he never became a superpatriot, never hated the French, and never liked war. In his *Freiheits-Büchlein* (Little Book on Liberty, 1805) Richter had written a forceful indictment of censorship. The occasion was a witty dedication of *Vorschule der Aesthetik* to the duke of Gotha which the censors, professors in Jena, may not have understood but in any case refused to pass. Richter published the relevant correspondence together with his own commentary. After 1807, with a general feeling of crisis in the air, he spoke out in *Friedens-Predigt an Deutschland* (Sermon for Peace to Germany, 1808) and then in the more extensive *Dämmerungen für Deutschland* (Twilights for Germany, 1809). Other essays and narrative texts, some of them first published in Cotta's *Morgenblatt,* were collected and updated in *Politische Fastenpredigten während Deutschlands Marterwoche* (Political Lenten Sermons during Germany's Passion Week, 1817).

Richter spoke to many but pleased few. He opposed the German patriots who supported rearmament; but Goethe, who admired Napoleon, made fun of Richter's apparent indecisiveness in a satirical poem. Richter tried to be impartial in a partisan atmosphere. He also insisted on a moral renewal at a time when people were thinking politically. He tried to maintain a Herderian liberal attitude and give a balanced view of the good and the bad the French occupation had brought to Germany. He was not blind to the progress in civil liberties and legal protection which the "Rhein-bund" (Rhenish Alliance) under Napoleon's protectorate introduced into western Germany. One of the most forceful sections of *Dämmerungen für Deutschland* is "Kriegserklärung gegen den Krieg" (Declaration of War against War), which holds that liberation of Germany should come through moral, cultural, economic, and political rather than military means. Richter warned against a new barbaric fanaticism and maintained that freedom comes with political maturity and can neither be imposed nor taken away.

In practical terms, the Rheinbund was good for Richter. Its leader, Karl Theodor von Dalberg, granted him an annual pension from 1808 to 1813. The pension was reinstated after 1815 by the king of Bavaria. Richter contributed some of his significant later essays to the *Museum* in Frankfurt, for instance his long essay on dream language and the subconscious. Compared to the political censorship after 1815, even in liberal Bavaria (Napoleon had made Bayreuth part of Bavaria), there was much freedom of opinion in the Napoleonic era. Richter maintained his liberal and cosmopolitan views, although he also felt touched by the new patriotism, especially in that beginning in October 1813 when Germany was evacuated by the French. But while the younger generation respected him as a great German and patriot, he was clearly out of place in the new era of nationalism.

There is much social criticism and a good measure of self-criticism in the narrative works after *Flegel-jahre;* a tone of satire and disillusionment is unmistakable. Still, they are humorous and even contain lofty moments. *Des Feldpredigers Schmelzle Reise nach Flätz mit fortgehenden Noten* (1808; translated as "Army Chaplain Schmelzle's Journey to Flaetz," 1827) is a character study of a coward whose too-vivid imagination makes him afraid of improbable dangers such as meteors raining down upon him. "Ehrlosigkeit" (lack of honor) was for Richter one of the major reasons for the German defeats and moral crisis. He included in this indictment a good part of the intelligentsia. Such intellectuals are depicted in *Dr. Katzenbergers Badereise* (Dr. Katzenberger's Trip to a Spa, 1809). While Dr. Katzenberger is a cold and cynical scientist who enjoys terrifying or nauseating others, the playwright Nieß is a vain and self-centered fraud. We should not look to such intellectuals for moral guidance but to simple, truthful, and courageous people like the mathematician and artillery captain Theudobach and Katzenberger's honest and loving daughter Theoda.

Even the idyllic village of Wuz and Fixlein is colored with satire in *Leben Fibels, des Verfassers der Bienrodi-schen Fibel* (Life of Fibel, the Author of the Bienroda Primer, 1812), in which Richter invents a biography for the author of a ridiculous primer. Fibel (whose name means primer in German) becomes wealthy from the sales of this primer; his vanity increases to absurd proportions and is reinforced by flattering biographers. Suddenly, however, he comes to his senses. The narrator Jean Paul, who reconstructs the biography from documents which are being used as grocery bags, finds Fibel himself: he is a very old man, reborn and far removed from earthly vanity.

A project of a large comic novel that was to be the crowning achievement of his career and a counterpart to Don Quixote went through many stages but never materialized as such. It produced, however, the three volumes of *Der Komet* (The Comet, 1820–1822) and a fragment of autobiography, *Selberlebensbeschreibung* (Description of My Own Life), written in 1818 and 1819 and published posthumously in 1826.

Der Komet, Richter's last novel, is unfinished, like *Die unsichtbare Loge* and *Flegeljahre.* It tells the story of Nikolaus Marggraf, a pharmacist who is made to believe that he is the illegitimate son of a prince. Suddenly becoming rich by producing artificial diamonds, he collects an entourage and sets out to look for his purported father, as well as for a princess whom he had seen in his childhood and whose wax bust he carries with him. His entourage of friends and spongers includes one Kandidat Richter from Hof, who can predict the weather (one of the author's lifelong hobbies). Kandidat Richter is one of the few people who see Marggraf as a real prince. The progress of Marggraf's party and his ridiculous princely demeanor give occasion for a series of comic scenes, mostly bordering on the grotesque. The grotesque becomes a central element, both in its funny and its frightful aspects, when Marggraf encounters the "Ledermensch" (leather man), who speaks at times with the voice of the devil. Though the work is subtitled *Eine komische Geschichte* (A Comic Story), it ends on a frightening note.

Richter liked to escape to a country inn outside of Bayreuth, the "Rollwenzelei," where he could work upstairs and Mrs. Rollwenzel would care for him. He felt isolated and out of place in Bayreuth but never moved; instead, he took summer trips to more lively cities. The most enjoyable of these trips was one in 1817 to Heidelberg, where he was given an honorary doctorate at the instigation of the philosopher G. W. F. Hegel. He had to write for money and produced many journal articles of uneven quality. He spent much time on revisions for new editions; *Siebenkäs,* in particular, was changed considerably. He also spent time defending dubious linguistic theories, like eliminating the *s* in the middle of compound nouns. Larger projects remained unfinished as he experienced increasing difficulties in writing. Among them was a plan to write against

"Über-Christentum" (Super Christianity), a new wave of emotional, fanatical, sometimes fundamentalist Christian faith which made the rounds of the younger generation after 1815. Richter's own son Max was affected by this movement when he went to Heidelberg to study philosophy. In the fall of 1821 Max fell ill, probably with typhoid fever, and came home to Bayreuth in a state of exhaustion but also with symptoms of a nervous breakdown. On 25 September 1821 Max died; he was not quite eighteen years old. After this blow Richter vowed to devote his time to writing about immortality.

Ever since the publication of *Das Kampaner Thal* he had thought of writing a revision or continuation of the work. Now he transplanted the same group of characters into the present and added to them a new generation of figures in *Selina oder Über die Unsterblichkeit* (Selina; or, On Immortality, 1827). From 1823 until his death on 14 November 1825 Richter devoted his main energy to this work, and he finished about two thirds of it; it was published posthumously in 1827. While it seems to represent a stubborn adherence to problems of the eighteenth century which the nineteenth century had laid aside, the work is interesting not only for its new arguments and perspectives but also for its introduction of social and historical reality, including events of the Greek war of liberation. The narrator Jean Paul, once more moving among his characters, wrote for himself a fitting testament with this combination of narration, philosophy, religion, and visions of a "second world."

Richter, who was sick and almost blind at the end, negotiated the publication of his collected works (1826–1838) with Reimer, Matzdorff's successor. Reimer had also published *Der Komet,* which had sold well, and had offered Richter a supplemental payment that Richter declined because he thought Reimer had been fair with him. The money from the collected works was substantial and was important for Richter's widow, who survived him by thirty-five years. The princely funeral in Bayreuth gave more honor to him than he had ever received in his lifetime. The most memorable eulogy was pronounced two weeks later in Frankfurt by Ludwig Börne, who saw Jean Paul as the prophet of the twentieth century, an age of liberty and justice.

German writers of the first half of the nineteenth century were clearly under the spell of Richter's work and style. Later, realists such as Gottfried Keller tried to distance themselves from him, and later in the century his major novels were seldom read; only "Das Leben des vergnügten Schulmeisterlein Wuz in Auenthal" seemed to survive. Literary historians had difficulties fitting his work into Classicism or Romanticism. At the turn of the century the neoclassicist Stefan George rediscovered the "sublime" Jean Paul, and around this time serious work began on editions of his work. Eduard Berend's critical edition (1927–1964), however, was interrupted by the Nazi takeover and then by the division of Germany after 1945 and may remain unfinished forever.

It is not difficult to discover modern features in Richter's work, and writers and scholars since 1945 have increasingly done so. It makes little sense, however, to overemphasize the political content of *Hesperus* and *Titan,* as Wolfgang Harich of the German Democratic Republic did in 1974; calling the novels a direct response to the French Revolution raises false expectations. Richter was, as many since Börne have noted, politically progressive, and he was sympathetic to the ideals of the French Revolution. But he dealt with the problems of his age on a human level and wanted to change people, not institutions.

There is no shortcut for the reader of Richter's works. Since they deal with the social reality of their time, the last decades of the Holy Roman Empire, the reader needs an encyclopedia to understand the facts and allusions. But the reader also needs to follow the game of the narrator, who demonstrates how he fashions the text and still remains in it. Heinrich Heine noted in *Die romantische Schule* (The Romantic School, 1836) that Richter offers a work in progress rather than a finished product, and that he includes the description of the process of narration. Thus the reader is invited to engage in a complex dialogue with the narrator which requires repeated readings and an agile mind. Such a writer cannot expect to be popular but will have a real impact on those readers who enter into such a dialogue. Richter's narrator Jean Paul has an unmistakable tone and voice within the tradition of the European humorous novel from Cervantes and Rabelais to Fielding, Sterne, Charles Dickens, Fyodor Dostoyevsky, Thomas Mann, Günter Grass, and Arno Schmidt.

Letters:

Jean Paul's Briefe an Friedrich Heinrich Jacobi (Berlin: Reimer, 1828);

Jean Pauls Briefwechsel mit seinem Freunde Christian Otto, 4 volumes, edited by Ernst Förster (Berlin: Reimer, 1829–1833; reprinted, 1 volume, Berlin & New York: De Gruyter, 1978);

Briefe an eine Jugendfreundin, edited by J. F. Täglichsbeck (Brandenberg: Müller, 1858);

Jean Paul's Blätter der Verehrung: Briefwechsel mit großen Männern, edited by Förster (Munich: Fleischmann, 1865);

Jean Paul's Briefwechsel mit seinen Freunden: Emanuel Osmund, Friedrich von Oertel und Paul Theriot (Munich: Fleischmann, 1865);

Jean Pauls Briefwechsel mit seiner Frau und Christian Otto, edited by Paul Nerrlich (Berlin: Weidmann, 1902);

Die Briefe Jean Pauls, 4 volumes, edited by Eduard Berend (Munich: Müller, 1922–1926);

Jean Paul und Frau von Krüdener im Spiegel ihres Briefwechsels, edited by Dorothea Berger (Wiesbaden: Limes, 1957);

Jean Paul und Herder: Der Briefwechsel Jean Pauls und Karoline Richters mit Herder und der Herderschen Familie in den Jahren 1785 bis 1805, edited by Paul Stapf (Bern: Francke, 1959).

Bibliographies:

Eduard Berend, *Jean-Paul-Bibliographie,* revised by Johannes Krogoll (Stuttgart: Klett, 1963);

Eike Fuhrmann, "Jean-Paul-Bibliographie 1963–1965," *Jahrbuch der Jean-Paul-Gesellschaft,* 1 (1966): 163–179;

Renate Merwald: "Jean-Paul-Bibliographie 1966–1969," *Jahrbuch der Jean-Paul-Gesellschaft,* 5 (1970): 185–219;

Sabine Müller, "Jean Paul-Bibliographie 1970–1983," *Jahrbuch der Jean-Paul-Gesellschaft,* 19 (1984): 137–205.

Biographies:

Paul Nerrlich, *Jean Paul: Sein Leben und seine Werke* (Berlin: Weidemann, 1889);

Walter Harich, *Jean Paul* (Leipzig: Haessel, 1925; reprinted, New York: AMS Press, 1971);

Günter de Bruyn, *Das Leben des Jean Paul Friedrich Richter* (Halle: Mitteldeutscher Verlag, 1975).

References:

Beate Allert, *Die Metapher und ihre Krise: Zur Dynamik der Bilderschrift Jean Pauls* (New York, Bern, Frankfurt am Main & Paris: Lang, 1987);

Heinz Ludwig Arnold, ed., *Jean Paul: Sonderband text & kritik* (Munich: Edition text & kritik, 1970; revised, 1983);

Hans Bach, *Jean Pauls Hesperus* (Berlin: Mayer & Müller, 1929);

Heidemarie Bade, *Jean Pauls politische Schriften* (Tübingen: Niemeyer, 1974);

Eduard Berend, *Jean Pauls Ästhetik* (Berlin: Dunkker, 1909);

Berend, ed., *Jean Pauls Persönlichkeit in Berichten der Zeitgenossen* (Berlin & Weimar: Akademie & Böhlau, 1956);

Dorothea Berger, *Jean Paul Friedrich Richter* (New York: Twayne, 1970);

Hendrik Birus, *Vergleichung: Goethes Einführung in die Schreibweise Jean Pauls* (Stuttgart: Metzler, 1986);

Ludwig Börne, *Denkrede auf Jean Paul* (Frankfurt am Main [actually Erfurt], 1826);

Bernhard Böschenstein, "Jean Pauls Romankonzeption," "Leibgeber und die Metapher der Hülle," in his *Studien zur Dichtung des Absoluten* (Zurich & Freiburg: Atlantis, 1968) pp. 25–50;

Heinrich Bosse, *Theorie und Praxis bei Jean Paul: Sektion 74 der "Vorschule der Ästhetik" und Jean Pauls erzählerische Technik, besonders im "Titan"* (Bonn: Bouvier, 1970);

Edward V. Brewer, "The New England Interest in Jean Paul Friedrich Richter," *University of California Publications in Modern Philology* 27, no. 1 (1943): 1–26;

Hans Esselborn, *Das Universum der Bilder: Die Naturwissenschaft in den Schriften Jean Pauls* (Tübingen: Niemeyer, 1989);

Ernst Förster, ed., *Denkwürdigkeiten aus dem Leben von Jean Paul Friedrich Richter: Zur Feier seines hundertjährigen Geburtstages herausgegeben,* 4 volumes (Munich: Fleischmann, 1863);

Marie-Luise Gansberg, "Welt-Verlachung und das 'rechte Land,'" *Deutsche Vierteljahrsschrift für Literaturwissenschaft und Geistesgeschichte,* 42 (1968): 373–398;

Hansjörg Garte, "Kunstform Schauerroman: Eine morphologische Begriffsbestimmung des Sensationsromans im 18. Jahrhundert von Walpoles 'Castle of Otranto' bis zu Jean Pauls 'Titan,'" dissertation, University of Leipzig, 1935;

Ursula Gauhe, *Jean Pauls Traumdichtungen* (Bonn: Scheur, 1936);

Jochen Golz, *Welt und Gegen-Welt in Jean Pauls "Titan"* (Stuttgart & Weimar: Metzler, 1996);

Käthe Hamburger, "Das Todesproblem bei Jean Paul," *Deutsche Vierteljahrsschrift für Literaturwissenschaft und Geistesgeschichte,* 7 (1929): 446–474;

Wolfgang Harich, *Jean Pauls Kritik des philosophischen Egoismus* (Frankfurt am Main: Suhrkamp, 1968);

Harich, *Jean Pauls Revolutionsdichtung: Versuch einer neuen Deutung seiner heroischen Romane* (Berlin: Akademie-Verlag, 1974);

Hesperus: Blätter der Jean-Paul-Gesellschaft, edited by Theodor Langemaier, nos. 1–30 (1951–1966);

Margaret R. Higonnet, "Jean Paul Richter: Kunstrichter," *Journal of English and German Philology,* 76 (1977): 471–490;

Jahrbuch der Jean-Paul-Gesellschaft, edited by Kurt Wölfel (1966–);

Jean-Paul-Blätter, edited by August Caselmann, Georg Regler, and Johannes Wirth, 1–19 (1926–1944);

Jean-Paul-Jahrbuch, edited by Eduard Berend, 1 (1925);

Herbert Kaiser, *Jean Paul lesen: Versuch über seine poetische Anthropologie des Ich* (Würzburg: Königshausen & Neumann, 1995);

Wulf Koepke, *Erfolglosigkeit: Zum Frühwerk Jean Pauls* (Munich: Fink, 1977);

Koepke, ". . . von den Weibern geliebt: Jean Paul und seine Leserinnen," in *Die Frau von der Reformation zur*

Romantik: Die Situation der Frau vor dem Hintergrund der Literatur- und Sozialgeschichte, edited by Barbara Becker-Cantarino (Bonn: Bouvier, 1980), pp. 217–242;

Max Kommerell, *Jean Paul* (Frankfurt am Main: Klostermann, 1933; fifth edition, 1977);

Burckhardt Lindner, *Jean Paul: Scheiternde Aufklärung und Autorrolle* (Darmstadt: Agora, 1976);

Peter Michelsen, *Laurence Sterne und der deutsche Roman des achtzehnten Jahrhunderts,* revised edition (Göttingen: Vandenhoeck & Ruprecht, 1972);

Götz Müller, *Jean Pauls Ästhetik und Naturphilosophie* (Tübingen: Niemeyer, 1983);

Müller, *Jean Pauls Exzerpte* (Würzburg: Königshausen & Neumann, 1988);

Ursula Naumann, *Predigende Poesie: Zur Bedeutung von Predigt, geistlicher Rede und Predigertum für das Werk Jean Pauls* (Nuremberg: Carl, 1976);

Eckart Oehlenschläger, *Närrische Phantasie: Zum metaphorischen Prozeß bei Jean Paul* (Tübingen: Niemeyer, 1980);

Hanns-Josef Ortheil, *Jean Paul in Selbstzeugnissen und Bilddokumenten* (Reinbek: Rowohlt, 1984);

Claude Pichois, *L'image de Jean-Paul dans les lettres françaises* (Paris: Cort, 1963);

Ulrich Profitlich, *Der seelige Leser: Untersuchungen zur Dichtungstheorie Jean Pauls* (Bonn: Bouvier, 1968);

Wolfgang Proß, *Jean Pauls geschichtliche Stellung* (Tübingen: Niemeyer, 1975);

Wolfdietrich Rasch, *Die Erzählweise Jean Pauls: Metaphernspiele und dissonante Strukturen* (Munich: Hanser, 1961);

Walther Rehm, *Jean Paul–Dostojewski: Eine Studie zur dichterischen Gestaltung des Unglaubens* (Göttingen: Vandenhoeck & Ruprecht, 1962);

Rehm, "Roquairol: Eine Studie zur Geschichte des Bösen," in his *Begegnungen und Probleme* (Bern: Francke, 1957); pp. 155–242;

Richard Rohde, *Jean Pauls Titan: Untersuchungen über Entstehung, Ideengehalt und Form des Romans* (Berlin: Mayer & Müller, 1920);

Heinz Schlaffer, "Epos und Roman: Tat und Bewußtsein. Jean Pauls Titan," in his *Der Bürger als Held: Sozialgeschichtliche Auflösungen literarischer Widersprüche,* third edition (Frankfurt am Main: Suhrkamp, 1981), pp. 15–50;

Wilhelm Schmidt-Biggemann, *Maschine und Teufel: Jean Pauls Jugendsatiren nach ihrer Modellgeschichte* (Freiburg & Munich: Alber, 1975);

Monika Schmitz-Emans, *Schnupftuchsknoten oder Sternbild: Jean Pauls Ansätze zu einer Theorie der Sprache* (Bonn: Bouvier, 1986);

Ferdinand Josef Schneider, *Jean Pauls Jugend und erstes Auftreten in der Literatur* (Berlin: Behr, 1905);

Rüdiger Scholz, *Welt und Form des Romans bei Jean Paul* (Bern: Francke, 1973);

Uwe Schweikert, *Jean Paul* (Stuttgart: Metzler, 1970);

Schweikert, *Jean Pauls Komet: Selbstparodie der Kunst* (Stuttgart: Metzler, 1971);

Schweikert, ed., *Jean Paul* (Darmstadt: Wissenschaftliche Buchgesellschaft, 1974);

Schweikert, Gabriele Schweikert, and Wilhelm Schmidt-Biggemann, eds., *Jean Paul Chronik: Daten zu Leben und Werk* (Munich: Hanser, 1975);

J. W. Smeed, "Jean Paul," in *German Men of Letters,* volume 5, edited by Alex Natan (London: Wolff, 1969), pp. 31–47;

Smeed, *Jean Paul's Dreams* (London, New York & Toronto: Oxford University Press, 1966);

Hans Michael Speier, *Die Ästhetik Jean Pauls in der Dichtung des deutschen Symbolismus* (Frankfurt am Main: Fischer, 1979);

Peter Sprengel, *Innerlichkeit: Jean Paul oder Das Leiden an der Gesellschaft* (Munich: Hanser, 1977);

Sprengel, ed., *Jean Paul im Urteil seiner Kritiker: Dokumente zur Wirkungsgeschichte Jean Pauls in Deutschland* (Munich: Beck, 1980);

Emil Staiger, "Jean Pauls 'Titan': Vorstudien zu einer Auslegung," in his *Meisterwerke deutscher Sprache aus dem neunzehnten Jahrhundert* (Zurich: Atlantis, 1943), pp. 39–81;

Gert Ueding, *Jean Paul* (Munich: Beck, 1993);

Engelhard Weigl, *Aufklärung und Skeptizismus: Untersuchungen zu Jean Pauls Frühwerk* (Hildesheim: Gerstenberg, 1980);

Waltraud Wiethölter, *Witzige Illumination: Studien zur Ästhetik Jean Pauls* (Tübingen: Niemeyer, 1979);

Gisela Wilkending, *Jean Pauls Sprachauffassung in ihrem Verhältnis zu seiner Ästhetik* (Marburg: Elwert, 1966);

Kurt Wölfel, *Jean-Paul-Studien,* edited by Bernhard Buschendorf (Frankfurt am Main: Suhrkamp, 1989);

Wölfel, ed., "Sammlung zeitgenössischer Rezensionen von Jean Pauls Werken," 4 installments, *Jahrbuch der Jean-Paul-Gesellschaft,* 13 (1978), 16 (1981), 18 (1983), 23 (1988);

Ralph-Rainer Wuthenow, *Jean-Paul-Aufsätze* (Frankfurt am Main: Insel, 1975).

Papers:

Johann Paul Friedrich Richter's papers are in the Staatsbibliothek Berlin and in the Eduard Berend Collection of the Deutsches Literaturarchiv, Marbach.

Rainer Maria Rilke

(4 December 1875 – 29 December 1926)

George C. Schoolfield
Yale University

This entry originally appeared in DLB 81: Austrian Fiction
Writers, 1875–1913.

BOOKS: *Leben und Lieder: Bilder und Tagebuchblätter*
(Strassburg & Leipzig: Kattentidt, 1894);
Wegwarten (Prague: Selbstverlag, 1896);
Larenopfer (Prague: Dominicus, 1896);
Todtentänze: Zwielicht-Skizzen aus unseren Tagen (Prague:
Löwit & Lamberg, 1896);
Im Frühfrost: Ein Stück Dämmerung. Drei Vorgänge (Vienna:
Theaterverlag O. F. Eirich, 1897);
Traumgekrönt: Neue Gedichte (Leipzig: Friesenhahn, 1897);
Advent (Leipzig: Friesenhahn, 1898);
Ohne Gegenwart: Drama in zwei Akten (Berlin: Entsch,
1898);
Am Leben hin: Novellen und Skizzen (Stuttgart: Bonz, 1898);
Zwei Prager Geschichten (Stuttgart: Bonz, 1899);
Mir zur Feier: Gedichte (Berlin: Meyer, 1899); republished
as *Die frühen Gedichte* (Leipzig: Insel, 1909; New
York: Ungar, 1943);
Vom lieben Gott und Anderes: An Große für Kinder erzählt
(Berlin & Leipzig: Schuster & Loeffler, 1900);
republished as *Geschichten vom lieben Gott* (Leipzig:
Insel, 1904; New York: Ungar, 1942); translated
by Nora Purtscher-Wydenbruck and M. D. Herter
Norton as *Stories of God* (London: Sidgwick &
Jackson, 1932; New York: Norton, 1932);
*Zur Einweihung der Kunsthalle am 15, Februar 1902:
Festspielszene* (Bremen, 1902);
Die Letzten (Berlin: Juncker, 1902);
Das tägliche Leben: Drama in zwei Akten (Munich: Langen,
1902);
Das Buch der Bilder (Berlin: Juncker, 1902; enlarged,
1906; New York: Ungar, 1943);
*Worpswede: Fritz Mackensen, Otto Modersohn, Fritz Overbeck,
Hans am Ende, Heinrich Vogeler* (Bielefeld & Leipzig:
Velhagen & Klasing, 1903);
Auguste Rodin (Berlin: Bard, 1903); translated by Jesse
Lemont and Hans Trausil (New York: Sunwise
Turn, 1919); translation republished as *Rodin*
(London: Grey Walls Press, 1946);

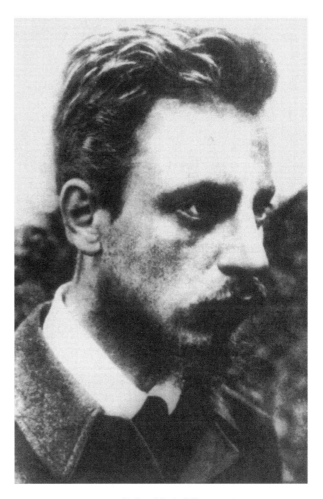

Rainer Maria Rilke

*Das Stunden-Buch enthaltend die drei Bücher: Vom mönchischen
Leben: Von der Pilgerschaft: Von der Armuth und vom
Tode* (Leipzig: Insel, 1905); translated by A. L.
Peck as *The Book of Hours; Comprising the Three
Books: Of the Monastic Life, Of Pilgrimage, Of Poverty
and Death* (London: Hogarth Press, 1961);

567

Die Weise von Liebe und Tod des Cornets Christoph Rilke (Berlin: Juncker, 1906); translated by B. J. Morse as *The Story of the Love and Death of the Cornet Christopher Rilke* (Osnabrück, 1927); translated by Herter Norton as *The Tale of the Love and Death of Cornet Christopher Rilke* (New York: Norton, 1932);

Neue Gedichte, 2 volumes (Leipzig: Insel, 1907–1908); translated by J. B. Leishman as *New Poems* (London: Hogarth Press, 1964; New York: New Directions, 1964);

Requiem (Leipzig: Insel, 1909);

Die Aufzeichnungen des Malte Laurids Brigge (Leipzig: Insel, 1910); translated by John Linton as *The Notebook of Malte Laurids Brigge* (London: Hogarth Press, 1930); translation republished as *The Journal of My Other Self* (New York: Norton, 1930);

Erste Gedichte (Leipzig: Insel, 1913; New York: Ungar, 1947);

Das Marien-Leben (Leipzig: Insel, 1913); translated by R. G. L. Barrett as *The Life of the Virgin Mary* (Würzburg: Triltsch, 1921); translated by C. F. MacIntyre as *The Life of the Virgin Mary* (Berkeley & Los Angeles: University of California Press, 1947); translated by Stephen Spender as *The Life of the Virgin Mary* (London: Vision Press, 1951; New York: Philosophical Library, 1951);

Poems, translated by Lemont (New York: Wright, 1918);

Aus der Frühzeit Rainer Maria Rilkes: Vers, Prosa, Drama (1894–1899), edited by Fritz Adolf Hünich (Leipzig: Bibliophilenabend, 1921);

Mitsou: Quarante images par Baltusz (Erlenbach-Zurich & Leipzig: Rotapfel, 1921);

Puppen (Munich: Hyperion, 1921);

Die Sonette an Orpheus: Geschrieben als ein Grab-Mal für Wera Ouckama Knoop (Leipzig: Insel, 1923; New York: Ungar, 1945); translated by Leishman as *Sonnets to Orpheus, Written as a Monument for Wera Ouckama Knoop* (London: Hogarth Press, 1936); translated by Norton as *Sonnets to Orpheus* (New York: Norton, 1942);

Duineser Elegien (Leipzig: Insel, 1923; New York: Ungar, 1944); translated by Vita Sackville-West and Edward Sackville-West as *Duineser Elegien: Elegies from the Castle of Duino* (London: Hogarth Press, 1931); translated by Leishman and Spender as *Duino Elegies* (New York: Norton, 1939; London: Hogarth Press, 1939);

Vergers suivi des Quatrains Valaisans (Paris: Éditions de la Nouvelle Revue Française, 1926); translated by Alfred Poulin as *Orchards* (Port Townsend, Wash.: Graywolf Press, 1982);

Les Fenêtres: Dix poèmes (Paris: Officina Sanctandreana, 1927); translated by Poulin as "The Windows," in

The Roses and the Windows (Port Townsend, Wash.: Graywolf Press, 1979);

Les Roses (Bussum: Stols, 1927); translated by Poulin as "The Roses," in *The Roses and the Windows* (Port Townsend, Wash.: Graywolf Press, 1979);

Gesammelte Werke, 6 volumes (Leipzig: Insel, 1927);

Erzählungen und Skizzen aus der Frühzeit (Leipzig: Insel, 1928);

Ewald Tragy: Erzählung (Munich: Heller, 1929; New York: Johannespresse, 1944); translated by Lola Gruenthal as *Ewald Tragy* (London: Vision, 1958; New York: Twayne, 1958);

Verse und Prosa aus dem Nachlaß (Leipzig: Gesellschaft der Freunde der Deutschen Bücherei, 1929);

Gesammelte Gedichte, 4 volumes (Leipzig: Insel, 1930–1933);

Über den jungen Dichter (Hamburg, 1931);

Gedichte, edited by Katharina Kippenberg (Leipzig: Insel, 1931; New York: Ungar, 1947);

Rainer Maria Rilke auf Capri: Gespräche, edited by Leopold von Schlözer (Dresden: Jess, 1931);

Späte Gedichte (Leipzig: Insel, 1934);

Bücher, Theater, Kunst, edited by Richard von Mises (Vienna: Jahoda & Siegel, 1934);

Der ausgewählten Gedichte anderer Teil, edited by Kippenberg (Leipzig: Insel, 1935);

Ausgewählte Werke, edited by Ruth Sieber-Rilke, Carl Sieber, and Ernst Zinn, 2 volumes (Leipzig: Insel, 1938);

Translations from the Poetry of Rainer Maria Rilke, translated by Herter Norton (New York: Norton, 1938);

Fifty Selected Poems with English Translations, translated by C. F. MacIntyre (Berkeley: University of California Press, 1940);

Selected Poems, translated by Leishman (London: Hogarth Press, 1941);

Tagebücher aus der Frühzeit, edited by Sieber-Rilke and Sieber (Leipzig: Insel, 1942);

Briefe, Verse und Prosa aus dem Jahre 1896, edited by Mises, 2 volumes (New York: Johannespresse, 1946);

Thirty-one Poems, translated by Ludwig Lewisohn (New York: Ackerman, 1946);

Freundschaft mit Rainer Maria Rilke: Begegnungen, Gespräche, Briefe und Aufzeichnungen mitgeteilt durch Elga Maria Nevar (Bümpliz: Züst, 1946);

Five Prose Pieces, translated by Carl Niemeyer (Cummington, Mass.: Cummington Press, 1947);

Gedichte, edited by Hermann Kunisch (Göttingen: Vandenhoeck & Ruprecht, 1947);

Gedichte in französischer Sprache, edited by Thankmar von Münchhausen (Wiesbaden: Insel, 1949);

Aus Rainer Maria Rilkes Nachlaß, 4 volumes (Wiesbaden: Insel, 1950); volume 1, *Aus dem Nachlaß des Grafen*

C. W., translated by Leishman as *From the Remains of Count C. W.* (London: Hogarth Press, 1952);

Werke: Auswahl in zwei Bänden (Leipzig: Insel, 1953);

Gedichte 1906–1926: Sammlung der verstreuten und nachgelassenen Gedichte aus den mittleren und späteren Jahren, edited by Zinn (Wiesbaden: Insel, 1953); translated, with additions, by Leishman as *Poems 1906 to 1926* (Norfolk, Conn.: Laughlin, 1957; London: Hogarth Press, 1957);

Selected Works, translated by G. Craig Houston and Leishman, 2 volumes (London: Hogarth Press, 1954; New York: New Directions, 1960);

Sämtliche Werke, edited by Zinn, 6 volumes (Wiesbaden & Frankfurt am Main: Insel, 1955–1966);

Angel Songs/Engellieder, translated by Rhoda Coghill (Dublin: Dolmen Press, 1958);

Die Turnstunde und andere Novellen, edited by Fritz Fröhling (Freiburg im Breisgau: Hyperion, 1959);

Poems, edited by G. W. McKay (London: Oxford University Press, 1965);

Werke in drei Bänden, 3 volumes (Frankfurt am Main: Insel, 1966);

Gedichte: Eine Auswahl (Stuttgart: Reclam, 1966);

Visions of Christ: A Posthumous Cycle of Poems, translated by Aaron Kramer, edited by Siegfried Mandel (Boulder: University of Colorado Press, 1967);

Das Testament, edited by Zinn (Frankfurt am Main: Insel, 1975);

Holding Out: Poems, translated by Rika Lesser (Omaha, Nebr.: Abbatoir Editions, 1975);

Possibility of Being: A Selection of Poems, translated by Leishman (New York: New Directions, 1977);

Werke: In 3 Bänden, edited by Horst Nalewski, 3 volumes (Leipzig: Insel, 1978);

Nine Plays, translated by Klaus Phillips and John Locke (New York: Ungar, 1979);

I Am Too Alone in the World: Ten Poems, translated by Robert Bly (New York: Silver Hands Press, 1980);

Selected Poems of Rainer Maria Rilke, translated by Bly (New York: Harper & Row, 1981);

Requiem for a Woman, and Selected Lyric Poems, translated by Andy Gaus (Putney, Vt.: Threshold Books, 1981);

An Unofficial Rilke: Poems 1912–1926, edited and translated by Michael Hamburger (London: Anvil Press, 1981);

Selected Poetry, edited and translated by Stephen Mitchell (New York: Random House, 1982);

Selected Poems, translated by A. E. Flemming (St. Petersburg, Fla.: Golden Smith, 1983);

The Unknown Rilke: Selected Poems, translated by Franz Wright (Oberlin, Ohio: Oberlin College, 1983);

Between Roots: Selected Poems, translated by Rika Lesser (Princeton: Princeton University Press, 1986).

TRANSLATIONS: Elizabeth Barrett Browning, *Sonette nach dem Portugiesischen* (Leipzig: Insel, 1908);

Maurice de Guérin, *Der Kentaur* (Leipzig: Insel, 1911);

Die Liebe der Magdalena: Ein französischer Sermon, gezogen durch den Abbé Joseph Bonnet aus dem Ms. Q I 14 der Kaiserlichen Bibliothek zu St. Petersburg (Leipzig: Insel, 1912);

Marianna Alcoforado, *Portugiesische Briefe* (Leipzig: Insel, 1913);

André Gide, *Die Rückkehr des verlorenen Sohnes* (Leipzig: Insel, 1914);

Die vierundzwanzig Sonette der Louise Labé, Lyoneserin, 1555 (Leipzig: Insel, 1918);

Paul Valéry, *Gedichte* (Leipzig: Insel, 1925);

Valéry, *Eupalinos oder Über die Architektur* (Leipzig: Insel, 1927);

Übertragungen (Leipzig: Insel, 1927);

Dichtungen des Michelangelo (Leipzig: Insel, 1936);

Gedichte aus fremden Sprachen (New York: Ungar, 1947);

Maurice Maeterlinck, *Die sieben Jungfrauen von Orlamünde* (Liege: Editions Dynamo, 1967).

PERIODICAL PUBLICATIONS: "Die goldene Kiste," *Unterhaltungs-Blatt der Nürnberger Stadt-Zeitung,* 2 February 1895, pp. 19–20;

"Eine Tote," *Deutsches Abendblatt* (Prague), 22–24 January 1896;

"Ihr Opfer," *Sommer-Beilage der "Politik"* (Prague) (28 June 1896);

"Der Apostel," *Die Musen,* 4 (1896): 24–28;

"Heiliger Frühling: Skizze," *Jugend,* 2, no. 19 (1897): 303–306;

"Leise Begleitung," *Das neue Jahrhundert,* 1, no. 4 (1898): 119–123;

"Masken," *Ver sacrum,* 1, no. 4 (1898): 12–13;

"Teufelsspuk," *Simplicissimus,* 3, no. 50 (1899): 395;

"Das Lachen des Pán Mráz," *Simplicissimus,* 4, no. 22 (1899): 170;

"Wladimir, der Wolkenmaler," *Revue franco-alle-mande,* 1 (1899): 378–380;

"Die Turnstunde," *Die Zukunft,* 10, no. 18 (1902): 211–214;

"Der Totengräber," *Österreichisches Novellenbuch,* 2 (1903): 59–81.

Rainer Maria Rilke is one of the major poets of twentieth-century literature. In the collections with which his early verse culminates, *Das Buch der Bilder* (The Book of Pictures, 1902; enlarged, 1906) and *Das Stunden-Buch* (1905; translated as *The Book of Hours,* 1961), he appears as a creator or discoverer of legends—his own and history's—and, particularly in the latter work, as a special brand of mystic. With the poems of his middle years, *Neue Gedichte* (1907–1908; translated as *New Poems,* 1964), he is an expert instructor in the art of "seeing" as well as a guide through Europe's cultural sites just before the onslaught of general war and, subsequently, mass tourism. Because of statements in *Duineser Elegien* (1923; translated as *Elegies from the Castle of Duino,* 1931) and *Die Sonette an Orpheus* (1923; translated as *Sonnets to Orpheus,* 1936) on the limitations and possibilities of the human condition, he has become something of a teacher and consoler to readers aware of the fragility and the potential of man. Long the prey of cultists and often obscure exegetes and regarded as the bearer of a "message" or "messages," he has more recently been seen as a brilliant verse tactician whose visions may be more original in their manner of perception than in their philosophical core. His novel *Die Aufzeichnungen des Malte Laurids Brigge* (1910; translated as *The Notebook of Malte Laurids Brigge,* 1930) was initially received as a belated product of European decadence or as an autobiographical document (neither opinion is wholly off the mark); later it was identified as a striking example of the "crisis of subjectivity and its influences on the traditional possibilities of narration," in Judith Ryan's formulation. Of all Rilke's works, the large body of stories he wrote has received the least attention; as a mature artist he himself grew condescending when he occasionally mentioned them in his letters—in striking contrast to *Die Aufzeichnungen des Malte Laurids Brigge,* which he continued to praise and explicate until his death. These tales and sketches, some seventy of them, fall into the beginning of his career, before the changes that took place in his life and production in the years from 1902 to 1905.

Rilke's attitudes toward Prague, where he was born René Karl Wilhelm Johann Josef Maria Rilke on 4 December 1875, were mixed, as were those toward his parents. His father, Josef, was a former warrant officer in the Austrian army who at the time of Rilke's birth was a railroad official—a job perhaps owed to the influence of Josef's well-to-do elder brother, Jaroslav. His mother, Sophie (Phia) Entz Rilke, homely and socially ambitious, was the daughter of a perfume manufacturer. Rilke was their only child; a daughter, born before him, had survived only a few days. The parents were divorced before Rilke's childhood was past. The epistolary evidence indicates that Rilke was devoted to his father, who was simple, gregarious, and a lady's man, but saw rather little of him, and that he nearly detested his mother; yet it was the latter who encouraged his literary ambitions. The complexity of his feelings for his mother may be indicated in his early verse and stories by the appearance of a dream mother, lovely and even desirable; his reaction to Phia's bigoted Roman Catholicism, the faith in which he was reared, is reflected both in the ambiguous allusions to a Roman

Catholic world in his early verse and *Das Marien-Leben* (1913; translated as *The Life of the Virgin Mary,* 1921) and in his much-proclaimed dislike of Christianity. Rilke's snobbery, which led him to cling obstinately to a family saga of age-old nobility, was encouraged by the genealogical researches of his uncle Jaroslav and by his mother's pretensions and prejudices; Phia Rilke was distinguished by her sense of extraordinary refinement and by her contempt for Jews and Czech speakers. Both the Rilkes and the Entzes were "Prague Germans," aware that they were up against an ever more aggressive Slavic majority in a city where German speakers were confronted, as the century wore on, by the rapid weakening of their social and political position.

At ten, after an elementary education, much interrupted by real or fancied illness, with the Piarist Brothers, Rilke was sent to the military school at Sankt Pölten in Lower Austria; save for summer vacations he remained there until 1890, when he was transferred to the military upper school at Mährisch-Weißkirchen in Moravia. The abrupt change from the cosseted existence at home to regimented boarding-school life cannot have been pleasant, even though his teachers encouraged him to read his poems aloud to his fellow students. As a young man Rilke planned to free himself from "jenes böse und bange Jahrfünf" (that evil and frightened half-decade) by writing a military-school novel, and in a letter of 1920 he made an extremely harsh reply to Major-General von Sedlakowitz, his German teacher at Sankt Pölten, who had written to congratulate him on his fame: "Als ich in besonneneren Jahren . . . Dostojewskis Memoiren aus einem Toten-Hause zuerst in die Hände bekam, da wollte es mir scheinen, daß ich in alle Schrecknisse und Verzweifelungen des Bagno seit meinem zehnten Jahre eingelassen gewesen sei" (When, in years of greater reflection . . . I first got hold of Dostoyevski's *Memoirs from the House of the Dead,* it seemed to me that I had been exposed to all the terrors and despairs of the prison camp from my tenth year on). After not quite a full year at the second school, from which he emerged, he told Sedlakowitz, "ein Erschöpfter, körperlich und geistig Mißbrauchter" (exhausted, abused in body and soul), he was discharged for reasons of health and went back to Prague—only to show off by wearing his cadet's uniform and bragging about a future return to the colors. His uncle Jaroslav then sent him to a commercial academy at Linz, an experience about which he later wrote that investigations were pointless, since he had not been himself at the time. Recent research indicates that he was a would-be bon vivant who persuaded a children's nurse to run away with him to a hotel in Vienna.

In 1892 Jaroslav agreed to finance private instruction leading to the qualifying examination at Prague's

German Charles-Ferdinand University, so that one day Rilke could take over his uncle's law firm. Not that Jaroslav was at all confident about the boy's future: "Renés Phantasie ist ein Erbteil seiner Mutter und durch ihren Einfluß, von Hause aus krankhaft angeregt, durch unsystematisches Lesen allerhand Bücher überheizt–[ist] seine Eitelkeit durch vorzeitiges Lob erregt" (René's imagination is an inheritance from his mother, abnormally excited through her influence from the very beginning, overheated by the unsystematic reading of all sorts of books–his vanity has been aroused by premature praise). Tutorial instruction was congenial to Rilke's temperament; by 1895 he was ready to matriculate. He was already avidly seeking an audience–his unbearably sentimental first book, *Leben und Lieder* (Life and Songs), had come out in 1894, dedicated to Valerie David-Rhonfeld, the niece of the Czech poet Julius Zeyer (Valerie had financed the book's publication). The twenty-one artificially simple poems of *Wegwarten* (Wild Chicory) appeared in January 1896. At the end of the summer of 1896 he moved to Munich, ostensibly for art history studies but with an eye to the cultural and publishing opportunities afforded by the Bavarian capital, which was then Berlin's equal as an artistic center. By this time he had considerably better proof of his lyric talent to display: *Larenopfer* (Offering to the Lares, 1896), with its tributes to Prague, was followed by *Traumgekrönt* (Crowned with Dreams, 1897), containing some turgid but striking erotic poems, and he was already a busy contributor to popular journals.

Some of Rilke's Munich acquaintanceships were plainly meant to further his career–for example, that with the dramatist Max Halbe. (Rilke's naturalistic drama *Im Frühfrost* [1897; translated as *Early Frost* in *Nine Plays,* 1979] was produced in Prague in July 1897 with the young Max Reinhardt in the role of the weak father.) Others were more important: the novelist Jakob Wassermann introduced him to the writing of the Danish author whose works became his vade mecum, Jens Peter Jacobsen. Another young friend, Nathan Sulzberger from New York, provided him with a second major object of cultural devotion: in March 1897, at Sulzberger's invitation, he visited Venice for the first time. He spent an April vacation on Lake Constance with "the mad countess," Franziska zu Reventlow, who was pregnant with another man's child; and in May 1897 he met Lou Andreas-Salomé, fifteen years his senior, the author and former friend of Nietzsche, and the wife (in name only, it would seem) of the Iranian scholar Friedrich Carl Andreas. The summer Lou and Rilke spent at Wolfratshausen in the Bavarian Alps wrought remarkable changes in him: he altered his name from René to Rainer, his handwriting became

firmer and clearer, and he gathered his passionate love poetry to Lou into the manuscript collection "Dir zur Feier" (In Celebration of You), which, at her request, he did not publish. (The title, transmuted into *Mir zur Feier* [In Celebration of Me], was used for a book of verse in 1899.) Some of these poems, estimated to have been about one hundred in number, were subsumed into published collections; others survived only in manuscript; others were destroyed. How long Lou and Rainer remained lovers is not known, but Rilke followed her and her husband to Berlin in the autumn of 1897.

The Prussian capital remained Rilke's home until the new century. His stay there was interrupted by trips that were to be of major importance for his poetic development: a springtime journey to Italy in 1898 (his verse play *Die weiße Fürstin* [published in *Mir zur Feier;* translated as *The White Princess* in *Nine Plays,* 1979] grew out of a stay at Viareggio); an excursion to Russia from April to June 1899 in the company of the Andreases; and a second and much more carefully prepared Russian trip from May to August 1900, again with Lou but without her husband. Rilke–who had learned Russian easily and quickly on the basis of his school training in Czech–visited the peasant poet Spiridon Drozhzhin and had an uncomfortable interview with Leo Tolstoy at his estate, Yasnaya Polyana. The Russian experience under the tutelage of Lou, a native of Saint Petersburg, provided him with new poetic material: following a fad of the time, he professed a mystic love for the great land in the east; he read its literature carefully and used Russian themes in the poems in *Das Buch der Bilder* and *Das Stunden-Buch,* in his tales, and in *Die Aufzeichnungen des Malte Laurids Brigge.* During a late-summer stay with the artist Heinrich Vogeler in the artists' colony at Worpswede, near Bremen, after his return from Russia, he wore a Russian peasant's blouse and a large Greek cross. In Worpswede, thus attired, he met the painter and sculptress Paula Becker and the sculptress Clara Westhoff. Rejected by Paula, he turned his affection to her statuesque friend. On 28 April 1901 Rilke and Clara were married.

The affair with Lou had been broken off, but their years together had been enormously productive for Rilke. Some of the poems in *Advent* (1898) are from the Wolfratshausen summer; Rilke came to regard *Mir zur Feier* as the first of his "admissible" books; his career as a dramatist had been encouraged by the publication of *Ohne Gegenwart* (1898; translated as *Not Present* in *Nine Plays,* 1979), with its Maeterlinckian suggestions of ineffable fears, but it concluded disastrously with *Das tägliche Leben* (1902; translated as *Everyday Life* in *Nine Plays,* 1979), a play written in 1900 about a painter caught between two loves. Produced at the Residenz Theater in Berlin in December 1901, it was greeted with laughter: Rilke resolved never to try the stage again.

The writing of stories had occupied much of Rilke's time: a first collection, *Am Leben hin* (Along Life's Course), had appeared in 1898. The book contains eleven tales, six of which can be identified as having been finished at Wolfratshausen during the summer with Lou. Some of the tales suffer from the mawkishness that beset Rilke during his early years, whether he was writing poems, plays, or narratives. In "Greise" (Old Men) a little girl brings a flower to her grandfather as he sits on a park bench. Other old men watch; one of them, Pepi, spits contemptuously as his companion, Christoph, picks up some stray blossoms from the street and carries them back to the poorhouse. Yet Pepi puts a glass of water on the windowsill of their room, waiting in the darkest corner for Christoph to place the scruffy bouquet in it. In "Das Christkind" (The Christ Child) a little girl, mistreated by her stepmother, takes the money her father has slipped to her as a Christmas gift, buys some paper ornaments, and adorns a young fir tree with them; then she lies down in the forest to die, imagining that she is in her mother's lap. Here Rilke ventures into a maudlin realm long since cultivated by certain nineteenth-century masters; in fact, he identifies one of them: in Elisabeth's dying dreams, "Die Mutter [war] schön, wie die Fee im Märchen von Andersen" (The mother [was] beautiful, like the fairy in the tale of Andersen). In "Weißes Glück" (White Happiness) a tubercular girl tells her sad life story to another traveler, a man hoping for erotic adventure at a railroad station in the middle of the night. A blind girl has a beautiful voice but will live out her life unloved in "Die Stimme" (The Voice). Gypsies fight over a girl, and the stronger, Král, slays the boyish flute player in "Kismet."

With such stories, save for his awareness of language and a certain psychological refinement, Rilke does not rise much above the level of, say, another popular writer from Prague, Ossip Schubin (pseudonym of Aloisia Kirschner, 1854–1934). Yet there are flashes of a brilliant satiric gift in the depiction of a moribund Prague-German family in "Das Familienfest" (The Family Festival) and "Sterbetag" (Death Day), and evidence of a keen insight into human relations in "Das Geheimnis" (The Secret), about the romantic dreams of two old maids, and "Die Flucht" (The Flight), about a schoolboy's plans for an escapade with a young girl and his failure—not hers—to carry through with them. In "Alle in Einer" (All in One Woman) Rilke shows a penchant for the shocking and the horrible which he shared with other Prague writers such as Gustav Meyrink and Paul Leppin: tormented by passion, a lame woodcarver makes one image after another of the same girl, until he ends by hacking at his own hands. The concluding story, "Einig" (United), has autobiographical tones: a son with artistic ambitions has returned home ill to his pious mother. It is spoiled by a contrived happy ending—each learns that the other has been sending money to the family's estranged father—but it offers a nice specimen for students of the Ibsen craze in Germany around the turn of the century: like Oswald in Henrik Ibsen's *Ghosts* (1881), Gerhard says that he is a "wurmfaule Frucht" (worm-eaten fruit), recalling Oswald's famous description of himself as *"vermoulu,"* and claims that his illness has been bestowed upon him by his father.

Zwei Prager Geschichten (Two Prague Stories, 1899) was composed at Berlin-Schmargendorf in 1897–1898. The foreword says: "Dieses Buch ist lauter Vergangenheit. Heimat und Kindheit—beide längst fern—sind sein Hintergrund" (This book is nothing but the past. Homeland and childhood—both far removed, long since—are its background). The two lengthy stories, however, have little to do with the Prague Rilke had known; rather, they take place in Czech milieus and are expressions of Rilke's brief flaring-up of interest in Czech nationalism (other evidence is to be found in *Larenopfer*). No doubt Rilke was also aware of the interest of German publishers and their public in Prague's semi-exotic world: Karl Hans Strobl (1877–1946), for example, launched his long career as a popular author by writing about the city and the tensions between its language groups. "König Bohusch" (King Bohusch) uses Prague's Czech-speaking artistic circles as a contrasting background for two outsiders who are far more energetic and tormented than the ineffectual aesthetes, actors, and dandies of the city's cafés: the student Rezek, detesting both German speakers and the Austrian government, organizes a terrorist band; Bohusch, a hunchback, loves his "Mütterchen" (little mother), Prague, and dreams of an affair with the prostitute Frantischka. Familiar with the city's nooks and crannies, the self-important Bohusch shows Rezek a hiding place for the latter's group; simultaneously, he falls into fantasies of his own power. The police capture all the plotters save Rezek, who kills the poor, addled Bohusch because he suspects him of betraying the gang to the authorities. In fact, it was Frantischka who did so; her high-minded sister, Carla, is a member of Rezek's group. Based on actual events in the Prague of Rilke's youth, the story is an attempt to provide a dispassionate view of what, for Rilke, was an alien world, however close at hand.

More loosely constructed, "Die Geschwister" (The Siblings) looks sympathetically at a Czech family that has moved to the capital from the countryside. The son, Zdenko, is at the university; the mother does washing for the arrogant German speakers, Colonel and Mrs. Meering von Meerhelm, the depiction of whom may be the most convincing part of the story. Zdenko takes up with the radical circles around Rezek, who is carried over from "König Bohusch," but dies of illness before he can be forced to participate in their activities. The daughter, Louisa, has aroused the interest of Rezek but falls in love with Ernst Land, a young Bohemian-German who rents the late Zdenko's room and stays on after the death of Louisa's mother. By the end it is plain that the Czech and the German, the representatives of two hostile camps, will marry. The simple plot is drawn out by allusions to Bohemia's history, especially to the legends surrounding Julius Caesar, the vicious illegitimate son of Rudolf II who was said to have driven a girl to her death as he attempted to rape her during a masked ball at Krummau Castle. Rilke describes the Daliborka, the "hunger tower" on the Hradcany, later to serve as the setting for the love and conspiratorial scenes in Gustav Meyrink's *Walpurgisnacht* (1917). These tidbits are not just window dressing but are used by Rilke in an attempt at psychological portraiture. Louisa mingles the tale of Julius Caesar with her impressions of Rezek: "Und sie konnte ihm nicht wehren, daß er auch in ihre Träume wuchs und endlich eines wurde mit dem dunklen Prinzen des alten Maskentraumes und nun für sie nicht mehr Rezek sondern Julius Cäsar hieß" (And she could not prevent him from entering into her dreams and finally becoming one with the dark prince of the old dream of the masked ball, and now for her he was no longer Rezek but Julius Caesar). When Zdenko, Rezek, and Louisa visit the Daliborka, the obsessive thought returns, and she imagines herself naked, fleeing before the advances of Julius Caesar. Her rescue from these fantasies by the calm presence of Land may indicate that Rilke naively thought his Czech compatriots could be saved from the destructive allure of a Rezek by good-natured German liberalism.

Plainly, Rilke is fascinated by sexuality; but he often shies away from addressing it directly. (One of the most linguistically tortuous and emotionally tormented poems in the whole of his work is "Das Bett" [The Bed] in *Neue Gedichte*.) It is surprising that in the title tale of his third story collection, *Die Letzten* (The Last, 1902), written in 1898–1899 under Lou's aegis, he can be as frank as he is in discussing a taboo theme: mother-son incest. (*Die Letzten* was the first of Rilke's books to be published by the Dane Axel Juncker, who shared, Rilke believed, his own interest in the physical makeup of books: a "quiet" text merited "quiet" and elegant printing and binding.) The first story, "Im Gespräch" (In Conversation), records the talk of a group of artists in the salon of the Princess Helena Pavlovna at Venice.

The speakers each have roles to play: the German painter is clumsy and loud, the gentleman from Vienna (a city Rilke, from provincial Prague, especially disliked) speaks with empty elegance, the Frenchman Count Saint-Quentin is still and polite, and the Pole Kasimir is the mouthpiece for Rilke's theories of artistic creation: "'Kunst ist Kindheit nämlich. Kunst heißt, nicht wissen, daß die Welt schon *ist,* und eine machen. Nicht zerstören, was man vorfindet, sondern einfach nichts Fertiges finden'" ("Art is childhood, you see. Art means not knowing that the world already *is,* and making [one]. Not destroying what one finds but rather simply not finding something finished"). Turning to the princess, Kasimir quotes her: "'Man muß, sagen Sie, dort muß man anfangen, wo Gott abließ, wo er müde wurde'" ("One must, you say, one must begin there where God left off, where He became tired"). At the end, having almost found a kindred soul, the Pole leaves, "wie einer der nicht wiederkommen wird an einen lieben Ort" (like someone who will not return to a beloved place).

A sensitive man is the central figure in the next story, "Der Liebende" (The Lover). the fragile Ernst Bang (his last name may allude to the adjective *bang* [anxious, afraid] or the Danish writer Herman Bang, whose works Rilke deeply admired) talks with his friend, the vigorous Hermann Holzer. Like Král in "Kismet," Holzer shuts out the light with his "schwarzen Rücken" (black silhouette; in Král's case it was "breite schwere Schultern" [broad, heavy shoulders]); Bang is in love with Helene, whom Holzer is going to marry; after many pauses (Rilke was captivated by Maeterlinck's use of silences onstage), Bang summons the courage to tell Holzer that the "latter will destroy Helene with his clumsy affection: "'Nimm mir's nicht übel, Hermann, aber . . . du . . . zerbrichst . . . sie . . . ' Pause" ("Don't take it amiss, Hermann, but . . . you . . . will shatter her . . . " Pause). The difficult conversation drifts along; affable and even respectful, Holzer asks what Bang thinks he should do. "'Sprich, die ganze Kultur steht hinter dir, bedenke'" ("Speak up—remember, the whole culture stands behind you"). The struggle may be not so much between two lovers of the same woman as between the subtle heir to an ancient tradition and the bluff bearer of contemporary strength: Holzer is a peasant's son and has his father's qualities—"Sowas Grades, Eichenes" (something straightforward, oaken). The juxtaposition of the two types is a common one in the fin de siècle, with its sense of the ending of an old Europe and the beginning of a less nuanced world. Helene enters, learns of the conversation, and weeps; taking her on his lap, Holzer tries to console her as she turns pale. The melodrama is obvious: she will stay with Holzer, but both she and Ernst know how sad her fate will be. Rilke's sympathy, however, is not wholly on the side of Bang and Helene; regarding himself as the spokesman of beleaguered refinement, he still looks with some admiration and envy at what is young and fresh and vigorous.

As Rezek turns up both in "König Bohusch" and "Die Geschwister," so an apparent relative of Hermann Holzer appears as the third person in the title story, "Die Letzten." Marie Holzer's grandfather was a peasant; more self-aware than Hermann, she has a sense of being "jünger in der Kultur" (younger in culture) than the members of the impoverished noble family to which she has become attached. She is engaged to Harald Malcorn, whom she met at a gathering of social reformers where he was the impassioned speaker. Now she and Harald's mother await his return from another speaking engagement amid the Malcorns' "Dinge" (things—a word to which Rilke attaches much significance), the great age of which Marie respects and yet cannot quite comprehend. Almost maternally concerned for little Frau Malcorn's well-being, Marie nonetheless senses a rival in the widow, and their competition for Harald comes to the surface in a long stichomythia. Returning home exhausted and ill, Harald decides to abandon his agitator's calling: he breaks with Marie and places himself in his mother's care.

In the story's second part the convalescent Harald and his mother talk of going to an uncle's estate, Skal; but the plan is dropped, in part because of a family curse: the death of a family member has always been presaged by the appearance of a "dame blanche," Frau Walpurga, at the castles the family once owned, and most frequently at Skal. Harald tells his mother about his misty notions of becoming an artist; after recalling circumstances that point to Frau Malcorn's having had a lover long ago and to his own role as a childish and unwitting surrogate for the lover, and after recalling his reaction to his father ("'Er hatte einen dichten weißen Bart. Er war alt'" ["He had a heavy white beard. He was old"]), Harald entices his mother into adorning herself like a bride: together they will celebrate a festival of beauty. Frau Malcorn reappears in a white dress, and Harald collapses; hitherto the room has been illuminated only by moonlight, but now someone lights a light, and the reader sees a terrifying tableau: "Harald sitzt entstellt in den Kissen, den Kopf noch vorgestreckt, mit herabhängenden Händen. Und vor ihm steht Frau Malcorn, welk, in Atlas, mit Handschuhen. Und sie sehen sich mit fremdem Entsetzen in die toten Augen" (Harald sits distorted in his cushions, his head still stretched forward, with his hands hanging down. And Frau Malcorn stands before him, withered, in satin, with her gloves. And they gaze into one another's dead eyes with strange horror).

"Die Letzten" is a grotesque and fascinating melange of themes: the "last of the line," unable to create the art that might have been born of his sensitivity; the mother who is led into a fatal attempt to recover her lost youth; the well-meaning outsider, "healthier" than the inhabitants of the old world to which she is drawn. The literary echoes are many: Ibsen's *Ghosts,* Maeterlinck (the numerous pauses, the subtle anxiety), Jacobsen (Frau Malcorn's *nom d'amour* is Edel, reminiscent of Edele Lyhne, the aunt of whom the adolescent Niels Lyhne becomes enamored in the novel *Niels Lyhne* [1880; translated, 1919]), the Gothic tale. What were Rilke's intentions with the story, which comes dangerously close to unintentional comedy with its "white lady" and its family curse? Did he mean to write a *conte cruel* to vie with the most exaggerated specimens of contemporary decadent literature? The decadent apparatus is plainly on display: the ancient family, incestuous eroticism, a shocking close. Did he intend to plumb the depths of an erotic mother-son relationship of whose existence he was aware in his own case (the psychiatrist Erich Simenauer thinks so) and then mix these personal problems with his theories on the creation of art? Does the story (as Egon Schwarz believes) show the young Rilke's swerve away from the social concerns with which he had flirted to the aesthetic vision of life he subsequently and adamantly maintained? "Die Letzten" is one of Rilke's most tantalizing works, a bizarre conclusion to his early fiction.

In the years between the start of his career in Prague and his removal from Berlin-Schmargendorf and the ambience of Lou in February 1901, Rilke wrote some thirty other tales and sketches: some of these appeared in journals; others were never printed during his lifetime. Exaggerated and often banal effects are common: in a painful specimen of naturalism, "Die Näherin" (The Seamstress, first published in volume 4 of Rilke's *Sämtliche Werke* [Collected Works] in 1961), the narrator is seduced by a lonely and physically unattractive woman; in the lachrymose "Die goldene Kiste" (The Golden Chest, 1895) little Willy admires a golden chest in an undertaker's window, and his dying words express his desire to be laid to rest in it; a beautiful girl is the victim of brain damage in "Eine Tote" (A Dead Girl, 1896); a wife kills herself so that her husband can devote himself fully to his art in "Ihr Opfer" (Her Sacrifice, 1896); a tubercular girl is used and then forgotten, after her death, by a robust male in "Heiliger Frühling" (Holy Spring, 1897); the young bride of a jovial and hearty older man falls in love with her husband's willowy and melancholy son in "Das Lachen des Pán Mráz" (The Laughter of Pán Mráz, 1899); the story of the masked ball at Krummau Castle from "Die Geschwister" is retold in "Masken" (Masks, 1898); a mother loves her son too well in "Leise Begleitung" (Soft Accompaniment, 1898) and vicariously experiences his disappointment in a love affair with a girl of his own age as she sits beside her unfeeling husband. There are stunted figures: the emotionally frigid man searching for an "event" in "Das Ereignis" (The Event, published in *Todtentänze* [Dances of Death, 1896]); the doctrinaire Nietzschean in "Der Apostel" (The Apostle, 1896); the dreamy would-be artist in "Wladimir, der Wolkenmaler" (Wladimir the Cloud-Painter, 1899)—in "Die Letzten," Harald planned to paint clouds, a subject quickly transmuted into his mother, clad in her white dress. Attempts are made at comedy: in "Teufelsspuk" (Devilment, 1899) the new owners of the estate of Gross-Rohozec are terrified by what they think is the castle ghost, but it is merely the former owner, a nobleman, who—slightly intoxicated—has groped his way back to his family's previous possessions. The story might seem to have anti-Semitic overtones, since the buyers of the castle are Jewish and Rilke implies that they are somehow ennobled by their midnight contact with nobility. "Teufelsspuk" was printed in the Munich journal *Simplicissimus* and intended for inclusion in a new volume of novellas Rilke outlined for the publisher Bonz in the summer of 1899; nothing came of the project.

Some of Rilke's best tales are autobiographical. One of the stories unpublished during his lifetime is "Pierre Dumont" (first published in Carl Sieber's biography *René Rilke,* 1932), about a boy parting from his mother at the military school's gate. Another is *Ewald Tragy* (written, 1898; published, 1929; translated, 1958), a long story in two parts about a watershed in the life of a young man. The first half consists of the cruel yet somehow affectionate depiction of his last dinner with the members of his Prague family (made up mainly of desiccated oldsters and eccentrics) and his difficult relation with his father, the bestower of uncomprehending love; in the second, Ewald moves away to the loneliness and freedom of Munich. "Die Turnstunde" (The Exercise Hour), published in *Die Zukunft* in 1902, pays painfully accurate attention to the petty obscenities and large emotional deformations of adolescence. Little Krix tells Jerome, Rilke's alter ego, that he has beheld the body of Gruber, a boy who had died during gymnastics: "'Ich hab ihn gesehen,' flüstert er atemlos und preßt Jeromes Arm und ein Lachen ist innen in ihm und rüttelt ihn hin und her. Er kann kaum weiter: 'Ganz nackt ist er und eingefallen und ganz lang. Und an den Fußsohlen ist er versiegelt. . . .' Und dann kichert er, spitz und kitzlich, kichert und beißt sich in den Ärmel Jeromes hinein" ("I have seen him," he whis-

pers breathlessly and presses Jerome's arm and a laughter is within him and shakes him back and forth. He can scarcely continue: "He's all naked and collapsed and very long. And there are wax seals on the soles of his feet. . . ." And then he giggles, in a sharp, tickling way, giggles and bites into Jerome's sleeve).

"Die Turnstunde" was written only four days before Rilke essayed another descent into physical and psychological horror in "Frau Blahas Magd" (Frau Blaha's Maid); like "Die Turnstunde," it was first set down in Rilke's diary in the autumn of 1899 at Berlin-Schmargendorf, but it remained in manuscript. An early Rilke biographer, Eliza M. Butler, called it a "truly ghastly tale," while a more sympathetic commentator, Wolfgang Leppmann, has characterized it as "one of the most impressive short stories we have from his hand." Annuschka, a simple-minded country girl leading a wretched life as kitchen help in Prague, gives birth to a child, throttles it with her apron, and puts the corpse away at the bottom of her trunk. Then she buys a puppet theater she has seen in a toy-store window: "Jetzt hatte Annuschka etwas für das Alleinsein" (Now Annuschka had something for her loneliness). Neighbor children cluster around the theater; Annuschka tells them she also has a very large doll. They want to see it, but when she comes back "mit dem großen Blauen" (with the large blue thing) they become frightened and run away. Annuschka wrecks her theater, and "als die Küche schon ganz dunkel war, ging sie herum und spaltete allen Puppen die Köpfe, auch der großen blauen" (when the kitchen was quite dark, she went around and split the heads of all the puppets, and of the large blue one too). Annuschka has found refuge in an imaginary world; then, at the intrusion of reality, she destroys it. More successfully than in "King Bohusch," Rilke demonstrates what he imagines goes on in a limited or disturbed mind.

Other stories from the diary seem almost compulsively to seek after gruesome effects: the title character in "Der Grabgärtner" (The Grave-Gardener) transforms a cemetery into a garden in full bloom; he has come from the outside world to take the place of the old gravedigger, who has died. During an outbreak of the plague the townspeople, believing that the stranger has caused the epidemic, try to murder him; they succeed in slaying Gita, the mayor's daughter, whom the gravedigger loves. He kills the leader of the mob and goes off into the night, "Man weiß nicht, wohin" (One knows not whither). The story's emphasis is not on the beauty and order the gravedigger has brought to the realm of death, but on mass hysteria and mass horror; Rilke was probably trying to emulate Jacobsen's story "Pesten i Bergamo" (The Plague in Bergamo, 1881; translated as "Death in Bergamo," 1971). Philippe Jullian has called attention to the popularity in late-nine-teenth-century art of what may be called necrophiliac scenes, with a superabundance of beautiful dead or dying bodies, as in Jean Delville's *Les Trésors de Sathan* (The Treasures of Satan, 1895) and Aristide Sartorio's *Diana d'Efeso e gli schiavi* (Diana of Ephesus and the Slaves, 1899): "eroticism and death have been blended with great skill." In the Rilke story, revised and published as "Der Totengräber" (The Gravedigger) in *Österreichisches Novellenbuch* (1903), the same public taste is fully met: "Der Wagen ist über und über mit Leichen beladen. Und der rote Pippo hat Genossen gefunden, die ihm helfen. Und sie greifen blind und gierig hinein in den Überfluß und zerren einen heraus, der sich zu wehren scheint. . . . Der Fremde schafft ruhig weiter. Bis ihm der Körper eines jungen Mädchens, nackt und blutig, mit mißhandeltem Haar, vor die Füße fällt" (The wagon is laden with corpses, pile upon pile. And the red-haired Pippo has found comrades who help him. And they reach blindly and greedily into this abundance, and pull out someone who seems to fend them off. . . . The stranger keeps calmly at his work. Until the body of a young girl, naked and bloody, with ill-treated hair, falls at his feet).

In the same autumn of 1899–as Rilke claimed, "in einer stürmischen Herbstnacht" (in a stormy autumn night)–he composed the initial version of the work that, in his lifetime, would make his name familiar to a broad public. It was called "Aus einer Chronik–der Cornet (1664)" (From a Chronicle–the Cornet [1664]); a revision made in Sweden in 1904 became "Die Weise von Liebe und Tod des Cornets Otto Rilke" (The Lay of the Love and Death of the Cornet Otto Rilke) and was published the same year in August Sauer's Prague journal *Deutsche Arbeit*. The final version, with the hero's name changed to Christoph, was published by Juncker in 1906; in 1912 it was the introductory number in Anton Kippenberg's series of inexpensive but handsome little books, "Die Inselbücherei," and made its way into thousands of romantically inclined hearts. In twenty-six brief poems in prose (reduced from twenty-nine in the first version and twenty-eight in the second) it gives an account of the last days of a noble officer from Saxony, eighteen years old, during an Austrian campaign against the Turks in western Hungary. Rilke had found a reference to this supposed ancestor in the genealogical materials assembled by his uncle Jaroslav; when he sent the manuscript of "Aus einer Chronik–der Cornet (1664)" to Clara Westhoff, he told her that it was "eine Dichtung . . . die einen Vorfahren mit Glanz umgiebt. Lesen Sie sie an einem Ihrer schönen Abende im weißen Kleid" (a poetic work that surrounds a forebear with splendor. Read it, on one of your beautiful evenings, in your white dress). The boy rides over the dusty plain; makes friends with a French marquis; sits by the campfire; observes the rough life of the bivouac; is presented to the commander, Johann von Sporck (of whom a portrait had hung in the military school at Sankt Pölten); and frees a girl tied nude to a tree–she seems to laugh when her bonds are cut, and the boy is horrified: "Und er sitzt schon zu Ross / und jagt in die Nacht. Blutige Schnüre fest in der Faust" (And he is already mounted on his steed / and gallops into the night. Bloody cords held tight in his grip). The cornet writes to his mother; sees his first dead man, a peasant; and senses that the enemy is near. The company comes to a castle, and the officers are feted– another of Rilke's festivals of beauty. Dressed in white silk (reminiscent of the dress uniform worn by Austrian officers in Viennese operettas), the virgin youth meets the lady of the castle, and shortly, "nackt wie ein Heiliger. Hell und schlank" (naked as a saint. Bright and slim), he spends a night of love with her. "Er fragt nicht: 'Dein Gemahl?' Sie fragt nicht: 'Dein Namen?'. . . Sie werden sich hundert neue Namen geben . . . " (He does not ask: "Your husband?" She does not ask: "Your name?" . . . They will give one another a hundred new names . . .). The Turks attack, and the troop rides out to meet them; the cornet, whose task is to bear the flag, is not present. But he appears in the nick of time, finds the banner–"auf seinen Armen trägt er die Fahne wie eine weiße, bewußtlose Frau" (he carries the flag in his arms, like a woman, white and unconscious)–and gallops into the midst of the foes; "die sechzehn runden Säbel, die auf ihn zuspringen, Strahl um Strahl, sind ein Fest. / Eine lachende Wasserkunst" (the sixteen curved sabers that leap at him, beam upon beam, are a festival. / A laughing fountain). The next spring, a courier brings the news of his death to his mother. That the tiny book captured a large readership is quite understandable: the impelling rhythms of its prose, the colorful settings, the theatrically simple situations, the amalgamation of eroticism and early heroic death were irresistible. That Rilke's view of war was hopelessly false, and a throwback to the worst extravagances of romanticism, is another matter.

A second book that also found a devoted audience, *Vom lieben Gott und Anderes* (Concerning Dear God and Other Matters), had also gotten under way in the busy autumn of 1899. These playfully "pious" tales were quickly delivered to the Insel publishing house, administered by Schuster and Loeffler in Berlin, and appeared just in time for the Christmas trade of 1900; a new edition, *Geschichten vom lieben Gott* (translated as *Stories of God*, 1932), came out in 1904, with a dedication to the Swedish feminist and pedagogical writer Ellen Key. The stories have held a prominent place among the "standard" items by the young Rilke, but the Rilke scholar Eudo C. Mason dismissed them as a reproduction of "much of the religious doctrine of *Das Stunden-Buch* in prose, in the form of whimsical little tales told to children by a lame cobbler." Professor Mason's statement might be refined to say that the stories reproduce in particular the message of the first part of *Das Stunden-Buch,* "Das Buch von mönchischen Leben" (The Book of Monkish Life), which Rilke also wrote in the early autumn of 1899. God is in a state of becoming, perceived by artists and repeatedly created in their works, or God is the mystery from which art emanates: "Du Dunkelheit, aus der ich stamme" (You darkness, out of which I come), as *Das Stunden-Buch* proclaims. Mason's indifference toward *Geschichten vom lieben Gott* is evidenced by his unwonted inaccuracy; the tales are told to several listeners—a neighbor lady, a visiting stranger, a priggish male schoolteacher, District Commissioner Baum, and an artistically inclined young man, as well as the lame cobbler Ewald.

Oddly, the gentle book delights in making fun of the establishment; amid the often sugary trappings and language a sense of rebellion can be detected. In the first tale, "Das Märchen von den Händen Gottes" (The Tale of the Hands of God), the Lord's hands let humankind loose from heaven before the Maker has had a chance to inspect His work; in "Der fremde Mann" (The Strange Man) God's right hand, long since out of favor with God, is cut off by Saint Paul and sent to earth in human form; in "Warum der liebe Gott will, daß es arme Leute gibt" (Why Dear God Wants There To Be Poor People) the shocked schoolteacher is informed that the poor are closest to the truth and so are like artists. (In *Das Stunden-Buch* Rilke coined the phrase that has garnered him some scorn from socially aware readers: "Denn Armuth ist ein großer Glanz aus Innen" [For poverty is a great shining from within].) The pompous Baum, with his bourgeois view of a "romantic" Venice, is told in "Eine Szene aus dem Ghetto von Venedig" (A Scene from the Venetian Ghetto) about the precarious lot of the Jews in that splendid city, and about the vision of one of them, old Melchisedech, whose daughter has just had a child by a Christian. The narrator wonders what Melchisedech has seen: "'Hat er das Meer gesehen oder Gott, den Ewigen, in seiner Glorie?'" ("Has he beheld the sea or God, the Eternal Being, in His glory?"), to which Baum confidently replies: "'Das Meer wahrscheinlich . . . es *ist* ja auch ein Eindruck'" ("The sea, probably . . . after all, *that's* an impression too"). As these examples show, the tales suffer from excessive archness; in "Wie der Fingerhut dazu kam, der liebe Gott zu sein" (How the Thimble Came To Be Dear God), the all too clear message is that God is to be found in the least significant of objects—as obvious a point as that made in "Ein Verein

aus einem dringenden Bedürfnis heraus" (A Club Created To Meet a Pressing Need), a long-winded formulaic narrative directed against artistic organizations.

The best of the stories are the three devoted to Russian themes, "Wie der Verrat nach Russland kam" (How Treachery Came to Russia), "Wie der alte Timofei singend starb" (How Old Timofei Died Singing), and "Das Lied von der Gerechtigkeit" (The Song of Justice). They are all told to the receptive Ewald and illustrate that Russia is a land that borders on God, a land of true reverence. The opportunity of making a thrust at dry scholarly authority is not allowed to slip by: the tales are based on *byliny* and *skazki,* epic folk songs and folktales long hidden away by learned men. According to the narrator, the tales have died out among the Russian people, and it seems to be his intention to bring them to life again. The first of the trio tells how a simple peasant demands from the czar not gold but truth and integrity (one more example of the poverty—and poverty of spirit in the biblical sense—that Rilke so admired); the second hopes for a continuation of the ancient line of folksingers and their songs, "darin die Worte wie Ikone sind und gar nicht zu vergleichen mit den gewöhnlichen Worten" (in which the words are like icons and not at all to be compared with ordinary words), even though such a continuation requires the singer to abandon his wife and child; the third is an historical tale from western Russia, in which a blind singer inspires his listeners to throw off the yoke of the Polish lords and the greed of the Jews.

There are also three tales from Italy: the Venetian ghetto story; a tribute to Michelangelo, "Von Einem, der die Steine belauscht" (Concerning Someone Who Eavesdropped on Stones); and another legend on the nature of true poverty, "Der Bettler und das stolze Fräulein" (The Beggar and the Proud Maiden), in which a Florentine noble disguises himself as a beggar and asks the prideful Beatrice to let him kiss the dusty hem of her garment. She is afraid of the strange beggar, but gives him a sack of gold. The experience transforms him: he remains in his beggar's rags, gives away all his possessions, and goes off barefoot into the countryside. Hearing the story, the teacher concludes that it is a tale of how a profligate becomes an eccentric tramp; the narrator rejoins that he has become a saint; and when the children hear the tale, they assert, "zum Ärger des Herrn Lehrer, auch in *ihr* käme der liebe Gott vor" (to the annoyance of the teacher, that dear God appeared in *this* story too). Like "Der Bettler und das stolze Fräulein," "Ein Märchen vom Tode" (A Tale about Death), with its glorification of "der alten schönen Gebärde des breiten Gebetes" (the beautiful old gesture of broad prayer), offers an example of the author's belief in the efficacy of a great or brave gesture that transforms its maker. Having begun with a double prologue set in heaven—the two tales about the hands of God—the collection harks back at its end to Rilke's more realistic stories with "Eine Geschichte, dem Dunkel erzählt" (A Story Told to the Darkness). Klara Söllner defies society's norms by divorcing her husband, a state official, and embarking on an affair with an artist; she rears their love child by herself. The narrator, twitting a narrow-minded public one last time, claims that nothing in the tale is unfit for children's ears; in fact, it reflects the scandalous independence of Rilke's friend, Franziska zu Reventlow.

Klara generously encourages her lover to leave her in pursuit of his art; Rilke himself was settling down to a life of considerably less freedom than he had known before. The young couple took up residence in Westerwede, near Worpswede; Rilke did reviews for a Bremen newspaper and larger periodicals and prepared *Die Letzten* and *Das Buch der Bilder* for publication. On 12 December 1901, their only child, Ruth (named after the heroine of a novel by Lou), was born. Home life could not long appeal to Rilke, and he began to conceive new plans. As a result of his Jacobsen enthusiasm, further readings of the Nordic works that were phenomenally popular in Germany at the time, and his association with Juncker, his interest in the north grew. Spending a month in the early summer of 1902 at Castle Haseldorf in Holstein as a guest of the poetaster Prince Emil von Schönaich-Carolath, he found in the archives sources that had to do with the great Danish-German Reventlow family: "Diese Wochen hier haben doch ihren Sinn, auch wenn sie nur im Lesen einiger Bücher bestehen" (These weeks here have their meaning after all, even though they consist only of the reading of some books). Simultaneously, he wrote a review of the Swedish reformer Ellen Key's *Barnets arhundrade* (1900; translated into German as *Das Jahrhundert des Kindes,* 1902; translated into English as *The Century of the Child,* 1909), with its recommendation for greater openness in the education of children; the review led to a correspondence with Key and, in time, to an invitation to the north.

But Rilke's immediate plan, the composition of a book about Auguste Rodin, led him to Paris in August 1902. The autumn weeks in the metropolis were difficult for him and formed the basis for several episodes in *Die Aufzeichnungen des Malte Laurids Brigge;* leaving Ruth in her parents' care, Clara also traveled to Paris to study with Rodin, but maintained a residence separate from her husband's so that each would have greater freedom. Rilke's production at the time was varied: he had completed his book on the Worpswede painters and the north German landscape in which they worked before he set out for Haseldorf; the Rodin book was written in Paris during November and December 1902 and was published in 1903; the second part of *Das Stunden-Buch,* "Das Buch von der Pilgerschaft" (The Book of Pilgrimage), had been completed at Westerwede in 1901; and in Paris he wrote verses that would be included in the augmented edition of *Das Buch der Bilder,* as well as "Der Panther" (The Panther), destined to become one of his best-known poems and the earliest of the items included in *Neue Gedichte.* A springtime trip to Viareggio in 1903 gave him the third part of *Das Stunden-Buch,* the upsetting mixture of eroticism and thoughts about death called "Das Buch von der Armuth und vom Tode" (The Book of Poverty and Death).

After a summer in Germany, the Rilkes set out in September 1903 for Rome; the poet's reaction to the city was one of discomfort. He found himself yearning for the north, and he sent pathetic letters to Key about the failure of the Roman winter and spring to be "real." In February 1904 Rilke made the first sketches for a novel about a young Dane in Paris: "An einem Herbstabende eines dieser letzten Jahre besuchte Malte Laurids Brigge, ziemlich unerwartet, einen von den wenigen Bekannten, die er in Paris besaß" (On an autumn evening of one of these last years Malte Laurids Brigge, rather unexpectedly, visited one of the few acquaintances he had in Paris). Malte tells his listener of a dinner interrupted by a ghostly apparition, an experience he had had when he was twelve or thirteen during a visit to his maternal grandfather's estate, Urnekloster, in the company of his father. The story would become one of the Danish episodes in the novel.

By the most skillful sort of hinting, Rilke arranged a Scandinavian stay from June to December 1904 to collect material for the book. The trip was spent largely with the artist and writer Ernst Norlind and Norlind's fiancée at a chateau, Borgeby, in south Sweden, and then at the home of an industrialist, James Gibson, at Jonsered near Gothenburg. The Gibsons were friends of Key, and a Sunday at the farmhouse of Key's brother, Mac Key (like the Gibsons, the family was of Scottish origin), in late November 1904 inspired another episode in *Die Aufzeichnungen des Malte Laurids Brigge,* the visit to the manor house of the Schulins, the center of which has been burned out. There, young Malte learns about fear. For a while Rilke toyed with the idea of preparing monographs on Jacobsen and on the Danish painter Vilhelm Hammershøj, but dropped both projects. He had learned to read Danish but could not speak it, and Copenhagen, which had initially charmed him as he passed through it, had come to seem ominous to him. He left Denmark on 8 December 1904 and never returned to the north; meeting a young Danish woman, Inga Junghanns, in Munich during the war, he rejoiced to think that the book about Malte would be returned to its "original language" in her translation. But Paris remained his true home, if so peripatetic a soul as Rilke may be said to have had a home.

In many ways 1905 marked a turning point in Rilke's career, just as the liaison with Lou had been the turning point in his personal development. Anton Kippenberg took over the Insel firm; in Kippenberg, Rilke discovered a skillful and usually generous manager of his literary fortunes and personal finances. His employment as Rodin's secretary began in September; it would end abruptly, in a dreadful scene, in May 1906. He made his first public appearances in Germany, reading from his works with a fire that was in contrast to his frail figure and exquisitely gloved hands. And, in part through the agency of the Rhenish banker Karl von der Heydt, he began to make the acquaintance of the noble ladies who would offer him so much solace and so many refuges. The relationship with Clara, whom he had to "keep at bay," in Miss Butler's malicious phrase, grew ever more tenuous, and Rilke developed the talent for swift wooing that would make the Princess Marie von Thurn und Taxis (happily married and, save intellectually, not one of his conquests) tell him that Don Juan was an innocent babe in comparison to him. Clara and Ruth briefly joined him on a trip to Belgium, sponsored by von der Heydt, late in the summer of 1906, but he much preferred to travel alone. Perhaps the first of his extramarital romances was with the Venetian Mimi Romanelli, whom he met at the pension of her brother in the autumn of 1907. He was the guest of Frau Alice Faehndrich at the Villa Discopoli on Capri in the winter and spring of 1906–1907 and again in the winter and spring of 1908; there he was surrounded by admiring ladies, among them the young and beautiful Countess Manon zu Solms-Laubach, for whom he wrote the poem "Migliera" (published in volume 2 of his *Sämtliche Werke,* 1956). With Frau Faehndrich, before her death in 1908, he translated Elizabeth Barrett Browning's *Sonnets from the Portuguese.* Some of the poems from the Capri days found their way into *Neue Gedichte;* the first part, dedicated to the von der Heydts, appeared in 1907, the second, dedicated "À mon grand ami Auguste Rodin," in 1908. The quarrel with the master had been patched up; Rilke remained grateful to Rodin for having taught him the doctrine of work: "Il faut travailler toujours, rien que travailler" (One must work always, nothing but work).

Capri was not the main growing ground for the *Neue Gedichte;* that was Paris, to which Rilke became more attached the more he was able to transform its beauties and horrors into literature. An apartment at the Hôtel Biron in the Rue de Varenne became Rilke's pied-à-terre in August 1908; Rodin liked the Louis-Qua-

torze mansion so much that he immediately moved his own Parisian studio there. In 1910, on a trip to Leipzig during which he stayed in the tower room of the Kippenbergs' home, Rilke looked after the final stages of *Die Aufzeichnungen des Malte Laurids Brigge.* The production of the slender book emptied him, he liked to declare, and no other major work came from his hand during the next twelve years, although the production of this so-called barren period includes some of his best verse.

Die Aufzeichnungen des Malte Laurids Brigge consists of seventy-one entries divided into two parts, with a break after entry thirty-nine. It has often been conjectured that the model for Malte was the Norwegian poet Sigbjørn Obstfelder (1866–1900), a devotee of Jacobsen who had lived for some time in Paris; his fragmentary novel *En prests dagbok* (1900; translated into German as *Tagebuch eines Priesters,* 1901; translated into English as *A Priest's Diary,* 1987), and a collection of his other prose, which Rilke reviewed in 1904, had come out in German translation. Much about Obstfelder does not fit, however, the picture of Malte in Rilke's novel: Obstfelder was of modest parentage, an engineer by calling, and had lived and had a nervous breakdown in the American Middle West; the aristocratic Malte–the last of his line–is fetched rather from Rilke's reading of Bang and his own musings about himself and his fancied background. The age of Rilke in February 1904, when the first sketches were made, is that of Malte as he looks back on his life as a man of letters: "Ich bin achtundzwanzig, und es ist so gut wie nichts geschehen. Wiederholen wir: ich habe eine Studie über Carpaccio geschrieben, die schlecht ist, ein Drama, das 'Ehe' heißt und etwas Falsches mit zweideutigen Mitteln beweisen will, und Verse. Ach, aber mit Versen ist so wenig getan, wenn man sie früh schreibt" (I am twenty-eight, and as good as nothing has happened. Let's repeat: I have written a study about Carpaccio, which is poor, a drama, called "Marriage," that tries to prove something false with ambiguous means, and verses. Oh, but how little is accomplished with verses when one writes them early in life). Rilke appears to have imagined that Malte was emotionally destroyed by the Parisian experience; he says in a letter of May 1906, after having heard the "inappropriate" laughter of a French audience at a performance of Ibsen's *Wild Duck:* "Und wieder begriff ich Malte Laurids Brigge und sein Nordischsein und sein Zugrundegehen an Paris. Wie sah und empfand und erlitt er es" (And once more I understood Malte Laurids Brigge and his Nordicness and his destruction by Paris. How he saw and felt and suffered it). Malte is undergoing a severe crisis: entry number twenty describes his visit to the Salpetrière Hospital, apparently for electrotherapy. (That Rilke sometimes feared that he would go insane is indicated by the "last will and testament" he sent to Nanny Wunderly-Volkart on 27 October 1925.)

The substance of the first part of *Die Aufzeichnungen des Malte Laurids Brigge,* on the one hand, is Malte's awareness of Paris: of "die Existenz des Entsetzlichen in jedem Bestandteil der Luft" (the existence of the horrible in every particle of the air)—the factory-like dying in the city's hospitals, the terrible street noises, the sordidness exposed on every side, coupled with the joy he feels while visiting an antiquarian bookseller's booth by the Seine, reading the poetry of Francis Jammes in the Bibliothéque Nationale, or viewing the tapestry "La dame à la licorne" in the Musée de Cluny. But intermingled with Parisian episodes are memories of his childhood in Denmark—a childhood of dramatic and terrifying scenes: the death of his paternal grandfather at Ulsgaard; ghost stories connected with Urnekloster, the maternal seat; hallucinations, such as a hand emerging from the wall, that he had while recovering from fever; his tender "Maman," his reserved father, and his maternal aunt Abelone, whom he loves in some never clearly defined way. He wishes he could show her the tapestries in the Parisian museum: "Ich bilde mir ein, du bist da" (I imagine that you are here). The kernel of the Parisian sections is Rilke's own observations, which he often put down in letters; save for quotations from Baudelaire's *Spleen de Paris* and the Book of Job, the Parisian material draws little on literary sources. The Danish components are more mixed, with strong echoes of the description of Danish estate life in the novels of Bang and Jacobsen and of Rilke's own childhood. Upon its appearance *Die Aufzeichnungen des Malte Laurids Brigge* was often treated by critics as another novel about the "decadent hero": the scion of the old family, disheartened, quiveringly sensitive, and suffering from an inability to act, yet admiring those beings—such as a man with Saint Vitus' dance trying to sustain his dignity by a tremendous act of will—who are undefeated. The book is also one of the several works of German fiction from the time that display a strong "Nordic" side.

The second and more difficult part of the novel again employs the main figures from the Danish past: Maman reappears, appreciating the careful work of anonymous lace-makers; young Malte visits the neighboring estate of the Schulins (based on the Key farm); birthdays are celebrated. A mature Malte returns to Copenhagen ("Ulsgaard war nicht mehr in unserm Besitz" [Ulsgaard was no longer in our possession]); witnesses the perforation of his dead father's heart lest he be buried alive; and ponders the death of Denmark's great baroque king, Christian IV, an account of which his father kept in his wallet. Among the Scandinavian figures, Abelone is the most important: taking dictation from her aged father, Count Brahe, for whom the past is part of the present, and introducing young Malte to one of the great "loving women," Bettina Brentano, who outdid Goethe, Malte claims, in the sheer strength of her emotion. Memories of Abelone come to Malte when he hears a Danish woman sing about "besitzlose Liebe" (possessionless love) and its splendors in a Venetian salon: "'weil ich dich niemals anhielt, halt ich dich fest'" ("since I never detained you, I hold you fast"); other salutes to splendid women—the Portuguese nun Heloise, Louise Labé, Sappho, and others—who know that "mit der Vereinigung nichts gemeint sein kann als ein Zuwachs an Einsamkeit" (with union nothing can be meant save an increase in loneliness) prepare for this last quasi-appearance by Abelone. Thus far it is relatively easy to follow Rilke's arguments on love; save in the artistry of the presentation, not much difference exists between the selfless Klara Söllner of the last story of *Geschichten vom lieben Gott* and the singer of the song in Venice. It is harder to grasp, however, what Rilke means when he speaks of Abelone's yearning to take everything that was transitive out of her love, to make it objectless loving, "absolutely, in complete loneliness," in Eudo C. Mason's words.

The horrors of Paris are still with the diarist: Malte—"Ich lerne sehen" (I am learning to see) is the way he describes his most imperative task—cannot shut his eyes to a girl who stands "mit ihrem dürren, verkümmerten Stück" (with her stunted, withered stump) of an arm or to a blind newspaper vendor. The fear of death is still overriding, not only in the story of the postmortem operation on Malte's father but even in the comical tale of Nikolaj Kusmitsch, Malte's neighbor in Petersburg, who, realizing how much time he had in his account (he assumed he would live another fifty years or so), resolved to use it sparingly. The Kusmitsch tale leads into stories about a mother who comes to console her disturbed son and about the rebelliousness of objects, followed by glosses on the dangers of loneliness and an intense and horrifying rehearsal of the temptations of Saint Anthony.

Other narratives are baffling, especially the stories recalled from the little green book Malte owned as a boy about the end of the false Dmitri, Grischa Otrepjow; the death of Charles the Bold of Burgundy; the mad Charles VI of France; John XXII, the Avignon pope; and the terrible fourteenth century, "Die Zeit, in der der Kuss zweier, die sich versöhnten, nur das Zeichen für die Mörder war, die herumstanden" (The time in which the kiss of reconciliation between two men was merely the signal for the murderers standing nearby). This awful reflection comes to Malte after he has remembered a trauma of his childhood, a time of similar insecurity, in which he thought himself pursued by another of those large and threatening male figures, like Král and Holzer of the early stories. Perhaps the historical exempla are meant to illustrate Rilke's thoughts on the human will, a will that is variously jeopardized or fails: just before the pistol shot that ends Grischa Otrepjow's life, the pretender experiences "noch einmal Wille und Macht . . . alles zu sein" (once more the will and power . . . to be everything). The will also sustains Eleonora Duse, to whom tribute is paid after a sideswipe at contemporary theater, but here the artist's will has made her overrun—magnificently and frighteningly—the limits of the art in which she must perform. Much of the second part of *Die Aufzeichnungen des Malte Laurids Brigge* could be presented as a statement, as oblique as the first part's is direct, on the strange heroism of the exceptional human who exceeds, or attempts to exceed, his own limitations, forever standing alone. The original ending of the novel, criticizing Tolstoy, who had abandoned his art and was beset by fears of death ("Es war kein Zimmer in diesem Haus, in dem er sich nicht gefürchtet hatte, zu sterben" [There was no room in this house in which he had not feared he would die]), was supplanted by the story of the Prodigal Son, retold as "die Legende dessen . . . der nicht geliebt werden wollte" (the legend of him . . . who did not wish to be loved)—a representation, as Joseph-François Angelloz thought, of Rilke's long search for the freedom that would enable him to apply his artistic will to the fullest. The final lines are cryptic: "Er war jetzt furchtbar schwer zu lieben, und er fühlte, daß nur Einer dazu imstande sei. Der aber wollte noch nicht" (He was now terribly difficult to love, and he felt that there was only One who was capable of it. He, however, did not yet want to). Mason suggests that this is a "hyperbolic way" of implying that there is no plane, "human or superhuman," on which the problem of love can be solved for one who, like the Prodigal Son, is "governed by a daemonic dread of his sacrosanct, isolated selfhood being encroached upon through the love of any other human being."

Die Aufzeichnungen des Malte Laurids Brigge is at once a profoundly satisfying and unsatisfying book. It presents in unforgettable language the tribulations of a sensitive being in an overwhelmingly beautiful and ugly world—the omnipresence of fear; the search for small joys ("Was so ein kleiner Mond alles vermag" [How much such a little moon can do]); the residual terrors of childhood, never to be overcome; the problems of loving; the profits and torments of being alone. Formally, the novel seems less daunting than it did to readers of the past; Rilke advertises his intention of writing a nonlinear novel: "Da man erzählte, wirklich erzählte, das muß vor meiner Zeit gewesen sein" (That people told

stories, really told stories, that must have been before my time). Just the same, in many episodes—the banquet at Urnekloster, the death of the chamberlain Brigge, the visit to the Schulins, the death of Charles of Burgundy—Rilke proved himself a master of the short story, in which he had served such a long apprenticeship. As Wolfgang Leppmann points out, the reader can become "frustrated": he is asked to know the obscure historical facts Rilke had stored away in the corners of his mind or culled directly from other texts; he may find some of the doctrines advanced (for example, intransitive love) hard to grasp, let alone embrace. What may be overlooked, in grappling with *Die Aufzeichnungen des Malte Laurids Brigge,* is that it is, after all, a feigned diary and also incomplete: Rilke told Lou Andreas-Salomé that he had ended it out of exhaustion. Furthermore, it is a personal document: Rilke made fun of Ellen Key for having identified Malte with him, yet she was by no means inaccurate in her naiveté. In Paris for his last visit, he would write to Nanny Wunderly-Volkart: "Je m'effraie comme, autrefois, Malte s'est effrayé . . . " (I am terrified, as, formerly, Malte was terrified . . .). In his letters, he could never let Malte go.

The post-*Malte* time was marked by flurries of frantic travel: to North Africa in the autumn of 1910; to Egypt in the spring of the next year with the mysterious Jenny Oltersdorf, about whom Rilke remained forever close-mouthed; to Castle Duino, near Trieste, a holding of the Thurn und Taxis clan, in 1911–1912 (here the "angel" of the Duineser Elegien is supposed to have spoken to him, inspiring the work that would not be complete until 1922); to Venice again, to spend much of the remainder of 1912–1913; to Spain in the winter of 1912–1913; and, in the summer of 1913, to Göttingen for a visit with Lou Andreas-Salomé. He spent October 1913 to late February 1914 in Paris and was in Munich when World War I broke out in August 1914. (The singer of the deeds of the cornet greeted the conflict with enthusiastic verse he soon regretted.) If the itinerary of these years is long, so is the list of feminine friends: the motherly and excitable Marie von Thurn und Taxis; the haughty Helene von Nostitz; the vivacious Sidonie Nádherný von Borutin, whom Rilke dissuaded from marrying the satirist Karl Kraus. On the passionate side, there was the simple Parisienne Marthe Hennebert, for a time Rilke's "ward"; and the pianist Magda von Hattingberg, or "Benvenuta," for both of whom he pondered a divorce from Clara. He could not do without the blue-blooded friends or the ones who became objects of his desire—such as the "douce perturbatrice," the phrase he bestowed on Marthe in one of the French poems he wrote more and more frequently.

The war years kept him far away from his Parisian books and papers, some of which were irretrievably lost, others saved through the good offices of his friend André Gide, whose *Le Retour de l'enfant prodigue* he had translated into German in 1913–1914. His principal residence was Munich, and his principal companion for a while was the painter Lulu Albert-Lasard. A rising tide of mainly erotic poetry in 1915 was interrupted by a draft call to the Austrian army at Christmas. He spent a wretched few weeks in basic training and was saved by powerful friends, including Princess Marie, who effected his transfer to the dull safety of the War Archive and comfortable quarters in Hietzing's Park-Hotel. Rilke continued to complain about his enforced residence in detestable Vienna and was released from service in June. The rest of the war went by in a kind of convalescence—mostly in Munich, but the summer of 1917 included a stay on an estate in Westphalia, and the autumn of the same year a stay in Berlin. There he saw both Walther Rathenau and Marianne Mitford (née Friedländer-Fuld), whose exceptionally wealthy family owned an estate in the vicinity of the capital: she received one of the first copies of his 1918 translation of the sonnets of the Lyonnaise poetess of the Renaissance, Louise Labé, whom he had ranked among the great lovers in *Die Aufzeichnungen des Malte Laurids Brigge*. Back in Munich, he lived first at the Hotel Continental and then in an apartment in the artists' quarter of Schwabing; observing the "Munich revolution," vaguely sympathizing with Kurt Eisner's idealistic socialism, and giving shelter for a night to the fugitive author Ernst Toller, Rilke was briefly suspected of leftist sympathies by the victorious "White" forces that took over the city on 1 May 1919. At the same time, he enjoyed the innocent attentions of Elya Maria Nevar, a young actress, and the less innocent ones of the would-be femme fatale Claire Studer ("Liliane"), shortly to become the mistress and then the wife of the expressionist poet and editor Iwan Goll.

Casting about for a refuge from postwar Germany's turbulence, Rilke was invited to undertake a reading tour in Switzerland. Once he had made fun of Switzerland and its scenic "Übertreibungen" (exaggerations), its "anspruchsvolle" (pretentious) lakes and mountains; now he was glad to cross the border. Some of his Swiss sanctuaries were much less satisfactory than he had hoped: at Schönenberg, near Basel, a summer home of the Burckhardt family, where he lived from March until May 1920, he liked neither the house's grounds nor its feeble stoves; at Castle Berg am Irchel, near Zurich, placed at his disposal by a Colonel Ziegler for the winter of 1920–1921, he was bothered by children at play and the noise of a sawmill—but at Berg there also appeared to him, he said, the phantom who dictated the double cycle of poems *Aus dem Nachlaß des Grafen C. W.* (1950; translated as *From the Remains of Count C. W.*, 1952). He quickly found new friends; the most important was "Nike," Nanny Wunderly-Volkart, the witty and self-controlled wife of the industrialist Hans Wunderly. Through her Rilke discovered and had rented for him a little tower at Muzot, near Sierre, in the canton of Valais; there—as literary histories never tire of repeating—he finished the *Duineser Elegien* and received the "additional gift" of *Die Sonette an Orpheus* in February 1922. (It is plain, though, that he knew the storm of inspiration was coming: he had some difficulty in persuading the great love of the first Swiss years, "Merline," or Baladine Klossowska, that he needed to be alone, cared for only by his competent housekeeper, Frida Baumgartner.)

Rilke announced the completion of his task with justifiable pride; the afterglow of accomplishment permeates his letters during the remainder of 1922. A sense of aging also came over him, however: his daughter married, and in 1923 he became a grandfather. (The birth of Ruth herself, he had told a friend years before, had given him a similar sense of "l'immense tristesse de ma propre futilité" [the immense sadness of my own futility].) His health declined: he spent time at a half-resort, half-hospital at Schöneck on the Lake of Lucerne, and then repeatedly at the sanatorium of Valmont above the Lake of Geneva. Rilke had always had a weakness for the restful weeks at a sanatorium or spa—for the sake of his nerves, he liked to say—and they brought useful and interesting contacts: in 1905 at the sanatorium "Weisser Hirsch" near Dresden he had met Countess Luise Schwerin, who had put him in touch with the von der Heydt and Faehndrich circles. Nevertheless, he had become hesitant about the efficacy of physicians in dealing with his ills, real or fancied, and regarded sleep as the great cure-all. The year 1924 opened and closed with stays at Valmont. From January to August 1925 he had his final sojourn in Paris—he was lionized during his stay there, but perhaps the most sincere of his many admirers was the Alsatian Maurice Betz, who was at work on a translation of *Die Aufzeichnungen des Malte Laurids Brigge*. By December he was back at Valmont, staying until May 1926. His last works were his translations of Paul Valéry's poetry and prose and three small volumes of his own French verse. Carl J. Burckhardt, a Swiss diplomat who possessed a keen eye for Rilke's weaknesses, recalled that Rilke did not understand how reserved and even condescending Valéry was toward the "German" poet who late in his career tried his hand at French. Rilke appears to have sought Valéry's company, chatting with him a last time in September 1926 at Anthy on the French side of Lake Geneva. A special issue of *Les Cahiers du Mois,* "Reconnaissance à Rilke," edited by the faithful Betz, had appeared at Paris in the summer of 1926–its opening a restrained salute from Valéry's own hand.

Also in September 1926 the critic Edmond Jaloux introduced Rilke to Nimet Eloui Bey, an Egyptian beauty of Circassian background. When Rilke was still viewed as the devoted and sensitive admirer of women but not an erotic adventurer, Jaloux's account of this "last friendship" seemed the perfect finale for the poet's romantic life; gathering white roses for her, Rilke pricked his hand, and the injury became infected, a harbinger of the final onslaught of his illness. It is now known that the Egyptian was but one of the women and girls who surrounded and attracted him almost to the end: the eighteen-year-old Austrian Erika Mitterer, who carried on a correspondence in poems with him from 1924 to 1926; the Russian poetess Marina Tsvetayeva, who wanted to visit and consume him; the pretty Lalli Horstmann, a friend of Marianne Mitford; the Dutch singer Beppy Veder; and the actress Elisabeth Bergner were among the many. What may be more significant about the "last friendship" with Nimet Eloui Bey, though, is that she wanted to meet the author of *Die Aufzeichnungen des Malte Laurids Brigge,* which she had just read in Betz's translation–the book of his that lay closest to his own heart.

Rilke returned to Valmont in November 1926. On 29 December he died of leukemia.

Letters:

Briefe an Auguste Rodin (Leipzig: Insel, 1928);

Briefe aus den Jahren 1902 bis 1906, edited by Ruth Sieber-Rilke and Carl Sieber (Leipzig: Insel, 1929);

Briefe an einen jungen Dichter (Leipzig: Insel, 1929); translated by M. D. Herter Norton as *Letters to a Young Poet* (New York: Norton, 1934); translated by K. W. Maurer as *Letters to a Young Poet* (London: Langley, 1943);

Briefe an eine junge Frau (Leipzig: Insel, 1930); translated by Maurer as *Letters to a Young Woman* (London: Langley, 1945);

Briefe aus den Jahren 1906 bis 1907, edited by Sieber-Rilke and Sieber (Leipzig: Insel, 1930);

Briefe und Tagebücher aus der Frühzeit, edited by Sieber-Rilke and Sieber (Leipzig: Insel, 1931);

Briefe aus den Jahren 1907 bis 1914, edited by Sieber-Rilke and Sieber (Leipzig: Insel, 1933);

Über Gott: Zwei Briefe (Leipzig: Insel, 1933);

Briefe an seinen Verleger 1906 bis 1926, edited by Sieber-Rilke and Sieber (Leipzig: Insel, 1934);

Briefe aus Muzot 1921 bis 1926, edited by Sieber-Rilke and Sieber (Leipzig: Insel, 1935);

Gesammelte Briefe, edited by Sieber-Rilke and Sieber, 6 volumes (Leipzig: Insel, 1936–1939);

Lettres a une Amie Vénitienne (Milan: Hoepli / Leipzig: Asmus, 1941);

Briefe an eine Freundin, edited by Herbert Steiner (Aurora, N.Y.: Wells College Press, 1944);

Briefe (Olten: Oltener Bücherfreunde, 1945);

Briefe an Baronesse von Oe, edited by Richard von Mises (New York: Johannespresse, 1945);

Letters of Rainer Maria Rilke, translated by Jane Bannard Greene and Herter Norton, 2 volumes (New York: Norton, 1945–1948);

Briefe an eine Reisegefährtin: Eine Begegnung mit Rainer Maria Rilke (Vienna: Ibach, 1947);

Briefe an das Ehepaar S. Fischer, edited by Hedwig Fischer (Zurich: Classen, 1947);

La dernière amitié de Rainer Maria Rilke: Lettres inédites de Rilke à Madame Eloui Bey, edited by Edmond Jaloux (Paris: Laffont, 1949); translated by William H. Kennedy as *Rainer Maria Rilke: His Last Friendship. Unpublished Letters to Mrs. Eloui Bey* (New York: Philosophical Library, 1952);

"So laß ich mich zu träumen gehen" (Gmunden & Bad Ischl: Mader, 1949); translated by Heinz Norden as *Letters to Benvenuta* (New York: Philosophical Library, 1951; London: Hogarth Press, 1953);

Briefe an seinen Verleger, edited by Sieber-Rilke and Sieber, 2 volumes (Wiesbaden: Insel, 1949);

Briefe, edited by Sieber-Rilke and Karl Altheim, 2 volumes (Wiesbaden: Insel, 1950);

Die Briefe an Gräfin Sizzo, 1921 bis 1926 (Wiesbaden: Insel, 1950); enlarged edition, edited by Ingeborg Schnack (Frankfurt am Main: Insel, 1977);

Briefwechsel in Gedichten mit Erika Mitterer 1924 bis 1926 (Wiesbaden: Insel, 1950); translated by N. K. Cruickshank as *Correspondence in Verse with Erika Mitterer* (London: Hogarth Press, 1953);

Lettres françaises à Merline 1919–1922 (Paris: Edition du Seuil, 1950); translated by Violet M. Macdonald as *Letters to Merline, 1919–1922* (London: Methuen, 1951);

Rainer Maria Rilke/Marie von Thurn und Taxis: Briefwechsel, edited by Ernst Zinn, 2 volumes (Zurich: Niehans & Rokitansky, 1951); translated by Nora Wydenbruck as *The Letters of Rainer Maria Rilke and Princess Marie von Thurn and Taxis* (London: Hogarth Press, 1958; Norfolk, Conn.: New Directions, 1958);

Rainer Maria Rilke/Lou Andreas-Salomé, Briefwechsel, edited by Ernst Pfeiffer (Zurich: Niehans / Wiesbaden: Insel, 1952; revised and enlarged edition, Frankfurt am Main: Insel, 1975);

Rainer Maria Rilke/André Gide: Correspondence 1909–1926, edited by Renée Lang (Paris: Corrêa, 1952);

Briefe über Cézanne, edited by Clara Rilke (Wiesbaden: Insel, 1952); translated by Joel Agee as *Letters on Cézanne* (New York: Fromm, 1986);

Die Briefe an Frau Gudi Nölke aus Rilkes Schweizer Jahren, edited by Paul Obermüller (Wiesbaden: Insel, 1953); translated by Macdonald as *Letters to Frau Gudi Nölke during His Life in Switzerland* (London: Hogarth Press, 1955);

Rainer Maria Rilke/Katharina Kippenberg: Briefwechsel, edited by Bettina von Bomhard (Wiesbaden: Insel, 1954);

Briefwechsel mit Benvenuta, edited by Kurt Leonhard (Esslingen: Bechtle, 1954); translated by Agee as *Rilke and Benvenuta: An Intimate Correspondence* (New York: Fromm, 1987);

Rainer Maria Rilke et Merline: Correspondence 1920–1926, edited by Dieter Basserman (Zurich: Niehans, 1954);

Lettres milanaises 1921–1926, edited by Lang (Paris: Plon, 1956);

Rainer Maria Rilke/Inga Junghanns: Briefwechsel, edited by Wolfgang Herwig (Wiesbaden: Insel, 1959);

Selected Letters, edited by Harry T. Moore (Garden City, N.Y.: Doubleday, 1960);

Briefe an Sidonie Nádherný von Borutin, edited by Bernhard Blume (Frankfurt am Main: Insel, 1973);

Über Dichtung und Kunst, edited by Hartmut Engelhardt (Frankfurt am Main: Suhrkamp, 1974);

Rainer Maria Rilke/Helene von Nostitz: Briefwechsel, edited by Oswalt von Nostitz (Frankfurt am Main: Insel, 1976);

Briefe an Nanny Wunderly-Volkart, 2 volumes, edited by Niklaus Bigler and Rätus Luck (Frankfurt am Main: Insel, 1977);

Lettres autour d'un jardin (Paris: La Delirante, 1977);

Hugo von Hofmannsthal/Rainer Maria Rilke: Briefwechsel, edited by Rudolf Hirsch and Ingeborg Schnack (Frankfurt am Main: Suhrkamp, 1978);

Briefe an Axel Juncker, edited by Renate Scharffenberg (Frankfurt am Main: Insel, 1979);

Briefwechsel mit Rolf Freiherrn von Ungern-Sternberg, edited by Konrad Kratzsch (Leipzig: Insel Verlag Anton Kippenberg, 1980);

Rainer Maria Rilke/Anita Forrer: Briefwechsel, edited by Magda Kérényi (Frankfurt am Main: Leipzig, 1982);

Rainer Maria Rilke/Marina Zwetajewa/Boris Pasternak: Briefwechsel, edited by Jewgenij Pasternak, Jelena Pasternak, and Konstantin M. Asadowskij (Frankfurt am Main: Insel, 1983); translated by Margaret Wettlin and Walter Arndt as *Letters Summer 1926* (New York: Harcourt Brace Jovanovich, 1985);

Rainer Maria Rilke: Briefe an Ernst Norlind, edited by Paul Åstöm (Partille: Paul Åströms Forlag, 1986);

Rilke und Rußland: Briefe, Erinnerungen, Gedichte, edited by Konstantin Asadowski, Russian texts translated by Ulrike Hirschberg (Frankfurt am Main: Insel, 1986);

Rainer Maria Rilke: Briefwechsel mit Regina Ullmann und Ellen Delp, edited by Walter Simon (Frankfurt am Main: Insel, 1987);

Rainer Maria Rilke/Stefan Zweig: Briefe und Dokumente, edited by Donald Prater (Frankfurt am Main: Insel, 1987).

Bibliographies:

Fritz Adolf Hünich, *Rilke-Bibliographie: Erster Teil: Das Werk des Lebenden* (Leipzig: Insel, 1935);

Walter Ritzer, *Rainer Maria Rilke: Bibliographie* (Vienna: Kerry, 1951);

Paul Obermüller, Herbert Steiner, and Ernst Zinn, eds., *Katalog der Rilke-Sammlung Richard von Mises* (Frankfurt am Main: Insel, 1966);

Karl Klutz, "Rilke-Bibliographie des Jubiläumsjahres 1975," *Blätter der Rilke-Gesellschaft,* 5 (1978): 63–79;

Klutz, "Rilke-Bibliographie für das Jahr 1976," *Blätter der Rilke-Gesellschaft,* 6 (1979): 62–85;

Klutz, "Rilke-Bibliographie für die Jahre 1977 und 1978," *Blätter der Rilke-Gesellschaft,* 7–8 (1980–1981): 143–168;

Klutz, "Rilke-Bibliographie für das Jahr 1979," *Blätter der Rilke-Gesellschaft,* 9 (1982): 128–151;

Klutz, "Rilke-Bibliographie für die Jahre 1980 und 1981," *Blätter der Rilke-Gesellschaft,* 10 (1983): 124–159;

Klutz, "Rilke-Bibliographie für das Jahr 1982," *Blätter der Rilke-Gesellschaft,* 11–12 (1984–1985): 137–164;

Klutz, "Rilke-Bibliographie für das Jahr 1983," *Blätter der Rilke-Gesellschaft,* 13 (1986): 155–175;

Klutz, "Rilke-Bibliographie für das Jahr 1984," *Blätter der Rilke-Gesellschaft,* 14 (1987): 201–217.

Biographies:

Carl Sieber, *René Rilke: Die Jugend Rainer Maria Rilkes* (Leipzig: Insel, 1932);

Sophie Brutzer, *Rilkes russische Reisen* (Königsberg: Klutke, 1934);

Eliza M. Butler, *Rainer Maria Rilke* (Cambridge: Cambridge University Press / New York: Macmillan, 1941);

Maurice Zermatten, *Les Années valaisannes de Rilke* (Lausanne: Rouge, 1941); translated by Waltrud Kappeler as *Der Ruf der Stille: Rilkes Walliser Jahre* (Zurich: Rascher, 1954);

F. W. van Heerikhuizen, *Rainer Maria Rilke: Leven en werk* (Bussum: Kroonder, 1946); translated by Fernand G. Renier and Anne Cliff as *Rainer Maria Rilke: His Life and Work* (London: Routledge &

Kegan Paul, 1952; New York: Philosophical Library, 1952);

Werner Kohlschmidt, *Rainer Maria Rilke* (Lübeck: Wildner, 1948);

Nora Wydenbruck, *Rilke: Man and Poet* (London: Lehmann, 1949);

Joseph-François Angelloz, *Rilke* (Paris: Mercure de France, 1952); translated by Alfred Kuoni as *Rainer Maria Rilke: Leben und Werk* (Munich: Nymphenburger Verlagsbuchhandlung, 1955);

J. R. von Salis, *Rainer Maria Rilkes Schweizer Jahre: Ein Beitrag zur Biographie von Rilkes Spätzeit* (Frauenfeld: Huber, 1952); translated by N. K. Cruickshank as *Rainer Maria Rilke: The Years in Switzerland* (London: Hogarth Press, 1964; Berkeley & Los Angeles: University of California Press, 1964);

Peter Demetz, *René Rilkes Prager Jahre* (Düsseldorf: Diederichs, 1953);

Erich Simenauer, *Rainer Maria Rilke: Legende und Mythos* (Bern: Haupt, 1953);

Else Buddeberg, *Rainer Maria Rilke: Eine innere Biographie* (Stuttgart: Metzler, 1955);

Ingeborg Schnack, *Rilkes Leben und Werk im Bild* (Wiesbaden: Insel, 1956);

Heinrich Weigand Petzet, *Das Bildnis des Dichters: Paula Becker-Modersohn und Rainer Maria Rilke. Eine Begegnung* (Frankfurt am Main: Societätsverlag, 1957);

Hans Egon Holthusen, *Rainer Maria Rilke in Selbstzeugnissen und Bilddokumenten* (Hamburg: Rowohlt, 1958);

H. F. Peters, *Rainer Maria Rilke: The Masks and the Man* (Seattle: University of Washington Press, 1960);

Eudo C. Mason, *Rainer Maria Rilke* (Edinburgh & London: Oliver & Boyd, 1963);

Mason, *Rainer Maria Rilke: Sein Leben und sein Werk* (Göttingen: Vandenhoeck & Ruprecht, 1964);

George C. Schoolfield, *Rilke's Last Year* (Lawrence: University of Kansas Libraries, 1969);

Leonid Certkov, *Rilke in Russland: Auf Grund neuer Materialien* (Vienna: Österreichische Akademie der Wissenschaften, 1975);

Schnack, *Rainer Maria Rilke: Chronik seines Lebens und seines Werkes,* 2 volumes (Frankfurt am Main: Insel, 1975);

Joachim W. Storck, ed., *Rainer Maria Rilke, 1875–1975: Katalog der Ausstellung des Deutschen Literaturarchivs im Schiller-National-museum Marbach* (Stuttgart: Klett, 1975);

Zermatten, *Les dernières années de Rainer Maria Rilke* (Fribourg: Le Cassetin, 1975); translated by Arthur Fibicher as *Rilkes letzte Lebensjahre* (Fribourg: Le Cassetin, 1975);

Horst Nalewski, *Rainer Maria Rilke* (Leipzig: VEB Bibliographisches Institut, 1981);

Wolfgang Leppmann, *Rilke: Sein Leben, seine Welt, sein Werk* (Bern & Munich: Scherz, 1981); translated by Leppmann, Russell S. Stockman, and Richard Exner as *Rilke: A Life* (New York: Fromm, 1984);

J. F. Hendry, *The Sacred Threshold: A Life of Rainer Maria Rilke* (Manchester, U.K.: Carcanet Press, 1983);

Richard Pettit, *Rainer Maria Rilke in und nach Worpswede* (Worpswede: Worpsweder Verlag, 1983);

Donald Prater, *A Ringing Glass: The Life of Rainer Maria Rilke* (Oxford & New York: Oxford University Press, 1986).

References:

Hans Aarsleff, "Rilke, Herman Bang, and Malte," in *Proceedings of the IVth Congress of the International Comparative Literature Association* (The Hague: Mouton, 1966), pp. 628–636;

Renate Adler, "Some Technical Problems in Translations of Rilke's *Notebooks of Malte Laurids Brigge,*" *Die neueren Sprachen,* new series, 12 (1963): 622–628;

Lou Andreas-Salomé, *Rainer Maria Rilke* (Leipzig: Insel, 1928);

Lydia Baer, "Rilke and Jens Peter Jacobsen," *PMLA,* 54 (1939): 900–932, 1133–1180;

Frank Baron, ed., *Rilke and the Visual Arts* (Lawrence, Kans.: Coronado, 1982);

Baron, Ernst S. Dick, and Warren R. Maurer, eds., *Rilke: The Alchemy of Alienation* (Lawrence, Kans.: Regents Press, 1981);

K. A. J. Batterby, *Rilke and France: A Study in Poetic Development* (London: Oxford University Press, 1966);

Marga Bauer, *Rainer Maria Rilke und Frankreich* (Bern: Haupt, 1931);

Ruth Bauer, "Rainer Maria Rilke: 'Der Bettler und das stolze Fräulein,'" in her *Interpretationen moderner Prosa: Anläßlich der Fortbildungstagung für Deutsch-und Geschichtslehrer* (Frankfurt, Berlin, Bonn & Munich: Diesterweg, 1968), pp. 55–63;

Hans Berendt, "Rainer Maria Rilke: Zu den *Aufzeichnungen des Malte Laurids Brigge,*" *Mitteilungen der literaturhistorischen Gesellschaft Bonn,* 6 (1911): 75–104;

Maurice Betz, *Rilke à Paris et Les cahiers de Malte Laurids Brigge* (Paris: Émile-Paul, 1941); translated and enlarged by Willi Reich as *Rilke in Paris* (Zurich: Arche, 1948);

Betz, *Rilke vivant* (Paris: Émile–Paul, 1937); enlarged and translated by Reich as *Rilke in Frankreich: Erinnerungen, Briefe, Dokumente* (Vienna, Leipzig & Zurich: Reichner, 1938);

Elaine Boney, "Love's Door to Death in Rilke's *Cornet* and Other Works," *Modern Austrian Literature,* 10, no. 1 (1977): 18–30;

Hans H. Borcherdt, "Das Problem des 'Verlorenen Sohnes' bei Rilke," in *Worte und Werte: Festschrift für Bruno Markwardt* (Berlin: De Gruyter, 1961), pp. 24–33;

Brigitte L. Bradley, *Zu Rilkes Malte Laurids Brigge* (Bern & Munich: Francke, 1980);

Bradley, "Rilke's *Geschichten vom lieben Gott:* The Narrator's Stance toward the Bourgeoisie," *Modern Austrian Literature,* 15 (1982): 1–24;

Patricia Pollock Brodsky, "The Military School: A Shared Source in Rilke and Musil," *Modern Language Studies,* 10 (1979–1980): 88–93;

Brodsky, *Russia in the Works of Rainer Maria Rilke* (Detroit: Wayne State University Press, 1984);

Brodsky, "The Russian Source of Rilke's 'Wie der Verrat nach Russland kam,'" *Germanic Review,* 5 (Spring 1979): 72–77;

Russell E. Brown, *Index zu Rainer Maria Rilkes Die Aufzeichnungen des Malte Laurids Brigge* (Frankfurt am Main: Athenäum, 1971);

Timothy J. Casey, *Rainer Maria Rilke: A Centenary Essay* (London: Macmillan, 1976);

Robert J. Clements, "Rainer Maria Rilke, Michelangelo and the *Geschichten vom lieben Gott,*" *Comparative Literature,* 6 (1954): 218–231; reprinted in *Studies in Germanic Languages and Literatures Presented to Ernst A. G. Rose,* edited by Robert A. Fowkes and Volkmar Sander (New York: New York University Press, 1967), pp. 57–70;

Charles Dédéyan, *Rilke et la France,* 4 volumes (Paris: Société d'édition d'enseignement supérieur, 1961);

Kirk Dethlefsen, "'Die Turnstunde': Rilkes Beitrag zu einer neuen Schule des Sehens," *Seminar,* 18 (1982): 236–260;

Eva Fauconneau Defresne, "Wirklichkeitserfahrung und Bewusstseinsentwicklung in Rilkes *Malte Laurids Brigge* und Sartres *La Nausée,*" *Arcadia,* 17 (1982): 258–273;

Reidar Ekner, "Rilke, Obstfelder och *Die Aufzeichnungen des Malte Laurids Brigge,*" in his *En sällsam gemenskap: Litteraturhistoriska essäer* (Stockholm: Norstedts, 1967), pp. 152–171;

Hartmut Engelhardt, ed., *Materialien zu Rainer Maria Rilkes 'Die Aufzeichnungen des Malte Laurids Brigge'* (Frankfurt am Main: Suhrkamp, 1974);

F. K. Feigel, *"Rilkes Geschichten vom lieben Gott,"* Pforte: *Monatsschrift für Kultur,* 6 (1954–1955): 228–245;

Diana Festa-McCormick, "Rilke's *Notebooks:* Paris and the Phantoms of the Past," in her *The City as Catalyst* (Rutherford, Madison & Teaneck, N.J.: Fairleigh Dickinson University Press, 1979), pp. 69–88;

Heinrich Gerhard Franz, "Wandlungen des Menschenbildes in Rainer Maria Rilkes *Die Aufzeichnungen des Malte Laurids Brigge*–Parall elen zur gleichzeitigen Malerei," in *Marginalien zur poetischen Welt: Festschrift für Robert Mühlher,* edited by Alois Eden, Hellmuth Himmel, and Alfred Kracher (Berlin: Duncker & Humblot, 1971), pp. 341–367;

Ulrich Fülleborn, "Form und Sinn der *Aufzeichnungen des Malte Laurids Brigge:* Rilkes Prosabuch und der moderne Roman," in *Unterscheidung und Bewahrung: Festschrift für Hermann Kunisch* (Berlin: De Gruyter, 1961), pp. 147–169;

Henry F. Fullenwider, *Rilke and His Reviewers: An Annotated Bibliography* (Lawrence: University of Kansas Libraries, 1978);

Rüdiger Görner, "Über die Fiktion des Täglichen: Das Diaristische moderner Literatur," in his *Das Tagebuch: Eine Einführung* (Munich & Zurich: Artemis, 1985), pp. 98–122;

Diego Hanns Goetz, *Der unsterbliche verlorene Sohn* (Vienna: Amandus, 1949);

Hartmann Goertz, *Frankreich und das Erlebnis der Form im Werke Rainer Maria Rilkes* (Stuttgart: Metzler, 1932);

Thomas Elwood Hart, "Simile by Structure in Rilke's *Geschichten vom lieben Gott,*" *Modern Austrian Literature,* 15, no. 3/4 (1982): 25–69;

Hildburg Herbst, "*Die Weise von Liebe und Tod des Cornets Christoph Rilke:* Ein Vergleich der Urfassung mit dem endgültigen Text," *German Quarterly,* 50 (January 1977): 21–31;

Ernst Fedor Hoffmann, "Zum dichterischen Verfahren in Rilkes 'Aufzeichnungen des Malte Laurids Brigge,'" *Deutsche Vierteljahresschrift für Literaturwissenschaft und Geistesgeschichte,* 42 (1968): 202–230;

Hermann von Jan, *Rilkes Aufzeichnungen des Malte Laurids Brigge* (Leipzig: Weber, 1938);

Rudolf Jancke, "Rilke und Kierkegaard," *Deutsche Vierteljahresschrift für Literaturwissenschaft und Geistesgeschichte,* 39 (1938): 314–329;

Klaus W. Jonas, "Die Rilke-Kritik 1950–1966," *Insel Almanach auf das Jahr 1967* (Frankfurt am Main: Insel, 1967), pp. 94–121;

Philippe Jullian, *Dreamers of Decadence: Symbolist Painters of the 1890s* (New York & Washington, D.C.: Praeger, 1971);

Wolfgang Kayser, "Eine unbekannte Prosaskizze von Rainer Maria Rilke," *Trivium,* 5 (1947): 81–88;

Byong-Ock Kim, *Rilkes Militärschulerlebnis und das Problem des verlorenen Sohnes* (Bonn: Bouvier, 1973);

Johannes Klein, "Die Struktur von Rilkes *Malte,*" *Wirkendes Wort,* 2 (1951–1952): 93–103;

H. R. Klieneberger, "Romanticism and Modernism in Rilke's *Die Aufzeichnungen des Malte Laurids Brigge,*" *Modern Language Review,* 74 (April 1979): 361–367;

Werner Kohlschmidt, "Rilke und Kierkegaard," in his *Entzweite Welt: Studien zum Menschenbild in der neueren Dichtung* (Gladbeck: Freizeiten, 1953), pp. 88–97;

Kohlschmidt, "Rilke und Obstfelder," in *Die Wissenschaft von deutscher Sprache und Dichtung: Methoden, Probleme, Aufgaben: Festschrift für Friedrich Maurer* (Stuttgart: Klett, 1963), pp. 458–477;

Kohlschmidt, ed., *Rilke: Interpretationen* (Lahr: Schauenburg, 1948);

Wilhelm Loock, *Rainer Maria Rilke: Die Aufzeichnungen des Malte Laurids Brigge* (Munich: Oldenbourg, 1971);

Claire Lucques, "La Chanson d'amour et de mort du cornette Christophe Rilke: Est-elle une exception d'art populaire dans l'ouvre de Rainer Maria Rilke?," in her *L'Absence ardente: Visages de Rilke* (Troyes: La Renaissance, 1977), pp. 19–31;

Lucques, "La Poétique de *Malte Laurids Brigge,*" *Blätter der Rilke-Gesellschaft,* 9 (1982): 22–32;

Børge Gedsø Madsen, "Influences from J. P. Jacobsen and Sigbjørn Obstfelder on Rainer Maria Rilke's *Die Aufzeichnungen des Malte Laurids Brigge,*" *Scandinavian Studies,* 26 (August 1954): 105–114;

Lorna Martens, "Reliable Narration: Rainer Maria Rilke's *Die Aufzeichnungen des Malte Laurids Brigge,*" in her *The Diary Novel* (London & New York: Cambridge University Press, 1985), pp. 156–172;

Fritz Martini, "*Die Aufzeichnungen des Malte Laurids Brigge,*" in his *Das Wagnis der Sprache: Interpretationen deutscher Prosa von Nietzsche bis Benn* (Stuttgart: Klett, 1954), pp. 137–175;

Eudo C. Mason, "Rilkes Humor," in *Deutsche Weltliteratur von Goethe bis Ingeborg Bachmann: Festschrift für J. Alan Pfeffer,* edited by Klaus W. Jonas (Tübingen: Niemeyer, 1972), pp. 216–244;

Gert Mattenklott, "Die Zeit der anderen Auslegung der 'Aufzeichnungen des Malte Laurids Brigge von Rilke,'" in *Methodische Praxis der Literaturwissenschaft: Modelle der Interpretation,* edited by Dieter Kimpel and Beate Pinkerneil (Kronberg im Taunus: Scriptor, 1975), pp. 117–157;

Josef Mayrhöfer, "Motivegeschichtliche Untersuchungungen zu Rainer Maria Rilkes 'Cornet,'" *Blätter der Rilke-Gesellschaft,* 2 (1975): 59–74;

Veronika Merz, "Die Gottesidee in Rilkes *Aufzeichnungen des Malte Laurids Brigge,*" *Jahrbuch der deutschen Schillergesellschaft,* 26 (1982): 262–295;

Armand Nivelle, "Sense et structure des 'Cahiers de Malte Laurids Brigge,'" *Revue d'Esthétique,* 12 (1959): 5–32;

Idris Parry, "Malte's Hand," *German Life and Letters,* new series 11 (1957): 1–12;

Wolfgang Paul, "R. M. Rilkes 'Die Weise von Liebe und Tod des Cornets Christoph Rilke' und die Schlacht von Mogersdorf," *Neue deutsche Hefte,* 11 (1964): 84–95;

Guenther C. Rimbach, "Zum Begriff der Aquivalenz im Werke Rilkes und zur Entsprechung zwischen den Künsten in der Poetik der Moderne," *Modern Austrian Literature,* 15, no. 3/4 (1982): 127–143;

Hugo Rokyta, *Das Schloß im "Cornet" von Rainer Maria Rilke* (Vienna: Bergland, 1966);

Inca Rumold, *Die Verwandlung des Ekels: Zur Funktion der Kunst in Rilkes "Malte Laurids Brigge" und Sartres "La Nausée"* (Bonn: Bouvier, 1979);

Judith Ryan, "'Hypothetisches Erzählen': Zur Funktion von Phantasie und Einbildung in Rilkes 'Malte Laurids Brigge,'" *Jahrbuch der deutschen Schillergesellschaft,* 15 (1971): 341–374;

Dieter Saalmann, *Rainer Maria Rilkes "Die Aufzeichnungen des Malte Laurids Brigge": Ein Würfelwerf nach dem Absoluten: Poetologische Aspekte* (Bonn: Bouvier, 1975);

Clementina di San Lazzaro, "'Die Aufzeichnungen des Malte Laurids Brigge' von R. M. Rilke im Vergleich mit Jacobsens 'Niels Lyhne' und A. Gides 'Nourritures Terrestres,'" *Germanisch-romanische Monatsschrift,* 29 (1941): 106–117;

Wolfgang Schneditz, *Rilkes letzte Landschaft* (Salzburg: Pallas, 1951);

George C. Schoolfield, "A Bad Story of Young Rilke," in *From Vormärz to Fin de Siècle: Essays in Nineteenth Century Austrian Literature,* edited by Mark G. Ward (Blairgownie: Lochee Publications, 1986), pp. 107–132;

Schoolfield, "Rilke's Ibsen," *Scandinavian Studies,* 51 (Autumn 1979): 460–501;

Walter Seifert, *Das epische Werk Rainer Maria Rilkes* (Bonn: Bouvier, 1969);

Walter Simon, "Philologische Untersuchungen zu Rainer Maria Rilkes 'Cornet,'" *Blätter der Rilke-Gesellschaft,* 2 (1975): 26–58;

Simon, ed., *Rainer Maria Rilke: Die Weise von Liebe und Tod. Texte und Dokumente* (Frankfurt am Main: Suhrkamp, 1974);

William Small, *Rilke-Kommentar zu den Aufzeichnungen des Malte Laurids Brigge* (Chapel Hill: University of North Carolina Press, 1983);

Walter H. Sokel, "Zwischen Existenz und Weltinnenraum: Zum Prozess der Ent-Ichung in Malte Laurids Brigge," in *Probleme des Erzählens in der Weltliteratur: Festschrift für Käte Hamburger,* edited by Fritz Martini (Stuttgart: Klett, 1971), pp. 212–233;

Ingeborg H. Solbrig and Joachim W. Storck, eds., *Rilke heute: Beziehungen und Wirkungen* (Frankfurt am Main: Suhrkamp, 1975);

August Stahl, *Rilke Kommentar: Zu den Aufzeichnungen des Malte Laurids Brigge, zur erzählerischen Prosa, zu den essayistischen Schriften und zum dramatischen Werk* (Munich: Winkler, 1979);

Steffen Steffensen, *Rilke und Skandinavien: Zwei Vorträge* (Copenhagen: Munksgaard, 1958);

Steffensen, "Rilkes Malte Laurids Brigges optegnelser: En førlober for den moderne roman," in *Romanproblemer: Teorier og analyser: Festskrift til Hans Sørensen,* edited by Merete Gerlach-Nielsen, Hans Hertel, and Morten Nøjgaard (Odense: Universitetsforlaget, 1968), pp. 254–263;

Anthony R. Stevens, *Rilkes Malte Laurids Brigge: Strukturanalyse des erzählerischen Bewusstseins* (Bern & Frankfurt am Main: Lang, 1974);

Gottfried Stix, "Das Geheimnis der Rose, Zu Rainer Maria Rilkes *Geschichten vom lieben Gott,*" *Literatur und Kritik,* 123 (1978): 171–180;

Ferenc Szasz, "Der Jugendstil als Weltanschauung am Beispiel Raines Maria Rilkes," *Blätter der Rilke-Gesellschaft,* 14 (1987): 11–20;

Marie von Thurn und Taxis-Hohenlohe, *Erinnerungen an Rainer Maria Rilke* (Munich, Berlin & Zurich: Oldenbourg, 1932);

Hermann Uyttersprot, "Rilkes *Weise von Liebe und Tod,*" *Nieuw Vlaams Tijdschrift,* 20 (1966): 2–21;

Alfred Vogt, "Ärztliche Betrachtung über 'Die Aufzeichnungen des Malte Laurids Brigge' von Rilke," *Deutsche Medizinische Zeitschrift,* 64 (1938): 457–459;

Karl E. Webb, *Rainer Maria Rilke and Jugendstil: Affinities, Influences, Adaptations* (Chapel Hill: University of North Carolina Press, 1978);

Felix Wittner, "Rilkes Cornet," *PMLA,* 44 (1929): 911–924;

Helmut Wocke, *Rilke und Italien* (Giessen: Von Münchow, 1940);

Wayne Wonderley, "An Analysis of Rilke's Novella 'Die Turnstunde,'" *Perspectives on Contemporary Literature,* 2 (1976): 134–139;

Eva C. Wunderlich, "Slavonic Traces in Rilke's *Geschichten vom lieben Gott,*" *Germanic Review,* 22 (1947): 287–297;

R. Zellweger, *Genèse et Fortune du "Cornette" de Rilke* (Neuchâtel: A la Baconnière, 1971);

Werner Zimmermann, "Rainer Maria Rilke: 'Der Bettler und das stolze Fräulein,'" in his *Deutsche Prosadichtung der Gegenwart* (Düsseldorf: Schwann, 1956), I: 145–154.

Papers:

Principal collections of Rainer Maria Rilke's papers are at the Rilke-Archiv, Gernsbach; the Rilke-Archiv of the Schweizerische Landesbibliothek, Bern; and the Deutsches Literaturarchiv, Marbach.

Hans Sachs

(5 November 1494 – 19 January 1576)

Eckhard Bernstein
College of the Holy Cross

This entry originally appeared in DLB 179: German Writers
of the Renaissance and Reformation, 1280–1580.

SELECTED BOOKS: *Von der Lieb. Ich bin genant der liebe streit. Sag von der liebe wunn vnd freyt. Darzu von schmertz vnd trawrickeit. So in der lieb verporgen leit* (Nuremberg: Wolfgang Formschneider, 1515?);

Ein kleglich lied von eines Fürsten tochter vnd einem Jüngling die von lieb wegen beyde jr leben haben verloren. Vnd ist in Fraw Eren thon zu singen (Nuremberg: Hans Guldenmundt, 1515?);

Die Wittenbergisch Nachtigall Die man yetz höret vberall. Ich sage euch wa diese schweygen so werden die stein schreyen Luce 19 (Nuremberg, 1523);

Disputation zwischen einem Chorherren vnd Schuchmacher darin das wort gottes vnnd ein recht Christlich wesen verfochten würdt (N.p., 1524);

Ein gesprech von den Scheinwercken der Gaystlichen, vnd jren gelübdten, damit sy zuverlesterung des bluts Christi vermaynen selig zu werden (N.p., 1524);

Ein Dialogus des inhalt: ein argument der Römischen wider das Christlich heüflein den Geytz auch ander offenlich laster betreffend (N.p., 1524);

Ain gesprech eins Ewangelischen Christen mit einem Lutherischen Darinn der ergerlich wandel etzlicher die sich Lutherisch nennen angezaigt vnd bruderlich gestrafft wirdt (N.p., 1524);

Eyn wunderliche Weyssagung von dem Babstumb wie es yhm biß an das endt der welt gehen sol, jn figuren oder gemäl begriffen, gefunden zu Nürmberg ym Cartheuser Closter vnd ist seher alt. Eyn vorred Andreas Osianders. Mit gutter verstendtlicher außlegung durch gelerte leut verklert. Welche Hans Sachs yn teutsche reymen gefast vnd darzu gesetzt hat (Nuremberg: Hans Goldenmund, 1527);

All Römisch Kaiser nach ordnung vnd wie lang yeder geregiert hat zu welcher zeit was sitten der gehabt vnd was todes er gestorben sey von dem ersten an biß auff den yetzigen groß mechtigsten Kaiser Carl (Nuremberg, 1530);

Ein lobspruch der statt Nürmberg. Der Stadt Nürmberg ordnung vnd wesen Findstu du in disem gdicht zulesen (Nuremberg: Kunegund Hergotin, 1530);

*Hans Sachs; portrait by Andreas Herneisen
(Germanisches Museum, Nuremberg)*

Ein kurtzweilig Faßnacht Spiell Vonn einem bösen Weib durch Hans Sachs (Nuremberg: Valentin Newber, 1530);

Ein vermanung Kayserlicher Mayestat sampt aller Stend des Römischen Reychs Eynes heerzugs wider den blutdurstigen Türcken (Nuremberg: Georg Wachter, 1532);

Clagred der Neün Muse oder künst vber Teütschlandt (Nuremberg, 1535);

Ein Gesprech mit dem schnöden Müssiggang vnd seynen acht schendtlichen Eygenschafften (Nuremberg: Jörg Merckel, 1535?);

589

Ein spruch von dem freüden fewer zu Nürnberg verbrent am xiij tag Septembris ob dem Keyserlichen erlangetn syg in Affrica am Königreich Thunis (Nuremberg: Hans Guldenmund, 1535);

Das Narren schneiden. Ein schön Faßnacht Spiel mit dreyen Personen (Nuremberg: Friedrich Gutknecht, 1536);

Anzeigung wider das schönd laster der Hurerey (Nuremberg: Hanns Wandereisen, 1540);

Kaiserlicher Mayestat Karoli der 5. einreyten zu Nürnberg in des heyligen Reychs Stat, Den 16. tag des 1541 jars (Nuremberg: Georg Wachter, 1541);

Ein war Contrafactur oder verzeychnuß der Königlichen stat Ofen in Vngern jr belagerung sampt dem vnglückhafftigen Scharmuetzel des pluturstigen Tüercken mit dem Königklichen heerleger im September des 1541 jars (Nuremberg: Steffan Hamer, 1541);

Das pitter süß Eelich leben (Nuremberg: Georg Wachter, 1541);

Der Todt ein Endt aller Yrdischen ding (Nuremberg: Georg Merckel, 1542);

Der gantz haußrat (Nuremberg: Hans Guldenmund, 1545);

Ein Epitaphium oder klagred ob der leich D. Martini Luthers (Nuremberg: Georg Wachter, 1546);

Ein Klagred Teutschen landts mit dem treuwen Eckhart (Nuremberg: Merckel, 1546);

Ein New Lied Wie Hertzog Johan Friderich vonn der Römi. Kaiserlichen Mayestät den 24.tag Aprils erlegt vnd gefangen worden ist (N.p., 1547);

Ein nutzlicher rath den jungen gsellen. So sich verheyraten wollen (Nuremberg: Hans Guldenmund, 1549);

Ein Faßnachtspiel der böß rauch im Hauß mit dreyen personen kurtzweylig zu hören (Nuremberg: Georg Merckel, 1551);

Ein Faßnacht Spil Die fünff Elenden wandrer mit sechs personen kurtzweylig zu hören (Nuremberg: Georg Merckel, circa 1551);

Ein schöne Comedi, mit xvj Personen zu recitieren, Die Judith, wie sie dem Holoferni das haupt, in seinem Zelt abschlegt, vnd hat Fünff Actus (Nuremberg: Friedrich Gutknecht, circa 1551);

Die Gemarthert Theologia. Mer das Klagent Ewangelium (Nuremberg: Georg Merckel, 1552);

Warhafftige Contrafactur der andern Schlacht so Margraff Albrecht der Jünger von Brandenburg verloren hat durch Hertzog Heynrich zu Braunschweig den XI tag Septembris Anno M.D.Iiij. Jar (Nuremberg: Steffan Hamer, 1553);

Ein ardlich gesprech der Götter die zwitracht des Römischen Reychs betreffende (Nuremberg: Georg Merckel, 1553);

Der Ehren spiegel der Zwölff Durchleuchtigenn Frawen des Alten Testaments (Nuremberg: Hermann Hamsing, 1553);

Die vier wunderbarlichen Eygenschafft und würckung des Weins, ein kurtzweylicher Spruch. Mehr ein Newer spruch von der Insel Bachi vnd jrer Eygenschafft (Nuremberg: Georg Merckel, 1553);

Der klagent Waldtbruder vber alle Stendt auff erden (Nuremberg: Georg Merckel, 1553);

Ein gesprech mit der Faßnacht von jrer eygenschafft (Nuremberg: Georg Merckel, 1554);

Ein gesprech der Götter ob der Edlen vnd Burgerlichen Kranckheit des Podagram oder Zipperlein (Nuremberg: Georg Merckel, 1554);

Der Teuffel lest kein Landtknecht mehr in die Helle faren (Nuremberg: Georg Merckel, 1555);

Ein Gesprech vnd klagred Fraw Arbeit vber den grossen müssigen hauffen (Nuremberg: Friedrich Gutknecht, 1556);

Ein klaggesprech vber das schwere Alter (Nuremberg: Valentin Neuber, 1558);

Sehr Herrliche Schöne vnd warhaffte Gedicht. Geistlich vnd Weltlich, allerley art, als ernstliche Tragedien, liebliche Comedien, seltzsame Spil, kurtzweilige Gesprech, sehnliche Klagreden, wunderbarliche Fabel, sampt andern lecherlichen schwencken vnd bossen [Folio I] (Nuremberg: Christoph Heußler, 1558);

Das ander Buch. Sehr Herrliche Schöne Artliche vnd gebundene Gedicht macherley art. Als Tragedi, Comedi, Spiel, Gesprech, Sprüch vnd Fabel, darinn auff das kürtzt vnd deutlichst an Tag gegeben werden, viel guter Christlicher vnd sittlicher Lehr, auch viel warhaffter vnd seltzamer Histori, sampt etlichen kurtzweyligen Schwencken, doch niemandt ergerlich, sondern jedermann nützlich vnnd gut zu lesen [Folio II] (Nuremberg: Christoph Heußler, 1560;

Ein Fasnacht Spiel. Der farend Schuler mit der Beurerin mit dreyen personen kurtzweylich zu hören (Nuremberg: Georg Merckel, 1560);

Tragedia des Jüngsten Geriechts vnnd Sterbenden Menschen einen Erbarn Raht der Churfürstlichen Statt Amberg zu gefallen gemacht durch Hanns Sachsen zu Nürnberg (Amberg: Wolff Guldenmund, 1560);

Zwey schöne Newe Geystliche Lieder, Das Erste, warumb betrübst du dich mein hertz. Ein Ander Geistlich Lied, Biß mir gnedig O Herre Gott (Nuremberg: Valentin Newber, circa 1560);

Das dritt vnd letzt Buch. Sehr Herrliche Schöne Tragedi, Comedi vnd schimpf Spil, Geistlich vnd Weltlich, viel schöner alter warhafftiger Histori, auch kurtzweiliger geschicht auff das deutlichst an tag geben. Welche Spil auch nit allein gut, nutzlich vnd kurtzweilig zu lesen sindt, sonder auch leichtlich aus diesem Buch spilweis anzurichten, weil es so ordenlich alle Person, gebärden, wort vnd werck, außgeng vnd eingeng aufs verstendigst anzeiget, durch alle Spil, der vormal keins im Truck ist außgangen, noch gesehen worden [Folio III] (Nuremberg: Christoph Heußler, 1561);

Eygentliche Beschreibung Aller Stände auff Erden Hoher vnd Nidriger, Geistlicher vnd Weltlicher, Aller Künsten, Handwercken vnd Händeln, vom grösten biß zum kleinesten. Auch von jrem Vrsprung, Erfindung vnd gebreuchen. Durch den weitberümptern Hans Sachsen Gantz fleissig beschrieben vnd in Teutsche Reimen gefasset. Sehr nutzbarlich vnd lustig zu lesen vnd auch mit kunstreichen Figuren deren gleichen zuvor niemands gesehen allen Ständen so in diesem Buch begriffen zu ehren vnd wolgefallen Allen Künstlern aber als Malern, Goldschmieden zu sonderlichen dienst in Druck verfertigt (Frankfurt am Main: Sigmund Feyerabend, 1568); translated as *The Book of Trades: Jost Amman and Hans Sachs*, introduction by Benjamin A. Rifkin (New York & London: Dover, 1973);

Zwey schöne newe kurtzweylige Faßnacht Spil. Das erste mit vier Personen Von eines Bawrn Son der zwey Weyber wolt haben. Das ander mit fünff Personen von dem Schwangern Bawrn (Nuremberg: Valentin Newber, circa 1570);

Drey kurtzweylicher Faßnacht Spiel. Das erste mit vier Personen Nemlich ein Richter ein Buler ein Spieler vnd ein Trincker. Das ander mit dreien personen Nemlich ein Kelner vnd zwen Bawrn die holen den Bachen im Teutschen Hoff. Das dritte auch mit dreien Personen Nemlich ein Burger vnd ein Bawer vnd ein Edelman die holen Krapffn (Nuremberg: Valentin Newber, 1570);

Valete, Des Weitberhümbten Teutschen Poeten Hans Sachsen zu Nürnberg Darinn er selbs im 71. Jar seines alters sein leben vnd inhalt, anzal vnd ordnung aller seiner Gedicht reimenweiz verfaß, gestelt vnd beschriben, im Jar nach Christi geburt 1567. Vorhin nie im Truck außgangen (Nuremberg: Katharina Gerlach & Johann vom Bergs heirs, 1576);

Hans Sachsen spruch damit er dem Maler sein Valete dediciert (Nuremberg: Katharina Gerlach & Johann vom Bergs heirs, 1576);

Ein new Lied Von eines Ritters Tochter der jr Bul an jren armen starb nach laut eines wunderlichen Traums (Nuremberg: Hans Guldenmundt, n.d.);

Das heyß Eysen und Der böse Rauch (Nuremberg: Valentin Neuber, 1576);

Das vierdt Poetisch Buch. Mancherley artliche Newe Stück, Schöner gebundener Reimen, in drey unterschiedliche Bücher getheylt [Folio IV] (Nuremberg: Leonhard Heußler, 1578);

Das fünfft vnd letzt Buch. Sehr Herrliche Schöne newe Stück artlicher, gebundener, Künstlicher Reimen, in drey unterschiedliche Bücher verfaßt [Folio V] (Nuremberg: Leonhard Heußler, 1579).

Editions and Collections: *Dichtungen von Hans Sachs,* 3 volumes, edited by Karl Goedeke and Julius Tittmann (Leipzig: Brockhaus, 1870–1871);

Hans Sachs Werke, 26 volumes, edited by Adelbert von Keller and Edmund Goetze (Stuttgart: Hiersemann, 1870–1908);

Sämtliche Fastnachtspiele von Hans Sachs, 7 volumes, edited by Goetze (Halle: Niemeyer, 1880–1887);

Sämtliche Fabeln und Schwänke von Hans Sachs, 6 volumes, edited by Goetze and Carl Drescher (Halle: Niemeyer, 1893–1913);

Die Prosadialoge von Hans Sachs, edited by Ingeborg Spriewald (Leipzig: VEB Bibliographisches Institut, 1970);

Hans Sachs: Werke in zwei Bänden, 2 volumes, edited by Reinhard Hahn (Berlin & Weimar: Aufbau, 1992).

Editions in English: *A Goodly dysputacion betwene a Christen Shomaker and a Popysshe Parson with two other parsones more, done within the famous citie of Noremborough,* translated by Anthony Scoloker (London: Anthony Scoloker & W. Seres, 1548);

Merry Tales and Three Shrovetide Plays, translated by William Leighton (London: Nutt, 1910) includes *The Horse Thief, The Hot Iron, The Travelling Scholar;*

The Wandering Scholar from Paradise: A Fastnachtspiel with 3 Persons, edited by Samuel A. Eliot Jr., in *Little Theatre Classics,* volume 4 (Boston: Little, Brown, 1922), pp. 115–137;

Seven Shrovetide Plays, translated and annotated by E. U. Ouless (London: Deane, 1930)—comprises *The Children of Eve, Dame Truth, The Wandering Scholar, The Old Game, The Horse Thief, Five Poor Travellers, Death in the Tree;*

Away with Surly Husbands, translated and annotated by Ouless (London: Deane, 1934; Boston: Baker, 1934);

The Glutton's Paradise, translated by Hans Hinrichs (Mount Vernon, N.Y.: Peter Pauper, 1955);

Nine Carnival Plays by Hans Sachs, translated, with an introduction and notes, by Randall W. Listerman (Ottawa: Dovehouse, 1990)—comprises *The Nose Dance, The Stolen Bacon, The Calf-Hatching, The Wife in the Well, The Farmer with the Blur, The Evil Woman, The Grand Inquisitor in the Soup, The Dead Man, The Pregnant Farmer.*

Although chiefly remembered today as the genial shoemaker-poet and leader of Nuremberg's Meistersinger Guild in Richard Wagner's opera *Die Meistersinger von Nürnberg* (1862; translated as *The Master-Singers of Nuremberg,* 1892), Hans Sachs was, in his time, one of Germany's best-known poets. A man of unparalleled literary productivity, he wrote more than 4,000 *Meister-*

lieder (master songs), almost 2,000 *Spruchgedichte* (poems), 85 *Fastnachtspiele* (carnival, or Shrovetide, plays), 128 other dramas, and 6 prose dialogues. A loyal champion of the Lutheran cause, he was, at the same, time, a critical and keen observer and chronicler of his times. Today only a small fraction of his enormous oeuvre is familiar to the general public. For anyone who is interested in the social history and mentality of early modern Germany, Sachs provides an inexhaustible source.

Sachs was born in Nuremberg on 5 November 1494 to the tailor Jörg Sachs, who had emigrated from Zwickau, and Christina Sachs, née Prunner. His relatively prosperous artisan family could afford to send its only son to one of the four Latin schools in the city, a school that awakened his lifelong passion for books. From 1509 to 1511 he was apprenticed to a shoemaker, and in the spring of 1512 he began his travels as a journeyman to Regensburg, Passau, Braunau, Otting, Burghausen, Wels, Salzburg, Munich, Frankfurt am Main, Koblenz, Cologne, and Aachen, and possibly also to Lübeck and cities in Saxony. In addition to getting to know large parts of Germany and becoming acquainted with the latest production techniques, he also made contacts with the Meistersinger, guild craftsmen who practiced the art of the *Meistergesang,* to which Sachs had been introduced as an apprentice by the Nuremberg linen weaver Lienhart Nunnenbeck. There is some evidence that he arranged his travels to take him to places where Meistersinger guilds existed. His earliest dated and preserved literary attempts come from this period: prompted by a love affair in Munich, Sachs wrote several texts, among them the moving *Buhlscheidlied Ach ungelück* (Song about the Pangs of Separation from a Loved One, 1513; printed in *Dichtungen von Hans Sachs,* 1870) and *Historia. Ein kleglich geschichte von zweyen liebhabenden. Der ermört Lorenz* (The Pitiful Story of Two Lovers. The Murdered Lorenz, 1515; printed in Folio I, 1558); and two carnival plays, *Das hoffgsindt Veneris* (Venus's Servants at the Court, 1517; printed in Folio III, 1561) and *Von der eygenschafft der lieb* (Love's Character, 1518; printed in Folio III). On 19 September 1519 Sachs married Kunigunde Kreutzer; the marriage would produce seven children and would last until Kunigunde's death forty-one years later. As a wedding gift his parents signed over their house in the Kotgasse, now Brunnengasse, to the young couple. In January 1520 Sachs became a master shoemaker.

Aside from a few trips to the trade fair in Frankfurt am Main, Sachs spent the remaining five and one-half decades of his life in Nuremberg, which at the beginning of the sixteenth century was one of the largest and most important of the free imperial cities in Germany. All political power lay in the hands of the forty patrician families who, through the *Rat* (council), regulated the lives of Nuremberg's citizens; Sachs, along with the vast majority of the population, was excluded from the political decision-making process. Since a failed revolt in 1348, the craftsmen were banned from organizing themselves into guilds. Nuremberg's wealth was based on commerce and manufacturing, and its products enjoyed an excellent reputation throughout Europe. Men such as Willibald Pirckheimer, Veit Stoß, Adam Krafft, and Albrecht Dürer made Nuremberg one of the centers of intellectual and artistic life in Germany.

Martin Luther's Ninety-five Theses, published in Latin in October 1517 and translated into German shortly thereafter by the Nuremberg patrician Kaspar Nützel, were well received in Nuremberg. Sachs, who had in his personal possession some forty Lutheran pamphlets, did not speak out on behalf of the Reformer until 1523, when he published the seven-hundred-verse poem *Die Wittenbergisch Nachtigall* (The Wittenberg Nightingale). An allegory in which the nightingale represents Luther, the lion Pope Leo X, and other animals bishops and prelates, the poem denounces the church, its institutions and representatives, its fiscal exploitation, the cults of relics, and the veneration of saints and expounds in simplified form Luther's teachings of justification through faith alone. Its catchy doggerels contributed to the poem's immediate success; it went through seven editions in short order and made the author famous throughout Germany.

In 1524, a year before the official introduction of the Reformation in Nuremberg, Sachs attempted to influence public opinion with four prose dialogues. Dealing with a wide spectrum of religious and social topics, these texts, with their lively discussions, vivid depiction of characters, and dramatic structure, represent some of the best prose of the sixteenth century. *Disputation zwischen einem Chorherren und Schuchmacher* (Disputation between a Canon and a Shoemaker), featuring an indolent canon and a Bible-quoting cobbler, clearly takes sides with the Lutheran cause. *Ein gesprech eins Ewangelischen Christen mit einem Lutherischen* (A Conversation of an Evangelical Christian with a Lutheran) articulates Sachs's uneasiness with some of the radical changes taking place. In this conversation between two friends, Hans attacks those whose new faith amounts to nothing more than a provocative rejection of centuries-old customs and rituals; and whereas Peter seeks confrontation with the Catholics, Hans pleads for a slow and deliberate process based on understanding, love, and patient persuasion. Social and economic problems posed by monasticism are the topics of *Ein gesprech von den Scheinwercken der Gaystlichen, und iren gelübdten* (A Conversation about the Phony Works of the Clergy and Their Vows), in which Sachs contrasts the productive lives of the craftsmen with the parasitic existence of the monks. Although Sachs never wavered in his commitment to the Lutheran cause, his initial hope that the acceptance of the Reformer's teachings would inaugurate a more just social order had been replaced with disillusionment. Nowhere is this attitude clearer than in his fourth dialogue, *Ein Dialogus des inhalt: ein argument der Römischen wider das Christlich heüflein den Geytzn . . . betreffend* (A Dialogue to the Effect: An Argument of the Romans against the Christian Crowd Concerning Excessive Profit Seeking and Other Public Vices), a criticism of the early capitalist economic system. Having the Catholic Romanus articulate these views against the Evangelical merchant Reichenburger may have been Sachs's way of distancing himself from this critique, thus circumventing Nuremberg's harsh censorship practices.

In 1527 Sachs experienced the narrow limits the patrician council set for its citizens when he collaborated with Andreas Osiander, the fiery preacher of Saint Lorenz Church, and the well-known woodcutter Erhard Schön on *Eyn wunderliche Weyssagung von dem Babstumb* (A Strange Prophecy of the Papacy). Although the pamphlet, in its antipapal thrust and skillful combination of illustration and text, did not differ markedly from other broadsheets flooding the German market, the Nuremberg censor banned the work, had all printed copies confiscated, censured Osiander and Hans Guldenmund (the printer), and ordered Sachs–literally–to stick to his trade of shoemaker and desist from further publishing. Such an action against a pro-Lutheran work by a Lutheran city council seems odd, but Nuremberg was dependent on trade with its Catholic neighbors and good relations with the Catholic emperor. Although Sachs observed the ban for the next three years, in the long run the perceptive and critical shoemaker-poet could not be prevented from interpreting critically the religious, social, and political issues of the day. He did so primarily in the form of Spruchgedichte of varying lengths, consisting of rhymed couplets commenting on topics from the Turkish threat to his increasing concern with the dissensions within the Protestant camp. Having experienced censorship at first hand, however, he couched his criticism increasingly in the form of allegories, dreams, and mythological stories. In *Die Gemarthert Theologia* (Tortured Theology), which was not published until 1552, it is the allegorical figure Theology who diagnoses *Eygennutz* (egotism), especially that of the territorial princes, as the root of all evil. In the poem "Der Interim" (The Interim), written in 1548, Sachs turned against the city council, which reluctantly favored adoption of the imperial mandate reintroducing Catholic holidays, aural confession, and fasting. But he

disguises his criticism by presenting the emperor as Jupiter, the Pope as Saturn, and the Reformer Philipp Melanchthon as Minerva. In addition, he pretends to have dreamed the whole episode, thus distancing himself twice from his criticism. Even in this encoded form, the poem was never published.

In the 1550s it was not the Catholic emperor but the Protestant margrave Albrecht Alcibiades of Brandenburg-Kulmbach who was a source of pain and suffering for Nuremberg. In 1552, in an attempt to annex parts of the extensive Nuremberg territory, Albrecht put the torch to castles, villages, and mills, terrorized the rural population with murder and lootings, and laid siege to the city itself. Only by paying the enormous sum of 200,000 gulden could the Nurembergers relieve themselves of the siege. But the threat continued to force the imperial city into costly war preparations and payments of tribute. Peace returned only with Albrecht's death in 1557, an event that prompted Sachs to one of his sharpest attacks. Presented as a dream vision, "Gesprech von der himelfart margraff Albrechts anno 1557" (The Conversation of the Ascension of Margrave Albrecht in the Year 1557) is by no means an apotheosis of the former enemy, as the title suggests, but a grim description of his descent into hell. In this poem Sachs creates scenes of oppressive gruesomeness. As the lonely figure walks silently through the valley of death, he is surrounded by a throng of burghers, women, and children whose demise he has caused. The contrast between the wailing victims and the solitary tyrant, as well as that between the ghostly darkness of purgatory and the blinding light of hell, is described in vivid detail. Like all of Sachs's poems having to do with Albrecht, however, this one was never printed. One day after the poet's death the ever-cautious city council would have the manuscripts for some of Sachs's unpublished works, including this poem, confiscated out of fear that they would bring harm to the city.

Sachs was not a revolutionary, as some Marxist critics have maintained; on the other hand, he was not the apolitical moralist portrayed by nineteenth-century critics. He was an independent, at times courageous man who did not hesitate to express his views on controversial and religious topics, albeit in masked fashion. Although these works did not appear in print, they were not written for the drawer but were circulated among friends. Even in manuscript form, however, some of them were considered too dangerous by the city authorities.

Today, thanks to Wagner, Sachs is primarily known as the Meistersinger of Nuremberg; and there is some historical justification for that image. For decades the composition and performance of Meisterlieder were at the center of Sachs's creative work, even during the years 1527 to 1530, when he was not allowed to publish: Meisterlieder, by statute, could not appear in print and, thus, were not subject to censorship. Sachs collected his more than four thousand Meisterlieder—two-thirds of his literary production—in sixteen handwritten volumes.

The Meistersinger were literary-musical artisans in Nuremberg and other southern German cities who organized themselves into associations. In their *Singschulen* (concerts), held on Sundays after the main church service, they competitively performed their songs, solo and unaccompanied, following, like every other trade, strict rules and conventions. The competitions were judged by four *Merker* (markers) on the basis not of originality and artistic merit but of strict conformance with the *Tabulatur* (the tablet on which the rules were written). Initiated into the art by Nunnenbeck, Sachs practiced it during his travels as a journeyman and joined the Nuremberg Meistersinger guild on his return. From 1524 to 1560 he was the guild's undisputed leader; by 1560 his interest in the genre had waned, but he remained the venerated master up to his death.

While in the *Hauptsingen* (Main Singing) part of the competition the Meistersinger concentrated on versifying Luther's translation of the Bible, in the *Freisingen* (Free Singing) part they treated a wide range of topics, from the sober and serious to the humorous and farcical, from ancient to modern, and from literary to anecdotal. All creation became the stuff of Sachs's songs. His curiosity was insatiable and his reading enormous, as is evidenced both by his sizable library and by the list of ancient, medieval, and contemporary sources on which he drew: Pliny, Plutarch, Ovid, Giovanni Boccaccio's *The Decameron* (1351–1353), the *Gesta Romanorum* (1472), Heinrich Steinhöwel's *Aesop* (1477), Herman Bote's *Dil Ulenspiegel* (1510 or 1511; translated, 1518), Johannes Pauli's *Schimpf und Ernst* (Jest and Seriousness, 1522), farces, histories, and chronicles. In reworking the themes found in these works Sachs skillfully sharpened points and condensed or expanded the stories. In the force of his personality, his indefatigable energy, his tuneful melodies, and his adroit handling of hundreds of meters he stood head and shoulders above his colleagues. His thousands of unprinted Meisterlieder still await analysis.

Although Sachs is known as the outstanding Meistersinger of Nuremberg, it is doubtful whether any of his Meisterlieder are actually read or sung today. His Fastnachtspiele, on the other hand, are still read and performed. The plays were an integral part of the pre-Lenten carnival celebrations, a time of ribaldry and boisterousness in which the world was turned upside down. Costumed journeymen went from street to street and from pub to pub performing skits that poked fun at social conventions. Among pre-Reformation Nuremberg carnival playwrights, the best known are Hans Rosenplüt and Hans Folz. Sachs surpassed his predecessors and contemporaries not only in the quantity but also in the quality of his plays. He wrote more than eighty Fastnachtspiele between 1517 and 1566—three-quarters of them between 1550 and 1560, a decade of unparalleled productivity during which he also wrote ninety-four comedies and tragedies, remained an active Meistersinger, commented on current events in Spruchgedichte, and practiced his trade as a shoemaker.

Though he wrote two carnival plays before the Reformation, Sachs did not really begin his career as an author of such plays until the mid 1530s. With the official introduction of the Reformation in 1525 the council abolished Lent, the season of penitence and fasting; thus, the pre-Lenten carnival, a time of officially sanctioned ribaldry, lost its meaning and came to be considered an undesirable interruption of work and a threat to morality, health, and the economy. For Sachs, the carnival plays assumed a didactic as well as an entertaining function; each of his plays ends with a moral.

Reliance on reason and the power of the mind, as well as belief in the improvability of humanity, lie at the core of Sachs's anthropology and of his self-concept as a poet: the poet's function is to help the individual to see his or her own foolishness. Whether Sachs used literary sources or drew on his own observations, he created a colorful crowd of figures: greedy merchants, simple-minded peasants, pathologically jealous husbands, wives who cheat on their husbands with the help of cunning matchmakers, young widows who console themselves with young lovers, and sexually deprived priests. There are cases of mistaken identity, intrigues, and, again and again, the theme of the deceived deceiver. Marriage, with its daily frictions, jealousies, and large and small deceptions, is an inexhaustible topic. Among Sachs's best-known carnival plays are *Das Narren schneiden* (The Foolectomy, 1536), *Der farendt Schuler im Paradeiss* (The Traveling Scholar in Paradise, 1550; translated as *The Travelling Scholar*, 1910), *Das Kelberbrüten* (1551; translated as *The Calf-Hatching*, 1990), *Das heyß eysen* (1551; translated as *The Hot Iron*, 1910), *Der bös rauch* (The Evil Smoke, 1551), *Der roßdieb zw Fünsing* (The Horse Thief of Fünsing, 1553; translated as *The Horse Thief*, 1910), and *Der Kremer Korb* (The Merchant's Basket, 1554). Of the thousands of works by Sachs, only his carnival plays have been translated into English.

Sachs also achieved undisputed mastery in the genre of the *Schwank* (farce). As in the carnival plays, with which the farces share many thematic and functional similarities, Sachs's message is a plea for tolerance and forgiveness. His laughter at the many foibles of his fellow human beings is mostly good-natured, rarely ironic, never sarcastic. Unlike the pessimist Sebastian Brant, whose *Das Narrenschiff* (The Ship of Fools, 1494; translated, 1509) held up a merciless mirror to his contemporaries, and Thomas Murner, whose *Narren bschwerung* (Exorcism of Fools, 1512) and *Der schelmen zunfft* (The Rogues' Guild, 1512) castigate his time in sharp words, Sachs tries to bring his contemporaries to a recognition of their mistakes and shortcomings through laughter.

Less well known today are Sachs's 128 tragedies and comedies, written to provide moral guidance and to contribute, as Sachs himself said, "zu anraitzung der guten tugendt unnd zu abschneidung der schendlichen laster" (to encourage good virtue and to cut out the bad vices). Drawing on the Bible and on ancient and medieval literature, each play follows the same pattern: a *Herolt* (announcer) greets the audience, names the literary source, briefly sums up the plot, and points to the moral. As in Bertolt Brecht's epic theater, the spectator is not allowed to be caught up in the action. The plot jumps boldly from place to place, occasionally from country to country, and extends over weeks, months, and sometimes decades. Unlike the carnival plays, the tragedies and comedies consist of acts, ranging from one to ten. After the actors exit, the Herolt reappears and establishes links between the play and the situation of contemporary Nuremberg. Since Sachs's primary intention was moral guidance, his characters are not unique individuals with all their contradictions and inner conflicts but paradigms for right and wrong behavior: a person is either good or bad. To get the audience to identify with the characters, Sachs gives them the features of burghers of sixteenth-century Nuremberg. This *Vernürnbergern* (Nurembergizing), as the nineteenth-century philosopher Georg Wilhelm Friedrich Hegel mockingly termed it, makes good, industrious, honest Nurembergers, or their opposites, out of Adam and Eve, Cain and Abel, the Old Testament prophets and patriarchs, the Homeric heroes, the half-mythical and historical figures of Livy, and the heroes of the chapbooks. The tragedies and comedies include *Tragedia von schöpfung, fal und auβtreibung Ade auβ dem paradeyβ*; (Tragedy of the Creation, Fall and Expulsion of Adam from Paradise, 1548), *Der wütrich könig Herodes* (The Tyrant King Herod, 1552), *Die mördisch königin Clitimestra* (The Murderous Queen Clytemnestra, 1554), *Tragedia könig Sauls* (The Tragedy of King Saul, 1557), *Von Alexander Magno* (Of Alexander the Great, 1558), *Die gedultig und gehorsam margräfin Griselda* (The Patient and Obedient Margravine Griselda, 1546), *Die ungeleichen kinder Eve* (The Unequal Children of Eve, 1553), *Tragedia des Jüngsten Geriechts* (The Trag-

edy of the Last Judgment, 1560), and *Die jung witfraw Francisca* (The Young Widow Francisca, 1560); with the exception of *Tragedia des Jüngsten Geriechts,* they were all first printed in the Nuremberg Folio editions.

All of Sachs's works, except the Meisterlieder and, of course, the prose dialogues, are written in *Knittelvers,* a rhymed couplet consisting of four stressed syllables and four to eleven unstressed syllables. That not every line is a masterpiece is not surprising, considering the enormous scope of Sachs's oeuvre: it is estimated that he wrote about half a million lines. But his mastery of this confining meter is superior to that of any other poet of the sixteenth century.

His awareness of his advancing age, along with a sense that his inspiration was drying up and the fear that his works might be dispersed and forgotten, prompted Sachs to edit and collect his works. The first volume appeared in 1558, volumes two and three in 1560 and 1561, and volumes four and five posthumously in 1578 and 1579. His *Generalregister,* a list of the fifty-four hundred works he had written to that time, also belongs to this period of personal and poetic stocktaking. The process was simplified by the fact that Sachs had, over the decades, faithfully copied all of his texts in thirty-three volumes. In the midst of this undertaking he lost his wife; he paid her a moving tribute in *Der wunderliche traum von meiner abgeschiden lieben gemahel Künigundt Sächsin* (The Strange Dream of My Dear Departed Wife Kunigunde Sachs, 1560; printed in Folio III). A year and a half later Sachs married Barbara Endres, née Harscher, a twenty-seven-year-old widow. Practical considerations may have been the primary reason for this alliance: she had six children and a small inheritance; he needed an efficient manager for his household, with its apprentices and journeymen. Barbara restored his optimism, revitalized his creativity, and turned the sixty-seven-year-old Sachs into a love poet. *Das künstlich frawen-lob* (The Artistic Praise of Women, 1562; printed in Folio V, 1579), a poetic homage to his young wife, is one of the most beautiful lyrical poems to come from his pen. After a description of her anatomical charms that approaches indiscretion, he hastens to add her chastity, humility, fidelity, and modesty to his portrayal.

In 1568 Sachs, at the request of the Frankfurt publisher Sigmund Feyerabend, collaborated on a book describing contemporary professions, trades, and crafts in word and picture. For each of the 117 woodcuts by Jost Amman, Sachs contributed four rhymed couplets sketching the artisan's work process and products or the human or mythological inventors of the craft. Published under the title *Eygentliche Beschreibung Aller Stnde auff Erden* (Exact Description of All Ranks on Earth, 1568; translated as *The Book of Trades,* 1973), it allows

Sachs, once again, to condemn egotism and *Müssiggang* (indolent leisure) and to emphasize a community-oriented work ethic. Today the work is a valuable document for the social history of sixteenth-century Germany.

Sachs died on 19 January 1576. He was buried outside the city gates in the Cemetery of Saint John. His grave site is not known.

Although Hans Sachs was never totally forgotten, the literary climate of the two centuries after his death did not favor artisan-poets. The ideal had become the *poeta doctus* (learned poet), who had studied the literary traditions of the Romans and Greeks at a university and composed poems after Latin and French models. A new appreciation of the Nuremberg poet began in Weimar on the two-hundredth anniversary of his death, when Christoph Martin Wieland dedicated a special issue of his *Teutscher Merkur* to Sachs; it featured an essay by Wieland and a poem by Johann Wolfgang von Goethe, "Hans Sachsens poetische Sendung" (Hans Sachs's Poetic Mission). For the Romantics, the image of the upright cobbler-poet merged with that of an idealized Nuremberg with its maze of medieval streets. In the nineteenth century Sachs became the subject of poems, dramas, and operas, of which Wagner's is the best and the one that has shaped the modern image of Sachs. The Sachs renaissance reached its high point in 1894 when Nuremberg celebrated the four-hundredth birthday of its native son with pageantry, essays, books, and speeches. Glorified as the pious, hardworking, patriotic, and loyal German, he became a model for the good citizen of Wilhelminian Germany.

Bibliographies:

Emil Weller, *Der Volksdichter Hans Sachs und seine Dichtungen: Eine Bibliographie* (Nuremberg: Sichling, 1868); republished, with a supplement, "Die Bibliothek Hans Sachs," by Erich Carlsohn (Wiesbaden: Martin Sändig, 1966);

Niklas Holzberg, *Hans-Sachs-Bibliographie: Schriftenverzeichnis zum 400-jährigen Todestag im Jahr 1976* (Nuremberg: Selbstverlag der Stadtbibliothek Nürnberg, 1976);

Holzberg, "Nachtrag zur Hans-Sachs-Bibliographie," *Mitteilungen des Vereins für Geschichte der Stadt Nürnberg,* 64 (1977): 333–343.

Biographies:

Salomon Ranisch, *Historisch-kritische Lebensbeschreibung Hanns Sachsens, ehemals berühmten Meistersängers zu Nürnberg* (Altenburg, 1765);

Charles Schweitzer, *Un poète allemand au XVI siècle: Étude sur la vie et les oeuvres de Hans Sachs* (Paris: Berger-Levrault, 1887);

Rudolph Genée, *Hans Sachs und seine Zeit* (Leipzig: Weber, 1894);

Klaus Wedler, *Hans Sachs* (Leipzig: Reclam, 1976);

Eckhard Bernstein, *Hans Sachs: Mit Selbstzeugnissen und Bilddokumenten* (Reinbek: Rowohlt, 1993).

References:

Roland Bainton, "Eyn wunderliche Weyssagung: Osiander–Sachs–Luther," *Germanic Review,* 21 (1946): 161–164;

Bernd Balzer, *Bürgerliche Reformationspropaganda: Die Flugschriften des Hans Sachs in den Jahren 1523–1525* (Stuttgart: Metzler, 1973);

Anne-Kathrin Brandt, *Die "tugentreich fraw Armut": Besitz und Armut in der Tugendlehre des Hans Sachs* (Göttingen: Gratia, 1979);

Neil C. Brooks, "The Artisan and Mastersinger Drama in Nürnberg," *Journal of English and Germanic Philology,* 17 (1918): 565–584;

Horst Brunner, Gerhard Hirschmann, and Fritz Schnelbögl, eds., *Hans Sachs und Nürnberg* (Nuremberg: Selbstverlag des Vereins für Geschichte der Stadt Nürnberg, 1976);

Eckehard Catholy, *Das deutsche Lustspiel* (Stuttgart: Kohlhammer, 1969), pp. 49–75;

Catholy, *Fastnachtspiel* (Stuttgart: Metzler, 1966);

Thomas Cramer and Erika Kartschoke, eds., *Hans Sachs: Studien zur frühbürgerlichen Literatur im 16. Jahrhundert* (Bern, Frankfurt am Main & Las Vegas: Peter Lang, 1978);

Ferdinand Eichler, *Das Nachleben des Hans Sachs vom XVI. bis ins XIX. Jahrhundert* (Leipzig: Harrassowitz, 1904);

Stephan Füssel and others, eds., *Hans Sachs: Katalog zur Ausstellung,* second edition (Göttingen: Gratia, 1979);

Eugen Geiger, *Der Meistergesang des Hans Sachs: Literarhistorische Untersuchung* (Bern: Francke, 1956);

Germanisches Nationalmuseum, ed., *Hans Sachs und die Meistersinger in ihrer Zeit* (Nuremberg: Germanisches Nationalmuseum, 1981);

Joseph E. Gillert, "The German Dramatist of the Sixteenth Century and the Bible," *PMLA,* 34 (1919): 465–493;

Reinhard Hahn, "Hans Sachs," in *Deutsche Dichter der frühen Neuzeit 1450–1600,* edited by Füssel (Berlin: Erich Schmidt, 1993), pp. 406–427;

Samuel Kinser, "Presentation and Representation: Carnival at Nuremberg 1450–1550," *Representations,* 13 (1986): 141;

Barbara Könneker, *Hans Sachs* (Stuttgart: Metzler, 1971);

Könneker, "Hans Sachs: Die Wittembergisch Nachtigall und die Reformationsdialoge," in her *Die deutsche Literatur der Reformationszeit: Kommentar zu einer Epoche* (Munich: Beck, 1975), pp. 148–157;

Helmut Krause, *Die Dramen des Hans Sachs: Untersuchungen zur Lehre und Technik* (Berlin: Hofgarten, 1979);

Georg F. Lussky, "The Structure of Hans Sachs' Fastnachtspiele in Relation to Their Place of Performance," *Journal of English and Germanic Philology,* 26 (1927): 521–565;

George R. Marek, "Nuremberg's Cobbler Poet," *Opera News,* 41 (18 December 1976): 1920;

Wolfgang F. Michael, *Das deutsche Drama der Reformationszeit* (Bern, Frankfurt am Main & Las Vegas: Peter Lang, 1984), pp. 323–356;

Bert Nagel, *Meistersang,* second edition (Stuttgart: Metzler, 1971);

Franz Otten, *Mit hilff gottes zw tichten . . . got zw lob und zw auspreittung seines heilsamen wort: Untersuchungen zur Reformationsdichtung des Hans Sachs* (Göppingen: Kümmerle, 1993);

Gerhard Pfeiffer, ed., *Nürnberg–Geschichte einer europäischen Stadt* (Munich: Beck, 1971), pp. 199–211;

Ralf Erik Remshardt, "The Birth of Reason from the Spirit of Carnival: Hans Sachs und Das Narrenschneyden," *Comparative Drama,* 23 (1989): 70–94;

Maximilian J. Rudwin, "The Origin of the German Carnival Comedy," *Journal of English and Germanic Philology,* 18 (1919): 402–454;

Richard Erich Schade, *Studies in Early German Comedy: 1500–1650* (Columbia, S.C.: Camden House, 1988);

Gottfried Seebass, "The Reformation in Nürnberg," in *The Social History of the Reformation,* edited by Lawrence P. Buck and Jonathan W. Zophy (Columbus: Ohio State University Press, 1972), pp. 1740;

Eli Sobel, "Martin Luther and Hans Sachs," *Michigan Germanic Studies,* 10 (1984): 129–141;

Ingeborg Spriewald, "Der Bürger ergreift das Wort: Luther und die Reformation im Werk von Hans Sachs," *Weimarer Beitrge,* 29 (1983): 1908–1927;

Spriewald, *Literatur zwischen Hören und Lesen: Wandel von Funktion und Rezeption im späten Mittelalter: Fallstudien zu Behaim, Folz und Sachs* (Berlin & Weimar: Aufbau, 1990);

Gerald Strauss, *Nuremberg in the Sixteenth Century: City Politics and Life Between Middle Ages and Modern Times* (Bloomington & London: Indiana University Press, 1976);

Archer Taylor, *The Literary History of Meistergesang* (New York & London: Oxford University Press, 1937);

Martin W. Walsh, "Quacks, Empirics, Spiritual Physicians: The Dramatic Function of the Medicus in the 15th and 16th Century Fastnachtspiele," *Fifteenth Century Studies,* 8 (1983): 239–274;

Friedrich Windolph, *Der Reiseweg Hans Sachsens in seiner Handwerksburschenzeit nach seinen eigenen Dichtungen* (Greifswald: Adler, 1911);

Dieter Wuttke, *Nuremberg: Focal Point of German Culture and History,* second edition (Bamberg: Wendel, 1988).

Papers:

Hans Sachs copied all of his *Meisterlieder* in sixteen volumes, of which seven have been lost; eight (numbers 2, 3, 4, 5, 8, 12, 13, and 15) are in the Ratsarchiv Zwickau, and one is in the Stadtbibliothek Nürnberg (Amb. 2° 784). Sachs also copied his *Spruchgedichte* in eighteen volumes; seven of these volumes have been lost, six (numbers 4, 11, 12, 13, and 16) are in the Ratsarchiv Zwickau, one is in the Staatsbibliothek Preußischer Kulturbesitz Berlin (Ms germ. 2° 591), one is in the Sächsische Landesbibliothek Dresden (M10*), two are in the Museum of German History Berlin (RA 52/3470), and one is in the Stadtbibliothek Nürnberg (Am 2° 784). The Ratsarchiv Zwickau also has, in Sachs's hand, a list of all of his works (the *Generalregister*), a list of the books he owned, and the *Singschulordnung* (statutes of the Nuremberg Meistersinger Guild) of 1540.

Friedrich Schiller

(10 November 1759 – 9 May 1805)

John D. Simons
Florida State University

This entry originally appeared in DLB 94: German Writers in the Age of Goethe:
Sturm und Drang to Classicism.

BOOKS: *Versuch über den Zusammenhang der thierischen Natur des Menschen mit seiner geistigen: Eine Abhandlung welche in höchster Gegenwart Sr. Herzoglichen Durchlaucht, während den öffentlichen akademischen Prüfungen vertheidigen wird Johann Christoph Friedrich Schiller, Kandidat der Medizin in der Herzoglichen Militair-Akademie* (Stuttgart: Cotta, 1780); translated by Kenneth Dewhurst and Nigel Reeves as "An Essay on the Connection between the Animal and Spiritual Nature of Man," in their *Friedrich Schiller: Medicine, Psychology, and Literature* (Berkeley: University of California Press, 1978), pp. 253–285;

Die Räuber: Ein Schauspiel, anonymous (Frankfurt am Main & Leipzig: Privately printed, 1781); revised as *Die Räuber: Ein Trauerspiel. Neue für die Mannheimer Bühne verbesserte Auflage,* as Schiller (Mannheim: Schwan, 1782); revised as *Die Räuber: Ein Schauspiel in fünf Akten* (Frankfurt am Main & Leipzig: Löffler, 1782); translated by Alexander F. Tytler as *The Robbers* (London: Robinson, 1792; New York: Printed for S. Campbell, 1793);

Elegie auf den frühzeitigen Tod Johann Christian Weckerlins: Von seinen Freunden, anonymous (Stuttgart: Mäntler, 1781);

Der Venuswagen, anonymous (Stuttgart: Metzler, 1781);

Anthologie auf das Jahr 1782, anonymous (Tobolsko: Gedruckt in der Buchdruckerei, 1782);

Todenfeyer am Grabe des hochwohlgebornen Herrn, HERRN Philipp Friderich von Rieger, Generalmajors und Chefs eines Infanterie-Bataillons, Kommandanten der Vestung Hohenasperg, und des herzoglich militairischen St. Karls Ordens Ritters, welcher im sechzigsten Jahr seines Alters am 15 ten May 1782 zu Hohenasperg an einem Schlagflusse seelig verschied, und den 18 ten des Monats feierlich zur Erde bestattet wurde, Ihm zum Ehrendenkmal geweyht von sämmtlicher Herzoglich-Wirtembergischen Generalität, anonymous (Stuttgart: Erhard, 1782);

*Friedrich Schiller; painting by Anton Graff, circa 1786–1791
(Deutsche Fotothek, Dresden)*

Die Verschwörung des Fiesko zu Genua: Ein republikanisches Trauerspiel (Mannheim: Schwan, 1783); translated by George Henry Noehden and Sir John Stoddart as *Fiesco; or, The Genoese Conspiracy* (London: Johnson, 1796);

Kabale und Liebe: Ein bürgerliches Trauerspiel in fünf Aufzügen (Mannheim: Schwan, 1784); translated by Matthew Gregory Lewis as *The Minister: A Tragedy in Five Acts* (London: Bell, 1797); translation revised as *The Harper's Daughter; or, Love and Ambition* (Philadelphia: Carey, 1813);

An die Freude: Ein Rundgesang für freye Männer. Mit Musik (N.p., 1786);

Dom Karlos, Infant von Spanien (Leipzig: Göschen, 1787); translated by Noehden and Stoddart as *Don Carlos, Infant of Spain* (London: Miller, 1798);

Der Geisterseher: Eine interessante Geschichte aus den Papieren des Grafen von O*** herausgegeben aus Herrn Schillers Thalia (Berlin & Leipzig, 1788); republished as *Der Geisterseher: Eine Geschichte aus den Memoires des Grafen von O*** (Leipzig: Göschen, 1789); translated by Daniel Boileau as *The Ghost-seer; or, The Apparitionist* (London: Vernor, 1795; New York: Printed for T. & J. Swords, 1796);

Geschichte des Abfalls der vereinigten Niederlande von der Spanischen Regierung: Erster Theil enthaltend die Geschichte der Rebellionen bis zur Utrechtischen Verbindung (Leipzig: Crusius, 1788); translated by Edward Backhouse Eastwick as *History of the Defection of the United Netherlands from the Spanish Empire* (Frankfurt am Main: Krebs, 1844);

Was heißt und zu welchem Ende studiert man Universal-geschichte?: Eine akademische Antrittsrede bey Eröffnung seiner Vorlesungen gehalten von Friedrich Schiller, Professor der Geschichte in Jena (Jena: Akademische Buchhandlung, 1789);

Historischer Calender für Damen für das Jahr 1791 (–1793): Geschichte des Dreißigjährigen Kriegs, 3 volumes (Leipzig: Göschen, 1791–1793); translated by William Blaquiere as *History of the Thirty Years' War,* 2 volumes (London: Miller, 1799);

Kleinere prosaische Schriften von Schiller: Aus mehrern Zeitschriften vom Verfasser selbst gesammelt und verbessert, 4 volumes (Leipzig: Crusius, 1792–1802);

Über Anmuth und Würde: An Carl von Dalberg in Erfurth, anonymous (Leipzig: Göschen, 1793);

Gedichte, 2 volumes (Leipzig: Crusius, 1800–1803);

Wallenstein: Ein dramatisches Gedicht, 2 volumes (Tübingen: Cotta, 1800)–comprises in volume 1, *Wallensteins Lager,* translated by F. L. Gower as *The Camp of Wallenstein* (London: Murray, 1830); *Die Piccolomini,* translated by Samuel Taylor Coleridge as *The Piccolomini; or, The First Part of Wallenstein, a Drama in Five Acts* (London: Longman & Rees, 1800); as volume 2, *Wallensteins Tod,* translated by Coleridge as *The Death of Wallenstein* (London: Longman & Rees, 1800);

Maria Stuart: Ein Trauerspiel (Tübingen: Cotta, 1801); translated by Joseph C. Mellish as *Mary Stuart: A Tragedy* (London: Printed by G. Auld, 1801);

Turandot, Prinzessin von China: Ein tragicomisches Mährchen nach Gozzi (Tübingen: Cotta, 1802);

Kalendar auf das Jahr 1802: Die Jungfrau von Orleans. Eine romantische Tragödie (Berlin: Unger, 1802); translated by Henry Salvin as *The Maid of Orleans* in his *Mary Stuart and The Maid of Orleans* (London: Longman, 1824);

Die Braut von Messina oder Die feindlichen Brüder: Ein Trauerspiel mit Chören (Tübingen: Cotta, 1803); translated by G. Irvine as *The Bride of Messina* (London: Macrone, 1837);

Wilhelm Tell: Ein Schauspiel. Zum Neujahrsgeschenk auf 1805 (Tübingen: Cotta, 1804); translated anonymously as *William Tell* (London: Bull, 1829);

Die Huldigung der Künste: Ein lyrisches Spiel (Tübingen: Cotta, 1805); translated by A. I. du Pont Coleman as "Homage to the Arts" in *The German Classics of the Nineteenth and Twentieth Centuries,* volume 3, edited by Kuno Francke and William G. Howard (New York: German Publication Society, 1913), pp. 366–377;

Theater, 5 volumes (Tübingen: Cotta, 1805–1807);

Friedrich v. Schillers sämmtliche Werke, 12 volumes, edited by Christian Gottfried Körner (Stuttgart & Tübingen: Cotta, 1812-1815; revised, 1835);

Schiller's erste bis jetzt unbekannte Jugendschrift: Die Tugend in ihren Folgen betrachtet. Rede zur Feier des Geburtsfestes der Frau Reichsgräfin von Hohenheim auf gnädigsten Befehl Seiner Herzoglichen Durchlaucht verfertigt vom Eleve Schiller (Amberg: Klöber, 1839);

Nachlese zu Schillers Werken nebst Variantensammlung: Aus seinem Nachlaß, 4 volumes, edited by Karl Hoffmeister (Stuttgart & Tübingen: Cotta, 1840–1841);

Aventuren des neuen Telemachs oder Leben und Exsertionen Koerners des decenten, consequenten, piquanten u.s.f. von Hogarth in schönen illuminierten Kupfern abgefaßt und mit befriedigenden Erklärungen versehen von Winkelmann: Rom, 1786, drawings by Schiller, texts by Ludwig Ferdinand Huber, edited by Carl Künzel (Leipzig: Payne, 1862);

Ich habe mich rasieren lassen: Ein dramatischer Scherz, edited by Künzel (Leipzig: Payne, 1862);

Schillers dramatische Entwürfe zum erstenmal veröffentlicht durch Schillers Tochter, edited by Emilie Freifrau von Gleichen-Rußwurm (Stuttgart: Cotta, 1867);

Schillers sämmtliche Schriften: Historisch-kritische Ausgabe, 16 volumes, edited by Karl Goedeke and others (Stuttgart: Cotta, 1867–1876);

Schiller's Werke: Nach den vorzüglichen Quellen revidirte Ausgabe, 16 volumes (Berlin: Hempel, 1868–1874);

Aus dem Schiller-Archiv: Ungedrucktes und unbekanntes zu Schillers Leben und Schriften, edited by J. Minor (Weimar: Böhlau, 1890);

Deutsche Größe: Ein unvollendetes Gedicht Schillers. 1801. Nachbildung der Handschrift im Auftrage des Vorstandes der Goethe-Gesellschaft, edited by Bernhard Suphan (Weimar, 1902);

Sämtliche Werke: Säkular-Ausgabe in sechzehn Bänden, 16 volumes, edited by E. von der Hellen (Stuttgart: Cotta, 1904–1905);

Werke: Nationalausgabe. Im Auftrag des Goethe-und Schiller-Archivs, des Schiller-Nationalmuseums und der Deutschen Akademie, 35 volumes to date, edited by Julius Petersen and Gerhard Fricke (Weimar: Böhlau, 1943–);

Sämtliche Werke, 5 volumes, edited by Fricke, Herbert G. Göpfert, and Herbert Stubenrauch (Munich: Hanser, 1958–1960).

Editions in English: *Historical Works,* 2 volumes, translated by George Moir (Edinburgh: Constable / London: Hurst, 1828);

Philosophical and Aesthetic Letters, translated by Joseph Weiss (London: Chapman, 1844);

Essays: The Aesthetic Letters, Essays, and the Philosophical Letters, translated by Weiss (Boston: Little, Brown, 1845);

Works, Historical and Dramatic, 4 volumes (London: Bohn, 1846–1849; New York: Harper, 1855);

Poems of Schiller, Complete, Including All His Early Suppressed Poems, translated by Edgar Alfred Bowring (London: Parker, 1851; revised edition, London: Bell, 1874, New York: Lovell, 1884);

Complete Works, 2 volumes, edited by Carl J. Hempel (Philadelphia: Kohler, 1861; revised, 1870);

Essays Aesthetical and Philosophical: Translated by Various Hands (London: Bell, 1875);

The Revolt of the United Netherlands, translated by Alexander James W. Morrison (London: Bell, 1889);

Works, 7 volumes (London: Bell, 1897–1903);

"The Sport of Destiny," translated by Marian Klopfer, in *Great German Short Novels and Stories,* edited by Victor Lange (New York: Random House, 1952), pp. 100–109;

William Tell, translated by Sidney E. Kaplan (Woodbury, N.Y.: Barron's Educational Series, 1954);

Wallenstein: A Historical Drama in Three Parts, translated by Charles E. Passage (London: Owen, 1958; New York: Ungar, 1958; revised edition, New York: Ungar, 1960);

Mary Stuart: A Tragedy, translated by Sophie Wilkins (Woodbury, N.Y.: Barron's Educational Series, 1959);

The Maiden of Orleans: A Romantic Tragedy, translated by John T. Krumpelmann (Chapel Hill: University of North Carolina Press, 1959; revised, 1962);

Don Carlos, Infante of Spain, translated by Passage (New York: Ungar, 1959);

Friedrich Schiller: An Anthology for Our Time, in New English Translations and the Original German. With an Account of His Life and Work by Frederick Ungar, translated by Passage, Jane Bannard Greene, and Alexander Godevon Aesch (New York: Ungar, 1959);

Mary Stuart; The Maid of Orleans: Two Historical Plays, translated by Passage (New York: Ungar, 1961);

The Bride of Messina; or, The Enemy Brothers: A Tragedy with Choruses; William Tell; Demetrius; or, The Blood Wedding in Moscow: A Fragment, translated by Passage (New York: Ungar, 1962);

Love and Intrigue; or, Louisa Miller, translated by Frederick Rolf (Great Neck, N.Y.: Barron's Educational Series, 1962);

Wilhelm Tell: A Verse Translation, translated by Gilbert J. Jordan (Indianapolis: Bobbs-Merrill, 1964);

On the Aesthetic Education of Man, in a Series of Letters, translated by Reginald Snell (New York: Ungar, 1965);

Naive and Sentimental Poetry, and On the Sublime: Two Essays, translated by Julius A. Elias (New York: Ungar, 1967);

On the Aesthetic Education of Man, in a Series of Letters, edited and translated by Elizabeth M. Wilkinson and Leonard A. Willoughby (Oxford: Clarendon Press, 1968);

Wilhelm Tell, translated by John Prudhoe (Manchester, U.K.: Manchester University Press / New York: Barnes & Noble, 1970);

Intrigue and Love: A Bourgeois Tragedy, translated by Passage (New York: Ungar, 1971);

William Tell, translated by William F. Mainland (Chicago & London: University of Chicago Press, 1972);

"The Philosophy of Physiology," translated by Kenneth Dewhurst and Nigel Reeves in their *Friedrich Schiller: Medicine, Psychology, and Literature* (Berkeley: University of California Press, 1978), pp. 149–167;

Love and Intrigue, translated and edited by Johanna Setzer and Elaine Gottesmann (Flushing, N.Y.: Setzer-Gottesmann, 1978);

The Robbers; Wallenstein, translated by F. J. Lamport (Harmondsworth, U.K. & New York: Penguin, 1979);

On the Naive and Sentimental in Literature, translated by Helen Wantanabe-O'Kelly (Manchester, U.K.: Carcanet New Press, 1981);

Plays, edited by Walter Hinderer (New York: Continuum, 1983).

OTHER: *Wirtembergisches Repertorium der Litteratur: Eine Vierteljahr-Schrift,* 2 volumes, edited by Schiller (N.p., 1782);

Rheinische Thalia: Erstes Heft, edited by Schiller (Mannheim: Auf dasigem kaiserl. freien R. Postamt & Schwan, 1785);

Thalia, 12 volumes, edited by Schiller (Leipzig: Göschen, 1786–1791);

Geschichte der merkwürdigsten Rebellionen und Verschwörungen aus den mittleren und neuern Zeiten: Bearbeitet von verschiedenen Verfassern. Erster Band, edited by Schiller (Leipzig: Crusius, 1788);

Euripides, *Iphigenie in Aulis: Ein Trauerspiel in fünf Aufzügen. Aus dem Griechischen,* translated by Schiller (Cologne: Langen, 1790);

Allgemeine Sammlung historischer Memoires vom zwölften Jahrhundert bis auf die neuesten Zeiten durch mehrere Verfasser übersetzt, mit den nöthigen Anmerkungen versehen, und jedesmal mit einer universalhistorischen Uebersicht begleitet, edited by Schiller, 7 volumes (Jena: Mauke, 1790–1792);

Geschichte des Maltheserordens nach Vertot von M. N. bearbeitet, 2 volumes, foreword by Schiller (Jena: Cuno, 1792–1793);

Merkwürdige Rechtsfälle als ein Beitrag zur Geschichte der Menschheit: Nach dem französischen Werk des Pitaval durch mehrere Verfasser ausgearbeitet und mit einer Vorrede begleitet, 4 volumes, edited by Schiller (Jena: Cuno, 1792–1795);

Neue Thalia, 4 volumes, edited by Schiller (Leipzig: Göschen, 1792–1793);

Die Horen: Eine Monatsschrift, 12 volumes, edited by Schiller (Tübingen: Cotta, 1795–1797);

Musen-Almanach für das Jahr 1796, edited by Schiller (Neustrelitz: Michaelis, 1796);

Musen-Almanach für das Jahr 1797, edited by Schiller (Tübingen: Cotta, 1797);

Musen-Almanach für das Jahr 1798, edited by Schiller (Tübingen: Cotta, 1798);

Musen-Almanach für das Jahr 1799, edited by Schiller (Tübingen: Cotta, 1799);

Musen-Almanach für das Jahr 1800, edited by Schiller (Tübingen: Cotta, 1800);

William Shakespeare, *Macbeth: Ein Trauerspiel,* translated and adapted by Schiller (Tübingen: Cotta, 1801);

Jean Racine, *Phädra: Trauerspiel,* translated by Schiller (Tübingen: Cotta, 1805);

Louis-Benoit Picard, *Der Parasit oder Die Kunst sein Glück zu machen: Ein Lustspiel nach dem Französischen,* adapted by Schiller (Tübingen: Cotta, 1806);

Picard, *Der Neffe als Onkel: Lustspiel in drey Aufzügen. Aus dem Französischen,* translated by Schiller (Tübingen: Cotta, 1807);

Johann Wolfgang von Goethe, *Goethe's Egmont für die Bühne bearbeitet,* adapted by Schiller (Stuttgart & Augsburg: Cotta, 1857).

A universal genius generally regarded as the greatest German dramatist, Friedrich Schiller dominates a period of German literary history as no one else

before or since. Schiller revealed more vividly than any of his predecessors the power of drama and poetry to convey a philosophy; his works contain the strongest assertions of human freedom and dignity and the worth of the individual in all German literature. After his death he rapidly became part of the cultural environment: streets and schools were named after him, statues and monuments were raised to his memory, his birthday was declared a national holiday, and his major works became part of the educational curriculum.

To modern English-speaking people the mystique surrounding Schiller may seem hard to fathom. Yet to study how Germans perceive Schiller is to study how they perceive themselves. He appeared at a time when German literature was dominated by the monumental achievements of England, France, and Italy; there was even serious debate about whether the German language was a fit vehicle for literary expression. Schiller furnished proof of Germany's high cultural achievement. His stature was recognized even in his lifetime: on 17 September 1801 he attended a performance of his *Kalendar auf das Jahr 1802: Die Jungfrau von Orleans. Eine romantische Tragödie* (1802; translated as *The Maid of Orleans,* 1824) at Leipzig. After the first act the audience exploded in shouts of "Es lebe Schiller!" (Long live Schiller), accompanied by cheers and applause. After the curtain fell on the last act, he was treated to a standing ovation. When he appeared at the exit, the throng fell silent. Baring their heads, they parted so as to form a corridor for him to pass. Here and there a parent lifted up a child and pointed out the honored man. Schiller had become, and remains, an icon.

Johann Christoph Friedrich Schiller was born in obscurity on 10 November 1759 in Marbach. His father, Johann Kaspar Schiller, was a captain in the army of Karl Eugen, duke of Württemberg. In 1749 he had married Elisabeth Dorothea Kodweiß, the daughter of a Marbach innkeeper. Though a captain's salary was not large, it provided the family with a modest standard of living and a happy home environment for the future poet. In later years Schiller looked back on his childhood as an idyllic time of simplicity and serenity. In 1762 the family moved to Ludwigsburg. In 1763 Johann Kaspar was sent to Schwäbisch-Gmünd as recruiting officer; the family followed in 1764. To save money they decided to live in the nearby hamlet of Lorch on the Rems. In 1766 the captain was posted back to Ludwigsburg. From 1767 to 1773 Schiller attended the local Latin school, where he received instruction in religion, Latin, Greek, Hebrew, and German.

Schiller's ambition in these early years was to become a clergyman. It was planned that he should attend the monastery school at Blaubeuren and then complete his studies at the Tübinger Stift (Tübinger

Seminary). These plans were abruptly terminated in 1773 when the duke, who was absolute dictator in all but name, forced the thirteen-year-old to enroll in his newly established military academy at Solitude, two miles west of Stuttgart. Founded in 1770 as the Militärwaisenhaus (Military Orphanage), the school had been renamed the Militär Pflanzschule (Military Cadet School) in 1771. As the duke's pedagogical designs became more grandiose, he moved the school to Stuttgart in 1775 and changed its name to the Herzogliche Militärakademie (Ducal Military Academy). The institution was generally known as the "Karlsschule" (Karl's School).

Thus began for Schiller eight grueling years of rigid discipline and petty rules. Cadets were forbidden to leave the school, receive visitors, or write letters; their activities were organized and monitored around the clock. This experience left its mark on Schiller's personality and on his literary productions. His hostility toward and contempt for arbitrary political power and despotic rulers runs like a leitmotif throughout his works.

The Karlsschule offered several subjects in which students could specialize. Schiller first chose law, then transferred to medicine when that subject was added in 1775. Determined to make his school the envy of Germany, Karl Eugen hired the best teachers he could find; consequently, Schiller received an excellent education. In addition to courses in medicine and military science, he received instruction in Greek, Latin, French, English, classical mythology, theology, philosophy, history, literature, physics, chemistry, botany, and mathematics. Since the Karlsschule aimed at producing officers and gentlemen, students received instruction in dance, horsemanship, fencing, and court etiquette. When Schiller graduated he would have the intellectual training and social graces necessary for entry into polite society.

In 1779 Schiller completed his course work and submitted a dissertation, "Die Philosophie der Physiologie" (translated as "The Philosophy of Physiology," 1978). The committee rejected it, primarily because he had had the temerity to dispute the teachings of some traditional authorities. Schiller was particularly incensed when told that he would have to spend another year at the school. In 1780 his second dissertation, *Versuch über den Zusammenhang der Rierischen Natur des Menschen mit seiner geistigen* (1780; translated as "An Essay on the Connection between the Animal and Spiritual Nature of Man," 1978), was accepted, and he was allowed to graduate and take up his duties as a regimental surgeon in Stuttgart. Since the Karlsschule was not a university Schiller could not be granted the title M.D. with the license to practice medicine; instead, he was

something like a paramedic, a position of little pay and less prestige. Schiller realized that all he could look forward to was the distasteful life of servitude laid out for him by the duke.

Schiller was delivered from his misery by his first drama, *Die Räuber* (1781; translated as *The Robbers*, 1792). Little is known about the genesis of the play other than that he had begun work on it when still a teenager. Once he was free of the academy he concentrated his energy and finished it in 1781. Unable to find a publisher, he borrowed the money and paid for the printing himself. Because of its many inflammatory passages, he decided to publish it anonymously outside the duchy. A vital, energetic, and troubling work, it soon caught the eye of Wolfgang Heribert von Dalberg, director of the Mannheim National Theater in the neighboring duchy of Hesse, who decided to bring it to the stage. Schiller left his post in Stuttgart without leave to attend the premiere on 13 January 1782. The play was a sensation. Much of its appeal resides in Schiller's choice of the archetypal theme of hostile brothers. The jealous and greedy Franz von Moor tricks his father, the ruling count, into disinheriting his elder brother, Karl, who is away at the university. He then imprisons his father and seizes the land and title for himself and tries to terrorize Karl's beloved, Amalia, into concubinage. Learning of his disinheritance, Karl drops out of school and becomes the leader of a band of robbers. No ordinary hoodlum, he is consumed by a demonic craving for justice; he has the noble but misguided notion that he can right the wrongs of the world by taking the law into his own hands. The frightening violence that attends each raid begins to plague his conscience. His final catastrophic effort to bring his brother to justice ends in Franz's suicide and the deaths of the count, Amalia, and Karl's closest friend. In the end Karl realizes that he has done more harm than good. His last act, turning himself in to the police, amounts to a cry from the heart for lost ideals.

The drama introduces two themes that were to occupy Schiller for the rest of his life. The first is that of the criminal hero, the man inspired by lofty goals who employs immoral methods to achieve them. The second is that of the idealistic reformer betrayed by institutionalized hypocrisy and greed; in his hero's fall Schiller consistently underscores the futility inherent in the pursuit of ideals. The play also reveals Schiller's innate grasp of what constitutes drama. As a piece of stagecraft *Die Räuber* has it all: sibling rivalry, armed robberies, an evil tyrant, a captive maiden, raging battles, tender love, and the conflict between good and evil. The language and the characterization are shamelessly overblown, but they matched the epic proportions of the action and struck a responsive chord in the viewers. The play was one of the most astonishing hits in the annals of the German stage, and the critics were no less enthralled than the public. In short order *Die Räuber* was playing all over the country. Since the production broke all house records at the Mannheim National Theater, Dalberg promised to produce any other play Schiller might write.

During the following months Schiller made several clandestine trips to Mannheim. The duke eventually learned of his secret life, jailed him for two weeks, and ordered him to cease all literary activity. Unwilling to sacrifice his talent to the duke's whim, on 22 September 1782 Schiller deserted the army–a capital offense–and fled to Mannheim. He was somewhat naive in expecting Dalberg's protection and assistance; frightened of the duke's wrath, the director refused to have anything to do with the young playwright until the matter was settled. The prospect of being kidnapped and returned to face the duke's capricious brand of justice forced Schiller into hiding under the alias Dr. Ritter at the Bauerbach estate of Frau Henriette von Wolzogen in distant Thuringia from December 1782 until July 1783. There he finished his second drama, *Die Verschwörung des Fiesko zu Genua* (1783; translated as *Fiesco: or, The Genoese Conspiracy,* 1796). Based on Count Fiesco's revolt against Andrea Doria in 1547, the play dramatizes the metamorphosis of an idealistic political reformer into an egotist hungry for power. Suspecting his ulterior motives, one of his coconspirators, the arch-republican Verrina, pushes Fiesko from a gangway, and he drowns. *Die Verschwörung des Fiesko zu Genua* is not a particularly deep or revealing examination of history, but it is a riveting drama. Nevertheless, when it premiered in Bonn on 20 July 1783 it received a mixed reception. The problem is that the hero is actually a villain involved in the ruthless pursuit of self-interest, and as Aristotle pointed out in his *Poetics,* if the hero is a villain it is not possible for the audience to experience the primary ingredients of tragedy, pity, and fear. Though *Die Verschwörung des Fiesko zu Genua* is much better constructed than *Die Räuber* is, it lacks both the idealistic fervor and the engaging characterizations of Schiller's first play.

By July 1783 it had become clear that Karl Eugen intended to ignore Schiller's desertion, and Dalberg decided that it was safe to hire Schiller as resident playwright to deliver three plays a year. Schiller assumed his new duties on 1 September, and *Die Verschwörung des Fiesko zu Genua* was produced at the National Theater on 11 January 1784. The first play Schiller wrote for Dalberg was *Kabale und Liebe* (Intrigue and Love, 1784; translated as *The Minister,* 1797). The play deals with one of the most controversial issues of the day: class discrimination. Ferdinand von Walter is the son of Presi-

dent von Walter, the unscrupulous chief administrator of a duchy. Ferdinand loves Luise Miller, the daughter of a lowborn musician. To break up the affair, which he regards as a threat to his political ambitions, the president employs the services of a slick opportunist, Wurm. Together they launch a cabal to convince Ferdinand that Luise is promiscuous. Believing the lies, Ferdinand poisons Luise and himself; he realizes the truth just before he dies. Justice–of a kind–is when the president and Wurm turn upon and destroy each other.

The most prominent theme of the play is the conflict between the decadent moral system of the aristocracy and the new morality emerging from the Enlightenment. Representative of the former is the president and his group, who treat the lower classes with contempt. They feel no obligation to respect laws, tradition, or even common decency in their pursuit of power and privilege. Luise, by contrast, represents traditional morality. She stands for custom, traditional values, honesty, and respect for the rights of others. Although the play ends with her death, the morality she represents triumphs.

The drama also displays another of Schiller's favorite themes, that of the hero who wears a mask of idealism to conceal motives of personal gain. Full of revolutionary enthusiasm, Ferdinand professes noble principles in defying his father, but the real reason is his passion for Luise. Furthermore, his idealism is selectively applied: he knows that his father gained power through mendacity and murder, but he feels no impulse to denounce him; nor does he object when his father's influence gets him the rank of major.

Schiller's year as official playwright was anything but serene: he quarreled with the actors and became involved in several intrigues. Dalberg was highly displeased with the failure of *Die Verschwörung des Fiesko zu Genua* and the poor attendance at *Kabale und Liebe.* When Schiller failed to deliver the third play he had promised, Dalberg refused to renew the contract, which expired in August 1784. Schiller found himself in serious financial trouble. He had borrowed heavily, and his creditors were pressing for payment. To support himself he decided to launch a literary journal, *Die rheinische Thalia,* later renamed *Thalia.* He hoped that it would bring him a thousand talers a year. The journal did not sell well, however, and he fell even further into debt. To complicate matters he had fallen deeply in love with Charlotte von Kalb, the wife of major Heinrich von Kalb. This affair, Benno von Wiese thinks, prompted Schiller more than anything else to leave Mannheim.

Help arrived from an unexpected source. Christian Gottfried Körner, a wealthy official in the Kingdom of Saxony, and some of his friends wrote Schiller expressing their admiration, offering support, and extending an invitation to live with them at Leipzig.

Schiller accepted. He wrote that his requirements were modest: a room to receive visitors, a place to work and sleep, and above all, companionship. Although he needed solitude for composition, he was gregarious by nature. He often said that he would rather not eat at all if he had to dine alone. His lifelong work habits began to emerge about this time. To avoid interruptions and still fulfill his duties as houseguest he decided to write at night, sustaining himself with large quantities of coffee. He worked usually until four o'clock in the morning and slept until eleven.

Schiller lived with the Körners from April 1785 until July 1787. His gratitude for their generosity and warm hospitality is reflected in *An die Freude* (To Joy, 1786). His best-known poem of this period, it is a paean to friendship, universal brotherhood, peace on earth, and good will to men; its appeal resides in its youthful vigor and in its image of an ideal world based on love. Ludwig van Beethoven immortalized the poem when he set it to music in the final movement of his Ninth Symphony. Besides other poetry of some merit, the chief product of this period was the drama *Dom Karlos, Infant von Spanien* (1787; translated as *Don Carlos, Infant of Spain,* 1798; in later German editions the spelling of the title character's name was changed to Don Carlos). The action is based loosely on the short life and mysterious death in 1568 of Don Carlos, son of Philip II and heir to the Spanish throne. Virtually everything is invented, including the central character, the Marquis Posa, an idealistic young man of uncommon abilities who tries to overthrow Philip II and place his intimate friend, Don Carlos, on the throne. Posa and Carlos plan to inaugurate a new order based on idealistic principles of freedom and dignity. These are noble goals, but Posa's devious means lead him ever deeper into a web of deception, secrecy, and betrayal involving not only Don Carlos but the queen–Carlos's stepmother, to whom Carlos was once engaged and whom he still loves–as well. Eventually, through a series of miscalculations, Posa loses control of events, and the king has him shot as a traitor. In the final scenes Philip turns his son over to the Inquisition.

This drama, with its ideal of freedom, its vision of a better future, and its merciless attack on political absolutism, earned a special place with the public, particularly the younger generation. For over a century Posa was hailed as the paragon of noble virtues, the perfect example of "the lionhearted German youth," as one early critic put it. This one-sided view has been considerably modified as critics have realized that Schiller's hero has serious flaws. Posa, like Fiesko and Ferdinand before him, uses idealism to conceal motives of self-aggrandizement. Although his dedication to the idea of freedom is genuine, he is also driven by the desire to go down in history as a great man. He pursues both aims in cold blood: he lies to and manipulates Carlos shamelessly, he maneuvers the queen into putting her life in danger, and he betrays the king in the most heartless way. In the final analysis, he tramples underfoot the very ideals he professes to uphold. Thus, the drama does not end on a note of moral triumph, for Schiller wanted to show how fanatical idealism is defeated by its own extreme. The drama premiered on 29 August 1787 in Hamburg; it was a success, and soon it was playing throughout the country. King Friedrich Wilhelm II attended a performance in Berlin and was deeply moved, especially by the scenes in which Philip's trust in Posa is betrayed. Despite the popular acclaim, the drama is seriously flawed technically. Directors had to edit it extensively, for it is constructed more like a thrilling novel than high tragedy.

Schiller was well aware that he needed both to perfect his craft and to think through certain fundamental philosophical principles; also, although the Körners were providing for his material needs, he wanted to regain his independence. On 20 July 1787 he moved to Weimar, which had the largest concentration of intellectual talent in Germany, and took up the study of history; he wrote no more plays and little poetry for the next ten years. It was widely held that there is a suprapersonal force at work within the phenomenal world directing the course of civilization; many, including Schiller, thought that this force could be grasped through the study of history. His study of the revolt of the Netherlands from Spain (1788; translated, 1844) attracted favorable attention and in January 1789 resulted in his appointment as an unsalaried professor of history at the university in nearby Jena. Schiller married Charlotte von Lengefeld on 22 February 1790. They had four children: Emilie, Ernst, Karl, and Karoline. Since the professorship carried no stipend, Schiller was forced to earn his living by writing popular histories, translating, and editing. One of his better-known literary products of this period is the unfinished novel *Der Geisterseher* (1788; translated as *The Ghost-seer; or, The Apparitionist,* 1795). It is his only effort in the colportage genre. With it he sought to capitalize on the contemporary fascination with the supernatural and the mysterious which was being promoted by such famous charlatans as Alessandro Cagliostro and Franz Mesmer. A German prince in Venice falls victim to the deceptions of a secret society which drives him to Catholicism and in the end is supposed to incite him to a crime disrupting the order of succession to the Austrian throne. Schiller himself had a low opinion of the project and before completing it decided his energy could be better employed elsewhere. The twentieth century judges the work more favorably than Schiller did: the language seems almost contemporary, and the novel is a masterpiece of suspense, adventure, and description.

Schiller's academic career came to an abrupt end in January 1791 when overwork and earlier privations brought on a pulmonary disorder, probably pneumonia, which was later complicated by pleurisy. He lay near death for weeks, and in the summer he traveled to the spas of Carsbad and Erfurt. He never fully recovered his health, and for the rest of his life he suffered a succession of illnesses, including whooping cough. Schiller was taller than six feet, with reddish-brown hair and blue eyes; before 1791 he had been robust and vigorous, but after the illness he became thin and bony with hollow cheeks and watery, bloodshot eyes. He suffered almost constantly from abdominal cramps, dyspnea, and insomnia. For months at a time he would not leave his house. Aside from trips to Württemberg from June 1793 to May 1794, to Leipzig in 1801, and to Berlin in May 1804, he never again left the vicinity of Weimar.

Although Schiller's body was wasted by disease, his mind and personality remained unaffected. In addition to his intellectual brilliance, the one trait virtually every visitor remarked upon was his enormous personal magnetism. He seems to have cast a spell over people, and the most independent-minded soon found themselves drawn into his orbit. The diplomat and linguist Wilhelm von Humboldt, who later founded the Humboldt University at Berlin, moved to Jena for the sole purpose of being near Schiller. Schiller, however, never seemed to be fully aware of his effect on people.

The severity of Schiller's illness had caused false reports of his death to circulate, and the loss of so great a talent was acutely felt by his admirers at the Danish court. When he learned that the rumor was false, Prince Christian Friedrich von Augustenburg of Denmark conferred upon Schiller a stipend of a thousand talers a year for three years, beginning in December 1791, so that he could convalesce properly. Freed from financial worries, Schiller took up the study of aesthetics and Kantian philosophy. This period marked the great intellectual and literary turning point of his life. He produced a series of analytical essays on tragedy, the sublime, spiritual rebirth, and grace and dignity, with his career culminating in two key essays on the role and nature of the fine arts: "Über die ästhetische Erziehung des Menschen in einer Reihe von Briefen"(On the Aesthetic Education of Man in a Series of Letters, 1795) and "Über naive und sentimentalische Dichtung" (On Naive and Sentimental Poetry, 1795-1796). Both essays were published in three parts in *Die Horen,* a monthly journal Schiller founded in 1795.

"Über die ästhetische Erziehung des Menschen in einer Reihe von Briefen" is a program for the improvement of man, society, and the state. Civilizations progress through three distinct stages, Schiller says: the natural state, the aesthetic state and the moral state. In the natural state individuals are ruled by their emotions and compelled by their physical needs. Since such people cannot be trusted to obey the law of their own free will, the state maintains order by brute force or the threat of it. Contemporary European society is near the end of the natural state but finds itself unable to take the next crucial step. An unsuccessful attempt to do so was under way in France: the French Revolution had begun with great promise but had turned into a bloodbath. The events in France proved that the average citizen was unable to cope with the freedom and the sophisticated moral principles promulgated by the reformers. Since political and social institutions emanate from the character of the citizenry, it follows that if society is to be changed for the better the citizen must be changed first.

To change the character of the modern individual it is necessary to harmonize the forces operating within the human psyche. In our daily activities we are compelled on the one hand by the impulses emanating from our animal side, which Schiller calls the *Stofftrieb* (sense-drive). The Stofftrieb includes sense perception, the emotions, and the appetites. The other force, which arises from the rational faculty, he calls the *Formtrieb* (form-drive). It is the source of such abstractions as duty, law, justice, and moral principles. At present these two drives are in conflict, pulling the individual in opposite directions, with the sense-drive usually dominant. This inner disharmony is the primary cause of individual and social misery and misfortune. For further progress to occur, the two drives must work in concert. Both must be developed equally so that neither infringes on the territory of the other. This harmonization can be achieved by cultivating the *Spieltrieb* (drive to play). Play involves both drives and satisfies the demands of each simultaneously. Schiller defines play as whatever is done for its own sake; it is an end in itself, devoid of any ulterior motive. We sing, dance, play games, or listen to music purely for the pleasure involved, and that pleasure is the sensation of harmony. The delight in play derives precisely from its non-utilitarian character: if something could be gained by it, our pleasure in it would cease, and play would become work. Work is goal-oriented, play is process-oriented. Play and work are equivalent to freedom and servitude, respectively.

Schiller draws a close parallel between play and beauty: both are compounded of the sense-drive and the form-drive, both are disinterested, and both exert the same synthesizing effect on the psyche. The aesthetic state is the condition of harmony between reason and feeling: we are transported into this state of mind both through play and through the enjoyment and creation of beauty. He coins the term, "ästhetische Freiheit" (aesthetic freedom) to signify our liberation from the one-sided compulsion of either drive. Schiller's innovation is in tying art and beauty to our mimetic faculty. Since human beings learn through imitation, imitate what they see, and so become what they imitate, he proposes the aesthetic education of man as the way to equalize the discordant elements of the psyche. When sense and reason compel us equally, the moral state is possible. Schiller defines this state as any political body whose organization derives from laws and principles. In such a state we obey the law of our own free will. Projecting this scheme into the future, he says that once we approximate ideal harmony, we ourselves become the state; political organizations as we know them will no longer exist. Public pressure will be the only force needed to insure conformity to the ideal.

In "Über naive und sentimentalische Dichtung" Schiller examines the problems raised in the essay on aesthetic education from a different angle. His purpose is to elucidate two fundamentally different modes of perceiving the world and the two types of poetry which spring from these modes. Children exemplify the naive mode of perception: they are characterized above all by their straightforwardness and lack of guile. There is no difference between what they are and what they seem to be. Furthermore, they make no distinction between the world as it is and as it appears to be. They exist in a state of oneness with nature and with themselves. This childlike unity also characterizes the ancient Greeks: both in their moral behavior and in their poetry there is a certain unreflective spontaneity, almost as if nature herself were whispering directions. The naive orientation to life and poetry recurs from time to time in the modern age, notably in Shakespeare and Goethe. Modern civilization is largely to blame for our separation from nature and the accompanying destruction of our inner unity. When, as children, we are forced to obey rules and social conventions which are contrary to nature, we find that the promptings of the heart are at odds with the dictates of duty. As a consequence we become "sentimentalisch" (sentimental), a word which Schiller uses in its older connotation of intellectual, rational activity: with nature no longer available to guide us, we must reflect on our actions. The sentimental poet's alienation is reflected in his poetry; every word is the result of calculation and choice. The metaphors and symbols are carefully woven into the poem according to a preconceived plan to achieve a calculated effect. Until the sentimental poet overcomes his alienation, he will be able to write in only two modes: the satirical and the elegiac. The poet writes in the first mode if he is either angered or amused by the discrepancy between the ideal and its translation into reality; his language is flavored with sarcasm, ridicule, or irony. The elegiac mode, by contrast, expresses sadness at something lost or unattainable; the language here is colored with nostalgia and lament. Once human beings have harmonized the discordant elements of the psyche and the ideal has become reality, the poet's language will be filled with praise and exclamations of satisfaction. These are the characteristics of the sentimental idyll, the art form of the Golden Age. Believing in the perfectibility of man, Schiller is convinced that we can attain the ideal—not by returning to a state of nature as advocated by some contemporaries but by going forward. He assigns to the poets of the world the task of showing the way.

Schiller's essay can be read as an analysis of himself and Goethe. Though the two poets had been introduced in 1788, they remained cool to each other for several years because of the great difference in their temperaments. Schiller's mind was bent toward the abstract, the theoretical, and the ideal, whereas Goethe was this-worldly, practical, and realistic—naive in Schiller's sense of the word. Writing, for Schiller, was hard work, involving careful planning and self-discipline; he bitterly resented Goethe's presumably spontaneous and effortless composition. For his part, Goethe was well aware that he had been born with an enormous natural talent and was himself somewhat mystified by its independent nature. In his twenties he had discovered that he was unable to compose by conscious effort; verse came to him automatically at irregular intervals. Goethe was at first cool to Schiller because the ten-year-younger Schiller reminded him of his own Sturm und Drang youth and outlook on life. In his essay Schiller identifies the difficulty he had in relating to the naive poets as his habit of separating the author from his work; one of his greatest insights was the realization that in naive poetry it is not possible to make this separation. The two are a unity. Once Schiller grasped the fundamental difference between himself and Goethe, the way to friendship was cleared. From July 1794 until Schiller's death each served as an inspiration to the other. The completion of Goethe's *Faust,* Part I (1808), for instance, was due largely to Schiller's prodding. The chief product of their relationship is a correspondence of about one thousand letters which deal primarily with literary matters. In 1796 they collaborated on "Xenien" (Xenia), a series of satirical distichs in which they put to scorching ridicule a host of literary philistines and pretentious, self-appointed critics. "Xenien" was published in Schiller's journal, the *Musen-Almanach für das Jahr 1797.*

By 1795 Schiller had developed the firm theoretical foundation he had sought, and he felt ready to take up poetry again. The contrast between the new verse and his earlier efforts is most striking. His development as a poet is usually divided into three periods. The productions of his early youth display all the faults of someone not yet in control of an immense talent. Typical is "Der Eroberer" (The Conqueror), first published in the *Schwäbisches Magazin* in 1777. Grandiloquent, emotionally excessive, and often bizarre, it is a moral condemnation of excessive ambition. Other pieces addressed to the fictitious "Laura" are written in the same superheated fashion and take the same delight in rhetorical embellishment. Above all, they are testimony to the youth's awakening libido. The second period covers the years 1785 to 1789. Although Schiller still indulges his gift for rhetoric, the language of the poems of this period is more refined and elevated, and the content inclines toward philosophical ideas. "Resignation," published in Schiller's journal *Thalia* in February 1786, focuses on true and false virtue. A man dies and appears before the judgment seat. He tells the judge that he had renounced all earthly pleasure in favor of compensation in the Hereafter; now he wants to collect his reward. Much to his distress he discovers that he has been laboring under a misapprehension. The judge tells him that humans can choose between hope and enjoyment; whoever picks the one must not covet the other. His reward for abstinence consisted in the pleasure he derived from self-denial. The poem ends with the remark that whatever we pass up in this life is not going to be waiting for us in eternity. A good deed performed with an eye toward a reward is not virtue. Like play, virtue is something we do purely for the pleasure involved. Another poem representative of the middle period is "Die Götter Griechenlandes" (The Gods of Greece), published in *Der Teutsche Merkur* in March 1788. It celebrates the ancient Greek view of religion and life to the detriment of the Christian. Schiller argues in the poem that if we look upon ourselves as helpless, sinful worms in a chain of being spiraling up to the Almighty, that simply makes Him the first and noblest worm. "Die Künstler" (The Artists), published in *Der Teutsche Merkur* in March 1789, is the last poem of the second period and probably the most significant. Schiller had by this time abandoned the study of history because it did not reveal the force responsible for social evolution. In this poem he says that art is this force, and he traces the role of art in civilization from earliest epochs to the eighteenth century. He went on to develop this idea in his essay on aesthetic education.

When Schiller resumed writing poetry in 1795 he was at the summit of his powers. His verse from this period has the ring of the self-confident master. Most of the poems are Gedankenlyrik (philosophical poetry); each is structured around a philosophical principle. Schiller believed that the poet's task is not to entertain but to inform, instruct, and improve the reader. The grand style is his mode of expression; his subjects are the rise and fall of civilizations, the destiny of mankind, the human condition. A particularly prominent motif is that of transcending through art and beauty the workaday world that inhibits the full development of our potential; only in the realm of ideals, truth, and beauty can we escape the enslaving forces of reality. He expresses this idea in such poems as "Der Tanz" (The Dance), published in the *Musen-Almanach für das Jahr 1796,* and particularly in his most profound philosophical poem, "Das Ideal und das Leben" (The Ideal and Life), published in *Die Horen* in September 1795,

in which he advises that one "fliehet aus dem engen, dumpfen Leben / In des Idealen Reich" (leave life's stupefying narrowness / For the realm of ideals).

Among Schiller's favorite subjects is the ascent of mankind from nomadism through the development of agriculture to the rise of cities. "Der Spaziergang" (The Walk), published in *Die Horen* in November 1795, focuses on the relation between nature and the development of civilization. In the beginning nature is our companion and protector. As we become more civilized, nature is made our servant. This is a positive development; trouble arises only when we try to dispense with nature altogether or when we act contrary to its laws. Without nature as its guiding principle, civilization loses its orientation and its roots. This kind of freedom is dangerous and can lead to social chaos. We must learn to live in harmony with nature.

In the *Musen-Almanach für das Jahr 1798* (1798) Schiller published a collection of ballads which included "Der Ring des Polykrates" (The Ring of Polykrates), "Die Kraniche des Ibykus" (The Cranes of Ibycus), "Der Taucher" (The Diver), and "Der Handschuh" (The Glove). The plot of "Der Ring des Polykrates" comes from a story found in the third book of Herodotus. As tyrant of Samos in the sixth century B.C. Polykrates, through dishonest means, dominated the eastern Aegean and amassed great wealth. In the poem the visiting Egyptian king warns him that the gods shower good fortune on those they have marked for destruction. To win their favor he should sacrifice his most esteemed possession. Polykrates agrees and casts his fabulous ring into the sea. The next day, while dressing a fresh fish, the cook finds the ring and returns it. Convinced that Polykrates' days are numbered, the Egyptian king hastily leaves Samos. By ending the ballad here, instead of going on to relate how Polykrates was soon lured to the mainland and crucified by the governor of Sardis, Schiller creates a mood of foreboding and doom.

"Die Kraniche des Ibykus" also dramatizes an incident from antiquity. The Greek poet Ibykus sets out to participate in the poetry competitions at Corinth. His journey happens to coincide with the migration of the cranes, whom he addresses as his friends. On the highway two robbers attack and murder him. With his dying breath he calls on the cranes to avenge him. The murderers continue to Corinth, where they enjoy the festival. One day, while they are attending a tragedy, a large flock of cranes suddenly flies over the ampitheater, provoking one of the murderers to exclaim without thinking: "Sieh da, sieh da, Timotheus, / Die Kraniche des Ibykus" (Look, look Timotheus, / The cranes of Ibykus). The robbers are arrested and brought to justice.

"Der Taucher" and "Der Handschuh" illustrate Schiller's concept of play. In the letters on aesthetic education, play is defined as any activity done merely for the pleasure involved without any thought of gain. If reward becomes the motivating factor the purity of the act is destroyed. In "Der Taucher" the king and his court are assembled on the cliffs of Messina overlooking the whirlpool known as Charybdis. Being in a playful mood, the king throws a golden goblet into the maelstrom and announces that whoever is intrepid enough to retrieve it can keep it as a symbol of his prowess. When none of the knights volunteers, a young squire steps forward, disrobes, and dives. A few minutes later he emerges with the goblet. Thrilled by the exploit and curious to hear more about the abyss and the gliding shadows the youth has described, the king announces that if he will dive a second time a fabulous ring and the king's beautiful daughter will be the reward. Even though the youth knows the danger, he dives. He never returns. Schiller's message is that when we act solely in accordance with reward, we corrupt not only the act but also ourselves.

In a letter to Goethe, Schiller referred to "Der Handschuh" as a sequel to "Der Taucher." In this ballad the king and his court are seated around an arena containing a lion, tiger, and two leopards. Lady Kunigunde tosses her glove among the beasts, turns to the knight Delorges, and tells him that he can prove his love for her by retrieving the glove. Delorges casually descends among the animals, picks up the glove, and returns amid shouts of praise and wonder. Lady Kunigunde greets him with an expression promising sweet reward. At that moment he throws the glove in her face with the words "Den Dank, Dame, begehr ich nicht" (Thanks, lady, I don't desire) and leaves her forever. As with the first dive in "Der Taucher," Delorges performs his feat as an end in itself; when he realizes that Kunigunde thinks he risked his life for her reward, his reaction is the natural and spontaneous expression of utter contempt for someone who has entirely misjudged him.

These ballads in the *Musen-Almanach für das Jahr 1798,* and others which soon followed, are more responsible than any other factor for Schiller's popularity among the general public. Drawing his material from the widest range of literature, myth, philosophy, and history, he deals with ultimate questions about truth, beauty, and justice. After reading one of his ballads, one has the sensation of having undergone an elevating experience. The ballads are uneven in quality. Many are set in the Middle Ages, and he was not entirely successful in capturing the spirit of that time. He is at his best when he takes his material from classical antiquity, a subject which had fascinated him for years. "Die Kraniche des Ibykus," generally regarded as his finest ballad, has the force of an Aeschylean chorus.

In 1797 Schiller began work on the trilogy *Wallenstein* (1800; translated, 1800, 1830), which is often cited as the greatest German tragedy. Of all Schiller's historical plays,

this one follows the actual events most closely. The play, which reflects his study of the Thirty Years' War (published in 1791-1793), has a fearful, paranoid, doom-laden feeling. Schiller portrays a cold, cruel, and murderous world where power is the medium of exchange and lies, betrayal, and intrigue are the norm. Against this somber background looms the protagonist, Albrecht von Wallenstein, commander in chief of the Catholic army. An ambiguous figure, he is an austere, ambitious man driven to become central Europe's most powerful warlord and to found a new dynasty, even if these goals require him to rebel against Ferdinand, the Hapsburg emperor, and to plunge the entire continent into civil war. When the action begins he has already won the allegiance of the army and most of the officer corps away from Ferdinand. Yet he hesitates to come out in open revolt because he is not sure that the time is ripe. His irresolution does not spring from any inner struggle between right and wrong, for he is amoral. In this respect he stands in sharp contrast to Schiller's earlier creations, Karl Moor and the Marquis of Posa. Though they, too, rebel against established authority, they do so in the name of humanity. Wallenstein believes in nothing. He is motivated neither by guiding principle nor moral law. Believing that necessity rules the universe, he denies the possibility of free choice and claims that all human actions are predictable.

It is precisely Wallenstein's amoral and deterministic philosophy that leads him to make the mistakes which end in his downfall. His failure to give Ferdinand his full moral support arouses the emperor's suspicion; his belief in the predictability of human behavior causes him to misjudge the loyalty of his most trusted general, Octavio Piccolomini, as well as that of the army. By the time he realizes the magnitude of his errors it is too late. Deserted by the army and abandoned by his friends, he knows that there is not much point in fighting on; yet he perseveres with increasing energy and determination, thus evoking the audience's admiration, even though it knows that General Buttler and his assassins are on the move and that the duke is doomed. Ultimately, it is Wallenstein's self-assertion in the face of fortune which makes his death tragic. The play made a massive impression throughout Germany. Until then German literature could not boast of a drama of such magnitude, depth, sweep, and excellence. For the most part, the critics were overawed and contented themselves with trying to outdo one another in praising the work.

Following *Wallenstein* Schiller chose another historical subject, the three days preceding the execution of Mary Stuart, Queen of Scots, in 1587. The action of *Maria Stuart* (1801; translated as *Mary Stuart,* 1801) begins when Maria learns that the royal commission appointed by Elisabeth I has found her guilty of conspiring with others to assassinate the English queen. While Elisabeth procrastinates in signing the order of execution, Maria frantically tries to avert her fate. After Maria's failure in act 3 to persuade Elisabeth to release her, Mortimer, her jailer's nephew, heads a conspiracy to free her by force; he is driven by his passion for Maria. Leicester informs on him, and Mortimer kills himself as he is arrested. After an attempt by one of Mortimer's allies to assassinate her, Elisabeth signs the order of execution. It is carried out the next day.

The historical events provide the background for a story about rage, crime, remorse, and spiritual rebirth. In the first four acts Maria is not a heroine with whom audiences are expected to sympathize. She is a petty, vain, and insulting woman consumed by hatred for Elisabeth. Because of the many crimes of her youth, especially her complicity in the murder of her husband, Lord Darnley, Maria's rage contains a quotient of self-condemnation; it is this remorse that eventually leads to her spiritual regeneration. One of Schiller's primary principles concerning the human condition, propounded in his theoretical writings on the sublime act, holds that a person who regrets a crime can regain peace of mind through voluntary self-punishment. The suffering brings about a change in character which amounts to a spiritual rebirth. For technical reasons, which he discusses in his theoretical writings, Schiller chose not to stage the moment of Maria's transformation but rather its effect on her character and bearing. To this end he uses the technique of contrast. First, he shows the unreconstructed Maria at her worst when she confronts Elisabeth in the third act. In this scene Maria loses her self-control and vents her pent-up hatred in a stream of verbal abuse culminating in the unparalleled and unforgivable insult: "Der Thron von England ist durch einen Bastard / Entweiht" (The throne of England is by a bastard / Profaned). Her transformation begins that night, when she realizes that the general uproar in the castle is not caused by her rescuers but by the workmen who are preparing her place of execution. Following an inner struggle, which happens offstage, she overcomes the negative qualities which led her not only into her earlier crimes but also into her present predicament. She even perceives a way to turn her execution for treason, of which she is innocent, into the means of her redemption: she chooses to regard her death as an atonement for her husband's murder. The effect of her inner transformation is seen through her serene speech and dignified bearing, which stand out in sharp contrast to the snarling shrew who called the queen of England a bastard. In the final scenes she projects an image of inner harmony and quiet tranquillity.

The first performance on 14 June 1800 at Weimar was a resounding success. After the play was issued in book form the following year, the literary critics spoke up. While praising the work's dramatic and linguistic qualities, they took its author to task for deviating from historical fact. They pointed out that the two queens had never met, that Elizabeth was not like Schiller's portrayal of her, that

Mortimer never existed, and so on. Schiller shrugged off the criticism, for he had long since come to the conviction that art is not in the service of history. It is the dramatist's business to tell how things could or should have been, not how they were.

For the subject of his next play Schiller turned to the Joan of Arc legend. Beneath the surface action of *Kalendar auf das Jahr 1802*, which follows the historical events fairly closely until the final act, there is a conflict between duty and inclination, spirit and flesh. In the prologue Schiller emphasizes the conditions of Johanna's mission, which she will later violate: she is to lead the French army against the English, liberate Rheims, and crown the dauphin King Charles VII, and she will be given divine power to accomplish the task; under no circumstances, however, is she to entertain erotic thoughts but is to live by spirit alone. Johanna pursues her object relentlessly until, at the peak of fortune, she is suddenly paralyzed by a blind infatuation for a handsome young English officer, Lionel. Her divine powers vanish, and she is plunged into misery. Overcome with shame, guilt, and remorse she submits to her father's misguided accusations and to her unjust banishment from court for witchcraft as the means to atone for breaking her vow to God. After putting herself through more suffering and hardship, she emerges purified. With her charisma and powers restored she breaks out of the English prison and leads the French to victory. Schiller digresses considerably from history when he has her die of wounds received in battle.

The play premiered on 11 September 1801 at Leipzig and swept the audience off its feet; the reaction was repeated in succeeding performances around the country. The critics, of course, were upset at his deviation from the facts, but hardly anyone paid any attention to them. *Kalendar auf das Jahr 1802* was Schiller's most popular play and remained in the permanent repertoires of almost all German theaters throughout the nineteenth century. The drama was largely responsible for overturning the prevailing notion–propounded in Voltaire's scurrilous *La Pucelle* (1755)–that Joan of Arc was a charismatic charlatan who whored her way through regiments to achieve dubious ends: such was the influence of this play that historians and the clergy reopened the case and got at the facts. That Joan of Arc was finally canonized in 1920 can be traced directly back to Schiller's drama.

Schiller's long fascination with classical antiquity inspired him to write a tragedy in the style of the Athenian tragic poets. *Die Braut von Messina oder Die feindlichen Brüder* (The Bride of Messina; or, The Enemy Brothers, 1803; translated as *The Bride of Messina*, 1837) incorporates such features as the chorus, pity and fear, recognition-reversal, tragic error, and catharsis. And, as in the ancient tragedies, within the classical structure unfolds a most unsavory tale of outrages against nature. An old king, enraged at his son's eloping with the woman he desired for himself, rapes her and then lays a curse on her progeny. Prophecies and dreams of doom foretell the birth of a daughter who will cause the dynasty's destruction. Transgressing against nature, the new king orders the infant, Beatrice, flung into the sea. Queen Isabella, however, spirits the child away to a convent, where she matures into a ravishing beauty. Ignorant of her true identity, her brothers Cesar and Manuel, who are divided by an unnatural and morbid hatred, meet and fall in love with her. In a jealous fury Cesar kills Manuel. The catastrophe is brought on not only by the abnormal deeds of the individual characters but also by the unnatural presence of the family in Messina. Several times the chorus complains that the ancestors of the ruling family came from across the seas to conquer and then to divide into warring camps a people who had lived in peaceful harmony with themselves and with nature. The play is one of Schiller's strongest depictions of what can happen when human beings violate the natural order. Structurally, *Die Braut von Messina* is the most carefully composed of Schiller's dramas; it is noted for its economy of form and its symmetry. Yet, he was unable to breathe life into it, and the play remains a passive experience. He avoided the very things in which he excelled: portraying vividly drawn characters in vigorous action and speaking virtuoso dialogue. Most critics agree that it is an interesting experiment which failed. It premiered on 19 March 1803 in Weimar and closed after a few performances.

After the cold, gray aloofness of *Die Braut von Messina,* Schiller wrote a hit noted for its color and warmth. *Wilhelm Tell* (1804; translated as *William Tell,* 1829) is his most widely known drama outside Germany. Few people have not heard the legend of how Geßler, the cruel Austrian governor of the Cantons Schwyz and Uri, places his hat atop a pole and commands the people to bow to it. Tell does not bow and as punishment must pierce with an arrow an apple on his son's head. Geßler arrests Tell by trickery, but Tell escapes from the prison ship and slays the tyrant. Parallel to Tell's adventure run two other independent plots. The first is known as the Rütli Confederacy. During the night of 7–8 November 1307 representatives from three cantons meet at a clearing in the forest called the Rütli to plan an armed revolt. They decide to strike after Christmas. The second plot involves the young Swiss nobleman Rudenz von Attinghausen, who has turned his back on his countrymen because he loves the beautiful Berta von Bruneck. When he learns that he can win her only through Swiss independence, he has a change of heart. The three independent plots come together in act 5: when the Rütli Confederacy learns of Geßler's death the leaders decide to launch the revolt immediately, and Rudenz joins them. Most of act 5 is devoted to the storming of the castles and the expulsion of the last Austrian governor. At this point Schiller added a scene which is extraneous to the action: Duke Johannes of Swabia, called Parricida in the play, has assassinated the Austrian emperor Ferdinand for withholding his inheritance. Pursued by soldiers, he seeks out Tell to beg for help because, as he explains, their deeds are similar. Tell stoutly denies any resemblance between them but gives assistance when he sees that Parricida is remorseful and wants to expiate his crime. This scene has often been criticized as gratuitous and out of harmony with the rest of the play, and it is almost always omitted when the play is performed. Yet Schiller felt compelled to justify Tell even more by contrasting his deed with Parricida's purely selfish, revengeful act.

The play dramatizes Schiller's thoughts on revolution (when it is justified, and that force should be applied without bloodshed) and his theory of social evolution. In his essay on aesthetic education he links civilization's upward course to the development of the rational faculty. In the figure of Wilhelm Tell he demonstrates how an individual, and by extension humanity, might progress from a naive state of oneness with nature through the moral state to the aesthetic state. In the first half of the play Tell displays the qualities of a person living in a state of nature: he is a unity within himself and lives at one with his environment. The basis of his morality is feeling, not reason. His actions are spontaneous and unpremeditated, as when he rescues Baumgarten from the pursuing soldiers in act 1. His naive simplicity is also apparent in his speech: a man of few words, he usually confines himself to proverbs. Tell's oneness is destroyed when Geßler orders him to risk his son's life, thereby forcing him to act contrary to his nature and to nature itself. At this point Tell is driven from the natural state into the moral state. In his essay "Über das Erhabene" (On the Sublime), written in 1793 and published in volume 3 of his *Kleinere prosaische Schriften* (Shorter Prose Writings, 1792–1802) in 1801, Schiller says that such an event always happens suddenly and without warning. From this point forward Tell is a different person. The change is at once apparent in his manner of speech: it is no longer a series of set phrases, as can be seen, for instance, in his vivid account of how he escaped from Geßler's ship and in his conversation with Johannes Parricida in act 5. As he awaits Geßler at the Hohle Gasse, Tell delivers a monologue in which he recalls his former inner unity and oneness with nature, then reflects upon how he has changed. He reasons that he must kill Geßler to protect not only his own family but also the Swiss people. He does not shoot Geßler in a blind fury as Cesar stabs his brother; rather, it is a premeditated act performed in full awareness of its necessity. In Schiller's terminology, Tell is forced to act sublimely; that is, he must overcome his natural feeling of revulsion at taking a human life and act solely according to what reason tells him is required. Tell's reason has been brought fully into play and can now operate in concert with his feelings. In the final scenes Tell has achieved that higher synthesis of the sense-drive and the form-drive that constitutes the aesthetic state.

For his next play Schiller turned to the life of Demetrius, the false czar. From the many fragments and notes he left behind it is possible to say that the work promised to be his crowning achievement; but he was unable to complete it. Early in 1805 his health began a rapid deterioration. On 1 May he contracted double pneumonia. Until his death on 9 May he drifted in and out of delirium. Among his last words, spoken in hallucination, were: "Ist das eure Himmel, ist das eure Hölle?" (Is that your heaven, is that your hell?). Schiller was first buried in the St. Jakobskirche cemetery in Weimar. From there his remains were removed to the Weimar Princes' Mausoleum. His coffin lies next to Goethe's.

Schiller's influence has been profound and far reaching. The psychologist Carl Gustav Jung, for example, devotes two chapters of his *Psychologische Typen* (Psychological Types, 1921) to a discussion of "Über Naive und sentimentalische Dichtung" and stresses the importance of Schiller's typology of human nature to the development of his own theory. Friedrich Nietzsche's distinction between the Apollonian and the Dionysian can be traced directly to Schiller's essay. In aesthetics, Georg Wilhelm Friedrich Hegel's *Phenomenologie des Geistes* (Phenomenology of Spirit, 1807) was deeply indebted to Schiller on the crucial point of the dialectical reconciliation of opposites and the dynamic concept of harmony, which Hegel formulates in his triad of thesis-antithesis-synthesis. Schiller's concept of art as aesthetic play has given rise to many play theories of art and education. In political theory Schiller's most notable influence is found in the early writings of Karl Marx. Schiller's remarks about the negative effect of the division of labor on the human psyche led Marx to work out his whole-man theory, according to which the task of the state is to create conditions which will promote the harmonious coordination of all of each person's forces and faculties; the ultimate result, as in Schiller's program, will be the gradual disappearance of the state as a political organization.

Schiller's life and works continue to be studied and analyzed with an intensity accorded those of few other writers. Essays and monographs number in the thousands. The average German citizen regards the author as something like a national monument. Schiller's legacy shows few signs of fading away.

Letters:
Briefwechsel zwischen Schiller und Goethe in den Jahren 1794 bis 1805, 4 volumes (Stuttgart & Tübingen: Cotta, 1828–1829);
Correspondence of Schiller with Körner, Comprising Sketches and Anecdotes of Goethe, the Schlegels, Wieland, and Other
Contemporaries, 3 volumes, translated by Leonard Simpson (London: Bentley, 1849);
Briefwechsel zwischen Schiller und Cotta, edited by Wilhelm Vollmer (Stuttgart: Cotta, 1876);
Briefe: Kritische Gesamtausgabe, 7 volumes, edited by Fritz Jonas (Stuttgart: Deutsche Verlags-Anstalt, 1892–1896);
Ausgewählte Briefe, edited by Henry B. Garland (Manchester, U.K.: Manchester University Press, 1959);
Der Briefwechsel zwischen Schiller und Goethe, edited by Paul Stapf (Berlin: Tempel, 1960);
Der Briefwechsel zwischen Friedrich Schiller und Wilhelm von Humboldt, 2 volumes, edited by Siegfried Seidel (Berlin: Aufbau, 1962);
Der Briefwechsel zwischen Schiller und Goethe, edited by Emil Staiger (Frankfurt am Main: Insel, 1966);
Briefe: In zwei Bänden, 2 volumes, edited by Karl-Heinz Hahn (Berlin & Weimar: Aufbau, 1968);
Briefe des jungen Schiller (1776–1789), edited by Karl Pörnbacher (Munich: Kösel, 1969);
Schillers Briefe, edited by Erwin Streitfeld (Königstein: Athenäum, 1983).

Bibliographies:
Wolfgang Vulpius, *Schiller Bibliographie 1893–1958* (Weimar: Arion, 1959);
Richard Pick, "Schiller in England 1787–1960: A Bibliography," *Publications of the English Goethe Society,* 30 (1961): 832–862;
Vulpius, *Schiller Bibliographie 1959–1963* (Berlin & Weimar: Aufbau, 1967);
Herbert Marcuse, ed., *Schiller-Bibliographie* (Hildesheim: Gerstenberg, 1971);
Peter Wersig, *Schiller Bibliographie 1964–1974* (Berlin & Weimar: Aufbau, 1977);
Ingrid Hannich-Bode, "Schiller Bibliographie 1974–1978 und Nachträge," *Jahrbuch der Deutschen Schillergesellschaft* (1979): 549–612.

Biographies:
Thomas Carlyle, *The Life of Friedrich Schiller* (London: Chapman & Hall, 1825);
Heinrich Düntzer, *Schillers Leben* (Leipzig: Fues, 1881); translated by Percey Pinkerton as *The Life of Schiller* (London: Macmillan, 1883);
Calvin Thomas, *The Life and Works of Friedrich Schiller* (New York: Holt, 1901);
Reinhard Buchwald, *Schiller: Leben und Werk,* 2 volumes (Leipzig: Insel, 1937);
Benno von Wiese, *Schiller: Einführung in Leben und Welt* (Stuttgart: Reclam, 1959);
Friedrich Burschell, *Schiller* (Hamburg: Rowohlt, 1968);
Peter Lahnstein, *Schillers Leben* (Munich: List, 1981);

Eike Middell, *Friedrich Schiller: Leben und Werk,* second edition (Leipzig: Reclam, 1982).

References:

Rainer Blesch, *Drama und wirkungsästhetische Praxis: Zum Problem der ästhetischen Vermittlung bei Schiller* (Frankfurt am Main: Fischer, 1981);

Paul Böckmann, *Strukturprobleme in Schillers "Don Karlos"* (Heidelberg: Winter, 1982);

Albert James Camigliano, *Friedrich Schiller and Christian Gottfried Körner: A Critical Relationship* (Stuttgart: Heinz, 1976);

Ronald L. Crawford, *Images of Transience in the Poems and Ballads of Friedrich Schiller* (Bern: Lang, 1977);

Hans-Dietrich Dahnke, *Goethe und Schiller: Werk und Wirkung* (Weimar: Nationale Forschungs-und Gedenkstätten der klassischen deutschen Literatur, 1981);

Peter M. Daly, *Text- und Variantenkonkordanz zu Schillers "Kabale und Liebe"* (Berlin: De Gruyter, 1976);

Kenneth Dewhurst, and Nigel Reeves, *Friedrich Schiller: Medicine, Psychology, and Literature* (Berkeley: University of California Press, 1978);

Christina Didier, *Das Schillerhaus in Weimar* (Weimar: Nationale Forschungs-und Gedenkstätten der klassischen deutschen Literatur, 1979);

Hermann Fähnrich, *Schillers Musikalität und Musikanschauung* (Hildesheim: Gerstenberg, 1977);

John R. Frey, ed., *Schiller 1759–1959: Commemorative American Studies* (Urbana: University of Illinois Press, 1959);

Friedrich Schiller: Kunst, Humanität und Politik in der späten Aufklärung: Ein Symposium (Tübingen: Niemeyer, 1982);

Henry B. Garland, *Schiller* (London: Harrap, 1949);

Dietrich Germann, *Ich habe dir also von Schiller zu erzählen: Dokumente und Zeugnisse aus Schillers Jenaer Jahren* (Jena: Stadtmuseum, 1982);

Alfons Glück, *Schillers Wallenstein* (Munich: Fink, 1976);

Ilse Graham, *Schiller's Drama: Talent and Integrity* (New York: Barnes & Noble, 1974);

André von Gronicka, "Friedrich Schiller's Marquis Posa: A Character Study," *Germanic Review,* 26 (1951): 196–214;

Hans Henning, ed., *Schillers "Kabale und Liebe" in der zeitgenössischen Rezeption* (Leipzig: Zentralantiquariat, 1976);

Walter Hinderer, *Der Mensch in der Geschichte: Ein Versuch über Schillers Wallenstein* (Königstein: Athenäum, 1980);

Hinderer, ed., *Schillers Dramen: Neue Interpretationen* (Stuttgart: Reclam, 1979);

Rolf Hochhuth, *Räuber-Rede: Drei deutsche Vorwürfe. Schiller, Lessing, Geschwister Scholl* (Reinbek: Rowohlt, 1982);

Renate Homann, *Erhabenes und Satirisches: Zur Grundlegung einer Theorie ästhetischer Literatur bei Kant und Schiller* (Munich: Fink, 1977);

Falk Horst, *Der Leitgedanke von der Vollkommenheit der Natur in Schillers klassischem Werk* (Cirencester: Lang, 1980);

Karl-Heinz Hucke, *Jene "Scheu vor allem Mercantilischen": Schillers "Arbeits-und Finanzplan"* (Tübingen: Niemeyer, 1984);

Rudolf Ibel, *Friedrich Schiller: Die Räuber* (Frankfurt am Main: Diesterweg, 1982);

Rolf-Peter Janz, *Autonomie und soziale Funktion der Kunst: Studien zur Ästhetik von Schiller und Novalis* (Stuttgart, 1973);

Gerhard Kaiser, *Von Arkadien nach Elysium: Schiller-Studien* (Göttingen: Vandenhoeck & Ruprecht, 1978);

Helmut Koopman, *Friedrich Schiller,* 2 volumes (Stuttgart: Metzler, 1966; revised, 1977);

Koopman, *Schiller-Forschung: 1970–1980. Ein Bericht* (Marbach am Neckar: Deutsche Schillergesellschaft, 1982);

Irmgard Kowatzki, *Der Begriff des Spiels als ästhetisches Phänomen: Von Schiller bis Benn* (Bern: Lang, 1973);

Herbert Kraft, *Um Schiller betrogen* (Pfullingen: Neske, 1978);

Fritz Kühnlenz, *Schiller in Thüringen: Stätten seines Lebens und Wirkens,* second edition (Rudolstadt: Greifenverlag, 1976);

Marietta Kuntz, *Schillers Theaterpraxis* (Zurich: Juris, 1979);

Eduard Lachmann, *Die Natur des Demetrius* (Hildesheim: Gerstenberg, 1975);

Rolf N. Linn, *Schillers junge Idealisten* (Berkeley & London: University of California Press, 1973);

William P. Mainland, *Schiller and the Changing Past* (London: Heinemann, 1957);

Heinrich Mettler, *Entfremdung und Revolution: Brennpunkt des Klassischen. Studien zu Schillers Briefen "Über die ästhetische Erziehung des Menschen" im Hinblick auf die Begegnung mit Goethe* (Bern: Francke, 1977);

Peter Michelsen, *Der Bruch mit der Vater-Welt: Studien zu Schillers "Räubern"* (Heidelberg: Winter, 1979);

Wolfgang Militz, *Friedrich Schiller: Ein Weg zum Geist* (Stuttgart, 1974);

R. D. Miller, *The Drama of Schiller* (Harrogate, U.K.: Duchy Press, 1963);

Horst Nitschack, *Kritik der ästhetischen Wirklichkeitskonstitution: Eine Untersuchung zu den ästhetischen Schriften Kants und Schillers* (Frankfurt am Main: Roter Stern, 1976);

Birgit Osterwald, *Das Demetrius-Thema in der russischen und deutschen Literatur: Dargestellt an A. P. Sumarokovs "Dimitrij Samozvanec," A. S. Puskins "Boris Godunov" und F. Schillers "Demetrius"* (Münster: Aschendorff, 1982);

Charles E. Passage, *Friedrich Schiller* (New York: Ungar, 1975);

Helmut Pillau, *Die fortgedachte Dissonanz: Hegels Tragödientheorie und Schillers Tragödie. Deutsche Antworten auf die Französische Revolution* (Munich: Fink, 1981);

Hans-Georg Pott, *Die schöne Freiheit: Eine Interpretation zu Schillers Schrift Über die ästhetische Erziehung des Menschen in einer Reihe von Briefen* (Munich: Fink, 1980);

Deric Regin, *Freedom and Dignity: The Historical and Philosophical Thought of Schiller* (The Hague: Nijhoff, 1965);

Vicky Rippere, *Schiller and "Alienation"* (Bern: Lang, 1981);

Henning Rischbieter, *Friedrich Schiller,* 2 volumes, second edition (Munich: Deutscher Taschenbuch Verlag, 1969–1975);

Willy Rosalewski, *Schillers Ästhetik im Verhältnis zur Kantischen* (Nendeln, Liechtenstein: Kraus, 1978);

Georg Ruppelt, *Schiller im nationalsozialistischen Deutschland: Der Versuch einer Gleichschaltung* (Stuttgart: Metzler, 1979);

Friedegard Schaefer, *Friedrich Schiller* (Berlin: Stadtbibliothek, 1980);

Joachim Schmidt-Neubauer, *Tyrannei und der Mythos zum Glück: Drei Essays zu Lessing, Schiller und Goethe* (Frankfurt am Main: Fischer, 1981);

Hans H. Schulte, *"Werke der Begeisterung": Friedrich Schiller–Idee und Eigenart seines Schaffens* (Bonn: Bouvier, 1980);

Lesley Sharpe, *Schiller and the Historical Character: Presentation and Interpretation in the Historiographical Works and in the Historical Dramas* (Oxford: Oxford University Press, 1982);

Sigrid Siedhoff, *Der Dramaturg Schiller, "Egmont": Goethes Text, Schillers Bearbeitung* (Bonn: Bouvier, 1983);

Andreas Siekmann, *Drama und sentimentalisches Bewußtsein: Zur klassischen Dramatik Schillers* (Frankfurt am Main: Haag-Herchen, 1980);

John D. Simons, *Friedrich Schiller* (Boston: Twayne, 1981);

E. L. Stahl, *Friedrich Schiller's Drama: Theory and Practice* (Oxford: Clarendon Press, 1954);

Emil Staiger, *Friedrich Schiller* (Zurich: Atlantis, 1967);

Staiger, Friedrich *Schlegels Sieg über Schiller* (Heidelberg: Winter, 1981);

Paul Steck, *Schiller und Shakespeare: Idee und Wirklichkeit* (Frankfurt am Main: Lang, 1977);

Gerhard Storz, *Der Dichter Friedrich Schiller* (Stuttgart: Klett, 1963);

Heinrich Teutschmann, *Schillers verborgene Schöpfung* (Dornach, Switzerland: Philosophisch-Anthroposophischer Verlag, 1977);

Peter Utz, *Die ausgehöhlte Gasse: Stationen der Wirkungsgeschichte von Schillers "Wilhelm Tell"* (Königstein: Forum Academicum, 1984;

Julia Wernly, *Prolegomena zu einem Lexikon der ästhetisch-ethischen Terminologie Friedrich Schillers* (Hildesheim: Gerstenberg, 1975);

Leonard P. Wessell, *The Philosophical Background to Friedrich Schiller's Aesthetics of Living Form* (Frankfurt am Main: Lang, 1982);

Benno von Wiese, *Friedrich Schiller,* fourth edition (Stuttgart: Metzler, 1978);

Kenneth Parmelee Wilcox, *Anmut und Würde: Die Dialektik der menschlichen Vollendung bei Schiller* (Bern: Lang, 1981);

Gero von Wilpert, *Schiller-Chronik: Sein Leben und Schaffen* (Stuttgart: Kröner, 1958);

Andreas Wirth, *Das schwierige Schöne: Zu Schillers Ästhetik. Auch eine Interpretation der Abhandlung "Über Matthissons Gedichte," 1794* (Bonn: Bouvier, 1975);

William Witte, *Schiller* (Oxford: Blackwell, 1949);

Wolfgang Wittkowski, ed., *Friedrich Schiller: Ein Symposium* (Tübingen: Niemeyer, 1982);

Helga Zepp-LaRouche, *Das geheime Wissen des Friedrich Schiller* (Wiesbaden: Campaigner, 1979);

Theodore Ziolkowski, *The Classical German Elegy* (Princeton: Princeton University Press, 1980), pp. 3–134.

Papers:

More than half of Friedrich Schiller's papers are in the Schiller National-Museum at Marbach am Neckar. The remainder are deposited in the Goethe-und-Schiller Archiv, Weimar. A selection from his personal library and memorabilia is on display at his house in Weimar, Schillerstraße 12, which is now a museum.

Arthur Schnitzler

(15 May 1862 – 21 October 1931)

Gerd K. Schneider
Syracuse University

This entry originally appeared in DLB 81: Austrian
Fiction Writers, 1875–1913.

BOOKS: *Anatol: Mit einer Einleitung von Loris* (Berlin:
   Bibliographisches Bureau, 1893); translated by
   Grace Isabel Colbron as *Anatol,* in *Anatol; Living
   Hours; The Green Cockatoo* (New York: Boni & Live-
   right, 1917), pp. 1–97;

Das Märchen: Schauspiel in drei Aufzügen (Dresden &
   Leipzig: Pierson, 1894; revised edition, Berlin:
   Fischer, 1902);

Sterben: Novelle (Berlin: Fischer, 1895); translated by
   Harry Zohn as "Dying," in *The Little Comedy and
   Other Stories* (New York: Ungar, 1977), pp. 147–
   234;

Liebelei: Schauspiel in drei Akten (Berlin: Fischer, 1896); trans-
   lated by Bayard Quincy Morgan as *Light-O'-Love: A
   Drama in Three Acts* (Chicago: Dramatic Publishing
   Co., 1912);

Die Frau des Weisen: Novelletten (Berlin: Fischer, 1898);

Freiwild: Schauspiel in drei Akten (Berlin: Fischer, 1898);
   translated by Paul H. Grummann as *Free Game*
   (Boston: Badger, 1913);

Der grüne Kakadu; Paracelsus; Die Gefährtin: Drei Einakter
   (Berlin: Fischer, 1899); translated by Horace B.
   Samuel as *The Green Cockatoo and Other Plays* (Chicago: McClurg, 1913)—comprises *The Green Cockatoo: Grotesque in One Act. The Mate, Paracelsus;*

Das Vermächtnis: Schauspiel in drei Akten (Berlin: Fischer,
   1899); translated by Mary L. Stephenson as *The
   Legacy: Drama in Three Acts, Poet Lore,* 22 (July–
   August 1911): 241–308;

Der Schleier der Beatrice: Schauspiel in fünf Akten (Berlin:
   Fischer, 1901);

Leutnant Gustl: Novelle (Berlin: Fischer, 1901); translated
   by Richard L. Simon as *None But the Brave* (New
   York: Simon & Schuster, 1926);

Frau Bertha Garlan: Novelle (Berlin: Fischer, 1901); translated by Agnes Jacques as *Bertha Garlan* (Boston:
   Badger, 1913); translated by J. H. Wisdom and

Arthur Schnitzler

Marr Murray as *Bertha Garlan: A Novel* (London:
   Goschen, 1914);

Lebendige Stunden: Vier Einakter (Berlin: Fischer, 1902);
   Die Frau mit dem Dolche: Schauspiel in einem Akt, pp.
   37–70, translated by Grummann as *Living Hours:
   Four One-Act Plays* (Boston: Badger, 1913);

Reigen: Zehn Dialoge geschrieben Winter 1896/97 (Vienna & Leipzig: Wiener Verlag, 1903); translated by L. D. Edwards and F. L. Glaser as *Hands Around: A Cycle of Ten Dialogues* (New York: Privately printed, 1920); translated by Eric Bentley as *La Ronde,* in *Arthur Schnitzler: Plays and Stories,* edited by Egon Schwarz (New York: Continuum, 1982), pp. 53–116; translated by Charles Osborne as *The Round Dance,* in *The Round Dance and Other Plays* (Manchester, U.K.: Carcanet New Press, 1982);

Der Einsame Weg: Schauspiel in fünf Akten (Berlin: Fischer, 1904); translated by Edwin Björkman as *The Lonely Way* (Boston: Little, Brown, 1904);

Die griechische Tänzerin: Novellen (Vienna & Leipzig: Wiener Verlag, 1905);

Marionetten: Drei Einakter (Berlin: Fischer, 1906);

Der Ruf des Lebens: Schauspiel in drei Akten (Berlin: Fischer, 1906);

Zwischenspiel: Komödie in drei Akten (Berlin: Fischer, 1906); translated by Björkman as *Intermezzo: A Comedy in Three Acts,* in *The Lonely Way; Intermezzo; Countess Mizzie: Three Plays* (New York: Kennerley, 1915), pp. 139–259;

Dämmerseelen: Novellen (Berlin: Fischer, 1907);

Der Weg ins Freie: Roman (Berlin: Fischer, 1908); translated by Samuel as *The Road to the Open* (New York: Knopf, 1932; London: Allen & Unwin, 1932);

Der tapfere Kassian: Singspiel in einem Aufzug, music by Oscar Straus (Leipzig & Vienna: Doblinger, 1909);

Der junge Medardus: Dramatische Historie in einem Vorspiel und fünf Aufzügen (Berlin: Fischer, 1910);

Der Schleier der Pierrette: Pantomime in drei Bildern, music by Ernst von Dohnanyi (Vienna & Leipzig: Doblinger, 1910);

Das weite Land: Tragikomödie in fünf Akten (Berlin: Fischer, 1911); translated by Edward Woticky and Alexander Caro as *The Vast Domain: A Tragi-Comedy in Five Acts, Poet Lore,* 324 (September 1923): 317–407; translated by Tom Stoppard as *Undiscovered Country* (Boston & London: Faber & Faber, 1980);

Masken und Wunder: Novellen (Berlin: Fischer, 1912);

Professor Bernhardi: Komödie in fünf Akten (Berlin: Fischer, 1912); translated by Hetty Landstone as *Professor Bernhardi: A Comedy in Five Acts* (London: Faber & Gwyer, 1927); translated by Mrs. Emil Pohli as *Professor Bernhardi,* in *A Golden Treasury of Jewish Literature,* edited by Leo W. Schwarz (New York & Toronto: Farrar & Rinehart, 1937), pp. 468–504;

Frau Beate und ihr Sohn: Novelle (Berlin: Fischer, 1913); translated by Jacques as *Beatrice: A Novel* (New York: Simon & Schuster, 1926);

Gesammelte Werke in zwei Abteilungen, 7 volumes (Berlin: Fischer, 1913–1914);

Komödie der Worte: Drei Einakter (Berlin: Fischer, 1915); translated, with additions, by Pierre Loving as *Comedies of Words and Other Play* (Cincinnati: Stewart & Kidd, 1917);

Fink und Fliederbusch: Komödie in drei Akten (Berlin: Fischer, 1917);

Doktor Gräsler, Badearzt: Erzählung (Berlin: Fischer, 1917); translated by E. C. Slade as *Dr. Graesler* (New York: Seltzer, 1923; London: Chapman & Hall, 1924);

Casanovas Heimfahrt: Novelle (Berlin: Fischer, 1918); translated by Eden and Cedar Paul as *Casanova's Homecoming* (New York: Seltzer, 1922; London: Brentano's, 1923);

Die Schwestern oder Casanova in Spa: Ein Lustspiel in Versen. Drei Akte in einem (Berlin: Fischer, 1919);

Komödie der Verführung: in drei Akten (Berlin: Fischer, 1924);

Fräulein Else: Novelle (Berlin, Vienna & Leipzig: Zsolnay, 1924); translated by Robert A. Simon as *Fräulein Else: A Novel* (New York: Simon & Schuster, 1925); translated by F. H. Lyon as *Fräulein Else* (London: Philpot, 1925);

Die Frau des Richters: Novelle (Berlin: Propyläen, 1925); translated by Peter Bauland as "The Judge's Wife," in *The Little Comedy and Other Stories,* pp. 85–145;

Traumnovelle (Berlin: Fischer, 1926); translated by Otto P. Schinnerer as *Rhapsody: A Dream Novel* (New York: Simon & Schuster, 1927; London: Constable, 1928);

Der Gang zum Weiher: Dramatische Dichtung in fünf Aufzügen (Berlin: Fischer, 1926);

Spiel im Morgengrauen: Novelle (Berlin: Fischer, 1927); translated by William A. Drake as *Day-break* (New York: Simon & Schuster, 1927);

Buch der Sprüche und Bedenken: Aphorismen und Betrachtungen (Vienna: Phaidon, 1927); partially translated by Dorothy Alden as "Aphorisms: From an Unpublished Book 'Proverbs and Reflections,'" *Plain Talk,* 2 (May 1928): 590; 3 (October 1928): 419; (December 1928): 733; edited and partially translated by Frederick Ungar as *Practical Wisdom: A Treasury of Aphorisms and Reflections from the German* (New York: Ungar, 1977);

Der Geist im Wort und der Geist in der Tat: Vorläufige Bemerkungen zu zwei Diagrammen (Berlin: Fischer, 1927); translated by Robert O. Weiss as *The Mind in Words and Action: Preliminary Remarks Concerning Two Diagrams* (New York: Ungar, 1972);

Therese: Chronik eines Frauenlebens (Berlin: Fischer, 1928); translated by Drake as *Therese: The Chronicle of a Woman's Life* (New York: Simon & Schuster, 1928);

Im Spiel der Sommerlüfte: in drei Aufzügen (Berlin: Fischer, 1930);

Flucht in die Finsternis: Novelle (Berlin: Fischer, 1931); translated by Drake as *Flight into Darkness: A Novel* (New York: Simon & Schuster, 1931);

Anatols Größenwahn: Ein Akt (Berlin: Fischer, 1932);

Die Gleitenden: Ein Akt (Berlin: Fischer, 1932);

Die kleine Komödie: Frühe Novellen (Berlin: Fischer, 1932);

Die Mörderin: Tragische Posse in einem Akt (Berlin: Fischer, 1932);

Abenteurernovelle (Vienna: Bermann-Fischer, 1937);

Über Krieg und Frieden (Stockholm: Bermann-Fischer, 1939); translated by Weiss as *Some Day Peace Will Return: Notes on Peace and War* (New York: Ungar, 1972);

Gesammelte Werke: Die Erzählenden Schriften, 2 volumes (Frankfurt am Main: Fischer, 1961–1962);

Gesammelte Werke: Die Dramatischen Werke, 2 volumes (Frankfurt am Main: Fischer, 1962);

Das Wort: Tragikomödie in fünf Akten. Aus dem Nachlaß, edited by Kurt Bergel (Frankfurt am Main: Fischer, 1966);

Aphorismen und Betrachtungen, edited by Weiss (Frankfurt am Main: Fischer, 1967);

Jugend in Wien: Eine Autobiographie, edited by Therese Nickl and Heinrich Schnitzler (Vienna, Munich & Zurich: Molden, 1968); translated by Catherine Hutter as *My Youth in Vienna* (New York & San Francisco: Holt, Rinehart & Winston, 1970);

Frühe Gedichte, edited by Herbert Lederer (Berlin: Propyläen, 1969);

Zug der Schatten: Drama in 9 Bildern. Aus dem Nachlaß, edited by Francoise Derré (Frankfurt am Main: Fischer, 1970);

Meisterdramen (Frankfurt am Main: Fischer, 1971);

Meistererzählungen (Frankfurt am Main: Fischer, 1975);

Ritterlichkeit: Fragment. Aus dem Nachlaß, edited by R. Schlein (Bonn: Bouvier, 1975);

Entworfenes und Verworfenes: Aus dem Nachlaß, edited by Reinhard Urbach (Frankfurt am Main: Fischer, 1977);

Gesammelte Werke in Einzelausgaben, 15 volumes (Frankfurt am Main: Fischer, 1977–1979);

Tagebuch 1909–1912, edited by Werner Welzig and others (Vienna: Verlag der Österreichischen Akademie der Wissenschaften, 1981);

Tagebuch 1913–1916, edited by Welzig and others (Vienna: Verlag der Österreichischen Akademie der Wissenschaften, 1983);

Tagebuch 1917–1919, edited by Welzig and others (Vienna: Verlag der Österreichischen Akademie der Wissenschaften, 1985);

Tagebuch 1879–1892, edited by Welzig and others (Vienna: Verlag der Österreichischen Akademie der Wissenschaften, 1987);

Beziehungen und Einsamkeiten: Aphorismen, edited by Clemens Eich (Frankfurt am Main: Fischer, 1987).

PERIODICAL PUBLICATIONS: "Er wartet auf den vazierenden Gott," *Deutsche Wochenschrift,* 4 (12 December 1886): 644;

"Amerika," *An der schönen blauen Donau,* 4, no. 1 (1889): 197; translated by Franzi Ascher as "America," *Decision,* 3 (January/February 1942): 35–36;

"Mein Freund Ypsilon: Aus den Papieren eines Arztes," *An der schönen blauen Donau,* 4, no. 2 (1889): 25–28;

"Der Andere: Aus dem Tagebuch eines Hinterbliebenen," *An der schönen blauen Donau,* 4, no. 21 (1889): 490–492;

Alkandis Lied: Dramatisches Gedicht in einem Aufzug, An der schönen blauen Donau, 5, no. 17 (1890): 398–400; no. 18 (1890): 424–426;

"Reichtum," *Moderne Rundschau,* 3 (1 September 1891): 385–391; (15 September 1891): 417–423; 4 (1 October 1891): 1–7; (15 October 1891): 34–40; translated by Helene Scher as "Riches," in *The Little Comedy and Other Stories* (New York: Ungar, 1977), pp. 37–73;

"Der Sohn: Aus den Papieren eines Arztes," *Freie Bühne für den Entwicklungskampf der Zeit,* 3 (January 1892): 89–94; translated by Peggy Stamon as "The Son," in *The Little Comedy and Other Stories,* pp. 75–83;

"Blumen," *Wiener Neue Revue,* 5 (1 August 1894): 151–157; translated by Frederick Eisemann as "Flowers," in *Viennese Idylls* (Boston: Luce, 1913), pp. 1–18; translated by Elsie M. Lang as "Flowers," in *Beatrice and Other Stories* (London: Laurie, 1926), pp. 121–136;

"Der Witwer," *Wiener Allgemeine Zeitung,* 25 December 1894, pp. 3–4; translated by Paul F. Dvorak as "The Widower," in *Illusion and Reality: Plays and Stories by Arthur Schnitzler* (New York, Bern & Frankfurt am Main: Lang, 1986), pp. 129–138;

"Die drei Elixiere," *Moderner Musen-Almanach auf das Jahr 1894: Ein Jahrbuch deutscher Kunst,* 2 (1894): 44–49;

"Die kleine Komödie," *Neue Deutsche Rundschau,* 6 (August 1895): 779–798; translated by George Edward Reynolds as "The Little Comedy," in *The Little Comedy and Other Stories,* pp. 1–36;

"Ein Abschied," *Neue Deutsche Rundschau,* 7 (February 1896): 115–124;

"Die überspannte Person," *Simplicissimus,* 1 (18 April 1896): 3, 6; translated by Dvorak as "The High-Strung Woman," in *Illusion and Reality: Plays and Stories of Arthur Schnitzler,* pp. 63–68;

"Die Frau des Weisen," *Die Zeit,* 2 January 1897, pp. 15–16; 9 January 1897, pp. 31–32; 16 January 1897, pp. 47–48; translated by Eisemann as "The Sage's Wife," in *Viennese Idylls,* pp. 19–52; translated by Lang as "The Wife of the Wise Man," in *Beatrice and Other Stories,* pp. 163–188;

Halbzwei: Ein Akt, Die Gesellschaft, 13 (April 1897): 42–49; translated by Dvorak as *One-Thirty,* in *Illusion and Reality: Plays and Stories of Arthur Schnitzler,* pp. 69–76;

"Die Toten schweigen," *Cosmopolis,* 8 (October 1897): 193–211; translated by Courtland H. Young as "The Dead are Silent," in *Short Story Classics: Foreign,* edited by William Patten (New York: Collier, 1907), III: 953–977;

"Der Ehrentag," *Die Romanwelt,* 5, no. 16 (1897): 507–516; translated by Agnes Jacques as "The Hour of Fame," in *Beatrice and Other Stories,* pp. 189–220; translated by Jacques as "The Jest," in *Rejections of 1927,* edited by Charles H. Baker (Garden City, N.Y.: Doubleday, Doran, 1928), pp. 171–194;

"Um eine Stunde," *Neue Freie Presse,* 24 December 1899, p. 29;

"Der blinde Gieronymo und sein Bruder," *Die Zeit,* 22 December 1900, pp. 190–191; 29 December 1900, pp. 207–208; 5 January 1901, pp. 15–16; 12 January 1901, pp. 31–32; translated by Eisemann as "Blind Geronimo and His Brother," in *Viennese Idylls,* pp. 53–106;

Lebendige Stunden: Schauspiel in einem Akt, Neue Deutsche Rundschau, 12 (December 1901): 1297–1306; translated by Helen Tracy Porter as "Living Hours: A Play in One Act," *Poet Lore,* 17 (Spring 1906): 36–45; translated by Colin Clements and Alice Ernst as "Living Hours," *Stratford Journal,* 4 (March 1919): 155–166;

Sylvesternacht, Jugend, 1, no. 8 (1901): 118–119, 121–122; translated by Dvorak as "New Year's Eve," in *Illusion and Reality: Plays and Stories of Arthur Schnitzler,* pp. 77–85;

"Andreas Thameyers letzter Brief," *Die Zeit,* 26 July 1902; translated by Eisemann as "Andreas Thameyer's Last Letter," in *Viennese Idylls,* pp. 107–120;

"Die Griechische Tänzerin," *Die Zeit,* 28 September 1902; translated by Pierre Loving as "The Greek Dancer," *Dial,* 71 (September 1921): 253–264;

"Exzentrik," *Jugend,* 2, no. 30 (1902): 492–493, 495–496;

"Dämmerseele," *Neue Freie Presse,* 18 May 1902, pp. 31–33; translated by Eric Sutton as "The Stranger," in *Little Novels* (New York: Simon & Schuster, 1929), pp. 39–54;

Der Puppenspieler: Studie in einem Aufzug, Neue Freie Presse, 31 May 1903;

"Die Grüne Krawatte," *Neues Wiener Journal* (25 October 1903);

"Das Schicksal des Freiherrn von Leisenbogh," *Neue Rundschau,* 15 (July 1904): 829–842; translated by Kenneth Burke as "The Fate of the Baron von Leisenbogh," *Dial,* 75 (December 1923): 565–582;

Der tapfere Cassian: Puppenspiel in einem Akt, Neue Rundschau, 15, no. 2 (1904): 227–247; translated by Adam L. Gowans as *Gallant Cassian: A Puppet Play in One Act* (London & Glasgow: Gowans & Gray, 1914); translated by Moritz A. Jagendorf as "Gallant Cassian: A Puppet Play," *Poet Lore,* 33 (December 1922): 507–520;

"Das neue Lied: Erzählung," *Neue Freie Presse,* 23 April 1905, pp. 31–34; translated by Burke as "The New Song," *Dial,* 79 (November 1925): 355–369;

Zum großen Wurstel: Burleske in einem Akt, Die Zeit, 23 April 1905;

"Die Weissagung," *Neue Freie Presse,* 24 December 1905, pp. 31–38; translated by Marie Bush as "The Prophecy," in *Selected Austrian Short Stories,* edited by Bush (London: Milford, 1928), pp. 246–279; translated by Sutton as "The Prophecy," in *Little Novels,* pp. 79–118;

"Die Geschichte eines Genies," *Arena,* 2 (March 1907): 1290–1292;

"Der tote Gabriel: Novelle," *Neue Freie Presse,* 19 May 1907, pp. 31–35; translated by Sutton as "Dead Gabriel," in *Little Novels,* pp. 195–217;

"Der Tod des Junggesellen: Novelle," *Österreichische Rundschau,* 15 (1 April 1908): 19–26; translated by Sutton as "The Death of a Bachelor," in *Little Novels,* pp. 259–279;

Die Verwandlungen des Pierrot: Pantomime in einem Vorspiel und sechs Bildern, Die Zeit, 19 April 1908;

Komtesse Mizzi oder der Familientag: Komödie in einem Akt, Neue Freie Presse, 19 April 1908, pp. 31–35; translated by Edwin Björkman as *Countess Mizzie* (Boston: Little, Brown, 1907);

"Der Mörder: Novelle," *Neue Freie Presse,* 4 June 1911, pp. 31–38; translated by O. F. Theis as "The Murderer," in *The Shepherd's Pipe and Other Stories* (New York: Brown, 1922), pp. 81–120;

"Die dreifache Warnung," *Die Zeit,* 4 June 1911; translated by Barrett H. Clark as "The Triple Warning," in *Great Stories of the World: A Collection of Complete Short Stories from the Literatures of All Periods and Countries,* edited by Clark and Maxim Lieber (New York: McBride, 1925), pp. 284–285;

"Die Hirtenflöte: Novelle," *Neue Rundschau,* 22 (September 1911): 1249–1273; translated by Theis as "The Shepherd's Pipe," in *The Shepherd's Pipe and Other Stories,* pp. 15–80;

"Das Tagebuch der Redegonda: Novellette," *Süddeutsche Monatshefte,* 9 (October 1911): 1–7; translated by Sutton as "Redegonda's Diary," in *Little Novels,* pp. 181–192;

"Wohltaten, still und rein gegeben," *Neues Wiener Tagblatt,* 25 December 1931, pp. 27–28; translated as "Charity's Reward," *Living Age,* 342 (March 1932): 48–52;

"Welch eine Melodie," *Neue Rundschau,* 43 (1932): 659–663;

"Der Sekundant," *Vossische Zeitung* (1–4 January 1932); translated by Dvorak as "The Second," in *Illusion and Reality: Plays and Stories of Arthur Schnitzler,* pp. 199–216;

"Der letzte Brief eines Literaten: Novelle," *Neue Rundschau,* 43 (January 1932): 14–37; translated by Dvorak as "The Last Letter of an Artist," in *Illusion and Reality: Plays and Stories by Arthur Schnitzler,* pp. 177–198;

"Die Nächste," *Neue Freie Presse,* 27 March 1932, pp. 33–39;

"Der Empfindsame: Eine Burleske," *Neue Rundschau,* 43 (May 1932): 663–669;

"Ein Erfolg," *Neue Rundschau,* 43 (May 1932): 669–678;

"Der Fürst im Hause," *Wiener Arbeiter Zeitung* (15 May 1932);

"Frühlingsnacht im Seziersaal: Phantasie," *Jahrbuch Deutscher Bibliophilen und Literatur-freunde,* 18–19 (1932–1933): 86–91;

"Boxeraufstand: Fragment. Entwurf zu einer Novelle," *Neue Rundschau,* 68, no. 1 (1957): 84–87;

"Über Psychoanalyse," edited by Reinhard Urbach, *Protokolle,* 2 (1976): 277–284.

Arthur Schnitzler was born on 15 May 1862 in Vienna, the first child of Johann Schnitzler, a laryngologist, and Louise Markbreiter Schnitzler, a physician's daughter. Johann Schnitzler, who wrote for the *Wiener Medizinische Presse* and in 1887 founded the *Internationale Klinische Rundschau,* was also one of the twelve founders of the Allgemeine Wiener Poliklinik (General Viennese Polyclinic), which he headed until his death in 1893. Johann Schnitzler did not have much impact on his son's literary work, which he did not fully understand and of which he occasionally disapproved. The family was Jewish, but nor orthodox, and Jewishness became for Arthur Schnitzler only a question of race, not one of religious commitment. His lengthy novel *Der Weg ins Freie* (1908; translated as *The Road to the Open,* 1932) contains many discussions on Jewish problems; a comment made by Heinrich Bermann, a character in this work, seems to reflect Schnitzler's view: "Was ist Ihnen Ihr 'Heitmatland' Palästina? Ein geographischer Begriff. Was bedeutet Ihnen 'der Glaube Ihrer Väter'? Eine

Sammlung von Gebräuchen, die sie längst nicht mehr halten und von denen Ihnen die meisten gerade so lächerlich und abgeschmackt vorkommen, als mir" ("What does your 'homeland' Palestine mean to you? A geographical concept. What meaning does 'the belief of your forefathers' have for you? A collection of customs to which they have not adhered for a long time and most of which appear as ridiculous and tasteless to you as to me").

In 1879 Schnitzler graduated with distinction from the Viennese Akademisches Gymnasium, and, following his father's wish, he enrolled in the School of Medicine of the University of Vienna. His heart, however, was in writing. His time was spent primarily in cafés or coffeehouses, which were the typical meeting places for young people of his social class. These cafés were also frequented by artists or would-be artists in need of like-minded people and of an audience interested in new ideas and approaches to literature. In 1885 Schnitzler completed his studies and became a doctor of medicine, working in residence at the General Hospital in Vienna until 1888. In 1886 he met Olga Waisnix, who was married and the mother of three sons. Her husband was the owner of the renowned Thalhof in Reichenau, where Schnitzler and his family occasionally spent a few weeks during their summer vacations. Schnitzler and Olga Waisnix fell in love; their relationship remained platonic, however, owing to Olga's scruples and to her fear of disclosure, which, according to the customs of the time, would surely have led to a duel. Olga recognized Schnitzler's poetic talent; she strengthened his belief in his creativity and encouraged him to write and submit his work to a publisher. Schnitzler did so in 1886, and a few aphorisms and a short story, "Er wartet auf den vazierenden Gott" (He Is Waiting for the Vacationing God), were printed. In the same year he became an assistant in his father's clinic; in 1887 he took over as editor of the *Internationale Klinische Rundschau,* a position he held until 1894. He contributed as many as twenty-five articles to the magazine, most of them book reviews.

Between 1888 and 1891 Schnitzler worked on *Anatol* (1893; translated, 1917), a cycle of seven one-act plays held together by Anatol, a young bachelor who discusses his views on women and other personal subjects with his friend Max. Each play in the cycle adds a new facet to his character; although kind and affable, he is basically superficial. Anatol is a "melancholischer Liebhaber" (melancholy lover) who prefers to hang on to his illusions rather than be disappointed by the facts. In the first play, *Die Frage an das Schicksal* (The Question of Fate; translated as *Ask No Questions and You'll Hear No Stories*), Anatol has the opportunity to ask his girlfriend Cora, whom he has hypnotized, whether she really loves him. He does not have the courage to do so, rationalizing his decision by doubting whether the real truth can ever be known. In the second play, *Weihnachtseinkäufe* (translated as *A Christmas Present*), Anatol meets Gabriele, a married high-society lady. She suggests a present for Cora, who, in contrast to Gabriele, is naive enough to love someone unconditionally. Anatol's feelings for Cora are nurtured not only by her devotion to him but also by her inability to use big words and to make promises and eternal vows.

Plays from the *Anatol* cycle were staged separately between 1893 and 1901; in December 1903 Otto Brahm produced five of the plays at the Berlin Lessing Theater and at the Vienna Deutsches Volkstheater. After 1910 the *Anatol* cycle was played more often, and today it is part of the repertoires of major theaters around the world. The reception of *Anatol* in the United States was positive, especially the 1912 premiere with John Barrymore; later, as Stephanie Hammer reports, "the play came increasingly to be dealt with as either a curio or a farce."

Between 1890 and 1891 Schnitzler finished his first full-length play, *Das Märchen* (The Fairy Tale, 1894), based on his relationship with the actress Mizi Glümer. She was passed on to him as a sixteen-year-old by his acquaintance Theodor Friedman, with whom he sometimes exchanged girls once they lost their charm or novelty. Schnitzler was Mizi's third affair, and thus she was considered a fallen woman who could not expect to be treated as a lady in a society that cherished appearance more than essence. Schnitzler, however, fell in love with her. Their affair was characterized by passion and extreme jealousy and proved to be an emotional roller coaster, but it was primarily Mizi who helped him to mature and become more productive. In 1925, having learned of her death, Schnitzler noted in his diary: "Am (7?) Juli 1889 lernte ich sie kennen, keinem Wesen verdankt mein Dichtertum so viel wie ihr. Keine hat mich geliebt wie sie (besonders nach ihrem 'Betrug')" (On (7?) July 1889 I made her acquaintance. My writing is indebted to her as to no one else. No one has loved me as she [especially after her "betrayal"]). Schnitzler thought of marrying her but rejected the idea for two reasons he recorded in his diary: "sie heiraten kann ich nicht. Es ist materiell unmöglich, und ich gesteh' es, in Wien mit ihr als mit meiner Frau zu leben bin ich noch zu feig.–Ich brauch das nicht näher auszuführen–es steht alles schon im Märchen" (I cannot marry her. It is impossible for material reasons, and I confess that I am still too much of a coward to live in Vienna with her as my wife.–I don't have to explain this further–everything is already contained in *Das Märchen*).

In *Das Märchen* the actress Fanny Theren has had two lovers before she meets Fedor Denner, who does not seem to be a slave to the rigid rules of society. Denner talks about the "fairy tale of the fallen woman," and his revolutionary words give Fanny new hope. Denner, however, is too weak to shake off the chains of convention, and he leaves her. Fedor's words at the end show the conflict Schnitzler suffered in his relationship with Mizi, a conflict not only between reason and emotion but also between emotional states: "und es gibt keinen Kuß keusch genug–und keine Umarmung glühend genug, und keine Liebe ewig genug, um die alten Küsse und die alte Liebe auszulöschen. Was war, ist!–Das ist der tiefe Sinn des Geschehenen" (and there is no kiss chaste enough–and no embrace scorching enough, and no love eternal enough, to extinguish the old kisses and the old love. What was, is!–that is the deeper significance of events). In his diary entry of 31 December 1922 Schnitzler wrote: "Was war, ist, das ist der tiefere Sinn des Geschehenen,–noch heute das Motto meines innern Lebens" (what was, is, that is the deeper significance of events,–today still the motto of my inner life).

The three versions of the play show Schnitzler's dissatisfaction with any one solution and his aversion to any one-sided dogma. As Sol Liptzin points out, "The apparent contradictions often encountered in Schnitzler's works result from his anxiety to view each problem from various angles. . . . After he has treated a problem from one angle and offered an apparently successful solution to it, he is tempted to revert to the same problem from another angle and to demonstrate the absurdity of the very same solution."

Schnitzler wrote several short stories between 1889 and 1892; the best known is *Sterben* (1895; translated as "Dying," 1977), which he began in February 1892 and finished five months later. It is a realistic portrayal of a young man, ironically called Felix (the happy one), who learns that he is soon to die. He does not want to die alone, so he is happy when his girlfriend Marie informs him that she intends to share his fate. During the weeks that follow deterioration sets in, not only in Felix's physical appearance but also in Marie's love for him. At the end she disassociates herself from him and follows her instinct to live. The story, sometimes referred to as an "Anti-Tristan," shows Schnitzler's mastery of clinical observation and his doubt about "eternal" promises.

In 1893 *Das Märchen* premiered at the Deutsches Volkstheater with the well-known actress Adele Sandrock as Fanny Theren; it was withdrawn after the second performance. The Viennese audience could not yet accept the daring thesis that a woman's value and honor were independent of the number of lovers she had had.

Schnitzler's breakthrough came in 1894, when *Liebelei* (1896; translated as *Light-O'-Love,* 1912) was performed. This play was based on Schnitzler's love affair with Marie Reinhard. Fritz has an affair with a married woman and is killed by the woman's husband in a duel. One irony is that he is no longer in love with the woman but, according to the social convention of his time, has to duel with the betrayed husband. The other irony is that Fritz had just met Christine, a so-called süßes Mädel (sweet girl) who is ignorant of her lover's other affair. Equally ironic is Christine's label *süßes Mädel,* a type Reinhard Urbach describes "as a loving and frivolous young thing from the outskirts who, during the flower of her youth, seeks pleasurable experience with the young men of better social class and then, in maturity, marries a workman–a good man." This definition much better fits Christine's friend Mizi, who, knowing the rules of the game, has an affair with Fritz's friend Theodor. When Christine learns of her lover's death, she feels betrayed and runs away. Christine's action is not motivated by Fritz's death; as J. P. Stern points out in his introduction to *Liebelei:* "The tragic conclusion lies not in Fritz's death in the duel, but in Christine's realization that she meant nothing to him: that *nothing* meant anything to him: and that she gave herself, all she was, to this nothing. The tragic conclusion lies in her realization of an absolute betrayal." Michaela L. Perlmann agrees with this verdict: "Im Duell mit dem Gatten der verheirateten Geliebten stirbt Fritz und zerstört damit das Selbstgefühl der schwächeren Partnerin, die sich um ihre Illusion von der wahren Liebe betrogen sieht" (Fritz dies in the duel with the husband of his married mistress, and thus he destroys the self-assurance of his weaker partner, who sees herself betrayed in her illusion of true love).

Liebelei premiered on 9 October 1895 with Adele Sandrock as Christine. A scandal was anticipated because Mizi and Christine daringly visit the apartment of a young man; the premiere, however, was a success, as were subsequent performances in the Deutsches Theater in Berlin, with Brahm directing. Successful performances were also staged in New York in 1905 under the title *Flirtation;* the American title was changed in 1907 to *The Reckoning.* More recent performances in the United States have not received the same acclaim; a possible explanation is suggested by Hammer: "*Liebelei* is generally not hedonistic, erotic, and amoral, that is to say, not European, not Austrian, and especially not Viennese enough to satisfy an American audience, which both craves and fears the artistic presentation of continental degenerateness. Sadly it seems that *Liebelei* must await the magic of Stoppardization in order to win the attention which it deserves on the U.S. stage."

Criticism of society is also the subject of Schnitzler's next play, *Freiwild* (1898; translated as *Free Game,* 1913). The title refers to actresses in summer theaters who were considered "free game" for officers stationed in nearby garrisons. Anna Riedel refuses to obey these rules because she is in love with Paul Rönner. Lieutenant Karinsky offends Anna and is slapped by Paul. Karinsky challenges Paul to a duel, which Paul declines as a matter of principle; to save his honor, Karinsky shoots him down. The tragic figure is Anna; when she is told to leave, her final word is "Wohin?" (Where to?). She has lost the man she loved, and she cannot go back to the theater after the scandal. Schnitzler's concern was not so much the duel itself but the obligation to fight a duel. Schnitzler also criticized such social pressure in *Das weite Land* (1911; translated as *The Vast Domain,* 1923) and the fragment *Ritterlichkeit* (Chivalry, 1975). The absurdity of having to fight a duel can be clearly seen in his comedy *Fink und Fliederbusch* (1917), in which a journalist writes under two different names for opposing newspapers, changing his point of view according to the philosophy of the paper. The situation climaxes when his personas attack each other's viewpoints so vehemently that he has to challenge himself to a duel.

Probably the most controversial play Schnitzler ever wrote was *Reigen* (Round Dance, 1903; translated as *Hands Around,* 1920, and *La Ronde,* 1982). This "dance" is executed by ten couples, consisting of ten persons, doubly linked by sex. The cycle begins with a streetwalker and a soldier; in scene 2 the soldier makes love to a parlormaid; in scene 3 the parlormaid sleeps with a young gentleman, then the gentleman with a married woman, the married woman with her husband, the husband with a "süßes Mädel," the süßes Mädel with a poet, the poet with an actress, the actress with a count, and the count with the prostitute from the beginning. This play is not only about sex but also about language: the characters carefully use language to achieve their goals; the language moves from the vernacular in the first two scenes to a highly elaborated code in the last episodes. The play was written in the winter of 1896–1897 and privately printed in 1900 with a preface expressing Schnitzler's intention not to publish the play because of possible misinterpretations.

Schnitzler was right in his pessimistic prediction. The first performances–scenes four to six were staged in Munich on 25 June 1903; the entire work was performed for the first time on 13 October 1912 in Budapest–received reviews which were based less on the artistic merits of the play than on the Jewish background of its author. Hermann Bahr, trying to rescue the work and its author, scheduled a public reading of *Reigen;* but the government objected, probably not on moral grounds as much as from fear of anti-Semitic demonstrations. The book version was confiscated by the prosecuting attorney's office in Berlin on 16 March 1904, and its sale was banned throughout Germany. This prohibition, however, did not deter various groups from giving performances of the work. After the German government lifted the ban, *Reigen* premiered on 23 December 1920 in Berlin and on 1 February 1921 in Vienna. Neither performance fared well. In Berlin nationalistic and anti-Semitic groups demonstrated during the performance of 22 February 1921. The director and the actors were prosecuted in a trial which lasted from 5 November to 18 November.

The transcript of this trial shows clearly the unstable situation in the Weimar Republic. Some comments indicate a genuine concern for the moral safety of young people who might be led into thinking that love is nothing but the pursuit of sexual satisfaction; other comments, however, reveal anti-Semitic sentiments. Pointing to the Jewish director and the Jewish author, the witnesses accused the Jews of demoralizing the German people, especially the young. Racial invectives came from Nazi groups and other right-wing organizations. "Für die Verteidigung kommt es darauf an, festzustellen, daß es sich gar nicht um einen Kampf gegen den *Reigen* handelt, sondern um einen Kampf gegen die Juden, daß man den *Reigen* nur benutzt hat, um in dieser Form eine antisemitische Aktion ins Werk zu setzen" (For the defense it is important to state that this trial is indeed not a battle against *Reigen* but one against the Jews, that *Reigen* was only used in order to bring about an anti-Semitic action). The trial ended with the acquittal of the defendants, but Schnitzler decided to withdraw the play in Germany and Austria. It was not until 1982 that *Reigen* could be seen again in those countries.

Reigen was not easily accepted in America, either. Translated into English by F. L. Glaser and L. D. Edwards as *Hands Around* in 1920, it was banned in New York State at the instigation of John S. Sumner, secretary of the New York Society for the Suppression of Vice. In 1929 charges were brought against a New York bookstore owner who had *Reigen* in stock; the case was dismissed with the following ruling: "Although the theme of the book is admittedly the quite universal literary theme of men and women, the author deals with it in a cold and analytical, one might even say scientific, manner that precludes any salacious interpretation. A careful scrutiny reveals not a single line, not a single word, that might be regarded as obscene, lewd, lascivious, filthy, indecent, or disgusting within the meaning of the statute." The French movie version of *Reigen*, titled *La Ronde* (1950) and directed by Max Ophuls, was banned in New York State; the United States Supreme Court, however, overturned the ban in 1954.

Personal tragedies in 1897–Olga Waisnix died and Marie Reinhard's child was stillborn–influenced Schnitzler in the writing of *Das Vermächtnis* (1899; translated as *The Legacy*, 1911), in which a dying man asks his family to accept his girlfriend and child into their home. The family agrees, but favors the child over the mother. When the child dies, the mother leaves the house because she feels unwelcome. The play premiered in Berlin in 1898, directed by Brahm. Although it was initially a success, it ran for only two weeks. The same happened in Vienna; it premiered in the Burgtheater on 30 November 1898 to good initial response; but the interest of the Viennese audience waned, and *Das Vermächtnis* was canceled after only ten performances.

In 1899 Schnitzler met the young actress Olga Gussmann, whom he married in 1903, the year after the birth of their son Heinrich. Also in 1899 the Burgtheater premiered three of his one-act plays: *Der grüne Kakadu* (1899; translated as *The Green Cockatoo*, 1913), *Die Gefährtin* (1899; translated as *The Mate*, 1913), and *Paracelsus* (1899; translated, 1913). The common element running through all of these plays is the blending of illusion and reality which becomes not only for the audience but for the characters as well. In *Der grüne Kakadu* the time is 14 July 1789, the eve of the outbreak of the French Revolution. In a tavern called Der grüne Kakadu extemporaneous plays are performed for members of the aristocracy. The actors make every attempt to present their illusion as reality; the audience is titillated by the thought that these exchanges could be true, even though it knows that they are not. What the audience does not realize is that the events acted out onstage will actually take place a little later on the streets of Paris, with some of the actors taking part in the real revolution. Illusion and truth are so finely interwoven that it is almost impossible to separate them. As William H. Rey comments: "Die bunte Fülle des Lebens–ist sie nicht nur gefälliger Schein, ausgebreitet über dem Abgrund des Todes? Die Wirklichkeit–ist sie nicht nur ein Traum, ein Spiel, ein Erzeugnis unserer Phantasie? Und wenn dem so ist, tritt dann nicht eine verwirrende Vertauschung der Gegensatzpole ein, so daß das Wirkliche zum Unwirklichen und das Unwirkliche zum Wirklichen wird? Eine klare Abgrenzung ist unter diesen Umständen kaum noch möglich" (The many-colored fullness of life–isn't it only a pleasing illusion, spread over the abyss of death? Reality–isn't it only a dream, a game, a product of our fantasy? And if this is so, does not then a confusing exchange of the opposite poles set in, so that the unreal becomes the real and vice versa? A clear demarcation under these circumstances is almost impossible). Adding to the confusion is that *Der grüne Kakadu* consists of three overlapping circles; as Robert Nelson remarks: "The frame or invisible play is the revolution taking place outside; the play within a play is all that we see going on in the tavern; the play within a play within a play is the 'entertainment' which Prosper offers his customers. . . . " In this mixture of reality and illusion all revolutionary efforts seem questionable: if actors are supporters of the revolution, then the revolutionaries are also actors, and the proclaimed political values thus appear in a doubtful light.

The juxtaposition of reality and unreality is also found in the verse drama *Paracelsus,* performed along with *Der grüne Kakadu* at the Deutsches Theater in Berlin in 1899. Paracelsus, the great illusionist, returns to Basel and visits Justinia, his former lover. She is now married to Cyprian, who is absolutely sure of Justinia's love. His certainty is shaken after Paracelsus hypnotizes Justinia and suggests to her that she is infatuated with a young nobleman. Awakened from the trance, Justinia asks her husband's forgiveness. Paracelsus hypnotizes her again and tells her to forget the event. When Justinia awakens the second time, she admits that she is in fact attracted to the young nobleman, but is also in love with her husband. As Martin Swales points out: "At the beginning Cyprian arrogantly asserts total possession of Justinia. As a result of Paracelsus's hypnotic arts, however, he comes to realize that he can never possess Justinia fully—there will always be memories, desires, longings in her heart of which he is not the object. But this is not to say that Justinia is incapable of fidelity; Paracelsus's hypnotism also reveals that she is happy with Cyprian and that she, at the deepest level of her being, does desire to remain faithful to him. Paracelsus's intervention does not destroy Cyprian's and Justinia's marriage. It puts it on a footing that is in one sense more precarious, because both partners are now aware of the possibility of desires and intentions that are in conflict with the marriage; and yet, in another sense, their marriage is more secure in that they know that moral certainty in relationships can only be partial, and that this partial certainty is yet a value by which man can live." The difficulty in distinguishing between inner and outer reality is expressed in *Paracelsus* in the often-quoted lines:

> Es fließen ineinander Traum und Wachen,
> Wahrheit und Lüge. Sicherheit ist nirgends.
> Wir wissen nichts von andern, nichts von uns;
> Wir spielen immer, wer es weiß, ist klug.

> (There flow together dream and waking time,
> Truth and deception. Certainty is nowhere.
> Nothing we know of others, of ourselves no more;
> We always play—and wise is he who knows.)

The theme of the nature of illusion and reality is also the basis of *Die Gefährtin.* Professor Pilgram knows that his wife, Eveline, who has just died, had an affair with his young assistant. Pilgram accepted this affair because he felt guilty about marrying someone much younger than himself. Pilgram is a man who, as he proudly announces, cannot be surprised: "Fur mich gibt es keine Überraschungen und Entdeckungen" (For me, there are no surprises and discoveries). He is wrong: he finds out that Eveline's lover was having a simultaneous affair with another woman whom he intends to marry and, worst of all, that Eveline had known of this double game all along. She had accepted this arrangement because it had provided her with emotional fulfillment she had not found in her marriage to Pilgram, whose work was more important to him than his wife. It becomes apparent that Pilgram did not know Eveline at all; as another character, Olga, points out: "wie unendlich fern von Ihnen diese Frau gelebt hat—die zufällig in diesem Hause gestorben ist" (how infinitely remote from you this woman lived—who, by coincidence, died in this house). At the end Pilgram is relieved; he smiles "wie befreit" (as if liberated), realizing that his wife's affair means that he no longer has to feel guilty.

The mixture of reality and illusion, of play and seriousness, dream and waking life points to a unity which lies outside time and space. Such a unity Schnitzler saw as an Urkraft (a primordial power) which unifies all seemingly polar elements. He believed that it was possible, under certain conditions, for the individual to transcend the limitations of time and space and to be part of this elemental power. The individual then experiences a feeling of simultaneity. This feeling occurs especially in music and in dreams.

Schnitzler shows this mystical experience in the novella *Fräulein Else* (1924; translated 1925), written in the form of an interior monologue. Else is pressured by her mother to ask the rich art dealer Dorsday for a large amount of money to help her father pay back money he borrowed from a trust fund and lost on the stock market. Dorsday promises to help on the condition that he be allowed to see Else naked for a few minutes. Else is in a state of great confusion—she wants to help her father, but her strong sense of decency forbids her succumbing to Dorsday's wish. At the same time, her sensuality is as strong as her modesty, and her love for her father includes resentment because his gambling placed her in this situation in the first place. Else has nobody to whom she can turn; Schnitzler stresses her existential loneliness in several passages. After an inner struggle, she goes to the hotel vestibule where Dorsday is sitting and shows herself in the nude to him and all the other guests. Afterward, she collapses and is carried to her room, where she takes an overdose of sleeping tablets. Before she dies, she experiences a musical vision which changes the motif of loneliness and anxiety to one of togetherness and cosmic harmony: "Ich habe ja Angst so allein. . . . Wo seid Ihr denn? . . . Was ist denn das? Ein ganzer Chor? Und Orgel auch? Ich singe mit, was ist es denn für ein Lied? Alle singen mit. Die Wälder auch und die Berge und die Sterne. Noch nie habe ich etwas so Schönes gesehen. Gib mir die Hand, Papa. Wir fliegen zusammen. So schön ist die Welt, wenn man fliegen kann" (I am afraid so alone. . . . Where are you? . . . What is this now? A complete choir? And also an organ? I am singing along, what kind of song is it? All are singing along. The forests, too, and the mountains and the stars. I have never seen anything so beautiful. Father, give me your hand. We will fly together. The world is so beautiful if one can fly). Else is in harmony with the cosmos, and out of this feeling of union she can forgive her father.

The verse drama *Der Schleier der Beatrice* (The Veil of Beatrice, 1901) is frequently cited to show that Schnitzler anticipated Freud's theory of the interpretation of dreams. The title character is a beautiful young woman who lives in Bologna during the Renaissance. Beatrice has just met the poet Filippo Loschi, and Loschi has fallen in love with her. When she tells him of a dream in which she has seen herself married to the duke, he condemns her. Later the dream comes true: Beatrice meets the duke and marries him. Then both discover the body of Loschi, who has taken his own life. Freudian dream analysis would point out that Beatrice had previously seen the duke, to whom she was unconsciously attracted. Beatrice is longing for a union of Loschi, the man of reflection, and the duke, the man of action. She also longs for death, which she regards as a transition to another existence.

Leutnant Gustl (1901; translated as *None But the Brave*, 1926), called by Swales "unquestionably the towering masterpiece of Schnitzler's prose narrative production," is written entirely in the form of an interior monologue. In a cloakroom after a concert Gustl gets into an argument with a baker who insults him and grabs his sword. Dishonored, Gustl must, according to the military code, commit suicide or quit the army. He wanders through Vienna; close to midnight he wishes that the baker would die of a stroke. When Gustl learns that this event has actually happened, a burden is removed from him. The entire experience is forgotten, along with the conviction that it was his duty to commit suicide. He returns to his aggressive nature and looks forward to a duel he knows he will win. Schnitzler's criticism of Gustl, who can be considered representative not only of Austria's army officers but of a military mentality just waiting for the outbreak of war, cost him his commission as lieutenant in the reserve. J. P. Stern, in the introduction to his edition of *Liebelei, Leutnant*

Gustl, Die letzten Masken (1966), characterizes Gustl as "a typical product of his military environment–that is, he is perfectly adjusted to it. In every one of his reactions and half-thoughts, urges, desires, fears, he conforms to and is protected by the military code, the social convention to which he conforms, and the convention is nothing more than a systematic manner of gratifying those desires and urges with the least possible bother, and of protecting him as best may be from his fears. . . . Gustl emerges as a recognizable type, as the portrait of a man in whom a number of historically significant qualities are combined in so powerful and concentrated a fashion that he becomes representative of a whole mode of life . . . the temper not only of a young Austrian lieutenant but of Europe in 1914 is encompassed." *Leutnant Gustl,* based on an experience Schnitzler's acquaintance Felix Salten had had in the foyer of the Musikvereinssaal in Vienna, not only caused one of the literary scandals of the year but led to strong anti-Semitic attacks such as this verse published in the Viennese periodical *Kikeriki* on 25 July 1901:

Leutnant Gustl, der vom Schnitzler
Als ein Feigling hingestellt,
Der nicht Mut noch Ehre kennet
Und als Kneifer sich gefällt:
War der etwa nicht ein Jude,
Wie es Schnitzler ist und bleibt?
Und wenn ja, warum dann klagen,
Daß ein Jud' "nen Jud" beschreibt?

(Lieutenant Gustl, who by Schnitzler
Is presented as a coward,
Bare of courage and of honor
And who shows himself a shirker:
Was he not himself a Jew,
Just as Schnitzler is and will be?
And if so, then why complain,
If one Jew describes another?)

In the one-act play *Die Frau mit dem Dolche* (1902; translated as *The Lady with the Dagger,* 1904) Pauline, who is married, and Leonhard, who desires her, look at a painting by an unknown Renaissance artist. Pauline points out to Leonhard that the two figures on the canvas resemble the two of them and mentions that her ancestors had come from Florence. She also says that she feels she has led a previous existence. When the bells start to ring noon, the scene on the canvas comes to life for Pauline: Paola, married to the painter Remigio, has spent the night with Lionardo. The lover boasts of the affair, but Paola makes it clear to him that a nighttime adventure does not count: "Zusammen wach sein, das allein bedeutet" (To be awake together, that alone is important). Because Lionardo brags of his adventure in front of the returned husband, Paola kills him with a dagger, and this scene is painted by Remigio. When the bells stop, Pauline returns to reality and, still in a dreamlike state, asks Leonhard: "Kommt alles wieder, was wir einst erlebt–Muß es wiederkommen?" (Does everything return that we have experienced–Must it return?). Because she is convinced of the inevitability of her fate, she will become Leonhard's lover.

Another work with a mystical basis is "Die Weissagung" (1905; translated as "The Prophecy," 1928), in which Marco Polo prophesies that a colonel who insulted him will die soon. This and another prophesied event both occur. Freud remarked about this story: "Bei uns bleibt ein Gefühl von Unbefriedigung, eine Art Groll über die versuchte Täuschung, wie ich sie besonders deutlich nach der Lektüre von Schnitzler's Erzählung *Die Weissagung* und ähnlichen mit dem Wunderbaren liebäugelnden Produkten verspürt habe" (A feeling of dissatisfaction remains with us, a kind of resentment about the attempted deception, such as I have felt, especially after having read Schnitzler's *Die Weissagung* and similar products which flirt with the supernatural).

Schnitzler's parable "Die dreifache Warnung" (1911; translated as "The Triple Warning," 1925) usually serves as the basis for a discussion of his views on free will versus determinism. A young hiker hears a voice warning him not to proceed unless he wants to commit a murder. Walking on, he hears the voice a second time, warning him not to cross a meadow unless he wants to bring disaster to his country. The youth heeds neither this warning nor a third one, to stop unless he is prepared to die. When he reaches the mountaintop, he accuses the voice of having erred. The voice now informs him of the consequences of his actions: when he crossed a meadow, he made a butterfly change its direction to the emperor's palace; it will lay an egg from which will hatch a caterpillar which will frighten the pregnant queen so that her unborn child will die. As a result, the emperor's evil brother will succeed to the throne and cause the destruction of the country. The last warning will also be fulfilled because the young man will perish on his way down from the mountaintop during the night. The youth curses the voice, which defines itself as "die Kraft, die am Anfang aller Tage war und weiter wirkt unaufhaltsam in die Ewigkeit durch alles Geschehen" (the power which was at the beginning of time and which is active in all eternity through all events). If this is true, the young man claims, then the power knew the outcome of all actions, and its warning was in vain. Were not the results of his actions, and the actions themselves, determined ahead of time? According to Rey, the youth comes to the wrong conclusion because he forgets that the same power which is outside him is also within him: "sein

Wille ist nichts anderes als eine individuelle Erscheinungsform der gleichen Lebensmacht und daher zur Mitwirkung im großen Spiel der Kräfte bestimmt" (his will is nothing else but an individual manifestation of the same vital force and therefore destined to partake in the huge play of forces). The young man had the choice to act or not to act, but once he had decided on a specific action, it had inevitable consequences.

In *Das weite Land,* which premiered in 1911, Friedrich Hofreiter accuses his wife, Genia, of fidelity! The consequence of his wife's moral character was that his friend, who wanted to have an affair with her, was driven to suicide. Hofreiter's resentment against his wife is strengthened by his own infidelity. When Genia finally enters into an affair with the young Lieutenant Otto, Hofreiter is relieved; but at the same time he invokes the social convention and kills Otto in a duel. The title is explained in the central statement of the play: "Sollt' es Ihnen noch nicht aufgefallen sein, was für komplizierte Subjekte wir Menschen im Grunde sind? So vieles hat zugleich Raum in uns–! Liebe und Trug . . . Treue und Treulosigkeit . . . Anbetung für die eine und Verlangen nach einer andern oder nach mehreren. Wir versuchen wohl Ordnung in uns zu schaffen, so gut es geht, aber diese Ordnung ist doch nur etwas Künstliches. . . . Das Natürliche . . . ist das Chaos. Ja . . . , die Seele . . . ist ein weites Land, wie ein Dichter es einmal ausdrückte. . . ." (Shouldn't you have observed what complex subjects we humans basically are? We can accommodate so many things at the same time–! Love and deception . . . faithfulness and infidelity . . . worship for one and desire for another one or others. We try to create order in us, as best we can, but this order is, to be sure, only something artificial. . . . The natural state . . . is chaos. Yes, . . . the soul . . . is a vast domain, as a poet once expressed it).

In his autobiography, *Jugend in Wien* (1968; translated as *My Youth in Vienna,* 1970), Schnitzler refers to *Das weite Land* and remarks: "Gefühl und Verstand schlafen wohl unter einem Dach, aber im übrigen führen sie in der menschlichen Seele ihren völlig getrennten Haushalt" (Feelings and understanding may sleep under the same roof, but they run their own completely separate households in the human soul). It would be wrong, though, to identify Schnitzler fully with this statement; there are some convictions which, in his view, are not subject to perspectivism. A case in point is *Professor Bernhardi* (1912; translated, 1927). Bernhardi is the director of the Elisabethinum Clinic in Vienna. A young woman patient is dying but is unaware of the fact. Since she is feeling euphoric, Bernhardi refuses to let her see a priest called in by the Catholic nurse. The nurse then informs the patient of her real condition, thus thwarting Bernhardi's attempt to make death easier for her. Because Bernhardi is a highly successful Jewish physician, the incident stirs up anti-Semitic prejudices which are fueled by the Catholic church. Bernhardi defends his action by declaring that it is his professional duty to reduce suffering and pain in any way he can. At the same time he fights against the opportunistic attacks of his colleagues, who hide their egotistical motives behind the masks of church and state ideology. Bernhardi's conviction and courage are also found in the figure of the priest, who has an unshakable belief in his mission. Schnitzler shows that understanding and a feeling of mutual tolerance are possible between opponents who are true to themselves and their callings.

Schnitzler's criticism of the prevailing attitudes in his society, especially of anti-Semitism, led the Austrian censorship to bar performance of the play in 1913. It was only after the collapse of the monarchy in 1918 that the work was allowed to be staged. Since then it has been performed many times in Europe and the United States, and many critics consider it to be one of the finest works Schnitzler ever created.

Schnitzler was a pacifist; the horrors of war are described realistically in his pamphlet *Über Krieg und Frieden* (1939; translated as *Some Day Peace Will Return*, 1972), written in 1915 during World War I:

Kriegsgreuel: Ein wehrloser Verwundeter wurde auf dem Schlachtfeld geblendet, verstümmelt, von einem Feind natürlich. Ich weiß noch Ärgeres zu erzählen: ein Dutzend Soldaten saßen in einem Schützengraben, ein Schrapnell kam, der eine wurde blind, dem anderen wurde der Bauch aufgeschlitzt, dem dritten der Kehlkopf zerfetzt, dem vierten das ganze Gesicht weggerissen, dem fünften zwei Arme und ein Bein zerschmettert und so weiter. Die nicht gleich tot waren, lagen stundenlang da in Durst, Martern, Höllenschmerzen, Todesangst. Auch sie waren wehrlos gewesen, vollkommen wehrlos. Es gab keine Möglichkeit, sich gegen das Schrapnell zu verteidigen. Auch davonlaufen durften sie nicht, dann wären sie mit Recht wegen Feigheit erschossen worden. Die Wehrpflicht hatte sie wehrlos gemacht

(War atrocity: a defenseless wounded man was blinded and mutilated on the battlefield–by an enemy, of course. I can tell a worse tale. A dozen soldiers were sitting in a trench when a shrapnel struck. One was blinded, another had his abdomen slit open, the third had his larynx shredded, the entire face of the fourth was torn off, the fifth had both arms and a leg shattered, and so forth. Those who were not immediately killed lay there for hours suffering thirst, torments, hellish pain, the fear of death. They too had been defenseless, completely defenseless. There was no possibility of defending themselves against the shrapnel. Also, they could not run off, for had they done so, they would have been shot for cowardice, justifiably. The obligation to defend their country had rendered them defenseless.)

In 1918 Schnitzler published *Casanovas Heimfahrt* (translated as *Casanova's Homecoming,* 1922), showing a morally disintegrated, aging adventurer, and in 1919 *Die Schwestern oder Casanova in Spa: Ein Lustspiel in Versen* (The Sisters; or, Casanova in Spa: A Comedy in Verse), which presents Casanova at the peak of his career as a respected diplomat, a famous mathematician, an eminent philosopher, a widely read author, and, above all, an admired amorous adventurer. *Casanovas Heimfahrt* is of greater interest than the comedy because it deals with aging, a problem Schnitzler addressed in various works. Schnitzler's concerns about the aging process are documented in his diaries. As early as 8 April 1900 he noted: "Frühlingsmorgen. Die Melancholie des Alterns. Ich weinte sehr" (Morning in springtime. The melancholy of getting old. I cried a lot). On 23 April he wrote: "Ich habe eine wachsende Angst vor dem Altwerden, ein ungeheures Bedürfnis nach Zärtlichkeit, Geliebt, Angebetet, Bewundertwerden. Nur das befreit mich zuweilen von meinem Angstgefühle" (I have a growing fear of becoming old, an immense need for tenderness, to be loved, adored, admired. Only this relieves me occasionally of my feelings of anxiety). And on 27 April he recorded his thoughts on old age in an entry which has special significance for *Casanovas Heimfahrt:* "Es gibt nur *ein* Erlebnis–das heit Altern. Alles andere ist Abenteuer" (There is only *one* experience– that is: getting old. Everything else is adventure). In the novella Casanova is fifty-three, Schnitzler's own age at the time of writing in 1915: "In seinem dreiundfünfzigsten Lebensjahre, als Casanova längst nicht mehr von der Abenteuerlust seiner Jugend, sondern von der Ruhelosigkeit nahenden Alters durch die Welt gejagt wurde, fühlte er in seiner Seele das Heimweh nach seiner Vaterstadt Venedig so heftig anwachsen, daß er sie, gleich einem Vogel, der aus luftigen Höhen zum Sterben nach abwärts steigt, in eng und immer enger werdenden Kreisen zu umziehen begann" (In his fifty-third year, when Casanova was no longer driven through the world by the adventurousness of youth but by the restlessness of approaching old age, he felt grow in his soul an intense homesickness for Venice, the city of his birth; and so, like a bird that slowly descends from the lofty heights to die, he began to approach the city in ever-narrowing circles). The metaphor of the slowly descending bird in its death flight indicates that Casanova's days are numbered. His main concern now is to return to the city of his youth, the city he loved and was forced to leave because of his political convictions, which were at variance with those of the Supreme

Council. While waiting for the letter informing him whether the Council will allow him to return, he accepts an invitation from an old benefactor to visit him and his wife Amalia, who was one of Casanova's former mistresses.

At the estate of his benefactor he meets Marcolina, who, he realizes, is the person he had sought all through his life. She has expert knowledge in philosophy, art, science, and mathematics, and she is ravishingly beautiful. Casanova's passion is inflamed; from now on his only thought is to win her favor. He could have Amalia, who implores him: "'Du bist nicht alt. Für mich kannst du es niemals werden. In deinen Armen hab' ich meine erste Seligkeit genossen . . .'" ("You are not old. For me you cannot be an old man. In your arms I had my first taste of bliss . . ."). Casanova, however, is realistic enough to see the signs of advancing old age and almost takes delight in pointing them out to Amalia:

"Sieh mich doch an, Amalia! Die Runzeln meiner Stirn. . . . Die Falten meines Halses! Und die tiefe Rinne da von den Augen den Schläfen zu! Und hier . . . ja, hier in der Ecke fehlt mir der Zahn,'—er riß den Mund grinsend auf. 'Und diese Hände, Amalia! Sieh sie doch an! Finger wie Krallen . . . kleine gelbe Flecken auf den Näglen. . . . Und die Adern da—blau und geschwollen—Greisenhände, Amalia!'"

("Look well, Amalia! The wrinkles on my forehead. . . . The loose folds of my neck! And the crow's-feet around my eyes. And, here . . . yes, here I have lost one of my eyeteeth,"–he opened his mouth in a grin. "And these hands, Amalia! Look at them! Fingers like claws . . . little yellow spots on the fingernails. . . . And the veins—blue and swollen—the hands of an old man, Amalia!").

Great disappointment comes for Casanova when he sees Marcolina with Lieutenant Lorenzi, who is described as a young Casanova; he has similar looks and the same lifestyle as the great Venetian adventurer. One night Casanova sees Lorenzi leave Marcolina's chamber. His rage is increased by a letter from the Council informing him that he can return to Venice provided that he agrees to spy for the state. In this state of mind he rapes Teresina, Amalia's thirteen-year-old daughter, who has come to summon him to dinner. The same evening Casanova wins at cards, and Lorenzi, the big loser, agrees to exchange places with Casanova so that the old adventurer can spend the night with Marcolina. Casanova enters Marcolina's chamber in the dark and takes Lorenzi's place. Marcolina, deceived, experiences a bliss which can be described as a mystical union:

An Marcolinens seufzendem Vergehen, an den Tränen der Seligkeit, die er ihr von den Wangen küßte, an der immer wieder erneuten Glut, mit der sie seine Zärtlichkeit empfing, erkannte er bald, daß sie seine Entzückungen teilte, die ihm als höhere, ja von neuer, andrer Art erschienen, als er jemals genossen. Lust ward zur Andacht . . .

(From Marcolina's sigh of surrender, from the tears of happiness which he kissed from her cheeks, from the ever-renewed warmth with which she received his caresses, he felt sure that she shared his rapture; and to him this rapture seemed more intense than he had ever experienced, seemed to possess a new and strange reality. Pleasure became worship . . .).

In the morning Marcolina discovers the betrayal, and in her terrified eyes Casanova reads "das Wort, das ihm von allen das furchtbarste war, da es sein endgültiges Urteil sprach: Alter Mann" (the word which to him was the most dreadful of all words, since it passed the final judgment upon him: old man). Leaving her room, he is confronted by Lorenzi, who challenges him to a duel. Casanova kills Lorenzi, but in the end it is questionable who has actually won: Lorenzi does not have to suffer the fate of Casanova, who will spend the rest of his life as a spy for the authorities he had detested in his younger days.

In the United States *Casanova's Homecoming* was considered obscene, and a seven-year legal battle followed its publication. Instrumental in banning the work was Sumner of the New York Society for the Suppression of Vice, who later brought charges of obscenity against *Reigen*. Sumner lost both cases in 1930. *Casanova's Homecoming* was cleared of the charge of obscenity in a ruling that said "that the book must be measured by living standards of our own time, not by those of the Mid-Victorian era" and called Schnitzler "one of the world's greatest writers and . . . *Casanova's Homecoming* . . . an incontestable contribution to literature."

At the beginning of *Traumnovelle* (1926; translated as *Rhapsody: A Dream Novel,* 1927), which is considered one of Schnitzler's best works, the physician Fridolin and his wife Albertine talk about the previous night's experiences at a fancy-dress ball. Memories of unfulfilled erotic opportunities as well as mutual mistrust are awakened. This mistrust can only be eliminated if both go through the zone of temptation. Fridolin has such an experience at a party, and Albertine lives out her desires in a dream which parallels Fridolin's adventures in detail. Fridolin and Albertine learn that they are susceptible to erotic temptations, but that their sexual drives are only one side of their human nature; equally important is the moral component which is present in both of their adventures. According to Dorrit Cohn (in Erika Nielsen, ed., *Focus on Vienna 1900* [1982]), both partners fulfill their unconscious wishes: "the erotic wish for an infinitely protracted sexual arousal by a partner who is simultaneously the familiar mate and a total stranger; and the destructive wish for that same partner's self-sacrificial death. What makes Fridolin's experience dreamlike—and not merely bizarre or horrific—is that it matches his secret desires no less exactly than Albertine's dream matches hers. Freed from the censuring precepts of conscience for the duration of a night, Fridolin literally lives his dream. It is as though Schnitzler had meant to demonstrate by a kind of limit case Schopenhauer's thesis that life and dream are cut from the same cloth."

In 1929 a collection of Schnitzler's fiction was published in the United States under the title *Little Novels;* it contained "The Fate of the Baron," "The Stranger," "The Prophecy," "Redegonda's Diary," "The Murderer," and "The Death of a Bachelor." The review in the *New Statesman* of 21 September 1929 said: "All these stories are told with a grace and delicacy that relieve them of the horror without depriving them of force. . . . In his stories Herr Schnitzler does not produce the gaiety of *Anatol*. Ten stories give us four suicides, two deaths in duels, two other sudden deaths, and a murder. But one ends, under the force of the author's persuasiveness, by believing with him that it does not much matter. For Herr Schnitzler is one of the most persuasive writers alive, and the mood into which he most often seeks to persuade us is this of attentive and interested detachment."

Schnitzler's pessimism and disillusionment were partly rooted in his health problems; in his later years he complained of frequent headaches and an increasingly severe ear ailment. He was also despondent over the suicide of his daughter Lily on 26 July 1928 in Venice. His diary entry for 15 September 1928 says: "Tolle Sehnsucht nach Lily.–Die Hoffnungslosigkeit in Hinsicht auf O[lga Schnitzlers] Wesen. Die triste Situation C[lara Katharina] P[ollaczeks], die finanz. Aussichtslosigkeit–die Unfähigkeit zu arbeiten–man müßte jünger sein, um all das zu ertragen" (Mad longing for Lily.–The hopelessness with regard to O[lga Schnitzler's] nature. The sad situation concerning C[lara Katharina] P[ollaczek], the lack of financ. prospects–the inability to work–one has to be younger to endure all this).

Schnitzler had met Clara Pollaczek (then known as Clara Loeb) in 1896; they had broken up soon afterward, and each had married someone else. Only after Schnitzler's divorce in 1921 and the death of Clara Pollaczek's husband did they see each other again, and they continued their relationship, which was marked by

Pollaczek's jealousy, from 1923 until Schnitzler's death. One of Schnitzler's last diary entries, dated 21 June 1931, points to the tension between them: "Um 9 kam C.P. . . . endlich sagte sie: sie gehe auf alles, ein, d.h. sie wird nichts dagegen haben, wenn ich Frauen empfange, so viel ich wolle, aber Aufrichtigkeit etc. . . . . Ich war ziemlich todt, als sie, auch ziemlich todt, ging. Ich fühle mich innerlich in mancher Hinsicht schuldig, u[nd] bin es doch nicht" (At 9 C.P. came. . . . finally she said: she would accept everything, that is, she would have no objections if I receive women, as many as I wanted, but honesty etc. . . . I was rather beat when she left, and she was, too. I feel guilty in some respects, but in other ways not).

It was during this difficult period that Schnitzler decided to publish his novella *Flucht in die Finsternis* (translated as *Flight into Darkness,* 1931), which he had written in 1913 and revised in 1915, 1916, and 1917. *Flucht in die Finsternis* was printed in May 1931 in the *Vossische Zeitung;* the book version appeared one day before Schnitzler's death in October. The novella concerns two brothers: Otto, a psychiatrist, and Robert, whose mind is deteriorating. Years earlier Robert had asked Otto to kill him in a painless fashion if madness were ever to befall him, and Otto had reluctantly agreed. Robert cannot forget the promise and interprets his brother's every action as threatening. In the final scene Otto visits Robert in a hotel room to assure him of his love and devotion. But Robert misunderstands the situation. In Otto's "Augen war Angst, Mitleid und Liebe ohne Maß. Doch dem Bruder bedeutete der feuchte Glanz dieses Blickes Tücke, Drohung und Tod. Otto wieder, von dem Ausdruck des Grauens in des Bruders Antliz im tiefsten erschüttert, beherrschte sich nicht länger, trat ganz nah an ihn heran, um ihn zu umarmen und ihn durch die rückhaltlose innigste Gebärde seiner brüderlichen Zärtlichkeit zu versichern. Robert aber, des Bruders kühle Hand an seinem Halse fühlend, zweifelte nun nicht mehr, daß der gefürchtete, daß der Augenblick der höchsten, der entsetzlichsten Gefahr gekommen sei, gegen die in jeder Weise sich zu wehren durch menschliche und göttliche Gesetze erlaubt, ja geboten war" (eyes were anxiety, sympathy, and love unbounded. But the twinkling moisture in those eyes meant to his brother malice, menace, and death. Otto, shaken to the depths by the expression of terror in his brother's face, could restrain himself no longer. He went up quite close to him, to embrace him and reassure him with the most tender, unreserved gestures of his brotherly affection. But Robert, feeling his brother's cool hands at his neck, could not doubt that the long-dreaded moment of supreme and unspeakable danger had come. He was permitted, commanded by all laws, human and divine, to defend himself as he could). Robert shoots Otto, who dies instantly; three days later Robert is found dead.

The tragicomedy *Das Wort* (The Word, 1966) remained a fragment although Schnitzler worked on it for thirty years, until his death. One of the central figures in *Das Wort* is the Literat (poetmaster) Anastasius Treuenhof, a Literat being the negative counterpart of the poet. What sets them apart from one another is their attitudes toward the word: while for the poet word and action are one and while he is guided by ethical considerations, the Literat is a sensationalist who is motivated by egotistical drives and opportunism. Treuenhof himself characterizes this type, whom Schnitzler criticized in many of his plays, as follows: "Sie werden an ihre Sargdeckel klopfen und den Totengräber um Papier und Bleistift bitten, um die Sensationen während des Begräbnisses aufzuzeichnen" (They will knock on their coffin lid and ask the undertaker for paper and pencil in order to record the sensations during their burial). The editor of the play, Kurt Bergel, sees its central problem as "die Verantwortung, die der Gebrauch der Sprache dem Menschen auferlegt" (the responsibility which the use of language imposes on man). Treuenhof is responsible for the death of a young man who is driven to suicide by Treuenhof's words. In an exchange between Treuenhof and Hofrat (Councillor) Winkler in the last act, the difference between the Literat and the human being becomes clear:

> Treuenhof: Worte sind nichts.
> Winkler: Worte sind alles. Wir haben ja nichts anderes.

> (Treuenhof: Words are nothing.
> Winkler: Words are everything. We have nothing else.)

Winkler's attitude toward the word is also Schnitzler's: words are important and one has to be careful in their usage. In many of his aphorisms Schnitzler points to the ethical, aesthetic, and psychological issues inherent in language. Words, as well as actions, have consequences, and sometimes the result is different from what one expects.

Schnitzler wrote at a specific time for a specific audience. The era was that of the Austro-Hungarian monarchy; the audience was the educated bourgeoisie of Vienna and Berlin. Schnitzler's work does not deal with the period after the end of World War I, which destroyed the culture he knew. But Schnitzler also transcends his time, as Frederick Ungar stresses in his foreword to the collection *The Little Comedy:* "His work has the validity of what is eternally human. Even though the world he captured with such charm and refinement has long since disappeared, Schnitzler's characters are still very much alive; they are true and original. And this is so because the questions he posed are timeless, as are the topics of his stories and plays—the lure of love, man's transitoriness, the incomprehensibility of fate. Nothing has gone stale—his work still speaks to us today."

Letters:

Briefwechsel mit Otto Brahm, edited by Otto Seidlin (Berlin: Gesellschaft für Theatergeschichte, 1953);

Sigmund Freud, "Briefe an Arthur Schnitzler," *Die neue Rundschau,* 66 (1955): 95–106;

Briefwechsel Georg Brandes und Arthur Schnitzler: Ein Briefwechsel, edited by Kurt Bergel (Bern: Francke, 1956);

Heinrich Schnitzler, "Briefwechsel Arthur Schnitzler und Rainer Maria Rilke," *Wort und Wahrheit,* 13, no. 4 (1958): 283–298;

"Unveröffentlichte Briefe Schnitzlers an Brahm," *Kleine Schriften der Gesellschaft für Theatergeschichte,* 16 (1958): 44–45;

Briefwechsel Hugo von Hofmannsthal-Arthur Schnitzler, edited by Therese Nickl and Heinrich Schnitzler (Frankfurt am Main: Fischer, 1964);

"Briefe an Josef Körner," *Literatur und Kritik,* 2, no. 12 (1967): 79–87;

"Karl Kraus und Arthur Schnitzler: Eine Dokumentation," edited by Reinhard Urbach, *Literatur und Kritik* (1970): 513–530;

Schnitzler and Olga Waisnix, *Liebe, die starb vor der Zeit: Ein Briefwechsel,* edited by Nickl and Heinrich Schnitzler (Vienna, Munich & Zurich: Molden, 1970);

"Briefwechsel Arthur Schnitzler-Franz Nabl," edited by Urbach, *Studium Generale,* 24 (1971): 1256–1270;

Briefwechsel Arthur Schnitzlers mit Max Reinhardt und dessen Mitarbeitern, edited by Renate Wagner (Salzburg: Müller, 1971);

The Correspondence of Arthur Schnitzler and Raoul Auernheimer with Raoul Auernheimer's Aphorisms, edited by Donald G. Daviau and Jorun B. Johns (Chapel Hill: University of North Carolina Press, 1972);

"The Correspondence of Arthur Schnitzler and Richard Beer-Hofmann," edited by Eugene Weber, *Modern Austrian Literature,* 6, no. 3/4 (1973): 40–51;

"Briefe: Arthur Schnitzler-Thomas Mann," edited by Hertha Krotkoff, *Modern Austrian Literature,* 7, no. 1/2 (1974): 1–33;

"Briefwechsel Richard Schaukal-Arthur Schnitzler," edited by Urbach, *Modern Austrian Literature,* 8, no. 3/4 (1975): 15–42;

"Vier unveröffentlichte Briefe Arthur Schnitzlers an den Psychoanalytiker Theodor Reik," edited by Bernd Urban, *Modern Austrian Literature,* 8, no. 3/4 (1975): 236–247;

Adele Sandrock und Arthur Schnitzler: Geschichte einer Liebe in Briefen, Bildern und Dokumenten, edited by Wagner (Vienna: Amalthea, 1975);

"Briefwechsel Fritz von Unruhs mit Arthur Schnitzler," edited by Ulrich K. Goldsmith, *Modern Austrian Literature,* 10, no. 3/4 (1977): 69–127;

"Arthur Schnitzler an Marie Reinhard (1896)," edited by Nickl and Urbach, *Modern Austrian Literature,* 10, no. 3/4 (1977): 23–68;

The Letters of Arthur Schnitzler to Hermann Bahr, edited by Daviau (Chapel Hill: University of North Carolina Press, 1978);

Briefe 1875–1912, edited by Nickl and Schnitzler (Frankfurt am Main: Fischer, 1981);

Briefe 1913–1931, edited by Peter Michael Braunwarth, Richard Miklin, and others (Frankfurt am Main: Fischer, 1984);

Briefe und Tagebücher: Hedy Kempny-Arthur Schnitzler. Das Mädchen mit den dreizehn Seelen (Reinbek: ro-ro-ro, 1984).

Bibliographies:

Richard H. Allen, *An Annotated Arthur Schnitzler Bibliography: Editions and Criticism in German, French and English* (Chapel Hill: University of North Carolina Press, 1965);

Jeffrey B. Berlin, *An Annotated Arthur Schnitzler Bibliography* (Munich: Fink, 1978).

References:

Friedbert Aspetsberger, "'Drei Akte in einem.' Zum Formtrieb von Schnitzlers Drama," *Zeitschrift für Deutsche Philologie,* 85 (1966): 285–308;

Joseph W. Bailey, "Arthur Schnitzler's Dramatic Work," *Texas Review,* 5, no. 4 (1920): 294–307;

Gerhart Baumann, *Arthur Schnitzler: Die Welt von gestern eines Dichters von morgen* (Frankfurt am Main: Athenäum, 1965);

Frederick J. Behariell, "Arthur Schnitzler's Range of Theme," *Monatshefte für deutschen Unterricht,* 43, no. 7 (1951): 301–311;

G. J. Carr and G. J. Eda Sagarra, eds., *Finde Siècle Vienna* (Dublin: Trinity College, 1985);

Giuseppe Farese, ed., *Akten des Internationalen Symposiums 'Arthur Schnitzler und seine Zeit'* (Bern, Frankfurt am Main & New York: Lang, 1985);

Alfred Fritsche, *Dekadenz im Werk Arthur Schnitzlers* (Bern: Herbert Lang / Frankfurt am Main: Peter Lang, 1974);

Barbara Gutt, *Emanzipation bei Arthur Schnitzler* (Berlin: Spiess, 1978);

Stephanie Hammer, "Fear and Attraction: *Anatol* and *Liebelei* Productions in the United States," *Modern Austrian Literature,* 19, no. 3/4 (1986): 63–74;

Michael Imboden, *Die surreale Komponente im erzählerischen Werk Arthur Schnitzlers* (Bern & Frankfurt am Main: Lang, 1971);

Rolf-Peter Janz and Klaus Laermann, *Arthur Schnitzler: Zur Diagnose des Wiener Bürgertums im Fin de Siècle* (Stuttgart: Metzler, 1977);

Gottfried Just, *Ironie und Sentimentalität in den erzählenden Dichtungen Arthur Schnitzlers* (Berlin: Schmidt, 1968);

Julius Kapp, *Arthur Schnitzler* (Leipzig: Xenien Verlag, 1912);

Klaus Kilian, *Die Komödien Arthur Schnitzlers. Sozialer Rollenzwang und kritische Ethik* (Düsseldorf: Bertelsmann, 1972);

Josef Koerner, *Arthur Schnitzlers Gestalten und Probleme* (Vienna: Amalthea, 1921);

Hans Landsberg, *Arthur Schnitzler* (Berlin: Gose & Tetzlaff, 1904);

Herbert Lederer, "Arthur Schnitzler's Typology: An Excursion into Philosophy," *PMLA,* 78 (1963): 94–406;

Hans-Ulrich Lindken, *Arthur Schnitzler: Aspekte und Akzente. Materialien zu Leben und Werk* (Frankfurt am Main & Bern: Lang, 1984);

Lindken, *Interpretationen zu Arthur Schnitzler: Drei Erzählungen [Spiel im Morgengrauen; Der blinde Geronimo und sein Bruder; Leutnant Gustl]* (Munich: Oldenbourg, 1970);

Sol Liptzin, *Arthur Schnitzler* (New York: Prentice-Hall, 1932);

Christa Melchinger, *Illusion und Wirklichkeit im dramatischen Werk Arthur Schnitzlers* (Heidelberg: Winter, 1968);

Gerhard Naumann and Jutta Müller, *Der Nachlaß Arthur Schnitzlers: Verzeichnis des im Schnitzler-Archiv der Universität Freiburg i. B. befindlichen Materials* (Munich: Fink, 1969);

Wolfgang Nehring, "Schnitzler, Freud's Alter Ego," *Modern Austrian Literature,* 10, no. 3/4 (1977): 179–194;

Robert James Nelson, *Play within a Play: The Dramatist's Conception of His Art from Shakespeare to Anouilh* (New Haven: Yale University Press, 1958), p. 118;

Erika Nielsen, ed., *Focus on Vienna 1900: Change and Continuity in Literature, Music, Art and Intellectual History* (Munich: Fink, 1982);

Ernst L. Offermanns, *Arthur Schnitzler: Das Komödienwerk als Kritik des Impressionismus* (Munich: Fink, 1973);

Michaela L. Perlmann, *Arthur Schnitzler* (Stuttgart: Metzler, 1987);

Heinz Politzer, "Arthur Schnitzler: Poetry of Psychology," *Modern Language Notes,* 78, no. 4 (1963): 353–372;

Herbert W. Reichert and Herbert Salinger, eds., *Studies in Arthur Schnitzler: Centennial Commemorative Volume* (Chapel Hill: University of North Carolina Press, 1963);

Theodor Reik, *Arthur Schnitzler als Psycholog* (Minden: Bruns, 1913);

William H. Rey, "Arthur Schnitzler," in *Deutsche Dichter der Moderne,* edited by Benno von Wiese, revised edition (Berlin: Schmidt, 1969), pp. 237–257;

Rey, *Arthur Schnitzler: Die späte Prosa als Gipfel seines Schaffens* (Berlin: Schmidt, 1968);

Heinz Rieder, *Das dramatische Werk* (Vienna: Bergland, 1973);

Felix Salten, "Arthur Schnitzler," in his *Gestalten und Erscheinungen* (Berlin: Fischer, 1913), pp. 49–63;

Hartmut Scheible, *Arthur Schnitzler in Selbstzeugnissen und Bilddokumenten* (Reinbek: Rowohlt, 1976);

Scheible, "Arthur Schnitzler–Figur-Situation-Gestalt," *Neue Rundschau,* 92, no. 2 (1981): 67–89;

Scheible, *Arthur Schnitzler und die Aufklärung* (Munich: Fink, 1977);

Scheible, ed., *Arthur Schnitzler in neuer Sicht* (Munich: Fink, 1981);

Otto P. Schinnerer, "The Early Works of Arthur Schnitzler," *Germanic Review,* 4 (1929): 153–197;

Schinnerer, "The Literary Apprenticeship of Arthur Schnitzler," *Germanic Review,* 5 (1930): 58–82;

Schinnerer, "Schnitzler and the Military Censorship: Unpublished Correspondence," *Germanic Review,* 5 (1940): 238–246;

Gerd K. Schneider, "The Reception of Arthur Schnitzler's *Reigen* in the Old Country and the New World: A Study in Cultural Differences," *Modern Austrian Literature,* 19, no. 3/4 (1986): 75–89;

Schneider, "Ton-und Schriftsprache in Schnitzlers Fräulein Else und Schumanns *Carnaval,*" *Modern Austrian Literature,* 2, no. 3 (1969): 17–20;

Heinrich Schnitzler, Christian Brandstätter, and Reinhard Urbach, eds., *Arthur Schnitzler: Sein Leben, sein Werk, seine Zeit* (Frankfurt am Main: Fischer, 1981);

Olga Schnitzler, *Spiegelbild der Freundschaft* (Salzburg: Residenz, 1962);

Carl E. Schorske, "Politics and the Psyche: Schnitzler and Hofmannsthal," in his *Fin-de-Siècle Vienna. Politics and Culture* (New York: Random House, 1981), pp. 3–23;

Schorske, "Schnitzler und Hofmannsthal: Politik und Psyche im Wien des Fin de Siècle," *Wort und Wahrheit,* 16 (1962): 367–381;

Herbert Seidler, "Die Forschung zu Arthur Schnitzler seit 1945," *Zeitschrift für Deutsche Philologie,* 95 (1976): 576–595;

Oskar Seidlin, "In Memoriam Arthur Schnitzler: May 15, 1862–Oct. 21, 1931," *American-German Review,* 28, no. 4 (1962): 4–6;

Richard Specht, *Arthur Schnitzler: Der Dichter und sein Werk. Eine Studie* (Berlin: Fischer, 1922);

Martin Swales, *Arthur Schnitzler: A Critical Study* (Oxford: Clarendon Press, 1971);

Petrus W. Tax and Richard H. Lawson, eds., *Arthur Schnitzler and His Age: Intellectual and Artistic Currents* (Bonn: Bouvier, 1984);

Reinhard Urbach, *Arthur Schnitzler* (Velber: Friedrich, 1968); translated by Donald G. Daviau (New York: Ungar, 1973); German version revised (Munich: Deutscher Taschenbuch Verlag, 1977);

Urbach, *Schnitzler-Kommentar: Zu den erzählenden Schriften und dramatischen Werken* (Munich: Winkler, 1974);

George S. Viereck, "The World of Arthur Schnitzler," *Modern Austrian Literature,* 5, no. 3/4 (1972): 7–17;

Marc Weiner, *Arthur Schnitzler and the Crisis of Musical Culture* (Heidelberg: Winter, 1986);

Robert O. Weiss, "Arthur Schnitzler's Literary and Philosophical Development," *Journal of the American Arthur Schnitzler Research Association,* 2, no. 1 (1963): 4–20;

Harry Zohn, "Schnitzler and the Challenge of Zionism," *Journal of the American Arthur Schnitzler Research Association,* 1, no. 4/5 (1962): 5–7.

Papers:

The Schnitzler Archive is in the Schiller-Nationalmuseum, Marbach am Neckar.

Anna Seghers
(Netty Reiling Radványi)
(19 November 1900 – 1 June 1983)

Gertraud Gutzmann
Smith College

This entry originally appeared in DLB 69: Contemporary
German Fiction Writers, First Series.

BOOKS: *Der Aufstand der Fischer von St. Barbara: Eine Erzählung* (Berlin: Kiepenheuer, 1928); translated by Margret Goldsmith as *The Revolt of the Fishermen* (London: Mathews & Marrot, 1929; New York: Longmans, Green, 1930);

Auf dem Wege zur amerikanischen Botschaft und andere Erzählungen (Berlin: Kiepenheuer, 1930);

Die Gefährten: Roman (Berlin: Kiepenheuer, 1932);

Der Kopflohn: Roman aus einem deutschen Dorf im Spätsommer 1932 (Amsterdam: Querido, 1933); translated by Eva Wulff as "A Price on His Head," in *Two Novelettes* (Berlin: Seven Seas, 1960);

Ernst Thaelmann, What He Stands For, by Seghers and others, translated by Michael Davidson (London: Workers' Bookshop, 1934);

Der Weg durch den Februar: Roman (Paris: Editions du Carrefour, 1935; Moscow: Verlagsgenossenschaft Ausländischer Arbeiter in der UdSSR, 1935);

Der letzte Weg des Koloman Wallisch: Erzählung (Paris: Editions du Carrefour, 1936);

Die Rettung: Roman (Amsterdam: Querido, 1937);

Die schönsten Sagen vom Räuber Wojnok (Moscow: Das Internationale Buch, 1940);

Das siebte Kreuz: Roman aus Hitlerdeutschland (Mexico City: El Libro Libre, 1942; Berlin: Aufbau, 1946); translated by James A. Galston as *The Seventh Cross* (Boston: Little, Brown, 1942; London: Hamilton, 1943);

Visado de tránsito, translated from German into Spanish by Angela Selke and Antonio Sánchez Barbudo (Mexico City: Nuevo Mundo, 1944); translated from the German by Galston as *Transit* (Boston: Little, Brown, 1944; London: Eyre & Spottiswoode, 1945); original German version published as *Transit: Roman* (Constance: Weller, 1948);

Anna Seghers in 1928 (Reclam Verlagsarchiv)

Der Ausflug der toten Mädchen und andere Erzählungen (New York: Aurora, 1946; enlarged edition, Berlin: Aufbau, 1948); "Der Ausflug der Toten Mädchen," translated by Elizabeth R. Hermann and Edna H. Spitz as "The Excursion of the Dead Girls," in *German Women Writers of the Twentieth Century,* edited

631

by Hermann and Spitz (Oxford & New York: Pergamon Press, 1978);

Sowjetmenschen: Lebensbeschreibungen nach ihren Berichten (Berlin: Kultur und Fortschritt, 1948);

Die Toten bleiben jung: Roman (Berlin: Aufbau, 1949); translated as *The Dead Stay Young* (Boston: Little, Brown, 1950; London: Eyre & Spottiswoode, 1950);

Die Hochzeit von Haiti: Zwei Novellen (Berlin: Aufbau, 1949);

Die Linie: Drei Erzählungen (Berlin: Aufbau, 1950);

Die Schule des Kampfes (Moscow: Verlag für fremdsprachige Literatur, 1950);

Crisanta: Mexikanische Novelle (Leipzig: Insel, 1951);

Die Kinder: Drei Erzählungen (Berlin: Aufbau, 1951);

Erzählungen (Berlin: Aufbau, 1952);

Der Mann und sein Name: Erzählung (Berlin: Aufbau, 1952);

Der Bienenstock: Ausgewählte Erzählungen, 2 volumes (Berlin: Aufbau, 1953);

Der Prozeß der Jeanne d'Arc zu Rouen 1431 (Berlin: Aufbau-Bühnen-Vertrieb, 1953; adapted for radio, Leipzig: Reclam, 1965);

Frieden der Welt: Ansprachen und Aufsätze, 1947–1953 (Berlin: Aufbau, 1953);

Über unsere junge Literatur: Diskussionsmaterial zur Vorbereitung des vierten Deutschen Schriftstellerkongresses, by Seghers and others (Berlin: Aufbau, 1955);

Die große Veränderung und unsere Literatur: Ansprache zum vierten Deutschen Schriftstellerkongreß, Januar 1956 (Berlin: Aufbau, 1956);

Hilfsmaterial für den Literaturunterricht an Ober-und Fachschulen, by Seghers, Hans Marchwitza, and Willi Bredel (Berlin: Volk und Wissen, 1957);

Brot und Salz: Drei Erzählungen (Berlin: Aufbau, 1958);

Die Entscheidung: Roman (Berlin: Aufbau, 1959);

Das Licht auf dem Galgen: Eine karibische Geschichte aus der Zeit der Französischen Revolution (Berlin: Aufbau, 1961);

Karibische Geschichten (Berlin: Aufbau, 1962);

Über Tolstoi, über Dostojewski (Berlin: Aufbau, 1963);

Die Kraft der Schwachen: Neun Erzählungen (Berlin: Aufbau, 1965);

Wiedereinführung der Sklaverei in Guadeloupe: Erzählung (Frankfurt am Main: Suhrkamp, 1966);

Das wirkliche Blau: Eine Geschichte aus Mexiko (Berlin: Aufbau, 1967); translated by Joan Becker as "Benito's Blue," in *Benito's Blue and Nine Other Stories* (Berlin: Seven Seas, 1973);

Das Vertrauen: Roman (Berlin & Weimar: Aufbau, 1968);

Ausgewählte Erzählungen (Hamburg: Rowohlt, 1969);

Glauben an Irdisches: Essays aus vier Jahrzehnten (Leipzig: Reclam, 1969);

Briefe an Leser (Berlin: Aufbau, 1970);

Über Kunstwerk und Wirklichkeit, 4 volumes, edited by Sigrid Bock (Berlin: Akademie, 1970–1979);

Überfahrt: Eine Liebesgeschichte (Neuwied: Luchterhand, 1971);

Sonderbare Begegnungen (Berlin: Aufbau, 1973);

Fünf Erzählungen, edited by Doris and Hans-Jürgen Schmitt (Stuttgart: Reclam, 1975);

Willkommen, Zukunft!: Reden, Essays und Aufsätze über Kunst und Wirklichkeit (Munich: Kürbiskern und Tendenzen Damnitz, 1975);

Steinzeit; Wiederbegegnung: 2 Erzählungen (Berlin & Weimar: Aufbau, 1977);

Die Macht der Worte: Reden, Schriften, Briefe, edited by Sina Witt (Leipzig & Weimar: Kiepenheuer, 1979);

Aufsätze, Ansprachen, Essays, 1927–1953 (Berlin: Aufbau, 1980);

Aufsätze, Ansprachen, Essays, 1954–1979 (Berlin: Aufbau, 1980);

Drei Frauen aus Haiti (Berlin: Aufbau / Darmstadt: Luchterhand, 1980);

Woher Sie kommen, wohin Sie gehen: Essays aus vier Jahrzehnten, edited by Manfred Behn (Darmstadt & Neuwied: Luchterhand, 1980);

Jude und Judentum im Werk Rembrandts (Leipzig: Reclam, 1981);

Bauern von Hruschowo und andere Erzählungen (Darmstadt: Luchterhand, 1982);

Überfahrt (Darmstadt & Neuwied: Luchterhand, 1982);

Ausgewählte Erzählungen, edited by Christa Wolf (Darmstadt: Luchterhand, 1983);

Vierzig Jahre der Margarete Wolf und andere Erzählungen (Darmstadt: Luchterhand, 1983);

Die Toten auf der Insel Djal: Sagen vom Unirdischen (Berlin: Aufbau, 1985);

Der gerechte Richter: Eine Novelle (Berlin: Aufbau, 1990).

OTHER: Nico Rost, *Goethe in Dachau,* translated from the Dutch by E. Rost-Blumberg, foreword by Seghers (Zurich: Universum, 1950);

Gustav Seitz, *Studienblätter aus China,* introduction by Seghers (Berlin: Aufbau, 1953);

L. N. Tolstoi: Bibliographie der Erstausgaben deutschsprachiger Übersetzungen und der seit 1945 in Deutschland, Österreich und der Schweiz in deutscher Sprache erschienenen Werke, introduction by Seghers (Leipzig: Deutsche Bücherei, 1958).

Anna Seghers was the most noted prose writer of the former German Democratic Republic (GDR) and, according to many critics, one of the most important German writers of the modern period. Such novels as *Das siebte Kreuz* (1942; translated as *The Seventh Cross,* 1942) and *Transit* (1948; originally published as *Visado de tránsito,* 1944; translated into English, 1944) and her stories "Der Ausflug der toten Mädchen"(1946; translated as "The Excursion of the Dead Girls", 1978), "Die Kraft der Schwachen" (The Strength of the Weak, 1965), and *Das wirkliche Blau* (1967; translated as "Benito's Blue," 1973) earned her a wide reading audience internationally as well, and the combined weight of her reputation at home and abroad established her as one of the great literary figures of the twentieth century.

Seghers's life and career were committed to the ideals of socialist humanism and the struggle for social change. Considering the political orientation of her writing, it is not surprising that Seghers chose to settle in East Germany rather than her native Rhineland after she returned from exile in Mexico in 1947. As she said: "Weil ich hier die Resonanz haben kann, die sich ein Schriftsteller wünscht. . . .Weil ich hier ausdrükken kann, wozu ich gelebt habe" (Here there is the resonance that an author needs. . . . Because here I can express what I have lived for). As a cofounder of the GDR's Academy of the Arts and as the long-term president of the East German Writers' Union, Seghers played a decisive role in the cultural life of her country and influenced and promoted the careers of many established and emerging writers. Recalling Seghers's address to the International Writers' Conference, Christa Wolf–a major contemporary German literary voice in her own right–captures the aura that surrounded Seghers whenever she spoke in public: "Es war still in jenem Saal in Weimar im Mai des Jahres fünfundsechzig, als sie die Bühne betrat, und es blieb still, solange sie sprach" (There was total silence when she appeared on the platform in that hall in Weimar in May 1965 as long as she spoke). Wolf says that all the writers present, young and old, probably felt that they had before them the best possible mentor. A similar view was expressed in the many letters of admiration sent to Seghers by writers from the GDR and abroad on the occasion of her eightieth birthday.

During the immediate postwar years Seghers's novels and stories were published in the West as well as in the East; but during the cold war she fell into disgrace among Western critics. Her steadfast loyalty to the Communist Party delayed the critical reception of her works in the West by more than two decades. But even then, while praised for her artistry, particularly in her exile writings, she was denounced for her official position in East German political and cultural life. Only recently has Seghers's substantial oeuvre received the critical attention it merits as a major body of writing on twentieth-century German social and political history.

Seghers was born Netty Reiling on 19 November 1900 to middle-class liberal Jewish parents in Mainz. Her youth was remarkably carefree and privileged, in contrast to those of many women of her generation. As

the only daughter of Isidor Reiling, a well-known art dealer who was also the curator of the art collection of Mainz Cathedral, she grew up in a climate of cultural refinement and learning. At home she was encouraged to read fairy tales and legends as well as the works of Johann Wolfgang von Goethe, Friedrich Schiller, Heinrich Heine, Honoré de Balzac, and Fyodor Dostoyevsky. Friends of her family, political refugees from czarist Russia, introduced her to *Crime and Punishment* and *The Brothers Karamazov,* which informed her own early literary efforts. She has also acknowledged the importance in her literary formation of John Dos Passos, Theodore Dreiser, Marcel Proust, Franz Kafka, and Fёdor Gladkov, as well as the cinema of Sergey Eisenstein.

In 1920, after receiving her diploma from a private secondary school for girls in Mainz, she left for Heidelberg, where she enrolled at Ruprechts-Karl University to study art, sinology, philology, and history. The years in Heidelberg, as well as a term at Cologne University, were hardly those of a carefree student existence, since they coincided with a period of intense political turmoil and economic instability. At Heidelberg Reiling came into contact with students from eastern and southeastern Europe who had been active in the revolutionary uprisings in their countries at the end of World War I. In her first novel, *Die Gefährten* (The Companions, 1932), she pays tribute to these young revolutionaries. One of them, the sociologist and political theorist László Radványi, was to become her husband in 1925. (Radványi later changed his name to Johann-Lorenz Schmidt.)

Reiling completed her four years at Heidelberg in 1924 with a doctoral dissertation entitled "Jude und Judentum im Werk Rembrandts" (The Jew and Judaism in the Works of Rembrandts). That year she wrote her first story, "Die Toten auf der Insel Djal" (The Dead of the Island of Djal), a fantastic tale about seafarers and their hero, a Dutch captain named Seghers. She signed the story with the pen name Anna Seghers. Wolf has called the adoption of this name an "undramatischer, doch nicht bedeutungsloser Akt einer Selbst-Taufe" (undramatic but not meaningless act of self-christening): in choosing Seghers, the name of a seventeenth-century Dutch etcher, as her pseudonym, the young author referred to her interest in Dutch art as well as to her childhood love for Holland. More important, she hoped that the unusual name would attract immediate attention to her stories and, at the same time, insure her anonymity.

In 1928, when her stories *Der Aufstand der Fischer von St. Barbara* (1928; translated as *The Revolt of the Fishermen,* 1929) and "Grubetsch" (published in the *Frankfurter Zeitung* in 1927) were awarded the Kleist Prize–the highest distinction a young writer could receive in the Weimar Republic—critics mistook Seghers for a man because the stories were written in a laconic, masculine style. But it soon became clear that the author was the twenty-eight-year-old Netty Reiling Radványi, a newly registered member of the Communist Party of Germany and mother of two young children. After her literary debut Seghers followed her husband to Berlin, where Radványi directed the Marxistische Arbeiter-Schule (Marxist Institute for Workers' Education). By marrying Radványi, who had committed his life to the party and was ready to carry out assignments wherever they might take him, Seghers had opted for a life of uncertainty and economic instability.

In 1929 Seghers joined the Bund Prole-tarisch-Revolutionärer Schriftsteller (BPRS [Association of Proletarian-Revolutionary Writers]). While she brought to her new associates a rich background in art and literature, they, in turn, introduced her to Marxist literary theory and included her in their debates about literature as an effective tool in politics.

In the fall of 1930 Seghers was a member of a delegation of the BPRS that traveled to Kharkov in the Soviet Union to attend the Second International Conference for Proletarian and Revolutionary Literature. During this trip Seghers visited major industrial sites and gained a firsthand impression of the country's efforts to strengthen its economy. She returned to Germany an admirer of the first socialist state and remained a staunch defender of the Soviet Union throughout her life, even refraining from commenting on the Stalinist purges in the late 1930s.

In the late 1920s and early 1930s Seghers made a name for herself with the publication of short stories such as *Der Aufstand der Fischer von St. Barbara,* "Grubetsch," "Die Ziegler" (The Ziegler Woman), and "Die Bauern von Hruschowo" (The Peasants of Hruschowo); the latter three stories appeared in her first collection, *Auf dem Wege zur amerikanischen Botschaft und andere Erzählungen* (On the Road to the American Embassy and Other Stories, 1930). They are tales of ordinary people who gradually learn to rebel against their social milieu and their economic misery. Although they are members of the lower classes, Seghers's characters do not represent the class-conscious proletariat, the collective hero in many of her later works. These stories, with their sparse and charged language, reveal Seghers's talent for writing fiction which is richly symbolic and ardent in its humanitarian commitment.

When the National Socialists came to power in Germany in January 1933, Seghers was triply condemned for being a woman author, a Communist, and a Jew; her name appeared on the list of forbidden authors. In April 1933 she was arrested but was released shortly thereafter because of her husband's Hungarian citizenship. The Radványis fled to France, where they took up residence in Bellevue, a suburb of Paris.

By the time of her arrival in France, Seghers had completed two novels. *Die Gefährten,* which had been banned shortly after publication in Germany, is an account of revolutionaries from various parts of the world who fight for socialism. Seghers's second novel, *Der Kopflohn* (The Bounty, 1933; translated as "A Price on His Head," 1960), completed in Paris and published in Amsterdam, is the first literary response to German fascism. It tells of life in a village in Seghers's native region before the Nazi takeover.

Seghers's seven years of exile in France were among the most politically active and productive of her career. It was there that she wrote some of her most important works. *Der Weg durch den Februar* (The Way through February, 1935) deals with the revolt of the working class against the Dollfu regime in Austria between November 1933 and February 1934. To gain firsthand impressions of the events, in the spring of 1934 Seghers traveled to cities in Austria where the fighting had been most violent. In her fictional account Seghers resorts to modernist techniques, such as simultaneity of events and frequent shifts in setting and narrative voice, to capture the frenzied quality of the uprising. *Die Rettung* (The Rescue, 1937) portrays life in a German mining town in the late 1920s and early 1930s, focusing on the economic and political crises that resulted in the gravitation of working-class people to the National Socialists. Both novels readily found publishers, albeit in countries other than the author's own: *Der Weg durch den Februar* was published in Paris and Moscow, *Die Rettung* in Amsterdam.

Seghers regarded France as a second home and frequently expressed her affection for the French people. As late as 1977, in a letter to her French publisher, she speaks of her admiration for the country that represented for her the best of Europe's progressive traditions. Most of her writing was done in the animated environment of Paris cafés, where friends and colleagues recall her sitting at an empty table filling page after page, oblivious to the confusion around her.

Much of Seghers's time in Paris was devoted to activities connected with the Schutzverband Deutscher Schriftsteller (Protective League of German Writers), where she met other exiles such as Rudolf Leonhard, Heinrich and Klaus Mann, and Ernst Bloch. She participated in lecture nights and contributed to political pamphlets and journals in hopes of enlightening the rest of Europe about National Socialism and encouraging the emergence of a resistance movement against Adolf Hitler in her homeland. Her faith in the potential for resistance against Nazism among the German people informs all of her writings of this period.

Through the Protective League of German Writers Seghers came into contact with famous French writers such as André Malraux and Louis Aragon. In August 1938 she published in the journal *Europe* excerpts from a diary in which she comments on her encounters with French writers and on her frustrated efforts to communicate to them her own artistic and political identity as well as that of other German exiles. In her speech on the theme of love for the fatherland at the First International Conference in the Defense of Culture in Paris in the fall of 1935, Seghers identified herself and her fellow exiles with a literary tradition represented by such figures as Gottfried Bürger, J. M. R. Lenz, Heinrich von Kleist, Friedrich Hölderlin, Karoline von Günderode, Heine, and Georg Büchner. In her view they had risked artistic greatness, as well as their lives, by taking a decisive stance on the political and social issues of their times. In her closing remarks she pays tribute to these writers and their concern for their troubled fatherland: "Diese deutschen Dichter schrieben Hymnen auf ihr Land, an dessen gesellschaftlicher Mauer sie ihre Stirnen wund rieben. Sie liebten gleichwohl ihr Land" (These German poets wrote hymns to their country on whose walls they beat their brows. But they loved their country nonetheless). Seghers's novels and stories written in exile are characterized by a similar commitment to Germany and its progressive traditions.

The late 1930s was also a time when Seghers freed herself from the aesthetic and theoretical dogmas that had characterized the debates on revolutionary art in leftist circles in the early years of the decade. When these issues once again became the focus of discussions among exiles such as Georg Lukács, Bertolt Brecht, and Hanns Eisler, Seghers came forth to articulate an independent position. In two letters to her friend Lukács she challenged his concept of realism and rejected the subordination of fiction writing to criteria based on a traditional literary canon and on scientific construction of reality. Instead, she advocated a realism that was open-ended and would allow for formal experimentation. Although Seghers later embraced Lukács's position on the social function of art, her exile writings show a closer affinity to the views of Brecht, Bloch, and Walter Benjamin than to those of her Hungarian mentor. In her novels *Das siebte Kreuz* and *Transit* and in "Der Ausflug der toten Mädchen" Seghers uses many of the modernist techniques that Lukács found objectionable, such as multiple plots, stream of consciousness, and frequent shifts in voice and setting. As a result, as much as Lukács valued Seghers as a friend, he never cared for these works.

Seghers hoped that *Das siebte Kreuz* would signal her breakthrough as a major writer, but its publication was delayed by the chaos that erupted soon after she finished the manuscript in 1939. Before escaping from occupied Paris she left copies of the manuscript with friends, sending other copies to the United States. Franz C. Weiskopf, a German-Czech exile in New York and a close friend of Seghers, brought the manuscript to the attention of Maxim Lieber, who found an interested publisher in Little, Brown and Company of Boston. Before the book appeared in the fall of 1942, the publisher offered American readers a blurb comparing Seghers to Dos Passos and Ernest Hemingway. The book was received with almost unanimous acclaim among critics; some went so far as to compare Seghers to Thomas Mann and Hermann Broch. The novel became the choice of the Book-of-the-Month Club in October 1943.

Das siebte Kreuz is the story of the escape of seven inmates from the concentration camp Westhofen in southwestern Germany in the fall of 1937. The camp commander sets up seven crosses on which the escapees are to be executed when they are caught. Six of the men are captured and die a cruel death at the hands of their captors; the seventh, a young Communist named George Heisler, eludes his pursuers and flees the country. His escape demonstrates to the remaining captives that the Third Reich is not omnipotent. Those who come in contact with Heisler–workers, a Jewish doctor, a priest, a chemist, and others–are confronted with a difficult choice: to help Heisler, thereby risking their own lives, or to turn him over to the state. Through this cross section of Germans Seghers meant to identify the potential for resistance against Nazism in her country. The idea of linking the flight motif with the panoramic depiction of German society had been suggested to her by Alessandro Manzoni's novel *I promesi sposi* (1827; translated as *The Betrothed*, 1834). An omniscient narrator functions as the collective voice of the camp inmates. It is he who, in a closing passage, articulates the faith in all that is "inviolable and unassailable" in mankind, echoing the author's lifelong credo.

With the advance of the German army the situation of exiles in Paris became untenable. Many of them fled overseas; others despaired and committed suicide. Seghers escaped to Pamiers, near Marseilles in unoccupied southern France; her husband was in an internment camp in nearby Le Vernet. She found a café where she could write or study Jean Racine and Balzac. There she began *Transit*, the Kafkaesque refugee story that she later completed in Mexico.

The narrator in *Transit*, an anonymous young worker, is a fugitive from Nazi Germany. Sitting in a harbor café in Marseilles in the spring of 1941, he tells the story of refugees from all parts of Europe who have come to southern France in the hope of leaving for a "promised land" abroad. They are caught in a nightmarish world of red tape, visas, functionaries, and consulates. Although he is initially not interested in leaving Europe, the worker's life begins to change when he finds a letter in a dead man's suitcase promising a visa to Mexico. He temporarily adopts the dead man's name, an act which becomes a threat to his very identity. But his friends—working-class people and other simple folk of Marseilles, none of whom has any intention of leaving the old world—tell him that he belongs with them and that he should share their fate. In his capacity as narrator, combining all the confusing stories into a coherent whole, he counts on the reader to participate in making sense out of the chaos. In telling his stories he captures the voice of the common people and their wisdom, and in so doing he conquers his feeling of isolation and displacement.

In contrast to the narrator of *Transit*, Seghers did leave Europe. With the help of the League of American Writers she obtained the papers and money necessary for her family's escape to their overseas exile. After a difficult journey, with holdovers in Martinique, Santo Domingo, and Ellis Island, they arrived in Mexico City in the summer of 1941. Speaking of the ordeal of that journey, Seghers confessed in a letter to her friend Bodo Uhse: "Ich habe das Gefühl, als wär ich ein Jahr lang tot gewesen" (I had the feeling of having been dead for a whole year).

In Mexico Seghers entered the company of a relatively large contingent of German-speaking Communists. Like Seghers, many of them had hoped for visas to the United States but were denied entry because of their affiliation with the Communist Party. They joined together in an effort to establish a center for antifascist activity in Mexico City while maintaining contact with the leadership of the German Communist Party in Moscow. Seghers was most active in her capacity as president of the Heinrich Heine Club, organizing cultural events for wider audiences. She also contributed extensively to the exile journal *Freies Deutschland*. The contact with a new continent and culture informed her subsequent writing, although she did not write about Mexico while living there."Mexico is ideal for the artist," she stated in an interview with the American journal *New Masses* in February 1943. "The atmosphere is stimulating. But I don't believe that I shall ever write about it. I know so little about the country. . . . Everything is so youthful and I have not quite absorbed it all." Later, after her return to East Germany, she paid tribute to Mexico in an essay on Mexican mural art and in the stories *Crisanta* (1951) and *Das wirkliche Blau*. The novels and essays Seghers wrote in Mexico deal almost

exclusively with Germany. Wolf has characterized Seghers's exile writings as "Leiden an Deutschland" (grieving for Germany). In light of the news from Germany that reached the exile community in Mexico, such grieving was understandable. The war crimes, mass deportation of Jews, and the construction of death camps where Seghers's mother perished caused her to wonder: "Ein Volk, das sich auf die andren Völker wirft, um sie auszurotten, ist das noch unser Volk?" (A people that attacks other peoples to destroy them—is that still our people?). Throughout those years she reflected on the question of the exiled writer's national identity, on which she wrote repeatedly in essays such as "Deutschland und Wir" (Germany and We, 1941), "Volk und Schriftsteller" (A People and Its Writers, 1942), and "Aufgaben der Kunst" (The Duty of Art, 1944). The theme of love for the homeland is further developed in "Der Ausflug der toten Mädchen," a story she began writing while recovering from injuries sustained in a hit-and-run accident in 1943.

One of the most beautiful modern German short stories, "Der Ausflug der toten Mädchen" is perhaps Seghers's most experimental work. Set in Mexico near the end of World War II, the story begins with the narrator, an exiled German woman writer, walking through the desolate, arid Mexican countryside toward a white wall she has seen in the distance. The wall turns out to be part of a deserted ranch. As the narrator goes through an open gate, the scenery changes and she finds herself back in the lush, green Rhine countryside in 1912 or 1913. It is the excursion day of a Mainz girls' school, and the narrator recognizes companions from an earlier, happier life. It is clear that she does not literally go back in time but that the past surfaces from her memory. As the title suggests, the schoolgirls are no longer alive. But in the narrator's visionary return to that day of her youth, the dead girls are resurrected out of her need to understand and communicate the meaning of their lives. As the narrator brings forward each of her schoolmates in their youthful innocence and promise in the idyllic setting on the Rhine, she interrupts with comments on their fates. Most of them end tragically in Nazi Germany, whether or not they supported the state. For example, the narrator says of her best friend Leni: "Ihr Gesicht war so glatt und blank wie ein frischer Apfel, und nicht der geringste Rest war darin, nicht die geringste Narbe von den Schlägen, die ihr die Gestapo bei der Verhaftung versetzt hatte, als sie sich weigerte, über ihren Mann auszusagen" (Her face was smooth and shiny and fresh as an apple, and not the slightest sign or scar could be detected of the blows that the Gestapo had inflicted on her at the time of her arrest, when she refused to give any information about her husband). In chronicling the lives of these women,

Seghers shows the morally and physically devastating effects of Nazism on the entire German people.

In January 1947 Seghers began a journey to Germany by way of Sweden and France. In April she arrived in Berlin, where she was stunned by the devastation she saw. Within a few months she had settled in East Berlin and became involved in political and cultural activities. She joined the world peace movement, attended meetings in Paris and Warsaw, and represented her country at international conferences. Among her extensive travels, several trips to the Soviet Union, where she spent time in archives studying Tolstoy and Dostoyevsky, were the most productive, resulting in publication of a 1963 collection of essays on the two Russian authors.

A novel with which she expected to contribute to the so-called antifascist reeducation program in postwar Germany was *Die Toten bleiben jung* (1949; translated as *The Dead Stay Young,* 1950), which treats German history from the November 1918 revolution to the defeat of Nazi Germany in 1945. The novel begins with the murder in a forest near Berlin of a young Communist worker by a group of officers and their subordinates. The killers represent various social groups and political interests of post–World War I Germany: the industrialists, the old nobility, the impoverished peasantry, and the lower middle class. Marie, the slain worker's bride, and her friends and neighbors speak for the working class and its concerns. Through the life stories and the personal and political choices of the characters Seghers points to the causes of the catastrophic course of recent German history. In shaping her vast subject matter into novel form, Seghers was probably influenced by Mexican mural art, which attracted her by its simultaneous simplicity and complexity. The novel has become a classic of socialist literature and history.

The novels *Die Entscheidung* (The Decision, 1959) and *Das Vertrauen* (Trust, 1968) deal with the choice many Germans faced in the immediate postwar era between the socialist society in the East and capitalist state in the West. Both novels revolve around the reconstruction of a steel mill in the Soviet Occupation Zone and the evolution of new social conditions in the GDR. The mill's former owners in the West and other enemies of the young socialist republic attempt to sabotage the rebuilding of the site–and by extension the entire East German economy–but the loyalty and efforts of many class-conscious socialists prevail in securing the future of the country. Seghers portrays the GDR as heir to all progressive German traditions and the West as a product of the capitalism and militarism of the past. Although these programmatic prosocialist novels are not Seghers's strongest pieces of fiction, they are more than mere political tracts, for they address the complex-

ities of the post–World War II era and their impact on individual lives.

Shortly before her return from Mexico, Seghers had said that artists who had come in contact with other cultures had the responsibility of introducing them to reading audiences in their own countries. *Karibische Geschichten* (Caribbean Stories, 1962) is an attempt at such a cross-cultural dialogue, telling of the eighteenth-century slave revolutions in the Caribbean and the proclamation of the first black republic in Haiti. The collection of stories *Die Kraft der Schwachen* (The Strength of the Weak, 1965) concentrates on common people, among them women and children in cultures other than Seghers's own. In critical moments they come to recognize their inner strength for enduring hardship and injustice as well as their potential for social and political change. Seghers's last collection of stories, *Drei Frauen aus Haiti* (Three Women from Haiti, 1980), traces the lives of three women from the time of the Spanish conquest to the Duvalier regime. These women are lauded for their capacity to suffer and to retain the ability to resist, to survive, and to regenerate life.

Among Seghers's later writings are some pieces in which she reflects on fantasy, imagination, and the creative process. "Das wirkliche Blau" (translated as "Benito's Blue," 1967) is a story about art, creativity, and the social identity of the artist. During World War II Benito, a Mexican potter, runs out of a unique blue color imported from Germany. He journeys into Mexico's interior to find his own true "color" among his people. Benito's quest for his inimitable blue is a metaphor for the author's lifelong search for human fulfillment, social justice, and artistic authenticity. "Reisebegegnung" (The Travel Encounter, 1973), which Seghers has called "Literatur-Geschichte" (a play on words suggesting "a story about literature" and "literary history"), depicts an encounter of E. T. A. Hoffmann, Nikolai Gogol, and Kafka, who engage in a dialogue about the relationship between fantasy, dreams, and historical time. Seghers makes a plea for infusing socialist literature with new visions and themes and articulates a concept of writing in which elements of the fantastic, of legends, and of fairy tales coexist with realistic settings.

Although Seghers was a prolific writer until her death, *Das siebte Kreuz, Transit,* and "Der Ausflug der toten Mädchen" stand out as her greatest literary achievements. These works encouraged writers in the GDR–most notably Christa Wolf–to break with the narrow constraints of socialist realism and to explore new possibilities of writing.

On the occasion of Seghers's eightieth birthday, symposia and colloquia were held to honor her both in the GDR and in the Federal Republic of Germany, including a conference at the university of her native city of Mainz. A year later, after extensive political controversy, Seghers was awarded the status of honorary citizen of Mainz. After her death on 1 June 1983 she was given a state burial at the Dorotheenstädtische Friedhof in East Berlin, the resting place of many high-ranking personages of the German Democratic Republic. Her life and works have been documented in several studies; chief among these are Kurt Batt's monograph *Anna Seghers: Versuch über Entwicklung und Werke* (1973), Klaus Sauer's *Anna Seghers* (1978) in the Beck series on modern authors, and Christiane Zehl Romero's richly documented monograph *Anna Seghers* (1987). The novel that brought the author international acclaim, *The Seventh Cross,* appeared in a new edition in 1987 with a foreword by Kurt Vonnegut and an afterword by Dorothy Rosenberg. *Über Kunstwerk und Wirklichkeit* (On Artistic Production and Reality, 1970–1979), the four-volume edition of Seghers's letters, speeches, and essays edited by Sigrid Bock for the GDR Academy Publishing House, documents Seghers's lifelong dedication to humanism and social change.

Letters:

Anna Seghers–Wieland Herzfelde: Ein Briefwechsel, edited by Ursula Emmerich and Erika Pick (Berlin: Aufbau, 1985);

"Anna Seghers: Briefe an F. C. Weiskopf," *Neue Deutsche Literatur,* 33, no. 11 (1985): 5–46.

Interview:

"Anna Seghers: An interview by John Stuart with the famous author of 'The Seventh Cross,'" *New Masses,* 46 (16 February 1943): 22–23.

Biography:

Frank Wagner, Ursula Emmerich, and Ruth Radványi, eds., *Anna Seghers: eine Biographie in Bildern* (Berlin: Aufbau, 1994).

References:

Anna Seghers, edited by Heinz Ludwig Arnold (Munich: Edition text + kritik, 1982);

Lowell Bangeter, *The Bourgeois Proletarian: A Study of Anna Seghers* (Bonn: Bouvier Verlag Herbert Grundmann, 1980);

Kurt Batt, *Anna Seghers: Versuch über Entwicklung und Werke* (Frankfurt am Main: Röderberg, 1973);

Batt, ed., *Über Anna Seghers: Ein Almanach zum 75. Geburtstag* (Berlin: Aufbau, 1975);

Kathleen J. LaBahn, *Anna Seghers' Exile Literature: The Mexican Years* (New York: Lang, 1986);

Christine Zehl Romero, *Anna Seghers* (Reinbek: Rowohlt, 1987);

Klaus Sauer, *Anna Seghers* (Munich: Beck & edition text + kritik, 1978);

Alexander Stephan, "Ein Exilroman als Bestseller: Anna Seghers' 'The Seventh Cross' in den USA," in *Exilforschung: Ein Internationales Jahrbuch,* edited by Thomas Koebner, Wulf Koepke, and Joachim Radkau (Munich: Edition text + kritik, 1985), pp. 238–259;

Christa Wolf, "Nachwort," in *Anna Seghers: Glauben an Irdisches (Essays aus vier Jahrzehnten),* edited by Wolf (Leipzig: Reclam, 1969), pp. 371–393; translated by Joan Becker as "Faith in the Terrestrial," in *Wolf, The Reader and the Writer: Essays, Sketches, Memories* (New York: International Publishers, 1977), pp. 111–137.

Papers:

The archives of Little, Brown and Company in Boston contain documents on the publication history of Seghers's *The Seventh Cross.*

Adalbert Stifter

(23 October 1805 – 28 January 1868)

Duncan Smith
Brown University

This entry originally appeared in DLB 133: Nineteenth-Century
German Writers to 1840.

BOOKS: *Studien,* 6 volumes (Pest & Leipzig: Heckenast, 1844–1850)—comprises in volume 1, "Der Condor," translated anonymously as "The Condor," *Democratic Review,* 27 (1850): 231; "Das Haidedorf," translated by Maria Norman as "The Village on the Heath," in *Rural Life in Austria and Hungary* (London: Bentley, 1850), III: 257–309; "Feldblumen"; in volume 2 (1844), "Der Hochwald," translated by Norman as "The Hochwald," in *Rural Life in Austria and Hungary,* II: 150–307; "Die Narrenburg," translated by Norman as "Crazy Castle," in *Rural Life in Austria and Hungary,* III: 1–159; in volume 3 (1847), "Die Mappe meines Urgroßvaters," translated by Norman as *My Great Grandfather's Notebook,* as volume 1 of *Rural Life in Austria and Hungary;* in volume 4 (1847), "Abdias," translated by Norman as "Abdias the Jew," in *Rural Life in Austria and Hungary,* II: 1–149; "Brigitta," translated by Edward Fitzgerald as Brigitta (London: Rodale, 1957); "Das alte Siegel"; in volume 5 (1850), "Der Hagestolz," translated by David Luke as "The Recluse," in *Limestone, and Other Stories* (New York: Harcourt, Brace & World, 1968); "Der Waldsteig"; in volume 6, "Zwei Schwestern," "Der beschriebene Tännling";

Bunte Steine: Ein Festgeschenck, 2 volumes (Pest & Leipzig: Heckenast, 1853)—comprises in volume 1, "Granit," "Kalkstein," translated by Luke as "Limestone; or, The Poor Benefactor," in *Limestone, and Other Stories;* "Turmalin," translated by Luke as "Tourmaline; or The Doorkeeper," in *Limestone, and Other Stories;* in volume 2, "Bergkristall," translated anonymously as *Mount Gars; or, Marie's Christmas-Eve* (Oxford: Parker, 1857); translated by Lee M. Hollander as "Rock Crystal," in *The German Classics of the Nineteenth and Twentieth Centuries,* volume 8, edited by Kuno Francke and William Guild Howard (New York:

Adalbert Stifter in 1863

German Publication Society, 1914), pp. 356–403; "Katzensilber," "Bergmilch";

Lesebuch zur Förderung humaner Bildung in Realschulen und in andern zu weiterer Bildung vorbereitenden Mittelschulen, by Stifter and Johannes Aprent (Pest: Heckenast, 1854);

Der Nachsommer: Eine Erzählung, 3 volumes (Pest: Heckenast, 1857); translated by Wendell Frye as *Indian Summer* (New York: Lang, 1985);

Der Weihnachtsabend (Pest: Hackenast, 1864);

Witiko: Eine Erzählung, 3 volumes (Pest: Heckenast, 1865–1867);

Erzählungen, 2 volumes, edited by Aprent (Pest: Heckenast, 1869);

Vermischte Schriften, 2 volumes, edited by Aprent (volume 1, Pest: Hackenast, 1870; volume 2, Leipzig: Amelang, 1870);

Früheste Dichtungen, edited by Heinrich Micko (Prague: Gesellschaft deutscher Bücherfreunde in Böhmen, 1937);

Sämtliche Werke, 23 volumes, edited by August Sauer, Gustav Wilhelm and Franz Hüller (Prague: Calve / Reichenberg: Kraus, 1901–1939);

Julius: Eine Erzählung, edited by Hüller (Augsburg: Kraft, 1950);

Erzählungen in der Urfassung, 3 volumes, edited by Max Stefl (Augsburg: Kraft, 1950–1952);

Die Schulakten Adalbert Stifters, edited by Kurt Vancsa (Graz: Stiasny, 1955);

Sämtliche Werke, 3 volumes, edited by Hannsludwig Geiger (Berlin: Tempel, 1959);

Gesammelte Werke, 6 volumes, edited by Stefl (Wiesbaden: Insel, 1959);

Pädagogische Schriften, edited by Theodor Rutt (Paderborn: Schöning, 1960);

Gesammelte Werke, 9 volumes, edited by Stefl (Darmstadt: Wissenschaftliche Buchgesellschaft, 1960–1963);

Documenta Paedagogica Austriaca. Adalbert Stifter, 2 volumes, edited by K. G. Fischer (Linz: Oberösterreichischer Landesverlag, 1961);

Werke und Briefe: Historisch-kritische Gesamtausgabe, 38 volumes, edited by Hermann Kunisch, Alfred Doppler, and Wolfgang Frühwald (Stuttgart: Kohlhammer, 1978);

Sämtliche Werke, 5 volumes, edited by Fritz Krökel and Karl Pörnbacher (Munich: Winkler, 1978);

Werke, 4 volumes, edited by Joachim Müller (Berlin: Aufbau, 1981).

OTHER: *Wien und die Wiener in Bildern aus dem Leben,* edited, with contributions, by Stifter (Pest: Nordmann, 1844).

Adalbert Stifter is the best-known nineteenth-century Austrian prose writer and is among the most highly regarded of all German and Austrian writers of the modern era. His work, along with that of such writers as Christian Dietrich Grabbe, Karl Immermann, Gottfried Keller, Wilhelm Raabe, and Theodor Storm, created the high reputation of the German novel and short story in the nineteenth century. Yet from the time of his earliest publications in the 1840s, Stifter's works have encountered a deeply divided critical response.

For some critics and readers, including the great Austrian playwright Franz Grillparzer and the musicians Clara and Robert Schumann, his works combine unsurpassed beauty with a unique ethical sensitivity. Others, led by the German dramatist Friedrich Hebbel, judged his writings as reactionary and boring, mannered in style, and lacking in integrity. Even during his lifetime Stifter's reputation declined steadily from an early popular and critical enthusiasm for his first works to a confused critical silence and the neglect of his later writings. After his death his fame declined still further, and Stifter was relegated by critics to the status of a regional writer who excelled in the descriptions of local natural landscapes. Toward the end of the nineteenth century and in the first decades of the twentieth, his work was rediscovered by such writers as Friedrich Nietzsche, Hugo von Hofmannsthal, Hermann Hesse, and Thomas Mann, who were admirers of the epic novels written in the latter half of his literary career. Attacked by critics Walter Benjamin and György Lukács, Stifter was dubiously rescued by the German nationalists of the 1920s and 1930s who attempted to see in him another glorifier of the German Fatherland and German virtues. Post–World War II reception included ringing endorsements of his modernity, even contemporaneity, as well as continuing disparagement of his literary ability and allegedly reactionary political stance. The debate about his novels and short stories continued into the late twentieth century, typified by the adamant opposition to Stifter by Arno Schmidt and endorsements from Thomas Bernhard and Peter Handke. The enthusiasm of Stifter's admirers is matched by those critics and writers who attack both the admirers and the author as exemplifying the worst kind of reactionary and inaccessible writing. Stifter's works continue to fascinate, puzzle, and challenge critics and readers.

The man around whom such strong reactions still circulate more than a century after his death was born on 23 October 1805 in the small town of Oberplan (today Horné Planà, Czech Republic) in what is still a rural area of Bohemia and was then part of the Hapsburg Empire. His father, Johann Stifter, was a linen weaver who had successfully turned to trading in flax, a principal crop of the region. His mother, Magdalena, née Friepess, was the daughter of an Oberplan butcher. Stifter was the oldest of two brothers and a sister. A half brother was born to his mother in a second marriage contracted after Stifter's father was killed in a road accident in 1817.

Stifter had already been singled out for his accomplishments in school by his first teacher, Josef Jenne, and plans had been made with his parents' encouragement to give the boy additional schooling. His father's death postponed these plans, but his maternal grandfather, Franz Friepess, arranged for Stifter to return to his studies and even to apply for admission to the well-known school at the Kremsmünster Benedictine abbey. Despite discouraging advice from the local priest, who had tutored Stifter in Latin and had judged him incompetent, the school's head teacher, Father Placidus Hall, recognized Stifter's talents and arranged for his immediate enrollment in 1822. He excelled in all his subjects—including Latin—and graduated in 1826 as one of the best pupils in his class. The third of a triumvirate of influential teachers, Georg Rietzlmayr encouraged Stifter's talents in drawing and painting. Stifter had early decided that painting was his vocation in the arts, and he would not devote himself seriously to literature until his mid thirties. He left a variety of mostly landscape paintings and drawings, some of which are still occasionally exhibited; they reveal a high level of skill. Some critics of Stifter's works have suggested that his highly descriptive and detail conscious literary style is the legacy of this first avocation as a painter, and there are several noteworthy studies of Stifter as a visual artist.

These three teachers had a lasting influence on Stifter's life; of equal importance were his two grandfathers, Friepess and Augustin Stifter, who provided the boy the support from older men that the early death of his father had interrupted. In many of his writings, most notably in "Die Mappe meines Urgroßvaters" (1847; translated as *My Great-Grandfather's Note-book,* 1850), Stifter has set a memorial to the figures of these influential older men of his youth.

In 1826 Stifter enrolled as a student of law at the University of Vienna. He received good grades but left the university without a degree, absenting himself from a mandatory final examination without satisfactory explanation. Willingly or not, therefore—and the evidence points to a deliberate decision—Stifter was spared the fate of becoming a bureaucrat in the Austrian administration, the certain result of a law degree, and devoted himself instead to his art while supporting himself as a private tutor to the wealthy families of Vienna. His familiarity with the world of Viennese aristocrats and patricians is portrayed in many of his works, including the early "Feldblumen" (Wildflowers, 1844), as well as his great novel *Der Nachsommer* (1857; translated as *Indian Summer,* 1985). For most of the 1830s Stifter led what appears to have been a comfortable life, concentrating on his painting; on his relationships with the wealthy families he served, including the family of Count Wenzel von Metternich, prime minister of

Austria and architect of post-Napoleonic European order; on his considerable circle of friends; and on walking tours of Austria. On visits back to Oberplan he fell in love with Fanny Greipl, whom he courted assiduously. Stifter, without means and even at times in straitened circumstances, was unacceptable to Greipl's parents unless he improved his situation; once again he escaped from the predicament by intentionally or accidentally failing to appear for an interview on which depended an appointment to an academic post at the University of Prague. He thereby forfeited both the post and Greipl. In 1835 he married the milliner Amalia Mohaupt, who came from a poor family.

Some of Stifter's biographers have dwelt on this strange union between the moody and brilliant young artist and author, who was clearly entering the world of recognized artistic achievement in Vienna and beyond, and a poorly educated young woman who brought her husband neither material nor class advantages. Although the letters Stifter sent to Amalia throughout their marriage reveal affection and devotion, they have been read by some biographers as portrayals of a relationship the writer wished he had rather than the prosaic and unsatisfying marriage he is alleged by some to have had. It is certain that following his marriage Stifter gradually settled into an outwardly bland domestic life from which the literary works that were to make him famous emerged.

He had some poems published in 1830 under the pseudonym Ostade but was otherwise still apparently dedicated to his private lessons, his painting, and the cultivation of his connections among the patrons of arts and letters in the Viennese upper classes. But in 1840 two stories, "Der Condor" (translated as "The Condor," 1850) and "Das Haidedorf" (translated as "The Village on the Heath," 1850), appeared under the name Adalbert Stifter in the literary journal *Iris,* published by Gustave Heckenast in Budapest. They were followed from 1841 to 1843 in *Iris* and other literary journals by "Feldblumen," "Die Mappe meines Urgroßvaters," "Der Hochwald" (translated as "The Hochwald," 1850), "Abdias" (translated as "Abdias the Jew," 1850), "Die Narrenburg" (translated as "Crazy Castle," 1850), the novella "Brigitta" (translated, 1957), and "Das alte Siegel" (The Ancient Seal). Between 1844 and 1850 Heckenast published six volumes of thoroughly revised versions of these stories under the title *Studien* (Studies). The volumes also include "Der Hagestolz" (translated as "The Recluse," 1968), "Der Waldsteig" (The Forest Path),

"Zwei Schwestern" (Two Sisters), and "Der beschriebene Tännling" (The Inscribed Fir Tree).

Both the original journal versions and the versions in *Studien* were greeted with critical acclaim.
Contemporary critics, however, ignored or missed
the odd contradictions between language and object
described and the element of looming catastrophe
that for many modern readers, beginning with
Nietzsche and Mann, are the hallmarks of Stifter's
writing. Instead, the young author was praised as an
example of the triumph of the aesthetic dimension
over the otherwise dominant and shrill voices of the
politically engaged writers of the period. Stifter's
indebtedness to the German writer Jean Paul was
noted, in general favorably, as was his distancing of
himself from still-fashionable Romanticism. The odd-
ities of Stifter's literary style were overlooked by
most readers, who responded with pleasure to his
brilliant descriptions of nature and the ethical dimension of his characterizations and plots. Stifter was
established as a promising writer.

Modern criticism of the best known of these
stories has tended to address the peculiarities of style
and the theme of alienation as well as the ethical and
aesthetic dimensions. Stories such as "Der Hagestolz" and "Brigitta" are viewed as examples of
Stifter's concern with the inexplicable and the tragic,
with accident and accommodation with the results
thereof. "Abdias," in which an elderly Jew is
deprived of his sight and finally his daughter in a violent natural accident after a life of adventure, greed,
and hatred, is a typical example of one of Stifter's
leading traits as a writer: the focus on the sudden
appearance of an uncompromising natural principle
that may or may not be associated with retributive
justice or divine guidance. Such terrors are described
with an impartiality of style and ethical attitude. Natural phenomena, of which human existence is but
one example, are simply what they are, though they
may strike an individual as wonderful or terrible.

Another frequent motif in Stifter's early works
is that of the father and son, or the older man,
related or not, and the younger man or boy. This
man-boy motif occurs in some of his finest works,
including "Die Mappe meines Urgroßvaters" and
"Der Hagestolz," as well as in the critically less
regarded novella "Das alte Siegel." In all of these stories the older men play significant roles in the development of the younger men's worldviews, assisting
the younger male figures with the entry into the
adult world as if in an initiation rite. In "Der Hagestolz" an isolated and lonely old bachelor is the
inspired initiator of his nephew into a bright and
broad world, helping the younger man to escape

from the narrow if safe world of the bureaucrat to
which his life with maternally loving women had led
him.

Stifter took part in the discussions and debates
that led to the short-lived revolutions throughout
Europe in 1848. His position was initially that of a
moderate liberal who supported the promulgation of
a constitution that would grant a greater measure of
political power to the prosperous middle class to
which he was himself steadily ascending. But 1848
was also the year of Karl Marx and Friedrich
Engels's *Manifest der kommunistischen Partei* (translated
as *Manifesto of the Communist Party,* 1888), and the specter of a seizure of power by the proletariat came to
haunt Stifter after the ouster of Metternich, the
apparent overthrow of the emperor, and the threat of
a "red republic" in Vienna. Stifter's liberalism did not
include accommodation with the masses. His doubts
increased with the increase in street violence and
what he regarded as the rule of the mob. He witnessed the heady moments of apparent triumph by
the moderate and loyalist liberals, among whose
number he reckoned himself. But he could not tolerate the overthrow of the feebleminded but popular
emperor, Ferdinand, who was forced into exile in
March 1848 and shortly thereafter was obliged to
abdicate in favor of his nephew Franz Josef. Stifter
left Vienna, ostensibly for the quiet he needed to pursue his literary work, and retired to the provincial
city of Linz, the capital of Upper Austria. There he
briefly took on the post of editor of a traditionalist
paper, writing in its pages and elsewhere a series of
political tracts deploring the growth of mob rule and
the accompanying violence and pleading for the restoration of order. These and other essays written in a
similar tone have been taken by Stifter's critics as evidence of his essentially conservative, even reactionary political position. In fact, Stifter had become far
more conservative during those years of tumult and
upheaval. His permanent settlement in Linz, where
old traditions still held sway, clearly expressed his
antagonism toward the changes that imperiled the
old order. Like many liberals who had risen from the
rural peasantry or the artisan class, Stifter saw
change as welcome only when it did not interrupt the
beneficial order of the state and society. Such
changes had to happen naturally and organically,
and Stifter refused to see in the changes he was witnessing any parallels to the violent interruptions of
natural order that his own fictional work so splen-
didly portrays. The contradictions such deeply held
feelings produced in Stifter marked all his work for
the rest of his life. It is from this point that Stifter's
writing changes to an espousal of moderation, preser-

vation, and loyalist conservatism. Stifter ceased being only an artist and chose to become a preacher of an ethical aesthetics that contains a deep political and social message as well as a deeper artistic contradiction.

Stifter's first post-1848 literary publication was a two-volume collection of stories, most of which were written prior to 1848 in a first version titled *Bunte Steine* (Colored Stones, 1853). This collection has become perhaps the best known of all his works and contains several stories that are regularly anthologized as classics of German literature: "Bergkristall" (Rock Crystal; translated as *Mount Gars; or, Marie's Christmas-Eve,* 1857), "Kalkstein" (translated as "Limestone, or, The Poor Benefactor," 1968), and "Granit" (Granite), all of which appeared in journal versions between 1845 and 1849. The remaining stories are "Bergmilch" (Aragonite), "Turmalin" (translated as "Tourmaline; or The Doorkeeper," 1968), and "Katzensilber" (Mica); the first of these appeared in a journal version in 1843, while "Kalkstein" appeared first in 1848, and "Katzensilber" appeared for the first time in the collection. The themes include infidelity in "Turmalin"; reconciliation and faith in "Bergkristall" and "Granit"; simplicity, justice, self-discipline, and right conduct in "Kalkstein"; disorder, catastrophe, art, and bourgeois values in "Katzensilber"; and war and pacifism in "Bergmilch." The use of a frame narrative in some of the stories serves to suggest universal truths, but the subject matter of the embedded stories is the small details of life, the apparently insignificant events from which true significance is derived. The tone of the stories is sober and instructive, and, since some of them were originally intended for children, they combine edification and rhetorical gentleness. Little violence is portrayed in the stories save for the occasional description of extreme natural phenomena at which Stifter excelled, most notably the snowstorm in "Bergkristall."

"Bergkristall" is the most critically acclaimed story in the collection. Two children from a mountain village are lost overnight in a terrible snowstorm as they attempt to return from a Christmas Eve visit with their grandparents in the village on the other side of the mountain. The search for the lost children by members of both villages forms the basis for reconciliation between the hostile communities. The plot is one of the utmost simplicity; but the descriptions of the children's experience and of the snowstorm itself have fascinated generations of readers and critics, the latter giving the story some of the most fulsome praise Stifter's work was ever to receive.

The somber "Turmalin" is set in Vienna, showing that Stifter was not only the consummate artist of the rural Austrian countryside but possessed equal skill in creating an atmosphere of urban change, which he portrays as part of the natural process. The story relates the changes that overcome the previously comfortable bourgeois lives of the characters: the father dies in the ruins of the house in which he had once lived; and the deformed daughter with whom he had fled after his wife and best friend ran off together is adopted by the narrator and his wife, who intend to counterbalance the strange education the girl had received from her father, but the reader is left with no doubt about the essential darkness of Stifter's vision in the story.

For critics and scholars the "Vorrede" (Introduction) of *Bunte Steine* has been the object of as much attention as the stories. Presumably written as a rebuttal to the already intense criticism of his earlier works by figures such as Hebbel, the "Vorrede" came to be regarded as the essential summation of Stifter's literary and personal philosophy. There are universal laws of justice and morality, Stifter says, but these laws are not to be grasped through any anthropocentric notions of causality. They may, however, be grasped by any reader who simply pays attention to the ways in which nature manifests itself. The "Vorrede" parallels ideas expressed by several contemporary thinkers, but it is an extremely bold statement in a time given over to belief either in God or in the ability of science completely to understand and control the world. It is a quite modern call for a holistic attitude as the best approach to healing a society beset by revolution and change.

But in explicitly stating these principles Stifter forced himself into the difficult task of carrying them out consciously. The style of his writing changed; the lengthy, convoluted sentence structures, the "litanesque" description of objects and events, the apparently straining causal conjunctions have provided challenging material for subsequent generations of critics, especially those interested in the field of narrative theory. Such stylistic phenomena also reduced his popularity with the reading public. Charges of inaccessibility and of readers' boredom with the often astonishing amount of descriptive detail were already current in his lifetime and have plagued his reputation ever since. His later work, including the epics *Der Nachsommer* and *Witiko* (1865–1867) as well as some of the shorter pieces he produced during the remainder of his life are all characterized by this apparent mannerism of literary style.

The years following the publication of *Bunte Steine* were filled with political and military crises in

Europe and in Austria. The Crimean War of 1853–1856; Austria's unsuccessful war in Italy against the nationalists supported by the French in 1859; the growing discord between Prussia under Otto von Bismarck and Austria, culminating in the defeat of Austria by Prussia in 1866; and the growth of capitalism formed the background of much of the literary work of the age. In his fiction Stifter remained aloof from these matters, though his personal dedication to the multinational empire and to the Hapsburg monarchy never wavered. In his career as inspector of primary and secondary schools in Upper Austria, a post he had requested and had received in 1850, he encouraged reforms and improvements. But the newly conservative empire had restored control of the schools to the Catholic church hierarchy, which opposed most of Stifter's suggestions. His textbook, written in collaboration with his Linz colleague Johannes Aprent and published in 1854, was rejected as too radical, and his subsequent career became more and more difficult. Plagued already by the symptoms of increasing ill health that was then more psychological than physiological in origin, he displayed in his reports and letters the considerable ability he possessed as an educator and as a mediator among people. His publisher and friend Heckenast remarked that he was completely at home with the common people, seeking them out in taverns and inns. Stifter received the Ritterkreuz des Franz-Josef Ordens (Knights Cross of Franz Josef) in 1854, honoring his work as one of Austria's foremost prose writers. The growing chorus of critical discontent from the more socially engaged writers was countered by the praise he received from those who valued his ethical and aesthetic stances. His personal life suffered a series of setbacks, beginning with the suicide of his adopted daughter, Juliana Mohaupt, in 1858. Stifter does not appear to have been close to this young woman, whose death may have been the result of a tragic love affair, but it occurred in the same year as the death of his mother, to whom he had remained devoted. The unexpected deaths of two newly discovered young relations, from whose company he had promised himself and his wife compensation for their childless marriage, weighed heavily on him as well. Combined with the increasing difficulties he was experiencing in his career—he was removed as school inspector for the secondary school at Linz in 1856—Stifter was undergoing difficult times. Yet he remained busy with civic tasks in Linz; visited Vienna on occasion, though with decreasing frequency; and continued to enjoy a growing if disputed national reputation as a writer and artist in German-speaking countries.

Der Nachsommer appeared in three volumes in 1857. Ideas for such epic undertakings had been advanced by Stifter to Heckenast before 1848; a lengthy treatment of Maximilien Robespierre is among the themes mentioned in his correspondence. But when the promised great epic actually appeared, after years of labor in the intervals of his professional work as an educator, it was not devoted to an event or a person of either historical or contemporary importance. In keeping with his profession of belief in the introduction to *Bunte Steine*, Stifter offered his publisher and public a work that is not really a novel at all. It has little actual plot within its hundreds of pages. It is assigned by perhaps desperate Germanists to the genre of the bildungsroman, whose model in German literature has been Johann Wolfgang von Goethe's *Wilhelm Meisters Lehrjahre* (1795–1796; translated as *Wilhelm Meister's Apprenticeship,* 1824). It resembles such novels only in the most general way, however. Instead, it is a mannered mass of didacticism about the good and the beautiful and the right path for a person to take to reach enlightenment and peace and do good in the world. Or it is a most modern work that uses photomontage to the most extraordinary advantage. Critical reactions range from Hebbel's splenetic offer of the crown of Poland to anyone who could say that he or she had, of his or her own free will, read the three volumes from cover to cover, to Nietzsche's, Mann's, and Hofmannsthal's praise of the work. The "story" is slight. Heinrich Drendorf, a young scientist, visits the home of a nobleman, von Risach; hears about von Risach's love affair with Mathilde, who now lives nearby; and falls in love with the nobleman's daughter Natalie, whom he eventually—many hundreds of pages later—marries. Surrounding these bones, however, is a depiction of that constant theme of Stifter's: the gradual and ritualistic maturing of a young man, a process that makes him truly cultured and civilized and, hence, an element of moderate but effective change in society. Each detail—whether dialogue on aesthetics, catalogue of objects in the nobleman's home, the dress of each of the characters, or an apparently endlessly didactic descent of a staircase—is lovingly and carefully recorded by the narrator.

The novel was not a commercial success. Stifter's reputation suffered a setback, and adherents of the Hebbel school of criticism grew in reaction to the work. This was, after all, the time of Charles Dickens and George Eliot in England and Honoré de Balzac in France; in Switzerland, Gottfried Keller was writing novels and novellas with abundant critical social themes combined with the ethical and the aesthetic; Raabe in Germany was narrating, with often biting irony, stories through which today the reader can still discern the social predicaments of the troubled times; Ivan Turgenev's work in Russia included novels and stories of great beauty that also contained direct societal relevance; in Paris, Heinrich Heine had earlier written poems and prose works that combined humor, irony, and beauty with the same topicality. In such a climate *Der Nachsommer* was reserved for the few faithful Stifter admirers who offered him cautious praise but spoke more affectionately and wistfully of his earlier stories. It was in the twentieth century that the novel found its first real critical response. Critics locate in Stifter's alleged mannerism an aesthetic undertaking in which ideology is made prominent by the very attempts of language to obscure it. It also appeals to readers and critics who see in Stifter's determined avoidance of the topical dedication to achieving a state of consciousness in which resistance to the dualistic norms of aesthetic and political discourse is more likely.

While writing *Der Nachsommer* Stifter had proposed to Heckenast the outline of a new epic work with more direct political and social relevance. *Witiko,* perhaps the strangest of all Stifter's writings, is a declaration of the author's views on history, politics, war and pacifism, the right relations of ruler to ruled, and the proper but difficult path to be taken in the achievement of both a just and ordered society and a just and civilized human being. With some retouching of twelfth-century history, Stifter re-creates the period in which Duke Wladyslaw became the ruler of Bohemia, warding off challenges from pretenders to the office whose political principles were permeated by selfishness, greed, and a lack of compassion for the subjects over whom they would rule. Witiko, a famous and just warrior, rallies to the support of the young duke, assisting him throughout the lengthy series of conflicts and providing the reader with a model of self-sacrificing service to a just historical cause. Duke Wladyslaw is victorious, and the novel ends with Witiko in attendance at the Parliament of Nobility held by the fabled Emperor Friedrich Barbarossa—the "King Arthur" of German legends—in 1184.

The epic reveals Stifter's most firmly held convictions about the importance of the maintenance of the Hapsburg Empire as a multinational state ruled by a just emperor to whom men and women should give their utmost loyalty. The work indicates that Stifter remained concerned about contemporary events and issues, though typically he chose not to engage in direct representation of those concerns. Instead, he tried to draw universal parallels. Far from being an expression of reactionary sentiments on the part of an aging writer, the epic may be read as a far-sighted work that endorses a vision of state and society not enmeshed in the nationalism that was to lead to the catastrophe of World War I. Stifter's sometimes ridiculed depictions of the virtues of manliness, courage, honor, and bodily strength detract only superficially from the essential themes of the horrors of war and the virtues of diplomacy and compassion. The many battle scenes are rendered in unrealistic fashion, and the greatest emphasis, to the bewilderment of critics and readers alike, is placed on the dialogues between the characters; the importance of the word as deed is stressed throughout.

In Stifter's time the novel was largely rejected, as it has been ever since, though its strangeness—Erik Lunding, one of Stifter's foremost modern interpreters, calls it the strangest prose fiction of the nineteenth century—has also exercised fascination for critics. It has never enjoyed popular success. Early reviews expressed invective or exasperation. Few contemporary readers and critics endorsed the work, which Heckenast nevertheless continued to produce for the steadily diminishing readership. Stifter was satisfied that the work contained a summation of his political and social philosophies and showed the means by which justice—personal and civil—could be approached.

Stifter's illness, a vaguely defined disorder attributed to diet and to job-related stress, worsened after 1863. Although he had concentrated almost exclusively on *Witiko,* he continued to produce such shorter pieces as "Nachkommenschaften" (Descendants), "Der Waldbrunnen" (The Forest Spring), "Der Kuß von Sentze" (The Kiss of Sentze), "Aus dem Bairischen Walde" (From the Bavarian Forest), and the final version of "Der fromme Spruch" (The Pious Saying). All of these stories were published in periodicals and were collected posthumously in 1869 by his friend Aprent in *Erzählungen* (Tales). In 1865 he obtained a provisional retirement from his education post, which became complete retirement with full pay shortly thereafter. He was named Hofrat (court councilor) in 1865 and received from the grand duke of Saxony-Weimar the Order of the White Falcon, First Class.

Contemporary reports of his life in these last years depict a tormented and unhealthy man who moved restlessly from one spa to another, seeking a cure for his still-undiagnosed ailment. He seemed unable to remain in Linz, leaving on any pretext to spend time in village retreats in the mountains or at various health resorts, most notably Kirchschlag and Carlsbad. Biographers have tried to link these flights to marital dissatisfactions, though Stifter's letters to

Amalia throughout this period are full of affection and expressions of his sorrow that his illness is making her life so difficult. He disregarded medical advice about his diet, which consisted of rich foods and heavy wines; he also frequently smoked cigars. He continued to write, working on the fourth version of his favorite story: "Die Mappe meines Urgroßvaters." This version was to have been a novel, but he died before completing the work. The final version was published in 1870 in *Vermischte Schriften* (Miscellaneous Writings), edited by Aprent.

"Die Mappe meines Urgroßvaters" is considered by many to be the finest of all of Stifter's works. He devoted more than twenty years to it, suggesting the central significance of its themes within the corpus of his writings. The narrator discovers the notebooks of his great-grandfather Augustinus, who as a young man in the eighteenth century leaves his home in southwestern Bohemia, becomes a doctor, and returns to the village to practice. He encounters a colonel and falls in love with the latter's daughter, Margarita. Through his jealousy, however, he loses her; he is prevented from suicide only by a chance encounter with the colonel, who points out to the despairing Augustinus the beauty of a nearby field, reminding the young man of the totality and the sacredness of all life. To further console him, the colonel tells him the story of his own previously stormy life and loves. Augustinus decides to dedicate himself to his calling as a healer and to write down in his notebooks a record of his experiences. He becomes a person whose identity is established in a near perfect harmony of the ethical individual with the natural world. Order results from acceptance, accommodation, and patient and nonanthropocentric observance of the world. Having become a universally respected man in the region, Augustinus accidentally meets Margarita again; she agrees to resume their engagement.

The four versions of the story record the author's growing shift of interest from descriptions of great events to depictions of ordinary life and the consolations of living life as it is rather than as it could be or ought to be. It is the premier example of the belief in acceptance and accommodation that was articulated in the "Vorrede" to *Bunte Steine*. Augustinus is gradually stripped of all apparent emotional responses to the vagaries of existence. "Die Mappe meines Urgroßvaters" enjoys a considerable following today among Stifter devotees and general readers alike. *Der Nachsommer,* the other work in which such a spiritual quest seems to be portrayed, contains a pedagogic element: it is a novel of instruction in which both Heinrich and the reader are asked to learn and to develop. Neither Augustinus nor the reader of "Die Mappe meines Urgroßvaters" is under such didactic duress. The story meanders from one event to another, with little or no distinction made between anecdotes, and in successive versions such distinctions as did exist are further minimized.

In January 1868 Stifter, in an excess of pain from what now appears to have been the final stages of cirrhosis of the liver, cut his throat with a razor. The doctor arrived in time to prevent him from bleeding to death; but the disease had already taken its toll, and Stifter died, aged sixty-two, on 28 January.

Letters:

Briefe, 3 volumes, edited by Johannes Aprent (Pest: Heckenast, 1869);

Ein Dichterleben aus dem alten Österreich: Ausgewählte Briefe, edited by Moriz Enzinger (Innsbruck: Wagnersche Universitäts-Buchdruckerei, 1947);

Briefe, edited by Hans Schumacher (Zurich: Manesse, 1947);

Briefe, edited by Gerhard Fricke (Nuremberg: Carl, 1949);

Adalbert Stifters Jugendbriefe (1822–1839): In ursprünglicher Fassung aus dem Nachlaß, edited by Gustav Wilhelm (Graz: Stiasny, 1954);

Adalbert Stifters Leben und Werk in Briefen und Dokumenten, edited by K. G. Fischer (Wiesbaden: Insel, 1962);

Adalbert Stifter in seinen Briefen, edited by Hanns-Ludwig Bachfeld (Hildesheim: Gerstenberg, 1973).

Bibliographies:

Werner Heck, *Das Werk Adalbert Stifters, 1840–1940: Versuch einer Bibliographie* (Vienna: Kerry, 1954);

"Adalbert Stifter bei den Tschechen in Übersetzungen und wissenschaftlichen Abhandlungen," *Vierteljahrsschrift des Adalbert-Stifter-Institutes des Landes Oberösterreich,* 6 (1957): 46–53;

W. A. Reichart and W. H. Grilk, "Stifters Werk in Amerika und England: Eine Bibliographie," *Vierteljahrsschrift des Adalbert-Stifter-Institutes des Landes Oberösterreich,* 9 (1960): 39–42;

Takashi Yoneda, "Stifters Werk in Japan: Eine Bibliographie," *Vierteljahrsschrift des Adalbert-Stifter-Institutes des Landes Oberösterreich,* 12 (1963): 64–66;

Eduard Eisenmeier, *Adalbert Stifter–Bibliographie* (Linz: Oberösterreichischer Landesverlag, 1964);

"Die Bibliographie der Veröffentlichungen zum 100. Todestag," *Vierteljahrsschrift des Adalbert-Stifter-Institutes des Landes Oberösterreich,* 18 (1969): 52–71;

"Das Adalbert-Stifter-Institut des Landes Oberösterreich," *Jahrbuch für Internationale Germanistik,* 8
(1976): 172–175.

Biographies:

Alois Raimund Hein, *Adalbert Stifter: Sein Leben und
seine Werke* (Prague: Calve, 1904);

Urban Roedl [Bruno Adler], *Adalbert Stifter: Geschichte
seines Lebens* (Berlin: Rowohlt, 1936; revised,
1948);

Emil Merkur, *Stifter* (Stuttgart: Cotta, 1942);

Karl Privat, *Adalbert Stifter: Sein Leben in Selbstzeugnissen, Briefen und Berichten* (Berlin: Tempelhof,
1946);

Roedl [Bruno Adler], *Adalbert Stifter in Selbstzeugnissen
und Bilddokumenten* (Reinbek: Rowohlt, 1965);

Alois Großschopf, *Adalbert Stifter: Leben, Werk, Landschaft* (Linz: Trauner, 1968).

References:

Ruth K. Angress, "Das Ehebruchmotiv in Stifters
'Das alte Siegel': Ein Beitrag zur Literaturge-
schichte der bürgerlichen Erotik," *Zeitschrift für
Deutsche Philologie,* 103 (1984): 481–502;

H. G. Barnes, "The Function of Conversations and
Speeches in *Witiko,*" in *German Studies: Presented
to H. G. Fiedler by Pupils, Colleagues and Friends*
(Oxford: Clarendon Press, 1938), pp. 1–25;

Ernst Bertram, *Studien zu Adalbert Stifters Novellentech-
nik,* second edition (Dortmund: Ruhfus, 1966);

Eric A. Blackall, *Adalbert Stifter: A Critical Study* (Cambridge: Cambridge University Press, 1948);

Barton W. Browning, "Cooper's Influence on Stifter:
Fact or Scholarly Myth?," *Modern Language
Notes,* 89 (October 1974): 821–828;

Walter Horace Bruford, "Adalbert Stifter: *Der Nachsommer,*" in his *The German Tradition of Self-Cultivation. Bildung from Humboldt to Thomas Mann*
(London: Cambridge University Press, 1975),
pp. 128–146;

Karen J. Campbell, "Toward a Truer Mimesis:
Stifter's 'Turmalin,'" *German Quarterly,* 57 (Fall
1984): 576–589;

Robert C. Conrad, "Heinrich Böll's Political Reevaluation of Adalbert Stifter: An Interpretation of
Böll's 'Epilog zu Stifters 'Nachsommer,'" *Michigan Academician: Papers of the Michigan Academy of
Sciences, Arts, and Letters,* 14, no. 1 (1981): 31–
39;

Gail Finney, "Garden Paradigms in Nineteenth-Century Fiction," *Comparative Literature,* 36, no. 1
(1984): 20–33;

Kurt Gerhard Fischer, *Die Pädagogik des Meschenmögli-
chen* (Linz: Landesverlag, 1962);

Gerald Gillespie, "Space and Time Seen through
Stifter's Telescope," *German Quarterly,* 37 (March
1964): 120–130;

H. A. Glaser, *Die Restauration des Schönen: Stifters
"Nachsommer"* (Stuttgart: Metzler, 1965);

Christian Godden, "Two Quests for Surety. A Com-
parative Interpretation of Stifter's 'Abdias' and
Kafka's 'Der Bau,'" *Journal of European Studies,* 5
(December 1975): 341–361;

Ulrich Greiner, "Der Tod des Nachsommers: Über
das Österreichische in der österreichischen Literatur," *Neue Rundschau,* 88, no. 3 (1977): 348–
361;

Margaret Gump, *Adalbert Stifter* (New York: Twayne,
1974);

Charles H. Helmetag, "The Gentle Law in Adalbert
Stifter's 'Der Hagestolz,'" *Modern Language Studies,* 16 (Summer 1986): 183–188;

Josef Heurkamp, "Das problematische Vorbild: über
das schwierige Verhältnis des Schriftstellers
Arno Schmidt zu Adalbert Stifter," *Vierteljahrsschrift des Adalbert-Stifter-Institutes des Landes
Oberösterreich,* 32 (1983): 163–178;

Hans Höller, "Die kapitalistische Gesellschaft aus der
Kirchturmperspektive? Anmerkungen zu
Stifters Ästhetik," *Germanica Wratislawiensia,* 32
(1978): 37–51;

Alan Holske, "Stifter and the Biedermeier Crisis," in
Studies in Honor of John Albrecht Walz (Lancaster:
Books for Libraries Press, 1941), pp. 256–290;

Konrad F. Kiensberger, "Mary Howitt und ihre
Stifter-Übersetzungen: zur Rezeption des Dichters im viktorianischen England," *Vierteljahrsschrift des Adalbert-Stifter-Institutes des Landes
Oberösterreich,* 25 (1976): 13–55;

Rosa Gudrun Klarner, *Pedagogic Design and Literary
Form in the Work of Adalbert Stifter* (Bern, Frankfurt am Main & New York: Lang, 1986);

Johann Lachinger, Alexander Stillmark, and Martin
Swales, eds., *Adalbert Stifter heute* (Linz: Landesverlag, 1985);

Dominique Lehl, "Realité et Penurie dans l'oeuvre
litteraire et picturale de Stifter: A Partir de la
Nouvelle Kalkstein et des tableaux de l'Epoque
de Bunte Steine," *Etudes Germaniques,* 40, no. 3
(1985): 297–310;

Dagmar Lorenz, "Stifters Frauengestalten," *Vierteljahrsschrift des Adalbert-Stifter-Institutes des Landes
Oberösterreich,* 32 (1983): 93–106;

Erik Lunding, *Adalbert Stifter: Mit einem Anhang über
Kierkegaard und die existentielle Literaturwissenschaft*
(Copenhagen: Nyt nordisk, 1946);

Eve Mason, "Stifter's 'Turmalin': A Reconsideration," *Modern Language Review,* 72 (1977): 348–358;

Joachim Müller, "Die Polemik zwischen Hebbel und Stifter und Stifters Ethos vom 'Sanften Gesetz,'" in *Gedenkschrift für F. J. Schneider (1879–1954),* edited by Karl Bischoff (Weimar: Böhlau, 1956);

Ursula Naumann, *Adalbert Stifter* (Stuttgart: Metzler, 1979);

Christine Oertel-Sjörgren, *The Marble Statue as Idea: Collected Essays on Adalbert Stifter's "Der Nachsommer"* (Chapel Hill: University of North Carolina Press, 1972);

Roy Pascal, "Adalbert Stifter: Indian Summer," in his *The German Novel Studies* (Manchester, U.K.: Manchester University Press, 1956), pp. 52–75;

Laurence A. Rickels, "Stifter's 'Nachkommenschaften': The Problem of the Surname, the Problem of Painting," *Modern Language Notes,* 100 (April 1985): 577–598;

D. C. Riechel, "Adalbert Stifter as Landscape Painter: A View from Cézanne's Mont Sainte-Victorie," *Modern Austrian Literature,* 20, no. 1 (1987): 1–20;

Arno Schmidt, ". . . und dann die Herren Leutnants! Betrachtungen zu 'Witiko' und Adalbert Stifter," in his *Adalbert Stifter, die Ritter, vom Geist: Von vergessenen Kollegen* (Karlsruhe: Stahlberg, 1965), pp. 282–317;

Herbert Seidler, "Die Adalbert Stifter Forschung der siebziger Jahre," *Vierteljahrsschrift des Adalbert-Stifter-Institutes des Landes Oberösterreich,* 30 (1981): 89–134;

Martin Selge, "Die Utopie im Geschichtsroman: Wie man A. Stifters 'Witiko' lesen kann," *Der Deutschunterricht,* 27 (1975): 86–103;

Lauren Small, "White Frost Configurations on the Window Pane: Adalbert Stifter's 'Der Nachsommer,'" *Colloquia Germanica: Internationale Zeitschrift für Germanische Sprach- und Literaturwissenschaft,* 18, no. 1 (1985): 1–17;

Lothar Stiehm, ed., *Adalbert Stifter: Studien und Interpretationen* (Heidelberg: Stiehm, 1968);

Alexander Stillmark, "Stifter's Early Portraits of the Artist: Stages in the Growth of an Aesthetic," *Forum of Modern Language Studies,* 11 (April 1975): 142–164;

Roman Struc, "The Threat of Chaos: Stifter's 'Bergkristall' and Thomas Mann's 'Schnee,'" *Modern Language Quarterly,* 24 (1963): 323–332;

Martin Swales and Erika Swales, *Adalbert Stifter: A Critical Study* (Cambridge: Cambridge University Press, 1984);

Erika Tunner, "Stifters Faszination auf österreichische Autoren der Gegenwart: Peter Handke, Peter Rosei, Jutta Schutting, Hermann Friedl und Reinhold Aumaier," *Vierteljahrsschrift des Adalbert-Stifter-Institutes des Landes Oberösterreich,* 36 (1987): 57–70;

Walter Weiss, "Antworten österreichischer Gegenwartsliteratur auf Adalbert Stifter," *Vierteljahrsschrift des Adalbert-Stifter-Institutes des Landes Oberösterreich,* 32 (1983): 133–143;

Rudolf Wildbolz, *Adalbert Stifter: Langeweile und Faszination* (Stuttgart: Kohlhammer, 1976);

Philip H. Zoldester, *Adalbert Stifter's Weltanschauung* (Bern: Lang, 1970).

Papers:

Adalbert Stifter's papers are at the Bayerische Staatsbibliothek (Bavarian State Library), Munich; the Stifter Archive, Prague; the Foundation Martin Bodmer, Cologny, Switzerland; the Adalbert-Stifter-Institut, Linz, Austria; and the Oberösterreichisches Landesarchiv (Upper Austrian National Archive), Linz.

Theodor Storm

(14 September 1817 – 4 July 1888)

A. Tilo Alt
Duke University

This entry was updated by Professor Alt from his entry in DLB 129:
Nineteenth-Century German Writers, 1841–1900.

BOOKS: *Liederbuch dreier Freunde,* by Storm, Theodor
  Mommsen, and Tycho Mommsen (Kiel: Schwers,
  1843);
Sommer-Geschichten und Lieder (Berlin: Duncker, 1851)–
  includes *Immensee,* translated by Helen Clark as
  Immensee, or the Old Man's Reverie (Münster:
  Brunn, 1863);
Gedichte (Kiel: Schwers, 1852; enlarged edition, Ber-
  lin: Schindler, 1856; enlarged, 1864; revised
  edition, Brunswick: Westermann, 1868; revised
  edition, Berlin: Paetel, 1875; enlarged, 1885);
Im Sonnenschein: Drei Sommergeschichten (Berlin:
  Duncker, 1854)–comprises "Im Sonnenschein";
  "Marthe und ihre Uhr"; "Im Saal," translated
  anonymously as *In the Great Hall* (London: Edu-
  cational Book, 1923);
Ein grünes Blatt: Zwei Sommergeschichten (Berlin: Schin-
  dler, 1855)–comprises "Angelika," "Ein grünes
  Blatt";
Hinzelmeier: Eine nachdenkliche Geschichte (Berlin: Paetel,
  1857);
In der Sommer-Mondnacht: Novellen (Berlin: Schindler,
  1860)–comprises "Auf dem Staatshof," "Wenn
  die Äpfel reif sind," "Posthuma";
Drei Novellen (Berlin: Schindler, 1861)–comprises
  "Veronica," "Späte Rosen," "Drüben am
  Markt";
Im Schloß (Münster: Brunn, 1863);
Auf der Universität (Münster: Brunn, 1863); repub-
  lished as *Lenore* (Münster: Brunn, 1865);
Zwei Weihnachtsidyllen (Berlin: Schindler, 1865)–com-
  prises "Abseits";
Drei Märchen (Hamburg: Mauke, 1866); republished
  as *Geschichten aus der Tonne* (Berlin: Paetel,
  1873)–comprises "Die Regentrude," "Bule-
  mann's Haus," "Der Speigel des Cyprianus";
Von Jenseit des Meeres: Novelle (Schleswig: Schulbuchhandlung, 1867);

Theodor Storm in 1887

In St. Jürgen (Schleswig: Schulbuchhandlung, 1868);
Novellen (Schleswig: Schulbuchhandlung, 1868)–com-
  prises "In St. Jürgen," "Von Jenseit des
  Meeres," "Eine Malerarbeit";
Sämmtliche Schriften, 19 volumes (Brunswick: Wester-
  mann, 1868–1869); enlarged as *Sämmtliche*

Werke, 12 volumes (Brunswick: Westermann, 1898–1916);

Zerstreute Kapitel (Berlin: Paetel, 1873);

Novellen und Gedenkblätter (Brunswick: Westermann, 1874)–comprises "Viola tricolor," "Beim Vetter Christian," "Von heut' und ehedem";

Waldwinkel; Pole Poppenspäler: Novellen (Brunswick: Westermann, 1875);

Ein stiller Musikant; Psyche; Im Nachbarhause links: Drei Novellen (Brunswick: Westermann, 1876);

Aquis submersus: Novelle (Berlin: Paetel, 1877); translated by Geoffrey Skelton as *Beneath the Flood* (London: New English Library, 1962);

Carsten Curator (Berlin: Paetel, 1878); translated by Frieda Voigt as *Curator Carsten* (London: Calder, 1956);

Renate (Berlin: Paetel, 1878); translated by James Millar as *Renate* (London: Gowans & Gray, 1909);

Eekenhof; Im Brauer-Hause: Zwei Novellen (Berlin: Paetel, 1880); "Eekenhof," translated by Millar as *Eekenhof* (London: Gowans & Gray, 1908);

Zur "Wald-und Wasserfreude": Novelle (Berlin: Paetel, 1880);

Der Herr Etatsrat; Die Söhne des Senators: Novellen (Berlin: Paetel, 1881); "Die Söhne des Senators," translated by E.M. Huggard as *The Senator's Sons* (London: Harrap, 1947);

Hans und Heinz Kirch (Berlin: Paetel, 1883);

Schweigen (Berlin: Paetel, 1883);.

Zur Chronik von Grieshuus (Berlin: Paetel, 1884);

John Riew'; Ein Fest auf Haderslevhuus: Zwei Novellen (Berlin: Paetel, 1885);

Bötjer Basch: Eine Geschichte (Berlin: Paetel, 1887);

Ein Doppelgänger: Novelle (Berlin: Paetel, 1887);

Ein Bekenntniß: Novelle (Berlin: Paetel, 1888);

"Es Waren zwei Königskinder" (Berlin: Paetel, 1888);

Der Schimmelreiter (Berlin: Paetel, 1888); translated by Muriel Almon as "The Rider of the Pale Horse," in *The German Classics of the Nineteenth and Twentieth Centuries,* volume 11 (New York: German Publication Society, 1914), pp. 225–342.

Editions in English: *Viola Tricolor, The Little Stepmother,* translated by Bayard Quincy Morgan; *Curator Carston,* translated by Frieda M. Voigt (London: Calder, 1956; New York: Ungar, 1956);

The Rider on the White Horse, and Selected Stories, translated by James Wright (New York: New American Library, 1964)–comprises "In the Great Hall," "Immensee," "A Green Leaf," "In the Sunlight," "Veronika," "In St. Jürgen," "Aquis Submersus," "The Rider on the White Horse."

OTHER: *Deutsche Liebeslieder seit Johann Christian Günther: Eine Codification,* edited by Storm (Berlin: Schindler, 1859);

Hausbuch aus deutschen Dichtern seit Claudius: Eine kritische Anthologie, edited by Storm (Hamburg: Mauke, 1870).

Theodor Storm is a prominent representative of the group of European writers known as "poetic" or "bourgeois" realists. The majority of his tales are set in his native region of Schleswig-Holstein, some of them in his hometown of Husum. His lyrical poetry also treats regional themes and motifs. This regionalism, however, is merely Storm's vehicle for treating themes of national and human significance. In his 1930 essay on Storm, Thomas Mann said that Storm's thematic innovations and craftsmanship were equal to those of such European contemporaries as Ivan Turgenev, Charles Dickens, and Gottfried Keller. Storm's novellas *Immensee* (Bee's Lake, 1851; translated as *Immensee, or The Old Man's Reverie,* 1863) and *Der Schimmelreiter* (1888; translated as "The Rider of the Pale Horse," 1914) are still widely known, and the line "die graue Stadt am Meer" (The gray town by the sea) from his poem "Die Stadt" (The Town, 1851) has entered the German language as a synonym for the poet's hometown. His major themes are love, family, death, and the transience of all things. Some of his stories have been adapted as films and television plays, and many of his poems have been set to music by eminent composers.

Storm's friend Ferdinand Tönnies outlined in his classic sociological text *Gemeinschaft und Gesellschaft* (Community and Society, 1887) the dilemma of the individual in postagrarian, industrial German society of the late nineteenth century. Storm was aware of this loss of community and the isolation of the individual in the impersonal, abstract organization of the body politic, and he turns to near-absolute love or to an idyllic past to counteract isolation and loneliness. He also points to the psychological stress that the impersonal society of isolated individuals has caused.

Theodor Woldsen Storm was born in Husum in the duchy of Schleswig on 14 September 1817, the son of Johann Kasimir Storm and his wife, Lucie Woldsen Storm. Since Schleswig then belonged to Denmark, Storm was a Danish citizen. On his mother's side he was descended from one of Husum's old patrician families, and the stately rococo house of his maternal grandparents made a lasting impression on him; the vignettes "Im Sonnenschein" (1854; translated as "In the Sunlight," 1964) and "Im Saal" (1854; translated as "In the Great Hall," 1923), which take place in the middle of the eighteenth century, were inspired by memories of his youth in the Woldsen house. On his father's side Storm was descended from a long line of millers and farmers. His father was a highly respected lawyer who had been decorated by the Danish king. The beauty of idyllic Westermühlen, his paternal grandparents' village, survives in many of Storm's poems.

Storm's secondary education at the Gelehrtenschule in Husum and the Katharineum in Lübeck was followed by his admission to the law school at the University of Kiel in 1837. His earliest attempts at writing poetry date from his student days, when he was under the influence of the lyrics of Heinrich Heine, Eduard Mörike, and Joseph von Eichendorff. Storm left Kiel after a year to join his friend Ferdinand Röse at the University of Berlin. Röse had introduced Storm to Johann Wolfgang von Goethe's *Faust* (1808, 1832) and to German poetry. Through Röse he met Emanuel Geibel, who was destined to become Germany's most celebrated poet in the nineteenth century and whom Storm in his later years was to call his poetic antithesis. In Berlin, Storm attended only the lectures of the jurist Karl von Savigny.

Röse's departure in 1839 prompted Storm to return to the University of Kiel, where he became a member of the circle around Theodor Mommsen, who was to become Germany's foremost classical historian and the world's first Nobel laureate in literature, and Mommsen's brother Tycho.

In 1842 Storm was admitted to the bar and went to work in his father's law office in Husum; the same year Bertha von Buchan, whom he had loved since his high-school days, refused his proposal of marriage. His poems reflecting his feelings for Bertha mark the point at which Storm found his individual style as a writer of love poetry. Some of the poems were included in *Liederbuch dreier Freunde* (Book of Songs by Three Friends, 1843), by Storm and the Mommsen brothers. Few of his poems in the book were included by him in his first separate collection of poetry.

Storm set up his own law practice in Husum in 1843. In 1846 he married his cousin Konstanze Esmarch, the daughter of the mayor of Seegeberg in Holstein and of the sister of Storm's mother. Many of Storm's twelve siblings and Konstanze's ten also intermarried, so that Storm's extended family was large indeed. Storm's views on family life were determined by this background: he saw the family as a bastion in a world that was becoming increasingly impersonal, isolating the individual from the traditional certainties of community life and religion. Nevertheless, during the first two years of his marriage Storm had an affair with Dorothea Jensen, who inspired some of his most outspoken love lyrics and also poems of remorse; some of

these sexually daring poems were not published until after his death. So as not to endanger his marriage, Dorothea left Husum in 1848. Storm confessed his infidelity to his wife, who magnanimously told him that if she should predecease him he should marry Dorothea. He also confessed to his friends Hartmuth and Laura Brinkmann in what came to be known posthumously as his "Beichtbrief" (Confessional Letter).

Storm's first prose work of note was *Immensee,* a tale of unfulfilled love that also concerns the separation of art and life and the middle-class valorization of austerity and frugality. It is a lyrical novella rich in poetic imagery and descriptive detail, especially about the psychological states of the protagonist. An atmosphere of tragic resignation permeates the story. In the frame of the novella Reinhard, an aging poet, is sitting in his lonely study remembering Elisabeth, his childhood companion and later his only love. In the main story Elisabeth's mother decides that the impractical Reinhard will never earn an adequate living, and Elisabeth is obliged to marry Erich, whom she does not love. Two years later Reinhard is invited to visit Erich and Elisabeth at their estate, Immensee. One evening Reinhard and his hosts are singing folk songs; Elisabeth's reaction to one of the songs reveals that she still loves him. The song's opening lines recall the reason for Elisabeth's marriage to Erich: "Meine Mutter hat's gewollt / Den andern ich, nehmen sollt" (My mother willed it / The other one I had to wed). In a gesture of utter hopelessness Elisabeth gets up and turns her back on the two men. Erich and Elisabeth must resign themselves to their unhappy marriage just as Reinhard and Elisabeth must accept their separate destinies. This state of affairs is symbolized by Reinhard's attempt to fetch a water lily in the Immen Lake: swimming toward it, he gets entangled in the stalks of the plants and has to turn back. Elisabeth, as delicate and beautiful as the water lily, is equally unattainable for him. When Reinhard takes his leave, Elisabeth realizes that he will never return.

The first separate edition of Storm's poetry, titled simply *Gedichte* (Poems, 1852), reflects the lyrical creed he was to elaborate later in his correspondence and in his two anthologies of German poetry. Storm has been regarded as the last of the great poets of the Sturm und Drang tradition that began in the eighteenth century. The poems in *Gedichte* are meant to be read consecutively, from cover to cover, for full effect; they were selected according to a set of criteria that included the requirement that a poem be the product of specific experience and be accompanied by a strong emotion. Storm favored the folk-song stanza, alternating rhyme schemes, and the iambic meter; he emphasized the untrammeled expression of an experience or subject matter and rejected intellectual or reflective lyrics. He also rejected the popular products of the Munich neoclassical school of poets, led by Geibel and Paul Heyse, as exercises in formalism. The themes of his poetry include love, nature, transiency, and death. The work includes "Die Stadt," the poem that made him famous and immortalized his hometown of Husum.

Storm's poetry at this point reflects his materialistic view of life, combined with a desire for a spiritual concept that would lend meaning to prosaic reality. This concept is that of absolute love, including love for the family and for one's native region. A materialistic philosophy brings into relief the transitory nature of all things, explaining the dominance of the motif of transiency in Storm's poems as well as in his prose. It is an entirely modern consciousness that stems from the loss of the anchor provided by commonly held religious beliefs. For Storm, sexual love is a substitute for divine love. "Schließe mir die Augen beide" (Close both my eyes), Storm's ultimate love poem, depicts a mystical union of two individuals that replaces the traditional Pietistic *unio mystica* with God.

On occasion, his poems violate the classical tenet of the exclusion of the aesthetically ugly from a work of art. The poem "Geh' nicht hinein" (Do Not Enter), for example, describes a dead body in vivid detail. To Storm it is the truth of art as measured against reality that gives it importance and provides aesthetic satisfaction.

Storm's political lyrics were based on his feeling of union with his homeland. Like absolute love, the homeland was to Storm a bastion against an impersonal and isolating universe; his political poems concern "verletztes Heimatgefühl" (violated sense of home). The struggle for independence from Denmark during the revolution of 1848 moved the poet deeply. Yet his poems are far from being tendentious or programmatic; rather, they are expressions of rage over the loss of personal freedom. He favored a semidemocratic order based on representation by the social estates, as was the tradition in Schleswig-Holstein. He loathed the unbridled power of the developing nation-state of his day. In addition, he could not abide the arrogance of the German aristocracy and their ideological allies, the clergy.

The duchies were reoccupied and reclaimed by Denmark in 1851. As an outspoken foe of Danish rule, Storm was denied renewal of his law license. In 1853, although unfamiliar with Prussian law, he became an assistant judge at the district court in Potsdam; since the position was unpaid, he had to depend on his and his wife's parents for financial support. In Potsdam he made the acquaintance of one of his poetic mentors, the Romantic poet Eichendorff, as well as the writers Heyse and Fontane and the painter Adolph Menzel. He joined two literary societies, Der Tunnel über der Spree (The Tunnel over the River Spree) and Rütli. In Potsdam he also found an outlet for his novellas and poems in the literary journal *Argo,* edited by Fontane. In 1855 Storm traveled to Heidelberg and Stuttgart with his parents. In Stuttgart they met Eduard Mörike, another of Storm's poetic mentors.

In 1856 Storm was offered a judgeship at the district court in Heiligenstadt, a provincial backwater in Thuringia. He founded a choir in the town, in which he sang. In Heiligenstadt, Storm prepared his important anthology of lyrical poetry, *Deutsche Liebeslieder seit Johann Christian Günther: Eine Codification* (German Love Lyrics since Johann Christian Günther: A Codification, 1859). The work aims to educate the reading public in the tradition of the lyric of personal experience that began in the eighteenth century, the tradition to which Storm's own poetic products belong. The book was intended to counteract the influence of the many anthologies on the market that advanced the kind of sentimental love poetry that Storm considered inferior.

It was also in Heiligenstadt that he entered the second phase of his prose-writing activity, in which he produced novellas focused on psychological problems. In his earlier works he had developed isolated situations taken from everday life into short vignettes. The novella *Im Schloß* (Inside the Chateau, 1863) concerns the then frequently treated theme of the love of an aristocratic young woman for her brother's tutor. A comparison has been made by scholars and by Storm himself of his story with Friedrich Spielhagen's novel *Problematische Naturen* (1861; translated as *Problematic Characters,* 1869). Both works attack the unwarranted status and power of the aristocracy, but Hinrich Arnold, Storm's self-assured protagonist, is proud of his humble origins, whereas Spielhagen's Oswald Stein suffers from feelings of inferiority because of his middle-class background. Since, however, Stein turns out to be the natural offspring of Baron von Grenwitz and thus a close relative of his aristocratic employer, Spielhagen defuses his social criticism and preaches what Storm calls the mystery of two kinds of blood. Spielhagen's protagonist dies on the barricades during the 1848 revolution; Storm did not feel that such an overly dramatic tragic ending was justified. For him the realities of the 1860s dictated that the middle class seek equality with the aristocracy by compromise rather than by forcibly removing the aristocracy from power. Storm shows a gradual process of ideological change within the characters toward a "reines Menschentum" (pure humanity). Thus, Anna's love for Arnold must be openly acknowledged; she cannot conceal her feelings for the sake of a convention that makes a liaison between the aristocracy and the bourgeoisie unsuitable. Predictably, the novella was received enthusiastically by middle-class readers and rejected by aristocratic ones.

In 1863 and 1864 Storm turned to the writing of fairy tales. The best of these tales is "Die Regentrude" (The Rain Maiden, 1866), which develops the theme of the interdependence of humanity and nature.

The Dano-Prussian war of 1863–1864 resulted in Schleswig-Holstein becoming a Prussian province. The people of Husum needed a replacement for the pro-Danish chief of police, who also held the office of judge. Because of his father's reputation in the area Storm was elected Landvogt (county provost), an ancient office combining police and judicial powers. He and his family moved to Husum in March 1864. The office of Landvogt was abolished by the Prussian government in 1867; Storm turned down a high administrative post that was offered him to become a lower court judge once again, a position he preferred because of the greater degree of independence it afforded. In 1865 Konstanze died after the birth of their seventh child. Later that year Storm traveled to Baden-Baden to meet the Russian novelist Turgenev, with whom he shared literary interests. In 1866 he married Dorothea Jensen. A child was born to them the following year. In 1868–1869 Storm's collected works were published by the firm of George Westermann in Brunswick.

In 1870 Storm's second anthology of lyrical poetry, *Hausbuch aus deutschen Dichtern seit Claudius: Eine kritische Anthologie* (Book for the Home of German Poets since Claudius: A Critical Anthology), was published. Unlike most anthologies popular at the time, Storm's book included only selections that met his personal criteria for lyrical poetry; it was also organized chronologically rather than thematically, with the intention of enabling his readers to arrive at their own conclusions about a poem (hence the words "Critical Anthology" in the title). It also contained biographical and bibliographical information on the poets whose works were included.

In *Von Jenseit des Meeres* (From across the Sea, 1867) Storm introduces the theme of the threat to the absolute values of family and home. Marriage and the family, he holds, are cultural inventions rather than natural law; as such, they are a counterpoise to the natural extinction of the individual. These institutions are inherently unstable and endangered. The protagonist of *Von Jenseit des Meeres* is a German businessman on the island of Saint Croix in the Caribbean. The novella is a racist tale of miscegenation in the tradition of nineteenth-century colonialism based on social Darwinism. The primitive instincts with which the natives are imbued threaten the civilized Europeans, whose culture is challenged by unbridled sexual instinct. In the end the businessman takes Jenni, the offspring of his liaison

with a black woman, to Germany; there she will be raised as a European in control of her instincts.

Storm's reaction to the outbreak of the Franco-Prussian War of 1870–1871 was that the primitive instincts of humanity are given an outlet in such wars. He wrote his son Ernst on 3 August 1870 that he believed that the stronger always devours the weaker, and since humanity has no predator to devour it, it devours itself. His ideology of social Darwinism even superseded Storm's contempt for the Prussian state: he considered the defense of the German way of life against a non-German way, to him, a moral imperative. Storm, however, did not rejoice in the Prussian victory; he feared that his countrymen might come to savor "gloire" (glory) in the manner of Napoleon. He hated war because it reduced humanity to a mere instrument of nature.

In 1877 appeared what was subsequently hailed as Storm's best prose effort to date, *Aquis submersus* (translated as *Beneath the Flood,* 1962). This novella is one of the so-called chronicle novellas or novellas of tragic fate, frame tales that were Storm's only genre in the last decade of his life. They are set in the fairly distant past in the duchy of Holstein. As a boy, the narrator of *Aquis submersus* had seen in a village church a seventeenth-century painting of a pastor and a boy holding a water lily. The picture was captioned "CPAS," an abbreviation of the Latin *culpa patris aquis submersus* (drowned through the fault of the father). As a student in search of a room, the narrator comes to a house that attracts his attention because of an inscription in Low German above the doorway: "Geliek as Rook un Stof verswindt, Also sind ook de Minschenkind" (Just as smoke and dust vanish, So does the human being). He enters and sees the same painting. The owner produces a seventeenth-century manuscript that contains the autobiographical account of the painter, Johannes. Johannes, a commoner, grew up on the estate of Squire Gerhardus, a friend of his dead father, with the squire's children, Wulf and Katharina. After the squire's death Johannes returns from a five-year apprenticeship in Holland and is commissioned by Wulf to paint a portrait of Katharina, who is about to be married to von der Risch, a country squire. During the sittings for the portrait the two fall in love. An encounter of Johannes, Wulf, and von der Risch in a tavern leads to an argument, and Wulf's bloodhounds pursue the painter back to the estate. Johannes finds refuge in Katharina's bedchamber, and he stays in the arms of his beloved until daybreak. He had been seen entering her room, and to head off scandal he asks Wulf for his sister's hand in marriage. Wulf's answer is a shot from his pistol. Badly wounded, Johannes flees and spends many weeks in the care of a friend. On his return he learns that von der Risch has married someone else, and that Katharina has vanished without a trace. Johannes and Katharina meet again when he is asked to paint the portrait of a pastor who turns out to be Katharina's husband; she had been forced to marry him because she was expecting Johannes's child. The painter and his beloved meet in the garden of the rectory; their child is playing nearby. As Johannes and Katharina embrace, the child drowns in the garden pond. At the pastor's request, Johannes adds the dead child to the picture of the pastor and places a water lily in his hand. Under the painting he places the letters *C.P.A.S.* After reporting Wulf's violent end from the bite of a rabid dog and of the passing of the estate into the hands of strangers, Johannes concludes his story. In the closing frame the narrator converts the motif of drowning into a metaphor of oblivion: Johannes's biography, he says, is nowhere to be found outside the autobiographical manuscript. Even in his native region he is not remembered; he is "aquis submersus," he has vanished in the flood.

The novella is a critique of an anachronistic feudal order that, according to Storm, destroys whatever is human and beautiful and, hence, justified. The aristocracy regards the artist as a mere servant. Storm's anticlerical stance also stands out in the negative characterization of Katharina's husband. In a comment on his novella Storm emphasized that he had not intended to locate tragic guilt in the passionate union of Johannes and Katharina; rather, guilt lies with the inherited power of the landed gentry, the force that drives the couple into each other's arms. Another important motif is that of heredity; the science of genetics was just emerging at the time of the novella's composition. Wulf's negative traits can be traced to a female ancestor beneath whose picture Johannes paints Katharina's portrait; the ancestor's picture periodically casts a pall over the otherwise happy sessions. The over-arching motif of the novella is articulated by the epigraph above the doorway: the transitoriness of all things and the demise of the individual.

A conscientious worker, Storm rose in the Prussian judicial hierarchy. In 1880 he built a house in the village of Hademarschen in Holstein, where he retired in 1881.

Storm's view that the family forms a bastion against the forces that threaten the individual extends to the state: ideally, the latter is the natural extension of the family. Political power, however, should be communal, not usurped as in a feudal or despotic state. Storm's contempt for the Prussian government was well known. Between 1877 and 1882 he wrote three novellas that deal with the collapse of the family because of hereditary factors, social values, and the Prussian state's per-

version of the idea of community. Storm suffered from guilt because of the alcoholism of his eldest son, Hans; in the last decade of his life a "culpa patris" motif runs through his correspondence as well as some of his novellas and poems. In *Carsten Curator* (1878; translated as *Curator Carsten,* 1956) the middle-aged Carsten Carstens, a solid citizen, marries the young and beautiful Juliane, his opposite in all essentials. She lends charm and excitement to his staid middle-class existence; but she dies when giving birth to their son, Heinrich, who turns out to be as morally weak, irresponsible, and reckless as his mother and ultimately drags his father down with him. An ineluctable hereditary mechanism destroys the family. Carsten's moral convictions demand that he stand by his son, no matter the consequences, and chaos overwhelms his world of middle-class prosperity and order. Anna, Carsten's foster child, although fully aware of Heinrich's irresponsible and morally weak character, accepts his marriage proposal. At the end of the story Heinrich is missing in a flood and has bankrupted his father. Carsten's house is auctioned off, and he, Anna, and her child are living in poverty. The novella ends on a hopeful note, however, since Heinrich's son resembles his grandfather and mother, thus promising the continuation of the middle-class traits that Storm and his age admired: trust, responsible behavior, self-reliance, and honesty.

In "Der Herr Etatsrat" (The State Councilor, 1881) the father is the destructive force in the family. Etatsrat Sternow, a Prussian government official in Schleswig-Holstein, destroys his wife, his son, his daughter, and his grandchild. The story is told in humorous tones; its tragic and horrific dimensions become manifest only gradually. The traits exhibited by this official are those that Storm had noted about the Prussian government in general: condescension toward the citizens, arbitrary decisions, and a general indifference toward people. The state is the extension of the family; but the Prussian state, as an extension of Sternow's family, is inhuman. In part, the fault lies with a perversion of the patriarchal order. Storm's ideal was the family governed by paternal love. The family is a bulwark against the untamed forces of nature, and traditionally the father is best suited to lead the family because of the middle-class tradition that prepares him for this duty. In the Sternow family the mother has died, and the masculinization of the family is a reflection of the heartlessness of a masculinized society. Presiding over this "Familie in der Zerstörung" (family in a state of disintegration), as Storm put it, is death. The Etatsrat has an altar to death in a large cabinet; at the foot of the black cross formed by the door frame of the cabinet lie a skull and crossbones carved from boxwood with horrifying realism. The Prussian state as symbolized by Sternow is life-destroying. To be sure, Prussia turned its death cult into one of positive value: to die for one's country was regarded as noble. To Storm, death signifies nothingness. Archimedes, Sternow's university-student son, has no sense of self; it has been destroyed by his father. Archimedes has adopted the habits of the enemy of humanity: the repetitious phrases typical of the Prussian officer class and the paraphernalia and rituals of the militant student fraternities. Phia, the weak and vulnerable daughter, has been seduced by her father's villainous assistant Käfer (the name means beetle or bug) and is expecting his child. She commits suicide and thereby destroys the weakest member of the family, her unborn baby. The entire society lives for the mindless pleasures of dancing and drinking. Archimedes' handmade patent leather shoes are a symbol of waste: he has had dozens of pairs of them made, using funds that were supposed to go for his studies. Archimedes relentlessly consumes alcohol, in keeping with the habits of the male members of the ruling classes in his society; he finally dies from the habit. He is unlamented by his father; Sternow's sole concern is with his son's debts, which he refuses to pay. In the end Sternow dies and Käfer disappears, and the townspeople scarcely remember them.

In *Hans und Heinz Kirch* (1883) a father is guilty of the demise of his son. The story is set in a small Baltic seaport where the father, Hans Kirch, is the owner and captain of a small merchantman; his son, Heinz, is a deckhand on the ship. The town is a middle-class cultural void whose sole interest is commerce. Patient, thrifty, hardworking, and devoted to his family, Hans embodies the ideals of his social class. There is, however, a tragic flaw in his character: his irascibility, which ultimately proves the undoing of both father and son. Wieb, the illegitimate daughter of a sailor and a washerwoman, was Heinz's childhood sweetheart, and they are now lovers. Wieb's family background is detrimental to Hans's plans for his son, which involve the accumulation of sufficient wealth to be accepted by the patrician families and become a senator. He forbids Heinz to continue his relationship with Wieb. Heinz does not reply, nor does he return to his father's ship; instead, he takes service on another ship. The father-son conflict turns into a contest of wills. The father expects the son to make the first move toward reconciliation, in keeping with the fourth commandment. At the end of two years a letter arrives with postage due; Hans refuses to accept it. Wieb offers to pay for it, but Hans remains adamant. Fifteen years later, Hans's wife has died of grief for her lost son, and Wieb has married a sailor. Hans hears that a man answering to the name of John Smidt and living in a cheap boarding house in Hamburg is Heinz. Hans decides to bring

his son home. But Heinz is different from what his family remembers: there are smallpox scars on his face; his manner is coarse; his speech is punctuated with English and Spanish phrases; and the anchor tattooed on his arm has disappeared. No reconciliation between father and son takes place, and rumors circulate that the man in Hans's house is not really his son. Hans leaves an envelope with a modest sum of money in Heinz's room and tells him to leave. On a stormy night some time after Heinz's departure, Hans has a vision of his son's death at sea. He remembers his wife's pleas not to reject their son's letter, and he seeks Wieb's company as an act of atonement for his wrongs. His death, his son-in-law's succession to his fortune, the arrival of a grandson, and his son-in-law's prospects of becoming a senator are listed laconically, and the narrator concludes the novella by saying that the question of Heinz's whereabouts remains unanswered.

Storm went to Berlin in 1884 at the invitation of many of his friends and admirers, including Theodor Mommsen, Fontane, Menzel, and Alexander von Wussow the former administrative head of the region around Heiligenstadt and then a high official in the Prussian ministry of culture. In 1886 he traveled to Weimar, accompanied by Tönnies, to take his daughter Elsabe to the school of music there; to visit with the writer Wilhelm Raabe, whose works he held in high esteem; and to accept invitations by the Goethe Gesellschaft (Goethe Society) and the grand duke of Saxe-Weimar. On both occasions, Storm was celebrated as one of Germany's outstanding writers. His son Hans, who was serving as a ship's doctor, died as a result of alcoholism in 1886.

In the winter of 1886–1887 Storm suffered his first bout with abdominal cancer. The protagonist of his novella *Ein Bekenntnis* (A Confession, 1888) is the gynecologist Franz Jebe, who loves his wife passionately and devotedly. She is suffering from cancer of the uterus. Unaware of a newly discovered method of treating that form of cancer, he gives her a lethal injection at her request. This act of euthanasia makes him guilty in a metaphysical sense: life is a sacred mystery, and no man of science has the right to end it. Jebe can only atone for his deed by serving life; no church or court of law can acquit him. Jebe renounces possible happiness with Hilda Rosen, the daughter of a woman he cures using the new procedure, and becomes a medical missionary in Africa. Jebe's confession to his friend, the narrator, just before his departure for Africa, is devoid of sentimentality or self-pity. Thirty years later, the narrator learns that Jebe had died in Africa in an epidemic. In Heyse's "Auf Tod und Leben" (A Matter of Life and Death, 1886), which also deals with euthanasia, the protagonist is reintegrated into society through understanding and love. The problem in Heyse's story is psychological rather than ethical, as it is in Storm's work.

On his seventieth birthday Storm was made an honorary citizen of Husum. Although he was seriously ill, Storm finished his last and most significant work, *Der Schimmelreiter*. The novella is based on a legend Storm had read in his youth; an early reference to it can be found in an 1843 letter from Storm to Theodor Mommsen. It is his longest novella; not only its length but also its concentration on the development of the hero rather than on a central event, as is typical of the novella genre, would justify the label "character novel" for this narrative.

The novella has three frames: the author recalls a tale he heard in his grandmother's house, in which a traveler in the 1830s took refuge from a storm with a schoolmaster who, in turn, told him the eighteenth-century story that forms the core of the narrative. Even as a youth Hauke Haien maintained that the construction of the dike protecting his village from the North Sea was faulty. Hauke enters the service of Tede Volkerts, the Deichgraf (dike reeve), as a handyman; he is able to make many suggestions for the improvement of the dike. It is no secret in the village that Volkerts was made Deichgraf because of his wealth rather than his ability; he comes to rely more and more on Hauke as his accountant and engineer. Hauke is promoted to foreman and marries Elke, Volkerts's daughter. When Volkerts dies, Hauke is appointed the new Deichgraf; his marriage to Elke brought him sufficient property to qualify for the position. Hauke draws up plans for a new dike and land-reclamation project, which are finally approved by the head Deichgraf. On the same day he acquires an emaciated white horse from a swarthy Slovak. Through patient care the horse is restored to health; it becomes inseparable from its new master and will tolerate no other rider. Hauke's men have a superstitious fear of the animal because it is rumored to have risen from a horse's skeleton on a sandbar off the coast; the skeleton had disappeared after Hauke's purchase of the horse.

To construct the new dike, Hauke has to struggle against the prejudice of the villagers, who are opposed to innovation and resent his superior intelligence. Hauke drives himself and his workers hard, and the dike is completed the following year. In a weakened state after an illness, however, he allows himself to be persuaded to carry out only superficial repairs on the old dike. During a severe storm in October 1756 he discovers a breach where he should have insisted on much more extensive repairs. His wife and child have gone out in the storm to look for him; he sees them driving toward the dike but cannot stop them. The waters rush through the gap in the old dike and carry them away. In despair he forces his horse into the waves, where both perish. Since that time, the villagers claim, the horse's skeleton has reappeared on the shoal, and during storms a ghostly figure on a white horse is seen riding on the dikes. After the schoolmaster finishes his story and the storm raging outside dies down, the traveler rides away across the Hauke Haien Dike.

Storm strikes a balance between the legendary character of the story and its realistic setting through a technique of deliberate ambiguity. Without committing himself, he presents reason and unreason, intelligence and ignorance, enlightenment and superstition in constant juxtaposition. He involves himself in the opening frame to indicate the importance he attaches to the search for a redemptive force, which he sees in the combining of reason, represented by the construction of the dike, and myth, represented by the legend to which Hauke's life and death have given rise. The novella is Storm's crowning achievement and ranks with the best literature of his country and time.

On 4 July 1888, four months after the completion of the novella, Storm died of abdominal cancer. He was buried in the family crypt in Husum. At his request, neither a priest nor a friend spoke at his grave. It was his ultimate acknowledgment that there is no answer to the power of death.

Letters:

"Briefwechsel zwischen Theodor Storm und Emil Kuh," edited by Paul R. Kuh, *Westermanns illustrierte deutsche Monatshefte,* 67 (1889–1890); 99–107, 264–274, 363–378, 541–554;

Briefe in die Heimat aus den Jahren 1853–64, edited by Gertrud Storm (Berlin: Curtius, 1907);

Briefe an seine Braut, edited by Storm (Brunswick: Westermann, 1915);

Briefe an seine Frau, edited by Storm (Brunswick: Westermann, 1915);

Briefe an seine Kinder, edited by Storm (Brunswick: Westermann, 1916);

Theodor Storms Briefwechsel mit Theodor Mommsen, edited by Hans-Erich Teitge (Weimar: Böhlau, 1966);

Theodor Storm und Iwan Turgenjew: Persönliche und literarische Beziehungen, Einflüsse, Briefe, Bilder, edited by Karl-Ernst Laage (Heide: Boyens, 1967);

Der Briefwechsel zwischen Theodor Storm und Gottfried Keller, edited by Peter Goldammer (Berlin: Aufbau, 1967);

Theodor Storm–Paul Heyse: Briefwechsel, 3 volumes, edited by Clifford A. Bernd (Berlin: Schmidt, 1969–1974);

Theodor Storm–Erich Schmidt: Briefwechsel, 2 volumes, edited by Laage (Berlin: Schmidt, 1972–1976);

"Theodor Storm und Hieronymus Lorm: Unveröffentlichte Briefe," edited by Arthur Tilo Alt, *Schriften der Theodor-Storm-Gesellschaft*, 27 (1978): 26–36;

Theodor Storm–Eduard Mörike; Theodor Storm–Margareth Mörike: Briefwechsel, mit Storms "Meine Erinnerungen an Eduard Mörike," edited by Hildburg and Werner Kohlschmidt (Berlin: Schmidt, 1978);

Theodor Storm–Ernst Esmarch: Briefwechsel, edited by Alt (Berlin: Schmidt, 1979);

Theodor Storm–Theodor Fontane: Briefwechsel, edited by Jacob Steiner (Berlin: Schmidt, 1981);

Theodor Storm–Wilhelm Petersen, Briefwechsel, edited by Brian Coghlan (Berlin: Schmidt, 1984);

Theodor Storm–Hartmuth und Laura Brinkmann: Briefwechsel, edited by August Stahl (Berlin: Schmidt, 1986);

Theodor Fontane über den "Eroticismus" und die "Husumerei" Storms: Fontanes Briefwechsel mit Hedwig Büchting, edited by Dieter Lohmeier, *Schriften der Theodor-Storm-Gesellschaft,* 39 (1990): 26–45;

Theodor Storm–Klaus Groth: Briefwechsel, edited by Boy Hinrichs (Berlin: Schmidt, 1990).

Bibliographies:

Hans-Erich Teitge, ed., *Theodor Storm Bibliographie* (Berlin: Deutsche Staatsbibliothek, 1967);

Kurt Meyer, "Storm Bibliographie: 1967–1973," *Schriften der Theodor-Storm-Gesellschaft,* 23 (1974): 72–81;

Meyer, "Storm Bibliographie: Neuerscheinungen," *Schriften der Theodor-Storm-Gesellschaft,* 24 (1975): 105–108;

Margarethe Draheim, "Storm Bibliographie: Neuerscheinungen," *Schriften der Theodor-Storm-Gesellschaft,* 25 (1976): 79–81; 26 (1977): 87–89; 27 (1978): 66–68; 28 (1979): 132–134; 29 (1980): 73–76; 30 (1981): 89–91; 31 (1982): 69–72; 32 (1983): 79–83; 33 (1984): 86–88; 34 (1985): 77–80; 35 (1986): 55–59; 36 (1987): 91–96;

Elke Jacobsen, "Storm Bibliographie: Neuerscheinungen," *Schriften der Theodor-Storm-Gesellschaft,* 38 (1989): 111–118; 39 (1990): 80–89; 40 (1991): 87–92.

Biographies:

Gertrud Storm, *Theodor Storm: Ein Bild seines Lebens,* 2 volumes (Berlin: 1912–1913);

Franz Stuckert, *Theodor Storm: Sein Leben und seine Welt* (Bremen: Schünemann, 1955);

Fritz Böttger, *Theodor Storm in seiner Zeit* (Berlin: Verlag der Nation, 1959).

References:

Arthur Tilo Alt, *Theodor Storm* (New York: Twayne, 1973);

Lore Amlinger, "Von 'Immensee' zum 'Schimmelreiter': Zur Entwicklung des Stormschen Helden," *Schriften der Theodor-Storm-Gesellschaft,* 38 (1989): 63–72;

David Artiss, *Theodor Storm: Studies in Ambivalence. Symbol and Myth in his Narrative Fiction* (Amsterdam: Benjamins, 1978);

Ralf Bartoleit, "Das Verhältnis von Ferdinand Tönnies' 'Gemeinschaft und Gesellschaft' zu Theodor Storm's Erzählwerk: Über die Fragwürdigkeit einer naheliegenden Interpretation," *Schriften der Theodor-Storm-Gesellschaft,* 36 (1987): 69–82;

Moritz Baßler, "Die ins Haus heimgeholte Transzendenz: Theodor Storms Liebesauffassung vor dem Hintergrund der Philosophie Ludwig Feuerbachs," *Schriften der Theodor-Storm-Gesellschaft,* 36 (1987): 43–60;

Clifford Bernd, *Theodor Storm's Craft of Fiction* (Chapel Hill: University of North Carolina Press, 1966);

Georg Bollenbeck, "Theodor Storm, verengter Horizont und vertiefter Blick," *Schriften der Theodor-Storm-Gesellschaft,* 39 (1990): 15–25;

Robert M. Browning, "Association and Disassociation in Storm's Novellen: A Study on the Meaning of the Frame," *PMLA,* 66 (June 1951): 381–404;

Ernst Feise, "Theodor Storm's 'Aquis submersus,'" in his *Xenion: Themes, Forms and Ideas in German Literature* (Baltimore: Johns Hopkins University Press, 1950), pp. 226–240;

Günter Häntzschel, "Storm als Anthologie-Herausgeber," *Schriften der Theodor-Storm-Gesellschaft,* 38 (1989): 39–51;

Lee B. Jennings, "Shadows from the Void in Theodor Storm's Novellen," *Germanic Review,* 37 (May 1962): 174–189;

Karl Ernst Laage, *Theodor Storm: Studien zu seinem Leben und Werk mit einem Handschriftenkatalog* (Berlin: Schmidt, 1985);

Ernst Loeb, *Faust ohne Transzendenz: Theodor Storms Schimmelreiter* (St. Louis: Washington University Press, 1963);

Thomas Mann, "Theodor Storm: 1930," in his *Adel des Geistes: Sechzehn Versuche zum Problem der Humanität* (Stockholm: Bermann-Fischer, 1945), pp. 518–542;

Allen McCormick, *Theodor Storm's Novellen: Essays on Literary Technique* (Chapel Hill: University of North Carolina Press, 1964);

Eckart Pastor, *Die Sprache der Erinnerung: Zu den Novellen von Theodor Storm* (Frankfurt am Main: Athenäum, 1988);

Willy Schumann, "Theodor Storm und Thomas Mann: Gemeinsames und Unterschiedliches," *Schriften der Theodor-Storm-Gesellschaft,* 13 (1964): 28–44;

Friedrich Sengle, "Storms lyrische Eigenleistung," *Schriften der Theodor-Storm-Gesellschaft,* 28 (1979): 9–33;

Walter Silz, "Theodor Storm: Three Poems," *Germanic Review,* 42 (November 1967): 293–300;

Silz, "Theodor Storm's Schimmelreiter," *PMLA,* 61 (September 1946): 762–783;

Silz, "Theodor Storm's 'Über die Heide,'" in *Studies in German Literature of the Nineteenth and Twentieth Centuries: Festschrift for Frederic E. Coenen,* edited by Siegfried Mews (Chapel Hill: University of North Carolina Press, 1970), pp. 105–110;

Lloyd Wedberg, *The Theme of Loneliness in Theodor Storm's Novellen* (The Hague: Mouton, 1964);

Benno von Wiese, "Theodor Storm: Hans und Heinz Kirch," in his *Die deutsche Novelle von Goethe bis Kafka,* volume 2 (Düsseldorf: Bagel, 1964), pp. 216–235;

Elmer Wooley, *Studies in Theodor Storm* (Bloomington: Indiana University Press, 1943);

Wooley, *Theodor Storm's World in Pictures* (Bloomington: Indiana University Press, 1954).

Papers:

Theodor Storm's papers are in the Schleswig-Holsteinische Landesbibliothek (Schleswig-Holstein Provincial Library), Kiel; and the Storm-Haus, Husum.

Ludwig Tieck

(31 May 1773 – 28 April 1853)

Donald H. Crosby
University of Connecticut

This entry originally appeared in DLB 90: German Writers
in the Age of Goethe, 1789–1832.

BOOKS: *Thaten und Feinheiten renommirter Kraft- und Kniff-genies,* 2 volumes (Berlin: Himburg, 1790–1791);

Abdallah: Eine Erzählung (Berlin & Leipzig: Nicolai, 1793);

Eine Geschichte ohne Abentheuerlichkeiten, as Peter Leberecht, 2 volumes (Berlin & Leipzig: Nicolai, 1795–1796);

Geschichte des Herrn William Lovell, 3 volumes (Berlin & Leipzig: Nicolai, 1795–1796);

Der betrügliche Schein, oder: Man muß nicht glauben, was man sieht (Berlin & Leipzig: Nicolai, 1796);

Ritter Blaubart: Ein Ammenmährchen, as Peter Leberecht (Berlin & Leipzig: Nicolai, 1797);

Herzensergießungen eines kunstliebenden Klosterbruders, by Tieck and Wilhelm Heinrich Wackenroder (Berlin: Unger, 1797); translated by Mary Hurst Schubert as "Confessions from the Heart of an Art-Loving Friar," in *Confessions and Fantasies* (University Park & London: Pennsylvania State University Press, 1971), pp. 79–160;

Der gestiefelte Kater: Ein Kindermärchen in drey Akten, mit Zwischenspielen, einem Prologe und Epiloge, as Peter Leberecht (Bergamo: Published by the author, 1797); translated by Lillie Winter as "Puss in Boots," in *The German Classics of the Nineteenth and Twentieth Centuries,* edited by Kuno Francke and W. G. Howard, volume 4 (New York: German Publications Society, 1913), pp. 194–293;

Die sieben Weiber des Blaubart: Eine wahre Familiengeschichte, as Gottlieb Färber (Berlin: Nicolai, 1797);

Der Abschied: Ein Traumspiel in zwey Aufzügen (Berlin: Langhoff, 1798);

Alla-Moddin (Berlin: Langhoff, 1798);

Ein Schurke über den andern oder die Fuchsprelle: Ein Lustspiel in drei Aufzügen (Berlin: Langhoff, 1798);

Franz Sternbalds Wanderungen: Eine altdeutsche Geschichte, 2 volumes (Berlin: Unger, 1798);

Ludwig Tieck (Bibliothèque Nationale, Paris)

Phantasien über die Kunst, für Freunde der Kunst, by Tieck and Wackenroder (Hamburg: Perthes, 1799); translated by Schubert as "Fantasies on Art for Friends of Art," in *Confessions and Fantasies,* pp. 161–197;

Sämmtliche Schriften, 12 volumes (Berlin & Leipzig: Nicolai, 1799);

Romantische Dichtungen, 2 volumes (Jena: Frommann, 1799–1800);

Das Ungeheuer und der verzauberte Wald: Ein musikalisches Mährchen in vier Aufzügen (Bremen: Wilmans, 1800);

Kaiser Octavianus: Ein Lustspiel in zwei Theilen (Jena: Frommann, 1804);

Phantasus: Eine Sammlung von Mährchen, Erzählungen, Schauspielen und Novellen, 3 volumes (Berlin: Realschulbuchhandlung, 1812–1816); translated by Julius C. Hare, James Anthony Froude, and others as *Tales from the Phantasus* (London: Burns, 1845);

Sämmtliche Werke, 30 volumes (Vienna: Grund, 1817–1824);

Leben und Tod der heiligen Genoveva: Ein Trauerspiel (Berlin: Reimer, 1820);

Gedichte, 3 volumes (Dresden: Hilscher, 1821–1823);

Der Geheimnißvolle: Novelle (Dresden: Hilscher, 1823);

Die Gemälde: Novelle (Dresden: Arnold, 1823); translated by G. Cunningham as *The Pictures in Foreign Tales and Traditions,* 2 volumes (Glasgow: Blackie, Fullarton, 1829);

Novellen, 7 volumes (Berlin: Reimer / Breslau: Max, 1823–1828); enlarged as *Gesammelte Novellen,* 14 volumes (Breslau: Max, 1835–1842); "Der blonde Eckbert"; "Der getreue Eckart"; "Der Runenberg"; "Die Elfen"; "Der Pokal," translated by Thomas Carlyle as "The Fair-Haired Eckbert"; "The Trusty Eckart"; "The Runenberg"; "The Elves"; "The Goblet," in *German Romance: Specimens of Its Chief Authors,* 4 volumes (London: Tait / New York: Scribner's, 1827);

Die Verlobung: Novelle (Dresden: Arnold, 1823);

Musikalische Leiden und Freuden: Novelle (Dresden: Arnold, 1824);

Die Reisenden: Novelle (Dresden: Arnold, 1824);

Dramaturgische Blätter, 3 volumes (Breslau: Max, volumes 1–2; Leipzig: Brockhaus, volume 3, 1825–1852);

Pietro von Abano oder Petrus Apone: Zaubergeschichte (Breslau: Max, 1825); translated anonymously as "Pietro of Abano," *Blackwood's Magazine,* 46 (1839): 288;

Der Aufruhr in den Cevennen: Eine Novelle in vier Abschnitten. Erster und zweiter Abschnitt (Berlin: Reimer, 1826); translated by Mme. Burette as *The Rebellion in the Cevennes: An Historical Novel,* 2 volumes (London, 1845);

Der Alte vom Berge, und: Die Gesellschaft auf dem Lande: Zwei Novellen (Breslau: Max, 1828); translated by J. C. Hare as *The Old Man of the Mountain* (London: Moxon, 1831);

Schriften, 28 volumes (Berlin: Reimer, 1828);

Novellenkranz, 5 volumes (Berlin: Reimer, 1831–1835);

Epilog zum Andenken Goethes: Nach Darstellung der Iphigenie in Dresden den 29. März 1832 (Dresden, 1832);

Der junge Tischlermeister: Novelle in sieben Abschnitten, 2 volumes (Berlin: Reimer, 1836); *Sämmtliche Werke,* 2 volumes (Paris: Tétot, 1837);

Vittoria Accorombona: Ein Roman in fünf Büchern, 2 volumes (Breslau: Max, 1840); translated anonymously as *The Roman Matron; or, Vittoria Accorombona: A Novel* (London: Bury St. Edmunds, 1845);

Gedichte: Neue Ausgabe (Berlin: Reimer, 1841);

Kritische Schriften, 4 volumes (Leipzig: Brockhaus, 1848–1852);

Bibliotheca Tieckiana (Berlin, 1849);

Epilog zur hundertjährigen Geburtsfeier Goethes (Berlin: Hertz, 1849);

Die Sommernacht: Eine Jugenddichtung (Frankfurt am Main: Sauerländer, 1853); translated by Mary C. Rumsey as *The Midsummer Night; or, Shakespeare and the Fairies* (London, 1854);

Nachgelassene Schriften: Auswahl und Nachlese, edited by Rudolf Köpke, 2 volumes (Leipzig: Brockhaus, 1855);

Werke: Kritisch durchgesehene und erläuterte Ausgabe, edited by G. L. Klee, 3 volumes (Leipzig: Bibliographisches Institut, 1892);

Das Buch über Shakespeare: Handschriftliche Aufzeichnung. Aus seinem Nachlaß herausgegeben, edited by Henry Lüdecke (Halle: Niemeyer, 1920).

Editions in English: *Puss in Boots (Der gestiefelte Kater),* edited and translated by Gerald Gillespie (Austin: University of Texas Press, 1974);

The Land of Upside Down (Die verkehrte Welt), translated by Oscar Mandel and Maria K. Feder (Rutherford, N.J.: Fairleigh Dickenson University Press, 1978).

OTHER: *Straußfedern,* edited by Tieck, Johann Karl August Musaeus, and Johann Georg Miller, 8 volumes (Berlin & Stettin: Nicolai, 1795–1798);

William Shakespeare, *Der Sturm: Ein Schauspiel, für das Theater bearbeitet,* translated and adapted by Tieck (Berlin & Leipzig: Nicolai, 1796)—includes Tieck's essay "Ueber Shakespeares Behandlung des Wunderbaren";

Volksmährchen, edited by Tieck as Peter Leberecht, 3 volumes (Berlin: Nicolai, 1797);

Miguel de Cervantes Saavedra, *Leben und Thaten des scharfsinnigen Edlen Don Quixote von La Mancha,* translated by Tieck, 4 volumes (Berlin: Unger, 1799–1801);

Poetisches Journal, edited by Tieck (Jena: Frommann, 1800);

Musen-Almanach für das Jahr 1802, edited by Tieck and August Wilhelm Schlegel (Tübingen: Cotta, 1802);

Friedrich von Hardenberg, *Novalis Schriften,* edited by Tieck and Friedrich Schlegel (Berlin: Realschulbuchhandlung, 1802–1805);

Minnelieder aus dem Schwäbischen Zeitalter, edited by Tieck (Berlin: Realschulbuchhandlung, 1803);

F. Müller, *Mahler Müller's Werke,* edited by Tieck, F. Batt, and Le Pique, 3 volumes (Heidelberg: Mohr & Zimmer, 1811);

Alt-Englisches Theater: Oder Supplement zum Shakespear, edited and translated by Tieck, 2 volumes (Berlin: Realschulbuchhandlung, 1811);

Frauendienst, oder: Geschichte und Liebe des Ritters und Sängers Ulrich von Lichtenstein, von ihm selbst beschrieben, revised and edited by Tieck (Stuttgart & Tübingen: Cotta, 1812);

Deutsches Theater, edited by Tieck, 2 volumes (Berlin: Realschulbuchhandlung, 1817);

Heinrich von Kleist, *Hinterlassene Schriften,* edited by Tieck (Berlin: Reimer, 1821);

Shakespeare's Vorschule, edited by Tieck, 2 volumes (Leipzig: Brockhaus, 1823–1829);

William Shakespeare: Dramatische Werke, translated by A. W. Schlegel and revised by Tieck and others (Berlin: Reimer, 1825–1833);

Kleist, *Gesammelte Schriften,* edited by Tieck, 3 volumes (Berlin: Reimer, 1826);

K. W. F. Solger, *Nachgelassene Schriften und Briefwechsel,* edited by Tieck and F. von Raumer, 2 volumes (Leipzig: Brockhaus, 1826);

Leben und Begebenheiten des Escudero Marcus Obregon: Oder Autobiographie des Spanischen Dichters Vicente Espinel, translated, with a foreword, by Tieck, 2 volumes (Breslau: Max, 1827);

F. von Uechtritz, *Alexander und Darius: Trauerspiel,* foreword by Tieck (Berlin: Vereinsbuchhandlung, 1827);

Braga: Vollständige Sammlung klassischer und volksthümlicher deutscher Gedichte aus dem achtzehnten und neunzehnten Jahrhundert, introduction by Tieck, 10 volumes (Dresden: Wagner, 1827–1828);

J. M. R. Lenz, *Gesammelte Schriften,* edited by Tieck, 3 volumes (Berlin: Reimer, 1828);

Johann Gottfried Schnabel, *Die Insel Felsenburg oder wunderliche Fata einiger Seefahrer: Eine Geschichte aus dem Anfange des achtzehnten Jahrhunderts,* edited by Tieck, 6 volumes (Breslau: Max, 1828);

F. L. Schröder, *Dramatische Werke,* introduction by Tieck, 4 volumes (Berlin: Reimer, 1831);

L. von Bülow, *Das Novellenbuch, oder hundert Novellen nach alten italiänischen, spanischen, französischen, lateinischen, englischen und deutschen bearbeitet,* foreword by Tieck, 4 volumes (Leipzig: Brockhaus, 1834–1836);

Sophie Bernhardi, née Tieck, *Evremont: Roman,* edited by Tieck, 3 volumes (Breslau: Max, 1836);

Shakespeare, *Vier Schauspiele,* translated by Tieck (Stuttgart & Tübingen: Cotta, 1836);

Cervantes Saavedra, *Die Leiden des Persiles und der Sigismunda,* introduction by Tieck, translated by Dorothea Tieck, 2 volumes (Leipzig: Brockhaus, 1838);

F. Berthold, *König Sebastian,* edited by Tieck, 2 volumes (Dresden & Leipzig: Arnold, 1839);

A. A. Afzelius, *Volkssagen und Volkslieder aus Schwedens älterer und neuerer Zeit,* foreword by Tieck, 3 volumes (Leipzig: Kollmann, 1842);

F. Berthold, *Gesammelte Novellen,* edited by Tieck, 2 volumes (Leipzig: Brockhaus, 1842);

K. Förster, *Gedichte,* edited by Tieck, 2 volumes (Leipzig: Brockhaus, 1843);

F. Laun, *Gesammelte Schriften,* revised, with a prologue, by Tieck, volume 1 (Stuttgart: Scheible, Rieger & Sattler, 1843);

Johann Wolfgang von Goethe, *Goethes ältestes Liederbuch,* edited by Tieck (Berlin: Schultze, 1844);

Sophocles, *Sämmtliche Tragödien,* foreword by Tieck (Berlin: Förstner, 1845);

Hardenberg, *Novalis Schriften: Dritter Theil,* edited by Tieck and E. von Bülow (Berlin: Reimer, 1846);

Norwegische Volksmährchen, foreword by Tieck (Berlin: Simion, 1847);

J. Ford, *Dramatische Werke,* volume 1, foreword by Tieck (Berlin: Simion, 1848);

D. Helena, *Lieder II,* foreword by Tieck (Berlin: Nicolai, 1848);

F. Lehmann, *Streit und Friede,* foreword by Tieck (Berlin: Paetel, 1851);

L. Wahl, *Mährchen,* foreword by Tieck (Berlin: Hollstein, 1852);

Mucedorus, ein englisches Drama aus Shakespeares Zeit, translated by Tieck (Berlin: Gronau, 1893).

Of the pioneers of the German Romantic movement around the turn of the nineteenth century, none was more daring—or more durable—than Ludwig Tieck. For more than five decades his name was virtually synonymous with German Romanticism; there was hardly a genre of this most multifarious of literary movements that he did not explore, if not actually inspire. Literary historians surveying the first half of the nineteenth century would be hard-pressed to name a German author who could not boast of a personal acquaintance with Tieck or who had not benefited from his conversation and counsel. Hailed by his youthful contemporaries as the founding poet of the Romantic movement, Tieck lived long enough to become its poet laureate as well. By the time he died in 1853 Romanticism had all but ceased to exist as a formal literary movement. Yet even to describe Tieck as the doyen of German Romanticism scarcely does justice to the esteem in which he was held for most of his long lifetime. Up to Goethe's death Tieck shared with the great poet recognition as Germany's preeminent man of letters; after Goethe's demise in 1832 the accolade was accorded to Tieck alone. Who else could have claimed to have conversed with Mozart, Beethoven, and Wagner; to have discussed philosophy with Fichte and Schelling, folklore with the Grimm Brothers, the art of translation with August Wilhelm Schlegel, poetry with Goethe, Novalis, and Kleist, and Shakespeare with Coleridge?

Johann Ludwig Tieck was born on 31 May 1773 into a middle-class family in Berlin, the capital of what was then the state of Prussia. His father, also named Johann Ludwig, was a ropemaker by trade. Well-read for his time and for his calling, he took an active interest in civic affairs and could lay claim to the honor of having been received by the King of Prussia, Frederick the Great. Tieck's mother, Anna Sophie Schale Tieck, was a sensitive, gentle, and pious woman who, while deferring to her ambitious and autocratic husband, nevertheless took an active part in the education of young Tieck. Evenings in the enlightened Tieck household were graced by readings and recitations either of biblical tales or contemporary German literature. One work which especially inflamed young Tieck's imagination was *Götz von Berlichingen* (1773), the popular "Storm and Stress" play by Johann Wolfgang von Goethe. Like Goethe, to whom he was later compared, Tieck was privileged to have a puppet theater at his disposal, and, like the older poet, he was soon captured by the magic of theatrical illusion. Although circumstances were to deny him his ambition of becoming a professional actor, Tieck never ceased to be a man of the theater.

Young Tieck's love of learning, evidenced at an early age and encouraged by his parents, mandated his enrollment at a progressive gymnasium, where his obvious academic gifts—especially his talent for foreign languages—could be developed. Among the friends he made at the gymnasium was Wilhelm Heinrich Wackenroder, who was later to write, with Tieck's collaboration, one of the most important works of early German Romanticism: *Herzensergießungen eines kunstliebenden Klosterbruders* (1797; translated as "Confessions from the Heart of an Art-Loving Friar," 1971). Despite the demands posed by his studies, Tieck found time to sample the abundant offerings of the many theaters which thrived in Berlin, where even a schoolboy's allowance sufficed to purchase inexpensive tickets. By the time he completed his gymnasium studies in 1792 Tieck was a passionate theatergoer and admirer of the dramas of Goethe, Schiller, and Shakespeare.

Scholarship has recorded more than thirty works written during Tieck's gymnasium years, among them dramas, comedies, farces, epic fragments, translations, and lyric poetry. While this juvenilia is predictably uneven in quality, its sheer volume clearly presaged the arrival of an uncommon literary talent. The young author's free play of fantasy, his fascination with the gruesome and the horrific, and his ventures into the realm of irrationality gave hints of the Romantic poet to come.

In the spring of 1792 Tieck matriculated at the Prussian university of Halle as a student of theology, but the separation from home, his beloved sister Sophie, and his friend Wackenroder, together with boredom brought on by academic routine, left him dispirited and restless. Late in the fall of the same year he transferred to the university at Göttingen, where he found the Anglophilic atmosphere of the province of Hannover more congenial and the curriculum at the university more stimulating. Theology, for which he evidently had little heart, was quickly forgotten in favor of philosophy, English literature, and writing. Although happy with his new university, whose excellent library was equal even to Tieck's passion for reading, and appreciative of the flexibility of a student's life at Göttingen, Tieck frequently fell victim to bouts of depression. Manic mood swings, episodes of melancholia, and even hallucinations posed a threat to his further development as a writer.

In 1793 Wackenroder and Tieck undertook a journey through Franconia which culminated in an extended sojourn in Nuremberg. The city of Albrecht Dürer and Hans Sachs made a powerful impression on the young friends. From this visit sprang that veneration of the German Middle Ages which, especially in Tieck's works, became one of the characteristics of German Romanticism. It was the spirit of Dürer, too, which sparked the proselytizing fervor of those pages of *Herzensergießungen eines kunstliebenden Klosterbruders* and of Tieck's novel *Franz Sternbalds Wanderungen* (Franz Sternbald's Journeys, 1798), dedicated to the praise of German art. A different but related source of inspiration awaited the friends in Dresden, where their sober Protestantism was all but overwhelmed by the richness of Roman Catholic rituals in the Dresden cathedral. This experience was to bear fruit both in Tieck's "Catholic" works, such as his play *Leben und Tod der heiligen Genoveva* (Life and Death of St. Genoveve, 1820), and in his prolonged flirtation with conversion to Catholicism.

The plethora of stimuli to which Tieck had been exposed soon translated into creative activity. Although only twenty-one, Tieck thought of himself as a student only in a formal sense; the professional writer was about to be born. In his final semester at Göttingen—a brief transfer to Erlangen had proved unsatisfying–Tieck undertook his first major translation project, a prose version, with embellishments, of Shakespeare's *The Tempest*. The translation was published in 1796 together with a perceptive essay, "Ueber Shakespeares Behandlung des Wunderbaren" (Shakespeare's Treatment of the Marvelous). This work marked the formal beginning of what was to become a lifetime preoccupation with Shakespeare.

In 1794 Tieck met the Berlin publisher Christoph Friedrich Nicolai, who offered the aspiring young writer employment as a sort of literary jack-of-all-trades. On the surface, the match would seem to have been an odd one: Nicolai was the Nestor of the waning Rationalist school of German literature, whereas Tieck's emerging literary persona was colored by the dawn of the new Romantic era. Yet the engagement turned out to be a productive one for both parties: Nicolai was happy to have in his employ a writer of Tieck's speed and adaptability, and Tieck was grateful for the opportunity to earn a living exclusively by his pen. It was during these early years of employment that Tieck found time to complete his first major opus, *Geschichte des Herrn William Lovell* (Story of Mr. William Lovell, 1795–1796). A rambling, often disjointed work, the three-volume epistolary novel follows the travels and adventures of a protagonist torn between sensual and spiritual love, between self-indulgence and the ordered discipline of nature. In a reversal of the developmental pattern common to so many German novels, Lovell's diverse experiences lead him ever deeper into a moral labyrinth. Like Goethe's Faust, Lovell belatedly tries to turn away from evil and to return to nature, but he is denied redemption, and, after a final series of sordid adventures, he is killed in a duel. Though by no means autobiographical, *Geschichte des Herrn William Lovell* reflects the dualism, the mood swings, and the adolescent instability of young Tieck. To that extent the novel, for all its flaws, was a necessary summing-up for Tieck, a literary catharsis which cleansed his psyche and prepared him for the tasks yet to come.

In 1797, though still in the employ of Nicolai, Tieck began the publication, under the pseudonym Peter Leberecht, of an extended series titled *Volksmährchen* (Folktales). Some of these tales were epic, some dramatic; some were derivative, some original. All of them flew in the face of Rationalist dogma, which held that folktales, like folk poetry, were too primitive or even barbaric to be subsumed under the rubric of literature. These seminal volumes, whose appearance roughly coincided with the publication of the founding journal of Romanticism, *Das Athenäum* (edited by August Wilhelm and Friedrich Schlegel), generated concepts now recognized as perdurable components of German Romanticism: reverence for indigenous literature; the depiction of the shifting moods of the German forest; the integration of hallucinations and dreams into story plots; the free play of fancy; and the effacement of the boundary between the rational and the irrational. Without being aware of it–Tieck was always a natural, unreflective writer rather than a theoretician–he became the progenitor of an entirely new genre, the Kunstmärchen (literary fairy tale), which was to become one of the most successful experiments essayed by Tieck and fellow Romantics such as Novalis, Clemens Brentano, and E. T. A. Hoffmann.

Among the tales found in Tieck's *Volksmährchen* are "Ritter Blaubart" (Sir Bluebeard), a new version of the ancient Bluebeard legend, and "Die schöne Magelone" (The Fair Magelone), a re-creation of a twelfth-century story which originated in Provence. Tieck interspersed throughout his tale seventeen poems, fifteen of which were selected by Johannes Brahms for his song cycle *Die Magelone-Lieder*. It is in the pages of the *Volksmährchen*, too, that one finds two of Tieck's best-known works: "Der blonde Eckbert" (Blond Eckbert) and *Der gestiefelte Kater* (1797; translated as "Puss in Boots," 1913). The former is an original tale which, although written hastily under the pressure of a publication deadline, has come to be regarded as a paradigm for the Romantic Kunstmärchen, especially in its blending of old and new elements. From the indigenous folktale Tieck borrowed the chronology of the indefinite past ("Once upon a time . . ."), the ambiance of the forest, a simple narrative style, and such commonplaces as a mysterious house deep in the woods, an old woman hobbling on a cane, and an enchanted bird which lays a jeweled egg. Building on this foundation Tieck made significant additions: a narrative frame distinguishing the real world from the world of enchantment, characters more complex than those found in the traditional folktale, syntactically complicated descriptive passages, a subplot, and a complex and somewhat ambiguous depiction of crime and punishment. Perhaps the most striking innovation in the tale is the mood Tieck creates, in part through detailed word pictures of the secluded forest refuge but chiefly through the songs sung by the enchanted bird, all of them variations on the theme of Waldeinsamkeit (meditative solitude in deep woods). The motif of Waldeinsamkeit, with its mysterious overtones, sometimes inviting, sometimes threatening, keynotes that mixture of awe and fear which was to become so characteristic of the Romantic perception of nature.

Like "Der blonde Eckbert," the play *Der gestiefelte Kater* was written with great speed; Tieck claimed to have finished it in one night. Yet, along with "Der blonde Eckbert," *Der gestiefelte Kater* has survived as his best-known literary creation. Based on a folktale retold by the seventeenth-century French writer Charles Perrault, the play centers around the story of the humanoid cat who gains a kingdom for his master. From this starting point Tieck embarks upon a far-ranging satire aimed in equal parts against the stuffy literalism of the Rationalists, the vapidity of popular playwrights of his day (especially August Wilhelm Iffland and August von Kotzebue), and the bad taste and intellectual shallowness of run-of-the-mill theater audiences. Withal, *Der gestiefelte Kater* is less a polemic than a spoof, and compared with the sharp attacks made by Goethe and Schiller against their contemporaries, the satire in *Der gestiefelte Kater* strikes today's reader as almost good-natured. Yet neither historical interest in the objects of Tieck's satire—most of the individuals targeted have passed into obscurity—nor the play's pervasive humor can account for its durability; what made the play unique for its time was Tieck's employment of a technique which can be broadly defined as Romantic irony. For as the fairy-tale plot of the *Der gestiefelte Kater*—intersecting with an apparently unrelated subplot—moves toward its conclusion, the illusion of a theatrical performance is constantly interrupted. The spectators become part of the performance by commenting aloud on the merits (or demerits) of the play; the actors fall out of their roles and rail at the spectators; the backstage technicians are integrated into the action; and even the fictive author of the play is called before the curtain to defend his creation. All the while the actual author—Tieck himself—toys both with the material and the reader, and by so doing asserts a new right claimed by the Romantic poet: the sovereign license to step outside (or inside) his creation and to regard it with detachment. Although playwrights before Tieck had ventured the experiment of inserting a "play within a play," none had ever attempted so ambitious a restructuring of the canonical relationship among actors, the audience, and the hitherto invisible author.

More serious in purpose than *Der gestiefelte Kater* were *Herzensergießungen eines kunstliebenden Klosterbruders; Phantasien über die Kunst, für Freunde der Kunst* (1799; translated as "Fantasies on Art for Friends of Art," 1971); and *Franz Sternbalds Wanderungen,* three works which also date from these highly productive years. Although Tieck's role in the composition of the *Herzensergießungen* was subordinate to that of his friend Wackenroder, he was in every sense a collaborator and fully deserves the recognition accorded him by posterity. The book consists of a series of short narratives connected by a common theme: the veneration of medieval painters and their paintings. Devoted chiefly to a discussion of Italian masters—among them Raphael, Leonardo da Vinci, and Michelangelo—the book is balanced by a lofty pane-

gyric to the German master Dürer. The volume concludes with two chapters written by Wackenroder depicting the life and career of a fictional musician, Joseph Berglinger. In these pages music is elevated to the exalted level of art and nature, because it, too, is deemed a divine language capable of mediating between God and man. Yet music, like nature, is Janus-faced: the intoxicating ecstasies described by Wackenroder barely conceal the destructive potential of music, a theme later taken up by such German authors as Kleist, Hoffmann, and Thomas Mann.

For *Phantasien über die Kunst,* published the year after Wackenroder's death, Tieck could claim a greater share of the joint effort, although the influence of his friend is apparent throughout. Here music, rather than painting, is given the highest rank among the arts because of its unique properties: intangible yet indisputably real, by turns emotional and cerebral, unlimited in its expressive qualities, music is seen as being universal in the wordless power of its divine language. Taken together with Wackenroder's depiction of the intoxicating effect of music in the Berglinger sections of the *Herzensergießungen eines kunstliebenden Klosterbruders,* the *Phantasien über die Kunst* forms the foundation of musical aesthetics for the Romantic movement. It is surely no coincidence that Tieck's other writings dating from this period, especially his lyric poetry, teem with musical effects: repeatedly Tieck combines assonance, rhyme, and rhythm to evoke the sounds and moods of music. This sort of verbal music would soon add a new dimension to the lyrics of Brentano, Heinrich Heine, and Joseph von Eichendorff.

Tieck's third important work of this period, *Franz Sternbalds Wanderungen,* was entirely of his own authorship. Several sources of inspiration can be described for this novel, which—setting a pattern for the open-ended Romantic novel—was never completed: Tieck's conscious attempt to write a Romantic counterpart to Goethe's classical developmental novel *Wilhelm Meisters Lehrjahre* (Wilhelm Meister's Apprenticeship, 1795–1796); his need of a literary outlet after the sudden death of Wackenroder; and his determination to propagate the veneration of German art in the spirit of *Herzensergießungen eines kunstliebenden Klosterbruders.* Set in the time of Dürer, the novel chronicles the adventures of a young painter who, after studying with the great master, leaves his native Nuremberg and journeys far and wide in the hope of rising to the level of his beloved mentor and model. Like Wilhelm Meister, Sternbald finds the path of human experience full of unforeseeable turns and twists; like Meister, too, he is educated through the vicissitudes of life, through encounters with confidantes, mentors, and lovers. Unlike Goethe's hero, however, Sternbald is denied a journey's end; when

Tieck's narrative breaks off, Sternbald is still a quester, still an unfinished artist. In form, too, Tieck's novel diverges from its model. In place of Goethe's taut design there is the rambling, ruminative narrative structure familiar from *Geschichte des Herrn William Lovell;* in place of the songs of Mignon and the harpist–which for all their atmospheric quality supply integral components to Goethe's plot–the reader finds long lyrical effusions which in fact retard the action. These diversions, made worse through Tieck's predilection for digressive polemics, weaken the novel's structure and give the work at times an almost improvisatory character. Tieck's strengths, on the other hand, emerge in stronger relief when his novel is not compared with its model; the reader can then savor the younger writer's ability to create musical verse, to conjure up marvelous varicolored landscapes, and to re-create the magic of the German forest. Above all, it is Tieck's limpid prose, imbued with music, color, and nature mysticism, which allows *Franz Sternbalds Wanderungen* to transcend its flaws and to assert its position as a landmark of early Romantic fiction.

Whatever its shortcomings, the novel established Tieck as an author to be reckoned with; his days of supplying hackwork to Nicolai were over. The appearance of *Franz Sternbalds Wanderungen* also led to a meeting with Goethe, who, despite understandable reservations about the novel, received its author with restrained cordiality. These two very different writers–often set against one another by malicious partisans–were to maintain a collegial, if somewhat distant relationship over the next thirty years. Most important for Tieck, however, was the fact that the immediate resonance that his novel found among like-minded literati of his own generation paved the way for his acceptance into that elite circle of poets, thinkers, theoreticians, and theologians who charged the final years of the eighteenth century with unparalleled intellectual dynamism: the so-called Jena Romanticists. Among their ranks were Friedrich Schlegel, August Wilhelm Schlegel, Friedrich Wilhelm Schelling, Johann Gottlieb Fichte, Friedrich Schleiermacher, and Novalis. Complementing this formidable male circle were two women intellectuals who were, by the standards of the day, emancipated: Caroline Schlegel, the wife of August Wilhelm, and Friedrich's wife, Dorothea Veit Schlegel. Although the circle of the Jena Romanticists was frequently broken by comings and goings, by mutual antipathies and even by infidelities, the intellectual energy generated in the few years of its precarious existence was sufficient to fuel the Romantic movement for decades to come.

For Tieck, his entrée into the Jena circle signaled the end of his increasingly tenuous relationship with the house of Nicolai, which had published an unauthorized edition of his writings. In a sense the break was only a formality, since Tieck's artistic development had been drawing him, independently but ineluctably, toward the new school of Romantic theory established by the Schlegel brothers. Although a warm personal friendship with the brothers was slow to flower, Tieck immediately felt a rapport with each. With the mercurial Friedrich–the premier theoretician of the Romantic movement–he shared a love of Goethe's poetry and an interest in Spanish literature, Shakespeare, and Dante; in the more reserved August Wilhelm he recognized a congenial admirer of Elizabethan poetry, a keen student of the art of translation, and, above all, a passionate exponent of the dramas of Shakespeare. One of the first fruits of Tieck's collaboration with the Schlegel brothers was his translation of Cervantes's *Don Quixote,* undertaken at the urging of August Wilhelm. Despite Tieck's less-than-perfect grasp of Spanish, the translation, in four volumes published from 1799 to 1801, turned out to be true to the spirit of the original and quickly gained acceptance as the standard German version of Cervantes's masterpiece. Tieck's interaction with the philosophers of the Jena circle–Fichte, Schelling, and the Danish-born Henrik Steffens–was less immediately productive, in part because Tieck was never much of an abstract thinker but chiefly because his poetic intuition had already anticipated, or at least paralleled, the abstract concepts of the theoreticians. Thus the unprepossessing *Der gestiefelte Kater* may be viewed as a farcical representation of Fichte's doctrine of the supremacy of the ego, and "Der blonde Eckbert" contains at least the germ of the philosophy of nature mysticism expounded by Schelling and Steffens.

Of this circle of newly found friends, colleagues, and fellow Romantics only one came close to filling the void left in Tieck's life by the death of Wackenroder: the fine-nerved mining engineer Friedrich von Hardenberg, who called himself Novalis. At the time of their meeting Novalis stood at the threshold of his career as a poet, a career which was to be cut short by his early death from tuberculosis. Although a year older than Tieck, Novalis looked up to the author of the *Volksmährchen* and *Franz Sternbalds Wanderungen* with something akin to reverence; in a remarkable letter to Tieck he praised his new friend's uncommon insight and sensitivity, and described their meeting as having opened a new book in his life. Tieck, for his part, was happy to escape the superheated atmosphere of Jena for occasional sojourns at Novalis's residence in Weißenfels, where the two men could exchange ideas at leisure. Although echoes of Tieck's language and thought can be heard in Novalis's *Geistliche Lieder* (Spiritual Songs) and his *Hymnen an die Nacht* (Hymns to the Night), it is his allegorical novel *Heinrich von Ofterdingen* (1802; translated as *Henry von Ofterdingen,* 1964) which most clearly bears Tieck's imprint. It was during the hours spent together at Weißenfels that Novalis filled out the plan of his ambitious novel, which, like Tieck's *Franz Sternbalds Wanderungen,* was to serve as a Romantic counterbalance to *Wilhelm Meisters Lehrjahre.* After Novalis's death in 1801 Tieck—once again mourning a beloved friend—gave some thought to completing the novel in line with Novalis's intentions, but wisely elected to give it to the world in its uncompleted form.

Inevitably, the daily contact with brilliant and original thinkers and artists supplied a powerful stimulus to Tieck's own creative energies. The years 1799 and 1800 brought the publication of Tieck's two-volume *Romantische Dichtungen* (Romantic Writings), much of which was conceived on his frequent visits to Jena during this time period. The collection includes two major dramas: *Prince Zerbino oder Die Reise nach dem guten Geschmack* (Prince Zerbino; or, The Trip in Search of Good Taste) and *Leben und Tod der heiligen Genoveva.* Described by Tieck as being something of a continuation of *Der gestiefelte Kater, Prinz Zerbino* does indeed share some of the characters, and much of the method, of the earlier play. Like most sequels, however, it falls short of the original, and today it is valued chiefly as a document showing Tieck at a turning point of his career, in what one might call his Jena phase. *Prinz Zerbino* is a far more ambitious work than *Der gestiefelte Kater,* and, unlike the earlier play, could hardly have been written "in one night." As a tour de force of form it invites admiration with its plays-within-plays, its constant creation and destruction of illusion, and a new technique, the "playback" or reversal of the action, which anticipates the theater of the absurd of the twentieth century. Unfortunately, in his attempt to outdo himself, or perhaps to impress the Schlegels, Tieck burdened the play with too many satires (including one on his bête noir Nicolai), too many lyrical interludes, and too many obscure topical references. In place of the organized chaos of *Der gestiefelte Kater*—which derives at least a modicum of coherence from the fairy tale which forms its frame—Tieck substituted chaos for the sake of chaos. Brilliant and witty in its individual sections, *Prinz Zerbino* never coheres as a whole work of art.

Leben und Tod der heiligen Genoveva, conceived of as a serious play from the start, has little in common with the rollicking *Prinz Zerbino.* Based on an old legend, it tells the story of a noblewoman who is falsely accused of adultery. Sentenced to death, she is spared by a kindly retainer. Abandoned in the woods, she gives birth to a son whom she nourishes with doe's milk. Eventually she is found by her husband, who, convinced of her innocence, restores her to her rightful position. There was much in this time-honored legend to appeal to Tieck: the medieval ambience; the fairy-tale plot; the faint echoes of mythology; and the suggestion of the inexplicable or miraculous. Rather than expound the subject matter with the dramatic tautness of, say, Schiller, Tieck bent his talents to re-creating the essence of what he perceived as medieval, that "Mondbeglänzte Zaubernacht" (moonlit magic night) he was to apostrophize in other works. In Tieck's hands *Leben und Tod der heiligen Genoveva* became a lyrical drama, with mood replacing action, and with musical effects softening conflicts and confrontations. As in "Der blonde Eckbert," nature is no mere backdrop but an organic component of the plot, always weaving its wondrous spell. Even Goethe, who was normally cool to the "new school" of literature and kept his distance from the Jena circle, was charmed by the prismatic colors of Tieck's verse, his shimmering images and beguiling rhymes. After Tieck had read the play aloud to him, the great poet praised the colors, flowers, mirrors, and magic arts Tieck had conjured up. As a lyrical drama *Leben und Tod der heiligen Genoveva* does, in fact, point the way to Goethe's *Faust, Part II* (1832), a work which often eschews the concreteness and confrontations of traditional drama in favor of long, atmospheric lyrical interludes. Like *Prinz Zerbino*—indeed, like virtually all Romantic dramas—*Leben und Tod der heiligen Genoveva* is what Germans call a *Lesedrama,* a play more likely to be read than to be performed onstage. There is every evidence that Tieck, a consummate man of the theater, had a reading public rather than theater audiences in mind when he wrote *Prinz Zerbino* and *Leben und Tod der heiligen Genoveva.* He politely declined offers from the theater director Iffland and from Goethe himself to produce altered stage versions of *Leben und Tod der heiligen Genoveva* and *Prinz Zerbino,* respectively. Keenly aware of his talents, Tieck was conscious of his limitations as well.

In the summer of 1800 Tieck's Jena phase came to an end. The Jena Romanticists were beginning to go their separate ways, and Tieck, who had enriched his mind as a houseguest of August Wilhelm Schlegel, now had to cope with the practical problem of supporting himself and his family. In April 1798 he had married Amalie Alberti, and the next year brought the birth of their daughter Dorothea, who would one day herself become a translator of Shakespeare. In addition to caring for his family, Tieck had to come to terms with his deteriorating physical condition: physically robust in his youth, he began to be subject to bouts of rheumatoid arthritis, the effects of which eventually distorted his once-handsome figure. The years 1800 to 1802 were spent in restless commuting among Hamburg, Berlin, and Dresden as Tieck fruitlessly sought some steady employment which would relieve him from the financial and psychological burden of having to live from manuscript to manuscript. Somehow his energies were adequate to producing, in these hectic years, another major work: the two-part drama *Kaiser Octavianus* (Emperor Octavian, 1804). In many ways a valedictory to early German Romanticism, the play would be Tieck's last large-scale literary work for years to come. In style and content the work suggests a synthesis of the two dramas immediately preceding it. The "open form" and frequent excursions into humor recall *Prinz Zerbino,* while the main plot–there are several identifiable plots– dealing with the slandering of a virtuous woman, her banishment, her trials, and her eventual exoneration, clearly harks back to *Leben und Tod der heiligen Genoveva.* What *Kaiser Octavianus* is really about, however, is the play of fancy itself, the sovereign freedom of the poet to be guided only by his creative whim. Taking full advantage of his license as a Romantic poet, Tieck carries the reader to exotic lands and peoples, summons up the chivalric spirit of the Middle Ages, invokes the shades of Shakespeare and Pedro Calderón de la Barca, and through the power of poetry pleads for the renewal of the era of miracles, mysticism, love, and faith. The play includes several now-familiar features: disjointed action, arbitrary transitions, and above all, long lyrical interludes marked by a stunningly virtuosic employment of verse forms and the evocation of shimmering, multi-hued images. Generations after the publication of *Kaiser Octavianus,* literary historians would be citing, as a motto for German Romanticism, the verses spoken by Romanze (Romance), the allegorical figure of the Prologue who symbolizes the spirit of poetry: "Mondbeglänzte Zaubernacht, / Die den Sinn gefangen hält, / Wundervolle Märchenwelt, / Steig' auf in der alten Pracht!" (Moonlit magic night, / Holding the mind in thrall, / Wondrous world of fairy tale, / Rise up in the splendor of old!). As a vehicle for stage performance, *Kaiser Octavianus*–like *Prinz Zerbino, Leben und Tod der heiligen Genoveva,* and indeed virtually every play by Tieck– was stillborn. Its value remains unquestioned, however, as a document which gives form, substance, and poetic realization to the theories and aspirations of an entire literary movement.

From 1802 until 1810 Tieck lived at Ziebingen, near Frankfurt an der Oder, where he and his family– another daughter, Agnes, was born in 1802–were in effect permanent houseguests of Wilhelm von Burgsdorff, an old friend from Tieck's university days. With the composition of *Kaiser Octavianus* brought to a close the extraordinary series of early Romantic works to which he owes his fame. Although he had another fifty years of life and literary productivity remaining, he would never again enjoy the accolades which had been accorded to the author of *Der gestiefelte Kater* and *Franz*

Sternbalds Wanderungen. From his new base in Ziebingen, Tieck continued his many literary projects, including co-editorship with Friedrich Schlegel of the writings of his departed friend Novalis and research on his long-planned work *Das Buch über Shakespeare* (The Book About Shakespeare)–a work he never completed, although portions were posthumously published in 1920. Gregarious as always, he also cultivated new friends, among them the young painter Philipp Otto Runge. The two men had much to give one another: Tieck, the collaborator on *Herzensergießungen eines kunstliebenden Klosterbruders,* was delighted to have a conversational partner to whom he could pour out his undiminished enthusiasm for the great Italian and German masters; Runge was fascinated to have before him in the flesh the author of *Franz Sternbalds Wanderungen.* Like the progenitors of literary Romanticism, Runge was searching for a new form of art, a method of pictorial representation which reflected the new spirit of the times; he sought a means of expression more reflective of spontaneity than of classical formalism. Because Runge–along with Caspar David Friedrich–became the leading exponent of the Romantic school of painting, the claim can be made that Tieck's influence, so easily documented in the works of the writers who came after him, lived on in the pictorial medium as well. A more immediate by-product of the friendship with Runge, however, was *Minnelieder aus dem Schwäbischen Zeitalter* (Minnesongs from the Swabian Era, 1803), edited by Tieck. Illustrated by Runge and introduced with a long essay by Tieck, the collection of 220 songs paid tribute to the outpouring of courtly-love poetry in the twelfth century, which, together with the epics *Parzival, Tristan und Isolde,* and *Das Nibelungenlied,* constitutes the literary glory of the German medieval era.

It was *Das Nibelungenlied,* sometimes called the national epic of the Germans, which next occupied Tieck during his residence in Ziebingen. Hampered by crippling bouts of rheumatism; often subjected to periods of depression, which had plagued him since his youth; always pressed for money; and feeling trapped in a deteriorating marriage, Tieck welcomed the opportunity to immerse himself in the distant world of medievalism he knew and loved so well. In the *Nibelungenlied* he found much to occupy him. The epic falls into two parts, with part one recounting the love story of the hero Siegfried–here portrayed as a mortal prince–and the Burgundian princess Kriemhild, the betrayal of Brünnhild, and the slaying of Siegfried by the scheming vassal Hagen; part two, "Kriemhilds Rache" (Kriemhild's Revenge), integrates the fiction of the Siegfried-Kriemhild-Brünnhild triangle with the historical slaughter of the Burgundian tribe at the hands of the Huns in 436 A.D. After centuries of neglect this amalgam of Germanic mythology, fiction, and history had surfaced around 1800 as part of the movement of revitalized nationalism which also placed emphasis on indigenous folk poetry and folktales. Eager to present his fellow Germans with a translation of the Middle High German epic, Tieck attacked the project with scholarly dedication, even journeying to Rome to study sources found in the Vatican Library. Like the complete *Buch über Shakespeare,* however, Tieck's edition never saw the light of day. A certain dilatory spirit which had crept into his writing habits, coupled with a perfectionist's mania for revision, consigned this work, too, to his unpublished papers. Highly praised by contemporaries (including the poet Clemens Brentano) who heard Tieck recite from his translation, the work lay discarded while inferior translations by Friedrich Heinrich von der Hagen and Karl Simrock gained recognition as the standard Modern High German renditions. Despite his growing physical handicap, Tieck managed to undertake extensive travels during the years 1811 to 1817; often he was away from Ziebingen for months at a time visiting Prague, Berlin, or Baden-Baden. In May 1817 Tieck fulfilled a lifetime's wish by visiting England, a trip instigated by his ever-useful friend and benefactor Burgsdorff. Tieck had scarcely set foot on English soil when he made straight for London and its theaters. For weeks he indulged his love for the stage, rarely missing an evening's performance. To his good fortune, the repertories of the various theaters were rich in Shakespeare productions: over the short period of his stay he saw performances of *Cymbeline, Julius Caesar, Henry IV,* part 1, *Hamlet, Macbeth, Coriolanus, The Merchant of Venice, Richard III* (with the celebrated actor Edmund Kean in the title role), and *Othello.* Yet his critical eye was not beguiled by the realization of his lifelong dream: he found the interpretations of Shakespeare ill-conceived and the acting style too pompous and rhetorical. All in all Tieck seems to have enjoyed himself more in the British Museum, where the firsthand information he gathered on Elizabethan literature was sufficient for *Shakespeare's Vorschule* (Pre-Shakespearean Drama), two volumes edited by Tieck and published in 1823 and 1829. Tieck's sojourn in London included a reunion with Samuel Taylor Coleridge, whom he had met some years before. Despite language difficulties on both sides, the two poets found enough collegial rapport to enjoy a meeting in which each expounded, at length, his views on poetry in general and English literature–of which Tieck by now had encyclopedic knowledge–in particular. Yet the real high point of the visit to England came with Tieck's trip to Shakespeare's birthplace, Stratford-upon-Avon, which Tieck felt was beckoning to him like a gleaming shrine. The pilgrimage made so deep an impression on Tieck that years later he was able to give

a fictional account of it in the novella "Der Mondsüchtige" (The Moonstruck One, 1831).

It was to fiction, specifically the newly emergent form of the novella, that Tieck turned in the middle years of his long career. In so doing he found himself, if not quite rejuvenated, revitalized as a writer. Already in the years 1812 to 1816 Tieck had published an extended collection of mixed works–plays and tales–under the title of *Phantasus.* Some of the works, such as *Der gestiefelte Kater* and "Der Runenberg" (The Runic Mountain), stem from his earlier Romantic period; others–two plays and three tales–are new. Both in the arrangement of the collection and in the content of the most recent works, especially the tales, Tieck gave evidence of essaying a new style of composition, if not indeed a new genre. Strictly speaking, the technique Tieck employed in organizing his collection was not new at all, since it is modeled after Boccaccio's *Decameron,* in which individual stories are framed by informal discussions held among cultured men and women. Nor was he the first German poet to borrow the Boccacian technique: Goethe had employed the same device in his *Unterhaltungen deutscher Ausgewanderten* (Conversations of German Émigrés, 1795). Typically, Tieck added a new dimension to the inherited technique: instead of using the conversations as mere transitional bridges between tales, he gave them a life of their own by extending them over many pages. As for the tales themselves, they do not entirely fit the accepted definitions of a novella as developed by later critics: the novella is shorter than the novel, with fewer characters and a more limited time frame; it has more dramatic tautness than the tale, often with what Tieck called a Wendepunkt (turning point) determining the direction of the plot; and it is basically realistic in content, with none of the fantastic excursions of the Kunstmärchen. Tieck claimed that he was moving toward a new, that is, un-Romantic, style in the tales of *Phantasus,* and there is some justification for his claim, provided that the reader overlooks "Die Elfen" (The Elves) a charming tale but one which might have been written in 1798: it is a throwback to Tieck's early Romantic period, full of fantasy and enchantment. The next tale, however, "Der Pokal" (The Goblet), meets in part Goethe's oft-quoted definition of a novella as an unheard-of event which might actually have taken place, since it is based on an experience Tieck had in Florence, where he came to the aid of a young woman who had stumbled on the steps of a church. This incident, though by no means "unheard-of," evidently left enough of an impression to serve as the factual germ of "Der Pokal." In the story Tieck expands the everyday incident into a love-at-first-sight romance and uses it as a starting point for an extended tale of thwarted love and wasted lives. By and large the story remains on the realistic plane associated with a novella, but Tieck tests the story's realism by adding supernatural properties to the goblet. The third tale in *Phantasus,* "Liebeszauber" (Love's Magic) is a horror story set in a realistic milieu; like E. T. A. Hoffmann's "Der Sandmann" (The Sandman), which appeared around the same time, it deals with the duplicity of the world of appearances. Despite unresolved contradictions and the intrusion of the uncanny—at one point a dragon materializes—the psychological realism of the story, especially in the blending of the themes of terror and guilt, is compelling.

It was from these tentative beginnings that Tieck evolved, in the course of the next two decades, into one of Germany's leading Novellendichter (novella writers). In 1819 Tieck moved to Dresden, where was appointed Dramaturg (literary historian and editor) of the Dresden theater, a position which at last assured him of a steady income. Relieved of the day-to-day pressure of finding means of support, Tieck was able to concentrate his energies on writing. The result was a steady stream of novellas, few of which one would label masterpieces, but most of them eminently readable. In their social orientation and restrained realism, novellas such as "Die Gemälde" (The Portraits, 1823) and "Die Verlobung" (The Betrothal, 1823) served as well-turned models of the new genre. One of the best-known—and most ambitious—of this series of novellas is *Der Aufruhr in den Cevennen* (The Uprising in the Cévennes Mountains, 1826). Based on the revolt of Calvinists in the south of France in the year 1703, the story in effect defines a subgenre of the novella, the historical novella, a form taken up later in the nineteenth century by Conrad Ferdinand Meyer. Of the later novellas—those written in the 1830s—only one has retained its popularity up to the present day: "Des Lebens Überfluss" (Life's Abundance). In a relaxed pace and with mellow humor Tieck unfolds the tale of a young couple, cut off from parental assistance, trying to live by their wits in the midst of a brutally cold winter. Making the most of their virtual imprisonment in a garret, they pass the time through enlightening conversations, always maintaining an exemplary civility toward one another. In a desperate attempt to keep warm, they begin sawing away at their staircase and using it for firewood, with predictably amusing complications. Having learned of their plight, the girl's parents end their estrangement and come to the couple's aid, thereby giving the story a happy ending. Reading this unprepossessing novella, the student of Tieck's life and works realizes that almost a full lifetime—more than forty years—separates the aging author of "Des Lebens Überfluss" from the youthful enthusiast who, before the turn of the nineteenth century, had penned the Volksmährchen and "Der blonde Eckbert."

In place of the enchanted landscapes of the early Tieck one finds the homely confines of an urban garret; replacing the symbolic "blue flower" of early German Romanticism are the frosted flowers the penurious couple find on their unheated window panes; instead of the unlimited poetic amplitude of the Kunstmärchen, the reader finds the modest parameters of realism of the novella. The world had changed greatly since the heady days of the Jena Romanticists, and Tieck had changed with it.

One more late work is of interest: *Vittoria Accorombona* (1840; translated as *The Roman Matron,* 1845), which was planned as a historical novella along the lines of *Der Aufruhr in den Cevennen* but which grew into a novel. Composed over a four-year period, the novel had its roots in Tieck's student days, when he had read John Webster's play *The White Devil* (1612). Set in sixteenth-century Italy, *Vittoria Accorombona* might almost be read today as a feminist statement. To escape the clutches of a lecherous cardinal, Vittoria agrees to marry his dissolute nephew. A liaison with a charismatic duke leads to dual murders and the arrest of Vittoria, but the duke is able to use his position and his wiles to free and then marry Vittoria. A change of popes results in a puritanical witch-hunt against sinners, however, and Vittoria is assassinated by a spurned suitor. Free of the discursiveness and slack form of Tieck's earlier novels, *Vittoria Accorombona* illustrates again the protean character of Tieck's literary persona, his lifelong ability to adapt to new trends, styles, and forms. The strictness of form in *Vittoria Accorombona* indicates that Tieck understood fully that the time for lyrical excursions, formal experiments, and open-ended novels had passed. Significantly, Tieck refused to beautify late-Renaissance Italy, to gloss over ugly political and social realities, as he had once idealized the Middle Ages: the corruption, cruelty, and bigotry of sixteenth-century Italy are unsparingly set forth. Even the theme of love, so tenderly developed in *Kaiser Octavianus,* is used in *Vittoria Accorombona* as a cipher for the destructive power of passion.

Tieck's declining years were spent in Berlin; thus in a sense his long life came full circle. Yet these years were not happy ones. Despite his stature as the last towering figure of Romanticism, indeed of the Age of Goethe, the aging poet had been treated shabbily in his last years in Dresden, and it was almost as a supplicant that he appealed to Wilhelm IV of Prussia for an appointment at the Prussian theaters. The appointment came, albeit grudgingly, and Tieck was to spend his final decade struggling against pain and infirmity to carry out his duties as Dramaturg and stage director. Amid many failures and frustrations one success stood out: his staging of Shakespeare's *A Midsummer Night's*

Dream in Potsdam in 1843. At last, the greatest Shakespeare authority of his day was able to bring his knowledge to bear on a practical realization of what he felt was the true Elizabethan spirit. Inevitably, Tieck had to make compromises, including the accommodation of Felix Mendelssohn's delightful but un-Elizabethan music, but the production met general acclaim and became a fixture of the repertory in Berlin and other cities for decades. It could be argued that only Max Reinhardt's dazzling production of the same play in Berlin early in the twentieth century eclipsed Tieck's authoritative interpretation.

Tieck died in Berlin on 28 April 1853, just a month before his eightieth birthday. To the end, despite illness and pain, he had kept up his reading, his correspondence, his editing, and even his writing. As always, his door remained open to aspiring artists and writers, some of whom came only to see the shell of a famous man, others who genuinely sought his counsel and support. Among the latter was that late-blooming Romantic Richard Wagner, whose opera *Tannhäuser* owed much to Tieck's tale "Der getreue Eckart und der Tannenhäuser" (1799), and who wished to discuss his planned opera *Lohengrin* with the aged man who had no peer as a re-creator of the spirit of the German Middle Ages. Visits such as Wagner's in 1847 were all the more welcome because Tieck's last years were spent in loneliness. His wife had died in 1837; his beloved daughter and literary protégée Dorothea in 1841; his brother Friedrich in 1851. Of his former friends, mentors, and colleagues, few were left: Wackenroder, Novalis, the Schlegels, and Goethe had long since passed into the realm of shadows and legends. Tieck had not only outlived these giants, he had in a sense outlived himself: he had become an anachronism in an era which, inexorably, was taking on a more "modern," more realistic coloration. Today Tieck occupies a position in German literature not unlike the one assigned to him in the declining years of his own time: he is regarded as an important author, but not a great one. He is remembered chiefly as the creator of "Der blonde Eckbert," *Leben und Tod heiligen Genoveva: Ein Trauerspiel, Der gestiefelte Kater,* and *Franz Sternbalds Wanderungen.* Of his volumes of lyric poetry, few have yielded poems for anthologies; of his many plays, none can be found in theater repertories; of his many novellas, only a few enjoy currency.

But Tieck deserves to be remembered for more than this scant handful of works. Just at a time when early German Romanticism was in danger of being overwhelmed by a surfeit of pure theory, Tieck, acting on poetic intuition alone, demonstrated that Romanticism "worked," that it was a viable form of literary creativity. Alone among the Jena Romanticists, Tieck remained an inspiration to the succeeding waves of middle and late Romantic writers, and to painters and musicians as well. Together with the Schlegel brothers he helped turn the gaze of his fellow Germans, in a nationalistic era, to the literary treasures of other nations: of Spain, Italy, and especially England. Unselfish in his dedication to literature, he helped rescue from obscurity the works of J. M. R. Lenz, Novalis, and Heinrich von Kleist. For more than fifty years, in fame and in obscurity, in good health and bad, this tireless *praeceptor Germaniae* stood as a living link to the greatness of Germany's literary past. His influence upon generations of German writers, as well as English, French, Danish, Russian, and American authors, has been enormous. Hence while it is true that the bulk of his works lies dormant on dust-covered library shelves, Ludwig Tieck cannot be measured against conventional standards of popularity. Like Romanticism itself, his spirit knows no chronological boundaries.

Biographies:

Rudolf Köpke, *Ludwig Tieck. Erinnerungen aus dem Leben des Dichters nach dessen mündlichen und schriftlichen Mitteilungen,* 2 volumes (Leipzig: Brockhaus, 1855; reprinted, 1 volume, Darmstadt: Wissenschaftliche Buchgesellschaft, 1970);

Roger Paulin, *Ludwig Tieck: A Literary Biography* (New York: Oxford University Press, 1985).

References:

Paul Johann Arnold, "Tiecks Novellenbegriff," *Euphorion,* 23 (1921): 258–278;

Richard Benz, *Die deutsche Romantik: Geschichte einer geistigen Bewegung* (Leipzig: Reclam, 1937);

Gordon Birrell, *The Boundless Present: Space and Time in the Literary Fairy Tales of Novalis and Tieck* (Chapel Hill: University of North Carolina Press, 1979);

Anneliese Bodensohn, *Ludwig Tiecks "Kaiser Octavian" als romantische Dichtung* (Frankfurt am Main: Diesterweg, 1937; reprinted, Hildesheim: Gerstenberg, 1973);

Richard Brinkmann, *Romantik in Deutschland: Ein interdisziplinäres Symposion* (Stuttgart: Metzler, 1978);

Walter Bruford, *Die gesellschaftlichen Grundlagen der Goethezeit* (Frankfurt am Main, Berlin & Vienna: Ullstein, 1975);

Pauline Bruny, "Ludwig Tiecks Künstlerdichtungen," dissertation, University of Vienna, 1934;

Willi Busch, *Das Element des Dämonischen in Ludwig Tiecks Dichtungen* (Delitzsch: Walter, 1911);

Alan Corkhill, *The Motif of "Fate" in the Works of Ludwig Tieck* (Stuttgart: Akademischer Verlag, 1978);

Corkhill, "Perspectives on the Language in Ludwig Tieck's Epistolary Novel *William Lovell*," *German Quarterly,* 58 (Spring 1985): 173–183;

Walter Donat, *Die Landschaft bei Ludwig Tieck und ihre historischen Voraussetzungen* (Hildesheim: Gerstenberg, 1973);

Kurt J. Fickert, "The Relevance of the Incest Motif in *Der blonde Eckbert,*" *Germanic Notes,* 13, no. 3 (1982): 33–35;

Gail Finney, "Self-Reflexive Siblings: Incest as Narcissism in Tieck, Wagner, and Thomas Mann," *German Quarterly,* 56, no. 2 (1983): 243–256;

Christa Franke, *Philipp Otto Runge und die Kunstansichten Wackenroders und Tiecks* (Marburg: Elwert, 1974);

Sonia Fritz-Grandjean, *Das Frauenbild im Jugendwerk von Ludwig Tieck als Mosaikstein zu seiner Weltanschauung* (Bern: Lang, 1980);

Lisa Galanski, "Romantische Ironie in Tiecks 'Verkehrter Welt': zum Verständnis einer artistischen Theaterkomödie aus Berliner Frühromantik," *Recherches Germaniques,* 14 (1984): 23–57;

Janis Gellinek, "*Der blonde Eckbert:* A Tieckian Fall from Paradise," in *Lebendige Form: Interpretationen zur deutschen Literatur. Festschrift für Heinrich E. K. Henel,* edited by Jeffrey L. Sammons and Ernst Schürer (Munich: Fink, 1970), pp. 147–166;

Hans Geulen, "Zeit und Allegorie im Erzählvorgang von Ludwig Tiecks Roman *Franz Sternbalds Wanderungen,*" *Germanisch-Romanische Monatsschrift,* 18 (July 1968): 281–298;

Frauke Gries, "Two Critical Essays by Ludwig Tieck: On Literature and its Sociological Aspects," *Monatshefte für den deutschen Unterricht, deutsche Sprache und Literatur,* 66 (Summer 1974): 157–165;

Reinhold Grimm, "Zur Vorgeschichte des Begriffs 'Neuromantik,'" in *Das Nachleben der Romantik in der modernen deutschen Literatur,* edited by Wolfgang Paulsen (Heidelberg: Stiehm, 1969), pp. 32–50;

Klaus Günzel, *König der Romantik: Das Leben des Dichters Ludwig Tieck in Briefen, Selbstzeugnissen und Berichten* (Tübingen: Wunderlich, 1981);

Dieter H. Haenicke, "Ludwig Tieck und 'Der blonde Eckbert,'" in *Vergleichen und Verändern: Festschrift für H. Motekat,* edited by Albrecht Goetze and Günther Pflaum (Munich: Hueber, 1970), pp. 170–187;

Rudolf Haym, *Die romantische Schule: Ein Beitrag zur Geschichte des deutschen Geistes* (Berlin: Gaertner, 1870; reprinted, Hildesheim: Olms, 1961);

Christoph Hering, "Die Poetisierung des Alltäglichen in Tiecks 'Peter Leberecht,'" *Monatshefte,* 49 (December 1957): 361–370;

Harvey W. Hewett-Thayer, "Tieck's Novellen and Contemporary Journalistic Criticism," *Germanic Review,* 3 (October 1928): 328–360;

Valentine C. Hubbs, "Tieck, Eckbert, und das kollektive Unbewusste," *Publications of the Modern Language Association,* 71 (September 1956): 686–693;

Hubbs, "Tieck's Romantic Fairy Tales and Shakespeare," *Studies in Romanticism,* 8 (Summer 1969): 229–234;

Ricarda Huch, *Die Romantik,* 2 volumes, seventh edition (Leipzig: Haessel, 1918);

Raymond M. Immerwahr, "*Der blonde Eckbert* as a Poetic Confession," *German Quarterly,* 34 (March 1961): 103–117;

Immerwahr, *The Esthetic Intent of Tieck's Fantastic Comedy* (St. Louis: Washington University, 1953);

Paul Kluckhohn, *Die deutsche Romantik,* 2 volumes (Bielefeld: Klasing, 1924);

Paul Gerhard Klussmann, "Die Zweideutigkeit des Wirklichen in Ludwig Tiecks Märchennovelen," *Zeitschrift für deutsche Philologie,* 83 (1964): 426–452;

Victor Knight, "The Perceptive Non-Artist: a Study of Tieck's *Der Runenberg,*" *New German Studies,* 10 (Spring 1982): 21–31;

Werner Kohlschmidt, "Der junge Tieck und Wackenroder," in *Die deutsche Romantik: Poetik, Formen und Motive,* edited by Hans Steffen (Göttingen: Vandenhoeck & Ruprecht, 1967), pp. 30–44;

Helmut Kreuzer, "Tiecks 'Gestiefelter Kater,'" *Deutschunterricht,* 15 (December 1963): 33–44;

Otto K. Liedke, "Tieck's 'Der blonde Eckbert.' Das Märchen von Verarmung und Untergang," *German Quarterly,* 44 (May 1971): 311–316;

W. J. Lillyman, "'Des Lebens Überfluß': The Crisis of a Conservative," *German Quarterly,* 46 (May 1973): 393–409;

Lillyman, "Ludwig Tieck's 'Der Runenberg,' The Dimension of Reality," *Monatshefte,* 62 (Fall 1970): 231–244;

Lillyman, *Reality's Dark Dream: The Narrative Fiction of Ludwig Tieck* (Berlin & New York: De Gruyter, 1978);

Percy Matenko, *Tieck and America* (Chapel Hill: University of North Carolina Press, 1954);

Robert Minder, *Un Poète romantique allemand: Ludwig Tieck (1773–1853)* (Paris: Societé d'édition Les Belles lettres, 1936);

Roger Paulin, "Der alte Tieck: Forschungsbericht," in *Zur Literatur der Restaurationsepoche 1815–1848: Forschungsreferate und Aufsätze,* edited by Jost Hermand and Manfred Windfuhr (Stuttgart: Metzler, 1970), pp. 247–262;

Paulin, "Ohne Vaterland kein Dichter: Bermerkungen über historisches Bewußtsein und Dichtergestalt beim späten Tieck," *Literaturwissenschaftliches Jahrbuch,* 13 (1972): 125–150;

Julius Petersen, *Die Wesensbestimmung der deutschen Romantik* (Leipzig: Quelle & Meyer, 1926; reprinted, Darmstadt: Wissenschaftliche Buchgesellschaft, 1968);

Helmut Prang, ed., *Begriffsbestimmung der Romantik* (Darmstadt: Wissenschaftliche Buchgesellschaft, 1968);

Wolfdietrich Rasch, "Blume und Stein. Zur Deutung von Ludwig Tiecks Erzählung 'Der Runenberg,'" in *The Discontinuous Tradition,* edited by Petrus F. Ganz (Oxford: Clarendon Press, 1971), pp. 113–128;

Rasch, "Die Zeit der Klassik und der frühen Romantik," in *Annalen der deutschen Literatur,* second edition, edited by Hans Otto Burger (Stuttgart: Metzler, 1971), pp. 465–550;

Victoria L. Rippere, "Ludwig Tieck's 'Der blonde Eckbert': A Psychological Reading," *Publications of the Modern Language Association,* 85 (May 1970): 473–486;

Gerhard Schneider, *Studien zur deutschen Romantik* (Leipzig: Koehler & Amelang, 1962);

Rolf Schröder, *Novelle und Novellentheorie in der frühen Biedermeierzeit* (Tübingen: Niemeyer, 1970);

Uwe Schweikert, "Jean Paul und Ludwig Tieck," *Jahrbuch der Jean-Paul-Gesellschaft,* 8 (1973): 23–77;

Wulf Segebrecht, ed., *Ludwig Tieck: Wege der Forschung* (Darmstadt: Wissenschaftliche Buchgesellschaft, 1976);

Friedrich Sengle, *Biedermeierzeit: Deutsche Literatur im Spannungsfeld zwischen Restauration und Revolution, 1815–1848,* 2 volumes (Stuttgart: Metzler, 1971–1972);

Emil Staiger, "Ludwig Tieck und der Ursprung der deutschen Romantik," in his *Stilwandel* (Zurich & Freiburg: Atlantis, 1963), pp. 175–204;

Ralf Stamm, *Ludwig Tiecks späte Novellen: Grundlage und Technik des Wunderbaren* (Stuttgart, Berlin, Cologne & Mainz: Kohlhammer, 1973);

Hans Steffen, ed., *Die deutsche Romantik: Poetik, Formen und Motive* (Göttingen: Vandenhoeck & Ruprecht, 1967);

Gerhard Storz, *Klassik und Romantik: Eine stilgeschichtliche Darstellung* (Mannheim, Vienna & Zurich: Bibliographischer Institut, 1972);

Fritz Strich, *Deutsche Klassik und Romantik oder Vollendung und Unendlichkeit* (Munich: Meyer & Jessen, 1922);

Marianne Thalmann, "Hundert Jahre Tieckforschung," *Monatshefte,* 46 (March 1953): 113–123;

Thalmann, *Ludwig Tieck, "Der Heilige von Dresden"* (Berlin: De Gruyter, 1960);

Thalmann, *Ludwig Tieck, der romantische Weltmann aus Berlin* (Bern: Francke, 1955);

Thalmann, *Das Märchen und die Moderne* (Stuttgart: Kohlhammer, 1961);

Thalmann, *Zeichensprache der Romantik* (Heidelberg: Stiehm, 1967);

James Trainer, "The Incest-Theme in the Works of Tieck," *Modern Language Notes,* 76 (December 1961): 819–824;

Trainer, *Ludwig Tieck: From Gothic to Romantic* (London, The Hague & Paris: Mouton, 1964);

Harry Vredeveld, "Ludwig Tieck's 'Der Runenberg': An Archetypical Interpretation," *Germanic Review,* 49 (May 1974): 200–214;

Karlheinz Weigand, *Tiecks William Lovell: Studie zur frühromantischen Antithese* (Heidelberg: Winter, 1975);

Benno von Wiese, "Ludwig Tieck: Des Lebens Überfluss," in *Die deutsche Novelle von Goethe bis Kafka* (Düsseldorf: Bagel, 1960), pp. 117–133;

Edwin H. Zeydel, "Die ersten Beziehungen Ludwig Tiecks zu den Brüdern Schlegel," *Journal of English and German Philology,* 27 (1928): 16–41;

Zeydel, "Ludwig Tieck und das Biedermeier," *Germanisch-romanische Monatsschrift,* 26 (1938): 352–358;

Zeydel, *Ludwig Tieck, The German Romanticist: A Critical Study* (Princeton: Princeton University Press, 1935; reprinted, Hildesheim & New York: Olms, 1971).

Papers:

Ludwig Tieck's papers are at the Staatsbibliothek Preußischer Kulturbesitz, Berlin.

Frank Wedekind

(24 July 1864 – 9 March 1918)

Steve Dowden
Brandeis University

This entry originally appeared in DLB 118: Twentieth-Century
German Dramatists, 1889–1918.

BOOKS: *Der Schnellmaler oder Kunst und Mammon: Große tragikomische Original-Charakterposse* (Zurich: Schabelitz, 1889);

Frühlings Erwachen: Eine Kindertragödie (Zurich: Gross, 1891); translated by Francis J. Ziegler as *The Awakening of Spring* (Philadelphia: Brown, 1909); translated by Samuel A. Eliot, Jr., as *Spring's Awakening,* in *Tragedies of Sex* (London: Henderson, 1923; New York: Boni & Liveright, 1923), pp. 1–110; translated by Frances Fawcett and Stephen Spender as *Spring's Awakening,* in *Five Tragedies of Sex* (London: Vision, 1952; New York: Theatre Arts, 1952), pp. 29–96; translated by Tom Osborn as *Spring Awakening* (London: Calder & Boyars, 1969); translated by Edward Bond as *Spring Awakening* (London: Methuen, 1980); translated by Eric Bentley as *Spring's Awakening,* in *Before Brecht,* edited by Bentley (New York: Applause, 1985);

Kinder und Narren: Lustspiel in vier Aufzügen (Munich: Warth, 1891); revised as *Die junge Welt: Komödie in drei Aufzügen und einem Vorspiel* (Paris: Langen, 1896);

Der Erdgeist: Eine Tragödie (Munich, Paris & Leipzig: Langen, 1895); translated by Eliot as *Erdgeist (Earth-Spirit): A Tragedy in Four Acts* (New York: Boni, 1914); translated by Spender as *Earth-Spirit,* in *Five Tragedies of Sex,* pp. 97–210; translated by Carl Richard Mueller as *Earth Spirit,* in *The Lulu Plays* (Greenwich, Conn.: Fawcett, 1967), pp. 27–106;

Die Fürstin Russalka (Munich: Langen, 1897); translated by Frederick Eisemann as *Princess Russalka* (Boston: Luce, 1919);

Der Liebestrank: Schwank in drei Aufzügen (Paris: Langen, 1899);

Der Kammersänger: Drei Szenen (Paris, Leipzig & Munich: Langen, 1899); translated by Albert Wilhelm

Frank Wedekind in 1894

Boesche as *The Court Singer,* in *The German Classics of the Nineteenth and Twentieth Centuries,* volume 20, edited by Kuno Francke and William G. Howard (New York: German Publication Society, 1914), pp. 360–397;

Der Marquis von Keith (Münchner Scenen): Schauspiel in fünf Aufzügen (Munich: Langen, 1901); translated by Beatrice Gottlieb as *The Marquis of Keith,* in *From the Modern Repertoire,* edited by Bentley, second series (Denver: University of Denver Press, 1952), pp. 123–176; translated by Mueller as *The Marquis of Keith,* in *Masterpieces of the Modern German Theater,* edited by Robert W. Corrigan (New York: Collier, 1967), pp. 236–310;

So ist das Leben: Schauspiel in fünf Akten (Munich: Langen, 1902); translated by Ziegler as *Such Is Life* (Philadelphia: Brown, 1912); revised as *König Nicolo oder So ist das Leben: Schauspiel in drei Aufzügen und neun Bildern, mit einem Prolog* (Munich: Müller, 1911); translated by Martin Esslin as *König Nicolo oder So ist das Leben: Schauspiel in drei Aufzügen und neun Bildern, mit einem Prolog,* in *The Genius of the German Theater,* edited by Esslin (New York: New American Library, 1968), pp. 459–522;

Mine-Haha oder Über die körperliche Erziehung der jungen Mädchen: Aus Helene Engels schriftlichem Nachlaß herausgegeben (Munich: Langen, 1903);

Die Büchse der Pandora: Tragödie in drei Aufzügen (Berlin: Cassirer, 1904; revised, 1906; revised edition, Munich: Müller, 1911); translated by Eliot as *Pandora's Box* (New York: Boni, 1914); translated by Spender as *Pandora's Box,* in *Five Tragedies of Sex,* pp. 211–302; translated by Mueller as *Pandora's Box,* in *The Lulu Plays,* pp. 107–166;

Hidalla oder Sein und Haben: Schauspiel in fünf Akten (Munich: Marchlewski, 1904); revised as *Karl Hetmann, der Zwerg-Riese (Hidalla): Schauspiel in fünf Akten* (Munich: Müller, 1911);

Die vier Jahreszeiten: Gedichte (Munich: Langen, 1905);

Totentanz: Drei Szenen (Munich: Langen, 1906); revised as *Tod und Teufel (Totentanz): Drei Szenen* (Berlin: Cassirer, 1909); translated by Eliot as *Damnation!,* in *Tragedies of Sex,* pp. 303–347; translated by Spender as *Death and Devil,* in *Five Tragedies of Sex,* pp. 303–336;

Feuerwerk: Erzählungen (Munich: Langen, 1906)–includes "Der greise Freier," translated by Ziegler as *The Grisley Suitor* (Philadelphia: Brown, 1911);

Die Zensur: Theodizee in einem Akt (Berlin: Cassirer, 1908);

Musik: Sittengemälde in vier Bildern (Munich: Langen, 1908);

Oaha: Schauspiel in fünf Aufzügen (Berlin: Cassirer, 1908); revised as *Till Eulenspiegel: Komödie in vier Aufzügen* (Munich: Müller, 1916);

Der Stein der Weisen: Eine Geisterbeschwörung (Berlin: Cassirer, 1909); revised as *Der Stein der Weisen oder Laute, Armbrust und Peitsche: Eine Geisterbeschwörung* (Munich: Müller, 1920);

In allen Satteln gerecht: Komödie in einem Aufzug (Munich & Leipzig: Müller, 1910);

Schauspielkunst: Ein Glossarium (Munich & Leipzig: Müller, 1910); translated by Mueller as "The Art of Acting: A Glossary," in *The Modern Theatre,* edited by Corrigan (New York: Macmillan, 1964), pp. 126–159;

In allen Sätteln gerecht: Komödie in einem Aufzug (Munich & Leipzig: Müller, 1910);

In allen Wassern gewaschen: Tragödie in einem Aufzug (Munich: Müller, 1910);

Mit allen Hunden gehetzt: Schauspiel in einem Aufzug (Munich: Müller, 1910);

Felix und Galathea (Berlin: Meyer, 1911);

Franziska: Ein modernes Mysterium in fünf Akten (Munich: Müller, 1912);

Schloß Wetterstein: Schauspiel in drei Akten (Munich: Müller, 1912); translated by Spender as *Castle Wetterstein,* in *Five Tragedies of Sex,* pp. 337–434;

Lulu: Tragödie in fünf Aufzügen mit einem Prolog (Munich & Leipzig: Müller, 1913);

Simson oder Scham und Eifersucht: Dramatisches Gedicht in drei Akten (Munich: Müller, 1914);

Bismarck: Historisches Schauspiel in fünf Akten (Munich: Müller, 1916);

Herakles: Dramatisches Gedicht in drei Akten (Munich: Müller, 1917);

Überfürchtenichts (Munich: Müller, 1917);

Lautenlieder: 53 Lieder mit eigenen und fremden Melodien, edited by Artur Kutscher (Berlin: Drei Masken, 1920);

Rabbi Esra (Munich: Müller, 1924);

Ein Genußmensch: Schauspiel in vier Aufzügen (Munich: Müller, 1924);

Das arme Mädchen: Ein Chanson (Lindau: Thorbecke, 1948);

Chansons (Munich: Desch, 1951);

Gedichte und Chansons (Frankfurt am Main & Hamburg: Bücherei, 1968);

Die Tagebücher: Ein erotisches Leben, edited by Gerhard Hay (Frankfurt am Main: Athenäum, 1986);

Die Büchse der Pandora: Eine Monstretragödie, edited by Peter Zadek (Hamburg: Programmbuch des Deutschen Schauspielhauses, 1988).

Collections: *Gesammelte Werke,* 9 volumes, edited by Artur Kutscher and Joachim Friedenthal (Munich: Müller, 1912–1921);

Ausgewählte Werke, edited by Fritz Strich (Berlin: Volksverband der Bücherfreunde, 1923); *Werke in drei Bänden,* 3 volumes, edited by Manfred Hahn (Berlin: Aufbau, 1969).

Editions in English: *Rabbi Ezra; The Victim: Two Stories,* translated by Francis J. Ziegler (Philadelphia: Brown, 1911);

Tragedies of Sex, translated by Samuel A. Eliot, Jr. (London: Henderson, 1923; New York: Boni & Liveright, 1923);

Five Tragedies of Sex, translated by Frances Fawcett and Stephen Spender (London: Vision, 1952; New York: Theatre Arts, 1952); reprinted without *Spring's Awakening* as *The Lulu Plays & Other Sex Tragedies,* translated by Spender (London: Calder & Boyars, 1972; New York: Riverrun, 1977);

The Lulu Plays, translated by Carl Richard Mueller (Greenwich, Conn.: Fawcett, 1967).

PLAY PRODUCTIONS: *Der Erdgeist,* Leipzig, Krystall-Palast, 25 February 1898;

Der Kammersänger, Berlin, Neues Theater, 10 December 1899;

Der Marquis von Keith, Berlin, Residenztheater, 11 October 1901;

So ist das Leben, Munich, Schauspielhaus, 22 February 1902; revised as *König Nicolo oder So ist das Leben,* Leipzig, Schauspielhaus, 15 January 1919;

Liebstrank, Nuremberg, Intimes Theater, 24 October 1903;

Die Büchse der Pandora: Eine Tragödie in drei Aufzügen, Nuremberg, Intimes Theater, 1 February 1904;

Karl Hetmann: Der Zwerg-Riese, Munich, Schauspielhaus, 18 February 1905;

Lulu, Nuremberg, Intimes Theater, 18 April 1905;

Totentanz, Nuremberg, Intimes Theater, 2 May 1906; revised as *Tod und Teufel,* Berlin, Künstlerhaus Werkstatt der Werdenden, 29 April 1912;

Frühlings Erwachen, Berlin, Kammerspiele des Deutschen Theaters, 22 November 1906;

Musik, Nuremberg, Intimes Theater, 11 January 1908;

Die junge Welt, Munich, Schauspielhaus, 22 April 1908;

Die Zensur, Munich, Schauspielhaus, 27 July 1909;

Der Stein der Weisen, Vienna, Kleine Bühne, 23 January 1911;

Oaha: Die Satire der Satire, Munich, Lustspielhaus, 23 December 1911; revised as *Till Eulenspiegel,* Munich, Kammerspiele, 1 December 1916;

Franziska, Munich, Münchner Kammerspiele, 30 November 1912;

Simson oder Scham und Eifersucht, Berlin, Lessing-theater, 24 January 1914;

Felix und Galothea, Munich, Unionsaal, 25 July 1914;

Der Schnellmaler oder Kunst und Mammon, Munich, Kammerspiele, 29 July 1916;

Schloß Wetterstein, Zurich, Pfauentheater, 17 November 1917;

Elins Erweckung, Hamburg, Kammerspiele, 16 March 1919;

Herakles, Munich, Prinzregententheater, 1 September 1919;

Das Sonnenspektrum, Berlin, Tribune, 23 September 1922;

Bismarck, Weimar, Deutsches Nationaltheater, 30 October 1926;

Die Büchse der Pandora: Eine Monstretragödie, Hamburg, Deutsches Schauspielhaus, 13 February 1988.

OTHER: "Die Furcht vor dem Tode," in *Frank Wedekind und das Theater* (Berlin: Drei Masken, 1915), pp. 83–84.

SELECTED PERIODICAL PUBLICATION–
UNCOLLECTED: *Die Büchse der Pandora: Eine Monstretragödie, Theater heute,* 17 (April 1988): 42–57.

From the standpoint of attitudes about women and eroticism, modernist sensibilities can be dated from Jack the Ripper's internationally notorious sex murders in 1888. His widely publicized crimes seized the imagination of all Europe, suddenly thrusting into public view a world that Wilhelmine Germany, like Victorian and Edwardian England, had passed over in silence. In the popular imagination the Ripper soon came to symbolize the demonic claims of sexual instinct, aggression, and domination, the destructive passions that seemed to threaten the orderly conduct of middle-class life. These same themes quickly spanned the geography of literary modernism, from D. H. Lawrence's England to Arthur Schnitzler's Austria-Hungary. In the German theater they are above all associated with the work of Frank Wedekind, whose well-known femme fatale, Lulu, dies horribly at the hands of Jack the Ripper.

In his most enduring works, *Frühlings Erwachen* (published, 1891; performed, 1906; translated as *The Awakening of Spring,* 1909) and the two Lulu plays, Wedekind probed sexual topics on the German stage with greater frankness and more humor than the naturalists had. Naturalism dominated German theater when Wedekind began making his mark in the 1890s, and its most celebrated representatives were Henrik Ibsen and Gerhart Hauptmann. But in its emphasis on social facts, detached objectivity, and a more or less scientistic realism, the naturalist movement belonged to the nineteenth century. Though Wedekind shared its spirit of enlightenment and demystification, his aesthetic is that of nascent modernism. Not only does he favor sexual instinct and the irrational as thematic material and alienated nonconformists as heroes but he also begins the modernist break with the conventions of realistic representation on the stage. Wedekind's mannered, tragicomic style helped cut a path toward the spiritual style of expressionism, the alienation effects of Bertolt Brecht, and the tragicomic satire of Friedrich Dürrenmatt and Max Frisch. Wedekind's antipsychological theater made effective use of various nonrealistic devices—such as the grotesque, the fantastic, and highly stylized and richly ambiguous dialogue—and he exploited a seriocomic tone that treats grave issues with all due gravity yet manages to generate an undercurrent of comic, usually satiric, irony.

Wedekind's social stance was that of an implacable Aufklärer (enlightener): his theater aims to unmask the mendacity and illusions of his culture. He was emphatically antibourgeois, a bohemian moralist opposed to the middle-class morality of imperial Germany and Austria. His drama characteristically satirizes the German bourgeoisie's most delicate subjects: sex and money. The spirit of liberal opposition seemed to run in Wedekind's family. His father, Friedrich Wilhelm Wedekind, a physician disenchanted with the failed revolutions of 1848, left Germany in 1849 for political reasons. He lived for a time in the United States, where he met Emilie Kammerer, an Austrian singer then engaged at the German Theater in San Francisco. They married and returned to Europe. Their son, named Benjamin Franklin Wedekind in memory of the American years, was born in Hannover on 24 July 1864; but he grew up at Schloß Lenzburg in the canton of Aargau, Switzerland, where the family moved in 1872. He attended school in Switzerland and went to the Universities of Lausanne and Munich, where he was a less than earnest student of law. After his father cut off his funds in 1886, Wedekind became the head of advertising for the Maggi food company of Zurich. By this time he was also consorting with the intellectuals, artists, and socialists of Zurich's lively bohemian scene, including the naturalist playwright Gerhart Hauptmann.

Though Wedekind shared the great naturalist's basic social sympathies, he showed little interest in exploiting the working class or rural poor as a literary theme. Instead, Wedekind was attracted personally and intellectually to artists, circus performers, pickpockets, prostitutes, and other inhabitants of the fringe of bourgeois culture. He was not interested in realistic portraiture of social and political concerns; nor did he claim insight into the individual souls of his slightly outlandish characters. Rather, Wedekind explored the ambiguous moral world that lies beneath social appearances and beyond the individual's inner life. He did not explore personal subjectivity so much as its foundations in nature and society. Human nature itself is Wedekind's basic theme. He shows it to be endlessly flexible, especially in its sexual, dominating, and acquisitive instincts. Because modern culture has been distorted by decadent values, human nature can only be represented in alienated, exaggerated types such as the sexual monster Lulu or the artist-swindler the Marquis of Keith and their clash with social and moral conventions. His

first play, *Kinder und Narren* (Children and Fools; published, 1891), written in 1889, lampoons the naturalist's obsession with impartial observation. The naturalist kisses his wife and makes notes for a play over her shoulder at the same time.

Wedekind perceived naturalism as the least truthful form of art. Art is by its nature not natural but reflective, at a critical remove from nature. (The play was first performed in its revised form as *Die junge Welt* [The Young World; published, 1896] in 1908.) The playwright Alwa Schön in *Die Büchse der Pandora* (performed, 1904; published, 1904; translated as *Pandora's Box,* 1914) speaks for Wedekind when he says, "Das ist der Fluch, der auf unserer jungen Literatur lastet, daß wir viel zu literarisch sind. Wir kennen keine anderen Fragen und Probleme als solche, die unter Schriftstellern und Gelehrten auftauchen. Unser Gesichtskreis reicht über die Grenzen unserer Zunftinteressen nicht hinaus. Um wieder auf die Fährte einer großen gewaltigen Kunst zu gelangen, müßten wir uns möglichst viel unter Menschen bewegen, die nie in ihrem Leben ein Buch gelesen haben, denen die einfachsten animalischen Instinkte bei ihren Handlungen maßgebend sind" (That's the curse that burdens present-day literature: we are much too literary. The only questions and problems we have are the ones that crop up among writers and scholars. Our field of vision doesn't reach beyond our vested interests. To get back on the track of a great and passionate art, we'd have to live as much as we can among people who have never in their lives read a book, among people whose actions are governed by the simplest animal instincts). Wedekind's own response to Alwa's injunction was to join the circus and travel throughout Europe, writing poems, skits, and stories. After his father died in 1888 Wedekind came into enough money to move to Munich in the summer of 1889 and take up residence among the people who interested him most: bohemians, cabaret artists, poets, and vamps.

His first published drama, *Frühlings Erwachen,* was written in the winter of 1890–1891. Children are a good example of people "governed by the simplest animal instincts," as Alwa Schön puts it. The play's theme is the disastrous results for children of middle-class prudery. In nineteen episodic scenes Wedekind follows several adolescents as they blunder toward sexual enlightenment through a maze of misapprehension, disinformation, and dimly understood emotions. Melchior Gabor seduces fourteen-year-old Wendla Bergmann, whose mother had been too embarrassed to tell her the facts of life. When she becomes pregnant her parents force her to undergo an abortion, which is botched, and Wendla dies. Melchior, the innocent seducer, is banished to reform school. Another boy, Moritz Stiefel, is driven to suicide by his teachers, grotesque and fatuous pedants who show Wedekind in his most satirical mode.

Frühlings Erwachen marked a distinct break with the theater of naturalism because of its mixture of lyrical, prosaic, and ironic language; its flights into the purely imaginary, as in the final scene when Moritz Stiefel returns from the dead; and its grotesque comedy, such as the high pathos of Hänschen Rilow, a masturbating bluebeard who takes pornographic photos of women with him into the lavatory, only to flush his discarded mistresses down the toilet—with a grand poetic flourish—once they have served him. But little Hänschen and his drowned Ophelias did not amuse everybody. The Wilhelmine authorities perceived in Hänschen and his friends an affront to public decency. *Frühlings Erwachen,* though a major theatrical success when it finally made its way past the censors onto the stage in 1906, still had to be presented in expurgated versions.

Between 1891 and 1895 Wedekind lived out his bohemian fantasies in Paris and worked on his Lulu plays. He originally composed the two dramas as a single five-act tragedy titled "Die Büchse der Pandora: Eine Monstretragödie" (Pandora's Box: A Monster Tragedy). But when he turned the manuscript over to Albert Langen, his Munich publisher, only the first half was accepted for publication; the second half no doubt seemed too violent and sexually charged to escape censorship. Wedekind revised the first half and added a fourth act, and it was published under the title *Der Erdgeist* (translated as *Erdgeist [Earth-Spirit],* 1914) in 1895; in later versions the title was shortened to *Erdgeist.* The original drama's final two acts, with a new first act added, were published in 1904 under the title *Die Büchse der Pandora.* The authorities speedily confiscated the edition and charged Wedekind and the publisher, Bruno Cassirer, with disseminating pornography, but the defendants were acquitted.

Wedekind's Lulu plays did not fare well at the beginning of their stage life. *Der Erdgeist* was only a modest success when it premiered in 1898, and the censors were unwilling to release *Die Büchse der Pandora* for public performance. The piece was seldom staged, and most of the few productions were private presentations. The best known of these private productions was organized in 1905 at Vienna's Trianon Theater by the satirist Karl Kraus, who sympathized with what he considered to be Wedekind's progressive outlook on women and sexuality and was eager to promote their shared views. Wedekind, who frequently acted in his own works, played Jack the Ripper in Kraus's production. The original 1895 version had to wait almost a century to be staged: in 1988 the West German director

Peter Zadek mounted a highly acclaimed production of the play in Hamburg and published the text, which had been available only in manuscript form, in the journal *Theater heute* (Theater Today).

Lulu has become an icon of fin de siècle feminine sexuality: a dangerous, man-devouring, mythical beast. In Wedekind's plays she is not strictly an embodiment of sexual instinct; rather, she is the embodiment of sexual instinct that has been conditioned by economic circumstance. In *Der Erdgeist* her chief antagonist is Dr. Schön, the manipulative newspaper tycoon whose wealth, success, and self-esteem are predicated on his cold-blooded rationality and pretense of bourgeois respectability. If he is to prosper he must exclude the irrational, indecent Lulu from his world, and he attempts to hold her in abeyance by marrying her off to other men. Naturally, marriage proves too flimsy a vessel to contain Lulu's tantalizing sexuality. Schön further tries to secure himself from her by marrying a respectable woman of high social rank, but in the end Lulu prevails: the intrusion of the irrational (Lulu's irrepressible sexuality) into the autonomous rationality of his world (the conventional but hypocritical values of business and family) upsets and finally destroys that world. In a jealous rampage the otherwise cool and rational businessman tries to murder Lulu. In the end she kills him in a scene that is a fine example of Wedekind's blackest comedy.

Die Büchse der Pandora finds Lulu in jail for the murder of Schön; her escape is arranged by some of her friends. Without Schön's economic protection, Lulu is led to her destruction by her sexuality. Sexual passion leads her to death because, in Wedekind's view, it belongs to nature and cannot be reconciled with civilization. With Schön's death even the pretense of civilization falls away, and Lulu finds herself among savage men eager to buy and sell her. She flees to London and becomes a prostitute. Lulu's yearning for release—she dreams of falling into the hands of a rapist-murderer—reveals Wedekind's antifeminist notion of sexual emancipation. Like Kraus and Sigmund Freud, Wedekind understands women to be less than fully rational creatures; they are determined by their sexual essence, a force that sits uneasily in civilization. Jack the Ripper serves as the exponentially heightened image of bourgeois morality exacting vengeance on Lulu for her transgressions. Wedekind's intention is the emancipation of female sexuality, but Lulu's decline and horrifyingly brutal death militate against his purpose. Jack's butchery, like Lulu's sexuality, seems to be a mythic force of nature that is beyond history and culture and inaccessible to reason. Whether Wedekind intends it or not, Lulu's murder has the effect of a cautionary tale, a warning for all right-minded people to beware the female lust and the male aggression it elicits. Wedekind purchases sexual freedom for women at the price of their humanity.

Under the pseudonyms "Hieronymus" and "Hermann" he was a frequent contributor to the satirical journal *Simplicissimus,* founded in 1896 by his publisher Langen. When Kaiser Wilhelm II became the butt of Wedekind's satirical poetry, a warrant was issued for his arrest. Wedekind fled to Zurich and then to Paris. He turned himself over to the police in June 1899 and spent seven months in jail, convicted of lèse-majesté for his poems "Meerfahrt" (Sea Journey) and "Im Heiligen Land" (In the Holy Land), in *Simplicissimus,* volume three, numbers 31 and 32, which satirized the Kaiser's trip to Palestine. After his release from confinement in March 1900 Wedekind turned his attention more and more to cabaret, a genre that had interested him since the mid 1890s. His act at the Elf Scharfrichter (Eleven Executioners), a cabaret that opened in Munich in 1901, was highly successful. It had been conceived as something of a nightclub counterpart to the irreverent journals *Simplicissimus* and *Jugend* (Youth) and featured political satire, social parody, pantomime, dancing, and songs. Wedekind, the "executioner" of Wilhelmine moral and sexual complacency, wrote and performed in skits and dialogues, sang his own compositions, and accompanied himself on the lute and guitar.

Wedekind's success as a cabaret performer kept him solvent and made his reputation with the public. But he regarded the work as a distraction from his true calling, writing plays. *Der Marquis von Keith* (1901; translated as *The Marquis of Keith,* 1952), which Wedekind finished during his house arrest, develops a theme that he had introduced in the Lulu plays: the collusion between commerce and art. The Marquis von Keith is a male version of Lulu. Her essence is sexual pleasure, which Wedekind links to art through her profession as a dancer. Keith's essence is similarly aesthetic: he is an amoral pleasure seeker involved in the business end of the art world. Both Lulu and Keith live from the illusions they create for rich men. The Marquis von Keith, who claims to be of noble Scottish descent, is a swindler who by trickery and deceit is trying to fund a center for the arts. But Keith, the aesthete, cannot compete with the brutal forces of commerce. The least artistic figures of the play, vulgar tycoons, discover that Keith is a con artist and take the project away from him. Keith loses everything because he is a true artist. His life and identity, like Lulu's, are works of art in the spirit of Friedrich Nietzsche's dictum that the world can be justified only as an aesthetic phenomenon. When

challenged to justify his existence, Keith exclaims to his moralist alter ego, Ernst Scholz: "Ich brauche keine Existenzberechtigung! Ich habe niemanden um meine Existenz gebeten und entnehme daraus die Berechtigung, meine Existenz nach meinem Kopfe zu existieren" (I don't need to justify my existence! I didn't ask to exist, which is precisely why I claim the right to exist as I choose). But an aesthetic life of the kind lived by Keith and Lulu is an illusion that founders on the reality principle of money.

Wedekind thought *Der Marquis von Keith* the best of all his plays, but when it premiered in 1901 it was received coolly. He complained that audiences, actors, and critics schooled in the conventions of naturalist theater failed to understand his analytic style. Wedekind argued that the psychological theater of naturalism did not require acting, since the performers were supposed to appear lifelike; the reason he frequently took to the stage in his own plays was to demonstrate the proper handling of them. But the critics failed to appreciate his style as an innovation, patronizingly regarding his exaggerated, mannered performance as dilettantish. Only gradually did the Wedekind style find acceptance. The major breakthrough came in 1906 when Max Reinhardt, one of the most prominent directors in Germany and Austria, staged the premiere of *Frühlings Erwachen* in Berlin. From that point Wedekind's fame and fortune rose. In 1906 he married the Austrian actress Tilly Newes, who had played Lulu in Kraus's Viennese production of *Die Büchse der Pandora.* Initially they lived in Berlin, but in 1908 they settled in Munich. The union produced two daughters, Pamela and Kadidja; but it was not a happy marriage, evidently because of Wedekind's possessive attitude toward Tilly.

The newfound success of the stage works taught the middle-aged bohemian that his fortune lay in play writing, which meant an end to his attempts at a major prose work. His novel *Mine-Haha* (1903), which deals with the sexual education of girls, remained a fragment. His copious output for the stage continued to explore variations on his main themes: art, sex, and money. Earlier works began to appear or reappear on stages around Germany and Austria, and new works were eagerly received—insofar as they were able to escape the censors. His popular comedy *Der Kammersänger* (1899; translated as *The Court Singer,* 1914) considers a philistine artist who panders to his adoring public. *So ist das Leben* (1902; translated as Such Is Life, 1912), which is in part Wedekind's reckoning with the lèse-majesté affair, also deals with the artist's life. After King Nicolo of Umbria is overthrown by a commoner, his aesthetic inner nature asserts itself, and he becomes a traveling performer. Unwilling to relinquish his right to the highest place in society, he is repeatedly mocked, jailed, and banished for claiming to be the true king. He dies as a court jester, struggling for recognition in a society that does not understand him. Like the unacknowledged King Nicolo, the scientist Karl Hetmann of *Hidalla* (1904; performed as *Karl Hetmann*, 1905) is a misunderstood artistic spirit. His grand design–a Nietzschean eugenics project that links sex, philosophy, and moral theory–is to create a race of physically and morally superior human beings. But Hetmann himself is a deformed dwarf–Wedekind's image of the alienated artist in late-nineteenth-century Germany. Betrayed by a businessman (modeled on Wedekind's publisher Langen), subjected to ridicule, declared insane, and institutionalized, Hetmann hangs himself when he is offered a job as a circus clown. Commentators have generally connected Wedekind's disillusioned artist figures with his own disillusionment over the role of art in society. Wedekind's never-ending wrangles with the censors and his conflicts with his publishers over money no doubt contributed to his pessimism.

Other dramas on the artist theme include *Die Zensur* (Censorship; published, 1908; performed, 1909), which measures the sensual claims of art against the claims of bourgeois culture, and *Oaha* (published, 1908; performed, 1911), which dramatizes the dealings of an opportunistic publisher who, once again, bears a strong resemblance to Langen. Still other plays of Wedekind's middle period stress his abiding interest in women and sexual morality. In *Totentanz* (Dance of Death, 1906; translated as *Damnation!*, 1923) a feminist attempts to liberate a prostitute from a bordello and is herself converted to sensuality, which is presented as a highly ambiguous value. Wedekind linked together three one-act plays to form *Schloß Wetterstein* (published, 1912; performed, 1917; translated as *Castle Wetterstein*, 1952), a meretricious farrago of the Lulu thematics in which the sensual prostitute Effie drinks acid to prove her love for the sadistic killer Tschamper. *Franziska* (1912) depicts an adventuress, a female Faustus, who experiments with the entire gamut of roles open to women. In the end she finds fulfillment in motherhood–a kind of mystical apotheosis promised in the play's subtitle, *Ein modernes Mysterium* (A Modern Mystery). Whether or not Wedekind intended the conclusion ironically has been a point of contention.

When World War I broke out in 1914, Wedekind was one of the few pacifists among German intellectuals. He supported the antiwar position of his friend Heinrich Mann, but he did not share Mann's republicanism; Wedekind believed that Germany was inherently disposed toward monarchy.

Late in 1914 a severe bout of appendicitis put Wedekind in the hospital. He was operated on at the end of December and again in April 1915. The wound could not be sutured and had to remain open. Wedekind's convalescence lasted until late in the summer of 1915, but even then the scar had not healed completely. By late fall it had become infected, forcing Wedekind back into bed until December. He returned to his acting and writing in 1916, responding to the nationalist fervor of the war years with his drama *Bismarck* (published, 1916; performed, 1926). The play takes a somewhat nostalgic view of Otto von Bismarck as the true German statesman, a clearsighted leader of the sort conspicuously absent in Wedekind's time. Bismarck's cunning statecraft, rich in intrigue, links him to Wedekind's trickster figures. Shortly after completing *Bismarck* in 1916 he began work on another heroic figure. *Herakles* (Hercules; published, 1917; performed, 1919), his last major drama, depicts the heroic struggle of the individual against his fate, which here takes the form of the passionate instincts of lust, violence, and revenge. Wedekind's friend and biographer Artur Kutscher emphasizes the element of autobiographical stylization in Wedekind's Hercules. The dramatist saw himself engaged in a similar heroic struggle over the years, not unlike King Nicolo and Karl Hetmann. During his career Wedekind fought for artistic self-determination, for his version of enlightened sexuality, and against hypocrisies of every sort.

By January 1917 another operation was necessary. Later in the year Wedekind seemed well enough to act and travel. By that time his marriage was breaking up; his wife attempted suicide, which was a severe blow to him. She recovered, but the incision from his operation still would not heal. On 2 March 1918 he was operated on for a final time. The operation was successful, but in his weakened state he caught a cold that developed into pneumonia. He died on 9 March.

Letters:

Gesammelte Briefe, 2 volumes, edited by Fritz Strich (Munich: Müller, 1924).

Bibliographies:

Ernst Stobbe, *Bibliographie der Erstausgaben Frank Wedekinds,* Almanach der Bücherstube auf das Jahr 1921 (Munich: Stobbe, 1920);

Hartmut Vinçon, *Frank Wedekind,* Sammlung Metzler, 230 (Stuttgart: Metzler, 1987).

Biographies:

Artur Kutscher, *Frank Wedekind: Sein Leben und seine Werke,* 3 volumes (Munich: Müller, 1922–1931);

Tilly Wedekind, *Lulu: Die Rolle meines Lebens* (Munich: Rütter & Loehning, 1969);

Günter Seehaus, *Frank Wedekind in Selbstzeugnissen und Bilddokumenten* (Reinbek: Rowohlt, 1974).

References:

Kathy Acker, "Lulu," *Performing Arts Journal,* 30, no. 10 (1986–1987): 102–117;

Theodor Adorno, "Über den Nachlaß Frank Wedekinds," in his *Gesammelte Werke,* volume 11 (Frankfurt am Main: Suhrkamp, 1974), pp. 627–633;

Ann Taylor Allen, *Satire and Society in Wilhelmine Germany: "Kladderadatsch" and "Simplicissimus" 1890–1914* (Lexington: University of Kentucky Press, 1984);

Peter von Becker, "Ästhetik und Ästhetisierung des Schreckens: Wie realistisch ist, wie präfaschistisch wirkt heute Wedekind?," *Theater heute,* 19 (1978): 21–26;

Alban Berg, *Lulu: Texte, Materialien, Kommentare,* edited by Attila Csampai and Dietmar Holland (Reinbek & Munich: Rowohlt/Ricordi, 1985);

Alan Best, *Frank Wedekind* (London: Wolff, 1975);

Gordon Birrell, "The *Wollen/Sollen* Equation in Wedekind's *Frühlings Erwachen," Germanic Review,* 57 (Summer 1982): 115–122;

Elizabeth Boa, *The Sexual Circus: Wedekind's Theatre of Subversion* (Oxford: Blackwell, 1987); Bertolt Brecht, "Frank Wedekind," in *Brecht on Theatre,* edited by John Willett (London: Methuen, 1964), pp. 3–4;

Angela Carter, "Femmes Fatales," in her *Nothing Sacred: Selected Writings* (London: Virago, 1982), pp. 119–123;

Edson Chick, *Dances of Death: Wedekind, Brecht, Dürrenmatt, and the Satiric Tradition,* Studies in German Literature, Linguistics and Culture, 19 (Columbia, S.C.: Camden House, 1984);

Carol Diethe, *Aspects of Distorted Sexual Attitudes in German Expressionist Drama: Wedekind, Kokoschka, Kaiser* (Bern: Lang, 1988);

Friedrich Dürrenmatt, "Bekenntnisse eines Plagiators," in *Deutsche Literaturkritik der Gegenwart,* edited by Hans Mayer (Stuttgart: Goverts, 1971), pp. 426–432;

Wilhelm Emrich, "Immanuel Kant und Frank Wedekind," in his *Polemik: Streitschriften, Pressefehden und kritische Essays um Prinzipien, Methoden und Maßstäbe der Literaturkritik* (Frankfurt am Main: Athenäum, 1968), pp. 56–60;

Gail Finney, *Women in Modern Drama* (Ithaca, N.Y.: Cornell University Press, 1989);

Sander Gilman, "The Nietzsche Murder Case," *New Literary History,* 14 (Winter 1983): 359–372;

Sol Gittleman, *Frank Wedekind* (New York: Twayne, 1969);

Friedrich Gundolf, *Frank Wedekind* (Munich: Langen/ Müller, 1954);

Edward Harris, "Freedom and Degradation: Frank Wedekind's Career as Cabaretist," in *The Turn of the Century: German Literature and Art 1890–1915,* edited by Gerald Chapple and H. H. Schulte, Modern German Studies, 5 (Bonn: Bouvier, 1981), pp. 493–506;

Wolfgang Hartwig, ed., *Der Marquis von Keith: Text und Materialien* (Berlin: De Gruyter, 1965);

J. L. Hibberd, "Frank Wedekind and the First World War," *Modern Language Review,* 82 (January 1987): 119–141;

Hibberd, "The Spirit of the Flesh: Wedekind's Lulu," *Modern Language Review,* 79 (April 1984): 336–355;

John Hibbert, "Frank Wedekind and Lassalle," *German Life and Letters,* 42 (January 1989): 113–128;

Hibbert, "'Die Wiedervereinigung von Kirche und Freudenhaus': Wedekind's *Die Zensur* and His Ideas on Religion," *Colloquia Germanica,* 19 (1986): 47–67;

Alfons Höger, "Hetärismus und bürgerliche Gesellschaft im Frühwerk Frank Wedekinds," *Text und Kontext,* Supplement 12 (1981): 1–208;

Hans-Jochen Irmer, *Frank Wedekind: Werk und Wirkung* (Berlin: Henschelverlag, 1975);

Peter Jelavich, *Munich and Theatrical Modernism: Politics, Playwriting, and Performance 1890–1914* (Cambridge, Mass.: Harvard University Press, 1985);

Volker Klotz, *Dramaturgie des Publikums* (Munich: Hanser, 1976);

Karl Kraus, "Die Büchse der Pandora," *Die Fackel,* 7, no. 182 (1905): 1–18;

Anna K. Kuhn, "Der aphoristische Dialog im *Marquis von Keith,*" in *Theatrum Mundi,* edited by Edward R. Haymes, Houston German Studies, 2 (Munich: Fink, 1980), pp. 80–92;

Robin Lenman, "Politics and Culture: The State and the Avant-Garde in Munich 1886–1914," in *Society and Politics in Wilhelmine Germany,* edited by Richard J. Evans (London: Croom Helm, 1978), pp. 90–111;

Heinrich Mann, "Erinnerungen an Frank Wedekind," in his *Essays* (Hamburg: Claasen, 1960), pp. 243–262;

Thomas Mann, "Über eine Szene von Wedekind," in his *Altes und Neues: Kleine Prosa aus fünf Jahrzehnten* (Frankfurt am Main: Fischer, 1961), pp. 31–36;

Kurt Martens, "Erinnerungen an Frank Wedekind, 1897–1900," *Der neue Merkur,* 4 (1920): 537–549;

Thomas Medicus, *"Die große Liebe": Ökonomie und Konstruktion der Körper im Werk Frank Wedekinds,* Reihe Metro, 11 (Marburg: Guttandin & Hoppe, 1982);

David Midgley, "Wedekind's Lulu: From 'Schauertragödie' to Social Comedy," *German Life and Letters,* 38 (April 1985): 205–232;

Libuse Monikova, "Das totalitäre Glück: Frank Wedekind," *Neue Rundschau,* 96 (1985): 118–125;

Marc Muylaert, *L'image de al femme dans l'ouvre de Frank Wedekind,* Stuttgarter Arbeiten zur Germanistik, 159 (Stuttgart: Heinz Akademischer Verlag, 1985);

Ronald Peacock, "The Ambiguity of Wedekind's Lulu," *Oxford German Studies,* 9 (1978): 105–118;

Henning Rischbieter, "Der wahre Wedekind: Lulu Furiosa," *Theater heute,* 17 (April 1988): 6–17;

Jeannie Schüler-Will, "Wedekind's Lulu: Pandora and Pierrot," *German Studies Review,* 7 (February 1984): 27–38;

Willy Schumann, "Frank Wedekind: Regimekritiker?," *Seminar,* 15 (1979): 235–243;

Günter Seehaus, *Wedekind und das Theater* (Munich: Laokoon, 1964);

Leroy Shaw, "Frank Wedekind's *Spring Awakening,*" in *Alogical Modern Drama,* edited by Kenneth White (Amsterdam: Rodopi, 1982), pp. 25–37;

Peter Skrine, *Hauptmann, Wedekind and Schnitzler* (London: Macmillan, 1989), pp. 72–110;

Colbert Stewart, "Comedy, Morality, and Energy in the Work of Frank Wedekind," *Publications of the English Goethe Society,* 56 (1987): 56–73;

Haucke Stroszeck, "'Ein Bild vor dem man verzweifeln muß': Zur Gestaltung der Tragödie in Wedekinds Lulu-Tragödie," in *Literatur und Theater im Wilhelminischen Zeitalter,* edited by Hans-Peter Bayerdörfer (Tübingen: Niemeyer, 1978), pp. 217–237;

Edward Timms, "Pandora and the Prostitute," in his *Karl Kraus: Apocalyptic Satirist* (New Haven: Yale University Press, 1986), pp. 63–93;

Hartmut Vinçon, "Wie Wedekinds Lulu entstand und unterdruckt wurde," *Theater heute,* 17 (April 1988): 16–17;

Klaus Völker, *Frank Wedekind,* Friedrichs Dramatiker des 20. Jahrhunderts, 7 (Velber bei Hannover: Friedrich, 1965);

Hans Wagener, *Frank Wedekind,* Köpfe des 20. Jahrhunderts, 90 (Berlin: Colloquium, 1979); Wagener, "Frank Wedekind: Politische Entgleisungen eines Unpolitischen," *Seminar,* 15 (1979): 244–250.

Androne B. Willeke, "Frank Wedekind und die Frauenfrage," *Monatshefte,* 72 (1980): 26–38.

Papers:

The Munich City Library has manuscripts and other documents of Frank Wedekind in its Wedekind Archive. Holdings are also available at the Wedekind Archive of the Aargau Canton Library in Switzerland.

Christa Wolf

(18 March 1929 –   )

Dieter Sevin
Vanderbilt University

This entry was updated by Professor Sevin from his entry in DLB 75:
Contemporary German Fiction Writers, Second Series.

BOOKS: *Moskauer Novelle* (Halle: Mitteldeutscher Verlag, 1961);

Der geteilte Himmel (Halle: Mitteldeutscher Verlag, 1963); translated by Joan Becker as *The Divided Heaven* (Berlin: Seven Seas, 1965; New York: Adler's Foreign Books, 1976);

Nachdenken über Christa T. (Halle: Mitteldeutscher Verlag, 1968); translated by Christopher Middleton as *The Quest for Christa T.* (New York: Farrar, Straus & Giroux, 1971; London: Hutchinson, 1971);

Lesen und Schreiben: Aufsätze und Betrachtungen (Berlin: Aufbau, 1972; enlarged, 1973); republished as *Lesen und Schreiben: Aufsätze und Prosastücke* (Darmstadt: Luchterhand, 1972); translated by Becker as *The Reader and the Writer: Essays, Sketches, Memories* (Berlin: Seven Seas, 1977; New York: Siguet, 1977);

Till Eulenspiegel: Erzählung für den Film, by Wolf and Gerhard Wolf (Berlin & Weimar: Aufbau, 1973);

Unter den Linden: Drei unwahrscheinliche Geschichten (Berlin: Aufbau, 1974);

Kindheitsmuster (Berlin: Aufbau, 1976); translated by Ursule Molinaro and Hedwig Rappolt as *A Model Childhood* (New York: Farrar, Straus & Giroux, 1980; London: Virago, 1982); republished as *Patterns of Childhood* (New York: Farrar, Straus & Giroux, 1984);

J'écris sur ce qui m'inquiète: Débat dans Sinn und Form sur son dernier Roman (Paris: Centre d'études et de recherches marxistes, 1977);

Fortgesetzter Versuch: Aufsätze, Gespräche, Essays (Leipzig: Reclam, 1979);

Kein Ort, nirgends (Berlin: Aufbau, 1979); translated by Jan van Heurck as *No Place on Earth* (New York: Farrar, Straus & Giroux, 1982; London: Virago, 1983);

Gesammelte Erzählungen (Darmstadt: Luchterhand, 1980);

Christa Wolf at the time her novel Kassandra *(1983) was published (Poly-Press—Ullstein Bilderdienst)*

Neue Lebensansichten eines Katers; Juninachmittag (Stuttgart: Reclam, 1981);

Kassandra: Vier Vorlesungen; Eine Erzählung (Berlin: Aufbau, 1983); translated by van Heurck as *Cassandra: A Novel and Four Essays* (New York: Farrar, Straus & Giroux, 1984);

Voraussetzungen einer Erzählung: Kassandra (Darmstadt: Luchterhand, 1983);

"Ins Ungebundene geht eine Sehnsucht": Gesprächsraum Romantik: Prosa, Essays, by Wolf and Gerhard Wolf (Berlin: Aufbau, 1985);

Die Dimension des Autors, edited by Angela Drescher (Darmstadt: Luchterhand, 1987);

Störfall: Nachrichten eines Tages (Darmstadt: Luchterhand, 1987); translated by Heike Schwarzbauer and Rick Takvorian as *Accident: A Day's News* (New York: Farrar, Straus & Giroux, 1989);

Ansprachen (Darmstadt: Luchterhand, 1988);

Sommerstück (Berlin: Aufbau, 1989);

Im Dialog: Aktuelle Texte (Berlin: Aufbau, 1990);

Reden im Herbst (Berlin: Aufbau, 1990);

Was bleibt: Erzählung (Frankfurt am Main: Luchterhand, 1990);

Auf dem Weg nach Tabou: Texte 1990–1994 (Cologne: Kiepenheuer & Witsch, 1994); translated by van Heurck as *Parting from Phantoms: Selected Writings, 1990–1994* (Chicago: University of Chicago Press, 1997);

Unsere Freunde, die Maler: Bilder, Essays, Dokumente, by Wolf and Gerhard Wolf, edited by Peter Böthig (Berlin: Janus, 1995);

Medea: Stimmen: Roman (Munich: Luchterhand, 1996); translated by John Cullen as *Medea: A Modern Retelling* (New York: Nan A. Talese, 1998);

Hierzulande, Andernorts: Erzählungen und andere Texte, 1994–1998 (Munich: Luchterhand, 1999);

Wüstenfahrt: Erzählung (Berlin: Gerhard Wolf, Luchterhand, 1999).

Editions in English: *The Author's Dimension: Selected Essays,* translated by van Heurck, edited by Alexander Stephan (New York: Farrar, Straus & Giroux, 1993); also published as *The Writer's Dimension* (London: Virago, 1993)—comprises essays from *Die Dimension des Autors, Ansprachen,* and *Im Dialog;*

What Remains and Other Stories, translated by Schwarzbauer and Takvorian (New York: Farrar, Straus & Giroux, 1993).

OTHER: *In diesen Jahren: Ausgewählte deutsche Prosa,* edited by Wolf (Leipzig: Reclam, 1957);

Proben junger Erzähler: Ausgewählte deutsche Prosa, edited by Wolf (Leipzig: Reclam, 1959);

Wir, unsere Zeit, edited by Wolf and Gerhard Wolf (Berlin: Aufbau, 1959);

Karoline von Günderode, Der Schatten eines Traumes, edited by Wolf (Berlin: Der Morgen, 1979);

Anna Seghers, Ausgewählte Erzählungen, edited by Wolf (Darmstadt: Luchterhand, 1983);

Historischer Verein für Hessen, 1934–1983: Vorträge, Exkursionen, Publikationen, edited by Wolf (Darmstadt: Verlag des Historischen Vereins für Hessen, 1983);

Anna Seghers: Eine Biographie in Bildern, edited by Frank Wagner, Ursula Emmerich, and Ruth Radvanyi, essay by Wolf (Berlin: Aufbau, 1994).

Christa Wolf is one of the most prominent postwar German writers. Her works were read and discussed widely in both Germanies prior to reunification in 1990. The intense interest in her works continues unabated as her reputation spreads beyond the German-speaking countries. In addition to her fiction, Wolf has done significant work in the essay form, providing a theoretical basis for her oeuvre.

Christa Ihlenfeld was born in 1929 in Landsberg an der Warthe (today Gorzów Wielkopolski, Poland). Her father, Otto Ihlenfeld, was a salesman. In 1945 the invading Red Army forced the German population in the territories east of the Oder-Neiße line to move to the West; the Ihlenfelds settled in Mecklenburg, where Christa worked as secretary to the mayor of Gammelin. After a stay in a tuberculosis sanatorium she finished school in 1949 in Bad Frankenhausen. She joined the Socialist Unity party and, from 1949 to 1953, studied German literature at the Universities of Leipzig and Jena. In 1951 she married the Germanist and essayist Gerhard Wolf; they have two daughters, Annette and Katrin. After receiving her degree with a thesis on problems of realism in the work of Hans Fallada, she worked as a technical assistant for the East German Writers' Union, as a reader for the Neues Leben publishing house in East Berlin, and as an editor of the periodical *Neue Deutsche Literatur.* From 1959 to 1962 she was a reader for the Mitteldeutscher Verlag in Halle, where she also worked in a boxcar factory. In 1962 she moved to Kleinmachnow, near Berlin, and turned to writing full time. She traveled widely in Europe, visited the Soviet Union, and made her first trip to the United States in 1974. In 1976 she and her husband moved to East Berlin; the same year she joined other prominent East German writers in signing a petition protesting the revocation of citizenship of the poet/singer Wolf Biermann. The publication of *Was bleibt: Erzählung* (1990) shortly after the reunification of East and West Germany precipitated an intense debate over the significance and role of East German literature, in which Wolf was severely criticized. The fact, however, that Wolf and her works were singled out by the mass media during this debate is an indication of the status she enjoys in Germany. In 1993 Wolf went to the United States as a visiting scholar at the Getty Center for the History of Art and Humanities in Santa Monica, California.

Wolf's first work of fiction, *Moskauer Novelle* (Moscow Novella, 1961), was received politely but did not enjoy great success. It is the story of an East Berlin doctor, Vera Brauer, who travels to Moscow in 1959 with a delegation from the German Democratic Republic; the interpreter assigned to the delegation turns out to be Pawel

Koschkin, whom she had met fifteen years before when, as a lieutenant in the Red Army, he had participated in the occupation of her hometown of Fanselow. Wolf's attempt to use their love affair as an allegory for international relations between Germany and the Soviet Union fails.

Her breakthrough as a writer came with the novel *Der geteilte Himmel* (1963; translated as *The Divided Heaven,* 1965). Published shortly after the building of the Berlin Wall, the book was an instant success and made Wolf, virtually overnight, the best-known author in the German Democratic Republic (GDR).

After an accident, education student Rita Seidel wakes up in a hospital bed and tries to analyze what has taken place. During her convalescence Rita examines the preceding two years of her life: her love for the chemist Manfred Herrfurth, her move from a small village to the city of Halle, her work in a railroad-car factory, her studies to become a teacher, Manfred's flight to the West just before the erection of the Berlin Wall on 13 August 1961, and her accident shortly thereafter. The sequence of events is primarily chronological, although there are flashbacks to Rita's and Manfred's early childhood. The third-person narrator seems to be almost omniscient but shares Rita's questioning attitude, thereby stimulating the reader to participate in the narrative process. The ambiguity of the text allows Wolf to deal with topics that otherwise could not have been discussed in published form in the GDR in the early 1960s.

The economic and political situation of the GDR was precarious at the time the novel was written: the prospering West German economy presented an enormous challenge to East German planners, who had to cope with the loss of thousands of skilled workers and professionals who crossed the open border to West Berlin. This problem was solved by the building of the Berlin Wall, but at a high price: the loss of international esteem for the GDR and of personal freedom for its population. The resulting intensification of the cold war and the fear that it might lead to actual war are woven into the background of Wolf's novel. Wolf's treatment of the "German Question"–the division of Germany–contributed to the enormous success of the book in both East and West.

Although the story takes place in the GDR, Wolf addresses general problems and concerns: the anxieties resulting from leaving the idyllic village for the big city–the feeling of being lost, lonely, and scared–are common in any industrialized nation. The same universality holds true for the love between Rita and Manfred and their separation by external forces. Nevertheless, Wolf's primary intended reader was East German, and she hoped to stimulate that reader to reflection. Hence, even though Halle is portrayed as a product of capitalism, which was replaced by socialism only fifteen years previously, Wolf points out that the water and air pollution produced by industry can

no longer be blamed on the old regime. In fact, Rita cannot find any positive aspect to the industrialized city, even though Manfred, who has lived there all his life, tries to show her its hidden beauty.

The village remains a place of refuge for Rita in times of crisis. But, when she returns there after some time away, she notices that it, too, is changing rapidly due to the forced collectivization of agriculture. Wolf is here touching on a topic which was, at the time she wrote the novel, taboo in the GDR: that the collectivization of farms precipitated an increase in the number of people leaving the country, which in turn led to the building of the Berlin Wall.

In depicting Rita's work in the railroad-car factory, Wolf was abiding by the call of the ruling Socialist Unity party to incorporate themes from the working world into literature, a doctrine formulated at the Bitterfeld Conferences in 1958 and 1959. The hope that workers would start writing about their own experiences did not materialize; authors such as Wolf, on the other hand, did respond by working in the fields and factories and gaining experiences which became part of their literary works.

Rita is portrayed as an emancipated woman: she selects the man she loves and lives with him; she leaves her village to pursue an education as a teacher in the big city, against the will of her mother; and she volunteers to work as the only woman in a large factory. Thus, she continually matures in understanding, self-confidence, and knowledge, eventually becoming intellectually equal to Manfred, who holds a doctorate in chemistry. In contrast to Rita, Manfred is emotionally stagnating. Ten years older than Rita, raised in the city and having experienced the Nazi era as a child, he is a skeptic and cynic who is less and less able to put up with the inadequacies of the socialist system. Finally, feeling that he is being treated unjustly in his job, he crosses the Berlin border. He assumes that Rita will follow him; but for her such a decision is more difficult: her loyalty to her country goes much deeper than his. Although she does follow him to West Berlin, she returns home the same day. Shortly thereafter, the Berlin Wall is built, precluding any further choice on her part. Then follows, at the novel's conclusion, her "accident," which may be an unconscious suicide attempt.

Suicide was not an acceptable topic in the GDR when the novel was written, and the book could not have been published there if Rita's attempt to take her own life had not been ambiguously disguised as an accident. The critical reception of the novel in the GDR tended to be apologetic, avoiding any mention of the suicide attempt and dwelling on Rita's remaining in the East as a demonstration of her commitment to the socialist state. In Western criticism, on the other hand, the building of the wall and the possibility of a suicide attempt were emphasized. Wolf received the prestigious East German Heinrich

Mann Prize for the novel. During the post-unification debate in the German media *Der geteilte Himmel* was one of the main works cited in the *Frankfurter Allgemeine Zeitung* to discredit Wolf as a willing servant of the East German state, ignoring the subtle subtext dictated by state censorship.

Wolf's next novel, *Nachdenken über Christa T.* (1968; translated as *The Quest for Christa T.*, 1971), presented the functionaries in the Ministry of Culture with an even greater headache than had *Der geteilte Himmel*. None of the criteria of the prevailing literary doctrine of socialist realism—the demands for a positive hero, for the setting of an example, for an appeal to the masses, and, most of all, for strict adherence to the policies of the party—seemed to have been met in the book.

At the beginning of the novel the narrator, contemplating the untimely death of her friend Christa T., an aspiring writer, decides that Christa's memory should not die and sets out to write about her. Her nonconformist subject fills the narrator with self-doubt and with skepticism about her own literary attempts. After all, who will read what she writes? Will it ever be published, and if it is, what good will it do? Furthermore, will she ever understand Christa T.'s secret vision of herself? Did the vision ever exist, or was the narrator just imagining or hoping for such meaning in the life of her friend? Why did Christa T. not write? The answer must be sought in her skepticism about her own ability; about language as a vehicle for conveying meaning; and, most important, about whether her subjective and personal concerns could be of interest to a society whose primary concern is to catch up economically with the West. Christa T., the narrator insists, had good intentions of contributing to the new society and possessed the kind of imagination needed to grasp and portray the concerns of that society.

The search for truth is a major theme in the novel. The narrator tries to discover the truth about the life of her dead friend. Like Christa T., she cannot write without speaking the truth; but in a collectivist society the truth is sometimes better not expressed. Christa T., in the final analysis, saw only two options for herself: to say everything or nothing. She knew that her half-hearted attempts to write were not in accordance with the prevailing literary principles; she was keenly aware that her subjective material and sensitive style would be frowned upon as lacking social relevance. Thus, she led the average life of a housewife and mother, unable to break the banal cycle of her existence, and that banality eventually destroyed her spiritually and physically. Dying of leukemia, she realized that her potential would be lost forever, and concluded that she had lived too early. The novel ends on an optimistic note: in the future young, inspired writers will not have to suffer Christa T.'s fate.

The response to *Nachdenken über Christa T.* in the GDR was notable for its absence, except for a few hesitantly critical reviews when the novel appeared. The reason for the neglect is easy to discern: the novel's implied criticisms of the GDR during its early years. The book was published in the GDR only intermittently and in small editions which were quickly sold out. In West Germany, on the other hand, the response in the media as well as in scholarly discussions has been intense.

In the collection of essays *Lesen und Schreiben: Aufsätze und Betrachtungen* (1972; translated as *The Reader and the Writer,* 1977) Wolf formulates her ideas about what she considers important in modern prose, as well as its function in her society and the world at large. Wolf believes that literature should provide the reader with stimuli for growth. In a technological age literature is more important than ever, but it also faces increased competition from the other media; therefore, it needs to find ways to be innovative and vital to its readers.

In the early 1970s Wolf wrote a film script, *Till Eulenspiegel* (1973), with her husband and published the short-story collection *Unter den Linden: Drei unwahrscheinliche Geschichten* (Under the Linden Trees: Three Improbable Stories, 1974). The title story uses a dream sequence to express social criticism; in "Neue Lebensansichten eines Katers" (New Perspectives of a Cat) a tomcat comments satirically on his scientist master's attempts to engineer human happiness; the protagonist of "Selbstversuch" (Self-Experiment) decides that she does not want to acquire masculine intellectual and emotional traits and calls a halt to an experimental sex-change procedure.

The autobiographical *Kindheitsmuster* (1976; translated as *A Model Childhood,* 1980), her longest novel to date, deals to a much lesser extent than her previous ones with the GDR. The narrator, Nelly Jordan, tells of her 1971 trip to her hometown—the former Landsberg, now part of Poland—with her husband, her brother, and her daughter Lenka; of her childhood during the Nazi period; of the three years she has spent writing the present book; and of her efforts to explain to Lenka how Nelly and her parents could have failed to oppose the Nazis. Daily middle-class life under fascism is described in detail, often by inserting authentic materials such as newspaper clippings. Such events as the limitation of the freedom of the press and the establishment of concentration camps do not really affect the family; they continue to operate their store and remain largely apolitical, as did so many Germans, not realizing that their disinterest is making possible the consolidation of Nazism.

Kindheitsmuster is daring in suggesting—contrary to the official dogma of the GDR—that East Germans as well as West Germans share in the guilt of the Nazi past. On the other hand, while problems of the 1970s, such as Vietnam, Chile, Greece, and the Middle East, are referred to, critical comments are limited to the non-Communist world, and no mention is made of such topics as the unrest in Poland. Restricting her work in this fashion might have been necessary in view of GDR censorship, but in previous and subsequent books Wolf was able to find indirect means of dealing with issues that could not be openly discussed in the GDR.

The reception of *Kindheitsmuster* was generally positive in both German states. While the novel's complicated structure, with its three levels of narration, was criticized, Wolf was praised for dealing openly and convincingly with the GDR's Nazi past. *Kindheitsmuster* is the one book of Wolf's which was easily obtainable in East Germany.

In 1979 Wolf published an experimental novel which, unlike her previous works, has little to do with either her own biography or the history of the GDR: *Kein Ort, nirgends* (No Place, Nowhere; translated as *No Place on Earth,* 1982). Wolf imagines a meeting of the German romantic writers Heinrich von Kleist and Karoline von Günderode at a tea party in the small town of Winkel am Rhein in June 1804. Kleist and Günderode feel out of place not only in society but also in an existential sense. Their struggle to discover new forms of human experience is not limited to theory and writing: they feel the need for productive dialogue, interaction with others of similar mind, friendship, and love. Kleist and Günderode seem destined to fulfill these needs for each other, but in the imaginary encounter they hardly have a chance to progress beyond superficialities. Incorporating quotations from documentary material into her novel—a technique first used by the nineteenth-century author Georg Büchner, whom Wolf admires greatly—helps to lend authenticity to her story, even though the historical figures are manipulated freely. The historical distance made it possible for Wolf to explore matters which in some instances were delicate subjects in the GDR, such as the relationship between the individual and the state, limitations on writing, and the danger of social alienation which may lead to despair and even to suicide—the ultimate fate of both main characters in real life. In spite of their affinity for each other, Kleist and Günderode are unable to break through the sexual and social barriers that separate them. The same problems Kleist and Günderode encounter—societal limitations and pressures; unsatisfactory relationships between men and women, both of whom need to be liberated from traditional roles; and possibly most important, the difficulty of writing freely and truthfully—still cry out for solutions which the socialist society failed to provide.

In 1980 Wolf became the first author living and writing in the GDR to receive the Federal Republic's most prestigious literary award, the Georg Büchner Prize. That Wolf should be selected for the Büchner Prize seemed particularly appropriate, since she had repeatedly mentioned her admiration and special feeling of affinity for the nine-

teenth-century author. She sees Büchner's writings as an expression of his sense of responsibility for the great issues that confronted his society and, ultimately, all of mankind. In her Büchner Prize address, published in *Die Dimension des Autors* (The Dimension of the Author, 1987), she pays special attention to Büchner's female characters, who show that only mature, liberated, yet loving women are capable of helping mankind to survive. This insight, Wolf proclaims, holds true even more in modern times. Women, she says, must not leave the responsibility for survival to men because of the male propensity for self-destruction, a tendency which is manifest in all of Büchner's male characters.

The concerns expressed in Wolf's Büchner Prize address are a major theme in her novel *Kassandra* (1983; translated as *Cassandra,* 1984). The novel begins with Kassandra, a prisoner of war awaiting execution, pondering the destruction of her city, Troy, and its civilization. How and why did it happen? What actions or inactions led up to this cataclysmic event? What role did she play in it? These are some of the questions Kassandra attempts to answer as she recapitulates what has happened. Wolf's main themes, expressed allegorically, are the threat of war in the nuclear age; the role, or better nonrole, women play in societies that seem to drift at an accelerating pace toward self-destruction; the unwillingness to negotiate to prevent war; the insane reliance on increasing armaments; economic interests; false concepts of honor and the fear of losing face; and industrialism as the Trojan horse which most societies embrace as a panacea but which might well carry the seeds of civilization's destruction. The novel shows that male- dominated power structures deny input not only from women like Kassandra but from anybody with differing ideas. As soon as Kassandra opposes the views and actions of her father, King Priamos, and his ruling clique, she is excluded from the inner circle and even thrown into the dungeon. Kassandra's plight has an autobiographical basis in Wolf's own need to speak and write the truth no matter what the official policy might be.

Although Kassandra's warnings are not heeded by the men in power, who ignore the truth and thereby bring about the destruction of Troy, the book's message should not be viewed as pessimistic. A thoughtful reader will be forced to ask: what would have happened if the male ruling clique had listened to Kassandra? Could she have saved Troy? The possibility of a positive response represents the optimistic component of this work about war, death, and destruction. That Wolf touched a central nerve of contemporary concerns is evident if one considers the appeal of the work in East Germany, where every new printing was immediately sold out, and in West Germany, where *Kassandra* was on the best-seller list for over a year after it appeared. The full meaning and autobiographical dimension of this work became more fully evident only after the sudden end of the East German state. Like the mythical Cassandra, Wolf was predicting the future, and her warnings went unheeded as well.

Simultaneously with the novel Wolf published *Voraussetzungen einer Erzählung: Kassandra* (Genesis of a Story: Kassandra, 1983), a series of lectures she delivered in Frankfurt am Main in 1982. Wolf describes in detail and without inhibition the impressions, concerns, and research–including a trip to Greece–which went into the writing of her novel. *Voraussetzungen einer Erzählung: Kassandra* was probably never intended for publication in the GDR because of its frankness, particularly in regard to the political issues only touched on allegorically in the novel. When the lectures were finally published in East Germany, certain passages were deleted.

The novel *Störfall: Nachrichten eines Tages* (1987; translated as *Accident: A Day's News,* 1989) appeared one year after the nuclear accident at Chernobyl in the Soviet Union. In this work Wolf juxtaposes the technical failure of the nuclear facility with the occurrence of a brain tumor in the narrator's brother. The novel poses searching questions about the future of humanity in view of man's frailty and the dangers as well as the positive developments of technology and science.

The autobiographical novel *Sommerstück* (Summer Play, 1989) describes events in the summer of 1975 that were actually written about seven years later, in 1982–1983. In the novel, a group of intellectual friends gathers in a village in Mecklenburg. Selected events are described in a series of vignettes by an omniscient, third-person narrator. Her impressions and reminiscences ultimately take on the character of a critical commentary concerning a way of life, which the narrator–distanced by time–is able to interweave with a certain nostalgia for a lost but memorable summer. This makes the book not just an "idyllic elegy," as the renowned German critic Fritz Raddatz asserted upon its first publication. There are also difficulties, such as tensions and friction, leading to real suffering among the amorous couples. A playful affinity to the works of the nineteenth-century Russian playwright and short-story writer Chekhov is detectable. Furthermore, a sense of guilt for the privileged, leisurely, and apolitical life of the group of friends becomes increasingly noticeable. Their withdrawal into a kind of Biedermeier existence–reflecting a tendency in East German society–coupled with the awareness of the transitory nature of life, even a sense of doom, are easily ascertainable from the comments of the narrator, who conveys to the reader a sense for urgent and necessary change.

During and shortly after reunification, Wolf stayed at the center of the German literary scene. At first she clung to her vision of a German socialist state, trying to persuade her fellow citizens of the GDR not to leave for the West, but to remain in the country. Many West Germans did not view this appeal favorably. The publication of the autobiographical story "Was bleibt" (1990; trans-

lated as "What Remains," in *What Remains and Other Stories,* 1993), in which she portrays a woman writer who is spied upon by the State Secret Police (Stasi), created an uproar in the media of western Germany, which branded the timing of the story as opportunistic. There is no question, however, that Wolf was indeed subjected to secret police surveillance, and prominent defenders, such as Günter Grass, wrote in magazines and newspapers in her support. Nevertheless, the controversy escalated into a general debate concerning the role of intellectuals in the former GDR and the significance of East German literature in the post-unification era.

In her major post-unification novel *Medea: Stimmen* (1996; translated as *Medea: A Modern Retelling,* 1998), Wolf successfully revised the enduring negative myth of the sorceress Medea. In the best-known version of the story, Euripides' tragedy *Medea* (431 B.C.), the sorceress kills her own children in a rage of jealousy. In Wolf's novel, Medea is no longer portrayed as a child-murderess, but rather as a loving mother who unsuccessfully tries to save her children, pleading for their life in a Corinthian temple; they are stoned to death by a fanatical mob, and Medea is wrongfully blamed. Allegorical implications between the two former German states are detectable in various ways. The Corinthians regard as inferior the society of Medea's home, Colchis, which in the novel is portrayed as being poorer than Corinth, but with more economic equality and a higher regard for women. This difference is symbolized by the hideous crime of King Creon of Corinth, who in order to prevent his daughter Iphinoe from succeeding him to the throne–thereby restoring the times when Corinth was ruled by women–has her hidden and eventually killed. By conveying subjective impressions through various voices concerning the events in the story and the personality of Medea, Wolf succeeds convincingly in overcoming the traditional image of Medea, casting her as a strong, morally and intellectually superior woman.

Letters:

Angela Drescher, ed., *Sei gegrüßt und lebe: Eine Freundschaft Briefen, 1964–1973,* by Wolf and Brigitte Reimann (Berlin: Aufbau, 1993);

Drescher, ed., *Monsieur, wir finden uns wieder: Briefe, 1968–1984,* by Wolf and Franz Fühmann (Berlin: Aufbau, 1995).

Bibliography:

Alexander Stephan, *Christa Wolf* (Amsterdam: Rodopi, 1980).

References:

Katharina von Ankum, *Die Rezeption von Christa Wolf in Ost und West: Von "Moskauer Novelle" bis "Selbstversuch"* (Amsterdam: Rodopi, 1992);

Thomas Anz, ed., *"Es geht nicht um Christa Wolf": Der Literaturstreit im vereinten Deutschland* (Frankfurt am Main: Fischer, 1995);

Franz Baumer, *Christa Wolf,* second edition (Berlin: Morgenbuch, 1996);

Manfred Behn, ed., *Wirkungsgeschichte von Christa Wolfs "Nachdenken über Christa T."* (Königstein: Athenäum, 1978);

Helga G. Braunbeck, *Autorschaft und Subjektgenese: Christa Wolfs "Kein Ort, nirgends"* (Vienna: Passagen, 1992);

George Buehler, *The Death of Socialist Realism in the Novels of Christa Wolf* (Frankfurt am Main: Lang, 1984);

Karl Deiritz and Hannes Krauss, eds., *Der deutsch-deutsche Literaturstreit oder "Freunde, es spricht sich schlecht mit gebundener Zunge": Analysen und Materialien* (Hamburg: Luchterhand, 1991);

Inta Ezergailis, *Woman Writers: The Divided Self: Analysis of Novels by Christa Wolf, Ingeborg Bachmann, Doris Lessing, and Others* (Bonn: Grundmann, 1982);

Helen Fehervary, "Christa Wolf's Prose: A Landscape of Masks," *New German Critique,* 27 (Fall 1982): 57–88;

Annette Firsching, *Kontinuität und Wandel im Werk von Christa Wolf* (Würzburg: Königshausen & Neumann, 1996);

Marilyn S. Fries, ed., *Responses to Christa Wolf: Critical Essays* (Detroit: Wayne State University Press, 1989);

Winfried Giesen, *Christa Wolf* (Frankfurt am Main: Universitätsbibliothek, 1982);

Ulrike Grow, *Erfinden und Erinnern: Typologische Untersuchungen zu Christa Wolfs Romanen "Kindheitsmuster," "Kein Ort, nirgends," und "Kassandra"* (Würzburg: Königshausen & Neumann, 1988);

Anne Herrmann, *The Dialogic and Difference: An/other Woman in Virginia Woolf and Christa Wolf* (New York: Columbia University Press, 1989);

Sonja Hilzinger, *Kassandra: Über Christa Wolf* (Frankfurt am Main: Haag & Herchen, 1982);

Therese Hörnigck, *Christa Wolf* (Göttingen: Steidl, 1989);

Karen H. Jankowsky, *Unsinn, anderer Sinn, neuer Sinn: Zur Bewegung im Denken von Christa Wolfs "Kasandra" über den Krieg und die "Heldengesellschaft"* (Berlin: Argument, 1989);

Charlotte W. Koerner, "'Divided Heaven' by Christa Wolf: A Sacrifice of Message and Meaning in Translation," *German Quarterly,* 57 (Spring 1984): 213–230;

Werner Krogmann, *Christa Wolf: Konturen* (Frankfurt am Main: Peter Lang, 1989);

Anna K. Kuhn, *Christa Wolf's Utopian Vision: From Marxism to Feminism* (Cambridge & New York: Cambridge University Press, 1988);

Myra Love, "Christa Wolf and Feminism: Breaking the Patriarchal Connection," *New German Critique,* no. 16 (Winter 1979): 31–53;

Love, *Christa Wolf: Literature and the Conscience of History* (New York: Peter Lang, 1991);

Wolfram Mauser, ed., *Erinnerte Zukunft: 11 Studien zum Werk Christa Wolfs* (Würzburg: Königshausen & Neumann, 1985);

Mechthild Quernheim, *Das moralische Ich: Kritische Studien zur Subjektwerdung in der Erzählprosa Christa Wolfs* (Würzburg: Königshausen & Neumann, 1990);

Klemens Renoldner, *Utopie und Geschichtsbewußtsein: Versuche zur Poetik Christa Wolfs* (Stuttgart: Akademischer Verlag, 1981);

Margit Resch, *Understanding Christa Wolf: Returning Home to a Foreign Land* (Columbia: University of South Carolina Press, 1997);

Martin Reso, ed., *"Der geteilte Himmel" und seine Kritiker: Dokumentation* (Halle: Mitteldeutscher Verlag, 1965);

Marion von Salisch, *Zwischen Selbstaufgabe und Selbstverwirklichung: zum Problem der Persönlichkeitsstruktur im Werk Christa Wolfs* (Stuttgart: Klett, 1975);

Klaus Sauer, ed., *Christa Wolf: Materialienbuch* (Darmstadt: Luchterhand, 1979);

Dieter Sevin, *Der geteilte Himmel, Nachdenken über Christa T.: Interpretationen* (Munich: Oldenbourg, 1982);

Colin E. Smith, *Tradition, Art, and Society: Christa Wolf's Prose* (Essen: Die Blaue Eule, 1987);

Alexander Stephan, *Christa Wolf,* fourth edition (Munich: Beck, 1991);

Christa Thomassen, *Der lange Weg zu uns selbst: Christa Wolfs Roman "Nachdenken über Christa T." als Erfahrungs- und Handlungsmuster* (Kronberg: Scriptor, 1977);

Hermann Vinke, ed., *Akteneinsicht Christa Wolf: Zerrspiegel und Dialog: Eine Dokumentation* (Hamburg: Luchterhand, 1993);

Ian Wallace, ed., *Christa Wolf in Perspective* (Amsterdam & Atlanta: Rodopi, 1994);

Heinz-Dieter Weber, *Über Christa Wolfs Schreibart* (Constance: Universitätsverlag, 1984);

John Whitley, "Quest for Christa T.," *Sunday Times* (London), 16 May 1971, p. 33;

Sabine Wilke, *Ausgraben und Erinnern: Zur Funktion von Geschichte, Subjekt und geschlechtlicher Identität in den Texten Christa Wolfs* (Würzburg: Königshausen & Neumann, 1993);

Christel Zahlmann, *Christa Wolfs Reise "ins Tertiär": Eine literaturpsychologische Studie zu "Kindheitsmuster"* (Würzburg: Königshausen & Neumann, 1986).

Wolfram von Eschenbach

(circa 1170 – after 1220)

Marianne Wynn
Queen Mary and Westfield College

This entry originally appeared in DLB 138: German Writers and Works
of the High Middle Ages: 1170–1280.

Seven Songs (circa 1200?)

Manuscripts: The songs are extant in three major manuscripts that date from the turn of the twelfth to the thirteenth century. There are four strophes in A, the Kleine Heidelberger Liederhandschrift (Heidelberg, Universitätsbibliothek, cpg 357), and three songs in B, the Weingartner Handschrift (Stuttgart, Württembergische Landesbibliothek, HB XIII, 1). Nine songs are attributed to Wolfram in C, the Manessische or Große Heidelberger Liederhandschrift (Heidelberg, Universitätsbibliothek, cpg 848), and two songs in G, the Munich manuscript of *Parzival* (Munich, Bayerische Staatsbibliothek, cgm 19).

First publication: Two songs in *Auswahl aus den Hochdeutschen Dichtern des dreizehnten Jahrhunderts: Für Vorlesungen und zum Schulgebrauch,* edited by Karl Lachmann (Berlin, 1820).

Standard edition: In *Die Lyrik Wolframs von Eschenbach: Edition Kommentar Interpretation,* edited by Peter Wapnewski (Munich: Beck, 1972).

Edition in modern German: In *Titurel; Lieder: Mittelhochdeutscher Text und Übersetzung,* edited and translated by Wolfgang Mohr (Göppingen: Kümmerle, 1978).

Editions in English: Translated by Arthur T. Hatto, in his *Eos: An Enquiry into the Theme of Lovers' Meetings and Partings at Dawn in Poetry* (London, The Hague & Paris: Mouton, 1965), pp. 448–455; translated by Olive Sayce, in *The Medieval German Lyric 1150–1300* (Oxford: Clarendon Press, 1982), pp. 211–216; translated by Marion E. Gibbs and Sidney M. Johnson, in their *Wolfram von Eschenbach: Titurel and the Songs. Texts and Translations with Introduction, Notes and Comments* (New York & London: Garland, 1988), pp. 70–111.

Parzival (circa 1200–1210)

Manuscripts: The work has been handed down in more than eighty manuscripts, sixteen of which

Illustration for Wolfram von Eschenbach's Parzival *in the Große Heidelberger Liederhandschrift (Heidelberg, Universitätsbibliothek, cpg 848, f. 149v)*

give the complete version; no other court romance has been transmitted in so many manuscripts. The main manuscripts on which the standard edition is based are D (Saint Gall, Stiftsbibliothek, 857) and G (Munich, Bayerische Staatsbibliothek, cgm 19).

First publication: *Parzival* (Strasbourg: Printed by Johann Mentelin, 1477).

Standard edition: In *Wolfram von Eschenbach,* edited by Karl Lachmann (Berlin: Reimer, 1833; revised, edited by Moriz Haupt, 1854).

Editions in modern German: *Parzival,* translated by Wolfgang Mohr (Göppingen: Kümmerle, 1977); *Parzival,* 2 volumes, translated by Wolfgang Spiewok (Stuttgart: Reclam, 1981).

Editions in English: Translated by Helen M. Mustard and Charles E. Passage as *Parzival* (New York: Vintage, 1961); translated by Arthur T. Hatto as *Parzival* (Harmondsworth, U.K.: Penguin, 1980).

Willehalm (circa 1210–1220)

Manuscripts: The transmission of this unfinished work comprises more than seventy manuscripts, twelve of which include as much of the work as Wolfram completed. The earliest of the latter, the Saint Gall manuscript (Saint Gall, Stiftsbibliothek, 857) dates from the thirteenth century and forms the basis for the three standard editions of the work. The oldest of the fragments can be dated to the first half of the thirteenth century (Munich, Bayerische Staatsbibliothek, cgm 193 III).

First publication: *Wilhelm der Heilige von Oranse: Zweyter Theil von Wolfram von Eschilbach, einem Dichter des schwäbischen Zeitpuncts,* edited by Wilhelm Johann Christian Gustav Casparson (Cassel, 1784).

Standard editions: In *Wolfram von Eschenbach,* edited by Karl Lachmann, sixth edition, edited by Eduard Hartl (Berlin & Leipzig: De Gruyter, 1926); in *Wolfram von Eschenbach,* edited by Albert Leitzmann, volumes 4–5, Altdeutsche Textbibliothek (Tübingen: Niemeyer, 1963); *Willehalm,* edited by Werner Schröder (Berlin & New York: De Gruyter, 1978); *Willehalm,* edited by Joachim Heinzle (Frankfurt am Main: Bibliothek deutscher Klassiker, 1991).

Edition in modern German: *Willehalm, aus dem Mittelhochdeutschen übertragen,* translated by Reinhard Fink and Friedrich Knorr (Jena: Diederichs, 1941).

Editions in English: Translated by Charles E. Passage as *The Middle High German Poem of Willehalm by Wolfram von Eschenbach* (New York: Ungar, 1977); translated by Marion E. Gibbs and Sidney M. Johnson as *Willehalm* (Harmondsworth, U.K.: Penguin, 1984).

Titurel (circa 1217)

Manuscripts: The work is extant in three manuscripts. The *Parzival* manuscript G (Munich, Bayerische Staatsbibliothek, cgm 19) contains both fragments. The first sixty-eight strophes of the first fragment are preserved in H, the Ambraser Heldenbuch (Vienna, Östereichische Nationalbibliothek, 2663), and forty-eight strophes of the same fragment are in M (Munich, Universitätsbibliothek, Ms 154).

First publication: *Titurel* (Strasbourg: Printed by Johann Mentelin, 1477).

Standard edition: In *Wolfram von Eschenbach,* edited by Karl Lachmann, sixth edition, revised by Eduard Hartl (Berlin & Leipzig: De Gruyter, 1926) in *Wolfram von Eschenbach,* edited by Albert Leitzmann, volume 5, Altdeutsche Textbibliothek (Tübingen: Niemeyer, 1963).

Edition in modern German: In *Titurel; Lieder: Mittelhochdeutscher Text und Übersetzung,* edited and translated by Wolfgang Mohr (Göppingen: Kümmerle, 1978).

Editions in English: Translated by Charles E. Passage, in his *Titurel: Wolfram von Eschenbach. Translation and Studies* (New York: Ungar, 1984); translated by Marion E. Gibbs and Sidney M. Johnson, in their *Wolfram von Eschenbach: Titurel and the Songs. Texts and Translations with Introduction, Notes and Comments* (New York & London: Garland, 1988).

One of the great poets of all time, Wolfram von Eschenbach was conscious of his stature and emphasizes it unashamedly in one of his major works: "ich bin Wolfram von Eschenbach unt kan ein teil mit sange" (114, 12–13 [all citations refer to the standard edition of Wolfram's works by Albert Leitzmann, 1963]: I am Wolfram von Eschenbach and do know a thing or two about poetry). Many of his contemporaries agreed with this self-assessment. Wirnt von Grafenberg, for example, maintained that "leien munt nie baz gesprach" (no layman's tongue has ever uttered finer poetry). His great rival, Gottfried von Straßburg, on the other hand, assigned Wolfram to the meretricious practitioners of literature, the paid hacks and obscurantists. Gottfried's crushing verdict did not gain wide currency. Wolfram was held in great reverence both by contemporary and later authors who refer to him or show themselves to have been influenced by him. Moreover, all three of his main works were seized on eagerly by poets who continued and enlarged them. That his works enjoyed widespread admiration among listeners and readers is borne out by the unusually large number of manuscripts that have been handed down.

Despite his fame, everything that is known about him has to be inferred from his work, from references to him in other works of literature, and from general information about his time. There is no direct documentary evidence about him. But at least one can be certain of his name, for he gives it several times, and other writers also mention it. His homeland was Franconia; he mentions several places in the vicinity of the Frankish town of Eschenbach (now Wolframs-Eschenbach), among them Abenberg, Nördlingen, and the Sant near Nuremberg. During his lifetime Eschenbach was a hamlet; like every other village in central Europe it cannot have consisted of more than a few wattle and daub cottages. There was a church, consecrated in the eleventh century, which means Wolfram would have had regular contact with a priest. A community like Eschenbach, however, could hardly have hoped to have the services of a learned clergyman. At some point Wolfram left the village, but he never traveled far. There is no evidence that he went on a pilgrimage to Rome or to the Holy Land, two of the main destinations of the medieval traveler, or that he joined a Crusade. It would appear that he never left the German-speaking territories.

One of the greatest magnates of his time, Hermann, Landgrave of Thuringia, seems to have been his patron for a while. The Thuringian court rivaled that of the emperor. The Wartburg at Eisenach was no mere castle; it was a palace. In a commanding position, high on a mountain promontory, it dominates the surrounding forests and valleys. Hermann kept a lavish court and was known to be an open-handed patron of the arts. At the Thuringian court Wolfram would have met the learned clerks of a first-rate chancery; great ladies, well versed in literature; political schemers; cavalrymen; foot soldiers; free lances; and entertainers of every conceivable sort—jesters, singers, and conjurers but also serious artists. Hermann's court had a reputation for rowdiness, yet it was also a cultural center, rather like the Babenberg court of Vienna. It is not difficult to recognize the ambience of this court in Wolfram's works—for example, in his portrayals of the court of King Arthur in *Parzival* (circa 1200–1210). Wolfram had connections with lesser courts as well. He was familiar with Wildenberg Castle, an imposing stronghold on a spur in the Odenwald near Amorbach owned by the rich lords of Durne. It was one of the finest castles of the Hohenstaufen period, though not as grand as the Wartburg. Wolfram's relationship with this family is unknown. The same is true of his connection with Count Wertheim, whose castle stood on the river Main. The Wertheims were neighbors of the Durnes and also had property in Eschenbach. Wolfram mentions Count Wertheim in a manner that leaves it unclear whether the two men knew one another. Wolfram also speaks of a patroness, whose name he does not reveal, three times in *Parzival;* he describes her as a *wîp* (woman), not as a *vrouwe* (noblewoman).

Wolfram, thus, had patrons, but he would hardly have been able to make a regular living from his poetry. A patron would commission a work, offer board and lodging to the poet while it was being composed, pay for the vellum, and supply a secretary for dictation. The poet might also receive a gift, but it would not be enough for him to live on, let alone to support a family. Wolfram begins to plead poverty early in his career, and although such hard-luck claims were a cliché among the beggar-poets of the Middle Ages, there is no reason to dismiss Wolfram's statements as nonautobiographical. The same applies to his mention of a wife and a daughter.

Proud as he was of his achievement as a poet, Wolfram was prouder still of his vocation as a soldier. He claims that he is a military man and offers the opinion that only a silly woman will love him for his poetry: love must be won in a passage of arms. His remark "schildes ambet ist min art" (115, 11) is ambiguous; its meaning could mean either "the office of the shield is my vocation" or "the office of the shield is mine by heredity." At any rate, he introduces himself as a shield-bearing man-at-arms. It has been argued that he assumes the guise of a knight for his persona as a narrator and that his self-description need bear no relation to his life. As the context in which this statement appears is neither ironic nor humorous, however, there seems little ground for disbelieving him.

He would not have been a foot soldier; they were the lowest social group among the fighting men, and Wolfram could hardly have expressed pride at belonging to their ranks. As a cavalryman he could have been a mercenary, a vassal, or a member of a magnate's household troop. His pride in his profession as a soldier points to the last possibility: mercenaries were considered unreliable because they followed the highest bidder, while vassals owed only forty days of military service a year and ignored the liege lord's summonses whenever they could. The elite group among the mounted shock troops in medieval warfare was a landowner's private army, and Wolfram may well have belonged to one. His knowledge of fighting techniques is considerable; throughout his works there are many descriptions of jousts, but unique in the literature of the time are his battle descriptions in his later epic, *Willehalm* (circa 1210–1220). They represent the first detailed strategic battle descriptions in medieval German literature.

He knew the work of Heinrich von Veldeke, Hartmann von Aue, Gottfried, Walther von der Vogelweide, and Neidhart von Reuental and was familiar with the *Kaiserchronik* (Emperor Chronicle, circa 1135–1150), the *Rolandslied* (Song of Roland, circa 1100) and the *Alexanderlied* (Song of Alexander circa 1130–1150) of Pfaffe Lamprecht, the *Nibelungenlied* (Song of the Nibelungs, circa 1200), and an early version of the Tristan story by Eilhart von Oberg. That he knew French is clear from his use of the source books for his two major narratives. He twice denies quite vehemently that he had any book learning, yet the disclaimer "ine kan decheinen buochstap" (115, 27: I cannot make out a single letter) is an exact rendering of the phrase in Psalm 70:15, "non cognovi litteraturam," and his use of it as a reverse-modesty topos shows that he understood its double meaning. Moreover, he betrays extensive knowledge of theology, the natural sciences, cosmology, astronomy, and medicine. A fair amount of such knowledge could have been picked up by sitting in on conversations among those who were better educated than he, so that Wolfram could have gathered a good deal of learning without knowing much Latin. Although there is some dispute as to whether Wolfram could read, it is extremely unlikely that he could have constructed narratives on so grand a scale, and of such detailed complexity, as *Parzival* and *Willehalm* if he were illiterate.

With the death of the emperor Heinrich VI in 1197, the Hohenstaufen and Welf dynasties embarked on a power struggle that lasted for two decades. For some of this period Germany had two rival kings, the Hohenstaufen Philip II and the Welf Otto IV. By the time the Hohenstaufen Friedrich II was crowned emperor in 1220 there had been twelve royal and imperial elections and coronations in the Holy Roman Empire. Twice the head of state was excommunicated, for the Holy See also claimed its share of political power. The civil wars meant destruction of villages and crops, burning and looting, and perpetual fear. In 1217 famine began in the northern German regions, moved southward to Bavaria and Austria, and finally spread as far as Bohemia and Hungary. Corpses in towns and fields would have been a familiar sight. Although Wolfram does not comment on these events, he shows himself acutely aware of their results. He is the poet of compassion par excellence, with a supreme understanding of human misery.

Wolfram also composed his works in an age of faith. Heresies, Crusades, the expansion of the Cistercian order, and the rise of a religious movement among women were all part of it, and much of this preoccupation with religion is reflected in his narratives. He portrays the personal dilemmas in which people find themselves trapped through their religious beliefs, and he also meditates on complex theological questions.

The German Wolfram wrote is Frankish, with some Bavarian characteristics. Often his syntax is emotional rather than grammatical, suggesting the impulsiveness and casual incoherence of spoken language. His imagery is extravagant and frequently obscure. His vocabulary embraces bold coinages of his own invention, loan words from French, and terminology generally encountered in the heroic epic rather than in the courtly romance. He constructed his longer narratives on the basis of a unit of thirty lines of rhymed couplets, with verses of three or four beats. Their division into books (chapters) may have been introduced by scribes.

Wolfram's first major work of fiction, *Parzival*, is based on the unfinished court romance by Chrétien de Troyes, *Perceval le Gallois ou Le Conte du Graal* (Perceval the Gaul; or, The Tale of the Grail, circa 1180), whose plot accounts for books 3 to 13. Wolfram completed and expanded Chrétien's work and added a long introductory section and a conclusion, but on the whole he follows the action as set out by Chrétien. Even while adopting some of Chrétien's stylistic devices and structural patterns, however, he changes the French romance fundamentally. Many of his changes can be categorized as closer narrative definition; thus, he gives proper names to figures not named in his source, such as the hero's cousin, Sigune, and his mentor, Trevrizent. Altogether there are 222 named characters in the German work, against a mere handful in the French source. Many of these characters he links with one another in a network of two great families, the Grail dynasty and the Arthurian clan. The mere belonging of a figure to one or the other family characterizes his or her fundamental nature. In addition, Wolfram gives place-names to his settings, creating a full-fledged fictional geography consistent within itself and endowing certain backgrounds with symbolic significance. This world of fiction is set in contrast, and at the same time linked, with the world of reality. Furthermore, while the hero of the French work is introduced as a boy, the German work begins before his birth and gives a detailed prehistory—including the biographies of the hero's parents, particularly that of the father, establishing a pattern of inherited characteristics that will come to the fore in his hero's development. Taken from Chrétien is the double-hero structure, which Wolfram enhances through immense elaboration and subtle annotation.

The most momentous change Wolfram effects is to give the narrative an overriding theme. He announces in his introduction that the story he is about to unfold has the leitmotiv of *triuwe* (loyalty or faithfulness), which he links with true femininity and manliness. The basic meaning of *triuwe* is a capacity for loving in total selflessness, with a love that is wholly directed toward its object. It denotes the bond between humanity and God and declares itself as maternal and paternal love, love in marriage, love among siblings, love between friends, feudal allegiance, and compassion. Its archetypal and perfect manifestation is God. Many of the characters in *Parzival* exhibit this capacity.

Parzival possesses it as his birthright, loses it, and must recover it. The poet says in the first words of the prologue that life will lead his hero through suffering, doubt, and despair but that by dint of single-mindedness and persistence he will find happiness and salvation.

The prologue is one of the most opaque passages in the work. Any interpretation of it will be controversial. It would appear that Wolfram was being deliberately cryptic: he speaks of a winged example that is much too quick for fools. He goes on to describe his style and the way in which it has been received by his public. Special instructions for women are given: they are to guard their honor and dignity and to bestow their love with care; outward beauty is less important by far than the beauty of character and soul. It is clear that Wolfram has his critics in mind, and one would assume, therefore, that this part of the prologue was written after large sections of the work had been made public. It seems reasonably certain that the instructions for women were aimed at the heroine of Gottfried's *Tristan und Isolde* (circa 1210). Gottfried sharply and brutally attacked Wolfram and his work, and Wolfram's counterattack pays Gottfried back in like coin. Gottfried's assault on Wolfram was couched in as mysterious a language and imagery as is Wolfram's response to it.

The third part of the prologue is the introduction proper to the narrative, stating its theme and introducing the hero. The story is as yet, however, not concerned with him.

The first two books are devoted to the hero's father, Gahmuret. When Gahmuret's father, the king, dies, the law of primogeniture leaves Gahmuret landless, and he becomes a free lance. He seeks his fortune in Europe, Asia, and Africa, achieving high distinction as a warrior. Reaching the besieged capital of a kingdom in Africa, he lifts the siege for its queen, Belakane. He falls in love with her, and they marry. Belakane conceives a son, but before he is born, Gahmuret grows restless. He leaves her by stealth, boarding a ship under cover of darkness. While he is at sea his son is born, a child of singular appearance, with checkered black and white skin, and hair colored like the feathers of a magpie. Belakane names him Feirefiz.

Gahmuret reaches Europe and makes his way to Seville and Toledo and then to the fictional kingdom of Waleis. The kingdom is in need of a ruler, and the young queen, Herzeloyde, has arranged a tournament to select one: she will marry the winner. Gahmuret enters the city in an eye-catching procession that proclaims his riches. He takes part in the exercises preliminary to the tournament and emerges clearly as the most skilled fighter among the participants. Herzeloyde

claims him in marriage, but Gahmuret advances three excuses to escape this unsought wedlock: he is married already, the queen of France has a prior claim on him, and he is in mourning, having just had news of his brother's death. When Herzeloyde brushes his excuses aside—pointing out in response to the first one that a Christian marriage supersedes marriage to a pagan—Gahmuret lights on yet another escape clause: the tournament proper has not taken place, so the rule regarding its outcome cannot be applied. Neither will give way, the matter is referred to a jury, and the verdict is in the queen's favor. They marry, but not long after the wedding Gahmuret leaves for the East, where he falls in battle. When the news of his death is brought to Herzeloyde, she faints in shock and hovers on the brink of death. But she rallies and proclaims to her people that she is carrying in her womb the heir to the kingdom. Shortly afterward, Parzival is born.

Herzeloyde's lands are overrun by a robber baron, and she flees with her son and a group of retainers into the magic wasteland of Soltane. Here Parzival is brought up in total ignorance of chivalry. One day, however, he meets a group of knights in the forest and learns about King Arthur. The knights' description kindles in him the desire to present himself at Arthur's court and become a knight himself. Herzeloyde lets him go, then dies of a broken heart. In the forest of Brizljan, the forest of Arthurian adventure, Parzival has a series of encounters, each of which will impinge decisively on his career and development. He stumbles on Jeschute, asleep alone in her pavilion; kisses her; and robs her of her ring. She is later accused of adultery by her husband. He next finds Sigune, his cousin on his mother's side and a member of the Grail family, cradling in her arms her lover, who has just been killed in a joust. She tells Parzival of his own lineage and his great inborn capacity for compassion. At Arthur's court Parzival kills the Red Knight in a joust, takes possession of the Red Knight's charger and accoutrements, and sets out again. Not being able to control the powerful horse, he rides on for two days in full armor until he comes to a castle. Its lord is Gurnemanz, who takes it upon himself to educate Parzival in horsemanship, fighting techniques, and rules of behavior, including one that will prove fatal—that he should not ask too many questions.

After leaving Gurnemanz, Parzival comes upon a kingdom under siege; its inhabitants are starving. He offers assistance to the young queen, Condwiramurs; defeats the opposing army; and marries her. After some time he takes leave of her to return to his mother, not knowing that she is dead.

On his way Parzival arrives at the Grail Castle. Its inhabitants are careworn and melancholy, and the Grail King, Anfortas, suffers from a crippling illness; huge fires and immense fur wrappings cannot allay his chill. Parzival witnesses the display of a bleeding lance accompanied by loud weeping and lamenting, followed by a mysterious procession of young women, one of whom is holding the Grail. The Grail possesses the magical quality of being able to supply any kind of sustenance in any quantity. Finally, a dazzling treasure, Anfortas's sword, is presented to Parzival as a gift from his host. Parzival accepts it, not understanding that by doing so he is acknowledging a close link with the giver. It should prompt him to inquire into the wretched fate that has befallen Anfortas, but, because of the reticence instilled in him by Gurnemanz, he does not do so. When he leaves the next morning, the castle is deserted. Riding through the forest he comes upon Sigune, who hails him as the Grail king-elect. When he confesses that he did not ask the healing question, she hurls violent abuse at him and refuses to have anything further to do with him. He next meets Jeschute, fights a joust with her husband, and reconciles husband and wife by testifying to her innocence. He takes his oath at Fontane la salvatsche, Trevrizent's hermitage.

Parzival's travels now take him out of Grail territory and back to the Arthurian world. Three drops of blood on the snow from a bird injured by a falcon remind him of the colors of Condwiramurs, and he falls into a trance of longing. Gawan, the most distinguished member of the Round Table, breaks the spell and takes him to Arthur's encampment, where he is received by the king and the nobles as an equal. Almost immediately, however, the Grail messenger, Cundrie, arrives and humiliates him before the assembled company for not having asked the vital question at the Grail Castle. Arthur and his court are degraded, she says, by his presence. Devastated by this public disgrace, Parzival despairs. He casts doubt on God's omnipotence, thereby committing the cardinal sin of *superbia* (pride). He and Gawan leave the court.

The secondary hero, Gawan, now moves into the foreground of the narrative. His first exploit takes him to a castle that is to be attacked by a large army because its lord's elder daughter has rejected the marriage proposal of a young king. The younger daughter, Obilot, still a child, captivates Gawan by her charm, and he agrees to fight in their defense. He captures the king, hands him over to Obilot, and she hands him over to her sister. They marry, and Gawan leaves.

At the next castle Gawan meets the irresistible Antikonie. Left alone with her, he makes immediate advances, to which she responds; they are, however, interrupted by a knight, who raises the alarm. At this point the story turns into farce. Gawan, who is unarmed, uses a chessboard as a shield, while Antiko-nie hurls chess pieces in their defense. A settlement is reached that obliges Gawan to seek the Grail.

The narrative returns to Parzival. He is once again on Grail territory, where he stumbles upon Sigune. This time he finds a sympathetic response from her, and she shows him the way to the Grail Castle. After winning a horse in a joust with a Grail knight, he loses his way and moves out of Grail country. Weeks later he is back. A group of pilgrims tells him that it is Good Friday and advises him to seek Trevrizent, the hermit, who turns out to be his maternal uncle. God guides him to the hermitage, where, in long and detailed discussions structured with great complexity, he is taught about love, mercy, the grace of God, and the sin of *superbia* and is led to sincere penitence and confession. He learns also of the secrets of the Grail and of his mother's death.

Meanwhile, Gawan reaches yet another country, whose beautiful and spirited liege lady, the duchess Orgeluse, treats him with disdain but accepts his offer to serve her. They ride on together, Orgeluse intent on testing Gawan's qualities as a knight, Gawan determined to carry his courtship of her to a successful conclusion. As they approach a river, beyond which rises a magnificent castle with ladies at every window, Gawan is challenged by a knight who is a rival for Orgeluse's favors. She leaves but promises to meet Gawan again, should he defeat his opponent. Gawan is victorious and spends the night in the ferryman's house.

The next morning Gawan is eager to hear about the castle he saw the day before. Gawan plies the ferryman and his daughter with questions and discovers that in the castle, Schastel Marveile, stands the great bed, Lit Marveile. A spell lies on the castle, and he who breaks the spell will become the castle's lord. Gawan enters the castle and faces the extraordinary bed, which charges about like a warhorse. He jumps on the bed, and as he rides it he has to protect himself against a shower of arrows and stones and kill a lion. The spell is broken, and Gawan, though wounded, survives. This episode also has elements of farce: that the womanizer Gawan should be riding a bed as if it were a horse and should be responsible for freeing four hundred women is a joke that would hardly be lost on the contemporary audience.

On the following morning Gawan inspects the castle and discovers a magic pillar in which the surrounding countryside may be seen. He catches a glimpse of Orgeluse, hurries to join her, and defeats her escort. Orgeluse offers her love if he will fight King Gramoflanz. To do so he must take a branch from the king's garden, which can only be reached by jumping a dangerous ravine on horseback. Gramoflanz appears the moment Gawan has picked the branch, declares himself to be in love with Gawan's sister, and announces that he nurses an unremitting hatred against Gawan. After they arrange a duel, Gawan returns to Orgeluse, who asks his forgiveness. The two ride back to Schastel Marveile.

The next day great celebrations take place at Schastel Marveile. Among the inhabitants of the castle are Gawan's two sisters, his mother, and his grandmother, but he has not revealed his identity to them. The festivities culminate in Gawan and Orgeluse's being led to their nuptial chamber. In the meantime Gawan has sent a messenger to ask Arthur to bring the court to Joflanze, where his joust with Gramoflanz is to take place. Gawan then sets out with the court of Schastel Marveile, as does Orgeluse with her own ducal court. The integration of the three courts is an important achievement, the more so because it allows Gawan to reunite the king with members of his family who had been imprisoned at Schastel Marveile.

Before the duel Gawan rides out to exercise his charger. On the plain he meets a knight who wears a garland made of branches from Gramoflanz's tree. Gawan takes him to be Gramoflanz and begins the joust. Soon it becomes clear that Gawan has found a dangerous opponent. He is, in fact, Parzival, who shows himself to be the superior fighter. Gawan is close to defeat when some passing pages call out his name. Parzival, in deep distress at having engaged in a duel with so close a friend, immediately reveals his identity and flings aside his sword, and they rejoin Arthur's court. Gawan's duel with Gramoflanz does not take place. Several weddings follow, among them the formal nuptials of Gawan and Orgeluse.

Witnessing the good fortune and happiness of those around him, Parzival concludes that his destiny is otherwise: "got wil miner freude niht" (733,8: God does not want happiness for me). With this thought he lays down defiance and rebellion and accepts what fate has decreed for him. He has moved from *superbia* to *humilitas,* from one of the cardinal sins to one of the cardinal virtues, and he can now be called to the Grail. He leaves Arthur's court and sets out alone.

The Gawan story is now at an end. Almost half the work is allotted to it, indicating its importance. Gawan is carefully contrasted with Parzival in personality, career, and fate. His conduct is without blemish; his faith never wavers; his actions are marked by courage and his thoughts by maturity. While Parzival's life is portrayed as exceptional, Gawan's is exemplary. Apart from its serious function, the Gawan story also introduces humor into the work. Witty and occasionally bawdy, it is entertaining in itself and serves, in addition, to throw Parzival's loneliness and misery into sharp relief.

Riding toward a large forest, Parzival meets a luxuriously accoutred pagan knight. Without speaking, they begin to fight. Parzival's sword splinters, and the stranger magnanimously throws his own aside and reveals his identity: he is Feirefiz, Parzival's half brother, and has arrived with an army to search for his father, Gahmuret. Overjoyed, the brothers exchange the kiss of peace, and Parzival takes Feirefiz to Arthur's court. Arthur makes Feirefiz a member of the Round Table and arranges a banquet in his honor. The festivities are interrupted by the arrival of the Grail messenger, Cundrie, who proclaims Parzival king of the Grail. Parzival and Feirefiz take leave of the court and, guided by Cundrie, ride to the Grail Castle.

Anfortas, in his agony, pleads for death but is kept alive by the Grail. Parzival, greatly moved, now asks the long-awaited question of pity: "oeheim, was wirret dier?" (795, 29: Uncle, what ails you?), and Anfortas is released from his misery. Parzival, now king of the Grail, rides out to meet Condwiramurs and sees his twin sons for the first time. There is one further meeting with Trevrizent, and on the return journey to the Grail Castle he passes Sigune's dead body. Feirefiz falls in love with the young woman who leads the Grail procession; after his baptism they marry and leave for the East. Parzival's son Loherangrin, a knight of the Grail, is sent to Brabant to help its liege lady against her enemies. He marries her on the condition that she never ask him who he is. She does ask the forbidden question, and he returns to the Grail. In a brief epilogue Wolfram names himself once more and concludes that a life led doing justice to both God and the world is a great achievement.

Alongside his epic work, Wolfram also composed seven songs. An eighth song handed down under his name is generally not considered genuine but may contain some strophes by him. Four of the songs are dawn songs, the standard subject of which is the parting of illicit lovers at daybreak. The genre is found in many civilizations, and a substantial corpus of it was developed in medieval Provençal. In Germany only two poets are known to have chosen this lyrical category before Wolfram. Dawn songs are miniature dramas, and in Wolfram's four examples the atmosphere is particularly highly charged. The yearning of the lovers for one another, the pain of parting, the fear of loss, and the menace of discovery make up a powerful poetic blend. The danger is ever present, and the suspense is sustained throughout.

Wolfram's dawn songs vary greatly in structure. In two of the songs only the lovers appear; in the others a third figure—the castle guard—enters the scene. Two of the songs are cast chiefly in dialogue; two are introduced by a monologue. One is a dispute between the woman and the castle guard; a large part of another is taken up by the castle guard's considering his function as protector of the lovers. This figure is given an important role. As he takes a considerable risk by waking the lovers at sunrise and thus enabling the knight to leave undetected, Wolfram makes him a friend of the lovers. The poet indicates this relationship by the use of the second-person singular, *du,* in the dialogue between the guard and the woman.

The identities of the lovers in the four songs are left vague. They could be married (though clearly not to one another), unmarried, young, or older. He could be a lord, a vassal, or a free lance living by his wits; she could be the lord's wife, one of the lord's legitimate or illegitimate daughters, or a cherished concubine of the lord. The constellation of identities in the songs, subtly left to the audience's imagination, makes for a variety of dramas.

These songs are distinguished by great artistic daring: in all of them Wolfram portrays the act of love. Descriptions of nudity, physical intimacy, and sex in serious literature constituted a breathtaking novelty. In all four dawn songs the lovers embrace in a last farewell before parting. This juxtaposition of union and separation invests the scene with maximum pathos.

Wolfram also composed an anti–dawn song in which the lovers' friend is not needed, for the lovers are married and are not forced to meet in secret. As regards poetic quality, the song is not to be compared with the dawn songs proper; it is probably a parody. Of the remaining songs, one ridicules the clichés of the conventional contemporary love lyric, referring to a song by Walther that, in turn, had as its target a song by Reinmar der Alte. The last song, a plea for love, is remarkable chiefly for the eccentric images the poet uses to describe the setting. Unusual also is the masterful stance the speaker of the poem takes in his wooing: in the opening section of the lyric his plea is a scarcely disguised command. It then dissolves in the second half into the standard begging attitude of the traditional courtly love song.

Wolfram's later verse narrative, *Willehalm,* is quite different from *Parzival.* While the central concern of the early work may be said to be the problem of the relationship of humanity to God, the main thrust of *Willehalm* is the disastrous nature of war. While the early work is a simple biography of two individuals, hero and counterpart, *Willehalm* is a highly elaborate, episodic work with a huge cast of characters. The action in *Willehalm* is diffuse, even confusing, and the work is, therefore, not as accessible as *Parzival.* The war in *Willehalm* involves not only the soldiers but also civilian men, women, and children. It is also a war of religion between Christianity and Islam, in which faith fuels

fanaticism and barbarity. The subject was highly topical at the time; by the end of the first decade of the thirteenth century four Crusades had been fought. In the first the religious fervor of the Christians had spilled over almost immediately into mindless brutality: in 1096 pogroms took place in the Rhineland, and hundreds of Jews were put to the sword in Mainz, Speyer, Worms, and Cologne; the Crusade was successful in that Jerusalem was captured, but the victory was a bloodbath–soldiers, it was said, waded through blood up to their knees–and even the Christians were appalled at the massacre. The Second Crusade, in 1147, was a fiasco, and the Third Crusade, in 1187, led by Friedrich Barbarossa, disintegrated on Barbarossa's death, with most of the German crusaders returning home and much of the Holy Land remaining in Muslim hands. With the sack of Constantinople in the Fourth Crusade, in 1204, war reached a new level of horror. For three days the crusaders committed murder, rape, and torture and looted or destroyed the city's artistic treasures. Constantinople's catastrophic fate reverberated throughout the world. So when audiences listened to a recitation of *Willehalm,* his portrayal of a war of religion and its implications held awesome meaning for them.

The war at the center of Wolfram's narrative has another dimension, also a deeply tragic one: it is a war between two great families that should be at peace because they are bound together by the marriage of the Christian margrave Willehalm and the Muslim Giburc, who has become a Christian. Members of the two families murder one another relentlessly. Their unremitting hostility reveals the pattern of a Germanic blood feud, in which the killing must go on until only one protagonist is left. More than half of *Willehalm* is devoted to war: books 1 and 2 are taken up with the portrayal of the first battle, and the last three, books 7, 8, and 9, with that of the second. The work is incomplete; several narrative strands are not followed to a proper conclusion. It is not known why Wolfram did not finish it, but the story is so full of problems that are unlikely ever to find a solution that he may have lost heart. The mood of resignation that pervades the work makes it unlikely that he would have ended it with the same confident optimism that marks the conclusion of *Parzival.*

The enmity between the warring families is counterbalanced by the love of Willehalm and Giburc. In two love scenes the strength of their emotional bond transcends the gloom cast by war and devastation. Yet their past constitutes one of the many problems that beset the epic: Willehalm abducted Giburc, the wife of the Muslim king Tybalt, whose territory he invaded and devastated; she accepted baptism out of love for Willehalm but also out of conviction. The twofold treachery—the abduction and the apostasy—provides the Muslims with a just grievance and a desire for revenge.

Wolfram's characterizations of Willehalm and Giburc are full of irony. While Willehalm, the Christian warrior, has a violent temper, is brutally vindictive, and gives no quarter to the enemy, refusing even to heed the pleas of the maimed, Giburc, the onetime "infidel," proclaims the Christian message of tolerance and pity in an impassioned speech that forms the ideological core of the work.

There are more than one hundred named characters in *Willehalm,* and they each attain a certain measure of individuality. Yet more important than their often sketchy individual identities is the mass they make up, for Wolfram's objective is to transmit the impression that hundreds upon hundreds suffer and are massacred in this war.

Willehalm has remote historical roots. In 793 Count Guillaume of Toulouse, a grandson of Charles Martel, fought against the Saracens in the area between Narbonne and Carcassonne; in 801 he fought them again, this time in Spain. In 804 he founded the monastery Gellone near Montpellier, entered it in 806, and died there six or seven years later. Gellone was renamed Saint Guilhem-le-Désert, the name it bears today.

Guillaume's courage and his saintly later life became the stuff of legend. In oral poetry, exploits of other warriors as well as fictitious episodes came to be linked with his name, and so the figure of real life gradually developed into a hero of fable. In the twelfth century a series of chansons de geste was composed on Guillaume and members of his family. The series grew into a cycle of more than twenty poems, of which *La Bataille d'Aliscans* (The Battle of Aliscans) forms the source of Wolfram's *Willehalm. La Bataille d'Aliscans* has been handed down in thirteen manuscripts, of which twelve are cyclic—that is, they also contain other epics of the Guillaume cycle. A comparison of the manuscripts has led to the view that the version from which Wolfram worked was close to manuscript M (now at Saint Mark's, Venice), the only extant noncyclic manuscript of *La Bataille d'Aliscans.*

According to Wolfram's own testimony it was the landgrave Hermann of Thuringia who made the story known to him. *La Bataille d'Aliscans* is believed to have been composed between 1180 and 1190; Wolfram worked on *Willehalm* between 1210 and 1220. No manuscripts of *La Bataille d'Aliscans* from that period have been handed down, and it is doubtful that any existed at that time: the chansons de geste were then still largely disseminated orally.

The prologue begins with a prayer in which the poet invokes God's help in telling the story of *Willehalm.*

He refers to his source and then asks Saint Willehalm to save him from perdition. He mentions his own name and invites the audience to listen to his new work.

Willehalm's father has disinherited his sons. Willehalm, the eldest, has sought his fortune in the East and has carried off the Muslim queen Arabel, who has converted to Christianity and been baptized in the name Giburc. A huge Muslim army commanded by her father, King Terramer, and her former husband, King Tybalt, has arrived in Provence to exact vengeance. On the field of Alischanz the twenty thousand Christians are vastly outnumbered by the Muslims, who inflict a crushing defeat on them. Willehalm's beloved nephew Vivianz is mortally wounded; an archangel speaks to him and protects his soul from the devil, and as he dies in Willehalm's lap, a miraculous fragrance rises, as if from a scented fire. Willehalm breaks away with his last fourteen men and tries to make his way to his castle at Oransche. In a final skirmish the other fourteen are killed, but Willehalm escapes into the mountains. Here he finds Vivianz, who briefly comes back to life and makes his confession. Willehalm holds vigil by the body throughout the night. The next day he meets eighteen Muslim kings and slays ten, among them Giburc's uncle, Arofel. From Willehalm's grief over Vivianz springs unbridled vengefulness. He cuts off Arofel's leg; helpless, Arofel, one of the richest and most powerful of the Muslim kings, offers untold treasure and pleads for his crippled life. In answer, Willehalm slaughters him in the most ignominious manner, cutting off his head and stripping the corpse. The scenes of Vivianz's death and the killing of Arofel are both intensely moving, and Wolfram clearly meant them to be considered together. Both episodes end with the same gesture of resignation on the part of the narrator: "waz hilfet, ob ichz lange sage?" (69, 17: What is the use, if I dwell on it any longer?) concludes the Vivianz episode, and "war umme solde ichz lange sagen?" (81, 11: What is the point of saying any more?) ends the Arofel scene. Willehalm spares Giburc's son, Ehmereiz. Wearing Arofel's armor and riding Arofel's charger, he reaches Oransche, where he has difficulty convincing Giburc of his identity. The poet is here implicitly condemning Willehalm's gratuitous cruelty to Arofel: his own wife takes him to be a heathen, not a Christian. The Muslim army besieges Oransche, and Willehalm leaves under cover of darkness to seek help at the court of the French king. As he speaks Arabic and is taken for Arofel by the Muslims, he rides unscathed through their lines.

Giburc has been left behind to defend Oransche. In a dialogue with her father he tells her that he despises the Christian faith and intends to heap dishonor on Jesus by giving his daughter a shameful death: he offers her the choice of being drowned, burned, or hanged. She refuses to surrender, although most of her men have been killed. In the meantime Willehalm, exhausted and unkempt, arrives at the French court. He is not made welcome: his sister, the queen, gives orders not to admit him, and Willehalm is forced to find lodgings with a merchant. The next day he enters the great hall fully armed and publicly upbraids the king, reminding him that he, Willehalm, has been the kingmaker. Despite Willehalm's insults and threats, the king is conciliatory, but the queen refuses to give him any help. Willehalm, in an uncontrollable rage, tears the crown from her head, seizes her by the hair, and raises his sword to decapitate her, but their mother separates them. In the end Willehalm's father offers military support, and his mother puts her fortune at his disposal. Willehalm's anger is calmed by the appearance of his niece, Princess Alice, who begs forgiveness for her mother's harshness.

When the queen learns of the many dead among her kin she decides that Willehalm must be helped, and she intercedes for him with the king. When the king is reluctant, Willehalm angrily threatens to return his fiefs. The king finally gives way, and a summons for military aid is proclaimed throughout the kingdom.

Willehalm notices a boy working in the kitchen, a Muslim who has refused to be baptized. He is Rennewart, Giburc's brother, but their kinship is not disclosed until later. Willehalm offers to equip Rennewart with arms, but he wants only a club. Rennewart is presumably introduced to relieve some of the tragedy and gloom that burden the narrative. He appears as a clumsy clown, but much of the humor associated with him is black humor; the farcical situations in which he is shown are mingled with cruelty. When he is teased by some young squires, he seizes one of them and hurls him against a pillar, bursting him open like rotten fruit. Later, when some of them knock over his club, he picks it up and hits out with such force at a boy who is hiding behind a pillar that although he misses the squire the club striking the stone sends flames flaring up to the roof. While he is asleep in the kitchen, the cook purposely singes his beard; on discovering his disgrace Rennewart ties up the cook and throws him alive into the kitchen fire. There is humor in Rennewart's uncouth bearing, but there is none in his menacing strength.

The king makes Willehalm supreme commander of the army. At this point the war against Islam takes on a new importance: the safety of the kingdom is at stake. Oransche is under siege. In a second conversation with Giburc, Terramer tries to win her back to Islam; this time he shows himself to be grief-stricken, declares his love for his daughter, and claims that he has been

forced to join the campaign against her. He is, however, adamant that Giburc must reconvert, but he is unable to persuade her to surrender. In a massive assault the town is set on fire, and the Muslims return to their fleet. The inner part of the castle is spared, and Willehalm arrives with the French army. A banquet is arranged to welcome the relief forces, during which Giburc reveals her deep distress to Willehalm's father. She tells him that, of her kin, twenty-three kings and countless other nobles have been killed. She is devastated by the loss of life on both sides and by the hatred shown to her by her countrymen and her kin: even her ten brothers had joined the attack.

A council of war is called; Willehalm outlines his desperate straits, but the French princes decline to help until a plea is made to them in the name of Christ. The scene culminates in Giburc's great speech: facing the all-male assembly, whose discussion has centered on fighting and revenge, she pleads for mercy. Should victory in the forthcoming struggle and, therefore, eternal salvation be theirs, let it be earned fittingly, she urges: "Hœrt eines tummen wîbes rât, / schônet der gotes hantgetât" (306, 27–28: Listen to the counsel of a simple, untutored woman, / Spare the handiwork of God). Although she calls herself simple, she grapples with problems that were highly topical in contemporary theological debates. Not all infidels can be meant for perdition; every child is born an infidel, even when born to a Christian mother, and the examples of Noah, Job, and the three Magi show that God does not consign all heathens to hell. Jesus even forgave those who took his life. Charity should be the Christians' lodestar. God and humanity form a vast family of Father and children; this realization throws the kin-versus-kin feud of the war between Christians and Muslims into sharp relief. At the end of her speech, the longest in the work, Giburc breaks down in tears.

This call for tolerance of those of different faith and for compassion for a defeated enemy would be remarkable at any time in history; that it should have been made during the period of the Crusades is even more astonishing. An unambiguous affirmation of intensely demanding moral values, it stands out not only in the work but in the whole of Western literature. Throughout the epic Wolfram is at pains to demonstrate the high level of civilization achieved by the non-Christians; time and again he points to similarities in fighting techniques and behavior toward women between knights of the East and the West. Knights from the East, richer and more resplendent than their counterparts of the West, are knights nevertheless; the ideals of chivalry unite them all. This concern to isolate the features that link opponents and opposing views permeates *Willehalm* and rises to its climax in the speech of the onetime Muslim, but now Christian, Giburc. The endeavor to establish a basis for tolerance, and the ultimate proclamation of tolerance as a guiding principle for human behavior, makes the work one of the great declarations of humaneness in Western culture.

Books 7, 8, and 9 are devoted to a detailed description of the second great battle, in which Rennewart plays a leading role. When the Christian troops reach a position close to the Muslim encampment and see the overwhelming force that confronts them, the French princes turn back; but they meet Rennewart, who kills many of them and forces the rest to return to the battlefield.

The portrayal of the battle represents the first detailed account of strategy and tactics in medieval German literature. References to place and time project a clear picture of the engagement. The Christian army is organized into six divisions, the Muslim army into ten. There are two parts to the battle: the first is dominated by the encounters of groups, the second by duels. The slaughter seems unending; Rennewart alone kills nine kings. When the bearer of the Muslim battle standard is cut down, Christian victory is assured. Many of the remaining Muslim soldiers are killed trying to flee. In individual combat between Willehalm and King Terramer, the latter is injured but is rescued by his men and carried to his ship. The victory the Christians celebrate has turned out to be a Pyrrhic one. There are countless dead, and Rennewart is missing. Among the twenty Muslim kings who have been taken captive is Matribleiz, a kinsman of Giburc. In a magnanimous gesture that contrasts favorably with Willehalm's initial stance toward the Muslims, he sets Matribleiz free and charges him to gather the bodies of the slain Muslim kings and have them buried according to the rites of their own faith. There the work breaks off.

Titurel (circa 1217), which was also left incomplete, is the first court romance cast in stanzas and the first not to be based on an earlier source. The work is preserved in two fragments. These fragments were enlarged in the latter half of the thirteenth century by a poet who calls himself Albrecht into a huge Grail narrative of more than 6,000 stanzas that is commonly referred to as *Der jüngere Titurel* (The Later Titurel). Wolfram's fragments consist of 131 and 39 stanzas, respectively. Stanzas were the metrical norm for the heroic epic and were traditionally of a rigid pattern. Wolfram seems occasionally to loosen the structure deliberately through the use of a mobile caesura; now and then this practice lends his stanzas a free-flowing rhythm. All stanzaic poetry in the Middle Ages was sung, but the melody for *Titurel* has not been preserved. The language Wolfram uses to tell his story displays an extravagance unusual even for him; it abounds in meta-

phors, unorthodox usages, ambiguities (possibly deliberate), coined words, and invented compounds. The combination of the novel rhythm, the music, and the eccentric language makes the work one of extreme sophistication and elegance.

Titurel presupposes knowledge of *Parzival.* The fragments represent, in the main, a partial biography of Sigune before her first appearance in the earlier work. Of the thirty-two named characters in *Titurel,* twenty-nine can also be found in *Parzival.* The theme Wolfram explores here is selfless love between the sexes. In what appears to be the early part of the story, the Grail king Titurel maintains in his abdication speech that one outstanding characteristic will mark all his descendants: "wâre minne mit triuwen" (strophe 4: true love and loyalty). The later Sigune, as portrayed in *Parzival,* is the epitome of selfless loving and, in this way, a model after which the hero is to strive. In *Titurel* she is shown experiencing the awakening of love in childhood and its changed nature in adolescence. Love is assessed in authorial comment, examined in discussions among the characters, and demonstrated in the behavior of the lovers. In both fragments the frame of reference is the code of manners that was expected to govern a love relationship in medieval aristocratic society.

In the first fragment Titurel abdicates in favor of his son, who has five grown children. One of the son's daughters dies while giving birth, and her husband decides to become a hermit. The province with which his brother, King Tampunteire, enfeoffed him is transferred to the baby, who is named Sigune. Tampunteire also has a daughter, Condwiramurs, and Sigune is brought up with her. After Tampunteire's death Sigune is taken to her aunt Herzeloyde, who marries Gahmuret. The latter has a boy named Schionatulander in his retinue. Sigune and Schionatulander fall passionately in love but are soon parted when Gahmuret leaves for the East and Schionatulander accompanies him. Sigune and Schionatulander suffer torments of longing and begin to ail visibly. Gahmuret, noticing the change in Schionatulander, presses for an explanation; when he hears of the boy's love for Sigune, he promises to help Schionatulander in his courtship. Herzeloyde also becomes aware of Sigune's love for Schionatulander and gives her approval as well.

At this point the poet apostrophizes the immense power of love. He fears for the children, as they are too young and inexperienced to endure the agony of a great passion. The love of Schionatulander and Sigune is cast in a conventional mold; indeed, it involves two conventions superimposed on one another. They keep their love secret not only from others but also from one another; they exhibit the physical symptoms of lovesickness when they are separated; and Sigune displays the characteristic behavior of the woman waiting for her lover—standing in the window, watching from the battlements. All three features—the secrecy, the lovesickness, and the waiting woman—are part of the stockpile of motifs of the contemporary love lyric. Their love also bends to the conventional demand of the courtly romance that a man earn a woman's love through deeds of valor in jousts and on the battlefield. Sigune makes this demand, and Schionatulander immediately accepts the obligation. Gahmuret and Herzeloyde subscribe to this code of behavior as well: Gahmuret exhorts Schionatulander to win Sigune's love with a long career in fighting, and Herzeloyde assumes that Schionatulander will do so.

In the second fragment Sigune and Schionatulander no longer have to hide their love because it has been sanctioned by their elders. They are encamped on a clearing in the middle of a forest, chaperoned by ladies-in-waiting and other attendants, when they hear the baying of a hound that is racing in their direction. Schionatulander catches the animal, which is wearing a magnificently jeweled collar with an extraordinary leash that is twelve fathoms (seventy-two feet) long and also set with precious stones. The gems form letters; the inscription on the collar says that the hound's name is Gardeviaz, which means "mind the trail!" (a command used in hunting), and it admonishes that human beings might well heed this warning, too: men and women must watch their path through life so that they may find favor in this world and salvation in the next. The message on the leash is from a young queen who is sending the hound as a gift to her husband-to-be. It relates the fate of her sister, Florie, who denied the man she loved nothing except her body. He set out to earn her love by deeds of arms and was killed in a joust, whereupon she died as well. To read the rest of the inscription, Sigune must untie the leash from the tent pole. As she undoes the knot, Gardeviaz breaks free and races off into the forest, dragging the leash behind him. Obsessed with the desire to read the inscription to the end, Sigune promises Schionatulander all he desires if he will bring back the leash to her. The story of Florie as told on the leash parallels that of Sigune: both love and are loved in return, and both postpone the fulfillment of their love until their lover has proved himself; the fate of Florie foreshadows tragedy for Sigune. The message began with advice; it might end with more. Sigune must have that ending. The urgency with which she clamors to have the leash restored to her, and the extravagant manner in which she expresses her need, clearly imply that she is filled with foreboding. Her demand is neither capricious nor unreasonable, as some scholars have labeled it. Neither in the two fragments nor in *Parzival* is such superficiality attributed to her. Wolfram, a master

at consistent characterization, would hardly have been guilty of such a lapse. Anxiety drives her, not whim. Schionatulander agrees at once to retrieve the leash.

And so Sigune unwittingly sends Schionatulander to his death. When she makes her appearance in *Parzival,* he has just been killed in a joust while on this mission, and she is holding his dead body. When first shown in *Parzival* Sigune is still in the world of the Arthurian court; she later moves to Grail country, where she finally becomes an anchorite living with Schionatulander's embalmed body. In *Titurel* and *Parzival* Wolfram charts Sigune's progress from childish love through adult love to love of God.

Wolfram's works were enlarged, imitated, and copied for hundreds of years. Ultimately, however, there came a break in this continuity of appreciation as the German language changed and the age of feudalism passed. By the sixteenth century Wolfram's works were no longer being read. It was not until 1753, when the Swiss poet Johann Jakob Bodmer translated *Parzival* into hexameters, that interest in Wolfram's poetry began to revive. His second rise to fame gathered momentum in the nineteenth century as scholars recognized the outstanding qualities of his work and made it accessible to a wider public through editions, commentaries, translations, and adaptations, yet knowledge of his poetry has largely remained restricted to cognoscenti. His thoughts are often movingly, wittily, or dramatically expressed, and many of the themes he treats are universal. He is one of the great visionary poets of Western civilization.

Bibliographies:

Ulrich Pretzel und Wolfgang Bachofer, *Bibliographie zu Wolfram von Eschenbach* (Berlin: Schmidt, 1968);

Joachim Bumke, *Die Wolfram von Eschenbach Forschung seit 1945: Bericht und Bibliographie* (Munich: Fink, 1970).

References:

David Blamires, *Characterization and Individuality in Wolfram's "Parzival"* (Cambridge: Cambridge University Press, 1966);

Joachim Bumke, *Wolfram von Eschenbach* (Stuttgart: Metzler, 1991);

Renate Decke-Cornill, *Stellenkommentar zum III. Buch des Willehalm Wolframs von Eschenbach* (Marburg: Elwert, 1985);

Dennis Howard Green and Leslie Peter Johnson, *Approaches to Wolfram von Eschenbach: Five Essays* (Bern, Frankfurt am Main & Las Vegas: Lang, 1978);

Erich Happ, "Kommentar zum zweiten Buch von Wolframs Willehalm," dissertation, University of Munich, 1966;

R. M. S. Heffner, ed., *Collected Indexes to the Works of Wolfram von Eschenbach* (Madison: University of Wisconsin Press, 1961);

Joachim Heinzle, *Stellenkommentar zu Wolframs Titurel* (Tübingen: Niemeyer, 1972);

Carl J. Lofmark, *Rennewart in Wolfram's "Willehalm"* (Cambridge: Cambridge University Press, 1972);

Ernst Martin, *Wolframs von Eschenbach Parzival und Titurel: Kommentar* (Halle: Waisenhaus, 1903);

Bodo Mergell, *Wolfram von Eschenbach und seine französischen Quellen,* 2 volumes (Münster: Aschendorff, 1936, 1943);

Benedikt Mockenhaupt, *Die Frömmigkeit im Parzival Wolframs von Eschenbach* (Darmstadt: Wissenschaftliche Buchgesellschaft, 1968);

Ingrid Ochs, *Wolframs Willehalm-Eingang im Lichte der frühmittelhochdeutschen geistlichen Dichtung* (Munich, 1968);

Linda B. Parshall, *The Art of Narration in Wolfram's "Parzifal" and Albrecht's "Jüngerer Titurel"* (Cambridge: Cambridge University Press, 1981);

Margaret Fitzgerald Richey, *Gahmuret Anschevin* (Oxford, 1923);

Richey, *Schionatulander and Sigune* (London, 1927; revised, 1960);

Richey, *Studies of Wolfram von Eschenbach* (Edinburgh & London: Oliver & Boyd, 1957);

Heinz Rupp, ed., *Wolfram von Eschenbach,* Wege der Forschung, no. 57 (Darmstadt: Wissenschaftliche Buchgesellschaft, 1966);

Hugh Sacker, *An Introduction to Wolfram's "Parzival"* (Cambridge: Cambridge University Press, 1963);

Ernst-Joachim Schmidt, *Stellenkommentar zum IX. Buch des "Willehalm" Wolframs von Eschenbach* (Bayreuth: University of Bayreuth, 1979);

Werner Schröder, *Die Namen im "Parzival" und im "Titurel" Wolframs von Eschenbach* (Berlin & New York: De Gruyter, 1982);

Schröder, ed., *Wolfram-Studien: Veröffentlichungen der Wolfram-von-Eschenbach-Gesellschaft* (Berlin: Schmidt, 1970–);

Marianne Wynn, "Book I of Wolfram von Eschenbach's *Willehalm* and Its Conclusion," *Medium Aevum,* 49 (1980): 57–65;

Wynn, "Orgeluse: Persönlichkeitsgestaltung auf Chrestienschem Modell," *German Life and Letters,* 30 (1977): 127–137;

Wynn, "Wolframs Dawnsongs," in *Festschrift Werner Schröder* (Tübingen: Niemeyer, 1989), pp. 549–558;

Wynn, *Wolfram's Parzival: On the Genesis of Its Poetry* (Frankfurt am Main & New York: Peter Lang, 1984).

Contributors

Dieter W. Adolphs . . . . *Michigan Technological University*

A. Tilo Alt . . . . *Duke University*

Ehrhard Bahr . . . . *University of California, Los Angeles*

Michael S. Batts . . . . *University of British Columbia*

Eckhard Bernstein . . . . *College of the Holy Cross*

Ruth B. Bottigheimer . . . . *State University of New York at Stony Brook*

Jane K. Brown . . . . *University of Washington*

Edson M. Chick . . . . *Williams College*

Roy C. Cowen . . . . *University of Michigan*

Donald H. Crosby . . . . *University of Connecticut*

Adrian Del Caro . . . . *University of Colorado*

Steve Dowden . . . . *Brandeis University*

Thomas H. Falk . . . . *Michigan State University*

Francis G. Gentry . . . . *Pennsylvania State University*

Glenn Guidry . . . . *Saint Meinrad Seminary*

Gertraud Gutzmann . . . . *Smith College*

Gail K. Hart . . . . *University of California, Irvine*

Will Hasty . . . . *University of Florida*

Gerd Hillen . . . . *University of California, Berkeley*

Charles W. Hoffmann . . . . *Ohio State University*

Robert C. Holub . . . . *University of California, Berkeley*

Jeffrey Jaynes . . . . *Methodist Theological School in Ohio*

Michael W. Jennings . . . . *Princeton University*

Alan Frank Keele . . . . *Brigham Young University*

Herbert Knust . . . . *University of Illinois at Urbana–Champaign*

Wulf Koepke . . . . *Texas A & M University*

Richard H. Lawson . . . . *University of North Carolina at Chapel Hill*

Paul Michael Lützeler . . . . *Washington University*

James K. Lyon . . . . *Brigham Young University*

James M. McGlathery . . . . *University of Illinois at Urbana–Champaign*

Phillip S. McKnight . . . . *University of Kentucky*

Joseph Mileck . . . . *University of California, Berkeley*

Brian Murdoch . . . . *University of Stirling*

William Arctander O'Brien . . . . *University of California, San Diego*

John Carson Pettey . . . . *University of Nevada, Reno*

Lawrence Ryan . . . . *University of Massachusetts, Amherst*
Steven Paul Scher . . . .*Dartmouth College*
Gerd K. Schneider. . . . . *Syracuse University*
George C. Schoolfield . . . . *Yale University*
Ernst Schürer. . . . . *Pennsylvania State University*
Egon Schwarz . . . . *Washington University*
Hinrich C. Seeba . . . . *University of California, Berkeley*
Dieter Sevin. . . . . *Vanderbilt University*
Monika Shafi . . . .*University of Delaware*
Robert K. Shirer . . . .*University of Nebraska at Lincoln*
John D. Simons . . . . *Florida State University*
Duncan Smith . . . . *Brown University*
Blake Lee Spahr. . . . . *University of California, Berkeley*
Carl Steiner . . . .*George Washington University*
Wiebke Strehl . . . . *Pennsylvania State University*
Rodney Taylor . . . . *Truman State University*
Hans Wagener . . . .*University of California, Los Angeles*
Michael Winkler . . . . *Rice University*
Marianne Wynn . . . . *Queen Mary and Westfield College*
Reinhard K. Zachau . . . . *University of the South*

Concise Dictionary of World
Literary Biography
Index

Index

ISBN 0-7876-4482-X

90000

9 780787 644826